WORLD SOCCER

THE DICTIONARY OF
FOOTBALL

WORLD SOCCER

THE DICTIONARY OF FOOTBALL

THE COMPLETE A-Z OF INTERNATIONAL FOOTBALL
FROM AJAX TO ZINEDINE ZIDANE

JOHN BALLARD AND PAUL SUFF

BⓈXTREE

First published 1999 by Boxtree
an imprint of Macmillan Publishers Ltd
25 Eccleston Place London SW1W 9NF
and Basingstoke

Associated companies throughout the world

ISBN 0 7522 2434 4

World Soccer is published monthly by IPC Magazines Limited,
Kings Reach Tower, Stamford Street, London SE1 9LS.
For subscription enquiries call: 01444 445555
(fax no: 01444 445599) or write to:
Quadrant Subscription Services, FREEPOST CY1061,
Haywards Heath, West Sussex RH16 3ZA.

9 8 7 6 5 4 3 2 1

A CIP catalogue record for this book is available from
the British Library.

Typeset by Blackjacks

Printed and bound by Mackays of Chatham Plc, Chatham, Kent

Dedication

This book is dedicated to football fans everywhere in the hope that the 'beautiful game' will continue to transcend the bigotry that divides nations and people within nations.

It is dedicated to our friends and families and most of all, to our fathers: Bill Ballard, who unwittingly turned John into a Chelsea fan, and Roy Suff, who took Paul to his first match.

Additional contributors

Jeanne Ballard, Jeremy Baugh, Mike Easterbrook,
Dr Mark Leigh-Howarth, Ezra Martin and Rachel Suff.

Foreword

Football is the new global language. Any fan who has travelled to another country will know that the most impenetrable language barrier can be breached by the mention of a few great footballing names. Even in the remotest corners of the world you can strike up a conversation based on common admiration of the great players, awe-inspiring teams and memorable international games. Football has pervaded virtually every sphere of life from theatre to politics and from washing powder advertisements to corporate finance. While very few can ever fulfil a dream of playing at Wembley or the Maracaná, anyone who has ever played can remember that great moment when they created a goal worthy of Pelé or made a save that Peter Schmeichel would have been proud of. The fact that the memory is far from the reality is of no consequence; such is the joy of football. Success or failure of a national team has been implicated in the state of the economy and even the national birth rate. In addition football has been at the centre – though not the cause – of tragedies that have left millions grief-stricken. It is, therefore, inevitable that football has invaded the language and, in every part of the world, has created its own terminology. This book is a description of the language of football, and a tribute to a game that has given so much to so many. It strives to provide answers for those who want to know more about football including the names of clubs or players, the bodies that govern the game, the rules, the technical and tactical terminology, or the plethora of international expressions that have grown out of the conversational use and abuse of language in the context of world's most-talked-about sport.

The Dictionary of Football is written from the perspective of nearly 140 years of organised football, while also charting its origins. Information and statistics are given for virtually every country with separate entries for the leading clubs of the major footballing nations. There is comprehensive coverage of the Laws of the game, with further examination of the regulations that govern domestic football in the United Kingdom, including detailed explanations of the transfer market and its complex history. There are records, feats and trivia from all over the world as well as data and histories for all English and Scottish league grounds and some of the most important grounds elsewhere in the world. *The Dictionary of Football* recognises the increasing popularity of women's football as well as the growth of games such as futsal and jorkyball. Football for those with visual impairments or learning disabilities is also covered. There is detailed coverage of the business of football including share issues, sponsorships and mergers.

The book is compiled in a traditional dictionary format in order to make access to information as easy as possible. If you want to know more about the former English Football League club **Southport**, you'll find it after **Southern League**, and before **Soviet Union**. It is as simple as that.

The book is written for everyone with an interest in football, from school children and the casual fan to coaches, journalists and academics. It has taken three years of detailed research to produce more than 6,000 definitions and encyclopaedic entries. The dynamic nature of the game will mean, inevitably, that some of the facts will date quicker than others. Reliable data from some parts of the world has proved more difficult to obtain than others; we welcome comments from readers of this first edition. Our e-mail address is dofootball@hotmail.com so that future editions can continue to provide the world's most comprehensive digest on football.

We hope that, whatever your perspective, you'll enjoy reading it.

John Ballard and Paul Suff, April 1999

Guide to Usage

GENERAL INFORMATION

The football leagues in England and Scotland have undergone several transformations, most notably with the inauguration of the FA Premier League, in England, and the Scottish Premier League. Where the dictionary refers to Division One (for example in a club's league record), this refers to the former top-flight division (ie before the formation of the Premier Leagues). First Division refers to the division immediately below the Premier League since reorganisation (Information specific to English and Scottish league clubs section for details).

All measurements are given in metric, with an imperial conversion in parentheses. It is important to note, however, that for pitch markings the **International FA Board** only uses an approximate imperial to metric conversion table.

Where the dictionary refers to the Laws of the game or league regulations, these are the interpretations of the authors and do not carry any official status. The Laws of the game have always been kept as simple as possible; their interpretation is decided by the International FA Board, which communicates its decisions to referees and governing bodies. *The Dictionary of Football* has striven to present these rules in lay person's terms; players and officials should always refer to the official advice of their governing bodies where a more critical interpretation is required.

Separate entries are given for all league clubs and former league clubs in the English Football League, FA Premier League, Scottish Football League and Scottish Premier League. For other countries, only the leading clubs are listed – based on historical performance tables. More clubs are included from the leagues of Ireland and Wales and from the world's leading footballing nations, such as from Germany, Spain, Brazil, Argentina, Italy and France. All United States Major League Soccer clubs and the founder members of the Japanese J-League clubs are listed. A number of clubs no longer in existence are included if they have some historical significance.

It was not practical to include all the world's leading players in the list of biographies. The dictionary does, however, have separate biographical entries for the **Football League Centenary 100**, the authors' choice of the world's top 100 players (based on a poll of polls), winners of most of the World and European players of the year and selected winners of the African, Asian and South American players of the year, and others noted for individual achievements, such as goal-scoring feats, longevity, record international appearances or, simply, because they have given special pleasure to the spectating public. The number of international appearances and goals scored by current players are recorded as close to publication as possible.

HEADWORD

The headword is the key word (or words) in bold type at the beginning of each separate entry. All headwords are listed in strict alphabetical order eg

Sporting Clube de Portugal, is followed by **Sporting Clube de Praia**, **Sporting Cristal**, **Sports Report**, **spot kick**, **spot-the-ball**, **Spotland** and **sprain**.

Where one headword has more than one meaning these are listed either as separate entries (in the case of clubs with the same name) or are numbered in the same entry. For example, there are separate entries for the various clubs named **Arsenal** whereas there are two possible interpretations for the verb **dive**, and these are listed under the single headword.

Proper nouns preceded by the abbreviated form of **Saint** – eg **St Johnstone**, **St Mirren** – are listed alphabetically under **Saint**.

Holland is listed and referred to as **Netherlands**.

Separate entries are given to the major women's footballing nations, such as **China, women**; **Germany, women**; **United States of America, women** and the British home nations. In all other cases, details on women's football are included under a country's main headword.

All clubs are listed under their most common name, with their country of origin given, for example:

Atlético Madrid *club* Spanish league.

A club's full name is, where appropriate, given in parentheses after the common name, eg:

Benfica (Sport Lisboa e Benfica) *club* Portuguese national league club . . .

Corinthians (Sport Club Corinthians Paulista) *club* Brazilian national league . . .

Club names beginning with 1.FC are all listed under the main part of the name followed by (1.FC), eg:

Kaiserslautern (1.FC) *club* German league.

Biographical entries are listed under the person's surname followed by their first or forenames, for example:

Moore, Bobby . . .

World, national, league or tournament records are listed under their most obvious headword: for example, 'record crowd' can be found under the headword **attendance, highest**, with various tournament records included under that entry. There are several records under **goals**, eg:

goals, fewest in one day *record* . . .

goals, most for one club *record* . . .

goals, most in one match (player) *record* . . .

CROSS-REFERENCES

Within an entry, cross-references are referred to in bold type. If a cross-referenced word appears more than once within an entry, it is only emboldened at the first time of mentioning. Common words, such as goal, foul or club, though defined, are only emboldened within an entry where there is a special relevance in cross-referring to such definitions.

LABELS

Each headword is followed by the appropriate part of speech (eg *n.*, *adj.*, *adv.*, *vb.*,) usage label (eg *informal*) or encyclopaedic label (eg *club*, *country*, *player*, *misc.*, *record*, *rule*) in italics. Foreign words are identified by their language of origin in italics: eg **spareggio** *Italian* . . .

1. Usage labels

informal   a conversational word or usage, eg **handbags**, **goalhang**, **yard short of pace**.

legal   civil actions and statutes, eg the **Safety of Sports Ground Act 1975**.

medical   all terms relating to injuries, drugs or treatments, eg **sprain**, **analgesic**, **RICE**.

2. Encyclopaedic labels

award   an honour or prize, such as the **Footballer of the Year**.

broadcaster   a person listed primarily because of their achievements as a commentator or other television or radio personality, such as John **Motson**, David **Mellor**.

club   a current or former football club, eg **Galatasaray**, **Plymouth Argyle**.

competition   a named tournament, such as the **World Cup**, **European Cup-winners Cup** and **Asian Champion Teams Cup**.

confederation   international, world, national and regional governing bodies, such as **FIFA**, the **Asian Football Confederation**, and the **Football Association of Wales**.

country   all nations and some former nations (such as **East Germany** and the **Soviet Union**). Where appropriate, this label is accompanied by the appropriate international affiliation (in its abbreviated form), eg **Portugal**   *country   UEFA* . . . If countries are not affiliated to FIFA or a continental federation, they are listed as having *no international affiliation*.

disaster   major incident at a football match involving substantial loss of life, eg **Hillsborough disaster**, **Superga aircrash**.

ground   club and national stadia, eg **Old Trafford** and **Stade de France**.

manager   a person listed primarily because of his or her record as a manager or coach, eg Rinus **Michels**, Bob **Paisley**.

misc.   miscellaneous or trivia headwords, such as **baked beans**, **dog** and **stamps**.

official   a person listed primarily because of his or her record as a referee, or as a club, national or international dignitary (such as the general secretary of a national governing body, or chairman of a club), eg Sepp **Blatter**, William **McGregor**.

player   a person listed primarily because of his or her record as a player, eg George **Best**, Diego **Maradona**.

player-manager   a person listed because of his or her record as a player and as a coach or manager, eg Kenny **Dalglish**, Mario **Zagallo**.

publication   current or former periodical or book, eg **Athletic News**, **Football Monthly**, **Rothmans Football Yearbook**, **World Soccer**.

radio   current or former radio programme or radio station.

record   a world, national, league or tournament record, eg **appearances**, **most for one club**, **oldest player**.

regulations   terms describing the specific rules of English and Scottish league football; where appropriate, these are accompanied by the relevant league statute in parentheses, eg **squad number** regulations . . . (FA Premier League rule F.1).

rules   the headword describes, or is directly related to one or more of the **Laws of the game** and the relevant law given in parentheses, eg **free kick** . . . (Law XIII), **charge an opponent** . . . (Law XI).

state   eg used for the 27 regional states of **Brazil**, each of which has its own **football league**.

tactics   a style of play or formation, eg **sweeper system**, **four-four-two**.

television   current or former television programme or station.

trademark   a registered symbol or label of a manufacture, eg **Barbie**, **Manfield Hotspur**.

NOTES WITHIN THE TEXT

Many of the encyclopaedic entries are annotated with summary information under a number of sub-headings.

1. General

Dossier formal information, such as the date of formation, team strip, ground capacity, dates of affiliation to FIFA and continental confederation (for nations), the names of the president and general secretary, first international match, approximate start and finish dates for the domestic season, record attendance, leading goalscorers, most-capped players, and biggest victory and defeat.

History a chronological summary of events in the development of a club, country, competition or rule, highlighting notable achievements, setbacks and star players.

Keynotes additional information included to illustrate a particular headword.

Website e-mail address or the official (or where indicated, unofficial) internet home page.

2. Information specific to countries

International tournament record a summary of the national team's achievements in major international competitions, including, where appropriate, age-restricted and women's tournaments.

Record against British and Irish national teams complete record of the number of games played, won, drawn and lost against the national teams of England, Northern Ireland, Scotland, Wales and the Republic of Ireland at senior level.

World Cup performance (leading countries only) number of games played, won, drawn and lost, goals scored and conceded, win rate (as a percentage of games played), and mean number of goals scored per game for all qualifiers and finals up to and including the 1998 tournament. Separate records for the qualifiers and the finals tournaments are given for the British and Irish home nations.

World Cup/European Championship winning/runners-up teams and scorers full teams given for any country that has reached the final of either the World Cup or the European Championship, with scorers indicated in parentheses, eg (1) = one goal; (2) = two goals.

13

League system   a brief description of the domestic league, including, where known, the number of clubs in the top divisions, number of points awarded for a win and draw, method of separating clubs level on points (such as goal difference or goals scored), and details of end-of-season playoffs and relegation/promotion criteria.

Record in international club tournaments   a summary of the achievements of a nation's leading clubs in continental and intercontinental club tournaments.

Other leading clubs: a list of the most successful domestic clubs, if these have not already been covered under *Record in international club tournaments*.

3. Information specific to English and Scottish league clubs

League record   a history of a club's league tenure. Note – up until the end of the 1991-92 season, the English Football League divisions are referred to as: Division One, Division Two, Division Three and, from 1958-59, Division Four. Between 1921-22 and 1957-58, the bottom division had a regional format: Division Three (North) and Division Three (South). Founder members of the Football League, prior to the establishment of Divisions One and Two in 1892-93, also have their league record included. Since the formation of the English Premier League in 1992-93, the classification is as follows: Premier League, First Division, Second Division and Third Division. In Scotland, the league format has changed on a number of occasions: the Scottish Football League ran for three seasons from 1890-91 and was re-established between 1915-16 and 1920-21. From 1946-47 to 1955-56 the two main divisions went under the title of A Division and B Division. The Premier Division was established in 1975-76, and thereafter the divisions are referred to as the First and Second, and, in 1994-95, with the creation of a new bottom tier, the Third Division. In 1998-99, the Scottish Premier League replaced the Premier Division.

Honours   a record of a club's major achievements at domestic and, where applicable, at European and World level.

Records   players who hold the club record for league goalscoring, appearances and international caps (the player's total caps are given in parentheses).

Team   full team line-up of FA Cup and major European tournament-winning sides, with scorers indicated in parentheses, eg (1) = one goal; (2) = two goals.

4. Information specific to players

Born   date of birth.

Club   chronological list of clubs played for at senior level.

Career ca.   approximate dates of career span.

Biographies also include the player's nationality (including adopted country, where appropriate), playing position, and number of international caps and goals.

LIST OF ABBREVIATIONS

a.e.t.   after extra time

AFC   Asian Football Confederation

agg.   aggregate score

CAF   Confédération Africaine de Football (African Football Confederation)

CONCACAF   Confederación Norte-Centroamericana y del Caribe de Fútbol (Caribbean, North and Central American Football Confederation)

CONMEBOL   Confederación Sudamericana de Fútbol (South American Football Confederation)

est.   estimated

FA   Football Association

FIFA   Fédération Internationale de Football Association

OFC   Oceania Football Confederation

pens.   penalties

St   Saint (as part of a proper noun)

UEFA   Union of European Football Associations

UK   United Kingdom

USA   United States of America

v   versus

A

Abahani Ltd *club* Bangladeshi national league club. Bangladesh national league champions 1974, 1977, 1981, 1983, 1984, 1985, 1990, 1992, 1993, 1994, 1995.

abandoned match *n.* match that is not completed. *Rules* A match which for reasons of inclement weather, public safety or public disorder, or for any other reason ruled by the **referee**, is not played for the normal duration (ie 90 minutes, unless extra time is being played). An abandoned match should normally be replayed, although individual **competition rules** may allow the result to stand (Law VII). *Regulations* If a **league** match does not last the full 90 minutes the **Premier League** Board, **Football League** Board or **Scottish Football League** Management Committee can decree that the result stands or that the match should be replayed (FA Premier League rules E.31 and 32, Football League regulation 30.2, Scottish Football League rules 27 and 84). This discretion can be useful if the match is abandoned owing to **crowd trouble**. In Scotland, if a match is abandoned and has to be replayed, then the **away club** receives its expenses, or about one-fifth of the **gate receipts** from the abandoned fixture (whichever is the lesser) (Scottish Football League rule 41). *History* The rule that an uncompleted match be replayed in full was set in 1899, after the English Football League had ordered **Sheffield Wednesday** and **Aston Villa** to replay the last 10 minutes of a game abandoned because of bad light on 26 November 1898. The 10 minutes were played on 13 March 1899 at Sheffield's Olive Grove ground, with 3,000 spectators (final score 4–1; Sheffield scoring its fourth goal in the replayed 10 minutes). *Keynotes* One of the first recorded incidents of a match being abandoned in Scotland occurred on 6 March 1875 when the **Scottish FA Cup** semi-final between **Dumbarton** and **Renton** was abandoned with 10 minutes of normal time remaining after the two **umpires** and the referee could not decide whether Renton had scored. The match was replayed and Renton won 1–0. On 12 December 1891, an English Football League Division One match between **Blackburn Rovers** and **Burnley** was eventually abandoned after the referee had sent off one player from each side for fighting. All of the Blackburn players, with the exception of goalkeeper Herbert Arthur, also left the field. Burnley immediately scored but Arthur claimed the player was offside, forcing the referee to abandon the match. On 20 April 1901, **Newcastle United**'s home Division One fixture against local rivals **Sunderland** at **St James' Park** was abandoned after fans invaded the pitch and, amid fighting, broke the goalposts. The match was replayed on 24 April and Sunderland won 2–0. This is the first recorded case of a Football League match being abandoned due to crowd trouble. The league governing body has discretion, however, to allow a score to stand: the score in an abandoned match between **Middlesbrough** and **Oldham Athletic**, at Ayresome Park, on Easter Monday 1915, was allowed to stand, with Middlesbrough leading 4–1. The game was stopped after 60 minutes when Oldham's Billy Cook was sent off but refused to leave the field of play. Cook was subsequently banned from football for one year (though, in fact, the league programme was suspended the following season because of **World War I**). Oldham was fined £350 and finished runners-up in Division One, a single point behind Everton. Denis **Law** scored six goals for **Manchester City** in a match that was subsequently abandoned (v Luton, 1961, at Kenilworth Road, FA Cup fourth round). A snowstorm forced the first leg of the 1973 **UEFA Cup** final between **Liverpool** and **Borussia Mönchengladbach** at **Anfield** to be abandoned after 27 minutes with the score goalless (May 1973). **Derby County**'s 1982-83 **Division Two** encounter with **Fulham** at the **Baseball Ground** was abandoned after 88 minutes, but the 1–0 scoreline in the home side's favour was allowed to stand. In April 1991, **AC Milan**'s players walked off the pitch complaining of bad light with three minutes remaining of a **European Cup** match with **Olympique de Marseille**. Milan was losing 0–1 at the time and facing elimination from the competition. The referee, Bo Karlsson, demanded that the Milan players return to the pitch, which they did, but **UEFA** subsequently banned the club from European competition the following season. The death of a **Genoa** supporter, Victor **Spagnulo**, following a clash between home supporters and AC Milan fans prior to a **Serie A** match between the clubs on 5 February 1995, forced the match to be abandoned at **half-time** (the police used water cannons to disperse the crowd). A number of Premier League matches during the 1997-98

16

season were abandoned due to floodlight failure, including Derby County's opening League fixture at its new **Pride Park** stadium (v **Wimbledon**, 13 August 1997), leading to an FA and later police inquiry (tampering in connection with a Far-Eastern gambling ring had been suspected). An **African Nations Cup** qualifier between **Libya** and **Algeria** in Tripoli on 2 August 1998 was abandoned after 75 minutes when the Libyan players protested against a second Algerian goal.

Abbey Stadium   *ground*   English football ground situated in Cambridge; home of **Cambridge United**. *Dossier* Ground capacity: 9,617. Record attendance: 14,000 v **Chelsea** (1 May 1970, friendly). Best average attendance: 7,078 (1991-92). Pitch dimensions: 100.5m x 68m. *History* Cambridge played its first match at the Abbey Stadium as Abbey United on 31 August 1932 (v Cambridge University Press, friendly). *Keynotes* The Abbey Stadium's record crowd recorded against Chelsea was the first occasion in which a record attendance was achieved for a friendly match. This match was also the first at the Abbey Stadium to be played under floodlights.

Abdullah, Majed   *player*   Striker. **Saudi Arabia** international (140 caps, 1978-94). *Keynotes* The World's all-time second-most capped player, after Thomas **Ravelli** of Sweden. Abdullah was originally credited with 157 caps, but these were not all in official top-grade internationals. He made his debut against **South Korea** in 1978 (friendly). Scored for Saudi Arabia in the 1988 Asian Cup of Nations final (2–0, v **China**). *Honours* **Asian Cup of Nations** (Saudi Arabia, 1984, 1988). Nicknamed 'the Desert Pelé'.

Abega Théophile   *player*   Striker. **Cameroon** international player. *Clubs* Lion Yaoundé, **Canon Yaoundé**. *Keynotes* Scored in the 1984 African Cup of Nations final (3–1, v Nigeria). *Honours* **African Cup of Nations** (Cameroon, 1984). *France Football*'s African Footballer of the Year 1984.

Abercorn   *club*   former Scottish league. *Dossier* Ground: Ralston Park, Paisley, Strathclyde. *Keynotes* Founder members of the Scottish League in 1890-91, finishing seventh in that inaugural season – the club's highest League position. After winning the Division Two title in 1895-96, Abercorn could muster only three points from 18 Division One fixtures the following season, scoring 21 goals and conceding 88. This is the lowest number of points ever recorded over a season by a UK club. Abercorn was a Scottish FA Cup semi-finalist on three occasions: 1888 (1–10 replay v **Cambuslang**), 1890 (0–2 v **Queen's Park**), 1891 (1–3 v **Dumbarton**). *League record* Division One 1896-97; Scottish League 1890-91 to 1892-93; Division Two 1893-94 to 1895-96, 1897-98 to 1914-15.

Aberdare Athletic   *club*   former English league. *Dossier* Ground: Athletic Ground, Aberdare, Mid Glamorgan. Record League attendance: 16,350 v **Bristol City** (2 April 1923, Division Three (South)). *Keynotes* Elected to Division Three (South) in 1921-22. Failed re-election in 1926-27 and was replaced by **Torquay United**. Aberdare's highest League position was eighth in Division Three (South), which the club achieved in 1921-22. *League record* Division Three (South) 1921-22 to 1926-27.

Aberdeen   *club*   Scottish league. *Dossier* Ground: **Pittodrie**, Aberdeen, Grampian, capacity: 21,634 all-seated. Strip: red shirts with white trim, red shorts, red socks with white trim. Nickname: Dons. Record attendance: 45,061 v **Heart of Midlothian** (13 March 1954, **Scottish FA Cup**, fourth round). Biggest win: 13–0 v Peterhead (9 February 1923, Scottish FA Cup). Biggest defeat: 0–8 **Celtic** (30 January 1965, Division One). *History* Founded in 1903 from an amalgamation of three clubs: Victoria United, Orion and Aberdeen. The latter, a teachers' club, was formed in 1881 and had settled at Pittodrie in 1899. The new club joined Division Two of the **Scottish Football League** from the Northeast Alliance League in 1904. The club finished seventh in its first season but, nevertheless, won election to the expanded Division One. *Keynotes* Aberdeen is one of three Scottish clubs never to have been relegated (others being Celtic and **Rangers**), although it dropped out of the League for two seasons during **World War I** (1917-18, 1918-1919). The club won its first major trophy, the Scottish FA Cup, in 1947 (2–1 v **Hibernian**), having been a finalist in 1937 (1–2 v Celtic). Aberdeen won the League Championship in 1954-55 and the following season the **Scottish League Cup** (2–1 v **St Mirren**). During the 1950s, Aberdeen also reached three Scottish FA Cup finals (1953, 0–1 replay v Rangers; 1954, 1–2 v Celtic; 1959, 1–3 v St Mirren). Aberdeen's most successful period was in the 1980s, when under the managership of Alex **Ferguson**, the club broke the Celtic-Rangers duopoly of Scottish football, winning the Scottish title on three occasions (1979-80, 1983-84, 1984-85) and achieving three consecutive Scottish FA Cup victories (1982, 4–1 a.e.t. v Rangers; 1983, 1–0 a.e.t. v Rangers; 1984, 2–1 a.e.t. v Celtic) – the three-in-a-row feat is matched only by **Queen's Park** (1876, 1882) and Rangers (1936, 1950, 1964). The club's 1983 Scottish FA Cup triumph meant it became the first club apart from Celtic or Rangers to retain the Scottish FA Cup in the 20th century. Also in 1983, Aberdeen won the **European Cup-winners Cup** (2–1 a.e.t. v **Real Madrid**). The following season, the club was successful in the **European Super Cup** (2–0 agg., v **Hamburg (SV)**) and it reached the semi-final of the Cup-winners Cup (0–2 agg., v **Porto**). In 1985-86, Aberdeen lifted the Scottish League Cup (3–0 v Hibernian). Since Ferguson left in 1986, Aberdeen has found it difficult to mount a serious challenge for the title. In 1990, it won a seventh Scottish FA Cup (0–0, 9–8 pens. v Celtic) and a fourth Scottish League Cup (2–1 v Rangers). A further League Cup was added in 1995-96 (2–0 v **Dundee**). Aberdeen only narrowly retained its Premier Division status in 1994-95, winning the end-of-season **playoff** against second-placed First Division finishers, **Dunfermline Athletic** (6–2 agg.). The club's Pittodrie ground became the UK's first **all-**

seater football stadium in 1978 when the final terracing, the south side, was seated. *League record* Premier League 1998-99; Premier Division 1975-76 to 1997-98; Division One (A Division) 1905-06 to 1914-15; 1921-22 to 1938-39, 1946-47 to 1974-75; Scottish League 1915-16 to 1916-17, 1919-20 to 1920-21 (did not compete between 1917-19); Division Two 1904-05. *Honours* Division One 1954-55; **Drybrough Cup** 1971 (2–1 Celtic), 1980 (2–1 St Mirren); European Cup-winners Cup 1983 (2–1 a.e.t. v Real Madrid) *Team* Leighton, Rougvie, McLeish, Miller, McMaster, Cooper, Strachan, Simpson, McGhee, Black (1), Hewitt (1), Weir; European Super Cup 1984 (2–0 agg., v Hamburg (SV)); Premier Division 1979-80, 1983-84, 1984-85; Scottish FA Cup 1947 (2–1 v Hibernian), 1970 (3–1 v Celtic), 1982 (4–1 a.e.t. v Rangers), 1983 (1–0 a.e.t. v Rangers), 1984 (2–1 a.e.t. v Celtic), 1986 (3–0 v Heart of Midlothian), 1990 (0–0, 9–8 pens. v Celtic); Scottish League Cup 1955-56 (2–1 v St Mirren), 1976-77 (2–1 v Celtic), 1985-86 (3–0 v Hibernian), 1989-90 (2–1 v Rangers), 1995-96 (2–0 v Dundee). *Records* Alex McLeish is Aberdeen's most capped player (77 for **Scotland**); Willie Miller holds the record for club appearances (556, 1973-90); Joe Harper is Aberdeen's record goalscorer (199, 1969-72, 1976-81).

Aberystwyth Town *club* Welsh league. *Dossier* Ground: Park Avenue, Aberystwyth, Dyfed, capacity: 2,500. Strip: green and black shirts, black shorts. Nickname: Seasiders. Formed in 1884. *Honours* **Welsh Cup** 1900 (3–0 v Druids).

Abide with me *misc.* hymn written by Henry Francis Lyte (1793-1847) and William Henry Monk (1823-1889) that was introduced at the **FA Cup** final at Wembley in 1927, following a suggestion from FA secretary Frederick Wall. Since then, only one final (1959) has taken place without the traditional cup final hymn.

AC Milan *club* Italian league. *Dossier* Ground: **San Siro**, Milan, Lombardy, capacity: 85,847 all seated. Strip: red and black striped shirts, white shorts. Website: *www.acmilan.it/* Nickname: Rossoneri. Biggest win: 9–0 v Palermo (1950-51, **Serie A**). Biggest defeat: 1–6 v Alessandria (1935-36, Serie A), v **Juventus** (1996-97, Serie A). *History* Formed in 1899 as the Milan Cricket and Football Club by Englishman Alfred Edwards. In 1905, the club changed its name to **Milan Football Club** and, in 1938, it adopted the Italian name Associazione Calcio Milan. Tyre magnate Piero Pirelli, a founder club member, bankrolled the construction of San Siro in 1926. After **World War II**, Milan bought three Swedish players, Gunnar **Gren**, Gunnar **Nordahl** and Nils **Liedholm**, collectively referred to as the Gre-no-li, and between 1948 and 1966 the club finished outside the top three in Serie A on only one occasion. Milan appeared in the 1958 **European Cup** final (2–3 a.e.t. v **Real Madrid**), winning the trophy for the first time in 1963. The club won the **European Cup-winners Cup** in 1968 and the following season it again lifted the European Cup. A second Cup-winners Cup success was recorded in 1973, but the club failed to retain the trophy the next year despite reaching the final (0–2 v **Magdeburg IFC**). Milan was relegated to **Serie B** in 1979-80 after the club was found guilty of fixing a 2–1 victory over **Lazio**. The then club president Felice Columbo and goalkeeper Ricky Albertosi were banned for life. Controversy occurred in 1991-92, when **UEFA** imposed a one-season ban from European competition on the club after its players refused to return to the pitch following floodlight failure during a match against **Olympique de Marseille** in a 1991 European Cup quarter-final. Between 1989 and 1995, Milan appeared in five European Cup finals, winning the trophy on three occasions. The club's 1993 defeat by Olympique de Marseille (0–1) was subsequently overturned following **match fixing** allegations against the French champions. Milan also lost in 1995 (0–1 v **Ajax**). Since Milan's Serie A title victory in 1995-96, the club has struggled to maintain consistency despite a glittering array of talent, missing lucrative European competition in 1998-99 after losing in the 1998 Italian Cup (2–3 agg., v Lazio). Aside from the Gre-no-li, a number of other foreign imports have starred for Milan over the years, including José Altafini, Juan **Schiaffino**, Karl-Heinz Schnellinger, Marco **Van Basten**, Ruud **Gullit**, Frank Rijkaard, Marcel **Desailly**, Zvonimir Boban, Jean-Pierre **Papin**, George **Weah** and Dejan **Savicevic**. Famous Italian players to wear the red and black of Milan include: Gianni **Rivera**, Cesare **Maldini** and his son Paolo, Giovanni **Trappatoni**, Franco **Baresi** and Roberto **Baggio**. *Honours* European Cup 1963 (2–1 v **Benfica**), 1969 (4–1 v **Ajax**), 1989 (4–0 v **Steaua Bucharest**), 1990 (1–0 v Benfica), 1994 (4–0 v **Barcelona**); European Cup-winners Cup 1968 (2–0 v **Hamburg SV**), 1973 (1–0 v **Leeds United**); **European Super Cup** 1989 (2–1 agg., v **Barcelona**), 1990 (3–1 agg., v **Sampdoria**), 1994 (2–0 agg., v **Arsenal**); Italian Cup 1967 (1–0 v Padova), 1972 (2–0 v **Napoli**), 1973 (1–1, 5–2 pens. v Juventus), 1977 (2–0 v **Internazionale**); Italian League 1901 (1–0 v **Genoa**), 1906 (playoff league), 1907 (playoff league); 1950-51, 1954-55, 1956-57, 1958-59, 1961-62, 1967-68, 1978-79, 1987-88, 1991-92, 1992-93, 1993-94, 1995-96, 1998-99; **World Club Cup** 1969 (4–2 agg., v Club **Estudiantes** La Plata), 1989 (1–0 a.e.t. v Club Deportivo **Atlético Nacional** Medellin), 1990 (3–0 v Club **Olimpia**).

AC Sodigraf (Athletic Club) *club* Congo Democratic Republic (formerly Zaire) national league club based in Kinshasa, founded 1989. Ground: 24 Septembre, capacity: 25,000. Strip: red shirts, blue shorts. **African Cup-winners Cup** runners-up 1996 (0–4 agg., v **Al Mokaouloon**, Egypt); Congo DR Cup 1995.

AC Sotema Morovoay (Athletic Club Sotema Morovoay) *club* Madagascar national league club, based in Mahajunga. Ground: Alexandre Rabemananjara, capacity: 3,000. Strip: orange shirts and black shorts. **African Cup of Champion Clubs**, second round 1992; Madagascar Cup 1978, 1979 and 1982; Madagascar League champions 1985, 1989, 1991 and 1992.

academies (football) *n.* place to develop and coach young players from the age of eight to 21. Brainchild of the **Football Association**'s technical director Howard Wilkinson to replace the national centre of excellence at **Lilleshall**. There are 34 academies throughout England, with each **Premier League** club, 10 First Division clubs and **Fulham**, **Millwall** and **Peterborough** operating one. Young players aged eight to 13 must live within one hour's travelling distance of the academy and older players within 90 minutes. Participants are split into four age groups with each academy allowed a minimum of eight and maximum of 16 in each grouping. Eight to 12 year-olds will spend three hours twice a week at the academies; 12 to 15 year-olds will attend three hours three times a week; and 15 to 16 year-olds three sessions five times a week. Older players will be full-time on club scholarships.

accident insurance *n.* accident insurance scheme operated by the **Professional Footballers' Association** under which players registered with the **Football League** and the **Premier League** are covered for retirement insurance in the event of serious injury. Members may also be eligible for a **testimonial** game and a lump sum payment worth at least six months' value of their contract. The PFA pays a subsidy to the Premier League and the Football League to make sure every player has private medical insurance and immediate access to medical treatment. Members registered with non-league clubs who are forced to retire through permanent disablement as a result of injury are covered by an insurance scheme administered by the PFA, from the Accident Fund.

Accrington *club* former English league. *Dossier* Ground: Accrington Cricket Ground, Accrington, Lancashire. Record League attendance: 9,000. *Keynotes* Founder members of the **Football League**. Folded in 1895-96 after resigning from the League in 1892-93. It was the first club to resign from the Football League (1893) due to lack of funds and was replaced by **Middlesbrough Ironopolis**. Accrington's highest League position was sixth in the Football League, which the club achieved in 1889-90. *League record* Football League 1888-89 to 1891-92; Division One 1892-93.

Accrington Stanley *club* former English league. *Dossier* Ground: Peel Park, Accrington, Lancashire. Record League attendance: 15,425 v **York City** (11 April 1955, Division Three (North)). *Keynotes* Formed as Stanley Villa around 1895, the club was a founder member of Division Three (North) in 1921-22. Stanley reached the Division Three (North) Cup final in 1938-39 (0–3 v **Bradford City**) and in 1945-46, the club won one of the wartime competitions, the League Three North (West section). Prior to the League being suspended in September 1939 due to the war, Stanley topped Division Three (North). On 13 October 1955, the BBC televised the Division Three (North) v Division Three (South) match at Peel Park, which was staged to commemorate the installation of **floodlights**. Stanley resigned from the Football League in 1961-62 because of financial

problems, after completing 33 Division Four fixtures (won five, drew eight, lost 20, scored 19, conceded 60) – results declared void. The final League match at Peel Park took place on 24 February 1962 (v **Rochdale**). The club folded in 1965-66 before reforming with the same name in 1968. Stanley play in the Northern League. Accrington Stanley's highest Football League position was second in Division Three (North), which the club achieved in 1957-58 – thus securing a place the following season in the newly established Division Three. *League record* Division Three 1958-59 to 1959-60; Division Three (North) 1921-22 to 1957-58; Division Four 1960-61).

Achilles tendon *medical* very strong and thick **tendon** at the back of the ankle, joining the gastrocnemius (calf muscle) and the heel bone (talus). It can be injured by a blow (such as a kick in a mistimed tackle causing a **contusion** or **haematoma**), overstretching or **overuse injury**. Minor injuries can be treated with RICE. Injuries can occur without contact when a player suddenly sprints or jumps, putting excessive load on the tendon as the player pushes down with the toes. A ruptured or partially ruptured Achilles tendon results in severely limited ability to bend the foot downwards at the ankle **joint** and can be very painful. An injured player should be taken to hospital for treatment.

Acre *state* one of the 27 state leagues in **Brazil**, founded 1947. Leading clubs: Rio Branco, Juventus (Rio Branco), Independiencia (Rio Branco), Vasco da Gama (Acre – not to be confused with **Vasco da Gama**, Rio de Janeiro).

action replay *n.* television replay of a match incident, especially a goal or goalscoring opportunity. Also slow-motion action replay in which the action appears much slower than usual.

Adams Park *ground* English football ground situated in High Wycombe, Buckinghamshire; home of **Wycombe Wanderers**. *Dossier* Ground capacity: 10,000. Record attendance: 9,002 v **West Ham United** (7 January 1995, **FA Cup**, third round). Pitch dimensions: 105m x 68.5m. *History* One of three **Football League** grounds to be named after an individual (the others being **Dean Court** and **Ninian Park**), Adams Park gets its title from Frank Adams who gave Wycombe its previous home, Loakes Park, in 1947. Wycombe played its first match at Adams Park on 9 August 1990 (v **Nottingham Forest**, friendly). *Keynotes* Adams Park was built at the cost of £3.5 million and the site was the 14th identified by the club as a potential future home since it first decided in the early 1970s to move from Loakes Park. The local council rejected all planning applications submitted by Wycombe over that period, and the club was only able to continue with the Adams Park project after an appeal.

Adams, Tony *player* Defender. **England** international (57 caps, 4 goals). Born 10 October 1966. Career ca. 1983–. *Clubs* **Arsenal**. *Keynotes* Joined Arsenal as an apprentice, turning professional in January 1984 having made his debut on 5 November 1983. Adams has remained a pivotal figure in the Arsenal defence ever since. In 1990, Adams was jailed for nine months for drink-driving and he later admitted to being an alcoholic. He made his England debut against **Spain** on 18 February 1987. Adams's book, *Addicted*, chronicling his personal problems as well as his football career, was the number one non-fiction bestseller in September 1998. Included in the **Football League Centenary 100 players**. *Honours* **FA Cup** (Arsenal 1993, 1998); **European Cup-winners Cup** (Arsenal 1994); **League Cup** (Arsenal 1987, 1993); League Championship (Arsenal 1988-89, 1990-91, 1997-98).

added time *rules* time added to the **duration of play**, at the discretion of the **referee**, in either period for all time lost due to **injuries** to **players** and their transport from the **field of play**, **time-wasting**, **substitutions** and other causes (Law VII). The amount of added time may be indicated at the end of each half by an electronic display board held by the fourth official; it does not, however, override the decision of a referee on how much time is actually added. Also called **injury time**.

Adelaide City *club* Australian national league club, based in Adelaide, formerly known as Adelaide City Juventus. *Dossier* Ground: Hindmarsh Stadium. Strip: black and white striped shirts, black shorts. *Honours* **Australian Cup** 1979, 1989, 1992; Australian league champions 1986, 1992, 1994. *Records* Adelaide's Damian Mori scored what may be the fastest goal in the world – or, at least, the fastest to be recorded on video – after four seconds (v **Sydney United**, 6 December 1995, Australian National League).

Admarc Tigers *club* Malawi Super League club, based in Blantyre (the largest city). Ground: Kanjizu, capacity: 35,000. Strip: red shirts and white shorts. Blantyne and District regional champions once; Chibuku Cup winners: once; **East and Central African Club Championship** runners-up 1983; Kamuzu Cup twice; Malawi National Super League champions 1989.

Admira-Wacker (VÄB Admira Wacker Mödling, formerly SC Niederösterreich Admira Wacker) *club* Austrian national league club, based in Vienna, founded in 1971 by the merger of two clubs: Admira Wien (founded 1905) and Wacker Wien (1908). Ground: Bundesstadion Südstadt, capacity: 12,000. Strip: black shirts, black shorts. Austrian Cup 1928, 1932, 1934, 1964, 1966 (Admira) and 1947 (Wacker); Austrian League Champions 1927, 1928, 1932, 1934, 1936, 1937, 1939, 1966 (Admira) and 1947 (Wacker); **Mitropa Cup** runners-up 1934.

admission price *n.* cost of admission to ground. *Regulations* **Premier League**, **Football League** and **Scottish Football League** clubs are not allowed to charge away club fans more than home fans for seats of comparable quality (FA Premier League rule I.20, Football League regulation 31.2, Scottish Football League rule 80). *Keynotes* In 1890, the Football League established a minimum entrance fee for league matches, of 6d. It was, however, permissible to lower the price for women and for boys under 14 years old.

ADO Den Haag *club* Netherlands national league club, based in The Hague, founded in 1905 (merged with Holland Sport in 1971, known as FC Den Haag from 1971 until ca. 1995). Ground: Zuiderparkstadion, capacity: 9,000. Strip: yellow shirts and green shorts. Dutch Cup 1968, 1975; Dutch league champions 1942, 1943.

advantage *rules* decision by the referee during a game of football to allow play to continue after a **foul** has been committed if, in his or her opinion, an advantage would be gained by the offending team should play be stopped to award a **free kick** or **penalty kick** (Law V). Referees can punish the original offence if the advantage does not materialise at the time. Even if the advantage is played, the original offending player or players can subsequently receive a **caution** or be **sent off**. **2.** *vb.* **apply the advantage**.

advertising *misc.* promotion/publicity of products using footballers and football imagery. Manufacturers of football strips not only have their logos on club shirts, shorts and socks, but often have their name or logo prominently displayed around the club's ground (such as the name *Umbro* spelled out in different coloured seating at **Manchester United's Stretford End** and **Chelsea's Shed** (south) Stand, and the *Reebok* symbol illustrated in a similar fashion at **Liverpool's** Anfield Road stand – see **seat lettering**); or the stadium/stand is named after the company (for example, **Bolton Wanderers' Reebok Stadium** and **Port Vale's** *Mizuno* Stand). The major sportswear companies also have their products endorsed by leading players. Footballers have frequently been used to advertise products other than football-related goods. **Liverpool** left-half and **England** international Tom Bromilow was one of the first players to endorse a non-football product. In the 1920s, he extolled the virtues of the tonic *Phosferine*. **Arsenal** winger Denis **Compton** advertised *Brylcreem* in the 1930s and 40s. Sixty years later **Manchester United** and England midfielder David Beckham endorses the same product, while Fulham and England captain Johnny **Haynes** had a £1,500 contract to endorse *Brylcreem* in the 1950s. Players/managers who have advertised non-football products include: Alan **Ball** – *Bisto*; George **Best** – eggs; Brian **Clough**, Jack Charlton, Glenn **Hoddle**, Paul **Gascoigne**, Gary **Lineker** – *Shredded Wheat*; Tommy **Docherty** (with Steve Coppell and Gordon Hill)– *Gillette* razors; 1998 England **World Cup** squad/Andy **Gray** – *Snickers*; Les Ferdinand – *Horlicks*; Ryan **Giggs** – *Konica* films and *Quorn* burgers; David Ginola – *L'Oreal* and *Renault*; Ruud **Gullit**, Stuart Pearce, Gareth Southgate, Chris Waddle – *Pizza Hut*; Ruud Gullit – *M&Ms*; Pat **Jennings** – *Solvite* ; Kevin **Keegan** – *Brut*; Kevin Keegan, Peter **Schmeichel** – *Danish* bacon, *Sugar Puffs*; Gary Lineker, Michael **Owen**, **Romario** – *Walkers Crisps*; Stanley **Matthews** – *Craven A* cigarettes; Jason McAteer – *Wash 'n' go*; Ally **McCoist** – *Vauxhall*; Alan **Shearer** – *Lucozade*, *McDonald's*;

Graham **Taylor** – *Vauxhall*; Kenny Dalglish Graham Taylor, Terry **Venables** – *BT*, *Yellow Pages*, Ray Wilkins – *Tango*; Ian Wright – *One 2 One*, *Thomas Cook*; Gianfranco **Zola** – *Tesco* pizza. (See also **shirt sponsorship**.)

AEK Athens *club* Greek national league club based in Athens, founded 1924. Ground: Nikos Goumas, capacity: 33,500. Strip: black shirts, black shorts. Greek Cup 1932, 1939, 1949, 1950, 1956, 1966, 1978, 1983, 1996, 1997; Greek league champions 1939, 1940, 1963, 1968, 1971, 1978, 1979, 1989, 1992, 1993,1994; **European Cup-winners Cup** quarter-final 1997; **UEFA Cup** semi-final 1977.

AEL Limassol *club* Cypriot national league club based in Limassol, founded 1930. Ground: Tsirion, capacity: 22,000. Strip: yellow shirts, yellow shorts. Cyprus Cup 1939, 1940, 1948, 1985, 1987, 1989; Cyprus league champions 1941, 1953, 1955, 1956, 1968.

aerial power *n.* team that has a number of players with renowned ability to **head** the ball.

Aerosport *club* Djibouti national league club based in the capital Djibouti. Djibouti Cup 1991; Djibouti league champions 1991.

a.e.t *abbrev.* **after extra time**. The abbreviation is often used in lists of results given in newspapers and other match reports.

AFC *abbrev.* **Asian Football Confederation**.

AFC Leopards *club* Kenyan national league club based in Nairobi, formed 1964 (formerly known as Abaluhya United and Abaluhya FC until 1981). Ground: City Ground, capacity: 18,000. Strip: blue shirts, white shorts. **African Cup of Champion Clubs** semi final 1968; **African Cup-winners Cup** semi-final 1985; **CAF Cup** quarter-final 1994, 1997; **East and Central African Club Championship** 1979 (as Abaluhya SC) 1982, 1983, 1984, 1997, runners-up 1974, 1980, 1985; Kenyan Cup 1967, 1985, 1991, 1994; Kenyan League champions 1966, 1967, 1970, 1973, 1980, 1981, 1982, 1986, 1988, 1989, 1992.

Afghanistan *country AFC* Islamic state in Southwest Asia, north and west of Pakistan, landlocked and mostly mountainous. Area: 652,225 sq km (251,773 sq miles). Extreme climatic variation: from 40°C in summer in lowlands, to -26°C in winter in mountainous areas. Population: 20,500,000 (1994 est.). Languages: Pashto, Farsi, Tadzhik and Dari. Capital: Kabul. Recent development hindered by war: invaded by Russian troops December 1979, withdrew by February 1989. *Dossier* Football association (the Football Federation of the National Olympic Committee, Kabul), founded in 1933 and affiliated to **FIFA** in 1948, founder member of the **Asian Football Confederation** in 1954; president Abuddin Osmani Zainul, general secretary Sultan Mohamad Najand. Season played from September to January. National stadium: Kabul, capacity: 25,000. National strip: white shirts with red lines, white shorts with red lines. *International tournament record* **Olympic Games** – played in the 1948 tournament in

London (0–6, v Luxembourg in the preliminary round). **World Cup** – never entered; **Asian Cup of Nations** – entered only three times, 1976, 1980 and 1984 (withdrew in 1956), last in each of its qualifying groups; **Asian Games** – semi-final/bronze medal of the first tournament in 1951 (0–3, v **India**, in New Delhi, semi-final). *Record against British and Irish national teams:* none played. *History* Afghanistan was a founder member of the AFC in 1954. After the Asian Games in 1954, however, the country did not play in any international tournaments until 1976. Afghanistan has not played a competitive international fixture since 1990; the 1984 Asian Cup was its last tournament. *League system* There are only around 30 registered clubs. *Record in international club tournaments* Afghani clubs have not entered international club tournaments.

Africa Sports Nationale *club* Ivory Coast national league club based in the capital Abidjan, founded 1936. Ground: Felix Houphouët-Boigny (the national stadium), capacity: 45,000. Strip: red shirts, green shorts. **African Cup of Champion Clubs** runners-up 1986 (2–2 agg., 2–4 pens., v **Zamalek**, Egypt); **African Cup-winners Cup** 1992 (5–1 agg., v **Vital'O**, Burundi), runners-up 1980 (1–4 agg., v **Toute Puissant Mazembe**, Congo Democratic Republic) and 1993 (1–2 agg., v **Al Ahly**, Egypt), semi-final 1998; **African Super Cup** 1992 (2–2, 5–3 pens., v **WAC Casablanca**, in Abidjan); French West African Cup 1958; Ivory Coast Cup 1961, 1964, 1977, 1978, 1979, 1981, 1982, 1985, 1986, 1989, 1991, 1998; Ivory Coast League champions 1967, 1968, 1971, 1977, 1978, 1982, 1983, 1985, 1986, 1987, 1988, 1989, 1996; Ivory Coast Super Cup (Coupe Houphouët-Boigny) 1979, 1981, 1982, 1986, 1987, 1988, 1989, 1991, 1993; **West African Football Union General Eyadema Cup** 1985, 1986 and 1991, runners-up 1995. Notable former player: Laurent **Pokou**.

African Cup of Champion Clubs *competition* (Sekou Toure Trophy) annual tournament for champion clubs of the member countries of the **Confédération Africaine de Football** (CAF). All matches in the preliminary, first and second rounds are played over two legs, the result decided on **aggregate score** and, if necessary, on **away goals** or **penalties**. Since 1997, the quarter-final stage has been played in two groups of four clubs, played as two mini-leagues with each club playing the other three in its group at home and away; three points are awarded for a win, and one for a draw; **goal difference** is used to separate clubs level on points. The group winners qualify for a two-leg final. The Cup winners gain automatic entry into the next year's tournament. *History* The tournament was first played in 1964, with 14 clubs participating. Four clubs qualified for a three-day finals tournament played in Accra, Ghana, the final won by **Oryx Douala**, from Cameroon. **Asante Kotoko** refused to take part in a replay in 1967, giving the Cup to TP Englebert after both games finished in draws. Thereafter, the final was decided on an home-and-away basis. The 1971 tournament was decided by a replay, after both **Canon Yaoundé** and Asante Kotoko had won a match (aggregate scores were not used in that edition), the Cup going to Canon Yaoundé. The 1976 final, won by **Mouloudia Chalia d'Algiers**, was the first to be settled on penalties. The biggest victory in the competition is 9–0 (**Kabwe Warriors** (Zambia) v Majanta Meseru (Lesotho), 1972, first round). *Winners, results and runners-up* 1964 Oryx Douala (Cameroon), 2–1, v **Stade Malien** (Mali) in Accra, Ghana; 1965 no tournament; 1966 **Stade Abidjan** (Ivory Coast), 5–4 agg., v **Real Bamako** (Mali); 1967 **Toute Puissant Mazembe** (known as TP Englebert, Congo Democratioc Republic), 3–3 agg., v **Asante Kotoko** (Ghana; Asante refused to take part in a playoff); 1968 Toute Puissant Mazembe (as TP Englebert) 6–4 agg., v **Etoile Filante** (Togo); 1969 **Ismailia Sporting Club** (Egypt), 5–3 agg., v Toute Puissant Mazembe (as TP Englebert); 1970 Asante Kotoko, 3–2 agg., v Toute Puissant Mazembe (as TP Englebert); 1971 **Canon Yaoundé** (Cameroon), 0–3, 2–0, 1–0 replay (aggregate scores not applied) v Asante Kotoko; 1972 **Hafia FC** (Guinea), 7–4 agg., v **Simba FC** (Uganda); 1973 **Vita Club Kinshasa** (Congo Democratic Republic), 5–4 agg., v Asante Kotoko; 1974 **CARA Brazzaville** (Congo), 6–3 agg., v **Mehalla Al Kubra** (Egypt); 1975 Hafia FC , 3–1 agg., v **Enugu Rangers** (Nigeria); 1976 **Mouloudia Chalia d'Algiers** (Algeria) 3–3 agg., 4–1 pens., v Hafia FC ; 1977 Hafia FC , 4–2 agg., v **Hearts of Oak** (Ghana); 1978 Canon Yaoundé, 2–0 agg., v Hafia FC; 1979 **Union Douala** (Cameroon), 1–1 agg., 5–3 pens., v Hearts of Oak; 1980 Canon Yaoundé, 5–2 agg., v **Amicale Sportive Bilima** (Congo Democratic Republic); 1981 **JE Tizi-Ouzou** (Algeria), 5–0 agg., v Vita Club Kinshasa; 1982 **Al Ahly** (Egypt), 4–1 agg., v Asante Kotoko; 1983 Asante Kotoko, 1–0 agg., v Al Ahly; 1984 **Zamalek** (Egypt), 2–0 agg., v **IICC Shooting Stars** (Nigeria); 1985 **FAR Rabat** (Morocco), 6–3 agg., v Amicale Sportive Bilima; 1986 Zamalek, 2–2 agg., 4–2 pens., v **Africa Sports** (Ivory Coast); 1987 Al Ahly, 2–0 agg., v **El Hilal** (Sudan); 1988 **Entente Setif** (Algeria), 4–1 agg., v **Iwuanyanwu Nationale** (Nigeria); 1989 **Raja Casablanca** (Morocco), 1–1 agg., 4–2 pens., v **Mouloudia Club d'Oran** (Algeria); 1990 **J S Kabylie** (Algeria), 1–1 agg., 5–3 pens., v **Nkana** (formerly Nkana Red Devils, Zambia); 1991 **Club Africain** (Tunisia), 6–2 agg., v **Nakivubo Villa** (Uganda); 1992 **WAC Casablanca** (Morocco); 2–0 agg., v El Hilal; 1993 Zamalek, 0–0 agg., 7–6 pens., v Asante Kotoko; 1994 **Espérance Tunis** (Tunisia), 3–1 agg., v Zamalek; 1995 **Orlando Pirates** (South Africa), 3–2 agg., v **ASEC Mimosas Abidjan** (Ivory Coast); 1996 Zamalek, 3–3 agg., 5–4 pens., v IICC Shooting Stars; 1997 **Raja Casablanca**, 1–1 agg., 5–4 pens., v **Obuasi Goldfields** (Ghana); 1998 ASEC Mimosas Abidjan, 4–2 agg., v **Dynamos Harare** (Zimbabwe).

African Cup of Nations *competition* biennial international nations tournament for member countries of the **Confédération Africaine de Football** (CAF, the African football federation), first played 1957. Qualification for the finals tournament takes place through seven regional groups of six or seven nations (though these have sometimes been diminished by withdrawals), played on a league basis, with each nation playing each other at home and away. The winners and runners-up from each group qualify for the finals tournament, along with the reigning champions and host nation. Sixteen nations compete in the finals tournament at a host country. The first round consists of four groups of four nations, played on a league basis. The winners and runners-up in each group qualify for the knockout quarter-finals, followed by semi-finals, third/fourth playoff and final. *History:* The first African Cup of Nations took place in Khartoum, **Sudan**, in 1957, with only three nations in the tournament: **Egypt**, **Ethiopia** and Sudan – a fourth nation, **South Africa**, withdrew before the tournament. Egypt beat Ethiopia in the first final (4–0). The same three entered in 1959; four nations took part in 1962; with six in 1963 (the first occasion that two first-round groups were played). A qualifying tournament was introduced in 1968 (six groups of three nations), with the finals tournament expanded to eight nations. The eight nations were divided into two first-round groups of four nations, before a knockout second phase. Although the number of nations entering the qualifying stages continued to increase, the format for the finals remained the same until 1992, when it was increased to 12 nations, playing in four groups of three at the first-round stage. Sixteen clubs qualified for the finals tournament in 1996, with four first-round groups of four nations before the knockout second stage. The first trophy, the Abdel Aziz Abdalla Salem Trophy, was donated to **Ghana** in 1978 after the country had won the competition for the third time. The current African Cup of Unity was presented the following year by the Supreme Council of Sport in Africa. The 1974 final was settled after a replay (**Congo Democratic Republic** eventually beating **Zambia**). The 1982 final was the first to be settled on penalties (Ghana beating **Libya** 7–6 on penalties after a 1–1 draw), while the 1992 final in **Senegal** went to a record 11–10 **penalty shoot-out** win for **Ivory Coast**, after a 0–0 draw with Ghana. Egypt and Ghana are the two most successful nations in the competition, with four championships each, by 1998. Egypt has appeared at more finals tournaments than any other country (16). Of 21 editions of the African Cup of Nations, the host country has won nine times. Ivory Coast won the 1992 edition without conceding a goal in the finals tournament. Laurent **Pokou** of the Ivory Coast is the tournament's all-time top scorer, with 14 goals in finals tournaments (1968, 1970), Rashidi **Yekini** is second with 13 (1988, 1990, 1992, 1994). The top scorer at a single tournament is Mulamba **Ndaye**, with nine for Zaire (now Congo Democratic Republic) at the 1974 finals in Cairo, including all four of his country's goals in the two-part final (a replay was required, and he scored two in both games). The fastest goal is thought to be 23 seconds, by Ayman Mansour for Egypt against **Gabon** (4–0, 28 March 1994, at the Zoulten Stadium, Tunis, first-round group). Record attendance: 100,000, International Stadium, Cairo, 21 March 1986 (Egypt v Cameroon, 0–0, 5–4 pens., final). *Winners, results, runners-up and venues* 1957 Egypt, 4–0, v Ethiopia, at the Khartoum Stadium, Khartoum, Sudan; 1959 Egypt, league of three nations, runners-up Sudan, at the Al Ahli Stadium, Cairo, Egypt; 1962 Ethiopia, 4–2, v Egypt, at the Haile Selassie Stadium, Addis Ababa, Ethiopia; 1963 Ghana, 3–0, v Sudan, at the Accra Stadium, Accra, Ghana; 1965 Ghana, 3–2, v **Tunisia**, at the Zouiten Stadium, Tunis, Tunisia; 1968 Congo Democratic Republic (as Congo Kinshasa), 1–0, v Ghana, at the Haile Selassie Stadium, Addis Ababa, Ethiopia; 1970 Sudan, 1–0, v Ghana, at the Municipal Stadium, Khartoum, Sudan; 1972 **Congo**, 3–2, v **Mali**, at the Omnisports Stadium, Yaoundé, **Cameroon**; 1974 Congo Democratic Republic (as Zaire), 2–2, 2–0 replay, v **Zambia**, at the International Stadium, Cairo, Egypt; 1976 **Morocco**, final-round league of four nations, runners-up Guinea, at the Addis Ababa Stadium, Ethiopia; 1978 Ghana, 2–0, v **Uganda**, at the Accra Stadium, Accra, Ghana; 1980 **Nigeria**, 3–0, v **Algeria**, at the Surulere Stadium, Lagos, Nigeria; 1982 Ghana, 1–1, 7–6 pens., v Libya, at the 11 June Stadium, Tripoli, Libya; 1984 Cameroon, 3–1, v Nigeria, at the Houphouët Boigny Stadium, Abidjan, Ivory Coast; 1986 Egypt, 0–0, 5–4 pens., v Cameroon, at the International Stadium, Cairo, Egypt; 1988 Cameroon, 1–0, v Nigeria, at the Mohammed V Stadium, Casablanca, Morocco; 1990 Algeria, 1–0, v Nigeria, at the Stade Olympique, Algiers, Algeria; 1992 Ivory Coast, 0–0, 11–10 pens., v Ghana, at the Stade de l'Amitié, Dakar, Senegal; 1994 Nigeria 2–1, v Zambia, at the Stade Olympique, El Menzah, Tunis, Tunisia; 1996 South Africa 2–0, v Tunisia, Soccer City, Johannesburg, South Africa; 1998 2–0, v South Africa, at the Stade du 4 Aout, Ouagadougou, **Burkina Faso**); 2000 tournament in Ghana and Nighera. *Top scorers* 1957 Ad El Diba (5, Egypt); 1959 Mohamed El Gohari (3, Egypt); 1962 Abdelfattah Badawi (3, Egypt) and Worku Menguistou (3, Ethiopia); 1963 Ahmed El Chazli (6, Egypt); 1965 Ben Acheampong and Abbrey Kofi (3 each, both Ghana) and Eustace Mangle (3, Ivory Coast); 1968 Laurent Pokou (6, Ivory Coast); 1970 Laurent Pokou (8, Ivory Coast); 1972 Salif Keita (5, Mali); 1974 Mulamba Ndaye (9, Congo Democratic Republic); 1976 William Njo'Lea (4, Guinea); 1978 Philip Omondi (4, Uganda); 1980 Khaled Labied (3, Morocco) and Segun Odegbemi (3, Nigeria); 1982 George Al Hassan (4, Ghana); 1984 Taleh Abou Zeid (4, Egypt); 1986 Roger **Milla** (4, Cameroon) and Abdoulaye **Traoré** (4, Ivory Coast); 1988 Lakhdar **Belloumi** (2, Algeria), Gamal Abdel Hamid (2, Egypt), Roger Milla (2, Cameroon) and Abdoulaye Traoré (2, Ivory Coast); 1990 Djamal Menad (4, Algeria); 1992 Rashidi Yekini (4, Nigeria); Rashidi Yekini (5, Nigeria);1996 Kalusha **Bwalya** (5, Zambia); 1998 Benedict McCarthy (7, South Africa) and Hossam Hassan (7, Egypt).

African Cup-winners Cup (Nelson Mandela Trophy) *competition* annual club tournament for national cup winners of the member countries of the **Confédération Africaine de Football** (CAF). The qualification berth goes to the national cup runners-up if the Cup winners have already qualified for the **African Cup of Champion Clubs**. All matches, including the final, are played over two legs, the result decided on **aggregate score** and, if necessary, on **away goals** or **penalties**. The Cup winners gain automatic entry into the next year's tournament. *History* The tournament was first played in 1975. **Al Ahly** is the most successful club in the competition, with four titles. The biggest victory is 12–1, by **Mwanza Pamba SC**, Tanzania (v Anse Boileau, Seychelles, 1990, preliminary round). *Winners, results and runners-up* 1975 **Tonnerres Yaoundé** (Cameroon), 5–1 agg., v **Stella Abidjan** (Ivory Coast); 1976 **IICC Shooting Stars** (Nigeria), 4–2 agg., v Tonnerre Yaoundé; 1977 **Ehugu Rangers** (Nigeria), 5–2 agg., v **Canon Yaoundé** (Cameroon); 1978 **Horoya AC** (Guinea), 5–2 agg., v **Milaha Athletic Hussein-Dey** (Algeria); 1979 Canon Yaoundé, 8–0 agg., v **Gor Mahia** (Kenya); 1980 **Toute Puissant Mazembe** (Congo Democratic Republic), 4–1 agg., v **Africa Sports** (Ivory Coast); 1981 **Union Douala** (Cameroon), 2–0 agg., v **Stationery Stores** (Nigeria); 1982 **Al Mokaouloon** (as Arab Contractors, Egypt), 4–0 agg., v **Power Dynamos** (Zambia); 1983 Al Mokaouloon, 1–0 agg., v **Agaza Lomé** (Togo); 1984 Al Ahly (Egypt), 1–1 agg., 4–2 pens., v Canon Yaoundé; 1985 Al Ahly, 2–1 agg., v **Leventis United** (Nigeria); 1986, Al Ahly, 3–2 agg., v **AS Sogara** (Gabon); 1987 Gor Mahia, 2–0 agg., v **Espérance Tunis** (Tunisia); 1988 **CA Bizerte** (Tunisia), 1–0 agg., v **Ranchers Bees** (Nigeria); 1989 **El Merreikh Sports Club** (Sudan), 1–0 agg., v **Bendel United** (Nigeria); 1990 **BCC Lions** (Nigeria), 4–1 agg., v **Club Africain** (Tunisia); 1991 Power Dynamos, 5–4 agg., v BCC Lions; 1992 Africa Sports, 5–1 agg., v **Vital'O** (Burundi); 1993 Al Ahly, 2–1 agg., v Africa Sports; 1994 **Daring Club Motema Pembe** (Congo Democratic Republic), 5–2 agg., v **Kenya Breweries** (Kenya); 1995 **JS Kabylie** (Algeria), 3–2 agg., v **Julius Berger** (Nigeria); 1996 Al Mokaouloon, 4–0 agg., v **AC Sodigraf** (Congo Democratic Republic); 1997 **ES Sahel** (Tunisia), 2–1, agg., v **FAR Rabat** (Morocco); 1998 **Espérance Tunis** (Tunisia), 4–2 agg., v **Primeiro de Agosto** (Angola).

African Footballer of the Year *award* annual award to the African national voted best player of the year by the **Confédération Africaine de Football** (CAF). The CAF award began in 1991; the list below includes the unofficial award made by the magazine *France Football* for the years 1970-90. *Winners and nationality* (*France Football*) 1970 Salif Keita (Mali); 1971 Ibrahim **Sunday** (Ghana); 1972 Chérif Souleymane (Guinea); 1973 Tshimimu **Bwanga** (Zaire); 1974 Paul **Moukila** (Congo); 1975 Ahmed **Faras** (Morocco); 1976 Roger **Milla** (Cameroon); 1977 Tarak

Dhiab (Tunisia); 1978 Abdul **Razak** (Ghana); 1979 Thomas **N'kono** (Cameroon); 1980 Jean **Manga-Onguene** (Cameroon); 1981 Lakhdar **Belloumi** (Algeria); 1982 Thomas N'kono (Cameroon); 1983 Mahmmoud **Al-Khatib** (Egypt); 1984 Téophile **Abega** (Cameroon); 1985 Mohammed **Timoumi** (Morocco); 1986 Badou **Zaki** (Morocco); 1987 Rabah **Madjer** (Algeria); 1988 Kalusha **Bwalya** (Zambia); 1989 George **Weah** (Liberia); 1990 Roger Milla (Cameroon); (CAF Award) 1991 Abedi Ayew **Pelé** (Ghana); 1992 Abedi Ayew Pelé (Ghana); 1993 Rashidi **Yekini** (Nigeria); 1994 Emmanuel Amunike (Nigeria); 1995 George Weah (Liberia); 1996 Nwankwo Kanu (Nigeria); 1997 Victor **Ikpeba Nosa** (Nigeria); 1998 Mustapha **Hadji** (Morocco).

African Games   competition see **All-Africa Games**.

African Super Cup (Felix Houphouët-Boigny Trophy) competition international African club tournament contested by the winners of the **African Cup of Champion Clubs** and the **African Cup-winners Cup**. Winners 1992 **Africa Sports** (Ivory Coast); 1993 **Zamalek SC** (Egypt); 1994 **Espérance Tunis** (Tunisia); 1995 **Orlando Pirates**; 1996 Zamalek SC; 1997 **Etoile du Sahel** (Tunisia); 1998-99 **ASEC Mimosas Abidjan** (Ivory Coast).

African Under-17 Championship competition biennial African nations tournament for players under-20 years of age, first played 1995. Serves as a qualifying tournament for the **Under-17 Championship**. Played in qualifying groups, with a finals tournament at a host nation. Winners, results, runners-up and venues 1995 **Ghana**, 3–1, v **Nigeria**, in Mali; 1997 **Egypt**, 1–0, v **Mali**, in Botswana.

African Women's Tournament competition international nations tournament for women, under the auspices of the **Confédération Africaine de Football** (CAF), first played 1998. Serves as a qualifier for the **Women's World Cup** (winners and runners-up qualify). Winners, results and venue 1998 **Nigeria**, 2–0, v **Ghana** in Lagos, Nigeria.

African Youth Cup competition biennial African nations tournament for players under 20 years of age, first played 1979. Serves as a qualifying tournament for the **World Youth Cup**. Also called the Junior African Nations Cup. Since 1991 it has been played in qualifying groups, with a finals tournament at a host nation. Winners, results, runners-up and venues 1979 **Algeria**, 4–4 agg., away goals, v **Guinea**; 1981 **Egypt**, 3–1 agg., v **Cameroon**; 1983 **Nigeria**, 4–3 agg., v **Ivory Coast**; 1985 Nigeria, 3–2 agg., v **Tunisia**; 1987 Nigeria, 4–1 agg., v **Mali**; 1989 Nigeria, 4–1 agg., v Mali; 1991 Egypt, 2–1, v Ivory Coast, in Egypt; 1993 **Ghana**, 2–0, v Cameroon, in Mauritius; 1995 Cameroon, 4–0, v **Burundi**, in Nigeria; 1997 **Morocco**, 1–0, v **South Africa**, in Morocco.

Afro-Asian Club Cup competition annual intercontinental club championship contested by the winners of the **African Cup of Champion Clubs** and the winners of the **Asian Champion Teams' Cup**, first played

1987. Winners 1986 **Daewoo Royals** (South Korea); 1987 **SC Zamalek** (Egypt); 1988 **Al Ahly** (Egypt); 1989 **Entente Setif** (Algeria); 1990 and 1991 not played; 1992 **Club Africain** (Tunisia); 1993 **WAC Casablanca** (Morocco); 1994 **Thai Farmers Bank** (Thailand); 1995 **Espérance Tunis** (Tunisia); 1996 **Ilhwa Chunma** (South Korea); 1997 SC Zamalek; 1998-99 **RAJA CA Casablanca**.

Afro-Asian Nations Cup competition biennial international nations tournament contested by the winners of the **African Cup of Nations** (held every two years) and either the **Asian Cup of Nations** or the **Asian Games** (whichever is the most recent, because both Asian tournaments are held every four years). It has been played as a single match (1993) or, more commonly, over two legs. The 1997 edition, between South African and Saudi Arabia was cancelled by the **Confédération Africaine de Football** (CAF). Winners (and results) 1985 **Cameroon** (5–3 agg., v **Saudi Arabia**); 1987 **South Korea** (1–1, 4–3 pens., v **Egypt**); 1991 **Algeria** (2–2 agg., **away goals**, v **Iran**); 1993 **Japan** (1–0, v **Ivory Coast**, in Tokyo); 1995 **Nigeria** (5–2 agg., v **Uzbekistan**); 1997 cancelled.

after 90 minutes   misc.   used in match reports and lists of results to indicate the final score after the normal **duration of play** but before any **extra time** has begun.

after extra time   misc.   used in match reports and lists of results to indicate the final score after an official period of **extra time** had been played. Abbrev. **a.e.t.**

afters   informal   a minor incident of aggression between two or more players retaliating after an incident such as a foul.

Agaza Lomé (full name: Omnisports Agaza Lomé) club   Togo national league club based in the capital Lomé. Ground: Stade Général Etienne Eyadema (the national stadium), capacity: 20,000. Strip: green shirts, yellow shorts. **African Cup-winners Cup** runners-up 1983 (0–1 agg., v **Al Mokaouloum**, Egypt), semi-final 1994; **CAF Cup** quarter-final 1995; Togo Cup 1979, 1981, 1988, 1989, 1993; Togo league champions 1980, 1984.

agent   regulations   person whose business is the representation and negotiation on behalf of a player, manager, club, or club official. Agents negotiate in **transfers**, and in contract negotiations of players and managers, but can only act for one party in any negotiation. Agents must hold either a "domestic licence" (in England this is granted by the **Football Association**, in conjunction with the boards of the **Premier League** and **Football League**) or "FIFA licence" (granted by **FIFA**), or be a barrister, solicitor or a close relative of the individual being represented. In 1997, there were 286 FIFA-approved licensed agents, operating in 35 countries. Each agent is required to post a £100,000 bond with FIFA before the world football governing body allows them to act as an agent. Agents must not have a significant financial interest (greater than 10%) in, or be an official of a club. It is illegal for individuals to appoint, or for clubs to negotiate with, an agent who does not fulfil one of the above criteria (FA Premier League rule 0.3, Football League regulation 43). In England and Wales, agents issued with a domestic licence are required to post a guarantee of £30,000 in favour of the Football Association (1997-98 figure). *Keynotes* In 1992, Rachel Anderson became the first FIFA-registered woman football agent, representing **West Ham United**'s Julian Dicks, among others. The banning of Anderson from the 1998 annual **Professional Footballers Association** dinner, because of her gender, led to British Sports Minister Tony Banks declining an invitation to attend.

ÅGF Åarhus (Åarhus Gimnastic Förening) *club* Danish national league club based in Åarhus, founded 1880. Ground: Åarhus, capacity: 19,500. Strip: white shirts, blue shorts. Danish Cup 1955, 1957, 1960, 1961, 1965, 1987, 1988, 1992, 1996; Danish league champions 1955, 1956, 1957, 1960, 1966; **European Cup** quarter-final 1961; **European Cup-winners Cup** quarter-final 1989.

aggregate score *competition rules* final or total score in a **two-leg** match. *Record* **Chelsea**'s 21–0 aggregate victory over Jeunesse Hautcharage (8–0 away and 13–0) in the first round of the 1971-72 **European Cup-winners Cup** competition is the record combined score in any European club tournament.

Aigle N'Kongsamba *club* Cameroon national league club based in N'Kongsamba. Ground: Omnisports, capacity: 6,000. Strip: blue shirts, red shorts. Cameroon league champions 1971, 1994.

AIK Bishkek (Allmänna Idrottsklubben) *club* Kyrgyzstan national league club based in the capital Bishkek, founded 1995. Ground: Spartak, capacity: 25,000 (the national stadium). Kyrgyzstan league champions 1995, runners-up 1996; Kyrgyzstan Cup 1996.

AIK Stockholm *club* Swedish national league club based in Solna, Stockholm, founded 1891. Ground: Råsunda Stadion (the national stadium), capacity: 36,000 all seated. Strip: yellow and black shirts, white shorts. *Keynotes* AIK won the 1998 Swedish league championship having scored only 25 goals in its 26 matches, fewer than any other club in the Swedish premier league. Swedish Cup 1949, 1950, 1976, 1985, 1996, 1997, 1999; Swedish league champions 1900, 1901, 1911, 1914, 1916, 1923, 1932, 1937, 1992, 1998.

air disaster *n.* aeroplane crash or accident involving football clubs/teams. see **Munich air crash**, **Superga air crash**, **Zambia**.

air travel *misc.* travelling to and from matches by aeroplane/helicopter. Although most British clubs travel to league games by road, air travel is frequently used for long distances and for international competitions. *Keynotes* The first player known to have flown to an English **Football League** game was Vivian **Gibbons**, a part-time **Bristol Rovers** player who flew from Romford to Bristol airport to play in a mid-week match

on 7 September 1932 (**Bristol Rovers** v **Southend United**). Plymouth Argyle denied permission by the Football League to fly to an away match in 1932 because the League's insurance did not cover air travel. It was not until 1957 that the Football League allowed clubs to fly their players to away matches: **Chelsea** flew to and from **Newcastle United** for a game on 9 April 1957 (Good Friday). Blackburn Rovers flew back from a match at Arsenal on the same day. Both Chelsea and Blackburn Rovers were scheduled to play home fixtures on the Saturday. Eight **Manchester United** players, and several club officials and journalists died in the **Munich air crash**, 6 February 1958. The entire team and staff of Peru club Alianza were killed in a plane crash in December 1987 after a game in Pucallpa. Eighteen members of Zambia's national team were killed in a plane crash in April 1993. See also **Superga Air crash**. Several players, notably **Arsenal**'s Dennis **Bergkamp**, have a phobia about air travel. Bergkamp refuses to travel by air and, in 1998-99, was absent from several of Arsenal's **Champions League** fixtures.

Airdrieonians *club* Scottish league. *Dossier* Ground: **Broadwood Stadium**, Airdrie, Strathclyde, capacity: 6,300 all seated. Strip: white shirt with red diamond, red shorts, red socks with white and black trim. Nickname: Diamonds or Waysiders. Record attendance: 24,000 v **Heart of Midlothian** (Broomfield Park, 8 March 1952, **Scottish FA Cup**). Biggest win: 15–1 v Dundee Wanderers (1 December 1894, Division Two). Biggest defeat: 1–11 v **Hibernian** (24 October 1959, Division One). *History* Founded in 1878. Between 1892 and 7 May 1994, Airdrie played at Broomfield Park. It was there, on 6 March 1891, that the first **penalty kick** was awarded – only three days after the ruling was adopted. However, it was awarded by mistake because the rule did not become law until the following season. Since the start of the 1994-95 season, Airdrie has shared **Clyde**'s Broadwood Stadium. Airdrie joined Division Two of the Scottish League, winning the title in 1902-03. During the 1920s, the club finished Division One runners-up in four consecutive seasons (1922-23 to 1925-26) and, in 1924, it won the Scottish FA Cup for the only time (2–0 v Hibernian). The club had to wait 51 years for a second appearance in the final (1975, 1–3 v **Celtic**). Airdrie was also a losing finalist in both 1992 (1–2 v **Rangers**) and 1995 (0–1 v Celtic). In 1994-95, the club were vicictorious in the **Scottish League Challenge Cup** (3–2 v **Dundee**). Airdrie narrowly failed to gain promotion to the Premier Division in 1996-97, losing the end-of-season **playoff** against second from bottom top-flight finishers, Hibernian (2–5 agg.). *League record* Premier Division 1980-81 to 1981-82, 1991-92 to 1992-93; First Division 1975-76 to 1979-80, 1982-83 to 1990-91, 1993-94–; Division One (A Division) 1903-04 to 1914-15, 1921-22 to 1935-36, 1947-48, 1950-51 to 1953-54, 1955-56 to 1964-65, 1966-67 to 1972-73, 1974-75; Scottish League 1915-16 to 1920-21; Division Two (B Division) 1894-95 to 1902-03, 1936-37 to 1938-39, 1946-47,

1948-49 to 1949-50, 1954-55, 1965-66, 1973-74. *Honours* Division Two 1902-03, 1954-55, 1973-74; Scottish FA Cup 1924 (2–0 v Hibernian); Scottish League Challenge Cup 1994-95 (3–2 v Dundee). *Records* Jimmy Crapnell is Airdrie's most capped player (9 for **Scotland**); Paul Jonquin holds the record for club appearances (523, 1962-79).

Ajax *club* Netherlands national league club. *Dossier* Based in Amsterdam, and founded in 1900. Ground: **Amsterdam ArenA**, capacity: 52,500 all seated. Strip: white shirts with a wide red stripe and white shorts. *Keynotes* Ajax is one of only four clubs to have won all three major European titles (along with **Juventus**, **Bayern Munich** and **Barcelona**). The club won the **European Cup** three years running in the early 1970s: Johan **Cruyff**, Gerry **Muhren** and Johan **Neeskens** playing in all three finals. Ajax has won 11 international club trophies (including the **World Club Cup** and **European Super Cup**); just two behind the European record holders **AC Milan**. Much of the club's success in the 1970s, and transformation into one of the world's leaders, is attributed to coach Rinus **Michels**, appointed in 1965, who pioneered the **total football** playing system. Michels was replaced in 1971 by Stefan Kovacs. Cruyff took over as coach in 1982-83, and led the club to a **European Cup-winners Cup** title in 1987. Cruyff signed the then 17-year-old Marco **van Basten**, who made his league debut in 1982-83, scoring in his first game. Van Basten scored 128 goals in 133 games in five years at the club. Van Basten and Cruyff both left the club after the Cup-winners Cup victory in 1987. In 1995, under club coach Louis Van Gaal, Ajax again won the European Cup (now the Champions League), with Patrick **Kluivert** scoring the only goal in the 85th minute. Ajax holds the record for the biggest victory in a **UEFA Cup** match (14–0, v **Red Boys**, Luxembourg, 1984-85, first round: the first leg finished 0–0). A new purpose-built stadium, the Amsterdam ArenA, was opened in 1996, replacing the De Meer stadium, built in the 1930s. In 1998, Ajax became the first club to float on the Amersterdam stock exchange. *Honours* Dutch Cup 1917, 1943, 1961, 1967, 1970, 1971, 1972, 1979, 1983, 1986, 1987, 1993, 1998, 1999; Dutch league champions 1918, 1919, 1931, 1932, 1934, 1937, 1939, 1947, 1957, 1960, 1966, 1967, 1968, 1970, 1972, 1973, 1977, 1979, 1980, 1982, 1983, 1985, 1990, 1994, 1995, 1996, 1998; European Cup 1971 (2–0, v **Panathinaikos**, at **Wembley Stadium**, London), 1972 (2–0, v **Internazionale**, at Feyenoord Stadium, Rotterdam), 1973 (1–0, v **Juventus,** in Belgrade), and 1995 (1–0, v **Milan**, in Vienna), runners-up 1969 (1–4, v Milan, in Madrid), 1996 (1–1, 2–4 pens., v Juventus, in Rome), semi-final 1980, 1997; European Cup-winners Cup – 1987 (1–0, v **Lokomotiv Leipzig**, in Athens), runners-up 1988 (0–1, v **KV Mechelen**, in Strasbourg); UEFA Cup/Fairs Cup – 1992 (2–2 agg., won on away goals, v **Torino**); European Super Cup – 1972 (6–3 agg., v **Rangers**), 1973 (6–1 agg., v Milan), 1995 (5–1 agg., v

Real **Zaragoza**); World Club Cup – 1972 (4–1 agg., v **Independiente**), 1995 (0–0, 4–3 pens., v **Gremio**, in Tokyo). Notable former players: Dennis **Bergkamp**, Frank and Ronald **de Boer**, Arie Haan, Ruud **Krol**, Johan **Neeskens**, Johnny **Rep**, Frank Rijkaard, Aaron Winter.

Ajax Cape Town *club* *see* **Cape Town Spurs**.

Akedemisk Boldklub København (AB København) *club* Danish national league club based in the capital Copenhagen, founded 1889. Ground: Gladsaxe Idraetspark, capacity: 10,000. Strip: green shirts, white shorts. Danish Cup 1999; Danish league champions 1919, 1921, 1937, 1943, 1945, 1947, 1951, 1952, 1967.

Akonangui FC *club* Equatorial Guinea national league club. Cup 1979, 1996; League champions 1992.

A-League *n.* United States professional football league, founded 1990 after merger of the **American Soccer League** (sense **3.**) and the Western Soccer League, originally named the American Professional Soccer League (current name adopted 1994). Officially the United States' second division (underneath the **Major League Soccer** – though there are no promotions from the A-League) after 1997 merger with the **Select League** – the former top division in the **United Systems of Independent Soccer Leagues** (USISL). The USISL administers the new A-League. Past winners: Fort Lauderdale Strikers (1990), San Francisco Bay Blackhawks (1991), Colorado Foxes (1992, 1993), Montreal Impact (1994), Seattle Sounders (1995, 1996).

Al Ahly *club* Qatar national league club. Qatar (Emir's) Cup 1973, 1981, 1987, 1991, 1992.

Al Ahly *club* Saudi Arabian national league club based in Jeddah. **Asian Champion Teams Cup** – runners-up 1985 (1–3 v **Daewoo Royals**, Korea, Jeddah, Saudi Arabia); Saudi Arabian league champions 1978, 1984; Saudi Arabian Cup 1963, 1966, 1970, 1971, 1972, 1973, 1974, 1978, 1979, 1983. Notable former player: **Tarak Dhiab**.

Al Ahly National Sporting Club *club* Egyptian national league club based in the capital Cairo, founded 1907 (Egypt's oldest major club). Ground: Mokhtar el Tetch (named after a famous Egyptian player of the 1920s), capacity: 20,000. Strip: red shirts, red shorts. *Keynotes* Al Ahly is the most successful club in the **African Cup-winners Cup**, with four titles, and has won a record six premier African club competitions (ie excluding **African Super Cup** and **Afro-Asian Club Cup**; compare record held by **Zamalek**). Before joining the inaugural national league in 1948, it played in the regional Cairo league. Al Ahly holds the national record of nine consecutive league titles (1949-51, 1953-54, 1956-59), though the run was punctuated by years when the league was not played. By 1999 it had won 29 domestic league titles – an African club record – and a record 30 domestic cups (only **Linfield FC, Northern Ireland** have won more national cups). *Honours* **African Cup of Champion Clubs** 1982 (4–1 agg., v **Asante Kotoko** Ghana), 1987 (2–0 agg., v **El Hilal** Sudan), runners-up 1983 (0–1 agg., v Asante Kotoko);

African Cup-winners Cup 1984 (1–1 agg., 4–2 pens., v **Canon Yaoundé** Cameroon), 1985 (2–1 agg., v **Leventis United** Nigeria), 1986 (3–2 agg., v **AS Sogara** Gabon), 1993 (2–1 agg., v **Africa Sports** Ivory Coast); Afro-Asian Club Cup 1987; **Arab Club Champions Cup** 1996, runners-up 1997); **Arab Cup-winners Cup** 1994; **Arab Super Cup** 1997, 1998; Cairo league champions 1939, 1942, 1943, 1948, 1950; Egyptian Cup 1924, 1925, 1927, 1928, 1930, 1931, 1937, 1940, 1942, 1943 (shared), 1945, 1946, 1947, 1949, 1950, 1951, 1953, 1956, 1958 (shared), 1961, 1966, 1978, 1981, 1983, 1984, 1985, 1991, 1992, 1993, 1996; Egyptian league champions 1949, 1950, 1951, 1953, 1954, 1956, 1957, 1958, 1959, 1961, 1962, 1975, 1976, 1977, 1979, 1980, 1981, 1982, 1985, 1986, 1987, 1989, 1990, 1994, 1995, 1996, 1997, 1998, 1999.

Al Ahly Benghazi *club* Libyan national league club, based in Benghazi. Ground: 28 March Stadium, capacity: 30,000. Strip: red shirts and red shorts. Libyan Cup 1980 and 1991; Libyan league champions 1970, 1972, 1975, 1992.

Al Ahly Tripoli (also known as Al Ahly National) *club* Libyan national league club, based in Tripoli. Ground: 7 October Stadium, capacity: 25,000. Strip: green shirts and white shorts. **African Cup of Champion Clubs** quarter-final 1972; African Cup-winners Cup: semi-final 1984; Libyan Cup 1975, 1976, 1983, 1985, 1988; Libyan league champions 1964, 1971, 1973, 1974, 1978, 1980, 1982, 1984, 1986, 1993, 1994. The club was disbanded in 1996 following crowd trouble, in which at least 20 people were shot dead, during a match against rivals **Al Ittihad** (see **Libya** – History).

Al-Ain *club* United Arab Emirates national league club. **Asian Champion Teams Cup** third place 1999; United Arab Emirates league champions 1977, 1981, 1984, 1993, 1998; UAE Super League champions 1995. Notable player: Abedi **Pelé**.

Al Ansar *club* Lebanese national league club. *Keynotes* Al Ansar won 10 consecutive domestic league titles, (1988, 1990-98; the league was not completed in 1989) – only **Al Faisaly** of **Jordan** has a better record. **Asian Champion Teams' Cup** quarter-final 1998; Lebanese Cup 1988, 1990, 1991, 1992, 1994, 1995, 1996; Lebanese league champions 1988, 1990, 1991, 1992, 1993, 1994, 1995, 1996, 1997, 1998.

Al Arabi *club* Kuwaiti national league club. **Asian Cup-winners Cup** quarter-finals 1992; Kuwaiti Cup 1962, 1963, 1964, 1966, 1969, 1971, 1981, 1983, 1992, 1996; Kuwaiti league champions 1962, 1963, 1964, 1966, 1967, 1970, 1980, 1982, 1983, 1984, 1985, 1988, 1989, 1993.

Al Arabi *club* Qatar national league club. **Asian Champion Teams Cup** – runners-up 1994 (0–1, v **Thai Farmers Bank**, in Bangkok, Thailand); **Asian Cup-winners Cup** – semi-final 1993; Qatar (Emir's) Cup 1978, 1979, 1980, 1983, 1984, 1989, 1990, 1993; Qatar league champions 1983, 1985, 1991, 1993, 1994, 1996, 1997.

Al Arabi *club* United Arab Emirates national league club. **Arab Club Champions Cup** runners-up 1993 (v **Al Shabab**, Saudi Arabia).

Al Faisaly *club* Jordanian national league club. *Keynotes* Al Faisaly holds the world record of 13 consecutive domestic league titles (1959-66, 1970-74; the run interrupted by years in which the league was not played). Its 23 titles is short of the Asian record (held by **Muharraq** Bahrain). **Arab Cup-winners Cup** runners-up 1996 (v Olympic Khourigba Morocco); Jordan Cup 1981, 1982, 1984, 1988, 1990, 1993, 1994, 1995; Jordan league champions 1944, 1945, 1959, 1960, 1961, 1962, 1963, 1964, 1965, 1966, 1970, 1971, 1972, 1973, 1974, 1976, 1977, 1983, 1985, 1986, 1990, 1992, 1993. Intense rivalry exists between Al Faisaly – an essentially ethnic Jordanian side – and **Wihdat FC** (Al Wahadat), the Palestinian club.

Al Fanja *club* Omani national league club. **Asian Champion Teams Cup** finals tournament 1989 (third in group of three, no points, Kuala Lumpur, Malaysia – winners of first-round group of four clubs); **Asian Cup-winners Cup** quarter-final 1992.

Al Foutoua *club* Syrian national league club based in Dayr az Zawr (Deir Ez-Zor). *Keynotes* Al Foutoua holds the Asian record of four consecutive domestic cup triumphs (1988 to 1991). Syrian league champions 1990, 1991, 1992; Syrian Cup 1988, 1989, 1990, 1991.

Al Hilal *club* Saudi Arabian national league club based in the capital Riyadh. **Arab Club Champions Cup** 1995 (v **Espérance Tunis**), runners-up 1992 (v **WAC Casablanca**, Morocco); **Asian Champion Teams Cup** – 1991 (1–1, 4–3 pens., v **Esteghlal Sports Club**, Iran, Doha, Qatar), runners-up 1986 (second in final group of four, final tournament in Riyadh), 1987 (withdrew from final after winning semi-final group in tournament in Riyadh – the cup was won by Yomiuri, **Japan**), semi-final/third 1998 (4–1 v **Piroozi**, Iran, in Hong Kong); **Asian Cup-winners Cup** – 1997 (3–1, v **Nagoya Grampus Eight** of Japan, in Riyadh, Saudi Arabia), semi-final 1990 (0–1 agg., v Piroozi); **Asian Super Cup** 1997 (2–1 agg., v **Pohang Steelers**, South Korea); Gulf Cup for Clubs 1998; Saudi Arabian Cup 1989; Saudi Arabian league champions 1977, 1979, 1985, 1986, 1988, 1990, 1996, 1998. Notable players: Saeed al-**Owairan**, Sami al-Jabir.

Al Ittifaq *club* Saudi Arabian national league club based in Dammam. **Arab Club Champions Cup** 1988; **Asian Champion Teams Cup** semi-final 1988; Saudi Arabian Cup 1969, 1985, 1987; Saudi Arabian league champions 1983, 1987.

Al Ittihad *club* Libyan national league club, based in Tripoli. Ground: 7 October Stadium, capacity: 25,000. Strip: blue shirts and red shorts. **African Cup of Champion Clubs** quarter-final 1967; Libyan Cup 1986; Libyan league champions 1965, 1969, 1988, 1989, 1990 and 1991. The club was disbanded in 1996 following crowd trouble, in which at least 20 people were shot dead, during a match against rivals **Al Ahly Tripoli** (see **Libya** – History).

Al Ittihad *club* Qatar national league club. **Asian Cup-winners Cup** quarter-final 1997; Qatar league champions 1992, 1998; Qatar (Emir's) Cup 1995, 1996, 1997.

Al Ittihad *club* Saudi Arabian national league club based in Jeddah. **Asian Cup-winners Cup** 1999 (3–2 v Chunnam Dragons, of South Korea, Toyko); third 1994 (1–1, 3–0 pens., v **TOT Thailand** of Thailand, Sharjah, United Arab Emirates, third/fourth playoff, 22 January 1995), semi-final 1992; Saudi Arabian Cup 1959, 1960, 1964, 1968, 1988, 1991; Saudi Arabian league champions 1982, 1997, 1999.

Al Ittihad *club* Syrian national league club based in Aleppo (Halab). **Asian Champion Teams Cup** fourth 1985 (0–1 v **Tiga Berlian** of Indonesia, Jiddah, Saudi Arabia, third/fourth playoff); Syrian Cup 1966, 1973, 1982, 1984, 1985, 1994; Syrian league champions 1967, 1968, 1977, 1993, 1995.

Al Jaish *club* Syrian national league club based in Damascus. **Arab Cup-winners Cup** runners-up 1998; Syrian Cup 1986, 1997, 1998; Syrian league champions 1973, 1976, 1979, 1985, 1986.

Al Kazma *club* Kuwaiti national league club. **Arab Club Champions Cup** runners-up 1988; **Asian Champion Teams Cup** finals tournament 1987 (third in group of four in Kuala Lumpur, Malaysia) and 1988 (third in group of four in tournament in Guangzhou, China); **Asian Cup-winners Cup** semi-final 1995, quarter-final 1991; Kuwaiti Cup 1982, 1984, 1990, 1997; Kuwaiti League champions 1986, 1987, 1994, 1996.

Al Khatib, Mahmoud *player* **Egypt** international. *Club* **Al Ahly**. *Honours* **African Cup of Champion Clubs** (Al Ahly, 1982, 1987); **African Cup of Nations** (Egypt, 1986); **African Cup-winners Cup** (Al Ahly, 1984, 1985, 1986); *France Football*'s African Footballer of the Year 1983.

Al Kuwait *club* Kuwaiti national league club. **Arab Cup-winners Cup** runners-up 1989; Kuwaiti Cup 1976, 1977, 1978, 1980, 1985, 1987, 1988; Kuwaiti league champions 1965, 1968, 1972, 1974, 1977, 1979.

Al Mokaouloum (also known as Arab Contractors) *club* Egyptian national league club based in the capital Cairo, founded 1962. Ground: Mokaouloum Stadium, capacity: 50,000. Strip: yellow shirts, black shorts. **African Cup-winners Cup** 1982 (4–0 agg., v **Power Dynamos**, Zambia), 1983 (1–0 agg. v **Agaza Lome**, Togo), 1996 (4–0 v **AC Sodigraf**, Congo Democratic Republic), quarter-final 1997; Egyptian Cup 1990, 1995; Egyptian league champions 1983.

Al Nasr *club* Libyan national league club, based in Benghazi. Ground: 28 March stadium, capacity: 30,000. Strip: green shirts and white shorts. **African Cup-winners Cup** semi-final 1985 (its opponents, and eventual winners, **Al Ahly Cairo**, Egypt, were given a **walkover** in the tie); Libyan Cup 1978, 1982 and 1984, 1998; Libyan league champions 1987.

Al Nasr *club* Omani national league club, based in Salala. **Asian Cup-winners Cup** quarter-final 1997; Omani league champions 1998.

Al Nasr *club* Saudi Arabian national league club based in the capital Riyadh. **Asian Champion Teams Cup** runners-up 1996 (0–1, v **Ilhwa Chumna**, South Korea), quarter-final 1997; **Asian Cup-winners Cup** – 1997-98 (1-0, v **Samsung**, South Korea, in Riyadh), runners-up 1991 (1–6 agg., v Nissan, Japan); Gulf Cup for Clubs 1997; Saudi Arabian Cup 1976, 1977, 1981, 1986, 1990; Saudi Arabian league champions 1976, 1980, 1981, 1989, 1994, 1995.

Al-Nasr *club* United Arab Emirates national league club. United Arab Emirates Cup 1985, 1986, 1989; United Arab Emirates league champions 1978, 1979, 1986; UAE Super League champions 1978, 1986, 1989, 1996.

Al Nijmeh *club* Lebanese national league club. Lebanese Cup 1971, 1987, 1989, 1997; Lebanese league champions 1973, 1975, 1996.

Al-Owairan, Saeed *player* Striker. **Saudi Arabia** international (55 caps). Born 1968. *Club* **Al Hilal**. *Keynotes* Considered by most observers to have scored the best goal of the 1994 **World Cup** finals tournament: a solo run from deep in the Saudi half (1–0, v **Belgium**, 29 June 1994, in Washington, USA, World Cup first round). Scored in the 1992 **Confederations Cup** final (1–3, v Argentina, in Riyadh, Saudi Arabia). Al-Owairan was suspended in 1996 – rumoured to be in connection with his controversial lifestyle – and consequently missed the 1996 **African Cup of Nations**, won by Saudi Arabia. Nicknamed the Desert Maradona. *Honours* **Asian Cup of Nations** runner-up (Saudi Arabia, 1992); Asian Footballer of the Year 1994 (the first year of the award); Confederations Cup runner-up (Saudi Arabia, 1992).

Al Qadisiyah *club* Kuwaiti national league club. Kuwaiti Cup 1965, 1967, 1968, 1972, 1974, 1975, 1979, 1989, 1994; Kuwaiti league champions 1969, 1971, 1973, 1975, 1976, 1978, 1992.

Al Qadisiyah *club* Saudi Arabian national league club based in Dammam. **Arab Cup-winners Cup** runners-up 1993; **Asian Cup-winners Cup** – 1993 (6–2 agg., v South China, Hong Kong); Saudi Arabian Cup 1992.

Al Ramthla *club* Jordanian national league club. **Asian Cup-winners Cup** – semi-final 1991 (1–3 agg., v **Al Nasr**, Saudi Arabia); Jordan Cup 1991, 1992; Jordan League champions 1981, 1982, 1989.

Al Rasheed *club* Iraqi league club. **Arab Club Champions Cup** 1985 , 1986 (v **CS Sfaxien**, Tunisia), 1987 (v **Espérance Tunis**, Tunisia); **Asian Champion Teams' Cup** runners-up 1988 (3–3 agg., lost on away goals, v **Al Saad**, Qatar), semi-final 1987, 1989; Iraq Cup 1986, 1988; Iraqi League champions 1985, 1987, 1988, 1989, 1990.

Al Rayyan *club* Qatar national league club. **Asian Champion Teams Cup** semi-final 1991, quarter-final 1997; Qatar league champions 1976, 1978, 1982, 1984, 1986, 1990, 1995.

Al Saad *club* Qatar national league club. **Arab Cup-winners Cup** runners-up 1992 (v **Olympique Casablanca**, Morocco); **Asian Champion Teams Cup** – 1988 (3–3 agg., v **Al Rasheed**, Iraq – Al Saad won on away goals); Qatar league champions 1974, 1979, 1980, 1981, 1987, 1988, 1989; Qatar (Emir's) Cup 1975, 1977, 1982, 1985, 1986, 1988, 1994.

Al Salmiyah *club* Kuwaiti national league club. Kuwaiti Cup 1993; Kuwaiti eague champions 1981, 1995.

Al Schurta *club* Iraqi national league club. Another name for **Police Club**.

Al Shabab *club* Saudi Arabian national league club based in the capital Riyadh. **Arab Club Champions Cup** 1993 (v **Al Arabi**, United Arab Emirates); **Arab Cup-winners Cup** runners-up 1994, 1997; **Arab Super Cup** 1995; **Asian Champion Teams' Cup** – runners-up 1992 (0–1 v Pass, Iran, Bahrain); Saudi Arabian Cup 1993; Saudi Arabian league champions 1991, 1992, 1993.

Al Shabab *club* United Arab Emirates (UAE) national league club. **Asian Champion Teams Cup** semi-final 1991; **Asian Cup-winners Cup** runners-up 1995 (1–2, v **As Flugels**, Japan, in Sharjah, UAE), semi-final 1990; United Arab Emirates Cup 1981, 1990, 1994, 1997; United Arab Emirates league champions 1990, 1995.

Al Sharjah *club* United Arab Emirates national league club based in Sharjah. Strip: white shirts, white shorts. United Arab Emirates Cup 1979, 1980, 1982, 1983, 1991, 1995, 1998; United Arab Emirates league champions 1987, 1989, 1994, 1996.

Al Talaba *club* Iraqi league club. **Asian Champion Teams Cup** semi final 1986; **Asian Cup-winners Cup** runners-up 1996 (1–2 v **Bellmare Hiratsuka**); Iraq League champions 1981, 1982, 1983, 1987, 1994.

Al Wasl *club* United Arab Emirates national league club. **Asian Champion Teams' Cup** semi-final 1992; United Arab Emirates league champions 1982, 1983, 1985, 1988, 1992.

Al Wehdat *club* Jordanian national league club. See **Wihdat FC**.

Al Zawra *club* Iraqi league club. **Asian Champion Teams Cup** semi-final/fourth 1996-97 (1–4, v **Piroozi**, Iran, in Malaysia); Iraqi league champions 1976, 1977, 1979, 1992, 1995, 1996; Iraq Cup 1976, 1979, 1981, 1982, 1989, 1990, 1991, 1993, 1994, 1995, 1996, 1998.

Alagoas *state* one of the 27 state leagues in **Brazil**, founded 1927. Leading clubs: CRB (Club de Regatas Brasil, Maceio), CSA (Centro Social Esportivo, Palmeira dos Indios).

Alajuelense (full name Liga Deportiva Alajuelense, or LD Alajuelense) *club* Costa Rican national league club based in Alajuela, founded 1919. Ground: Estadio Alejandro Morera Soto, capacity: 12,000. Strip: red and black striped shirts, black shorts. **CONCACAF Champions Cup** 1986 (5–2 agg., v Transvaal, Surinam), runners-up 1971 (1–5, v Cruz Azul, Mexico,

Mexico City, final playoff), 1992, (0–1, v América, Mexico), third 1995 (league of four in San José, Costa Rica), quarter-final 1998; Costa Rica champions 1928, 1939, 1941, 1945, 1949, 1950, 1958, 1959, 1960, 1966, 1970, 1971, 1980, 1983, 1984, 1991, 1992, 1996, 1997; **Torneo Grandes de Centroamerica** 1996 (league of four), semi-final 1997.

Åland Islands *country* *no affiliation* self-governing province of **Finland** consisting of more than 6,000 islands on the Gulf of Bothnia. Area: 1,505 sq km (581 sq miles). Population: 24,993. Capital: Mariehamn. Hosted 1991 **Island Games** (which includes a football tournament). Finish name: Ahvenanmaa.

Alania Vladikavkaz *club* Russian national league and former-Soviet Union league club based in Vladikavkaz, founded in 1921 as SK Terksoi Oblasti (later known as ORK Imeni Lenina, known as Spartak Ordzhonikidze from 1937, Spartak-Alania from 1995, and Alania from 1996). Ground: Spartak, capacity: 38,000. Strip: red and yellow striped shirts, white shorts. Russian league champions 1995, runners-up 1992, 1996; no Soviet Union League or Cup honours.

Albania *country* *UEFA* European republic on the eastern seaboard of the Adriatic Sea. Area: 28,750 sq km (11,100 sq miles). Population: 3,420,000 (1996 est.). Language: Albanian. Capital Tirana. *Dossier* Football association (Fédération Albanaise de Football, Tirana) founded in 1930, affiliated to **FIFA** in 1932 and **Union of European Football Associations** (UEFA) in 1954; president Edmond Spaho, general secretary Eduard Dervishi. Season played from September to May. National stadium: Qemel Stafa, Tirana, capacity: 18,000. National strip: red shirts, red shorts. First international game: 7 October 1946 v Yugoslavia (2–3, Tirana, **Balkan Cup**). Most capped player: Sulejman Demollari (43 caps). *International tournament record* **Olympic Games** – first entered 1964, never qualified for finals tournament; **Women's World Cup** – never entered; **World Cup** – first entered 1966, never qualified for finals tournament; **Balkan Cup** (1946); **European Championship** – first entered 1964, second round 1964 (no qualifying tournament), never qualified for finals tournament; **European Championship for Women** – never entered. *Record against British and Irish national teams* v **England**, played two, lost two; v **Northern Ireland**, played eight, won one, drawn two, lost five; v **Wales**, played two, drawn one, lost one; v **Republic of Ireland**, played two, lost two. *History* The Albanian national league started in 1929; the Cup was first played in 1947. The league and Cup have been dominated by four clubs, **SK Tiranè**, **Vllaznia Shkodèr**, **Olimpik Tiranè** and **Partizani Tiranè**. However, the best achievement in a European club competition was by **Flamurtari Vlorè**, which reached the third round of the **UEFA Cup** in 1988. Albanian clubs were barred from European competitions in 1997-98 owing to civil war; however, two clubs, 1998 champions Vllaznia Shkodèr and 1997 champions SK Tiranè, entered the 1998-99 edition. Albania's first international match was in 1946, in the Balkan Cup: its triumph in the tournament that year gave the country its only international trophy. A self-imposed exile from the rest of Europe meant that, with the exception of a friendly against East Germany, Albania played no internationally recognised matches between 1953 and 1963 (it played a non-FIFA game against China in Beijing, in 1957). It took part in the Olympic Games qualifying tournament in 1963, followed, in the same year, by an appearance in the second round of the European Championship (after a walkover against **Greece** in round one): it lost 0–5 (agg.) against **Denmark**. It entered the World Cup for the first time in the 1996 tournament, losing in the qualifying tournament after gaining just one point (a 1–1 draw at home to **Northern Ireland**) in its six games. Albania's 1998 World Cup qualifying home ties were played in Spain because of the civil war. Albania's final qualifier in the 1998 World Cup campaign was a memorable game against Germany: Albania was defeated by a single goal, 3–4, with Germany scoring a winner in the 90th minute to guarantee its World Cup finals place (12 October 1997, in Germany). *League system* Eighteen clubs compete in the national first division, with three points awarded for a win and one for a draw; **goal difference** is used to separate clubs level on points. The civil war in 1996 so disrupted the season that a temporary system was used. The season was played in two phases: in the first phase, the 18 clubs played each other only once. In the second phase, the top six clubs played each other once, at a neutral ground, to determine the championship (combining the points totals from both phases). The remaining 12 clubs were divided into two groups of six clubs, again playing each other once. *Record in international club tournaments* **European Cup** – SK Tiranè (as 17 Nèntori, second round 1983, 1989, 1990); **European Cup-winners Cup** – **Partizani Tiranè** (second round 1971), Besa Kavajè (second round 1973), SK Tiranè (as 17 Nèntori, second round 1987), **Vllaznia Shkodèr** (second round 1988); **UEFA Cup** – **Flamurtari Vlorè** (third round 1988). Other leading club: **Olimpik Tiranè**.

Albert, Florian *player* Striker. **Hungary** international (31 goals, ca. 1958-69). Born 15 September 1951. *Clubs* **Ferencvaros**. *Honours France Football's* European Footballer of the Year 1967; Hungarian league championship (Ferencvaros) 1963, 1964, 1967, 1968; **World Cup Golden Goal** (joint top-scorer in final, 1962 with four goals).

Albion Rovers *club* Scottish league. *Dossier* Ground: **Cliftonhill Stadium**, Coatbridge, Strathclyde, capacity: 1,238. Strip: yellow shirt with black chestband and white collar with black trim, black shorts, black socks. Nickname: Wee Rovers. Record attendance: 27,381 v **Rangers** (8 February 1936, **Scottish FA Cup**, second round). Biggest win: 12–0 v Airdriehill (3 September 1887, Scottish FA Cup). Biggest defeat: 1–11 v **Partick Thistle** (11 August 1993, Scottish FA Cup). *History* Founded in 1882. The club joined Division Two of the **Scottish League** in 1903-04 and

it has rarely appeared in the top flight – only seven seasons in total. In 1920, Rovers finished bottom of the post-war Scottish League, but reached the Scottish FA Cup final (2–3 v Kilmarnock), having beaten Rangers over three matches in the semi-final (2–0 replay). Rovers' only major honour was achieved in 1933-34, when the club won the Division Two Championship. Jock **Stein** was a Rovers player in the 1940s. *League record* Scottish League 1919-20 to 1920-21; Second Division 1975-76 to 1988-89, 1990-91 to 1993-94; Division Two (B Division) 1903-04 to 1914-15, 1923-24 to 1933-34, 1937-38, 1946-47 to 1947-48, 1949-50 to 1974-75; Third Division 1994-95–. *Honours* Division Two 1933-34. *Records* Jock White is Albion's most capped player (1 (2) for **Scotland**); Murdy Walls holds the record for club appearances (399, 1921-36); Bunty Weir is Albion's record goalscorer (105, 1928-31).

Alcock, Charles *player-official* Born 1842 in Sunderland. Alcock was appointed Honorary Secretary of the **Football Association** in 1870 and proposed the **FA Cup**. He was captain of the first FA Cup winning club, **Wanderers** (1–0 v **Royal Engineers**) in 1872.

alcohol *medical* any beverage containing ethanol, produced by fermentation (includes wines, beers, spirits and various fortified drinks). Although legally bought and consumed, alcohol has short-term effects on coordination and judgement. It can lead to long-term health effects, such as alcohol dependency (alcoholism) and cirrhosis of the liver. Several top players have admitted to being alcoholics during and/or after their playing careers. *Keynotes* Hughie **Gallacher**, the former **Newcastle United**, **Chelsea** and **Derby County** striker, was allegedly addicted to whisky before his death by suicide in May 1957. Jimmy **Greaves's** autobiography, *This One's On Me*, which was published in 1979, contained an admission of alcoholism. **Brazil's** 1958 and 1962 **World Cup** star **Garrincha** died of alcohol poisoning in 1983. Former **Bayern Munich** striker Gerd **Müller**, scorer of 62 goals in 68 international appearances for West **Germany**, admitted to being an alcoholic in the early 1990s. **Arsenal's** Tony Adams and Paul Merson both admitted to having an alcohol problem before resurrecting their respective careers. Paul **Gascoigne** entered a rehabilitation clinic in October 1998 partly to recover from alcohol addiction.

Aldershot *club* former English league. *Dossier* Ground: Recreation Ground, Hampshire. Record attendance: 19,138 v **Carlisle United** (28 January 1970, **FA Cup**, fourth round replay). *History* Founded in December 1926. The club joined Division Three (South) in 1932-33 in place of **Thames**. Aldershot was wound up at a High Court hearing on 18 March 1992 with debts of £1.2 million, having survived a similar crisis in July 1990. Although the club was allowed to fulfil a Division Four fixture at **Cardiff City** the following day, it was expelled from the League on 25 March 1992. The club re-formed as Aldershot Town and plays in the Isthmian Premier League. Aldershot's highest League position was eighth in Division Three, which the club achieved in

1973-74. *League record* Division Three 1973-74 to 1975-76, 1987-88 to 1988-89; Division Three (South) 1932-33 to 1957-58; Division Four 1958-59 to 1972-73, 1976-77 to 1986-87, 1990-91 to 1991-92.

Aldridge, John *player-manager* Striker. **Republic of Ireland** international (64 caps, 19 goals, 1986-96). Born 18 September 1958. Career ca. 1979–1998. *Clubs* **Newport County, Oxford United, Liverpool, Real Sociedad, Tranmere Rovers** (player-manager). *Keynotes* Aldridge holds the unfortunate record of being the first player to miss a penalty in an **FA Cup** final at **Wembley** (for Liverpool v **Wimbledon**, 1988, 0–1); Aldridge had already scored 11 penalties that season. He was not, however, the first to miss a penalty in a final; Charlie Wallace missed one for Aston Villa in 1913 (v Sunderland, at Crystal Palace, 1–0). Aldridge's last goal for Liverpool also came from a penalty; this time, however, he was brought on as a 69th minute substitute in his farewell game at Anfield to score a penalty with his first kick (Liverpool won the match 9–0, v Crystal Palace, 12 September 1989, Division One). *Honours* Aldridge scored 474 senior goals – a record for player predominantly based in England. He scored 329 goals in the **Football League**, 81 goals in English cup competitions, 45 goals for Real Sociedad and 19 goals for the Republic of Ireland. Aldridge scored two in his last ever game (3 May 1998, v **Wolverhampton Wanderers**, First Division). He is Tranmere's most capped player, having won 29 caps while at the club; he is also the Republic of Ireland's second-highest goalscorer, behind Frank Stapleton (with 20).

Alfred McAlpine Stadium *ground* English football ground situated in Huddersfield, West Yorkshire; home of **Huddersfield Town**. *Dossier* Ground capacity: 24,000 all seated. Pitch dimensions: 105m x 69m. Record attendance: 20,741 v **Sunderland** (21 October 1998, First Division). *History* Huddersfield played its first match at the stadium on 20 August 1994 (v **Wycombe Wanderers**, Second Division), having relocated from **Leeds Road**, the club's home for 86 years. *Keynotes* The ground's design is based on a blueprint entitled "A Stadium for the Nineties", which had been developed by two architects, Rod Sheard and Geraint John, and structural engineer Stephen Morley, and was exhibited at the NEC in 1991. The local council finally approved planning permission for a new stadium based on the blueprint, which would be home to both Huddersfield Town and Huddersfield Rugby League Club, in August 1992. The initial three-sided stadium cost around £15 million. Finance came from several quarters, including a £2.5 million grant from the **Football Trust** and a £2 million contribution from contractors Alfred McAlpine, which granted the company naming rights. The stadium won the Royal Institute of British Architects' Building of the Year award in 1995 – the first time it had gone to a sports stadium.

Algarve Cup *competition* women's international nations' tournament played in the Algarve on the south coast of **Portugal**, organised by the Scandinavian foot-ball associations (**Denmark, Norway** and **Sweden**) in collaboration with the Portuguese association, with other nations invited to take part. It was first played in 1989. The fifth tournament in March 1998 involved eight nations: **China**, Denmark, **Finland**, **Netherlands**, **Norway**, Portugal, **Sweden**, **USA**. Norway beat Denmark 4–1 in the final. The 1999 final was won by China (2–1, v **USA**).

Algeria *country CAF* Republic in Northwest Africa on Mediterranean Sea, between Morocco, Libya and Tunisia, and north of Mauritania, Mali and Niger. Former French colony, gained independence in 1962. Area: 2,381,745 sq km (919,355 sq miles). Landscape varies from the North Saharan Desert in the south, to the Atlas Mountains and a fertile coastal plain. Climate is mainly hot, though more temperate on coast. Population: 28,580,000 (1995 est.). Languages: Arabic, French and Berber. Capital: El Djezaïr (Algiers). *Dossier* Football association (Fédération Algérienne de Foot-ball, El Djezaïr) formed in 1962 (year of independence), affiliated to **FIFA** in 1963, **Confédération Africaine de Football** (CAF) in 1964, member of **Arab Football Union**, general secretary Faouzi Boubaha. Season played from September to June. National stadium: Stade Cheraga, El Djezaïr, capacity: 74,000 (9,000 seated). National strip: green shirts, white shorts. Nickname of national team: Desert Warriors. First international match: 1 June 1957 v **Tunisia** (2–1, friendly, Tunis). Biggest victory: 15–1 v South **Yemen** (17 August 1973, friendly, neutral venue). Biggest defeat: 0–5 v **East Germany** (21 April 1976, in Cottbus, Germany, friendly). *International tournament record* **Olympic Games** – quarter-final 1980; **Women's World Cup** – never entered; **World Cup** – first entered 1970 (lost in first round of qualifying tournament), qualified for finals tournament in 1982 and 1986 (first round); **African Cup of Nations** – first entered 1969, 1990 (1–0, v **Nigeria**, in Algiers), runners-up 1980 (0–3, v host nation **Nigeria**, in Lagos), semi-finalists/third place 1984, fourth place 1982, 1988, also qualified for finals tournament 1998 (lost all three first-round group matches), hosts 1990, disqualified in 1994 qualifying tournament for fielding an **ineligible player**; **African Youth Cup** – 1979; **Afro-Asian Cup of Nations** – 1991 (2–2 agg., won on **away goals**, v **Iran**); **All-Africa Games** – 1978 (v Nigeria, in Algiers); Mediterranean Games – 1975, runners-up 1993; *Record against British and Irish national teams* **Northern Ireland** – played one, drawn one, **Republic of Ireland** – played one, won one. *History* Three regional leagues operated before independence in 1962: Algiers from 1920, Oran from 1920 and Constantine from 1922. National league started in 1962-63. Algerian Cup first played 1962-63. The clubs have won the **African Cup of Champion Clubs, J S Kabylie, Mouloudia Chalia d'Algiers** and **Entente Setif**. Algeria has twice qualified for the World Cup finals (1982 and 1986). Its 1986 campaign was noted for the victory over West **Germany** (2-1, in Gijon, Spain).

Rabah Madjer scored after 54 minutes and Lakhdar Belloumi scored the 70th minute winner, just one minute after Germany had equalised. Algeria only failed to qualify for the second stage on its goal record (Austria, Germany and Algeria were tied on four points). Hosted and won African Cup of Nations in 1990. *Record in international club competitions* African Cup of Champion Clubs – **Mouloudia Chalia d'Algiers** (1976), **J S Kabylie** (formerly JE Tizi-Ouzou, 1981 and 1990, semi-final 1996), **Entente Setif** (1988), **Mouloudia Club d'Oran** (runners-up 1989), **USM Algiers** (quarter-final "champions league" stage 1997); **African Cup-winners Cup** – **Milaha Athletic Hussein-Dey** (runners-up 1978), J S Kabylie (1995, quarter-final 1993), **C R Belouizdad** (semi-final 1996), Mouloudia Club d'Oran (quarter-final 1997), USM Algiers (quarter-final 1998); **African Super Cup** – J S Kabylie (1996); **Afro-Asian Club Cup** – Entente Setif (1989); **Arab Club Champions Cup** – J S Kabylie (semi-final 1994), WA Tlemcen (winners 1998); **Arab Cup-winners Cup** – Mouloudia Club d'Oran (1997, 1998); **Arab Super Cup** – Mouloudia Club d'Oran (1999); **CAF Cup** – Mouloudia Club d'Oran (quarter-final 1996), USM Ain Beida (quarter-final 1997); **Maghreb Champions Cup** – **C R Belouizdad** (formerly C R Belcourt, 1970, 1971 and 1972); **Maghreb Cup-winners Cup** – Mouloudia d'Algiers (1971 and 1973). Other leading clubs: CS Constantine (league champions 1997), MO Constantine (league champions 1991), USM El Harrach (league champions 1998). Notable players: Salah **Assad**, Ali **Bencheikh**, Lakhdar **Belloumi**, Rabah **Madjer**, Cherif El Quazani.

Alianza *club* Peruvian national league club based in the capital Lima, founded in 1901. Ground: Estadio Alejandro Villanueva, capacity: 35,000. Strip: dark blue and white striped shirts, dark blue shorts (the club strip is changed to purple and white in October, in honour of a saint). *Keynotes:* Peru's best-supported club with an average league attendance of around 10,000. The entire team and staff was killed in a plane crash in December 1987 after a game in Pucallpa. **Copa Libertadores** semi-final 1976, 1978; Peru League champions 1927, 1928, 1931, 1932, 1933, 1948, 1952, 1954, 1955, 1962, 1963, 1965, 1975, 1977, 1978, 1997.

Alianza Fútbol Club *club* El Salvador national league club based in the capital San Salvador, founded 1959. Ground: Estadio Cuscatlan (shared with **Atlético Marte**), capacity: 47,000. Strip: white shirts, white shorts. **CONCACAF Champions Cup** 1967 (1–2, 3–0, 5–3 playoff, v **Jong Colombia** of Netherlands Antilles), semi-final 1994; El Salvador league champions 1966, 1967, 1986, 1989, 1994, 1997; **Torneo Grandes de Centroamerica** 1997 (1–0, v **Saprissa**, Costa Rica), runners-up 1996 (league of four).

All-Africa Friendship Games *competition* ephemeral former sports and athletics tournament for French-speaking African states, former French territo-

ries and a French representative team, included a football tournament. *Winners* 1960, 1961 French amateur team, 1962 **Cameroon**.

All-Africa Games *competition* sports and athletics tournament for African nations restricted to players under 19 years of age. *Keynotes* The 19654 tournament final was won on corners after the match between Congo and Mali finished 0–0; Congo had won seven corners, compared with Mal's two. *Winners* 1965 **Congo**, 1973 **Nigeria**, 1978 **Algeria**, 1987, 1995 **Egypt**, 1991 **Cameroon**; 1999 tournament held in Johannesburg, South Africa; 2003 tournament in Lagos, Nigera.

all-seater stadium *n.* ground that consists entirely of seated spectator accommodation. **Aberdeen**'s **Pittodrie** ground became the UK's first all-seater football stadium in 1978 when the final terracing, the South Side, was seated. **Coventry City**'s **Highfield Road** ground followed the Pittodrie example, becoming the **Football League**'s first all-seater stadium in 1981 with a capacity of 20,616. Rangers' Ibrox ground was the first purpose-built all-seater stadium in the UK when the ground was completely redeveloped, beginning in 1978. During summer 1992, **Ipswich Town**'s **Portman Road** stadium became the first Premier League ground to become all seated. See also **Taylor Report**.

all-seater stadiums deadline *misc.* time period in which English and Scottish Premier/Football League clubs should establish all-seater stadiums. *Keynotes* Initially, Premier League and First Division clubs were given until August 1994 to remove all terrace accommodation, and their lower-level counterparts until August 1999. However, one Premier League club (**Newcastle United**) and five First Division clubs (**Derby County**, **Grimsby Town**, **Middlesbrough**, **Portsmouth** and **Sunderland**) were granted one-year extensions to the deadline, while, in July 1992, the government announced that clubs in the lower divisions could retain some terracing after all, subject to ensuring that whatever standing accommodation was preserved met specified standards by the original date. Clubs promoted were given additional time – three seasons in England and five in Scotland – to bring their grounds up to the required standard. A further measure recommended by the **Taylor Report** and implemented by the British government in 1990 was to reduce the tax on pools betting from 42.5% to 40% to free additional money to help redevelop grounds. This released around £100 million over a five-year period to assist in the redevelopment of stadiums (see **Football Trust**).

all-ticket *adj.* match for which all tickets are sold in advance, with no gate sales. Matches may be designated as all-ticket by the police in order to discourage travelling fans for security reasons. *Keynotes* **FA Cup** finals have been all-ticket affairs since the crowd problems encountered at the first **Wembley** final in 1923 (see **White horse final**). The **Football Association** was forced to return almost £3,000 to ticket holders who were unable to get into the stadium because of the vast crowds. The first all-ticket match is believed to have been the 1884 international between **Scotland** and **England** at Cathkin Park. Some 10,000 tickets were sold for the match which took place on 15 March.

Allchurch, Ivor   *player*   Inside-forward. **Wales** international (68 caps, 23 goals). Born 16 October 1929. Career ca. 1948–1967. *Clubs* **Swansea** Town (twice), **Newcastle United**, **Cardiff City**. *Keynotes* Transferred to Newcastle United from Swansea Town for £27,000 in 1958, having made 330 appearances in his first spell with the south Wales club. *Honours* Division Three (South) (Swansea Town 1948-49); Welsh Cup (Swansea Town 1950, 1966; Cardiff City 1964, 1965). Allchurch's 166 overall **Football League** goal tally with Swansea remains a club record. He scored 46 goals in 143 appearances for Newcastle and 39 goals in 103 outings for Cardiff. He played in 692 League games and scored 251 goals. Allchurch starred for Wales in the 1958 **World Cup**, scoring twice as his country reached the quarter-finals. His 23 goals for Wales remained a record until surpassed by Ian **Rush** in 1993. Included in the **Football League Centenary 100 players**.

Alliance Premier League   *competition*   former name of the **Football Conference**.

Allison, George   *broadcaster*   BBC Radio's first football commentator. Allison, an A**rsenal** director, commentated on the first match to be broadcast in **England** (Arsenal v **Sheffield United**, 22 January 1927, Division One). He was supported by Derek ("Uncle Mac") McCulloch who plotted the position of the ball against a plan of the pitch, which was divided into eight numbered squares and published in the *Radio Times*. In this way listeners were able to follow the ball as it moved around the pitch. Matches were broadcast from portable sound-proof huts.

Alloa Athletic   *club*   Scottish league. *Dossier* Ground: **Recreation Park**, Alloa, capacity: 4,111. Strip: gold shirt with black sleeves, black shorts with gold trim, gold socks with black tops. Nickname: Wasps. Record attendance: 15,467 v **Celtic** (February 1955, **Scottish FA Cup**). Biggest win: 9–2 v **Forfar Athletic** (18 March 1933, Division Two). Biggest defeat: 0–10 v **Dundee** (8 March 1947, Division Two), v **Third Lanark** (8 August 1953, **Scottish League Cup**). *Keynotes* Founded in 1883. The club has played at Recreation Park since 1895 and joined Division Two of the **Scottish League** in 1921-22, winning the title in some style (by 13 points) in its first season – the club's only major honour. The following season was Alloa's only one in the top flight. *League record* First Division 1977-78, 1982-83 to 1983-84, 1985-86, 1989-90; Second Division 1976-77, 1978-79 to 1981-82, 1984-85, 1986-87 to 1988-89, 1990-91 to 1993-94; Division Two (B Division) 1921-22 to 1974-75; Third Division 1994-95–. *Honours* Division Two 1921-'22. *Records* Jock Hepburn is Alloa's most capped player (1 for **Scotland**).

Almondvale Stadium   *ground*   Scottish football ground situated in Livingstone, Lothian; home of **Livingston**. *Dossier* Ground capacity: 6,100. Pitch

dimensions: 96m x 66m. Record attendance: 4,148 v **East Stirlingshire** (11 November 1995, Third Division). *History* Meadowbank Thistle moved to the Scottish new town, Livingston, in 1995, and adopted the town's name. Thistle's lease of Meadowbank Stadium ended that year and Livingston Development Corporation offered the club £2 million towards the new £5.1 million Almondvale Stadium. The club played its final game as Thistle on 6 May 1995 (v **Stenhousemuir**), continuing to play at Meadowbank, but as Livingston, until the new ground was ready in November 1995. Livingston's first League match at Almondvale took place on 11 November (v **East Stirlingshire**) before a record crowd of 4,148.

alphabetical letters   *misc.*   method of relaying the half-time scores. Before grounds had **electronic scoreboards**, half-time scores were generally communicated to spectators by placing the score with the relevant match letter, as found in the match **programme**. The letters were placed on a scoreboard or on the perimeter wall.

Altay Spor Kolübü   *club*   Turkish national league club based in Izmir, founded 1914. Ground: Alsancak, capacity: 20,000. Strip: white shirts, white shorts. Turkish Cup 1967, 1980.

Alternative Investment Market (AIM)   *n.*   UK alternative equity market to a full stock market flotation. AIM is less regulated than the official Stock Exchange listing; AIM companies require no past trading record – a full listing requires published accounts covering a three-year period and there are tax advantages for investors. Small to medium-size companies typically opt for an AIM listing to secure investment rather than float on the official list. At the start of the 1998-99 season, eight UK football clubs were listed on the AIM: **Birmingham City**, **Celtic**, **Charlton Athletic**, **Chelsea** (Chelsea Village), **Nottingham Forest**, **Preston North End**, **Queens Park Rangers** (Loftus Road) and **West Bromwich Albion**.

altitude   *medical*   height above sea level. The amount of oxygen in the air decreases with increasing altitude and, at high altitude, people can suffer from oxygen deficiency – a lack of oxygen in the blood, which particularly affects the brain – a condition sometimes experienced by mountaineers. Playing at high altitude is thought to be advantageous to a team that has acclimatised to the conditions; athletes training or living at altitude tend to compensate for the reduced oxygen by producing more blood cells, thus boosting the blood's oxygen-carrying capacity. *Keynotes* **Bolivia** plays the majority of its international matches at La Paz (3,600 metres above sea level – 1,500 m higher than Mexico City) and Cochabamba (2,559 metres above sea level). While the evidence is clearly circumstantial, it is worth noting that Bolivia is the only nation ever to have beaten **Brazil** in a **World Cup** qualifier (2–0, 25 July 1993), and the game was played in La Paz. The victory was followed by a 0–6 defeat away from home. Bolivia's only international tournament success – winners of the **Copa**

America in 1963 – was as tournament hosts. It was runner-up in the Copa America in 1997, again when the tournament was played in Bolivia. Athletes have sometimes attempted to mimic the effects of training at altitude by **blood doping** (now outlawed).

Amapa *state* one of the 27 state leagues in **Brazil**, founded 1944. Leading clubs: EC Macapa (Macapa), Amapa Clube (Macapa).

Amarilla, Raul Vicente *player* Striker. **Paraguay** international. *Clubs* **Olimpia**. *Keynotes* Scored twice in Olimpia's 3–1 agg. victory in the 1990 Copa Libertadores final v **Barcelona** of Peru, and twice in Olimpia's 6–3 agg win over **Nacional Montevideo** of Uruguay in the Supercopa final, scoring seven goals in that tournament, and helping his team to an unprecedented South American double. Amarilla was equal top scorer with 10 goals in the 1989 Copa Libertadores when Olimpia lost on penalties in the final to **Atlético Nacional Medellín** of Colombia. *Honours* **Copa Libertadores** (Olimpia, 1990); **Supercopa** (Olimpia, 1990); *El Pais* journal's South American Footballer of the Year 1990.

Amateur Football Alliance *n.* governing body of English amateur football between 1907 and 1914. *Keynotes* A breakaway association (originally called the Amateur Football Association, abbrev. AFA) from the **Football Association** that was formed in 1907 by long-established clubs who wanted to retain their amateur status and who believed that the FA was more interested in the growing professional game. Clubs present at the inaugural meeting of the AFA, which took place at a Holborn restaurant, included Cambridge University, Clapham Rovers, Corinthians, Old Carthusians, Old Etonians, Old Westminsters and Swifts. Delegates adopted the following resolution: "It is essential for the good of the game of Association football as played by amateurs that an Amateur Football Association is formed". The AFA also established a Senior Cup competition. In 1914, the FA and AFA resolved their differences, and although amateur clubs agreed to recognise the FA as the governing body of English football, the AFA retained its independence. In May 1934, the AFA changed its name to the Amateur Football Alliance.

amateur player *regulations* a player who does not receive remuneration from a club for playing football. **Scottish Football League** clubs must **register** their amateur players and include their names in the **club list of players** submitted to the league at the end of each season (Scottish Football League rule 50(a)). Once registered with a Scottish Football League club, an amateur player cannot be transferred to another club without his club's consent, or that of the league management committee (Scottish Football League rule 52). Compare **professional player**.

Amazonas *state* one of the 27 state leagues in **Brazil**, founded 1914. Leading clubs: Nacional Fast Clube (Manaus), Atlético Rio Negro (Manaus).

America FC *club* Nicaraguan national league club, based in the capital Managua. Strip: red shirts and red shorts.

América (full name: Club de Fútbol América) *club* Mexican national league club, based in Mexico City and founded in 1916 (merger of Record FC and Colón FC). Ground: Estadio Azteca, capacity: 110,000. Strip: yellow and blue shirts and yellow shorts. Nickname: the Eagles. **CONCACAF Champion Clubs Cup** – 1977 (1–0 agg., v **Robin Hood**, Surinam), 1987 (3–1 agg., v **Defence Force**, Trinidad and Tobago), 1990 (8–2 agg., v Pina del Rio, Cuba) and 1992 (1–0, v **LD Alajeulense**, Costa Rica, in Santa Ana); **Copa Inter Americana** 1977, 1990; Mexican Cup (Copa Mexico) 1938, 1954, 1955, 1964, 1965 and 1974; Mexican league champions 1925, 1926, 1927, 1928, 1966, 1971, 1976, 1984, 1985, 1985 (a short, autumn-only league programme to accommodate World Cup finals hosted by Mexico), 1988 and 1989.

América de Cali (Corporación Deportiva América) *club* Colombian national league club based in Cali, founded 1918 (as Deportivo America). Ground: Estadio Pascual Guerrero, capacity: 45,750 (shared with **Deportivo Cali**). Strip: red shirts, red shorts. *Keynotes* América de Cali holds the national league record of five consecutive league titles (1982 to 1986). Colombian league champions 1979, 1982, 1983, 1984, 1985, 1986, 1990, 1992, 1997; **Copa CONMEBOL** semi-final 1997, quarter-final 1997; **Copa Libertadores** runners-up 1985 (0–1, 1–0, 1–1 playoff in Asuncion, 4–5 pens, v **Argentinos Juniors**), 1986 (1–2, 0–1, v **River Plate**, Argentina), 1987 (2–0, 1–2, 0–1 playoff in Santiago, v **Peñarol**, Uruguay), 1996, (1–2 agg., v River Plate), semi-final 1988, 1992, 1993, second-round group stage 1980, 1983.

American Cup *competition* former United States domestic Cup competition, founded in 1885 by the **American Football Association**. The Cup was first won, in 1885, by Kearny O N T (1–0, v New York). The last known winner was Providence Gold Bugs, in 1929 (2–2, 4–2, replay, v New York Nationals). The Cup was overshadowed in importance by the **US Open Challenge Cup**, founded 1914.

American football *n.* form of **football** played chiefly in the **United States of America** and **Canada**. It is also played as a minority sport in some other countries, including **Australia**, **England**, **Finland**, **Germany**, **Japan**, the **Netherlands** and **New Zealand**. The game is played with eleven players on each side, using an oval ball. Players are heavily protected with body padding and full-face helmets. The pitch is marked with a series of lines, five yards (4.57 metres) apart, running parallel with the goal-line, giving rise to the sport's informal name, gridiron. The ball can be passed forward (contrasting rugby football), with the ultimate aim of scoring a **touchdown**, by being in possession of the ball in the opposition's end zone (the playing area behind the goal-line). The game is punctuated by time-outs, at which the entire team may be substituted (ie an attacking "offence" being replaced by a "defence"). Points are also scored by kicking the ball over a crossbar between two posts following a touchdown (similar to rugby football). The sport is administered in the US and Canada by the National Football League, with its membership divided into two "conferences", the National Football Conference and the American Football Conference (originally an independent league). Each conference is divided into regions, Central, East and West. The so-called World Series Championship, or Super Bowl, is played between the winners of the two conferences (first played in 1967, and won by the Green Bay Packers). *History* The sport has its origins in both **association** and **rugby football** and was first codified in 1876, at the Massasoit Convention. The first American football game was probably that between Rutgers and Princeton Colleges, although the game was also developing in Canada. Like rugby union, American college games were originally played with 15 players on each side. A game between the Canadian McGill University and the US Harvard College was played with only 11 players on each side, because four of the McGill players were too sick to travel; the precedent of only 11 players on each side was thus set. The five-yard pitch markings, exclusive to American football, were introduced by Walter Camp, responsible for revising the early rules.

American Football Association *n.* former football federation of the United States, formed in 1884, later affiliated to the **Football Association** in England. The United States played its first international game on 28 November 1885 (0–1, v **Canada**, Newark, US, friendly). It organised the first US domestic Cup, the **American Cup** (1885-1929). Superseded in 1913 by the **United States Football Association**.

American League of Professional Football *competition* former United States professional football league, founded 1894 by the former **American Football Association**. The league folded after one season. Only winner: Baltimore Orioles.

American Professional Soccer League *competition* former name of the **A-League**.

American Samoa *country associate member OFC* part of Samoan Islands to Northeast of Fiji, administered by the **United States**. Area: 197 sq km (76 sq miles). Tropical climate. Population: 132,726. Capital: Pago Pago. *Dossier* Associate member of the **Oceania Football Confederation** (OFC). Biggest defeat: 0–12, v **French Polynesia/Tahiti** (Oceania Cup, Polynesian qualifying group, 7 September 1998). *International tournament record* **Oceania Women's Tournament/ Women's World Cup** – first entered 1998 (did not qualify for 1999 World Cup finals); **World Cup** – never entered; **Oceania Cup** – first entered 1998. See also **Western Samoa**.

American Soccer League *competition* **1.** former United States professional football league, founded 1921, replaced the **National Association Football League** (NAFL). The league, which was not truly national (operating only in the northeast) folded in 1933. The first winner was Bethlehem Steel (playing under the assumed name of Philadelphia FC; Bethlehem was the last winner of the NAFL, and went on to win the league again in 1928). The last known championship winner was Fall River FC (1932). Fall River Marksmen was the most successful team with six championships. **2.** former United States professional football league, founded 1933, folded 1983. First won by Irish Americans (1934). The Jacksonville Tea Men won the last title in 1983. The most successful clubs were the Philadelphia Americans (later known as the Uhrik Truckers, winners seven times) and the Ukrainian Nationals (five championships). **3.** former United States professional football league, founded 1988, merged with the **Western Soccer League** in 1990 to form the **A-League**. Won by Washington Diplomats (1988) and Fort Lauderdale Strikers (1989).

Amicale Sportive Bilima *club* Congo Democratic Republic (formerly Zaire) national league club based in the capital Kinshasa, founded 1938. Ground: 24 Septembre, capacity: 25,000. Strip: red shirts, white shorts. **African Cup of Champion Clubs** runners-up 1980 (2–5 agg., v **Canon Yaoundé**, Cameroon), 1985 (3–6 agg., v **FAR Rabat**, Morocco); Congo DR Cup 1965 (as FC Dragons Kinshasa); Congo DR league champions 1965, 1979, 1982, 1984.

Amilcar Cabral Cup *competition* West African regional nations' tournament. **Senegal** won the first competition in 1979 (1–0 v **Mali**, held in Guinea-Bissau). Participating nations are **Cape Verde**, **Gambia**, **Guinea**, **Guinea-Bissau**, **Mali**, **Mauritania**, **Senegal** and **Sierra Leone**. *Winners* 1979, 1980, 1983, 1984, 1985, 1986, 1991 Senegal; 1981, 1982, 1987, 1988 Guinea; 1993, 1995 Sierra Leone; 1989, 1997 Mali.

Amokachi, Daniel Owefin *player* Striker. **Nigeria** international (45 caps, 14 goals). Born 30 December 1972. *Clubs* Ranchers Bees (of Nigeria), **Club Brugge**, **Everton**, **Besiktas**. *Keynotes* Amokachi scored in the Olympic Games final against Argentina (3–2, in Athens, Georgia, USA). *Honours* **Olympic Games** gold medal (Nigeria, 1996).

Amoros, Manuel *player* Defender. **France** international (82 caps, 1982–92). Born 1 February 1961. *Clubs* AS **Monaco**, **Olympique de Marseille**, Olympique Lyonnais. *Keynotes* Played in the 1991 European Cup final, missing the crucial first penalty that led to a shoot-out defeat by **Red Star Belgrade** (0–0, 3–5 pens., in Bari, Italy). *Honours* **World Cup** fourth place (France, 1982); **European Championship** (France, 1984); French Championship (AS Monaco, 1982, 1988, Olympique de Marseille, 1991, 1992). France's all-time most capped player, Amoros made his international debut on 23 February 1982 (2–0, v **Italy** in Paris, friendly). He had Spanish parents but chose to play for France, the country of his birth.

amphetamine *medical* a stimulant drug medically used to treat various illnesses such as Parkinson's disease, epilepsy and narcolepsy. The most commonly misused amphetamine is amphetamine sulphate, which can be swallowed, injected or sniffed. Users experience euphoria, excitation and boundless energy – hence their misuse in sport – and occasional aggressiveness, with after-effects of depression and irritability. Users can become psychologically, though not physiologically, dependent. Other amphetamines include dexamphetamine sulphate, methylamphetamine and benzadrine.

amputation *medical* the surgical removal of all or part of a limb, because of injury or infection. *Keynote* **Sheffield Wednesday**'s 23-year-old centre-forward Derek Dooley broke his right leg in a collision with **Preston North End**'s goalkeeper in a league match at **Deepdale** on 14 February 1953 (Division One); the leg became gangrenous while Dooley was recovering in hospital and it had to be amputated. He had scored 62 goals in 59 first-team games for Wednesday and had been on the verge of an **England** call-up.

Amsterdam ArenA *ground* Dutch stadium situated in Amsterdam; home of **Ajax**. Ground capacity: 51,700 all seated. *Keynotes* Built at a cost of 250 million Dutch guilders and officially opened in August 1996 (**Netherlands** v **Brazil**, friendly). The ArenA has a retractable roof and 46,000 **season ticket** holders. Situated in the Bijlmer district of Amsterdam and developed by a consortium consisting of Ajax, the city council and private sector investors, the surrounding complex includes De Toekomst (the future), an area housing Ajax's famed soccer school for young talent. The ArenA was the venue for the 1998 **European Cup** final (**Real Madrid** v **Juventus**, 47,500). Ajax's previous ground, the 30,000-capacity Ajax Stadion, was opened in 1934 and was commonly known as De Meer.

Amunike, Emmanuel *player* Striker. **Nigeria** international. Born 25 December 1970. *Clubs* Nigerlux, Concorde FC, **Julius Berger** (all Nigeria), **Sporting Lisbon**, **Barcelona**. *Keynotes* Amunike scored in the Olympic Games football tournament final against Argentina in 1996 (3–2, in Athens, Georgia, USA). *Honours* **Olympic Games** gold medal (Nigeria, 1996); **CAF Footballer of the Year** 1994.

An impossible job *television* title of the *Cutting Edge* programme, first shown on *Channel 4* on 24 January 1994, that followed former **England** manager Graham **Taylor** through England's qualifying matches for the 1994 **World Cup**. The programme is renowned for Taylor's liberal use of the expletive "fucking", the phrase "do I not like that" and his remark to the linesman – "you've just cost me my job" – who had failed to adjudge that a foul by the Dutch defender Ronald Koeman on England midfielder David Platt during the final and decisive qualifying match in Rotterdam occurred inside the penalty area.

anabolic steroid *medical* a class of drugs that encourages the synthesis of new tissue, particularly muscle. Steroidal hormones – such as the male sex hormone testosterone – are produced naturally by the body; most anabolic steroids mimic the anabolic effects of natural testosterone. They are outlawed in most sports. Examples include stanozolol, stanolone, propetandrol, oxymetholone, atamestane, bolenol, bolasterone, nan-

drolone, norboletone, drostanolone, enestebol, epostane, furazabol, methandienone and oxymesterone.

analgesic *medical* class of pain-killing drugs that induce analgesia (reduction in pain without loss of consciousness). Analgesics range from mild over-the-counter drugs, such as aspirin and paracetamol, and non-steroidal anti-inflammatory drugs (which inhibit the formation of prostaglandins), such as ibuprofen and diclofenac, to controlled **opioid** drugs. Analgesics can be misused by sports players by masking the pain of an ongoing injury (risking permanent damage), or to increase their pain threshold. Opioid drugs may also be misused for their euphoric effects. Some analgesics and all opioids are banned substances in sport.

Anderlecht *club* Belgium. See **RSC Anderlecht**.

Andorra *country UEFA* principality in the Pyrenees between France and Spain. Area: 465 sq km (180 sq miles). Alpine climate – long winter, warm summer. Population: 62,500 (1994 est.). Languages: Catalan, Spanish, French. Capital Andorra la Vella. *Dossier:* Football association (Federació Andorrana de Fútbol, Saint Julia de Loria), founded 1994, affiliated to **FIFA** 1996, and to **Union of European Football Associations** (UEFA) 1996, president Francesc Vila Circuns, general secretary Tomas Gea. National stadium: Coronal, Andorra la Vella, capacity: 800. National strip: yellow shirts, red shorts. First international match: 13 November 1996, v **Estonia** (1–6, Andorra la Vella, friendly). First international tournament: **European Championship** 2000. *Record against British and Irish national teams* none played. *History* In 1996, Andorra became the 51st member of UEFA, entering its first tournament in 1998 (the qualifiers for the European Championships of 2000). In 1996-97, one of its clubs, Spordany Juvenil, lost all 22 of its league games, conceding 137 goals, and scoring only 23. 1996-97 champions **Charlot Principat** became the first Andorran club to qualify for Europe (UEFA Cup preliminary round). *League system* Twelve clubs compete in the Andorran league. Three points are awarded for a victory, with one for a draw; final positions for clubs level on points are determined by **goal difference**. Leading clubs: Charlot Principat, Veterans d'Andorra, Santa Colona.

Andrade, 1. José Leandro *player* Midfield **Uruguay** international (41 caps, one goal). Born 20 November 1898. Career ca. 1918–1933. *Clubs* Bella Vista, **Nacional**. *Keynotes* Andrade helped Uruguay win the first World Cup final (4-2, v **Argentina**, in Montevideo). He scored his only international goal at a Copa America match against Peru in 1929 (his team won 4-1). *Honours* **Olympic Games** gold medal (Uruguay, 1920, 1924); **World Cup** (Uruguay, 1930); **Copa America** (Uruguay, 1923, 1924, 1926). **2.** His nephew, Victor Rodriguez *player* Midfield. Uruguay international. Born 1930. *Clubs* **Peñarol** *Keynotes* Andrade played in the 1954 World Cup finals, at which Uruguay finished fourth. *Honours* World Cup (Uruguay, 1950); Copa America (Uruguay, 1956). Uruguayan league championship (Peñarol, 1949, 1951, 1953, 1954).

Anfield *ground* English football ground situated in Liverpool, Merseyside; home of **Liverpool**. *Dossier* Ground capacity: 45,362 all seated. Pitch dimensions: 101m x 68m. Record attendance: 61,905 v **Wolverhampton Wanderers** (2 February 1952, **FA Cup**, fourth round). Best average attendance: 48,127 (1972-73). *History* **Everton** had been tenants of **Anfield** for eight years when in 1892, following a disagreement with the ground's owner, John Houlding, the club decided to depart to a site on the other side of Stanley Park. The ground had staged an international on 2 March 1889 (v **Ireland**) and prior to Everton's departure it could accommodate around 20,000 spectators. Liverpool played its first match at Anfield on 1 September 1892 (v **Rotherham** Town, friendly) and paid £100 a year rent. Major ground developments, including the construction of an Archibald **Leitch**-designed main stand, and the erection of **turnstiles**, occurred after Liverpool won its second League Championship in 1905-06. In addition, a new, and very large, south end terracing was built and within weeks of its opening (1 September 1906) it had been christened the **Spion Kop**, or more commonly the **Kop** after a Boer War battle site where many Merseysiders had died. At this time, a 50-foot flagpole that was originally a mast on the iron ship, Great Eastern, was erected at the ground. The Kop was roofed in 1928 and became the UK's largest covered terrace, with room for 28,000 people. There was no major redevelopment of the ground until 1963, when the Kemlyn Road stand was replaced. This development coincided with the beginning of Liverpool's 25-year period of success and consistency on the pitch that would be unparalleled in English football. On 22 August 1964, Anfield was the location for the first **Match of the Day** (then on BBC2, and featuring Liverpool v **Arsenal**). The proximity of terraced housing on the Kemlyn Road side of the ground initially prevented Liverpool from constructing a second tier on the stand. The club gradually bought the houses in order to proceed with the development, which it finally began in November 1990 after the last tenants – sisters Joan and Nora Mason – agreed an out-of-court financial settlement. The stand was called the Centenary Stand because it opened on 1 September 1992, 100 years after Liverpool played its first match at Anfield. However, the club faced resistance from supporters, including a 10,000-signature petition, to its plans to redevelop the Kop into an all seated facility. The stand was demolished after the club's final home match of the 1993-94 season (30 April, v **Norwich City**) and a concert featuring 1960s Merseybeat bands, such as Gerry and the Pacemakers and The Searchers, the following day. It was replaced by a 12,000-seater stand, which houses a club shop and the first branch of the fast-food outlet McDonalds at a UK sports stadium. During the 1997-98 season, a second tier to the Anfield Road stand was completed, to bring the ground's capacity up to more

than 45,000. Anfield has staged surprisingly few important international and domestic fixtures. In addition to the 1889 international noted earlier, the ground has been the venue for only four other **England** internationals (v **Wales**, 27 March 1905, v Wales 13 March 1922, v **Northern Ireland**, 20 October 1926, v Wales, 18 November 1931). Anfield also staged the **Scotland** v Wales **World Cup** qualifying tie on 12 October 1977 (the match was switched from **Cardiff City**'s **Ninian Park** due to capacity restrictions). In 1995, Anfield staged the 1996 **European Championship** qualification **playoff** between **Netherlands** and the **Republic of Ireland**. The ground was also selected as a venue for the competition, hosting group C matches (**Italy** v **Russia**; **Czech Republic** v Italy; Czech Republic v Russia) and a quarter-final (**France** v Netherlands). Anfield has also been the venue for five FA Cup semi-finals, and various Rugby Union and Rugby League fixtures. The first floodlit match at Anfield took place on 30 October 1957 (v Everton, Liverpool County FA Cup).

Anglo-Italian Cup *competition* knockout competition involving **Football League** clubs and **Serie A** (now **Serie B**) sides. Launched in 1970 and initially involving English and Italian League clubs that had failed to qualify for European competition; later (1993) revived for minor league clubs with the previous **two-leg** final replaced by a **Wembley Stadium** showdown. *Final results* 1970 **Swindon Town** 3–0 v **Napoli** (match **abandoned** after 79 minutes – result stood); 1971 **Blackpool** 2–1 v **Bologna** (a.e.t.); 1972 **Roma (AS)** 3–1 v Blackpool; 1973 **Newcastle United** 2–1 v **Fiorentina**; 1974 Fiorentina 2–0 v **West Ham United**; 1975 Napoli 4–1 v **Southampton**; 1993 Cremonese 3–1 v **Derby County**; 1994 Brescia 1–0 v **Notts County**; 1995 Notts County 2–1 v Ascoli; 1996 **Genoa** 5–2 v **Port Vale**.

Anglo-Italian League Cup-winners Cup *competition* former competition between the winners of the **League Cup** and its Italian equivalent, launched in 1969 largely as a way of rewarding **Swindon Town**, who won the **League Cup** in that year but was barred from competing in the **UEFA** (Fairs) **Cup** because of the club's **Division Three** status. The competition lasted for three seasons. *Final results* 1969 Swindon Town 5–2 agg., v **Roma (AS)**; 1970 **Bologna** 3–2 agg., v **Manchester City**; 1971 **Tottenham Hotspur** 3–0 agg., v **Torino**.

Anglo-Scottish Cup *competition* former knockout competition that in 1975-76 replaced the **Texaco Cup**. Initially an early-season competition involving clubs from both the English and Scottish Leagues that had failed to qualify for European competition and subsequently consisting of clubs with the highest aggregate number of goals scored. Later the competition became the preserve of **Division Two** clubs. Ties were played over two legs up to 1980-81. **Newcastle United** was banned in 1977 after the club failed to field a **full-strength team** against **Ayr United**. The competition ended, as an all British affair, in 1981, when the Scottish clubs withdrew after only one of their number had won the trophy, including the Texaco Cup, in the previous 11 seasons – it was replaced by the **Football League Group Cup** and, later, the **Football League Trophy**. *Final results* 1975-76 **Middlesbrough** 1–0 agg., v **Fulham**; 1976-77 **Nottingham Forest** 5–1 agg., v **Orient**; 1977-78 **Bristol City** 3–2 agg., v **St Mirren**; 1978-79 **Burnley** 4–1 agg., v **Oldham Athletic**; 1979-80 St Mirren 5-1 agg., v Bristol City; 1980-81 **Chesterfield** 2–1 **Notts County**.

Angola *country CAF* republic in Southwest Africa on Atlantic coast. Independence from Portugal in 1975, followed by civil war which had a huge and damaging impact on the economy. Area: 1,246,700 sq km (481,225 sq miles). Climate varies from areas of comparatively high rainfall in coastal plain to semi-desert in Southeast. Population: 11,500,000 (1995 est.). Languages: Portuguese, tribal languages and dialects. Capital: Luanda. Football association (Fédération Angolaise de Football, Luanda) founded in 1979, affiliated to **FIFA** and to **Confédération Africaine de Football** (CAF) in 1980, president Armando Machado, general secretary Victor Barros. Season played from April to January. National stadium: Citaddela, Luanda, capacity: 60,000. National strip: red shirts, black shorts. Nickname of national team: Black Panthers. First international match: June 1977 v **Cuba** (1–0, Luanda, friendly). Biggest victory: 4–0 v **Gabon** (26 November 1982, Luanda, African Nations Cup qualifier), 4–0 v **Botswana** (30 July 1995, Luanda, African Nations Cup qualifier). Biggest defeat: 0–6 v **Portugal** (29 March 1989, Lisbon, friendly). *International tournament record* **Olympic Games** – first entered 1984, never qualified for finals tournament; **Women's World Cup** – semifinal of the African qualifying group for 1995 tournament; **World Cup** – first entered 1986, never qualified for finals tournament, second in second-round qualifying group stage 1998; **African Cup of Nations** – first entered 1982, qualified for finals tournament 1996 (last in its first-round group of four nations), 1998 (third in its group of four); Central African Games – runners-up 1987; *Record against British and Irish teams* none. *Record in international club tournaments* **African Cup of Champion Clubs** – Petro Atlético (quarter-final 1996), **Primeiro de Agosto** (quarter-final "champions-league" stage 1997); **African Cup-winners Cup** – Primeiro de Agosto (runners-up 1998), Ferroviario de Lubango (quarter-final 1988); **CAF Cup** – **Primeiro de Maio** (runners-up 1994), **Petro Atlético** (runners-up 1997), **AS Aviacao** (CAF Cup semi-final 1993.

Anguilla *country CONCACAF* island in the West Indies, in the Leeward Islands, UK dependent territory. Area: 115 sq km (60 sq miles). Population: 8,960. Capital: The Valley. *Dossier* Anguilla Football Association (The Valley), affiliated to **FIFA** and **Confederación Norte-Centroamerican y del Caribe de Fútbol** (CONCACAF) in 1996, president John Martin, general secretary Claus Lippert. National

strip: blue shirts, blue shorts. *International tournament record* **World Cup** – never entered; **CONCACAF Championship/Gold Cup** – never qualified; **Caribbean Nations Cup** – never finished in top four places.

ankle injury *medical* any injury to the ankle, including to the **ankle ligaments**, **Achilles' tendon**, **talus** and ankle **joint**. See **anterior talofibular ligament**, **lateral ankle ligament**, **medial deltoid ligament**, **lateral deltoid ligament**, **lateral malleolus**, **medial malleolus**, **tibiofibular ligament**, **eversion injury**, **inversion injury**.

ankle ligament *medical* any of the **ligaments** of the ankle, including the **medial deltoid ligament** and **lateral deltoid ligament**. Injuries can occur when the ankle is twisted into a plantar flexion and inversion, overstretching the ligaments.

annual subscription *regulations* yearly payment made to retain an ongoing service or membership of an organisation. The **Scottish Football League** requires its member clubs to pay an annual membership fee of £10 plus value-added tax (VAT) (Scottish Football League rule 37). Any club joining the league must pay an entrance fee of £1,000 plus VAT (Scottish Football League rule 36).

Anorthosis Famagusta *club* Cypriot national league club based in Larnaca (formerly in Famagusta, but moved to Larnaca because of the political divide between southern and northern Cyprus), founded 1911. Ground: Antonis Papadopoulos, capacity: 15,000. Strip: blue and white striped shirts, blue shorts. Cyprus Cup 1949, 1962, 1971, 1975, 1998; Cyprus league champions 1950, 1957, 1958, 1960, 1962, 1963, 1995, 1997, 1998j, 1999.

anterior talofibular ligament *medical* part of the **lateral deltoid ligament** joining the **lateral malleolus** of the **fibula** forward to the **talus**. An **inversion injury** (such as a **sprain**, **tear** or **rupture**) at this site is the most common ankle injury in footballers.

Antigua and Barbuda *country CONCACAF* islands in the West Indies, in the Leeward Islands. Commonwealth state. Area: 442 sq km (171 sq miles). Population: 63,900 (1995 est.). Language: English. Capital: St John's (Antigua). Economy centred around tourism and rum production. *Dossier* Antigua Football Association (St John's) founded in 1928, affiliated to **FIFA** in 1970 (three years after independence from Britain) and **Confederación Norte-Centroamerican y del Caribe de Fútbol** (CONCACAF) in 1980, president Ralph Potter, general secretary Chet Greene. Season played from August to December. National stadium: The Recreation Ground, capacity: 12,000. National strip: gold shirts, black shorts. *International tournament record* **Olympic Games** – never beyond qualifying tournament. **World Cup** – first, entered 1974, never beyond first qualifying round; **Caribbean Nations Cup** – semi-final/fourth 1998 (2–3, v **Haiti**, in Trinidad, third/fourth playoff; 0–1, v Jamaica, semifinal), also played in finals tournaments in 1992, 1995 (finished last in group in both years); **Gold Cup** – never qualified. *Record against British and Irish national teams* none played. Leading clubs: J & J Construction, Empire/Gray's Farm (league champions 1992, 1998); English Harbour (league champions 1995, 1996, 1997). Notable former player: Viv **Richards**.

apertura *n.* first of the two domestic league seasons played in **Argentina**, **Bolivia**, **Chile**, **Colombia**, **Ecuador**, **Mexico**, **Paraguay**, **Uruguay** and **Venezuela**. The "season of two halves" maintains spectator interest throughout the year and, depending on the league system in each country, may be followed by a championship playoff or final tournament involving the best-placed clubs from each half. Two regular league seasons (the Apertura followed by the **Clausura**) are played in Argentina, Bolivia, Colombia, Paraguay, Uruguay and Venezuela, followed by an end-of-season tournament. In Ecuador the Apertura is followed by a complex system of group-based tournaments to determine the championship and relegation places. In Chile, the Apertura is a group-based tournament (the **Copa Chile**) with a knockout stage, followed by a regular league season.

Apoel Nicosia *club* Cypriot national league club based in the capital Nicosia, founded 1926. Ground: Makarion, capacity: 20,000. Strip: yellow shirts, blue shorts. Cyprus Cup 1937, 1941, 1947, 1951, 1963, 1968, 1969, 1973, 1976, 1978, 1979, 1984, 1993, 1995, 1996, 1997; Cyprus league champions 1936, 1937, 1938, 1939, 1940, 1947, 1948, 1949, 1952, 1965, 1973, 1980, 1986, 1990, 1992, 1996; **European Cup** second round 1987 (withdrew from tournament after drawing Turkish club **Besiktas** in second round); **European Cup-winners Cup** second round 1964, 1977.

Apollon Limassol *club* Cypriot national league club based in Limassol, founded 1954. Ground: Tsirion, capacity: 22,000. Strip: blue shirts, blue and white shorts. Cyprus Cup 1966, 1967, 1986, 1992; Cyprus league champions 1991, 1994; **European Cup** second round 1992; **UEFA Cup** second round 1994).

appearances, most for national team *record* see **caps, most**.

appearances, most for one club *record* **Football League**: 770 matches, John **Trollope** (Swindon Town, ca. 1961-1980); the previous record, 764 matches, was held by Jimmy **Dickinson** (Portsmouth, 1946-65); the goalkeepers' record is held by Alan **Knight** with 662 league matches, also for Portsmouth (1976-98).

appearances, most in league matches *record* the **Football League** record for the most games by a single player is held by Peter **Shilton**, with 1,005 matches in a playing career that spanned more than 30 years (**Leicester City**, **Stoke City**, **Nottingham Forest**, **Southampton**, **Derby County**, **Plymouth Argyle**, **Bolton Wanderers**, **Leyton Orient**, 1966-97); the record for an outfield player is held by Tony Ford, 838 (1975-99).Ford broke the previous record of

824 held by Terry P**aine**, while playing for **Mansfield Town**. Ford's previous clubs include **West Bromwich Albion**, **Grimsby**, **Barrow**, **Scunthorpe United** and **Bradford City**. Graham Armstrong holds the **Scottish Football League** record for an outfield player; the fulll-back made his 1,000th league appearance in 1998 while playing for **Stenhousemuir**. His first game was in 1975.

appearances, most in succession *record* **1.** **Football League**: 401 consecutive matches, all in Division 3 (North), by Harold Bell of **Tranmere Rovers** (1946-55); Bell played 459 consecutive games in various competitions. **2.** Division One/FA **Premier League**: 366 consecutive league matches, Phil Neal for **Liverpool** (1974-83); Dave Beasant played 394 consecutive league games for **Wimbledon**, **Newcastle** and **Chelsea** (1981-90), but not all were in the top flight.

apply the advantage *rules* see **advantage**.

apprentice *regulations (Scotland)* players who, when aged under 18 and over 16, sign a "contract of apprenticeship" with a **Scottish Football League** club; the contract must be for at least two seasons and for a maximum of three years (Scottish Football League rule 63). An apprentice benefits from training and coaching at the club, but must also be allowed, if desired, to continue with an outside profession, trade, or further education.

approach *vb. regulations* to attempt to persuade a player to leave his registered club and sign for a new club. **1. England**: clubs in England are normally prohibited from approaching **contract players**, either directly or indirectly, except by written permission of the club where he is registered (FA **Premier League** rule J.1, Football League regulation 57). A club is allowed to approach an **out-of-contract player** at any time (FA Premier League rule J. 1.1). A Premier League club is also allowed to approach a contract player, after the third Saturday in May and before 1 July, if that player's contract is shortly to end and he has either not been offered or has declined a new contract (FA Premier League rule J.2). A club is prohibited from expressing an interest in public (for example, by a statement to the press) in any contract player registered at another club, unless the approach falls within the above criteria (FA Premier League rule J.7, Football League regulation 65.2). Contract players, or their agents on their behalf, are normally prohibited from approaching another club without written consent from their present club (FA Premier League rule J.5, Football League regulation 65.4). Premier League contract players whose contracts are about to expire, and who have not been offered, or have declined a new contract, are entitled to approach another club, but only after the third Saturday in May and before 1 July (FA Premier League rule J.6). Out-of-contract players are free to approach another club at any time (FA Premier League rule J.4). **2. Scottish Football League** clubs may approach and sign any player whose name appears on an official **transfer list**, without seeking the consent of the player's original club, provided that the new club pays the **transfer fee** stipulated by the player's original club (Scottish Football League rule 52). Scottish Football League clubs cannot approach a player (professional or amateur) whose name is not on the transfer list without first gaining permission from the player's club. Within this context, any public statement of a club's interest in signing a player is also considered as an unauthorised approach. Players under contract with one club, and their agents, are also prohibited from approaching other clubs with the idea of negotiating a transfer; breaching this rule can lead to a fine, suspension or even expulsion (Scottish Football League rule 52). Compare **inducement**.

April 25th *club* North Korean national league club. **Asian Champion Teams Cup** – third place 1990 (2–2, 7–6 pens., v **Pelita Jaya**, Indonesia, finals tournament in Dhaka, Bangladesh, third/fourth playoff), finals tournament 1988 (two groups of five in a tournament in Kuantan Malaysia; finished third in its group). April 25th has represented North Korea in the Asian Champion Teams Cup more than any other club.

April fool's day *misc.* April 1, a day on which tricks are traditionally played. Football has regularly been used to play April Fool hoaxes. *Keynotes* In 1998, Portuguese national radio told its listeners that the national football team, which had failed to qualify for that summer's **World Cup** in **France**, had been selected by **FIFA** to replace **Iran**, which had decided not to compete for "security reasons". The radio station used actors pretending to be FIFA officials to "confirm" the story. Also in 1998, a German commentator claimed that the world's richest man, the Sultan of Brunei, would be financing the reconstruction of Berlin's Olympic Stadium to boost the country's bid for the 2006 World Cup finals.

aqsaqtuk *n.* early and rudimentary form of football played on ice by various Eskimo peoples in Alaska and Canada. The balls were made of skin and stuffed with animal hair, grass or moss. The goals could be kilometres apart, with whole villages involved.

Arab Club Champions Cup *competition* international club tournament for champion clubs of member nations of the **Arab Football Union**. *Winners* 1982 **Al Schurta** (Iraq); 1983 not played; 1984 **Al Ittifaq** (Saudi Arabia); 1985 **El Rasheed** (Iraq); 1986 El Rasheed; 1987 El Rasheed; 1988 Al Ittifaq; 1989 **WAC Casablanca** (Morocco); 1990 abandoned; 1991 not played; 1992 **Al Shabab** (Saudi Arabia); 1993 **Espérance** (Tunisia); 1994 **Al Hilal** (Saudi Arabia); 1995 Al Hilal; 1996 **Al Ahly** (Egypt); 1997 **Club Africain** (Tunisia), 1998, WA Tlemcem (Algeria).

Arab Contractors *club* Egypt see **Al Mokaouloum**.

Arab Cup of Nations *competition* international nations tournament for member countries of the **Arab Football Union**. *Winners* 1962 **Tunisia**; 1964, 1966, 1985, 1988 **Iraq**; 1992 **Egypt**; 1998 **Saudi Arabia**. Kuwait host the 2001 tournament.

Arab Cup-winners Cup *competition* international club tournament for the national club cup winners of

member nations of the **Arab Football Union**. *Winners* 1989 **Stade Tunisien** (Tunisia); 1990 not played; 1991 **Olympique Casablanca** (Morocco); 1992 Olympique Casablanca; 1993 Olympique Casablanca; 1994 **El Ahly** (Egypt); 1995 **Club Africain** (Tunisia); 1996 **Olympique Club Khourigba** (Morocco); 1997 **Mouloudia Club d'Oran** (Algeria); 1998 Mouloudia Club d'Oran.

Arab Football Union (AFU) *confederation* international football association of Arab nations (from North Africa and the Middle East), based in Riyadh, Saudi Arabia, founded 1974. Member countries: **Algeria, Bahrain, Egypt, Iran, Iraq, Jordan, Kuwait, Lebanon, Libya, Morocco, Oman, Qatar, Saudi Arabia, Sudan, Syria, Tunisia, United Arab Emirates, Yemen**. *Nations tournaments* **Arab Cup of Nations**. *International club tournaments* **Arab Club Champions Cup**, **Arab Cup-winners Cup**, **Arab Super Cup**.

Arab Super Cup *competition* international club tournament contested by the four finalists in the **Arab Club Champions Cup** and **Arab Cup-winners Cup**. It is played as a round-robin mini-league, each club playing three games in a single host nation. *Winners* 1995 **Al Shabab** (Saudi Arabia); 1996 **Espérance** (Tunisia); 1997 **Al Ahly** (Egypt); 1998 **Al Ahly**; 1999 **Mouloudia Club d'Oran** (Algeria).

Arabian Gulf Cup *competition* biennial regional nations tournament held over two weeks, open to the nations of the Persian/Arabian Gulf: **Bahrain, Iraq, Iran, Kuwait, Oman, Qatar, Saudi Arabia** and the **United Arab Emirates**. First played 1970. Now played on a league basis, with the top nation declared champions. Iraq was dismissed from the competition in 1992 for its invasion of Kuwait. *Winners* 1970, 1972, 1974, 1976, 1982, 1986, 1990, 1996 Kuwait; 1979, 1984, 1988 Iraq; 1992 Qatar; 1994, 1998 Saudi Arabia.

Ararat Yerevan *club* Armenian national league club, based in the capital Yerevan, founded 1937 (as Dynamo Yerevan until 1954 when name changed to Spartak Yerevan, adopting current name in 1962). Ground: Razdan (the national stadium), capacity: 50,000. Strip: red shirts, blue shorts. Armenian cup 1993, 1994, 1995, 1997; Armenian league champions 1993; **European Cup** quarter-final 1975; former-Soviet Union Cups 1973, 1975 (including the "**double**" in 1973); former-Soviet Union league championship 1973. The club was eighth in the former-Soviet Union all-time order of merit.

Arbroath *club* Scottish league. *Dossier* Ground: **Gayfield Park**, Arbroath, Tayside, capacity:6,488. Strip: maroon shirt with white collar and maroon and white stripes on sleeve, maroon shorts with white trim, maroon socks with sky blue hoops. Nickname: Red Lichties. Record attendance: 13,510 v **Rangers** (23 February 1952, **Scottish FA Cup**, third round). Biggest win: 36–0 v Bon Accord (12 September 1885, Scottish FA Cup). Biggest defeat: 1–9 v **Celtic** (25 August 1993, **Scottish League Cup**, third round). *History* Founded in 1878, Arbroath moved to Gayfield Park two years later. Arbroath's 36–0 Scottish FA Cup victory over Bon Accord in September 1885 remains the biggest score in a UK senior match. The previous season Arbroath had humbled Rangers in a fourth-round Cup match at Gayfield, only for the Scottish FA to order the game to be replayed because the pitch was too small. Rangers won the replay 8–1. Arbroath's 11th place in Division One in 1937-38 is the club's highest finish. In 1947, Arbroath was a Scottish FA Cup semi-finalist (0–2 v **Aberdeen**). Gayfield Park is closer to the sea than any other senior football ground in the UK and the club's nickname, Red Lichties, is derived from the red light that is cast by the Bell Rock lighthouse. *League record* First Division 1975-76 to 1979-80; Division One 1935-36 to 1938-39, 1959-60, 1968-69, 1972-73 to 1974-75; Second Division 1980-81 to 1993-94; Division Two (B Division) 1921-22 to 1934-35, 1946-47 to 1958-59, 1960-61 to 1967-68, 1969-70 to 1971-72; Third Division 1994-95–. *Records* John "Ned" Doig is Arbroath's most capped player (2 (5) for **Scotland**); Tom Cargill holds the record for club appearances (445, 1966-81); Jimmy Jack is Arbroath's record goalscorer (120, 1966-71).

Ardiles, Ossie (Osvaldo) *player-manager* Midfield. **Argentina** international (42 caps, 8 goals). Born 3 August 1952. Career ca. 1970–1988. *Clubs* (player) Instituto Cordoba, **Huracan**, **Tottenham Hotspur**, **Paris St-Germain**, **Blackburn Rovers**, **Queens Park Rangers**; (manager) **Swindon Town**, **Newcastle United**, **West Bromwich Albion**, Tottenham Hotspur, **Shimizu S-Pulse**, **America** (Mexico). *Keynotes* Joined Tottenham Hotspur for around £325,000 in a double £700,000 transfer which also brought fellow Argentina World Club squad member Ricardo Villa to **White Hart Lane**. Ardiles went on to make 238 **Football League** appearances for Tottenham, although the Falklands War interrupted his Spurs career. Ardiles did not play in Spurs' 1982 **FA Cup** final victory because of the war and he also started the 1982-83 season on loan with Paris St-Germain. He became Swindon manager in 1989 and won promotion to the top flight via the Division Two end-of-season **playoffs** in his first full season (1–0 v **Sunderland**), but the club's elevation was denied by the Football League after an investigation uncovered financial irregularities committed during the mid-1980s. Ardiles moved to Newcastle in 1991 but was sacked and replaced by Kevin **Keegan** in February 1992. As West Bromwich Albion manager, Ardiles led to club to promotion, again via the playoffs (3–0 v **Port Vale**) from the Second Division, but quit to become boss at Tottenham only to be dismissed 16 months later. *Honours* FA Cup (Tottenham Hotspur 1981); **UEFA Cup** (Tottenham Hotspur 1984); **World Cup** (Argentina 1978) Included in the **Football League Centenary 100 players**.

Ards FC *club* Northern Irish national league club based in Newtownards, Ards, County Down, founded 1902. Ground: Castlereagh Park, capacity: 10,000. Strip: red and blue striped shirts, blue shorts. **Irish FA**

Cup 1927, 1952, 1969, 1974; Northern Ireland league champions 1958.

area *n.* shortened term for **penalty area**.

Argentina *country* CONMEBOL republic in south and central South America. Area: 2,766,889 sq km (1,068,302 sq miles). Large climatic variation: from the Andes Mountains in the West – with altitudes above 6,000 m (19,500 feet) through the fertile plains or Pampas, hot tropics in the north, to the much colder, wetter climate of the deep south. Population: 34,770,000 (1995 est.). Language: Spanish. Capital: Buenos Aires. *Dossier* Football association (Asociación del Fútbol Argentino, Buenos Aires) formed in 1893, joined **FIFA** in 1912 and founder member of the **Confederación Sudamericana de Fútbol** (CONMEBOL) in 1916, president Julio Grondona, general secretary Fernando Da Miele. Domestic season played in two parts: August to December (**Apertura**) and February to May (**Clausura**). National stadium: **Antonio Liberti "Monumental" de Nunez**, Buenos Aires, capacity: 76,000 (59,000 seated). National strip: light blue and white striped shirts, black shorts. Website http://www.afa.org.ar (official site). First international match: 16 May 1901, v **Uruguay** (3–2, in Montevideo, friendly). Biggest victory: 12–0 v **Ecuador** (22 January 1942, Montevideo, **Copa America**). Biggest defeat: 1–6 v **Czechoslovakia** (15 June 1958, Halsingbord, Sweden, World Cup first round). Most capped players: Oscar Ruggeri (98 appearances, 1983-94); Diego **Maradona** (90 appearances, 1977-94), Diego Simeone (76 appearances, 1989-), Amerigo Gallego (73 appearances, 1975-82), Daniel **Passarella** (70 appearances, 1976-86), Gabriel **Batistuta** (68 appearances, 1991-) Alberto Tarantini (61 appearances). Leading international goalscorers: Gabriel Batistuta (49 goals, 1991-); Diego Maradona (34 goals), Luis Artime (24 goals), Daniel Passarella (22 goals). Other leading players: Norberto Alonso, Osvaldo **Ardiles**, Daniel Batista, Jorge Burruchaga, Claudio Caniggia, Ubaldo Fillol, Sergio Goycochea, Mario **Kempes**, Norberto **Mendez**, Antonio Rattin, Omar **Sivori**. *International tournament record* **Olympic Games** – runners-up/silver medal 1928 (1–2 v Uruguay, in Amsterdam, the Netherlands), 1996 (2–3, v Nigeria, Atlanta, USA); **World Cup** – entered first tournament in 1930, 1978 (3–1, v **Netherlands**, in Buenos Aires, 25 June 1978) and 1986 (3–2, v West **Germany**, in Mexico City, Mexico, 29 July 1986), runners-up 1930 (2–4, v host-nation Uruguay, in Montevideo, 30 July 1930) and 1990 (0–1, v West Germany, in Rome, 8 July 1990), quarter-final 1966, 1998, also qualified for finals tournament 1934, 1958, 1962, 1974, 1982, 1994 (did not enter in 1938, 1950 or 1954), hosts 1978; **Women's World Cup** – first entered 1995, second in its four-nation qualifying group (including a 12–0 victory over **Bolivia**), failed to qualify for 1999 finals tournament after losing CONMEBOL/CONCACAF playoff (3–6 agg., v Mexico); **Atlantic Cup** – runners-up 1956, 1960, 1976; **Confederations Cup** – 1992 (3–1, v **Saudi Arabia**, in Riyadh, Saudi Arabia 20 October 1992), runners-up 1995 (0–2, v **Denmark**, in Riyadh, 13 January 1995); Copa America – 1910, 1921, 1925, 1927, 1929, 1937, 1941, 1945, 1946, 1947, 1955, 1957, 1959, 1991, 1993, runners-up 1916, 1917, 1920, 1923, 1924, 1926, 1935, 1942, 1959, and 1967 (see Copa America for full results), third 1919, 1956, 1963, 1989, semi-final 1987, quarter-final 1995, 1997; FIFA **Under-17 World Championship** – third 1991 (1–1, 4–1 pens., v **Qatar**, in Italy, third/fourth playoff), 1995 (2–0, v Oman, in Guayaquil, Ecuador, third/fourth playoff), quarter-final 1997; **Lipton Cup** – 1906, 1907, 1909, 1913, 1915, 1916, 1917, 1937, 1962; **Newton Cup** – 1906, 1907, 1908, 1911, 1916, 1918, 1924, 1927, 1928, 1937, 1942, 1945, 1968, 1971, 1975; **Pan-American Championship** – 1960 (tournament held in San José, Costa Rica), runners-up 1956 (the tournament was played only three times, from 1952 to 1960); **Pan-American Games** (amateur) – 1937, 1951, 1955, 1959, 1971, 1995 (0–0, 5–4 pens., v **Mexico**, in Mar del Plata, Argentina); **South American Under-17 Championship** 1985; **South American Women's Championship** (World Cup qualifier) – runners-up 1995 (league of five nations, in Uberlândia, Brazil), 1998 (1–7, v Brazil, in Mar del Plata, Argentina); **South American Youth Cup** (under-20) – 1967, 1997; **World Youth Cup** (under-20) – 1979 (3–1, v **Soviet Union**, in Tokyo, Japan), 1995 (2–0, v **Brazil**, in Qatar), 1997 (2–1, v Uruguay, in Kuala Lumpur, Malaysia), runners-up 1983 (0–1, v Brazil, in Mexico City), qualified 1999. *World Cup performance* (finals and qualifiers to end of 1998 tournament) played 105, won 57, drawn 22, lost 26, scored 187 goals, conceded 112 goals. Win rate: 54%. Goals scored per game: 1.78. *Record against British and Irish national teams* v **England**, played 12, won three, drawn four, lost four, with one match abandoned (1953, Buenos Aires); v **Northern Ireland**, played one, won one; v **Scotland**, played three, won one, drawn one, lost one; **Wales**, played one, won one; v **Republic of Ireland**, played four, won three, drawn one. *History* Football is said to have been introduced by British sailors in the 1860s. It was initially played by British and other European expatriates, who founded many of the first clubs, but became popular with Argentineans by the end of the 19th century. The oldest clubs still in existence are **Quilmes Athletic Club** and **Gimnasia y Esgrima La Plata** (both formed 1887). Buenos Aires Football Club was founded in 1865, but no longer exists. The strong British link to the early development of football in Argentina is clear from the English spelling of some of the most famous clubs – such as **Boca Juniors**, **Newell's Old Boys** and **Racing Club** – while the national league club, Club Atlético Douglas Haig, of Pergamino, founded in November 1918, bears the name of the commander-in-chief of the British forces in Europe in World War I. The Argentinean domestic league is the oldest in the world outside Britain and Ireland. The first league, the Argentine Association

Football League, was founded in 1891 and lasted only one season. It involved six clubs: Belgrano FC, Buenos Aires FC, Buenos Aires to Rosario Railway, Hurlingham FC, Old Caledonians and Saint Andrews Scotch School, the first champions. It was replaced by a new championship, the Argentine Football Association League, founded in 1893 by a Scotsman, Alexander **Watson Hutton**. The new league involved five clubs, Buenos Aires Railway, English High School (where Hutton was director), Flores AC, Lomas AC and Quilmes Rovers, and was first won by Lomas Athletic. The entirely amateur competition increased in size, but included clubs from a relatively small area of the country, from the four major cities on the Rio de la Plata and the Paraná River – Buenos Aires, La Plata, Rosario and Santa Fe – excluding other large cities such as Córdoba, Mendoza and Santiago del Estero, where separate regional leagues were organised. English High School, later known as Alumni (an old boys' club), were the most successful early club, winning 10 championships between 1900 and 1911. Professional football was introduced in 1931. A National Championship was created in 1967, running parallel to the original league. It included clubs from the professional Primera A league and the leading provisional league clubs. Both competitions continued to run until 1985 when a formal national league was established. Historically, the most successful clubs in the various forms of the national championship are, in order, River Plate (24 titles to 1998), Boca Juniors (20), Racing Club (15), **Independiente** (11), Alumni (10) and **San Lorenzo de Almagro** (nine). Racing Club's seven consecutive domestic league titles (1913 to 1919) is a joint South American club record (matched by **Robin Hood** of **Surinam**). Argentinean clubs have been the most successful in the **World Club Cup**, winning the trophy seven times, as well having the best record in the **Copa Libertadores**, with 17 wins and seven- imes runners-up. Independiente, the most successful club in the tournament, has won the Copa Libertadores on seven occasions, and has never lost in the final. **Estudiantes La Plata** won three tournaments in succession (1968, 1969, 1970) and was runner-up in 1971. The trophy also has been won by Racing Club, Boca Juniors, **Argentinos Juniors**, River Plate and **Velez Sarsfield**. In 1996, Argentinean clubs completed a clean sweep, winning all three South American club tournaments (Copa Libertadores, **Copa CONMEBOL** and **Supercopa**. Argentina's first international match, in 1901 against Uruguay (above), was the first international match played outside the United Kingdom. The regular fixture against Uruguay became, in 1905, the **Lipton Cup**, given by Sir Thomas Lipton, the English tea importer, last played in 1973. Argentina won the first Copa America in 1910, and is the most successful nation in the tournament's history. It has won the Copa 15 times, one more than Uruguay, and 10 more than Brazil. It has won the World Cup twice, the first time as hosts in 1978, and was beaten finalists in the first World Cup of 1930 (by the host nation Uruguay, in front of 93,000 spectators at the **Centenario Stadium**, Montevideo). The 1978 final, at the Monumental Stadium, Buenos Aires, was watched by 77,000 spectators. Mario **Kempes** (2), and Bertoni scored Argentina's goals in an extra-time victory over Netherlands. Kempes was the tournament's top scorer, with six goals. Argentina won the tournament again in 1986, with a 3-2 victory over West Germany, at Azteca Stadium in Mexico City; Brown, Valdano and Burrachaga scoring for Argentina. In Britain, however, the 1986 tournament will be remembered for Diego Maradona's infamous **"Hand of God"** goal, in Argentina's 2-1 defeat of England in the quarter-final (22 June, Azteca Stadium). The goal, after 51 minutes, was followed four minutes later by what is widely considered the finest goal of all time: Maradona made a stunning individual run from inside his own half, beating the entire England defence before dummying the goalkeeper, Peter **Shilton**, and side-footing the ball into the empty net. Maradona scored five goals in the tournament, one short of Gary **Lineker**'s **World Cup Golden-Boot** winning tally. Maradona captained a comparatively lacklustre Argentine side to another World Cup final in 1990, this time losing to West Germany, at the Olimpico Stadium in Rome, Argentina finishing the match with only nine players after Monzon and Dezotti were sent off. Maradona was sent home from the 1994 World Cup finals after failing a drug test. Argentina were knocked out in the second round by Romania (2-3). A strong Argentine side, featuring Gabriel **Batistuta** (Argentina's all-time top scorer) and Ariel **Ortega**, reached the quarter-final of the 1998 World Cup. Alongside Maradona in Argentina's list of all-time most talented players, is Alfredo **di Stefano**. Di Stefano scored six goals for Argentina in its 1947 Copa America winning side – including a hat-trick against Colombia. He played only eight games for Argentina before moving to Spain, where he joined **Real Madrid**. Di Stefano scored 23 goals for his adopted country in only four years (1957-61), and is still Spain's second-highest scorer. Argentina was runner-up in the first International Blind Sports Federation Football World Championships in São Paulo in 1998 (see **visually impaired football**). *World Cup final teams and scorers* 1930 (runners-up): Botasso (goalkeeper), Della Torre, Paternóster, J Evaristo, Monti, Suárez, Peucelle (1), Varallo, Stábile (1), Ferreira, M Evaristo; 1978: Fillol (goalkeeper), Olguin. Galván, Passarella, Tarantini, Ardiles (Larrosa), Gallego, Kempes (2), Bertoni (1), Luque, Ortiz (Houseman); 1986: Pumpido (goalkeeper), Cuciuffo, Brown (1), Ruggeri, Olarticoechea, Batista, Giusti, Enrique, Burruchaga (1) (Trobbiani), Maradona, Valdano (1). *1990* (runners-up): Goycochea (goalkeeper), Ruggeri (Monzon), Simón, Serrizuela, Sensini, Basualdo, Burruchaga (Calderon), Troglio, Lorenzo, Maradona, Dezotti. *League system* There are two national divisions – Primera A and Nacional B – with regional feeder leagues. The Primera B, C and D divisions are restricted to teams around Buenos Aires. There

are 20 clubs in the Primera A and, since 1996-97, 32 clubs in the Nacional B. The Primera A league Apertura and Clausura tournaments are separate, with no playoffs; each season thus has two champions. Relegation from the Primera A is determined by average points over the previous three seasons. The first promotion place from the Nacional B league is decided by a playoff between the winners of the Apertura and Clausura tournaments. The second promotion place is decided by an eight-nation tournament involving the beaten playoff finalists, the top six teams (over the whole season) and the champions of the Primera B league. Similar playoffs and end-of-season eight-club tournaments determine the promotion issues in the Primera C and D leagues. Another tier, of provincial clubs, plays in the Argentina A league; a tournament played by four groups of eight teams; the top four in each group playing in a championship tournament, while the bottom four in each group play in a relegation tournament. The winning club is automatically promoted to the Nacional B division. *Record in international club tournaments* **World Club Cup** – Independiente (1973, 1984), **Estudiantes La Plata** (1968), **Boca Juniors** (1977), **Racing Club** (1967), **River Plate** (1986), **Velez Sarsfield** (1994); **Copa Libertadores** – Argentinos Juniors (1985), Boca Juniors (1977, 1978, runners-up 1963, 1979, semi-final 1965, 1991), Estudiantes La Plata (1968, 1969, 1970, runners-up 1971), Independiente (1964, 1965, 1972, 1973, 1974, 1975, 1984), Racing Club (1967, semi-final 1968, 1997), River Plate (1986, 1996, runners-up 1966, 1976, semi-final 1970, 1990, 1995, 1998), Velez Sarsfield (1994), **Newell's Old Boys** (runners-up 1988, 1992), **San Lorenzo de Almagro** (semi-final 1960, 1988); **Copa CONMEBOL** – **Rosario Central** (1995, semi-final 1996, runners-up 1998), **Lanús** (1996, runners-up 1997), **Gimnasia y Esgrima** (semi-final 1992), San Lorenzo de Almagro (semi-final 1993), Club Colon (semi-final 1997); **Supercopa** – Boca Juniors (1989, runners-up 1994), Independiente (1994, 1995), Racing Club (1988, runners-up 1992), Velez Sarsfield (1996), River Plate (1997, runners-up 1991, 1996, semi-final 1988), Argentinos Juniors (semi-final 1989) Estudiantes La Plata (semi-final 1991); **Recopa** – Boca Juniors (1989), Independiente (1994); Vélez Sarsfield (1997); **Copa Mercosur** – **San Lorenzo de Almagro** (semi-final 1998); **Copa Inter Americana** – Estudiantes (1968), Independiente (1972, 1974, 1976), Argentinos Juniors (1986), River Plate (1987); Velez Sarsfield, (1996). Other leading club: **Huracán**.

Argentinos Juniors (Asociacion Atlética Argentinos Juniors) *club* Argentinean national league club, based in Buenos Aires, founded 1904. Ground: Estadio Martin de Gainza, capacity: 24,000. Strip: red shirts, red shorts. Argentinos Juniors won the longest penalty shoot-out on record, eventually beating **Racing Club** 20–19 in a cup match in 1988. Argentinean league champions 1984; Argentinean National Championship (a pre-national-league tournament operating from 1967 to 1985) 1985; **Copa Libertadores** 1985 (1–0, 0–1, 1–1 playoff, 5–4 pens., v **America Cali**); **Supercopa** semi-final 1989. Notable former player Diego **Maradona**.

Aris Salonica *club* Greek national league club based in Thesalonika (Salonika), founded 1914. Ground: Harilaou, capacity: 27,000. Strip: yellow shirts, black shorts. Greek Cup 1970; Greek league champions 1928, 1932, 1946.

Armadale *club* former Scottish league. *Dossier* Ground: Volunteer Park, Lothian. *Keynotes* Armadale joined Division Two in 1921-22, finishing third – the club's highest League position. Armadale was a **Scottish FA Cup** quarter-finalist in 1920 (1–2 v **Kilmarnock**). The club was expelled from the Scottish League in November 1932 after failing to produce the financial guarantees (£50) required by the Scottish football authorities. *League record* Division Two 1921-22 to 1932-33 (did not complete fixtures).

Armenia *country UEFA* republic in West Asia, former republic of the Soviet Union, declared independence 1991, recognised 1992. Joined the ephemeral **Commonwealth of Independent States** in 1991. Area: 11,580 sq miles (29,800 sq km). Population: 3,740,000 (1995 est.). Languages: Armenian, Russian. Capital: Yerevan. *Dossier* Football Federation of Armenia (Yerevan), originally founded 1934, with the independent association reformed in 1992 when the country was also affiliated to FIFA and the **Union of European Football Associations** (UEFA), president Armenak Sargsyan, general secretary Pavel Katchatrian. Season from September to May. National stadium: Razdan, Yerevan, capacity: 69,500. National strip: red shirts, blue shorts. Website http://www.ffa.arminco.co (official site). First international 15 May 1994 v **USA** (0–1, Fullerton, USA, friendly). Most capped players: Sarkis Hovsepyan (29 appearances, 1992–), Artur Petrosyan (29 appearances, 1992–). *International tournament record* **Women's World Cup** – never entered; **World Cup** – first entered 1998, never qualified for finals tournament; **European Championship** – first entered 1996, never qualified for finals tournament; European Championship for Women – never entered. *World Cup performance* (finals and qualifiers to end of 1998 tournament) played 10, won 1, drawn 1, lost 8, scored 7 goals, conceded 20 goals; win rate 10%; goals scored per game 0.7. *Record against British and Irish national teams* v **Northern Ireland**, played two drawn two. *History* Top clubs played in the Soviet leagues prior to independence. **Ararat Yerevan** won both the Soviet league and cup competitions, including the "**double**" in 1973. Independent Armenian national league and cup competitions started 1991-92. *League system* Ten clubs compete in the national first division, with three points awarded for a win and one for a draw; **goal difference** is used to separate clubs level on points. The bottom two clubs are relegated. The domestic Cup final is played at the end of May. *Record in international club tournaments* **European Cup** – **Ararat Yerevan** (quar-

ter-final 1975). Other leading clubs: Banants Abovyan (Armenian Cup 1992), **Erebuni Yerevan**, FK Yerevan (Armenian league champions 1998), **Pyunik Yerevan**, **Shirak Gyumri**. Notable players: Oganesian, Andreasian (both played for the former-**Soviet Union**).

Armfield, Jimmy *player-manager/broadcaster* Right-back. **England** international (43 caps). Born 21 September 1935. Career ca. 1951–1971. *Clubs* (player) **Blackpool**; (manager) **Bolton Wanderers**, **Leeds United**. *Keynotes* Joined Blackpool as an amateur in 1951, turning professional in September 1954. Armfield made 568 **Football League** appearances. He captained England on 15 occasions. Bolton manager between 1971 and 1974, becoming Leeds boss and taking the club to the 1975 **European Cup** final (0–2 v **Bayern Munich**). Prior to Glenn **Hoddle**'s appointment as England manager in 1996, the **Football Association** asked Armfield to identify a possible successor to Terry **Venables**. Currently a **Radio 5 Live** commentator/pundit. Included in the **Football League Centenary 100 players**. *Honours* Division Three (Bolton Wanderers 1972-73).

Arsenal *club* English league. *Dossier* Ground: **Highbury Stadium**, north London, capacity: 38,500 all seated. Strip: red shirts with white sleeves, white shorts, red socks with white hoops. Website: *www.arsenal.co.uk* Nickname: Gunners. Record attendance: 73,295 v **Sunderland** (9 March 1935, Division One). Best average attendance: 54,982 (1947-48). Biggest win: 12–0 v **Loughborough Town** (12 March 1900, Division Two). Biggest defeat: 0–8 v Loughborough Town (12 December 1896, Division Two). *History* Formed in 1886 by workers employed at the Royal Arsenal, Woolwich, in South-east London. Initially the club was named Dial Square FC, after one of the workshops at the weapons manufacturer, and the players wore an all-red strip, which continued to be worn until 1933. The jerseys and a ball were supplied by **Nottingham Forest**, responding to a request from a former player, Fred Beardsley, to help the fledgling club. Officially known as Royal Arsenal, a name it retained until 1891 when the club acquired professional status and became Woolwich Arsenal. The club were the first London-based team to turn professional and the only club south of Birmingham at the time to be members of the **Football League**. After playing at several local venues, including Plumstead Common and Manor Field, where the club played between 1888 and 1890, Royal Arsenal moved to the purpose-built Invicta Ground, which was owned by George Weaver, of the Weaver Mineral Water Company. Weaver's proposed rent increase, to coincide with the club's election to Division Two in 1893, resulted in Woolwich Arsenal returning to Manor Field (later Ground), which it subsequently bought. In 1896, the club was forced to play a league fixture and an **FA Cup**-tie on the same day: the reserves beat Leyton 5-0 in the Cup, while the first team lost 0-8 to Loughborough Town – the club's heaviest defeat. In 1904, the club was promoted to Division One.

The extra demands placed on workers at the Royal Arsenal by the Boer War meant that they had less time to devote to the club, and this, coupled with high mortgage repayments and low attendances, led to increasing debts and eventual liquidation. **Fulham** director, Member of Parliament and property developer Henry Norris stepped in and proposed a merger between Woolwich Arsenal and Fulham, which had just joined the League, but the authorities refused. Relegation followed in 1913, after the club won only one home game all season – a record that no other senior-level club has matched. This is the only time Arsenal has been relegated in its history. By the following season, Norris had moved the club to a new venue in north London, at Highbury, although the ground did not become a major stadium until 1930s. The move sparked an outrage: local professional teams **Tottenham Hotspur** and Clapton **Orient** did not want the competition, while Islington Borough Council and local residents campaigned against the club settling in their area. Woolwich Arsenal became The Arsenal, a name retained until 1927, when "The" was dropped. The Arsenal's first match at Highbury was played on 6 September 1913 v **Leicester Fosse**. Financial problems continued to plague the club despite the move across the Thames. In 1919, with the expansion of the League, Norris engineered a place for Arsenal in the extended Division One, largely at the expense of neighbours Tottenham Hotspur. Precedent (from earlier league expansions) suggested that Tottenham should have retained its place in Division One, having finished 20th. Arsenal was awarded first-division status following a poll of the Football League clubs, allegedly heavily influenced by Norris. Arsenal's election, rather than promotion, was the beginning of the club's unbroken spell in the top flight. As a result, Arsenal holds two unique records: the only club with continuous membership of Division One (Premier League) since 1919; and the only league club to have been promoted other than on playing merit. By the 1930s, Arsenal, under the management of Herbert **Chapman**, was the dominant force in English football, winning the League Championship on five occasions and the FA Cup twice during the decade. In 1932 London Underground acknowledged the club's success by renaming Gillespie Road station as Arsenal station. Arsenal won the **UEFA** (Fairs) **Cup** in 1970 (4–3 agg., v **Anderlecht**) and, in 1971, the club became only the second club this century to win the League Championship and the FA Cup (**double**). Arsenal completed a unique cup double in 1993, defeating **Sheffield Wednesday** 2-1 in both the FA Cup final and the **League Cup** final. In 1994, Arsenal won the **European Cup-winners Cup** (1–0 v **Parma**) and the following season the club reached the final of the same competition (1–2 v **Real Zaragoza**). George **Graham**'s nine years as Arsenal manager (1986-95) included six major trophies, but he was dismissed in February 1995 amid accusations of financial irregularities. The club is currently managed by Frenchman Arséne **Wenger**, who, in only his second season in

English football, led the Gunners to a **Premiership** title and FA Cup (2–0 v **Newcastle United**) double in 1997-98. In the process, Wenger became the first foreigner to manage a championship-winning side in England. Arsenal has played all but 13 seasons in the top division during its history. Although Arsenal withdrew a £125 million bid in 1998 to buy **Wembley**, the club was granted permission in July 1998 by both the Football Association and UEFA to stage its forthcoming **Champions League** fixtures at the national stadium. *League record* Premier League 1992-93 to present; Division One 1904-05 to 1912-13, 1919-20 to 1991-92; Division Two 1893-94 to 1903-04, 1913-14 to 1918-19. *Honours* League 1930-31, 1932-33, 1933-34, 1934-35, 1937-38, 1947-48, 1952-53, 1970-71, 1988-89, 1990-91; Premiership 1997-98; FA Cup 1930 (2–0 v **Huddersfield Town** – *Team* Preedy, Parker, Hapgood, Baker, Seddon, John, Hulme, Jack, Lambert (1), James (1), Bastin); 1936 (1–0 v **Sheffield United** – *Team* Wilson, Male, Hapgood, Crayston, Roberts, Copping, Hulme, Bowden, Drake (1), James, Bastin); 1950 (2–0 v **Liverpool** – *Team* Swindin, Scott, Barnes, Forbes, L Compton, Mercer, Cox, Logie, Goring, Lewis (2), D Compton); 1971 (2–1 a.e.t. v Liverpool – *Team* Wilson, Rice, McNab, Storey (Kelly (1)), McLintock, Simpson, Armstrong, Graham, Radford, Kennedy, George (1)); 1979 (3–2 v **Manchester United** – *Team* Jennings, Rice, Nelson, Talbot (1), O'Leary, Young, Brady, Sunderland (1), Stapleton (1), Price (Walford), Rix); 1993 (2–1 a.e.t/replay v Sheffield Wednesday – *Team* Seaman, Dixon, Winterburn, Linighan, Adams, Parlour (Smith), Davis, Merson, Jensen, Wright (1) (O'Leary), Campbell; replay Seaman, Dixon, Winterburn, Linighan (1), Adams, Davis, Jensen, Merson, Smith, Wright (1) (O'Leary), Campbell); 1998 (2–0 v Newcastle United – *Team* Seaman, Dixon, Keown, Adams, Winterburn, Vieira, Parlour, Petit, Overmars (1), Anelka (1), Wreh (Platt)); League Cup 1987 (2–1 v Liverpool), 1993 (2–1 v Sheffield Wednesday); **FA Charity Shield** 1930 (2–1 v Sheffield Wednesday), 1931 (1–0 v **West Bromwich Albion**), 1933 (3–0 v **Everton**), 1934 (4–0 v **Manchester City**), 1938 (2–1 v **Preston North End**), 1948 (4–3 v Manchester United), 1953 (3–1 v **Blackpool**), 1991 (0–0 v Tottenham Hotspur (each club held the trophy for six months)), 1998 (3–0 v Manchester United); **Sheriff of London's Charity Shield** 1931 (5–3 v **Corinthians**), 1933 (9–2 v Corinthians), 1965 (7–0 v Corinthian Casuals), 1966 (5–2 v Corinthian Casuals); **European Cup-winners Cup** 1994 (1–0 v **Parma** – *Team* Seaman, Dixon, Winterburn, Davis, Bould, Adams, Campbell, Morrow, Smith (1), Merson (McGoldrick), Selley); UEFA (Fairs) Cup 1970 (4–3 agg., v Anderlecht – *Team* first leg (away) Wilson, Storey, McNab, Kelly, McLintock, Simpson, Armstrong, Sammels, Radford, George (Kennedy (1)), Graham; second leg (home) Wilson, Storey, McNab, Kelly (1), McLintock, Simpson, Armstrong, Sammels (1), Radford (1), George, Graham). *Records* Kenny **Sansom** is Arsenal's most capped player (77 (86) for **England**); David **O'Leary** holds the record for club appearances (558, 1975-93); Ian Wright is Arsenal's record goalscorer (185, 1991-98). **2.** *club* English Women's League club. *Dossier* Ground: Bromley FC, south-east London. Strip: red shirts with white sleeves, white shorts, red socks with white hoops. Biggest win: 12–0 v **Canary Racers** (11 January 1998, **FA Women's Challenge Cup**). Biggest defeat: 1–3* v Everton (16 November 1997, Premier League (*since National League)). *Keynotes* Formed in 1987 from a merger of Aylesbury Ladies and local women. *Honours* FA Cup 1993 (3–0 v **Doncaster Belles**), 1995 (3–2 v Liverpool), 1999 (2–0 v Southampton Saints); FA Women's Premier League Cup 1993, 1994, 1998 (0–0, 4–3 pens. v Croydon); Premier League 1992-93, 1994-95, 1996-97.

Arsenal, Lesotho *club* Lesotho national league club, based in Maseru (capital of Lesotho) founded 1983. Strip: red shirts and white shorts. Ground: Pitso, capacity: 6,000. Founded by supporters of English league side, **Arsenal FC**. Nickname: the Gunners. **African Cup of Champion Clubs** second round 1990; **African Cup-winners Cup** second round 1993; CAF Cup second round 1995; Lesotho Cup 1989 and 1991, 1998; Lesotho league champions 1989, 1991, 1993.

art *misc.* football as the subject of fine art. Despite being the national game, football is not well-represented in UK's national galleries. However, the National Portrait Gallery in London has a portrait of Sir Bobby **Charlton**, painted by Peter Edwards in 1991. A portrait of ex-**Celtic** and **Scotland** international Danny **McGrain**, by Humphrey Ocean, hangs in the Scottish National Portrait Gallery in Edinburgh (oil on canvas, 1989). In the summer of 1996 two galleries staged entire exhibitions on football art: "Offside!", a fine art installation at City Art Gallery, Manchester, and "Life's a pitch" at Cornerhouse Gallery, Manchester. Peter Howson's pre-World Cup 1998 exhibition, "Football Paintings", comprised 36 paintings described by Rachel Campbell-Johnston in *The Times* (25 May 1998) as spontaneous: "the vibrant smears, the looser than usual brushstrokes, the unmixed colour. This, and the way the big brawny figures can scarcely be contained within their small frames make for an energetic display. Bodies dive and twist, hands splay, shoulders shunt into the foreground, knees smash against the picture frame." The exhibition was staged at the Flowers East gallery in East London.

arthroscopy *medical* the procedure in which a surgeon will look into the inside of a **joint** with fibre optic equipment to get a direct view of any damage. This is done using an arthroscope through a very small hole made into the joint. The knee is very commonly examined in this way, and in some cases **torn cartilages** (see **meniscus**) can be removed without having to cut the knee joint open.

Arthurlie *club* former Scottish league. *Dossier* Ground: Dunterlie Park, Barrhead, Strathclyde. *Keynotes* Arthurlie joined Division Two in 1901-02. The club won the short-lived (only three years) Division Three title in 1923-24. Arthurlie striker Owen McNally, on loan from **Celtic**, scored eight goals in the club's 10–0 victory over **Armadale** on 1 October 1927 (Division Two). Arthurlie was a **Scottish FA Cup** quarter-finalist in 1927 (0–3 v **East Fife**). The club resigned from the Scottish League in 1928-29, having compeleted 32 of the 36 fixtures that season. The authorities allowed Arthurlie's record to stand. *League record* Division Two 1901-02 to 1914-15; 1924-25 to 1928-29. *Honours* Division Three 1923-24.

artificial pitch *n.* a playing surface constructed of synthetic material. *Regulations* an artificial playing surface for football pitches, ie without grass. Artificial pitches are banned by the **Premier League**, **Football League** and **Scottish Football League** (FA Premier League rule I.14, Football League regulation 16, Scottish Football League rule 72), but may be used in other tournaments where **competition rules** permit. *Keynotes* **Colchester United** was the first **Football League** club to apply to use a synthetic pitch – this was refused in 1980 by the **Football League Management Committee**. Queens Park Rangers was the first **Football League** club to install an artificial pitch at its ground. The **Loftus Road** pitch (Omniturf) cost £350,000 when it was installed in 1981. **Oldham Athletic**, Luton Town, **Preston North End** and **Stirling Albion** all followed QPR's lead. Andy King scored the first Football League goal on an artificial pitch, for Rangers during a Division Two fixture with Luton Town at **Loftus Road** in September 1981. QPR, however, was prohibited from using its pitch in the 1984-85 UEFA Cup, and switched its ties to **Highbury**. The first **World Cup** match to be played on artificial turf took place in Vancouver between **Canada** and **United States of America** (24 September 1976). **Luton Town**'s **Kenilworth Road** staged the first English representative match on an artificial pitch (**England** U15 v **Northern Ireland U15**). The Football Association banned the use of synthetic pitches for cup ties in 1985. Preston North End's **Deepdale** was granted a four-year extension to the deadline to remove artificial pitches, with the final League match ever played on plastic occurring on 18 May 1994 (v **Preston North End**, Third Division **playoff** semi-final).

Artmedia Petrzalka *club* Slovakian national league club based in Bratislava founded in 1892 as Pozsonyi Torna Egyesulet - an ethnic Hungarian club - later known as Polgari. Merged with Inter Bratislava in 1986, regained its independence in 1993 (as 1. FC Petrzalka). Slovakia's oldest professional club. Ground: Petrzalka, capacity: 12,000. Strip: green and black shirts, black shorts.

Aruba *country CONCACAF* island in West Indies off coast of Venezuela. Former part of **Netherlands Antilles**, and still under Dutch realm. Self-governing since 1986 and has its own national football status. Area: 193 sq km (75 sq miles). Population 68,897. Capital: Oranjestad. *Dossier* Football association (Arubaanse Voetbal Bond, Oranjestad), formed in 1932 (then part of Netherlands Antilles), joined FIFA and the **Confederación Norte-Centroamerican y del Caribe de Fútbol** (CONCACAF) in 1988, president Charles Marchena, general secretary Merrill Robles. Season played from May to November. National stadium: Guillermo Trinidad, Orenjestad, capacity: 10,000. National strip: yellow shirts, blue shorts. *International tournament record* **Olympic Games** – never qualified for finals tournament; **World Cup** – first entered 1998, lost in first round of qualifying tournament (3–6 agg., v **Dominican Republic**); **Gold Cup** – never qualified. *Record against British and Irish national teams* none played. Leading clubs: the following teams have represented Aruba in the **CONCACAF Champions Cup**: Racing Club (1993 and 1994) and River Plate (1994).

AS Aviacao (Gruppo Desportivo Atlético Sport Aviacao, ASA) *club* Angolan national league club, based in the capital Luanda. Formerly known as Transports Aeriens Angolaise (TAAG). Ground: ASA, capacity: 8,000. Strip: white shirts, red shorts. **CAF Cup** semifinal 1993; Angolan cup 1981, 1993, 1995.

AS Capoise *club* Haitian national league club based in Cap Haïtien, founded 1930. Strip: red shirts, white shorts.

AS Cheminots *club* Congo league club based in Lubomo. Ground: Pont, capacity: 10,000. Congo Cup 1982, 1984; Congo league champions 1995.

AS Dragons de l'Oueme *club* Benin national league club based in Porto Novo. Ground: Municipale, capacity: 15,000. Strip: blue shirts, white shorts. **African Cup-winners Cup** semi-finalists 1987; Benin Cup 1984, 1985, 1986, 1990; Benin league champions 1978, 1979, 1982, 1983, 1986, 1989, 1994, 1998.

AS Monaco (Association Sportive) *club* French national league club based in the principality of Monaco, formed 1924. Ground: Louis II, capacity: 18,500. Strip: red and white diagonal halved shirts, red shorts. **European Cup/Champions League** semifinal 1994 (lost 0–3 to eventual winners Milan, having qualified from its quarter-final group); semi-final 1998; **European Cup-winners Cup** runners-up 1992 (0–2, v **Werder Bremen** of Germany, in Lisbon, semi-final 1990 (2–4 agg., v eventual winners **Sampdoria**); **UEFA Cup** semi-final 1997; (2–3 agg., v **Internazionale**); French Cup 1960, 1963, 1980, 1985, 1991, runners-up 1974, 1984, 1989; French league champions 1961, 1963, 1978, 1982, 1988, 1997, runners-up 1964, 1984, 1991, 1992. Notable former players: Manuel **Amoros**, Glenn **Hoddle**. Former coach: Arséne Wenger.

AS Police (Association Sportive) *club* Mauritanian national league club, based in the capital Nouakchott. Ground: Capitale, capacity: 6,000. *Keynotes* AS Police holds the national league record of five consecutive championships (1986 to 1991). Mauritanian Cup 1985; Mauritanian league champions 1981, 1982, 1986, 1987, 1988, 1990 and 1991.

AS Sogara *club* Gabon national league club based in Port Gentile, founded 1958. Ground: Mosquee,

capacity: 5,000. Strip: white shirts, green shorts. **African Cup of Champion Clubs** quarter-final 1993, 1994; **African Cup-winners Cup** runners-up 1986 (2–3 agg., v **Al Ahly Cairo**, Egypt); Gabon Cup 1985; Gabon league champions 1984, 1989, 1991, 1992, 1993, 1994.

AS Somasud *club* Madagascar national league Club, based in Toliara. **African Cup of Champion Clubs** second round 1982 (withdrew after winning first leg against eventual runners-up El Hilal, Sudan); Madagascar league champions 1981.

AS Tempeta Mocaf (Association Sportif) *club* Central African Republic national league club based in the capital Bangui. Ground: Barthelmy Boganda (the national stadium), capacity: 35,000. Strip: red shirts, black shorts. **African Cup of Champion Clubs** second round 1994; **African Cup-winners Cup** quarterfinal 1975; Central African Republic Cup 1974, 1982, 1985, 1992; Central African Republic league champions 1976, 1984, 1990, 1993, 1996, 1997.

AS Vita Club *club* Congo Democratic Republic (formerly Zaire) see **Vita Club Kinshasa**.

Asante Kotoko *club* Ghanaian professional league club based in Kumasi, founded 1926 (as Rainbow, and later Titanics). Ground: Kumasi Sports, capacity: 55,000. Strip: red shirts, white shorts. Said to be the first club in the country to wear football boots, apparently after a tour to the UK in 1955. **African Cup of Champion Clubs** 1970 (3–2 agg., v **Tout Puissant Englebert**, Zaire), 1983 (1–0 agg., v **Al Ahly**, Egypt), runners-up 1967 (3–3 agg., v Tout Puissant Englebert – Asante refused to take part in a replay, Tout Puissant was given a walkover), 1971 (3–0, 0–2, 0–1 replay, v **Canon Yaoundé**, Cameroon), 1973 (4–5 agg., v **AS Vita Club**, Zaire), 1982 (1–4 agg., v Al Ahly), 1993 (0–0 agg., 6–7 pens., v **Zamalek**, Egypt); Ghanaian Cup 1958, 1960, 1976, 1978, 1984, 1990, 1991; Ghanaian league champions 1959, 1963, 1964, 1965, 1967, 1969, 1970, 1972, 1975, 1980, 1981, 1982, 1983, 1986, 1987, 1988, 1989, 1991, 1992, 1993. Notable former players: Karim **Abdoul Razak**, Ibrahim **Sunday**.

asbestos *misc.* fibrous mineral formerly used as a building material, now known to cause lung disease and cancer. *Keynotes* In May 1996, **Aston Villa** was fined £17,500 by Birmingham Crown Court after the particularly dangerous blue asbestos was released during demolition work on the club's Doug Ellis stand, carried out at the end of May 1995. The club pleaded guilty to a breach of the Health and Safety at Work etc Act 1974, for failing to protect contractors and members of the public from possible exposure to the hazardous material. The incident was so serious that a scheduled international match between **Brazil** and **Sweden** could not be staged at the ground because the terracing had to be sealed with polythene sheeting until the asbestos could be safely dealt with.

ASC Diaraf (Association Sportive Culturelle) *club* Senegal national league club, based in Dakar, founded

1969. Ground: Stade de l'Amité, capacity: 60,000 (national stadium). Strip: green shirts, white shorts. **African Cup of Champion Clubs** semi-final 1983, quarter-final 1996; Senegal Cup 1970, 1973, 1975, 1982, 1983, 1985, 1991, 1993, 1994, 1995; Senegal league champions 1968, 1970, 1975, 1976, 1977, 1982, 1989, 1995.

ASC Garde Nationale (Association Sportive Culturelle) *club* Mauritanian national league club, based in the capital Nouakchott. Ground: Olympique, capacity: 15,000. **African Cup-winners Cup** first round 1978 (having won preliminary round); Mauritanian Cup 1981, 1986, 1989; Mauritanian league champions 1976, 1977, 1978, 1979, 1984, 1994, 1998.

ASC Jeanne d'Arc (Association Sportive Culturelle) *club* Senegal national league club, based in Dakar, founded 1921. Ground: Demba Diop, capacity: 30,000. Strip: blue shirts, white shorts. **African Cup of Champion Clubs** semi-final 1974; **African Cup-winners Cup** semi-final 1975; **CAF Cup** runners-up 1998 (0–4, v **CS Sfaxien**, Tunisia); Senegal Cup 1962, 1969, 1974, 1980, 1984, 1987; Senegal league champions 1960, 1969, 1973, 1985, 1986, 1988.

ASC Ksar Sonader (Association Sportive Culturelle) *club* Mauritanian national league club, based in the capital Nouakchott. Ground: Ksar, capacity: 5,000. Mauritanian Cup 1979, 1993; Mauritanian league champions 1983, 1985, 1992, 1993.

ASC Ndiambour (Association Sportive Culturelle) *club* Senegal national league club, based in Louga. Ground: Albouryndiaye, capacity: 3,000. Strip: black shirts, white shorts. Senegal league champions 1992, 1994, 1998.

ascenseur *misc.* French term for a club which constantly moves between two divisions.

Ascension *country no affiliation* volcanic island and dependency of St Helena (UK dependent territory) in the south-east Atlantic. Area 88 sq km (34 sq miles). Population: 1,117. Capital: Georgetown. Neither Ascension nor St Helena is affiliated to any international football federation. Leading club: Harts (league champions 1999).

ASCOT (Association Sportive Cotton Tchad) *club* Chad national league club based in the capital N'Djamena, also known as Cottonchad. Ground: Moursel, capacity: 2,000. **African Cup of Champion Clubs** first round 1997 (after preliminary round); **CAF Cup** quarter-final 1998; Chad Cup 1995; Chad league champions 1996.

ASDR Fatima (Association Sportive Diables Rouges de Fatima) *club* Central African Republic national league club based in the capital Bangui. Ground: Fatima, capacity: 1,500. Strip: red shirts, white shorts. **African Cup-winners Cup** second round 1974; Central African Republic Cup 1980, 1981, 1991, 1993; Central African Republic league champions 1974, 1978, 1983, 1988.

Asean Tiger Cup *competition* international tournament for member countries of the **Association of South East Asian Nations Football Federation**

(Asean FF), sponsored by the Tiger Beer company. The first tournament was held in 1996, in Singapore. All 10 members of the Asean FF took part. The 1998 edition was marred by a farcical group game between **Indonesia** and **Thailand**, with both teams deliberately trying to lose to avoid playing against hosts **Vietnam** in the semi-final in Hanoi, Vietnam (both had already qualified; the loser was set to face **Singapore** in Ho Chi Minh City). The game was settled by an own goal from Indonesia's Mursyid Effendi who shot deliberately – and obviously – into his own net (Thailand thus "won" the match 3–2). The Thailand coach resigned, both nations were fined, and both lost in the semi-final. *Final results (and venues)* 1996 Thailand v **Malaysia**, 1–0 (in Singapore); 1998 Singapore v Vietnam, 1–0 (in Hanoi, Vietnam).

ASEC Mimosas Abidjan (Association Sporting Employees Commercials) *club* Ivory Coast national league club based in the capital Abidjan, founded 1948. Ground: Felix Houphouët-Boigny (the national stadium), capacity: 45,000. Strip: yellow shirts, black shorts. *Keynotes* ASEC holds the world record of 108 consecutive league games without defeat (1988 to 19 June 1994). Its six consecutive league titles (1990 to 1995) is a national club record. **African Cup of Champion Clubs** 1998 (4–2 agg., v **Dynamos Harare** of Zimbabwe), runners-up 1995 (2–3, agg, v **Orlando Pirates** of South Africa), semi-final 1971, 1976 and 1993; **African Cup-winners Cup** semi-final 1983; **African Super Cup** 1998-99 (3–1, v **Espérance Tunis** of Tunisia); Ivory Coast Cup 1962, 1967, 1968, 1969, 1970, 1972, 1973, 1983, 1992, 1995, 1997; Ivory Coast league champions 1964, 1970, 1972, 1973, 1974, 1975, 1980, 1990, 1991, 1992, 1993, 1994, 1995, 1997, 1998; Ivory Coast Super Cup (Coupe Houphouët-Boigny) 1975, 1980, 1983, 1990, 1994, 1995, 1997; **West African Football Union General Eyadema Cup** 1990, runners-up 1989. Notable former players: Laurent **Pokou**, Abdoulaye **Traoré**.

ASFA Yennenga (Association Sportive du Faso) *club* Burkina Faso national league club based in Ouagadougou, founded 1947. Stadium: Camp Militaire, capacity: 5,000. Strip: green shirts, yellow shorts. Burkina Faso league champions 1989, 1995.

ASFAG (Association Sportive Forces Armees Guineen) *club* Guinea national league club based in Conakry. Ground: Stade du 28 Septembre (the national stadium), capacity: 40,000. Strip: blue shirts, white shorts. Guinea Cup 1987, 1991, 1996; West African Football Union club cup 1988.

ASFAN (Association Sportive Forces Armees Niger) *club* Nigerian national league club, based in the capital Niamey. Ground: Muselman, capacity: 1,500. Niger Cup 1995; Niger league champions 1971 and 1975; **West African Football Union Cup** runners-up 1996 (0–7 agg., v **East End Lions**, Sierra Leone).

Ashington *club* former English league. *Dossier* Ground: Portland Park, Ashington, Northumberland.

Record League attendance: 8,824 v **Wolverhampton Wanderers** (5 January 1924, Division Three (North). *Keynotes* Founder members of Division Three (North) in 1921-22. The club failed to get re-elected in 1928-29 and was replaced by **York City**. Ashington's highest League position was eighth in Division Three (North), which the club achieved in 1923-24. *League record* Division Three (North) 1921-22 to 1928-29.

Ashton Gate *ground* English football ground situated in Bristol; home of **Bristol City**. *Dossier* Ground capacity: 21,479. Pitch dimensions: 105m x 69m. Record attendance: 43,335 v **Preston North End** (16 February 1935, **FA Cup**, fifth round). Best average attendance: 26,575 (1955-56). *History* Originally known as Bedminster Athletic Ground, Ashton Gate was first used by Bristol City on 27 August 1904 (1st XI v 2nd XI) following the club's earlier merger with Bedminster, whose home it had been since 1896. The merged City and Bedminster used both clubs' grounds, St John's Lane and Ashton Gate, during its first full season and the club designated the former as its home on election to the **Football League** in 1901-02. Once City established Aston Gate as its principal home, the ground became the region's foremost sports venue, staging both Rugby Union (1908) and Rugby League (1911) fixtures, and in 1913, a second **England** international (v **Wales**, 17 March 1913) – it was first used for an England international on 23 March 1899 (v Wales). In 1929, the ground's number two stand was completely gutted by fire and, in 1941, its counterpart, the number one stand, was destroyed by a bomb. The building of the Dolman Stand (named after an earlier club chairman), which opened in 1970 at a cost of £285,000, almost bankrupted the club, forcing it to sell a number of club-owned properties and to rely on financial pledges from the club sponsors and the **Football Association** to survive. Ashton Gate's first floodlights were rather primitive, with each of the 14 lights, which had to be switched on by hand, mounted on poles. The lights were first used on 27 January 1953 (first game v **Wolverhampton Wanderers**, friendly) and were later sold to non-League Burton Albion. Conventional corner pylon-mounted floodlights were erected in 1965 (v Wolverhampton Wanderers, Division Two) and, in June 1992, these were removed by **Wigan Athletic** and re-erected at its **Springfield Park** ground. The installation of new floodlights on both side stands in the early 1990s led to the then club chairman being banned by the Football Association for nine months for failing to adopt proper tendering procedures for the work. Aside from rugby fixtures, Ashton Gate has staged several other non-football events, including a Rolling Stones concert (1982) and a meeting by American preacher Billy Graham (1984). **Bristol Rovers** was forced to play five matches at Ashton Gate during the 1980-81 season after fire destroyed a stand at the club's **Eastville** stadium.

Asian Champion Teams Cup *competition* annual international club tournaments for Asian national champions (league champions or other national championship winners). The tournament is initially regionalised with the first round divided into east and west zones. It climaxes with a semi-finals and final tournament staged by a host nation (since 1995 played in the following spring). Geographically, it is the biggest club tournament in the world, with clubs representing countries as far apart as Syria and Indonesia. *History* The Cup was first played in 1967 (it took five years to launch the competition from the initial decision by the **Asian Football Confederation** in 1962). Originally known as the Asian Champion Clubs Tournament. Only six clubs took part in the first tournament held in Bangkok and won by Israeli club **Hapoel Tel-Aviv**. Israeli clubs dominated the early tournaments, with **Maccabi Tel-Aviv** winning in 1968 and 1971, and Hapoel runners-up in 1970. Maccabi Tel-Aviv, however, were declared champions in 1971 after Iraq side Al Schurta (**Police Club**) refused to play in the final. It was not played in 1969, nor from 1972 to 1984. *Results (and venues)* 1967 Hapoel Tel Aviv (Israel) v **Salangor** (Malaysia) 2–1 (in Bangkok, Thailand); 1968 Maccabi Tel Aviv (Israel) v **Yangzee** (Korea) 1–0 (in Bangkok, Thailand); 1970 **Taj Club** (Iran) v Hapoel Tel Aviv, 2–1 (in Tehran, Iran); 1971 Maccabi Tel Aviv, walkover, v Police Club (Iraq) (in Bangkok, Thailand); 1972–1985 not played; 1986 **Daewoo Royals** (South Korea) v **Al Ahly** (Saudi Arabia), 3–1 (in Jeddah, Saudi Arabia); 1987 **Jeff United** (as Furukawa FC) (Japan) v **Al Hilal** (Saudi Arabia) 4–3 (in Riyadh, Saudi Arabia); 1988 **Verdy Kawasaki** (as Yomiuri) (Japan) v Al Hilal (Saudi Arabia), walkover; 1989 **Al Saad** (Qatar) v **Al Rashed** (Iraq) 5–3 agg.; 1990 **Liaoning** (China) v **Nissan** (Japan) 3–2 agg.; 1991 **Esteghlal SC** (Iran) v Liaoning 2–1 (in Dhaka, Bangladesh); 1992 Al Hilal (Saudi Arabia) v Esteghlal SC 1–1, 4–3 pens. (in Doha, Qatar); 1993 **Pas Club** (Iran) v **Al Shabab** (Saudi Arabia) 1–0 (in Bahrain); 1994 **Thai Farmers Bank** (Thailand) v **Omani Club** (Oman) 2–1 (in Thailand); 1995 Thai Farmers Bank v **Al Arabi** (Qatar) 1–0 (in Bangkok, Thailand); 1996 **Ilhwa Chunma** (South Korea) v **Al Nasr** (Saudi Arabia) 1–0 (in Riyadh, Saudi Arabia); 1997 **Pohang Steelers** (South Korea) v Ilhwa Chunma 2–1 (in Kuala Lumpur, Malaysia); 1998 Pohang Steelers v **Dalian** (China) 0–0, 6–5 pens. (in Hong Kong); 1999 **Julibo Iwata** (Japan) 2–1 v Esteghlal SC (in Tehran).

Asian Club Championship *competition* another name for the **Asian Champion Teams Cup**.

Asian Cup *competition* official name for the **Asian Cup of Nations**.

Asian Cup of Nations *competition* international tournament for member countries of the **Asian Football Confederation** (AFC), held every four years. Originally a round-robin league of four nations, now played in 10 qualifying groups followed by a finals tournament of the 10 group winners, the host nation and the reigning champions. Forty-two nations entered the 2000 qualifying tournament. The countries in each qualifying group tend to be from the same geographical area. The finals tournament has three groups of four nations; the top two in each group, plus the two best third-place nations qualify for a straight knockout finale. Officially entitled the Asian Cup. It has always been open to both professional and amateur players. *History* First held in 1956 with seven of the then 12 members of the AFC: **Cambodia, Hong Kong, Malaysia, Philippines, South Korea, South Vietnam** and **Taiwan** (Chinese Taipei). Hong Kong hosted the first finals tournament of four nations (Hong Kong, **Israel**, South Korea and South Vietnam) in September 1956, won by South Korea. By 1996 it had grown to 37 competing nations from the AFC's then 42 member countries; 44 of the AFC's member countries entered the 2000 tournament. Taiwan was expelled from the AFC from 1975 to 1990 and was unable to compete in the tournament during that period. *Final results (and venues)* 1956 South Korea (final group tournament in Hong Kong; runners-up Israel); 1960 South Korea (final group tournament in South Korea; runners-up Israel); 1964 Israel (final group tournament in Hong Kong; runners-up **India**); 1968 **Iran** (final group tournament in Hong Kong; runners-up Burma (**Myanmar**)); 1972 Iran v South Korea, 2–1 (in Thailand); 1976 Iran v **Kuwait** 1–0 (in Iran); 1980 Kuwait v South Korea, 3–0 (in Kuwait); 1984 **Saudi Arabia**, 2–0 (in Singapore); 1988 Saudi Arabia v South Korea, 0–0, 4–3 pens. (in Qatar); 1992 **Japan** v Saudi Arabia, 1–0 (in Japan); 1996 Saudi Arabia v **United Arab Emirates**, 0–0, 4–2 pens. (in United Arab Emirates); 2000 tournament in Beirut, Lebanon.

Asian Cup-winners Cup *competition* international club tournaments for Asian nations cup winners (or cup runners-up if one club wins both the cup and the national championship, thus qualifying for the **Asian Champion Teams Cup**). Qualifying matches are played over two legs (home and away) with a final tournament (semi-finals, third/fourth place and final) played in a host city. *History* The competition started in 1990 with 18 clubs taking part (though five withdrew before the start of the competition). Twenty-six clubs took part in the 1994 competition. Prize money for semi-finalists was introduced in 1993. The finals were played over two legs until 1993; a last-four final tournament in a host city was introduced in 1994. The 1996 final was watched by 50,000 spectators in Saudi Arabia's King Fahd Stadium in Riyadh. *Final results (and venues from 1994)* 1991 **Piroozi** (Iran) v **Al Muharraq** (Bahrain) 1–0 agg.; 1992 **Yokohama Marinos** (as Nissan) (Japan) v **Al Nasr** (Saudi Arabia) 6–1 agg.; 1993 Yokohama Marinos (as Nissan) v Piroozi, 2–1 agg.; 1994 **Al Qadisiyah** (Saudi Arabia) v **South China** (Hong Kong) 6–2 agg.; 1995 **Yokohama Flugels** (Japan) v **Al Shabab** (United Arab Emirates) 2–1 (in Sharjah, United Arab Emirates); 1996 **Bellmare Hiratsuka** (Japan) v **Al Talaba** (Iraq) 2–1 (in Yokohama, Japan); 1997 **Al Hilal** (Saudi Arabia) v **Nagoya Grampus Eight** (Japan) 3–1 (in Riyadh, Saudi Arabia); 1998 **Al Nasr** (Saudi Arabia) v **Suwon Samsung Bluwings** (South Korea) 1–0 (in Riyadh, Saudi Arabia); 1999 **Al Ittihad** (Saudi Arabia) v Chunnam Dragons (South Korea) 3–2 (in Yokyo, Japan).

Asian Football Confederation (AFC)   *confederation* international football association for Asia, based in Kuala Lumpur, Malaysia. *Dossier* Founded 8 May 1954, affiliated to **FIFA** 21 June 1954. President: HRH Sultan Ahmed Shah (Malaysia). General secretary: Dato' Peter Velappan. Website: http://www.asian-football.com (official site). *Full member countries* **Afghanistan, Bahrain, Bangladesh, Brunei Darussalam, Cambodia, China, Guam, Hong Kong, Indonesia, India, Iran, Iraq, Japan, Jordan, Kazakhstan, Kuwait, Kyrgyzstan, Laos, Lebanon, Macao, Malaysia, Maldives, Myanmar** (Burma)**, Nepal, North Korea, Oman, Pakistan, Palestine, Philippines, Qatar, Saudi Arabia, Singapore, South Korea , Sri Lanka, Syria, Taiwan** (Chinese Taipei)**, Tajikistan, Thailand, Turkmenistan, United Arab Emirates, Uzbekistan, Vietnam, Yemen**. *Associate members* **Bhutan, Mongolia**. *Competitions (selection)* **Asian Under-17 Championship**; **Asian Youth Cup** (under 20); **Asian Women's Football Championship**; **Asian Cup of Nations**; **Asia Under-23 Championship**; **Asian Under-16 Tournament**; **Asian Champion Teams' Cup, Asian Cup-winners Cup**. *History* Asian Confederation first mooted in 1952 at the **Olympic Games** in Finland. Formal meetings held at the 1954 **Asian Games** in the Philippines, chaired by John Clelland of the Philippine Football Federation. Originally based in Hong Kong, its headquarters moved to Kuala Lumpur in 1965. *Keynotes* The AFC's member countries account for more than half the world's population. The AFC has four places at the 2002 World Cup finals – including the two co-hosts Japan and South Korea – and had three/four places allocated at the 1998 World Cup finals (the fourth place for the 1998 finals was decided by a playoff with the winner of the **Oceania Football Confederation** qualifying tournament). It was allocated two places at the 1999 **Women's World Cup** finals.

Asian Games   *competition* international sports tournament for Asian nations, held every four years since 1951. The football tournament is open to member countries of the **Asian Football Confederation** (AFC) and has been included in the games since its inception. It includes a women's tournament. *History* Six nations entered the football tournament of the first Asian Games, held in New Delhi, India: **Afghanistan, Myanmar** (then known as Burma), **India, Indonesia, Iran, Japan**. The games were originally played over 80, rather than 90 minutes. Although **Taiwan** – calling itself "China" – won the event in 1954 and 1958, its players were all based in **Hong Kong**. In 1962, host nation Indonesia withdrew the invitations for **Israel** and Taiwan, for political reasons. Taiwan was expelled from the AFC from 1975 to 1990 and was unable to compete in the Games football tournament during that period. Seventeen nations entered the football tournament in 1994 and 23 in 1998. *Winners (results and host cities)* 1951 India (1–0, v Iran, in New Delhi); 1954 Taiwan

(5–2, v **South Korea**, in Manila, the Philippines); 1958 Taiwan (3–2, v South Korea, in Tokyo, Japan); 1962 India (2–1, v South Korea, in Djakarta, Indonesia); 1966 Myanmar (as Burma, 1–0, v Iran, in Bangkok, Thailand); 1970 Myanmar and South Korea shared the gold medal (0–0, in Bangkok); 1974 Iran (1–0, v Israel, in Tehran, Iran); 1978 South Korea and **North Korea** shared the gold medal (0–0, in Bangkok); 1982 **Iraq** (1–0, v **Kuwait**, in New Delhi); 1986 South Korea (2–0, v **Saudi Arabia**, in Seoul, South Korea); 1990 Iran (0–0, 4–1 pens., v North Korea, in Beijing, China); 1994 **Uzbekistan** (4–2, v **China**, in Hiroshima, Japan); 1998 Iran (2–0, v Kuwait, in Bangkok). *Women's tournament winners* 1994 China; 1998 China.

Asian Footballer of the Year *award* annual award for the best individual Asian player, now sponsored by Sanyo. *Winners* 1994 Saeed **Owairan** (**Saudi Arabia** and **Al Hilal**); 1995 Masami **Ihara** (**Japan** and **Yokohama Marinos**); 1996 Khodadad **Azizi** (**Iran** and FC **Cologne**); 1997 Hidetoshi **Nakata** (Japan and **Bellmare Hiratsuka**).

Asian Super Cup *competition* annual international club tournament contested over two legs by winners of the **Asian Champion Teams Cup** and the **Asian Cup-winners Cup**, organised by the **Asian Football Confederation** (AFC), first played 1995. The winners of the 1997 tournament received a trophy and $100,000 prize money. *Results* 1995 **Yokohama Flugels** (Japan) v **Thai Farmers Bank** (Thailand), 4–4 agg.; 1996 **Ilhwa Chunma** (South Korea) v **Bellmare Hiratsuka** (Japan), 6–3 agg.; 1997 **Al Hilal** (Saudi Arabia) v **Pohang Steelers** (South Korea), 2–1 agg.;1998 Pohang Steelers v Al Nasr (Saudi Arabia) 1–1 aggr. (away goals).

Asian Under-16 Championship *competition* biennial youth tournament (under-16 years) for Asian national teams, organised by the **Asian Football Confederation** (AFC), first played 1984 (18 nations competed). Qualifying tournament for the FIFA **Under-17 World Championship** (three places go to AFC members). *Winners* **Saudi Arabia** (1984, 1988), **South Korea** (1986), **Qatar** (1990), **China** (1992), **Japan** (1994), **Oman** (1996).

Asian Under-23 Championship *competition* international youth (under-23) tournament for Asian nations: Asian qualifying tournament for the **Olympic Games**.

Asian Women's Football Championship *competition* biennial international Asian nations tournament for women, under the auspices of the **Asian Football Confederation** (AFC), first played 1975 in Hong Kong. *History* The tournament was mooted after a meeting of representatives from **Taiwan** (Chinese Taipei), **Hong Kong**, **Malaysia**, and **Singapore**, when the former Asian Ladies Football Confederation was formed. The first tournament took place in 1975, in Hong Kong, with just six participating nations: **Australia**, Hong Kong, Malaysia, **New Zealand**, Singapore and **Thailand**. New Zealand won the first event, in the only year it has entered. The tournament came under the AFC in 1986. China first entered in 1986, winning at the first attempt. China has won in five successive tournaments. In 1991 and 1997, the championship constituted the Asian qualifying tournament for the **Women's World Cup** (three qualify). *Final results (and hosts)* 1975 New Zealand v Thailand 3–1 (in Hong Kong); 1977 Taiwan v Thailand 3–1 (in Taiwan); 1979 Taiwan beat **India** (in India); 1981 Taiwan v Thailand 5–0 (in Hong Kong); 1985 Thailand v India 3–0 (in Thailand); 1986 China v **Japan** 2–0 (in Hong Kong); 1987 China v Taiwan 1–0 (in Hong Kong); 1991 China v Japan 5–0 (in Japan); 1993 China v **North Korea** 3–0 (in Malaysia); 1995 China v Japan 2–0 (in Malaysia); 1997 China v North Korea 3–0 (in China).

Asian Youth Champtionship *competition* biennial (formerly annual) youth tournament (under-19 years) for Asian national teams, organised by the **Asian Football Confederation** (AFC), first played 1959. Serves as qualifier for the FIFA **World Youth Cup** (under-20) (winners and runners-up qualify). Most AFC member countries compete in the qualifying stages, with 10 going through to a final tournament in a host nation. *History* Founded by Tunku Abdul Rahman Putra Al-Haj, former president of Malaysia and fifth president of the AFC, to promote youth football in Asia. Twelve nations entered the first tournament in 1959, in **Malaysia** (originally it was an under-20 tournament). Contested annually until 1978, then every two years to fit in with the World Youth Cup. *Winners* **South Korea** (1959, 1960, 1980, 1982, 1990, 1996, joint 1963, 1978, 1998), **Indonesia** (joint 1961), **Myanmar** (formerly known as Burma, 1968, 1970, joint 1961, 1963, 1964, 1969), **Thailand** (1962, joint 1966), **Israel** (1965, 1967, 1971, 1972, joint 1964, 1966), **Iran** (1973, joint 1974, 1975, 1976), India (joint 1974), **Iraq** (1977, 1988, joint 1975, 1978), **North Korea** (joint 1976), **China** (1984), **Saudi Arabia** (1986, 1992), **Syria** (1994).

ASKO Kara (Association Sportive de Kozah Lama Kara) *club* Togo national league club based in Lama Kara. Ground: Kara, capacity: 7,000. Strip: yellow shirts, black shorts. Togo Cup 1975, 1976, 1987, 1994, 1995, 1996; Togo league champions 1988, 1989, 1996.

ASMO/FC 105 (AS Militaire Omnisports/Football Canon) *club* Gabon national league club based in Libreville, founded by merger of FC 105 and Vautour Club Mangoungou. The club of the army and police. Ground: Omar Bongo (the national stadium), capacity: 30,000. Strip: orange shirts, white shorts. **African Cup of Champion Clubs** quarter-final 1984, 1988; **CAF Cup** quarter-final 1992; Gabon Cup 1984 (FC 105), 1986 (FC 105), 1988 (Vautour Club), 1996; Gabon league champions 1976, 1977 (as Vautour Club), 1978, 1982, 1983, 1985, 1986, 1987, 1997.

Asociation Sportive Nianan *club* Mali national league club, based in Koulikoro. Ground capacity: 7,000. **African Cup-winners Cup** second round 1995; **CAF Cup** – second round 1994; Mali Cup runners-up 1994.

Asprilla, Faustino *player* Striker. **Colombia** international (39 caps, 15 goals). Born 10 November 1969. *Clubs* Cuetua Deportivo, **Atlético Nacional Medellin**, **Parma** (twice), **Newcastle United**. *Keynotes* Arrested in 1995 on a gun-related charge. After a brief period in the English Premier League, Asprilla returned to his former club Parma in Italy's **Serie A**. *Honours* **European Cup-winners Cup** runner-up (Parma, 1994).

Assad, Salah *player* **Algeria** international. *France Football*'s African Footballer of the Year runner-up 1982.

assist *n.* any significant contribution made by a player towards a goal or goalscoring opportunity.

assistant manager/coach *n.* individual with partial responsibility for team affairs, especially coaching. Compare **manager**.

assistant referee *rules* (formerly **linesman**) qualified match official whose job is to assist the referee. The assistant referee's primary functions (Law VI), are to indicate when the ball is out of play, which side should be awarded a **corner-kick**, **throw-in** or **goal-kick**, when a player may be penalised for being in an **offside** position (the player may be penalised only when **interfering with play**), where an offence or other incident has occurred but was not seen by the referee, and when a team wishes to make a **substitution**. Assistant referees may also be asked to give an opinion on an incident if consulted by the referee. In all cases the assistant referee's opinion is subordinate to that of the referee, and the referee shall not consider the intervention of an assistant if he or she was in a better position to judge the incident concerned. A referee may, however, change a decision – including cancel a **goal** – if he or she considers that the assistant's information is relevant and that the assistant was better placed to make a judgement. A decision can be changed only if play has not restarted. The referee has a duty to act on information of an assistant referee if this concerns an incident which he or she had not noticed. The assistant referee may also help to organise a **penalty shoot-out**. Two assistant referees are appointed at each match. Unlike the referee, they perform their duties from outside the boundaries of the pitch. Their decisions are indicated by hand-held **assistant referees flags** provided by the clubs on whose ground the match is being played. *Keynotes* "Linesmen" were introduced in 1891, when a decision was made to replace the old system of matches being adjudicated by two **umpires**, one appointed by each club. One of the assistant referee's most important functions has always been to indicate when a player is offside. Curiously, it was only in 1996 that the **International FA Board** (IFAB) actually wrote this responsibility into the text of the **Laws of the game**. The term linesman was dropped for qualified officials by the IFAB before the 1996–97 season to more accurately reflect the duties of the official and, as the Board stated at the time, because "it does not reflect the fact that there are also women who are active in this function." The term club linesman is still used for unqualified personnel (usually attached to the clubs taking part) appointed by the referee in some local league and junior games; the job of the club linesman is largely restricted to indicating when the ball has gone out of play and which team should be awarded a throw-in. See **club linesman; electronic bleeper, neutral assistant referees, woman referee**.

assistant referee's flag *rules* hand-held flag used by an **assistant referee** to indicate to the **referee** when the ball has gone out of play, which side is entitled to a **throw-in**, **corner-kick** or **goal-kick**, when a player may be penalised for being in an **offside position**, calling the attention of the referee in response to **unsporting behaviour**, **violent conduct** or other illegal incident that the referee may not have seen, and to indicate to the referee that a **substitution** is requested.

Associate Member *n.* formerly, a member club of the English **Football League** without full voting rights; a status originally given to clubs in divisions three and four. Associate membership was created when the Football League expanded from two to three divisions in 1920-21. The term became redundant in 1992, after the breakaway of the **Premier League**. Every club in the Football League (First, Second and Third Divisions) now has equal voting rights as a **Member of the Football League**. Compare **Full Member**.

Associate Members Cup *competition* knockout competition that in 1983-84 replaced the **Football League Trophy**. Unlike its predecessors it was open only to clubs from Divisions Three and Four (see **Associate Member**). In this way, the competition was a revival of the pre-war **Third Division Cup** that had almost been resurrected on several occasions, including in 1972 when a **pools** promoter, offering £100,000 in sponsorship, suggested an end-of-season competition involving clubs from Divisions Three and Four, and clubs from the Southern League and the Northern Premier League, but the League clubs refused to compete against non-league opposition. The Associate Members Cup began in January 1984, but in its first season the competition was poorly supported and it was relaunched the following season with sponsorship and retitled the **Freight Rover Trophy**, with every Division Three and Four club taking part. Matches were played on a regional basis, with two regional finals – just like the pre-war competition – and the winners, from 1984-85, meeting in a **Wembley** showdown. The competition was retitled the **Sherpa Van Trophy** in 1987-88, the **Leyland Daf Cup** in 1989-90, the **Autoglass Trophy** in 1991-92 and, in 1994-95, it became the **Auto Windscreens Shield**. *Final results* 1983-84, **Bournemouth (AFC)** 2–1 **Hull City**; 1984–85, **Wigan Athletic** 3–1 Brentford; 1985-86, **Bristol City** 3–0 **Bolton Wanderers**; 1986-87, **Mansfield Town** 1–1 Bristol City (5–4 pens.); 1987-88, **Wolverhampton Wanderers** 2–0 **Burnley**; 1988-89, Bolton Wanderers 4–1 **Torquay United**; 1989-90, **Tranmere Rovers** 2–1 **Bristol Rovers**; 1990-91, **Birmingham City** 3–2 **Stoke City**; 1991-92, Stoke City 1–0 **Stockport County**; 1992-93, **Port Vale** 2–1

Stockport County; 1993-94, **Swansea City** 1–1 **Huddersfield Town** (3–1 pens.); 1994-95, Birmingham City 1–0 **Carlisle United** (**golden goal overtime**); 1995-96, **Rotherham United** 2–1 **Shrewsbury Town**; 1996-97, Carlisle United 0–0 **Colchester United** (4–3 pens.); 1997-98, **Grimsby Town** 2–1 **Bournemouth (AFC)** (golden goal overtime).

associated schoolboy *regulations* young male player, aged 14 years or over, and in full-time education, whose **registration** is held by a **Football League** or **Scottish Football League** club. The term was replaced in England for the 1998-99 season by a broader definition of **student** player, though players registered as associated schoolboys before 31 July 1998 continued to come under the previous regulations.

Association of Football Players with Learning Disabilities *confederation* British football federation for youth and senior players with **learning disabilities**, based in Leicester, founded August 1994. Organised the first **European Championships for Players with Learning Disabilities** in 1996 and the first **World Football Championships for Players with Learning Disabilities** in 1998.

Association of Football Statisticians *n.* body for individuals/organisations concerned with collecting footballing facts and figures. The AFS has more than 1,400 members in 38 countries.

Association of Scottish Youth Football Clubs *confederation* see **Scottish Youth Football Association**.

Association of South East Asian Nations Football Federation (Asean FF) *confederation* regional football association founded in 1984, affiliated to the **Asian Football Confederation** (AFC). Member countries: **Brunei**, **Cambodia**, **Indonesia**, **Laos**, **Malaysia**, **Myanmar**, the **Philippines**, **Singapore**, **Thailand**, **Vietnam**. Organises the **Asean Tiger Cup**, first played 1996.

association football *n.* sport whereby two teams attempt to strike the ball into their opponent's goal. With the exception of the **goalkeeper**, who may handle the ball in his/her **penalty area**, players are prohibited from controlling the ball with their hands or arms. Association football is generally played with 11 players on each side, though youth games, and variants, such as **five-a-side**, **seven-a-side**, **jorkyball** and **futsal**, have fewer players. The game is played according to the **Laws of the game**, originally drawn up by the **Football Association**, and is presided over by a **referee** and **assistant referees**. Association football is the world's most popular spectator and participative sport: by the end of the 20th century, more than 20 million organised 11-a-side matches were played every year around the world. There are more than 150 million registered players – including 10 million women – and more than 1 million referees. *History* There are many accounts of early forms of football played all around the world, including **aqsaqtuk**, **episkyros**, **giuoco del**

calcio Fiorentino, **kemari**, **harpastum**, **pasuck-quakkohowog**, **pilimatun**, la **soule**, **tchoekah**, and **Tsu Chu**. Some form of football may have been introduced to Britain by the Romans. It was certainly played in the Middle Ages, though the games consisted of great gangs of people simply trying to take the ball towards the opponents' end by any means possible: the goal could be almost anything, a river for example. The violent nature of these mob games led to the sport being outlawed at various times. Edward II is known to have banned mob football from being played in London in 1314. Whole villages might take part in games organised on feast days, such as at Shrovetide, though they were often frowned upon by the authorities which tried to have them stopped. The Justice of the Peace Act 1361 was one of the first statutes to be used to control football in Britain, the Highways Act 1835 barred any football on a public highway and, in 1847, the Riot Act 1715 was used to disperse an annual Shrovetide match between two parishes in Derby. Organised football – contrasting **mob football** – was developed in the English Public schools in the early 19th century; rules varied from school to school but generally involved more kicking then handling. Players were allowed to control the ball with their hands, or if they made a clean catch they could take a free kick from the point at which they caught the ball. The rules of the game were first formally codified at Rugby School in 1846 and Eton College in 1847. The principal difference was that, in the Rugby School rules, if the ball was caught cleanly, the player had the option of running with the ball. An attempt at unifying the rules led to the drafting of the **Cambridge Rules** in 1848, revised in 1856 and again in 1863. The newly formed **Football Association** adopted the first rules of Association Football (a code of 13 rules) at a meeting on 1 December 1863. These were broadly in line with the Cambridge Rules, prohibiting players from holding the ball and running with it. The rules retained the principle that a player could catch the ball – a clean catch rewarded with a free kick. A ball that was kicked over the goal line could be touched down by a defender or an attacker; a free kick awarded to the side that made the touch-down. Goal width was settled at eight yards (7.3 metres, with no **cross bar**), but neither the number of players in a team nor the size nor shape of the ball was stipulated. The first match under the new rules was played at Mortlake, London, on 19 December 1863 (Barnes v Richmond, 0–0). In 1867, the FA adopted a modified **offside** rule whereby a player would be offside only if he was both in front of the ball and the last two defending players when the ball was played (until 1867, an attacking player would be offside simply by being in front of the ball when it was passed). The goalkeeper's right to handle the ball was established in 1870, but only while defending his goal (it was not until 1909 that goalkeepers were required to wear different coloured shirts from the rest of the team). The FA adopted two elements of the previously independent **Sheffield rules**: replacing touchdowns behind the goal with the forerunners of the modern **corner kick** and **goal kick** (1872); and introducing **free-kicks** for offside and illegal handling (1873). A cross bar (actually, a cross-tape) was stipulated in the rules at a meeting of the FA in February 1886, stretched between the posts at a height of eight feet (2.44 metres). By March 1877, the Association rules were effectively unified; the Sheffield FA had amended the Sheffield rules in line with the FA's, adopting the latter's version of offside, throw-ins, free-kicks and 11-a-side matches. Compare **rugby football**, **American football**, **Australian rules**, **Gaelic football**.

Aston Villa *club* English league. *Dossier* Ground: **Villa Park**, Birmingham, west Midlands. Strip: claret shirts with sky blue trim, white shorts, claret socks with sky blue trim. Website: *www.astonvilla-fc.co.uk* Nickname: Villans or Villa. Ground capacity: 40,310 all seated. Record attendance: 76,588 v **Derby County** (2 March 1946, **FA Cup**, sixth round). Best average attendance: 47,320 (1948-49). Biggest win: 13–0 v Wednesbury Old Athletic (30 October 1886, FA Cup, first round). Biggest defeat: 1–8 v **Blackburn Rovers** (16 February 1889, FA Cup, third round). *History* Formed in 1874 by cricket enthusiasts of Villa Cross Wesleyan Chapel in the Aston area of Birmingham. The club's first game was against Aston Brook St Mary's Rugby team and had the novelty of being played as one half football and the other rugby. Villa won the association half 1–0 and chose the association code. The club played its first matches on a pitch that is now part of Aston Park and is across the road from the club's present venue, Villa Park. In 1876, Villa moved to the nearby Birmingham suburb of Perry Barr, where the club played on a field rented from a local butcher for £5 a year. Scotsman George Ramsay joined the club as captain in the same year and Villa went on to become one of the most powerful teams in the country. The club was a founder member of the **Football League** in 1888. The Perry Barr pitch had very few facilities, yet Villa enjoyed much success while playing at the venue, including winning the FA Cup for the first time in 1887, and again in 1895, as well as the League Championship in 1894 and 1896. Perry Barr also witnessed one of the first incidents of **crowd trouble** in the UK when Villa played **Preston North End** in the FA Cup. The crowd of 27,000 twice invaded the pitch and Villa, the cupholders, were subsequently disqualified from the competition. In 1897, Villa built its own stadium at Aston Lower Grounds, a site that previously had been a Victorian amusement park. Villa's first season at its new home coincided with the club becoming only the second to win the FA Cup and League in the same season (1897) (**double**). Villa won the Championship title again in 1899, 1900 and 1910. This was the last major success the club enjoyed until it won the FA Cup in 1957 and the **League Cup** in 1961, the competition's inaugural season. Villa remained in the top flight until 1936 when the club was relegated to Division Two. In 1970, the club was relegated to Division Three before returning to the Division One in 1975, following the appointment of Ron Saunders as manager. He succeeded eminent managers such as Joe **Mercer** and Tommy **Docherty**, who had both failed to turn round the club's fortunes. Two League Cup triumphs, in 1975 and 1977, were followed in 1981 by Villa's first Championship for 71 years. A year later, the club won the **European Cup**. Villa spent a further season in Division Two (1987-88) before lifting the League Cup again in 1994. In May 1997, Villa became a plc and was floated on the stock market (flotation price = 1,100p). *League record* Premier League 1992-93–; Division One (including Football League) 1888-89 to 1935-36, 1938-39 to 1958-59, 1960-61 to 1966-67, 1975-76 to 1986-87, 1988-89 to 1991-92; Division Two 1936-37 to 1937-38, 1959-60, 1967-68 to 1969-70, 1972-73 to 1974-75, 1987-88; Division Three 1970-71 to 1971-72. *Honours* European Cup 1982 (1–0 v **Bayern Munich** – *Team* Rimmer (Spink), Swain, Evans, McNaught, Williams, **Bremner**, Cowans, Mortimer, Shaw, Withe (1), Morley); **European Super Cup** 1982-83 (3–1 agg., v **Barcelona**); FA Cup 1887 (2-0 v **West Bromwich Albion**), 1895 (1–0 v West Bromwich Albion), 1897 (3–2 v **Everton**), 1905 (2–0 v **Newcastle United**), 1913 (1–0 v **Sunderland**), 1920 (1–0 a.e.t. v **Huddersfield**), 1957 (2–1 v **Manchester United** – *Team* Sims, Lynn, Aldis, Crowther, Dugdale, Saward, Smith, Sewell, Myerscough, Dixon, McParland (2)); League Cup 1961 (3–2 agg., v **Rotherham United**), 1975 (1–0 **Norwich City**), 1977 (3–2, second replay/a.e.t. v Everton), 1994 (3–0 v **Leeds United**); **FA Charity Shield** 1981 (2–2 v **Tottenham Hotspur** (each club held the trophy for six months)); League 1893-94, 1895-96, 1896-97, 1898-99, 1899-00, 1909-10, 1980-81; **Sheriff of London's Charity Shield** 1899 (1–1 v **Queen's Park** (each club held the trophy for six months)), 1901 (1–0 v **Corinthians**). *Records* Paul **McGrath** is Villa's most capped player (45 (76) for **Republic of Ireland**); Charlie **Aitken** holds the record for club appearances (561, 1961-75); Harry Hampton is Villa's record league goalscorer (215, 1904-15).

Aston Villa plc *n.* publicly-quoted business which owns **Aston Villa**. The club became a fully listed company on the London Stock Exchange in May 1997 (floatation price = 1,100p). Aston Villa had a market capitalisation – the market value of the company's issued share capital (eg, the quoted price of its shares multiplied by the number of shares outstanding) – of £125.9 million on floatation.

astro turf *n.* artificial playing surface first developed by Monsanto in 1966 to provide a pitch for Houston's sports stadium where grass would not grow. See **artificial pitch**.

athlete's foot *medical* fungal infection of the foot caused by a yeast-like microbe, such as *Trichophyton* or *Epidermophyton*. Athlete's foot is characterised by peeling and broken skin, particularly between the toes. Over-the-counter foot powders are available from chemists; footballers should take care to dry their feet properly and change into clean socks frequently. Also called tineapedis.

Athletic Bilbao *club* Spanish league. *Dossier* Ground: **San Mamés**, Bilbao, Basque region, capacity: 46,223. Strip: red and white striped shirts, black shorts with red and white trim. Website: *www.athletic-club.es History* Formed in 1898 by local merchants and mining engineers from the North-east of England. The club is heavily influenced by its English origins with the team strip modelled on the colours of **Sunderland**. The club retains the English spelling of Athletic, although Spain's former dictator, Francisco Franco, enforced the Spanish spelling, Atlético, during his rule. Officially the club is known as Athletic Club de Bilbao. Athletic allow only players of Basque ethnic origin to play for the club, and did not sign its first non-Spanish Basque player, **France** international Bixente Lizarazu from **Bordeaux**, until 1996. Several foreign managers, however, including Jean Fernandez, Jupp Heynckes, Guus Hiddink and Howard Kendall, have been in charge at San Mamés. Athletic won the Spanish Cup (**Copa del Ray**) for a then record 23rd time in 1984 (it was surpassed, in 1998, when **Barcelona** recorded its 24th cup victory). The club has not won a major honour since that 1984 Cup triumph was coupled with winning the **Primera Liga**. In 1997-98, Athletic pipped **Real Madrid** to the second spot in the Primera Liga, thus qualifying for the **European Cup**. Athletic reached the 1977 **UEFA Cup** final, losing on the **away goal** rule (2–2 agg., v **Juventus**). *Honours* Spanish Cup 1903 (3–2 v Real Madrid), 1904 (walkover), 1910 (1–0 v Basconia), 1911 (3–1 v **Espanyol RCD**), 1914 (2–1 v España Barcelona), 1915 (5–0 v Espanyol RCD), 1916 (4–0 Real Madrid), 1921 (4–1 v **Atlético Madrid**), 1923 (1–0 v Europa Barcelona), 1930 (3–2 v Real Madrid), 1931 (3–1 **Real Betis Balompié**), 1932 (1–0 v Barcelona), 1933 (2–1 v Real Madrid), 1943 (1–0 v Real Madrid), 1944 (2–0 v **Valencia**), 1945 (3–2 Valencia), 1950 (4–1 Real Valladolid), 1955 (1–0 v **Sevilla**), 1956 (2–1 v Atlético Madrid), 1958 (2–0 v Real Madrid), 1969 (1–0 v Elche), 1973 (2–0 v Castéllon), 1984 (1–0 v Barcelona); Spanish league 1929-30, 1930-31, 1933-34, 1935-36, 1942-43, 1955-56, 1982-83, 1983-84.

Athletic News *misc.* former weekly sports newspaper published by Hulton Newspapers in Manchester and dating back to the 1880s. Effectively, the chronicle of the **Football League**.

Athlone Town FC *club* Republic of Ireland national league club based in Athlone, County Westmeath, in the centre of the Republic, founded 1887. Ground: St Mels Park, capacity: 6,000. Strip: blue and black striped shirts, black shorts. Republic of Ireland **FAI Cup** 1924 (Athlone's only appearance in the final); Republic of Ireland league champions 1981, 1983; **UEFA Cup/Fairs Cup** second round 1976.

Atlante (full name: Club de Fútbol Atlante) *club* Mexican national league club, based in Mexico City and founded (as Sinaloa) in 1916 (current name since

1920). Ground: Estadio Azulgrana, capacity: 39,000. Strip: maroon and blue striped shirts and blue shorts. *Keynotes* Atlante has a traditionally working-class following. It was originally called Sinaloa after a street near to where the club first played. The club was later known as U-53 (the name of a German U-boat), before adopting the current name. **CONCACAF Champion Clubs Cup** – 1983 (6–1 agg., v **Robin Hood** of Surinam), runners-up 1994 (2–3, v **CS Cartagines** of Costa Rica, in San Jose, California, USA); Mexican Cup (Copa Mexico) 1942, 1951 and 1952; Mexican league Champions 1932, 1941, 1947 and 1993.

Atlantic Cup *competition* former occasional tournament between **Argentina**, **Uruguay** and **Brazil** – the South American nations bordering the Atlantic Ocean – later to include **Paraguay**. Won on all three occasions by Brazil (1956, 1960, 1976). Argentina was runner-up, on each occasion.

Atlético Junior (Corporación Popular Atlético Junior) *club* Colombian national league club based in Barranquila, founded 1948. Ground Estadio Metropolitano "Roberto Melendez", capacity: 60,000. Strip: red and white striped shirts, blue shorts. Colombian league champions 1977, 1980, 1993, 1995; **Copa CONMEBOL** quarter-final 1992; **Copa Libertadores** semi-final 1994, quarter-final 1996.

Atlético Madrid *club* Spanish league. *Dossier* Ground: **Vincente Calderón** (Estadio), Castille, capacity: 62,000. Strip: red and white striped shirts, blue shorts. Website: *www.at-madrid.es/*. Nickname: los Colchomeros (mattress makers). *History* Formed in 1903 by a breakaway group of Madrid FC members (Madrid FC would later become **Real Madrid**). The official name of the club is Club Atlético de Madrid. Between 1939 and 1946 it was known as Atlético Aviación following the club's merger with the Spanish air force club, Aviación. Atlético won its first Spanish League (**Primera Liga**) titles as Aviación in 1940 and 1941. Atlético won the Primera Liga in 1966, which was the club's last season while based at its former ground, Metropolitano. The new venue, originally called the Estadio Manzanares, was, in 1971, named after the club's former president, Vincente Calderón, who made its construction possible by giving substantial financial assistance. Atlético got its nickname – los Colchomeros (mattress makers) – from its red and white striped shirts which is modelled on the colours of **Athletic Bilbao**. Atlético's only European honour was achieved in 1962, when it lifted the **UEFA** (Fairs) **Cup**. The club did reach the **European Cup** final in 1974 (0–4 replay v **Bayern Munich**) and was a **European Cup-winners Cup** finalist in both 1963 (1–5 v **Tottenham Hotspur**) and 1986 (0–3 v **Dinamo Kiev**). It reached the semi-final of the UEFA Cup in 1999. *Honours* **European Cup-winners Cup** 1962 (3–0 replay v **Fiorentina**); Spanish Cup 1960 (3–1 v Real Madrid), 1961 (3–2 v Real Madrid), 1965 (1–0 v **Real Zaragoza**), 1972 (2–1 v **Valencia**), 1976 (1–0 v Real Zaragoza), 1985 (2–1 v **Athletic Bilbao**), 1991 (1–0 v Mallorca RCD),

1992 (2–0 v Real Madrid), 1996 (1–0 a.e.t. v **Barcelona**); Spanish league 1939-40, 1940-41, 1949-50, 1950-51, 1965-66, 1969-70, 1972-73, 1976-77, 1995-96; **World Club Championship** 1974 (2–1 agg., v **Independiente** – Madrid had qualified as European Cup runners-up, when the winners, Bayern Munich, declined to take part).

Atlético Malabo *club* Equatorial Guinea national league club based in the capital Malabo. Ground: Estadio La Paz (the national stadium, also shared with **Clube Deportivo Ela Nguema**), capacity: 15,000. Equatorial Guinea Cup 1985, 1987, 1988, 1990, 1991; Equatorial Guinea league champions 1981, 1982.

Atlético Marte *club* El Salvador national league club based in the capital San Salvador, founded 1950 by the merger of CD Libertad and CD Alacranes. Ground: Estadio Cuscatlan (shared with **Alianza**), capacity: 47,000. Strip: blue shirts, white shorts. **CONCACAF Champions Cup** runners-up 1981 (1–2 agg., v **Transvaal** of Surinam); **CONCACAF Cup-winners Cup** 1991; El Salvador league champions 1954, 1955, 1956, 1969, 1970, 1980, 1982, 1985.

Atlético Mineiro *club* Brazilian national league and **Minas Gerais** state league club based in Belo Horizonte, founded 1908. Ground: Governador Magalhaes Pinto "Mineirao", capacity: 130,000. Strip: black and white shirts, black shorts. **Campeonato Brasileiro** champions 1971, São Paulo Tournament 1937; **Copa CONMEBOL** 1992 (2–1 agg., v **Olimpia** of Paraguay), 1997 (5–2, v **Lanús**), runners-up 1995 (4–4 agg., 3–4 pens., v **Rosario Central**) semi-final 1993, 1998; **Copa Libertadores** second-round group stage 1978; **Master de la Copa CONMEBOL** runners-up 1996 (0–3, v São Paulo); state league champions 35 times (to 1998).

Atlético Nacional Medellin (Club Deportivo) *club* Colombian national league club based in Medellin, founded 1936 (as Atlético Municipal, known as Independiente Nacional from 1958 to 1960). Ground Estadio Atanasio Girardot, capacity: 53,700 (shared with **Independiente Medellin**). Strip: white and green striped shirts, white shorts. Colombian league champions 1954, 1973, 1976, 1981, 1991, 1994; **Copa Inter Americana** 1990 (6–1 agg., v **UNAM** of Mexico), 1997 (3–2, v **Deportivo Saprissa** of Mexico); **Copa Libertadores** 1989 (2–2 agg., 5–4 pens., v **Olimpia** of Paraguay), runners-up 1995 (2–4 agg., v **Grêmio**), semi-final 1990, 1991; **Copa Merconorte** 1998 (4–1 agg., v **Deportivo Cali**); **Supercopa** semi-final 1993, 1997, quarter-final 1996.

Atlético Zulia *club* Venezuelan national league club based in Mérida, founded 1977 as Universidad de Los Andes. Originally based in Mérida, the club moved to Maracaibo in 1997 and adopted its current name. Ground: Estadio Guillermo Soto Rosas, capacity: 15,000. Strip: blue and white striped shirts, blue shorts. **Copa Libertadores** semi-final 1984; **Copa Venezuela** 1996, 1997; Venezuelan league champions (**Torneo Clausura**) 1983, 1991, 1998.

attacker *n.* another word for **striker**.

attacking player *rules* member of an **attacking team**. Compare: **attacker**.

attacking team *rules* term used in the **Laws of the game** to describe the team that is playing *towards* a particular **goal area**, **goal line** or **penalty area**. It is important to distinguish the attacking team from the defending team with regard to rules governing **penalty kicks**, **free kicks**, **corner kicks** and **goal kicks**. Examples: *A goal kick is awarded if a player from the attacking team is the last player to make contact with the ball before it crosses the goal line. A penalty kick is awarded if a player from the attacking team is fouled in the penalty area by a player from the defending team.*

attendance *n.* aggregate total number of spectators at a match. *Keynotes* When the **Football League** began in 1888, the average attendance was 4,500. Up to World War II, and in its immediate aftermath, attendance at League matches, especially in the top two divisions, rose substantially. From 1951, until the creation of the **Premier League** and, with the exception of a period following **England**'s 1966 **World Cup** success, attendances have generally declined. Between 1946-47 and 1949-50, attendances at English football grounds were at an all-time high. The 1948-49 season set a record for the English game as a whole, with 41,248,808 people watching football over the nine-month League campaign, when 1,848 matches were played. The average attendance at a Division One match that season was 36,217. The average gate at Premier League grounds during the 1997-98 season was 29,189, an increase of 2.65% on the previous campaign. Some 11,092,106 people watched Premier League football in 1997-98 – the first time since the division was reduced to 20 clubs in 1995 that the aggregate total was above 11 million. Only **Everton** and **Tottenham Hotspur** experienced a fall in support, while **Derby County** recorded an increase of more than 62%. **Manchester United** was the biggest box office draw, with 1,048,185 people going through **Old Trafford**'s turnstiles during the season. The 1997-98 season also showed a resurgence in people attending football matches elsewhere in Europe. The 1997-98 French league season saw the highest aggregate league attendance. The biggest crowd at a French league match was recorded on 8 April 1998 when 56,478 spectators watched **Olympique de Marseille** play **Paris Saint-Germain** at Stade **Vélodrome**. Also in 1997-98, the German **Bundesliga** attendances topped the 10 million mark – a record (overall = 10,009,529; average attendance = 32,711).

attendance, highest *record* **1.** World/**World Cup**: 199,854 spectators (**Brazil** v **Uruguay**, 1–2, 16 July 1950, at **Maracaná**, Rio de Janeiro, Brazil, World Cup final round). There is some doubt about the validity of this record – see Maracaná for details. **2.** World Cup qualifier: 120,000 (**Cameroon** v **Morocco**, 2–1, 29 November 1981, at Ahmadou Ahidjo, Yaoundé). **3. England**: 126,047 (official; but the unofficial figure has been estimated at 150,000-200,000, **Bolton Wanderers** v **West Ham United**, 2–0, 28 April, 1923, **Wembley Stadium**). **4. FA Cup**: 126,047 (as above); the record for a non-final tie is 84,569 (**Manchester City** v **Stoke City**, 1–0, 3 March 1934, at **Maine Road**, Manchester, quarter-final). **5. Football League**: 83,260 (**Manchester United** v **Arsenal**, 1–1, 17 January 1948, at Maine Road, Division One). **Hillsborough** stadium recorded the highest-ever attendance at a Division Three match when 49,309 saw **Sheffield Wednesday** entertain local rivals **Sheffield United** (26 December 1979). The record attendance for a single day's matches in the Football League is 1,272,185 (27 December 1949; all divisions, 44 matches; 28,913 per match). **6.** 55,316 (Manchester United v **Southampton**, 2–1, 27 February 1999, at Old Trafford, Manchester). **7. Scotland**: 149,547 (official, the actual crowd is estimated at 160,000 as many spectators are known to have entered the ground without paying, Scotland v England, 3–1, 17 April 1937, at **Hampden Park**, Glasgow, **Home International Championship** – this is also the record for an international involving a British or Irish home nation). **8. Scottish FA Cup**: 144,433 (**Celtic** v **Aberdeen**, 2–1, 24 April 1937, at Hampden Park); the record for a non-final game (also a British record) is 143,570 (**Rangers** v **Hibernian**, 1–0, 27 March 1948, at Hampden Park, semi-final). **9. Scottish Football League** 118,567 (Rangers v Celtic, 2 January 1939, at Ibrox Park, Glasgow). **10.** British midweek match: 133,570 (Rangers v **Morton**, 1–0, 21 April 1948, at Hampden Park, Scottish FA Cup final replay). **11. European Championship**: (finals) 105,000 (**Spain** v **Soviet Union**, 2–1, 21 June 1964, at Bernabeu, Madrid); (qualifiers) 134,000 (Scotland v England, 1–1, 24 February 1968, at Hampden Park, qualifying group match). **12. Copa America**: 170,000 (Brazil v Uruguay, 1–0, 16 July 1989, at Maracaná, final round). **13. African Cup of Nations**: 100,000 (**Egypt** v Cameroon, 0–0, 5–4 pens., 21 March 1986, International Stadium, Cairo, final). **14. Olympic Games** football tournament (men): 120,000 (**Soviet Union** v **Yugoslavia**, 1–0, 8 December 1956, at Melbourne Cricket Ground, Melbourne, Australia, final). **15.** Olympic Games football tournament (women): 76,481 (**United States of America** v **China**, 2–1, 1 August 1996, at Sanford Stadium, Athens, Georgia, USA, final). **16. World Club Cup**: 150,000, (**Santos** v **AC Milan**, 4–2, 14 November 1963, at Maracaná); the scheduled two-leg final required a playoff at Maracaná, and the total attendance for the three games was 351,000, the largest ever for a cup final. **17. European Cup**: 135,826 (Celtic v **Leeds United**, 2–1, 15 April 1970, at Hampden Park, semi-final second leg; Celtic won 3–1 agg.). **18. Copa Libertadores**: 114,000 (**Flamengo** – using the Maracaná for its home leg – v **Cobreloa**, 2–1, 13 November 1981, at the Maracaná, final first leg). **19. World Club Match** (all competitions): 177,656 (Flamengo v **Flumineuse**,

1963, at Maracaná. **20. Women's football**: 76,481 (Olympic Games, as above); this is also the largest crowd to watch a women's sports event. **21. World Youth Cup**: 110,000 (Brazil v **Argentina**, 1–0, 19 June 1983, at Azteca Stadium, Mexico City, Mexico). **21. Friendly** (club): 104,679 (Rangers v **Eintracht Frankfurt**, 17 October 1961, at Hampden Park). **23.** British **non-league**: 100,000 (Pegasus v Harwich and Parkeston, 11 April 1953, at Wembley Stadium, **FA Amateur Cup** final).

attendance, lowest *record* **1. World Cup**: 300 spectators (**Romania** v **Peru**, 14 July 1930, at Pocitos stadium, Montevideo, Uruguay, first round). **2. Football League** (not including games played **behind closed doors**): 450 (**Rochdale** v **Cambridge United**, at **Spotland**, 5 February 1974, Division Three) – the match was played on a Tuesday afternoon because a miners' strike had resulted in power cuts and a limit on floodlit games. **Thames**' home match with **Luton Town** at West Ham Stadium on 6 December 1930, which attracted only 469 spectators, is thought to be the lowest attendance at a Football League match played on a Saturday afternoon. **3.** Division One (since 1946): 3,121 (**Wimbledon** v **Sheffield Wednesday**, 2 October 1991, at **Selhurst Park**). **4.** FA **Premier League**: 3,039 (Wimbledon v Everton, 26 January 1993, at Selhurst Park). **5.** British or Irish international: 2,315 (**Wales** v **Northern Ireland**, 27 May 1982, at **Racecourse Ground**, Wrexham).

Åtvidabergs FF (Fotboll Förening) *club* Swedish national league club based in Åtvidaberg, founded 1907. Ground: Kopparvallen, capacity: 11,000. Strip: blue shirts, white shorts. **European Cup-winners Cup** quarter-final 1972; Swedish Cup 1970, 1971; Swedish league champions 1971, 1973.

August 1 FC (Ba Yi) *club* Chinese national league club based in Xi'an (Sian), Shaanxi province; an army club. **Asian Champion Teams' Cup** semi-final 1987; Chinese league champions 1953, 1959, 1974, 1977, 1981, 1986.

Aurora Fútbol Club *club* Guatemala national league club based in Guatemala City, founded 1945. Ground: Estadio de Ejercito. Strip: yellow and black striped shirts, black shorts. **CONCACAF Cup-winners Cup** runners-up 1994 (0–3, v **Necaxa** of Mexico, in Miami, USA); Guatemala national champions 1959, 1965, 1967, 1968, 1986, 1994.

Australia *country* *OFC* federal nation, with British monarch as Head of State, situated between the Indian and Pacific Oceans, the sixth largest country (by area) in the world. Area 7,682,300 sq km (2,965,370 sq miles). Landscape ranges from arid plateaux and deserts in the west, to fertile lowlands. Around half the land mass is desert, with the population largely concentrated in cities in the south east coastal area. Climate varies from temperate to tropical monsoon. Population 18,300,000 (1996 est.). Language: English. Capital: Canberra. Prosperous economy. Hosts for Olympic Games in Sydney, 2000. *Dossier* Football association (Soccer

Australia, Sydney) founded in 1882, reconstituted in 1961, affiliated to **FIFA** in 1963 and **Oceania Football Confederation** (OFC) in 1966, president David Hill, general secretary David Woolley. Season played from October to May. National stadium: National Stadium, Canberra, capacity: 30,000; international matches also played at Melbourne Cricket Ground, capacity: 100,000, and in Sydney. National strip: gold shirts, green shorts. Website: http://www.ausport.gov.au/socer/home.html (official site). Nickname of national team: Socceroos. Biggest victory: 16–0, v **Cook Islands** (28 September 1998, in Australia, Oceania Cup finals tournament). Best victory: 4–1 v **Argentina** (14 July 1988, Sydney, four-nation tournament – along with Brazil and Saudi Arabia – to celebrate Australia's bi-centenary). Highest attendance: 100,000, v **Iran** (29 November 1997, 2–2, in Melbourne, Australia, World Cup qualifier playoff). Most capped player: Alex Tobin (87 appearances, to 1998). Notable players: Marc Bosnich, Frank Farina, Jim **Mackay**. *International tournament record* **Olympic Games** – semi final/fourth 1992 (0–1 v **Ghana**, Barcelona, Spain, third/fourth playoff), also played in finals tournament 1956 (qualified as hosts, first round), 1996 (first round); **Women's World Cup**: qualified for finals tournament 1995, though lost all three group games, qualified for finals tournament 1999; **World Cup** – first entered 1966, qualified for finals tournament 1974 (first round), Oceania/Asia qualifying tournament 1970, OFC qualifying tournament winners 1978, 1986, 1994, 1998 (lost in final playoffs in each of these); **Asian Women's Championship** – has entered on one occasion, the first tournament in 1971; **Confederations Cup** – runners-up 1998 (0–6, v **Brazil**, in Riyadh, Saudi Arabia); **Oceania Cup** – first entered 1980, 1980 (4–2 v **Tahiti**, in Noumea, New Caledonia), 1996 (World Cup qualifier, 11–0 agg., v **French Polynesia/Tahiti**), runner-up 1998 (0–1, v **New Zealand**, in Australia); **Oceania Women's Tournament** – 1998 (3–1, v New Zealand); **Under-17 World Championship** – quarter-final 1985, 1987, 1991, 1993; **World Youth Cup** (under 20) – semi-final 1991 (0–1, v tournament winners and host nation Portugal), semi-final and hosts 1993, (0–2 v **Brazil**, semi-final; beat **Uruguay** 2–1 in the quarter-final), quarter-final 1981, 1995, qualified 1999, hosts 1981. *World Cup performance* (finals and qualifiers to end of 1998 tournament) played 77, won 37, drawn 23, lost 17, scored 163 goals, conceded 74; win rate 48%; goals scored per game 2.12. *Record against British and Irish national teams* v **England**, played five, drawn two, lost three; v **Northern Ireland**, played three, drawn one, lost two; v **Scotland**, played three, drawn one, lost two. *History* Although football is not the major sport in Australia – trailing in popularity behind rugby league and union, cricket and **Australian Rules** – the large number of comparatively recent immigrants from Europe has maintained a core level of interest. The first football association, in New South Wales, was founded in 1882: the equal-first football association outside the UK (with that of the then-British colony of Natal, South Africa). The first club was formed in Sydney in 1880. State leagues operated prior to the inauguration of the Australian National League in 1977. The **Australian Cup** has been played since 1977. Australia reached the finals of the World Cup in 1974, but has since lost at the final qualifying stages, generally after winning its regional qualification tournaments. It has won the Oceania, Asia or Asia/Oceania qualifying tournaments on five occasions (1970, 1974, 1986, 1994, 1998) but has lost at the last playoff stage in four of these. In 1970, Australia lost to **Israel**; in 1986 to **Scotland** (runner-up in one of the **UEFA** qualifying groups); in 1994 against **Argentina** (a **CONMEBOL** group runner-up) – having already won its qualifying tournament first round group, its second-round knock-out *and* the Oceania v **CONCACEF** playoff; and in 1998 against Iran. Australia has scored an average 2.12 goals per game in all its World Cup matches – and, in this respect, is joint-sixth in the all-time list, behind **Germany**, Brazil, New Zealand, Macedonia and Hungary, and level with France. The 1998 World Cup squad was coached by Terry **Venables**. Australia won the Oceania Cup in 1980 and 1996, was fourth in the 1992 Olympic Games in Spain, and was beaten finalist in the 1998 Confederations Cup (the Intercontinental Championship). In 1980, Australia played England and Northern Ireland in a tournament to recognise 100 years of association football in the country. It lost 1–2 to England in Sydney, lost twice to Northern Ireland (1–2 in Sydney and 1–2 in Adelaide) and drew 1–1 with Northern Ireland in Melbourne. Along with Brazil, Australia shares the world record of 14 consecutive international victories (27 October 1996 to 22 November 1997). *League system* Fifteen clubs compete in the national A-League, playing each other at home and away. Three points are awarded for a victory, with one for a draw: final positions for clubs level on points are determined by **goal difference**. The top six clubs enter a championship playoff. State leagues act as feeders. Tasmania and Western Australia are not part of the National league set-up. Leading clubs: **Adelaide City, Brisbane Strikers, Marconi Fairfield, Melbourne Knights, Perth Glory, South Melbourne, Sydney United**.

Australian Cup *competition* annual knockout competition for Australian clubs, first played 1977. *Winners* 1977 Brisbane City; 1978 Brisbane City; 1979 **Adelaide City**; 1980 **Marconi Fairfield**; 1981 Brisbane Lions; 1982 Apia; 1983 Sydney Olympic; 1984 Newcastle Rosebud; 1985 Sydney Olympic; 1986 **Sydney City Hakoah**; 1987 Sydney CSC; 1988 Apia; 1989 Adelaide City; 1990 **South Melbourne**; 1991 Parramatta Eagles; 1992 Adelaide City; 1993 Heidelberg United; 1994 Parramatta Eagles; 1995 **Melbourne Knights**; 1996 South Melbourne; 1997 Collingwood Warriors; the competition was not played in the 1997-98 season.

Australian Rules *n.* a variant of football with broad similarities to **rugby football**. Chiefly played in

Australia. The game is played between two competing teams of 18 players on an oval pitch. The ball is also oval (similar to a rugby ball). Players attempt to kick the ball between two goalposts, which, unlike in rugby, do not have crossbars – this scores maximum points. Points can also be scored for kicking the ball between either of two outer posts and the main goalposts. The ball can be kicked or punched, and players can run with the ball provided that they bounce it every 9.1 metres (10 yards).

Austria *country UEFA* central European federal republic, around three-quarters in the Alps, with lowlands drained by the River Danube. Became an independent republic in 1919 but forcibly incorporated in the German Reich in 1938, liberated in 1945 and regained full independence in 1955. Area 32,370 sq miles (83,850 sq km). Population: 8,050,000 (1995 est.). Language: German. Capital: Vienna. *Dossier* Football association (Österreichischer Fussball-Bund, Vienna), founded in 1904, affiliated to **FIFA** in 1905 and **Union of European Football Associations** (UEFA) in 1954, president Beppo Mauhart, general secretary Alfred Ludwig. Season played from July to December and February to June (includes a **winter break**). National stadium: **Ernst Happel Stadion**, Vienna, capacity: 47,500. National strip: white shirts, black shirts. Website: http://www.asn.or.at/oefb (official site). First international match: 12 October 1902 v **Hungary** (5–0 v Vienna, friendly). Biggest victories: 9–1 v **Portugal** (27 September 1953, Vienna) and 9–0 v **Malta** (30 April 1977, Salzburg). Biggest defeat: 1–11 v **England** (8 June 1908, Vienna). Most capped players: Toni **Polster** (94 appearances, 1982–), Gerhard **Hanappi** (93 appearances, 1948–1962), Karl Koller (86 appearances, 1952-65). Leading international goal scorers: Toni Polster (44 goals, 1982–), Hans Krankl (35 goals, 1973–1985), Matthias **Sindelar** (27 goals, 1926-37). Other notable player: Ernst **Ocwirk**. *International tournament record* **Olympic Games** – runners-up/silver medal 1936 (1–2, v **Italy**, Berlin); **World Cup** – first entered 1934, semi-final 1934 (fourth place, 2–3 v **Germany**, Naples, third/fourth playoff), 1954 (third place, 3–1 v **Uruguay**, Zurich, third/fourth playoff), also reached finals tournament in 1958, 1978, 1982, 1990, 1998; **European Championship** – quarter-final 1960, failed to progress beyond qualifying tournament in all subsequent years; **International Cup** 1931-32, runners-up 1927–30 and 1933-35; **Under-17 World Championship** – qualified for finals tournament 1997; **World Youth Cup** (under-20) – never qualified for finals. *World Cup performance* (finals and qualifiers to end of 1998 tournament) played 101, won 49, drawn 19, lost 33, scored 177 goals, conceded 118 goals. Win rate: 48.5%. Goals scored per game: 1.75. *Record against British and Irish national teams* v **England**, played 15, won four, drawn three, lost eight; v **Northern Ireland**, played six, won one, drawn two, lost three; v **Scotland**, played 17, won seven, drawn five, lost four, abandoned one; v **Wales**, played five,

won three, drawn one, lost one; v **Republic of Ireland**, played 11, won seven, drawn two, lost two. *History* An Austrian knockout tournament ("Der Challenge-Cup") dates back to 1897, which included invited clubs from Hungary, with the current Austrian Cup starting in 1919. The League was formed in 1912, but, until 1949 was restricted to clubs from Vienna. Austrian clubs played in German competitions during years of incorporation in German Reich, with **Rapid Vienna** winning the German Cup in 1938 and championship in 1941, and **First Vienna** winning the Cup in 1943. No Austrian clubs have won any of the three modern European club competitions, though **Austria Vienna**, Rapid Vienna and First Vienna FC all won the prestigious **Mitropa Cup** in the late 1920s and 1930s. Austria Vienna and Rapid Vienna have reached the final of the **European Cup-winners Cup**, while **SV Austria Salzburg** was a finalist in the **UEFA Cup**. Austria's first international match, on 12 October 1902, against Hungary (above), was the first international match to be played in Continental Europe. Although Austria has qualified for the World Cup finals in the 1970s, 80s and 90s – including the 1998 finals in France – its best performances were in 1934 and 1954: semi-finalists in both years. Austria was not able to compete in the 1938 World Cup; the nation having been absorbed into Germany's Third Reich. The highly successful Austrian team of the 1930s, the so-called **Wunderteam**, won the silver medal at the 1936 Olympic Games. Under the management of Hugo Meisl and Scottish trainer Jimmy Hogan, Austria scored 101 goals in 30 games from 1931-34. Star players included Johann Horvath, Anton Schall, Matthias Sindelar and Karl Zischek. Austria's worst defeat is probably its 0–1 defeat v **Faeroe Islands** (12 September 1990, in Landskrona, Sweden, European Championship qualifier): the Faeroes' first senior international game.It also lost 0–9 in a European Championship 2000 qualifier against Spain (27 March 1999, in Madrid). *League system* The first division has 10 clubs playing each other four times. Three points are awarded for a win, with one for a draw; **goal difference** is used to separate clubs level on points. The bottom side is automatically relegated and replaced by the top club in the second division. The second promotion/relegation place is decided by a playoff between the second-bottom club in the first and the runners-up in the second division. Three clubs are relegated from the 16-club second division. Below the second division are three regional leagues (East, West and Central). *Record in international club tournaments* **European Cup** – FK Austria Vienna (semi final 1979), SK Rapid Vienna (semi-final 1961), **SK Sturm Graz** (champions-league stage 1998-99); European Cup-winners Cup – FK Austria Vienna (runners-up 1978, semi-final 1983), SK Rapid Vienna (runners-up 1985); Mitropa Cup – FK Austria Vienna (1933, 1936, runners-up 1931), SK Rapid Vienna (1930, runners-up 1927 and 1928), **First Vienna FC** (1931), **Admira-Wacker** (runners-up 1934), FC Tirol Innsbruck (1975,

1976);. UEFA Cup – SV Austria Salzburg (runners-up 1994), **FC Tirol Innsbruck** (semi final, 1987).

Austria Vienna (FK Austria-Memphis Vienna) *club* Austrian national league club, based in Vienna founded 1911 as Amateure (until 1926). Merged with Wiener Athletic Club (founded 1896) in 1969. Ground: Franz Horr, capacity: 10,500. Strip: violet shirts with white sleeves, white shorts. Austrian Cup 1931, 1938, 1959 (Wiener AC), 1921, 1924, 1925, 1926 (Amateure), 1933, 1935, 1936, 1948, 1949, 1960, 1962, 1963, 1967, 1971, 1974, 1977, 1980, 1982, 1986, 1990, 1992, 1994; Austrian league Champions 1914 (Wiener AC), 1924, 1926 (Amateure), 1949, 1950, 1953, 1961, 1962, 1963, 1969, 1970, 1976, 1978, 1979, 1980, 1981, 1984, 1985, 1986, 1991, 1992, 1993; Der Challenge-Cup 1901, 1903, 1904 (Wiener AC); **European Cup** semi-final 1979; **European Cup-winners Cup** runners-up 1978, semi-final 1983; **Mitropa Cup** 1933 and 1936, runners-up 1931. Notable former player: Matthias **Sindelar**.

Auto Windscreens Shield *competition* name given to the former **Associate Members Cup** from 1994-95, and a competition open only to clubs from the English **Football League** Second and Third Divisions. *Final results* 1994-95 **Birmingham City** 1–0 **Carlisle United** (**golden goal overtime**); 1995-96, **Rotherham United** 2–1 **Shrewsbury Town**; 1996-97, Carlisle United 0–0 **Colchester United** (4–3 pens.); 1997-98, **Grimsby Town** 2–1 **Bournemouth (AFC)** (golden goal overtime); 1998-99 **Wigan** 1–0 **Millwall**.

Autoglass Trophy *competition* name of the former **Associate Members Cup** between 1991-92 and 1993-94, and a competition open only to clubs from English **Football League** Divisions Three and Four (later Second and Third Divisions). *Final results* 1991-92, **Stoke City** 1–0 **Stockport County**; 1992-93, **Port Vale** 2–1 Stockport County; 1993-94, **Swansea City** 1–1 **Huddersfield Town** (3–1 pens.).

automatic promotion *n.* assured progression to a higher level of a league system. *Keynotes* Automatic promotion and relegation was not introduced into the **Football League** until 1898-99. **Manchester City**, as Division Two Champions, and **Glossop** were the first two clubs to be automatically promoted to the higher level, replacing **Bolton Wanderers** and The Wednesday (later **Sheffield Wednesday**) in Division One. Previously, promotion and relegation issues had been resolved via a series of **test matches**. In 1986-87, Scarborough became the first non-League club to gain automatic entry to the Football League when, as **Football Conference** champions, it replaced **Lincoln City** in Division Four. In Scotland, automatic promotion between the divisions was not introduced until 1921-22, although the bottom Division One club had to seek **re-election**, and several **playoffs**, similar to the Football League's test matches, were played. The first Scottish club to win automatic promotion from Division Two was **Alloa**, which replaced **Dumbarton**. Both **Queen's Park** and **Clydebank** finished below Dumbarton and

also were relegated in order to reduce size of Division One to 20 clubs.

automatic relegation *n.* assured demotion to a lower level of a league system. *Keynotes* Automatic promotion and relegation was not introduced into the **Football League** until 1898-99. **Bolton Wanderers** and The Wednesday (later **Sheffield Wednesday**) were replaced by **Manchester City**, as Division Two Champions, and **Glossop** in Division One. Previously, promotion and relegation issues had been resolved via a series of **test matches**. In 1986-87, **Lincoln City** became the first League club automatically to lose its status, being replaced by **Conference Football** champions **Scarborough**. Previously, clubs finishing bottom of Division Four had applied for **re-election**.

automatic suspension *n.* match ban meted out to a player who has been **cautioned** a set number of times in a competition or who has been **sent off**; the length of the ban and the trigger point depends on individual **competition rules**; the length of the suspension may depend on the severity of the offences committed. In the FA **Premier League** and **Football League**, automatic suspensions are given to players who have been cautioned five times – and after every three subsequent cautions – or for being **sent off**. Suspensions begin 14 days after the last caution or sending off. Players can circumvent the three-subsequent-caution rule if, after a suspension, they complete five games without a further card.

Auxerre (Association de la Jeunesse Auxerroise) *club* French national league club based in Auxerre, formed 1905. Ground: Abbé Deschamps, capacity: 22,000. Strip: white shirts, white shorts. **European Cup/Champions League** quarter-final 1997; French Cup 1994, 1996; French league champions 1996; **UEFA Cup** quarter-final 1998. Notable former player: Eric **Cantona**.

avulsion *medical* the forcible separation of two separate tissues normally joined to each other such as ligament from bone or tendon from bone.

awarded results *n.* match result awarded by the football authorities to one team because of infringement(s) by the opposition. *Keynotes* In 1992, **UEFA** awarded **Leeds United** a 3–0 victory over **Stuttgart (VfB)**, although it had lost the **European Cup** tie on **away goals** (4–4), because the German club had fielded an **ineligible player**. During the 1998 **World Cup** qualifying competition, **FIFA** initially awarded **Scotland** a 3–0 victory over **Estonia** after the Balkan country had failed to fulfil its home tie in Tallinn because the timing of the **kick-off** had been rearranged due to the poor state of the ground's **floodlights**. At the proposed time and place the Scotland side kicked off but there were no opponents. Eventually, FIFA ordered a replay at a **neutral ground**.

away club *n.* In a league or cup fixture, the club that is not playing at its own ground. If a fixture is between two clubs that share a stadium, the away team is the one that is named second. The distinction is important: in deciding which team should play in its first-choice **strip** (the home team always wears its **home strip**); if **competition rules** stipulate that **away goals** may be counted as a premium in the event of a drawn tie; for gate receipts; and with regards to policing and security.

away goal *n.* goal scored by the **away club** in a fixture. Away goals have special significance in **two-leg** matches in some cup competitions: if the **aggregate** scores are level at the end of the second leg, then the team that has scored most away goals is declared the winner. For example, if a team wins its home leg 2–1 and loses the away leg 2–3 it will win the tie because it has scored two away goals compared with its opponent's one. If the aggregate and away-goal scores are level, the tie may be decided on **penalties**, or a **replay** (depending on **competition rules**). The two-leg knockout stages of all **UEFA**, **CONCACAF**, **CAF** and **AFC** continental club tournaments are decided on away goals if the aggregate scores are level. The **Copa CONMEBOL**, however, does not use the away-goals rule; tied rounds are decided directly on penalties. Away goals are used in the **League Cup**, and in the **Football League** divisional **playoffs**, but only if the aggregate score remains level after **extra time** has been played.

away strip *n.* a club's second-choice **strip**. *Regulations* **Premier League** clubs can only use their away strip for league matches if they are playing away from home and if their normal **home strip** would clash with that of the opposition; otherwise they should always play in their home strip (Premier League rule F.17). Football League clubs playing away from home must wear colours that are "clearly distinguishable from those of their opponents" (Football League regulation 35.2). See also **third strip**.

away win *n.* in **pools** betting, a match ending in victory for the **away** side.

Ayew, Abedi *player* real name of Abedi **Pelé**.

Ayr United *club* Scottish league. *Dossier* Ground: **Somerset Park**, Ayr, Strathclyde, capacity: 12,128. Strip: white shirt with black sleeves and red and blue side panels, black shorts with white trim and red stripe, black socks with white hoops. Nickname: Honest Men. Record attendance: 25,225 v **Rangers** (13 September 1969, Division One). Biggest win: 11–1 v **Dumbarton** (13 August 1952, **Scottish League Cup**). Biggest defeat: 0–9 v Rangers (1929, Division One), v **Heart of Midlothian** (1931, Division One), v **Third Lanark** (1954, Division Two (B)). *History* Founded in 1910 from a merger with Ayr Parkhouse, although its forerunner Ayr FC had played at Somerset Park since 1888 and had joined the Scottish League in 1897-98. United won the Scottish Division Two Championship in both 1911-12 and 1912-13, earning election to Division One on the second occasion (there was no automatic promotion in Scotland until 1921-22). The club won the Division Two title a further four times (1927-28, 1936-37, 1958-59, 1965-66) before the League structure was altered prior to the start of the 1975-76 season. United's sixth place in 1972-73 (Division One) and 1975-76 (Premier

Division) is the club's highest League position. Also in 1972-73, the club was a Scottish FA Cup semi-finalist (0–2 v **Rangers**). The club has reached the last four of the Scottish League Cup on three occasions: 1950-51 (3–4 v **Motherwell**), 1969-70 (1–2 replay v **Celtic**), 1980-81 (3–4 agg., v **Dundee**). It was a **Scottish League Challenge Cup** finalist in both 1990-91 (2–3 v **Dundee**) and 1991-92 (0–1 v **Hamilton Academicals**). The club's nickname, Honest Men, derives from a Robert Burns poem which refers to Ayr as being full of "honest men and bonnie lasses". *League record* Premier Division 1975-76 to 1977-78; First Division 1978-79 to 1985-86, 1988-89 to 1993-94, 1997-98–; Division One 1913-14 to 1914-15, 1921-22 to 1924-25, 1928-29 to 1935-36, 1937-38 to 1938-39, 1956-57, 1959-60 to 1960-61, 1966-67, 1969-70 to 1974-75; Scottish League 1915-16 to 1920-21; Second Division 1986-87 to 1987-88, 1994-95 to 1996-97; Division Two (B Division) 1897-98 to 1912-13 (as Ayr FC until 1910-11), 1925-26 to 1927-28, 1936-37, 1946-47 to 1955-56, 1957-58 to 1958-59, 1961-62 to 1965-66, 1967-68 to 1968-69. *Honours* Division Two 1911-12, 1912-13, 1927-28, 1936-37, 1958-59, 1965-66; Second Division 1987-88, 1996-97. *Records* Jim Nisbet is Ayr's most capped player (3 for **Scotland**); John Murphy holds the record for club appearances (459, 1963-78); Peter Price is Ayr's record goalscorer (213, 1955-61).

Ayresome Park *ground* former English football ground that was situated in Middlesbrough; former home of **Middlesbrough**. *Dossier* Capacity (in 1995): 24,000. Pitch dimensions (1995): 105m x 68.5m. Record attendance: 53,596 (v **Newcastle United**, Division One, 27 December 1949). Best average attendance: 36,123 (1950-51). *History* Middlesbrough settled at Ayresome Park in 1903. It was the club's home for 92 years until the building of the new **Riverside** (Cellnet) **Stadium** in 1995. The club played its first match at Ayresome Park on 1 September 1903 (v **Celtic**, friendly) and its final game on 30 April 1995 (v **Luton Town**, First Division) – the same day that the club celebrated winning the First Division Championship. Ayresome Park was closed on 1 August 1983, when the club went into liquidation, forcing club to play at **Hartlepool United**'s **Victoria Ground** on 23 August 1983 (v **Port Vale**, Division Three), after the home side had entertained **Cardiff City** in Division Four earlier in the day. In 1966, Ayresome Park was used as a **World Cup** venue; Newcastle United's **St James' Park** was initially selected as the north-east's venue but failed to install the necessary extra seating. Ayresome Park staged three group 4 matches (**North Korea** v **Soviet Union**; **Chile** v North Korea; **Italy** v North Korea) – total attendance 54,627; average attendance 18,209. The ground staged three **England** internationals (v Ireland, 25 February 1905; v Ireland, 14 February 1914; v **Wales**, 17 November 1937). Ayresome Park also was the venue for several **Inter-League** matches between the **Football League** and the **Scottish League** (eg, 17 February 1912, 22 March 1950, 20 March 1968 and 15 March 1972) and nine **FA Amateur Cup** finals or final replays (1912 Stockton v Eston United and replay; 1921 Bishop Auckland v Swindon Victoria; 1922 Bishop Auckland v South Bank; 1928 Leyton v Cockfield; 1935 Bishop Auckland v Wimbledon; 1954 second replay Crook Town v Bishop Auckland; 1956 replay Bishop Auckland v Corinthian Casuals; 1962 replay Crook Town v Hounslow Town). The ground's first floodlit match took place on 16 October 1957 (v **Sunderland**, friendly).

AZ 67 Alkmaar *club* Netherlands national league club, based in Alkmaar, and founded in 1967. Ground: Alkmaarderhoot, capacity: 10,500. Strip: red shirts and white shorts. Dutch Cup 1978, 1981, 1982; Dutch league champions 1981; **UEFA Cup** runners-up 1981 (4–5 agg., v **Ipswich Town**).

Azerbaijan *country UEFA* republic and former-Soviet state. Gained independence from former-Soviet Union in 1991. On Caspian Sea and border of Iran, separated from Irani provinces of Eastern and Western Azerbaijan by the Aras River. Area:, 87,000 sq km (33,580 sq miles). Dry subtropical steppes surrounded by the Caucasus Mountains. Population: 7,430,000 (1995 est.). Languages: Azeri (majority), Armenian and Russian. Capital: Baku. *Dossier* Association of Azerbaijan Football Federations (Baku) founded in 1991, joined FIFA and **Union of European Football Associations** (UEFA) in 1994, president Fuad Musayev, general secretary Çingiz Ismayilov. Season played from May to November. National Stadium: National Tofik Bakhramov, Baku, capacity: 37,000. (Continuous territorial disputes with Armenia have meant the venues of some international matches have been switched to neutral countries.) National strip: white shirts with blue stripes, blue shorts. First international match: 19 April 1994, v **Malta** (0–5, in Ta'Qali, Malta, friendly). Best international performance: 1–0 v **Switzerland** (31 August 1996, in Baku, **World Cup** qualifier). Biggest defeat 0–10 v **France** (1996, in France, **European Championship** qualifier). Leading international goalscorer: Anatoly Banishevski (formerly of Neftchi Baku, 19 goals for former-Soviet Union, 1965-72, equal seventh in all-time Soviet goalscoring list). *International tournament record* **World Cup** – first entered 1998 (finished last in its group of five nations); **Women's World Cup** – never entered; European Championship – first entered 1996 (last in its six-nation qualifying group, with only one point from 10 games). *Record against British and Irish national teams* none played. *History* The Azerbaijan national league championship and domestic cup competitions started in 1992. War with Armenia over the disputed territory of Nagorno-Karabakh meant that Azerbaijan played all three of its home ties in the 1996 European Championship qualifiers in Turkey (at Trabzon). Its short league history has been noted for the unorthodox method of deciding the championship. In 1995-96, its season was divided into championship and relegation

rounds (rather like some South American leagues): the second stage involved the top six clubs and the bottom five clubs in two mini-leagues. In the 1996-97 season, the Association of Azerbaijan Football Federations ruled that the championship would be decided by adding the total Premier League points to the average points in the under-15 and under-16 leagues. The top junior club was awarded 15 championship points, the runners-up 14, third-place 13, and so on. For example, **Neftchi Baku**'s junior sides finished eighth and third in their respective leagues: they thus gained 10.5 championship points (the average of 8 and 13). The senior side had won 74 points, so the total championship points were 74 + 10.5 = 84.5 (1.5 points behind the total for **Karabakh Agdam**). UEFA did not accept this formula and ruled that the Premier League winners Neftchi Baku should qualify for the 1997-98 **European Cup** rather than second-placed Karabakh Agdam, the "combined-points champions". Azerbaijan's national stadium is named after its controversial 1966 World Cup final linesman Tofik **Bakhramov**. *League system* Sixteen clubs compete in the national Premier League, each playing each other at home and away. Three points are awarded for a win and one for a draw. The bottom two clubs are automatically relegated, with the 13th and 14th clubs entering a playoff. The first division has nine clubs, and the second division 12. The Azerbaijan Cup final is played in mid-May. *Record in international club tournaments* never beyond first round. Leading clubs: **Neftchi Baku** (third in former-Soviet Union League Championship 1966), **Karabakh Agdam**, **Kyapaz Gyandzha**, **Turan Tauz**.

Azizi, Khodadad *player* Striker. **Iran** international (30 caps, 10 goals). Born 1972. *Clubs* **Piroozi**, FC **Cologne**. *Keynotes* Scored the goal that took Iran to the 1998 **World Cup** finals, an 80th-minute equaliser against **Australia** that gave his country an **away-goals** victory (29 November 1997, 2–2, in Australia, World Cup qualifier playoff). Names **Liverpool**'s Ian **Rush** and John Barnes as his childhood heroes. *Honours* Sanyo **Asian Footballer of the Year** 1996.

Azores *country no separate affiliation* self-governing region of **Portugal**, comprising three groups of islands in mid-Atlantic 1,440 km west of Lisbon. Area: 2,335 sq km (901 sq miles). Population: 237,100. Capital: Ponta Delgada.

Azteca (Estadio Guillermo Cañedo) *ground* Mexican football ground situated in Mexico City; home of **Mexico** national team and club sides Club de Fútbol **America**, Club Deportivo Social y Cultural **Cruz Azul** and Club Impulsora del Deportivo **Necaxa**. Ground capacity: 111,258. *Keynotes* Three-tier stadium built as one of the sporting facilities for the 1968 **Olympic Games** and opened in June 1966. The Azteca is around 2,240 metres (7,350 feet) above sea level. The stadium was officially renamed in 1997 after the former **FIFA** vice-president and long-serving Federación Mexicana de Fútbol Asociación AC (Mexican FA) official Guillermo Cañedo. The stadium was quickly given a facelift after

Mexico stepped in at short notice to stage the 1986 **World Cup** finals following **Colombia**'s sudden withdrawal as hosts. During the 1970 World Cup, Azteca staged all six group 1 fixtures (Mexico v **Soviet Union**, **Belgium** v **El Salvador**, Soviet Union v Belgium, Mexico v El Salvador, Soviet Union v El Salvador, Mexico v Belgium) a quarter-final tie (**Uruguay** v Soviet Union), a semi-final (**Italy** v West **Germany**), the 3rd place playoff (West Germany v Uruguay) and the final (**Brazil** v Italy) – total attendance 879,015; average attendance 87,901. Aside from the 1986 World Cup final (**Argentina** v West Germany), the Azteca staged a further eight matches (**Bulgaria** v Italy, group A; Mexico v Belgium, Mexico v **Paraguay**, Mexico v **Iraq**, group B; Mexico v Bulgaria, **England** v Paraguay, second round; Argentina v England, quarter-final; Argentina v Belgium, semi-final) – total attendance 976,251; average attendance 108,472. The stadium hosted the second **Confederación Norte-Centroamericana y del Caribe de Fútbol** (CONCACAF) **Gold Cup** in 1993 (Mexico v USA, 120,000) and the 1968 Olympic Games final (**Hungary** v Bulgaria).

Azuri   *n.*   *Italian* nickname for the Italian national side.

B

B'36 Tórshavn (Boltfelagid 36) *club* Faeroe Islands national league club based in the capital Tórshavn, founded 1936. Ground: Gundadular, capacity: 8,000. Strip: white shirts, black shorts. Faeroe Islands league champions 1936, 1948, 1950, 1959, 1962, 1997; Cup winners 1991.

B'68 Toftir *club* Faeroe Islands national league club based in Toftir, founded 1962. Ground: Svangaskard, capacity: 6,000. Strip: red and black striped shirts, black shorts. Faeroe Islands league champions 1984, 1985, 1992.

Babayaro, Celestine *player* Defender. **Nigeria** international. Born 26 December 1978. *Clubs* Plateau United (Nigeria), **Anderlecht**, **Chelsea**. *Honours:* **Olympic Games** gold medal (Nigeria, 1996), European Cup-winners Cup (Chelsea 1998), European Super Cup (Chelsea, 1998). Babayaro scored in the Olympic Games football tournament final against Argentina in 1996 (3–2, in Athens, Georgia, USA).

back foot *n.* *informal* of a defence under continuous pressure from the opposition. A team can thus be described as: on the back foot.

back four *tactics* four defenders (right-back, right centre-back, left centre-back, left-back) in a playing **formation**.

back-heel *vb.* to strike the ball with the back of the foot; a technique used rarely, but which can be effective because the opposing players may not be expecting such an action. *n.* the execution of this.

backpass 1. *n.* a **pass** played back down the field of play to the **defence** or **goalkeeper**. *vb.* to make such a pass. **2.** *rules* informally, the word backpass is used to describe any pass to the goalkeeper which, under Law XII, cannot be handled (see **pass to the goalkeeper**).

backstick *n.* *informal* another term for **far post**.

Baggio, Roberto *player.* Striker. **Italy** international (55 caps, 27 goals, 1988-). Born 18 February 1967. *Clubs* Vicenza, **Fiorentina**, **Juventus**, **AC Milan**, Bologna, **Internazionale**. *Keynotes* Baggio made his senior debut for Italy on 16 November 1988 (1–0, v **Netherlands**, in Rome, friendly), and scored his first international goal in a friendly against **Uruguay** (1–1, 22 April 1989, in Verona, friendly). By the end of 1998, Baggio was fourth in Italy's all-time list of international goalscorers. Baggio was transferred to Juventus for a then world record £7.7 million in 1990 and, in 1995, for £10 million to AC Milan. Nicknamed "Il Codino Divino", the Divine Ponytail, because of the **hairstyle** he once adopted. Baggio missed the vital final penalty in the shoot-out at the 1994 World Cup final against **Brazil**. *Honours* **World Cup** runner-up 1994; Italian **Serie A** championship (Juventus 1995, AC Milan 1996), Italian Cup (Juventus 1995); **UEFA Cup** (Juventus 1993); *World Soccer* World Footballer of the Year 1993, runner-up 1995; **FIFA World Footballer of the Year** 1993; *France Football* European Footballer of the Year 1993, runner-up 1994.

Bagheri, Karim *player* Striker. **Iran** international (41 caps, 33 goals). Born 1974. *Clubs* (include) Arminia Bielefeld (German **Bundesliga**). *Keynotes* Bagheri was top scorer in the 1998 **World Cup** qualifying competition, with 19 goals from 17 qualifying games. He scored the first of two late goals that took Iran to the 1998 World Cup finals: Bagheri's goal was followed three minutes later by an 80th minute equaliser by Khodadad **Azizi**, against **Australia** that gave his country an **away-goals** victory (29 November 1997, 2–2, in Australia, World Cup qualifier playoff).

Bahamas *country* CONCACAF Commonwealth nation comprising more than 700 coral islands (only about 30 of which are inhabited) stretching from the coast of Florida to **Cuba** and **Haiti**. Area: 13,865 sq km (5,350 sq miles). Subtropical climate with 1,000 mm of rain, falling mostly in the summer. Population: 276,000 (1995 est.). About 70% of the working population are employed in tourism. Language: English. Capital: Nassau. *Dossier* Bahamas Football Association (Nassau) formed in 1967, affiliated to **FIFA** in 1968 and **Confederación Norte-Centroamerican y del Caribe de Fútbol** in 1981, president Anton Sealey, general secretary Lionel Haven. Season played form October to May. National stadium: Thomas Robinson, Nassau, capacity: 15,000. National strip: yellow shirts, black shorts. *International tournament record* **Women's World Cup** – never entered; **World Cup** – first entered 1998; **Gold Cup** – never qualified. *Record against British and Irish National teams:* none played.

Bahia *state* one of the 27 state leagues in **Brazil**, founded 1904 (the second-oldest league in Brazil). Leading clubs: Vitória (of Salvador), **EC Bahia**.

Bahrain *country AFC* independent sheikhdom, consisting of several islands on the Persian Gulf. Declared independence from Britain in 1971. Rich oil reserves account for 60% of revenue. Area: 661 sq km (225 sq miles). Barren climate with less than 80 mm (3 inches) average rainfall. Can be very hot. Population: 586,000 (1995 est.). Languages: Arabic, English. Capital: Al Manamah. *Dossier* Bahrain Football Association (Manama) formed in 1951, affiliated to **FIFA** in 1966 and **Asian Confederation** (AFC) in 1970, president Shaikh Mohamed bin Isa Al-Khalifa, general secretary Mubarak Bin-Daina. Season played from November to April. National stadium: Isa Town Stadium, Al Manamah, capacity: 16,000. National strip: Red shirts, red shorts. *International tournament record* **Olympic Games** – won its qualifying tournament first-round group stage in 1992, but lost in the final qualifying round group; **World Cup** – first entered 1978, qualifying tournament second round 1986, never reached finals tournament (last in three-nation qualifying group 1998); **Arab Cup of Nations** – runners-up 1995 (0–1, v **Iraq**, in Saudi Arabia); **Arabian Gulf Cup** – never won, hosts 1998; **Asian Cup of Nations** – first entered 1972, qualified for finals tournament in 1988 but finished last in the first-round group stage; **Asian games** – never progressed beyond first round; **Asian Under-16 Championship** – runners-up 1988, third 1996; **Asian Youth Cup** (under-19) – runners-up 1986; **Under-17 World Championship** – qualified for finals tournament 1997; **World Youth Championship** (under-20) – qualified for finals tournament in 1987, gaining a draw against **Scotland** in the group matches. *Record against British and Irish national teams* none played. *League system* Ten clubs play in the national first division (18 games in total). *Record in international club tournaments* **Asian Cup-winners Cup** – **Muharraq** (runners-up 1990); **Arab Club Champions Cup** – Muharraq (runners-up 1994). Other leading clubs: Al Ahli, Al Hilal, Bahrain Club, **West Refa'a**.

baked beans *misc.* baked beans were banned by **England** coach Glenn **Hoddle** from the diet of the 1998 England **World Cup** squad, apparently because the tomato sauce contained too much sugar. The wisdom of the decision was questioned by dieticians.

Bakhramov, Tofik *official* **linesman** from **Azerbaijan** who gave **England** striker Geoff **Hurst**'s controversial second goal in the 1966 **World Cup** final against West **Germany**. Bakhramov adjudged that Hurst's **shot**, which came down off the **crossbar**, had crossed the line. Subsequent studies, using computer technology, have suggested that the whole of the ball did not cross the line and should not have been allowed. Bakhramov died on 27 March 1993. The national stadium of Azerbaijan is named in his honour.

balance of payments *n.* figure showing the difference between the value of goods and services exported by a country and those imported from outside. Traditionally, transfer fees for players bought from abroad were not included in the UK's national accounts. However, the increasing number of foreign players joining British clubs – valued at around £70 million over the summer 1998 period – led to a change in August 1998. For the first time the Office of National Statistics, the body which calculates the country's balance of payments, included transfer market dealings in its figures.

Balbo, Abel *player* Striker. **Argentina** international (30 caps, 11 goals). Born 1 June 1966. *Clubs* **Roma (AS)** – later **Parma** – striker who became the first **overseas player "stranieri"** in Italian **Serie A** to score 100 goals since Italy's **ban on foreign players**, that had been introduced in 1964, was lifted in 1980. Balbo scored a hat-trick in Roma's 6–2 victory over **Napoli** (5 October 1997) to achieve his century of Serie A goals.

Balboa, Marcelo *player* Defender. **United States of America** international (125 caps, 13 goals, 1988-). Born 8 August 1967. *Clubs* San Diego Nomads, San Francisco Bay Blackhawks, Colorado Foxes, **León** (Mexico), **Colorado Rapids**. *Keynotes* Balboa is the United States' most capped player, and one of the 10 most-capped players in the world. He made his international debut on 10 January 1988 (0–1, v **Guatemala**). He was the first US player (male or female) to achieve 100 caps for his country (11 June 1995, 3–2 v **Nigeria**). Played in the 1990, 1994 and 1998 **World Cup** finals teams. Captained the United States to the semi-final of the 1995 **Copa America**. *Honours* **Gold Cup** (USA, 1991); US Soccer male athlete of the year 1992, 1994.

baldies *misc.* players/managers with very little or no hair. Recently it has become common for footballers, especially those with receding hairlines, to shave their heads. **Chelsea** player-manager Gianluci **Vialli**, his teammate, French international Frank Leboeuf, and Ian Wright of West Ham are only three of the high-profile "baldies" to have played in the **Premier League**. **Ronaldo** famously shaved his head and during the 1997 **Confederations Cup** tournament, his Brazilian teammates also shaved their heads in his honour. Elsewhere, Channel Four's *Football Italia* has made the bald-headed **Serie A** and 1998 **World Cup** referee, Pierluigi Collina, an instantly recognisable figure.

Balkan Cup *competition* former tournament contested by the Balkan countries, **Albania** (winners 1946), **Bulgaria** (1932, 1935, 1976), **Hungary** (1947), **Romania** (1931, 1936, 1980), and **Yugoslavia** (1934).

Ball, Alan *player-manager* Midfield. **England** international (72 caps, 8 goals). Born 12 May 1945. Career ca. 1960–1983. *Clubs* (player) **Blackpool**, **Everton**, **Arsenal**, **Southampton** (twice), **Bristol Rovers**; (manager) Blackpool (player-manager), **Portsmouth** (twice), **Exeter City**, Southampton, **Manchester City**. *Keynotes* Had a spell as an amateur with **Bolton Wanderers** – told he was too small to make it as a professional player – before joining Blackpool in 1961 and turning professional in May 1962. Transferred to

Everton for a record £110,000 in August 1966, having played a key role in England's 1966 World Cup victory. Ball made 208 **Football League** appearances with Everton and he played a further 177 League games for Arsenal following his record £220,000 move to **Highbury** in December 1971. Ball is the only player to have been sent off on two occasions when playing for England (Under-23 v **Austria**, 1965; v **Poland**, 1973). Moved into management after retiring as a player in 1983, taking Portsmouth to Division One in 1987-88. Included in the **Football League Centenary 100 players**. *Honours* (player) League Championship (Everton 1969-70); **World Cup** (England 1966).

ball *rules* hollow sphere constructed of leather and/or polymers – the fundamental piece of equipment for a game of football. Official match balls must have an outer casing of leather or other suitable materials, measure 68–70 cm (27–28 inches) in circumference ("size 5") and, at the start of the game, must weigh 410–450 grams (14–16 ounces), with an internal pressure of 0.6–1.1 atmospheres (8.5–15.6 lb/square inch) at sea level (Law II). The match ball must be approved by the **referee**. The ball cannot be changed during a match unless authorised by the referee. If the ball bursts during play, then the game is stopped immediately and restarted by dropping a new ball at the place where the ball burst (except if the incident occurred within the **goal area**, in which case the ball is dropped on the goal line at a point nearest to the incident). If the ball bursts during a **free kick**, **penalty**, **throw-in**, **corner kick** or **goal kick**, then the kick or throw must be retaken. Balls used for international nation and international club competition matches must be designated as "**FIFA approved**", "**FIFA inspected**" or of "**International matchball standard**". Balls must not display any commercial advertising, other than the logo of the competition, the organiser of the competition, and the trademark of the ball manufacturer. *Keynotes* Rudimentary forms of football were played with inflated bladders from animals such as sheep or pigs, later surrounded by a shell made of leather pieces sewn together. The size and shape of the ball was not stipulated in the first rules of Association Football; the **Football Association** first ruled that a standard size ball should be used for **FA Cup** matches at a meeting in October 1872. Pigs' bladders were used inside the first official match balls, but were eventually replaced by "synthetic bladders" made of rubber. All-synthetic balls were first manufactured in the 1960s. **São Paulo FC** is thought to have pioneered the white ball for evening games; it had a brown leather ball painted white for a floodlit match. White balls were introduced to **Football League** matches in the 1950s. The Football League also pioneered the use of high-visibility yellow balls in the 1998-99 season; initially on an experimental basis. A different ball was used in each half of the first **World Cup** final in 1930 owing to a disagreement between the two finalists, **Uruguay** and **Argentina**. The first World Cup finals

to use a synthetic ball was the 1986 tournament in Mexico, when FIFA chose the "Adidas Azteca". The "Adidas **Tricolore**" for the 1998 finals in France also was all-synthetic, and featured a syntactic foam layer under the main shell. A ball was designed specifically for the 1999 **Women's World Cup** – in 1991 and 1995, the ball from the men's World Cup had been employed – the "Icon" (manufactured by Adidas) features an icon representing each of the seven host venues (Boston, Chicago, Los Angeles, New York/New Jersey, Portland, San Francisco Bay and Washington DC).

ball skills *n. pl.* impressive control of the ball, such as ball juggling and disguised turns and tricks to beat an opposition player.

ball watching *n.* term applied to players (usually defenders) who watch the ball rather than the movement of an opposing player, allowing the opponent to move into space or to get **goal-side** and gain an advantage.

ball-winner *n.* player who is adept at winning the ball and who usually plays in front of the **back-four** (also known as a front **sweeper**).

ballboy/ballgirl *n.* one of a number of youths positioned around, but at a distance from, the pitch whose job is to collect the ball if it goes out of play. *Regulations* Their clothing must not clash with the colour of either of the clubs involved in the game (Football League regulation 35.7).

Ballyclare Comrades *club* Northern Ireland national league club based in Ballyclare, County Antrim. Strip: red shirts, black shorts.

Ballymena United *club* Northern Ireland national league club based in Ballymena, County Antrim, founded 1928 as Ballymena FC. Ground: the Showgrounds, capacity: 8,000. Strip: sky blue shirts, sky blue shorts. **Irish FA Cup** 1929 (as Ballymena FC), 1940, 1958, 1981, 1984, 1989; Northern Ireland league runners-up 1939, 1980. Notable former players: Jim Platt (23 caps for Northern Ireland, 1976-86).

balompié *n.* former Spanish name for football – now fútbol. Of the major Spanish clubs, only **Real Betis Balompié** and Albacete Balompié retain the name in their official titles.

Baltic Championship *competition* annual international nations tournament for the three Baltic countries: **Estonia** (winners 1929, 1931, 1938), **Latvia** (1928, 1932, 1936, 1937, 1940, 1993, 1995) and **Lithuania** (1930, 1935, 1991, 1992, 1994, 1996, 1997, 1998). First played 1928 (until 1940), revived 1991, now played on a home-and-away basis. Also called Baltic Cup.

Baltic League *competition* ephemeral league competition involving club sides from the newly independent Baltic States of **Latvia**, **Estonia** and **Lithuania** in 1990. After only one season, the league was replaced by national leagues in the three countries. The only winner was **Zalgiris Vilnius** of Latvia.

Baltika Liepaja *club* Latvian national league club based in Liepaja, founded 1996 (formerly known as DAG Liepaja and FK Liepaja). Ground: Daugava, capacity: 8,000.

ban clubs *legal* prohibition of clubs from playing in official tournaments/competitions etc. *Keynotes* English clubs attempted to lift the **UEFA** ban imposed on them after the **Heysel Stadium tragedy** in the courts. The High Court refused the application on the grounds that the **Football Association** was acting beyond its power (*ultra vires*) by attempting to enforce an application outside its jurisdiction (*Liverpool FC and others v Football Association, 1985*). Following the formation of the **League of Wales** in 1992, three Welsh clubs, **Caernarfon Town**, **Colwyn Bay** and Newport AFC, refused to join the new league and were subsequently banned by the **Association of Wales** (FAW) from playing matches in the principality (see **Exiles**). The clubs took the FAW to court alleging an illegal **restraint of trade**. In April 1995, the clubs, which had been granted an interim injunction against the FAW's decision at a previous hearing in July 1994, won their case.

ban fans *legal* prohibition of supporters from attending football matches and stadiums. Several clubs have banned disruptive and violent supporters from their grounds in accordance with national law. *Keynotes* In 1978, **Bristol City** was granted an injunction preventing a fan the club had banned for the rest of the season from entering or attempting to gain access to its **Ashton Gate** ground. The ban had been instigated after the supporter had been convicted in the courts of an offence under the Public Order Act (*Bristol City v Milkins, 1978*). **Brighton & Hove Albion** banned five supporters from its **Goldstone Ground** for life after they were convicted of various Public Order Act offences following crowd trouble at **Portsmouth**'s **Fratton Park** ground on 8 April 1985 (*R v Clark and Ors, 1985*). Following crowd disturbances after **Chelsea**'s **FA Cup** fourth round **penalty shoot-out** defeat by **Millwall** at **Stamford Bridge**, six home supporters were banned for life (8 February 1995). **Rangers** banned several season ticket holders in the early 1990s following racist abuse of Mark Walters. In April 1998, 11 **Bristol City** supporters were banned from every football ground in the world for five years after being arrested for rioting following a local derby with **Bristol Rovers** at **Ashton Gate** (15 December 1996, Second Division). **Celtic** imposed life bans on two supporters in August 1998 after they were identified by fellow spectators of shouting pro-IRA slogans during a one-minute silence for those who died in the Omagh bombing (v **Dundee United**, Scottish Premier League, 22 August).

ban players *legal* prohibition of club officials, players, managers and other officials from engaging in official football-related activities. There have been several court cases relating to such bans. *Keynotes* The **Football Association** banned Don **Revie** from the game for 10 years after he quit as England manager in July 1977. The courts later ruled that the FA had acted contrary to natural justice and overturned the ban (*Revie v Football Association, 1979*). **Brighton & Hove Albion** captain Steve Foster challenged his ineligibility for the 1983 **FA Cup** final in the courts because of the

points total he had accumulated for disciplinary offences. The court refused to intervene on the basis of no breach of natural justice or other unlawful act (*Foster v Football Association, 1983*).

Bangkok Bank *club* Thailand national league club, based in Bangkok. **Asian Champion Teams Cup** – qualified for finals tournament 1967 (the first ever tournament), 1968, 1971, 1985, 1987, 1991; Thailand professional league champions 1994,1996, 1997.

Bangladesh *country AFC* republic in South Asia, formerly Eastern Province of **Pakistan**. Independence from Pakistan in 1971 after civil war. One of the poorest and most densely populated countries in the world. Area: 144,000 sq km (55,585 sq miles). Plains and vast deltas of the Ganges and Brahmaputra Rivers, monsoon climate. Population: 118,700,000 (1993 est.). Languages: Bengali, Bihari, Hindi and English. Capital: Dhaka. *Dossier* Bangladesh Football Federation (Dhaka) formed in 1972 (one year after independence), affiliated to **FIFA** and to the **Asian Confederation** (AFC) in 1974, president Mohammad Hanif, general secretary Rashid Harunur. Season played from March to December. National stadium: Dhaka Stadium, Dhaka, capacity: 55,000. National strip: orange shirts, white shorts. First international match: 27 July 1973 v **Vietnam** (1–1). Record attendance: 35,000, v **South Korea** (1–1, 5–3 pens., in Dhaka). Biggest victory: 8–0, v **Philippines**. Most capped player: K M Salahuddin (1969-84). Leading international goalscorer: SK Mohammad Aslam (1973-96). *International tournament record* **Olympic Games** – entered 1992 (fourth in its five-nation group); **Women's World Cup** – never entered. **World Cup** – first entered 1986, never past first round of qualifying tournament (last of four nations in first round of 1998 qualifying tournament with one win and five defeats in its six matches); **Asian Cup of Nations** – first entered 1980, qualified for finals tournament in 1980 (first round); **Asian Games** – first entered 1978, never past first round; **South Asian Gold Cup** – runners-up 1999 (0–2, v India, in Margoa, India). *Record against British and Irish national teams* none played. *History* A Dhaka league began in 1948; the Cup started in 1973, shortly after independence. Tthe league became a national championship in 1997. More than 70,000 players are now registered. There are at least 1,500 clubs registered at junior and senior level. Bangladesh hosted the finals tournament of the 1991 **Asian Champion Teams Cup** (Dhaka). Although international football began in 1973, Bangaladesh won its first international game in 1979 (3–2, v **Afghanistan**, Asian Cup qualifier). Football **hooliganism** hit Bangladesh in 1998 when fighting between rival fans of **Mohammedan Sporting** and **Abahani Ltd** during the national Major Cup led to the match being abandoned after 70 minutes; around 40 people were injured. *League system* Ten clubs play in the national league. After each club has played each other at home and away, the top five enter a 'Super League' playing a further four games for the championship (points from the first 18 games are carried over to the championship phase). The bottom five clubs enter a similar relegation league, with the bottom two clubs relegated to the regional league. Three points are awarded for a win, with one for a draw. *International tournament record* **Asian Champion Teams Cup** – **Mohammedan Sporting** (finals tournament 1988, 1990, 1991); **Asian Cup-winners Cup** – Mohammedan Sporting (second round 1990, 1992, 1993). Other leading clubs: **Abahani Ltd**, Dhaka University (Bangladesh Cup 1997), Muktijoddha Sangshad KC (Dhakha) (Bangladesh National league champions 1997, 1998).

Bangor City *club* Welsh league. *Dossier* Ground: The Stadium, Bangor, Gwynedd. Strip: blue shirts, blue shorts. Nickname: Citizens. Ground capacity: 2,000. *Keynotes* Formed in 1876. Bangor City lost in a preliminary round replay of the **European Cup-winners Cup** after drawing against **Napoli** over two legs (2–0, 1–3; 1–2 replay, 1962-63). Bangor would have won had the modern **away-goals** rule been applicable at the time. Bangor was involved in another glamorous Cup-winners tie in 1985: having reached the second round, the club lost against **Atlético Madrid** (0–3 agg.). *Honours* Welsh League 1927-28 (Northern Division); League of Wales 1993-94, 1994-95; **Welsh Cup** 1889 (2–1 v Northwich Victoria), 1896 (3–1 v **Wrexham**), 1962 (0–3, 2–0, 3–1 v Wrexham).

Bangor FC *club* Northern Ireland national league club based in Bangor, County Down, founded 1918. Ground: Clandeboye Park, capacity: 5,000. Strip: yellow shirts, blue shorts. **Irish FA Cup** 1993; Northern Ireland league runners-up 1991.

Banik Ostrava (FC Banik Ostrava OKD) *club* Republic and former-Czechoslovakia league club based in Ostrava, founded 1922 (as Slezska). Ground: Bazaly, capacity: 18,700. Strip: light blue shirts, blue shorts. **European Cup-winners Cup** semi-final 1979; former-Czechoslovakia league champions 1976, 1980, 1981; former-Czechoslovakia Cup 1973, 1978, 1991; **Mitropa Cup** 1987.

Bankrupting of English *misc.* report produced in 1991 by independent consultant Simon Pitt. He claimed that **Football League** clubs were, at that time, collectively in debt in the order of £130 million and that a number of clubs were close to bankruptcy; at least three-quarters of league clubs were in debit. He also blamed the "financial crisis" on a disproportionate rise in players' wages, transfer fees, signing-on fees, policing and security costs, compared with a much slower growth in revenue. Football, he said was "undercapitalised and over-borrowed".

Banks, Gordon *player* Goalkeeper. **England** international (73 caps). Born 30 December 1937. Career ca. 1955–73. *Clubs* **Chesterfield**, **Leicester City**, **Stoke City**. *Keynotes* Transferred to Leicester City from Chesterfield for £6,000 in May 1959, going on to make 293 **Football League** appearances for the club before joining Stoke for £52,000 in April 1967. Overall, Banks

made 510 League appearances in a career that was tragically curtailed in August 1972 when he lost an eye in a car crash. Banks' 73 international appearances included 35 **clean sheets** – seven of them in succession before the 1966 World Cup semi-final against **Portugal**. During the 1970 World Cup he produced one of the greatest saves of all time, scooping a header from **Pelé** up and over the bar. In 1970, Banks was awarded the OBE and, in 1972, he was voted **Footballer of the Year**. Included in the **Football League Centenary 100 players**. *Honours* **League Cup** (Leicester City 1964; Stoke City 1972); **World Cup** (England 1966).

Barbados *country* CONCACAF island in the West Indies in the East Lesser Antilles. Independent commonwealth state since 1966, having been a British colony since 1628. Area: 430 sq km (166 sq miles). Pleasant climate with temperatures ranging from 25° to 28°C, though with much rainfall (1,270–1,900 mm per year). Population: 264,000 (1994 est.). One third of working population is employed in tourism. Language: English. Capital: Bridgetown. *Dossier* Barbados Football Association (Bridgetown) founded in 1910, affiliated to **FIFA** and **Confederación Norte-Centroamerican y del Caribe de Fútbol** (CONCACAF) in 1968, president George Lascaris, general secretary Patrick Beckles. Season played from January to May. National stadium: National Stadium, Bridgetown, capacity: 12,000. National strip: royal blue shirts, gold shorts. *International tournament record* **Women's World Cup** – never entered; **World Cup** – first entered 1978, reached second round of qualifying tournament in 1998; **Caribbean Nations Cup** – qualified for finals tournament 1994, hosted final in 1989 (in Bridgetown); **Gold Cup** – never qualified. *Record against British and Irish national teams* none played. *Record in international club tournaments* **CONCACAF Cup-winners Cup** – **Lambada** (fourth place 1994); **Caribbean Club Championship** – Notre Dame SC (quarter-final 1998).

Barbie *trademark* female doll. In 1998, Barbie's makers Mattel introduced a souvenir "Women's World Cup Barbie", modelled on US star striker Mia **Hamm**.

Barcelona (FC) *club* Spanish league. *Dossier* Home: **Nou Camp**, Catalonia. Strip: red and blue stripes, blue shorts with red trim. Website: *www.fcbarcelona.es* Nickname: Barça. Ground capacity: 115,000. *History* Formed in 1899 by a Swiss national and bank worker, Hans Gamper. Barcelona's blue and red colours are based on the flag of the Swiss canton where Gamper was born. The club's first president was an Englishman, Walter Wild. It was the first club in Spain to turn professional. Between 1922 and 1957, Barça played at Les Corts before moving to the Nou Camp. Barcelona was the first winner of the Spanish league (**Primera Liga**) in 1929 and the club was also five-times winners of the Spanish Cup (**Copa del Ray**) in the 1920s. Barça's 1998 Spanish Cup victory was the club's 24th in the competition – a record. Spain's former dictator Francisco Franco's policy to forge a nationwide Spanish identity led to the appointment of a Castillian and Francoist, Enric

Piñeyro, as club president in 1940. He changed the club's name from the Catalonian, Fútbol Club Barcelona, to the Castillian, Club de Fútbol Barcelona. Only after the dictator's death in 1975 could the club revert to its original Catalonian name. *Keynotes* Barça has been a **European Cup** finalist on four occasions, winning the trophy in 1992 (see below) and losing in 1961 (2–3 v **Benfica**), 1986 (0–0, 0–2 pens. v **Steaua Bucharest**) and 1994 (0–4 v **AC Milan**). The club's 1992 European Cup success meant it joined a select group to have won all three European club competitions (the others being **Ajax**, **Bayern Munich** and **Juventus**). Barcelona has won the **European Cup-winners Cup** four times and been a finalist on two further occasions: 1969 (2–3 v **Slovan Bratislava**) and 1991 (1–2 v **Manchester United**. It won the first two **UEFA** (Fairs) **Cup** competitions, added a further trophy in 1966, and was a losing finalist in 1962 (3–7agg., v **Valencia**). Barcelona has a tradition of appointing foreign managers, including Helenio **Herrera**, Rinus **Michels**, Terry **Venables**, Johan **Cruyff**, Bobby **Robson** and Louis Van Gaal. Under Van Gaal, the club won its first League and Cup **double** for 39 years in 1998. *Honours* **European Cup** 1992 (1–0 a.e.t. v **Sampdoria**); **European Cup-winners Cup** 1979 (4–3 a.e.t. v **Fortuna Düsseldorf**), 1982 (2–1 v **Standard Liege**), 1989 (2–0 v Sampdoria), 1997 (1–0 v **Paris Saint-Germain**; **European Super Cup** 1992 (3–2 agg., v **Werder Bremen**), 1998 (3–1 agg., v **Borussia Dortmund**); Spanish Cup 1910 (3–2 v Español Madrid), 1912 (2–0 v Gimnástica Madrid), 1913 (2–1 second replay v **Real Sociedad**), 1920 (2–0 v **Athletic Bilbao**), 1922 (5–1 v Real Union Irún), 1925 (2–0 v Arenas Guecho Bilbao), 1926 (3–2 v **Atlético Madrid**), 1928 (3–1 second replay v Real Sociedad), 1942 (4–3 v Athletic Bilbao), 1951 (3–0 Real Sociedad), 1952 (4–2 v **Valencia**), 1953 (2–1 v Athletic Bilbao), 1957 (1–0 v **Espanyol RCD**), 1959 (4–1 v Granada), 1963 (3–1 **Real Zaragoza**), 1968 (1–0 v **Real Madrid**), 1971 (4–3 v Valencia), 1978 (3–1 v Las Palmas), 1981 (3–1 v Real Sporting Gijón), 1983 (2–1 v Real Madrid), 1988 (1–0 v Real Sociedad), 1990 (2–0 v Real Madrid), 1997 (3–2 v **Real Betis Balompié**), 1998 (1–1, 5–4 pens. v Mallorca (RCD)); Spanish league 1928-29, 1944-45, 1947-48, 1948-49, 1951-52, 1952-53, 1958-59, 1959-60, 1973-74, 1984-85, 1990-91, 1991-92, 1992-93, 1993-94, 1997-98, 1998-99; **UEFA** (Fairs) **Cup** 1958 (8–2 agg., v London), 1960 (4–1 agg., v **Birmingham City**), 1966 (4–3 agg., v Real Zaragoza).

Barcelona Foundation *misc.* an institution founded in 1994 by **Barcelona** president Josep Lluis Nunez to ensure that all sections of Catalan society are involved in the club and can take advantage of its facilities. The foundation is sponsored by a number of major corporations and provides financial support for all kinds of sporting and cultural activities. It has 22,000 individual members who each paid 9000 pesetas to join.

Barcelona Sporting Club *club* Ecuador national Primera league club based in Guayaquil. Founded 1925.

Ground: Estadio Monumental "Isidro Romero Carbo", capacity: 75,000. Strip: yellow shirts, black shorts. **Copa Libertadores** runners-up 1990 (1–3 agg., v **Olimpia** of Paraguay), 1998 (1–4 agg., v **Vasco da Gama** of Brazil), semi-final 1971, 1972, 1986, 1987, 1992, quarter-final 1996; Ecuador league champions 1960, 1963, 1966, 1970, 1971, 1980, 1981, 1985, 1987, 1989, 1991, 1995, 1997. Notable former player: Alberto **Spencer**.

Barclays League *competition* title given to the English **League** from 1987-90, when sponsored by Barclays Bank. The deal was worth about £4.55 million over three seasons.

Baresi, Franceschino (Franco) *player* Defender. **Italy** international (81 caps, one goal, 1982-94). Born 8 May 1960. *Club* **Milan**. *Keynotes* Baresi captained the Italian national side in the 1994 World Cup, but missed the opening penalty in the shoot-out against **Brazil** in the final (Baresi shot over the bar); Italy lost the shoot-out 2–3 (0–0 after extra time, Rose Bowl, Los Angeles, USA). *Honours* **World Cup** runner-up (Italy, 1994); **European Cup** (Milan, 1989, 1990); Italian **Serie A** championship (Milan, 1988, 1992, 1993, 1994).

Barnes FC *club* former English club. *Keynotes* Football club founded in South London in 1862, played at Mortlake. Took part in the first match ever played under the rules of Association Football (see **Laws of the game**: *Keynotes*, (19 December 1863, Barnes FC v Richmond FC, 0-0, Mortlake).

Barnes, John *player* Midfield. **England** international (79 caps, 11 goals). Born 7 November 1963. Career ca. 1981– . *Clubs* **Watford**, **Liverpool**, **Newcastle United**, **Charlton Athletic**. *Keynotes* Joined Watford in July 1981 and a member of the side which finished Division One runners-up in 1982-83. In 1984, he also played in Watford's only FA Cup final (0–2 **Everton**). He played 233 **Football League** games for Watford and scored 65 goals. Barnes was transferred to Liverpool for £900,000 in June 1987. He teamed up with his former Liverpool manager Kenny **Dalglish** at Newcastle in 1997, moving from **Anfield** on a **free transfer** and making an appearance as a substitute in the 1998 FA Cup final; he is the only player to appear on the losing side in FA Cup finals with three clubs. Barnes made his international debut for England against **Northern Ireland** on 28 May 1983 at the age of 19. Voted **Footballer of the Year** in both 1988 and 1990, and **PFA Footballer of the Year** in 1988. Included in the **Football League Centenary 100 players**. *Honours* League Championship (Liverpool 1987-88, 1989-90); **FA Cup** (Liverpool 1989); **League Cup** (Liverpool 1995).

Barnet *club* English league. *Dossier* Ground: **Underhill Stadium**, Barnet, Hertfordshire. Strip: amber and black striped shirts, black shorts, black socks. Nickname: Bees. Ground capacity: 4,057. Record league attendance: 5,090 v **Crewe Alexandra** (17 August 1991, Division Four). Best average: 3,643 (1991-92). Biggest win: 6–0 v **Lincoln City**

(4 September 1991, Division Four). Biggest defeat: 1–9 v **Peterborough United** (5 September 1998, Third Division). *History* A Barnet FC was formed in 1888 but was forced to disband in 1901 after a **Football Association** inquiry. Barnet Avenue emerged in 1903, while Alston Works, a dental company's team, changed its name to Barnet Alston in 1906 and moved to Underhill. Avenue and Alston merged as Barnet Alston in 1912, becoming Barnet FC in 1919. Barnet won the FA Amateur Cup at **Stamford Bridge** in 1946 (3–2 v **Bishop Auckland**). During the early-1970s, the club, then a non-league entity, enjoyed some FA Cup success, reaching the third round on two occasions: 1971 (0–1 v **Colchester United**), 1973 (0–3 replay v **Queens Park Rangers**). The club's 1971 FA Cup campaign included a record-equalling victory margin by a non-league side over a **Football League** club (6–1 v **Newport County**, first round). In 1979-80, Barnet was one of 13 Southern League clubs which were founder members of the Alliance Premier League (later the **Football Conference**), finishing runners-up in three out of four seasons (1986-87,1987-88, 1989-90) before securing promotion to the Football League as Champions in 1990-91. In the club's first season in the League, it narrowly failed to secure promotion to the Second Division via the end-of-season **playoffs**, reaching the semi-final stage. In 1992-93, Barnet won an automatic promotion place but its tenure in the Second Division lasted for only one season. The club was again a playoff semi-finalist in 1997-98. Barnet, with debts of £80,000, almost folded in 1985 but was saved by chairman and former **ticket tout** agent Stan Flashman. He and manager Barry Fry, appointed in 1978, enjoyed an uneasy relationship with the latter being sacked and reinstated on three occasions between March 1992 and April 1993, when, with the club again heavily in debt, Flashman left the club. *League record* Second Division 1993-94; Third Division 1992-93, 1994-95–; Division Four 1991-92. *Honours* Football Conference 1990-91; FA Amateur Cup 1946 (3–2 v Bishop Auckland). *Records* Paul Wilson holds the record for club League appearances (213, 1991-98); Sean Devine is Barnet's record League goalscorer (46, 1991-98).

Barnsley *club* English league. *Dossier* Ground: **Oakwell**, Barnsley, south Yorkshire. *Dossier* Strip: red shirts with white trim, white shorts, red socks. Nickname: Tykes, Reds or Colliers. Ground capacity: 18,806 all seated. Record attendance: 40,255 v **Stoke City** (15 February 1936, **FA Cup**, fifth round). Best average attendance: 21,262 (1947-48). Biggest win: 9–0 v **Loughborough Town** (28 January 1899, Division Two), 9–0 v **Accrington Stanley** (3. February 1934, Division Three (North)). Biggest defeat: 0–9 v **Notts County** (19 November 1927, Division Two). *History* Formed in 1887 as Barnsley St Peter's by the Reverend Tiverton Preedy, the club turned professional a year later and changed its name to Barnsley. The club became a **limited company** in 1899. Barnsley played

its first matches on a pitch that is behind the Brewery Stand of the club's present ground, Oakwell, where it moved in 1895. Three years later, Barnsley was elected to Division Two, where it has spent more time than any other club. Until the 1997-98 season, Barnsley had never played in the top division, although the club missed promotion to Division One on **goal average** in 1922. The club's stay in the top flight lasted only one season. Barnsley's only honour was achieved in the FA Cup, which it won in 1912, following defeat in the final of the same competition two years earlier. The club became known as "Battling Barnsley" during its 1912 FA Cup success, playing 12 matches on the way to winning the trophy, including six 0-0 draws, five one-goal victories and a 3-1 win over **Birmingham**. Barnsley's victory in the 1912 FA Cup final was only the third by a team from Division Two (overall seven Division Two clubs have won the FA Cup: Barnsley, Notts County (1894), **Wolverhampton Wanderers** (1908), **West Bromwich Albion** (1931), **Sunderland** (1973), **Southampton** (1976), **West Ham United** (1980)). Between 1959 and 1981, Barnsley experienced its worst period, floundering in the bottom two divisions and suffering several financial crises before rising to the Premiership in 1997. *League record* Premier League 1997-98; First Division 1992-93 to 1996-97, 1998-99–; Division Two 1898 to 1931-32, 1934-35 to 1937-38, 1946-47 to 1952-53, 1955-56 to 1958-59, 1981-82 to 1991-92; Division Three 1959-60 to 1964-65, 1968-69 to 1971-72, 1979-80 to 1980-81; Division Three (North) 1932-33 to 1933-34, 1938-39, 1953-54 to 1954-55; Division Four 1965-66 to 1967-68, 1972-73 to 1978-79. *Honours* Division Three (North) 1933-34, 1938-39, 1954-55; FA Cup 1912 (1–0, replay/a.e.t. v West Bromwich Albion). *Records* Gerry Taggart is Barnsley's most-capped player (35 (45) for **Northern Ireland**); Barry Murphy holds the record for club appearances (514, 1962-78); Ernie Hine is Barnsley's record league goalscorer (123, 1921-26, 1934-38).

Barrow *club* former English league. *Dossier* Ground: Holker Street, Barrow, Cumbria. Record attendance: 16,874 v **Swansea** Town (9 January 1954, FA Cup, third round). *History* Founder members of Division Three (North) in 1921-22. The club failed to get re-elected in 1971-72 and was replaced by **Hereford United**. Barrow's highest League position was fifth in Division Three (North), which the club achieved in 1931-32. In 1998, Barrow was promoted to the **Football Conference**. *League record* Division Three 1967-68 to 1969-70; Division Three (North) 1921-22 to 1957-58; Division Four 1958-59 to 1966-67, 1970-71 to 1971-72.

Barry Town *club* Welsh league. *Dossier* Ground: Jenner Park, Barry, South Glamorgan. Strip: yellow shirts, blue shorts. Nickname: Dragons. Ground capacity: 6,500. *Keynotes* Formed in 1893. Barry completed a Welsh domestic treble by winning the **League of Wales**, the **Welsh Cup**, and the League of Wales Cup in 1996-97. The club won the title with a record number of points (105), losing only one match (0–1 v Llansantffraid (**Total Network Solutions**)) during the season. Barry qualified for the 1997-98 **UEFA Cup** competition, beating Dinaburg Daugavpils of Latvia (2–1 agg.) in the first preliminary round; BVSC of Hungary, 4–4 agg., 4–2 pens., in the second preliminary round, before losing 4–6 agg., v **Aberdeen**). The club failed to qualify for the **Champions League** in 1997-98, losing to **Dinamo Kiev** (0–6 agg.) in the **European Cup** qualifiers. *Honours* League of Wales 1995-96, 1996-97, 1998-99; Welsh Cup 1955 (5–4 agg., v **Chester**), 1994 (2–1 v **Cardiff City**), 1997 (2–1 v **Cwmbran Town**); Welsh league 1982-83.

Baseball Ground *ground* English football ground in Derby; former home of **Derby County**. *Dossier* Capacity when Derby County vacated the ground: 19,500. Pitch dimensions: 100.5m x 65m. Record attendance: 41,286 v **Tottenham Hotspur** (20 September 1969, Division One). Best average: 35,924 (1969-70). *Keynotes* The ground was so named because it was built to stage baseball. It was founded in 1889 (it had previously been a works' sports ground) by Derby foundry owner Francis Ley, following his return from the US where he had come to love the game of baseball. Derby moved to the Baseball Ground in 1895, although the club had played one match at the ground in March 1892 (v **Sunderland**). The club switched from its previous home, the Racecourse Ground, because it was regularly forced to move venues when games clashed with race meetings. Derby's first game at the Baseball Ground was also against Sunderland (14 September 1895, Division One). In March 1924, Derby bought the ground from Ley for £10,000 and proceeded to rebuild it completely between 1925 and 1933. In its early years, baseball was regularly played, and in 1944 locally-based American service personnel played an exhibition match at the ground. In 1953, the Baseball Ground was one of the first English league grounds to experiment with **under soil heating**. The ground was one of only four English club grounds in the late 1960s to contain seated and standing accommodation on all four sides of the ground (the others being **Goodison Park**, **Old Trafford**, **White Hart Lane**). Throughout Derby's 102 year tenure of the Baseball Ground, the club had three opportunities to relocate elsewhere. In 1923, the local council proposed a municipally-owned stadium. In 1945, another council-owned stadium was on the drawing-board; both were turned down. A third chance to move came in 1991, when funding from the then government's "City Challenge" initiative offered the club the opportunity to become part of a public and private sector consortium to build a new stadium. In January 1995 the club decided, once again, to remain at the Baseball Ground and embark on a redevelopment programme. Derby was within two weeks of starting the ground's redevelopment when it announced its decision to relocate to the proposed **Pride Park** after all. At the start of the 1997-98 season, with Derby second in the Premier League, the club moved to the new stadium. Derby con-

tinued to play their reserve matches at the Baseball Ground for a period. The first floodlit match at the ground was staged on 16 March 1953 (v **Notts County**, friendly). The Baseball Ground was the venue for one international (v **Ireland**, 11 February 1911) and two **FA Cup** semi-finals (1899, 1901).

Bassett, Billy (William Isiah) *player* Winger. **England** international (16 caps, 7 goals). Born 27 January 1869. Career ca. 1886–1899. *Clubs* **West Bromwich Albion**. *Keynotes* Retired from playing in April 1899, having made around 450 appearances for WBA and scored 125 goals. He became a WBA director in 1905 and club chairman from 1908. Bassett was a member of both the **Football Association** Council and the **Football League Management Committee** between 1930 and his death in 1937. Included in the **Football League Centenary 100 players**. *Honours* **FA Cup** (WBA 1888, 1892).

Bastia *club* see **SC Bastia**.

Bastin, Cliff *player* Winger/striker. **England** international (30 caps, 12 goals). Born 14 March 1912. Career ca. 1926–1947. *Clubs* **Exeter City**, **Arsenal**. *Keynotes* One of the youngest FA Cup finalist this century, aged 18 years 43 days, when he appeared for Arsenal in the 1930 final (v **Huddersfield Town**). He scored a winger's record 33 goals in 42 League matches as outside-left for Arsenal in 1932-33. Bastin's tally of 150 League goals in a Arsenal career spanning 18 years was a club record until surpassed by Ian Wright in 1997-98. Bastin died in 1991. Included in the **Football League Centenary 100 players**. *Honours* League Championship (Arsenal 1930-31, 1932-33, 1933-34, 1934-35, 1937-38); **FA Cup** (Arsenal 1930, 1936).

Bata Bullets *club* Malawi Super League club based in Blantyre (the largest city) – the most successful Malawi club. Ground: Kanjizu, capacity: 35,000. Strip: red shirts and white shorts. **African Cup of Champion Clubs** – second round 1975; **African Cup-winners Cup** – second round 1977; Blantyne and District regional champions six times (regional leagues operated before the Super League); Chibuku Cup nine times; **East and Central African Club Championship** – semi-final 1979 and 1987; Kamuzu Cup seven times; Malawi National Super League champions 1986, 1991, 1992 and 1993 (the Super League has only been in operation since 1986).

Bathgate *club* former Scottish league. *Dossier* Ground: Mill Park, Bathgate, Lothian. *Keynotes* Bathgate joined Division Two in 1921-22, twice finishing fifth and, in 1923-24, third – the club's highest league position. The club resigned during the 1928-29 season. *League record* Division Two 1921-22 to 1928-29 (did not complete fixtures).

Batistuta, Gabriel *player* Striker. **Argentina** international (68 caps, 49 goals, 1991-). Born 1 February 1969. *Clubs* **Newell's Old Boys**, **River Plate**, **Boca Juniors**, **Fiorentina**. *Keynotes* Batistuta is Argentina's all-time top goalscorer. He made his international debut against **Brazil** on 27 June 1991 (1–1, in Curitiba, friendly). He scored both Argentina's goals in the final of the 1993 Copa America (2–1, v **Mexico**). He was top scorer in the 1991 and 1995 (joint) Copa America (six goals, four goals respectively), and leading scorer in the Italian **Serie A** in 1995. By November 1998, Batistuta had become the most prolific overseas goalscorer in Italy's Serie A since the ban on foreign players was lifted in 1980. Batistuta scored in each of **Fiorentina**'s first 11 matches in the 1994-95 Italian season – a record.*Honours* **Copa America** (Argentina, 1991 1993); *El Mundo* South American Footballer of the Year 1991.

Battle of Berne   *misc.*   match between **Hungary** and **Brazil** at the 1954 **World Cup** finals (27 June 1954, at **Wankdorf Stadium**, Berne, Switzerland, quarter-final). The fixture had been billed as a match between two of the best sides in the world but, unfortunately, was shrouded in violence, both on and off the field. Two Brazilians and Hungary's captain for the day, József **Bozsik**, were **sent off**. Hungary won the match 4–2.

Battle of Highbury   *misc.*   alleged friendly match between **England** and **Italy** (playing its first game since winning the 1934 **World Cup**) at **Highbury** on 14 November 1934; England, including seven Arsenal players, won 3–2. The match attracted its infamous nickname due to the actions of the Italian team, who, promised exemption from military service in the event of victory, resorted to physical confrontation, leaving a number of English players injured (including Arsenal's Eddie **Hapgood** with a broken nose) and provoking retaliation.

Battle of Santiago   *misc.*   World Cup finals first-round group match in Santiago, 2 June 1962, between Chile and Italy. Noted for serious on-pitch violence in which the referee was nearly forced to abandon the match because of persistent foul play and violent conduct by players from both sides. Chile won the match 2–0, Ramirez and Toro scoring the goals. Two Italians, Ferrini and David, were sent off.

Bayern Munich (Bayern München) (FC)   *club* German league. *Dossier* Home: **Olympiastadion**, Munich, Bavaria. Strip: red and blue striped shirts, blue shorts. Ground capacity: 64,000. *History* Formed in 1900. The club's official title is FC Bayern München, meaning Bavaria Munich. Until October 1998, when the German football authorities altered its rules to allow clubs to become **limited companies**, Bayern was a non-profit making sports club, run for the benefit of its estimated 74,000 members. The club previously played at the Grünwalder Stadium until it moved to the Olympic venue in 1972 and it is currently planning to build a new purpose-built stadium elsewhere in the city. By 1998, Bayern was the most successful club in Germany, winning one German Championship (1932), 13 **Bundesliga** titles and eight German Cup finals. Aside from Bayern's 1932 German title, all of the club's honours have come in the post-**World War II** period. Its previous lack of success, meant that Bayern was not invited to join the Bundesliga when the league

was established in 1964, although the club was promoted within two years, winning the league and Cup **double** in 1968-69. A second domestic double was achieved in 1985-86. Bayern has twice won the Bundesliga title on three successive occasions (1971-72, 1972-73, 1973-74 and 1984-85, 1985-86, 1986-87). Bayern's first success in European competition occurred in 1967 with victory in the **European Cup-winners Cup**. It has since appeared in five **European Cup** finals, winning three successive trophies between 1974 and 1976. It was the beaten finalist in 1982 in 1982 (0–1 v **Aston Villa**) and 1987 (1–2 v FC **Porto**). Its 1974 European Cup triumph was the first by a German club in Europe's premier club competition. In 1996, Bayern won the **UEFA Cup**, thus becoming one of only four clubs to win each of the three major European club competitions (the others being **Ajax**, **Barcelona** and **Juventus**). It reached the final of the 1999 European Cup (2–1 v **Manchester United**, **Nou Camp**). Franz **Beckenbauer** was a star of the Bayern teams between 1964 and 1976, and became club president. Other notable (West) **Germany** internationals to appear for Bayern include: Paul **Breitner**, Uli Hoeness, Jürgen **Klinsmann**, Sepp **Maier**, Lothar **Matthäus**, Gerd **Müller** and Karl-Heinz **Rummenigge**. *Honours* Bundesliga 1968-69, 1971-72, 1972-73, 1973-74, 1979-80, 1980-81, 1984-85, 1985-86, 1986-87, 1988-89, 1989-90, 1993-94, 1996-97; European Cup 1974 (4–0 replay v **Atlético Madrid**), 1975 (2–0 v **Leeds United**), 1976 (1–0 v St-Etienne), finalist 1999 (v Manchester United); European Cup-winners Cup 1967 (1–0 a.e.t. v **Rangers**); German league 1932 (2–0 v **Eintracht Frankfurt**); UEFA Cup 1996 (5–1 agg., v **Bordeaux**); West German Cup 1957 (1–0 v Fortuna Düsseldorf), 1966 (4–2 v MSV Duisburg), 1967 (4–0 v **Hamburg SV**), 1969 (2–1 v **Schalke 04** (FC)), 1971 (2–1 v **Cologne** (1.FC)), 1982 (4–2 v **Nuremberg** (1.FC)), 1984 1–1, 7–6 pens. v **Borussia Mönchengladbach**), 1986 (5–2 v **Stuttgart** (VfB)), 1998 (2–1 v MSV Duisburg); World Club Championship 1976 (2–0 agg., v **Cruzeiro**).

Bayview Park   *ground*   former Scottish football ground situated in Methil, Fife; former home of **East Fife**. *Dossier* Ground capacity (1998): 5,385. Pitch dimensions: 100.5m x 65m. Record attendance: 22,515 v **Raith Rovers** (2 January 1950, **Division One**). *Keynotes* East Fife played at Bayview Park since the club was formed in 1903, playing its first match there in August (v **Heart of Midlothian**). East Fife agreed to sell the ground to property developers in 1995. The first floodlit match at Bayview took place on 7 March 1954 (v **Leeds United**, friendly). Bayview, together with Hibernian's Easter Road ground, was the setting, on 8 February 1956 (v **Stenhousemuir**), for the first **Scottish FA Cup** tie to be played under floodlights. East Fife's final match at Bayview Park took place on 31 October 1998 (v **Livingston**, Second Division) before moving to the new **Bayview Stadium**.

Bayview Stadium *ground* Scottish football ground situated in Methil, Fife; home of **East Fife**. *Dossier* Capacity: 2,000. *Keynotes* A £2 million stadium built in the dock area of Methil and having the fourth largest playing surface in the **Scottish Football League**. East Fife played its first match at the ground on 14 November 1998 (v **Forfar Athletic**, Second Division), having vacated its former home **Bayview Park** on 31 October 1998.

BCC Lions (Benue Cement Club) *club* Nigerian national league club based in Gboko. Ground capacity: 30,000. Strip: sky blue shirts, white shorts. **African Cup-winners Cup** 1990 (4–1 agg., v **Club Africain** of Tunisia), runners-up 1991; Nigerian FA Challenge Cup 1989, 1993, 1994; Nigerian league champions 1994.

beach football *n.* variant form of football played on sand or beaches, usually barefoot. Around 10,000 people enter beach football competitions in Brazil, most famously at Copacabana Beach, organised by the Confederação Brasileira de Futebol (the Brazilian Football Association), with matches lasting 60 minutes.

Beaujoire (Stade de la) *ground* French football ground situated in Nantes, Pays des la Loire; home of **FC Nantes Atlantique**. Ground capacity: 39,500 all seated. *Keynotes* Built for the 1984 **European Championship** and opened on 8 May 1984 (FC Nantes v **Romania**, friendly). Refurbished for the 1998 **World Cup** at a cost of more than £4 million. During the tournament, Stade de la Beaujoire staged one match from each of groups A (**Brazil** v **Morocco**), B (**Cameroon** v **Chile**), D (**Nigeria** v **Spain**), F (**United States** v **Yugoslavia**), and H (**Croatia** v **Japan**); and a quarter-final (Brazil v **Denmark**) – total attendance 219,023; average attendance 36,503.The ground was one of only two (the other being the **Stade Geoffroy-Guichard**, St-Etienne) that retained its **perimeter fencing** for the competition.

Bebeto Real name: José Roberto Gama de Oliveira *player* Striker. **Brazil** international (75 caps, 38 goals, 1985-1998). Born 16 February 1964. *Clubs* **Flamengo**, **Vasco da Gama**, **Deportivo de la Coruña**, **Botafogo**, **Cruzeiro**, **Vitoria**. *Keynotes* Top scorer at the 1989 Copa America (six goals); scored three in the 1994 World Cup finals. Top scorer in the 1996 Olympic Games football finals tournament (six goals). *Honours* **World Cup** (Brazil, 1994); **Copa America** (Brazil, 1989); **Olympic Games** silver medal (Brazil, 1988); **World Club Cup** (Cruzeiro, 1997); Spanish Cup (Deportivo de la Coruña, 1995; *El Pais* **South American Footballer of the Year** 1989.

Beckenbauer, Franz *player-manager* Defender/mid-fielder. West **Germany** international (103 caps, 13 goals, 1965-77). Born 11 September 1945. Career ca. 1962–1982. *Clubs* **Bayern Munich**, New York Cosmos, **Hamburg (SV)**. *Keynotes* Nicknamed Der Kaiser, Beckenbauer was a renowned sweeper who went on to become West Germany's most-capped player (Lothar **Matthäus** has since won more caps, but for Germany and West Germany). Beckenbauer joined Bayern Munich as a junior in 1959, and stayed with the club until 1976. Beckenbauer was the first person to captain and manage a World Cup winning team, captaining West Germany in 1974 and managing Germany in 1990 (1–0 v **Argentina**). He made his international debut on 26 September 1965 (2–1, v **Sweden**). He scored four goals in the 1966 World Cup finals (equal third highest in the tournament), including West Germany's second in the 2–1 semi-final victory over the **Soviet Union** (at **Goodison Park**). Beckenbauer gained some revenge for the 1966 World Cup final defeat by **England** when spearheading West Germany's recovery from a 0–2 deficit against England in the 1970 quarter-final; he scored his country's first after 68 minutes, with West Germany going on to a memorable 3–2 victory after extra time. He coached the national team from 1984 to 1990 and was club manager at **Olympique de Marseille**. He became manager of Bayern Munich in 1994 and later club president. Beckenbauer was voted *France Football*'s European Footballer of the Year twice and appeared in the top seven in 11 consecutive years (1966-76) – a unique achievement that indicated the consistently high *Honours* **World Cup** (West Germany 1974, runner-up 1966, third 1970; and as a manager 1990, runner-up 1986); **European Championship** (West Germany 1972); **European Cup** (Bayern Munich 1974, 1975, 1976); **European Cup-winners Cup** (Bayern Munich 1967); **World Club Championship** (Bayern Munich 1976); German **Bundesliga** championship (Bayern Munich 1969, 1973, 1974; and as a manager 1994); German Cup (Bayern Munich 1966, 1967, 1969, 1971); **North American Soccer League** Soccer Bowl (New York Cosmos, 1977, 1978, 1980); *France Football* **European Footballer of the Year** in 1972 and 1976, runner-up 1974, 1975. standard to which he continued to play.

behind closed doors *regulations* match played without admitting spectators. A match may occasionally be played behind closed doors as a disciplinary measure imposed by a governing body or for reasons of public safety. **Football League** matches must always be open to the public, except by special permission of the league or as a disciplinary sanction (Football League regulation 30.1). *Keynotes* In 1898, **Middlesbrough** became the first club to play a home match behind closed doors. The quarantine regulations during the smallpox epidemic that year led to the club's **FA Amateur Cup** semi-final being played with no spectators – Boro went on to win the trophy (2–1 v Uxbridge). A number of matches have been played behind closed doors by order of the football authorities, as a result of previous **crowd trouble**. In November 1992, for example, the goalkeeper of non-league Kingstonian was hit by a coin thrown from the crowd during an **FA Cup** replay against **Peterborough United** at **London Road**. The FA subsequently ordered the match to be replayed behind closed doors. In European games, these include: **West Ham United** v Castilla (of Spain) (1 October 1980, 5–1, **UEFA Cup**); and **Aston Villa** v **Besiktas** (15 September 1982, 3–1, **European Cup**).

Beijing Guo'an *club* Chinese national league club based in the national capital Beijing (Peking). Ground: Beijing Workers' Stadium, capacity: 70,000 (national stadium). **Asian Cup-winners Cup** semi-final/third 1998 (4–1, v **Kopetdag Ashkhabad** of Turkmenistan, in Riyadh, Saudi Arabia, third/fourth playoff); Chinese league champions 1958, 1973, 1976, 1982, 1984; Chinese Cup 1996, 1997.

Beitar Jerusalem *club* Israeli national league club based in Jerusalem, founded 1939. Ground: "Teddi" Malcha, capacity: 13,000. Strip: yellow and black striped shirts, black shorts. **European Cup** first round 1994; Israel Cup 1976, 1979, 1985, 1986, 1989; Israel league champions 1987, 1993, 1997, 1998.

Belanov, Igor *player* Striker. **Ukraine**-born former-**Soviet Union** international (eight goals, ca. 1985-1988). *Club* **Dinamo Kiev**. *Keynotes* Scored four goals in the 1986 **World Cup** finals, including a hat-trick in the 3–4 defeat by Belgium in the second round. *Honours* **European Championship** runner-up (Soviet Union, 1988); **European Cup-winners Cup** (Dinamo Kiev, 1986); Soviet Union league championship (Dynamo Kiev, 1985, 1986); *World Soccer* **World Footballer of the Year** runner-up 1986; *France Football* **European Footballer of the Year** 1986.

Belarus *country UEFA* republic and former Soviet Republic, independence from former-**Soviet Union** in 1991. Comparatively poor country, suffered decline in industrial output. Many people exposed to radioactive contamination following Chernobyl nuclear power station disaster. Old name: Belorussia or White Russia. Area: 208,000 sq km (80,290 sq miles). Continental climate with cold winters (-7° C). Population: 10,400,000 (1994 est.). Languages: Belorussian and Russian. Capital: Minsk. *Dossier* Belorussian Football Federation (Minsk), formed in 1992, affiliated to **FIFA** in 1992 and **UEFA** in 1993, president Yevgeni Shuntov, general secretary Vadim Zhuk. Season played from April to November. National stadium: Dinamo Stadium, Minsk, capacity: 50,000. National strip: White shirts, red shorts. First international game: 28 October 1992, v Ukraine (1–1, Minsk, friendly). Best international result: 1–0 v **Netherlands** (Gerisamets, 7 June 1995, **European Championship** qualifying tournament). Most capped players: Sergei Aleinikov (of **Dinamo Minsk**, **Juventus**, Lecce; 77 appearances for the former-Soviet Union, 1984-92); Sergei Gurenko (26 appearances for Belarus, to 1998). *International tournament record* **Women's World Cup** – first entered 1999; **World Cup** – first entered 1998, last in its six-nation qualifying group with four points from its 10 games); **European Championship** – first entered 1996 (fourth in its six-nation qualifying group). *World Cup performances* (finals and qualifiers to end of 1998 tournament): played 10, won one, drawn one, lost eight, scored five goals, conceded 21 goals; win rate 10%;

goals scored per game 0.5. *Record against British and Irish national teams* v **Scotland**, played two, lost two; v **Wales**, played one, lost one. *History* The Belarus league and cup were first played in 1992. Its season is now played from April to November; the new format introduced in 1996 (the former league season was played from July to June, with a **winter break** from November to March). The leading club Dinamo Minsk won the first five league championships after independence, the run finally broken by **MPKC Mozyr** in 1996. Dinamo won the former-Soviet Union league championship in 1982, and reached the final of the former-Soviet Union Cup in 1965 and 1987. The club has reached the quarter-finals of all three major European club competitions. *League system* The Belarus national league first division consists of 16 clubs, playing each other twice in a season. Two clubs are relegated. *Record in international club tournaments* **European Cup** – Dinamo Minsk (quarter-final 1984); **European Cup-winners Cup** – Dinamo Minsk (quarter-finalists 1988); **UEFA Cup** – Dinamo Minsk (quarter-final 1985). Other leading clubs: **Belshina Bobruisk**, **Neman Grodno**, MPKC Mozyr, **Dinamo-93 Minsk**.

Belfast Celtic *club* former all-Ireland/Northern Ireland national league club based in Belfast. *Keynotes* Belfast Celtic was founded in 1891, but ceased playing league football in 1949. The club was generally associated with a Catholic following; the club withdrew from the league after politically-oriented violence between its fans and those of **Linfield FC** in 1948. Former strip: green shirts, white shorts. All-Ireland league champions 1900, 1915, 1916, 1920; **Irish FA Cup** (all-Ireland) 1918; (Northern Ireland) 1926, 1937, 1938, 1941, 1943, 1944, 1947; Northern Ireland league champions 1926, 1927, 1928, 1929, 1933, 1936, 1937, 1938, 1939, 1940, 1948. Notable former players: Elisha Scott (31 caps for Northern Ireland).

Belgium *country UEFA* monarchy in North-western Europe, independent since 1830. Member of the European Union. Rich economy based on industry, commerce and intensive farming. Area: 30,520 sq km (11,780 sq miles). Low-lying region of sands, wood and heath in the Northwest, and a central undulating plain, rising to forested Ardennes Mountains in the South East. Mild, maritime climate with 720–1,200 mm (28–47 inches) rainfall each year. Population: 10,400,000 (1994 est.). Language: French, Flemish (Dutch), with English and German spoken widely. Capital: Brussels. *Dossier* Football association (Union Royale des Sociétés de Football Association, Brusells), formed in 1895, founder member of **FIFA** (1904) and of **UEFA** (1954), president: Michel D'Hooghe, general secretary Jan Peeters. Season played from August to May. National stadium: Stade du Roi Baudouin (formerly Heysel Stadium), capacity: 41,000 all seated. National strip: red shirts, red shorts. Website: http://users.skynet.be/sky40428/engl.htm (unofficial). First international game: 1 May 1904, v **France** (3–3 in Brussels, friendly). Biggest victory: 9–0, v **Zambia** (4 June 1994, in Brussels, friendly); Biggest defeat: 2–11, v **England** Amateurs (17 April 1909, in London, friendly). Most capped players: Jan **Ceulemans** (96 appearances, 1977–91); Eric Gerets (86 appearances, 1975–91); Franky van der Elst (86 appearances, 1984-), Enzo **Scifo** (84 appearances, 1984-). Leading international goalscorers: Bernhard Voorhoof (30 goals, 1925–40); Paul van Himst (30 goals, 1960–74). Other notable players: Raymond **Braine**, Jean-Marc **Bosman**. *International tournament record* **Olympic Games** – first entered 1920, 1920 (2–0, v **Czechoslovakia**, in Antwerp), quarter-final 1928; **Women's World Cup** – never qualified for finals tournament; **World Cup** – entered first tournament in 1930, semi-final/fourth 1986 (2–4, v France, third/fourth playoff in Puebla, Mexico), second round 1982, 1990, 1994, also qualified for finals tournament 1930 (no qualifying tournament), 1934, 1938, 1954, 1970, 1998; **European Championship** – first entered 1964, runners-up 1980 (1–2 v West **Germany**, in Rome), semi-final/third 1972 (2–1, v **Hungary**, in Liège, third/fourth playoff; 1–2 v eventual winners West Germany, in Antwerp, semi-final), quarter-final 1976, also qualified for finals tournament 1964 (no qualifying tournament), 1984; **European Championship for Women** – first entered 1984, never beyond first-round group stage; **Under-17 World Championship** – never qualified for finals tournament; **World Youth Cup (under-20)** – never qualified for finals tournament. *World Cup performance* (finals and qualifiers to end of 1998 tournament) played 115, won 56, drawn 23, lost 36, scored 200 goals, conceded 150 goals; win rate: 49%; goals scored per game: 1.74. *Record against British and Irish national teams* v **England**, played 28, won three, drawn five, lost 20 (includes nine games against English amateur sides to 1923, accounting for two wins, one draw, six defeats); v **Northern Ireland**, played two, won one, lost one; v **Scotland**, played 13, won seven, drawn two, lost four; v **Wales**, played eight, won four, drawn one, lost three; v **Republic of Ireland**, played 14, won five, drawn five, lost four. *History* Outside the UK, Belgium has the joint-oldest football league in Europe (along with **Sweden**), founded in 1896. The oldest of the current clubs, **Royal Antwerp**, was founded in 1880, with the first Belgium league championship won by RC Liègeois of Liège. Football remained an amateur game until late 1950s when it became clear that the country and its leading sides had fallen behind the standards of other European nations and clubs. The game did not turn fully professional until 1972 – **RSC Anderlecht**'s subsequent success in the 1976 **European Cup-winners Cup** was the first international trophy won by a Belgium club or national side since Belgium's gold medal in the 1920 Olympic Games. Traditional rivalry exists between the French-speaking Walloons in Brussels (eg RSC Anderlecht) and the South and East (eg **Standard Club Liège**) and the Flemish-speaking Flanders regions of the North and West (eg Club Brugge, Antwerp and **KV Mechelen**). Belgium clubs have won the European Cup-winners Cup, **UEFA Cup** and **European Super Cup**. Belgium hosted the 1920 Olympic Games, with the quarter-finals, semi-finals and final played at the Olympic Stadium in Antwerp. The final, on 5 September, attracted 35,000 people, with Belgium beating Czechoslovakia 2–0. Belgium was one of four European nations to take part in the first World Cup in 1930, along with France, **Romania** and **Yugoslavia**. Belgian referee Jean Langenus was referee at the first World Cup Final. The country finished fourth in the 1986 World Cup in Mexico. In the final group game of the 1998 World Cup finals tournament in France (1–1, v **South Korea**, 25 June 1998, in Paris), two milestones were reached: Luc Nilis's goal after seven minutes was Belgium's 200th World Cup goal (qualifiers and finals matches); Sang-chul Yoo's 70th minute equaliser for South Korea was the 150th goal Belgium had conceded. Belgium hosted the 1972 semi-finals and final of the European Championship. It reached the final in 1980, losing to West Germany at the Olympic Stadium in Rome. Belgium is joint hosts (with Netherlands) of the European Championship finals tournament in 2000. After the **Heysel Stadium disaster** of 29 May 1985 (**European Cup** final, **Liverpool** v **Juventus**), at which 39 people died and more than 400 were hurt, the stadium was rebuilt and renamed Stade du Roi Baudouin. The stadium is the venue of the opening match in the 2000 European Championship. Belgium was runners-up at the first **European Championships for Players with Learning Disabilities** (2–4, v Poland, in Leicester, England). In 1992, the Belgium football association received FIFA's **Fairplay Award** for sportsmanship. *League system* Eighteen clubs compete in the Belgium first division, with three points awarded for a win and one for a draw; if points are level, final places are decided on the **number of victories** ahead of **goal difference**. The bottom two clubs are automatically relegated from the first division. Two clubs are promoted from the 18-club second division: the top team automatically, the other place going to the winners of a six-club playoff. Two clubs are automatically relegated from the second division. *Record in international club tournaments* European Cup – Club Brugge (runners-up 1978); European Cup-winners Cup – RSC Anderlecht (1976, 1978, runners-up 1977, 1990), KV Mechelen (1988), Royal Antwerp (runners-up 1993), Standard Club Liège (runners-up 1982); UEFA Cup – RSC Anderlecht (1983, runners-up 1970, 1984), Club Brugge (runners-up 1976); European Super Cup – RSC Anderlecht (1976, 1978), KV Mechelen (1988). Other leading clubs: **KRC Genk**, KAA Gent, **Lierse SK**.

Belize *country CONCACAF* Independent republic and member of the Commonwealth in Central America on Caribbean Sea, former name British Honduras. British colony from 1638, self-governing since 1964, full independence in 1981. Area: 22,965 sq km (8,865 sq miles). Heavily forested, with only about 15% of land under cultivation. Sub-tropical climate dominated by heavy rainfall with occasional hurricanes. Population: 209,500 (1994 est.). Languages: English, Spanish, Maya. Capital: Belmopan. *Dossier* Belize National Football Association (Belize City) formed in 1980, affiliated to **FIFA** and to **Confederación Norte-Centroamerican y del Caribe de Fútbol** (CONCA-CAF) in 1986, general secretary Dr Bertie Chimilio. National stadium: People's Stadium, Orange Walk, capacity: 10,000. National strip: red, white and blue shirts, red, white and blue shorts. *International tournament record* **Olympic Games** – never qualified for finals tournament; **World Cup** – first entered 1998 (lost in first round of qualifying tournament v **Panama**, 2–6 agg.); **Gold Cup** – never qualified. *Record against British and Irish national teams* none played. *League system* The league championship (Championship Liguilla) is decided by a playoff between the top two teams in the league. *Leading clubs* Acros, Cemcol Crown, Duurly's, **Juventus Caribbean**, LA Victoria, Real Verdes, San Pedro.

Bell, Colin   *player*   Midfield. **England** international (48 caps). Born 26 February 1946. Career ca. 1963–79. *Clubs* **Bury**, **Manchester City**. *Keynotes* Bell had trials with both **Newcastle United** and **Sunderland** before joining Bury in July 1963. He moved to Manchester City for £47,500 in March 1966. Bell suffered a serious injury in 1976 which forced him to retire in August 1979. After making his England debut against **Sweden** on 22 May 1968, he became a regular international player. Bell replaced Bobby **Charlton** during England's 1970 **World Cup** quarter-final match against West **Germany** (14 June) – Charlton's final game for his country. Included in the **Football League Centenary 100 players**. *Honours* **European Cup-winners Cup** (Manchester City 1970); **FA Cup** (Manchester City 1969); League Championship (Manchester City 1967-68); **League Cup** (Manchester City 1970).

Bella Vista   *club*   Uruguayan Primera League club based in Montevideo, founded 1920. Ground: Parque José Nasazzi, capacity: 7,000. Strip: gold and white halved shirts, blue shorts. **Copa Uruguaya** (Uruguay's professional league) champions 1990; **Pre-Libertadores Liguilla** 1998.

Bellmare Hiratsuka   *club*   Japanese **J-League** club based in Hiratsuka, formerly Fujita Football Club (1968-1992). Ground: Hiratsuka Stadium, capacity: 18,500. Strip: yellow shirts, green shorts. **Asian Cup-winners Cup** 1996 (2–1, v **Al Talaba** of Iraq), quarter-final 1997.

Belloumi, Lakhdar   *player*   Striker. **Algeria** international. *Honours France Football* **African Footballer of the Year** 1981. *Keynotes* Scored the winning goal in Algeria's victory over West **Germany** in the 1982 **World Cup** finals (2–1, in Gijon, Spain, first round).

Belshina Bobruisk   *club*   Belarus national league club based in Bobruisk, founded 1996. Ground: Spartak Stadium, capacity: 4,800. Belarus Cup 1997.

bench   *n.*   area on the side of the pitch, with seating for the the manager/coach, substitutes and other club offi-

cials. *Rules* another name for the **designated seating area**. *Regulations* **Premier League** clubs must ensure that there are separate areas for both home and away clubs, and marked as such, that they are located at equal distance from the halfway line, capable of seating at least eight people and covered (FA Premier League rule I.15). No more than eight people are allowed to sit on the bench in **Football League** games (Football League regulation 31.1). **On the bench**   *informal* term used to describe a player who is named as a **substitute**.

Bencheikh, Ali   *player*   **Algeria** international. *France Football* **African Footballer of the Year** runner-up 1978.

Bendel Insurance   *club*   Nigerian National league club based in Benin City. Ground: Ogbe, capacity: 40,000. Strip: yellow shirts, blue shorts. **African Cup of Champion Clubs** semi-final 1980; **African Cup-winners Cup** semi-final 1979; **CAF Cup** 1994 (3–1 agg., v **Primeiro de Maio** of Angola); Nigerian FA Challenge Cup 1972, 1978, 1980; Nigerian league champions 1973, 1979; **West African Union General Eyadema Cup** 1993, 1994, 1995.

Benevolent Fund   *n.*   fund operated by the **Professional Footballers' Association** which provides temporary financial assistance for any member or dependant, past or present, who in the opinion of the PFA's Management Committee, may require it. The fund also provides a death benefit payable to the next-of-kin of any member in the event of his death.

Benfica (Sport Lisboa e Benfica)   *club*   Portuguese national league club based in Lisbon, founded in 1904. Ground: **Estádio da Luz** (known as the "Stadium of Light", despite the fact that the stadium's name comes from the suburb of Luz in which it is situated), capacity: 92,000. Strip: red shirts, white shorts. *Keynotes* Benfica has appeared in European club competitions every season since 1960-61, a record bettered only by **Barcelona**. Benfica won two **European Cups** in succession (1961 and 1962). Its 5–3 defeat of **Real Madrid** in the 1962 final was achieved thanks to two goals from the club's most famous former player, **Eusébio**, in reply to a hat-trick by Real's **Puskás**. *Honours* European Cup – 1961 (3–2 v Barcelona, Berne, Switzerland), 1962 (5–3 v **Real Madrid**, Amsterdam, Netherlands), runners-up 1963, 1965, 1968 (1–4 v **Manchester United**, London), 1988, 1990; **European Cup-winners Cup** quarter-final 1997; Portuguese Cup 1930, 1931, 1935, 1940, 1943, 1944, 1949, 1951, 1952, 1953, 1955, 1957, 1959, 1962, 1964, 1969, 1970, 1972, 1980, 1981, 1983, 1985, 1986, 1987, 1993; Portuguese league champions 1936, 1937, 1938, 1942, 1943, 1945, 1950, 1955, 1957, 1960, 1961, 1963, 1964, 1965, 1967, 1968, 1969, 1971, 1972, 1973, 1975, 1976, 1977, 1981, 1983, 1984, 1987, 1989, 1991, 1994; **UEFA Cup** – runners-up 1983.

Benfica Sport   *club*   Guinea-Bissau national league club based in the capital Bissau. Strip: red shirts, white shorts. Ground: Lino Correia, capacity 8,000. Guinea-Bissau Cup 1985, 1992; Guinea-Bissau league champions 1977, 1979, 1980, 1982, 1988, 1989.

Benin *country CAF* republic in West Africa on the Gulf of Guinea. French colony from 1893, gained independence in 1960. Before colonisation it was famed for its women warriors. Former name (until 1975): Dahomey. Area: 112,620 sq km (43,470 sq miles). Benin is characterised by coastal lagoons and swamps in the south, with fertile plains in the centre and the wooded savannah hills and Atakora Mountains in the northwest. Offshore oil has added to the agriculture-based economy. Population: 5,460,000 (1995 est.). Languages: French, Fon and Adja. Capital: Porto Novo. *Dossier* Football association (Fédération Béninoise de Football, Cotonou) formed in 1968, affiliated to **FIFA** and **Confédération Africaine de Football** (CAF) in 1969, president Moucharafou Gbadamassi, general secretary Edmond Annie Dossa. Affiliated to the **West African Football Union**. Season played from November to June. National stadium: Stade de l'Amitie, Cotonou (the chief port), capacity: 35,000. National strip: yellow shirts, green shorts. First international game: 17 November 1963 v **Tunisia**, (2–2, home, **Olympic Games** qualifier). *International tournament record* Olympic Games – entered 1964, 1984 (qualifying stages only); **Women's World Cup** – never entered; **World Cup** – first entered 1974, has never progressed beyond first round of qualifying tournament; **African Cup of Nations** – first entered 1972, never past first round of qualifying tournament. *Record against British and Irish national teams* none played. *Record in international club tournaments* **African Cup-winners Cup** – AS Dragons de l'Oueme (semi-final 1987); **West African Club Cup** – Requins de L'Atlantique (semi-final 1983), **Mogas 90** (semi-final 1990). Other leading clubs: **Buffles de Borgou**, Energie Sport (of Cotonou, Benin Cup 1997), Postel Sport (league champions 1991), Toffa (league champions 1995), 1996 Université Nationale du Benin (of Porto Novo, Benin Cup 1996).

Bennett v Football Association Ltd and Nottinghamshire FA *legal* precedent English civil case in 1978 at which Theresa Bennett, then a 12-year-old schoolgirl, contended that she had been unfairly discriminated against by the **Football Association** and her local **county FA**, Nottinghamshire Football Association. Bennett had been banned from playing football with boys of her own age in a local youth league. At the original hearing, the county FA was ordered to overturn the ban, on grounds that it had failed to provide her with recreational facilities. The FA successfully appealed against the decision; the court ruled that the circumstances of the discrimination were, in fact, lawful under section 44 of the **Sex Discrimination Act 1975**.

Bentley, John J *official* founder committee member and second chairman of the English **Football League**, elected 1892. Born 1860. Former secretary of **Bolton**

Wanderers and councillor of the **Football Association**.

Berger, Patrik *player* Striker/midfield **Czech Republic** international (26 caps, 12 goals, 1994-). Born 10 November 1973. *Clubs* (include) **Liverpool**. *Keynotes* Scored the Czech Republic's goal in the 1996 European Championship final (1–2 a.e.t., v **Germany**, at **Wembley Stadium**). *Honours* **European Championship** runner-up (Czech Republic, 1996).

Bergkamp, Dennis *player* Striker. **Netherlands** international (68 caps, 36 goals). Born 18 May 1969. Career ca. 1986– . *Clubs* **Ajax**, **Internazionale**, **Arsenal**. *Keynotes* Made his debut for Ajax at the age of 17 and moved to Internazionale for £8 million in 1992 following his performance for Netherlands in the 1992 **European Championship**. Transferred to Arsenal for a club record £7.5 million in July 1995 after a disappointing period in Italy. As an Arsenal striker, Bergkamp became the first player to make a clean sweep (first, second and third place) in **Match of the Day**'s **goal of the month** competition, in August/September 1997. Bergkamp missed Arsenal's 1998 **FA Cup** final victory through injury. Voted **World Footballer of the Year** and **PFA Footballer of the Year** in 1998. Twice runner-up in the *World Soccer* **Footballer of the Year** award (1992, 1993). Chosen for **FIFA**'s 22-man all-star squad of the 1998 **World Cup** finals. Included in the **Football League Centenary 100 players**. *Honours* Dutch Cup (Ajax 1986, 1987); Dutch league (Ajax 1989-90); **European Cup-winners Cup** (Ajax 1987); **UEFA Cup** (Ajax 1992; Internazionale 1994); League Championship (Arsenal 1997-98).

Berlin FC *club* German regional league club and former-East German national league club based in Berlin. Founded in 1952 as Dynamo Berlin (until 1990). Ground: Sportforum, capacity: 15,000. Strip: white shirts, white shorts. *Keynotes* Jointly holds the World record for 10 consecutive national league championships in 10 years with **Dynamo Tbilisi** of Georgia (**Al Faisaly** of **Jordan**, has 13 consecutive titles, but its run was interrupted by years when the league championship was not played). Before German reunification, Dynamo Berlin was said to have been linked to the former East German hard-line police, the Stasi, and historians have questioned the fairness by which it achieved its 10-year league domination. *Honours* **European Cup** quarter-final 1980, 1984; former-East German Cup 1959, 1988, 1989; former-East German league champions 1979, 1980, 1981, 1982, 1983, 1984, 1985, 1986, 1987, 1988.

Bermuda *country CONCACAF* self-governing British Crown Colony, consists of 360 coral islands (20 inhabited) in the northwest Atlantic, 1,120 km east of South Carolina, USA. Colonised by British in 1684. Area: 54 sq km (21 sq miles). Population: 60,100 (1996 est.). Language: English. Capital: Hamilton. *Dossier* Bermuda Football Association (Hamilton) formed in 1928, affiliated to **FIFA** in 1962 and **Confederación Norte-Centroamerican y del Caribe de Fútbol**

(CONCACAF) in 1966, president Neville Tyrrell, general secretary David Sabir. Season played from September to April. National stadium: National Stadium, Hamilton, capacity: 10,000. National strip: royal blue shirts, white shorts. *International tournament record* **Women's World Cup** – never entered; **World Cup** – first entered 1970, never qualified for finals tournament, reached second round of qualifying tournament in 1994; **Gold Cup** – never qualified. *Record against British and Irish national teams* none played. *League system* Ten clubs compete in the national first division, playing each other at home and away. Three points are awarded for a victory, with one for a draw: final positions for clubs level on points are determined by **goal difference**. The bottom two clubs are automatically relegated. Bermuda is grouped with the northern nations within CONCACAF for club competitions. *Leading clubs* **Devonshire Colts**, **Vasco Volcanoes**, Dandy Town Hornets, North Village Red Devils.

Bernabéu (Estadio Santiágo) *ground* Spanish football ground situated in Madrid, Castille; home of **Real Madrid**. Ground capacity: 106,000. *Keynotes* Real Madrid's original home, Chamartin, was severly damaged during the Spanish Civil War and when Don Santiágo Bernabéu became club president in 1943 a new stadium, which today bears his name, was constructed, largely financed by public subscription. Nuevo Chamartin, as it was initially called, opened, with a 75,000 capacity, in December 1947 (Real Madrid v Belenenses (Portugal), **testimonial** for Jesus Alonso). Bernabéu was redeveloped for the 1982 **World Cup**. In 1998, **UEFA** instructed Real to play its next two home European ties at least 190 miles away from Bernabéu and fined the club £512,000 after fencing at the south end (Fondo Sur area) of the ground gave way under the weight of supporters climbing on it, forcing the goal to collapse and delaying, by 75 minutes, the kick-off at the **Champions League** semi-final first leg match with **Borussia Dortmund** (1 April 1998) – the fine was later reduced on appeal. The stadium underwent a further revamp before the start of the 1998-99 season, with **perimeter fencing** replaced by barriers and several terrace sections, including the Fondo Sur area, converted to seating. During the 1982 World Cup, it staged all three second-round group B fixtures (**England** v West **Germany**, West Germany v **Spain**, England v Spain) and the final (**Italy** v West Germany) – total attendance 320,178; average attendance 80,044. Bernabéu was also the venue for the 1964 **European Championship** final (Spain v **Soviet Union**, 105,000) and it has staged three **European Cup** finals (1957, Real Madrid v **Fiorentina**, 124,000; 1969 **AC Milan** v **Ajax**, 50,000; 1980 **Nottingham Forest** v **Hamburg SV**, 50,000).

Bernabéu, Don Santiágo *official* president of **Real Madrid** between 1943 and his death in 1978. Bernabéu had played for the club as a youngster and was a pivotal figure in making Real Madrid the dominant team in Europe in the second half of the 1950s. Real's ground at Chamartin, which was partly destroyed during the Spanish Civil War and rebuilt in the 1940s after Bernabéu took over, was later renamed in his honour.

Berwick Rangers *club* Scottish league. *Dossier* Ground: **Shielfield Park**, Berwick-upon-Tweed, Northumberland, capacity: 4,131. Strip: black shirt with gold diamonds/gold stripes, black shorts with gold trim, black socks with gold tops. Nickname: Borderers. Record attendance: 13,365 v **Rangers** (28 January 1967, **Scottish FA Cup**, first round). Biggest win: 8–1 v **Forfar Athletic** (25 December 1965, Division Two), v Vale of Leithen (December 1966, Scottish FA Cup). Biggest defeat: 1–9 v **Hamilton Academicals** (9 August 1980, First Division). *History* Founded in 1881, Berwick Rangers is the only English-based club playing in the **Scottish League**, which the club joined in 1955-56. The only major honour, the Second Division Championship, was won in 1978-79 and the club spent two seasons at the higher level. Berwick reached the semi-final stage of the **Scottish League Cup** in 1963-64 (1–3 v Rangers). The club's most famous victory, a 1–0 win over Rangers in the Scottish FA Cup, was also the occasion when Shielfield Park recorded its biggest ever crowd. *League record* First Division 1979-80 to 1980-81; Second Division 1975-76 to 1978-79, 1981-82 to 1996-97; Division Two (B Division) 1955-56 to 1974-75; Third Division 1997-98–. *Honours* Division Two 1978-79. *Records* Eric Tait holds the record for club appearances (435, 1970-87); he is also Berwick's record goalscorer (115, 1970-87).

Bescot Stadium *ground* English football ground situated in Walsall, West Midlands; home of **Walsall**. *Dossier* Ground capacity: 9,000. Pitch dimensions: 100.5m x 68m. Record attendance: 10,628 **England** v **Switzerland** (20 May 1991, **'B' International**). *History* Walsall moved to the Bescot Stadium in 1990, with the stadium officially opened on 18 August (v **Aston Villa**, friendly). Built on the site of a former sewage works at a cost of £4.5 million, Bescot Stadium was first owned by the ground's developers, Denglen, before Walsall and the stadium were reunited under the same ownership in 1991 with the club renting it at an index-linked £75,000 a year. Aston Villa Reserves played at the ground for two seasons and, in June 1991, the rock band the Wonder Stuff performed there in front of 18,000 fans. The **Football League** staged its 1993 and 1994 annual general meetings at the Bescot. The stadium complex includes an **artificial pitch** which is widely used by the local community. The club has also exploited the stadium's proximity to the M6 motorway by selling advertising space on an illuminated hoarding mounted on its roof.

Besiktas (Besiktas Jimnastik Kolübü) *club* Turkish national league club based in Istanbul, founded 1903. Ground: Inönü, capacity: 45,000. Strip: black and white striped shirts, white shorts. **European Cup** Qualified for **Champions League** 1998; Istanbul league (regional league operated from 1924 to 1958) champions 1924 (the first championship), 1934, 1939, 1940,

1941, 1942, 1943, 1945, 1946, 1950, 1951, 1952, 1954; Turkish Cup 1975, 1989, 1990, 1994, 1998; Turkish league champions 1960, 1966, 1967, 1982, 1986, 1990, 1991, 1992, 1995; **UEFA Cup** third round 1997.

Best, George *player* Winger. **Northern Ireland** international (37 caps, 9 goals). Born 22 May 1946. Career ca. 1963–84. *Clubs* **Manchester United**, Dunstable Town, **Stockport County**, Los Angeles Aztecs, **Cork Celtic, Fulham**, Fort Lauderdale Strikers, **Motherwell, Hibernian**, San Jose Earthquakes, **Bournemouth AFC**. *Keynotes* Considered to be the greatest UK player of the post-**World War II** period and often described as a "wayward genius". He made his debut for Manchester United at the age of 17 years and 4 months in 1963, going on to make 361 **Football League** appearances for the club and scoring 137 goals. Best holds the United record for individual scoring achievement; he scored six against **Northampton Town**, away, in the **FA Cup** on 7 February 1970 (8–2, fifth round). Best quit United in 1973 after being dropped by manager Tommy **Docherty** and having regularly missed training and been disciplined by the club over the previous two years. **FIFA** banned Best from playing anywhere in the world after he walked out on United, but this was rescinded when the club released him to join Stockport County in 1975 – the first of numerous comebacks. Voted both **European Footballer of the Year** and **Footballer of the Year** in 1968. Included in the **Football League Centenary 100 players**. *Honours* **European Cup** (Manchester United 1968); League Championship (Manchester United 1964-65, 1966-67).

Best Mover of the Year *award* **FIFA** international award based on a country's performance over the previous 12 months. The Best Mover of the Year result is achieved by multiplying a country's total amount of points at the end of a year by the number of points gained during the 12-month period. The method of calculation, however, takes into account the number of points that a country already has, so that it is more difficult for high ranking countries to accumulate points. The winner of the 1997 award was **Yugoslavia**, which amassed 56.90 points over the year after losing only one of 13 matches, and that on penalties. An award is also given to the Best Mover in each of the six international football confederations.

beta-blockers *medical* a class of drugs, more properly called beta-adrenergic blocking agents. These inhibit certain types of nerve activities and are used to treat certain cardiovascular conditions. They are sometimes misused in sports where a steady hand is required – such as shooting and snooker – because of their ability to reduce tremor induced by anxiety. They are banned in most sports, though are rarely misused in football.

beton *tactics* French term, meaning all-out defence.

betting *regulations* it is an offence for any player, referee, assistant referee or club official to place a bet on football, other than the football **pools** (Football Association rules, and Scottish Football League rule 74).

betting shop *n.* licensed office where wagers can be placed; bookmaker. Many clubs now lease space within their stadiums to one or more of the major betting shop chains. *Regulations* the rules of the **Scottish League** specifically allow betting shops at football grounds (Scottish Football League rule 73).

between the sticks *informal* reference to the goalkeeper, as in **Shilton** is between the sticks.

BFV Mahanjunga (Bankin Fampandrosuo NY Vareta) *club* Madagascar national league club, based in Mahanjunga and formed in 1978. Ground: Alexandre Rabemananjara, capacity: 3,000. Strip: blue shirts and white shorts. **African Cup-winners Cup** semi-finalist 1989 (1–4 agg., v **Bendel United** of Nigeria); Madagascar Cup 1988 and 1990; Madagascar league champions 1996.

Bhutan *country associate member of AFC* small kingdom situated between China and India in the foothills of the Himalayas, east of Nepal. Area: 46,000 sq km (17,995 sq miles). Population: 600,000 (1996 est.). Languages: Dzongkha, Nepali and English. Capital Thimphu. Bhutan Football Federation (Thimphu) affiliated to **FIFA** and the **Asian Confederation** (AFC) in 1998, president Dasho Ugyen Dorji, general secretary RK Chetri. Strip: red and yellow shirts, red and yellow shorts. *International tournament record* **Asian Cup of Nations** – first entered 2000. *Record against British and Irish national teams* none played. *History* Football introduced in the 1960s by Bhutan students returning from universities in India and Nepal.

bib *n.* piece of coloured material that goes over the head and arms and is used to distinguish one player or group of players from others. **Substitutes** generally wear bibs over their strip so as not to confuse on-field players. During training matches, one side will wear bibs. It is common for match photographers to wear distinguishing bibs.

bicycle kick *n.* overhead shot, usually made facing away from the goal and with both legs off the ground.

Big Match *television* programme of recorded highlights, formerly broadcast by London Weekend Television on Sunday afternoons, with commentary/presentation from Brian **Moore**. Peak audiences in the 1970s reached nine million.

big freeze *misc.* the unusually cold weather that severely affected the British football league programme from 2 December 1962 until 9 March 1963; the worst winter in the history of British football. The weather caused 29 of 32 **FA Cup** third-round ties to be postponed on 5 January, with the tie between **Lincoln City** and **Coventry** postponed a record 15 times. Only five games were played in the **Football League** programme of 2 February. On 9 February, only seven Football League matches were played, with all matches in Scotland called off; 64 games in England and Scotland were postponed. Although the winter was not nearly as cold as that of 1962-63, the fixture list on 27

January 1996 was severely hit by freezing weather: only three FA Cup ties, one Football League game, five **Scottish FA Cup** ties and one **Scottish Football League** match were played, and 55 games in England and Scotland were postponed.

Bingham, Billy *player-manager* Winger. **Northern Ireland** international (56 caps). Born 5 August 1931. Career ca. 1949–64. *Clubs* (player) **Glentoran**, **Sunderland**, **Luton Town**, **Everton**, **Port Vale**. *Clubs/country* (manager) **Southport**, **Plymouth Argyle**, Everton, **PAOK Salonika**, **Mansfield Town**, Northern Ireland, **Greece**. *Keynotes* as a player, Bingham was a **FA Cup** finalist with Luton in 1959 (1–2 v **Nottingham Forest**). He moved to Everton for £20,000 (plus players) in 1960, helping the club win the League title in 1962-63. Bingham is the most successful manager in Northern Ireland history, taking the country to the finals of two **World Cups** (1982 and 1986). In 1982, Northern Ireland qualified for the second round by defeating the host nation, **Spain** (1–0, 25 June). Bingham had played in the 1958 World Cup finals, when Northern Ireland reached the quarter-final stage. *Honours* (player) League Championship (Everton 1962-63).

'B' international *n.* an international representative match between the competing nations' second choice-players; used as an opportunity to experiment with new squad players.

birds of prey *misc.* birds which hunt animals for food. Several football clubs use birds of prey to stop pigeons nesting/fouling grounds. *Keynotes* In 1998, **Crewe Alexandra** employed a trio of birds of prey – a hawk, a kestrel and an eagle owl – at its **Gresty Road** ground to scare off roosting pigeons. Also, **Wolverhampton Wanderers** employ the services of "Harry" the Hawk to eradicate pigeons from **Molineux**.

Birmingham City *club* English league. *Dossier* Ground: **St Andrews**, Birmingham, West Midlands, capacity: 25,812. Strip: blue shirts with white trim, white shorts, blue socks with white trim. Nickname: Blues. Record attendance: 66,844 v **Everton** (11 February 1939, **FA Cup**, fifth round). Best average attendance: 38,453 (1948-49). Biggest win: 12–0 v **Walsall Town Swifts** (17 December 1892, Division Two). Biggest defeat: 1–9 **Sheffield Wednesday** (13 December 1930, Division One), v **Blackburn Rovers** (5 January 1895, Division One). *History* Founded in 1875 as Small Heath Alliance by, in the main, cricketing members of Trinity Church, Bordesley. The club played its matches at Muntz Road between 1877 and 1906, before moving to St Andrews. As Small Heath, the club was a founder member of Division Two in 1892. The club reached the semi-finals of the FA Cup in 1886 (0–4 v **West Bromwich Albion**). In the club's first season in the Football Lague, Small Heath finished top of Division Two but failed to gain promotion via the **test matches** that between 1892-93 and 1897-98 were used to determine promotion and relegation. Thereafter it has mainly alternated between the top two divisions, a situation that

was graphically illustrated at the turn of the century when the club was promoted, relegated and promoted again in the three seasons between 1900-01 and 1902-03. For the 1905-06 season, the club adopted the name Birmingham – City was added in 1945. The club reached its first FA Cup final in 1931 (1–2 v West Bromwich Albion). A second FA Cup final appearance occurred in 1956 (1–3 v **Manchester City**). In 1955, Birmingham became the first English club to play in a European competition, and later the first to reach a European final, when it entered the Inter-City Industrial Fairs Cup (see **UEFA Cup**). In the first tournament, Birmingham reached the semi-final stage before losing in a **playoff** (4–4 agg., v **Barcelona**, 1–2). The club reached the final of the following two competitions (1960, 1–4 agg., v Barcelona; 1961, 2–4 agg., v **Roma (AS)**). Birmingham's only major trophy was won in 1963 when the club defeated arch-rivals **Aston Villa** (3–1 agg.) in a two-legged **League Cup** final. In 1991, the club won the **Leyland Daf Cup** (3–2 v **Tranmere Rovers**) and four years later it lifted the **Auto Windscreens Shield** (1–0 a.e.t. v **Carlisle United** – the first time an English final had been settled by a **golden goal**). Birmingham achieved its highest-ever League position in 1955-56, sixth in Division One. In 1988-89, Birmingham was relegated to Division Three. Birmingham holds two Football League records: it is the only club to reach double figures in goals five times (12–0 twice, 11–1, 10–2, 10–1) and has used the most players in its first team in a single season (46 players, 1995-96). It was the first Football League club to appoint a woman – Karen Brady – as chief executive. The club was floated on the **Alternative Investment Market** in March 1997 (floatation price = 50p), which is a precursor to full floatation on the stock market. *League record* Division One 1894-95 to 1895-96, 1901-02, 1903-04 to 1907-08, 1921-22 to 1938-39, 1950-51, 1955-56 to 1964-65, 1971-72 to 1978-79, 1980-81 to 1983-84, 1985-86; First Division 1992-93 to 1993-94, 1995-96–; Division Two 1892-93 to 1893-94, 1896-97 to 1900-01, 1902-03, 1908-09 to 1920-21, 1946-47 to 1949-50, 1951-52 to 1954-55, 1965-66 to 1970-71, 1979-80, 1984-85, 1986-87 to 1988-89; Second Division 1994-95; Division Three 1989-90 to 1991-92. *Honours* Second Division 1994-95; Division Two 1892-93, 1920-21, 1947-48, 1954-55; League Cup 1963 (3–1 agg., v Aston Villa); Leyland Daf Cup 1991 (3–2 v Tranmere Rovers); Auto Windscreens Shield 1995 (1–0 a.e.t. v Carlisle United). *Records* Malcolm Page is Birmingham's most capped player (28 for **Wales**); Frank Womack holds the record for club appearances (491, 1908-28); Joe Bradford is Birmingham's record league goalscorer (249, 1920-35).

Birmingham City plc *n.* publicly-quoted business which owns **Birmingham City**. The club became a listed company on the **Alternative Investment Market** in March 1997 (floatation price = 50p). Birmingham had a market capitalisation – the market value of the company's issued share capital (eg, the quoted price of its shares multiplied by the number of shares outstanding) – of £25 million when it joined the AIM.

Birra Moretti tournament *competition* close season triangular tournament held at Udinese's Stadio Friuli on 7 August 1998. The three competing clubs were **Internazionale**, **Juventus** and Udinese. The tournament was notable for including a number of playing experiments: each game lasted for 45 minutes; **kick-ins** replaced **throw-ins**; **short corners** were used; and **shoot-outs** replaced the penalty shoot-out for drawn matches. The shoot-out involved a player making a run on goal from 35 metres, with seven seconds in which to score. Udinese won the tournament.

Bisham Abbey *n.* **England** base camp situated in Buckinghamshire where the squad congregate/train prior to international fixtures.

Black Aces *club* Zimbabwe national league club based in Harare. Ground: National Sports (shared with **CAPS United** and **Blackpool**), capacity: 30,000. Strip: white shirts, blue shorts. Zimbabwe Cup runners-up 1992; Zimbabwe league champions 1992.

Black Africans Nashua (also known as Black Africa) *club* Namibian national league club, based in Windhoek. Ground: Khomasdal. Namibian Cup 1993, 1997; Namibian league champions 1989, 1994, 1995, 1998.

Black Rhinos *club* Zimbabwe national league club based in Mutare, founded 1983. Ground: Mutare, capacity: 8,000. Strip: light blue shirts, dark blue shorts. **African Cup of Champion Clubs** quarter-final 1985; Zimbabwe league champions 1984, 1987; Zimbabwe Cup 1984.

Blackburn Rovers *club* English league. *Dossier* Ground: **Ewood Park**, Blackburn, Lancashire, capacity: 31,367 all seated. Strip: blue and white quartered shirts, white shorts, white socks with blue stripe. Website: *www.rovers.co.uk* Nickname: Rovers. Record attendance: 61,783 v **Bolton Wanderers** (2 March 1929, **FA Cup**, sixth round). Best average attendance: 30,544 (1958-59). Biggest win: 11–0 v Rossendale (13 October 1884, FA Cup, first round). Biggest defeat: 0–8 v **Arsenal** (25 February 1933, Division One). *History* Formed in 1875 by a group of ex-public schoolboys, the club turned professional in 1880. In its first year, Blackburn did not have a home and played, and won, its matches "away". The club played at several venues, including Oozehead, Pleasington Cricket Ground, Alexandra Meadows and Leamington Road, before finally settling at Ewood Park in 1890 (the club had played four matches at its present home in April 1881). Blackburn appeared in six FA Cup finals between 1882 and 1891, winning the trophy on five occasions (1884, 1885, 1886, 1890, 1891). The club was a founder member of the **Football League**. On 12 December 1891, Blackburn was involved in a bizarre incident; 10 of the team (all except goalkeeper Herbert Arthur) left the field of play in protest at the referee's dismissal of one of their team-mates during a match against local rivals

Burnley, forcing the referee to **abandon** the game – the football authorities insisted that the 3–0 scoreline in Burnley's favour would stand. Rovers won the League Championship in 1911-12 and 1913-14, and was captained by England international, and the club's most revered player, Bob **Crompton**. Local textiles' manufacturer, Laurence Cotton, who became Rovers' chairman in 1905, spent considerable sums of money on both the ground and players (including a then-record £2,000 for **West Ham United**'s Danny Shea in 1912). Blackburn won its sixth FA Cup in 1928. Thereafter the club's fortunes declined. It was relegated for the first time in 1936. Under the management of Johnny **Carey**, it returned to Division One in 1958-59 and reached the FA Cup final in 1960 (0–3 v **Wolverhampton Wanderers**). In 1971, Blackburn, along with fellow Lancastrian founder members of the Football League, Bolton Wanderers, was relegated to Division Three. The club did not return to the top flight until the formation of the **Premier League** in 1992-93. Blackburn secured promotion via the **playoffs** at the end of the 1991-92 season (1–0 v **Leicester City**), having failed on three previous occasions (1987-88, 1988-89, 1989-90). Steel magnate, Jack Walker, a long-time Rovers fan (whose business, Walkersteel, was bought by British Steel for £330 million in 1990), provided the financial resources to help rebuild Blackburn's team and ground. He bought a 62% share of the club in January 1991. Kenny **Dalglish**, the former Liverpool boss, was appointed manager in 1991 and bought **Southampton**'s Alan **Shearer** in July 1992 for a then record £3.6 million, and Chris Sutton for £5 million, another record, prior to breaking **Manchester United**'s stranglehold on the Premiership by winning the title in 1994-95. It was relegated just four seasons later. Both Dalglish and Shearer have since departed. *League record* Premier League 1992-93 to 1998-99; Division One (including Football League) 1888-89 to 1935-36, 1946-47 to 1947-48, 1958-59 to 1965-66; First Division 1999-00; Division Two 1936-37 to 1938-39, 1948-49 to 1957-58, 1966-67 to 1970-71, 1975-76 to 1978-79, 1980-81 to 1991-92; Division Three 1971-72 to 1974-75, 1979-80. *Honours* Division Two 1938-39; Division Three 1974-75, 1979-80; **FA Charity Shield** 1912 (2–1 v **Queens Park Rangers**); FA Cup 1884 (2–1 v **Queen's Park**), 1885 (2–0 v Queen's Park), 1886 (2–0 v **West Bromwich Albion**), 1890 (6–1 v **Sheffield Wednesday**), 1891 (3–1 v **Notts County**), 1928 (3–1 v **Huddersfield Town**); **Full Members Cup** 1987 (1–0 v **Charlton Athletic**); League 1911-12, 1913-14; Premiership 1994-95. *Records* Bob Crompton is Blackburn's most capped player (41 for **England**); Derek Fazackerley holds the record for club appearances (596, 1970-86); Simon Garner is Blackburn's record league goalscorer (168, 1978-92).

Blackpool *club* English league. *Dossier* Ground: **Bloomfield Road**, Blackpool, Lancashire, capacity: 11,295. Strip: tangerine shirts with white trim, white shorts, tangerine socks with navy blue trim. Nickname:

Seasiders. Record attendance: 38,098 v **Wolverhampton Wanderers** (17 September 1955, Division One). Best average attendance: 26,336 (1949-50). Biggest win: 7–0 v **Reading** (10 November 1928, Division Two), **Preston North End** (1 May 1948, Division One), v **Sunderland** (5 October 1957, Division One). Biggest defeat: 1–10 **Small Heath** (2 March 1901, Division Two), v **Huddersfield Town** (13 December 1930, Division One) *History* Founded in 1887 by old boys of St John's School. The club was a founder member of the Lancashire League and joined Division Two in 1896-97, only to lose League status in 1899. Thereafter the club merged with South Shore, at who's ground (eventually called Bloomfield Road) the newly-amalgamated club settled, before being readmitted to the League in 1900-01. Following almost three decades of under-achievement, which included only one notable moment, an **FA Cup** quarter-final appearance in 1925 (0–1 v **Blackburn Rovers**), Blackpool won the Division Two Championship and promotion to the top flight in 1929-30. Division One tenure lasted only three seasons, with the club narrowly avoiding relegation in both 1930-31 and 1931-32 before returning to Division Two in 1932-33. Under the managership of the former **Bolton Wanderers** and **England** inside-forward Joe Smith (1935-58), Blackpool again secured a place in the top flight in 1936-37. After World War II, with Smith still in charge and with a team which included England internationals Harry Johnston, Stanley **Matthews** (bought from **Stoke City** for £11,500 in 1947) and Stanley **Mortensen**, Blackpool entered its most successful period. The club reached three FA Cup finals between 1947-48 and 1952-53, losing the first two (1948 2–4 v **Manchester United**, 1951 0–2 v **Newcastle United**) before lifting the trophy in the so-called **Matthews Final** of 1953 (4–3 v Bolton Wanderers). In addition, Blackpool finished Division One runners-up in 1955-56 – the club's highest-ever League placing. Its tenure in Division One, which at the time was second only to **Arsenal**, ended in 1966-67. Although Blackpool returned to the top flight for one season in 1970-71, the club went into decline, dropping to Division Three for the first time in 1977-78. Blackpool's brief return to Division One coincided with its victory in the **Anglo-Italian Cup** (2–1 a.e.t. v **Bologna**), a competition in which the club would be finalists again the following year (1–3 v **Roma (AS)**). By 1980-81, the club was playing in the bottom Division. In 1990-91, Blackpool missed promotion from Division Four, losing the end-of-season **playoff** final on penalties (2–2, 4–5 pens. v **Torquay United**). The following season the club won at the same stage (1–1, 4–3 pens. v **Scunthorpe United**) to secure a place in the newly established Second Division. Blackpool missed promotion to the First Division in 1995-96, losing at the semi-final stage of the Second Division playoffs. *League record* Division One 1930-31 to 1932-33, 1937-38 to 1966-67, 1970-71; Division Two 1896-97 to 1898-99 (failed re-election), 1900-01 to 1929-30, 1933-34 to

1936-37, 1967-68 to 1969-70, 1971 -72 to 1977-78; Second Division 1992-93–; Division Three 1978-79 to 1980-81, 1985-86 to 1989-90; Division Four 1981-82 to 1984-85, 1990-91 to 1991-92. *Honours* Division Two 1929-30; FA Cup 1953 (4–3 v Bolton Wanderers – *Team* Farm, Shimwell, Garrett, Fenton, Johnston, Robinson, Matthews, Taylor, Mortensen (3), Mudie, Perry (1)); Anglo-Italian Cup 1971 (2–1 a.e.t. v Bologna). *Records* Jimmy **Armfield** is Blackpool's most capped player (43 for England); he also holds the record for club League appearances (568, 1952-71); Jimmy Hampson is Blackpool's record League goalscorer (246, 1927-38).

Blackpool *club* Zimbabwe national league club based in the capital Harare, founded 1994 from a former club Dynamos United. Ground: National Sports (shared with **CAPS United** and **Black Aces**), capacity: 30,000. **African Cup-winners Cup** semi-final 1995; Zimbabwe Cup 1994; Zimbabwe league runners-up 1995.

Blanchflower, Danny *player-manager* Midfielder. **Northern Ireland** international (56 caps, 2 goals). Born 10 February 1926. Career ca. 1945–64. *Clubs* (player) **Glentoran, Barnsley, Aston Villa, Tottenham Hotspur;** (manager) **Chelsea.** Also Northern Ireland manager. *Keynotes* Transferred to Barnsley from Glentoran for £6,500 in 1949, making 68 **Football League** appearances for the club before moving to Aston Villa for £15,000 two years later. Joined Tottenham Hotspur for £30,000 in 1954, becoming captain and leading the club to the first League and FA Cup **double** of the 20th century. He went on to make 337 League appearances for Spurs, scoring 15 goals. Blanchflower was the first English club skipper to lift a European club trophy when Spurs won the European Cup-winners Cup in 1963 (5–1 v **Atlético Madrid**). Overall Blanchflower played 553 League matches. He was voted **Footballer of the Year** in both 1958 and 1961. Had a brief spell as Chelsea manager (1978-79). Died on 9 December 1993. Included in the **Football League Centenary 100 players**. *Honours* (player) League Championship (Tottenham Hotspur 1960-61); **FA Cup** (Tottenham Hotspur 1961, 1962); **European Cup-winners Cup** (Tottenham Hotspur 1963).

Blatter, Sepp *official* **FIFA** president. Born 10 March 1936. Blatter was elected FIFA president in June 1998 at the 51st Ordinary Congress, held in Paris prior to the **World Cup**. Blatter defeated Lennart **Johansson**, **UEFA** president, by 111 to 80 with each of the 191 members casting one vote. Although Blatter did not receive the required 128 votes to win outright in the first ballot, Johansson withdrew his candidature before a second vote was taken. Blatter is a Swiss national and first worked for FIFA as director of technical development programmes in 1975, becoming general secretary in 1981. Blatter never played professional football, but was striker and player-coach of Swiss club Visp (1964-65).

Blaxnit Cup *competition* early 1970s sponsored competition between the leading clubs from **Northern**

Ireland and the **Republic of Ireland**. *Winners* 1971-72, **Cork Hibernians**; 1972-73, Cork Hibernians; 1973-74, **Ards**. Escalating political problems in the Northern Ireland in the mid-1970s ended the competition.

bleachers *n.pl.* tier of cheaper, uncovered seats in a stadium.

blind football see **visually impaired football**.

blind-side *n.* player's run made outside of an opponents' line of vision and into an area not easily covered by defenders. Also known as ghosting.

blister *medical* accumulation of fluid underneath the epidermis (outermost layer) of the skin. Caused by continuous abrasion and pressure on the skin. Blood can sometimes leak into the blister if the area has been crushed or pinched excessively (blood blister). Football players can suffer blisters on the souls, heels and underside of the toes, made more likely by wearing poorly fitted footwear. Treatment very much depends on the size of the blister, which should be lightly dressed. A padded dressing can sometimes make a blister worse as it causes more rubbing. The mainstay of treatment involves keeping the blister clean to avoid infection.

block tackle *n.* a **tackle** executed in order to prevent a player from shooting or passing by using full body weight to stop the ball at the same time as the opposing player attempts to play it.

Blokhin, Oleg *player* Winger. **Soviet Union** international (101 caps, 35 goals, 1972-88; excludes Olympic Games). Born 5 November 1952. *Clubs* **Dinamo Kiev**, Vorwärts Steyr (Austria). *Keynotes* Blokhin holds the record for the most appearances for his country and is the record Soviet international goalscorer. He scored in Dinamo Kiev's 1975 **European Cup-winners Cup** final win against **Ferencváros** (3–0, Basle, Switzerland), the 1986 European Cup-winners Cup final win against **Atlético Madrid** (3–0, Lyon, France), and scored all three goals in Kiev's 1975 **European Supercup** victory against **Bayern Munich** (3–0 agg.). Blokhin was a renowned sprinter, recording a 100-metre time of 10.8 seconds. He made his international debut on 16 July 1972 (1–1, v Finland) and played for the Soviet Union in the 1982 and 1986 **World Cup** finals tournaments. Became manager of **Olympiakos** and, later, a member of the Ukraine parliament. *Honours France Football* **European Footballer of the Year** 1975; **Olympic Games** bronze medal (Soviet Union, 1972); European Cup-winners Cup (Dinamo Kiev, 1975, 1986); European Supercup (Dinamo Kiev, 1975); Soviet Union league championship (Dinamo Kiev, 1974, 1975, 1977, 1980, 1981, 1985, 1986).

blood blister *medical* see blister.

blood-doping *medical* method of increasing the amount of oxygen that can be carried by the blood. It can be achieved by artificially increasing the blood count by infusing with freeze-preserved blood previously taken from the same individual. The blood count can also be increased by drugs such as erythropoietin (EPO), medically used to treat some kinds of anaemia. Both techniques have been used by endurance athletes to boost their performance, but are outlawed in most sports. There have been rumours of EPO misuse among some footballers in Italy, though there has been no evidence. See also **altitude**.

Bloomer, Steve *player* Inside-forward. **England** international (23 caps, 28 goals). Born 20 January 1874. Career ca. 1892–1914. *Clubs* **Derby County** (twice), **Middlesbrough**. *Keynotes* Scorer of 353 goals in 598 League appearances for Derby County and Middlesbrough. He also scored 28 goals for England in 23 international matches – a record which stood until 1956. Bloomer scored five goals for England in a 9–1 victory over **Wales** (16 March 1896) and six goals for Derby County against **Sheffield Wednesday** (21 January 1899, Division One). Died 16 April 1938. Included in the **Football League Centenary 100 players**. *Honours* Division Two (Derby County, 1911-12).

Bloomfield Road *ground* English football ground situated in Blackpool, Lancashire; home of **Blackpool**. *Dossier* Ground capacity: 11,295. Pitch dimensions: 102m x 68m. Record attendance: 38,098 v **Wolverhampton Wanderers** (17 September 1955, Division One). Best average attendance: 26,336 (1949-50). *History* Blackpool began its residence of Bloomfield Road in 1899 after merging with the ground's tenants, South Shore. Formerly known as Gamble's Field, Bloomfield Road was used as an army training ground during **World War II** and its south stand has interior wood panelling derived from Nelson's former flagship HMS Foudroyant. South Shore played its first match at Bloomfield Road on 21 October 1899 (v South Lancashire Regiment). The ground has staged one **England** international (v **Northern Ireland**, 17 October 1932), six **Inter-League** fixtures between the **Football League** and Irish League (23 September 1931; 25 September 1935; 6 October 1937; 11 October 1941; 18 October 1950; 12 October 1960), and an RAF benefit match in 1941. The first floodlit match at Bloomfield Road took place on 13 October 1958 (v **Heart of Midlothian**, friendly).

Blue Waters *club* Namibian national league club, based in Walvis Bay. Ground: Kuisebmord. Namibian Cup 1994; Namibian league champions 1988 and 1996.

Blueprint for the Future of Football *n.* **Football Association** document published in April 1991 that included plans for an 18-club "Super League", which would, in time, become the **Premier League**. Initially, the smaller top flight was favoured by the FA as a way of allowing the national side more time to prepare for international fixtures, but eventually the FA Council gave its approval to a 22-club Premier League to begin on 15 August 1992.

Blundell Park *ground* English football ground situated in Cleethorpes, Lincolnshire; home of **Grimsby Town**. *Dossier* Ground capacity: 8,870 all seated. Pitch dimensions: 101m x 69m. Record attendance: 31,657 v **Wolverhampton Wanderers** (20 February 1937, **FA**

Cup, fifth round). Best average attendance: 18,056 (1949-50). *History* Blundell Park is located in nearby Cleethorpes and built on the site of a former brick works. The club played its first fixture at Blundell Park on 2 September 1899 (v **Luton Town**, Division Two). The ground's first main stand, opened in 1901, was financed by 150 supporters each paying £10 and this still forms the basis of the current facility. During **World War II**, Grimsby played its matches at **Scunthorpe United**'s previous home, the Old Showground. Although Blundell Park first installed floodlights in 1953 (v **Gainsborough Trinity**, Midland League), it was not until 20 September 1960 that the lights were of sufficient standard to illuminate a **Football League** match (v **Newport County**, Division Three). The opening of the Findus Stand in August 1982 was beset by financial problems which prevented the interior furbishment of the **executive boxes** and the construction of new changing rooms, so that the new stand's players' tunnel was never used. The club was granted a one year extension to the **all-seater stadiums deadline** following the announcement in 1994 of plans to relocate to a 12,000 capacity stadium which would form part of out-of-town retail and leisure development. These plans collapsed and, in May 1995, Grimsby began converting Blundell Park into an all-seater stadium.

Bo'ness *club* former Scottish league. *Dossier* Ground: Newton Park, Bo'ness, Lothian. *Keynotes* Bo'ness joined Division Two in 1921-22, winning the title in 1926-27 but lasting only one season at the higher level. The club was a **Scottish FA Cup** quarter-finalist on three occasions: 1923 (2–4 v **Motherwell**), 1927 (2–5 v **Celtic**), 1931 (0–5 replay v **Kilmarnock**). The club was expelled from the Scottish League in November 1932 after failing to produce the financial guarantees (£50) required by the Scottish football authorities. *League record* Division One 1927-28; Division Two 1921-22 to 1926-27, 1928-29 to 1932-33 (did not complete fixtures). *Honours* Division Two 1926-27.

Boavista FC *club* Portuguese national league club based in Oporto, founded in 1903. Ground: Estádio do Bessa, capacity: 26,000. Strip: black and white checked shirts, black shorts. Portuguese Cup 1975, 1976, 1979, 1992, 1997; Portuguese league runners-up 1976; **UEFA Cup** third round 1997.

Bobek, Stjepan *player* Striker. **Former-Yugoslavia** international (38 goals, 63 caps, 1946-56). *Club* **Partizan Belgrade**. *Keynotes* Former-Yugoslavia's all-time top goalscorer. Played in the 1950 **World Cup** finals. Won two **Olympic Games** silver medals and scored Yugoslavia's goal in the 1948 final (1–3, v **Sweden**). *Honours* Olympic Games silver medal (Former-Yugoslavia, 1948, 1952); Former-Yugoslavia league championship (Partizan Belgrade, 1947, 1949,

Boca Juniors (Club Atlético) *club* Argentinean national league club, based in the Boca district of Buenos Aires, founded 1905. Ground: La Bombonera (the "Chocolate Box"), capacity: 58,750. Strip: blue

shirts with a yellow hoop, blue shorts. *History* Founded in 1905 by three students at the National School of Commerce. Joined the Argentine Football Association League (for the Buenos Aires metropolitan area) in 1913. Boca won the first professional championship in 1931, and the **Copa Libertadores** in 1977 and 1978. Its **World Club Cup** victory in 1977 was against the European Cup runners-up, **Borussia Mönchengladbach**; the European champions, Liverpool, boycotted the match. *Honours* Argentinean league champions 1919, 1920, 1923, 1924, 1926 (two leagues operated prior to 1927), 1930, 1931, 1934, 1935, 1940, 1943, 1944, 1954, 1962, 1964, 1965, 1976, 1981 1993 (**apertura**), 1998 (apertura); Argentinean National Championship (a pre-national-league tournament operating from 1967 to 1985) 1969, 1970, 1976; Copa Libertadores 1977 (1–0, 0–1, 0–0 playoff, 5–4 pens., v **Cruzeiro**), 1978 (0–0, 4–0, v Deportivo Cali), runners-up 1963 (2–3, 1–2, v **Santos**), 1979 (0–2, 0–0, v **Olimpia**), semi-final 1965, 1991; **Copa Mercosur** quarter-final 1998; **Recopa** 1989 (1–0, v **Atlético Nacional Medellin**); **Supercopa** 1989 (0–0 agg., 5–3 pens., v **Independiente**), runners-up 1994 (1–2 agg., v Independiente); World Club Cup 1977 (5–2 agg., v Borussia Mönchengladbach). Notable players: Gabriel **Batistuta**, Diego **Maradona**, Oscar **Ruggeri**.

body check *n.* a **foul** committed by impeding the progress of an opponent by using the body to obstruct. *vb.* to execute such a foul.

bogey team *n.* opponents against which a club is rarely successful. *Keynotes* up to and including 1997-98, in 55 League visits to **Anfield, Chelsea** had lost on 39 occasions. **Tottenham Hotspur** had also fared poorly against Liverpool at Anfield, recording only four wins in 55 visits in the same period. **Coventry City**, also, has an unenviable record against Liverpool at Anfield, winning on only three occasions by 1998, although the club's performances at **West Ham United**'s **Upton Park** are equally bad, having lost 22 times in 28 visits. **Newcastle United**'s League record at **Wolverhampton Wanderers' Molineux** ground reads 38 visits, 25 defeats.

Boghead Park *ground* cottish football ground situated in Strathclyde; home of **Dumbarton** and **Clydebank**. *Dossier* Ground capacity: 5,503. Pitch dimensions: 100.5m x 62m. Record attendance: 18,000 v **Raith Rovers** (2 March 1957, **Scottish FA Cup**). *Keynotes* Boghead Park is Scotland's oldest football ground. Dumbarton first played there in 1879. Clydebank moved in at the start of the 1996-97 season. Cash-strapped Dumbarton have since sold Boghead to a property developer for £1.75 million and at the start of the 1999-00 season moved to a ground near Dumbarton Castle. Clydebank, meanwhile, which had hoped to move to Dublin, is uncertain of its future.

Bohemia *former country* former monarchy in central Europe, now in the **Czech Republic**, part of the Hapsburg empire until 1918. Bohemia became part of **Czechoslovakia** in 1918, though during World War II it was part of the German protectorate of Bohemia-Moravia. *Dossier* Bohemia played seven international games between 1903 and 1908, all but one against **Hungary**. Its last fixture on 13 June 1908, was against **England** (0–4, in Prague, friendly).

Bohemians FC *club* Republic of Ireland national league club based in the capital Dublin, on the east coast, founded 1890. Ground: **Dalymount Park**, capacity: 25,000. Strip: red and black striped shirts, black shorts. *Honours* **European Cup-winners Cup** second round 1977; **Irish FA Cup** (all-Ireland) 1908, runners-up 1895 (lost 1–10 to **Linfield** – the highest ever score in an Irish FA Cup final), 1900, 1903, 1909, 1911; Republic of Ireland **FAI Cup** 1928, 1935, 1970 (one of only two FAI Cup finals to require two replays, Bohemians winning 0–0, 0–0, 2–1 against **Sligo Rovers**), 1976, 1992, runners-up 1929, 1945, 1947, 1982, 1983; Republic of Ireland league champions 1924, 1928, 1930, 1934, 1936, 1975, 1978. Notable former players: Mick Martin (52 caps for the Republic of Ireland, later with **Manchester United**, **West Bromwich Albion**, and **Newcastle United**).

Bohemians Prague *club* Czech Republic and former-Czechoslovakia league club based in Prague, founded 1905. Ground: V D'olicku, capacity: 17,200. Strip: green and white shirts, green shorts. former-Czechoslovakia league champions 1983; **UEFA Cup** semi-final 1983).

Bohr, 1. Niels *player* **Denmark** international player (one cap). Born 1885, died 1962. *Keynotes* Nobel Prize for physics 1922. **2.** his brother Harald **Bohr**, Denmark international. *Keynotes* Played for Denmark in the 1908 Olympic Games football tournament final (0–2 v **England**, White City, London). He became an acclaimed mathematician. *Honours* **Olympic Games** silver medal (Denmark, 1908).

Bolivar Independiente Unificada *club* Bolivian national league club based in La Paz, founded 1927. Ground: Estadio Nacional Olimpico de Hernándo Siles (the national stadium), capacity: 55,000. Strip: sky blue shirts, sky blue shorts. Bolivian national league champions 1966, 1968, 1976, 1978, 1982, 1983, 1985, 1987, 1988, 1991, 1992, 1994, 1996, 1997; **Copa Libertadores** semi-final 1986, quarter-final 1997, 1998; Torneo Integrado champions 1956; eight-times winners of the former La Paz regional league.

Bolivia *country* CONMEBOL landlocked republic in South America, stretching from the Eastern Andes to the Amazon basin. Area 1,098,575 sq km (424,050 sq miles). Population: 8,070,000 (1995 est.). Languages: Spanish, Quenchua and Aymara. Capital: La Paz – the highest capital city in the world at 3,626 m (11,897 feet) above sea level (technically, Sucre is the capital, though the seat of Government is at La Paz). *Dossier* Football association (Federación Boliviana de Fútbol, Cochabamba) founded in 1925, affiliated to **FIFA** and **Confederación Sudamericana de Fútbol** (CONMEBOL) in 1926, president José Saavedra Banzer, general secretary Dr Oliverio Irjarte Lafuente. Season played

from February to December. National Stadium: Estadio Nacional Olimpico de Hernándo Siles, capacity: 55,000 (29,000 seated). National team strip: green shirts with white borders, white shorts with green borders. First international game: 12 October 1926, v **Chile** (1–7, in Santiago, Chile, **Copa America**). Best international victories: 2–0 v **Brazil** (25 July 1993, La Paz, **World Cup** qualifier – the only team ever to beat Brazil in a World Cup qualifying match); 7–0 v **Venezuela** (22 August 1993, La Paz, World Cup qualifying tournament). Worst defeat: 1–10 v Brazil (10 April 1949, Sao Paulo, Brazil, Copa America). Most capped player: José Soruco (89 appearances). Other notable players: Victor Ugarte , Marco Etcheverry. *International tournament record* **Olympic Games** – last in South American qualifying group for 1992 tournament; **Women's** World Cup – finished last in the 1995 qualifying tournament after losing all four matches letting in 44 goals with only one scored; World Cup – played in first World Cup in 1930 (no qualification), in 1954 (walkover in qualifying stages) and qualified for finals tournament in 1994, never progressed beyond first round of finals tournament; Copa America – 1963 (finished top of seven-nation league, staged in Bolivia), runners-up 1997 (1–3, v Brazil, in La Paz), quarter-finalist 1995; Simon Bolivar Games – 1938 (v **Venezuela**, in Colombia); **South American Under-17 Championship** 1986; **Under-17 World Youth tournament** – qualified for finals tournament 1987 (first round). *Record against British and Irish national teams* v **Republic of Ireland**, played one, lost one (friendly in Dublin, 24 May 1994). *History* Football has been played in Bolivia since the end of the 19th century with the first club, Oruro Royal Club, founded in 1896. **The Strongest**, Bolivia's oldest current major club, was founded in 1908. A league based in the capital, La Paz, was formed in 1914 (becoming semi-professional in 1950), with other regional leagues formed later. From 1954 to 1957, the winners of the La Paz, Cochabamba and Oruro leagues competed in the Torneo Integrado to decide the national championship. A national league was formed in 1958; the current fully national and structured professional league started in 1977. No Bolivian clubs have won a South American club tournament, although **Club Blooming**, **Club Jorge Wilsterman** and **Bolivar Independiente Unificada** have all reached the semi-final of the **Copa Libertadores**. Bolivia's first international match was in 1926. It entered the first World Cup, but has never progressed beyond the first round of the finals tournament. Bolivia has won the Copa America only once, in 1963, when it hosted the tournament. It finished top of a seven-nation league, beating Brazil 5–4 in a crucial match at Felix Capriles stadium, Cochabamba, on the last day of the tournament. A crowd of 25,000 watched Ugarte (2), Camacho, Garcia and Alcocer score the Bolivian goals and secure the country's only major international tournament triumph. Bolivia was hosts and runners-up in the 1997 tournament, losing to Brazil in the final in La Paz. International matches are generally played at La Paz (3,626 metres above sea level) and Cochabamba (2,559 metres above sea level) at high altitude (La Paz is 1,500 m higher than Mexico City), potentially giving the national side an advantage over visiting teams unused to the rarefied atmosphere (see **altitude**). Bolivia's two appearances in the final of the Copa America have been when the tournament was staged at home. International matches are occasionally played at Santa Cruz – a mere 457 metres above sea level. *League system* The national league comprises one division of 12 clubs, fed by eight regional leagues: Cochabamba, Chiquisaca (Sucre), La Paz, Orudo, Potosi, Santa Cruz, Tarija, Trinidad (Beni). The championship is played in two half-seasons: the Torneo **Apertura** and the Torneo **Clausura**. The Apertura tournament is decided by a playoff semi-final and final. The finalists in the Apertura playoffs join the top four teams in the Clausura tournament in a "final hexagonal" league (each of the six clubs playing each other twice). The first- and second-placed clubs in the final hexagonal playoff for the championship. Promotion from the regional leagues is decided by a knockout tournament (the Torneo Simon Bolivar) of the 16 first- and second-placed clubs from the regional leagues. The winners are automatically promoted, while the runners-up must play the second-bottom club in the national league. *Record in international club tournaments* Copa Libertadores – Club Blooming (semi-final 1985), Club Jorge Wilsterman (semi-final 1981), Bolivar Independiente Unificada (semi-final 1986). Other leading clubs: **Oriente Petrolero**, **Real Santa Cruz**, **San José**, The Strongest.

Bologna (FC) *club* Italian league. *Dossier* Ground: **Stadio Renato Dall'Ara**, Emila-Romagna, capacity: 40,572. Strip: red and blue striped shirts, white shorts with red and blue trim. Record victory: 8–0 v Triestina (**Serie A**, 1931-32). Record defeat: 2–8 v **Lazio** (Serie A, 1948-49); 0–6 v **Internazionale** (Serie A 1988-89). *History* Formed in 1909. The club's official title is Bologna 1909 Football Club. Bologna was one of the main clubs in Italian football during the inter-war period, winning the League Championship four times (1935-36, 1936-37, 1938-39, 1940-41) and finishing outside the Serie A top three on only three occasions between 1930-31 and 1940-41. In 1963-64, Bologna won a further title in a **playoff** against Internazionale (2–0) after the two clubs had finished level on points (54). In the 1962-63 season, the Italian football authorities docked Bologna – then top of the league – three points after five of its players tested positive during a routine **drug test**; the five were found to have taken **amphetamines**. The three-point penalty was subsequently overturned after medical evidence suggested that the alleged levels of amphetamine found in the urine samples would have been fatal. Bologna reached the semi-final of the **UEFA Cup** in 1999. *Honours* Italian Cup 1970 (league basis), 1974 (0–0, 5–4 pens. v Palermo); Italian league 1925 (6–0 agg., v Alba), 1929 (4–2 agg., v **Torino**), 1935-36, 1936-37, 1940-41, 1963-64 (2–0 v Internazionale, playoff).

Bolton Wanderers *club* English league. *Dossier* Ground: **Reebok Stadium**, Bolton, Greater Manchester, capacity: 25,000 all seated. Strip: white shirts with black and red trim, black shorts with white and red stripe, black socks with red and white trim. Website: *www.boltonfc.co.uk* Nickname: Trotters. Record attendance: 25,000 (several occasions; first, v **Manchester United**, 20 September 1997, **Premier League**). Best average attendance: 35,832 (**Burnden Park**, 1951-52). Biggest win: 13–0 v **Sheffield United** (1 February 1890, **FA Cup**, second round). Biggest defeat: 1–9 v **Preston North End** (10 December 1887, FA Cup, second round). *History* Initially formed in 1874 as Christ Church FC, Bolton Wanderers emerged three years later following a disagreement with the church's vicar. The club adopted the name "Wanderers" because in its early years it kept changing headquarters. Bolton was at the forefront of moves towards professionalism and one of the first English clubs to recruit Scottish players. The club was a founder member of the **Football League**. Wanderers played its first matches at Pikes Lane before agreeing a 14-year lease with Bolton Corporation in 1894 for some wasteland, that would eventually become Burnden Park. The ground's freehold was purchased by the club for just over £8,000 in 1914. Bolton has appeared in some memorable FA Cup finals, including the first Wembley final in 1923 (the **White horse final**) and the 1953 encounter (the **Matthews Cup final**). Between 1923 and 1929, Bolton won the FA Cup three times without conceding a goal in the final. Five men played in all three finals – Butler, Haworth, Nuttall, Pym and Seddon – and only 17 players were used in the three finals. The club won the Cup again in 1958. Between 1888 and 1971, Bolton spent only 14 seasons outside the top flight. Relegation to Division Three in 1971 was followed by one season in Division Four (1987-88). Bolton finally returned to the top division, the Premier League, in 1995, although for only one season. The club also reached the **League Cup** final (1–2 v **Liverpool**) that year. Wanderers moved the 25,000 all-seater Reebok Stadium at the start of the 1997-98 season, a move that coincided with the club's return to the Premier League. The club was relegated on goal difference in 1997-98 failing to make an immediate return by losing the final of the 1998-99 First Division playoff (0–2 v **Watford**). Bolton, under the name of Burnden Leisure, was floated on the stock market in April 1997 (floatation price = 52p). In 1946, 33 spectators were killed and more than 400 injured when barriers at Burnden Park broke during Bolton's FA Cup-tie against **Stoke City** (**Burnden Park disaster**). *League record* Premier League 1995-96, 1997-98; Division One (including Football League) 1888-89 to 1898-99, 1900-01 to 1902-03, 1905-06 to 1907-08, 1909-10, 1911-12 to 1932-33, 1935-36 to 1963-64, 1978-79 to 1979-80; First Division 1993-94 to 1994-95, 1996-97, 1998-99–; Division Two 1899-00, 1903-04 to 1904-05, 1908-09, 1910-11, 1933-34 to 1934-35, 1964-65 to 1970-71, 1973-74 to 1977-78,

1980-81 to 1982-83; Second Division 1992-93; Division Three 1971-72 to 1972-73, 1983-84 to 1986-87, 1988-89 to 1991-92; Division Four 1987-88. *Honours* First Division 1996-97; Division Two 1908-09, 1977-78; Division Three 1972-73;**FA Charity Shield** 1958 (4–1 v **Wolverhampton Wanderers**); **FA Cup** 1923 (2–0 v **West Ham United** – *Team* Pym, Haworth, Finney, Nuttall, Seddon, Jennings, Butler, Jack (1), J R Smith (1), J Smith, Vizard), 1926 (1–0 v **Manchester City** – *Team* Pym, Haworth, Greenhalgh, Nuttall, Seddon, Jennings, Butler, Jack (1), JR Smith, J Smith, Vizard), 1929 (2–0 v **Portsmouth** – *Team* Pym, Haworth, Finney, Kean, Seddon, Nuttall, Butler (1), McClelland, Blackmore (1), Gibson, Cook), 1958 (2–0 v **Manchester United** – *Team* Hopkinson, Hartle, T Banks, Hennin, Higgins, Edwards, Birch, Stevens, Lofthouse (2), Parry, Holden); **Sherpa Van Trophy** 1989 (4–1 v **Torquay United**). *Records* Nat **Lofthouse** is Bolton's most capped player (33 for **England**); Eddie Hopkinson holds the record for club appearances (519, 1956-70); Lofthouse is also Bolton's record league goalscorer (255, 1946-61).

Bombe *misc.* German nickname for a prolific goalscorer (sometimes also used in Italy). Gerd **Müller**, who appeared for **Bayern Munich** and West **Germany** in the late 1960s and 1970s, was the first to be given the title.

bone *medical* a hard connective tissue that is composed of cells embedded in a matrix of collagen, calcium phosphate and other inorganic salts. About three-quarters of the weight of bones is inorganic material. There are about 200 bones in the human skeleton (not including the auditory bones of the ear). See **fracture**.

Bonev, Hristo *player-manager* Striker. **Bulgaria** international (87 caps, 45 goals, 1967–1979, excludes Olyimpic Games). Clubs: **Lokomotiv Plovdiv**. *Keynotes* Bulgaria's highest scorer and most-capped player. Later became his country's national coach. *Honours* Bulgarian Cup runner-up (Lokomotiv Plovdiv, 1971).

Boniek, Zbigniew *player* Striker. **Poland** international (80 caps, 24 goals, ca. 1977–1985). Born 3 March 1956. *Clubs* Zawisza Bydgoszcz, **Widzew Lódz**, **Juventus**. *Keynotes* Boniek was the third-highest scorer in the 1982 World Cup finals, with four goals, including a hat-trick against Belgium in the second round (3–0, 28 June 1982, at **Nou Camp**, Barcelona). He scored twice in the 1978 finals. Transferred to Juventus in 1982 for £1.1 million (a former Polish record transfer). He scored the 41st-minute winner for Juventus in the 1984 European Cup-winners Cup final (2–1, v FC **Porto**). Boniek played in the ill-fated European Cup final 1985 (the **Heysel Stadium disaster**). Boniek was voted tenth in the *World Soccer* **World Footballer of the Year** award for 1982, and third in *France Football* **European Footballer of the Year** 1982. *Honours* **World Cup** third place (Poland, 1982); **European Cup-winners Cup** (Juventus , 1984); **European Cup** (Juventus, 1985); Polish league

championship (Widzew Lódz, 1981, 1982); Italian **Serie A** championship (Juventus, 1984, 1986).

Boniperti, Giampiero *player* Striker. **Italy** international (38 caps, eight goals, ca. 1949–1960). Born 4 July 1928. *Clubs* Momo, **Juventus**. *Keynotes* Signed by Juventus in 1946 and played 444 matches for the club. In a match at Wembley Stadium in 1953, 97,000 spectators watched Boniperti score twice for the "Rest of Europe" against **England** in a match to celebrate the 90th birthday of the **Football Association**; the match finished 4–4. Later became president of Juventus. *Honours* Italian **Serie A** Championship (Juventus, 1950, 1952, 1958, 1960, 1961).

bonus *n.* additional payment made to a player or players, for example, for scoring a goal or for winning a match. Bonuses were outlawed by the **Football Association** in 1900, though were re-introduced by a payments formula in 1910. From 1910, clubs could distribute a prescribed maximum sum of money to its players for success in the Cup or league. **Win bonuses** were introduced in 1920. Players are now free to negotiate their own bonus arrangements as part of their contracts.

bonus point *n.* additional point awarded to clubs in some South American leagues depending on their league position. The bonus point is carried over to a second stage of the league, such as the championship or relegation leagues. In **Paraguay**, for example, the eight clubs qualifying for the second stage championship mini-leagues carry over bonus points from the first stage: 3.0 bonus points for the club finishing first in the league, 2.5 for the second, 2.0 for the third, and so on. Bonus points are also awarded in, for example, **Colombia** and **Ecuador**, and Tunisia in Africa.

booking *n.* another word for a **caution** of a player for an infringement of the **Laws of the game**. Literally, record of the name of the offending player in the referee's notebook. **2. book** *vb.* to caution a player.

bookmaker *n.* see **betting shop**

books, football *misc.* What is now the*News of the World football annual* was the first annual football statistics book; first published in 1887 and produced every season since. It was originally published as the *Athletic News football supplement and club directory*, and was taken over by the *News of the World* in 1961. See also **Rothmans Yearbook**.

Bootham Crescent *ground* English football ground situated in York, north Yorkshire; home of **York City**. *Dossier* Ground capacity: 9,534. Pitch dimensions: 105m x 68m. Record attendance: 28,123 v **Huddersfield Town** (5 March 1938, **FA Cup**, sixth round). Best average attendance: 10,412 (1948-49). *History* York City took over Yorkshire County Cricket Club's Bootham Crescent ground in 1932, playing its first match there on 31 August (v **Stockport County**, Division Three (North)). The cricketers had used the ground since at least 1880. York bought the freehold for £4,075 in 1948. In 1985, one of Bootham Crescent's biggest gates for years, 11,347, watched York Rugby

League Club play Leeds in a Challenge Cup match. When the Shipton End terrace was covered in 1991, with partial funding from the **supporters' club**, the stand was renamed in memory of York striker David Longhurst, who collapsed and died during a match against **Lincoln City** on 8 September 1990. The first floodlit match at Bootham Crescent took place on 7 September 1959 (v **Queens Park Rangers**, Division Three).

Boothferry Park *ground* English football ground situated in Kingston upon Hull, Humberside; home of **Hull City**. Ground capacity: 12,996. Pitch dimensions: 105m x 68.5m. Record attendance: 55,019 v **Manchester United** (26 February 1949, **FA Cup**, sixth round). Best average: 37,319 (1949-50). *History* Hull bought Boothferry Park in 1930, but did not move there until after **World War II**, having abandoned its development due to financial difficulties in 1939. The club played its first match at the ground on 31 August 1946 (v **Lincoln City**, Division Three (North)). Hull intended to build a 80,000 capacity stadium at Boothferry Park with its own railway station and car parks. Although the station, Boothferry Park Halt, was established, much of the rest of the plan was never realised. The first **penalty shoot-out** to decide the outcome of a UK football match took place at the ground on 5 August 1970; Hull City lost to **Manchester United** (4–5) in a **Watney Cup** semi-final. Because of political troubles in Ireland, Boothferry Park staged an international between **Northern Ireland** and **Spain** on 16 February 1972 (Northern Ireland also used **Craven Cottage**, **Goodison Park**, **Highfield Road** and **Hillsborough**, and switched its home matches against **Scotland** to **Hampden Park** during this period). The ground hosted an **Inter-League** match between **Football League** and League of Ireland on 27 October 1965. The Rugby League club Hull Kingston Rovers staged several local derby matches against rival club Hull at Boothferry Park between 1953 and 1959, including, in April 1953, a game watched by a club record 27,670. It has also staged a number of England Rugby League international fixtures. The first floodlit match at Boothferry Park took place on 19 January 1953 (v **Dundee**, friendly).

Bootle *club* former English league. *Dossier* Ground: Hawthorne Road, Liverpool, Merseyside. Record League attendance: 3,000. *Keynotes* Bootle was a founder member of the Football Alliance, which was set up in 1899 by northern clubs denied entry to the **Football League**, and in 1892-93, Division Two. After only one season, it was the first club to resign Football League membership. The club was an **FA Cup** quarter-finalist in 1889-90 (0–7 v **Blackburn Rovers**). Bootle finished eighth in Division Two in the club's only season in the Football League. *League record* Division Two 1892-93.

boots *n.pl* see **football boots**.

Borac Banja Luka *club* former-Yugoslavia national league club based in Banja Luka, founded 1926. Ground: Gradski, capacity: 18,000 (pre-civil war). Strip: red shirts, blue shorts. **European Cup-winners Cup**

second round 1975-76; former-Yugoslavia Cup 1988, runners-up 1975; **Mitropa Cup** 1992.

Bordeaux (Girondins de Bordeaux) *club* French national leauge club based in Bordeaux, formed 1881. Ground: Parc Lescure, capacity: 36,500. Strip: blue shirts with a white chevron, blue shorts. French Cup 1941, 1986, 1987; French league champions 1950, 1984, 1985, 1987, 1998; **UEFA Cup** runners-up 1996 (1–5 agg., v **Bayern Munich**).

Borussia Dortmund *club* German league. *Dossier* Ground: **Westfalenstadion**, Nordheim-Westfalen. Strip: yellow shirts with black trim, black shorts. Ground capacity: 69,000. *History* Formed in 1909 from a merger of several clubs (Britannia, Rhenania and disaffected Trinity members). Officially called Ballspiel Verein 09 Borussia Dortmund and commonly referred to as BVB. Dortmund was a non-profit making club until October 1998, when the German football authorities altered its rules to allow clubs to become limited companies. The club reached its first West German League national **playoff** final in 1949 (2–3 v VfR Mannheim). It won the title in 1956, 1957 and 1963, and was a finalist again in 1961 (0–3 v **Nuremberg** (1.FC)). Dortmund's 1963 title success, the last to be decided on a playoff basis, coincided with the club's first appearance in the final of the West German Cup (0–3 v **Hamburg SV**). The following season, it became the first German victors of a European club competition, winning the **European Cup-winners Cup**. After winning consecutive **Bundesliga** titles in 1994-95 and 1995-96, Dortmund won the **European Cup** (Champions' League) in 1997 – the third German club to win the trophy – and it reached the semi-final stage of the same competition the following season (0–2 agg., **Real Madrid**). *Honours* Bundesliga 1994-95, 1995-96; European Cup (Champions League) 1997 (3–1 v **Juventus**); European Cup-winners Cup 1966 (2–1 a.e.t. v **Liverpool**); West German Cup 1965 (2–0 v Alemannia Aachen), 1989 (4–1 v **Werder Bremen**); West German League 1956 (4–2 v Karlsruher SC), 1957 (4–1 v Hamburg SV), 1963 (3–1 v Cologne (1.FC)).

Borussia Mönchengladbach (VfL 1900) *club* German league. *Dossier* Ground: Bökelberg, Mönchengladbach. Strip: white shirts with two green stripes, white shorts. Ground capacity: 34,500. *History* Formed in 1900 and officially entitled Verein für Leibsuebung 1900 Borussia Mönchengladbach. The club's most successful period occurred in the 1970s. During that decade, Mönchengladbach won five **Bundesliga** titles, including three consecutive Championships between 1974-75 and 1976-77, one domestic cup and the **UEFA Cup** on two occasions. In the decade between 1967-68 and 1977-78, the club finished outside the Bundesliga top three only once. It also appeared in the 1977 **European Cup** final (1–3 v **Liverpool**) and 1973 UEFA Cup final (2–3 agg., v Liverpool). The club again reached the UEFA Cup final in 1980, losing on the **away goals** rule (3–3 agg. v Eintracht Frankfurt) in the first all-German final of a European club competition. Before the club's 1969-70

Bundesliga title, Mönchengladbach's only silverware was won in 1960, when it lifted the West German Cup. Since winning the UEFA Cup in 1979, the club's only success has come in the domestic Cup, appearing in three finals: winning in 1995 and being defeated in both 1984 (1–1, 6–7 pens. v **Bayern Munich**) and 1992 (0–0, 3–4 pens. v Hannover 96). The club was relegated from the Bundesliga in 1998-99. *Honours* Bundesliga 1969-70, 1970-71, 1974-75, 1975-76, 1976-77; German Cup 1995 (3–0 v VfL Wolfsburg); UEFA Cup 1975 (5–1 agg. v **Twente** (FC)), 1979 (2–1 agg. v **Red Star Belgrade**); West German Cup 1960 (3–2 v Karlsruher SC), 1973 (2–1 v **Cologne** (1.FC).

Bosman, Jean-Marc *player* Born 1964. Bosman, a Belgian national, is famous for bringing a legal case which led to the removal of restrictions on the movement of players within the **European Union** (EU) (see **restraint of trade**). He successfully argued that the rules on transfers of players and the limits on the number of EU nationals allowed to play in club matches were contrary to the **Treaty of Rome** – the founding articles of the European Community. The European Communities Court of Justice ruled in Bosman's favour on 15 December 1995 (Case C-415/93 Bosman). It concluded that **UEFA** rules governing the number of non-domestic EU nationals eligible to play during a club match were contrary to the freedom of movement of workers within the EU as contained in article 85 of the Treaty of Rome. The Court also found that free circulation of players was constrained by the UEFA system of transfers, which prevented a player employed by a club in one member state moving to a new club in another member state unless a transfer fee was paid for his or her services even when the player's contract had expired. Bosman agreed a £312,000 settlement with the Belgian FA in December 1998. *Keynotes* Bosman had brought the case after his two-year contract as a professional with Belgium club RC Liège expired on 30 June 1990 and the one-year extension offered by the club included a 75% wage reduction. He refused to sign the contract and was placed on the **transfer list**, with the fee set at 11,743,000 Belgian francs. Eventually, the French Division Two club US Dunkerque offered to take Bosman on an initial one-year contract with an option to sign the player permanently. The agreement involved US Dunkerque paying RC Liège an initial fee of 1,200,000 Belgian francs and a further 4,800,000 should the club exercise the full transfer option. The deal was conditional on US Dunkerque receiving the transfer papers from the Belgian FA by 2 August 1990, but RC Liège was doubtful that the French club could finance the deal and refused to sanction their issue. As a result, Bosman was left in limbo, with neither the US Dunkerque or the RC Liège contract in operation. Also, on 31 July 1990, the Belgian club suspended Bosman, an act which prevented his playing for the whole of the 1990-91 season. Bosman took his case to the Belgian courts and the Court of Appeal in Liège subsequently asked the European Court of Justice to rule on various questions relating to articles 85 and 86 of the Treaty of Rome.

Bosman *n.* informal term for a **free transfer** (after Jean-Marc **Bosman**).

Bosman ruling *legal* European Communities Court of Justice ruling in 1995 which outlawed the existing rules on transfers and the limits on the number of **European Union** (EU) nationals playing for club in another EU country. *Keynotes* Jean-Marc **Bosman**, a Belgian national, successfully argued that the rules on transfers of players and the limits on the number of EU nationals allowed to play in club matches were contrary to the Treaty of Rome – the founding articles of the European Community. The European Communities Court of Justice ruled in Bosman's favour on 15 December 1995 (Case C-415/93 Bosman). It concluded that **UEFA** rules governing the number of non-domestic EU nationals eligible to play during a club match were contrary to the freedom of movement of workers within the Union as contained in article 85 of the Treaty of Rome. The Court also found that free circulation of players was constrained by the UEFA system of transfers, which prevented a player employed by a club in one member state moving to a new club in another member state unless a transfer fee was paid for his or her services. In the UK, the home football associations attempted to stave off further legal challenge to the **compensation-fee** system by introducing the principle of compensation fees for out-of-contract players aged under-24. Such fees, it was argued, should be paid on the transfer of young players as compensation for training and development. The principle was introduced at the end of the 1997-98 season. See **freedom of contract**, **transfer**, **transfer fee**.

Bosnia-Herzegovina *country* UEFA republic of the former-Yugoslavia, gained independence in 1992. Area: 51,130 sq km (19,736 sq miles). Continental and Mediterranean climate. Population: 4,370,000 (1991 census). Language: Serbo-Croat. Capital: Sarajevo. *Dossier* Bosnia and Herzegovina Football Federation (Sarajevo) founded 1992, affiliated to **FIFA** 1996 and **Union of European Associations** (UEFA) 1996, president Jusuf Pusina, secretary Ivan Mioc. National stadium: Kosevo, Sarajevo, capacity: 20,000. Strip: white shirts, blue shorts. Most capped player: Faruk **Hadzibegic** (61 caps for former-Yugoslavia, 1982-92, fifth in former-Yugoslavia's all-time list). *International tournament record* **Women's World Cup** – first entered 1999; **World Cup** – first entered 1998, fourth of five-nation qualifying group (three wins, five defeats in its eight matches); **European Championship** – first entered 2000. *World Cup performance* (finals and qualifiers to end of 1998 tournament) played eight, won three, drawn none, lost five, scored nine goals, conceded 14 goals; win rate 37%; goals scored per game 1.12. *Record against British and Irish national teams* none played. *History* Before independence, a number of clubs from Bosnia and Herzegovina were successful in the **Former-Yugoslavia** league - FK **Sarajevo** were league champions twice, Velez Mostar won the Yugoslavian Cup twice, **Borac Banja Luka** were cup winners once, while FK **Zeljeznicar Sarajevo** won the league once and reached the semi-final of the **UEFA Cup** in 1985. Civil war in Bosnia hampered development of organised football since independence. However, league football restarted in 1995-96. One of Bosnia's first international games was against **Paraguay** in Asunción (21 April 1996, 0–3, friendly). In the same year, Bosnia played **Brazil** at Estadio Manaus in Brazil (18 December 1996, 0–1, friendly). *League system* Leagues in Bosnia are organised predominantly along ethnic groupings. Sixteen clubs play in the Muslim league first division, 14 in the Croat Leauge and 18 in the Serbian League. Three points are awarded for a victory, with one for a draw: final positions for clubs level on points are determined by **goal difference** and, if necessary, by **goals scored**. The national championship is decided by a playoff of the top two Muslim league first division clubs, along with the top two clubs from each of the Croat and Serbian leagues. Herzegovina has its own regional league. *Record in international club tournaments* **European Cup** – FK Sarajevo (second round 1967/68); **European Cup-winners Cup** – Borac Banja Luka (second round 1976), FK **Velez Mostar** (second round 1982, 1987); **UEFA Cup** – FK Zeljeznicar Sarajevo (semi-final 1985, quarter-final 1972), Velez Mostar (quarter-final 1975); **Mitropa Cup** – FK **Celik Zenica** (1971, 1972), Borac Banja Luka (1992).

Botafogo de Futebol e Regatas *club* Brazilian national league and **Rio de Janeiro** state league club based in **Rio de Janeiro**, founded 1904. Ground: Marechal Hermes "Mane Garrincha", capacity: 18,000. Strip: black and white striped shirts, black shorts. **Campeonato Brasileiro** runners-up 1971, 1972, 1992; **Copa CONMEBOL** 1993 3–3 agg., 3–1 pens., v **Peñarol**); **Copa do Brasil** 1969; **Copa Libertadores** semi-final 1963; São Paulo Tournament 1962, 1964 (shared), 1966 (shared); state league champions 16 times (to 1998). Notable former player: **Jairzinho**.

Botev Plovdiv *club* Bulgarian national league club based in Plovdiv, formed 1912, (known as Trakia Plovdiv from 1967-90). Ground: Hristo Botev, capacity: 21,000. Strip: yellow and black chequered shirts, black shorts. Bulgarian Cup/Soviet Army Cup 1962, 1981; Bulgarian league champions 1929, 1967; Republic Cup runners-up 1991, 1993, 1995.

Botswana *country CAF* landlocked republic in southern Africa, stretching from the Orange River to the Zambesi River, between the Kalahari desert in the south-west and Okavango swamps in the northwest. Formerly the British protectorate of Bechuanaland, becoming an independent Commonwealth state in 1966. Area: 582,000 sq km (224,652 sq miles). Population: 1,330,000 (1991 census). Languages: Tswana (Setswana) and English. Capital: Gaborone. *Dossier* Botswana Football Association (Gaborone) formed in

1970, affiliated to **FIFA** and **Confédération Africaine de Football** (CAF) in 1976, president Ismail Bhamjee, general secretary Ashford Mamelodi. Season played from February to October. National stadium: Botswana National Stadium, Gaborone, capacity: 20,000. National strip: blue and white shirts, blue, white and black shorts. Nickname of national team: Zebras. First international game: 18 April 1981 v **Malawi** (2–5, away, friendly). *International tournament record* **Olympic Games** – lost in preliminary round in 1992 qualifying tournament; **Women's World Cup** – never entered; **World Cup** – first entered 1994 (last in its first round qualifying group); **African Cup of Nations** – first entered 1994, never qualified for finals tournament; **Under-17 World Championship** – never entered; World Youth Cup (under-20) – never qualified. *Record against British and Irish national teams* none played. *League system* There are 12 clubs in the national league. Leading clubs: **Botswana Defence Force**, **LCS Gunners**, **PG Notwane**, **Township Rollers**.

Botswana Defence Force (BDF XI) *club* Botswana national league club based in the capital Gaborone. Ground: the National Stadium, capacity: 20,000. Botswana Cup 1998; Botswana league champions 1981, 1988, 1989, 1991, 1997.

Boundary Park *ground* English football ground situated in Oldham, Greater Manchester; home of **Oldham Athletic**. *Dossier* Ground capacity: 13,559 all seated. Pitch dimensions: 100.5m x 68m. Record attendance: 47,671 v **Sheffield Wednesday** (25 January 1930, **FA Cup**, fourth round). Best average attendance: 18,075 (1920-21). *History* Originally called the Athletic Ground, and home of the town's first professional club, Oldham County, since 1896. Pine Villa, as Oldham Athletic was initially called, took over the ground for a short spell in 1899 when County folded. Oldham returned on a permanent basis in 1906. Fifteen supporters were taken to hospital after crush barriers gave way during a 1962 third round FA Cup tie against **Liverpool** watched by 41,733. The club won the £70,000 first prize in the one-season **Ford Sporting League** competition, which awarded points on the basis of good behaviour on the pitch and the number of goals scored. The rules of the competition stipulated that prize money should be spent on ground improvements and Oldham chose to replace the Broadway Stand at Boundary Park. **Undersoil heating** was installed in 1980, enabling Oldham to switch its 1981 Boxing Day fixture against **Blackburn Rovers**, which had been scheduled for **Ewood Park**, to Boundary Park – this was the first occasion that the **League** allowed such a change. In 1986, Oldham followed **Queens Park Rangers'** lead and installed an **artificial pitch**, enabling the ground's traditional 5.5 metre slope to be levelled. Oldham copied **Luton Town** and made the artificial pitch the focal point of a community sports centre, earning the club an additional £50,000 to £60,000 income each year. Oldham replaced its artificial pitch with a Fibreturf (a mixture of natural and synthetic grass) pitch in 1991. It was the last

Football League ground in Lancashire to install floodlights, which were financed by £18,000 public appeal. Boundary Park staged its first floodlit match on 3 October 1961 (v **Burnley**, friendly). Boundary Park staged an **Inter-League** fixture between the **Football League** and Irish League on 9 October 1909.

Bournemouth (AFC) *club* English league. *Dossier* Ground: **Dean Court**, Bournemouth, Dorset. Strip: red and black striped shirts, black shorts, and black socks. Nickname: Cherries. Ground capacity: 10,770. Record attendance: 28,799 v **Manchester United** (2 March 1957, **FA Cup**, sixth round). Best average attendance: 16,854 (1947-48). Biggest win: 11–0 v **Margate** (20 November 1971, FA Cup, first round). Biggest defeat: 0–9 v **Lincoln City** (18 December 1982, Division Three). *History* Although a Bournemouth FC was established in 1875 (which still exists), AFC Bournemouth has no connection, being founded in 1890 as Boscombe St John's. The club was refounded in 1899 as Boscombe FC, a name it retained until 1923 when the title Bournemouth & Boscombe Athletic FC was adopted to coincide with the club's election to the **Football League** (Division Three (South)). A further change of name occurred in 1972 when the club adopted the AFC prefix and dropped Boscombe Athletic FC. Bournemouth's FA Cup **giantkilling** exploits in 1956-57 included victories over Division One opponents **Wolverhampton Wanderers** (1–0, fourth round) and **Tottenham Hotspur** (3–1, fifth round), before losing to **Manchester United** in the quarter-finals (1–2). Bournemouth's relegation on **goal average** from Division Three in 1969-70 ended the longest tenure in that division of any club. Under the managership of John Bond and with a team which contained prolific striker Ted MacDougall, the club bounced back at the first attempt, narrowly missing promotion to Division Two the season after. Harry Redknapp was appointed manager in 1983 and during his nine-year reign the club enjoyed some success. In 1984, the club lifted its first trophy, winning the newly-established **Associate Members Cup** (2–1 v **Hull City**). In the same season, Bournemouth defeated the FA Cup-holders Manchester United in the third round of the competition (2–0). Three years later, Bournemouth won the Division Three Championship, although the club's tenure in Division Two lasted for only three seasons. In January 1997, the club, more than £3.5 million in debt, was put into receivership by its bankers. Supporters raised sufficient funds to convince the club's creditors that financial restructuring was possible. A fans' trust was set up which holds a 51% share in the club, making Bournemouth the UK's first community-owned football club. The club also adopted the official title, Bournemouth & Boscombe Athletic Community Football Club Limited. In 1998, Bournemouth made its first appearance at **Wembley**, reaching the final of the **Auto Windscreens Shield** 1998 (1–2 **golden goal** v **Grimsby Town**). *League record* Division Two 1987-88 to 1989-90; Second Division 1992-93–; Division

Three 1958-59 to 1969-70, 1971-72 to 1974-75, 1982-83 to 1986-87, 1990-91 to 1991-92; Division Three (South) 1923-24 to 1957-58; Division Four 1970-71, 1975-76 to 1981-82. *Honours* Associate Members Cup 1984 (2–1 v Hull City); Division Three 1986-87. *Records* Gerry **Peyton** is Bournemouth's most capped player (7 (33) for **Republic of Ireland**); Sean O'Driscoll holds the record for club League appearances (423, 1984-95); Ron Eyre is Bournemouth's record League goalscorer (202, 1924-33).

box *informal* another term for **penalty area** (a shortened form of "penalty box").

Bozsik, József *player* Midfield. **Hungary** international (100 caps, 11 goals, 1947-1962). Born 28 September 1929. *Club* **Kispest-Honvéd FC**. *Keynotes* One of the **Magnificent Magyars**, Bozsik is the most capped player in Hungary's history. He made his international debut against **Bulgaria**, on 17 August 1947, a game which Hungary won 9-0. He played in the 1954 **World Cup** final v West **Germany** (2–3) and was a member of Hungary's Olympic gold medal winning side of 1952. His former club, Kispest-Honvéd, named its stadium, the József Bozsik Stadium, in his honour. Bozsik was sent off in the notorious **Battle of Berne** at the 1954 World Cup finals. He became a member of Parliament in Hungary – while still playing – and coached the Hungarian national team in 1974. *Honours* World Cup runner-up (Hungary, 1954); **Olympic Games** gold medal (Hungary, 1952); Hungarian league championship (Honvéd, 1952, 1954, 1955).

Bradford City *club* English league. *Dossier* Ground: **Valley Parade**, West Yorkshire, capacity: 18,018. Strip: claret and amber striped shirts, black shorts, black socks with amber trim. Nickname: Bantams. Record attendance: 39,146 v **Burnley** (11 March 1911, **FA Cup**, fourth round). Best average attendance: 22,585 (1920-21). Biggest win: 11–1 v **Rotherham United** (25 August 1928, Division Three (North)). Biggest defeat: 1–9 v **Colchester United** (30 December 1961, Division Four). *History* Founded in 1903 by Manningham Rugby Club. Bradford was a Northern Union (later Rugby League) stronghold, but the **Football League** was so keen to establish football in that part of Yorkshire that Manningham, a club with mounting financial problems, was strongly encouraged to switch codes from rugby to football. Indeed, Manningham was accepted into Division Two before it had played a match or assembled a team, and a few days later the club became Bradford City. In only its fifth season in the League, City won the Division Two Championship. In 1911, the club became the first winners of the third FA Cup trophy (1–0 replay v **Newcastle United**). This is still the club's only major trophy; ironically the new cup had been made at Bradford-based Fattorini & Sons. In that 1910-11 season City also achieved its highest-ever League position, fifth in Division One. The club has never been able to regain a place in the top flight since it was relegated in 1921-22, although it only narrowly missed promotion to

Division One in 1988 when it lost at the **playoff** stage. City reached the FA Cup sixth round in 1976 (0–1 v **Southampton**), a joint record for a Division Four team (along with **Cambridge United**, **Colchester United** and **Oxford United**), and in 1984-85 the club won the Division Three title. It was at the final match of that season (v **Lincoln City**, 11 May 1985), with 11,000 supporters ready to celebrate the team's success, that a fire engulfed Valley Parade's main stand, killing 56 people and injuring more than 200 others (see **Bradford fire**). The club won promotion to the First Division in 1996 via the Second Division end-of-season **playoffs** (2–0 v **Notts County**). Bradford was promoted to the Premier League after finishing as First Division runners-up in 1998 – a return to the top flight after a 77-year absence. *League record* Premier League 1999-00–; Division One 1908-09 to 1921-22; First Division 1996-97 to 1998-99; Second Division 1992-93 to 1995-96; Division Two 1903-04 to 1907-08, 1922-23 to 1926-27, 1929-30 to 1936-37, 1985-86 to 1989-90; Division Three 1958-59 to 1960-61, 1969-70 to 1971-72, 1977-78, 1982-83 to 1984-85, 1990-91 to 1991-92; Division Three (North) 1927-28 to 1928-29, 1937-38 to 1957-58; Division Four 1961-62 to 1968-69, 1972-73 to 1976-77, 1978-79 to 1981-82. *Honours* Division Two 1907-08; Division Three 1984-85; Division Three (North) 1928-29; FA Cup 1911 (1–0 replay v Newcastle United). **Division Three (North) Cup** 1939. *Records* Harry Hampton is Bradford City's most capped player (9 for **Northern Ireland**); Cec Podd holds the record for club appearances (502, 1970-84); Bobby Campbell is the record league goalscorer (121, 1981-84, 1984-86).

Bradford fire *disaster* stadium disaster at **Bradford City**'s ground, **Valley Parade**, 11 May 1985. A crowd of 11,000 were hoping to celebrate Bradford City's promotion. During the game, fire swept through the 76-year-old stand in less than five minutes. The stand had wooden floorboards and debris had accumulated beneath. It is thought that a lighted match or cigarette fell through a gap in the floor on to the debris. Fifty-six people died and 200 others suffered burns. The Bradford fire – and the subsequent inquiry by Mr Justice **Popplewell** – led to the Fire Safety and Safety of Places of Sport Act 1987. Provisions of the Act included new enforcement and prohibition powers and extended the safety certificate requirement of the **Safety of Sports Grounds Act 1975** to any ground where this was considered necessary, regardless of ground capacity.

Bradford Park Avenue *club* former-English league. *Dossier* Ground: Park Avenue, Bradford. Record attendance: 32,421 v **Leeds United** (25 December 1931, Division Two). *History* Founded in 1907 by members of Bradford Rugby FC. The club immediately joined the Southern League before being elected to Division Two in 1908-09. Bradford was an **FA Cup** quarter-finalist in 1912-13 (0–5 v **Aston Villa**) and 1919-20 (1–4 v **Chelsea**). During **World War I**, Bradford won one of the wartime competitions, the Midland Subsidiary Tournament. The club failed to be **re-elected** in 1969-

70, after four consecutive applications, and was replaced by **Cambridge United**. The club folded at the end of the 1973-74 season after a period in the Northern Premier League following the loss of League status. Bradford Park Avenue's highest League position was ninth in Division One, achieved in 1914-15. It holds the record of 25 successive home victories in the **Football League** (the last 18 in 1926-27, and the first seven in 1927-28, Division Three (North)). *League record* Division One 1914-15 to 1920-21; Division Two 1908-09 to 1913-14, 1921-22, 1928-29 to 1949-50; Division Three 1961-62 to 1962-63; Division Three (North) 1922-23 to 1927-28, 1950-51 to 1957-58; Division Four 1958-59 to 1960-61, 1963-64 to 1969-70. *Honours* Division Three (North) Champions 1927-28.

Brady, Liam   *player-manager*   Midfield. **Republic of Ireland** international (54 caps, 3 goals). Born 13 February 1956. Career ca. 1973–90. *Clubs* (player) **Arsenal**, **Juventus**, **Sampdoria**, **Internazionale**, Ascoli, **West Ham United**; (manager) **Celtic**, **Brighton & Hove Albion**. *Keynotes* Made his Arsenal debut at the age of 17, eventually making 235 **Football League** appearances for the Gunners and scoring 43 goals. He appeared in four finals – **FA Cup** 1978, 1979, 1980 and **European Cup-winners Cup** 1980 – with Arsenal but gained only one winner's medal. During the 1980-81 close season, Brady turned down a £1.5 million move to **Manchester United**, opting instead to join Juventus for £600,000. Brady spent seven years in Italy before returning to England with West Ham United in March 1987. He retired in 1990, having made 89 appearances for the Hammers, and in June 1991 became the first Celtic manager who had never played for the club. He later managed Brighton and, after his resignation in November 1995, he fronted a consortium which attempted to buy the club. He became Arsenal youth team coach in 1996. PFA **Footballer of the Year** in 1979 and Ireland Footballer of the Year in 1976. Included in the **Football League Centenary 100 players**. *Honours* (player) FA Cup (Arsenal 1979); Italian League (Juventus 1980-81, 1981-82).

brain injury *medical* physical and physiological damage to the brain as a result of an accident or severe blow. Scientists have also speculated that injury to the brain could occur among footballers as a result of cumulative trauma from heading the ball – professional players are estimated to head the ball on average about 800 times in a season, and up to 1,500 times for defenders. Research from the Netherlands has suggested that the frequent impact may lead to mild brain injury causing slight loss of cognitive skills. The cummulative effect of heading the ball over many years at professional level has also been implicated in causing Parkinson's Disease – a chronic disorder of the central nervous disease, characterised by tremor and loss of muscular control – though the evidence is not conclusive.

Braine, Raymond   *player*   Midfield. **Belgium** international (54 caps, 26 goals, ca. 1925-39). Born 28 April

1907. *Clubs* Beerschot (twice), **Sparta Prague**. *Keynotes* Braine won four league titles with Belgian side Beerschot in 1920s. Because Belgium would not allow professional football, Braine applied to work abroad; he was refused a **work permit** to play in England, so went to Sparta Prague in 1931 in the **Czechoslovakia** professional league. He returned to play for Beerschot in 1938. Braine is Belgium's fifth-highest all-time goalscorer. His brother Pierre also played for Beerschot and Belgium (five goals, ca. 1924-30). *Honours* Belgium league championship (Berschot, 1924, 1925, 1926, 1928); Czechoslovakian league championship (Sparta Prague, 1936).

Bramall Lane *ground* English football ground situated in Sheffield, South Yorkshire; home of **Sheffield United**. *Dossier* Ground capacity: 30,370 all seated. Pitch dimensions: 102m x 66m. Record attendance: 68,287 v **Leeds United** (15 February 1936, **FA Cup**, fifth round). Best average attendance: 35,094 (1947-48). *History* Sheffield United was formed in September 1889 by the ground committee to make better use of Bramall Lane's facilities and generate additional income. The ground had been a cricket venue since 1855 and, since December 1862, it was regularly used for football, including the staging of an international on 10 March 1883 (**England** v **Scotland**) and a 1889 FA Cup semi-final (**Preston North End** v .**West Bromwich Albion**). It was also used by The Wednesday (later **Sheffield Wednesday**) until 1887. More significantly, Bramall Lane staged the first experiment with **floodlights** on 14 October 1878 when two representative Sheffield sides met. The pitch was illuminated by four lamps, each powered by dynamos driven by engines located behind each goal, mounted on four wooden towers. The architect, Archibald **Leitch**'s first English commission was the John Street stand at Bramall Lane, which opened in 1902. In 1912, Bramall Lane was the venue of the **FA Cup** final replay (**Barnsley** v **West Bromwich Albion**). Bramall Lane also staged a **Football League** representative match (only the third such game) between a side made up of players from clubs in the North and one from Midlands-based teams (North v South, 24 October 1892), although United was unable to charge the League for hiring the ground. During **World War II**, 10 bombs hit the ground, destroying part of the Leitch stand. Until August 1975, when the new south stand opened, Bramall Lane was a three-sided stadium sharing its facilities with the cricket club. After 188 years of cricket at Bramall Lane, the final Yorkshire County Cricket match took place on 7 August 1973. The £1 million cost of the new south stand almost ruined the club, especially with attendances declining as United fell to Division Four. A club proposal to turn the ground into a multi-sports and leisure facility, to be called Bramall Centre, was rejected by both the local council and the Department of Environment. Leitch's stand was demolished in 1994 and for the next two years, until its replacement was built, the ground was again three-sided. Apart from the 1883 England v

Scotland match, Bramall Lane has been the venue for four other England international games (v **Wales**, 5 February 1887, 29 March 1897; v Scotland, 4 April 1903; v **Northern Ireland**, 20 October 1930). It has also hosted several FA Cup semi-final ties. Sheffield United's first floodlit match at Bramall Lane took place on 16 March 1954 (v **Rotherham United**, friendly).

brawls *misc.* a scuffle or fight involving several players. *Keynotes* In 1950, an Argentine league encounter between **Huracan** and **Velez Sarsfield** was abandoned after all 22 players were dismissed following a mass brawl. **Pelé** was one of seven players sent off for fighting during the 1965 Brazilian Championship (**Campeonato Brasileiro**) decider between **Santos** and **Vasco de Gama**. Following a brawl during the 1969 **World Club Cup** second leg match between **AC Milan** and **Estudiantes** de la Plata, two players with the Argentine club, Poletti and Suarez, were imprisoned for 30 days on the orders of Argentina's president. During the 1995-96 season, Brazilian club side **Cruzeiro**'s match with **São Paulo** was abandoned after two players were sent off and three others departed the field, leaving the team with only six players – Brazilian rules state that a match must be abandoned if one team has fewer than six players on the pitch (**International FA board** recommends seven players). In the UK, **Arsenal** and **Manchester United** were fined £50,000 each following a mass brawl at **Old Trafford** on 20 October 1990. Several Arsenal players also received individual fines. **Rangers**' Chris Woods, Graham Roberts and Terry Butcher, with **Celtic**'s Frank McAvennie, were charged with "behaviour likely to cause a breach of the peace" following a brawl during the **Old Firm** derby in 1987. The April 1988 court case was the first time players faced criminal proceedings for their actions on the pitch. **Albania** club **Skenderbeu Korce** was docked three points in October 1998, following a brawl involving players, club officials, the referee and supporters. See also **Battle of Santiago**.

Brazil *country CONMEBOL* federal republic and largest country in South America, comprising about half of the land area and population of the continent. Independent nation since 1822, following Portuguese rule. Brazil is divided into 27 states, each with its own state football league (see below). It is the fifth largest country by area in the world. Area: 8,511,965 sq km (3,285,620 sq miles). One third of the country is covered by the Amazon rainforest. Population: 155,800,000 (1995 est.). Language: Portuguese. Capital: Brasilia. *Dossier* Football association (Confederação Brasileira de Futebol, Rio de Janeiro) founded in 1980 (previously football was administered by the Confederação Brasileira de Desportos, founded in 1914), affiliated to **FIFA** in 1923 and a founder member of **Confederación Sudamericana de Fútbol** (CONMEBOL) in 1916, president Ricardo Terra Teixeira, general secretary Marco António Teixeira. Season played in two halves: February to June and September to December (see below). National stadium: **Maracaná**,

Rio de Janeiro, capacity: 140,000 (70,000 seated). National strip: yellow shirts with green collars and cuffs, blue shorts. Website http://users.sti.com.br/lele/ (unofficial site). First international game: 20 September 1914, v **Argentina** (0–3, Buenos Aires, friendly) – though Brazil played a warm-up game against **Exeter City** on 21 July 1914 (2–0). Biggest victory: 10–1 v **Bolivia** (10 April 1949, São Paulo, **Copa America**) and 9–0 v **Colombia** (24 March 1957, Lima, Peru, Copa America). Biggest defeat: 0–6 v Uruguay (18 September 1920, Vina del Mar, Chile, Copa America). Most-capped players: Claudio Taffarel (101 appearances, 1987-98), Djalma **Santos** (98 appearances, 1952-68), Gilmar I (94 appearances, 1953-69), Roberto **Rivelino** (92 appearances, 1965-78) **Pelé** (92 appearances, 1957-71), Dunga (91 appearances, 1982-98), **Jairzinho** (87 appearances, 1963-82). Leading international goalscorers: Pelé (77 goals), **Zico** (54 goals), **Romario** (44 goals, 1987-98), **Bebeto** (38 goals, 1985-98), Jairzinho (38 goals). Other notable players: Cafu, Careca, Carlos Alberto, Clodoaldo, **Denilson**, Didi, Falcao, Artur **Friedenreich** (allegedly the world record goalscorer at club and national senior level, with 1,329 goals between 1909 and 1934), **Garrincha**, **Gerson**, **Juninho**, Roberto Carlos (see **swerve**), **Ronaldo**, Nilton **Santos**, Socrates, Tostao, Vava, Zagallo, Zito. *International tournament record* **Olympic Games** – runners-up (silver medal) 1984 (0–2 v **France**, in Pasadena, Los Angeles) and 1988 (1–2, v **Soviet Union**, in Seoul, South Korea), third/bronze medal 1996 (5–0, v **Portugal**, in Athens, Georgia, USA); **Women's World Cup/South American Women's Championship/Olympic Games** (women) – see **Brazil, women**; **World Cup** – entered first tournament in 1930, Brazil is the only nation to have played in all the finals tournaments since the competition began, 1958 (5–2 v **Sweden**, in Stockholm, Sweden), 1962 (3–1 v **Czechoslovakia**, in Santiago, Chile), 1970 (4–1 v **Italy**, in Mexico City, Mexico), 1994 (0–0, 3–2 pens., v Italy, in Los Angeles, USA), runners-up 1950 (finished second to **Uruguay** in a four-nation final round), runners-up 1998 (0–3, v **France**, at Stade de France, St-Denis, Paris), semi-final 1938 (finished third), quarter-final 1954 and 1982; **Atlantic Cup** 1956, 1960 and 1976 (all three years in which the tournament has been played); **Caribbean Nations Cup** – Brazil's Under-20 team was the guest nation at the 1999 tournament; **Confederations Cup** – 1998 (6–0, v **Australia**, in Riyadh, Saudi Arabia); **Copa America** – first entered 1916, 1919, 1922, 1949, 1989, 1997 (3-1, v Bolivia, in La Paz), runners-up 1921, 1925, 1937, 1945, 1946, 1953, 1957, 1959, 1983, 1991, 1995 (see Copa America for full results); **Futsal World Championship** – 1989, 1992, 1996; **Gold Cup** – first invited 1996 (the Gold Cup is a **CONCACAF** tournament, with guest nations), runners-up 1996 (0–2, v **Mexico**, in Los Angeles, USA), semi-final/third 1998 (0–1, v **Jamaica**, in California, USA, third/fourth play-off); **Pan-American Championship** – 1952, 1956,

runners-up 1960; **Pan-American Games** – 1963, 1979, 1987; **Rio Branco Cup** 1931, 1932, 1947, 1958; **South American Under-17 Championship** – 1988, 1991; **South American Youth Cup** (under-20) – 1974, 1983, 1985, 1988, 1991, 1992, 1995; **Under-17 World Championship** – 1997 (2–1, v Ghana, in Cairo, Egypt), runners-up 1995 (2–3, v Ghana, in Guayaquil, Ecuador), third place 1985; **World Youth Cup** (under-20) – 1983 (1–0, v Argentina, in Mexico City), 1985 (1–0, v **Spain**, in Moscow), 1993 (2–1, v **Ghana**, in Sydney, Australia), runners-up 1991 (0–0, 2–4 pens., v Portugal in Lisbon), 1995 (0–2, v Argentina, in Doha, Qatar), third place 1977,1989, quarter-final 1999. *World Cup performance* (finals and qualifiers to end of 1998 tournament) played 118, won 82, drawn 22, lost 14, scored 272 goals, conceded 93 goals; win rate: 69%; goals scored per game: 2.31. *Record against British and Irish national teams* v **England** – played 18, won eight, drawn seven, lost three; v **Northern Ireland** – played one, won one; v **Republic of Ireland** – played three, won two, lost one; v **Scotland** – played nine, won seven, drawn two; v **Wales** – played eight, won six, drawn one, lost one. *History* Along with **Germany**, Brazil is one of the two most successful nations in the history of international football, having won the World Cup four of the 15 times the tournament has been played. In 1970, it was allowed to keep the **Jules Rimet Trophy**, having won it three times. In addition to the four World Cups, Brazil has won the Copa America five times. Its **World Cup win rate** of 69% is the best in the world, while its **World Cup goal-scoring average** (2.31 goals per game) is second only to that of Germany (2.48). It has produced some of the greatest names in football, most notably Pelé, but also Garrincha, Jairzinho, Zico, and Rivelino, and more recently Bebeto and Ronaldo. Its World Cup side of 1970 (see below) is considered one of the greatest teams of all time. Brazil hosted the World Cup in 1950, the only year a final was not played, the tournament being decided by a final-round league involving four nations (Uruguay, Brazil, Sweden and Spain). Brazil lost the deciding game on 16 July at Maracaná Stadium in front of the highest recorded crowd in world football, 199,854 (although there is some dispute as to the final tally). Brazil holds the world record of 36 consecutive internationals without defeat (16 December 1993 to 21 January 1996). With Australia, it holds the world record of 14 consecutive victories (10 June 1997 to 14 December 1997). Organised football started in the late 19th century, probably introduced by British railway workers; although other accounts attribute the introduction to British and Dutch sailors. Charles Miller, a Brazilian-born, English-educated innovator, is thought to have imported the first football equipment from England, on his return to Brazil in 1894. Many of the early clubs had strong links with immigrant communities: particularly English, Portuguese, Italian and German. The first recorded match took place in São Paulo in 1894. Associaçao Atlética, of Mackenzie

College in São Paulo, is the first known club in the country, founded in 1898. The first league tournament, the Campeonato Paulista de Futebol – a championship based in **São Paulo** – was set up in 1901, followed by the **Bahia** state league (1904) and **Rio de Janeiro** league (1905). By 1920, there were 15 separate state leagues. An interstate select tournament was played from 1913, but this was not open to all state leagues. The first floodlit match took place on 23 June 1923 (AA República v SE Linhas e Cabos, 2–1): the lights provided by the headlamps of the city trams. **Vasco da Gama** installed floodlights in 1928. Professionalism was introduced in 1933. In 1950 a Rio-São Paulo championship was organised for the leading teams from the Rio de Janeiro and São Paulo state leagues. This was replaced in 1967 by the Roberto Gomez Pedroso Tournament with wider state representation. A Brazilian National Championship began in 1971, with 94 teams taking part by 1979. Clube Atlético Paulistano was the first Brazilian club to tour Europe; in 1927 it played 10 matches in France, Switzerland and Portugal, winning nine and losing one. The Brazilian Cup, the **Copa do Brasil**, started in 1959. The first football association (Confederação Brasileira de Desportos) was set up in 1914, in charge of a number of team and individual sports, athletics and swimming. Confederação Brasileira de Futebol took separate control of football in 1980. At club level, Brazil has not been dominated by one or two clubs, unlike many other countries. Four of its clubs, **Santos**, **São Paulo FC**, **Flamengo** and **Grêmio**, have won the **World Club Cup** while these, plus **Cruzeiro**, have each won the **Copa Libertadores**, South America's premier club competition. **Vasco da Gama** won the first South American club tournament, the ephemeral **Campeonato Sudamericano de Campeones**, in 1948; the tournament was played only once. Two Brazilian clubs, Cruzeiro and **Palmeiras**, competed in the first final of the **Copa Mercosur** – the South America "super league" in 1998. Brazil won the first International Blind Sports Federation Football World Championships in São Paulo in 1998 (v Argentina in the final; see **visually impaired football**). Brazil was runner-up in the first **World Championships for Players with Learning Disabilities** (0–4, v Poland, in Leicester, 1998). *World Cup final teams and scorers 1950* World Cup (runners-up – the following team played against Uruguay in the final game of the league-based finals competition): Barbosa (goalkeeper), Augusto, Juvenal, Bauer, Danilo Alvim, Bigode, Friaça (1), Zizinho, Ademir Menezes, Jair Pinto, Chico; *1958*: Gilmar (goalkeeper), Djalma Santos, Bellini, Orlando Peçanha, Nilton Santos, Zito, Didi, Garrincha, Vavá (2), Pelé (2), Zagallo (1); *1962*: Gilmar (goalkeeper), Djalma Santos, Mauro Oliveira, Zózimo, Nilton Santos, Zito (1), Didi, Garrincha, Vavá (1), Amarildo (1), Zagallo; *1970*: Félix (goalkeeper), Carlos Alberto (1), Brito, Piazza, Everaldo, Clodoaldo, Gérson (1), Jairzinho (1), Tostao, Pelé (1), Rivelino. *1994* World Cup: Taffarel (goalkeeper), Jorghino (Cafu),

Marcio Santos, Aldair, Branco, Mazinho, Mauro Silva, Dunga, Zinho (Viola), Bebeto, Romario; *1998 (runners-up):* Taffarel (goalkeeper), Roberto Carlos, Aldair, Junior Baiano, Cafu, Cesar Sampaio (Edmundo), Dunga, Leonardo (Denilson), Rivaldo, Ronaldo, Bebeto. *League system* Brazil's league system is complex, with each of the 27 states having its own league: **Acre**, **Alagoas**, **Amapa**, **Amazonas**, **Bahia**, **Ceara**, **Distrito Federal de Brasilia**, **Espirito Santo**, **Goias**, **Maranhao**, **Mato Grosso do Sul**, **Mato Grosso**, **Minas Gerais**, **Para**, **Paraiba**, **Parana**, **Pernambuco**, **Piaui**, **Rio de Janeiro**, **Rio Grande do Norte**, **Rio Grande do Sul**, **Rondonia**, **Roraima**, **Santa Catarina**, **São Paulo**, **Sergipe**, **Tocantins**. The Brazilian season is played in two parts, with state leagues played in the first half and the national league in the second (the **Campeonato Brasileiro**). The most prestigious leagues are Rio de Janeiro (with Flamengo, **Botofogo**, Vasco da Gama and **Fluminense** among the top teams), Rio Grande do Sul (Grêmio, **Internacional**), Minas Gerais (**Atlético Mineiro**, Cruzeiro) and São Paulo (Palmeiras, Santos, São Paulo FC, **Corinthians**, **Portuguesa**). Each league has its own format, but the competitions are generally played in two stages. Most leagues have a knock-out finale, involving best-placed clubs in each of the two league stages. The first stage of the Rio Grande do Sol league is contested in two groups, with a complicated formula for deciding which clubs go on to the second-stage league, followed by a championship final. Minas Gerais has a final hexagonal (six-club league), while São Paulo has a four-club final tournament, unless one club has won both stages. The Rio de Janeiro league also involves a championship final, unless one club wins both stages. The national championship has three divisions: Campeonato Brasileiro, Serie B and Serie C. The Campeonato has 24 clubs, all playing each other once. The top eight qualify for a straight knockout tournament, with the bottom two relegated to Serie B. Serie B is divided into eight regionalised groups of five clubs, playing each other twice. The top three in each group and the best fourth-placed club qualify for a 16-club knockout tournament with a four-club final group. The winners and runners-up are promoted to the Campeonato. Serie C has 16 regional groups of three, four or five clubs, each playing each other twice. The top two in each group qualify for a 32-club straight knockout tournament. The champions and runners-up are promoted to Serie B. *Record in international club tournaments:* World Club Cup – Santos (1962, 1963), São Paulo FC (1992, 1993), Flamengo (1981), Grêmio (1983), Cruzeiro (runners-up 1976, 1997); Copa Libertadores – Santos (1962, 1963, semi-final 1964, 1965), Cruzeiro (1976, 1997, runners-up 1977), Flamengo (1981), Grêmio (1983, 1995, runners-up 1984, semi-final 1996), São Paulo FC (1992, 1993, runners-up 1974, 1994), Vasco da Gama (1998), Palmeiras (runners-up 1961, 1968), Internacional (runners-up 1980, semi-final 1989), Botofogo (semi-final 1963),

Atlético Mineiro (second-round group stage 1978), Portuguesa (second-round group stage 1977); **Supacopa** Cruzeiro (1991, 1992, runners-up 1988, 1996, semi-final 1994), São Paulo FC (1993, semi-final 1994), Flamengo (runners-up 1993, 1995, semi-final 1992), Grêmio (semi-final 1989), Santos (semi-final 1996); **Copa CONMEBOL** – Atlético Mineiro (1992, 1997, runners-up 1995, semi-final 1993, 1998), Botafogo (1993), São Paulo FC (1994), Santos (1998), Corinthians (semi-final 1994), Vasco da Gama (semi-final 1996), Sampaio Corrêa (semi-final 1998); **Recopa** – São Paulo (1992, 1993), Grêmio (1995); **Copa Mercosur** – Palmeiras (1998), Cruzeiro (runners-up 1998); **Master de la Copa CONMEBOL** – São Paulo (1996), (Atlético Mineiro (runners-up 1996); **Campeonato Sudamericano de Campeones** – Vasco da Gama (1948).Other leading clubs: **Fluminense**, **EC Bahia** (see separate state league entries for leading regional clubs: note that many Brazilian clubs share a name).

Brazil, women *country/women* women's football in Brazil is administered by the Confederação Brasileira de Futebol, Rio de Janeiro. *History* Brazilian women's football increased dramatically in popularity in the 1990s: in 1991 there were only 20 clubs registered with the national association, by 1995, this had risen to more than 420 clubs. The national team finished third in the first FIFA women's tournament in Guangzhou, China, in 1988. Brazil was fourth in the first **Olympic Games** women's football tournament in 1996. Women's **beach football** has been increasingly popular since the first Copacabana Beach women's tournament in 1981. *Dossier* First international match: 1982, v **Spain**. *International tournament record* **Olympic Games** – semi-final/fourth 1996 (0–2, v **Norway**, third/fourth playoff, in Atlanta, USA); **Women's World Cup** – qualified for finals tournament in 1991 and 1995, losing in first round group stage on both occasions, also qualified 1999; **South American Women's Championship** – 1991 (league of three, in Maringa, Brazil), 1995 (league of five, in Uberlândia, Brazil), 1998 (7–1, v **Argentina**, in Mar del Plata, Argentina).

Brazilian Cup *competition* see **Copa do Brasil**.
break *n. vb.* another world for counter-attack.
Brechin City *club* Scottish league. *Dossier* Ground: **Glebe Park**, Brechin, Angus, capacity: 3,980. Strip: red shirt with white and blue stripe on shoulder, red shorts with blue waistband, red socks with white trim. Nickname: City. Record attendance: 8,122 v **Aberdeen** (28 January 1967, **Scottish FA Cup**, third round). Biggest win: 12-1 v Thornhill (28 January 1928, Scottish FA Cup, first round). Biggest defeat: 0–10 v **Airdrieonians** (12 February 1938, Division Two), **Albion Rovers** (15 January 1938, Division Two), **Cowdenbeath** (20 November 1937, Division Two). *Keynotes* Founded in 1906, Brechin is the smallest town in the UK in terms of population (7,600) to support a senior football league club. Brechin moved to Glebe Park in 1919 and joined the **Scottish League** in 1929-

30. The club won the short-lived C Division Championship in 1953-54 and won the Second Division title in both 1982-83 and 1989-90. *League record* First Division 1984-85 to 1986-87, 1990-91, 1993-94 to 1994-95; Second Division 1975-76 to 1983-84, 1987-88 to 1989-90, 1991-92 to 1992-93, 1995-96–; Division Two (B Division) 1929-30 to 1938-39, 1954-55 to 1974-75; C Division 1946-47 to 1953-54; Third Division 1997-98 to present. *Honours* C Division 1953-54; Division Two 1982-83, 1989-90. *Records* David Watt holds the record for club appearances (459, 1975-89); Ian Campbell is Brechin's record goalscorer (131, 1970-87).

Breitner, Paul *player* Defender/midfield. West **Germany** international (10 goals, 1971-82). Born 5 September 1951. *Clubs* **Bayern Munich** (twice), **Real Madrid**, Eintracht Braunschweig. *Keynotes* Breitner is one of only three players to have scored in two **World Cup** finals (1974, 1982), along with **Pelé** and **Vava**. His 25th-minute penalty against the **Netherlands** in the 1974 final brought West Germany level; his side won with a goal by Gerd **Müller** just before half-time. His 82nd-minute goal in the 1982 final was only a consolation for West Germany in its 1–3 defeat by **Italy** in Madrid. Breitner did not play in the 1978 World Cup finals, the 1976 or 1980 European Championship finals. In 1974, Breitner played in Bayern Munich's **European Cup** winning side (4-0 v **Atlético Madrid**, in Brussels) and, later that year was transferred to Real Madrid. He eventually returned to Germany and played in the 1982 European Cup final, for Bayern Munich (0–1, v **Aston Villa**, in Rotterdam). *Honours* World Cup (West Germany, 1974, runner-up 1982); **European Championship** (West Germany, 1972); European Cup (Bayern Munich, 1974); German **Bundesliga** championship (Bayern Munich, 1972, 1973, 1974, 1981); Spanish league championship (Real Madrid, 1975, 1976, 1978, 1979).

Bremner, Billy *player-manager* Midfield. **Scotland** international (54 caps, 3 goals). Born 9 December 1942. Career ca. 1959–1981. *Clubs* (player) **Leeds United**, **Hull City**, **Doncaster Rovers**; (manager) Doncaster Rovers (twice), Leeds United. *Keynotes* Bremner made 585 appearances for Leeds United after joining the club as an amateur in 1958. He remains the club's most-capped player. Bremner holds the unenviable distinction, together with Kevin **Keegan**, of being one of the first domestic players to be sent off at **Wembley**, when both were dismissed during the 1974 **Charity Shield** match between Leeds and **Liverpool**. He left Leeds in September 1976 to play for Hull City, before becoming the player-manager at **Doncaster Rovers**. He led Rovers to promotion from Division Four on two occasions (1980-81, 1983-84). In 1985, Bremner was appointed manager of Leeds United, but was sacked three years later. He later returned to the **Belle Vue Ground** for a second spell, which lasted until 1992. Bremner's autobiography, *You get nowt for being second*, was published in 1969. A jury awarded Bremner

£100,000 in libel damages in 1982 over allegations that he had tried to bribe players. Voted **Footballer of the Year** in 1970. Bremner died on 7 December 1997. Included in the **Football League Centenary 100 players**. *Honours* (player) League Championship (Leeds United 1968-69, 1973-74); Division Two (Leeds United 1963-64); **FA Cup** (Leeds United 1972); **League Cup** (Leeds United 1968); **UEFA** (Fairs) **Cup** (Leeds United 1968, 1971).

Brentford *club* English league. *Dossier* Ground: **Griffin Park**, west London, capacity: 12,763. Strip: red and white striped shirts, red shorts and red socks. Nickname: Bees. Record attendance: 39,626 v **Preston North End** (5 March 1938, **FA Cup**, sixth round). Best average attendance: 25,768 (1946-47). Biggest win: 9–0 v **Wrexham** (15 October 1963, Division Three). Biggest defeat: 0–7 v **Swansea Town** (8 November 1926, Division Three (South)), v **Walsall** (19 January 1957, Division Three (South)). *History* Founded in 1889 by members of a local rowing club. Brentford initially sported the rowing club's colours of pink, claret and light blue. The club played at several venues, including Clifden Road, Benn's Field and Shotter's Field, before settling at Griffin Park in 1904. Until 1903, the club had no manager, with team affairs handled by a committee. Brentford was a founder member of Division Three in 1920-21, having previously played in the **Southern League**. In 1932-33, the club won the Division Three (South) Championship, having been runners-up the previous season after winning all of its 21 home fixtures. Brentford won the Division Two title in 1934-35. In its first season in Division One, Brentford finished fifth – the club's highest-ever League placing. Either side of **World War II**, Brentford reached the FA Cup quarter-finals on three occasions – 1937-38 (0–3 v **Preston North End**), 1945-46 (4–9 agg. v **Charlton Athletic**) and 1948-49 (0–2 v **Leicester City**) – although the club was relegated at the end of the first full League season after the war (1946-47). By 1953-54, the club was again playing in Division Three (South). In 1961-62, Brentford was relegated to Division Four, although the club bounced back as champions the following season. Brentford's year in Division Four meant that it became the first **Football League** club to play all 91 other League sides. Brentford almost ceased to exist in January 1967, when chairman Jack Dunnett announced that **Queens Park Rangers** would take over Griffin Park; a move that was eventually defeated. The club made its first **Wembley** appearance in 1985, reaching the final of the **Freight Rover Trophy** (1–3 v **Wigan Athletic**). Brentford again reached the FA Cup quarter-final stage in 1988-89 (0–4 v **Liverpool**), beating **Manchester City** (3–1, fourth round), then of Division One, and **Blackburn Rovers** (2–0, fifth round) on the way. Brentford was a Division Three end-of-season **playoff** semi-finalist in 1991. In 1997, the club narrowly missed promotion to the First Division, losing in the playoff final (0–1 v **Crewe Alexandra**). The following season the club was relegated to the Third

Division. In June 1998, former **Crystal Palace** and **Wimbledon** chairman Ron Noades was confirmed as the club's new chairman and manager; he took the club to the Third Division championship in his first season. *League record* Division One 1935-36 to 1946-47; First Division 1992-93; Division Two 1933-34 to 1934-35, 1947-48 to 1953-54; Second Division 1993-94 to 1997-98, 1999-00; Division Three 1920-21, 1958-59 to 1961-62, 1963-64 to 1965-66, 1972-73, 1978-79 to 1991-92; Division Three (South) 1921-22 to 1932-33, 1954-55 to 1957-58; Third Division 1998-99–; Division Four 1962-63, 1966-67 to 1971-72, 1973-74 to 1977-78. *Honours* Division Two 1934-35; Division Three 1991-92; Division Three (South) 1932-33; Division Four 1962-63; Third Division 1998-2000. *Records* John Buttigieg is Brentford's most capped player (63 for **Malta**); Ken Coote holds the record for club League appearances (514, 1949-64); Jim Towers is Brentford's record League goalscorer (153, 1954-61).

Brighton & Hove Albion *club* English league. *Dossier* Ground: **Withdean Stadium**, Brighton, East Sussex, capacity: 6,000. Strip: blue and white striped shirts, blue shorts, white socks. Nickname: Seagulls. Record attendance: 36,747 v **Fulham** (**Goldstone Ground**, 27 December 1958, Division Two). Best average attendance: 25,265 (Goldstone Ground, 1977-78). Biggest win: 10–1 v Wisbech (13 November 1965, **FA Cup**, first round). Biggest defeat: 0–9 v **Middlesbrough** (23 August 1958, Division Two). *History* Brighton United was formed in 1897 and played at Sussex County Cricket Ground. The club folded in 1900 and Brighton & Hove Rangers was formed in its place, initially playing its home fixtures at Home Farm, Withdean, before moving to the County Ground under the name Brighton & Hove Albion in 1901. At the same time, another club, Hove FC, was playing at Goldstone Bottom. In February 1902, Hove invited Brighton to use their Goldstone ground because the County Ground was double booked. By that summer , the two clubs had reached a formal **groundshare** agreement and in 1904, Brighton bought the Goldstone Ground's lease and Hove moved elsewhere. The club won the **Southern League** Championship in 1910. It was as Southern League Champions that Brighton won the 1910 **Charity Shield** (1–0 v **Aston Villa**). Brighton was a founder member of Division Three in 1920-21, but it took the club 31 seasons to win promotion to a higher level, taking the Division Three (South) title in 1957-58. During the inter-war period, the club reached the FA Cup fifth round on three occasions: 1930 (0–3 **Newcastle United**), 1933 (0–1 replay v **West Ham United**) and 1946 (1–10 agg. v **Derby County**). Brighton was forced to compete in the qualifying rounds of the 1932 FA Cup competition because the club had failed to submit its application for exemption, as is required of **Football League** clubs. Brighton again reached the FA Cup fifth round in 1959-60 (1–2 v **Preston North End**) and in 1964-65, the club won the Division Four Championship. Ex-Derby County boss Brian **Clough**

was appointed manager in 1973, following the club's relegation from Division Two after only one season (1972-73). His reign was short-lived and included a first round FA Cup exit, courtesy of non-League Walton & Hersham (0–4 replay), and Brighton's heaviest home defeat (1 December 1973, 2–8 v **Bristol Rovers**, Division Three). Under the managership of former **England** international Alan **Mullery**, Brighton won promotion to the top flight for the first time in 1978-79, as well as reaching the last eight of the **League Cup** (1–3 v **Nottingham Forest**). Brighton's finest football moment came in 1983 when it reached the FA Cup final (0–4 replay v **Manchester United**). Jimmy Melia's team had gone close to winning the trophy during the first encounter, with Gordon Smith missing a golden opportunity in the closing minutes of extra time. Albion's defeat in the replay, meant that it joined a group of clubs who have appeared in the final and been relegated in the same season (others are **Leicester City** (1968-69), **Manchester City** (1925-26), **Middlesbrough** (1996-97)). After one season in Division Three in 1987-88, Brighton returned to Division Two and, in 1990-91, the club narrowly missed a return to the top flight, losing in the end-of-season **playoff** final (1–3 v **Notts County**). Thereafter Brighton's fortunes declined significantly. On the pitch, Brighton was relegated in consecutive seasons, so that by 1996-97 the club was back playing in the bottom division. The club narrowly avoided a hat-trick of consecutive demotions by drawing away at **Hereford United** on the final day of the 1996-97 season, ensuring continued League status and sending Hereford into the **Football Conference** (1–1, 3 May 1997). Off the pitch, the club was forced to vacate its Goldstone Ground in May 1997 without finding an alternative venue at which to play home fixtures the following season – several planning applications for a new stadium were refused by the local council. Eventually the club agreed a groundshare deal with **Gillingham** (**Priestfield Stadium**) for the 1997-98 season. Average attendance at League matches plummeted from 5,877 at the Goldstone during 1996-97 to 2,327 at Priestfield in 1997-98. A catalogue of events led to this state of affairs. In October 1993, the club, heavily in debt, was saved from collapse by Greg Stanley, who had been a board member since the mid-1980s. The Goldstone Ground was subsequently sold to property developers for £7.4 million on condition that the club leave in May 1996 (later extended by one year). Towards the latter end of the 1995-96 and throughout the 1996-97 campaign, Brighton fans protested against the club's board. A demonstration by supporters led to the abandonment of Brighton's home match against **York City** in May 1996; as punishment the club was instructed by the **Football Association** to play one home fixture **behind closed doors** and it would also face the possibility of losing three points if further disturbances took place. Following three pitch invasions at the Goldstone during the match against **Lincoln City** (10 October 1996) and further crowd trouble during the **Fulham**

game (26 October), the FA enforced the three-point deduction. Brighton's final match at the Goldstone took place on 26 April 1997 (1–0 v **Doncaster Rovers**). During the 1997-98 season, the club's presence in Brighton was limited to a club shop in the town centre, while Albion's official "home" – club offices, treatment room and training facilities – was at the Sussex University's Sports Pavilion and grounds. The club overcame substantial opposition from local residents to win approval (from the local council and the government) to use the town's Withdean Stadium as a temporary venue for three seasons from 1999. *League record* Division One 1979-80 to 1982-83; Division Two 1958-59 to 1961-62, 1972-73, 1977-78 to 1978-79, 1983-84 to 1986-87, 1988-89 to 1991-92; Second Division 1992-93 to 1995-96; Division Three 1920-21, 1962-63, 1965-66 to 1971-72, 1973-74 to 1976-77, 1987-88; Third Division 1996-97–; Division Three (South) 1921-22 to 1957-58; Division Four 1963-64 to 1964-65. *Honours* Division Three (South) 1957-58; Division Four 1964-65; FA Charity Shield 1910 (1–0 v Aston Villa); Southern League 1910. *Records* Steve Penney is Brighton's most capped player (17 for **Northern Ireland**); "Tug" Wilson holds the record for club League appearances (509, 1922-36); Tommy Cook is Brighton's record League goalscorer (114, 1922-29).

Brisbane Road *ground* English football ground situated in east London; home of **Leyton Orient**. *Dossier* Ground capacity: 13,842. Pitch dimensions: 100.5m x 73m. Record attendance: 34,345 v **West Ham United** (25 January 1964, **FA Cup**, fourth round). Best average: 17,254 (1956-57). *History* Originally Brisbane Road (or Osborne Road as it was initially known) was the home of Leyton FC, which first played there on 1 September 1905. It became the works ground of matchmakers Bryant & May in the 1920s, before Leyton returned in 1929 only to be evicted by the local council for rent arrears and replaced by Clapton Orient, as Leyton Orient was then known, in 1937. Orient played its first match at the ground on 28 August 1937 (v **Cardiff City**, Division Three (South)). In 1994, Orient unveiled a £9.25 million plan – Orient 2000 – to turn Brisbane Road into a 16,000 capacity all-seater stadium which would be realised only if the pitch was shifted by 90 degrees and if funding could be found. The first floodlit match at Brisbane Road took place on 10 September 1959 (v **Brighton & Hove Albion**).

Brisbane Strikers *club* Australian national league club, based in Brisbane. Ground: Perry Park. Strip: white shirts, white shorts. Australian league champions 1997.

Bristol City *club* English league. *Dossier* Ground: **Ashton Gate**, Bristol, capacity: 21,479. Strip: red shirts, white shorts and red and white socks. Nickname: Robins. Record attendance: 43,335 v **Preston North End** (16 February 1935, **FA Cup**, fifth round). Best average attendance: 26,575 (1955-56). Biggest win: 11–0 v Chichester City (5 November 1960, FA Cup, first round). Biggest defeat: 0–9 v **Coventry City** (28 April 1934,

Division Three (South)). *History* Founded in 1894 as Bristol South End, before adopting the name Bristol City and becoming a limited company in 1897. In April 1900, City merged with Bedminster, whose ground Ashton Gate became the club's home in 1904. Following the amalgamation between City and Bedminster, the new club played its home matches during the 1900-01 season alternatively at both grounds (St John's Lane and Ashton Gate). The following season, City's first in the **Football League**, the club played at St John's Lane because the League authorities allowed only one home venue to be registered. City won the Division Two Championship in 1905-06 and finished runner-up in Division One the following season – the club's highest-ever League placing. In 1909, City reached its only **FA Cup** final (0–1 v **Manchester United**). After City was relegated in 1910-11, the club did not regain a top-flight place until 1976. City was a FA Cup semi-finalist in 1919-20 (1–2 v **Huddersfield Town**). The club was relegated to Division Three (South), returned to Division Two as Champions and was relegated again in three consecutive seasons between 1921-22 and 1923-24. Further Division Three (South) Championship success was achieved in 1926-27 and 1954-55 but, until City won promotion to the top flight under the managership of Alan Dicks in 1975-76, it had spent more than 50 years alternating between Divisions Two and Three. During that period the club's only notable successes came in the **Welsh Cup**, which City won in 1934 (3–0 replay v **Tranmere Rovers**), and a **League Cup** semi-final appearance in 1971 (1–3 agg. v **Tottenham Hotspur**). In 1974, the club reached the quarter-final of the FA Cup (0–1 v **Liverpool**), having defeated **Leeds United** (1–0 replay, fifth round) on the way and, in 1978, City won the **Anglo-Scottish Cup** (3–1 agg. v **St Mirren**). The Division One tenure lasted only four seasons, with the club dropping from the top flight to Division Four in four consecutive seasons between 1979-80 and 1982-83. City, £700,000 in debt, was still paying eight of its players Division One wages despite its fall to the bottom tier. The ensuing financial crisis almost caused the demise of City, but the 1897 club was wound up and a new limited company, Bristol City FC 1982, was established. City reached the final of the **Freight Rover Trophy** in 1986 and 1987, winning the trophy on the first occasion (3–0 v **Bolton Wanderers**) and losing on the second (1–1, 4–5 pens. v **Mansfield Town**). In 1988, City narrowly missed promotion to Division Two via the end-of-season **playoffs**, losing to **Walsall** in the final (0–3 replay). City reached a second League Cup semi-final in 1989 (1–2 a.e.t. agg. v **Nottingham Forest**). The club won promotion to the First Division in 1997-98, having failed to progress the previous season after reaching the semi-final stage of the playoffs. City's players were awarded First Division runners-up medals rather than Second Division medals by mistake (following the match v **Preston North End**, 2 May 1998). The club was relegated after just one season. *League record* Division One 1906-07 to 1910-11, 1976-77 to 1979-80;

First Division 1992-93 to 1994-95, 1998-99–; Division Two 1901-02 to 1905-06, 1911-12 to 1921-22, 1923-24, 1927-28 to 1931-32, 1955-56 to 1959-60, 1965-66 to 1975-76, 1980-81, 1990-91 to 1991-92; Second Division 1995-96 to 1997-98, 1999-00; Division Three 1960-61 to 1964-65, 1981-82, 1984-85 to 1989-90; Division Three (South) 1922-23, 1924-25 to 1926-27, 1932-33 to 1954-55; Division Four 1982-83 to 1983-84. *Honours* Anglo-Scottish Cup 1978 (3–1 agg. v St Mirren); Division Two 1905-06; Division Three (South) 1922-23, 1926-27, 1954-55; Freight Rover Cup 1986 (3–0 v Bolton Wanderers); Welsh Cup 1934 (3–0 replay v Tranmere Rovers). *Records* Billy Wedlock is City's most capped player (26 for **England**); John Atyeo holds the record for club League appearances (597, 1951-66); he is also City's record League goalscorer (314, 1951-66).

Bristol Rovers *club* English league. *Dossier* Ground: **Memorial Ground**, Bristol, capacity: 9,173. Strip: blue and white quartered shirts, white shorts, blue socks. Nickname: Pirates. Record attendance: 9,173 v **Northampton Town** (10 May 1998, Second Division playoff semi-final, first leg). Best average attendance: 24,662 (**Eastville**, 1953-54). Biggest win: 7–0 v **Brighton & Hove Albion** (29 November 1952, Division Three (South)). Biggest defeat: 0–12 v **Luton Town** (13 April 1936, Division Three (South)). *History* Founded in 1883 as the Black Arabs, before becoming Eastville Rovers in 1884, Bristol Eastville Rovers in 1897 and, finally, Bristol Rovers in 1898. The club has played at numerous venues throughout its history, including **Eastville** between 1894 and 1986, followed by a groundshare with non-League Bath City at **Twerton Park**, before settling at Bristol Rugby Football Club's Memorial Ground in 1996. Rovers was a founder member of Division Three in 1920-21. By 1939, the club was £16,000 in debt and seeking **re-election**, forcing the sale of Eastville to a greyhound company (the ground had been used for greyhound racing since 1932), which would eventually cause the club to quit the ground. After more than 30 years in Division Three, the club, under the managership of Bert Tann, won the Division Three (South) Championship in 1952-53, having reached the **FA Cup** quarter-finals the previous season (1–3 replay v **Newcastle United**). Another FA Cup quarter-final was reached in 1958 (1–3 v **Fulham**). The club spent a further 11 seasons in Division Three after being relegated in 1961-62, before returning to Division Two in 1973-74. Rovers reached the quarter-final stage of the **League Cup** in 1971 (0–1 replay v **Aston Villa**) and 1972 (2–4 v **Stoke City**). Following a fire at Eastville on 16 August 1980, which destroyed the south stand, the club was forced to play its next five home fixtures at Bristol City's **Ashton Gate** – both clubs were relegated to Division Three at the end of that season. Rovers played its final match at Eastville on 26 April 1986 (v **Chesterfield**). In 1989, the club narrowly missed promotion to Division Two via the end-of-season **playoffs**, losing in the final (1–2 agg. v **Port Vale**). The same outcome occurred in 1995 when

Rovers lost in the final of the Second Division playoffs (1–2 v **Huddersfield Town**). Rovers reached the semi-final stage of the playoffs in 1998. In 1997-98, Rovers established a no-swearing terrace at the club's Memorial Ground. *League record* First Division 1992-93; Division Two 1953-54 to 1961-62, 1974-75 to 1980-81, 1990-91 to 1991-92; Second Division 1993-94–; Division Three 1920-21, 1962-63 to 1973-74, 1981-82 to 1989-90; Division Three (South) 1921-22 to 1952-53. *Honours* Division Three 1989-90; Division Three (South) 1952-53; **Division Three (South) Cup** 1935 (3–2 v **Watford**); Southern League 1905; **Watney Cup** 1972 (0–0, 7–6 pens. v **Sheffield United**). *Records* Neil Slatter is the club's most capped player (10 (22) for **Wales**); Stuart Taylor holds the record for club League appearances (546, 1966-80); Geoff Bradford is record League goalscorer (242, 1949-64).

Britannia Stadium *ground* English football ground situated in Stoke-on-Trent, Staffordshire; home of **Stoke City**. *Dossier* Ground capacity: 24,054 all seated. Pitch dimensions 106m x 66m. Record attendance: 26,664 v **Manchester City** (3 May 1998, First Division). Best average attendance: 15,105 (1997-98). *History* . Stoke moved to the Britannia Stadium at the start of the 1997-98 season, having played at the **Victoria Ground** since 1883. The club's first match at Britannia took place on 30 August (v **Swindon Town**, First Division) and attracted a crowd of 23,000. The new ground was built at a cost of £25 million (ground and infrastructure) and with funding from a number of quarters, including the club, the local council, the **Football Trust** and a government quango, the Stoke Regeneration Company. At the end of Stoke's first season there, the club was relegated to the Second Division along with final-day opponents **Manchester City** – a match which set the ground's attendance record.

British League Cup *competition* 1902 knockout tournament to raise financial assistance for the victims of the first **Ibrox Park disaster** and involving four invited clubs – **Celtic**, **Everton**, **Rangers** and **Sunderland**. *Winner* Celtic 3–2, v Rangers. The trophy was the **Glasgow Exhibition Cup** that Rangers had won previously and which the club donated to the competition.

British Virgin Islands *country* CONCACAF part of the Virgin Islands, a group of around 100 small islands, in the Leeward Islands of the West Indies. The British Virgin islands comprise Anegada, Jost van Dykes, Tortola, Virgin Gorda and another 40 or so islets. Area: 153 sq km (59 sq miles). Population: 16,750. Languages: English. Capital: Road Town (on Tortola). *Dossier* British Virgin Islands Football Association affiliated to FIFA and **Confederación Norte-Centroamericana y del Caribe de Fútbol** (CONCACAF) in 1996, president: Kenrick Grant; general secretary: John Lewis. *International tournament record* **Olympic Games** – never entered; **Women's World Cup** – never entered; **World Cup** – never entered; **Caribbean Nations Cup** – never qualified; **Gold Cup** – never qualified. *Record against British and Irish*

national teams none played. *Record in international club tournaments* never entered. Leading club: HBA Panthers (league champions 1998).

Broadwood Stadium *ground* Scottish football ground situated in Cumbernauld, Strathclyde; home of **Airdrieonians** and **Clyde**. *Dossier* Ground capacity: 6,300 all seated. Pitch dimensions: 102m x 69m. Record attendance: 24,000 v **Heart of Midlothian** (Broomfield Park, 8 March 1952, **Scottish FA Cup**). *Keynotes* Opened on 5 February 1994 (Clyde v **Hamilton Academicals**) and built at a cost of £6 million for the Cumbernauld Development Corporation and Dumbartonshire Enterprise. The ground's corner areas house various sporting activities, including a gymnastics academy. Airdrieonians moved to the stadium at the start of the 1994-95 season. Broadwood is the highest senior football ground in Scotland. It also has the largest playing surface of any senior football ground in Scotland.

Brockville Park *ground* Scottish football ground situated in Falkirk, Lothian; home of **Falkirk**. *Dossier* Ground capacity: 9,706. Pitch dimensions: 100.5m x 66m. Record attendance: 23,100 v **Celtic** (21 February 1953, **Scottish FA Cup**, third round). *Keynotes* Falkirk first played at Brockville Park in 1876, when the club was formed and when the ground was little more than a field. The club returned in 1882. Brockville's town centre location has prevented any large-scale redevelopment in line with the requirements of the **Taylor Report**. As a result, the club has been attempting to find an alternative out-of-town location for a new stadium. The first floodlit match at Brockville was in October 1953 (v **Newcastle United**, friendly).

broken collarbone *medical* fracture of the clavicle (**collarbone**) caused by a direct blow or a fall. Hospitalisation is not usually required. A broken collarbone is treated using a sling. This allows the bone to rejoin of its own accord. If the bone resets in a deformed way, surgical treatment may be required.

broken finger *medical* fracture of one of the bones of a finger. The injury can occur, for example, by one or more fingers being bent backwards into involuntary hyperextension – the bone may break if the finger is struck with sufficient force or if the player falls on the outstretched finger, subjecting the bone to the whole weight of the player. Broken fingers are common among goalkeepers and can be caused by the player attempting to stop a fiercely struck shot or falling on an outstretched hand while attempting to make a save. First aid involves **ice** and support; broken fingers should be examined in hospital.

broken neck *medical* fracture of one of the cervical vertebrae (see **spinal injury**).

broken rib *medical* fracture of one of the ribs. Footballers, particularly goalkeepers, can suffer fractured ribs from a heavy fall, or even from a heavy blow from a fiercely struck shot or kick to the chest.

broken toe *medical* fracture in one of the toe bones. Caused by a direct blow and indicated by severe swelling, pain and discomfort. All suspected fractures should be referred to hospital. Fractures of the big toe are the most serious since this toe is very important for balance and running.

Brøndby IF *club* Danish national league club based in Brøndby (a suburb of Copenhagen), founded 1964. Full name: Brøndbyernes Idraetsförening. Denmark's first full-time **professional** club. Ground: Brøndby Stadion, capacity: 22,000. Strip: yellow shirts, blue shorts. Danish Cup 1989, 1994, 1998; Danish league champions 1985, 1988, 1990, 1991, 1996, 1997, 1998; **UEFA Cup** semi-final 1991. Notable former players: Peter **Schmeichel**, Brian **Laudrup**.

brothers *record* there have been a number of note-worthy brothers in World football history. A selection is presented here. **1. World Cup** match: two brothers, Fernando and Manuel Rosas, played for **Mexico** in the first World Cup match (13 July 1930, Mexico, v **France**, 1–4, Pocitos Stadium, Montevideo, Uruguay). **2.** World Cup winners: West **Germany's** Fritz and Otmar **Walter** were the first brothers to play in a World Cup winning team (1954, 3–2, v **Hungary** in Berne, Switzerland). Bobby and Jack **Charlton** of **England** repeated the feat in 1966 (4–2, v West Germany, at **Wembley**). **3.** World Cup runners-up: Rene and Willy Van der Kerkhof played for the **Netherlands** in the 1978 World Cup final (1–3, v **Argentina**, in Buenos Aires). **4.** World Cup goalkeepers: brothers Viktor and Vyacheslav Chanov were both goalkeepers in the **Soviet Union**'s World Cup squad in 1982. **5.** World Cup coaches: Zeze Moreira managed the Brazilian World Cup team in 1954, and his brother Aimore Moreira was coach of the 1962 squad. **6.** England inter-nationals (dates show first and last appearance of either brother, the list includes all brothers who have played for England, irrespective of whether they appeared in the same team): Arthur, Ernest and Charlie Bambridge (1876-87); Charles and William Clegg (1872-79); Herbert and William Rawson (1875-77); Frank and Hubert Heron (1873-78); Alfred and Edward Lyttelton (1877-78); Arthur and Harry Cursham (1876-84); Arthur and Percy Walters (1885-90); Alf and Charlie Dobson (1882-86); Alf and Charlie Shelton (1888-92); Arthur and Robert Topham (1893-94); Charlie and Tom Perry (1890-98); Frank and Fred Forman (1898-1903); Charles and Geoffrey Wilson (1884-1900); Bertie and Rex Corbett (1901-03); Frank and Reg Osborne (1922-27); Clem and George Stephenson (1924-31); Jack and Sep Smith (1931-35); Bobby and Jack Charlton (1958-70 – the brothers played 28 times together); Gary and Philip Neville (1995-). **7. FA Cup** winners: only four sets of brothers have won FA Cup winners medals in the same team at **Wembley** stadium: Leslie and Denis **Compton** (of **Arsenal** v **Liverpool**, 1950), George and Ted Robledo (of **Newcastle United** v Arsenal, 1952), Brian and Jimmy Greenhoff (of **Manchester United** v Liverpool 1977), and Gary and Philip Neville (of Manchester United v Liverpool 1996). In 1876, Frank and Hubert Heron played for **Wanderers** in its 3–0 FA Cup final defeat of Old Etonians, which included the

brothers Alfred and Edward Lyttelton. This is the only time that two sets of brothers have played in the same FA Cup Final. **8. Football League**: three brothers appeared for **Southampton** on 22 October 1988: Danny, Ray and Rod Wallace (Division One). Eddie and Frank **Gray** both played for **Leeds United** and **Scotland**, although the two never appeared in the same international. **9. Scottish FA Cup**: two brothers hold the highest and second-highest goal tally record for a Scottish Cup match in the 20th century: Gerry Baker scored 10 for **St Miren** in its first-round defeat of Glasgow University on 30 January 1960 (15–0); his brother Joe scored nine for **Hibernian** the following season against Peebles Rovers in the second round (15–1). **10. Referees**: brothers Graham and David Laws, from Whitley Bay, became the first siblings on the Football League national list of referees in 1996-97.

Brown, Harry *official* the first public relations officer of the **Football League** and first editor of the former *Football League Review*.

Broxburn United *club* former Scottish league. *Dossier* Ground: Sports Park, Broxburn, Lothian. *Keynotes* Broxburn joined Division Two in 1921-22, fin-ishing sixth that season – the club's highest League position. The club was a **Scottish FA Cup** quarter-finalist in 1925 (1–0 v **Dundee**). *League record* Division Two 1921-22 to 1925-26.

Brugge *club* see **Club Brugge KV**.

bruise *medical* see **contusion**.

bruised toe nail *medical* common injury to the toe caused either by a direct blow – such as by being stamped on – or by the player's toe being squashed against his or her boot. The injury results in a **haematoma** or bruise developing under the toenail; it can be quite painful owing to the build-up of pressure under the nail.

Brunei *country AFC* sultanate on northwest coast of Borneo and bordered by Sarawak. British protectorate from 1888, self-governing since 1971. Two separate areas on the South China Sea. Area: 5,765 sq km (2,225 sq miles). Tropical climate. Population: 276,000 (1993 est.). Language: Malay, English and Chinese. Capital: Bandar Seri Begawan. *Dossier* The Football Association of Brunei Darussalam (Bandar Seri Begawan) formed in 1959 affiliated to **FIFA** in 1969 and **Asian Confederation** (AFC) in 1970, president Pehin Dato Hj Hussain Yussoff, general secretary Pengiran Haji Matusin Matasan. Season played from September to March. National stadium: Hassanal Bolkiah, Bandar Seri Begawan, capacity: 40,000. National strip: yellow shirts, black shorts. Notable international players: Liew Chuan Fue (national team captain). *International tournament record* **Women's World Cup** – never entered; **World Cup** – entered 1986 (eliminated in first qualifying round); **Asean Tiger Cup** – played in first tournament in 1996 (fourth in its five-nation first round group); **Asian Cup of Nations** – entered 1976 (eliminated in first qualifying round). *Record against British and Irish national teams* none played. *League system* There is no national league. Clubs play in four regional leagues (each with two divisions): Brunei/Muara, Belait, Tutong and Temburong. The regional winners playoff for the national championship. *Record in international club tournaments* **Asian Champion Teams Cup** – no Brunei club has reached the finals tournament. Leading club sides: Kota Rangers, Belait, Daerah Brunei, Angkata Persenjata, Muara FC. Brunei plays in the Malaysian M League.

Brunton Park   *ground*   English football ground situated in Carlisle, Cumbria; home of **Carlisle United**. *Dossier* Ground capacity: 16,651. Pitch dimensions: 107m x 66m. Record attendance: 27,500 v **Birmingham City** (5 January 1957, **FA Cup**, third round), v **Middlesbrough** (7 February 1970, FA Cup, fifth round). Best average attendance: 14,530 (1974-75). *History* Carlisle United played its first match at Brunton Park on 2 September 1909 (**Newcastle United** reserves, friendly), having raised around £1,000 to develop the site. The club bought the ground for £2,000 when it was elected to the **Football League** in 1928-29. Brunton Park became one of the first grounds outside the South East to install **floodlights**, staging its first floodlit game on 24 February 1953 (v **Blackburn Rovers,** friendly). A fire destroyed the ground's main stand in 1953, forcing the club to borrow a kit from **Newcastle United** and the players to change in the nearby swimming baths. Brunton Park was flooded in October 1967 when the nearby River Petteril broke its banks, enabling the ground's pronounced slope to be estimated at around 2.5 metres because one goal was almost entirely submerged whereas the goal at the other end of the pitch was only partially under water.

BSC Young Boys Bern (Berner Sport Club) *club* Swiss national league club based in the capital Berne, founded 1898. Ground: **Wankdorf Stadium** (the national stadium), capacity: 37,551. Strip: yellow shirts, yellow shorts. **European Cup** semi-final 1959; BSC Young Boys **European Cup-winners Cup** quarter-final 1988; Swiss Cup 1930, 1945, 1953, 1958, 1977, 1987; Swiss national champions 1903, 1909, 1910, 1911, 1920, 1929 (three regional leagues operated until 1933, with the national championship decided by an inter-league playoff), 1957, 1958, 1959, 1960, 1986.

BTM Antananarivo (Bankin NY Tantsaha Mpamokatra) *club* Madagascar national league club, based in Antananarivo (the capital city). Ground: Mahamasina, capacity: 25,000. **African Cup of Champion Clubs**, second round 1994; Madagascar Cup 1991; Madagascar league champions 1986 and 1993.

Buchan, Charles *player* Striker. **England** international (6 caps). Born 22 September 1891. Career ca. 1908–1928. *Clubs* Leyton, **Sunderland**, **Arsenal**. *Keynotes* Buchan joined Arsenal in July 1925 for a fee of £2,000 plus £100 for every goal he scored for the club during his first Highbury season (he scored 22). Buchan had previously been registered as an amateur at Woolwich Arsenal in December 1908. At Sunderland Buchan was a member of the famed triangle along with

Frank Cuggy and Jackie Mordue, and he scored 27 goals in the club's 1912-13 Championship-winning season. In 1922-23, he was the top scorer in Division One with 30 goals. Buchan is credited with making the roving centre-half into a permanent defender in the aftermath of the change to the **offside** law in 1925-26. Buchan retired from playing when he was 36 years old, having made 506 **Football League** and **Southern League** appearances and having scored 258 goals for Sunderland and Arsenal, and immediately moved into journalism, becoming football correspondent for the *Daily News* (later the *News Chronicle*), a post he held until 1956. Buchan had earlier come up with the idea for a monthly football magazine and Charles Buchan's **Football Monthly** was first published in 1951. Included in the **Football League Centenary 100 players**. *Honours* League Championship (Sunderland 1912-13).

Buducnost Podgorica   *club*   Yugoslavian and **for-mer-Yugoslavia** national league club based in the Montenegron capital Podgorica, founded 1925 (known as FK Buducnost Titograd from 1946-92) . The leading club from the republic of Montenegro. Ground: Pod Goricom, capacity: 15,000. Strip: blue and white striped shirts, blue shorts. Former-Yugoslavian Cup runners-up 1965, 1977.

Buenos Aires Club   *club*   former Argentinean club from Buenos Aires, the first known club in the country, founded in 1865 (no longer exists).

Buffles de Borgou   *club*   Benin national league club based in Parakou. Ground: Borgou, capacity: 8,000. Strip: white shirts, black shorts. Benin Cup 1979, 1982; Benin league champions 1980, 1992.

Bulawayo Highlanders   *club*   Zimbabwe national league club based in Bulawayo. Ground: Barbour Fields (shared with **Zimbabwe Saints**), capacity: 10,000. Strip: black shirts, white shorts. Zimbabwe Cup 1986, 1990; Zimbabwe league champions 1974, 1990, 1993. Former notable players: Peter Ndlovu, Bruce **Grobbelaar**.

Bulgaria   *country*   UEFA republic in Southeast Europe in the Balkan peninsula and the Black Sea. Former communist country and former close ally of the former-**Soviet Union**. Area: 110,910 sq km (42,810 sq miles). Population: 8,463,000 (1995 est.). Language: Bulgarian and minority Turkish. Capital: Sofia. *Dossier* Football association (Bulgarski Futbolen Soius, Sofia) formed in 1923, affiliated to **FIFA** in 1924 and founder member of the **Union of European Football Associations** (UEFA) in 1954, president Ivan Slavkoc, general secretary Ivan Vutzov. Season played from August to December and February to June, with a **winter break**. National stadium: Vasilij Levski, capacity: 70,000. National strip: white shirts, green shorts. Website: http://www.online.bg/sport/football/bfu e/bfs e.htm (official site). First international game: 21 May 1924, v **Austria** (0–6, Vienna, friendly). Biggest victory: 7–0 v **Norway** (3 November 1937, Sofia, **World Cup** qualifier) and 7–0 v **Malta** (14 October 1982, Sofia, friendly). Biggest defeat: 0–13 v **Spain** (21 May 1933, Madrid, friendly). Most capped players: Borislav **Mikhailov** (102 appearances, 1983–), Dimitar Penev (90 appearances, 1964–1977), Hristo **Bonev** (87 appearances, 1967–1979). Leading goalscorers: Hristo Bonev (45 goals), Hristo **Stoichkov** (37, 1987–), Emil **Kostadinov** (26 goals, 1988-), Lubomir Angelov (25 goals, 1931–1940), Ivan **Kolev** (25 goals, 1950–1963). Other notable international players: Yordan Letchkov. *International tournament record* **Olympic Games** – runner-up/silver medal 1968 (1–4 v **Hungary**, Mexico City – Bulgaria won its quarter-final v **Israel** on the **toss of a coin** after a 1–1 draw), third place/bronze medal 1960 (3–0 v **India**, Melbourne, Australia, third/fourth playoff); **Women's World Cup** – never qualified; **World Cup** – first entered 1934, semi-final/fourth 1994 (1–2 v **Italy**, Giants Stadium, New York, semi-final; 0–4 v **Sweden**, Rose Bowl, Los Angeles, third/fourth playoff), also qualified for finals tournament 1962, 1966, 1970, 1974, 1986, 1998; **Balkan Cup** – 1932, 1934-35, 1973-76; **European Championship** – entered first tournament in 1960, quarter-final 1968, also qualified for finals tournament 1996; **European Championship for Women** – first entered 1987-89, never beyond first-round group stage; **European Junior Championship** (under-18) 1959, 1969, 1974; **Under-17 World Championship** – never qualified; **World Youth Cup** (under-20) – quarter-final 1985, 1987. *World Cup performance* (finals and qualifiers to end of 1998 tournament) played 105, won 44, drawn 20, lost 41, scored 155 goals, conceded 157 goals; win rate: 42%; goals scored per game: 1.48. *Record against British and Irish national teams* v **England** played seven, drawn three, lost four; v **Northern Ireland** played four, won one, drawn one, lost two; v **Republic of Ireland** played six, won three, drawn one, lost two; v **Scotland** played five, drawn three, lost two; v **Wales** played four, won three, lost one. *History* Organised football is thought to have started as a schoolboy sport in the late 19th century. **Slavia Sofia** was formed in 1913, with **Levski Sofia** formed one year later. The Bulgarian Football Federation was formed in 1923 as part of the National Sports Federation. Two regional leagues – in Sofia (10 clubs) and Varna – were formed in 1921. Four other regional leagues were formed and, in 1924, a national tournament involved the winners of the six regional leagues. The national tournament continued until 1937 when a national league of 10 clubs was formed. The Bulgarian Cup (now known as the Profi-Liga Kupa – Bulgarian League Cup) started in 1938 (known as the Soviet Army Cup from 1946-1991). The league was suspended in 1940 because of **World War II**, restarted in 1945 and reconstituted in 1948 with a **pyramid system** of leagues that included all clubs in the country, including junior sides. Domestic football was dominated in the 1950s by the army club **CSKA Sofia**. A second cup competition (Kupa Na Bulgariya – the Republic Cup) began in 1981. Bulgaria's fourth place in the 1994 World

Cup was its best international achievement. Yordan Letchkov scored the winning goal in a famous victory over World champions **Germany** in the quarter-final (9 July 1994, Giants Stadium, New York, USA). Prior to the 1994 finals, Bulgaria had appeared in five finals tournaments without a single victory in 16 games. Bulgaria has a silver medal (1968) and bronze medal (1960) in the Olympic Games. In September 1998, the Bulgarian Government controversially took the responsibility of running the national team away from the Bulgarian football association and placed it in the hands of the Bulgarian Professional Football League. A possible suspension from international football by FIFA was averted after the Bulgarian Sports Ministry reversed its decision; Bulgaria's European Championship qualifying match against England had been under threat. *League system* There are two national divisions: A Grupa (16 clubs) and B Grupa (20 clubs), with three points awarded for a win and one for a draw; goal difference separates clubs level on points. There is direct promotion and relegation of the top three of the B Grupa and bottom three of the A Grupa. There are four regional sections in the V Grupa, with each regional winner promoted to the B Grupa at the expense of the bottom four B clubs. *Record in international club tournaments* **European Cup** – CSKA **Sofia** (semi-final 1967, 1982); **European Cup-winners Cup** – **Slavia Sofia** (semi-final 1967), CSKA Sofia (semi-final 1989); **UEFA Cup** – **Levski Sofia** (quarter-final 1976), **Lokomotiv Sofia** (quarter-final 1980). Other leading clubs: **Botev Plovdiv, Etar Veliko Tarnovo, Liteks Lovech**.

Bundesliga *competition (German)* The German national league, founded in West **Germany** in 1963. West Germany was, with the exception of the now-independent former-Soviet republics, the last European country to have a full national league: regional leagues had operated from 1898 to 1963 with an end-of-season playoff to decide the national champions. **Cologne** (1.FC) was the first Bundesliga winner in 1964. Only two places in the Bundesliga first division were awarded to East German clubs after reunification in 1990: **Hansa Rostock** and **Dynamo Dresden**. The Bundesliga has two divisions of 18 clubs. The bottom three clubs in the first division are automatically relegated and replaced by the top three in the second division. The bottom four clubs are relegated to the German regional leagues. Three points are awarded for a victory, with one for a draw: final positions for clubs level on points are determined by **goal difference**.

bung *n. informal* an unauhorised payment or bribe. See **illegal payments**.

Burkina (Burkina Faso) *country CAF* landlocked republic in West Africa on the southern edge of the Sahara, bordered by **Niger, Mali, Ivory Coast, Ghana, Togo** and **Benin**. Formerly Upper Volta. One of the poorest countries in the world. Independence from **France** in 1960. Burkina Faso means the "land of upright men". Area: 274,122 sq km (105,811 sq miles). Population: 10,000,000 (1994 est.). Languages: Mossi

(Moré), Dyula and about 50 local languages. Capital: Ouagadougou. *Dossier* Football association (Fédération Burkinabe de Foot-Ball, Ouagadougou) formed in 1960, affiliated to **FIFA** in 1964 and **Confédération Africaine de Football** (CAF) in 1964, member of the West African Football Union, president Nabéré Traore, general secretary Robert Korahire. Season played from October to July. National stadium: Stade du 4 Aout, Ouagadougou, capacity: 40,000. National strip: red shirts, green shorts with a yellow star. Nickname of national team: les Etalions (the stallions). First international game 1960 v **Madagascar** (1–6, in Madagascar, friendly). Biggest victory: 3–0 v Ghana (25 May 1988, Ouagadougou, friendly). Biggest defeat: 0–7 v **Algeria** (30 August 1981, in Algeria, **African Cup of Nations** qualifier). Notable international players: Mamadou **Zongo**. *International tournament record* **Olympic Games** – entered 1976 and 1996 (never qualified for finals tournament); **Women's World Cup** – never entered; **World Cup** – first entered 1978, qualified for group stage in 1998 (after preliminary round victory v **Mauritania**, 2–0 agg.; lost all six of its group matches); **African Cup of Nations** – first entered 1968, semi-final/fourth 1998 (4–4, lost on penalties, v **Congo**, in Ouagadougou, third/fourth playoff; 0–2, v **Egypt**, Ouagadougou, semi-final), qualified for finals tournament 1978 (first round), hosts 1998; **CSSA Zone 3 Tournament** (West African Championship) third place 1994; **Under-17 World Championship** – never qualified; **World Youth Cup** (under-20) – never qualified. *Record against British and Irish national teams* none played. *History* Burkina Faso hosted the 1998 African Cup of Nations and surprised many people by reaching the semi-final and finishing fourth in only its second finals appearance. In the third/fourth playoff against Congo, Burkina had been winning 4–1 with only four minutes left: Congo scored three goals to tie the score at 4–4 and force a penalty shoot-out which went in favour of Congo. Burkino Faso took part in the first **World Championships for Players with Learning Disabilities**, in Leicester in 1998. *Record in international club tournaments* **African Champion Clubs Cup** – Silures (quarter-final 1978); **African Cup-winners Cup** – Rail Club Nationaux Kadiogo (semi-final 1978, 1980); **West African Football Union Cup** – USFA (third 1998).Other leading clubs: **ASFA Yennenga**, **Etoile Filante**, Racing (of Bobo Dioulasso; league champions 1987, 1996).

Burma *country* former name of **Myanmar**.

Burnden Leisure plc *n.* publicly-quoted business which owns **Bolton Wanderers**. Burnden Leisure became a fully listed company on the London Stock Exchange in April 1997 (floatation price = 52p). Burnden, which also includes the manufacture of spirit measures and other bar catering equipment within its portfolio of companies, had a market capitalisation – the market value of the company's issued share capital (eg, the quoted price of its shares multiplied by the number of shares outstanding) – of £63.4 million on floatation.

Burnden Park *ground* English football ground situated in Bolton, Greater Manchester; former home of **Bolton Wanderers**. *Dossier* Capacity: 20,500 (1997). Pitch dimensions: 103m x 69m. Record attendance: 69,912 v **Manchester City** (18 February 1933, FA Cup fifth round). Best average attendance: 35,832 (1951-52). *History* Burnden Park was built on the site of a former gas works. Wanderers agreed a 14-year lease with Bolton Corporation for the site in 1894 and eventually bought the ground's freehold for just over £8,000 in 1914. Initially, the ground was developed into a multi-purpose sports stadium. It opened on 17 August 1895, staging the town's annual Athletics Festival. Bolton's first match at Burnden Park took place on 11 September 1895 (v **Preston North End**, friendly). The club's first league fixture at the ground occurred three days later and was preceded by a cycle race. In 1899, Burnden Park staged an FA Cup semi-final (three other semi-finals were staged at the ground over the years). Three years later (1901) it was the venue for the **FA Cup** final replay (**Sheffield United** v **Tottenham Hotspur**), but the match attracted the lowest recorded final attendance (officially 20,740). During World War II, Burnden Park's stands were used to store supplies by the Ministry of Supply. In 1946, the ground was the scene of the first major football stadium disaster in the England; 33 spectators were killed and more than 400 injured when barriers collapsed during Bolton's FA Cup-tie against **Stoke City** (**Burnden Park disaster**). The ground's Railway End features in the 1954 film, *Love Match*. Burnden Park staged its first floodlit match on 10 October 1957 (v **Heart of Midlothian**, friendly). During its 102-year existence as a major stadium, Burnden Park was sometimes used to stage Rugby League Challenge Cup semi-finals and Regal Trophy finals. Bolton's final league fixture at Burnden Park took place on 25 April 1997 (v **Charlton Athletic**, First Division) and was watched by a crowd of 22,024. The club has retained the old centre-spot from Burnden Park at its new ground, **Reebok Stadium**.

Burnden Park disaster *disaster* stadium disaster at **Bolton Wanderers'** **Burnden Park** stadium, 9 March 1946. Thirty-three people died and 400 were injured at an FA Cup sixth round, second-leg match between Bolton and **Stoke City** when overcrowding in a section of a terrace caused a number of crush barriers to collapse. Around 65,000 people were inside the ground, with another 20,000 locked outside. Under the recommendation of the police, the match was restarted – in order to avoid panic. It finished goalless. A Home Office inquiry followed, which recommended more rigorous inspection and licensing of grounds.

Burnley *club* English league. *Dossier* Ground: **Turf Moor**, Burnley, Lancashire. Strip: claret shirts with sky blue sleeves, white shorts and white socks. Nickname: the Clarets. Ground capacity: 22,546. Record attendance: 54,775 v **Huddersfield Town** (23 February 1924, **FA Cup**, third round). Best average attendance: 33,621 (1947-48). Biggest win: 9–0 v **Darwen** (9

January 1892, Division One), v **Crystal Palace** (10 February 1909, FA Cup, second round replay). Biggest defeat: 0–10 v **Aston Villa** (29 August 1925, Division One), v **Sheffield United** (19 January 1929, Division One). *History* Formed as a **rugby** club called Burnley Rovers in 1881, the club switched to association football in May 1882 and dropped the "Rovers" from its name. Burnley played its first match at Turf Moor on 17 February 1883 (only two other **Football League** clubs (**Preston North End** and **Stoke City**) have played continuously at their present grounds longer than Burnley). The club was a founder member of the Football League in 1888. Relegation in 1896-97, via the **test matches** which between 1892-93 and 1897-98 were used to determine promotion and relegation between the two divisions, was followed by an immediate return as Division Two Champions the following season. In 1914, Burnley won the FA Cup (1–0 v **Liverpool**), having reached the semi-final stage the previous season (2–3 replay v **Sunderland**), a year in which the club also won promotion back to the top flight after a 13-season absence. Under the managership of John Haworth and with a team captained by England international Tommy Boyle, the club won the League Championship in 1920-21. During its Championship-winning season the club went 30 Division One matches without defeat (6 September 1920 to 25 March 1921), a run which included 21 victories (a Division One record until surpassed by **Leeds United** in 1969-70 with a 34-match unbeaten run). The club reached a further two FA Cup semi-finals, in 1924 (0–3 v **Aston Villa**) and 1935 (0–3 v **Sheffield Wednesday**), before again reaching the final in 1947 (0–1 a.e.t. v **Charlton Athletic**). That season the club also won promotion. Burnley won the League title for a second time in 1959-60 and, in 1961-62, the club finished runners-up and reached its third FA Cup final (1–3 v **Tottenham Hotspur**). The previous season, Burnley was a semi-finalist in the inaugural **League Cup** competition, losing in a playoff at **Old Trafford** (1–2 v Aston Villa), and the club reached the quarter-final stage of the **European Cup** (4–5 agg., v **Hamburg (SV)**). In 1966-67, it got to the quarter-finals of the **UEFA** (Fairs) **Cup** (2–3 agg. v **Eintracht Frankfurt**). Between 1947-48 and 1965-66, Burnley finished in the top half of Division One in all but three seasons; however, by 1971-72, the club was again playing in Division Two, returning to the top flight as Champions for a two-season spell in 1972-73, before entering a period which culminated in relegation to Division Three for the first time in the club's history in 1979-80. Burnley's short return to Division One also coincided in 1974 with a further FA Cup semi-final appearance (0–2 v **Newcastle United**). In 1979, the club won the **Anglo-Scottish Cup** (4–1 agg. v **Oldham Athletic**). Burnley won the Division Three title in 1981-82, was relegated the following season, although the club did reach the semi-final of the League Cup (1–3 agg. v Liverpool) that year. By 1985-86, the club was playing in the bottom divi-

sion, requiring victory in the last game of the 1986-87 season to avoid the possibility of losing its League status. Burnley made its first **Wembley** appearance for 26 years in 1988 when the club reached the final of the **Sherpa Van Trophy** (0–2 v **Wolverhampton Wanderers**). Having failed to gain promotion to Division Three via the end-of-season **playoffs** in 1990-91, the club won the Division Four title the following season. In 1993-94, Burnley was successful at the play-off stage (2–1 v **Stockport County**), although the club's stay in the new First Division lasted only one season. Ex-**England** international Chris Waddle was appointed player-manager in May 1997, but he resigned the following May after the club narrowly avoided relegation. *League record* Division One (including Football League) 1888-89 to 1896-97, 1898-99 to 1899-00, 1913-14 to 1929-30, 1947-48 to 1970-71, 1973-74 to 1975-76; First Division 1994-95; Division Two 1897-98, 1900-01 to 1912-13, 1930-31 to 1946-47, 1971-72 to 1972-73, 1976-77 to 1979-80, 1982-83; Second Division 1992-93 to 1993-94, 1995-96–; Division Three 1980-81 to 1981-82, 1983-84 to 1984-85; Division Four 1985-86 to 1991-92. *Honours* Anglo-Scottish Cup 1979 (4–1 agg. v Oldham Athletic); Division Two 1897-88, 1972-73; Division Three 1981-82; Division Four 1991-92; **FA Charity Shield** 1960 (2–2 v **Wolverhampton Wanderers** (each club held the trophy for six months)); FA Cup 1914 (1–0 v Liverpool); League 1920-21, 1959-60. *Records* Jimmy McIlroy is Burnley's most capped player (51 (55) for **Northern Ireland**); Jerry Dawson holds the record for club League appearances (522, 1907-28); George Beel is the record League goalscorer (178, 1923-32).

Bursaspor Kolübü *club* Turkish national league club based in Bursa, founded 1963. Ground: Atatürk, capacity: 24,000. Strip: green and white striped shirts, white shorts. **European Cup-winners Cup** quarter-final 1975; Turkish Cup 1986.

bursitis *medical* swelling of a bursa (hollow components of fibrous tissue containing fluid to aid the free movement of a **joint** and acting as cushions between **bones** and their **tendons**). Bursitis in the knee joint can be caused if a player receives a direct injury or repeated irritation at the joint.

Burton Swifts/Burton United *club* former English league. *Dossier* Ground: Peel Croft, Burton, West Midlands. Record League attendance: 10,000 (as Burton United). *Keynotes* Swifts was a founder member of Division Two in 1892-93. Prior to the start of the 1901-02 season, the club merged with **Burton Wanderers** to form Burton United, taking the Swifts' place in the **Football League**. The club was an **FA Cup** quarter-finalist in 1878-79 (1–8 v Clapham Rovers) and a semi-finalist in 1885-86 (1–2 v **Blackburn Rovers**). Burton Swifts' highest League position was sixth in Division Two, which the club achieved in both 1892-93 and 1893-94. United's highest League position was 10th in Division Two (1901-02). The club failed to get **re-elected** in 1906-07 and joined the Birmingham and

District League before folding in 1909-10. *League record* Division Two 1892-93 to 1906-07.

Burton Wanderers *club* former English league. *Dossier* Ground: Derby Turn, Burton, West Midlands. Record League attendance: 5,000. *Keynotes* The club was elected to Divison Two in 1894-95, finishing seventh in the first season. Before the start of the 1901-02 season, Wanderers merged with **Burton Swifts** to form Burton United. At the time of the amalgamation, Wanderers claimed to be the fourth oldest club in England. Wanderers highest League position was fourth in Division Two, which the club achieved in 1895-96. *League record* Division Two 1894-95 to 1896-97.

Burundi *country CAF* republic in east central Africa, on Lake Tanganyika, bordered by Rwanda, Zaire, Tanzania. Separated from Ruanda-Urundi in 1962. Civil war and poverty since early 1990s. Area: 27,835 sq km (10,745 sq miles). Population: 5,360,000 (1996 est.). Languages Kirundi, French and Kiswahili. Capital: Bujumbura. *Dossier* Football association (Fédération de Football du Burundi, Bujumbura) formed in 1948, affiliated to **FIFA** in 1972 and **Confédération Africaine de Football** (CAF) in 1972, member of the **Confederation of East and Central African Football Associations**, president Daniel Kigali, general secretary Dr André Gakwavu. Season played from October to July. National stadium: Stade Prince Louis Rwigasore, Bujumbura, capacity: 20,000. National strip: red shirts, white shorts. First international game: 5 December 1971 v **Tanzania** (1–4, Dar Es Salaam, Tanzania, friendly). Biggest victory: 6–2 v **Rwanda** (29 June 1976, tournament in Gabon, Central African Games). Biggest defeat: 0–5 v **Cameroon** (10 July 1976, in Gabon, Central African Games). *International tournament record* **Olympic Games** – first entered 1996, never qualified for finals tournament; **Women's World Cup** – never entered; **World Cup** – first entered 1994, never progressed beyond first qualifying round; **African Cup of Nations** – first entered 1976, never qualified for finals tournament; **African Under-20 Youth Championship** – runners-up 1995 (0–4 v Cameroon in final, tournament in Nigeria); **Under-17 World Championship** – never qualified; **World Youth Cup (under-20)** – qualified for finals tournament 1995. *Record against British and Irish national teams* none played. *History* Burundi league championship started in 1971-72. Cup first played in 1991. Burundi has entered the World Cup in 1994 and 1998. In the 1998 tournament, it won its first round against Sierra Leona (2–0 agg.), but then withdrew from the tournament; its second-round group place was given to Sierra Leone. *Record in international club tournaments* **African Cup of Champion Clubs** – Vital'O Sports Club (quarter-final 1985), **International Stars** (quarter-final 1986); **African Cup-winners Cup** – Inter Star (semi-final 1991); East and Central African Club Championship – Vital'O Sports Club (fourth 1999). Other leading clubs: **Fantastique Express**, **Prince Louis**, Maniema (league champions 1997).

Bury *club* English league. *Dossier* Ground: **Gigg Lane**, Bury, Greater Manchester, capacity: 11,841. Strip: white shirts, blue shorts and blue socks. Nickname: Shakers. Record attendance: 35,000 v **Bolton Wanderers** (9 January 1960, **FA Cup**, third round). Best average attendance: 19,500 (1924-25). Biggest win: 12–1 v **Stockton** (2 February 1897, FA Cup, first round replay). Biggest defeat: 0–10 v **Blackburn Rovers** (1 October 1887, FA Cup Preliminary round), v **West Ham United** (25 October 1983, **League Cup**, second round 2nd leg). *History* Bury was founded in April 1885 by, in the main, members of two other clubs in the town, Bury Wesleyans and Bury Unitarians. The club has always played at Gigg Lane and it joined the **Football League** in 1894, finishing top of Division Two in its first season; it was promoted to the top-flight via the **test matches** that between 1892-93 and 1897-98 determined promotion and relegation. The club enjoyed its most successful period at the turn of the century. In 1900, Bury won the FA Cup (4–0 v **Southampton**), the following season the club finished fifth in Division One – its highest-ever position – and in 1903, it won the FA Cup for the second time. Bury's 6–0 victory over **Derby County** in the 1903 FA Cup final is the record winning margin. Following relegation from Division One in 1911-12, Bury, despite a brief return to the top flight in the mid-1920s, has struggled in the lower divisions. Between 1990 and 1995, Bury reached the end-of-season Division Three (Second Division) **playoffs** on four occasions: the club was a losing semi-finalist in 1990, 1991, 1993 and a losing finalist in 1995 (0–2 **Chesterfield**). In 1996-97, the club won the Second Division Championship, so returning to the First Division – although no longer the top flight – after a 68-year absence. *League record* Division One 1895-96 to 1911-12, 1924-25 to 1928-29; First Division 1997-96 to 1998-99; Division Two 1894-95, 1912-13 to 1923-24, 1929-30 to 1956-57, 1961-62 to 1966-67, 1968-69; Second Division 1996-97, 1999-00; Third Division 1992-93 to 1995-96; Division Three 1958-59 to 1960-61, 1967-68, 1969-70 to 1970-71, 1974-75 to 1979-80, 1985-86 to 1991-92; Division Three (North) 1957-58; Division Four 1971-72 to 1973-74, 1980-81 to 1984-85. *Honours* Division Two 1894-95; Division Three 1960-61; FA Cup 1900 (4–0 v Southampton); 1903 (6–0 v Derby County – record score); Second Division 1996-97. *Records* Bill Gorman is Bury's most capped player (11 (13) for **Republic of Ireland**, (4) for **Northern Ireland**); Norman Bullock holds the record for club appearances (506, 1920-35; Craig Madden is Bury's record league goalscorer (129, 1978-86).

bury *vb.* to shoot decisively into the goal net.

Busby, Matt *player-manager* Defender. **Scotland** international (one cap). Born 26 May 1909; died 20 January 1994. *Clubs* (player) **Manchester City**, **Liverpool**; (manager) **Manchester United**. *Keynotes* Became United manager in 1945, having played as a half-back for Manchester City and won an **FA Cup** winner's medal in 1934 (2–1 v Portsmouth). He won his only Scottish cap in 1993 (v **Wales**). As a manager, Busby transformed United into one of the great club sides, creating first the so-called **Busby babes**, eight of whom perished in the **Munich air disaster**, and later a successful side around the brilliant but wayward George **Best**. Busby only narrowly avoided death at Munich, spending several months in hospital before returning to **Old Trafford**. In 1968, United became the first English side to win the European Cup (v **Benfica**) for which Busby received a knighthood. He became general manager at United in 1969, resuming control of first-team affairs for one season after his replacement as manager, Wilf McGuinness, was dismissed. Busby was later club president. He was temporarily in charge of the Scotland national team in 1958. *Honours* (player) FA Cup (Manchester City 1934); (manager) **European Cup** (1968); FA Cup (1948, 1963); League Championship (1951-52, 1955-56, 1956-57, 1964-65, 1966-67).

Busby babes *misc.* **Manchester United's** side of the mid-1950s was known as the **Busby babes** after the club's manager, Matt Busby, who fashioned a highly-talented young team, including Roger **Byrne**, Eddie Colman, Bobby **Charlton**, Duncan **Edwards**, Tommy Taylor and Dennis Viollet. Tragedy struck on 6 February 1958, when the plane transporting the side back to Manchester after a **European Cup** quarter-final second leg match against **Red Star Belgrade** (5–4 agg.) crashed on take-off at Munich Airport, where it had stopped to refuel. In total 23 people died, including eight United players: Byrne, Geoff Bent, Colman, Edwards, Mark Jones, David Pegg, Taylor and Bill Whelan. Busby sustained serious injuries. In addition, two other players, Jackie Blanchflower and Johnny Berry, never played again. Former **Manchester City** goalkeeper Frank **Swift** was one of eight journalists who died in the crash. See **Munich air disaster** and **disasters**.

Butragueño, Emilio *player* Striker. **Spain** international (69, caps, 26 goals, 1984-92). Born 22 July 1963. *Clubs* Castilla, **Real Madrid**. *Keynotes* Spain's all-time top goalscorer. Butragueño scored on his international debut on 17 October 1984 against **Wales** (3–0, in Seville, **World Cup** qualifier). He was the joint second-highest goalscorer, with five goals, in the 1986 World Cup finals, including four in Spain's second-round victory over **Denmark** (5–0, in Querétaro, Mexico). *Honours* **UEFA Cup** (Real Madrid, 1985, 1986); Spanish championship (Real Madrid, 1986, 1987, 1988, 1989,1990).

butt *n.* serious foul and criminal offence by a player striking an opponent with the forehead. *Keynotes* Former-**Rangers** striker Duncan Ferguson was imprisoned for three months in May 1995 for assaulting (head-butting) **Raith Rovers'** John McStay during a 1994 match. Ferguson, then of **Everton**, appealed, but failed to get the conviction overturned.

Bwalya, Kalusha *player* Midfield/striker. **Zambia** international. Born 16 August 1963. *Clubs* **Mufulira Wanderers**, Cercle Brugge, **PSV Eindhoven**, **América** (Mexico), **Necaxa** (Mexico). *Keynotes* Joined Cercle Brugge from Mufulira Wanderers in 1985; transferred to PSV Eindhoven in 1989 and América of Mexico in 1994. He moved to Necaxa in 1996. Bwalya featured in the top 10 African footballers, as polled by *France Football*, in six consecutive years (1988-94). He played a major part in Zambia's 4–0 victory over Italy in the 1988 **Olympic Games** finals first round in Seoul, South Korea. *Honours* **African Cup of Nations** runner-up (Zambia, 1994; third 1990); Netherlands league championship (PSV Eindhoven, 1991,1992); *France Football* **African Footballer of the Year** 1988.

Bwanga, Tshimen *player* Defender. Zaire (now **Congo Democratic Republic**) international. *Club* **Toute Puissant Mazembe**. *Honours* **African Cup of Nations** (Zaire, 1974); *France Football* **African Footballer of the Year** 1973, runner-up 1972.

bye *n.* situation where a club wins a round of a knock-out tournament simply because it has no opposition – for example, because there were insufficient entrants to make up the full complement in the competition draw. Compare **walkover**.

by-line *rules* another word for **goal-line**.

Byshovets, Anatoly *player* Striker. **Soviet Union** international (15 goals, 1966-72). *Club* **Dinamo Kiev**. *Keynotes* Scored four goals in four games in the 1970 **World Cup** finals in Mexico. National team coach 1990-92, and again for six months in 1998. *Honours* Soviet Union league championship (Dinamo Kiev, 1966, 1967, 1968, 1971).

C

C R Belcourt *club* former name (1962-80) of **C R Belouizdad**.

C R Belouizdad (Chabab Riadi) *club* Algerian national league club, based in the capital El Djezaïr (Algiers), founded 1962 as C R Belcourt (changed to CM Belcourt in 1980, current name adopted 1993). Ground: 20 Aout, capacity: 30,000. Strip: red shirts, white shorts. **African Cup-winners Cup** semi-final 1996; Algerian Cup 1966, 1969, 1970, 1978, 1995; Algerian league champions 1965, 1966, 1969, 1970; **Maghreb Champions Cup** 1970, 1971 and 1972.

CA Bizerte (Club Athletique) *club* Tunisian national league club based in Bizerte, founded 1928. Ground: Olympique a Bsiri, capacity: 18,000. Strip: yellow shirts, black shorts. **African Cup-winners Cup** 1988 (1–0 agg., v **Ranchers Bees** of Nigeria); **Arab Club Champions Cup** semi-final 1994; **CAF Cup** semi-final 1992; Tunisian Cup 1982, 1987; Tunisian league champions 1944, 1945, 1948, 1984.

Cadets Club *club* Mauritius national league club, based in Trianon Quarte Bornes. Ground: Guy Rozemont, capacity: 2,000. **African Cup-winners Cup** second round 1995; Mauritius Cup runners-up 1992, 1995.

Caernarfon Town *club* Welsh league. *Dossier* Ground: The Oval, Caernarfon, Gwynedd. Strip: yellow shirts, green shorts. Nickname: the Canaries. Ground capacity: 3,678. Formed in 1876. *Honours* Welsh League 1926-27 (Northern Division), 1929-30 (Northern Division).

Caersws *club* Welsh league. Ground: Recreation Ground, Caersws, Powys. Strip: blue shirts, white shorts. Nickname: Blue Birds. Ground capacity: 3,000. Formed in 1887.

CAF *abbrev.* **Confédération Africaine de Football**.

CAF Cup *competition* (Moshood Abiola Cup). Annual tournament for national league runners-up in the member countries of the **Confédération Africaine de Football** (CAF), first played 1992. The CAF Cup berth goes to the next-placed club in the respective national league if the runners-up have already qualified for one of the other African club competitions (eg the **African Cup of Champion Clubs** or the **African Cup-winners Cup**). All matches, including the final, are played over two legs, the result decided on **aggregate score** and, if necessary, on **away goals** or **penalties**. The champions gain automatic entry into next year's tournament. *Winners, results and runners-up* 1992 **IICC Shooting Stars** (of Nigeria), 3–0 agg., v **Nakivubo Villa** (of Uganda); 1993 **Stella Abidjan** of Ivory Coast), 2–0 agg., v **Simba SC** (of Tanzania); 1994 **Bendel Insurance** (of Nigeria), 3–1 agg., v **Primeiro de Agosto** (of Angola); 1995 **ES Sahel** (of Tunisia), 2–0, agg., v **AS Kaloum Stars** (of Guinea); 1996 **KAC Marrakesh** (of Morocco) 3–3 agg., away goals, v ES Sahel; 1997 **Espérance** (of Tunisia), 2–1 agg, v **Petro Atlético** (of Angola); 1998 **CS Sfaxien** (of Tunisia), 4–0 agg., v **ASC Jeanne d'Arc** (of Senegal).

calcaneum *medical* a large block-like **bone** that projects backwards beyond the bones of the leg to form what is commonly known as the heel bone.

calcio fiorentino *n.* *Italian* see **giuoco del calcio Fiorentino**.

Caledonian Stadium *ground* Scottish football ground situated in Inverfness; Highland region; home of **Inverness Caledonian Thistle**. *Dossier* Ground capacity: 5,600. Pitch dimensions: 104m x 68m. Record attendance: 5,525 v **Ross County** (15 March 1997, **Third Division**). *Keynotes* Built under the auspices of the Inverness and Nairn Enterprise board at a cost of more than £5 million. The Caledonian Stadium staged its first **Scottish League** fixture on 17 August 1996 (v **Cowdenbeath**, Third Division).

call-up *n.* an invitation to play for a team, such as one's national team or any one of a club's teams. *vb.* **call up**.

Cambodia *country. AFC* kingdom in southeast Asia on South China sea, bordered by **Thailand, Laos** and **Vietnam**. Former names: Khmer Republic, Kampuchea. Independence from France 1953. Civil war 1970–1975, invaded by Vietnam in 1979 whose forces finally withdrew in 1989. Area: 182,000 sq km (69,865 sq miles). Population: 9,860,000 (1996 est.). Languages: Khmer and French. Capital: Phnom Penh. *Dossier* Football association (Fédération Khmère de Football Association, Phnom-Penh), formed in 1933 affiliated to FIFA in 1953 and **Asian Football Confederation** (AFC) in 1957, president Sin Sok, general secretary Keo Sarin. Season played from November to October.

National stadium: Complex Sportif National, Phnom Penh, capacity: 60,000. National strip: blue, red and white shirts, white and blue shorts. **Indonesia** (1995, in Chiang Mai, Thailand, South East Asian Games). *International tournament record* **Women's World Cup** – never entered; **World Cup** – first entered 1998 (finished last in its four-nation qualifying group with one draw and five defeats in its six matches); **Asean Tiger Cup** – entered first tournament in 1996 (last in its first-round group of five nations, losing all its matches); **Asian Championship** – entered first tournament in 1956, semi-final (fourth) 1972 (1–2 v **Iran**, in Bangkok, semi-final; 2–2, 3–5 pens., v **Thailand**, Bangkok, third/fourth playoff); **Asian Games** – entered in 1970 (first round) and 1998 (last in its first-round group of three nations); **Under-17 World Championship** – never qualified; **World Youth Cup (under-20)** – never qualified. *Record against British and Irish national teams* none played. *History* Football introduced by the French at the beginning of the 20th century. National association formed in 1933. Semi-professional national league started in 1996. *League system* Eight clubs compete in the national league.

Cambridge Rules *n.pl.* early set of football rules, established in 1848 at Cambridge University. The rules were drawn up by a committee comprising two representatives each from six Public schools and two others, including H C Malden, who hosted the group. The Cambridge Rules were revised in 1856 (giving a code of 10 rules) and again in 1863, this time following a number of meetings at Trinity College with representatives of Eton, Harrow, Rugby, Marlborough, Shrewsbury and Westminster schools. Its 15 rules included that the goal width should be five yards (4.6 metres) wide but that, so long as the ball went between the posts, a goal would be scored no matter how high it was kicked. Although players could catch the ball – entitling them to a free kick if caught cleanly – they could not run with it. Cambridge Rules formed the basis of the first rules of Association Football adopted by the newly formed **Football Association** in 1863. Cambridge University continued with its own rules until the 1870s when it set up separate Association and **Rugby football** clubs playing their respective codes (see **association football**: history).

Cambridge United *club* English league. *Dossier* Ground: **Abbey Stadium**, Cambridge, capacity: 9,617. Strip: amber and black striped shirts, black shorts with amber trim, black and amber socks. Nickname: U's. Record attendance: 14,000 v **Chelsea** (1 May 1970, friendly). Best average attendance: 7,078 (1991-92). Biggest win: 6–0 v **Darlington** (18 September 1971, Division Four). Biggest defeat: 0–6 v **Aldershot** (13 April 1974, Division Three), v Darlington (28 September 1974, Division Four), v Chelsea (15 January 1983, Division Two). *History* Founded as Abbey United in 1912, the club played its first matches on Midsummer Common and later at Parker's Piece (where the first codified rules of football had been posted in 1848), before settling at Abbey Stadium in 1934. In the aftermath of

World War II, Cambridge became professional and in 1951, the club changed its name to Cambridge United, joining the **Southern League** in 1958. The club won the Southern League Championship in 1968-69 and 1969-70. In 1970, Cambridge replaced **Bradford Park Avenue** in Division Four – securing its place in the **Football League** by 31 votes to 17. Under the managership of Ron Atkinson (1974-78), Cambridge won the Division Four title in 1976-77, having spent one season in Division Three in 1973-74, and the following year the club achieved further elevation, finishing runners-up and securing a place in Division Two. In 1983-84, the club achieved an unenviable League record: the longest run of matches without a victory (31). By 1985-86, Cambridge was back playing in the bottom division. The club achieved a notable double in 1989-90. It was an **FA Cup** quarter-finalist (0–1 v **Crystal Palace**) – a joint record for a Division Four team (shared with **Bradford City**, **Colchester United** and **Oxford United**) – and it won promotion to Division Three via the end-of-season **playoffs** (1–0 v **Chesterfield**). The following season the club again reached the FA Cup quarter-finals (1–2 v **Arsenal**), having defeated several higher-level opponents in earlier rounds (1–0 v **Wolverhampton Wanderers**, third round; 2–0 v **Middlesbrough**, fourth round; 4–0 v **Sheffield Wednesday**, fifth round). In 1991-92, Cambridge narrowly missed promotion to the top flight, reaching the semi-final stage of the Division Two playoffs, but the following season the club was relegated – although it was also a **League Cup** quarter-finalist (2–3 v **Blackburn Rovers**). Further demotion followed in 1994-95, with a return to the Second Division after promotion in 1998-99. *League record* First Division 1992-93; Division Two 1978-79 to 1983-84, 1991-92; Second Division 1993-94 to 1994-95, 1999-00–; Division Three 1973-74, 1977-78, 1984-85, 1990-91; Third Division 1995-96 to 1998-99; Division Four 1970-71 to 1972-73, 1974-75 to 1976-77, 1985-86 to 1989-90. *Honours* Division Three 1990-91; Division Four 1976-77; Southern League 1969, 1970. *Records* Tom Finney is Cambridge's most capped player (7 (15) for **Northern Ireland**); Steve Spriggs holds the record for club League appearances (416, 1975-87); John Taylor is Cambridge's record League goalscorer (75, 1988-92 and 1997–).

Cambuslang *club* former Scottish league. *Dossier* Ground: Whitefield Park, Cambuslang, Strathclyde. *Keynotes* Cambuslang was a founder member of the **Scottish Football League** in 1890-91, finishing fourth in that inaugural season. The club was a **Scottish FA Cup** finalist in 1887-88 (1–6 v **Renton**), having won its semi-final replay against **Abercorn** 10–1. *League record* Scottish League 1890-91 to 1891-92.

Cameroon *country CAF* republic in West Africa on the Atlantic, bordered by **Nigeria**, **Chad**, the **Central African Republic**, **Congo**, **Gabon** and **Equatorial Guinea**. Area: 475,500 sq km (188,545 sq miles).

Population: 12,200,000 (1992 est.). Languages: French, English, pidgin. Capital: Yaoundé. *Dossier* Football association (Fédération Camerounaise de Football, Yaoundé) formed in 1960 affiliated to FIFA in 1962 and **Confédération Africaine de Football** (CAF) in 1963, member of the **Union of Football Associations of Central Africa**, president Vincent Onana, general secretary Robert Penne. Season played from November to July. National stadium: Ahmadou Ahidjo, Yaoundé, capacity: 55,000 (15,000 seated). National strip: green shirts, red shorts. Nickname of national team: the "Indomitable Lions". First international game: 1960, v **Somalia** (9–2, neutral venue, friendly). Biggest victory: 9–2 v Somalia (as above) Biggest defeat: 1–6, v **Norway** (31 October 1990, Oslo, friendly), 1–6 v **Russia** (28 June 1994, Detroit, **World Cup** finals first round). Highest crowd: 120,000 v **Morocco** (29 November 1981, 2–1, Yaoundé, World Cup qualifier – the world-record attendance for a World Cup qualifier). Most capped players: Francois **Omam-Biyik** (76 appearances). Leading goalscorers: Francois Omam-Biyik (50 goals). Notable international players: Théophile **Abega**, Emmanuel Kunde, Roger **Milla**, Thomas **N'Kkono**, Jean **Manga-Onguene**, Pierre Nlend **Wome**. *International tournament record* **Olympic Games** – qualified for finals tournament 1984 (first round); **Women's World Cup** – entered first tournament in 1991, reached final of African qualifying tournament 1991 (0–6 agg., v Nigeria); World Cup – first entered 1970, quarter-final 1990, also qualified for finals tournament 1982, 1994, 1998; **African Cup of Nations** – first entered 1968, 1984 (3–1 v Nigeria, Abidjan, Ivory Coast, final), 1988 (1–0, v Nigeria, Casablanca, Morocco, final), runners-up 1986 (0–0, 4–5 pens., v **Egypt**, Cairo, Egypt, final), semi-final/third 1972, semi-final/fourth 1992, quarter-final 1998, also qualified for finals tournament 1970, 1982, 1990; **African Women's Tournament** (World Cup qualifier) – fourth 1998 (3–3, 1–3 pens., v **Congo Democratic Republic**, in Nigeria, third/fourth playoff); **African Youth Cup** (under-20) – 1995 (4–0 v **Burundi**, in Nigeria), runners-up 1981, 1993; **Afro-Asian Cup of Nations** – 1985 (5–3 agg., v **Saudi Arabia**); **All-Africa Friendship Games** – 1962 (tournament in Senegal); **All-Africa Games** (under 19) – 1991 (final v **Tunisia**, in Egypt); **UDEAC Tournament** – 1984, 1986, 1987, 1989, runners-up 1988, 1990, hosts 1988; **Under-17 World Championship** – never qualified; **World Youth Cup (under-20)** – quarter-final 1995, qualified 1999. *World Cup performance* (finals and qualifiers to end of 1998 tournament) played 53, won 23, drawn 16, lost 14, scored 74 goals, conceded 62 goals; win rate: 43%; goals scored per game: 1.40. *Record against British and Irish national teams* v **England**, played three, lost three. *History* The national league of Cameroon began in 1961; first won by **Oryx Douala**, which had been the first winner of the Cameroon cup in 1955, and was the first club to win Africa's premier club competition, the **African Cup of**

Champion Clubs; the competition also has been won by **Canon Yaoundé** (three times) and **Union Douala**. Cameroon is the first African country to have qualified for three successive World Cup finals tournaments. It shares, with Morocco, the African record of four appearances in the World Cup finals. It has won the African Cup of Nations twice, and was the first African nation to reach the quarter-final of the World Cup, losing to England in the 1990 tournament, having led with only eight minutes to play in normal time (2–3 after extra time, Naples, quarter-final). Roger Milla is both the oldest player to have played in the World Cup finals and the oldest to score. He did so in the 1994 finals at the age of 42. Issa Hayatou of Cameroon has been president of CAF since 1988. In 1998, the president of the Cameroon FA, Vincent Onana, was detained in Cameroon over alleged ticket irregularities for the World Cup finals. *Record in international club tournaments* African Cup of Champion Clubs – Canon Yaoundé (1971, 1978, 1980) Oryx Douala (1964), Union Douala (1979); **African Cup-winners Cup** – Canon Yaoundé (1979, runners-up 1977, 1984, semi-final 1996), Union Douala (1981), **Diamant Yaoundé** (semi-final 1988); **Tonnerre Yaoundé** (1975, runners-up 1976); **CAF Cup** – Unisport Bafang (quarter-final 1996), **Cotonsport** (quarter-final 1997).Other leading clubs: **Racing Bafoussam**, **Prevoyance Yaoundé**, **Aigle N'Kongsamba**.

Campeonato Brasileiro *competition* the national club championship of Brazil, played in the second half of the season. The Campeonato has 24 clubs, each playing each other once. The top eight qualify for a straight knockout tournament, with the bottom two relegated to Brazil's national division two (Serie B). The championship final is played over two legs; if the aggregate score is level, the club with the best record over the season is declared champions.

Campeonato Sudamericano de Campeones *competition* ephemeral club tournament for champion clubs of the South American nations; the first international club tournament in the continent. Played only once, in 1948, in Chile. *Winner* 1948 **Vasco da Gama**.

Campeonisimo *n.* champion of champions. In Honduras, a club that wins both stages of the league tournament – the main league and the final tournament – is declared the Campeonisimo. Only two clubs have achieved this since 1974: **Olimpia** (1982, 1984 and 1993) and **Real España** in 1994.

Campionat de Catalunya *competition* see **Catalonia Championship**.

Campionato Nazionale *competition* the first Italian national championship, founded in 1898 and played until 1928. It was replaced by the Liga Calcio **Serie A** in 1929. The championship was decided either by a single **playoff** or a round-robin tournament between the winners of regional competitions. It was first won by **Genoa 1893** (playing as Genoa Football and Cricket Club, 2–1 v Internazionale Torino – a forerunner of present-day **Torino**).

Campos, Jorge *player* Goalkeeper and occasional striker. Mexico international (100 caps). Born 15 October 1966. *Club* **UNAM, Atlante**. *Keynotes* Played in the 1994 and 1998 **World Cup** finals; in 1994 he was registered for the finals as an outfield player *and* a goalkeeper! He has also played as a striker for Atlante. *Honours* **Gold Cup** (Mexico, 1993, 1996, 1998); **Copa America** runner-up (Mexico, 1993).

Camsell, George *player* Striker. **England** international (9 caps). Born 27 November 1902. Died 7 March 1966. Career ca. 1923–1940. *Clubs* Tow Law Town, **Durham City, Middlesbrough**. *Keynotes* Camsell cost Middlesbrough £800 when the club signed him from **Durham City** in October 1925. His 59 **Football League** goals for Middlesbrough in 1926-27 remained on the record books for only a short time – Dixie **Dean** went one better the following season – although Camsell's scoring feat is still a Division Two record and the nine hat-tricks he scored that season remains the highest ever in one League campaign. Camsell scored 344 goals in 444 League appearances with Durham and Middlesbrough, and 18 in only nine games for England. Included in the **Football League Centenary 100 players**. *Honours* Division Two (Middlesbrough 1926-27, 1928-29).

Canada *country CONCACAF* Commonwealth nation in North America, bordered by USA and Alaska (USA). World's second largest country by area. Area: 9,922,385 sq km (3,8330,840 sq miles). Population: 29,960,000 (1996 census). Languages: English and French. Capital: Ottawa. *Dossier* The Canadian Soccer Association (Ottawa) formed in 1912 (known then as the Dominion of Canada Football Association), affiliated to **FIFA** in 1912 and **Confederación Norte-Centroamericana y del Caribe de Fútbol** (CONCACAF) in 1978, president Terry Quinn, general secretary Kevan Pipe. Season played from May to November. National stadium: Commonwealth Stadium, Montreal, capacity: 60,000 all seated. National strip: red shirts, red shorts. Website: http://www.canoe.ca/soccercan (official site). First international game: 28 November 1885 v **United States of America** (1–0, Newark, USA, friendly) – the first international game played outside Great Britain and Ireland. Biggest victory: 6–0 v **Bermuda** (8 May 1983, in Burnaby, Canada, Olympic Games qualifier). Biggest defeat: 1–8 v **Poland** (6 July 1975, Montreal, friendly). Notable international players: Craig Forrest, Paul Peschisolido. *International tournament record* **Olympic Games** – a Canadian representative side (Galt FC of Ontario) won an unofficial football tournament of the 1904 games in St Louis, USA, took part in finals tournament as hosts in 1976 (in Montreal); **Women's World Cup** – entered first tournament in 1991, qualified for finals tournament 1995 (third in four-nation first-round group); **World Cup** – first entered 1958, finals tournament first round 1986, reached CONCACAF final qualifying round in 1998 (last in group of six nations); **CONCACAF Championship** (World Cup qualifying tournament) – 1985 (first of three-nation final group, ahead of **Honduras** and **Costa Rica**); **CONCACAF Women's Championship** – 1998 (1–0, v **Mexico**, at the Centennial Stadium, Etobicoke, Canada), runners-up 1991 (0–5 v USA), 1995 (league of five nations), hosts 1998; **CONCACAF Youth Championship** (under-20) – 1986; **Gold Cup** – reached finals tournament 1991, 1993; **Under-17 World Championship** – qualified for finals tournament 1987, 1989, 1993 (though Canada lost all its group games in each of the three tournaments); **World Youth Cup (under-20)** – qualified for finals tournament 1979, 1985, 1987. *Record against British and Irish national teams* v **England**, played one, lost one; v **Northern Ireland**, played two, won one, drawn one; v **Scotland**, played four, lost four; v **Wales**, played two, won one, lost one; v **Republic of Ireland**, none played. *History* Association football lags behind ice hockey, baseball, basketball and **American football** in spectator popularity. Nevertheless, the number of people playing association football has increased making football the number-one participative sport in the country: in 1995 there were 536,488 registered players, compared with 533,571 registered ice hockey players. There is a long history of association football in the country, with one of the first clubs, Montreal FC, founded in 1868. International matches date back to 1885 (the first outside Britain and Ireland; see above). Cup football began in 1912, with the launch of the Canadian Challenge Cup (a trophy was donated by the Duke of Connaught), contested by the champions of each provincial league. A **Canadian National Soccer League** was founded in 1922. Several of the early club names reflected associations with the various immigrant communities, such as Toronto Ulster, Toronto Scottish, Toronto Ukraine, Polish White Eagles, Montreal Hungaria and **Toronto Italia**. Two leading current clubs, **Toronto Croatia** and Kosova Albanians (from North York), are among the many clubs that retain this tradition. The **Eastern Canada Professional Soccer League** was formed in 1961, lasting only five seasons. A genuinely national professional league, the Canadian Professional Soccer League, lasted just one season (1983 – won by Edmonton Eagles). Canadian clubs played in the ephemeral **North American Soccer League** (1967–84) – the championship won by a Canadian club in 1976 (Toronto Metros) and 1979 (Vancouver Whitecaps). A professional **Canadian Soccer League** was formed in 1987. It was, however, disbanded in 1992, with the two leading clubs, **Montreal Impact** and **Vancouver 86ers**, now playing in the **American A-League** (along with **Toronto Lynx**). In 1997, the Canadian National Soccer League was replaced by the **Canadian Professional Soccer League (Ontario Division)**, with the hope that other regional divisions eventually would form a nationwide structure. A national cup for professional sides started in 1999. Canada's lack of a truly national league was used as an excuse to persuade the national side to withdraw from the 1998 CONCACAF **Gold Cup** to make way for non-qualifiers **Jamaica** (a qualifier for the 1998 World Cup finals). Canada hosted and won the 1998 **CONCACAF Women's Championship** (though the United States of America was absent), beating Mexico 1–0 in the final. In the first-round group, Canada beat **Puerto Rico** 21–0; it scored a total of 40 goals in four matches, with none conceded. *League system* There is no national league. There are semi-professional regional leagues, including the Canadian Professional Soccer League (Ontario Division) which, in 1997, replaced the misleadingly titled Canadian National Soccer League, and comprises seven clubs in southern Ontario. This is played in two parts: the regular season and a "League Cup" (also played in a league format). The combined tables decide which two clubs will compete for the championship playoff. The Canadian Challenge Cup involves top amateur clubs from all the main provincial leagues. A professional national cup started in 1999. *Record in international club tournaments* Canadian clubs do not compete in CONCACAF tournaments. Other leading club: **St Catherine's Wolves**.

Canadian National Soccer League *n.* former regional semi-professional league for clubs in South Ontario, Canada, founded 1922. Replaced in 1997 by the **Canadian Professional Soccer League (Ontario Division)**.

Canadian Professional Soccer League (Ontario Division) *n.* regional professional football league in Canada, founded 1997, replacing the **Canadian National Soccer League**. Contested by clubs from Ontario, with the hope that other regional divisions eventually would form a nationwide structure. Each club has a fixed, standard budget to spend on players. There are seven clubs: **St Catherine's Roma Wolves** (the inaugural league winners), Hamilton White Eagles, London City, Kosova Albanians (from North York), North York Talons, **Toronto Croatia** and Toronto Supra.

Canadian Soccer League *n.* former national professional football league in Canada, founded 1987, disbanded 1992.

Canary Islands *country no international affiliation (Spanish football association)* island provinces of Spain – group of volcanic islands 100 km (60 miles) off the northwest coast of Africa, comprising Gran Canaria, Tenerife, La Palma, Gomera, Hierro, Fuerteventura and Lanzarote. Forms the two provinces of Las Palmas and Santa Cruz de Tenerife. Area: 7,275 sq km (2,810 sq miles). Population: 1,494,000. Language: Spanish. Capitals: Las Palmas (Gran Canaria) and Santa Cruz (Tenerife). *Dossier* The Canary Islands are affiliated to the Spanish football association (Real Fedeación Española de Fútbol in Madrid). *Record in international club tournaments* **UEFA Cup** – **CD Tenerife** (semifinal 1997). Other leading club: UD **Las Palmas**. See **Spain**.

cannabis *medical* a type of **drug** comprising the dried female flower tops of the hemp plant (*Cannabis sativa*). It contains various cannabinoids, which when smoked or ingested induce various psychological and behavioural effects, such as euphoria, hallucinations and drowsiness. Although there are no obvious performance-enhancing benefits, cannabis is outlawed in football and most other sports. It is one of the most frequent drugs identified in **drug tests** and a common reason for drug-related suspensions. Its purified resin form is known as hashish. Also called, grass, ganja, pot. See also **marijuana**.

Canon Yaoundé (Canon Sportif Yaoundé) *club* Cameroon national league club based in the capital Yaoundé, founded 1930. Ground: Ahmadou Ahidjo (national stadium), capacity: 60,000. Strip: red shirts, green shorts. **African Cup of Champion Clubs** 1971 (0–3, 2–0, 1–0 playoff in Yaoundé, v **Asante Kotoko** of Ghana), 1978 (2–0 agg., v **Hafia Conakry** of Guinea), 1980 (5–2 agg., v **AS Bilima** of Zaire); **African Cup-winners Cup** 1979 (8–0 agg., v **Gor Mahia** of Kenya), runners-up 1977 (2–5 agg., v **Enugu Rangers** of Nigeria), 1984 (1–1 agg., 2–4 pens., v **Al Ahly Cairo** of Egypt), semi-final 1996; Cameroon Cup 1957, 1967, 1973, 1975, 1976, 1977, 1978, 1983, 1986, 1993, 1995; Cameroon league champions 1970, 1974, 1977, 1979, 1980, 1982, 1985, 1986, 1991. Notable former players: Roger **Milla**, Thomas **N'Kono**, Jean **Manga-Onguene**, Pierre Nlend **Wome**.

cantilever stands *misc.* covered **stand** where the roof is not supported by view-restricting columns. *Keynotes* Although popular in the design of stadiums in continental Europe from the 1930s, the first cantilevered stand to be built at a UK football ground was at **Scunthorpe United**'s former home, the **Old Show Ground**. Scunthorpe's stand was opened 23 August 1958 with seats for 2,200 people. In 1961, **Sheffield Wednesday** built a much larger cantilevered stand at its **Hillsborough** ground. A year later, a unique L-shaped cantilever stand was built at **Dundee United**'s **Tannadice Park.**

Cantona, Eric *player* Striker. **France** international (45 caps, 19 goals). Born 24 May 1966. Career ca 1983–97. *Clubs* Martigues, Auxerre, **Olympique de Marseille**, Bordeux, Montpelier, Nimes, **Leeds United**, **Manchester United**. *Keynotes* Transferred to Leeds United for £900,000 in February 1992 and sold to Manchester United for £1.2 million in November 1992. First player to win consecutive English Championships (**Football League** and **Premier League**) with different clubs, in 1991-92 and 1992-93. Cantona scored United's winner in the 1996 FA Cup final, securing the club's second **double** in three years. Voted the **PFA Footballer of the Year** in 1994 and the **Footballer of the Year** in 1996. Cantona was banned from the game for eight months, fined £10,000 by the **Football Association** (plus £20,000 by United) and ordered by the courts to perform 120 hours of **community service**, after leaping a barrier and making a "kung fu" style lunge at **Crystal Palace** supporter Matthew Simmonds following his sending off during a Premiership encounter at **Selhurst Park** on 25 January 1995. Cantona was banned from the French national side for 12 months for insulting the coach Henri Michel, and, before resurrecting his career in England with Leeds United, he also "quit" the game after an acrimonious appearance before a French disciplinary committee. Before the start of the 1997-98 season, Cantona retired from football to pursue an acting career. Cantona has appeared in three feature films: Le Bonheur est dans le Pré (Rural Bliss); Elizabeth; and Mookie. Included in the **Football League Centenary 100 players**. *Honours* League Championship (Leeds United 1991-92; Manchester United 1992-93, 1993-94, 1995-96, 1996-97), **FA Cup** (Manchester United 1994, 1996).

cap *n.* emblematic hat awarded to a player for representing his or her country in an official international match. Caps are awarded for each appearance though the player must take part in the match. Non-playing substitutes are not awarded caps. Caps have been awarded since 1886. *vb.* to award a player with an international appearance.

capacity *n.* the number of spectators officially allowed into a football stadium. Numbers are determined as much by health and safety legislation as the physical size of the stadium, and local authorities assess ground capacity based on these criteria. The **Bradford fire** and the **Hillsborough disaster** led to capacity reductions and a revision of the health and safety requirements covering football stadiums (see **Taylor Report**). *adj.* usage: capacity crowd.

Cape Town Spurs *club* South African **National Soccer League** club based in Cape Town, founded 1969. Ground: Greenpoint. Strip: red shirts, white shorts. *Keynotes* The club changed its name in 1994 to Ajax Cape Town after a **nursery club** deal with Dutch club **Ajax** and merger with another club, Seven Stars. South African Cup ("Super Bowl") 1995; South Africa National Soccer League champions 1995.

Cape Verde *country CAF* republic comprising a group of islands in the Atlantic Ocean, 500 km west of **Senegal**. Former Portuguese colony, independent since 1975. Area: 4,035 sq km (1,560 sq miles). Population: 420,000 (1996 est.). Languages: Portuguese and Creole. Capital: Praia. *Dossier* Football association (Federação Cabo-Veriana de Futebol, Praia), formed in 1982, affiliated to **FIFA** and **Confédération Africaine de Football** (CAF) in 1986, member of the **West African Football Union**, president Luis Lopes de Almeida, general secretary Francisco João Evora. Season played from October to July. National stadium: Estadio da Varzea, Praia, capacity: 15,000. National strip: green shirts, green shorts. First international game: 7 January 1979 v **Guinea Bissau** (0–3, in Guinea Bissau, **Amilcar Cabral (Zone 2) Cup**). Biggest victory: 3–0 v Guinea Bissau (7 February 1981, in Mali, Amilcar Cabral Cup). Biggest defeat: 1–5 v Senegal (12 February 1981, in Mali, Amilcar Cabral Cup). *International tournament record* **Olympic Games** – never entered; **Women's World Cup** – never entered; **World Cup** – never entered; **African Cup of Nations** – first entered 1994, never

qualified for finals tournament; Amilcar Cabral Cup runners-up 1991 (0–1, v Senegal, tournament in Senegal). *Record against British and Irish national teams* none played. *History* League championship dates back to 1960. *Record in international club tournaments* **African Cup of Champions Clubs – Sporting Clube de Praia** (first round 1992, after preliminary round); **Travadores de Praia** (first round 1995) Other leading clubs: Sporting Club de Praia, Boavista Praia FC (league champions 1995), Acedemio Sal (league champions 1993), Academico Mindelo (league champions 1988), CS Mindelense (league champions 1998).

Cappielow Park *ground* Scottish football ground situated in Greenock, Strathclyde; home of **Greenock Morton**. *Dossier* Ground capacity: 14,267. Pitch dimensions: 100.5m x 65m. Record attendance: 23,500 v **Celtic** (1921-22, Division One). *Keynotes* Morton (the club did not adopt its present title until 1993-94) first played at Cappielow Park in 1879. Apart from one season (1882-83) it has remained the club's home ever since. In its early days, Cappielow Park staged athletics, cycling and **women's football** matches. In 1923, Cappielow Park was the first UK football ground to provide blind spectators with match commentary. The first floodlit match at Cappielow Park took place on 4 November 1958 (v **Third Lanark**).

caps, most *record* the 15 all-time most-capped players in the world (full international matches only) are: Thomas **Ravelli** (Sweden) 143 caps, 1981-1997; Majed **Abdullah** (Saudi Arabia) 140 caps, 1978-1995; Lothar **Matthäus** (Germany and West Germany) 135 caps, 1980-1999; Andoni **Zubizarreta** (Spain) 126 caps, 1985-1998; Marcelo **Balboa** (USA) 125 caps, 1988-1998; Peter **Shilton** (England) 125 caps, 1970-1990; Masami **Ihara** (Japan) 121 caps, 1988-1998; Pat **Jennings** (Northern Ireland) 119 caps, 1964-1986; Heinz Hermann (Switzerland) 117 caps, 1978-1991; Gheorghe **Hagi** (Romania) 115 caps, 1983-1998; Björn Nordqvist (Sweden) 115 caps, 1963-1978; Cobi **Jones** (USA) 114 caps, 1992–; Claudio Suárez (Mexico) 114 caps, 1992–; Soon Ho Choi (South Korea) 113 caps, 1980-91. Four of the top 10 are goalkeepers.

CAPS United *club* Zimbabwe national league club based in the capital Harare. Ground: National Sports (shared with **Blackpool** of Harare and **Black Aces**), capacity: 30,000. Strip: green shirts, green shorts. **African Cup-winners Cup** quarter-final 1982, 1983; Zimbabwe Cup 1980, 1981, 1982, 1983, 1987, 1992, 1997; Zimbabwe league champions 1979, 1996.

captain *n.* player designated to lead a team on the field of play (compare **manager, coach**). Apart from the formal duty of taking part in **tossing the coin** at the start of a match, captains play an important part in encouraging their team-mates and in trying to ensure discipline when tempers are frayed. *Regulations* The captain of a winning side in a cup final usually accepts the trophy. The team captain must be distinguished by wearing an armband (eg FA Premier League rule F.10, Football League regulation 30.9). *Keynotes* Two players have captained their countries in two **World Cup** finals: Karl-Heinz **Rummenigge** (1982, 1986) and Diego **Maradona** (1986, 1990).

captain's armband *regulations* band that, according to **competition rules** is worn to indicate which of the players is designated as captain. They are obligatory in **Premier League** and **Football League** matches (FA Premier League rule F.10, Football League regulation 30.9).

CARA Brazzaville (Club Athletique Renaissance Aiglons) *club* Congo league club based in the capital Brazzaville, founded 1951 from the merger of two older clubs, Old Renaissance FC (founded ca. 1927) and Ecole St Vincent. Ground: A M Deba, capacity: 50,000. Strip: orange shirts, black shorts. *Keynotes* Its five consecutive league titles (1971 to 1975) is a national record. **African Cup of Champion Clubs** 1974 (6–3 agg., v **Mehalla Al Kubra** of Egypt); Congo Cup 1981, 1986; Congo league champions 1969, 1971, 1972, 1973, 1974, 1975, 1980, 1982, 1984. Notable former player: Paul **Moukila**.

Caracas FC *club* Venezuelan national league club based in the capital Caracas, founded 1967. Ground: Estadio Nacional Brigido Iriarte, capacity: 15,000. Strip: red shirts, red shorts (or all white). **Copa CONMEBOL** quarter-final 1993; **Copa Venezuela** 1988, 1993, 1994, 1995; Venezuelan league champions (**Torneo Clausura**) 1992, 1994, 1995, 1997.

Carbajal, Antonio *player* Goalkeeper. **Mexico** international. *Keynotes* Played in five successive **World Cup** finals tournaments, 1950, 1954, 1958, 1962, 1966; a record matched only by Lothar **Matthäus** of Germany.

Cardiff City *club* English league. *Dossier* Ground: **Ninian Park**, Cardiff, South Glamorgan, capacity: 14,660. Strip: blue shirts with white trim, white shorts, blue socks. Nickname: Bluebirds. Record attendance: 57,893 v **Arsenal** (22 April 1953, Division One). Best average attendance: 37,933 (1952-53). Biggest win: 8–0 v **Enfield** (28 November 1931, **FA Cup**, first round). Biggest defeat: 2–11 v **Sheffield United** (1 January 1926, Division One). *History* Founded as the football section of the Riverside Cricket Club in 1899. Cardiff's elevation to city-status in 1905 led to a formal request to the local football association in 1906 to allow the club to change its name to Cardiff City. The association refused, declaring that the title should go to the first Cardiff club to turn professional, which Riverside did in 1910 when it moved to Ninian Park, although it was granted permission to use the name Cardiff City in 1908. Cardiff is the most successful of six Welsh clubs playing in the English **pyramid system** (**Swansea City**, **Wrexham**, and non-league Colwyn Bay, Merthyr Tydfil and Newport AFC). The club was elected to Division Two in 1920-21, winning promotion as runners-up in its first **Football League** season and finishing fourth in Division One the following year. In 1923-24, Cardiff finished League runners-up. Both Cardiff and **Huddersfield Town** finished the season on 57 points. Cardiff had an inferior **goal average**

(1.794 v 1.818), identical **goal difference** (+27), but superior **goals scored** (61 v 60). Cardiff City missed a penalty on the last day of the season which, had it been scored, would have increased its goal average to 1.824, marginally above that of Huddersfield (goal average was replaced by goal difference and goals scored in 1976 as the method of deciding **Football League** positions). Cardiff is the only non-English club to win either the **FA Cup** or the **FA Charity Shield**. In 1927, the club lifted the FA Cup (1–0 v **Arsenal**), having been a finalist in 1925 (0–1 v **Sheffield United**), and the Charity Shield (2–1 v Corinthians). Cardiff's first **Welsh Cup** victory occurred in 1912 (3–0 replay v Pontypridd) and the club has subsequently won the trophy on a further 21 occasions (see below). The club was relegated in 1928-29 and suffered further demotion, to Division Three (South), in 1930-31. Cardiff won the Division Three (South) Championship immediately after **World War II** (1946-47) and narrowly missed a return to the top flight in 1950-51, before securing a place in Division One as runners-up the following season. Cardiff spent five seasons back in the top flight before being relegated in 1956-57. The club enjoyed a further two-season spell in Division One between 1960 and 1962. Cardiff's success in the Welsh Cup has enabled it to qualify for the **European Cup-winners Cup** (ECWC) competition on 15 occasions. In the club's first ECWC appearance in 1964-65, it reached the quarter-final stage (2–3 agg., v **Real Zaragoza**). In 1967-68, under the managership of former **Portsmouth** and **Newcastle United** defender and **Scotland** international Jimmy Scoular (died 19 March 1998), Cardiff, then of Division Two, was a semi-finalist (3–4 agg., v **Hamburg (SV)**) and in 1970-71, it again reached the quarter-final stage (1–2 agg., v **Real Madrid**). In 1965-66, Scoular's Cardiff was also a **League Cup** semi-finalist (3–10 agg., v **West Ham United**). By 1986-87, Cardiff was playing in Division Four for the first time in the club's history, having suffered two consecutive demotions. The club won the Third Division Championship in 1992-93, but returned to the bottom tier after only two seasons. Cardiff was a Third Division end-of-season **playoff** semi-finalist in 1996-97 and won promotion automatically in 1998-99. In 1991, Cardiff was saved from collapse after millionaire Rick Wright bought an 84% share in the club, declaring that he would sell once its financial affairs were in order. In 1995, former **Birmingham City** chairman Samesh Kumar bought the club. *League record* Division One 1921-22 to 1928-29, 1952-53 to 1956-57, 1960-61 to 1961-62; Division Two 1920-21, 1929-30 to 1930-31, 1947-48 to 1951-52, 1957-58 to 1959-60, 1962-63 to 1974-75, 1976-77 to 1981-82, 1983-84 to 1984-85; Second Division 1993-94 to 1994-95, 1999-00–; Division Three 1975-76, 1982-83, 1985-86, 1988-89 to 1989-90; Third Division 1992-93, 1995-96–; Division Three (South) 1931-32 to 1946-47; Division Four 1986-87 to 1987-88, 1990-91 to 1991-92. *Honours* Division Three (South) 1946-47; FA Charity Shield

1927 (2–1 v Corinthians); FA Cup 1927 (1–0 v **Arsenal** – *Team* Farquharson, Nelson, Watson, Keenor, Sloan, Hardy, Curtis, Irving, Ferguson (1), Davies, McLachlan); Third Division 1992-93; Welsh Cup 1912 (3–0 v Pontypridd), 1920 (2–1 v **Wrexham**), 1922 (2–0 v Ton Pentre), 1923 (3–2 v Aberdare Athletic), 1927 (2–0 v Rhyl), 1928 (2–0 v Bangor), 1930 (4–2 replay v Rhyl), 1956 (3–2 v Swansea Town), 1959 (2–0 v Lovells Athletic); 1964 (5–3 agg., v **Bangor City**), 1965 (8–2 agg., v Wrexham), 1967 (4–3 agg., v Wrexham), 1968 (6–1 agg., v Hereford United), 1969 (5–1 agg., v Swansea Town), 1970 (5–0 agg., v **Chester**), 1971 (4–1 agg., v Wrexham), 1973 (5–1 agg., v Bangor City) 1974 (2–0 agg., v Stourbridge), 1976 (6–5 agg., v Hereford United), 1988 (2–0 v Wrexham), 1992 (1–0 v Hednesford Town), 1993 (5–0 v Rhyl). *Records* Alf Sherwood is Cardiff's most capped player (39 (41) for **Wales**); Phil Dwyer holds the record for club League appearances (471, 1972-85); Len Davies is Cardiff's record League goalscorer (128, 1920-31).

caretaker manager   *n.* coach who takes temporary charge of a team before a permanent manager is appointed.

Carey, Johnny   *player-manager* Defender. **Republic of Ireland** (28 caps) and **Northern Ireland** international (7 caps). Born 23 February 1923. Career ca. 1936–53. *Clubs* (player) **Manchester United**; (manager) **Blackburn Rovers** (twice), **Everton**, **Leyton Orient**, **Nottingham Forest**. *Keynotes* Signed by Manchester United from League of Ireland club St James's Gate for £250 in October 1937. Carey went on to make 304 **Football League** appearances for United, captaining the club to its 1948 FA Cup final success and its 1951-52 League Championship. Carey was voted **Footballer of the Year** in 1949 and Sportsman of the Year in 1950. He retired from playing at the end of the 1952-53 season, having scored 16 goals for Manchester United. Under Carey's managership, Blackburn Rovers won promotion back to Division One in 1957-58. He later went on to manage Everton and Leyton Orient, where he achieved the same success that he had at Blackburn, by taking the club to the top flight for the first time in its history in 1961-62. Included in the **Football League Centenary 100 players**. *Honours* (player) **FA Cup** (Manchester United 1948); League Championship (Manchester United 1951-52).

Caribbean Club Championship *competition* annual club tournament for the champion clubs of the Caribbean section of the **Confederación Norte-Centroamericana y del Caribe de Fútbol**, first played 1998. The winners qualify for the **CONCACAF Champions Cup**. *Winners* 1998 **Joe Public**, 1–0, v Courts Caledonia AIA (both clubs from Trinidad and Tobago).

Caribbean Nations Cup (Copa Caribe) *competition* annual international nations tournament, competed by the Caribbean member countries of the **Confederación Norte-Centroamericana y del**

Caribe de Fútbol, CONCACAF); known until 1999 as the Shell Caribbean Cup. The tournament also serves as the regional qualifier for the **Gold Cup**; 1997 winners **Trinidad and Tobago** qualified automatically for the 1998 Gold Cup, while 1996 runners-up **Cuba** played off with 1997 runners-up **St Kitts and Nevis** for the second berth. The 1999 edition comprised five preliminary-round matches to finalise the line-up for five round-robin groups of four or five nations. The winners of each group qualified for the final tournament, where they were joined by the holders **Jamaica**, the hosts Trinidad and Tobago, and the Brazilian under-20 team as the guest nation; the finals tournament was played in two round-robin groups of four nations; the group winners and runners-up qualifying for knockout semi-finals and final. The losing semi-finalists playoff for third place. *Winners, scores, runners-up and venue* 1989 Trinidad and Tobago, 2–1, v **Grenada**, in Barbados; 1991 Jamaica, 2–0, v Trinidad and Tobago, in Jamaica; 1992 Trinidad and Tobago, 3–1, v Jamaica, in Trinidad; 1993 **Martinique**, 0–0, 6–5 pens., v Jamaica, in Jamaica; 1994 Trinidad and Tobago, 7–2, v Martinique, in Trinidad; 1995 Trinidad and Tobago, 5–0, v **St Vincent** (in Cayman Islands and Jamaica); 1996 Trinidad and Tobago, 2–0, v Cuba (in Trinidad and Tobago); 1997 Trinidad and Tobago, 4–0, v St Kitts and Nevis (in Antigua and St Kitts and Nevis); 1998 Jamaica, 2–1, v Trinidad and Tobago (in Trinidad and Tobago and Jamaica); 1999 tournament in Trinidad and Tobago.

Carl Zeis Jena   *club* German and former-East German national league club based in Jena, formed 1946 as SG Ernst Abbe. Ground: Ernst Abbe Sportfeld, capacity: 9,000. Strip: blue shirts, white shorts. East German Cup 1960, 1972, 1974, 1980; East German league champions 1963, 1968, 1970; **European Cup** quarter-final 1971; **European Cup-winners Cup** runners-up 1981 (1–2, v **Dynamo Tbilisi**, Dusseldorf).

Carling Report   *misc.* annual survey of supporters; the results of which were first published in 1994. The first Carling Report was the largest survey of football fans ever carried out in the UK, with more than 10,500 fans questioned. The survey was conducted by the **Sir Norman Chester Centre for Football Research**.

Carlisle United   *club* English league. *Dossier* Ground: **Brunton Park**, Carlisle, Cumbria. Strip: blue shirts, white shorts, blue socks. Nickname: Cumbrians or the Blues. Ground capacity: 16,651. Record attendance: 27,500 v **Birmingham City** (5 January 1957, FA Cup, third round), v **Middlesbrough** (7 February 1970, FA Cup, fifth round). Best average attendance: 14,530 (1974-75). Biggest win: 8–0 v **Hartlepool United** (1 September 1928, Division Three (North)), 8–0 v **Scunthorpe United** (25 December 1952, Division Three (North)). Biggest defeat: 1–11 v **Hull City** (14 January 1939, Division Three (North)). *History* Formed around the turn of the century as Shaddongate United, becoming Carlisle United in 1904. The club played its first matches at Milholme Bank and later at Devonshire Park before settling at Brunton Park in 1909.

In 1928-29, Carlisle was elected to Division Three (North) in place of **Durham City**. After 26 continuous seasons in the bottom division, Carlisle won promotion to Division Three in 1961-62. The club was relegated after one season, but bounced straight back the following year, with Hugh McIlmoyle scoring 39 goals, before winning the Division Three Championship in 1964-65. In 1966-67, Carlisle finished third in Division Two and the club was a **League Cup** semi-finalist in 1970 (2–4 agg., v **West Bromwich Albion**). Under the managership of Alan Ashman, in his second spell in charge of the club, Carlisle won promotion to Division One. The club's tenure in the top flight lasted only one season and by 1987-88 it was again playing in Division Four. Carlisle's brief stay in Division One also coincided with the club's best performance in the FA Cup, when it was quarter-finalist (0–1 v **Fulham**). Despite finishing bottom of Division Four in 1991-92 the club was spared relegation from the **Football League** because of **Aldershot**'s demise. Nonetheless, Carlisle's perilous financial situation resulted in the club being put up for sale and serious consideration given to a return to part-time status. Michael Knighton, who in August 1989 had attempted to buy **Manchester United**, purchased Carlisle and, in 1994-95, the club won the Third Division title, having failed to gain promotion to the Second Division via the end-of-season **playoffs** the previous season. Carlisle also made its first **Wembley** appearance in 1995, losing in the final of the **Auto Windscreens Shield** (0–1 **golden goal** v **Birmingham City**). The club won the same competition two years later (0–0, 4–3 pens. v **Colchester United**), the same season as it again secured promotion to the Second Division. The 1997-98 season finished in the club's demotion to the bottom division, and during the year Mervyn Day was dismissed as manager and Knighton took control of team affairs. Carlisle retained its long history of Football League football with virtually the last kick of the 1998-99 season. It needed a win in its home game against **Plymouth Argyle** while hoping for an inferior result by relegation rivals **Scarborough** in its home game against **Peterborough United**. With both matches level at 1–1 and the Scarborough match at full time, Carlisle was in the relegation position. However, in the 94th minute, Carlisle's **on-loan** goalkeeper Jimmy Glass joined the Carlisle attack for a corner. Glass scored from the edge of the penalty area and Carlisle stayed in the Third Division. *League record* Division One 1974-75; Division Two 1965-66 to 1973-74, 1975-76 to 1976-77, 1982-83 to 1985-86; Second Division 1995-96, 1997-98; Division Three 1962-63, 1964-65, 1977-78 to 1981-82, 1986-87; Third Division 1992-93 to 1994-95, 1996-97, 1998-99–; Division Three (North) 1928-29 to 1957-58; Division Four 1958-59 to 1961-62, 1963-64, 1987-88 to 1991-92. *Honours* Auto Windscreens Shield 1997 (0–0, 4–3 pens. v Colchester United); Division Three 1964-65; Third Division 1994-95. *Records* Eric Welsh is Carlisle's most capped player (4 for **Northern**

Ireland); Alan Ross holds the record for club League appearances (466, 1963-79); Jimmy McConnell is Carlisle's record League goalscorer (126, 1928-32).

Carlsberg Tournament *competition* four-team pre-season tournament staged at Lansdowne Road, Dublin in July/August 1998. The tournament involved **Lazio**, **Leeds United**, **Liverpool** and **St Patrick's Athletic**. Liverpool was victorious (2–0 v Leeds United).

Carmarthen *club* Welsh league. Ground: Richmond Park, Carmarthenshire. Strip: Old Gold shirts, black shorts. Nickname: Town. Ground capacity: 3,000. Formed in 1953.

Carrick Rangers FC *club* Northern Ireland national league club based in Carrickfergus, County Antrim, founded 1939. Ground: Taylor's Avenue, capacity: 5,000. Strip: light brown shirts, black shorts. **Irish FA Cup** 1976.

Carrow Road *ground* English football ground situated in Norwich, Norfolk; home of **Norwich City**. *Dossier* Ground capacity: 21,994 all seated. Pitch dimensions: 104m x 68m. Record attendance: 43,984 v **Leicester City** (30 March 1963, **FA Cup**, sixth round). Best average attendance: 28,420 (1972-73). *History* Norwich City played its first match at Carrow Road on 31 August 1935 (v **West Ham United**, Division Two), having used a venue known as the Nest since 1908. Mustard manufacturer's Colmans owned Carrow Road and it was the sports ground of local engineering company Boulton Paul. City initially sub-let the ground from the engineers, eventually buying the freehold in 1972. King George VI visited the ground on 29 October 1938 during a match with **Millwall** – this was the first occasion a British monarch watched a Division Two game. Fire destroyed part of the Main Stand on 25 October 1984. The ground became an **all-seater stadium** in 1992. Carrow Road staged an **Inter-League** match on 31 October 1962 (**Football League** v Irish League) and on 23 September 1970 (Football League v Irish League). The first floodlit match took place on 17 October 1956 (v **Sunderland**).

cartel, football *n.* informal association of clubs to gain the biggest price for televised matches. In 1999, the **Office of Fair Trading** (OFT) took a case to the Restrictive Practices Court alleging that the **Premier League** acted as a cartel in collectively agreeing to sell the exclusive rights to televise live matches. The case had serious implications for televised sport in Britain.

Carter, Raich (Horatio Stratton) *player-manager* Inside-forward. **England** international (13 caps, 7 goals). Born 21 December 1913. Career ca. 1930–53. *Clubs* (player) **Sunderland**, **Derby County**, **Hull City** (player/assistant manager), Cork Athletic; (manager) Hull City (player-manager); **Leeds United**, **Mansfield Town**, **Middlesbrough**. *Keynotes* Scorer of 216 goals in 451 **Football League** matches in a playing career spanning 23 years. Carter had distinctive silver hair and during **World War II** he appeared 17 times for England in wartime or Victory internationals (not counted as full internationals). Carter scored in the first minute of **England**'s first post-World War II international fixture (v **Northern Ireland**, 28 September 1946). He scored one of Sunderland's three goals in the club's 1937 FA Cup final triumph (3–1 v **Preston North End**). Carter became assistant manager at Hull City after signing for the club for £6,000 in March 1948. He went on to make 136 appearances for Hull, scoring 52 goals. Aside from winning the Division Three (North) title with Hull in 1948-49, Carter's managerial career also included winning promotion to Division One with Leeds United in 1955-56. Included in the **Football League Centenary 100 players**. *Honours* League Championship (Sunderland 1935-36); Division Three (North) (Hull City 1948-49); **FA Cup** (Sunderland 1937; Derby County 1946); Irish FA Cup (Cork Athletic 1953).

Carter, Philip *official* twelfth president of the **Football League** (appointed 1986), former chairman of **Everton** and protagonist of the proposal for a **Super League**.

cartilage *medical* connective tissue found at the part of a **bone** that forms a **joint**. It is very tough, yet flexible and elastic so that it can act as a shock absorber and allow two bone surfaces to move smoothly against each other. The two cartilages of most significance in football injuries are the medial (inner) and lateral (outer) cartilages of the knee joint. These are attached to the **tibia** and work like shock absorbers, stabilising the knee joint during activity. Injuries occur when the cartilage is torn, usually due to a rotational force. A torn knee cartilage can cause discomfort usually along the line of the joint and may make straightening the leg difficult. In extreme cases the knee joint can become locked.

cartilage operation *medical* operation to repair or replace damaged **cartilage**. Cartilage damage is particularly common in footballers' knees.

Caszely, Carlos *player* Striker. **Chile** international (29 goals, ca. 1972-85). *Club* **Colo Colo**. *Keynotes* formerly Chile's all-time leading goalscorer. Top scorer in the 1973 **Copa Libertadores** with nine goals for Colo Colo.

Catalonia Championship (Campionat de Catalunya) *competition* former regional league championship competed by clubs from the Catalonia region of **Spain**; the first league in Spain. It was founded in 1901 by Alfons Macaya, as the Macaya Cup. From 1904 it was organised by the then Catalan Football Association (Associacio Catalana de Clubs de Fútbol). No championship was played in 1938-39 owing to the Spanish Civil War. The competion was abolished by the new military government in 1940. The two most successful clubs were **Barcelona** (22 championships) and **RCD Espanyol** (seven championships).

catenaccio defence *tactics* defensive system. Catenaccio means "bolt" or "chain" in Italian, where the system was widely adopted. A highly defensive/cautious system based on a four-three-three formation which involves a team denying its opponents scoring opportunities by defending the **scoring space** and adopting **man-to-man** marking, supported by a **sweeper**. Teams adopting the catenaccio approach rely on **counter-attack**s and breakaways, using fast forwards, to score. A variation of the catenaccio system is favoured today by teams defending **set plays**, such as free-kicks and corners. A forerunner of catenaccio was developed by Austrian Karl Rappan as manager of **Switzerland** in the late 1930s. Rappan's approach, called **verrou** (bolt), used a rudimentary sweeper system and relied on the counter-attack, something that had rarely been seen before. Switzerland adopted the system during the 1938 **World Cup**. However, it was the Italian club sides of the 1950s and 1960s which perfected the system, most notably **Internazionale** under the managership of Helenio **Herrera** – during his spell at Internazionale the club appeared in three **European Cup** finals in four years, winning the trophy on two occasions (1964, 1965), with a team that included the Italian international defensive trio, Tarcisio Burgnich, Armando Picchi and Giacinto **Facchetti**).

caution *rules* also called **booking.** Recorded punishment meted out to an individual player by a referee during a game of football for any one of a number of offences listed in the **Laws of the game** (Law XII). A caution may be administered in addition to a punishment delivered to the offending player's team by way of a **free kick** or **penalty kick**. A player in receipt of a caution is shown a **yellow card** by the referee and his or her name is recorded in the **referee's notebook**. A player may be cautioned for **unsporting behaviour**; persistently infringing the Laws of the game; entering or leaving the **field of play** during a game without permission of the referee; failing to retreat 9.15 metres (10 yards) from the ball when a **free-kick** is taken; for delaying the **restart** of play; or for showing **dissent** (by word or deed) against a referee's decision. A player can be cautioned for a foul even when the referee chooses to apply the **advantage**; the caution given when play eventually stops. A player who receives two cautions in a single match, or who commits a **second cautionable offence** before the referee has recorded the first caution, should be **sent off**. If a player commits two different infringements at the same time, the referee must punish the more serious offence. The implication of a caution varies according to the rules of a particular competition. *Keynotes* Vinnie Jones of **Chelsea** was cautioned only three seconds after the start of an **FA Cup** fifth-round match against **Sheffield United** (15 February 1992, at **Stamford Bridge**). **Mansfield Town** had 10 of its players booked in one match – an English league and cup record (v **Crystal Palace**, at **Selhurst Park**, January 1963, FA Cup third round). In the 1998 **World Cup** finals tournament in France, 244 cautions were meted out in 64 matches (3.81 per match). *vb.* to penalise a player with a caution. See **Fair Play League**.

cautionable offence *rules* infringement of the **Laws of the game** that warrants a **caution** (Law XII).

Cayman Islands *country* CONCACAF British dependent territory in the West Indies. Area: 259 sq km (100 sq miles). Population: 29,000 Language: English.

Capital: George Town. *Dossier* Cayman Islands Football Association (George Town) formed in 1966, affiliated to **FIFA** and **Confederación Norte-Centroamericana y del Caribe de Fútbol** (CONCACAF) in 1992, president Jeffrey Webb, general secretary Mark White. National stadium: National Stadium, George Town, capacity: 8,000. National strip: red shirts, blue shorts. Biggest defeat: 2–9 v **Trinidad** (July 1995, **Caribbean Nations Cup** semi-final). *International tournament record* **Olympic Games** – never qualified for finals tournament; **Women's World Cup** – never entered; **World Cup** – first entered 1998 (first qualifying round); Caribbean Nations Cup – semi-final/fourth 1995 (0–3 v **Cuba**, third/fourth playoff); **Gold Cup** – never qualified. *Record against British and Irish national teams* none played. *Record in international club tournaments* no major successes in CONCACAF tournaments. Leading clubs: International, Scholars, Strikers.

CCCF Championship *competition* former tournament of nations affiliated to the former **Confederación Centroamericana y del Caribe de Fútbol** (CCCF), held approximately every two years. Replaced in 1962 by the **CONCACAF Championship**. The first tournament was held in San José, **Costa Rica**, in May 1941, and won by the host nation, which won a league of five nations, ahead of **El Salvador**, Curacao (the largest island of the **Netherlands Antilles**), **Panama** and **Nicaragua**. Costa Rica won the tournament seven times. The only other winners were El Salvador (1943), Panama (1951) and **Haiti** (1957). *Winners and venues (where known)* 1941 Costa Rica (in San José); 1943 El Salvador (in San Salvador, El Salvador); 1946 Costa Rica (in San José); 1948 Costa Rica (in Guatemala City, Guatemala); 1951 Panama; 1953 Costa Rica; 1955 Costa Rica; 1955 Costa Rica; 1957 Haiti (in Curacao, Netherlands Antilles); 1960 Costa Rica (in Havana, Cuba); 1961 Costa Rica (in San José).

CD Plaza Amador *club* Panama national league club based in Panama City. Ground: Estadio Revolución (the national stadium), capacity: 22,000. Strip: blue shirts, red shorts.

CD Tenerife *club* Spanish national league club based in Santa Cruz de Tenerife in the **Canary Islands**, founded 1922. Ground: Heliodoro Rodríguez, capacity: 24,000. Strip: white shirts, blue shorts. **UEFA Cup** semi-final 1997 (1–2, agg., v **FC Schalke 04**). Arguably, one of only two clubs in Africa (with **CS Maritimo** of Madiera/Portugal) to play in a major European club competition.

CDE (Association Sportive Compagne Djiboutie-Ethiopie) *club* Djibouti national league club based in the capital Djibouti. Djibouti Cup 1992; Djibouti league champions 1988.

Cea, Pedro *player* Striker. **Uruguay** international player. *Keynotes* The first player to have scored in both a **World Cup** final (1930, 4–2, v **Argentina**, in Montevideo) and **Olympic Games** final (1924, 3–0, v **Switzerland**, in Paris). Only Ferenc **Puskas** and Zoltan **Czibor** have equalled this feat. Cea was the sec-

ond highest scorer in the first World Cup tournament with five goals (three behind Guillermo **Stábile** of Argentina). *Honours* Olympic Games (Uruguay, 1924); World Cup (Uruguay, 1930); **Copa America** (Uruguay, 1923, 1924).

Ceara *state* one of the 27 state leagues in **Brazil**, founded 1920. Leading clubs: Fortaleza Esporte Clube (Fortaleza), Ceara Sporting Club (Fortaleza).

CEDEAO Tournament *competition* (Tournament of the Communaut-Economique des Etats de Afrique de l'Ouest.) Regional championship for nations in the **West African Football Union** (more specifically, the West African economic trading community), first played 1983 when **Ivory Coast** beat **Togo** 1–0 in the final. Participating nations are **Benin**, **Burkina Faso**, **Cape Verde**, **Gambia**, **Ghana**, **Guinea**, **Guinea-Bissau**, Ivory Coast, **Liberia**, **Mali**, **Mauritania**, **Niger**, **Nigeria**, **Senegal**, **Sierra Leone** and Togo. *Winners* Ivory Coast (1983, 1987, 1991), Senegal (1985), Nigeria (1989).

Celik Zenica *club* Bosnia and former-Yugoslavia league club based in Zenica, founded 1945. Ground: Bilino Polje, capacity: 22,000 (pre-civil war). Strip: red shirts, black shorts. Bosnian league champions 1996, 1997; Mitropa Cup 1971, 1972.

Celtic *club* Scottish league. *Dossier* Ground: **Celtic Park** (Parkhead), Glasgow, Strathclyde, capacity: 60,294 all seated. Strip: green and white-hooped shirts, white shorts with green trim, white socks with green hoops. Website: *www.celticfc.co.uk* Nickname: Bhoys. Record attendance: 92,000 v **Rangers** (1 January 1938, Division One). Biggest win: 11–0 v **Dundee** (26 October 1896, Division One). Biggest defeat: 0–8 v **Motherwell** (30 April 1937, Division One). *History* Founded in 1887 as a charitable trust by Glasgow's large Catholic community as a way of raising money for the poor of the city's East End. Celtic was a founder member of the **Scottish Football League** in 1890-91 and, in 1892, the club moved to its present home. In Celtic's first season at Parkhead, the club won its first League Championship. Celtic's first appearance in the final of the **Scottish FA Cup** was in 1889 (1–2 replay v **Third Lanark**), winning the trophy for the first time in 1892 (5–1 replay v **Queen's Park**). In the first 49 seasons of the Scottish Football League/Division One, prior to its suspension during **World War II**, Celtic never finished outside the top five, winning the title on 19 occasions. In the immediate post-war period, Celtic struggled to regain its former supremacy, finishing as low as 12th in 1947-48 and not winning the Championship again until 1953-54. The appointment as manager of Jock **Stein**, who had been a member of Celtic's **double** winning side in 1953-54, began a period of unparalleled success for the club. Stein rejoined the club in 1965 and won his first Scottish Championship as manager in 1965-66, beginning a run of nine straight League titles between (a world record at the time and one not equalled by Rangers until 1996-97). He also led the club to its greatest triumph, in the 1967 **European Cup** final (2–1 v **Internazionale**) – the first UK club to win the trophy. That season, Celtic also made a clean sweep of the domestic honours. Celtic reached the final of the European Cup again in 1970 (1–2 a.e.t. v **Feyenoord**) and was a semi-finalist in both 1972 (0–0, 4–5 pens. v Internazionale) and 1974 (0–2 v **Atlético Madrid**). Between 1965-66 and 1997-98, Celtic only once finished outside the top four in Division One/Premier Division. However, Rangers' ascendancy from the late-1980s meant that Celtic, which had won the Championship in 1987-88, had to wait until 1997-98 to win another title. Overall Celtic trail Rangers in the number of League title successes, having won 36 Championships up to the start of the 1998-99 season compared to its rival's 47 victories. Celtic's 1995 Scottish FA Cup triumph (1–0 v **Airdrieonians**), its first since 1989, was the club's 30th and a competition record. Celtic's and Rangers' nine-year runs in the league are one short of the World-record 10-year run held by **Berlin FC** and **Dynamo Tbilisi**. By 1998, only three clubs in the world had won more league championships than Celtic (Rangers, **Peñarol** and **Linfield**). By 1998, just two clubs in the world had won more domestic cups than the 30 triumphs by Celtic: Linfield (35) and **Al Ahly** (31). In March 1994, Canadian businessman Fergus McCann bought a controlling interest (51%) in Celtic (after an acrimonious power struggle – see Celtic Park) and, in September 1995, the club became a listed company on the **Alternative Investment Market** (floatation price = 6,600p). At one point, Celtic's shares, which were originally sold at around £60, were trading above £450 and more than 10,000 supporters are shareholders. In September 1998, Celtic announced plans to become a fully listed business on the London Stock Exchange. Since McCann took control of the club, he has presided over a complete redevelopment of Parkhead and, at the start of the 1998-99 season, the ground's 60,294 capacity made it the UK's biggest club football stadium. *League record* **Premier League**; Premier Division 1975-76 to 1997-98; Division One (A Division) 1893-94 to 1914-15, 1921-22 to 1974-75; Scottish League 1890-91 to 1892-93, 1915-16 to 1920-21. *Honours* Division One 1893-94, 1895-96, 1897-98, 1904-05, 1906-07, 1907-08, 1908-09, 1909-10, 1913-14, 1921-22, 1925-26, 1935-36, 1937-38, 1953-54, 1965-66, 1966-67, 1967-68, 1968-69, 1969-70, 1970-71, 1971-72, 1972-73, 1973-74; **European Cup** 1967 (2–1 v **Internazionale** – Simpson, Craig, McNeill, Gemmell (1), Murdoch, Clark, Johnstone, Wallace, Chalmers (1), Auld, Lennox); Premier Division 1976-77, 1978-79, 1980-81, 1981-82, 1985-86, 1987-88, 1997-98; Scottish FA Cup 1892 (5–1 replay v **Queen's Park**), 1899 (2–0 v Rangers), 1900 (4–3 v Queen's Park), 1904 (3–2 v Rangers), 1907 (3–0 v **Heart of Midlothian**), 1908 (5–1 v **St Mirren**), 1911 (2–0 replay v **Hamilton Academicals**), 1912 (2–0 v **Clyde**), 1914 (4–1 replay v **Hibernian**), 1923 (1–0 v Hibernian), 1925 (2–1 v **Dundee United**), 1927 (3–1 v **East Fife**), 1931 (4–2 replay v **Motherwell**), 1933 (1–0 v Motherwell), 1937 (2–1 v **Aberdeen**), 1951 (1–0 v Motherwell), 1954 (2–1 v Aberdeen), 1965 (3–2 v **Dunfermline Athletic**), 1967 (2–0 v Aberdeen), 1969 (4–0 v Rangers), 1971 (2–1 replay v Rangers), 1972 (6–1 v Hibernian), 1974 (3–0 v Dundee United), 1975 (3–1 v **Airdrieonians**), 1977 (1–0 v Rangers), 1980 (1–0 v Rangers), 1985 (2–1 v Dundee United), 1988 (2–1 v Dundee United), 1989 (1–0 v Rangers), 1995 (1–0 v Airdrieonians); Scottish League 1892-93, 1915-16, 1916-17, 1918-19; Scottish League Cup 1956-57 (3–0 replay v **Partick Thistle**), 1957-58 (7–1 v Rangers), 1965-66 (2–1 v Rangers), 1966-67 (1–0 v Rangers), 1967-68 (5–3 v Dundee), 1968-69 (6–2 v Hibernian), 1969-70 (1–0 **St Johnstone**), 1974-75 (6–3 v Hibernian), 1982-83 (2–1 v Rangers), 1997-98 (3–0 v Dundee United). *Records* Paul McStay is Celtic's most capped player (76 for **Scotland**), Billy McNeill holds the record for club appearances (486, 1957-77); James McGrory is Celtic's record goalscorer (397, 1922-39).

Celtic Park (Parkhead) *ground* Scottish football ground situated in Glasgow, Strathclyde; home of **Celtic**. *Dossier* Ground capacity: 60,294 all seated. Pitch dimensions: 105m x 68.5m. Record attendance: 92,000 **Rangers** (1 January 1938, **Division One**). *History* Celtic played its first match at Parkhead – named after the district of Glasgow in which ground is situated and the name by which it is commonly known – on 20 August 1892 (v **Renton**). The ground staged the first of many **Scotland** internationals on 28 March 1891 (v **Ireland**). A Scotland v **England** international fixture on 7 April 1894 earned record takings of £46,000 for such a match. Celtic bought the ground for £10,000 in 1897 and, in its early years, Parkhead was used for a host of sports including athletics, cycling and speedway. The club experimented with floodlights during 1893, staging a night match on Christmas Day against **Clyde** with lights suspended on wires above the pitch together with lamps on poles around the ground. In 1894, Parkhead became the first ground to construct its own **press box**. By 1967, the ground had more covered **terrace** accommodation (three sides) than any other League ground in the UK, but less seated areas than most. When the **Taylor Report** recommended **all-seater stadium**s, Parkhead's facilities were well behind those of other club grounds. At one stage, with the club more than £6 million in debt, Celtic considered moving to a new purpose-built 52,000 capacity stadium in Cambuslang. Parkhead's "Jungle" end – Celtic's equivalent of **Liverpool**'s **Kop** – was seated in summer 1993. The following season, supporters, protesting against the running of the club by the board, boycotted matches and attendance at one stage dropped below 11,000. In March 1994, the board, unable to raise the money to finance the Cambuslang scheme and facing a demand from its bankers to reduce the club's overdraft, was saved from putting the club into receivership by Canadian businessman Fergus McCann who purchased a controlling interest (51%). McCann rejected the proposed move to Cambuslang, deciding, instead, to redevelop Parkhead. In the summer of 1994, Parkhead's three terraces were demolished and the club played the following League campaign at **Hampden Park**, returning to a partially-finished stadium on 5 August 1995 (v **Newcastle United**, friendly). At the start of the 1998-99 season, the ground's redevelopment had been completed and the 60,294 plus capacity made it the UK's biggest club football stadium. The first floodlit match at Parkhead took place on 12 October 1959 (v **Wolverhampton Wanderers**, friendly). Parkhead staged its first **Scottish FA Cup** final in 1902 (**Hibernians** v Celtic).

Celtic plc *n.* publicly-quoted business which owns **Celtic**. The club became a listed company on the **Alternative Investment Market** (floatation price = 6,600p) in September 1995. Celtic had a market capitalisation – the market value of the company's issued share capital (eg, the quoted price of its shares multiplied by the number of shares outstanding) – of £19.8 million when it joined the AIM. At one point, Celtic's shares, which were originally sold at around £66, were trading above £450. More than 10,000 Celtic supporters are shareholders. In September 1998, Celtic announced plans to become a fully listed business on the London Stock Exchange.

Cemaes Bay *club* Welsh league. Ground: School Lane Stadium, Cemaes, Anglesey, Gwynedd. Strip: gold and black shirts, black shorts. Nickname: none. Ground capacity: 3,000. Formed in 1976.

Cendrillon *misc.* French term (literally) Cinderella, given to the club from the lowest division still left in the French domestic cup (la Coupe de France).

Centenario (Estadio) *ground* Uruguayan football ground situated in Montevideo; home of **Uruguay** national side and the club sides Club Atletico **Peñarol** and Club **Nacional** de Football. Ground capacity: 80,000. *History* A large open-air bowl built to commemorate the country's centenary in 1930 (hence the name) and to stage the inaugural **World Cup** final (Uruguay v **Argentina**). Aside from the final, Centenario was the venue for nine other fixtures during the first World Cup tournament (**Chile** v **France**, Argentina v **Mexico**, Argentina v Chile, group 1; **Brazil** v **Bolivia**, group 2; Uruguay v **Peru**, Uruguay v **Romania**, group 3; **Paraguay** v **Belgium**, group 4; Argentina v **USA**, Uruguay v **Yugoslavia**, semi-finals) – total attendance 508,981; average attendance 50,898. Centenario staged the **Copa America** in 1942 (18th edition), 1956 (25th edition) and 1967 (30th edition). It was also the venue for several matches during the 1983 (33rd edition) and 1995 (38th edition) tournaments, including the final on both occasions (1983 Uruguay v Brazil, first leg, 65,000; 1995 Uruguay v Brazil, 60,000), and was an occasional venue during the 1975 (31st edition) and 1979 (32nd edition) series. The stadium was the setting for the first **World Club Cup** match (1960 Peñarol v **Real Madrid**, 75,000) and has hosted the home legs for both Nacional and Peñarol when either

has qualified (1961 Peñarol v **Benfica**, 56,000; + **play-off**, 62,000; 1966 Peñarol v Real Madrid, 70,000; 1971 Nacional v **Panathinaikos**, 70,000) as well as the 1967 playoff (**Racing Club** v Celtic, 65,000).

Central African Republic *country CAF* land-locked country in central Africa, bordered by Sudan, **Zaire**, **Congo**, **Cameroon** and **Chad**. Independent from France in 1960. Area: 624,975 sq km (241,240 sq miles). Population: 3,070,000 (1994 est.). Languages: Sango and French. Capital: Bangui. *Dossier* Football association (Fédération Centrafricaine de Football Amateur, Bagui) formed in 1937, affiliated to **FIFA** in 1963 and **Confédération Africaine de Football** (CAF) in 1965, member of the **Union of Football Associations of Central Africa**, president Jonathan N'Kouet, general secretary Gervais Mboe. Season played from October to July. National stadium: Barthelemy Boganda, Bangui, capacity: 35,000. National strip: grey blue shirts with the national emblem and star, white shorts. First international game: 1960 v **Mali** (3–4, in Madagascar, friendly). Biggest victory: 4–1 v Congo (**UDEAC Tournament**, in Gabon). Biggest defeat: 1–7 v **Cameroon** (17 December 1984, in Congo, UDEAC Tournament). *International tournament record* **Olympic Games** – never entered; **Women's World Cup** – never entered; **World Cup** – never entered; **African Nations Cup** – first entered 1974, never beyond first qualifying round; **UDEAC Tournament** – runners-up and hosts 1989; **Under-17 World Championship** – never entered; **World Youth Cup (under-20)** – never entered. *Record against British and Irish national teams* none played. *History* National league dates back to 1968; all the national leagues clubs are based around the capital Bangui. Its best international achievement was as runners-up in the 1989 UDEAC Tournament contested by six countries in Central Africa (along with Cameroon, Chad, Congo, **Equatorial Guinea** and **Gabon**). *League system* There are 12 clubs in the national league – predominantly from the capital Bangui – as well as regional leagues. *Record in international club tournaments* **African Cup of Champion Clubs** – **AS Tempeta Mocaf** (second round 1994), **Real Olympique Castel** (second round 1974), **SCAF Tocages** (second round 1985); **African Cup-winners Cup** – AS Tempeta Mocaf (quarter-final 1975), **ASDR Fatima** (second round 1974). Other leading club: **FACA** .

Central American and Caribbean Games *competition* multi-sports competition for nations of Central America and Caribbean, held every four years. Includes a football competition, first staged 1926. *Winners (football tournament):* **Colombia** (1946), **Cuba** (1930, 1970, 1974, 1978, 1986), **El Salvador** (1954), **Mexico** (1926, 1935, 1938, 1959, 1966, 1990), **Venezuela** (1982).

Central Park *ground* Scottish football ground situated in Cowdenbeath, Fife; home of **Cowdenbeath**. *Dossier* Ground capacity: 5,268. Pitch dimensions: 98m x 60m. Record attendance: 25,586 v **Rangers** (21 September 1949, **Scottish League Cup**, quarter-final). *Keynotes* Cowdenbeath played its first matches at Central Park in 1917, having previously played at Jubilee Park and North End Park. The first floodlit match at Central Park occurred in October 1968 (v **Celtic**, friendly). Central Park is widely known as a stock car circuit, staging several world championships since 1970.

Central Sport *club* Tahiti national league club based in the capital Papeete. *Keynotes* Central Sport's 19 league titles is an Oceania club record. It also holds the Oceania club record of eight consecutive national league titles (1972 to 1979). Tahiti Cup – 18 times to 1998; Tahiti league champions 1958, 1962, 1963, 1964, 1965, 1966, 1967, 1972, 1973, 1974, 1975, 1976, 1977, 1978, 1979, 1981, 1982, 1983, 1985.

centre back *n.* defender playing in the middle of a defensive formation. Compare **wing back**.

centre circle *rules* circle of 9.15 metres (10 yards) marked out at the centre of the **field of play**. The circle line must be no more than 12 cm (5 inches) wide (Law I). *Keynotes* When **Bolton Wanderers** moved to a purpose-built **Reebok Stadium** in 1997, the centre circle turf from its old ground **Burnden Park** was transferred to the new pitch.

centre forward *n.* **striker** who occupies the central position of the attacking players. Traditionally, the centre forward wears the number nine shirt; though the introduction of **squad numbers** has reduced this tradition.

centre half *n.* **defender** who plays in the centre of the defence.

centre of excellence *regulations* a licensed football training and development centre for **student** players. The centres are operated by **Football League** or **Premier League** clubs in accordance with **Football Association** rules (FA Premier League rule M.3, Football League regulation 53). FA rules require that the establishments employ only qualified staff and offer suitable coaching and education facilities, as well as medical treatment and hygiene areas. There are about 145 centres of excellence in England.

centre spot *rules* centre of the field of play, indicated by a suitable mark (Law I) See: **kick-off** and **start of play**.

Cerro Porteño (Club Cerro Porteño) *club* Paraguay national league club based in the capital Asuncion, founded in 1912. The name is derived from a 19th-century military victory by Paraguay over Argentina. Ground: Estadio General Pablo Rojas ("El Olla"), capacity: 30,000. Strip: blue and maroon broad striped shirts, white shorts. **Copa Libertadores** semi-final 1993, 1998, quarter-final 1992, second round group 1973, 1978; Paraguay league champions 1913, 1915, 1918, 1919, 1935, 1939, 1940, 1941, 1944, 1950, 1954, 1961, 1963, 1966, 1970, 1972, 1973, 1974, 1977, 1987, 1990, 1992, 1994, 1996, 1998.

Ceulemans, Jan *player* Striker/midfield. **Belgium** international (96 caps, 23 goals, 1977–91). Born 28 February 1957. *Clubs* Lierse SK, **Club Brugge**.

Keynotes Belgium's all-time most-capped player; scored three goals in the 1986 **World Cup** finals. Transferred to Club Brugge in 1978 for a then Belgian record fee of £250,000. Belgium league top scorer 1980 (29 goals). *Honours* World Cup fourth place (Belgium, 1986); Belgium league championship (Club Brugge, 1980, 1988, 1990, 1992).

CF Uniao (Clube de Futebol) *club* Portuguese national league club, from Funchal on the island of **Madeira** and formed in 1913. Ground: Estádio dos Barreiros, capacity: 16,000. Strip: yellow and blue striped shirts and blue shorts.

Cha Bum Kun *player* **South Korea** international (41 caps). Born 21 May 1953. *Clubs* (include) Darmstadt, **Eintracht Frankfurt**, **Bayer Leverkusen**. Career ca. 1975-86. *Keynotes* South Korean national coach at the 1998 World Cup finals and 1998 Asian manager of the year. *Honours* **UEFA Cup** (Bayer Leverkusen, 1988).

Chad *country CAF* vast republic in central Africa, with a large area in the Sahara desert, bordered by Libya, Sudan, the Central African Republic, Cameroon, Nigeria and Niger. Former French colony, independent in 1960. Area: 1,284,000 sq km (495,625 sq miles). Very poor country with frequent droughts and increasing desertification. Population: 6,280,000 (1993 census). Languages: French and Arabic. Capital: N'Djamena. *Dossier* Football association formed in 1962 affiliated to **FIFA** and **Confédération Africaine de Football** (CAF) in 1988, member of the **Union of Football Associations of Central Africa**, president Djibrine Adoum, general secretary Daouda Ramadane. National stadium: Stade Concorde N'Djamena, capacity: 25,000. National strip: blue shirts, yellow shorts. First international game 29 June 1976 v **Sao Tome e Principe** (5–0, in Gabon, Central African Games). Biggest victory: 5–0 (above). Biggest defeat: 1–5 v **Egypt** (12 July 1991, in Egypt, **African Nations Cup**). *International tournament record* **Olympic Games** – never entered; **Women's World Cup** – never entered; **World Cup** – never entered; **African Nations Cup** – first entered 1992, never qualified for finals tournament; **UDEAC Cup** – runners-up 1986 (1–4 v **Cameroon**, in Equatorial Guinea), 1987 (0–1 v Cameroon, in Chad); **Under-17 World Championship** – never entered; **World Youth Cup** (under-20) – never entered. *Record against British and Irish national teams* none played. *League system* Regional leagues operate: the Chari-Baguirmi league for clubs around the capital N'Djamena is considered as the national premier league. *Record in international club tournaments* **African Cup of Champion Clubs** – **Tourbillon** (first round 1992, 1998 – victory in preliminary rounds), **Postal 2000** (first round 1996), **ASCOT** (first round 1997); **CAF Cup** – ASCOT (quarter-final 1998), Tourbillon (first round 1993, victory in preliminary round); **African Cup-winners Cup** – **Renaissance** (first round 1997 – victory in preliminary round). Other leading clubs: **Elect Sport**, Gazelle (from N'Djamena, Chad Cup 1997).

chairman-manager *n.* person who combines being club chairman with team management. *Keynotes* Ron Noades (**Brentford**), Michael Knighton (**Carlisle United**) and John Reames (**Lincoln City**) have all combined the twin roles of club ownership/chairmanship with management.

challenge *vb., n.* another term for **tackle**.

Champions League *competition* see **European Cup**.

championship winners as players and managers *record* nine men have won a **Football League** championship as a player and as a manager (nobody has achieved this in the FA **Premier League**): Ted **Drake** (player, **Arsenal** 1934, 1935, 1938; manager, **Chelsea** 1955); Bill **Nicholson** (player, **Tottenham Hotspur** 1951; manager, Tottenham Hotspur 1961); Alf **Ramsey** (player, Tottenham Hotspur 1951; manager, **Ipswich Town** 1962); Joe **Mercer** (player, **Everton** 1939; Arsenal 1948, 1953; manager, **Manchester City** 1968); Dave **Mackay** (player, Tottenham Hotspur 1961; manager, **Derby County** 1975); Bob **Paisley** (player, **Liverpool** 1947; manager, Liverpool 1976, 1977, 1979, 1980, 1982, 1983); Howard **Kendall** (player, Everton 1970; manager, Everton 1985, 1987); Kenny **Dalglish** (player, Liverpool 1979, 1980, 1982, 1983, 1984; manager, Liverpool 1986, 1988, 1990); **Blackburn Rovers** 1995); George **Graham** (player, Arsenal 1971; manager, Arsenal 1989, 1991). Dalglish was the first to win the title as a player and as a **player-manager** and to win the English league and Cup **double** (1986, Liverpool).

chance *n.* a goal-scoring opportunity.

Channel Islands *country no international affiliation* British Crown dependency. Group of islands in the English channel, off northwest France, including Jersey, Guernsey, Alderney, Great Sark and Little Sark. Area: 194 sq km (75 sq miles). Population: 146,000. Language: English. Capitals: St Hélier (Jersey) and St Peter Port (Guernsey). *Dossier* Football associations not directly affiliated to **FIFA** or **Union of European Football Associations** (UEFA). Season played from August to May. Notable international players: Graham Le Saux, Matthew Le Tissier (both were born in the Channel Islands, though selected to play for **England**). *International tournament record* ineligible for major international tournaments; however, Jersey and Guernsey play each other regularly and have competed in the **Island Games**. *History* The annual Channel Islands Championship (the **Upton Park Cup**), has been played almost continuously since 1907 (except in 1911 and during the two World Wars); it is contested by the champions of Jersey and Guernsey. Clubs from Jersey have won the title outright on 40 occasions; Guernsey's clubs have won the trophy 37 times; the title has been shared twice (1921 and 1968). *Leading clubs* Northerners AC St Sampsons (of Guernsey, 16 Upton Park Cup championships to 1998, including one shared title), First Tower United St Hélier (of Jersey, 12 championships), Jersey Wanderers St Hélier (of Jersey, 11

championships, including two shared titles); also Sylvans SC St Peters (of Guernsey, three championships, 1996, 1997, 1998) and Jersey Scottish (of Jersey, two championships).

channels *n.pl.* nominal area/space either side of the **penalty area**, into which the ball is often played for attackers to exploit.

Chapman, Herbert *player-manager* Born 19 January 1878; died 6 January 1934. Career ca. 1898–09. *Clubs* (player) **Northampton Town** (also player-manager), **Notts County, Tottenham Hotspur**; (manager) **Leeds City, Huddersfield Town, Arsenal**. *Keynotes* Chapman, the first of the great football managers, was an amateur player with several clubs, including Stalybridge Rovers, **Swindon** and **Grimsby** before turning professional with Northampton Town in 1901. He moved to Notts County for £300 in 1903 and, in 1905, to Tottenham Hotspur, where he spent most of his time in the reserves. Chapman returned to Northampton as player-manager in 1907. He was appointed secretary-manager of Leeds City in 1912 and the club's most successful season was in 1913-14 when it finished fourth in Division Two. During **World War I**, Leeds City won a number of wartime tournaments: Midland Tournament (North) 1915-16, Midland Regional Tournament 1916-17, 1917-18. Leeds City was expelled from the **Football League** on 4 October 1919 for failing to co-operate with the football authorities which had accused the club of making **illegal payments** to players during the war, and Chapman was temporarily banned from football. He returned in 1921 as manager of Huddersfield Town, where he won two League titles and an FA Cup. In 1925, he took charge of Arsenal after replying to the club's advert in the **Athletic News** for a manager. Chapman turned Arsenal into the most formidable club in England in the 1930s, but died after a short illness in January 1934 as Arsenal was on course for its third title under his managership. During his spell at **Highbury**, Chapman is credited with having persuaded London Transport to rename the club's local tube station from Gillespie Road to Arsenal. He was also an advocate of floodlit football, numbered shirts and the use of a white ball. *Honours* League Championship (Huddersfield Town 1923-24, 1924-25; Arsenal 1930-31, 1932-33); **FA Cup** (Huddersfield Town 1922; Arsenal 1930); **Southern League** (Northampton Town).

charging an opponent *rules* **1.** one of the offences listed as a **foul** under the **Laws of the game** (Law XII). The offence is committed if a player uses his or her body weight to push an opponent out of the way, and does so carelessly, recklessly or with excessive force (Law XII). The punishment for charging an opponent is for the opposing team to be awarded a **direct free kick,** taken from the point where the foul was committed (unless within the opponents' **goal area**, in which case it is taken from anywhere within that area). If the foul is committed in the offending side's penalty area, then the opponents are awarded a **penalty kick. 2.** careful use of a player's body weight, without excessive force, to push past an opponent, when in playing distance of the ball (eg **fair shoulder charge**). This is not an offence, though, if the ball is not within playing distance then the player will be guilty of **obstruction**.

charity match   *n.* fixture played to raise money for a charity. One of the first known charity games was held in Sheffield at Bramall Lane in 1862 between **Sheffield FC** and Hallam FC, with the proceeds going to the Lancashire Distress Fund. See **FA Charity Shield** and **Sheriff of London's Charity Shield**.

Charity Shield *competition* see **FA Charity Shield**.

Charles, John *player* Striker/defender. **Wales** international (38 caps, 15 goals). Born 27 December 1931. Career ca. 1948–66. *Clubs* **Leeds United**, **Juventus**, **Roma (AS)**, **Cardiff City**. *Keynotes* Joined Leeds United in 1948, going on to make 308 **Football League** appearances for the club and scoring 153 goals. His 42 Division Two goals in season 1953-54 remain a club record. Charles moved to Juventus for a UK record transfer fee of £65,000 in summer 1957. Known in Italy as "Il buon gigante" (the Gentle Giant), Charles made 155 League appearances for Juventus, scoring 93 goals and winning three **Serie A** titles and two **Coppa Italia** winner's medals. Charles finished his playing career with Cardiff City, scoring 18 goals in 70 appearances. Overall Charles scored 243 goals in 543 matches, as well as playing many games in central defence. John was joined by his brother Mel in the 1958 Welsh **World Cup** squad. Included in the **Football League Centenary 100 players**. *Honours* Italian Championship (Juventus 1957-58, 1959-60, 1960-61); Italian Cup (Juventus 1959, 1960); Welsh Cup (Cardiff City 1964, 1965).

Charlot Principat *club* Andorran national league club. The first Andorran club to qualify for a European club competition (1998 **UEFA Cup** preliminary round). CE dropped only five points in the 1996-97 season (one defeat, one draw), and was unbeaten in 1997-98. Andorran league champions 1997, 1998.

Charlton Athletic *club* English league. *Dossier* Ground: The **Valley**, south London, capacity: 20,000. Strip: red shirts with white trim, white shorts, red socks with white trim. Website: *www.charlton-athletic.co.uk* Nickname: Valiants. Record attendance: 75,031 v **Aston Villa** (12 February 1938, **FA Cup**, fifth round). Best average attendance: 40,216 (1948-49). Biggest win: 8–1 v **Middlesbrough** (12 September 1953, Division One), 7–0 v **Burton Albion** (7 January 1956, FA Cup, third round). Biggest defeat: 1–11 v **Aston Villa** (14 November 1959, Division Two). *History* Founded in June 1905 by a group of teenagers in south-east London close to where the Thames Barrier is now located. After playing at numerous grounds, including Siemens Meadow, Woolwich Common, Pound Park and Horn Lane, Charlton finally settled at The Valley in 1919 – local supporters helped to raise the finance to purchase the site and to prepare it for football (the area had

been left without a football club following Woolwich **Arsenal**'s move to north London before **World War I**). The club turned professional in 1920 and joined the **Southern League**. The following year the club was elected to the **Football League** (Division Three (South)). The club reached the quarter-finals of the FA Cup in its second League season (0–1 v **Bolton Wanderers**). In December 1923, the club moved to a new ground, The Mount, at Catford, although it continued to use The Valley for reserve games and, owing to the lack of seating, FA Cup ties. Lack of support forced the club to return to The Valley by the start of the 1925-26 season, having played only 13 first-team matches at The Mount. In 1928-29, Charlton won the Division Three (South) Championship on goal average from fellow south-Londoners, **Crystal Palace**. A second Division Three (South) title was achieved in 1934-35 and the following season the club won promotion to the top flight, finishing second in Division One in 1936-37 – the club's highest-ever position. The club reached the FA Cup final in the first two seasons after **World War II**, losing in 1946 (1–4 a.e.t. v **Derby County**) before winning the trophy the following year (1–0 a.e.t. v **Burnley**). By 1972, the club was back in Division Three. Charlton almost ceased to exist in 1984, when the club, more than £1.5 million in debt, was only 35 minutes away from failing to meet the deadline for the payment of the financial guarantees demanded by the Football League. In September 1985, the Charlton board made a decision to leave the Valley and **groundshare** with neighbours Crystal Palace. The move provoked anger among Charlton supporters, some of whom campaigned to return the club to The Valley – something which eventually occurred in December 1992 (see **Valley Party**). Charlton returned to Division One for four seasons in the 1980s (1986-87 to 1989-90), retaining its place in the top-flight via the **playoffs** in 1987 (2–1 replay v **Leeds United**). In 1996, the club narrowly missed promotion to the **Premier League**, losing at the semi-final stage of the **playoffs**. The club was victorious at the playoff stage in 1997-98 (4–4, 7–6 pens. v **Sunderland**), returning to the top flight for the first time in almost a decade. To commemorate Charlton's **Wembley** playoff triumph, the players were granted the freedom of the London Borough of Greenwich by the local council. The club was floated on the **Alternative Investment Market** in March 1997 (floatation price = 80p), which is a precursor to full floatation on the stock market. *League record* Premier League 1998-99; Division One 1936-37 to 1956-57, 1986-87 to 1989-90; First Division 1992-93 to 1997-98, 1999-00–; Divsion Two 1929-30 to 1932-33, 1935-36, 1957-58 to 1971-72, 1975-76 to 1979-80, 1981-82 to 1985-86, 1990-91 to 1991-92; Division Three 1972-73 to 1974-75, 1980-81; Division Three (South) 1921-22 to 1928-29, 1933-34 to 1934-35. *Honours* Division Three (South) 1928-29, 1934-35; FA Cup 1947 (1–0 a.e.t. v Burnley – *Team* Bartram, Croker, Shreeve, Johnson, Phipps,Whittaker, Hurst, Dawson, Robinson,

Welsh, Duffy (1)). *Records* John Hewie is Charlton's most capped player (16 for **Scotland**); Sam Bartram holds the record for club appearances (583, 1934-56); Stuart Leary is Charlton's record league goalscorer (153, 1953-62).

Charlton Athletic plc *n.* publicly-quoted business which owns **Charlton Athletic**. The club became a listed company on the **Alternative Investment Market** (floatation price = 80p) in March 1997. Charlton had a market capitalisation – the market value of the company's issued share capital (eg, the quoted price of its shares multiplied by the number of shares outstanding) – of £17.5 million when it joined the AIM.

Charlton, Bobby *player-manager* Striker/midfield. **England** international (106 caps, 49 goals). Born 11 October 1937. Career ca. 1953–75. Player *Clubs* (player) **Manchester United**, **Preston North End**, (manager) Preston North End, **Wigan Athletic**. *Keynotes* Joined Manchester United as an amateur in 1953, turning professional in October 1954. Charlton scored 198 goals for United in 606 **Football League** appearances, the last of which took place at **Stamford Bridge** on 28 April 1973. He played a further 38 League fixtures as Preston's player-manager. Charlton survived the **Munich air crash** in 1958 and, in 1968, he became the first captain of an English club to lift the **European Cup**, scoring twice in the club's **Wembley** triumph (4–1 v **Benfica**). Charlton's 49 international goals is an England record. With his brother Jack Charlton, he played in England's World Cup winning team of 1966 (4–2 a.e.t. v West **Germany**, Wembley): they were the second set of **brothers** to play in a World Cup final winning side (after Fritz and Otmar **Walter** of West Germany, 1954). Voted both **Footballer of the Year** and **European Footballer of the Year** in 1966. Awarded the OBE in 1969 and a knighthood in 1994. Became a Manchester United director. Matt **Busby** once said of Charlton: "He was idolised from his 20th year on. There has never been a more popular footballer. He was as near perfection as man and player as it is possible to be". Included in the **Football League Centenary 100 players**. *Honours* (player) League Championship (Manchester United 1956-57, 1964-65, 1966-67), **FA Cup** (Manchester United 1963), **European Cup** (Manchester United 1968), **World Cup** (England 1966).

Charnley, Tom *official* second secretary of the **Football League** (1902-33) and former secretary of **Preston North End**. Born 1860, died 1936.

Charter for Quality *misc.* **Football Association** plan of action for the education and training of young foootballers that was adopted in November 1997. Developed by the FA's **technical director** and ex-**Notts County**, **Sheffield Wednesday** and **Leeds United** manager Howard Wilkinson, the plan creates a network of football **academies** and **centres of excellence**, run in partnership with **Premier League** and **Football League** clubs, to educate and coach youngsters from the age of eight to 21. The FA's national

centre of excellence at **Lilleshall** closed as part of the shift to local provision.

Château Eric *misc.* British red wine named after French international Eric **Cantona**. Produced by the Lamberhurst vineyard in Kent to coincide with the 1996 **European Championship**.

Chelsea *club* English league. *Dossier* Ground: **Stamford Bridge**, west London, capacity: 35,000 all seated (42,000 planned). Strip: blue shirts with white/yellow trim, blue shorts with white trim, white socks with blue trim. Website: *www.chelseafc.co.uk* Nickname: Blues. Record attendance: 82,905 v **Arsenal** (12 October 1935, Division One). Best average attendance: 48,260 (1954-55). Biggest win: 13–0 v Jeunesse Hautcharage (29 September 1971, **European Cup-winners Cup**, first round 2nd leg). Biggest defeat: 1–8 v **Wolverhampton Wanderers** (26 September 1953, Division One). *History* Formed in 1905, Chelsea is unusual in that the club had a ground before it existed (only **Plymouth Argyle** and **Sheffield United** have a similar beginning) and was elected to the **Football League** without playing a match. Gus **Mears** acquired the home of the London Athletic Club, Stamford Bridge, in 1904 with the aim of creating a sporting venue that would include not only athletics, but cycling, and provide a home for **Fulham**. Fulham turned down the offer to rent the ground and Mears, and his colleague Fred Parker, decided to form their own football club. They chose the name Chelsea, although other suggestions included Kensington FC and London FC. In May 1905, the Chelsea Football and Athletic Company was established. A formidable squad of players, including **Sheffield United**'s 22-stone goalkeeper Willie Foulke, was assembled and this, coupled with a ground that was England's second largest venue after **Crystal Palace**, meant that Chelsea was easily elected to Football League (although admission to the **Southern League** had been denied). The club's first match was on 2 September 1905 (v **Stockport County**, away) and two days later Chelsea played its first game at Stamford Bridge (v **Liverpool**, friendly). Chelsea had a highly successful first season, finishing third in Division Two and attracting the highest average gate (including a crowd of 67,000 v **Manchester United**) in the division. The following season, the club won promotion to the top flight. Chelsea's defeat in the 1915 FA Cup final (0–3 v **Sheffield United**) – known as the **Khaki cup final** – meant that the club became the first to reach the final and be "relegated". Chelsea was only technically relegated because the club was subsequently re-elected to Division One when it was extended after **World War I** in 1919-20. In 1928, Chelsea, along with Arsenal, was the first to introduce **shirt numbers** for a Football League match (25 August, v **Swansea**). Chelsea did not win a major honour until, under Ted **Drake**'s management, it won the League Championship in 1955 – the club's golden jubilee. In 1957, Chelsea became the first English club to travel by air to a Football League match (v **Newcastle United**, 9 April

– Good Friday). Despite one season in Division Two at the beginning of the decade, the 1960s was the beginning of the club's most successful period. Drake's successor, Tommy **Docherty**, developed a young side that included Peter Bonetti, Charlie **Cooke**, George **Graham**, Peter Osgood, Bobby Tambling and Terry **Venables**. In 1965, Chelsea won the League Cup and a year later the club reached the **UEFA** (Fairs) **Cup** semi-final (0–5 replay v **Barcelona**). Chelsea played in three consecutive FA Cup semi-finals in the mid-1960s, eventually reaching the final in 1967 before losing to **Tottenham Hotspur** (1–2) in the first all-London FA Cup final. Dave Sexton replaced Docherty as Chelsea's manager in October 1967 and three years later the club won the FA Cup in a replay; the first match against **Leeds United** was the first Wembley final to finish in a draw. The next year the club won the **European Cup-winners Cup**, also in a replay. In 1972, Chelsea reached Wembley again, this time in the League Cup final, but lost to **Stoke City**. Thereafter the club entered a period of decline both on and off the pitch. The proposed £5.5 million redevelopment of Stamford Bridge – that resulted only in the construction of the 11,500 seat East stand (the largest single stand that had been built in England at the time) – caused the club severe financial problems. At the end of its first season of use (1974-75), Chelsea was relegated. In April 1982, the former **Oldham Athletic** chairman Ken Bates bought the club for a nominal amount (see Stamford Bridge). The club won the Division Two Championship with a record number of points (99 (three points for a win)) in 1988-89. Glenn **Hoddle** was appointed **player-manager** in 1993, and in his first season in charge he took the club to the FA Cup final (0–4 v Manchester United). The following year, Chelsea reached the European Cup-winners Cup semi-final (3–4 agg., v **Real Zaragoza**) and, in the next, the FA Cup semi-final (1–2 v Manchester United). Hoddle's successor in 1996, following his appointment as **England** manager, was the Dutch international and former **AC Milan** player Ruud **Gullit**, who had spent the previous season as a player with the club. In Gullit's first season, the club won the FA Cup, its first major trophy in 26 years (2–0 v **Middlesbrough**). Chelsea's victory in the 1997 FA Cup final was also the club's first **Wembley** win in a major competition. Gullit was sensationally dismissed on 12 February 1998, after protracted negotiations failed to reach an agreement on a new contract, and was replaced as player-manager by Chelsea striker and former Italian international, Gianluca **Vialli**. Chelsea won the League Cup in March 1998 (2–0 a.e.t. v Middlesbrough) and, in May, the European Cup-winners Cup for a second time (1–0 v VfB **Stuttgart**). In August 1998, the club won its fourth trophy in fifteen months by lifting the **European Super Cup** (1–0 v Real Madrid). It reached the semi-final of the European Cup-winners Cup in 1999. The club, under the ownership of **Chelsea Village plc**, was floated on the **Alternative Investment Market** in March 1996

(floatation price = 55p), which is a precursor to full floatation on the stock market. *League record* Premier League 1992-93–; Division One 1907-08 to 1909-10, 1912-13 to 1923-24, 1930-31 to 1961-62, 1963-64 to 1974-75, 1977-78 to 1978-79, 1984-85 to 1987-88, 1989-90 to 1991-92; Division Two 1905-06 to 1906-07, 1910-11 to 1911-12, 1924-25 to 1929-30, 1962-63, 1975-76 to 1976-77, 1979-80 to 1983-84, 1988-89. *Honours* Division Two 1983-84, 1988-89; European Cup-winners Cup 1971 (2–1 replay/a.e.t. v Real Madrid – *Team* Bonetti, Boyle, Dempsey, Webb, R Harris, Hollins (Mulligan), Hudson, Cooke, Weller, Osgood (1) (Baldwin), Houseman; replay Bonetti, Boyle, Dempsey (1), Webb, R Harris, Cooke, Hudson, Weller, Baldwin, Osgood (1) (Smethurst), Houseman), 1998 (1–0 v VfB Stuttgart – *Team* De Goey, Clarke, Duberry, Leboeuf, Granville, Petrescu, **Di Matteo**, Wise, Poyet (Newton), Vialli, Flo (**Zola** (1)); European Super Cup 1998-99 (1–0 v Real Madrid); **FA Charity Shield** 1955 (3–0 v **Newcastle United**); FA Cup 1970 (2–1 replay v Leeds United – *Team* Bonetti, Webb, McCreadie, Hollins, Dempsey, R Harris (Hinton), Baldwin, Houseman (1), Osgood, Hutchinson (1), Cooke; replay Bonetti , R Harris, McCreadie, Hollins, Dempsey, Webb (1), Baldwin, Cooke, Osgood (1) (Hinton), Hutchinson, Houseman), 1997 (2–0 v Middlesbrough – *Team* Grodås, Sinclair, Leboeuf, Clarke, Minto, Petrescu, Di Matteo (1), Newton (1), Wise, Zola (Vialli), M Hughes); **Full Members Cup** 1986 (5–4 v Manchester City); League 1954-55; League Cup 1965 (3–2 agg., v **Leicester City**), 1998 (2–0 a.e.t. v Middlesbrough); **Zenith Data Systems Cup** 1990 (1–0 v Middlesbrough). *Records* Dan **Petrescu** is Chelsea's most capped player (31 (79) for **Romania**); Ron Harris holds the record for club appearances (655, 1962-80); Bobby Tambling is Chelsea's record league goalscorer (164, 1958-70).

Chelsea Village plc *n.* publicly-quoted business which owns **Chelsea**. Chelsea Village became a listed company on the **Alternative Investment Market** (floatation price = 55p) in March 1996. Chelsea Village, which is also involved in property management, the operation of catering and function facilities, travel and publishing, had a market capitalisation – the market value of the company's issued share capital (eg, the quoted price of its shares multiplied by the number of shares outstanding) – of £71.5 million when it joined the AIM.

Cheltenham Town *club* English league. Ground Waddon Road, Cheltenham, Gloucestershire, capacity: 6,000. Strip: red and white striped shirts, black shorts. Nickname: Robins. *Keynotes* Founded in 1892. Won the **FA Challenge Trophy** in 1998 (1–0 v **Southport**). Joined the **Football League** as Football Conference Champions in 1990-2000, replacing **Scarborough**. This was only two years after winning promotion to the Conference from the **Southern League**. Former **Chelsea** and **Sunderland** forward Clive Walker was a key figure in Cheltenham's Championship winning side.

League record Third Division 1990-2000–. *Honours* FA Challenge Trophy 1998 (1–0 v Southport); Football Conference 1998-99.

Chernomorets Odessa *club* Ukraine national league and former-Soviet Union league club based in Odessa, founded 1958. Ground: Central, capacity: 42,000. Strip: white shirts, white shorts. Never won former-Soviet Union Cup; former-Soviet Union league third place 1974; Ukraine cup 1992, 1994; Ukraine league runners-up 1995, 1996.

chest trap *n.* the act of controlling the ball using the chest, effectively bringing the ball to a standstill. *vb.*

Chester City *club* English league. *Dossier* Ground: **Deva Stadium**, Chester, Cheshire, capacity: 6,000. Strip: blue and white striped shirts, blue shorts, blue socks. Nickname: Blues or City. Record attendance: 5,638 v **Preston North End** (2 April 1994, Third Division). Biggest win: 12–0 v **York City** (1 February 1936, **Division Three (North)**). Biggest defeat: 2–11 v **Oldham Athletic** (19 January 1952, Division Three (North)). *History* Formed as Chester (not becoming City until 1983) in 1884 from a merger between King's School Old Boys and Chester Rovers. Chester played its first matches at Faulkner Street, later moving to a ground at Whipcord Lane before settling in 1906 at **Sealand Road**, the club's home until 1990. Chester's first major honour was achieved in 1908 when the club won the **Welsh Cup** (3–1 v **Connah's Quay**). Chester was elected to Division Three (North) in 1931-32, finishing third in its first **Football League** season, fourth the following year, third in 1934-35, runners-up 1935-36 and third again in 1936-37. Chester won its second Welsh Cup in 1933 (2–0 v **Wrexham**) and a third victory in the competition was achieved in 1947 (5–1 replay v Merthyr Tydfil). The club finished bottom of Division Three (North) in consecutive seasons (1953-54, 1954-55) and, in 1958-59, it was allocated to the newly-formed Division Four. In 1974-75, Chester won promotion to Division Four on **goal average** and the club was a **League Cup** semi-finalist (4–5 agg., v **Aston Villa**). The club's League Cup run included victories over **Leeds United** (3–0, fourth round) and **Newcastle United** (1–0, fifth round). Further cup success was achieved in the FA Cup, with Chester reaching the fifth round in 1977 (0–1 v **Wolverhampton Wanderers**) and 1980 (1–2 v **Ipswich Town**). By 1982-83, Chester was back playing in Division Four and, in 1986, the club faced a **winding-up order** by the Inland Revenue for non-payment of taxes. Property developers BCH bought a controlling interest in Chester with a view to redevelop land behind one of the Sealand Road stands and relocate the club to a purpose-built stadium elsewhere. The local council rejected BCH's proposal and the company sought to retrieve its investment by offering potential buyers vacant possession of Sealand Road from May 1990. The club approached a number of nearby clubs, including **Manchester City** and Northwich Victoria, to arrange a **groundshare**, eventually agreeing a move to (then) non-League

Macclesfield Town's **Moss Rose** ground. Sealand Road staged its final match on 28 April 1990 (v **Rotherham United**, Division Three). Chester's two-year tenure of Moss Rose resulted in losses of around £1 million and, in 1990-91, the average attendance of 1,564 was the lowest in the League. On 25 August 1992, Chester played its first match at the new Deva Stadium - though situated within the town's boundaries most of the ground lies over the Welsh border. In 1996-97, the club was a Third Division end-of-season **playoff** semi-finalist. In an attempt to boost attendance, Chester offered free entry, in November and December 1997, to **season-ticket** holders with **Premier League**, Division One and Division Two teams. Continuing financial difficulties led to an offer from Chester supporters to pay the travelling expenses of the first-team squad in August 1998. *League record* Second Division 1992-93, 1994-95; Division Three 1975-76 to 1981-82, 1986-87 to 1991-92; Third Division 1993-94, 1995-96–; Division Three (North) 1931-32 to 1957-58; Division Four 1958-59 to 1974-75, 1982-83 to 1985-86. *Honours* **Division Three (North) Cup** 1936 (2–1 v **Darlington**), 1937 (3–1 v **Southport**); Welsh Cup 1908 (3–1 v Connah's Quay), 1933 (2–0 v Wrexham) 1947 (5–1 replay v Merthyr Tydfil). *Records* Bill Lewis is Chester's most capped player (13 (27) for **Wales**); Ray Gill holds the record for club League appearances (406, 1951-62); Stuart Rimmer is Chester's record League goalscorer (135, 1985-88, 1991-98).

Chester Report *misc.* government report published in 1968 following an inquiry into the state of Association Football in Great Britain. The 11-member inquiry team was chaired by Sir Norman Chester, then warden of Nuffield College, Oxford. The report took two years to compile. Its recommendations included a proposal to restructure the English **Football League** with fewer clubs in the top flight and a regional Fourth Division. It also proposed a levy on **transfer fees** to raise cash for improvements to stadiums and a pools levy to improve footballing facilities. It was widely dismissed by the Football League clubs.

Chesterfield *club* English league. *Dossier* Ground: **Recreation Ground**, Chesterfield, Derbyshire. Strip: blue shirts with white trim, white shorts and blue socks with white trim. Nickname: Blues or Spirerites. Ground capacity: 8,880. Record attendance: 30,968 v **Newcastle United** (7 April 1939, Division Two). Best average attendance: 15,372 (1947-48). Biggest win: 10–0 v **Glossop** (17 January 1903, Division Two). Biggest defeat: 0–10 v **Gillingham** (5 September 1987, Division Three). *History* Founded in 1866 as Chesterfield Town (making the club the fourth oldest in the **Football League**). Chesterfield is thought to have played its earliest matches at the Recreation Ground, which would make it the Football League's oldest venue, although the club played at a ground in Spital for several seasons in the 1880s before returning to its present home around 1887. The club joined the Football League as Chesterfield Town in 1899-00, but failed to win

re-election in 1908-09 before returning as Chesterfield and membership of Division Three (North) in 1921-22. Until the club bought the Recreation Ground in 1921, it was owned by the local corporation. The close links between the council and the football club reached a high-point in 1918 when the club adopted the name Chesterfield Municipal FC. The club was forced to drop the title because of the Football League's rules on club ownership and become plain Chesterfield when it joined Division Three (North). Chesterfield won the Division Three (North) Championship on two occasions in the 1930s, in 1930-31 and 1935-36, and was a runner-up in 1933-34. In the first season after **World War II**, Chesterfield achieved its highest-ever League position, finishing fourth in Division Two. Following relegation in 1950-51 the club has alternated between the two lower divisions, twice winning the Division Four Championship (1969-70 and 1984-85) and occasionally, as in 1979-80, narrowly missing promotion to Division Two. The club won the **Anglo-Scottish Cup** in 1981 (2–1 agg., v **Notts County**). Chesterfield narrowly missed promotion in 1989-90, losing in the final of the end-of-season Division Four **playoffs** (0–1 v **Cambridge United**), in what was the club's first appearance at **Wembley**. In 1994-95, the club had a more successful Wembley experience, winning the Third Division playoff (2–0 v **Bury**). Chesterfield's most exciting footballing moment occurred in 1997 when the club reached the semi-final stage of the **FA Cup**, losing in a replay to **Middlesbrough** (0–3) after a memorable 3–3 draw in the first encounter. *League record* Division Two 1899-00 to 1908-09 (failed re-election), 1931-32 to 1932-33, 1936-37 to 1950-51; Second Division 1995-96–; Division Three 1958-59 to 1960-61, 1970-71 to 1982-83, 1985-86 to 1988-89; Third Division 1992-93 to 1994-95; Division Three (North) 1921-22 to 1930-31, 1933-34 to 1935-36, 1951-52 to 1957-58; Division Four 1961-62 to 1969-70, 1983-84 to 1984-85, 1989-90 to 1991-92. *Honours* Anglo-Scottish Cup 1981 (2–1 agg., v Notts County); Division Three (North) 1930-31, 1935-36; Division Four 1969-70, 1984-85. *Records* Walter McMillen is Chesterfield's most capped player (4 (7) for **Northern Ireland**); Dave Blakey holds the record for club League appearances (613, 1948-67); Ernie Moss is Chesterfield's record League goalscorer (161, 1969-76, 1979-81, 1984-86).

Chicago Fire *club* United States football club and member of **Major League Soccer** (joined league in 1998), based in Chicago, Illinois. Member of the league's **Western Conference**. Founded: 1997. Ground: Soldier Field, capacity: 66,946. Major League Soccer Championship (MLS Cup) 1998; **US Open Challenge Cup** 1998.

Chief Santos *club* Namibian national league club, based in Tsumeb. Ground: Nomtsoub. Namibian Cup 1991, 1998; Namibian League Champions 1993.

chief scout *n.* a club's most senior scout.

Chilavert, José Luis *player* Goalkeeper. **Paraguay** international (41 caps, four goals). Born 1967. *Clubs* (include) **Velez Sarsfield.** *Keynotes* Captained Paraguay at the 1998 **World Cup** finals. Noted – as a goalkeeper – for taking free-kicks and penalties for his club and the national side. For example, he scored in Paraguay's 1–1 draw with Argentina in the 1998 World Cup qualifying campaign, and for his club Velez Sarsfield when it won the South American **Recopa** in 1997 (1–1, 4–2 pens, v **River Plate**). He has scored 40 senior goals, 27 in the league and four for his country. In his club's 1999 victory over Independiente (2–0) Chilavert saved one penalty and scored another. He is also known for placing a "lucky" medal on his goal line at each match. Chosen as one of two goalkeepers in **FIFA**'s 22-man all-star squad of the 1998 World Cup finals. *Honours* Argentinean league champions (Velez Sarsfield, 1993 (**Clausura**), 1996 (**Apertura**) 1996 (Clausura)); **Copa Inter America** (Velez Sarsfield, 1996); **Copa Libertadores** (Velez Sarsfield, 1994); *El Pais* **South American Footballer of the Year** 1996, runner-up 1994; Recopa (Velez Sarsfield, 1997); **Supercopa** (Velez Sarsfield, 1996); **World Club Cup** (Velez Sarsfield, 1994).

children's football *regulations* in England, boys and girls aged under-nine are prohibited from playing in organised games with more than seven players on each side (Football Association rule 21a.iii). This rule applies to schools, clubs **football academies** and **centres of excellence**. Players aged over-nine and under-14 are prohibited from taking part in games with players more than two years their senior (Football Association rule 21a.iv). The age bands for junior games are: over-nine to under-11; over-10 to under-12; over-11 to under-13; and over-12 to under-14. Boys and girls up to the age of 11 years can play in mixed competitive matches; this is the only age-group in England where mixed competitive football is allowed. See **English Schools' Football Association**

Chile *country* CONMEBOL republic in southwest South America on the Pacific Ocean, bordered by **Peru**, **Argentina** and **Bolivia**. Area: 751,625 sq km (290,125 sq miles). Population: 14,660,000 (1997 est.). Language: Spanish. Capital: Santiago. *Dossier* Football association (Federación de Fútbol de Chile, Santiago), formed in 1895, affiliated to **FIFA** in 1912 and founder member of **Confederación Sudamericana de Fútbol** (CONMEBOL) in 1916, president Ricardo Abumohor, general secretary Cristián Lyon. Season played from February to October. National stadium: Estadio Nacional, Santiago, capacity: 78,000 (58,000 seated) National strip: red shirts with white collar and cuffs, blue shorts. Website: http://www.anfp.cl (official site). First international game: 27 May 1910 v Argentina (1–3, Buenos Aires, friendly). Biggest victory: 7–0 v **Venezuela** (29 August 1979, Santiago, **Copa America** first round). Biggest defeat: 0–7 v **Brazil** (17 September 1959, Rio de Janeiro, O'Higgins Cup). Most capped players: Leonel Sánchez (85 appearances, ca. 1956-68), Alberto Fouilloux (70 appearances, ca. 1960-72). Leading goalscorers: Marcelo **Salas** (31 goals, ca.

1994-), Carlos Caszely (29 goals, ca. 1972-85), Ivan Zamorano (28 goals in 46 games, ca. 1989-), Leonel Sánchez (24 goals, ca. 1956-68). Other notable international players: Elias **Figueroa**, Raul Toro. *International tournament record* **Olympic Games** – first entered 1928, quarter-final 1984; **Women's World Cup** – entered first tournament in 1991, never qualified for finals tournament; **World Cup** – entered first tournament in 1930 (first round), semi-final/third 1962, also qualified for finals tournament 1950, 1966, 1974, 1982, 1998, hosts 1962; **Copa America** – entered first tournament in 1910, runners-up 1955 (second in six-nation league), 1956 (second in six-nation league), 1979 (0–3, 1–0, 0–0, v **Paraguay**, home and away legs, with playoff in Buenos Aires), 1987 (0–1 v **Uruguay**, Buenos Aires); **Pan-American Championship** runners-up and hosts 1952; **South American Women's Championship** – runners-up 1991 (league of three, in Maringa, Brazil), third 1995 (league of five in Uberlândia, Brazil); **Under-17 World Championship** – semi-final/third 1993 (1–1, 4–2 pens., v **Poland**, in Japan, third/fourth playoff) also qualified for finals tournament 1997; **World Youth Cup** (under-20) – semi-final/fourth 1987 (1–1, 1–3 pens., v **East Germany**, in Chile, third/fourth playoff). *Record against British and Irish national teams* v **England**, played five, won one, drawn two, lost two; v **Northern Ireland**, played two, won two; v **Scotland**, played two, lost two; v **Wales**, played one, won one; v **Republic of Ireland** played five, won two, drawn one, lost two. *History* An early and rudimentary form of football known as pilimatun was played in Chile before the arrival of the modern game. The Federación de Fútbol de Chile is the second oldest football association in South America (behind the Argentinian FA). Football is thought to have been introduced by British immigrants in Valparaiso and Viña del Mar in the late 19th century. One of the first clubs, Valparaiso, was formed in 1889. Regional leagues operated in the early years of organised club football, with a national cup tournament, the Copa Arturo Allesandri, introduced in 1910 as a competition for the regional league champions. A national league began in 1933. In 1997, the league format was changed and split into two championships per year (there were, thus, two champion clubs in 1997, similar, for example, to the league in Argentina). In 1998 it reverted to its previous format. The domestic cup, the **Copa Chile**, was first played in 1958, with various interruptions (notably 1962–73 when it was not played at all); it was first won by **Colo Colo**. Chile has played international matches since 1910, though it did not win its first match until 1926 (7–1, v Bolivia, Santiago, Copa America – its 34th competitive game). Arguably the worst moment in Chile's football history was the so-called **Battle of Santiago** in 1962, during the World Cup which Chile hosted. Two Chileans, Luis Valenzuela (1939–1955) and Carlos Dittborn Pinto (1955-57), have been presidents of CONMEBOL. *World Cup performance* (finals and qualifiers to end of 1998 tournament): played 82, won 32, drawn 19, lost 31, scored 126 goals, conceded 112 goals; win rate: 39%; goals scored per game: 1.54. *League system* The league season is played in two stages, the apertura and clausura, with 16 clubs in the Primera (first) and Segunda (second) divisions. Three points are awarded for a victory, with one for a draw: final positions for clubs level on points are determined by **goal difference**. In the second part of the season, the top eight clubs enter a championship playoff; the bottom eight compete to avoid relegation. Promotions and relegations are decided as follows: the top two clubs from the Segunda division are automatically promoted, the bottom two clubs from the Primera relegation league are automatically relegated; the other two promotion/relegation places are determined by playoffs between the fourth and third clubs in the Segunda division and the 13th and 14th clubs, respectively, in the Primera division. There are four regional Tercera (third divisions): north, central, and south and south-central. *Record in international club tournaments* Copa Libertadores – Colo Colo (1991, runners-up 1973, semi-final 1964, semi-final 1997), **Cobreloa** (runners-up 1981, 1982), **Union Española** (runners-up 1975), **Universidad Catolica** (runners-up 1993, semi-final 1962, 1969), **Universidad de Chile** (semi-final 1970, 1996); **Copa CONMEBOL** – Universidad de Chile (semi-final 1994), Cobreloa (quarter-final 1995); **Supercopa** – Colo Colo (semi-final 1996, 1997, quarter-final 1994); **Recopa** – Colo Colo (1991); **Copa Inter Americana** – Colo Colo (1992); Universidad Catolica (1994).Other leading clubs: **Santiago Wanderers**, **Club Palestino**, **Everton** (CD Everton Vina del Mar), **O'Higgins**.

Chile Cup see **Copa Chile**.

China *country AFC*. People's Republic of China. Situated in southeast Asia on the South China Sea and East China Sea, China is bordered by **Mongolia**, **Kazakhstan**, **Russia**, **India**, **Nepal**, **Myanmar** (Burma), **Bhutan**, **Laos**, **North Korea** and **Vietnam**. Third largest country by area, and most populous with around one-quarter of the world's population. The majority of the population live in the east. China has the oldest continuous civilisation, dating to before 2000 BC. People's Republic established in 1949. China is divided into municipalities and provinces; the largest, Sichuan (Szechwan) has more than 109 million people. Area: 9,597,000 sq km (3,704,440 sq miles). Population: 1,199,000,000 (1995 est.). Languages: Mandarin Chinese, Cantonese and many regional dialects. Capital: Beijing. *Dossier* Football association of the People's Republic of China (Beijing) formed in 1924, affiliated to **FIFA** in 1931 (resigned 1958, rejoined 1979) and **Asian Football Confederation** (AFC) in 1974, president Yuang Weimin, general secretary Wang Junsheng. Season played from February to September National stadium: Workers' Stadium, Beijing, capacity: 70,000 (international matches also played at **Dalian**). National strip: white shirts, white shorts. First international game: February 1913 v the **Philippines** (1–2, in Manila, **Far Eastern Games**). *International tourna-*

ment record **Olympic Games** – first entered 1936, qualified for finals tournament 1936 (0–2, v **Great Britain**, first round), 1948, 1988 (first-round group stage, in Seoul, South Korea); **Women's World Cup/Olympic Games (Women)/Asian Women's Football Championship** – see **China, women**; **World Cup** – first entered 1982, never qualified for finals tournament, but reached second qualifying round after winning first-round groups stages in 1982 (lost in a playoff for the final qualifying place, v **New Zealand**, 1–2, in Singapore), 1990 (fourth in its six nation second-round group) and 1998 (five wins and one draw in its six first-round games, but finished third of five nations in the second stage); **Asian Cup of Nations** – first entered in 1976, runners-up 1984 (0–2, v **Saudi Arabia**, in Singapore), semi-finals/third 1976 (1–0, v **Iraq**, in Iran, third/fourth playoff), 1992 (1–1, 4–3 pens., v **United Arab Emirates**, in Hiroshima, Japan, third/fourth playoff), semi-final/fourth 1988 (0–0, 0–3 pens., v **Iran**, in Qatar, third/fourth playoff), quarter-final 1996; **Asian Games** – first entered 1978, runners-up 1994 (2–4, v **Uzbekistan**, in Hiroshima, Japan), semi-final/third 1978 (1–0, v **Iraq**, in Bangkok, third/fourth playoff), 1998 (3–0, v **Thailand**, in Bangkok, third/fourth playoff), quarter-final 1982, 1986, 1990; **Asian Under-16 Tournament** – 1992 (v **Qatar**, in Saudi Arabia); **Asian Youth Cup** (under-19) – 1984 , runners-up 1996 (0–3, v South Korea, in Seoul, South Korea); **Dynasty Cup** – hosted first and second tournaments in 1990 and 1995, runners-up 1990 (1–1, 4–5 pens., v **South Korea**, in Beijing; **Far Eastern Games** – 1915, 1917, 1919, 1921, 1923, 1925, 1927, 1930 (joint-winners), 1934; **Under-17 World Championship** – hosted first championship in 1985 (reached quarter-final), also qualified for finals tournament 1989, 1991, 1993; **World Youth Cup** (under-20) – qualified for finals tournament 1985. *World Cup performance* (finals and qualifiers to end of 1998 tournament) played 54, won 33, drawn 7, lost 14, scored 106 goals, conceded 44 goals; win rate 61%; goals scored per game 1.96. *Record against British and Irish national teams* v **England**, played one, lost one. *History* A rudimentary form of football, **tsu chu**, was played during the Han Dynasty, (206 BC to 221 AD). A China representative side played the Philippines as part of the Far Eastern Games in 1913 – this was the first international played in Asia. National league competition started 1926; a professional league (sponsored by Marlboro) was launched in 1993. Although China has never reached a World Cup finals tournament, its overall performance in qualifying games is one of the best records in the world; it has won 61% of all its World Cup matches and, in this respect, is fourth in the tournament's all-time list, behind **Brazil** (69%), **Germany** (65%), and **Italy** (64%). Its best international achievements was as runner-up in the 1984 Asian Cup of Nations, and runner-up in the 1994 Asian Games. China dominates women's international football in Asia with an almost unblemished record in the Asian Women's Football Championship since its first entry in 1986. China won all six tournaments from 1986 to 1997, without conceding a goal in any of the six finals. The 1997 campaign included a 16-0 victory over the Philippines. China is one of the leading nations in world women's football. *League system* The national league has two divisions: Division 1A has 14 clubs, with 12 clubs in Division 1B. Two clubs are relegated automatically. Three points are awarded for a win, with one for a draw. Teams level on points are separated according to the respective results of games between those clubs. China's league season overlaps the Asian club tournaments; champions and cup winners from the previous year, therefore, qualify for the **Asian Cup of Champion Teams** and the **Asian Cup-winners Cup**. *Record in international club tournaments* **Asian Champion Teams Cup** – Liaoning (1989, runners-up 1990, semi-final 1986, 1993), **Dalian Wanda** (runners-up 1998, fourth 1999), **August 1 FC** (semi-final 1987), **Guangzhou** (semi-final 1988); **Asian Cup-winners Cup** – Dalian (quarter-final 1990), **Beijing Guo'an** (semi-final/third 1998).Other leading clubs: **Guangdong Honguyan, Kunming Army Unit**, Shangdong Taishan (Chinese Cup 1995); **Shanghai Shenua, Tianjin Football Club**. See also Hong Kong.

China, women *country/women* Women's football in China is administered by the Football Association of the People's Republic of China, Beijing. *Dossier* First international: 1983 (**International Women's Football Tournament**, Guangzhou, China). Biggest victory: 16–0 v the **Philippines** (1997 **Asian Women's Football Championship**). *International tournament record* **Olympic Games** (Women) – runners-up (silver medal) 1996 (1–2, v **United States of America**, in Athens, Georgia, United States of America); **Women's World Cup** – hosted first tournament in 1991 (reached quarter-final), semi-final/third 1995 (0–2 v United States of America, in Sweden, third/fourth playoff), qualified for finals tournament in 1999; **Algarve Cup** 1999 (2–1, United States of America); **Asian Games** women's football tournament – 1994, 1998 (1–0, v North Korea, in Thailand); **Asian Women's Football Championship** – first entered 1986, 1986 (2–0, v **Japan**, in Hong Kong), 1987 (1–0, v **Taiwan**, in Hong Kong), 1991 (5–0, v Japan, in Japan), 1993 (3–0 v **North Korea**, in Malaysia), 1995 (2–0 v Japan, in Malaysia), 1997 (3-0, v North Korea, in China); Goodwill Games women's football tournament – runners-up 1998, (0–2, v USA, in New York, USA); **US Women's Cup** runners-up 1994, 1996.*History* Women are known to have played the rudimentary football **tsu chu** as far back as the first century AD. Modern women's football dates back to the 1920s when girls were encouraged to play football in some schools. A national league was founded in 1986. China, very much a leader in women's football at international level, launched the International Women's Football Tournament in Guangzhou, in 1983, the first of China's now regular invitation tournaments. In 1986, China organised the first national under-16 championship, while its senior team became the first to tour Europe. China's regional supremacy was demonstrated by its triumph in the sixth Asian Women's Championship in 1986, the first time it had entered the competition. It won all six tournaments from 1986 to 1997, without conceding a goal in any of the six finals. China also won the women's football tournament of the Asian Games in 1994. China hosted the first **FIFA** women's tournament, at Guangzhou in 1988 and hosted the first Women's World Cup in 1991 (reaching the quarter-final). It reached the semi-finals of the 1995 Women's World Cup in Stockholm. China won the silver medal at the 1996 Olympic Games in Atlanta, USA, the first Olympic women's football tournament. *League system* Twelve teams play in the national First Division. There are regional Second, Third and Fourth Divisions.

Chinese Taipei *country AFC* another name for **Taiwan** (Taiwan is, in fact, registered with **FIFA** as Chinese Taipei).

chip *vb.* lofted pass/shot made without excessive force with the instep. A chip is often played with backspin, which makes the ball hang longer in the air and drop shorter than a ball struck without backspin; it also tends not to bounce so far forward. *n.* the execution of this. Compare **lob**.

Chiquita Cup *competition* original name of the **US Women's Cup**.

Chivadze, Aleksander *player* Defender **Soviet Union** international. *Club* **Dynamo Tbilisi**. *Keynotes* Former national coach of **Georgia** (1994-96) and vice-president of the Georgian Football Federation. *Honours* **European Cup-winners Cup** (Dynamo Tbilisi, 1981); Soviet Union league championship (Dynamo Tbilisi, 1978).

Chocolate Box *ground* informal name of the Estadio La Bombonera, the stadium of Argentinean club **Boca Juniors**, capacity: 58,750, built 1940.

Christchurch United *club* New Zealand national league club based in Christchurch. (New Zealand) Chatham Cup 1972, 1974,1975, 1976, 1989, 1991; New Zealand national league champions 1973, 1975, 1978, 1987, 1988, 1991.

Christmas Island *country no international affiliation* external territory of **Australia**. Island in the Central Pacific. Area: 135 sq km (52 sq miles). Population: 1,275.

Christmas tree *tactics* system of play/formation. A system consisting of four defenders, five midfielders and one striker arranged in a Christmas tree (4–3–2–1) shape. The formation involves a lone striker (**target man**) who is supported in attack by two midfield players, playing as inside-forwards and making forward runs into the penalty area. Two midfielders play wide pushing forward when the team is in possession and tracking back to hold midfield when the opposition has the ball, while a third midfield player operates as a holding player in front of the back four. Terry **Venables**

used the Christmas tree formation on occasions during his time as **England** manager.

Chunan Ilhwa Chunma *club* South Korean Pro-Football League club, based in Ch'unyang, joined South Korean Pro-Football League in 1988. Adidas Korea Cup 1992; **Afro-Asian Club Championship** – 1996 (v **Orlando Pirates** of South Africa); **Asian Champion Teams Cup** 1995-6 (1–0, v **Al Nasr** of Saudi Arabia), runners-up 1996-97 (1–2, v **Pohang Steelers** of South Korea, in Malaysia), semi-final/fourth 1994 (0–1, v **Neftchi Fergana** of Uzbekistan, final tournament in Bangkok, Thailand, third/fourth play off); **Asian Super Cup** 1996 (6–3 agg., v **Bellmare Hiratsuka** of Japan); South Korean Pro-Football League champions 1993, 1994, 1995.

CIS Cup *competition* annual indoor competition for the league champions of the former-**Soviet Union** republics. Held in Moscow. *Winners* 1997, Dinamo Kiev.

cinema *misc.* French and Italian term which refers to a player who is play-acting.

CIS *abrev.* **Commonwealth of Independent States**.

City Ground *ground* English football ground situated in Nottingham; home of **Nottingham Forest**. *Dossier* Ground capacity: 30,602 all seated. Pitch dimensions 106m x 70m. Record attendance: 49,946 v **Manchester United** (28 October 1967, Division One). Best average attendance: 32,715 (1967-68). *History* Forest played its first match at City Ground on 3 September 1898 (v **Blackburn Rovers**, Division One), having played at several venues, including Forest Recreation Ground (from where the club derives its name) and Trent Bridge Cricket Ground. Nestling on the banks of the River Trent and across the water from **Notts County**'s **Meadow Lane** ground, City Ground remained fairly basic until the 1950s. In 1922, the ground was the first to use elliptically-shaped (regular oval) **goalposts**. The ground was severely flooded in both 1947 and 1968. Also in 1968, the main stand caught fire during a Division One match, forcing spectators on to the pitch (v **Leeds United**, 24 August) and the club subsequently to share **Meadow Lane** for six games. The Executive Stand, which was opened in August 1980, has the name "FOREST" picked out in white seats against a backdrop of red seating. This is thought to be the first occasion that **seat lettering** was used. City Ground is owned by Nottingham City Council and, in 1964, the club agreed a 50-year lease at a rent of £750 a year for the 11-acre site. The club was forced to pay an additional £22,000 a year for 1,121 square yards of land behind the Trent End in order to construct a new all-seater stand. At the opposite end, the Bridgford Stand, which opened in 1992, has an oddly stepped roof in one corner as a result of objections from local residents, who complained of loss of light if the roof continued at the same elevation. City Ground was selected as a venue for the 1996 **European Championship**, staging group D matches

(**Croatia** v **Turkey**; **Portugal** v Turkey; Croatia v Portugal). The ground also has been the venue for several **FA Cup** semi-finals. The first floodlit match at the City Ground took place on 11 September 1961 (v **Gillingham**, **League Cup**) – at the time, the ground was the second from last in Division One to install floodlights.

Ciudad Havana   *club*   Cuba national league club based in the capital Havana. Strip: red shirts, white shorts. Cuban league champions 1998.

Clackmannan   *club*   former Scottish league. *Dossier* Ground: Chapelhill Park, Clackmannan, Clackmannanshire. *Keynotes* Joined the reformed and enlarged Scottish Division Two in 1921-22, finishing bottom of the league and failing to gain re-election. *League record* Division Two 1921-22.

classified results   *n.pl.*   official match results and summary of their **pools** value, broadcast on national television and radio after a full league and cup programme.

clausura   *n.*   second of the two domestic league seasons played in **Argentina**, **Bolivia**, **Colombia**, **Mexico**, **Paraguay**, **Uruguay** and **Venezuela**. The "season of two halves" maintains spectator interest throughout the year and, depending on the league system in each country, may be followed by a championship playoff or final tournament involving the best placed clubs from each half. See **Apertura**.

clean sheet   *n.*   a match where a goalkeeper/team does not concede a goal (also called shutout in the United States of America and Canada). Usage: *The goalkeeper kept a clean sheet in his team's 3–0 victory.*

clean sheet, duration   *record*   **1.** World (senior): 1,275 minutes, Abel Resino for **Atletico Madrid** (to 17 March 1991). **2.** International: 1,142 minutes, Dino **Zoff** for **Italy** (September 1972 to June 1974). **3.** Britain (senior leagues): 1,196 minutes, Chris Woods for **Rangers** (26 November 1986 to 31 January 1987). **4. Football League**: 1,103 minutes, Steve Death for **Millwall** (1978-79, Division Four). **5.** British youth football: 1,417 minutes, Thomas McKenna for Folkestone Invicta Under-13s (25 September 1995 to 5 May 1996).

clean sheet, most in a season   *record*   **1. Football League**: 29 clean-sheets in 46 matches, Jim Stannard for **Gillingham** (1995-96, Football League Third Division). **2.** Division One/FA **Premier League**: 28 in 42 matches, Ray Clemence for **Liverpool** (1978-79, Division One).

clear   *vb.*   to kick the ball swiftly out of defence in order to relieve the pressure of an attack.

clearance   *n.*   ball kicked out from a defensive position to relieve pressure on the defence rather than to set up any tactical opportunity.

Clegg,   Charles   *player/referee/official*   **England** international (1 cap). Born 15 June 1850; died 26 June 1937. *Club* The Wednesday (now **Sheffield Wednesday**). *Keynotes* Clegg played in the first official international match (0–0 v **Scotland**, in Partick) on 30 November 1872. After retiring, Clegg became a referee, officiating at both the 1882 and 1892 **FA Cup** finals. He was a member of the **Football Association** Committee from 1885 and its chairman from 1889. Clegg was FA vice-president between 1889 and 1923, when he became president until his death in 1937. He was a club official at both **Sheffield United** and Sheffield Wednesday. Clegg developed the idea of the **FA Charity Shield** and was knighted in 1927, the first footballer to receive the honour.

Clemence, Ray   *player*   Goalkeeper. **England** international (61 caps). Born 5 August 1948. Career ca. 1965–87. *Clubs* **Scunthorpe United**, **Liverpool**, **Tottenham Hotspur**. Also **Barnet** manager. *Keynotes* Transferred to Liverpool from Scunthorpe United for £18,000 in June 1967, going on to make 470 **Football League** appearances for the club and winning a host of honours. He also played in 77 European club competition matches for Liverpool. He moved to Tottenham Hotspur for £300,000 in August 1981, playing 240 League games. Clemence joined Glenn **Hoddle**'s coaching staff when the ex-Spurs midfielder was appointed England manager in 1996. Awarded the MBE in 1987. Included in the **Football League Centenary 100 players**. *Honours* **European Cup** (Liverpool 1977, 1978, 1981); **FA Cup** (Liverpool 1974; Tottenham Hotspur 1982); League Championship (Liverpool 1972-73, 1975-76, 1976-77, 1978-79, 1979-80); **League Cup** (Liverpool 1981); **UEFA Cup** (Liverpool 1973, 1976).

Cliff, the   *ground*   **Manchester United**'s training ground.

Cliftonhill Stadium   *ground*   Scottish football ground situated in Coatbridge, Strathclyde; home of **Albion Rovers**. *Dossier* Ground capacity: 1,238. Pitch dimensions: 100.5m x 64m. Record attendance: 27,381 v **Rangers** (8 February 1936, **Scottish FA Cup**, 2nd). *Keynotes* Opened on 24 December 1919. The first floodlit match at Cliftonhill took place in October 1968 (v **Airdrieonians**).

Cliftonville FC   *club*   Northern Ireland national league club based in north Belfast, founded 1879. Ground: Solitude, capacity: 17,000. Strip: red shirts, white shorts. *Keynotes* Generally associated with a Catholic following. Cliftonville was barred from playing its matches against rival Belfast club **Linfield**, with its large Protestant fan base, at either of the two clubs' home venues from 1970 until 1998, with the fixtures moved to a **neutral ground**, Windsor Park. On 21 November 1998, police allowed the league fixture to be played at Solitude, but restricted the crowd to just 1,500. Clitonville was disqualified from the 1999 **Irish FA Cup** final (against **Portadown**) for playing a **cup-tied** player, Simon Gribben, in the semi-final replay against **Linfield**. *Honours* All-Ireland league champions 1906, 1910; **Irish FA Cup** (all-Ireland) 1883, 1888, 1897, 1900, 1901, 1907, 1909; (Northern Ireland) 1979; Northern Ireland league champions 1998.

close season   *regulations*   the period outside the main club league and cup **season** (as defined by the relevant football authority). In the UK the close season is from mid May until the beginning of September.

close-season tournament *n.* a series of competitive fixtures that are held at the end of a season. In contrast to **pre-season tournaments**, which are usually contested by club sides, close-season tournaments tend to be between national sides. See **King Hussan II Cup**, **Tournoi de France**, **Umbro International tournament**.

closed fracture *medical* broken bone where the skin remains intact. Also called simple fracture. Compare **compound fracture**.

closed-circuit television *n.* **1.** crowd surveillance by television cameras. **2.** match action relayed to a separate venue (for exampe, to the away team's ground) and, usually transmitted on a big screen. *Keynotes* The first **Football League** match to be transmitted via closed-circuit television, was the 1965 Division Two encounter between **Cardiff City** and **Coventry City** at **Ninian Park**, which Coventry relayed to fans at the club's **Highfield Road** ground. A crowd of 40,149 watched an **FA Cup** match between **Everton** and **Liverpool** (1–0) which was relayed to **Anfield** on closed-circuit television on 11 March 1967; 64,851 attended the match at **Goodison Park**. It was the first FA Cup match relayed by closed-circuit television.

Clough, Brian *player-manager* Striker. **England** international (2 caps). Born 21 March 1935. Career ca. 1951–1964. *Clubs* (player) **Middlesbrough**, **Sunderland**, (manager) Sunderland (coach), **Hartlepool United**, **Derby County**, **Brighton & Hove Albion**, **Leeds United**, **Nottingham Forest**. *Keynotes* Exceptional striker, scoring 251 goals in 274 League appearances (leading scorer in the **Football League** in 1957-58 with 40 goals and in 1958-59, scoring 42 times), who was forced to retire from playing through injury in November 1964. Became manager of Hartlepool United with his long-time assistant Peter Taylor in October 1965. After moving to Derby County in July 1967, he, and Taylor, took the club to the Division Two title and, in 1971-72, its first League title. Appointed manager of Brighton & Hove Albion in 1973, his reign was short-lived and he, but not Taylor, moved on to Leeds United, a club he had often criticised in the past for "gamesmanship" under Don **Revie**. He survived only 44 days in charge before being dismissed. Established a highly successful side at Nottingham Forest, where he was manager for 18 years between 1975 and 1993, winning the European Cup in consecutive seasons in 1979 (v **Malmö FF**) and 1980 (v **Hamburg SV**). He was a forthright television football pundit with ITV. In January 1998, the **Football Association**'s inquiry into transfer dealings found that Clough had accepted unauthorised payments while manager of Nottingham Forest. *Honours* League Championship (Derby County 1971-72, Nottingham Forest 1977-78); Division Two (Derby County 1968-69); **League Cup** (Nottingham Forest 1978, 1979, 1989, 1990); **Simod Cup** (Nottingham Forest 1989); **Zenith**

Data Systems Cup (Nottingham Forest 1992); **European Cup** (Nottingham Forest 1979, 1980); **European Super Cup** (Nottingham Forest 1980).

Club Africain *club* Tunisian national league club based in the capital Tunis, founded 1920. Ground: Chedly Zouiten, capacity: 35,000. Strip: red shirts, white shorts. **African Cup of Champion Clubs** 1991 (6–2 agg., v **Nakivubo Villa** of Uganda), quarter-final "champions-league" stage 1997; **African Cup-winners Cup** runners-up 1990 (1–4 agg., v **BCC Lions** of Nigeria); **Afro-Asian Club Cup** 1992 (4–3 agg., v **Al Hilal** of Saudi Arabia); **Arab Club Champions Cup** 1997; **Arab Cup-winners Cup** 1995; Tunisian Cup 1965, 1967, 1968, 1969, 1970, 1972, 1973, 1976, 1992, 1998; Tunisian league champions 1946, 1947, 1964, 1967, 1973, 1974, 1979, 1980, 1990, 1992, 1996. Notable former player: Adel **Sellimi**.

Club Blooming *club* Bolivian national league club based in Santa Cruz de la Sierra, founded 1946. Ground: Estadio Ramon "Tahuichi" Aguilera Costas, capacity: 40,000. Strip: sky blue shirts, white shorts. Bolivian national league champions 1984, 1998; **Copa Libertadores** semi-final 1985.

Club Brugge KV *club* Belgium national league club based in Bruges, founded 1891. Ground: Olympiastadion, capacity: 18,000 (shared with KSV Cercle Brugge). Strip: blue and black striped shirts, black shorts. Belgium Cup 1968, 1970, 1977, 1986, 1991, 1995, 1996; Belgium league champions 1920, 1973, 1976, 1977, 1978, 1980, 1988, 1990, 1992, 1996, 1998; **European Cup** runners-up 1978 (0–1, v **Liverpool**, **Wembley**, London); **UEFA Cup** runners-up 1976 (2–3 agg., v Liverpool).

Club Deportivo El Nacional *club* Ecuador national Primera league club based in the capital Quito. Founded 1964. Ground: Estadio Olimpico Atahualpa, capacity: 46,000. Strip: grey shirts with red and blue sash, red shorts. **Copa CONMEBOL** semi-final 1992; **Copa Libertadores** semi-final 1985; **Copa Merconorte** semi-final 1998; Ecuador league champions 1967, 1973, 1976, 1977, 1978, 1982, 1983, 1984, 1986, 1992, 1996.

Club Deportivo FAS (Fútbolistas Asociados Santanecos) *club* El Salvador national league club based in Santa Ana, founded 1947 (by merger of four clubs: Excelsior, Fuerte 22, Mecca and Olimpic). Ground: Estadio Oscar Alberto Quiteno, capacity: 15,000. Strip: blue and red halved shirts, white shorts. **CONCACAF Champions Cup** 1979 (9–0 agg., v **Jong Colombia** of Netherlands Antilles); El Salvador league champions 1951, 1953, 1959, 1962, 1963, 1977, 1978, 1981, 1984, 1995, 1996.

Club Deportivo Los Millonarios *club* Colombian national league club based in Bogota, founded 1938. Ground Estadio Distrital Nemesio Camacho "El Campin", capacity: 51,300 (shared with **Independiente Santa Fé**). Strip: blue shirts, white shorts. The club qualified for the first **Copa Libertadores** in 1960. Colombian league champions

1949, 1951, 1952, 1953, 1961, 1962, 1963, 1964, 1972, 1978, 1987, 1988; Copa Libertadores quarter-final 1989, second-round group stage 1973, 1974; **Copa Merconorte** semi-final 1998.

Club Homentmen *club* Lebanese national league club. **Asian Champion Teams Cup** semi-final/third place 1970 (1–0 v **PSMS** of Indonesia, in Tehran, Iran, third/fourth play-off); Lebanese Cup 1943, 1948, 1962; Lebanese league champions 1944, 1945, 1946, 1948, 1951, 1954, 1955, 1957, 1961, 1963, 1969.

Club Jorge Wilsterman *club* Bolivian national league club based in Cochabamba, founded 1949. Ground: Estadio Felix Capriles, capacity: 35,000. Strip: dark red shirts, blue shorts. It qualified for the first **Copa Libertadores** in 1960. Bolivian national league champions 1958 (the first national champions), 1959, 1960, 1967, 1972, 1973, 1980, 1981; Copa Libertadores semi-final 1981.

Club Palestino *club* Chilean national league club based in Santiago, founded 1920. Ground: Estadio Municipal de la Cisterna, capacity: 12,000. Strip: white, red and green striped shirts, black shorts. Chilean Cup (**Copa Chile**) 1978; Chilean league champions 1955.

Club Sport Emelec (Empressa Electrica del Ecuador) *club* Ecuador national Primera league club based in Guayaquil. Founded 1929. Ground: Estadio George Capwell, capacity: 28,000. Strip: blue shirts with grey sash, grey shorts. **CONMEBOL Cup** semi-final 1995, quarter-final 1996; **Copa Libertadores** quarter-final 1990; Ecuador league champions 1957, 1961, 1965, 1972, 1979, 1988, 1993, 1994.

Club Sport Herediano *club* Costa Rica national league club based in Heredia, founded 1921. Ground: Estadio Eladio Rosabel Cordero, capacity: 12,000. Strip: yellow shirts with a red sash, black shorts. Costa Rica champions 1921, 1922, 1924, 1927, 1930, 1931, 1932, 1933, 1935, 1937, 1947, 1948, 1951, 1955, 1961, 1978, 1979, 1981, 1985, 1993.

club colours *misc.* colour of club strip. Fans also sport club (national) colours, wearing scarves and hats, and, more recently replica shirts. The colours worn by several clubs today are quite different from those adopted by their founders. *Keynotes* **Brentford** initially sported the pink, claret and light blue colours of the local rowing club, whose members had helped to form the soccer club. Similarly, **Derby County** first turned out in the amber, chocolate brown, light blue of the Derbyshire County Cricket club, whose members had formed the club. **Liverpool** first wore blue and white quartered shirts, before adopting the now famous all-red, while neighbours **Everton** once wore salmon pink. **Bolton Wanderers** took to the field in white shirts and red spots in 1884. **Manchester United**, as Newton Heath, wore yellow and green halved shirts. White shirts were popular among many clubs in the early years because they were easy to come by. Arsenal's red – all-red until the 1930s – was adopted because the jerseys were supplied by **Nottingham Forest**, which responded to a request from a former player, Fred

Beardsley, to help the London club when it was formed. **Juventus** adopted its famous black and white striped shirts from the colours of **Notts County**. The English influence also is evident in Spain, where **Athletic Bilbao**'s red and white striped shirts and black shorts are modelled on the strip worn by **Sunderland**.

club fines and suspensions *regulations* disciplinary action taken by a club on one of its own players for misconduct or a breach of its disciplinary rules. **Premier League** clubs that impose fines or suspensions on any player must send a copy of the written notice to the League and Football Association (FA Premier League rule J.20).

club linesman *rules* an unqualified match official that assists the referee in games where qualified **assistant referees** are not appointed (such as in many local games). Club linesmen are appointed by the participating clubs (usually one from each side). Club linesmen's duties are generally restricted to indicating to the referee when the ball has crossed the touchline and which team is entitled to the subsequent throw-in. Club linesmen should always consult with the referee before a match so that their duties are clear.

club list of players *regulations* document containing the names of players at a club for **registration** with the league, submitted at the end of the season (in England this is taken as the third Saturday in May; in Scotland, the list must be forwarded no later than 15 May). **Premier League** and **Football League** clubs must include in their lists of players: all **contract players** (even if they have not been offered new contracts and whose contracts are due to expire before the next season, or who have not accepted new terms); and **non-contract players** (FA Premier League rule K.24, Football League regulation 60). Football League clubs must also register **associated schoolboys** – until this class of registration is phased out – and **trainees**. Premier League clubs must also include **students** and "any other player whose registration the club holds". **Scottish Football League** clubs must include: all **professional players** currently under contract (even if they have not been offered new contracts and whose contracts are due to expire before the next season, or who have not accepted new terms); **delayed transfer players**; **apprentices** who are under contract; **trainees** (sense **2.**); associated schoolboys and **amateur players** (Scottish Football League rule 50 (a)).

club *n.* see **football club**.

Clube Deportivo Ela Nguema *club* Equatorial Guinea national league club based in the capital Malabo. Ground: Estadio La Paz (the national stadium, also shared with **Atletico Malabo**), capacity: 15,000. *Keynotes* Its eight league titles in eight years is a national record and just one behind the African record held by **Hafia FC** of **Guinea**. **African Cup-winners Cup** first round 1993 (having won its preliminary round against Gazelle of Chad); Equatorial Guinea Cup 1980, 1981, 1982, 1983, 1992; Equatorial Guinea league champions 1984, 1985, 1986, 1987, 1988, 1989, 1990, 1991.

Clube Desportivo Nacional *club* Portuguese national league Club, from Funchal on the island of **Madeira** and formed in 1910. Ground: Estádio dos Barreiros, capacity: 16,000. Strip: black and white striped shirts and black shorts.

Clyde *club* Scottish league. *Dossier* Ground: **Broadwood Stadium**, Cumbernauld, Strathclyde, capacity: 8,200 all-seater. Strip: white shirt with black, red and white trim, white shorts with red and black stripe, white socks with red and black trim. Nickname: Bully Wee. Record attendance: 52,000 v **Rangers** (21 November 1908, Division One). Biggest win: 11–1 v **Cowdenbeath** (6 October 1951, Division Two)). Biggest defeat: 0–11 v **Dumbarton** (22 November 1879, **Scottish FA Cup**, fourth round), v Rangers (13 November 1880, Scottish FA Cup, fourth round). *History* Founded in 1878 in the Rutherglen district of Glasgow and taking its name from the river which flows through the city. Clyde joined the expanded **Scottish League** in 1891-92. Despite finishing third in Division Two in 1893-94, Clyde was elected to the top flight. The club has won the Division Two Championship on five occasions and, since the re-formation of the Scottish League in 1974-75, the Second Division title three times. The last Second Division Championship success, in 1977-78, was achieved on goal difference from **Raith Rovers**. Clyde's third place in Division One in 1908-09, 1911-12 and 1966-67 is the club's highest League position. Clyde reached the **Scottish FA Cup** final in both 1910 (1–2 second replay v **Dundee**) and 1912 (0–2 v **Celtic**), finally winning the trophy at the third attempt in 1939 (4–0 v **Motherwell**). In 1949, the club appeared in another final (1–4 v Rangers). Clyde has enjoyed a further two Cup successes: 1955 (1–0 replay v Celtic) and 1958 (1–0 v **Hibernian**). After **World War II**, Clyde played for a time in Khaki coloured shirts. In 1995, Clyde moved to a new ground, Broadwood Stadium, in Cumbernauld, having left its previous ground, Shawfield, in 1991 and having spent three seasons sharing **Hamilton Academical**'s **Firhill Park** ground. *League record* First Division 1975-76, 1978-79 to 1979-80, 1982-83 to 1990-91, 1993-94; Division One (A Division) 1894-95 to 1899-00, 1906-07 to 1914-15, 1921-22 to 1923-24, 1926-27 to 1950-51, 1957-58 to 1960-61, 1962-63, 1964-65 to 1971-72, 1973-74 to 1974-75; Scottish League 1891-92 to 1892-93, 1915-16 to 1920-21; Second Division 1976-77 to 1977-78, 1980-81 to 1981-82, 1991-92 to 1992-93, 1994-95–; Division Two 1893-94, 1900-01 to 1905-06, 1924-25 to 1925-26, 1956-57, 1961-62, 1963-64, 1972-73. *Honours* Division Two 1904-05, 1951-52, 1956-57, 1961-62, 1972-73, 1977-78, 1981-82, 1992-93; Scottish FA Cup 1939 (4–0 v Motherwell), 1955 (1–0 replay v Celtic), 1958 (1–0 v Hibernian). *Records* Tommy Ring is Clyde's most capped player (12 for **Scotland**), Brian Ahern holds the record for club appearances (428).

Clydebank 1. *club* Scottish league. *Dossier* Ground: **Boghead Park**, Dumbarton, Strathclyde,

capacity: 5,503. Strip: red and white striped shirts with black trim, black shorts, black with red trim. Nickname: Bankies. Record attendance: 14,900 v **Hibernian** (New Kilbowie Park, 10 February 1965, **Scottish FA Cup**, first round). Biggest win: 8–1 v **Arbroath** (3 January 1977, First Division). Biggest defeat: 1–9 v Gala Fairydean (15 September 1965, Scottish FA Cup, qualifying round). *History* Founded in 1966 out of Clydebank Juniors which was formed in 1899 and following a controversial 12-month merger with **East Stirlingshire** under the name East Stirlingshire Clydebank. ES Clydebank played one season in the **Scottish Football League** (1964-65) before the club lost a legal battle brought by East Stirling in the courts and both clubs reverted to their original names. Clydebank returned to **junior football** before securing a place of its own in Division Two in 1966-67. The current Clydebank is no relation to the club of the same name which played in the Scottish League in the inter-war period (see Clydebank **2**). The club's only major honour, the Second Division Championship, was won in 1975-76. The following season, Clydebank won further promotion and a place in the top flight for the first time. Clydebank reached the semi-finals of the **Scottish FA Cup**. In 1993, the rock band Wet, Wet, Wet, Clydebank supporters, sponsored the club. The club left its New Kilbowie Park ground, where it had first played in 1939, in 1996 and currently shares **Dumbarton**'s **Boghead Park** ground. Clydebank's future remains uncertain, especially as its current owners have suggested moving the club to Dublin. *League record* Premier Division 1977-78, 1985-86 to 1986-87; First Division 1976-77, 1978-79 to 1984-85, 1987-88 to 1996-97; Second Division 1975-76, 1997-98–; Division Two 1966-67 to 1974-75. *Honours* Second Division 1975-76. *Records* Jim Fallon holds the record for club appearances (620, 1968-86); Ken Eadie is Clydebank's record goalscorer (138, 1988-95). **2.** *club* former Scottish League. *Dossier* Ground: Clydeholm Park, Yoker, Strathclyde. *Keynotes* Unconnected to the present Clydebank, this club joined Scottish Division Two in 1914-15. In the post-**World War I** period, Clydebank competed in the Scottish Football League, finishing fifth in 1919-20. With the reformation of Division's One and Two in 1921-22, the club alternated between the two levels for five consecutive seasons. The club disbanded after the 1930-31 season. *League record* Division One 1921-22, 1923-24, 1925-26; Division Two 1914-15, 1922-23, 1924-25, 1926-27 to 1930-31; Scottish League 1917-18 to 1920-21.

coach *n.* club official responsible, at least in part, for first-team training, tactics and team selection, without the added responsibility of club affairs. The term coach is, however, sometimes interchangeable with that of the club **manager** (particularly so outside Great Britain). *rules* The coach is allowed to convey tactical information to the players provided that he or she remains within the **technical area** (if provided). Only one person at a time can convey instructions to the player, and he or she must return to the **designated seating area** afterwards. *vb.* to train players in footballing skills, tactics and fitness.

coaching qualification *regulations* a certified qualification to lead or assist in the teaching of footballing skills and development. In England, the **Football Association** has five levels of coaching qualification: level one, FA Junior Team Managers' Award (for coaching players aged seven- to 16-years-old); level two, FA Coaching Certificate (also for youth-level coaching); Level three, FA Coaching Licence (for coaching teenagers and young adults); level 4, FA Advanced Coaching Licence (there are separate youth and senior licences); and level five, FA Coaching Diploma. The **UEFA** "B", "A" and "Pro" Coaching Awards are at equivalent levels three, four and five, respectively. Course content varies with the coaching level. The level-one award, for example, includes sessions in attitude and ethics for young players, first aid, understanding football, organising small-sided games, "fitting the game to the needs of players", organising training sessions, development, fitness, preventing injuries and a final assessment. There are about 10 hours' tuition involved. At the opposite end of the spectrum, the UEFA "Pro" Licence covers everything from squad training and video analysis, to performance psychology, business management and media relations; the trainees will already have an advanced-level coaching licence. In addition to any previous tuition to attain the required entry level, it takes about 60 hours' learning to achieve the FA Coaching Certificate, about 120 hours to qualify for the FA Advanced Coaching Licence/UEFA "A" Coaching Award, and about 240 hours to reach the UEFA Pro Licence. The Football Association is registered as an "approved centre" for the awarding of National Vocational Qualifications at various coaching levels. The **Scottish Football Association** (SFA) has five adult coaching qualification levels: SFA C (Club Coach) Certificate; UEFA/SFA B (basic) Licence Diploma; SFA A (introductory) Intermediate Certificate; UEFA/SFA (Advanced) Licence Diploma; and UEFA Pro Licence. The SFA also operates the SFA G (goalkeeping) Licence Diploma and Certificate as well as various youth and children's coaching qualifications and a **National Youth Training Scheme** for young players at senior clubs.

Cobh Ramblers *club* Republic of Ireland national league club based in Cobh, County Cork on the south coast of Ireland. Strip: sky blue shirts, white shorts.

Cobreloa *club* Chilean national league club based in Calama, founded 1952. Ground: Estadio Municipal de Calama, capacity: 30,000. Strip: orange shirts, orange shorts. Chilean Cup (**Copa Chile**) 1986; Chilean league champions 1980, 1982, 1985, 1988, 1992; **Copa CONMEBOL** quarter-final 1995; **Copa Libertadores** runners-up 1981 (1–2, 1–0, 0–2 play-off, v **Flamengo**), 1982 (0–0, 0–1, v **Peñarol**).

cocaine *medical* a naturally occurring alkaloid drug, also called benzoylmethylecgonine, derived from the coca plant (*Erythroxylon coca*).It can also be manufactured synthetically. It can be used as an anaesthetic, though its main misuse-effects are intense exhilaration and euphoria. Its after-effects include anxiety and delusions. In sport, it can be used illegally as a stimulant, and is universally banned. Cocaine hydrochloride (its usual form) is taken by sniffing a powder preparation, and is thus absorbed into the blood via the nasal mucous membrane. Cocaine hydrochloride does not cause physiological dependence (addiction), though users can become psychologically dependent on it (ie, they perceive a need to take it regularly in order to perform well). Another form of the drug, crack cocaine, can be smoked. *Keynotes* Until 1903, cocaine was a constituent of the soft drink Coca-Cola. A number of footballers, including Diego **Maradona** and Claudio Cannigia (of **Roma** and **Argentina**) have been suspended after failing **drug tests** for cocaine.

Colchester United *club* English league. *Dossier* Ground: **Layer Road**, Colchester, Essex, capacity: 7,556. Strip: blue and white striped shirts, blue shorts, white socks. Nickname: the U's. Record attendance: 19,072 v **Reading** (27 November 1948, **FA Cup**, first round). Best average attendance: 10,573 (1950-51). Biggest win: 9–1 v **Bradford City** (30 December 1961, Division Four). Biggest defeat: 0–8 v **Leyton Orient** (15 October 1989, Division Four). *History* Founded in 1937 as a successor to Colchester Town, an amateur club which had been formed in 1873. United is the youngest club in the **Football League**. The club plays at Layer Road, a former army parade ground which Colchester Town first began using in 1909. United won the **Southern League** Championship in 1939 and in 1948, it became the first non-League club to reach the FA fifth round (0–5 v **Blackpool**), having disposed of three League opponents: **Huddersfield Town** 1–0, of Division One; **Wrexham**, 1–0, Division Three (North), and **Bradford Park Avenue**, 3–2, Division Two. United's 1948 FA Cup successes were among the first of many **giant-killing** feats, but its Football League career has been less memorable. The club joined the League with the expansion of Division Three (South) in 1950-51 and narrowly missed promotion to Division Two in 1956-57. Thereafter, the club has alternated between the bottom two divisions. United's most celebrated moment came in 1971 when the club produced arguably the FA Cup's biggest shock by defeating Don **Revie**'s **Leeds United** (3–2, fifth round). Although Colchester lost in the quarter-finals (0–5 v **Everton**), it joined a small band of Division Four clubs that have reached the last eight of the FA Cup (along with **Bradford City**, **Cambridge United** and **Oxford United**). That summer United won the close-season **Watney Cup** tournament (4–4, 4–3 pens. v **West Bromwich Albion**) and in 1974-75, the club was a **League Cup** quarter-finalist (1–2 v **Aston Villa**). It was the first club to apply to use an **artificial pitch** – this was refused in 1980 by the **Football League management committee**. United was an end-of-season Division Four **playoff**

semi-finalist in 1986-87 but, in 1989-90, the club finished bottom of the division, losing its League status to **Darlington**. The club returned to the League as **Football Conference** Champions in 1991-92. In the same season, United made its first **Wembley** appearance, winning the **FA Challenge Trophy** (3–1 v Witton Albion), and, in 1997, made a return trip in the final of the **Autoglass Windscreens Shield** (0–0, 3–4 pens. v **Carlisle United**). In 1997-98, Colchester won promotion to the Second Division via the end-of-season **playoffs** (1–0 v **Torquay United**), having been a losing semi-finalist two years earlier. One unenviable record which Colchester holds is that it was the first Football League club to have its goalkeeper (John Keeley) and substitute goalkeeper (Nathan Munson) sent off in the same match – both for **professional fouls** (16 October 1993, 0–5, v **Hereford United**, Third Division). *League record* Second Division 1998-99–; Division Three 1958-59 to 1960-61, 1962-63 to 1964-65, 1966-67 to 1967-68, 1974-75 to 1975-76, 1977-78 to 1980-81; Third Division 1992-93, 1992-93 to 1997-98; Division Three (South) 1950-51 to 1957-58; Division Four 1961-62, 1965-66, 1968-69 to 1973-74, 1976-77, 1981-82 to 1989-90 (relegated to Football Conference). *Honours* FA Challenge Trophy 1992 (3–1 v Witton Albion); Football Conference 1991-92; Southern League 1939; Watney Cup 1971 (4–4, 4–3 pens. v West Bromwich Albion). *Records* Micky Cook holds the record for club League appearances (613, 1969-84); Martyn King is Colchester's record League goalscorer (130, 1956-64).

Coleraine FC *club* Northern Ireland national league club based in Coleraine, County Antrim, founded 1927. Ground: the Showgrounds, capacity: 8,000. Strip: blue and white striped shirts, blue shorts. **Irish FA Cup** 1965, 1972, 1975, 1977; Northern Ireland league champions 1974; **UEFA Cup** second round 1970, 1971. Notable former players: Terry Cochrane (26 caps for **Northern Ireland**, 1976-84), Bertie Peacock (31 caps for Northern Ireland, 1952-62), Jim Platt (23 caps for Northern Ireland, 1976-86).

collarbone *medical* the bone that joins the shoulder to the sternum. Otherwise known as the clavicle.

collateral ligament *medical* either of two **ligaments** around the knee joint, attached to the bottom of the **femur**. More specifically, these are the **medial collateral ligament** and the **lateral collateral ligament**.

Colo Colo (Club Social y Deportivo Colo Colo) *club* Chilean national league club based in Santiago, founded 1925. Ground: Estadio Monumental "David Arellano", capacity: 62,000. Strip: white shirts, white shorts. Chilean Cup (**Copa Chile**) 1958, 1974, 1981, 1982, 1985, 1988, 1989, 1990, 1994, 1996; Chilean league champions 1937, 1939, 1941, 1944, 1947, 1953, 1956, 1960, 1963, 1970, 1972, 1979, 1981, 1983, 1986, 1989, 1990, 1991, 1993, 1996, 1997 (**Clausura** tournament), 1998; **Copa Inter Americana** 1992; **Copa Libertadores** 1991 (3–0 agg., v **Olimpia**), runners-up

1973 (1–1, 0–0, 1–2 playoff, v **Independiente**), semi-final 1964, 1997; **Recopa** 1991 (0–0, 5–4 pens., v **Cruzeiro**); **Supercopa** semi-final 1996, 1997, quarter-final 1994.

Cologne (Köln) (1.FC) *club* German league. *Dossier* Ground: Müngersdorfer Stadion, Cologne, capacity: 47,000. Strip: white shirts with red shoulder flashing, white shorts with red trim. *History* Formed in 1948 from a merger of two pre-**World War II** clubs, Kölner Ballspiel-Club and FC Sülz. The club is officially called 1.FC Köln, meaning the first football club of Cologne. The club won its first title, the West German Championship, in 1962, having appeared in the 1960 national **playoff** (2–3 v **Hamburg SV**). Köln won the inaugural **Bundesliga** Championship in 1963-64 and a second title in 1977-78, a year in which it was also victorious in the West German Cup. Köln's last piece of silverware, the West German Cup, was achieved in 1983, although it was a finalist again in 1991 (1–1, 3–4 pens. v **Werder Bremen**). The club was **European Cup** semi-finalist in 1978 (3–4 agg., v **Nottingham Forest**) and a **UEFA Cup** finalist eight years later (3–5 agg., v **Real Madrid**). *Honours* Bundesliga 1963-64, 1977-78; West German Cup 1968 (4–1 v VfL Bochum), 1977 (1–0 replay v Hertha BSC Berlin), 1978 (2–0 v Fortuna Düsseldorf), 1983 (1–0 v Fortuna Köln); West German League 1962.

Colombia *country CONMEBOL* republic in north-west South America, on the Caribbean Sea and Pacific Ocean. Republic since 1886. Area: 1,138,915 sq km (439,620 sq miles). Almost half the country is covered by the Amazon forest, with mountainous areas in the Andes. Population: 34,500,000 (1994 est.). Language: Spanish. Capital: Bogotá. *Dossier* Football association (Federación Colombiana de Fútbol, Bogotá) formed in 1971 (though an earlier federation was founded in 1924, replaced by the Associacion Colombiana de Fútbol in 1938), affiliated to **FIFA** in 1936, and the **Confederación Sudamericana de Fútbol** (CONMEBOL) in 1940, president Dr Alvaro Fina, general secretary Celina Sierra. Season played from March to October, in four stages. National stadium: El Campin, Bogota, capacity: 60,000 (47,000 seated). National strip: yellow shirts with tricolour borders, blue shorts. Website: http://www.geocities.com/-colfutbol (official site). First international game: 10 February 1938 v **Mexico** (1–3, in Panama City, Panama, **Central American and Caribbean Games**). Biggest victory: 5–0 v **Argentina** (5 September 1993, in Buenos Aires, **World Cup** qualifier). Biggest defeat: 0–9 v **Brazil** (24 March 1957, in Lima, **Copa America**). Most capped players: Carlos **Valderrama** (111 appearances, 10 goals, 1985-98). Other notable international players: Bernardo Redin, Rene **Higuita**, Alberto Iguaran, Faustino **Asprilla**, Freddy Rincon, Andres **Escobar**. *International tournament record* **Olympic Games** – qualified for finals tournament 1968, 1972, 1980, 1992, never beyond first round group stage; **Women's World Cup** – first entered 1999 tournament; World Cup

– first entered 1958, second round 1990, also qualified for finals tournament 1962, 1994, 1998; Central American and Caribbean Games 1946; Copa America – first entered 1945, runners-up 1975 (1–0, 2–0, 0–1 playoff in Caracas, v Peru), semi-final/third 1987 (2–1 v **Argentina**, in Buenos Aires, third/fourth playoff), 1993 (1–0 v **Ecuador**, in Portoviejo, Ecuador, third/fourth playoff), 1995 (4–1, v **United States of America**, in Maldonad, Uruguay, third/fourth playoff), quarter-final 1997; **South American Youth Cup** (under-20) 1987; **Under-17 World Championship** – qualified for finals tournament 1993 (first round group stage); **World Youth Cup** (under-20) – quarter-final 1985, 1989, also qualified for finals tournament 1987, 1993. *Record against British and Irish national teams* v **England**, played four, drawn two, lost two; v **Northern Ireland**, played one, won one; v **Scotland**, played three, won one, drawn two; v **Wales**, none played; v **Republic of Ireland**, none played. *History* A rudimentary form of football is thought to have been played from the sixth century. Modern football was introduced around 1880, with first recorded game in 1888. Liga de Football del Atlantico founded in Barranquilla in 1924, with a national professional league championship started in 1948. Professionalism encouraged the import of foreign players, such as Alfredo **Di Stefano**, even though the national association was suspended by FIFA from 1950 to 1954. The current national association, the Federación Colombiana de Fútbol, was formed in 1971. The league was reorganised in 1968, with the introduction of an **apertura, clausura** and final league tournaments (see below), replacing a straightforward European-style league championship. The 1989 league season abandoned after the assassination of a referee. The league format was changed in 1996-97, with the league season starting in September: **América de Cali** emerging as champions in May 1997. However, after experimenting with a September-May season, it was decided to revert to the original February-December format. Colombia thus staged an interim "Torneo Adecuacion" to bridge the gap before the start of the next regular season in 1998. The league has been dominated by América de Cali, **Club Deportivo Los Millonarios, Deportivo Cali** and **Atlético Nacional Medellin**. Atlético Nacional is the only Colombian club to have won the **Copa Libertadores** (1989), though Deportivo Cali and América have reached the final. Three Colombian clubs reached the semi-finals of the first **Copa Merconorte** – the weaker of the South American "super leagues" – with Atlético Nacional Medellin beating Deportivo Cali 4–1 over the two-leg final in 1998; Millonarios reached the semi-final. Colombia's best international achievement was runners-up in the 1975 Copa America. It has qualified four times for the World Cup finals and reached the second round in 1990. The 1994 campaign was tragically marred by the murder of Andres Escobar in Medellin, shortly after Colombia returned home after the finals. Escobar had scored an own goal in the first-round defeat by the United States of America. Former Federación de Fútbol president Juan Jose Bellini was sentenced to six years in prison for accepting money from drug traffickers. *World Cup performance* (finals and qualifiers to end of 1998 tournament) played 77, won 25, drawn 22, lost 30, scored 88 goals, conceded 101 goals; win rate: 32%; goals scored per game: 1.14. *League system* There are two national divisions – the first division (Dimayor) of 16 clubs, and a second division (Copa Concasa) also of 16 clubs – and provincial leagues. The Dimayor is played in stages: the apertura, clausura and "championship liguilla". Three points are awarded for a win, with one for a draw. **Bonus points** are also awarded to the top four clubs in the first stage, and these are carried forward to the next stage. The clubs with the most points (total for apertura and clausura stages, plus bonus points) enter a "championship liguilla": the winners of this mini-league are the champions (the "Copa Mustang"). The champions of the Copa Concasa are also determined by a final mini-league. *Record in international club tournaments* Copa Libertadores – Atlético Nacional Medellin (1989, runners-up 1995, semi-final 1990, 1991), Deportivo Cali (runners-up 1978), América de Cali (runners-up 1985, 1986, 1987, 1996, semi-final 1988, 1992, 1993, second-round group stage 1980, 1983), **Independiente Santa Fé** (semi-final 1961), **Atlético Junior** (semi-final 1994, quarter-final 1996), Club Deportivo Los Millonarios (quarter-final 1989, second-round group stage 1973, 1974), **Independiente Medellin** (quarter-final 1994), **Deportes Tolima** (second-round group stage 1982); **Supercopa** – Atlético Nacional Medellin (semi-final 1993, 1997, quarter-final 1996); **Copa CONMEBOL** – Atletico Junior (quarter-final 1992), Independiente Santa Fé (runner-up 1996), América de Cali (semi-final 1995, quarter-final 1997), Deportes Tolima (quarter-final 1997); Copa Merconorte – Atlético Nacional Medellin (1998), Deportivo Cali (runner-up 1998), Club Deportivo Los Millonarios (semi-final 1998); **Copa Inter Americana** – Atlético Nacional Medellin (1990, 1997). Other leading club: Once Caldas (of Manizales, Colombian league champions 1950, 1998).

Colorado Rapids *club* United States football club and founder member of **Major League Soccer**, based in Denver, Colorado. Member of the league's **Western Conference**. Founded: 1996 Ground: Mile High Stadium, capacity: 76,123. Notable players: Chris Woods (former **England** goalkeeper), Roy Wegerle (became club coach).

coloured ball *regulations* match ball of distinctive colour (eg orange) made available in case of snow. **Premier League** home clubs are required to have a coloured ball available: this to be checked by the referee (FA Premier League rule G.10.6). *Keynotes* An orange ball was introduced to English football by the **Football League** in 1954; a high-visibility ball was piloted in the Football League in 1998-99.

coloured boots *misc.* non-black football boots. Although former **Arsenal** manager Herbert **Chapman**

was believed to have worn yellow boots as a player, **Everton**'s Alan **Ball**, **Derby County**'s Alan Hinton and **Leeds United**'s Terry Cooper were among the first players to sport coloured boots, wearing white ones in the early-1970s. Nowadays it is commonplace for players to wear different coloured boots, especially ones that match their kit. In 1996, **Liverpool**'s John **Barnes** was the first player to sport white boots in a FA Cup final. During the 1996 **African Nations** tournament, the entire **Liberia** squad wore red boots.

Columbus Crew *club* United States football club and founder member of **Major League Soccer**, based in Columbus, Ohio. Member of the league's **Eastern Conference**. Founded: 1996, Ground: Ohio Stadium, capacity: 89,840. Notable former player: Brad **Friedel**. Major League Soccer Championship runners-up 1997.

Coluna, Mário Esteves *player* Striker/midfield. **Portugal** international (57 caps, 1955-68). Born 6 August 1935 in **Mozambique**. *Clubs* **Gruppo Desportivo de Maputo** (Mozambique), **Benfica**, Olympique Lyonnais (France). *Keynotes* Noted for his fierce left-foot shot. Joined Benfica from Gruppo Desportivo de Maputo in 1954. Coluna appeared in Benfica's first five **European Cup** finals (1961, 1962, 1963, 1965, 1968), scoring in the winning sides of 1961 and 1962. Captained the Portuguese national team in the 1966 World Cup. Later became minister of sport in his native Mozambique. *Honours* World Cup third place (Portugal, 1966); European Cup (Benfica, 1961, 1962); Portuguese league championship (Benfica, 1955, 1957, 1959, 1962, 1964).

Combination *competition* short-lived English football competition set up as a rival to the **Football League** in 1888. Founded by J G Hall of **Crewe Alexandra**. Membership of 20 clubs. Lasted just one season. It was replaced by the **Football Alliance**.

combination defence *tactics* defensive system that combines features of the **man-to-man** and **zone defensive** formations. Typically a combination defence will be used to counteract an opposition team which includes a player(s) of exceptional ability. Under such circumstances a defender/midfielder will be assigned a close man-marking role, while the other defenders adopt a zone defence. A further example of a combination defence, and one commonly adopted by **Germany**, involves a **sweeper** supporting the nine outfield players, who are each assigned a man-marking role on a zone defence basis.

commissario tecnico *n.* title give to club/national coach in Italian football.

Commission of Inquiry into Playing Surfaces *n.* joint **Football League/Football Association** body established to examine **artificial pitches** that reported in May 1989.

Common, Alf *player* Striker. **England** international (3 caps). Born 25 May 1880. Career ca. 1900–1914. *Clubs* **Sunderland** (twice), **Sheffield United**, **Middlesbrough**, Woolwich **Arsenal**, **Preston North End**. *Keynotes* Middlesbrough paid Sunderland £1,000

for Common in February 1905 – the first four figure transfer fee – provoking a special commission to investigate the deal. Sunderland had earlier paid a then record fee for Common when the club signed him from Sheffield United for £520 in 1904. Within a few weeks of signing for Middlesbrough, Common scored the only goal in the club's victory over Sheffield United, its first away win for two years. Included in the **Football League Centenary 100 players**. *Honours* Division Two (Preston North End 1912-13); FA Cup (Sheffield United 1902).

Commonwealth of Independent States (CIS) *n.* body which succeeded the former-**Soviet Union** (Union of Soviet Socialist Republics) following the demise of Communist rule. Formed on 21 December 1991, consisting of 11 republics: **Azebaijan**, **Belarus**, **Kazakhstan**, **Krgyzstan**, **Moldova**, the Russian Federation (**Russia**), **Tajikistan**, **Turkmenistan**, **Ukraine** and **Uzbekistan**. **Georgia** did not join the new Commonwealth, while the Baltic States – **Latvia**, **Lithuania** and **Estonia** – had already declared independence from the former-Soviet Union. Its headquarters were in Minsk, Belarus. *Dossier* First international game: 25 January 1992, v the **United States of America** (1–0, in Miami, USA, friendly). Last international game: 18 June 1992, v **Scotland** (0–3, in Norrköping, Sweden, **European Championship** finals first round). *International tournament record* European Championship – first round 1992; no other tournaments. *Record against British and Irish national teams* v England, played one, drawn one; v Scotland played one, lost one. *History* Twelve international matches were played by the CIS, between 25 January and 18 June 1992, including games against **England** (Moscow, 29 April, 2–2, friendly) and **Scotland** (above). It inherited the 1992 European Championship finals berth of the former-Soviet Union. The CIS drew its first two games in the tournament (1–1, v **Germany**, and 0–0, v **Netherlands**) and lost the last against Scotland (0–3). Dobrovolski's goal in the match against Germany was the last of only 13 goals scored by the ephemeral Commonwealth.

Community Awards scheme *competition* annual competition to promote community activities/links by **Football League** clubs, which was established by the **Football Trust** in 1988-89. In its first season, 57 Football League clubs entered the first competition. In 1995, **Sunderland** was voted Community Club of the Year for its involvement with youth clubs, schools, senior citizens groups, hospitals and social centres. The club operates a Football-in-the-Community scheme which includes the club's Childlink project. This is designed to encourage access to the club for the youth of the area.

community service *misc.* period of unpaid work imposed on a convicted offender. *Keynotes* Former **Manchester United** captain Eric **Cantona** was ordered by the courts to perform 120 hours of community service after leaping the barrier and making a "kung fu" style lunge at **Crystal Palace** supporter Matthew Simmonds following his sending off during a **Premier League** encounter at **Selhurst Park** on 25 January 1995. **Queens Park Rangers**' player-coach and former **Wales** international Vinnie Jones was ordered by the courts in June 1998 to perform 100 hours of community service following his conviction for assault.

community-owned football club   *n.*   club of which the majority shareholding is owned by supporters. *Keynotes* In January 1997, **Bournemouth**, more than £3.5 million in debt, was put into receivership by its bankers. Supporters raised sufficient funds to convince the club's creditors that a financial restructuring was possible. A fans' trust was set up which holds a 51% share in the club, making Bournemouth the UK's first community-owned football club. The club also adopted the official title, Bournemouth & Boscombe Athletic Community Football Club Limited.

Comoros *country no international affiliation* Comoro Islands. Group of volcanic islands in the Indian Ocean, off northwest coast of **Madagascar**, independent from **France** in 1976. Area: 1,860 sq km (718 sq miles). Tropical climate. Population: 490,000 (1995 est.). Languages: French, Arabic, Comoran. Capital: Moroni. *Dossier* Football association (Federation Comorienne de Football, Moroni) founded in 1982, affiliated to French Football Federation, no independent affiliation to **FIFA**, not affiliated to **Confédération Africaine de Football** (CAF). Season played from April to December. National stadium: Moroni, capacity: 5,000. National strip: green shirts, white shorts. First international game: 31 August 1979 v **Réunion** (1–6, in Réunion, **Indian Ocean Games**). *International tournament record* **Olympic Games** – never entered; **Women's World Cup** – never entered; **World Cup** – never entered; **African Cup of Nations** – never entered; Indian Ocean Games – first entered 1979, third 1985; **Under-17 World Championship** – never entered; **World Youth Cup** (under-20) – never entered. *Record against British and Irish national teams* none played. *League system* Separate tournaments are played in each of the three main islands – Anjouan, Grande Comoro and Mohali – with the winners competing for the national championship. *Record in international club tournaments* never entered major African club tournaments. Leading clubs: Etoile de Sud, Faigaff, Papillon Bleu, Rapid Moroni, US Zlimadjou (league champions 1998).

Compensation Tribunal *regulations (Scotland)* tribunal of the **Scottish Football League** set up to adjudicate on **compensation fees** where the two clubs involved in the transaction cannot agree on the size of the fee. Its rulings are binding (Scottish Football League rule 60.13). The Committee has an independent chairman and includes one representative each from the Scottish Professional Footballers Association and the Scottish Football League.

compensation fee *regulations* **1. Premier League** Fee paid by a club for the **transfer** of a player's registration. There are two circumstances under which a Premier League club may be entitled to seek a compensation fee for the transfer, or "sale" of one of its players: (i) for the transfer of a **contract player**, transferred during the period of his contract – the compensation fee agreed between the two clubs and set out in the **transfer agreement** (FA Premier League rule L.22); and (ii) for the transfer of an **out-of-contract player** who is under 24 years of age, providing that the current club has offered the player a new contract which is on terms at least as good as the expired one (the fee is considered as compensation for the training and development of young players). The value of the compensation fee is either agreed between the two clubs or, if no agreement is reached, settled by the **Football League Appeals Committee** (FA Premier League rules L.12 and L.23). The compensation fee is paid directly to the Premier League "Compensation Fee Account", for immediate forwarding to the player's original club (FA Premier League rules L.25 and 26). If a transfer agreement has been reached, at least half the full fee must be received before the Premier League will register a player with the new club, and the balance paid within 12 months (FA Premier League rule L.27); if the fee is settled by the appeals committee, half the fee must again be paid at the outset, with the balance paid over a timescale determined by the committee (rule L.28). If a player is transferred before the balance is paid, then any subsequent transfer fee must be used immediately to settle the outstanding balance (FA Premier League rule L.29). The principle of compensation fees for out-of-contract players aged under 24 years was introduced at the end of the 1997-98 season in an effort to stave off any legal challenge to the British compensation-fee system under the **Bosman ruling**. **2. Football League** Fee paid by a club for the transfer of an out-of-contract player's registration, provided that the player is under 24-years of age (Football League regulation 59.3). The selling club will only be entitled to seek a compensation fee if it has made a written offer of a contract to the player which is at least as good as the previous contract (if one existed) (Football League regulation 59.3). The compensation fee is paid directly to the league for immediate forwarding to the player's original club (Football League regulation 44.1). The club paying the fee must pay a deposit to the league when the relevant transfer documents are submitted. The rules of the Football League require that full payment must be made within a timescale agreed by the clubs, and certainly within the period of a player's contract (Football League regulation 44.2). If a player is transferred before the balance is paid, then any subsequent transfer fee must be used immediately to settle the outstanding balance. If clubs cannot agree a compensation fee, a fee may be set by the Football League Appeals Committee (Football League regulation 59.5). **3. Scottish Football League** Fee paid by a club for the transfer of an out-of-contact player's registration, provided that the player is under 24 years of age (Scottish Football league rule 60). The selling club will only be entitled to seek a compensation fee if it has made a written offer of a contract to the player that, in the opinion of the Scottish Football League Management Committee, is at least as good as the previous contract (Scottish Football League rule 60). The club must also continue to pay the player's basic wage for a period of 31 days after the contract has expired (Scottish Football League rule 60.7) and, during this 31-day period, offer the player a continuing **monthly contract** (Scottish Football League rule 60.7(2)). If a monthly contract is not offered, then the club loses its right to a compensation fee. The full details of the compensation agreement, signed by both clubs, must be given to the league secretary along with the registration documents (Scottish Football League rule 60.6). At least half of the fee must be paid on the date of registration, and the balance paid within 12 months (Scottish Football League rule 60.6.ii). If the two clubs cannot reach an agreement on the size of the compensation fee, then it is determined by the Scottish Football League **Compensation Tribunal** (Scottish Football League rule 60.6(b)). Compare **transfer fee** (senses **2.** and **3.**), **free transfer**.

competition rules *n.pl.* set of rules stipulated for a particular league or tournament in addition to the **Laws of the game**. Competition rules may, for example, state the number of **substitutes** allowed by each side, whether or not **extra-time** or **penalties** are to be played and whether or not **away goals** will be a premium in a drawn two-leg tie.

compliance officer *n.* individual charged with ensuring compliance with codes of conduct/best practice. The **Football Association** appointed its first compliance officer, Graham Bean, a policeman, **Football Supporters Association** chairman and member of the **Football Taskforce**, in November 1998 – Bean took up his position in January 1999. His remit is to oversee issues of financial malpractice, drug abuse, racism and general misconduct within football.

compound fracture *medical* a **fracture** where the skin is also broken (either by the bone protruding through the skin, or by the skin being broken by the blow that caused the injury). Compare **closed fracture**.

compression *medical* application of gentle pressure to a **soft-tissue injury** to limit the extent of damage to the tissue. Compression is applied by applying a bandage or by direct pressure.

Comunale (Stadio Artemio Franchi) *ground* Italian football ground situated in Florence, Tuscany; home of **Fiorentina**. Ground capacity: 45,000 all seated. *History* Designed by Pier Luigi Nervi and originally named Stadio Comunale Giovanni Beta, after a local fascist leader, the stadium opened on 13 September 1931 (v **Admira-Wacker** (Austria)). Nervi's design included the construction of one of the world's first **cantilever stands** and a tall thin tower. The fascist name was dropped after **World War II** and the ground was partially redeveloped for the 1990 **World Cup**. During the tournament, the Stadio Comunale staged three group A

matches (**Czechoslovakia** v **USA**, Czechoslovakia v **Austria**, Austria v USA) and a quarter-final tie (**Argentina** v **Yugoslavia**) – total attendance 146,056; average attendance 36,514. The ground was also a 1934 World Cup venue, hosting three matches in all (**Germany** v **Belgium**, round one; **Italy** v **Spain** (plus replay), quarter-final) – total attendance 88,000; average attendance 29,333.

Comunicaciones Fútbol Club *club* Guatemala national league club based in Guatemala City, founded 1950. Ground: Estadio Mateo Flores, capacity: 50,000. Strip: cream shirts, white shorts. **CONCACAF Champions Cup** 1978 (in 1978, there were three regional winners to the CONCACAF Champions Cup; Comunicaciones won the Central region), runners-up 1962 (the first ever tournament, 0–6 agg., v **Guadalajara CD** of Mexico), 1969 (0–1 agg., v **Cruz Azul** of Mexico), third 1996, quarter-final 1997; Guatemala Cup 1992; Guatemala national champions 1956, 1958, 1960, 1969, 1971, 1972, 1978, 1980, 1981, 1982, 1985, 1987, 1988, 1991, 1995, 1997, 1998, 1999.

CONCACAF *abbrev.* **Confederación Norte-Centroamericana y del Caribe de Fútbol**.

CONCACAF Champions Cup (Copa de Campeones CONCACAF) *competition* international club tournament for the champion clubs (and some runners-up) of the member nations of the **Confederación Norte-Centroamericana y del Caribe de Fútbol**, started 1962. The competition starts with regional qualifiers, in the Caribbean, North and Central America, followed by a finals tournament in a host nation. Originally played over two legs, the finals tournament now culminates in a one-match final at a host country, with **extra time** and **penalties** if necessary. In some years, the champions have been decided by a final-tournament mini-league. *Winners, runners-up and scores* 1962, **Guadalajara CD** of Mexico v **Comunicaciones** of Guatemala, 6–0 agg.; 1963, **Racing Club** of Haiti v Guadalajara CD (walkover); 1967, **Alianza** of El Salvador v **Jon Colombia** of Netherlands Antilles, 1–2, 3–0, 5–3 playoff; 1968, **Toluca** of Mexico (walkover); 1969, **Cruz Azul** of Mexico v Comunicaciones, 1–0 agg.; 1970, Cruz Azul (walkover); 1971 Cruz Azul v **Liga Deportiva Alajuelense** of Costa Rica, 5–1; 1972 **Olimpia** of Honduras v **Robin Hood** of Surinam, 2–0 agg.; 1973, **Transvaal** of Surinam (walkover); 1974, **Municipal** of Guatemala v Transvaal, 4–2 agg.; **Atlético Español** of Mexico v Transvaal, 5–1 agg.; 1976, **Aguila** of El Salvador v Robin Hood (walkover); 1977, **América** of Mexico v Robin Hood, 1–0 agg.; 1978, **Universidad Guadalajara** of Mexico, Comunicaciones and **Defence Force** of Trinidad and Tobago (joint winners); 1979, **Deportivo FAS** of El Salvador v Jong Colombia, 9–0 agg.; 1980, **UNAM** of Mexico (three-club final tournament in Tegucigalpa, Honduras; runners-up, **Universidad de Honduras** of Honduras); 1981, Transvaal v **Atlético Marte** of El Salvador, 2–1 agg.;

1982, UNAM v Robin Hood, 5–2 agg.; 1983, **Atlante** of Mexico v Robin Hood, 6–1 agg.; 1984, **Violette** of Haiti (walkover); 1985 Defence Force v Olimpia, 2–1 agg.; 1986, Liga Deportiva Alajuelense v Transvaal, 5–2 agg.; 1987 América v Defence Force, 3–1 agg.; 1988, Olimpia v Defence Force, 4–0 agg.; 1989, UNAM v **Piñar del Rio** of Cuba, 4–2 agg.; 1990, América v Piñar del Rio, 8–2 agg.; 1991, **Puebla** of Mexico v **Police FC** of Trinidad and Tobago, 4–2 agg.; 1992, América v Liga Deportiva Alajuelense, 1–0 agg.; 1993, **Deportivo Saprissa** of Costa Rica (four-club final league in Guatemala City; runners-up, **Leon** of Mexico); 1994 **CS Cartagines** of Costa Rica v Atlante, 3–2, final in San José, California; 1995 Deportivo Saprissa (league of four), in San José, Costa Rica; 1996 Cruz Azul (league of four), in Guatemala (1996 finals tournament played in July 1997); 1997 Cruz Azul, v **Los Angeles Galaxy** of USA, 5–3, in Washington DC, USA; 1998 **DC United** of USA, v Toluca, 1–0, in Washington DC.

CONCACAF Championship *competition* former international nations tournament for member countries of the **Confederación Norte-Centroamericana y del Caribe de Fútbol**, first played in 1963 to replace the previous **CCCF Championship**. The **CONCACAF Championship** was played every two years as a separate event until 1971, after which it was replaced by the CONCACAF World Cup qualifying tournament, played every four years; the winners of the World Cup qualifying tournament were declared CONCACAF champions. It was replaced, in 1991, by the CONCACAF **Gold Cup**. *Winners (and venue, where applicable)* 1963 **Costa Rica** (tournament in San Salvador, El Salvador); 1965 **Mexico** (in Guatemala City, Guatemala); 1967 **Guatemala** (in Tegucigalpa, Honduras); 1969 Costa Rica (in San José, Costa Rica); 1971 Mexico (in Port of Spain, Trinidad); 1973 **Haiti** (World Cup qualifying competition in Haiti); 1977 Mexico (World Cup qualifying competition in Mexico); 1981 **Honduras** (World Cup qualifying competition in Tegucigalpa); 1985 **Canada** (World Cup qualifying competition); 1989 Costa Rica (World Cup qualifying competition).

CONCACAF Cup-winners Cup (CONCACAF Recopa) *competition* international club tournament for the cup winners of the member nations of the **Confederación Norte-Centroamericana y del Caribe de Fútbol**, started 1991. *Winners* 1991, **Atlético Marte** of El Salvador (finals tournament mini-league); 1992 not played; 1993, **Monterrey** of Mexico (finals tournament mini-league); 1994, **Necaxa** of Mexico, 3–0, v **Aurora Fútbol Club** of Guatemala; 1995 **Universidad Autonoma de Guadelajara** of Mexico, 2–1, v **Luis Angel Firpo** of El Salvador; 1996 competition not completed; 1997 **Olimpia** of Honduras and Necaxa qualified for the final, (not played); tournment abandoned 1998.

CONCACAF Recopa *competition* see **CONCACAF Cup-winners Cup**.

CONCACAF Under-17 Championship *competition* biennial youth tournament (under-17 years) for North and Central America and Caribbean national teams (member countries of **Confederación Norte-Centroamericana y del Caribe de Fútbol**, CONCACAF). *Winners* **Costa Rica** (1994), **Cuba** (1988), **Mexico** (1985, 1987, 1990), **United States of America** (1983, 1992).

CONCACAF Women's Championship *competition* international nations tournament for women, contested by member countries of the **Confederación Norte-Centroamericana y del Caribe de Fútbol**, CONCACAF). Since 1990, the championship has served as North and Central American and Caribbean qualifying tournament for the **Women's World Cup**. The United States of America did not enter the 1998 tournament; as hosts, it had already qualified for the 1999 Women's World Cup. *Winners, scores and runners-up* 1991 **United States of America** (USA), 5–0, v **Canada**; 1994 USA (league of five nations), runners-up Canada; 1998 Canada, 1–0 v **Mexico** (in Toronto).

CONCACAF Youth Championship *competition* biennial youth tournament for players under-20 years of age, for North and Central America and Caribbean national teams (member countries of **Confederación Norte-Centroamericana y del Caribe de Fútbol**, CONCACAF). *Winners* **El Salvador** (1964), **Canada** (1986), **Costa Rica** 1988), **Honduras** (1994), **Mexico** (1962, 1970, 1973, 1974, 1976, 1978, 1980, 1984, 1990, 1992), **United States of America** (1982).

concussion *medical* the possible consequence of a blow to the head which may result in transient dizziness, loss of memory, disorientation and nausea.

condyle *medical* a rounded surface at the end of a **bone** that is covered in **cartilage**.

Confederación Centroamericana y del Caribe de Fútbol (CCCF) *confederation* former federation of nations formed in 1938, comprising countries in the Caribbean and Central America. Replaced in 1961 by the **Confederación Norte-Centroamericana y del Caribe de Fútbol** (CONCACAF). *Former tournaments* **CCCF Championship**.

Confederación Norte-Centroamericana y del Caribe de Fútbol (CONCACAF) *confederation* international football association for Central and North America and the Caribbean; it also includes **Guyana** and **Surinam**, which are geographically in South America. The headquarters are in New York, United States of America. It was founded in 1961. President: Jack Warner (**Trinidad and Tobago**). General secretary: Chuck Blazer (**United States of America**). The CONCACAF has 33 full members, plus two associate members, and has three places allocated at the 2002 **World Cup** finals; the same as for the 1998 finals. It was allocated three automatic places at the 1999 **Women's World Cup** finals (including the United States, which qualified as hosts); a possible fourth place was decided by a playoff between the CONMEBOL runners-up and the CONCACAF third-placed nation (**Mexico** beat **Argentina** 6–3 agg. in the playoff).

History CONCACAF was founded in 1961, replacing the former **Confederación Centroamericana y del Caribe de Fútbol** (CCCF), which dated back to 1938. *Full member countries* **Anguilla, Antigua and Barbuda, Aruba, Bahamas, Barbados, Belize, Bermuda, British Virgin Islands,** Canada, Cayman Islands, Costa Rica, Cuba, Dominica, **Dominican Republic, El Salvador, Grenada,** Guatemala, Guyana, Haiti, Honduras, Jamaica, Mexico, **Montserrat, Netherlands Antilles, Nicaragua, Panama, Puerto Rico, Saint Lucia, St Kitts and Nevis, St Vincent and the Grenadines, Surinam,** Trinidad and Tobago, United States of America. *Associate members* **Turks and Caicos Islands, US Virgin Islands.** *Tournaments (selection)* **Gold Cup, CONCACAF Youth Championship, CONCACAF Under-17 Championship, CONCACAF Champion Clubs' Cup, CONCACAF Cup-winners Cup, CONCACAF Women's Championship** (Women's World Cup qualifying tournament) and a CONCACAF Veteran's Championship.

Confederación Sudamericana de Fútbol (CONMEBOL) *confederation* international football federation for South America, excluding **Guyana** and **Surinam** – which are geographically in South America but affiliated to the **Confederación Norte-Centroamericana y del Caribe de Fútbol** (CONCACAF) – and **French Guiana**, which is only affiliated to the French Football Federation. The headquarters are in Asuncion, **Paraguay**. It was founded in 1916 and is the world's oldest continental federation. President: Dr Nicolás Leóz (Paraguay). General secretary: Eduardo Deluca (**Argentina**). The CONMEBOL has 10 members and was allocated five places at the 1998 World Cup finals (including **Brazil**, which qualified as champions). It has four automatic berths for the 2002 World Cup finals, with a fifth possible place depending on a playoff against the winners of the **Oceania Football Confederation** (OFC) qualifying tournament. The decision to award a fifth possible berth was made after drawing lots with the **Union of European Football Associations** on which should face a playoff with the OFC. It was allocated one automatic place at the 1999 **Women's World Cup** finals; a possible second place was decided by a playoff between the CONMEBOL runners-up and the CONCACAF third-placed nation (Argentina lost to Mexico in the playoff). *Full member countries* Argentina, **Bolivia**, Brazil, **Chile, Colombia, Ecuador,** Paraguay, **Peru, Uruguay, Venezuela.** *Associate members* none. *Competitions (selection)* **Copa America, South American Women's Championship, Copa Libertadores, Supercopa, Copa CONMEBOL, Copa Merconorte, Copa Mercosur, Recopa, South American Youth Cup** (under-20), **South American Under-17 Championship.** Website: www.conmebol.com/

Confederation of East and Central African Football Associations (CECEFA) *confederation* international football association of east and central

Africa, based in Nairobi, **Kenya**, founded 1970. *Member countries:* **Djibouti, Ethiopia,** Kenya, **Rwanda, Seychelles, Somalia, Sudan, Tanzania, Uganda** and **Zanzibar.** *Nations tournaments* **East and Central African Championship.** *International club tournaments* **East and Central African Club Championship.**

Confederation of Southern African Football Associations (COSAFA) *confederation* international football association of southern Africa, based in Kitwe, **Zambia,** founded 1982. Member countries: **Botswana, Lesotho, Malawi, Mozambique, Namibia, South Africa, Swaziland,** Zambia, **Zimbabwe.** *Nations tournaments* **COSAFA Cup**; COSAFA Youth Tournament (under 20), COSAFA Under-17 Championship. *International club tournaments* COSAFA Club Championship.

Confédération Africaine de Football (CAF) *confederation* international football federation of Africa (continental and island nations), based in Cairo, **Egypt.** *Dossier* CAF was founded in 1957 and has 51 full members and two associate members. President: Issa Hayatou (Cameroon). General secretary: Mustapha Fahmy (Egypt). *Founder member countries* **Egypt, Ethiopia, South Africa, Sudan.** *Other member countries* **Algeria, Angola, Benin, Botswana, Burkina Faso, Burundi, Cameroon, Cape Verde, Central African Republic, Chad, Congo, Djibouti, Equatorial Guinea, Gabon, Gambia, Ghana, Guinea, Guinea-Bissau, Ivory Coast** (Côte d'Ivoire), **Kenya, Lesotho, Liberia, Libya, Madagascar, Malawi, Mali, Mauritania, Mauritius, Morocco, Mozambique, Namibia, Niger, Nigeria, Rwanda, São Tomé and Principe, Senegal, Seychelles, Sierra Leone, Somalia, Swaziland, Tanzania, Togo, Tunisia, Uganda, Zaire, Zambia, Zimbabwe.** Associate members: **Eritrea, Réunion. Zanzibar** is affiliated via Tanzania. **Comoros, Mayote** and **Western Sahara** are not members of CAF. *Nations tournaments (senior level)* **African Cup of Nations.** *International club tournaments* **African Cup of Champion Clubs, African Cup-winners Cup** (Nelson Mandela Trophy), **CAF Cup, African Super Cup** (Mahood Abiola Cup). Website: http://www.cafonline.com (official site). *Keynotes* The CAF is allocated five places at the 2002 **World Cup** finals. It was awarded five places at the 1998 finals, and two places at the 1999 **Women's World Cup** finals. Its first president was Abdelaziz Salem (Egypt, 1957-58); the first general secretary was Mourad Fahmy (Egypt, 1961-82). CAF member nations, affiliated and associated members are also members of the five regional federations, which organise regional international and club tournaments. The five federations are: the **Arab Football Union** (which includes countries in north Africa and in the Middle East), the **Confederation of East and Central African Football Associations** (CECEFA), the **Confederation of Southern African Football**

Associations (COSAFA), the **Union of Football Associations of Central Africa** (UFACA), and the **West African Football Union** (WAFU). Sudan is in both the AFU and CECEFA.

Confederations Cup *competition* international nations tournament supposedly played between, the various Confederations champions (**UEFA**, **CONCACAF**, **CONMEBOL**, **CAF**, **AFC** and **OFC**), with the tournament holders and hosts. *History* The first three editions of the tournament were played at the King Fahd Stadium, Riyadh, **Saudi Arabia**, and began in 1992; the nations competed for the King Fahd Cup. It became an official **FIFA** tournament in 1997. Eight nations took part in the third edition, played between 12 and 21 December 1997: Australia, **Brazil**, **Czech Republic** (the **European Championship** runners-up), **Mexico**, Saudi Arabia, **South Africa**, **United Arab Emirates** and **Uruguay**. The fourth edition was originally scheduled to take place in January 1999, but was rescheduled to July 1999 after World Cup winners **France** had initially pulled out because of the disruption the tournament would have caused had it been played midway through the main European league season. *Winners, result and runners-up* 1992 **Argentina** (3–1, v Saudi Arabia); 1995 **Denmark** (2–0, v Argentina); 1997 Brazil (6–0, v Australia); 1999 tournament in Mexico.

Conferación Panamericana de Football *confederation* former federation of nations of South, Central and North America, founded 1946 in Colombia. Organised the former **Pan-American Championship**.

Conference *n.* see **Football Conference**.

Congo *country CAF* republic in West Central Africa on the Atlantic Ocean, bordered by **Cameroon**, the **Central African Republic**, **Congo Democratic Republic** (Zaire) and **Gabon**. Area: 342,000 sq km (132,010 sq miles). Population: 2,940,000 (1995 est.). Languages: French, Kongo, Teke and other local languages. Capital: Brazzaville. *Dossier* Football association (Fédération Congolaise de Football, Brazzaville), formed in 1962, affiliated to **FIFA** in 1962 and **Confédération Africaine de Football** (CAF) in 1966, president Sylvestre M'Bongo, general secretary Charles Loubassou. Season played from November to August. National stadium: Stade de la Révolution/Alphonse Massemba Deba, Brazzaville, capacity: 50,000. National strip: red shirts, red shorts (the national side is nicknamed the Red Devils). First international game: 18 July 1965, v **Mali**, (1–1, Brazzaville, African Games). Biggest victory: 11–0, v **São Tomé and Príncipe** (7 July 1976, in Gabon, Central African Games). Biggest defeat: 1–7, v Cameroon (14 March 1971, in Cameroon, friendly). Notable international players: Francois M'Pele, Paul **Moukila**. *International tournament record Olympic Games* – never qualified for finals tournament; **Women's World Cup** – entered first tournament in 1991, but withdrew, entered 1999, never qualified for finals tournament; **World Cup** – first entered 1974,

reached second round of qualifying tournament in 1978, second-round group stage 1998 (second behind South Africa in four-nation group, with 10 points from six games), never reached finals tournament; **African Cup of Nations** – first entered 1968, 1972 (3–2, v **Mali**, in Yaoundé, Cameroon), semi-final/fourth 1974 (0–4, v the hosts **Egypt**, in Cairo, third/fourth playoff), quarter-final 1992, also qualified for finals tournament 1968, 1978; **All Africa Games** – 1965 (v Mali, in Brazzaville); **Central African Games** – runners-up 1976 (2–3, v Cameroon, in Gabon), 1981 (second in league tournament in Congo Democratic Republic (Zaire)); **UDEAC Tournament** – 1990 (2–1, v Cameroon, in Brazzaville), runners-up 1984 (2–2, 4–5 pens., v Cameroon, in Brazzaville), 1985 (0–3, v host nation **Gabon**); **Under-17 World Championship** – qualified for finals tournament 1985 (last in first round group); **World Youth Cup** (under-20) – never qualified. *Record against British and Irish national teams* none played. *League system* Eight clubs qualify from regional leagues to play in an annual national league championship. *Record in international club tournaments* **African Cup of Champion Clubs** – CARA **Brazzaville** (1974); **African Cup-winners Cup** – **Inter Club** (semi-final 1988); **CAF Cup** – Inter Club (semi-final 1995). Other leading clubs: **Etoile du Congo**, **Diables Noirs**, **AS Cheminots**, Munisport (of Pointe-Noire, league champions 1996).

Congo Democratic Republic (formerly Zaire) *country CAF* republic in central Africa. Its large landmass is bordered by **Angola**, **Burundi**, **Central African Republic**, **Congo**, **Rwanda**, **Sudan**, **Tanzania** and **Zambia**. Congo DR is connected to the Atlantic Ocean by a corridor through Angola. Independence from Belgium in 1960 (as the Republic of Congo). Changed name to Zaire in 1971; adopted new name of Congo Democratic Republic ca. 1996 (with which it is now registered with **FIFA**). Other former names: Congo Free State (1885-1908), Belgian Congo (1908-60), Democratic Republic of the Congo or Congo-Kinshasa (1960-71). Area: 2,345,410 sq km (905,330 sq miles). Population: 45,260,000 (1996 est.). Languages: French, Lingala, Kiswahili, Tshiluba, Kikongo. Capital: Kinshasa. *Dossier* Football association (Fédération Congolaise de Football-Association, Kinshasa) formed in 1919, affiliated to FIFA in 1962 and **Confédération Africaine de Football** (CAF) in 1963, president: Kyasenge Bwabadeke; general secretary: Biangany Gomani Tamp'wo. Season played from August to May. National stadium: Stade Kamanyola, Kinshasa, capacity: 24,000 (8,750 seated). National strip: green shirts, yellow shorts. Nickname of national team: the Leopards. First international game: 1965 v **Ghana** (1–4, in Ghana, friendly). Biggest victory: 10–1 v Zambia (22 November 1969, Kinshasa, friendly). Biggest defeat: 0–9 v **Yugoslavia** (18 June 1974, in Gelsenkirchen, Germany, World Cup first round). Notable international players: Tshimen **Bwanga**, Mwamba **Kazadi**, **Lobilo**, Pierre Mulamba, **Ndaye**. *International tournament* *record* **Olympic Games** – first entered 1976, never qualified for finals tournament;**Women's World Cup** – first entered 1999, did not qualify for finals; **World Cup** – first entered 1974, qualified (as Zaire) for finals tournament 1974 (first round: 0–2 v **Scotland**; 0–9 v Yugoslavia; and 0–3 v **Brazil**), qualifying tournament third round 1982; **African Cup of Nations** – first entered 1965 as (Congo-Kinshasa), 1968 (as Congo-Kinshasa, 1–0, v Ghana, in Addis Ababa, Ethiopia), 1974 (2–2, 2–0 replay, v Zambia, in Cairo, Egypt), semi-final 1972 (fourth, 2–5 v **Cameroon**, in Yaoundé, Cameroon, third/fourth playoff), quarter-final 1992, 1994, also qualified for finals tournament 1970 (as holders), 1976 (as holders), 1988; **African Women's Tournament** (Women's World Cup qualifier) – third 1998 (3–3, 3–1 agg., v Cameroon, third/fourth playoff, in Lagos, Nigeria); **Central African Games** – 1981 (tournament in Angola); **Under-17 World Championship** – never qualified; **World Youth Cup** (under-20) – never qualified. *Record against British and Irish national teams* v **Scotland**, played one, lost one. *History* Congo DR's football association, was founded in 1919 (as the Association Royale Sportive Congolaise) and is the second oldest football association in Africa, after **South Africa**. Football league started in 1916 in Kinshasa (then Leopoldville). A championship involving clubs from the former-Belgium Congo and the former Middle Congo (now Congo), started in 1923. Known as the Pool Championship (after Stanley Pool, now Pool Malebo, the lake formed by the widening of the Congo river separating the capitals of the two countries, Kinshasa and Brazzaville), it lasted until 1950. **Toute Puissant Mazembe** (formerly known as Toute Puissant Englebert) reached four successive finals of the **African Cup of Champion Clubs** (1967-70), winning the first two. It has also won the **African Cup-winners Cup** (1980). Congo DR has won the African Cup of Nations twice, and qualified for the World Cup finals tournament in 1974. *Record in international club tournaments* African Cup of Champion Clubs – Toute Puissant Mazembe (1967, 1968, runners-up 1969, 1970), **Vita Club Kinshasa** (1973, runners-up 1981), **Amicale Sportive Bilima** (runners-up 1980, 1985), **Daring Club Motema Pembe** (semi-final 1979); African Cup-winners Cup – Toute Puissant Mazembe (1980), Daring Club Motema Pembe (1994, quarter-final 1993), **AC Sodigraf** (runners-up 1996); **CAF Cup** – **Mbongo Sports** (quarter-final 1992), Vita Club Kinshasa (semi-final 1996), Daring Club Motema Pembe (semi-final 1998); **African Super Cup** – Daring Club Motema Pembe (runners-up 1994). Other leading clubs: FC **Kalumu**, Association Sportive Bantous (of Mbuji Mayi, league champions 1995).

Congo-Kinshasa *country* former name (until 1971) for **Congo Democratic Republic** (formerly Zaire). Played under this name in the 1965, 1968 and 1970 **African Cup of nations**, winning in 1968.

Congreso Deportivo Centroamericano *confederation* former sporting federation of nations in Central America, founded 1924. Later becoming the Organizacion Deportiva Centroamericano y del Caribe. Organised the **Central American and Caribbean Games**, including the football competitions. The football organisation was replaced in 1938 by the **Confederación Centroamericana y del Caribe de Fútbol**.

CONMEBOL *abbrev* **Confederación Sudamericana de Fútbol**.

CONMEBOL Women's Championship *competition* see **South American Women's Championship**.

Connah's Quay Nomads *club* Welsh league. Ground: **Halfway Ground**, Connah's Quay, North Wales. Strip: white shirts, black shorts. Nickname: Westenders. Ground capacity: 2,000. Reformed in 1946. *Honours* **Welsh Cup** 1929 (3–0 v **Cardiff City**); Welsh League 1928-29 (Northern Division).

Constructorul Chisinau *club* Moldovan national league side based in Chisinau, founded 1993. Ground: Republican, capacity: 22,000, or Dinamo, capacity: 5,000. **European Cup-winners Cup** first round 1997; Moldovan Cup 1996; Moldovan league champions 1997, runners-up 1998.

continuity play *tactics* the retention of the ball through continuous passing (forwards, backwards and across the pitch) in order to penetrate the opposition's defence.

contract player *regulations* professional footballer who has a **full contract** or **monthly contract** with a club that holds his **registration**. **Premier League** and **Football League** clubs are required to provide private medical insurance for such players (FA Premier League rule H.11, Football League regulation 50.1). Contract players cannot be **released** within the period of their contracts except for reasons of permanent disability or by mutual consent of the club and player. However, they can be dismissed for serious misconduct or breach of contract. No player under-17 years of age can be given a contract (FA Premier League rule J.4, Football League regulation 55.1). Contracts for players under-18 years must be for three years or less (FA Premier League rule J.10.1). Compare **non-contract player**, **out-of-contract player**, **student**. In the rules of the **Scottish Football League**, the term **professional player** is used instead of "contract player"; players must be at least 16 years of age before being registered as professional players (Scottish Football League rule 44).

contract *regulations* **1.** A written employment agreement under which a player is registered as a professional for a club for an agreed time period. In the United Kingdom, players' contracts must be approved by the appropriate governing body. See **full contract**, **monthly contract**, **registration**; compare **non-contract**. **2.** The written terms of employment agreed between a club and an individual employee, such as the manager, coaching and administrative staff. Managers' contracts must also be approved by the relevant governing body in the UK.

contre-pied *tactics* French term for **counter-attack**.

control *vb.* to check the motion of a fast moving ball, usually with the feet or chest, thus enabling the player to execute a **dribble**, **shot**, or **pass**. *n* the act of controlling the ball; the ability to control the ball, as in "he has good control".

control play *tactics* system of play which involves retaining the ball, usually in a team's own half and with an **overload** of defenders, to draw out the opposition in order to mount a swift **counter-attack** or, simply to waste time towards the end of a match.

contropiede *tactics* Italian term for **counter-attack**.

contusion *medical* soft tissue injury commonly known as a bruise. Treated by **RICE**. Contusions to the foot are common football injuries, caused, for example, by the player's foot being kicked or stamped on.

Conwy United *club* Welsh league. Ground: Morfa Ground, Conwy, Gwynedd. Strip: tangerine shirts, black shorts. Nickname: the Musselmen. Ground capacity: 2,000. Formed in 1977.

Cook Islands *country OFC* self-governing overseas territory of, in free association with, **New Zealand**. Group of Polynesian Islands around 2,000 km northeast of New Zealand. Self-governing since 1965. Area: 233 sq km (90 sq miles). Population: 18,600. Languages: English, indigenous languages. Capital: Avarua on the island of Rarotonga. *Dossier* Cook Islands Football Association (Avarua) formed in 1971 affiliated to **FIFA** and **Oceania Football Confederation** (OFC) in 1994, president Lee Harmon, general secretary Allen Parker. Season played from October to December. National strip: green shirts with golden stripes, green shorts with golden stripe. Biggest defeat: 0–16, v **Australia** (28 September 1998, in Australia, **Oceania Cup** finals tournament). Association football lags behind rugby in popularity. *International tournament record* **Olympic Games** – never entered; **Women's World Cup** – never entered; **World Cup** – first entered 1998 (finished last in the OFC Polynesian qualifying group of three countries, behind **Tonga** and **Western Samoa**); Oceania Cup – first entered 1996, qualified for final stages 1998; **Under-17 World Championship** – never entered; **World Youth Cup** (under-20) – never entered. *Record against British and Irish national teams* none played. Leading clubs: Tupapa FC (league champions 1992, 1993, 1999), Avatiu (league champions 1994, 1996, 1997).

Cooke, Charlie *player* inside forward/winger. **Scotland** international (16 caps). Born 14 October 1942. Career ca. 1959–79. *Clubs* **Aberdeen**, **Dundee**, **Chelsea** (twice), **Crystal Palace**, Memphis Rogues, California Surf. *Keynotes* Outstanding dribbling winger/inside forward who began his playing career with Aberdeen in October 1959. He moved to Dundee for a then Scottish record £44,000 in December 1964. Tommy **Docherty** took Cooke to Chelsea in April 1966,

paying Dundee £72,500 to secure his services. Cooke made 373 appearances for Chelsea in two spells with the club. He was sold to Crystal Palace by manager Dave Sexton for £85,000 in September 1972, returning to Stamford Bridge 18 months later for £17,000. Cooke played only 16 times for Scotland, and his most memorable performance was against **England** at **Hampden Park** on 24 February 1968. Now lives in the USA. *Honours* **FA Cup** (Chelsea 1970); **European Cup-winners Cup** (Chelsea 1971).

cooling-off period *misc.* a period of reflection to allow players/club officials a change of mind; to take the heat out of a situation. *Keynotes* In November 1964, the match between **Everton** and **Leeds United** was suspended for a time when the referee, Ken Stokes, took the players off the pitch for a cooling-off period. On 13 March 1974, referee Clive Thomas sent off **Manchester United**'s Lou Macari and **Manchester City**'s Mike Doyle, but both players refused to leave the pitch. Thomas took both teams off until the players accepted his decision.

Copa America (South American Championship) *competition* biennial international nations tournament for member countries of **Confederación Sudamericana de Fútbol** (CONMEBOL, the South American confederation) and, since 1993, has invited two guest nations. The first official CONMEBOL championship took place in 1917, in Montevideo, Uruguay. Many different formats have been played (see below). The competition is now played over three weeks at various venues in a single host nation. The 12 competing nations are divided into three groups of three, playing each other once. The top two from each qualify for the knockout quarter-finals, along with the two third-placed nations with the most points. The quarter-finals, semi-finals, third/fourth place playoff and final may be decided by a **penalty shoot-out** if there is no result in normal time. *History* Although the Copa America officially started in 1917, two championships were played before the foundation of CONMEBOL in 1916: the first in 1910, in Buenos Aires, **Argentina**, with only three nations – the hosts, **Chile** and **Uruguay**. **Brazil** joined these three for a second unofficial tournament in 1916, again in Buenos Aires. The tournament was initially played as a league, with all countries playing each other once in a single host nation. If nations were level on points, irrespective of goal difference, then a playoff match decided the overall champions. In 1975, the competition was divided into three first-round groups of three nations, with the reigning champions (Uruguay) joining at the semi-final stage. The first-round matches, semi-final and final played over two legs, home and away (a playoff final was, in fact, required in this first year of the new format, because the result was decided on points, rather than on the aggregate score). The format was repeated at the next tournament in 1979 (again a playoff final was required) and in 1983. The group system was retained for the next edition in 1987, but the whole championship was, once again, played in a single host nation

(Argentina). In 1989, at the tournament in Brazil, the first round was played in two groups of five nations (with no first-round bye for the reigning champions). The winners and runners-up in each group entered a final-round group; the championship going to the winners of this mini-league. This format was repeated in 1991. In 1993, the competition was expanded to include two representatives from CONCACAF: **Mexico** and the **United States of America**. The first round consisted of three groups of four nations, with the top two from each group, plus the two best third-placed nations, qualifying for knockout quarter-finals, semi-finals and final. The format was repeated in 1995 (again with Mexico and USA) and 1997. In 1997, **Costa Rica** joined Mexico as invited representatives from CONCACAF. **Japan** and Mexico were invited for the 1999 tournament. The biggest attendance for a single match in the Copa America, was 170,000 at **Maracaná**, Rio de Janeiro, for the final round, and decisive, match between Brazil and Uruguay (1–0, 16 July 1989). Norberto Méndez of Argentina and Zizinho of Brazil share the tournament record of 17 goals. Three players have scored a record nine goals at a single tournament: Jair R Pinto (Brazil, 1949), Humberto Maschio (Argentina, 1957) and Javier Ambrois (Uruguay, 1957). *Winners, result, runners-up and venue (plus playoff results where indicated)* 1910 (unofficial) Argentina (league of three, runners-up Uruguay, in Buenos Aires, Argentina);1916 (unofficial) Uruguay (league of four, runners-up Argentina, in Buenos Aires); 1917 (first official CONMEBOL tournament) Uruguay (league of four, runners-up Argentina, in Montevideo, Uruguay); 1919 Brazil (league of four, runners-up Uruguay, in Rio de Janeiro, Brazil; Brazil v Uruguay, 1–0, final playoff); 1920 Uruguay (league of four, runners-up Argentina, in Viña del Mar, Chile); 1921 Argentina (league of four, runners-up Brazil, in Buenos Aires); 1922 Brazil (league of five, runners-up **Paraguay**, in Rio de Janeiro; Brazil v Paraguay, 3–1, final playoff); 1923 Uruguay (league of four, runners-up Argentina, in Montevideo); 1924 Uruguay (league of four, runners-up Argentina, in Montevideo); 1925 Argentina (league of three – each nation played each other twice – runners-up Brazil, in Buenos Aires); 1926 Uruguay (league of five, runners-up Argentina, in Santiago, Chile); 1927 Argentina (league of four, runners-up Uruguay, in Lima); 1929 Argentina (league of four, runners-up Paraguay, in Buenos Aires); 1935 (unofficial) Uruguay (league of four, runners-up Argentina, in Lima); 1937 Argentina (league of six, runners-up Brazil, in Buenos Aires; Argentina v Brazil, 2–0, final playoff); 1939 **Peru** (league of five, runners-up Uruguay, in Lima); 1941 (unofficial) Argentina (league of five, runners-up Uruguay, in Santiago); 1942 Uruguay (league of seven, runners-up Argentina, in Montevideo); 1945 (unofficial) Argentina (league of seven, runners-up Brazil, in Santiago); 1946 (unofficial) Argentina (league of six, runners-up Brazil); 1947 Argentina (league of eight, runners-up Paraguay, in Guayaquil, Ecuador); 1949 Brazil (league of eight, runners-up Paraguay, in São Paulo, Rio de Janeiro, Santos and Belo Horizonte, Brazil; Brazil v Paraguay, 7–0, final playoff in Rio de Janeiro); 1953 Paraguay (league of seven, runners-up Brazil, in Lima; Paraguay v Brazil, 3–2, final playoff); 1955 Argentina (league of six, runners-up Chile, in Santiago); 1956 (unofficial) Uruguay (league of six, runners-up Chile, in Montevideo); 1957 Argentina (league of seven, runners-up Brazil, in Lima); 1959 (official tournament March/April) Argentina (league of seven, runners-up Brazil, in Buenos Aires); 1959 (unofficial tournament, December) Uruguay (league of five nations, runners-up Argentina, in Guayaquil); 1963 **Bolivia** (league of seven, runners-up Paraguay, in Cochabamba and La Paz, Bolivia); 1967 Uruguay (league of six, runners-up Argentina, in Montevideo); 1975 Peru (v **Colombia**, 0–1 in Bogota, 2–0 in Lima, 1–0 playoff in Caracas, Venezuela); 1979 Paraguay (v Chile, 3–0 in Asuncion, 0–1 in Santiago, 0–0 playoff in Buenos Aires, Paraguay won on aggregate scores); 1983 Uruguay (v Brazil, 2–0 in Montevideo, 1–1 in Salvador, Brazil); 1987 Uruguay (1–0, v Chile, at the Monumental Stadium, Buenos Aires); 1989 Brazil (final round group of four, runners-up Uruguay, all final-round matches played at the Maracaná, Rio de Janeiro); 1991 Argentina (final-round group of four, runners-up Brazil, all final-round matches played at the Estadio Nacional, Santiago); 1993 Argentina (2–1, v Mexico, at the Monumental Stadium, Guayaquil); 1995 Uruguay (1–1, 5–3 pens., v Brazil, at the Centenario, Montevideo); 1997 Brazil (3–1, v Bolivia, at the Estadio Nacional Olimpico de Hernándo Siles, La Paz); 1999 tournament in Paraguay. *Top scorers* 1910 Susan (three, Argentina); 1916 Isabelino Gradin (three, Uruguay); 1917 Angel Romano (four, Uruguay); 1919 Artur **Friedenreich** and Neco (four each, both of Brazil); 1920 José Perez and Angel Romano (four each, both of Uruguay), 1921 Julio Libonatti (three, Argentina); 1922 Juan Francia (four, Argentina); 1923 Valdino Aguirre (three, Argentina) and Pedro Petrone (three, Uruguay); 1924 Pedro Petrone (four, Uruguay); 1925 Manuel Seoane (six, Argentina); 1926 Hector Castro, Hector **Scarone** (six each, both Uruguay) and Guillermo Subiabre (six, Chile); 1927 Alfredo Carricaberry, Segundo Luna, Manuel Seoane (three each, all Argentina), Roberto Figueroa, Pedro Petrone and Hector Scarone (three each, all Uruguay); 1929 Aurelio González (five, Paraguay); 1935 Herminio Masantonio (four, Argentina); 1937 Raul Toro (seven, Chile); 1939 Teodoro Fernández (seven, Peru); 1941 Marvezzi (five, Argentina); 1942 Herminio Masantonio and José Moreno (five each, both Argentina); 1945 Helenio de Fretes (six, Brazil) and Norberto Méndez (six, Argentina); 1946 Medina (seven, Uruguay); 1947 Nicolas Falero (seven, Uruguay); 1949 Jair R Pinto (nine, Brazil); 1953 Francisco Molina (seven, Chile); 1955 Rodolfo Michelli (eight, Argentina); 1956 Enrique Hormazabal (four, Chile); 1957 Javier Ambrois (nine, Uruguay) and Humberto Maschio (nine, Argentina); 1959 (March/April) **Pelé** (eight, Brazil); 1959 (December) José Sanfilippo (six, Argentina); 1963

Carlos Raffo (six, Ecuador); 1967 Luis Artime (five, Argentina); 1975 Ernesto Diaz (four, Colombia) and Leopoldo Luque (four, Argentina); 1979 Eugenio Morel (four, Paraguay) and Jorge Peredo (four, Chile); 1983 Carlos Aguilera (three, Uruguay), Jorge Burruchaga (three, Argentina), Roberto Dinamite (three, Brazil) and Eduardo Malasquez (three, Peru); 1987 Arnaldo Iguarán (four, Colombia); 1989 **Bebeto** (six, Brazil); 1991 Gabriel **Batistuta** (six, Argentina); 1993 Dolgetta (four, Venezuela); 1995 Gabriel Batistuta (four, Argentina) and Luis Garcia (four, Mexico); 1997 Luis Hernandez (six, Mexico).

Copa Caribe *competition* Spanish name of the **Caribbean Nations Cup** (formerly the Shell Caribbean Cup).

Copa Chile *competition* annual cup competition Chile, first played 1958, not played 1962-73; last played 1998. *Winners and results* 1958 **Colo Colo**, 2–2, v **Universidad Católica**; 1959 **Santiago Wanderers**, 5–1, v Deportes La Serena; 1960 not played; 1961 Santiago Wanderers, 2–0, v Universidad Católica; 1962-73 not played; 1974 Colo Colo, 3–0, v Santiago Wanderers; 1975 **Club Palestino**, 4–0, v Lota Schwager; 1976 not played; 1977 Club Palestino, 4–3, v **Union Española**; 1978 not played; 1979 **Universidad de Chile**, 2–1, v Colo Colo; 1980 Deportes Iquique, 2–1, v Colo Colo; 1981 Colo Colo, 5–1, v Audax Italiano; 1982 Colo Colo, 2–0, v Universidad Católica; 1983 Universidad Católica, 1–0, v **O'Higgins**; 1984 **Everton**, 3–0, v Universidad Católica; 1985 Colo Colo, 1–0, v Club Palestino; 1986 Cobreloa, 0–1, 2–0, 3–0 playoff, v Fernandez Vial; 1987 Cobresal, 2–0, v Colo Colo; 1988 Colo Colo, 1–0, v Union Española; 1989 Colo Colo, 2–2, 1–0 replay, v Universidad Católica; 1990 Colo Colo, 3–2, v Universidad Católica; 1991 Universidad Católica, 1–0, v Cobreloa; 1992 Union Española, 3–1, v Colo Colo; 1993 Union Española, 3–1, v Cobreloa; 1994 Colo Colo, 1–1 (4–2 pens.) v O'Higgins; 1995 Universidad Católica, 4–2, v Cobreloa; 1996 Colo Colo, 0–0, 1–0, replay, v Rangers; 1997 not played; 1998 Universidad de Chile, 1–1, 2–0 replay, v Audax Italiano.

Copa CONMEBOL *competition* annual South American club tournament for leading clubs of the member countries of the **Confederación Sudamericana de Fútbol** (CONMEBOL, the South American confederation), first played 1992. Sixteen clubs compete in a straight knockout tournament, with all fixtures, including the final, played over two legs. The competition is contested by each nation's next-best clubs after those that take the country's two berths in the **Copa Libertadores** (similar, therefore, to the **UEFA Cup** in Europe). There are different numbers of qualifying berths: Brazil has four places, Colombia, and Uruguay two, while Argentina, Bolivia, Chile, Ecuador, Paraguay, Peru and Venezuela have one each. The sixteenth berth goes to the reigning champions. Because each national league in South America has a different format, the method of determining the Copa CONMEBOL qualifiers

also differs: in Uruguay, for example, the two Copa CONMEBOL places are decided from the **Pre-Libertadores Liguilla**. Unlike the system in Europe, there is nothing to stop any club competing in more than one South American club competition, as long as it qualifies. In 1994, for example, **São Paulo** took part in the Copa CONMEBOL by virtue of its performance in the 1993 Brazilian national championship, in the **Supercopa** – as a former winner of the **Copa Libertadores** – and in the Copa Libertadores as reigning champions. The club went on to win the Copa CONMEBOL, lost in the final of the Copa Libertadores and reached the semi-final of the Supercopa. *Winners, scores and runners-up* 1992 **Atlético Mineiro**, 3–1 agg., v **Olimpia**; 1993 **Botofogo**, 3–3 agg., 3–1 pens., v **Peñarol**; 1994 São Paulo, 6–4 agg., v Peñarol; 1995 **Rosario Central**, 4–4 agg., 4–3 pens., v Atlético Mineiro; 1996 **Lanús**, 2–1 agg., v **Independiente Santa Fé**; 1997 Atlético Mineiro, 5–2 agg., v Lanús; 1998 **Santos**, 1–0 agg., v Rosario Central.

Copa de Campeones CONCACAF *competition* see **CONCACAF Champions Cup**.

Copa de Oro *competition* former South American club knockout tournament contested by the winners of the **Copa Conmebol**, **Copa Libertadores**, **Supercopa Masters** and **Supercopa**, first played 1993. *Winners and scores* 1993 **Boca Juniors**, 1–0 agg., v **Atlético Mineiro**; 1994 not played; 1995 **Cruzeiro** 1–1 agg., 4–1 pens., v **São Paulo**; 1996 **Flamengo**, 3–1 São Paulo (in Manaus, Brazil). See also **Copa Iberoamericana**.

Copa del Rey *competition* annual Spanish knockout competition founded in 1902. All matches, with the exception of the final, which is a one-off match played in June at a **neutral venue**, are played over two-legs. Primera Liga and Segunda A clubs enter the second round of the competition, with the exception of those clubs playing in European club competitions, which receive a bye until the last 16 or fourth round. *History* The first match in 1902 was played to mark the coronation of King Alfonso XIII. In 1931, with the establishment of the Spanish Republic, the competition was renamed the Copa del Presidente de la República. Both the 1937 and 1938 competitions were cancelled due to the Spanish civil war and following the defeat of the Republican forces, the cup was again renamed, this time as the Copa del Generalísimo in honour of the fascist leader, General Francisco Franco. He awarded **Sevilla**, as the newly named competition's first winners, the trophy (the fifth) in perpetuity. With the restoration of the monarchy following Franco's death in 1976, the competition was renamed the Copa del Rey Don Juan Carlos I. Prior to the establishment of the national Spanish league in 1929, qualification to the Copa del Rey was on a regional league basis. Thus, winners were considered national champions. *Records* (Up to and including 1998) **Barcelona**'s victory in the 1998 competition was the club's 24th, putting it one ahead of **Athletic Bilbao**. The Basque club and **Real Madrid** have both appeared in the final a record 34 times, while Barcelona has been a finalist on 33 occasions. Real Madrid won the first trophy outright following its third consecutive victory in 1907. The club, as five-time winners of the ninth trophy in 1989, was able to keep it permanently. Athletic Bilbao did likewise after a third straight win in 1916, 1932, 1945. Following Barcelona's fifth victory in the competition in 1925, and again in 1971, the club kept the trophy. It also kept the trophy (the sixth) in 1953 after winning the competition for the third year running. The first **penalty shoot-out** to settle the final occurred in 1975 after a Madrid derby, between Real and Atlético, ended goalless. *Final results* 1902, Vizcaya Bilbao 2-1 Barcelona; 1903, Athletic Bilbao 3-2 Real Madrid; 1904, Athletic Bilbao (walkover); 1905, Real Madrid 1-0 Athletic Bilbao; 1906, Real Madrid 4-1 Athletic Bilbao; 1907, Real Madrid 1-0 Vizcaya Bilbao; 1908, Real Madrid 2-1 Vigo Sporting; 1909, Ciclista San Sebastián (**Real Sociedad**) 3-1 Español Madrid; 1910, Barcelona 3-2 Español Madrid; 1910, Athletic Bilbao 1-0 Vasconia San Sebastián; 1911, Athletic Bilbao 3-1 Espanyol (RCD); 1912, Barcelona 2-0 Gimnastica Madrid; 1913, Racing Irún 1-0 Athletic Bilbao (replay); 1913, Barcelona 2-1 Real Sociedad (second replay); 1914, Athletic Bilbao 2-1 España Barcelona; 1915, Athletic Bilbao 5-0 Espanyol (RCD); 1916, Athletic Bilbao 4-0 Real Madrid; 1917, Real Madrid 2-1 Arenas Guecho (replay); 1918, Real Unión Irún 2-0 Real Madrid; 1919, Arenas Guecho 5-2 Barcelona; 1920, Barcelona 2-0 Athletic Bilbao; 1921, Athletic Bilbao 4-1 **Atlético Madrid**; 1922, Barcelona 5-1 Real Unión Irún; 1923, Athletic Bilbao 1-0 CD Europa Barcelona; 1924, Real Unión de Irún 1-0 Real Madrid; 1925, Barcelona 2-0 Arenas Guecho; 1926, Barcelona 3-2 Atlético Madrid; 1927, Real Unión Irún 1-0 Arenas Guecho; 1928, Barcelona 3-1 **Real Sociedad** (second replay); 1929, Espanyol (RCD) 2-1 Real Madrid; 1930, Athletic Bilbao 3-2 Real Madrid; 1931, Athletic Bilbao 3-1 Real Betis; 1932, Athletic Bilbao 1-0 Barcelona; 1933, Athletic Bilbao 2-1 Real Madrid; 1934, Real Madrid 2-1 **Valencia**; 1935, Sevilla 3-0 Sabadell; 1936, Real Madrid 2-1 Barcelona; 1939, **Sevilla** 6-2 Racing Ferrol; 1940, Espanyol (RCD) 3-2 Real Madrid; 1941, Valencia 3-1 Espanyol (RCD); 1942, Barcelona 4-3 Athletic Bilbao; 1943, Athletic Bilbao 1-0 Real Madrid; 1944, Athletic Bilbao 2-0 Valencia; 1945, Athletic Bilbao 3-2 Valencia; 1946, Real Madrid 3-1 Valencia; 1947, Real Madrid 2-0 Espanyol (RCD); 1948, Sevilla 4-1 RC Celta (RC); 1949, Valencia 1-0 Athletic Bilbao; 1950, Athletic Bilbao 4-1 Real Valladolid; 1951, Barcelona 3-0 Real Sociedad; 1952, Barcelona 4-2 Valencia; 1953, Barcelona 2-1 Athletic Bilbao 1954, Valencia 3-0 Barcelona; 1955, Athletic Bilbao 1-0 Sevilla; 1956, Athletic Bilbao 2-1 Atlético Madrid; 1957, Barcelona 1-0 Espanyol (RCD); 1958, Athletic Bilbao 2-0 Real Madrid; 1959, Barcelona 4-1 Granada; 1960, Atlético Madrid 3-1 Real Madrid; 1961, Atlético Madrid 3-2 Real Madrid; 1962, Real Madrid 2-1 Sevilla; 1963,

Barcelona 3-1 Real Zaragoza; 1964, **Real Zaragoza** 2-1 Atlético Madrid; 1965, Atlético Madrid 1-0 Real Zaragoza; 1966, Real Zaragoza 2-0 Athletic Bilbao; 1967, Valencia 2-1 Athletic Bilbao; 1968, Barcelona 1-0 Real Madrid; 1969, Athletic Bilbao 1-0 Elche; 1970, Real Madrid 3-1 Valencia; 1971, Barcelona 4-3 Valencia; 1972, Atlético Madrid 2-1 Valencia; 1973, Athletic Bilbao 2-0 Castellón; 1974, Real Madrid 4-0 Barcelona; 1975, Real Madrid 0-0 Atlético Madrid (4-3 pens.); 1976, Atlético Madrid 1-0 Real Zaragoza; 1977, **Real Betis** 2-2 Athletic Bilbao (8-7 pens.); 1978, Barcelona 3-1 Las Palmas; 1979, Valencia 2-0 Real Madrid; 1980, Real Madrid 6-1 Castilla; 1981, Barcelona 3-1 Sporting Gijón; 1982, Real Madrid 2-1 Sporting Gijón; 1983, Barcelona 2-1 Real Madrid; 1984, Athletic Bilbao 1-0 Barcelona; 1985, Atlético Madrid 2-1 Athletic Bilbao; 1986, Real Zaragoza 1-0 Barcelona; 1987, Real Sociedad 2-2 Atlético Madrid (4-3 pens.); 1988, Barcelona 1-0 Real Sociedad; 1989, Real Madrid 1-0 Real Valladolid; 1990, Barcelona 2-0 Real Madrid; 1991, Atlético Madrid 1-0 Mallorca; 1992, Atlético Madrid 2-0 Real Madrid; 1993, Real Madrid 2-0 Real Zaragoza; 1994, Real Zaragoza 0-0 Celta (RC) (5-4 pens.); 1995, Deportivo 2-1 Valencia; 1996, Atlético Madrid 1-0 Barcelona; 1997,Barcelona 3-2 Real Betis; 1998, Barcelona 1-1 Mallorca (5-4 pens.).

Copa do Brasil (Brazilian Cup) *competition* annual knockout competition for Brazilian clubs, first played 1959. It was not played between 1970 and 1988. The final is over two legs (playoffs were used until 1969 if both sides had won or drawn one game each, regardless of the aggregate score). *Results* 1959 **EC Bahia**, 3-2, 0-2, 3-1 playoff, v **Santos**; 1960 **Palmeiras**, 3-1, 8-2, v Fortaleza; 1961 Santos, 1-1, 5-1, v EC Bahia; 1962 Santos, 4-3, 1-3, 5-0 playoff, v **Botafogo**; 1963 Santos, 6-0, 2-0, v EC Bahia; 1964 Santos, 4-1, 0-0, v **Flamengo**; 1965 Santos, 5-1, 1-0, v **Vasco da Gama**; 1966 **Cruzeiro**, 6-2, 3-2, v Santos; 1967 Palmeiras, 3-1, 1-2, 2-0, v Nautico; 1968 not played; 1969 Botafogo, 2-2, 4-0, v Fortaleza; 1970-88 not played; 1989 **Grêmio**, 2-1 agg., v Sport Recife; 1990 **Flamengo**, 1-0 ag., v Goiás; 1991 Criciúma 1-1 agg., v Grêmio; 1992 **Internacional**, 2-2 agg., v **Fluminense**; 1993 Cruzeiro, 2-1 agg., v Grêmio; 1994 Grêmio 1-0 agg., v Ceará; 1995 **Corinthians**, 3-1 agg., v Grêmio; 1996 Cruzeiro 3-2 agg., v Palmeiras; 1997 Grêmio, 2-2, v Flamengo; 1998 Palmeiras 2-1 agg., v Cruzeiro.

Copa Iberoamericana *competition* former intercontinental club tournament contested by the winner of the Spanish Cup (Copa del Rey) and the **Copa de Oro**. Only one edition has been played (1994). *Winner and score* 1994 **Real Madrid**, 4-3 agg., v **Boca Juniors**.

Copa Inter Americana *competition* annual intercontinental club tournament, first played 1968. The competition was conceived as a match between the champion clubs from South America and of the Caribbean, Central and North America: ie the winners of the **Copa Libertadores** and the **CONCACAF**

Champions Cup. South America's entrant, however, no longer seems to represent the best club from the continent. In 1996, **Velez Sarsfield** were the winners of the South American **Supercopa**, while in 1997, the continent was represented by **Atlético Nacional Medellin**, which reached merely the semi-final of the Supercopa. The Copa Inter Americana has generally been played over two legs. In the early editions, if both clubs had won one of the two matches, or if both games finished in a draw, then the cup was decided by a replay. Aggregate scores, and, if necessary penalties, were introduced later. In 1997, the competition was decided as a single fixture. In several years, the tournament was not played. *Winners, result and runners-up* 1968 **Estudiantes**, 1–2, 2–1, 3–0 replay (in Montevideo), v **Toluca**; 1971 **Nacional** (Montevideo), 1–1, 2–1, v **Cruz Azul**; 1972 **Independiente**, 2–1, 2–0, v **Olimpia** (Honduras); 1974 Independiente, 1–0, 0–2, 4–2 pens., v **Municipal**; 1976 Independiente, 2–2, 0–0., 4–2 pens., v **Atlético Español**; 1977 **América** 0–3, 1–0, 2–1 replay (in Mexico City), v **Boca Juniors**; 1979 Olimpia, 3–3, 5–0, v **Deportivo FAS**; 1980, **UNAM**, 3–1, 1–3, 2–1 replay (in Los Angeles), v Nacional; 1981-85 no tournament; 1986 **Argentinos Juniors**, 1–0 (in Port of Spain), v **Defence Force**; 1987, **River Plate**, 0–0, 3–0, v **LD Alajeulense**; 1988 not played; 1989 Nacional, 1–1, 4–0, v Olimpia; 1990 **Atlético Nacional Medellin**, 2–0, 4–1, v UNAM; 1991 América, 1–1, 2–1, v Olimpia; 1992 **Colo Colo**, 4–1, 3–1, v **Puebla**; 1994 **Universidad Catolica**, 6–4 agg., v **Deportivo Saprissa**; 1995 not played; 1996 **Velez Sarsfield**, 2–0 agg., v **Cartagines** (Costa Rica); 1997 **Atlético Nacional Medellin**, 3–2 (only one leg played), v **Deportivo Saprissa**; 1998 **DC United**, 2–1 agg., v **Vasco da Gama**.

Copa Intercontinental *competition* the Spanish name for the **World Club Cup**.

Copa Libertadores (full title: Copa Libertadores de América) *competition* annual South American club championship for champion clubs of the member countries of the **Confederación Sudamericana de Fútbol** (CONMEBOL, the South American confederation), first played in 1960. Each country has two berths in the tournament. Different systems exist in each country to determine which two clubs qualify – reflecting the different league systems employed by CONMEBOL member countries. In Brazil, for example, the two berths go to the champions of the overall **Campeonato Brasileiro**, along with the club that finishes top of the first (league) phase of the season. In Uruguay, the two places are determined by a dedicated end-of-season **Pre-Libertadores Liguilla**; involving the top six clubs from Uruguay's **Primera A**, plus two clubs qualifying from the country's interior leagues (the mini-league also determines Uruguay's two berths in the **Copa CONMEBOL**). The winners of this mini-league take the first Copa Libertadores berth automatically. The runners-up then playoff against the national league

champions (ie the winners of the **Copa Uruguaya**) to decide the second place. In Chile, the national Primera A champions qualify automatically, while the second-, third-, fourth- and fifth-placed clubs playoff in an end-of-season knockout tournament to determine the second berth. The first stage of the Copa Libertadores is played in a league format: with five groups of four clubs. The top three from each group progress to the knockout second round, along with the reigning champions, which receive a bye in the first stage. The second-round matches, quarter-finals, semi-finals and final are all played over two legs. If the **aggregate score** is level at the end of the second leg then the fixture is decided by a **penalty shoot-out**. *History* Champion clubs from seven countries took part in the first tournament in 1960: **Club Deportivo Los Millonarios** (Colombia), **EC Bahia** (Brazil), **Club Jorge Wilsterman** (Bolivia), **Olimpia** (Paraguay), **Peñarol** (Uruguay), **San Lorenzo** (Argentina), **Universidad de Chile** (Chile). It was played as a straight knockout, each round played over two legs. Since 1962, the first stage of the final has been played on a league basis, initially with three groups of three champion clubs; the group winners qualified for knockout semi-finals, along with the reigning champions, which received a bye in the first stage. The number of entrants was expanded in 1966, with each country given two qualifying berths; there were 16 clubs, in three groups. The semi-finals were also played as two mini-leagues. By 1968, the competition had changed again to five groups of four, with the quarter-finals played as three mini-leagues. The format was changed to the current system in 1988; a first stage of five groups of four clubs, followed by a straight knockout format. From 1960 to 1987, the final was decided on points, rather than the aggregate score: a playoff was staged if both legs finished in a draw or if each club had won one leg (irrespective of the scores). However, as happened in 1977, in the final between **Boca Juniors** and **Cruzeiro**, the playoff was goalless and penalties were used for the first time (Boca Juniors won 5–4 in the shoot-out); penalties also decided the playoff in 1985. In 1988, the final was decided on the aggregate score, along with the decision to have the tie settled over two legs, with penalties if necessary, and no playoffs. In 1989, **Atlético Nacional** beat Olimpia after a penalty shoot-out at the end of the second leg in Bogota (5–4 pens., after a 2–2 aggregate score). The biggest attendance for a final match was 114,000, at **Maracaná** Stadium, Rio de Janeiro, on 13 November 1981, between **Flamengo** (using Maracaná for its home leg) and **Cobreloa**; the 1981 tournament also produced the biggest total attendance for a final, 210,000, which included a playoff in Montevideo, Uruguay. Alberto **Spencer** of **Barcelona Sporting Club** and Peñarol is the tournament's record scorer with 54 goals (all but four of these for Peñarol). Spencer scored the opening goal in the first final in 1960. The biggest victory in the competition is 11–2, (Peñarol v Valencia of Venezuela, 1970, first-round group). *Winners, scores* *and runners-up* 1960 Peñarol, 1–0, 1–1, v Olimpia; 1961 Peñarol, 1–0, 1–1,v **Palmeiras**; 1962 **Santos** 2–1, 2–3, 3–0 playoff, v Peñarol; 1963 Santos, 3–2, 2–1, v **Boca Juniors**; 1964 **Independiente**, 0–0, 1–0, v **Nacional** (Uruguay); 1965 Independiente, 1–0, 1–3, 4–1 playoff, v Peñarol; 1966 Peñarol, 2–0, 2–3, 4–2 playoff, v **River Plate**; 1967 **Racing Club**, 0–0, 0–0, 2–1, v Nacional; 1968 **Estudiantes**, 2–1, 1–3, 2–0 playoff, v Palmeiras; 1969 Estudiantes 1–0, 2–0, v Nacional; 1970 Estudiantes, 1–0, 0–0, v Peñarol; 1971 Nacional, 0–1, 1–0, 2–0 playoff, v Estudiantes; 1972 Independiente, 0–0, 2–1, v **Universitario**; 1973 Independiente, 1–1, 0–0, 2–1 playoff, v **Colo Colo**; 1974 Independiente 1–2, 2–0, 1–0 playoff, v **São Paulo**; 1975 Independiente, 0–1, 3–1, 2–0 playoff, v **Union Española**; 1976 **Cruzeiro**, 4–1, 1–2, 3–2 playoff, v River Plate; 1977 Boca Juniors, 1–0, 0–1, 0–0 playoff, 5–4 pens., v Cruzeiro; 1978 Boca Juniors, 0–0, 4–0, v **Deportivo Cali**; 1979 Olimpia, 2–0, 0–0, v Boca Juniors; 1980 Nacional, 0–0, 1–0, v **Internacional**; 1981 **Flamengo**, 2–1, 0–1, 2–0 play-off, v **Cobreloa**; 1982 Peñarol, 0–0, 1–0, v Cobreloa; 1983 **Grêmio**, 1–1, 2–1, v Peñarol; 1984 Independiente, 1–0, 0–0, v Grêmio; 1985 **Argentinos Juniors**, 1–0, 0–1, 1–1 playoff, 5–4 pens., v **America Cali**; 1986 River Plate, 2–1, 1–0, v America Cali; 1987 Peñarol, 0–2, 2–1, 1–0 playoff, v America Cali; 1988 Nacional 3–1 agg., v **Newell's Old Boys**; 1989 **Atlético Nacional Medellin**, 2–2 agg., 5–4 pens., v Olimpia; 1990 Olimpia 3–1 agg., v Barcelona Sporting Club; 1991 Colo Colo 3–0 agg., v Olimpia; 1992 São Paulo, 1–1 agg., 3–2 pens., v Newell's Old Boys; 1993 São Paulo, 5–3 agg., v **Universidad Catolica**; 1994 **Velez Sarsfield** 1–1 agg., 5–3 pens., v São Paulo; 1995 **Grêmio**, 4–2 agg., v Atlético Nacional Medellin; 1996 River Plate 2–1 agg., v América de Cali; 1997 Cruzeiro, 1–0 agg., v **Sporting Cristal**; 1998 **Vasco da Gama**, 4–1 agg., v Barcelona Sporting Club.

Copa Libertadores, top scorers *record* tournament top goal scorers, by season (number of goals and club in parentheses): 1960 Alberto **Spencer** (seven goals, Peñarol); 1961 Walter Perazzo (five, Indepente Santa Fé); 1962 Coutinho (six, Santos); 1963 José Sanfilippo (seven, Boca Juniors); 1964 Mario Rodríguez (six, Independiente); 1965 **Pelé** (seven, Santos); 1966 Daniel Onega (seven, River Plate); 1967 Norberto Raffo (four, Rácing Club); 1968 Tupazinho (11, Palmeiras); 1969 Alberto Ferrero (nine, Santiago Wanderers); 1970 Francisco Bertocchi Ldu (nine, Quito); 1971 Raúl Castronovo (10, Peñarol); Luis Artime (10, Nacional); 1972 Toninho (six, São Paulo); Teófilo **Cubillas** (six, Alianza Lima); 1973 Carlos **Caszely** (nine, Colo Colo); 1974 Terto (seven, São Paulo); Fernando **Morena** (seven, Peñarol); 1975 Oswaldo Ramírez (eight, Universitario); 1976 Palinha (13, Cruzeiro); 1977 Néstor Scotta (five, Deportivo Cali); 1978 Néstor Scotta (eight, Deportivo Cali); Guillermo Larrosa (eight, Alianza Lima); 1979 Miltao (six, Guarani); Juan José Oré (six, Universitario); 1980 Waldemar Victoriano (six,

Nacional); 1981 **Zico** (11, Flamengo); 1982 Fernando Morena (seven, Peñarol); 1983 Arsenio Luzardo (eight, Nacional); 1984 Tita (eight, Flamengo); 1985 Juan Carlos Sánchez (11, Club Blooming); 1986 Juan Carlos De Lima (nine, Deportivo Quito); 1987 Ricardo Gareca (seven, América De Cali); 1988 Arnoldo Iguarán (five, Millonarios); 1989 Carlos Aguilera (10, Peñarol); Raúl **Amarilla** (10, Olimpia); 1990 Adriano Samaniego (seven, Olimpia); 1991 Gaucho (eight, Flamengo); 1992 Palinha (seven, São Paulo); 1993 Juan Carlos Almada (nine, Universidad Católica); 1994 Stalin Rivas (seven, Minervén); 1995 Jardel (12, Grêmio); 1996 Anthony De Ávila (11, América De Cali); 1997 Alberto Acosta (11, Universidad Católica).

Copa Merconorte *competition* Central American "super league" for clubs in the nominally northern countries of the **Confederación Sudamericana de Fútbol** (CONMEBOL) – **Bolivia**, **Colombia**, **Ecuador**, **Peru**, and **Venezuela** – **Mexico** and the **United States of America**, first played in 1998. The first edition was reduced to 12 clubs (after Mexico withdrew its entrants and United States teams were excluded), playing in three mini-leagues of four clubs. The group winners and two runners-up with the best records qualified for knock-out semi-finals and final. Clubs from the southern CONMEBOL countries compete in the richer **Copa Mercosur**. *Winners* 1998 **Atlético Nacional Medellin**, 4–1 agg., v **Deportivo Cali** (both of Colombia).

Copa Mercosur *competition* South American "super league" for the top clubs in the nominally southern countries of **Confederación Sudamericana de Fútbol** (CONMEBOL): **Argentina**, **Brazil**, **Chile**, **Paraguay** and **Uruguay**. It was first played in 1998. The initial stage of the competition is played in five mini-league groups of four clubs, followed by knockout stages and a final. There is a system of relegation and promotion to the Copa Mercosur: the club from each country that has the weakest record in the group stages is eliminated from the following season's tournament, and is replaced by the national champions of that country. *History* The first season of the new league was blighted by fixture congestion: top South American clubs were already playing large numbers of domestic and international fixtures. Some clubs were forced to field second-choice teams. A match at **Maracaná** Stadium, Rio de Janeiro, for example, attracted only 791 spectators for the Copa Mercosur game between **Flamengo** of Brazil and **Boca Juniors** of Argentina (2 September 1998). Clubs from the southern CONMEBOL countries compete in the **Copa Merconorte**. *Winners* 1998 **Palmeiras** 1–0 **Cruzeiro** (playoff; both of Brazil).

Copa Uruguaya *competition* the league championship of Uruguay, decided automatically or, if necessary, by a **playoff** of the top teams from the **Apertura** and **Clausura** league tables (there may be no need, if one team wins both league stages). Compare: **Pre-Libertadores Liguilla**.

Copa Venezuela *competition* national club tournament of Venezuela, played in the first half of the season (the **Apertura**) The Copa Venezuela is played by geographical region: the Grupo Centro Oriental and the Grupo Centro Occidental. Each has nine teams, playing each other twice. The Copa is decided by a two-leg playoff between the winners of each group. The top six teams in each group qualify for the **Torneo Clausura**.

Coppa Italia *competition* annual Italian club knockout competition founded in 1922. All **Serie A** and Serie B clubs plus 10 sides from Serie C are involved in the competition, with the top-flight teams entering the second round. All ties, including the final which usually takes place in June, are played over two legs. *History* First played in 1922, la Coppa Italia is not taken seriously by many of the bigger clubs or its supporters (crowds are often very low for the mid-week encounters) unless, having reached the latter stages, it provides the only route into European competition. The format of the competition has changed several times, with the first final to be played over two legs staged in 1938. Between 1968 and 1971, the cup was decided on a league basis. It reverted to a one-off match for the final in 1971, before the present two-legged arrangement was introduced in 1982. The competition was suspended during Mussolini's fascist dictatorship (1923-35), and, although its was staged during **World War II**, the competition was not played between 1944 and 1957. *Records* (Up to and including 1998) **Juventus** has won la Coppa a record nine times, while **Roma** (AS) has won the trophy on seven occasions. The first final to be decided on penalties was the 1971 match between **Torino** and **AC Milan**. Both clubs had finished with seven points in the league format and had drawn 0–0 in the playoff. *Final results* 1922, Vado 1–0 Udinese; 1935-36, Torino 5–1 Alessandria; 1936-37, **Genoa** 1–0 Roma; 1937-38, Juventus 5–1 Torino (agg.); 1938-39, **Internazionale** 2–1 Novara; 1939-40, **Fiorentina** 1–0 Genoa; 1940-41, Venezia 1–0 Roma (AS) (replay); 1941-42, Juventus 4–1 AC Milan; 1942-43, Torino 4–0 Venezia; 1958, **Lazio** 1–0 Fiorentina; 1958-59, Juventus 4–1 Internazionale; 1959-60, Juventus 3–2 Fiorentina; 1960-61, Fiorentina 2–0 Lazio; 1961-62, **Napoli** 2–1 Spal Ferrara; 1962-63, Atalanta 3–1 Torino; 1963-64, Roma (AS) 1–0 Torino (replay); 1964-65, Juventus 1–0 Internazionale; 1965-66, Fiorentina 2–1 Catanzaro; 1966-67, AC Milan 1–0 Padova; 1967-68, Torino (9 points, AC Milan 7, Internazionale 4, Bologna 4); 1968-69, Roma (AS) (9 points, Cagliari 6, Foggia 5, Torino 4); 1969-70, Bologna (9 points, Torino 8, Cagliari 5, Varese 2); 1970-71, Torino 0–0 AC Milan (5–3 pens. playoff/replay; Torino 7 points, AC Milan 7 points, Fiorentina 6, Napoli 4); 1971-72, AC Milan 2–0 Napoli; 1972-73, AC Milan 1–1 Juventus (5–2 pens.); 1973-74, Bologna 0–0 Palermo (5–4 pens.); 1974-75, Fiorentina 3–2 AC Milan; 1975-76, Napoli 4–0 Verona; 1976-77, AC Milan 2–0 Internazionale; 1977-78, Internazionale 2–1 Napoli; 1978-79, Juventus 2–1 Palermo; 1979-80, Roma (AS) 0–0 Torino (3–2 pens.); 1980-81, Roma (AS) 1–1 Torino (second replay, 5–3 pens.); 1981-82, Internazionale 2–1 Torino (agg.); 1982-83, Juventus 3–2 Verona (agg.); 1983-84, Roma (AS) 2–1 Verona (agg.); 1984-85, **Sampdoria** 3–1 AC Milan (agg.); 1985-86, Roma (AS) 3–2 Sampdoria (agg.); 1987-88, Sampdoria 3–2 Torino (agg.); 1988-89, Sampdoria 4–1 Napoli (agg.); 1989-90, Juventus 1–0 AC Milan (agg.); 1990-91, Roma (AS) 4–2 Sampdoria (agg.); 1991-92, Parma 2–1 Juventus (agg.); 1992-93, Torino 5–5 Roma (AS) (away goals); 1993-94, Sampdoria 6–1 Ancorta (agg.); 1994-95, Juventus 3–0 Parma (agg.); 1995-96, Fiorentina 3–0 Atalanta (agg.); 1996-97, Vicenza 3–1 Napoli (agg.); 1997-98, Lazio 3–2 AC Milan (agg.); 1998-99, Parma 3–3 (agg., away goals) Fiorentina.

Copping, Wilf *player* Left-half. **England** international (20 caps). Born 17 August 1907. Career ca. 1929–1940. *Clubs* **Leeds United** (twice), **Arsenal**. *Honours* League Championship (Arsenal 1934-35, 1937-38); **FA Cup** (Arsenal 1936). *Keynotes* Known as a "hard man" for his ferocious tackling and shoulder charging, Copping cost Arsenal £6,000 when he moved from Leeds United in June 1934. He returned to Leeds in March 1939, retiring as a player during **World War II** and later becoming a trainer at **Southend United**, **Bristol City** and **Coventry City**. Included in the **Football League Centenary 100 players**.

Corinthians (Sport Club Corinthians Paulista) *club* Brazilian national league and **São Paulo** state league club based in São Paulo, founded 1910, after a visit by the English amateur club of the same name. Ground: Alfredo Schuring "Parque Sao Jorge", capacity: 15,000. Strip: white shirts, black shorts. **Campeonato Brasileiro** champions 1990, 1998; **Copa CONMEBOL** semi-final 1994; **Copa do Brasil** 1995; São Paulo Tournament 1950, 1953, 1954, 1966; state league champions 22 times (to 1998). Notable former player: Sócrates.

Cork Athletic *club* former Republic of Ireland national league club based in Cork, founded 1912 as Fordsons FC, dissolved in 1957. Also known as Cork FC (1930-38), Cork City (1938-40), Cork United (1940–48). Republic of Ireland **FAI Cup** (as Fordsons FC) 1926, (as Cork FC) 1934, (as Cork United) 1941, 1947, (as Cork Athletic) 1951, 1953, runners-up (as Fordsons) 1924, (as Cork FC) 1936, (as Cork United) 1942, 1943, (as Cork Athletic) 1950 (one of only two FAI Cup finals to require two replays, Cork Athletic losing 2–2, 2–2, 1–3 v Transport), 1952, 1956; Republic of Ireland league champions (as Cork United) 1941, 1942, 1943, 1945, 1946, as (Cork Athletic) 1950, 1951.

Cork Celtic *club* former Republic of Ireland national league club based in Cork. Founded 1935 (as Evergreen United), dissolved 1979. **European Cup** second round 1975; Republic of Ireland **FAI Cup** runners-up 1953 (as Evergreen), 1964, 1969; Republic of Ireland league champions 1974.

Cork City *club* **1.** Republic of Ireland national league club based in Cork, in the South coast, in Cork County, founded 1984. Ground: Turner's Cross. Strip: white shirts with red and green stripes, green shorts. FAI League Cup runners-up 1997; Republic of Ireland **FAI Cup** 1989, 1992, 1998; Republic of Ireland league champions 1993. **2.** Previous name (1938-40) of the former Republic of Ireland national league club **Cork Athletic**.

Cork FC *club* previous name (1930-38) of the former Republic of Ireland national league club **Cork Athletic**.

Cork Hibernians *club* former Republic of Ireland national league club based in Cork, dissolved 1976. **European Cup-winners Cup** second round 1973; Republic of Ireland **FAI Cup** 1972, 1973, runners-up 1960, 1963; Republic of Ireland league champions 1971.

Cork United *club* **1.** former Republic of Ireland national league club (1946-82). **2.** previous name (1940-48) of the former Republic of Ireland national league club **Cork Athletic**.

corner arc *rules* ninety degree sector (quarter circle) marked out at each corner of the **field of play** with a radius of 1 metre (1 yard) (Law I). Note: the **International FA Board** has agreed an approximate imperial to metric conversion table that does not follow exact measurements.

corner flagpost *rules* flag on a post marking the four corners of the **field of play** (Law I). Posts must be no less than 1.5 metres (5 feet) high with a non-pointed top. The corner flag must not be moved in order for a **corner kick** to be taken (Law XVII). Note: the **International FA Board** uses an approximate imperial to metric conversion table that does not follow exact measurements.

corner kick *rules* method of restarting a game after the ball has crossed a defending team's **goal line** where a goal has not been scored and where a member of the **defending team** was the last player to touch the ball (Law XVII). A corner kick is awarded if the ball crosses the goal line between a **corner flagpost** and its nearest goal post. The rule applies even if the ball curves out of play and back in without touching the ground – it does not, therefore, have to bounce outside the **field of play**. A corner kick is also awarded if the ball crosses the goal line *between* the goal posts if it had been thrown directly into the goal from a **throw in**, or kicked into the goal directly from an **indirect free kick**, taken by the defending team. The game is restarted by an **attacking team** player kicking the ball into play from the **corner arc** at the nearest corner flagpost. The whole of the ball must be within the corner arc. A goal may be scored directly from a corner kick – but only against the opposing team – without it touching another player. Opposition players must remain at least 9.15 metres (10 yards) from the ball when it is kicked – an optional mark may be included on the outside of the goal line to indicate this distance. The corner kick taker must not contact the ball twice until it has been touched by another player (of either side) – failure to observe this rule results in an **indirect free kick** awarded to the

defending side. The corner flagpost must not be moved in order to take the kick. *Keynotes* The only recorded **Football League** match where no corner kicks were awarded was the Division One game between **Newcastle United** and **Portsmouth** (5 December 1931, 0–0, at **St James Park**). Corners were used to determine the outcome of the 1965 **All-Africa Games** football tournament. **Congo** won 7–2 on corners after its final against **Mali** finished 0–0.

corner *rules* abbreviated term for **corner kick**.

Coronation Cup *competition* 1953 knockout tournament organised to celebrate the crowning of Queen Elizabeth II and involving eight invited English and Scottish League clubs – **Aberdeen**, **Arsenal**, **Celtic**, **Hibernian**, **Manchester United**, **Newcastle United**, **Rangers** and **Tottenham Hotspur**. *Final result* Celtic 2–0 Hibernian.

COSAFA Cup *competition* regional nations tournament for member countries of the **Confederation of Southern African Football Associations** (COSAFA). It culminates in a final round-robin league of five nations. *Winners* 1997, **Zambia**; 1998, Zambia.

Costa Rica *country* CONCACAF republic in Central America on the Caribbean and Pacific Ocean, bordered by **Nicaragua** and **Panama**. Area: 50,900 sq km (19,650 sq miles). High central plateau and tropical coastline. Population: 3,370,000 (1995 est.). Language: Spanish. Capital: San José. *Dossier* Football association (Federación Costarricense de Fútbol, San José) formed in 1921, affiliated to **FIFA** in 1921 and **Confederación Norte-Centroamericana y del Caribe de Fútbol** (CONCACAF) in 1962, president E Echeverria Calzada, general secretary Raúl Chacon Bonilla. Season played from August to May. National stadium: Saprissa Stadium, San José, capacity: 26,000 (7,500 seated). National strip: red and white shirts, blue shorts. Website http://www.intnet.co.cr/sports/fedefutbol/fede.html (official site). Notable international players: Cayasso (scored against **Scotland** in 1990 **World Cup** first round), Paulo Wanchope. *International tournament record* **Olympic Games** – qualified for finals tournament 1980 (last in its first-round qualifying round), 1984 (last in its first-round qualifying round); **Women's World Cup** – entered first tournament in 1991, reached qualifying playoff 1999 (v **CONMEBOL** runners-up **Argentina**); World Cup – first entered 1958, finals tournament second round 1990, reached final qualifying round in 1998 (fourth of six nations in final round of qualifying tournament); **CCCF Championship** – 1941 (five-nation league, in San José), 1946 (six-nation league, in San José), 1948 (five-nation league, in Guatemala City, Guatemala), 1953, 1955, 1960 (five-nation league, in Havana, Cuba), 1961 (nine nations, four-nation final-group league in San José), runners-up 1943 (four-nation league, in San Salvador, El Salvador); **CONCACAF Championship** – 1963 (nine nations in tournament, four-nation final-group league in San Salvador), 1969 (six-nation league-based final tournament, in San José), 1989 (World Cup qualifying tournament; five-nation final round league), third 1965 (six-nation league in Guatemala City); **CONCACAF Under-17 Championship** – 1994; **CONCACAF Women's Championship** – first entered 1991, third 1998 (4–0, v **Guatemala**, in Toronto, third/fourth playoff); **CONCACAF Youth Championship (under-20)** – 1988; **Copa America** (South American Championship) – invited to take part 1997 (first round); **Gold Cup** – semi-final/third-equal 1993 (1–1, v **Jamaica**, in Jamaica, third/fourth playoff), qualified for finals tournament 1998, 2000; **Pan-American Championship** – third place 1956; **UNCAF Cup** – and host nation 1991 (the first tournament, held in San José), 1999 (tournament in San José), runners-up 1993 (finals tournament in Tegucigalpa, Honduras); **Under-17 World Championship** – qualified for finals tournament 1997; **World Youth Cup** (under-20) – qualified for finals tournament 1995, 1999. *Record against British and Irish national teams* v **Scotland**, played one, won one; v **Wales**, played one, lost one. *History* League tournament started in 1922. Three clubs have won the **CONCACAF Champions Cup** (see below). Costa Rica reached the second round of the World Cup in 1990, and has won the various Central America/North America/Caribbean international competitions on 10 occasions. It was third in the 1993 Gold Cup. Costa Rica was invited to participate in the 1997 Copa America, though gained just one point from its three first-round group games. In 1998, Costa Rica's Paulo Wanchope – based in England with **Derby County** – scored four goals in the country's 7–2 victory against **Cuba** in the 1998 Gold Cup finals tournament. *League system* Twelve clubs compete in the Primera division, playing each other four times in the first stage of the season. The league is followed by a second-stage knockout tournament featuring the top eight clubs in the league. Unless the same club has won both stages, there will be a final playoff for the championship. There are national second and third divisions. *Record in international club tournaments* **CONCACAF Champions Cup** – Liga Deportiva **Alajuelense** (1986, runners-up 1971, 1992, third 1995), **Deportivo Saprissa** (1993, 1995, semi-final/third 1998); **CS Cartagines** (1994, quarter-final 1997); **Torneo Grandes de Centroamerica** – Alajuelense (1996, semi-final 1997), Deportivo Saprissa (runners-up 1997, finalists 1998). Other leading club: **Club Sport Herediano** (Heredia).

Cote d'Ivoire *country CAF* see **Ivory Coast**.

Cotonsport *club* Cameroon national league club based in Garoua. Ground: Garoua, capacity: 50,000. **CAF Cup** quarter-final 1997; Cameroon league champions 1997, 1998.

Cotton Club *club* Ethiopian national league club based in Dire Dawa. Ground: Dire Dawa, capacity: 30,000. **African Cup of Champion Clubs** semi-final 1964; Ethiopian league champions 1960, 1962, 1963, 1965, 1983.

Cottonchad *club* another name for **ASCOT**.

Coultard, Gillian *player* **England** women's international

(102 caps, 1981-97). *Clubs* **Doncaster Belles**. *Keynotes* England's captain and most-capped player.

counter-attack *n.* a swift attack mounted after regaining possession of the ball from a defensive position.

county football association *confederation* one of 43 football governing bodies that administer amateur football at regional level in England. The county FAs are affiliated to the **Football Association** and are responsible for the day-to-day running of senior football in their areas as well as disciplinary matters and county tournaments. Each association has affiliated leagues and regional competitions in both men's and women's football. More than 2,000 regional and local leagues are affiliated to the county FAs, with in excess of 60,000 teams playing at this level.

County Ground *ground* English football ground situated in Northampton; former home of **Northampton Town**. Dossier Pitch dimensions: 110m x 68.5m. Record attendance: 24,523 v **Fulham** (23 April 1966, Division One). Best average attendance: 18,633 (1965-66). *History* Northampton shared the County Ground with Northamptonshire County Cricket Club and cricket was first played there in 1885. Initially, the club, formed in 1897, was able to use the ground on the condition that no football be staged before September and after April. The club played its first match at the ground on 18 August 1897 (Earls Barton, friendly). At 110 metres, the County Ground was the longest **Football League** ground in the country. It was also the bumpiest, with half the pitch used as a picnic area and car park during the cricket season. In addition, the County Ground was the last three-sided ground in the Football League when Northampton decamped to the purpose-built **Sixfields Stadium** in 1994. Only once in Northampton's 97-year tenancy of the County Ground was the ground a fully enclosed venue. This occurred in 1970 when a full-length temporary stand was erected for the club's 5th round FA Cup encounter with **Manchester United**. Northampton's final game at the County Ground was scheduled to be the last home fixture of the 1993-94 season (30 April 1994) but it actually took place on 11 October 1994 (v **Mansfield Town**, Third Division) because the Sixfields Stadium was not ready. The County Ground staged its first floodlit match on 10 October 1960 (v **Arsenal**, friendly).

County Ground *ground* English football ground situated in Swindon, Wiltshire; home of **Swindon Town**. *Dossier* Ground capacity: 15,728. Pitch dimensions 100.5m x 64m. Record attendance: 32,000 v **Arsenal** (15 January 1972, **FA Cup**, third round). Best average attendance: 20,075 (1969-70). *History* Swindon played its first match at the County Ground on 5 September 1896 (v Uxbridge, friendly). The ground is owned by the local council. During **World War II**, the ground was used to hold prisoners of war. In 1951, the County Ground became the first League ground to install **floodlights** (floodlights had been installed at **Oxford United**'s **Manor Ground** in 1950, but the club was, at that time, in the **Southern League**). The lights were first used on 2 April 1951 (v **Bristol City**, friendly). After plans to build a new stadium collapsed in 1992, the club pursued the all-seater redevelopment of the County Ground, including the construction in 1994 of the Intel stand.

county schools' football association *confederation* a governing body of association football for schools in an English county. County schools' FAs are affiliated to the **English Schools' Football Associations**.

Court of Arbitration in Sport *legal* tribunal set up by the International Olympic Committee to settle legal disputes in Sport. *Keynotes* In 1998, the tribunal overturned a 12-month ban on Belgian club **RSC Anderlecht** for bribing a referee in a 1984 **UEFA Cup** semi-final (v **Nottingham Forest**). The court ruled that the UEFA executive committee was not empowered to impose such a ban.

Coventry City *club* English league. *Dossier* Ground: **Highfield Road**, Coventry, Warwickshire, capacity: 23,611 all seated. Strip: sky blue shirts with dark blue and white panels, sky blue shorts, sky blue socks. Website: *www.ccfc.co.uk* Nickname: Sky Blues. Record attendance: 51,455 v **Wolverhampton Wanderers** (29 April 1967, Division Two). Best average attendance: 34,705 (1967-68). Biggest win: 9–0 v **Bristol City** (28 April 1934, Division Three). Biggest defeat: 2–10 v **Norwich City** (15 March 1930, Division Three (South)). *History* Formed in 1883 by workers at the Singers bicycle factory. The club remained Singers FC until 1898, when it became Coventry City. Coventry became a limited company in 1907 and, in 1908, it joined the **Southern League**. Singer/Coventry played at a number of different venues in the club's early years, including Dowells Field and Stoke Road, before settling on a piece of land that eventually became Highfield Road. The club secured its **Football League** status in 1919, joining Division Two. Coventry alternated between Division Two and Division Three (except for one season in Division Four, 1958-59) until the club was promoted to Division One in 1967. It has subsequently become ever-present in the top division. In the 1960s Coventry introduced a number of innovations, particularly in terms of pre-match entertainment and ground developments. Highfield Road witnessed the introduction of an electric scoreboard and the establishment of the league's first executive club in 1964. At the same time, Coventry developed a range of pre-match and half-time entertainment, including Radio Sky Blue, introduced by Kent and England cricketer Godfrey Evans, as well as netball matches and dog handling displays. These pioneering developments were followed, in 1965, with the club's away fixture at Cardiff's **Ninian Park** transmitted via **closed-circuit television** live to spectators at Highfield Road. Jimmy **Hill** became manager of Coventry in November 1961, following his retirement from playing. He took the club from Division Three to Division One in eight seasons. It was Hill and

chairman Derrick Robbins who were largely responsible for the club's sky blue image, that not only included the club strip (the old one was blue and white), but also special sky blue trains for fans travelling to away games. After winning the Division Two Championship in 1967-68, Coventry suffered a series of setbacks. Hill resigned as manager (although he became a board member) and Highfield Road's main stand was destroyed by fire. Coventry's innovative reputation was enhanced further when the club established the first **all-seater stadium** in England. Every home game was virtually **all-ticket**, with only a few seats available on match days. The club revised both the ticketing policy and the all-seater nature of the ground when attendance slumped and several pitch invasions occurred. Coventry had to wait 104 years to win its first major trophy when, under John Sillett's management, the club won the **FA Cup** in 1987. In 1996, Gordon Strachan became **player-manager**. By the 1997-98 season, only **Arsenal**, **Everton** and **Liverpool** had a longer tenure in the top division than Coventry. The club has frequently battled against relegation from the top division and its highest placing was 6th in the 1969-70 season. Coventry is the only club to have played in all seven divisions (Premier and Divisions One, Two, Three, Three (North), Three (South) and Four). *League record* Premier League 1992-93–; Division One 1967-68 to 1991-92; Division Two 1919-20 to 1924-25, 1936-37 to 1951-52, 1964-65 to 1966-67; Division Three 1959-60 to 1963-64; Divsion Three (North) 1925-26; Division Three (South) 1926-27 to 1935-36, 1952-53 to 1957-58; Division Four 1958-59. *Honours* Division Two 1967-68; Division Three 1963-64; Division Three (South) 1935-36; **Division Three (South) Cup** (5–2 agg., v **Swindon Town**); FA Cup 1987 (3–2 a.e.t. v **Tottenham Hotspur** – *Team* Ogrizovic, Phillips, Downs, McGrath, Kilcline, (Rodger),Peake, Bennett (1), Gynn, Regis, Houchen (1), Pickering, plus 1 o.g.). *Records* Roland Nilsson is Coventry's most capped player (94 for **Sweden**); George Curtis holds the record for club appearances (486, 1956-70); Clarrie Bourton is Coventry's record league goalscorer (171, 1931-37).

Coverciano *n* Italian FA's national headquarters located outside Florence. The facility includes a swimming pool, gymnasium and tennis courts and the **Azzuri** regularly prepare for international matches at the site.

covered stadium *n.* stadium with a fixed or retractable roof. *Regulations* a British league club would require permission from its league governing body, after consultation with league members, before a match could be played in a stadium where all or part of the pitch is covered (FA Premier League rule I.4, Football League regulation 15, Scottish Football League rule 71).

covering centre-back *n.* one of a centre-back pairing or trio who covers for his partner(s). See **stopper**.

covering *n.* aspect of play which involves one player covering a team-mate who is marking/engaging an **onball** attacker. The **sweeper** provides the ultimate cover in defensive situations. See also **sagging**.

Cowdenbeath *club* Scottish league. *Dossier* Ground: **Central Park**, Cowdenbeath, Fife, capacity: 5,268. Strip: blue and white striped shirts with red piping, white shorts with blue trim, blue socks. Nickname: Bankies. Record attendance: 25,586 v **Rangers** (21 September 1949, **Scottish League Cup**, quarter-final). Biggest win: 12–0 v **St Johnstone** (21 January 1928, **Scottish FA Cup**, first round). Biggest defeat: 1–11 v **Clyde** (6 October 1951, **Division Two**). *History* Founded in 1881 from an amalgamation of three miners' teams. Cowdenbeath joined Division Two in 1905-06 and won promotion to the top flight in 1924-25. Cowdenbeath was a **Scottish FA Cup** quarter-finalist in 1931 (0–1 v **Motherwell**). The club won the Division Two title by a 12-point margin in 1938-39, but when League football resumed after **World War II** there was no place for the club in Division One. Cowdenbeath enjoyed one season in the top flight again in 1970-71, a season in which the club also reached the semi-finals of the **Scottish League Cup** (0–2 v **Rangers**). The club had also been a semi-finalist in 1959-60 (3–9 v **Heart of Midlothian**). *League record* First Division 1992-93; Division One 1924-25 to 1933-34, 1970-71; Second Division 1975-76 to 1991-92, 1993-94; Division Two (B Division) 1905-06 to 1923-24, 1934-35 to 1969-70, 1971-72 to 1974-75; Third Division 1994-95–. *Honours* Division Two 1913-14, 1914-15, 1938-39. *Records* Jim Paterson is Cowdenbeath's most capped player (3 for **Scotland**); Ray Allan holds the record for club appearances (491, 1972-75, 1979-80); Willie Devlin is Cowdenbeath's record goalscorer (127, 1922-26, 1929-30).

Cowlairs *club* former Scottish league. *Dossier* Ground: Springvale Park, Glasgow, Strathclyde. *Keynotes* Founder members of the **Scottish League** in 1890-91, finishing bottom in that inaugural season with only six points and failing to gain re-election. *League record* Scottish League 1890-91.

Cracovia *club* Polish national league side based in Krakow, founded in 1906. Ground: Cracovia, capacity: 12,000. Strip: red and white striped shirts, white shorts. *Keynotes* Cracovia is Poland's oldest club. Pope John Paul II (himself a former goalkeeper) is the club's most famous fan. Poland's first league champions. Polish league champions 1921, 1930, 1932, 1937, 1948.

cramp *medical* painful spasm or involuntary contraction of a muscle or muscle group. Duration is variable. Cramp can be treated by the physiotherapist or trainer gently stretching and holding the player's muscle against the contraction until the pain is relieved.

Craven Cottage *ground* English football ground situated in west London; home of **Fulham**. *Dossier* Ground capacity: 19,250. Pitch dimensions: 100.5m x 68.5m. Record attendance: 49,335 v **Millwall** (8 October 1938, Division Two). Best average attendance: 33,030 (1949-50). *History* Fulham bought Craven Cottage in 1894 on a 125-year leasehold from the Church Commissioners. The ground gets its name from the original Craven Cottage, which had been built by Baron Craven VI in 1780 and which was destroyed by fire in 1888. Fulham played its first match at Craven Cottage on 10 October 1896. Scottish architect and engineer Archibald **Leitch** remodelled Craven Cottage in 1905. In 1985, Fulham bought the freehold to Craven Cottage for £940,000 with money borrowed from property company Kilroe Enterprises in a deal which involved part of the ground being redeveloped for housing. Kilroe's initial plans for Craven Cottage were scuppered by the local council, which pledged to keep football at the ground. One year later, Marler Estates (another property company that at the time also owned **Stamford Bridge**) bought a majority shareholding in Fulham. The club was saved from a merger with **Queens Park Rangers** when a consortium headed by Jimmy **Hill** bought the Fulham name and the players' contracts in return for limited redevelopment of Craven Cottage. Marler Estates was taken over by another property developer, Cabra Estates, in 1989, a company which sought to develop the ground for housing. The local council dismissed Cabra's development plans, insisting that the venue should be retained as a football ground, and in January 1990 the matter went to a public inquiry. At the eleventh-hour Cabra offered Fulham a financial package worth up to £13 million, on condition that the club vacate the ground at the end of a three-year period or before if the company's development proposals were passed, which the board accepted. The public inquiry failed to endorse either the local council's, or Cabra's, redevelopment plans. Fulham started talks with Chelsea in June 1991 to use Stamford Bridge but the clubs failed to agree a **groundshare**. Cabra was placed in the hands of liquidators in November 1992, with Craven Cottage (and Stamford Bridge) becoming the property of the company's main creditors, the Royal Bank of Scotland. In May 1997, Fulham exercised its right to purchase the ground when the club was bought by Mohamed Al Fayed. During 1997-98, partial redevelopment of the ground raised the capacity from just under 15,000 to more than 19,000. Craven Cottage has staged one **England** international (v **Wales**, 18 March 1907). Because of political troubles in the north of Ireland, Craven Cottage staged an international match between **Northern Ireland** and **Cyprus** on 8 May 1973 (Northern Ireland also used **Boothferry Park**, **Goodison Park**, **Highfield Road** and **Hillsborough**, and switched its home matches against **Scotland** to **Hampden Park** during this period). Craven Cottage was the last Divsion One club (at the time) to install **floodlights**, with the first floodlit match played on 19 September 1962 (v **Sheffield Wednesday**, Division One).

creatine *medical* naturally occurring amino acid produced in the liver and kidneys which can boost performance by quickly replenishing muscle energy. Creatine has been artificially manufactured and is available in powder/tablet form and can be used as a restorative to help players cope with increased workload and to build muscle. Although the Italian Olympic Committee's

1998 investigation into drug abuse among **Serie A** players found no evidence of "doping", it recommended that the use of creatine should be either banned or restricted (see **drug**).

creative *adj.* of a style of play that lends itself to providing goal-scoring opportunities.

crèche *n.* nursery for babies and young children. *Keynotes* In 1985, **Millwall** established the first ever crèche at a British football ground when the club introduced childcare facilities at its Den ground following a sponsorship deal with Lewisham Council. At the beginning of the 1998-99 season, only two **Premier League** clubs, **Chelsea** and **Leeds United**, provided crèche facilities, while a third, **Charlton Athletic,** planned to open one during the season.

credit card *misc.* card which authorises the purchase of goods. *Keynotes* All but one Premier League club (**Wimbledon**) offers a credit card. The majority of club cards are backed by either the Royal Bank of Scotland and the American bank MBNA. Only the cards offered by **Chelsea** (Co-operative Bank) and **Southampton** (Beneficial Bank) are backed by different companies. Other financial services offered by clubs include the following savings accounts: **Birmingham City** (The Blues Bonus); **Leicester City** (Foxer Saver Account); **Leeds United** (The Leeds United Privilege Account); **Norwich City** (The Canary Account); **West Bromwich Albion** (Albion Account). **Wolverhampton Wanderers** also offers mortgages through the Bradford and Bingley Building Society.

Crewe Alexandra *club* English league. *Dossier* Ground: **Gresty Road**, Crewe, Cheshire, capacity: 6,000. Strip: red shirts, white shorts, red socks. Nickname: Railwaymen. Record attendance: 20,000 v **Tottenham Hotspur** (30 January 1960, **FA Cup**, fourth round). Best average attendance: 9,065 (1949-50). Biggest win: 8–0 v **Rotherham United** (1 October 1932, Division Two). Biggest defeat: 2–13 v Tottenham Hotspur (3 February 1960, FA Cup, fourth round replay). *History* Founded in 1877 as the footballing section of Alexandra Athletic Club, which had been formed in 1866. The name "Alexandra" was adopted in honour of Princess Alexandra, who married the future Edward VII. In 1888, the club reached the FA Cup sem-final (0–4 **Preston North End**). Crewe was a founder member of Division Two in 1892, but the club failed in its bid for re-election in 1896 and it did not return to the **Football League** (Division Three (North)) until 1921-22. In the mid-1930s, the club won the **Welsh Cup** on two occasions (1936 (2–0 v **Chester**), 1937 (4–2 agg., v **Rhyl**)). Crewe has spent most of its history in the lower divisions, but in 1996-97 it won promotion to the First Division via the end-of-season playoffs (1–0 v **Brentford**). This was the club's first playoff success following four previous attempts between 1992 and 1996: 1992 Third Division playoff semi-finalists; 1993 Second Division playoff finalists (1–1, 3–5 pens. v **York City**); 1995 Second Division playoff semi-finalists; 1996 Second Division playoff semi-finalists. Crewe's long-

serving manager, Dario Gradi, was appointed in 1983 after the club finished level bottom of Division Four and was still in the post in 1999. *League record* First Division 1996-97–; Division Two 1892-93 to 1895-96; Second Division 1994-95 to 1996-97; Division Three 1963-64, 1968-69, 1989-90 to 1990-91; Division Three (North) 1921-22 to 1957-58; Third Division 1992-93 to 1993-94; Division Four 1958-59 to 1962-63, 1964-65 to 1967-68, 1969-70 to 1988-89, 1991-92. *Honours* Welsh Cup 1936 (2–0 v Chester), 1937 (4–2 agg., v Rhyl). *Records* Bill Lewis is Crewe's most capped player (9 (27) for **Wales**); Tommy Lowry holds the record for club appearances (436, 1966-78); Bert Swindells is Crewe's record league goalscorer (126, 1928-37).

cricket score *n.* *informal* a high score. For example: the team won by a cricket score.

criminal liability *legal* football-related incident in which a crime is committed. *Keynotes* As early as 1878, a case came before Leicester Assizes in which a player was charged with manslaughter for causing the death of another player during a friendly match (*R v Bradshaw*). The player was acquitted by the jury after one of the game's **umpires** reported that no foul play had occurred. The court's decision contained a rider that football authorities should tighten the **Laws of the game** relating to tackling. In 1898, also at Leicester Assizes, two players were found guilty of manslaughter after it was proved that they had committed a deliberate and/or reckless tackle that was outside the Laws of the game, causing the death of another player (*R v Roberts and Ors*). At Maidstone Assizes in 1969, a player was prosecuted for murder after striking another player during an amateur match in Essex (*R v Southby*). The player was found guilty of manslaughter on the grounds that the accused had made a deliberate and/or reckless blow outside the Laws of the game. In the professional game, a **Football Association** tribunal heard a case in 1985 in which a player was accused of assault and, under FA rule 35 (a), of bringing the game into disrepute. Although the FA found the case not proven, the tribunal did establish that there was a prime facie case and returned the complainant's deposit. Also in 1985, an amateur woman footballer was found guilty at Clacton Magistrates Court of assaulting an opponent and breaking her jaw during a friendly match. The guilty party was fined £250 plus costs.

Croatia *country* *UEFA* republic in southern Europe on the Adriatic Sea and bordered by **Slovenia, Hungary, Yugoslavia** and **Bosnia-Herzegovina**. Former part of the Federal Republic of Yugoslavia (see: **former-Yugoslavia**), declared independent in 1991. Independent before 1918 (when became part of the Kingdom of Serbs, Croats and Slovenes – which formed Yugoslavia in 1929), and nominally as a Nazi puppet state after German invasion of 1941 until 1945 when again became part of Yugoslavia. Area: 56,540 sq km (21,825 sq miles). Climate varies from Mediterranean to continental. Population: 4,840,000 (1995 est.). Language: Serbo-Croat. Capital: Zagreb. *Dossier*

Croatian Football Federation (Zagreb) formed in 1912 and again in 1991. Affiliated to **FIFA** and **Union of European Football Associations** in 1992, president Branko Miksa, general secretary Josip Cop. Season played from August to June, with **winter break** from December to February. National stadium: Maksimir, Zagreb, capacity: 60,000. National strip: red and white shirts, white shorts. Website: http://www.geocities.com/Colosseum/Field/2146/ (unofficial site). First international game 2 May 1940 v **Hungary** (0–1, in Budapest, friendly). Biggest victory: 7–1 v **Estonia** (1996, in Zagreb, **European Championship** qualifier). Biggest defeat: 1–5 v Germany (18 June 1941 in Vienna, friendly; 1 November 1942, in Stuttgart, friendly). Most capped players: **1.** *Croatians who played for former-Yugoslavia* Zlatko Vujovic (70 appearances, 24 goals, for former-Yugoslavia), Ivan Horvat (60 appearances for former-Yugoslavia), Bernard Vukas (59 appearances, 22 goals, for former-Yugoslavia); **2.** *For Croatia* Drazen Ladic (52 appearances for Croatia, to 1998); Davor Suker (50 appearances 1992–). Leading goalscorer: Davor **Suker** (41 goals, 1992-). Other notable international players: Zvonimir Boban, Alen Boksic, Robert **Prosinecki**. *International tournament record* **Women's World Cup** – first entered 1995, never qualified for finals tournament; **World Cup** – first entered 1998, qualified for finals tournament 1998, third (2–1, v Netherlands, at the **Parc des Princes**, Paris); **European Championship** – first entered 1996, quarter-final 1996; **European Championship for Women** – first entered 1995, second in its four-nation first-round group 1995; **World Youth Cup** (under-20) – qualified for finals tournament 1999. *World Cup performance* (finals and qualifiers to end of 1998 tournament) played 17, won 10, drawn four, lost two, scored 31 goals, conceded 18 goals; win rate: 59%; goals scored per game: 1.82. *Record against British and Irish national teams* v **England**, played one, drawn one.; v **Republic of Ireland**, played one, lost one. *History* A separate Croatian league operated during the semi-independent years from 1940-44. A new national league and cup competition began after independence from former-Yugoslavia in 1991-92. **Croatia Zagreb** is the only Croatian club to have won a European club competition, winning the **UEFA** (Fairs) **Cup** in 1967 (as Dynamo Zagreb). Croatia finished third in its first World Cup in 1998 (the first nation since Portugal, in 1966, to reach the semi-final at its first finals tournament). Croatian striker Davor Suker won the 1998 World Cup **Golden Boot**, with six goals. *League system* Twelve clubs compete in the national first division (Prva A HNL), reduced from 16 clubs in 1996-97. The 12 first division clubs play each other three times (33 games). Three points are awarded for a win and one for a draw; **goal difference** separates clubs level on points. A complex two-stage season, with separate end-of-season championship and relegation groups was scrapped before the 1999-00 season. There are five regional second divisions. The champions of each regional league qualify for an end-of-season tournament to decide two

promotion places. The domestic Cup final is played in May. *Record in international club tournaments* **European Cup** – Hajduk Split (quarter-final 1976, 1980, 1995); **European Cup-winners Cup** – Croatia Zagreb (as Dynamo Zagreb, semi-final 1961), Hajduk Split (semi-final 1973); **UEFA Cup/Fairs Cup** – Croatia Zagreb (1967, runners-up 1963 – as Dynamo Zagreb). Other leading clubs: **Zagreb**, **NK Rijeka**, **NK Osijek**, **INKER Zapresic**.

Croatia Zagreb *club* Croatia national league and former-Yugoslavia league club based in the capital Zagreb, founded 1945 (as Dynamo Zagreb 1945–1991, known as HASK Gradanski Zagreb 1991–92). Formed by the merger of two older clubs: Gradanski Zagreb dating from 1911, and HASK Zagreb). Ground: Maksimir, capacity: 56,500 all seated. Strip: blue shirts, blue shorts. Croatia Cup 1994, 1996, 1997, 1998; Croatia league champions 1993, 1996, 1997, 1998; Croatia Super Cup (league champions v Cup winners) 1993, 1996 (automatic), 1997 (automatic); **European Cup-winners Cup** semi-final 1961 (as Dynamo Zagreb); former-Yugoslavia Cup 1951, 1960, 1963, 1965, 1969, 1973, 1980, 1983; former-Yugoslavia league champions 1948, 1954, 1958, 1982; **UEFA Cup/Fairs Cup** 1967 (2–0 agg., v **Leeds United**), runners-up 1963 (1–4 agg., v **Valencia**) (both times as Dynamo Zagreb). Notable former players: Ivan **Horvat**, Zvonimir **Boban**.

Croker, Ted *official* former secretary of the **Football Association**.

Crompton, Bob *player* Right-back. **England** international (41 caps). Born 26 September 1879. Career ca. 1896–1920. *Clubs* **Blackburn Rovers**. *Keynotes* Crompton spent 23 years and seven months with Blackburn, signing for Rovers in October 1896 and playing the last of his 528 games for the club in May 1920. He was later a Blackburn director and team manager, before spending a year as manager at Bournemouth & Boscombe Athletic (**Bournemouth** (AFC)). Included in the **Football League Centenary 100 players**. *Honours* League Championship (Blackburn Rovers 1911-12, 1913-14).

cross bar *rules* horizontal bar joining the two upright posts of the **goal** (sense **1**) (Law I). Crossbars may be made of wood, metal or any material approved by the **International FA Board**. They may be square, rectangular, round, half-round or elliptical in cross section and must be painted white. If a crossbar is broken or displaced, then play must be stopped until it is repaired or replaced. If this is not possible, then the match must be **abandoned**. Use of a rope as a crossbar is not allowed, even for friendly matches. *Keynotes* A cross tape, at a height of eight feet, was adopted by the **Football Association** in February 1886; the tape was stretched between the posts. **Hit the crossbar** vb. to **shoot** or **head** the ball against the crossbar.

cross *vb.* to strike the ball from either side of the field of play towards a colleague or team-mates near to the opposition's goal; the aim is to create an opportunity for a header of shot towards goal. *n.* the execution of this.

crossover play *tactics* interchange of players/positions while maintaining a basic pattern, such as a three-player passing triangle.

crowd doctor *regulations* doctor employed by a **home club** in case medical attention is required by a spectator. Crowd doctors appointed after the beginning of the 1998-99 season are required to hold an FA Diploma in Immediate Medical Care or its equivalent (FA Premier League rule H.2, Football League regulation 32.4).

crowd trouble *misc.* disruptive and violent acts by football supporters. *Keynotes* Crowd trouble associated with football matches is virtually as old as the game itself. Football was banned in London in 1314 because of the public disorder associated with the rudimentary game of the day (see **association football** (*History*)). In March 1884, **Wrexham** was forced to disband after being expelled from the English **Football Association** following crowd trouble at an **FA Cup** tie with Oswestry (3–4, December 1883, second round). A 1901 Good Friday derby match between **Newcastle United** and **Sunderland** at **St James' Park** contained a pitch battle among rival supporters, while a linesman, Charles **Sutcliffe**, was forced to don a policeman's uniform to escape angry supporters at **Roker Park**. Also at Roker Park, **Sheffield Wednesday** players were stoned by **Sunderland** fans as they left the ground following a 1903 game. In Scotland, the 1892 **Scottish FA Cup** final between **Celtic** and **Queen's Park** was replayed after crowd trouble disrupted the first match (1–1, **Ibrox**, 12 March; 5–1, Ibrox, 9 April). The 1919-20 **Irish Cup** final was not played after riots at the replayed semi-final between **Belfast Celtic** and **Glentoran**. In more recent times, crowd unrest at **Leeds United**'s **Elland Road** ground in 1971 (16 April), following a controversial refereeing decision during a League game against **West Bromwich Albion**, which effectively cost Leeds the league title that season, led to the ground being closed for the club's first four matches of the 1971-72 season (see **Leeds United**). **Manchester City** received a suspended £50,000 fine in 1993 following crowd trouble at an FA Cup tie at which **Maine Road**'s new Umbro Stand was opened (v **Tottenham Hotspur**, 6th round). Following a Division Two match between **Gillingham** and **Fulham** at **Priestfield Stadium**, a Fulham supporter (Matthew Fox) died from head injuries sustained as a result of a fight between rival supporters (28 March 1998). On the same day, the **Premier League** fixture between **Barnsley** and **Liverpool** at **Oakwell** was suspended for a short time after several fans invaded the field of play in protest at refereeing decisions. The Football Association charged Barnsley with failing to control the crowd, while the club banned indefinitely those supporters arrested as a result of the disturbances. Police figures show that, during the 1997-98 season, 258 people were arrested at football matches for violent conduct, including assault, violent disorder and missile-throwing. Also, 31 were arrested for racist or indecent chanting. Total arrests at football

matches that season were 3,307 (down from 3,557 the previous season): **Premier League** 1,438 (inside and outside stadiums); First Division 1,173 arrests; Second Division and Third Division 696 arrests. **Millwall** holds the unenviable record of having its previous ground, the **Den**, closed by the Football Association on more occasions than any other **Football League** ground; the Den was closed in 1920, 1934, 1947, 1950, 1978 as a result of crowd trouble. *European keynotes* Crowd trouble at the 1975 **European Cup** final (0–2 v **Bayern Munich**), resulted in **Leeds United** receiving a seven-year **UEFA**-imposed ban from European competition. In October 1977, Manchester United was forced to play a **European Cup-winners Cup** match at **Plymouth Argyle**'s **Home Park** after UEFA ordered the club to play the return leg against **St Etienne** at least 200 miles from **Old Trafford** following crowd trouble during the first game in France. **Chelsea** was fined £30,000 by UEFA after its supporters were involved in crowd disorder at the first leg of the club's 1995 European Cup-winners Cup semi-final against Real Zaragoza in Spain. **UEFA** instructed **Gotënberg (IFK)** to play its 1996 **European Cup** qualifier against **Ferencváros** at the Idrottsparken in Norrköping following several incidents of crowd trouble at the Nya **Ullevi**. In 1998, **UEFA** instructed **Real Madrid** to play its next two home European ties at least 190 miles away from its **Bernabéu** stadium, and fined the club £512,000, after fencing at the south end of the ground gave way under the weight of supporters climbing on it, forcing the goal to collapse and delaying, by 75 minutes, the kick-off of the European Cup Champions League semi-final first leg match with **Borussia Dortmund** (1 April 1998). *International keynotes* More than 100 arrests were made in the French city of Marseille after two consecutive nights of trouble involving **England** and **Tunisia** supporters (and locals) prior to the 1998 **World Cup** group G encounter between the two countries on 15 June at the **Stade Velodrome**. Ninety-six people were arrested, mainly German nationals, before and after the group F match between **Germany** and **Yugoslavia** at the **Stade Felix-Bollaert** in Lens on 21 June. A pitch invasion at **Cardiff City**'s **Ninian Park** on 22 May 1976 (Wales v Yugoslavia, **European Championship** qualifier) led to **UEFA** banning its use for international matches for two years. The Argentinean League was suspended for three weeks in May 1998 following escalating crowd problems at football matches. See also **hooliganism, football**.

cruciate ligament *medical* either of two **ligaments** joining the **tibia** to the **femur**: known as the anterior and posterior cruciate ligaments. The two cross over the inside the knee **joint** and, as such, are vital to the overall stability of the knee. If either of them rupture the femur becomes able to move horizontally over the top of the tibia and the knee becomes unstable. Physiotherapy to build up leg muscles can overcome this, but surgery may ultimately be required.

Cruyff, Johan *player-manager* Striker. **Netherlands** international (48 caps, 33 goals, 1966-77). Born 25 April 1947. *Career* 1963–1984. *Clubs* **Ajax** (twice), **Barcelona**, Los Angeles Aztecs, Washington Diplomats, Levante (Spain), **Feyenoord**. *Keynotes* Cruyff joined Ajax as a junior in 1959. Having made his debut for Ajax in 1965, Cruyff scored 33 goals in 34 matches for the club the following season (1966-67). He won three consecutive European Cup winner's medals with Ajax, winning the trophy again two decades later as a manager with Barcelona. He was transferred to Barcelona in 1973 for a then world record fee of £922,300 (of which £400,000 was reported to be Cruyff's signing-on fee). He returned to Ajax in 1982 after playing in the **North American Soccer League** and a brief spell at Spanish club Levante. He joined Feyenoord for a season, winning the Dutch league championship for the last time as a player. Cruyff scored on his international debut (7 September 1966, 2–2, v **Hungary**, in Rotterdam, **European Championship** qualifier), but was sent off in a match two months later against **Czechoslovakia**; the first Dutch international to be sent off while playing for his country. He captained Netherlands to the 1974 World Cup final, (1–2 v West **Germany**); Cruyff withdrew from the 1978 World Cup, prematurely ending an international career after only 48 appearances; in which he became Holland's equal-second highest goalscorer with 33 goals. Cruyff was voted *France Football* **European Footballer of the Year** three times, and appeared in the top seven for nine consecutive years (1969-77); a record bettered only by Franz **Beckenbauer**. Cruyff was a heavy smoker throughout his playing days and early coaching career; which probably contributed to his developing a serious heart condition. His reign as coach at Barcelona ended in 1996, after which he worked as a television sports pundit. *Honours* **World Cup** runner-up (Netherlands, 1974); **European Cup** (Ajax, 1971, 1972, 1973; and as a manager 1992, with Barcelona), **European Super Cup** (Ajax, 1972, 1973; and as a manager 1992, with Barcelona), **World Club Cup** (Ajax, 1972); **European Cup-winners Cup** (as a manager, with Ajax 1987; Barcelona 1989); Dutch League championship (Ajax, 1966, 1967, 1968, 1970, 1972, 1973, 1983, Feyenoord 1984; and as a manager 1985, with Ajax), Dutch Cup (Ajax, 1967, 1968, 1970, 1972, 1973, 1983; and as a manager 1986, 1987, with Ajax), Spanish League (Barcelona, 1974; and as a manager 1991, 1992, 1993, 1994, with Barcelona); Spanish Cup (Barcelona, 1978; and as a manager 1988, 1990, with Barcelona); *France Football* European Footballer of the Year in 1971, 1973 and 1974.

Cruz Azul (Club Deportivo Social y Cultural Cruz Azul) *club* Mexican national league club, based in Mexico City, founded in 1927. Ground: Estadio Azteca, capacity: 110,000. Strip: blue shirts and white shorts (or white shirts and blue shorts). *Keynotes* The club was founded by the Mexican Cooperative Society in Jasso, and was originally known as Cruz Azul Jasso. It moved to Mexico

City from Jasso in 1970, after being bought by a cement company. **CONCACAF Champion Clubs Cup** 1969 (1–0 agg., v **Comunicaciones** of Guatemala), 1970 (walkover in final), 1971 (5-1, v **LD Alajuelense** of Costa Rica, in Mexico City), 1996 (final league of four, in Guatemala), 1997 (5–3, v **Los Angeles Galaxy**, in Washington DC, USA); Mexican Cup (Copa Mexico) 1969; Mexican League Champions 1969, 1970 (short league programme to accommodate Mexico's hosting of the **World Cup**), 1972, 1973 and 1974, 1979, 1980, 1997 (Apertura).

Cruzeiro Esporte Clube *club* Brazilian national league and **Minas Gerais** state league club based in Belo Horizonte, founded 1902. Ground: Governador Magalhaes Pinto "Mineirao", capacity: 130,000. Strip: blue shirts, white shorts. **Copa de Oro** 1995; **Campeonato Brasileiro** runners-up 1975; **Copa do Brasil** 1966, 1993, 1996; state league champions 25 times (to 1998); **Copa Libertadores** 1976 (4–1, 1–2, 3–2 playoff in Santiago, Chile, v **River Plate**), 1997 (1-0 agg., v **Sporting Cristal**, of Peru), runners-up 1977 (0–1, 1–0, 0–0 playoff in Montevideo, Uruguay, 4–5 pens., v **Boca Juniors**); **Supacopa** 1991 (3–2 agg., v River Plate), 1992 (4–1 agg., v **Racing Club**), runners-up 1988 (2–3 agg., v Racing Club), 1996 (0–3 agg., v **Velez Sarsfield**), semi-final 1994; **World Club Championship** runners-up 1976 (0–2 agg., v **Bayern Munich**, in Tokyo), 1997 (0-2 v **Borussia Dortmund**).

Crvena Zvezda Beograd *club* Serbo-Croat name for **Red Star Belgrade**.

Crvena Zvezda Stadion *ground* Yugoslvaia's National stadium situated in Belgrade; home of **Red Star Belgrade**. Ground capacity: 97,000. *History* The ground was built in 1945 on a site originally occupied by the pre-**World War II** club Jugoslavija. Crvena Zvezda was completely rebuilt in the early 1960s and the 97,000 capacity bowl immediately earned the nickname Maracaná after the famous Rio stadium. The stadium staged the 1976 **European Championship** final (**Czechoslovakia** v West **Germany**, 45,000) and the 1973 **European Cup** final (**Ajax** v **Juventus**, 93,500) – the only time a major European club competition final was held in an Eastern bloc country.

crying *misc.* Paul **Gascoigne**'s tears following his booking against West **Germany** in the semi-final of the 1990 **World Cup**, which would have kept him out of the final had **England** won, endeared him to the nation. That year, he was voted BBC television's Sports Personality of the Year.

Crystal Palace *club* **1.** English league. *Dossier* Ground: **Selhurst Park**, south London, capacity: 26,400 all seated. Strip: blue and red striped shirts, white shorts, white socks. Website: *www.cpfc.co.uk* Nickname: the Eagles. Record attendance: 51,482 v **Burnley** (11 May 1979, Division Two). Best average attendance: 30,167 (1972-73). Biggest win: 9–0 v **Barrow** (10 October 1959, Division Four). Biggest defeat: 0–9 v Burnley (10 February 1909, **FA Cup**, second round replay). *History* Although a football club with the name Crystal Palace had been formed in 1861 by staff working at the Great Exhibition (see below, **2.**), it was not until 1905 that a professional club with the name was formed. This delay was owing to the fact that the **Football Association** opposed the establishment of a club that could, if it reached the FA Cup final, play the match on its home ground. The club became a tenant of **Crystal Palace stadium** and played its first match in September 1905. In 1915, Palace moved to Herne Hill when the Admiralty took over Crystal Palace stadium for the duration of **World War I**. The club never returned to Crystal Palace stadium and played at a number of venues – including The Nest where the club made its league debut (1920) – between 1915 and 1924 when it settled at its permanent home, Selhurst Park. Palace won the Division Three Championship in its first season, but it was not until 1969 that the club, under the management of Bert Head (appointed in April 1966), would play in the top flight. The club finished in the bottom five of Division One for three seasons before being relegated in 1973, despite the appointment of Malcolm Allison as manager in March of that year. He changed the club's strip – from claret and sky blue to red and blue stripes – to resemble **Barcelona,** and took the club to its first FA Cup semi-final in 1976 (0–2 v **Southampton**). Palace won promotion to Division One in 1979 under Allison's former assistant Terry **Venables**. The club was relegated again two years later, so that in 12 seasons the club went from Division One to Division Three, then back to the top flight, then down to Division Two. The club returned to Division One in 1989 under the management of Steve Coppell. The following season Palace reached its first FA Cup final (0–1 replay v **Manchester United**; following a 3–3 draw). Coppell resigned in 1993, but returned to manage the club in 1997. Since the formation of the Premier League in 1992 Palace has regularly moved between the top flight and Division One. In 1997, the club returned to the top flight via the end-of-season playoffs (1–0 v **Sheffield United**), having failed at the same stage the previous year (1–2 v **Leicester City**). On 13 March 1998, with the club bottom of the Premier League, Coppell became **director of football**, with responsibility for first-team affairs switching to former Italian international Attilio Lombardo. He resigned after Palace's relegation to the First Division was confirmed on 27 April 1998. Terry Venables began a second spell as Palace manager in summer 1998, following Mark Goldberg's purchase of the club but resigned after just six months in charge and with the club heavily in debt. *League record* Premier League 1992-93, 1994-95, 1997-98; Division One 1969-70 to 1972-73, 1979-80 to 1980-81, 1989-90 to 1991-92; Division Two 1921-22 to 1924-25, 1964-65 to 1968-69, 1973-74, 1977-78 to 1978-79, 1981-82 to 1988-89; First Division 1993-94, 1995-96 to 1996-97, 1998-99–; Division Three 1920-21, 1961-62 to 1963-64, 1974-75 to 1976-77; Division Three (South) 1925-26 to 1957-58; Division Four

1958-59 to 1960-61. *Honours* Division Two 1978-79; Division Three 1920-21; First Division 1993-94; **Zenith Data Systems Cup** 1991 (4–1 v Everton). *Records* Eric Young is Palace's most capped player (19 (21) for **Wales**); Jim Cannon holds the record for club appearances (571, 1973-88); Peter Simpson is Palace's record league goalscorer (153, 1930-36). **2.** former football club founded in South London in 1861, not connected to **Crystal Palace (1.)**. The team consisted of staff at the Great Exhibition, and played at Penge. It helped form the **Football Association** in 1863 and reached the 1871 FA Cup semi-final, v **Royal Engineers**.

Crystal Palace stadium *ground* sports ground situated in south London; burnt down in 1936. Crystal Palace stadium staged the **FA Cup** final on 20 occasions, the first being the 1895 game between **Aston Villa** and **West Bromwich Albion**. It was also the setting for the 1902 final replay.

CS Cartagines (Club Sport) *club* Costa Rica national league club based in Cartago, founded 1906. Ground: Estadio Jose Rafael "Fello" Meza Ivankovich, capacity: 18,000. Strip: blue shirts with white sleeves, white shorts. **CONCACAF Champions Cup** 1994 (3–2, v Atlante of Mexico, final in San José, California), quarter-final 1997; Costa Rica champions 1923, 1936, 1940.

CS Maritimo (Clube Sport) *club* Portuguese national league club, from Funchal on the island of **Madeira** and formed in 1910. Ground: Estádio dos Barreiros, capacity: 16,000. Strip: red and green striped shirts and white shorts. One of just two clubs geographically in Africa (with **CD Tenerife** of the Canary Islands/Spain) to play in a major European club competition. Portuguese Cup 1926, runners-up 1995; **UEFA Cup** second round 1995 (lost 1–3 to eventual runners-up **Juventus**).

CS Sfaxien (Club Sportif) *club* Tunisian national league club based in Sfax. Ground: Taieb Mehiri, capacity: 18,000. Strip: black shirts, white shorts. **Arab Club Champions Cup** runners-up 1986; **CAF Cup** finalist 1998 (4–0 agg., v **ASC Jeanne d'Arc** of Senegal); Tunisian Cup 1971, 1995; Tunisian league champions 1969, 1971, 1978, 1981, 1983, 1995.

CS spray *n.* (o-chloro-benzal malononitrile) gas used by the police and military to control civil disturbances. *Keynotes* The first police use of CS spray at an English football ground occurred when crowd trouble erupted at the **FA Cup** second round match between **Scunthorpe United** and non-league, Ilkeston Town (6 December 1997). Four people were subsequently charged with violent disorder.

CSKA Moscow (Centralnyi Sportivny Klub Armii) *club* Russian national league and former-**Soviet Union** league club, founded in 1923 as OPPV (formerly known as Olls, OPPV, CDKA, CDSA, CSK-MO, adopting current name in 1959). Ground: Dinamo (ground share with **Dinamo Moscow**), capacity: 52,000. Strip: red shirts, red shorts. *Keynotes* Formerly associated with the

Soviet army. CSKA won a Russian league record 12 consecutive games at the end of the 1998 season, though this was not enough to win the championship. **European Cup** quarter-final group stage 1993 (bottom of its league of four); Russian Cup runners-up 1992, 1993, 1994; Soviet Union Cup 1945, 1948, 1951, 1955, 1991; Soviet Union League champions 1946, 1947, 1948, 1950, 1951, 1970, 1991 (the last Soviet Union League champions).

CSKA Sofia *club* Bulgarian national league club based in the capital Sofia formed 1948 as the army club. Ground: Bulgarska Armia, capacity: 30,000. Strip: red shirts, red shorts. *Keynotes* CSKA's record unbroken sequence of nine championships (1954-1962) equals that of **Celtic** and **Rangers**, though is one behind the joint World record of **Berlin FC and Dynamo Tbilisi** (**Al Faisaly** of **Jordan** has 13 consecutive titles, but its record was punctuated by years in which the league championship was not played). It does, however, hold the world record for the most national league championships since World War II (26 titles to 1998). The club was forced to change its name to CFKA Sredets in 1985-89 after players from both sides fought in front of the Communist Party leadership at the 1985 Cup final against **Levski Sofia**. Bulgarian Cup/Soviet Army Cup 1951, 1954, 1955, 1960, 1961, 1965, 1969, 1972, 1973, 1974, 1985, 1986, 1989, 1990; Bulgarian league champions 1948, 1951, 1952, 1954, 1955, 1956, 1957, 1958, 1959, 1960, 1961, 1962, 1966, 1969, 1971, 1972, 1973, 1975, 1976, 1980, 1981, 1982, 1983, 1987, 1989, 1990, 1992, 1997; **European Cup** semi-final 1967, 1982; **European Cup-winners Cup** semi-final 1989; Republic Cup 1981, 1983, 1985, 1987, 1988, 1989, 1993, 1997. Notable former players: Ivan **Kolev**, Hristo **Stoichkov**.

CSSA Zone 3 Tournament *competition* (Tournament of the Conseil Supérieure du Sport en Afrique, West African Championship.) Former regional championship for certain nations in West Africa – **Benin**, **Burkina Faso**, **Ghana**, **Ivory Coast**, **Liberia**, **Niger** and **Togo**. Won on every occasion by Ghana (1982, 1983, 1984, 1986, 1987), with Togo runners-up 1982-86, and Liberia runners-up in 1987.

Cuba *country* CONCACAF republic and island (plus more than 1,500 small islands) in the Caribbean, in the Greater Antilles, off south coast of Florida in the Gulf of Mexico. Independence from **Spain** in 1901, communist state since 1960. Area: 114,525 sq km (44,205 sq miles). Population: 10,980,000 (1994 est.). Language: Spanish. Capital: Havana. *Dossier* Football association (Associación de Fútbol de Cuba, Havana) formed in 1924, affiliated to FIFA in 1931 and **Confederación Norte-Centroamericana y del Caribe de Fútbol** (CONCACAF) in 1961, president José Reinoso Zayas, general secretary Antonio Garces Segura. Season played from July to November. National stadium: Juan Abrantes, Havana, capacity: 18,000. National strip: white shirts with red collars and cuffs, dark blue shorts. *International tournament record*

Olympic Games – quarter-final 1980, also qualified for finals tournament 1976; **Women's World Cup** – never entered; **World Cup** – first entered 1934, quarter-final 1938 (the only occasion Cuba qualified for the finals tournament); **Caribbean Nations Cup** – runners-up 1996 (0–2, v **Trinidad and Tobago**, in Trinidad), semi-final/third 1995 (3–0, v **Cayman Islands**, in Cayman Islands, third/fourth playoff), semi-final/fourth 1992 (1–1, 3–5 pens., v **Martinique**, in Trinidad, third/fourth playoff); **CCCF Championship** – last place 1957, 1960, 1961 (last in its group), hosts 1960; **Central American and Caribbean Games** 1930, 1970, 1974, 1978, 1986; **CONCACAF Championship** – first entered 1971, fourth 1971 (six nation tournament in Port of Spain, Trinidad); **CONCACAF Under-17 championship** – 1988; **Gold Cup** – qualified for 1998 tournament (after a playoff with **St Kitts and Nevis**); **Under-17 World Championship** – qualified for finals tournament 1989, 1991; **World Youth Cup (under-20)** – never qualified for finals tournament. *Record against British and Irish national teams* none played. *Record in international club tournaments* **CONCACAF Champions Cup** – **Piñar del Rio** (runners-up 1989, 1990). Other leading clubs: **Ciudad Havana**, **Deportivo Central FAR**.

Cubillas, Teófilo *player* Striker. **Peru** international striker (81 appearances, 26 goals, 1968-1982). Born 8 March 1949. *Clubs* **Alianza**, Basel (Switzerland), **Porto**, Fort Lauderdale Strikers (USA). *Keynotes* Cubillas began his international career at the age of 19, against **Brazil**, on 17 July 1968 (0–4, in Lima, friendly). He scored his first international goal the following year (8 May 1969, 3–1, v **Colombia**, in Bogota, friendly). Second-highest scorer in 1978 **World Cup** finals with five goals; third-highest in the 1970 finals, also with five goals. Cubillas is the only player to have scored five goals in two World Cup finals tournaments. A talented striker, with a fierce shot, Cubillas scored a memorable goal against soon-to-be World Champions Brazil, after a run by striking partner Hugo Sotil (2–4, in Guadalajara, Mexico). He scored a hat-trick against **Iran** at the 1978 finals. Cubillas scored two of the goals in Peru's 1975 **Copa America** semi-final away-leg victory against Brazil (3–1, in Belo Horizonte, Brazil) that helped his country to the South American championship for only the second time in its history; Cubillas missed the two scheduled legs of the final but returned to play in the final playoff in Caracas (1–0, v **Colombia**). *Honours* Copa America (Peru, 1975).

Cuff, William *official* (1868-1949). Former chairman of **Everton** (1921-38). Member of the **Football League management committee** (1895-1901 and 1925-38), secretary (1901-18), vice-president (1936-39), president (1939-49), life member 1945. In 1935, Cuff put forward a proposal for **two referees** to officiate at matches – the scheme was tested at a number of friendly matches.

Cullis, Stan *player-manager* Defender. **England** international (12 caps). Born 25 October 1916. Career ca.

1934–47. *Clubs* (player) **Wolverhampton Wanderers**, (manager) Wolverhampton Wanderers, **Birmingham City**. *Keynotes* Joined Wolverhampton Wanderers in February 1934. In 1939, Cullis was an **FA Cup** finalist (1–4 v **Portsmouth**) with the club and, in both 1937-38 and 1938-39, he was a member of the Wolves side that finished **Football League** Division One runners-up. Cullis moved into management in August 1947 when he was appointed Wolves' assistant manager. In June 1948, Cullis was given the grand title of secretary-manager. Cullis, renowned as a disciplinarian, built Wolves' most successful side. Under his managership Wolves won three League titles and two FA Cups. His sides used a "kick and rush" style of play which depended on the pace and stamina of the players. Cullis claimed that the quicker and more often the ball was played into the opposition's penalty area the more likely it would be for his side to score. It was Cullis' idea to stage a series of floodlit friendlies against continental opposition in the 1950s. Following Wolves' victories over both **Spartak Moscow** (4–0) and Honvéd (now **Kispest-Honvéd**) (3–2), Cullis proclaimed the club: "The Champions of the world". *Honours* League Championship (Wolverhampton Wanderers 1953-54, 1957-58, 1958-59); FA Cup (Wolverhampton Wanderers 1949, 1960).

Cup rules *n.pl.* early set of laws by the **Football Association**. Adopted as the rules of the new **Football League** in 1888.

cup-tied *regulations* player who, under some **competition rules**, is not entitled to play in a cup fixture because he/she has played for a different club in the same competition in the same season (for example, **League Cup** rule 15, **Scottish Football League Cup** rule 8). It is the responsibility of the club to make sure that its players are eligible. *Keynotes* **Cliftonville** was disqualified from the 1999 **Irish FA Cup** final against **Portadown** after fielding a cup-tied player, Simon Gribben, in the semi-final replay v **Linfield**.

cups, consecutive final appearances *record* **FC Vaduz** appeared in a world-record 17 successive **Liechtenstein** Cup finals (1946-62), the first nine against the same club, FC Triesen (also a world record). It won the last seven of these finals, a joint world record for consecutive domestic cup triumphs.

cups, consecutive trophies *record* The following statistics are for premier national domestic cups only. **1.** World: **Djoliba Athletic Club**, seven consecutive Mali Cups (1973-79); and **FC Vaduz**, seven Liechtenstein Cups (1956-62). **2.** Europe: FC Vaduz (as above). **3.** Africa: Djoliba AC (as above). **4.** South America: **Santos**, four consecutive **Copas do Brasil** (1961-65). **5.** Asia: **Al Foutoua**, four Syrian Cups (1988-91).

cups, total *record* the following clubs have won more domestic cups than any other clubs (the statistics are for premier national domestic cups only). **1.** World/Europe: **Linfield FC** 35 **Irish FA Cups** (includes all-Ireland and Northern Ireland). **2.** Africa: **Al Ahly**, 31 Egyptian Cups. **3.** Asia: **Selangor FA**, 29 Malaysia Cups (plus two shared titles).

Curacao *country* self-governing island of the **Netherlands Antilles** in the West Indies. See: **Netherlands Antilles**.

curler *n. informal* pass, shot or cross that **swerves** in flight.

curtain-raiser *n.* game which precedes the main competition. For example, the **Charity Shield** is considered as a preliminary to the FA **Premier League**. A decision by the **International FA Board** means that curtain raisers to international matches – for example between teams of veteran internationals – are allowed only following agreement, on the day of the main match, between representatives of the relevant national associations and the **referee**, and must take into account the condition of the **field of play**.

Cwmbran Town *club* Welsh league. *Dossier* Ground: Cwmbran Stadium, Cwmbran, Gwent. Strip: white with blue trim shirts, blue with white trim shorts. Nickname: the Town. Ground capacity: 8,201. *Keynotes* Formed in 1950. Cwmbran won the inaugural **League of Wales** title in 1992-93. It qualified for the 1997-98 **European Cup-winners Cup**, losing in the qualifying round to **National Bucharest** (2–11 agg.). *Honours* League of Wales 1992-93.

Cyprus 1. *country* UEFA republic and island in the Mediterranean off the south coast of Turkey. Independence from Britain in 1960, now essentially divided between the unilaterally declared independent Turkish Republic of Cyprus in the north (see below) and the largely Greek-Cypriot community to the south. Area: 9,250 sq km (3,570 sq miles). Population: 730,000 (1995 est.). Languages: Greek, Turkish and English. Capital: Nicosia. *Dossier* Cyprus Football Association (Nicosia) formed in 1934, affiliated to FIFA in 1948 and founder member of **Union of European Football Associations** (UEFA) in 1954: president, Marios Lefkaritis; general secretary, Lambros Adamou. Season played from September to May. National stadium: Makarion Athletic Centre, Nicosia, capacity: 20,000. National strip: blue shirts, white shorts. First international game 30 July: 1949 v **Israel** (1–3, in Tel Aviv, friendly). Biggest defeat: 0–12 v West **Germany** (21 May 1969, in Essen, **World Cup** qualifier). Most capped players: Pambos Pittas (69 appearances, ca. 1988-), Yiannakis Yiangoudakis (68 appearances). Leading goalscorers: Pambos Pittas (7 goals). *International tournament record* Olympic Games – never qualified for finals tournament; **Women's World Cup** – never entered; World Cup – first entered 1962, never qualified for finals tournament (best performances: fifth of six-nation group 1994, and fourth in five-nation group 1998); **European Championship** – first entered 1968, never qualified for finals tournament, last in all qualifying groups except 1996 (fifth of six nations); **European Championship for Women** – never entered. *World Cup performance* (finals and qualifiers to end of 1998 tournament) played 64, won 6, drawn 3, lost 51, scored 39 goals, conceded 203 goals; win rate 9%; goals scored per game 0.61. *Record* *against British and Irish national teams* v **England**, played two, lost two; v **Scotland**, played four, lost four; v **Northern Ireland**, played four, won one, lost three; v **Wales**, played two, lost two; v **Republic of Ireland**, played two, lost two. *History* League and Cup introduced in 1935. Cyprus FA was formerly affiliated to the English **Football Association**. Cyprus hosted, and played in the very last game of the former-**Soviet Union**, on 13 November 1991 (0-3, in Larnaca, European Championship qualifier). One of its best results was a 1–1 home draw against the defending European champions **Denmark** in the 1996 European Championship qualifiers. *League system* Fourteen clubs compete in the national league first division, playing each other home and away, with three relegated each season to the national second division. Three points are awarded for a win and one for a draw; goal difference separates clubs level on points. There are 14 clubs in the second division. *Record in international club tournaments* **European Cup** – Omonia Nicosia (second round 1973, 1980, 1986, 1988), **Apoel Nicosia** (second round 1987), **Apollon Limassol** (second round 1992); **European Cup-winners Cup** – Apoel Nicosia (second round 1964, 1977); **UEFA Cup** – Omonia Nicosia (second round 1991), Apollon Limassol (second round 1994). Other leading clubs: **AEL Limmassol, Anorthosis of Famagusta** (Larnaca, formerly of Famagusta, but moved because of divide between north and south). **2. Turkish Republic of Northern Cyprus** *country no international affiliation* unilaterally declared independent republic in northern Cyprus. *Dossier* Football association not recognised by FIFA .

Czechoslovakia *former country (formerly)* UEFA former communist republic in central Europe, formed by union of Czech and Slovak regions of former Austro-Hungarian Empire. Communist regime fell in 1989, country divided into **Czech Republic** and **Slovakia** in 1993. Area: 127,870 sq km (49,371 sq miles). Population: 14,686,000 (1974). Languages: Czech and Slovak. Capital: Prague. *Dossier* former football association formed in 1922 affiliated to FIFA in 1922 (until 1993) and founder member of the **Union of European Football Associations** (UEFA) in 1954 (until 1993). First international game: 28 August 1920, v **former-Yugoslavia** (7–0, in Antwerp, **Olympic Games**, first round). Biggest victory: 7–0 (as above; and v former-Yugoslavia, 28 October 1925, in Prague, friendly). Biggest defeat: 3–8 v **Hungary** (19 September 1937, in Budapest, **Dr Gerö/International Cup**) Most capped players: Zdenek **Nehoda** (90, 1971–87), Ladislav Novák (75, 1952–66), Marián Masny (75, 1974–82). Leading goalscorers: Antonin **Puc** (34, 1926–1938), Zdenek Nehoda (31), Oldrich **Nejedly** (28, 1931–38). Other notable players: Josef **Masopust**, Ivo Viktor. *International tournament record* Olympic Games – winners/gold medal 1980 (1–0 v **East Germany**, in Moscow), runners-up/silver medal 1964 (1–2, v **Hungary** in Tokyo), disqualified in the 1920 final (v

Belgium); **Women's World Cup** – never qualified; **World Cup** – first entered 1934, runners-up 1934 (1–2 a.e.t., v **Italy**, in Rome), 1962 (1–3 v **Brazil**, Santiago), quarter-final 1938, 1990, also qualified for finals tournament 1954, 1958, 1970, 1982; Dr Gerö/International Cup – 1960, runners-up 1953; **European Championship** – first entered 1960, 1976 (2–2, 5–3 pens., v West **Germany**, Belgrade), semi-final/third 1960 (2–0, v **France**, in Marseille, third/fourth playoff), 1980 (1–1, 9–8 pens., v Italy, in Naples, third/fourth playoff), failed to qualify for other finals tournaments; **European Championship for Women** – first entered 1989, quarter-final 1989; **European Junior Championship/European Youth Championship** – 1968, runners-up 1982, 1983; **European Under-16 Championship** – 1990; **European Under-23 Championship** – 1972 (5–3 agg., v **Soviet Union**); **Under-17 World Championship** – quarter-final 1993; **World Youth Cup (under-20)** – quarter-final 1983. *Record against British and Irish national teams* v **England**, played 12, won one, drawn three, lost seven, one abandoned; v **Northern Ireland**, played two, lost two; v **Scotland**, played 10, won four, drawn one, lost five; v **Wales**, played 12, won six, lost three, drawn three; v **Republic of Ireland**, played 12, won seven, lost four, drawn one. *History* A national league of Czechoslovakia began in 1925, with a Cup played from 1961. The league was dominated by the three leading Czech clubs, **Sparta Prague** (19 championships), **Dukla Prague** (11 championships) and **Slavia Prague** (nine championships), and the leading Slovakian club **Slovan Bratislava** (eight championships). Sparta Prague won the prestigious **Mitropa Cup** in 1927 – the first year the tournament was played – and again in 1935, while Slavia Prague won the trophy in 1938. Slovan Bratislava is the only former-Czechoslovakian club to have won a modern European club tournament; in 1969 it won the **European Cup-winners Cup** (3–2, v **Barcelona**, in Basle, Switzerland). Czechoslovakia was Olympic Games gold medalists in 1980 and silver medalists in 1964. It was disqualified in the 1920 final against Belgium, having left the pitch with the match score at 0–2, accusing the referee of cheating. The country reached the final of the World Cup in 1934, losing 1–2 to the home nation Italy. Oldrich Nejedly was the top scorer in the 1934 finals tournament with five goals (see World Cup **Golden Boot**). Czechoslovakia reached the World Cup final again in 1962 when it was beaten by Brazil in Santiago. Its finest achievement, however, was in winning the European Championship in 1976: a penalty shoot-out victory over West Germany at the final in Belgrade. Czechoslovakia were 2–0 ahead after 25 minutes: extra time was forced by an 89th minute equaliser from Holzenbein. The game went to penalties: Panenka scored Czechoslovakia's fifth penalty, securing the trophy after Uli Hoeness had put Germany's fourth penalty high and wide. Czechoslovakia's last ever game was played on 17 November 1993, a 0–0 draw against

Belgium in Brussels, in the 1994 World Cup qualifiers. Skuhravy was the last to score for the former country (27 October 1993, 3–0, v **Cyprus** in Kosice, World Cup qualifier). *World Cup final teams and scorers* 1934: World Cup (runners-up)- Plánicka (goalkeeper), Zenisek, Ctyroky, Kostálek, Cambal, Krcil, Junek, Svoboda, Sabotka. Nejedly, Puc (1). 1962: World Cup (runners-up): Schrojf (goalkeeper), Tichy, Pluskal, Popluhár, Novák, Kvasnák, Masopust (1), Pospíchal, Scherer, Kadraba, Jelínek. *European Championship winning team and scorers* 1976: Viktor (goalkeeper), Pivarník, Ondrus, Capkovic, Gögh, Dobiás (1) (Vesely), Móder, Panenka, Masny, Svehlík (1) (Jurkemik), Nehoda. *Record in international club tournaments* **European Cup** – Dukla Prague (semi-final 1967), **Spartak Trnava** (semi-final 1969); European Cup-winners Cup – Slovan Bratislava (1969), Sparta Prague (semi-final 1973), **Banik Ostrava** (semi-final 1979), Dukla Prague (semi-final 1986); **UEFA Cup** – **Bohemians Prague** (semi-final 1983); Mitropa Cup – Sparta Prague (1927, 1935, runners-up 1930, 1936), Slavia Prague (1938, runners-up 1929), Spartak Trnava (1967) **Inter Bratislava** (1969), Tatran Presov (1981), Banic Ostrava (1987). Other leading clubs: (from former-Czechoslovakia): **Lokomotiva Kosice**, **Viktoria Zizkov**.

Czech Republic *country UEFA* federal republic in east central Europe, bordered by **Germany**, **Poland**, **Slovakia** and **Austria**. Independent from Austro-Hungarian Empire after **World War I**, joined Slovakia to form independent **Czechoslovakia** (1918), existed as a Czech Socialist Republic within Czechoslovakia from 1968 until 1989. Became independent state in January 1993. Area: 127,870 sq km (49,360 sq miles). Population: 10,330,000 (1996 est.). Language: Czech. Capital: Prague. *Dossier* Football Association of the Czech Republic (Prague), originally formed in 1901 (until 1922), and, in the new republic, in 1990, affiliated to FIFA in 1907 (until 1922) and again in 1994, and to the **Union of European Football Associations** (UEFA) in 1993, president Frantisek Chvalovsky, general secretary Dr Zdenek Sivek. Season played from August to June, with **winter break** from December to February. National stadium: Strahov, Prague, capacity: 20,000. National strip: red shirts, white shorts. First international game: 23 February 1994 v **Turkey** (4–1, in Istanbul, friendly). Biggest victory: 6–0 v **Malta** (18 September 1996, Teplice, **World Cup** qualifier). Most capped players: Miroslav Kadlec (64 appearances for the Czech Republic and former-Czechoslovakia, ca. 1985-), Pavel Kuka (64 appearances for the Czech Republic and former-Czechoslovakia, ca. 1990-), Jiri Nemec (60 appearances, ca. 1991-), Lubos Kubik (56 appearances for the Czech Republic and former-Czechoslovakia, ca. 1985-97). Other notable international players: Patrik **Berger**, Ludek Miklosko, Karel Poborsky. Leading goalscorer: Pavel Kuka (23 goals). *International tournament record* **Women's World Cup** – never qualified for finals; World Cup – first entered 1998 (third in six-nation

qualifying group, with five wins, one draw and four defeats from its 10 games); **Confederations Cup** – third 1998 (1–0, v **Uruguay**, in Riyadh, Saudi Arabia, third/fourth playoff); **European Championship** – first entered 1996, runners-up 1996 (1–2 a.e.t/**golden goal**, v Germany, at **Wembley**); **European Championship for Women** – first entered 1995 (last in its first-round group of four nations). *Record against British and Irish national teams* (Czech Republic only) v **England**, played one, lost one; v **Republic of Ireland**, played three, won three. *History* The Football Association of the Czech Republic is the oldest in Eastern Europe, originally founded in 1901, eight years ahead of the Romanian FA, and 11 years before that of Russia. The two oldest existing clubs, **Sparta Prague** and **Slavia Prague**, were founded in 1893, with a Czech league dating from 1896 and a Czech cup from 1906. Czech regional competitions continued during the existence of Czechoslovakia and, from 1970 to 1993, the Czechoslovakia Cup was a playoff between the winners of the two regional cups: the Czech Cup and the Slovak Cup. Separate Czech leagues operated from 1896 to 1913, 1918 to 1924, 1939 to 1944 (**World War II**), and from 1994 (after independence). A team representing **Bohemia** (a Czech region) played international matches from 1903 to 1908. The Czech Republic's performance in the 1996 European Championship meant that the country was runner-up in its first senior international tournament as an independent nation. It finished third in the 1998 Confederations Cup (Intercontinental Championship), held in Riyadh, Saudi Arabia. *World Cup performance* (finals and qualifiers to end of 1998 tournament – includes all results for the former-Czechoslovakia) played 111, won 56, drawn 22, lost 33, scored 204 goals, conceded 114 goals; win rate 50%; goals scored per game 1.84. *League system* Sixteen clubs compete in the national first division (1 fotbalová liga) and national second division (2 fotbalová liga), with three points awarded for a win and one for a draw; **goal difference** separates clubs level on points. The bottom two clubs in the first division are relegated, replaced by the top two in the second division. There are two semi-professional regional "third" divisions: the Czech (18 clubs) and Moravian (16 clubs) regional leagues; one club from each is promoted to the second division. There are five provincial "fourth" divisions. *Record in international club tournaments* **European Cup** – **Dukla Prague** (semi-final 1967) Sparta Prague (champions-league stage 1998); **European Cup-winners Cup** – Sparta Prague (semi-final 1973), **Banik Ostrava** (semi-final 1979), Dukla Prague (semi-final 1986), Slavia Prague (quarter-final 1998); **UEFA Cup** – **Bohemians Prague** (semi-final 1983); **Mitropa Cup** – Sparta Prague (1927, 1935, runners-up 1930, 1936), Slavia Prague (1938, runners-up 1929), Banik Ostrava (1987). Other leading club: **Viktoria Zizkov**.

Czibor, Zoltan *player* Striker. **Hungary** international (43 caps, 1951-1957). Born 1929, died September 1997. *Career* ca. 1950-62. *Clubs* **Ferencvaros**,

Csepel, **Kispest-Honvéd**, **Barcelona**, **Espanyol RDC**. *Keynotes* One of the **Magnificent Magyars**. Czibor is one of only three players to have scored in both a **World Cup** final (1954) and **Olympic Games** final (1952). Only Ferenc **Puskas** (in the same years) and Pedro **Cea** have equalled this feat. Czibor scored for Barcelona in the 1961 European Cup final, his side losing 2–3 to Benfica (at **Wankdorf** stadium, Berne) - the same ground where he lost a World Cup final, by the same score. He played in the second leg of the Fairs Cup (now UEFA Cup) final in 1960, scoring two goals in the 4–1 aggregate defeat of **Birmingham City**. *Honours* World Cup runner-up (Hungary, 1954); Olympic Games gold medal (Hungary, 1952); **UEFA cup** (Fairs Cup) (Barcelona, 1960); Hungarian league championship (Honvéd 1954, 1955); Spanish league championship (Barcelona, 1959, 1960).

D

D *rules* another name for **penalty arc**.

Daewoo Royals *club South Korea* former name, until 1996, of **Pusan Daewoo Royals**.

Dalglish, Kenny *player-manager* Striker. **Scotland** international (102 caps, 30 goals). Born 4 March 1951. Career ca. 1967–90. *Clubs* (player) **Celtic, Liverpool**; (manager) Liverpool (player-manager), **Blackburn Rovers, Newcastle United**. *Keynotes* Joined Celtic in 1967, scoring 112 goals in 204 Scottish League Championship appearances for the club before moving to Liverpool for a UK record fee of £440,000 in August 1977. Dalglish played in 354 **Football League** games for Liverpool and scored on 118 occasions. He was the first player to score more than 100 goals for a single club in both the Football League and the **Scottish Football League**. Appointed Liverpool's player-manager in June 1985, he led the club to the **double** in his first season – the first player-manager to both win the League and the double. Dalglish sensationally resigned as Liverpool boss on 22 February 1991, six months after he played his 516th and final game for the club. He came out of self-imposed retirement on 12 October 1991 to become manager of Blackburn Rovers, taking the club to the Premier League via the end-of-season **playoffs** (5–4 v **Derby County**) in his first season. In 1994-95, he led the club to its first title in 81 years, but before the start of the following season Dalglish moved "upstairs" to become **director of football**. He succeeded Kevin **Keegan**, just as he had as a player with Liverpool, by becoming Newcastle United manager in February 1997. Under Dalglish's managership, Newcastle reached its first major final in 24 years, contesting the 1998 FA Cup (0–2 v **Arsenal**). He was replaced by Ruud **Gullit** in September 1998. Dalglish played at schoolboy, youth, Under-23 and full international level for Scotland. Voted **Footballer of the Year** in 1979 and **PFA Footballer of the Year** in 1983. Included in the **Football League Centenary 100 players**. *Honours* (player) League Championship (Liverpool 1978-79, 1979-80, 1981-82, 1982-83, 1983-84); **FA Cup** (Liverpool 1986); **League Cup** (Liverpool 1981, 1982, 1983, 1984); **European Cup** (1978, 1981, 1984); Scottish League (Celtic 1971-72, 1972-73, 1973-74, 1976-77); **Scottish FA Cup** (Celtic 1972, 1974, 1975, 1977); **Scottish League Cup** (Celtic 1975), (manager) League Championship/ Premiership (Liverpool 1985-86; 1987-88, 1989-90; Blackburn Rovers 1994-95); FA Cup (Liverpool 1989).

Dalian Wanda *club* Chinese national league club based in Dalian, Liaoning province. Ground: Jinzhou Stadium, Dalian, capacity: 30,000 (hosts some of China's international fixtures). *Keynotes* Dalian holds the Asian club record of 55 consecutive domestic league games without defeat (1996 to 1997) – the seventh longest unbeaten run in the world by a national league club. **Asian Champion Teams Cup** runners-up 1998 (v **Pohang** of Korea, 0–0, 5–6 pens.), fourth 1999; **Asian Cup-winners Cup** quarter-final 1990; Chinese league champions 1994, 1996, 1997, 1998; **Far East Club Championship** runners-up 1998 (2–3, v **Rotor Volgograd**).

Dallas Burn *club* United States football club and founder member of **Major League Soccer**, based in Dallas, Texas. Member of the league's **Western Conference**. Founded: 1996. Ground: The Cotton Bowl, capacity: 67,000. **National Open Challenge Cup** 1997.

damages *legal* financial award made to an individual as a result of injuries sustained through foul play on a football pitch. *Keynotes* The first recorded award of substantial damages (£4,500) for injuries caused by foul play on a football pitch was made in 1970 to a Sussex amateur player after his leg was broken by a foul tackle (*Lewis v Brookshaw*). In October 1998, **Bradford City** striker Gordon Watson sued **Huddersfield Town** and its defender Kevin Gray on the grounds of negligence following a tackle by Gray which resulted in a double fracture of his opponent's leg during a First Division encounter on 1 February 1997. Watson was supported by his club which brought similar action for recklessness against both Gray and Huddersfield. Watson was unable to play first-team football for 18 months following the incident, having joined the club for a then club record fee of £575,000 from **Southampton** only a few weeks earlier. Watson's complaint was upheld although the action brought by his club was dismissed. The 27-year-old Watson's victory meant he became the first player to win damages (he received an interim payment of £50,000) as a result of the actions of a fellow professional.

DANA Cup *competition* annual tournament held in **Denmark** for young players aged from 10 to 18 and one of the biggest events of its kind in the world. Teams are placed in eight age groups and generally over 50 countries are represented.

dangerous play *rules* one of the offences listed as a **foul** under the **Laws of the game** (Law XII). A foul is committed if a player acts in a manner that the referee considers is dangerous. This might include, for example, raising a foot high with studs showing, or kicking the ball when held firmly by the goalkeeper (Law XII). The punishment for non-specific dangerous play is for the opposing team to be awarded an **indirect free kick** from the spot where the offence took place (unless within the opponents' **goal area** – in which case it is taken from anywhere within that area – or within the offending side's goal area, in which case it must be taken from the **goal line** at the point nearest to where the foul was committed). Other forms of dangerous play may be covered by fouls specifically listed in the **Laws of the game** as warranting a **direct free kick** or **penalty kick** (see: **kicking an opponent, tripping an opponent, charging at an opponent, striking an opponent** and **jumping at an opponent**). Persistent dangerous play can also be punished by the player receiving a **caution**. If the player is guilty of **violent conduct** or **serious foul play**, he or she is liable to be **sent off**.

Danubio *club* Uruguayan Primera League club based in Montevideo, founded 1932. Ground: Estadio Jardins del Hipodromo, capacity: 18,000. Strip: white shirts with black sash, white shorts. **Copa Uruguaya** (Uruguay's professional league) champions 1988; **Pre-Libertadores Liguilla** 1983.

Daring Club Motema Pembe *club* Congo Democratic Republic (formerly Zaire) national league club based in the capital Kinshasa, founded 1936 (formerly known as Cercle Sport Imana). Ground: 20 Mai, capacity: 60,000. Known as the "Clean Hearts". Strip: green shirts, white shorts. **African Cup of Champion Clubs** semi-final 1979; **African Cup-winners Cup** 1994 (5–2 agg., v **Kenya Breweries** of Kenya, quarter-final 1993; **African Super Cup** runners-up 1994 (0–3, v **Espérance Tunis** of Tunisia, in Alexandria, Egypt); **CAF Cup** semi-final 1998; Congo DR Cup 1964, 1974, 1978, 1984, 1985, 1990, 1991, 1993, 1994; Congo DR league champions 1963, 1964, 1974, 1978, 1989, 1994.

Darlington *club* English league. *Dossier* Ground: **Feethams Ground**, Darlington, Durham; capacity: 8,500. Strip: black and white striped shirts, black shorts, black socks. Nickname: Quakers. Record attendance: 21,023 v **Bolton Wanderers** (14 November 1960, **League Cup**, third round). Best average attendance: 10,234 (1948-49). Biggest win: 9–2 v **Lincoln City** (7 January 1928, Division Three (North)). Biggest defeat: 0–10 v **Doncaster Rovers** (25 January 1964, Division Four). *History* Founded in 1883, sharing Darlington Cricket Club's Feethams home, and turning professional

in 1908. Darlington reached the third round of the **FA Cup** (equivalent to the fifth round today) in 1911 (0–3 v **Swindon Town**), defeating League opposition in earlier rounds (1–0 v **Sheffield United**, first round; 2–1 v **Bradford Park Avenue**, second round). The club amalgamated with Darlington Forge Albion (1917), a local works team, prior to becoming founder members of Division Three (North) in 1921-22. Darlington won promotion as Division Three (North) Champions in 1924-25. The two seasons that Darlington spent in Division Two is the only time in the club's history it has played in one of the two top divisions. In 1925-26, the club finished 15th in Division Two – its highest ever **Football League** position. In 1958, the club again reached the FA Cup fifth round (1–6 v **Wolverhampton Wanderers**), having beaten Division One opponents in the previous round (4–1 replay v **Chelsea**). The club was a *League Cup* quarter-finalist in 1968 (4–5 v **Derby County**). Darlington won promotion in 1966-67 and 1984-85, but the club's tenure in Division Three was short-lived on both occasions. In 1988-89, the club finished bottom of Division Four and was replaced by **Maidstone United**. Darlington immediately restored its League status, winning the **Football Conference** Championship the following season, and in 1990-91, the club lifted the Division Four title. In 1995-96, Darlington was an end-of-season Third Division **playoff** finalist (0–1 **Plymouth Argyle**). *League record* Division Two 1925-26 to 1926-27; Division Three 1966-67, 1985-86 to 1986-87, 1991-92; Third Division 1992-93–; Division Three (North) 1921-22 to 1924-25, 1927-28 to 1957-58; Division Four 1958-59 to 1965-66, 1967-68 to 1984-85, 1987-88 to 1988-89 (relegated to Football Conference), 1990-91. *Honours* Division Three (North) 1924-25; **Division Three (North) Cup** 1934 (4–3 v **Stockport County**); Division Four 1990-91; Football Conference 1989-90. *Records* Ron Greener holds the record for club League appearances (442, 1955-68); Alan Walsh is Darlington's record League goalscorer (90, 1978-84).

Darwen *club* former-English league. *Dossier* Ground: Barley Bank, Darwen, Lancashire. Record League attendance: 10,000. *Keynotes* Darwen was a founder member of the **Football Alliance** in 1899, which was set up by northern clubs denied entry to the **Football League**. The club was elected to the Football League in 1891-92, but resigned in 1898-99 and joined the Lancashire Combination. In its final Football League season, Darwen lost all but one of its 17 away fixtures, scoring only six goals and conceding 109. The club was an **FA Cup** semi-finalist in 1880-81 (1–4 v Old Carthusians), and a quarter-finalist in 1886-87 (2–3 v **Aston Villa**) and 1892-93 (0–5 v **Wolverhampton Wanderers**). Darwen scored 67 goals during the 1896-97 season, of which 12 were scored against an eight-man **Walsall** Town Swifts' team on 26 December 1896 (12–0). The club holds the League record for the most goals conceded in a season: 141 goals in 34 games (1898-99).

Darwen's highest League position was 14th in the Football League, which the club achieved in 1891-92. *League record* Football League 1891-92; Division One 1893-94; Division Two 1892-93, 1894-95 to 1898-99.

Daugava Riga *club* Latvian national league club based in the capital Riga, founded 1995 (as Amstrig Riga): a club of the same name was founded in 1948 and played in the former-**Soviet Union** first division 1948-1949. Ground: Daugava, capacity: 15,000. The original Daugava won the Latvian regional cup in 1990. Latvian league runners-up 1996.

Davies, Barry *broadcaster* Born 24 October 1940. BBC television commentator who joined BBC Sport in 1969 after spells with the British Forces Network, BBC Radio Sport and ITV. He made his TV debut in February 1966, commentating on **Chelsea**'s Inter City Fairs (**UEFA**) **Cup** clash with **AC Milan** from **Stamford Bridge**. Later that year he was a member of ITV's team at the 1966 **World Cup** finals and, in 1994, he commentated on the final between **Brazil** and **Italy** for the BBC. Also regularly provides tennis commentary from Wimbledon.

DC United *club* United States football club and founder member of **Major League Soccer**, based in Washington, District of Columbia. Member of the league's **Eastern Conference**. Founded: 1996. Ground: RFK Memorial Stadium, capacity: 56,500. *Keynotes* The first winners of the Major League Soccer Championship (MLS Cup) 1996 (3–2 after sudden-death overtime, v **Los Angeles Galaxy**, at Foxboro Stadium, Foxboro, Mass.), and the first US club to win an international club tournament (below). **CONCACAF Champions Cup** 1998 (1–0, v **Toluca** of Mexico, in Washington DC, USA), semi-final 1997; **Copa Inter Americana** 1998 (2–1 agg., v **Vasco da Gama** of Brazil); MLS Cup 1996, 1997, runners-up 1998; **US Open Challenge Cup** 1996, 1997. Notable former player: John Harkes.

dead-ball line *n.* another word for **goal line**.

Dean Court *ground* English football ground situated in Bournemouth, Dorset; home of **Bournemouth** (AFC). *Dossier* Ground capacity: 10,770. Pitch dimensions: 102m x 69m. Record attendance: 28,799 v **Manchester United** (2 March 1957, **FA Cup**, sixth round). Best average attendance: 16,854 (1947-48). *History* Situated on the site of a former gravel pit owned by Cooper Dean (hence the name), Dean Court was revamped in the late-1920s with fixtures and fittings bought from the Empire Exhibition which had been staged at **Wembley**. These articles included a steel cafe, which the club developed into a 3,700 seated stand, and turnstiles. On several occasions, the club has put forward proposals to redevelop the Dean Court site, one of which included a 1995 plan to turn the pitch by 90 degrees, but a lack of money (see Bournemouth AFC) and local council objections scuppered these plans. Bournemouth played its first match at Dean Court on 31 December 1910 (v **Southampton** Reserves) and the ground staged its first floodlit fixture on 27 September 1961 (v **Northampton Town**, Division Three).

Dean, Dixie (William) *player* Striker. **England** international (16 caps, 18 goals). Born 22 January 1907. Career ca. 1923–1940. *Clubs* **Tranmere Rovers**, **Everton**, **Notts County**, Sligo Rovers. *Keynotes* Dean holds the record for the most **Football League** goals in one season, scoring 60 in 1927-28 for Everton: with England internationals and Cup games his total tally for the season was 82. Overall he scored 473 goals in 502 League, FA Cup, international and representative appearances in a career which began with Tranmere Rovers in November 1923 and ended with Sligo Rovers in January 1939. His goal tally included 37 hat-tricks, and his 349 League goals for Everton between 1925 and 1937 remains the most scored by one man for one club. Dean scored one of Everton's three goals in the club's 1933 FA Cup final victory (v **Manchester City**) – the first final in which players' shirts were numbered; Dean wore number nine. Dean's death on 1 March 1980 occurred at **Goodison Park** following an Everton v **Liverpool** Derby. Included in the **Football League Centenary 100 players**. *Honours* League Championship (Everton 1927-28, 1931-32); Division Two (Everton 1930-31); FA Cup (Everton 1933).

death, players *medical* fatality directly linked to playing football. *Keynotes* Each year, there are around five recorded deaths to players in the UK occurring on the football pitch or from health conditions which start during play (these figures are for all players – at all levels of the game). However, the fatal-injury rate in football is comparatively small compared with, say, horse riding (10–20 deaths per year). Around 1 million people play association football in the UK, and it accounts for around 40% of non-fatal sports injuries recorded in hospital accident and emergency departments. Of 98 deaths recorded between 1963 and 1983 (both amateur and professional players), 35 resulted from head injuries – usually due to collisions between players – and seven from spinal injuries. Deaths from playing football were recorded in the early rudimentary forms of the game: an early example is that of Henry de Ellington, fatally wounded on Trinity Sunday 1280 in Ulkham, as he collided with his friend David le Keu, his wounds sustained from an unsheathed knife worn on le Keu's belt. Sam Wynne (pneumonia) is the first recorded player to die during an English league match (**Sheffield United** v **Bury**, 1927). In 1892, **St Mirren**'s James Dunlop died after contracting tetanus from a gash to the leg. A similar fate befell **Port Vale**'s Tom Butler in 1923. He died in hospital from tetanus eight days after breaking an arm in a match against Clapton **Orient**. Ex-**England** international Bobby Benson died in 1916 after playing for his old club **Arsenal** at **Reading**. Benson, who had been out of the game for over a year, was asked to play because the Gunners was short of players, but the exertion killed him. **Scotland** international and **Hibernian** right back James Main died in December 1909, four days after sustaining internal injuries from an accidental kick to the stomach. In 1934, Gillingham striker Sim Raleigh died of a brain haemorrhage after a clash of heads with **Brighton & Hove Albion**'s Paul Mooney. More recently, in 1973 **Sevilla**'s Pedro Berruezo collapsed on the pitch and died of heart failure. **York City** striker David Longhurst died during a match against **Lincoln City** at **Bootham Crescent** on 8 September 1990. A stand at the ground was renamed in his memory. Goalkeepers are particularly vulnerable to fatal injuries. John Thomson of **Celtic** and Scotland died following a collision with the **Rangers** striker Sam English during an **Old Firm** match in 1931. Thomson fractured his skull diving for a 50-50 ball at his opponent's feet. English, devastated by the incident, later moved to **Liverpool** and then back to his native Ireland. **Hungary** keeper Gabor Zsiboras died as a result of a blood clot on the brain during an international training session in 1993.

death, fans *misc.* fatalities have occurred to spectators, predominantly through crowd incidents, building collapse or fire. *Keynotes* Notable UK examples include the **Burnden Park disaster** (33 fatalities in 1946), the **Ibrox Stadium disaster** (66 fatalities in 1971), the **Bradford fire** (56 deaths in 1985) and the **Hillsborough disaster** (95 deaths, in 1989). Individual fans have died, usually as a result of **crowd trouble**. On 4 April 1995, a **Crystal Palace** fan died after fighting broke out between rival supporters outside a Walsall pub before the Palace v **Manchester United** FA Cup semi-final at **Villa Park**. The attendance at the replay – after a 2–2 draw in the first match – was the lowest (17,987) for a post-**World War II** FA Cup semi-final, largely due to the fact that Palace fans boycotted the game after the FA refused to postpone it for one week as a mark of respect for the deceased fan. Following a **Division Two** match between **Gillingham** and **Fulham** at **Priestfield Stadium** a Fulham supporter (Matthew Fox) died from head injuries sustained as a result of a fight between rival supporters (28 March 1998). **Genoa** supporter Victor **Spagnulo** died following a clash between home supporters and **AC Milan** fans, including members of a Milan gang called *Barbour*, prior to a **Serie A** match between the clubs on 5 February 1995. In Spain, **Real Sociedad** supporter Aitor **Zabaleta** died from a stab wound to the heart before the start of an away **UEFA Cup** game against **Atlético Madrid** in January 1998.

debenture *misc.* mechanism used by several clubs to raise funds from supporters by offering bonds that give them the future right to purchase a season ticket or discounted tickets. **Arsenal**, **Charlton Athletic**, **Leeds United**, **Millwall**, **Rangers** and **West Ham United**, among others, have used debentures to help redevelop stadiums, but not all have been successful. *Keynotes* In 1990, to help fund the £20 million development of **Ibrox**, Rangers introduced a debenture scheme – the first in the UK – which entitled the purchaser to the right to buy a season ticket in the new facility for the next 30 years. The price of the 6,800 debentures on offer ranged from £1,000 to £1,650 and they sold out within a few weeks, raising £8.5 million. In 1992, at Arsenal's

Highbury ground, the North Bank was demolished and replaced with a 12,400 **all-seater stadium**. The finance was funded in part by the sale of debentures to fans, allowing them to buy season tickets in the new stand. The scheme, along with proposals for the new North Bank, provoked controversy and led to the formation of the **Group for an Alternative Arsenal Stand**. West Ham United's bond scheme (Hammers Bond), launched in 1991 at a cost of between £500 and £975, was a disaster with only 5% of fans buying one, forcing the club to extend its borrowings in order to finance the construction of a new West Stand at **Upton Park**. Millwall established the so-called Lion Cards to help finance the construction of its **New Den** stadium. The cards, costing £250 each, entitled the buyer to subsequent reductions on future tickets up to £275 worth over six years. The club raised around £400,000 from the cards.

de Boer *players* Frank (Defender, 67 caps, six goals, 1990-) and Ronald (Striker/midfield, 50 caps, 12 goals, 1993-) **Netherlands** internationals. Born 15 May 1970 (twin brothers). *Clubs* both: **Ajax** and **Barcelona**. *Keynotes* Frank de Boer made his international debut on 26 September 1990 (0–1, v **Italy**, in Palermo, friendly). His twin brother Ronald scored on his international debut, a 6–0 victory over **San Marino** on 24 March 1993 (in Utrecht, **World Cup** qualifier). Both played in the 1998 World Cup finals in France – Ronald in midfield and Frank in defence – and both took penalties in the semi-final defeat by **Brazil** (1–1, 2–4 pens., in Marseille): Frank scored, but Ronald's kick was saved. Frank was chosen for **FIFA**'s 22-man all-star squad of the 1998 World Cup finals. *Honours* – both: **European Cup** (Ajax, 1995); **European Supercup** (Ajax, 1995); Dutch league championship (Ajax, 1994, 1995, 1996); Frank – **UEFA Cup** (Ajax, 1992).

debut *n.* the first appearance by a player, such as for a club (club debut), country (international debut) or in a league (league debut).

decided on penalties *misc.* match where the outcome is decided by a **penalty shoot-out**.

decoy play *tactics* aspect of play which involves an attacker making a run in order to draw a defender(s) away from a space for a team-mate to exploit.

Deepdale *ground* English football ground situated in Preston, Lancashire; home of **Preston North End**. *Dossier* Ground capacity: 21,412. Pitch dimensions: 100.5m x 70m. Record attendance: 42,684 v **Arsenal** (23 April 1938, Division One). Best average attendance: 33,226 (1948-49). *History* Deepdale is the oldest ground in the **Football League** in continuous use. Preston North End first moved to Deepdale as a cricket club in 1875. Originally an all-purpose sports venue, football was first played there in 1879, becoming Deepdale's sole activity from 1881. Despite its success on the pitch, the club was unable to build a larger stadium in the mid-1890s when a share issue failed to raise sufficient finance. In the inter-war period, developments at Deepdale included the construction of two pavilions and stained glass windows in the boardroom. During **World War II**, Deepdale became an army base and a transit facility for prisoners of war, forcing Preston to use the Leyland Motors' ground. The club later was forced to raise finance by selling Deepdale to the local council. This move led in 1986 to the installation of an **artificial pitch** to open the ground up to community use. Deepdale was granted a four-year extension to the Football League deadline to remove artificial pitches, with the final League match ever played on plastic occurring on 18 May 1994 (v **Torquay United,** Third Division **playoff** semi-final). In 1995, Preston was granted a 125-year lease to the ground at a one-off cost of £350,000. The purchase of Preston by the employee-owned boiler manufacturer Baxi in October 1994, was followed by the beginnings of Deepdale's transformation into a 27,000 **all-seater stadium**, which started with the construction of the Tom **Finney** stand. The stand, which bears a picture of Finney picked out in white seating, houses the **National Football Museum**. Deepdale's first floodlit match took place on 20 October 1953 (v **Bolton Wanderers**, Lancashire Cup). It staged an **Inter-League** fixture on 4 October 1933 (Football League v Irish League). See also **Dick, Kerr's Ladies**.

defeats, most in succession   *record*   **1.** Britain (all senior levels): 39 league and cup games, Stockport United (September 1976 to February 1978, Stockport Football League), and Poole Town (1995-96 season, Southern League, Southern Division). **2. Football League**: 18 matches, **Darwen** (1898-99, Division One); the longest run of defeats in the 20th century was 15 matches, by **Walsall** (1988-89, Division Two); **Manchester United** lost the opening 12 matches of the 1930-31 season (Division One); **Nelson** holds the unfortunate league record of 24 consecutive away defeats (1929-30/1930-31, Division Three North). **3.** FA **Premier League**: eight, **Ipswich Town** (1994-95), **Manchester City** 1995-96) and **Crystal Palace** (1997-98).

Defence Force   *club*   Trinidad and Tobago league club based in Chaguanas (Trinidad). Strip: gold shirts, blue shorts. **CONCACAF Champions Cup** 1985 (2–1 agg., v **Olimpia** of Honduras, joint-1978, runners-up 1987 (1–3 agg., v **América** of Mexico), 1988 (0–4 agg., v Olimpia of Honduras); Trinidad and Tobago league champions 1997 (no earlier records).

defender   *n.*   player who operates in defence and whose role is primarily to prevent opponents scoring.

defending deep   *tactics*   strategy whereby the **defenders** maintain a line relatively close to their own goal rather than, for example, defending from the half-way line (see **offside trap**). The strategy invites the opposition to attack the goal but has the effect of reducing the amount of space available to **attacking player**s to create scoring opportunities. It is often employed to defend a winning score, to play for a draw or to rely on an opportunity to score from a sudden breakaway.

defending player   *rules*   member of a **defending team**. A defending player includes the goalkeeper; important because the **offside** rule does not distinguish between outfield players and the goalkeeper when determining whether an **attacking player** may be penalised for being in an offside position. Compare: **defender**.

defending team   *rules*   term used in the **Laws of the game** to describe the team that is playing *away from* a particular **goal area**, **goal line** or **penalty area**. It is important to distinguish the attacking team from the defending team with regard to rules governing **offside, penalty kicks, free kicks, corner kicks** and **goal kicks**. *For example:* A corner kick is awarded if a player from the defending team is the last player to make contact with the ball before it crosses the goal line.

defensive   *adj.*   pertaining to the defence of the goal; such as a defensive position or defensive play.

defensive wall   *n.*   two or more players in a line ten yards from a free-kick with the intention of covering the near side of the goal (the goalkeeper generally covers the far side). The goalkeeper tends to decide how many players stand in the wall, which usually consists of attackers and midfielders freeing the defenders to perform **man-to-man marking** of the opposition. The goalkeeper takes up a position at the far post, while the wall's anchorman is aligned with the near post. The wall reduces the size of the target for the player taking the kick, though it may also reduce the goalkeeper's field of view, particularly where the ball is swerved over or around the defenders. *Rules* All defending players in the wall must be at least 9.15 metres (10 yards) from the ball when the free kick is taken (Law VIII).

Defensor-Sporting Club   *club*   Uruguayan Primera League club based in Montevideo, originally founded 1913 by workers from a glass factory, relaunched 1923. *Keynotes* Defensor merged with Sporting Club de Montevideo in 1989. In 1976, became the first club to take the Uruguayan professional league championship away from Uruguay's "big two", **Peñarol** and **Nacional**. Ground: Estadio Luis Franzini, capacity: 13,000. Strip: violet shirts, white shorts. **Copa Uruguaya** (Uruguay's professional league) champions 1976, 1987, 1991; **Pre-Libertadores Liguilla** 1976, 1979, 1981, 1989, 1991.

deflection   *n.*   pass or shot which riochets off another player or even the referee.

delayed transfer player   *regulation   (Scotland)* special **registration** by a **Scottish Football League** club of a player currently playing for a member club of the **Scottish Junior Football Association**; the player's contract is already agreed and signed, but the player may continue to play for his junior club until the transfer is complete (Scottish Football League rule 56). The new club must include delayed transfer players in its **club list of players** (Scottish Football League rules 50(a) and 59).

delaying the restart of play   *rules*   a **cautionable offence** under the **Laws of the game** (Law XII). A player who deliberately delays the restart of play is liable to receive a **caution**. This illegal tactic is often used by players in an attempt to **waste time**, particularly towards the end of a game, and may involve not returning to the correct half after a goal has been scored, preventing a throw-in or free kick from being taken, or kicking the ball away after play has stopped.

de León, Hugo *player* **Uruguay** international. *Clubs* (include) **Grêmio** and **Nacional**. *El Mundo* **South American Footballer of the Year** runner-up 1988.

deliberate *rules* of a **handball** which, in the opinion of the referee, is committed with intent. A handball decision is not given if the ball simply strikes an opponent's arm or hand, and who has no opportunity to avoid such contact. Also called **intentional**. See: **unintentional**.

Dell, The *ground* English football ground situated in Southampton, Hampshire; home of **Southampton**. *Dossier* Ground capacity: 15,300 all seated. Pitch dimensions: 100.5m x 66m. Record attendance: 31,044 v **Manchester United** (8 October 1969, Division One). Best average attendance: 25,527 (1966-67). *History* Southampton played its first match at The Dell on 3 September 1898 (v Boston United, **Southern League**). The club moved to the ground after it failed to buy the freehold to the Antelope Cricket Ground where it had played since 1886. A local fish merchant, George Thomas, bought the site, granting the club an eight-year lease at £250 per annum. Southampton eventually bought the freehold to the ground for £26,000 in April 1926. In January 1928, the Archibald **Leitch** designed west stand was opened, but a year later the east stand was destroyed by fire. The Dell suffered bomb damage during **World War II** because of its proximity to Southampton docks. As a result, the club was forced to use alternative venues, including the Pirelli sports ground at Eastleigh and **Portsmouth**'s **Fratton Park**. In 1951, Southampton became one of the first English clubs to erect floodlighting, with the first floodlit match taking place on 1 October (v **Tottenham Hotspur** Reserves, Football Combination). Although The Dell's capacity was around 33,000 in 1920s, the current all seated 15,300 total is the smallest in the **Premier League**. Over the years – since the late 1940s – the club has regularly considered relocating to a greenfield site away from the physical constraints that prevent expansion at The Dell. Southampton has sought permission to develop an all-purpose 25,000 sports venue at Stoneham on the outskirts of the city, but the proposed multi-facility development, including retail outlets and a multiplex cinema, was rejected by Eastleigh Council in October 1998. An alternative proposal to develop an inner-city ground at St Mary's, the location of the club's founders, has also been explored. The Dell has hosted one **England** men's international (v **Ireland**, 9 March 1901). On 31 October 1978, The Dell hosted the first **women's football** match on a First Division ground since the Football Association introduced a ban on women playing at FA-affiliated grounds in 1921 (**England** v **Belgium**, 3–0). The attendance of 5,471 is the record home attendance for an official England women's match.

Delle Alpi (Stadio) *ground* Italian football ground situated in Turin, Piemonte; home of **Juventus** and **Torino**. Ground capacity: 71,000 all seated. *History* Built for the 1990 **World Cup** at a cost of over L180 billion, Stadio delle Alpi is situated in the northern suburbs of Turin. The stadium will become a concert venue in 2000, leaving Juventus to return to its Stadio Comunale and Torino to Campo Filadelfia – if enough money can be found to rebuild the decaying stadium. The first sell-out for a **Serie A** fixture occurred on 28 April 1998 when Juventus entertained **Internazionale** in what was effectively the 1997-98 championship decider. On 27 October 1998, Juventus recorded its lowest crowd at delle Alpi for a first-team fixture when only 561 spectators saw the club's Italian Cup (**Coppa Italia**) match with Venezia. During the 1990 World Cup, Stadio delle Alpi staged three group C matches (**Brazil** v **Sweden**, Brazil v **Costa Rica**, Brazil v **Scotland**), one second-round game (**Argentina** v Brazil) and a semi-final (West **Germany** v **England**) – total attendance 289,139; average attendance 57,827.

deltoid ligament *medical* see **lateral deltoid ligament**, **medial deltoid ligament**.

demotion *regulations* enforced **relegation** by a disciplinary ruling. *Keynotes* In 1967-68, the **Football League Management Committee** ruled that **Peterborough United** be relegated to the Fourth Division for making **illegal payments** to players and infringing the rules on **signing-on** fees. The punishment was later reduced to a 19-point deduction; but the club was still relegated. See also **Swindon Town**

Den, The *ground* English football ground situated in south London; former home of **Millwall**. Pitch dimensions: 102m x 68m. Record attendance: 48,672 v **Derby County** (20 February 1937, FA Cup, fifth round). Best average attendance: 27,387 (1938-39). *History* Millwall decamped south of the River Thames from the Isle of Dogs to more densely populated Bermondsey in 1910. The club played its first match at The Den on 22 October 1910 (v **Brighton & Hove Albion**, **Southern League**). The ground was developed by Archibald **Leitch** and, in the 1930s, most of the ground was partially covered. It was damaged by a bomb during **World War II**. The club bought the freehold to the ground for £30,000 in 1951. The ground held the unenviable record of having been closed by the **Football Association**, because of crown trouble, on more occasions than any other **Football League** ground; The Den was closed in 1920, 1934, 1947, 1950, 1978. It was also the first UK football ground to have a **crèche** when childcare facilities were introduced in 1985. Following Millwall's elevation to the top flight in 1988-89, the club and the local council actively pursued relocation plans. The Den was sold to Fairview Homes for £5.2 million and the final match at the ground took place on 8 May 1993 (v **Bristol Rovers**, First Division). The Den staged one full **England** international fixture (v **Wales**, 13 March 1911) and an **inter-League** match (Football League v Southern League, 9 February 1914). It also hosted six **FA Amateur Cup** finals (1915 Clapton v Bishop Auckland; 1920 Dulwich Hamlet v Tufnell Park; 1924 Clapton v Erith & Belvedere; 1925 Clapton v Southall; 1927 Leyton v Barking Town; 1938 Bromley v Erith & Belvedere). The first floodlit match at the Den took place on 5 October 1953 (v **Manchester United**, friendly).

Denilson *player* full name: Denilson de Oliveira. Striker. **Brazil** international (18 caps, 1996-). Born 24 August 1977. *Clubs* **São Paulo**, **Real Betis**. *Keynotes* Denilson made his international debut for Brazil against **Cameroon** in November 1996 (friendly). Denilson's £23 million transfer from São Paulo to Real Betis in July 1997 was a world record **transfer fee**. *Honours* **Copa America** (Brazil, 1997); **Copa CONMEBOL** (São Paulo, 1994); **World Cup** runner-up (Brazil, 1998).

Denmark *country* UEFA monarchy in northern Europe, on the North Sea, Skagerrak and Kattegat in Scandinavia. Comprises a peninsula, bordered by **Germany** to the south, and 400 islands only about a quarter of which are inhabited. Area: 43,075 sq km (16,625 sq miles). Population: 5,300,000 (1996 census). Language: Danish. Capital: Copenhagen. *Dossier* Danish Football Association (Brøndby) formed in 1889, founder member of **FIFA** in 1904 and founder member of **Union of European Football Associations** (UEFA) in 1954, president Poul Hyldgaard, general secretary Jim Stjerne Hansen. Season played from August to June, with **winter break** from December to February. Season played in two phases: **Grundspil** (late July to November) and **Slutspil** (early March to end of May). National stadium: Idraetsparken, Copenhagen, capacity: 40,000. National strip: red shirts, white shorts. Website: http://www.geocities.com/Colosseum/Loge/8240/landshold.htm (unofficial site). First international game: 19 October 1908 v **France** (9–0, in London, **Olympic Games** first round). Biggest victories: 17–1 (22 October 1908, v France, in London, Olympic Games semi-final), and 14–2 v **Iceland** (23 August 1967, in Copenhagen, friendly). Biggest defeat: 0–8 v Germany (16 May 1937, in Wroclaw (now in Poland), friendly). Most capped players: Peter **Schmeichel** (110 appearances, 1987–), Michael **Laudrup** (104 appearances, 1982-98), Morten Olsen (102 appearances, 1970-89). Leading goalscorers: Poul **Nielsen** (52 goals in 38 appearances, 1910-25), Pauli Jorgensen (44 goals, in 47 appearances, 1925-39), Ole Madsen (43 goals, 1958-69), Preben **Elkjaer-Larsen** (38 goals, 1977-88), Michael Laudrup (37 goals). Other notable international players: Allan **Simonsen**, Niels **Bohr**, Harald **Bohr**, Brian **Laudrup**, Sophus **Nielsen**, Nils **Middelboe**. *International tournament record* Olympic Games – runners-up/silver medal 1908 (0–2, v **England**, White City, London), 1912 (2–4, v England, in Stockholm), 1960 (1–3, v **Yugoslavia**, in Rome), semi-final/bronze medal 1948 (5–3, v **Great Britain**, **Wembley**, London, third/fourth playoff); **Women's World Cup/European Championship for Women**/Olympic Games/**Algarve Cup** – see

Denmark, women; **World Cup** – first entered 1958, quarter-final 1998, second round 1968; **Confederations Cup** – 1995 (2–0, v **Argentina**, in Riyadh, Saudi Arabia); **European Championship** – 1992 (2–0, v Germany, in Gothenburg), semi-final 1964 (fourth, 1–3, v **Hungary**, in Barcelona, third/fourth playoff), 1984 (1–1, 4–4 pens., v **Spain**, in Lyon, semi-final); **European Under-16 Championship** – runners-up 1994 (0–1, v **Turkey**); **Scandinavian Championship** 1928; **Under-17 World Championship** – never qualified; **World Youth Cup** (under-20) – never qualified. *Record against British and Irish national teams* v England, played 14, won one, drawn four, lost nine; v **Scotland**, played 12, won four, drawn none, lost eight; v **Northern Ireland**, played seven, won four, drawn two, lost one; v **Wales**, played six, won three, drawn none, lost three; v **Republic of Ireland**, played 11, won three, drawn five, lost three. *History* Football became popular in mid to late 19th century, with a football association formed in 1889 – one of the oldest in the world; Denmark was one of the founder members of FIFA in 1904. The Danish national side achieved success in the early part of the 20th century, with two Olympic Games silver medals in 1908 and 1912. It persisted with a rule that barred players from the national squad if they were playing for clubs outside Denmark; the rule was dropped in 1976. Professionalism was not introduced in the domestic league until 1978; a factor which had led to the exodus of many of the country's leading players. Denmark created a professional premier division (Superliga) in 1991, originally with only eight clubs playing each other four times in each season. The league was increased to 12 clubs in 1995. Denmark's greatest achievement was to become European Champions in 1992. John Jensen and Kim Vilfort scored in the 2–0 victory over Germany, in Gothenburg, Sweden. Ironically, Denmark was invited to compete in the tournament only at the last minute: qualifiers Yugoslavia was barred from the competition owing to the civil war there. Denmark had finished as runners-up in Yugoslavia's group (one point behind). It won the 1995 Confederations Cup, with a victory over South American champions Argentina, Michael Laudrup and Rasmussen scoring the goals. *World Cup performance* (finals and qualifiers to end of 1998 tournament) played 77, won 34, drawn 13, lost 30, scored 127 goals, conceded 110 goals. Win rate: 44%; goals scored per game: 1.65. *European Championship winning team and scorers* 1992 Schmeichel (goalkeeper), Sivebaek (Christiansen), K Nielsen, L Olsen, Piechnik, Christofte, J Jensen (1), Vilfort (1), H Larsen, Povlsen, B Laudrup. *League system* Twelve clubs compete in the national Superliga, with each club playing each other three times. Three points are awarded for a victory, with one for a draw: final positions for clubs level on points are determined by **goal difference**. The bottom two clubs at the end of each season are relegated to the national first division. The first division has 16 clubs, the bottom four of which are automatically relegated to the two regional second divisions (east and west regions). Beneath the third division are provincial leagues. *Record in international club tournaments* **European Cup** – **ÅGF Åarhus** (quarter-final 1961; **European Cup-winners Cup** – **Randers Freja** (quarter-final 1969), **Vejle BK** (quarter-final 1978), ÅGF Åarhus (quarter-final 1989); **UEFA Cup** – **Brøndby IF** semi-final 1991. Other leading club: **Akedemisk Boldklub København, FC Copenhagen** (FC København), **OB Odense**.

Denmark, women *country/women* women's football in Denmark is administered by the Danish Football Association in Brøndby. *Dossier* First official international match: 1974 v **Sweden** (Denmark had taken part in non-UEFA international tournaments as early as 1969). *International tournament record* **Olympic Games** (women) – played in the first tournament in 1996 (first round, Atlanta, USA); **Women's World Cup** – entered first tournament in 1991, quarter-final 1991, 1995; **Algarve Cup** – runners-up 1998 (1–4, v Norway); **European Championship for Women** – entered first tournament in 1984, semi-final/third 1991 (2–1, v **Italy**, in Denmark, third/fourth playoff), 1993 (3–1 v **Germany**, in Italy, third/fourth playoff), semi-final 1984 (1–3 agg., v **England**), quarter-final 1995. *History* Compared with other European nations, Denmark took an early lead in the development of women's football, at club and national level. The first national championship took place in 1969, as a playoff between the winners of the East and West divisions (won by Femina). In 1972, the Danish FA set up a women's committee, and a true national league was established the following year (first won by Ribe Boldklub). Denmark was runner-up in the **Federation of Independent European Female Football** (FIEFF) European tournament in Italy in 1969 (1–3, v Italy, in Turin). It also won the FIEFF unofficial world competitions in 1970 (2–0, v Italy, in Italy) and 1971 (2–0, v **Mexico**). Denmark competed in the first Olympic Games women's football tournament in 1996, in Atlanta, USA. It has around 40,000 registered players, at youth and senior level. *League system* Ten clubs compete in the national Super League. There are 10 clubs in the national First Division, and 20 clubs divided into two east and west Second Divisions. Leading clubs: B1909, Fortuna Hjorring, Hjortshoj-Ega IF.

Dens Park *ground* Scottish football ground situated in Dundee, Tayside; home of **Dundee**. *Dossier* Ground capacity: 14,177. Pitch dimensions: 100.5m x 66m. Record attendance: 43,024 v **Rangers** (1953, **Scottish FA Cup**). *History* Dundee first played at Dens Park on 19 August 1899 (v **St Bernards**), having previously played at several grounds, including Craigie Park and Carolina Port. Dundee bought the ground for £5,000 in 1919 and Archibald **Leitch** presided over its £60,000 development. The redeveloped Dens Park opened on 17 September 1921. In 1990, the local authority proposed that Dundee and **Dundee United** should share a council-developed new stadium at Caird Park. Both clubs declined the offer. Dundee was bought for £600,000 by

Canadian businessman Ron Dixon, who, in 1992, planned a £8.5 million stand at Dens Park which would incorporate a home for the town's ice hockey club, Tayside Tigers. But his plans floundered and, in 1994, redevelopment of Dens Park began, which included the introduction of greyhound racing. The first floodlit match at Dens Park took place in March 1960 (v **Liverpool**, friendly). Dens Park has staged three full **Scotland** internationals (12 March 1904, v **Wales**; 7 March 1908, v Wales; 2 December 1936,v Wales).

Denver Sundowns *club* Swaziland national league club based in the capital Mbabane. Ground: Somholo, capacity: 15,000. Strip: white shirts, blue shorts. Swaziland Cup 1991, 1992; Swaziland league champions 1989, 1990, runners-up 1996.

Deportes Tolima (Corporacion Club) *club* Colombian national league club based in Ibague, founded 1955. Ground Estadio Manuel Murillo Toro, capacity: 15,000. Strip: yellow shirts with a maroon and white striped upper section, maroon shorts. **Copa CONMEBOL** quarter-final 1997; **Copa Libertadores** second-round group stage 1982.

Deportivo Aguila (Club Deportivo) *club* El Salvador national league club based in San Miguel, founded 1926 (though a football section was only formed in 1958 by merging with CD Alacranes). Ground: Estadio Juan Francisco "Cariota" Barraza. Strip: orange shirts, black shorts. **CONCACAF Champions Cup** 1976 (walkover in final against **Robin Hood** of Surinam); El Salvador league champions 1960, 1961, 1964, 1965, 1968, 1972, 1975, 1976, 1983, 1987.

Deportivo Cali *club* Colombian national league club based in Cali, founded 1943 (from the former club Cali Futebol Club, founded 1908). Ground Estadio Pascual Guerrero, capacity: 45,750 (shared with **América de Cali**). Strip: green shirts, white shorts. Colombian league champions 1965, 1967, 1969, 1970, 1974, 1995, 1996, 1998; **Copa Libertadores** runners-up 1978 (0–0, 0–4, v **Boca Juniors**); **Copa Merconorte** runners-up 1998 (1–4 agg., v **Atlético Nacional Medellin**).

Deportivo Central FAR *club* Cuba national league club based in the capital Havana. Strip: blue and black striped shirts, black shorts.

Deportivo Independiente Medellin *club* see **Independiente Medellin**

Deportivo Italia *club* Venezuelan national league club based in the capital Caracas, founded 1952. Ground: Estadio Nacional Brigido Iriarte, capacity: 15,000. Strip: blue shirts, white shorts. **Copa Venezuela** 1961, 1962, 1970; Venezuelan league champions (**Torneo Clausura**) 1961, 1963, 1966, 1972.

Deportivo Mongomeyen *club* Equatorial Guinea national league club, based in Mongomo. Ground: La Libertad, capacity: 12,000. League champions 1980, 1997.

Deportivo Municipal *club* Peruvian national league club based in the capital Lima, founded in 1935.

Ground: Estadio Municipal de Chorillos. Strip: white shirts with red sash, black shorts. Peru League champions 1938, 1940, 1943, 1950.

Deportivo Quito *club* Ecuador national Primera league club based in the capital Quito. Founded 1955. Ground: Estadio Olimpico Atahualpa, capacity: 46,000. Strip: red and blue striped shirts, blue or white shorts. Ecuador league champions 1964, 1968.

Deportivo Saprissa *club* Costa Rica national league club based in the capital Saprissa, founded 1935. Ground: Estadio Ricardo Saprissa Ayma, capacity: 34,000. Strip: maroon shirts, white shorts. *Keynotes* Deportivo holds the national league record of six consecutive championships (1972 to 1977). **CONCACAF Champions Cup** 1993 (four-club final league in Guatemala City), 1995 (league of four in San José, Costa Rica), semi-final/third 1998; Costa Rica champions 1952, 1953, 1957, 1962, 1964, 1965, 1967, 1968, 1969, 1972, 1973, 1974, 1975, 1976, 1977, 1982, 1988, 1989, 1994, 1995, 1998; **Torneo Grandes de Centroamerica** runners-up 1997 (0–1, v **Alianza** of El Salvador), finalist 1998 (v **Municipal** of Guatemala.

Derby County *club* English league. *Dossier* Ground: **Pride Park**, Derby, capacity: 33,000 all seated. Strip: white shirts with black trim, black shorts, white socks with black trim. Website: www.dcfc.co.uk Nickname: Rams. Record attendance at (Pride Park): 32,913 v **Liverpool** (13 March 1999, **Premier League**). Record at the club's former **Baseball Ground** 41,286 v **Tottenham Hotspur**, Division One, 20 September 1969. Best average attendance: 35,924 (Baseball Ground, 1969-70). Biggest win: 12–0 v **Finn Harps** (15 September 1976, **UEFA Cup**, first round 1st leg). Biggest defeat: 2–11 v **Everton** (18 January 1890, **FA Cup**, first round). *History* Formed in 1884 by members of the Derbyshire County Cricket Club. Initially Derby sported the amber, chocolate and pale blue colours of their founders and played at the cricket club's ground, which was part of the town's racecourse. Derby moved to the Baseball Ground in 1895 because the club was angry at having to reschedule matches that clashed with race meetings. The club was a founder member of the **Football League**. Between 1896 and 1909 the club reached three FA Cup finals (1898 v **Nottingham Forest**, 1899 v **Sheffield United**, 1903 v **Bury**) and eight semi-finals (1896, 1897, 1898, 1899, 1902, 1903, 1904, 1909). However, Derby had to wait until the first post-**World War II** final before it won the Cup, a victory that secured the club's first major trophy. The successful 1946 Cup final team included the forward pairing of Raich **Carter** and Peter **Doherty**. During World War II, the club was suspended for making **illegal payments** to players. In 1955, Derby was relegated to Division Three (North) and it was not until 1969 that the club was again playing in the top flight. This was the beginning of a golden period for the club. Derby's return to Division One was achieved under the managership of the ex-**Middlesbrough** and **England** player Brian **Clough,** and his assistant Peter Taylor. The managerial duo

signed, among others, Roy McFarland, Dave **Mackay**, Colin Todd and Archie Gemmill. The club finally won the League Championship in 1971-72, the players learning of their triumph only while on holiday in Majorca following the failure of both **Leeds United** and **Liverpool** to win their final fixtures. The following season Derby reached the semi-final of the **European Cup** (1–3 agg. v **Juventus**). Three years later, this time with Mackay as manager, the club won its second Championship. The second title-winning side included Kevin Hector, Francis Lee, David Nish and Bruce Rioch. In 1980, Derby was relegated and four years later, in its centenary year, the club was back playing in Division Three. At the time, Derby was also suffering severe financial difficulties, with a big debt and the Baseball Ground's deeds being held by the club's bankers, that led to a **winding-up** petition from the Inland Revenue. In 1984, the club was bought by the publisher Robert Maxwell. Despite returning to Division One in 1987, and building a team containing internationals Dean Saunders, Peter **Shilton** and Mark Wright, the club was relegated four years later. At the start of the 1997-98 season, Derby's second in the Premier League, the club moved to a new stadium, Pride Park. *League record* Premier League 1996-97–; Division One (including Football League) 1888-89 to 1906-07, 1912-13 to 1913-14, 1919-20 to 1920-21, 1926-27 to 1952-53, 1969-70 to 1979-80, 1987-88 to 1990-91; First Division 1992-93 to 1995-96; Division Two 1907-08 to 1911-12, 1914-15, 1921-22 to 1925-26, 1953-54 to 1954-55, 1957-58 to 1968-69, 1980-81 to 1983-84, 1986-87, 1991-92; Division Three 1984-85 to 1985-86; Division Three (North) 1955-56 to 1956-57. *Honours* League 1971-72, 1974-75; Division Two 1911-12, 1914-15, 1968-69, 1986-87; Division Three (North) 1956-57; FA Cup 1946 (4–1 a.e.t. v **Charlton Athletic** – *Team* Woodley (goalkeeper), Nicholas, Howe, Bullions, Leuty, Musson, Harrison, Carter, Stamps (2), Doherty (1), Duncan); **FA Charity Shield** 1975 (2–0 v **West Ham United**); **Watney Cup** 1970 (4–1 v Manchester United); **Texaco Cup** 1972 (2–1 agg., v **Airdrieonians**). *Records* Peter Shilton is Derby's most capped player (34 (125) for **England**); Kevin Hector holds the record for club appearances (486, 1966-78, 1980-82); Steve **Bloomer** is Derby's record league goalscorer (292, 1892-06, 1910-14).

derby *n.* match between two clubs in close proximity (town, county, region). The word derby is thought to derive from the annual Shrovetide football matches played between the parishes of St Peter's and All Saints, in Derby, England. Hundreds of people were involved in the rudimentary game, which was last played in 1846 (see **football** *history*). *Keynotes* In England, there are three main derby meetings: **Everton** v **Liverpool** (the Merseyside derby); **Manchester City** v **Manchester United**; and **Arsenal** v **Tottenham Hotspur** (the North-London derby). Brian Kidd, Paul Stewart and Paul Walsh are the only players to have played in the Manchester, Liverpool and North London derbies. The North-east derby between **Newcastle United** and

Sunderland and the Bristol derby between **Bristol City** and **Rovers** also are considered significant fixtures which attract great rivalry. Other derbies include: **Port Vale** v **Stoke City** (Potteries derby); **Cardiff City** v **Swansea City** (South Wales derby); **Nottingham Forest** v **Notts County** (Nottingham derby); and **Sheffield United** v **Sheffield Wednesday**. In Scotland, the so-called Old Firm derby between **Celtic** and **Rangers** is one of the most passionate of derby encounters, which is fuelled by the historical and religious foundations of each club. The term "Old Firm" was given to the Glasgow duo to reflect their dominance of Scottish football. Elsewhere in Scotland, the 200th Deesside derby between **Dundee** and **Dundee United** took place at **Dens Park** on 19 September 1998 (2–2). Derby matches in other parts of the world are also passionate affairs. The derby games between **AC Milan** and **Internazionale** reflect an intense rivalry, which began on 9 March 1908 when several disaffected members of the Milan Cricket and Football Club (AC) established Inter. Moreover, Internazionale's fan base is mainly drawn from the higher social classes, whereas AC Milan supporters typically come from Milan's working class. **Galatasaray** v **Fenerbahçe**, the Istanbul derby, is always a highly charged affair because of the great rivalry between the two clubs, which – along with a third Istanbul side **Besiktas** – have dominated Turkish football. When Galatasaray beat its rivals in the 1996 Turkish Cup final, manager Graeme **Souness** became a hero and villainafter planting his club's flag in the centre circle, provoking a riot among spectators. In Argentina, the big derby is the game between **Boca Juniors**, which attracts a largely working class following from the docks area, and **River Plate**, the self-styled millionaires of Argentine football. The Tehran derby between **Piroozi** (Persepolis) and **Estghal Sports Club** is the biggest football match in **Iran** and regularly attract capacity crowds of 100,000 at the Azadi Stadium. The Asuncion derby in Paraguay between **Olimpia** and Club **Guarani** dates from 1903 and is known as the Viejo Clasico.

Derry City *club* Republic of Ireland national league, and former Northern Ireland league club based in Derry (also known as Londonderry). Geographically in Northern Ireland though plays in the Republic of Ireland league. Founded 1892 (as Derry Celtic). Ground: Brandywell Park, capacity: 11,000. Strip: red and white striped shirts, black shorts. *History* Derry City has a largely Catholic support base; it withdrew from the Northern Ireland league in 1972, owing to continued political troubles in the province, and has since played its competitive football in the Republic of Ireland. **Irish FA Cup** (all-Ireland) runners-up 1904; Irish FA Cup (Northern Ireland) 1949, 1954, 1964, runners-up 1936, 1957, 1971; Northern Ireland league champions 1965, runners-up 1932, 1935, 1936, 1937, 1938, 1966, 1969; Republic of Ireland **FAI Cup** 1989, 1995, runners-up 1988, 1994, 1997; Republic of Ireland league champions; 1989, 1997, runners-up 1990, 1992.

Desailly, Marcel *player* Defender/midfield. **France** international (54 caps, two goals, 1993-). Born 7 September 1968. *Clubs* **Nantes**, **Olympique de Marseille**, **AC Milan**, **Chelsea**. *Keynotes* Desailly made his international debut on 22 August 1993 (1–1, v **Sweden**, in Stockholm, World Cup qualifier). He was the first player to win the European Cup with different clubs in consecutive seasons. He was transferred to Chelsea for £4.6 million in June 1998, just before his World Cup triumph with France. He was chosen for **FIFA**'s 22-man all-star squad of the 1998 World Cup finals. Desailly launched his own range of clothing in 1998. *Honours* **World Cup** (France 1998); **European Cup** (Olympique de Marseille, 1993, AC Milan 1994); **European Super Cup** (AC Milan, 1994, Chelsea 1998); French championship (Nantes, 1992); Italian **Serie A** championship (AC Milan, 1994, 1995, 1996).

designated seating area *rules* part of the **technical area** where coaching staff, physiotherapists or medical staff and the **substitutes** must sit during the match. Informally known as the **bench**.

designated stadiums *misc.* selected stadiums which meet specific criteria in terms of capacity, access, safety etc. The finals of European club competitions are awarded only to stadiums which are rated by **UEFA** as either five-star or four-star grounds. Only five-star stadiums can host the **European Cup** (Champions League) final, whereas four-star grounds are eligible to stage **European Cup-winners Cup** or **UEFA Cup** finals. On UEFA's 1998 list of five-star stadiums were (UEFA capacities): **Nou Camp** (Barcelona, 92,000); **San Siro** (Milan, 85,700); **Luzhniki** (Moscow, 84,745); **Olimpico** (Rome, 82,307); **Wembley** (77,800); **Delle Alpi** (Turin, 69,041); **Olympiastadion** (Munich, 63,573); **Old Trafford** (53,810); **Feyenoord** (52,000); **Amsterdam ArenA** (51,620); **Ibrox** (50,500); **Ernst-Happel Stadion** (Vienna, 50,000). Its four-star stadiums were: Louis Spiros (Athens, 74,084); San Nicola (Bari, 58,000); **Roi Baudouin** (Brussels, 50,000); **Parc des Princes** (Paris, 48,700); **Gottlieb-Daimler** (Stuttgart, 46,886); Parken (Copenhagen, 41,752); **Anfield** (41,000); **Villa Park** (39,339); **Råsunda Stadion** (Stockholm, 37,285); Anoeta (San Sebastian, 30,000). The **Football Association** has a list of designated "category A" stadiums which could stage fixtures as part of **England**'s formal bid to stage the 2006 **World Cup**. The list (and projected capacities) was: Villa Park (51,000); **Ewood Park** (40,000); **Stamford Bridge** (42,000); **Highfield Road** (40,000); **Pride Park** (40,000); **Goodison Park** (40,100); **Elland Road** (45,000); Leicester (40,000 – new stadium); Anfield (45,369); Old Trafford (67,5000); Manchester (50,000 – new stadium); **Riverside Stadium**, Middlesbrough (42,000); **St James' Park** (51,000); **Hillsborough** (40,000); **Stadium of Light** (64,000); Wembley (80,000).

Desportes Costa do Sol *club* Mozambique national league club based in the capital Maputo. Ground capacity: 20,000. Strip: yellow shirts and green shorts. **African Cup of Champion Clubs** second round 1993 and 1994, **African Cup-winners Cup** quarter-final 1996, 1997; Mozambique Cup 1980, 1984, 1988, 1992, 1995, 1997; Mozambique League champions 1979, 1980, 1991, 1992, 1993, 1994, 1998.

Desportivo Guadeloupe *club* Sao Tomé and Principe national league club based in Guadeloupe. Ground: Guadeloupe, capacity: 3,000. Strip: yellow shirts, blue shorts. Sao Tomé and Principe Cup 1981; Sao Tomé and Principe league champions 1980, 1981.

Deva Stadium *ground* English football ground situated in Cheshire; home of **Chester City**. *Dossier* Ground capacity: 6,000. Pitch dimensions: 105m x 68.5m. Record attendance: 5,638 v **Preston North End** (2 April 1994, Third Division). *Keynotes* Chester played its first match at the new Deva Stadium on 25 August 1992 (v **Stockport County**, **League Cup**). "Deva" is the Latin name for Chester. Although situated within the town's boundaries, most of the ground lies over the Welsh border. Built at a cost of £3 million, the club was granted a 125-year lease by the local council at an annual rent of £20,000.

Devonshire Colts *club* Bermuda Cup 1999. Bermuda national league champions 1997.

Deyna, Kazimierz *player* Midfield. **Poland** international (83 caps, 33 goals, excluding **Olympic Games**). Born 23 October 1947. Career ca. 1969–1978. *Clubs* Starogard, Sportowy Lodz, **Legia Warsaw**, **Manchester City**, San Diego (USA). *Keynotes* Poland's second-most capped player, and joint-second highest goalscorer. Deyna appeared in two Olympic Games finals, and scored both Poland's goals in the 2–1 defeat of Hungary in 1972. Top scorer in the 1972 Olympic Games football finals tournament (nine goals). He was voted third in the *France Football* **European Footballer of the Year** 1974. *Honours* Olympic Games gold medal (Poland, 1972), silver medal (Poland 1976); **World Cup** third place (Poland, 1974); Polish league championship (Legia Warsaw, 1969, 1970).

DFB Pokal *competition* annual German knockout competition first founded in 1935 under the auspices of the German football association (Deutscher Fussball-Bund). All ties are one-off matches and the first round is seeded so that clubs from the same division cannot meet and to ensure that smaller clubs, which are also given home advantage, can potentially play one of the bigger sides. The first rounds of the competition are finished by November each year, with the semi-finals played in the following April and the final staged at the Olympic Stadio in Berlin each June. *History* First staged in 1935, the Pokal was suspended after 1943. The division of Germany after **World War II** led to the establishment of a separate cup competition in the East (from 1949). The Pokal resumed in the West in 1953. A harmonised competition was founded in 1992 following the unification of the country. Between 1938 and 1944 (during **Austria's** incorporation into Hitler's Third Reich), Austrian clubs competed for the Pokal and, in 1938, **Rapid Vienna** won the trophy. *Records* (Up to and including 1998)

Bayern Munich has won the Pokal a record nine times, although it was not until 1957 that the club won its first cup. **Cologne** (1.FC) and **Eintracht Frankfurt** have each won the trophy on four occasions. The first final to be settled on penalties was the 1984 encounter, between Bayern Munich and **Borussia Mönchengladbach**. *Final results* 1934-35, **Nuremberg** (1.FC) 2–0 FC Schalke 04; 1935-36, VfB Leipzig 2–1 FC Schalke 04; 1936-37, FC Schalke 04 2–1 Fortuna Düsseldorf; 1937-38, Rapid Vienna 3–1 FSV; 1938-39, Nuremberg (1.FC) 2–0 SV Waldhof Mannheim Frankfurt; 1939-40, Dresdner SC 2–1 1. FC Nuremburg (1.FC); 1939-49, Dresdner SC 2–1 FC Schalke 04; 1940-41, 1860 Munich 2–0 FC Schalke 04; 1941-42, First Vienna 3–2 **Hamburg** (SV); 1952-53, Rot-Weiss Essen 2–1 Alemannia Aachen; 1953-54, **Stuttgart** (VfB) 1–0 Cologne (1.FC); 1955-56, Karlsruher 3–2 FC Schalke 04; 1955-56, Karlsruher 3–1 Hamburg SV; 1956-57, Bayern Munich 1–0 Fortuna Düsseldorf; 1957-58, Stuttgart (VfB) 4–3 Fortuna Düsseldorf; 1958-59, Schwarz-Weiss Essen 5–2 Borussia Neunkirchen; 1959-60, Borussia Mönchengladbach 3–2 Karlsruher SC; 1960-61, **Werder Bremen** 2–0 Kaiserslautern (1.FC); 1961-62, Nuremberg (1.FC) 2–1 Fortuna Düsseldorf; 1962-63, Hamburg (SV) 3–0 **Borussia Dortmund**; 1963-64, 1860 Munich 2–0 Eintracht Frankfurt; 1964-65, Borussia Dortmund 2–0 Alemannia Aachen; 1965-66, Bayern Munich 4–2 Meidericher SV; 1966-67, Bayern Munich 4–0 Hamburg (SV); 1967-68, Cologne (1.FC) 4–1 VfL Bochum; 1968-69, Bayern Munich 2–1 FC Schalke 04; 1969-70, Kickers Offenbach 2–1 Cologne (1.FC); 1970-71, Bayern Munich 2–1 Cologne (1.FC); 1971-72, FC Schalke 04 5–0 Kaiserslautern (1.FC); 1972-73, Borussia Mönchengladbach 2–1 Cologne (1.FC); 1973-74, Eintracht Frankfurt 3–1 Hamburg (SV); 1974-75, Eintracht Frankfurt 1–0 MSV Duisburg; 1975-76, Hamburg (SV) 2–0 Kaiserslautern (1.FC); 1975-76, Cologne (1.FC) 1–0 Hertha BSC Berlin (replay); 1977-78, Cologne (1.FC) 2–0 Fortuna Düsseldorf; 1978-79, Fortuna Düsseldorf 1–0 Hertha BSC Berlin; 1979-80, Fortuna Düsseldorf 2–1 Cologne (1.FC); 1980-81, Eintracht Frankfurt 2–1 Kaiserslautern (1.FC); 1981-82, Bayern Munich 4–2 Nuremberg (1.FC); 1982-83, Cologne (1.FC) 1–0 Fortuna Cologne; 1983-84, Bayern Munich 1–1 Borussia Mönchengladbach (7–6 pens.); 1984-85, Bayer Uerdingen 2–1 Bayern Munich; 1985-86, Bayern Munich 5–2 Stuttgart (VfB); 1986-87, Hamburg 3–1 Stuttgart Kickers; 1987-88, Eintracht Frankfurt 1–0 VfL Bochum; 1988-89, Borussia Dortmund 4–1 Werder Bremen; 1989-90, Kaiserslautern (1.FC) 3–2 Werder Bremen; 1990-91, Werder Bremen 1–1 Cologne (1.FC) (4–3 pens.); 1991-92, Hannover 96 0–0 Borussia Mönchengladbach (4–3 pens.); 1992-93, Bayer Leverkusen 1–0 Hertha BSC Berlin Amat.; 1993-94, Werder Bremen 3–1 Rot-Weiss Essen; 1994-95, Borussia Mönchengladbach 3–0 VfL Wolfsburg; 1995-96, Kaiserslautern (1.FC) 1–0 Karlsruher; 1996-97, Stuttgart (VfB) 2–0 Energie Cottbus; 1997-98, Bayern Munich 2–1 MSV Duisburg.

Dhiab, Tarak *player* **Tunisia** international. *Clubs* **Espérance**, **Al Ahly** (of Saudi Arabia). *France Football* **African Footballer of the Year** 1977.

Di Matteo, Roberto *player* Midfielder. **Italy** (34 caps, 12 goals). Born 29 May 1970. *Clubs* Schaffausen, FC **Zurich**, FC Arau, **Lazio**, **Chelsea**. *Keynotes* Signed for Chelsea in summer 1996 for £4.9 million. Scorer of the fastest-ever FA Cup final goal at **Wembley**, after 43 seconds against **Middlesbrough** in 1997. *Honours* **FA Cup** (Chelsea 1997), **League Cup** (Chelsea, 1998), **European Cup-winners Cup** (Chelsea, 1998); **European Super Cup** (Chelsea, 1998).

Di Stefano, Alfredo *player* Striker. **Argentina** (8 caps, 6 goals, 1947) and **Spain** international (31 caps, 23 goals, 1957-61). Born 4 July 1926 in Barracas, Buenos Aires. Career ca. 1943–1965. *Clubs* Los Cardales (youth team); **River Plate** (twice), **Hurácan** (loan), **Club Deportivo Los Millonarios**, **Real Madrid**, Español. *Keynotes* Di Stefano is widely regarded as one of the greatest players of all time. Although technically a centre forward for most of his career, Di Stefano's brilliance was attributed to the way he dictated the pattern of the game, collecting and distributing the ball from his own defence and running into key positions and, crucially, his excellent finishing. He made his senior club debut, as an outside-right, for River Plate (his father's club) in 1943, aged 17 years. After a loan period with Hurácan, he returned to River Plate in 1946 and, as centre forward, was Argentinean league top scorer in 1947 (25 goals, with River Plate). During his spell in Colombia with Millonarios, Di Stefano was the league top goalscorer in 1951 and 1952 (31 and 20 goals, respectively). Di Stefano was the second player to score a **hat-trick** in a European Cup final (1960, Real Madrid 7–3 Eintracht Frankfurt; completing his hat-trick just 15 minutes after his team-mate Ferenc **Puskás** had completed the first). Di Stefano won five consecutive European Cup winner's medals, and scored in all five finals (1956, 1957, 1958, 1959 and 1960 (three goals). He scored 428 goals in 510 games for Real Madrid, including 49 in the European Cup, which is the record for the competition. He was top scorer in the 1958 edition with 10 goals, and joint top in 1962 with seven, although this time he was on the losing side in the final (3–5, v Benfica). Di Stefano was twice voted **European Footballer of the Year**, and was runner-up to Stanley **Matthews** in the first award in 1956. He was able to play for both his native Argentina and his adopted Spain because of the more flexible rules on nationality in place at the time. In 1947, he helped Argentina to victory in the Copa America, and scored a hat-trick in the 6–0 defeat of Colombia; all six of Di Stefano's goals for Argentina were scored in the 1947 Copa. He scored 23 goals in only 31 appearances for his adopted country; making him Spain's second-highest goalscorer of all time. He scored three goals in the two first-round games of the 1960 **European Championship** against Poland (4–2, 3–0); but any further opportunity was quashed when Spain withdrew

from the quarter-final, refusing to travel to the away leg against the **Soviet Union**. Di Stefano did not play for Spain in the 1962 **World Cup** finals in Chile due to injury. He later became manager of Boca Juniors, Valencia – where he won the Spanish League championship in 1971 – and Real Madrid (twice). *Honours* **Copa America** (Argentina 1947); **European Cup** (Real Madrid 1956, 1957, 1958, 1959, 1960), **World Club Cup** (Real Madrid 1960); Argentinean league championship (River Plate, 1947); Colombian league championship (Millonarios 1951, 1952); Spanish League championship (Real Madrid 1954, 1955, 1957, 1958, 1961, 1962, 1963, 1964; as a manager, 1971 with Valencia); Spanish Cup (Real Madrid 1962); *France Football* European Footballer of the Year 1957, 1959, runner-up 1956.

Diables Noirs *club* Congo league club based in the capital Brazzaville, founded 1940. Ground: A M Deba, capacity: 50,000. Strip: yellow shirts, black shorts. Cup 1989, 1990; Congo league champions 1965, 1976, 1991; Congo.

diagonal ball *n.* forward ball played from one side of the pitch to the other.

diagonal system of control *refereeing* common and recommended strategy adopted by **referee** and **assistant referees** to control a **match** and effectively implement the **Laws of the game**. The system is based around imaginary diagonals. According to where the ball is in play, the referee will take up a position running from the near-top left to the near-bottom right of the **field of play** (looking up field from one **goal line** to the other), thus keeping a close watch on the game while minimising the amount of running required. Assistant referees will stand just outside the opposite **touchlines** and will, generally, stay in the opposing halves. When the referee is in his/her half, the assistant referee will be on the opposite side of the field of play and will run along the touchline keeping up with the most forward attacking player. The assistant referee's diagonal thus runs almost at right-angles to the referee's diagonal, with this official taking up a position where his/her diagonal crosses the touchline. Exceptions to this general guidance occurs at **corner kicks**, where the nearest assistant referee should take up a position just behind the goal line near to the corner flag, and **penalty kicks**, where the assistant will usually stand behind the goal line, observing the goalkeeper (to see if he/she moves before the kick is taken) and the ball (to judge if it crosses the line).

Diamant Yaoundé *club* Cameroon national league club based in the capital Yaoundé. Ground: Ahmadou Ahidjo (national stadium), capacity: 60,000. Strip: white shirts, blue shorts. **African Cup-winners Cup** semi-final 1988; Cameroon Cup 1964, 1971, 1972; Cameroon league champions 1966.

Diamond Stars *club* Sierra Leone national league club based in Kono. Ground: Koidu Field, capacity: 15,000. Strip: green shirts, white shorts. **CAF Cup** – quarter-final 1994; Sierra Leone Cup 1992.

diamond system *tactics* system of play/formation. A system in which the formation of the midfield players is in the shape of a diamond. One player operates at the tip in a half-midfielder, half-striker role; two players play behind in wider positions, pushing forward when in possession and tracking back when the opposition has the ball; and at the base of the diamond is the anchor midfielder who sits in front of the defence, linking defensive and attacking play and preventing opponents from exploiting the space between the **back four**.

Dick, Kerr's Ladies *club* formerly England's most successful women's club, founded during **World War I** by women from W B Dick and John Kerr's engineering firm in Preston, Lancashire. *Dossier* Founded 1917, disbanded 1964. Strip: white shirts, black shorts, black and white hooped socks. Club record: played 828, won 758, drawn 46, lost 24. Top scorer: Lily Parr (believed to have scored more than 1,000 goals). *History* Dick and Kerr's was a tramway and railway equipment works which, during World War I, was manufacturing munitions and, in common with many firms in the UK, had taken on large numbers of women to replace male employees who had joined the British armed forces. Grace Sibbert is credited with organising the team's first match. Alfred **Frankland**, a draughtsman at the firm, was the team's trainer (he remained as club manager until his death in 1957). Fixtures were arranged between women's teams from other firms, with the money raised going to help war victims and their families. Ten thousand spectators watched a match at **Preston North End**'s **Deepdale** ground on 25 December 1917, against the Arundel Coulthard Foundry women's team, also from Preston: the fixture raised £600 for charity. Fixtures were regularly played at Deepdale until 1920, when the club moved to its own ground, Ashton Park, owned by the factory. Dick, Kerr's Ladies played its first international club match against a French representative side on 30 April 1920, winning 2–0 in front of 25,000 spectators at Deepdale. It was one of a series of five matches against the French, including one at **Stamford Bridge**, London, and one in Paris watched by 22,000 spectators. A match at **Anfield** Stadium, Liverpool, against a rest-of-Britain representative side in 1921 was watched by 25,000 people (Dick, Kerr's won 9–1). The club also played in front of the biggest ever attendance for a women's match in England: 53,000, 26 December 1920, v St Helen's Ladies (4–0, at **Goodison Park**). The **Football Association's** ban on women teams from playing at Football League grounds in December 1921 (see **women's football**) hastened the demise of the club's most successful period – at least with regard to attendances and fund-raising. It enjoyed another successful spell after **World War II**, dominating women's football in the post-war years. The club eventually folded in 1964. (A more detailed history of the club is given in *Women on the ball*, by Sue **Lopez** published by Scarlet Press, London.)

Dickinson, Jim *player-manager* Left-half. **England** international (48 caps). Born 6 October 1919. Career ca.

1935–1957. *Clubs* **Portsmouth**. Also, Portsmouth manager (1977-79). *Keynotes* Joined Portsmouth as a amateur in 1943, turning professional in January 1944. He made 764 **Football League** appearances for Portsmouth before retiring in April 1965 – still a club record and, at the time, a League record. Dickinson played in both the 1950 and 1954 **World Cup** finals for England. His only international goal was in his own net against **Belgium** during the 1954 World Cup finals in **Switzerland** (group 4, 17 June). Included in the **Football League Centenary 100 players**. *Honours* League Championship (Portsmouth 1948-49, 1949-50); Division Three (Portsmouth 1961-62).

Didi *player* real name Waldir Pereira. Midfield. **Brazil** international (85 caps, 31 goals). Born 8 October 1928. Career ca. 1952–1962. *Clubs* Rio Branco, Lencoes, Madureiro, **Fluminense**, **Botafogo** (twice), **Real Madrid**, **Valencia**, **Sporting Cristal**. *Keynotes* As well as winning **World Cup** medals in 1958 and 1962, Didi also played in the 1954 finals in Switzerland, scoring twice. He scored in Brazil's 5-2 defeat of France in the 1958 World Cup semi-final (at **Råsunda**, Stockholm); a match in which team-mate **Pelé** scored a **hat-trick**. He later became coach of the **Peru** national team. Noted as a free-kick specialist. *Honours* World Cup (Brazil, 1958, 1962); **Copa America** runner-up (Brazil, 1953, 1957, 1959).

dig *vb. informal* a shot, generally used to describe a speculative shot rather than a clear goalscoring opportunity.

Dinamo Batumi *club* Georgian national league club based in Batumi, founded 1923. Ground: Dinamo, capacity: 25,000. Georgian Cup 1998, runners-up 1993, 1995, 1996, 1997.

Dinamo Bishkek *club* Kyrgyzstan national league club based in the capital Bishkek, founded 1934. Ground: Spartak, capacity: 25,000 (the national stadium). Kyrghizian Cup runners-up 1995; Kyrgyzstan league champions 1997.

Dinamo Bucharest *club* Romanian national league club based in the capital Bucharest, founded in 1948 as a merger of two former clubs. Dinamo was originally a police club. Ground: Dinamo, capacity: 18,000. Strip: red shirts, red shorts. **European Cup** semi-final 1984 (1–3 agg., v **Liverpool**); **European Cup-winners Cup** – semi-final 1990, quarter-final 1989); Romanian Cup 1959, 1964, 1968, 1982, 1984, 1986, 1990; Romanian League champions 1941 (as Unirea Tricolor), 1955, 1962, 1963, 1964, 1965, 1971, 1973, 1975, 1977, 1982, 1983, 1984, 1990, 1992. Notable former players: Dudu Georgescu, Florin Raducioiu.

Dinamo Dushanbe *club* Tajikistan national league club based in the capital Dushanbe. Ground: Dinamo Stadium, capacity: 5,000. **Asian Champion Teams Cup** second qualifying round 1997; Tajikistan league champions 1996.

Dinamo Kiev *club* Ukraine national league and former-**Soviet Union** league club based in the capital Kiev, founded 1927. Ground: Central Republikanski

Stadium (national stadium), capacity: 100,000, or Dinamo Stadium, capacity: 18,000. Strip: white shirts, white shorts. *Keynotes* Dinamo was the most successful club in the former-Soviet Union with 13 league championships and nine cup wins. It was the first club from outside Moscow to win the Soviet league championship and, with **Dynamo Tbilisi**, was one of only two Soviet clubs to win a European club trophy. Since the independence of Ukraine, Dinamo has continued to dominate the domestic league and Cup. **European Cup** semi-final 1977, 1987, 1999; Champions League and quarter-final 1998; **European Cup-winners Cup** 1975 (3–0, v **Ferencvaros**, in Basle, Switzerland), 1986 (3–0, v **Atlético Madrid**, in Lyon, France); **European Supercup** 1975 (3–0, agg., v **Bayern Munich**); former-Soviet Union Cup 1954, 1964, 1966, 1974, 1978, 1982, 1985, 1987, 1990; former-Soviet Union league champions 1961, 1966, 1967, 1968, 1971, 1974, 1975, 1977, 1980, 1981, 1985, 1986, 1990; Ukraine cup 1993, 1998; Ukraine league champions 1993, 1994, 1995, 1996, 1997, 1998. Notable players: Oleg **Blokhin**, Oleg **Protasov**, Igor **Belanov**, Andriy Shevchenko.

Dinamo Minsk 1. *club* Belarus national league and former-Soviet Union league club based in the capital Minsk, founded 1927. Ground: Dinamo Stadium, capacity: 50,000. Strip: violet shirts with white sleeves, white shorts. Belarus Cup 1992, 1994; Belarus League champions 1992, 1993, 1994, 1995, autumn 1995 (a mini-season played as a stopgap when the Belarus league format changed to a new April-November season in 1996), 1997; **European Cup** – quarter final 1984; **European Cup-winners Cup** quarter final 1988; former-Soviet Union Cup runners-up 1965 and 1987; former-Soviet Union League Championship 1982, third place 1954 (as Spartak Minsk), 1963 and 1983; **UEFA Cup** quarter final 1985.   **2.** its sister club **Dinamo-93 Minsk** (the two clubs share the same address and president), founded 1993. Ground: also plays at Dinamo Stadium. Belarus Cup 1995.

Dinamo Moscow *club* Russian national league and former-Soviet Union league club, founded in 1923. Ground: Dinamo Stadium (ground share with **CSKA Moscow**), capacity: 52,000. Strip: blue shirts with thin white stripes, blue shorts. *History* Dinamo was the club of the electrical workers union in the Soviet era, but it grew out of a pre-Soviet club, Morozov, set up in 1887 by two Lancashire cotton mill owners in the late 19th century, and playing in the blue and white team colours of English club **Blackburn Rovers**. The mill club moved to Moscow (renamed Orekhovo Klub Sport) and was officially founded as Dinamo Moscow in 1923. **European Cup-winners Cup** runners-up 1972; Russian Cup 1995, runners-up 1997; Russian league runners-up 1994; Soviet Union Cup 1937, 1953, 1967, 1970, 1977, 1984; Soviet Union League champions 1936 (the first Soviet League championship), 1937, 1940, 1945, 1949, 1954, 1955, 1957, 1959, 1963, 1976. Notable former player: Lev **Yashin**.

direct *adj. rules* of a **direct free kick**, **penalty kick** or **corner kick,** where, according to the **Laws of the game** a goal can be scored directly from the kick into the goal without a second player (of either side) making contact with the ball. The term is used in the Laws only to describe a direct free kick.

direct free kick *rules* method of restarting a game after it has been stopped in order to punish a team for a **foul** or **handball** as specified in the **Laws of the game** (Law XII and XIII). A direct free kick can be struck directly into an opponent's goal and a goal is scored even if no other player touches the ball first (compare **indirect free kick**). The referee will signal that the free kick is direct by leaving his or her arms in a lowered position. A free kick is taken, by the non-offending side, from the point where the offence was committed unless it is awarded to a defending team in its own **goal area**, in which case it can be taken from anywhere within that goal area. All opposition players must be at least 9.15 metres (10 yards) from the ball when a free kick is taken, or outside the **penalty area** if the free kick is awarded inside the defending team's penalty area. See **free kick** for full details on rules on how the kick is taken. Offences resulting in direct free kicks include when a player is guilty of **tripping**, **jumping at**, **pushing** or **charging at an opponent** in a reckless or careless manner, or with excessive force; **holding an opponent**; **striking an opponent** or attempting to strike an opponent; **spitting at an opponent**; **kicking an opponent** or attempting to kick an opponent; or **deliberately** handling the ball (**handball**) – except for the **goalkeeper** who may handle the ball in his or her own penalty area (unless the ball has been passed by a team mate). See **penalty kick**.

director of football *n.* individual charged with overall management responsibility, but with little input into first-team affairs other than to arrange/negotiate transfers and wages. *Keynotes* Kenny **Dalglish** was appointed director of football at **Blackburn Rovers** in 1995-96, following the club's **Premier League** triumph, with Ray Harford taking sole charge of first-team affairs. Kevin **Keegan**'s initial role at Fulham was in a similar capacity, although his official job title was chief operating officer. He later replaced Ray Wilkins as club manager.

directors' box *regulations* a stadium enclosure or designated seating area, invariably in the best part of the stand, reserved for the directors of both clubs involved in a match and their guests. **Scottish Football League** clubs must provide the visiting club with 10 complimentary tickets for the directors' box (Scottish Football League rule 80). Directors' boxes are mandatory under the **ground criteria** of the **Football League**; they must have clearly marked home and away areas, with a minimum of 16 seats for visiting directors and 24 for the home club.

Diriangen FC *club* Nicaraguan national league club, based in the small town of Diriamba. Strip: black and white striped shirts and white shorts. *Keynotes* It is the country's most successful club in recent years and has represented Nicaragua in the **CONCACAF Champions Cup** more than any other club from the country. Nicaraguan champions 1996, 1997, 1999 (no previous records); Nicaraguan Cup 1997 (no previous records).

disabled facilities *regulations* facilities, including wheelchair spaces and commentary for the visually impaired, available to disabled supporters at football grounds. **Premier League** clubs must provide "sufficient and adequate" facilities for the disabled supporters (FA Premier League rule 21). *Keynotes* At the start of the 1998-99 season, Premier League grounds offered the following disabled facilities: **Arsenal** (92 wheelchair spaces; 56 seats for visually impaired; 30 headsets); **Aston Villa** (41 disabled spaces; 22 seats with commentary for visually impaired); **Blackburn Rovers** (280 wheelchair spaces); **Charlton Athletic** (52 wheelchair spaces); **Chelsea** (57 seats/spaces); **Coventry City** (54 wheelchair spaces); **Derby County** (200 wheelchair spaces; 40 seats for visually impaired; spaces for 100 mobile disabled and 20 deaf supporters); **Everton** (61 wheelchair spaces; 20 seats for visually impaired); **Leeds United** (101 wheelchair spaces, 26 seats for visually impaired, spaces for 180 mobile disabled); **Leicester City** (45 wheelchair spaces, also visually impaired facilities); **Liverpool** (84 wheelchair spaces); **Manchester United** (70 wheelchair spaces, 20 seats for visually impaired); **Middlesbrough** (70-seat disabled enclosure); **Newcastle United** (95 wheelchair spaces, 20 seats for visually impaired); **Nottingham Forest** (wheelchair spaces, seats for visually impaired); **Sheffield Wednesday** (135 wheelchair spaces, 66 spaces for mobile disabled); **Southampton** (23 wheelchair spaces, 33 spaces for deaf/visually impaired); **Tottenham Hotspur** (27 wheelchair spaces); **West Ham United** (102 wheelchair spaces, 18 seats for mobile disabled, six commentary seats for visually impaired); **Wimbledon** (58 wheelchair spaces, 18 seats for visually impaired with commentary headsets).

disability football *n.* see **learning disability**, **European Soccer Championships for Players with Learning Disabilities**, **World Football Championships for Players with Learning Disabilities**, **visually impaired football**.

disabled supporter *n.* person who, because of impaired physical or mental ability, requires special facilities to attend football matches. *Keynotes* In 1923, **Cappielow Park**, home to **Greenock Morton**, then called Morton, was the first UK football ground to provide blind spectators with match commentary. Facilities for disabled fans at football grounds have been the subject of a report by the **Football Task Force**. The **Taylor Report** recommended that the redevelopment of football stadiums should make the needs of disabled supporters "integral to planning", yet the Task Force report found that many new stands, including **Old Trafford**'s North Stand and **Anfield**'s Centenary Stand, failed to provide a single space for wheelchair users.

Aston Villa's **Villa Park** was found to have the worst ratio of wheelchair spaces to ground capacity (41 places out of a capacity of 39,339) and **Swansea City**'s **Vetch Field** had the worst record among **Football League** grounds, providing only six wheelchair spaces in a 11,155 capacity stadium. On a positive note, **Blackburn Rovers**, **Derby County** and **Northampton Town** were all praised for their attitude to disabled fans, with **Pride Park**, for example, designed in consultation with the disabled supporters' club. The report's main recommendations were that disabled fans are fully consulted about new ground developments; legislation should be brought in to ensure all new sports stadiums include a specified number of wheelchair spaces; minimum requirements for ambulant (non-wheelchair) disabled, blind and deaf supporters; incentives for clubs to upgrade their **disabled facilities**; and an annual audit of disabled facilities at grounds.

disaster *n.* accident or malicious incident that involves loss of life. *Keynotes* There have been a number of football related tragedies, one of the worst of which occurred in 1982, at **Luzhniki Stadium** in Moscow, Russia. A total of 340 spectators were crushed to death at **Spartak Moscow**'s **UEFA Cup** second round match against Dutch club Haarlem (a match that Spartak had won 2–0). The tragedy was kept quiet by the Soviet authorities for several years. A century of disasters at British football grounds – **Ibrox Park disasters** (26 deaths in 1902, and 66 deaths in 1971), **Burnden Park disaster** (33 deaths in 1946), **Bradford fire** (56 deaths in 1985) and **Hillsborough disaster** (95 deaths in 1989) – led to the loss of 276 lives. Adding a further 39 fatalities at the 1985 **Heysel Stadium disaster**, a total of 315 people were killed in six major disasters involving British teams in the 20th century. A large component of the tragedies can be attributed to poorly designed and/or ageing stadiums and inadequate crowd control, however, it took many years before the lessons were learned and effective action taken. The **Wheatley Report** into the 1971 Ibrox Park Disaster lead to the **Safety of Sports Ground Act 1975**, while the **Popplewell Inquiry** into the Bradford Fire resulted in the Fire Safety and Safety of Places of Sport Act 1987: both statutes lead to some ground-safety improvements. Far-reaching changes to stadium safety, however, were not implemented until after the most serious UK tragedy, the Hillsborough disaster, and the resulting **Taylor Report**. There have been a number of serious football disasters throughout the world, see **France** (*History*), **Fútbol war**, **Guatemala** (*History*), **Libya** (*History*), **Lima disaster**, **Mexico** (*History*), **Munich air crash**, **Nepal** (*History*), **Nigeria** (*History*), **Olympiakos**, **River Plate**, **South Africa** (*History*), **Superga aircrash**, **Turkey** (*History*), **Zamalek**, **Zambia** (*History*).

dislocated shoulder *medical* **dislocation** of the glenohumeral **joint** in which the ball of the humerus (upper arm bone) comes out of the cavity in the shoulder blade (the glenoid). The injury is characterised by severe pain with the arm tending to hang down if not supported. The shoulder appears clearly deformed if compared to the opposite side. First aid treatment should be to immobilise and support the arm; the player may require resetting of the joint under anaesthetic. The injury can occur if the arm is suddenly pulled outwards or from direct impact such as a shoulder charge or hitting the ground with the shoulder in a heavy fall.

dislocation *medical* abnormal displacement of the bones from their normal position in a **joint**. A **dislocated shoulder** can occur through a heavy fall. Footballers can also occasionally dislocate their elbows, an extremely painful condition that will normally require hospital treatment. *vb.* dislocate.

dismiss *vb.* rules another word for **send off**.

dismissal *n.* the act of being **sent off**.

dissent *rules* infringement of the **Laws of the game** where a player demonstrates – by word or deed – an unwillingness to accept the referee's decision (Law XII). The offending player will receive a **caution**.

dissolved club *regulations* club that has ceased to operate, for example due to financial insolvency. If this were to happen to a **Premier League** or **Football League** club during the season, then any fixtures already played by that club would be removed from the league record. There would be one fewer club relegated that season (FA Premier League rule B.29, Football League regulation 13.2). This has never happened in the Premier League. If a Premier League club goes out of business during the **close season**, the Premier League Board can invite the highest-placed relegated club back into the league, provided that the season's fixtures had not already been set (FA Premier League rule B.30). By contrast, if a Football League club ceases to operate during the close season, the Football League Board has the discretion to promote an additional club from the division below (Football League regulation 13.4). See **lost clubs**.

Distillery FC *club* Northern Ireland national league club based in Belfast, founded 1880. Ground: New Grosvenor, capacity: 14,000. Strip: white shirts with blue sleeves, blue shorts. All-Ireland league champions 1896, 1899, 1901, 1903; **Irish FA Cup** (all-Ireland) 1884, 1885, 1886, 1889, 1894, 1896, 1903, 1905, 1910; (Northern Ireland) 1925, 1956, 1971; Northern Ireland league champions 1963. Notable former players: Martin O'Neill (64 caps, nine goals for Northern Ireland), J Peden (24 caps for Northern Ireland), O M Stanfield (30 caps for Northern Ireland).

Distrito Federal de Brasilia *state* one of the 27 state leagues in **Brazil**, based around the capital Brasilia, founded 1959. Leading clubs: Brasilia Esporte Clube (Brasilia), Taguatinga Esporte Clube (Taguatinga).

diuretics *medical* a substance or drug that increases the amount of urine excreted. Diuretic drugs are used to help remove fluids from the body (used medically to treat certain kidney, heart and liver diseases). They are misused in sport as **masking agents**, and to promote rapid temporary weight loss (in such sports as boxing and weight-lifting). Misuse can cause cramp and dizziness; in the long term diuretics can damage the heart and kidneys.

dive *vb.* **1.** a lunge in mid-air or on the ground by a goalkeeper in an effort to execute a **save**. **2.** to mimic being tripped, to give the referee the impression that the player has been fouled and thus gain a **direct free kick** or **penalty kick**. A player guilty of this should receive a **caution** for **unsporting behaviour** (under Law 12).

dividend *n.* in **pools** betting, the distribution of pay-outs to winners. The size of the dividend depends on the number of winners and the amount of money in the pool. Where there are few possible maximum-points combinations (in most pools systems this would occur when there are around eight **score-draws** on the coupon) the pool is likely to be shared by very few entrants; each receiving a large share of the prize money or dividend. Conversely, where there are many possible maximum-points combinations – usually when there are many score-draws – the dividend is low because many participants will share the pool.

dividend forecast *n.* in **pools** betting, the predicted spread of payouts to winners, released shortly after all the football results have been collated. The forecast is based purely on the results of matches, without any knowledge of how many participants have entered winning coupons. See **dividend**, **jackpot**, **telegram claims**.

diving header *n.* **header** executed by a player lunging in mid-air.

division *n.* one of the tiers of a **league** system.

divot *n.* a small piece of turf accidentally lifted from the pitch during play.

Djibouti *country CAF* (also Jibouti.) Republic in east Africa at the mouth of the Red Sea. Bordered by **Somalia**, **Ethiopia**. Independence from France in 1977. Area: 23,000 sq km (8,800 sq miles). Consists almost entirely of desert, with mountains in the north. Very hot climate all year with very little rainfall. Population: 586,000 (1995 est.; nearly half of the population live in the capital). Languages: French, Somali, Afar, Dankali, Arabic. Capital: Djibouti. *Dossier* Football association (Fédération Djiboutienne de Football, Djibouti), formed in 1977, affiliated to FIFA and **Confédération Africaine de Football** (CAF) in 1994, member of the **Confederation of East and Central African Football Associations** (CECAFA); president Fadoul Houssein, general secretary Kamil Ali. Season played from October to June. National stadium: Hassan Gouled, Djibouti, capacity: 10,000. National strip: green shirts, white shorts. First international game: 29 March 1983 v Ethiopia (2–4, Addis Ababa, friendly). Biggest victory: 4–1 v **South Yemen** (26 February 1988, Djibouti, friendly) Biggest defeat: 1–7 v **Madagascar** (9 August 1986, Djibouti, **All-Africa Games** qualifier). *International tournament record* **Olympic Games** – never entered; **Women's World Cup** – never entered; **World Cup** – never entered;

African Cup of Nations – never entered; **East and Central African Championship** – first entered 1994 (last in its group); **World Youth Cup** (under-20) – never entered; **Under-17 World Championship** – never entered. *Record against British and Irish national teams* none played. *Record in international club tournaments* Djibouti clubs first entered 1995, no major success. Leading club: **FNS**, **Aerosport**, **CDE**.

Djoliba Athletic Club *club* Mali national league club, based in the capital Bamako. Ground: Mamadou Konate, capacity: 10,000. Strip: red shirts and white shorts. *Keynotes* Djoliba AC holds the African and joint world record of seven consecutive domestic cup triumphs (1973 to 1979). Djoliba AC has won 14 domestic cups, a national record shared with rivals **Stade Malien**. **African Cup of Champion Clubs** semifinal 1967; **African Cup-winners Cup** semi-final 1981 and 1982; **CAF Cup** quarter-final 1995; Mali Cup 1965, 1971, 1973, 1974, 1975, 1976, 1977, 1978, 1979, 1981, 1983, 1993, 1996, 1998; Mali League champions 1960, 1966, 1967, 1968, 1971, 1973, 1974, 1975, 1976, 1979, 1982, 1985, 1988, 1990, 1992, 1996, 1997, 1998; **West African Club Champions Cup** runners-up 1990.

Djurgårdens IF Stockholm (Idrottsförening) *club* Swedish national league club based in Stockholm, founded 1891. Ground: Olympiastadion, capacity: 12,500. Strip: light and dark blue striped shirts, dark blue shorts. Swedish Cup 1990; Swedish league champions 1912, 1915, 1917, 1920, 1955, 1959, 1964, 1966.

Dnepr Dnepropetrovsk *club* Ukraine national league and former-Soviet Union league club based in Dnepropetrovsk, founded 1936 (as Stal, became Metallurg in 1948, present name adopted 1962). Ground: Meteor, capacity: 30,000. Strip: red shirts, red shorts. Former-Soviet Union Cup 1989; former-Soviet Union league champions 1983, 1988; **UEFA Cup** third round 1986; Ukraine cup runners-up 1995, 1997; Ukraine league runners-up 1993. Notable former player: Oleg **Protasov**.

Docherty, Tommy *player-manager* Wing-half. **Scotland** international (25 caps). Born 24 April 1928. Career ca. 1948–1961. *Clubs* (player) **Celtic**, **Preston North End**, **Arsenal**, (manager) **Chelsea**, **Rotherham United**, **Queens Park Rangers** (twice), **Aston Villa**, **Porto** (FC), **Hull City**, **Manchester United**, **Derby County**, Sydney Olympic (twice), Preston North End, South Melbourne, **Wolverhampton Wanderers**, Altrincham. Also Scotland manager. *Keynotes* Docherty had a highly controversial managerial career, having been a powerful wing-half in his playing days, which included being captain of Scotland on eight occasions. Known as "The Doc", he created a highly talented young side at Chelsea, his first management position, taking them to the 1967 **FA Cup** final (v **Tottenham Hotspur**). In 1967, he moved to Rotherham United, then of Division Two, but could not prevent the club's relegation. He

became manager of Queens Park Rangers in 1968, only to be dismissed 28 days after his arrival. In 1970, Docherty, in his second season at Aston Villa, was sacked with the club on the brink of relegation. Prior to taking control at **Old Trafford** in 1972, Docherty spent 14 months as manager of the Scottish national side. Having presided over Manchester United's relegation to Division Two in 1973-74, he proceeded to take the club to two consecutive FA Cup finals (1976, v **Southampton**; 1977, v **Liverpool**), but left under a cloud soon after the second **Wembley** appearance. At Derby County he was subject of a police investigation and was eventually cleared of perjury charges. His brief spell at Wolves also coincided with relegation. Docherty is now an after-dinner speaker. *Honours* (player) Division Two (Preston North End 1950-51); (manager) Division Two (Manchester United 1974-75); FA Cup (Manchester United 1977).

doctor *regulations* **home club**s in the **Premier League** and **Football League** are required to provide a qualified medical practitioner to attend to injured players or officials (FA Premier League rule H.6.1, Football League regulation 32.1). The doctor must examine any player who leaves the field because of a **head injury**; the player can only resume playing with the permission of the doctor (FA Premier League rule H.8, Football League regulation 32.2). Similarly, players with head injuries sustained in training can only resume training with clearance from the medical practitioner. *Keynotes* **Yugoslavia**'s national team doctor died of a heart attack during his country's match against **France** (19 June 1984, 2–3, in St Etienne, **European Championship** finals first round).

dog *misc.* a dog is credited with assisting the automatic relegation of **Lincoln City** from the **Football League** Division Four to the **Football Conference**. **Torquay United** was losing 1–2 in the closing minutes of its game against **Crewe Alexandra** on the final day of the 1986-87 season. A dog bit Torquay's Jim McNichol, delaying play and forcing **injury time**. Torquay equalised in injury time and so gained enough points to stay up; instead Lincoln City was relegated, after losing 0–2 at **Swansea City**. A dog named Pickles is famous for finding the **World Cup trophy** in 1966 after it had been stolen from a philatelic exhibition before the tournament that year.

Doherty, Peter *player-manager* Forward. **Northern Ireland** international (16 caps). Career ca. 1933–1954. *Clubs* (player) **Blackpool**, **Manchester City**, **Derby County**, **Huddersfield Town**, **Doncaster Rovers**, (manager) **Northern Ireland**, **Bristol City** and Doncaster Rovers manager. *Keynotes* Doherty signed for Manchester City from Blackpool for £10,000 in 1936 and joined Eric Brook in attack in the club's Championship-winning side of 1936-37. Doherty also struck up a fruitful attacking partnership with Raich **Carter** at Derby County after **World War II**, scoring one of the club's four goals in its 1946 FA Cup success (4–1 v **Charlton Athletic**). After hanging up his boots,

Doherty managed Northern Ireland in the 1958 **World Cup** finals. Previously he led Doncaster Rovers, as player-manager, to promotion to Division Two, winning the Division Three (North) title in 1949-50. Doherty scored 26 League goals for Rovers that season. Included in the **Football League Centenary 100 players**. *Honours* League Championship (Manchester City 1936-37); **FA Cup** (Derby County 1946).

Domagnano *club* San Marino league club based in Domagnano, founded 1966. Ground: Domagnano, capacity: 500. San Marino Cup 1988, 1990, 1992, 1996; San Marino League champions 1989.

Dominica *country CONCACAF* Commonwealth state in the Windward Islands of the east Caribbean, between **Guadeloupe** and **Martinique**. Independence from Britain in 1978. Area: 751 sq km (290 sq miles). Tropical rainforest covers half the island. Population: 74,000 (1994 est.). Languages: English and Dominican patois (a French dialect). Capital: Roseau. *Dossier* Dominica Football Association (Roseau) formed in 1970, affiliated to **FIFA** and **Confederación Norte-Centroamericana y del Caribe de Fútbol** (CONCACAF) in 1994, president Patrick John, general secretary Edgar Hunter. National strip: emerald green shirts, green shorts. *International tournament record* **Olympic Games** – never entered; **Women's World Cup** – never entered; **World Cup** – first entered 1998 (qualifying tournament, Caribbean zone second round – beat Antigua and Barbuda in first round, 6–4 agg.); **Caribbean Nations Cup** – played in the finals tournament in 1994 and 1998 (last in its first-round group of four nations in both years); **Gold Cup** – never qualified; **Under-17 World Championship** – never entered; **World Youth Cup** (under-20) – never entered. *Record against British and Irish national teams* none played. Leading clubs: Black Rocks, **Harlem Bombers** (holds the CONCACAF club record of 11 domestic cups), ACS zebians (league champions 1998).

Dominican Republic *country CONCACAF* Republic in the West Indies, in the Caribbean Sea. The country is in the eastern two-thirds of the island of Hispaniola (with **Haiti** in the west). Independent from **Spain** in 1821. Area: 48,440 sq km (18,700 sq miles). Mountainous rainforests with fertile lowlands. Population: 7,770,000 (1994 est.). Language: Spanish. Capital: Santo Domingo. *Dossier* Football association (Federación Dominicana de Fútbol, Santo Domingo) formed in 1953, affiliated to FIFA in 1958 **Confederación Norte-Centroamericana y del Caribe de Fútbol** (CONCACAF) in 1964, president Rodolfo Guzman Lara, general secretary Osiris Guzman. Season played from March to December. National stadium: Olimpico Juan Pablo Duarte, Santo Domingo, capacity: 30,000. National strip: blue shirts, white shorts. Biggest defeat: 0–8 v **Trinidad and Tobago** (15 June 1996, **World Cup** qualifying tournament). *International tournament record* **Olympic Games** – never entered; **Women's World Cup** – never entered; World Cup – first entered 1978, reached the Caribbean zone qualifying tournament third round in 1998; **Caribbean Nations Cup** – finals tournament 1991 (last in its first-round group of four nations); **Gold Cup** – never qualified; **Under-17 World Championship** – never entered; **World Youth Cup** (under-20) – never entered. *Record against British and Irish national teams* none played. *Record in international club tournaments* no major success. Leading clubs: Catolica, Don Bosco, San Cristobel.

Doncaster Belles *club* English women's league club. *Dossier* Ground: Armthorpe Welfare, Doncaster. Strip: yellow and blue shirts, blue shorts, blue socks. Biggest win: 44–0 (unknown). Biggest defeat: 1–4 v Croydon (1996-97, Premier League). *History* Formed by female **Doncaster Rovers** supporters in 1969, going on to play in the local south Yorkshire leagues. The club reached its first national final, the **FA Women's Challenge Cup** finals, in 1983, winning the first of its six cups. Overall, Belles has appeared in a record 11 finals, though it has only managed to retain the trophy on one occasion, 1988. Belles players have regularly provided the nucleus of the national women's team. *Honours* FA Women's Challenge Cup 1983, 1987, 1988, 1990, 1992 (4–2 v Southampton Saints), 1994 (1–0 v Knowlsey United); **FA Women's Premier League** 1991-92, 1994-95.

Doncaster Rovers *club* former-English league. *Dossier* Ground: Belle Vue, Doncaster, south Yorkshire. Record attendance: 37,149 v **Hull City** (2 October 1948, Division Three (North)). Best average attendance: 22,838 (1950-51). Biggest win: 10–0 v **Darlington** (25 January 1964, Division Four). Biggest defeat: 0–12 v Small Heath (11 April 1903, Division Two). *History* Founded in 1879 to play a one-off match against the Yorkshire Institute of the Deaf. The club was elected to Division Two in 1901-02 and failed **re-election** twice in three seasons (1902-03 and 1904-05). Darlington finished seventh in its first **Football League** season, which is the club's highest position. The club re-formed in 1920 and joined Division Three (North) in 1923-24. Rovers played at the Intake Ground and at Bennetthorpe prior to settling at Low Pasture, which eventually would become Belle Vue, in 1922. Doncaster won the Division Three (North) Championship in 1934-35 and 1946-47, but the club's tenure in Division Two was short-lived on both occasions. Doncaster's 1946-47 Division Three (North) Championship was won with a record 72 points, during which the club lost only three matches and scored 123 goals. The club won a further Division Three (North) title in 1949-50, this time retaining a place in Division Two for eight seasons before being relegated in 1957-58. Thereafter Doncaster alternated between the bottom two divisions until in 1997-98 the club lost its League status (replaced by **Halifax Town**). During the 1950s, the club reached the fifth round of the **FA Cup** on four occasions: 1952 (0–4 v **Portsmouth**), 1954 (1–3 v **Leyton Orient**), 1955 (1–2 v **Birmingham City**), 1956 (0–2 v **Tottenham Hotspur**). The club was a **League Cup** quarter-finalist in 1976 (2–7 v

Tottenham Hotspur). Doncaster's final League season in 1997-98 included several low-points. On 3 March 1998, only 739 fans turned up to watch Doncaster in a Division Three match against Barnet – the club's lowest League attendance. Also in March, the club informed the players that they should turn up only on match days; there would be nobody to coach them at other times. The club played its first season in the **Football Conference**. *League record* Division Two 1901-02 to 1902-03 (failed re-election), 1904-05 (failed re-election), 1935-36 to 1936-37, 1947-48, 1950-51 to 1957-58; Division Three 1958-59, 1966-67, 1969-70 to 1970-71, 1981-82 to 1982-83, 1984-45 to 1987-88; Third Division 1992-93 to 1997-98; Division Three (North) 1923-24 to 1934-35, 1937-38 to 1946-47, 1948-49 to 1949-50; Division Four 1959-60 to 1965-66, 1967-68 to 1968-69, 1971-72 to 1980-81, 1983-84, 1988-89 to 1991-92. *Honours* Division Three (North) 1934-35, 1946-47, 1949-50; Division Four 1965-66, 1968-69.

donkey *n. informal* derogatory term for a player accused of being too slow or lacking in creative play.

double *informal* winning both of the two major domestic competitions. The term may also apply to various other combinations of success in two competitions in the same season. *Keynotes* 1. England: winning both the League Championship and the **FA Cup** in the same season. Only six clubs have managed to win the double: **Preston North End** (1888-89); **Aston Villa** (1896-97); **Tottenham Hotspur** (1960-61); **Arsenal** (1970-71, 1997-98); **Liverpool** (1985-86); **Manchester United** (1993-94, 1995-96, 1998-99). 2. Italy: winning both the Italian Championship and the **Coppa Italia**. **Juventus** has twice won the double (1959-60, 1994-95), while **Napoli** (1986-87) and **Torino** (1942-43) have both achieved the feat just once.

double-double *informal* 1. England: winning both the League Championship and the **FA Cup** in the same season on two occasions. **Manchester United** became the first team to achieve this feat in 1996 when, having won the Championship, it beat **Liverpool** 1–0 in the FA Cup final. The club had secured its first **double** in 1994. 2. Scotland: winning both the Scottish League Championship and the **Scottish FA Cup** in two consecutive seasons. **Rangers** have won the double-double on four occasions (1934–35, 1949–50, 1963–64 and 1992–93). **Celtic** have achieved this twice (1907–08 and 1971–72). See **grand-slam, treble**.

double teaming *tactics* situation in which two defenders work in unison, one **marking** and one providing cover, against an **onball** attacker.

Dr Gerö Cup *competition* former international nations tournament, played over two, and later five, years, contested by **Austria** (1932), **Czechoslovakia** (1960), **Hungary** (1953), **Italy** (1929, 1935), **Switzerland** and, in the final tournament, **former-Yugoslavia**. The tournament was played on a league basis, with each nation playing each other at home and away. Switzerland finished bottom of the league in each

of the tournament's six editions, winning just five games and drawing eight of the 50 games it played. By contrast Hungary won 25 of its 49 matches (the 1936-37 tournament was unfinished). Records for the other countries were: Czechoslovakia – 22 wins from 49 played; Italy – 21 wins, 46 played; Austria – 21 wins, 48 played; Yugoslavia – three wins, 10 played (1955-60 tournament only). Also called the International Cup.

Drake, Ted *player-manager* Striker. **England** international (5 caps, 6 goals). Born 16 August 1912. Career ca. 1931–1945. *Clubs* (player) **Southampton, Arsenal**; (manager) **Reading, Chelsea, Barcelona** (assistant manager). *Keynotes* Signed by Arsenal from Southampton for £6,000 in March 1934. Drake scored 42 League goals in Arsenal's 1934-35 League Championship winning season – a club record – and 136 goals in his six-year career with the north London club. He scored a Division One record seven goals against **Aston Villa** (14 December 1935). Drake retired from playing through injury in 1945, becoming Reading manager in June 1947. Drake established a successful youth policy at Chelsea, leading the club to its first League Championship in 1954-55 with a team that became known as "Drake's Ducklings". Thus, Drake became the first Championship-winning player also tomanage a title winning team. On 23 January 1963, Drake was a member of the first **pools panel** assembled to forecast the results of postponed matches. He also played cricket for Hampshire County Cricket Club in the 1930s. Included in the **Football League Centenary 100 players**. *Honours* (player) FA Cup (Arsenal 1936); League Championship (Arsenal 1934-35, 1937-38); (manager) League Championship (Chelsea 1954-55).

draw 1. *n.* game of football at which both teams score the same number of goals, or fail to score at all. *vb.* to finish a game with the same number of goals as the opposing team. **2.** *n.* the method by which teams are allocated to play each other in a **knockout competition**. *vb.* to be allotted to play [a particular team] in a knockout competition. *Usage* the different senses are illustrated in the following example: "In the draw for the third round of the **FA Cup, Arsenal** was drawn to play **Manchester United**. The match ended in a draw. The two teams drew 1–1." *Keynotes* The record highest-scoring draw in the **Football League** is 6–6 (**Leicester City** v Arsenal, 21 April 1930, Division One; and **Charlton Athletic** v **Middlesbrough**, 22 October 1960, Division Two).

drawing lots *competition rules* **1.** method of deciding the outcome of a drawn match in a **knockout competition** by allocating the names of the two clubs to slips of paper and picking one at random (the winner). This method was largely repealed in 1970 when the **International FA Board** adopted the **penalty shoot-out**. Drawing lots or **tossing a coin** may still be used to decide a match if the light fails before a penalty shoot-out is completed. *Keynotes* **Turkey** qualified for the 1954 **World Cup** finals after winning the home leg

(1–0) and losing the away leg (1–4) of its qualifying match with **Spain**; a playoff in Rome finished 2–2, and Turkey went through to the finals in Switzerland after a blind Italian boy drew lots from a hat. **2.** method to establish home advantage when no neutral venue is available. *Keynote* After Glasgow rivals, **Celtic** and **Rangers** were drawn against each other in the Scottish FA Cup the clubs drew lots to decide which ground the tie would be played at. Celtic won the right to stage the match at its **Celtic Park** ground on 5 April 1998.

draws, most in succession *record* the **Football League** record for consecutive league drawn matches is eight, held by **Torquay United** (1969-70, Division Three).

Dream Team *television* football-based soap opera that was first screened on Sky television on 14 October 1997. Features the fictional team Harchester United and has included cameo appearances of real-life football people, including Ron Atkinson, John Hollins and Harry Redknapp.

dressing room *n.* room for players/officials to change their clothing before and after a match, and to clean themselves following a game. *Keynotes* The players' changing facilities at **Arsenal's Highbury** ground contain individual player's baths.

dressing room music *misc.* the playing of music in the players' dressing room before a match. *Keynotes* **Wimbledon** players are believed to have started playing music before a game in the 1980s, but the practice is rarely found in other countries. **Newcastle United** manager Ruud **Gullit** banished music from his team's dressing room in December 1998, commenting that: "I like a lively dressing room, but I want the players to talk about the game. If there's music, it distracts them."

Drewery, Eileen *misc.* faith-healer who uses prayer rather than conventional medicine to aid the healing process. **England** manager Glenn **Hoddle** controversially used faith-healer Eileen Drewery to help players during preparations for the 1998 **World Cup**. Several players, including Les Ferdinand and Darren Anderton, have endorsed the work of Drewery despite cynicism about her work within the **Football Association**.

Drewry, Arthur *official* (1891-1961) former president of the **Football League** (1949-55), president of **FIFA** (1956-61). Former chairman of **Grimsby Town**.

dribble *vb.* to run with the ball, evading an opponent's challenge by screening it, **feint**ing to pass or to move in one direction while moving in another, stepping over the ball and by riding tackles.

Drogheda United FC *club* Republic of Ireland national league club based in Drogheda, County Louth, in the east of Ireland, founded 1919 as Drogheda FC (until 1975). Ground: United Park, capacity: 10,000. Strip: blue shirts, white shorts. Republic of Ireland **FAI Cup** runners-up 1971, 1976; Republic of Ireland league runners-up 1983.

drop ball *rules* method of restarting a game after a temporary suspension of play (perhaps due to a serious injury or burst or defective ball), where the ball has not crossed either the **touch-lines** or **goal-lines** (Law VIII). Play starts with the **referee** dropping the ball at the spot where it was when play was suspended – except if the ball was in either of the two **goal-areas,** when it is dropped on the **goal area line**. Play restarts as soon as the ball touches the ground. A goal can be scored directly from a drop ball. *Keynotes* An unofficial players' code exists that, if play is stopped because of a serious injury to a player and subsequently restarted with a drop ball, only one player will take part and will kick the ball back to the opposition's goalkeeper or defence.

drug *medical* substance which can enhance mental or physical performance or to treat injuries. Players are banned from taking, injecting or administering performance-enhancing or recreational/social drugs by the football authorities and are subject to random drug testing. **FIFA** states that "doping contravenes the ethics of sport and constitutes an acute or chronic health hazard to players with possible fatal consequences". FIFA has attempted to eradicate drugs from football since 1966 and the **World Cup** that year was the first to involve drug testing. Banned substances and prohibited methods of doping fall into two categories. Category one relates to substances and includes all stimulants, narcotic **analgesics, anabolic steroids, beta-blockers, diuretics** and **polypeptide** and glycoprotein hormones and related substances. The second category relates to methods of doping and includes all **blood doping** and pharmacological, chemical and physical manipulation. A further list of substances are subject to partial restriction and traces or excessive traces in a player's urine sample may lead to sanctions (see **drug test**). These are: **alcohol, marijuana, local anaesthetics** (especially **cocaine**-based) and corticosteriods (with the exception of local applications). FIFA only decided in September 1997 to add **cannabis** to its list of banned substances. Sanctions, including lengthy bans, are applied to players who test positive. Several players have fallen foul of this ruling. *Keynotes* Scottish international Willie Johnston was sent home from the 1978 **World Cup** in **Argentina** after failing a routine drug test. Johnston had been prescribed the drug Reactivan for a nasal condition by his club doctor (**West Bromwich Albion**). Unknown to Johnston the pills contained banned stimulant Fencamsamin, traces of which were found in his urine sample. Diego **Maradona** has twice tested positive for banned substances, once in March 1991 (cocaine) and again during the 1994 World Cup (cocktail of five **ephedrine**-based substances). He was banned for 15 months on both occasions. In the UK, between 1995 and 1997 five **Charlton Athletic** players were found to have taken prohibited substances. Four – Lee Bowyer and Dean Chandler (cannabis), Jay Notely (cocaine, ecstasy and marijuana) and Jamie Stuart (cocaine and marijuana) – failed drug test performed by the FA's doping control unit, while Craig Sloan admitted to having taken cocaine. **Barnsley's** Dean Jones was banned in December 1997 for three months by the FA for failing a drug test. **Leyton Orient**'s Roger Stanislaus was banned for one year in 1996 after testing positive for cocaine, while **Huddersfield Town**'s Craig Whittington was sacked by his club after becoming the first English player to test positive twice for cannabis. Paul Merson has admitted to using cocaine. In **France**, Toulouse's Dominique Arribage has twice tested positive for taking steroids. His second positive test was announced in November 1997. France international goalkeeper Bernard Lama has tested positive for cannabis, as has his colleague and rival for the French goalkeeping shirt Fabien Barthez, who was banned for two months in 1996. In Italy, seven **Napoli** players tested positive in 1963, four of whom were banned for three weeks. Also in Italy in 1963, five **Bologna** FC players were found to have taken amphetamines. Although the players were let off, the club was docked three points (later rescinded) and manager Fulvio Bernardini was banned for two years. In 1990, Andrea Carnevale and future Italian international goalkeeper Angelo Peruzzi, both then of **Roma (AS)**, were banned from football for a year after testing positive for the drug Fenermina. Argentina international Claudio **Cannigia**, then also playing for Roma (AS), tested positive for cocaine in 1993 and was banned for a year. Two players (Farshad Falahai and Naeim Saabavi) of Iranian club side **Piroozi** FC were suspended for 12 months each by the **Asian Football Confederation** in May 1997 after testing positive for the anabolic steroid Nandrolone following a routine doping test at the 16th **Asian Champion Teams Cup** in Kuala Lumpur. **Colombia** international Alverio Usuriaga was banned for two years in October 1997 after testing positive for cocaine while playing for Argentinian club side Club Atlético **Independiente**. In October 1997, Den Bosch goalkeeper Maikel Aerts became the first player in **Netherlands** to fail a drug test. Aerts tested positive for cocaine and was banned for one year. **Ukraine** defender Serhiy Nahornyak was the first player to test positive for drugs during a World Cup qualifying campaign. Nahornyak failed a doping test after Ukraine's 1998 World Cup **playoff** first-leg defeat against **Croatia** in Zagreb (29 October 1997) and was banned until 2000. Former **Argentina** international and **Pénarol** player Carlos Aguilera was banned for two years in July 1998 after he tested positive for cocaine. Didier Deschamps, Alessandro Del Piero and Ginaluca **Vialli**, among others, were summoned to testify before the Turin state prosecutor, Rafaele Guariniello, in August 1998 as part of an inquiry into alleged drug abuse by footballers in Italy. A similar investigation was mounted by the Bologna state prosecutor. A third inquiry, under the auspices of the Italian Olympic Committee and headed by Ugo Longo, ran in tandem with the Turin and Bologna investigations and several London-based former-**Serie A** players, including Vialli, Pierluigi Casiraghi, Roberto **Di Matteo** and Gianfranco **Zola**, were interviewed. Although the Italian Olympic Committee's inquiry found no evidence of "doping", it recommended that the use of

creatine, a muscle-building agent, should be either banned or restricted. The inquiries were prompted by allegations in an Italian weekly magazine, *L'Espresso*, by Roma (AS) coach Zdenêk Zeman, who expressed surprise at the muscular development of certain **Juventus** players.

drug test *medical* officially sanctioned analysis of blood or urine to identify the presence of illegal or performance-enhancing substances (see **drug**). Drug tests may be carried out on professional footballers without prior notification according to rules laid down by football's governing bodies. The rules also list which substances are banned – many may be present in over-the-counter medications, such as cold remedies. Misuse of drugs in sport is thought to date back to before **World War II**, though it was not until 1967 that the International Olympic Committee first banned certain drugs known to enhance performance, strength or training stamina. More than 3,700 drugs are currently banned by sporting authorities. During competitions, the **FIFA** doping co-ordinator will select two players from each team for testing by drawing lots at half-time. Occasionally additional players will be tested if they are suspected of contravening the doping rules. Selected players are tested as soon as they leave the field of play. They are required to produce a urine sample (usually at least 75ml) which is then split into two containers (A = 50ml; B = 25ml). The remaining drops of urine are subject to a pH test (measure of acidity or alkalinity) and the two containers sent for laboratory analysis. A tested player must also declare any medicines taken or administered to him or her in the 72 hours preceding the match. The laboratory tests sample A and if that proves negative sample B is disposed of within 24 hours of the test. *Keynotes* Whereas, the Italian football authorities first used drug testing during the 1961-62 season, such arrangements were first introduced in England in January 1980, with eight players from two matches (**Swindon Town** v **Brentford**, Division Three; **West Ham United** v **Cardiff City**, Division Two) tested. The **Football Association** doubled its random dope testing at the start of the 1996-97 season. Most testing is performed at training grounds with around 20% carried out after matches. Out of 300 random tests performed by the Football Association's doping control unit in 1995-96 only two were positive. Between 1994-95 and 1997-98, 27 players tested positive. Elsewhere, the US **Major Soccer League** has a policy of blanket testing of players. Coaches and League administrators are also tested. Random testing was introduced in **Croatia** at the start of the 1998-99 season. Banned drugs include **anabolic steroids**, some **analgesics** (including all **opioids**), **beta-blockers**, **cannabis**, **cocaine**, **diuretics**, **stimulants** and **polypeptide hormones**. See also **alcohol** and **drug**.

Drumcondra *club* former Republic of Ireland national league club based in Dublin, merged in 1972 with Home Farm FC (now playing as **Home Farm Everton FC**). Republic of Ireland **FAI Cup** 1927, 1943,

1946, 1954, 1957, runners-up 1928, 1948, 1955, 1961; Republic of Ireland league champions 1948, 1949, 1958, 1961, 1965; **UEFA Cup/Fairs Cup** second round 1963. See Home Farm for records after 1972. Notable former players: Alan Kelly (47 caps for the Republic of Ireland, later with **Preston North End**).

Drybrough Cup *competition* former pre-season sponsored Scottish knockout tournament and the Scottish equivalent of the **Watney Cup.** Final results: 1971 **Aberdeen** 2–1 **Celtic**, 1972 **Hibernian** 5–3 Celtic, 1973 Hibernian 1–0 Celtic, 1974 Celtic 2–2 (4–2 pens) **Rangers**, 1975–1978 not contested, 1979 Rangers 3–1 Celtic, 1980 Aberdeen 2–1 **St Mirren**.

DSA Antanarivo (Domoina Soavino Atsimandravo) *club* Madagascar national league club, based in the capital Antanarivo. **CAF Cup** quarter-final 1997, 1998; Madagascar league champions 1997, 1998.

dual nationality *misc.* nationality of birth and of country of residence. *Keynotes* Four players have played for different countries in the **World Cup**: Luis Monti (**Argentina** 1930, **Italy** 1934); Ferenc **Puskás** (**Hungary** 1954, **Spain** 1962); José Santamaria (**Uruguay** 1954, Spain 1962); José **Mazzola** (**Brazil** 1958, Italy 1962).

dug-out *n.* covered box/area by the touchline where managers, coaches, substitutes and other club officials sit during a match. **Aberdeen** coach Donald Colman is credited with creating the first dug-out. He liked to study the players' footwork and so, in the 1920s, had a sunken area built next to the touchline at **Pittodrie**, which was referred to as the dug-out. **Everton** copied the idea at **Goodison Park** and other clubs soon followed. See also **designated seating area**.

Dukla Prague *club* Czech Republic and former-Czechoslovakia league club based in Prague, founded 1948. Ground: Na Julisce, capacity: 28,800 (11,000 seated). Strip: yellow shirts, yellow shorts. **European Cup** semi-final 1967); **European Cup-winners Cup** semi-final 1986; former-Czechoslovakia Cup 1961, 1965, 1966, 1969, 1981, 1983, 1985, 1990; former-Czechoslovakia league champions 1953, 1956, 1958, 1961, 1962, 1963, 1964, 1966, 1977, 1979, 1982. Notable former players: Zdenek **Nehoda**, Josef **Masopust**. The club received an unusual accolade in the United Kingdom in the 1988 song by cult band Half Man Half Biscuit: *All I want for Christmas is a Dukla Prague away kit.*

Dumbarton *club* Scottish league. *Dossier* Ground: **Boghead Park**, Dumbarton, Strathclyde, capacity: 5,503. Strip: white shirt with yellow edge and black chest hoop, white shorts with black trim, white socks with black hoops. Nickname: Sons. Record attendance: 18,000 v **Raith Rovers** (2 March 1957, **Scottish FA Cup**). Biggest win: 13–1 v Kirkintilloch Central (1 September 1888, Scottish FA Cup, first round). Biggest defeat: 1–11 v **Albion Rovers** (30 January 1926, **Division Two**), v **Ayr United** (13 August 1952, **Scottish League Cup**). *History* Formed in 1872 and founder members of the **Scottish Football League**.

The club was a formidable force in Scottish football in its early years, winning the first two Scottish League Championships in 1890-91 (shared with **Rangers** following a 2–2 draw in the **playoff**) and 1891-92. Dumbarton appeared in five Scottish FA Cup finals between 1881 and 1891 – 1881 (1–3 replay v **Queen's Park**), 1882 (1–4 v Queen's Park), 1883 (2–1 replay v **Vale of Leven**), 1887 (1–2 v **Hibernian**), 1891 (0–1 v **Heart of Midlothian**) – but winning the trophy only once. The 1881 final was replayed because the **Scottish Football Association** upheld Dumbarton's complaint about spectators invading the pitch. The club reached a further final in 1897 (1–5 v Rangers). With the exception of two Division Two Championships, in 1910-11 and 1971-72, and a Second Division title in 1991-92, the club has won no major honour since its 1883 Cup victory. Boghead Park, which the club moved to in 1879, is Scotland's oldest football ground, but cash-strapped Dumbarton has sold it to a property developer for £1.75 million and at the start of the 1999-00 season the club moved to a ground near Dumbarton Castle. *League record* Premier Division 1984-85; First Division 1975-76 to 1983-84; 1985-86 to 1987-88, 1992-93 to 1993-94, 1995-96; Division One 1893-94 to 1895-96; 1913-14 to 1914-15, 1921-22, 1972 to 1974-75; Scottish League 1890-91 to 1892-93, 1915-16 to 1920-21; Second Division 1988-89 to 1991-92, 1994-95, 1996-97; Division Two (Division B) 1896-97 (failed **re-election**), 1906-07 to 1912-13, 1922-23 to 1971-72; Third Division 1997-98–. *Honours* Scottish FA Cup 1883 (2–1 replay v Vale of Leven); Scottish League 1890-91 (shared with Rangers after a drawn (2–2) playoff), 1891-92; Division Two 1910-11, 1971-72; Second Division 1991-92. *Records* James McAulay is Dumbarton's most capped player (9 for **Scotland**), Andy Jardine holds the record for club appearances (297, 1957-67); Hughie **Gallacher** is Dumbarton's record goalscorer (169, 1954-62).

dummy *n.* pretending to pass or receive a pass without actually doing so.

Dünamo Tallinn *club* former Estonian national league club based in the capital Tallinn, founded 1940, dissolved 1997. Estonian Cup 1946, 1947, 1949, 1953, 1980, 1983; Estonian regional league champions 1945, 1947, 1949, 1950, 1953, 1954, 1978, 1980, 1981, 1983.

Dundalk FC *club* Republic of Ireland national league club based in Dundalk, County Louth, on the east coast of Ireland, founded 1919. Ground: Oriel Park, capacity: 20,000. Strip: white shirts, black shorts. **European Cup** second round 1980; **European Cup-winners Cup** second round 1982; Republic of Ireland **FAI Cup** 1942, 1949, 1952, 1958, 1977, 1979, 1981, 1988, runners-up 1931, 1935, 1938, 1987, 1993; Republic of Ireland league champions 1933, 1963, 1967, 1976, 1979, 1982, 1988, 1991, 1995.

Dundee *club* Scottish league. *Dossier* Ground: **Dens Park**, Dundee, Tayside, capacity: 14,177. Strip: navy blue shirts with white sleeves and white trim, white shorts with navy blue trim, navy blue socks with white trim. Nickname: Dark Blues/Dees. Record attendance: 43,024 v **Rangers** (1953, **Scottish FA Cup**). Biggest win: 10–0 v **Alloa** (9 March 1947, **Division Two**), v **Dunfermline Athletic** (22 March 1947, Division Two). Biggest defeat: 0–11 v **Celtic** (26 October 1895, Division One). *History* Founded in June 1893 from an amalgamation of two Dundee clubs, Our Boys and East End. The club joined Division One in 1893-94. Dundee won the Scottish FA Cup in 1910 (2–1 second replay v **Clyde**) and it has been a finalist a further three times: 1925 (1–2 v Celtic), 1952 (0–4 v **Motherwell**) and 1964 (1–3 v Rangers). Dundee has won the **Scottish League Cup** on three occasions: 1951-52 (3–2 v Rangers), 1952-53 (2–0 v **Kilmarnock**), 1973-74 (1–0 v Celtic). It was also a finalist in 1967-68 (3–5 v Celtic), 1980-81 (0–3 v **Dundee United**) and 1995-96 0–2 v **Aberdeen**). The club's only League Championship was won in 1961-62. The following season, Dundee reached the **European Cup** semi-final (2–6 agg., v **AC Milan**) and, in 1968, the club was a **UEFA** (Fairs) **Cup** semi-finalist (1–3 agg., v **Leeds United**). Dundee lost seven out of seven Scottish FA Cup encounters, including five semi-final defeats, with Celtic during the 1970s (semi-finals 1970 1–2, 1973 0–3 replay, 1974 0–1, 1975 0–1, 1977 0–2). Until 1976-77, Dundee had spent only two seasons, either side of **World War II**, outside the top flight, before being relegated from the newly formed Premier Division in 1976-77. Despite a nine-season run in the Premier Division in the 1980s, the club has twice dropped out of the top flight since, returning as First Division Champions on both occasions (1991-92 and 1997-98). Dundee won the inaugural **Scottish League Challenge Cup** in 1991 (3–2 v **Ayr United**) and reached the final again in 1995 (2–3 v **Airdrieonians**). Dundee was bought for £600,000 by Canadian businessman Ron Dixon, and, in 1993, his share was purchased for £3 million by vice-chairman Malcolm Reid. *League record* Premier League 1998-99–; Premier Division 1975-76, 1979-80, 1981-82 to 1989-90, 1992-93 to 1993-94; First Division 1976-77 to 1978-79, 1980-81, 1990-91 to 1991-92, 1994-95 to 1997-98; Division One (A Division) 1893-94 to 1914-15, 1921-22 to 1937-38, 1947-48 to 1974-75; Scottish League 1915-16 to 1920-21; Division Two (B Division) 1938-39, 1946-47. *Honours* Division One 1961-62; Division Two 1946-47; First Division 1978-79, 1991-92; Scottish FA Cup 1910 (2–1 2nd replay v Clyde); Scottish League Challenge Cup 1990-91 (3–2 v Ayr United); Scottish League Cup 1951-52 (3–2 v Rangers), 1952-53 (2–0 v Kilmarnock), 1973-74 (1–0 v Celtic). *Records* Alex Hamilton is Dundee's most capped player (24 for **Scotland**), Doug Cowie holds the record for club appearances (341, 1945-61); Alan Gilzean is Dundee's record goalscorer (113, 1957-64).

Dundee United *club* Scottish league. *Dossier* Ground: **Tannadice Park**, Dundee, Tayside, capacity: 12,616 all seated. Strip: tangerine shirts with black sleeves and trim, black shorts with tangerine trim, black

socks with tangerine and white trim. Nickname: Terrors. Record attendance: 28,000 v **Barcelona** (16 November 1966, **UEFA** (Fairs) **Cup**). Biggest win: 14–0 v Nithsdale Wanderers (17 January 1931, **Scottish FA Cup**, first round). Biggest defeat: 1–12 v **Motherwell** (23 January 1954, Division Two). *History* Founded in 1909 as Dundee Hibernian as the club of Dundee's catholic community, which had once supported Dundee Harps – an amateur club which, in 1885, enjoyed a 35–0 victory over Aberdeen Rovers. Dundee Hibernian joined Division Two in 1910-11, but almost ceased to exist in 1922 and was saved by a consortium of local business people who changed the club's name to Dundee United. The club rejoined the League in 1923-24, winning promotion as Champions the following season and securing a further Division Two title in 1928-29. United has been a Scottish FA Cup finalist on seven occasions, winning only once (1994, 1–0 v **Rangers**) – 1974 (0–3 v **Celtic**), 1981 (1–4 replay v Rangers), 1985 (1–2 v Celtic), 1987 (0–1 a.e.t. v **St Mirren**), 1988 (1–2 v Celtic), 1991 (3–4 a.e.t. v Motherwell). United's most successful period was in the 1980s. That decade the club won the **Scottish League Cup** in both 1979-80 (3–0 replay v **Aberdeen**) and 1980-81 (3–0 v **Dundee**) and, in 1982-83, it secured its only League Championship. United was also a Scottish League Cup runners-up twice during that time, in 1981-82 (1–2 v Rangers) and 1984-85 (0–1 v Rangers), and, in 1984, it reached the **European Cup** semi-finals (2–3 agg., v **Roma (AS)**). And, in 1986-87, Dundee was a UEFA Cup finalist (1–2 agg., v **IFK Gothenburg**). After one season in the First Division in 1995-96, United returned to the Premier Division via the end-of-season **playoffs** against the second from bottom top-flight side, **Partick Thistle** (3–2 agg.). The club was a Scottish League Cup finalist in 1997-98 (0–3 v Celtic). In 1987, the club was awarded FIFA's **Fairplay Award** for sportsmanship. *League record* Premier League 1998-99–; Premier Division 1975-76 to 1994-95, 1996-97 to 1997-98; First Division 1995-96; Division One 1925-26 to 1926-27, 1960-61 to 1974-75; Division Two (B Division) 1910-11 to 1924-25, 1927-28 to 1928-29, 1930-31 to 1959-60. *Honours* Division Two 1924-25, 1928-29; Premier Division 1982-83; Scottish FA Cup 1994 (1–0 v Rangers); Scottish League Cup 1979-80 (3–0 replay v Aberdeen), 1980-81 (3–0 v Dundee). *Records* Maurice Malpas is United's most capped player (55 for **Scotland**); Dave Narey holds the record for club appearances (612, 1973-94); Peter McKay is United's record goalscorer (158).

Dunfermline Athletic *club* Scottish league. *Dossier* Ground: **East End Park**, Dunfermline, Lothian, capacity: 12,500 all seated. Strip: black and white striped shirts, black shorts, black socks with white hoops. Nickname: Pars. Record attendance: 27,816 v **Celtic** (30 April 1968, Division One). Biggest win: 11–2 v **Stenhousemuir** (27 September 1930, Division Two). Biggest defeat: 1–11 v **Hibernian** (26 October 1889, **Scottish FA Cup**, third round replay). *History* Founded in 1885 by members of a local cricket club. The club joined Division Two in 1912-13, winning the title and securing promotion in 1925-26. The 1960s were Dunfermline's most successful period. The club was a Scottish FA Cup finalist on three occasions during the decade, winning the trophy twice, in 1961 (2–0 replay v Celtic) and 1968 (3–1 v **Heart of Midlothian**), and losing in 1965 (2–3 v Celtic). Twice in five years, Dunfermline reached the **UEFA** (Fairs) **Cup** quarter-finals – 1961-62 (3–5 agg., v **Ujpest Dozsa**) and 1965-66 (3–4 agg., v **Real Zaragoza**) – and, in 1969, the club was a **European Cup-winners Cup** semi-finalists (1–2 agg., v **Slovan Bratislava**). Dunfermline's first appearance in a major final took place in 1949-50, when the club reached the final of the **Scottish League Cup** (0–3 v **East Fife**). A second appearance in the final occurred in 1991-92 (0–2 v Hibernian). The club failed to win promotion to the Premier Division via the end-of-season **playoffs** against the second bottom finisher in the top flight, **Aberdeen**, in 1994-95 (2–6 agg.). The following season, Dunfermline won the First Division title but was relegated from the new Scottish Premier League in 1998-99. *League record* Premier League 1998-99–; Premier Division 1987-88, 1989-90 to 1991-92, 1996-97 to 1997-98; First Division 1975-76, 1979-80 to 1982-83, 1986-87, 1988-89, 1992-93 to 1995-96, 1999-00; Division One (A Division) 1926-27 to 1927-28, 1934-35 to 1936-37, 1955-56 to 1956-57, 1958-59 to 1971-72, 1973-74 to 1974-75; Second Division 1983-84 to 1985-86; Division Two (B Division) 1912-13 to 1925-26, 1928-29 to 1933-34, 1937-38 to 1954-55, 1957-58, 1972-73, 1976-77 to 1978-79. *Honours* Division Two 1925-26; First Division 1988-89, 1995-96; Second Division 1985-86; Scottish FA Cup 1961 (2–0 replay v Celtic), 1968 (3–1 v Heart of Midlothian). *Records* Colin Miller is Dunfermline's most capped player (15 (59) for **Canada**); Norrie McCathie holds the record for club appearances (497, 1981-96); Charles Dickson is Dunfermline's record goalscorer (154).

Dunnett, Jack Jacob *official* Eleventh president of the **Football League** (1981-1986), former Labour MP for Nottingham East, board member of **Brentford** (1961-67; he resigned in 1967 after proposing a failed **ground share** deal with **Queens Park Rangers**) and chairman of **Notts County** (from 1968-1987). Credited with spearheading Notts County's revival from Division Four to the Division One in 13 seasons.

Dupont, Jean-Louis *misc.* Brussels-based lawyer who represented Jean-Marc **Bosman** in his European Court case to free players from unfair contract restraint. In January 1998 he prepared English **Premier League** club **Wimbledon**'s case for a proposed relocation to Dublin in the **Republic of Ireland**, potentially permitted under the rules of the **Treaty of Rome**.

duration of play *rules* total time allocated for a game of football. Unless otherwise agreed – and within the rules of a particular competition – there are two equal periods of 45 minutes (Law VII) (less for youth matches).

Additional time may be added, at the discretion of the **referee**, in either period for all time lost due to the assessment of **injuries** to players and their transport from the field of play, **time-wasting**, **substitutions** and other causes. Time must also be extended in either period in order that a penalty be taken at or after the expiration of the normal period of play. See **extra time**.

Durham City *club* former-English league. *Dossier* Ground: Kepier Haughs and Holiday Park, Durham. Record League attendance: 6,000 (at Kepier Haughs). *Keynotes* The club was a founder member of Division Three (North) in 1921-22. It failed in its bid for **re-election** in 1927-28 and was replaced by **Carlisle United**. After losing its **Football League** status in 1927-28, the club joined the North Eastern League and folded in 1938. Durham's highest League position was 11th in Division Three (North) in 1921-22. *League record* Division Three (North) 1921-22 to 1927-28.

Dynamo Berlin *club* former-East Germany see **Berlin FC**.

Dynamo de Fima *club* Madagascar national league club, based in Antananarivo (the capital city) and owned by a transport company. Ground: Municipal, capacity: 14,000. Madagascar Cup 1981 and 1983; Madagascar League champions 1982 and 1983.

Dynamo Dresden *club* German regional league club and former-East German national league club based in Dresden. Founded in 1945 as VP Dresden (until 1953). Ground: Rudolf Harbig Stadion, former capacity: 32,000. Strip: yellow shirts, black shorts. *Keynotes* Dynamo Dresden was the most successful club in the former-East Germany winning eight league titles, seven domestic cups and a **UEFA Cup** semi-final place in 1989. It was one of only two East German clubs (with **Hansa Rostock**) to win a place in the German **Bundesliga** first division after reunification in 1990. The club, however, failed to prosper in the unified Germany. By 1995 the club was in financial difficulties and its professional licence was withdrawn by the Deutscher Fussball-Bund (the German FA). The club now plays in the semi-professional regional league. **European Cup** quarter-final 1977, 1979; former-East German Cup 1952 (as VP Dresden), 1971, 1977, 1982, 1984, 1985, 1990; former-East German league champions 1953, 1971, 1973, 1976, 1977, 1978, 1989, 1990; **UEFA Cup** semi-final 1989.

dynamo (midfield) *n informal* midfield player who exhibits a high workrate, constantly linking defence and attack and covering a significant amount of the pitch during a match.

Dynamo Tbilisi *club* Georgian national league and former-**Soviet Union** league club based in the capital Tbilisi, founded 1925 (known as Dynamo Iberiya from 1990–93). Ground: Boris Paichadze (the national stadium), capacity: 75,000. Strip: white shirts, blue shorts. *Keynotes* Dynamo won six consecutive Georgian league and cup doubles 1992-1997. It won 10 straight championships (1990-99); a joint world record with **Berlin FC** (as Dynamo Berlin). It was the sixth most successful side in former-Soviet Union and one of only two former-Soviet clubs to win a European club tournament (with **Dinamo Kiev**). **European Cup** – second round 1980; **European Cup-winners Cup** – 1981 (2–1, v **Carl Zeiss Jena** of East Germany, in Dusseldorf; Dynamo beat **West Ham United** in the quarter-final); former-Soviet Union Cup 1976, 1979; former-Soviet Union league champions 1964, 1978; Georgian Cup 1992, 1993, 1994, 1995, 1996, 1997; Georgian league champions 1990, 1991, 1992, 1993, 1994, 1995, 1996, 1997, 1998, 1999; **UEFA Cup** – third round 1974, 1978, 1988. Notable former players: Aleksander **Chivadze**; Murtaz Khurtsilava (67 caps for USSR while at Dynamo Tbilisi from 1965–73).

Dynamo Zagreb *club*   see **Croatia Zagreb**.

Dynamos Harare   *club*   Zimbabwe national league club based in Harare, founded 1962. Ground: Rufaro Stadium (the national stadium), capacity: 60,000. Strip: white shirts, blue shorts. **African Cup of Champion Clubs** runners-up 1998 (2–4 agg., v **ASEC Mimosas Abidjan** of Morocco), quarter-final 1981, 1984, 1987, 1995; **African Cup-winners Cup** quarter-final 1991; Zimbabwe Cup 1976, 1985, 1988, 1989, 1996; Zimbabwe league champions 1963, 1965, 1970, 1976,

1978, 1980, 1981, 1982, 1983, 1985, 1986, 1988, 1989, 1991, 1994, 1995, 1997.

Dynasty Cup   *competition*   regional nations tournament contested by **China**, **Japan**, **South Korea** and either **North Korea** (1990, 1992), or **Hong Kong** (1995). under the auspices of the **Asian Football Confederation** (AFC). First competed 1990 in Beijing, China, over one week. *Winners (and host city)* 1990 South Korea (in Beijing); 1992 Japan (in Beijing); 1995 Japan (in Hong Kong).

Dzajic, Dragan   *player*   Striker **former-Yugoslavia** international (85 appearance, 23 goals, 1964-79). *Clubs* **Red Star Belgrade** (twice), SEC Bastia (France). *Honours* **European Championship** runner-up (former-Yugoslavia, 1968); former-Yugoslavian league championship (Red Star Belgrade, 1964, 1968, 1969, 1970, 1973). *Keynotes* Former-Yugoslavia's all-time most-capped player. As a left winger, Dzajic scored the opening goal in the 1968 European Championship final (1–1, v **Italy**, in Rome; former-Yugoslavia lost the replay 0–2). Voted third in the *France Football* **European Footballer of the Year** award in 1975. Later became general manager of Red Star Belgrade.

E

Earle, Robbie *player* Midfield. **Jamaica** international (9 caps, 1 goal). Born 27 January 1965. *Clubs* **Port Vale**, **Wimbledon**. *Keynotes* Earle was the first player to score for Jamaica in a **World Cup** finals match (v **Croatia**, in Lens, France, 14 June 1998). Earle had been in the **England** squad on four occasions but never played, entitling him to play for Jamaica by his parents' birthright.

early ball *n.* pass played quickly in order to surprise the defending team or to beat an **offside trap**.

early bath *informal* reference to a player dismissed from the field of play, as in "to take an early bath".

early doors *informal* the early stages in a match.

East and Central African Championship *competition* annual international nations tournament, first played in 1973, between member nations of the **Confederation of East and Central African Football Associations – Djibouti, Ethiopia, Kenya, Rwanda, Seychelles, Somalia, Sudan, Tanzania, Uganda** and **Zanzibar**. The island of Zanzibar still competes separately, though it is part of Tanzania. Three former participants, **Malawi, Zambia** and **Zimbabwe**, are now part of the **Confederation of Southern African Football Associations** and no longer eligible. The championship replaced the **Gossage Cup**. It was not held in 1993. *Winners* Ethiopia (1987), Kenya (1975, 1981, 1982, 1983), Malawi (1978, 1979, 1988), Sudan (1980), Tanzania (1974, 1994), Uganda (1973, 1976, 1977, 1989, 1990, 1992, 1996), Zambia (1984, 1991), Zanzibar (1995) and Zimbabwe (1985).

East and Central African Club Championship *competition* international club tournament for the champion or nominated clubs of member nations of the **Confederation of East and Central African Football Associations – Djibouti, Ethiopia, Kenya, Rwanda, Seychelles, Somalia, Sudan, Tanzania, Uganda, Zanzibar –** and formerly **Malawi, Zambia** and **Zimbabwe**. The tournament has been won by **Simba SC** (Tanzania, 1974, 1991, 1992, 1995, 1996), **Young Africans SC** (Tanzania, 1975, 1993, 1999), **Luo Union** (Kenya, 1976, 1977), **Kampala City Council** (Uganda, 1978), **Abaluhya SC** (Kenya, 1979), **Gor Mahia** (Kenya, 1980, 1981, 1985), **AFC Leopards** (Kenya, 1982, 1983, 1984,

1997), **El Merreikh** (Sudan, 1986, 1994), **Nakivubo Villa** (Uganda, 1987, 1990), and **Kenya Breweries** (Kenya, 1988, 1989); not played 1998.

East Asian Games *competition* international sports tournament for East Asian nations, run by the East Asian Games Association and held every four years. The first games were held in Shanghai, **China** in May 1993, with 15 different sports. The football tournament comes under the auspices of the **Asian Football Confederation** (AFC) and is for players under 23 years of age "with the idea of giving young players international experience". Six countries entered the first football tournament. The second tournament, in May 1997, was held in Pusan (a venue for the 2002 **World Cup** finals), **South Korea**. Nine countries took part: South Korea, China, **Japan, Taiwan** (Chinese Taipei), **Mongolia, Macau, Hong Kong, Kazakhstan** and **Guam**. It was Mongolia's first international football tournament.

East Bengal *club* Indian club based in Calcutta. Ground: Salt Lake Stadium (the national stadium), capacity: 120,000. **Asian Cup-winners Cup** second round 1991; Calcutta League champions 1942, 1945, 1946, 1949, 1950, 1952, 1961, 1966, 1970, 1971, 1972, 1973, 1974, 1975, 1977, 1982, 1985, 1987, 1988, 1989, 1991, 1993; Federation Cup 1978, 1980, 1985, 1996 (the first two shared with **Mohun Bagan**).

East End Lions *club* Sierra Leone national league club based in the capital Freetown, founded 1926. Ground: Siaka Stevens (national stadium), capacity: 30,000. Strip: red shirts, black shorts. Sierra Leone league champions 1980, 1985, 1992, 1993, 1994; **West African Football Union General Eyadema Cup** 1996.

East End Park *ground* Scottish football ground situated in Dunfermline, Lothian; home of **Dunfermline Athletic**. *Dossier* Ground capacity: 12,500 all seated. Pitch dimensions: 105m x 62m. Record attendance: 27,816 v **Celtic** (30 April 1968, Division One). *Keynotes* Dunfermline has played at East End Park since the club was founded in 1885. Originally owned by the North British Railway Company, Dunfermline bought the ground for £3,500 after **World War I**. In the 1930s, the ground staged greyhound racing. The first floodlit match at East End Park took place in October 1959 (v **Sheffield United**, friendly).

East Fife *club* Scottish league. *Dossier* Ground: **Bayview Stadium**, Methil, Fife, capacity: 2,000 all seated. Strip: black shirts with gold stripes, white shorts with black trim, black socks with gold top. Nickname: Fifers. Record attendance: 22,515 v **Raith Rovers** (**Bayview Park**, 2 January 1950, Division One). Biggest win: 13–2 v **Edinburgh City** (11 December 1937, Division Two). Biggest defeat: 0–9 v **Heart of Midlothian** (5 October 1957, Division One). *History* Founded in 1903 as East of Fife. The club joined the re-formed Division Two in 1921-22. East Fife reached its first **Scottish FA Cup** final in 1927 (1–3 v **Celtic**), and in 1938 the club lifted the trophy (4–2 replay v **Kilmarnock**) – the only Division Two club to do so. The club reached four Cup finals in seven years between 1947 and 1954, winning the **Scottish League Cup** on three occasions – 1947-48 (4–1 v **Falkirk**), 1949-50 (3–0 v **Dunfermline Athletic**), 1953-54 (3–2 v **Partick Thistle**) – and was again a Scottish FA Cup finalist in 1950 (0–3 v **Rangers**). East Fife won the Division Two Championship in 1947-48, finishing third in Division A in two consecutive seasons (1951-52, 1952-53) – the club's highest League position. It moved to the Bayview new purpose-built Stadium in September 1998. *League record* First Division 1975-76 to 1977-78, 1984-85 to 1987-88, 1996-97; Second Division 1978-79 to 1983-84, 1988-89 to 1995-96, 1997-98 to 1998-99; Division One (A Division) 1930-31, 1948-49 to 1957-58, 1971-72 to 1973-74; Division Two (B Division) 1921-22 to 1929-30, 1931-32 to 1947-48, 1958-59 to 1970-71, 1974-75. Third Division 1999-00. *Honours* Division Two 1947-48; Scottish FA Cup 1938 (4–2 replay v Kilmarnock); Scottish League Cup 1947-48 (4–1 v Falkirk), 1949-50 (3–0 v Dunfermline Athletic), 1953-54 (3–2 v Partick Thistle). *Records* George Aitken is East Fife's most capped player (5 (8) for **Scotland**); David Clarke holds the record for club appearances (517, 1968-86); Phil Weir is East Fife's record goalscorer (225).

East Germany *country (formerly) UEFA* (German Democratic Republic). Former communist republic in north central Europe on the Baltic. Established in 1949 from the partition of **Germany** after **World War II**. Became a sovereign state in 1954, reunited with West Germany in October 1990. Area: 108,178 sq km (42,189 sq miles). Former population: 16,850,000 (1975). Language: German. Former capital: East Berlin. Abbrevs: DDR; GDR. *Dossier* Former football associa-tion (Deutscher Fussball-Verband de DDR (Berlin) founded in 1948, affiliated to **FIFA** in 1952 (until 1990) and founder member of the **Union of European Football Associations** (UEFA) in 1954. Former national stadium: Olympia-Stadion, Berlin, capacity: 76,000. First international game: 21 September 1952 v **Poland** (0–3, friendly, Warsaw). Last international game: 12 September 1990, v **Belgium** (2–0, friendly, Brussels). Biggest victory: 12–1 v **Sri Lanka** (then known as Ceylon, 12 January 1964, Colombo, friendly). Biggest defeats: 1–4 v **Wales** (25 September 1957,

Cardiff, **World Cup** qualifier), 1–4 v **Czechoslovakia** (27 October 1957, Leipzig, World Cup qualifier), 1–4 v **Denmark** (8 May 1985, Copenhagen, friendly) and v **Sweden** (13 January 1988, Las Palmas, friendly). Most capped players: Joachim **Streich** (98 appearances, 1969–1984), Hans-Jürgen Dörner (96, 1969–1985), Jürgen Croy (94, 1967–1981), Konrad Weise (86, 1970–1981). Leading goalscorers: Joachim Streich (55 goals, 1969–1984), Hans-Jürgen Kreische (25, 1968–1975), Eberhard Vogel (25, 1962–1976). Other notable international players: Andreas Thom, Matthias **Sammer**, Jurgen Sparwasser. *International tournament record* **Olympic Games** – winners/gold medal 1976 (3–1, v Poland, in Montreal), runners-up/silver medal 1980 (0–1, v Czechoslovakia, in Moscow), third place/bronze medal 1964 (3–1, v **Egypt**, in Tokyo, third/fourth playoff), joint bronze medal 1968 (2–2, v **Soviet Union**, in Munich, third/fourth playoff); **Women's World Cup** – not applicable (first tourna-ment started after reunification); World Cup – first entered 1958, qualified for finals tournament 1974, sec-ond round; **European Championship** – entered first tournament in 1960, second round 1964, failed to reach finals tournaments 1968–1988; **European Championship for Women** – never entered; **European Junior Championship/European Youth Championship** (under-18) – 1965, 1970, 1986; **European Under-16 Championship** – runners-up 1989; **European Under-21 Championship** – run-ners-up 1978, 1980; **European Under-23 Championship** – runners-up 1974; **Under-17 World Championship** – quarter-final 1989; **World Youth Cup** (under-20) – third place 1987 (1–1, 3–1 pens., v **Chile**, in Santiago, Chile, third/fourth playoff), also qualified for finals tournament 1989. *World Cup perfor-mance* (finals and qualifiers to end of 1990 tournament) played 53, won 24, drawn 10, lost 19, scored 92 goals, conceded 70 goals; win rate 45%; goals scored per game 1.74. *Record against British and Irish national teams* v **England**, played four, drawn one, lost three; v **Northern Ireland**, none played; v **Scotland**, played six, won three, drawn one, lost two; v Wales, played four, won three, lost one; v **Republic of Ireland**, none played. *Record against West Germany* 8 September 1972 (3–2, in Munich, Olympic Games second round); 22 June 1974 (1–0, in Hamburg, World Cup finals first-round group stage). *History* The East German league championship was played from 1948 (first won by SG Planitz) until 1991 (last won by **Hansa Rostock**). Hansa Rostock also won the last East German Cup final, in 1991. The cup was first played in 1948-1949 (won by Waggonbau Dessau). 1.FC **Dynamo Dresden**, Dynamo Berlin (now known as **Berlin FC**), **Magdeburg (1.FC)**, FC Vorwärts Frankfurt/Oder (now known as **FC Victoria 91**) and FC **Carl Zeiss Jena** were the top five clubs in league and cup football. Dynamo Berlin won 10 championships in succession, from 1979 to 1988: a World record. The club was said to be linked to the East German Stasi – the former hard-line secret police force – and football historians have cast doubt on the fairness by which it achieved its 10-year league dominance. East German club successes in European tournaments were largely restricted to the **European Cup-winners Cup**. Magdeburg (1.FC) won the tournament in 1974, with a 2–0 victory over **AC Milan** in Rotterdam. Carl Zeis Jena (1981) and Lokomotive Leipzig (now **VfB Leipzig**) (1987) were both beaten finalists. Only two East German clubs, Hansa Rostock and Dynamo Dresden, won places in the German **Bundesliga** first division after reunification in 1990. East Germany won the Olympic Games gold medal in 1976, the silver medal in 1980, and the bronze medal in 1964 and 1968 (shared). East Germany's 1–0 victory over West Germany in the 1974 World Cup finals tournament was the only professional international played between the two former countries. The match, in Hamburg, was watched by 60,000 spectators and was West Germany's only defeat on its way to winning the tournament. Jürgen Sparwasser scored East Germany's goal. East Germany won the Olympic Games match between the two countries in 1972 and went on to share the bronze medal with the former-Soviet Union. East Germany played its last international game on 12 September 1990, a friendly against Belgium in Brussels. Matthias Sammer scored both East Germany's goals in the 2–0 victory. *Record in international club tournaments* **European Cup** – Wismut Karl-Marx-Stadt (now Chemnitzer FC, quarter-final 1959), Vorwärts Berlin (now FC Victoria 91, quarter-final 1970), Carl Zeis Jena (quarter-final 1971), Dynamo Dresden (quarter-final 1977, 1979), Dynamo Berlin (now Berlin FC, quarter-final 1980, 1984); European Cup-winners Cup – Magdeburg (1.FC) (1974), Carl Zeis Jena (runners-up 1981), Lokomotive Leipzig (now VfB Leipzig, runners-up 1987); **UEFA Cup** – Lokomotive Leipzig (semi-final 1974), Dynamo Dresden (semi-final 1989). Other notable club: Hansa Rostock. See Germany.

East of Scotland League *competition* Scottish amateur and semi-professional league for **senior football clubs** in the East of Scotland. The league is affiliated to the **Scottish Football Association**. Although the league is, technically, at a level directly below the **Scottish Football League** there is no direct promotion. Member clubs compete in the **Scottish Qualifying Cup** (southern section); the semi-finalists qualifying for the **Scottish FA Cup**.

East Stirlingshire *club* Scottish league. Ground: **Firs Park**, Falkirk, Lothian, capacity: 1,880. Strip: black and white striped shirts, black shorts, black socks and amber hoops. Nickname: Shire. Record attendance: 12,000 v **Partick Thistle** (19 February 1921, **Scottish FA Cup**, third round). Biggest win: 11–2 v Vale of Bannock (22 September 1888, Scottish FA Cup, second round). Biggest defeat: 1–12 v **Dundee United** (13 April 1936, Division Two). *History* Founded in 1880, East Stirling joined Division Two in 1900-01. The club has played only two seasons in the top flight (1932-33, 1963-64) since it entered the **Scottish Football**

League. Only on the first occasion did the club enter the top flight as Division Two Champions – this is the club's only honour. The board agreed a controversial merger with **Clydebank** under the name East Stirlingshire Clydebank in 1964-65. ES Clydebank played that one season in the Scottish League before the club's shareholders won a legal battle brought against Clydebank in the courts and both clubs reverted to their original names. *League record* First Division 1980-81 to 1981-82; Division One 1932-33, 1963-64; Second Division 1975-76 to 1979-80, 1982-83 to 1993-94; Third Division 1994-95 to present; Division Two (B Division) 1900-01 to 1931-32, 1933-34 to 1938-39, 1948-49, 1955-56 to 1962-63, 1964-65 to 1974-75; C Division 1946-47 to 1947-48, 1949-50 to 1954-55. *Honours* Division Two Champions 1931-32. *Records* Humphrey Jones is East Stirlingshire's most capped player (5 (14) for **Wales**); Gordon Simpson holds the record for club appearances (379, 1968-88).

Easter Road *ground* Scottish football ground situated in Edinburgh; home of **Hibernian**. *Dossier* Ground capacity: 16,218. Pitch dimensions: 102m x 68m. Record attendance: 65,860 v **Heart of Midlothian** (2 January 1950, Division One). *History* Hibernian played its first match at Easter Road, officially called Hibernian Park, in February 1893. Hibernian almost moved to a new ground at Piershill in 1909, but the club's plans were scuppered by a counter proposal from the North British Railway Company which never materialised. At the time, Easter Road was owned by the local council and, in 1922, Hibernian agreed a 25-year lease of the ground. At this time, industrial action by the builders held up redevelopment work and the club was forced to share Tynecastle on two occasions. In October 1998, Hibernian repurchased the ground for £2.5 million and is planning extensive redevelopment. Easter Road and the club had been separated by the Official Receiver in 1991 when the club almost folded. Easter Road staged its first floodlit match on 18 October 1954 (v Heart of Midlothian). Easter Road, together with **East Fife's Bayview Park** ground, was the setting, on 8 February 1956 (v **Raith Rovers**) for the first **Scottish FA Cup** tie to be played under floodlights. Scotland's 1998 **World Cup** warm-up match against **Finland** at Easter Road on 22 April 1998 was the first international to be staged at the ground for more than 110 years and the first to be held in Edinburgh, the Scottish capital city, since 1938 when **Tynecastle** was used on 9 November (v **Wales**). The only previous international match to be played at Easter Road took place on 10 March 1888 (v Wales).

Eastern Canada Professional Soccer League *competition* former regional professional football league in Canada, founded 1961, disbanded 1967.

Eastern *club* Hong Kong league club. Hong Kong Cup 1984, 1993, 1994; Hong Kong league champions 1956, 1993, 1994,1995.

Eastern Conference *competition* one of the two regional divisions of the United States **Major League**

Soccer. Its clubs are: **Columbus Crew** (Columbus, Ohio), **DC United** (Washington, District of Columbia), **Miami Fusion** (Miami, Florida), **Metrostars** (New York City), **New England Revolution** (Boston, Massachusetts), **Tampa Bay Mutiny** (Tampa, Florida). The first four clubs in the conference contest a playoff competition. The winners of this play a championship final with the winners of the **Western Conference**. Conferences and conference playoffs are also in operation in the other US football leagues, eg the **A-League/Select League**, **Pro-League** and **Premier Leagues**.

Eastern-Bloc boycott *misc.* mass withdrawal-in-protest by many of the former-communist eastern European countries from the **European Cup-winners Cup** and **European Cup** in 1968-69. The boycott had been proposed by the **Soviet Union** following a decision by **Union of European Football Associations** to regionalise the early rounds of both competitions into Communist Europe and Western Europe - apparently prompted by the Soviet invasion of **Czechoslovakia** in 1968. Spartak Sofia (**Bulgaria**), Union Berlin (**East Germany**), **Gornik Zabrze** (**Poland**), Vasas ETO Györ, now **Györ ETO FC** (**Hungary**) and **Dinamo Moscow** (**Soviet Union**) withdrew from the Cup-winners Cup. However, **Slovan Bratislava** (Czechoslovakia), FK Bor (**Yugoslavia**) and **Dinamo Bucharest** (**Romania**) decided against the boycott, and Slovan went on to win the cup. In the European Cup, **Levski Sofia** (Bulgaria), **Ferencváros** (Hungary), **Dinamo Kiev** (Soviet Union), **Ruch Chorzow** (Poland) and **Carl Zeiss Jena** (East Germany) all withdrew, while **Red Star Belgrade** (Yugoslavia), **Steaua Bucharest** (Romania) and **Spartak Trnava** (Czechoslovakia) elected to play. **AC Milan** won the tournament. The **UEFA** (Fairs) **Cup** was unaffected.

Eastville *ground* English football ground situated in Bristol; former home of **Bristol Rovers**. *Dossier* Capacity (1986): 12,500. Record attendance: 38,472 v **Preston North End** (30 January 1960, FA Cup fourth round). Best average attendance: 24,662 (1953-54). *History* Bristol Rovers played its first match at Eastville on 3 April 1897 (v **Aston Villa**, friendly), adopting the name Bristol Eastville Rovers for a short time. Rovers paid £150 for the site which had first been used by the Bristol Harlequins Rugby Club in the early-1890s. In 1940, the ground was sold to a greyhound racing company for £12,000. Eastville's main stand was mysteriously destroyed by fire on 16 August 1980. Following extensive negotiations between the club and the ground's owners, the Bristol Stadium Company, the threat of High Court action and the collapse of a **groundshare** with **Bristol City**, Rovers were forced to agree a five-year lease of Eastville at an annual rent of £50,000. Rovers' final match at Eastville took place on 26 April 1986 (v **Chesterfield**, Division Three). Eastville staged its first floodlit match on 7 September 1959 (v **Ipswich Town**, Division Two) and it hosted an **inter-League** fixture on 11 October 1961 (**Football League** v **League of Ireland**).

Ebbw Vale *club* Welsh league. Ground: Eugene Cross Park, Ebbw Vale. Gwent, capacity: 8,000. Strip: amber shirts, black shorts. Nickname: the Cowboys. Formed in 1888. *Honours* **Welsh Cup** 1926 (3–2 v Swansea Town); Welsh League 1952-53.

ebola *medical* a serious viral infection that nearly always results in death. An outbreak of ebola in **Congo Democratic Republic** (formlery Zaire) at the time of qualification to the 1996 **African Cup of Nations** led to **Lesotho** being disqualified for refusing to host a match involving the Congo DR team. In addition, **Zimbabwe**'s top players, including Bruce **Grobbelaar**, refused to play a qualifier in Congo DR and a second XI fulfilled the fixture in their place.

EC Bahia (Esporte Clube) *club* Brazilian national league and **Bahia** state league club based in Salvador, founded 1931 (merger of A A de Bahia and Baiano de Tênis). Ground: Octavio Mangabeira "Fonte Nova", capacity: 100,000. Strip: white shirts, blue shorts. EC Bahia qualified for the first **Copa Libertadores** in 1960. **Campeonato Brasileiro** champions 1988; **Copa do Brasil** 1959; state league champions 43 times (to 1998).

Ecuador *country* CONMEBOL republic of South America, on Pacific Ocean, bordered by **Colombia** and **Peru**. Includes Galápagos Islands in the Pacific. Independence from **Spain** in 1830. Area: 283,560 sq km (109,483 sq miles). Coastal plain in west separated from Amazon rainforest by Andes mountains. Population: 11,700,000 (1996 est.). Languages: Spanish, Quechua, Jivaro and other native languages. Capital: Quito. *Dossier* Football association (Federación Ecuatoriana de Fútbol, Guayaquil), founded in 1957 (predated by the Federación Deportiva Guayaquil, formed in 1925 – see below), affiliated to **FIFA** in 1926 and the **Confederación Sudamericana de Futbol** (CSF) in 1930 – president Galo Roggiero, general secretary Carlos Rodriguez. Season played from March to December. National stadium: Estadio Modelo, Guayaquil, capacity: 48,775 (40,000 seated). National strip: yellow shirts, blue shorts. First international game 8 August 1938 v **Bolivia** (1–1, in Bogota, Bolivar Games). Biggest victory: 6–0 v **Peru** (22 June 1975, in Quito, friendly). Biggest defeat: 0–12 v **Argentina** (22 January 1942, in Montevideo, **Copa America**). Leading goalscorer: Alberto **Spencer**. *International tournament record* **Olympic Games** – final qualifying round 1992, never qualified for finals tournament; **Women's World Cup** – first entered 1995, never qualified for finals tournament; **World Cup** – first entered 1962, never qualified for finals tournament; Copa America – first entered 1939, semi-final/fourth 1993 (0–1 v Colombia, in Portoviejo, Ecuador, third/fourth playoff), quarter-final 1997, hosts 1947, 1959, 1993; **South American Women's Championship** – fourth 1998 (3–3, 4–5 pens, v Peru, in Mar del Plata, Argentina, third/fourth playoff); **Under-17 World Championship** – qualified for finals tournament 1987, and 1995 as hosts; **World**

Youth Cup (under-20) – never qualified for finals tournament. *Record against British and Irish national teams* v England, played one, lost one; v **Northern Ireland**, none played; v **Scotland**, played one, lost one; v **Wales**, none played; v **Republic of Ireland**, played one, lost one. *History* Football in Ecuador first came under the auspices of the Federación Deportiva Guayaquil, formed in 1925, which become the Federación Deportiva Nacional del Ecuador. The current Federación Ecuatoriana de Fútbol was founded in 1957: a national league was started in the same year, replacing the previous regional structures. Although Ecuador has been involved in international football since 1938, it was not until April 1970 that it played a match outside South America: Ecuador played a friendly against **Mexico** in Leon, Mexico (2–4). **England** provided the first international opposition from outside the Americas (24 May 1970, 0–2, in Quito, friendly). Ecuador won only two international matches in its first 59 games, spanning more than 21 years. Both victories were against Colombia (2–1 in 1938 and 3–2 in 1949). It has never won a major international tournament, though it finished fourth when it hosted the 1993 Copa America, and no club has won a South American club tournament, though **Barcelona Sporting Club** reached the final of the **Copa Libertadores** in 1990 and 1998. *League system* There are two national divisions, Primera A and Primera B. Twelve clubs compete in the Primera A, playing each other home and away in the **Apertura** tournament. The winners of the Apertura tournament qualify for the Copa Libertadores. The second part of the season is played in two periods. The 12 Primera A clubs are divided into three groups of four clubs, organised according to their final positions in the Apertura (each group thus includes one club from the top three, one from the next three, one from the next three and one from the bottom three clubs in the Apertura). Each club plays each other twice, home and away. The final phase of the league (the "finalizacion" tournament) involves two leagues of six clubs: the top two clubs from each of the second-phase groups qualify for the championship league, while the bottom two clubs from each group play in the relegation league. Clubs again play each other at home and away in these final tournaments. The final tournaments are complicated further by the introduction of bonus and minus points: the winners of the Apertura take three **bonus points** into the championship league, with the second-placed club taking two points forward. Similarly, the bottom and second-bottom clubs in the Apertura take forward minus-three and minus-two points, respectively, into the relegation league. The bottom two clubs in the relegation league (taking into account the minus points from the Apertura) are relegated to the Primera B. The winners of the championship league play the winners of the Apertura to decide the overall Ecuador league championship (the championship playoff is played over two legs, home and away). The eight clubs in the Primera B play each other four times, with a conventional league format, two clubs

automatically promoted, and two clubs relegated to the Segunda divisions. There are 12 provincial leagues within the Segunda division. The two Segunda division promotion places are decided by end-of-season playoffs involving the champions and runners-up from each provincial league. *Record in international club tournaments* Copa Libertadores – Barcelona Sporting Club (runners-up 1990, 1998, semi-final 1971, 1972, 1986, 1987, 1992, quarter-final 1996), **Liga Deportivo Universitaria** (semi-final 1975, 1976), **Club Deportivo El Nacional** (semi-final 1985), **Club Sport Emelec** (semi-final 1995, quarter-final 1990); **Copa CONMEBOL** – Club Deportivo El Nacional (semi-final 1992), Club Sport Emelec (quarter-final 1996); **Copa Merconorte** – Club Deportivo El Nacional (semi-final 1998). Other leading clubs: **Deportivo Quito**, Deportivo Cuenca.

Edgeley Park　*ground*　English football ground situated in Stockport, Greater Manchester; home of **Stockport County**. *Dossier* Ground capacity: 11,540. Pitch dimensions 101m x 66m. Record attendance: 27,833 v **Liverpool** (11 February 1950, **FA Cup**, fifth round). Best average attendance: 14,399 (1937-38). *History* Edgeley Park was first used for rugby in 1891 and County shared the ground with a rugby club when it moved there in 1902. The rugby club folded a year later, leaving County to develop the ground as a football stadium. County played its first match there on 13 September 1902 (v **Gainsborough Trinity**, Division Two). In July 1935, the main stand and 12 nearby houses were destroyed by fire. Rugby returned to Edgeley Park during **World War II**, when Broughton Park played there. Edgeley Park was sold to the local council in 1964 but ownership was later returned to the club. For almost 10 years, the ground was only three-sided; the Cheadle End stand was demolished in 1985 on the orders of safety inspectors and its 6,000 all seated replacement did not open until August 1995. The first floodlit match at Edgeley Park took place on 16 October 1956 (v Fortuna 54 Geleen, friendly).

Edinburgh City　*club*　former Scottish League. *Dossier* Ground: City Park, Edinburgh. *Keynotes* Founded in 1928 and joining Scottish Division Two in 1931-32. The club played at several grounds before settling at City Park in 1937. In eight seasons prior to **World War II**, Edinburgh never finished higher than 15th in Division Two and bottom on six occasions. The club's worst performance was in 1936-37, when it accumulated just seven points and conceded 120 goals in 34 fixtures. With the resumption of football after the war, Edinburgh spent three seasons in the short-lived C Division before disbanding in 1949. *League record* Division Two 1931-32 to 1938-39; C Division 1946-47 to 1948-49.

Edwards, Duncan　*player*　Midfield. **England** international (18 caps, 5 goals). Born 1 October 1936. Career ca.1952–1958. *Clubs* **Manchester United**. *Keynotes* Joined Manchester United as an amateur in May 1952, turning professional in October 1953. Edwards made his

United debut at the age of 16 years and 285 days – a club record – and he won his first England cap when he was only 18 years and 183 days (v **Scotland**, 2 April 1955). Edwards made 175 **Football League** appearances for United in a career that was ended in 1958 when he was involved in the **Munich air crash** and died after fighting for his life for 15 days – the last of the eight United players to die. A stained glass window depicting Edwards is in the Parish Church of St Francis in Dudley, his home town. Included in the **Football League Centenary 100 players**. *Honours* League Championship (Manchester United 1955-56, 1956-57).

Egypt *country CAF* Arab republic in northeast Africa on Mediterranean and Red Sea. Bordered by **Sudan**, **Libya** and **Israel**. The nation of Egypt dates back some 5,000 years, occupied by the British in 1882, became a kingdom in 1922, full independence from Britain in 1936, and a republic in 1953. Area: 1,000,250 sq km (386,095 sq miles). Around 96% of the land mass is desert. Population: 60,240,000 (1996 est.). Language: Arabic, Berber, Nubian, English and French. Capital: Cairo (El Qahira). *Dossier* Egyptian Football Association (Cairo) formed in 1921, affiliated to **FIFA** in 1923, founder member of the **Confédération Africaine de Football** (CAF) in 1957, member of the **Arab Football Union**, president Samir Zaher, general secretary General Khalil Mohamed El Deeb. Season played from September to June. National stadium: Nasser International Stadium, Cairo, capacity: 100,000 all seated. National strip: red shirts, white shorts. Nickname of national team: the Pharoahs. First international game: 29 August 1920 v **Italy** (1–2, in Gent, Belgium, **Olympic Games** first round). Biggest victory: 10–0 v **South Korea** (October 1964, Olympic Games first round). Biggest defeat: 3–11 v Italy (10 June 1928, in Amsterdam, Netherlands, Olympic Games third/fourth place playoff). Highest crowd: 100,000, International Stadium, Cairo, 21 March 1986 (v **Cameroon**, 0–0, 5–4 pens., **African Cup of Nations** final). Notable international players: Mahmoud **Al Khatib**, Ibrahim Youssef, Hany Ramzy. *International tournament record* Olympic Games – first entered 1920 (the first African nation to play in the finals tournament), semi-final/fourth 1928, 1964, quarter-final 1984, also played in finals tournament 1920, 1924, 1936, 1948, 1952, 1960, 1992; **Women's World Cup** – first entered 1999; **World Cup** – first entered 1934 (the first African nation to play in the finals tournament; first round), also qualified for finals tournament 1990 (first round); African Cup of Nations – entered first tournament in 1957, 1957 (4–0, v **Ethiopia**, in Khartoum, Sudan), 1959 (maximum points in the three-nation tournament in Cairo), 1986 (0–0, 5–4 pens., v Cameroon, in Cairo), 1998 (2–0, v **South Africa**, in Ouagadougou, Burkina Faso, runners-up 1962 (2–4, v Ethiopia, in Addis Ababa, Ethiopia),third 1963 (3–0 v Ethiopia, in Accra, Ghana, third/fourth playoff), semi-final/third 1970 (3–1, v **Ivory Coast**, in Khartoum, third/fourth playoff), 1974 (4–0, v **Congo**, in Cairo, third/fourth

playoff), fourth 1976, semi-final/fourth 1984, quarter-final 1994, 1996, hosts 1959, 1974, 1986; **African Under-20 Youth Championship/Junior Nations Cup** – 1981 (3–1 agg., v Cameroon), 1991 (2–1 v Ivory Coast); **Afro-Asian Cup of Nations** – runners-up 1987 (1–1, 3–4, pens., v South Korea); **All Africa Games** – 1987 (v host nation **Kenya**), 1995 (v host nation **Zimbabwe**); **Arab Cup of Nations** – 1992 (3–2, v **Saudi Arabia**, in Syria); Arab Games – 1953; **Under-17 World Championship** – quarter-final 1997, also qualified for finals tournament 1987, hosts 1997; **World Youth Cup** (under-20) – quarter-final 1981, qualified for finals tournament 1991. *Record against British and Irish national teams* v **England**, played two, lost two; v **Northern Ireland**, none played; v **Scotland**, played one, won one; v **Wales**, none played; v **Republic of Ireland**, played one, drawn one. *History* Football was introduced in the 19th century. Egypt was the first nation from Africa to join FIFA and the first to play in the World Cup (1934). It was Africa's sole representative in the World Cup until Sudan entered in 1958. A domestic cup competition has been played virtually every year since 1922 (as the Farouk Cup; replaced by the Cup of Egypt in 1949). Regional leagues operated from 1938, in Cairo, Alexandria, and Bahary and Canal. The national league championship started in 1948. Egypt won the first African Cup of Nations in 1957 and its win in the 1998 final equalled **Ghana**'s record of four championships. It has appeared in more African Cup of Nations finals tournaments than any other country (16, to 1998). Egypt's Ayman Mansour is thought to hold the record for the fastest goal scored at an African Cup of Nations finals tournament: 23 seconds, v **Gabon** (28 March 1994, at the Zoulten Stadium, Tunis, first-round group). Cairo is the headquarters of CAF, Egypt also providing two past presidents: Abdelaziz Abdallah Salem (1957-58), and Abdelaziz Mostafa (1958-68), and all four general secretaries. The **Al Ahly** club was formed in 1907. Domestic football has been dominated by Al Ahly and **Zamalek**, winning 36 of the first 43 league championships between them from 1949 to 1999 (the league was not played in all years). Zamalek is the most successful club in the **African Cup of Champion Clubs** with four titles (to 1998), while Al Ahly is the most successful club in the **African Cup-winners Cup**, with four titles (to 1999). *World Cup performance* (finals and qualifiers to end of 1998 tournament) played 48, won 21, drawn 13, lost 14, scored 67 goals, conceded 45 goals; win rate 44%; goals scored per game 1.40. *League system* Sixteen clubs compete in the national league (increased from 14 in 1996), playing each other home and away in each season. Three points are awarded for a win and one for a draw. *Record in international club tournaments* African Cup of Champion Clubs – **Ismailia Sporting Club** (1969, semi-final 1995), Al Ahly (1982, 1987, runners-up 1983), Zamalek (1984, 1986, 1993, 1996, runners-up 1994, quarter-final "champions-league" stage 1997), **Mehalla Al Kubra** (runners-up 1974); African Cup-winners Cup – **Al Mokaouloum** (Arab Contractors, 1982, 1983, 1996, quarter-final 1997), Al Ahly (1984, 1985, 1986, 1993), Mansoura (semi-final 1997); **African Super Cup** – Zamalek (1993, 1997); **Afro-Asian Club Cup** – Zamalek (1987, 1997), Al Ahly (1987); **Arab Club Champions Cup** – Al Ahly (1996, runners-up 1997); **Arab Cup-winners Cup** – Al Ahly (1994); **Arab Super Cup** – Al Ahly (winers 1997, 1998). Other leading club: Al-Masry (of Port Said, Egyptian Cup 1998).

Eintracht Frankfurt (SG) *club* German league. *Dossier* Ground: Waldstadion Stadion, Frankfurt, capacity: 61,000. Strip: red shirts and black shirts, black shorts. *History* Formed in 1899, merging with Kicker & Viktoria Frankfurt and Frankfurter FV in 1911. Officially called Sport Gemeinde Eintracht Frankfurt. The club was Germany's first finalist in a European club competition, playing in the classic **European Cup** final of 1960 (3–7 v **Real Madrid**), having won its only (West) German League title the previous season. Eintracht reached the German League national **playoff** final in 1932 (0–2 v **Bayern Munich**) and other than its 1959 West German Championship triumph, most of the club's success has come in the domestic cup competition. Since **World War II**, Eintracht has been a German Cup (**DFB Pokal**) finalist on five occasions, winning the trophy in 1974, 1975, 1981 and 1988, and having been defeated in its first appearance in 1964 (0–2 v TSV München 1860). Eintracht won the **UEFA Cup** in 1980, defeating fellow **Bundesliga** club **Borussia Mönchengladbach** on the **away goals** rule in the first all-German European club final. The club was a **European Cup-winners Cup** semi-finalist in 1976 (3–4 agg. v **West Ham United**) and a quarter-finalist in both 1982 (1–4 agg. v **Tottenham Hotspur**) and 1989 (0–1 agg. v **KV Mechelen**). *Honours* UEFA Cup 1980 (3–3, away goals v Borussia Mönchengladbach); West German Cup 1974 (3–1 v **Hamburg SV**), 1975 (1–0 v MSV Duisburg), 1981 (3–1 v **Kaiserslautern** (1.FC)), 1988 (1–0 v VfL Bochum); West German League 1959 (5–3 v Kickers Offenbach).

Ekranas Panevezys *club* Lithuanian national league club, based in Panevezys, founded 1962. Ground: Aukstaitija, capacity: 10,000. Lithuanian Cup 1998, runners-up 1994; Lithuanian league champions 1993; Lithuanian regional Cup 1985; Lithuanian regional league champions 1985.

El Hilal *club* Sudanese Khartoum-Omdurman league club based in Omdurman, formed 1930. Ground: Hilal, capacity: 45,000. Strip: blue shirts, white shorts. **African Cup of Champion Clubs** runners-up 1987 (0–2 agg., v **Al Ahly Cairo** of Egypt), 1992 (0–2 agg., v **Wydad AC Casablanca** of Morocco); **CAF Cup** quarter-final 1998; **East and Central African Club Championship** – semi-final 1988; Sudanese Cup 1977, 1993; Sudanese league champions 1962, 1964, 1965, 1966, 1967, 1973, 1974 (there were two championships in 1974), 1980, 1981, 1983, 1984, 1986, 1987, 1988, 1989, 1991, 1994, 1995, 1996, 1998.

El Merreikh Sports Club *club* Sudanese Khartoum-Omdurman league club based in Omdurman, formed 1931. Ground: Omdurman, capacity: 38,000. Strip: red shirts, yellow shorts. **African Cup-winners Cup** 1989 (1–0 agg., v Bendel United of Nigeria), semi-final 1990; **East and Central African Club Championship** – 1986, 1994, runners-up 1987, 1993; Sudanese Cup 1970, 1971, 1972, 1983, 1984, 1985, 1986, 1988, 1991, 1992, 1994, 1996; Sudanese league champions 1970, 1971, 1972, 1973, 1974 (there were two championships in 1974), 1975, 1977, 1978, 1982, 1985, 1990, 1993, 1997.

El Mourada *club* Sudanese Khartoum-Omdurman league club based in Omdurman, formed 1930. Ground: Mourada, capacity: 15,000. Strip: red shirts, blue shorts. **CAF Cup** semi-final 1994; **East and Central African Club Championship** – third place 1995; Sudanese Cup 1989, 1995; Sudanese league champions 1968.

El Nacional *club* see **Club Deportivo El Nacional**.

El Pichichi *misc.* **Spain**'s top goalscorer (all competitions) each season. It is named after the former **Athletic Bilbao** striker Rafael Moreno, who was nicknamed Pitxitxi (Pichichi in Castillian Spanish), and who played for the Basque club in its early years.

El Salvador *country* CONCACAF republic in central America on Pacific Ocean. Bordered by **Honduras** and **Guatemala**. Area: 21,395 sq km (8,260 sq miles). Population: 5,050,000 (1992 census). Languages: Spanish and Nahuatl. Capital: San Salvador. *Dossier* Football association (Federación Salvadoreña de Fútbol, San Salvador) founded in 1935, affiliated to **FIFA** in 1938 and **Confederación Norte-Centroamericana y del Caribe de Fútbol** (CONCACAF) in 1962, president Juan Torres Polanco, general secretary Fidel António Gonzalez. Season played from January to November. National stadium: Estadio Nacional de Flor Blanca, San Salvador, capacity: 60,000. National strip: blue shirts, white shorts. Biggest defeat: 1–10 v **Hungary** (15 June 1982, in Elche, Spain, **World Cup** first round). *International tournament record* **Olympic Games** – qualified for finals tournament in 1968 (first round); **Women's World Cup** – did not enter first two tournaments in 1991 and 1995; World Cup – first entered 1970, qualified for finals tournament 1970 and 1982, reached final qualifying round of 1998 tournament; **CCCF Championship** – 1943 (four-nation league, in San Salvador), runners-up 1941 (second, behind **Costa Rica**, in five-nation league, in San José, Costa Rica), 1961 (second, behind Costa Rica, in four-nation final-round group, in San José, Costa Rica); **Central American and Caribbean Games** 1954; **CONCACAF Championship** – runners-up 1963 (second, behind Costa Rica, in four-nation final-round group, in San Salvador); **CONCACAF Youth Championship** (under-20) – 1964; **Gold Cup** – qualified 1998 (fifth in six-nation group); **Under-17 World Championship** – never qualified; World Youth Cup (under-20) – never qualified. *Record against British and Irish national teams* none played. *History* The El Salvador national league started in 1926, though the oldest major league club, Club Deportivo **Luis Angel Firpo**, was founded in 1923 (the club was named after an Argentinean boxer). The current Federación Salvadoreña de Fútbol was formed in 1935; El Salvador was a founder member of the Confederación Centroamericana y del Caribe (CCCF, the forerunner of CONCACAF) in 1938. Former El Salvador team Club Deportivo Hercules won seven consecutive league championships (1928 to 1934), which remains a record for Central America and is matched only by **Robin Hood** of **Surinam** among clubs from the CONCACAF nations. Three clubs have won the **CONCACAF Champions Cup**, the region's premier international club competition: **Alianza**, **Deportivo Aguila** and **Club Deportivo FAS**. **Atlético Marte** won the **CONCACAF Cup-winners Cup** in 1991. El Salvador played in the first CCCF Championship in 1941, finishing second in the five-nation tournament in Costa Rica. The most notorious point in the history of football in El Salvador was in 1969 – the so-called **Fútbol War**. El Salvador defeated Honduras in a World Cup qualifier playoff (3–2, in Mexico City, second-round playoff; the two countries had both won their home match in the two-leg tie). The playoff was the final trigger in a climate of continued border disputes and troubles involving migrants from El Salvador working in Honduras. El Salvador troops invaded Honduras and 2,000 people were killed in the ensuing fighting. El Salvador went on to qualify for the World Cup finals in Mexico, but lost all three of its first-round group games, conceding nine goals, with none scored. El Salvador again qualified for the World Cup finals of 1982 but again lost all its group matches. *League system* Ten teams compete in the national Primera Division, each club playing each other four times a season. The top six clubs compete in an end-of-season straight knockout tournament; the championship is decided by a playoff between the winner of the first phase league and the end-of-season tournament (no playoff is required if one side wins both phases). The bottom club in the main league is automatically relegated to the second division. *Record in international club tournaments* CONCACAF Champions Cup – Alianza (1967, semi-final 1994), Deportivo Aguila (1976), Club Deportivo FAS (1979), Atlético Marte (runners-up 1981), Luis Angel Firpo (quarter-final 1997, 1998); CONCACAF Cup-winners Cup – Atlético Marte (1991), Luis Angel Firpo (runners-up 1995, third 1993); **Torneo Grandes de Centroamerica** – Alianza (1997, runners-up 1996).

Elect Sport *club* Chad national league club based in the capital N'Djamena. Ground: Concorde (the national stadium), capacity: 25,000. Chad Cup runners-up 1993; Chad league champions 1990, 1992.

election *n.* see **re-election**.

electric fence *misc.* low-voltage electric fence (similar to those used for cattle and sheep fencing) was erected at **Stamford Bridge** in 1985 under the instructions of **Chelsea** chairman Ken Bates, designed to keep spectators from running on to the pitch. He was prevented from using it by the local authority environmental health officers.

elevation *medical* raising of an injured limb so that fluid can drain backwards rather than accumulate due to gravity. The leg has to be raised above the level of the pelvis; the arm has to be raised above the shoulder.

Eleven Men In Flight *club* Swaziland national league club based in Thabankulu. Ground: Mayaluka, capacity: 10,000. The first professional club in Swaziland. **African Cup-winners Cup** second round 1994; Swaziland Cup 1993; Swaziland league champions 1994, 1996, runners-up 1995.

Elimai Semipalatinsk *club* Kazakhstan national league club based in Elimai (Yelimai), founded 1964 (as Tsementnik, later Spartak, current name since 1994). Ground: Spartak, capacity: 15,000. Kazakhstan Cup 1995; the club won the cup again in 1996, but refused to accept the trophy as a protest against Kazakhstan football authorities (the cup was awarded to **Kairat Alma-Ata**); Kazakhstan league champions 1995, 1998.

Elkjaer-Larsen, Preben *player* Striker **Denmark** international (38 goals, ca. 1977-87). *Clubs* **Cologne (1.FC)**, Lokeren, Verona. *Honours* **European Championship** semi-final (Denmark, 1984); *World Soccer* **World Footballer of the Year** runner-up 1985; *France Football* **European Footballer of the Year** runner-up 1985.

Elland Road *ground* English football ground situated in Leeds, West Yorkshire; home of **Leeds United**. *Dossier* Ground capacity: 40,000 all seated. Pitch dimensions: 100.5m x 66m. Record attendance: 57,892 v **Oldham Athletic** (15 March 1967, **FA Cup**, fifth round replay). Best average attendance: 39,204 (1970-71). *History* Originally the home of Leeds Rugby Club and later Holbeck Rugby Club, which bought the ground for £1,000. Elland Road staged its first major football match on 23 April 1898 (Hunslet AFC v Harrogate, West Yorkshire Cup Final). In August 1904, members of Hunslet AFC formed **Leeds City** and became Holbeck's tenants at Elland Road, leasing it for £75 a year before the club exercised its option to purchase the ground. City played its first match at the ground on 15 October 1904 (v **Hull City**, friendly). When Leeds City was expelled from the **Football League** in October 1919 (see Leeds City), Elland Road's fixtures and fittings, such as goalposts and nets, were auctioned along with the club's players. Various plans as to the future use of Elland Road were put forward at the time and included its purchase by a brick manufacturer, a home for the Yorkshire Amateurs club, or a new venue for the financially-strapped **Huddersfield Town**. Eventually a new club, Leeds United, was formed to replace City and Elland Road's new inhabitants gradually developed the ground. Disaster struck on 18 September 1956, when an electrical fault started a fire that destroyed the west stand. The replacement stand, which opened on 31

August 1957, was partly funded by a public appeal that raised a third of the £180,000 cost. The ground has suffered a number of crowd problems over the years. An FA Cup quarter-final replay (**Barnsley** v **Bradford City**), for example, was **abandoned** in March 1912 after thousands of fans broke down the gates to the ground, forcing others to spill on to the pitch. Fifty-five years later, 30 people were taken to hospital when crush barriers collapsed during an FA Cup fifth round replay (Leeds United v **Sunderland**), a match that attracted Elland Road's record attendance. Following this incident, the ground was extensively modernised, including the building of new north (Kop) and south stands. Crowd unrest at the ground in 1971 (16 April) following a controversial refereeing decision during a League game against **West Bromwich Albion**, that effectively cost Leeds the title, led to Elland Road being closed for the club's first four matches of the 1971-72 season (see Leeds United). In 1982, Hunslet Rugby League club became tenants of Elland Road and, in 1985, Leeds, heavily in debt, sold the ground to the local council for £2.5 million. As part of the deal, Leeds agreed a 125-year "licence" with the council that involved a yearly rent of £160,000 plus 20% of all the club's annual receipts. The licence was renegotiated in 1991; a higher rent and a cap on the council's share of receipts. To fund the ground's conversion into an **all-seater stadium** following the **Taylor Report**, the club issued a bond in January 1992, which would enable investors to receive **season ticket** price discounts over the following seven years. The switch to all seated accommodation was completed by the start of the 1994-95 season. Over the years, Elland Road has staged a number of important football matches and has been regularly used as a venue for other sporting events, particularly Rugby League fixtures, including Challenge Cup final replays and semi-finals, and Great Britain internationals. The ground was selected as a **European Championship** venue in 1996, hosting group B matches (**Spain** v **Bulgaria**; **France** v Spain; **Romania** v Spain). Elland Road also staged the **England** v **Sweden** fixture (8 June 1995) as part of the 1995 **Umbro tournament**, that also included **Brazil** and **Japan**. The ground has hosted eight FA Cup semi-finals and the 1914 **Amateur Cup** Final (Bishop Auckland v Northern Nomads). The first floodlit match to take place at Elland Road occurred on 9 November 1953 (v **Hibernian**, friendly).

Elm Park *ground* former English football ground situated in Reading, Berkshire; former home of **Reading**. *Dossier* Capacity when closed: 15,000. Pitch dimensions 102m x 70m. Record attendance: 33,042 v **Brentford** (19 February 1927, **FA Cup**, fifth round). Best average attendance: 15,973 (1950-51). *History* Elm Park is built on a former gravel pit and it became Reading's home in 1896. The club played its first match there on 5 September (v Mr Roston Bourke's XI, friendly), but the game was abandoned due to torrential rain and the club was fined by the **Football Association** because the opposing team was not

officially recognised. In 1995, with backing from multi-millionaire auto magazine publisher John Madejski, who bought the club in September 1990, Reading announced plans to relocate to a new £37 million **Madejski Stadium** alongside the M4 at Smallmead. Reading played its final **Football League** match at Elm Park on 3 May 1998 (v **Norwich City**). The first floodlit match at Elm Park, which was also broadcast by BBC television, took place on 6 October 1954 (v Racing Club de Paris, friendly).

employment tribunal *legal* statutory body that makes binding judgements on disputes between employers and employees. There are a number of football-related incidents going to employment tribunals. *Keynotes* In October 1997, **Manchester City** admitted unfairly terminating the employment of youth development officers Colin **Bell** and Terry Farrell. The two former City players had taken the club to an employment tribunal claiming unfair dismissal. In November 1997, **Chester City** manager Kevin **Ratcliffe** was found guilty of racial discrimination by an employment tribunal. The tribunal ruled that Ratcliffe had verbally abused a former Chester apprentice, James Hussaney. Female coach Vanessa Hardwick took the **Football Association** to an employment tribunal in September 1997 alleging that she had been failed in an examination for the FA's advanced coaching licence due to sexual discrimination. The tribunal found the FA guilty and awarded Hardwick £5,000 damages plus compensation. Former **Lincoln City** manager John Beck took the club to an employment tribunal in August 1998 claiming unfair dismissal after he was dismissed from his post. The club claimed that Beck's unauthorised absence (a skiing holiday) at a time when it was challenging for promotion was a breach of contract and the culmination of a difficult period in which the relationship between the club's board and Beck deteriorated. Beck lost the case. Formerly called industrial tribunal.

England *country* UEFA the largest constituent country of **Great Britain**, bordered by **Scotland** to the north and **Wales** to the west. Area: 130,360 sq km (50,320 sq miles). Mild, wet and variable climate; with the highest rainfall in the Lake District, and lowest in East Anglia. Population: 46,400,000 (1991 census). Language: English. Capital: London. *Dossier* The **Football Association** (FA, London) founded 1863, affiliated to FIFA 1905, permanent member of the **International FA Board**, and founder member of the **Union of European Football Associations** (UEFA) in 1954, president: Keith Wiseman ; general secretary: RH Graham Kelly(awaiting appointment). Season played from August to May. National stadium: **Wembley** Stadium, London, capacity: (under reconstruction). National strip: white shirts with navy blue collar, navy blue shorts, white socks with light blue top. First official international game: 30 November 1872 v Scotland (0–0, Glasgow, friendly); an unofficial game was played on 5 March 1870 (1–1 v Scotland representative side, London). First game v Wales 18 January 1879 (2–1,

London, friendly); v **Ireland** 18 February 1882 (13–0, Belfast, friendly); v **Northern Ireland** 22 October 1924 (3–1, **Goodison Park**, Liverpool, **Home International Championship**); v **Republic of Ireland** 30 September 1946 (1–0, Dublin, friendly). Biggest victory: 13–0 v Ireland (above); England beat **France** 15–0 in an amateur game on 1 November 1906 (Paris, friendly). Biggest defeat: 1–7 v **Hungary** (23 May 1954, Budapest, friendly). Most capped players: Peter **Shilton** (125 appearances, 1970-90), Bobby **Moore** (108 appearances, 1962-73), Bobby **Charlton** (106 appearances, 1958-70), Billy **Wright** (105 appearances, 1946-59), Bryan **Robson** (90 appearances, 1980-91),Kenny Sansom (86 appearances, 1979-88), Ray Wilkins (84 appearances, 1976-86), Gary **Lineker** (80 appearances, 1984-92), John **Barnes** 79 appearances, 1983-96). Leading goalscorers: Bobby Charlton (49 goals in 106 appearances), Gary Lineker (48 goals in 80 appearances), Jimmy **Greaves** (44 goals in 57 appearances, 1959-67), Tom **Finney** (30 goals in 76 appearances, 1946-58), Nat **Lofthouse** (30 goals in 33 appearances, 1950-58), Vivian **Woodward** (29 goals in 23 appearances, 1903-11), David **Platt** (28 goals in 62 appearances, 1990-96). National team coaches/managers: Walter Winterbottom (1946-62), Sir Alf **Ramsey** (1962-74), Joe **Mercer** (**caretaker manager**, 1974), Don **Revie** (1974-77), Ron Greenwood (1977-82), Bobby **Robson** (1982-90), Graham **Taylor** (1990-94), Terry **Venables** (1994-96), Glenn **Hoddle** (1996-99), Kevin **Keegan** (1999-). *International tournament record* **Olympic Games** – winners/gold medal 1908 (2–0, v **Denmark**, White City, London), 1912 (4–2, v Denmark, in Stockholm, Sweden) (see also Great Britain); **Women's World Cup** – see **England, women**; **World Cup** – first entered 1950, 1966 (4–2, a.e.t., v West **Germany**, Wembley Stadium, London), fourth 1990 (1–1, 3–4 pens., v Germany, Turin, semi-final 1–2, v **Italy**, Bari, third/fourth playoff), quarter-final 1954, 1962, 1970, 1986, second round 1982, qualified for finals tournament 1950, 1958, 1998, hosts 1966; **European Championship** – first entered 1964 (the second tournament), third 1968 (0–1, v **former-Yugoslavia,** in Florence, Italy, semi-final; 2–0, v **Soviet Union**, Rome, third/fourth playoff), semi-final 1996 (1–1, 5–6 pens., v Germany, Wembley Stadium, semi-final), quarter-final 1972, qualified for finals tournament 1980, 1988, 1992, hosts 1996; **European Championship for Women** – see **England, women**; **European Junior Championship/ European Under-18 Youth Championship** 1948, 1963, 1964, 1971, 1972, 1973, 1975, 1980, 1993; **European Under-21 Championship** – 1982, 1984; **Home International Championship** (British Championship) 54 times; **Under-17 World Championship** – never qualified; **World Youth Cup** (under-20) – third 1993 (1–2, v **Ghana**, in Sydney, Australia, semi-final; 2–1 v **Australia**, in Sydney, third/fourth playoff); fourth 1981 (1–2 v **Qatar**, in Sydney, Australia, semi-final; 0–1 v **Romania**, in

Sydney, third/fourth playoff), qualified for finals 1999. *Record against other British and Irish national teams* v all-Ireland 31 wins, three defeats, four draws; v Northern Ireland 43 wins, three defeats, 12 draws; v Republic of Ireland five wins, two defeats, six draws, one abandoned match; v Scotland 44 wins, 40 defeats, 24 draws; v Wales 62 wins, 14 defeats. 21 draws. *History* A rudimentary form of football (**harpastum**) is thought to have been introduced to England by the Romans. **Mob football** – often involving whole villages trying to get the ball to their opponents' end by any means possible – was played from the Middle Ages and, because of its violent nature, was outlawed at various times. Organised football began early in the 19th century, chiefly developed by the English public schools. Rules varied according to where the game was played, but involved a combination of kicking and some handling. The first formal sets of rules were produced at Rugby School in 1846 and Eton College in 1847, with the **Cambridge Rules** drawn up at Cambridge University in 1848 in an attempt to unify the playing codes (see **Laws of the Game**, *history*). The Football Association was set up at a meeting on 26 October 1863, at the **Freemasons Tavern**, Great Queen Street, London. It was the world's first national association. The meeting comprised members of 10 London-based clubs (see Football Association for details). The new association adopted a set of rules broadly based on a revised version of the Cambridge rules; these outlawed players from holding and running with the ball, and retained the principle that a player could make a clean catch and take a free kick from the point (or mark) of the catch. The goals were to be eight yards (7.3 metres) wide, not five as stipulated at Cambridge. There were 13 original rules of association football. The first match under the new rules was played at Mortlake, London, on 19 December 1863 (Barnes v Richmond, 0–0). The world's first national cup competition, the FA Challenge Cup (see **FA Cup**) was proposed by the FA's honorary secretary, Charles **Alcock**, and agreed at a meeting of the FA on 20 July 1871. The first final, in 1872, was won by **Wanderers** (captained by Alcock). Professional football was introduced in the early 1880s and made legal in 1885. The world's first national league, the **Football League**, was founded in 1888 (see Football League for the history of English league football). The Football Association joined FIFA in 1905 but resigned its membership in 1920 (until 1924) and again in 1928 (see **Football Association** for details). The five most successful clubs in the history of English domestic football are: **Liverpool** (18 Premier League/Division One championships, five FA Cups, five League Cups); **Manchester United** (11 championships, nine FA Cups, one League Cup); **Arsenal** (11 championships, seven FA Cups, two League Cups); **Everton** (nine championships, five FA Cups); and **Aston Villa** (seven championships, seven FA Cups, five League Cups). English clubs were not represented at the first **European Cup**; the Football League advising the 1955 Division One champions **Chelsea** to decline the invitation to participate. The first English teams to enter European club competitions were **Birmingham City** and the **London Select XI**; both entered the first Inter Cities Fairs Cup (the original version of the **UEFA Cup**) which ran from 1955 to 1958. London was beaten 2–8 (agg.) by **Barcelona** in the final. Birmingham City was beaten finalist in the next two tournaments, 1960 and 1961. Manchester United was the first English club to enter the European Cup, competing in the second tournament in 1956-57. It won its first round against **RSC Anderlecht** 2–0 away and 10–0 at home, but lost to eventual champions **Real Madrid** in the semi-final (3–5 agg.). Manchester United reached the semi-final again in 1958; but the competition was tragically marred by the **Munich air crash** on 6 February 1958, in which 23 people were killed, including eight Manchester United players. United was travelling back from its quarter-final away leg against **Red Star Belgrade**. **Tottenham Hotspur** was the first English club to win a European club competition, the **European Cup-winners Cup** in 1963, with a 5–1 victory over **Atlético Madrid** at the final at the **Feyenoord Stadion**, Rotterdam. Jimmy Greaves scored two of Tottenham's goals. Manchester United became the first English club to win the European Cup, beating **Benfica** 4–1 (after extra time) in the 1968 final at Wembley Stadium. Bobby Charlton, a survivor of the Munich Air Crash, scored two of the goals, with the others from George **Best** and Brian Kidd. Although English clubs had considerable success in the European Cup-winners Cup and Fairs Cup/UEFA Cup competitions of the late 1960s and early 1970s (see records below), the English domination of European football was at its peak in the late 1970s and early 1980s. Perhaps the best European club side of the period, Liverpool, won the European Cup four times (1977, 1978, 1981, 1984) and was beaten finalist in 1985. In between Liverpool's successes, **Nottingham Forest** (1979, 1980) and Aston Villa (1982) gave English clubs victory in the European Cup in seven out of eight seasons from 1977 to 1984. The most successful period in English club football came to an end at the 1985 European Cup final between Liverpool and **Juventus** at Heysel Stadium, Brussels. Rioting inside the stadium led to the deaths of 39 people as a wall collapsed (see **Heysel Stadium disaster**). The incident led to a lengthy ban of English clubs from all European competitions (see **hooliganism**). Having dominated European club competitions for more than a decade, English clubs did not win again until Manchester United's victory in the 1991 European Cup-winners Cup. English clubs are second in the "league table" of European club trophies: by 1999, English clubs had won 26 European trophies, compared with 26 by Italian clubs, and 23 by Spanish clubs. English clubs had appeared in 39 finals, compared with 42 by Spanish clubs, and 50 finals by Italian clubs. England has had mixed fortunes in international nations' football, although, with Scotland, it will forever hold the distinction of taking part in the first ever international

fixture. England's first international match took place at the Oval on 5 March 1870, against Scotland (1–1, with Baker scoring for England), but the sides were "representative" rather than truly international (all the Scotland players played for London-based clubs and some had only tenuous connections to Scotland). The first official international, also against Scotland, was played on 30 November 1872 (St Andrew's Day), at the West of Scotland Cricket Club, Partick, Scotland (0–0). The match was organised by the Scottish club **Queen's Park**, and watched by 4,000 spectators, with gate receipts of £103. The first victory in an official international match went to England in a rematch the following year (4–2, v Scotland, 8 March 1873, at the Oval, London): England's Alexander Bonsor scored the first official international goal. An England representative side played an unofficial game against Germany on 21 September 1901 (12–0, London, friendly). England played its first official game outside the United Kingdom on 6 June 1908 (6–1 v **Austria**, Vienna, friendly). Its first international tournament triumph (apart from the Home International Championships) came in October of the same year, with England beating Denmark 2–0 to take the gold medal in the Olympic Games at White City, London. England won the Olympic gold medal again in 1912, beating Denmark 4–2 at the Stockholms Stadion in Stockholm. As a consequence of its resignation from FIFA in 1928, England's international fixtures between the wars were confined to the Home International Championship and friendlies against, for example, France, Belgium, Germany and **Spain**. It was not eligible to enter the first three World Cup tournaments (1930-38), and thus missed the opportunity to keep abreast of developing techniques and skills in South America. By the late 1930s, however, a number of highly skilled players were beginning to emerge in England, including Stanley **Matthews**, Denis **Compton**, Raich **Carter**, Cliff **Bastin** and Tommy **Lawton**. One of England's last overseas fixtures before the outbreak of **World War II** was a friendly against Germany at the Olympic Stadium in Berlin; the game is remembered, in part, because the England team – persuaded by the British ambassador – gave a Nazi salute in front of the 110,000 crowd. England went on to win the game 6–3 (14 May 1938), with Matthews and Bastin among the scorers. England played a number of friendly matches against the home nations during World War II. All four home nations rejoined FIFA in 1946 and celebrated their return to true international status with a one-off Great Britain v Rest of Europe friendly match at Hampden Park, Glasgow; Matthews and Lawton were outstanding in a 6–1 win. One of the stars of the post-war England sides was Billy Wright, who made 105 international appearances between 1946 and 1959 and played 70 consecutive games from October 1951 to May 1959. He missed only three games in his international career, and captained the national side for a record 90 games. England first entered the World Cup in 1950, and qualified for the finals tournament in each of its first four entries; the Home International Championship acting as a qualifying group in 1950 and again in 1954. It qualified as hosts in 1966 and went on to win the tournament, with a dramatic 4–2 extra-time victory over West Germany in the final on 30 July 1966. A crowd of 96,000 spectators at Wembley Stadium watched Geoff Hurst (19, 100 and 119 minutes) and Martin Peters (77 minutes) score England's goals. Haller (13 minutes) and Weber (89 minutes) scored for West Germany. England's third and decisive goal was hotly disputed, Hurst's shot hitting the crossbar and bouncing down; the Swiss referee, Gottfried Dienst, after conferring with the Soviet linesman, Tofik **Bakhramov**, ruled that the ball had crossed the goal line. Computer simulation some 30 years later indicated that the goal should never have been allowed. Hurst wrapped up the game, however, and completed the only hat-trick in a World Cup final, with a shot from a breakaway clearance with just one minute left to play. England's World Cup final captain, Bobby Moore, captained the national side on 90 occasions, equalling the record set by Billy Wright. Moore won 108 caps between 1962 and 1973. West Germany avenged its 1966 World Cup final defeat at the 1970 finals tournament in **Mexico**, defeating England 3–2, again after extra time, in the quarter-final at Guanajuato stadium in León; England had been 2–0 ahead after 49 minutes. England failed to qualify for the World Cup in 1974, losing out to **Poland** in the qualifying tournament, and again in 1978; this time missing the finals on goal difference to Italy. Both nations had won five of their six matches and had beaten each other 2–0 in their home legs. Italy went through having scored more goals than England in their game against **Finland** and **Luxembourg**. England qualified in 1982 and again in 1986. England reached the quarter-final of the 1986 World Cup in Mexico, and was beaten 1–2 by Argentina; a game noted for Diego Maradona's infamous "**hand-of-god**" goal and his impudent second, which is generally regarded as one of the finest individual goals ever scored. England reached the semi-final of the World Cup in 1990, losing to Germany in a **penalty shoot-out** after a 1–1 draw in Turin. Stuart Pearce and Chris Waddle missed the crucial penalties in the shoot-out. England has twice reached the semi-final of the European Championship, losing in 1968, 0–1 to the runners-up former-Yugoslavia, in Florence, and when hosting the championships in 1996. This defeat was again by penalties, Germany winning 6–5 after a 1–1 draw at Wembley Stadium: Gareth Southgate missed the crucial **sudden-death** penalty. England's ill fortune in penalty shoot-outs continued in the 1998 World Cup finals in France, when England lost 3-4 to **Argentina** in the second round at the stade **Geoffroy-Guichard** Saint Etienne, this time after a 2–2 draw, with Paul Ince and David Batty failing to convert their penalty kicks (30 June 1998). More than half the population of England is thought to have watched the match on television. UK prime minister Tony Blair described England after the defeat as having "a mountain of courage and a molehill

of luck." *World Cup performance* Finals and qualifiers to end of 1998 tournament: played 109, won 60, drawn 29, lost 20, scored 221 goals, conceded 85 goals; win rate 55%; goals scored per game 2.02. Qualifiers: played 64, won 40, drawn 16, lost eight, scored 159 goals, conceded 43 goals; win rate 62%; goals scored per game 2.48. Finals tournaments: played 45, won 20, drawn 13, lost 12, scored 62 goals, conceded 42 goals; win rate 44%; goals scored per game 1.38. England *World Cup final team and scorers 1966* (winners) **Banks** (goalkeeper), Cohen, Jack Charlton, Moore, Wilson, Stiles, Bobby Charlton, **Ball**, Hunt, **Hurst** (3), **Peters** (1). *League system* The top flight of the English league system is the FA **Premier League**, with 20 clubs. Three points are awarded for a victory, with one for a draw: final positions for clubs level on points are determined by **goal difference**. If clubs are level on points and goal difference then positions are decided on **goals scored**; if clubs are still level, and are involved in relegation, the championship or in qualification for a European competition, the clubs **playoff** at a **neutral venue**. At the end of the season, the bottom three clubs in the Premier League are relegated to the Football League First Division, replaced by the top two clubs in that division plus the winner of the playoff between the third, fourth, fifth and sixth clubs. There are 24 clubs in each of the Football League First, Second and Third Divisions. The final positions at the end of each season are determined by the number of points won by each club, with three points awarded for a win and one for a drawn match. If clubs are level on points, however, their league position is determined by goals scored (not goal difference as in the Premier League); if clubs are level on points and goals scored, they are separated by **goals conceded**; if they remain level, their final league ranking can be decided by a playoff at a neutral ground (although this is extremely unlikely). The bottom three clubs in the First Division are relegated automatically, and replaced by the top two clubs in the Second Division along with the winner of a playoff competition between the third- to sixth-ranked clubs. The bottom four clubs from the Second Division are relegated to the Third Division, to be replaced by the top three clubs in the third division and the winner of a playoff competition. Finally, the bottom club in the Third Division is replaced by the champions of the semi-professional **Football Conference**, provided that the champion club meets the Football League's **ground criteria**. Underneath the Football Conference are three semi-professional contributory leagues: the Northern Premier League, Southern Premier League and Isthmian League. A **pyramid structure** provides a system beneath these so that, in theory, any club in the pyramid could eventually make it to the Football League and Premier League. *Record in international club tournaments* European Cup – Manchester United (1968, 1999, semi-final 1957, 1958, 1966, 1969, 1997), Liverpool (1977, 1978, 1981, 1984, runners-up 1985, semi-final 1965), Nottingham Forest (1979, 1980), Aston Villa (1982), **Leeds United** (runners-up 1975, semi-final 1970), Tottenham Hotspur (semi-final 1962), **Derby County** (semi-final 1973), **Burnley** (quarter-final 1961); European Cup-winners Cup – Tottenham Hotspur (1963, semi-final 1982), **West Ham United** (1965, runners-up 1976, semi-final 1966), **Manchester City** (1970), Chelsea (1971, 1998, semi-final 1995, 1999), Everton (1985), Manchester United (1991, semi-final 1984), Arsenal (1994, runners-up 1980, 1995) Liverpool (runners-up 1966, semi-final 1997), Leeds United (runners-up 1973); UEFA Cup/Fairs Cup – Leeds United (1968, 1971, runners-up 1967, semi-final 1966), **Newcastle United** (1969), Arsenal (1970), Tottenham Hotspur (1972, 1984, runners-up 1974, semi-final 1973), Liverpool (1973, 1976, semi-final 1971), **Ipswich Town** (1981), London Select XI (runners-up 1958), Birmingham City (runners-up 1960, 1961, semi-final 1958), **Wolverhampton Wanderers** (runners-up 1972), Manchester United (semi-final 1965), Chelsea (semi-final 1966), Nottingham Forest (semi-final 1984); **European Supercup** – Liverpool (1977), Nottingham Forest (1980), Aston Villa (1983), Manchester United (1991), Chelsea (1998).

England manager *official* individual charged with coaching the national team. Prior to Kevin **Keegan**'s appointment in 1999, there had been nine England managers: Walter Winterbottom (1946-62) – record played 139, won 78, drawn 33, lost 28, goals for 383, goals against 196; Alf **Ramsey** (1963-74) – record played 113, won 69, drawn 27, lost 17, goals for 224, goals against 99; Joe **Mercer** (1974) – record played seven, won three, drawn three, lost one, goals for nine, goals against 7; Don **Revie** (1974-77) – record played 30, won 15, drawn eight, lost seven, goals for 52, goals against 16; Ron Greenwood (1977-82) – record played 55, won 33, drawn 12, lost 10, goals for 93, goals against 40; Bobby **Robson** (1982-90) – record played 95, won 47, drawn 30, lost 18, goals for 154, goals against 60; Graham **Taylor** (1990-93) – record played 38, won 18, drawn 13, lost seven, goals for 62, goals against 32; Terry **Venables** (1994-96) – record played 23, won 11, drawn 11, lost one, goals for 35, goals against 13; Glenn **Hoddle** (1996-99) – record played 28, won 17, drawn six, lost five, goals for 42, goals against 13; Kevin Keegan (1999–). On 28 November 1998, the first-ever meeting between two clubs managed by ex-England managers took place when Terry Venables' **Crystal Palace** met Graham Taylor's **Watford** at **Selhurst Park**.

England, women *country/women* women's football in England comes under the auspices of the Football Association; the headquarters of the women's section is in Potters Bar, Hertfordshire. The national women's team has a dedicated manager, coach, physiotherapist, team doctor and administrator. Ted Copeland was the first FA-appointed national team coach (1995-). *Dossier* First official international match: 19 November 1972, 3–2, v **Scotland**, in Greenock. Record attendance: 5,471, 31 October 1978, at the **Dell**, Southampton (v **Belgium**,

3–0). *International tournament record* **Women's World Cup** – first qualified for finals tournament 1995, quarter-final 1995 (0–3 v **Germany**, in Sweden), failed to qualify 1991, 1999; **European Championship for Women** entered first tournament in 1984, runners-up 1984 (1–1 agg., 3–4 pens., v **Italy**), fourth 1987 (2–2, 2–3 pens., v **Sweden**, in Norway, semi-final; 1–2 v Italy, in Norway, third/fourth playoff), semi-final 1995 (2–6, agg., v Germany), quarter-final 1991, 1993, failed to qualify for finals 1997 (lost in qualifying group play-off). *History* See **women's football** for historical notes on the development of women's football in England. *League system* There are three divisions of the **FA Women's Premier League** (FAWPL): National Division, Northern Division and Southern Division, each has 10 clubs. Beneath the FAWPL are 10 regional leagues. There are two top-level cup competitions: **FA Women's Challenge Cup** – open to all women's clubs – and the **FA Women's Premier League Cup**, restricted to clubs in the three FAWPL divisions.

English disease *misc* see **hooligans, football**.

English Ladies Football Association *confederation* former association for women's football in England, founded 10 December 1921; representatives from 25 clubs attended the first meeting in Blackburn.

English National Investment Company (ENIC) *misc.* UK-based investment company that owns **AEK Athens** as well as a stake in FC Basle, **Slavia Prague** and Vicenza. At the beginning of 1998, ENIC was also seeking to invest £10 million in the French club, **Bordeaux (FC)**. ENIC board member, Joe Lewis also holds a substantial stake in **Rangers**.

English Schools' Football Association *confederation* governing body for schools football in England, founded 1904. Its headquarters are in Stafford. Chair: John Robson. Chief executive: Malcolm Berry. Individual **county schools' football associations** are affiliated to the ESFA which itself is affiliated to the **Football Association**. **Local schools' football associations** or, in exceptional cases, individual schools, are affiliated to their county associations. Headteachers are responsible for disciplinary matters involving individual pupils when they are representing schools, but any sanctions should be in line with the ESFA guidelines. Misconduct at inter-association matches is dealt with by the appropriate schools football association (ie local, county or national). Disciplinary guidelines and the various competition rules are laid down in the ESFA's annual handbook. The ESFA encourages competition in youth football, but warns that "those participating, coaching, organising and watching should always be aware of the dangers which might ensue from too great a commitment to a competitive approach." Schools football, it says, should provide many other opportunities, including: attaining certain standards; representing the school or area; being part of a team; travelling to other schools and areas; experiencing different environments; meeting players from other schools and areas; playing within the laws and "spirit" of the game; experiencing the pleasure of victory; experiencing the disappointment of defeat; accepting victory or defeat in the appropriate way; self and team discipline; appreciating the efforts of others; improving fitness; and making firm and lasting friendships. In 1990, the English Schools Football Association ruled that mixed competitive matches could be played in schools, by children up to the age of 11 years; the only age-group where mixed football is sanctioned (see **Bennett v Football Association Ltd and Nottinghamshire FA**). ESFA tournaments include the **ESFA Under-15 Inter-Association Trophy**, the ESFA Premier League Under-16 Inter County Competition; the ESFA Trophy (under-16, schools representing County Associations); the ESFA (Schools and Colleges) Under-19 Trophy (under-19, schools representing County Associations); the ESFA Individual Schools Under-19 Trophy; the ESFA Premier League Under-19 Inter County Competition; the **ESFA Girls' Under-16 Trophy**; the **ESFA Five-a-side Competition**; and the ESFA Six- and Seven-a-side Competitions (for boys and girls aged under-11, mixed teams).

Englische woche *misc.* German term for a mid-week league match – a rare feature of German football.

Entente Setif (Entente Sportive de Setif) *club* Algerian national league club, based in Setif, founded 1945. Ground: 8 de Mai (the date of the club's foundation), capacity: 30,000. Strip: white shirts, black shorts. **African Cup of Champion Clubs** 1988 (4–1 agg., v **Iwuanyanwu Nationale** of Nigeria); **Afro-Asian Club Cup** 1989 (5–1 agg., v **Al Saad** of Qatar); Algerian Cup 1963, 1964, 1967, 1968, 1980, 1990; Algerian league champions 1968, 1987.

Enugu Rangers International *club* Nigerian national league club based in Enugu, formed 1970. Ground: Nnamdi Azikiwe, capacity: 50,000. Strip: white shirts, red shorts. **African Cup of Champion Clubs** – runners-up 1975, semi-final 1976, 1978, 1982; **African Cup-winners Cup** 1977 (5–2 agg., v **Canon Yaoundé** of Cameroon); Nigerian FA Challenge Cup 1974, 1975, 1976, 1981, 1983; Nigerian league champions 1974, 1975, 1977, 1981, 1982, 1984.

ephedrine *medical* a stimulant drug medically used to treat bronchial spasm and airway obstruction. Misusers experience similar effects to **amphetamines**.

episkyros *n.* early form of football played in ancient Greece, competed by two teams.

equaliser *n.* goal that levels the score in a match.

Equatorial Guinea *country CAF* republic in west Central Africa on the Atlantic Ocean, bordered by **Cameroon** and **Gabon**. Includes the island of Bioko off the coast of Cameroon. Area: 28,050 sq km (10,825 sq miles). Population: 420,000 (1992 est.). Languages: Spanish, pidgin English, Pagulu (a Portuguese dialect). Capital: Malabo. *Dossier* Football association (Federación Ecuatoguineana de Fútbol, Malabo), formed in 1976 affiliated to **FIFA** in 1986 and **Confédération Africaine de Football** (CAF) in 1986, member of the

Union of Football Associations of Central Africa, president Bonifacio Manga Obiang, general secretary Domingo Mbela Echela. Season played from October to June. National stadium: Estadio La Paz, Malabo, capacity: 15,000. National strip: red shirts, red shorts. First international game: 9 December 1984 v **Congo** (0–5, in Congo, **UDEAC Tournament**). Biggest victory: no recorded victory. Biggest defeat: 0–6 v Congo (13 December 1990, 0–5, in Congo, UDEAC Tournament). *International tournament record* **Olympic Games** – never entered; **Women's World Cup** – never entered; **World Cup** – never entered; **African Cup of Nations** – first entered 1982, never past first qualifying round; **Under-17 World Championship** – never entered; **World Youth Cup** (under-20) – never entered. *Record against British and Irish national teams* none played. *Record in international club tournaments* **African Cup-winners Cup** – Clube Deportivo Ela Nguema (first round 1993; having won a preliminary round). Other leading clubs: **Akonangui FC, Atletico Malabo, Deportivo Mongomeyen**, Cafe Band Sportif (of Malabo, league champions 1996).

equipment *n.* see **players' equipment**.

Erebuni *club* Armenian national league club (formerly Erebuni Homenetmen), based in the capital Yerevan. Armenian league champions 1992.

Eritrea *country CAF* republic in East Africa on the Red Sea, bordered by **Ethiopia** and **Sudan**. Independence from Ethiopia in 1993. Civil war and drought have caused considerable poverty in the country. Area: 91,600 sq km (35,370 sq miles). Population: 3,530,000 (1994 est.). Language: Arabic, English, Amharic and Tigrinya. Capital: Asmara. *Dossier* Eritrean Football Association (Asmara) formed in 1992, affiliated to **FIFA** in June 1998, affiliated to the **Confédération Africaine de Football** (CAF) in 1994, member of the **Confederation of East and Central African Football Associations**, president Negasi Selassie, general secretary Eyob Gebre Kristes. Season played from November to June. National stadium: Ras Asula (Asmara), capacity: 25,000. National strip: red shirts, yellow shorts. First international game: 29 November 1994 v **Seychelles** (1–0 **East and Central Africa Championship**, in Kenya). *International tournament record* **Olympic Games** – never entered; **Women's World Cup** – never entered; **World Cup** – never entered; **African Cup of Nations** – first entered 1998. *Record against British and Irish national teams* none played. *History* Eritrea became FIFA's 199th member in June 1998; it played its first African Cup of Nations tournament match on 4 October 1998, a group one qualifier against **Mozambique** (1–3, in Maputo). *Record in international club tournaments* **African Cup of Champion Clubs** – Tele Sporting Club (second round 1970, 1974). Other leading club: **Eritrea Shoe Factory**.

Eritrea Shoe Factory *club* Eritrea national league club, based in the capital Asmara, formerly in the Ethiopian national league. Ground: Ras Asula (the national stadium, and shared with **Tele Sporting Club**), capacity: 25,000. Ethiopian Cup 1984, 1985, 1986.

Ernst Happel-Stadion *ground* Austrian football ground situated in Vienna; national stadium, occasionally used by Austrian clubs **Rapid Vienna**, **FK Austria** and **Salzburg**. Ground capacity: 49,000 all seated. *History* Opened in 1931 and known as the Prater (after the Prater Park in which it is situated) until 1992, when it was renamed in honour of Austrian international and national team manager Ernst **Happel** who died in 1992. The ground has been developed over the years, and in 1986 a roof costing more than £17 million was erected. The stadium has staged four **European Cup** finals (1964 **Internazionale** v **Real Madrid**, 74,000; 1987 **Porto** v **Bayern Munich**, 59,000; 1990 **AC Milan** v **Benfica**, 57,500; 1995 **Ajax** v AC Milan, 49,730) and a **European Cup-winners Cup** final (1970 **Manchester City** v **Gornik Zabrze**, 10,000).

ES Sahel (Etoile Sportive du Sahel) *club* Tunisian national league club based in Sousse, founded 1925. Ground: Olympique, capacity: 22,000. Strip: red shirts, white shorts. **African Cup of Champion Clubs** quarter-final "champions-league" stage 1998; **African Cup-winners Cup** 1997 (2–1, agg., v **FAR Rabat** of Morocco; **Arab Cup-winners Cup** runners-up 1995; **African Super Cup** 1997 (2–2, 4–2 pens., v **Raja Casablanca** of Morocco; **CAF Cup** 1995 (2–0 agg., v **AS Kaloum Stars** of Guinea), runners-up 1996 (3–3, away goals, v **Kawkab Marrakesh** of Morocco); Tunisian Cup 1959, 1963, 1974, 1975, 1981, 1983, 1991, 1996; Tunisian league champions 1949, 1958, 1959, 1960, 1963, 1966, 1972, 1986, 1987, 1997.

Escobar, Andres *player* Defender. **Colombia** international player. *Clubs* (include) **Atlético Nacional Medellin**. *Keynotes* Escobar was a member of Colombia's 1994 **World Cup** team, and was shot dead shortly after the tournament. He had scored an **own goal** in Colombia's match against **United States of America** (1–2, in Los Angeles, USA); the defeat effectively cost Colombia a place in the second round. Various possible explanations have been advanced about Escobar's murder, including that he was punished because of a failed match-fixing scandal. *Honours* **Copa Libertadores** (Atlético Nacional Medellin 1989), Colombian league championship (Atlético Nacional Medellin, 1991).

Escobar, Pablo *misc.* former Colombian "drug baron" (deceased), said to have been financially linked with the Colombian club **Atlético Nacional Medellin**.

ESFA Five-a-side Competition (boys' and girls' teams) *competition* annual national five-a-side knockout competition for English schools' teams whose players are, at some point during the normal school year (1 September to 31 August) aged over-11 and under-12 years of age. The tournament is run by the **English Schools' Football Association** (ESFA). All matches last 10 minutes (in two halves of five minutes, with no half-time interval). The tournament comprises local and

area qualifying competitions and national finals. The boys' competition started in 1991-91, while the girls' tournament started in 1995-96. A total of 2,345 teams entered the 1997-98 tournament: 1,660 schools from 164 local associations in the boys' competition; and 685 schools from 99 local associations in the girls' tournament. *Winners, boys* 1992 Wood Green High School, Wednesbury (West Midlands SFA); 1993 St Benedict's School, Upton (Wirral SFA) and Pelton Roseberry School SFA (Chester-le-Street SFA) (trophy shared); 1994 Hadrian Park Middle School, Wallsend (Northumberland SFA); 1995 no competition; 1996 Bradon Forest School (Swindon SFA); 1997 Audenshaw High School (Tameside SFA); 1998 Nicholas Chamberlaine School (Nuneaton and District SFA). *Winners, girls* 1996 Queens Park School (Brent SFA); 1997 ADT College (West London SFA); 1998 Mountain Ash School (Cynon Valley SFA).

ESFA Girls' Under-16 Trophy *competition* annual national knockout girls' football competition for English and Welsh schools representing their **county schools football associations** whose players are, at some point during the normal school year (1 September to 31 August) aged over-13 and under-16-years-old. The tournament is run by the **English Schools' Football Association** (ESFA) and was first played in 1995-96. All matches last for 70 minutes (35 minutes each way), with a half-time interval of 10 minutes. A size-4 ball is used, unless it is mutually agreed that the standard size-5 ball be used. The rules are virtually identical to those of the **ESFA Under-15 Inter-Association Trophy** (for boys), except that the final is played as a single match at a **neutral venue**. If the score is level at the end of normal playing time in the final then **extra time**, but not a **penalty shoot-out**, is played; the trophy is shared if the score is level at the end of extra time. *Winners* 1996 West Bridgford Comprehensive School (representing the Nottinghamshire SFA); 1997 Montgomery High School, Blackpool (Lancashire SFA); 1998 Valley School, Mansfield (Nottinghamshire SFA).

ESFA Under-15 Inter-Association Trophy (boys) *competition* annual national knockout competition for English and Welsh **local schools football associations** whose players are, at some point during the normal school year (1 September to 31 August) aged over-13 and under-15-years-old. The tournament is run by the **English Schools' Football Association** (ESFA). All matches last for 70 minutes (35 minutes each way), with a half-time interval of 10 minutes. Twenty minutes' **extra time** is played in the event of a draw. If the score remains level, then the match is replayed. If at the end of normal playing time in the replay, the scores remain level, then 20 minutes of extra time is played; if the score remains equal, the result is decided by a **penalty shoot-out**. The final is played over two legs. Neither extra time nor penalties is played in the final; if the **aggregate score** is tied then the trophy is shared. Teams can use three from five nominated substitutes. The **field of play** must be at least 82.3 metres (90 yards) long and 54.9 metres (60 yards) wide. The ball must be a size 5. The team strip must bear **shirt numbers**; shirts can carry advertising, as long as it does not conflict with the interests of the tournament sponsors (the sponsor for the 1998-99 tournament was Heinz Ketchup). *History* The tournament was first played in 1905 and carried on through **World War I**, but was suspended during **World War II**. The first final was won by London, against Sheffield. The most successful associations in the competition's history are: Liverpool (14 wins), Sheffield (nine), Manchester (seven), Barnsley (five) and Swansea (five). *Winners* 1905 London; 1906 Sheffield; 1907 West Ham; 1908 Derby; 1909 Sheffield; 1910 Sunderland; 1911 Chester-le-Street; 1912 West Ham; 1913 Watford; 1914 Sheffield; 1915 Cardiff; 1916 Bradford; 1917 West Ham; 1918 Liverpool; 1919 Grimsby; 1920 Reading; 1921 Liverpool; 1922 South London; 1923 Sheffield; 1924 North Staffordshire; 1925 Sheffield; 1926 Grimsby; 1927 East Northumberland; 1928 North Staffordshire; 1929 South Northumberland; 1930 Newcastle; 1931 Islington; 1932 Manchester and Southampton (joint); 1933 Sunderland; 1934 Manchester; 1935 Manchester; 1936 Preston and West Ham (joint); 1937 Liverpool; 1938 Manchester; 1939 Swansea; 1946 Leicester; 1947 Salford; 1948 Liverpool and Stockport (joint); 1949 Barnsley; 1950 Swansea; 1951 Liverpool; 1952 Ilford; 1953 Swansea; 1954 Liverpool; 1955 Swansea; 1956 Liverpool; 1957 Barnsley and Southampton (joint); 1958 Bristol; 1959 Brierley Hill/Sedgley Hill/Tipton and Doncaster (joint); 1960 Manchester; 1961 Barnsley; 1962 Stoke; 1963 Stoke; 1964 Erdington and Saltley; 1965 Leicester and Swansea (joint); 1966 East London; 1967 Liverpool; 1968 Manchester and Waltham Forest (joint); 1969 Liverpool; 1970 Liverpool; 1971 Huyton; 1972 Chelmsford and Mid-Essex; 1973 Liverpool; 1974 Manchester; 1975 Barking; 1976 Liverpool; 1977 South London; 1978 Newham; 1979 Bristol; 1980 Middlesbrough; 1981 High Wycombe; 1982 Sheffield; 1983 Middlesbrough and Sunderland (joint); 1984 Sheffield; 1985 Doncaster; 1986 Hull and Middlesbrough (joint); 1987 South London; 1988 Cambridge and West London (joint); 1989 Saint Helens; 1990 Sheffield; 1991 Barnsley; 1992 Leeds; 1993 Liverpool; 1994 Sheffield; 1995 Islington and Camden; 1996 Bury; 1997 Liverpool; 1998 Barnsley and Bristol (joint).

Espanyol (RCD) (Castillian: Español) *club* Spanish league. *Dossier* Ground: Estadi Olimpic du Montjuïch, Barcelona, Catalonia. Strip: blue and white striped shirts, white shorts. Nickname: Los Periquitos (the "Parakeets"). Ground capacity: 55,000 (30,000 for Espanyol matches). *History* Formed in 1900 by local students, calling the club Espanyol – "Spanish" – a snipe at **Barcelona**'s Swiss origins. The club is officially called Real Club Deportivo Espanyol de Barcelona. Espanyol's home between 1923 and summer 1997 was **Sarriá Estadia**, but it was forced to sell the ground owing to to financial difficulties and, at the start of the 1997-98 season, it moved to Estadia Olimpic du

Montjuïch, using the areas behind the goals for advertising rather than spectators. Espanyol's traditional fan base has been drawn from those hostile to the Catalan nationalism exhibited across the city at **Nou Camp**. Only in 1994 did the club replace the Castillian spelling of its name, Español, with the Catalan, Espanyol. The club's only honours have come in the Spanish Cup (**Copa del Ray**), which it has won on two occasions (1929 and 1940). It has also been finalist four times: 1915 (0–5 v **Athletic Bilbao**), 1941 (1–3 v **Valencia**), 1947 (0–2 v **Real Madrid**) and 1957 (0–1 v Barcelona). Espanyol reached the **UEFA Cup** final in 1988 (3–3, 2–3 pens. v Bayer Leverkusen). *Honours* Spanish Cup 1929 (2–1 v Real Madrid), 1940 (3–2 v Real Madrid).

Espérance (Espérance Sportive Tunis, ES Tunis) *club* Tunisian national league club based in the capital Tunis, founded 1910. Ground: Stade Olympique El Menzah (the national stadium), capacity: 50,000. Strip: red shirts, gold shorts. **African Cup of Champion Clubs** 1994 (3–1 agg., v **Zamalek** of Egypt); **African Cup-winners Cup** 1998 (4–2 agg., v **Primeiro de Agosto** of Angola), runners-up 1987 (0–2 agg., v **Gor Mahia** of Kenya); **African Super Cup** – 1994 (3–0 v **Daring Club Motema Pembe** of Congo Democratic Republic (Zaire), in Alexandria, Egypt); **Afro-Asian Club Cup** 1995 (v **Farmers Club** of Thailand); **Arab Club Champions Cup** 1994, runners-up 1987, 1995; **Arab Super Cup** 1996; **CAF Cup** 1997 (2–1 agg, v **Petro Atlético** of Angola); Tunisian Cup 1938, 1957, 1964, 1979, 1980, 1986, 1989, 1997; Tunisian league champions 1941, 1970, 1975, 1976, 1982, 1985, 1988, 1989, 1991, 1993, 1994, 1998, 1999. Notable former player: Tarak **Dhiab**.

Espirito Santo *state* one of the 27 state leagues in **Brazil**, founded 1917. Leading clubs: Rio Branco Atletico Clube (of Vitória), Desportiva Ferroviaria (Cariacica).

Estádio da Luz *ground* Portuguese football ground situated in Lisbon; home of **Benfica** (Sport Lisboa e Benfica). Ground capacity: 92,000 all seated. *History* Benfica's "Stadium of Light" was opened in 1954 as a 60,000 two-tier ground. A further tier was added in 1960. The stadium's name is derived from the Lisbon suburb, Luz, in which the ground and its surrounding sports facilities are situated. There are currently plans to completely renovate the stadium, which in the late-1970s had a capacity of 120,000 and was one of Europe's largest football venues.

Estádio Nacional *ground* Portuguese sports ground situated on the outskirts of Lisbon; venue of the Portuguese cup final (La Taça de Portugal). Ground capacity: 60,000 all seated. *History* The stadium was the setting for **Celtic**'s 1967 **European Cup** final victory (v **Internazionale**, 56,000). It has also staged a **European Cup-winners Cup** final (1992 **Werder Bremen** v **Monaco**, 16,000). The ground also hosted the last match played by the celebrated **Torino** side, which perished in the 1949 **Superga aircrash**.

Esteghlal Sports Club *club* Iranian league club based in the capital Tehran, changed name from Taj Club in 1979, after Islamic revolution. **Asian Champion Teams Cup** 1970 (as Taj, 2–1, v **Hapoel Tel-Aviv**, in Tehran), 1990 (as Esteghlal, 2–1, v **Liaoning** of China, in Dhaka, Bangladesh), runners-up 1991 (1–1, 3–4 pens., v **Al Hilal** of Saudi Arabia, in Doha, Qatar), 1999 (1–2 v **Jubilo Iwata** of Japan), semi-final 1971 (as Taj); **Asian Cup-winners Cup** semi-final/fourth 1992 (0–1, v **Ulsan Hyundai** of South Korea); Iranian League champions (as Taj) 1970, 1974, 1975, (as Esteghlal) 1990, 1995, 1998; **Turkmenistan President's Cup** 1998.

Estonia *country* UEFA republic of north-east Europe on the Baltic Sea. Bordered by **Latvia** and the Russian Federation. Independence from **Russia** in 1918, but incorporated into the **Soviet Union** in 1940. Full independence from Soviet Union in 1991 after declaration as an autonomous state in 1988. Area: 45,100 sq km (17,413 sq miles). Languages: Estonian and minority Russian. Population: 1,600,000 (1994 est.). Capital: Tallinn. *Dossier* Estonian Football Association (Tallinn) formed in 1921 (until 1943), and again in 1989, affiliated to **FIFA** in 1923 (until 1943) and again in 1992. Affiliated to **Union of European Football Associations** (UEFA) in 1992, president Peeter Küttis, general secretary Tönu Sirel. Season played from April to October. National stadium: Kadriorg, Tallinn, capacity: 6,000 – technically, Estonia has no national football stadium; Kadriorg does not meet international standards and a new stadium is planned, finances permitting. National strip: blue shirts, black shorts. First international game: 17 October 1920 v **Finland** (0–6, in Helsinki, friendly). Biggest victory: 6–0 v Latvia (26 July 1928, in Tallinn, **Baltic Cup**). Biggest defeat: 2–10 v Finland (11 August 1922, in Helsinki, friendly). Most capped players: Marko Kristal (70 appearances, ca. 1993-), Martin Reim (65 appearances, ca. 1993–), Mart Poom (59 appearances, ca. 1993-). Leading goalscorers: Edward Ellman-Eelma (18, 1920-1935), Richard Kuremaa (18, 1933-1939), Arnold Pihlak (17, 1925-1929). *International tournament record* **Olympic Games** – first entered 1924 (lost in preliminary round, 0–1 v **United States of America** in Paris), never since qualified for finals tournament; **Women's World Cup** – first entered 1999; **World Cup** – first entered 1934 (also 1938, but not again until 1994), never qualified for finals tournament (finished fifth of six-nation group in 1998, with one win and one draw in its 10 games); Baltic Cup 1929, 1931, 1938; **European Championship** – first entered 1996 (last in its six-nation qualifying group, with 10 defeats, conceding 31 goals with three scored); **European Championship for Women** – first entered 1998; **Under-17 World Championship** – never qualified; **World Youth Cup** (under-20) – never qualified. *Record against British and Irish national teams* v **England**, none played; v **Northern Ireland**, none played; v **Scotland**, played six times, one draw, four defeats and one abandoned match; v **Wales**, played one, lost one; v **Republic of Ireland**, none played. *History* Football was imported to Estonia at the beginning of 20th century by English merchant seamen – credited with teaching the game to Estonian boys. The first known games, in 1906, were those between various boys' gangs. By 1908 gang football led to the formation of the first clubs. The oldest recorded club, Meteor, was formed in 1909 by three players – Abrams, Reinans and Isak – in the capital Tallinn. The club's 40-strong membership was largely comprised of schoolboys and coached by an Englishman named Urchard who lived in Tallinn. Urchard even ordered a team strip from England. A second team, Merkuur, was formed shortly afterwards by Tallinn printing workers and financed by a wealthy businessman named Orlov. The first official football match took place on 6 June 1909 – Meteor beat Merkuur 4–2. At the same time, football became popular in three other cities: Narva, Pärnu and Tartu. In the university town of Tartu, players were mostly German, Russian and Latvian students; while in Narva the main club comprised workers of a big textile manufacturer, Kreenholm. Football in Narva was played under the then-Russian rules; in Tallinn they were played according to the English rules; and in Tartu by the German rules. By **World War I**, there were tens of active clubs in Estonia, but football almost died out during the war years. The Tallinn Football League was formed in 1916 by the Kalev, Sport and Olimpia clubs. An Estonian championship final was held on 7 November 1920; though the Estonian Football Association, formed in 1921, does not consider this game as the first "official" championship. Officially, the league started in 1921, with a cup competition dating from 1938. The Kadriorg Stadium was built in 1926. After absorption into the Soviet Union, Estonia continued to operate its own regional league; the true Estonian national championship restarting in 1991. Until the 1999 season, the national league had been played from August to June, with a **winter break** from November to March. A complex league system had been formulated to accommodate the long winter break, with the league played in two phases. In the autumn phase, clubs played each other at home and away. The top six clubs at the end of the phase competed in the spring tournament, again playing each other twice, to decide the championship. The system was slightly complicated because the clubs in the second phase carried forward half their league points from the autumn phase (rounded up to an integer). The team with the highest total points was declared national champions. The bottom two Premier Division clubs from the autumn phase competed in a second-phase tournament with the four top clubs from the First Division in a six-club league to decide the two promotion/relegation places. The 1997-98 season was the last full season played under this format; the new format began in spring 1999. The national team won the Baltic Cup three times between 1929 and 1938, while its post-independence international record was noted most for a game that lasted just a few seconds. Estonia's

World Cup qualifier against Scotland at the Kadriorg Stadium on 9 October 1996 was abandoned shortly after Scotland kicked off: the Estonian team was still at its training ground. Scotland had earlier protested that the **floodlights** – imported specially from Finland – were inadequate; the FIFA representative agreed to bring the match forward to a lunchtime kickoff. Estonia refused to turn up for the game, arguing that insufficient notice had been given. FIFA overturned its original decision to award a 3–0 **walkover** to Scotland, and the match was ordered to be replayed, this time at a neutral venue (0–0, in Monaco, 11 February 1997). *World Cup performance* (finals and qualifiers to end of 1998 tournament) played 24, won 2, drawn 2, lost 20, scored 11 goals, conceded 60 goals; win rate 8%; goals scored per game 0.46. *League system* Eight clubs compete in the national Premier Division. Three points are awarded for a win and one for a draw; **goal difference** separates clubs level on points. *Record in international club tournaments* never beyond preliminary rounds. Leading clubs: **Flora Tallinn, Lantana Tallinn, Tallinna Sadam, Dünamo Tallinn** (now defunct), **Norma Tallinn** (now defunct).

Estudiantes La Plata *club* Argentinean national league club, based in La Plata, founded 1905, sometimes known simply as Estudiantes, or Estudiantes LP. Ground: Estadio Jorge Luis Hirsch, capacity: 26,000. Strip: red and white striped shirts, black shorts. *Keynotes* Formed in 1905 by former members of rival club **Gimnasia y Esgrima La Plata**. The club's hat-trick of victories in the **Copa Libertadores** in 1968, 1969 and 1970 was characterised by a hard-line disruptive style of play. The club's notoriously ill-mannered performances against **Manchester United, AC Milan** and **Feyenoord**, in the **World Club Cup** fixtures of 1968, 1969 and 1970, respectively, were instrumental in the partial boycott of the competition by **European Cup** champions in the 1970s. Argentinean league champions 1913 (two leagues operated prior to 1927), 1967, 1982; Argentinean national championship (a pre-national-league tournament operating from 1967 to 1985) 1983; Copa Libertadores 1968 (2–1, 1–3, 2–0 playoff, v **Palmeiras**), 1969 (1–0, 2–0, v **Nacional**); 1970 (1–0, 0–0, v **Peñarol**), runners-up 1971 (0–1, 1–0, 2–0 playoff, v Nacional, of Uruguay); **Supercopa** semi-final 1991; World Club Cup 1968 (1–0, 1–1, v Manchester United).

Etar Veliko Tarnovo *club* Bulgarian national league club based in Tarnovo, formed 1924. Ground: Ivailo, capacity: 18,000. Strip: purple shirts, purple shorts. Bulgarian Cup/Soviet Army Cup 1991; Bulgarian league champions 1991.

Ethiopia *country CAF* republic in east Africa on the Red Sea. Bordered by **Djibouti, Somalia, Sudan, Kenya** and **Eritrea**. Area: 1,023,050 sq km (394,895 sq miles). Population: 55,000,000 (1994 est.). Languages: Amharic, Tigrinya, Orominga, Arabic and English. Capital: Addis Ababa. *Dossier* Ethiopian Football Federation (Addis Ababa) formed in 1943,

affiliated to **FIFA** in 1953 and founder member of the **Confédération Africaine de Football** (CAF) in 1957, member of the **Confederation of East and Central African Football Associations** (CECEFA), president Gizaw Teklemariam, general secretary Nega Liku Afework. Season played from September to June. National stadium: Addis Ababa Stadium, capacity: 30,000. National strip: green shirts, yellow shorts. First international game: January 1956 v **Egypt** (1–4, Addis Ababa, friendly). Biggest victory: 8–1, v *Djibouti* (27 March 1983, Addis Ababa, friendly). Biggest defeat: 0–6 v **Nigeria** (24 July 1993, in Lagos, **African Cup of Nations** qualifier). *International tournament record* **Olympic Games** – first entered 1956, never qualified for finals tournament; **Women's World Cup** – never entered; **World Cup** – first entered 1962, never qualified for finals tournament; African Cup of Nations – entered first tournament in 1957, 1962 (4–2, v Egypt, in Addis Ababa), runners-up 1957 (0–4 v Egypt, in Khartoum, Sudan), third 1959 (group of three), fourth 1963 (0–3, v Egypt, in Accra, Ghana, third/fourth playoff), semi-final/fourth 1968, also played in finals tournament 1965, 1970, 1976, 1982, hosts 1962, 1968, 1976; CECAFA Youth Cup (under-18) 1995; **East and Central Africa Championship** (CECAFA Tournament) – 1987 (1–1, 5–4 pens., v **Zimbabwe**, in Addis Ababa), semi-final 1995; **Under-17 World Championship** – never qualified; **World Youth Cup** (under-20) – never qualified. *Record against British and Irish national teams* none played. *History* Football is said to have been introduced by British schoolteachers and Italian workers in the 1930s. Ethiopia was one of the first nations in Africa to establish national-league football. Its football association and national league were formed in 1943; the league championship was first won by the British Military Mission (from Addis Ababa). Ethiopia won the third African Cup of Nations in 1962, and has hosted the finals in 1962, 1968 and 1976. *Record in international club tournaments* **African Cup of Champion Clubs** – **Cotton Club** (semi-final 1964), **St Georges** (semi-final 1967); **African Cup-winners Cup** – **Mechele Army** (quarter-final 1976); **CAF Cup** – **Ethiopian Insurance Corporation FC** (semi-final 1993). Other leading clubs: Ethiopian Bunna (from Addis Ababa, league champions 1997, Cup 1998), **Mebrat Hail**.

Ethiopian Insurance Corporation FC *club* Ethiopian national league club based in Addis Ababa, also known as Medhin. Ground: Saba, capacity: 20,000. **CAF Cup** semi-final 1993; Ethiopian Cup 1995.

Etincelles *club* Rwandan national league club based in Gisenyi. Ground: Umaganda, capacity: 10,000. **African Cup-winners Cup** – second round 1989; Rwandan Cup 1988.

Etoile du Congo *club* Congo league club based in the capital Brazzaville, formerly known as Ngok Imperial. Ground: A M Deba, capacity: 50,000. Strip: yellow shirts, black shorts. Congo Cup 1983, 1995; Congo league champions 1967, 1978, 1979, 1981, 1985, 1987, 1989, 1992, 1994.

Etoile du Sahel *club* see **ES Sahel**.

Etoile Filante ("Shooting Star") *club* Togo national league club based in the capital Lomé. Ground: Stade Général Etienne Eyadema (the national stadium), capacity: 20,000. Strip: blue shirts, white shorts. **African Cup of Champion Clubs** runners-up 1968 (4–6 agg., v **Tout Puissant Englebert** of Congo Democratic Republic (Zaire)); never won Togo Cup; Togo league champions 1965, 1967, 1968, 1992.

Etoile Filante *club* Burkina Faso national league club based in Ouagadougou, founded 1955. Stadium: 4 August (national stadium), capacity: 45,000. Strip: green shirts, red shorts. Burkina Faso Cup 1990, 1991, 1992, 1993, 1996; Burkina Faso league champions 1965, 1985, 1988, 1990, 1991, 1992, 1993, 1994.

European Championship *competition* four-yearly international nations tournament involving member countries from the **Union of European Football Associations** (UEFA). The tournament comprises qualifying groups played over two years, and a final tournament played at a host country or countries. The 1996 tournament finals ("Euro '96") were played in **England**. **Belgium** and the **Netherlands** jointly host the 2000 finals, both qualifying automatically as hosts. *History* Originally entitled the European Nations Cup, the idea for a European Championship, bringing together the various regional tournaments throughout Europe, including the British **Home International Championship**, came from Henri Delaunay, secretary of the French football federation. The European Championship trophy bears his name, although he died before the first tournament was held in 1960. The **Soviet Union** was the first winner, defeating **former-Yugoslavia** in the final. Only 17 countries entered the first tournament and several prominent nations, including the four British home countries, Netherlands, **Italy**, **Sweden** and West **Germany**, declined to participate. The first tournament was a straight knockout competition, with matches played on a home and away basis to establish the four semi-finalists. **France** hosted the two semi-finals and the final. **Spain** staged the 1964 final stages (this time including a third-place playoff as well as the semi-finals and the final) and emerged victorious. Group qualifying matches were introduced for the renamed European Championship in 1968 – the Home International Championship acting as the UK qualifying group. The finals, held in Italy, followed the same format as the preceding tournament. The host nation won the trophy, but required a replay against former-Yugoslavia to do so. The 1972 tournament, the finals of which were staged in Belgium, was won by West Germany, which had defeated England over a two-legged quarter-final on its way to the final. A number of high-profile nations, including England and Italy, failed to qualify for the final stages of the 1976 tournament in former-Yugoslavia, and **Czechoslovakia** won the final against West Germany in a **penalty shoot-out** – the first time it was used to determine the outcome of a major international nations competition. UEFA altered the format of the 1980 tournament, so that eight nations, in two groups of four, contested the final stages, with the group winners meeting in the final. Also, for the first time, the host nation, on this occasion Italy, received a bye to the last eight. West Germany won the tournament for a second time. The format was altered again for the 1984 tournament, with the top two teams in each group contesting the semi-finals. France, as hosts, won, defeating Spain in the final. Netherlands won the 1988 tournament, hosted by West Germany. In 1992, **Denmark** was a late entrant to the finals, replacing former-Yugoslavia, which was suspended by UEFA due to the civil war engulfing the Balkans and in line with United Nations sanctions against the country over breaches of human rights. The Danes emerged as surprise victors, defeating Germany in the final with two goals scored on the **counter-attack**. Euro'96 was the largest European Championships to date, and Germany, finalists on four previous occasions and victors twice, won the Henri Delaunay trophy for a third time, Oliver Bierhoff's **golden goal** five minutes into extra time beating the **Czech Republic**. *Records* West Germany has appeared in a record five finals and its three tournament victories is also a record. The former-Soviet Union has been a finalist on four occasions, winning once. Michel **Platini**'s eight goals during the 1984 tournament is a record for the final stages. Davor **Suker** (**Croatia**) holds the record as top overall scorer in the competition (17). The largest attendance for a European Championship match was 134,000 at **Hampden Park** on 24 February 1968 to watch the qualifer between **Scotland** and England (1–1). *Final results* 1960, Soviet Union 2–1 former-Yugoslavia (Paris); 1964, Spain 2–1 Soviet Union (Madrid); 1968, Italy 2–0 former-Yugoslavia (replay; Rome); 1972, West Germany 3–0 Soviet Union (Brussels); 1976, Czechoslovakia 2–2 West Germany (5–4 pens.; Belgrade); 1980, West Germany 2–1 Belgium (Rome); 1984, France 2–0 Spain (Paris); 1988, Netherlands 2–0 Soviet Union (Munich); 1992, Denmark 2–0 West Germany (Stockholm); 1996, Germany 2–1 Czech Republic (London).

European Championship for Women *competition* international women's tournament for member nations of the **Union of European Football Associations** (UEFA), first played 1982-84. Participating nations are divided into qualifying groups of four, playing each other at home and away on a league basis. The top nations qualify for a finals tournament. The groups are divided into two streams; only those in the first stream can qualify for the finals. Second-stream group winners playoff against the bottom nations in the first-stream groups for promotion/relegation to/from the first stream for the next international tournament (the group seedings apply to both the European Championship for Women and the **Women's World Cup**). *History* Sixteen nations took part in the first tournament, 1982-84. The European Championship for Women served as the European qualifying tournament for the first two Women's World Cup (1991, 1995); a separate European qualifying tournament was staged for the 1999 finals. Sixteen nations took part in 1987, 17 in 1989, 18 in 1991, 23 in 1993, 30 in 1995 and 33 in 1997. *Winners, scores, runners-up* 1984 **Sweden**, 1–1 agg., 4–3 pens., v **England**; 1987 **Norway**, 2–1 v Sweden; 1989 **Germany**, 4–1 v Norway; 1991 Germany 3–1, v Norway; 1993 Norway, 1–0 v **Italy**; 1995 Germany, 3–2 v Sweden.

European Championships for Players with Learning Disabilities *competition* international European nation's tournament for players with **learning disabilities**, first played 1996, in Leicester, **England**. Ten teams competed in the first championships: **Belgium**, **Denmark**, England, **Germany**, **Netherlands**, **Poland**, **Portugal**, **Scotland**, **Sweden** and AFPLD XI (a side representing the organisers, the **Association of Football Players with Learning Disabilities**). *Winners* 1996 Poland, 4–2, v Belgium. Denmark was awarded the **Fairplay award**. *Top scorer* Olivier Lambeau (14 goals, Belgium).

European Cup (Champions League) *competition* European-wide club competition which began in 1956. Originally a straight knockout competition involving the national League Champions of member countries of the **Union of European Football Associations** (UEFA), it has, since 1992, featured a league phase (now called the Champions League) and a knockout stage. The reigning European Cup holders have always qualified automatically for the next season's tournament. The format was altered in 1992 with the quarter-final and semi-final stages replaced by two groups of four clubs, with the two group winners going on to the final. In 1994-95, the format changed again, with the semi-finals reinstated and the last four teams coming from the winners and runners-up in two Champions League groups. The following season, the top eight seeded teams – the holders plus the League Champions from the strongest European Leagues – automatically entered the Champions League phase (four groups of four) along with eight qualifiers from a preliminary round of clubs ranked from eight to 23 in the UEFA list. League Champions from "lesser" countries entered the **UEFA Cup**. Winners of the group sections entered a knockout quarter-final phase and the final was renamed the Champions League Cup final. The competition was expanded again for the 1999-00 season: the Champions League format consisting of eight leagues of four teams instead of the previous six leagues of four teams. The top two teams in each section qualify for the second stage, which consists of four groups of four clubs, with the top two in each group going forward to the knockout quarter-final phase. The top two England **Premier League** clubs qualify automatically for the initial group stage, while the third-placed club enters the qualifying rounds, switching to the UEFA Cup should it fail to qualify. The three most successful European nations, in terms of recent club competitions – **Germany**, **Italy** and **Spain** – each has four representatives in the tournament. *History* The idea for a European club tournament had been regularly aired since the 1920s. It was finally established in 1956, after the former **France** international and then editor of the French sports newspaper *L'Equipe*, Gabriel Hanot, had invited representatives of the continent's leading clubs to a meeting in Paris a year earlier. Fifteen clubs, including **Chelsea**, the current English League Champions, and **Hibernian** (which was considered to have a superior recent record than current Scottish Champions **Aberdeen**) attended the Paris meeting and agreed to begin the competition the following season. **FIFA** formally sanctioned the tournament on 8 May 1955 with the stipulation that all entrants should be approved by their national governing bodies. Sixteen teams entered the first competition, although not all (such as Hibernian, which reached the semi-finals) were national League Champions. Chelsea was drawn to play the Swedish club Djurgaarden in the opening round but the **Football League** refused to give the club permission to participate and the Londoners were forced to withdraw. **Real Madrid** was the first winner of the competition and the Spanish club went on to win the trophy for the next four years. The 1958 final between Real Madrid and **AC Milan** was the first to go to extra time, while the first **penalty shoot-out** to settle the final took place in 1984 after **Liverpool**, the eventual winners, had drawn 1–1 with **Roma** (AS). Only one final has required a replay, the 1974 encounter between **Bayern Munich** and **Atlético Madrid**. English clubs, having dominated the competition in the previous eight years (with seven victories) were banned from competing following the **Heysel Stadium tragedy** in 1985. **Olympique de Marseille** was subsequently stripped of its 1993 title after club officials were found guilty of **match fixing**. *Records* Real Madrid has won a record seven European Cups and has appeared in 10 finals. The club also holds the record for consecutive apearances in the competition, qualifying for 15 consecutive seasons between 1955 and 1970. By 1998, Italian clubs had won the trophy on nine occasions (AC Milan with five victories; and **Internazionale** and **Juventus** twice each) and been finalists 21 times. **Celtic** was the UK's first winner, lifting the trophy in 1967, while England's first winner, **Manchester United**, achieved its success the following season. The six consecutive victories achieved by English clubs (**Aston Villa**, Liverpool and **Nottingham Forest**) between 1977 and 1982 is a record sequence. The biggest victory in a European Cup match is **Feyenoord**'s 12–2 victory over **KR Reykjavik** in the first round of the 1969-70 competition. *Final results* 1956, Real Madrid 4–3 **Stade de Reims** (Paris); 1957, Real Madrid 2–0 **Fiorentina** (Madrid); 1958, Real Madrid 3–2 AC Milan (Brussels); 1959, Real Madrid 2–0 Stade de Reims (Stuttgart); 1960, Real Madrid 7–3 **Eintracht Frankfurt** (Glasgow); 1961, **Benfica** 3–2 **Barcelona** (Berne); 1962, Benfica 5–3 Real Madrid (Amsterdam); 1963, AC

Milan 2–1 Benfica (London); 1964, Internazionale 3–1 Real Madrid (Vienna); 1965, Internazionale 1–0 Benfica (Milan); 1966, Real Madrid 2–1 **Partizan Belgrade** (Brussels); 1967, Celtic 2–1 Internazionale (Lisbon); 1968, Manchester United 4–1 Benfica (London); 1969, AC Milan 4–1 **Ajax** (Madrid); 1970, **Feyenoord** 2–1 Celtic (Milan); 1971, Ajax 2–1 **Panathinaikos** (London); 1972, Ajax 2–0 Internazionale (Rotterdam); 1973, Ajax 1–0 Juventus (Belgrade); 1974, Bayern Munich 4–0 Atlético Madrid (replay; Brussels); 1975, Bayern Munich 2–0 **Leeds United** (Paris); 1976, Bayern Munich 1–0 **St Etienne** (Glasgow); 1977, **Liverpool** 3–1 **Borussia Mönchengladbach** (Rome); 1978, Liverpool 1–0 **Club Brugge KV** (London); 1979, Nottingham Forest 1–0 **Malmö** (Munich); 1980, Nottingham Forest 1–0 **Hamburg** (SV) (Madrid); 1981, Liverpool 1–0 Real Madrid (Paris); 1982, Aston Villa 1–0 Bayern Munich (Rotterdam); 1983, Hamburg (SV) 1–0 Juventus (Athens); 1984, Liverpool 1–1 **Roma** (AS) (4–2 pens., Rome); 1985, Juventus 1–0 Liverpool (Brussels); 1986, **Steaua Bucharest** 0–0 Barcelona (2–0 pens., Seville); 1987, **Porto** 2–1 Bayern Munich (Vienna); 1988, **PSV Eindhoven** 0–0 Benfica (pens., Stuttgart); 1989, AC Milan 4–0 Steaua Bucharest (Barcelona); 1990, AC Milan 1–0 Benfica (Vienna); 1991, **Red Star Belgrade** 0–0 Olympique de Marseille (5–3 on pens., Bari); 1992, Barcelona 1–0 **Sampdoria** (London); 1993, Olympique de Marseille* 1–0 AC Milan (Munich; *subsequently stripped of title); 1994, AC Milan 4–0 Barcelona (Athens); 1995, Ajax 1–0 AC Milan (Vienna); 1996, Juventus 1–1 Ajax (4–2 pens., Rome); 1997, **Borussia Dortmund** 3–1 Juventus (Munich); 1998, Real Madrid 1–0 Juventus (Amsterdam); 1999, Manchester United v Bayern Munich (Barcelona).

European Cup-winners Cup *competition* former European-wide club knockout competition which began in 1961 for the winners of domestic cup competitions, last played 1999. All ties up to the final were played over two legs, home and away. From 1962, the final was played as a one-off match at a **neutral venue**. The competition was open to clubs of member countries of the **Union of European Football Assocations** (UEFA). Thirty-two sides qualified for the 1998-99 competition proper, comprising: the holders; the cup winners (or finalists) from the 14 strongest Leagues in the UEFA confederation; and 17 other domestic cup winners which came through the qualifying stages. The competition was replaced in 1999-00 by the revamped **UEFA Cup**. *History* Developed by the committee responsible for the **Mitropa Cup** (which had been established in the inter-war period) following the success of the **European Cup**. The first competition, in 1960-61, was contested by 10 clubs, with four – **Ferencváros**, **Rangers**, Red Star Brno (now known as FC Boby Brno) and Vorwärts Berlin (now known as **FC Victoria 91**) – playing a qualifying round to join the six other entrants – **Borussia Mönchengladbach**, **Dynamo Zagreb**, FC Luzern, **Fiorentina**, **Austria Vienna**,

Wolverhampton Wanderers. Fiorentina, which had qualified for the competition as losing Italian Cup finalists, won the competition, beating Rangers 4–1 over two legs. The Florence club also got to the final the following season, when 23 clubs entered the competition, but was beaten by **Atlético Madrid**. No club ever won the trophy in successive years. The 1962, 1964 and 1971 finals all went to replays, while the 1980 encounter between **Valencia** and **Arsenal** was the first major European club competition final to be decided by a **penalty shoot-out**. Aside from Fiorentina, **RSC Anderlecht** (1978), **Barcelona** (1997) and **Dynamo Tbilisi** (1981) have all won the ECWC despite losing in the final of their respective domestic cup competitions. *Records* Barcelona won the ECWC a record four times and appeared in the final on six occasions. The club's 4–3 extra-time victory over Fortuna Düsseldorf in 1979 is the highest-scoring final. Barcelona is one of only five clubs to have qualified for the ECWC for four consecutive seasons (others being RSC Anderlecht, **Dinamo Batumi**, **Dinamo Bucharest** and **Shamrock Rovers**). **Cardiff City** and **Reipas Lahti** hold the record for having appeared in the competition in five consecutive seasons. **Chelsea**'s 21–0 aggregate victory over Jeunesse Hautcharage (8–0 and 13–0) in the first round of the 1971-72 competition is the record combined score in any European club tournament. The UK has been represented in 17 finals. Chelsea has twice won the competition. **Tottenham Hotspur**'s 1963 triumph was the first by an English team in a European club competition. The very last Cup-winners Cup was won by **Lazio**, 2–1 winners over Real Mallorca at **Villa Park**, Birmingham (19 May 1999). *Final results* 1961, Fiorentina 4–1 Rangers (agg.); 1962, Atlético Madrid 3–0 Fiorentina (replay; Stuttgart); 1963, Tottenham Hotspur 5–1 Atlético Madrid (Rotterdam); 1964, **Sporting Lisbon** 1–0 **MTK Hungária FC** (as MTK Budapest) (replay; Antwerp); 1965, **West Ham United** 2–0 Munich 1860 (London); 1966, **Borussia Dortmund** 2–1 **Liverpool** (Glasgow); 1967, **Bayern Munich** 1–0 Rangers (Nuremberg); 1968, AC Milan 2–0 **Hamburg** (SV) (Rotterdam); 1969, **Slovan Bratislava** 3–2 Barcelona (Basle); 1970, **Manchester City** 2–1 **Gornik Zabrze** (Vienna); 1971, Chelsea 2–1 Real Madrid (replay; Athens); 1972, Rangers 3–2 **Dinamo Moscow** (Barcelona); 1973, AC Milan 1–0 **Leeds United** (Salonika); 1974, **Magdeburg** (1.FC) 2–0 AC Milan (Rotterdam); 1975, **Dinamo Kiev** 3–0 **Ferencváros** (Basle); 1976, RSC Anderlecht 4–2 West Ham United (Brussels); 1977, Hamburg (SV) 2–0 RSC Anderlecht (Amsterdam); 1978, RSC Anderlecht 4–0 **Austria Vienna** (Paris); 1979, Barcelona 4–3 Fortuna Düsseldorf (Basle); 1980, Valencia 0–0 Arsenal (5–4 pens., Brussels); 1981, Dynamo Tbilisi 2–1 **Carl Zeiss Jena** (Dusseldorf); 1982, Barcelona 2–1 **Standard Club Liege** (Barcelona); 1983, **Aberdeen** 2–1 Real Madrid (Gothenburg); 1984, **Juventus** 2–1 **Porto** (Basle); 1985, **Everton** 3–1 **Rapid Vienna** (Rotterdam); 1986, Dinamo Kiev 3–0 Atlético Madrid

(Lyon); 1987, **Ajax** 1–0 **Lokomotiv Leipzig** (Athens); 1988, **KV Mechelen** 1–0 Ajax (Strasbourg); 1989, Barcelona 2–0 **Sampdoria** (Berne); 1990, Sampdoria 2–0 RSC Anderlecht (Gothenburg); 1991, **Manchester United** 2–1 Barcelona (Rotterdam); 1992, **Werder Bremen** 2–0 **Monaco** (Lisbon); 1993, **Parma** 3–1 **Royal Antwerp** (London); 1994, Arsenal 1–0 Parma (Copenhagen); 1995, **Real Zaragoza** 2–1 Arsenal (Paris); 1996, **Paris St Germain** 1–0 Rapid Vienna (Brussels); 1997, Barcelona 1–0 Paris St Germain (Rotterdam); 1998, Chelsea 1–0 **Stuttgart** (VfB) (Stockholm); 1999, Lazio 2–1 Real Mallorca (Villa Park, Birmingham).

European Economic Area *n* **Iceland**, **Liechtenstein** and **Norway** – countries that are outside the **European Union** but whose citizens are not counted as **foreign players** by the **Premier League**, **Football League** and **Scottish Football League**.

European Footballer of the Year *award* annual accolade to the top player in European football, as voted for by readers of the magazine *France Football*. *Winners* 1956, Stanley **Matthews** (**Blackpool**); 1957, Alfredo **di Stefano** (**Real Madrid**); 1958, Raymond **Kopa** (Real Madrid); 1959, Alfredo di Stefano (Real Madrid); 1960, Luis **Suarez** (**Barcelona**); 1961, Omar **Sivori** (**Juventus**); 1962, Josef **Masopust** (**Dukla Prague**); 1963, Lev **Yashin** (**Moscow Dinamo**); 1964, Denis **Law** (**Manchester United**); 1965, **Eusébio** (**Benfica**); 1966, Bobby **Charlton** (Manchester United); 1967, Florian **Albert** (**Ferencváros**); 1968, George **Best** (Manchester United); 1969, Gianni **Rivera** (**AC Milan**); 1970, Gerd **Muller** (**Bayern Munich**); 1971, Johan **Cruyff** (**Ajax**); 1972, Franz **Beckenbauer** (Bayern Munich); 1973, Johan Cruyff (Barcelona); 1974, Johan Cruyff (Barcelona); 1975, Oleg **Blokhin** (**Dinamo Kiev**); 1976, Franz Beckenbauer (Bayern Munich); 1977, Allan **Simonsen** (**Borussia Mönchengladbach**); 1978, Kevin **Keegan** (**Hamburg** (SV); 1979, Kevin Keegan (Hamburg (SV); 1980, Karl-Heinz **Rummenigge** (Bayern Munich); 1981, Karl-Heinz Rummenigge (Bayern Munich); 1982, Paolo **Rossi** (Juventus); 1983, Michel **Platini** (Juventus); 1984, Michel Platini (Juventus); 1986, Michel Platini (Juventus); 1986, Igor **Belanov** (Dinamo Kiev); 1987, Ruud **Gullit** (AC Milan); 1988, Marco **Van Basten** (AC Milan); 1989, Marco Van Basten (AC Milan); 1990, Lothar **Matthäus** (**Internazionale**); 1991, Jean-Pierre **Papin** (**Olympique de Marseille**); 1992, Marco Van Basten (AC Milan); 1993, Roberto **Baggio** (Juventus); 1994, Hristo **Stoichkov** (Barcelona); 1995, George **Weah** (AC Milan); 1996, Matthias **Sammer** (**Borussia Dortmund**); 1997, **Ronaldo** (Barcelona and Internazionale); 1998, Zinedine **Zidane** (Juventus).

European Golden Boot *award* annual award made by the European Sports Magazines group (including *France Football* – the organisers of the **European Footballer of the Year** award) to the player who scores the most goals in top-flight league matches in any European country. Since 1997, the criteria have been modified to weight in favour of the major European leagues. Players in the top eight leagues (according to UEFA rankings) are awarded two points for every goal scored, compared with 1.5 points for scorers in the lower leagues. The official Golden Boot was not awarded from 1993 to 1996, however, the statistics below include the top scorers for those years. *Winners* 1967-68 **Eusébio** (42 goals for **Benfica**); 1968-69 Petar Jekov (36 goals for **CSKA Sofia**); 1969-70 Gerd **Müller** (38 goals for **Bayern Munich**); 1970-71 Joseph Skoblar (44 goals for **Olympique de Marseille**); 1971-72 Gerd Müller (40 goals for Bayern Munich); 1972-73 Eusébio (40 goals for Benfica); 1973-74 Hector Yazalde (46 goals for **Sporting Clube de Portugal**); 1974-75 Dudu Georgescu (31 goals for **Dinamo Bucharest**); 1975-76 Sotiris Kaiafas (39 goals for **Omonia Nicosia**); 1976-77 Dudu Georgescu (37 goals for Dinamo Bucharest); 1977-78 Hans Krankl (41 goals for **Rapid Vienna**); 1978-79 Kees Kist (34 goals for **AZ 67 Alkmaar**); 1979-80 Erwin Vandenbergh (39 goals for **Lierse SK**); 1980-81 Georgi Slavkov (31 goals for **Botev Plovdiv**); 1981-82 Wim Kieft (32 goals for **Ajax**); 1982-83 Fernando Gomez (36 goals for **Porto**); 1983-84 Ian **Rush** (32 goals for **Liverpool**); 1984-85 Fernando Gomez (39 goals for Porto); 1985-86 Marco **van Basten** (37 goals for Ajax); 1986-87 Rodion Camataru (44 goals for Dinamo Bucharest); 1987-88 Tanju Colak (39 goals for **Galatasaray**); 1988-89 Dorin Mateut (43 goals for Dinamo Bucharest); 1989-90 Hugo **Sanchez** (38 goals for **Real Madrid**), jointly with Hristo **Stoitchkov** (38 goals for CSKA Sofia); 1990-91 Darko **Pancev** (34 goals for **Red Star Belgrade**); 1991-92 Ally **McCoist** (34 goals for **Rangers**); 1992-93 (unofficial) Ally McCoist (34 goals for Rangers); 1993-94 David Taylor (43 goals for **Porthmadog**); 1994-95 Arsen Avetisyan (39 goals for **Erebuni-Homenetmen Yerevan**); 1995-96 Zviad Endeladze (40 goals for Margveti Zestafoni of Georgia); 1996-97 **Ronaldo** (34 goals for **Barcelona**); 1997-98 Nikos Mahlas (34 goals for Vitesse Arnhem, Netherlands).

European Nations Cup *competition* former name, until 1968, of the **European Championship**.

European Super Cup *competition* annual competition between the winners of the **European Cup** (Champions League) and the **European Cup-winners Cup** established by the **Union of European Football Associations** (UEFA) in 1972-73. With the demise of the European Cup-winners Cup in 1999, the tournament will be competed by the European Cup and **UEFA Cup** winners from 2000. *History* Until the winners of the 1998 club competitions, **Real Madrid** and **Chelsea** respectively, met in a one-off match in Monaco's Louis II stadium (21 August 1998), the Super Cup was (with the exception of the 1984-85, 1986-87 and 1991-92 competitions) played over two legs. The 1998-99 competition was also the first to be staged at the beginning of the season rather than in the post-Christmas period. The Cup was not contested in either 1974-75 or 1981-82. The 1985-86 competition did not take place owing to UEFA's ban on English clubs participating in Europe following the **Heysel Stadium disaster** In 1993-94, **AC Milan** replaced **Olympique de Marseille** after the French European Cup winner was stripped of the title for **match fixing**. *Records* (Up to and including 1998) **Liverpool** was England's first Super Cup victors (1976-77) and **Aberdeen** first lifted the trophy for Scotland (1982-83). AC Milan (1988-89, 1989-90, 1993-94) and **Ajax** (1972-73, 1973-74, 1994-95) have each won the trophy a record three times. *Final results* 1972-73, Ajax 6–3 **Rangers** (agg.); 1973-74, Ajax 6–1 AC Milan (agg.); 1974-75, not contested; 1975-76, **Dinamo Kiev** 3–0 **Bayern Munich** (agg.); 1976-77, **RSC Anderlecht** 5–3 Bayern Munich (agg.); 1977-78, Liverpool 7–1 **Hamburg** (SV) (agg.); 1978-79, RSC Anderlecht 4–3 Liverpool (agg.); 1979-80, **Nottingham Forest** 2–1 **Barcelona** (agg.); 1980-81, **Valencia** 2–2 Nottingham Forest (agg. Valencia won on **away goal**); 1981-82, not contested; 1982-83, **Aston Villa** 3–1 Barcelona (agg.); 1983-84, Aberdeen 2–0 Hamburg (SV) (agg.); 1984-85, **Juventus** 2–0 Liverpool; 1985-86, not contested; 1986-87, **Steaua Bucharest** 1–0 Dinamo Kiev; 1987-88, **Porto** (FC) 2–0 Ajax (agg.); 1988-89, **KV Mechelen** 3–1 **PSV Eindhoven** (agg.); 1989-90, AC Milan 2–1 Barcelona (agg.); 1990-91, AC Milan 3-1 **Sampdoria** (agg.); 1991-92, **Manchester United** 1–0 **Red Star Belgrade**; 1992-93, Barcelona 3–2 **Werder Bremen** (agg.); 1993-94, **Parma** 3–0 AC Milan (agg.); 1994-95, AC Milan 2–0 **Arsenal** (agg.); 1995-96, Ajax 5–1 **Real Zaragoza** (agg.); 1996-97, Juventus 9–2 **Paris St-Germain** (agg.); 1997-98, Barcelona 3–1 **Borussia Dortmund** (agg.); 1998-99, Chelsea 1–0 Real Madrid.

European Team of the Year *award* annual award for the national team judged to be the best in Europe, organised by the journal *France Football*. **Germany** (including West Germany) has won the award most times (10), followed by **England** (five). *Winners* 1959 **Hungary**; 1960 **Soviet Union**; 1961 **Austria**; 1962 **Czechoslovakia**; 1963 **Sweden**; 1964 Hungary and **Spain** (shared); 1965 England; 1966 England; 1967 Soviet Union; 1968 West Germany; 1969 England; 1970 **Italy**; 1971 England and Soviet Union (shared); 1972 West Germany; 1973 Italy; 1974 West Germany and **Netherlands** (shared); 1975 Czechoslovakia; 1976 West Germany; 1977 West Germany; 1978 Netherlands; 1979 **Yugoslavia**; 1980 West Germany; 1981 West Germany; 1982 Italy; 1983 **Denmark**; 1984 **France**; 1985 Soviet Union; 1986 Spain; 1987 England; 1988 Netherlands; 1989 Netherlands; 1990 West Germany; 1991 France; 1992 Denmark; 1993 Germany; 1994 Italy and Sweden (shared); 1995 Spain; 1996 Germany; 1997 Spain; 1998 France.

European Under-21 Championship *competition* biennial tournament (predominately for players under 21), which began in 1978 and now serves as the European qualifier for the **Olympic Games**. *Winners* 1978, **Yugoslavia**; 1980, **Soviet Union**; 1982, **England**; 1984, England; 1986, **Spain**; 1988, **France**; 1990, Soviet Union; 1992, **Italy**; 1994, **Portugal**; 1996, Italy; 1998, Spain.

European Union *n.* political, economic and judicial alliance of 15 countries of Western Europe, founded 1957 (as the European Economic Community). The United Kingdom and the Republic of Ireland joined in 1973. The member countries are: **Austria**, **Belgium**, **Denmark**, **Finland**, **France**, **Germany**, **Greece**, **Italy**, **Luxembourg**, the **Netherlands** (Holland), **Portugal**, the **Republic of Ireland**, **Spain**, **Sweden** and the **United Kingdom**. European Union citizens are not counted as **foreign players** by the **Premier League**, **Football League** and **Scottish Football League**. See **Bosman ruling**.

European Under-18 Youth Championship *competition* annual tournament, first established in 1948 as the European Junior Championship for Under-18s, adopting its present format and name in 1981. Between 1984 and 1992 the competition was a biennial event. *Winners* 1948, **England**; 1949, **France**; 1950, **Austria**; 1951, **Yugoslavia**; 1952, **Spain**; 1953, **Hungary**; 1954, Spain; not held in 1955 or 1956; 1957, Austria; 1958, **Italy**; 1959, **Bulgaria**; 1960, Hungary; 1961, **Portugal**; 1962, **Romania**; 1963, England; 1964, England; 1965, **East Germany**; 1966, **Soviet Union** and Italy (shared trophy); 1967, Soviet Union; 1968, **Czechoslovakia**; 1969, Bulgaria; 1970, East Germany; 1971, England; 1972, England; 1973, England; 1974, Bulgaria; 1975, England, 1976, Soviet Union; 1977, **Belgium**; 1978, Soviet Union; 1979, Yugoslavia; 1980, England; 1981, West **Germany**; 1982, **Scotland**; 1983, France; 1984, Hungary; 1986, East Germany; 1988, Soviet Union; 1990, Soviet Union; 1992, **Turkey**; 1993, England; 1994, Portugal; 1995, Spain; 1996, France; 1997, France; 1998, **Ireland, Republic of**.

Eusébio *player* Full name: Eusébio Da Silva Ferreira. Striker. **Portugal** international (64 caps, 41 goals 1961-73). Born 25 January 1942, in Maputo, Mozambique. *Clubs* **Gruppo Desportivo de Maputo**, **Benfica**, Boston Minutemen (USA), Toronto Metros-Croatia (Canada), Las Vegas Quicksilver (USA), **Monterrey** (Mexico). *Keynotes* Eusébio, known simply by his first name, started his career as a junior at Mozambique club Gruppo Desportivo de Maputo, before moving to Benfica in 1961. Because Mozambique was, at that time, a Portuguese colony, Eusébio was eligible to play for Portugal rather than his country of birth. He scored on his international debut on 8 October 1961, a 2–4 defeat by Luxembourg (in Luxembourg, **World Cup** qualifier) and went on to become Portugal's highest all-time goalscorer in an international career that spanned 12 years. Eusébio was top scorer at the 1966 World Cup finals, with nine goals, including four goals in his country's memorable 5–3 defeat of **North Korea** – the Koreans had gone 3–0 ahead after just 22 minutes

– and the opening goal in the third/fourth playoff against the **Soviet Union** (2–1, at **Wembley** Stadium). Eusébio had already scored seven goals in Portugal's six qualifying games, including a hat-trick against **Turkey** (5–1). He scored his last international goal on 28 March 1973, in a World Cup qualifier against **Northern Ireland** (1–1, in Coventry, England). He appeared in **Benfica**'s first five **European Cup** finals (1961, 1962, 1963, 1965, 1968), scoring twice in the 5–2 defeat of **Real Madrid** in 1962, and was tournament top scorer in 1966 (eight goals) and 1968 (six goals). Eusébio was nicknamed the "Black Panther" by the British press. Eusébio scored 47 goals for Benfica in European Cup matches; only two behind the all-time tournament record held by Alfredo **di Stefano**. *Honours* World Cup **Golden Boot** 1966; World Cup third place (Portugal, 1966); European Cup (Benfica, 1961, 1962); Portuguese league championship (Benfica, 1963, 1964, 1965, 1967, 1968, 1969, 1971, 1972, 1973); **European Golden Boot** 1968 (42 league goals for Benfica), 1973 (40 goals for Benfica); *France Football* **European Footballer of the Year** 1965, runner-up 1962, 1967.

eversion injury *medical* a **sprain**, **tear** or **rupture** injury to the **medial deltoid ligament** resulting from the ankle being overstretched either downwards or upwards. See **inversion injury**.

Everton (Club de Deportes Everton Vina del Mar) *club* Chilean national league club based in Valparaiso, founded 1909. Ground: Estadio Sausalito, capacity: 18,000. Strip: blue shirts with a single yellow hoop, blue shorts. Chilean Cup (**Copa Chile**) 1984; Chilean league champions 1950, 1952, 1976.

Everton *club* English league. *Dossier* Ground: **Goodison Park**, Liverpool, Merseyside, capacity: 40,200 all seated. Strip: blue shirts with white/black trim, white shorts, blue socks with white/black trim. Website: *www.evertonfc.com* Nickname: Toffees. Record attendance: 78,299 v **Liverpool** (18 September 1948, Division One). Best average attendance: 51,603 (1962-63). Biggest win: 11–2 v **Derby County** (18 January 1890, **FA Cup**, first round). Biggest defeat: 4–10 v **Tottenham Hotspur** (11 October 1958, Division One). *History* Formed in 1878 as St Domingo's FC, the club played its first matches in Stanley Park (which is situated between Goodison Park and **Anfield**) before moving to a venue in Priory Road and then off Anfield Road before finally settling at Goodison Park in 1892. The name Everton was adopted in the club's second season and is derived from the district of Liverpool in which the club began its life. The players initially wore black shirts with a white sash, before adopting the now-traditional royal blue in 1901. The club's first major backer was a local brewer named John Houlding and it was he who partly owned the field off Anfield Road that Everton used between 1884 and 1892 (the ground would eventually be the home of Liverpool). Everton was a founder member of the **Football League** and won the League Championship in 1890-91. The club was unhappy with the arrangement with Houlding and, despite being offered the Anfield site for £6,000, Everton decided to move and sever its link with the man who would go on to form Liverpool; Houlding formed the Everton FC and Athletic Club but the football authorities insisted that Everton should retain the name, and so Liverpool was founded. Everton established the first major club football ground in England at Goodison Park. In 1905, the club won the FA Cup. Everton won its third League title in 1927-28 with Dixie **Dean** scoring a record 60 goals in one season. Two years later, following a 42-year tenure in Division One (and Football League), the club was relegated for the first time. However, the club bounced straight back at its first attempt, winning the Division Two title and the League Championship in successive seasons – a feat matched only by **Ipswich Town** (1960-61, 1961-62), Liverpool (1904-05, 1905-06), and **Tottenham Hotspur** (1949-50, 1950-51) – and earning Goodison Park the nickname the School of Science, to describe the team's methodical style of play. Everton won a further title in 1938-39 with Dean's striking role taken by the young Tommy **Lawton**. In 1951, Everton (along with **Sheffield Wednesday**) was relegated on **goal average**, but took only three seasons to regain its place in the top flight. In the 1960s, under the managership of Harry Catterick (1961 to 1973), the club finished outside the top six on only one occasion, winning the league title twice (1962-63, 1969-70) and the FA Cup once (1966) during the decade (the club also lost the 1968 final, 0–1 v **West Bromwich Albion**). The second title-winning team included the midfield trio Alan **Ball**, Colin Harvey and Howard Kendall. The appointment of Kendall as Everton manager in 1981 ushered in another successful period for the club, winning the League Championship twice in three years (1984-85, 1986-87) and, in the process, breaking its neighbour Liverpool's stranglehold on the title. It also won the FA Cup in 1984, appeared in two further finals in 1985 and 1986, and won the **European Cup-winners Cup** in 1985. Despite a succession of managers, including former Everton players Colin Harvey and Joe Royle and the return of Kendall (twice), the club has won only one trophy, the FA Cup (1995, 1–0 v **Manchester United**), since its 1986-87 title success. In 1997-98, the club narrowly avoided relegation (goal difference) for the first time since dropping from **Division One** in 1950-51. Ex-**Rangers** manager Walter Smith was appointed manager in summer 1998. In the wake of the controversial transfer of captain Duncan Ferguson to **Newcastle United** in November 1998 apparently without Smith's knowledge, club chairman Peter Johnson resigned his position after four-and-a-half years and put his 68% shareholding up for sale. *League record* Premier League 1992-93–; Division One (including Football League) 1888-89 to 1929-30, 1931-32 to 1950-51, 1954-55 to 1991-92; Division Two 1930-31, 1951-52 to 1953-54. *Honours* Division Two 1930-31; European Cup-winners Cup 1985 (3–1 v **Rapid Vienna** – *Team* **Southall**, Stevens, Van den Hauwe,

Ratcliffe, Mountfield, Reid, Steven (1), Bracewell, Sheedy (1), Gray (1), Sharp); **FA Charity Shield** 1928 (2–1 v **Blackburn Rovers**), 1932 (5–3 v Newcastle United), 1963 (4–0 v Manchester United), 1970 (2–1 v **Chelsea**), 1985 (2–0 v Manchester United), 1987 (1–0 v **Coventry City**); FA Cup 1906 (1–0 v **Newcastle United**), 1933 (3–0 v **Manchester City** – *Team* Sagar, Cook, Cresswell, Britton, White, Thomson, Geldard, Dunn (1), Dean (1), Johnson, Stein (1)), 1966 (3–2 v Sheffield Wednesday – *Team* West, Wright, Wilson, Gabriel, Labone, Harris, Scott, Trebilcock (2), Young, Harvey, Temple (1)), 1984 (2–0 v **Watford** – *Team* Southall, Stevens, Bailey, Ratcliffe, Mountfield, Reid, Steven, Heath, Sharp (1), Gray (1), Richardson), 1995 (1–0 v Manchester United – *Team* Southall, Jackson, Watson, Unsworth, Ablett, Horne, Parkinson, Hinchcliffe, Stuart, Limpar (Amokachi), Rideout (1) (Ferguson)); League (including Football League) 1890-91, 1914-15, 1927-28, 1931-32, 1938-39, 1962-63, 1969-70, 1984-85, 1986-87. *Records* Neville Southall is Everton's most capped player (92 for **Wales**); He also holds the record for club appearances (578, 1981-97); Dixie Dean is Everton's record league goalscorer (349, 1925-37).

Ewood Park *ground* English football ground situated in Blackburn, Lancashire; home of **Blackburn Rovers**. *Dossier* Ground capacity: 31,367 all seated. Pitch dimensions: 105m x 66m. Record attendance: 61,783 v **Bolton Wanderers** (2 March 1929, **FA Cup**, sixth round). Best average attendance: 30,544 (1958-59). *History* Blackburn Rovers had six homes in 15 years before settling at Ewood Park in 1890 (including four matches at Ewood Bridge, the site of Ewood Park, in April 1881). The club's first official match at the ground was on 13 September 1890 (v **Accrington**, **Football League**). Rovers bought the ground for £2,500 in 1893. After a stand collapsed at the ground in 1896 the club was found guilty, and club committee members personally liable, of negligent construction. Between 1905 and 1914, Ewood Park was transformed with the financial support of textiles manufacturer and club chairman Laurence Cotton. In the 1990s, steel magnate Jack Walker's millions helped to turn the ground into an **all-seater stadium**. First the Walkersteel stand was opened in 1988 and between March 1993 and November 1994 three new stands were built at an estimated cost of £25 million. In March 1998, the club announced plans to increase the capacity of the ground to 40,000. A floodlit match was first tried at Ewood Park in 1892 (v **Darwen**), although the first official game under floodlights was not until 10 November 1958 (v **Werder Bremen**, friendly). Ewood Park has staged two **England** internationals (v **Scotland**, 4 April 1891, v **Wales**, 3 March 1924) and six FA Cup semi-finals (1893–1947).

executive box *misc.* private match viewing area usually set behind glass and with television and other facilities, including bar and meal services. **Manchester United**'s **Old Trafford** was one of the first UK football stadiums to have executive boxes when the £350,000 two-tier United Road Stand opened in August 1965. The 20,000 capacity stand included 55 five-seater executive boxes. At around the same time, **Chelsea**'s newly constructed West Stand at **Stamford Bridge** also included six executive boxes. In the mid-1980s, **Aberdeen**'s **Pittodrie** Stadium became the first Scottish ground to install executive boxes.

Exeter City *club* English league. *Dossier* Ground: **St James' Park**, Exeter, Devon, capacity: 10,570. Strip: red and white striped shirts, black shorts, red socks. Nickname: Grecians. Record attendance: 20,984 v **Sunderland** (4 March 1931, **FA Cup**, sixth round replay). Best average attendance: 10,339 (1952-53). Biggest win: 9–1 v **Aberdare** (26 November 1927, FA Cup, first round). Biggest defeat: 0–9 v **Notts County** (16 October 1948, Division Three (South)), v **Northampton Town** (12 April 1958, Division Three (South)). *History* Exeter United was founded around 1890 and in 1904, it merged with St Sidwell's Old Boys to form Exeter City. The new club continued to play at St James' Park, where United had first played in 1894. Exeter turned professional in 1908 and joined the **Southern League**. The club was a founder member of Division Three in 1920-21, but it was not until 1963-64 that it was promoted for the first time. The club also won promotion in 1976-77 and 1989-90, winning the Division Four Championship – the club's only honour – on the second occasion. Exeter was a FA Cup quarter-finalist in 1931 (2–4 replay v **Sunderland**) and 1981 (0–2 v **Tottenham Hotspur**). During the 1973-74 season, Exeter's away match against **Scunthorpe United** was not played because the club failed to arrive (2 April 1974); Scunthorpe was awarded two points as a result. *League record* Second Division 1992-93 to 1993-94; Division Three 1920-21, 1964-65 to 1965-66, 1977-78 to 1983-84, 1990-91 to 1991-92; Third Division 1994-95–; Division Three (South) 1921-22 to 1957-58; Division Four 1958-59 to 1963-64, 1966-67 to 1976-77, 1984-85 to 1989-90. *Honours* Division Four 1989-90; **Division Three (South) Cup** 1934 (1–0 v **Torquay United**). *Records* Dermot Curtis is Exeter's most capped player (1 (17) for **Republic of Ireland**); Arnold Mitchell holds the record for club League appearances (495, 1952-66); Tony Kellow is Exeter's record League goalscorer (129, 1976-78, 1980-83, 1985-88).

Exhibition Cup *competition* 1938 knockout tournament that was played to coincide with a major Glasgow exhibition and involving eight invited English and Scottish League clubs – **Aberdeen**, **Brentford**, **Chelsea**, **Celtic**, **Everton**, **Heart of Midlothian**, **Rangers** and **Sunderland**. *Final result* Celtic 1–0 Everton.

exiles *misc.* four Welsh-based clubs that continued to play in English non-league football after refusing to join the newly created **League of Wales** (LoW) in 1992. The four clubs were **Caernarfon Town** (which has since entered the LoW), Colwyn Bay (which plays in the Northern League), Merthyr Tydfil and Newport AFC (which play in the **Southern League**). Although the **Football Association of Wales** (FAW) granted Merthyr permission to continue in the English **pyramid system**, it effectively barred Caernarfon, Colwyn Bay and Newport from playing in the principality – hence the exiles name. The clubs took the FAW to court alleging an illegal restraint of trade. In April 1995, the clubs, which had been granted an interim injunction against the FAW's decision at a previous hearing in July 1994, won their case.

exploratory *medical* a preliminary surgical examination to ascertain the extent of an injury and whether further surgery is required. See **arthroscopy**.

Express Red Eagles *club* Ugandan national league club based in the capital Kampala, founded as Uganda Express FC. Ground: Nakivubo, capacity: 20,000. Strip: red shirts, white shorts. Banned from playing 1977-79 by Uganda's military dictatorship under Idi Amin. **African Cup of Champion Clubs** semi-final 1995; East African Super Cup 1997; **East and Central African Club Championship** runners-up 1994, 1995; Ugandan Cup 1985, 1991, 1992, 1994, 1995, 1997; Ugandan league champions 1966, 1974, 1975, 1988, 1989, 1993, 1994, 1995, 1996.

extra time *rules* two equal periods added at the end of some competition matches in order to facilitate a winning score. If the rules of a competition allow it, extra time is added at the end of **normal time** if the scores are level. *Keynotes* Different competitions have different rules on its use. For example, in the **European Championship** and **World Cup** finals, the extra time period is terminated as soon as one of the sides scores a goal (see **golden goal**). In the English **League Cup**, extra time is played if the **aggregate** score is level after the end of normal time. If the scores remain level after extra time, then the **away goals** rule applies. If that fails to decide the match then there will be a **penalty shoot-out**. In other competitions – the knockout stages of all European club competitions, for example – the away goals rule takes precedence over the extra time period and extra time is played only if the scores are level after taking account of the away-goals rule. Compare **added time**.

F

F'91 Dudelange *club* Luxembourg national league club, based in Dudelange and formed in 1991 from three clubs, Stade Dudelange, Alliance Dudelange and US Dudelange (clubs which dated back to 1912–16). Ground: Jos Nosbaum, capacity: 5,000. Strip: yellow shirts and yellow shorts. Luxembourg Cup runners-up 1993, 1994. Stade Dudelange were Luxembourg league champions in 1939, 1940, 1945, 1946, 1947, 1948, 1950, 1955, 1957, 1965, runners-up six times, and Luxembourg Cup winners in 1938, 1948, 1949, 1956, runners-up seven times. Alliance Dudelange won the Cup in 1961 and 1962. US Dudelange won the cup in 1939.

FA *abbrev.* **Football Association**.

FA Amateur Cup *competition* former annual English knockout competition for non-league clubs, first played in 1894 (old Carthusians 2–1 v Casuals). The competition ended in 1974 (Bishops Stortford 4–1 v Ilford). Wimbledon is the only club to have won both the Amateur Cup (1963, 4–2 v Sutton United) and the FA Cup (1988, 1–0 v Liverpool). *Keynotes* The record attendance for an Amateur Cup Final was 100,000 (Pegasus v Harwich and Parkeston, 11 April 1953, **Wembley**).

FA Challenge Trophy *competition* annual English knockout tournament founded in 1969 and contested by non-League professional/semi-professional clubs. The final is played at **Wembley**. Clubs cannot enter both the Challenge Trophy and the **FA Vase**. Several clubs which became members of the **Football League** have won the competition, including **Barnet**, **Macclesfield Town**, **Scarborough** and **Wycombe Wanderers**. In 1995-96, the competition attracted 176 entrants. *Final results* 1970, Macclesfield Town 2–0 Telford United; 1971, Telford United 3–2 Hillingdon Borough; 1972, Stafford Rangers 3–0 Barnet; 1973, Scarborough 2–1 **Wigan Athletic**; 1974, Morecambe 2–1 Dartford; 1975, Matlock Town 4–0 Scarborough; 1976, Scarborough 3–2 Stafford Rangers; 1977, Scarborough 2–1 Dagenham; 1978, Altrincham 3–1 Leatherhead; 1979, Stafford Rangers 2–0 Kettering Town; 1980, Dagenham 2–1 Mossley; 1981, Bishop's Stortford 1–0 Sutton United; 1982, Enfield 1–0 Altrincham; 1983, Telford United 2-1 Northwich Victoria; 1984, Northwich Victoria 2–1 **Bangor City** (replay; **Victoria Ground**,

Stoke); 1985, Wealdstone 2-1 Boston United; 1986, Altrincham 1–0 Runcorn; 1987, Kidderminster Harriers 2–1 Burton Albion (replay; **Hawthorns**); 1988, Enfield 3–2 Telford United 2 (replay; Hawthorns); 1989, Telford United 1–0 Macclesfield Town; 1990, **Barrow** 3–0 Leek Town; 1991, Wycombe Wanderers 2–1 Kidderminster Harriers; 1992, Colchester United 3–1 Witton Albion; 1993, Wycombe Wanderers 4–1 Runcorn; 1994, Woking 2–1 Runcorn; 1995, Woking 2–1 Kidderminster; 1996, Macclesfield Town 3-1 Northwich Victoria; 1997, Woking 1–0 Dagenham and Redbridge; 1998, Cheltenham 1–0 **Southport**; 1999 Kingstonian 1–0 Forest Green Rovers.

FA Charity Shield *competition* annual one-off match founded in 1908 which is (usually) played between the **Premier League** (previously **Football League**) Champions and the **FA Cup** winners and is traditionally regarded as the curtain-raiser to the new season. The idea for the annual encounter to raise funds for charity came from Charles **Clegg**, vice-president and later president of the **Football Association**. Initially the match was between the Football League Champions and the **Southern League** winners or between two select XIs, and the first game, in 1908 (**Manchester United** v **Queens Park Rangers**), raised £1,275 for charitable causes. The 1921 game (**Burnley** v **Tottenham Hotspur**) was the first between the League Champions and the FA Cup win-ners, although several subsequent matches were played between selected professional and amateur sides. When clubs have won the **double**, the FA generally invites the League runners-up to participate, although in 1961 double-winners Tottenham Hotspur played a select XI. An earlier variation was the 1950 match, which was played between the **England** World Cup XI and an FA XI which had toured **Canada** earlier that year. The Charity Shield was transferred to **Wembley** Stadium in 1974 (**Liverpool** v **Leeds United**), a match that was marred by the sending-off of Kevin **Keegan** and Billy **Bremner** – the first dismissal of UK players at Wembley. By 1996 around £5 million pounds had been distributed to some 1,000 charities since the Shield was first played for in 1908. The two participating clubs also receive an allocation of money to give to nominated charities. By 1998-99, Manchester United had secured

12 victories, Liverpool had won the trophy 10 times and **Arsenal** and **Everton** had each won it on nine occasions. *Final results* 1908, Manchester United 1–1,4–0 Queens Park Rangers (replay); 1909, **Newcastle United** 2–0 **Northampton Town**; 1910, **Brighton & Hove Albion** 1–0 **Aston Villa**; 1911, Manchester United 8–4 **Swindon Town**; 1912, **Blackburn Rovers** 2–1 Queens Park Rangers; 1913, Professionals 7–2 Amateurs; 1920, **West Bromwich Albion** 2–0 Tottenham Hotspur; 1921, Tottenham Hotspur 2–0 Burnley; 1922, **Huddersfield Town** 1–0 Liverpool; 1923, Professionals 2–0 Amateurs; 1924, Professionals 3–1 Amateurs; 1925, Amateurs 6–1 Professionals; 1926, Amateurs 6–3 Professionals; 1927, **Cardiff City** 2–1 Corinthians; 1928, Everton 2–1 Blackburn Rovers; 1929, Professionals 3–0 Amateurs; 1930, Arsenal 2–1 **Sheffield Wednesday**; 1931, Arsenal 1–0 West Bromwich Albion; 1932, Everton 5–3 Newcastle United; 1933, Arsenal 3–0 Everton; 1934, Arsenal 4–0 **Manchester City**; 1935, Sheffield Wednesday 1–0 Arsenal; 1936, **Sunderland** 2–1 Arsenal; 1937, Manchester City 2–0 Sunderland; 1938, Arsenal 2–1 **Preston North End**; 1948, Arsenal 4–3 Manchester United; 1949, **Portsmouth** 1–1 **Wolverhampton Wanderers** (shared trophy); 1950, England World Cup XI 4–2 FA Canadian Tour Team; 1951, Tottenham Hotspur 2–1 Newcastle United; 1952, Manchester United 4–2 Newcastle United; 1953, Arsenal 3–1 **Blackpool**; 1954, Wolverhampton Wanderers 4–4 West Bromwich Albion (shared trophy); 1955, **Chelsea** 3–0 Newcastle United; 1956, Manchester United 1–0 Manchester City; 1957, Manchester United 4–0 Aston Villa; 1958, **Bolton Wanderers** 4–1 Wolverhampton Wanderers; 1959, Wolverhampton Wanderers 3–1 **Nottingham Forest**; 1960, Burnley 2–2 Wolverhampton Wanderers (shared trophy); 1961, Tottenham Hotspur 3–2 FA XI; 1962, Tottenham Hotspur 5–1 **Ipswich Town**; 1963, Everton 4–0 Manchester United; 1964, Liverpool 2–2 **West Ham United** (shared trophy); 1965, Manchester United 2–2 Liverpool 2–2 (shared trophy); 1966, Liverpool 1–0 Everton; 1967, Manchester United 3–3 Tottenham Hotspur (shared trophy); 1968, Manchester City 6–1 West Bromwich Albion; 1969, Leeds United 2–1 Manchester City; 1970, Everton 2–1 Chelsea; 1971, **Leicester City** 1–0 Liverpool; 1972, Manchester City 1–0 Aston Villa; 1973, Burnley 1–0 Manchester City; 1974, Liverpool 1–1 Leeds United (6–5 pens.); 1975, **Derby County** 2–0 West Ham United; 1976, Liverpool 1–0 **Southampton**; 1977, Liverpool 0–0 Manchester United (shared trophy); 1978, Nottingham Forest 5–0 Ipswich Town; 1979, Liverpool 3–1 Arsenal; 1980, Liverpool 1–0 West Ham United; 1981, Aston Villa 2–2 Tottenham Hotspur (shared trophy); 1982, Liverpool 1–0 Tottenham Hotspur; 1983, Manchester United 2–0 Liverpool; 1984, Everton 1–0 Liverpool; 1985, Everton 2–0 Manchester United; 1986, Everton 1–1 Liverpool (shared trophy); 1987, Everton 1–0 Coventry City; 1988, Liverpool 2–1 **Wimbledon**; 1989, Liverpool 1–0

Arsenal; 1990, Liverpool 1–1 Manchester United (shared trophy); 1991, Arsenal 0–0 Tottenham Hotspur (shared trophy); 1992, Leeds United 4–3 Liverpool; 1993, Manchester United 1–1 Arsenal (5–4 pens.); 1994, Manchester United 2–0 Blackburn Rovers; 1995, Everton 1–0 Blackburn Rovers; 1996, Manchester United 4–0 Newcastle United; 1997, Manchester United 1–1 Chelsea (4–2 pens.); 1998, Arsenal 3–0 Manchester United.

FA Cup *competition* annual English knockout competition and the oldest football tournament in the world. In 1998-99, 588 clubs entered the competition (compared with a record 674 entrants in 1920-21), each paying a £75 entry fee. Qualifying rounds, of which there are currently four, are regionalised. The first round proper – the draw for which in 1998-99 was nationwide following several years of being conducted on a regional basis – includes non-League qualifiers and all **Football League** Second and Third Division sides, while clubs from the top two tiers enter at the third-round stage. In September 1998, the **Football Asssociation** announced that, after 127 years, from May 1999, the final would no longer be resolved by a **replay** should the teams remain level after **normal playing time** plus **extra time**; the match would, instead, be settled by a **penalty shoot-out**. Replays were retained for the other rounds of the competition. Clubs entering the Cup must meet the following criteria: correct League status; play on an enclosed pitch with a protected walkway for players and officials; floodlights; a match programme; and have the ability to collect admission money (minimum £3 in 1998-99). In September 1994, the FA announced that **pools** company Littlewoods would have its name attached to the FA Cup (and **FA Charity Shield**) as part of a £14 million four-year sponsorship deal. Since 1998-99, financial services company AXA has sponsored the competition. *History* Officially called the Football Association Challenge Cup, the competition was the brainchild of FA secretary Charles **Alcock**, an old Harrovian who had seen a knockout competition for the honour of being the "Cock House" while at school and decided to adapt the idea for the newly-formed FA. The decision to stage the FA Cup was taken at a meeting of the FA on 16 October 1871 and the inaugural competition finally attracted 15 clubs – Barnes, Civil Service, Clapham Rovers, **Crystal Palace (2.)**, Donnington School, Great Marlow, Hampstead Heathens, Harrow Chequers, Hitchin, Maidenhead, **Queen's Park**, Reigate Priory, **Royal Engineers**, Upton Park and **Wanderers**. The first final was played on 16 March 1872 at Kennington Oval with the Wanderers, captained by Charles Alcock, 1–0 victors over Royal Engineers (see **FA Cup venues**). The trophy, the first of four, was not presented to the winning team on the day, but at the Pall Mall Restaurant on 11 April (see **FA Cup trophies**). Extra time was first played in 1875. **Manchester United** has won the trophy on 10 occasions, including a record eight Wembley victories. **Tottenham Hotspur** has won the Cup eight times, and is one of only three clubs to have won the Cup in consecutive seasons, a feat it has achieved twice (1961 and 1962, 1981 and 1982 – others: **Blackburn Rovers**, 1890 and 1891; **Newcastle United**, 1951 and 1952). Seven Division Two clubs – **Notts County** (1894), **Wolverhampton Wanderers** (1908), **Barnsley** (1912), **West Bromwich Albion** (1931), **Sunderland** (1973), **Southampton** (1976) and **West Ham United** (1980) – have won the Cup. In addition, Tottenham Hotspur's 1901 triumph was achieved when it was a **Southern League** club. Lord Kinnaird (Wanderers and Old Etonians), Charles Wollaston (Wanderers) and James Forrest (Blackburn Rovers) each won five winner's medals. Mark **Hughes** (Manchester United and **Chelsea**) has won more winner's medals at Wembley than any other player, having been on the winning side on four occasions. **Cardiff City**'s 1927 FA Cup final triumph (1–0 v **Arsenal**) is the only occasion on which the trophy has gone outside England. **Wimbledon** is the only Football League club to have won both the FA Cup (1988) and the **FA Amateur Cup** (1963). **Bury**'s 6–0 defeat of **Derby County** in 1903 remains the record winning margin in a final. *Final results* 1872, The Wanderers 1–0 Royal Engineers (at Kennington Oval, London); 1873, The Wanderers 2–1 Oxford University (at Lillie Bridge, London); – at Kennington Oval, London – 1874, Oxford University 2–0 Royal Engineers; 1875, Royal Engineers 2–0 replay Old Etonians; 1876, The Wanderers 3–0 Old Etonians (replay); 1877, The Wanderers 2–1 Oxford University; 1878, The Wanderers 3–1 Royal Engineers; 1879, Old Etonians 1–0 Clapham Rovers; 1880, Clapham Rovers 1–0 Oxford University; 1881, Old Carthusians 3–0 Old Etonians; 1882, Old Etonians 1–0 Blackburn Rovers; 1883, Blackburn Olympic 2–1 Old Etonians; 1884, Blackburn Rovers 2–1 Queen's Park; 1885, Blackburn Rovers 2–0 Queen's Park; l886, Blackburn Rovers 2–0 West Bromwich Albion (replay at the **Racecourse Ground**); 1887, **Aston Villa** 2–0 West Bromwich Albion; 1888, West Bromwich Albion 2–1 Preston North End; 1889, **Preston North End** 3–0 Wolverhampton Wanderers; 1890, Blackburn Rovers 6–1 The Wednesday; 1891, Blackburn Rovers 3–1 Notts County; 1892, West Bromwich Albion 3–0 Aston Villa ; 1893, Wolverhampton Wanderers 1–0 **Everton** (at Fallowfield, Manchester); 1894, Notts County 4–1 **Bolton Wanderers** (at Goodison Park); – at **Crystal Palace stadium**, London – 1895, Aston Villa 1–0 West Bromwich Albion; 1896, The Wednesday 2–1 Wolverhampton Wanderers; 1897, Aston Villa 3–2 Everton; 1898, **Nottingham Forest** 3–1 Derby County; 1899, **Sheffield United** 4–1 Derby County; 1900, Bury 4–0 Southampton; 1901, Tottenham Hotspur 3–1 Sheffield United (replay at **Burnden Park**); 1902, Sheffield United 2–1 replay Southampton (replay at Crystal Palace stadium); 1903, Bury 6–0 Derby County; 1904, **Manchester City** 1–0 Bolton Wanderers; 1905, Aston Villa 2–0 Newcastle United; 1906, Everton 1–0 Newcastle United; 1907, The

Wednesday 2–1 Everton; 1908, Wolverhampton Wanderers 3–1 Newcastle United; 1906, Manchester United 1–0 **Bristol City**; 1910, Newcastle United 2–0 Barnsley (replay at Goodison Park); 1911, **Bradford City** 1–0 Newcastle United (replay at **Old Trafford**); 1912, Barnsley 1–0 West Bromwich Albion (replay at **Bramall Lane**); 1913, Aston Villa 1–0 Sunderland; 1914, **Burnley** 1–0 **Liverpool**; 1915, Sheffield United 3–0 Chelsea (at Old Trafford); 1920, Aston Villa 1–0 **Huddersfield Town** (at **Stamford Bridge**); 1921, Tottenham Hotspur 1–0 Wolverhampton Wanderers (at Stamford Bridge); 1922, Huddersfield Town 1–0 Preston North End (at Stamford Bridge); – at **Wembley Stadium** – 1923, Bolton Wanderers 2–0 West Ham United; 1924, Newcastle United 2–0 Aston Villa; 1925, Sheffield United 1–0 Cardiff City; 1926, Bolton Wanderers 1–0 Manchester City; 1927, Cardiff City 1–0 Arsenal; 1928, Blackburn Rovers 3–1 Huddersfield Town; 1929, Bolton Wanderers 2–0 **Portsmouth**; 1930, Arsenal 2–0 Huddersfield Town; 1931, West Bromwich Albion 2–1 **Birmingham**; 1932, Newcastle United 2–1 Arsenal; 1933, Everton 3–0 Manchester City; 1934, Manchester City 2–1 Portsmouth; 1935, Sheffield Wednesday 4–2 West Bromwich Albion; 1936, Arsenal 1–0 Sheffield United; 1937, Sunderland 3–1 Preston North End; 1938, Preston North End 1–0 Huddersfield Town; 1939, Portsmouth 4–1 Wolverhampton Wanderers; 1946, Derby County 4–1 **Charlton Athletic**; 1947, Charlton Athletic 1–0 Burnley; 1948, Manchester United 4–2 **Blackpool**; 1949, Wolverhampton Wanderers 3–1 **Leicester City**; 1950, Arsenal 2–0 Liverpool; 1951, Newcastle United 2–0 Blackpool; 1952, Newcastle United 1–0 Arsenal; 1953, Blackpool 4–3 Bolton Wanderers; 1954, West Bromwich Albion 3–2 Preston North End; 1955, Newcastle United 3–1 Manchester City; 1956, Manchester City 3–1 Birmingham City; 1957, Aston Villa 2–1 Manchester United; 1958, Bolton Wanderers 2–0 Manchester United; 1959, Nottingham Forest 2–1 **Luton Town**; 1960, Wolverhampton Wanderers 3–0 Blackburn Rovers; 1961, Tottenham Hotspur 2–0 Leicester City; 1962, Tottenham Hotspur 3–1 Burnley; 1963, Manchester United 3–1 Leicester City; 1964, West Ham United 3–2 Preston North End; 1965, Liverpool 2–1 Leeds United; 1966, Everton 3–2 Sheffield Wednesday; 1967, Tottenham Hotspur 2–1 Chelsea; 1968, West Bromwich Albion 1–0 Everton; 1969, Manchester City 1–0 Leicester City; 1970, Chelsea 2–1 Leeds United (replay at Old Trafford); 1971, Arsenal 2–1 Liverpool; 1972, Leeds United 1–0 Arsenal; 1973, Sunderland 1–0 Leeds United; 1974, Liverpool 3–0 Newcastle United; 1975, West Ham United 2–0 **Fulham**; 1976, Southampton 1–0 Manchester United; 1977, Manchester United 2–1 Liverpool; 1978, **Ipswich Town** 1–0 Arsenal; 1979, Arsenal 3–2 Manchester United; 1980, West Ham United 1–0 Arsenal; 1981, Tottenham Hotspur 3–2 Manchester City (replay); 1982, Tottenham Hotspur 1–0 **Queens Park Rangers** (replay); 1983, Manchester United 4–0

Brighton & Hove Albion (replay); 1984, Everton 2–0 Watford; 1985, Manchester United 1–0 Everton; 1986, Liverpool 3–1 Everton; 1987, **Coventry City** 3–2 Tottenham Hotspur; 1988, Wimbledon 1–0 Liverpool; 1989, Liverpool 3–2 Everton; 1990, Manchester United 1–0 **Crystal Palace** (replay); 1991, Tottenham Hotspur 2–1 Nottingham Forest; 1992, Liverpool 2–0 Sunderland; 1993, Arsenal 2–1 Sheffield Wednesday (replay); 1994, Manchester United 4–0 Chelsea; 1995, Everton 1–0 Manchester United; 1996, Manchester United 1–0 Liverpool; 1997, Chelsea 2–0 **Middlesbrough**; 1998, Arsenal 2–0 Newcastle United; 1999, Manchester United 2–0 v Newcastle United.

FA Cup hat-trick *record* **Blackburn Rovers**' outside left, William Townley, became the first player to score a **hat-trick** in a FA Cup final when Rovers defeated The Wednesday (now **Sheffield Wednesday**) 6–1 at Kennington Oval in 1890.

FA Cup, longest tie *record* Alvechurch's **FA Cup** fourth qualifying round tie against Oxford City took five replays before the match was settled (1971; Alvechurch won the fifth replay 1–0); the record cannot be beaten as, since 1992-93, ties have been restricted to one replay, with extra-time and penalties if necessary. There have been several ties in the main competition that have required four replays, the last taking place in 1979 (**Arsenal** v **Sheffield Wednesday**, third round; Arsenal won the fourth replay 2–0 and went on to win the cup).

FA Cup third-place playoff *competition* third-place playoff match between the two losing **FA Cup** semi-finalists which was introduced by the **Football Association** in 1970 and played on the eve of the final. The playoffs were 1970, **Manchester United** 2–0 **Watford**; 1971, **Stoke City** 3–2 **Everton**; 1972, not contested; 1973, **Wolverhampton Wanderers** 3–1 **Arsenal**; 1974, **Burnley** 1–0 **Leicester City**.

FA Cup trophies *misc.* trophy awarded to the **FA Cup** winners. The winners retain the trophy until the following March when it is prepared for the new victors. Since the competition began in 1872, there have been four trophies. The first trophy, made by Martin, Hall & Company for £20 was stolen in 1895 from the shop of W Shillcock, a Birmingham boot manufacturer, while on display; **Aston Villa** was the holder and the trophy was never recovered. The second trophy, produced by Vaughtons of Birmingham, was presented to Lord Kinnaird on 6 February 1911 in honour of his 21-year spell as President of the **Football Association** and the fact that he had played in more finals than any other individual – nine of the first 12 finals for either **Wanderers** or Old Etonians. Bradford-based Fattorini & Sons made the third trophy at a cost of £52.50, and ironically, in 1911, **Bradford City** was its first winners. This trophy was replaced before the 1992 final; with the original now held at the FA's head office, **Lancaster Gate**. Wanderers won the first trophy outright following the club's fifth victory in 1878 (v **Royal Engineers**), but returned it to the FA on condition that no team could keep the trophy.

FA Cup venues *misc* ground staging the **FA Cup** final. Eight grounds have staged FA Cup finals since the competition began in 1872. Up to and including the 1999 final, after which the original stadium was demolished for complete rebuilding, **Wembley** had staged 71 finals, the first of which took place on 28 April 1923 (**Bolton Wanderers** v **West Ham United**, see **White horse final**). In addition, Wembley has also been the venue for five final replays (1981, 1982, 1983, 1990, 1993). Kennington Oval staged 20 finals, including the first between Wanderers and **Royal Engineers** on 16 March 1872. The ground was also the venue for the final replay on two occasions (1875, 1876). **Crystal Palace stadium** also staged the final 20 times, the first being the 1895 game between **Aston Villa** and **West Bromwich Albion**. It was also the setting for the 1902 final replay. **Stamford Bridge** was the final venue in 1920, 1921 and 1922. Four other grounds have each staged the final once: **Goodison Park** (1894 final); Lillie Bridge (1873); Fallowfield (1893); and **Old Trafford** (1915). The latter was also the setting for both the 1911 and 1970 replays, as was Goodison Park in 1910. Three other grounds have also staged final replays: **Racecourse Ground** (1886); **Burnden Park** (1901); and **Bramall Lane** (1912).

FA Trophy *competition* see **FA Challenge Trophy**.

FA Vase *competition* annual English knockout competition founded in 1974 for clubs from Leagues that had previously been considered as amateur. All finals are played at **Wembley** and clubs cannot enter both the FA Vase and the **FA Challenge Trophy**. *Keynotes* Officially entitled the Football Association Challenge Vase, the competition was a successor to the **FA Amateur Cup**, which had started in 1893-94 but was abolished by the FA in 1974 along with the distinction between professional and amateur. In 1995-96, the competition attracted 473 entrants. *Final results* 1975, Hoddesdon Town 2–1 Epsom and Ewell; 1976, Billericay Town 1–0 Stamford; 1977, Billericay Town 2–1 Sheffield 1 (replay; Nottingham); 1978, Blue Star 2–1 Barton Rovers; 1979, Billericay Town 4–1 Almondsbury Greenway; 1980, Stamford 2–0 Guisborough Town; 1981, Whickham 3–2 Willenhall Town; 1982, Forest Green Rovers 3–0 Rainworth Miners' Welfare; 1983, VS Rugby 1–0 Halesowen Town; 1984, Stansted 3–2 Stamford; 1985, Halesowen Town 3–1 Fleetwood Town; 1986, Halesowen Town 3–0 Southall; 1987, St Helens Town 3–2 Warrington Town; 1988, Colne Dynamos 1–0 Emley; 1989, Tamworth 3–0 Sudbury Town 0 (replay; Peterborough); 1990, Yeading 1–0 Bridlington (replay; **Elland Road**); 1991, Guiseley 3–1 Gresley Rovers (replay; **Bramall Lane**); 1992 Wimbome Town 5–3 Guiseley; 1993, Bridlington Town 1–0 Tiverton Town; 1994 Diss Town 2–1 Taunton Town; 1996, ArleseyTown 2–1 Oxford City; 1996 Brigg Town 3–0 Clitheroe; 1997 Whitby Town 3–0 North Ferriby United; 1998 Tiverton Town 1–0 Tow Law Town; 1999, Tiverton Town 1–0 Bedlington Terriers.

FA Women's Challenge Cup *competition* knockout tournament for English women's clubs, formerly the

Women's Football Association National Cup until 1992-93. First played 1971, originally run by the now defunct **Women's Football Association**. *Winners; result and runners-up (where available)* 1971 **Southampton WFC** 4–1, v Stewarton and Thistle (from Scotland), at Crystal Palace National Sports Centre, London; 1972 Southampton WFC 3–2, v Stewarton and Thistle (known then as Lees Ladies), at Burton Albion FC; 1973 Southampton WFC, 2–0, v Westthorn United (from Scotland), at Bedford Town FC; 1974 Fodens, 2–1, v Southampton WFC; 1975 Southampton WFC, 4–2, v Warminster Town, at Dunstable Town FC; 1976, Southampton WFC, 2–1, v Queens Park Rangers Ladies, at Bedford Town FC; 1977 Queens Park Rangers Ladies, 1–0, v Southampton WFC, at Dulwich Hamlet FC; 1978 Southampton WFC, 8–2, v Queens Park Rangers Ladies, at Slough Town FC; 1979 Southampton WFC; 1980 St Helens; 1981 Southampton WFC, 4–2 v St Helens; 1982 Lowestoft; 1983 **Doncaster Belles**; 1984 Howbury Grange; 1985 Friends of Fulham; 1986 Norwich; 1987 Doncaster Belles; 1988 Doncaster Belles; 1989 Leasowe Pacific; 1990 Doncaster Belles; 1991 Millwall Lionesses; 1992 Doncaster Belles, 4–2, v Southampton Saints, at **Prenton Park**; 1993 **Arsenal (2.)**, 3–0, v Doncaster Belles; 1994 Doncaster Belles, 1–0, v Knowsley United; 1995 Arsenal, 3–2, v Liverpool; 1996 Croydon, 1–1, 3–2 pens., v Liverpool; 1997 Millwall Lionesses, 1–0 v Wembley (at **Upton Park**); 1998 Arsenal, 3–2, v Croydon (at the **New Den**, Millwall); 1999 Arsenal, 2–0 v Southampton Saints.

FA Women's Premier League Cup *competition* annual knockout tournament for clubs in the **Football Association Women's Premier League**. *Winners, (result and runners-up)* 1993 Arsenal; 1994 Arsenal; 1995 Wimbledon, 2–0 v Villa Aztecs; 1996 Wembley, 2–2, 5–3 pens., v **Doncaster Belles**; 1997 Millwall Lionesses, 2–1 v Everton; 1998 Arsenal, 0–0, 4–3 pens., v Croydon; 1999 Arsenal, 3–1 v Everton.

FA Youth Cup *competition* annual English knockout competition for the youth sides which was founded in 1953. The competition resembles the format of the **FA Cup**, with the youth sides of non- and lower-League clubs contesting the preliminary and qualifying rounds and their counterparts from the top two tiers entering the competition at a later stage. The finals (with the exception 1978) are played over two legs. *Keynotes* First played in 1952-53, devised by the then **Football League** president Joe **Richards**. The trophy was donated by the Football League, having been bought – but never used – during **World War II**. The 1995 final between **Manchester United** and **Tottenham Hotspur** was the first to be settled by a penalty shootout, with United winning 4–3. The following season, the competition attracted 261 entrants. **West Ham United**'s 9–1 aggregate win over Coventry City in the 1999 final was the largest margin of victory. *Winners* 1953, Manchester United; 1954, Manchester United; 1955, Manchester United; 1956, Manchester United; 1957, Manchester United; 1958, **Wolverhampton Wanderers**; 1959,

Blackburn Rovers; 1960, **Chelsea**; 1961, Chelsea; 1962, **Newcastle United**; 1963, West Ham United; 1964, Manchester United; 1965, **Everton**; 1966, **Arsenal**; 1967, **Sunderland**; 1968, **Burnley**; 1969, Sunderland; 1970, Tottenham Hotspur; 1971, Arsenal; 1972, **Aston Villa**; 1973, **Ipswich Town**; 1974, Tottenham Hotspur; 1975, Ipswich Town; 1976, **West Bromwich Albion**; 1977, **Crystal Palace**; 1978, Crystal Palace; 1979, **Millwall**; 1980, Aston Villa; 1981, West Ham United; 1982, **Watford**; 1983, **Norwich City**; 1984, Everton; 1985, Newcastle United; 1986, **Manchester City**; 1987, **Coventry City**; 1988, Arsenal; 1989, Watford; 1990, Tottenham Hotspur; 1991, Millwall; 1992, Manchester United; 1993, **Leeds United**; 1994, Arsenal; 1995, Manchester United; 1996, **Liverpool**; 1997, Leeds United; 1998 Everton; 1999 West Ham United.

FACA *club* Central African Republic national league club based in the capital Bangui. Central African Republic Cup 1990; Central African Republic league champions 1991, 1995.

Facchetti, Giacinto *player* Defender/midfield. **Italy** international (94 caps, three goals, 1963-77). Born 1942. *Clubs* Trevigliese, **Internazionale**. *Keynotes* Facchetti made his international debut on 27 March 1963 (1–0, v **Turkey**, in Istanbul, European Championship). Italy's third-most-capped player. He played in three World Cup finals tournaments 1966, 1970, and 1974 and was captain at the 1970 World Cup final against **Brazil**. He scored 60 league goals for Inter. *Honours* **World Cup** runner-up (Italy, 1970); **European Championship** 1968; **European Cup** (Inter, 1964, 1965); Italian Serie A championship (Inter, 1963, 1965, 1966, 1971); *France Football* **European Footballer of the Year** runner-up 1965.

Faeroe Islands (or Faroe Islands, Faeroes) *country* *UEFA* self-governing island region of **Denmark** in the North Atlantic between the Shetland Islands and **Iceland**. Comprises 22 islands, 19 of which are inhabited. Area: 1,399 sq km (540 sq miles). Population: 47,000. Languages: Faeroese and Danish. Capital: Torshavn (on Strømø). *Dossier* Faroe Islands Football Association (Torshavn) formed in 1979, affiliated to **FIFA** in to **Union of European Football Associations** (UEFA) in 1988, president Torleif Sigudsson, general secretary Isak Mikladal. Season played from April to October. National stadium: Gundadular, Torshavn, capacity: 8,000. National strip: white shirts, blue shorts. First international game: 1930, v Iceland (0–1, in Thorshavn, friendly). Biggest victory: 7–2 v Shetland Islands (9 July 1951, in Lerwick, Shetland Islands, friendly). Biggest defeat: 0–9 v Iceland (10 July 1985, in Keflavik, Iceland, friendly). *International tournament record* **Olympic Games** – never entered; **Women's World Cup** – never entered; **World Cup** – first entered 1994 (last in its six-nation qualifying group), finished fifth of six nations in its 1998 qualifying group (defeating **Malta** at home and away); **European Championship** – first entered 1992 (last in its six-nation qualifying group), finished fifth of six nations in its 1996 qualifying group (defeating **San Marino** at home and away); **Under-17 World Championship** – never entered; **World Youth Cup (under-20)** – never entered. *World Cup performance* (finals and qualifiers to end of 1998 tournament) played 20, won 2, drawn 0, lost 18, scored 11 goals, conceded 69 goals; win rate 10%; goals scored per game 0.55. *Record against British and Irish national teams* v **England**, none played; v **Northern Ireland**, played two, drawn one, lost one; v **Scotland**, played three, lost three; v **Wales**, played two, lost two; v **Republic of Ireland,** none played. Most capped players: Jens Martin Knudsen (51 appearances, ca. 1990–1997, the country's goalkeeper, also famous for playing while wearing a bobble hat). Leading goalscorers: Jens Rasmussen (12 goals, 1989-). *History* The country's oldest major club, **TB Tvoroyri**, was founded in 1892, with **HB Torshavn** and KI Klsksvik formed in 1904. Prior to 1990, the Faeroe Islands' international competition was restricted to the **Island Games** and to the former North Atlantic Cup (against the Orkney Islands and Shetland Islands). It played its first major competition match in 1990: a 1–0 victory over **Austria** in the European Championship qualifying tournament (12 September 1990, in Landskrona, Sweden). Torkil Nielsen – a timber-shop worker – scored the Faroes' goal after 61 minutes, in front of 1,544 spectators at the Swedish ground (the Faroes was barred, under UEFA competition rules, from playing on one of its 12 artificial pitches). The national squad was later coached by the 1977 **European Footballer of the Year** Allan **Simonson**; Simonson was in charge for the 2000 European Championship qualifiers. *League system* Ten teams compete in the national First Division, each club playing each other at home and away. Three points are awarded for a win, and one for a draw; final positions are decided on **goal difference** if clubs are level on points. The bottom club is automatically relegated, and replaced by the top club in the Second Division. The second-bottom placed club in the First Division and the second and third clubs in the Second Division compete in an end-of-season playoff to decide the second promotion/relegation place. Ten teams also compete in the second division, with the bottom club automatically relegated. The second-bottom joins the top clubs in the next division for an end-of-season playoff. *Record in international club tournaments* Never beyond first round. Leading clubs: **B'36 Torshavn, B'68 Toftir, GI Gotu** (Gotu Itrottarfelag), **HB Torshavn** (Havnar Boltfelag), KI Klaksvik (Klaksvikar Itrottarfelag) and TB Tvoroyri (Tvoroyrar Boltfelag).

Faetano *club* San Marino league club based in Faetano, founded 1962. Ground: Faetano, capacity: 500. San Marino Cup 1993, 1994, 1998; San Marino League champions 1986 (the first San Marino championship), 1991, 1999.

FAI Cup (Football Association of Ireland Cup) *competition* the knock-out competition of the Republic of Ireland. First played in 1922 and won by **St James's Gate FC** of Dublin (1–1, 1–0 replay, v **Shamrock Rovers**). Finals played at **Dalymount Park**, Dublin. Shamrock Rovers is by far the most successful club in the competition, having won the Cup 24 times by 1998, 16 more than nearest rivals **Dundalk**.

failure to play a match *regulations* if a club causes a match to be postponed without permission of the referee or governing body, or by the order of the police or other statutory body, it may be punished under **competition rules**. **Premier League** clubs, for example, which fail to play a match without permission can be punished by a Premier League commission; this has the power to impose a fine, deduct points from, or reprimand the club at fault (FA Premier League rules E.13 and section P).

Fair Play award *award* award given to a team/supporters with the best disciplinary record/behaviour over the season or during a tournament. **Denmark** fans won the UNESCO-sponsored supporters Fair Play award at the 1984 **European Championship** in **France**. **Republic of Ireland** supporters won the 1997 **FIFA** Fair Play award for their collective behaviour during the **World Cup** qualifying campaign. Since the 1995-96 season the **Union of European Football Associations** has awarded three additional **UEFA Cup** places to clubs in countries that head its **Fair Play League** – based on the number of **caution**s and **dismissal**s picked up by both national sides and clubs playing in international competition (clubs in **England**, **Luxembourg** and **Norway** were the first beneficiaries). Each season the **Premier League** presents a team and a fans' Fair Play award. In 1997-98, **Liverpool** won the club award and **Blackburn Rovers**' supporters received the fans' honour. England and France shared FIFA's 1998 World Cup Fair Play award, which was open only to countries progressing to the second round. *Previous winners of the FIFA Fairplay award* 1987 fans of **Dundee United**; 1988 Frank Ordenewitz, and the spectators at the **Olympic Games** football tournament in Soeul, **South Korea**; 1989 the spectators of **Trinidad and Tobago**; 1990 Gary **Lineker**; 1991 the Spanish football association, and Jorginho; 1992 the **Belgium** football association; 1993 Nandor **Hidgekuti**, and the Football Association of **Zambia**; 1994 no award; 1995 Jacques Glassmann; 1996 George **Weah**; 1997 **Republic of Ireland supporters**.

fair shoulder charge *rules* careful use of a player's shoulder, without excessive force, to push an opponent at his or her shoulder, when within **playing distance** of the ball, in order to make further progress. This is not an offence. If, however, the charge is reckless, careless or with excessive force then a **foul** will have been committed and the **referee** will award a **direct free kick**. If the shoulder charge is made when the ball is not within playing distance then the player will be guilty of **obstruction** and an **indirect free kick** will be awarded.

Fairplay League *competition* **UEFA** scheme that ranks nations on the basis of the number of **cautions** and **dismissals** picked up by both national sides and clubs playing in international competition. Since the 1995-96 season, UEFA has awarded three additional **UEFA Cup** places to clubs in countries that head the League.

Fairs Cup *competition* former name, until 1972, of the **UEFA Cup**. *Keynotes* **Barcelona** is the permanent holder of the original Fairs Cup trophy after the club, as the competition's first winner in 1958, defeated the holders, **Leeds United**, in a 1971 **playoff** match (2–1, 22 September).

Falkirk *club* Scottish league. *Dossier* Ground: **Brockville Park**, Falkirk, Lothian, capacity: 9,706. Strip: navy blue shirt with navy blue and white chequered sleeves, white with navy blue and white chequered band; navy blue socks with navy blue and white chequered bands. Nickname: Bairns. Record attendance: 23,100 v **Celtic** (21 February 1953, **Scottish FA Cup**, third round). Biggest win: 12–1 Laurieston (23 September 1893, Scottish FA Cup, second round). Biggest defeat: 1–11 v **Airdrieonians** (28 April 1951, Division One). *History* Founded in 1876. Falkirk joined Division Two in 1902-03, three seasons after its local neighbours, **East Stirlingshire**. After finishing runners-up in 1904-05, the club was elected to Division One. In 1907-08 and 1909-10, Falkirk finished as runners-up in the top flight and, in 1913, the club won the **Scottish FA Cup** (2–0 v **Raith Rovers**). Following relegation from the top flight in 1934-35, the club made an immediate return as Division Two Champions. Further Division Two titles were added in 1969-70 and 1974-75. On the second occasion, Falkirk was not promoted to the newly-formed Premier Division but was, instead, placed in the new First Division. Falkirk was a **Scottish League Cup** finalist in 1947-48 (1–4 v **East Fife**) and, in 1957, the club won the Scottish FA Cup for the second time (2–1 replay v **Kilmarnock**). The club reached its third Scottish FA Cup final in 1997 (0–1 v Kilmarnock), having won the **Scottish League Challenge Cup** in 1993-94 (3–0 v **St Mirren**). In 1997-98, Falkirk won the final Scottish League Challenge Cup competition (1–0 v **Queen of the South**). Falkirk's nickname Bairns, is derived from the adage "Better meddle wi' the Devil than the Bairns o' Falkirk". *League record* Premier Division 1986-87 to 1987-88, 1991-92 to 1992-93, 1994-95 to 1996-97; First Division 1975-76 to 1976-77, 1980-81 to 1985-86, 1988-89 to 1990-91, 1993-94, 1997-98–; Division One (A Division) 1905-06 to 1914-15, 1921-22 to 1934-35, 1936-37 to 1950-51, 1952-53 to 1958-59, 1961-62 to 1968-69, 1970-71 to 1973-74; Scottish League 1915-16 to 1920-21; Second Division 1974-75, 1977-78 to 1979-80; Division Two (B Division) 1902-03 to 1904-05, 1935-36, 1951-52, 1959-60 to 1960-61, 1969-70, 1974-75. *Honours* First Division 1990-91, 1993-94; Second Division 1979-80; Division Two 1935-36, 1969-70, 1974-75; Scottish FA Cup 1913

(2–0 v Raith Rovers), 1957 (2–1 replay v Kilmarnock); Scottish League Challenge Cup 1993-94 (3–0 v St Mirren); 1997-98 Scottish League Challenge Cup (1–0 v Queen of the South). *Records* Alex Parker is Falkirk's most capped player (14 (15) for **Scotland**); George Watson holds the record for post-war club appearances (353, 1975-87); Dougie Moran is Falkirk's record goalscorer (86).

Falkland Islands *country no affiliation* United Kingdom Crown Colony in South Atlantic, comprises East and West Falkland and around 200 small islands. Area: 12,175 sq km (4,700 sq miles). Population: 2,121. Language: English. Capital: Stanley. *Dossier* Football association not affiliated to **FIFA**.

fan *n* another term for **supporter**.

fan projekt *misc.* German scheme to develop close links between clubs and local youth groups.

fans' surveys *misc.* annual national survey of fans' views partly funded by the **Premier League** and its sponsors Carling. The first Carling Premiership Fan survey was conducted in 1993-94 and produced responses from 10,651 supporters of Premier League clubs. The 1994-95 survey, produced 15,170 responses. Some of the surveys' findings show that season ticket holders are more likely to view their club as more important than the national side; 60% believe that **all-seater stadium**s are a major benefit; and 40% say that the game has improved its "attractiveness".

Fantastique Express *club* Burundi national league club based in the capital Bujumbura. Burundi league champions 1982, 1994, 1995.

fantasy football 1. *misc.* annual competition run predominantly through national newspapers. Earliest leagues organised in 1990. Subscribers choose their "fantasy team" from a published list of more than 300 contemporary players (sometimes including a manager). The teams must comprise a goalkeeper, defenders, midfielders and strikers from the list of players at given transfer values. The overall value of the team must be equal to or less than the competition's limit. Points are awarded for goals scored by the players in real matches, **assists** or – in the case of goalkeepers and defenders – for conceding no goals in a game. Points are deducted for defenders or goalkeepers whose teams concede goals. Performances of all the players in the league are published periodically by the participating newspapers, along with a list of the most successful "fantasy" teams. The *Daily Telegraph* was the first national newspaper to publish a fantasy football league. Its first season, in 1993, attracted around 300,000 entries. **2.** *television* BBC television comedy presented by David Baddiel and Frank Skinner, first broadcast 1993. It was resurrected by ITV during the 1998 **World Cup**.

fanzine *n.* pamphlet or magazine produced by supporters. One of the earliest football fanzines was *Foul*, first published in 1972. Later football fanzines were heavily influenced by similar publications emerging from the punk rock music scene, especially *Sniffin'*

Glue. Club fanzines, the number of which increased substantially from the mid-1980s, were often the only vehicles available to fans in which they could voice their concerns and make clubs more accountable. Also in the mid-1980s, two national football fanzines, *Off the Ball* and **When Saturday Comes** (first published in March 1986) were launched. By 1995, it was estimated that more than 600 fanzines existed in the UK. Some fanzines are curiously named, including: *The Ugly Inside* (**Southampton**); *Hanging on the Telephone* (**Huddersfield Town**); *The 69er* (**Swindon Town**); *Brian Moore's Head* (**Gillingham**); and *Greasy Chip Buttie* (**Sheffield United**).

far post *n.* the **goal post** that is furthest away from the ball as it is played from the wing (for example at a **corner kick**). *adj.* **far-post**. Compare **near post**.

FAR Rabat (Forces Armees Royale) *club* Moroccan national league club based in the capital Rabat and nicknamed "Les Militaires". Ground: Prince Moulay Abdallah, capacity: 35,000. Strip: red shirts and black shorts. **African Cup of Champion Clubs** – winners 1985, beat AS Bilima, Congo Democratic Republic 6–3 in final over two legs); **African Cup-winners Cup** runners-up 1997 (1–2, agg., v **ES Sahel**, Tunisia), quarter-final 1987; **Afro-Asian Club Cup** – runners-up 1985 (lost 0–2 to **Daewoo Royals**, Korea); Moroccan Cup 1959, 1971, 1984, 1985, 1986; Moroccan League champions 1961, 1962, 1963, 1964, 1967, 1968, 1970, 1984, 1987, 1989; Notable former player: Mohamed **Timoumi**.

Far East Club Championship *competition* annual international club championship contested by champion clubs from East Asia, first played 1998. *Winners* **Rotor Volgograd** (of Russia), 3–2, v **Dalian** (of China, in Shanghai, China).

Far Eastern Games *competition* former international sports event for nations of the Far East, initially held every two years. A football tournament was held from 1913 to 1934. The opening tournament in 1913 consisted of a single challenge match between the **Philippines** and **China**, and is thought to be the first international football match held in Asia (the Philippines beat China 2–1 in Manila). China won nine of the 10 tournaments played (sharing it with **Japan** in 1930). The competing nations were China, the Philippines, Japan and (in 1934) **Indonesia** (then known as Dutch East Indies).

Faras, Ahmed *player* Striker. **Morocco** international. *Club* Chabab Mohammedia (of Morocco). *Keynotes* Scored three goals in the 1976 African Cup of Nations final tournament in Ethiopia. *Honours* **African Cup of Nations** (Morocco, 1976); *France Football* **African Footballer of the Year** 1975.

far post *n.* the **goal post** that is furthest away from the ball as it is played from the wing (for example at a **corner kick**). *adj.* **far-post**. Compare **near post**.

fastest goal record see **goal, fastest**.

fathers and sons *misc.* players whose sons have played in the same match or who have replicated their

father's footballing achievements. *Keynotes* After 125 years of the tournament, a father and son played on opposite teams in an **FA Cup** match: 21-year-old Nick Scaife of Bishop Auckland played opposite his 41-year-old father Bobby Scaife of Pickering (first qualifying round September 1996). Bishop Auckland won the tie 3–1. Scaife senior had been a professional with **Hartlepool**, **Middlesbrough** and **Rochdale**. **Iceland**'s then 35-year-old Arnor **Gudjohnsen** was substituted by his then 17-year-old son Eidur in his country's friendly international against **Estonia** (4–0, 16 August 1984, in Akureyri, Iceland). Domingas da Guia played for **Brazil** in the 1938 **World Cup**; his son, Ademir da Guia played for Brazil in the 1950 tournament.

Fazekas, László *player* Midfield. Hungarian international (92 caps, ca. 1968-1981). *Clubs* Ujpesti Dózsa (now **Ujpesti Torna Egylet**), **Royal Antwerp**. *Honours* **Olympic Games** gold medal (Hungary, 1968); Hungarian league championship (Ujpesti Dózsa, 1969, 1970, 1971, 1972, 1973, 1974, 1975, 1978, 1979). *Keynotes* Hungary's all-time second-most capped player. Played for Ujpesti Dózsa in the final of the **Fairs Cup** (now **UEFA Cup**) in 1969 (2–6, v **Newcastle United**).

FC Balzers *club* club from Liechtenstein, but playing in Swiss League. Reached the first round of the **European Cup-winners Cup** in 1993–94, having beaten Albpetrol Patosi (Albania) 4–1 over two legs in the preliminary round. Liechtenstein Cup winners 11 times (to 1998).

FC Copenhagen (FC København) *club* Danish national league club based in the capital Copenhagen, founded 1992 by the merger of two of Denmark's oldest (and, at that time, amateur) clubs: KB København (formed 1876) and B 1903 København (formed 1903). Ground: Idraetsparken, capacity: 40,000. Strip: white shirts, white shorts. Danish league champions 1993; Danish Cup 1995, 1997. KB København were Danish league champions 15 times, and Cup winners once; B 1903 København were Danish league champions 10 times, and Cup winners once. Notable player: Brian **Laudrup**.

FC Euro Kickers *club* Panama national league club based in Panama City. Panama league runners-up 1996, 1997.

FC Groningen *club* Dutch national league club, based in Groningen, and founded in 1921, as GVAV (until 1971 when adopted present name). Ground: Oosterpark, capacity: 18,000. Strip: green and white striped shirts and white shorts.

FC Haka (FC Haka Valkeakoski) *club* Finnish national league club based in Valkeakoski, founded 1932. Ground: Tehtaankenttä, capacity: 6,000. Strip: white shirts, black shorts. **European Cup-winners Cup** quarter-final 1984; Finnish Cup 1955, 1959, 1960, 1963, 1969, 1977, 1982, 1985, 1988, 1997; Finnish league champions 1960, 1962, 1965, 1977, 1995, 1998.

Pelé and Bobby **Moore** swap shirts after the Brazil v England World Cup match on 7 June 1970.

50ᵀᴴ FOOTBALLER OF THE YEAR AWARD

Gianfranco **Zola** receives the 50th Footballer of the Year Award from Stanley **Matthews**, the first winner of the title, 1997.

George **Best** celebrates with the European Cup after Manchester United's 4–1 victory over Benfica, 29 May 1968.

Eusébio (Benfica) on his way to score in the 1963 European Cup Final against AC Milan at Wembley.

The world's oldest football rivals: fixtures between England and Scotland date back to St Andrew's Day 1872 when they thrashed out a 0–0 draw in a match organised by **Queen's Park**.

Johann **Cruyff** scores the Netherlands' fourth goal in the 1974 World Cup match against Argentina.

Champion of champions: Farid Mondragon and Nestor Clausen of Independiente (Argentina) celebrate winning the 1995 **Supercopa** after beating Flamengo (Brazil) 2–1 on aggregate.

Ronaldo in action for Brazil against Denmark in the 1998 World Cup.

Mia **Hamm** (USA) and Wang Liping (China) compete for the ball in the finals of the 1996 Olympic Games.

The Brazilian team triumphs in the 1994 World Cup.

Zinedine **Zidane** scores France's opening goal in the 1998 World Cup final.

Tony **Adams** and the Arsenal team celebrate their FA Cup triumph – the second part of the 1997-98 double.

The **White horse** final, 1923.

An English disease? Football **hooliganism** hits the Netherlands as fans riot following
Feyenoord's triumph in the 1999 Dutch football league championship.

FC Jazz *club* Finnish national league club based in Pori (venue of a summer jazz festival), founded 1934 (as PPT Pori, a post office club, adopting current name in 1992). Ground: Porin, capacity: 10,000. Strip: red shirts, white shorts. Finnish league champions 1993, 1996. Notable players: Luis António.

FC Lugano (Football-Club) *club* Swiss national league club based in Lugano, founded 1908. Ground: Comunale Cornaredo, capacity: 15,000. Strip: black shirts with a white "V" on the chest, white shorts. Swiss Cup 1931, 1968, 1993; Swiss league champions 1938, 1941, 1949.

FC Luzern (Fussball-Club) *club* Swiss national league club based in Lucerne, founded 1879. Ground: Allmend, capacity: 24,000. Strip: blue shirts, white shorts. Swiss Cup 1960, 1992; Swiss league champions 1989.

FC Nantes Atlantiques *club* French national league club based in Nantes, formed 1943. Ground: La Beaujoire Louis Fonteneau, capacity: 40,000 all seated. Strip: yellow and green striped shirts, yellow shorts. French Cup 1979, 1999; French league champions 1965, 1966, 1973, 1977, 1980, 1983, 1995.

FC Porto *club* see **Porto**.

FC Tirol Innsbruck *club* Austrian national league club, based in Innsbruck, founded 1913 (as Wacker Innsbruck). Ground: Tivoli, capacity: 16,000. Strip: red and green striped shirts, green shorts. Austrian Cup 1970, 1973, 1975, 1978, 1979, (Wacker),1989, 1993; Austrian League 1971, 1972, 1973, 1975, 1977 (Wacker), 1989, 1990; **Mitropa Cup** 1975, 1976; **UEFA Cup** semi final 1987.

FC Twente Enschede *club* Dutch national league club, based in Enschede, and founded in 1965 by merger of SC Enschede (founded 1910) and Enschede Boys Honours. Ground: Het Diekman, capacity: 13,000. Strip: red shirts and red shorts. Dutch Cup 1977; **European Cup-winners Cup** semi-final 1978; **UEFA Cup** runners-up 1974-75 (1–5 agg., v **Borussia Mönchengladbach** – FC Twente drew the opening away leg 0-0), semi-final 1973.

FC Utrecht *club* Dutch national league club, based in Utrecht, and founded in 1970 by merger of DOS Utrecht (founded 1902) and Elinkwijk Utrecht (founded 1919). Ground: Nieuw Galgewaard, capacity: 14,000. Strip: red shirts with a white sash and white shorts. Dutch Cup 1985.

FC Vaduz *club* club from Liechtenstein, but playing in Swiss League. *Keynotes* FC Vaduz holds the European and joint world record of seven consecutive domestic cup triumphs (1956 to 1962). It also holds the world record of appearing in 17 consecutive domestic cup finals (1946 to 1962). **European Cup-winners Cup** first round 1997 (won its preliminary round v **Universitate Riga** of Latvia, 2–2 agg., 5–3 pens.; it lost the first round 0–7 agg., v **Paris St-Germain**); Liechtenstein Cup winners 27 times (to 1999).

FC Victoria 91 *club* German regional league club and former East German national league club based in

Frankfurt-an-der-Oder. Founded 1951 (formerly known as Vorwärts Leipzig until 1953, Vorwärts Berlin until 1971 and Vorwärts Frankfurt/Oder until 1991). Ground: Freundschaft, capacity: 16,000. Strip: yellow shirts, white shorts. Played in the very first **European Cup-winners Cup** tournament in 1960-61. East German Cup 1954, 1970; East German league champions 1958, 1960, 1961, 1965, 1966, 1969; **European Cup** quarter-final 1970).

FC Zurich (Fussball-Club) *club* Swiss national league club based in Zurich, founded 1896. Ground: Letzigrund, capacity: 27,000. Strip: blue and white striped shirts, blue shorts. **European Cup/Champions League** semi-final 1964, 1977; **European Cup-winners Cup** quarter-final 1974; Swiss Cup 1966, 1970, 1972, 1973, 1976; Swiss national champions 1902, 1924 (three regional leagues operated until 1933, with the national championship decided by an inter-league playoff), 1963, 1966, 1968, 1974, 1975, 1976, 1981.

Federation of Independent European Female Football *confederation* former European **women's football** federation founded in Italy in the late 1960s, before the **Union of European Football Associations** took overall control of women's football in 1971. The federation organised a woman's tournament in Italy in November 1969, involving teams from **Denmark**, **England**, **France** and **Italy**, and a world tournament, the "Mundialito", in 1970 (in Italy) and again in 1971 (hosted by **Mexico**). The 1970 final attracted 35,000 spectators. *FIEFF international women's tournaments winners, result and runners-up* 1969 (Europe only) Italy, 3–1, v Denmark, at the Stadio Communale, Turin; 1970 (world tournament) Denmark, 2–0, v Italy, in Italy; 1971 (world tournament) Denmark, 2–0, v Mexico, in Mexico.

Fédération Internationale de Football Association *confederation* see **FIFA**.

feeder league *n.* one of a number of regional leagues that feed into a national league or wider-regional league; they are linked by automatic **promotion** and **relegation**. See **pyramid system**.

Feethams Ground *ground* English football ground situated in Darlington, County Durham; home of **Darlington**. *Dossier* Ground capacity: 8,500. Pitch dimensions: 100.5m x 68m. Record attendance: 21,023 v **Bolton Wanderers** (14 November 1960, **League Cup**, third round). Best average attendance: 10,234 (1948-49). *Keynotes* Darlington played its first match at the Feethams Ground, then, as now, home of the local cricket club, in September 1883. The ground has its own **twin towers**, which, as at **Wembley**, act as a gateway. Feethams staged three **FA Amateur Cup** final replays: 1897 Old Carthusians v Stockton; 1903 Stockton v Oxford City; 1933 Kingstonian v Stockton. The first floodlit match at Feethams took place on 19 September 1960 (v **Millwall**, Division Four). That night, the west stand was destroyed by fire.

feint *n.* the act of pretending to go one way, while moving and taking the ball in another direction in order to deceive an opponent. *vb.* to feint. See **dribble**.

Felix-Bollaert (Stade) *ground* French football ground situated in Lens; home of Racing Club de Lens (see **Lens RC**). Ground capacity: 41,649 all seated. *History* Opened in June 1934. Refurbished for the 1998 **World Cup** at a cost of more than £14 million. During the tournament, the Stade Felix-Bollaert staged one match from each of group's C (**Denmark** v **Saudia Arabia**), D (**Bulgaria** v **Spain**), F (**Germany** v **Yugoslavia**), G (**Colombia** v **England**), and H (**Croatia** v **Jamaica**); and a second round match (**France** v **Paraguay**) – total attendance 240,023; average attendance 40,003.

Fellows Park *ground* English football ground situated in Walsall, west Midlands; former home of **Walsall**. Capacity (1990): 16,000. Pitch dimensions: 100.5m x 67m. Record attendance: 25,453 v **Newcastle United** (August 1961, Division Two). Best average attendance: 12,089 (1949-50). *History* Walsall first played at Fellows Park on 1 September 1896 (v **Glossop**, friendly) and the club's final League match there took place on 1 May 1990 (v **Rotherham United**, Division Three). The ground was originally known as Hillary Street. The club was evicted in December 1900 for non-payment of rent, returning there in 1903 after agreeing a new lease. In 1930, the ground was renamed after the club's chairman Len Fellows – at that time, making Fellows Park one of only four **Football League** grounds to be named after individuals (the others being **Dean Court**, **Ninian Park** and **Adams Park**). The ground was sold for £5.75 million and demolished in summer 1990, having staged 1,577 competitive matches between 1896 and 1990. Fellows Park's final football match occurred on 11 May 1990 (v **West Bromwich Albion**, Peter Hart testimonial). The first floodlit match at Fellows Park took place on 16 December 1957 (v **Falkirk**, friendly).

female fans see **spectators, women**.

femur *medical* the long **bone** of the thigh, jointed with the pelvis above and the knee below. It is the longest and the thickest bone in the body.

Fenerbahçe Spor Kolübü *club* Turkish national league club based in Istanbul – on the Asian side of the Bosphorus, in Istanbul's Kadikoy district – founded 1907. Claims to be Turkey's most supported club. Ground: Fenerbahçe, capacity: 30,000. Strip: blue and yellow striped shirts, yellow shorts. **European Cup** qualified for Champions League 1996 (won two of its six matches, including a 1–0 victory over **Manchester United** at **Old Trafford**); **European Cup-winners Cup** quarter-final 1964; Istanbul League (regional league operated from 1924 to 1958) champions 1930, 1933, 1935, 1936, 1937, 1944, 1947, 1948, 1953; Turkish Cup 1968, 1974, 1979, 1983; Turkish league champions 1959 (the first national league championship), 1961, 1964, 1965, 1968, 1970, 1974, 1975, 1978, 1983, 1985, 1989, 1996. Notable former players: **Lefter** Kücükandonyadis, Tanju Colak.

Ferencváros Torna Club *club* Hungarian national league club based in Budapest, founded 1899, formerly known as ÉDOSZ (1950-51) and Budapest Kinizsi (1951-56). Nickname: Fradi (an abbreviation of the German translation of the club's name, Franzstadt). *Keynotes* In the 1950s, Ferencváros was forced to play in red and adopt the name Kinizsi (a Hungarian folk hero adopted by the Hungarian communists) by the country's then Stalinist government; Ferencváros had been the favoured club of the **World War II** pro-Nazi right-wing government. Ferencvaros won the 1909 Austrian Der Challenge Cup. Ground: Üllöi Út Stadium, capacity: 18,000 all seated. Strip: green and white striped shirts, white shorts. Austrian Cup 1909; **European Cup** – qualified for the Champions League 1995-96; **European Cup-winners Cup** – runners-up 1975 (0–3, v **Dinamo Kiev**, in Basle, Switzerland); **Fairs Cup/UEFA Cup** – winners 1965 (1–0, v **Juventus**, in Turin), runners-up 1968 (0–1 agg., v **Leeds United**); **Mitropa Cup** – winners 1928, 1937, runners-up 1935, 1938, 1939; Hungarian Cup 1913, 1922, 1927, 1928, 1933, 1935, 1942, 1943, 1944, 1958, 1972, 1974, 1976, 1978, 1991, 1993, 1994, 1995; Hungarian league champions 1903, 1905, 1907, 1909, 1910, 1911, 1912, 1913, 1926, 1927, 1928, 1932, 1934, 1938, 1940, 1941, 1949, 1963, 1964, 1967, 1968, 1976, 1981, 1992, 1995, 1996. Notable former players: Sándor **Kocsis**, Florian **Albert**.

Ferguson, Alex *manager* Born 31 December 1941. *Clubs* **East Stirlingshire**, **St Mirren**, **Aberdeen**, **Manchester United**. Also **Scotland** manager and assistant coach. *Keynotes* Former striker who played for **Queen's Park**, **St Johnstone**, **Dunfermline Athletic**, **Rangers**, **Falkirk** and **Ayr United**. He finished his playing career as player-manager of, first East Stirlingshire, and then St Mirren before moving to **Pittodrie** to take charge of Aberdeen. Ferguson successfully broke the **Celtic**-Rangers duopoly of Scottish football, winning the Scottish title with Aberdeen on three occasions between 1980 and 1985. He also led the Dons to three consecutive **Scottish FA Cup** victories and, in 1983, the **European Cup-winners Cup** (v **Real Madrid**). Ferguson joined Manchester United in 1986 after unsuccessfully managing Scotland during the 1986 **World Cup** finals. Although Ferguson had to wait four years to secure his first trophy with United (1990 FA Cup, v **Crystal Palace**), he has subsequently become the most successful manager of his generation in the English game. In 1996, he became the first manager to win the **double-double** and, in 1999, Ferguson's United became the first English club to win the treble – Premiership, FA Cup and **European Cup**. *Honours* Premiership (Manchester United 1992-93, 1993-94, 1995-96, 1996-97, 1998-99); FA Cup (Manchester United 1990, 1994, 1996, 1999); **League Cup** (Manchester United 1992); Scottish League (Aberdeen 1979-80, 1983-84, 1984-85); Scottish FA Cup (Aberdeen 1982, 1983, 1984, 1986); **Scottish League Cup** (Aberdeen 1986); Scottish First Division (St Mirren 1976-77); European Cup (Manchester United 1999); European Cup-winners Cup (Aberdeen 1983,

Manchester United 1991); **European Super Cup** (Manchester United 1991).

Ferrer, Albert *player* Defender. **Spain** international (35 caps, no goals, ca. 1993-). Born 6 June 1970. *Clubs* **Barcelona**, **Chelsea**. *Keynotes* Transferred to Chelsea for £2.2 million in June 1998 and, soon after, became the first player to win the **European Super Cup** in consecutive seasons with different clubs: Barcelona in 1997 and Chelsea in 1998. He was the first Spaniard to play in the FA **Premier League**. *Honours* **Olympic Games** gold medal (Spain, 1992); **European Cup** (Barcelona, 1992); **European Cup-winners Cup** (Barcelona, 1989, 1997); European Super Cup (Barcelona, 1992, 1997, Chelsea 1998); Spanish League (Barcelona, 1991, 1992, 1993, 1994, 1998); Spanish Cup (Barcelona, 1990, 1997, 1998).

Ferreyra, Bernabe *player* Striker. **Argentina** international. Born 1909. *Clubs* Tigre, **River Plate**. *Keynotes* Transferred to River Plate in 1932 – one of the first transfers under the new Argentinean professional league – and scored 43 league goals in his first season; the second-highest tally in Argentine league history. He was renowned for his powerful shooting. *Honours* **Copa America** (Argentina, 1927, 1929); Argentinean league championship (River Plate, 1932).

Ferroviário Maputo *club* Mozambique national league club based in the capital Maputo. Ground: Estadio de Machava, Maputo, capacity: 60,000 (national stadium). **African Cup of Champion Clubs** quarter-final "champions-league" stage 1997; **CAF Cup** semi-final 1992 (eliminated on penalties to eventual runners-up **Nakivubo Villa** of Uganda, after 2–2 aggregate score); Mozambique Cup 1982 and 1989; Mozambique league champions 1982, 1989, 1996, 1997.

Fever Pitch *publication* novel by **Arsenal** supporter Nick **Hornby**, first published in 1992 by Victor Gollancz Ltd. It tells the story of Hornby's obsessive support for Arsenal between 1968 and 1992. It has been adapted as a stage play and **film**.

Feyenoord *club* Dutch national league club, based in Rotterdam, founded 1908. Ground: Stadion Fiejenoord, capacity: 51,000 all seated. Strip: red and white halved shirts and black shorts. *History* Founded by a Dutch mining businessman as Wilhelmina, became Hellesluis in 1910, Celeritas in 1911 and Feijenoord in 1912. In the late 1960s, the club changed its name from Feijenoord to Feyenoord, apparently to make pronunciation easier for foreigners. In 1970, it became the first Dutch club to win a European club competition – the **European Cup** – while coached by former Austrian international (and later Austrian national coach) Ernst **Happel**. Happel created a fluid playing style which, it is claimed, was adapted by **Ajax** and Netherlands coach Rinus **Michels** to create the legendary **total football** playing system. Feyenoord holds the record for the biggest victory in a European Cup match (12–2, v **KR Reykjavik**, 1969-70, first round). Dutch Cup 1930, 1935, 1965, 1969, 1980, 1984, 1991, 1992, 1994, 1995; Dutch league champions 1924, 1928, 1936,

1938, 1940, 1961, 1962, 1965, 1969, 1971, 1974, 1984, 1993; European Cup – winners 1970 (2–1, v **Celtic**, in **San Siro** Stadium, Milan), semi-final 1963; **European Cup-winners Cup** – semi-final, 1981, 1992; **UEFA Cup** – winners 1974 (4–2 agg., v **Tottenham Hotspur**); **World Club Cup** – winners 1970 (3–2 agg., v **Estudiantes**). Notable former players: Johann **Cruyff** (joined Feyenoord from Ajax in 1983, at the age of 37), Ruud **Gullit**, Ronald **Koeman**.

fibula *medical* the smaller if the two long **bones** in the part of the leg between the knee and the foot.

Fiejenoord (Stadion) *ground* Dutch football ground situated in Rotterdam; occasional venue of **Netherlands** internationals and home of **Feyenoord**. Ground capacity: 51,000. *History* Opened in 1937 and known locally as de Kuip (the Tub). The stadium underwent extensive renovation in 1994, funded by the local council, which included the construction of an executive area called the Maastribune. Feyenoord was fined £10,500 by **UEFA** following crowd trouble during the club's **European Cup** fixture against **Manchester United** on 5 November 1997. The stadium has staged two European Cup finals (1972 **Ajax** v **Internazionale**, 67,000; 1982 **Aston Villa** v **Bayern Munich**, 46,000); and five **European Cup-winners Cup** finals (1963 **Tottenham Hotspur** v **Atlético Madrid**, 25,000; 1968 **AC Milan** v **Hamburg** (SV), 60,000; 1974 **Magdeburg** v AC Milan, 5,000; 1985 **Everton** v **Rapid Vienna**, 30,000; 1991 **Manchester United** v **Barcelona**, 45,000; 1997 Barcelona v **Paris St Germain**, 40,000). Feyenoord Stadion was also the venue of the 1993 **World Cup** qualifier between Netherlands and **England** which was featured in the *Channel 4* film, "**An impossible job**". The stadium is the venue for the 2000 **European Championship** final.

Field Mill *ground* English football ground situated in Mansfield, Nottinghamshire; home of **Mansfield Town**. *Dossier* Ground capacity: 6,905. Pitch dimensions: 105m x 64m. Record attendance: 24,467 v **Nottingham Forest** (10 January 1953, **FA Cup**, third round). Best average attendance: 12,128 (1949-50). *History* Originally home of Greenhalgh Cricket Club, which first played there in 1840, the ground became the home of Greenhalgh FC in 1861 – making it the second oldest football ground in the world after Hallam FC's Sandgate. After Greenhalgh FC departed in 1894, Mansfield Amateurs and Mansfield Town Cricket Club moved in and, in 1912, the football club was replaced by another called Mansfield Mechanics. Mansfield Town moved to Field Mill in 1921 following the ground's purchase for £500 by a group of local businessmen, including members of the club's committee. The club bought the freehold after **World War II**, although this situation altered in July 1993 when Mansfield's then owners, Abacus, sold the club but retained ownership of the ground. Field Mill hosted greyhound racing in the late 1920s, which meant the installation of one of the first **public-address system**s at a **Football League**

ground. Field Mill staged an experimental floodlit match on 22 February 1930 with the pitch illuminated by 76 1,000 watt lamps supplied by the Dutch company Philips. The match, the North Nottinghamshire Senior Cup final (Ollerton Forest v Welbeck Athletic), is thought to be the first competition game – rather than a friendly – to be played under floodlights and it was attended by representatives of the **Football Association** and several clubs. Permanent floodlights were erected at Field Mill in 1961 and Mansfield Town's first floodlit match took place on 5 October (v **Cardiff City**, **League Cup**).

field of play *rules* the playing area of a football match. The **Laws of the game** state that the playing area for senior matches must be an oblong of dimensions 90 metres (100 yards) to 120 metres (130 yards) length by 45 metres (50 yards) to 90 metres (100 yards) width (Law I). The field of play for international matches must be 100 metres to 110 metres length by 64 metres to 75 metres width – national football associations must give prior notice of the exact dimensions to the visiting association. The field of play must be marked with clear **lines** and – where appropriate, **flagposts** – delineating the **touchlines**, **goal lines**, **halfway line**, **centre**, **centre circle**, **goal area**, **goal area lines**, **goals**, **penalty area**, **penalty spots** and **corner areas**. Note: the **International FA Board** uses an approximate imperial to metric conversion table that does not follow exact measurements. *Regulations* FA **Premier League** and **Football League** clubs are required to maintain their pitches in good order (FA Premier League rule I.13, Football League regulation 14.4). Premier League and Football League pitches must be 100 to 110 metres (110-120 yards) in length and 64 to 75 metres (70-80 yards) wide (FA Premier League rule I.9, Football League regulation 14.2). Premier League, Football League and **Scottish Football League** clubs must register their pitch dimensions with the league at the start of the season and can only change the pitch dimensions during a season with the permission of the Leauge (FA Premier League rule I.10, Football League regulation 14.3, Scottish Football League rule 70). Pitch dimensions of Premier League, Football League and Scottish Football League clubs are published in the **league handbooks**. Scottish Football League clubs must keep their pitches exclusively for the playing of football and cannot allow them to be used for any other activity that, in the opinion of the League Management Committee, could be detrimental to the field of play (Scottish Football League rule 72). *Keynotes* At the West Country Derby between **Torquay United** and **Plymouth Argyle** on 3 October 1998 (1–1, at Torquay), the Torquay substitute Andy MacFarlane was **sent off** for entering the field of play without permission; he went on in an attempt to separate two fighting players.

FIFA (Fédération Internationale de Football Association) *confederation* world governing body of association football, founded 21 May 1904. *Dossier* FIFA's headquarters are in Zurich, Switzerland. It has 201 member nations and six member confederations: **Asian Football Confederation** (AFC), **Confederación Norte-Centroamericana y del Caribe de Fútbol** (CONCACAF), **Confédération Africaine de Football** (CAF), **Confederación Sudamericana de Fútbol** (CONMEBOL), **Oceania Football Confederation** (OFC) and **Union of European Football Associations** (UEFA). President: Joseph Sepp **Blatter**. General secretary: Michael Zen-Ruffinen. Website: http://www.fifa.com (official site). *Keynotes* Although FIFA is the umbrella body over all international confederations and national associations, it does not dictate the **Laws of the game**. These are set by the **International FA Board**. FIFA holds a biennial congress, with each member country given one vote. FIFA organises, and stipulates the **competition rules** for, the **World Cup**, the **Under-17 World Championship**, the **World Youth Championship** (under-20), the **Women's World Cup**, the **Olympic Games** Football Tournament (under-23), the Olympic Games Women's Football Tournament, and the **Futsal** World Championship. Since 1991 it has awarded an annual FIFA **World Footballer of the Year** and, from 1987, has awarded a FIFA **Fairplay award**. *History* FIFA was established in 1904 to "promote the game of association football, to foster friendly relations among national associations, confederations, and their officials and players, by promoting the organisation of football matches at all levels; and to control every type of association football by taking steps as shall be deemed necessary or advisable." The seven founder members, **France**, **Belgium**, **Denmark**, **Netherlands** (Holland), **Spain**, **Sweden** and **Switzerland**, were brought together by Robert **Guérin**, a French journalist, for the first meeting in Paris. Guerin was elected as first president. At its 45th Congress in 1986, FIFA created an ad hoc committee on **women's football**. The committee was fully constituted within FIFA at its Congress in 1990. *Past presidents* Robert Guérin (1904-06); Daniel **Woolfall** (1906-18); Jules **Rimet** (1921-54); Rodolphe **Seeldrayers** (1954-55); Arthur **Drewry** (1956-61); Stanley **Rous** (1961-74); João **Havelange** (1974-1998); Joseph Sepp Blatter (1998-).

FIFA approved *misc.* indication on a **ball** that it has been tested and found to meet certain technical standards, not only required by the **Laws of the game** (Law II), but additionally approved by the **International FA Board** for international matches (either club or inter-nation competitions). It is one of three designated labels for an international match ball, the other two being: **FIFA inspected** and **International matchball standard**. **National Associations** may also require balls manufactured and tested to these standards.

FIFA inspected *misc.* one of three designated labels for an international match ball. See **FIFA approved**.

FIFA president *official* head of football's world governing body, **FIFA**. Swiss-national Sepp **Blatter** was elected FIFA president on 8 June 1998, defeating UEFA president Lennart Johansson by 111 votes to 80 at the 51st Ordinary Congress of football's governing body. Blatter, a FIFA official for 18 years and its general secretary since 1981, succeeded João **Havelange**, who was elected before the 1974 **World Cup** in succession to Stanley **Rous**. Blatter is FIFA's eighth president since 1904. Each of the full FIFA members (there were 191 in 1998) has one vote in the presidential election and a successful candidate must secure at least two thirds of the vote to win outright or further ballots take place. In 1998, Johansson withdrew his candidature following the first vote and installing Blatter as president. The 191 votes at the 1998 Congress were split among the confederations as follows: **Asian Football Confederation** (AFC) 41; **Confédération Africaine de Football** (CAF) 44; **Union of European Football Associations** (UEFA) 51; **Confederación Norte-Centroamericana y del Caribe de Fútbol** (CONCACAF) 35; **Confederación Sudamericana de Fútbol** (CONMEBOL) 10; **Oceania Football Confederation** (OFC) 10.

FIFA Under-17 World Championship *competition* see **Under-17 World Championship**.

FIFA World Footballer of the Year *award* annual accolade to the top player in world football, as voted by national team coaches. *Winners* 1991, Lothar **Matthäus**; 1992, Marco **Van Basten**; 1993, Roberto **Baggio**; 1994, **Romario**; 1995, George **Weah**; 1996, **Ronaldo**; 1997, **Ronaldo**; 1998, Zinedine **Zidane**.

fifty-fifty ball *n.* a loose ball that two opposing players have an equal chance of reaching with, for example, a shot or clearance.

Figueroa, Elias *player* Defender. **Chile** international. *Clubs* (include) **Internacional** (Brazil). *Honours* **Copa America** runner-up (Chile, 1979); Brazil **Campeonato Brasileiro** championship 1975, 1976; *El Mundo* **South American Footballer of the Year**, 1974, 1975 and 1976.

Fiji *country OFC* republic in the southwest Pacific, comprising 844 islands, 110 of which are inhabited. Independence from UK in 1970. Area: 18,330 sq km (7,075 sq miles). Population: 803,500 (1996 est.). Languages: Fijian, English and Hindi. Capital: Suva. *Dossier* Fiji Football Association formed in 1938, affiliated to **FIFA** and **Oceania Football Confederation** (OFC) in 1963, president Dr Muhammad Sahu Khan, general secretary Bob Sant Kumar. Season played from February to October. National stadium: National Sports Stadium, Suva, capacity: 25,000. National strip: white shirts, blue shorts. *International tournament record* **Olympic Games** – entered 1992 Oceania qualifying tournament (third of four nations), never qualified for finals tournament; **Oceania Women's Tournament/Women's World Cup** – first entered 1998 (did not qualify for 1999 World Cup finals); **World Cup** – first entered 1982, never beyond first qualifying round; **Oceania Cup** – entered first tournament in 1973, third place 1980 (1–2, v **New Caledonia**, in Noumea, New Caledonia, third/fourth playoff), 1998

(4–2, v **Tahiti/French Polynesia**, in Australia, third/fourth playoff); **Under-17 World Championship** – never qualified; **World Youth Cup** (under-20) – never qualified. *Record against British and Irish national teams* none played. Leading clubs: Ba (Fiji league champions 1992, 1994, 1995), Nadi (league champions 1998), Suva (league champions 1996. 1997).

Filbert Street *ground* English football ground situated in Leicester; home of **Leicester City**. *Dossier* Ground capacity: 22,517 all seated. Pitch dimensions: 100.5m x 69m. Record attendance: 47,298 v **Tottenham Hotspur** (18 February 1928, **FA Cup**, fifth round). Best average attendance: 31,359 (1957-58). *History* Leicester Fosse (the previous name of Leicester City), began playing at the ground that is today known as Filbert Street, but was then referred to as Walnut Street, on 7 November 1891 (v **Nottingham Forest**, friendly). Ground developments in the 1920s, during a period of success on the pitch, meant that Filbert Street began to resemble its present look. During **World War II**, part of the ground's main stand was destroyed by fire, although its cause is unknown. City bought the ground from the local council in 1960. The next stage of ground development took place following City's return to the top flight in 1971. It was at this time that City introduced an innovative method – that involved polythene sheeting inflated with hot-air blowers – to protect the Filbert Street pitch during adverse weather. The club stopped using the "balloon" in 1982. Turning Filbert Street into an **all-seater stadium**, following the recommendations of the **Taylor Report**, proved difficult owing to the lack of surrounding space into which the ground could expand. Various options, including relocation to a new stadium on the outskirts of Leicester and turning the pitch by 90 degrees, were considered, before the club decided to build a new main stand (the Carling Stand), which includes 9,300 seats, 28 boxes, a club shop and conference rooms. The club's aim has been to generate additional income by encouraging businesses to use Filbert Street's facilities and this has led to the ground being officially named City Stadium. In 1991, Leicester became the world's first "Environment City" and, as a result, Filbert Street was subjected to a "Green Audit" that has led to rainwater from the stands being used to irrigate the ground, and the use of organic fertiliser and low-energy light bulbs. Over the years, Filbert Street occasionally has been used to stage **FA Amateur Cup** finals (1896 Bishop Auckland v R A (Portsmouth), 1900 Bishop Auckland v Lowestoft Town), Amateur international matches and FA Cup semi-finals (1928, 1962, replay). The first floodlit match to take place at Filbert Street occurred on 23 October 1957 (v **Borussia Dortmund**, friendly). The ground also hosted an **inter-League** match (Football League v Scottish League, 19 March 1927).

film, football and *misc.* cinema films that have football as the main theme. Examples of the genre include: Harry the Footballer (1911); Pimple on Football (1914); The Footballers' Honour (1914); Ball of Fortune (1926);

The Great Game (1930); The Arsenal Stadium Mystery (1939); Small Town Story (1953); The Love Match (1954); Ket Felido a Pokolban (Hungary, 1961); Tretiy Taym (USSR, 1963); Bloomfield (aka the Hero) (1969); La Vida Sigue Igual (Spain, 1969); The Goalkeeper's Fear of The Penalty (1971); Yesterday's Hero (1979); Gregory's Girl (1980); Escape to Victory (1981); The Glory Glory Days (1983); Young Giants (1983); Appuntamento a Liverpool (Italy, 1987); Games Men Play (1988); Ultra (Italy, 1990); When Saturday Comes (1996); and Fever Pitch (1997). Despite notable exceptions, such as The Arsenal Stadium Mystery, transferring football to the big screen has not generally proved successful. Although **Pelé** stars in both Escape to Victory and Young Giants, they are not considered to be two of director John Huston's best cinematic presentations. Since the 1966 tournament, the **World Cup** finals have been filmed in their entirety, with the first film entitled "Goal". Former **Manchester United** and **France** striker Eric **Cantona**, who retired from football in 1997, has appeared in three feature films: Le Bonheur est dans le Pré (Rural Bliss); Elizabeth; and Mookie.

final 22   *n.*   the **squad** (sense **2.**) selected for an international finals tournament that restricts the number of eligible players to 22 (such as the 1998 **World Cup** finals). The final 22 is usually selected from a much larger preliminary squad.

final ball   *n.*   player's final contact with the ball, usually after dribbling or running with the ball, and executed as a **cross** or **pass**.

Finance and Revenue   *club*   Myanmar national league club. **Asian Champion Teams Cup** quarter-final 1998; Myanmar league champions 1997, 1998.

fine   *n.*   amount of money exacted as a punishment for a breach of regulations. Fines can be imposed on players, clubs or even national associations. *Keynotes* The first English **Football League** fines were meted out on 2 December 1889, when **Wolverhampton Wanderers**, **Bolton Wanderers** and **Stoke City** were penalised for fielding **ineligible players**. In the same year, **Notts County** was fined £25 for fielding an ineligible player, Tinsley Lindley, after successfully appealing against a one-point penalty.

finger injury   *medical*   damage to the fingers, for example by one or more finger being bent backwards into involuntary hyperextension, stressing the interphalangeal joints. The injury is common among goalkeepers and can be caused by the player attempting to stop a ball struck with great force. The fingers can be similarly injured by a fall onto an outstretched hand. Although **sprains** are common, in more severe instances the finger/s may be broken. First aid involves **ice** and support; severe sprains, with suspected torn finger **ligaments**, and broken fingers should be examined in hospital.

finish   *vb.*   to shoot or head the ball towards goal.

finishing   *n.*   a player's or team's general execution of goalscoring opportunities (usually preceded by a superlative).

Finland   *country*   *UEFA*   republic in Scandinavia on the Baltic Sea, bordered by **Norway**, the Russian Federation and **Sweden**. Independence from **Russia** in 1917. Area: 337,030 sq km (130,095 sq miles). One third of the country is within the Artic Circle; temperatures in the north fall to -30°C, rising to +27°C in the summer. Population: 5,120,000 (1995 census). Languages: Finnish and Swedish, as well as some Russian and Lapp. Capital: Helsinki. *Dossier* Football association formed in 1907 affiliated to **FIFA** in 1908 and founder member of **Union of European Football Associations** (UEFA) in 1954, president Pentti Seppälä, general secretary Pertti Alaja. Season played from April to October. National stadium: Olympiastadion, Helsinki, capacity: 50,000. National strip: white shirts, blue shorts. Website: http://www.palloliitto.fi (official site). First international game: 22 October 1911, v Sweden (2–5, in Helsinki, friendly). Biggest victory: 10–2, v **Estonia** (11 August 1922, in Helsinki, friendly). Biggest defeat: 0–10, v **Soviet Union** (15 August 1957, in Helsinki, World Cup qualifier). Most capped players: Ari Hjelm (100 appearances, 1983–1996), Erkka Petäjä (83, 1980-1995) and Arto Tolsa (76, 1962–81). Leading goalscorers: Ari Hjelm (21 goals, 1983-96), Verner Eköff (17, 1919–27), Mika-Matti (Mixu) Paatelainen (16 goals, 1983–). Other notable international players: Jari Litmanen (58 appearances, 13 goals, 1991–, **European Cup** winners' medal with **Ajax**, 1994). *International tournament record* **Olympic Games** – first entered 1912, semi-final/fourth (0–9, v **Netherlands**, in Stockholm, Sweden, third/fourth playoff), qualified for finals tournament 1936, 1980, hosts 1952 (first round); **Women's World Cup** – never qualified; **World Cup** – first entered 1938, never qualified for finals tournament; **European Championship** – first entered 1968, never qualified for finals tournament; **European Championship for Women** – entered first tournament in 1984, never progressed beyond first-round group stage (though finished second in its four-nation group in 1995, including a draw against reigning European champions Norway); **Scandinavian Championship** – winners 1963; **Under-17 World Championship** – never qualified; **World Youth Cup** (under-20) – never qualified. *Record against British and Irish national teams* v **England**, played nine (seven in Helsinki), drawn one, lost eight; v **Northern Ireland**, played three, won one, lost two; v **Scotland**, played eight, drawn two, lost six; v **Wales**, played six, won one, drawn two, lost three; v **Republic of Ireland**, played three, drawn two, lost one. *History* Finland's oldest league club, **Repas Lahti**, was founded in 1891. Football league founded in 1908, though initially based in and around the capital Helsinki. A Finnish Cup has been played since 1955. Although the national side first entered the World Cup in 1938, and has competed ever since, it finished last or second-last in 13 consecutive qualifying groups up to and including 1994. However, in the 1998 tournament it was prevented from qualifying for the **playoff** matches only by a 90th-minute equaliser in its final group match, at home against **Hungary**, in front of nearly 32,000 spectators (1–1, 13 October 1997). *World Cup performance* (finals and qualifiers to end of 1998 tournament) played 81, won 15, drawn 10, lost 56, scored 73 goals, conceded 225 goals; win rate 19%; goals scored per game 0.90. *League system* Ten clubs compete in the Finnish National League (the Veikkausliiga); reduced from 14 clubs in 1995. The season is played in two phases; the opening phase (April to August) involves all clubs playing each other at home and away. The league is then split into two equal groups: a championship group and a relegation group. The clubs in each respective group play each other once; the total points (from both phases) determine the championship and the relegation places. One club is automatically relegated to the First Division, with the second-bottom club entering a playoff. The First Division is divided into northern and southern section; the top five in each section amalgamating for a second-phase group to decide the promotion places (each club plays each other just once). The top club is automatically promoted, while the second-placed club plays against the second-bottom club from the National League to decide the remaining promotion/relegation place. Three points are awarded for a victory and one for a draw; **goal difference** is used to separate clubs that are level on points. *Record in international club tournaments* **European Cup** – **Kuusysi Lahti** (quarter-final 1986), **HJK Helsinki** (qualified for Champions League 1999); **European Cup-winners Cup** – **FC Haka** (quarter-final 1984), **RoPS Rovaniemi** (quarter-final 1988); **UEFA Cup** – **TPS Turku** (third round 1989). Other leading clubs: **FC Jazz**, **FinnPa**, **HJK Helsinki**, Reipas Lahti.

Finn Harps FC *club* Republic of Ireland national league club based in Ballybofey, founded 1954. Ground: Finn Park, capacity: 10,000. Strip: white shirts, blue shorts. Republic of Ireland **FAI Cup** 1974; Republic of Ireland league runners-up 1973, 1976, 1978.

Finney, Tom *player* Winger. **England** international (76 caps, 30 goals). Born 5 April 1922. Career ca. 1937–1960. *Clubs* **Preston North End**. *Keynotes* Known as the "Preston plumber" because that was his trade when he joined Preston North End as an amateur in 1937. He turned professional in January 1940. Finney made 433 **Football League** appearances for Preston, scoring 187 goals – still a club record. He was an **FA Cup** finalist in 1954 (2–3 v **West Bromwich Albion**). He was voted **Footballer of the Year** in both 1954 and 1957 (the first player to win the accolade twice). He was awarded the OBE in 1961. Finney was a member of the first **pools panel**, which sat on 26 January 1963. Finney became Preston vice-president and, later, president. His outline is depicted in the different coloured seating at Preston's **Deepdale** ground and the stand, which opened in March 1996, is named in his honour. Included in the **Football League Centenary 100**

players. *Honours* Division Two (Preston North End 1950-51).

FinnPa *club* Finnish national league club based in the capital Helsinki, founded 1965. Ground: Pallokenttä, capacity: 10,000 (or Olympiastadion – the national stadium – capacity: 45,0000). Strip: blue shirts, blue shorts. Finnish Cup winners; Finnish league champions. Notable player: Jallo Rantanen.

Fiorentina *club* Italian league. *Dossier* Ground: **Stadio Comunale Artemio Franchi**, Florence, Tuscany, capacity: 47,495. Strip: lilac shirts with yellow and white trim, lilac shorts with yellow and white trim. Website: *www.cecchigori.com/fiorentina/index.htm*. Nickname: Viola. Record win: 7–0 v Udinese (**Serie A** 1958-59). Record defeat: 0–8 v **Juventus** (Serie A, 1952-53). *History* Formed in 1926 from the merger of two Florence clubs, Palestra Ginnastica Libertas and Club Sportivo Firenze. The club is officially known as Associazione Sportiva Fiorentina. Fiorentina was first promoted to Serie A in 1931-32 and moved to the new Stadio Comunale. The club's first trophy was the **Coppa Italia** (Italian Cup), which it won in 1940 (1–0 v **Genoa**). Fiorentina remained unbeaten until the final game of the season when it won the League Championship in 1955-56. The club reached the second **European Cup** final in 1957 (0–2 v **Real Madrid**) and was the first winner of the **European Cup-winners Cup** in 1961 (4–1 agg., v **Rangers**). The club was runner-up the following season (1–4 agg., v **Atlético Madrid**) and, in 1990, Fiorentina was defeated in an all-Italian **UEFA Cup** final (1–3 agg., v Juventus). Fiorentina narrowly lost the 1981-82 Serie A title to Juventus; while the Viola could manage only a goalless draw in Cagliari on the final day of the season, the Turin club secured victory over Catanzaro with a disputed penalty. Gabriel **Batistuta**, who had helped Fiorentina secure an immediate return to Serie A following relegation in 1992-93, scored in each of the club's first 11 League matches in the 1994-95 season – a Serie A record. Fiorentina was expelled from the 1998-99 UEFA Cup competition following the throwing of a firecracker at its second round second leg fixture with **Grasshopper Zurich**, which was played in Salerno after crowd trouble at the club's own Comunale the previous season. It reached the final of the 1998-99 Coppa Italia, but lost on away goals (3–3 agg., v **Parma**). *Honours* League Champions 1955-56, 1968-69; Italian Cup 1940 (1–0 v Genoa), 1961 (2–0 v **Lazio**), 1966 (2–1 v Catanzaro), 1975 (3–2 v **AC Milan**), 1996 (2–1 agg., v Atalanta); European Cup-winners Cup 1961 (4–1 agg., v Rangers); **Anglo-Italian Cup** 1974 (2–0 v **West Ham United**).

Fiorucci International Challenge *competition* pre-season club tournament between **Internazionale**, **Real Madrid** and **Tottenham Hotspur** that took pace at **White Hart Lane** in 1993. Matches lasted just 45 minutes.

Fir Park *ground* Scottish football ground situated in Motherwell, Strathclyde region; home of **Motherwell**.

Ground capacity: 13,742 all seated. Pitch dimensions: 100.5m x 68.5m. Record attendance: 35,632 v **Rangers** (12 March 1952, **Scottish FA Cup**, fourth round replay). *Keynotes* Motherwell first played at Fir Park in 1895 (v **Celtic**). In 1929, the club introduced advertising at the ground. The club financed the building of a new main stand in 1962 by selling two players, including Ian St John. Fir Park staged its first floodlit match in February 1956 (v **Preston North End**, friendly).

Fire Brigade SC (Sports Club) *club* Mauritius national league club, based in Port Louis. Ground: Rose Hill, capacity: 12,000. Strip: red shirts and black shorts. **African Cup of Champion Clubs** second round 1989 and 1995; Mauritius Cup 1980, 1981, 1982, 1983, 1986, 1989, 1990, 1991, 1994, 1995, 1997, 1998; Mauritius League champions 1973, 1974, 1980, 1983, 1984, 1985, 1988, 1993, 1994.

Fire Safety and Safety of Places of Sport Act 1987 *legal* see **Bradford fire**.

Firhill Park *ground* Scottish football ground situated in Glasgow; home of **Partick Thistle**. Ground capacity: 20,876. Pitch dimensions: 100.5m x 68m. Record attendance: 49,838 v **Rangers** (18 February 1922, Division One). *Keynotes* Partick first played at Firhill in September 1909, although it had been due to open on 21 August (v **Queen's Park**) – the match was postponed at the last moment, much to the annoyance of the fans locked out. Partick had been unable to stage the game because the club had not received planning consent to develop a football ground. The site had previously been waste ground owned by the Caledonian Railway Company and the club eventually bought it for £5,500. Firhill was the setting, in 1986, for the first modern **groundshare** in Scottish League football. **Clyde** shared the ground between 1986 and 1991, and, in 1994, **Hamilton Academicals** moved in. The first floodlit match at Firhill took place in November 1955 (v **Tottenham Hotspur**, friendly).

firm *misc.* an organised gang of football **hooligans**, unofficially associated with a particular club or national team.

Firs Park *ground* Scottish football ground situated in Falkirk, Lothian; home of **East Stirlingshire**. Ground capacity: 1,880. Pitch dimensions: 102m x 66m. Record attendance: 12,000 v **Partick Thistle** (19 February 1921, **Scottish FA Cup**, third round). *Keynotes* East Stirlingshire first played at Firs Park in August 1921 (v **Heart of Midlothian**, friendly). As part of the board's agreed merger with **Clydebank** in 1964, Firs Park lost its floodlights. New lights were installed after the club's shareholders won a 12-month legal battle brought against Clydebank in the courts.

first aid *regulations* immediate medical treatment administered in an emergency. The **home club** in a **Scottish Football League** or **Scottish League Cup** match is required to ensure that a qualified first aider is present throughout the game (Scottish Football League rule 28). Home clubs in the **Premier League**

and **Football League** are required to provide a qualified medical practitioner to attend to injured players or officials (FA Premier League rule H.6.1, Football League regulation 32.1). See also **stretcher**, **crowd doctor**, **physiotherapist**.

first-choice strip *regulations* see **home strip**.

first class league *n.* original name of the English **Football League** First Division.

first half *n.* see **half** (sense 1).

first refusal transfer *misc.* agreement between two clubs which allows one club first refusal on the other's players in the event of a **transfer**. *Keynotes* Several Spanish clubs have agreed first refusal transfer deals with Brazilian clubs, including **Deportivo** and **Palmeiras**, **Real Madrid** and **Portuguesa**, **Valencia** and **Flamengo**. Such deals allow the Spanish clubs first refusal on any players the Brazilian clubs are willing to sell.

first team *n.* players selected by the manager or coach to play in a senior league or cup game. *Regulations* **Premier League**, **Football League** and **Scottish Football League** rules state that clubs should field their **strongest side** in all matches played under the auspices of their league, and not withdraw first-choice players simply because of fixture congestion (FA Premier League rule E.17, Football League regulation 21, Scottish Football League rule 68). Proving that a club has breached this regulation, however, is difficult.

first touch *n.* player's initial contact with a **pass** or **cross**. The quality of the first touch is often significant: good control may mean that the player can set up a shot or take the ball past the opponent; a poor touch may allow an opposing player to make a good tackle or to take up a good defensive position.

First Vienna FC *club* Austrian national league club, based in Vienna, founded 1894. Ground: Hohe Warte, capacity: 12,000. Strip: yellow shirts, blue shorts. Austrian Cup 1929, 1930, 1937; German Cup 1943; Austrian League Champions 1931, 1933, 1942, 1943, 1944, 1955; Der Challenge-Cup 1898, 1899, 1900; **Mitropa Cup** 1931.

first Wembley FA Cup final goal *record* David **Jack**, **Bolton Wanderers** 1923 (v **West Ham United**).

five-a-side football *n.* variant form of **association football** where the two sides are restricted to only five players each. The match is played on a small pitch, often with walled sides (such that there are no **throw-ins**) and small goals. The **offside** rule does not apply. Some competition rules restrict the play to balls played under head height (an **indirect free-kick** awarded for a breach of this rule). Five-a-side tournaments date back to the late 1950s, such as the *Evening Standard* tournament among London clubs. See **futsal**.

fixed odds *n. pl.* wager where the **odds** are fixed in advance. Fixed-odds betting coupons are commonly issued at bookmakers operating at a football match, usually listing a range of betting options, such as final score, half-time score and name of first player to score. The system contrasts one of the betting options commonly seen in horse racing, where bets may be settled according to fixed odds (as above) or as the final odds given at the start of the race (starting price). Compare **pools**.

fixture *n.* a match, the date of a match.

fixture, rearranged *n.* match which take place at a time other than originally specified but which is not postponed due to the weather. **Fixture congestion**, excessive injury problems, special occasions, political unrest are just some of the reasons why a match might be re-arranged for another date. *Keynotes* **Rangers** agreed to a two-day delay in the staging of its 1998 **UEFA Cup** second-leg match against Beitar Jerusalem at **Ibrox** to allow the Israeli club more time to celebrate a Jewish holiday, Yom Kippur. The game was due to be played on 29 September but was switched to 1 October. **Manchester United** agreed to a 30-minute delay in the kick-off of the club's Premiership encounter with **Liverpool** at Old Trafford on 10 April 1998 after the Roman Catholic Archbishop of Liverpool and the bishops of Salford and Manchester objected to the original time because it coincided with the traditional moment of Christ's death on the cross. The **European Cup** (Champions League) group B fixture between **Juventus** and **Galatasaray** was postponed for a week – from 25 November 1998 to 2 December – following a diplomatic row between **Italy** and **Turkey** over the extradition of Kurdish leader Abdullah Ocalan. UK clubs involved in the **European Cup-winners Cup**, in which matches are generally played on a Thursday, are allowed to switch the following Saturday games to a Sunday to allow players more time to recover. Occasionally the football authorities refuse a request to move a match. The **Premier League** refused **Chelsea**'s application to play its final 1997-98 Premier League fixture against **Bolton Wanderers** on 9 May rather than 10 May. The club had wanted an extra day to prepare for the European Cup-winners Cup final on 13 May.

fixture congestion *misc.* difficulty in scheduling fixtures, usually at the end of a season, because of a club's commitment to several competitions (e.g. Cup, League and international club competitions).

fixture list *n.* schedule of matches of all teams in a league or for a single club. In most leagues, this requires that every club plays each other once at home and away. Fixture lists are usually drawn up such that neighbouring clubs do not play their home matches on the same day (see **pairing**), taking account of cup rounds and international fixtures, with regard to other non-football events (such as the Aintree Grand National horse race in Liverpool) and public holidays (Boxing Day fixtures are traditionally arranged to reduce travelling distance for visiting clubs and supporters), and such that clubs play no more than three home fixtures in a row. The copyright of a fixture list is generally owned by the relevant league. *Regulations* **Football League** clubs are allowed to rearrange up to three Saturday

matches for the preceding Friday or following Sunday, but only with the prior agreement of the away club (this does not include matches rescheduled by agreement with the League for television) (Football League regulation 24.2). In every season, the **Premier League** and **Football Association** agree four dates reserved for international matches; no league or cup fixtures are arranged in any of the six days preceding these dates (FA Premier League rule E.2). *History* The first English Football League fixture list was drawn up on 1 May 1888 at the Grand Hotel, Birmingham. In this first season (1888-89), the 12 member clubs held a ballot to determine which would play the first match at home; the rest of the fixtures were arranged between the clubs. A formal system devised by W F **Fletcher** was adopted in 1898. *Fletcher's simplex tables for the arrangement of fixtures* were used up to the 1914-15 season. From 1919 (after **World War I**) to 1967, league fixtures were arranged using a series of charts drawn up by Charles **Sutcliffe**; they were so devised that no two seasons would be alike. Sutcliffe's system also enabled clubs to nominate pairings. Computer-generated lists have been used by the Football League since 1968; though modifications can be made by the League secretary and at the request of clubs and for live television coverage. The Football League fixtures are compiled by SEMA (based in Cheshire). A Fixtures Working Party, with representatives from league clubs and from other football bodies (such as the FA) attempts to prevent fixtures conflicts.

FK Sarajevo *club* Bosnia-Herzegovina and former-Yugoslavia league club based in Sarajevo, founded 1946. Ground: Kosevo, capacity: 45,000 (pre-civil war). Strip: claret shirts, claret shorts. Bosnian Cup 1997, 1998; Bosnian league runners-up 1997; **European Cup** second round 1967-68 (lost 0–0, 1–2 over two legs against the eventual winners **Manchester United**); former-Yugoslavia Cup runners-up 1967, 1983; former-Yugoslavia league winners 1967, 1985, runners-up 1965, 1980. Notable former player: Faruk **Hadzibegic**.

FK Vardar Skopje *club* Macedonian national league club, based in the capital Skopje, formed in 1947. Ground: Gradski, capacity: 25,000. Strip: red and black striped shirts and black shorts. *Keynotes* A successful court appeal by **Partizan Beograd** (and other clubs) in 1987 – after the season had finished – overturned a six-point league penalty which, in the event, cost FK Vardar Skopje the former-Yugoslav League championship. Macedonian Cup 1993 and 1995; former Yugoslavian Cup 1961; Macedonian League champions 1993, 1994, 1995, 1998; **UEFA Cup** second round 1986 (lost to **Dundee United**, 1–3 agg.).

flag *n.* see **flagpost** and **assistant referee's flag**.

flagpost *rules* flag on a post used to mark the four corners of the **field of play** (the corner flags) and, optionally, the halfway line. Posts must be no less than 1.5 metres (5 feet) high with a non-pointed top (Law I). The two flags on the halfway lines must be at least 1 metre (1 yard) outside the touch line. The corner flag must not be moved in order for a **corner kick** to be taken (Law XVII). Note: the **International FA Board** uses an approximate imperial to metric conversion table that does not follow exact measurements.

Flamengo (Club de Regatas Flamengo) *club* Brazilian national league and **Rio de Janeiro** state league club based in Rio de Janeiro, founded 1895. Ground: Da Gavea, capacity: 22,500 (Flamengo also use **Maracaná Stadium** for major games). Strip: red and black hooped shirts, white shorts. **Campeonato Brasileiro** champions 1980, 1982, 1983, 1987, 1992; **Copa Libertadores** 1981 (2–1, 0–1, 2–0 playoff in Montevideo, v **Cobreloa** of Chile); **Copa de Oro** 1996; **Copa do Brasil** 1990; São Paulo Tournament 1961; state league champions 24 times (to 1998); **Supacopa** runners-up 1993 (4–4 agg., 3–5 pens., v **São Paulo FC**), 1995 (1–2 agg., v **Independiente**), semi-final 1992; **World Club Cup** 1981 (3–0, v **Liverpool**, Tokyo). Notable former players: Junior, **Zico**, Nunes, Marinho.

Flamurtari Vlorè (Klubi Sportiv) *club* Albanian national league club, based in Vlorè, founded 1923. Ground: Flamurtari, capacity: 8,200. Strip: white shirts, white shorts. Albanian Cup 1985, 1988; Albanian league champions 1991; **UEFA Cup** third round 1988.

flank *n.* another term for wing.

flanker *n.* another term for winger.

flat back-four *tactics* four defenders (right back, right centre-back, left centre-back, left back) playing in a line across the defence with no **sweeper**, but often moving as a unit to catch an opposing forward **offside**.

Fletcher, W F *official* author of the first system for arranging the **fixture list** of the **Football League**. *Fletcher's simplex tables for the arrangement of fixtures* were used up to the 1914-15 season.

flick-on *n.* light forward header into space for a team-mate to run on to.

Flint Town United *club* Welsh league. Ground: Cae-y-Castell, Flint, Flintshire. Strip: black and white stripes on shirts, black shorts. Nickname: Silkmen. Ground capacity: 3,000. Formed in 1886. *Honours* Welsh Cup 1954 (2–0 v **Chester**).

float *vb.* to strike the ball long and high but without excessive force, usually with the intention of making a slow lofted **cross** into the opposition's **goalmouth**.

floodlight failure *n.* occasion when floodlights fail and a match is plunged into darkness. *Keynotes* In December 1997, the **Football Association** decided to convene a study of floodlighting at the 19 **Premier League** grounds, following the abandonment of a third 1997-98 fixture (**Wimbledon** v **Arsenal**, 22 December) due to floodlight failure (the two other failures were: **Derby County** v Wimbledon, 13 August (see **Pride Park**) and **West Ham United** v **Crystal Palace**, 24 November. In the aftermath of the **Selhurst Park** floodlight failure, the Premier League denied that it was the result of interference or sabotage linked to Far East gambling syndicates. However, four people were arrested for allegedly tampering with the floodlights at **Charlton Athletic**'s Valley ground prior to the Premier League encounter with **Liverpool** on 13 February 1999. The four were believed to be linked with a Far Eastern betting syndicate (see **spread betting**).

floodlights *n. pl.* artificial lighting that illuminates the field of play and allows matches to be played in the evenings and in other periods when natural light is poor. Floodlights have traditionally been positioned in the four corners of the ground on pylons, although the redevelopment of many stadiums has led to lights being incorporated into the roofs of stands. *Regulations* In England, **Premier League** clubs must have floodlights that give an average 800 **lux**, with a minimum of 500 lux at any point on the field of play (FA Premier League rule I.18). The minimum standard for floodlighting in the **Football League** (e.g. the criteria for admission to the league from the **Football Conference**) is an average of 250 lux. However, the club must have an average illumination of 350 lux by the end of its second season in the Football League. A higher average lux value is required for clubs in Division One (500 lux). These criteria are obligatory; a Football League club that does not meet the floodlighting criteria for its division by a particular date can be relegated to the division in which it does meet the criteria (Football League regulation 9.3) *History* The first experiment with floodlights took place at **Bramall Lane** on 14 October 1878 between two representatives Sheffield sides. The pitch was illuminated by four lamps, each powered by dynamos driven by engines located behind each goal, mounted on four wooden towers. This experiment was followed by further trials around the country. *Keynotes* On 30 November 1878, **Notts County** entertained a Derbyshire XI under floodlights at Trent Bridge. Also in 1878, **Crewe Alexandra**'s former-home, Nantwich Road staged a floodlit match. **Grimsby Town**'s first ground Clee Park staged two experimental floodlit matches in 1889, while, in September 1894, a ground at Hermit Road in Canning Town (later the first home of Thames Ironworks (later **West Ham United**)) staged an exhibition floodlit match between Woolwich **Arsenal** and **West Bromwich Albion**. In March 1889, Gregory Ground, at the time **Nottingham Forest**'s home, was the venue of a floodlit game using Wells lights (oil-fired lights). In February 1890, **Stoke City**'s **Victoria Ground** also hosted a floodlit match with Wells lighting (Stoke City v **Crewe Alexandra**). **Celtic** experimented with floodlights at its **Celtic Park** ground during 1893, staging a night match on Christmas Day against **Clyde** with lights suspended on wires above the pitch together with lamps on poles around the ground. **Mansfield Town**'s **Field Mill** ground staged an experimental floodlit match on 22 February 1930 with the pitch illuminated by 76 1,000 watt lamps supplied by the Dutch company Philips and the ball was painted white – five balls were used during the game as the paint kept wearing off. The match, the North Nottinghamshire Senior Cup final (Ollerton Forest v Welbeck Athletic), is thought to be the first competition game to be played under floodlights and it was attended by representatives of the **Football Association** and several clubs. The Football League reprimanded **Watford** for switching on trackside lighting used to illuminate greyhound racing at **Vicarage Road** in December 1930. **Highbury** also experimented with the use of floodlights, holding a public demonstration in November 1932. White City stadium, in west London, staged an exhibition floodlit football match between two London XIs in January 1933. Nonetheless, in 1930, the Football Association banned floodlit football, a situation which continued until 1950. In the early-1950s **Wolverhampton Wanderers** staged a serious of exhibition floodlit friendlies against foreign opposition, the first of which took place in September 1953 against a South African XI, with the Wolves players sporting luminous shirts and Molineux illuminated by 60 lamps. **Oxford United**, then Headington United, was the first club currently playing in the Football League to install floodlights, mounting two lamps each on 18 poles at the **Manor Ground** and staging a floodlit match on 18 December 1950 (v Banbury Spencer, friendly). In 1951, Highbury became the first Division One ground to install floodlights (v **Hapoel Tel Aviv**, 19 September, friendly). The first **FA Cup** tie to be staged under floodlights took place on 14 September 1955, when Kidderminster Harriers played Brierley Hill Alliance in a preliminary round replay. The first competition match between two Football League clubs to be played under floodlights occurred on 28 November 1955, when **Carlisle United** met **Darlington** in an FA Cup first round replay at **Newcastle United**'s **St James' Park**. **Fratton Park**, home of **Portsmouth**, staged the first floodlit Football League match on 22 February 1956 (v Newcastle United, Division One), although **kickoff** was delayed for 30 minutes after the lights failed. Chesterfield's Recreation Ground was the last Football League venue to install floodlights, finally staging its first floodlit match on 18 October 1967 (**Sheffield Wednesday**, friendly) after two previous attempts ended in failure. **Stenhousemuir**'s **Ochilview Park** has the distinction of being the setting for the first modern floodlit match in **Scotland**. This took place on 7 November 1951 (v **Hibernian**, friendly). By contrast, in August 1981, **Stranraer**'s **Stair Park** became the last senior football ground in the UK to install floodlights. In **Brazil**, the first floodlit match (A.A. República 2–1 S.E. Linhas e Cabostook) took place on the 23rd June 1923 with the pitch illuminated by tram headlights. **Vasco da Gama**'s São Januário stadium was the first to install floodlights on 31 April 1928.

Flora Tallinn *club* Estonian national league club based in the capital Tallinn, founded 1990. Ground: Kadriorg, capacity: 6,000. Strip: green shirts, white shorts. Traditionally, the club's support is associated with ethnic Estonians, thus creating a rivalry with **Lantana Tallinn**, with the latter's ethnic Russian support, and **Tallinna Sadam**. Estonian Cup 1995, 1998; Estonian league champions 1994, 1995, 1998, runners-up 1996, 1997. Notable former player: Mart Poom.

Floriana FC *club* Maltese national league club, based in Floriana and formed in 1900. Ground: Ta'Qali Stadium, Valletta, capacity: 18,000 (all Maltese premier league games are played here). Strip: green and white striped shirts and green shorts. Maltese FA Trophy 1938, 1945, 1947, 1949, 1950, 1953, 1954, 1955, 1957, 1958, 1961, 1966, 1967, 1972, 1976, 1981, 1993, 1994; Maltese league champions 1910 (the first championship), 1912, 1913, 1921, 1922, 1925, 1927, 1928, 1929, 1931, 1935, 1937, 1950, 1951, 1952, 1953, 1955, 1958, 1962, 1968, 1970, 1973, 1975, 1977, 1993.

Fluminense Football Club *club* Brazilian national league and **Rio de Janeiro** state league club based in Rio de Janeiro, founded 1902. Ground: Laranjeiras, capacity: 8,000 (Fluminense also use the **Maracaná Stadium** for major games). Strip: maroon, green and white striped shirts, white shorts. **Campeonato Brasileiro** champions 1984; **Copa do Brasil** runners-up 1992; Roberto Gomez Pedrosa Tournament 1970; São Paulo Tournament 1957, 1960; state league champions 27 times (to 1998). Notable former player: **Rivelino**.

flute playing *misc.* Paul **Gascoigne** has twice engaged in mock flute-playing during matches for **Rangers** against **Celtic**. Gascoigne's flute-playing was seen as a provocative act because it may be interpreted as a symbol of Protestantism or loyalism and therefore likely to inflame the sectarianism that exists between some fans of the two Glasgow rivals. On the first occasion, Gascoigne claimed he was unaware of the reaction that his actions could provoke. The second incident occurred as Gascoigne was warming up before going on as substitute in the 1998 New Year Old Firm **derby** (2 January). He was subsequently reported to Strathclyde police and was substantially fined by Rangers. On 18 March 1998, the **Scottish Football Association** severely reprimanded Gascoigne but did not administer any further punishment because he already had been heavily fined by Rangers.

flying substitute *rules* a temporary substitution. Under the **Laws of the game**, once a player has been substituted he or she can take no further part in the game (Law 3). However, where a national association agrees, in women's, veteran's and under-16 matches, the rules may be relaxed to allow "flying substitutes", whereby players can be substituted and later return to the game as a substitute for another player. This flexibility to the Laws was introduced as a decision of the **International FA Board** and came into effect on 1 July 1999.

FNS (Forces Nationale Securite) *club* Djibouti national league club based in the capital Djibouti. **African Cup of Champion Clubs** first round 1995; Djibouti Cup 1993; Djibouti league champions 1994.

Folgore *club* San Marino league club based in Falciano, founded 1972. Ground: Falciano, capacity: 500. San Marino League champions 1998.

Fontaine, Just *player* Striker **France** international (21 caps, 30 goals, 1953–60). Born 18 August 1933.

Clubs **KAC Marrakesh** (Morocco), **Olympique Gymnaste Club de Nice**, **Stade de Reims**. *Keynotes* Fontaine was born in Marrakesh, Morocco (his mother was Spanish and father was French). Fontaine scored a **hat-trick** on his international debut for France, an 8–0 victory over **Luxembourg** (17 December 1953, in Paris, **World Cup** qualifier). He is joint third in France's all-time list of goalscorers. Scored 13 goals in the 1958 World Cup finals, the most in a World Cup finals tournament. He scored in all six of France's games in the tournament, including a hat-trick in its opening match (7–3, v **Paraguay**, in Norrköpping, Sweden), and four in the 6–3 defeat of West **Germany** in the third/fourth place playoff (in Gothenburg). Fontaine scored a hat-trick in his country's opening game in the 1960 **European Championship** (5–2, v **Czechoslovakia**, in Paris). He played for Stade de Reims in the 1959 European Cup final (0–2, v Real Madrid, in Stuttgart) and was tournament top scorer with 10 goals. His career was ended in 1961 by a fractured **tibia**. He was voted third in the *France Football* **European Footballer of the Year** award for 1958. France national team coach 1967. *Honours* World Cup third place (France, 1958); World Cup **Golden Boot** 1958; European Championship fourth place (France, 1960); French league championship (OGC Nice, 1956, Stade de Reims, 1958, 1960).

foot injury *medical* any one of a number of injuries to the foot, common among footballers. These include **contusion**, **fracture**, **sprain**, **strain** and **tenosynovitis**.

foot ligament *medical* any of the **ligaments** of the foot. A common injury to football players is a **sprain** of the ligaments of the upper foot caused by the foot being bent too far downwards at the ankle, for example when a player attempts to strike the ball but it is blocked by an opponent's foot. The ligaments can also be partially **torn** or **ruptured**.

football *n.* **1.** any of a number of games played between two teams, using either a round or oval ball, where the principal object is to propel or carry the ball into the opposition team's goal or goal area. See **association football** (soccer), **American football**, **Australian rules**, **Gaelic football**, **Rugby football**. **2.** the **ball** used to play football.

football academy *regulations* a licensed football training centre for **student** players. The academies are operated by **Football League** or **Premier League** clubs in accordance with **Football Association** rules (FA Premier League rule M.2, Football League regulation 53). FA rules require that the establishments employ only qualified staff and offer suitable coaching and education facilities, as well as medical treatment and hygiene areas. The Football Association opened a football academy for young women in 1998: the Women's Football Academy of the North, in Peterlee, County Durham.

Football Alliance *competition* former English club competition set up in the wake of the **Combination**.

Football Association, the *confederation* the national football federation of England, based in Lancaster Gate, London W2, formed in 1863, first affiliated to FIFA in 1905, permanent member of the **International FA Board**, and founder member of the **Union of European Football Associations** (UEFA) in 1954, president awaiting appointment, general secretary awaiting appointment. *Keynotes* It is the only national association with no mention of the country in its name. The FA is the governing body for all domestic football in England. It is responsible for the recruitment and training of referees, disciplinary maters and appeals, international affairs, player's registrations, coaching and development. It also runs eight national competitions: the **FA Cup**, **FA Trophy**, **FA Vase**, **FA Women's Cup**, **FA Women's Premier League Cup**, FA Sunday Cup, FA Youth Cup and FA County Youth Cup. Although the **Football League** and FA **Premier League** run as independent bodies, they come under the ultimate jurisdiction of the FA. The FA is the governing body for both men's and women's football. It is also the umbrella body for the **English Schools Football Association** and 43 **Country Football Associations**. There are around 90 members of the FA Council, the FA's governing body, which includes representatives from the leagues, clubs and County Football Associations. *History* The Football Association is the oldest national association in the world. It was established at a meeting on 26 October 1863, at the **Freemasons Tavern**, Great Queen Street, London. The meeting comprised members of 10 London-based clubs: **Barnes**, Blackheath, Blackheath School, Crusaders, **Crystal Palace (2.)**, **Forest**, **No Names**, Kensington School, Perceval House School and Surbiton. The representatives accepted a proposal, by Ebeneza C Morley (of Barnes club) and seconded by A W MacKenzie (of Forest), to set up a national association; Morley was elected as honorary secretary. Any club could join, provided that it had been in existence for at least a year and could pay the membership fee of one guinea (21 shillings, equivalent to £1.05). Morley presented a draft set of 14 rules to the new Football Association on 24 November 1863. His draft was based on the various sets of rules played by the public schools, universities and the clubs, and included elements that have survived in the modern game, such as the **throw-in**, the **kick-off** at the start of the match and after a goal is conceded, the **toss of a coin** at the start of the game, and that opposition players should be 10 yards (9.1 metres) from the kick-off. The goals were to be eight yards (7.3 metres) wide, but would have no cross bar. However, he also proposed that the teams change ends after a goal, that the pitch could be up to 200 yards (183 metres) long and that players could catch the ball and run with it; players running with the ball could be charged, held, tripped or hacked. The meeting also considered the latest version of the **Cambridge Rules** which, though similar, prohibited catching then running with the ball. An FA meeting on 1

December 1863, adopted 13 rules of Association Football, having redrafted Morley's original proposals in line with the Cambridge Rules, though choosing an eight-yard goal width (not five as stipulated at Cambridge). At the same meeting, Blackheath FC resigned from the FA, unable to accept that handling and running with the ball would be prohibited (Blackheath became one of the 21 founder members of the Rugby Football Union, founded in January 1871). The first match under the new rules was played at Mortlake, London, on 19 December 1863 (Barnes v Richmond, 0–0). On 20 July 1871, the FA voted in favour of a proposal by Charles **Alcock**, the FA's honorary secretary, for a challenge cup competition: the FA Challenge Cup (FA Cup). The FA became a limited company in 1903. The Football Association was originally affiliated to FIFA in 1905, but resigned in 1920, along with the other home nations (**Scotland**, **Wales**, **Ireland**); Britain was unable to tolerate dealings with its former enemies from **World War I**. It rejoined in 1924 and resigned again in 1928 (with the other home nations), this time over a dispute concerning the definition of amateur status in the **Olympic Games**. It rejoined in 1946. The FA was a founder member of the UEFA in 1954. In 1992, it supervised the creation of the FA Premier League, the biggest change to the organisation of professional league football in England since the foundation of the Football League in 1888.

Football Association of Ireland *confederation* the national football federation of the **Republic of Ireland** founded in 1921 after the division of Ireland into the Republic and **Northern Ireland**. Headquarters in Merrion Square, Dublin. Affiliated to **FIFA** in 1923 and a founder member of the **Union of European Football Associations** (UEFA) in 1954. President: Paul Quigley; general secretary: Bernard O'Byrne. See also **Irish Football Association**.

Football Association of Wales *confederation* the national football federation of Wales, headquarters in Plymouth Chambers, Westgate Street, Cardiff. Formed in 1876, affiliated to **FIFA** in 1910. The FA of Wales resigned from FIFA in 1920 along with the other home nations (**England**, **Scotland**, **Ireland**); Britain did not want to associate with its enemies from **World War I**. It rejoined in 1924, but was, once again, part of an en-bloc resignation in 1928 as the home nations protested against the flexible interpretation of "amateur status" in the **Olympic Games** football tournament. It rejoined FIFA in 1946. The FA of Wales is a permanent member of the **International FA Board**, and founder member of the **Union of European Football Associations** (UEFA) in 1954, president: John Hughes; general secretary: David Collins. See **High Court action**.

Football Association Women's Premier League *competition* the national league of English women's football, under the auspices of the **Football Association**. The league was founded in 1991 as the Women's Football Association National League, initially with eight clubs in each of three divisions: Premier

Division, Northern Division and Southern Division. Membership was expanded in 1994-95, to 10 clubs in each division. *League champions* 1992 **Doncaster Belles**; 1993 **Arsenal (2.)**; 1994 Doncaster Belles; 1995 Arsenal (2.); 1996 Croydon; 1998 Everton; 1999 Croydon.

Football Association, women's section *confederation* women's football in England is administrated by the women's section of the Football Association, based in Potters Bar, Hertfordshire. The FA took full control of women's football in 1993, taking over from the former **Women's Football Association**. At senior level, it runs the **FA Women's Challenge Cup**, the **Football Association Women's Premier League** and the **FA Women's Premier League Cup**.

football boots *n. pl* footballers' shoes; essential and compulsory components of the **players' equipment** (law IV). Football boots are made of leather and synthetic fabric uppers, with moulded synthetic soles and screw-in or integral **studs**. Boots are secured to the feet by laces. The term "boot" is a misnomer because modern football boots do not cover the ankle: ankle protection was sacrificed by the mid-20th century to meet the demands of a faster, more athletic game. *History* The evolution of the football boot dates from the 1880s, with the establishment of organised competitions in Great Britain; players had, hitherto, worn their work boots. Early boots were made of leather and had hard toecaps and ankle protectors. Early manufacturers included Walker, Kempson and Stevens of Leicester, whose "Stevens'" boots, dating from the 1880s, were designed for both **rugby** and association football codes, and Benetfink & Co, of London. Leather studs or bars were officially sanctioned in 1891 and, by 1900, referees were examining players' boots before the match to check for illegal, dangerous appendages. Boot leather was improved in the 1890s, with advances in tanning technology to improve suppleness and strength. Two of the most successful early boot designs were the "McGregor" (named after William **McGregor**), by the Birmingham manufacturers Shillcocks, popular in the 1900s, and the "**Manfield Hotspur**", the market leader by the 1920s. There were many boot manufacturers in the early 20th century, each attempting to outdo each other with innovations and improvements, such as "ankle grips", "non-skid toes" and "lock-riveted studs". While manufacturers were tinkering with traditional designs in Britain, South American players were already using football shoes, ie with no ankle support: the style dates back at least to the 1920s in Argentina. It was not until after the 1950 **World Cup** finals in Brazil that British manufacturers began to follow the South American example. England international player Stanley **Matthews** had been impressed with the football technique of the Brazilian players at the 1950 finals: he also noted their light, soft football shoes without the hard toecaps featured on all British-made boots. Matthews asked the Cooperative Wholesale Society (CWS) boot manufacturers to create a lightweight boot similar to those worn by the Brazilians. The CWS **"Stanley Matthews" football boots** became one of the most popular on the market, and set a trend in British boot design. **Screw-in studs** were legalised in 1951. Another major advance came with the development of moulded soles, made of plastic or rubber rather than leather. These had a huge advantage over traditional leather soles in that they did not absorb moisture as the game went on. The first moulded soles were those produced in 1949 by the German manufacturers Adidas. Its boots had integral **moulded studs**. Boot design continued to embrace developments in materials technology, though the basic shape established in the 1950s has been retained. Leather remains the predominant material for football boot uppers, though it is very often combined with synthetic fabrics. Retailers continue to offer a choice of screw-in and moulded studs. Manufacturers also have developed a vast range of footwear for use on training pitches and **artificial grass**, as well as for **five-a-side football**. While technology has continued to improve boot design, the real battle among manufacturers such as Adidas, Asics, Diadora, Nike, Puma, Reebok and Umbro is on fashion and brand imaging; winning the endorsement of star players and teams is as much the key to market success as quality. Footwear manufacturers used the 1998 World Cup finals as a marketing vehicle, through direct advertising and by signing key players to wear their brands. The *Financial Times*, in July 1998, analysed and rated the manufacturers according to their "media exposure" during the finals. Adidas and Nike were clear leaders, followed by Umbro, Reebok, Puma and Lotto. The two biggest brands were Nike's "R9", worn by **Ronaldo** (Brazil), Marcelo **Salas** (Chile) and Christian Vieri (Italy), and the Adidas "Predator", worn by David Beckham (England), Alessandro Del Piero (Italy) and Zinedine **Zidane** (France). The first heated boots were developed in the late 1990s by Blackburn-based company, S Reed and Co. Using a rechargeable battery in the heel the centrally-heated boot is designed to keep the player's foot warm for the full 90 minutes playing time. The heating element is integrated into the sole.

football club *n.* sporting organisation registered with a football league for the purposes of entering a team in association football competitions. A club consists of players and officials. *Regulations* Clubs may have more than one team, but **Premier League**, **Football League** and **Scottish Football League** clubs are restricted to one senior team, as well as reserve, youth and junior teams. Football clubs may be registered as limited companies with shareholders. Except with written permission of the league, no club is allowed to own a stake or shares in another club (FA Premier League rules section S, Football League regulation 82.1, Scottish Football League rule 88.1). No club official can be involved in managing the affairs of another club (FA Premier League rules section S, Football League regulation 83, Scottish Football League rule 88.2). Directors, club officials and their associates are not allowed to

hold more than a 10% financial stake in another club, except by written permission of the league – these shares must be for investment purposes only (FA Premier League rules section S, Football League regulation 83). *History* Aside from the English Public Schools and universities, among the first clubs to be established were: **No-Names** (ca. 1859), **Forest** (1859), **Crystal Palace** (**2.**) (1861), Lincoln FC (1861), **Barnes** (1862), **Sheffield FC** (1862), Civil Service FC (1862), Nottingham FC (1864, later **Notts County**), Old Etonians FC (1865), Stoke Ramblers (1867, later **Stoke City**) and The Wednesday (1867, later **Sheffield Wednesday**).

Football Conference *competition* (formerly the Alliance Premier League and Gola League). Semi-professional English league immediately under the **Football League** with direct promotion and relegation to Division Three (provided that promoted clubs meet Football League **ground criteria**). The top club in the Conference replaces the bottom club in the Football League. The bottom three clubs in the Conference are replaced by the top clubs in the Isthmian, Southern and Northern Premier Leagues. See also **pyramid system**. *History* Originally proposed by Alan **Hardaker** in 1971 in discussions with the Northern League and **Southern League**. It was launched in 1979-80 as the Alliance Premier League, under the presidency of Bob **Lord** (then vice-president of the Football League). Twenty clubs were elected from the Northern and Southern Leagues, vetted by the **Football League management committee** for their ground conditions and financial status. From 1998-99, sponsored by the Nationwide Building Society, replacing previous sponsors Vauxhall (General Motors).

Football Grounds Improvement Trust *misc.* trust established in 1975 to help finance ground improvements to meet the standards of the **Wheatley Report** as required by the **Safety of Sports Ground Act 1975**. The fund was generated by a levy on **spot-the-ball** competitions run by **pools** companies.

Football in the community *misc.* designed to develop club-community (schools, youth clubs and other local groups) links. The scheme was developed from a joint **Professional Footballers' Association (PFA)** and Manpower Services Commission initiative, "Football and the Community".

Football Italia *television* Channel 4 programme that shows live Italian League matches. Channel 4 first began screening **Serie A** games from the start of the 1993-94 season after agreeing a £1.5 million two-year deal. The programme's accompanying monthly magazine is also entitled *Football Italia*. Channel 4 coverage of Italian football also includes a news and preview programme, Gazetta Football Italia.

Football League *competition* English national league competition founded 22 March 1888, began 8 September the same year. It is the oldest football league in the world. The Football League has, since 1992, been the second tier of English senior league football, directly beneath the FA **Premier League**. Its headquarters moved from Lytham St Anne's, Lancashire, to Preston in 1998; secretary J D Dent. It has 72 member clubs. The Football League is a registered company and has 100 shares, valued at 5 pence each. Each member club is issued with one share: there are thus 72 shares issued to the member clubs. *League system* The Football League is limited by its current constitution to 72 clubs: 24 clubs in each of the First, Second and Third Divisions (Football League regulation 6.1). The final positions at the end of each season are determined by the number of **points** won by each club, with three points awarded for a win and one for a drawn match. If clubs are level on points, their league position is determined by **goals scored**; if clubs are level on points and goals scored, they are separated by **goals conceded**; if they remain level, their final league ranking can be decided by a **playoff** at a neutral ground (Football League regulation 10.1). The Football League Championship is awarded to the club that finishes first in the First Division; there are divisional championship trophies for each of the divisions. Championship trophies are held until the end of the following season, but must be given back to the Football League by 1 May in the following season (Football League regulation 34). Nineteen "souvenirs" or medals are given to the League and divisional champions; 14 for the players, one for the secretary, one for the manager, one for the physiotherapist and two for other non-playing staff (additional medals may be awarded with the permission of the Football League Board). *Promotion/relegation* At the end of each season, the bottom three clubs in the FA Premier League are relegated to the Football League First Division (the number of clubs relegated/promoted is determined by agreement between the Football League First Division and the Premier League). The first two clubs in the First Division are automatically promoted to the Premier Division along with the winner of a playoff competition involving the third-, fourth-, fifth- and sixth-ranked clubs at the end of the season: third v sixth and fourth v fifth over two legs (home and away), with the two winners playing a final match at a **neutral venue** (e.g. **Wembley** Stadium) (Football League regulation 11.1). The bottom three clubs are relegated from the First Division, replaced by the top two clubs in the Second Division and the winner of a playoff competition between the third- to sixth-ranked clubs, as above. The bottom four clubs from the Second Division are relegated to the Third Division, to be replaced by the top three clubs in the Third Division and the winner of a playoff competition (as for the First and Second Divisions). Finally, the bottom club in the Third Division is replaced by the champions of the **Football Conference**, provided that the latter meets Football League **ground criteria** (Football League regulation 11.1.3). In the event that the two-leg playoff matches are tied, **away goals** will count double; but only after **extra time** has been played. If the score is still level, then the winner will be determined by a **penalty shoot-**out. Extra time and penalties may be played in the playoff final. If a club drops out of the league partway through a season (e.g. through bankruptcy), one fewer club will be relegated from that club's division (Football League regulation 13.2); the club's league record will be erased. The Football League Board has discretion to promote an extra club to replace a club that has been relegated as a disciplinary measure (see, for example, **Swindon Town**); the extra promotion place is decided on league ranking at the end of the normal season (ie not counting the playoffs) (Football League regulation 12.2). If a club drops out of the league during the **close season**, then the Football League can promote an extra club from the lower division, again on the basis of final league positions (Football League regulation 13.4). *History* The name "Football League" was formally adopted at a League committee meeting on 11 January 1889 ("English" was not included in the title because it was felt that Scottish clubs might be invited in future years). A Scotsman, William **McGregor**, is widely credited with the idea for the league. On 2 March 1888, McGregor circulated his ideas to five major English clubs: **Blackburn Rovers**, **Bolton Wanderers**, **Preston North End**, **West Bromwich Albion**, and his own club, **Aston Villa**. Drawing attention to a disorganised club fixture list, interrupted by cup-ties and cup replays, his letter advocated that "10 or 12 of the most prominent clubs in England combine to arrange home and away fixtures each season, the said fixtures to be arranged at a friendly conference." A meeting was convened at the Anderton Hotel in London on 22 March, the eve of the 1888 **FA Cup** final. Along with McGregor, those officially attending were: Arthur T Ashwell (representing **Notts County** – a solicitor), John T Birtwistle (Blackburn Rovers – an inspector of factories), William Allt (**Wolverhampton Wanderers** – a bootmaker), George Armistead (**Burnley** – an auctioneer), Thomas Smith (West Bromwich Albion – a former player with the club) and Harry Lockett (**Stoke** – a printer). Twelve clubs were invited to join the new league: **Accrington**, Aston Villa, Blackburn Rovers, Bolton Wanderers, Burnley, **Derby County**, **Everton**, Notts County, Preston North End, Stoke, West Bromwich Albion, Wolverhampton Wanderers. All twelve were professional, with six from the Midlands and six from Lancashire. One of the rules proposed at the meeting was that each club should field its **full-strength team** for each league game; a principle that has remained in the League's regulations. A second conference involving the 12 clubs was held at the Royal Hotel, Manchester on 17 April 1888. This second meeting was attended by McGregor, Lockett, Allt, William **Sudell** (Preston North End), John Bentley (Bolton), John Lewis (Blackburn), Alex Nisbet (Everton), Edwin Browne (Notts County), J H Richardson (Derby), George Armistead (Burnley) and a representative of Accrington. McGregor had proposed that clubs shared the **gate receipts** of all league fixtures, but this was rejected with the visitors to be paid a fee of £15 (later reduced to £12). Membership of the league would be £2 and 2 shillings. Players from one club would not be permitted to play for another in the same season except with permission from the League committee. Halliwell, **Nottingham Forest** and **Sheffield Wednesday** applied to join the new league but were rejected. The first **fixture list** was drawn up on 1 May 1888 at the Grand Hotel, Birmingham. The League started on Saturday 8 September 1888: Bolton v Derby (3–6); Everton v Accrington (2–1); Preston v Burnley (5–2); Stoke v West Bromwich Albion (0–2); Wolverhampton Wanderers v Aston Villa (1–1). The system for awarding **points** was formalised on 21 November 1888, some way into the season: a win would be worth two points, with one for a draw. This was formalised at the first sub-committee of the league on 11 January 1889 when it was decided that **goal average** would decide league positions if clubs were on the same points total. The principle of a "second class" league or Division Two was agreed at the same meeting, though was not put into effect until 1892 (see **re-election**). The first league season was won by Preston North End (40 points – 18 wins, four draws, no defeats) from Aston Villa (29) and Wolverhampton Wanderers (28). The number of member clubs was increased from 12 to 14 for the 1891-92 season. Stoke (which had been relegated in 1890) and **Darwen** entered the League from the old Alliance League. The formation of the English Football League Division Two, with 12 clubs, was agreed at a League meeting in April 1892, with the following clubs elected: Ardwick (later **Manchester City**), **Bootle**, Burslem Port Vale (later known simply as **Port Vale**), **Burton Swifts**, **Crewe Alexandra**, Darwen (which had failed to be re-elected to the First Division), **Grimsby Town**, **Lincoln City**, **Northwich Victoria**, **Sheffield United**, Small Heath Alliance (now called **Birmingham City**) and **Walsall** Town Swifts. At the same time, the number of clubs in Division One was increased to 16; Newton Heath (now **Manchester United**), Nottingham Forest and Sheffield Wednesday joining from the Alliance League. Promotion and relegation between the divisions was initially decided by a series of **test matches** involving the top three clubs in Division Two and the bottom three in Division One (this was later reduced to two teams from each division). Four more clubs, **Woolwich Arsenal**, **Liverpool**, **Newcastle United** and **Rotherham**, joined Division Two in 1893-94, creating two divisions of 16 teams. Two divisions of 18 were created in 1898. Test matches were replaced by automatic promotion and relegation in 1898-99. The Football League became a limited company in 1904. In 1905, the League expanded again, to two divisions of 20 clubs. The Football League programme (along with those of the **Southern League**, **Scottish Football League** and Irish League) was suspended before the start of the 1915-16 season due to the prolongation of **World War I** – though the Football League management committee continued to hold its annual meetings. The programme restarted in 1919, with the two divisions expanded to 22

clubs. In 1920-21, **Cardiff City** became the first Welsh club in the Football League when it was elected from the Southern League to Division Two. A third tier, Division Three, of 22 clubs was created in 1920-21, from the remaining 21 clubs of the Southern League first division – which included three other clubs from Wales, **Merthyr Town**, **Newport County** and Swansea Town (now **Swansea City**), – and one other: Grimsby Town had failed in its re-election to the Division Two and became the only northern club in the new Division Three. Division Three clubs were not given full voting rights (see **Associate Member**, **Full Member**). Another division, the Division Three North, was created in 1921-22 with a further 20 clubs (Grimsby moved to the northern section). The number of clubs in this northern section was increased to 22 in 1923-24. During the period of regional third divisions, any club relegated from Division Two joined whichever Division Three was appropriate to its geographic location. The bottom two clubs from each of the third divisions were required to apply for re-election. A fourth tier, Division Four, was launched in 1958-59, steered by the then League president Joe **Richards**. The top half of the two regional third divisions joined a new united Division Three, with the remainder entering Division Four (all the current clubs were re-elected). In 1965, all League clubs except **Chelsea** resigned from the Football Association in protest at an FA directive on club finances, deemed to be interfering in League affairs. Chelsea did not resign because its chairman, Joe Mears, was also chairman of the FA. The clubs rejoined shortly after when the FA relented. **Goal difference** replaced goal average in the 1976-77 season. The change was prompted by Arsenal at the annual meeting of the Football League in 1976 and remains in use in the FA Premier League (since 1992, the Football League has favoured the system of goals scored). The allocation of points was revised at a meeting of the League in February 1981. From the beginning of the 1981-82 season three points would be awarded for a win; a draw remaining as one point. A proposal, in 1985, for a breakaway **Super League** (sense **2.**) was quashed by a compromise deal between the Division One clubs and the rest of the Football League. The compromise was accepted at a Football League Extraordinary General Meeting on 28 April 1986. It led, however, to a major restructuring of the League. From the 1986-87 season, Division One was reduced to 20 clubs (the reduction achieved over two seasons through playoffs), with 24 clubs in Divisions Two, Three and Four. Division One clubs were given enhanced voting rights (1.5 votes each, against one each for Division Two clubs and eight votes for all the Associate Members combined). Division One clubs also were given greater representation the Management Committee and 50% of the League's **sponsorship** and **television** revenue. The Football League's levy of gate receipts was reduced from 4% to 3%. Automatic promotion and relegation was introduced between Division Four and the Football Conference (**Scarborough** being the first beneficiary at the expense of Lincoln City). Playoffs between the Divisions One and Two remained in force after 1988-89. The Football League celebrated its centenary with a representative match on 8 August 1987: Football League v Rest of the World. The "rest" team was picked by Terry **Venables**, then manager of **Barcelona**, and included Gary **Lineker** (also of Barcelona), Diego **Maradona** and Michel **Platini**. A crowd of 61,000 watched the Football League win 3–0 at Wembley Stadium. The top flight of the Football League resigned in 1992 to join the newly formed Premier League; the old Division Two becoming the Football League First Division (for the purposes of this dictionary, the restructured divisions are referred to as First, Second and Third Divisions, replacing Divisions Two, Three and Four). After the breakaway of the Premier League clubs, full and equal voting rights were given to all remaining members of the Football League: all league clubs are now **Members of the Football League** (there are no Full or Associate Members). *Keynotes* The record **attendance** for a single day's matches in the Football League is 1,272,185 (27 December 1949; all divisions, 44 matches; 28,913 per match). There has been only one season in the history of English league football when two clubs have finished level in every respect: Blackburn Rovers and Woolwich Arsenal in 1907-08 (36 points, scored 51 goals, conceded 63 goals; both clubs had won 12 games, drawn 12 and lost 14; they finished joint 14th). See also **pyramid system**.

Football League Appeals Committee *regulations* tribunal in **England**, set up to adjudicate in disputes. Its rulings are binding. Common disputes are those that arise between two clubs over the transfer of **non-contract players**, and the size of **compensation fees** for **out-of-contract players** who are under-24 years' old (FA Premier League rules section R, Football League regulation 63). It also rules on fees relating to the transfer of players from clubs that cease to operate, and on other contract disputes. The Committee is chaired by the chairman of the Professional Football Negotiating Committee (casting vote), and includes one representative each from the **Professional Footballers Association** (PFA), the Institute of Football Management and Administration, the FA **Premier League** (but only if matters involve Premier League clubs), and the **Football League** (only if matters involve Football League clubs). Players can request a personal hearing and may be represented by the PFA. In **Scotland**, **compensation fees** (sense 3.) may be determined by the Scottish Football League **Compensation Tribunal**, if the two clubs involved in the transaction cannot agree the size of the fee. All other disputes are settled by the **Scottish Football League Appeals Committee**.

Football League Board of Directors *n.* elected committee of the **Football League**, comprising seven members, including the chairman. The Football League secretary, historically, is not one of the directors. Football League management committee.

Football League Centenary 100 players *misc.* top 100 players to have graced the **Football League** throughout its then 100-season history. The list was selected by football journalists as part of the Football League centenary season celebrations in 1998. It includes players from all eras: 34 whose careers began before **World War II**; 37 who had playing careers between the end of the war and 1980; and 29 who played during the 1980s and into the 1990s.

Football League championship, fewest defeats *record* **Arsenal**'s 1990-91 League Championship-winning side set a **Football League** Division One record for the 20th century, losing only one of its 38 fixtures all season (against **Chelsea**). Statistically, only **Preston North End**'s 22-match undefeated sequence throughout the 1888-89 season surpasses Arsenal's achievement.

Football League Group Cup *competition* competition involving 24 clubs from **Football League** Division's Two, Three and Four that replaced the defunct **Anglo-Scottish Cup**. Participants were split into six regional groups of four clubs with each team playing three matches. The group winners then went into the knockout stage. The Football League Group Cup was replaced by the **Football League Trophy** after only one season. *Final result* 1982 **Grimsby Town** 3–2 **Wimbledon**.

Football League management committee *n.* former name (until 1992) of the **Football League Board of Directors**.

Football League regulations *regulations* the rules of the English **Football League** that exist alongside the **Laws of the game**. Published annually in the *Football League Handbook*, they establish the special rules of Football League tournaments – such as, how league points are allocated, how teams on the same points are separated in the league table, fixture priorities, promotions and relegations, players' registration, fines and transfer deadlines – that must be adhered to in addition to the Laws.

Football League Review *publication* former magazine of the **Football League**, launched in August 1966 (previously existed as the independent *Soccer Review*). Inserted into club programmes. Circulation peaked at 250,000. Renamed *League Football* in 1972. Last printed on 31 December 1974.

Football League Trophy *competition* replacement competition for the **Football League Group Cup**, and the last of a series of cup competitions that began with the **Texaco Cup** in 1970-71. The format of the Football League Trophy was basically the same as that of its predecessor with the exception that two Division One clubs, **Norwich City** and **Watford**, joined 30 clubs drawn from the other three divisions and with clubs scoring three or more goals in a match awarded a bonus point. Participants were split into eight regional groups of four. The competition lasted for only one season, after which clubs from Divisions Three and Four entered their own competition, the **Associate Members Cup**, which was retitled the **Frieght Rover Trophy** in 1984-85. *Final result* 1983 **Millwall** 3–2 **Lincoln City**.

Football League (War) Cup Competition *competition* organised by the English Football League during **World War II**, when the national leagues were suspended.

Football Licensing Authority *misc.* body established by the Football Spectators Act (1989) which regulates football ground safety. The FLA is due to be replaced with a new body to be called the Sports Ground Safety Authority. The new body will also be responsible for sports grounds other than football stadiums.

Football Monthly *publication* original football magazine. *Football Monthly* was the idea of ex-**Arsenal**, **Sunderland** and **England** captain Charles **Buchan**. Stanley **Matthews** appeared on the front cover of the first *Football Monthly* in September 1951. In its heyday, the magazine sold around 350,000 copies a month. In 1973, the magazine was renamed *Football Monthly Digest* and later the *Football Magazine*, before the original name was revived in 1980. The magazine was relaunched in August 1997.

Football Mutual Insurance Federation *misc.* mutual society set up in 1907 by the **Football League**, **Scottish Football League** and the **Southern League** to provide insurance cover to football players in the event of injury.

football pools *n.pl.* see **pools**.

football special *n.* train specially chartered to convey supporters to away matches. *Keynotes* The very first football special is believed to have carried supporters to the 1881 **Scottish FA Cup** final between **Dumbarton** and **Queen's Park** at Kinning Park. In **Italy**, the **tifosi** – club-sponsored travelling supporters – often travel by train. Vandalism and violent incidents aboard football specials have curtailed their use in Britain and now such modes of transport tend to operate only to ferry supporters to major matches, such as **Wembley** Cup finals. Following the destruction of a train carrying **Chelsea** fans back to London from Luton and trouble on another train at Crewe, British Rail, the former state-run rail company, stopped running football specials and refused to sell cheap-day return tickets until after 3pm on a Saturday only a few weeks into the 1975-76 season. Although newspaper pictures of smashed trains were common in the 1970s, there are earlier press reports of football specials being damaged by supporters. A riot ensued at the end of **Scottish Football League** Division One Championship decider between **Morton** and **Celtic** at **Cappielow Park** in 1921-22 in which several trains carrying Celtic fans back to Glasgow town centre were severely damaged. On 19 March 1934, following a match between **Birmingham City** and **Leicester City**, the *Leicester Mercury* newspaper reported of the football special carrying Leicester fans back from the game that "Windows were smashed, seats cut and torn and the leather window straps slashed with knives."

Football Spectators Act 1989 *legal* legislation primarily designed to prevent crowd trouble. The Act was in response to growing crowd disturbances in the mid- to late-1980s, such as the **Heysel Stadium tragedy** and rioting by **Millwall** supporters at **Luton Town**'s **Kenilworth Road** ground in March 1985 (**FA Cup**, sixth round). Introduced to Parliament in 1988, the two-part legislation covered the domestic game, and included provision for a **national identity-card scheme** for fans, and restrictions on fans travelling abroad to matches. *Keynotes* Individuals convicted of a football-related offence can be required to report to a police station at the time of matches.

Football Stadia Advisory Design Council (FSADC) *misc.* former body made up of architects and construction specialists, established in August 1990 at the recommendation of the **Taylor Report** to examine the design of football stadia and ensure safety standards and comfort for spectators. The FSADC was funded jointly by the **Football Association** and the **Football League** at a cost of £80,000 a year. It was replaced in 1993 by a Department of National Heritage body called the Football Stadia Development Committee, which meets twice a year and consists of representatives from, among others, the FA, **Premier League** and the **Football Trust**.

Football Supporters Association *misc.* national body representing the interests of football supporters and independent supporters' clubs. Formed in 1985 in the aftermath of the **Heysel Stadium disaster**. It differs from the **National Federation of Football Supporters Clubs** in that it attempts to represent supporters at a national level rather than as a loose affiliation of supporters' clubs. The FSA was instrumental in campaigning against the proposed **national identity-card scheme**, collecting more than 250,000 signatures on a petition opposing its introduction. The FSA has also campaigned to increase the **FA Cup** final ticket allocation to participating clubs and, during major tournaments, it has provided "fan embassies" (for example, at the 1998 **World Cup**), which give out information and help fans in trouble. See also **Independent Supporters Associations**.

Football Taskforce *misc.* UK body established in 1997 by the newly elected Labour Government to examine issues of concern within the game, such as hooliganism, racism and supporters' facilities. Chaired by ex-Conservative minister and radio presenter David **Mellor**.

Football Trust *misc.* trust fund founded in 1979 to help develop football in Britain. The fund originally was generated by a levy on **spot-the-ball** competitions run by **pools** companies (Littlewoods, Vernons and Zetters). More recently it has received direct funding by the British Government to help implement the recommendations of the **Taylor Report**, mainly to put in place ground improvements. One of the remits of the Football Trust is to assist projects aimed at tackling **hooliganism**, as well as safety and community programmes. It also funds, in its entirety, the **Sir Norman Chester Centre for Football Research**. Since its inception, the Football Trust has distributed around £256 million and by 1998, it had contributed some £139 million towards ground developments. Over the same period, more than £38 million has been allocated to non-professional football.

Footballer of the Year (England) *award* **1.** annual award by the **Football Writers Association** to the top player in English league football, as voted by the association's membership (football journalists). *Winners* 1948, Stanley **Matthews** (**Blackpool**); 1949, Johnny **Carey** (**Manchester United**); 1950, Joe **Mercer** (**Arsenal**); 1951, Harry Johnston (Blackpool); 1952, Billy **Wright** (**Wolverhampton Wanderers**); 1953, Nat **Lofthouse** (**Bolton Wanderers**); 1954, Tom **Finney** (Preston); 1955, Don **Revie** (**Manchester City**); 1956, Bert **Trautmann** (Manchester City); 1957, Tom Finney (Preston); 1958, Danny **Blanchflower** (**Tottenham Hotspur**); 1959, Syd Owen (**Luton Town**); 1960, Bill Slater (Wolverhampton Wanderers); 1961, Danny Blanchflower (Tottenham Hotspur); 1962, Jimmy Adamson (**Burnley**); 1963, Stanley Matthews (**Stoke City**); 1964, Bobby **Moore** (**West Ham United**); 1965, Bobby Collins (**Leeds United**); 1966, Bobby **Charlton** (Manchester United); 1967, Jack Charlton (Leeds United); 1968, George **Best** (Manchester United); 1969, Tony Book (Manchester City)/Dave **Mackay** (**Derby County**); 1970, Billy **Bremner** (Leeds United); 1971, Frank McLintock (Arsenal); 1972, Gordon **Banks** (Stoke City); 1973, Pat **Jennings** (Tottenham Hotspur); 1974, Ian Callaghan (Liverpool); 1975, Alan **Mullery** (Fulham); 1976, Kevin **Keegan** (Liverpool); 1977, Emlyn Hughes (Liverpool);1978, Kenny Burns (**Nottingham Forest**); 1979, Kenny **Dalglish** (Liverpool);1980, Terry McDermott (Liverpool); 1981, Frans Thijssen (**Ipswich Town**); 1982, Steve Perryman (Tottenham Hotspur); 1983, Kenny Dalglish (Liverpool); 1984, Ian **Rush** (Liverpool); 1985, Neville **Southall** (**Everton**); 1986, Gary **Lineker** (Everton); 1987, Clive Allen (Tottenham Hotspur); 1988, John **Barnes** (Liverpool); 1989, Steve Nicol (Liverpool); 1990, John Barnes (Liverpool); 1991, Gordon Strachan (Leeds United); 1992, Gary Lineker (Tottenham Hotspur); 1993, Chris Waddle (**Sheffield Wednesday**); 1994, Alan **Shearer** (**Blackburn Rovers**); 1995, Jürgen **Klinsmann** (Tottenham Hotspur); 1996, Eric **Cantona** (Manchester United); 1997, Gianfranco **Zola** (**Chelsea**); 1998, Dennis **Bergkamp** (**Arsenal**); 1999, David Ginola (Tottenham Hotspur). **2. PFA Footballer of the Year award** top player in English league football as voted by members of the **Professional Footballers Assiociation**. *Winners* 1974, Norman **Hunter** (Leeds United); 1975, Colin Todd (Derby County); 1976, Pat Jennings (Tottenham Hotspur); 1977, Andy **Gray** (**Aston Villa**); 1978, Peter **Shilton** (Nottingham Forest): 1979, Liam **Brady** (Arsenal); 1980, Terry McDermott (Liverpool); 1981, John Wark (Ipswich Town); 1982, Kevin Keegan (**Southampton**); 1983, Kenny Dalglish (Liverpool);

1984, Ian Rush (Liverpool); 1985, Peter Reid (Everton); 1986, Gary Lineker (Everton); 1987, Clive Allen (Tottenham Hotspur); 1988, John Barnes (Liverpool); 1989, Mark **Hughes** (Manchester United); 1990, David Platt (Aston Villa); 1991 Mark Hughes, (Manchester United); 1992, Gary Pallister (Manchester United); 1993, Paul **McGrath** (Aston Villa); 1994, Eric Cantona (Manchester United); 1995, Alan Shearer (Blackburn Rovers); 1996, Les Ferdinand (**Newcastle United**); 1997, Alan Shearer (Newcastle United); 1998, Dennis Bergkamp (Arsenal); 1999, David Ginola (Tottenham Hotspur). *Keynotes* Ipswich Town players were voted in first, second and third place in the 1981 PFA award: John Wark, Frans Thijssen and Paul Mariner, respectively. **3. FA Women's Footballer of the Year award** top women's player in England, awarded by the **Football Association**. *Winner* 1999, Sue Smith (Tranmere Rovers).

Footballer of the Year (Scotland) *award* **1.** annual award by the **Scottish Football Writers Association** to the top player in Scottish league football, as voted by the association's membership (eg, football journalists). *Winners* 1965, Billy McNeill (**Celtic**); 1966, John Greig (**Rangers**); 1967, Ronnie Simpson (Celtic); 1968, Gordon Wallace (**Raith Rovers**); 1969, Bobby Murdoch (Celtic); 1970, Pat Stanton (**Hibernian**); 1971, Martin Buchan (**Aberdeen**); 1972, David Smith (Rangers); 1973, George Connelly (Celtic); 1974 – award was given to Scotland's 1974 World Cup squad); 1975, Sandy Jardine (Rangers); 1976, John Greig (Rangers); 1977, Danny McGrain (Celtic); 1978, Derek Johnstone (Rangers); 1979, Andy Ritchie (Greenock **Morton**); 1980, Gordon Strachan (Aberdeen); 1981, Alan Rough (**Partick Thistle**); 1982, Paul Sturrock (**Dundee United**); 1983, Charlie Nicholas (Celtic); 1984, Willie Miller (Aberdeen); 1985, Hamish McAlpine (Dundee United); 1986, Sandy Jardine (**Heart of Midlothian**); 1987, Brian McClair (Celtic); 1988, Paul McStay (Celtic); 1989, Richard Gough (Rangers); 1990, Alex McLeish (Aberdeen); 1991, Maurice Malpas (Dundee United); 1992, Ally **McCoist** (Rangers); 1993, Andy Goram (Rangers); 1994, Mark Hateley (Rangers); 1995, Brian **Laudrup** (Rangers); 1996, Paul **Gascoigne** (Rangers); 1997, Brian Laudrup (Rangers); 1998, Craig Burley (Celtic). **2. Scottish Professional Footballers' Association** accolade to the top player in Scottish league football as voted by members of the association. *Winners* 1978, Derek Johnstone (Rangers); 1979, Paul Hegarty (Dundee United); 1980, Davie Provan (Celtic); 1981, Mark McGee (Aberdeen); 1982, Sandy Clarke (**Airdrieonians**); 1983, Charlie Nicholas (Celtic); 1984, Willie Miller (Aberdeen); 1985, Jim Duffy (Morton); 1986, Richard Gough (Dundee United); 1987, Brian McClair (Celtic); 1988, Paul McStay (Celtic); 1989, Theo Snelders (Aberdeen); 1990, Jim Bett (Aberdeen); 1991, Paul Elliott (Celtic); 1992, Ally McCoist (Rangers); 1993, Andy Goram (Rangers); 1994, Mark Hateley (Rangers); 1995, Brian Laudrup

(Rangers); 1996, Paul Gascoigne (Rangers); 1997, Paulo di Canio (Celtic); 1998, Jackie McNamara (Celtic).

Footballers Battalion *misc.* informal name of a **World War I** army battalion, the 17th (Service) Battalion, the Duke of Cambridge's Own Middlesex Regiment (Football), formed in December 1914. By March 1915, 122 professional footballers had joined the battalion, including 41 players and officials of Clapton Orient. Football players and clubs were criticised, however, because this represented less than 10% of the players registered in the **Football League** and **Southern League**.

Footballers Further Education & Vocational Training Society *n.* registered charity formed in 1980 and jointly financed by the **Professional Footballers Association**, the **Football Association**, the **Premier League** and the **Football League,** which provides assistance for players preparing for a career when their playing days are over. Assistance also is given to ex-professional players. The Society provides education grants to unemployed members and those under 21 years of age. In conjunction with local education colleges, the Society helps to arrange various academic and practical courses for professional footballers. The Society is the managing agent for the Government-sponsored Youth Training Scheme in the football industry since 1983 and the Football Club and the Community Programme since 1986.

footwork *n.* the control of the ball with the feet.

Ford Sporting League *competition* 1970-71 English League competition sponsored by Ford (UK) that awarded clubs points throughout the season based on League results and the number of **goals scored**, with points deducted for **bookings** and **sendings off**. Total prize money amounted to £100,000, with the winners receiving £50,000 and the runners-up £30,000. A further £20,000 was divided into eight monthly awards of £2,500 each. The rules of the competition stipulated that prize money could be spent only on ground improvements. **Oldham Athletic**, then of Division Four, easily won the competition, receiving £70,000 in prize money, with **Crewe Alexandra**, also of Division Four, taking the rest of the financial rewards. The competition lasted only one season.

Ford, Trevor *player* Striker. **Wales** international (38 caps, 23 goals). Career ca. 1946–1961. *Clubs* **Swansea** Town, **Aston Villa**, **Sunderland**, **Cardiff City**, **Newport County**. *Keynotes* Ford moved to Sunderland from Aston Villa for a then-record £30,000 in 1950. Included in the **Football League Centenary 100 players**.

Fordsons FC *club* original name (1912-30) of former Republic of Ireland national league club **Cork Athletic**.

forechecking *tactic* ice hockey term commonly used in German football to describe a style of play that involves putting the opposition under constant pressure. See also **pressing**.

foreign players *misc.* players of a different nationality to that of the country in which they are playing.

Italian and Spanish clubs have a long tradition of importing overseas players, especially South American talent. *Keynotes* Foreign players sometimes take **dual nationality** or became naturalised citizens, allowing them to play for the country of residence. In **Spain**, for example, Alfredo **Di Stéfano** and Ferenc **Puskás**, along with Martínez of **Paraguay** and Santamaría of **Uruguay**, were members of Spain's 1962 **World Cup** squad. However, Italy banned new overseas players from playing in the Italian League between 1964 and 1980. Spain too, banned overseas players from the League for a spell, only lifting their exclusion in 1973. English clubs do not have the same tradition of importing overseas players, although foreign players have played in the English league for many years. **Chelsea**, for example, whose squad at the start of the 1998-99 season included 15 players of non-UK origin, signed its first overseas player, the half-back, amateur and **Denmark** captain, Nils **Middelboe**, in 1913. **Liverpool** fielded the first side to win the **FA Cup** without an Englishman. The club's team for its 1986 FA Cup final triumph contained only one player born in England, Mark Lawrenson, born in Preston, but he played for the **Republic of Ireland**. Although **Tottenham Hotspur**'s signing of two Argentinians, Osvaldo **Ardiles** and Ricardo Villa, in 1978, attracted much publicity, **Barrow** had recruited two players from **Argentina** (Augustus Corpa and Casco Rinaldi) in October 1937. Since the **Bosman ruling** the number of overseas players in the major European domestic Leagues has increased substantially. At the start of the 1998-99 season, 184 (or 38.5%) of the 577 professionals playing in the **Spanish Primeria Liga** were overseas players. By contrast, in 1996-97 only 17% were foreign. The influx of overseas players has provoked criticism, especially from players' unions (the Spanish players' union threatened strike action in 1997-98).

foreigners rule *misc.* regulations covering non-**European Union** (EU) players. English and German clubs are only allowed to field three non-EU players at any one time. By contrast, Spanish legislation, in the wake of the **Bosman-ruling**, allows Spanish clubs to register six non-EU foreigners and play four on the pitch at any one time. Elsewhere, the US **Major Soccer League** limits each team to five foreign players, in an effort to develop American players. This contrasts with the defunct **North American Soccer League** that required only three American players on the field of play. Free movement of players from Scottish to English teams was established in 1889 when the **Football League** abandoned its rule of residency for league players. Nowadays, to qualify to play in the UK, a player from outside the EU or **European Economic Area** must have played around 75% of his country's internationals in the year preceding the proposed move. Once in the UK, they must also play in the majority of club games or their **work permit** is unlikely to be renewed. *Regulations* players who, for the purposes of the Premier League and Scottish Football League are not citizens of the EU or the European Economic Area, or who have not been resident in the United Kingdom for five years continuously. **Premier League clubs** may not play more than three such players in any match, unless by permission of their respective league boards (FA Premier League rule E24). The restriction on the number of foreign players allowed at **Football League** clubs was removed from the Football League regulations prior to the 1998-99 season. The **Scottish Football League** restricts the number of players from outside the EU/European Economic Area to 20 in the whole league, with no single club allowed to register more than three players (Scottish Football League rule 62). All foreign players are required to have a work permit, issued by the Department of Education and Employment. See **foreign players**.

Forest   *club*   former-English club. *Keynotes* Founded in Snaresbrook, East London by former pupils of Harrow School in 1859, one of the first clubs outside of the Public Schools to formally adopt **Cambridge University Rules**. Forest FC moved to Battersea Park in 1864, with a new name **Wanderers** FC.

Forfar Athletic   *club* Scottish league. *Dossier* Ground: **Station Park**, Forfar, Tayside, capacity: 8,732. Strip: sky blue shirts with navy blue trim, navy blue shorts with sky blue trim, navy blue socks with white hoops. Nickname: Loons. Record attendance: 10,780 v **Rangers** (2 February 1970, **Scottish FA Cup**, second round). Biggest win: 14–1 v Lindertis (1 September 1988, Scottish FA Cup, first round). Biggest defeat: 2–12 v **King's Park** (2 January 1930, Division Two). *History* Members of Angus Athletic's reserve side established a separate club in May 1885, calling itself Forfar. The club joined the reformed Division Two in 1921-22. Forfar has never played in the top flight of Scottish football. Its first major honour, the Second Division Championship, was not achieved until 1983-84. Forfar reached the **Scottish League Cup** semi-finals in 1977-78 (2–5 v Rangers) and was a Scottish FA Cup semi-finalist four years later (1–3 replay v Rangers). Forfar was Third Division Champions in 1994-95. *League record* First Division 1984-85 to 1991-92; Division Two (B Division) 1921-22 to 1938-39, 1949-50 to 1974-75; Second Division 1975-76 to 1983-84, 1992-93 to 1993-94, 1995-96, 1997-98 to 1998-99; C Division 1946-47 to 1948-49; Third Division 1994-95, 1996-97, 1999-00. *Honours* Second Division 1983-84; Third Division 1994-95. *Records* Ian McPhee holds the record for club appearances (480, 1978-79, 1991-97).

formations   *tactics*   the arrangement and roles of outfield players/systems of play. Playing formations have tended to change over the years, adjusting to the current footballing style. For example, the emphasis of the Italian game in the 1960s and 1970s was on defending (**catenaccio defence**), while the "return" of the **wing-backs** in the English game of the 1990s has led to a resurgence of wing-play after it was largely discarded by the **four–four–two** formation's emphasis on midfield prowess. There are many playing formations besides

four–four–two, including **four–two–four**, **three–five–two**, **four–three–three** and **four–five–one**. *History* In the early years of football's development, the accent was on attack and players would primarily **dribble** with the ball, rather than pass it to a team-mate. "Offball" players simply supported their "**onball**" team-mate as the player dribbled up the pitch, protecting him from opposition tackles. The tactic was dictated by the first **offside** rule which prohibited any team-mate from being in front of the ball when it was passed. The rule was modified in 1867 (see offside: *History*) so that forward passing became a feature of the game for the first time, with a consequent change in formations. Early playing formations mirrored the attacking emphasis of the game and teams would typically line up with a goalkeeper, two full-backs, one half-back (midfielder) and seven forwards (two–one–seven). The full-backs would rarely venture forward and would kick the ball as far upfield as possible after successfully dispossessing an opponent. The **Royal Engineers** are credited with introducing formations into football tactics. The Royal Engineers played in an innovative one–two–four–three formation, comprising a three-quarter back (in front of the goalkeeper), two half-backs, four wingers and three centres. The club also adopted a strategy of short passes. The influx into English football in the 1880s of Scottish professionals led to a more widespread development of the passing game. **Preston North End**, a club which dominated the first two **Football League** seasons, adopted the passing approach with great success. The advent of the passing game led to the first real change in playing formations. Two forwards were brought back into midfield to bolster and protect the defence. Hence a typical playing formation would consist of a goalkeeper, two full-backs, centre-back and two half-backs, and five forwards (two–three–five). The two full-backs would mark the opposing inside-forwards and the half-backs would cover the wingers. The centre-half would be free to roam the pitch, defending and attacking, rather than specifically marking the centre-forward as is the main role of such a player in the modern game. a second change in the offside rule in 1925 led to a further development in playing formations. Since 1865, three opposing players had to be between the attacker and the **goal line** when the ball was played. Quick full-backs, such as **Newcastle United** and **Ireland** international Bill McCracken, had perfected the art of catching opposing forwards offside. This effectively confined play to a narrow strip either side of the **centre line** and resulted in fewer goals being scored. The new offside rule reduced the minimum number of players between the forward and the goal line to two. As a result, the centre-half's free role was curtailed, with the position converted into that of an out-and-out defender (a centre-back or stopper) responsible for marking the opposing centre-forward. In addition, one of (later both) the inside-forwards was brought back to support the midfield and cover for the departed centre-half. Thereafter, full-backs, rather than the wing-backs, became responsible for marking the wingers. This is the classic **W–M formation** (or three–two–two–three), which was the first, and the most popular, of the modern systems of play. The idea to change the roving centre-half to a permanent defender is attributed to Charles **Buchan**, who first suggested the switch to the **Arsenal** manager Herbert **Chapman** at the start of the 1925-26 season. But it was only after a 0–7 defeat by Newcastle United at **St James' Park** in early October that Jack Butler, the Arsenal centre-half, was moved to a defence-only role. In the 1950s, the Hungarian national side introduced the twin striker positions, supported by a deep-lying centre-forward. For example, the **Hungary** team that, on 25 November 1953, inflicted a 3-6 home defeat on **England** included **Puskàs** and **Koscis** as the forward pairing, with **Hidegkuti** playing slightly behind them. At **Wembley**, England's centre-back, Henry Johnston, was constantly pulled out of position trying to mark Hidegkuti, while the two supporting wing-halves, Billy **Wright** and Jimmy Dickinson, were unused to dealing with twin strikers. Don **Revie** successfully replicated Hidegkuti's deep centre-forward role for **Manchester City** during the mid-1950s. To counteract two centre-forwards the twin centre-back roles were developed, which led to the four–two–four formation. The **Brazil** side that won the 1958 **World Cup** adopted the four–two–four formation, with a deep-lying centre-forward and a wing-half in midfield, linking defence and attack. **Ipswich Town**'s 1961-62 League Championship winning side adopted a different formation, with one winger moving into midfield (four–three–three). Alf **Ramsey**, the Ipswich manager, took this move one stage further, when he became England manager in April 1963: he discarded wingers entirely, although the full-backs were encouraged to attack along the wings. The removal of traditional wingers established the four–four–two formation and greater emphasis on midfield play. In the mid-1960s, the catenaccio (meaning "bolt" or "chain" in Italian) defensive system, which involves a team denying its opponents scoring opportunities by defending the **scoring space**, was developed and was successfully adopted by, among others, **Internazionale**. During the 1974 World Cup, **Netherlands** adopted a playing system – **total football** – which allowed all outfield players to take part in an attack, with their regular position covered by a team-mate. This enabled the team to alter its formation several times during a match. Some teams have adopted a style of play known as the long-ball game which involves getting the ball forward to a **target player** as quickly as possible. This system is based on the view (supported by research) that most goals are scored from moves involving fewer than four passes. Stan **Cullis' Wolverhampton Wanderers** adopted a highly-effective "kick and rush" **long-ball game** that depended on pace and stamina in the 1950s, when the club won three League Championships and one **FA Cup**. More recently, Watford (during the club's climb from Division Four to Division One between 1977-78

and 1982-83 and an FA Cup final appearance in 1984) used the long-ball game with two central attackers supported by two quick wingers. A further development is the three–five–two system, which consists of three defenders, five midfielders and two attackers. The defensive line is made up of two central defenders and a free player – known as a **sweeper** – who plays behind the other two, covering any open space, forward runs by opponents and through passes. The five midfield players will typically include two wing-backs, who push forward down the flanks when the team is attacking, but who also provide defensive cover. The **Christmas tree** formation (four–three–two–one) was used on occasion during Terry **Venables**' reign as England manager. The system involves a lone striker (target player) who is supported in attack by two midfield players, playing as inside-forwards and making forward runs into the penalty area. Two midfielders play wide pushing forward when the team is in possession and tracking back to hold midfield when the opposition has the ball, while a third midfield player operates as a holding player in front of the back-four. See **Zone 14**.

former-Yugoslavia (Socialist Federal Republic of Yugoslavia) *country formerly affiliated to UEFA* former communist federal republic of South-east Europe, on the Adriatic Sea, consisting of the former-republics of Bosnia, Croatia, Herzegovina, Macedonia, Montenegro, Serbia and Slovenia, and the autonomous regions of Kosovo and Vojvodina. Established in 1918 from the states of Macedonia and Montenegro and regions of Austria-Hungary (Bosnia, Croatia, Herzegovina and Slovenia). Originally known as the Kingdom of Serbs, Croats and Slovenes; adopted name of Yugoslavia in 1929. Invaded by Nazi Germany during **World War II**. Communist republic declared in 1945 by the former resistance leader Tito (real name Josip Broz). Civil war started in 1991 precipitated by the breakdown of the communist system and growing ethnic unrest. Independence of the constituent republics of **Croatia**, **Slovenia**, **Macedonia** and **Bosnia-Herzegovina** recognised in 1992. New Federal Republic of Yugoslavia, consisting of Serbia and Montenegro, including the autonomous regions of Kosovo and Vojvodina, declared in 1992. Area: 255,804 sq km (98,766 sq miles). Former population: 23,400,000 (1987 est.). Languages: Serbo-Croat, Slovene, Macedonian. Former capital: Belgrade. *Dossier* Football association formed in 1919, affiliated to **FIFA** in 1919 and founder member of the **Union of European Football Associations** (UEFA) in 1954. First international game: 28 August 1920 v **Czechoslovakia** (0–7, Antwerp in Belgium, **Olympic Games** first round). Biggest victory: 10–0 v **Venezuela** (14 June 1972, Curitiba in Brazil, Brazilian tournament to celebrate 150th anniversary of its independence). Biggest defeat: 0–7 v Czechoslovakia (as above), v **Uruguay** (26 May 1924, in Paris, Olympic Games first round), v Czechoslovakia (28 October 1925, Prague, friendly). Most appearances for former-

Yugoslavia: Dragan **Dzajic** (85 appearances, 1964-79), Zlatko Vujovic (70 appearances, 1979-90). Former-Yugoslavia's leading goalscorers: Stjepan **Bobek** (38 goals, 1946-56), Milan Galic (37 goals, 1959-65), Blagoje Marjanovic (36, 1926-38). Other notable players: Dusan Bajevic, Faruk Hadzibegic, Darko **Pancev**, Robert **Prosinecki**. *International tournament record* (records to 1991 only) Olympic Games – first entered 1920, winners/gold medal 1960 (3–1, v Denmark, in Rome, Italy), runners-up/silver medal 1948 (1–3, v **Sweden**, at **Wembley** Stadium, London), 1952 (0–2, v **Hungary**, in Helsinki, Finland), 1956 (0–1 v **Soviet Union**, at Melbourne Cricket Ground, Melbourne, Australia), semi-final 1980 (fourth, 0–2 v Soviet Union, in Moscow, third/fourth playoff), sixth 1964; **World Cup** – first entered 1930, semi-final 1930 (1–6, v eventual winners Uruguay, Montevideo), 1962 (fourth, 0–1, v **Chile**, in Santiago, third/fourth playoff), quarter-final 1954, 1958, 1990, second round 1974, also qualified for finals tournament 1950, 1986; **Balkan Cup** – 1934; **Dr Gerö Cup** – fourth 1955-60; **European Championship** – first entered 1960, runners-up 1960 (1–2, v Soviet Union, in Paris, France), 1968 (0–2, v **Italy**, in Rome), semi-final 1976 (fourth, 2–3, v **Netherlands**, in Belgrade), quarter-final 1972, second round 1964, also qualified for finals tournament 1984, 1992 (though did not play in finals tournament due to civil war – place taken by eventual winners **Denmark**); **European Championship for Women** - never entered; **European Junior Championship/ European Youth Championship** (under-18) – 1951, runners-up 1979; **European Under-16 Championship** – runners-up 1990; **European Under-21 Championship** – 1978, runners-up 1990; **Under-17 World Championship** – never qualified; **World Youth Cup** (under-20) – qualified for finals tournament 1979 (first round group stage). *Record against British and Irish national teams* v **England**, played 14, won four, drawn five, lost five; v **Northern Ireland**, played seven, won five, drawn one, lost one; v **Scotland**, played eight, won one, drawn five, lost two; v **Wales**, played seven, won four, drawn three, lost none; v **Republic of Ireland**, played two, won one, drawn none, lost one; *History* The two oldest clubs from the former country, Croatian club **Hajduk Split** and Serbian club **OFK Beograd**, were both founded in 1911. The original national league was founded in 1923, with the Cup founded in 1947. Professionalism introduced in the 1970s. The two most successful clubs were both from the Serbian capital Belgrade: **Red Star Belgrade** (Serbo-Croat name FK Crvena Zvezda Beograd) won the former-Yugoslavia league 18 times and Cup 12 times; **Partizan Belgrade** was league champions 11 times, and Cup winners five times. Croatian club Hajduk Split won nine league titles (though was runner-up 10 times) and was Cup winners on nine occasions. Dynamo Zagreb (now known as **Croatia Zagreb**) was league champions four times, and Cup winners eight times. All Croatian and Slovenia

clubs left the league at the end of the 1990-91 season. At the end of the following season, all clubs from Macedonia and Bosnia had also resigned, effectively ending the former Yugoslavian national league. Two former Yugoslavian clubs won European club championships: Red Star Belgrade won the **European Cup** in 1991, while Croatia Zagreb (as Dynamo Zagreb) won the **Fairs Cup** (now **UEFA Cup**) in 1967. Red Star also won the 1991 **World Club Cup**. Partizan reached the quarter-final of the first European Cup in 1955-56, losing 3-4 (agg.) to the eventual winners **Real Madrid**. A representative Zagreb Select XI took part in the first Inter Cities Fairs Cup (the forerunner of the UEFA Cup) in 1955-58, while a Belgrade Select XI reached the semi-final of the same tournament in 1958-1960. Former Yugoslavia was runners-up in the 1960 and 1968 European Championships. The country qualified for the finals tournament in 1992, but was barred from playing owing to the civil war; its place was taken by eventual winners Denmark. Yugoslavia won gold medal at the 1960 Olympic Games, and was silver medalist in 1948, 1952 and 1956: its 0–1 defeat by the Soviet Union in the 1956 final was watched by 120,000 spectators at Melbourne Cricket Ground in Australia. The former Yugoslavia's last game was played on 25 March 1992 (0–2, v Netherlands, in Amsterdam, friendly). Dejan **Savicevic** was the last player to score for former Yugoslavia (13 November 1991, 2-0, v Austria, in Vienna, European Championship qualifier; Lukic scored the other goal). *Record of former-Yugoslavia clubs in international club tournaments* (records to 1991 only) World Club Cup – Red Star Belgrade (FK Crvena Zvezda Beograd) (1991); European Cup – Red Star Belgrade (1991, semi-final 1957, 1962, 1971, quarter-final 1958, 1974, 1981, 1982, 1987, quarter-final group 1992), Partizan Belgrade (FK Partizan Beograd) (runners-up 1966, quarter-final 1956, 1964), **Vojvodina Novi Sad** (quarter-final 1967), Hajduk Split (quarter-final 1976, 1980, 1995); **European Cup-winners Cup** – Croatia Zagreb (as Dynamo Zagreb) (semi-final 1961, quarter-final 1965, 1970), OFK Beograd (semi-final 1963), Hajduk Split (semi-final 1973, quarter-final 1978), Red Star Belgrade (semi-final 1975, quarter-final 1972, 1986), Partizan Belgrade (quarter-final 1990); UEFA Cup/Fairs Cup – Croatia Zagreb (as Dynamo Zagreb) (1967, runners-up 1963), Red Star Belgrade (runners-up 1979, quarter-final 1963), Belgrade Select XI (a Belgrade representative side – semi-final 1960, quarter-final 1961), **Radnicki Nis** (semi-final 1982), Hajduk Split (semi-final 1984, quarter-final 1986), **Zeljeznicar Sarajevo** (semi-final 1985, quarter-final 1972), Red Star Belgrade (quarter-final 1963), Vojvodina Novi Sad (quarter-final 1968), OFK Beograd (quarter-final 1973), **Velez Mostar** (quarter-final 1975*); **Mitropa Cup** – Red Star Belgrade (1968), **Celik Zenica** (1971, 1972), Vojvodina Novi Sad (1977), Partizan Belgrade (1978).

Forsdick, Elizabeth *referee* the first woman **assistant referee** (then known as "linesman") at an **FA Cup** match (October 1981).

Forthbank Stadium *ground* Scottish football ground situated in Stirling, Stirlingshire; home of **Stirling Albion**. Ground capacity: 3,808. Pitch dimensions: 100.5m x 68m. Record attendance: 3,808 v **Aberdeen** (15 February 1996, **Scottish FA Cup**, fourth round). *Keynotes* Stirling played its first match at the £4 million Forthbank Stadium on 24 April 1993 (v **Clydebank**). The club's previous ground, Annfield Road, was the only Scottish football ground to have installed an **artificial pitch**. The three-year plastic-pitch experiment between 1987 and 1990 had been largely at the behest of the local council which had purchased the ground from the club for £180,000 in 1983 and wanted to make more community use of the facility. When grass returned in 1990, the local authority decided to sell Annfield Road for housing and develop a community stadium elsewhere. Stirling moved to the new purpose-built Forthbank Stadium in April 1993, having been forced to share **Stenhousemuir**'s **Ochilview Park** for most of the 1992-93 season. Forthbank boasts the second largest (after **Clyde**'s **Broadwood Stadium**) playing surface of any senior football ground in Scotland. The ground derives its name Forth Bank ground of the city's previous League club, **King's Park**, which had been destroyed in 1940 by a wartime bomb.

Fortior Côte Ouest (Fortior Mahajunga) *club* Madagascar national league club, based in Mahajunga. Ground: Alexandre Rabemananjara, capacity: 3,000. Strip: blue shirts and white shorts. **African Cup of Champion Clubs** second round 1973; Madagascar Cup 1974, 1975, 197 and 1985; Madagascar League champions 1972 and 1979.

foul *rules* violation of the **Laws of the game**. A foul is committed if a player: **1.** kicks, **2.** trips or attempts to trip, **3.** pushes, **4.** jumps at, or **5.** charges an opponent recklessly, carelessly or with excessive force; **6.** holds an opponent; **7.** strikes or attempts to strike an opponent; **8.** spits at an opponent; **9.** makes a tackle but contacts the opponent before the ball; **10.** deliberately handles the ball (handball) – except for the goalkeeper who may handle the ball in his or her own penalty area; **11.** is guilty of **dangerous play** (including raising a foot head-high with studs showing, and kicking the ball when held firmly by the goalkeeper); **12.** unfairly impedes a player from making progress (**obstruction**); or **13** prevents the goalkeeper from releasing the ball back into play (Law XII). Additionally, a goalkeeper commits a foul if he or she: **14.** takes more than four **steps** in any direction while in possession of the ball with his or her hands, and before releasing it back into play; **15.** releases the ball back into play, but then re-handles it; **16.** handles a **pass to the goalkeeper**; **17.** handles a ball directly from a **throw-in** from a team-mate; or **18.** is guilty of **time-wasting**. The punishment for any of the fouls 1–10 listed above is for the opposing team to be awarded a **direct free kick,** taken from the point where the foul is committed (unless within the opponent's **goal area**, in which case it is taken from anywhere within that area).

If, however, the foul is committed in the offending side's penalty area, then the opponents are to be awarded a **penalty kick**. The punishment for any of the fouls 11-19 is for the opposing team to be awarded an **indirect free kick** taken from the point where the foul was committed (unless within the opponents' goal area – in which case it is taken from anywhere within that area – or within the offending side's goal area in which case it must be taken from the edge of the goal area parallel to the **goal line** at the point nearest to where the foul was committed). Players can also receive a **caution** or be **sent off** for serious or persistent fouling. A player is not guilty of tripping an opponent if he or she plays the ball first and only trips the opponent during the same movement, unless the player is considered by the referee to have made a reckless or dangerous tackle with excessive force (see also **tackle from behind**). *vb.* to commit such an offence.

foul or abusive language *rules* obsolete term for **offensive or abusive language**.

foul play *rules* see **serious foul play**.

foul throw *rules* a **throw-in** taken improperly (Law XV). A foul throw is committed if, when the throw is taken, the thrower does not have both feet on the ground – either on the touchline or outside it – does not use both hands, is not facing the field of play, or if the ball is not thrown from behind and over the thrower's head. The sanction for a foul throw is for the throw in to be retaken by the opposite team.

Foulke, Billy (William) *player* Goalkeeper. **England** international (one cap). Born 12 April 1874. Career ca. 1894–1907. *Clubs* **Sheffield United**, **Chelsea**, **Bradford City**. *Keynotes* Nicknamed "Fatty" because of his size: 187m (6ft 2ins) and 140kg (22st). Sheffield United paid a Derbyshire colliery side (Blackwell Colliery) £19 to take him to **Bramall Lane** in 1894. Foulke moved from Sheffield United to the newly established Chelsea in 1905. He made four appearances for Derbyshire County Cricket Club. Included in the **Football League Centenary 100 players**. *Honours* League Championship (Sheffield United 1897-98); **FA Cup** (Sheffield United 1899, 1902).

four-five-one *tactics* system of play/**formation**. A system consisting of four defenders, five midfielders and one striker. A defensive/cautious formation which relies for its success on the ability of the lone striker to hold the ball up to enable team-mates to join the attack. The 4-5-1 system is a variation of the **three-five-two** formation. The **Tottenham Hotspur** side which reached the 1987 **FA Cup** final used the 4-5-1 formation, with a midfield quintet of Paul Allen, Osvaldo **Ardiles**, Glenn **Hoddle**, Steve Hodge and Chris Waddle supporting a lone striker, Clive Allen.

four-four-two **1.** *tactics* system of play/**formation**. A system consisting of four defenders (right-back, right centre-back, left centre-back, left -back), four midfield players and two strikers. Within the system the formation of the midfield can resemble a diamond pattern with the front player supporting the two attackers. The anchor midfielder sits in front of the defence, linking defensive and attacking play and preventing opponents from exploiting the space between the **back four**. **2. Four-four-two** *publication* monthly football magazine first published in September 1994.

four–three–three *tactics* system of play/**formation**. A system consisting of four defenders, three midfielders and three attackers. The four–three–three formation is a variation of both the **W–M formation** and the **four–two–four** system. Given the right players, the system can be rapidly modified to become either more defensive (**four–four–two**) or more attacking (three–three–four). See also **catenaccio defence**.

four–two–four *tactics* system of play/**formation**. A system consisting of four defenders (right back, right centre-back, left centre-back, left back), two midfielders and four attackers (right wing, right striker, left striker, left winger). The two midfielders are pivotal to the system, linking defensive and attacking play, but they also have to cover a considerable amount of space. The four–two–four system's origins lie with the Hungarian national side's innovation of twin strikers with a deep-lying centre-forward playing behind them (for example, the 1953 Hungarian team which defeated **England** 6–3 at **Wembley** included **Puskàs** and **Kocsis** in the twin attacker positions and **Hidegkuti** playing the deep centre-forward role). Twin centre-back roles (right and left) were introduced to counteract the threat posed by two centre-forwards. The Brazilian side which won the 1958 **World Cup** adopted the four–two–four formation.

fourth official *rules* match official appointed in some competitions – particularly internationals – to assist the **referee** in any administrative duties before, during and after the match. They may be required to assist with substitutions – including checking the **substitutes**' boots and other kit prior to their entering the field of play – and in controlling the replacement of the match ball. The fourth official may submit a report to the appropriate football authority on any misconduct or incident which the referee or **assistant referees** have not seen. The fourth official is also empowered to inform the referee of any irresponsible behaviour by anyone in the **technical area**. The official also may be called on to take over in the event that the referee or an assistant referee is unable to continue. Fourth officials must be distinguished from reserve (or standby) officials. Fourth officials are recommended for all national league top-flight divisions.

fracture *medical* a broken **bone**. Fractures usually result from a direct blow to the limb, but can be caused by rotational stress, for example when a player falls and twists on a leg which is supporting the entire body weight. Fractures can be caused by direct violence – where the bone breaks at the site of the blow or kick – or indirect violence where the break occurs at a site away from the point of contact (such as a broken arm sustained by a fall following a trip). *vb.* to break a bone. See **stress fracture**, **compound fracture**, **closed fracture**, **joint fracture**, **fracture dislocation**.

fracture dislocation *medical* serious injury where a bone is broken and a **joint** becomes dislocated.

fractured rib *medical* a break in one of the bones of the rib cage, usually caused by a heavy blow to the rib cage from another player.

fractured skull *medical* a **fracture** of the neurocranium (the bony case surrounding the brain) – a very serious head injury that requires hospital examination. *Keynotes* Twenty-five-year-old **Celtic** goalkeeper John Thomson died after fracturing his skull in a game against **Rangers** on 25 September 1931. Thomson dived to intercept the ball but collided with a Rangers striker; he died five hours later.

fractured vertebrae *medical* see **spinal injury**.

Fram (Knattspyrnufélagid Fram) *club* Icelandic national league club based in Reykjarvik, founded 1908. Ground: Laugardalsvöllur, capacity: 7,000. Strip: blue shirts, white shorts. *Keynotes* Fram holds the national league record of six consecutive titles (1913 to 1918). **European Cup-winners Cup** second round 1986, 1991; Icelandic Cup 1970, 1973, 1979, 1980, 1985, 1987, 1989; Icelandic League 1913, 1914, 1915, 1916, 1917, 1918, 1921, 1922, 1923, 1925, 1939, 1946, 1947, 1962, 1972, 1986, 1988, 1990, runners-up 17 times (to 1996).

France *country* UEFA republic in west Europe on the Atlantic Ocean and Mediterranean Sea, bordered by **Belgium**, **Germany**, **Switzerland**, **Italy**, **Spain** and **Andorra**. Area: 543,965 sq km (209,970 sq miles). Population: 58,000,000 (1995 est.). Languages: French, with Breton, Catalan and Provençal dialects. Capital: Paris. *Dossier* Football association (Fédération Française de Football, Paris) formed in 1918, founder member of **FIFA** in 1904, and founder member of **Union of European Football Associations** (UEFA) in 1954, president Claude Simonet, general secretary Gérard Enault. Season played from August to June with **winter break** from December to January. National stadium: **Stade de France**, Saint Denis (a suburb to the north of Paris), capacity: 80,000 all seated. (The former national stadium was Le **Parc des Princes**, Paris, capacity: 49,000.) National strip: blue shirts, white shorts. Website: http://www.fff.asso.fr (official site). First international game 1 May 1904, v Belgium (3–3, in Brussels, friendly). Biggest victory: 10–0 v **Azerbaijan** (1996, in France, **European Championship** qualifier). Biggest defeats: 1–17 v **Denmark**, (22 October, in London, **Olympic Games** semi-final), 1–13, v **Hungary** (12 June 1927, in Budapest, friendly) Most capped players: Didier Deschamps (84 appearances, 1989-), Manuel **Amoros** (82 appearances, 1982–92), Laurent Blanc (80 appearances, 1989-), Maxime Bossis (76 appearances, 1976–86), Michel **Platini** (72 appearances, 1976–87), Marius Tresor (65, 1971–83), Roger Marche (63, 1947–1959). Leading goalscorers: Michel Platini (41 goals), Jean-Pierre **Papin** (30 goals, 1986–95), Just **Fontaine** (30 goals, 1953–60), Yourri Djorkaeff (20 goals, 1993-), Jean Nicolas (20, 1922–39), Paul Nicolas (20, 1920–31), Jean Vincent

(22 goals, 1953–61), Eric **Cantona** (19 goals, 1987–1995). Other notable international players: Marcel **Dessailly**, Alain **Giresse**, Raymond **Kopa**, Zinedine **Zidane**. *International tournament record* Olympic Games – played in first tournament 1908, winners/gold medal 1984 (2–0, v **Brazil**, Rose Bowl stadium, Pasadena, Los Angeles – 101,000 spectators), semi-final 1908 (received a bye in the first round, result above), 1920 (1–4, v Czechoslovakia, in Antwerp, semi-final), quarter-final 1924, 1968, 1976, 1996, also qualified for finals tournament 1928, 1952; **Women's World Cup/European Championship for Women** – see **France, women**; **World Cup** – first entered 1930, has entered every tournament to date, 1998 (3–0, v Brazil, in the Stade de France, St-Denis, Paris), semi-final/third 1958 (6–3, v West Germany, in Gothenburg, Sweden, third/fourth playoff), 1986 (4–2, v Belgium, in Puebla, Mexico, third/fourth playoff), semi-final/fourth 1982 (2–3, v **Poland**, in Alicante, Spain, third/fourth playoff), second round 1938, also qualified for finals tournament 1930 (no qualifying tournament), 1934, 1954, 1966, 1978, hosts 1938, 1998; European Championship – entered first tournament in 1960, 1984 (2–0, v Spain, in Paris), semi-final/fourth 1960 (0–2, v **Czechoslovakia**, in Paris, third/fourth playoff), semi-final 1996 (0–0, 5–6 pens., v **Czech Republic**, at **Old Trafford**, Manchester, semi-final), quarter-final 1964, 1968, also qualified for finals tournament 1992, hosts 1960 (semi-finals and final only), 1984; **European Junior Championship/European Youth Championship** (under-18) – 1949, 1983, 1996, 1997; **European Under-21 Championship** – 1988 (3–0 agg., v **Greece**); **Under-17 World Championship** – qualified 1997; **World Youth Cup** (under-20) – qualified for first finals tournament in 1977 (first-round groups stage). *Record against British and Irish national teams* v **England**, played 24, won five, drawn three, lost 16 (this figures does not include six defeats against England amateur sides before **World War I**); v **Northern Ireland**, played seven, won four, drawn three; v **Scotland**, played 11, won five, drawn none, lost six; v **Wales**, played four, won two, drawn one, lost one; v **Republic of Ireland**, played 11, won four, drawn three, lost four. *History* Rudimentary forms of football – similar to the games played in Britain – were played from the seventh century in Brittany, Normandy and Picardy. Modern football in France dates back to the mid-late 19th century, spreading first from northern France. The country's oldest football club, **Le Havre Athletic Club**, was founded in 1872 (though it did not adopt association football until 20 years later). Other early clubs included Les Girondins de **Bordeaux** (1881), **Red Star 93** (Paris, founded by Jules **Rimet** in 1897) and Nimes Olympique (1901). Football was originally run by a number of organisations, operating their own league competitions. The French domestic Cup was first played in 1918 and first won by Olympique de Pantin (3–0 v FC Lyon); it was played continuously through **World War II**. The only year the competition

was not completed was 1992, when 15 spectators were killed in the semi-final between Sporting Club Bastia and **Olympique de Marseille** (5 May 1992, in Bastia). Around 1,300 others were injured when a temporary stand collapsed; the tournament was abandoned. The current national league championship dates back to 1933 (first won by Olympique Lille). French club **Stade de Reims** played in the first **European Cup** final, losing 3–4 to **Real Madrid** at Parc des Princes, Paris, in June 1956. In 1959 Reims against reached the European Cup final and again lost to Real Madrid, this time 0–2 in Stuttgart. Olympique de Marseille won the tournament in 1993 but was later stripped of the title for **match-fixing** in the French league. It reached the UEFA Cup final in 1999. **Paris St Germain** is the only other French club to have won a European club trophy: the **European Cup-winners Cup** in 1996. France's domestic league was restructured prior to the 1997-98 season, reducing the top-flight Division 1 from 20 to 18 clubs, and creating a brand new semi-professional and amateur league structure. France made a considerable contribution to the early development of international football. It was a founder member of FIFA in 1904, while a Frenchman, Robert **Guérin**, was FIFA's first president. Two other Frenchmen, Jules Rimet (then president of FIFA) and Henri Delaunay (as general secretary of the Fédération Française de Football) proposed the organisation of the FIFA World Cup (the trophy was designed by yet another Frenchman, Albert **Lafleur**). Delaunay also founded the European championship, while Gabriel Hanot is credited with creating the European Cup. France's first match against a full-England side took place in May 1923 (1–4, in Paris, friendly). The six previous fixtures against England were all against England amateur sides: France lost all six, conceded 55 goals and scored just two, including a 0–15 scoreline in 1906 (1 November 1906, in Paris, friendly). It entered the first World Cup in 1930, and won the first ever World Cup match (4–1 v Mexico, 13 July 1930, Pocitos Stadium, Montevideo, Uruguay) in front of 1,000 spectators. The 1980s became France's most successful international period, winning the European Championship in 1984, and finishing fourth and third, respectively, in the 1982 and 1986 World Cup finals tournaments. All three campaigns featured the country's record goalscorer, Michel Platini, who also scored the opening goal in the 1984 European Championship final victory over Spain. France was hosts to the 1938 World Cup, with the final played at Stade Colombe in Paris. From 16 February 1994 to 9 November 1996, France played 30 consecutive games without defeat, just one behind the record for a European nation, held by Spain, and six behind the world record held by Brazil. France hosted and won the 1998 World Cup finals tournament, with the final played at a purpose-built 80,000 **all-seater stadium**, Stade de France, in the Paris suburb of Saint-Leu-Saint-Denis. France beat favourites Brazil 3–0 in the final (12 July 1998), with Zinidine Zidane scoring two goals after 27 and 45 minutes, and Emmanuel Petit scoring the third in injury time. France scored the first ever **golden goal** in a World Cup match (1–0, v **Paraguay**, 28 June 1998, in Lens). Following its World Cup triumph in 1998, the French government awarded all the squad players its highest civilian honour, the Legion of Honour. *World Cup performance* (finals and qualifiers to end of 1998 tournament) played 109, won 61, drawn 15, lost 33, scored 231 goals, conceded 119 goals; win rate: 56%; goals scored per game: 2.12. *World Cup final team and scorers 1998 (winners)* Barthez (goalkeeper), Lizarazu, Desailly (sent off after two cautions), Leboeuf, Thuram, Petit (1), Deschamps, Karembeu (Boghossian), Zidane (2), Guivarc'h (Dugarry), Djorkaeff (Vieira). *European Championship winning team and scorers 1984* Bats (goalkeeper), Battiston (Amoros), Le Roux, Bossis, Domergue, Giresse, Tigana, Fernandez, Platini (1), Lacombe (Genghini), Bellone (1). *League system* France has two professional divisions (la Ligue Nationale). Eighteen clubs compete in Division 1 (reduced from 20 after the 1996-97 season, when four clubs were relegated, and replaced by just two promoted clubs). The bottom three clubs are automatically relegated to Division 2. Twenty-two clubs compete in Division 2. Three points are awarded for a win, with one for a draw; clubs level on points are separated on **goal difference**. Below the national league is a 20-club semi-professional National Open; below this, the Championnat de France Amateurs is divided into four regional divisions. *Record in international club tournaments* European Cup – Olympique de Marseille (1993, runners-up 1991, semi-final 1990), Stade de Reims (runners-up 1956, 1959), **Saint Étienne** (runners-up 1976; **Auxerre** (quarter-final 1997), **AS Monaco** (semi-final 1998); European Cup-winners Cup – Paris St Germain (1996, runners-up 1997), AS Monaco (runners-up 1992); **UEFA Cup – SC Bastia** (runners-up 1978), Girondins de Bordeaux (runners-up 1996), Olympique de Marseille (finalist 1999). Other clubs: **RC Lens, Racing Club de Paris, Olympique Gymnaste Club de Nice, FC Nantes Atlantiques, Olympique Lyonnais**.

France, women *country/women* football in France is administered by the Fédération Française de Football, in Paris. *International tournament record* **Women's World Cup** – entered first tournament in 1991, never qualified for finals tournament; **European Championship for Women** – entered first tournament in 1982, quarter-final 1989. *History* Organised women's football in France dates back to **World War I**, with a number of clubs formed in Paris. In 1920, a French representative side played five games against the top English women's club **Dick, Kerr's Ladies**: a 1–1 draw in Paris was watched by 22,000 spectators. Two of the French players later joined the English club.

Francescoli, Enzo *player* Striker. **Uruguay** international (65 caps, 1982-). Born 12 November 1961. *Clubs* **Wanderers** (Uruguay), **River Plate** (twice), Matra Racing/**Racing Club de Paris, Olympique de Marseille**, Cagliari, **Torino**. *Keynotes* Argentinean

league top scorer 1984 (24 goals), 1986 (25 goals), 1995 Apertura (12 goals) – all with River Plate. *Honours* **South American Footballer of the Year** (*El Mundo*) 1984, runner-up 1985; **Copa Libertadores** (River Plate, 1996); **Supercopa** (River Plate, 1997).

franchise *n.* authorisation granted by a football association to an operator to run a club in its league. *Keynotes* Franchising is used in professional football in the **United States of America** where, for example, **Major League Soccer** is owned collectively by the club operators ("single-entity ownership"). Individual club operators buy a share of the whole league, not just their own club.

Francis, Trevor *player-manager* Striker. **England** international (52 caps, 12 goals). Born 19 April 1954. Career ca. 1969–1994. *Clubs* (player) **Birmingham City, Nottingham Forest, Manchester City, Sampdoria**, Atalanta (Italy), **Rangers**, (manager) **Queens Park Rangers** (player-manager), **Sheffield Wednesday** (player-manager), Birmingham City. *Keynotes* Joined Birmingham City as an apprentice in 1969, turning professional in April 1971 and going on to score 118 goals in 278 **Football League** appearances for the club. In February 1979, Francis became the UK's first £1 million player when he moved to Nottingham Forest for £1.1 million. Francis scored Forest's winner in the 1979 European Cup final having been ineligible for the earlier rounds (1–0 v **Malmö FF**). Manchester City paid £1.2 million for Francis but his stay at **Maine Road** lasted for only 10 months before he was transferred to Sampdoria for £900,000 in July 1982. As a manager, Francis took Sheffield Wednesday to both the FA Cup final (1–2 a.e.t. replay v **Arsenal**) and the League Cup final (1–2 v Arsenal) in 1993. Included in the **Football League Centenary 100 players**. *Honours* **Scottish League Cup** (Rangers 1988); Italian Cup (Sampdoria 1985); **European Cup** (Nottingham Forest 1979).

Frankland, Alfred *coach* first trainer and manager of the celebrated women's club **Dick, Kerr's Ladies**, born 1882, died 1957. Frankland was the club's trainer for 40 years from its foundation in 1917, during which the club played 748 matches, losing only 13. He was affectionately known as the "father of women's football".

Franklin, Neil (Cornelius) *player-manager* Defender. **England** international (27 caps). Born 24 January 1922. Career ca. 1936–1962. *Clubs* (player) **Stoke City, Independiente Santa Fé, Hull City, Crewe Alexandra, Stockport County**, (manager) **Colchester United**. *Keynotes* Turned professional with Stoke City in January 1939, moving to Hull City for £22,500 in February 1951. He joined Crewe Alexandra for £1,250 in February 1956 and Stockport County for the same amount in October 1957. Prior to the 1950 **World Cup**, Franklin joined the Colombian club Independiente Santa Fé of Bogota, returning to the UK after a few months. On his return, he was suspended for four months for walking out on Stoke. Franklin made 323 **Football League** appearances. He and Billy

Wright played in England's first 27 international matches after **World War II**, starting against **Northern Ireland** on 28 September 1946. Included in the **Football League Centenary 100 players**.

Fratton Park   *ground*   English football ground situated in Portsmouth, Hampshire; home of **Portsmouth**. *Dossier* Ground capacity: 19,179. Pitch dimensions 104m x 66m. Record attendance: 51,385 v **Derby County** (26 Febraury 1949, **FA Cup**, sixth round). Best average attendance: 37,082 (1948-49). *History* Portsmouth played its first match at Fratton Park on 2 March 1899 (v **Southampton**, friendly). The club's founders had bought the land, which is near Fratton station, for £4,950 in 1898. The ground was extensively developed, including the construction of an Archibald **Leitch**-designed south stand, during the inter-war period, which coincided with Pompey's heyday. Fratton Park has the distinction of staging the first floodlit **Football League** match on 22 February 1956 (v **Newcastle United**, Division One), although kick-off was delayed for 10 minutes after the lights failed. Later, the Portsmouth **supporters' club** provided the finances to erect **floodlights** on corner pylons. After Jim Gregory bought the club in May 1988, Portsmouth pursued plans to build a new £10 million stadium on adjacent railway land, but it was unable to reach agreement with British Rail (the UK's former state rail company) and began redeveloping Fratton Park. In 1993, following consultation with the local authority, the club announced plans to build a new stadium, the Parkway Stadium, on council-owned land at Farlington. Fratton Park was granted a one year extension to the August 1994 **all-seater stadium deadline** while the Department of Environment (DoE) studied the club's Parkway Stadium plans, only for the DoE to reject the proposal in December 1994. Since then, Portsmouth has pursued the redevelopment of Fratton Park. The ground has staged one full **England** international (v **Wales**, 2 March 1903). The first floodlit match at Fratton Park took place on 2 March 1953 (v Southampton, friendly).

Fredrikstad FK (Fotball Klubb) *club* Norwegian league club based in Fredrikstad, founded in 1903. Ground: Fredrikstad, capacity: 16,000. Strip: white shirts, red shorts. **European Cup** second round 1961. Norwegian Cup 1932, 1935, 1936, 1938, 1940, 1950, 1957, 1961, 1966, 1984; Norwegian league champions 1938, 1939, 1949, 1951, 1952, 1954, 1957, 1960, 1961.

free   *n.*   **free transfer**.

free kick   *rules*   method of restarting a game after it has been stopped in order to punish a team for a **foul**, **handball** or other infringement of the **Laws of the game** (Law XIII). The kick is awarded by the referee to the side that did not commit the offence, and is either **direct** – where a goal can be scored directly from the free kick – or **indirect** (where a second player must contact the ball before a goal can be scored), depending on the nature of the offence (see **direct free kick** and

indirect free kick for list of offences). The referee will signal which type of free kick has been awarded: by raising his hand above his head for an indirect kick. Where appropriate, a referee may additionally punish an individual player for the offence with a **caution** or **sending off**. With two exceptions (below), a free kick is taken from the point where the offence was committed. All opposition players must be at least 9.15 metres (10 yards) from the ball when a free kick is taken, or outside the **penalty area** if the free kick is awarded inside the defending team's penalty area. Failure to observe the 9.15-metre rule may receive a caution or may be sent off for a repeated offence. A free kick taken from a defending team's penalty area must be kicked directly outside that area and all opposition players must not enter the penalty area until the ball has left the area. The kick must be retaken if the ball fails to leave the penalty area. Goalkeepers must not handle free kicks passed directly to them (see **pass to the goalkeeper**). A free kick awarded to a defending team in its own **goal area** can be taken from anywhere within that goal area. An indirect free kick awarded to an attacking side within the goal area must be taken on the **goal area line** parallel to the **goal line** from the point nearest to the offence. The ball must be still when a free kick is taken. A player taking a free kick cannot touch the ball again until another player, from either team, has touched the ball. In this event, an indirect free kick will be awarded to the opposition. When a free kick is taken, players, from either side, are not allowed to unfairly distract the opposition players. Players who do so may be cautioned for **unsporting behaviour**. If a player kicks the ball into his or her own goal directly from a free kick, then a **corner kick** is awarded to the opposition, unless the ball had not left a player's own penalty area (as above) in which case the free kick would be retaken. If an indirect free kick results in the ball going into the opponent's goal without it touching another player, then a goal kick is given to the opposition.

Free State League   *competition*   former name (until 1936) of the League of Ireland.

free transfer   *regulations*   **transfer** of a player's **registration** to a new club where no **transfer fee** or **compensation fee** is involved. There are several scenarios where free transfers arise. **1.** A club may decide to offer a **contract player** to another club for no fee if the player is considered surplus to requirements: the financial incentive to the club is that it will no longer have to pay the player's wages and other overheads. The player can, of course, refuse to sign for the new club, or sue for breach of contract if he is not retained on his contractual terms. **2.** An **out-of-contract player** who is at least 24 years of age is automatically entitled to a free transfer (FA Premier League rule L.10, Football League regulation 59.1, Scottish Football League rule 60.1): this avoids the kind of contractual entrapment that players were previously forced to endure (see **Bosman ruling**) and offers the player the chance to negotiate better terms with a new club. **3.** An out-of-contract player who is under-24-years' old is entitled to a free transfer only if the club has not offered a new contract, or the contract is on terms inferior to the previous one (FA Premier League rule L.12, Football League regulation 59.6, Scottish Football League rule 60): the under-24 rule allows clubs the chance to gain some compensation for the training and development of their youth players and was introduced at the end of the 1997-98 season in an effort to stave off any legal challenge, under the Bosman ruling, to the British compensation-fee system. **4.** Any player who has been released by a club (ie whose registration has been cancelled) is entitled to a free transfer, unless the registration was cancelled because of a permanent disability (in which case the player will not play again) **5.** Any out-of-contract player (regardless of age) in the United Kingdom, is free to join any club outside the United Kingdom on a free transfer. However, a player cannot re-register with the **Football League** or **Scottish Football League** within 12 months, except with the permission of the Football League Board/Scottish Football League management committee (Football League regulation 59.15, Scottish Football League rule 60.12). If a player returns to the UK, the previous Football League club may be entitled to a **compensation fee** (decided by the **Football League Appeals Committee**).

freedom of contract *regulations* the freedom of a player to transfer to any club after the expiry of his/her previous contract. In principle, the player's former club has no right to determine where the player moves to and is not entitled to a **transfer fee**. The club, may, however, be entitled to a **compensation fee** if the player is under-24 years of age and is transferred within the United Kingdom (FA Premier League rule L.12, Football League regulation 59.6, Scottish Football League rule 60). *History* Freedom of contract was introduced in England and Wales in 1978 by the **Football League** in agreement with the **Professional Footballers' Association**, to allow a player to **transfer** to a new club at the end of his contract, whilst allowing the player's former club to receive financial compensation for its supposed investment in the training and development of the player. The 1978 scheme replaced *in toto* the **retain and transfer system** (first outlawed in 1963). Under the 1978 system, a transfer fee was – and still is – payable during a player's contract. However, at the end of a player's contract, if a club wanted to retain the player or receive a compensation fee then it would be obliged to offer a new contract on terms at least as good as before and to continue to pay the player's wages. If an inferior contract was offered, then the player would be entitled to a **free transfer**. If the clubs failed to agree on a compensation fee, then it would be settled by the **Football League Appeals Committee**. The 1978 system was flawed because a club offering a new contract could still prevent a player from moving if a second club was not able to match the asking price: in other words, it still had some "ownership" of an out-of-contract player. Greater freedom of contracts emerged in

1995 as a result of the **Bosman ruling** that, technically, means that players should become free agents at the end of their contracts. The British and Northern Ireland football associations were slow to adopt the full implications of the ruling such that, initially, this free-agent status was restricted to players moving overseas (ie away from the registration rules of their own leagues): Michael Hughes became the first *British* player to be signed on a free transfer under the Bosman ruling; he moved from **Strasbourg** to **West Ham United** in July 1996. An attempt to stave off a legal challenge to what remained of the compensation-fee system was made at the end of the 1997-98 season. The British football associations introduced the principle of compensation fees for **out-of-contract players** aged under 24 years. Such fees, it was argued, should be paid on the transfer of young players as compensation for training and development.

Freemasons Tavern *n.* now the Freemasons Hall, Great Queen Street, London WC2. Birthplace and venue of the first meeting of the **Football Association**, 26 October 1863.

Freight Rover Trophy *competition* the renamed **Associate Members Cup** between 1984-85 and 1986-87, and a competition only open to clubs from Divisions Three and Four. *Final results* 1984–85 **Wigan Athletic** 3–1 **Brentford**, 1985-86 **Bristol City** 3–0 **Bolton Wanderers**, 1986-87 **Mansfield Town** 1–1 Bristol City (a.e.t. Mansfield won 5–4 pens.).

French Guiana (Guyane Française) *country affiliated to French Football Federation* overseas region of France on the north coast of South America, bordered by **Surinam** and **Brazil**. Area: 91,000 sq km 35,125 sq miles). Population: 114,808. Languages: Creole, French and some American Indian languages. Capital: Cayenne. *Dossier* Football association (Ligue Guyanaise de Football, Cayene), neither affiliated to **FIFA**, **CONCACAF** nor **CONMEBOL**, but is affiliated to the French Football Federation (Fédération Française de Football). Season played from March to December. The national team competes in the **Caribbean Nations Cup** (despite being in South America), while clubs compete in the **CONCACAF Champions Cup** (in the Caribbean qualifying tournament). *International tournament record* **Olympic Games** – never entered; **Women's World Cup** – never entered; **World Cup** – never entered; **Caribbean Nations Cup** – third of four in the first round group stage of the 1995 finals tournament; **CONCACAF Championship/Gold Cup** – never qualified. *Record against British and Irish national teams* none played. Leading clubs: US Sinnamary (based in Sinnamary), FC AK Regina, Geldar Kourou (based in Kourou).

French Polynesia *country OFC* see **Tahiti/ French Polynesia**.

fresh legs *informal* substitute brought on to the field late in a match to replace a tired (rather than an injured) player.

Friedel, Brad *player* Goalkeeper. **United States of America** international (53 caps, 1992-). Born 18 May

1971. Clubs **Brøndby**, **Galatasaray**, **Columbus Crew**, **Liverpool**. *Keynotes* Bought by Liverpool for £1 million in December 1997 from Columbus Crew. Friedel's contract was owned by the **Major League Soccer**, which received the transfer fee. He played in the 1998 **World Cup** finals. A **work-permit** restriction placed by the UK Department for Education and Employment required him to play 75% of games for Liverpool in his first season. He had previously signed provisionally for **Newcastle United** in 1994, but was not granted a work permit. *Honours* Pan-American Games gold medal (USA, 1991).

Friedenreich, Artur *player* Striker. **Brazil** international (17 caps, eight goals, 1914-30). Born 1892. Career 1909–1935. *Clubs* Germania, Ipiranga, Americao, Paulistano, **São Paulo FC**, **Flamengo**. *Keynotes* Friedenreich was born of mixed parents; his father was German and his mother Brazilian. Friedenreich played for the first-ever Brazilian national side; in a warm-up game against **Exeter City** on 21 July 1914 (2–0). He is thought to be the world record goalscorer at club and national senior level, with 1,329 goals between 1909 and 1935.

friendly *n.* fixture that is not part of a formal competition, such as a league or cup. They may be arranged for pre-season practice, for a player's **testimonial** or for charity. *Regulations* **Premier League** clubs must not arrange friendlies until the League fixture list has been published; friendlies must not interfere with a League match (FA Premier League rule E.8). **Football League** clubs must, with the exception of officially sanctioned matches (e.g. **FA Cup** ties), always give priority to League matches, and must not play other matches that would interfere with League matches (Football League regulation 29). **Scottish Football League** clubs must obtain permission from the League Management Committee before staging a friendly; such matches must not interfere with the other club's home fixtures (Scottish Football League 83). *Keynotes* The record attendance for a club friendly match is 104,679 (**Rangers** v **Eintracht Frankfurt**, 17 October 1961, **Hampden Park**, Glasgow).

Fuchs, Gottfried *player* Striker. **Germany** international. *Keynotes* Scored 10 goals in one game when Germany beat **Russia** 16–0 in the Stockholm **Olympic Games** in 1912.

Fulham *club* English league. *Dossier* Ground: **Craven Cottage**, west London, capacity: 19,250. Strip: white shirts with red and black trim, black shorts and white socks with red and black trim. Nickname: the Cottagers. Record attendance: 49,335 v **Millwall** (8 October 1938, Division Two). Best average attendance: 33,030 (1949-50). Biggest win: 10–1 v **Ipswich Town** (26 December 1963, Division One). Biggest defeat: 0–10 **Liverpool** (23 September 1986, **League Cup**, second round, 1st leg. *History* Formed in 1879 by two clergymen as Fulham St Andrew's Sunday School FC. The present name was adopted in 1888. Fulham played at several venues, including the Ranelagh Club, Purser's

Cross and Eelbrook Common, and a ground-share with Wasps Rugby Club before buying Craven Cottage in 1894. The club turned professional in 1898, becoming a limited company in 1903. In 1907, Fulham was elected to the Second Division after the club won the **Southern League** Championship twice, in 1902 and 1903. Fulham's most successful period occurred in the 1960s, when the club spent nine consecutive seasons in Division One. Fulham was an **FA Cup** semi-finalist twice in five seasons, in 1958 (3–5 replay v **Manchester United**) and 1962 (1–2 replay v **Burnley**), having only once before reached the last four of the competition (1936, 1–2 v **Sheffield United**). Fulham has never won a major trophy although the club did contest the second all-London FA Cup Final in 1975 (0-2 v **West Ham United**). In 1988-89, Fulham reached the semi-final stage of the end-of-season Division Three **playoffs**. The club was reformed in 1987 after it almost ceased to exist: only the refusal of the **Football League management committee** stood between Fulham and a merger with nearby **Queens Park Rangers**. A group formed by the ex-Fulham inside-forward, former chairman of the **Professional Footballers Association** and TV pundit Jimmy **Hill** finally bought the Fulham name and the players' contracts. Hill remained in control until May 1997, when Mohamed Al Fayed, owner of the London retail store Harrods, acquired the club for £9 million. In September 1997, Kevin **Keegan** was appointed chief operating officer and Ray Wilkins became team manager. Keegan replaced Wilkins as manager in May 1998, three days before the first leg of the end-of-season Second Division **playoff** semi-final against **Grimsby Town**. After taking Fulham to the Second Division title in 1998-99, Keegan resigned to take charge of the **England** national team. Fulham became the first club to be sponsored by a trade union when the London Region of the General, Municipal and Boilermakers Union (GMB) agreed financial support in 1993. The club was the last Divsion One club (at the time) to install **floodlights** (September 1962). *League record* Division One 1949-50 to 1951-52, 1959-60 to 1967-68; First Division 1998-99; 1999-00–; Division Two 1907-08 to 1927-28, 1932-33 to 1948-49, 1952-53 to 1958-59, 1968-69, 1971-72 to 1979-80, 1982-83 to 1985-86; Second Division 1992-93 to 1993-94; 1997, 1998-99; Division Three 1969-70 to 1970-71; Third Division 1994-95 to 1996-97; Division Three (South) 1928-29 to 1931-32. *Honours* Second Division 1998-99; Division Two 1948-49; Division Three (South) 1931-32; Southern League 1906, 1907. *Records* Johnny **Haynes** is Fulham's most capped player (56 for England); he also holds the record for club League appearances (592); Gordon Davies is Fulham's record League goalscorer (159, 1978-84, 1986-91).

full contract *regulations* long-term **contract** and **registration** of a player. Contracts must be within the rules of the relevant league governing body (such as the FA **Premier League**, **Football League**, **Scottish**

Premier League or **Scottish Football League**). Full contracts may be for any period provided that it expires on 30 June in a specified year (FA Premier League rule J.10, Football League regulation 55.2, Scottish Football League rule 54; see also **part-time contract**). The Football League and Premier League prohibit contracts being given to players under 17 years of age (Football League regulation 55.1, FA Premier League rule K.4); the Scottish Football League allows professional contracts for players over 16 years of age (Scottish Football League rule 44). Premier League and Scottish Football League clubs are prohibited from offering contracts lasting more than three years to players under 18 years old (FA Premier League rule J.10.1, Scottish Football League rule 54). Clubs are free to renegotiate or amend the contract, on terms agreeable to both parties, provided that the new contract is set to expire at least 12 months after the previous one (FA Premier League rule J.27, Football League regulation 55.2). Premier League clubs must not seek to amend a contract between the **transfer deadline** and the end of the season. Scottish Football League clubs must ensure that players under 21 who are on contracts lasting more than one year undergo a formal course of approved training (the training is provided jointly by the Scottish Football Association, Scottish Football League and Scottish Professional Footballers Association) (Scottish Football League rule 54.4). Compare **monthly contract**, **non-contract**

full-back *n.* **defender**, especially the left or right back.

Full Member *n.* formerly, a member club of the English **Football League** with full voting rights; full membership originally given just to clubs in Divisions One and Two. The term became redundant in 1992, after the breakaway of the FA **Premier League**. All clubs in the Football League (First, Second and Third Divisions) now have equal voting rights as **Members of the Football League**. Compare **Associate Member**.

Full Members Cup *competition* former knockout competition involving clubs from **Football League** Divisions One and Two (**Full Members**) that was launched in the aftermath of the **Heysel Stadium disaster** and the UEFA-imposed ban on English clubs competing in Europe. In its first season (1985-86), only 21 of the 44 Full Members, including only five from Division One, participated in the competition. The following season 37 clubs took part, although average attendances of 5,140 were only a marginal improvement on the previous year's 4,223. The competition was renamed the **Simod Cup** in 1988 after the sportswear company agreed a £120,000 sponsorship deal, which included a prize of £60,000 for the winners. All but four Full Members competed in the 1987-88 season and attendances improved 16% on average. In 1990, the competition became the **Zenith Data Systems Cup** before it ceased in 1992. *Final results* 1985-86 **Chelsea** 5–4 **Manchester City**, 1986-87 **Blackburn Rovers** 1–0 **Charlton Athletic**, 1987-88 **Reading**

4–1 **Luton Town**, 1988-89 **Nottingham Forest** 4–3 **Everton**, 1989-90 Chelsea 1–0 **Middlesbrough**, 1990-91 **Crystal Palace** 4–1 Everton, 1991-92 Nottingham Forest 3–2 **Southampton**.

full-strength team *regulations* a team comprising the best available players at a club (ie excluding only those who are injured or ineligible to play in the particular fixture). **Premier League**, **Football League** and **Scottish Football League** rules state that clubs should field their strongest side in all matches played under the auspices of their league (FA Premier League rule E.17, Football League regulation 21, Scottish Football League rule 68). *Keynotes* The principle that a club should field its strongest team was established at the founding of the Football league in 1888. This was reinforced in 1890 when the League ruled that the offence would be punishable by a fine of £50. Seven clubs were fined on 21 occasions between 1909 and 1912, all for fielding weak sides close to crucial **FA Cup** games. Burnley was fined £1,000 for fielding a team with nine players from outside its regular first team for a league game in March 1961. Burnley was scheduled to play a **European Cup** game and FA Cup semi-final shortly after.

full-time score *n.* the **score** or goal-tally at **full-time** in a game of football. See **result**.

full-time whistle *rules* blast on the referee's whistle to indicate that the **duration of play** has ended.

Fútbol war *n.* a war between **El Salvador** and **Honduras** in 1969, triggered by a football match, which lead to the deaths of more than 2,000 people. El Salvador had defeated Honduras in a **World Cup** qualifier playoff (3–2, in Mexico City). The playoff was the final trigger in a climate of continued border disputes and troubles involving migrant workers from El Salvador in Honduras. El Salvador troops invaded Honduras and 2,000 people were killed in the ensuing fighting. El Salvador went on to qualify for the World Cup finals in Mexico.

Futre, Paolo *player* **Portugal** international (1983-). Born 28 February 1966. *Clubs* **Sporting Clube de Portugal**, FC **Porto**, **Atlético Madrid**, **Benfica**, **Olympique de Marseille**, Reggiana (Italy). *Keynotes* Futre made his international debut aged only 17, and scored his first goal for Portugal on 30 January 1985 (2–3, v **Romania**, in Lisbon, friendly). He was voted fifth in *World Soccer* **World Footballer of the Year** 1987. Transferred to Reggiana for £8 million in 1993. *Honours* **European Cup** (Porto, 1987); Portuguese league champions (Porto, 1985, 1986); Spanish Cup (Atlético Madrid, 1991, 1992); *France Football* **European Footballer of the Year** runner-up 1987.

Futsal *n.* type of **indoor football** played on a pitch about the size of a basketball court. Unlike other forms of indoor football, the pitch is not directly bounded by walls; the ball can, therefore, go out of play. There are five players, including the goalkeeper. Players can be substituted – and returned to the play – at any time. Futsal is popular in a number of countries, including **Argentina**, **Belgium**, **Brazil**, **China**, **Italy**,

Netherlands, **Peru**, **Russia Spain**, **Ukraine** and **USA**. Brazil has the best record, having won the FIFA **Futsal World Championship** in 1989, 1992 and 1996. Other international tournaments include the European Futsal Championship, the African Futsal Championship and, since 1999, the Asian Futsal Championship.

Futsal World Championship *competition* international nations indoor football tournament (see **Futsal**) – the only indoor tournament hosted by **FIFA**. First played 1989 in the Netherlands. *Finals* 1989 **Brazil** beat **Netherlands**, in the Netherlands; 1992 Brazil beat **USA** in Hong Kong; 1996 Brazil beat **Spain**, in Spain. The fourth tournament is in 2000.

G

Gabon *country* *CAF* republic in central Africa on the Atlantic Ocean and equator, neighbouring **Cameroon**, **Congo** and **Equatorial Guinea**. Comparatively wealthy country, rich in natural resources, including oil. Independence from **France** in 1960. Area: 267,665 sq km 103,320 sq miles). Hot and wet all year, with average temperatures of 25°C. Population: 1,012,000 (1993 census). Languages: French, Fang, and Bantu dialects. Capital: Libreville. *Dossier* Football association (Fédération Gabonaise de Football, Libreville), formed in 1962, affiliated to **FIFA** in 1963 and **Confédération Africaine de Football** (CAF) in 1967, member of the **Union of Football Associations of Central Africa**, president Adrien Nkoghe-Essingone, general secretary Robert Mangollo-M'Voulou. Season played from October to July. National stadium: Omar Bongo Omnisport, Libreville, capacity: 30,000. National strip: green shirts, yellow shorts. First international game: 1960, v **Burkina Faso** (4–5, in Madagascar, friendly). Biggest victory: 7–0, v **Benin** (2 April 1995, in Libreville, friendly). Biggest defeat: 1–6, v **Guinea** (9 July 1967, in Conakry, Guinea, **Olympic Games** qualifier). *International tournament record* Olympic Games – first entered 1968, never qualified for finals tournament; **Women's World Cup** – never entered; **World Cup** – first entered 1990, qualifying tournament second round 1990, 1998; **African Nations Cup** – first entered 1972, quarter-final 1996 (lost to tournament runners-up **Tunisia** on penalties after a 1–1 draw in Durban, South Africa), also qualified for finals tournament 1994; **UDEAC Tournament** – 1985 (3–0, v Congo, in Libreville), 1988 (1–0, v Cameroon, in Cameroon); **Under-17 World Championship** – never qualified; **World Youth Cup** (under-20) – never qualified. *Record against British and Irish national teams* none played. *History* National league championship began 1968 (Olympique Sportif of Libreville won the first title). Gabon has twice won the UDEAC Tournament, the regional tournament of the Central African Customs and Economic Union (also contested by Cameroon, **Central African Republic**, **Chad**, Congo and Equatorial Guinea) It has never won the African Nations Cup. Gabon's 1998 World Cup qualifier with **Morocco** (6 April 1997, in Libreville) was abandoned after 55 minutes following a pitch invasion by the home fans.

Morocco was leading 4–0 when the match was stopped: the score was allowed to stand. *Record in international club tournaments* **African Cup of Champion Clubs** – **US Mbila Nzambi** (quarter-final 1981), **ASMO/FC 105** (quarter-final 1984, 1988), **Mbilinga** (quarter-final 1995), **AS Sogara** (quarter-final 1993, 1994; **African Cup-winners Cup** – AS Sogara (runners-up 1986), Mbilinga (semi-final 1994, quarter-final 1998); **CAF Cup** – ASMO/FC 105 (quarter-final 1992), Mbilinga (quarter-final 1993) .

Gaelic football *n.* a type of football played in the **Republic of Ireland**, **Northern Ireland** as well as some parts of the **United States of America**, **Canada**, **Australia**, **Scotland**, **England** and some other parts of Europe. The game is played with 15 players on each side using a round ball. The goals resemble **rugby football** posts, though there is a net under the crossbar; points can be scored under or over the posts. Players can kick, punch ("hand-pass") and bounce the ball to retain possession; players can carry the ball for four steps, after which they must kick, bounce or release it. There is no **offside** rule. As in **association football**, there is a **goalkeeper**. The game has the same origins as association football, rugby football and **Australian rules**, though is most closely aligned with the latter. It is played throughout the year and has remained as a strictly amateur game. In Ireland, it is played at club and county level. The All-Ireland Championship, for county sides, is played on a knock-out basis, with the final in September at Croke Park, Dublin, the headquarters of the sport.

Gainsborough Trinity *club* former-English league. *Dossier* Ground: Northolme, Gainsborough, Lincolnshire. Record League attendance: 7,000. *Keynotes* Founded in 1872, the club was elected to Division Two in 1896-97. It failed to get re-elected in 1911-12, having finished in the bottom three in the previous three seasons, and was replaced by neighbours **Lincoln City**. Trinity's highest League position was sixth in Division Two, which the club achieved in 1904-05. The club play in the Northern League. *League record* Division Two 1896-97 to 1911-12.

Galatasaray Spor Kolübü *club* Turkish national league club based in Istanbul (on the main European side of the Bosphorus), founded 1905. Ground: Ali Sami

Yen, capacity: 40,000. Strip: red and yellow shirts, red shorts. **European Cup** semi-final 1989 (1–5 agg., v **Steaua Bucharest**), quarter-final league 1994 (after beating **Manchester United** 3–3 agg., **away goals**, in the second round), qualified for Champions League 1995, 1998; **European Cup-winners Cup** quarter-final 1992; Istanbul League (regional league operated from 1924 to 1958) champions 1925, 1926, 1927, 1929, 1931, 1949, 1955, 1956, 1957, 1958; Turkish Cup 1963, 1964, 1965, 1966, 1973, 1976, 1982, 1985, 1991, 1993, 1996, 1999; Turkish league champions 1962, 1963, 1969, 1971, 1972, 1973, 1987, 1988, 1993, 1994, 1997, 1998. Notable players: Tanju Colak, **Hakan** Sükür, Gheorghe **Hagi**.

Gallacher, Hughie   *player*   Striker. **Scotland** international (20 caps, 22 goals). Born 2 February 1903. Career ca. 1921–1939. *Clubs* **Queen of the South, Airdrieonians, Newcastle United, Chelsea, Derby County, Notts County, Grimsby Town, Gateshead**. *Honours* League Championship (Newcastle United 1926-27); **Scottish FA Cup** (Airdrieonians 1924). *Keynotes* Scorer of 387 goals in 541 League appearances in England and Scotland. Gallacher scored 22 goals in 20 matches for Scotland, including a Scottish record five goals in one match against **Northern Ireland** (23 February 1929). Chelsea paid £10,000 for Gallacher in May 1930 and his cumulative transfers fees totalled £23,000 – a record for the period. Committed suicide in 1957. Included in the **Football League Centenary 100 players**.

Galloping Major   *player*   affectionate nickname for Ferenc **Puskás**.

Galway United FC   *club*   Republic of Ireland national league club based in Galway, county Galway on the west coast, founded 1976. Ground: Terryland Park, capacity: 5,000. Strip: maroon shirts, white shorts. FAI League Cup 1997; Republic of Ireland **FAI Cup** 1991, runners-up 1985; Republic of Ireland league runners-up 1986.

Gambia, The   *country*   CAF   republic in west Africa, on Atlantic Ocean, surrounded by **Senegal**. Smallest country in Africa, just 470 km (292 miles) long and, on average, 24 km (15 miles) wide. Independence from United Kingdom in 1965. Area: 10,690 sq km (4,125 sq miles). Monsoon rainfall from July to October. Population: 1,090,000 (1995 est.). Languages: English, Mandinka, Fula and Wolof. Capital: Banjul. *Dossier* Gambia Football Association formed in 1952, affiliated to **FIFA** in 1966 and **Confédération Africaine de Football** (CAF) in 1962, member of the **West African Football Union**, president Ousman Conateh, general secretary Allasana Jitteh. Season played from November to July. National stadium: Box Bar Stadium, Banjul, capacity: 10,000. National strip: white shirts, white shorts. Nickname of national team: the Scorpions. First international game: 16 November 1968, v **Sierra Leone** (1–2, friendly in Freetown, Sierra Leone); the Gambia played an earlier international match against a French amateur side (1963, 1–5, in Senegal). Biggest victory: 4–1 v **Guinea** (21 July 1983, in Mauritania,

Amilcar Cabral Cup) Biggest defeat: 0–8, v Guinea (1972, **All-Africa Games** qualifier). *International tournament record* **Olympic Games** – first entered 1976, never qualified for finals tournament; **Women's World Cup** – never entered; **World Cup** – first entered 1982, never beyond first qualifying round; **African Nations Cup** – first entered 1976, never qualified for finals tournament; **Amilcar Cabral Cup** – runners-up 1980 (0–1, v Senegal, in Banjul), 1985 (0–1, v Senegal, in Banjul); **Under-17 World Championship** – never qualified; **World Youth Cup** (under-20) – never qualified. *Record against British and Irish national teams* none played. *Record in international club tournaments* **African Cup of Champion Clubs** – **Real Olympique Banjul** (second round 1979, 1995); **African Cup-winners Cup** – **Wallidan Leader** (second round 1995). Other leading clubs **Mass Sosseh, Hawks**.

game plan   *n.*   team strategy for a particular match.

game of two halves   *informal*   hackneyed expression to describe a match where the two halves are characterised by different styles of play, e.g. defensive/all-out attack; or domination by one team in the first half, and the other in the second; or where the first half is dull, and the second is more exciting.

Garcia, Atilio   *player*   Striker. **Uruguay** international (seven goals, ca. 1943-45). *Club* **Nacional**. *Keynotes* Top scorer in the Uruguayan league for a record seven times in a row: 1938 (20 goals), 1939 (22 goals), 1940 (18 goals), 1941 (23 goals), 1942 (19 goals), 1943 (18 goals), 1944 (21 goals), and again in 1946 (21 goals). He played few games for Uruguay, but scored a **hat-trick** in the 5–1 defeat of **Ecuador** in the 1945 **Copa America** (24 January 1945, in Santiago, Chile).

Garrincha   *player*   Winger. Real name: Manoel Francisco dos Santos. Striker. **Brazil** international (50 caps, 12 goals, 1958-66). Born 28 October 1933, in Pau Grande, Brazil, died 1983. *Clubs* Pau Grande, **Botafogo, Corinthians, Atlético Junior** (Colombia), **Flamengo**, Red Star (now **Red Star 93**, Paris, France). *Keynotes* Garrincha, named after a small bird, was a gifted outside right in the Brazilian teams of the late 1950s and 1960s. He had required corrective surgery on deformed legs as a child and was considered lucky to walk. Garrincha provided the crosses for both of Vavà's goals in the 1958 World Cup final against Sweden in Stockholm; both preceded by runs down the right wing (Brazil went on to win 5–2). Garrincha played in Brazil's **Copa America** runners-up team of 1959. He was equal-top goalscorer at the 1962 World Cup finals, with four goals, and scored twice in both the 3–1 quarter-final victory over **England** and the 4–2 semi-final victory over the host nation **Chile**. Garrincha was sent off in the semi-final in Santiago, for pushing a Chilean player in retaliation, apparently after opposition players had spat at, sworn at, and pushed him. Despite the sending off, **FIFA** ruled that Garrincha could compete in the final against **Czechoslovakia** (3–1). Garrincha scored his last international goal in the 1966 World Cup finals in England, in a 2–0 victory over **Bulgaria** at **Goodison Park**, Liverpool (Brazil was eliminated after the first round). He died of alcohol poisoning in 1983. *Honours* **World Cup** 1958, 1962; World Cup **Golden Boot** (joint) 1962.

Gascoigne, Paul *player* Midfield. **England** international (57 caps, 9 goals). Born 25 May 1967. Career ca. 1985–. *Clubs* **Newcastle United**, **Tottenham Hotspur**, **Lazio**, **Rangers**, **Middlesbrough**. *Keynotes* Gascoigne made 92 **Football League** appearances for Newcastle United before moving to Tottenham Hotspur for £2 million in 1988. An ebullient performance for England at the 1990 **World Cup** and his tears after being booked in the semi-final against West **Germany** transformed him into a star and he was voted BBC television's Sports Personality of the Year. After agreeing a £8.5 million move to Lazio, Gascoigne badly damaged knee ligaments following a rash tackle in the 15th minute of the 1991 FA Cup final and was out of the game for over a year. In April 1994, he broke a leg during a Lazio training session and in three seasons with the Rome club he made only 42 **Serie A** appearances. He moved to Rangers for £4.3 million in 1995 and although he was voted Footballer of the Year (Scotland) in 1996 he spell in Glasgow was accompanied by several controversial incidents, including twice being reprimanded for mock **flute playing** – which was considered provocative. Gascoigne transferred to Middlesbrough for £3.45 million in March 1998. His first appearance for the club was in the 1998 **League Cup** final when he went on as substitute (0–2 v **Chelsea**). Gascoigne made his debut for England against **Denmark** on 14 September 1988. He was controversially omitted from England's final 22-man squad for the 1998 World Cup. Included in the **Football League Centenary 100 players**. *Honours* **FA Cup** (Tottenham Hotspur 1991); Scottish League (Rangers 1995-96, 1996-97); **Scottish FA Cup** (Rangers 1996); **Scottish League Cup** (Rangers 1996-97).

gastrocnemius *medical* the calf muscle that joins the back of the knee to the calcaneum (heel bone).

gate compensation money *regulations* monies paid out to a home club whose match is postponed for a compensable reason in lieu of reduced gate receipts for the rearranged fixture. **Premier League** and **Football League** clubs whose home league matches are postponed because of a clash with the away club's **League Cup** of **FA Cup** tie are able to claim such compensation: the sum paid out is calculated as the difference between the actual gate receipts for the rearranged league match and the average gate receipt for all the club's home league fixtures for the season (FA Premier League rules C3 and C4, Football League Article 68). Compensation for Premier League clubs is paid from a pool held by the Football Association (for FA Cup ties) and a pool agreed with the Football League and Football Association for League Cup games. Football League clubs receive money from the **Pool account** (income from the Football Association's FA Cup pool is paid into

this account). The moneys are not paid, however, for Saturday matches rearranged for another Saturday.

gate receipts *n.pl.* total proceeds from admitting spectators to the ground for a football match (usually including an appropriate share of the **season ticket** revenue). Net gate receipts are the gate receipts after expenses have been deducted – such as for policing, printing and advertising, admissions personnel, floodlighting, security and tax. Gate receipts from league matches usually go to the **home club**, whereas receipts from cup matches played as a single tie are generally divided between the participating clubs (after the home club's expenses). Although in the **Scottish Football League**, the home club normally retains the entire gate receipts for a league match (Scottish Football League rule 40), if a match is abandoned and a replay is required, then the visitors must receive either its incurred expenses or about one-fifth of the gate receipts from the abandoned match, whichever is the lesser (Scottish Football League rule 41). *Keynotes* In 1983, the **Football League** rules were changed to allow the home club to keep all the receipts from home matches, bar a 4% League levy. The rules had, hitherto, required that a percentage be given to the away club. This did not affect gate-receipt rules on cup games.

Gateshead *club* former-English league. *Dossier* Ground: Horsley Hill and Redheugh Park. Record attendance: 21,000 v **Luton Town** (Horsley Hill, 29 January 1921, **FA Cup**, second round). *Keynotes* Founded as South Shields Adelaide in 1899, the club became Gateshead in 1930 when it moved to a new ground, Redheugh Park. The club was elected to Division Two in 1919-20. Gateshead was an FA Cup quarter-finalist in 1952-53 (0–1 v **Bolton Wanderers**). The club failed to get re-elected in 1959-60 and was replaced by **Peterborough United**, despite having gained more points than either **Oldham Athletic** or **Hartlepool United**. Gateshead's highest League position was achieved as South Shields in 1921-22, when the club finished sixth in Division Two. In 1931-32, Gateshead finished second in Division Three (North), losing the title on **goal average**. The club folded in 1973. It reformed in 1977 and plays in the Northern League. *League record* Division Two 1919-20 to 1927-28; Division Three (North) 1928-29 to 1957-58; Division Four 1958-59 to 1959-60.

Gay Games *competition* international sports tournament organised for homosexual and lesbian teams, held every four years. Includes a "Gay World Cup" football tournament. Played in Amsterdam in July 1998.

Gay Meadow *ground* English football ground situated in Shrewsbury, Shropshire; home of **Shrewsbury Town**. *Dossier* Ground capacity: 8,000. Pitch dimensions: 104m x 68m. Record attendance: 18,917 v **Walsall** (26 April 1961, Division Three). Best average attendance: 9,799 (1951-52). *History* Shrewsbury moved to Gay Meadow in 1910, playing its first match there on 10 September (v **Wolverhampton Wanderers** reserves, Birmingham League). The club leased the ground from the local council which had purchased the site for £1,365 in 1909. The club bought the ground's freehold for £6,750 in 1959 on condition it was used only for "sporting and cultural" purposes. Much of the work to enclose the ground during the 1930s was funded by the **supporters' club**. Gay Meadow's existence was threatened in 1984 when an attempt to place a compulsory purchase order on parts of the ground to enable a new road to be built was defeated only after a three-hour debate in the House of Commons. The first official floodlit match at Gay Meadow took place on 25 November 1959 (v **Stoke City**, friendly), although they were first used during the second half of a Division Three game on 21 November (v **Queens Park Rangers**).

Gay World Cup *n.* see **Gay Games**.

Gayfield Park *ground* Scottish football ground situated in Arbroath, Tayside; home of **Arbroath**. *Dossier* Ground capacity: 6,488. Pitch dimensions: 105m x 65m. Record attendance: 13,510 v **Rangers** (23 February 1952, **Scottish FA Cup**, third round). *Keynotes* Arbroath first played at Gayfield Park in 1880. The ground was the setting for the biggest score in an official UK football match: Arbroath beat Bon Accord 36–0 in September 1885 (Scottish FA Cup, first round). In 1884, Arbroath beat Rangers in the Scottish FA Cup, only for the **Scottish Football Association** to order the match to be replayed because the pitch was too small. **Floodlights** were first installed in 1955. Gayfield is closer to the sea than any other senior football ground in the UK.

Gençlerbirligi Spor Kolübü *club* Turkish national league club based in the capital Ankara, founded 1923. Ground: 19 Mayis (shared with **MKE Ankaragücü**), capacity: 24,000. Strip: red and black striped shirts, black shorts. Turkish Cup 1987.

General Eyadema Cup *competition* see **West African Football Union General Eyadema Cup**.

Genoa (1893) *club* Italian league. *Dossier* Ground: **Luigi Ferraris**, Liguria, capacity, 42,000 all seated. Strip: red and blue halved shirts, blue shorts. Nickname: Grifone (Griffins). *History* Formed in 1893 as the Genoa Football and Cricket Club. In 1899, the club changed its name to Genoa FC and, in 1926, it adopted the current title Genoa 1893. Mussolini's Fascist **World War II** government, which disliked the English sounding Genoa, forced the club to switch to the Italian Genova 1893 between 1929 and 1945. James Spensley, a principal figure in the club's formation, played in goal for Genoa when it won five of the first seven Italian League championships. The club was relegated for the first time in 1934 and it has since regularly alternated between **Serie A** and Serie B, even dropping to Serie C in 1970. Genoa's most recent major trophy, the Italian Cup, was won in 1937 (1–0 v **Roma (AS)**). Following a fourth place Serie A finish in 1990-91, the club reached the semi-final stage of the **UEFA Cup** the following season (3–4 agg., v **Ajax**). *Honours* Italian League 1898 (2–1 v **Internazionale**), 1899 (2–0 v Internazionale), 1900

(1–0 v FC Torinese), 1902 (2–0 v **AC Milan**), 1903 (3–0 v **Juventus**), 1904 (1–0 v Juventus), 1915 (declared winners), 1923 (6–1 agg., v **Lazio**), 1924 (4–2 agg., v Savio); Italian Cup 1937 (1–0 v Roma (AS)); **Anglo-Italian Cup** 1996 (5–2 v **Port Vale**).

gentleman's agreement *n.* an understanding between players over their conduct following an injury to a player; it is not bound by the **Laws of the game**. If a player is lying injured on the pitch, but the referee has not stopped play, the players' custom is for the ball to be kicked over the touchline so that the injured player can receive medical attention. When the match is restarted it is generally accepted that the ball is thrown back to the other team, for example to a defender, or kicked on to the goalkeeper. Similarly, if the referee has stopped play because of an injury to a player, and restarts the game with a **drop-ball**, it is customary for only one player to take part in the restart and kick the ball to the opposition's defending players or goalkeeper. *Keynotes* One of the most unusual reasons for a **rematch** was the **FA Cup** fifth-round tie between **Arsenal** and **Sheffield United** in 1998-99. The first match, at **Highbury** (13 February 1999), finished with a 2–1 victory for Arsenal. The club's second goal, however, was controversially scored after the game had been stopped so that an injured Sheffield player could receive medical attention. Arsenal's Ray Parlour restarted the match with a throw-in and, following custom, dutifully threw the ball towards the Sheffield goalkeeper. The ball was intercepted by Arsenal's Nwankwo Kanu, who passed for Marc Overmars to shoot into the net. The match was delayed for several minutes as Sheffield players protested; the referee, Peter Jones, allowed the goal as no rule had been breached. After the match, Arsenal manager Arsene Wenger offered the game to be replayed, unhappy at the unsporting manner of the victory. The **Football Association** was called to adjudicate and made the unprecedented decision to arrange a rematch at Highbury (Arsenal again won 2–1, 23 February 1999). Earlier incidents of this breach of the "gentleman's agreement" include Arsenal's key **Premier League** match at Highbury against **Blackburn Rovers** in 19 April 1997. After play had been stopped because of an injury, the subsequent throw-in was chased by Blackburn's Chris Sutton and an Arsenal defender was forced to give away a **corner-kick**. This led to an 89th minute goal by Gary Flitcroft, earning Blackburn a 1–1 draw. The goal helped Blackburn in its quest to avoid relegation and, arguably, prevented Arsenal from gaining a place in the **European Cup** (losing out on goal difference to Premier League runners-up **Newcastle United**). On 30 January 1999 (Football League Second Division, **Racecourse Ground**), Jeff Whitley of **Wrexham** scored directly from a drop-ball following a player's injury in his club's game against **Preston North End**. On this occasion, the referee, Brian Coddington, disallowed the goal for unsporting behaviour; Preston won the match 5–0.

Gento, Francisco (Paco) *player* Left winger. **Spain** international (43 caps, five goals, ca. 1955-67). Born 22 October 1933. *Clubs* Nueva Montana, Astillero, Santander, **Real Madrid**. *Keynotes* Gento scored the extra-time winner for Real Madrid in the 1958 **European Cup** final against **AC Milan** (3-2, Heysel Stadium, Brussels). He appeared in all eight of Real's European Cup finals in the 1950s and 1960s and was only twice on the losing side. Gento played an instrumental part in the 1960 European Cup triumph over **Eintracht Frankfurt**; his 50 metre run and subsequent cross set up a header for **Puskas** to complete his hattrick (7-3, at **Hampden Park**, Glasgow). Gento played 800 games for Real, and scored 256 goals for his club. His six European Cup winner's medals is a tournament record. *Honours* European Cup (Real Madrid, 1956, 1957, 1958, 1959, 1960, 1966); Spanish league championship (Real Madrid, 1955, 1957, 1958, 1961, 1962, 1963, 1964, 1965, 1967, 1968, 1969).

Geoffroy-Guichard (Stade) *ground* French football ground situated in St Etienne; home of Association Sportive Saint-Etienne (see **Saint Etienne**). Ground capacity: 35,924 all seated. *History* Opened on 13 September 1931. Refurbished for the 1998 **World Cup** at a cost of nearly £10 million. During the tournament, the Stade Geoffroy-Guichard staged one match from each of groups A (**Morocco** v **Scotland**), B (**Austria** v **Chile**), D (**Spain** v **Paraguay**), G (**Mexico** v **Netherlands**), F (**Iran** v **Yugoslavia**); and a second round game (**Argentina** v **England**) – total attendance 197,184; average attendance 32,864.

George, Kim *referee* The first woman to **referee** an **FA Cup** match (February 1989, preliminary round).

Georgia *country UEFA* republic in south east Europe on the Black Sea, next to **Armenia**, **Azerbaijan**, **Turkey** and the Russian Federation. Existed as an independent republic from 1918 to 1921, established as part of the **Soviet Union** in 1921. Georgia was, initially, a component of the Transcaucasian Republic of the Soviet Union until 1936, when it became a Soviet Republic in its own right. Independence from Soviet Union in 1991. Area: 69,700 sq km (26,905 sq miles). Population: 5,430,000 (1994 census). Languages: Georgian, Russian, Armenian and Azeri. Capital: Tbilisi. Georgian Football Federation (Tbilisi) formed in 1991, affiliated to **FIFA** in 1992 and **Union of European Football Associations** (UEFA) in 1993, president Nodar Akhalkatsi, general secretary David Kvinikadze. Season played from August to May, with a four-month **winter break** from mid-November to mid-March. National stadium: Boris Paichadze, Tbilisi, capacity: 75,000. National strip: white shirts, black shorts. First international game: 8 February 1994, v **Slovenia** (0-1, in Ta'Qali, Malta, "Rothmans' tournament"). Biggest victory: 7-0, v Armenia (30 March 1997, in Tbilisi, friendly). Biggest defeat: 1-5 v **Nigeria** (11 June 1994, in Ibadan, Nigeria, friendly). Most capped players: Giorgi Nemsadze (33 appearances, 1994-), Georgi Kinkladze (29 appearances, 1994-),

Temur Ketsbaia 29 appearances, 1984-). Leading goalscorers: Revaz Arveladze (12 goals, 1994-), Shota Arveladze (11 goals in 28 appearances, 1994-), Temur Ketsbaia (10 goals, including Georgia's first-ever international goal, 1994-). Other notable international players: Aleksander **Chivadze**, Ramas Shengelia. *International tournament record* **Women's World Cup** – first entered 1999; **World Cup** – first entered 1998 (fourth in its five-nation qualifying group with three victories, one draw and four defeats); **European Championship** – first entered 1996 (third in its six-nation qualifying group, with five victories and five defeats); **European Championship for Women** – first entered 1998; **Under-17 World Championship** – never qualified; **World Youth Cup (under-20)** – never qualified. *World Cup performance* (finals and qualifiers to end of 1998 tournament) played eight, won three, drawn one, lost four, scored seven goals, conceded nine goals; win rate 37%; goals scored per game 0.87. *Record against British and Irish national teams* v **England**, played two, lost two; v **Wales**, played two, won two. *History* The Georgian national league and cup competitions started in 1990, with both competitions dominated by **Dynamo Tbilisi**; the club won six consecutive league and cup doubles from 1992 to 1997, and 10 straight championships from 1990-99; equalling the world record held by **Berlin FC** (**Al Faisaly** of **Jordan** has 13 consecutive league titles, but the run was broken by years in which the league was not played). Dynamo was the sixth most successful club in the former Soviet Union, winning two league championships and two Soviet Cups. It also won the **European Cup-winners Cup** in 1981; the most easterly club to win a major European competition. Georgia's national side played its first game in 1994 and won its first World Cup match on 7 June 1997 (2-0, v **Moldova**, in Tbilisi). Its 5-0 victory against Wales (16 November 1994, in Tbilisi, European Championship) was its first competition victory. *League system* Sixteen clubs compete in the national first division, with the bottom two clubs automatically relegated to the second division; the 13th- and 14th-placed clubs playoff with the third- and fourth-placed clubs in the second division for a possible third promotion/relegation place. Three points are awarded for a victory, with one for a draw; **goal difference** is used to separate clubs level on points. The national second division was, until 1996-97 divided into an Eastern and a Western Zone, with 37 clubs between them; a national second division of 16 clubs was introduced in 1997-98. *Record in international club tournaments* **European Cup** – Dynamo Tbilisi (second round 1980; European Cup-winners Cup – Dynamo Tbilisi (1981); **UEFA Cup** – Dynamo Tbilisi (third round 1974, 1978, 1988). Other leading clubs: **Dinamo Batumi**, **Guriya Lanchkuti**, **Kolkheti 1913 Poti**.

Gerland (Stade de) *ground* French football ground situated in Lyon, Rhône-Alpes; home of **Olympique Lyonnais**. Ground capacity: 43,895 all seated. *History*

Opened in 1926. The stadium is a listed building. Refurbished for the 1998 **World Cup** at a cost of £8.7 million. During the tournament, Stade de Gerland hosted one match from each of groups C (**Denmark** v **France**), E (**Mexico** v **South Korea**), F (**Iran** v **United States**), G (**Colombia** v **Romania**) and H (**Jamaica** v **Japan**); and a quarter-final (**Germany** v **Croatia**) – total attendance 245,260; average attendance 40,876. Stade de Gerland also hosted the 1986 **European Cup-winners Cup** final (**Dinamo Kiev** v **Atlético Madrid**, 39,300).

German Democratic Republic *former country* see **East Germany**.

Germano De Figureido *player* Defender. **Portugal** international (20 caps). Born 1933. *Clubs* Atlético Clube Portugal, **Benfica**. *Keynotes* Germano played in goal in the second half of the **European Cup** final in 1965 against Internazionale; he kept a **clean sheet**, though Benfica lost 0–1. *Honours* European Cup (Benfica, 1961, 1962); Portuguese league championship (Benfica, 1960, 1961, 1963, 1964, 1965).

Germany *country UEFA* republic in central Europe on the North Sea and Baltic Sea. Bordered by **Austria**, **Switzerland**, **France**, **Belgium**, **Luxembourg**, the **Netherlands**, **Denmark**, **Poland** and the **Czech Republic**. Germany's turbulent history during the 20th century includes the division into **East Germany** and West Germany in 1949. The country was reunited in October 1990 following the break-up of the Soviet bloc in eastern Europe. Area: 356,840 sq km (137,740 sq miles). Population: 81,540,000 (1995 est.). Language: German. Capital: Berlin. *Dossier* Football association (Deutscher Fussball-Bund, Frankfurt-am-Main) formed in 1900, founder member of **FIFA** in 1904, president Egidius Braun, general secretary Horst Schmidt. Germany remained affiliated to FIFA until 1946. West Germany rejoined FIFA in 1950, and joined the **Union of European Football Associations** (UEFA) as a founder member in 1954. East Germany joined FIFA in 1950, and became assimilated into the unified German association in 1990. Season played from August to May, with a winter break from mid-December to mid-February. National stadium: **Olympiastadion**, Munich, capacity: 64,000. National strip: white shirts, black shorts. First international game: 5 April 1908 v Switzerland (3–5, in Basle, Switzerland, friendly); first international game by West Germany: 22 November 1950, v Switzerland (1–0, in Stuttgart, friendly); see also East Germany. Biggest victories: 16–0, v **Russia** (1 July 1912, Stockholm, **Olympic Games** consolation tournament) and 13–0 v **Finland** (1 September 1940, in Leipzig, friendly). Biggest defeats: 0–9 v **England** (16 March 1909, in Oxford, friendly: the status of this match is disputed) and (as West Germany) 3–8 v **Hungary** (20 June 1954, in Basle, Switzerland, **World Cup** first round). Most capped players (West Germany and Germany combined): Lotthar **Matthäus** (135 appearances, 1980-99), Jürgen **Klinsmann** (108 appearances, 1987), Jurgen Kohler (105 appearances,

1986–1998), Franz **Beckenbauer** (103 appearances, 1965–77), Berti Vogts (96 appearances, 1967–78), Sepp **Maier** (95 appearances, 1966–79), Thomas Hassler (97 appearances, 1988–1998), Karl-Heinz **Rummenigge** (95 appearances, 1976–86). Leading goalscorers (West Germany and Germany combined): Gerd **Müller** (68 goals, 1966–74), Jürgen Klinsmann (47 goals), Rudi Völler (47 goals, 1982–95), Karl-Heinz Rummenigge (45 goals), Uwe **Seeler** (43 goals, 1954–70), Fritz Walter (33 goals, 1940–1958), Klaus Fischer (32 goals, 1977–82). Other notable international players: Helmut **Schön**, Wolfgang Overath, Gunter Netzer, Uli Hoeness, Paul **Breitner**, Pierre **Littbarski**, Gottfried **Fuchs**. *International tournament record* (Germany and West Germany only; see East Germany for its results) Olympic Games – first entered 1912, bronze medal/third 1988 (3–0, v Italy, in Seoul, South Korea, third/fourth playoff), semi-final/fourth 1952 (0–2, v **Sweden**, in Helsinki, Finland), quarter-final 1928, 1936, 1984, second round 1972, hosts, 1936, 1972; **Women's World Cup/European Championship for Women/Olympic Games** – see **Germany, women**; World Cup – first entered 1934, 1954 (3–2, v Hungary, in Berne, Switzerland), 1974 (2–1, v Netherlands, at the Olympiastadion, Munich), 1990 (1–0, v **Argentina**, in Rome, Italy), runners-up 1966 (2–4 after extra time, v England, at **Wembley Stadium**, London), 1982 (1–3, v **Italy**, in Madrid, Spain), 1986 (2–3, v Argentina, in Mexico City, Mexico), semi-final/third 1934 (3–2, v Austria, in Naples, Italy, third/fourth playoff), 1970 (1–0, v **Uruguay**, in Mexico City, Mexico), semi-final/fourth 1958 (3–6, v France, in Gothenburg, Sweden), quarter-final 1962, 1994, 1998, also qualified for finals tournament 1938, 1978 (did not enter 1930, 1950), hosts 1974; **European Championship** – first entered 1968, 1972 (3–0, v **Soviet Union**, in Brussels, Belgium), 1980 (2–1, v Belgium, in Rome), 1996 (2–1, after extra time, v Czech Republic, Wembley Stadium, London), runners-up 1976 (2–2, 3–5 pens., v **Czechoslovakia**, in Belgrade, Yugoslavia), 1992 (0–2, v Denmark, in Gothenburg, Sweden), semi-final 1988, also qualified for finals tournament 1984 (did not enter 1960, 1964); **European Under-21 Championship** – runners-up 1982; **European Youth Championship** (under 18) – 1981, runners-up 1994; **Under-17 World Championship** – runners-up 1985 (0–2, v **Nigeria**, in Beijing, China), semi-final/third 1997 (2–1, v **Spain**, in Egypt, third/fourth playoff, in Cairo, Egypt), quarter-final 1991; **World Youth Cup** (under-20) – 1981 (4–0, v **Qatar**, in Sydney, Australia), runners-up 1987 (1–1, 4–5 pens., in Santiago, Chile), also qualified 1999. *World Cup performance* (finals and qualifiers to end of 1998 tournament, includes Germany and West Germany) played 130, won 84, drawn 29, lost 17, scored 323 goals, conceded 141 goals. win rate: 65%; goals scored per game: 2.48. Germany has scored more goals and heads the all-time **World Cup goal-scoring averages**; it is second only to **Brazil** in its **World**

Cup win rate. *Record against British and Irish national teams* (Germany/West Germany only; see East Germany for its matches) v England, played 22, won eight, drawn five (includes two draws won by Germany on penalties), lost nine (does not include the three defeats and one draw in pre-**World War I** fixtures of disputed status); v **Northern Ireland**, played 12, won six, drawn four, lost two; v **Scotland**, played 13, won five, drawn four, lost four; v **Wales**, played 13, won six, drawn five, lost two; v **Republic of Ireland**, played 14, won seven, drawn two, lost five. *History (see also East Germany)* Football was introduced to Germany in the mid to late 19th century. SC Germania Hamburg, founded in 1887, is thought to be one of the first clubs set up to play football. Two regional leagues, in southern Germany and around Berlin started in 1898, with a playoff to determine the "national championship" starting in 1902 (**VfB Leipzig** won the first playoff, 7–2 v DFC Prague). The regional leagues and championship playoffs continued in Germany and West Germany through to 1963, when it was replaced by the national **Bundesliga**: **Cologne** (1.FC) was the first Bundesliga winner in 1964. East Germany abandoned the playoff final after just two seasons, adopting a conventional league championship in the 1949-50 season. West Germany was, with the exception of the now-independent Soviet republics, the last European country to organise a full national league. The German Cup (the Deutscher Fussball-Bund Pokal (**DFB Pokal**)) was first played in 1935 (**Nuremberg** 1.FC beat **Schalke 04** in the first final – 2–0). Austrian clubs played in the German championship and Cup from 1938 to 1944, when Austria was incorporated into Hitler's Third-Reich Germany: **Rapid Vienna** was German champion in 1941, while Admira Wien (now playing as **Admira-Wacker**) was runner-up in 1939, and **First Vienna** was runner-up in 1942; Rapid Vienna won the German cup in 1938, while First Vienna triumphed in 1942. After the reunification in 1990, the disbanded East German league was awarded just two places in the Bundesliga first division: **Hansa Rostock** and **Dynamo Dresden**. Of the former-East Germany, only Hansa Rostock, **Carl Zeiss Jena** and VfB Leipzig have survived in the Bundesliga: **Dynamo Dresden** lost its professional licence in 1995 after financial difficulties. German clubs have, en masse, been successful in international club tournaments. By 1999, German clubs had appeared in 69 European semi-finals, second only to Italian clubs; though, in terms of tournaments won (15 in total, by 1998), they lagged some way behind clubs from England (25), Italy (26) and Spain (23). **Bayern Munich** is one of an elite group of clubs to have won all three European club tournaments and the **World Club Cup**. Although the German national team lost its first game in April 1908 (see above), it has become the most successful European footballing nation and, with Brazil, is one of the two most successful countries in the world. Germany/West Germany has qualified in every edition of the World Cup that it has entered, and all but one of the European

Championships, winning each on several occasions (see above). Germany played England representative sides four times before World War I, although, the first official match between the two countries took place on 10 May 1930 (3–3, in Berlin, friendly). West Germany lost its only professional international match against East Germany: the first round group match in the 1974 World Cup (0–1, in Hamburg). Despite the setback, West Germany went on to win the tournament. The two former countries met once in the Olympic Games, the result again going in favour of East Germany (2–3, in Munich, second round, 8 September 1972). Germany first won the World Cup in 1954, with a 3–2 victory against Hungary in Berne; Morlock and Rahn (two) scored West Germany's goals, after it had gone 0–2 behind after just eight minutes (with **Puskás** and **Czibor** scoring for Hungary). It won again in 1974, this time as hosts. The 1974 final at the Olympiastadion in Munich was watched by 77,000 spectators: West Germany, under the captaincy of Franz Beckenbauer, beat the "**total football**" Netherlands 2–1, with goals from Breitner and Müller. From 2 May 1979 to 17 June 1980, West Germany won 12 consecutive matches, a joint-European record for the 20th century, equalled by France (Scotland completed 13 successive victories from 1879 to 1885). The World Cup triumph of 1990 – the last major tournament under the West German banner – was achieved with a lacklustre 1–0 victory over an ill-disciplined Argentina in Rome: Argentina had two players sent off; Brehme scored the only goal, after Völler was fouled in the penalty area in the 85th minute. West Germany/Germany won the European Championship in 1972, 1980 and 1996. The 1996 victory, at Wembley, was the first major triumph as the unified Germany and was also the first time that a tournament was settled by a **golden goal**: Germany beat the Czech Republic 2–1, with an extra-time golden goal from Oliver Bierhoff (adding to his goal after just two minutes). After the final, the Deutscher Fussball-Bund paid £20,000 for a full-page advertisement in *The Times* expressing thanks "for the great hospitality in England; for the fair-play shown by the English public; and for the smooth organisation of Euro '96 – football came home and England felt like home." Lotthar Matthäus, Germany's all time most-capped player, has appeared in an all-time record 22 World Cup finals-tournament matches, having played in all five tournaments from 1982 to 1998. Germany finished third in the first **European Championships for Players with Learning Disabilities** (4–1, v Netherlands, in Leicester, England, 1996), and third in the first **World Football Championships for Players with Learning Disabilities** (5–3, v Portugal, in Leicester, 1998). *World Cup final teams and scorers* 1954 (winners) Turek (goalkeeper), Posipal, Liebrich, Kohlmeyer, Eckel, Mai, Rahn (2), Morlock (1), O Walter, F Walter, Schäfer; 1966 (runners-up): Tilkowski (goalkeeper), Höttges, Schulz, Weber (1), Schnellinger, Haller (1), Beckenbauer, Seeler, Held, Overath, Emmerich; 1974 (winners): Maier (goalkeeper), Vogts, Schwarzenbeck, Beckenbauer, Breitner (1), Bonhof, Hoeness, Overath, Grabowski, G Müller (1), Hölzenbein; 1982 (runners-up): Schumacher (goalkeeper), Kaltz, Stielike, K-H Förster, B Förster, Breitner (1), Breigel, Dremmler (Hrubesch), Rummenigge (H Müller), Littbarski, Fischer; 1986 (runners-up): Schumacher (goalkeeper), Jakobs, K-H Förster, Breigel, Brehme, Eder, Berthold, Matthaus, Magath (D Hoeness), Rummenigge (1), Allofs (Völler (1)); 1990 (winners): Illgner (goalkeeper), Berthold (Reuter), Kohler, Augenthaler, Buchwald, Brehme (1), Hässler, Matthäus, Littbarski, Völler, Klinsmann. *European Championship winning teams and scorers* (West Germany) 1972 Maier (goalkeeper), Höttges. Schwarzenbeck, Beckenbauer, Breitner, Wimmer (1), Hoeness, Netzer, Heynckes, G Müller (2), Kremers; 1980 Schumacher (goalkeeper), Kaltz, Stielike, K-H Förster, Schuster, Briegel (Cullmann), H Müller, Rummenigge, Hrubesch (2), Allofs; 1996 Kopke (goalkeeper), Helmer, Sammer, Babbel, Struntz, Scholl (Bierhoff), Eilts (Bode), Hassler, Klinsmann, Ziege, Kuntz. *League system* The Bundesliga has two divisions of 18 clubs. The bottom three clubs in the first division are automatically relegated and replaced by the top three in the second division. Three points are awarded for a win and one for a draw; clubs level on points are separated on **goal difference**. The bottom four clubs in the second division are relegated to the four regional leagues that make up the third tier of the league system. In order to win promotion from the regional leagues, clubs must win their leagues and meet the standards set by the Deutscher Fussball-Bund in order to be granted a mandatory professional licence. *Record in international club tournaments* (winners and runners-up only) *World Club Cup* – *Bayern Munich* (1976, 1999); **European Cup** – Bayern Munich (1974, 1975, 1976, runners-up 1982, 1987), **Hamburg SV** (1983, runners-up 1980), **Borussia Dortmund** (1997), **Eintracht Frankfurt** (runners-up 1960), **Borussia Mönchengladbach** (runners-up 1922); **European Cup-winners Cup** – Borussia Dortmund (1966), Bayern Munich (1967), **Magdeburg** (1.FC) (1974), SV Hamburg (1980, runners-up 1968), **Werder Bremen** (1992), TSV 1860 Munich (runners-up 1965), Fortuna Düsseldorf (runners-up 1979), Carl Zeis Jena (runners-up 1981), Lokomotive Leipzig (now VfB Leipzig, runners-up 1987), **Stuttgart VfB** (runners-up 1998); **UEFA Cup** – Borussia Mönchengladbach (1975, 1979, runners-up 1973, 1980), Eintracht Frankfurt (1980), Bayer Leverkusen (1988), Bayern Munich (1996), Schalke 04 (1997), SV Hamburg (runners-up 1982), **Cologne** (runners-up 1986), Stuttgart VfB (runners-up 1989), Borussia Dortmund (runners-up 1993). Other leading clubs – from former-West Germany: **Nuremberg**, **Kaiserslautern** – and from former-East Germany: **FC Victoria 91**, **Berlin FC**, **Hansa Rostock**.

Germany, women *country/women* women's football in Germany is administered by the German football association, the Deutscher Fussball-Bund (DFB).

Dossier First international: September 1956, v the **Netherlands**, 2–1, in Essen (18,000 spectators). First official international: 1982, v **Switzerland**, 5-1. Most capped player: Sylvia Neid (111 appearances). *International tournament record* **Olympic Games** (women) – played in the first tournament in 1996 (first round, Atlanta, USA); **Women's World Cup** – qualified for first tournament in 1991, runners-up 1995 (0–2, v **Norway**, in Stockholm), semi-final/fourth 1991 (0–4,v **Sweden**, in China), qualified for finals tournament 1999; **European Championship for Women** – entered first tournament in 1984, 1989 (4–1, v **Norway**, in Osnabruck, Germany), 1991 (3–1, v Norway, in Aalborg, Denmark), 1995 (3–2, v Sweden, in Kaiserslautern, Germany), fourth place 1993. *History* Women's football in Germany dates back to the 1900s. Its early development was hampered by the negative attitude displayed by the country's national association. In an almost identical move to the **Football Association** in England, the DFB, in 1955, banned women's clubs from playing on grounds belonging to clubs affiliated to the DFB; the ban remaining in place until October 1970. The women's game continued despite the DFB's ban, and the former West German Women's Football Association was founded in 1955, in Essen. A European women's tournament, organised by the former **International Ladies Football Association**, was held in Berlin in 1957. The final between a German representative side and the English women's club **Manchester Corinthians** attracted a crowd of 37,000 (the visitors won 4–0). By 1971, there were more than 1,000 senior and junior women's football teams. The first German women's club championship was played in 1974, with a woman's cup commencing in 1981 (first won by Bergisch Gladbach). Germany has won the European Championship for Women on three occasions (see *International tournament record*), and was runner-up in the second Women's World Cup in 1995. An estimated 5.97 million people in Germany watched the 1995 final live on German television. By 1995, there were 4,415 women's teams and 612,000 registered female players (senior and youth level) in Germany. *League system* The German national women's championship has two regional First Divisions of 10 clubs each (northern and southern sections). Leading clubs: FSV Frankfurt, Grun-Weis Brauweiler, TSV Siegen.

Gerson *player* Midfield. **Brazil** international (83 caps). Born 1974 in Niteroi, Brazil. *Clubs* **Flamengo**, **Botafogo**, **São Paulo**. *Keynotes* Gerson scored with a famous left-footed shot in the 1970 **World Cup** final (4–1, v **Italy**, at the Azteca, Mexico City). *Honours* World Cup (Brazil, 1970).

Geylang United *club* Singapore S-League club, based in Singapore, formerly known as Geylang International. *Keynotes* Geylang holds the national league record of six consecutive titles (1988 to 1993). It has had no success in international club tournaments, though has played in the **Asian Champion Teams Cup** and the **Asian Cup-winners Cup**. Singapore league 1975, 1976, 1977, 1988, 1989, 1990, 1991, 1992, 1993, 1996.

Ghana *country CAF* republic in West Africa (formerly known as the Gold Coast), on the Gulf of Guinea. Bordered by **Burkina Faso**, **Ivory Coast** and **Togo**. Independence from UK in 1957. Area: 238,305. sq km (91,985 sq miles). Population: 16,470,000 (1995 est.). Languages: English and various tribal languages. Capital: Accra. *Dossier* Ghana Football Association (Accra) formed in 1957 affiliated to **FIFA** and **Confédération Africaine de Football** (CAF) in 1958, member of the **West African Football Union**, president Samuel Brew-Butler, general secretary Fred Osam-Duodu. Season played from January to November. National stadium: The Accra Sports Stadium, capacity: 45,000 (5,000 seated). National strip: yellow shirts, yellow shorts. Nickname of national team: Black Stars. First international game: October 1950, v **Nigeria** (1–0, in Accra, friendly). Biggest victory: 12–0, v **Malawi** (15 October 1962, in Blantyre, Malawi, friendly). Biggest defeat: 2–8 v **Brazil** (27 March 1996, in Brazil, friendly). Notable international players: Abedi **Pelé**, Karim **Abdoul Razak** , Ibrahim **Sunday**, Antony Yeboah, Opoku Afriyie, Ossey Coffie, Nii Lamptey, Malik, Yaw Sam. *International tournament record* **Olympic Games** – semi-final/bronze medal 1992 (1–0, v **Australia**, in Spain), quarter-final 1964, 1996, also qualified for finals tournament 1968, 1972; **Women's World Cup** – first entered 1991, qualified for finals tournament 1999; **World Cup** – first entered 1962, never qualified for finals tournament, reached third qualifying round in 1974 and 1986; **African Cup of Nations** – 1963 (3–0, v **Sudan**, in Accra), 1965 (3–2, v **Tunisia**, in Tunis), 1978 (2–0 v **Uganda**, in Accra), 1982 (1–1, 7–6, pens., v **Libya**, in Tripoli, Libya), runners-up 1968 (0–1, v **Congo Democratic Republic** – formerly Zaire, then known as Congo Kinshasa – in Addis Ababa, Ethiopia), 1970 (0–1, v Sudan, in Khartoum, Sudan), 1992 (0–0, 10–11 pens., v Ivory Coast, in Dakar, Senegal), semi-final/fourth 1996 (0–1, v **Zambia**, in Johannesburg, third/fourth playoff), quarter-final 1994, also qualified for finals tournament 1980, 1984, 1998, hosts 1963, 1978, joint hosts 2000; **African Under-17 Junior Championship** – 1995; **African Under-20 Youth Championship** – 1993, fourth place 1997; **African Women's Tournament** – runners-up 1998 (0–2, v Nigeria, in Lagos); **All-Africa Games** – runners-up 1973; CSSA Zone 3 (West Africa) Tournament – 1982,1983, 1984, 1985, 1986, 1987; **Under-17 World Championship** – 1991 (1–0, v **Spain**, in Florence, Italy), 1995 (3–2, v Brazil, in Guayaquil, Ecuador), runners-up 1993 (1–2, v Nigeria, in Tokyo, Japan), 1997 (1–2, v Brazil, in Cairo, Egypt); **World Youth Cup** (under-20) – runners-up 1993 (1–2, v Brazil, in Sydney, Australia), semi-final/fourth 1997 (1–2, v **Republic of Ireland**, in Kuala Lumpur, Malaysia, third/fourth playoff), quarter-final 1999. *Record against British and Irish national teams* none played. *History* Football introduced around 1900, with

the country's oldest club, **Hearts of Oak**, founded in 1911. The Gold Coast Football Association was founded in 1922, replaced, after independence in 1957, by the Ghana Football Association. National league started in 1956, first won by Hearts of Oak. Ghanaian Cup introduced in 1958. The league became professional in 1993. Ghanaian club **Asante Kotoko** is twice winners of the **African Cup of Champion Clubs** and has appeared in seven finals. Ghana was bronze medalists at the 1992 Olympic Games and has won the African Cup of Nations four times, a record shared with **Egypt**. It has also appeared in a record seven finals. As the most successful nation in Africa, in continental competitions at least, it is surprising that Ghana has never qualified for the World Cup finals. *World Cup performance* (finals and qualifiers to end of 1998 tournament) played 34, won 11, drawn 11, lost 11, scored 41 goals, conceded 33 goals; win rate 32%; goals scored per game 1.21. *League system* Twelve clubs compete in national IKAM Ghana FA Premier League, each club plays each other at home and away, with three points for a win and one for a draw. The bottom club is automatically relegated to the First Division; the second-bottom club plays off against the First Division runners-up. *Record in international club tournaments* African Cup of Champion Clubs – Asante Kotoko (1970, 1983, runners-up 1967, 1971, 1973, 1982, 1993), Hearts of Oak (runners-up 1977, 1979, quarter-final "champions-league" stage 1998), **Great Olympics** (semi-final 1971), **Obuassi Goldfields** (runners-up 1997, quarter-final 1995); **African Cup-winners Cup** – **Sekondi Hasaacas** (semi-final 1981), Hearts of Oak (semi-final 1982, quarter-final 1995); **West African Football Union General Eyadema Cup** – Sekondi Hasaacas (1982), Cornerstone (1987), Ghapoha (of Tema, 1997). Other leading club: **Okwawu United**.

GÍ Gotu (Gotu Itrottarfelag) *club* Faeroe Islands national league club based in Gotu, founded 1926. Ground: Gotu, capacity: 3,000. Strip: yellow shirts, blue shorts. Faeroe Islands Cup 1983, 1985, 1996, 1997; Faeroe Islands league champions 1983, 1986, 1993, 1994, 1995, 1996.

giant-killing *n.* victory by a lower division or non-league side over a higher-placed, top-flight or more celebrated club in a knockout competition. The term may also be applied to a victory by a low-ranked country over an illustrious national team. *Keynotes* Notable giant killers include the German amateur league club Eintracht Trier. In 1996-97 it beat two European club champions in the **German Cup**: 1997 **UEFA Cup** winners **Schalke 04** (1–0) and **European Cup** and **World Club Cup** winners **Borussia Dortmund** (2–1). In English football, **Leeds United** has been on the receiving end of some famous **FA Cup** giant-killing acts, including defeat in the 1973 final by Division Two opponent's **Sunderland** (0–1), and, perhaps more dramatically, losing a 1971 fifth-round tie against Division Four side **Colchester United** (2–3). Besides the Leeds United upset, Colchester United has also recorded a number of other famous giant-killing victories, including the 1948 FA Cup triumphs over **Huddersfield Town** (1–0, third round) and **Bradford Park Avenue** (3–2, fourth round), when the club was in the **Southern League**. **Bournemouth AFC**'s FA Cup giant-killing exploits in 1956-57 included victories over Division One opponents' **Wolverhampton Wanderers** (1–0, fourth round) and **Tottenham Hotspur** (3–1, fifth round), before losing to **Manchester United** in the quarter-finals (1–2). **Norwich City** also has a history of FA Cup giantkilling: 1909 (3–2 v **Liverpool**, second round); 1911 (3–1 v **Sunderland**, first round), 1915 (3–2 v **Tottenham Hotspur**, second round), 1935 (2–1 replay v **Leeds United**, fourth round), 1951 (3–1 v Liverpool, third round), 1954 (2–1 v **Arsenal**, fourth round). Norwich's most famous FA Cup giantkilling run occurred in 1958-59. The club, then of Division Three and under the managership of Archie Macaulay, with a team that included the striking partnership of Terry Bly and Terry Allcock, reached the FA Cup semi-finals (0–1 replay v **Luton Town**), defeating **Manchester United** (3–0, third round) and Tottenham Hotspur (1–0 replay, fifth round) on the way. Prominent FA Cup non-league victories over League opposition include: **Corinthians**, 1–0, v **Blackburn Rovers** (1924, first round); **Wolverhampton Wanderers**, 0–1, v **Mansfield Town** (1929, third round); **Yeovil Town**, 2–1 v **Sunderland** (1949, fourth round); **Derby County**,1–6 v Boston (1955-56, second round); Worcester, 2–1, v **Liverpool** (1959, third round); **Coventry City**, 1–2, v King's Lynn (1961, second round); Tamworth, 2–1, v **Torquay United** (1969, first round); Barnet, 6–1, v **Newport County** (1971, first round); **Hereford United**, 2–1, v **Newcastle United** (1972 replay, third round); **Burnley**, 0–1 v **Wimbledon** (1975, third round); Coventry Sporting, 2–0 v **Tranmere Rovers** (1975, first round); **Stoke City**, 2–3, v Blyth Spartans (1978, fourth round); Harlow Town, 1–0, v **Leicester City** (1980, replay, third round); **Brighton & Hove Albion**, 0–4, v Walton & Hersham (1982, second round); Slough, 1–0, v **Millwall** (1982, first round); **Birmingham City**, 1–2, v Altrincham (1986, third round); Chorley, 3–0, v Wolverhampton Wanderers (1986, second replay, first round); Sutton, 2–1, v Coventry City (1989, third round); **West Bromwich Albion**, 2–4, v Woking (1991, third round); Birmingham City, 1–2 v Kidderminster Harriers (1994, third round). Notable examples in the **Scottish FA Cup** include: Fraserburgh, 1–0, v **Dundee** (1958-59, first round); **Berwick Rangers**, 1–0, v **Rangers** (1967, first round); Elgin City, 1–0 v **Ayr United** (1966-67); Tarff Rovers, 1–0, v **Alloa Athletic** (1969, first round). One of the most celebrated **World Cup** upsets occurred in the 1950 finals when the **United States of America** defeated **England** (1–0, in group 2). The England side included Alf **Ramsey**, Billy **Wright**, Tom **Finney**, Roy Bentley and Stanley **Mortensen**. Other World Cup shocks include: **Northern Ireland**, 1–0, v **Czechoslovakia** (1958, group 1); **North Korea** 1–0,

v **Italy** (1996, group 4); **Tunisia**, 3–1, v **Mexico** (1978, group 2); **Algeria**, 2–1, v **West Germany** (1982, group 2); Northern Ireland, 1–0, v **Spain** (1982, group 5); **Cameroon**, 1–0, v **Argentina** (1990, group B); and **Saudi Arabia**, 1–0, v **Belgium** (1994, group F). **Iran**'s 2–0 victory over the USA at the 1998 World Cup was more of a political giant-killing act than a footballing one.

giant screen   *n.*   large television erected at some grounds to display team information and recorded highlights. *Regulations* Screens are only permitted at **Premier League** or **Scottish Football League** clubs with the pro written consent of the governing body (FA Premier League rule I.25, Scottish Football League rule 71). If screens are used in the Premier League, they must be positioned such that they do not distract players or officials and, while live action is permissible, action replays can only be shown when the ball is out of play and must not be of controversial or negative incidents (e.g. fouls, violent conduct or potentially disputed referee's decisions) (FA Premier League rule I.26). It is also prohibited to show pictures of substitutes warming up (unless the **substitute board** has already been held up). Giant screens can also be used to relay closed-circuit coverage of games, for example at the home ground of a club playing an away fixture: Premier League and Scottish Football League clubs require written permission from their respective governing body (FA Premier League rule I.24, Scottish Football League rule 71).

Gibbons, Vivian   *player*   the first English player to travel to an English **Football League** game by air (7 September 1932, **Bristol Rovers** v **Southend United**). A part-time player and London schoolteacher, Gibbons flew from Romford to Bristol airport to play in a mid-week match for the home club.

Gibraltar   *country*   *no international affiliation*   British dependency consisting of a small limestone promontory on the tip of Spain. Area: 6.5 sq km (2.5 sq miles). Population: 31,000. Languages: English and Spanish. Capital: City of Gibraltar.

Gigg Lane   *ground*   English football ground situated in Bury, Greater Manchester; home of **Bury**. *Dossier* Ground capacity: 11,841. Pitch dimensions: 102m x 66m. Record attendance: 35,000 v **Bolton Wanderers** (9 January 1960, **FA Cup**, third round). Best average attendance: 19,500 (1924-25). *History* Bury has played at Gigg Lane since the club's formation in April 1885. The first football match at the ground, an exhibition game between **Accrington** and a church XI, took place on 6 June 1885. Gigg Lane was originally part of the Earl of Derby's estate and, in 1922, he made a gift of the ground to Bury, enabling the club to partially redevelop it by rebuilding the two end terraces and raising the capacity to 41,600. In order to finance essential safety work at Gigg Lane, the club launched the Shakers' Incentive Scheme in 1992, which offered participants £700 savings on season tickets on a initial £500 down payment. The scheme raised £130,000 of the £275,000 required, with the remainder coming from the gate receipts from a fortuitous cup tie against **Manchester United** in January 1993. Bury was the first club in the north-west to erect floodlights, and the first floodlit match occurred on 6 October 1953 (v **Wolverhampton Wanderers**, friendly).

Giggs, Ryan   *player*   Winger. **Wales** international (22 caps, 4 goals). Born 29 November 1973. Career ca. 1991–. *Clubs* **Manchester United**. *Keynotes* Joined Manchester United as a trainee in December 1990, making his first team debut as a substitute against **Everton** on 2 March 1991. When he made his Wales debut as a substitute against **Germany** on 16 October 1991, Giggs was the country's youngest debutant at 17 years and 332 days. Previously he had appeared for **England** schoolboys as Ryan Wilson, his father's surname. Giggs scored the last ever goal in a **FA Cup** semi-final replay against **Arsenal** at **Villa Park** on 14 April 1999. Giggs' extra-time winner was a remarkable solo effort, with Giggs collecting the ball in his own half, beating several Arsenal players before shooting past goalkeeper David **Seaman** (2–1). Semi-final replays were abolished at the end of the 1999 FA Cup competitions. Included in the **Football League Centenary 100 Players**. *Honours* League Championship (Manchester United 1992-93, 1993-94, 1995-96, 1996-97, 1998-99); FA Cup (Manchester United 1994, 1996, 1999); **League Cup** (Manchester United 1992); **European Cup** (Manchester United 1999); **European Super Cup** (Manchester United 1991).

Giles, Johnny   *player*   Midfield. **Republic of Ireland** international (59 caps, 5 goals). Born 6 January 1940. Career ca. 1957–1979. *Clubs* (player) **Manchester United**, **Leeds United**. *Clubs/country* (player-manager) **West Bromwich Albion**; **Shamrock Rovers**; Republic of Ireland. *Keynotes* Known as "Mr Availability" because he often found space, Giles signed professionally for Manchester United in November 1957. He made 98 appearances for United before moving to Leeds United for £32,000 in August 1963. Giles played 383 **Football League** games for Leeds and his last appearance for the club was the 1975 **European Cup** final (0–2 v **Bayern Munich**). In June 1975, he became player-manager at West Bromwich Albion, taking the club back to Division One in his first season in charge. He later became player-manager at Shamrock Rovers and won his final international cap at the age of 39. Included in the **Football League Centenary 100 Players**. *Honours* League Championship (Leeds United 1968-69, 1971-72); Division Two (Leeds United 1963-64); **FA Cup** (Manchester United 1963; Leeds United 1972); **League Cup** (Leeds United 1968); **FAI Cup** (Shamrock Rovers 1978); **UEFA** (Fairs) **Cup** (Leeds United 1968, 1971).

Gillingham   *club*   English league. *Dossier* Ground: **Priestfield Stadium**, Kent, capacity: 10,600. Strip: blue shirts, white shorts, white socks. Nickname: the Gills. Record attendance: 23,002 v **Queens Park Rangers** (10 January 1948, **FA Cup**, third round). Best average attendance: 12,576 (1951-52). Biggest win:

10–0 v **Chesterfield** (5 September 1987, Division Three). Biggest defeat: 2–9 **Nottingham Forest** (18 November 1950, Division Three (South)). *History* Founded in the early 1890s as Excelsior before becoming New Brompton FC in 1893, when the club purchased a piece of land near Gillingham Road which would eventually become the Priestfield Stadium. The club adopted the name Gillingham in 1913 and was a founder member of Division Three in 1920-21. After finishing bottom of Division Three (South) in 1937-38, Gillingham, having previously applied for re-election on four occasions, was replaced by **Ipswich Town**. Two **Southern League** Championships in three seasons, in 1947 and 1949, led to the club's return to the **Football League** in 1950-51 with the expansion of the two regional bottom divisions. Gillingham won the Division Four Championship in 1963-64 on **goal average**, before returning to the bottom division in 1970-71 after seven seasons in Division Three. The club secured a place in Division Three in 1973-74 and in 1978-79, 1984-85 and 1986-87 it only narrowly missed further elevation. On the last occasion, Gillingham reached the final of the end-of-season **playoffs** (2–2 agg., 0–2 replay v **Swindon Town** at **Selhurst Park**), but three seasons later the club was back playing in Division Four. In 1995-96, the club finished runners-up in the Third Division, achieving a Football League record for the number of clean sheets (20) over 46 games during the season. The club made its first **Wembley** appearance in 1999, reaching the 1998-99 Second Division playoff final (v **Manchester City**) – lost playoff final (2-2, 1-3 pens. v Manchester City. *League record* Second Division 1996-97 to–; Division Three 1920-21, 1964-65 to 1970-71, 1974-75 to 1988-89; Third Division 1992-93 to 1995-96; Division Three (South) 1921-22 to 1937-38 (failed re-election), 1950-51 to 1957-58; Division Four 1958-59 to 1963-64, 1971-72 to 1973-74, 1989-90 to 1991-92. *Honours* Division Four 1963-64; Southern League 1947, 1949. *Records* Tony Cascarino is Gillingham's most capped player (3 (70) for **Republic of Ireland**); John Simpson holds the record for club League appearances (571, 1957-72); Brian Yeo is Gillingham's record League goalscorer (135, 1963-75).

Gimnasia y Esgrima La Plata   *club*   Argentinean national league club, based in La Plata, founded 3 June 1887. Ground: Estadio Jorge Zerillo, capacity: 25,000. Strip: white shirts with a dark blue hoop, blue shorts. *History* Gimnasia is the oldest Argentinean club still in existence, formed five months before **Quilmes Athletic Club**. Some club members left to form **Estudiantes La Plata** in 1905. Argentinean league champions 1929; **Copa CONMEBOL** semi-final 1992.

Giresse, Alain   *player*   **France** international. *Club* Girondins de Bordeaux. *Honours* **European Championship** (France, 1984); *France Football* **European Footballer of the Year** runner-up 1982.

Girondins de Bordeaux   *club*   see **Bordeaux.**

giuoco del calcio Fiorentino   *n.*   *Italian* early form of football played in the 16th century in Florence.

In a version similar to the **mob football** played in Britain, crowds of players fought for possession of a ball, or as some accounts claim, a severed head. A slightly more refined version was played by the Italian upper classes – traditionally between the Christian festivals of Epiphany and Lent. The principal aim was to score by throwing the ball over a certain fixed point marked on the edge of the field. An exhibition of calcio was performed at the 1980 **European Championship** opening ceremony in Rome. Calcio is the name by which football is commonly known in Italy and several clubs include it in their official names. These include Piacenza Calcio, Udinese Calcio, Vicenza Calcio and Associazione Calcio Milan or **AC Milan**.

glancing header　*n.*　light header into space for a team-mate to run on to.

Glanford Park　*ground*　English football ground situated in Scunthorpe, Humberside; home of **Scunthorpe United**. *Dossier* Ground capacity: 9,183. Pitch dimensions: 100.5m x 65m. Record attendance: 8,775 v **Rotherham United** (1 May 1989, Division Four). *History* Built at a cost of £2.1 million, Glanford Park bears the name of Scunthorpe's neighbouring town where it is situated and which also agreed a £200,000 10-year sponsorship deal with the club when it moved. Scunthorpe played its first match at Glanford Park on 14 August 1988 (v **Football League** XI, friendly) and the opening ceremony was performed by Princess Alexandra. Local Labour councillors boycotted the event in protest at the South African coaching activities of guest player Kevin **Keegan**, who began his career at Scunthorpe United.

Glebe Park　*ground*　Scottish football ground situated in Brechin, Angus; home of **Brechin City**. *Dossier* Ground capacity: 3,980. Pitch dimensions: 100.5m x 61m. Record attendance: 8,122 v **Aberdeen** (28 January 1967, **Scottish FA Cup**, third round). *Keynotes* Brechin City, which had been founded in 1906, moved to Glebe Park in 1919. Floodlights were installed in 1977 (v **Hibernian**).

Glenavon FC　*club*　Northern Ireland national league club based in Lurgan, founded 1889. Ground: Mourneview Park, capacity: 15,000. Strip: blue shirts, white shorts. **Irish FA Cup** 1957, 1959, 1961, 1992, 1997; Northern Ireland league champions 1952, 1957, 1960. Notable former players: Wilbur Cush (26 caps for Northern Ireland, 1951-62).

Glentoran　*club*　Northern Ireland national league club based in Belfast, founded 1882. Ground: the Oval, capacity: 30,000. Strip: green shirts with red sleeves, black shorts. Largely Protestant support base. all-Ireland league champions 1894, 1897, 1905, 1912, 1913; **European Cup-winners Cup** quarter-final 1974; **Irish FA Cup** (all-Ireland) winners; 1914, 1917, 1921 (the last year the cup was played throughout Ireland); Irish FA Cup (Northern Ireland) 1932, 1933, 1935, 1951, 1966, 1973, 1983, 1985, 1986, 1987, 1988, 1990, 1996, 1998; Northern Ireland league champions 1921, 1925, 1931, 1951, 1953, 1964, 1967,

1968, 1970, 1972, 1977, 1981, 1988, 1992. Notable former player: Con Martin (30 caps for the **Republic of Ireland**, 1946-56).

Glossop North End　*club*　former-English league. *Dossier* Ground: North Road, Derbyshire. Record League attendance: 9,000. *Keynotes* Glossop joined the **Football League** in 1898-99 and the town is the smallest in England to have supported a top-flight club. Glossop dropped North End from its name in 1903 and resigned from the League in 1914-15 – replaced by **Stoke City**. Glossop was an FA Cup quarter-finalist in 1908-09 (0–1 replay v **Bristol City**). *League record* Division One 1899-00; Division Two 1898-99, 1900-01 to 1914-15.

GM Vauxhall Conference　former name, until 1997-98 of the **Football Conference**.

Go Ahead Eagles　*club*　Netherlands national league club, based in Deventer, and founded in 1902. Ground: De Adelaarshorst, capacity: 11,000. Strip: red and yellow striped shirts and red shorts. Dutch league champions 1917, 1922, 1930, 1933.

go over on the ankle　*medical*　informal injury to the **lateral ligament** of the ankle when it is twisted into a plantar flexion and inversion.

goal　*rules*　**1.** structures consisting of two upright **goalposts** and a **crossbar** 2.44 metres (8 feet high) – measured at the lower edge – situated on the **goal line** on the **field of play** (Law I). The two posts are 7.32 metres (8 yards) apart and equidistant from the corner flags. For safety reasons, the goalposts must be secured to the ground. The goalposts and crossbars must be of the same width and no more than 12 cm (5 inches) wide. The goal line must be of the same width as the width of the goal posts and crossbar. **Nets** may be attached to the posts and crossbars. Goal posts and crossbars may be made of wood, metal or any material approved by the **International FA Board.** They may be square, rectangular, round, half-round or elliptical in cross section and must be painted white. **2.** a point scored in a game of football. A goal is scored when the whole of the ball has crossed the goal line, under the **crossbar** and between the goalposts, assuming no other infringements had taken place prior to this (Law X). The team scoring the most goals in a game wins the match. If no goals are scored or each side scores the same number of goals then the game is a **draw** (sense **1.**). A goal cannot be scored if the ball has been prevented from crossing the line by some external object, person or animal. If this happens, the game must be restarted by a **drop ball** (except in the case of a **penalty kick** which would be retaken). **in goal** (Scottish dialect: **in goals**) *informal* to take up the role and position of a goalkeeper, as in: *David went in goal.*

goal area　*rules*　small area in front of each **goal** of the **field of play** delineated by **lines**. Two lines of 5.5 metres (6 yards) length run at right angles to the **goal line**, 5.5 metres (6 yards) from each **goalpost**. They are joined by a line running parallel to the goal line (**goal area line**) (Law I). Also called six-yard area.

goal area line *rules* line running parallel to, and 5.5 metres (6 yards) out from, the **goal line** on the **field of play**, forming part of the **goal area**.

goal average *n.* former method of deciding the league position of two or more clubs with the same **points** total. Calculated by dividing the goals scored by an individual club by the goals it conceded. *Keynotes* Goal average was introduced to the English **Football League** in its first season (1888-89) at a League sub-committee meeting on 11 January 1889 convened to formalise league rules. It was replaced by **goal difference** in 1976. Several League Championships have been decided by goal average. In 1923-24, **Hudersfield Town** and **Cardiff City** both finished with 57 points, but Huddersfield won the title because the club's goal average of 1.818 was superior to Cardiff's 1.794. Similarly, in 1952-53, **Arsenal** won the Championship because its goal average of 1.515 was better than **Preston North End**'s 1.416. Three clubs, **Chelsea**, **Everton** and **Sheffield Wednesday**, all finished the 1950-51 season with 32 points. Chelsea escaped relegation to **Division Two** because the club's goal average of 0.815 bettered that of both Wednesday (0.771) and Everton (0.558).

goal celebration *misc.* manner in which a player commemorates the scoring of a goal. Excessive goal celebrations may be construed under the laws of the game as **delaying the restart of play** (**cautionable offence**). In 1975-76 season, the **Football League** attempted to outlaw extravagant goal celebrations stating that "kissing and cuddling should be stopped and players continuing to act this way should be charged with bringing the game into disrepute." Referees tend to curtail "over exuberant" celebrations, especially those which involve spectators. A **FIFA** technical committee in 1982 recommended that the "excessive demonstrative attitude of some players" after a goal has been scored and the "exuberant outbursts of several players at once jumping on top of each other, kissing and embracing, should be banned from the football pitch", and that this should be enforced by national associations. **Arsenal** suspended its defender Sammy Nelson for two weeks and fined him two weeks' wages for lowering his shorts to the home crowd after scoring an equaliser against Coventry City on 3 April 1979 (1–1, at Highbury, Division One); Nelson had scored an own-goal in the first half, to the consternation of the Arsenal fans. Goal celebrations have become more elaborate, with players engaging in "choreographed" routines. **Chelsea** players, for example, engaged in a depiction of an Italian renaissance painting following Roberto **Di Matteo**'s first goal for the club against **Middlesbrough** on 21 August 1997. At the 1994 **World Cup**, the **Brazil** national side would all accompany **Bebeto** in his cradle-rocking routine after the striker had scored. Individual players tend to celebrate their strikes in a certain manner. Fabrizio Ravanelli inspired numerous copycats with his shirt-over-the-head celebration, while Cameroon's Roger **Milla** would dance with the corner flag after scoring at the 1990 **World Cup** in **Italy**. During the 1997-98 season, several **Premier League** players uncovered t-shirt messages after scoring. Ian Wright, then of Arsenal unveiled the message "Just done it" (a play on Nike's "Just do it" slogan) after he scored his 179th goal for the club against **Bolton Wanderers** on 13 September 1997, thereby breaking Cliff **Bastin**'s 58-year-old record (178). In March 1997, **Liverpool** striker Robbie Fowler wore a t-shirt with a message of support for the striking Liverpool dock workers during a **European Cup-winners Cup** match against Brann Bergen at **Anfield**. Fowler was subsequently fined £900 by UEFA because his t-shirt message was deemed to be "politically motivated". Fowler was again in the news in 1999 for a controversial celebration following his 15th minute penalty equaliser in the Premier League Merseyside derby against Everton at Anfield (4 April 1999, 3–2). Fowler crawled along the **penalty area line** pretending to sniff the paint, mimicking the actions of cocaine abuse. He was fined two weeks' wages by his club – the maximum allowed – and punished by the **Football Association**. Fowler was fined a record £32,000 by the FA and suspended for four matches. **Chelsea** captain Dennis Wise exposed a t-shirt after scoring against **Derby County** on 18 January 1997 with the message "Cheer-up Luca, we love you. XX", which was reference to teammate Gianluca **Vialli**'s continued place on the substitute's bench. **West Ham United**'s Ian Wright and Neil Ruddock celebrated the striker's Premier League goal against **Southampton** on 28 September 1998 with a comical re-enactment of the Paul Alcock–Paolo Di Canio incident from two days earlier. Di Canio had pushed referee Alcock to the ground after the official had dismissed the **Sheffield Wednesday** player. While Diego **Maradona** and Claudio **Caniggia** were both playing for **Boca Juniors** in 1997-98 they celebrated goals by kissing each other full on the lips. This led to complaints from Caniggia's wife, Mariana Nannis, who had agreed to her husband's return to Argentinian football in 1997 from Europe only on condition that when players score they hug not kiss. One unusual goal celebration was performed by **Atlético Mineiro**'s Edmilson. After scoring against local rivals America-Belo Horizonte in September 1998, Edmilson ate a carrot he had hidden in his shorts. His actions were directed at the opposition fans who are commonly known as "The Rabbits".

goal difference *n.* a method of deciding the league position of two or more clubs with the same **points** total. Calculated by subtracting the goals conceded by a club from the goals it has scored. *Regulations* Goal difference is used to determine the league position of clubs in the **Premier League** or **Scottish Football League** that are level on points; if the teams are still level, the position is determined on **goals scored** (FA Premier League rule B.22, Scottish Football League rule 30). A **playoff** (sense **2.**) would decide the final ranking if the goal difference and goals scored are identical for two teams). *Keynotes* Goal difference replaced **goal**

average in English league football in the 1976-77 season. The change was prompted by **Arsenal** at the annual meeting of the **Football League** in 1976 and remains in use in the FA Premier League. The Football League separates clubs level on points by goals scored (those still level are separated by **goals conceded**). *Keynotes* Only one English league championship before 1976 would have had a different outcome had goal average been replaced by the goal difference system: Huddersfield Town won the 1923-24 championship ahead of Cardiff City, with both clubs finishing the season on 57 points; Cardiff had an inferior goal average (1.794 v 1.818) identical goal difference (+27), but superior goals scored (61 v 60). Cardiff have never won the championship. See also **number of victories**.

goal drought   *n.*   period experienced by a team or player when few or no goals are scored

goal, fastest   *record*   **1.** World: there are various claims for goals scored in under four seconds after the kick-off, including several by British footballers. Damian Mori's goal after four seconds for **Adelaide City**, however, was recorded on video (v **Sydney United**, 6 December 1995, Australian National League). **2. World Cup**: 8.3 seconds, Davide **Gualtieri** (for **San Marino** v **England**, 17 November 1993, in Bologna, qualifier). **3.** World Cup finals: 25 seconds, Vaclav Masek (for **Czechoslovakia** v **Mexico**, 7 June 1962, 1–3, in Viña del Mar, Chile, first round), two seconds faster than Brian **Robson**'s goal after 27 seconds (for England **v France,** 16 June, 3–1, in Bilbao, Spain, first round). **4. Football League**: four seconds (unconfirmed), Jim Fryatt for **Bradford Park Avenue, v Tranmere**, 25 April 1965, Fourth Division – timed by the referee); six seconds, Albert Mundy (for **Aldershot, v Hartlepool United**, in Hartlepool, 25 October 1958, Fourth Division); six seconds, Barrie Jones (for **Newport County** v **Torquay United**, 31 March 1962, Third Division); and six seconds, Keith Smith (for **Crystal Palace,** v **Derby Count**y, in Derby, 12 December 1964, Second Division). **5. FA Cup** final (at **Wembley** stadium): 43 seconds, Roberto **Di Matteo** (for Chelsea, v **Middlesbrough**, May 1997). **6. Scottish Cup** 9.6 seconds, John Hewitt, for Aberdeen (v **Motherwell**, in Motherwell, 23 January 1982, third round). **7.** Friendly: five seconds Malcolm Macdonald, for **Newcastle United** (v **St Johnstone**, at St Johnstone, 29 July 1972). **8.** African Cup of Nations 23 seconds, Ayman Mansour for **Egypt** (v Gabon, 1994).

goal-hang   *vb.*   *informal*   to wait near the opposition team's goal for a break-away opportunity to score. In practice, "goal-hanging" only applies in informal games, **five-a-side** and seven-a-side games where the **offside** rule does not apply. *n.* **goal-hanger**.

goal kick   *rules*   method of restarting a game after the ball has crossed a **defending team's goal line** where a goal has not been scored and where a member of the **attacking team** was the last player to touch the ball (Law XVI). A goal kick is awarded if the ball crosses the goal line between a **corner flagpost** and its nearest

goal post. The rule applies even if the ball curves out of play and back in without touching the ground – it does not, therefore, have to bounce outside the **field of play**. A goal kick is also awarded if the ball crosses the goal line between the goal posts if it had been thrown directly into the goal from a **throw in**, or kicked into the goal directly from an **indirect free kick**, taken by the attacking team. The game is restarted by a player from the defending team kicking the ball into play from a point anywhere within the **goal area**. The ball must be kicked beyond the **penalty area** (failure to do so will result in the kick being retaken). All opposition players must remain outside the penalty area until the kick has left that area. The player taking the kick must not touch the ball a second time until it has come into contact with another player – a breach of this rule will result in an indirect free kick awarded to the opposition from where the player made the second contact (unless the second contact is made with the ball still inside the penalty area, in which case the kick is retaken). A referee must signal that the goal kick is to be taken. A goal can be scored directly from a goal kick, but only against the opposition (if the defending side kicks the ball directly into its own net from a goal kick, then the kick is retaken). This rule was changed before the 1997-98 season; hitherto, a goal could not be scored directly. See **corner kick**.

goal line   *rules*   either of the two shorter boundary **lines** of the **field of play** (Law I). They run at right angles to the **touchlines**. The goal line must be of the same width as the width of the **goal posts** and **crossbar**. See **goal**.

goal nets   *n.*   see **net**.

goal-poach   *vb.*   *informal*   another word for **goalhang**. *n.* **goal-poacher**.

goal post   *rules*   either of the upright posts situated on the goal line which, along with the **crossbar** make up the **goal** (sense **1**) (Law I). Goal posts may be made of wood, metal or any material approved by the **International FA Board** and must be firmly secured for safety reasons. They may be square, rectangular, round, half-round or elliptical in cross-section (though the cross-section may be dictated by **competition rules**) and must be painted white. *History* In 1922, **Nottingham Forest**'s **City Ground** became the first to use elliptically-shaped (regular oval) goal posts, replacing the previous square and round posts. The new oval posts, which became widely used, were manufactured by the Nottingham-based company, Standard Goals. The English **Football League** ruled in 1939 that all league goal posts should be elliptical in cross-section. In 1997, the goal posts for **Spartak Moscow**'s home **UEFA Cup** match against **Sion** of Switzerland (1 October 1997, Lokomotiv Stadium, Moscow) were 2 cm taller than permitted. The **Union of European Football Associations** (UEFA) ruled that the match should be replayed. The following season, **Hearts** lodged a formal complaint with UEFA that the goal posts in its **European Cup-winners Cup** second leg against Real Mallorca (1 October 1998, in Mallorca) were too high in one of the goals; UEFA did not uphold the complaint and the result was allowed to stand. Hearts drew the match 1–1, but lost 1–2 on **aggregate**.

goal-shy *adv.* afraid to **shoot**.

goal-side *adv., adj.* of a player standing nearer to the goal than the opponent. Defenders are often advised to stand goal-side of an attacker in defensive situations, such as **corner kicks**.

goal-tally *n* another word for **score**.

goalkeeper *rules* a player whose primary duty is to prevent the ball entering his/her team's goal. Goalkeepers are the only players who are permitted to handle the ball (except for outfield players when taking a **throw-in**), but only when the ball is in their own **penalty area** and not when the ball is kicked to them from a team-mate or received directly from a throw-in (Law XII). Goalkeepers must wear a shirt that distinguishes them from the other players and officials (Law IV). Any player can change places with the goalkeeper, providing that the referee is notified of the change, and the change is made during a stoppage in play (Law III). The player must change into a goalkeeper's shirt, ie one distinct from the other players and the officials. *Keynotes* In the early years of **association football**, goalkeepers were allowed to handle the ball anywhere in their own half. The restriction to handling in the penalty area was introduced in 1912. Goalkeepers were first required to wear shirts of a different colour to their team mates in 1909 (though the idea had first been proposed in 1898). They were given a choice from scarlet, blue or white, with green added to the list in 1912. The most goals conceded by a goalkeeper in a **World Cup** match is 17, by Iqbal Mohamed of the **Maldives** (2 June 1997, 0–17, v **Iran**, in Damascus, Syria, first round qualifier).

goalkeepers' shirts *rules* the **shirt** worn by goalkeepers. It must be of a colour that distinguishes the goalkeeper from the other players and officials (Law IV). *Keynotes* Initially **goalkeepers** wore the same colours as their teammates, but at the **Football Association**'s annual meeting on 8 June 1909 it was decided that in order to assist the **referee** a goalkeeper's shirt should be of a distinctive colour – either royal blue, scarlet or white, with royal green added to the list four years later. On 3 June 1921, the **Football Association** ruled that goalkeepers in international matches should wear yellow shirts; a rule that remained for many years. Goalkeepers playing in **Scottish FA Cup** matches were also required to wear yellow shirts. The rules governing the colours of goalkeepers' shirts remained largely unaltered until the 1980s when sportswear manufacturers, unable to radically alter the first kits of the major football clubs, were given the freedom to experiment with the design of goalkeepers' kit. Some of the most flamboyant goalkeepers' shirts have belonged to **Mexico** international Jorge Campos, who designs his own kit.

goalmouth *n.* the area in front of the goal; it is not a technical definition with regards to dimensions and layout of the field of play, but refers to the small area from

where many goals are scored by strikers heading or striking a cross.

goals conceded *n.pl.* the number of goals that a club has conceded in its league games. *Regulations* Goals conceded are used to separate clubs in the **Football League** that are level on **points** and on **goals scored**; if they are still level at the end of the season they will **play off** at a **neutral venue** (Football League regulation 10.1).

goals, fewest conceded in one season (club) *record* **1. Football League**: 16 goals in 42 games, **Liverpool** (1978-79, Division One) – Liverpool conceded only four goals at home. **2.** Division One: 16 in 42 games, Liverpool (as above). **3.** FA **Premier League**: 17 in 38 games, Arsenal (1998-99); Manchester United conceded just four goals in 21 Premier League games at Old Trafford in 1994-95. **4. Scottish Football League**: 14 goals in 38 games, Celtic (1913-14, Division One); Dundee conceded only 12 goals in 1902-03 (Division One), but in a season of only 22 games. **5.** Scottish Premier Division/League: 19 in 36 games, **Rangers** (1989-90).

goals, fewest in one day *record* the fewest number goals ever scored on one day in a normal English top-flight league programme (**Football League** Division One or FA **Premier League**) is 10, in 10 matches (28 April 1923). All were scored by clubs playing at home.

goals, fewest scored in one season (club) *record* **1.** Football League: 24 in 42 matches, **Watford** (1971-72, Division Two). **2.** Division One: 24 in 42 matches, **Stoke City** (1984-85). **3.** FA Premier League: 28 in 38 matches, **Leeds United** (1996-97 – remarkably, Leeds finished 11th in the table). *Keynotes* **Hartlepool United** played 1,227 minutes, more than 13 games, without scoring (2 January to 6 March 1993; 11 league and two cup games). Swedish club **AIK Stockholm** scored only 25 goals in its 26 games of the 1998 league season – the fewest in the league – and still won the championship. **Trabzonspor** won the 1980 Turkish league championship despite scoring just 25 goals in its 30 games: the goals-per-game ratio of 0.833 is a world record low for a top-flight championship winning club.

goals, most at international level *record* the 12 all-time top goalscorers at full international level are: Ferenc **Puskás** (**Hungary**), 83 goals in 84 games, 1945-56; **Pelé** (**Brazil**), 77 goals in 92 games, 1957-71; Sándor **Kocsis** (Hungary), 75 goals in 68 games, 1948-56; Gerd **Müller** (West **Germany**) 68 goals in 62 matches, 1966-1974; Imre Schlosser (Hungary) 60 goals in 68 matches (1906-1927); Joachim **Streich** (**East Germany**) 55 goals in 102 matches, 1969-1984; Kazuyoshi Miura (Japan) 54 goals in 86 matches, 1990-1998; Poul **Nielsen** (**Denmark**) 52 goals in 38 matches, 1910-1925; Kunishige Kumamoto (**Japan**), 51 goals in 59 matches, 1964-77; Bobby **Charlton** (**England**) 49 goals in 106 matches, 1958-1970; Sven Rydell (**Sweden**) 49 goals in 43 matches 1923-1932; Lájos Tichy (Hungary) 49 goals in 71 matches, 1955-1964.

goals, most conceded in one season (club) *record* **1. Football League**: 141 goals in 34 games, **Darwen** (1898-99, Division Two). **2.** Division One: 125 goals in 42 games, **Blackpool** (1930-31). **3.** FA **Premier League**: 100 goals in 42 games, **Swindon Town** (1993-94). **4. Scottish Football League**: 146 in 38 games, **Edinburgh City** (1931-32, Division Two). **5. Scottish Premier Division/League**: 100 in 36 games, **Morton** (1984-85); and 100 in 44 games, Morton (1987-88).

goals, most for one club *record* **1.** World: **Pelé** scored 1,090 goals for **Santos** in 1,114 matches (though many were in friendlies). **2. Football League**: 349 Dixie **Dean** (**Everton**, 1925-37).

goals, most in cup football *record* **1. World Cup** finals: 14, Gerd **Müller** (1970, 1974). **2. Copa America**: Norberto **Mendez**, 17 goals (1945, 1946, 1947). **3. European Cup**: Alfredo **Di Stefano**, 49 (1956–62). **4. FA Cup**: 48, Henry Cursham for **Notts County** (1880-87); 44, Ian **Rush** for **Chester**, **Liverpool**, **Newcastle United** (1979-98; including two in both the 1986 (3–1 v **Everton**) and 1989 (3–2 v Everton) finals and one in the 1992 (2–0 v **Sunderland**) final); 41, Denis **Law** for **Huddersfield Town**, **Manchester City** and **Manchester United**.

goals, most in league football *record* **1. Football League**: 434, Arthur **Rowley** (1947-65, **West Bromwich Albion** 4, **Fulham** 27, **Leicester City** 251, **Shrewsbury Town** 152). **2.** First Division: 357, Jimmy **Greaves** (1957-71, **Chelsea**, **Tottenham Hotspur**, **West Ham United**). **3.** FA **Premier League**: 145, Alan **Shearer** (1992-, **Blackburn Rovers**, **Newcastle United** (figure to the end of 1998). **4. Scottish Football League**: 410, Jimmy McGrory (1922-38, **Celtic** 397, **Clydebank** 13).

goals, most in one day *record* **1. Football League**: 209 goals in 44 league matches, 1 February 1936 (Division One – 46; Division Two – 46; Division Three (South) 49; Division Three (North) 68), including 12 **hat-tricks**. Only one match ended goalless (**Aldershot** v **Bristol City**, Division Three (South)). **2.** Division One: 66 goals in 10 matches (26 December 1963). **3.** FA **Premier League**: 47 goals in nine matches (8 May 1993).

goals, most in one match (player) *record* **1. Football League**: 10, Joe Payne of **Luton Town** (v **Bristol Rovers**, 13 April 1936, Division Three South). **2.** FA **Premier League**: five, Andy Cole of **Manchester United** (v **Ipswich Town**, 4 March 1995). **3. FA Cup**: nine, Ted MacDougall of **Bournemouth** (v Margate, 20 November 1971, first round). **4. England** international: seven, Vivian **Woodward** (for England Amateurs, 1 November 1906, 15–0, v France, in Paris); five, Oliver Vaughton (18 February 1882, 13–0, v Ireland, in Belfast); five, Steve **Bloomer** (16 March 1896, 9–1, v **Wales**, in Cardiff); five, Willie Hall (16 November 1938, 7–0, v **Ireland**, at **Old Trafford**, Manchester); five, Malcolm Macdonald

for **England** (16 April 1975, 5–0, v **Cyprus**, at **Wembley** Stadium, London, **European Championship** qualifying group). **5. Scottish League**: several players have scored eight in one game; the first to do so was Owen McNally of Arthurlie (v Armadale, 1 October 1927, Scottish Division One), followed by Jimmy McGrory of **Celtic** (v **Dunfermline Athletic**, 14 January 1928, Scottish Division One). **6. Scottish Premier Division/League**: five, Paul Sturrock of **Dundee United** (v Morton – now **Greenock Morton**– 20 November 1984, 7–0, at Tannadice Park); five Marco Negri of **Rangers** (v Dundee United, 23 August 1997, 5–1, at Ibrox). **7. Scottish FA Cup**: 13, John Petrie of **Arbroath** (v Bon Accord, 12 September 1885, Scottish FA Cup first round); Gerry Baker scored 10 for **St Mirren** in its 15–0 first-round defeat of Glasgow University on 30 January 1960 – the Scottish Cup record in the 20th century; Baker's brother Joe scored nine for **Hibernian** the following season against Peebles Rovers in the second round (15–1). **8. Scotland** international: five, Hughie **Gallacher** (23 February 1929, 7–3, v Ireland, in Belfast). **9. Ireland** international: six, Joe Bambrick (1 February 1930, 7–0, v Wales, in Belfast); **10. World Cup**: Oleg **Salenko** of **Russia** scored a World Cup finals record of five goals in one game (6–1, v **Cameroon**, 28 June 1994, in Detroit, USA, first round). **11. European Championship**: five, Malcolm Macdonald (as above). **12.** European club competition: six, Lothar Emmerich, for **Borussia Dortmund** (v **Floriana FC**, 8–0, **European Cup-winners Cup**, first round, 1965). **13. FA Women's Challenge Cup** 22, Linda Curl for Norwich (40–0, v Milton Keynes, 1983).

goals, most in one season (club) *record* **1. Football League**: 134 goals in 46 matches, **Peterborough United** (Division Four 1960-61) – it was Peterborough's debut season in the Football League, with centre-forward Terry Bly scoring a post-war record of 52 goals in the season. **2.** Division One: 128 goals in 42 games, **Aston Villa** (1930-31) 3. **Premier League**: 82 goals in 42 games, **Newcastle United** (1993-94). **3. Scottish Football League** 142 goals in 34 matches, **Raith Rovers** (1937-38, Scottish Second Division). **4.** Scottish Division One: 132 goals in 34 matches, **Hearts** (1957-58). **5.** Scottish Premier Division/League: 101 goals in 44 matches, **Rangers** (1991-92).

goals, most in one season (player) *record* **1. Football League**: 60, Dixie **Dean** (**Everton**, Division One, 1927-28, in 39 games); 59 George Camsell (**Middlesbrough**, Division Two, 1926-27, in 37 games). **2.** FA **Premier League**: 34, Andy Cole (**Newcastle United**, 1993-94, in 40 games); 34, Alan **Shearer** (**Blackburn Rovers**, 1994-95, 42 games). **3. Scottish Football League**: 66, Jimmy Smith (**Ayr United**, 1927-28, Scottish Division Two, in 38 games). **4. Scottish Premier Division/League**: 35, Brian McClair (**Celtic**, 1986-87, in 44 games).

goals, most in senior career *record* **1.** World: Former **Brazil** international Artur **Friedenreich** is thought to be the world record goalscorer at club and national senior level, with 1,329 goals between 1909 and 1935, for Brazil, Germania, Ipiranga, Americao, Paulistano, **São Paulo FC** and **Flamengo**; **Pelé** is credited with 1,282 career goals in 1,365 matches (1956-77), including 1,090 goals for **Santos** in 1,114 matches, and 77 goals in 92 appearances for Brazil (1957-71). **2.** Players predominantly based in England: 474, John **Aldridge** (1979-98, **Newport County**, **Oxford United**, **Liverpool**, **Tranmere Rovers**, and including 45 goals for **Real Sociedad** and 19 goals for the **Republic of Ireland**; Aldridge scored two in his last game, on 3 May 1998, v **Wolverhampton Wanderers**, First Division); 464, Arthur **Rowley** (1947-65, **West Bromwich Albion**, **Fulham**, **Leicester City**, **Shrewsbury Town**); 410, Jimmy **Greaves** (1957-71, **Chelsea**, **Tottenham Hotspur**, **West Ham United**, and includes nine league goals for **ACMilan** and 44 goals for **England**); **3.** Player based in Scotland: 550, Jimmy **McGrory** (1922-38, **Celtic** and **Clydebank**, including six goals for **Scotland**). *Keynotes* McGrory's 550 goals is a UK record in first-class football, made during a playing career spanning 15 years between 1922 and 1937. His total includes 410 goals in 408 **Scottish League** matches, of which 397 were scored for Celtic in 378 League games. McGrory scored eight against **Dunfermline Athletic** in January 1928 and he holds the Scottish League record for the fastest hat-trick, scoring three times in three minutes against **Motherwell** in March 1936.

goals, most scorers in one match *record* **1.** **Football League**: eight players scored for **Liverpool** in its 9–0 victory over **Crystal Palace** (12 September 1989, at **Anfield**, Division One): Nicol (two), McMahon, **Rush**, Gillespie, Beardsley, **Aldridge** (in his last game for the club), **Barnes** and Hysen. **2.** European club competition: nine players scored for Liverpool in a **European Cup-winners Cup** match against Norwegian club Stromsgodset (17 September 1974, 11–0, at Anfield, first round). **3.** **Scottish Football League**: nine players scored for **Stirling Albion** in its 20–0 victory over Selkirk (8 December 1984, Scottish Cup first round).

goals scored *n. pl.* the number of goals that a club has scored in its league games. *Regulations* Goals scored are used to separate clubs in the **Football League** that are level on **points**; if they are still level, the final position will be decided on the basis of **goals conceded** (Football League regulation 10.1). Goals scored are used to determine the league position of clubs in the **Premier League** or **Scottish Football League** that are level on both points and **goal difference** (FA Premier League rule B.23, Scottish Football League rule 30). If Premier League or Scottish Football League clubs are still level at the end of the season, and if their respective positions are important to determine the championship, relegation or qualification for other competitions (such as the **UEFA Cup**), they will **play off** at a **neutral venue** (FA Premier League rule A.31, Scottish Football League rule 30). See also **goal average**, **number of victories**.

goals, top scorer in successive seasons *record* **1.** World: Atilio **Garcia** was top scorer in the Uruguayan league for a record seven times in a row: 1938, 1939, 1940, 1941, 1942, 1943 and 1944 with a grand total of 141 goals (he was top scorer again in 1946, with a further 21 goals). **2.** FA **Premier League**: Alan **Shearer** was top scorer in three consecutive seasons (31 in 1993-94; 34 in 1994-95; and 31 in 1995-96). *Keynotes* David Halliday scored more than 30 goals in four consecutive seasons for Sunderland, all in **Football League** Division One (38 in 1925-26; 36 in 1926-27; 36 in 1927-28; and 49 in 1928-29). Jimmy **Greaves** was Division One top scorer six times in 11 years, including three in succession: 32 in 1958-59, 41 in 1960-61, 37 in 1962-63, 35 in 1963-64, 29 in 1964-65 (joint top) and 27 in 1968-69. Greaves was transferred to **AC Milan** in 1961.

goalscoring position *n.* position from which it is possible to shoot or head at goal.

Goias *state* one of the 27 state leagues in **Brazil**, founded 1944. Leading clubs: Vila Nova (Goiânia), Atlético Goianense (Goiânia), Goiâs Esporte Clube (Goiânia).

Gola League *competition* former name (ca. 1981) of the **Football Conference**.

Gold Cup *competition* international nations tournament for member countries of the **Confederación Norte-Centroamericana y del Caribe de Fútbol**, first played in 1991. It was the first separate championship for CONCACAF countries since the **CONCACAF Championship** was last played as a discrete tournament in 1971 (from 1971 it was replaced by the CONCACAF World Cup qualifying tournament; the winners simply being declared CONCACAF champions). From 1996, the Gold Cup organisers have invited Brazil. *Winners, results and runners-up* 1991 **United States of America** (0–0, 4–3 pens., v **Honduras**, in Los Angeles, USA); 1993 **Mexico** (4–0, v United States of America, in Mexico City); 1996 Mexico (2–0, v Brazil, in Los Angeles); 1998 Mexico (1–0 v USA, in Los Angeles).

golden boot *award* any of the annual awards for the leading goalscorer in an English, British or European season. The traditional trophy is a replica gold-coloured boot. See also **European Golden Boot**.

golden goal *n.* the sudden-death first goal scored in **extra time**. The match is finished as soon as a golden goal is scored. Golden goals were introduced in major competitions in an effort to increase the likelihood that a knock-out match would reach a conclusion during playing time, without having to resort to a **penalty shoot-out**. *Keynotes* **Germany** striker Oliver Bierhoff became the first player to score a golden goal in a major international tournament, in the 94th minute of the 1996 **European Championship** final against the **Czech**

Republic at **Wembley**. **France**'s second round 1998 **World Cup** encounter with **Paraguay** became the first World Cup finals match to be settled by a golden goal, when French captain Lauren Blanc scored in the 114th minute of the game at **Stade Felix-Bollaert** in Lens on 28 June. In England, two **Auto Windscreens Shield** finals have been settled by a golden goal: 1994-95 Birmingham City 1–0 **Carlisle United**, 1997-98 **Grimsby Town** 2–1 **Bournemouth (AFC)**. The 1995 final, when Paul Tait scored in the 103rd minute, was the first occasion that a golden goal decided a match in England.

Goldstone Ground *ground* former English football ground situated in Hove, East Sussex; former home of **Brighton & Hove Albion**. Demolished Summer 1997. *Dossier* Capacity (1997): 10,952. Pitch dimensions: 104m x 68.5m. Record attendance: 36,747 v **Fulham** (27 December 1958, Division Two). Best average: 25,265 (1977-78). *History* A club called Hove FC first played at Goldstone Bottom on 7 September 1901 (v Clapton, friendly) and, in February 1902, it invited Brighton & Hove Albion to use the ground because the latter's County Ground was double booked. By that summer, the two clubs had reached a formal **groundshare** agreement and, in 1904, Brighton bought the ground's lease and Hove moved elsewhere. When Brighton joined the **Football League** in 1920-21, the Goldstone required extensive development. The club purchased the ground for £8,000 in 1926 on condition that the views of houses on Goldstone Lane should not be obstructed. The club was forced to vacate the Goldstone in May 1997 without finding an alternative venue at which to play home fixtures the following season – several planning applications for a new stadium were refused by the local council. Eventually the club agreed a groundshare deal with **Gillingham** (**Priestfield Stadium**) for the 1997-98 season. A catalogue of events led to this state of affairs. In October 1993, the club, heavily in debt, was saved from collapse by Greg Stanley, who had been a board member since the mid-1980s. The Goldstone Ground was subsequently sold to property developers, Chartwell Development Properties, for £7.4 million on condition that the club leave in May 1996 (later extended by one year). Chartwell subsequently sold the fully-developed site to Abbey Life Assurance for £24 million in a deal concluded in September 1997. Towards the latter end of the 1995-96 season and throughout the 1996-97 campaign, the Goldstone was the setting for several protests by Brighton fans against the club's board. A demonstration by supporters led to the abandonment of Brighton's home match against **York City** in May 1996; as punishment the club was instructed by the **Football Association** to play one home fixture **behind closed doors** and it would also face the possibility of losing three points if further disturbances took place. Following three pitch invasions at the Goldstone Ground during the match against **Lincoln City** (10 October 1996) and further crowd trouble during the **Fulham** game (26 October), the FA enforced the three-point deduction. Brighton's final match at the Goldstone Ground took place on 26 April 1997 (1–0 v **Doncaster Rovers**). Both **Tottenham Hotspur** and **Wimbledon** played their **Intertoto Cup** matches at the Goldstone in July 1995. The first floodlit match at the Goldstone took place on 10 April 1961 (v Danish club Frem, friendly). The site is now home to several retail superstores.

goleador *misc.* Spanish term for an ace goalscorer.

Goodall, John *player* Striker. **England** international (14 caps). Born 19 June 1863. Career ca. 1880–1913. *Clubs* **Preston North End**, **Derby County**, **New Brighton Tower**, **Glossop North End**, **Watford** (player-manager). *Keynotes* A Londoner who developed his game in Scotland, playing for Kilmarnock Burns and Kilmarnock Athletic and Great Lever before joining Preston North End. Goodall scored one of Preston's three goals in the club's 1889 FA Cup final victory over **Wolverhampton Wanderers** (3–1). As a Preston player, Goodall famously scored nine goals against Dundee Strathmore and 16 in a 26–0 victory over Hyde FC. Made his final playing appearance in January 1913 at the age of 50, turning out for Maerdy against Swansea Town (now **Swansea City**). Goodall also twice played cricket for Derbyshire County Cricket Club. Included in the **Football League Centenary 100 Players**. *Honours* Football League Championship (Preston North End 1888-89), **FA Cup** (Preston North End 1889).

Goodison for Everton *misc.* campaign group set up by **Everton** supporters opposed to the club's plans to decamp to a new purpose-built stadium on the outskirts of **Liverpool**. The club had claimed that redevelopment to increase the capacity of **Goodison Park** is restricted by nearby housing. A feasibility study by an independent architect, and financed by the group, suggests that Goodison could be redeveloped to accommodate 50,000 plus. Following Peter Johnson's resignation as club chairman in 1998, the club shelved plans to move from Goodison.

Goodison Park *ground* English football ground situated in Liverpool, Merseyside; home of **Everton**. *Dossier* Ground capacity: 40,200 all seated. Record attendance: 78,299 v **Liverpool** (18 September 1948, Division One). Best average attendance: 51,603 (1962-63). Pitch dimensions: 102m x 71m. *History* Everton had been tenants of **Anfield** for eight years when in 1892, following a disagreement with the ground's landlord and club backer, John Houlding, the club decided to buy a site at Mere Green in Liverpool for £8,090. The ground is named Goodison Park because one entrance is on Goodison Road. The club spent around £3,000 clearing the site and building two uncovered stands. Goodison is considered to be the first major English club ground. Everton played its first match at the ground on 1 September 1892 (v **Bolton Wanderers**, friendly), although Goodison had staged an athletics meeting as its opening ceremony eight days earlier. In its first decade, Goodison had the highest average gate each season of any **Football League** club ground. In 1906, Archibald **Leitch** designed the ground's main stand (at the same time he also designed Anfield's **Kop**), a bigger stand in 1909 and a further double-decker stand in 1926. In July 1913, Goodison Park became the first Football League ground to be visited by a British monarch when George V met local school children at the ground. In 1938, with the opening of the Gladwys Street stand (also designed by Leitch), Goodison became the first league ground to have seated and standing accommodation on all four sides of the ground. The ground was one of the first to experiment with **under soil heating**, installing a system in 1958. No major redevelopment of the ground took place between then and 1969, when a £1 million three-tier stand, that included escalators in the public walkways, replaced Leitch's 1926 stand. By August 1994, with the opening of the Park Road stand, Goodison had become an **all-seater stadium**. Nonetheless, the then Everton chairman, Peter Johnson, held a "vote" of supporters at the end of the 1996-97 season to ascertain whether they would support a move to an all-purpose stadium on the outskirts of Liverpool. At the time, he received an affirmative vote, but following his departure in 1998 the plan was shleved. One **FA Cup** final (1894 **Notts County** v **Bolton Wanderers**) and one FA Cup final replay (1910 **Newcastle United** v **Barnsley**) have been staged at Goodison Park. In 1966, Goodison Park was used as a **World Cup** venue. The ground staged group 3 matches (**Brazil** v **Bulgaria**; Brazil v **Hungary**; Brazil v **Portugal**); a quarter-final (Portugal v **North Korea**); and a semi-final (**Soviet Union** v **West Germany**) – total attendance 235,695; average attendance 47,139. Because of political troubles in Ireland, Goodison Park hosted two **Northern Ireland** international matches in 1973 (v **England**, 12 May, v **Wales**, 19 May – Northern Ireland also used **Boothferry Park**, **Craven Cottage**, **Highfield Road** and **Hillsborough**, and switched its home matches against **Scotland** to **Hampden Park** during this period). The ground also staged the Brazil v **Japan** fixture as part of the 1995 **Umbro International Tournament**, that also included England and **Sweden** (6 June 1995). Goodison also hosted one England "victory international" after **World War I** (v **Scotland**, 26 April 1919) and a wartime international (v Wales, 16 September 1944). Goodison Park was also the setting for one of three matches in 1935 that experimented with **two referees** (**Football League** v Wales & Ireland, 11 May 1935) – the match also celebrated the Jubilee of King George V. Goodison Park hosted the record attendance for a **women's football** match in England: 53,000, 26 December 1920, **Dick, Kerr's Ladies** v St Helen's Ladies (4–0).

Gor Mahia (Golf Olympic Rangers Mahia) *club* Kenyan national league club based in Nairobi, founded 1968. Mahia is a tribal name; the club is associated with the Luos. Ground: Nyayo, capacity: 35,000. Strip: green shirts, white shorts. **African Cup-winners Cup** 1987 (3–3 agg., v **Esperance Sportive Tunis** of Tunisia; Gor Mahia won on **away goals**; the only all-Africa competition won by a Kenyan club), runners-up 1979 (0–8 agg., v **Canon Yaoundé** of Cameroon); **CAF Cup** quarter-final 1993; **East and Central African Club Championship** 1980, 1981, 1985, runners-up 1984; Kenyan Cup 1976, 1981, 1983, 1986, 1987, 1988, 1995;Kenyan league champions 1969, 1974, 1976, 1979, 1983, 1984, 1985, 1990, 1991, 1993, 1995.

Gordon, James Alexander *broadcaster* reader of the **classified results** on BBC radio's **Sports Report** and later BBC **Radio 5 Live**.

Górnik Zabrze *club* Polish national league side based in Kotowice, founded in 1948. Ground: Górnik, capacity: 23,000. Strip: red shirts, red shorts. *Keynotes* Górnik Zabrze has won more league titles than any other club in Poland. Its five consecutive titles (1963 to 1967) is a national record. **European Cup** quarter-final 1968; **European Cup-winners Cup** runners-up 1970 (1–2 v **Manchester City**, Vienna, Austria), quarter-final 1971; Polish Cup 1965, 1968, 1969, 1970, 1971, 1972; Polish League champions 1957, 1959, 1961, 1963, 1964, 1965, 1966, 1967, 1971, 1972, 1985, 1986, 1987, 1988 (more than any other Polish club). Notable former player: Wlodzimierz **Lubanski**.

Gossage Cup *competition* former international nations tournament participated by **Kenya** (12-times), Tanganyika (now part of **Tanzania**, four wins), **Uganda** (26 wins) and **Zanzibar** (now part of Tanzania, one win). Played from 1927 (won by Kenya) to 1972 when it was replaced by the **East and Central African Challenge Cup**. Named after a former governor.

Gottlieb-Daimler stadion *ground* German football ground situated in Stuttgart, Baden-Württemberg; home of **Stuttgart VfB**. Ground capacity: 47,000. *History* Built in 1933 and completely redeveloped for the 1974 **World Cup**. Initially called the Adolf Hitler Kampfbahn and later the Neckarstadion. In 1950, it hosted West **Germany**'s first international fixture (v **Switzerland**, 22 November). During the 1974 World Cup, Gottlieb-Daimler staged three group 4 matches (**Poland** v **Argentina**, Argentina v **Italy**, Poland v Italy) and one second-round group B fixture (Poland v **Sweden**) – total attendance 213,055; average attendance 53,263. The stadium was also a venue for the 1988 **European Championship**. It has staged two **European Cup** finals (1958 **Real Madrid** v **AC Milan**, 67,000; 1988 **PSV Eindhoven** v **Benfica**, 70,000) and the replay of the 1962 **European Cup-winners Cup** final (**Atlético Madrid** v **Fiorentina**, 45,000).

Göztepe Izmir (Göztepe Spor Kolübü) *club* Turkish national league club based in Izmir, founded 1925. Ground: Alsancak, capacity: 17,000. Strip: red and green shirts, red shorts. **European Cup-winners Cup** quarter-final 1969; Turkish Cup 1969, 1970, runners-up 1967; Turkish league – third 1971; **UEFA Cup** semi-final 1969 (1–8 agg., v **Ujpesti Dózsa**).

Graham, George *player-manager* Midfield. **Scotland** international (12 caps). Born 30 November 1944. Career ca. 1962–1980. *Clubs* (player) **Aston Villa**, **Chelsea**, **Arsenal**, **Manchester United**, **Portsmouth**,

Crystal Palace, Queens Park Rangers, (manager) Queens Park Rangers (coach), **Millwall**, Arsenal, **Leeds United, Tottenham Hotspur**. *Keynotes* Joined Chelsea from Aston Villa for £6,000 in June 1964, making 72 appearances and scoring 35 goals for the club. He moved to Arsenal for £50,000 (with Tommy Baldwin going to Chelsea in an exchange deal) in September 1966 and was a member of the 1970-71 **double** winning side. Manchester United paid £125,000 for him in December 1972. As a manager, Graham has been one of the most successful in the post-**World War II** period. During his nine years as Arsenal manager (1986-95), the club won six major trophies. He was dismissed by the club in February 1995 amid allegations of transfer irregularities. A **Football Association** inquiry found Graham guilty of accepting money from Norwegian agent Rune Hauge and he was banned from football for one year. Graham became Leeds United manager in September 1996. Amid some controversy and compensation of around £3 million he was appointed manager of Tottenham Hotspur on 1 October 1998, winning the **League Cup** in his first season (1–0 v **Leicester City, Wembley**). *Honours* (player) League Championship (Arsenal 1970-71); **FA Cup** (Arsenal 1971); League Cup (Aston Villa 1963, Chelsea 1965); **UEFA** (Fairs) **Cup** (Arsenal 1970), (manager) League Championship (Arsenal 1988-89, 1990-91); FA Cup (Arsenal 1993); League Cup (Arsenal 1987, 1993, Tottenham Hotspur 1999); **European Cup-winners Cup** (Arsenal 1994); League Cup (Tottenham Hotspur 1999); **Football League Trophy** (Millwall 1983).

grand-slam *informal* victory in the domestic league, all domestic cups and the **European Cup**. The only British team to have achieved this is **Celtic**, winning the **Scottish League** Championship, **Scottish FA Cup** (2–0 v **Aberdeen**), **Scottish League Cup** (1–0 v **Rangers**) and the European Cup (2–1 v **Internazionale**) in 1966-67.

Grasshopper-Club Zurich *club* Swiss national league club based in Zurich, founded 1886. Ground: Hardturm, capacity: 22,000 all seated. Strip: blue and white halved shirts, white shorts. **European Cup-winners Cup** quarter-final 1990; **Mitropa Cup** quarter-final 1937; Swiss Cup 1926 (the first competition), 1927, 1932, 1934, 1937, 1938, 1940, 1941, 1942, 1943, 1946, 1952, 1956, 1983, 1988, 1989, 1990, 1994; Swiss national champions 1898 (the first championship), 1900, 1901, 1905, 1921, 1927, 1928, 1931 (three regional leagues operated until 1933, with the national championship decided by an inter-league play-off), 1937, 1939, 1942, 1943, 1945, 1952, 1956, 1971, 1978, 1982, 1983, 1984, 1990, 1991, 1995, 1996, 1998; **UEFA Cup/Fairs Cup** semi-final 1978. Notable former player: Kubilay Türkyilmaz.

Gray, Andy *player/broadcaster* Striker. **Scotland** international (20 caps, 7 goals). Born 30 November 1955. Career ca. 1973–1989. *Clubs* **Dundee United**, Aston Villa (twice), **Wolverhampton Wanderers**,

Everton, Notts County, West Bromwich Albion, Rangers. Joined Dundee United as a schoolboy, signing professional forms in May 1973. He made 62 League appearances for Dundee United, and scoring 36 goals before being transferred to Aston Villa for £110,000 in September 1975. In his first spell with Villa, Gray netted 54 goals in 113 **Football League** matches, moving to Wolves for a then UK record £1.46 million. During his time at **Villa Park**, Gray became the first, and so far only, player to win both the PFA's **Footballer of the Year** award and its Young Footballer of the Year accolade in the same season (1977). Gray scored the winning goal for Wolves in the 1980 **League Cup** final victory over **Nottingham Forest**. In November 1983, Gray was transferred to Everton for £200,000. Gray retired in 1989, becoming assistant to manager Ron Atkinson at Villa Park before moving in 1991 into television as pundit for BSkyB. Gray turned down the chance to become Everton manager before the start of the 1997-98 season, preferring to stay in television. In 1998, *Flat Back Four*, a guide to football tactics written by Gray, was published. *Honours* League Championship (Everton 1984-85); **FA Cup** (Everton 1984); League Cup (Wolverhampton Wanderers 1980); **European Cup-winners Cup** (Everton 1985).

Gre-no-li *players* nickname given to the post-war Swedish forwards Gunnar **Gren**, Gunnar **Nordhal** and Nils **Liedholm**. The name, derived from their surnames, was given by fans of **AC Milan**, after the three were transferred to the Italian club in 1949. Between them, they scored 329 goals for Milan. All three played in Sweden's **Olympic Games** Gold medal winning side of 1948: a 3–1 defeat of **Yugoslavia** at **Wembley** Stadium, with Gren (2) and Nordahl getting the goals. Liedholm and Gren played in the 1958 **World Cup** final, with Liedholm scoring after only four minutes (2–5 v **Brazil**, Stockholm). The Gre-no-li were barred from the 1950 and 1954 World Cup squad, with Sweden placing a ban on professional players. Curiously, all three were born in October.

Great Britain *country* *no unified affiliation* monarchy in north-west Europe consisting of **England, Scotland** and **Wales**. With **Northern Ireland**, it forms the United Kingdom of Great Britain and Northern Ireland. It does not include the Channel Islands or the Isle of Man. Northern Ireland was created in 1921 – with the separation of the Irish Free State (now the **Republic of Ireland**) – and has remained a constituent part of the United Kingdom. It joined the European Union in 1973. Britain's colonial past started around 1600. Between the two World Wars, the British empire covered more than a quarter of the World's land mass and population. Virtually all former colonies are now independent nations, most remaining in the Commonwealth. Area: 244,755 sq km (94,475 sq miles). Population: 58,738 (total for UK, 1996 est.). Languages: English, Welsh, Gaelic, various Asian languages. Capital: London. *Dossier* Great Britain is neither affiliated to **FIFA** nor to the **Union of European Football Associations** (UEFA) – separate football associations exist for England, Northern Ireland, Scotland and Wales – though Great Britain has fielded amateur sides in the **Olympic Games**. Biggest victory: 9–0 v **Thailand** (November 1956, in Melbourne, Australia, Olympic Games preliminary round). Biggest defeat: 1–6 v **Bulgaria** (November 1956, in Melbourne, Olympic Games first round). *International tournament record* Olympic Games – fourth place 1948 (3–5 v **Denmark**, London, third/fourth playoff), quarter-final 1936, first round 1952, 1956, 1960; Great Britain finished fifth in the first International Blind Sports Federation Football World Championships in São Paulo in 1998 (see **visually impaired football**). *History* Although England entered the Olympic Games football tournament in 1908, 1912 and 1920, since then neither England, Northern Ireland, Scotland nor Wales, has been allowed to enter separate teams. Amateur Great Britain sides entered the Olympic Games from 1936 to 1960. Aside from these Olympic Games amateur squads, a full-strength Great Britain XI played a one-off friendly against the "Rest of Europe" to celebrate the rejoining of the four home nations to FIFA in 1946 (they had resigned en bloc in 1928). The match, at Hampden Park, Glasgow, was won 6–1 by Great Britain, in front of 135,000 spectators, with Wilf **Mannion**, Tommy **Lawton** (2), scoring five of the goals between them. Scotland's Billy Steel scored the other for the home side. The team comprised five English, three Scots, two Welsh, and one Northern Irish: **Swift** (goalkeeper), Hardwick, Hughes, Macaulay, Vernon, Burgess, Matthews, Mannion, Lawton, Steel and **Liddell**. See England, Northern Ireland, Scotland, Wales.

Great Olympics *club* Ghanaian professional league club based in the capital Accra, founded 1954. Accra Sports Stadium (the national stadium), capacity: 45,000 (5,000 seated). Strip: blue shirts, white shorts. **African Cup of Champion Clubs** semi-final 1971; Ghanaian Cup 1975, 1983; Ghanaian League champions 1974.

Greaves, Jimmy *player* Striker. **England** international (57 caps, 44 goals). Born 20 February 1940. Career ca. 1955–71. *Clubs* **Chelsea, AC Milan, Tottenham Hotspur, West Ham United**. *Keynotes* Joined Chelsea juniors in 1955, turning professional in May 1957. Transferred to AC Milan for £80,000 in June 1961, but he made only 14 appearances – although he scored nine goals – before returning to England with Tottenham Hotspur for £99,999 seven months later. Greaves scored 124 goals in 157 **Football League** appearances for Chelsea and 220 in 321 matches for Spurs – a club record. One of his most remarkable achievements was to score on his **debut** for England, England Under-23s, Chelsea, AC Milan, Spurs and West Ham. His international debut was against **Peru** (17 May 1959, lost 1–4) and he recorded a hat-trick in England's 9–3 demolition of Scotland (15 April 1961). Although Greaves played in England's early 1966 **World Cup** fixtures, he lost his place through injury and was left out of

the team for the final stages. In 1970, he took part in the **World Cup rally** (London to Mexico), finishing sixth. He is England third all-time record goalscorer – behind Bobby **Charlton** and Gary **Lineker** – with 44 goals in 57 appearances. Overall, Greaves scored 357 goals in 516 League matches. He later co-hosted a television programme, *The Saint and Greavsie Show*, with former **Liverpool** and **Scotland** international Ian St John. Included in the **Football League Centenary 100 Players**. *Honours* **FA Cup** (Tottenham Hotspur 1962, 1967); **European Cup-winners Cup** (Tottenham Hotspur 1963).

Greece *country UEFA* republic in south-east Europe on the Mediterranean, Ionian and Aegean Seas, includes the South Balkan Peninsula and many islands (154 inhabited). Bordered by **Macedonia**, **Bulgaria**, **Turkey** and **Albania**. Area: 131,985 sq km (50,945 sq miles). Population: 10,400,000 (1994 est.). Language: Greek. Capital: Athens. *Dossier* Hellenic Football Federation (Athens) formed in 1926, affiliated to **FIFA** in 1927 and founder member of **Union of European Football Associations** (UEFA) in 1954, president Sotiris Alimissis, general secretary Vassilis Gagatsis. Season played from September to June. National stadium: Stadio OAKA Spiros Louis, Athens, capacity: 76,000 all seated. National strip: white shirts, blue shorts. First international game: 28 August 1920, v **Sweden** (0–9, in Antwerp, **Olympic Games** first round). Biggest victory: 8–0, v **Syria** (25 November 1949, in Athens, friendly). Biggest defeat: 0–9 (as above). Most capped players: Efstratios Apostolakis (95, 1986-), Dimitrios Saravakos (78, 1982-97), Anastasios Mitropoulos (76, 1978–1994). Leading goalscorers: Nikolaos Anastopoulos (29 goals), Dimitrios Saravakos (22 goals), Dimitrios Papaioanou (21 goals, 1963–78). *International tournament record* Olympic Games – first entered 1920, never passed first round; **Women's World Cup** – never qualified; **World Cup** – first entered 1934, qualified for finals tournament 1994 (first round); **European Championship** – entered first tournament in 1960 (first round, no qualifying tournament), qualified for finals tournament 1980 (first round); **European Championship for Women** – first entered 1993, never past first-round group stage; **Under-17 World Championship** – never qualified; **World Youth Cup** (under-20) – never qualified. *Record against British and Irish national teams* v **England**, played six, drawn one, lost five; v **Northern Ireland**, played three, won two, lost one; v **Scotland**, played two, won one, lost one; v **Wales**, played two, won one, lost one; v **Republic of Ireland**, none played. *History* The ancient Greeks are thought to have played a rudimentary form of football, episkyros. The modern game, however, was introduced in the late nineteenth century. Representative sides from the two largest cities, Athens and Salonica, competed in a match in 1906: a game marred by an outbreak of violence. A league competition involving clubs from Athens and Salonica started in 1928, with the national championship decided through playoffs with clubs from the other regional leagues. Regional leagues continued to operate until 1960, when a truly national Greek championship started. It did not become full-time professional until 1979. The league competitions have been dominated by "big-three" clubs from Athens, **Olympiakos**, **AEK Athens**, and **Panathinaikos**: from 1928 to 1999, the league championship had been won only six times by other clubs. Panathinaikos was **European Cup** finalists in 1971. The Greek Cup dates back to 1932. The Greek national side has had only limited success. After entering the World Cup in 1934, Greece waited 60 years for its first appearance in the World Cup finals, in 1994, unbeaten in its five-nation qualifying group. Greece went close to qualifying for the finals in 1998. However, its 0–0 draw with **Denmark** in the last game in the qualifying tournament, in front of 70,000 spectators in Athens, allowed Denmark to qualify automatically and **Croatia** (winners in **Slovenia**) to progress to the playoff stages, and thence to the finals tournament. A win would have put Greece top of the group, and automatic qualifiers for France '98. Disgruntled Greek fans threw flares on to the pitch during the game. *World Cup performance* (finals and qualifiers to end of 1998 tournament) played 75, won 25, drawn 15, lost 35, scored 82 goals, conceded 129 goals; win rate 33%; goals scored per game 1.09. *League system* There are 18 clubs in the Greek First Division (A'Ethniki); clubs play each other home and away. Three points are awarded for a win, and one for a draw; if clubs are level on points, the final positions are determined by the results of the matches between them; **goal difference** is used to separate clubs level on points and fixture parity. The bottom three clubs are automatically relegated to the second division (B'Ethnikis). The second division has 18 clubs, four being relegated into the regional (north and south) third divisions. The fourth division is also regionalised. *Record in international club tournaments* European Cup – Panathinaikos (runners-up 1971, semi-final 1985); **European Cup-winners Cup** – PAOK Salonica (quarter-final 1974), **Larissa FC** (quarter-final 1985), Olympiakos (quarter-final 1993), AEK Athens (quarter-final 1997); **UEFA Cup** – AEK Athens (semi-final 1977). Other leading club: **Aris Salonica**.

Green, Alan *commentator* **Radio 5 Live** sports commentator who began as a journalist on local Belfast newspaper before joining the BBC in 1975. Later joined BBC Radio Sport as senior sports broadcaster. Green won the Sony Awards Sports Broadcaster of the Year accolade in 1998.

Green Buffaloes *club* Zambian national league club based in the capital Lusaka, founded as Zambia Army (adopted current name 1975). Ground: Independence (the national stadium), capacity: 30,000. Strip: green shirts, white shorts. **East and Central African Cup** semi-final 1980; Zambian Cup 1982; Zambian league champions 1973, 1974, 1975, 1977, 1979, 1981.

Green Guide *legal* former voluntary code for ground safety at sports stadiums, brought in by the **Wheatley**

Report in the wake of the 1971 **Ibrox disaster**. Superceded by the mandatory requirements of the **Safety of Sports Ground Act 1975**.

Greenland (Kalaalit Nunaat) *country no international affiliation* self-governing island region of **Denmark** – Greenland is largely within the Arctic Circle, off the northeast coast of North America. Area: 2,175,600 sq km (836,780 sq miles). Almost 85% of the island is under a permanent ice cap. Population: 55,558. Languages: Greenlandic and Danish. Capital: Godthaab (Nuuk). *Dossier* The football association is affiliated to neither the **Union of European Football Associations** (UEFA) nor to **FIFA**. *International tournament record* **World Cup** – never entered; **European Championship** – never entered; tournament matches restricted to the **Island Games**. *Record against British and Irish national teams* none played (though **Jersey**, Shetland and Anglesey have competed with Greenland in the Island Games). *History* A national league has been played since 1971. *Leading clubs* B-67 (of Godthaab/Nuuk, league champions 1993, 1994, 1996), Grønlands Seminarius Sportklub (of Godthaab/Nuuk, league champions 1972, 1973, 1975, 1976), Kissaviarsuk 1933 (of Qaqortoq, league champions 1987, 1990, 1991), Nagdlunguaq 48 (league champions 1977, 1978, 1980, 1982, 1983, 1984).

Greenock Morton *club* Scottish league. *Dossier* Ground: **Cappielow Park**, Greenock, Strathclyde, capacity: 14,267. Strip: blue and white hooped shirts, white shorts with blue trim, blue and white hooped socks. Nickname: Ton. Record attendance: 23,500 v **Celtic** (1921-22, Division One). Biggest win: 11–0 v Carfin Shamrock (13 November 1886, **Scottish FA Cup**, first round). Biggest defeat: 1–10 v **Port of Glasgow** (5 May 1894, **Division Two**), v **St Bernards** (14 October 1933, Division Two). *History* Founded as Morton, name derived from the street, Morton Terrace, where some of the founder members lived. The club did not adopt its present title until the start of the 1993-94 season. The club, which in 1896 was the first **Scottish Football League** club to become a **limited company**, joined the newly-formed Division Two in 1893-94, finishing runners-up in 1899-00 and winning election to Division One. During the 1912–13 season, every Morton player scored, including the goalkeeper who converted a penalty. In 1916-17, the club was runners-up in the **World War I** Scottish League structure. Morton won the Scottish FA Cup in 1922 (1–0 v **Rangers**) and was a finalist again in 1948 (0–1 replay v Rangers). The club was a **Scottish League Cup** finalist in 1963-64 (0–5 v Rangers) and, in the same season, won the Second Division title with 67 points out of a possible 72. Morton was one of the first UK clubs to recruit Scandinavian players, starting with Danish goalkeeper Eric Sorenson in 1964. In 1968-69, Morton qualified for the European competition for the only time (3–9 agg., v **Chelsea**, UEFA (Fairs) **Cup**, first round). The club was a **Scottish League Challenge Cup** finalist in 1992-93 (2–3 v **Hamilton**

Academicals) and, in 1994-95, the first season after the expansion of the League, Morton was Second Division champions. The occasion of its biggest crowd, 23,500 against Celtic in 1921-22, was marred by a riot at the end of the match. The game was effectively a championship decider for the visitors and several trains carrying Celtic fans back to Glasgow's city centre were severely damaged. *League record* Premier Division 1978-79 to 1982-83, 1984-85, 1978-88; Division One (A Division) 1900-01 to 1914-15, 1921-22 to 1926-27, 1929-30 to 1932-33, 1937-38, 1946-47 to 1948-49, 1950-51 to 1951-52, 1964-65 to 1965-66, 1967-68 to 1974-75; First Division 1975-76 to 1977-78, 1983-84, 1985-86 to 1986-87, 1988-89 to 1993-94, 1995-96–; Scottish League 1915-16 to 1920-21; Division Two (B Division) 1893-94 to 1899-00, 1927-28 to 1928-29, 1933-34 to 1936-37, 1938-39, 1949-50, 1952-53 to 1963-64, 1966-67; Second Division 1994-95. *Honours* First Division 1977-78, 1983-84, 1986-87; Division Two 1949-50, 1963-64, 1966-67; Second Division 1994-95; Scottish FA Cup 1922 (1–0 v Rangers). *Records* Jimmy Cowan is Morton's most capped player (25 for **Scotland**); David Hayes holds the record for club appearances (358, 1969-84).

Grêmio Foot-Ball Porto-Alegrense *club* Brazilian national league and **Rio Grande do Sul** state league club based in Porto Alegre, founded 1903. Ground: Olimpico Monumental, capacity: 55,000. Strip: blue, black and white striped shirts, black shorts. **Campeonato Brasileiro** champions 1981, 1996; **Copa do Brasil** 1989, 1994, 1997; **Copa Libertadores** 1983 (1–1, 2–1, v **Peñarol**), 1995 (4–2 agg., v **Atlético Nacional Medellin**), runners-up 1984 (0–1, 0–0, v **Independiente**), semi-final 1996; **Recopa** 1995 (4–1, v Independiente, in Japan); state league champions 32 times (to 1998); **Supacopa** semi-final 1989; **World Club Cup** 1983 (2–1 v **Hamburg (SV)**, Tokyo), runners-up 1995 (0–0, 3–4 pens., v **Ajax**).

Gren, Gunnar *player* Striker. **Sweden** international (57 caps, 32 goals, ca. 1940-58). Born 31 October 1920, died November 1990. *Clubs* Garda BK, **IFK Göteborg**, **Ögryte Idrottssälskap**, **AC Milan**, **Fiorentina**, GAIS Göteborg. *Honours* **Olympic Games** gold medal (Sweden, 1948); **World Cup** runner-up (Sweden, 1958); Swedish championship (IFK, 1942), Italian Serie A championship (AC Milan, 1950). *Keynotes* Sweden's third-highest all-time goalscorer. Gren was one of the **Gre-no-li** trio, and affectionately known as "the Professor". He joined AC Milan in 1949.

Grenada *country CONCACAF* island state in the Caribbean in the Windward Islands. Includes the southern section of the Grenadines, a group of 600 islands in the Caribbean Sea. Independent from UK in 1974. Area: 345 sq km (133 sq miles). Population: 96,000 (1995 est.). Languages: English, French Patois. Capital: St George's. *Dossier* Grenada Football Association (St Georges) formed in 1924, affiliated to **FIFA** in 1976 and **Confederación Norte-Centroamericana y del**

Caribe de Fútbol (CONCACAF) in 1969, president A S P Smith Roberts, general secretary Carl Phillip. Season played from July to December. National stadium: Queen's Park, St Georges, capacity: 8,000. National strip: green and yellow striped shirts, red shorts. *International tournament record* **Olympic Games** – never qualified for finals tournament; **World Cup** – first entered 1982, did not enter again until 1998 when reached second round of qualifying tournament; **Caribbean Nations Cup** – fourth 1997 (1–4, v **Jamaica**, in Antigua and St Kitts, third/fourth playoff); **Gold Cup** – never qualified; **Under-17 World Championship** – never qualified; **World Youth Cup** (under-20) – never qualified. *Record against British and Irish national teams* none played. *Record in international club tournaments* no major success. Leading club: Fontenoy United (league champions 1998).

Gresty Road *ground* English football ground situated in Crewe, Cheshire; home of **Crewe Alexandra**. *Dossier* Ground capacity: 6,000. Pitch dimensions: 102m x 68m. Record attendance: 20,000 v **Tottenham Hotspur** (30 January 1960, **FA Cup**, fourth round). Best average attendance: 9,065 (1949-50). *History* Crewe played its first match at Gresty Road some time in 1906, having earlier played at several venues, including at one stage a ground at nearby Nantwich Road. Crewe won £30,000 second prize in the one-season **Ford Sporting League** in 1970-71, enabling the club to rebuild Gresty Road's Popular Side. In 1998, Crewe employed a trio of birds of prey – a hawk, a kestrel and an eagle owl – to scare off roosting pigeons. The first floodlit match, under floodlights bought from **Coventry City** and mounted on telegraph poles, took place on 29 October 1958 (v All Star XI).

gridiron *n.* informal name for **American football**, so-called because of the parallel lines marked out on every five yards (4.6 metres) of the pitch.

Griffin Park *ground* English football ground situated in west London; home of **Brentford**. *Dossier* Ground capacity: 12,763. Pitch dimensions: 101m x 68m. Record attendance: 39,626 v **Preston North End** (5 March 1938, **FA Cup**, sixth round). Best average attendance: 25,768 (1946-47). *History* Brentford played its first match at Griffin Park on 1 September 1904 (v **Plymouth Argyle**, Western League). Situated on a former orchard, Brentford leased the site from the brewers Fuller, Smith and Turner on a 21-year lease at an annual rent of £40. In 1967, the then club chairman Jack Dunnett planned to move **Queens Park Rangers** to Griffin Park and disband Brentford. The club also considered moving to the nearby local authority sports ground, Leas Stadium, and in February 1983 a section of the ground's main stand was destroyed by fire. Griffin Park is the only ground in the **Football League** to have a public house in each of its four corners. Rugby League club London Broncos has played at Griffin Park on several occasions. The first floodlit match at Griffin Park took place on 5 October 1954 (v **Chelsea**, friendly).

Grimsby Town *club*   English league. *Dossier* Ground: **Blundell Park**, Cleethorpes, Lincolnshire, capacity: 8,870. Strip: black and white striped shirts, black shorts, white socks. Nickname: the Mariners. Record attendance: 31,657 v **Wolverhampton Wanderers** (20 February 1937, **FA Cup**, fifth round). Best average attendance: 18,056 (1949-50). Biggest win: 8–0 v **Darlington** (21 November 1885, FA Cup, second round). Biggest defeat: 1–9 v **Arsenal** (28 January 1931, Division One). *History* Founded in September 1878 as Grimsby Pelham FC before adopting the Grimsby Town name a year later. Despite the club's name, and a 10-year residence in Grimsby between 1889 and 1899, the club has always played in nearby Cleethorpes. Grimsby's first ground was Clee Park, where two experimental floodlit matches were staged in 1889, and after a spell at Abbey Park the club settled at Blundell Park. Grimsby was a founder member of Division Two and in the division's first five seasons the club never finished outside of the top five, narrowly missing participation in the **test matches**, which between 1892-93 and 1897-98 determined promotion and relegation, on several occasions before winning the title and automatic promotion in 1900-01. Grimsby's tenure in Division One lasted only two seasons and the club did not regain a place in the top flight until 1929-30. The club failed in its bid for **re-election** in 1909-10, spending one season outside the **Football League**. The 1930s was the club's most successful period. It was relegated to Division Two in 1931-32, before returning to the top flight as champions two seasons later. It was also an FA Cup semi-finalist on two occasions, in 1936 (0–1 v Arsenal) and 1939 (0–5 v **Wolverhampton Wanderers**). Grimsby was relegated in 1947-48, dropping to Division Three (North) in 1950-51. Since then the club has alternated between the bottom two divisions interspersed with brief spells in Division Two. In 1968-69, Grimsby was forced to seek re-election. Three seasons later the club won the Division Four title. Grimsby was a **League Cup** quarter-finalist in 1980 (0–2 second replay v Wolverhampton Wanderers) and 1985 (0–1 v **Norwich City**). In 1982 the club won the **League Group Cup** (3–2 v **Wimbledon**), which had replaced the **Anglo-Scottish Cup** the previous year after the Scottish clubs withdrew. Grimsby's first **Wembley** appearance took place in 1998, when the club lifted the **Auto Windscreens Shield** (2–1 **golden goal** v **Bournemouth** (AFC)), and was rapidly followed by a return visit as the club won the end-of-season Division Two **playoff** final (1–0 v **Northampton Town**). Along with **Coventry City**, it is one of only two clubs to have played in all six former Football League divisions: Division One, Two, Three, Four, Division Three South and Division Three North. *League record* Division One 1901-02 to 1902-03, 1929-30 to 1931-32, 1934-35 to 1947-48; First Division 1992-93 to 1996-97, 1998-99–; Division Two 1892-93 to 1900-01, 1903-04 to 1909-10 (failed re-election), 1911-12 to 1919-20, 1926-27 to 1928-29, 1932-33 to 1933-34, 1948-49 to 1950-51, 1956-57 to 1958-59, 1962-63 to 1963-64, 1980-81 to 1986-87, 1991-92; Second Division 1997-98; Divsion Three 1920-21, 1959-60 to 1961-62,1964-65 to 1967-68, 1972-73 to 1976-77, 1979-80, 1987-88, 1990-91; Divsion Three (North) 1921-22 to 1925-26, 1951-52 to 1955-56; Divsion Four 1968-69 to 1971-72, 1977-78 to 1978-79, 1988-89 to 1989-90. *Honours* Divsion Two 1900-01, 1933-34; Divsion Three 1979-80; Divsion Three (North) 1925-26; 1955-56; Divsion Four 1971-72; Auto Windscreens Shield (2–1 golden goal v Bournemouth (AFC)); League Group Cup 1982 (3–2 v Wimbledon). *Records* Pat Glover is Grimsby's most capped player (7 for **Wales**); Keith Jobling holds the record for club League appearances (448, 1953-69); Pat Glover is also the club's record League goalscorer (180, 1930-39).

groin strain   *medical*   general term for a range of **sprain, strain** or **tear** injuries to the **muscles** and/or **tendons** of the groin (the part of the body where the legs join the abdomen; it includes the upper part of the front of the thighs and the lower part of the abdomen). The symptoms of groin strain are pain or stiffness on one or both sides of the groin, especially when running, or even when walking or trying to sit down. It may be accompanied by some swelling and tenderness. Typically, groin strain is caused by a tearing or bruising of the muscles that run from the pelvis down the thighs; it also may involve a torn tendon. It may be caused by over-exertion, particularly to players who have not warmed up sufficiently. Players should not attempt to play through the injury and should apply an ice pack – to reduce swelling – to the tender area as soon as possible. Players should rest and not exert themselves until the muscles can be used without pain. Minor strains heal in a day or so, more serious muscle injuries can take a week or several weeks. Minor injuries also can be helped by non-steroidal anti-inflammatory drugs (see **analgesics**), though professional players must be aware of which drugs can legally be taken. In extreme cases, where a muscle or tendon is completely torn, surgery may be required. Also called groin pull. Compare **hernia**.

ground   *n.*   a football stadium. *Regulations* Clubs are required to register their grounds with their league and require permission to move to another ground (FA Premier League rule I.1, Football League regulation 14.1, Scottish Football League rule 70).

ground criteria   *regulations*   minimum standards on stadium structure and facilities which must be met in order to be a member of a league. Criteria can cover floodlighting, seating, ground capacity, the quality of the pitch and safety aspects, for example. The **Football League** has strict ground criteria which must be met by clubs promoted from the **Football Conference**: criteria which have prevented clubs from promotion – Kidderminster Harriers were Conference champions in 1993-94 but had not met the ground criteria, thus reprieving Football League bottom club **Northampton**

Town. The promoted club's ground must have, for example: a minimum capacity of 6,000 spectators (as certified by its local authority), that is capable of being increased to 10,000 in the future; a minimum number of seats equivalent to at least 10% of the ground capacity or at least 1,000 seats, whichever is greater; terracing that conforms to government safety standards; solid boundary walls that would deter anyone from climbing over; measures available to segregate home and away fans; a sufficient number of ground exits that meet safety/fire requirements; a closed-circuit television surveillance system; a ground-safety control room; emergency lighting; a **directors' box** and directors' room; turnstiles; adequate toilet facilities for men and women; a designated first-aid room; separate dressing rooms for players and officials, with safe passage onto the pitch; a medical treatment room near to the dressing rooms; facilities for the press; a **public address system**; parking facilities; and adequate refreshment facilities for spectators, players and visitors. In addition, there are requirements on the playing facilities – such as a pitch with high-standard grass and a slope no more that 1:41 (1.4 degrees) – and minimum standards for **floodlights**. All clubs in the Football Conference must have their grounds graded by the Football League Board: the gradings are carried out in August. The club can submit plans for improving its ground and these will be taken into account by the inspectors; the Football League may then confirm that a club will meet its minimum standards (or "A" grading), conditional on the ground improvements being made. Any club hoping to be promoted from the Football Conference must have all its ground improvements completed by 1 April in order to have its A grading confirmed. Without an A grading, the Conference champions will not be entitled to join the Football League. The rules of the **Scottish Football League** require that clubs promoted to a higher division must have grounds that meet the standards set by the league management committee; if a promoted club's ground is not suitable for the higher league, it will remain in its division and there will be one fewer club relegated from the higher division.

ground improvement levy *regulations* levy charged to clubs by the **Football League** to fund ground improvements. The Football League may charge clubs a 10% levy on club's merit payments (see **Pool account**) (Football League Article 66.1) and a 5% levy on **transfer fees** and **compensation fees**, though clubs which already meet the requirements of the **Taylor Report** will not be charged the levy (Football League regulation 44.2.11 and Article 66.2).

grounds named after individuals *misc.* only four current **Football League** grounds are named after individuals. These are: **Bournemouth AFC**'s **Dean Court**, **Cardiff City**'s **Ninian Park**, **Reading**'s **Madejski Stadium** and **Wycombe Wanderers**' **Adams Park**. **Walsall Town**'s former **Fellows Park** ground was also named after an individual, in this case the club's former chairman, Les Fellows.

groundshare *n.* formal agreement between two clubs for one to share the other's ground. In September 1985, **Charlton Athletic** announced a groundshare with **Crystal Palace** at **Selhurst Park**, a move which lasted until 1990-91 when Charlton spent one season (1991-92) sharing **West Ham United**'s **Upton Park**. After Charlton left Selhurst Park, **Wimbledon** – which was forced to leave **Plough Lane**, the club's home since 1912, because there was no prospect of the ground being redeveloped to meet the requirements of the **Taylor Report** – agreed a seven-year groundshare with Crystal Palace. **Partick Thistle**'s **Firhill Park** was the setting in 1986 for the first modern groundshare in **Scottish League** football. **Clyde** shared the ground between 1986 and 1991, and, in 1994, **Hamilton Academical** moved in. On the continent, especially in Italy where stadiums are generally owned by the local authorities, it is more common for clubs to share facilities. **Internazionale** moved to **AC Milan**'s **San Siro** stadium after **World War II**. **Juventus** and **Torino** both share Stadio **Delle Alpi** in Turin, while **Lazio** and **Roma (AS)** both play at Stadio **Olimpico** in Rome.

Group for an Alternative Arsenal Stand *misc.* group formed in 1991 by disgruntled **Arsenal** fans who objected to the club's initial plans to redevelop the North Bank. See **Highbury**.

group of death *informal* mini-league stage of a tournament in from which at least one of the big-name teams is certain to be eliminated. An example was the 1998-99 **European Cup** (Champions League) group comprising **Barcelona**, **Bayern Munich**, **Brøndby** and **Manchester United**: only one would definitely qualify for the knockout stage of the tournament. Eventually, both Bayern and Manchester United progressed to the knockout stage, while Barcelona was eliminated. The 1998 **World Cup** "group of death" comprised **Bulgaria**, **Nigeria**, **Paraguay** and **Spain**; from which Spain, one of the tournament favourites, and 1994 semi-finalists Bulgaria failed to qualify. Most tournaments involving a qualifying group stage have a "group of death".

grundspil *n. Danish* first of the two phases in the Danish football league season, from August to November, before the winter break. See **slutspil**.

Gruppo Desportivo de Maputo *club* Mozambique national league club based in the capital Maputo. Ground: Desportivo, capacity: 13,000. Strip: black shirts and white shorts. **African Cup-winners Cup** semi-final 1990 (3–7 v eventual winners **BCC Lions** of Nigeria over two legs); Mozambique Cup 1983; Mozambique League champions 1977, 1978, 1983, 1988, 1995; Notable former players: **Eusébio** Da Silva Ferreira, Mario Esteves **Coluna**.

Guadalajara (full name: Club Deportivo Guadalajara) *club* Mexican national league club, based in Guadalajara and founded in 1906 (formerly Union Guadalajara, until 1908). Ground: Estadio Jalisco, capacity: 66,000. Strip: red and white striped shirts and blue shorts. *Keynotes* The club was founded by a

Belgian, Edgar Evaraert. **CONCACAF Champion Clubs Cup** – 1962 (6–1 agg., v **Comunicaciones** of Guatemala), runners-up 1963 (withdrew from final against **Racing Club** of Haiti), semi-final 1997; Mexican Cup (Copa Mexico) 1963, 1970; Mexican League Champions 1957, 1959, 1960, 1961, 1962, 1964, 1965, 1970, 1987, 1997 (clausura).

Guadeloupe *country no international affiliation* group of islands in the Leeward Islands in the West Indies, east Caribbean. Overseas department of **France**. Consists of Basse-Terre, Grande-Terre, Marie-Galante and other islands. Area: 1,780 sq km (687 sq miles). Population: 406,000. Language: French. Capital: Basse-Terre (on Basse-Terre island) *Dossier* Football association (Ligue de Football Guadeloupe, Basse-Terre), neither affiliated to **FIFA** nor to the **Confederación Norte-Centroamericana y del Caribe de Fútbol** (CONCACAF), though is affiliated to the French Federation. National strip: green shirts, white shorts. *International tournament record* **Olympic Games** – never entered; **Women's World Cup** – never entered; **World Cup** – never entered; **Caribbean Nations Cup** – semi-final/third 1994 (2–0, v **Surinam**, in Trinidad, third/fourth playoff); **Gold Cup** – never qualified; **Under-17 World Championship** – never qualified; **World Youth Cup** (under-20) – never qualified. *Record against British and Irish national teams* none played. *Record in international club tournaments* **CONCACAF Champions Cup** – Moulien (fourth place 1995). Other leading clubs: Cygne Noir (Basses-Terre), Olympique (Morne-a-l'Eau, league champions 1998), Etoile Filante (Morne-a-l'Eau, league champions 1998), Solidarité Scolaires (Point-a-Pitre) and Red Star (Point-a-Pitre).

Gualtier, Davide *player* Striker. **San Marino** international. *Keynotes* Scorer of the fastest goal in a **World Cup** match, after 8.3 seconds (1–7 v **England**, 17 November 1993, Bologna – technically a home match for San Marino – World Cup qualifier).

Guam *country AFC* external territory of the **United States of America**, in the Mariana Islands in the West Pacific. Area: 450 sq km (174 sq miles). Population: 140,000. Languages: English, Chamorro. Capital: Agaña. *Dossier* Guam Soccer Association (Agaña), formed in 1975, affiliated to **FIFA** and **Asian Football Confederation** (AFC) 1996, president Carl Wegner, general secretary Randall Cunliffe. National strip: blue shirts, white shorts. Biggest defeat: 0–9 v **South Korea** and v **Vietnam** (both 1997, **Asian Cup of Nations**, qualifiers). Notable international players: Ryan Stepp (thought to be the youngest player ever to score in the Asian Cup of Nations, at just 16 years of age, v **Taiwan**, 1996). *International tournament record* **Olympic Games** – never entered; **Women's World Cup** – first entered 1999, last in its qualifying group (conceding 32 goals in four games, scoring none); **World Cup** – never entered; Asian Cup of Nations – first entered 1996 (lost all three group games); **Asian Women's Championship** – never entered; **East Asian Games**

(under-23) – first entered 1997; **Under-17 World Championship** – never qualified; **World Youth Cup** (under-20) – never qualified. *Record against British and Irish national teams* none played. *History* Organised games first recorded in the 1960s, influenced by the American military presence. Guam played its first international tournament in 1996, the Asian Cup of Nations. *League system* Only five clubs contest the national First Division. However, by 1998 there were around 650 registered players. Leading club: Island Carlgo (league champions 1998).

Guangdong Honguyan Football Club *club* Chinese national league club based in Guangzhou (Canton), Guangdong province in South China. Ground: People's Stadium. **Asian Champion Teams Cup** semi-final 1988; Chinese league champions 1979, 1987.

Guangzhou Football Club *club* Chinese national league club based in Guangzhou (Canton), Guangdong province in South China. Ground: New Stadium, Guiyang, capacity: 20,000.

Guarani (Club Guarani) *club* Paraguay national league club based in the capital Asuncion, founded in 1903. Ground: Estadio Rogelio Lorenzo Livieres, capacity: 20,000. Strip: yellow and black striped shirts, black shorts. Nickname: the Aborigines (the Guarani are the South American Indians of Paraguay, Bolivia and southern Brazil). Traditional rivalry with Club **Olimpia**, dating back to 1903 (the game between the two is known as the "Viejo clasico", or Old Classic). **Copa Libertadores** second round group 1966, 1968, 1970, 1979, 1997; Paraguay League champions 1906, 1907, 1921, 1923, 1949, 1964, 1967, 1969, 1984.

Guatemala *country* CONCACAF republic in Central America, straddling the central American isthmus, on the Caribbean Sea and Pacific Ocean, bordered by **Mexico**, **Belize**, **Honduras** and **El Salvador**. Independence from **Spain** in 1839. Area: 108,890 sq km (42,030 sq miles). High annual rainfall (up to 5,000 mm, 200 inches in lowland areas). Rainy season from May to October. Population: 10,620,000 (1995 est.). Languages: Spanish and 18 Indian languages. Capital: Guatemala City. *Dossier* Football association (Federación Nacional de Fútbol de Guatemala, Guatemala City), formed in 1926, affiliated to **FIFA** in 1946 and **Confederación Norte-Centroamericana y del Caribe de Fútbol** (CONCACAF) in 1961, president Rolando Piñeda Lam, general secretary Hugo Hernadez Cane. Season played from January to December. National stadium: Mateo Flores, Guatemala City, capacity: 45,000. National strip: blue shirts, white shorts. *International tournament record* **Olympic Games** – quarter-final 1968, also qualified 1976, 1988; **Women's World Cup** – first entered 1999; **World Cup** – first entered 1958, never qualified for finals tournament (third of four nations in its second round qualifying group 1998); **CCCF Championship** – first entered 1943, runners-up 1946 (six-nation league in San José, Costa Rica), 1948 (five-nation league in Guetemala City); **CONCACAF Championship** –

entered first tournament in 1963, 1967 (first in the league of six nations, in Tegucigalpa, Honduras), runners-up 1965 (six-nation league in Guatemala City), 1969 (six-nation league in San José); **CONCACAF Women's Championship** – first entered 1998, fourth 1998 (0–4, v **Costa Rica**, in Etobicoke, Canada, third/fourth playoff); **Gold Cup**, qualified for first tournament in 1991, semi-final/fourth 1996 (0–3, v **United States of America**, in Guatemala, in California, USA), also qualified 1998, 2000; **Under-17 World Championship** – never qualified; **World Youth Cup** (under-20) – never qualified. *Record against British and Irish national teams* none played. *History* A national championship dates from 1919. Since the 1940s the league has been dominated by three clubs: **Aurora Fútbol Club**, **Municipal** and **Comunicaciones Fútbol Club**. Municipal is the only Guatemalan club to have won the **CONCACAF Champions Cup** outright (1974). Comunicaciones was declared winners in 1978, a year in which there were three regional winners; Comunicaciones won the Central region. The national Cup has been played since 1991, first won by Comunicaciones. At international level, Guatemala's best achievements are in winning the CONCACAF Championship in 1967 and finishing fourth in the 1996 Gold Cup. Its worst day was the 1998 World Cup qualifier against **Costa Rica** (16 October 1996, at the Mateo Flores stadium, Guatemala City): 81 spectators died from crushing before the start of the match as a crowd of 60,000 (allegedly swollen by forged tickets) tried to get into the 45,000-capacity stadium. The disaster was exacerbated by **perimeter fencing** that prevented the crowd from spilling on to the pitch. *League system* Twelve clubs compete in the national Primera Division, playing each other twice in the first stage of the season. The top six from the first stage qualify for the second-stage championship league, with the clubs again playing each other twice. Three points are awarded for a victory, with one for a draw: final positions for clubs level on points are determined by **goal difference**. The bottom six clubs from the first stage enter a relegation league (Liga Permanencia); the bottom club is relegated automatically, while the second-, third- and fourth-from-bottom clubs enter the end-of-season playoffs to decide the second relegation place. The 14-club Segunda Division is also played in two stages; the top eight clubs after the first stage enter a promotion league, (Liga de Ascenso), while the bottom six enter the relegation league (Liga de Descenso). The winner of the promotion league is automatically promoted, the next three enter the playoffs. Relegation from the Segunda Division is decided by a playoff between the club at the bottom of the league at the end of each stage (unless, of course, one club finishes bottom of both phases). *Record in international club tournaments* CONCACAF Champions Cup – Municipal (1974), Comunicaciones Fútbol Club (joint-1978 see above), runners-up 1962, 1969), third 1996; **CONCACAF Cup-winners Cup** – Aurora Fútbol Club (runners-up 1994), **Torneo**

Grandes de Centroamerica – Municipal (finalist 1998, semi-final 1997); Other leading clubs: **Suchitepequez**, **Xelaju MC**.

Gudjohnsen, Arnór *player* Striker. **Iceland** international (73 caps, 14 goals, 1979-98). Born 30 July 1961. *Clubs* Lokeren, **RSC Anderlecht**, **Bordeaux**, Hacken, **Örebro SK**. *Keynotes* Gudjohnsen is the second-most capped Icelandic player, and the second highest goalscorer. He went on as a substitute for Anderlecht in the second leg of the 1984 **UEFA Cup** final against **Tottenham Hotspur**, and missed the vital fifth penalty in the shoot-out which gave the match to Spurs. Gudjohnsen, then 35, was substituted by his then 17-year-old son Eidur in his country's friendly international against Estonia (4–0, 16 August 1984, in Akureyri, Iceland): the only known case of a **father and son** playing in the same international match.

Guérin, Robert *official* first president and co-founder of **FIFA** (president 1904-06). Nationality: French.

Guernsey *country no international affiliation* the second-largest of the **Channel Islands**, a British Crown dependency. The Bailiwick of Guernsey includes Alderney, Great Sark and Little Sark, Herm and Jethou. Area: 63 sq km (24 sq miles). Population: 56,000. Languages: English, French. Capital: St Peter Port. *Dossier/History/Leading clubs* see Channel Islands, **Upton Park Cup**.

Guinea *country CAF* republic in west Africa, on the Atlantic Ocean bordered by **Senegal**, **Mali**, the **Ivory Coast**, **Liberia**, **Sierra Leone** and **Guinea-Bissau**. Independence from **France** in 1958. Area: 245,855 sq km (94,900 sq miles). Hot and humid climate in coastal areas, temperate inland in highland regions. Population: 6,500,000 (1994 est.). Languages: French, Susu, Manika. Capital: Conakry. *Dossier* Football association (Federación Guinéenne de Football, Conakry) formed in 1959, affiliated to **FIFA** in 1961, and **Confédération Africaine de Football** (CAF) in 1962, president Dr Baba Sakho, general secretary Altafini Aly Bangoura. Season played from November to July. National stadium: Stade du 28 Septembre, Conakry, capacity: 40,000. National strip: red shirts, yellow shorts. First international game: 16 December 1962, v **East Germany** (B squad) (2–2, in Conakry, friendly). Biggest victory: 14–0, v **Mauritania** (1972, neutral venue, **African Games** qualifier). Biggest defeat: 2–6, v **Ghana** (14 December 1975, in Accra, **Olympic Games** qualifier). Notable international players: N'Jolea (*France Football* **African Footballer of the Year** runner-up 1975), Papa Camara (*France Football* African Footballer of the Year runner-up 1976 and 1977). *International tournament record* Olympic Games – qualified for finals tournament 1968 (first round); **Women's World Cup** – entered first tournament 1991, never qualified for finals tournament; **World Cup** – first entered 1974, never qualified for finals tournament (in 1998, Guinea missed out by one point to **Nigeria**, finishing second of four nations in its second-round qualifying group, winning four of its six games, losing two);

African Cup of Nations – first entered 1968, runners-up 1976 (second in a final-round league of four nations, behind **Morocco**, in Addis Ababa, Ethiopia), also qualified for finals tournament 1970, 1974, 1980, 1994, 1998; **African Under-17 Championship** – third place 1995; **African Youth Championship** (under-20) – runners-up 1979, qualified for finals tournament 1995; **Amilcar Cabral Cup** – 1981 (0–0, 6–5 pens., v Mali, in Mali), 1982 (3–0, v Senegal, in Cape Verde), 1987 (1–0, v Mali, in Guinea), 1988 (0–0, 4–2 pens., v Mali, in Guinea-Bissau), runners-up 1989 (0–3, v Mali, in Mali), hosts 1987; **Under-17 World Championship** – semi-final/fourth 1985 (1–4, v **Brazil**, in Beijing, China, third/fourth playoff), also qualified for finals tournament 1989, 1995; **World Youth Cup** (under-20) – qualified for finals tournament 1979 (first round group stage). *Record against British and Irish national teams* none played. *History* Guinea became FIFA's 100th member when it joined on 28 May 1962. The national league dates from 1965, and the Cup from around 1985. The league championship was cancelled for the 1997 season. **Hafia FC** is three-times winners of the **African Cup of Champion Clubs**. Guinea was runners-up in the 1976 African Cup of Nations and has won the regional Amilcar Cabral Cup on four occasions. Although it has never qualified for the World Cup finals, it finished fourth in the 1985 Under-17 World Championship and has qualified on three occasions. *World Cup performance* (finals and qualifiers to end of 1998 tournament) played 35, won 17, drawn 4, lost 14, scored 50 goals, conceded 39 goals; win rate 49%; goals scored per game 1.43. *Record in international club tournaments* African Cup of Champion Clubs – Hafia FC (1972, 1975 and 1977, runners-up 1976, 1978); **African Cup-winners Cup** – **Horoya AC** (1978), **Kaloum Star** (semi-final 1970, 1981); **African CAF Cup** – Kaloum Stars (runners-up 1995). Other leading club: **ASFAG**.

Guinea-Bissau *country CAF* republic in west Africa on the Atlantic Ocean, bordered by **Senegal** and **Guinea**. Independence from **Portugal** in 1974 (including separation from former Portuguese colonial link with Cape Verde). Area: 36,125 sq km (13,945 sq miles). Hot and humid climate. Interior includes large areas of rain forest. Population: 1,006,000 (1994 est.). Languages: Portuguese, Crioulo (a Portuguese Creole) and local languages. Capital: Bissau. *Dossier* Football association (Federação de Futebol da Guiné-Bissau, Bissau), formed in 1974, affiliated to **FIFA** and **Confédération Africaine de Football** (CAF) in 1986, president Dr Augusto Viegas, general secretary José Lobo de Pina. Season played from October to July. National stadium: 24 Septembre, (Bissau), capacity: 25,000. National strip: red shirts, red shorts. First international game: 7 January 1979, v **Cape Verde** (3–0, in Bissau, Zone 2 **Amilcar Cabral Cup**). *International tournament record* **Olympic Games** – never entered; **Women's World Cup** – never entered; **World Cup** – first entered 1998 (lost in first qualifying round, 4–5, v **Guinea**);

African Cup of Nations – first entered 1994, never qualified for finals tournament; Amilcar Cabral Cup – runners-up 1983 (0–3, v Senegal, in Mauritania), hosts 1979 (the first tournament) and 1988; **Under-17 World Championship** – never qualified; **World Youth Cup** (under-20) – never qualified. *Record against British and Irish national teams* none played. *History* League championship started 1974-75, first won by Os Balantas (of Mansoa). *Record in international club tournaments* **African Cup of Champion Clubs** – **Sporting Clube Bissau** (second round 1984); **African Cup-winners Cup** – Sporting Clube Bissau (second round 1977) Other leading clubs: **Benfica Sport**, Porto FC (of Bissau, league champions 1994).

Gulf Cup *competition* see **Arabian Gulf Cup**.

gullies *n.pl. informal* the space either side of the **penalty box**.

Gullit, Ruud *player-manager* Sweeper/midfielder/striker. **Netherlands** international (64 caps, 16 goals, 1981-92). Born 1 September 1962, in Amsterdam, of Dutch and **Surinam** parents. *Clubs* FC Amsterdam (dissolved 1983), Haarlem, **Feyenoord**, **PSV Eindhoven**, **AC Milan** (twice), **Sampdoria** (twice), **Chelsea**. *Keynotes* Gullit was transferred from PSV Eindhoven to Milan in June 1987 for a then world record £6 million. Gullit scored the opening goal in the 1988 European Championship final in Munich; his Milan partner Marco **Van Basten** scored the second in the 2–0 defeat of the **Soviet Union**. The following May, Gullit and Van Basten scored two goals each in the 4–0 victory over **Steaua Bucharest** in the 1989 European Cup final at **Nou Camp**, Barcelona. Gullit had been carried off injured in the semi-final second leg five weeks previously; he had required surgery on a damaged knee cartilage and was lucky even to play in the final (he was substituted after 59 minutes). He scored in the 1990 European Super Cup (3–1 agg., v **Sampdoria**). Gullit made his international debut on 1 September 1981 (1–2, v **Switzerland**, in Zurich, friendly). He refused to play for the Dutch **World Cup** squad in 1994, after a dispute with the coach, Dick Advocaat. He was voted both European Footballer of the Year and World Footballer of the Year in 1987; awards he dedicated to imprisoned ANC leader Nelson **Mandela**. After his distinguished club career in Netherlands and Italy, Gullit joined Chelsea on a **free transfer** in summer 1995. He was appointed player-manager in May 1996, succeeding Glen **Hoddle**, becoming the first foreigner to manage an FA Cup-winning team 12 months later. Chelsea dismissed Gullit on 12 February 1998, after protracted negotiations had failed to reach an agreement on a new contract. He was appointed manager of Newcastle United in September 1998, succeeding Kenny **Dalglish**. *Honours* **European Championship** (Netherlands 1988); Dutch league championship (Feyenoord 1984, PSV Eindhoven 1986, 1987), Dutch Cup (Feyenoord 1984); Italian **Serie A** championship (AC Milan 1988, 1992, 1993); **European Cup** (AC

Milan 1989, 1990); **World Club Cup** (AC Milan, 1990); **European Super Cup** (Milan, 1989, 1990); **FA Cup** (Chelsea 1997 – as manager); *World Soccer* **World Footballer of the Year** in 1987, 1989, runner-up 1988; *France Football* **European Footballer of the Year** 1987, runner-up 1988.

Guriya Lanchkuti *club* Georgian national league club based in Lanchkhuti, founded 1952. Ground: Central, capacity: 22,000. Georgian Cup 1990; Georgian league runners-up 1990, 1991.

Guyana (formerly British Guiana) *country CONCACAF* republic of north-east South America on the Atlantic Ocean. Bordered by **Surinam**, **Brazil** and **Venezuela**. Self-governing from 1961, full independence from UK in 1966; became a Commonwealth republic in 1970. Area: 214,970 sq km (82,980 sq miles). Tropical, hot and wet climate. Population: 808,000. Languages: English, Hindi, Urdu, South American Indian dialects. Capital: Georgetown. *Dossier* Guyana Football Association (Georgetown) formed in 1902, affiliated to **FIFA** in 1968 and **Confederación Norte-Centroamericana y del Caribe de Fútbol** (CONCACAF) in 1969, president Colin Klass, general secretary Colin Erskine. Despite being in South America (and south of Venezuela), Guyana is affiliated to CONCACAF: the country and clubs play in the Caribbean sections of CONCACAF tournaments. Season played from March to December. National stadium: Cricket Cub, Georgetown, capacity: 15,000. National strip: green shirts, green shorts. *International tournament record* **Olympic Games** – never qualified for finals tournament; **Women's World Cup** – never entered; **World Cup** – first entered 1978, never progressed beyond first qualifying round; **Caribbean Nations Cup** – semi-final/fourth 1991 (1–4, v **St Lucia**, in Jamaica, third/fourth playoff); **Gold Cup** – never qualified; **Under-17 World Championship** – never qualified; **World Youth Cup** (under-20) – never qualified. *Record against British and Irish national teams* none played. *History* The domestic Cup – the Kashif and Shanghai Knockout Tournament – has been played since 1990-91; first won by Milerock. *Record in international club tournaments* no major success. Leading clubs: Santos (of Georgetown, league champions 1999), ASL Sport, Beacons (of Georgetown, Guyana Cup 1996), Milerock (Guyana Cup 1991, 1998), Topp XX (Guyana Cup 1995, 1997), Omar Goal Sackers.

Györi ETO FC (Egyetértés Torna Osztálya) *club* Hungarian national league club based in Györ, founded 1904 (as ETO Györ (1904-46), later known as Vasas ETO Györ (1946-68) and Györi Raba ETO (1968-93). Ground: Györi, capacity: 26,000. Strip: white shirts, white shorts. **European Cup** – semi-final 1965; Hungarian Cup 1965, 1966, 1967, 1979; Hungarian league champions 1963, 1982, 1983.

H

hacking *n.* deliberately kicking at an opponent on the shin. Hacking was defined by the **Football Association** in the rules of the game adopted at its foundation in 1863 as "kicking an opponent intentionally"; rule 10 stated that "neither **tripping** nor hacking shall allowed and no player shall use his hands to hold an adversary".

Hadji, Mustapha *player* Midfield. **Morocco** international (45 caps). Born 16 November 1971. *Clubs* Nancy (of France), **Sporting Clube de Portugal,** Deportivo de la Coruña. *Keynotes* Scored a memorable individual goal for Morocco in the 1998 **World Cup** finals against Norway (2–2, 10 June 1998, first round, in Montpelier), considered one of the best goals of the tournament. **African Footballer of the Year** 1998.

haematoma *medical* a swelling composed of blood that has leaked into the body of a **muscle** or other soft tissue. Often the result of direct trauma which has damaged blood vessels. Treated by **RICE. 1.** intramuscular haematoma: localised bruising. **2.** intermuscular haematoma: bruising some distance from the original site of the injury owing to blood passing down the intermuscular fascial planes.

Hafia FC *club* Guinea national league club based in Conakry, formerly known as Conakry II. Ground: Cloah, capacity: 8,000. Strip: green shirts, white shorts. *Keynotes* Its nine straight championships (1971 to 1979) is an African club record. **African Cup of Champion Clubs** 1972 (7–4 agg., v **Simba FC** of Uganda), 1975 (3–1 agg., v **Enugu Rangers** of Nigeria) and 1977 (5–2 agg., v **Canon Yaoundé** of Cameroon), runners-up 1976 (3–3 agg., 1–4 pens., v **Mouloudia Chalia d'Algiers** of Algeria), 1978 (0–2 agg., v Canon Yaundé); Guinea Cup 1992, 1993; Guinea league champions 1966, 1967, 1968, 1971, 1972, 1973, 1974, 1975, 1976, 1977, 1978, 1979, 1982, 1983, 1985.

Hagi, Georghe *player* Striker. **Romania** international (113 caps, 32 goals, 1983-). Born 5 February 1965. *Clubs* Sportul Studentesc, **Steaua Bucharest**, **Real Madrid**, Brescia (Italy), **Barcelona, Galatasaray**. *Keynotes* Romania's most-capped player and 10th in the world's all-time list of most-capped players. Hagi made his international debut on 10 August 1983 (0-0, v **Norway**). He scored three goals in the 1994 **World Cup** finals in USA and was one of the outstanding players of the tournament. He captained his country in the 1996 **European Championship** and 1998 World Cup finals in France. Voted fourth in the FIFA **World Footballer of the Year** 1994, *World Soccer* **World Footballer of the Year** 1994, and equal fourth in the *France Football* **European Footballer of the Year** 1994. Hagi helped his first major club Sportul Studentesc to third in the Romanian league in his first season in 1983, and runner-up in 1986. Hagi was the Romanian league top scorer in 1985 (20 goals) and 1986 (31 goals). He was transferred to Steaua in 1986 and scored in the European Super Cup the following February (1–0, v **Dinamo Kiev**). He was a beaten finalist with Steaua in the 1989 **European Cup** final (0–4, v **AC Milan**). In 1990, he moved to Real Madrid jand later to Galatasaray in Turkey. *Honours* **European Super Cup** (Steaua Bucharest, 1986-87); Romanian league championship 1987, 1988, 1989.

hairline fracture *medical* **fracture** where the bone does not separate.

hairstyle *misc.* characteristic haircut of an individual player or team. Notable examples of the "footballer's hairstyle" are the long-at-the-back/short-on-top cut of the 1970s – sported by legendary players, such as Kevin **Keegan** and Charlie George – and the famous dreadlocks of Ruud **Gullit**. More recent styles include the many colours of Paul **Gascoigne**'s close-cropped cut, the long curly blonde locks of Colombian international Carlos **Valderrama**, and the entire Wimbledon team which started the 1995-96 season with a traditional barber's "number one", close-cropped all round. **Romania**'s 1998 **World Cup** squad all (with the exception of goalkeeper Bogdan Stelea, whose head is shaved) dyed their hair peroxide blonde after qualifying for the second stage of the tournament; the players had made a wager with coach Anghel Iordanescu. The 1998 squad was not the first side from the country to be noted for its hairstyles. Leading club **National Bucharest**, known from 1954-89 as Progresul, was the official club of the Romanian union of hairdressers during the communist years. The players of Icelandic side **IBK Keflavik** boasted peroxide hair for their 1997 Icelandic Cup final replay against **IBV Vesmannaeyjar**. Hair has also caused problems for several players.

Argentina and **Real Madrid** midfielder Redondo was apparently left out of his country's 1998 World Cup squad after refusing to have his hair cut in accordance with Argentine coach Daniel Passarella's instruction to trim his locks. Taribo West regularly sports blue ribbons in his hair when playing for **Internazionale**, and green and white ribbons when appearing for **Nigeria**. In his playing days, Bobby **Charlton** had continually to flick or place his thinning hair back over his balding head. **Burnley**'s Ralph Coates suffered from a similar problem. See also **baldies**.

Haiti *country CONCACAF* republic of the Caribbean, the western part of the island of Hispaniola (to the east is the **Dominican Republic**). A mountainous country with tropical climate. Economically poor. Area: 27,750 sq km (10,710 sq miles). Population: 6,764,000 (1992 est.). Languages: French and Creole. Capital: Port-au-Prince. *Dossier* Football association (Fédération Haïtienne de Football, Port-au-Prince), formed in 1904, affiliated to **FIFA** in 1933 and **Confederación Norte-Centroamericana y del Caribe de Fútbol** (CONCACAF) in 1957, president Dr Jean Marie Kyss, general secretary Jean Elie. Season played from November to May. National stadium: Stade Sylvio Cator, Port-au-Prince, capacity: 25,000. National strip: blue and red shirts, blue shorts. Notable international players: Sanon (Sanon is the only Haitian ever to score at a World Cup finals; see below). *International tournament record* **Olympic Games** – never qualified for finals tournament; **Women's World Cup** – entered first tournament in 1991, never qualified for finals tournament; **World Cup** – first entered 1934, qualified for finals tournament 1974 (first round, lost all three group games against **Poland**, **Argentina** and **Italy**); **Caribbean Nations Cup** – first entered 1994, semi-final/third 1998 (3–2, v **Antigua and Barbuda**, in Trinidad, third/fourth playoff; **CCCF Championship** – 1957 (five-nation league format in Curacao; Haiti won all its four games, scoring 14 goals and conceding only four), final-round/fourth 1961; **CONCACAF Championship** – 1973 (six-nation league format in Haiti; World Cup qualifying tournament), runners-up 1971 (six-nation league format in Port of Spain, Trinidad), 1977 (six-nation league format; **CONCACAF Women's Championship** – semi-final/fourth 1991 (2–4, v **Trinidad and Tobago**, third/fourth playoff; 0–10 v **United States of America**, semi-final), hosts 1998; **Gold Cup** – never qualified; **Under-17 World Championship** – never qualified; **World Youth Cup** (under-20) – never qualified. *Record against British and Irish national teams* none played. *History* There is a long tradition of football in the country, with an association founded in 1904, the first association in the Caribbean. Haiti became FIFA's 50th member when it joined on 8 October 1932. Haiti was the first Caribbean country to qualify for the World Cup finals (1974). Sanon scored both of Haiti's goals in the 1974 finals tournament in Munich, including his first which gave Haiti the lead against Italy; Italy eventually won 3–1. The country's two

most successful clubs, **Violette AC** and **Racing Club**, were founded in 1918 and 1923, respectively. Haiti finished fourth in the 1991 CONCACAF Women's Championship: having finished second in its first-round group of four nations, it lost 0–10 to the United States of America in the semi-final, and 2–4 to Trinidad and Tobago in the third/fourth place playoff. It competed again in 1998, at the tournament in Canada, but finished bottom of its first-round group with no points. Haiti finished fourth in 1991. *Record in international club tournaments* **CONCACAF Champions Cup** – Racing Club (1963); Violette AC (1984). Other leading clubs: **AS Capoise**, **Tempete**.

Hajduk Split (NK Hajduk Split) *club* Croatia national league and **former-Yugoslavia** league club based in Split, founded 1911. Ground: Stadion Poljud, capacity: 37,000. Strip: white shirts, blue shorts. Croatia Cup 1993, 1995; Croatia league champions 1992, 1994, 1995; Croatia Super Cup (league champions v Cup winners) 1992, 1994, 1995 (automatic); **European Cup** quarter-final 1976, 1980, 1995; **European Cup-winners Cup** semi-final 1973; former-Yugoslavia Cup 1967, 1972, 1973, 1974, 1976, 1977, 1984, 1987, 1991; former-Yugoslavia league champions 1927, 1929, 1950, 1952, 1955, 1971, 1974, 1975, 1979. Notable former players: Zlatko Vujovic, Bernard Vukas, Alen Boksic.

Haka Valkeakoski *club* see **FC Haka**.

Hakan, Sükür *player* Striker. **Turkey** international striker (41 caps, 22 goals, 1992-). Born 1 September 1971. *Clubs* (include) **Torino**, **Galatasaray**. *Keynotes* His tally of 38 goals in the 1996-97 season, was one short of Tanju Colak's all-time Turkish league record. He is Turkey's all-time top international goalscorer.

half *rules* **1.** either of the two periods of the **duration of play**, known as the first half and second half. **2.** either of the two parts of the **field of play** either side of the **halfway line**. The section of the field nearest to a team's goal is its own half, distinguishing it from the opposition's half – a point crucial to the **offside** law.

half time *rules* official break in play to allow players and officials to rest (Law VII). Players have a right to an interval, but this shall not exceed 15 minutes (as stipulated by the rules of a particular competition). After half time, the game is restarted with the teams changing ends, with the **kick-off** taken by the team that did not take the kick-off in the first half. The half time interval is 15 minutes for most domestic and international fixtures. See **start of play**.

half-time oranges *n.pl.* traditional snack given to players at the half-time intervals, usually consisting of pre-cut segments of oranges. Half-time oranges are popular at non-league and junior matches.

half-time score *n.* the **score** or goal-tally at **half time** in a game of football.

half-time whistle *rules* blast on the referee's whistle to indicate that the first half of the **duration of play** has ended.

half-volley *vb.* to kick a moving ball immediately after it hits the ground. *n.* the execution of this.

halfway line *rules* one of the **lines** of the **field of play**. It runs across the field of play, at right angles to the **touchlines**, marking the halfway point on the field (Law I). It may be further delineated by two **flagposts**.

Halifax Town *club* English league. *Dossier* Ground: **Shay**, Halifax, West Yorkshire, present capacity: 7,449. Strip: blue shirts with white trim, white shorts with blue trim, blue socks. Nickname: Shaymen. Record attendance: 36,885 v **Tottenham Hotspur** (14 February 1953, **FA Cup**, fifth round). Best average attendance: 10,525 (1922-23). Biggest win: 6–0 v **Bradford Park Avenue** (3 December 1955, Division Three (North)). Biggest defeat: 0–13 v **Stockport County** (6 January 1934, Division Three (North)). *Keynotes* Founded in 1911. The club played at Sandhall and at Exley before it settled at the Shay in 1921; the same year that the club was a founder member of Division Three (North). Halifax was an FA Cup quarter-finalist in 1933 (0–2 v **Luton Town**) and 1953 (0–3 v **Tottenham Hotspur**). The latter FA Cup campaign included victories over Division One opponents' **Stoke City** (1–0, fourth round) and **Cardiff City** (3–1, third round) in earlier rounds. Halifax's most successful **Football League** season was in 1970-71, when the club narrowly missed promotion to Division Two, finishing third in Division Three. In 1992-93, Halifax was relegated from the League, following five consecutive seasons in which the club finished in the bottom five of Division Four (Third Division), and was replaced by **Wycombe Wanderers**. The club regained its League status in 1997-98, winning the **Football Conference** Championship. *League record* Division Three 1958-59 to 1962-63, 1969-70 to 1975-76; Third Division 1992-93, 1998-99 to present; Division Three (North) 1921-22 to 1957-58; Division Four 1963-64 to 1968-69, 1976-77 to 1991-92. *Honours* Football Conference Champions 1997-98. *Records* John Pickering holds the record for club League appearances (367, 1965-74); Ernie Dixon is Halifax's record League goalscorer (129, 1922-30).

Hall of fame *n.* museum dedicated to some of English football's most famous players, including George **Best**, Bobby **Charlton**, Stanley **Matthews** and Bobby **Moore**, and situated at the former County Hall in London. The museum opened in March 1999.

Halmstads BK (Bollklubb) *club* Swedish national league club based in Halmstad, founded 1914. Ground: Örjans Vall, capacity: 20,000. Strip: blue shirts, white shorts. Swedish Cup 1995; Swedish league champions 1976, 1979, 1997.

Hamburg (SV) (Hamburger Sport-Verein) *club* German league. *Dossier* Ground: Volksparkstadion, Hamburg, capacity: 58,000. Strip: white shirts with red and black flashing, white shorts. *History* Origins date from 1897. The current club was formed in 1919 from a merger of three amateur sides – Falke '87, Germania '87 and Hamburger SC '87. The club's official name is Hamburger Sport-Verein. It won the German League title in 1923. Since 1953, the club has played at the Volksparkstadion (People's Park Stadium), having pre-

viously played at a city centre ground, the Rotherbaum. Hamburg reached consecutive West German Championship finals in 1957 (1–4 v **Borussia Dortmund**) and 1958 (0–3 v **Schalke 04**) before securing the title in 1960. It was a **European Cup-winners Cup** finalist in 1968 (0–2 **AC Milan**). The club's was most successful spell occurred between 1977 and 1983, during which it won three **Bundesliga** titles, the 1983 **European Cup** and the European Cup-winners Cup. Also in that period, Hamburg was a European Cup finalist (1980, 0–1 v **Nottingham Forest**) and a **UEFA Cup** runner-up (1982, 0–4 agg., v **IFK Göteborg**). Since then Hamburg has only won one trophy, the German Cup (**DFB Pokal**) in 1987. *Honours* Bundesliga 1978-79; European Cup 1983 (1–0 v **Juventus**); European Cup-winners Cup (2–0 v **RSC Anderlecht**); German League 1923 (3–0 v Union Berlin), 1928 (5–2 v Hertha BSC Berlin); West German Cup 1963 (3–0 v Borussia Dortmund), 1976 (2–0 v Kaiserslautern (1.FC)), 1987 (3–1 v Stuttgart Kickers); West German League 1960 (3–2 v **Cologne** (1.FC)).

Hamilton Academicals *club* Scottish league. *Dossier* Ground: **Firhill Park**, Glasgow, Strathclyde, capacity: 1,238. Strip: red and white hooped shirts, red shorts with white trim, red socks with white top. Nickname: Accies. Record attendance: 28,690 v **Heart of Midlothian** (Douglas Park, 3 March 1937, **Scottish FA Cup**, third round). Biggest win: 11–1 v Chryston (28 November 1885, Lanarkshire Cup, first round). Biggest defeat: 1–11 v **Hibernian** (6 November 1965, Division One). *History* Founded in 1874 at local Hamilton Academy. The club joined Division Two in 1897-98, winning election to the expanded Division One in 1906-07, retaining its top-flight status until relegation from the A Division in 1946-47. Since then, Hamilton has spent only four seasons in the top flight (1953-54, 1965-66, 1986-87, 1988-89). Hamilton was a Scottish FA Cup finalist in both 1911 (0–2 replay v **Celtic**) and 1935 (1–2 v **Rangers**). Hamilton's best League position was achieved in 1934-35, when the club finished fourth in Division One. The club has reached the **Scottish League Cup** semi-final stage on three occasions: 1948-49 (0–2 v **Raith Rovers**), 1960-61 (1–5 v **Kilmarnock**), 1979-80 (2–6 v **Dundee United**). Hamilton won the **Scottish League Challenge Cup** in consecutive seasons in 1991-92 (1–0 v **Ayr United**) and 1992-93 (3–2 v **Morton**). The club left Douglas Park, its home since 1888, in 1994 and entered a groundshare with **Partick Thistle** at Firhill Park. *League record* Premier Division 1986-87, 1988-89; Division One (A Division) 1906-07 to 1914-15, 1921-22 to 1946-47, 1953-54, 1965-66; First Division 1975-76 to 1985-86, 1987-88, 1989-90 to 1995-96, 1997-98 to 1998-99; Scottish League 1915-16 to 1920-21; Division Two (B Division) 1897-98 to 1905-06, 1947-48 to 1952-53, 1954-55 to 1964-65, 1966-67 to 1974-75; Second Division 1996-97, 1999-00. *Honours* First Division 1985-86, 1987-88; Scottish League Challenge Cup 1991-92 (1–0 v Ayr United), 1992-93 (3–2 v

Morton). *Records* Colin Miller is Hamilton's most capped player (29 for **Canada**); Rikki Ferguson holds the record for club appearances (447, 1974-88); David Wilson is Hamilton's record goalscorer (246, 1928-39).

Hamm, Mia *player* full name: Mariel Margaret Hamm. Striker. **United States of America, women** international (145 caps, 1987-). Born 17 March 1972. *Keynotes* Hamm was the youngest player ever to play for the US national team, at 15 years old. She was the leading US international goalscorer in 1995, 1996 and 1997 – in the latter scoring 18 goals in just 16 games, including a hat-trick against **England, women** (9 May 1997). She is one of just seven US players to have more than 100 caps for the national side and one of the most successful woman players of all time. Hamm scored fher 100th international goal in September 1998 (4–0 v Russia, **US Women's Cup**.) In 1997, Hamm was voted in *People Magazine*'s "Fifty most beautiful women". The 1999 souvenir "Women's World Cup Barbie" doll was modelled on Hamm. *Honours* **Olympic Games** gold medal (USA, 1996); US Soccer female athlete of the year 1994, 1995, 1996, 1997; Women's Sports Foundation athlete of the year 1997.

Hampden Park *stadium* Scottish football stadium situated in Glasgow; home of **Queen's Park** and **Scotland** national side and venue for both the **Scottish FA Cup** final (since 1904) and the **Scottish League Cup** final (since 1969-70). Current capacity: 52,000 all seated. *History* Opened on 31 October 1903 (Queen's Park v **Celtic**, Division One) and the third ground to bear the Hampden name. A £60 million redevelopment of the stadium began in May 1992. Hampden Park was originally fashioned by Archibald **Leitch** and its initial 65,000 capacity was gradually increased so that by 1937 it could accommodate 150,000 people. Until the early-1950s, when the near 200,000 capacity **Maracaná** stadium opened in Rio de Janeiro, Hampden was the largest football ground in the world. It still holds a number of attendance records, including the highest ever official crowd for a football match in the UK, when, on 17 April 1937, 149,415 people watched Scotland entertain **England**. On 24 April 1937, a record crowd for a UK club fixture (and at the time a world record) was set when 147,365 people saw Celtic defeat **Aberdeen** in the Scottish FA Cup final. A further attendance record was achieved at Hampden, this time for a UEFA club competition match, on 15 April 1970, when the **European Cup** semi-final second-leg between Celtic and **Leeds United** attracted a crowd of 136,505. The 135,000 people who saw **Real Madrid** beat **Eintracht Frankfurt** in the 1960 European Cup final is the record attendance for a European final. The first official **floodlit match** at Hampden on 17 October 1961, set a record attendance for a match played under lights in the UK and for a friendly club game, with 104,494 people watching **Rangers** play Eintracht Frankfurt. Over the years, Hampden's capacity was drastically reduced; first to 135,000 following the **Burnden Park disaster**; and to 81,000 after the **Safety at Sports**

Grounds Act was implemented in 1977. A National Stadium Committee, consisting of Queen's Park, the **Scottish Football Association** and the **Scottish Football League**, began the first phase of the development of an **all-seater stadium** in May 1992, partly financed by a government grant and an award from the **Football Trust**. A partially redeveloped Hampden was opened with a capacity of almost 37,000 on 23 March 1994 (Scotland v **Netherlands**, friendly). Following the announcement of a £23 million grant from the National Lottery's Millennium Commission, the second phase of Hampden's redevelopment began at the start of 1996. In September 1998, the UK telecoms company BT agreed a £5 million 10-year sponsorship deal of the stadium. Hampden Park staged its first Scotland international on 7 April 1906 (v England). Aside from the 1960 European Cup final, the stadium also staged the 1976 final between **Bayern Munich** and St Etienne (54,864). It was also the venue for the **European Cup-winners' Cup** final in 1962 (**Atlético Madrid** v **Fiorentina**, 27,389; not the replay) and 1966 (**Borussia Dortmund** v **Liverpool**, 41,657).

Hamrun Spartans FC *club* Maltese national league club, based in Hamrum and formed in 1907. Ground: Ta'Qali Stadium, Valletta, capacity: 18,000 (all Maltese premier league games are played here). Strip: red and black striped shirts and red shorts. **European Cup-winners Cup** second round 1985 (beat Ballymena United 3–1 agg., in first round); Maltese FA Trophy 1983, 1984, 1987, 1988, 1989, 1992; Maltese league champions 1914, 1918, 1947, 1983, 1987, 1988, 1991.

hamstring *medical* a group of **tendons** behind the knee, linking the thigh muscles to the bones of the lower leg.

hamstring muscle *medical* the group of muscles at the back of the thigh that are responsible for bending the knee and extending the gluteus maximus (one of the muscles in the buttock). The **hamstring** (tendons) and hamstring muscles can be **strained** or **sprained**, particularly by a sudden sprint when the muscle has not been sufficiently warmed-up. An injured player will usually have to be substituted and should be treated with **RICE**. *Keynotes* It is not just the players that have suffered a pulled hamstring. At the 1998 **World Cup** finals in France, **Yugoslavia** coach Slobodan Santrac damaged his hamstring while running just five metres out of his dug-out to celebrate Dragan Stojkovic's goal, and second for Yugoslavia, against **Germany** (21 June 1998, in Lens, first round; final score: 2–2).

Hanappi, Gerhard *player* Midfield. **Austria** international (93 caps, 12 goals, 1948–1962). Born 9 July 1929, in Vienna. Career ca. 1947-63. *Clubs* Wacker Wien (now **Admira-Wacker**) and **Rapid Vienna**. *Keynotes* Joined Rapid Vienna from Wacker Vienna in 1950. Represented Austria in the 1954 **World Cup** finals in Switzerland. Of the 12 goals scored by Hanappi in his international career, five were scored against the British home nations (four against Scotland and one against Wales). Hanappi later designed Rapid Vienna's stadium (the 19,000 capacity Gerhard Hanappi Stadium). *Honours* World Cup third place (Austria, 1954); Austria league champions (Wacker 1947; Rapid 1951, 1952, 1954, 1956, 1957, 1960); Austrian Cup (Wacker, 1947; Rapid 1961).

Hand of God *misc.* 51st minute goal scored by Argentine international Diego **Maradona** in Argentina's 2–1 defeat of England in the 1986 World Cup quarter-final (22 June, **Azteca Stadium**, Mexico City, Mexico). Maradona quite clearly handled the ball into the net, punching a high ball ahead of England's goalkeeper Peter **Shilton**. Maradona said afterwards that the goal was "a little bit of Maradona's head, a little bit of the hand of God."

handbags *informal* a minor scuffle between two or more players. The term derives from the hackneyed expression "handbags at 10 paces" (ie a duel with hand-bags rather than guns).

handball *rules* one of the offences listed as a **foul** under the **Laws of the game** (Law XII). The foul is committed if a player carries, strikes or controls the ball with his or her hands. The punishment for deliberately handling the ball is for the opposing team to be awarded a **direct free kick,** taken from the point where the foul was committed (unless within the opponents' **goal area**, in which case it is taken from anywhere within that area). If the foul is committed in the offending side's **penalty area**, then the opponents are awarded a **penalty kick**. The **goalkeeper**, may handle the ball in his or her own penalty area unless it has been received from a **pass to the goalkeeper**, directly from a **throw-in**, or if he or she rehandles the ball after releasing it into play: the punishment for any of these three offences is for the opposition to be awarded an **indirect free kick** (taken from the point of the offence, or from the **goal area line** parallel to the **goal line** if the offence was committed within the goal area). **2.** *vb.* **handle**: to commit such an offence.

handcuffs *misc.* lockable rings that fit around the wrists, used by police to secure a person under arrest. *Keynotes* On 21 March 1998, the Scottish Division Two match between **Stenhousemuir** and **Clydebank** at **Ochilview Park** was delayed for a period after a visiting supporter, protesting against Clydebank's proposed move to Dublin, handcuffed himself to a goal post. A hacksaw had to be found to free him before the game could continue.

handshake *misc.* traditional greeting between captains before the toss-of-the-coin. *Keynotes* During the 1998 **World Cup**, **FIFA** instructed the players of the lower ranked side to shake hands with each of their opponents prior to the start of a match. **Iran**'s players pre-empted this by moving along the line of **United States of America** players, shaking hands and proffering flowers as a gesture of goodwill before the nations' group F encounter at the Stade de **Gerland** in Lyon on 21 June.

hang up one's boots *vb. informal* to retire as a player.

Hansa Rostock *club* German national league (**Bundesliga**) club and former-East German national league club based in Rostock near the Baltic coast, formed 1965 (though existed earlier as Rostock, Empor Lauter and SC Empor). Ground: Ostseestadion, capacity: 26,000. Strip: white shirts, white shorts. One of just two East German clubs (with **Dynamo Dresden**) to win a place in the German Bundesliga first division after reunification in 1990. East German Cup 1991; East German league champions 1991.

Hansen, Alan *player/broadcaster* Defender. **Scotland** international (22 caps). Born 13 June 1955. Career ca. 1973–91. *Clubs* **Partick Thistle**, **Liverpool**. *Keynotes* Joined Partick Thistle in 1973, moving to Liverpool for £100,000 in April 1977. Hansen made 434 **Football League** appearances for Liverpool, captaining the club to its 1985-86 **double** triumph. Joined BBC television as a **Match of the Day** pundit. Included in the **Football League Centenary 100 players**. *Honours* League Championship (Liverpool 1978-79, 1979-80, 1981-82, 1982-83, 1983-84, 1985-86, 1987-88, 1989-90); **FA Cup** (Liverpool 1986, 1989); **League Cup** (Liverpool 1981, 1982, 1983, 1984); Scottish Division One (Partick Thistle 1975-76); **European Cup** (Liverpool 1978, 1981, 1984).

Hansen, John *player* Midfield/striker. **Denmark** international. Born 1924, died 1990. *Clubs* Frem (twice), **Juventus**, **Lazio**. *Keynotes* Hansen played in the Danish team that beat **Great Britain** 5–3 in the bronze-medal playoff match in the 1948 **Olympic Games** in London. *Honours* Olympic Games bronze medal 1948; Italian **Serie A** Championship 1950, 1952 (with Juventus).

Hapgood, Eddie (Edris) *player* Left-back. **England** international (30 caps). Born 24 September 1908. Career ca. 1927–1944. *Clubs* Kettering Town, **Arsenal**, **Shrewsbury Town** (player-coach). *Keynotes* Cost Arsenal £750 when he joined the club from Kettering Town in October 1927. Hapgood was one of a record seven Arsenal players in the England team which played Italy at **Highbury** on 14 November 1934 (Cliff **Bastin**, Ray Bowden, Wilf Copping, Ted **Drake**, George Male, Frank Moss). During **World War II**, Hapgood also guested for both **Luton Town** and **Chelsea**, and after hostilities ceased he managed **Blackburn Rovers**. Later he was manager of both **Watford** and **Bath City**. Included in the **Football League Centenary 100 players**. *Honours* League Championship (Arsenal 1930-31, 1932-33, 1933-34, 1934-35, 1937-38); **FA Cup** (Arsenal 1930, 1936).

Hapoel Petach-Tikva *club* Israeli national league club based in Petach-Tikva, Tel Aviv, formed 1930. Ground: Hapoel Petach-Tikva, capacity: 7,500. Strip: blue and black striped shirts, black shorts. *Keynotes* The club holds the Israeli league record of five consecutive league titles (1959 to 1963). Israel Cup 1957, 1992; Israel league champions 1955, 1959, 1960, 1961, 1962, 1963.

Hapoel Tel Aviv *club* Israeli national league club based in Tel Aviv, founded 1927. Ground: Bloomfield, capacity: 28,000. Strip: red shirts, white shorts. **Asian Champion Teams' Cup** 1967, (2–1, v FA **Selangor** of Malaysia, in Bangkok), runners-up 1970 (1–2, v **Taj Club** of Iran, final in Tehran); former-Palestine Cup 1928, 1934, 1937, 1938, 1940; former-Palestine League champions 1934, 1935, 1936, 1938, 1940, 1943; Israel Cup 1960, 1972; Israel league champions 1957, 1966, 1969, 1981, 1986, 1988.

Happel, Ernst *player and manager* Striker. **Austria** international (51 caps, ca. 1952-58). Born 29 June 1925, died 1992. *Clubs* **Rapid Vienna**, **First Vienna FC**, **Racing Club de Paris**. *Keynotes* Coached **Feyenoord** to its **European Cup** success in 1970 (2–1, v **Celtic**, in **San Siro** Stadium, Milan) – the first European success by a Dutch club. Happel created a fluid playing style which, it is claimed, was adapted by **Ajax** and **Netherlands** coach Rinus **Michels** to create the legendary **total football** playing system. Happel succeeded Rinus Michels as manager of the Netherlands, guiding the country to the 1978 **World Cup** final (1–3 v **Argentina**). He became national coach of Austria from 1991 until his death in 1992. Happel continued to coach the national squad despite suffering from cancer; after his death he was honoured in Austria through the naming of the national stadium: the all-seater **Ernst Happel Stadion** in Vienna, capacity: 49,000.

Happy Valley *club* Hong Kong league club. **Asian Cup-winners Cup** quarter-final 1999; Hong Kong league champions 1965, 1989.

Hardaker, Alan *player and official* former secretary of the **Football League** 1956-1980. Born 1912, died 1980. Hardaker was born in Kingston upon Hull and signed as an amateur player for **Hull City** (though he never turned professional). Devised the **League Cup**, first played in 1960. Proposed the **Alliance Premier League** in 1971 (started 1979-80; later known as the **Football Conference**). Co-author, with Joe **Richards**, of the **Pattern for Football**.

Hardwick, George *player-manager* Left-back. **England** international (13 caps). Born 2 February 1920. Career ca. 1935–56. *Clubs* **Middlesbrough**, **Oldham Athletic** (player-manager). Manager **Sunderland**, Gateshead. *Keynotes* Turned professional with Middlesbrough in May 1937, becoming Oldham Athletic's player-manager in November 1950 following his £15,000 transfer. Hardwick also made 17 appearances for his country in wartime or "Victory" internationals. Included in the **Football League Centenary 100 players**. *Honours* Division Three (North) (Oldham Athletic 1952-53).

Hardy, Sam *player* Goalkeeper. **England** international (21 caps). Born 26 August 1883. Career ca. 1903–1925. *Clubs* **Chesterfield** Town, **Liverpool**, **Aston Villa**, **Nottingham Forest**. *Keynotes* Hardy made around 600 League appearances during a career which spanned 22 years from 1903 to 1925. Included in the **Football League Centenary 100 players**. *Honours* League Championship (Liverpool 1905-06);

Division Two (Nottingham Forest 1921-22); **FA Cup** (Aston Villa 1913, 1920).

Harlem Bombers *club* Dominica national league club. *Keynotes* Harlem's 11 domestic cup triumphs is a **CONCACAF** record. Dominica Cup 1970, 1971, 1973, 1974, 1976, 1978, 1980, 1984, 1992, 1994, 1997; Dominica league champions 1970, 1972, 1973, 1974, 1982, 1983, 1985 (joint winners), 1989, 1992, 1995, 1997.

harpastum *n.* early form of football played in ancient Rome, competed by two teams.

Hartlepool United *club* English league. *Dossier* Ground: **Victoria Park**, Hartlepool, Cleveland, capacity: 7,229. Strip: blue and white striped shirts, blue shorts, blue socks. Nickname: Pool. Record attendance: 17.426 v **Manchester United** (5 January 1957, **FA Cup**, third round). Best average attendance: 9,265 (1951-52). Biggest win: 10–1 v **Barrow** (4 April 1959, Division Four). Biggest defeat: 1–10 v **Wrexham** (3 March 1962, Division Four). *History* Founded in 1908 as Hartlepools United (a name the club retained until 1968 when it became plain Hartlepool; a title it dropped in 1977 in favour of the current name). The club took over the Victoria Ground, which had been the home of West Hartlepool rugby club since 1886. Hartlepool was a founder member of Division Three (North) in 1921-22 and the club has spent all but four (1968-69, 1991-92 to 1993-94) of its 72-season **Football League** career in the bottom division. The club has applied for **re-election** on a record 11 occasions, including finishing bottom, or second from bottom, of Division Four in five consecutive seasons between 1959-60 and 1963-64. One of Hartlepool's most celebrated moments came in 1993 when the club defeated **Premier League** opponent's **Crystal Palace** (1–0) in the third round of the FA Cup. *League record* Second Division 1992-93 to 1993-94; Division Three 1968-69, 1991-92; Third Division 1994-95–; Division Three (North) 1921-22 to 1957-58; Division Four 1958-59 to 1967-68, 1969-70 to 1990-91. *Records* Ambrose Fogarty is Hartlepool's most capped player (1 (11) for **Ireland, Republic of**); Wattie Moore holds the record for club League appearances (447, 1948-64); Ken Johnson is Hartlepool's record League goalscorer (98, 1949-68).

hat-trick *n.* three goals scored by the same player in a single match (derived from the same expression used in cricket to describe the taking of three wickets in consecutive balls). *Keynotes* Argentine international Guillermo **Stábile** scored the first hat-trick in the **World Cup** (19 July 1930, **Argentina** v **Mexico**, 6–3, at Centenario, Montevideo, first round). The only hat-trick in a World Cup final was scored by Geoff **Hurst**, for **England** against West **Germany** (30 July 1966, **Wembley** Stadium, 4–2). Ernst Willimowski was the first player to score a hat-trick in a World Cup finals fixture and be on the losing side: Willimowski scored four for **Poland** in its 5–6 defeat by **Brazil** (first round, in Strasbourg, France, 5 June 1938; his fourth goal was in extra time); Igor **Belanov** also scored three goals for the losing side; for the Soviet Union in its 3–4 defeat by **Spain** (second round, in León, Mexico, 15 June 1986). **Pelé** was the first player to score a hat-trick in the **World Club Cup** (5–2, for **Santos** v **Benfica**, in Lisbon, 11 October 1962; he also scored two in the 3–2 first leg victory at **Maracaná**, Rio de Janeiro). **Real Madrid**'s Ferenc **Puskás** was the first player to score a hat-trick in a **European Cup** final (he actually scored four); his team-mate Alfredo **Di Stefano** also completed his hat-trick 15 minutes later in the same game (7–3, v **Eintracht Frankfurt**, at **Hampden Park**, Glasgow). Three players have scored hat-tricks in the **FA Cup** final: Billy Townley for **Blackburn Rovers** (1890, 6–1, v **Sheffield Wednesday**); Jimmy Logan for **Notts County** (1894, 4–1, v **Bolton Wanderers**); and Stan **Mortensen** for **Blackpool** (1953, 4–3, v Bolton Wanderers). Wilf **Mannion** (28 September 1946, v **Northern Ireland**, **Home International Championship**), Stan Mortenson (four goals, 25 May 1947, v Portugal), v **United States of America** (in New York, friendly) and Luther Blissett (15 December 1982, 9–0, v **Luxembourg**, at Wembley Stadium, European Championship) have scored hat-tricks for England on their international debuts. The world's fastest reported hat-trick was scored by Maglioni for the Argentinean club **Independiente** in only 110 seconds (v **Gimnasia y Esgrima La Plata**, 18 March 1973). The fastest international hat-trick was scored by Willie Hall for England in under four minutes (16 November 1938, 7–0, v **Ireland**; Hall scored five goals). **Motherwell** (and later **Liverpool**) striker Ian St John scored a hat-trick in 150 seconds on 15 August 1959 (v **Hibernian**, Scottish League Cup). Dixie **Dean**, of **Tranmere** and **Everton**, holds the **Football League** record for the most hat-tricks in his league career (37, 1924-38); George Camsell of **Middlesbrough** holds the record for the most hat-tricks in one season (nine, 1926-27, Division Two); Jimmy **Greaves**, while playing for **Chelsea**, holds the post-war top-flight record (six, 1960-61, Division One); Alan **Shearer** of **Blackburn Rovers** scored a record five hat-tricks in one season of the FA **Premier League** (1995-96); Shearer was also the youngest player to score a top-flight hat-trick, at 17 years 240 days, for **Southampton** (4–2, v **Arsenal**, 9 April, 1988, Division One – the first time he had started a match for Southampton). Cliff Holton of **Watford** was the first player to score hat-tricks on consecutive days (15 April 1960, v **Chester**, 4–2; and 16 April, v **Gateshead**, 5–0; Division Four). **Charlton Athletic**'s Clive Mendoca became the first player to score a hat trick in an end-of-season Wembley **playoff** when his side defeated **Sunderland** on penalties to win promotion to the Premier League on 25 May 1998 (4–4, 7–6 pens.).

hats *misc.* headgear, sometimes worn by players, managers and spectators. *Keynotes* **Sunderland** manager Bob Stokoe sported a red-and-white bowler hat when the club won the FA Cup in 1973. Malcolm

Allison's fedora was a familiar sight, along with a cigar, during his managership of **Crystal Palace** and **Manchester City**. **Croatia** manager Miroslav Blazevic was presented with a French gendarme's cap before his side faced **Romania** in the second round of the 1998 **World Cup** and it became something of a lucky charm as the team reached the third-place **playoff**. Jens Martin Knudsen, the **Faroe Island**'s most capped player, is famed for wearing a bobble hat during matches. **Arbroath**, Sunderland and **Liverpool** goalkeeper Ned (John Edward) Doig wore a cap held in place by an elastic band throughout his career, which included five appearances for **Scotland** between 1887 and 1903.

Havelange, João *official* the seventh **FIFA** president (1974-1998). Born 8 May 1916. Havelange was elected in 1974 at a Frankfurt meeting prior to the **World Cup**, defeating the then president Stanley **Rous** over two ballots. He was replaced by Sepp **Blatter** following the 1998 World Cup. Nationality: Brazilian.

Haverfordwest   County *club* Welsh league. Ground: The Bridge Meadow Stadium, Pembrokeshire, capacity: 2,000. Strip: blue shirts, blue shorts. Nickname: the Bluebirds. Formed in 1899. *Honours* Welsh League 1956-57, 1980-81.

Hawks *club* Gambian national league club based in the capital Banjul. Strip: maroon shirts, white shorts. Ground: Friendship Stadium, capacity: 5,000. Gambian Cup 1983; Gambian league champions 1993, 1996.

Hawthorns *ground* English football ground situated in West Bromwich, west Midlands; home of **West Bromwich Albion**. *Dossier* Ground capacity: 25,396 all seated. Pitch dimensions 105m x 69m. Record attendance: 64,815 v **Arsenal** (6 March 1937, **FA Cup**, sixth round). Best average attendance: 38,910 (1949-50). *History* Albion played its first match at the Hawthorns on 3 September 1900 (v **Derby County**, Division One), having previously played at several venues, including Four Acres and Stoney Lane. The ground gets its name from the hawthorn hedges that had once bordered the area. The club originally signed a 14-year contract to lease the ground at £70 a year, eventually buying the freehold for £5,350 in 1913. A 600-capacity grandstand, dubbed Noah's Ark, which had been built at Albion's previous ground, Stoney Lane, was re-erected at the Hawthorns only to be destroyed by fire in 1904. A nearby railway station, called Hawthorns Halt, was opened in 1931 (it was closed in 1968) and, in 1949, the ground became one of the first to install electronic **turnstile** counters. In 1935, the ground was the setting for an experiment using **two referees**; an idea that had first been proposed by **Everton** chairman William **Cuff** at the 1935 annual meeting of the **Football League**. Two matches were held at the Hawthorns using the dual control plan (**England** v The Rest, 27 March 1935 and Football League XI v West Bromwich Albion, 8 May 1935). The Hawthorns staged a Football League v Irish League match on 7 October 1914. The Hawthorns has staged two full England international fixtures (v **Northern Ireland**, 21 October 1922; v **Belgium**, 8

December 1924). It was also the venue for a **World War II** "Victory" international (England v Wales, 20 October 1945) and a B international (v **Chile**, 10 February 1998). The ground has twice been used as a n FA Cup semi-final venue. The first floodlit match at the Hawthorns took place on 18 September 1957 (v **Chelsea**, Division One), although the lights were officially unveiled on 29 October (v **Soviet Union** army side, friendly) – an event televised by the BBC.

Haynes, Johnny *player* Midfield. **England** international (56 caps, 18 goals). Born 17 October 1934. Career ca. 1952-70. *Clubs* **Fulham**, Durban City (South Africa). Also, Fulham's caretaker manager (1968). *Keynotes* Joined Fulham in 1950 and after spells with various non–League sides, turned professional in May 1952. He scored 145 goals in 594 **Football League** appearances for Fulham. He became the first £100-a-week player in 1961 following the lifting of the **maximum wage**. Haynes captained England on 22 occasions. In 1962, Haynes was injured in a car crash and never appeared for England again. His first full international appearance (v **Northern Ireland**, 2 October 1954) meant that Haynes became the first player to be capped at six age levels, including as a schoolboy. Moved to South Africa in 1970 where he both played and coached Durban City. Included in the **Football League Centenary 100 players**.

Hazard United *club* Jamaica league club based in May Pen. Strip: blue shirts, yellow shorts. Jamaica League champions 1993.

HB Torshavn (Havnar Boltfelag) *club* Faeroe Islands national league club based in the capital Torshavn, founded 1904. Ground: Gundadular, capacity: 8,000. Strip: black and red striped shirts, black shorts. Faeroe Islands Cup 1955, 1957, 1959, 1962, 1963, 1964, 1968, 1969, 1971, 1972, 1973, 1975, 1976, 1978, 1979, 1980, 1981, 1982, 1984, 1987, 1988, 1989, 1992, 1995, 1998; Faeroe Islands League champions 1955, 1960, 1963, 1964, 1965, 1971, 1973, 1974, 1975, 1978, 1981, 1982, 1988, 1990, 1998.

head *vb.* to strike the ball with the head. *n.* **header** The execution of this. *Keynotes* The practice of heading the ball is believed to have originated in Sheffield, and became common practice in the south of England only in the 1870s. The world record for non-stop heading the ball, without it touching the ground, or any other part of the body, is eight hours, 12 minutes, 25 seconds, by Goderdzi Makharadze, from **Georgia** (26 May 1996, in Tbilisi, Georgia, as recorded by the *Guinness Book of Records*).

Heart of Midlothian *club* Scottish league. *Dossier* Ground: **Tynecastle Park**, Edinburgh, capacity: 18,300. Strip: maroon shirts, white shorts with maroon trim, maroon socks with white top and maroon hoops. Nickname: Hearts. Record attendance: 53,396 v **Rangers** (13 February 1932, **Scottish FA Cup**, third round). Biggest win: 21–0 v Anchor (30 October 1880). Biggest defeat: 1–8 v **Vale of Leven** (Scottish FA Cup, 1888). *History* Founded in 1874 and taking its name

from a local dance club (which itself had been named after Edinburgh's old tollbooth). The club was a founder member of the **Scottish Football League** in 1890-91. Hearts won its first League Championship in 1894-95 and a second in 1896-97. Between 1891 and 1907, Hearts appeared in six Scottish FA Cup finals. It won the trophy in 1891 (1–0 **Dumbarton**), 1896 (3–1 v The **Hibernian**), 1901 (4–3 v Celtic), 1906 (1–0 v **Third Lanark**) and was also a finalist in both 1903 (0–2 second replay v Rangers), 1907 (0–3 v **Celtic**). The club enjoyed a successful decade from the mid-1950s. During that spell, Hearts won the League Championship twice (1957-58, 1959-60) and was runners-up on four occasions (1953-54, 1956-57, 1958-59, 1964-65). In addition, Hearts also lifted the Scottish FA Cup (1956, 3–1 v Celtic) and four **Scottish League Cup** trophies (1954-55, 4–2 v **Motherwell**; 1958-59, 5–1 v **Partick Thistle**; 1959-60, 2–1 v Third Lanark; 1962-63, 1–0 v **Kilmarnock**). It also appeared in a fifth League Cup final (1961-62, 1–3 v Rangers). Hearts was relegated from the top flight for the first time in 1976-77 and over the following six seasons the club alternated between the Premier and First Divisions. Between the club's 1956 Scottish FA Cup triumph and its 1998 victory (2–1 v Rangers), Hearts was defeated in three finals: 1968 (1–3 v **Dunfermline Athletic**), 1976 (1–3 v Rangers), 1986 (0–3 v **Aberdeen**), 1996 (1–5 v Rangers). It was also a Scottish League Cup runner-up in 1996-97 (3–4 v Rangers) and, in 1988-89, the club reached the quarter-final stage of the **UEFA Cup** (1–2 agg., v **Bayern Munich**). Hearts was floated on the London Stock Exchange in May 1997 (flotation price = 140p) – see **Heart of Midlothian plc**. *League record* Premier Leauge 1998-99–; Premier Division 1975-76 to 1976-77, 1978-79, 1983-84, 1997-98; Division One (A Division) 1893-94 to 1914-15, 1921-22 to 1974-75; Scottish League 1890-91 to 1892-93; 1915-16 to 1920-21; First Division 1977-78, 1979-80, 1981-82 to 1982-83. *Honours* Division One 1894-95, 1896-97, 1957-58, 1959-60; First Division 1979-80; Scottish FA Cup 1891 (1–0 Dumbarton), 1896 (3–1 The Hibernian), 1901 (4–3 v Celtic), 1906 (1–0 Third Lanark), 1956 (3–1 v Celtic), 1998 (2–1 v Rangers); Scottish League Cup 1954-55 (4–2 v Motherwell), 1958-59 (5–1 v Partick Thistle), 1959-60 (2–1 v Third Lanark), 1962-63 (1–0 v Kilmarnock). *Records* Bobby Walker is Hearts' most capped player (29 for **Scotland**); Gary Mackay holds the record for club appearances (515, 1980-97); John Robertson is Hearts' record goalscorer (214, 1983-98).

Heart of Midlothian plc *n.* publicly-quoted business which owns **Heart of Midlothian**. The club became a fully listed company on the London Stock Exchange in May 1997 (flotation price = 140p). Hearts had a market capitalisation – the market value of the company's issued share capital (e.g. the quoted price of its shares multiplied by the number of shares outstanding) – of £14.2 million on flotation.

Hearts of Oak *club* Ghanaian professional league club based in the capital Accra, formed 1911, Ghana's oldest club. Ground: Accra Sports Stadium (the national stadium), capacity: 45,000 (5,000 seated). Strip: red shirts, blue shorts. **African Cup of Champion Clubs** runners-up 1977 (2–4 v **Hafia FC** of Guinea), 1979 (1–1 agg., 3–5 pens., v **Union Douala** of Cameroon), quarter-final "champions-league" stage 1998; **African Cup-winners Cup** semi-final 1982, quarter-final 1995; Ghanaian Cup 1973, 1974, 1979, 1981, 1987, 1988, 1989, 1994, 1995, 1996; Ghanaian League champions 1956, 1958, 1962, 1971, 1973, 1976, 1977, 1978, 1979, 1984, 1985, 1990, 1997, 1998.

Heathrow Agreement *misc.* proposed settlement to end the dispute over the proposed **Super League** breakaway from the English **Football League**. Agreed on 18 December 1985 at the Post House Hotel at Heathrow Airport. Although it was not immediately approved, it formed the basis of the agreement that eventually prevented the breakaway. It gave a greater share of the revenue to the First Division clubs. It also involved a smaller First Division (20 clubs), promotion and relegation **playoffs**, automatic promotion and relegation from the **Football Conference** (at that time known as the Gola League) to and from the Fourth Division, and greater representation of First Division clubs on the **Football League Management Committee**.

Helsingborgs IF (Idrottsförening) *club* Swedish national league club based in Helsingborg, founded 1907. Ground: Olympia, capacity: 16,000. Strip: red shirts, blue shorts. *Keynotes* Helsingborg won the first ever Swedish Cup in 1941, (3–1, v IK Sleipner). Swedish Cup 1941, 1998; Swedish league champions 1929, 1930, 1933, 1934, 1941; **UEFA Cup** third round 1997.

Hereford United *club* former English league. *Dossier* Ground: Edgar Street, Hereford, capacity: 9,022. Record attendance: 18,114 v **Sheffield Wednesday** (4 January 1958, **FA Cup**, third round). Biggest win: 6–0 v **Burnley** (24 January 1987, Division Four). Biggest defeat: 1–7 v **Mansfield Town** (26 December 1994, Division Three). *Keynotes* Joined the **Football League** in 1972-73, replacing **Barrow**. The club won promotion to Division Three in its first League season, winning a place to Division Two for one season in 1976-77. Hereford recorded its most famous victory as a non-League side in the season before enterng the League. Following a 2–2 draw at **St James' Park**, Hereford defeated **Newcastle United** 2–1 in the third round of the FA Cup. Hereford lost its League status in 1996-97, after drawing at home on the last day of the season against **Brighton & Hove Albion** (1–1, 3 May 1997), its only competitors for the drop. *League record* Division Two 1976-77; Division Three 1973-74 to 1975-76, 1977-78; Third Division 1992-93 to 1996-97; Division Four 1972-73, 1978-79 to 1991-92. *Honours* Division Three (1975-76); **Welsh Cup** (2–1 v **Wrexham**).

hernia *medical* technically, the protrusion of an organ through the lining of the cavity in which it is situated. It commonly refers to the protrusion of the intestine through the front wall of the abdominal cavity, caused by muscular strain or injury; symptoms include discomfort in the abdomen during exertion, and discomfort brought on by coughing and sneezing. More often than not a hernia is painless.

Herrera, Helenio *manager* Born 17 April 1917; died 9 November 1997. *Clubs* Puteaux (France), **Red Star 93**, Stade Francais, **Atlético Madrid**, Malaga, Valladolid, **Sevilla** FC, **Barcelona**, **Internazionale**, **Roma (AS)**. Also **Spain** and **Italy** manager. *Keynotes* Nicknamed Il Mago ("The Magician"), Herrera, an Argentine, built Il Grande Inter, the "Great Inter" side of the 1960s, which included Luis **Suárez,** Mario Corso and Sandro **Mazzola**. It was at Internazionale that Herrera perfected the **catenaccio** defensive system in the mid-1960s, using the Italian international defensive trio, Tarcisio Burgnich, Armando Picchi and Giacinto **Facchetti**. He is also credited with establishing the **tifosi** – travelling flag-waving supporters. Herrera took **Spain** to the 1962 **World Cup** finals having been a member of **Italy**'s coaching staff during the qualifying rounds. *Honours* **European Cup** (Internazionale 1964, 1965); Italian Cup (Roma (AS) 1970); Italian League (**Serie A**) (Internazionale 1963, 1965, 1966); Spanish League (Atlético Madrid 1950, 1951, Barcelona 1959); **World Club Cup** (Internazionale 1964, 1965).

Heysel Stadium disaster *disaster* stadium disaster at the Heysel Stadium, Brussels, Belgium, on 29 May 1985, sparked by rioting between rival fans before the start of the **European Cup** Final between **Liverpool** and **Juventus**. Thirty-nine spectators died and more than 350 were injured. Most of the victims were supporters of the Italian club, who fell, were crushed or were trampled to death when a wall collapsed as they tried to escape the fighting. In a move tragically reminiscent of the **Burnden Park disaster**, the match was eventually started, 85 minutes after the scheduled kick-off, on the advice of the police in an attempt to restore order. Although the tragedy was clearly caused by football **hooliganism**, a Belgium parliamentary investigation also held the police and football organisations as partly to blame for the scale of the disaster. On 8 April 1989, 24 Liverpool fans were found guilty of manslaughter by a Brussels court, and sentenced to three years in prison (18 months suspended). They were each fined £1,000. The football authorities and Brussels officials were cleared of any negligence. Following the disaster, all English clubs were banned from European competitions for an indefinite period by the **Union of European Football Associations**, a move endorsed by **FIFA** which increased the sanction to include a ban on other English clubs playing clubs from any other country. Liverpool was initially banned for a further three years, to start after the lifting of the ban on English clubs; the ban interpreted as meaning any three years in which Liverpool qualified for a European competition. English clubs were readmitted to European competitions in 1990; Liverpool were allowed back in 1991. The Heysel Stadium was rebuilt and renamed the Stade du **Roi**

Baudouin. It is a venue for the 2000 **European Championship**.

Hibbs, Harry (Henry) *player* Goalkeeper. **England** international (25 caps). Born 27 May 1906. Career ca. 1924–1940. *Clubs* **Birmingham City**. *Keynotes* Played almost 400 matches for Birmingham City, appearing in one **FA Cup** final (1931 v **West Bromwich Albion**). Hibbs retired in April 1940, going on to manage **Walsall** (1944 to 1951). Included in the **Football League Centenary 100 players**.

Hibernian *club* Scottish league. *Dossier* Ground: **Easter Road**, Edinburgh., capactity: 16,218. Strip: green shirts with white sleeves, white shorts with green trim, green socks with white hoops. Nickname: Hibees. Record attendance: 65,860 v **Heart of Midlothian** (2 January 1950, **Division One**). Biggest win: 22–1 v 42nd Highlanders (3 September 1881). Biggest defeat: 0–10 v **Rangers** (24 December 1898, Division One). *History* Founded in 1875. The club won the **Scottish FA Cup** in 1887 (2–1 v **Dumbarton**). Despite the club's success, in 1891 it disbanded after losing many of its players to **Celtic** and its ground to developers. The club explored the possibilities of, first moving to **Aberdeen** and then taking over **Motherwell**. The club reformed and joined the newly-established Division Two in 1893-94, winning the title that season and again in 1894-95, but only gaining election to the top flight on the second occasion because automatic promotion/relegation was not introduced in Scotland until 1921-22. The club won a second Scottish FA Cup, as The Hibernian, in 1902 (1–0 v Celtic), having been a finalist again in 1896 (1–3 v Heart of Midlothian). The 1896 final was played at Logie Green in Edinburgh and is the only occasion it has been played outside of Glasgow. **Hibs** reached the final on a further seven occasions following its 1902 success: 1914 (1–4 v Celtic), 1923 (0–1 v Celtic), 1924 (0–2 v **Airdrieonians**), 1947 (1–2 v Aberdeen), 1958 (0–1 v **Clyde**), 1972 (1–6 v Celtic), 1979 (2–3 second replay v Rangers). Aside from two seasons in 1931-32 and 1932-33, Hibs retained its top-flight status until relegation from the Premier Division in 1979-80, although the club made a immediate return as First Division Champions. Hibernian won consecutive League Championships in 1950-51 and 1951-52 to add to the two titles achieved in 1902-03 and 1947-48. Despite finishing fifth in Division One in 1954-55, Hibernian was the UK's first representatives in the **European Cup** in the following season, reaching the semi-final stage (0–3 agg., v **Stade de Reims**). In 1960-61, the club reached the semi-finals of the UEFA (Fairs) Cup, losing a replay against **Roma (AS)** after the aggregate score finished level (5–5 agg; 0–6 replay). Two years later, Hibernian reached the quarter-final stage of the same competition (2–6 agg., v **Valencia**). Following the club's appearance in the 1972 Scottish FA Cup final, Hibernian entered the **European Cup-winners Cup** competition as losing finalists, reaching the last four (4–5 agg., v **Hadjuk Split**). The club won the **Scottish League Cup** in 1972-73 (2–1 v Celtic) and

1991-92 (2–0 v **Dunfermline Athletic**). In addition, Hibernian has been a finalist a further five times: 1950-51 (0–3 v Motherwell), 1968-69 (2–6 Celtic), 1974-75 (3–6 v Celtic), 1984-85 (0–3 v Aberdeen) and 1993-94 (1–2 v Rangers). Hibernian narrowly retained its Premier Division status in 1996-97, winning the end-of-season playoff against second-placed First Division finishers, Airdrieonians (5–2 agg.). Only relegation from the Premier Division in 1997-98 prevented the club from becoming a founder member of the new Premier League, though it won promotion to the top flight the following season. *League record* Premier League 1999-00; Premier Division 1975-76 to 1979-80, 1981-82 to 1997-98, 1999-00; Division One (A Division) 1895-96 to 1914-15, 1921-22 to 1930-31, 1933-34 to 1974-75; First Division 1980-81, 1998-99–; Division Two 1893-94 to 1894-95, 1931-32 to 1932-33; Scottish League 1915-16 to 1920-21. *Honours* First Division 1980-81; Division Two 1893-94, 1894-95, 1932-33; League Champions 1902-03, 1947-48, 1950-51, 1951-52; Scottish FA Cup 1887 (2–1 v Dumbarton), 1902 (1–0 v Celtic); Scottish League Cup 1972-73 (2–1 v Celtic), 1991-92 (2–0 v Dunfermline Athletic). *Records* Lawrie Reilly is Hibernian's most capped player (38 for **Scotland**); Arthur Duncan holds the record for club appearances (446).

Hibernians FC *club* Maltese national league club, based in Paola, and formed in 1931. Ground: Ta'Qali Stadium, Valletta, capacity: 18,000 (all Maltese premier league are games played here). Strip: white shirts and black shorts. Maltese FA Trophy 1962, 1970, 1971, 1980, 1982, 1998; Maltese league champions 1961, 1967, 1969, 1979, 1981, 1982, 1994, 1995.

Hibs *abbrev.* for Scottish league club **Hibernian**.

Hidegkuti, Nandor *player* Striker. **Hungary** international (39 goals, 1951-1958). Born 1922. *Clubs* **MTK Budapest** (the club was known as Vörös Logobó from 1953 to 1956). *Keynotes* One of the **Magnificent Magyars**, Hidegkuti scored a hat-trick against **England** at **Wembley** Stadium in Hungary's 6–3 victory, his first after 90 seconds (25 November 1953, friendly). He played in the 1954 **World Cup** final against West **Germany** (2–3) and was Hungary's sixth highest all-time goalscorer. He became coach of **Vasas DH** and **Fiorentina**. In 1993, he was awarded FIFA's **Fairplay Award** for sportsmanship. *Honours* **Olympic Games** gold medal (Hungary, 1952); World Cup runner-up (Hungary, 1954); Hungarian league championship (MTK, 1953, 1958).

High Court action *legal* dispute that comes before the supreme court of justice (England) or high court of justiciary (Scotland). In the UK, both players and clubs have taken cases to the High Court. *Keynotes* Following the formation of the **League of Wales** in 1992, three Welsh clubs, **Caernarfon Town**, **Colwyn Bay** and Newport AFC, refused to join the new league and were subsequently barred by the **Football Association of Wales** (FAW) from playing matches in the principality (see **Exiles**). The clubs took the FAW to court alleging an illegal restraint of trade. In April 1995, the clubs, which had been granted an interim injunction against the FAW's decision at a previous hearing in July 1994, won their case. Caernarfon later joined the League of Wales, while Colwyn Bay and Newport continue to play in the English non-league. Several players have attempted to seek redress through the courts for on-the-pitch incidents. In December 1992, Gary Blissett was acquitted of grievous bodily harm following a clash with **Torquay United**'s John Uzzell, that left Uzzell with a smashed cheek. **Chelsea**'s Paul Elliott sought redress (£1 million in damages) through the courts in 1994 after his career was prematurely ended following a tackle by Dean Saunders during a match against **Liverpool** at **Anfield** in September 1992. Elliott lost his case. Ian Knight, a former **Sheffield Wednesday** defender, whose leg was broken in seven places following a tackle by Gary Bennett, then of **Chester City**, went to the High Court in October 1997 claiming £1.5m in damages as a result of the injury. The case was eventually settled out of court. At the time of the case, Knight was a coach with **Grimsby Town**. Former Sunderland player and **Ireland, Replublic of** youth team member, Kieron Brady lost his claim for £2.4 million compensation from the club in April 1998. Brady had claimed during an 11-day High Court hearing that the club had failed to respond satisfactorily to his repeated complaint of serious leg pains. The court decided that neither the then Sunderland manager Malcolm Crosby nor its physiotherapist Steve Smelt had been negligent and costs were awarded against Brady. In October 1998, **Bradford City** striker Gordon Watson sued **Huddersfield Town** and its defender Kevin Gray on the grounds of negligence following a tackle by Gray that resulted in a double fracture of his opponent's leg during a First Division encounter on 1 February 1997. Watson was supported by his club which brought similar action for recklessness against both Gray and Huddersfield. Watson was out for 18 months following the incident, having joined the club for a then record fee of £575,000 from **Southampton** only a few weeks earlier. Watson's complaint was upheld although the action brought by his club was dismissed. The 27-year-old Watson's victory meant he became the first player to win damages (he received an interim payment of £50,000) as a result of the actions of a fellow professional.

high tackle   *n.*   a tackle where the player's foot is dangerously high, liable to cause injury, and invariably ruled as a **foul** (see **dangerous play**). Also called high challenge.

Highbury   *ground*   English football ground situated in north London; home of **Arsenal**. *Dossier* Ground capacity: 38,500 all-seater. Pitch dimensions: 100.5m x 67m. Record attendance: 73,295 v **Sunderland** (9 March 1935, **Division One**). Best average attendance: 54,982 (1947-48). *History* Arsenal switched to Highbury from south-east London after the close of 1912-13 season. The move was initially opposed by the local council and residents, as well as the two existing north London clubs,

Tottenham Hotspur and Clapton **Orient**. Arsenal paid £20,000 for a 21-year lease on the land for the new ground from the Ecclesiastical Commission. The agreement stipulated that the club should not play home matches on Good Friday or Christmas Day. One of the main attractions of the ground's location was its close proximity to Gillespie Road (later renamed Arsenal) underground station. Scottish architect and engineer, Archibald **Leitch** designed the new venue which, although incomplete, opened on 6 September 1913. Arsenal's owner, Henry **Norris**, bought the ground's freehold for £64,000 in 1925 and arranged for the Good Friday and Christmas Day restriction on matches to be lifted. Arsenal's dominance of English football in the 1930s enabled the club to completely rebuild Highbury. The ground's west stand was designed by celebrated architect Claude Waterlow Ferrier, at a cost of £45,000 and includes an electric lift. At the same time the name of the ground changed from Highbury to Arsenal Stadium (although it is still commonly referred to by its former name), while a 12-feet diameter, 45-minute clock was erected, despite the objections of the football authorities, at the northern end of the ground (it was subsequently moved to the southern end, which thereafter became known as the Clock End). Aside from early experiments with **floodlights** at several grounds before the turn of the century, Arsenal, and especially manager Herbert **Chapman**, became one of the first clubs to promote the benefits of floodlit football, holding a public demonstration in November 1932. Highbury was later the first Division One ground to install floodlights. In October 1936, the east stand opened at a cost of £130,000 and was very similar to its western counterpart, although it included individual player baths, a wood-panelled boardroom and a marbled entrance hall. The interior was designed by Ferrier's partner, William Binnie. In 1992, the "NorthBank" was demolished and replaced with a 12,400 all-seater stand. Original plans for the stand were opposed by some local residents and supporters (see **Group for an Alternative Arsenal Stand** (**GAAS**)). The finance was raised in part by the sale of **debentures** to fans, allowing them to purchase future **season tickets**. While the stand was being constructed, the club erected a specially commissioned mural depicting a crowd scene. The mural had to be repainted after it was criticised for omitting any black or distinctly female faces. Prior to the redevelopment of the NorthBank, Highbury was one the largest club grounds in England with a capacity of 47,000 in 1991, although the pitch is the smallest at a League football ground in London. In July 1997, Highbury's east stand was awarded listed-building status. Arsenal plans to redevelop parts of the ground to bring capacity up to more than 50,000. In March 1998, Arsenal submitted a £125 million bid to buy **Wembley**, and although it withdrew the bid the club was granted permission in July 1998 by the **Football Association** and the **Union of European Football Associations** (UEFA) to stage its forthcoming **European Cup** Champions League fixtures at the national stadium. The three games were watched by a total of more than 200,000 people. The club made the move because UEFA regulations regarding advertising hoardings and press facilities would have reduced Highbury's capacity by around 6,000. Highbury staged its first floodlit match in September 1951 (v **Hapoel Tel Aviv**, friendly) and, in 1964, was one of the first grounds to install **undersoil heating**. Highbury was the scene of the inaugural radio broadcast of a football match on 22 January 1922 (v **Sheffield United**) and the first trial televised match (v Arsenal Reserves) on 16 September 1937. Highbury was also the setting for the 1939 feature film, "The Arsenal Stadium Mystery". The ground staged its first international match on 15 March 1920 (v **Wales**) and three years later Highbury became the first English venue to host an international against foreign opposition (v **Belgium**, 19 March 1923). Highbury has also staged **FA Cup** semi-final matches and has been the venue for **FA Amateur Cup** finals (1929, 1931, 1947). The ground was also the venue for the **England** v Football League XI match that celebrated the Centenary of the Football Association and the 75th Anniversary of the **Football League** on 24 May 1963.

highest club *record* there is no official record of the highest club in the world, but **Bolivia**'s top two clubs, **Bolivar Independiente Unificada** and **The Strongest**, are situated in the World's highest capital city, La Paz, at 3,800 m (12,400 feet) above sea level. While geographically not the highest, **Ecuador** national league club Club Everest, from Guayaquil, can lay claim to be the highest in name. See **altitude**.

highest crowd see **record attendance**.

Highfield Road *ground* English football ground situated in Coventry, Warwickshire; home of **Coventry City**. *Dossier* Ground capacity: 23,611 all seated. Pitch dimensions: 100.5m x 68.5m. Record attendance: 51,455 v **Wolverhampton Wanderers** (29 April 1967, Division Two). Best average attendance: 34,705 (1967-68). *History* Coventry City played its first match at Highfield Road on 9 September 1899 (v **Shrewsbury Town**). The field on which the ground was built had been used by Craven Cricket Club and the club rented it for £60 per year. In 1936, Coventry bought the ground's freehold after receiving a loan from the chairman of local engineering company Armstrong-Siddeley. The appointment of Jimmy **Hill** as Coventry's manager in 1961 signalled the start of major ground development at Highfield Road with the introduction of an electric scoreboard and the establishment of the league's first executive club in 1964. At the same time, Coventry developed a range of pre-match and half-time entertainment, including Radio Sky Blue, introduced by Kent and England cricketer, Godfrey Evans, as well as netball matches and dog-handling displays. These pioneering developments were followed in 1965, with the club's away fixture at Cardiff's **Ninian Park** being transmitted via **closed-circuit television** live to spectators at Highfield Road. In March 1968, the ground's main stand was destroyed by fire. The replacement stand included a

further innovation for a football ground, a restaurant. Coventry's innovative reputation was enhanced further when, in 1981, the club established the first **all-seater stadium** in England. Every home game was virtually all-ticket, with only a few tickets available on match days. The club revised both the ticketing policy and the all-seater nature of the ground a few years later when attendances slumped and several pitch invasions occurred. Highfield Road's first floodlit match took place on 21 October 1953 (v **Queen of the South**, friendly). Because of political troubles in Ireland, Highfield Road staged an international between **Northern Ireland** and **Portugal** on 28 March 1973 (Northern Ireland also used **Boothferry Park**, **Craven Cottage**, **Goodison Park** and **Hillsborough**, and switched its home matches against **Scotland** to **Hampden Park** during this period). The ground also hosted FA Cup semi-final third replay replay in 1980 between **Arsenal** and **Liverpool**.

Highland League *competition* Scottish amateur and semi-professional league for **senior football clubs** in the Scottish Highlands, affiliated to the **Scottish Football Association**. The sixteen member clubs are: Brora Rangers, Buckie Thistle, Clachnacuddin, Cove Rovers, Deveronvale, Elgin City, Forres Mechanics, Fort William, Fraserburgh, Huntly, Keith, Lossiemouth, Nairn County, Peterhead, Rothes, Wick Academy. The Highland League lost three of its leading clubs before the start of the 1994-95 season: **Ross County** and **Inverness Caledonian Thistle** (formed by a merger of Inverness Thistle and Inverness Caledonian) joined the **Scottish Football League** as part of the latter's restructuring and expansion. Member clubs compete for the **Scottish Qualifying Cup** (northern section); the semi-finalists qualifying for the **Scottish FA Cup**. *League system* Sixteen clubs compete in the league, playing each other at home and away. Three points are awarded for a victory, with one for a draw: final positions for clubs level on points are determined by **goal difference**. There is no promotion and relegation, although the league is, technically, directly below the Scottish Football League.

Highways Act 1835 *legal* British legislation that once outlawed the playing of football on the public highway.

Higuita, Rene *player* Goalkeeper. **Colombia** international. Clubs (include) **Atlético Nacional Medellin**, Independiente Medellin. *Keynotes* Voted third in the **South American Footballer of the Year** (*El Mundo*) 1990. Achieved international fame for his novel **scorpion kick** and for his imprisonment in 1993 for his middle-man role in a kidnapping incident. Higuita has also scored 46 senior goals – mostly from penalties. *Honours* Colombian league champions 1991, 1994; **Copa Inter America** (Atlético Nacional Medellin, 1990, 1997); **Copa Libertadores** (Atlético Nacional Medellin, 1989).

Hill, Jimmy *broadcaster/player/manager/official* Striker. Born 22 July 1928. Career ca. 1949-60. *Clubs*

Brentford, **Fulham**, **Coventry City**. As the youngest ever chairman of the **Professional Footballers Association** in 1961, Hill was instrumental (along with secretary Cliff **Lloyd**) in forcing clubs to remove the ceiling on players' wages (see **maximum wage**). Hill became Coventry City manager in 1961 and successfully led the club from Division Three to the top flight, winning the Division Three and Division Two titles in 1963-64 and 1966-67 respectively. Hill and club chairman Derrick Robbins were largely responsible for Coventry's "Sky Blue" image, that not only included the club strip (the old one was blue and white), but also special Sky Blue trains for fans travelling to away games. Hill resigned as Coventry manager following the club's 1967 Division Two Championship success (although he became a board member) and moved into television as head of ITV Sport. He joined the BBC as **Match of the Day** presenter in 1973, making over 600 appearances on the Saturday night highlights programme and later becoming a regular pundit at live broadcasts. Hill was a member of a consortium which bought his former club Fulham in 1987, becoming club chairman. After the 1998 **World Cup**, Hill joined BSkyB to present his own show, *The Last Word*.

Hillsborough *ground* English football ground situated in Sheffield, south Yorkshire; home of **Sheffield Wednesday**. *Dossier* Ground capacity: 39,859 all seated. Pitch dimensions: 105m x 68m. Record attendance: 72,841 v **Manchester City** (17 February 1934, **FA Cup**, fifth round). Best average attendance: 42,634 (1952-53). *History* The Wednesday (Sheffield Wednesday's name until 1929) moved to a site in Owlerton (eventually named Hillsborough) in 1899 after the club's lease at Olive Grove, its previous ground where Wednesday had first played on 12 September 1887 (v **Blackburn Rovers**), expired. The club initially sought to share **Sheffield United**'s **Bramall Lane** – Wednesday had played its major matches at the ground since the club was founded in 1867 and before United had been formed – but talks broke down, while an attempt to buy another former venue, Sheaf House, also failed. Eventually the club bought the 10-acre site at Owlerton for £5,000 and a former Olive Grove stand was erected at the new ground, which along with other developments cost a further £5,000. Wednesday played its first match at Owlerton on 2 September 1899 (v **Chesterfield**, Division Two). Major developments, which began in 1913, including the erection of an Archibald **Leitch**-designed south stand and the construction of the **Spion Kop** embankment, brought the ground's capacity up to more than 50,000. On 4 February 1914, 75 supporters were hurt, including three who were critically injured, after a wall at the Kop end collapsed (v **Wolverhampton Wanderers**, FA Cup). Also, in 1914, the Owlerton district of Sheffield became part of the Hillsborough parliamentary constituency and the ground's name was changed to reflect this development. In 1961, the largest **cantilever stand** at a UK football was built at Hillsborough – only **Scunthorpe**

United's former home, the Old Show Ground, had a cantilever stand before this, but it was much smaller. Further development of the ground took place after Hillsborough was chosen as a venue for the 1966 World Cup, and, as a result, the ground had more seats (23,250) than any other club ground at the time. The ground recorded the highest-ever attendance at a Division Three match in 1979 when a crowd of 49,309 saw Wednesday play local-rivals Sheffield United (26 December). On 15 April 1989, the worst disaster in the history of British football occurred when 95 **Liverpool** supporters lost their lives (another died some months later) at the Leppings Lane end at the FA Cup semi-final between Liverpool and **Nottingham Forest** (see **Hillsborough disaster**, **Taylor Report**). Hillsborough's only full **England** international took place 3 October 1962 (v **France**, **European Championship**). In 1966, Hillsborough was used as a **World Cup** venue, staging group 2 matches (**Switzerland** v **West Germany**; **Spain** v Switzerland; **Argentina** v Switzerland) and a quarter-final (West Germany v **Uruguay**) – total attendance 140,289; average attendance 35,072. Hillsborough was also selected as a **European Championship** venue in 1996, staging group D matches (**Denmark** v **Portugal**; **Croatia** v Denmark; Denmark v **Turkey**). Because of political troubles in Ireland, Hillsborough staged an international between **Northern Ireland** and **Bulgaria** on 26 September 1973 (Northern Ireland also used **Boothferry Park**, **Craven Cottage**, **Goodison Park** and **Highfield Road**, and switched its home matches against **Scotland** to **Hampden Park** during this period). Hillsborough was also the venue for the 1977 League Cup final replay (**Aston Villa** v **Everton**) and the 1997 final replay (**Leicester City** v **Middlesbrough**). The ground is regularly used as an FA Cup semi-final venue, the first of which took place in 1912. The first floodlit match at Hillsborough occurred on 9 March 1955 and was a benefit game for ex-Wednesday player and future club manager, Derek Dooley who had lost a leg following an injury (Sheffield XI v International XI). The match attracted a crowd of more than 55,000.

Hillsborough disaster *disaster* stadium disaster at Hillsborough Stadium, Sheffield, 15 April 1989, during an **FA Cup** semi-final between **Liverpool** and **Nottingham Forest**. It was the worst disaster in British football history: 95 spectators were killed and nearly 200 were injured. The deaths and injuries resulted as spectators at the Leppings Lane end of the ground – where Liverpool fans were standing – were crushed when a gate was opened to let more fans in at the top of the terrace. Police had opened the gate in a flawed attempt to ease congestion because many fans were still trying to get into the stadium with only 10 minutes to go before kick-off. As more spectators poured in, fans at the front of the terrace were crushed against the **perimeter fencing**, erected to prevent **pitch invasions**. In addition to the 200 people who sustained physical injuries, many others suffered **post-traumatic stress disorder**. An investigation into the disaster was led by Lord Justice **Taylor** (see **Taylor Report**). There followed years of civil actions against the police, club and stadium designers by injured parties and the families of the victims. The 1989 FA Cup final was delayed because of the Hillsborough disaster, with Liverpool ironically facing Merseyside neighbours **Everton**. Liverpool won the match 3–2, dedicating its triumph to the Hillsborough victims. The League season was also delayed, finishing on 26 May; when **Arsenal** took the title with a 2–0 victory over runners-up Liverpool (at Anfield), thus preventing a Liverpool double. Aside from the impact on British football, the Hillsborough disaster led **FIFA** to rule, in 1990, that all **World Cup** matches (finals and qualifiers) should be all seated, starting with the 1994 tournament.

Himst, Paul van *player* Striker. **Belgium** international (82 caps, 30 goals, 1960–74) *Club* **RSC Anderlecht**. *Honours* Belgium league championship (Anderlecht, 1962, 1964, 1965, 1966, 1967, 1968, 1972, 1974). *Keynotes* Belgium's joint-all-time leading goalscorer with Bernhard Voorhoof.

hit the post *vb.* to **shoot** or **head** the ball against the **goal post**.

HJK Helsinki (Helsingin Jalkapallo Klubi) *club* Finnish national league club based in the capital Helsinki, founded 1907. *Keynotes* The most successful side in the history of Finnish domestic football. In 1998-99, HJK Helsinki became the first Finnish club to qualify for the **European Cup** Champions League, following its 2–1 aggregate victory over Metz in the qualifying phase. Ground: Pallokenntä, capacity: 10,000 (or Olympiastadion – the national stadium – capacity: 45,0000). Strip: blue and white striped shirts, blue shorts. Finnish Cup 1966, 1981, 1984, 1993, 1996, 1998; Finnish league champions 1911, 1912, 1917, 1918, 1919, 1923, 1925, 1936, 1938, 1964, 1973, 1978, 1981, 1985, 1987, 1988, 1990, 1992, 1997.

hobby kicker *misc.* German phrase for a part-time footballer.

Ho Chi Minh City Police *club* Vietnamese national league club based in Ho Chi Minh City (Saigon). Vietnam league champions 1995.

Hoddle, Glenn *player-manager* Midfield. **England** international (53 caps, 8 goals). Born 27 October 1957. Career ca. 1975–95. *Clubs* (player) **Tottenham Hotspur**, **Monaco**, **Chelsea**, (manager) **Swindon Town** (player-manager), Chelsea (player-manager), England (record played 28, won 17, drawn six, lost five, goals for 42, goals against 13). *Keynotes* Joined Tottenham Hotspur as an apprentice in 1974, turning professional in April 1975. Hoddle made 377 **Football League** appearances for Spurs and he scored 88 goals. He scored the winning goal (penalty) in the 1982 **FA Cup** final replay (1–0 v **Queens Park Rangers**), having also scored in the first match. He made his international debut against **Bulgaria** on 6 June 1979 and scored. Hoddle moved to Monaco for £750,000 in 1987, where, in 1987-88, he became the first Englishman to be part of a French championship winning-team. While at Monaco, Hoddle was inspired by the manager Arséne Wenger to take up coaching. He "retired" through injury in 1991 but became a **non-contract player** with Chelsea, before moving to Swindon Town as player-manager. Under Hoddle's managership, Swindon won promotion to the Premier League via the First Division **playoffs** (4–3 v **Leicester City**) in 1992-93. He joined Chelsea as player-manager and, in his first season in charge, took the club to its first major final (1994 FA Cup) in 22 years, and, the following season, to the **European Cup-winners Cup** semi-finals. Hoddle succeeded Terry **Venables** as England manager in 1996 and took the national side to the 1998 **World Cup**. He was dismissed on 2 February 1999, following the controversy sparked by his alleged remarks about disabled people. Included in the **Football League Centenary 100 players**. *Honours* FA Cup (Tottenham Hotspur 1981, 1982); French League (Monaco 1987-88).

hold *vb.* **1.** to keep **control** of the ball while supporting players find suitable positions to receive the ball. **2.** a **foul** where the instigator illegally pulls at the opponent with his hands (see **holding an opponent**).

holding an opponent *rules* one of the offences listed as a **foul** under the **Laws of the game** (Law XII). The punishment for deliberately holding an opponent is for the opposing team to be awarded a **direct free kick**, taken from the point where the foul was committed (unless within the opponents' **goal area**, in which case it is taken from anywhere within that area). If the foul is committed in the offending side's **penalty area**, then the opponents are awarded a **penalty kick**.

hole *n.* space into which a ball is placed or into which a player moves. For example, "put the ball into the hole". See **zone 14**.

Holland *country UEFA* see **Netherlands**.

home advantage *n.* supposed advantage of a side playing at its own ground. Familiarity with the conditions, having no need to travel and the support of its own fans are generally considered to favour the home club.

home club *n.* the club whose ground a league or cup match is played on. Where clubs share a stadium, the home club is the one that is named first in the fixture list. This can be important: in deciding which team should play in its **home strip** (the home team always wears the home strip, the away team may need to use its **away strip** if there is a clash of colours); where **competition rules** incorporate **away goals** in two-leg ties; with regard to **gate receipts**; and in relation to security and policing. *Regulations* In the **Scottish Football League**, the home club must provide a set number of complimentary tickets for the visitors: 10 for the **directors' box**, 40 for the stands and 15 for the players; no player or committee member from the visiting club is allowed into the home club's ground without a ticket (Scottish Football League rule 80).

Home Farm Everton FC *club* Republic of Ireland national league club based in Dublin on the east coast, founded 1928, merged in 1972 with **Drumcondra** as Home Farm FC. Ground: Tolka Park (shared with **Shelbourne FC**), capacity: 9,000. Strip: blue and white hooped shirts, white shorts. Republic of Ireland **FAI Cup** 1975 (see Drumcondra for pre-1972 cups); Republic of Ireland league champions (see Drumcondra).

Home International Championship *competition* former annual international tournament contested by the four United Kingdom "home" nations: **England**, **Scotland**, **Northern Ireland** (**Ireland** until 1923) and **Wales**. The tournament was played on a round-robin, mini-league format (each nation played three games; the home venue of the corresponding fixture was alternated annually). The first tournament was played in 1884 (won by Scotland) and the last in 1984 (won by Northern Ireland). Home Internationals were the qualifying group for the **World Cup** during the 1950s. The highest crowd for a championship fixture was officially recorded as 149,547 (Scotland v England, 3–1, 17 April 1937, at **Hampden Park**, Glasgow); the actual crowd is estimated at 160,000 as many spectators were known to have entered the ground without paying. The lowest crowd was 2,315 (Wales v Northern Ireland, 27 May 1982, at Racecourse Ground, Wrexham); low crowds and fixture congestion led to the demise of the championships in 1984. *Winners (summary)* England 54 championships (including 19 shared titles); Scotland 40 (including 15 shared); Northern Ireland/Ireland eight (including five shared); Wales 12 (including five shared). Most home international appearances: Pat **Jennings** (Northern Ireland) 48; Billy **Meredith** (Wales) 48; Billy **Wright** (England) 38. Top goalscorer: Steve **Bloomer** (England) 28. Oldest player: Billy Meredith (Wales, aged 45). Biggest victories: Wales 11–0, v Ireland (1888); England 13–2, v Ireland (1899); Scotland 11–0, v Ireland (1901). Highest aggregate score: England 13–2, v Ireland (1899).

Home Park *ground* English football ground situated in Plymouth, Devon; home of **Plymouth Argyle**. *Dossier* Ground capacity: 19,630. Pitch dimensions: 100.5m x 66m. Record attendance: 43,596 v **Aston Villa** (10 October 1936, Division Two). Best average attendance: 23,375 (1946-47). *History* Plymouth Argyle settled at Home Park in 1901, playing its first senior match on 5 September 1903 (v **Northampton Town**, **Southern League**). The ground had staged rugby fixtures since 1894. Home Park hosted a number of exhibition football matches, including one between The Wednesday (later **Sheffield Wednesday**) and **Notts County** on 24 April 1903. Home Park's proximity to the naval base at Devonport meant it suffered extensive bomb damage during **World War II**, including the complete destruction of the main stand in 1941. **Manchester United** played the home leg of its 1977 **European Cup-winners Cup** tie against **Saint Etienne** at Home Park after the **Union of European**

Football Associations (UEFA) instructed the club to play the match at least 200 miles from **Old Trafford** following crowd trouble at the first match in France. Home Park staged an **inter-League** fixture in 1966 (**Football League** v Irish League, 21 September). The first floodlit match at Home Park took place on 28 September 1953 (v **Bournemouth (AFC)** Reserves) with the lights officially inaugurated several weeks later (v **Exeter City**, friendly).

home strip *n.* the first-choice colour and design of club shirts, shorts and socks. *Regulations* **1. Premier League** clubs are required to register both their home and **away strips** (FA Premier League rule 15), as well as any **third strip**. They must, however, use their home strip for all league games (home and away) unless their colours would clash with the opposition; in the event of a clash the **away club** wears its away strip, or a combination of its home and away strips (FA Premier League rule F.17). **2. Football League** clubs are required to register their home strip with the Football League during the **close season**. They must play all their home games in this strip (Football League regulation 35). When playing at a **neutral venue**, Football League clubs decide which will wear its home strip either by mutual agreement, or by the **toss of a coin**. **3. Scottish Football League** clubs must register and submit for approval with the league their first-choice strip before 1 June each year and are required to play in their first-choice strip wherever possible (Scottish Football League rule 66). The home club uses its first-choice kit in the event that both clubs in a fixture have similar playing colours. Each club is allowed to play up to four of its home league matches in a second- or third-choice strip provided that the league and match officials are notified at least two days in advance of the game. Where two clubs are engaged in a match at neutral venue both clubs must change their strips if their colours are similar.

home win *n.* in **pools** betting, a match ending in victory for the home side.

homer *n. informal* derogatory term for a **referee**, suggesting that he or she makes decisions in favour of the **home club**.

Honduras *country* CONCACAF republic in Central America on the Caribbean Sea and Pacific Ocean. Bordered by **Nicaragua**, **El Salvador** and **Guatemala**. Sparsely populated and economically poor. Area: 112,085 sq km (43,265 sq miles). Mountainous, high plateaux and hot and humid coastal plains with high annual rainfall. Population: 5,290,000 (1994 est.). Languages: Spanish, English and American Indian languages. Capital: Tegucigalpa. *Dossier* Football association (Federación Nacional Autónoma de Fútbol de Honduras, Tegucigalpa) formed in 1935, affiliated to **FIFA** in 1946 and **Confederación Norte-Centroamericana y del Caribe de Fútbol** (CONCACAF) in 1961, president Frixione Jorge Abudoj, general secretary Allan Ramos. Season played from September to May. National stadium: Estadio Nacional

"Tiburcio Carias Andino", Tegucigalpa, capacity: 35,000. National strip: blue shirts, white shorts. *International tournament record* **Olympic Games** – never qualified for finals tournament (reached third round/final stage of qualifying tournament in 1992); **Women's World Cup** – had not entered before 1999; **World Cup** – first entered 1962, qualified for finals tournament 1982 (last in its group of four nations, with two draws, against **Spain** and **Northern Ireland**, and one defeat, against **Yugoslavia**); **CCCF Championship** – first entered 1946, third 1957, 1960, 1961; **CONCACAF Championship** – entered first tournament in 1963, 1981 (World Cup qualifying tournament; first of six-nation league, in Tegucigalpa), runners-up 1986 (World Cup qualifying tournament), third 1967, final round/fourth 1963; **Gold Cup** – qualified for first tournament in 1991, runners-up 1991 (0–0, v **United States of America**, 3–4 pens., in Los Angeles, USA), also qualified 1993, 1998, 2000; **UNCAF Cup** winners and host nation 1992 (finals tournament in Tegucigalpa), runners-up 1991 (finals tournament in San José, Costa Rica); **Under-17 World Championship** – never qualified; CONCACAF Youth Championship (under-20) – 1994; **World Youth Cup** (under-20) – qualified 1977 (second in its first-round group of four), 1995 (last in its first-round group of four), 1999. *Record against British and Irish national teams* v Northern Ireland, played one, drawn one. *History* The country's oldest current league clubs, **Marathon** and **Real España** were founded in 1925, followed by **Olimpia** (1926) and **Motagua** (1928). The national championship was first played in 1965. There have been two changes to the league season: it was originally played from August to May; in 1973 it changed to February to December, changing to the current September to May in 1991. Olimpia is the only Honduran club to have won the **CONCACAF Champions Cup**. Honduras qualified for the World Cup finals in 1982. It won the CONCACAF Championship in 1981 (played as the World Cup qualifying tournament), and was runners-up in the first Gold Cup (1991). See also **Fútbol War**. *League system* Ten clubs play in the national Primera Division, playing each other three times in the first stage of the season: three points are awarded for a win, with one for a draw; **goal difference** determines the positions of clubs level on points. The winner of the first stage wins the Honduras Cup (in 1992 and 1993, the Cup was played as a separate pre-season tournament). The top six clubs in the first stage playoff (first v sixth, second v fifth, third v fourth) to determine which three clubs enter a final mini-league tournament (the three clubs play each other at home and away). The winner of the mini-league plays the winner of the first-stage to determine the national championship, unless, of course, one club wins both stages: in which case it is declared the **Campeonisimo.** There are two regional Segunda Divisions of 10 to 12 clubs. The top four in each regional division in the first stage of the season enter a

second-stage tournament. The top four clubs from the second stage enter a mini-league: the winner is promoted, at the expense of the bottom club in the Primera Division. A separate domestic cup was played from 1992 to 1994; since 1995 it has been awarded to the winners of the first stage of the Primera Division. *Record in international club tournaments* CONCACAF Champions Cup – Olimpia (1972, 1988, runners-up 1985), **Universidad Nacional Autonoma de Honduras** (runners-up 1980), **CONCACAF Cup-winners Cup** – Marathon (semi-final/third 1995), Olimpia (finalist 1998); **Torneo Grandes de Centroamerica** – Olimpia (semi-final 1998), Real España (semi-final 1998). Other leading clubs: Platense (Honduras Cup 1996, 1997), Motagua, **Victoria**.

Honey Monster *misc.* fictitious character created to advertise the breakfast cereal Sugar Puffs. He has "played" for two teams in television commercials, as a striker for **Newcastle United** and as a replacement for **Manchester United**'s goalkeeper Peter **Schmeichel**.

Hong Kong *country AFC* Special Administrative Region of China and former UK Crown colony until 1997, comprising Hong Kong Island, Kowloon Peninsula, the New Territories and several small islands in the South China Sea. After a 99-year lease, Hong Kong was returned to China in 1997. Area: 1,067 sq km (412 sq miles). Population: 5,920,000. Languages: Chinese and English. Capital: formerly Victoria (Hong Kong City). *Dossier* The Hong Kong Football Association (Homantin, Kowloon) formed in 1914, affiliated to **FIFA** in 1954 (and has remained affiliated as an independent association) and founder members of **Asian Football Confederation** (AFC) in 1954, president Timothy Tsun Ting Fok, general secretary Vincent Yuen. Season played from August to May. Provincial stadium: Hong Kong Stadium, capacity: 40,000. National strip: red shirts, red shorts. *International tournament record* **Olympic Games** – never qualified for finals tournament; **Women's World Cup** – first entered 1991, never qualified for finals tournament (third of four nations in the 1999 qualifying tournament); **World Cup** – first entered from 1974, never progressed beyond second round of qualifying stage (did win first round qualifying group in 1978 and 1986, but on both occasions lost in knockout stage); **Asian Cup of Nations** – entered first tournament in 1956, third 1956 (four-nation final-round group), fourth 1964 (four-nation final-round group), fifth 1968 (five-nation final-round group), has not reached finals tournament since 1968, hosts 1956; **Asian Games** – quarter-finals 1958; **Asian Women's Championship** – entered first tournament (as hosts) 1975, also hosted the tournament in 1986 and 1989; **Dynasty Cup** – first entered 1995 (last of four nations); **Under-17 World Championship** – never qualified; **World Youth Cup** (under-20) – never qualified. *Record against British and Irish national teams* none played. *History* National league began in 1945-46, along with the Hong Kong Senior Shield. The Hong Kong league is the oldest professional league in Asia and was first won by the Royal Air Force. The Hong Kong Cup began in 1974-75. The Hong Kong Viceroy Cup started in 1970. Both Bobby **Moore** and George **Best** played in the Hong Kong league after retiring from English league football. The Hong Kong Football Association has remained independent of the association on mainland China (the Football Association of the People's Republic of China), though there is no principle objection to Hong Kong clubs playing in the mainland leagues. Hong Kong has been assured autonomy in sport for 50 years after its reunification with China. The first four presidents of the **Asian Football Confederation** were from Hong Kong (Man Kam-Lo (1954), Kwok Chan (1954–56), S T Loney (1956–57), and N C Chan (1957–58). The first general secretary (1954–65), Lee Wai-Tong, was also from Hong Kong. *League system* Eight clubs compete in the national First Division. At the end of the first phase of the season, the top four clubs enter a championship mini-league, taking half of their original points total into the second phase. The bottom four clubs enter a relegation mini-league to determine the two automatic relegation places. Three points are awarded for a win, one for a draw; clubs level on points are divided on **goal difference**. *Record in international club tournaments* **Asian Cup-winners Cup** – **South China** (runners-up 1993, quarter-final 1997), **Happy Valley** (quarter-final 1999). Other leading clubs **Eastern**, **Rangers**, **Instant Dict**, **Seiko**, Sing Tao.

Honvéd *club* former name, until 1991, of **Kispest-Honuéd FC**.

hoof *vb.* to kick the ball high and long from a defensive position, with no other aim than to relieve pressure on the defence.

hooligan, football *n.* person who causes and incites crowd violence at a football match.

hooligan hotline *n.* free telephone line set up by the National Criminal Intelligence Service to collect information about **football hooliganism**.

hooliganism, football *misc.* the act of causing trouble in football crowds. Football hooligans are almost exclusively male. Alcohol is seen as a major factor in exacerbating the risk of hooliganism, though organised violence has much deeper sociological, psychological and even political elements. The sheer popularity of football, coupled with traditional rivalries and the continued predominance of male spectators are factors as to why football, more than other organised activities, is a focus for hooliganism. Hooliganism has also been linked with racial abuse. *History* Football hooliganism has a history as long as the game itself. Football was banned in London in 1314 because of the public disorder associated with the rudimentary game of the day (see **association football**: *History*). Crowd trouble was first noted by the **Football League management committee** at a meeting in December 1891. Ungentlemanly behaviour by **Derby County** supporters was reported to the **Football League** in 1895, with the League subsequently threatening that matches be with-

drawn from Derby's ground. Assaults on referees were reported as early as 1895. In 1895, clubs were encouraged to put railings around the pitch rather than ropes in order to prevent spectators entering the field of play. Sporadic incidents of crowd trouble continued through the first half of the 20th century. In the 1960s, however, it entered a more sophisticated phase, with gangs or "firms" beginning to use football fixtures as venues for organised public disorder. Violence in the 1970s at Football League matches became so prevalent that it earned the reputation of the "English disease", arguably reaching a peak in the 1975-76 season. More than 100 **Chelsea** fans were arrested only two weeks into the season, following crowd violence and a **pitch invasion** at the club's Division Two match at **Luton Town**. Luton's goalkeeper was struck by coins thrown from the terraces, and the violence continued after the match and even on the trains back to London. On the same day, 50 **Manchester United** fans were arrested at **Stoke City** with another 60 arrested at **Rangers' Ibrox Stadium**. **Perimeter fencing** was introduced at many league grounds as a result of the persistent crowd violence. Crowd violence by supporters of Manchester United in the club's away leg **European Cup-winners Cup** first-round match at **Saint Etienne** in 1977-78 (3–1 agg.) led to the club being temporarily barred from the tournament. United was reinstated but ordered to play its next home leg at **Plymouth Argyle's Home Park** stadium on 2 November 1977 (v **Porto**, 5–6 agg.). Crowd violence was so bad at Chelsea's home second-leg **League Cup** semi-final match against **Sunderland** in 1984-85 that referee Alan Gunn ordered the teams into the centre circle while mounted police tried to restore order. Chelsea's former player, Clive Walker, then with Sunderland, was attacked by one of the fans and had to be protected by the Chelsea players; Walker's second goal in the 72nd minute was the trigger for a pitch invasion. Sunderland won the tie 5–2 on aggregate. A match on 29 April 1985, at **Kenilworth Road**, between Luton Town and **Millwall**, was nearly abandoned after fans invaded the pitch. After the match Millwall fans went on the rampage within and outside the ground. The match was described by then Football Association chairman Bert Millichip as "probably the worst in the long catalogue that has blighted our game over the last 20 years." In response to the violence, Luton announced a ban on visiting supporters at Kenilworth Road – the first such ban in British football – and compulsory computerised membership cards for home fans; Luton chair David Evans MP had the support of Prime Minister Margaret Thatcher for his scheme. On the last day of the same season, crowd trouble among travelling **Leeds United** fans is thought to have caused a retaining wall to collapse at a stand in **Birmingham City's** ground **St Andrews**; a teenager was killed in the incident. The game was marred by a pitch invasion and pre- and post-match violence in the city; around 150 were injured and 125 arrested. Hooliganism even hit pre-season friendlies in 1986: a ferry between Harwich and the Hook of

Holland had to return to port when fighting broke out on board between Manchester United and **West Ham United** fans en route to matches on the continent. Fourteen fans were arrested and four taken to hospital with knife wounds. One of the worst examples of crowd violence occurred at the 1985 **European Cup** final at the Heysel Stadium in Brussels, Belgium: 39 spectators were killed when a wall collapsed after rioting by rival fans of **Liverpool** and **Juventus**. More than 350 people were injured (see **Heysel Stadium disaster**). Twenty-four Liverpool fans were later found guilty of manslaughter by a Belgium court. The disaster also led all English clubs to be banned from all European club competitions until 1990. In 1987, two members of the so-called hooligan firm the Chelsea Head-hunters were jailed for 10 years each at the Inner London Crown Court (11 May 1997). Their sentences followed a six-year campaign of organised violence. Three other gang members were also jailed. The mob were caught after an undercover police programme, "Operation own goal". The 18-week trial is estimated to have cost £3 million. Other notorious organised gangs in the 1980s included the Inter-City Firm (West Ham) and F-Troop (Millwall). With increased ground security in the late 1980s and 1990s, match-day confrontations between rival gangs increasingly took place in the vicinities of, rather than inside stadiums. The 1990s was characterised by clubs implementing measures to create "family-friendly" atmosphere in an effort to break the link between football matches and organised violence. Ground improvements triggered by the **Taylor Report**, have created improved facilities, again encouraging a wider spectator audience. There has also been a steady rise in **closed-circuit television**, private security firms and stewarding at matches. Between 1986 and 1992 (prior to the foundation of the **Premier League**), there were an average 5,500 arrests per season at Football League grounds (all four divisions), though this represents only about 2.5 arrests per match. By 1997-98, the total arrests at English league matches had fallen to 3,307. Football hooliganism is not exclusive to England: neo-fascist hooligans following the German national team at the 1998 **World Cup** in France allegedly used mobile phones to orchestrate pre-match violence, while serious incidents of crowd violence and hooliganism have occurred in **Russia**, **Greece**, **Italy**, **Spain**, **Turkey** and South America. On 25 May 1964, more than 300 spectators died during rioting at **Peru**'s home match against **Argentina** in Lima (see **Lima disaster**). On 22 October 1986, fans of the Dutch club **Feyenoord** caused one of the most serious incidents of football-related violence in Germany during and after the club's **UEFA Cup** match at **Borussia Mönchengladbach**. Seventy-one arrests were made after looting, vandalism, arson and rioting by the visiting spectators. Thirty-eight arrests followed rioting in Verona, Italy, as **Napoli** fans rioted after the club's 0–3 defeat at the end of the 1986-87 season. **Poland**'s national stadium at Chorzow was closed in 1993 following crowd violence and, in 1996,

hooliganism at rival clubs **Widzew Lodz** and **Legia Warsaw** led to the closure of their stadiums for the remainder of the season. Hooliganism in **Romania** is very much a post-communism phenomena, with strong rivalries between fans from the leading clubs; much of the baiting is racially oriented. Gangs include the "Ultra Army" (**Steaua Bucharest**), Violet legion (**Rapid Bucharest**) and "Red Dogs" (**Dinamo Bucharest**). Spectators rioted in Beijing on 19 May 1985 after **China**'s World Cup qualifying match against **Hong Kong** (1–2, at the Workers' Stadium) and were controlled by riot police. *Regulations (Scotland)* **Scottish Football League** clubs are specifically required to "take all such steps as are reasonably practicable to ensure the good conduct and behaviour of its supporters on any ground." If the Management Committee decides that crowd trouble has had a "material effect on the result of a match", it can rule that the result be declared void and order a replay, or deduct three points from the offending club (Scottish Football League rule 84). See also **pitch invasion**, **crowd trouble**.

Hornby, Nick *misc.* author, born 1957, noted for his autobiographical account of his love affair with Arsenal FC, **Fever Pitch**. His other books include the novel High Fidelity.

Horoya AC (Athletic Club) *club* Guinea national league club based in Conakry. Ground: Stade du 28 Septembre (the national stadium), capacity: 40,000. Strip: white shirts, red shorts. **African Cup-winners Cup** 1978 (5–2 agg., v **Milaha Athletic Hussein-Dey** of Algeria); Guinea Cup 1989, 1994, 1995; Guinea league champions 1986, 1988, 1989, 1990, 1991, 1992, 1994.

Horsed *club* Somalia national league club based in the capital Mogadishu. Ground: Cons (the national stadium), capacity: 40,000. *Keynotes* Horsed holds the Somalia league record of five consecutive titles (1976 to 1980). **African Cup of Champion Clubs** second round 1981; **African Cup-winners Cup** second round 1988; **East and Central African Club Championship** runners-up 1977 (v **Luo Union** of Kenya); Somalia league champions 1972, 1973, 1974, 1976, 1977, 1978, 1979, 1980.

hospital ball *n. informal* badly executed pass that puts team members (usually defenders or the goalkeeper) in a risky situation.

Howarth, Fred *official* former secretary of the Football League (1933-56). Born 1888, died 1972. Co-author, with J A Brierley and Charles **Sutcliffe**, of *The Story of the Football League* (1938).

Huddersfield Town *club* English league. *Dossier* Ground: **Alfred McAlpine Stadium**, Huddersfield, West Yorkshire, capacity: 24,000 all-seater. Strip: blue and white striped shirts, white shorts, white socks. Nickname: Terriers. Record attendance: 22,129 v **Derby County** (13 February 1999, **FA Cup**, 5th round). Best average attendance: 30,820 (Leeds Road, 1953-54). Biggest win 10–1 v **Blackpool** (13 December 1930, Division One). Biggest defeat 1–10 v **Manchester City**

(7 November 1987, Division Two). *History* Huddersfield was founded in September 1908 by the Huddersfield Association Football Ground Company, which had been searching for a ground to stage football matches since 1905 when an initial decision was taken to form a football club. Lack of money and the Northern Union's (later Rugby League) policy of discouraging **groundsharing** between the two codes had prevented the formation of a club any earlier. Financial support was eventually forthcoming from Hilton Crowther (who later played a part in the formation of **Leeds United** following the expulsion of **Leeds City** from the **Football League**) and a site at **Leeds Road** was successfully turned into a football ground in March 1908 – six months before the club was formed. Huddersfield Town was elected to the Football League in 1910-11 replacing **Grimsby Town**. The cost of bringing the ground up to Football League standards led to liquidation in May 1912. The financial problems continued and in 1919 a plan was hatched to move the club to Leeds, replacing the recently defunct Leeds City at **Elland Road**. Protests and fundraising by supporters prevented the move and the following decade is the most successful in the club's history. In 1919-20, Huddersfield won promotion to Division One and the club reached the FA Cup final (0–1 a.e.t. v **Aston Villa**). Two years later, under the managership of Herbert **Chapman**, the club lifted the FA Cup (1–0 v **Preston North End**) for the only time in its history. The club won three consecutive League Championships (1923-24, 1924-25, 1925-26) and finished **runners-up** in the next two seasons (1926-27, 1927-28). Three further FA Cup finals were reached in 1928 (1–3 v **Blackburn Rovers**), 1930 (0–2 v **Arsenal**) and 1938 (0–1 a.e.t. v Preston North End). The club was relegated in 1951-52, and although it bounced straight back, finishing third in season 1953-54, relegation followed again in 1955-56. Thereafter, the club has spent only two seasons in the top flight (1970-71, 1971-72), slipping from Division One to Division Four in four seasons between 1971-72 and 1974-75. Huddersfield won promotion to the First Division via the end-of-season **play-offs** in 1995 (2–1 v **Bristol Rovers**). The previous year, the club had reached the **Autoglass Trophy** final (1–1, 1–3 pens. v **Swansea City**). Also, in 1994, the club played its final match at Leeds Road (v Blackpool, Division Two, 30 April) before departing to the new purpose-built Alfred McAlpine Stadium. *League record* Division One 1920-21 to 1951-52, 1953-54 to 1955-56, 1970-71 to 1971-72; First Division 1995-96 to present; Divsion Two 1910-11 to 1919-20, 1952-53, 1956-57 to 1969-70, 1972-73, 1983-84 to 1987-88; Second Division 1992-93 to 1994-95; Division Three 1973-74 to 1974-75, 1980-81 to 1982-83, 1988-89 to 1991-92; Division Four 1975-76 to 1979-80. *Honours* League 1923-24, 1924-25, 1925-26; Division Two 1969-70; Division Four 1979-80; **FA Charity Shield** 1922 (1–0 v Liverpool); FA Cup 1922 (1–0 v Preston North End). *Records* Jimmy Nicholson is Huddersfield's most capped player (31 (41) for **Northern Ireland**); Billy

Smith holds the record for club appearances (520, 1914-34); George Brown (142, 1921-29) and Jimmy Glazzard (142, 1946-56) are jointly Huddersfield's record league goalscorer.

huddle *n.* close circle/grouping of players. Several teams, notably **Celtic**, **Germany**, **Iran** and the **United States**, employ a huddle prior to the start of a match to generate enthusiasm and promote team cohesion.

Hughes, Mark *player* Striker. **Wales** international (70, 16 goals). Born 1 November 1963. Career ca. 1983–. *Clubs* **Manchester United** (twice), **Barcelona**, **Bayern Munich**, **Chelsea**, **Southampton**. *Keynotes* In two spells with Manchester United, which he joined as a schoolboy, Hughes made 345 **Football League** appearances and scored 119 goals. He moved to Chelsea for £1.5 million before the start of the 1995-96 season, eventually playing 108 (+14 as substitute) matches for the club and scoring 39 goals. Hughes has appeared in six **Wembley** FA Cup finals, sharing the modern record with four others, and his four winner's medals is an individual record for the 20th century. He scored both of Manchester United's goals in the 1991 European Cup-winners Cup final against his former club Barcelona, and, in 1998, he received another winner's medal in the same competition despite being a non-playing substitute in Chelsea's triumph. Voted **PFA footballer of the Year** in both 1989 and 1991. He was awarded the MBE in 1997. *Honours* League Championship (Manchester United 1992-93, 1993-94); **FA Cup** (Manchester United 1985, 1990, 1994; Chelsea 1997); **League Cup** (Manchester United 1991; Chelsea 1998); **European Cup-winners Cup** (Manchester United 1991; Chelsea 1998).

Hull City *club* English league. *Dossier* Ground: **Boothferry Park**, Kingston upon Hull, Humberside, capacity: 12,996. Strip: amber and black striped shirts, black shorts, amber socks with black hoops. Nickname: Tigers. Record attendance: 55,019 v **Manchester United** (26 February 1949, **FA Cup**, sixth round). Best average attendance: 37,319 (1949-50). Biggest win: 11–1 v **Carlisle United** (14 January 1939, Division Three (North)). Biggest defeat: 0–8 v **Wolverhampton Wanderers** (4 November 1911, Division Two). *History* Hull City was formed in 1904 and joined Division Two in 1905-06. At first the club shared Hull Rugby League Club's Boulevard ground but the rugby authorities closed the ground following crowd trouble at a rugby match. Between March 1906 and 1943, Hull played at a venue known as Anlaby Road. Hull folded in 1943, reforming a year later and eventually settling at Boothferry Park (which the club had bought in 1930) after **World War II**. The club finished third in Division Two in 1909-10 – Hull's highest League position – missing promotion to Division One only on goal average (·286 of a goal). Hull produced a major FA Cup shock in 1921, defeating **Burnley** (3–0), the soon-to-be League Champions, in the third round. In 1929-30, Hull was relegated to Division Three (North) and was a FA Cup semi-finalist (0–1 replay v **Arsenal**). Hull won the

Division Three (North) Championship in 1932-33 and 1948-49, and the Division Three title in 1965-66. The club spent 12 consecutive seasons in Division Two between 1966-67 and 1977, finishing fifth in 1970-71. In the mid-1970s, Hull reached the last 16 of the **League Cup** on three occasions: 1973-74 (1–3 replay v **Liverpool**), 1975-76 (1–2 v **Doncaster Rovers**), 1977-78 (1–5 v Arsenal). The club's League Cup exploits included victories over the following higher-level opposition: 1973-74 **Leicester City** (3–2 replay, second round); 1975-76 **Sheffield United** (2–0, third round). By 1981-82, Hull was playing in Division Four for the first time in the club's history and in February 1982, receivers were appointed and, thereafter, the club has lurched from one financial crisis to another. On the pitch, the club reached the final of the **Associate Members Cup** (1–2 v **Bournemouth AFC**) in 1984. Ex-tennis player and fitness club entrepreneur David Lloyd bought the club in the mid-1990s and prior to the start of the 1997-98 season, former **England** international Mark Hateley was appointed manager. In November 1998, a consortium of businessmen bought a controlling interest in the club following Lloyd's decision to sell. The club finished third-bottom of the Third Division in 1997-98 – the club's lowest ever League position. *League record* Division Two 1905-06 to 1929-30, 1933-34 to 1935-36, 1949-50 to 1955-56, 1959-60, 1966-67 to 1977-78, 1985-86 to 1990-91; Second Division 1992-93 to 1995-96; Division Three 1958-59, 1960-61 to 1965-66, 1978-79 to 1980-81, 1983-84 to 1984-85,1991-92; Third Division 1996-97–; Division Three (North) 1930-31 to 1932-33, 1936-37 to 1948-49, 1956-57 to 1957-58; Division Four 1981-82 to 1982-83. *Honours* Division Three 1965-66; Division Three (North) 1932-33, 1948-49. *Records* Terry Neill is Hull's most capped player (15 (59) for **Northern Ireland**); Andy Davidson holds the record for club League appearances (520, 1952-67); Chris Chilton is Hull's record League goalscorer (195, 1960-71).

Hungary *country* UEFA landlocked republic in central Europe, bordered by **Austria**, **Macedonia**, **Romania**, the Slovak Republic and **Ukraine**. Hungary is bisected by the River Danube which runs north to south through the country. Communist country from 1946, with reformist government established in 1989. Area: 93,030 sq km (35,910 sq miles). Humid, continental climate. Population: 10,210,000 (1996 est.). Language: Hungarian (Magyar). Capital: Budapest. *Dossier* Hungarian Football Federation (Budapest) formed in 1901, affiliated to **FIFA** in 1906 and founder member of **Union of European Football Associations** (UEFA) in 1954, president Dr Mihály Laczko, general secretary Lajos Czékus. Season played from August to June, with **winter break** from late November to early March. National stadium: Népstadion, Budapest, capacity: 72,000. National strip: red shirts, white shorts. First international game: 12 October 1902, v Austria (0–5, in Vienna, friendly). Biggest victories: 13–1 v **France** (12 June 1927, in Budapest, friendly), 12–0, v **Russia** (14 July 1912, in Moscow, friendly), 12–0 v **Albania** (24 September 1950, in Budapest, friendly). Biggest defeat: 0–7, v **England** (10 June 1908, in Budapest, friendly), 0–7 v **Germany** (6 April 1941, in Cologne, friendly). Most capped players: József **Bozsik** (100 appearances, 1947-62), László **Fazekas** (92 appearances, 1968-1981), Gyula Grosics (86 appearances), and Ferenc **Puskás** (84 appearances, 1945-56; Puskas later played for **Spain**). Leading goalscorers: Ferenc Puskás (83 goals), Sándor **Kocsis** (75 goals, 1948-56), Imre Schlosser-Lakatos (60 goals in 68 appearances, 1906-27). Other notable international players: Florian **Albert**, Nandor **Hidegkuti**, Zoltan **Czibor**. *International tournament record* **Olympic Games** – first entered 1912 (the second football tournament – lost in first round, but won the "consolation tournament", 3–0, v Austria, in Stockholm), winners/gold medal 1952 (2–0, v **Yugoslavia**, in Helsinki, Finland), 1964 (2–1, v **Czechoslovakia**, in Tokyo, Japan), 1968 (4–1, v **Bulgaria**, in Mexico City, Mexico), runners-up/silver medal 1972 (1–2, v **Poland**, in Munich, Germany), semi-final/third/bronze medal 1960 (2–1, v Italy, in Rome, third/fourth playoff), also played in finals tournament 1924, 1996; **Women's World Cup** – entered first tournament in 1991, never qualified for finals tournament; **World Cup** – first entered 1934, runners-up 1938 (2–4, v **Italy**, in Paris,France), 1954 (2–3, v Germany, in Berne, Switzerland: Hungary was 2–0 ahead after just eight minutes), quarter-final 1934, 1962, 1966, also qualified for finals tournament 1958, 1978, 1982, 1986, reached playoff stage of 1998 qualifying tournament, after finishing as runners-up in its group of five nations (lost 1–12 agg., v Yugoslavia in playoffs); **Dr Gerö Cup** – 1953 (league of five nations), runners-up 1960 (behind **Czechoslovakia**, league of six nations); **European Championship** – entered first tournament in 1960, semi-final/third 1964 (3–1, v **Denmark**, in Barcelona, Spain, third/fourth playoff), semi-final/fourth 1972 (1–2, v **Belgium**, in Liège, Belgium, third/fourth playoff), quarter-final 1968, has not qualified for finals tournament since 1972; **European Championship for Women** – first entered 1987-89, quarter-final 1991; **European Junior Championship/European Youth Championship** (under-18) – 1953, 1960, 1984 (0–0, 3–2 pens., v **Soviet Union**); **European Under-23 Championship** – 1974 (6–3 agg., v **East Germany**); **Under-17 World Championship** – quarter-final 1985 (the first tournament); **World Youth Cup** (under-20) – qualified for first tournament in 1977, also qualified 1979, 1985, never beyond first-round group stage. *World Cup performance* (finals and qualifiers to end of 1998 tournament) played 106, won 53, drawn 21, lost 32, scored 231 goals, conceded 151; win rate 50%; goals scored per game 2.18. *Record against British and Irish national teams* v England, played 20, won two, drawn one, lost 13; v **Northern Ireland**, played two, won two, drawn none, lost none; v **Scotland**, played seven, won three, drawn two, lost two; v **Wales**, played eight, won three, drawn two, lost three; v **Republic of Ireland**, played 10, won four, drawn four, lost two. *History* Modern football was introduced to Hungary in the mid to late 19th century, with the first of the modern clubs, **Újpesti Torna Egylet**, founded in 1885 (as Ujpest TE), followed by **MTK Budapest** (now **MTK Hungária FC**) in 1888. A league was formed in 1901, with a Cup competition first played in 1910. In 1996 the national Division One was increased to 18 clubs. The national league also had a major change at the end of the 1997-98 season when the old-style Division Two, previously divided into two regional divisions, east and west, was replaced by a single 16-club division: clubs finishing in the top half of the old regional divisions qualified for the new division. **Ferencváros** is the only Hungarian club to have won a modern European club competition: **Fairs Cup** (now **UEFA Cup**) winners in 1965. Ferencváros and **MTK Budapest** were both finalists in the **European Cup-winners Cup**, while Újpesti Dózsa (now Újpesti Torna Egylet), and **Videoton FC Fehérvar** have reached the final of the **UEFA/Fairs Cup**. Ferencváros and Újpesti Dózsa were winners of the prestigious **Mitropa Cup** in the 1920s and 1930s. In October 1902, Hungary played the first international game in continental Europe (0–5 v **Austria**). Professional football was introduced in 1926, although under the post-**World War II** communist regime Hungary was able to enter full-strength state-sponsored sides in the ostensibly "amateur" Olympic Games football tournaments. The national side of the 1950s was known by the UK press as the "**Magnificent Magyars**", with notable players Sándor Kocsis, Ferenc Puskás, Zoltan Czibor, Nandor Hidegkuti and József Bozsik. Its record was impressive: in 50 matches from 14 June 1950 to 17 November 1955 Hungary recorded 42 wins, seven draws and one defeat. It scored 215 goals (an average of 4.3 per game), conceding just 58 (1.16 per game). The only defeat was the 1954 World Cup final against West Germany, in Berne, Switzerland: a match that Hungary lost 2–3, despite being 2–0 ahead after just eight minutes. Hungary's 6–3 defeat of England (25 November 1953, at Wembley Stadium, friendly), followed by a 7–1 thrashing six months later (23 May 1954, in Budapest, friendly) served to notify England that it was beginning to lag behind in international football. After the first defeat in 1953, England captain Billy **Wright** said: "The Hungarians produced some of the finest, most brilliantly applied football it has ever been my privilege to see. The ball did precisely what they wanted . . . They were relentless. They were superb" (as recorded in the *Daily Telegraph*). In 1958, Hungary scored 27 goals in five games in the World Cup finals tournament in Switzerland, conceding 10. Sándor Kocsis was the tournament's top scorer, with 11 of Hungary's goals. Hungary holds the record for the biggest victory in a World Cup finals match (10–1 v **El Salvador**, 15 June 1982, in Elche, Spain, first round); it also beat South Korea 9–0 in the 1958 finals (17 June

1954, in Zurich, first round). Hungary has scored an average 2.18 goals per game in all its World Cup matches (qualifiers and finals) – and is fifth in the all-time list of **World Cup goal-scoring averages**, behind Germany, Brazil, **New Zealand** and Macedonia. Hungary is the most successful nation in Olympic Games football, with three gold medals (1952,1964, 1968), one silver medal (1972) and one bronze medal (1960). Three of the world's six highest goalscorers are Hungarian (see **goals, most at international level**). *World Cup final teams and scorers 1938* (runners-up): Szabó, Polgar, Bíró, Szalay, Szücs, Lázár, Sas, Vincze, Sárosi (1), Zsengellér, Titkos (1); *1954* (runners-up): Grosics (goalkeeper), Buzánszky, Lóránt, Lantos, Bozsik, Zakariás, Czibor (1), Kocsis, Hidegkuti, Puskás (1), J Tóth. *League system* Eighteen clubs compete in the national Division One (NB1), with 20 clubs in Division Two (NB2). Three points are awarded for a victory, with one for a draw: final positions for clubs level on points are determined by **goal difference**. The bottom two clubs from Division One are automatically relegated to Division Two; the 15th- and 16th-placed clubs enter a playoff with the third- and fourth-placed clubs from Division Two. Divisions Three and Four are regionalised and largely made up of amateur or semi-professional clubs. *Record in international club tournaments* **European Cup** – **Vasas DH** (semi-final 1958), **Györi ETO FC** (semi-final 1965), Újpesti Torna Egylet (semi-final 1974, then known as Újpesti Dózsa), Ferencváros Torna Club (qualified for the Champions League 1995/96); European Cup-winners Cup – MTK Hungária FC (as MTK Budapest, runners-up 1964), Ferencváros Torna Club (runners-up 1975); Fairs Cup/UEFA Cup – Ferencváros (winners 1965, runners-up 1968), Újpesti Torna Egylet (runners-up 1969, as Újpesti Dózsa), Videoton FC Fehérvar (runners-up 1985); Mitropa Cup – Ferencváros (1928, 1937, runners-up 1935, 1938, 1939), Újpesti Torna Egylet (1929, 1939, as Újpesti Dózsa), Vasas DH (1956, 1957, 1960, 1962, 1965, 1970, 1983), **Kispest-Honuéd FC** (1959), MTK Hungária FC (1963), Tatabánya Bányász (1973, 1974).

Hunt, Rev. Kenneth *player* last amateur to win an **FA Cup** winners medal, for **Wolverhampton Wanderers** in 1908 (3–1, v **Newcastle United**). Hunt scored the first goal.

Hunter, Archie *player* Striker. Career ca. 1888–91. *Clubs* **Aston Villa**. Died prematurely in 1894 at the age of 35. As Villa's captain, Hughes wrote a regular football column for the local *Birmingham Weekly Mercury*. Included in the **Football League Centenary 100 players**.

Hunter, Norman *player* Defender. **England** international (28 caps). Born 29 October 1943. Career ca. 1960–83. *Clubs* **Leeds United**, **Bristol City**, **Barnsley** (also manager). *Keynotes* Known as Norman "Bites yer legs" Hunter because of his uncompromising tackling, he joined Leeds United in November 1960, enjoying a 16-year career with the Yorkshire club before moving to Bristol City for £40,000 in October 1976.

Later, Hunter moved to Barnsley, becoming club manager. Hunter appeared in 11 finals for Leeds, including two **European Cup** finals, but he was only a winner three times. Prior to the 1966 **World Cup** there was speculation that Hunter would replace Bobby **Moore** in England's defence after the **West Ham United** player fell out with manager Alf **Ramsey**. Voted **PFA Footballer of the Year** in 1974. Included in the **Football League Centenary 100 players**. *Honours* League Championship (Leeds United 1968-69, 1973-74); Division Two (Leeds United 1963-64); **FA Cup** (Leeds United 1972); **League Cup** (Leeds United 1968); **UEFA** (Fairs) **Cup** (Leeds United 1968, 1971).

Huracán (Club Atlético) *club* Argentinean national league club, based in Buenos Aires, founded 1908. Ground: Estadio Tomas Alfonso Duco, capacity: 48,300. Strip: white shirts, white shorts. Argentinean league champions 1921, 1922, 1925 (two leagues operated prior to 1927), 1928, 1973. Notable player: Alfredo **Di Stefano** (on loan 1944-46).

Hurst, Geoff *player* Striker. **England** international (49 caps, 24 goals). Born 8 December 1941. Career ca. 1958–76. *Clubs* (player) **West Ham United**, **Stoke City**, **West Bromwich Albion**, **Cork Celtic**, (manager) Telford United (player-manager), **Chelsea** (1979-81). *Keynotes* Joined West Ham in 1958, turning professional in April 1959 and going on to make 410 **Football League** appearances for the Hammers. In all competitions Hurst scored 240 goals for West Ham in his 13-year career with the club before departing to Stoke City for £80,000 in August 1972. On one occasion, Hurst scored six times for West Ham against **Sunderland**, although he later admitted that the first should have been disallowed for handball (October 1968, Division One). He set the record for the all-time highest scorer in the **League Cup** competition with 49 goals (equalled by Ian **Rush** in October 1997). Hurst found lasting fame as the first, and only, player to have scored a hat-trick in a **World Cup** final, scoring three times in England's 1966 victory (4–2 v West **Germany**). Hurst received a kighthood in 1998. Included in the **Football League Centenary 100 players**. *Honours* **FA Cup** (West Ham United 1964); **European Cup-winners Cup** (West Ham United 1965); **World Cup** (England 1966).

Hyundai *club* see **Ulsan Hyundai Horang-i** .

IA Akranes (Idróttabandelag) *club* Iceland national league club based in Akranes, founded 1946. Ground: Akranesvöllur, capacity: 3,000. Strip: yellow shirts, black shorts. **European Cup** second round 1976; Icelandic Cup 1978, 1982, 1983, 1984, 1986, 1993, 1996; Icelandic League champions 1951, 1953, 1954, 1957, 1958, 1960, 1970, 1974, 1975, 1977, 1983, 1984, 1992, 1993, 1994, 1995, 1996.

IBK Keflavik (Idrótta Bandelag) *club* Icelandic national league club based in Keflavik, founded 1929. Ground: Keflavikurvöllur, capacity: 2,000. Strip: blue shirts, white shorts. Icelandic Cup 1975, 1997; Icelandic League champions 1964, 1969, 1971, 1973; **UEFA Cup** second round 1980. See also **hairstyle**.

Ibrox Park disaster *disaster* either of two stadium disasters at **Ibrox Park**, Glasgow. The first, in April 1902, occurred when the new West Stand, constructed of wooden planks on steel pylons, collapsed six minutes into an international match between **Scotland** and **England**. Twenty-six people fell to their deaths, with over 500 injured. More than 100,000 people had crammed into a stadium designed to accommodate around 80,000. The match continued, ending in a 1–1 draw (the match was later replayed, with the proceeds going to a fund to help the victims' families). The second disaster occurred on 2 January 1971, towards the end of the "Old Firm" derby between **Rangers** and **Celtic**. Thousands of spectators had started to leave the ground, with Rangers trailing 0–1 with only a few minutes to play: Rangers equalised and spectators on the stairway attempted to return to the terraces. The crush barriers on the stairway collapsed under the weight of the crowd. Sixty-six people died and 145 were injured in the ensuing crush. See **Wheatley Report**.

Ibrox Stadium *ground* Scottish football ground situated in Glasgow, in the Strathclyde region; home of **Rangers**. Ground capacity: 50,500 all-seater. Pitch dimensions: 105m x 71m. Record attendance: 118,567 v **Celtic** (2 January 1939, Division One). *History* Rangers first played at the current Ibrox Park on 30 December 1899, having previously played at another ground called Ibrox Park (after the district of Glasgow in which it was situated) on 20 August 1887 (v **Preston North End**, friendly). The first Ibrox Park staged three **Scotland** internationals (v **Ireland**, 9 March 1889; v England, 2 April 1892; v Ireland, 27 March 1897) and the 1890 **Scottish FA Cup** final (**Queen's Park** v **Vale of Leven**). The current Ibrox is situated next the former ground. The ground holds the record for the largest attendance at a League match in the UK, when on 2 January 1939, 118,567 people saw the traditional New Year "Old Firm" derby between Rangers and Celtic. At the time, Ibrox was the second largest ground after Hampden Park in the country. The ground has twice been the scene of large-scale fatalities among spectators: on 5 April 1902 (Scotland v **England**), 26 people died and 500 were injured when a wooden terrace collapsed; and on 2 January 1971 (Rangers v Celtic) 66 people were killed and 145 injured on a stairway (number 13) – see **Ibrox Park disaster**. Several years after the second tragedy, Rangers embarked on an ambitious redevelopment of Ibrox, which included the construction of three all-seater stands at a cost of £10 million. The new 45,000-capacity Ibrox, by now named Ibrox Stadium, opened on 19 September 1981 (v Celtic). In 1994, the final piece of terracing, a 7,500-capacity enclosure, was converted to seating with the construction of a third-tier on the South Stand, designed by Archibald **Leitch**. To help fund the £20 million development, Rangers introduced a **debenture** scheme – the first in the UK – which entitled the purchaser to the right to buy a season ticket in the new facility for the next 30 years. The price of the 6,800 debentures on offer ranged from £1,000 to £1,650 and they sold out within a few weeks, raising £8.5 million towards the proposed development. The first floodlit match at Ibrox took place on 8 December 1953 (v **Arsenal**, friendly). The second Ibrox staged its first Scotland international on 15 March 1909 (v Ireland) and its first Scottish FA Cup final on 14 April 1900 (Celtic v Queen's Park).

IBV Vestmannaeyjar (Idrótta Bandelag) *club* Icelandic national league club based in Vestmannaeyjar, founded 1946. Ground: Hásteinsvöllur, capacity: 1,500. Strip: white shirts, white shorts. Icelandic Cup 1968, 1972, 1981, 1998; Icelandic League champions 1979, 1997, 1998; **UEFA Cup** second round 1979.

ice *medical* frozen water. Ice is used for the first-aid treatment of **soft-tissue injuries** to reduce the extent of swelling and inflammation as well as reducing pain. Ice cubes or crushed ice are often kept by the **physiotherapist** or **trainer** in an ice bucket, or can be generated from a chemical ice pack. It is important not to place ice directly on to skin as this can cause a freezing injury such as frostbite. See **RICE**.

Iceland *country UEFA* island republic in the North Atlantic, just south of the Arctic Circle between **Greenland** and **Norway**, 798 km (530 miles) north-west of **Scotland**. Independence from Denmark in 1944. Area: 102,820 sq km (39,690 sq miles). Volcanic landscape. Population: 267,800 (1995 census). Language: Icelandic. Capital: Reykjavik. *Dossier* The Football Association of Iceland (Knattspyrnusamband Islands, Reykjavik) formed in 1929, affiliated to **FIFA** in 1947 and founder member of **Union of European Football Associations** (UEFA) in 1954, president Eggert Magnusson, general secretary Geir Thorsteinsson. Season played from April to October. National stadium: Laugardalsvöllur, Reykjavik, capacity: 14,000. National strip: blue shirts, blue shorts. First international game: 17 July 1946 v **Denmark** (0–3, in Reykjavik, friendly). Biggest victory: 9–0, v **Faeroe Islands** (10 July 1985, in Keflavik, friendly). Biggest defeat: 2–14, v Denmark (23 August 1967, in Copenhagen, friendly). Most capped players: Gudni Bergsson (77 appearances, 1984-98), Arnór **Gudjohnsen** (73 appearances, 1979–98), Atli Edvaldsson (70 appearances 1976-91). Leading goalscorers: Rikhardur Jónsson (17 goals, 1947–65), Arnór Gudjohnsen (14 goals, 1979–98), Pétur Pétursson (11, 1978–1990). Other notable international players: Asgeir Sigurvinsson, Marteinn Geirsson (67 appearances, 1971–1982), Bjarni Gudjónsson. *International tournament record* **Olympic Games** – never qualified for finals tournament; **Women's World Cup** – first entered 1995, never qualified for finals tournament; **World Cup** – first entered 1958, never qualified for finals tournament; **European Championship** – first entered 1964 (first round, no qualifying tournament), has since never qualified for finals tournament; **European Championship for Women** – entered first tournament in 1982-84, quarter-final 1995 (won its first-round group of three nations, ahead of **Netherlands** and **Greece**, with four straight wins; narrowly lost in quarter final v **England**, **women** 2–4 agg.); **Under-17 World Championship** – never qualified; **World Youth Cup** (under-20) – never qualified. *Record against British and Irish national teams* v **England**, played one, drawn one; v **Northern Ireland**, played two, won one, lost one; v Scotland, played two, lost two; v **Wales**, played five, won one, drawn one, lost three; v **Republic of Ireland**, played seven, won none, drawn two, lost five. *History* Modern football has been played in Iceland since the end of the 19th century, with the first club **KR Reykjavik** founded in 1899. Early club football was concentrated in the capital Reykjavik. The national league started in 1912, with the Cup first played in 1960. *World Cup performance* (finals and qualifiers to end of 1998 tournament) played 56, won 10, drawn 11, lost 35, scored 48 goals, conceded 131 goals; win rate 18%; goals scored per game 0.86. *League system* Only 10 clubs compete in the national First Division. The bottom two clubs are automatically relegated to the 10-club Second Division. Three points are awarded for a victory, with one for a draw: final positions for clubs level on points are determined by **goal difference**. The Iceland Cup final is played in August. *Record in international club tournaments* **European Cup** – Knattspyrnufélagid **Valur** (second round 1968), **IA Akranes** (second round 1976); **European Cup-winners Cup** – Knattspyrnufélagid **Fram** (second round 1986, 1991); **UEFA Cup** – **IBV Vestmannaeyjar** (second round 1979), **IBK Keflavik** (second round 1980). Other leading clubs: KR Reykjavik, Knattspyrnufélagid **Vikingur**.

identity card n. see **national identity card scheme**.

IFK Göteborg (IFK Gothenburg) (Idrottsföreningen Kamraterna) *club* Swedish national league club based in Gothenburg, founded 1904. Ground: league games played at Gamla Ullevi Stadium, capacity: 18,000; European games played at the Nya Ullevi Stadium, capacity: 52,000. Strip: blue and white striped shirts, blue shorts. *Keynotes* IFK's **European Cup** record has included notable victories against three of Europe's leading clubs: in 1995, it recorded home wins against **Barcelona** (2–1) and **Manchester United** (3–1) in the Champions League); and in 1997 it defeated **AC Milan** 2–1 in the home leg of the Champions League (although it lost its remaining five group matches). **European Cup** quarter-final 1995, also qualified for Champions League 1996, 1997, 1998; **UEFA Cup** 1982 (4–0 agg., v **SV Hamburg**), 1987 (2–1 agg., v **Dundee United**); **European Cup-winners Cup** quarter-final 1980; Swedish Cup 1979, 1982, 1983, 1992; Swedish league champions 1908, 1910, 1918, 1935, 1942, 1958, 1969, 1982, 1983, 1984, 1987, 1990, 1991, 1993, 1994, 1995, 1996, 1997.

IFK Norrköping (Idrottsföreningen Kamraterna) *club* Swedish national league club based in Norrköping, founded 1897. Ground: Idrottspark, capacity: 15,000. Strip: white shirts, blue shorts. Swedish Cup 1943, 1945, 1969, 1988, 1991, 1994; Swedish league champions 1943, 1945, 1946, 1947, 1948, 1952, 1956, 1957, 1960, 1962, 1963, 1989.

Ihara, Masami *player* Defender. **Japan** international defender (119 caps, five goals, 1988-). Born 12 June 1968. *Club* **Yokohama Marinos**. *Keynotes* Ihara made his international debut on 27 January 1988 (1–1, v **United Arab Emirates**), is Japan's most capped player and the all-time sixth-most-capped player in the world. He was captain of Japan's 1998 **World Cup** finals team. *Honours* **Asian Cup of Nations** (Japan, 1992); **Dynasty Cup** (Japan, 1992); **Asian Cup-winners Cup** (Yokohama Marinos, 1991); Japanese **J-League** championship (Yokohama Marinos, 1995). **Asian Footballer of the Year** 1995.

IICC Shooting Stars (Industrial Investment Credit Corporation) *club* Nigerian national league club based in Nigeria's second largest city Ibadan, founded 1963 (formerly known as Ibadan Lions until 1971). Ground: Lekan Salami, capacity: 30,000. Strip: blue shirts, white shorts. **African Cup of Champion Clubs** runners-up 1984 (0–2 agg., v **Zamalek** of Egypt), 1996 (3–3 agg., 4–5 pens., v Zamalek); **African Cup-winners Cup** 1976 (4–2 agg., **Tonnerre Yaoundé** of Cameroon); **CAF Cup** 1992 (3–0 agg., v **Nakivubo Villa** of Uganda); Nigerian FA Challenge Cup 1959, 1961, 1966, 1969, 1971, 1977, 1979, 1995.; Nigerian league champions 1976, 1980, 1983, 1995, 1998; **West African Football Union General Eyadema Cup** 1998. Notable former player: Rashidi **Yekini**.

Ikpeba Nosa, Victor *player* Striker. **Nigeria** international (19 caps, 2 goals). Born 12 June 1973. *Clubs* ACB Lagos (of Nigeria), RC Liegeois (of Belgium), **Monaco**. *Honours* **Olympic Games** gold medal (Nigeria, 1996); CAF Footballer of the Year 1997.

Ilhwa Chunma *club* former name of **Chunan Ilhwa Chunma**.

illegal payment *n.* financial inducement or incentive paid by clubs/officials or agents to players or officials. *Keynotes* **Football Association** and **Football League** investigations into alleged illegal payments date back to the 1890s - mostly for paying **signing-on fees** to players over the £10 limit in force at the time. **Leeds City** was the first club to be expelled by the Football League and FA, for failing to allow the inspection of its accounts following allegations of illegal payments. An early case of financial malpractice involved **Manchester City**, whose 1904 successes (won **FA Cup**, second in League), were marred by allegations of illegal payments to players arising from the transfers of Irvine Thornley and Frank Nogrove from **Glossop** (a club being investigated for financial irregularities by the FA at the time). As a result, City was fined £250 and five of its directors and Thornley were suspended. More allegations of illegal payments to City players surfaced in the following season. In total 17 players were found guilty of accepting illegal payments and they each received a suspended fine and were banned from ever playing for the club again. Also, Tom Maley, City's manager, received a life ban from the game (later rescinded) and the club was forced to auction its players – raising a sum of £2,600. **Sunderland** was fined £250 in 1904 for making illegal payments to players and several of the club's directors were banned for three years. **Derby County** and **Leicester City** were both fined by the Football League in 1941 for making illegal payments to players dating back over several seasons. Both clubs were fined £500 with a number of directors suspended, including the Derby County chairman Walter Bendle Moore. Derby's manager George Jobey was banned, while former Leicester manager Frank Womack was suspended from the game for 12 months. In June 1969, **Manchester United** was found guilty of making illegal payments and, along with a £7,000 fine, the Football League banned the club from playing friendly matches against overseas clubs for two seasons. **Peterborough United** received one of the harshest penalties for making illegal payments to players when in 1967-68 it was fined 19 points, which effectively condemned the club to Division Four football

the following season. **Swindon Town** almost suffered a similar fate in 1989-90. The club won promotion to Division One for the first time, but was prevented from taking its place in the top flight after an investigation found financial irregularities which mainly concerned illegal payments to players. Swindon's punishment was relegation to Division Three, although this was reduced on appeal and the club retained its place in Division Two (though lost out on promotion). In 1991, **Chelsea** was fined a record £105,000 for making illegal payments to players. Financial irregularities emerged at **Tottenham Hotspur** in June 1992, following an investigation by the Inland Revenue. It found that a number of players, including **Belgium** international Nico Claesen, had benefited from undisclosed payments. In addition, Chris Waddle and Paul **Gascoigne** were both promised ex-gratia payments up to £120,000 should they leave the club, while three transfers – Mitchell Thomas from **Luton Town**, Paul Allen from **West Ham United** and Chris Fairclough from **Nottingham Forest** – also involved irregular payments concerning undisclosed loans. The FA Commission of Inquiry found Spurs guilty of 40 charges, half of which related to transfer irregularities. The club was fined £600,000, had 12 points deducted and was banned from the 1994-95 FA Cup competition. An appeal later lifted the FA Cup suspension and the points reduction, although the club still had to pay a £1.5 million fine for financial misdemeanours. A four-year Football Association investigation into the alleged "bungs" made to individuals following transfers arranged by a Scandinavian agent, Rune Hauge, found that former Nottingham Forest manager Brian **Clough**, his assistant Ronnie Fenton and former **Arsenal** chief scout Steve Burtenshaw had received illegal payments. At a FA disciplinary hearing on 16 September 1998, Burtenshaw apologised for contravening regulations and accepting £35,000 from Hauge two months after John Jensen moved to **Highbury** from **Brøndy IF**. He was later fined £7,500. Arsenal manager George **Graham** had earlier been banned from the game for one year for receiving money from Hauge.

impede *vb. rules* see **obstruction**.

in play *rules* of a match that is actively in progress: the ball is in play while it remains inside the **field of play** and play has not been stopped by the **referee** (Law IX). The ball can be kept in play by the **goal posts**, **crossbar**, **flagposts** and even the referee, as long as it has not crossed a **goal-line** or **touchline**. The ball is in play from a **goal-kick** only when it has travelled beyond the **penalty area** (Law XVI). The ball is in play when a **drop-ball** touches the ground (Law VII). It is in play from a **free kick** or **corner kick** when it moves after being kicked (Laws XIII and XVI). A free-kick taken within the penalty area by the **defending team** is only in play when it has travelled beyond the penalty area (Law XIII). A ball is in play from a penalty kick as soon as it has been kicked and moves forward (Law XIV). It is in play from a **kick-off** when it moves forward after being kicked (Law VIII).

independent supporters associations (ISAs) *n.* supporters' groups set up independently of a club and, in general, to campaign on a specific issue. *Keynotes* **Queens Park Rangers** (QPR Loyal Supporters Association) established one of the first ISAs in 1986 to campaign against plans to merge the club with neighbours **Fulham**. **West Ham United** fans formed an independent association to protest against the club's ill-fated **debenture** scheme. An ISA established by **Leeds United** supporters has been instrumental, with the support of the local trades union council, the police and the club's players, in isolating racist supporters at **Elland Road**.

Independiente (Club Atlético) *club* Argentinean national league club, based in Avellaneda, Buenos Aires, founded 1905. Ground: Estadio Cordero, capacity: 69,000. Strip: red shirts, dark blue shorts. *History* The club was founded by staff at the "City of London", a British-owned store in Buenos Aires. The club became independent from the company, thus adopting the name Independiente. It did not have its own stadium until 1928. Independiente has won the **Copa Libertadores** seven times and has never lost in the final. By 1998, it had won 11 South American club titles, five more than its nearest rivals **Peñarol** of Uruguay and **São Paulo** of Brazil. It has won a record 15 international tournaments, including the **World Club Cup** twice and the **Copa Inter Americana** three times. *Honours* Argentinean league champions 1922, 1926 (two leagues operated prior to 1927), 1938, 1939, 1948, 1960, 1963, 1970, 1971, 1983, 1990, 1994 (**Clausura**); Argentinean National Championship (a pre-national-league tournament operating from 1967 to 1985) 1967, 1977, 1978; Copa Inter Americana 1973, 1974, 1976; Copa Libertadores 1964 (0–0, 1–0, v **Nacional** of Uruguay), 1965 (1–0, 1–3, 4–1 playoff, v Peñarol), 1972 (0–0, 2–1, v **Universitario**), 1973 (1–1, 0–0, 2–1 playoff, v Colo Colo), 1974 (1–2, 2–0, 1–0 playoff, v São Paulo), 1975 (0–1, 3–1, 2–0 playoff, v Union Española), 1984 (1–0, 0–0, v **Grêmio**); **Supercopa** 1994 (2–1 agg., v **Boca Juniors**), 1995 (2–1 agg., v **Flamengo**), runners-up 1989 (0–0 agg., 3–5 pens., v Boca Juniors); World Club Cup 1973 (1–0, v **Juventus**, in Rome), 1984 (1–0, v **Liverpool**); **Recopa** 1994 (1–0, v **Velez Sarsfield**, in the National Stadium, Tokyo).

Independiente Medellin (Club Deportivo) *club* Colombian national league club based in Medellin, founded 1913 (as Medillin Fútbol Club, until 1951). Ground, Ground Estadio Atanasio Girardot, capacity: 53,700 (shared with **Atlético Nacional Medellin**). Strip: red shirts, blue shorts. Colombian league champions 1955, 1957; **Copa Libertadores** quarter-final 1994.

Independiente Santa Fé *club* Colombian national league club based in Bogota, founded 1941. Ground Estadio Distrital Nemesio Camacho "El Campin", capacity: 51,300 (shared with **Club Deportivo Los Millonarios**). Strip: red shirts with white sleeves, white shorts. Colombian league champions 1948, 1958, 1960,

1966, 1971, 1975; **Copa CONMEBOL** runners up 1996 (1–2 agg., v **Lanús** of Argentina); **Copa Libertadores** semi-final 1961. Notable former player: Neil **Franklin**.

India (Hindi name: Bharat) *country AFC* federal republic in south Asia on the Indian Ocean, bordered by **China**, **Nepal**, **Bhutan**, **Myanmar**, **Pakistan**, and **Bangladesh**. Comprises 22 states. India is the second most populated country in the world – which is growing at around 2% a year – and has widespread poverty, particularly among the subsistence farming communities. Area: 3,166,830 sq km (1,22,395 sq miles). Wide geographical and climatic variation: including the Himalayas to the north (the world's highest mountains), the lush Himalayan foothills, the vast plains around the Brahmaputra, Ganges and Indus rivers – with their fertile land and monsoon climate (though susceptible to drought) – the Daccan plateau to the south, and the Thar Desert in northwest. Population: 913,200,000 (1996 est.). Languages: 854 known languages or dialects, including Hindi, English and 12 other official languages. Capital: New Delhi. *Dossier* All India Football Federation (Guwahati, Assam) formed in 1937, affiliated to **FIFA** in 1948 and founder member of **Asian Football Confederation** (AFC) in 1954, president Priya Ranjan Das Munshi, general secretary K N Mour. Season played from November to March. National stadium: Salt Lake, Calcutta, capacity: 120,000. National strip: orange shirts, white shorts. *International tournament record* **Olympic Games** – fourth 1956 (0–3 v **Bulgaria**, in Melbourne, Australia, third/fourth playoff), also played in finals tournament 1948, 1952 (lost 1–10 v **former-Yugoslavia** in the preliminary round), 1960; **Women's World Cup** – first entered 1999 (second in its four-nation qualifying group); **World Cup** – first entered 1986, never beyond first qualifying round; **Asian Cup of Nations** – first entered 1960, runners-up 1964 (second in the four-nation final tournament in Israel), also qualified for finals tournament 1984; **Asian Games** – winners/gold medal 1951 (1–0, v **Iran**, in New Delhi) and 1962 (2–1, v **South Korea**, in Jakarta, Indonesia), third place (bronze medal) in 1970 (1–0, v **Japan**, in Bangkok, Thailand, third/fourth playoff) and fourth place in 1958 (1–4, v **Indonesia**, in Tokyo, third/fourth playoff), second round 1998; **Asian Women's Championship** – runners-up 1979 (six-nation group, in India), 1983 (0–3, v **Thailand**, in Thailand); **Asian Youth Championship** (under-19) – joint 1974 (with Iran); **South Asian Gold Cup** – entered first tournament in 1993, 1993 (v **Sri Lanka**, in Lahore, Pakistan), 1997 (5–1, v **Maldives**, in Kathmandu, Nepal), 1999 (2–0, v Bangladesh, in Margoa, India), runners-up 1995 (0–1, v Sri Lanka, in Colombo, Sri Lanka); **Under-17 World Championship** – never qualified; **World Youth Cup** (under-20) – never qualified. *Record against British and Irish national teams* none played. *History* Football has been played in India since the latter quarter of the 19th century, introduced by British colonials. Cup football dates from 1892, and the regional Calcutta league championship has been played since 1898: first won by the

Gloucestershire Regiment, with 17 of the first 20 championships going to British army regiments. The National Football League started in 1998. There are two national knockout competitions: the Santosh Trophy (started 1941 – for state teams and the army) and the Federation Cup (first played in 1977). Bengal has won the Santosh Trophy 28 times, including five successive trophies from 1993 to 1998. India's best international achievement was finishing in fourth place at the 1956 Olympic Games. It has won the football tournament of Asian Games twice and was runners-up in the 1964 Asian Cup of Nations. One of the worst incidents of football-related vandalism occurred in the 1998 season when the offices of the Calcutta Referees Association were attacked by fans retaliating at the dismissal of a player during a league game. A few days before the incident, a referee had been knocked unconscious by a player angry at being sent off. *League system* The 12 leading clubs are professional and play in the National Football League (extended to 14 in 2000). These clubs are divided into two groups of six (seven from 2000). At the end of the first phase, the top three clubs in each group enter the "Super League" – these clubs playing each other at home and away. The bottom club in each of the first-stage groups is relegated to one of the regional leagues. Three points are awarded for a win, with one for a draw. Many regional leagues operate. *Record in international club tournaments* Asian Champion Teams Cup – Mysore State (semi-final 1968), **Mohun Bagan** (semi-final 1988); Asian Cup-winners Cup – **East Bengal** (second round 1991). Other leading clubs: **Mohammedan Sporting**, **Salgaocar**, Eastern Railway, JCT Mills.

Indian Ocean Games *competition* international sports tournament for African nations of the Indian Ocean, first played 1947. The football tournament has been won by **Madagascar** (1947, 1958, 1963, 1983, 1990, 1993, 1998), **Mauritius** (1948, 1949, 1950, 1951, 1952, 1953, 1954, 1955, 1956, 1957, 1982, 1985). **Reunion** 1979 1999. The **Seychelles** was runner-up in 1979.

indicator board *n.* electronic number boards used by the **fourth official** to indicate the amount of **added time** to be played and which players are being substituted and by which team. The **Premier League** began using electronic indicator boards at the start of the 1998-99 season following their successful use at the 1998 **World Cup** finals.

indirect free kick *rules* method of restarting a game after it has been stopped in order to punish a team for a **foul** or other infringement specified in the **Laws of the game** (Laws XII and XIII). A goal cannot be scored from an indirect free kick unless another player (from either team) contacts the ball before it crosses the **goal line** (compare **direct free kick**). The referee will signal that the free kick is indirect by raising a hand above his or her head. If an indirect free kick results in the ball going into the opponent's goal without it touching another player, then a goal kick is given to the opposition. A free kick is taken, by the non-offending side, from the point where the offence was committed unless it is awarded to a defending team in its own **goal area**, in which case it can be taken from anywhere within that goal area. An indirect free kick awarded to an attacking side in the goal area must be taken on the **goal area line** parallel to the **goal line** from the point nearest to the offence. All opposition players must be at least 9.15 metres (10 yards) from the ball when a free kick is taken, or outside the **penalty area** if the free kick is awarded inside the defending team's penalty area. (See **free kick** for full details on rules.) Offences resulting in indirect free kicks include where a player: is guilty of **dangerous play** (including raising a foot head-high with studs showing, and kicking the ball when held firmly by the goalkeeper); prevents the **goalkeeper** from releasing the ball; impedes an opposition player such that he or she is prevented from making progress (**obstruction**); and if a player taking a **kick-off**, free kick, penalty kick, **throw in** or **corner kick** touches it twice before another player has made contact with the ball. An indirect free kick also results if a player takes a **goal kick**, which goes out of the penalty area, but then touches it a second time before another player has made contact with the ball. An indirect free kick may also be awarded if the referee stops the game in order to **caution** a player for entering or re-entering the field of play without his or her permission; or for any other offence where the referee stops play in order to caution or **send off** a player. An indirect free kick is awarded specifically against a goalkeeper if he or she: takes more than four **steps** in any direction while holding, bouncing or throwing and catching the ball after taking control of it, but before releasing it back into play; releases the ball back into play after holding it, but then re-handles it; handles a **pass back to the goalkeeper** or a ball received directly from a throw in; or is guilty of **time-wasting** (sense **1.**).

indirect *adj. rules* of an **indirect free kick**, where, according to the **Laws of the game** a goal cannot be scored if the ball is kicked directly into the goal without a second player (of either side) making contact with the ball. Compare: **direct**, **direct free kick**.

Indonesia *country AFC* republic in the Malay Archipelago, in south-east Asia, comprising thousands of islands straddling the equator, and running over 4,800 km. Indonesia includes: Kalimantan (central and southern Borneo), Sumatera (Sumatra), Bali, Sumbawa, Flores, Sumba, Irian Jaya (the western half of New Guinea), Sulawesi (Celebes), Lombok, Flores, the Moluccas, Timor, Java and more than 13,600 small islands in the Indian and Pacific Oceans. The large population – the fourth largest in the world – is concentrated along the river valleys and coast of Java. There are more than 300 ethnic groups. Formerly Dutch East Indies – gained independence in 1949, with Irian Jaya ceded by Netherlands in 1963 and East Timor (a former Portuguese colony) annexed in 1976. Area: 1,919,445 sq km (740,905 sq miles). Tropical climate, with monsoons. Population: 195,280,000 (1995 est.). Languages include: Bahasa Indonesian, Dutch and Javan. Capital:

Jakarta (Djakarta, on Java). *Dossier* All Indonesia Football Federation (Jakarta) formed in 1930, affiliated to **FIFA** in 1952, and founder member of **Asian Football Confederation** (AFC) in 1954, president Dr Azwar Anas, general secretary Dr Nugraha Besoes. Season played from June to April. National stadium: Senayan, Jakarta, capacity: 110,000. National strip: red shirts, white shorts. *International tournament record* **Olympic Games** – played in finals tournament 1956 (first round); **Women's World Cup** – first entered 1999, but withdrew before the qualifying tournament; **World Cup** – first entered 1938, first round of finals tournament 1938 (after walkover in qualifying tournament), won first stage of qualifying tournament (first of four in group) in 1986, but knocked out in second qualifying round; **Asean Tiger Cup** – entered first tournament in 1996, third 1996 (2–3, v **Vietnam**, in Singapore, third/fourth play-off); **Asian Cup of Nations** – first entered 1968, qualified for finals tournament 1996 (last in its first round group); **Asian Games** – first entered 1951, semi-final/third (bronze medal) 1958 (4–1, v **India**, in Japan, third/fourth playoff), semi-final/fourth 1954 (4–5, v Burma – now **Myanmar** – in the Philippines, third/fourth playoff), 1986 (0–5, v **Kuwait**, in South Korea, third/fourth playoff), hosts 1962; **Asian Women's Championship** – first entered 1977; **Asian Youth Championship** (under-19) – joint-1961 (shared with Burma now Myanmar); **South East Asian Games** – winners/gold medal 1997 (1–1, 4–2 pens., v **Thailand**); **Under-17 World Championship** – never qualified; **World Youth Cup** (under-20) – never qualified.` *Record against British and Irish national teams* none played. *History* An estimated 5 million people play football in Indonesia. Football association established in 1930 from seven regional associations. The first Asian nation to compete in the World Cup finals tournament (1938, as Dutch East Indies). Indonesia was fined £25,000 and suspended from international competition by the AFC for deliberately losing an Asean Tiger Cup group match against Thailand (2–3); both nations had already qualified for the semi-final, but neither wanted to play hosts Vietnam in Hanoi. The game was a farce with both sides trying to lose – Indonesia's Mursyid Effendi eventually scoring a deliberate own goal in injury time to hand the tie to Thailand. *League system* The huge geographical spread of Indonesia makes national competition difficult: there are around 350 regional amateur associations. A national league, however, has been played since 1980, with a professional league introduced in the 1994/95 season. The Premier League is played in five regional groups of five or six clubs in each. The top two in each group qualify for two championship groups of five clubs. The top two in each of the championship groups enter a knockout semi-final and final to decide the title. The bottom club in each of the regional groups enter a relegation playoff league. Indonesia has 17 professional clubs. *Record in international club tournaments* **Asian Champion Teams Cup** – PSMS (semi-final 1970), **Tiga Berlian** (semi- final 1985); **Pelita**

Jaya (semi-final 1989, 1990); **Asian Cup-winners Cup** Pupuk Kaltin (semi-final 1991), Petrokemia Putra (quarter-final 1996), **PSM Ujung** (quarter-final 1998). Other leading clubs: Semen Padang (Indonesian Cup 1992), NIAC Mitra (Indonesian national champions 1982, 1983, 1988), Aresto (national champions 1992, Cup 1985), Persebaya (national champions 1997), PSIS (of Semerang, national champions 1999).

indoor football *n.* football played inside a building. *Keynotes* Although indoor football is, generally, five- or seven-a-side, played on small pitches, the world's first (albeit ephemeral) indoor, 11-a-side league, played on a full-size pitch, was started in 1923, in Boston, USA. The first **World Cup** match to be played indoors was in Seattle, for the **United States of America**'s qualifying tournament game against **Canada** (20 October 1976). See also **CIS Cup**, **futsal**, **jorkyball**, **visually-impaired football**.

inducement *regulations* any unauthorised payment or other benefit offered by a club to a player, his agent or his associate, to entice that player to sign a contract with that club: such payments are strictly prohibited (FA Premier League rule J.8, Football League regulation 65, Scottish Football League rule 53). **Scottish Football League** clubs are similarly prohibited from trying to induce a manager, coach or trainer to break a written contract with another club (Scottish Football League rule 89). Compare **approach**.

industrial action *misc.* strike action or other form of protest involving the full or partial withdrawal of labour or cooperation, taken by players or match officials against their employers or the football authorities. *Keynotes* **Newcastle United** players threatened strike action prior to the 1910 **FA Cup** final (v **Barnsley**) if striker Albert Shepherd, who had been forced to miss the semi-final (v **Swindon Town**) because of bribery allegations, was not picked for the team; Shepherd played in the final – and scored both Newcastle's goals in the replay. Before the start of the 1922-23 season, **Football League** players threatened to strike after the football authorities agreed a £1 cut in the maximum wage, from £9 to £8, but they eventually took no action. A players' strike in **Argentina** precipitated Alfredo **Di Stefano**'s exile when he moved to Colombian **Club Deportivo Los Millonarios** in 1951 to continue playing. Uruguayan professional players went on strike in 1949 over wages. Many players also left to play in **Colombia**. In **Italy**, the first matches of the 1993-94 league season (29 August 1993) kicked off 30 minutes late as part of the Italian players' union's protest at the new owners of **Bologna** and Livorno, who, it was claimed, had reneged on the players' existing contracts. In October 1997, Chilean players embarked on a three-week strike in protest at the poor condition of some club facilities, late payment of wages and the lack of proper contracts. The strike immediately resumed after it was lifted when Division Two (Segunda Division) side Club de Deportes Arica dismissed its entire first team squad. The second strike was called off after one day when Arica agreed to reinstate the sacked players. In March 1998, **Chester City**'s players were contemplating strike action because of non-payment of wages. In August 1998, **Celtic**'s first-team squad refused to participate in off-the-field activities, including non-attendance at a photo-call to launch the club's new away strip and a collective refusal to talk to the media, as a protest against the club's proposed **European Cup** bonus system, which the players claimed was inferior to that offered by rival clubs because no bonuses had been offered for points won in the competition. In October 1998, the Italian players' union proposed a six-month strike to protest against the handling of the investigation into drug use among players (see **drugs**). In **Bolivia**, players of champion's **Bolivar** took over the club's stadium to demand payment of unpaid wages amounting to £135,000 in November 1998. On an individual basis, Pierre van Hooijdank engaged in a three-month one-man strike, when he refused to return to **Nottingham Forest** at the start of the 1998-99 season. His action followed criticism of the club's sale of his striking partner Kevin Campbell. The **De Boer** brothers, Ronald and Frank, did not play their first match of the 1998-99 season for **Ajax** until 20 September, following a court case instigated by the players to free them from their contracts , which would allow them to join **Barcelona**. The Dutch FA's appeal court turned down the twins' request. Referees have also threatened or staged protest strikes. In 1989, Greek referees went on strike to protest against violence to match officials. A strike, or "day of reflection", by Spanish **Primera Liga** referees over the weekend 29-30 November 1997 in a protest at being pilloried by club officials and the media; their place was taken by referees from the Spanish Division Three (Segunda B). Bulgarian referees only called off their threatened strike action in October 1997 after they were promised more protection from disgruntled spectators. Industrial action by staff outside of football can significantly affect match/tournament attendance. Pilots at Air France, the official 1998 **World Cup** airline, staged a series of strikes in the run-up to the competition, posing enormous potential travel difficulties. A strike by London Underground employees was the main reason for **England**'s lowest **Wembley** crowd for a full international, on 23 May 1989, when only 15,628 spectators turned up to see the national side play **Chile**. Industrial action may also affect football in other ways. For example, the 1926 General Strike delayed the opening of a new main stand at **Reading**'s **Elm Park** ground that year.

ineligible player *regulations* a player who is not entitled to play in a match, either because: (a) the player is not registered with the appropriate governing body (see **registration**); (b) the player is **cup-tied**; (c) the player is under a **suspension**; (d) the player is over the age limit for an age-restricted competition (eg a youth tournament); or (e) the player is of the wrong sex for the competition (women are not allowed to play in men's matches, and vice versa; see **Sex Discrimination Act**). It is the responsibility of the club to make sure that its players are eligible. Clubs fielding ineligible players may be punished by their governing body: the **Scottish Football League**, for example, may deduct points from such clubs or impose other penalties (Scottish Football League rule 44). *Keynotes* A fine of £25 and the loss of two league points for fielding ineligible players was introduced by the English **Football League** in 1890. The earliest example of a club being punished for fielding an ineligble player occurred during the 1890-91 season when **Sunderland** fielded goalkeeper John Edward Doig before he was eligble in a match against **West Bromwich Albion** (20 September 1890, Football League). As a result, Sunderland was penalised two points. In season 1926-27, **Stockport County**, then of Division Three (North), was penalised two points for fielding Joe Smith without permission against **Stoke City** (19 March 1927). In season 1973-74, **Preston North End**, then of Division Two, and **Newport County**, then of Division Four, each had one point deducted for fielding an ineligble player. **Aldershot**, then of Division Three, suffered a similar punishment in 1974-75 for the same offence. The **Union of European Football Associations** awarded **Leeds United** a 3-0 victory over **Stuttgart (VfB)** after the German side fielded an ineligible player during their **European Cup** first round second-leg encounter at **Elland Road** (30 September 1992). Although the match ended 4-1 in Leeds' favour, Stuttgart would have qualified for the next round on **away goals** after winning the first-leg 3-0. The UEFA-imposed 3-3 **aggregate** scoreline resulted in a playoff at a neutral ground which Leeds won 2-1 (9 October 1992). Meadowbank Thistle (now **Livingston**) was deducted three points in 1994-95 for fielding an ineligble player in the club's Second Division encounter against **Brechin City** on 13 August 1994 (the goals from the game were eliminated from the records). In March 1998, Division Three club, **Leyton Orient** was fined £20,000 (£12,500 suspended) by the Football League for fielding three players – Simon Clark, Stuart Hicks, Mark Warren – while banned. The club also had three points deducted after the **Football Association** upheld the League's decision. Liverpool FC Ladies was banned from the 1997-98 **FA Women's Cup** competition, after reaching the semi-final stage, for fielding a player, Jody Handley, who was no longer registered with the club, in the quarter-final tie with Millwall Lionesses (3-1, 22 March 1998) – Millwall was awarded the tie. **Mexico** was suspended from the 1990 **World Cup** for fielding an over-age player in the **World Youth Cup**.

infringement *n.* any breach of the **Laws of the game**. See **foul**.

Inglis, Simon *misc.* sports journalist and writer, author of *League Football and the Men who Made It* (1988) and *The Football Grounds of Great Britain* (1983, 1987, 1996).

ingrown toenail *medical* condition whereby the tissue on the outer edge of the toenail overgrows the nail causing pain and infection. It can be extremely disabling and should be prevented by paying close attention to foot care: cutting the nails flat and using a nail file for the corners. Correctly fitting footwear is vital. An infected ingrown toe nail is likely to require medical attention. The big toe is most susceptible to the condition.

injection of pace *informal* a fillip provided for a team by the introduction (for example by a substitution) of a player of renowned speed and fitness.

injury *n.* physical damage to a player, generally requiring medical attention and sometimes substitution. Injuries range from cuts and bruises to **fractures**, **torn ligaments** and **concussion**. A player who is bleeding must leave the field of play and have the wound dressed before returning to the pitch. The player can only re-enter the field with the permission of the referee (who will signal). If the ball is **in play**, the player can only re-enter from the **touch line**. If the ball is **out of play**, then he or she can enter from any of the boundary lines. *Keynotes* An unofficial players' code exists that, if play is stopped because of a serious injury to a player and subsequently restarted with a **drop-ball**, only one player will take part and kick the ball back to the opposition's goalkeeper or defence. Similarly, if the ball is deliberately kicked out of play so that an injured player can receive attention, the team taking the subsequent **throw-in** will generally ensure that the ball goes to the opposition goalkeeper or defence. An "Audit of Injuries in professional football" is being carried out by the **Football Association**'s Medical Education Centre at Lilleshall Hall National Sports Centre in Shropshire. It is based on questionnaires completed by 91 of the 92 **Football League** and **Premier League** clubs in England and Wales. Preliminary findings suggest that the 2,500 footballers in the Premier League and Football League suffer more than 3,000 injuries per season. Injury ends the careers of around 50 players each season. The study began at the beginning of the 1996-97 season. Interim findings indicated: on average, each injury causes a player to miss four matches; about two-thirds of injuries are sustained in the course of competitive games, the rest occur during training sessions; players lose around 22 training days each season through injury; 30% of injuries are healed within one week, while 50% last one week to one month, and 20% are serious injuries causing the player to be out of action for more than a month; and muscle **strains** are the largest single cause of injury, responsible for about one-third of injuries. When complete, it is hoped that the study will determine if players in certain positions are at increased risk of injury; the effect of training on injury risk; the value of **shin guards**; and whether players return to competitive football too soon after injury. See also **head injury**.

injury risk *medical* the risk of sustaining injury is relatively high in football when compared with other sports. *Keynotes* An analysis of injuries based on accidents recorded in United Kingdom hospital accident and emergency (A and E) departments, carried out by Middlesex University in London, placed association football second only to **rugby football** in injury risk. For every 100,000 hours of play, 290 rugby players would be expected to

sustain an injury requiring treatment at an A and E department; football has 130 injuries per 100,000 hours of play, followed by hockey (90), netball (80) cricket, basketball, squash and skiing (all at 40), athletics and motorsport (both 20), and tennis (15). Among the safest sports are table tennis (one injury per 100,000 hours) and snooker (0.1 per 100,000 hours). Association football, however, accounts for 44% of all sports-related injuries requiring hospital treatment – around 250,000 per year in the UK, compared with 60,000 for rugby. Football rarely results in fatal accidents – there are around two deaths per 100 million hours play – and is much safer in this respect than horse riding (10 per 100 million hours' riding) and mountaineering (30-60 per 100 million hours' climbing).

injury time *rules* another name for **added time**.

Inkaras Kaunas *club* Lithuanian national league club, based in Kaunas, founded 1947. Ground: Darius ir Girenas, capacity: 15,000. Lithuanian Cup 1995, runners-up 1996, 1997; Lithuanian League Champions 1995, 1996; Lithuanian regional Cup 1948, 1949, 1951, 1954, 1965, 1969; Lithuanian regional league champions 1950, 1951, 1954, 1964, 1965.

INKER Zapresic *club* Croatia national league and former-Yugoslavia league club based in Zapresic, founded 1929. Ground: Inker, capacity: 15,000. Strip: yellow shirts, blue shorts. Croatia Cup 1992.

inside forward *n.* either of two players alongside the **centre forward**.

inside left *n.* player just to the left of the **centre forward**.

inside right *n.* player just to the right of the **centre forward**.

Instant Dict *club* Hong Kong league club. Hong Kong league champions 1996, 1998.

insulting gesture *misc.* use of the hands/arms to convey an abusive message or to support an offensive remark (eg, V-sign). *Keynotes* **Tottenham Hotspur** striker Mark Falco was reported to the **Football Association** by the Metropolitan Police in 1986 for allegedly making inflammatory gestures to visiting **Aston Villa** supporters during a Division One match at **White Hart Lane**. Falco admitted the offence and was fined £1,500 and suspended for two matches (subsequently halved on appeal). The **Professional Footballers Association** criticised the FA for acting judicially on a police complaint rather than allowing the matter to be resolved in the courts. Mark **Bosnich**, the Aston Villa and **Australia** goalkeeper, apologised for making a Nazi-style salute to home fans during a **Premier League** encounter between Tottenham Hotspur and Villa at White Hart Lane on 12 October 1996. Although the Football Association accepted Bosnich's explanation that his gestures were a joke, it fined him £1,000 and warned him about his future conduct. Ian Wright was reported to the Crown Prosecution Service for allegedly baring his bottom to **Arsenal** fans after a match in which some sections of the **Highbury** crowd had criticised his performance. In November

1997, **Barcelona**'s Giovanni was banned for two matches after being found guilty by the Spanish football authorities of making obscene gestures to **Real Madrid** fans. **Germany**'s Stefan Effenberg was sent home from the 1994 **World Cup** for gesturing to the crowd. Paul Ince was accused of directing a V-sign at Swedish supporters following his dismissal during **England**'s opening 2000 **European Championship** qualifier against **Sweden** in Stockholm on 5 September 1998. Ince received an automatic one-match ban for his dismissal and **UEFA** subsequently suspended him for an additional two matches. Arsenal's Patrick Vieira was alleged to have made a V-sign to **Sheffield Wednesday** supporters following a Premiership clash between the two clubs at **Hillsborough** on 26 September. He was subsequently fined £20,000 by the FA. See **offensive or abusive language**.

insurance   n.   see **private medical insurance**.

inswinger   n.   cross or corner that, because of the spin imparted on it, swings towards the goal. A right-footed player crossing the ball from the right side of the pitch with the *outside* of the foot will tend to make the ball swing inwards. compare **outswinger**, see **swerve**.

intentional   adj. rules   of a **handball** which, in the opinion of the referee, was committed with intent (Law XII of the **Laws of the game**). *Keynotes* If the referee considers that a player handled the ball by accident – "ball to hand", rather than "hand to ball" – and was unable to avoid hand contact, then a foul will not be ruled. The terms "intentional" or "unintentional" are no longer used with reference to the offence of **tripping an opponent**. Technically, a foul will always be given if a player trips an opponent before making contact with the ball, regardless of intent. In practice, referees tend to show some leniency, particularly with respect to **cautions** or **dismissals**, if a minor infringement is clearly made without intent. Also called **deliberate**. See **unintentional**, **prfessional foul**.

Inter Bratislava (ASK Inter Slovnaft Bratislava)   *club*   Slovakian national league club, based in the capital Bratislava, founded 1942, formerly known as CH Bratislava (Red Star), Slovnaft, TJ Internacionál, Internacionál ZTS (after merger with ZTS Petrzalka in 1986: demerged 1993). Ground: Pasienky, capacity: 15,000. Strip: yellow shirts, black shorts. Czechoslovakian Cup runners-up 1984, 1988, 1990; former Czechoslovakian league 1959 (as CH Bratislava); **Mitropa Cup** 1969; Slovakian Cup 1984, 1988, 1990, 1995. Slovakian league runners-up 1994, 1998; **UEFA Cup** third round 1976.

Inter CableTel   *club*   Welsh league. Ground: Cardiff Athletic Stadium, Cardiff, South Glamorgan. Strip: white shirts, black shorts. Nickname: Seagulls. Ground capacity: 2,500. *Keynotes* Formed in 1990. Inter played in the **UEFA Cup** in 1997-98, losing to **Celtic** in the first preliminary round (0–8 agg.). Welsh Cup 1999.

Inter-Cities Fairs Cup   *competition*   former official name, until 1972, of the UEFA Cup.

Inter Club   *club*   Congo league club based in the capital Brazzaville. Ground: A M Deba, capacity: 50,000. Strip: yellow shirts, red shorts. **African Cup-winners Cup** semi-final 1988; **CAF Cup** semi-final 1995; Congo Cup 1985, 1987; Congo league champions 1977, 1988, 1990.

inter-League match   n.   any of the **representative** matches between teams selected by the **Football League** management committee and representative sides from other leagues, such as the **Scottish Football League**, former **Alliance League**, **Southern League** and Irish League. Inter-League games date from 20 April 1891 (Football League v Football Alliance, 1–1, at Olive Grove, Sheffield). The first Football League v Scottish Football League match was played on 11 April 1992 (2–2, at Pike's lane, Bolton). The early matches provided much of the income of the Football League. A crowd of 90,000 attended the Scottish League v Football League match of 23 March 1949 (0-3, **Ibrox Park**), with Stan **Mortensen** (2) and Tom **Finney** scoring for the Football League. Matches continued on a regular basis until 1977. A centenary game between the Irish League and the Football League was played in Belfast on 8 September 1987 (2–2).

intercept   vb.   to prevent an opponent's pass from reaching its dfestination.   n. interception.

Intercontinental Championship   *competition*   see **Confederations Cup**.

interfering with play   *rules*   ruling that dictates whether a player can be penalised for being in an **offside** position (Law XI). A player is interfering with play if he or she is considered to be actively involved in a particular playing situation such that he or she would gain an advantage from being in that position. An offside player is not interfering with play if, for example: he or she is injured and not in the path of the ball; if a teammate shoots and scores but he/she is not interfering with the vision of the goalkeeper or a defending player. In the last example, however, if the ball rebounds (say off the goalkeeper or post) to the offside player, then that player is now deemed to be interfering with play and the referee should stop play and award an **indirect free kick**.

Internacional (Sport Club Internacional Porto Alegre)   *club*   Brazilian national league and **Rio Grande do Sul** state league club based in Porto Alegre, founded 1909. Ground: Jose Pinheiro Borba "Beira Rio", capacity: 90,000. Strip: red shirts, white shorts. **Campeonato Brasileiro** champions 1975, 1976, 1979; **Copa do Brasil** 1992; **Copa Libertadores** runners-up 1980 (0–0, 0–1, v **Nacional Montevideo**), semi-final 1989; state league champions 33 times (to 1998). Notable former players: Batista, Falcao, Claudio Taffarel.

international call-up   n.   an invitation to play for one's national team.

International Cup   *competition*   another name for **Dr Gerö Cup**.

international duty   *regulations*   FIFA rules require that clubs release players selected by national squads for stipulated competitions. **Scottish Football League**

clubs who lose three or more players on international duty may call for the match to be postponed (Scottish Football League rule 68). Four dates are set aside in every English **Premier League** season especially for international matches; no league or cup fixtures are arranged in any of the six days preceding these dates (FA Premier League rule E.2); the **Football League** programme is not affected.

International FA Board *confederation* eight-member authority that governs the **Laws of the game**. Founded in 1886 following annual meetings of the English, Irish, Welsh and Scottish **Football Associations** held since 1882. The international body **FIFA** has four votes, with the remaining four going to each of the British and Northern Ireland Football Associations. The IFAB meets annually and its decisions are binding on all national Football Associations. No alteration to the rules of the game may be made by any Association until they have been passed by the Board. The IFAB generally takes the view that the rules of the game should be kept simple and that, where possible, differences of application should be resolved by rulings or decisions, rather than new laws or wider definitions. See **Manchester Conference**.

International Football League Board *n.* official adjudicating and enforcing body comprising two representatives each of the FA **Premier League**, the **Football League**, the **Scottish Premier League**, the **Scottish Football League** and the Irish Football League. It has the power to "enforce and carry into effect any agreement, rules, resolutions, provisos or bye-laws made, entered into, or agreed upon by the leagues represented thereon." It deals with matters affecting the represented leagues, such as players' **registrations** and **transfers** between leagues: its decisions are binding on all parties involved. Compare **International FA Board**.

International Gay and Lesbian Football Association *confederation* international football federation for homosexual and lesbian football clubs. Organises a European championship and the football tournament of the **Gay Games**.

International Hall of Fame *n.* FIFA forum honouring the world's greatest players. Those inducted include: **Pelé**, Franz **Beckenbauer**, Bobby **Charlton**, Ferenc **Puskás**, Johan **Cruyff**, Alfredo Di **Stefano**, Bobby **Moore**, Just **Fontaine**, **Garrincha** and Stanley **Matthews**.

International Ladies Football Association *confederation* former women's international football association, based in Luxembourg, founded August 1957. Organised a European women's championship in 1957: with representative sides from **Austria**, **England**, **Germany**, **Luxembourg** and the **Netherlands**. **Manchester Corinthians**, representing England, won the final 4–1, at the Poststadium, Berlin (attendance, 37,000).

international match *n.* fixture between teams selected from players of a particular nationality to represent the football association of that country. Eligibility rules dictate that a player may be entitled to selection for one country despite being a citizen of another. For example, the nationality of single grandparent is often used by a player wishing to play for that country rather than his/her own country of birth. *History* The first international match took place at the Oval in London on 5 March 1870, between **England** and **Scotland** (1–1), but the sides were "representative" rather than truly international (all the Scotland players played for London-based clubs and some had only tenuous connections to Scotland). The first official international, again between England and Scotland, was played on 30 November 1872 (St Andrew's Day), at the West of Scotland Cricket Club, Partick, Scotland (0–0). The match was organised by Scottish club **Queen's Park**, and was watched by 4,000 spectators, with gate receipts of £103. The first victory in an official international match went to England in a rematch the following year (4–2, v Scotland, 8 March 1873, at the Oval, London): England's Alexander Bonsor scored the first international goal. The first international game in continental Europe was played on 12 October 1902: **Austria** v **Hungary** (5–0, in Vienna, friendly). Compare **representative match**.

International matchball standard *n.* indication on a **ball** that it has been tested and found to meet certain technical standards, not only required by the **Laws of the game** (Law II), but additionally approved by the **International FA Board** for international matches (either club or inter-nation competitions). It is one of three designated labels for an international match ball, the other two being: **FIFA approved** and **FIFA inspected**. **National Associations** may also require balls manufactured and tested to these standards.

international referee *n.* a **referee** who adjudicates over an **international match**. For all senior professional internationals, unless otherwise agreed by the countries concerned, the international referee must be from a neutral country and chosen from the official list of international referees. **FIFA** ruled, in 1992, that international referees must be able to speak English.

International Soccer League *competition* former football competition founded in 1960 in the **United States of America**, contested by the New York Americans and 11 overseas clubs. The first season's competition was won by Bangu of Brazil, with **Kilmarnock** the runners-up. Disbanded in 1965.

International Stars (FC Inter Stars) *club* Burundi national league club based in the capital Bujumbura. Stadium: Prince Louis Rwigasore (national stadium), capacity: 20,000. Strip: white shirts, black shorts. *Keynotes* The club holds the national record of five consecutive league titles (1985 to 1989). **African Cup of Champion Clubs** quarter-final 1986; **African Cup-winners Cup** semi-final 1991; Burundi league champions 1974, 1985, 1986, 1987, 1988, 1989, 1991.

International Women's Football Tournament *competition* women's international nation's invitation tournament played in Guangzhou, China, first played 1983.

Internazionale (Inter Milan) *club* Italian league. *Dossier* Ground: **San Siro**, Milan, Lombardy, capacity: 85,847 all-seater. Strip: blue and black striped shirts, black shorts. Website: *www.inter.it* Nickname: Nerazzurri. Biggest win: 9–0 v Casale (1933-34, **Serie A**). Biggest defeat: 1–9 v **Juventus** (1960-61, Serie A). *History* Formed in 1908 by a breakaway group of **AC Milan** members. Inter merged with the US Milanese club in 1928. Mussolini's Fascist **World War II** government forced the club to change its name (from the Leninist connotations of Internazionale) to Ambrosiana-Inter after Ambrosio, the patron saint of Milan. The club's first Italian Championship was achieved via a 10–3 playoff victory over Pro Vercelli, which fielded a junior side because most of its first team was on military service. Inter won the inaugural Serie A title as Ambrosiana-Inter in 1929-30. In the 1960s, manager Helenio **Herrera** fashioned a formidable Inter team, which appeared in three **European Cup** finals in four years between 1964 and 1967, and won two consecutive **World Club Cup**s. Herrera's team included foreign stars Luis *Suárez* and Jair, as well as home-grown talent such as Sandro *Mazzola* and Giacinto **Facchetti**. Aside from Suárez and Jair other foreign players to star for Inter include: Lennart Skoglund, Faas Wilkes, Karl-Heinz **Rummenigge**, Lothar **Matthäus**, Jürgen **Klinsmann**, Paul Ince, Youri Djorkaeff and **Ronaldo**. Between 1991 and 1998, Inter appeared in four **UEFA Cup** finals, lifting the trophy on three occasions. *Honours* European Cup 1964 (3–1 v **Real Madrid**), 1965 (1–0 v **Benfica**); Italian Cup 1939 (2–1 v Novara), 1978 (2–1 v **Napoli**), 1982 (2–1 agg., v **Torino**); Italian League 1910 (won playoff 10–3 v Pro Vercelli), 1920 (3–2 v Livorno), 1929-30, 1937-38, 1939-40, 1952-53, 1953-54, 1962-63, 1964-65, 1965-66, 1970-71, 1979-80, 1988-89; UEFA Cup 1991 (2–1 agg., v **Roma**), 1994 (2–0 agg., v **Salzburg**), 1998 (3–0 v **Lazio**); World Club Cup 1964 (3–1 agg., v Club Atlético **Independiente**), 1965 (3–0 agg., v Club Atlético Independiente).

Intertoto Cup *competition* summer tournament established by the **Union of European Football Associations** in 1961 and relaunched in 1995 as an additional route to **UEFA Cup** qualification. *Keynotes* Initially known as the Rappan Cup (after its founder Karl Rappan) and contested by invited clubs, the tournament provided fixtures for football **pools** during the close season. Since 1966, when the playoff final between the group winners was abandoned, there have been no overall champions, merely group winners. In 1995, UEFA revamped the competition, attempting to make it more attractive to clubs from the higher-ranked countries by offering the top two clubs entry to the UEFA Cup. The format was changed in 1996 and, since then, three of the six finalists from the 12 groups have been awarded entry to the first round of the UEFA Cup. Although **Bordeaux**, which qualified for the UEFA Cup via the Intertoto in 1995-96, reached the UEFA Cup final against **Bayern Munich,** the Intertoto remains a marginal competition. Both **Tottenham Hotspur** and **Wimbledon** received

European suspensions for fielding under-strength sides during their Intertoto fixtures in 1995-96, although the one-season punishment was overturned on appeal. *Results* (Playoff winners to 1966-67) 1961-62, **Ajax**; 1962-63, **Slovan Bratislava**; 1963-64, Slovan Bratislava; 1964-65, Polonia Bytom; 1965-66, **Lokomotive Leipzig**; 1966-67, **Eintracht Frankfurt**; (UEFA Cup qualifiers) 1995-96, Bordeaux, Strasburg ; 1996-97, Karlsruhe, Guingamp, Silkeborg; 1997-98, **SC Bastia**, **Olympique Lyonnaise**, **Auxerre**; 1998-99, **Bologna**, **Valencia**, **Werder Bremen**.

Inverness Caledonian Thistle *club* Scottish league. *Dossier* Ground: **Caledonian Stadium**, Inverness, capacity, 5,600. Strip: blue and thin red striped shirts, blue shorts with red and white trim, red socks with black tops. Record attendance: 5,525 v **Ross County** (15 March 1997, Third Division). Biggest win: 6–1 v **Albion Rovers** (21 October 1995, Third Division). Biggest defeat: 0–4 v **Queen's Park** (20 August 1994, Third Division), v **Montrose** (14 February 1995, Third Division) *History* Founded amid much controversy in 1994 from a merger between Inverness Caledonian and Inverness Thistle (both formed in 1885). The amalgamation, which had first been suggested in 1937, was promoted by the Inverness and Nairn Enterprise board and was especially attractive at the time because of the proposed expansion of the **Scottish Football League** from 38 to 40 clubs. The club joined the League in 1994-95, playing its first match as Caledonian Thistle at Caledonian's Telford Street ground in August 1994. The club adopted the name Inverness Caledonian Thistle at the start of the 1996-97 season to coincide with its move to the new purpose-built 5,600 capacity Caledonian Stadium. The club reached the quarter-final stage of the **Scottish FA Cup** in 1996 and, in 1996-97, it won the Third Division Championship. It was promoted to the First Division at the end of the 1998-99 season. *League record* First Division 1999-00; Second Division 1997-98, 1998-99; Third Division 1994-95 to 1996-97. *Honours* Third Division Champions 1996-97. *Records* Michael Noble holds the record for club appearances (91, 1994-97); Ian Stewart is the record goalscorer (50, 1995-97).

inventive *adj.* of a style of play that creates goal-scoring opportunities through variation and imaginative play.

inversion injury *medical* **sprain**, **tear** or **rupture** injury to the **lateral ligaments** of the ankle resulting from the foot being forced inwards, straining the ligament. This is the most common form of sprain injury among footballers. It may be possible for a player with a mild sprain to continue to play; he or she can be treated later with **RICE**. Partial tears and more serious injuries require clinical assessment: players cannot remain on the field of play. A rupture requires hospital treatment. Ruptured ankle ligaments cause severe pain. See **eversion injury**.

Invincible Eleven *club* Liberian national league club, based in the capital Monrovia. Ground: Antoinette Tubman, capacity: 10,000. Strip: yellow shirts, blue shorts. **African Cup of Champion Clubs** second round 1982; Liberian Cup 1991, 1998; Liberian national league champions 1965, 1966, 1980, 1981, 1983, 1984, 1985, 1987; 1999. Notable former players: George **Weah**, Christopher Wreh.

Ipswich Town　*club* English league. *Dossier* Ground: **Portman Road**, Ipswich, Suffolk. Strip: blue shirts with white trim, white shorts, blue socks. Nickname: Blues or Town. Ground capacity: 22,600. Record attendance: 38,010 v **Leeds United** (8 March 1975, **FA Cup**, sixth round). Best average attendance: 26,672 (1976-77). Biggest win: 10–0 v **Floriana** (25 September 1962, **European Cup**, preliminary rd). Biggest defeat: 1–10 v **Fulham** (26 December 1963, Division One). *History* Founded in 1878 following a meeting at the Town Hall and initially named Ipswich Association Football Club to differentiate it from the rugby club, which was called Ipswich Football Club. The two clubs merged as Ipswich Town in September 1888 and the club moved to the Corporation-owned Portman Road ground, although it played on what is now the training pitch until 1907. Until May 1936 the club retained its amateur status – making Ipswich, at the time, the biggest town in England not to have a professional football club. The club joined the **Southern League** that year, winning the title in its first season but failing to get elected to the **Football League**. Ipswich eventually was elected to Division Three (South) in 1938-39. The club won the Division Three Championship in 1953-54, but immediately came back down, only to win the title again in 1956-57, this time under the managership of former **Tottenham Hotspur** double-winner and future **England** manager Alf **Ramsey**. In 1960-61, Ipswich won the Division Two title and the following season the club took the League Championship – a feat matched only by **Everton** (1930-31, 1931-32), **Liverpool** (1904-05, 1905-06), Tottenham Hotspur (1949-50, 1950-51). Ramsey's Championship-winning side included strikers Ray Crawford and Ted Phillips, who between them scored 61 of the club's 93 goals during the League campaign. Only two seasons after the title success, and with Ramsey gone, the club was relegated, before regaining its top-flight status as Division Two Champions in 1967-68. Another future England manager, Bobby **Robson**, was appointed manager in 1969 and a further period of success followed. In 1972-73, Ipswich finished fourth in Division One, thus qualifying for the following season's **UEFA Cup** competition in which the club reached the quarter-final stage before going out on away goals (1–1 agg., v **Lokomotive Leipzig**). Between 1973-74 and 1981-82 (when Robson departed) Ipswich only once finished outside of the top-six in Division One. Ipswich won the FA Cup for the first and only time in 1978 (1–0 v **Arsenal**) and in 1981 the club triumphed in Europe, winning the UEFA Cup (5–4 agg., v **AZ67 Alkmaar**). The following season, Ipswich reached the **League Cup** semi-finals (2–4 agg., v Liverpool). The club was relegated in 1985-86 and since the creation of the **Premier League** in 1991-92, it has spent only three seasons in the top division. It lost in the semi-final of the end-of-season First Division **playoffs** in three consecutive seasons (1996-97, 1997-98, 1998-99). *League record* Premier League 1992-93 to 1994-95; Division One 1961-62 to 1963-64, 1968-69 to 1985-86; First Division 1995-96–; Division Two 1954-55, 1957-58 to 1960-61, 1964-65 to 1967-68, 1986-87 to 1991-92; Division Three (South) 1938-39 to 1953-54, 1955-56 to 1956-57. *Honours* Division Two 1960-61, 1967-68, 1991-92; Division Three (South) 1953-54, 1956-57; FA Cup 1978 (1–0 v Arsenal – *Team* Cooper (goalkeeper), Burley, Mills, Talbot, Hunter, Beattie, Osborne (1) (Lambert), Wark, Mariner, Geddis, Woods); League 1961-62; Southern League 1937; **Texaco Cup** 1973 (4–2 agg., v **Norwich City**); UEFA Cup 1981 (5–4 agg., v AZ67 – *Team* first leg (home) Cooper, Mills, Osman, Butcher, McCall, Thijssen (1), Wark (1), Muhren, Mariner (1), Brazil, Gates; second leg (away) Cooper, Mills, Osman, Butcher, McCall, Thijssen (1), Wark (1), Muhren, Mariner, Brazil, Gates). *Records* Allan Hunter is Ipswich's most capped player (47 (53) for **Northern Ireland**); Mick Mills holds the record for club appearances (591, 1966-82); Ray Crawford is Ipswich's record league goalscorer (203, 1958-63).

Iran (Islamic Republic of)　*country AFC* Islamic republic in southwest Asia on the Gulf of Oman, the Persian Gulf and Caspian Sea. Bordered by **Turkey**, **Iraq**, **Azerbaijan**, **Afghanistan** and **Pakistan**. Former name, until 1935: Persia. Islamic Republic created by the Ayatollah Khomeini in 1979. At war with Iraq from 1980 to 1988. More than one million Kurds sought refuge in Iran after fleeing Iraq in 1991. Area: 1,648,000 sq km (636,130 sq miles). Much of the country is desert. Population: 63,200,000 (1994 est.). Languages: Farsi, Arabic, Kurdish, Turkish, English and French. Capital: Tehran. *Dossier* IR Iran Football Federation (Tehran) formed in 1920, affiliated to **FIFA** in 1945 and **Asian Football Confederation** (AFC) in 1958, president Dariush Mostafavi, general secretary Sayed Reza Eftekhari. Season played from September to May. National stadium: Azadi, Tehran, capacity: 120,000. National strip: white shirts, white shorts. Website: http://www.Iranfootball.com/ (unofficial). Biggest victory: 17–0 v the **Maldives** (2 June 1997, in Damascus, Syria, **World Cup** qualifier). Highest crowd: 110,000 eg 19 September 1997, v **Saudi Arabia** (1–1, Azadi Stadium, World Cup qualifier) and 22 November 1997, v **Australia**(1–1, Azadi Stadium, World Cup qualifier playoff). *International tournament record* **Olympic Games** – quarter-final 1976, also qualified for finals tournament 1964, 1972; **Women's World Cup** – never entered; World Cup – first entered 1974, qualified for finals tournament 1978, 1998, never passed first round; **Afro-Asian National Cup** – runners-up 1991 (2–2 agg., away goals, v **Algeria**); **Asian Cup of Nations** – first entered 1960, 1968 (five-nation final group, in Tehran), 1972 (2–1, v **South Korea**, in Bangkok, Thailand), 1976 (1–0, v **Kuwait**, in Tehran), semi-final/third 1980 (3–0, v **North Korea**, in Kuwait City, third/fourth playoff), 1988 (0–0, 3–0 pens., v **China**, in Doha, Qatar, third/fourth playoff), 1996 (lost to eventual winners Saudi Arabia on penalties in semi-final), semi-final/fourth 1984 (1–1, 3–5 pens., v Kuwait, in Singapore, third/fourth playoff); Asian Futsal Championship 1999 (9–1 v South Korea, in Kuala Lumpur, Malaysia); **Asian Games** – entered first tournament in 1951, 1974 (1–0, v **Israel**, in Tehran), 1990 (0–0, 4–1 pens., v North Korea, in Beijing, China), 1998 (2–0, v Kuwait, in Bangkok, Thailand), runners-up 1951 (0–1, v **India**, in New Delhi, India), 1966 (0–1, v Burma, in Bangkok), quarter-final 1982, 1986, also entered 1958, 1970, 1994; **Asian Women's Championship** – never entered; **Asian Youth Championship** (under-19) – 1973, 1974 (shared with India), 1975 (shared with Iraq), 1976 (shared with North Korea); **Under-17 World Championship** – never qualified; **World Youth Cup** (under-20) – qualified for finals tournament 1977. *Record against British and Irish national teams* v **Scotland**, played one, drawn one; v **Wales**, played one, lost one; v **Republic of Ireland**, played one, lost one. Most capped players: Nader Mohammadkhani (93). Leading goalscorers: Ali Daei (38 goals, in 55 games), Karim **Bagheri** (33 goals, in 41 games) Other notable international player: Khodadad **Azizi**. *History* Iran's football association was founded in 1924. Its league dates from 1960, but was suspended during the 1978 season because of the Islamic revolution. The national championship was not played from 1978 to 1989. Two clubs have won the **Asian Champion Teams Cup**: **Esteghlal Sports Club** (the first time under its former name Taj Club) and **Pas Club**. Iran's other major club, **Piroozi**, has won the **Asian Cup-winners Cup**. Iran entered the first Asian Games football tournament in 1951 (runners-up) and has won the tournament three times. Iran won the Asian Cup of Nations at its second attempt, and won three tournaments in succession (1968, 1972, 1976), followed by three successive third placings. It has qualified for two World Cup finals tournaments and holds the record for the biggest victory in the tournament's history (17–0, v Maldives, above). It was also the top scorer in the 1998 World Cup qualifying tournament with 57 goals in 17 games; Bagheri was the qualifying tournament's top scorer with 19 goals. Iran was the best supported nation in the qualifying tournament, hosting the highest crowd for a qualifier (110,000, v Saudi Arabia, in Tehran, September 1997); its lowest home crowd was 50,000 (v Kuwait, October 1997). Iran's route to the 1998 finals included winning its first-round group of four nations; finishing second in the second-round group of five nations; losing to Japan (2–3) in the AFC playoff; and finally beating Australia on away goals in the OFC-AFC playoff (3–3 agg.) – Iran was 0–2 behind with only 14 minutes to play in the second leg against Australia. In the 1998 World Cup finals tournament in **France**, Iran finished third of four nations in the first-round group, with one win in its three games. Iran's victory was against the **United States of America** (2–1, 21 June 1998, in Lyon: Hamid-Reza Estili and

Mehdi Mahdavikia scored Iran's goals). The enhanced diplomatic, political and national significance of the match was demonstrated by gestures of goodwill on the pitch before the start of the game – including the presentation of flowers by each member of the Iranian team to their opponents and a joint team photograph – and, later, by a statement from the Iranian leader Ayatollah Khomeini (issued after the match through Iranian television): "In the name of God, the Merciful, the Compassionate. My dear ones. In tonight's honourable and brave game, which was technical and strong, you defeated strong opponents . . . This was a beautiful picture of the struggle of the Iranian nation in all . . . its revolutionary existence. A combination of intelligence, strength and dedicated and co-ordinated efforts in a paradise of remembering God and relying on him. It was this unprecedented struggle which bestowed victory and honour on our nation during the revolution and in all the conflicts between the Iranian nation and the Great Satan. Tonight, once again, the strong and arrogant opponent felt the bitter taste of defeat at your hands. Be happy because you made the Iranian nation happy." Iran's record of 2.08 goals per game in all World Cup qualifiers and finals matches puts the country in the top 10 of the all-time **World Cup goal-scoring averages**, behind **Germany** (2.48), **Brazil** (2.31), **New Zealand** (2.20), **Macedonia** (2.20), **Hungary** (2.18), Australia (2.12), France (2.12) and Iraq (2.11), and level with **Netherlands**. Although Iran has never entered the Women's World Cup or the Asian Women's Championship, in 1971 an Iranian women's side hosted two international games against the Italian national women's team (0–2, 0–5, in Tehran). *World Cup performance* (finals and qualifiers to end of 1998 tournament) played 60, won 34, drawn 13, lost 13, scored 125 goals, conceded 56 goals; win rate: 57%; goals scored per game: 2.08. *League system* Sixteen clubs play in the Premier League, three points are awarded for a win with one for a draw. Clubs level on points are separated on **goal difference**. The bottom four clubs are relegated. *Record in international club tournaments* Asian Champion Teams' Cup – Esteghlal Sports Club (as Taj Club, 1970, semi-final 1971, as Esteghlal, 1990, runners-up 1991, 1999), Pas Club (1992), Piroozi (semi-final/third 1997, semi-final/fourth place 1998), Saipa Tehran (semi-final/fourth 1996); Asian Cup-winners Cup – Piroozi (1990, runners-up 1992), Esteghlal (semi-final/fourth). Other leading club: Saypa (of Tehran, league champions 1993, 1994).

Iraq *country AFC* republic of southwest Asia on the Persian Gulf, bordered by **Turkey**, **Iran**, **Kuwait**, **Saudi Arabia**, **Jordan** and **Syria**. Iraq has a short coastline on the Persian Gulf with its only port at Basra. Became a republic in 1958, at war with Iran from 1980 to 1988. Its invasion of Kuwait in 1990 precipitated the Gulf War of 1991 in which Iraq was quashed by a 28-nation alliance including **USA**, United Kingdom, **France** and **Egypt**. Area: 438,317 sq km (169,235 sq miles). There are fertile plains along the Tigris and Euphrates rivers (which become the Shatt al Arab, flowing into the Persian Gulf). Most of the country, however, is desert. Population: 19,410,000 (1993 est.). Languages: Arabic, Kurdish, Assyrian, Armenian, Turkoman. Capital: Baghdad. *Dossier* Iraqi Football Association (Baghdad) formed in 1948, affiliated to **FIFA** in 1950 and **Asian Football Confederation** (AFC) in 1971, president Udai Saddam Hussein, general secretary Dr Kamil Shamil. Season played from September to May. National stadium: Sha'ab, Baghdad, capacity: 50,000. National strip: white shirts, green shorts. *International tournament record* **Olympic Games** – quarter-final 1980, also qualified for finals tournament 1984, 1988; **Women's World Cup** – never entered; **World Cup** – qualified for finals tournament in 1986 (after winning a group stage and two knock-out rounds – but did not progress beyond first round group of finals tournament), second qualifying round 1994; **Arab Cup of Nations** – 1964 (league of five in Kuwait), 1966 (2–1, v Syria), 1985 (1–0, v **Bahrain**), 1988 (1–1, 4–3 pens, v Syria); Pan-Arab Games – 1985; **Arabian Gulf Cup** – 1979, 1984, 1988; **Asian Cup of Nations** – semi-final/fourth 1976 (0–1,v **China**, in Iran, third/fourth playoff); **Asian Games** – 1982 (1–0, v Kuwait, in New Delhi, India), semi final/fourth 1978 (0–1, v China, in Bangkok, Thailand, third/fourth playoff), reached second group stage in 1974 (third in its four-nation group); **Asian Women's Championship** – never entered; **Asian Youth Championship** (under-19) – 1975 (shared with Iran), 1977, 1978 (shared with South Korea), 1988; **Under-17 World Championship** – never qualified; **World Youth Cup** (under-20) – qualified 1977 (first round). *Record against British and Irish national teams* none played. *History* Football association formed in 1948; the national league and Cup date back to 1974. Qualified for World Cup finals tournament in 1986, but lost all three first-round games. Rhadi has the honour of being Iraq's only goalscorer in a World Cup finals, in the defeat by **Belgium** (1–2, in Toluca, Mexico, first round). Iraq's record of 2.11 goals per game in all World Cup qualifiers and finals matches puts the country in the top 10 of the all-time list of **World Cup goal-scoring averages**, behind **Germany** (2.48), **Brazil** (2.31), **New Zealand** (2.20), **Macedonia** (2.20), **Hungary** (2.18), **Australia** (2.12), France (2.12). Iraq won the Asian Games in 1982. Iraq was temporarily suspended from FIFA and international tournaments in 1991 after the Gulf War. Two clubs have reached the final of the **Asian Champion Teams Cup, Police Club** and **Al Rasheed**. *World Cup performance* (finals and qualifiers to end of 1998 tournament) played 44, won 23, drawn 9, lost 12, scored 93 goals, conceded 49 goals; win rate 52%; goals scored per game 2.11. *League system* Sixteen clubs compete in the national First Division. Three points are awarded for a win with one for a draw. The bottom three clubs are relegated. The league was suspended from 1992 to 1994. *Record in international club tournaments* Asian Champion Teams' Cup – Police Club (runners-up 1971), Al Rasheed (runners-up 1988, semi-final 1987, 1989),

Al Talaba (semi final 1986), **Al Zawra** (semi-final/fourth 1996-97); **Asian Cup-winners Cup** – Police Club (quarter-final 1998), Al Talaba (runners-up 1996, third 1999); **Arab Club Champions Cup** – Al Schurta (1982), Al Rasheed (1985, 1986, 1987). Other leading club: Air Force (league champions 1993, 1997, Cup 1992, 1997).

Ireland (all-Ireland) *country* former country now divided into the Republic of Ireland (see **Ireland, Republic of**) and **Northern Ireland** (a constituent region of the United Kingdom). Geographically, Ireland is an island in the British Isles, to the west of Britain. It comprises four provinces, Ulster (mostly in Northern Ireland), Leinster, Munster and Connacht. It was conquered at various times by England in the 16th and 17th centuries and became part of the United Kingdom in 1801. The Irish Free State (now the Republic of Ireland) was created in 1921, with Northern Ireland remaining as a constituent part of the United Kingdom: a division which has created continuous political tension ever since. Area: 83,937 sq km (32,370 sq miles). Languages: English, Irish Gaelic. *Dossier* **Irish Football Association** (Belfast) formed in 1880, affiliated to **FIFA** 1911, remaining as the association of Northern Ireland after the south became a republic (see **Football Association of Ireland**). First international game: 18 February 1882 v **England** (0–13, Belfast, friendly). Biggest victory: 7–2 v **Wales** (7 February 1891, Belfast, **Home International Championship**). Biggest defeat: 0–13 (above). Notable international players: Billy **McCracken**, Elisha **Scott**. *International tournament record* Home International Championship 1914, shared 1903. *Record against British national teams* v England, played 38, won three, drawn four draws, lost 31; v **Scotland** played 36, won one, drawn four, lost 31; v Wales, played 37, won 13, drawn seven, lost 17. *History* The **Irish FA Cup** began in 1881, and was first won by Moyola Park (1–0, v Cliftonville). Although it is now restricted to clubs in Northern Ireland, it has been played continuously since its inception and is thus the longest continuously running football competition in the world (competitions in England, Scotland and Wales were suspended during the World Wars). The Irish League (now the Northern Ireland league) is the third oldest league competition in the world, founded in 1890-91. It was first won by **Linfield**. The League and Cup were dominated by clubs from the north during the all-Ireland period: only **Shelbourne** and **Bohemians** from the south had ever won the Irish FA Cup, while no club from what is now the Republic of Ireland had ever won the all-Ireland league. The all-Ireland national team never played a game against a country from outside the British Isles, and only ever entered the Home International Championship.

Ireland, Republic of (Eire, Southern Ireland, the Irish Republic) *country* UEFA Republic of northwest Europe occupying the southern, central and north-western part of the island of Ireland (four fifths of Ireland is in the Republic), on the Irish Sea and Atlantic Ocean, lying north-west of the United Kingdom, bordered by **Northern Ireland**. Established as the Irish Free State in 1921 (a British dominion), with independence from the UK in 1937. The Republic of Ireland became a republic in 1949. Area: 68,895. sq km (26,595 sq miles). Maritime climate, influenced by the Gulf Stream. Population: 3,620,000 (1996 census). Languages: Irish Gaelic and English. Capital: Dublin. *Dossier* The **Football Association of Ireland** (Dublin) was formed in 1921, affiliated to **FIFA** in 1923 and a founder member of the **Union of European Football Associations** (UEFA) in 1954. President: Paul Quigley; general secretary: Bernard O'Byrne. Season played from August to May. National stadiums: Landsdowne Road (technically, the stadium of the Irish Rugby Union), Dublin, capacity: 49,000; and **Dalymount Park**, Dublin, capacity: 22,000. National strip: green shirts, white shorts (reserve colours: white shirts, green shorts). First international game (as the Republic): 28 May 1924 v **Bulgaria** (1–0, in Paris, **Olympic Games** first round). First game v **England**: 30 September 1946 (0–1, Dublin, friendly); v **Scotland**: 3 May 1961 (1–4, Glasgow, **World Cup** qualifier); v **Wales** 28 September 1960 (2–3, Dublin, friendly); v **Northern Ireland** 20 September 1978 (0–0, Dublin, **European Championship** qualifier). Biggest victory: 8–0 v Malta (16 November 1983, in Dublin, European Championship qualifier). Biggest defeat: 0–7 v **Brazil** (27 May 1982, Uberlândia, Brazil, friendly). Most capped players: Paul **McGrath** (83 appearances, 1985–97), Pat Bonner (80 appearances, 1981–94), Tony Cascarino (77 appearances, 1986–), Steve Staunton (75 appearances, 1988–), Ray Houghton (73 appearances, 1986–97), Liam **Brady** (72 appearances, 1975–90), Kevin Moran (71 appearances, 1980–94), Frank Stapleton (71 appearances, 1977–90), John **Aldridge** (69 appearances, 1986–97), David O'Leary (68 appearances, 1977–93). Leading goalscorers: Frank Stapleton (20 goals), John Aldridge (19 goals), Tony Cascarino (19 goals), Don Givens (19 goals, 1969–82), Niall Quinn (16 goals, 1986–), Noel Cantwell (14 goals, 1954–67), Jimmy Dunne (13 goals, 1930–39), Gerry Daly (13 goals, 1973–1987). Other notable international player: Johnny **Carey** (also played for Northern Ireland). National team coaches/managers: Mick Meagan (1968–71), Liam Tuohy (1971–73), Sean Thomas (1973), Johnny **Giles** (1973–80), Alan Kelly (1980), Eoin Hand (1980–85), Jack Charlton (1986– 96), Mick McCarthy (from 1996). *International tournament record* Olympic Games – first entered 1924, quarter-final 1924 (1–2 v **Netherlands** in Paris – the only occasion Ireland qualified for the finals tournament); **Women's World Cup/European Championship for Women** – see **Ireland, Republic of, women**; World Cup – first entered 1934, first qualified for finals tournament 1990, quarter-final 1990, second round 1994, qualifying tournament playoff 1998; European Championship – first entered 1960, quarter-final 1964, did not qualify for finals tournament again until 1988 (first round), did not qualify 1992 or 1996 (lost in playoff, 0–2 v Netherlands

at **Anfield**, Liverpool); **European Under-18 Youth Championship** – 1998; **Under-17 World Championship** – never qualified; **World Youth Cup** (under-20) – third 1997 (2–1, v **Ghana**, in Kuala Lumpur, Malaysia, third/fourth playoff), also qualified 1991 (third in its first-round group of four nations), 1999. *Record against British and Northern Ireland national teams* v England, played 14, won two, drawn six, lost five, one abandoned; v Northern Ireland, played eight, won three, drawn four, lost one; v Scotland, played six, won two, drawn two, lost two; v Wales, played nine, won three, drawn one, lost five. *History* Association football in the Republic of Ireland dates back to the mid 19th century, though Ireland's equally popular sport **Gaelic football** is probably closer to the early codes (see **association football**, *History*). The oldest of the current clubs were founded towards the end of the century: **Athlone Town** (1887), **Bohemians FC** (1890), **Shelbourne** (1895), **University College Dublin FC** (1895) and **Shamrock Rovers** (1899). Prior to the establishment of the Irish Free State in 1921, clubs in the South had played in all-Ireland league and cup competitions (see **Ireland**); though, with the exception of Bohemians, Shamrock Rovers and Shelbourne, few clubs had been successful. Only Shelbourne and Bohemians from the south had ever won the **Irish FA Cup**, which began in 1881, while no club from what is now the Republic of Ireland had ever won the all-Ireland league, which ran from 1891 to 1920. The Republic of Ireland FAI League and **FAI Cup** started in 1922, both won by **St James's Gate FC** of Dublin. The most successful clubs are Shamrock Rovers, with 15 league championships and 24 Cup wins by 1998, **Dundalk**, with nine league championships and eight cup wins, and Shelbourne, with eight championships and nine cup wins (includes three Irish FA Cup triumphs). One club which has enjoyed recent success in the FAI national league is, in fact, from Northern Ireland. Political expediency, led **Derry City** (founded in 1892) to cease playing football in Northern Ireland in 1972. Derry City has a largely Catholic following; the sectarian conflict in Northern Ireland, at a peak in the 1970s, forced the club to withdraw from football in the north where football clubs inevitably became linked with a Protestant or Catholic support base. Derry City, previously successful in Northern Ireland, has won the FAI league championship and Cup twice each. Club football has been hampered by the departure of top players to English and Scottish clubs and no club from the Republic has ever progressed beyond the second round of a European club competition. The Republic has entered all but the first World Cup tournament. It qualified for the finals for the first time in 1990, under manager Jack Charlton, having lost only one of its eight qualifying tournament games (0–2 against Spain). The Republic drew the first four of its final tournament games, winning a place in the quarter finals 5–4 on penalties after a 0–0 draw with **Romania** in the second round; David O'Leary scored the deciding penalty. The Republic lost to **Italy** in the quarter-final (0–1, Olympic Stadium in Rome, Italy). The Republic of Ireland qualified for the finals tournament again in 1994, and reached the second round (it lost 0–2 v Netherlands, at the Citrus Bowl stadium, Orlando, USA). The country finished second in its qualifying group for the 1998 World Cup tournament and lost in the qualifying tournament playoffs (2–3 agg., v **Belgium**. Although Ireland reached the quarter-final of the second European Championship in 1964, it did not qualify for the finals tournament again until 1988 when it was beaten in the first round. It failed to qualify for the 1996 finals tournament, losing in a playoff (0–2 v Netherlands at Anfield, Liverpool); the last match under Jack Charlton. He had been in charge for 93 matches and was the most successful manager in the history of the national team. *World Cup performance* (finals and qualifiers to end of 1998 tournament) played 94, won 32, drawn 26, lost 36, scored 123 goals, conceded 126 goals; win rate 34%; goals scored per game 1.31. *League system* There are 12 clubs in the National Premier Division, playing each other three times in a season. Three points are awarded for a victory, with one for a draw: final positions for clubs level on points are determined by **goal difference**. The bottom two clubs are automatically relegated to the 10-club second division. A third promotion/relegation place is decided by a playoff between the third-bottom club from the first division and the third-placed club in the second division. *Record in international club tournaments* **European Cup** – **Waterford United** (second round 1971), **Cork Celtic** (second round 1975), Dundalk (second round 1980); **European Cup-winners Cup** – Shamrock Rovers (second round 1963, 1967, 1979), **Cork Hibernians** (second round 1973 – note, the club folded in 1976), Bohemians FC (second round 1977), Waterford United (second round 1981), Dundalk (second round 1982); **UEFA Cup/Fairs Cup** – Drumcondra (second round 1963), Shelbourne (second round 1965), Shamrock Rovers (second round 1966, 1983), Athlone Town (second round 1976). Other leading clubs: **Home Farm-Everton FC**, **St Patrick's Athletic**, **Sligo Rovers**, Derry City, **Cork City**, University College Dublin FC, **Finn Harps**, **Kilkenny City**, **Drogheda United**, **Bray Wanderers** (FAI Cup 1990, 1999).

Ireland, Republic of, women *country/women* women's football in the Republic of Ireland is administered by the Ladies' Football Association of Ireland (LFAI), in Dublin, founded 1973. *Dossier* First international match: 1973, 4–1, v **Northern Ireland**. *International tournament record* **Women's World Cup** – never qualified for finals tournament; **European Championship for Women** – entered first tournament in 1984 (its first-round group also comprised England 0–1, 0–6; Scotland 1–1, 0–3; and Northern Ireland 3–2, 2–1 – the Republic finished third in the group), first round 1989, 1991, 1993, did not compete 1995, first-round group runners-up 1997. *History* Organised women's league football started in the early 1970s, with leagues based in Dublin, Galway and Limerick. The LFAI

Cup was founded in 1975. The Republic of Ireland women's team played its first match in 1973, against Northern Ireland, and its first match in the European Championship for Women in 1982 (0–3, v **Scotland**). The LFAI becaame affiliated to the **Football Association of Ireland** (FAI) in 1991. In 1992, the national side was beaten 0–10 by **Sweden, women** in the European Championship for Women. The defeat led to a major initiative by the LFAI to rejuvenate the national game. The Republic did not enter the following edition of the European Championship, choosing to concentrate on a redevelopment programme. In 1994, the LFAI and FAI set up a development programme for young women's football and introduced under-16, under-18 and under-20 sides to the national team structure. It also created football academies for girls under 18 years of age, with FAI coaches running weekend courses. In 1995, the under-18 team won the Gothia Cup (a women's international youth competition) in Sweden. An FAI Census of Soccer Teams in the Republic of Ireland in 1996 identified 317 women's teams, from 236 clubs, with 6,214 registered players. At the start of the 1998-99 season, Siobhan Furlong, an international with the Republic of Ireland's women's team, was appointed coach of men's club **Limerick FC** – the first woman in the Irish League to achieve the position. *League system* There are 11 women's leagues affiliated to the LFAI: Clare, Cork, LSCAI, Donegal, Dublin, Galway, Inishowen, Limerick, North Eastern, Roscommon and District, and Sligo/Leitrim and District. Each year, the various league champions compete in the inter-league President's Cup. Representative sides from each league compete in the Bracken Trophy (founded 1975).

Irish FA Cup *competition* annual knockout competition played in **Northern Ireland**. *Keynotes* The Irish FA Cup has had an unbroken annual sequence since the first tournament was held in 1881. Founded by JM McAlery, the Irish FA Cup attracted only seven participants in its inaugural season, but now consists of nine rounds, including the final, which is played at Windsor Park, Belfast. It was originally the knockout competition for the whole of Ireland. The first winner was Moyola Park (1–0, v **Cliftonville**). The tournament has been restricted to clubs from Northern Ireland since 1921 (when the former all-Ireland was split into Northern Ireland and **Ireland, Republic of**). The first Northern Ireland Cup final, in 1922, was won by **Linfield** (2–0, v **Glenavon**). *Records* Linfield has the won the trophy on a record 35 occasions. *Cup winners* 1881 Moyola Park; 1882 Queen's Island; 1883 **Cliftonville**; 1884 **Distillery**; 1885 Distillery; 1886 Distillery; 1887 Ulster; 1988 Cliftonville; 1889 Distillery; 1890 Gordon Highlanders; 1891 **Linfield**; 1892 Linfield; 1893 Linfield; 1894 Distillery; 1895 Linfield; 1896 Distillery; 1897 Cliftonville; 1998 Linfield; 1899 Linfield; 1900 Cliftonville; 1901 Cliftonville; 1902 Linfield; 1903 Distillery; 1904 Linfield; 1905 Distillery; 1906 **Shelbourne** 1907 Cliftonville; 1908 **Bohemians**; 1909 Cliftonville; 1910 Distillery; 1911 Shelbourne;

1912 Linfield; 1913 Linfield; 1914 **Glentoran**; 1915 Linfield; 1916 Linfield; 1917 Glentoran; 1918 **Belfast Celtic**; 1919 Linfield; 1920 Shelbourne; 1921 Glentoran; 1922 Linfield; 1923 Linfield; 1924 Queen's Island; 1925 Distillery; 1926 Celtic; 1927 **Ards**; 1928 Willowfield; 1929 Ballymena (now **Ballymena United**); 1930 Linfield; 1931 Linfield; 1932 Glentoran; 1933 Glentoran; 1934 Linfield; 1935 Glentoran; 1936 Linfield; 1937 Belfast Celtic; 1938 Belfast Celtic; 1939 Linfield; 1940 Ballymena; 1941 Belfast Celtic; 1942 Linfield; 1943 Belfast Celtic; 1944 Belfast Celtic; 1945 Linfield; 1946 Linfield; 1947 Belfast Celtic; 1948 Linfield; 1949 **Derry City**; 1950 Linfield; 1951 Glentoran; 1952 Ards; 1953 Linfield; 1954 Derry City; 1955 Dundela; 1956 Distillery; 1957 **Glenavon**; 1958 Ballymena; 1959 Glenavon; 1960 Linfield; 1961 Glentoran; 1962 Linfield; 1963 Linfield; 1964 Derry City; 1965 **Coleraine**; 1966 Glentoran; 1967 Crusaders; 1968 Crusaders; 1969 Ards; 1970 Linfield; 1971 Distillery; 1972 Coleraine; 1973 Glentoran; 1974 Ards; 1975 Coleraine; 1976 **Carrick Rangers**; 1977 Coleraine; 1978 Linfield; 1979 Cliftonville; 1980 Linfield; 1981 Ballymena United; 1982 Linfield; 1983 Glentoran; 1984 Ballymena United; 1985 Glentoran; 1986 Glentoran; 1987 Glentoran; 1988 Glentoran; 1989 Ballymena United; 1990 Glentoran; 1991 **Portadown**; 1992 Glenavon; 1993 **Bangor FC**; 1994 Linfield; 1995 Linfield; 1996 Glentoran; 1997 Glenavon; 1998 Glentoran; 1999 Portadown (walkover).

Irish Football Association *confederation* the national football federation of **Northern Ireland** (and formerly of **Ireland**), founded in 1880. Headquarters in Windsor Avenue, Belfast. Affiliated to **FIFA** in 1911, remained a member until 1920 when, along with the other home nations (**England**, **Scotland** and **Wales**) it resigned; the United Kingdom did not wish to associate with its former enemies from **World War I**. The Irish FA rejoined in 1924 (as the association representing Northern Ireland), but resigned again in 1928 when all four home nations protested at the flexible definition of "amateur" status in the **Olympic Games**. The association rejoined FIFA in 1946. It is a permanent member of the **International FA Board**, and founder member of the **Union of European Football Associations** (UEFA) in 1954. President: Jim Boyce; general secretary: David Bowen. Compare **Football Association of Ireland**.

Irish International tournament *competition* four-team pre-season tournament staged at Lansdowne Road, Dublin during summer 1997. The tournament involved **Celtic**, **Derry City**, **Newcastle United** and **PSV Eindhoven**. *Winners* Newcastle United.

Irtysh Pavlodar (formerly, Ansat Pavlodar, Traktor Pavlodar) *club* Kazakhstan national league club based in Pavlodar, founded 1965. Ground: Central Stadium, capacity: 15,000. Kazakhstan Cup 1998; Kazakhstan league champions 1993, 1997, runner-up 1996.

Island Games *competition* multi-sports tournament held every two years for islands with fewer than 125,000 inhabitants. Islands can come from anywhere in the world (20 competed in the 1997 games held in **Jersey**). Jersey, Anglesey, Shetland Islands, Orkney Islands, **Aland Islands** and **Faeroe Islands** and **Greenland** have all played in the Island Games football tournaments. Jersey won the football tournament of the seventh games in 1997 (1–0 a.e.t., v Anglesey (Ynys Mon), Springfield Stadium, St Helier, Jersey).

Ismailia Sporting Club *club* Egyptian national league club based in Ismâ'ilîya. Ground: Municipal, capacity: 30,000. Strip: gold shirts, green shorts. **African Cup of Champion Clubs** 1969, semi-final 1995; Egyptian Cup 1997; Egyptian league champions 1967, 1991.

Israel *country* *UEFA* state of southwest Asia on the Mediterranean Sea and Gulf of Aqaba, bordered by **Lebanon**, **Syria**, **Jordan** and **Egypt**. Established, by international treaty, as an independent Jewish state in 1948 in the former British mandate of **Palestine (2.)**. Sporadic disputes and wars with Arab neighbours. In 1993, an accord was established for the mutual recognition between Israel and the Palestinian Liberation Organisation, giving partial autonomy to Palestinian areas within the state (see **Palestine (1.)**). Area: 20,770 sq km (8,015 sq miles). Varied landscape, from the coastal plain, to the interior hills, Dead Sea and the semi-desert of the Negev. Population: 5,710,000 (1996 est.). Languages: Hebrew, Arabic, Yiddish, English and some European and Asian languages. Capital: Jerusalem. *Dossier* Israel Football Association, based in Tel Aviv, formed in 1948, affiliated to **FIFA** in 1948 and **Union of European Football Associations** (UEFA) in 1992, president: Gavriel Levi, general secretary Jacob Erel. Season played from September to June. National stadium: Ramat-Gan Stadium, Tel Aviv, capacity: 55,000. National strip: blue shirts, white shorts. First international game: 16 March 1934, v Egypt (1–7, in Cairo, **World Cup** qualifier). Biggest victory: 7–0, v **Sri Lanka** (17 March 1968, in Tel Aviv, **Olympic Games** qualifier). Biggest defeats: 0–6, v **former-Yugoslavia** (21 August 1949, in Belgrade, World Cup qualifier); and v **Italy** (4 November 1961, in Turin, World Cup qualifier). Most capped players: Nir Klinger (83 appearances, 1987-97), Mordechai Spiegler (79, 1963–77), Itzak Shum (75, 1969–81). Leading goalscorers: Mordechai Spiegler (24 – including one in the 1970 World Cup finals in Mexico), Nahum Stelmach (22, 1956–68), Yoshua Feygenbaum (22, 1966–77). Other notable international players: Ronny Rosenthal (60 appearances, 11 goals, from 1983, , clubs include **Liverpool** and **Tottenham Hotspur**), Eyal Berkovic (43 appearances, clubs include **Southampton** and **West Ham United**). *International tournament record* Olympic Games – first entered 1956, quarter finals 1968 (lost to silver-medal winners **Bulgaria** on the toss of a coin, after drawing 1–1) and 1976 (lost 1–4 to **Brazil**); **Women's World Cup** – first entered 1999; World Cup – first entered 1934 (as "Palestine"), qualified for finals tournament in Mexico in 1970 (lost one and drew two of its first-round group matches), lost in qualifying tournament play-off in 1958 (0–4 agg., v **Wales**, see below) and 1990 (won Oceania qualifying tournament, but lost 0–1 agg., v **Colombia** in the playoff); **Asian Cup** – first entered 1956, 1964 (2–0, v **India**, in Jaffa, Israel), runners-up 1956 (1–2 v **South Korea**, in Hong Kong) and 1960 (0–3 v South Korea, in Seoul, South Korea), third place 1968; **Asian Games** – first entered 1958, runners-up 1974 (0–1, v **Iran**, in Tehran, Iran), quarter finals 1958; **Asian Womens' Championship** – never entered; **Asian Youth Championship** (under-19) – 1964 (joint, with Burma (**Myanmar**)), 1965, 1966 (joint, with Burma (Myanmar)), 1967, 1971, 1972; **European Championship** – first entered 1996 (fifth in its six-nation qualifying group); **European Championship for Women** – first entered 1997; **Under-17 World Championship** – never qualified; **World Youth Cup** (under-20) – never qualified. *Record against British and Irish national teams* v **England**, played two, won none, drawn one, lost one; v **Northern Ireland**, played six, won none, drawn three, lost three; v **Scotland**, played three, won none, drawn none, lost three; v Wales, played four, won none, drawn two, lost two; v **Republic of Ireland**, played three, won one, drawn one, lost one. *History* The current football association, founded in 1948, was preceded by a Palestine Football Association, founded in 1928, in the former British mandate (see Palestine 2.). A championship was first played in Israel in 1932, 16 years before it became an independent state. The first champion was the British Police club. A Cup tournament has been played since 1928 (first won by **Hapoel Tel Aviv**, with **Macabi Tel Aviv** winning in 1929). Israeli clubs have competed in Asian and European club tournaments, with Hapoel Tel Aviv winning the **Asian Champion Teams Cup** in 1967, and Maccabi Tel Aviv winning in 1969 and 1971. The club competitions have been affected by regional politics: Maccabi Tel Aviv was awarded the 1971 trophy by default as **Al Schurta** of Iraq refused to play them in the final. Israeli clubs have had less impact in European competitions, though **Maccabi Haifa** qualified for the second round of the **European Cup-winners Cup** in 1993-94 having won its preliminary round match against Stade Dudelange (now **F'91 Dudelange**) of Luxembourg, followed by a first-round victory over **Torpedo Moscow** (3–2 agg.), losing to eventual runners-up **Parma** only on penalties in the second round (1–1 agg., 1–3 pens.). It reached the quarter-final of the same tournament in 1998-99, losing to **Lokmotiv Moscow** (0–4 agg.), having beaten **Paris Saint Germain** in the first round (4–3 agg.). Israel's international appearances have been dogged by Middle-East politics. Before becoming a permanent member of UEFA in 1992, it had been a member of the **Asian Football Confederation** – it was expelled in 1975 – and an associate member of the **Oceania Football Confederation**. As a consequence, it is the only nation to have played a World Cup qualifying match in five different continents: Africa (1934 v Egypt, 1962 v **Ethiopia**); Asia (1974 v **Japan**, South

Korea, **Malaysia**, **Thailand**, 1978 v Japan and South Korea, 1986 v **Taiwan**); Europe (1938 v **Greece**, 1950 v former-Yugoslavia, 1954 v Greece and former-Yugoslavia, 1958 v Wales, 1962 v **Cyprus** and **Italy**, 1966 v **Belgium** and Bulgaria, 1982 v **Northern Ireland**, **Sweden**, **Portugal** and **Scotland**, 1994 v Bulgaria, Sweden, **Finland**, **France** and **Austria**, and 1998 v Bulgaria, **Russia**, Cyprus and **Luxembourg**); Oceania (1970, 1986 and 1990 v **New Zealand** and **Australia**); and South America (1990 v Colombia: OFC/CONMEBOL playoff). Israel's one appearance at the finals was, ironically, in the only remaining football-playing continent, North America (the 1970 tournament in Mexico). In the 1958 World Cup tournament, Israel was given walkovers in all its qualifying tournament matches as its various opponents refused to play them: **Turkey** withdrew in the first round, **Indonesia** and Egypt withdrew in the second round, and **Sudan** withdrew in the third round. FIFA, however, ruled that a team could not qualify for the finals without playing a match, so Israel was forced to meet Wales in a play-off (Israel lost 0–4 agg.). Similarly, in the 1974 Asian Games, at which Israel finished as runners-up, both **North Korea** and **Kuwait** refused to play Israel in the semi-final group stage. *World Cup performance* (finals and qualifiers to end of 1998 tournament) played 73, won 22, drawn 18, lost 33, scored 89 goals, conceded 110 goals; win rate 30%; goals scored per game 1.22. *League system* Sixteen clubs compete in the national First Division. The bottom two clubs are automatically relegated to the 16-club Second Division. Three points are awarded for a victory, with one for a draw; final positions for clubs level on points are determined by **goal difference**. *Record in international club tournaments* Asian Champion Teams' Cup – Hapoel Tel Aviv (1967, runners-up 1970); Maccabi Tel Aviv (1969 and 1971); **European Cup** – Maccabi Tel Aviv (first round 1993), **Beitar Jerusalem** (first round 1994), Maccabi Haifa (first round 1995); European Cup-winners Cup – Maccabi Haifa (second round 1994, quarter-final 1999). Other leading clubs: **Hapoel Petach Tikva**, **Maccabi Netanya**, Hapoel Haifa (League champions 1999).

Isthmian League *competition* one of the three leagues directly below the **Football Conference** (see **pyramid structure**). The Isthmian League was a pioneer of league sponsorship, with a deal from the paint firm Berger in the late 1970s.

Italy *country* UEFA republic in southern Europe, on the Adriatic, Tyrrhenian, Ionian and Mediterranean Seas, bordered by **France**, **Switzerland**, **Austria** and **Slovenia**. Includes the islands of Sicily and Sardinia. The country is three-quarters hilly or mountainous – including the Alps, Dolomites and the Apennines – and is separated from the rest of Europe by the Alps. There is an economical imbalance between the more prosperous north and those living in the south. Italy has been a united country since 1861 and has been a republic since 1946. Area: 301,245 sq km (116,280 sq miles). The climate is Mediterranean in the south and more temperate in the north. Population: 57,270,000 (1995 est.). Languages: Italian, with some German, French and minority Slovene and Albanian. Capital: Rome. *Dossier* Football association (Federazione Italiana Giuoco Calcio, Rome) formed in 1898, affiliated to **FIFA** in 1905 and founder member of **Union of European Football Associations** (UEFA) in 1954, president Luciano Nizzola, general secretary Pietro Renato Corsini. Season played from September to June. National stadium: Stadio Olimpico, Rome, capacity: 80,000; international matches also played at major club stadiums. National strip: blue shirts, white shorts. Website: http://www.mclink.it/com/ ies/calcio/indice.htm (unofficial). First international game: 15 May 1910, v France (6–2, in Milan, friendly). Biggest victory: 9–0, v **United States of America** (August 1948, in London, **Olympic Games** first round) and 11–3, v **Egypt** (10 June 1928, in Amsterdam, Olympic Games third/fourth playoff). Biggest defeat: 1–7, v **Hungary** (6 April 1924, in Budapest, friendly). Most capped players: Dino **Zoff** (112 appearances, 1968–83), Paolo **Maldini** (100 appearances, 1988-), Giacinto **Facchetti** (94 appearances, 1963–77), Giuseppe Bergomi (81 appearances, 1982-98) Marco Tardelli (81 appearances, 1976–85), Franco **Baresi** (81 appearances, 1982–94). Leading goalscorers: Luigi **Riva** (35 goals, 1965–74), Giuseppe **Meazza** (33 goals, 1930–39), Silvio **Piola** (30 goals, 1935–52; the Lazio and Italian international striker scored more Serie A goals, 290, than any other player), Roberto **Baggio** (27 goals, 1988-), Alessandro Altobelli (25 goals, 1980–88), Adolfo Baloncieri (25 goals, 1920–1930). Other notable international players: Paolo **Rossi** (20 goals, 1977–86), Gianfranco **Zola**, Gianluca **Vialli**, Omar **Sivori**, Gianni **Rivera**, Gaetano **Scirea**. *International tournament record* Olympic Games – first entered 1912, winners/gold medal 1936 (2–1, v Austria, in Berlin, Germany), semi-final/third/bronze medal 1928 (11–3, v Egypt, in Amsterdam, third/fourth playoff), semi-final/fourth 1960 (1–2, v Hungary, in Rome, third/fourth playoff; Italy lost in the semi-final after **drawing lots**, following a 1–1 draw), 1988 (0–2, v West Germany, in Seoul, South Korea, third/fourth playoff), quarter-final 1920, 1924, 1948, 1992, also played in finals tournament 1952, 1996, hosts 1960; **Women's World Cup/European Championship for Women** – see **Italy, women**; **World Cup** – first entered 1934, 1934 (2–1 after extra time, v **Czechoslovakia**, in Rome), 1938 (4–2, v Hungary, in Paris, France), 1982 (3–1, v West **Germany**, in Madrid, Spain), runners-up 1970 (1–4, v **Brazil**, in Mexico City, Mexico), 1994 (0–0, 2–3, pens., v Brazil, in Los Angeles, USA: Baresi, Massaro and Roberto Baggio missed Italy's penalties), semi-final/third 1990 (2–1, v **England**, in Bari, Italy, third/fourth playoff), second-round/fourth 1978 (1–2, v Brazil, in Buenos Aires, Argentina, third/fourth playoff), second round 1986, also qualified for finals tournament 1950, 1954, 1962, 1966, 1974 (it has failed to qualify just once, in 1958), hosts 1934, 1990; **Dr Gerö Cup/International Cup** – 1930 (league of five

nations), 1935 (league of five nations), runners-up 1932 (behind Hungary in a league of five nations); **European Championship** – first entered 1964, 1968 (1–1, 2–0 replay, both games in Rome), fourth 1980 (1–1, 8–9 pens., v **Czechoslovakia**, in Rome, third/fourth play-off), semi-final 1988, quarter-final 1972, second round 1964, also qualified for finals tournament 1996, hosts 1968, 1980; **European Junior Championship/ European Youth Championship** (under-18) – 1958, runners-up 1986; **European Under-16 Championship** – 1982 (the first tournament), runners-up 1986, 1993 (Italy's victory in 1987 was overturned when it was discovered that it had fielded over-age play-ers); **European Under-21 Championship** – 1992, 1994, runners-up 1986; **Under-17 World Championship** – qualified for first championship in 1985, fourth 1987 (1–2, v **Ivory Coast**, in Canada, third/fourth playoff), also qualified 1991, 1993; **World Youth Cup (under-20)** – qualified for first champi-onship in 1977, quarter-final 1987, also qualified 1981. *Record against British and Irish national teams* v England, played 20, won seven, drawn six, lost seven; v **Northern Ireland**, played five, won three, drawn one, lost one; v **Scotland**, played six, won four, drawn one, lost one; v **Wales**, played five, won four, drawn none, lost one; v **Republic of Ireland**, played eight, won seven, drawn none, lost one. *History* A rudimentary form of football, **harpastum**, was played in ancient Rome: two opposing teams would attempt to take the ball over the opposition's line. An even rougher early form of foot-ball, **giuoco del calcio Fiorentino**, was played in the 16th century in Florence where crowds fought for pos-session of a ball, or as some accounts claim, a severed head. A slightly more refined version was played by the Italian upper classes – traditionally between the Christian festivals of Epiphany and Lent. The principal aim was to score by throwing the ball over a certain fixed point marked on the edge of the field. Modern football was introduced by English merchant traders in the mid to late 19th century, although its introduction to Turin is attrib-uted to Edoardo Bisio, an Italian businessman. The ear-liest clubs were formed in the 1880 and 1890s, includ-ing: **Palestra Ginnastica Libertas** (formed in 1887; merged with **Club Sportivo Firenze** in 1926 to form **Fiorentina**), Internazionale Torino (formed in 1890, became **Torino Calcio** after merger with FC Torinense), **Pro Vercelli** (founded in 1892) and **Genoa 1893** (formed in 1893 as the Genoa Football and Cricket Club). The "big three" of Italian football, **Juventus** (Turin), **AC Milan**, and **Internazionale** (also Milan) were founded in 1897, 1899 and 1908, respectively. The Federazione Italiana Giuoco Calcio was founded in 1898 and affiliated to FIFA in 1905. The national championship, the "Campionato Nazionale", was introduced in 1898, though only three games were played: Genoa beat Internazionale Torino in the "final" (2–1). Regional com-petitions operated in the early years, with the national championship determined by round-robin playoffs between the provincial winners. A national league was played in 1910 – the same year as the Italian national side played its first game (against France, above) – but regional competitions continued until 1929. By 1921, 18 regional leagues were in operation. A true national league, **Lega Calcio**, was formed in 1929. Club football grew in the 1930s with the new national league and with the enthusiastic support of Italy's dictatorial prime minister, Benito Mussolini. The influence of Mussolini's Fascist Government stretched even as far as the clubs' names: in 1929, Genoa 1893 was forced to changed its name to Genova 1893 – the English spelling of Genoa was disliked by the government – reverting to its original title in 1945. Similarly, Internazionale was known as **Ambrosiana-Inter** between 1929 and 1946, owing to the government's dislike of the Leninist connotations of its original name (the revised name came from St Ambrose, the fourth-century bishop of Milan). Internazionale won the first league championship in 1929-30 as Ambrosiana-Inter. The league resumed immediately after World War II but, in 1949, disaster struck Italy's then-leading club **Torino**. A plane transporting the team – including 10 members of the national side – from Lisbon crashed into the **Superga Hill** outside Turin. A drugs scandal rocked the domestic football scene in the 1962-63 season when the Italian football authorities docked three league points from league leaders Bologna, after five of its players allegedly tested positive during a routine drug test; the five were supposed to have taken amphetamines. The three-point penalty was subsequently overturned after medical evidence suggested that the alleged levels of amphetamine found in the urine samples would have been fatal. In the 1950s and 1960s many star players from overseas, particularly from South America, Denmark and Sweden, joined the top Italian clubs. At the same time, however, the national side was seen to be under-achieving and, in 1964, in an effort to improve the quality of Italian footballers, the country introduced a ban on signing foreign players (though existing foreigners were allowed to continue with their clubs). The ban lasted until 1980, after which Serie A flourished with huge financial backing and a new influx of foreign stars, including Marco **Van Basten**, Ruud **Gullit**, Diego **Maradona** and Michel **Platini**. Maradona's influence helped **Napoli** win Serie A for the first time in 1987 – the first time that the championship had travelled south of Rome on mainland Italy (Sardinian club Cagliari had won in 1970 – the only time the title has left the mainland). Napoli completed an Italian league and Cup double in 1987 and won the championship again in 1990. By 1997, Serie A had picked up 14 **European Footballer of the Year** awards – far more than the national leagues of Germany (nine), Spain (seven) and England (four). The national champion wears a championship shield, the **Scudetto**, on its shirts for the following season (the championship is informally called the Scudetto). A club that wins the championship 10 times is granted the right to wear a gold star above its club badge: an honour granted to the big three clubs, Juventus, AC Milan and Internazionale.

Juventus now has the right to wear two stars following a league title. Juventus holds the Italian league record of five consecutive league titles (1931 to 1935). The feat was matched by Torino (1943, 1946-49), though its run was punctuated by **World War II**). Italian clubs dominated European club tournaments in the 1990s and, together, have appeared in more **European Cup**, **UEFA Cup/Fairs Cup** and **European Cup-winners Cup** finals than clubs from any other country (48 finals, ahead of Spanish clubs with 41, and English clubs with 38: by 1998, however, English clubs had won 25 cups, Italian clubs 24, and Spanish clubs 23). Juventus appeared in three consecutive European Cup finals between 1996 and 1998, winning the first (1–1, 4–2 pens. v **Ajax**) but losing in 1997 (1–3 v **Borussia Dortmund**) and 1998 (0–1 v **Real Madrid**) – thus becoming the first club to lose two consecutive finals. AC Milan has won 13 international club competitions (including three **World Club Cup**s and three **European Super Cup**s) – more than any other club in Europe (two more than Ajax). Italy is the only European country whose clubs won all three premier European club competition in a single season: in 1990, AC Milan won the European Cup, **Sampdoria** the European Cup-winners Cup, and Juventus the UEFA Cup. At international level, the country has been very successful, perhaps on a par with Argentina, and lagging only behind Brazil and Germany. Italy has won the World Cup three times, winning at its first attempt in 1934, and has appeared in five finals (see records, above). Italy's triumph in 1934 also was the only occasion that the host country has had to qualify for the finals tournament (it played a single match against Greece, winning 7–0). In the final it beat Czechoslovakia 3–1 in front of 55,000 spectators at the PNF stadium, Rome. Orsi scored an 81st-minute equaliser for Italy, with Schiavio scoring the winner in extra time (95 minutes). Italy has failed to qualify for the finals tournament only once (1958) since it first entered the tournament and, with the exception of a second-round defeat in 1986, has either finished in the top four or has been eliminated in the first round (as has happened in five tournaments). Luigi Di Biagio scored Italy's 100th World Cup finals goal in the 3–0 defeat of **Cameroon** in the 1998 tournament (17 June, in Montpellier, France, first round). Surprisingly, Italy has won the European Championship only once, in 1968. The national side's low point was in 1982-83 when it failed to qualify for the 1984 European Championship finals, finishing a distant fourth behind **Romania**, **Sweden** and **Czechoslovakia**, and just three points ahead of **Cyprus**; it won only one of its qualifying games (3–1, v Cyprus, in Perugia), lost four and drew three (including a 1–1 draw v Cyprus in Limassol). The Italian Women's side has not matched the success of the men, but was runner-up in the 1993 European Championship for Women, and reached the quarter finals of the first Women's World Cup in 1991. It was the first European nation to qualify for the Women's World Cup in 1999. *World Cup performance* (finals and qualifiers to end of 1998 tournament) played 124, won 79, drawn 28, lost

17, scored 234 goals, conceded 91 goals. win rate: 64%; goals scored per game: 1.89. *League system* Italy's premier division, Lega Calcio Serie A, has 18 clubs, playing each other twice (home and away) in a season. Three points are awarded for a victory, with one for a draw: final positions for clubs level on points are determined by **goal difference**. The bottom three clubs are automatically relegated, while the fourth relegation place is determined by a **playoff** (spareggio) between the 14th and 15th placed club at a neutral venue. Twenty clubs compete in Serie B, with the top four clubs automatically promoted to Serie A, and the bottom four automatically relegated to Serie C1 (there is no playoff). Serie C1 is divided into two regional divisions of 18 clubs (Girone A and B). The four clubs promoted to Serie B are decided as follows: the two divisional champions are promoted automatically, with one further place in each division decided by a playoff series between the second-, third-, fourth- and fifth-placed clubs. Below Serie C1 is the Serie C2, comprising three regional divisions. *World Cup final teams and scorers* 1934 Combi (goalkeeper), Monzeglio, Allemandi, Ferraris, Monti, Bertolini, Guaita, Meazza, Schiavio (1), Ferrari. Orsi (1); 1938 Olivieri (goalkeeper), Foni, Rava, Serantoni. Andreolo, Locatelli, Biavati, Meazza, Piola (2), Ferrari, Colaussi (2); 1970 (runners-up): Albertosi (goalkeeper), Burgnich, Cera, Rosato, Facchetti, Bertini (Juliano), Mazzola, De Sisti, Domenghini, Boninsegna (1) (Rivera), Riva; 1982 Zoff (goalkeeper), Cabrini, Scirea, Gentile, Collovati, Oriali, Bergomi, Tardelli (1), Conti, Rossi (1), Graziani (Altobelli (1) (Causio)); 1994 (runners-up): Pagliuca (goalkeeper), Mussi (Apolloni), Maldini, Baresi, Benarrivo, Donadoni, Albertini, D Baggio (Evani), Berti, R Baggio, Massaro. *European Championship winning team and scorers* 1968 Zoff (goalkeeper), Burgnich, Guarneri, Facchetti, Ferrini, Castano, Domenghini (1), Juliano. Anastasi, Lodetti, Prati; replay: Zoff, Burgnich, Guarneri, Facchetti, Rosato, Salvadore, Domenghini, Mazzola, Anastasi (1), De Sisti, Riva (1). *Record in international club tournaments (winners and runners-up only)* World Club Cup – Internazionale (1964, 1965), AC Milan (1969, 1989, 1990, 1958, 1993, 1995), Juventus (1985, 1996); European Cup – AC Milan (1963, 1969, 1989, 1990, 1994, runners-up 1995), Internazionale (1964, 1965, runners-up 1967, 1972), Juventus (1985, 1996, runners-up 1973, 1983, 1997, 1998), Fiorentina (runners-up 1957), **Roma (AS)** (runners-up 1984), Sampdoria (runners-up 1992); European Cup-winners Cup – Fiorentina (1961, runners-up 1961), Juventus (1984), AC Milan 1968, 1973, runners-up 1974), Sampdoria (1990, runners-up 1989), **Parma** (1993, runners-up 1994); UEFA Cup/Fairs Cup – Roma (1961, runners-up 1991), Juventus (1977, 1990, 1993, runners-up 1965, 1971, 1995), Napoli (1989), Internazionale (1991, 1994, 1998, runners-up 1997), Parma (1995 finalist 1999), Fiorentina (runners-up 1990), Torino (runners-up 1992), **Lazio** (runners-up 1998); European Super Cup – Juventus (1984, 1997), AC Milan (1989, 1990, 1994), Parma (1993); **Mitropa Cup** – Bologna (1932, 1934),

Fiorentina (1966), Udinese (1980), AC Milan (1982), Pisa (1986), Bari (1990), Torino (1991), Internazionale (playing as Ambrosiana-Inter, runners-up 1933), Lazio (runners-up 1937); **Anglo-Italian Cup** – Fiorentina (1974), Genoa 1893 (1996), Napoli (1975), Roma (1972). Other leading clubs: Venezia, Atalanta, Cagliari Calcio, Calcio, Perugia, Brescia, Piacenza, Palermo, Bari, Verona, Cremonese.

Italy, women *country/women* women's football in Italy is administered by the Federazione Italiana Giuoco Calcio Femminile, under the auspices of the Italian football association, the Federazione Italiana Giuoco Calcio, in Rome. *Dossier* First official international match: 22 February 1968, v **Czechoslovakia**, 2–0, in Viareggio. Most capped player: Carolina Morace (138 appearances, to 1997). *International tournament record* **Women's World Cup** – qualified for first tournament in 1991, quarter-final 1991, also qualified for finals tournament 1999; **European Championship for Women** – entered first tournament in 1984, runners-up 1993 (0–1, v **Norway, women**, in Cesena, Italy), semi-final 1984, semi-final/third 1987 (2–1, v **England, women**, in Norway, third/fourth playoff), semi-final/fourth 1989 (1–2, v **Sweden, women**, in West Germany, third/fourth playoff), 1991 (1–2, v Denmark, in Denmark, third/fourth playoff), quarter-final 1995, hosts 1993. *History* An Italian women's football association, the Federazione Italiana Calcio Femminile (FICF), in Viarregio, was founded in 1968. A schism in Italian women's football led to the formation of a second national body in 1970, the Federazione Femminile Italiana Giuoco Calcio (FFIGC), based in Rome. However, the FICF and the FFIGC united in 1972, to form the Federazione Femminile Italiana Unificate Autonome Giuoco Calcio: known from 1976 as the Federazione Italiana Giuoco Calcio Femminile (FIGCF). The FIGCF became an associate member of the national football association in 1980, with the association taking full control of women's football in 1986. The Italy-based **Federation of Independent European Female Football** (FIEFF) organised a European tournament in 1969: the host nation beat Denmark, women in the final (3–1, at the Stadio Comunale, Turin). Italy also hosted an FIEFF world tournament, the "Mundialito", in 1970 – it lost to Denmark in the final (0–2). Italy was host and runner-up in the 1993 European Championship for Women. The first FICF club championship was played in 1968, with a northern and southern division: Genoa won the first championship playoff against Roma. A national league of 14 clubs was established in 1971. By 1972, the league had grown to 46 clubs, playing in four regional leagues (the championship decided by a playoff between the regional champions). By 1995, there were an estimated 350 women's clubs, with around 11,000 registered players. *League system* Sixteen clubs compete in the national Serie A. There are three regional Serie B divisions. Leading clubs: Lazio, Verona Ginther, Zambelli Reggiana.

Ivory Coast (Côte d'Ivoire) *country CAF* republic in west Africa on the Gulf of Guinea, bordered by **Mali**, **Burkina Faso**, **Ghana**, **Liberia** and **Guinea**. Independence from **France** in 1960 (formerly part of French West Africa). Subsistence agriculture predominates. Area: 322,465 sq km (124,470 sq miles). Tropical, hot and humid climate, with two rainy seasons in the south. Population: 13,720,000 (1994 est.). Languages: French and at least 60 tribal languages and dialects. Capital: Yamoussoukro (replaced Abidjan as capital in 1983). *Dossier* Football association (Fédération Ivoirienne de Football, Abidjan), formed, affiliated to **FIFA**, and to **Confédération Africaine de Football** (CAF) in 1960, president Ousseynou Dieng. Season played from December to August. National stadium: Felix Houphouet-Boigny, Abidjan, capacity: 45,000. National strip: orange shirts, white shorts. Nickname of national team: the Elephants. First international game: 1962 v **Senegal** (1–1, in Senegal, friendly). Biggest victory: 6–0 v Mali (31 March 1985, in Abidjan, African Nations Cup qualifier) and 6–0 v **Botswana** (11 October 1992, in Abidjan, **World Cup** qualifier). Biggest defeat: 2–6, v **Ghana** (2 May 1971, in Abidjan, friendly). *International tournament record* **Olympic Games** – never qualified for finals tournament; **Women's World Cup** – never qualified; World Cup – first entered 1974, never qualified for finals tournament, third (penultimate) qualifying round 1974, 1978, final qualifying group 1994 (lost out to Nigeria on goal difference for a place in the 1994 finals); **African Cup of Nations** – 1992, quarter-final 1998; **African Under-20 Youth Championship** – third place 1997 (2–0, v Ghana, in Morocco, third/fourth playoff); **Afro-Asian Nation's Cup** – runners up 1993 (0–1, v **Japan**, in Tokyo); **Confederations Cup** – fourth 1992 (2–5, v **United States of America**, third/fourth playoff, in Riyadh, Saudi Arabia); **Under-17 World Championship** – semi-final/third 1987 (2–1, v **Italy**, in Canada, third/fourth playoff); **World Youth Cup** (under-20) – qualified for finals tournament 1977, 1983, 1991, 1997 (never beyond first round). *Record against British and Irish national teams* none played. *History* Football was introduced by French and British workers. The earliest clubs, **Stella Abidjan**, **Africa Sports Nationale** and **Stade Abidjan**, were all founded in 1936, in Abidjan. **ASEC Mimosas Abidjan** was founded in 1948. The "big four" clubs have dominated the national league and cup competitions, which began in 1960, the year of independence. ASEC holds the world record of 108 consecutive league games without defeat (1988 to 19 June 1994). The Ivory Coast Super Cup (Coupe Houphouët-Boigny) has been played since 1975. Internationally, the Ivory Coast's greatest achievement was winning the 1992 African Cup of Nations. Ivory Coast clubs have won the **African Cup of Champion Clubs** and the **CAF Cup**. *League system* The national league comprises two regional First Divisions of eight clubs. The top three clubs from each of the regional divisions compete in a second-stage "Super Division", playing each club at home and away. The national champions are the winners of the Super Division. Three points are awarded for a victory, with one for a draw: final positions for clubs level on points are determined by **goal difference**. The bottom club in each of the regional First Divisions is relegated automatically to one of the two regional Second Divisions. The winners of the two regional Second Divisions are automatically promoted. A third promotion/relegation place is decided by a playoff tournament involving the two seventh-placed clubs in each of the First Divisions and the second placed clubs in the Second Divisions. *Record in international club tournaments* African Cup of Champion Clubs – Stade Abidjan (1966), ASEC Mimosas Abidjan (1998, runners-up 1995, semi finals 1971, 1976 and 1993), Africa Sports Nationale (runners-up 1986); **African Cup-winners Cup** – Africa Sports Nationale (1992, 1993, semi-final 1998), Stella Abidjan (runners-up 1975), ASEC Mimosas Abidjan (semi-finals 1983), SO de l'Armee (quarter-final 1997); CAF Cup – Stella Abidjan – (1993); **African Super Cup** – Africa Sports Nationale (1992); ASEC Minosas Abidjan (1998-99); **West African Football Union General Eyadema Cup** – Stade Abidjan (1977), Stella Abidjan (1981, runners-up 1987), Africa Sports Nationale (1985, 1986, 1991, runners-up 1995), ASEC Mimosas Abidjan (1990); French West African Cup – Africa Sports Nationale (1958). Notable international players: Laurent **Pokou**, Abdoulaye **Traoré**.

Iwuanyanwu Nationale *club* Nigerian national league club based in Owerri, founded 1972 (as Spartan Owerri). Ground: Dan Anyian, capacity: 25,000. Strip: red shirts, white shorts. In 1994, two Iwuanyanwu players were killed in an air crash in Algeria (returning from an **African Cup of Champion Clubs** match in Tunisia). African Cup of Champion Clubs runners-up 1988 (1–4 agg., v **Entente Setif** of Algeria), semi-final 1990; Nigerian league champions 1987, 1988, 1989, 1990, 1993; Nigerian FA Challenge Cup 1988. Notable former player: Nwankwo **Kanu**.

J

JS Kabylie *club* (Jeunesse Sportive de Kabylie, JSK, formerly **JE Tizi-Ouzou** and JS Kawkabi). Algerian national league fclub, basedin Tizi-Ouzou, founded 1946. Ground: 1 Novembre, capacity: 35,000. Strip: yellow shirts, green shorts. **African Cup of Champion Clubs** winners 1981 (5–0 agg., v **AS Vita Club Kinshasa** of Zaire), and 1990 (1–1 agg., 5–3 pens., v **Nkana Red Devils** of Zambia), semi-final 1996; **African Cup-winners Cup** 1995 (3–2 agg., v **Julius Berger** of Nigeria), quarter-final 1993; **Arab Club Champions Cup** semi-final 1994; Algerian National League champions 1973, 1974, 1977, 1980, 1982, 1983, 1985, 1986, 1989, 1990, 1995; Algerian Cup 1977, 1986, 1992, 1994.

J-League *competition* Japan Professional Football League, founded in 1991. *History* The league was set up by the former Japan Soccer League (JSL) with the Football Association of Japan (FAJ) in order to reinvigorate Japanese football. A working party was set up in 1988 with the blueprint announced in 1990. Twenty business consortia expressed an interest in the proposed professional league and, in February 1991, the FAJ announced that 10 clubs would participate in the new Japan Professional Football League, the "J-League". The 10 founding clubs were under the control of the J-League. The league got under way on 15 May 1993, though the J-League Cup started the previous September. The league increased to 12 clubs by 1994, 14 for the start of the 1995 season, 16 by 1996 and 17 by 1997. A second division was established in 1999 with the First Division reduced to 16 clubs. Relegation **playoffs** were introduced in 1998 as part of the establishment of the second tier. The clubs are all linked to former JSL clubs, and owned by major Japanese businesses. For example, **Jubilo Iwata** was set up by the Yamaha Corporation, Shizuoka Shimbun and the Shizuoka Broadcasting System, **Urawa Red Diamonds** was established by Mitsubishi Motors, while **Nagoya Grampus Eight** was set up by a consortium of 20 local companies. *League system* Sixteen clubs compete in the J-League, playing each other at home and away. Three points are awarded for a normal-time win (ie at 90 minutes); two points for a **golden goal** win in extra-time, and one point for a draw after extra time (penalty shoot-outs were abolished for league matches at the end of the 1998 season). If clubs are level on points, they are separated by **goal difference** and, if necessary, by **goals scored**.

Jablah *club* Syrian national league club based in the port of Jablah. Syrian league champions 1987, 1988, 1989.

Jack, David *player* Inside-forward. **England** international (9 caps). Born 3 April 1899. Career ca. 1916–1934. *Clubs* **Plymouth Argyle, Bolton Wanderers, Arsenal.** *Keynotes* One of three brothers (Donald and Robert being the others) who played for Plymouth in 1920 and for Bolton Wanderers in 1923. Their father Bob Jack had earlier played for Bolton and was manager of Plymouth between 1910 and 1938. Jack scored in both of his victorious FA Cup final appearances for Bolton, including the first goal in a **Wembley** final (1923 2–0 v **West Ham United**). He was the subject of the first five-figure transfer fee when he moved from Bolton to Arsenal for £10,890 in October 1928. Included in the **Football League Centenary 100 players**. *Honours* League Championship (Arsenal 1930-31, 1932-33, 1933-34); **FA Cup** (Bolton Wanderers 1923, 1926; Arsenal 1930).

jackpot *n.* in **pools** betting, when the pool is shared by few winning entrants and the **dividend** is consequently large. In most pools systems this occurs when there are around eight score-draws on the coupon.

Jairzinho, *player* Real name Jair Ventura Filho. Striker. **Brazil** international (87 caps, 38 goals, 1963-82). Born 25 December 1944. Career ca. 1960-82. *Clubs* **Botafogo, Olympique de Marseilles, Cruzeiro, Portuguesa FC.** *Keynotes* Jairzinho is the only player to have scored in all six games on the way to winning a World Cup final; despite this feat, he was only second-highest goalscorer in the 1970 finals, with seven goals (three behind Gerd **Müller**). Jairzinho was noted for his swerving free kicks. *Honours* **World Cup** (Brazil, 1974; **Copa Libertadores** (Cruzeiro, 1976).

Jamaica *country* CONCACAF Commonwealth state. Island in the Greater Antilles chain of the Caribbean, south of **Cuba** and west of **Haiti**. Self governing from 1944, full independence from Britain in 1962. Area: 11,425 sq km (4,410 sq miles). Population: 2,500,000 (1995 est.). Languages: English and patois. Capital: Kingston. *Dossier* Jamaica Football Confederation

(Kingston) formed in 1910, affiliated to **FIFA** in 1962 and **Confederación Norte-Centroamericana y del Caribe de Fútbol (CONCACAF)** in 1963, president: Captain Horace Burrell; general secretary: Horace Reid. Season played from August to April. National stadium: National Stadium, Kingston, capacity: 33,000. National strip: gold shirts, black shorts and gold socks. Website: *http://www.uwimona.edu.jm/sports/football/jff.html* (official). Nickname: Reggae Boyz. Most capped players (these are unofficial records and include national team games against club sides) Warren Barrett (112 appearances), Durrant Brown (111 appearances), Linval Dixon (92 appearances). Other notable international players: Deon Burton (of **Derby County**), Robbie **Earle**, Marcus Gayle (both of **Wimbledon**), Frank Sinclair (of **Chelsea** and **Leicester City**). *International tournament record* **Olympic Games** – never qualified for finals tournament; **Women's World Cup** – entered first tournament in 1991, never qualified for finals tournament; **World Cup** – first entered 1966, qualified for finals tournament 1998; **Caribbean Nations Cup** – winners 1991 (2–0, v **Trinidad and Tobago**, in Jamaica), 1998 (2–1, v Trinidad and Tobago, in Trindad); runners-up 1992 (0–2,v Trinidad and Tobago, in Trinidad), 1993 (0–0, 5–6 pens., v **Martinique**, in Jamaica), third 1996 (4–1, v **Grenada**, third/fourth playoff); **CONCACAF Championship** – entered first CONCACAF Championship 1963, **CONCACAF Women's Championship** – entered first tournament in 1991, did not win a game in either of its first two qualifying group tournaments (1991, 1994), did not enter 1998; **Gold Cup** – semi-final/fourth 1993 (1–1 v **Costa Rica**, in Mexico City, third/fourth playoff), 1998 (0–1 v **Brazil**, in Los Angeles, USA, third/fourth playoff); **Under-17 World Championship** – never qualified; **World Youth Cup** (under-20) – never qualified. *World Cup performance* (finals and qualifiers to end of 1998 tournament) played 51, won 20, drawn 12, lost 19, scored 54 goals, conceded 79 goals; win rate 39%; goals scored per game 1.06. *Record against British and Irish national teams* v **Wales**, played one, drawn one. *History* Football in Jamaica dates back to the 19th century; the football association was founded in 1910. Jamaica won the Caribbean Nations Cup in 1991 and again in 1998, and has twice finished fourth in the Gold Cup. In qualifying for the 1998 World Cup finals, Jamaica became the first English-speaking Caribbean nation to progress beyond the qualifying stages, and the first Caribbean nation since Haiti in 1974. Robbie Earle was the first player to score for Jamaica in a World Cup finals match (v **Croatia**, 14 June 1998). The 1998 World Cup squad was coached by a Brazilian, Rene Simoes. The father of **England** international player John **Barnes** captained Jamaica in the 1950s (Barnes junior played 79 times for England 1983-96). *League system* Sixteen clubs compete in the national first division. The leading eight clubs after the first stage of the season qualify for a championship league tournament, culminating in two-leg semi-finals and a two-leg final.

The bottom eight clubs play off in a relegation tournament. *Record in international club tournaments* **Caribbean Club Championship – Waterhouse** (semi-final 1998). Other leading clubs: **Hazard United**, **Reno FC**, **Santos**, **Seba United**, Tivoli Gardens (of Kingston, league champions 1983), **Violet Kickers**, **Whadadah**.

James, Alex *player* Inside-forward. Scottish international (33 caps, 8 goals). Born 14 September 1901. Career ca. 1922-1937. *Clubs* **Raith Rovers**, **Preston North End**, **Arsenal**. *Keynotes* Known as the "Wee wizard" due to being only 5ft 6ins tall – a reason why **Heart of Midlothian** turned him down early in his career. James scored the first of Arsenal's two goals in the club's 1930 FA Cup final victory (v **Huddersfield Town**), having joined the club for £8,750 from Preston in June 1929. Included in the **Football League Centenary 100 players**. *Honours* League Championship (Arsenal 1930-31, 1932-33, 1933-34, 1934-35); **FA Cup** (Arsenal 1930, 1936).

Japan *country AFC* Constitutional monarchy. Group of islands in east Asia in the north Pacific, the largest being Hokkaido, Honshu, Kyushu and Shikoku, stretching over 1,600 km. Wealthy nation following economic recovery after World War II. Area: 369,700 sq km (142,705 sq miles). Population: 125,570,000 (1995 census). Language: Japanese. Capital: Tokyo. *Dossier* The Football Association of Japan (Tokyo) formed in 1921 affiliated to **FIFA** in 1929 and founder member of **Asian Football Confederation** (AFC) in 1954, president: Ken Naganuma; general secretary: Junji Ogura. Season played from March to December. National stadium: National Stadium, Tokyo, capacity: 62,000. National strip: blue shirts, white shorts and blue socks. Website: *www.jfa.or.jp/html/jfa_e.htm* Most capped players: Masami **Ihara** (121 appearances, 1988-). Leading goalscorers: Kunishige Kamamoto (51 goals in 59 games, 1964-77, Kazuyoshi Miura (54 goals in 86 games, 1990-). Other notable international player: Hidetoshi **Nakata**. *International tournament record* **Olympic Games** – first entered 1936 (quarter-final), third/bronze medal 1968 (2–0, v **Mexico**, in Mexico City, third/fourth playoff), also qualified for finals tournament 1956, 1964 (hosts), 1996; **World Cup** – first entered 1954, qualified for finals tournament 1998, reached final stage of qualifying tournament in 1986, co-hosts (with **South Korea**) 2002; **Afro-Asian Nations Cup** – winners 1993 (1–0, v **Ivory Coast**, in Tokyo); **Asian Cup of Nations** – first entered 1968, 1992 (1–0, v **Saudi Arabia**, in Hiroshima, Japan), also qualified for finals tournament 1988, 1996, hosts 1992; **Asian Games** – entered first tournament in 1951, semi-final/third 1966 (2–0, v **Singapore**, in Bangkok, Thailand, third/fourth playoff), semi-final/fourth 1970 (0–1, v **India**, in Bangkok, third/fourth playoff), semi-final 1951 (2–3 v **Iran**, in New Delhi, India), quarter-final 1982, 1990, 1994, hosts 1958, 1994, second round 1998; **Asian Under-16 Championship** – winners 1994; **Copa America** – guest nation 1999;

Dynasty Cup – entered first tournament in 1990, winners 1992 (2–2, 6–4 pens., v South Korea), 1995 (2–2, 5–3 pens., v South Korea); **Under-17 World Championship** – quarter-final 1993; Asian Youth Cup – runners-up 1998; **World Youth Cup** (under-20) – runner-up 1999 (0-4, v Spain, in Lagos, Nigeria); **Women's World Cup/Asian Women's Championship/Olympic Games** (women) – see **Japan, women**. *World Cup performance* (finals and qualifiers to end of 1998 tournament) played 64, won 28, drawn 16, lost 20, scored 125 goals, conceded 58 goals; win rate: 44%; goals scored per game: 1.95. *Record against British and Irish national teams* v **England**, played one, lost one; v **Scotland**, played one, drawn one; v **Wales**, played one, lost one. *History* A rudimentary form of football, kenari, was played in Japan from the fifth century. The modern game has been long-established in Japan, with the Football Association of Japan founded in 1921. An "English FA Cup" was played from 1921 (first won by Tokyo FC) until the outbreak of World War II. It was replaced by the Emperor's Cup from 1946. Japan has had a national league since 1965. However, in 1988, the former Japan Soccer League and the Football Association of Japan (FAJ) set up a study group to consider ways to revitalise domestic football. In 1990, the JFA announced a blueprint for a professional league: the Japan Professional Football League (the **J-League**). Ten clubs started the first J-League season on 15 May 1993. By 1997, the league had increased in size to 17 clubs. A second division was introduced in 1999 while the First Division was reduced to 16 clubs. The Japan Soccer League Cup was introduced in 1976, becoming the J-League Cup in 1992. **JEF United Ichihara** (as JR East Furukawa Football Club) and **Verdy Kawasaki** (as Yomiuri Nippon) have both won the **Asian Champion Teams Cup**. Three clubs, **Bellmare Hiratsuka**, **Yokohama Marinos** (as Nissan FC) and **Yokohama Flugels** have won the **Asian Cup-winners Cup**. Japan won the Asian Cup of Nations in 1992 and was bronze medalist at the 1968 Olympic Games. Japan qualified for the World Cup finals for the first time in 1998, losing its first game 0–1 against **Argentina**. Japan is scheduled to co-host, with South Korea, the World Cup finals in 2002. At the 1996 Olympic Games in Atlanta, USA, Japan's under-23 side beat **Brazil** 1–0. Japan was the guest nation at the 1999 Copa America (the South American Championship). The under-20 team was runner-up at the 1999 World Youth Cup in Nigeria; losing 0-4 in the final against Spain. *League system* Sixteen clubs compete in the J-League, playing each other at home and away. Three points are awarded for a normal-time win (ie at 90 minutes); two points for a **golden goal** win in extra time, and one point for a draw after extra time (penalty shoot-outs were abolished for league matches at the end of the 1998 season). If clubs are level on points, they are separated by **goal difference** and, if necessary, by **goals scored**. *Record in international club tournaments* Asian Champion Teams Cup – JEF United (winners 1987, as JR East Furukawa Football Club), Verdy Kawasaki (winners 1988, as Yomiuri Nippon, semi-final/third 1993, semi-final/fourth 1992, quarter-final 1998), **Jubilo Iwata** (winners 1999), Yokohama Marinos (runners-up 1989, as Nissan FC, quarter-final 1997), **Sanfrecce Hiroshoma FC** (semi final/third 1968), **Kashima Antlers** (quarter-final 1998); Asian Cup-winners Cup – Bellmare Hiratsuka (winners 1996, quarter-final 1997), Yokohama Marinos (winners 1992, 1993, as Nissan FC, semi-final 1994), Yokohama Flugels (winners 1995, semi-final 1996); **Nagoya Grampus Eight** (runners-up 1997), Kashima Antlers (fourth 1999), Verdy Kawasaki (quarter-final 1998); **Asian Super Cup** – Yokohama Flugels (winners 1995). Other leading clubs: **Urawa Red Diamonds**, **Kashiwa Reysol**, **Shimizu S-Pulse**.

Japan, women   *misc.*   Women's football in Japan is governed by the Football Association of Japan, based in Tokyo. *Dossier* First international match: 1981, v **Taiwan** (0–1, **Asian Women's Championship**). *International tournament record* **Olympic Games** (women) – played in the first tournament in 1996 (first round, Atlanta, USA); **Women's World Cup** – entered first tournament 1991, qualified for finals tournament 1991, 1995, failed to progress beyond first-round group stage in either year; **Asian Games** (women) – 1998 third place (2–1, v **Taiwan**, in Thailand, third/fourth playoff); **Asian Women's Championship** – first entered 1981, runners-up 1986 (0–2, v **China**, **women**, in Hong Kong), 1991 (0–5, v China, **women**, in Fukuoka, Japan), 1995 (0–2, v China, in Malaysia), hosts 1991. *History* Japan was the first country in the world to establish a national women's full-time professional league, founded in 1992; the original national championship was founded in 1980, with 16 clubs. By 1996, there were around 1,000 women's clubs in Japan, with 20,000 registered players.

JD Sports Cup   *competition*   four-team pre-season tournament staged at **Middlesbrough**'s **Riverside Stadium** in August 1998. Aside from Boro, the tournament also involved **Benfica**, Empoli and **Newcastle United**. Benfica won (1–1, 7–6 pens. v Empoli).

JE Tizi-Ouzou (Jeunese Electronique) *club* former name (1977-89) of Algerian club **J S Kabylie**. Sponsored by Algeria's national electricity company.

JEF United Ichihara   *club*   Japanese **J-League** club based in Urayasu, formerly JR East Furukawa Football Club (1946-91). Ground: Ichihara Stadium, capacity: 15,400. Strip: yellow shirts, green shorts. **Asian Champion Teams Cup** 1986 (as Furukawa, finished first in a four-team final tournament in Riyadh, Saudi Arabia); Japanese National League champions 1985, 1986; Emperor's Cup 1977; Japanese League Cup 1977, 1982, 1986.

Jennings,   Pat *player* Goalkeeper.   **Northern Ireland** international (119 caps). Born 12 June 1945. Career ca. 1960-86. *Clubs* Newry Town, **Watford**, **Tottenham Hotspur**, **Arsenal**. *Keynotes* Joined Watford from Newry Town for £6,000 in 1963, moving to

Tottenham Hotspur for £27,000 a year later. Jennings made 472 **Football League** appearances for Spurs before departing to north-London rivals Arsenal for £45,000 in 1977. He played 237 League matches for Arsenal, and appeared in three successive FA Cup finals gaining a second winner's medal. Jennings was the first UK player to make 1,000 first-class appearances: he played his first match for Watford in May 1963 and his 1,000th for Arsenal in February 1983. Retired from playing after Northern Ireland's participation in the 1986 **World Cup**, where Jennings won his 119th and final international cap (v **Brazil**) on 12 June – his 41st birthday. Voted **Footballer of the Year** in 1973 and **PFA Footballer of the Year** in 1976. Famously scored for Tottenham in the 1967 **Charity Shield** match against Manchester United; his clearance beat Alex Stepney in the opposing goal. Included in the **Football League Centenary 100 players**. Honours **FA Cup** (Tottenham Hotspur 1967; Arsenal 1979); **League Cup** (Tottenham Hotspur 1971, 1973); **UEFA Cup** (Tottenham Hotspur 1972).

Jersey country the largest of the **Channel Islands**, a British Crown dependency. Area: 117 sq km (45 sq miles). Population: 80,000. Capital: St Hélier. Dossier/History/Leading clubs see **Channel Islands**, **Upton Park Cup**.

jersey n. another name for **shirt.**

Jeunesse d'Esch (AS La Jeunesse d'Esch) club Luxembourg's most successful national league club, based in Esch-sur-Alzette, founded 1907. Ground: De la Frontiere, capacity: 7,000. Strip: black and white striped shirts, white shorts. European Cup second round 1964; Luxembourg League Champions 1921, 1937, 1951, 1954, 1958, 1959, 1960, 1963, 1967, 1968, 1970, 1973, 1974, 1975, 1976, 1977, 1980, 1983, 1985, 1987, 1988, 1995, 1996, 1997, 1998; Luxembourg Cup 1935, 1937, 1946, 1954, 1973, 1974, 1976, 1981, 1988, 1997, 1999.

jewellery rules players are forbidden, under the **Laws of the game**, from wearing any kind of jewellery while taking part in a match (Law IV). Jewellery is considered to pose a hazard to the wearer and other players.

jockeying n. preventing an opponent from passing/shooting by closing down, restricting space and steering them to a weaker position.

Joe Public club Trinidad and Tobago league club. **CONCACAF Champions Cup** quarter-final 1998; **Caribbean Club Championship** winners 1998 (1–0, v Courts Caledonia AIA, also of Trinidad and Tobago); Trinidad and Tobago league runners-up 1997.

Johansson, Lennart official **Union of European Football Associations** president and **FIFA** vice-president. Born 5 November 1929. Johansson was elected UEFA president in 1990, having first been a member of the 1988 **European Championship** committee (1984-88) and then the UEFA executive committee (1988-90). Johansson, a Swedish national, was chairman of **AIK Stockholm** (1962-80), a board member of the Swedish Football League (1979-84) and later chairman of the Swedish Football Association (1984-91). He was also vice-chairman of the 1998 **World Cup** organising committee. Johansson is an **Arsenal** supporter and did much to help English clubs return to European competition following the ban imposed after the **Heysel Stadium disaster**.

Johnstone club former-Scottish league. Dossier Ground: Newfield Park, Renfrewshire. Keynotes Unconnected to **St Johnstone**, this club joined Scottish **Football League** Division Two in 1911-12. Johnstone finished fifth in its first League season, the club's highest position. After Divisions One and Two were re-formed in 1921-22, Johnstone rejoined the League before failing to gain re-election in 1924-25. League record Division Two 1911-12 to 1914-15, 1921-22 to 1924-25.

joint capsule medical the fibrous tissue that holds a **joint** together. Injury can occur if the fibres are **sprained**.

joint fracture medical broken **bone** where the fracture extends as far as the **cartilage** of a **joint**. Also known as fracture dislocation. This is a serious injury that will require hospital treatment.

joint medical the connection between two **bones**; the two bones are connected by **cartilage** so that they cannot be separated. Joints vary in flexibility, from the nearly fixed connections between bones of the skull, to the hinged joints of the ankle and elbow, the ball-and-socket joint of the hip and compound joint of the knee. Flexible or synovial joints contain synovial fluid inside a synovial membrane, which keep the joint lubricated, slightly separated (so that there is no direct bone-to-bone contact) and free to move. Cartilaginous joints – where the bones are kept rigidly in place, such as the pubic bones at the front of the pelvis – do not contain synovial fluid. Joints are susceptible to injury by heavy tackles and falls, or in goalkeepers' fingers, by being bent beyond their normal range by the force of a shot. See **dislocation**.

joker misc. French term to describe a player who joins a club during a season.

jolly misc. Italian term for a **utility player.**

Jomo Cosmos club South African national league club based in Johannesburg. Formerly the all-white club Highlands Park – franchise bought by former New York Cosmos player Jomo Sono in 1983. Sono remains the coach. Grounds: Tembisa, Rustenburg and Western Deep. Strip: navy blue shirts, navy blue shorts. **African Cup-winners Cup** semi-final 1993, quarter-final 1997; South Africa National Soccer League champions 1980 (as Highlands Park); South African Cup ("Super Bowl") 1990. Highlands Park were also winners of the former all-white **National Professional Football League** (NPFL) in 1960, 1962, 1964, 1965, 1966, 1968, 1975, 1977 (the last season of the NPFL) and NPFL Cup 1961, 1965, 1966, 1967, 1973, 1975, 1977 (the last NPFL Cup).

Jones, Cliff player Winger. **Wales** international (59 caps, 15 goals). Born 7 February 1935. Career ca. 1952-70.

Clubs **Swansea** Town, **Tottenham Hotspur**, **Fulham**. *Keynotes* Transferred to Tottenham from Swansea Town for a record £35,000 in 1958. Recovered from a broken leg to become a leading member of the club's 1960-61 **double** winning side. Scored 134 goals in 318 League matches for Spurs – a remarkable record for a winger. Included in the **Football League Centenary 100 players**. *Honours* League Championship (Tottenham Hotspur 1960-61); **FA Cup** (Tottenham Hotspur 1961, 1962); **European Cup-winners Cup** (Tottenham Hotspur 1963).

Jones, Cobi *player* Midfield. **United States of America** international (114 caps, eight goals 1992-). Born 16 June 1970. *Clubs* **Los Angeles Galaxy**. *Keynotes* Jones made his international debut on 3 September 1992 (2–0, v **Canada**) and is the second-most capped player in his country's history. He played in the United States' 1994 and 1998 **World Cup** finals teams.

Jong Colombia *club* Netherlands Antilles national league club based in the capital Willemstad on the island of Curacao. Strip: yellow shirts with blue sleeves and blue shorts. **CONCACAF Champions Cup** runners-up 1967 (3–5 agg., v **Alianza** of El Salvador in final replay) and 1979 (0–9 agg., v **Deportivo FAS** of El Salvador); **CONCACAF Cup-winners Cup** – semi-final/fourth 1995 (0–12, v **Marathon** of Honduras, in Miami, USA, third/fourth playoff).

Jordan *country AFC* Kingdom in southwest Asia, on the Gulf of Aqaba, bordered by **Syria**, **Iraq**, **Saudi Arabia** and **Israel**. Jordan is mostly desert, with temperatures rising to 49°C (120°F) in the east. Independence from Britain in 1946. Dispute with Israel since 1967 over Israeli-occupied West Bank territory – though in 1988 Jordan ceded responsibility for the claims over the area to the Palestine Liberation Organisation. Area: 90,650 sq km (35,000 sq miles). Population: 4,100,000 (1995 est.). Language: Arabic. Capital: Amman. *Dossier* Jordan Football Association formed in 1949, affiliated to **FIFA** in 1958 and **Asian Football Confederation** (AFC) in 1970, member of the **Arab Football Union**, president: HRH Prince Abdullah Al-Hussein; general secretary: Mohammed Hamdan. Season played from April to October. National stadium: International Stadium, Amman, capacity: 30,000. National strip: white and red shirts, white and red shorts and white and red socks. *International tournament record* **Olympic Games** – never qualified for finals tournament; **Women's World Cup** – never entered; **World Cup** – first entered 1986, never beyond first-round group stage of qualifying tournament; Arab Games – winners/gold medal 1997 (1–0, v Syria); **Asian Cup of Nations** – first entered 1984, never qualified for finals tournament; **Asian Games** – never entered; **Asian Women's Championship** – never entered; Pan-Arab Games – winners/gold medal 1997 (1–0, v Syria, in Beirut, Lebanon); **Under-17 World Championship** – never qualified; **World Youth Cup** (under-20) – never qualified. *Record against British and*

Irish national teams none played. *History* The Jordanian national league has been played since 1944. The Jordanian Cup was started in 1981. Domestic club football has been dominated by three clubs: **Al Faisaly**, **Wihdat FC** (Al Wahadat) and **Al Ramtha**. Al Faisaly has won the Jordan league championship 23 times, including a world record of 13 consecutive titles (159-66, 1970-74; the run interrupted by years in which the league was not played). Intense rivalry exists between Al Faisaly – an essentially ethnic Jordanian club – and Wihdat FC, the Palestinian club. Jordan's only international success was in winning the 1997 Pan-Arab Games. Jirius Tadras scored the winning goal in the final against Syria. *League system* Ten clubs play in the top-flight Premier Division, with 14 in Division One and 17 in Division Two. The bottom two clubs are relegated from the Premier Division. There is a regional Division Three, with 64 clubs playing at this level. *Record in international club tournaments* **Asian Champion Teams Cup** – Wihdat FC (finals tournament 1989); **Asian Cup-winners Cup** – Al Ramtha (semi final 1991); **Arab Cup-winners Cup** – Al Faisaly (runners-up 1996).

jorky-ball *n.* variant form of football played by only two players on each side. *Keynotes* The game is played in a 10 metres by five metres closed court, usually of transparent plastic walls, with a net roof. The goals are just one metre high and one metre wide. The ball is continually in play unless a goal is scored or a foul committed. The pitch is delineated by five lines: two goal area lines, one metre from each goal; a centre line and two "contact-area lines", one metre either side of the centre line. Goals can be scored from any point on the pitch, either directly or rebounded off the walls. Each side nominates an attacker and defender; the attacker can go anywhere on the pitch apart from the opponent's goal area, while the defender must stay in his/her own half. The game is played as the best of three sets, a set being won by the first team to score seven goals. A team must, however, be two clear goals ahead – unless the score reaches 9–9, at which point it is decided by "sudden death" (eg the first to score the 10th goal). The attacker and defender must swap roles for the second set, though if a third set is played the team may, once again, nominate the attacker. Players are not allowed to handle the ball in any position and must not stop the ball. The kick off is taken with all players in their own goal areas, and must cross the halfway line without bouncing. A penalty is awarded if a payer handles the ball – deliberately or not – and is taken from the middle of the contact-area line closest to the goal. Penalties are also awarded for deliberate fouls; in which case, the attacking team has three penalty attempts (though if a penalty is scored the remaining attempts are not used). Free kicks are awarded if the defender crosses the halfway line, if the ball is stopped, if the attacker enters the opposition goal area, if a player reverses into an opponent, or keeps the ball in the goal area for more than five seconds. Free kicks are taken by the attacker from the middle of the centre line. Jorky-ball is thought to have originated in Italy, becoming popular there and in Spain and France in the 1980s. Italy has a national championship. The first UK tournament was played in London's Spitalfields Market sport centre in February 1998. Also called two-a-side football.

Jubilee Fund *misc.* fund set up in 1937, initially timed to coincide with the 50th anniversary of the English **Football League** in 1938, to assist players and clubs at times of financial hardship. Early fund-raising included pre-season friendly matches played by all 88 Football League clubs. The fund was later bolstered by the donation of club fines and a share of the **Charity Shield** receipts. The fund remained active and, in 1979, was incorporated into the Footballers' Further Education Vocational Training Society, a trust run jointly by the **Professional Footballers Association** and the Football League.

Jubilo Iwata *club* Japanese **J-League** club based in Iwata, formerly Yamaha Motors Football Club (1972-92). Ground: Jubilo Iwata Stadium, capacity: 19,200. Strip: blue shirts and blue shorts. **Asian Champion Teams Cup** 1999; Japanese National League winners 1988; J-League champions 1997.

Julius Berger *club* Nigerian national league club based in Lagos, founded 1972. Ground: Onikan. Strip: green shirts, white shorts. **African Cup-winners Cup** runners-up 1995 (2–3 agg., v **JS Kabylie** of Algeria); Nigerian league champions 1991; Nigerian FA Challenge Cup Winners 1996. *Notable former player* Emmanuel **Amunike**.

jumping at an opponent *rules* one of the offences listed as a **foul** under the **Laws of the game** (Law XII). A player is guilty of a foul for jumping at an opponent carelessly, recklessly or with excessive force. The punishment for the offence is for the opposing team to be awarded a **direct free kick**, taken from the point where the foul was committed (unless within the opponents' **goal area**, in which case it is taken from anywhere within that area). If the foul is committed in the offending side's penalty area, then the opponents are awarded a **penalty kick**.

Juninho *player* **1.** Real name: Giulio Botelho. Striker. **Brazil** international. Born 1929 in São Paulo. *Clubs* **Portuguesa, Fiorentina**. *Honours:* Italian **Serie A** championship (Fiorentina, 1956).

junior football club *n.* **1. Scotland** A Scottish club that is outside the Scottish senior league system, and is a member of the **Scottish Junior Football Association**. Clubs are termed junior by league status rather than age (compare **Scottish Youth Football Association**); a description that dates back to the 19th century merely to distinguish major from minor clubs. Historically, junior clubs tended to be village sides, contrasting the city- and town-based clubs of the senior leagues; the distinction is less clear now. Compare senior football club. **2. England** Technically, the term junior football club also applies to adult football clubs at the lower levels of English football, though the expression is rarely used except in football administration.

Juventus Caribbean *club* Belize national league club based in Orange walk. In 1998-99, the club was renamed Juventus Pepsi. Belize league champions 1996, 1997, 1998, 1999.

Juventus *club* Italian league. *Dossier* Ground: **Delle Alpi** (Stadio), Turin, Piemonte. Strip: black and white striped shirts, white shorts,black socks. Website: *http://www.juventus.it/* Nickname: La Vecchia Signora (The Old Lady) or La Juve. Ground capacity: 71,012 all seated. Biggest win: 9–1 v **Internazionale** (1960-61, Serie A). Biggest defeat: 1–7 v **AC Milan** (1949-50, Serie A), 0–6 v Internazionale (1953-54, Serie A). *History* Formed in 1897 by pupils of the Massimo d'Azeglio Grammar School, the club took the name Football Club Juventus in 1899. Juventus has won the Italian League on more occasions than any other club, winning its first title in 1905. Former AC Milan player Giovanni **Trapattoni** became manager in 1977 and went on to win six Serie A titles in 10 years. Juve's 1985 **European Cup** success meant the club became the first in Europe to win all three major club competitions (three others, **Ajax, Barcelona** and **Bayern Munich**, have since achieved the same feat). The club moved to Stadio delle Alpi in 1990 and after Roberto Bettega's side won the **UEFA Cup** in 1993, Marcello Lippi took over as coach and, despite buying and selling star players with much regularity, created a series of formidable teams. Under Lippi, Juventus appeared in three consecutive European Cup finals 1996-1998, winning the first (1–1, 4–2 pens. v **Ajax**) but losing in 1997 (1–3 v **Borussia Dortmund**) and 1998 (0–1 v **Real Madrid**) – thus becoming the first club to lose two successive finals. Foreign players who have sported the black and white shirts of Juventus include Raimundo Orsi, Luisito Monti, John Hansen, Karl Præst, John **Charles**, Omar Sivori, Liam **Brady**, Michel **Platini**, Zbigniew **Boniek**, Jürgen Kohler, Andreas Möller, Zinedine **Zidane** and Alen Boksic. Domestic stars include Luigi Bertolini, Giovanni Ferrari, Giampiero **Boniperti**, Pietro Anastasi, Dino **Zoff**, Claudio Gentile, Marco Tardelli, Roberto **Baggio**, Gianluca **Vialli**, Fabrizio Ravanelli and Alessandro del Piero. *Honours* Italian League 1905 (league playoff), 1926 (12–1 agg. v Alba), 1930-31, 1931-32, 1932-33, 1934-35, 1949-50, 1951-52, 1959-60, 1960-61, 1966-67, 1971-72, 1972-73, 1974-75, 1976-77, 1977-78, 1980-81, 1981-82, 1983-84, 1985-86, 1994-95, 1996-97, 1997-98; Italian Cup 1938 (5–1 agg. v **Torino**), 1942 (4–1 agg. v AC Milan), 1959 (4–1 agg. v Internazionale), 1960 (3–2 v **Fiorentina**), 1965 (1–0 v Internazionale), 1979 (2–1 v Palermo), 1983 (3–2 agg. v Verona), 1990 (1–0 v Milan), 1995 (3–0 agg. v **Parma**); European Cup (including Champions League) 1985 (1–0 v **Liverpool**), 1996 (1–1, 4–2 pens. v Ajax); **European Cup-winners Cup** 1984 (2–1 v **Porto**); UEFA Cup 1977 (2–2 away goals v **Athletic Bilbao**), 1990 (3–1 agg. v Fiorentina), 1993 (6–1 agg. v Borussia Dortmund); **European Super Cup** 1984 (2–0 v Liverpool), 1997 (9–2 agg. v **Paris St Germain**);

World Club Championship1985 (2–2, 4–2 pens. v Asociacion Atlética **Argentinos Juniors**), 1996 (1–0 v Club Atlético **River Plate**).

Juventus FC *club*ⁱ Nicaraguan national league club, based in the capital Managua. Strip: red and white striped shirts and white shorts.

K

Kabwe Warriors *club* Zambian national league club based in Kabwe. Ground: Railways Stadium, capacity: 10,000. Strip: blue shirts, blue shorts. *Keynotes* Kabwe holds the record for the biggest victory in the **African Cup of Champion Clubs** (9–0, v Majanta Meseru of Lesotho, 1972, first round). **East and Central African Cup** semi-final 1981; Zambian league champions 1968, 1970, 1971, 1972, 1987; Zambian Cup 1982.

KAC Marrakesh (Kawkab Athletic Club) *club* Moroccan national league club based in Marrakesh. Ground: Harti, capacity: 20,000. Strip: red shirts and white shorts. **CAF Cup** 1996 (3–3 agg., won on away goals, v **ES Sahel** of Tunisia); Moroccan League champions 1958 and 1992; Moroccan Cup 1963, 1964, 1965, 1987 and 1993.

Kairat Alma-Ata *club* Kazakhstan national league club based in the capital Almaty (Kairat means "power"), founded 1954 (formerly Lokomotiv Almaty). Former-Soviet Union First Division club (24 years in the top flight). Ground: Central Respublikanski, capacity: 30,000. *Keynotes* Kairat Alma-Ata won the first Kazakhstan Cup, and won the trophy again in 1996; this time, however, after losing in the semi-final – original winners **Elimai Semipalatinsk** refused to accept the trophy. Kazakhstan league champions 1992; Kazakhstan Cup 1992, 1996 1997; twice winners of the "International Railway Union Cup" (a former-Eastern Europe competition for railway workers' clubs).

Kaiserslautern (1.FC) *club* German league. *Dossier* Ground: Fritz-Walter Stadion, Kaiserslautern Strip: red shirts with black trim, black shorts, red socks. Ground capacity: 38,500. *History* Formed in 1900. The club is officially called the First Club of Kaiserslautern. Between 1948 and 1955, Kaiserslautern won two West German titles (1951 and 1953) and reached the national **playoff** final on three other occasions: 1948 (1–2 v **Nuremberg** (1.FC)), 1954 (1–5 v Hannover 96) and 1955 3–4 v Rot-Weiss Essen). Prior to the club 's first (West) German Cup victory in 1990, it had reached the final four times: 1961 (0–2 v **Werder Bremen**), 1972 (0–5 v **Schalke 04**), 1976 (0–2 v **Hamburg SV**), 1981 (1–3 v **Eintracht Frankfurt**). The club's best performance in European club competition was achieved in the **European Cup** in 1991-92 when reaching the second round (1–5 agg. v **Barcelona**). Kaiserslautern won

the Second Division Championship and the **Bundesliga** title in consecutive seasons in 1996-97 and 1997-98. *Honours* West German League 1951 (2–1 v Preussen Munster), 1953 (4–1 v **Stuttgart** (VfB)); Bundesliga 1990-91, 1997-98; West German Cup 1990 (3–2 v Werder Bremen), 1996 (1–0 v Karlsruher).

Kaizer Chiefs *club* South African National Soccer League club based in Johannesburg, founded 1970. Ground: Johannesburg Stadium. Strip: gold shirts, black shorts. South Africa National Soccer League champions 1974, 1976, 1977, 1979, 1981, 1984, 1989, 1991, 1992; South African Cup ("Super Bowl") winners 1979, 1981, 1982, 1984, 1987, 1992; South African **Top Eight Cup** 1974, 1976, 1977, 1981, 1982, 1985, 1987, 1989, 1991, 1992, 1994.

Kaloum Star (Association Sportive) *club* Guinea national league club based in Conakry, formerly known as Conakry I. Ground: Cloah, capacity: 8,000. Strip: yellow shirts, green shorts. **African CAF Cup** runners-up 1995 (0–2 agg., v **ES Sahel** of Tunisia); **African Cup of Champion Clubs** semi-final 1970, 1981; Guinea league champions 1965, 1969, 1970, 1980, 1981, 1984, 1987, 1993, 1995, 1996, 1998; Guinea Cup 1985, 1997, 1998.

Kalumu (FC Kalumu) *club* Congo Democratic Republic (formerly Zaire) national league club based in Kinshasa. Ground: 20 Mai, capacity: 60,000. Zaire league champions 1985; Zaire Cup 1986, 1987, 1988, 1989.

Kampala City Council SC *club* Ugandan national league club based in the capital Kampala. Ground: Nakivubo, capacity: 20,000. Strip: yellow shirts, blue shorts. **African Cup-winners Cup** quarter-final 1985; **CAF Cup** semi-final 1997; **East and Central African Club Championship** winners 1978; Ugandan league champions 1976, 1977, 1978, 1981, 1983, 1985, 1986, 1991,1997; Ugandan Cup 1979, 1980, 1982, 1984, 1987, 1990, 1993.

Kansas City Wiz *club* United States football club and founder member of **Major League Soccer**, based in Kansas City, Missouri. Member of the league's **Western Conference**. Founded: 1996. Ground: Arrowhead Stadium, capacity: 79,000. Notable player: Mo Johnston.

Kanu, Nwankwo *player* Striker. **Nigeria** international (11 caps, 2 goals). Born 1 August 1976. *Clubs* Fed

Works, **Iwuanyanwu Nationale** (both of Nigeria), **Ajax, Internazionale, Arsenal**. *Honours* **Olympic Games** gold medal (Nigeria, 1996); **CAF Footballer of the Year** 1996.

Karabakh Agdam *club* Azerbaijan national league club, based in Agdam, founded 1986. Ground: Karabakh, capacity: 15,000. Azerbaijan League Champions 1993, 1997 (technically, the 1997 championship should have been awarded to **Neftchi Baku**, but the Azerbaijan football association awarded the championship to Karabakh by basing the title on junior league results as well as the national league; a decision not accepted by **UEFA**, which awarded the **European Cup** place to Neftchi Baku); Azerbaijan Cup 1993.

Karama *club* Syrian national league club based in Hims (Homs). Syrian league champions 1975, 1983, 1984, 1996.

Kareda Siauliai *club* Lithuanian national league club, founded in 1960 (as Siauliai-Sakalas), based in Siauliai. Ground: Zalgiris, capacity: 8,000. Lithuanian league champions 1997, 1998; Lithuanian Cup 1996.

Kashima Antlers *club* Japanese **J-League** club based in Kashima, formerly Sumitomo (until 1991). Ground: Kashima Soccer Stadium, capacity: 15,900. **Asian Champion Teams Cup** quarter-final 1998; Asian Cup-winners Cup fourth 1999; J League champions 1996, 1998. Notable former player: **Zico**.

Kashiwa Reysol *club* Japanese **J-League** club based in Kashiwa, formerly Hitachi (until 1992). Ground: Hitachi Kashiwa Stadium, capacity: 15,900. Japanese National League winners 1972; Emperor's Cup 1973, 1976; Japanese League Cup 1976.

Kazadi, Mwamba *player* Goalkeeper. Zaire (now **Congo Democratic Republic**) international. *Club* **Toute Puissant Mazembe**. *Honours* **African Cup of Nations** (Zaire, 1968, 1974); *France Football* **African Footballer of the Year** runner-up 1973.

Kazakhstan *country AFC* vast republic in north Asia on the Caspian and Aral Seas, bordered by the Russian Confederation, **China, Kyrgyzstan, Uzbekistan** and **Turkmenistan**; more than 10 times the size, by area, of the United Kingdom. Continental climate with hot summers. Kazakhstan became an autonomous republic within the **Soviet Union** in 1920 and a full Soviet republic in 1936. Anti-Russian riots in 1991 were followed by the setting up of an autonomous government. Joined **Commonwealth of Independent States** in 1991, with full independence in 1992. Area: 2,717,300 sq km (1,048,880 sq miles). Population: 16,500,000 (1996 est.). Languages: Kazakh and Russian. Capital: Alma-Ata. *Dossier* The Football Association of the Republic of Kazakhstan (Alma-Ata) formed in 1914 affiliated to **FIFA** and **Asian Football Confederation** (AFC) in 1994, president: Kuralbek Ordabaev; general secretary: Timur Segizbaev. Season played from April to November. National stadium: Central Stadium, Almaty, capacity: 30,000. National strip: yellow shirts, yellow shorts and yellow socks. Biggest victory: 7–0, v **Pakistan** (11 June 1997, in Lahore, Pakistan, World Cup qualifier). *International tournament record* **World Cup** – first entered 1998 (won its first-round qualifying group of three nations, with four out of four victories, scoring 15 goals and conceding only two; in the second round it finished last in its five-nation group); **Asian Cup of Nations** – first entered 1996 (last in its qualifying group); **Olympic Games** – first entered 1996 (reached final stage of the qualifying tournament); **Women's World Cup** – first entered 1999; **Asian Games** – first entered 1998 (second round); **World Youth Cup** (under-20) – qualified 1999; **Under-17 World Championship** – never qualified; **Asian Women's Championship** – first entered 1995. *Record against British and Irish national teams* none played. *History* There is a long history of organised football in Kazakhstan, with a football association established in 1914. One of the leading clubs, **Kairat Alma-Ata** (formerly known as Lokomotiv Almaty), competed in the former Soviet Union national league, with 24 years in the top flight. The club was also twice winners of the "International Railway Union Cup" (a former-Eastern Europe competition for railway workers' clubs). Kazakhstan national league and cup started in 1992. The Kazakhstan Cup final has been played since 1992; first won by Kairat Alma-Ata. The club won the Cup again in 1996, despite being eliminated in the semi-final. The actual winners **Elimai Semipalatinsk** (2–1, v Munaishi Aktau) refused to accept the trophy, as a protest against the Kazakhstan football authorities. The beaten semi-finalists, Kairat Alma-Ata and Vostok Ust-Kamenogorsk, were ordered to play a new final; Kairat Alma-Ata won 2–0. The independent Kazakhstan entered international competition in 1993. *League system* The national professional league has two divisions. Eighteen clubs compete in the Premier Division, playing each other twice in a season. Three points are awarded for a victory, with one for a draw; if two or more clubs are level on points, the one with the most victories is placed first; **goal difference** is used to separate clubs level on points and victories. Because the season overlaps with the Asian club tournaments, champions and cup winners from the previous year qualify for the **Asian Champion Teams Cup** and **Asian Cup-winners Cup**. *Record in international club tournaments* Asian Champion Teams Cup – **Taraz Dzhambul** (second round 1998); Asian Cup-winners Cup – Ordabassy (quarter-final 1997). Other leading clubs: **Irtysh Pavlodar** (formerly, Ansat Pavlodar and Traktor Pavlodar), Kairat Alma-Ata, Elimai Semipalatinsk.

Keegan, Kevin *player-manager* Striker. **England** international (63 caps, 21 goals). Born 14 February 1951. Career ca. 1967–84. *Clubs* (player) **Scunthorpe United, Liverpool, Hamburg (SV), Southampton, Newcastle United**. *Keynotes* Joined Scunthorpe United as an apprentice in 1967, turning professional in December 1968 and moving to Liverpool for £33,000 in May 1971. Keegan made 230 **Football League** appearances for Liverpool and scored 68 goals. He left **Anfield** for Hamburg in June 1977 in a £500,000 deal.

Keegan won a **Bundesliga** title with Hamburg and reached the 1980 European Cup final with the club (0–1 v **Nottingham Forest**). Keegan holds the unenviable distinction, together with Billy **Bremner**, of being one of the first domestic players to be sent off at **Wembley**, when both were dismissed during the 1974 **Charity Shield** match between Liverpool and **Leeds United**. He sensationally resigned as Newcastle manager after five years in January 1997 and was replaced, just as he had been as a player at Liverpool, by Kenny **Dalglish**. Appointed "chief operating officer" at Fulham in 1997, taking charge of first-team affairs after the dismissal of Ray Wilkins in May 1998, and guiding the club to promotion to the First Division the following season. In February 1999, he agreed to become temporary England coach for four matches, including three Euro 2000 qualifiers, while retaining his role at Fulham. Twice winner of the **European Footballer of the Year** (1978, 1979) and, in 1976, he received the domestic **Footballer of the Year** accolade. Keegan made a pop record in 1978, *Head over heels*, which reached the Top Ten in the music charts. Included in the **Football League Centenary 100 players**. *Honours* League Championship (Liverpool 1972-73, 1975-76, 1976-77); **FA Cup** (Liverpool 1974); **European Cup** (Liverpool 1977); **UEFA Cup** (Liverpool 1973, 1976); German Bundesliga (Hamburg (SV) 1978-79). *Clubs* (manager) Newcastle United, **Fulham,** England.

keep-ups *record* the world record for juggling a regulation-size football off the ground without handling the ball is 19 hours, five minutes 31 seconds, by Ricardinho Neves, from Brazil, (15-16 July 1994, in Los Angeles, USA, as recorded by the *Guinness Book of Records*). The woman's record is held by Brazilian Milene Domingues, who achieved a world record 55,187 touches in nine hours and six minutes in December 1997. She beat the previous record held by Claudio Martini, also from Brazil, with seven hours, five minutes, 25 seconds (12 July 1996, in Caxias do Sul, Brazil).

keeper *n.* another name for **goalkeeper**.

Kelly, Graham *official* secretary of the **Football Association** between 1989 and 1998 and former secretary of the **Football League**. Kelly resigned his FA post in December 1998, following allegations that he was involved in an unsanctioned £3.2 million "loan" to the **Football Association of Wales**.

kemari *n.* early form of football played in **Japan** in the fifth century.

Kempes, Mario Alberto *player* Striker. **Argentina** international (43 caps, 20 goals, 1973-82). Born 15 July 1954, in Cordoba. *Clubs* Instituto Cordoba, **Rosario Central**, **Valencia** (Spain), **River Plate**, Hercules, **First Vienna**, **SV Austria Salzburg**. *Keynotes* Kempes scored two goals in Argentina's 3–1 victory over **Netherlands** in the 1978 World Cup final (**Monumental** Stadium, Buenos Aires) and was tournament top scorer with six goals. Argentinean league top scorer 1976 (21 goals, with Rosario Central). His

plans to manage **Albania**'s Klubi Sportiv Lushnjë in 1997 were ruined by civil unrest prompting him to leave the country. *Honours* **World Cup** (Argentina, 1978); World Cup **Golden Boot** 1978.

Kenilworth Road *ground* English football ground situated in Luton, Bedfordshire; home of **Luton Town**. *Dossier* Ground capacity: 9,975 all seated. Pitch dimensions: 100.5m x 66m. Record attendance: 30,069 v **Blackpool** (4 March 1959, **FA Cup**, sixth round replay). Best average attendance: 21,455 (1955-56). *History* Luton played its first match at Kenilworth Road on 4 September 1905 (v **Plymouth Argyle**, **Southern League**). Originally called Ivy Road, the ground adopted its familiar title after **World War I**. In 1921, the main stand was destroyed by fire and, in 1933, the club bought the freehold to the ground. Emergency centre-forward Joe Payne set an English league football scoring record by netting 10 goals in April 1936, and is commemorated at Kenilworth Road, where a lounge is named after him. Kenilworth Road was the scene of a riot by **Millwall** supporters in March 1985. This led to the club's banning of away supporters, as well as inspiring Margaret Thatcher's government to pursue a **national identity-card scheme**. Later that year the club installed an **artificial pitch**, earning an estimated £300,000 from its use by the surrounding community during its six-year lifespan. During this period, Kenilworth Road staged the first English representative match on an artificial pitch (**England** U-15 v **Northern Ireland** U-15). Both the artificial pitch and the ban on away fans were discarded in 1991, with most of the plastic pitch given to Whipsnade Zoo. Luton Council bought the freehold to Kenilworth Road for £3.25 million in February 1989 and granted the club a seven-year lease. Luton has, over the years, pursued several alternative sites, leading to a proposal in April 1995 from former club chairman David Kohler to build a £30 million indoor stadium with a retractable roof – provisionally entitled the Kohlerdome. The Department for Environment provisionally rejected the Kohlerdome plan on 20 August 1998; a decision affirmed the following November. Kenilworth Road staged its first floodlit match on 7 October 1953 (v **Fenerbahçe**, friendly).

Kenya Breweries *club* Kenyan national league club based in Nairobi. Ground: Nyayo, capacity: 35,000. Strip: yellow shirts, black shorts. **African Cup of Champion Clubs** semi-final 1973; **African Cup-winners Cup** runners-up 1994 (2–5, v **Daring Club Motema Pembe** of Zaire); **CAF Cup** semi-final 1996; **East and Central African Club Championship** winners, 1988, 1989; **East African Super Cup** 1994 1995; Kenyan League champions 1972, 1977, 1978, 1994, 1996; Kenyan Cup 1975, 1989, 1992, 1993.

Kenya *country CAF* Republic in east Africa, on the equator and the Indian Ocean. Bordered by **Ethiopia**, **Sudan**, **Somalia**, **Tanzania** and **Uganda**. Hilly and mountainous interior. Seven provinces. Independence from Britain in 1963. High population growth rate

(3.5% per year). Area: 582,645 sq km (224,900 sq miles). Population: 26,440,000 (1995 est.). Languages: Kiswahili, English, Kikuyu and Luo. Capital: Nairobi. *Dossier* Kenya Football Confederation (Nairobi) formed in 1932, affiliated to **FIFA** in 1960 and **Confédération Africaine de Football** (CAF) in 1968, member of the **Confederation of East and Central African Football Associations** (CECEFA), president Peter Kenneth; general secretary: Sam Nyamweya. Season played from February to November. National stadium: Nyayo, Nairobi, capacity: 35,000; though a new stadium, the Arap Moi Kaseran in Nairobi, is being built, with a projected capacity of 65,000. National strip: red, green and white shirts, red, green and black shorts, red, green and black socks. Nickname of national team: the Harambee Stars. First recorded international game: 1930, v Uganda (0–0, friendly – earlier games may have been played in the **Gossage Cup**, which started in 1927); post-independence 12 October 1963, v Ethiopia (4–3, in Nairobi, **Olympic Games** qualifier). Biggest victory: 6–0 v **Zanzibar** (4 October 1967, in Nairobi, **East and Central Africa Championship**). Biggest defeat: 0–9 v **Zambia** (13 November 1978, in Malawi, East and Central Africa Championship). *International tournament record* Olympic Games – first entered 1964, never qualified for finals tournament; **Women's World Cup** – first entered 1999; **World Cup** – first entered 1974, never qualified for finals tournament, third qualifying round 1974, second round of qualifying tournament 1998 (third in four-nation group); **African Cup of Nations** – first entered 1968, qualified for finals tournament 1972, 1988, 1990, 1992, never past first round; **African Games** – runners-up 1987 (v Egypt, in Kenya); East and Central African Championship – winners 1975, 1981, 1982, 1983; Gossage Cup – 12-times winners between 1927 and 1972 (the first tournament was won by Kenya); **Under-17 World Championship** – never qualified; **World Youth Cup** (under-20) – never qualified; CECEFA Youth Cup (under-18) – winners 1975. *Record against British and Irish national teams* none played. *History* There is a long history of football in Kenya; one club, Mombassa FC, was founded in 1906 and international matches were played long before independence, with Kenya taking part in the Gossage Cup, along with Uganda and Tanzania, from 1927. The Kenya Football Confederation was founded in 1932. The national league of Kenya dates from 1963 (first won by Nakuru All Stars). **Gor Mahia** won the **African Cup-winners Cup** in 1987, the country's only club success in all-Africa club competitions. Kenya should have hosted the African Cup of Nations in 1996, but had to relinquish the tournament owing to a lack of funds. *League system* Eighteen clubs compete in the national league first division, playing each other at home and away. Three points are awarded for a victory, with one for a draw: final positions for clubs level on points are determined by **goal difference**; if clubs are still level,

final positions are determined by **goals scored**. *Record in international club tournaments* **African Cup of Champion Clubs** – **AFC Leopards** (semi-final 1968), **Kenya Breweries** (semi final 1973); African Cup-winners Cup – Gor Mahia (1987, runners-up 1979), Kenya Breweries (runners-up 1994), AFC Leopards (semi-final 1985); **CAF Cup** – Kenya Breweries (semi-final 1996), Gor Mahia (quarter-final 1993), AFC Leopards (quarter-final 1994, 1997); East and Central African Club Championship – **Luo Union** (winners 1976, 1977), Gor Mahia (winners 1980, 1981, 1985, runners-up 1984), AFC Leopards (winners 1979, 1982, 1983, 1984, runners-up 1974, 1980, 1985), Kenya Breweries (, 1988, 1989); **East African Super Cup** – Kenya Breweries (1994 and 1995). Other leading clubs: 1998 Mathare United (Kenya Cup 1998), Mumias Sugar (Kenyan Cup 1996), Shabana Kisii (league champions 1987), Utalii (league champions 1997).

Khaki Cup final *misc.* name given to the **FA Cup** final of 1915, played after the outbreak of **World War I**. The Cup was won by Sheffield United (3–0, v **Chelsea**), in front of 50,000 spectators at **Old Trafford**. The name was coined because of the large number of servicemen in uniform in the crowd. At the presentation of the trophy, Lord Derby said that it was "now the duty of everyone to join with each other and play a sterner game for England."

KI Klaksvik (Klaksvikar Itrottarfelag) *club* Faeroe Islands national league club based in Klaksvik, founded 1904. Ground: Klaksvik, capacity: 4,000. Strip: blue and white hooped shirts, blue shorts. *Keynotes* KI holds the national league record of five consecutive titles (1966 to 1970). Faeroe Islands League champions 1942, 1945, 1952, 1953, 1954, 1956, 1957, 1958, 1961, 1966, 1967, 1968, 1969, 1970, 1972, 1991; Cup 1966, 1967, 1990, 1994.

kick-in *rules* short-lived experimental method for restarting play in place of a **throw-in**; instead of throwing the ball back into play, the ball was kicked from the **touch-line**. The idea was attributed to Sepp **Blatter** – who later became **FIFA** secretary general – and was piloted at a number of tournaments in 1994-95, including the **Isthmian League** in England. Although it was designed to create more of an advantage to the team taking the throw-in, it led to confusion for many of the players who concurrently had to adapt to other competition rules where conventional throw-ins were played.

kick-off *rules* also called place-kick. A kick of the ball while it is stationary on the **centre spot** taken at **start of play** or after a **goal** (Law VIII). It must be kicked into the opposing team's half of the **field of play**, with every player in his or her own half of the field and with all opposition players at least 9.15 metres (10 yards) from the ball. The game starts or restarts as soon as the ball has moved. It must then be kicked by a different player (ie not the player taking the kick-off). A goal can be scored directly from a kick-off (this rule was changed prior to the 1997-98 season; previously a goal could not be scored directly). If the kick-off is incorrectly taken – for example, if opposition players are within 9.15 metres, or if players are not in their own halves – then it must be retaken. If the player taking the kick-off touches the ball twice before another player makes contact, then play is stopped by the referee and an **indirect free-kick** is awarded to the opposition team, taken from the position of the infringement. The team that loses the toss at the **start of play** will take the first kick-off (see **tossing a coin**). The team that wins the toss will take the kick-off after the **half-time** interval.

kick-off time *regulations* advertised time that a fixture is due to start. In the **Premier League**, the **home club** must normally fix the kick-off time; it must be between 11 am and 3 pm for league matches played on a Saturday or public holiday, and between 11 am and 8 pm for Sunday and midweek matches (FA Premier League rule E.26). The kick-off times for televised matches are decided by the Premier League Board, in consultation with the two clubs (FA Premier League rule E.25). Any club delaying the kick-off without good reason can be fined (FA Premier League rule 29). **Football League** clubs must fix Saturday matches to kick off between noon and 3.15 pm, and not later than 8 pm for midweek games; again the home club is responsible for fixing the time and, once set, can alter it only by agreement with both the league and the away club (Football League regulation 24.1.1). League permission and the consent of the away club are required before any matches can be scheduled outside the above kick-off times. Away clubs in the Football League can claim necessary overnight expenses for games kicking off before 12 noon (Football League regulation 24.6).

kicking an opponent *rules* one of the offences listed as a **foul** under the **Laws of the game** (Law XII). The offence is also committed if an *attempt* is made to kick the opponent. The punishment for deliberately kicking or attempting to kick an opponent is for the opposing team to be awarded a **direct free-kick**, taken from the point where the foul was committed (unless within the opponents' **goal area**, in which case it is taken from anywhere within that area). If the foul is committed in the offending side's penalty area, then the opponents are awarded a **penalty kick**.

kidnap *misc.* the abduction of a person usually for ransom or political gain. There have been several football-related kidnapping incidents. *Keynotes* Alfredo **Di Stefano** was kidnapped in February 1964 while on a tour of Venezuela with **Real Madrid**. Di Stefano's abductors, the Armed Front for National Liberation, took the player from his hotel room to publicise their cause. He was held for 57 hours before being released outside the Spanish embassy in Caracas. Colombian international Rene **Higuita** was imprisoned in 1993 for his middle-man role in a kidnapping incident. The costume of **Chelsea**'s mascot, Stamford the Lion, disappeared from the club's **Stamford Bridge** ground following the Premiership match against **Nottingham Forest** on 12 September 1998. The costume, packed in a box, was eventually found outside BSkyB's Isleworth head office, addressed to Tim Lovejoy, presenter of the televsion programme *Soccer AM*. The plot to kidnap a star striker before a big match was the storyline of the pre-**World War I** football **film**, Harry the Footballer (1911).

Kilkenny City *club* Republic of Ireland national league club based in Kilkenny, County Kilkenny in the south-east of Ireland, founded 1966. Ground: Buckley Park, capacity: 7,000.

Kilmarnock *club* Scottish league. *Dossier* Ground: **Rugby Park**, Kilmarnock, capacity: 18,128 Strathclyde. Strip: white shirts with broad yellow chest band with blue trim, blue shorts with red and white trim, blue socks with white trim. Nickname: Killie. Ground capacity: 18,128. Record attendance: 35,995 v **Rangers** (10 March 1962, **Scottish FA Cup**). Biggest win: 11–1 v Paisley Academical (18 January 1930, Scottish FA Cup). Biggest defeat: 1–9 v **Celtic** (13 August 1938, Division One), v **Montrose** (14 February 1995, Third Division). *History* Originally formed as a cricket club, Kilmarnock began playing football in 1873. The club joined Division Two in 1895-96, winning the title in both 1897-98 and 1898-99 and gaining election to the top flight on the second occasion. In a six-season spell from 1959-60, Kilmarnock finished second in Division One on four occasions and won its first League Championship in 1964-65. The club won the Scottish FA Cup twice in the 1920s: 1920 (3–2 v **Albion Rovers**) and 1929 (2–0 v Rangers), having first appeared in the final in 1898 (0–2 v Rangers). Kilmarnock reached the final on a further four occasions, in 1932 (0–3 replay v Rangers), 1938 (2–4 replay v **East Fife**), 1957 (1–2 v **Falkirk**) and 1960 (0–2 v Rangers), before it lifted the trophy for a third time in 1997 (1–0 v Falkirk). The club has also made three appearances in **Scottish League Cup** finals: 1952-53 ((0–2 v **Dundee**), 1960-61 (0–2 v Rangers) and 1962-63 (0–1 v **Heart of Midlothian**). In 1966-67, Kilmarnock reached the semi-final stage of the **UEFA** (Fairs) **Cup** (2–4 agg. v **Leeds United**). The club spent much of the 1980s in the First Division, even dropping to the Second Division for one season in 1989-90, before regaining its place in the top flight in 1993-94. *League record* Premier League 1998-99–; Premier Division 1976-77, 1979-80 to 1980-81, 1982-83, 1993-94 to 1997-98; Division One (A Division) 1899-00 to 1914-15, 1921-22 to 1946-47, 1954-55 to 1972-73, 1974-75; First Division 1975-76, 1977-78 to 1978-79, 1981-82, 1983-84 to 1988-89, 1990-91 to 1992-93; Scottish League 1915-16 to 1920-21; Division Two (B Division) 1895-95 to 1898-99, 1947-48 to 1953-54, 1973-74; Second Division 1989-90. *Honours* Division One 1964-65; Division Two 1897-98, 1898-99; Scottish FA Cup 1920 (3–2 v **Albion Rovers**), 1929 (2–0 v Rangers), 1997 (1–0 v Falkirk). *Records* Joe Nibloe is Kilmarnock's most capped player (11 for **Scotland**); Alan Robertson holds the record for club appearances (481, 1972-88); William Culley is Kilmarnock's record goalscorer (148, 1912-23).

King Baudouin Stadium *stadium* see **Stade du Roi Baudouin**.

King Fahd Stadium *stadium* national stadium of **Saudi Arabia**, in Riyadh, capacity: 70,000. Venue for the first three editions of the **Confederations Cup** (1992, 1995, 1997).

King Hassan II Cup *competition* friendly four-nation pre-1998 **World Cup** tournament held in **Morocco** between 20 May and 22 May 1998. *Results* Morocco 0–0 **England**; **Belgium** 0–1 **France**; Belgium 0–0 (4–3 pens.) England; France 1–0 Morocco.

King's Cup *competition* international nations tournament held in **Thailand** for invited nations. Four countries took part in the 28th tournament in 1997 – Thailand, **Sweden**, **Romania** and **Japan** – played as a mini-league with a final between the group leaders and runners-up. Sweden beat Thailand 3–1 in the final, watched by 25,000 spectators at the national stadium in Bangkok (Sweden's squad was made up of players based in Sweden rather than those playing for clubs in other countries). Brazil under-20 beat North Korea 7–1 in the 1999 tournament.

King's Park *club* former-Scottish league. *Dossier* Ground: Forthbank Park, Stirling, Central. *Keynotes* Joined the reformed Scottish Division Two in 1921-22. The club's third place finish in Division Two in 1927-28 was its highest League position. King's Park folded after a bomb badly damaged the club's ground in 1940 – it was the only bomb dropped on the city during the war. *League record* Division Two 1921-22 to 1938-39.

Kirghizia *country AFC* see **Kyrgyzstan.**

Kiribati *country no international affiliation* Republic in the central and west Pacific Ocean. Four groups of islands (the Gilbert, Phoenix and Line Islands and Ocean Island), spread over 5 million sq km. Warm climate. Area: 717 sq km (277 sq miles). Population: 80,000 (1995 est.). Languages: I-Kirbati and English. Capital: Bairiki (on Tarawa Atoll). *Dossier* Football association is not affiliated to **FIFA**.

Kispest-Honvéd FC *club* Hungarian national league club based in Budapest, founded 1909, previously known as Kispest AC (1909-49) and Honvéd SE (1949-91). Originally the Hungarian Army side. Ground: József Bozsik (after the star player from the 1950s), capacity: 15,000. Strip: red and black striped shirts, black shorts. **Mitropa Cup** 1959; Hungarian league champions 1950 (both the spring and autumn championships), 1952, 1954, 1955, 1980, 1984, 1985, 1986, 1988, 1989, 1991, 1993; Hungarian Cup 1926, 1964, 1985, 1989, 1996. Notable former players: Ferenc **Puskás**, Sándor **Kocsis**, József **Bozsik**.

kit *n.* another name for the **players' equipment**.

Kiyovou Sports *club* Rwandan national league club based in the capital Kigali. Ground: Mumena, capacity: 5,000. Rwandan league champions 1983, 1992, 1993; Rwandan Cup 1985.

klassiker *misc.* German and Dutch term for a derby match – eg, **Borussia Dortmund** v **Schalke 04** (the Ruhr derby) and **Ajax** v **Feyenoord** matches.

Klinsmann, Jürgen *player* Striker. **Germany** international (108 caps, 47 goals, 1987-98). Born 30 July 1964. *Clubs* Stuttgart Kickers, **Stuttgart (VfB)**, **Internazionale**, **Monaco**, **Tottenham Hotspur** (twice), **Bayern Munich**, **Sampdoria**. *Keynotes* Klinsmann made his international debut on 12 December 1987 at the age of 23 (1–1, v Brazil, in Brasilia, friendly) and scored his first international goal on 27 April 1988 (1–0, v Switzerland, in Kaiserlautern, friendly). He is Germany's second highest scorer (behind Gerd **Müller**) and only three players have scored more goals in World Cup finals: Müller, Just **Fontaine** and **Pelé**. Klinsmann scored three goals in Germany's successful 1990 World Cup campaign, five in USA 1994 and three in France 98. He also scored three times in Germany's triumphant 1996 European Championship campaign, and set up Oliver Bierhoff for the first **golden goal** in a European Championship final (2–1, v **Czech Republic**, at **Wembley**). Klinsmann reached the UEFA Cup final with Stuttgart (VfB) in 1989 (4–5 agg., v **Napoli**), and won the trophy with Internazionale in 1991 and Bayern Munich in 1996. He scored in every round of the 1996 UEFA Cup campaign for Bayern Munich; his 15 goals is the highest ever by one man in one season in a single European club tournament campaign. He was **Bundesliga** top scorer in 1988 with 19 goals. Klinsmann had a successful season with Tottenham Hotspur in 1994-95, when he was voted **Footballer of the Year**, and returned to Spurs at the end of 1997-98 to help the club avoid relegation. *Honours* **Olympic Games** bronze medal (West Germany, 1988); **World Cup** (West Germany, 1990); **European Championship** (Germany, 1996; runner-up 1992); **UEFA Cup** (Internazionale, 1991, Bayern Munich 1996); German **Footballer of the Year** 1988; Football Writers Association Footballer of the Year 1995.

Klubi Sportiv Tiranè *club* see **SK Tirana**.

KMKM Zanzibar *club* Zanzibar league club, club of the Zanzibar Navy. Ground: Amaan, capacity: 10,000. Strip: light blue shirts, dark blue shorts. **African Cup-winners Cup** quarter-final 1977; **East and Central African Club Championship** semi-final 1983; Tanzania and Zanzibar Union League champions 1984 (the first Zanzibar club to achieve this); Zanzibar Island League champions 1982, 1985.

knee injury *medical* any injury to the knee, for example **bursitis**, **osteochondritis**, **osteoarthritis**, **torn cartilage** and **ligament** injuries. See **cruciate ligament**, **lateral deltoid ligament**, **medial deltoid ligament**, **medial collateral ligament**, **lateral collateral ligament**, **medial knee ligament**, **patella**.

knickerbockers *n.* shorts/breeches that cover, and are gathered at, the knee. In 1904, **Football Association** rules were changed to ensure that players wore "knickerbockers" long enough to cover their knees. At the time it was thought that the current fashion for short-length shorts was causing an offence.

Knight, Alan *player* Goalkeeper. Born 3 July 1961. Career ca. 1976-. *Club* **Portsmouth**. *Keynotes* Knight played 662 league matches for Portsmouth, a **Football League** record for the most games by a goalkeeper for a single club. He won two caps for **England** at under-21 level.

knighthood *misc.* non-hereditary rank in recognition of services to the country or for personal achievements. British and Commonwealth citizens awarded knighthoods are given the title Sir before their names. Charles **Clegg**, former president of the **Football Association**, was the first former footballer to be knighted (1927). A number of other prominent footballers have been knighted, including Stanley **Matthews** (who received his award while still playing), Tom **Finney**, Alf **Ramsey**, Bobby **Charlton**, and Geoff **Hurst**. **Pelé** was given an honorary knighthood in December 1997 (honorary knights are not given the title Sir).

knock *medical* an informal term for a minor injury, such as a mild **sprain** or **contusion**.

knock-back *n.* header down to a supporting teammate.

knock-down *n.* header down into space for a teammate to run on to.

Kocsis, Sándor *player* Striker. **Hungary** international (68 caps, 75 goals, 1948-56). Born 30 September 1929, in Budapest, died 21 July 1978. Career ca. 1948-63. *Clubs* KTC, **Ferencváros**, Honvéd SE (now **Kispest-Honvéd FC**), Young Fellows (Switzerland), **Barcelona**. *Keynotes* One of the **Magnificent Magyars**. Kocsis scored twice on his international debut (9–0, v **Romania**, in Budapest, **Balkan Cup**). He is Hungary's second-highest goalscorer, eight behind Ferenc **Puskás** and the third-highest all-time international goalscorer in the world (two behind **Pelé**). His strike rate of 1.1 goals per game was better than both Puskas and Pelé. Kocsis was top scorer in the 1954 World Cup finals, with 11 goals (five clear of his nearest rival in the tournament). He played in the 1954 World Cup final v West **Germany** (2–3). Kocsis left Hungary in 1956 (after the **Soviet Union** suppressed a nationalist uprising in the country) and, after a brief spell in Switzerland, signed for Barcelona. He played in the 1961 European Cup final; his goal, with that of Hungarian team-mate Czibor, however, was not enough to prevent Barcelona's 2–3 defeat by **Benfica**. Kocsis played in the first leg of the Fairs Cup final in 1960 (4–1 agg., v **Birmingham City**). He also played in the 1962 Fairs Cup final and scored all three of Barcelona's goals in the 3–7 aggregate defeat by **Valencia**. Died in a fall from a hospital window. *Honours* **Olympic Games** gold medal (Hungary, 1952); **World Cup** runner-up (Hungary, 1954); World Cup **Golden Boot** 1954; **Fairs Cup (UEFA Cup)** (Barcelona, 1960); Hungarian league championship (Ferencváros, 1949, Honvéd SE, 1952, 1954, 1955); Spanish league championship (Barcelona, 1959).

Kolev, Ivan *player* Striker. **Bulgaria** international (75 caps, 25 goals, 1950–1963). Born 1 November 1930.

Clubs CDNA Sofia (now **CSKA Sofia**). *Keynotes* Considered one of the greatest players in Bulgarian history. A key member of the CSKA Sofia side of the 1950s that won nine consecutive league championships (1954-1962): a European league record until 1988 when it was bettered, controversially, by **Dynamo Berlin**. *Honours* Bulgarian league championship (CDNA Sofia, 1951, 1952, 1954, 1955, 1956, 1957, 1958, 1959, 1960, 1961, 1962).

Kolkheti 1913 Poti *club* Georgian national league club based in Poti, founded 1913. Ground: Fazisi, capacity: 10,000. Georgian league runners-up 1997.

Kop *n.* terrace at a stadium, usually behind a goal, named after the Boer War battle of **Spion Kop**. The most famous Kop is at **Liverpool**'s **Anfield**, which was built in 1906 and at one time had a capacity for 28,000 supporters. The idea for the title Spion Kop at Anfield is believed to have come from Ernest Edwards, who was sports editor of the Liverpool Daily Post, although the original Kop was established at **Arsenal**'s Plumstead ground in 1904. Several other grounds also had Kops. **Birmingham**'s Tilton Road end was nicknamed the Spion Kop, and was the largest such terrace, with a estimated capacity for 48,000 fans, when it opened at **St Andrews** in 1906. **Bradford City**'s **Valley Parade** ground had a Nunn's Kop after one of the club's founders.

Kopa, Raymond *player* real name: Raymond Kopaczeski. Striker. **France** international (45 caps, 18 goals, 1952-62). Born 13 October 1931, the son of a Polish immigrant. *Clubs* Angers, **Stade de Reims** (twice), **Real Madrid**. *Keynotes* Originally a right-winger at Angers, Kopa became a centre-forward at Stade de Reims after his transfer in 1950. He played for Stade de Reims in the first European Cup final in 1956, against Real Madrid (3–4, in Paris)). Kopa subsequently was transferred to Real Madrid and played for the Spanish club in the next three European Cup finals; the last of which was against his old club (1957, 2–0, v Fiorentina; 1958, 3–2, v Milan; 1959, 2–0, v Stade de Reims). He returned to Reims in 1959, helping it to win the French championship in his first season back. Kopa made his international debut on 5 October 1952 (3–1, v West **Germany**, in Paris, friendly) and played for France in the 1958 World Cup finals in Sweden, scoring three goals, including one in the third-place playoff against West Germany – a match in which he and his four-goal strike partner Just **Fontaine** were dominant (6–3, in Gothenburg). He was one of only two French players to score in the unsuccessful squad at the 1954 finals in Switzerland. Kopa also played in the first **European Championship**, scoring two goals for France en route to the semi-final (France finished fourth). *Honours* **World Cup** third place 1958; *France Football* **European Footballer of the Year** 1958, runner-up 1959; **European Cup** (Real Madrid, 1957, 1958, 1959); French league championship (Stade de Reims, 1953, 1959, 1960, 1962); Spanish league championship (Real Madrid, 1957, 1958).

Kopetdag Ashkhabad *club* Turkmenistan national league club based in the capital Ashkhabad. **Asian Cup-winners Cup** semi-final/fourth 1998 (1-4, v **Beijing Guoan** of China, in Riyadh, Saudi Arabia, third/fourth playoff); Turkmenistan league champions 1992, 1993, 1994, 1995, 1998, runners-up 1996; Turkmenistan Cup 1992, 1993, 1996, 1997.

Korea DPR *country* see **North Korea.**

Korea *country* see **North Korea** and **South Korea.**

Kosice (1.FC) *club* Slovakian national league club, based in Kosice, founded 1952 as Spartak Kosice, formerly known as ZTS Kosice and Jednota VSS Kosice. Ground: Vsesportovy Areál, capacity: 30,000. Strip: orange shirts, blue shorts. **European Cup** – qualified for Champions League 1997, 1998 (lost all six matches in both seasons); Former Czechoslovakian Cup 1993 (the last Czechoslovakian Cup tournament before independence, beating **Sparta Prague** of the now Czech Republic 5–1 in the final); Slovakian league champions 1997, 1998; Slovakian Cup 1973, 1980, 1993.

KR Reykjavik (Knattspyrnufélagid Reykjavikur) *club* Icelandic national league club based in Reykjavik, founded 1899. Ground: KR-Vollur, capacity: 2,500. Strip: black and white striped shirts, black shorts. Icelandic League winners 1912, 1919, 1926, 1927, 1928, 1929, 1931, 1932, 1934, 1941, 1948, 1949, 1950, 1952, 1955, 1959, 1961, 1963, 1965, 1968; Icelandic Cup 1960, 1961, 1962, 1963, 1964, 1966, 1967, 1994, 1995.

KRC Genk (Racing Club Genk) *club* Belgium national league club based in Hasselt, founded 1988 by merger of Waterschei THOR and SV Winerslag. Ground: Thyl Gheyselinckstadium, capacity: 16,500. Strip: yellow shirts, white shorts. Belgium league champions 1999, runners-up 1998; Belgium Cup 1980, 1982 (both as Waterschei THOR), 1998.

Krol, Ruud *player* Defender. **Netherlands** international (83 caps, four goals, 1969-83). Born 1949 in Amsterdam. *Clubs* Root Wit, **Ajax,** Vancouver Whitecaps (Canada), **Napoli.** *Keynotes* Krol is the Netherlands' most-capped player of all time, making his international debut on 5 November 1969 (0–1, v **England,** in Amsterdam, friendly). Krol joined Ajax in 1967 – becoming part of the legendary **total football** Ajax and Dutch national teams under Rinus **Michels** – and won two consecutive European Cup winners' medals with Ajax (2–0 against **Internazionale** in Rotterdam in 1972, and 1–0 v **Juventus** in Belgrade the following year). Krol played in two World Cup finals, on the losing side in both. One of his four goals for the national team came in the 4–0 defeat of **Argentina** in the second round of the 1974 World Cup finals (26 June 1974, in Gelsenkirchen, Germany). Krol left Ajax towards the end of his career and joined Napoli in 1980 after a brief period in **Canada.** *Honours* **World Cup** runner-up (Netherlands, 1974, 1978); **European Cup** (Ajax, 1972, 1973); Dutch league championship 1968, 1970, 1972, 1973, 1977, 1979.

Kuala Lumpur FA *club* Malaysian national league football team, based in Cheras, Kuala Lumpur. Ground: Kuala Lumpur Stadium, capacity: 15,000. Strip: red and white shirts, white and red shorts. **Asian Champion Teams Cup** – reached final tournament 1989 (came second in its group of three); Malaysia Cup 1987, 1988 and 1989.

Kunming Army Unit *club* Chinese national league club based in Kunming, the capital of Yunnan province, southwest China.

Kuusysi Lahti *club* Finnish national league club based in Lahti, founded 1934 (as UP Lahti). Ground: Keskusurheilukenttä (shared with **Repas Lahti**), capacity: 15,000. Strip: white shirts, white shorts. **European Cup** quarter-final 1986; Finnish league champions 1982, 1984, 1986, 1989, 1991; Finnish Cup 1983, 1987.

Kuwait *country AFC* State of southwest Asia, on the Persian Gulf, bordering **Iraq** and **Saudi Arabia**. Former British colony, recognised as an independent state in 1914, with full independence in 1961. Invaded by Iraq in 1990, resulting in the Gulf War and eventual liberation by United Nations forces. Area: 24,280 sq km (9,370 sq miles). Population: 1,590,000 (1995 census). Language: Arabic, Kurdish, Farsi and English. Capital: Kuwait (Al Kuwayt). *Dossier* Kuwait Football Association (Safat) formed in 1952 affiliated to **FIFA** in 1962 and **Asian Football Confederation** (AFC) in 1964, president: Sheikh Ahmed Fahad A. Al-Sabah; general secretary: Mohammad O T Al-Failakawi. Season played from October to May. National stadium: Al Qadesseyah, Kuwait City capacity: 25,000. National strip: blue shirts, white shorts and blue socks. Most-capped player: Wail Sulaiman Al-Habashi (109 appearances). Other notable international players: Al Dakhil (scorer of the equaliser (1–1) against **Czechoslovakia** in the 1982 **World Cup** finals tournament in Spain, Kuwait's only point); Al Bouloushi (scorer of Kuwait's other World Cup Finals goal, in the same tournament during the 1–4 defeat by **France**). *International tournament record* **Olympic Games** – quarter-final 1980; **Women's World Cup** – never entered; World Cup first entered 1974, qualified for finals tournament 1982 (first round, Kuwait drew 1–1 v Czechoslovakia, but lost against **England** and France); **Arab Cup of Nations** – never won, hosts the 2001 tournament; **Arabian Gulf Cup** – played in first tournament in 1970, winners 1970, 1972, 1974, 1976, 1982, 1986, 1990, 1996 (2–1, v Qatar, in Muscat, Oman); **Asian Cup of Nations** – first entered 1972, winners 1980 (3–0 v **South Korea**, in Kuwait), runners-up 1976 (0–1, v **Iran**, in Iran), semi-final/third 1984, semi-final 1996 (0–1, v United Arab Emirates, semi-final in Saudi Arabia), also qualified for finals tournament 1972, 1988; **Asian Games** – first entered 1974, runners-up 1982 (0–1, v Iraq, in New Delhi, India), 1998 (0–2, v Iran, in Bangkok, Thailand), semi-final/third 1986 (5–0, v **Indonesia**, in Seoul, South Korea, third/fourth playoff), 1994 (2–1, v South Korea, in Hiroshima, Japan, third/fourth playoff), quarter-final 1990, second-stage 1974, 1978; **Asian Women's Championship** – never entered; **Under-17 World Championship** – never qualified; **World Youth Cup** (under-20) – never qualified. *World Cup performance* (finals and qualifiers to end of 1998 tournament) played 56, won 26, drawn 9, lost 17, scored 101 goals, conceded 48 goals; win rate 46%; goals scored per game 1.80. *Record against British and Irish national teams* v England, played one, lost one; v **Wales**, played two, drawn two (no goals in either match). *History* The Kuwaiti national league and cup competitions began in 1962, the year that Kuwait affiliated to FIFA. There are fewer than 3,000 registered players, a remarkable figure considering the country's relative success in the World Cup and Olympic Games, victory in the 1980 Asian Cup of Nations, twice runners-up in the Asian Games and domination of the Arabian Gulf Cup. *League system* Fourteen clubs play in the national first division. *Record in international club tournaments* **Asian Champion Teams Cup** – **Al Kazma** (finals tournament 1987, 1988); **Asian Cup-winners Cup** – Al Kazma (semi-final 1995, quarter-final 1991), **Al Arabi** (quarter finals 1992); **Arab Club Champions Cup** – Al Kazma (runners-up 1988); **Arab Cup-winners Cup** – **Al Kuwait** (runners-up 1989). Other leading clubs: **Al Qadisiyah**, **Al Salmiyah**.

KV Mechelen *club* Belgium national league club based in Mechelen, founded 1904. Ground: Achter de Kazerne, capacity: 14,000. Strip: red and yellow striped shirts, black shorts. **European Cup-winners Cup** 1988 (1–0, v **Ajax**, Strasbourg); **European Super Cup** 1988 (3–1 agg., v **PSV Eindhoven**); Belgium league winners 1943, 1946, 1948, 1989; Belgium Cup 1987.

Kyapaz Gyandzha *club* Azerbaijan national league club, based in Gyandzha, founded 1959. Ground: Shekhar, capacity: 25,000. Azerbaijan League champions 1998, 1999; Azerbaijan Cup 1997, 1998.

Kyrgyzstan (Kirghizia) *country AFC* Republic in northern Asia, bordered by **Kazakhstan**, **China**, **Tajikistan** and **Uzbekistan**. Mountainous country. Former republic in the **Soviet Union**. Joined **Commonwealth of Independent States** in 1991 and gained full independence in 1992. Area: 198,500 sq km (76,620 sq miles). Population: 4,460,000 (1994 est.). Languages: Kirghizian and Russian. Capital: Bishkek (formerly Frunze). *Dossier* Football Confederation of the Kyrgyz Republic (Bishkek) formed in 1992, affiliated to **FIFA** and **Asian Football Confederation** (AFC), president Amangeldi Muraliev, general secretary Klichbek Berdybekov. Season played from April to November. National stadium: Spartak, Bishkek, capacity: 20,000. National strip: red shirts, white shorts and red socks. Biggest victory: 6–0 v **Maldives** (13 June 1997, in Tehran, Iran, **World Cup** qualifier). Biggest defeat: 0–7 v **Iran** (4 June 1997, in Damascus, Syria, World Cup qualifier). *International tournament record* **Olympic Games** – never qualified for finals tournament; **Women's World Cup** – never entered; World Cup – first entered 1998 (second in its four-nation qualifying group); **Asian Cup of Nations** – first entered 1996 (failed to qualify for finals tournament); **Asia Women's Championship** – never entered; **Under-17 World Championship** – never qualified; **World Youth Cup** (under-20) – never qualified. *Record against British and Irish national teams* none played. *History* National league and cup competitions started in 1992. *League system* There are 12 clubs in the national First Division, playing each other twice in a season. Three points are awarded for a victory, with one for a draw. Because the season overlaps with the Asian club tournaments, champions and cup winners from the previous year qualify for the **Asian Cup of Champion Teams** and **Asian Cup-winners Cup**. *Record in international club tournaments* no major successes. Leading clubs: **AiK Bishkek**, **SKA-PVO Bishkek**, **Dinamo Bishkek**, **Metallurg Kadamzhai**.

L

La Fiorita *club* San Marino league club based in Montegiardino, founded 1967. Ground: Montegiardino, capacity: 200. San Marino League champions 1987, 1990; San Marino Cup 1986.

ladder principle *regulations* see **pool account**; **Scottish Football League Trading Account**.

Lafleur Albert *misc.* French sculptor and designer of the **Jules Rimet Trophy**, the original **World Cup**.

Lambada *club* **Barbados** club side. **CONCACAF Cup-winners Cup** fourth place 1994 (0–1 v **Real Maya** of Honduras, in Miami, USA, third/fourth playoff).

Lantana Tallinn *club* Estonian national league club based in the capital Tallinn, founded 1995 (in place of former club Nikol Tallinn, formed in 1951, once known as VMV Tallinn, absorbing former club **Norma Tallinn**). Ground: Viimsi, capacity: 3,000. Strip: black and white striped shirts, black shorts. Estonian regional league champions 1990, 1991 (as VMV Tallinn); Estonian league champions 1996, 1997; Estonian Cup 1991, 1992 (as VMV Tallinn), 1993 (as Nikol Tallinn).

Lanús (Club Atlético) *club* Argentinean national league club, based in Lanus, Buenos Aires, founded 1916. Ground: Estadio Lanús, capacity: 33,000. Strip: maroon shirts, white shorts. **Copa CONMEBOL** winners 1996 (2–1 agg., v **Independiente Santa Fe**), runners-up 1997 (2–5 agg., v **Atlético Mineiro**).

Laos *country AFC* Landlocked republic of southeast Asia, bordered by **China**, **Cambodia**, **Thailand** and **Vietnam**. Independence from France in 1954. Area: 236,725 sq km (91,375 sq miles). Population: 4,580,000 (1995 census). Languages: Lao, French and tribal languages. Capital: Vientiane (Viangchan). *Dossier* Football association (Fédération Lao de Football, Vientiane) formed in 1951, affiliated to **FIFA** in 1952 and **Asian Football Confederation** (AFC) in 1968, president: Dr Vannaret Rajpho; general secretary: Kasem Inthara. Season played from October to May. National stadium: Stade National, Vientiane, capacity: 11,000. National strip: red shirts, white shorts and blue socks. *International tournament record* **Olympic Games** – never entered; **Women's World Cup** – never entered; **World Cup** – never entered; **Asean Tiger Cup** – entered first tournament in 1996, fourth in its first-round group of five nations (it beat neighbours Cambodia, 1–0, and drew with Vietnam, 1–1, in Singapore); **Asian Cup of Nations** – never entered; **Asian Games** – first entered 1998 (first round); **Asian Women's Championship** – never entered; **South East Asian Games** – played in the 1995 football tournament (two victories, one draw and one defeat at the tournament in Chiang Mai, Thailand); **Under-17 World Championship** – never entered; **World Youth Cup** (under-20) – never entered. *Record against British and Irish national teams* none played. *History* A new national league championship was inaugurated in 1997 (won by Lao Army). *League system* There are 76 clubs in the national league structure; the national championship is competed by four teams from the capital Vientiane and four provincial clubs. *Record in international club tournaments* no major success. Leading clubs: Lao Army (based in Vientiane, national champions 1997), Pakse (league champions 1995), Savannakhet (league champions 1993), Sayaboury (league champions 1997).

Larissa FC *club* Greek national league club based in Larissa, founded 1964. Ground: Alkazar, capacity: 18,000. Strip: white shirts, white shorts. **European Cup-winners Cup** quarter-final 1985; Greek league champions 1988; Greek Cup 1985.

Larne FC *club* Northern Ireland national league club based in Larne, County Antrim, founded 1889. Ground: Inver Park, capacity: 12,000. Strip: red shirts, white shorts. **Irish FA Cup** (Northern Ireland) finalists 1928, 1935, 1987, 1989.

Las Palmas (UD Las Palmas) *club* Spanish national league club based in Las Palmas in the **Canary Islands**, founded 1949. Ground: Insular, capacity: 20,000. Strip: yellow shirts, blue shorts. Spanish league runners-up 1969; Spanish Cup runners-up 1978

last man *n.* the only outfield defending player between an opposition player and the goal. *Rules* The "last man" is significant where, under Law XII of the **Laws of the game**, and in the opinion of the referee, a player commits a **foul** or **handball** that prevents an opposition player from taking a clear opportunity to score a goal and is thus guilty of **serious foul play**. The guilty player would be **sent off**. If another outfield player is between the attacker and the goal, and could have covered the position, then the referee is likely to rule that there was not a clear goal scoring opportunity and, unless a more serious offence had been committed, the player would not be sent off (the player may, however, receive a **caution**). The goalkeeper could also be the "last man", and would thus be sent off for serious foul play if the attacking player is prevented from taking a clear opportunity to score, either by the goalkeeper committing a foul or by handling the ball outside the penalty area. If a player handles the ball illegally, but it still goes into the net, a goal is awarded and the player is not sent off for serious foul play, but should be cautioned for the lesser offence of **unsporting behaviour**. See **moving away from goal**.

lateral   *misc.*   Spanish name for a **wing-back**.

lateral collateral ligament   *medical*   a **ligament** in the knee joint that is attached to the bottom of the **femur** at the lateral (outside) **condyle** to the top of the **fibula**. Injury can occur if the knee is bent outwards under force.

lateral deltoid ligament   *medical*   a **ligament** that provides support to the ankle, preventing the foot from being bent inwards; attached to the lateral malleolus of the **fibula**, and down, in three ligament bands, to join the **talus** (anterially and posterially) and the **calcaneum**. Injury to this ligament is common in footballers, particularly to the **anterior tallofibular ligament** band. See **medial deltoid ligament**, **inversion injury**.

lateral ligament   *medical*   a **ligament** on the outside of a **joint**.

lateral malleolus   *medical*   the bottom end of the **fibula** that forms the bony, protuberant part of the ankle on the outside of the foot. Frequently injured by direct trauma from a tackle.

late tackle   *n.*   a mistimed **tackle** executed after the ball has been played and where contact is made with the opponent rather than the ball. Late tackles are always ruled as **foul**s and can be dangerous. Players guilty of such fouls are sometimes described as "going in late".

Latin Cup   *competition*   former international club tournament contested by the champion clubs of **France**, **Italy**, **Portugal** and **Spain**, first played 1949 and last played in 1957, shortly after the introduction of the **European Cup**. It was played annually in a single host city and, although there were nominal club winners, the trophy was awarded at the end of a four-year edition to the nation whose clubs had accumulated the most points. Spain won both editions (1949-52 and 1953-57). *Individual annual club winners* 1949 **Barcelona**; 1950 **Benfica**; 1951 **Milan**; 1952 Barcelona; 1953 **Stade de Reims**; 1955 **Real Madrid**; 1956 Milan; 1957 Real Madrid.

Lato, Grzegorz   *player*   Striker/midfield. **Poland** international (95 caps, 42 goals, 1971-80; excluding Olympic Games). Born 8 April 1950. *Clubs* **Stal Mielec**, Lokeren (Belgium), **Atlante** (Mexico). *Keynotes* Lato made his international debut against West **Germany**, on 17 November 1971 (0-0, in Hamburg, **European Championship** qualifier), but

did not score his first goal for Poland until 1973 – two against **Bulgaria** (19 August, friendly, in Varna, Bulgaria). He is Poland's all-time most capped player and second-highest goalscorer. Lato played on the right wing and later as a midfielder. *Honours:* World Cup **Golden Boot** winner 1974 (seven goals – no World Cup player since has scored more than six); **Olympic Games** gold medal (Poland, 1972); **World Cup** third place (Poland, 1974); Polish league championship (Stal Mielec, 1973, 1976).

Latvia   *country UEFA*   Republic in northeast Europe on the Baltic Sea and the Gulf of Riga, neighbouring **Belarus**, **Estonia**, the Russian Confederation and **Lithuania**. The country is characterised by forests and around 4,000 lakes. Incorporated into the former **Soviet Union** in 1940, occupied by **Germany** 1940-44, regained by the Soviet Union in 1944; unilateral declaration of independence 1990. Area: 63,700. sq km (24,590 sq miles). Population: 2,490,000 (1996 census). Languages: Latvian, Lithuanian and Russian. Capital: Riga. *Dossier* Latvian Football Confederation formed in 1921, affiliated to **FIFA** in 1922 (until 1943) and again in 1991, and **Union of European Football Associations** (UEFA) in 1992, president: Guntis Indriksons; general secretary: Janis Mezeckis. Season played from April to October. National stadium: Daugava, Riga, capacity: 15,000. National strip: carmine red shirts, white shorts and carmine red socks. First international game: 24 September 1922, v Estonia (1–1, in Riga, friendly). Biggest victory: 8–1, v Estonia (18 August 1942, in Tallinn, friendly) Biggest defeat: 0–12, v **Sweden** (29 May 1927, in Stockholm, friendly). Most capped players: Eriks Pétersons (63 appearances, 1929-40), Jánis Lidmanis (58 appearances, 1931-40), Alberts Seibelis (54 appearances, 1925–39), Valery Astafyev (53 appearances, ca. 1990-), Valery Ivanov (51 appearances, ca 1990-), Mikhail Zemlinsky (46 appearances, 1992-). Leading goalscorers: Eriks Pétersons (24 goals, 1929-40), Alberts Seibelis (14 goals, 1925-39), Aleksandrs Vanags (13 goals, 1937-42) and Ilja Vestermans (13 goals, 1935-38). *International tournament record* **Olympic Games** – first entered 1924 (lost 0–7 v **France** in first round, in Paris); **Women's World Cup** – first entered 1995, never qualified for finals tournament; **World Cup** – first entered 1938, and then again from 1994, never qualified for finals tournament (in 1998, Latvia finished fourth in its six-nation group with three wins, one draw and six defeats); **Baltic Cup** – winners 1928, 1932, 1936, 1937, 1940, 1993, 1995, 1997; **European Championship** – first entered 1996 (fifth in six-nation group); **European Championship for Women** – first entered 1995 (last in its first-round group of three nations); **Under-17 World Championship** – never qualified; **World Youth Cup** (under-20) – never qualified. *World Cup performance* (finals and qualifiers to end of 1998 tournament) played 25, won 5, drawn 6, lost 14, scored 24 goals, conceded 40 goals; win rate 20%; goals scored per game 0.96. *Record against British and Irish national* *teams* v **England**, none played; v **Northern Ireland**, played four, won one, drawn none, lost three; v **Scotland**, played two, won none, drawn none, lost two; v **Wales**, none played; v **Republic of Ireland**, played four, won none, drawn none, lost four. *History* The original Latvian league championship dates back to 1922, and operated through to 1940. The league continued to operate on a regional basis during the Soviet years from 1942 to 1990. **Daugava Riga** was the only club to compete in the former-Soviet Union First Division (1948-49). The national league and cup competitions restarted in 1991, with **Skonto Riga** winning the first eight championships (1991-1998). Although Latvia entered the World Cup in 1938 (it reached the second round of the qualifying tournament, with victory over Lithuania, 9–3 agg., before losing 1–2 v **Austria**), its incorporation into the Soviet Union meant that it did not enter again until 1994. Latvia won the first Baltic Cup in 1928. *League system* Eight clubs compete in the national Premier Division. Each club plays each other four times. Three points are awarded for a victory, with one for a draw; positions for clubs level on points are determined by **goal difference**. A more complex system involving 10 clubs playing in two phases was dropped in 1999. Thirteen clubs play in the First Division which is played in a conventional single-phase format. The bottom two clubs are automatically relegated to the regional Second Divisions. Promotion from the three regional Second Divisions are decided by a promotion playoff league involving the six top clubs. The Latvian Cup final is played in June. *Record in international club tournaments* **European Cup** – Skonto Riga (first round, after winning preliminary round, 1993 and 1994); **European Cup-winners Cup** – Dinaburg Daugavpils (first round 1998); **UEFA Cup** – Skonto Riga (first round 1995). Other leading clubs: Daugava Riga; **Universitate Riga**, **Baltika Liepaja**.

Laudrup, 1. Brian *player* Striker. **Denmark** international (82 caps, 21 goals, 1987-98). Born 22 February 1969. *Clubs* **Brøndby IF**, Bayer 05 Uerdingen (of Essen, Germany), **Bayern Munich**, **Fiorentina**, **AC Milan**, **Rangers**, **Chelsea**, **FC Copenhagen**. *Keynotes* Brian Laudrup was voted joint fifth in the **FIFA World Footballer of the Year** 1992, and fifth in the *World Soccer* **World Footballer of the Year** 1992. *Honours* **European Championship** (Denmark, 1992); **European Super Cup** (Chelsea, 1998), Danish league championship (Brøndby, 1987, 1988); Italian **Serie A** championship (AC Milan, 1994), Scottish League Championship (Rangers, 1995, 1996, 1997); Footballer of the Year (Scotland) (while at Rangers, 1995, 1997). **2.** His brother Michael, Midfielder. Denmark international (104 caps, 37 goals, 1982-98). Born 16 June 1964. *Clubs* Brøndby, **Lazio**, **Juventus**, **Barcelona**, **Real Madrid**, **Ajax**. *Keynotes* Michael Laudrup made his international debut on his 18th birthday, and scored (15 June 1982, 1–2, v **Norway**). He went on to become Denmark's most capped outfield player. He was voted eighth in the *World Soccer* World Footballer of the Year

1989 and ninth in 1993. He scored a late equaliser in the 1985 World Club Cup final for Juventus against **Argentinos Juniors**, a match his club won on penalties. Michael did not play in the 1992 Danish European Championship winning team after a dispute with the coach, Richard Moller-Nielsen. *Honours* **World Club Cup** (Juventus, 1985); **European Cup** (Barcelona, 1992); **European Cup-winners Cup** runner-up (Barcelona, 1991); Italian Serie A championship (Juventus, 1986); Spanish league championship (Barcelona, 1991, 1992, 1993, 1994, Real Madrid, 1995), Netherlands league championship (Ajax, 1998); Dutch Cup (Ajax, 1998). Both brothers were chosen for **FIFA**'s 22-man all-star squad of the 1998 World Cup finals. **3.** Their father, Finn Laudrup, Denmark international (six goals, ca. 1966-73).

Laurent, Lucien *player* Winger/inside forward. **France** international. *Clubs* Sochaux, Athletic Club Paris, Mulhouse, Rennes, Strasbourg. *Keynotes* Scorer of the first-ever **World Cup** goal, in 13 July 1930 in the opening game of the first World Cup(**France** v **Mexico**, 4–1, Pocitos Stadium, Montevideo, Uruguay). Laurent scored in the 19th minute.

Lausanne-Sports *club* Swiss national league club based in Lausanne, founded 1896 (as Montriond Lausanne, which merged with Hygrénique in 1920 to form Lausanne Sports). Ground: Stade Olympique La Pontaise, capacity: 16,000. Strip: blue shirts, blue shorts. **European Cup-winners Cup** quarter-final 1965; **UEFA Cup/Fairs Cup** semi-final 1958; Swiss national champions 1913 (as Montriond Lausanne), 1932 (three regional leagues operated until 1933, with the national championship decided by an inter-league playoff), 1935, 1956, 1944, 1951, 1965; Swiss Cup 1935, 1939, 1944, 1950, 1962, 1964, 1981, 1998.

Lavori Publici *club* Somalia national league club based in the capital Mogadishu. **African Cup-winners Cup** second round 1981; Somalia league champions 1969, 1970, 1971, 1981.

Law, Denis *player* Striker. **Scotland** international (55 caps, 30 goals). Born 24 February 1940. Career ca. 1955-74. *Clubs* **Huddersfield Town**, **Manchester City** (twice), **Torino**, **Manchester United**. *Keynotes* Joined Huddersfield Town as an amateur in 1955, turning professional in February 1957. Transferred to Manchester City for a record £53,000 in March 1960 and then to Torino for £100,000 in June 1961. Law appeared alongside Joe Baker in the Torino attack. United paid £116,000 in July 1962 to bring Law back to Manchester. Law scored 171 goals in 309 **Football League** appearances for United. He missed United's **European Cup** triumph in 1968 through injury. Only Ian Rush scored more FA Cup goals in the 20th century than Law (41 goals), who scored one of United's three goals in its 1963 final victory (3–1 v **Leicester City**). Law was Scotland's youngest post-**World War II** debutant, making his first international appearance against **Wales** (18 October 1958) and scoring one goal. He twice scored four goals for Scotland, exactly a year apart (v **Northern Ireland**, 7 November 1962; v **Norway**, 7 November 1963). Voted **European Footballer of the Year** in 1964. Law moved to City in July 1973, famously scoring against United on 27 April 1974; a goal which helped to relegate his former club to Division Two. Law later said: "I didn't want to play in the match but as a professional I had to. After 11 years with United most of the people there were my friends, and I certainly didn't want to put the nail in their coffin. I have seldom felt so depressed as I did that weekend." Included in the **Football League Centenary 100 players**. *Honours* League Championship (Manchester United 1964-65, 1966-67); **FA Cup** (Manchester United 1963).

Laws of the game *rules* the essential rules of **association football** as designated by the **International FA Board** (IFAB). There are seventeen Laws, governing: **field of play** (Law I); **ball** (Law II); number of **players** (Law III); **players' equipment** (Law IV); **referee** (Law V); **assistant referee** (Law VI); **duration of play** (Law VII); **start of play** and **restart of play** (Law VIII); when the ball is **in play** or **out of play** (Law IX); how to **score** (Law X); **offside** (Law XI); **fouls** and misconduct (Law XII); **free kick** (Law XIII); **penalty kick** (Law XIV); **throw-in** (Law XV); **goal kick** (Law XVI); and **corner kick** (Law XVII). The Laws of the game have deliberately been kept brief and straightforward, with their interpretation decided on by the IFAB – as "decisions of the IFAB" – rather than a continuous redrafting and expansion of the regulatory framework. The Laws of the game apply to all member countries of **FIFA**. Issues such as how league points are allocated, how teams on the same points are separated in league tables, fixture priorities, number of substitutions, promotions and relegations, players' registrations, fines and transfer regulations are kept out of the Laws and are, instead, dealt with by the regulations of the particular governing body, league or competition (see **competition rules**, **Football League regulations**). *History* Thirteen original laws of association football were adopted at a meeting of the **Football Association** on 1 December 1983, though they have their origins in the earlier **Cambridge rules**. See **Football Association** (*History*), **association football** (*History*) and **Sheffield rules**.

Lawton, Tommy *player-manager* Striker. **England** international (23 caps, 22 goals). Born 6 October 1919. Career ca. 1935-1957. *Clubs* (player) **Burnley**, **Everton, Chelsea, Notts County, Brentford, Arsenal**. *Keynotes* Scorer of 231 goals in 390 **Football League** appearances. Signed professional with Burnley in 1936, moving to Everton for £6,500 in January 1937 as successor to Dixie **Dean**. While at Everton, Lawton played for two Football League clubs on the same day. On 25 December 1940, he appeared for his own club (v Liverpool) in the morning and he guested for **Tranmere Rovers** (v **Crewe Alexandra**) in the afternoon, scoring twice. Also at Everton, Lawton was Division One top scorer in both 1937-38 (28) and 1938-39 (34). Lawton twice scored four times for

England (v **Netherlands**, 27 November 1946; v **Portugal**, 25 May 1947 – his first after 17 seconds is the quickest goal ever scored by England) and his tally of 16 goals in 15 matches remains a post-**World War II** record. Lawton also made 23 appearances for his country in wartime or Victory internationals, scoring four times against **Scotland** on 16 October 1943. During World War II, Lawton guested for **Aldershot** and, while on honeymoon, for **Morton**. Lawton was the first Division Three player in the post-World War II period to play for England (v **Scotland**, 10 April 1948). Lawton's November 1947 transfer from Chelsea to Notts County for £20,000 was a record fee at the time. Despite being in his mid-30s, Lawton played for Arsenal, having been signed for £10,000, for three seasons in the mid-1950s. Included in the **Football League Centenary 100 players**. *Honours* League Championship (Everton 1938-39); Division Three (South) (Notts County 1949-50). *Clubs* (manager) **Brentford** (player-manager), Notts County, Kettering Town (player-manager).

lay-off *vb.* to deflect or pass the ball to a team-mate, particularly one in a better position to shoot or cross the ball; often as part of a **one-two**. *n.* pass made by a player to an overlapping team-mate who has made a penetrating run.

Layer Road *ground* English football ground situated in Colchester, Essex; home of **Colchester United**. *Dossier* Ground capacity: 7,556. Pitch dimensions: 100.5m x 65m. Record attendance: 19,072 v **Reading** (27 November 1948, **FA Cup**, first round). Best average attendance: 10,573 (1950-51). *History* Layer Road is a former army parade ground which the amateur Colchester Town first began using on 4 November 1909 (v Shepherds Bush). The club bought the ground in 1919. Colchester United, founded in 1937, was the professional successors to Town. Before United was formed, Layer Road was given to the local council on condition it was never used for anything other than football. Layer Road's record attendance (see above) was achieved for a match that lasted only 35 minutes: fog forced it to be abandoned. In 1986, Colchester followed **Luton Town**'s example and banned away fans from attending Layer Road, leading to a big fall in attendances over the 1987-88 season. Colchester sold the ground to the local council to help clear its debts after dropping to the **Football Conference** in 1990. The first floodlit match at Layer Road took place on 3 August 1959 (v **Norwich City**, friendly).

Lazio (SS) *club* Italian league. *Dossier* Ground: **Olimpico** (Stadio), Rome, Lazio. Strip: sky blue shirts, white shorts, white socks. Website: *http://www. sslazio.it/* Nickname: Biancocelesti (White and skies). Ground capacity: 82,922 all seated. Biggest win: 9–1 v Nodena (**Serie A** 1931-32). Biggest defeat: 1–8 v **Internazionale** (Serie A 1933-34). *History* Formed in 1900 as SP Lazio by Luigi Bigiarelli, who based the club strip on the colours of the Greek flag. The club retained the SP Lazio name until 1925 when it adopted the present title Società Sportivo Lazio. In 1931, Lazio moved to Stadio del Partito Nazionale Fascista (PNF) from its Rodinella ground. Lazio's first major trophy, the Italian Cup **(Coppa Italia)**, was won in 1958 (1–0 v **Fiorentina**), but it had to wait another 40 years to lift the Cup a second time (1998, 3–2 agg. v **AC Milan**). The **Union of European Football Associations** banned the club from European competition for one year following crowd trouble during a **UEFA Cup** (second round, 2nd leg) match against **Ipswich Town** at Olimpico in 1972-73. In 1973-74, under the managership of Giorgio Chinaglia, Lazio won its first League Championship, but because of the ban the club was unable to take its place in the **European Cup**. The club narrowly avoided relegation to Serie C1 in 1986-87, winning an end-of-season playoff against Campobasso (1–0). Paul **Gascoigne** spent three seasons at Lazio between 1992 and 1995, but played only 42 games. The club, which since February 1992, has been owned by Sergio Cragnotti, became the first Italian club to become a public limited company when it was floated on the Milan stock market in May 1998. Lazio invested an estimated £72 million on players, including Marcelo **Salas**, Ivan Del La Pena, Dejan Stankovic and Christian Vieri before the start of the 1998-99 season. Lazio won its first European trophy in 1999 – the very last edition of the **European Cup-winners Cup**. *Honours* European Cup-winners Cup 1998-99 (2–1 v Real Mallorca, **Villa Park**); Italian League 1973-74; Italian Cup 1958 (1–0 v Fiorentina), 1998 (3–2 agg. v AC Milan).

LCS Gunners (Lobatse Cash Stores) *club* Botswana national league club based in Lobatse, formerly known as Extension Gunners. Ground: Lobatse, capacity: 5,000. Strip: black shirts, white shorts. Botswana league champions 1992, 1993, 1994; Botswana Cup 1992.

league *n.* a round-robin competition whereby the participating clubs play each other at least once during the season or duration of the tournament.

league table *n.* document displaying the positions of each club in a **league** or **division**.

Le Havre Athletic Club *club* France's oldest football club founded in 1872 (though it did not adopt association football until 20 years later). Ground: Jules Deschaseaux, capacity: 21,000. Strip: blue shirts and shorts. French Cup 1959.

lead marking *tactics* defensive system whereby the defender marks an attacker's forward run or run towards the ball in order to prevent the player receiving a through pass.

lead pass *n.* pass into the space in which a teammate has made a run, potentially creating a scoring opportunity.

League Cup *competition* English knockout tournament involving **Football League** and **Premier League** clubs. *History* The idea for a league cup competition was first raised in 1892 (a firm called Hudson & Co offered to donate a cup worth £500 to the winners of a competition contested solely by Football League

clubs), but the Football League authorities did not want to compete with the established **FA Cup**. During **World War II** various cup competitions involving only League clubs operated (see **Wartime Football**), largely because the FA Cup was suspended, and after the war Stanley **Rous**, then secretary of the **Football Association**, raised the idea of a League Cup and several trial tournaments were staged (see **Anglo-Scottish Floodlit League** and the **Southern Professional Floodlit Cup**). The League Cup was officially launched in 1960 and formed part of the "**Pattern for Football**" promoted by Football League secretary Alan **Hardaker**, who originally wanted the competition played at the beginning of the season (as is the **Scottish League Cup**). Initially, the competition was not a geat success, and with clubs not compelled to enter, several of the leading Division One clubs refused to take part for the first six seasons. For example, **Arsenal**, **Sheffield Wednesday**, **Tottenham Hotspur** and **Wolverhampton Wanderers** first entered the competition in 1966. In 1967, the final, which had been a two-legged home and away affair, was moved to **Wembley**. The Wembley final, plus the introduction of an automatic **UEFA** (Fairs) **Cup** place for the winners, made the competition more attractive to the bigger clubs. Semi-finals remained two-legged. The UEFA Cup place was restricted to Division One clubs. To generate more income for the lower-level clubs, the format of the competition was changed on several occasions. In 1975, two-legged first-round ties were introduced and, in 1979, the second-round matches were also made two-legged, while seeding was established in 1983 so that smaller clubs had a better chance of drawing one of their bigger counterparts. Clubs involved in European competition received a second round bye from season 1997-98. The UEFA Cup place was withdrawn by UEFA before the start of the 1997-98 competition but, following protestations by the Football League and the threat of court proceedings, the decision was rescinded. The League Cup was first sponsored in 1981-82, when the competition became the **Milk Cup**. The sponsorship deal was only agreed half way through the 1981-82 season, so **Liverpool**, the winners in March 1982, received both the existing Football League Cup and the new Milk Cup. Since 1982, the Cup has had several different sponsors and titles: **Littlewoods Challenge Cup** (1986-87 to 1989-90), **Rumbelows Cup** (1990-91 to 1991-92), **Coca-Cola Cup** 1992-93 to 1997-98 and **Worthington Cup** 1998-99–. *Records* (Up to and including 1999) **Aston Villa** and **Liverpool** have each won the League Cup on five occasions. Both **Queens Park Rangers** (1967) and **Swindon Town** (1969) were Division Three clubs when they won the trophy. **Norwich City**'s 1985 victory coincided with relegation to Division Two, making it the only club to have won a major honour and been relegated in the same season. Ian **Rush** has won more winner's medals (five) than any other individual. *Final results* 1960-61 Aston Villa 3–2 **Rotherham United** (agg.); 1961-62 **Norwich City**

4–0 **Rochdale** (agg.); 1962-63 **Birmingham City** 3–1 Aston Villa (agg.); 1963-64 **Leicester City** 4–3 **Stoke City** (agg.); 1964-65 **Chelsea** 3–2 Leicester City (agg.); 1965-66 **West Bromwich Albion** 5–3 **West Ham United** (agg.); 1966-67 **Queens Park Rangers** 3–2 West Bromwich Albion; 1967-68 **Leeds United** 1–0 **Arsenal**; 1968-69 **Swindon Town** 3–1 Arsenal; 1969-70 **Manchester City** 2–1 West Bromwich Albion; 1970-71 **Tottenham Hotspur** 2–0 Aston Villa; 1971-72 Stoke City 2–1 Chelsea; 1972-73 Tottenham Hotspur 1–0 Norwich City; 1973-74 **Wolverhampton Wanderers** 2–1 Manchester City; 1974-75 Aston Villa 1–0 Norwich City; 1975-76 Manchester City 2–1 **Newcastle United**; 1976-77 Aston Villa 3–2 **Everton** (second replay); 1977-78 **Nottingham Forest** 1-0 Liverpool (replay); 1978-79 Nottingham Forest 3–2 **Southampton**; 1979-80 Wolverhampton Wanderers 1–0 Nottingham Forest; 1980-81 Liverpool 2–1 West Ham United (replay); 1981-82 Liverpool 3–1 Tottenham Hotspur; 1982-83 Liverpool 2–1 **Manchester United**; 1983-84 Liverpool 1–0 Everton (replay); 1984-85 Norwich City 1–0 **Sunderland**;1985-86 **Oxford United** 3–0 Queens Park Rangers; 1986-87 Arsenal 2–1 Liverpool; 1987-88 **Luton Town** 3–2 Arsenal; 1988-89 Nottingham Forest 3–1 Luton Town; 1989-90 Nottingham Forest 1–0 **Oldham Athletic**; 1990-91 **Sheffield Wednesday** 1–0 Manchester United; 1991-92 Manchester United 1–0 Nottingham Forest; 1992-93 Arsenal 2–1 Sheffield Wednesday; 1993-94 Aston Villa 3–1 Manchester United; 1994-95 Liverpool 2–1 **Bolton Wanderers**; 1995-96 Aston Villa 3–0 Leeds United; 1996-97 Leicester City 1–0 **Middlesbrough** (replay); 1997-98 Chelsea 2–0 Middlesbrough; 1998-99 Tottenham Hotspur 1–0 Leicester City.

League Cup, most goals *record* Geoff **Hurst** and Ian **Rush** jointly hold the record for the most goals scored in **League Cup** matches. By the end of 1998 both players had scored 49 goals apiece, with Rush, then **Wrexham**'s player-manager, still with the opportunity to increase his tally.

League Managers' Association (LMA) *n.* the association representing the interests of all league managers, founded in 1980. The Association is open to the managers of all 92 **Premier League** and **Football League** clubs as well as international managers of the British and Northern Ireland home countries. The LMA is run by an elected management committee of eight members. Before it was founded in 1980, league managers had been part of the Secretaries and Managers Association, which held an annual dinner during which the Football League would hold its Annual General Meeting with representation from all club secretaries, managers and chairmen. The LMA is one of four constituent organisations – together with the Commercial and Marketing Managers Association, the Football Administrators Association, and the Managerial Staffs Association – represented by the Institute of Football Management and Administration (IFMA). The IFMA has

a governing committee comprising a representative from each of the four constituent organisations whose principal objective is to "make a positive contribution to the welfare of the game and, by doing that, improve the working environment of their members".

League of Wales *competition* Welsh national league started in 1992-93, initially sponsored by Konica. The three major Welsh clubs, **Cardiff City**, **Swansea City** and **Wrexham**, remained in the English **Football League**, with some **non-league** Welsh clubs choosing to remain in the English lower leagues. The league was first won by **Cwmbran Town**. *League system* Seventeen clubs compete in the national Premier Division, with three points awarded for a win and one for a draw; clubs level on points are separated on **goal difference**. The bottom two clubs are relegated. The First Division is divided into two regional leagues, north and south. Each has 20 clubs, with the champions in each promoted to the Premier Division, subject to meeting League of Wales ground and financial criteria.

league championship *n.* title and trophy awarded to the team that wins the top level of a football league (rather than the divisional winners). *Keynotes* An English **Football League** championship trophy was first awarded in 1891, to **Everton**. Originally presented to the chairman of the winning club at the League annual meeting, from 1920 it was presented, whenever possible, to the winning club after one of the final league matches. **West Bromwich Albion** was the first club to receive the trophy in this way, at its home ground after its match against **Chelsea** (1 May 1920).

league goals, most in one season *record* see **goals, most in one season** (separate records for clubs and players).

league handbook *publication* annual publication produced by all football leagues detailing the financial, administrative and competition rules as well as a club directory, fixture list and rules for referees. They are issued to all league clubs and referees but usually can be obtained from the league secretary (a fee may be charged).

league matches, most by a club *record.* **Notts County** became the first club to play 4,000 **Football League** matches, on 10 January 1998 (v **Rochdale**, Third Division).

league titles, successive *record* the following statistics are for the top-flight domestic league championships. **1.** World: **Al Faisaly** of **Jordan** won 13 consecutive league championships (1959-66, 1970-74), although the sequence was broken by years in which the league was either not played or incomplete. **Berlin FC** (as Dynamo Berlin) set the world record of 10 consecutive titles in 10 years in the former **East Germany** league (1979-88); though some historians have questioned the fairness by which the club achieved its records, suggesting interference by the East German authorities. The record has been matched by **Dynamo Tbilisi** of Georgia (1990-99). **2.** Asia: Al Faisaly (as above). **3.** Europe: Berlin FC and Dynamo Tbilisi (as above). **4.** Africa: **Hafia FC** of **Guinea**, nine successive championships (1971-79). **5.** Oceania: **Central Sport** of **Tahiti**, eight consecutive titles (1972-79). **6.** South America/**CONMEBOL: Racing Club** of **Argentina**, seven consecutive titles (1913-19). **7. CONCACAF: Robin Hood** of **Surinam**, seven (1983-89).

league titles, total *record* the following statistics are for the top-flight domestic league championships. **1.** World/Europe: **Rangers** of **Scotland**, 48 league titles. **2.** South America/**CONMEBOL: Peñarol** of **Uruguay**, 45 titles. **3.** Africa: **Al Ahly** of **Egypt**, 29 titles. **4.** Asia: **Muharraq** of **Bahrain**, 24 titles. **5. CONCACAF: Robin Hood** of **Surinam**, 23 titles. **6.** Oceania: **Central Sport** of **Tahiti**, 19 titles.

learning disability *n.* a recognised cognitive disability, generally requiring special or additional help in schools and the workplace. Football is a growing sport for children and adults with learning disabilities, with many clubs throughout the world. In Britain, it is organised by the **Association of Football Players with Learning Disabilities**. The British learning disabilities charity Mencap also has football development officers. *History* The first international invitation tournament for players with learning disabilities was played in 1989, in Sweden, with sides from the Netherlands and Germany. A more ambitious tournament was staged in Netherlands in 1994. The first 11-a-side league in Britain was founded in 1994, in Leicestershire. The Association of Football Players with Learning Disabilities was founded in 1994 and has helped to organise five-a-side and 11-a-side leagues throughout the United Kingdom. Britain hosted the first **European Championships for Players with Learning Disabilities** in 1996 and the first **World Football Championships for Players with Learning Disabilities** in 1998.

Lebanon *country AFC* Republic in west Asia on the Mediterranean Sea, bordered by **Syria** and **Israel**. Mediterranean climate. Independence from **France** in 1944. Original home of the Palestine Liberation Organisation. Civil war in 1970s and 1980s. Area: 10,400 sq km (4,015 sq miles). Population: 2,840,000 (1991 est.). Language: Arabic, French, English. Capital: Beirut. *Dossier* Football association (Fédération Libanaise de Football-Association, Beirut) formed in 1933 affiliated to **FIFA** in 1935 and **Asian Football Confederation** (AFC) in 1964, president: Dr Al Rae'E Nabil; general secretary: Rahif Alameh. Season played from October to May. National stadium: Camille Champum, capacity: 60,000. National strip: red shirts, white shorts and red socks. First international game: – 1934, against a Romanian club side. *International tournament record* **Olympic Games** – never qualified for finals tournament; **Women's World Cup** – never entered; **World Cup** – first entered 1994, never progressed beyond first-round qualifying group (in 1998, Lebanon finished second in its three-nation group); **Asian Cup of Nations** – first entered 1980, then again

in 1996, never qualified for finals tournament (losing out to **Kuwait** by a single point in 1996) hosts 2000; **Asian Games** – first entered 1998 (second round); **Asian Women's Championship** – never entered; **Under-17 World Championship** – never qualified; **World Youth Cup** (under-20) – never qualified. *Record against British and Irish national teams* none played. *History* Football introduced in 1908 by students at Beirut's American University: in 1910 the university played a match against a British naval side, the crew of HMS Durham. The Lebanese football association was formed on 22 March 1933, with 13 member clubs. The national league started in 1933, with nine clubs (Al Nahda was the first winner). The league was suspended from 1976 to 1987 due to the civil war. The domestic Cup was first played in 1938 (first won by Al Nahda). Former **Wales** manager Terry Yorath coached the national side in the mid 1990s. *League system* Twelve clubs compete in the national first division; the bottom two are relegated. Three points are awarded for a win, with one for a draw. *Record in international club tournaments* **Asian Champion Teams Cup – Club Homentmen** (semi- final/third 1970), **Al Ansar** (quarter-final 1998). Other leading club: **Al Nijmeh**.

Lech Poznan *club* Polish national league side based in Poznan, founded in 1922. Ground: Lech, capacity: 15,000. Strip: blue shirts, blue shorts. Polish League champions 1983, 1984, 1990, 1992, 1993 (awarded the 1993 championship after **Legia Warszawa** and **LKS Lódz** had two points deducted for alleged match-fixing on last day of season); Polish Cup 1982, 1984, 1988.

Leeds City *club* former-English league club. *Dossier* Ground: **Elland Road**, Leeds, west Yorkshire. Best average attendance: 15,845 (1913-14). *History* Formed in August 1904 by members of Hunslet AFC, the club was nicknamed the Peacocks due to its blue and gold strip. City played its first match on 15 October 1904 (v **Hull City**, friendly) and six months later the club became a limited company. City finished sixth in Division Two in its first season, and the club's most successful season was in 1913-14 when, under the managership of Herbert **Chapman**, it finished fourth. During **World War I**, City's teams contained numerous guest players, including many internationals, and won a number of wartime tournaments: (see **wartime football**) Midland Tournament (North) 1915-16, Midland Regional Tournament 1916-17, 1917-18. City was expelled from the **Football League** on 4 October 1919 for failing to co-operate with the football authorities which had accused the club of making **illegal payments** to players during the war. At the time, the club had completed eight matches and accumulated 10 points (winning four games, drawing two and losing two, and scoring 17 goals and conceding 10), and its place in Division Two was taken by **Port Vale**. The club's final League match took place against **Wolverhampton Wanderers** at **Molineux** (City won 4–2). The team travelled overnight by bus to the match due to a rail strike. City's players were sold at auction for a total of £10,150 and a new club, **Leeds United**, was formed. *League record* Division Two 1905-06 to 1919-20 (expelled on 4 October 1919).

Leeds Road *ground* former-English football ground that was situated in west Yorkshire; former home of **Huddersfield Town**. *Dossier* Capacity when ground closed (1994): 16,500. Pitch dimensions: 105m x 69m. Record attendance: 67,037 v **Arsenal** (27 February 1932, **FA Cup** sixth round). Best average attendance: 30,820 (1953-54). *History* Leeds Road was successfully turned into a football ground in March 1908, some six months before Huddersfield Town was formed. The club was forced to play two matches at **Leeds United's Elland Road** ground in April 1950 following a fire at Leeds Road which destroyed the schoolboy enclosure and damaged the West Stand. During the 1950s, Leeds Road had one of the first electronic scoreboards – a gift from Dutch electronics company Philips – at an English sporting venue. Huddersfield Rugby League Club played its first match at Leeds Road on 30 August 1992 as part of a groundshare which would continue as Town's new **Alfred McAlpine Stadium**. Huddersfield played its final League game at Leeds Road on 30 April 1994 (v **Blackpool**, Second Division). Leeds Road staged an **England** international on 27 November 1946 (v **Netherlands**, 8–2) and hosted several FA Cup semi-finals. The first floodlit match took place on 11 January 1961 (v **Wolverhampton Wanderers**, FA Cup, third round replay).

Leeds Sporting plc *n.* publicly-quoted business which owns **Leeds United**. Leeds Sporting became a fully listed company on the London Stock Exchange in August 1996 (flotation price = 19p). Leeds Sporting, which also has media interests, had a market capitalisation – the market value of the company's issued share capital (eg, the quoted price of its shares multiplied by the number of shares outstanding) – of £52.7 million on flotation.

Leeds United *club* English league. *Dossier* Ground: **Elland Road**, Leeds west Yorkshire. Strip: white shirts, white shorts, white socks. Website: *http://www.lufc.co.uk* Nickname: United. Ground capacity: 40,000 all seated. Best average attendance: 39,204 (1970-71). Record attendance: 57,892 v **Oldham Athletic** (15 March 1967, **FA Cup**, fifth round replay). Biggest win: 10–0 v Lyn (Oslo) (17 September 1969, **European Cup**, first round first leg). Biggest defeat: 1–8 v **Stoke City** (27 August 1934, Division One). *History* Leeds United was formed in 1919 to replace **Leeds City**, which had, it was alleged by the authorities, made **illegal payments** to players and was expelled from the **Football League** for failing to co-operate with the subsequent inquiry. United was elected to the League in 1920 and the club received considerable backing from former **Huddersfield Town** benefactor Hilton Crowther, who initially wanted the club to merge with its financially-strapped Yorkshire neighbours. Although Leeds won the Division Two title in its fourth

season (1923-24), the club was relegated three years later (1926-27) and thereafter it regularly moved between the two divisions, never finishing higher than fifth in the top flight until the mid-1960s, when a golden period began. Don **Revie** became player-manager in 1961, after the club finished only three points clear of relegation to Division Three. Revie introduced the club's all-white strip (similar to **Real Madrid**) and over the following 13 years, Leeds won six major trophies: League Championship (1968-69, 1973-74); FA Cup (1972); **League Cup** (1968); **UEFA** (Fairs) **Cup** (1968, 1971). The club's 1968-69 Championship triumph was achieved with a record number of points (67 (two points for a win, eventually surpassed by **Liverpool in** 1978-79)). During Revie's period, the club went close to winning the **double** on three occasions: in 1965, the club finished equal on points at the top of Division One with **Manchester United**, but lost the title on **goal average**, as well as losing the FA Cup final (1–2 a.e.t. v Liverpool); in 1970, the club finished second in Division One and again lost the FA Cup final (1–2 replay/a.e.t. v **Chelsea**); and in 1972, Leeds won the FA Cup, but finished one point behind champions **Derby County** in the League. The club also failed to win the title in 1970-71 due largely to a 1–2 home defeat against **West Bromwich Albion** (16 April 1971). The result rested on a controversial refereeing (Ray Tinkler) decision that allowed Albion striker Jeff Astle's goal to stand although his team-mate, Colin Suggett, had been flagged offside, and Astle was in an offside position when Tony Brown played him in to score. Crowd unrest at this match – 30 spectators were arrested – led to Elland Road being closed for the club's first four matches of the following season. Revie's reign also included an appearance in the 1973 **European Cup-winners Cup** final (0–1 v **AC Milan**) and the semi-final of the 1970 European Cup (1–3 agg. v **Celtic**). The Leeds side of this period included Jack Charlton, Allan Clarke, Billy **Bremner**, Johnny **Giles** and Peter Lorimer. Revie left Leeds in 1974 to manage **England** and was replaced by Brian **Clough**, who had often criticised Leeds in the past for "gamesmanship". The former **Derby County** manager survived only 44 days in charge of the club before being dismissed. However, Leeds won a second League title in 1973-74 and reached the European Cup final in 1975 (0–2 v **Bayern Munich**). Crowd trouble at the final resulted in a seven-year UEFA-imposed ban from European competition. Seven years later, Leeds was relegated and financial difficulties forced it to sell Elland Road in 1985 to the local council, with the club granted a 125-year "licence" (see Elland Road) on the ground. Howard Wilkinson was appointed manager in 1988 and, in 1989-90, the club returned to the top flight. Leeds was the last club to win the League Championship (1991-92) before the establishment of the Premier League. The title-winning team included Frenchman Eric **Cantona**, but he departed the following season and the club has since failed to maintain a serious challenge for honours, losing in the 1996 League Cup Final in a one-sided encounter against **Aston Villa** (0–3). Wilkinson, who was later appointed the Football Association's **technical director**, was sacked after the club made a poor start to the 1996-97 season and replaced by George **Graham,** who had recently completed a 12-month ban from the game, imposed for financial impropriety. Graham departed amid controversy in October 1998 and was replaced by his assistant David O'Leary. In August 1996, Leeds, under the name Leeds Sporting, floated on the stock market (flotation price = 19p). *League record* Premier League 1992-93; Division One 1924-25 to 1926-27, 1928-29 to 1930-31, 1932-33 to 1946-47, 1956-57 to 1959-60, 1964-65 to 1981-82, 1990-91 to 1991-92; Division Two 1920-21 to 1923-24, 1927-28, 1931-32, 1947-48 to 1955-56, 1960-61 to 1963-64, 1982-83 to 1989-90. *Honours* League 1968-69, 1973-74, 1991-92; Division Two 1923-24, 1963-64, 1989-90; FA Cup 1972 (1–0 v **Arsenal** – *Team* Harvey, Reaney, Madeley, Bremner, Charlton, Hunter, Lorimer, Clarke (1), Jones, Giles, E Gray; League Cup 1968 (1–0 v Arsenal); **FA Charity Shield** 1969 (2–1 v **Manchester City**), 1992 (4–3 v Liverpool); UEFA (Fairs) Cup 1968 (1–0 agg. v **Ferencváros** – *Team* first leg (home) Sprake, Reaney, Cooper, Bremner, Charlton, Hunter, Lorimer, Madeley, Jones (1) (Belfitt), Giles (Greenhoff), E Gray; second leg (away): Sprake, Reaney, Cooper, Bremner, Charlton, Hunter, O'Grady, Lorimer, Jones, Madeley, Hibbitt (Bates)), 1971 (3–3, away goals v **Juventus** – *Team* first leg (away) Sprake, Reaney, Cooper, Bremner, J Charlton, Hunter, Lorimer, Clarke, Jones (Bates (1)), Giles, Madeley (1); second leg (home): Sprake, Reaney, Cooper, Bremner, Charlton, Hunter, Lorimer, Clarke (1), Jones, Giles, Madeley (Bates)). *Records* Billy Bremner is United's most capped player (54 for **Scotland**); Jack Charlton holds the record for club appearances (629, 1953-73); Peter Lorimer is the record league goalscorer (168, 1965-79, 1983-86).

Left On The Shelf (LOTS) *misc.* campaign group formed by **Tottenham Hotspur** supporters in 1988 to prevent the club from replacing the middle terrace area of the East Stand (known as The Shelf and constructed in the early-1930s) with seating and **executive box**es. The campaign delayed the work, which meant that Tottenham was unable to play its opening fixture of the 1988-89 season against **Coventry City**. As a result, the club had two points deducted, although this was later commuted to a £15,000 fine. LOTS and the club eventually reached a compromise, albeit a short-lived one, whereby some of the area would be retained for standing supporters. The recommendations of the **Taylor Report** eventually prevented the retention of the terrace, which in the summer of 1994 was converted to seating.

left back *n.* **defender** who plays on the left side of a **formation**.

left half *n.* **midfielder** who plays on the left side of a **formation**.

left wing *n.* the left side of a **formation**.

left winger *n.* **attacker** who plays on the left side of a **formation**.

Lefter, Kücükandonyadis *player* Striker **Turkey** international (21 goals, 46 caps, 1948-62). *Club* **Fenerbahçe**. *Keynotes* Record scorer for the Turkish national side; scored twice in Turkey's famous 3–1 victory which ended **Hungary's** two-year unbeaten run (19 February 1956, Istanbul, friendly).

Legia Warsaw *club* Polish national league side based in the capital Warsaw, founded in 1916 (Polish name: Legia Warszawa). Ground: Wojska Polskiego, capacity: 18,000. Strip: green shirts, green shorts. *Keynotes* Legia was deducted two points for alleged **match fixing** on the last game of the season in 1993, thus losing the league championship to **Lech Poznan**. Three other clubs, **LKS Lódź**, Olimpia Poznan and **Wisla Krakow** were also deducted three points for their alleged involvement. **European Cup** semi-final 1970, quarter-final 1971; **European Cup-winners Cup** quarter-final 1982; **Fairs Cup/UEFA Cup** third-round 1969, second round 1997 (including two preliminary round victories); Polish League champions 1955 and 1956 (as CWKS Warszawa), 1969, 1970, 1994, 1995; Polish Cup 1955, 1956 (as CWKS Warszawa), 1964, 1966, 1973, 1980, 1981, 1989, 1990, 1994, 1995, 1997 (more than any other Polish club). Notable former players: Jan **Tomaszewski**, Kazimierz **Deyna**.

Leicester City *club* English league. *Dossier* Ground: **Filbert Street**, Leicester. Strip: blue shirts with white/yellow trim, blue shorts with white trim, blue socks. Website: http://www.lcfc.co.uk Nickname: Foxes. Ground capacity: 22,517 all seated. Record attendance: 47,298 v **Tottenham Hotspur** (18 February 1928, **FA Cup**, fifth round). Best average attendance: 31,359 (1957-58). Biggest win: 10–0 v **Portsmouth** (20 October 1928, Division One). Biggest defeat: 0–12 (as **Leicester Fosse**) v **Nottingham Forest** (21 April 1909, Division One). *History* The club began life as Leicester Fosse in 1884, when a dozen former Wyggeston School students paid nine pence each to buy a football and a further nine pence as a subscription. The club's original name was inspired by the part of Leicester – Roman Fosse Way – from which most of the team came. Fosse played its first matches at Victoria Park, which, at the time, was also the home of Leicester Rugby Club, before settling at the club's present Filbert Street ground in 1891. Fosse was elected to the **Football League** in 1894, finishing fourth in Division Two in the club's first season. The club won promotion to the top flight in 1908, but was relegated the following season. In 1912, Fosse finished a match (v **Grimsby Town**, 6 January, Division Two) with only five players after the rest of the team had left the pitch due to the bad weather conditions. At the start of the 1919-20 season, Leicester Fosse became Leicester City. Leicester has never been out of the top two divisions and the club's best position in Division One was achieved in 1928-29, when it finished one point behind the championship winners, The Wednesday (later **Sheffield Wednesday**). City just avoided relegation from the Second Division in

1949 but reached the **FA Cup Final** that year for the first time. The club's longest spell in the top flight occurred between 1957 and 1969, and for most of this period Leicester was under the managership of Matt Gillies. The 1960s was also Leicester's most successful period in cup competition. City won the **League Cup** in 1964 (4–3 agg. v **Stoke City**), lost in the final of the same competition a year later (2–3 agg. v **Chelsea**) and appeared in three **FA Cup** finals during the 1960s: 1961 (0–2 v **Tottenham Hotspur**), 1963 (1–3 v **Manchester United**), 1969 (0–1 v **Manchester City**). The victorious League Cup team included England goalkeeper Gordon **Banks**. Leicester's defeat in the 1969 FA Cup final meant that the club joined a unique group of clubs which have appeared in the final and been relegated in the same season (others are **Brighton & Hove Albion** (1982-83), **Manchester City** (1925-26), **Middlesbrough** (1996-97)). The club returned to the top flight in 1971 but continued to yo-yo between the top two divisions despite having teams that over the years included a number of talented individual players, such as Allan Clarke, Gary **Lineker**, Peter **Shilton**, Alan Smith, Keith Weller and Frank Worthington. In 1994, having twice failed to win promotion to the top flight at the end-of-season **playoff** stage (1992 0–1 v **Blackburn Rovers**; 1993 3–4 v **Swindon Town**), the club secured a place in the Premier League via the playoffs (2–1 v **Derby County**), only to be relegated again the following season. Again, the club returned to the Premier League the next season after Steve Claridge's last-minute goal in the playoffs (2–1 v **Crystal Palace**). Leicester not only consolidated its position in the top flight in 1996-97 by finishing ninth, the club also won its first major trophy for 33 years – a League Cup final replay victory over **Middlesbrough**. The victory also secured the club a place in Europe (**UEFA Cup**) for the first time since 1961 – in that year, the club had played in the **European Cup-winners Cup** as losing FA Cup finalists because **double** winners Tottenham Hotspur entered the **European Cup**. In 1997-98, Leicester was defeated over two legs by **Atlético Madrid**, just as the club had been 36 years previously. In October 1997, Leicester floated on the stock market (flotation price = 93p). *League record* Premier League 1994-95; 1996-97 to present; Division One 1908-09, 1925-26 to 1934-35, 1937-38 to 1938-39, 1954-55; 1957-58 to 1968-69, 1971-72 to 1977-78, 1980-81, 1983-84 to 1986-87; First Division 1992-93 to 1993-94, 1995-96; Division Two 1894-95 to 1907-08, 1909-10 to 1924-25, 1935-36 to 1936-37, 1946-47 to 1953-54, 1955-56 to 1956-57, 1969-70 to 1970-71, 1978-79 to 1979-80, 1981-82 to 1982-83, 1987-88 to 1991-92. *Honours* Division Two 1924-25, 1936-37, 1953-54, 1956-57, 1970-71, 1979-80; League Cup 1964 (4–3 agg. v Stoke City), 1997 (1–0 replay/a.e.t. v Middlesbrough); **FA Charity Shield** 1971 (1–0 v **Liverpool**). *Records* John O'Neill is Leicester's most capped player (39 for **Northern Ireland**); Adam Black holds the record for club appearances (528, 1920-35); Arthur Chandler is Leicester's record league goalscorer

(259, 1923-35) but he did NOT score in 16 successive games, as so many books claim.

Leicester City plc *n.* publicly-quoted business which owns **Leicester City**. The club became a fully listed company on the London Stock Exchange in October 1997 (flotation price = 93p). Leicester had a market capitalisation – the market value of the company's issued share capital (eg, the quoted price of its shares multiplied by the number of shares outstanding) – of £30.6 million on flotation.

Leicester University *misc.* English university and home of the **Sir Norman Chester Centre for Football Research**. The University also offers post-graduate courses in the sociology of sport, and has links with university departments in other European countries such as Germany and Italy. The Centre for Research into Sport and Society, runs a campus-based Master of Arts in the Sociology of sport and a Master of Science by distance learning on the Sociology of sport and sports management. Components of the course include the development of major sports such as football, the political and cultural significance of sport, the relationship between sport, gender, class and race, and issues such as health, drugs and violence.

Leitch, Archibald *architect/engineer* Glasgow-based architect/engineer (1866 to 1939) who was the principal designer of football grounds and stands throughout the UK from the turn of the century. Leitch was popular because he made the limited budgets of clubs stretch. His trademark was two-tier stands with a centre gable on the roof and later double-decker stands with a balcony and criss-crossed steelwork. Leitch's first English commission was the John Street stand at **Sheffield United**'s **Bramall Lane** ground, which opened in 1902. He also was responsible for designing **Middlesbrough**'s **Ayresome Park** in 1903 at the same time as developing a huge bowl in Glasgow called **Hampden Park**. Leitch was hired to redevelop **Stamford Bridge** after Gus Mears and Fred Parker had visited grounds that he had designed, including Hampden Park, **Ibrox** and Parkhead (**Celtic Park**) in Glasgow. He also designed **Arsenal**'s new ground, **Highbury**, which opened in 1913, and was responsible for the development of **Selhurst Park**, home of **Crystal Palace**, in the 1920s. Leitch designed **Goodison Park**'s main stand (at the same time he also planned Anfield's **Kop**), a bigger stand in 1909 and a further double-decker stand in 1926. **Old Trafford**, built at a cost £60,000, was created by Leitch, as was the south stand at **Sheffield Wednesday**'s **Hillsborough** ground, which was constructed before World War I. **Portsmouth**'s **Fratton Park** also has a Leitch-designed south stand, opened in 1925, which includes his trademark balcony. Further along the south coast, Leitch designed the west stand at **Southampton**'s **Dell** ground, which was opened in January 1928 and was destroyed by fire a year later. The Leitch-designed stand at **White Hart Lane**, which was opened for the visit of **Manchester United** on

11 September 1909, had a spurred cockerel perched on a ball on its roof – chosen to reflect the fact that fighting cocks wore spurs, as did Shakespeare's Harry Hotspur character from whom the club drew its name – and the east stand, which opened in September 1934 at a cost of £60,000, was his most expensive design. One of Leitch's most distinctive designs was the seven-gable **Molineux** Street stand at **Wolverhampton Wanderers**' ground, which was opened in 1932 and demolished in 1978. Leitch was responsible for the 36,000-capacity west end terrace at Ibrox which collapsed on 5 April 1902 (Scotland v England), killing 26 people and injuring a further 500. Leitch later avoided using wooden terracing, opting, for example, to use reinforced concrete for the construction of the Roker End at **Sunderland**'s **Roker Park** in 1911. He also engineered a complete redevelopment of **Bradford City**'s **Valley Parade** ground from 1908, including the construction of the Main Stand. This stand burned down on 11 May 1985, during the club's final match of the season (v **Lincoln City**), with 11,000 supporters celebrating the team's Division Three Championship: 56 people were killed and more than 200 injured (see **Bradford City fire**).

Leith Athletic *club* former Scottish league. *Dossier* Ground: Old Meadowbank (now Meadowbank Stadium), Lothian. *Keynotes* Joined the expanded **Scottish League** in 1891-92, finishing fourth that season – the club's highest position. Following relegation in 1894-95, the club did not regain its top-flight status until 1930-31 after winning the Division Two title for a third time. On the first two occasions (1905-06 and 1909-10), Leith was denied a place in Division One because automatic promotion/relegation did not begin in Scotland until 1921-22. The club was involved in a series of **test matches** (together with **Cowdenbeath** and **St Bernards**) in 1914-15 to decide the Division Two Championship, which Cowdenbeath won. *League record* Division One 1891-92 to 1894-95, 1930-31 to 1931-32; Division Two 1896-97 to 1914-15, 1927-28 to 1929-30, 1932-33 to 1938-39; C Division 1924-25 to 1925-26; 1946-47. *Honours* Division Two 1905-06, 1909-10, 1929-30.

leitwolf *misc.* German term (meaning wolf) for an inspirational player.

Lens *club* see **RC Lens**.

Leo Victor SV *club* Surinam national league club based in the capital Paramaribo, founded 1934. Strip: orange shirts, orange shorts. Surinam league champions 1963, 1978, 1982.

León (full name: Club Social y Deportivo León) *club* Mexican national league club, based in León and founded in 1920 (as León Atlético until 1944). Ground: Estadio Nou Camp, capacity: 40,000. Strip: green shirts and white shorts. **CONCACAF Champion Clubs Cup** – runners-up 1993 (finished second in a four-club final league in Guatemala City, behind **Deportivo Saprissa** of Costa Rica), semi-final/fourth 1998; Mexican League Champions 1948, 1949, 1952, 1956 and 1992; Mexican Cup (Copa Mexico) 1949, 1958, 1967, 1972 and 1973.

Lesotho *country CAF* Kingdom in southern Africa, an enclave within South Africa, formerly Basutoland. Rugged and mountainous. Independence in 1966. Area: 30,345 sq km (11,715 sq miles). Population: 2,110,000 (1996 est.). Languages: Sethotho and English. Capital: Maseru. *Dossier* Lesotho Football Association (Meseru) formed in 1932, affiliated to **FIFA** in 1962 and **Confédération Africaine de Football** (CAF) in 1964, member of the **Confederation of Southern African Football Associations** (COSAFA), president: Morapeli Motaung; general secretary: Salemane Phafane. Season played from January to October. National stadium: Setsotho Stadium, Maseru, capacity: 20,000. National strip: blue shirts, green shorts and white socks. Nickname of national team: the Crocodiles. First international game: 7 March 1971 v **Madagascar** (1–2, friendly, home). Biggest victory: 4–0 v **Botswana** (28 June 1991, away, **African Cup of Nations** qualifier). Biggest defeat: 0–7 v **Zaire** (25 July 1993, away, African Cup of Nations qualifier) *International tournament record* **Olympic Games** – first entered 1980, never qualified for finals tournament; **Women's World Cup** – first entered 1999; **World Cup** – first entered 1974, never past first round of qualifying tournament (entered only in 1974 and 1982); African Cup of Nations – first entered 1974, never qualified for finals tournament; **Under-17 World Championship** – never qualified; **World Youth Cup** (under-20) – never qualified. *Record against British and Irish national teams* none played. *History* Lesotho's football association was founded in 1932. The national league championship has been played since 1970 and was first won by **Maseru United Brothers**. *Record in international club tournaments* **African Cup of Champion Clubs** – **Matlama FC** (quarter-final 1979); Arsenal (see **Arsenal, Lesotho**, second round 1990); **African Cup-winners Cup** – Maseru United Brothers (second round 1979), Arsenal (second round 1993); **CAF Cup** – Arsenal (second round 1995) Other leading clubs: Chelsea, **Royal Lesotho Defence Force** (RLDF), Majanja (of Mohales Hoek, league champions 1971, 1995), Roma Rovers (of Roma, previously Roma University, league champions 1996).

Let's kick racism out of Football *misc.* campaign launched by the Campaign for Racial Equality (CRE) and **Professional Footballers Association** (PFA) at the start of the 1994-95 season to combat racism in the game. Initially the campaign was supported by 91 of the 92 professional clubs, with only **York City** declining to participate. The campaign includes a nine-point action plan for clubs to combat racism, including publishing a statement highlighting the clubs' support for the campaign and how it will deal with racist supporters. By 1998, some 87% of supporters said that they were aware of the campaign. There have been similar campaigns on the continent. In Italy, players in both **Serie A** and Serie B paraded banners proclaiming "No al razzimo" ("No to racism") before the start of matches on 13 December 1992. This action followed the racial abuse of two Dutch players, Ruud **Gullit** and Aaron Winter. A similar protest by players occurred in Germany in December 1992, with all players' shirts displaying the slogan "Mein freund ist Auslander" ("My friend is a foreigner").

Leventis United *club* Former Nigerian national league club based in Ibadam, defunct since 1987. **African Cup-winners Cup** runners-up 1985 (1–2 agg., v **Al Ahly** of Egypt); Nigerian league champions 1986; Nigerian FA Challenge Cup 1984, 1986.

Levski Sofia *club* Bulgarian national league club based in the capital Sofia, formed 1914 (known as Dinamo from 1949-57 and Levski Spartak from 1969-85). Ground: Georgi Asparuchov, capacity: 45,000 (Levski also play at the national stadium, capacity: 70,000). Strip: blue shirts, blue shorts. *Keynotes* The club was forced to change its name to Vitosha (the name of the mountain adjacent to the city) from 1985-89 after players from both sides fought in front of the Communist Party leadership at the 1985 Cup final against **CSKA Sofia**. **UEFA Cup** quarter-final 1976; Bulgarian league champions 1933, 1937, 1942, 1946, 1947, 1949, 1950, 1953, 1965, 1968, 1970, 1974, 1977, 1979, 1984, 1985, 1988, 1993, 1994, 1995; Bulgarian Cup/Soviet Army Cup 1942, 1946, 1947, 1949, 1950, 1956, 1957, 1959, 1967, 1970, 1971, 1976, 1977, 1979, 1984, 1987, 1988; Republic Cup 1982, 1984, 1986, 1991, 1991, 1992, 1994, 1998.

Lewis, John *player/referee* former player, referee and founder member of the **Football League** committee in 1888. Born 1855, died 1926. *Keynotes* Refereed **FA Cup** finals in 1895, 1897 and 1898. Believed to have refereed more than 1,000 games in 25 years. Lewis refereed the controversial 1920 **Olympic Games** football final in Antwerp (**Belgium** v **Czechoslovakia**) when aged 65. Belgium won by default, the Czech team having walked out in protest after Lewis sent off one of its players.

Leyland Daf Trophy *competition* name given to the former **Associate Members Cup** between 1989-90 and 1990-91, and a competition open only to clubs from Divisions Three and Four. *Final results* 1989-90, **Tranmere Rovers** 2–1 **Bristol Rovers**, 1990-91, **Birmingham City** 3–2 **Stoke City**.

Leyton Orient *club* English league. *Dossier* Ground: **Brisbane Road**, east London, capacity: 13,842. Strip: red shirts with thin white stripes, white shorts, red socks. Nickname: Os. Record attendance: 34,345 v **West Ham United** (25 January 1964, **FA Cup**, fourth round). Best average attendance: 17,254 (1956-57). Biggest win: 8–0 v **Crystal Palace** (12 November 1955, Division Three (South)), v **Doncaster Rovers** (28 December 1997, Division Three). Biggest defeat: 0–8 v **Aston Villa** (30 January 1929, FA Cup, fourth round replay). *History* Founded in 1888 as the football section of Eagle Cricket Club (previously Glyn Cricket Club), eventually adopting the name Orient at

the suggestion of a player who was employed by the Orient Steam Navigation Company. In 1898, the prefix Clapton was added, which was used until 1946, when the club became Leyton Orient. Between 1966 and 1977 the club was known simply as Orient, after which it reverted to Leyton Orient. The club played at several venues, including Whittles Athletic Ground and a ground at Lea Bridge Road, before finally settling at Osborne Road, which later became Brisbane Road. Orient was elected to Division Two in 1905-06, finishing fourth in 1910-11 and 1911-12. Orient's most successful League season came in 1962-63 when it won promotion to the top flight for the first and only time. The following season, Orient finished bottom of Division One – the club's highest League position – 10 points adrift of the next placed team, having lost 27 games and conceded 81 goals. By 1966-67, Orient was playing in Division Three and, with the club more than £100,000 in debt, it almost folded. Generous financial support from supporters helped to halve the debt and the club's position was further helped by the sale of Tommy Taylor to West Ham United for £80,000 in 1970; a year in which the club also won the Division Three Championship. Orient was relegated to Division Four in 1984-85, returning to a higher grade via the end-of-season **playoffs** in 1988-89 (2–1 agg. v **Wrexham**). Orient has enjoyed several FA Cup **giantkilling** achievements over the years. In 1978, the club was an FA Cup semi-finalist (0–3 v **Arsenal**), having defeated **Chelsea** (1–2 replay, fifth round) and **Norwich City** (1–0 replay, third round). Aside from 1978, the club has reached the quarter-final stage of the FA Cup on three occasions: 1926 (1–6 v **Manchester City**), 1954 (0–1 v **Port Vale**), 1972 (0–1 v Arsenal). Orient's 1972 FA Cup campaign included a fifth-round victory over Chelsea (3–2). In 1962-63, the club was a **League Cup** quarter-finalist (0–2 v **Bury**). Orient faced further financial problems in 1995, but was saved when boxing promoter Barry Hearns took control of the club. In 1997-98, Orient had three points deducted for fielding suspended players. Orient failed to gain promotion in 1998-99, losing in the Third Division playoff (0-1 v **Scunthorpe United**). *League record* Division One 1962-63; Division Two 1905-06 to 1928-29, 1956-57 to 1961-62, 1963-64 to 1965-66, 1970-71 to 1981-82; Second Division 1992-93 to 1994-95; Division Three 1966-67 to 1969-70, 1982-83 to 1984-85, 1989-90 to 1991-92; Third Division 1995-96–; Division Three (South) 1929-30 to 1955-56; Division Four 1985-86 to 1988-89. *Honours* Division Three 1969-70; Division Three (South) 1955-56. *Records* John Chiedozie is Orient's most capped player (8 (10) for **Nigeria**); Peter Allen holds the record for club League appearances (432, 1965-78); Tom Johnston is Orient's record League goalscorer (121, 1956-58, 1959-61).

Liaoning Football Club *club* Chinese national league club based in Shen-yang (Mukden), the capital of Liaoning province in north-east China. *Keynotes* Liaoning FC holds the Chinese league record of six consecutive championships (1988 to 1993). **Asian Champion Teams Cup** 1989 (3–2 agg., v **Nissan** of Japan), runners-up 1990 (1–2, v **Esteghlal Sports Club** of Iran, in Dhaka, Bangladesh), semi-final 1986, 1993; Chinese league champions 1978, 1985, 1988, 1989, 1990, 1991, 1992, 1993.

Liberia *country CAF* Republic in west Africa on the Atlantic Ocean. Bordered by **Guinea**, **Ivory Coast** and **Sierra Leone**. Founded as an independent republic in 1847. Civil War 1989–92. Area: 111,370 sq km (42,990 sq miles). Population: 2,830,000 (1993 est.). Language: English and more than 20 tribal languages. Capital: Monrovia. *Dossier* Liberia Football Association formed in 1936, affiliated to FIFA and **Confédération Africaine de Football** (CAF) in 1962, member of the **West African Football Union**, president: Edwin Snowe; general secretary: Sackie Kennedy. Season played from January to October. National stadium: National Complex, Monrovia, capacity: 35,000. National strip: red shirts, white shorts and blue socks. Nickname of national team: Lone Star. First international game: 18 January 1964 v **Ghana** (home, 4–5, Olympic Games qualifying tournament). Biggest victory: 4–0 v **Gambia** (home, 23 June 1996, World Cup qualifier). Biggest defeat: 0–6 v Ghana (away, 6 April 1975, World Cup qualifier). Notable international players: George **Weah**, Christopher Wreh. *International tournament record* **Olympic Games** – first entered 1964, never qualified for finals tournament; **Women's World Cup** – never entered. **World Cup** – first entered 1982, never progressed beyond second round of qualifying tournament (second round group stage in 1998, finished third of four nations); **African Cup of Nations** – first entered 1968, qualified for finals tournament 1996 (failed to progress beyond its first round group on **goal difference**); **CEDEAO Tournament** – runners-up 1987 (1–2, v **Ivory Coast**); **Under-17 World Championship** – never qualified; **World Youth Cup** (under-20) – never qualified. *Record against British and Irish national teams* none played. *History* The Liberian national league dates from 1965, with the Cup played since 1974. Most of the major clubs are from the capital Monrovia. The league has been dominated by **Invincible Club** and **Mighty Barolle**. In 1995 George Weah became the first African to be voted **FIFA World Footballer of the Year**. Neither the national side nor any of Liberia's club sides has won a major international tournament. *Record in international club tournaments* **African Cup of Champion Clubs** – **Invincible Eleven** (second round 1982), **Mighty Barolle** (second round 1987); **African Cup-winners Cup** – **LPRC Oilers** (quarter-final 1989); **West African Cup** – St **Joseph Warriors** (semi final 1984). Other leading clubs: Junior Professional (Monrovia, league champions 1996).

libero *n.* player who combines a defensive **sweeper** role (either in front or behind the defence) with initiating, and participating in, attacks (also referred to as a sweeper-cum-schemer). The libero role requires a high degree of tactical awareness, excellent (long and short) passing skills and the ability to bring the ball out of defence. The former West **Germany** international Franz **Beckenbauer** often fulfilled the libero role for his country.

Libertad (Club Libertad) *club* Paraguay national league club based in the capital Asuncion, founded in 1905. Ground: Estadio Alfredo Stroessner, capacity: 45,000. Strip: black and white striped shirts, black shorts. **Copa Libertadores** second round group 1977; Paraguay League champions 1910, 1917, 1920, 1930, 1943, 1945, 1955, 1976.

Libertas *club* San Marino league club based in Borgomaggiore, founded 1928. Ground: Fonte dell'Ovo, capacity: 500. San Marino League champions 1996; San Marino Cup 1937, 1950, 1954, 1958, 1959, 1961, 1987, 1989, 1991.

Liberté *club* Niger national league club, based in the capital Niamey. Ground: Stade 29 Juillet, Niamey, capacity: 30,000 (Niger's national stadium). Strip: blue shirts and black shorts. Niger Cup 1975, 1976, 1988 and 1990.

Libya *country CAF* Republic in north Africa on the Mediterranean Sea, bordering **Egypt**, **Sudan**, **Chad**, **Niger**, **Algeria** and **Tunisia**. Italian colony until 1942, then controlled by Britain and France. Independence in 1951. Libya is heavily dependent on oil for its revenue, though this has suffered due to sanctions for alleged terrorist activities against other countries in 1980s and early 1990s. Area: 1,759,540 sq km (679,180 sq miles). Population: 5,590,000 (1996 est.). Languages: Arabic, Italian and English. Capital: Tripoli. *Dossier* Libyan Arab Football Confederation (Tripoli) formed in 1962, affiliated to FIFA in 1963 and **Confédération Africaine de Football** (CAF) in 1965, member of the Arab Football Union, president: Bel-Eied Ali El-Meshairi; general secretary: Othman Saied Ali Zentani. Season played from September to April. National stadium: 11 June Stadium, Tripoli, capacity: 45,000. National strip: green shirts, white shorts and green socks. First international game: 1958, v Tunisia (friendly, 0–4). Biggest victories: 4–0, v **Indonesia** 26 July 1977, (neutral venue, friendly); 4–0, v **Malta** 9 October 1983, (in Tripoli, friendly); and 4–0, v Sudan 8 March 1985 (in Tripoli, World Cup qualifier). Biggest defeat: 0–5 v **Poland** (19 August 1979, in Slupsk, Poland, friendly). *International tournament record* **Olympic Games** – first entered 1968, never qualified for finals tournament; **Women's World Cup** – never entered; **World Cup** – first entered 1970, reached fourth and final round of the 1986 qualifying tournament (1–3 agg., v **Morocco**), never qualified for finals tournament (did not enter 1994, 1998); **African Cup of Nations** – first entered 1968, runners-up 1982 (1–1, 6–7 pens., v **Ghana**, in Tripoli), hosts 1982 (Libya has qualified for the finals tournament only as hosts); **Arab Cup of Nations** – runners-up 1964 (league of five, in Kuwait); **Under-17 World Championship** – never qualified; **World Youth Cup (under-20)** – never qualified. *Record against British and Irish national teams* none played. *History* National league championship started 1963-64, first won by **Al Ahly Tripoli**. On 9 July 1996, at a derby match between Libya's top clubs, Al Ahly Tripoli and **Al Ittihad**, at least 20 people were reported killed and many more injured when shooting broke out between armed guards and fans. The incident happened when the referee ruled in favour of one of the clubs, supposedly controlled by a son of Libyan leader Colonel Gadafy. Fans were shouting anti-Gadafy slogans and were shot by armed guards of Gadafy's sons. Other fans invaded the pitch and the referee was stabbed. The Libyan government declared a day of national mourning and the two clubs – both innocent of any provocation – were disbanded. Al Ahly had won the match 1–0. *Record in international club tournaments* **African Cup of Champion Clubs** – Al Ittihad (quarter-final 1967), Al Ahly Tripoli (quarter final 1972), **African Cup-winners Cup**: Al Ahly Tripoli (semi-final 1984), **Al Nasr** (semi-final 1985). Other leading clubs: **Al Ahly Benghazi**, Al Tahaddy (of Benghazi, league champions 1967, 1977, 1998).

licensing system *legal* permit ensuring that a football ground meets the current safety regulation. *History* Two UK government reports – one produced as a result of the crowd problems (1,000 casualties) at the first Wembley **FA Cup** final in 1923 (Cmnd 2088, 1924) and the other after 33 supporters were killed at **Bolton Wanderers**' **Burnden Park** ground in 1946 (Cmnd 6846, 1947) – recommended stadium licensing systems and fire precautions but they were largely ignored. A third report (Cmnd 4952, 1972), as result of the inquiry chaired by Lord Wheatley into the 1971 **Ibrox Park disaster**, in which 66 people died, led to the **Safety of Sports Ground Act** 1975. Both Lord Justice **Popplewell**'s final report on the **Bradford City fire** and the **Taylor Report** examining the **Hillsborough disaster** have influenced changes to safety regulations covering sports grounds in the UK.

Liddell, Billy *player* Winger. **Scotland** international (28 caps). Born 10 January 1922. Career ca. 1938-61. *Club* **Liverpool**. *Keynotes* Joined Liverpool in 1938, turning professional in April 1939. He made 495 **Football League** appearances for Liverpool, scoring 216 goals. Liddell was an FA Cup finalist in 1950 (0–2 v **Arsenal**). He played for **Great Britain** against the Rest of Europe in both 1947 and 1955 (only Stanley **Matthews** also appeared in both sides). Still revered as one of Liverpool's greatest. Included in the **Football League Centenary 100 players**. *Honours* League Championship (Liverpool 1946-47).

Liechtenstein *country UEFA* Landlocked principality in the central Alps between Switzerland and Austria. Sovereign state since 1342. Customs and currency union with Switzerland. Area: 160 sq km (62 sq miles). Population: 30,900 (1995 est.). Languages: Alemannish and German. Capital: Vaduz. *Dossier* Football association (Liechtensteiner Fussball-Verband, Vaduz) formed in 1934, affiliated to FIFA and **Union of European Football Associations** (UEFA) in 1974, president:

Otto Biedermann; general secretary: Antoine Lemaire. Season played from August to June. National stadium: Sportplatz, Eschen, capacity: 5,000. National strip: blue shirts, red shorts and blue socks. First international game: 14 June 1981 v **Malta** (1–1, Seoul, Korea, Presidents Cup). Biggest victory: 2–0 v **China** (6 June 1982, Vaduz, friendly). Biggest defeat: 1–11 v **Macedonia** (9 November 1996, World Cup qualifier). Most capped players: Daniel Hasler (22 appearances, ca. 1994-), Daniel Telser (22 appearances, ca. 1994-). Other notable international players: Moser (scored both goals in the victory over China, above). Website: *http://www.lie-net.li* (official). *International tournament record* **Women's World Cup** – never entered; **World Cup** – entered for the first time in the 1998 tournament (finished last of six nations, losing all 10 matches, scoring three goals and conceding 52); **European Championship** – entered for the first time in the 1996 tournament (finished last of six nations, losing all but one game – a 0–0 draw with the **Republic of Ireland** – finishing with one point, one goal scored and 40 conceded); **European Championship for Women** – never entered. *World Cup performance* (finals and qualifiers to end of 1998 tournament) played 10, won 0, drawn 0, lost 10, scored 3 goals, conceded 51 goals; win rate 0%; goals scored per game 0.3. *Record against British and Irish national teams* v **Republic of Ireland** – played four drawn one, lost three; v **Northern Ireland** – played two lost two. *History* The Liechtenstein Cup is the country's only domestic tournament and has been in existence since 1946. It has been largely dominated by **FC Balzers**, **FC Vaduz**, and FC Triesen. FC Vaduz holds the European and joint-world record of seven consecutive domestic cup triumphs (1956 to 1962). It also holds the world record of appearing in 17 consecutive domestic cup finals (1946 to 1962). FC Vaduz and FC Triesen competed in nine consecutive cup domestic cup finals (1946 to 1954), also a world record. Until the 1996 European Championship, Liechtenstein had only played friendly matches or invitation tournaments. In 1981 it played three matches in Korea, against Malta, Thailand and Indonesia (winning 3–2 against the latter). A year later it beat China in a friendly match in Vaduz (see above). Liechtenstein played its first senior tournament game on 20 April 1994 (1–4, v Northern Ireland, in Belfast, European Championship qualifier). Its best result in championship matches was a 0–0 draw against the **Republic of Ireland** (3 June 1995, Eschen, European Championship qualifier). The country has the unfortunate distinction of conceding more goals than any other European nation in the 1998 World Cup qualifying tournament: 52 goals in 10 games, scoring only three; however it was beaten to the world record by **Maldives**, with 59 goals from six matches. *League system* Liechtenstein has only a handful of registered clubs, these playing in the Swiss League. It has, however, a domestic cup competition, with the final played in mid May (the winners qualify for the **European Cup-**

winners Cup). *Record in international club tournaments* European Cup-winners Cup – FC Balzers (first round 1994), FC Vaduz (first round 1997); Liechtenstein clubs have no automatic entry to the **European Cup** or **UEFA Cup**. Other leading clubs: FC Triesen (Liechtenstein Cup eight times to 1998), USV Eschen (Cup four times to 1998).

Liedholm, Nils *player* Striker/midfield. **Sweden** international (18 caps, 12 goals). Born 8 October 1922. Career ca. 1946-58 *Clubs* **IFK Norköpping**, **Milan**. *Keynotes* One of the **Gre-no-li** trio. Liedholm scored the opening goal in the 1958 **World Cup** final, after four minutes: a superb dribble and shot, later described by Pelé as the best goal ever scored against Brazil. Liedholm may well have scored many more goals than the dozen he struck for Sweden, had his country not barred professional players from its squad in the early 1950s; Leidholm and his Gre-no-li partners, Gunnar **Gren** and Gunnar **Nordhal**, were omitted from Sweden's 1950 and 1954 World Cup squads. He was transferred to Milan in 1949, and scored 60 goals in 367 games. Played for Milan in the 1958 European Cup (2-3, v Real Madrid). In 1964 Liedholm became coach of Milan; he was later the coach at **Fiorentina** and **Roma**. *Honour:* **Olympic Games** gold medal (Sweden, 1948); World Cup runner-up (Sweden, 1958); Swedish league championship (IFK Norköpping 1945, 1946, 1947, 1948); Italian Serie A championship 1951, 1955, 1957.

Lierse SK *club* Belgium national league club based in Lier, founded 1906. Ground: Herman Vanderpoortenstadion, capacity: 14,000. Strip: yellow shirts with black sleeves, yellow shorts. **European Cup** Champions League 1998; Belgian league champions 1931, 1942, 1960, 1997; Belgian Cup 1969.

Liga Calcio *competition* The Italian national football league. See **Serie A**.

Liga Deportiva Alajuelense *club* see **Alajuelense.**

Liga Deportivo Universitaria (Quito) *club* Ecuador national Primera league club based in the capital Quito. Founded 1930. Ground: Estadio Olimpico Atahualpa, capacity: 46,000. Strip: white shirts with a red "U" on the chest, white shorts. **Copa Libertadores** semi-final 1975, 1976; Ecuador league champions 1969, 1974, 1975, 1990, 1998.

Liga Mediterrania *competition* see **Mediterranean League.**

Liga Santiaguena de Futbol *competition* one of the former and oldest of the regional leagues of **Argentina**, set up, in 1906, in the city and state of Santiago del Estero in northern Argentina. Clubs from areas outside the four major cities on the Rio de la Plata and the Paraná River (Buenos Aires, La Plata, Rosario and Santa Fe) were excluded from the official national championships until 1967.

ligament *medical* a tough, thickened band of fibrous tissue that connects **bones** and forms the protective capsule surrounding **joints**. Ligaments have a very rich blood supply. If they snap or **rupture,** bleeding can be considerable. Ligament injuries occur when the liga-

ments are over-stretched, resulting in a minor **sprain**, or in a moderate sprain if some of the fibres are torn, or in the complete rupture of the ligament. Surgery may be required to repair a ruptured ligament, but otherwise should be treated by **RICE**. It is important to allow ligaments to rest for six weeks and to avoid the temptation of returning to full training or playing too early. Common injuries are to the knee and foot ligaments, in particular the **cruciate ligaments**, the **collateral ligaments** and the **anterior talofibular ligament**.

lightning *misc.* a flash of light in the sky caused by a discharge of electricity in the atmosphere. People struck by lightning can suffer severe burns or even death. Several footballers have been hit by lightning while playing. *Keynotes* John White, the **Tottenham Hotspur** and **Scotland** (22 caps) forward, was killed by lighting on 21 July 1964, while playing golf in Enfield. He was only 27 years old. Five players were struck by lightning in an Amateur Cup quarter-final match on 25 February 1967 (Highgate v Enfield Town); 23-year-old Tommy Allden died of his injuries. Eleven players from a village side in the **Congo Democratic Republic** were struck by lightning and killed in October 1998. Around 30 fans were injured at the match, played in the province of Eastern Kaasai. Also, in October 1998, several players were injured when struck by lightning during a match in **South Africa** between Jomo Cosmos and Moroka Swallows.

Lilleshall National Sports Centre *misc.* home of the **Football Association**'s National School, a football academy for the training and development of leading young players, located near Newport, Shropshire. Founded in 1984.

Lillestrøm SK (Sporstklubb) *club* Norwegian national league club based in Lillestrøm, founded in 1917. Ground: Åråsen, capacity:, 15,000. Strip: yellow shirts, black shorts. **European Cup** second round 1979; Norwegian league champions 1959, 1976, 1977,1986, 1989; Norwegian Cup 1977, 1978, 1981, 1985.

Lima disaster *disaster* Stadium disaster at the Estadio Nacional in Lima, **Peru** on 25 May 1964. More than 300 people were killed following a riot at the end of Peru's match against **Argentina**. The riot was triggered by a disallowed goal by the home side. More than 500 spectators were injured.

Limbe Leaf Wanderers *club* Malawi Super League club, based in Limbe. Also known as Telecom Wanderers, formerly known as Yamaha Wanderers. Ground: Limbe, capacity: 11,000. Strip: green shirts and white shorts. **East and Central African Club Championship** semi-final 1980 and 1981; Malawi National Super League champions 1990, 1996, 1997, 1998; Blantyre and District regional champions twice (regional leagues operated before the Super League started in 1986); Kamuzu Cup four times; Chibuku Cup five times.

Limerick FC *club* Republic of Ireland national league club based in Limerick, County Limerick in the south-west of Ireland. Founded 1937, known as Limerick United 1979-83, Limerick City 1983-92, current name readopted 1993. Ground: Rathbane, capacity: 10,000. Strip: blue shirts, white shorts. *Keynotes* At the start of the 1998-99 season, Limerick appointed Siobhan Furlong, a Republic of Ireland women's international, as its coach – the first woman in the Irish League to achieve the position. Republic of Ireland league champions 1960, 1980 (as United); Republic of Ireland **FAI Cup** 1971, 1982 (as United), runners-up 1965, 1966, 1977.

limited company (Ltd) *misc.* a company whose owners have only limited liability for its debts. Many football clubs became limited companies before the turn of the century to prevent the owners incurring financial penalties as a result of stadium incidents. For example, one fan, injured when a stand collapsed at **Blackburn Rovers**' **Ewood Park** ground in 1897, was awarded £25 compensation after the club was judged to have been negligent. In 1885, Burslem **Port Vale** became the first club to adopt limited company status. Several other clubs, including Small Heath (later **Birmingham City**) in 1888, quickly followed. In 1896, (**Greenock**) **Morton**, then called Morton, was the first club in **Scotland** to become in limited company.

Lincoln City *club* English league. *Dossier* Ground: **Sincil Bank**, Lincolnshire, capacity: 10,918. Strip: red and white striped shirts, black shorts, red socks with white trim. Nickname: Red Imps. Record attendance: 23,196 v **Derby County** (15 September 1967, **League Cup**, fourth round). Best average attendance: 16,775 (1952-53). Biggest win: 11–1 v **Crewe Alexandra** (29 September 1951, Division Three (North)). Biggest defeat: 3–11 v **Manchester City** (23 March 1895, Division Two). *History* Founded in 1884. Lincoln was a **founder member** of Division Two in 1892-93, finishing fifth in 1901-02 – the club's highest League position – before failing re-election on three occasions (1907-08, 1910-11, 1919-20). The club settled at Sincil Bank in 1894 after playing its first matches at a venue known as John O'Gaunt's. Lincoln reached the **FA Cup** fifth round (or today's equivalent) in 1887 (0–3 v **Rangers**), 1890 (0–4 v **Preston North End**), 1902 (1–3 v Derby County). The club has won the Division Three (North) Championship three times (1931-32, 1947-48, 1951-52) since rejoining the League in 1921-22. Relegation from Division Two in 1960-61 was immediately followed by further demotion, to Division Four for the first time in the club's history, in 1962-63. Thereafter the club alternated between the bottom two divisions until, in 1986-87, it became the first club to be automatically demoted to the Vauxhall Conference (replaced by **Scarborough**). Lincoln regained its League status straight away, winning the Vauxhall Conference Championship the following season. In 1997-98, Lincoln won automatic promotion to the Second Division. *League record* Division Two 1892-93 to 1907-08 (failed re-election), 1909-10 to 1910-11 (failed re-election), 1912-13 to 1919-20

(failed re-election), 1932-33 to 1933-34, 1948-49, 1952-53 to 1960-61; Second Division 1998-99 to present; Division Three 1961-62, 1976-77 to 1978-79, 1981-82 to 1985-86; Third Division 1992-93 to 1997-98; Division Three (North) 1921-22 to 1931-32, 1934-35 to 1947-48, 1949-50 to 1951-52; Division Four 1962-63 to 1975-76, 1979-80 to 1980-81,1986-87 (relegated to GM Vauxhall Conference), 1988-89 to 1991-92. *Honours* Division Three (North) 1931-32, 1947-48, 1951-52; Division Four 1975-76; GM Vauxhall Conference 1987-88. *Records* David Pugh (3 (7) for **Wales**) and George Moulson (3 for **Republic of Ireland**) are Lincoln's most capped players; Tony Emery holds the record for club League appearances (402, 1946-59); Andy Graver is Lincoln's record League goalscorer (144, 1950-55, 1958-61).

Lineker, Gary *player/broadcaster* Striker. **England** international (80 caps, 48 goals). Born 30 November 1960. Career ca. 1978-94. *Clubs* **Leicester City**, **Everton**, **Barcelona**, **Tottenham Hotspur**, **Grampus Eight**. *Keynotes* Joined Leicester City as a apprentice in 1977, turning professional in November 1978 and going on to score 95 goals in 194 **Football League** appearances for the club. He transferred to Everton for £800,000 (plus a percentage of profit from a subsequent move), scoring in the club's 1986 FA Cup final defeat (1–3 v **Liverpool**). Lineker moved to Barcelona for £2.75 million in July 1986, winning Spanish Cup and **European Cup-winners Cup** winner's medals before returning to England with Tottenham Hotspur for £1.1 million in 1989. Lineker played in 105 League games for Spurs and scored 67 goals. He joined the Japanese club Grampus Eight at the end of the 1991-92 season. Lineker won the **Golden Boot** at the 1986 **World Cup** by scoring six goals. He scored four more at the 1990 finals and 16 of his international goals were the only ones of the match. In his first 25 appearances for England, Lineker scored 23 goals. During his international career, Lineker scored five hat-tricks, the first against **Turkey** on 16 October 1985. He is England's second highest goalscorer behind Bobby **Charlton**. Lineker was never booked at either club or international level. Voted **Footballer of the Year** and **PFA Footballer of the Year** in 1986, and awarded the OBE in 1992. Now a BBC Sports presenter, fronting *Football Focus*, **Match of the Day** and programmes on **Radio 5 Live**, as well as appearing in the comedy sports quiz show *They think it's all over*. Included in the **Football League Centenary 100 players**. *Honours* Division Two (Leicester City 1979-80); **FA Cup** (Tottenham Hotspur 1991); Spanish Cup (Barcelona 1988); European Cup-winners Cup (Barcelona 1989).

lines *rules.* clear lines which mark out the **field of play**. Lines must be no more than 12 cm (5 inches) wide (Law I(2).

linesman *rules* former name for **assistant referee**. The term was dropped by the **International FA Board** before the 1996-97 season to more accurately reflect the duties of the official, and, as the Board stated at the time, because "it does not reflect the fact that there are also women who are active in this function." The term has been retained, however, for unqualified persons assisting the referee in matches without appointed assistant referees (see **club linesman**).

Linfield FC *club* Northern Ireland national league club based in Belfast, founded 1886. Ground: Windsor Park (national stadium), capacity: 28,000. Strip: blue shirts, white shorts. *Keynotes* Generally associated with Protestant supporters. Linfield was barred from playing its matches against rival Belfast club **Cliftonville**, with its large Catholic support, at either of their home venues from 1970 until 1998; the fixtures were moved to a neutral ground, Windsor Park. By 1998, Linfield had won the Ireland/Northern Ireland league championship 42 times; only two clubs in the world had won more domestic league championships: **Rangers** (47) and **Peñarol** (45). Linfield holds the world record for the most domestic cup triumphs (35 by 1998, five more than **Al Ahly** of Egypt) and five more than **Celtic**). It also holds the Northern Ireland national league record of six consecutive titles (1982- 87) **European Cup** quarter-final 1967; all-Ireland league champions 1891 (the first season), 1892, 1893, 1895, 1898, 1902, 1904, 1907, 1908, 1909, 1911, 1914; **Irish FA Cup** (all-Ireland) winners 1891, 1892, 1893, 1895, 1898, 1899, 1902, 1904, 1912, 1913, 1915, 1916, 1919; Northern Ireland league champions 1922, 1923, 1930, 1932, 1934, 1935, 1949, 1950, 1954, 1955, 1956, 1959, 1961, 1962, 1966, 1969, 1971, 1975, 1978, 1979, 1980, 1982, 1983, 1984, 1985, 1986, 1987, 1989, 1993, 1994; Irish FA Cup (Northern Ireland) 1922, 1923, 1930, 1931, 1934, 1936, 1939, 1942, 1945, 1946, 1948, 1950, 1953, 1960, 1962, 1963, 1970, 1978, 1980, 1982, 1994, 1995. Notable former players: David Walsh (20 caps for the **Republic of Ireland**, 1946-54).

Links Park *ground* Scottish football ground situated in the Tayside region; home of **Montrose**. *Dossier* Ground capacity: 4,338. Pitch dimensions: 103m x 64m. Record attendance: 8,983 v **Dundee** (17 March 1973, **Scottish FA Cup**, third round). *Keynotes* Montrose first played at a ground called Links Park on 12 August 1885 (v **Arbroath**). In 1887, the club opened the current Links Park with a game against the Perth club Caledonia Rangers. Montrose was unable to afford its own goal nets until 1920 so it borrowed those of a local junior side. Although lights were erected in the 1960s, these were not of League standard and were replaced in the 1970s.

Linthouse *club* former-Scottish league. *Dossier* Ground: Langlands Park/Govandale Park, Strathclyde. *Keynotes* Joined Scottish Division Two in 1895-96. The club had four points deducted for fielding an **illegible player** in 1896-97. Linthouse finished fifth the following season, its highest League position. *League record* Division Two 1895-96 to 1899-00.

Lipton Cup *competition* former annual and later occasional fixture between **Uruguay** and **Argentina**,

first played 1905, when it was drawn and the trophy – donated by Thomas Lipton, the English tea producer – was shared. Considered to be the first regular international football tournament outside the United Kingdom. Uruguay won the trophy seven times (1910, 1911, 1912, 1919, 1922, 1927, 1968); Argentina won it nine times (1906, 1907, 1909, 1913, 1915, 1916, 1917, 1937, 1962). The fixture was tied on 11 occasions. It was last played in 1973 (tied). See also **Newton Cup**.

list of players *regulations* see **teamsheet**, **club list of players**.

Liteks Lovech *club* Bulgarian national league club based in Lovech, formed 1921. Ground: Lovech, capacity: 7,000. Bulgarian league champions 1998 (after promotion from second division in 1997).

Lithuania *country UEFA* Republic on the Baltic Sea, bordered by **Latvia**, **Belarus** and **Poland**. Independence declared in 1918, but incorporated into the former **Soviet Union** in 1940. Lithuania was occupied by Germany during World War II and, once again, became part of the Soviet Union in 1944. Unilateral declaration of independence in 1990, with full recognition as independent state a year later. Area: 65,200 sq km (25,174 sq miles). Population: 3,710,000 (1996 census). Languages: Lithuanian, Russian and Polish. Capital: Vilnius. *Dossier* Lithuanian Football Confederation formed in 1922, originally affiliated to FIFA in 1923 (until 1943) and rejoined in 1992, affiliated to the **Union of European Football Associations** (UEFA) in 1992, president: Vytautas Dirmeikis; general secretary: Pranas Miezelis. Season played from August to May, with a winter break from November to March. National stadium: Central Stadium, Vilnius, capacity: 15,000. National strip: yellow shirts, green shorts and yellow socks. First international game: 24 June 1923, v **Estonia** (0–5, in Kaunas, Lithuania, friendly). Biggest victory: 7–0, v Estonia (20 May 1995, Riga, Baltic Cup). Biggest defeat: 0–9 v **Switzerland** (25 May 1924, Paris, Olympic Games preliminary round). Most capped players: Andrius Tereskinas (50 appearances, 1991-), Tomas Ziukas (45 appearances, 1991-), Virginijus Baltusnikus (42 appearances, 1991-), Raimondas Vainoras (41, 1991-), Romualdas Marcinkus (41 appearances, 1927–38). Leading goalscorers: Antanas Lingois (13 goals, 1928-38 in 34 appearances), Virginijus Baltusnikus (8 goals). *International tournament record* **Olympic Games** – first entered 1924 (lost 0–9 v **Switzerland**, first round, in Paris); **Women's World Cup** – first entered 1995, never qualified for finals tournament; **World Cup** – first entered 1934, also entered in 1938 but did not compete again as an independent nation until 1994, never qualified for finals tournament (third of six nations in 1998, with five wins, two draws and three defeats; missing the qualifying playoffs by only one point, behind the **Republic of Ireland**); **Baltic Cup** 1930, 1935, 1991, 1992, 1994, 1996, 1997, 1998; **European Championship** – first entered 1996 (third in its six-nation qualifying group); **European Championship for Women** – first entered 1993-95 (last in its first-round group of three nations); **Under-17 World Championship** – never qualified; **World Youth Cup** (under-20) – never qualified. *World Cup performance* (finals and qualifiers to end of 1998 tournament) played 25, won 7, drawn 5, lost 13, scored 22 goals, conceded 40 goals; win rate 28%; goals scored per game 0.88. *Record against British and Irish national teams* v **England**, played none; v **Northern Ireland**, played two, won none, drawn one, lost one; v **Scotland**, played none; v **Wales**, played none; v **Republic of Ireland**, played four, won none, drawn one, lost three. *History* Lithuanian clubs played in a Lithuanian league from 1922–1938. After the country became part of the Soviet Union, some teams played in the Soviet League, while the remainder played in a Lithuanian regional league and regional Cup. **Zalgiris Vilnius** qualified for the former-Soviet Union first division in 1982 and was third in 1987. A new national league and cup were started in 1991. In 1996-97 the league was restructured into two phases: a preliminary phase with all 16 clubs and a final phase in which the top eight clubs competed for the championship and the bottom eight competed to avoid relegation (Divisions 1A and 1B, respectively). After one season, however, the league returned to its original format. Lithuania has won the Baltic Cup five times, three of these in the 1990s, when the tournament was rekindled following the Baltic nations' departure from the former-Soviet Union. *League system* Sixteen clubs compete in the national Premier Division, playing each other at home and away. Three points are awarded for a victory, with one for a draw; final positions for clubs level on points are determined by **goal difference**; the bottom three clubs are relegated. There are 13 clubs in the First and 16 in the Second Division. The Lithuanian Cup final is played in June. *Record in international club tournaments* **UEFA Cup** – Zalgiris Vilnius (second round 1990); **Baltic League** – Zalgiris Vilnius (winners 1990; the only season it was played). Other leading clubs: **Kareda Siauliai, Ekranas Panevezys, Inkaras Kaunas**.

Littbarski, Pierre *player* Striker. **West Germany** and **Germany** international (18 goals, ca. 1981-90). Born 16 April 1960. *Clubs* Hertha Zehlendorf, **Cologne** (1.FC) (twice), **Racing Club de Paris, JEF United**. *Keynotes* Littbarski played in the 1982 World Cup final, when Germany were beaten 1–3 by **Italy**, missed the 1986 final, but played in the 1990 final and helped Germany to a 1–0 victory over Argentina. He played for Cologne (1.FC) in the 1986 UEFA Cup final (3–5 agg., v Real Madrid). *Honours* **World Cup** (Germany, 1990, runner-up 1982).

Liverpool   *club*   English league. *Dossier* Ground: Anfield, Merseyside, capacity: 45,362 all seated. Strip: red shirts with white trim, red shorts with white trim, red socks. Nickname: Reds. Record attendance: 61,905 v **Wolverhampton Wanderers** (2 February 1952, **FA Cup**, fourth round). Best average attendance: 48,127 (1972-73). Biggest win: 11–0 v Stromsgodset Drammen (17 September 1974, **European Cup-win-**

ners Cup, first round 1st leg). Biggest defeat: 0–8 v **Huddersfield Town** (10 January 1934, Division One), 1–9 v **Birmingham City** (11 December 1954, Division Two). *History* Liverpool owes its existence to a disagreement in 1892 between **Everton** and the club's first major backer, a local brewer named John Houlding, who later became the city's mayor. The Houlding-Everton falling-out led to the club decamping from the ground that is now Anfield to a site on the other side of Stanley Park and severing all links with its previous landlord. Houlding formed the Everton FC and Athletic Club but the football authorities insisted that Everton should retain the name, and so he founded Liverpool Association FC on 15 March 1892. Liverpool's first eleven players were mainly Scots, and in its first match (v **Rotherham** Town, 1 September 1892, friendly) the club played not in red, but in blue and white quartered shirts. Liverpool was elected to Division Two in 1893-94 and the club won the title, and promotion to the top flight, at its first attempt without losing a game. Less than 10 years after Liverpool's foundation, in 1900-01, the club won its first League Championship. Since then Liverpool has won the title a further 17 times and its 18 League Championships is a record. Despite relegation in 1903-04, Liverpool bounced straight back to Division One, and became the first club to win the Division Two title and the League Championship in successive seasons (1904-05, 1905-06) – a feat matched only by Everton (1930-31, 1931-32), **Ipswich Town** (1960-61, 1961-62), **Tottenham Hotspur** (1949-50, 1950-51). The club won two more Championships in 1921-22 and 1922-23 and a further title immediately after **World War II** in 1946-47, with a side that included Scottish international Billy Liddell. Relegation in 1954 was followed by the arrival of a new manager, Bill **Shankly**, in 1959, and thereafter began almost 25 years of unparalleled success and consistency. Liverpool won two more League Championships, in 1963-64 and 1965-66, and finished outside the top three on only five occasions between 1963-64 and 1990-91. Shankly's 1960s Liverpool sides included Ian Callaghan, Roger **Hunt**, Ian St John, Tommy Lawrence, Tommy **Smith**, Peter Thompson and Ron Yeats. Surprisingly, Liverpool had to wait until 1965 to win its first FA Cup (2-1 v Leeds United), although the club had appeared in two previous finals (1914, 0–1 v **Burnley**, 1950, 0–2 v **Arsenal**), but thereafter it reached another eight finals, winning the trophy on a further four occasions (1971 1–2 a.e.t. v Arsenal, 1974 3–0 v **Newcastle United**, 1977 1–2 v **Manchester United**, 1986 3–1 v Everton, 1988 0–1 v Wimbledon, 1989 3–2 a.e.t. v Everton, 1992 2–0 v Sunderland, 1996 0–1 v Manchester United). Shankly's Liverpool reached the European Cup-winners Cup final in 1966 (1–2 v **Borussia Dortmund**), a year after it was an unsuccessful semi-finalist in the European Cup (3–4 agg. v **Internazionale**), and the **UEFA** (Fairs) **Cup** semi-final in 1971 (0–1 v **Leeds United**). In 1973, Shankly, with a side that included goalkeeper Ray Clemence and defender Emlyn Hughes, and the striking partnership of Kevin **Keegan** and John Toshack, finally won a European trophy by defeating **Borussia Mönchengladbach** in the UEFA Cup final. The club had also won the League Championship, making it the first English club to win the domestic title and a European competition in the same season. Bob **Paisley**, starting a Liverpool tradition of promoting people from within the club to the manager's position, replaced Shankly, who retired at the start of the 1974-75 season, and went on to become the most successful club manager in the history of English football, winning 20 trophies, including six League Championships and three European Cups, between 1974 and 1983. Liverpool's 1978-79 Championship was won with a record number of points – (68 (two points for a win)). Paisley, who had played in Liverpool's 1946-47 Championship-winning side, signed two players who would later manage the club; Kenny **Dalglish** from **Celtic** for £440,000 at the start of the 1977-78 season, and Graeme **Souness** from **Middlesbrough** for £352,000 in January 1978. Joe Fagan, who had joined Liverpool as assistant trainer in 1958, took over when Paisley stepped down at the end of the 1982-83 season and steered the club to three majors honours in his first season: the League Championship for a record-equalling (Huddersfield Town 1923-24, 1924-25, 1925-26, Arsenal 1932-33, 1933-34, 1934-35) third successive season; **European Cup**; and **League Cup** for a record-breaking fourth consecutive time (1–0 replay v Everton; 1981 2–1 replay/a.e.t. v **West Ham United**, 1982 3–1 a.e.t. v Tottenham Hotspur, 1983 2–1 a.e.t. v Manchester United). Fagan relinquished the managership in 1985 following the **Heysel Stadium tragedy**, at which 39 people, mainly Italians, were trampled or crushed to death before the European Cup final between Liverpool and **Juventus** (29 May). Liverpool supporters, who had rioted and invaded a section of the ground reserved for Juventus fans, were held responsible for the disaster and UEFA subsequently banned English clubs from European competition (**FIFA** later extended the ban worldwide) for an indefinite period that lasted until 1990, while Liverpool received an additional three-year ban, later reduced to one. A second tragedy befell the club four years later, when 95 Liverpool supporters were crushed to death at the FA Cup semi-final against **Nottingham Forest** at Hillsborough on 15 April 1989 (another died some months later; see **Hillsborough disaster**). Dalglish had become **player-manager** (with Paisley acting as team consultant) following Fagan's departure and he led the club to its first **double** in his first season (1985-86). Dalglish steered the club to two further Championships before suddenly resigning in 1991, citing the pressure of the job for his decision. Former Liverpool and **Scotland** playing colleague Souness became manager, and, despite an FA Cup triumph in 1992 (2–0 v Sunderland), he was dismissed in 1994 after three years in charge and was replaced by another of Liverpool's backroom staff and a former player, Roy Evans. In 1995, Liverpool won a

record fifth League Cup (2–1 v **Bolton Wanderers**). Gérard Houllier was appointed joint-manager with Evans in summer 1998 and in the following November he took sole responsibility for first-team affairs. *League record* Premier League 1992-93 to present; Division One 1894-95, 1896-97 to 1903-04, 1905-06 to 1953-54, 1962-63 to 1991-92; Division Two 1893-94, 1895-96, 1904-05, 1954-55 to 1961-62. *Honours* League 1900-01, 1905-06, 1921-22, 1922-23, 1946-47, 1963-64, 1965-66, 1972-73, 1975-76, 1976-77, 1978-79, 1979-80, 1981-82, 1982-83, 1983-84, 1985-86, 1987-88, 1989-90; Division Two 1893-94, 1895-96, 1961-62; FA Cup 1965 (2–1 a.e.t. v Leeds United – Team Lawrence, Lawler, Byrne, Strong, Yeats, Stevenson, Callaghan, Hunt (1), St John (1), Smith, Thompson), 1974 (3–0 v Newcastle United – Team Clemence, Smith, Lindsay, Thompson, Cormack, Hughes, Keegan (2), Hall, Heighway (1), Toshack, Callaghan), 1986 (3–1 v Everton – Team Grobbelaar, Lawrenson, Beglin,Nicol, Whelan, Hansen, Dalglish, Johnston (1), Rush (2), Molby, MacDonald), 1989 (3–2 a.e.t. v Everton – Team Grobbelaar, Ablett, Staunton (Venison), Nicol, Whelan, Hansen, Beardsley, Aldridge (1) (Rush (2)), Houghton, Barnes, McMahon), 1992 (2–0 v Sunderland – Team Grobbelaar, Jones, Burrows, Nicol, Molby, Wright, Saunders, Houghton, Rush (1), McManaman, Thomas (1)); League Cup 1981 (2–1 replay/a.e.t. v West Ham United), 1982 (3–1 a.e.t. v Tottenham Hotspur), 1983 (2–1 a.e.t. v Manchester United), 1984 (1–0 a.e.t. v Everton) 1995 (2–1 v Bolton Wanderers); **FA Charity Shield** 1964 (2–2 v West Ham United (each club held the trophy for six months)), 1965 (2–2 v Manchester United (each club held the trophy for six months)), 1966 (1–0 v Everton), 1974 (1–1, 6–5 pens. v Leeds United), 1976 (1–0 v **Southampton**), 1977 (1–1 v Manchester United (each club held the trophy for six months)), 1979 (3–1 v Arsenal), 1980 (1–0 v West Ham United), 1982 (1–0 v Tottenham Hotspur), 1986 (1–1 v Everton (each club held the trophy for six months)), 1988 (2–1 v Wimbledon), 1989 (1–0 v Arsenal), 1990 (1–1 v Manchester United (each club held the trophy for six months)). **Sheriff of London's Charity Shield** 1906 (5–1 v Corinthians); European Cup 1977 (3–1 v Borussia Mönchengladbach – *Team* Clemence, Neal (1), Jones, Smith (1), Hughes, Case, R Kennedy, Callaghan, McDermott (1), Keegan, Heighway), 1978 (1–0 **FC Brugge** – *Team* Clemence, Neal, Thompson, Hansen, Hughes, McDermott, R Kennedy, Souness, Case (Heighway), Fairclough, Dalglish (1)), 1981 (1–0 v **Real Madrid** – *Team* Clemence, Neal, Thompson, Hansen, A Kennedy (1), Lee, McDermott, Souness, R Kennedy, Dalglish (Case), Johnson), 1984 (1–1, 4–2 pens. v **Roma (AS)** – *Team* Grobbelaar, Neal (1), Lawrenson, Hansen, A Kennedy, Johnston (Nicol), Lee, Souness, Whelan, Dalglish (Robinson), Rush); UEFA Cup 1973 (3–0 agg. v Borussia Mönchengladbach – *Team* first leg (home) Clemence, Lawler, Lindsay, Smith, Lloyd (1), Hughes, Keegan (2), Cormack, Toshack, Heighway (Hall), Callaghan; second leg (away)

Clemence, Lawler, Lindsay, Smith, Lloyd, Hughes, Cormack, Heighway (Boersma), Toshack, Callaghan.), 1976 (3–2 agg. v FC Brugge – *Team* first leg (home) Clemence, Smith, Neal, Thompson, Hughes, Keegan (1), R Kennedy (1), Callaghan, Fairclough, Heighway, Toshack (Case (1)); second leg (away) Clemence, Smith, Neal, Thompson, Hughes, Keegan (1), R Kennedy, Callaghan, Case, Heighway, Toshack (Fairclough)); **European Super Cup** 1977 (6–1 agg. v **Hamburg (SV)**). *Records* Ian **Rush** is Liverpool's most capped player (67 (73) for **Wales**); Ian Callaghan holds the record for club appearances (640, 1960-78); Roger Hunt is Liverpool's record league goalscorer (245, 1959-69).

Liverpool *club* Namibian national league club, based in Okahandja. Ground: Okahandja. Strip: red shirts and white shorts. Namibian Cup 1992.

Liverpool FC *club* Uruguayan Primera League club based in Montevideo, founded 1915. Ground: Estadio Belvedere, capacity: 10,000. Strip: blue and black striped shirts, white, blue or black shorts. **Copa Uruguaya** (Uruguay's professional league) third place 1971, 1974, 1975.

Liverpool University *misc.* English university. Runs a Masters in Business Administration (MBA) postgraduate course on Football Industries. The aim of the course is to combine professional development in the field of football industries with a critical awareness of the issues involved in management, marketing and the administration of football. Part of the course is taught by staff from the Football Research Unit at the University and covers the relationships between football and society, structures of football administration, and football in the media. One of the University's most famous footballing alumnae – though not a graduate of the MBA – was **Manchester United** and **England** player and **Crystal Palace** manager Steve Coppell.

Livingston *club* Scottish league. *Dossier* Ground: **Almondvale Stadium**, Lothian, capacity: 6,100. Strip: gold shirts with black and gold striped side panels, gold shorts with black trim, black socks with gold trim. Nickname Livvy Lions. Record attendance: 4,000 v **Albion Rovers** (9 September 1974, **Scottish League Cup**, first round). Biggest win: 6–0 v **Raith Rovers** (9 November 1985, Second Division). Biggest defeat: 0–8 v **Hamilton Academical** (14 December 1974, Division Two). *History* Founded in 1943 as works club Ferranti Thistle and becoming Meadowbank Thistle in 1974 when it joined the Scottish League and moved to councilowned Meadowbank Stadium. The club moved to the Scottish new town, Livingston, in 1995, and adopting the town's name. Thistle's Meadowbank lease ended that year and the Livingston Development Corporation offered the club £2 million towards a new stadium, Almondvale Stadium, which the club moved to in November 1995. The club played its final game as Thistle on 6 May 1995 (v **Stenhousemuir**), continuing to play at Meadowbank, but as Livingston, until the new ground was ready. As Thistle, the club won the Second Division

Championship in 1986-87. It reached the semi-final stage of the Scottish League Cup in 1984-85. It was also a Scottish League Challenge Cup semi-finalist in both 1992-93 and 1993-94. The club had three points deducted during the 1994-95 season for fielding an ineligible player against **Brechin City** on 14 August 1994 and the goals scored in the match were deleted from the records. *League record* First Division 1983-84 to 1984-85, 1987-88 to 1992-93; Division Two 1974-75; Second Division 1975-76 to 1982-83, 1985-86 to 1986-87, 1993-94 to 1994-95, 1996-97 to present; Third Division 1995-96. *Honours* Second Division 1986-87; Third Division 1995-96. *Records* Walter Boyd holds the record for club appearances (446, 1979-80); David Roseburgh is Livingston's record goalscorer (64, 1986-93).

LKS Łódź (Lodzki Klub Sportowy) *club* Polish national league side based in Łódź, founded 1908. Ground: LKS, capacity: 30,000. Strip: red shirts, red shorts. Polish league champions 1957, 1998; Polish Cup 1957.

Lloyd, Cliff *official* former secretary of the **Professional Footballers Association**, who, with Jimmy **Hill**, played a major role in the overturning of the **maximum wage** rule in 1961.

loan *regulations* another word for **temporary registration**.

lob *vb.* to strike the ball in a high arc over the opposition players, often with the intention of going over the goalkeeper and into the opponent's goal. If the ball is struck with topspin it will tend to rise and drop faster and then bounce forward, making it more difficult for a goalkeeper or defender to intercept the lob in time to prevent a goal. *n.* the execution of this. Compare **chip**.

Lobilo *player* **Congo Democratic Republic** (formerly Zaire) international. *Club* **Vita Club Kinshasa**. *Honours* **African Cup of Nations** (Zaire, 1974); **African Cup of Champion Clubs** (Vita Club Kinshasa, 1973); Zaire league championship (Vita Club Kinshasa, 1970, 1971, 1972, 1973, 1975) *France Football* **African Footballer of the Year** runner-up 1974.

local anaesthetic *medical* a drug applied topically (ie to a single part of the body) causing loss of sensation in a certain part of the body only. It has advantages over general anaesthetic because treatment can be applied to an injury without the loss of consciousness experienced with a general anaesthetic.

local schools' football association *confederation* a governing body of association football for schools in a particular area of England. Local schools' FAs are affiliated to **county schools' football associations**.

Lochgelly United *club* former-Scottish league. *Dossier* Ground: Recreation Ground, Fife. *Keynotes* Joined Scottish Division Two in 1914-15, returning to the League in 1921-22 with the reformation of the two tier-structure. Lochgelly's highest League position was 10th, which it achieved in both 1914-15 and 1922-23. *League record* Division Two 1914-15, 1921-22 to 1923-24.

Lockett Harry *official* first honorary secretary of the **Football League** in 1888. Resigned in 1901 after financial irregularities; borrowing Football League funds to finance his own business. Lockett led the refinancing of **Stoke City** which, in 1908, had resigned from the Football League and gone into liquidation.

Lofthouse, Nat (Nathaniel) *player* Striker. **England** international (33 caps, 30 goals). Born 27 August 1925. Career ca. 1939-61. *Clubs* **Bolton Wanderers**. Also Bolton manager (1968-70, 1971). *Keynotes* Joined Bolton Wanderers as an amateur in September 1939, turning professional in 1942-43. He scored 255 goals for Bolton in 452 **Football League** appearances. In 1953, Lofthouse scored in every round of the **FA Cup**, including the final (3–4 v **Blackpool**), but finished with only a loser's medal. Lofthouse scored both Bolton's goals in the club's 1958 **Wembley** triumph (2–0 v **Manchester United**). Lofthouse scored two goals on his England debut against **Yugoslavia** (22 November 1950). After scoring another two against **Austria** on 25 May 1952, he became known as the "Lion of Vienna" – largely because he was unconscious when his second goal crossed the goal line. Overall, Lofthouse scored two goals for his country on 12 separate occasions. He was voted **Footballer of the Year** in 1953. Included in the **Football League Centenary 100 players**. *Honours* FA Cup (Bolton Wanderers 1958).

Loftus Road *ground* English football ground situated in west London; home of **Queens Park Rangers**. *Dossier* Ground capacity: 19,148 all seated. Pitch dimensions 102m x 66m. Record attendance: 35,353 v **Leeds United** (27 April 1974, Division One). Best average attendance: 23,850 (1975-76). *History* Officially entitled the "Rangers Stadium", it has always been commonly referred to as Loftus Road after the highway on which one end of the ground is situated. QPR moved to Loftus Road in 1917 after amateur club Shepherd's Bush FC, whose home it had been since 1904, disbanded during **World War I**. Loftus Road was QPR's 12th venue, which is greater than that of any other **Football League** club. The club played its first match at Loftus Road on 8 September 1917 (v **West Ham United**, London Cup). The ground was closed for one match in 1930 following **crowd trouble**, forcing QPR to play at **Highbury** before deciding to decamp to the nearby White City stadium. It was at White City that QPR recorded its highest ever home attendance of 41,097 on 9 January 1932 (v Leeds United, **FA Cup**). Following three seasons at White City, QPR returned to Loftus Road, buying the ground's freehold in 1948. Nonetheless, in 1962-63, the club played further matches at White City, but soon returned to Loftus Road. Between 1968 and 1980, the ground was completely redeveloped. In 1981, QPR became first club to install an **artificial pitch** (Omniturf), which endured for six seasons before grass returned in 1987. QPR share the ground with rugby club Wasps, which is also owned by Rangers' parent company, **Loftus Road plc**. On 22 March 1998, Loftus Road

staged a testimonial game for QPR defender Simon Barker between the home side and the Jamaican national team, a match that was also part of the Reggae Boyz (as the Jamaican side was commonly known) preparations for the 1998 **World Cup**. The first floodlit match at Loftus Road took place on 5 October 1953 (v **Arsenal**, friendly).

Loftus Road plc *n.* publicly-quoted business which owns **Queens Park Rangers** (and Wasps Rugby Union club). Loftus Road became a listed company on the **Alternative Investment Market** in October 1996 (flotation price = 72p). Loftus Road had a market capitalisation – the market value of the company's issued share capital (eg, the quoted price of its shares multiplied by the number of shares outstanding) – of £28.8 million when it joined the AIM.

Lokomotiv Moscow *club* Russian national league and former-Soviet Union league club, founded in 1923 as Kor (later known as Kazanka, adopted current name in 1936). In Soviet era, it was the club of the railway workers. Ground: Lokomotiv (now shared with **Spartak Moscow**), capacity: 24,000. Strip: red shirts with white sleeves, white shorts. **European Cup-winners Cup** semi-final 1998; Russian league runners-up 1995; Russian Cup 1996, 1997; Soviet Union League runners-up 1959; Soviet Union Cup 1936 (the first Soviet Cup), 1957.

Lokomotiv Sofia *club* Bulgarian national league club based in the capital Sofia, formed 1929. Ground: Lokomotiv Stadium, capacity: 25,000. Strip: red and black striped shirts, white shorts. **UEFA Cup** quarter-final 1980; Bulgarian league champions 1940, 1945, 1964, 1978; Bulgarian Cup/Soviet Army Cup 1948, 1953, 1982, 1983; Republic Cup 1995.

Lokomotiva Kosice (FK Lokomotiva Kosice) *club* Slovakian national league club, based in Kosice, founded 1946 (as Zeleznicari), formerly known as Sparta Kosice and Dinamo Kosice. Ground: Lokomotiva, capacity: 28,000. Strip: blue and white striped shirts, white shorts. Former Czechoslovakian Cup 1977, 1979; Slovakian Cup 1977, 1979, 1985.

Lokomotive Leipzig *club* see **VfB Leipzig.**

London Combination League *competition* London-regional league in operation during **World War I**, after suspension of the English **Football League** programme in 1915.

London Road *ground* English football ground situated in Cambridgeshire; home of **Peterborough**. *Dossier* Ground capacity: 15,314. Pitch dimensions: 102m x 68.5m. Record attendance: 30,096 v **Swansea Town** (20 February 1965, **FA Cup**, fifth round). Best average attendance: 14,203 (1960-61). *History* Football was first played at London Road by a number of clubs between 1900 and 1910, including Fletton United, which eventually became Peterborough & Fletton United in 1923. Peterborough United emerged in May 1934 from the remnants of Peterborough & Fletton and continued playing at the council-owned ground. When Peterborough was elected to the **Football League** in

1960-61, London Road was an impressive ground, but by 1985, when it became designated under the Safety of Sports Grounds Act, its 28,000 capacity was reduced substantially to only 9,000. Safety work enabled the capacity to be restored to around 20,000 and subsequent development has led to the construction of the 4,700 capacity Freemans Family Stand. The first floodlit match at London Road took place on 8 February 1960 (v **Arsenal**, friendly).

London Select XI *misc.* former select team made up of players from London-based **Football League** clubs; runners-up in the first Inter-Cities Fairs Cup (the forerunner of the **UEFA Cup**), played from 1955 to 1958. Lost 2–2 (home, **Stamford Bridge**), 0–6 (away, **Nou Camp**) in the two-leg final against **Barcelona**. The London team for the final comprised: home – Kelsey, Sillett, Langley, **Blanchflower**, Norman, Coote, Groves, **Greaves**, R Smith, **Haynes** and Robb; away – Kelsey, Wright, Cantwell, Blanchflower, Brown, Bowen, Medwin, Groves, R Smith, Bloomfield and Lewis. England was never again represented by a London Select side in the competition.

long ball *n.* ball passed/played over a considerable distance, usually from a player in a defensive position to an **attacker**. *Adj.* usage: **long-ball game**.

long throw *n.* tactic adopted by some players to use a **throw-in** to create a goal-scoring opportunity. The ball is thrown, often with a run-up, into or near to the opponent's goal area with the aim that a colleague will head the ball into the goal or into the path of a team mate to score. One of the most famous exponents of the long throw was **Chelsea**'s Ian Hutchinson in the 1970s.

long throw *record* the *Guinness Book of Records* lists Andy Legg of **Birmingham City** as holding the world record distance for a **throw-in** of 44.54 metres (146 feet 1 inch), November 1996.

long-ball game (kick and rush) *tactics* style of play which involves getting the ball forward to a **target player** as quickly as possible, circumventing the need for a slow build-up of short passes. This system is based on the view (supported by research) that most goals are scored from moves involving fewer than four passes. Stan **Cullis'** **Wolverhampton Wanderers** adopted a highly-effective "kick and rush" long-ball game that depended on pace and stamina in the 1950s, when the club won three League Championships and one **FA Cup**. More recently, **Watford** (during the club's climb from Division Four to Division One between 1977-78 and 1982-83 and an FA Cup final appearance in 1984) used the long-ball game with two central attackers supported by two quick wingers. **Wimbledon**, among others, have also adopted the long-ball game with some success.

longest unbeaten run *record* see **unbeaten in league matches**.

Longford Town *club* Republic of Ireland national league club based in Longford, County Longford, in the centre of Ireland.

loose ball *n.* a ball which, during the course of play,

is not in the possession of either team.

Lopez, Sue *player* **England women**'s international player (22 appearances, 1973-79). *Clubs* **Southampton WFC** (1966-71, 1972-86), Roma (1971). *Keynotes* The first English woman to play semi-professional football (in Italy, 1971). Manager of the Welsh national women's team 1995-96. Author, in 1997, of *Women on the ball: a guide to women's football*.

Lord Bob *official* former vice-president of the **Football League** (1974-81) and acting president in 1981 (the year of his death). Member of the **Football League Management Committee** from 1967. Former chairman of **Burnley** (from 1955) and credited with transforming the club into one of the top English teams of the 1960s with a modern stadium (ironically, the heavy investment in the **Turf Moor** stadium was blamed for the team's subsequent decline). Noted for attacking the Football League Management Committee in 1956 for its policy of banning clubs from allowing pensioners to attend matches at reduced prices. Attained notoriety for his outspoken views and an allegedly anti-Semitic speech at a charity dinner. President of the **Alliance Premier League** (the former name of the **Football Conference**) from 1979: the League's Bob Lord Challenge Trophy was named after him.

Lorimer, Peter *player* Striker. **Scotland** international (21 caps). Born 14 December 1946. Career ca. 1962-1986. *Clubs* **Leeds United** (twice), Toronto Blizzard, **York City**, Vancouver Whitecaps, Whitby Town, Hapoel Haifa. *Keynotes* Lorimer scored more goals than any other UK player in European club competitions, with 31 in nine seasons. Lorimer's European record includes eight goals during Leeds United's 1968 **UEFA** (Fairs) **Cup** success and four in the club's progress to the 1975 **European Cup** final. He is the club's record League scorer, with 168. *Honours* League (Leeds United, 1968-69, 1973-74); **FA Cup** (Leeds United, (1972); **League Cup** (Leeds United, 1968); UEFA (Fairs) Cup (Leeds United 1968, 1971).

Los Angeles Galaxy *club* United States football club and founder member of **Major League Soccer**, based in Los Angeles, California. Member of the league's **Western Conference**. Founded: 1996. Ground: Rose Bowl, Pasadena (the national stadium), capacity: 100,090. *Keynotes* Finished first in the 1996 Western Conference final table; winners of the Western Conference final (beating Kansas City); Major League Soccer Championship runners-up 1996 (2–3 after-sudden-death overtime, v **DC United**, at Foxboro Stadium, Foxboro, Mass.). **CONCACAF Champions Cup** runners-up 1997 (3–5, v Cruz Azul, in Washington DC, USA).

Los Angeles Wolves *club* former United States club, technically based in Los Angeles, California, USA. Only winners of the ephemeral **United Soccer Association** league in the United States of America (6–5, v Washington Whips, playoff final). The team was a representative side composed of players loaned from **Wolverhampton Wanderers**.

lost clubs *misc.* clubs that have gone out of business, usually owing to financial difficulties. UK football is littered with clubs that at one time were members of either the **Football League** or the **Scottish Football League** but which no longer exist. English lost clubs: **Aberdare Athletic**, **Accrington**, **Aldershot** (later resurrected as Aldershot Town), **Bootle**, **Burton United**, **Burton Wanderers**, **Durham City**, **Loughborough Athletic**, **Maidstone United**, **Merthyr Town**, **Middlesbrough Ironopolis**, **New Brighton**, **New Brighton Tower**, **Thames**. Scottish lost clubs: **Abercorn**, **Armadale**, **Arthurlie**, **Bathgate**, Beith, **Bo'Ness**, **Broxburn United**, **Cambuslang**, **Clackmannan**, **Cowlairs**, Dumbarton Harp, Dykehead, **Edinburgh City**, Galston, Helensburgh, **Johnstone**, **King's Park**, **Leith Athletic**, **Linthouse**, **Lochgelly United**, Mid-Annandale, **Nithsdale Wanderers**, **Northern**, Peebles Rovers, **Port Glasgow Athletic**, **Renton**, Royal Albert, **St Bernards**, Solway Star, **Third Lanark**, **Thistle**, **Vale of Leven**. *Keynotes* A similar story occurs elsewhere. In **Italy** before the start of season 1993-94, for example, the following six clubs failed to meet the financial conditions stipulated by the football authorities and went out of business: Casertana, Catania, Messina, Taranto, Ternana and Vis Pesaro. At the end of the 1992-93 campaign, two Serie C2 clubs, Casale (Italian Championship winners in 1913-14) and Varese went into voluntary liquidation, as did Arezzo during the season. Japanese clubs also have disappeared due to financial difficulties. At the end of the 1997-98 season, **Yokohama Flugels**, a founder member of the **J League**, and winners of both the **Asian Cup-winners Cup** and **Asian Super Cup** in 1995, ceased to function as a separate club, merging with neighbours Yokohama Marinos after losing around £5 million.

Loughborough Athletic *club* former-English league. *Dossier* Ground: Athletic Ground, Loughborough, Leicestershire. Record League attendance: 5,000. Best average attendance: 3,025 (1898-99). *Keynotes* Joined the **Football League** Division Two in 1895-96, finishing 12th that season, the club's higest League position. During the 1899-00 season, the club scored only 18 goals in 34 matches – a Division Two record – and won only one home fixture. Financial difficulties led to the club folding following its failure to gain **re-election** in 1899-00. *League record* Division Two 1895-96 to 1899-00.

lowest attendance *record* see **attendance, lowest**.

loyalty bonus *n.* financial incentive to encourage players not to ask for a transfer.

LPRC Oilers (Liberia Petroleum Refining Company) *club* Liberian national league club, based in the capital Monrovia. Strip: yellow shirts and black shorts. **African Cup-winners Cup** – quarter finals 1989; Liberian National League champions 1991 and 1992; Liberian Cup – 1988, 1989, 1993, 1999.

Lubanski, Wlodzimierz *player* Striker. **Poland** international (65 caps, 44 goals, 1963-80; excluding **Olympic Games**). Born 28 February 1947. *Clubs* GKS Gliwice, **Gornik Zabrze**, Lokeren (Belgium), Valenciennes, Quimper (both France). *Keynotes* Poland's all-time top scorer and captain of the Olympic Games gold medal team. He scored on his international debut on 4 September 1963, a 9–0 victory over **Norway** (in Szczecin, friendly) – he was only 16 years, 188 days old. His international career lasted more than 17 years. Lubanski missed the 1974 **World Cup** finals through injury, but played in the 1978 finals when Poland reached the second round group stage. He was top scorer in the 1970 **European Cup-winners Cup** tournament, with eight goals, and played in the final for Gornik Zabrze (1–2, v **Manchester City**). He was voted joint seventh in the *France Football* **European Footballer of the Year** award for 1972. *Honours* Olympic Games gold medal (Poland, 1972); Polish league championship (Gornik Zabrze, 1959, 1961, 1963, 1964, 1965, 1966, 1967).

Luigi Ferraris (Stadio) *ground* Italian football ground situated in Genoa, Liguria; home of **Genoa** and **Sampdoria**. Ground capacity: 42,000 all seated. *History* Opened in 1910 as the home of Genoa and rebuilt on three occasions since, including a redevelopment by Vittorio Gregotti for the 1990 **World Cup** which involved the construction of a red-brick tower in each corner of the ground. In the 1920s, the venue adopted the name Luigi Ferraris, after a former Genoa player who was killed during **World War I**. Sampdoria Unione Calcio, a merger of two Genoese clubs, Andrea Doria and Sampierdarenese, moved to Stadio Luigi Ferraris after **World War II**. There are two plaques outside Stadio Luigi Ferraris: one dedicated to Dr James Spensley, who helped to found Genoa and was the club's goalkeeper; the other is a tribute to Genoa fan Vincenzo **Spagnolo**, who was killed during a clash with Milan fans in 1995. During the 1990 World Cup, the stadium staged three group C matches (**Costa Rica** v **Scotland**, Scotland v **Sweden**, Costa Rica v Sweden) and one second-round fixture (**Republic of Ireland** v **Romania**) – total attendance 124,731; average attendance 31,182. It was also the venue for one 1934 World Cup first round match (**Spain** v **Brazil**, 30,000).

Luis Angel Firpo (Club Deportivo Luis Angel Firpo) *club* El Salvador national league club based in Ursulután. Ground: Estadio Usuluteco. Strip: white shirts, white shorts. El Salvador's oldest club, founded in 1925 and named after an Argentinean heavyweight boxer. **CONCACAF Champions Cup** quarter-final 1997, 1998; **CONCACAF Cup-winners Cup** runners-up 1995 (1–2, v **Universidad Autonoma de Guadalajara** of Mexico), third 1993 (final tournament group of four); El Salvador league champions 1988, 1990, 1991, 1992, 1993, 1998.

Luo Union *club* Kenyan national league club based in Mombassa, founded 1973. Ground: Mombassa, capacity: 15,000. **East and Central African Club Championship** winners 1976, 1977; Kenya league champions 1964, 1975.

Luton Town *club* English league. *Dossier* Ground: **Kenilworth Road**, Luton, Bedfordshire, capacity: 9,975. Strip: white shirts with blue sleeves and orange and white trim, blue shorts with orange and white trim, white socks with orange trim. Nickname: the Hatters. Record attendance: 30,069 v **Blackpool** (4 March 1959, **FA Cup**, sixth round replay). Best average attendance: 21,455 (1955-56). Biggest win: 12–0 v **Bristol Rovers** (13 April 1936, Division Three (South)). Biggest defeat: 0–9 v Small Heath (now **Birmingham City**, 12 November 1898, Division Two). *History* Founded in April 1885 from a merger between Luton Town Wanderers and Excelsior, a works side. The club turned professional in 1890, making it the first in the south to abandon amateurism. Luton was forced to vacate its first ground at Dallow Lane because there was no room to expand, moving to Dunstable Road in 1897 before settling at Kenilworth Road in 1905. Luton joined **Football League** Division Two in 1897-98, but failed its bid for **re-election** in 1899-00 after finishing second bottom. The club had to wait until the creation of Division Three in 1920-21 to regain its League status. Luton won the Division Three (South) Championship in 1936-37, a season in which the club recorded its biggest win, 12-0 against Bristol Rovers – with emergency centre-forward Joe Payne setting an English league football record by netting 10 goals (his feat is marked by the Joe Payne Lounge at Luton's Kenilworth Road ground). Luton won promotion to Division One on **goal average** in 1954-55 and, in 1959, the club reached the FA Cup final (1–2 v **Nottingham Forest**). Relegation to Division Two in 1959-60 was followed by further demotions in rapid succession, to Division Three in 1962-63 and to Division Four in 1964-65. After winning the Division Four Championship in 1967-68, the club progressed gradually through the divisions so that by 1974-75 it was back playing in the top flight. A further period in Division Two culminated in 1981-82 in the Division Two Championship under the managership of David Pleat. The following year the club avoided relegation in dramatic style on the last day of the season by defeating **Manchester City**, sending the opposition down instead. Luton enjoyed considerable Cup success in the second half of the 1980s. The club was an FA Cup semi-finalist in 1985 (1–2 v **Everton**). In 1988, Luton reach two **Wembley** finals, winning the **League Cup** (3–2 v **Arsenal**) and losing in the final of the **Simod Cup** (1–4 **Reading**). In the same season, Luton also reached the last four of the FA Cup (1–2 v **Wimbledon**). The following season the club again got to the League Cup final (1–3 v Nottingham Forest). A further FA Cup semi-final was achieved in 1994 (0–2 v **Chelsea**), with the club beating **Newcastle United** (2–0 replay, fourth round) and **West Ham United** (3–2 replay, sixth round) on the way. In 1996-97, the club reached the semi-final stage of the end-of-season Second Division **playoffs**. The club banned all away supporters from its Kenilworth Road ground in 1986-87 in an attempt to prevent football-related **hooliganism**.

As a result, it was banned from the League Cup, the rules of which required 25% of tickets to be available to away supporters. Prime Minister Margaret Thatcher urged the Football League to reinstate Luton Town in the competition, but it did not rescind its decision. It did, however, offer Luton the chance to play its home leg against **Cardiff City** at a **neutral venue**; Luton refused and withdrew from the tournament. *League record* Division One 1955-56 to 1959-60, 1974-75, 1982-83 to 1991-92; First Division 1992-93 to 1995-96; Division Two 1897-98 to 1899-00 (failed re-election), 1937-38 to 1954-55, 1960-61 to 1962-63, 1970-71 to 1973-74, 1975-76 to 1981-82; Second Division 1996-97–; Divsion Three 1920-21, 1963-64 to 1964-65, 1968-69 to 1969-70; Division Three (South) 1921-22 to 1936-37; Divsion Four 1965-66 to 1967-68. *Honours* Division Two 1981-82; Division Three (South) 1936-37; Divsion Four 1967-68; League Cup 1988 (3–2 v Arsenal). *Records* Mal Donaghy is Luton's most capped player (58 (91) for **Northern Ireland**); Bob Morton holds the record for club League appearances (494, 1948-64); Gordon Turner is also the club's record League goalscorer (243, 1949-64).

lux *n.* the international standard (SI) unit of illumination. *Regulations* Lux values are important for measuring **floodlight** efficiency: **Premier League** clubs must have floodlights that give an average 800 lux, with a minimum of 500 lux at any point on the field of play (FA Premier League rule I.18). Minimum **ground criteria** for admission to the **Football League** require that a club's floodlights must produce an average illumination of 250 lux; this must be increased to 350 lux by the end of its second season in the league. The minimum average illumination requirement for a Football League Division One club is 500 lux.

Luxembourg *country UEFA* Grand Duchy in west Europe, neighbouring **Belgium**, **France** and **Germany**. Existed as a duchy since 1354, ruled by France from 1797 to 1815, then Dutch rule until 1830. Area: 2,585 sq km 998 sq miles). Population: 412,800 (1996 census). Temperate climate and prosperous economy. Languages: Letzeburgish, French (official) and German. Capital: Luxembourg. *Dossier* Football association (Fédération Luxembourgeoise de Football, Luxembourg), formed in 1908 affiliated to **FIFA** in 1910 and founder member of **Union of European Football Associations** (UEFA) in 1954, president: Norbert Konter; general secretary: Joël Wolff. Season played from August to May. National stadium: Stade Municipal, Luxembourg, capacity: 9,200. National strip: red shirts, red shorts and red socks. First international game: 29 October 1911, v France (1–4, Luxembourg, friendly). Biggest victory: 6–0 v **Afghanistan** (26 July 1948, **Olympic Games** first round, London). Biggest defeats: 0–9 v Germany (4 August 1936, in Luxembourg, **World Cup** qualifier); 0–9 v **England** (19 October 1960, in Luxembourg, World Cup qualifier) and 0–9 v England (15 December 1982, in London, **European Championship** qualifier). Best wins: v **Czech**

Republic (1–0, 7 July 1995, in Luxembourg, European Championship qualifier, see below); v **Netherlands** (2–1, 30 October 1963, European Championship second round, second leg, Rotterdam, see below); and v **Portugal** (4–2, 19 March 1961, in Luxembourg, World Cup qualifier). Most capped players: Carlo Weiss (86 appearances, ca. 1983-97), Francois Konter (77 appearances), Roby Langers (70 appearances, nine goals, 1985-). Leading goalscorers: Léon Mart (16 goals, ca. 1936–45), Gustave Kemp (15 goals, ca. 1938–45). *International tournament record* Olympic Games – first entered 1920, played in finals tournament 1920, 1924, 1928, 1948, 1952, never beyond first round (though it did beat **Great Britain** 5–3 in the 1952 preliminary round at the Helsinki games); **Women's World Cup** – never entered; World Cup – has entered every World Cup tournament since 1934 but failed to get beyond the qualifying tournament, finishing last of its group in all of its 15 attempts (in the 1998 qualifying tournament it lost all its eight games, conceding 22 goals with only two scored); European Championship – first entered 1964, quarter final 1964, Luxembourg finished last in each of its qualifying groups from 1968 to 1992, and fifth of six nations in 1996; **European Championship for Women** – never entered; **Under-17 World Championship** – never qualified; **World Youth Cup** (under-20) – never qualified. *World Cup performance* (finals and qualifiers to end of 1998 tournament) played 82, won 2, drawn 2, lost 78, scored 41 goals, conceded 275 goals; win rate 2%; goals scored per game 0.50. *Record against British and Irish national teams* v England, played eight, lost eight; v **Northern Ireland**, played none; v **Scotland**, played three, drawn one, lost two; v **Wales**, played four, lost four; v **Republic of Ireland**, played five, lost five. *History* There is a long tradition of football in Luxembourg: its football association was formed in 1908; the national league dates back to 1910 and the domestic cup to 1922; its first international was played in 1911; and it has entered the World Cup on every occasion since the second tournament was held in 1934. Luxembourg's best international achievement was as quarter-finalists in the 1964 European Championship. It eventually went out of the tournament 0–1 v **Denmark** in a playoff at a neutral venue (the previous home and away ties finished 3–3 and 2–2 respectively); Luxembourg had already beaten Netherlands in the second round (2–3 agg.). Despite finishing second-last in its 1996 qualifying tournament group, one of its three wins was against the eventual championship runners-up the Czech Republic (1–0, in Luxembourg): Luxembourg was the only nation, aside from champions Germany, to beat the Czech Republic in the entire Euro 96 tournament. The national team had a sequence of 78 games without a win (and only five draws), from 1980 to 1994, including 32 straight defeats from 11 May 1980 to 27 March 1985 – the sequence was broken by a 0–0 draw with **Iceland** on 24 April 1985, with a victory not coming until 22 February 1995 (1–0 v **Malta**, Ta'Qali, Malta, European Championship qualifier). *League system* Twelve clubs compete in the national first division, the bottom two are automatically relegated. Clubs play each other at home and away. Three points are awarded for a victory, with one for a draw: final positions for clubs level on points are determined by **goal difference**. There are 14 clubs in the second division, the top two are promoted automatically, while the bottom three are relegated. Clubs are largely amateur. The national cup final is played at the end of May. *Record in international club tournaments* **European Cup** – **Jeunesse d'Esch** (second round 1964); **European Cup-winners Cup** – Alliance Dudelange (second round 1962), Aris Bonnevoie (second round 1980). Other leading clubs: **Spora Luxembourg**, **Red Boys Differdange**, **Union Sportive Luxembourg** and **F'91 Dudelange**.

Luzhniki Stadium *ground* national stadium of Russia and, since 1997, the home ground of **Torpedo Moscow**, capacity: 96,000. Largely rebuilt in the 1990s. Original home of **Spartak Moscow**. In 1982 it was the scene of a major stadium disaster: 340 spectators were crushed to death at Spartak Moscow's **UEFA Cup** second round match against Dutch club Haarlem (a match which Spartak won 2–0). Hosted the 1999 UEFA Cup final.

Lynam, Des *broadcaster* born 17 September 1942. Regular presenter of **Match of the Day** and live televised football for the BBC. Began in local radio journalism before joining BBC Radio Sport in 1969. His first major tournament was the 1972 **European Championship** in **Belgium** which he presented for BBC Radio. Voted Royal Television Society's Sports Presenter of the Year in 1995 and, in 1996, he received the viewers' accolade of Most Popular Presenter as part of the 60th anniversary of BBC television. Lynam played a cameo role in the pre-1998 World Cup television play, *My Summer with Des*.

Lytham St Annes *n.* town in Lancashire, England, and the former location of the **Football League**'s headquarters. The League moved to Lytham, and its new offices, formerly a hotel, in 1959, and stayed for 40 years before moving to Preston.

M

Macau (Macao) *country AFC* Chinese territory under Portuguese administration until December 1999. Situated on the south coast of **China**, about 65 km west of **Hong Kong**. The territory comprises a peninsula and the islands of Taipa – linked by a bridge – and Coloane. Return to Chinese administration 20 December 1999. Area: 16 sq km (6 sq miles). Population: 374,000. Languages: Cantonese and Portuguese. Capital: Macau. *Dossier* Football association (Associação de Futebol de Macau, Macau) formed in 1939 affiliated to **FIFA** and **Asian Football Confederation** (AFC) in 1976, president: Chui Vai Pui Andy; general secretary: João Dos Santos Lopes. Season played from September to June. National stadium: Campo Desportivo, Macau, capacity: 12,000. National strip: red and green shirts, red shorts and red socks. Biggest defeat: 0–10 v **Japan** (twice: 25 March 1997, in Muscat, Oman, World Cup qualifier; and 22 June 1997, Tokyo, World Cup qualifier). *International tournament record* **Olympic Games** – never qualified for finals tournament; **Women's World Cup** – never entered; World Cup – entered since 1982, its best achievement finishing third of four teams in the 1986 and 1998 first-round qualifying groups; **Asian Cup of Nations** – first entered 1980, runner-up in the 1992 qualifying tournament (group of four nations); **Asian Women's Championship** – never entered; **Under-17 World Championship** – never qualified; **World Youth Cup** (under-20) – never qualified. *Record against British and Irish national teams* none played. *History* Football association established in 1939. Macau has been assured autonomy in sport for 50 years after reunification with China in 1999. *League system* Six clubs compete in the national First Division, with 11 in the Second Division. Record *in international club tournaments* **Asian Champion Teams Cup** – Hap Kuan (finished bottom of its second-round qualifying group in 1986 – a walkover allowed its progress to the second round, despite losing its only other game – and bottom of its first-round group in 1987 and 1989, with no wins), Wa Seng (finished bottom of the qualifying group in 1988, also winning no games), Leng Ngan (won its two-leg East Asia preliminary round in 1993 – against Pa Team of the Philippines – but lost the next round 3–15 over two legs against **Liaoning Football Club** of China), GD Artilheiros (withdrew in 1996).

Maccabi Haifa *club* Israeli national league club based in Haifa, formed 1919. Ground: Kiriat Eliezer, capacity: 18,000. Strip: green shirts, green shorts. **European Cup** first round 1995; **European Cup-winners Cup** quarter final 1999 (it lost 0-4 agg. v **Lokomotiv Moscow**, having already beaten **Paris St Germain** 4-3 agg. in the first round), second round 1994 (the club won its preliminary round match against Stade Dudelange (now **F'91 Dudelange**) of Luxembourg, followed by a first round victory over **Torpedo Moscow**, 3–2 agg., losing only to eventual runners-up **Parma** on penalties in the second round, 1–1 agg., 1–3 pens.); Israel league champions 1984, 1985, 1989, 1991, 1994; Israel Cup 1962, 1991, 1993, 1995, 1998.

Maccabi Netanya *club* Israeli national league club based in Netanya, formed 1942. Ground Maccabi Netanya, capacity: 14,000. Strip: yellow shirts, black shorts. Israel league champions 1971, 1974, 1978, 1980, 1983; Israel Cup 1978.

Maccabi Tel Aviv *club* Israeli national league club based in Tel Aviv, formed 1906. Ground: Bloomfield, capacity: 28,000. Strip: white shirts with blue sleeves, blue shorts. **Asian Champion Teams' Cup** 1969 (1–0,v **Yangzee** of Korea, in Bangkok) and 1971 (walkover in the final after Iraq's **Al Schurta** refused to play them); **European Cup** first round 1993; former-Palestine league champions 1937, 1939, 1941, 1947; Israel league champions 1949, 1950, 1951, 1952, 1954, 1956, 1968, 1970, 1972, 1977, 1979, 1992, 1995, 1996; former-Palestine Cup 1929, 1930, 1933, 1941, 1946, 1947; Israel Cup 1954, 1955, 1958, 1959, 1964, 1965, 1967, 1970, 1977, 1987, 1988, 1994, 1996; Israel League Cup 1999.

Macclesfield Town *club* English league. *Dossier* Ground: **Moss Rose**, Macclesfield, Cheshire, capacity: 6,028. Strip: blue shirts with white trim, white shorts, blue socks with white trim. Nickname: Silkmen. Record League attendance: 5,982 v **Chester City** (25 April 1998, Third Division). Biggest win: 15–0 v Chester St Marys (16 February 1886, Cheshire Senior Cup, second round). Biggest defeat: 1–13 v **Tranmere Rovers** reserves (3 May 1929). *History* Macclesfield began playing football in 1874, having previously been a rugby club. The club moved to the Moss Road ground in 1891 and was a founder member of the Cheshire County League in 1919. The club won the **FA Challenge Trophy** in 1969-70 (2–0 v Telford United) and 1995-96 (3–1 v Northwich Victoria). Macclesfield lifted the Northern Premier League Championship in 1968-69, 1969-70 and 1986-87 and won the **Football Conference** title in 1994-95 and 1996-97. The club was unable to take its place in the Third Division after winning the Conference in 1994-95 because its ground did not comply to the **ground criteria** laid down by the **Football League**. In 1997-98, Macclesfield replaced **Hereford United** and won automatic promotion to the Second Division by finishing runners-up in the Third Division. The club finished the season undefeated at home, winning 19 of its 23 home fixtures. It was relegated after just one season. *League record* Second Division 1998-99 to present; Third Division 1997-98, 1999–. *Honours* Football Conference 1994-95, 1996-97; Northern Premier League 1968-69, 1969-70, 1986-87; FA Challenge Trophy 1970 (2–0 v Telford United); 1996 (3–1 v Northwich Victoria).

Macdonald, Malcolm *player* Striker. **England** international (14 caps). Born 7 January 1950. Career ca. 1968-79. *Clubs* **Fulham**, **Luton Town**, **Newcastle United**, **Arsenal**. Also Fulham and **Huddersfield Town** manager. *Keynotes* Macdonald was known as "Supermac" on Tyneside following his £180,000 move to Newcastle from Luton Town in May 1971. He was transferred to Arsenal for £333,333 in July 1976 before being forced to retire through injury in August 1979. Macdonald played in three **Wembley** finals, but never won a winner's medal: **FA Cup** (Newcastle United 1974; Arsenal 1978) and **League Cup** (Newcastle 1976). He scored a post-war record five goals for England against **Cyprus** on 16 April 1975. During Macdonald's spell as Fulham manager (1980-84) he was also made a club director – the first one to be paid in England. Included in the **Football League Centenary 100 players**.

Macedonia, Former Yugoslav Republic of *country UEFA* landlocked republic in east Europe, on the border of **Greece**, **Albania**, **Bulgaria** and **Yugoslavia**. Continental climate with hot summers and very cold winters. The country emerged from the Balkan Wars of 1912–13 when the ancient territory of Macedonia was divided between Serbia, Bulgaria and Greece; the Serbian territory forming part of the **former-Yugoslavia** in 1918 and created as a republic within former-Yugoslavia in 1945. Independence from Yugoslavia in 1992 – its full name, embracing the words "Former Yugoslav Republic of", was established to appease Greece so as not to imply any claims over the ancient Macedonian territory. (Not, therefore, to be confused with Greek Macedonia, a region in northern Greece and home of the Greek League sides **PAOK Salonica** and **Aris Salonica**.) Area: 25,715 sq km (9,925 sq miles). Population: 1,950,000 (1994 census). Languages: Macedonian, Albanian. Capital: Skopje. *Dossier* Football Association of the Former Yugoslav Republic of Macedonia, Skopje, formed in 1908,

affiliated to **FIFA** and **Union of European Football Associations** (UEFA) in 1994, president: Ljubisav Ivanov; general secretary: Ilija Atanasovski. Season played from August to May. National stadium: Gradski, Skopje, capacity: 25,000. National strip: red shirts, red shorts and red socks. First international game: 13 October 1993, v **Slovenia** (4–1, in Kranj, friendly). Biggest victory: 11–1 v **Liechtenstein** (9 June 1996, in Eschen, Liechtenstein, **World Cup** qualifier). Biggest defeat: 0–5, v **Belgium** (7 June 1995, **European Championship** qualifier, Skopje). Most capped players: Ljupco Markovski (29 appearances, 1994-), Mitko Stojkovski (25 appearances, 1994-), Zoran Jovanovski (21 appearances, 1993-), Toni Micevski (24 appearances, 1994-). Leading goalscorers: Georgi Hristov (eight goals, 1993-), Mitko Stojkovski (five goals, 1994-). Other notable players: Darko **Pancev**. *International tournament record* **Women's World Cup** – never entered; World Cup – entered for the first time in the 1998 tournament, finishing fourth of six nations (four wins, one draw, five defeats, scored 22 goals, conceded 18); European Championship – first entered for the 1996 tournament, finishing fourth of six teams (one win, four draws, five defeats); **World Youth Cup** (under-20) – never qualified; **Under-17 World Championship** – never qualified; **European Championship for Women** – never entered. *World Cup performance* (finals and qualifiers to end of 1998 tournament) played 10, won 4, drawn 1, lost 5, scored 22 goals, conceded 18 goals; win rate 40%; goals scored per game 2.20. *Record against British and Irish national teams* v **England**, none played; v **Northern Ireland**, none played; v **Scotland**, none played; v **Wales**, none played; v **Republic of Ireland**, played two, won one, lost one. *History* Macedonia was the 49th member of UEFA, joining in 1994. It played its first international competition match on 7 September 1994 (1–1, v **Denmark**, in Skopje, European Championship qualifier). **FK Vardar Skopje** was former Yugoslavia Cup in 1961. The independent Macedonian league and cup competitions started in the 1992-93 season. Macedonia's average of 2.20 goals per game in all its World Cup matches – takes fourth place in the all-time **World Cup goal-scoring averages**, behind Germany, Brazil and **New Zealand** (it has, however, entered only one edition of the tournament – 1998). *League system* Fourteen clubs compete in the national first division, playing each other at home and away. Three points are awarded for a victory, with one for a draw: final positions for clubs level on points are determined by **goal difference**. The bottom two clubs are automatically relegated. The national Cup final is played at the end of May. *Record in international club tournaments* UEFA Cup – FK Vardar Skopje (second round 1986). Other leading clubs: **Sileks Kratovo**, **Pelister Bitola** and **Sloga Jugomagnat Skopje**.

Mackay, Dave *player-manager* Defender. **Scotland** international (22 caps). Born 14 November 1934. Career ca. 1952-71. *Clubs* (player) **Heart of Midlothian**,

Tottenham Hotspur, **Derby County**, (manager), **Swindon Town** (player-manager), **Nottingham Forest**, Derby County, **Walsall**, Arabic Sporting Club (Kuwait), **Doncaster Rovers**, **Birmingham City**. *Keynotes* Transferred to Tottenham Hotspur from Heart of Midlothian for £32,000 in March 1959. During his Spurs career, which spanned almost a decade, Mackay made 268 **Football League** appearances. He twice broke his left leg, and another injury kept him out the 1963 **European Cup-winners Cup** final (though he did receive a winner's medal). He captained the club to its third FA Cup success in six years in 1967 (2–1 v **Chelsea**). Voted **Footballer of the Year (Scotland)** in 1958 and joint **Footballer of the Year** with **Manchester City**'s Tony Book in 1969 – the only occasion on which the award has been shared. Replaced Brian **Clough** as Derby manager in 1974, leading the club to the League Championship in his first season in charge. Included in the **Football League Centenary 100 players**. *Honours* League Championship (Tottenham Hotspur 1960-61); **FA Cup** (Tottenham Hotspur 1961, 1962, 1967); Division Two (Derby County 1968-69); Scottish Football League (Heart of Midlothian 1957-58); **Scottish FA Cup** (Heart of Midlothian 1956); **Scottish League Cup** (Heart of Midlothian 1955, 1959); European Cup-winners Cup (Tottenham Hotspur 1963); League Championship (as manager, Derby County 1974-75).

Mackay Jim *player* Striker. **Australia** international. *Keynotes* Scored Australia's goal in its group playoff to win through to 1974 **World Cup** finals tournament – the only occasion in which Australia has progressed to the finals (1–0 v **South Korea**, in Hong Kong, Asia World Cup qualifying group playoff).

Madagascar *country CAF* a republic. The world's fourth largest island. Situated in the Indian Ocean off east Africa, about 400 km from **Mozambique**. Independence from **France** in 1960. Area: 594,180 sq km (229,345 sq miles). Population: 13,500,000 (1994 est.). Languages: Malagasy, French and English. Capital: Antananarivo. *Dossier* Football association (Fédération Malagasy de Football, Antananarivo) formed in 1961 affiliated to **FIFA** in 1962 and **Confédération Africaine de Football** (CAF) in 1963, president: Jacques Benony; general secretary: Léon Maurice Rakotoarison. Season played from February to November. National stadium: Municipal de Mahamasina, Antananarivo, capacity: 15,000. National strip: red shirts, white shorts and green socks. Nickname: Club M. First international game: 1947, v **Reunion** (4–2, home, **Indian Ocean Games**); first international game (post-independence): 1960, v **Burkina Faso** (then Upper Volta, 6–1, home, friendly). Biggest victory: 7–1 (v **Djibouti**, 9 August 1986, away, **African Games**) and 6–0 (v **Seychelles**, 27 August 1990, neutral venue, Indian Ocean Games). Biggest defeat: 0–5 (v **Ivory Coast**, 21 July 1965, neutral venue, African Games) and 3–8 (v Ethiopia, 17 December 1967, **Olympic Games** qualifier).

International tournament record Olympic Games – first entered 1968, never qualified for finals tournament; **Women's World Cup** – first entered 1999; **World Cup** – first entered 1982, never qualified for finals tournament; **African Cup of Nations** – first entered 1972, never qualified for finals tournament; Indian Ocean Games winners 1947, 1958, 1963, 1983, 1990, 1993, runners-up 1948, 1949, 1950, 1951, 1952, 1953, 1955, 1956, 1998, hosts 1947 (the first tournament), 1950, 1953, 1956, 1963, 1983, 1990; **Under-17 World Championship** – never qualified; **World Youth Cup** (under-20) – never qualified. *Record against British and Irish national teams* none played. *Record in international club tournaments* **African Cup of Champion Clubs** – AC Sotema Morovoay (second round 1992), **AS Somasud** (second round 1982), **BTM Antananarivo** (second round 1994), **Fortior Cote Ouest** (second round 1973), **MMM Tamatave** (second round 1971); **African Cup-winners Cup** – BFV **Mahanjunga** (semi-finalist 1989); **CAF Cup** – DSA **Antanarivo** (quarter-final 1997, 1998). Other leading clubs: **Dynamo de Fima**. FC Fobar (of Toliara, league champions 1995), FC Djivan (Farafangana Madagascar Cup 1998).

Madeira *country affiliated to Portuguese FA* self-governing group of islands forming autonomous region of **Portugal**. Situated off north west coast of Africa, 420 km north of the **Canary Islands**. Madeira and Porto Santo are the only inhabited islands of the group. Partial autonomy from Portugal in 1976. Area: 796 sq km (307 sq miles). Population: 253,400. Language: Portuguese. Capital: Funchal. Madeira is neither affiliated to **FIFA** nor to the **Confédération Africaine de Football** (CAF). However, clubs do play in the Portuguese National League. Leading clubs: **CS Maritimo** (**UEFA Cup** second round 1995; Portuguese Cup 1926, runners-up 1995), **Clube Desportivo Nacional** and **CF Uniao**.

Madejski Stadium *ground* English football ground situated in Berkshire; home of **Reading**. *Dossier* Ground capacity: 25,000 all seated. Record attendance: 20,055 v **Manchester City** (27 March 1999, Second Division). *History* Named after Reading chairman and multi-millionaire auto magazine publisher John Madejski, who bought the club in September 1990, and built on a former-contaminated rubbish tip at a cost of £37 million. Work on the new stadium was halted on 8 September 1997 when builders uncovered an unexploded **World War II** bomb. The opening fixture at Madejski Stadium attracted 18,108 spectators and took place on 22 August 1998 (v **Luton Town**, Second Division). Reading share the ground with Richmond Rugby Union Club.

Madjer, Rabah *player* Striker. **Algeria** international Clubs (include) FC **Porto**. *Keynotes* Scored the opening goal in Algeria's victory over West **Germany** in the 1982 **World Cup** finals (2–1, in Gijon, Spain, first round). Madjer was voted 10th in *World Soccer* **World Footballer of the Year** 1987. *Honours* **European**

Cup-winners Cup (Porto, 1987);*France Football African Footballer of the Year* 1987 and runner-up 1985. In 1999 Madjer coached Qatar club **Al Wakra** to its first ever league championship.

Magdeburg (1.FC) *club* German regional league club and former East German national league club based in Magdeburg. Founded in 1951 as Einheit Sudenburg, adopted current name 1965. Ground: Ernst Grube Stadion. Strip: white shirts, white shorts. **European Cup-winners Cup** 1974 (2–0 v **Milan**, at **Feyenoord** Stadion, Rotterdam); former-East German league champions 1972, 1974, 1975; former-East German Cup 1964, 1965, 1969, 1973, 1978, 1979, 1983.

Maghreb Champions Cup *competition* former North African regional club tournament for national league champions.

Maghreb Cup-winners Cup *competition* former North-African regional club tournament for national cup winners.

magic sponge *n.* wet sponge traditionally wielded by the trainer when administering aid to an injured player. Concern over the risk of blood-borne infections has outlawed the sponge. Largely replaced by ice packs, "deep-heat" treatment and muscle sprays.

Magnificent Magyars *misc.* name given by the British press to **Hungary**'s national side of the early 1950s. With notable players Sandor **Kocsis**, Ferenc **Puskás**, Zoltan **Czibor**, Nandor **Hidegkuti** and Jozsef **Bozsik**, its record was impressive: in 50 matches from 14 June 1950 to 17 November 1955 Hungary recorded 42 wins, seven draws and one defeat (2-3 v West **Germany**, in the 1954 **World Cup** final in Berne). It scored 215 goals (an average of 4.3 per game), conceding 58 (1.16 per game). The nickname was endorsed by the 6–3 defeat of **England** (25 November 1953, at **Wembley** Stadium, friendly), followed by a 7–1 thrashing six months later (23 May 1954, in Budapest, friendly). The Magnificent Magyars were Olympic Gold medal winners in 1952. Also known as Magic Magyars, Mighty Magyars.

Maidstone United *club* former English league. *Dossier* Ground: Watling Street, Dartford, Kent. Record attendance: 5,006 v **Carlisle United** (5 May 1990, Division Four). Best average attendance: 2,427 (1989-90). *Keynotes* Promoted to the **Football League** in place of **Darlington** in 1989-90. Maidstone narrowly missed promotion to Division Three in its first League season, finishing fifth – the club's highest position – and competing in the end-of-season **playoff** semi-finals (1–3 agg. v **Cambridge United**). Before achieving League status, the club reached the third round of the **FA Cup** in 1979 (1–2 replay v **Charlton Athletic**). Maidstone resigned its League membership on 17 August 1992 due to mounting debts and continued problems with finding a suitable venue of its own. *League record* Division Four 1989-90 to 1991-92.

Maier, Sepp *player* full name Josef Maier. Goalkeeper. West t **Germany** international (95 caps), 1966–79). Born 28 February 1944. Clubs TSV Haar,

Bayern Munich. Career ca. 1960-79. *Keynotes* Played an unbroken sequence of 422 games for Bayern Munich. Maier was the first goalkeeper to face a penalty shoot-out in the **European Championship**: unfortunately he failed to stop any of **Czechoslovakia**'s penalties in the 1976 final (West Germany lost 2–2, 3–5 pens.). *Honours* **World Cup** (West Germany, 1974); European Championship (West Germany, 1972, runner-up 1976); **European Cup** (Bayern Munich, 1974, 1975, 1976); **World Club Cup** (Bayern Munich, 1976); West German **Bundesliga** championship (Bayern Munich, 1969, 1972, 1973, 1974); German Cup – **DFB Pokal** – (Bayern Munich, 1969, 1971).

Maine Road *ground* English football ground situated in Manchester; home of **Manchester City**. *Dossier* Ground capacity: 31,458 all seated. Pitch dimensions: 107m x 71m. Record attendance: 84,569 v **Stoke City** (3 March 1934, **FA Cup**, sixth round). Best average attendance: 42,725 (1947-48). *History* Manchester City played at several grounds, including Pink Bank Lane, Reddish Lane and Hyde Road, as well as turning down an offer to share **Old Trafford**, before settling at Maine Road in 1923. The club bought the land, a former claypit, for £5,500 and the developed Maine Road was the largest club ground in England with a estimated capacity of between 80,000 and 90,000. A crowd of 60,000 watched City's first match there, on 25 August 1923 (v **Sheffield United**, Division One). Maine Road's record attendance of 84,569 (v Stoke City, above) is the biggest in England for a club match outside **Wembley**. In March 1946, Maine Road set a further English attendance record, the highest for a midweek afternoon match, when 80,407 watched the FA Cup semi-final replay between **Birmingham City** and **Derby County**. **Manchester United** was forced to use Maine Road between 1941 and 1949 because Old Trafford, which was close to Trafford Park docks, had suffered extensive bomb damage during **World War II** – it was while United was at Maine Road that a another attendance record was established; the biggest **Football League** attendance (83,260 United v **Arsenal**, 17 January 1948). In the early 1950s, Maine Road had more seated accommodation (around 18,500) than any other League ground. The club received a suspended £50,000 fine in 1993 following crowd trouble at an FA Cup-tie at which the new Umbro Stand was opened (v **Tottenham Hotspur**, sixth round). City attracted its lowest crowd to Maine Road on 8 December 1998, when only 3,007 people turned up to watch the club play **Mansfield Town** in the **Auto Windscreens Shield**. City has plans to move to a new 50,000-capacity stadium on the outskirts of Manchester, which is being built for the Commonwealth Games. Maine Road has staged three **England** internationals (v **Northern Ireland**, 16 November 1938; v **Wales**, 13 November 1946; and a **World Cup** qualifier v Northern Ireland, 16 November 1949). The ground has been the venue for three **inter-League** matches (Football League v **Scottish Football League**, 9 November 1932;

Football League v League of Ireland, 10 February 1954; Football League v Scottish Football League, 20 March 1974). The ground hosted the **League Cup** final replay in 1984 (**Liverpool** v **Everton**) and has also staged several FA Cup semi-finals, including the 1994 semi-final replay (Manchester United v **Oldham Athletic**). The first floodlit match took place on 14 October 1953 (v **Heart of Midlothian**, friendly).

Major League Soccer *competition* top-flight professional football league of the **United States of America** – the US's official "First Division". *Keynotes* Launched after the 1994 **World Cup**, under the guidance and approval of the **United States Soccer Confederation**, in 1996. All 12 clubs are owned by the league itself, with the club operators owning a franchise or share of the whole league. The initial membership of 10 clubs had grown to 12 by 1998. There are two regional "conferences", each with six clubs in six cities: **Western Conference** – **Chicago Fire** (Chicago, Illinois – joined league in 1998), **Colorado Rapids** (Denver, Colorado), **Dallas Burn** (Dallas, Texas), **Kansas City Wiz** (Kansas City, Missouri), **Los Angeles Galaxy** (Los Angeles, California), **San Jose Clash** (San Jose, California); and **Eastern Conference** – **Columbus Crew** (Columbus, Ohio), **DC United** (Washington, District of Columbia), **Metrostars** (New York City, though the stadium is in New Jersey), **Miami Fusion** (Miami, Florida – joined league in 1998), **New England Revolution** (Boston, Massachusetts), **Tampa Bay Mutiny** (Tampa, Florida). Each team plays 32 league games in a season (excluding the playoffs), biased towards its own conference (each team plays the other five teams in its own conference four times, and the six teams in the other conference twice). Three points are awarded for a victory, with one point awarded for a "**shoot-out win**". There are no drawn games. The first-, second-, third- and fourth-placed clubs in each conference contest best-of-three semi-finals, the "playoffs", (with the first-placed club playing the fourth-placed etc). There is a best-of-three final for each conference and then a "championship final" with the winners of each conference playing off in a single match at a neutral venue. **Sudden-death overtime** may be used in the playoffs and championship final, but not in the normal league games. The league allocates players to each club, though clubs express a preference for particular players. Players' contracts are owned by Major League Soccer; **transfer fees** to overseas clubs are paid to the league, not the club (see Brad **Friedel**). The league arranges for replacement players to be allocated to clubs that lose players through overseas transfers. Individual club operators own a stake in the whole league, not just their own clubs. Players' wages are restricted to $1.5 million per team, though individual players can earn more through **signing-on fees** and **endorsements**. There is no relegation from or promotion to Major League Soccer. Average attendance in the first season (1996) was 17,286, about 5,000 more than the average for the

defunct **North American Soccer League**. Attendances fell to around 14,600 in the second season (1997). The first season's championship (1996) was won by DC United, against Los Angeles Galaxy (3–2 after sudden-death overtime, Foxboro, Mass.) in front of 34,643 spectators (the ground holds 60,000). DC United won the championship again in 1997 (2–1, v Colorado Rapids, in Washington, DC), when the attendance had risen to 57,431, and was a finalist in 1998 (0–2, v Chicago Fire, at **Rose Bowl**, Pasadena; attendance 51,350). See **United Systems of Independent Soccer Leagues**.

Makita Cup *competition* pre-season knockout tournament sponsored by the Japanese electrical tool manufacturer and involving four invited club sides. The 1994 tournament took place at **Highbury** and **White Hart Lane** was the venue for the 1995 edition.

malaria *medical* fever caused by protozoan parasite and spread via the bite of a mosquito. *Keynotes* **West Ham United** striker Samassi Abou's proposed £900,000 transfer to **Bradford City** in August 1998 fell through after a medical found he was suffering from malaria, which he had contracted during a holiday in his native **Ivory Coast**. Malaria also has affected the playing careers of several other African players, including Tijjani Babangida (**PSV Eindhoven** and **Nigeria**), Alexander Nyarko (Karlsruhe and **Ghana**), Kingsley Obiekulu (**Go Ahead Eagles** and Nigeria) and George **Weah** (then of **Paris Saint-Germain** and **Liberia**).

Malawi *country CAF* a republic in south-east Africa at the southern end of the east African Rift Valley, bordered by **Tanzania**, **Mozambique** and **Zambia**. More than 95% of the population work in agriculture. Formerly known as Nyasaland, part of the Central African Confederation under British rule. Independence from Britain in 1964. In 1986–89 more than 1 million Mozambican refugees entered the country. Area: 94,080 sq km (35,315 sq miles). Population: 11,000,000 (1996 est.). Languages: Chichewa and English. Capital: Lilongwe. *Dossier* Football Association of Malawi (Blantyre) formed in 1966, affiliated to **FIFA** in 1967 and **Confédération Africaine de Football** (CAF) in 1968, member of the **Confederation of Southern African Football Associations** (COSAFA), president G R C Gondwe, general secretary Y S Osman. Season played from March to December. National stadium: Kamazu, Blantyre, capacity: 50,000. National strip: red shirts, red and green shorts and green socks. First international game: 15 October 1962 v **Ghana** (0–12, Blantyre, friendly). Biggest victory: 8–1 v **Botswana** (13 July 1968, neutral venue, friendly). Biggest defeat: 0–12, v Ghana, (see above). Notable international player: Clifton Msiya (voted 10th in the 1984 *France Football* **African Footballer of the Year Award**). *International tournament record* Olympic Games – first entered 1972, never qualified for finals tournament; **Women's World Cup** – never entered; **World Cup** – first entered 1978, never qualified for finals tournament; **African Cup of Nations** – first entered 1976, qualified for finals tournament 1984 (first round); All-African Games – third place 1987; **East and Central African Championship** – winners, 1978, 1979 and 1988; **Under-17 World Championship** – never qualified; **World Youth Cup** (under-20) – never qualified. *Record against British and Irish national teams* none played. *History* Prior to independence, football was racially segregated, with the Nyasaland African FA for black players, and a Nyasaland FA for white players. Black players played in regional leagues. The Blantyre and District and Lilongwe and District regional leagues were formed in 1974, finally being replaced by a national Super League in 1986 and fed by regional leagues. A number of cup competitions have been played, including the Chibuku Cup and Kamuzu Cup. Malawi's best achievements in international football were in winning the East and Central African Championship in 1978, 1979 and 1988. *League system* National Super League started in 1986. Three regional leagues, Blantyre, Lilongwe and Mzuzu, act as feeders. *Record in international club tournaments* **African Cup of Champion Clubs** – **Bata Bullets** (second round 1975); **African Cup-winners Cup** – Bata Bullets (second round 1977); **East and Central African Club Championship** – **Admarc Tigers** (runners-up 1983); Bata Bullets (semi-final 1979 and 1987). **MDC United** (semi-final 1984); **Limbe Leaf Wanderers** (semi-final 1980 and 1981).

Malaysia *country AFC* a federation (includes states of Peninsular Malaysia, Sabah and Sarawak. The Federation is divided into two distinct parts, and three states: Peninsular Malaysia (West Malaysia), on the Malay Peninsula; and Sabah and Sarawak (East Malaysia) on the northern part of the island of Borneo – about 700 km from the Peninsula, across the South China Sea. Peninsular Malaysia is bordered by **Thailand**, while Sabah and Sarawat are bordered by South Borneo (part of **Indonesia**). Malysia is a former British colony. The Federation of Malaysia was formed in 1963 (at that time including **Singapore**, which later withdrew). Area: 332,665 sq km (128,405 sq miles). Population: 21,300,000 (1996 est.) (more than 15 million on Peninsular Malaysia). Languages: Bahasa Malaysian, English, Chinese and local languages. Capital: Kuala Lumpur (on Peninsular Malaysia). *Dossier* Football Association of Malaysia (Persatuan Bolasepak Malaysia, based in Petaling Jaya, Selangor) formed in 1933, affiliated to **FIFA** in 1956 and founder member of the **Asian Football Confederation** (AFC) in 1954, president: HRH Sultan Ahmad Shah; general secretary: Dato' Paul Mony Samuel. Home of the AFC; Sultan Ahmad Shah has been the president of the AFC since 1994, with Dato' Peter Velappan its general secretary since 1978. Season played from one month after Ramadan (a month of fasting), lasting about nine months and finishing in the same calendar year. National stadium: Shah Alam, Petaling Jaya, Selangor, capacity: 80,000. National strip: yellow and black shirts, yellow and black shorts and yellow and black socks. First international game: 14 May 1958, v **Pakistan** (4–2). Highest crowd: 45,000. Most capped players: Soh Chin Aun (credited with 250 appearances by the Football Association of Malaysia, although these are not all recognised as full internationals). Leading goalscorer: Mokhtar Dahari (scorer of more than 500 goals at club and international level). Website: *http://www.fam.org.my/welcome/welcome.htm* (official site). *International tournament record* **Olympic Games** – qualified for finals tournament 1972 (third in its four-nation first-round group); **Women's World Cup** – entered first tournament in 1991, never reached finals tournament; **World Cup** – first entered 1974, has not progressed beyond the first-round group stage of the qualifying tournament; **Asean Tiger Cup** – played in first tournament 1996, runners-up (0–1, v Thailand, in Singapore); **Asian Cup of Nations** – first entered 1956, reached first round of finals tournament (having won its qualifying group of five nations) in 1976 and again in 1980 (second of seven in its qualifying group), but in both cases did not progress beyond first round, failed to reach the finals tournament in 1996 on goal difference; **Asian Games** – first entered 1958, semi-final/third 1962 (4–1, v **South Vietnam**, in Djakarta, Indonesia, third/fourth playoff) and 1974 (2–1, v **North Korea**, in Tehran, Iran, third/fourth playoff), second round group stage 1978; **Asian Women's Championship** – entered first tournament in 1975, hosts 1993, 1995; South East Asian Games – winners 1961, 1977, 1979, 1989; **Under-17 World Championship** – never qualified; **World Youth Cup** (under-20) – hosts 1997 (tournament in Kuala Lumpur). *Record against British and Irish national teams* v **England**, played one, lost one. *History* Football introduced by British soldiers in the mid 19th century. Malaysian national league and cup competitions played since 1921. The national league and cup is played mainly by state teams, eg Pahang FA, Penang FA, Sabah FA, Sarawak FA and **Selangor FA**, along with **Kuala Lumpur FA**; Singapore also plays in the national league and cup, despite being an independent country since 1965. Selangor was runner-up in the first **Asian Champion Teams Cup** in 1967. Malaysia was a founder member of the AFC in 1954, and of the Asian Ladies Football Confederation in 1968. Malaysia's former prime minister, Tunku Abdul Rahman Putra Al-Haj, was the fifth president of the AFC (1958-77). There are more than 200,000 registered players in Malaysia. Malaysia's best international achievements are third place in the 1962 and 1974 Asian Games football tournaments, and runners-up in the first Asean Tiger Cup in 1996. It also qualified for the 1972 Olympic Games football tournament finals in Munich. It played a friendly game against England in Kuala Lumpur in 1991 (12 June, 2–4), at which Gary **Lineker** scored all four of England's goals. *League system* The national M-League has 12 clubs. Three points are awarded for a win, with one for a draw. *Record in international club tournaments* Asian Champion Teams Cup: Selangor (runners-up 1967); Federal Territory (final tournament 1987), Pehang FA (final tournament 1988) and Kuala Lumpar FA (final tournament 1989). Asian Cup-winners Cup - Sarawak FA (quarter-final 1999).

Maldini 1. Cesare *player* Defender. **Italy** international (16 caps). *Club* **AC Milan**. *Keynotes* Maldini was a **European Cup** winner with AC Milan in 1963 (2–1, v **Benfica**), and a beaten finalist in 1958 (2–3, v **Real Madrid**). Became Italy's national coach. *Honours* European Cup (AC Milan, 1963); Italian **Serie A** championship (AC Milan 1957, 1959, 1962). **2.** his son Paolo *player* Defender. Italy international (100 caps, six goals, 1988-). Born 26 June 1968. *Clubs* AC Milan. *Honours* Italian Serie A championship (AC Milan 1988, 1992, 1993, 1994, 1996), European Cup (AC Milan 1989, 1990, 1994). Maldini made his international debut on 31 March 1988 (1–1, v **Yugoslavia**, in Split, friendly). He is Italy's second most-capped player of all time.

Maldives *country AFC* a republic in the Indian Ocean comprising more than 2,000 coral islands (215 inhabited) stretching 885 km. Area: 298 sq km 115 sq miles). Population: 253,300 (1996 est.). A former British protectorate, gaining full independence in 1965. Language: Dhivehi (a dialect of Sinhalese) and English. Capital: Male. *Dossier* Football Association of Maldives (Male) formed in 1982 affiliated to **FIFA** in 1986 and **Asian Football Confederation** (AFC) in 1983, president: Ibrahim Manik; general secretary: Ali Ibrahim Ismail. Season played from November to February. National stadium: National Stadium, Male. National strip: green shirts, white shorts and red socks. Best victory: 2–1 v **Sri Lanka** (September 1997, in Nepal, **South Asian Gold Cup** semi-final). Biggest defeat: 0–17 v **Iran** (2 June 1997, in Damascus, Syria, **World Cup** qualifier – the largest margin of victory in any World Cup Match in the tournament's history). *International tournament record* World Cup – first entered 1998 (last in its qualifying group, losing all its games); **Asian Cup of Nations** – first entered 1996 (last in its qualifying group, losing all its games); **Asian Games** – first entered 1998 (last in first-round group of three nations); South Asian Gold Cup – runners-up 1997 (1–5 v **India**, in Nepal); third 1999 (2-0 v Nepal, India). *Record against British and Irish national teams* none played. *History* Football was said to be introduced to the islands in 1970, by a visitor from Sri Lanka. National league started in 1983. The Maldives' first appearance in the World Cup, in the 1998 qualifying tournamen,t was disappointing. It lost all its six matches, conceding 59 goals (the most goals conceded by any nation in the 1998 qualifying tournament) with none scored, including the worst ever performance in a World Cup match: 0–17 (above). *League system* Only six clubs compete in the national first division. *Record in international club tournaments* **Asian Champion Teams Cup: New Radiant** (quarter-final 1997); **Victory Soccer Club** (second round 1997-98); **Asian Cup-winners Cup** – New Radiant (quarter-final 1996).

Other leading club: Valencia (league champions 1983, 1984, 1985, 1994, 1998, Maldives Cup 1988, 1996, 1997, 1998).

Mali *country CAF* a republic in north west Africa, bordered by **Algeria**, **Burkina Faso**, **Guinea**, the **Ivory Coast**, **Mauritania**, **Niger** and **Senegal**. Area: 1,240,140 sq km (478,695 sq miles). Population: 9,200,000 (1996 est.). Over half the country is desert. The population is mostly congregated around the Niger valley. Independence from **France** in 1960. Languages: French, Bambara and other native languages. Capital: Bamako. *Dossier* Football association (Fédération Malienne de Foot-Ball, Bamako) formed in 1960 affiliated to **FIFA** in 1962 and **Confédération Africaine de Football** (CAF) in 1963, president: Amadou Diakite; general secretary: Tidiani Niambele. Season played from 1 October to 31 July. National stadium: Mobido Keita, Bamako, capacity: 30,000. National strip: green shirts, yellow shorts and red socks. Nickname of national team: the Eagles. First international game: 11 November 1960 v **Nigeria** (3–1, in Nigeria, friendly). Biggest victory: 5–1 v **Uganda** (21 July 1965, **African Games**, neutral venue) and 5–1 v Burkina Faso (7 April 1991, home, friendly). Biggest defeat: 0–6 v Ivory Coast (31 March 1985, away, African Cup of Nations qualifier). Highest crowd: 40,000 (1972, v Guinea, 2–2). Notable international player: Salif Keita (formerly of **Stade Malien**, AS **Real Bamako** and **Saint-Etienne** of France: he was voted *France Football* **African Footballer of the Year** in 1970). *International tournament record* **Olympic Games** – never qualified for finals tournament; **Women's World Cup** – never entered; **World Cup** – never entered; **African Cup of Nations** – runner-up 1972 (2–3, v **Congo**, in Yaoundé, Cameroon); and semi-final/fourth 1994 (1–2, v Ivory Coast, in Tunis, Tunisia, third/fourth play-off); African Games runner-up 1965; **Amilcar Cabral Cup** (Africa zone 2) – winners 1989, 1997 (1–0, v Senegal), runners-up 1979, 1981, 1987 and 1988; **Under-17 World Championship** – quarter-final 1997; **World Youth Cup** (under-20) – semi-final/third 1999, also qualified 1989 (first round). *Record against British and Irish national teams* none played. *History* The Mali national league and Cup were first played in 1961. Both tournaments have been dominated by three clubs: Real Bamako, Stade Malien and **Djoliba Athletic Club**. Djoliba AC holds the African and joint world record of seven consecutive domestic cup triumphs (1973 to 1979). Only one African club, **Al Ahly** of Egypt, has won more domestic cups than the 14 by Djoliba AC and its rivals Stade Malien. Mali was runner-up in the 1972 African Cup of Nations. Its under-17 youth team reached the quarter-final of the seventh Under-17 World Championship in 1997 (tournament in Egypt). Mali's under-20 side has qualified twice for the World Youth Cup finals tournament. In 1999, it reached the semi-final in Nigeria (1–3 v Spain). It beat **Uruguay** in the third/fourth playoff (1–0). *Record in international club tournaments* **African Cup of Champion Clubs** – Stade Malien (runner-up in the first tournament of

1964), Real Bamako (runners up 1966), Djoliba Athletic Club (semi-final 1967); **African Cup-winners Cup** – Djoliba AC (semi-finalists 1981 and 1982), **Asociation Sportive Nianan** (second round 1995); **CAF Cup** – Djoliba AC (quarter final 1995), Asociation Sportive Nianan second round 1994); **West African Club Champions Cup** – Stade Malien (runner-up 1984), Djoliba AC (runner-up 1990.

Malindi Sports Club *club* Zanzibar league club. Ground: Amaan, capacity: 10,000. **African Cup-winners Cup** – quarter-final 1994; **CAF Cup** – semi-final 1995; Tanzania and Zanzibar Union League champions 1989, 1992; Zanzibar League champions 1990, 1992.

Malmö FF (Fotboll Förening) *club* Swedish national league club based in Malmö, founded 1910. Ground: Malmö, capacity: 26,000. Strip: sky blue shirts, white shorts. **European Cup** runners-up 1979 (0–1, v **Nottingham Forest**, at **Bernabéu**, Madrid); **European Cup-winners Cup** quarter-final 1975, 1987; Swedish league champions 1944, 1949, 1950, 1951, 1953, 1965, 1967, 1970, 1971, 1974, 1975, 1977, 1986, 1988; Swedish Cup 1944, 1946, 1947, 1951, 1953, 1967, 1973, 1974, 1975, 1978, 1980, 1984, 1986, 1989.

Malta *country UEFA* an island republic in the Mediterranean Sea, between Sicily, **Tunisia** and **Libya**. Area: 316 sq km (122 sq miles). Population: 376,300 (1995 census). Language: Maltese, English and Italian. Capital: Valletta. Self-government, after British rule, in 1947 and full independence in 1964. *Dossier* Malta Football Association (Valletta) formed in 1900, affiliated to **FIFA** in 1959 and **Union of European Football Associations** (UEFA) in 1960, president: Dr Joseph Mifsud; general secretary: Joseph Sacco. Season played from September to May. National stadium: Ta'Qali Stadium, Valletta, capacity: 18,000 (also the ground for all Maltese premier league games). National strip: red shirts, white shorts and red socks. First international game: 8 March 1959, v Tunisia (0–0, Tunis, friendly). Biggest victory: 5–0 v **Azerbaijan** (19 April 1994, friendly, Valletta). Best victory, 1–0 v **Belgium** (16 February 1994, friendly, Valletta). Biggest defeat: 1–12, v **Spain** (21 December 1983, Seville, Spain, **European Championship** qualifier). Most capped players: Carmel Busuttil (90 appearances, 1982-), Silvio Vella (84 appearances, ca. 1987-). Leading goalscorer: Carmel Busuttil (21 goals). Website: *http://www.mfa. com.mt* (official site). *International tournament record* **Olympic Games** – first entered 1960 (in 1960 Malta played in an African qualifying group), never qualified for finals tournament; **Women's World Cup** – never entered; **World Cup** – first entered 1974, finished last in each of its qualifying groups, except 1994, when finished fifth of six nations, no points from 10 games in 1998 tournament; European Championship – first entered 1964 when lost in first round (no qualifying groups), finished last in each of its qualifying groups from 1972–96; **European Championship for Women** – never entered; **Under-17 World Championship** – never qualified; **World**

Youth Cup (under-20) – never qualified. *Record against British and Irish national teams* v **England**, played two, lost two; v **Northern Ireland**, played two, lost two; v **Scotland**, played five, drawn one, lost four; v **Wales**, played four, lost four; v **Republic of Ireland**, played six, lost six. *History* League formed in 1910, with the Maltese FA Trophy played from 1935. The league was extended in 1996-97 so that each club now plays each other three times in a season. *League system* Ten clubs compete in the national Premier League. Clubs play each other three times in a season (27 games in total – all played at Ta'Qali National Stadium). Three points are awarded for a victory, with one for a draw: final positions for clubs level on points are determined by **goal difference**. The bottom two clubs are automatically relegated to the First Division, which has 10 clubs, playing each other twice. The top two are promoted automatically; the bottom two are relegated. The Maltese Trophy final takes place in late May. Clubs also compete for the Löwenbräu, Super Five and Super Cups. *Record in international club tournaments* **European Cup** – **Sliema Wanderers** (second round 1971/72); European Cup-winners Cup – Sliema Wanderers (second round 1968/69), **Hamrun Spartans** (second round 1984/85). Other leading clubs: **Floriana**, **Hibernians FC**, **Valletta FC**.

Mamelodi Sundowns *club* South African **National Soccer League** club based in Pretoria, founded 1970, formerly known as Mamelodi United. Ground: HM Pitje. Strip: yellow shirts, blue shorts. South Africa National Soccer League champions 1988, 1990, 1993, 1998; South African **Top Eight Cup** 1990.

Man, Isle of *country no international affiliation* British Crown Dependency (not part of the UK). Island in the Irish Sea between Cumbria and Northern Ireland. Tax haven and partially self-governing. Area: 588 sq km (227 sq miles). Population: 71,000. Language: English and some Manx. Capital: Douglas. *Dossier* Football association neither affiliated to **FIFA** nor to the **Union of European Football Associations**. Season played from August to May. *History* An Isle of Man club championship has been played since 1896, first won by Peel AFC. Leading clubs: Peel AFC (26 championships to 1998), Ramsey FC (11), Rushen United (nine), Castletown FC (seven), Douglas Gymnasium (seven), Douglas High School Old Boys (six), Bradda (four), Pulrose United (four), St. George's FC (four), St Mary's AFC (three).

management committee *n.* see **Football League management committee**.

manager *n.* the club official responsible for selecting the club's first team and dealing with other club matters such as players' transfers. In some countries the term is interchangeable with **coach**. *Regulations* **Premier League** manager's contracts must be registered with the league (FA Premier League rules section N).

manager of the year *award* accolade, originally sponsored by Bell's Whisky, awarded to the most outstanding UK manager each season. *Winners* 1966, Jock **Stein** (**Celtic**); 1967, Jock Stein (Celtic); 1968,

Matt **Busby** (**Manchester United**); 1969, Don **Revie** (**Leeds United**); 1970, Don Revie (Leeds United); 1971, Bertie Mee (**Arsenal**); 1972, Don Revie (Leeds United); 1973, Bill **Shankly** (**Liverpool**); 1974, Jack Charlton (**Middlesbrough**); 1975, Ron Saunders (**Aston Villa**); 1976, Bob **Paisley** (**Liverpool**); 1977, Bob Paisley (Liverpool); 1978, Brian **Clough** (**Nottingham Forest**); 1979, Bob Paisley (Liverpool); 1980, Bob Paisley (Liverpool); 1981, Ron Saunders (Aston Villa); 1982, Bob Paisley (Liverpool); 1983, Bob Paisley (Liverpool); 1984, Joe Fagan (Liverpool); 1985, Howard Kendall (**Everton**); 1986, Kenny Dalglish (Liverpool); 1987, Howard Kendall (Everton); 1988, Kenny Dalglish (Liverpool); 1989, George **Graham** (Arsenal); 1990, Kenny Dalglish (Liverpool); 1991, George Graham (Arsenal); 1992, Howard Wilkinson (Leeds United); 1993, Alex **Ferguson** (Manchester United); 1994, Alex Ferguson (Manchester United); 1995, Kenny Dalglish (Blackburn); 1996, Alex Ferguson (Manchester United); 1997, Alex Ferguson (Manchester United); 1998, Arséne Wenger (Arsenal); 1999, Alex Ferguson (Manchester United). **2.** *award* the manager in English league football who has made the best use of available resources, as voted by members of the **League Managers Association**. *Winners* 1993, Dave Bassett (**Sheffield United**); 1994, Joe Kinnear (**Wimbledon**); 1995, Frank Clark (Nottingham Forest); 1996, Peter Reid (**Sunderland**); 1997, Danny Wilson (**Barnsley**); 1998, David Jones (**Southampton**)

Managers Arbitration Tribunal *regulations* body set up to rule on disputes over **Premier League** managers' contracts, including the cancelling of contracts and the awarding of compensation. Its rulings are binding. It has three members: a legally qualified independent chair, an official of the Premier League and a appointee of the **League Managers Association** (FA Premier League rules section N). Parties can be represented by qualified legal advisers.

Manchester City *club* English league. *Dossier* Ground: **Maine Road**, Manchester. Ground capacity: 31,458 all seated. Strip: sky blue shirts, white shorts, sky blue socks. Nickname: City. Record attendance: 84,569 v **Stoke City** (3 March 1934, **FA Cup**, sixth round). Best average attendance: 42,725 (1947-48). Biggest win: 10–1 v **Huddersfield Town** (7 November 1987, Division Two), v **Swindon Town** (29 January 1930, FA Cup, fourth round). Biggest defeat: 1–9 v **Everton** (3 September 1906, Division One). *History* Founded in 1880 as a church team, the club changed its name on several occasions in its early years. First it was known as West Gorton, shortening the name to Gorton in 1884-85 after merging with Gorton Athletic, before becoming Ardwick in 1892, when the club became founder members of **Football League** Division Two. Although the club finished fifth in its first season in the Football League, it was beset by financial difficulties and folded. It was reformed as Manchester City in 1894. The club has played at several grounds, including at Pink Bank Lane, Reddish

Lane and Hyde Road, as well as turning down an offer to share **Old Trafford**, before setttling at Maine Road in 1923. City missed promotion to Division One in 1895-96 after heavily losing two of the **test match** series that, between 1892-93 and 1897-98, determined promotion and relegation. In 1898-99, the club gained promotion to the top-flight as Division Champions, and in 1904 it won the FA Cup (1–0 v **Bolton Wanderers**), finishing as Division One runners-up and narrowly missing the **double**. In between, City was relegated and promoted – again as Champions. The club achieved the same feat between 1908-09 and 1909-10; relegation immediately followed by promotion and the Division Two title. City's 1904 League and FA Cup winning success was marred by allegations of **illegal payments** to players arising from the **transfers** of Irvine Thornley and Frank Nogrove from **Glossop North End** (a club being investigated for financial irregularities by the **Football Association** at the time). As a result, City was fined £250 and five of its directors and Thornley were suspended. The following season more allegations of illegal payments to City players surfaced the following season. In total 17 players were found guilty of accepting illegal payments and they each received a suspended fine and were banned from ever playing for the club again. Tom Maley, City's manager, received a life ban from the game (later rescinded) and the club was forced to auction it players – raising a sum of £2,600. City reached a second FA Cup final in 1926, ironically losing to the club it had beaten 22 years earlier (0–1 v Bolton Wanderers). City's defeat in the 1926 FA Cup Final meant that the club joined a unique group of clubs that have appeared in the final and been relegated in the same season (others are **Brighton & Hove Albion** (1982-83), **Leicester City** (1968-69), **Middlesbrough** (1996-97). A further FA Cup final defeat followed in 1933 (0–3 v Everton), before the club lifted the trophy for the first time a year later (2–1 v **Portsmouth**). In 1936-37, City won its first League Championship, but the club was relegated the following season (having scored 80 goals – more than any other in Division One), thus becoming the only club to win the title and be relegated in consecutive seasons. City is also the only club to have scored and conceded a century of goals in a season: in 1957-58, the club scored 104 goals and conceded 100. Also in the 1950s, the club again reached consecutive FA Cup finals, losing in 1955 (1–3 v **Newcastle United**) and winning in 1956 (3–1 v **Birmingham City**). After winning the Division Two Championship in 1965-66, under the partnership of Joe **Mercer** as manager and Malcolm Allison as coach, the club enjoyed one of its most successful periods. With a squad that included Colin **Bell**, Tony Book, Mike Doyle, Francis Lee, Mike Summerbee and Neil Young, City won its second League Championship in 1967-68 (by two points from **Manchester United**), the FA Cup in 1969 (1–0 v **Leicester City**) and, in 1970, both the **League Cup** (2–1 v **West Bromwich Albion**) and the **European**

Cup-winners Cup (2–1 v **Gornik Zabrze**). In 1971, the club reached the semi-final of the same European competition, losing the all-English encounter to **Chelsea** (0–2 agg.). Since the Mercer-Allison partnership ended in 1973, and despite a succession of managers, including Alan **Ball**, John Bond, Tony Book, Howard Kendall, Billy **McNeill** and Ron Saunders, success has been relatively rare. City has won only one trophy, the League Cup in 1976 (2–1 v Newcastle United), since its European triumph in 1970, although the club did reach the **UEFA Cup** quarter-finals in 1979 (2–4 agg. v **Borussia Mönchengladbach**) and the FA Cup final in 1981 (2–3 replay v **Tottenham Hotspur**). In January 1994, with the club heavily in debt and struggling to meet the deadline for converting Maine Road into an all-seater stadium, a consortium led by former player Francis Lee wrested control from long-time chairman Peter Swales (see Maine Road). Between 1990 and 1998, City apointed seven managers, including Steve Coppell, whose reign lasted only 32 days. The club was relegated from the **Premier League** in 1995-96. In March 1998, with City third bottom of the First Division, manager Frank Clark was replaced by former City and England striker Joe Royle, and Lee resigned as chairman and as a director. City was relegated to the lowest level in the club's 111-year history in 1997-98. The club returned to the First Division via the 1998-99 Second Division playoffs (2-2, 3-1 pens. v **Gillingham**). *League record* Premier League 1992-93 to 1995-96; Division One 1899-00 to 1901-02, 1903-04 to 1908-09, 1910-11 to 1925-26, 1928-29 to 1937-38, 1947-48 to 1949-50, 1951-52 to 1962-63, 1966-67 to 1982-83, 1985-86 to 1986-87, 1989-90 to 1991-92; First Division 1996-97, 1997-98, 1999-00; Division Two 1892-93 to 1898-99, 1902-03, 1909-10, 1926-27 to 1927-28, 1938-39 to 1946-47, 1950-51, 1963-64 to 1965-66, 1983-84 to 1984-85, 1987-88 to 1988-89; Second Division 1998-99. *Honours* League 1936-37, 1967-68; Division Two 1898-99, 1902-03, 1909-10, 1927-28, 1946-47, 1965-66; FA Cup 1904 (1–0 v Bolton Wanderers), 1934 (2–1 v Portsmouth – *Team* **Swift**, Barnett, Dale, **Busby**, Cowan, Bray, Toseland, Marshall, Tilson (2), Herd, Brook), 1956 (3–1 v Birmingham City – *Team* **Trautmann**, Leivers, Little, Barnes, Ewing, Paul, Johnstone (1), Hayes (1), **Revie**, Dyson (1), Clarke), 1969 (1–0 v Leicester City – *Team* Dowd, Book, Pardoe, Doyle, Booth, Oakes, Summerbee, Bell, Lee, Young (1), Coleman); League Cup 1970 (2–1 v West Bromwich Albion), 1976 (2–1 v Newcastle United); **FA Charity Shield** 1937 (2–0 v **Sunderland**), 1968 (6–1 v West Bromwich Albion), 1972 (1–0 v **Aston Villa**); European Cup-winners Cup 1970 (2–1 v Gornik Zabre – *Team* Corrigan, Book, Booth, Heslop, Pardoe, Doyle, (Bowyer), Towers, Oakes, Bell, Lee (1), Young (1)). *Records* Colin Bell is City's most capped player (48 for **England**); Alan Oakes holds the record for club appearances (565, 1959-76); Tommy Johnson is City's record league goalscorer (158, 1919-30).

Manchester Corinthians *club* former English women's football club based in Manchester and formed in 1949. Corinthians played charity matches throughout Great Britain and overseas in the 1950s and 1960s. The **Football Association**'s ban on women's clubs playing at **Football League** grounds (see **women's football**) prevented Corinthians from gaining the level of success enjoyed by **Dick, Kerr's Ladies** in the post-**World War I** period. The clubs' best result was, perhaps, its 4–0 defeat of a German representative side in the final of a European women's tournament, organised by the former **International Ladies Football Association**, in Berlin in 1957, a match that attracted 37,000 spectators. Corinthians and its reserve side, Nomads, played many overseas exhibition fixtures organised by the International Red Cross, including a 12-week tour of South America and matches in North Africa. The club folded ca. 1973.

Manchester United *club* English league. *Dossier* Ground: **Old Trafford**, Manchester. Strip: red shirts with black and white trim, white shorts with red trim, black socks. Website: *http://www.manutd.com* Nickname: Red Devils. Ground capacity: 56,387 all seated. Club record attendance: 70,504 v **Aston Villa** (27 December 1920, Division One). Best average attendance: 57,552 (1967-68). Biggest win: 10–0 v **RSC Anderlecht** (26 September 1956, **European Cup**, preliminary round second leg). Biggest defeat: 0–7 v **Blackburn Rovers** (10 April 1926, Division One), v Aston Villa (27 December 1930, Division One), v **Wolverhampton Wanderers** (26 December 1931, Division Two). *History* Originally known as Newton Heath Lancashire and Yorkshire Cricket and Football Club, the club was founded in 1878 by staff employed by the Lancashire and Yorkshire Railway Company and joined the **Football League** in 1892 – United adopted the green and yellow colours of Newton Heath as a second kit during the 1992-93 centenary season. Newton Heath finished bottom of Division One in both its first two seasons but was relegated only on the second, never appearing in the top flight again under the club's original name. Following the bankruptcy of Newton Heath in 1902, the club was relaunched with the help of a local brewer, John Davies, and renamed Manchester United. United "rejoined" the league in 1904-05, and two years later the club won its first League Championship in 1907-08, and the **FA Cup** the following season, Davies moved it from the ground that it had occupied since 1893 – Bank Street at Clayton – to a new site five miles away that would become Old Trafford. United won a further Championship in 1910-11, its second season at Old Trafford, but thereafter the club had to wait a further 41 years before winning the title again. As Manchester United, the club has spent only 11 seasons outside the top flight, although in 1933-34 it narrowly avoided relegation to the then Division Three (North). In 1931, only the financial support of James Gibson, who paid off the club's £30,000 debts, prevented the club from a second bankruptcy. The appointment of former

Manchester City player Matt **Busby** as United manager in October 1945 was the beginning of new era for the club that culminated in 1968 when it became the first English club to win the European Cup. Before winning the League Championship in 1951-52, Busby's United finished second in four of the five previous seasons and had won the FA Cup for a second time in 1948. United's **Wembley** triumph was achieved with a side that contained Johnny **Carey**, Stan Pearson and Jack Rowley. The club was forced to use Manchester City's **Maine Road** ground between 1941 and 1949 because Old Trafford, which was close to Trafford Park docks, had suffered extensive bomb damage during **World War II**. It was while United was at Maine Road that the biggest-ever Football League attendance was recorded (83,260 United v **Arsenal**, 17 January 1948). United won the title again in 1955-56 and 1956-57. Following the first of these Championships, United became the first English club to enter the European Cup, winning its first home tie 10–0 on 29 September, 1956 (12–0 agg. v RSC Anderlecht, preliminary round). The United side of the mid-1950s was known as the **Busby Babes**, and included players such as Roger Byrne, Eddie Colman, Bobby **Charlton**, Duncan **Edwards**, Tommy Taylor and Dennis Viollet. Tragedy struck on 6 February 1958, when the plane transporting the side back to Manchester after a European Cup quarter-final second leg match against **Red Star Belgrade** (5–4 agg.) crashed on take-off at Munich Airport, where it had stopped to refuel (see **Munich air crash** and **disasters**). Altogether 23 people died, including eight United players – Byrne, Geoff Bent, Colman, Edwards, Mark Jones, David Pegg, Taylor and Bill Whelan. Busby sustained serious injuries. During the 1960s, however, Busby built a third great team that included George **Best**, Charlton, Denis **Law** and Nobby Stiles. After winning the FA Cup in 1963 and two further Championships in 1964-65 and 1966-67, United finally won the European Cup in 1968, having reached the semi-final on three previous occasions (1956-57, 3–5 agg. v **Real Madrid**, 1957-58, 2–5 agg. v **AC Milan**, 1965-66, 1–2 agg. v **Partizan Belgrade**) that the club had qualified for the competition – and again the following season (1968-69, 1–2 v AC Milan). Busby stepped down as United's manager a year after the European Cup triumph, having received a knighthood in the same year. He became general manager (and in 1971 a club director and later president) with Wilf McGuinness in charge of first-team affairs, but Busby resumed control again for a time in 1970 after McGuinness was sacked. Despite a succession of high-profile managers – Frank O'Farrell, Tommy **Docherty**, Dave Sexton and Ron Atkinson – during the 1970s and early 1980s, United's only success came in the FA Cup, which the club won on three occasions - 1977, 1983 and 1985. The appointment of ex-**Aberdeen** manager Alex **Ferguson** to the managership was the beginning of a period of further success for United, although the club had to wait four years before he won his first trophy, the FA Cup in 1990. Thereafter, Ferguson's teams,

which at various times contained players such as Eric **Cantona**, Mark **Hughes**, Paul Ince, Andrei Kanchelskis, Bryan **Robson**, and later David Beckham, Nicky Butt, Andy Cole, Gary and Phil Neville and Paul Scholes, as well as almost ever-present Ryan **Giggs** and Peter **Schmeichel**, have won a succession of trophies, including four out of the first five **Premier League** titles and the League and FA Cup **double** twice in three seasons (1993-94, 1995-96) – something no other club has achieved. It won the double again in 1998-99. United reached the semi-final of the European Cup in 1997 (0–2 agg. v **Borussia Dortmund**) and the quarter-finals the following year, losing on away goals (1–1 v **Monaco**). United won a unique treble in 1998-99, becoming the first English club to win the Premier League title, the FA Cup and, fulfilling Ferguson's long-held goal, the European Cup (2–1 v **Bayern Munich**). In June 1991, United became a public limited company when it floated on the London Stock Exchange (flotation price = 385p). United 's board agreed a £623.4 million takeover of the club by television company BSkyB in September 1998, but the takeover was blocked by the Competition Commission (formerly, the Monopolies and Mergers Commission) in April 1999. The planned takeover was ruled "anti-competitive". *League record* Premier League 1992-93–; Division One 1892-93 to 1893-94, 1906-07 to 1921-22, 1925-26 to 1930-31, 1936-37, 1938-39 to 1973-74, 1975-76 to 1991-92; Division Two 1894-95 to 1901-02 (resigned from League following bankruptcy), 1904-05 to 1905-06, 1922-23 to 1924-25, 1931-32 to 1935-36, 1937-38, 1974-75. *Honours* Premier League 1992-93, 1993-94, 1995-96, 1996-97, 1998-99; Football League 1907-08, 1910-11, 1951-52, 1955-56, 1956-57, 1964-65, 1966-67; Division Two Champions 1935-36, 1974-75; FA Cup 1909 (1–0 v **Bristol City**), 1948 (4–2 v **Blackpool** – *Team* Crompton, Carey, Aston, Anderson (1), Chilton, Cockburn, Delaney, Morris, Rowley (2), Pearson (1), Mitten), 1963 (3–1 v **Leicester City** – *Team* Gaskell, Dunne, Cantwell, Crerand, Foulkes, Setters, Giles, Quixall, Herd (2), Law (1), Charlton), 1977 (2–1 v **Liverpool** – *Team* Stepney, Nicholl, Albiston, McIlroy, B Greenhoff, Buchan, Coppell, J Greenhoff (1), Pearson (1), Macari, Hill (McCreery)), 1983 (4–0 replay v **Brighton & Hove Albion** – *Team* Bailey, Duxbury, Albiston, Wilkins (1), Moran, McQueen, Robson, Muhren, Stapleton (1), Whiteside, Davies; replay Bailey, Duxbury, Albiston, Wilkins, Moran, McQueen, Robson (2), Muhren (1, pen.), Stapleton, Whiteside (1), Davies), 1985 (1–0 a.e.t. v **Everton** – *Team* Bailey, Gidman, Albiston (Duxbury), Whiteside (1), McGrath, Moran, Robson, Strachan, Hughes, Stapleton, Olsen), 1990 (1–0 replay v **Crystal Palace** – *Team* Leighton, Ince, Martin, Bruce, Phelan, Pallister (Robins). Robson (1). Webb, McClair, Hughes (2), Wallace; replay Sealey, Ince, Martin (1), Bruce, Phelan, Pallister, Robson, Webb, McClair, Hughes, Wallace), 1994 (4–0 v **Chelsea** – *Team* Schmeichel, Parker, Bruce, Pallister, Irwin (Sharpe), Kanchelskis

(McClair (1)), Keane, Ince, Giggs, Cantona (2, pens), Hughes (1)), 1996 (1–0 v Liverpool – *Team* Schmeichel (goalkeeper), Irwin, May, Pallister, P Neville, Beckham (G Neville), Keane, Butt, Giggs, Cantona (1), Cole (Scholes)); **League Cup** 1992 (1–0 v **Nottingham Forest**); **FA Charity Shield** 1908 (4–0 replay v **Queens Park Rangers**), 1911 (8–4 v **Swindon Town**), 1952 (4–2 v **Newcastle United**), 1956 (1–0 v Manchester City), 1957 (4–0 v Aston Villa), 1965 (2–2 v Liverpool (each club held the trophy for six months)), 1967 (3–3 v **Tottenham Hotspur** (each club held the trophy for six months)), 1977 (0–0 v Liverpool (each club held the trophy for six months)), 1983 (2–0 v Liverpool), 1990 (1–1 v Liverpool (each club held the trophy for six months)), 1993 (1–1, 5–4 pens. v Arsenal), 1994 (2–0 v Blackburn Rovers), 1996 (4–0 v Newcastle United), 1997 (1–1, 4–2 pens. v Chelsea), 1999 (2-0 v Newcastle United - *Team* Schmeichel (goalkeeper), G Neville, May, Johnsen, P Neville, Beckham, Keane, (Sheringham (1)), Scholes (1), (Stam), Giggs, Solskjaer, Cole (Yorke)); European Cup 1968 (4–1 a.e.t. v Benfica – *Team* Stepney, Brennan, Dunne, Stiles, Foulkes, Crerand, Charlton (2), Sadler, Best (1), Kidd (1), Aston), 1999 (2-1 v Bayern Munich – *Team* Schmeichel, G Neville, Johnsen, Stam, Irwin, Giggs, Beckham, Butt, Blomqvist (Sheringham (1)), Cole (Solskjaer (1)), Yorke); European Cup-winners Cup 1991 (2–1 v **Barcelona** – *Team* Sealey, Irwin, Bruce, Pallister, Blackmore, Phelan, Robson, Ince, Sharpe, Hughes (2), McClair), finalist 1999 (v Bayern Munich); **European Super Cup** 1991 (1–0 v Red Star Belgrade). *Records* Bobby Charlton is United's most capped player (106 appearances for **England**); he also holds the record for United appearances (606, 1956-73), and league goals (199, 1956-73).

Manchester United plc *n.* publicly-quoted business which owns **Manchester United**. The club became a fully listed company on the London Stock Exchange in June 1991 (flotation price = 385p). United had a market capitalisation – the market value of the company's issued share capital (eg the quoted price of its shares multiplied by the number of shares outstanding) – of £46.8 million on flotation. Supporters own around 22% of shares. United's board agreed a £623.4 million takeover of the club by television company BSkyB in September 1998, but it was blocked by the Competition Commission (formerly the Monopolies and Mergers Commission) in April 1999.

Mandela, Nelson *misc.* former South Africa president (1994-99) and former political dissident. In 1988, **Netherlands** international Ruud **Gullit** dedicated his **World Footballer of the Year** and **European Footballer of the Year** awards to the then still-imprisoned Mandela.

Manfield Hotspur *trademark* an early, and commercially very successful **football boot** manufactured by the Northampton firm Manfield & Sons Ltd. The boot was endorsed by **Tottenham Hotspur**; its manufacturers claimed that it was worn by more than 100,000

players and was by far the most successful boot of the 1910s and 1920s. A rival "Genuine Hotspur" boot (trademarked in 1894) was manufactured by another Northampton firm, Read, Myall & Read, also endorsed by Tottenham Hotspur. Its manufacturers also claimed sales in excess of 100,000 pairs.

Manga-Onguene, Jean *player* **Cameroon** international. *Club* **Aigle N'Kongsamba, Canon Yaoundé.** *Keynotes* Cameroon national coach for 1998 **African Cup of Nations** and **World Cup**; dismissed later that year. *Honours* **African Cup of Champion Clubs** (Canon Yaoundé, 1978, 1980); *France Football* **African Footballer of the Year** 1980.

Manning Rangers *club* South African **National Soccer League** club based in Durban, founded 1928. Ground: Chatsworth. Strip: yellow shorts, blue shorts. Nickname: the Mighty Maulers. **African Cup of Champion Clubs** quarter-final "champions-league" stage 1998; South African league champions 1997.

Mannion, Wilf *player* Inside-forward. **England** international (26 caps, 11 goals). Born 16 May 1918. Career ca. 1937-1962. *Clubs* **Middlesbrough, Hull City,** Poole Town, **Cambridge United.** *Keynotes* Scorer of 100 goals in 357 League appearances for Middlesbrough and Hull City. Mannion "retired" from playing in June 1954, but resumed his career with Hull after joining the club from Middlesbrough for £5,000 in the following December. Mannion refused to play for Boro for a period in 1948 in a dispute over wages. He departed from Hull in 1955 amid allegations of **illegal payments**. Mannion scored a hat-trick on his England debut, against **Northern Ireland** (28 September 1946). Following England's shock 1–0 defeat by the USA in the 1950 **World Cup**, Mannion is reported to have said: "Bloody ridiculous. Can't we play them again tomorrow?" Included in the **Football League Centenary 100 players**.

Manor Ground *ground* English football ground situated in Oxford; home of **Oxford United**. *Dossier* Ground capacity: 9,572 all seated. Pitch dimensions 100.5m x 68.5m. Record attendance: 22,750 v **Preston North End** (29 February 1964, **FA Cup**, sixth round). Best average attendance: 11,637 (1968-69). *History* Oxford, then called Headington United, played its first match at Manor Ground (originally known as Mattock's Field or Sandy Lane) in 1925, but only after **World War II** did the ground come to resemble its current form. Since 1949, United and the local council have considered around 30 sites for a new stadium and the club has made 12 separate planning applications. In June 1995, the council finally granted permission for a new stadium to be built at Minchery Farm, although construction work was suspended in 1997 due to financial problems, which also forced the club to put a number of players up for sale. United was the first club currently playing in the **Football League** to install **floodlights**, mounting two lamps each on 18 poles at the Manor Ground and staging a floodlit match on 18 December 1950 (v Banbury Spencer, friendly).

Mansfield Town *club* English league. *Dossier* Ground: **Field Mill**, Mansfield, Nottinghamshire. Strip: amber and blue striped shirts, blue shorts, white socks. Nickname: Stags. Ground capacity: 6,905. Record attendance: 24,467 v **Nottingham Forest** (10 January 1953, **FA Cup**, third round). Best average attendance: 12,128 (1949-50). Biggest win: 8–0 v **Scarborough** (22 November 1952, FA Cup, first round). Biggest defeat: 1–8 v **Walsall** (19 January 1933, Division Three (North)). *History* Founded in 1897 as Mansfield Wesleyans, a boys brigade team, becoming Mansfield Town (a team with the same name had folded in 1894) in 1910. The club played at several venues, including at Kate Moody Lane, Newgate Lane and Ratcliffe Gate, before settling at Field Mill in 1919. The club won the Midland League Championship in 1924, 1925 and 1929. Mansfield also produced a major FA Cup shock in 1929, defeating **Wolverhampton Wanderers** (1–0, third round) before going out to **Arsenal** (0–2, fourth round). Mansfield produced a further FA Cup **giantkilling** feat in 1969, beating **West Ham United** (3–0, fifth round) and in 1976, the club was a **League Cup** quarter-finalist (2–4 v **Manchester City**). Mansfield was elected to **Football League** Division Three (South) in 1931-32, replacing Walsall, which switched to Division Three (North). The club narrowly missed winning promotion to Division Two in 1950-51 and again in 1964-65 (failing on **goal average**). The club won the Division Four Championship in 1974-75 and followed this by winning the Division Three title two seasons later, although the club enjoyed only one season in the higher grade before being relegated. Mansfield made its first **Wembley** appearance in 1987, lifting the **Freight Rover Trophy** (1–1, 5–4 pens. v **Bristol City**). The club won promotion to the newly-established Second Division in 1991-92, but again the club's elevation lasted only one season. In 1994-95, Mansfield was an end-of-season Third Division **playoff** semi-finalist. *League record* Division Two 1977-78; Second Division 1992-93; Division Three 1958-59 to 1959-60, 1963-64 to 1971-72, 1975-76 to 1976-77, 1979-80, 1986-87 to 1990-91; Third Division 1993-94–; Division Three (North) 1932-33 to 1936-37, 1947-48 to 1957-58; Division Three (South) 1931-32, 1937-38 to 1946-47; Division Four 1960-61 to 1962-63, 1972-73 to 1974-75, 1980-81 to 1985-86, 1991-92. *Honours* Division Three 1976-77; Division Four 1974-75; Freight Rover Trophy 1987 (1–1, 5–4 pens. v Bristol City). *Records* John McClelland is Mansfield's most capped player (6 (53) for **Northern Ireland**); Rod Arnold holds the record for club League appearances (440, 1970-83); Harry Johnson is Mansfield's record League goalscorer (104, 1931-36).

man on *informal* instruction issued by a coach, team-mate or spectator to indicate that a player is being marked on his/her **blindside**.

man-to-man marking *tactics* form of defence which involves each defender marking a designated, or the nearest, attacker/opponent. The effect is to minimise the space available to attacking players, thereby frustrating the opportunities for creative passing play.

Manzini Wanderers *club* Swaziland national league club based in Manzini. Ground: Salesian, capacity: 9,000. Strip: maroon shirts, white shorts. **CAF Cup** second round 1993; Swaziland league champions 1983, 1985, 1987; Swaziland Cup 1984.

Maracané (Estadio Mario Filho) *ground* Brazilian football ground situated in Rio de Janeiro; home for most **Brazil** internationals and occasional venue for club sides Club de Regatas **Flamengo** (normal ground: Estadio Da Gavea) and **Fluminense** Futebol Clube (Estadio Laranjeiras). Ground capacity: 180,000. *History* Built for the 1950 **World Cup** and officially opened in June 1950 (Rio v São Paulo) but not completed until 1965. Maracanã resembles a huge oval-shaped bowl complete with a cantilevered roof and a moat separating the stands from the pitch. The stadium is officially named Mario Filho, after the Rio de Janeiro mayor who presided over its construction. Although it is alleged that a World Cup record attendance of 199,854 watched the 1950 final pool match (**Uruguay** v Brazil) at Maracané this figure has been questioned and a crowd of 183,341 to see a World Cup qualifying game in 1969 (Brazil v **Paraguay**) is now thought to have been the stadium's largest. In 1963, the stadium held a world record attendance for a club match (177,656 Flamengo v Fluminense). League fixtures still regularly attract more than 100,000 spectators. After undergoing partial repairs and with part of the stadium still closed, Maracaná staged its first major fixture in five years on 29 April 1998, when Brazil entertained local rivals **Argentina** in a 1998 World Cup warm-up. Aside from the final pool match, Maracaná hosted seven other fixtures during the 1950 World Cup tournament (Brazil v **Mexico**, Brazil v **Yugoslavia**, group 1; **England** v **Chile**, **Spain** v Chile, Spain v England, group 2; Brazil v **Sweden**, Brazil v Spain, final pool) – total attendance (including final) 839,541; average attendance 104,942. **Santos** played its **World Club Cup** matches at Maracaná in both 1962 (v **Benfica**, 90,000) and 1963 (v **AC Milan**, 150,000; and the **playoff**, 121,000). The stadium also hosted the 1989 (35th edition) **Copa America** final group matches involving Argentina, Brazil, Uruguay and Paraguay.

Maradona, Diego *player* Striker. **Argentina** international (90 caps, 34 goals). Born 30 October 1960, in Lanus, Buenos Aires. *Clubs* **Argentinos Juniors**, **Boca Juniors** (twice), **Barcelona**, **Napoli**, **Sevilla FC**, **Newell's Old Boys**, **Quilmes Athletic Club**. *Keynotes* Maradona, one of eight children, and brought up in a poor district of Buenos Aires, became one of the most talented and controversial players in football history. His senior playing career began at the age of 15, when he played for Argentinos Juniors (20 October 1976, v Talleres), and he made his international debut at 16 on 27 February 1977 (5–1, v **Hungary**, in Buenos Aires, friendly). Although Maradona was dropped from manager Cesar Menotti's final squad for Argentina's

1978 **World Cup** winning campaign, he was named player of the tournament in the **World Youth Cup** (under-20) in September 1979; he scored the final goal in the 3–1 triumph over the **Soviet Union** in Tokyo. He was top scorer in the Argentinean professional league in 1978 (22 goals), 1979 (22 goals) and 1980 (25 goals) – all with Argentinos Juniors – and the Argentinean national championship (which ran in parallel to the professional league from 1967 to 1985) in 1979 (12 goals) and 1980 (18 goals), also with Argentinos Juniors. Maradona was three-times transferred for a world record fee: sold to Boca Juniors for £1 million in 1980, a record for a teenager; transferred to Barcelona for £4.2 million in 1982; and to Napoli for £6.9 million in 1984. His career at Napoli peaked with the club winning its only two Serie A championships in its history. Maradona also scored the opening goal in Napoli's 5–4 aggregate defeat of Stu**ttgart VfB** in the 1989 UEFA Cup final. Maradona enjoyed mixed fortunes at World Cup finals: he was sent off against **Brazil** in 1982, for a dangerous challenge on Batista; captained Argentina to victory in 1986; was a runner-up in 1990 after having been reduced to tears following Argentina's semi-final victory over hosts **Italy**, which took place in his club's stadium in Naples; and was sent home from the 1994 tournament after failing a **drug test**. Maradona was voted Player of the Tournament at the 1986 World Cup and his second goal against **England** (quarter-finals) in Mexico is acknowledged as one of the greatest individual goals ever scored (see **Argentina**, *History*); his first being the infamous "**Hand of God**". Maradona was joint second-highest goalscorer in the 1986 finals, with five goals, and scored both in the 2–0 semi-final victory over **Belgium** – including another memorable solo run. Maradona has twice (1991, 1994) tested positive for banned substances and each time he has been suspended from the game for 15 months. Maradona has coached Deportivo Mandiyu and **Racing Club**. *Honours* World Cup (Argentina, 1986, runner-up 1990), World Youth Cup (Argentina, 1979); **UEFA Cup** (Napoli, 1989); Argentinean professional league championship (Boca Juniors, 1981); Spanish Cup (Barcelona, 1983), Italian **Serie A** championship (Napoli 1987, 1990), Italian Cup (**Coppa Italia**) (Napoli, 1987); *World Soccer* **World Footballer of the Year** 1986, runner-up 1987; *El Mundo* **South American Footballer of the Year** 1979, 1980, 1986, 1989, 1990, 1992, runner-up 1981.

Maranhao *state* one of the 27 state leagues in **Brazil**, founded 1918. Leading clubs: Sampaio Correa FC (Sao Luis), Maranhao AC (Sao Luis), Moto Clube (Sao Luis).

Marathon (Club Deportivo) *club* Honduras national league club based in San Pedro Sula, formed 1925. Ground: Estadio Francisco Morazan, capacity: 20,000. Strip: green shirts, white shorts. Honduras League champions 1979, 1985; Honduras Cup 1994.

Marconi Fairfield *club* Australian national league club, based in Sydney. Ground: Marconi Stadium. Strip:

green shirts, white shorts. Australian league champions 1979, 1988, 1989, 1993; **Australian Cup** 1980.

Maribor Teatanik (formerly Maribor Branik) *club* Slovenian national league club based in Maribor, founded 1958. Ground: Ljudski Vrt, capacity: 15,000. Strip: violet shirts with yellow trim, violet shorts. **UEFA Cup** – second round 1994; pre-independent Slovenian league champions 1961, 1976, 1982, 1984, 1986; Slovenian league champions 1997, 1998, runners-up 1992, 1993, 1995; pre-independent Slovenian Cup 1965, 1966, 1968, 1973, 1974, 1978, 1980, 1982, 1984, 1986, 1987, 1989, 1990; Slovenian Cup 1992, 1994.

marijuana *medical* the dried leaves and flowers hemp plant (*Cannabis sativa*). Used as an illegal recreational drug, banned in sport (see **cannabis**).

marking *n.* keeping an opponent in close proximity in order to tackle them, or to prevent them passing, shooting or running into **space**. *vb.* to **mark**.

Marseille *club* see **Olympique de Marseille**.

Marshall Islands *country no affiliation* island nation in the West Pacific, consists of two groups of islands (Ralik and Radak), includes the Bikini and Eniwetok atolls (formerly used for United States nuclear bomb testing programme). Area: 180 sq km (69 sq miles). Population: 58,500 (1996 est.). Capital: Majuro. Football association not affiliated to **FIFA**.

Martinique *country no international affiliation (affiliated to French Confederation)* overseas department of France. Island in the West Indies, in the Windward Islands, part of the Lesser Antilles. Became a French colony in 1635, an overseas department since 1972. Area: 1,079 sq km (417 sq miles). Population: 373,000. Language: French. Capital: Fort-de-France. *Dossier* Football association (Ligue Martiniquaise de Football) affiliated to the French Confederation, neither affiliated to **FIFA** nor **Confederación Norte-Centroamericana y del Caribe de Fútbol (CON-CACAF)**. *International tournament record* **Women's World Cup** – entered first tournament in 1991, never qualified for finals tournament; **World Cup** – has not entered; **Gold Cup** – qualified in 1993 (the second Gold Cup), finishing last in its first-round group of four; **Caribbean Nations Cup** – winners 1993 (0–0, 6–5 pens., v **Jamaica**, in Jamaica), runners-up 1994 (2–7, v **Trinidad and Tobago**, in final in Trinidad), third place 1992 (1–1, 5–3 pens., v **Cuba**, in Trinidad, third/fourth play-off), 1996 (1–1, 3–2 pens., v **Surinam**); **CONCACAF Women's Championship** – entered first tournament in 1991 (finished bottom of its first-round group of four, with just one point) and again in 1998 (third in its first-round group of four nations); **Under-17 World Championship** – never qualified; **World Youth Cup** (under-20) – never qualified. *Record against British and Irish national teams* none played. *Record in international club tournaments* **Caribbean Club Championship** L'Aiglons (of Le Lamentin, semi-final 1998); **CONCACAF Champions Cup** – US Robert (semi-final/fourth 1994), Club

Franciscain (of Le Francois, Caribbean section semi-final 1994). Other leading clubs: Olympique Marin (Fort-de-France) and Golden Star (Fort-de-France).

mascot *misc.* young supporter who accompanies the team on to the pitch; or individual clothed in fancy dress/costume; or figure designed to promote a tournament. *Keynotes* Every **World Cup** finals tournament since 1966, when it was World Cup Willie, has been accompanied by an official mascot. For example, Tip and Tap were joint mascots of the 1974 event, while in 1978 the organising committee adopted Guachito. Footix, a cockerel, was used for the 1998 World Cup and, in 1999, the Womens' World Cup in the US was represented by a fox named Nutmeg. Mascots have long been a tradition among football clubs. At the turn of the century, **Wolverhampton Wanderers** boasted a wolf (sporting a flat cap). Most clubs have mascots dressed as animals, for example: **Arsenal** (a dinosaur named Gunnersaurus); **Chelsea** (Stamford the lion); **Crewe Alexandra** (Gresty Lion); **Bradford City** (Billy Bantam, a cockerel); **Leicester City** (Filbert the fox); **West Bromwich Albion** (Baggie Bird); Wolverhampton Wanderers (Wolfie). Pottermus, **Stoke City**'s hippo mascot was voted seventh by supporters in the club's 1997-98 Footballer of the Year award.

Maseru United Brothers *club* Lesotho national League team, based in the capital Maseru. Ground: Pitso, capacity: 6,000. Strip: gold shirts, black shorts. **African Cup-winners Cup** second round 1979; Lesotho league champions 1970, 1976.

masking agent *medical* any illegal drug used to prevent the detection of a banned substance in a **drug test**. **Diuretics** are used as masking agents by increasing the volume of urine produced by the player thus reducing the concentration of the drug in a urine test.

Masopust, Josef *player* Midfield. **Czechoslovakia** international (63 caps, 10 goals, 1954-66). Born 9 February 1931 *Club* **Dukla Prague** (known as UDA Prague until 1955). *Keynotes* Scored the first goal in the 1962 **World Cup** final, which his country lost 1–3 to **Brazil**. *Honours* World Cup runner-up (Czechoslovakia, 1962); **European Championship** third place (Czechoslovakia, 1960; **Dr Gerö Cup** (Czechoslovakia, 1960); Czechoslovakian league championship (Dukla Prague, 1953, 1956, 1958, 1961, 1962, 1963, 1964, 1966); *France Football* **European Footballer of the Year** 1962.

Mass Sosseh *club* Gambian national league club based in the capital Banjul, formerly known as Ports Authority. Ground: Box Bar (the national stadium), capacity: 10,000. Strip: blue shirts, white shorts. Gambian league champions 1973, 1982, 1984; Gambian Cup 1975.

Master de la Copa CONMEBOL *competition* South American club tournament for past winners of the Copa CONMEBOL, played in 1996. *Winner, result, runners-up:* 1996 **São Paulo**, 3–0, v **Atlético Mineiro**.

Match of death *informal* match played between Kiev and German army side, Flakelf, during **World War II**. Eight Kiev players subsequently were executed after the team had disobeyed German orders to lose the "friendly". Two players were sent to a labour camp and another escaped.

Match of the Day *television* BBC **television** show of recorded *Premier League* and **FA Cup** football highlights on Saturday night. The original agreement between the BBC and the **Football League**, signed in August 1964, allowed for up to 55 minutes' of one match; the BBC paid £20,000 for the rights. First shown on BBC 2 on 22 August 1964 (**Liverpool** v **Arsenal**). The estimated audience was only 75,000 (BBC 2 was a new channel on a transmission format that meant that most television owners were not able to tune in). Match of the Day was switched to BBC1 in 1966. By 1969, the BBC had to pay £100,000 for continued rights to show highlights. See **Snatch of the Day**.

match fee *regulations* fee paid to an official for adjudicating over a match. **Referees** and **assistant referees** receive match fees for senior level matches. In the 1998-99 season, **Football League** referees were paid £195 per match, rising to £275 for cup matches at and beyond the quarter-final stage and for the league **play-offs**. Football League assistant referees were paid £95 per match, rising to £135. Until the end of the 1998-99 season, referees in the **Premier League** were paid a fixed rate determined by the Premier League Board: in the 1997-98 season they were paid £375 per match plus travelling and hotel expenses; assistant referees were paid £165 per match plus travelling and hotel expenses. A Premier League referee could also be paid additional, discretionary, payments "in recognition of his performance and his commitment to training, education and development". Full professional referees were introduced in the Premier League for the start of the 1999-00 season. Clubs are barred from offering any payment or benefit to referees (FA Premier League rule G.9, Football League standing orders for referees rule 4).

match fixing *n.* actions by players/club officials or referees to influence the result of a match. *Keynotes* The first recorded allegations of match-fixing occurred in 1900 when the **Burnley** goalkeeper Jack Hillman is said to have offered a bribe to the captain of **Nottingham Forest**. Burnley needed to win the match (on 30 April) to avoid relegation from Division One. Hillman was made to answer the charge in front of a joint **Football League** and **Football Association** commission in Manchester on 9 May 1900. He was banned for one year. Nine players, including **Manchester United**'s Enoch West, received bans after suspicion was cast on **Liverpool**'s 0–2 defeat at **Old Trafford** on 2 April 1915. A Liverpool player later admitted that the result had been agreed in a Manchester pub prior to the match. For his part in the scam, West was banned for life, although this punishment was later rescinded – when he was 62! In December 1962, **Ipswich Town** beat **Sheffield Wednesday** 2–1 at **Portman Road**. It was later revealed in a newspaper article by former **Everton**

player, Jimmy Gauld, that the result was fixed as part of a staged betting coup. He also revealed that the Division Three clash between **Lincoln City** and **Brentford** and the Division Four match between **York City** and **Oldham Athletic** on the same day also had been rigged. The police subsequently interviewed over 60 players, and 33 appeared in court charged with "conspiracy to defraud". Gauld and nine others were imprisoned. Three Wednesday players, Tony Kay, David Layne and Peter Swan, were also banned from football for their part in the scandal. On 14 March 1995, Bruce Grobbelaar was arrested, together with **Wimbledon** duo John Fashanu and Hans Segers (and Fashanu's wife Melissa Kassa-Mapsi and Malaysian businessman Heng Suan Lim), for allegedly being involved in match-fixing as part of a Far Eastern betting syndicate. All of the defendants were subsequently cleared following two protracted High Court trials. Both Grobbelaar and Segers were later found guilty by an **Football Association** tribunal of contravening its betting regulations. The FA suspended both players from the game for six months and fined each £10,000, although the punishment was suspended for two years in both cases. Elsewhere, **AC Milan** was relegated to Serie B in 1979-80 after the club was found guilty of fixing a 2–1 victory over **Lazio**. As a result, the then club president Felice Columbo and goalkeeper Ricky Albertosi, as well as Lazio goalkeeper Massimo Cacciatori, were banned for life. In addition, Lazio was fined £6,000. The case was part of a much bigger betting scandal, involving a host of top players, which was disclosed by two members of a Rome-based gambling syndicate. Included on the list of 27 players who were allegedly involved in match fixing ,was future Italy **World Cup** star Paolo **Rossi**. Eventually, 10 players were banned as a result of the investigation, including Rossi, who received a three-year ban (later reduced to two years, making him eligible for Italy's 1982 World Cup squad). In **France**, the millionaire owner of **Olympique de Marseille**, Bernard Tapie, was imprisoned for one year as part of a match fixing scandal, and the club was stripped of both its French League title and the 1993 **European Cup** title. Marseille's 1–0 League victory over Valenciennes in 1993, which ensured the club the French title, had been rigged, with an opponent, Christophe Robert, paid 250,000 ff. to "take it easy" during the game. The **CSKA Moscow** coach, Gennadi Kostylev, also claimed that his players were offered money before the club's European Cup fixture against Marseille. In September 1993, **Dynamo Tiblisi** was dismissed from the European Cup qualifying stage for allegedly trying to bribe the match officials before its tie with **Linfield**. The Italian Football Confederation opened an investigation into bribery allegations after referee Stefano Farina received a telephone call asking him to favour Empoli in the club's away **Serie A** fixture against **Sampdoria** on 25 October 1998. Another referee took control of the match which Sampdoria won

3–0. In November 1998, five **Hong Kong** internationals were charged with fixing matches, including the 1998 World Cup qualifier with **Thailand** in March 1997, following an investigation by the Independent Commission Against Corruption. Striker Alan Chan Tsz-kong was jailed for one year in July 1998 after pleading guilty to match fixing. Wai Kwan-lung was charged with accepting HK$30,000 from Tsz-kong for failing to perform to the best of his ability against Thailand, while Lee Wai-man, Kevin Lok Kar-win and Philip Chan Chi-keung were also charged with conspiring to obtain HK$200,000 from a bookmaker following the 0–2 defeat. In addition, Lau Chi-yuen was charged with fixing four matches involving the Hong Kong club Sing Tao in 1995-96.

match observer *regulations* person appointed by the FA **Premier League** to attend and report on each Premier League match. The observer must be given a good seat and access to all areas of the ground (FA Premier League rule E.14).

match programme *n.* official publication released by the home club usually on the day of a match. It contains details about the opposition and both sets of players, as well as general information and news. Match programmes are commonly collected by football hobbyists. *Regulations* every club in the **Premier League** and **Football League** must allocate the **Football Trust** half a page of free advertising or editorial in its match programme (FA Premier League rules section S, Football League regulation 69).

Matchedje *club* Mozambique national league club based in the capital Maputo. Ground: Estadio de Machava, capacity: 60,000 (national stadium). Strip: green shirts and white shorts. **African Cup of Champion Clubs** quarter final 1988; Mozambique League champions 1987 and 1990; Mozambique Cup 1990.

Matlama FC *club* Lesotho national League team, based in Maseru (capital of Lesotho). Ground: Pitso, capacity: 6,000. Strip: blue shirts and white shorts. **African Cup of Champion Clubs** quarter-final 1979 (lost to eventual winners of the tournament, **Union Douala** of Cameroon); **African Cup-winners Cup** second round 1980; Lesotho League champions 1974, 1977, 1978,1982, 1986, 1988, 1992; Lesotho Cup 1976, 1979, 1980, 1987, 1992, 1994.

Mato Grosso do Sul *state* one of the 27 state leagues in **Brazil**, founded 1979 when the state of **Mato Grosso** was divided into two separate states. Leading clubs: Operario FC (of Campo Grande), Comercial FC (Campo Grande).

Mato Grosso *state* one of the 27 state leagues in **Brazil**, founded 1943. Leading clubs: Mixto Esporte Clube (Cuiaba), Clube Esportivo Operario (Varzea Grande).

Matthäus, Lothar *player* Defender. **West Germany** and Germany international (135 caps 1980-99, 2). Born 21 March 1961. *Clubs* **Borussia Mönchengladbach**, **Bayern Munich** (twice), **Internazionale**. *Keynotes*

Matthäus made his international debut on 14 June 1980, aged 19 (3–2, v **Netherlands**, in Naples, **European Championship** first round). He played in five World Cup finals (equalling the record) and broke the record for the most games in World Cup finals when playing his 22nd such game, on 21 June 1998). Matthäus, who scored four goals in the 1990 tournament, is Germany's most-capped player of all time and the world's third-most capped player of all time. Despite his lengthy career, Matthäus missed the finals of the 1980, 1992 and 1996 European Championships – against **Belgium**, **Denmark** and **Czech Republic**, respectively – although he scored for West Germany in the 1–2 defeat by Netherlands in the 1988 semi-final. He was transferred to Bayern Munich in 1984 – for a then German record of £650,000 – and Internazionale in 1988; returning to Bayern in 1992. He played for Bayern in the 1987 European Cup final (1–2 v FC **Porto**), and scored the opening goal for Internazionale in the 1991 UEFA Cup final (2–1 agg., v **Roma**). *Honours* **World Cup** (West Germany, 1990, runner-up 1986); **UEFA Cup** (Internazionale, 1991, Bayern Munich 1996); German **Bundesliga** championship (Bayern Munich, 1985, 1986, 1987, 1994, 1997, 1999); Italian **Serie A** championship (Internazionale, 1989); **FIFA World Footballer of the Year** 1991 (the first year of the award); *France Football* **European Footballer of the Year** 1990.

Matthews final   *misc.*   1953 **FA Cup** final between **Blackpool** and **Bolton Wanderers** (4–3). The final is commonly referred to as The Matthews Final in honour of Stanley **Matthews**'s contribution to Blackpool's victory. Blackpool, 3–1 behind with only 22 minutes remaining, staged a remarkable comeback: only one other club, **Everton** in 1966, has won a Wembley FA Cup final from two down. Matthews, cutting in from the right, provided the pass which set up Bill Perry to score the winner in the final minute. For a brief moment, the Wembley scoreboard mistakenly read Blackpool 4 Bolton 4.

Matthews, Stanley   *player*   Winger. **England** international (54 caps). Born 1 February 1915. Career ca. 1932-1965. *Clubs* **Stoke City** (twice), **Blackpool**. *Keynotes* Known as the "Wizard of the dribble", Matthews had a career that spanned 33 years. He made his debut for Stoke City on 19 March 1932 and played his last game for the same club on 6 February 1965. His final appearance for England was at the age of 42 (v **Denmark**, 15 May 1957). Matthews was twice a losing **FA Cup** finalist before he won with Blackpool in 1953, a match that became known as the **Matthews final** (v **Bolton Wanderers**). In 1947-48, he was the first winner of the Football Writers **Footballer of the Year** award, an accolade he won again in 1962-63. He was the first recipient of the **European Footballer of the Year** award in 1956. Matthews was knighted in 1965 (the first serving player to receive the honour), having received a CBE in 1957. A statue of Matthews stands in the town of his birth, Hanley, and bears the following

inscription: "His name is symbolic of the beauty of the game, his fame timeless and international, his sportsmanship and modesty universally acclaimed. A magical player, of the people, for the people". Included in the **Football League Centenary 100 players**. See **Stanley Matthews Football Boots**. *Honours* Division Two (Stoke City 1932-33, 1962-63); FA Cup (Blackpool 1953).

Mauritania   *country CAF*   Islamic Republic in north-west Africa on the Atlantic Ocean and bordered by **Algeria**, **Mali**, **Western Sahara** and **Senegal**. A large part of the country is desert. Independence from France in 1960. Area: 1,030,700 sq km (397,850 sq miles). Population: 2,330,000 (1996 est.). Languages: Hasaniya Arabic, French and some native languages. Capital: Nouakchott. *Dossier* Football association (Fédération de Foot-Ball de la République de Mauritanie, Nouakchott) formed in 1961 affiliated to **FIFA** in 1964 and **Confédération Africaine de Football** (CAF) in 1968, president Mohamed Lemine Cheiguer, general secretary Mohamed Vall. Season played from November to July. National stadium: Fode Capi Camara, Nouakchott, capacity: 15,000. National strip: green and yellow shirts, yellow shorts and green socks. First international game: 1967, v **Tanzania** (1–1, home, friendly). Biggest victory: 3–0 v **Liberia** (23 November 1984, home, **African Cup of Nations** qualifier). Biggest defeat: 0–14 v **Guinea** (1972, away, **All-Africa Games** qualifier). *International tournament record* Olympic Games – played in qualifying tournaments since 1980, but has never qualified for finals tournament; **Women's World Cup** – never entered; **World Cup** – has entered twice, in 1978 (lost in the African group preliminary round) and 1998 (lost in first round); African Cup of Nations – first entered 1980, never beyond qualifying tournament; **Amilcar Cabral Cup** – runners-up 1995 (0–0, 2–4 pens., v **Sierra Leone**); **Under-17 World Championship** – never qualified; **World Youth Cup** (under-20) – never qualified. *Record against British and Irish national teams* none played. *Record in international club tournaments* **African Cup of Champion Clubs** – Espoirs (second round 1977); **African Cup-winners Cup** – ASC Garde Nationale (first round 1978, having won a preliminary round); **CAF Cup** – ASC Air Mauritanie (second round 1993, having won through a preliminary and first round). Other leading clubs: **AS Police**, **ASC Ksar Sonader**, Sonalec (of Nouakchott), Mauritanian Cup 1997, 1998).

Mauritius   *country CAF*   republic.   Mountanous island in the Indian Ocean, east of **Madagascar**; includes the island of Rodrigues and other small islands. Independence from Britain in 1968, became a republic in 1990. Area: 1,865 sq km (720 sq miles). Population: 1,130,000 (1995 est.). Languages: English, French Creole, Hindi and Bhojpuri. Capital: Port Louis. *Dossier* Mauritius Football Association (Port Louis) formed in 1952, affiliated to **FIFA** in 1962 and **Confédération Africaine de Football** (CAF) in 1963, president: Ravindra Chetty; general secretary:

Ananda Vuddamalay. Season played from September to June. National stadiums: King George V, Curepipe, capacity: 19,000; and Sir Anerood Jugnauth, Port Louis, capacity: 18,000. National strip: red shirts, white shorts and red socks with white tops. First international game: 1947, v **Réunion** (its nearest neighbours, 2–0, in Madagascar, **Indian Ocean Games**). Biggest victory: 15–2 v Réunion (1950, in Madagascar, Indian Ocean Games). Biggest defeat: 0–5 v **Zambia** (4 May 1975, away, **Olympic Games** qualifier). *International tournament record* Olympic Games – first entered 1976, but has failed to progress beyond qualifying tournament); **Women's World Cup** – never entered; **World Cup** – took part in 1974, 1986 and 1998 qualifying tournaments, but has not won any of its first-round games; **African Cup of Nations** – qualified for final tournament in 1974 (beat **Tanzania** on penalties in its final qualifying match, but finished bottom of its group of four in the first round of the finals tournament, losing all its three matches); **All-Africa Games** – qualified for finals tournament in 1991 and 1995; Indian Ocean Games – winners 1948, 1949, 1950, 1951, 1952, 1953, 1954, 1955, 1956, 1957, 1982, 1985, runners-up 1947, 1958, 1990, third place 1983; **Under-17 World Championship** – never qualified; **World Youth Cup** (under-20) – never qualified. *Record against British and Irish national teams* none played. *Record in international club tournaments* **African Cup of Champion Clubs – Sunrise Flacq United SC** (second round 1988, 1990, 1991 and 1993), **African Cup-winners Cup – Cadets Club** (second round 1995); **Fire Brigade SC** (second round 1989 and 1995). Other leading club: **Police Club**.

Maxaquene (Clube Desportes Maxaquene) *club* Mozambique national league club based in the capital Maputo. Ground: Maxaquene, capacity: 17,000. Strip: blue shirts and red shorts. **African Cup-winners Cup** semi-final 1995; Mozambique League champions 1984, 1985, 1986; Mozambique Cup 1978, 1981, 1987, 1994, 1996.

maximum wage *n.* ceiling on players' wages formerly imposed by the **Football Association**. *Keynotes* The suggestion of a maximum wage for players was first mooted in English league football in 1891, though the proposals were not taken up until 1900, when the **Football Association** ruled that, from the 1901-02 season, wages would be restricted to £4 per week (£208 per annum). **Bonus payments** also were outlawed, though this rule was amended in 1910. The maximum wage was raised in 1910 to £5 per week, but only for players who had remained at a club for four years (players would be paid £4 10s after two years). The figure was raised again in 1920, to £9 per week (again after four years' service), but this time payable throughout the year, and not just for the season and weeks of pre-season training. The maximum wage was reduced to £8 per week in 1922, with a lower wage of £6 paid in the summer (**summer wages**). Wage disputes continued after **World War II** and in 1946 a dispute between the **Football League** and the Players' Union was settled at a National Arbitration Tribunal, with a maximum wage agreed at £12 (£10 for the **close season**) with a minimum of £6. The maximum wage reached £20 in 1958. A long-running battle between the Players Union – renamed the **Professional Footballers Association** (PFA) in 1958 – and the Football League came to a head in 1960. The PFA, under the chairmanship of Jimmy **Hill**, wanted to abolish the maximum wage. In December 1960, the Football League management committee, with the approval of the FA, offered to raise the maximum to £30 with freedom to negotiate contracts of up to three years (compared with the one-year contracts that operated at that time) and an increase of the **signing-on fee** to £150. The package was rejected. A revised offer, with the abolition of the maximum wage, was turned down in January 1961: the revision still offered no change to the **retain-and-transfer system**. The PFA voted to stage strike action on Saturday 21 January 1961. The action was called off on 18 January, after a meeting between the League and the FA, in the presence of the Minister of Labour, John Hare. The maximum wage was abolished, with some compromises tabled on the transfer system. Soon after, Johnny **Haynes** became the first £100-a-week player in the English Football League.

Mayotte *country no international affiliation (affiliated to French Confederation)* Territorial collectivity of **France**. Volcanic island in the Indian Ocean, northwest of Madagascar. Remained a French territory when, in 1976, the **Comoro** Islands gained independence. Area: 376 sq km (145 sq miles). Population: 85,000. Languages: French and Comoran. Capital: Dzaoudzi. *Dossier* Football association (Ligue Regionale de Football de Mayotte, Dzaoudzi) formed in 1979, affiliated neither to **FIFA** nor to the **Confédération Africaine de Football**, but to the French Confederation, president: Inzoudine Abdouraiimane. Season played from April to December. National stadium: Kavani, capacity: 5,000. National strip: white shirts, white shorts and white socks. *International tournament record* none entered (including the **Indian Ocean Games**). *Record against British and Irish national teams* none played. Leading club: Association Sportive Sada (league champions 1998) and Ouragan Labbatoir.

Mazurkiewicz, Ladislao *player* Goalkeeper. **Uruguay** international. *Club* **Peñarol**. *Honours* **World Cup** fourth place (Uruguay, 1970). **Copa America** (Uruguay, 1967); **Copa Libertadores** (Peñarol, 1966); **World Club Championship** (Peñarol, 1966).

Mazzola, 1. Alessandro (Sandro) *player* Striker/midfield. **Italy** international (70 caps, 22 goals, 1963-74). Born 7 November 1942. *Clubs* **Internazionale**. *Keynotes* Mazzola scored twice for Internazionale in the 1964 **European Cup** final against **Real Madrid** (3–1, in Vienna). Mazzola started out as a striker and later moved into midfield. He made his international debut on 12 May 1963 (3–0, v **Brazil**, in Milan, friendly). *Honours* **World Cup** runner-up (Italy, 1970);

European Championship (Italy, 1968); European Cup (Inter, 1964, 1965); Italian **Serie A** championship (Inter, 1963, 1965, 1966, 1971); *France Football* European **Footballer of the Year** runner-up 1971. **2.** His father, Valentino *player* Striker. Italy international (12 caps, four goals). Born 26 January 1919, died 4 May 1949. Career ca. 1937-49. *Clubs* Tresoldi, Venezia, **Torino**. *Keynotes* Transferred from Venezia to Torino in 1942; he was captain and Italian national team captain. Mazzola was killed in the 1949 **Superga aircrash**, when his son Alessandro was only six years old. *Honours* Italian Serie A championship 1943, 1946, 1947, 1948, 1949.

Mbabane Highlanders *club* Swaziland national league club based in the capital Mbabane. Ground: Somholo, capacity: 15,000. Strip: black shirts, white shorts. **African Cup-winners Cup** second round 1986; COSAFA Club Championship winners 1992; Swaziland league champions 1976, 1980, 1982, 1984, 1986, 1988, 1991, 1992, 1995, 1997; Swaziland Cup 1983, 1985, 1990.

Mbilinga *club* Gabon national league club based in Port Gentil, founded 1962. Ground: Mosquee, capacity: 5,000. Strip: yellow shirts, red shorts. **African Cup of Champion Clubs** quarter-final 1995; **African Cup-winners Cup** semi-final 1994, quarter-final 1998; **CAF Cup** quarter-final 1993; Gabon league champions 1996; Gabon Cup 1990, 1995, 1997.

Mbongo Sports *club* Congo Democratic Republic (formerly Zaire) national league. **CAF Cup** quarter-final 1992; Congo DR Cup runners-up 1995.

McBain, Neil *player-manager* oldest player ever to play in a **Football League** fixture – 51 years 120 days, for **New Brighton** (lost 0–3 v **Hartlepool United**, 15 March 1947, Division Three North). McBain acted as an emergency replacement goalkeeper (he was the **New Brighton** manager, and a former **Scotland** centre-half). He was also one of the few men to play for both **Everton** and **Liverpool**.

McCain Stadium *ground* English football ground situated in Scarborough, north Yorkshire; home of **Scarborough**. *Dossier* Ground capacity: 6,899. Pitch dimensions: 104m x 68m. Record attendance: 11,130 v **Luton Town** (8 January 1938, **FA Cup**, third round). Record League attendance: 7,314 v **Wolverhampton Wanderers** (15 August 1987, Division Three). Best average attendance: 2,962 (1988-89). *History* Commonly known as Seamer Road (officially called the Athletic Ground) until it became the McCain Stadium after the club sold the name rights to a frozen food company in 1988, Scarborough first played there on 22 October 1898 (v Loftus, Cleveland Senior Cup). The ground's only stand was destroyed by fire in 1927. Scarborough's first **Football League** fixture on 15 August 1987 resulted in Wolverhampton Wanderers supporters causing £25,000 worth of damage to the ground. The first floodlit match at Seamer Road took place on 16 September 1970 (v Boston, Northern Premier League).

McCoist, Ally *player* Striker. **Scotland** international (60 caps, 19 goals). Born 24 September 1962. Career ca. 1978-. *Clubs* **St Johnstone**, **Sunderland**, **Rangers**, **Kilmarnock**. *Keynotes* Turned professional with St Johnstone in August 1978, moving to Sunderland for £350,000 in August 1981. Joined Rangers for £180,000 in June 1983, scoring a hat-trick in his first major final for the club, the 1983-84 Scottish League Cup final (3–2 v **Celtic**). His 250-goal Scottish League tally with Rangers is a club record and in both 1992 and 1993 he was Europe's leading goalscorer. McCoist made his Scotland debut in 1986. He moved to Kilmarnock on a **free transfer** before the start of the 1998-99 campaign. He was controversially omitted from Craig Brown's 1998 Scotland **World Cup** squad. Voted **Footballer of the Year (Scotland)** in 1992. He was awarded the MBE in 1994. Regularly appears on television, most notably as a captain on BBC's *Question of Sport* and as co-host of the Saturday night show, *McCoist and MacAulay*. *Honours* Scottish Football League (Rangers 1986-87, 1988-89, 1989-90, 1990-91, 1991-92, 1992-93, 1993-94, 1994-95, 1995-96, 1996-97); **Scottish FA Cup** (Rangers 1992, 1996); **Scottish Football League Cup** (Rangers 1983-94, 1984-85, 1986-87, 1987-88, 1988-89, 1990-91, 1992-93, 1993-94, 1996-97).

McCracken, Bill *player* Full-back. **Ireland** international (15 caps). Career ca. 1904-24. *Clubs* **Newcastle United**. *Keynotes* McCracken's speed and intelligent positional play, along with that of his Newcastle United colleague Frank Hudspeth, led to the change in the **offside** law in 1925. As a scout, McCracken discovered the future **Northern Ireland** goalkeeper Pat **Jennings**. McCracken died aged 95 on 20 January 1979. Included in the **Football League Centenary 100 players**.

McDiarmid Park *ground* Scottish football ground situated in Perth, Tayside region; home of **St Johnstone**. Ground capacity: 10,673 all seated. Pitch dimensions: 105m x 68.5m. Record attendance: 10,504 v **Rangers** (20 October 1990, Premier Division). *Keynotes* St Johnstone moved to McDiarmid Park in August 1989, having previously played at Muirton Park since 1924. The Muirton Park site, which had staged its first match on 25 December 1924 (v **Queen's Park**), was sold to Asda to build a supermarket. The retail chain paid the whole £4.9 million cost of building McDiarmid Park, which was completed in 10 months after work began in October 1988. The ground gets its name from a farmer, Bruce McDiarmid, who donated the 16 acres of land on which the stadium is built. Aside from St Johnstone's games, McDiarmid Park has staged a number of other football matches, including under-21 international fixtures. It has also hosted several Rugby Union games.

McGrath, Paul *player* Defender. **Republic of Ireland** international (83 caps). Born 4 December 1959. Career ca. 1981-98. *Clubs* **St Patrick's Athletic, Manchester United, Aston Villa, Derby County**. *Keynotes* Signed by Manchester United from

Republic of Ireland club St Patrick's Athletic for an initial £35,000 in June 1981, he went on to make 163 **Football League** appearances for the club. His seven seasons at **Old Trafford** were interrupted by eight knee operations and, in 1989, he was advised to retire but chose instead to move to Aston Villa. Despite his problems he played in 253 League games for Villa between 1989-90 and 1995-96, before moving to Derby County for £200,000 in October 1996. Voted **PFA Footballer of the Year in 1993**. Included in the **Football League Centenary 100 players**. *Honours* **FA Cup** (Manchester United 1983, 1985); **League Cup** (Aston Villa 1994, 1996).

McGregor William *official* First chairman of the English **Football League** and credited with its original concept in 1888. Born 1847, in Braco, Perthshire, Scotland. McGregor owned a drapery at 306-307 Summer Lane, in Newtown, Birmingham. In addition to more traditional clothing, the shop also sold "football jerseys". McGregor's idea for a league is believed to have been gleaned from the English County Cricket league system. He was an early supporter of professionalism. He was the first Life Member of the Football League, a former vice-president of **Aston Villa** and a former councillor of the **Football Association**. One of the most successful football boot designs of the 1900s was named after him – the "McGregor" by Birmingham footwear manufacturers Shillcock – though there is no evidence of his actually endorsing the boot. McGregor died in 1911 aged 65.

McGrory, Jimmy *player* Striker. *Clubs* **Celtic** and **Clydebank**. 550, Career ca. 1922-38. *Keynotes* McGrory scored 550 goals in his career, a Scottish record. See details under **goals, most in senior career.**

McIlroy Jimmy *player* Striker. **Northern Ireland** international (55 caps). Career ca. 1950-67. *Clubs* **Burnley, Stoke City, Oldham Athletic**. *Keynotes* Member of the Burnley side that won the League title in 1959-60 and reached the 1962 **FA Cup** final (1–3 v **Tottenham Hotspur**). Appeared in the 1958 **World Cup** for Northern Ireland. Later became a journalist in Lancashire. Included in the **Football League Centenary 100 players**. *Honours* **Football League** Championship (Burnley 1959-60).

McKenna, John *official* third and longest-serving president of the **Football League** (1910-36) and director of **Liverpool**. Born 1854 in County Monaghan, Ireland, died 1936 (while still in office). Credited with getting Liverpool elected to the Football league in 1893. Made a life member of the Football League in 1922.

McLintock, Frank *player-manager/broadcaster* Defender. **Scotland** international (9 caps). Born 28 December 1939. Career ca. 1956-77. *Clubs* (player) **Leicester City, Arsenal, Queens Park Rangers**, (manager) Leicester City, **Brentford**. *Keynotes* Transferred to Arsenal from Leicester City for £80,000 in October 1964, captaining the north-London club to the **double** in 1970-71. McLintock appeared in six **Wembley** finals, but won only one (1971 v **Liverpool**): he was twice an FA Cup beaten finalist with Leicester (1961, 1963) and once with Arsenal (1972); also with Arsenal, he was twice a losing League Cup finalist (1968, 1969). McLintock retired from playing in May 1977, and was Leicester manager between June 1977 and April 1978. He later managed Brentford, taking the club to the 1985 **Freight Rover Trophy** final (1–3 v **Wigan Athletic**). Awarded the MBE in 1972. Included in the **Football League Centenary 100 players**. *Honours* League Championship (Arsenal 1970-71); **FA Cup** (Arsenal 1971); **UEFA** (Fairs) **Cup** (Arsenal 1970).

MDC United *club* Malawi Super League club based in Lilongwe (the capital city). Ground: Muzu, capacity: 17,000. Strip: red shirts and white shorts. **East and Central African Club Championship** semi-final 1984; Malawi National Super League champions 1988; Lilongwe and District League champions 1983 (regional leagues operated before the Super League started in 1986).

Meadow Lane (County Ground) *ground* English football ground situated in Nottingham; home of **Notts County**. *Dossier* Ground capacity: 20,300. Pitch dimensions: 104m x 68m. Record attendance: 47,310 v **York City** (12 March 1955, **FA Cup**, sixth round). Best average attendance: 35,176 (1949-50). *History* Notts County, the **Football League**'s oldest club, moved to the council-owned Meadow Lane in 1910, playing its first match there on 3 September (v **Nottingham Forest**, Division One). The club spent around £10,000 developing the site for football. Bombs destroyed part of the main stand during **World War II** and, in the winter of 1946-47, the River Trent burst its banks and flooded the ground. It also flooded the **City Ground**, home of Nottingham Forest, across the river, forcing Forest to use Meadow Lane for a time because the water subsided more quickly there. In January 1992, County unveiled plans to build three new stands seating 13,400 people during the 1992-93 close season. A fourth new stand was added at the end of the 1994 season, so that within two years Meadow Lane was transformed into a 20,300 **all-seater stadium** at a cost of around £8 million. Meadow Lane staged an FA Cup semi-final in both 1912 and 1925. The first floodlit match at Meadow Lane took place on 23 March 1953 (v **Derby County**, friendly).

Meazza, Giuseppe *player* Striker. **Italy** international (53 caps, 33 goals, 1930-39). Born 23 August 1910, died 1979. Career ca. 1927-47. *Clubs* **Internazionale, AC Milan, Juventus**, Varese FC (Italy), Atalanta (Italy) *Keynotes* Meazza scored 355 goals in a career spanning nearly 20 years. He scored two goals on his international debut for Italy (9 February 1930, 4–2, v **Switzerland**, Rome, friendly), a hat-trick three months later against **Hungary** in the **Dr Gerö Cup**, and another three the following January in a friendly against France; he had scored 10 goals in his first year of international football and is Italy's second highest scorer of all time. He and Giovanni Ferrari were the only two players to appear for

Italy in both the 1934 and 1938 **World Cup** winning teams. He scored the winning goal in the 1–0 defeat of **Spain** in the 1934 quarter-final replay, and was captain of the 1938 team, scoring in the semi-final (2–1 v **Brazil**). He did not play in the 1936 **Olympic Games** gold-medal winning team. At club level, Meazza scored 33 goals – then an Italian league record – in his first full season, 1928-29 (at Internazionale). He was transferred from Internazionale to AC Milan in 1938. Meazza temporarily joined Juventus and Verese FC during World War II, and finished his career at Atalanta. Joint coach of the Italian national team 1952-53. *Honours* World Cup (Italy, 1934, 1938); Italian **Serie A** championship (Internazionale, 1930, 1938).

Mebrat Hail (formerly known as Ethiopia Electric Power Authority, EELPA, Electric Sports) *club* Ethiopian national league club based in Addis Ababa. Ground: Saba, capacity: 20,000. Strip: red shirts, blue shorts. Ethiopian league champions 1993, 1998; Ethiopian Cup 1976.

Mechele Army *club* Ethiopian national league club based in Mechele. Ground: Army Stadium, capacity: 7,000. Strip: green shirts, red shorts. **African Cup-winners Cup** quarter-final 1976; Ethiopian league champions 1949, 1951, 1952, 1953, 1954, 1956, 1976, 1982, 1984, 1988; Ethiopian Cup 1975, 1990.

medal *n.* souvenir medallion (or sometimes a plaque or trophy) given to the players and team officials of competition winners and runners-up. *Regulations* in the **Premier League**, 21 championship medals are given to players, managers and club officials, awarded at the club's discretion. Players must have played at least 10 games during the season (FA Premier League rule B27). Additional medals may be given, but only with the consent of the Premier League Board. In the **Football League** 19 "souvenirs" or medals are given to the League and divisional champions; 14 for the players, one for the secretary, one for the manager, one for the physiotherapist and two for other non-playing staff (additional medals may be awarded with the permission of the Football League Board) (Football League regulation 34). Sixteen gold medals are presented to each of the Scottish Football League divisional champions (Scottish Football League rule 34). *Keynotes* Players of the beaten finalists in the **FA Cup** final collect their medals before the winning team. In 1992, however, the winners' medals were presented to the losing team, **Sunderland**, instead of **Liverpool**.

medial collateral ligament *medical* **ligament** in the knee join that is attached to the bottom of the **femur** at the medial (inside) **condyle** to the medial cartilage and medial (inside) condyle of the **tibia**. Injury can occur if the knee is bent too far inwards due to excessive force.

medial deltoid ligament *medical* very strong **ligament** providing support to the ankle and arch of the foot; attached to the medial malleolus of the **tibia**, and then down, in three ligament bands, to join the navicular bone, the back of the **talus** and the middle of the

spring ligament. See **lateral deltoid ligament**, **eversion injury**.

medial knee ligament *medical* a **ligament** inside the knee **joint**. Injuries to the medial knee ligament generally occur when the knee is knocked inwards (**valgus** position) thus over-stretching the fibres.

medial malleolus *medical* the bottom end of the tibia that forms the bony, protuberant part of the ankle on the inside of the foot. Often injured by direct trauma from a tackle.

medical insurance *n.* see **private medical insurance.**

Mediterranean League (Liga Mediterrania) *competition* ephemeral league competition played for one season, 1936-37, during the Spanish Civil War. Contested by leading clubs from Catalonia and Valencia. *Winners* **Barcelona** (1937).

megastore, football *n.* large club shop selling branded club merchandise. *Keynotes* **Chelsea**'s South Stand (former Shed End) houses the largest club store in England, with 975 square metres (10,500 square feet) of floor space. Around 500,000 customers visited the store in its first 18 months. In September 1998, Chelsea announced plans to open a second megastore in Guildford, Surrey. At the same time, **Manchester United**, which pioneered the megastore format, announced plans to open 150 United shops around the world, with the first outlet at Dublin airport. The shops operate under a United subsidiary, Manchester United International.

Mehalla Al Kubra *club* Egyptian national league club based in Mehalla Al Kubra. Ground: Mehalla Textiles, capacity: 22,000. Strip: green and yellow shirts, yellow shorts. **African Cup of Champion Clubs** runners-up 1974; Egyptian league champions 1973.

meister *misc.* German term for champion.

Melbourne Knights *club* Australian national league club, based in Melbourne (formerly Melbourne Croatia). Ground: Croatian Sports Centre. Strip: red shirts, white shorts (same as the Croatian national side). Australian league champions 1995, 1996; **Australian Cup** 1995.

Mellor, David *broadcaster/official* former-Conservative MP and former presenter of the **Radio 5 Live** Saturday evening football phone-in programme, **Six-O-Six**. Mellor, a **Chelsea** supporter, was appointed chair of the **Football Taskforce** in 1997. He is also a newspaper columnist.

Member of the Football League *n.* a member club of the English **Football League** with full voting rights. All clubs in the Football League (First, Second and Third Divisions) have equal voting rights, replacing the pre-1992 system of **Full Members** and **Associate Members**.

membership scheme *n.* system operated by most clubs to allow fans to become members and be entitled to preferential treatment in terms of access to match tickets and to specific areas of a ground. It also provides the clubs with the potential sanction of card withdrawal should an individual misbehave. The first schemes involving **Football League** clubs were introduced in 1985. *History* **Leicester City** established a partial membership scheme in January 1985 in response to growing supporter complaints that troublemakers were increasingly entering seated sections of the club's **Filbert Street** ground. Leicester's scheme converted one side of the ground into a membership-only area. Following rioting by **Millwall** supporters at **Luton Town**'s **Kenilworth Road** ground in March 1985 (**FA Cup** sixth round), the **Football Association** ordered the club to install **perimeter fencing** in front of its Family Stand. Luton preferred to introduce a home-fans-only membership scheme which excluded all away supporters (this scheme heavily influenced later government proposals to establish a **national identity-card scheme** for all football supporters). At the beginning of the 1987-88 season, the **Football League Management Committee** recommended that all League clubs establish partial membership schemes – designating part of the ground as home-members-only sections. The proposal was not widely supported (one club refused to comply in any way) and the then government decided to pursue a legislative route and tried to establish a national identity-card scheme. The plans were never approved in Parliament.

Memorial Cecchi Gori tournament *competition* pre-season triangular club event staged at **Fiorentina**'s Stadio **Coumunale** (Artemio Franchi) on 3 September 1998. In addition to Fiorentina, **Monaco** and **Roma (AS)** also participated. The tournament consisted of 45-minute matches.

Memorial Ground *ground* English football ground situated in Bristol; home of **Bristol Rovers**. *Dossier* Ground capacity: 9,300. Pitch dimensions: 92m x 62m. Record attendance: 9,274 v **Leyton Orient** (23 January 1999, FA Cup, fourth round). *History* Bristol Rovers moved to the Memorial Ground, home of Bristol Rugby Club, at the start of the 1996-97 season, having played at non-League Bath City's **Twerton Park** since leaving its original ground, **Eastville**, in 1986. The club played its first League fixture at the Memorial Ground on 17 August 1996 (v **Peterborough United**, Second Division). In 1997, Rovers established a "no-swearing terrace" at the ground.

Mendez, Norberto *player* Striker. **Argentina** international (19 goals, 1945-47). *Keynotes* Mendez scored 19 international goals for Argentina in three years and is the all-time top scorer in the **Copa America** with 17 goals in three editions (1945, 1946, 1947). He was all-time top scorer at the 1945 championship with six goals. *Honours* Copa America (Argentina, 1945, 1946, 1947).

meniscus *medical* another word for the area of **cartilage** at the top of the **tibia** on which the **femur** rests. There are two within the knee **joint**, known as the medial meniscus and the lateral meniscus. They are prone to tearing. *pl.* **menisci.**

Mercato *misc.* Italian transfer market held twice yearly in a Milan hotel. These occasions, which last for several weeks and are the only periods when transfers can be arranged, bring together coaches, clubs and agents. See also **transfer window.**

Mercer, Joe *player-manager* Defender. **England** international (5 caps). Born 9 August 1914. Career ca. 1931-1955. *Clubs* (player) **Everton, Arsenal.** *Honours* League Championship (Everton 1938-39; Arsenal 1947-48, 1952-53); **FA Cup** (Arsenal 1950). Manager *Clubs* (manager) **Sheffield United, Aston Villa, Manchester City, Coventry City** (general manager). Also, temporary **England manager** (record played 7, won 3, drawn 3, lost 1, goals for 9, goals against 7). *Keynotes* Career began as an attacking wing-half with Everton but was curtailed by **World War II** – he guested for **Aldershot** during the war – which limited his international appearances to only five. Signed by Arsenal for £7,000 in 1946 and was immediately made captain. He was voted **Footballer of the Year** in 1949-50. Mercer retired from playing in 1955 after suffering a double fracture of the leg. Mercer's managership of Manchester City (1965-71; general manager until 1972), in tandem with Malcolm **Allison**, was the club's most successful period. "Uncle Joe" died on his 76th birthday. Included in the **Football League Centenary 100 players**. *Honours* League Championship (Manchester City 1967-68); Division Two (Aston Villa 1959-60; Manchester City 1965-66); FA Cup (Manchester City 1969); **League Cup** (Aston Villa 1961; Manchester City 1970); **European Cup-winners Cup** (Manchester City 1970).

Meredith, Billy *player* Winger. **Wales** international (48 caps, 11 goals). Born 30 July 1874. Career ca. 1894-1924. *Clubs* **Northwich Victoria, Manchester City** (twice), **Manchester United.** *Keynotes* Known as the "Welsh Wizard", Meredith made 669 League appearances for the two Manchester clubs between 1984 and 1924. Meredith claimed to have played 1,568 games, scoring 470 goals, although his figures are hard to verify. He scored the only goal in the 1904 FA Cup final, and, coming from a Welsh mining background, was a major figure in the creation of the **Players' Union.** Meredith made his last appearance for Wales at the age of 45 (v **England**, 15 March 1920) and appeared for Manchester City in an FA Cup semi-final when he was 49 years and eight months (v **Newcastle United**, 29 March 1924) – the oldest player to appear in a FA Cup match outside the qualifying rounds. Meredith missed a complete season after he was banned amid allegations of bribery and **match-fixing**. Included in the **Football League Centenary 100 players**. *Honours* League Championship (Manchester United 1907-08, 1910-11); Division Two (Manchester City 1898-99, 1902-03); FA Cup (Manchester City 1904, Manchester United 1909).

merger *n.* amalgamation of two clubs or more to form one new club under single ownership. The merger may or may not result in a new name and must be approved by the relevant governing body. Several prominent clubs have been established from the merger of two or more teams. *Keynotes* **Sampdoria** was formed in 1946 from the merger of Andrea Doria and Sampierdarenese. **Internazionale** amalgamated with the US Milanese club in 1928. Fans tend to react angrily to mergers. Supporters of both clubs campaigned against the proposed merger of **Fulham** and **Queens Park Rangers** in 1987 to form "Fulham Park Rangers", while Robert Maxwell's proposal in April 1983 to create one club, Thames Valley Royals, from the merger of **Oxford United** and **Reading**, was vehemently opposed by fans. More recently, the merger in 1994 of **Inverness Caledonian** and **Inverness Thistle** to form **Caledonian Thistle** provoked controversy among supporters. Similarly, the fans of Japanese **J League** sides **Yokohama Flugels** and **Yokohama Marinos** have protested against a merger of the two clubs. At other times, the football authorities have refused to sanction the merger of two clubs. For example, before **World War I** Henry **Norris** proposed a merger between the cash-strapped Woolwich **Arsenal** and **Fulham**, which had just joined the League, but the **Football Association** refused permission.

Merthyr Town *club* former English league. *Dossier* Ground: Penydarren Park, Mid Glamorgan. Record attendance: 21,686 v **Millwall** Athletic (27, Decmber 1921, Division Three (South). Best average attendance: 12,300 (1920-21). *Keynotes* Founder members of **Football League** Division Three in 1920-21, finishing eighth in the division's inaugural season – the club's highest League position. The club was a **Welsh Cup** finalist in 1924 (0–1 replay v **Wrexham**). Merthyr failed in its bid for **re-election** in 1929-30, following three consecutive seasons in which the club finished in the bottom three of Division Three (South), and was replaced by **Thames**. Merthyr Town folded in 1930 and, in 1945, reformed as Merthyr Tydfil. *League record* Division Three 1920-21; Division Three (South) 1921-22 to 1929-30.

Metalist Kharkov *club* Ukraine national league and former Soviet Union league club based in Kharkov, founded 1944. Ground: capacity: 25,000. Strip: white shirts, blue shorts. Ukraine cup runners-up 1992; former-Soviet Union Cup 1988, runners-up 1983 (never won former Soviet league).

Metallurg Kadamzhai *club* Kyrgyzstan national league club, based in Kadamzhai, founded 1996. Ground: Surmyanoi Stadium. **Kyrgyzstan** league champions 1996; Kyrgyzstan Cup runners-up 1996.

metatarsal *medical* any of the five long bones in the foot between the toes and the **tarsus**. **Stress fractures** to the second metatarsal are relatively common footballing injuries.

Metrostars *club* United States football club and founder member of **Major League Soccer**, based in New York City. Member of the league's **Eastern Conference**. Founded: 1996. Ground: Giants Stadium (in East Rutherford, New Jersey), capacity: 77,000. Notable player: Roberto Donadoni.

Mexican wave *n.* a travelling wave of spectators created by the sequential and synchronised rising (with raised arms) and sitting of the crowd at a sports stadium. Popularised at the 1986 **World Cup** in Mexico.

Mexico *country CONCACAF* federal Republic in Central America on the Pacific Ocean and the Gulf of Mexico, bordered by **Belize**, **Guatemala** and the **United States of America**. Mountainous country with arid north, tropical and humid south. High population growth (about 1.8% per year). Area: 1,972,545 sq km (761,400 sq miles). Population: 91,120,000 (1995 est.). Languages: Spanish, Nahuatl, Maya and Mixtec. Capital: Mexico City (Ciudad de México) – 2,255 metres (7,400 feet) above sea level. Independence from **Spain** in 1821. *Dossier* Football association (Federación Mexicana de Fútbol, Mexico City) formed in 1927 affiliated to **FIFA** in 1929 and founder member of **Confederación Norte-Centroamericana y del Caribe de Fútbol** (CONCACAF) in 1961, president: Juan Leano Alvarez Del; general secretary: Dr Edgardo Codesal Mendez. Season played from July to June in two phases (**apertura** and **clausura**). National stadium: **Azteca**, Mexico City, capacity: 111,258. National strip: green shirts with white collars, white shorts and red socks. First international game: 1 January 1923 v Guatemala (3–2, Guatemala City, friendly). Biggest victory: 11–0 v **St Vincent** (6 December 1992, Mexico City, **World Cup** qualifier). Biggest defeat: 0–8 v **England** (10 May 1961, London, friendly). Highest crowd: 120,000, v United States of America (Azteca Stadium, 26 July 1993, **Gold Cup** final – Mexico won 4–0). Most capped players: Claudio Suarez (114 appearances, 1992), Jorge **Campos** (100 appearances, 1991-), Ramón Ramirez (91 appearances, 1991-). Leading goalscorers: Carlos Hermosillo (33 goals, 1985-1997), Enrique Borja (31 goals, 1966-75), Luis Garcia (29 goals, 1991-), Luis Zague (28 goals, 1988-97), Hugo **Sanchez** (26 goals, 1977-1998), Luis Hernandez (24 goals, to 1998). Other notable international player: Antonio **Carbajal**. Website: *http://www.gdl.uag.mx/fmf/femex.htm* (official site). *International tournament record* World Cup – quarter-finals 1970 (host nation) and 1986 (host nation), second round 1994, 1998, also qualified for finals tournament in 1930 (no qualifying tournament), 1950, 1954, 1958, 1962, 1966 and 1978 (in each of these losing in the first-round group stage); **CONCACAF Championship** – winners 1965 (won six-nation finals league in Guatemala City, Guatemala), 1971 (won six-nation finals league in Port of Spain, Trinidad), 1977 (World Cup qualifier, six-nation final tournament in Mexico), runners-up 1967, third 1973 (six-nation final tournament in Haiti), 1981 (six-nation final tournament in Tegucigalpa, Honduras); Gold Cup – qualified for first tournament in 1991, winners 1993 (4–0, v United States of America, in Mexico City), 1996 (2–0, v **Brazil**, in Los Angeles, USA), 1998 (1–0, v USA), third place 1991 (2–0, v **Costa Rica**, in Los Angeles, third/fourth place play-off); **Copa America** – Mexico invited to take part from 1993, runners-up 1993 (4 July, 1–2 v **Argentina** in the final in Guayaquil, Ecuador), semi-final/third

1997 (1–0, v **Peru**, in Oruro, Bolivia, third/fourth play-off), quarter-final 1995; **Olympic Games** – fourth place 1968 (0–2, v **Japan**, in Mexico City, third/fourth playoff), quarter-final 1996, finals tournament second round 1972; **Central American and Caribbean Games** – winners 1926 (the first tournament), 1935, 1938, 1959, 1966, 1990; **Confederations Cup** – third place 1995 (1–1, 5–4 pens., v **Nigeria**, in Riyadh, Saudi Arabia, third/fourth playoff); **World Youth Cup** (under-20) – qualified for first tournament 1977, runners-up 1977 (2–2, 8–9 pens., v **Soviet Union**, in Tunis, Tunisia), quarter-final 1985, 1991, 1993, 1999 also qualified 1979, 1981, 1983, hosts 1983; **Under-17 World Championship** – qualified for first tournament in 1985, also qualified 1987, 1991, 1993, 1997; **CONCACAF Youth Championship** – winners 1962, 1970, 1973, 1974, 1976, 1978, 1980, 1984, 1990, 1992; **CONCACAF Under-17 Championship** – winners 1985, 1987, 1990; **Women's World Cup** – entered first tournament in 1991, qualified for finals tournament 1999 (6–3 agg., v Argentina, CONMEBOL/CONCACAF playoff); **CONCACAF Women's Championship** – entered first tournament in 1991, runners-up 1998 (0–1, v **Canada**, in Haiti), third 1994 (league of five nations); **Federation of Independent European Female Football** unofficial world tournament – runners-up 1971 (0–2, v **Denmark, women**, in Mexico). *World Cup performance* (finals and qualifiers to end of 1998 tournament) played 125, won 64, drawn 31, lost 30, scored 243 goals, conceded 140 goals; win rate: 51%; goals scored per game: 1.94. *Record against British and Irish national teams* v England, played seven, won two, lost four, drawn one; v **Northern Ireland**, played two, won one, lost one; v **Scotland**, none played; v **Wales**, played two, won one, drawn one; v **Republic of Ireland**, played four, won one, drawn three. *History* Football was introduced in the late 19th century. The first club was founded by British workers in Pachuca around 1900. Most of the early clubs were founded by Britons or other European expatriates. They included Athletic, British Club, Mexico CCC, Reforma and Rovers. A league championship was first played in 1903, originally based around the capital, Mexico City. The first championship involved only five clubs and was won by Orizaba Athetic Club. Mexico's two best-supported clubs were formed soon after: Club Deportivo **Guadalajara**, from Guadalajara, was founded in 1906 as Union FC (adopting the current name in 1908); and Club de Fútbol **América**, from Mexico City, was founded in 1916 from a merger of Record FC and Colón FC. Professionalism was introduced in 1930s, with the professional league officially started in 1944. The end-of-season championship playoffs were introduced in the mid 1970s. The various national cup competitions began in 1908: Copa Tower 1908-1921; Copa Eliminatoria 1922-36; Copa Mexico, from 1933. Rival clubs América and Guadalajara have won 21 Mexican championships between them, with **Cruz Azul**, **Necaxa** and **UNAM** also having good records in the professional league. América, Necaxa and Atlanté are all owned by the national television company Televisa. Mexican clubs have dominated CONCACAF club championships, with Gadalajara winning the first **CONCACAF Champion Clubs Cup** in 1962. América, **Atlante**, Cruz Azul, Necaxa, **Toluca**, UNAM and **Puebla** also have won the tournament outright, while Club Universidad de Guadalajara (withdrew from professional league in 1994) were joint winners in 1978 and **León** were runners-up in 1993. One of the worst days in Mexican football occurred at the Mexican Cup final on 26 May 1985: 10 spectators died and 29 were injured from crushing at Azteca (UNAM v América). Mexico played its first international tournament match in 1928 (1–7, v Spain, in Amsterdam, Olympic Games first round). It entered the first World Cup in 1930, and played in the first ever World Cup match (1–4 v **France**, 13 July 1930, Pocitos Stadium, Montevideo, Uruguay, in front of 1,000 spectators). It hosted the World Cup finals in 1970 and 1986, with both finals staged at the impressive Azteca Stadium (also the main venue of the 1968 Olympic Games). Mexico won the second CONCACAF Gold Cup in 1993, a 4–0 victory over United States of America, in front of 120,000 spectators at the Azteca. Mexico was suspended from the 1990 World Cup for fielding an over- age player in **World Youth Cup**. The country has been invited to participate in the South American Championship (Copa America) since 1993. Mexico hosted, and was runners-up in, the second Federation of Independent European Female Football's unofficial world tournament in 1971. *League system* Since August 1996, the Mexican league has been divided into two phases, an apertura (played from August to December) and a clausura (from January to June). There are two separate championship titles in each season. The system for deciding the championship, promotion and relegation is complex. Eighteen clubs compete in the national Primera Division, which is divided into four groups of four or five clubs. Each club, however, plays all 17 other clubs at home *or* away (17 games in each phase of the league). Three points are awarded for a victory, with one for a draw: final positions for clubs level on points are determined by **goal difference**. Although each club plays all the other Primera Division clubs, the championship is determined by a series of playoffs rather than a "European-style" league. The top two clubs from each of the four groups qualifies for the next stage, unless any third-placed team has a better record (in which case their will be an additional repechage playoff between the runners-up with the least points and the third-placed club with the most points). The winners of the repechage join the automatic qualifiers in the quarter-final for a straight knockout competition to decide the national champions. The repechage, knockout rounds and championship final are all played over two legs, and may be determined on **away goals** if the aggregate score is level. The club with the lowest points total over the past *two* seasons is relegated. There are 16 clubs in the second flight (Primera A Division), also played in groups of four with a final knockout tournament. The Primera A apertura and clausura champions playoff for promotion to the Primera Division. The Segunda Division (third tier) is also played in groups. Beneath the Segunda Division is a regional league structure involving 84 clubs (Tercera Division). *Record in international club tournam*ents CONCACAF Champion Clubs Cup – Club Deportivo Guadalajara (winners 1962, runners-up 1963), Club Deportivo Toluca (winners 1968, runners-up 1998), Cruz Azul (winners 1969, 1970, 1971, 1996, 1997), Club Impulsora del Deportivo Necaxa (winners 1975, known at the time as Atlético Espanol), Club de Fútbol América (winners 1977, 1987, 1990 and 1992), Club Universidad de Guadalajara (joint winners 1978), UNAM (Club Universidad Nacional Autónoma de Mexico, winners 1980, 1982 and 1989), Club de Fútbol Atlante (winners 1983, runners-up 1994), and Club de Fútbol Puebla de la Franja (winners 1991), Club Social y Deportivo León (runners-up 1993, semi-final/fourth 1998); **CONCACAF Cup-winners Cup** – Club de Fútbol **Monterrey** (winners 1993), Necaxa (winners 1994, finalist 1998), **Universidad Autonoma de Guadalajara "Los Tecos"** (winners 1995); **Copa Inter Americana** – América (winners 1977, 1990), UNAM (winners 1980). Other leading clubs: Club Deportivo **Universidad Autonoma de Nuevo León**, Santos Laguna (Mexican league champions 1996 apertura).

MHSK Tashkent *club* Uzbekistan and former Soviet Union league club based in the capital Tashkent, founded 1979 (as FKA Pachtakor – current name adopted 1993). Ground: MHSK Stadium, capacity: 17,500. Uzbekistan league champions 1997, runners-up 1995; Uzbekistan Cup runners-up 1995.

Miami Fusion *club* United States football club and member of **Major League Soccer** (joined league in 1998), based in Miami, Florida. Member of the league's **Eastern Conference**. Founded: 1997. Ground: Lockhart Stadium, Fort Lauderdale, capacity: 20,000.

Michels, Rinus (Marinus) *manager* born 9 February 1928. *Clubs* **Ajax**, **Barcelona**, Los Angeles Aztecs, **Bayer Leverkusen**. Also **Netherlands** coach. *Keynotes* Ex-Netherlands international striker who became Ajax coach in 1965. He is credited with developing the concept of **total football** (totaal voetbal) and of nurturing the talent of the young Johan **Cruyff**. Michels took Netherlands to the **World Cup** final in 1974 (1–2 v West **Germany**), returning as national coach to lead the Dutch side that included **Gullit**, Rijkaard and **Van Basten** to success in the 1988 European Championship. *Honours* Dutch League (Ajax 1966, 1967, 1968, 1970); Dutch Cup (Ajax 1967, 1970, 1971); **European Cup** (Ajax 1971); **European Championship** (Netherlands 1988).

Micronesia, Federated States of *country no international affiliation* self-governing federation of states. Six hundred and seven islands and atolls over 3,200 km in the Pacific Ocean. Area: 702 sq km (271 sq miles).

Population: 105,000 (1994 census). Languages: English and eight indigenous languages. Capital: Palikir. *Dossier* Football association neither affiliated to **FIFA** nor to **Oceania Football Confederation**.

Middelboe, Nils *player* Defender/striker. **Denmark** international. **Olympic Games** silver medal (Denmark, 1908). Middelboe joined **Chelsea** in 1913.

Middlesbrough *club* English league. *Dossier* Ground: **Riverside** (Cellnet) **Stadium**, Middlesbrough. Strip: red shirts with white trim, white shorts, red and white socks. Nickname: Boro. Ground capacity: 35,000 all seated. Record attendance (at the Riverside Stadium): 34,687 v **Tottenham Hotspur** (20 February 1999, **Premier League**). Previous ground: Ayresome Park, 53,596 v **Newcastle United** (27 December 1949, Division One). Best average attendance: 36,123 (**Ayresome Park** 1950-51). Biggest win: 9–0 v **Brighton & Hove Albion** (23 August 1958, Division Two). Biggest defeat: 0–9 v **Blackburn Rovers** (6 November 1954, Division Two). *History* Founded in February 1876, Middlesbrough turned professional in 1889 following the breakaway of some members to form **Middlesbrough Ironopolis**. Boro reverted to amateur status in 1892, going on to win the **FA Amateur Cup** on two occasions later in the decade (1895, 2–1 v Old Carthusians, 1898, 2–1 v Uxbridge) before turning professional once again in 1899. Until **Wimbledon** joined the **Football League** in 1977, Boro was the only League club to have won the Amateur Cup. The club was elected to the Football League in 1899 and, in 1903, Boro settled at Ayresome Park, which would be the club's home for 92 years until it switched to the new Riverside Stadium in 1995. In 1901, the club reached the quarter-final stage of the **FA Cup** (0–1 v **West Bromwich Albion**) and the following season Boro won promotion to Division One. Although the club only narrowly avoided relegation in 1905-06 and 1909-10, Boro maintained its position in the top-flight, finishing third in 1913-14, until 1923-24. The club was the first to pay a four-figure transfer fee when Alf **Common** joined from **Sunderland** for £1,000 in 1905. In 1926-27, Boro set two Division Two records: the club scored 122 goals, of which centre-forward George **Camsell** scored 59. The club enjoyed another an extended run in the top flight between 1929-30 and 1953-54 but, in 1965-66, Boro was relegated to Division Three for the first time. Under the managership of former **Leeds United** and **England** defender Jack Charlton, the club regained its Division One place in 1973-74, and in the process became the first since **World War II** to achieve promotion in March. Boro almost went out of business in the summer of 1986 after the Inland Revenue was granted a **winding-up order** for non-payment of tax arrears, and an official receiver was appointed who sacked manager Bruce Rioch and the entire non-playing staff. A new board of directors, including millionaire Steve Gibson (who took control in March 1994), saved the club from bankruptcy by reforming it and paying off its debts. The club was forced to play the first "home" game of the 1986-87 season at **Hartlepool United**'s **Victoria Ground**. Boro spent a further season in Division Three in 1986-87 before gaining promotion to Division One in 1988 via the end-of-season **playoffs** (2–1 agg. v **Chelsea**). Since then the club has alternated between the top two divisions. Bryan **Robson**'s appointment as manager in May 1994 was followed by the First Division Championship in 1995. Although Robson bought some high-profile players, including the Brazilian duo Emerson and Juninho, and the Italian Fabrizio Ravanelli, and led Boro to the first major finals in its history, the club was relegated in 1996-97. Middlesbrough's defeat in the 1997 FA Cup final (0–2 v Chelsea) meant that the club joined a unique group of clubs who have appeared in the final and been relegated in the same season (others are Brighton & Hove Albion (1982-83), **Leicester City** (1968-69), **Manchester City** (1925-26)). Middlesbrough is only one of two clubs to have lost both the FA Cup final and the League Cup final (0–1 replay v Leicester City) in the same season (the other is **Sheffield Wednesday**, 1993). Boro's relegation plight in 1996-97 was exacerbated when the Football Association docked the club three points for failing to fulfil a League fixture against Blackburn Rovers at **Ewood Park**. Boro reached a third consecutive **Wembley** Cup final in 1998, again losing in the League Cup final in a repeat of the 1997 FA Cup final (0–2 a.e.t. v Chelsea). The club regained its Premier League status in 1997-98. *League record* Premier League 1992-93, 1995-96 to 1996-97, 1998-99–; Division One 1902-03 to 1923-24, 1927-28, 1929-30 to 1953-54, 1974-75 to 1981-82, 1988-89; First Division 1993-94 to 1994-95, 1997-98; Division Two 1899-00 to 1901-02, 1924-25 to 1926-27, 1928-29, 1954-55 to 1965-66, 1967-68 to 1973-74, 1982-83 to 1985-86, 1987-88, 1989-90 to 1991-92; Division Three 1966-67, 1986-87. *Honours* First Division 1994-95; Division Two 1926-27, 1928-29, 1973-74; FA Amateur Cup 1895 (2–1 v Old Carthusians), 1898 (2–1 v Uxbridge); **Anglo Scottish Cup** 1976 (1–0 agg. v **Fulham**). *Records* Wilf **Mannion** is Middlesbrough's most capped player (26 for England); Tim Williamson holds the record for club appearances (563, 1902-23); George Camsell is Boro's record league goalscorer (326, 1925-39).

Middlesbrough Ironopolis *club* former English league. *Dossier* Ground: Paradise Ground, Middlesbrough. Record League attendance: 2,000. *Keynotes* Founded in 1885 as a professional club by former members of **Middlesbrough** (formed in 1876). The club was elected to Division Two in 1893-94, but folded after one season due to financial problems. Prior to joining the **Football League**, Ironopolis was an **FA Cup** quarter- finalist in 1893 (0–7 replay v **Preston North End**) and the following year, the club reached the last 16 of the competition (0–2 v **Nottingham Forest**). The club finished 11th in its only League season. *League record* Division Two 1893-94.

midfield *n.* collective name given to those players who play between defence and attack.

midfielder *n.* player whose chief job is to control play in the centre of the field and to create opportunities for the strikers. They generally occupy positions in the middle of the **formation**.

Mighty Barolle *club* Liberian national league club, based in the capital Monrovia. Ground: Antoinette Tubman, capacity: 10,000. Strip: red shirts and white shorts **African Cup of Champion Clubs** second round 1987; Liberian National League champions 1967, 1972, 1973, 1974, 1986, 1988, 1989, 1993 and 1995; Liberian Cup – 1974, 1981, 1983, 1984, 1985 and 1986. Notable former player: George **Weah**.

Mighty Blackpool *club* Sierra Leone national league club based in the capital Freetown, founded 1954 (as Sokro Eleven, later renamed in honour of Stanley **Matthews** – former player with English league club **Blackpool**). Ground: Siaka Stevens (national stadium), capacity: 30,000. Strip: orange shirts, white shorts. **African Cup of Champion Clubs** quarter-final 1989; Sierra Leone league champions 1967, 1974, 1978, 1979, 1988, 1991; Sierra Leone Cup 1983, 1988.

Mighty Magyars *misc.* another name for the **Magnificent Magyars**

Mijatovic, Predrag *player* Striker. **Yugoslavia** international (37 caps, 16 goals, 1994-). Born 19 January 1969. *Clubs* **Partizan Belgrade**, **Real Madrid**. *Keynotes* Mijatovic scored seven of the goals in Yugoslavia's 12–1 aggregate victory over **Hungary** in the 1998 **World Cup** qualifying tournament playoffs, giving him a tally of 14 for the qualifiers (the top scorer in the UEFA qualifying groups: he added another goal in the finals tournament). He scored the 66th-minute goal in Real Madrid's 1–0 victory over favourites **Juventus** in the 1998 European Cup final. *Honours* **European Cup** (Real Madrid, 1998).

Mikhailov, Borislav *player* Goalkeeper. **Bulgaria** international (102 caps, 1983-). *Clubs* **Levski Sofia**, Belenenses, Mulhouse, **Reading**. *Keynotes* Bulgaria's most capped player. *Honours* **World Cup** fourth place (Bulgaria, 1994).

Milaha Athletic Hussein-Dey (also known as Nasr Athletic Hussein-Dey) *club* Algerian national league club, based in the capital El Djezaïr (Algiers), founded 1946. Ground: Zioui, capacity: 25,000. Strip: gold shirts, red shorts. **African Cup-winners Cup** runners-up 1978 (2–5 agg., v **Horoya Conakry** of Guinea); Algerian league champions 1967; Algerian Cup 1979.

Milan *club* see **AC Milan**.

Milburn, Jackie (John) *player-manager* Striker. **England** international (13 caps, 10 goals). Born 11 May 1924. Career ca. 1943-1960. *Clubs* (player) **Newcastle United**, (manager) **Linfield** (player-manager), **Ipswich Town**. *Keynotes* Known in the Northeast as "Wor Jackie". Milburn joined Newcastle United in August 1943, making 354 **Football League** appearances and scoring 179 goals – a club record. Scored two in Newcastle's 1951 **FA Cup** final triumph (2–0 v **Blackpool**) and his goal after 45 seconds in 1955 (3–1 v **Manchester City**) was the quickest ever in a **Wembley** final until **Chelsea**'s Roberto **Di Matteo** scored after 43 seconds in 1997. Milburn scored in every round of the 1951 FA Cup competition. He became Ipswich Town manager for a season (1963–64), following a successful spell in **Northern Ireland** with Linfield. He later became a sports journalist. His sister Cissie was the mother of Bobby and Jackie **Charlton**. Milburn was made a Freeman of the City of Newcastle and a bronze statue of him stands in the city centre. Died on 9 October 1988. Included in the **Football League Centenary 100 players**. *Honours* FA Cup (Newcastle United 1951, 1952, 1955); **Irish FA Cup** (Linfield 1960).

Milla, Roger *player* Striker. **Cameroon** international. Born 20 May 1952. *Clubs* (include) Leopard Douala, Olympique Mvolye, **Tonnerrre Yaoundé**, **St Denis** (Reunion), **Monaco**, Bastia (France), Montpellier (France). *Keynotes* Milla is both the oldest player to have played in the **World Cup** finals and the oldest to score. He played in the 1994 finals at the age of 42 and scored in the first-round match against **Russia**: ironically, the match in which Oleg **Salenko** scored a World Cup finals record five goals in one game (Russia won 6–1). Milla also scored four goals in the 1990 World Cup finals in Italy; two pairs, both as a substitute. He was voted eighth in the 1990 *World Soccer* **World Footballer of the Year**. He was equal top scorer at the 1986 and 1988 **African Cup of Nations** with four and two goals respectively. Milla is reported to have changed his name from Miller, allegedly to sound less European. *Honours* **African Cup of Nations** (Cameroon, 1984, 1988; runner-up 1986); *France Football* **African Footballer of the Year** 1976, 1990.

Millmoor Ground *ground* English football ground situated in Rotherham, south Yorkshire; home of **Rotherham United**. *Dossier* Ground capacity: 11,514. Pitch dimensions: 105m x 68.5. Record attendance: 25,170 v **Sheffield United** (13 December 1952, Division Two). Best average attendance: 18,770 (1951-52). *Keynotes* Rotherham County, which would merge with Rotherham Town in 1925 to form Rotherham United, first played at Millmoor on 2 September 1907 (v **Leeds City** Reserves, Midland League). Rotherham bought the ground from its owners, a railway company, for £5,500 in 1949. The first floodlit match at Millmoor took place on 23 November 1960 (v **Bristol Rovers**, League Cup).

Millonarios *club* see **Club Deportivo Los Millonarios.**

Millwall *club* English league. *Dossier* Ground: the **New Den**, south London. Strip: blue shirts, white shorts and blue socks. Nickname: Lions. Ground capacity: 20,146 all seated. Record attendance (at the New Den): 20,093 v **Arsenal** (10 January 1994, **FA Cup**, third round). Record attendance at previous ground, the Den: 48,672, v Derby County (20 February 1937, FA Cup, fifth round). Best average attendance: 27,387 (The Den, 1938-39). Biggest win: 9-1 v **Torquay United**

(29 August 1927, Division Three (South)). Biggest defeat: 1–9 v **Aston Villa** (28 January 1946, FA Cup, fourth round). *History* Founded in 1885 as Millwall Rovers by jam workers employed by Morton & Co on the Isle of Dogs. The club played at several venues on the north side of the Thames, including at Glengall Road, at East Ferry Road and at North Greenwich, before decamping to New Cross on the south side in 1910 and a ground at Cold Blow Lane. Millwall replaced "Rovers" with "Athletic" in 1889, a name it retained until 1925. Millwall was a founder member of the **Southern League**, winning the title in the League's first two seasons (1895 and 1896). Millwall was an FA Cup semi-finalist in both 1900 (3–0 replay v **Southampton**) and 1903 (3–0 v **Derby County**). The club was also a founder member of Division Three in 1920-21 and, in 1927-28, Millwall won promotion to Division Two by taking the Division Three (South) Championship, scoring a then record 127 goals. In 1937, Millwall became the first Division Three side to reach the **semi-final** of the FA Cup (1–2 v **Sunderland**). The club defeated **Chelsea** (3–0, fourth round), Derby County (2–1, fifth round) and **Manchester City** (2–0, sixth round) on its way to the last four. The following season Millwall again won the Division Three (South) title, having suffered relegation from Division Two in 1933-34. In 1949-50, Millwall finished bottom of Division Three (South) and for the next 14 seasons, until it won the Division Four Championship in 1961-62, the club remained in the bottom tier. A further season in the bottom division (1964-65) was followed by promotion to Division Two in 1965-66. Between 1964 (24 August, Division Four) and 1967 (14 January 1967, Second Division), the club established a League record of 59 consecutive home matches without defeat. Millwall reached the quarter-final stage of the **League Cup** in both 1974 (1–2 replay v **Norwich City**) and 1977 (0–2 v **Aston Villa**), and won the **Football League Trophy** in 1983 (3–2 v **Lincoln City**). In 1987-88, Millwall, the only London club never to have played in the top flight, won promotion to Division One. The club finished tenth in 1988-89, its highest-ever League position, spearheaded by the striking partnership of Tony Cascarino and Teddy Sheringham. That year the club became a plc named Millwall Holdings, which was floated on the stock market with a £5 million share issue. In both 1990-91 and 1993-94, the club narrowly missed a return to the top flight, losing in semi-finals of the Division Two/First Division end-of-season **playoffs**. Millwall reached the final of the Auto Windscreens Shield in 1999 (0–1 v **Wigan Athletic**). The requirements of the **Taylor Report** coupled with considerable support from Lewisham Council convinced the club to proceed with the construction of a new all-seater stadium on land 400 yards from the Den. The final match at the Den took place on 8 May 1993 (v **Bristol Rovers**, First Division) and the new venue, entitled the New Den, was opened on 4 August 1993 (v **Sporting Lisbon**, friendly). Millwall holds the unenviable record of having its previous

ground closed by the **Football Association** on more occasions than any other League ground; the Den was closed in 1920, 1934, 1947, 1950, 1978 as a result of crowd trouble. *League record* Division One 1988-89 to 1989-90; First Division 1992-93 to 1995-96; Divsion Two 1928-29 to 1933-34, 1938-39 to 1947-48, 1966-67 to 1974-75, 1976-77 to 1978-79, 1985-86 to 1987-88, 1990-91 to 1991-92; Second Division 1996-97–; Division Three 1920-21, 1962-63 to 1963-64, 1965-66, 1975-76, 1979-80 to 1984-85; Divsion Three (South) 1921-22 to 1927-28, 1934-35 to 1937-38, 1948-49 to 1957-58; Division Four 1958-59 to 1961-62, 1964-65. *Honours* Division Two 1987-88; Division Three (South) 1927-28, 1937-38; Division Four 1961-62; Southern League 1895, 1896; Football League Trophy 1983 (3–2 v Lincoln City); Division Three (South) Cup 1937 (1–1 v **Watford** (shared trophy)). *Records* Eamonn Dunphy is Millwall's most capped player (22 (23) for **Republic of Ireland**); Barry Kitchener holds the record for club League appearances (523, 1967-82); Teddy Sheringham is Millwall's record League goalscorer (93, 1984-91).

Millwall Holdings plc *n.* publicly-quoted business which owns **Millwall**. The club became a fully listed company on the London Stock Exchange in October 1989 (flotation price = 20p). Millwall had a market capitalisation – the market value of the company's issued share capital (eg, the quoted price of its shares multiplied by the number of shares outstanding) – of £13 million on flotation.

Minas Gerais *state* one of the 27 state leagues in **Brazil**, founded 1916. Leading clubs: América (Belo Horizonte), Clube **Atlético Mineiro** (Belo Horizonte), Esporte Clube **Cruzeiro** (Belo Horizonte), Uberlandia Esporte Clube (Uberlandia).

Minerven FC *(Futbol Club) club* former Venezuelan national league club based in El Callao, founded 1985, dissolved 1999. Ground: Estadio Hector Thomas, capacity: 5,000. Strip: blue shirts, blue shorts. **Copa CONMEBOL** quarter-final 1994; Venezuelan league champions (**Torneo Clausura**) 1996.

minimum wages *regulations* lowest weekly remuneration payable by clubs employing **contract players**. **Football League** clubs are required to pay their contract players at least the minimum wage (in 1998-99 this was set at £90 per week, Football League regulation 56). British legislation introduced in 1999 ensured that all employers in the United Kingdom paid all employees at least the national minimum wage.

minute's silence *n.* sixty seconds of organised silence before the **kick-off** of a match out of respect for the death of an individual. The individual may have had a particular significance for one of the clubs – a former player, chairman or manager – or of wider significance to football (eg Bobby **Moore**) or society (eg Diana, Princess of Wales). A minute's silence also has been held at all league grounds to respect the dead in tragedies such as the **Hillsborough disaster**. Over the weekend of 23–26 October 1998, all 46 **Premier** and **Football League** matches played a recorded message by BBC sports presenter Des **Lynam** and held a minute's silence to help launch the 1998 **Poppy Appeal**.

miskick *vb.* to kick the ball badly so that it skews. *n.* the execution of such a kick.

missile throwing *misc.* throwing objects, such as bottles, coins and stones at players and officials. *History* In March 1897, a spectator was jailed for one month after being found guilty of throwing a stone at a match between **Burnley** and **Wolverhampton Wanderers** (Division One). The stone struck Wolves' player Hilary Griffiths on the head. In 1947, the **Football Association** circulated to all member clubs a statement highlighting the growing incidence of missile throwing at football matches. It stated that: "The FA is disturbed at the growing practice of throwing missiles at officials and players at football grounds. All clubs are asked therefore to inform the spectators through the medium of the programmes or speaker apparatus of the serious consequences which may result from such disorderly conduct and to emphasise that such is likely to bring both clubs and the game generally into disrepute". In that year, a **linesman** at the **Division Two** match between **Millwall** and **Barnsley** was hit in the chest by a pellet fired from an airgun. **Celtic** goalkeeper Ronnie Simpson was injured by a missile thrown from the crowd before the second leg of the club's 1967 **World Club Cup** match with **Racing Club** in Avellanada. The 1965 World Club Cup match between **Independiente** and **Internazionale** at Avellanada in Buenos Aires also was marred by missile throwing. On that occasion, several Inter players and coach Helenio **Herrera** were struck by flying objects. A firework thrown into the players' tunnel at half-time during a match in Turin between **Juventus** and Cesena in January 1988 at Stadio **Comunale** injured Cesena's Dario Sanguin. Cesena lost the match but was awarded the points. **Roma (AS)** goalkeeper Franco Tancredi suffered cardiac arrest after he was hit by a firework thrown on to the pitch during a match at Milan's **San Siro** stadium in February 1988. Tancredi was resuscitated by the Roma team doctor. In November 1992, the goalkeeper of non-league Kingstonian was hit by a coin thrown from the crowd during an FA Cup replay against **Peterborough** at **London Road**. The FA subsequently ordered the match to be replayed **behind closed doors**. **Scottish Football League** referee Martin Clark was injured when coins thrown from the crowd hit him during a Scottish Division Three match between **Montrose** and **Arbroath** at **Links Park** on 27 December 1997. The game had been interrupted earlier when a **streaker**, wearing only socks and shoes, ran across the pitch. **Aston Villa** goalkeeper Mark Bosnich was pelted with objects during the club's **UEFA Cup** quarter-final first leg match against **Atlético Madrid** at Estadio **Vincente Calderón** (3 March 1998). In November 1997, the Argentinian league match between Club Atlético **Rosario Central**

and Club Atletico **Boca Juniors** at Estadio Gigante de Arroyito Cordiviola was abandoned midway through the second half after missiles were thrown on the pitch. Referee Matt Messias made reference to coin-throwing in his match report on the Millwall v **Manchester City** encounter at the **New Den** on 29 September 1998. Italy and **Parma** midfield player Dino Baggio required several stitches to a head wound after being struck by a knife thrown from the crowd during a UEFA Cup second-round fixture against **Wisla Kraków** in **Poland** on 20 October 1998. **Fiorentina**'s second-round UEFA Cup tie with **Grasshopper Zurich** on 3 November 1998, which had been moved to Salerno following crowd trouble at the club's Stadio Comunale the previous season, was abandoned after an assistant referee was injured by a firecracker thrown from the crowd.

Mission Viejo *n.* **United States of America** national squad training base for the 1994 **World Cup** finals, near Los Angeles, southwest California. The US national team's biggest victory was played here (8–1 v **Cayman Islands**, 14 November 1993, friendly).

mission statement *n.* brief statement of the key aims or philosophy of a business or organisation. *Keynotes* The **Football League** is one such organisation with a mission statement: "The role of the Football League is to provide a nationwide membership organisation and structure for professional football through which the Football League can facilitate financial success, stability and development of professional football clubs, administer and regulate the professional game and promote the values,and contribution of the professional game to our national life." It lists a number of ways through which this will be achieved. The mission statement of the 1999 **Women's World Cup** was: "To stage a breakthrough for women's sport and inspire the next generation of female athletes."

mister *misc.* Italian name for manager. Stems from the English influence on the Italian game.

mistimed tackle *n.* a badly executed tackle that usually results in a **foul**, with the executor making contact with the opposition player before the ball.

Mitropa Cup *competition* annual inter-war competition between clubs from **Austria**, **Czechoslovakia**, **Hungary** and **Italy**, and occasionally **Romania**, **Switzerland** and **Yugoslavia** that was revived after **World War II**. *History* Officially entitled the Mittel Europa, the competition was established in 1927 by Hugo Meisl. Initially it consisted of the League Champions from each country, but its status declined with the introduction of the **European Cup**. In 1980, the competition was open only to the champions of the second tier divisions in each country and the political upheaval in the **former-Yugoslavia** led to its suspension in the early-1990s. *Winners* 1927, **Sparta Prague**; 1928, **Ferencváros**; 1929 **Ujpest Dozsa**; 1930, **Rapid Vienna**; 1931, **First Vienna**; 1932 **Bologna**; 1933 **FK Austria**; 1934, Bologna; 1935 Sparta Prague; 1936, FK Austria; 1937, Ferencváros; 1938, **Slavia Prague**; 1939, Upjest Dozsa; 1951,

Rapid Vienna; 1955, Voros Lobogo; 1956, Vasas Budapest (now **Vasas DH**); 1957, Vasas Budapest; 1959, **Kispest-Honvéd**; 1960, Vasas Budapest; 1961, Bologna; 1962, Vasas Budapest; 1963, **MTK Budapest**; 1964, Spartak Sokolovo; 1965, Vasas Budapest; 1966, **Fiorentina**; 1967, **Spartak Trnava**; 1968, **Red Star Belgrade**. 1969, TJ Internacional (now **Inter Bratislava**); 1970, Vasas Budapest; 1971, **Celik Zenica**; 1972, Celik Zenica; 1973, Tatabánya; 1974, Tatabánya; 1975, Wacker Innsbrück (now **FC Tirol Innsbruck**); 1976, Wacker Innsbrück; 1977, **Vojvodina**; 1978, **Partizan Belgrade**; 1980, Udinese; 1981, Tatran Presov; 1982, **AC Milan**; 1983, Vasas Budapest; 1984, SC Eisenstadt; 1985, Iskra Bugojno; 1986, Pisa; 1987, **Banik Ostrava**; 1990, Bari;1991, **Torino**; 1992, **Borac Banja Luka**.

MKE Ankaragücü Kolübü (Makina Kimya Endüstrisi) *club* Turkish national league club based in the capital Ankara, founded 1910. Ground: 19 Mayis (shared with **Gençlerbirligi**), capacity: 24,000. Strip: yellow and blue striped shirts, white shorts. Turkish Cup 1972, 1981.

MMM Tamatave (Mpiasa Mpianatra Miraka) *club* Madagascar national league club, based in Tomasina. Ground: Tamatava, capacity: 5,000. **African Cup of Champion Clubs**, second round 1971; Madagascar League champions 1970 and 1980.

mob football *n.* forerunner of modern football, involving as many as 1,000 people, usually from neighbouring villages, carrying or kicking a ball through entire villages to a specified point. Games usually took place on feast days and could last all day. An annual Shrovetide match dating at least to the early 19th century is known to have taken place in Derby between the rival parishes of St Peter's and All Saints, giving rise to the term **derby**.

modifications *rules* the **Laws of the game** may only be changed by the **International FA Board**. However, subject to agreement of the national football association concerned, and provided that the principles of the game are maintained, the Laws may be modified for youth, women's and veteran's football. The following may be modified: size of the **field of play**; size weight and material of the **ball**; width between **goal posts** and height of **crossbar**; **duration of play**; and number of **substitutions**.

Mogadishu Municipality *club* Somalia national league club based in the capital Mogadishu. Ground: Cons (national stadium), capacity: 40,000. Somalia league champions 1975, 1986, 1989.

Mogas 90 *club* Benin national league club based in Porto Novo. Ground: De Gaulle, capacity: 15,000. Strip: yellow shirts, green shorts. **West African Club Cup** semi-final 1990; Benin League champions 1996, 1997; Benin Cup 1991, 1992, 1994, 1995.

Mohammedan Sporting *club* Bangladesh national league club. **Asian Champion Teams Cup** finals tournament 1988, 1990 (the finals were actually played in July 1991), 1991; Dhaka League champions 1957,

1959, 1961, 1963, 1965, 1966, 1969; Bangladesh National League champions: 1975, 1976, 1978, 1980, 1982, 1986, 1987, 1988, 1989, 1996.

Mohammedan Sporting *club* Indian club based in Calcutta. Ground: Salt Lake Stadium (the national stadium), capacity: 120,000. Calcutta League champions Mohammedan 1934, 1935, 1936, 1937, 1938, 1940, 1941, 1948, 1957, 1967, 1981; Confederation Cup 1983, 1984.

Mohun Bagan *club* Indian club based in Calcutta. Ground: Salt Lake Stadium (the national stadium), capacity: 120,000. **Asian Champion Teams' Cup** semi-final 1988; Indian National League Champions 1998; Calcutta League champions 1939, 1943, 1944, 1951, 1954, 1955, 1956, 1959, 1960, 1962, 1963, 1964, 1965, 1969, 1976, 1978, 1979, 1983, 1984, 1986, 1990, 1992, 1994; Confederation Cup 1978, 1980, 1981, 1982, 1986, 1987, 1992, 1993, 1994, 1997 (shared with **East Bengal** in 1978 and 1980).

Moldova *country UEFA* republic in southeast Europe, bordered by **Romania** to the south and **Ukraine** to the north. Independence from the former **Soviet Union** claimed in 1991 and recognised in 1992. Close ethnic, cultural and linguistic ties to Romania. Area: 33,700 sq km (13,010 sq miles). Population: 4,400,000 (1996 est.). Languages: Moldovan, Russian and Romanian. Capital: Chisinau (Kishinev). *Dossier* Moldavian Football Association (Chisinau), formed in 1991, affiliated to **FIFA** and **Union of European Football Associations** in 1994, president, Pavel Ciobanu, general secretary Vigil Inculet. Season played from the first week in August to mid June with **winter break** from December to mid March. National stadium: Republican, Chisinau, capacity: 22,000. National strip: blue shirts, red shorts and yellow socks. First international game: 16 April 1994 v **United States of America** (1–1, Jacksonville, USA, friendly). Most capped player: Sergei Secu (27 appearances, 1994), Serghei Clescenco (26 appearances 1994-). Leading goalscorers: Iurie Miterev (7 goals, 1994-), Serghei Clescenco (6 goals, 1994-). *International tournament record* **World Cup** – first entered 1998 (finished bottom of its qualifying group – **England**'s group – no points from eight matches, with just two goals scored and 21 conceded; **European Championship** – first entered 1996 (finished fourth of six nations – ahead of **Wales** – with nine points from 10 games); **Under-17 World Championship** – never qualified; **Women's World Cup** – never entered; **World Youth Cup** (under-20) – never qualified. *World Cup performance* (finals and qualifiers to end of 1998 tournament) played 8, won 0, drawn 0, lost 8, scored 2 goals, conceded 21 goals; win rate 0%; goals scored per game 0.25. *Record against British and Irish national teams* v England, played two, lost two; v **Northern Ireland**, none played; v **Scotland**, none played; v Wales, played two, won one, lost one; v **Republic of Ireland**, none played. *History* A national league and cup competition started in 1991-92. The

Premier League and First Divisions have been reduced in size since the 1995-96. The league and cup competitions have been largely dominated by three clubs, **Constructorul Chisinau**, **Zimbru Chisinau** and **Tiligul Tiraspol**. In the 1997 season, international striker Iurie Miterev scored nine goals in one league match for his club Zimbru Chisinau in a league-record 15–1 victory over Ciuhur Ocnita (19 June 1997, in Chisinau); Miterev scored 18 in the last three matches of the season. Also in the 1997 season, CSA Victoria Cahul avoided playing in the Premier Division end-of-season relegation playoffs by special dispensation of the league: several of its players had been killed in a road accident earlier in the season. Moldova played its first match in a major international competition on 7 September 1994 (1–0, v **Georgia**, in Tbilisi, European Championship qualifier). *League system* Ten clubs (reduced from 12 in 1997-98) compete in national Premier Division. Three points are awarded for a victory, with one for a draw. After the first phase of the season (18 games), the top five clubs enter a championship league, with the bottom five entering a relegation league; clubs keep their points records from the first phase. Two clubs are relegated to the national First Division. The Second Division is divided into Northern, Southern and Central zones. *Record in international club tournaments* **European Cup-winners Cup** – Constructorul Chisinau (first round 1997); **UEFA Cup** – never progressed beyond preliminary rounds. Its principal club, AS Monaco, is one of the top-five clubs in the French league.

Moldovan, Dinu Viorel *player* Striker. **Romania** international. Born 1972 (29 caps, 11 goals). *Clubs* **Grasshopper Zurich**, **Coventry City, Fenerbahce**. *Keynotes* Moldovan scored the 2,000th goal in the 1998 **World Cup** tournament (finals and qualifiers) (2–1, v **England**, 22 June, in Toulouse, France) – the first tournament that this landmark was reached.

Molineux *ground* English football ground situated in Wolverhampton, West Midlands; home of **Wolverhampton Wanderers**. *Dossier* Ground capacity: 28,525. Pitch dimensions 100.5m x 68.5m. Record attendance: 61,315 v **Liverpool** (11 February 1939, **FA Cup**, fifth round). Best average attendance: 45,466 (1949-50). *History* Molineux began life as a sports venue in the late 1860s and takes its name from Molineux House – home of local merchant Benjamin Molineux – which later became Molineux Hotel and the setting for many **Football League Management Committee** meetings. Wolverhampton Wanderers made the ground its home in 1889, with the club playing its opening fixture there on 2 September (v **Aston Villa**, friendly). Wolves had first played a cup-tie at Molineux in March 1886 (v **Walsall** Town). The ubiquitous architect Archibald **Leitch** began an extensive ten-year development of Molineux in the 1920s, including the building of a new main stand and in 1932, the construction of the famous Molineux Street stand with its distinctive seven gables. Success on the pitch led to record gates before **World War II** and Wolves signalled its intention to move from Molineux by placing an advert to buy 10 acres of land, but the plan was scuppered. In the 1950s, Molineux staged a series of floodlit matches against foreign opposition, including a South African XI, **Moscow Spartak** and **Kispest-Honvéd** (the latter match televised live in December 1954). Leitch's Molineux Street stand was demolished in 1978 and replaced by a stand with a capacity for more than 9,000 seated spectators plus 2,140 square metres (23,000 square feet) of office space (which was rented to Wolverhampton Polytechnic). Building this stand, named the John Ireland Stand after the club chairman, almost bankrupted the club (see Wolverhampton Wanderers, *History*). For a time, the ground was limited to two sides and a capacity of only 25,000. In April 1991, Jack Hayward bought the club for £2.1 million, allowing Molineux to be redeveloped as an **all-seater stadium**, a process which included the construction in 1993 of the Billy **Wright** Stand. The new Molineux was officially unveiled on 7 December 1993 (v Kispest-Honvéd, friendly), although the match was almost called off after power failure, which lasted until 10 minutes before kick-off, plunged the ground into darkness. In the 1990s, Wolves has employed the services of "Harry" the Hawk to eradicate pigeons from Molineux. The ground has staged four full **England** international fixtures (v Ireland, 7 March 1891, 14 February 1903; v **Wales**, 5 February 1935; v **Denmark**, 5 December 1956) and three **inter-League** matches (**Football League** v **Scottish Football League**, 2 November 1938: Football League v League of Ireland, 15 February 1950; Football League v League of Ireland, 24 September 1952). Molineux has also been the setting for numerous FA Cup semi-final ties. The first floodlit match took place on 30 September 1953 (v South African XI, friendly).

Monaco *country no international affiliation (club plays in French league)* Principality on the Mediterranean Sea, forming an enclave of southeast **France**, near to **Italy**. It is the world's second-smallest independent state, after the **Vatican City**. Comprises four towns: Monaco, Monte Carlo, la Condamine and Fontvieille. A constitutional monarchy under French protection. Area: 1.6 sq km (0.6 sq miles). Population: 30,000 (1990 census). Languages: French, Monegasque, Italian and English. Capital: Monaco-Ville. *Dossier* No independent football association. See *Club* **AS Monaco**.

Monaghan United *club* Republic of Ireland national league club based in Monaghan, County Monaghan, in the north of the Republic, close to the border with Northern Ireland. Strip: blue shirts, white shorts.

Moneni Pirates *club* Swaziland national league club based in Manzini. Ground: Salesian, capacity: 9,000. Strip: white shirts, black shorts. **CAF Cup** second round 1994; Swaziland league runners-up 1993; Swaziland Cup 1988.

Mongolia *country AFC* landlocked republic in east Central Asia, sandwiched between the Russian Confederation to the north and **China** to the south. Area: 1,565,000 sq km (604,090 sq miles). Characterised by high undulating plateau reaching 1,500 m (4,920 feet) in some areas, by mountain ranges in the north (up to 4,231 m, 13,881 feet) and the Gobi Desert in the south. Population: 2,310,000 (1996 est.) – one of the lowest national population densities in the world. Language: Khalka Mongolian. Capital: Ulan Bator. *Dossier* Football Federation of the Mongolian People's Republic (Ulan Bator), affiliated to **FIFA** 1998, member of the **Asian Football Confederation** (AFC), president S Jamts, general secretary Ch Vladimir. National strip: red shirts, blue shorts and red socks. Biggest victory: 4–0 v **Guam** (1997, **East Asian Games**, in Pusan, South Korea). Biggest defeat: 0–15 v **Uzbekistan** (1998, **Asian Games**). *International tournament record* **Olympic Games** – never entered; **Women's World Cup** – first entered 2000; **World Cup** – has not entered; **Asian Cup of Nations** – never entered; **Asian Games** – first entered 1998, (last in first-round group of three nations); **Asian Women's Championship** – never entered; East Asian Games (under-23) – first entered 1997. *History* Mongolia's first international tournament was the 1997 East Asian Games. It competed in the 1998 Asian Games in Thailand, but lost its two first-round group games (0–11, v **Kuwait**; and 0–15, v Uzbekistan. *League system* Ten clubs compete in the Ulan Bator championship. The top four clubs take part in a championship playoff. Three points are awarded for a win, with one for a draw. Leading clubs: Derger (Ulan Bator, league champions 1997, cup winners 1998), Erchim (Ulan Bator, cup winners 1997).

Monterrey (full name: Club de Fútbol Monterrrey) *club* Mexican national league club, based in Monterrey and founded in 1945. Ground: Estadio Tecnologico, capacity: 39,000. Strip: blue and white striped shirts and blue shorts. **CONCACAF Cup-winners Cup** 1993 (four-club final tournament); Mexican League Champions 1986 (a short league programme to accommodate **World Cup** finals hosted in Mexico); Mexican Cup (Copa Mexico) 1991.

Montevideo Wanderers *club* Uruguayan Primera League club based in Montevideo, founded 1902. Ground: Parque Alfredo Victor Viera, capacity: 12,000. Strip: black and white striped shirts, black shorts. Uruguayan amateur league (played from 1900-31) champions 1906, 1909, 1923, 1931; **Copa Uruguaya** (Uruguay's professional league, started in 1932) runners-up 1980, 1985; **Pre-Libertadores Liguilla** winners 1987.

monthly contract *regulations* short-term **contract** and **registration** of a player lasting one calendar month. **1. Premier League** and **Football League** players can be registered any number of times in this way, provided that their club gives notice of its intention to renew the contract at least seven days before it expires (FA Premier League rule K.18, Football League regulation 54). **2. Scottish Football League** clubs must offer players under 24 years of age a "continuing monthly contract" at the end of their normal contract if the club wishes to retain its right to a **compensation fee** (sense **3.**) (Scottish Football League rule 60.7.2). Compare **full contract**, **non-contract**.

Montreal Impact *club* Canadian club playing in the **American A-League**. Based in Montreal, Quebec, founded 1993. Ground: Centre Claude-Robillard, capacity: 7,500. Strip: blue shirts, white shorts. A-League champions 1994.

Montrose *club* Scottish league. *Dossier* Ground: **Links Park**, Montrose, Tayside, capacity: 4,338. Strip: blue shirts with blue and white striped sleeves, white shorts with blue trim, blue socks. Nickname: Gable Endies. Record attendance: 8,983 v **Dundee** (17 March 1973, **Scottish FA Cup**, third round). Biggest win: 12–0 v Vale of Leithen (4 January 1975, Scottish FA Cup, second round). Biggest defeat: 0–13 v **Aberdeen** (17 March 1951, Scottish FA Cup). *History* Founded in 1879 and alter amalgamating with Montrose United. The club joined Division Two in 1929-30. It has never played in the top flight of Scottish football. Montrose reached the quarter-final stage of the Scottish FA Cup in 1973 (1–4 v Dundee) and 1976 (1–2 second replay v **Heart of Midlothian**). It was also a **Scottish League Cup** semi-finalist in 1975-76 (1–5 v **Rangers**) and, in 1992-93, it reached the last four of the **Scottish League Challenge Cup**. In 1984-85, Montrose won the Second Division Championship. *League record* First Division 1975-76 to 1978-79, 1985-86 to 1986-87, 1991-92; Division Two (B Division) 1929-30 to 1938-39, 1955-56 to 1974-75; Second Division 1979-80 to 1984-85, 1987-88 to 1990-91, 1992-93, 1995-96; C Division 1946-47 to 1954-55; Third Division 1994-95, 1996-97–. *Honours* Second Division Champions 1984-85. *Records* Alexander Keillor is Montrose's most capped player (2 (6) for **Scotland**); David Larter holds the record for club appearances (426, 1987-98).

Montserrat *country CONCACAF* UK Crown Colony. A volcanic island in the West Indies and part of the Leeward Islands. Much of the country has been destroyed by a hurricane in 1989 and a volcanic eruption in 1997. Area: 106 sq km (41 sq miles). Population: 11,000. Language: English. Capital: Plymouth. *Dossier* Montserrat Football Association (Plymouth) affiliated to **FIFA** and **Confederación Norte-Centroamericana y del Caribe de Fútbol** (CONCACAF) in 1996, president: Lionel Nanton; general secretary: St Claire Thornhill. *International tournament record* has not entered **World Cup**, **Caribbean Nations Cup** or **Gold Cup**.

Monumental (Estadio Antonio Vespucio Liberti "Monumental" de Nunez) *ground* Argentinian football ground situated in Buenos Aires; home of **Argentina** national side and Club Atletico **River Plate**. Ground capacity: 76,000. *History* Originally a two-tier horseshoe-shaped stadium with a 100,000 capacity which opened "officially" in May 1938 (River

Plate v **Peñarol**). Prior to its official opening, the stadium staged one match during the 1937 (15th edition) **Copa America** tournament which was held in Buenos Aires (Argentina v **Brazil**, 80,000). Monumental was not completed until 1957 when River Plate invested much of the £91,000 transfer fee it received from **Juventus** for inside-left Omar **Sivori** in finishing the stadium. In June 1968, 74 people died and a further 113 were injured at Monumental when Club Atlético **Boca Junior** fans dropped lighted torches onto a section of the ground containing mainly River Plate supporters. The stadium was completely redeveloped for the 1978 **World Cup**. Monumental is famous for its ticker tape celebrations. Aside from the 1978 World Cup final (Argentina v **Netherlands**), Monumental staged eight other fixtures during the tournament (Argentina v **Hungary**, Argentina v **France**, **Italy** v Argentina, group 1; **Poland** v **West Germany**, group 2; Italy v West Germany, Italy v **Austria**, Netherlands v Italy, second round group A; Brazil v Italy, 3rd place playoff) – total attendance 627,684; average attendance 76,618. Monumental hosted four of the 1946 (20th edition) Copa America tournament matches (Argentina v **Paraguay**, 70,000; Paraguay v **Bolivia**, 80,000; Argentina v **Chile**, 80,000; Argentina v Brazil, 80,000) and several fixtures during the 1987 (34th edition), including the final (1987 **Uruguay** v Chile, 35,000). It was the venue for all 21 matches at the 1959 (27th edition) Copa America tournament.

Moore, Bobby *player* Defender. **England** international (108 caps, 2 goals). Born 12 April 1941. Career ca. 1958-77. *Clubs* **West Ham United**, **Fulham**, Herning FC (Denmark), San Antonio Thunder, Seattle Sounders, Team America. Also, managed **Southend United** (1984-86). *Keynotes* Joined West Ham United as a amateur, turning professional in June 1958. Moore played 544 **Football League** games for West Ham before moving across London to Fulham for £25,000 in March 1974, making 124 League appearances. Ironically, Moore's Fulham played West Ham in the 1975 **FA Cup** final (0–2). Moore was voted **Footballer of the Year** in 1964 and captained England to its greatest triumph, the **World Cup** in 1966, in which he received the Player of the Tournament accolade. In the build-up to the 1970 World Cup in **Mexico**, Moore was falsely arrested in Bogota for allegedly stealing a bracelet from a jewellery shop. Aside from his 108 full international caps (he was captain 90 times), Moore also played for England Youth on 18 occasions and made eight appearances for the Under-23 side. He was awarded the OBE in 1967. Moore died of cancer on 24 February 1993. **Pelé** once described Moore as "the best defender in the world". Included in the **Football League Centenary 100 players**. *Honours* FA Cup (West Ham United 1964); **European Cup-winners Cup** (West Ham United 1965); World Cup (England 1966).

Moore, Brian *commentator* born 28 February 1932. ITV television commentator who began his career in radio broadcasting in 1961. He joined the ITV team in

1968 and throughout the 1970s and early 1980s he fronted the Sunday afternoon football highlights programme, the **Big Match**. Retired from commentating after the 1998 **World Cup**.

Morena, Fernando *player* Striker. **Uruguay** international (21 goals, 1971-78). *Clubs* **Peñarol**, Rayo, Vallecano, **Flamengo**. *Keynotes* Morena was top scorer in the Uruguay league six seasons running: 1973 (23 goals), 1974 (27 goals), 1975 (34 goals), 1976 (18 goals), 1977 (19 goals), 1978 (26 goals), and again in 1982 (17 goals); all for Peñarol. However, he did not achieve the goal-scoring record set by Atilio **Garcia**. He was voted third in the 1975 *El Mundo* **South American Footballer of the Year**; fourth in 1973, 1982 and 1983; and sixth in 1974, 1976 and 1979; and 10th in 1984. He was in the Peñarol side that beat **Aston Villa** 2–0 in the 1982 **World Club Cup**, and scored the only goal in the club's 1–0 aggregate victory over **Cobreloa** in the 1982 **Copa Libertadores** and was top scorer with seven goals. Morena scored both goals in the 1983 Copa Libertadores final, but Peñarol lost 2–3 on aggregate to Gremio. *Honours* **Copa America** (Uruguay, 1983); World Club Cup (Peñarol, 1982); Copa Libertadores (1982); Uruguay championship/**Copa Uruguaya** (Peñarol, 1973, 1974, 1975, 1978, 1979, 1981, 1982); Uruguay **Pre-Libertadores Liguilla** championship (Peñarol, 1974, 1975, 1977, 1978, 1980).

Morocco *country CAF* kingdom in north Africa on the Mediterranean Sea and bordered by **Algeria** and **Mauritania**. The territory of **Western Sahara** is in dispute: some countries recognise its independence as the Saharan Arab Democratic Republic. Established in 1912 as a French and Spanish protectorate, with independence from **France** achieved in 1956. Area: 710,895 sq km (274,414 sq miles). Population: 26,100,000 (1994 census). Languages: Arabic, French, Spanish and Berber. Capital: Rabat. *Dossier* Football association (Fédération Royale Marocaine de Football, Rabat) formed in 1955 affiliated to **FIFA** in 1956 and **Confédération Africaine de Football** (CAF) in 1966, member of the **Arab Football Union**, president: General Benslimane Housni; general secretary: Mohamed El Amrani. Season played from September to June. National stadium: Mohamed V, Casablanca, capacity: 80,000. National strip: red shirts, red shorts and red socks. Nickname of national team: the Atlas Lions. First international game: 3 April 1958, v Libya (2–1, home, friendly). Biggest victory: 7–0, v **Congo Democratic Republic** (former Zaire) (29 August 1996, home, friendly). Biggest defeat: 0–5, v **former-Yugoslavia** (1 January 1960, home, friendly) and 0–5, v **Poland** (38 September 1972, Munich, Germany, **Olympic Games** finals tournament). Highest crowd: 90,000 v **Ivory Coast** (19 March 1988, Mohammed V Stadium, Casablanca, **African Cup of Nations**, first round group match); 90,000 v **Ghana** (1–0, 8 June 1997, Mohammed V Stadium, World Cup qualifier). Most capped players:

Noureddine Naybet (94 appearances, to 1998). Other notable international players: Ahmed **Faras**, Mustapha **Hadji**, Mohamed **Timoumi**, Badou **Zaki**. *International tournament record* **Olympic Games** – finals tournament second round group 1972, also qualified for finals tournament in 1964, 1984 and 1992; **Women's World Cup** – never entered; **World Cup** –first entered 1962, qualified for finals tournament in 1970 (in Mexico, finished bottom of its first round group), 1986 (in Mexico, finished top in its first round group, ahead of **England**, Poland and **Portugal**, losing 0–1 to West **Germany** in the second round, through an 89th-minute goal), 1994 (in USA, finished bottom in first round group) and 1998 (in France, finished third of four nations in the first round group, in spite of a 3–0 victory over **Scotland** and a 2–2 draw with **Norway**), lost in the fourth and final qualifying round in 1982 (1–4 agg., v **Cameroon**); African Cup of Nations – first entered 1970, winners 1976 (won the final round league of four nations at the tournament in Addis Ababa, Ethiopia), third place 1980 (2–0, v **Egypt**, third/fourth play-off in Lagos, Nigeria), fourth 1986 (2–3, v Ivory Coast, third/fourth play-off in Cairo, Egypt), fourth 1988 (1–1, 3–4 pens., v Algeria, third/fourth play-off in Casablanca), quarter-final 1998, also qualified for finals tournament 1972, 1978, 1992; **African Youth Cup** – winners 1997 (1–0, v **South Africa**, in Meknes, Morocco); All-Arab Games – runners-up 1985; Mediterranean Games – winners 1983; **Under-17 World Championship** – never qualified; **World Youth Cup** (under-20) – qualified for finals tournament 1997 (first round). *World Cup performance* (finals and qualifiers to end of 1998 tournament) played 79, won 33, drawn 25, lost 21, scored 98 goals, conceded 63 goals; win rate: 42%; goals scored per game: 1.24. *Record against British and Irish national teams* v England, played two, drawn one, lost one; v **Northern Ireland**, played one, lost one; v Scotland, played one, won one; v **Wales**, none played; v **Republic of Ireland**, played one, lost one. *History* League championship first played 1916, with a Cup competition from 1957. Moroccan clubs have performed well in African club competitions: **FAR Rabat** (1985), **RAJA CA Casablanca** (1989 and 1997) and **WAC Casablanca** (1992) have won the **African Cup of Champion Clubs**, Africa's premier club tournament. US Marocaine holds the national league record of six consecutive league titles (1938 to 1943). Morocco has qualified for four World Cup finals tournaments and won the African Nations Cup in 1976. The most famous Moroccan-born player, Just **Fontaine** – the highest goalscorer in any single World Cup finals tournament – was a French international. *League system* Sixteen clubs compete in the national league first division. Three points are awarded for a victory, with one for a draw: final positions for clubs level on points are determined by **goal difference**. *Record in international club tournaments* African Cup of Champion

Clubs – FAR Rabat (winners 1985), RAJA CA Casablanca (winners 1989, 1997, quarter-final "champions-league" stage 1998), WAC Casablanca (winners 1992), COD Meknes (quarter-final 1996); **African Cup-winners Cup** – Diffaa Hassani El Jadida (quarter-final 1986) and FAR Rabat (runners-up 1997, quarter-final 1987), FUS Rabat (quarter-final 1996), WAC Casablanca (semi-final 1998); **CAF Cup – KAC Marrakesh** (winners 1996), Renaissance Settat (quarter-final 1998); **Afro-Asian Club Cup** – WAC Casablanca (winners 1992), RAJA CA Casablanca (winners 1998-99) FAR Rabat (runners-up 1985); **Arab Club Champions Cup** – WAC Casablanca (winners 1992), Raja CA Casablanca (runners-up 1996); **Arab Cup-winners Cup – Olympique Casablanca** (winners 1991, 1993 and 1994; the club was dissolved in 1995), Olympic Khourigba (winners 1996).

Mortensen, Stan *player-manager* Striker. **England** international (25 caps, 23 goals). Born 26 May 1921. Career ca. 1937-62. *Clubs* (player) **Blackpool, Hull City, Southport**, Bath City, Lancaster City, (manager) Blackpool. *Keynotes* Mortensen scored 197 goals for Blackpool in 320 League appearances. He scored a hat-trick in Blackpool's only **FA Cup** success, the 1953 final (4–3 v **Bolton Wanderers**). In 1948 he scored in every round of the FA Cup, including the final (2–4 v **Manchester United**). He was Division One top scorer with 30 goals in 1950-51. Mortensen scored four goals for England on his international debut against **Portugal** on 25 May 1947. Later that year, he hit a hat-trick against **Sweden** (19 November). Mortensen's final match for England was the infamous 3–6 defeat by **Hungary**. During **World War II**, Mortensen was a RAF bomber pilot. He unofficially played for **Wales** against England before making his international debut, replacing an injured Welsh player in a **wartime** fixture on 25 September 1943. Included in the **Football League Centenary 100 players**. *Honours* FA Cup (Blackpool 1953).

Moss Rose Ground *ground* English football ground situated in Macclesfield, Cheshire; home of **Macclesfield Town**. *Dossier* Ground capacity: 6,028. Pitch dimensions: 91m x 60m. Record League attendance: 5,982 v **Chester City** (25 April 1998, Third Division). *Keynotes* The highest-ever attendance at Moss Rose was recorded on 4 February 1948, when 9,008 saw Macclesfield entertain Winsford in the second round of the Cheshire Senior Cup.

Mosson (Stade de la) *ground* French football ground situated in Montpellier, Languedoc-Roussillon; home of Montpellier Hérault Sports Club. Ground capacity: 35,500 all seated. *History* First opened in 1900 and renovated between 1987 and 1990. Refurbished for the 1998 **World Cup** at a cost of more than £9 million. During the tournament, Stade de la Mosson staged one match from each of groups A (**Morocco v Norway**), B (**Cameroon v Italy**), D (**Bulgaria v Paraguay**), F (**Germany v Iran**) and G (**Colombia v Tunisia**); and

a second-round game (Germany v **Mexico**) – total attendance 197,900; average attendance 32,983.

most expensive player *record* see **transfer fee, highest** .

Motagua (Club Deportivo) *club* Honduras national league club based in the capital Tegucigalpa, formed 1928. Ground: Estadio Nacional "Tiburcio Carias Andino", capacity: 35,000. Strip: blue shirts, blue shorts. Honduras League champions 1968, 1970, 1973, 1978, 1992, 1998.

Motherwell *club* Scottish league. *Dossier* Ground: **Fir Park**, Motherwell, Strathclyde. Strip: claret and amber halved shirts, claret and amber halved shorts, claret socks with amber tops. Nickname: Well. Ground capacity: 13,742 all seated. Record attendance: 35,632 v **Rangers** (12 March 1952, **Scottish FA Cup**, fourth round replay). Biggest win: 12–1 v **Dundee United** (23 January 1954, Division Two). Biggest defeat: 0–8 v **Aberdeen** (26 March 1979, Premier Division). *History* Founded in May 1886 from a merger between two local clubs, Alpha and Glencairn. The club joined **Scottish Football League** Division Two in 1894-95, replacing **Thistle** and finishing second in that first season. Motherwell won election to Division One in 1902-03. The inter-war period is the club's most successful. Between 1926-27 and 1931-32, when the club won its only League Championship, Motherwell finished either second or third in the League. In the two seasons after its title triumph the club finished as runners-up. Also in this period, Motherwell played in three Scottish FA Cup finals: 1931 (2–4 replay v **Celtic**), 1933 (0–1 v Celtic), 1939 (0–4 v **Clyde**). Motherwell enjoyed more Cup success in the early-1950s. It won the Scottish FA Cup in 1952 (4–0 v **Dundee**), having reached the final the previous season (0–1 v Celtic). It also won the **Scottish League Cup** in 1950-51 (3–0 v **Hibernian**) and, in 1954-55, it again was a finalist (2–4 v **Heart of Midlothian**). Motherwell won its second Scottish FA Cup in 1991 (4–3 a.e.t. v Dundee United). After finishing Premier Division runners-up in 1994-95, the club qualified for European competition (**UEFA** Cup) for the first time the following season (0–3 agg. v **Borussia Dortmund**, first round). *League record* Premier League 1998-99–; Premier Division 1975-76 to 1978-79, 1982-83 to 1983-84, 1985-86 to 1997-98; Division One (A Division) 1903-04 to 1914-15, 1921-22 to 1952-53, 1954-55 to 1967-68, 1969-70 to 1974-75; First Division 1979-80 to 1981-82, 1984-85; Scottish League 1915-16 to 1920-21; Division Two (B Division) 1894-95 to 1902-03, 1953-54, 1968-69. *Honours* Division One 1931-32; First Division 1981-82, 1984-85; Division Two 1953-54, 1968-69; Scottish FA Cup 1952 (4–0 v Dundee), 1991 (4–3 a.e.t. v Dundee United); Scottish League Cup 1950-51 (30 v Hibernian). *Records* George Stevenson (12 for **Scotland**) and Tommy Coyne (13 for **Republic of Ireland**) are Motherwell's most capped players; Bobby Ferrier holds the record for club appearances (626,

1918-37); Hugh Ferguson is Motherwell's record goalscorer (283, 1916-25).

Motson, John *commentator* born 7 October 1945. BBC television commentator who made his broadcasting debut reporting on football, boxing and tennis for BBC Radio Sport, moving to **Match of the Day** in 1971. His first **World Cup** finals was in Germany in 1974. He became the youngest **FA Cup** final commentator in 1977, at the age of 31. The BBC paid Motson a tribute in 1998 by broadcasting *The Full Motty*, a programme featuring Motson and a celebrity audience.

Moukila, Paul *player* Striker. **Congo** international. *Club* **CARA Brazzaville**. *Honours* **African Cup of Nations** (Congo, 1972; third place 1974); **African Cup of Champion Clubs** (CARA Brazzaville, 1974); Congo league champions 1970, 1971, 1972, 1973, 1974, 1975; *France Football* **African Footballer of the Year** 1974.

moulded studs *n. pl.* type of **studs** that are an integral part of a moulded synthetic sole of a **football boot**. Moulded studs date from 1949, in boots manufactured by the German company Adidas; made from a rubber resin. Compare **screw-in studs**.

Mouloudia Chalia d'Algiers *club* Algerian national league club, based in the capital El Djezaïr (Algiers). The oldest club in Algeria, founded 1921. Formerly known as Mouloudia des Petroliers d'Algiers. Ground: Bologhine, capacity: 30,000. Strip: red shirts, green shorts. **African Cup of Champion Clubs** 1976 (3–3 agg., 4–1 pens., v **Hafia Conakry** of Guinea; **Maghreb Cup-winners Cup** 1971 and 1973; **Arab Super Cup** 1999; Algerian league champions 1972, 1975, 1976, 1978, 1979; Algerian Cup 1971, 1973, 1976, 1983; Algiers regional league winners 1944.

Mouloudia Club d'Oran (MC Oran) *club* Algerian national league club, based in Oran, founded 1946. Ground: 19 June 65, capacity: 60,000. Strip: red shirts, white shorts. **African Cup of Champion Clubs** runners-up 1989 (1–1 agg., v **Raja Casablanca** of Morocco); **CAF Cup** quarter-final 1996; **African Cup-winners Cup** quarter-final 1997; **Arab Cup-winners Cup** 1997, 1998; **Arab Super Cup** 1999; Algerian League champions 1971, 1988, 1992, 1993; Algerian Cup 1975, 1984, 1985.

Mount Wellington *club* New Zealand national league club based in Wellington. New Zealand National League champions 1972, 1974, 1979, 1980, 1982, 1986; (New Zealand) Chatham Cup 1973, 1980, 1982,1983, 1990.

moving away from goal *rules* of an **attacking player** who is fouled by a **defending player** or the **goalkeeper** when not moving in the direction of the goal. This is important in rule XII of the **Laws of the game** where a defending player can be sent off for **serious foul play** if a clear opportunity to score a goal had been prevented by a foul or by illegally handling the ball. If the attacking player is moving away from the goal, then no obvious goalscoring opportunity exists.

Mozambique *country CAF* republic in southeast Africa on the Indian Ocean, bordered by **Malawi, South Africa, Swaziland, Tanzania, Zambia** and **Zimbabwe**. Independence from **Portugal** in 1975. Large coastal plains with mountain ranges in the north. Area: 784,755 sq km (302,915 sq miles). Population: 16,000,000 (1995 est.). Languages: Portuguese and 16 tribal languages. Capital: Maputo. *Dossier* Football association (Federacao Mocambicana de Futebol, Maputo) formed in 1975, affiliated to **FIFA** and **Confédération Africaine de Football** (CAF) in 1978, member of the **Confederation of Southern African Football Associations** (COSAFA), president Mário Gomes Guerreiro, general secretary: António Carvalho. Season played from February to November. National stadium: Estadio de Machava, Maputo, capacity: 60,000. National strip: red shirts, black shorts and black and red socks. Nickname of national team: the Mambas (snakes). First international game: December 1977, v **Tanzania** (1–2, Maputo, friendly). Biggest victory: 6–1 v **Lesotho** (10 August 1980, home, **African Cup of Nations** qualifier). Biggest defeat: 0–6 v Zimbabwe (May 1979, Harare, friendly). *International tournament record* **Olympic Games** – first entered 1984, never qualified for finals tournament; **Women's World Cup** – first entered 1999; **World Cup** – first entered 1982, then again in 1994 and 1998, never progressed beyond first qualifying round; African Cup of Nations – qualified for finals tournament in 1986 (last in its first-round group of four nations) and 1996 (last in its first round group of four nations); COSAFA Under-17 Championship – runners-up 1994; **Under-17 World Championship** – never qualified; **World Youth Cup** (under-20) – never qualified. *Record against British and Irish national teams* none played. *History* National championship played since 1976, first won by Textafrica (of Chimoio), with the cup competition played since 1978, first won by Clube Desportivo **Maxaquene**. Mozambique's first major international tournament match was a World Cup qualifier against **Congo Democratic Republic** (as Zaire) on 13 July 1980 (2–5, in Kinshasa, Congo DR). The country's greatest player, Portuguese international **Eusébio** Da Silva Ferreira, was born in Maputo and started his career at **Gruppo Desportivo de Maputo**, along with another Portuguese international, Mario Esteves **Coluna**, before moving to **Benfica** in 1961. Because Mozambique was a Portuguese colony, both Eusébio and Coluna were eligible to play for Portugal. *League system* National championship determined by a tournament involving the winners of 11 regional leagues and the bigger clubs based in Maputo. *Record in international club tournaments* **African Cup of Champion Clubs** – **Matchedje** (quarter final 1988), **Ferroviário Maputo** (quarter-final "champions-league" stage 1997), **Desportes Costa do Sol** (second round 1993 and 1994); **African Cup-winners Cup** – Gruppo Desportivo de Maputo (semi-final 1990), Maxaquene (semi-final 1995), Desportes Costa do Sol (quarter-final

1996, 1997); **CAF Cup** – Ferroviário Maputo (semi-final 1992).

MP Tigers (Mukorob Pelagic) *club* Namibian national league club, based in Windhoek and formed in 1942 (the oldest club in the Namibian league). Ground: Showgrounds, capacity: 3,500. Namibian Cup 1995 and 1996.

MPKC Mozyr *club* Belarus national league club based in Mozyr, founded 1995. Ground: Yunost, capacity: 7,500. Belarus league champions 1996; Belarus cup 1996.

MTK Budapest *club* former name, until 1998, of Hungarian club **MTK Hungária FC**

MTK Hungária FC (Magyar Testgyakorlók Köre) *club* Hungarian national league club based in Budapest, founded in 1888 as MTK Budapest. Ground: Hungária Úti, capacity: 25,000. Strip: blue and white shirts, white shorts. *Keynotes* MTK won the Hungarian league championship 10 times in succession (1914, 1917-25; the run punctuated by **World War I**). This was a world record that lasted until 1972 when it was bettered by **Al Faisaly** of **Jordan**. Much of MTK's pre-**World War II** success is attributed to the former **Bolton Wanderers** player Jimmy Hogan, a former prisoner of War in Vienna. Hogan coached a side that won seven consecutive titles (1919–1925). The club adopted the name MTK Hungária FC in 1998. **European Cup-winners Cup** – runners-up 1964 (3–3, 0–1 replay, v **Sporting Clube de Portugal**, in Brussels and replay in Antwerp, Belgium); Hungarian league champions 1904, 1908, 1914, 1917, 1918, 1919, 1920, 1921, 1922, 1923, 1924, 1925, 1929, 1936, 1937, 1951, 1953, 1958, 1987, 1997, 1999; Hungarian Cup 1910, 1911, 1912, 1914, 1923, 1925, 1932, 1952, 1968, 1997. Notable former player: Nandor **Hidegkuti**.

Mufulira Wanderers *club* Zambian national league club based in Mufulira. Ground: Shinde, capacity: 12,000. Strip: white shirts, green shorts. **African Cup of Champion Clubs** semi-final 1977; Zambian league champions 1963, 1965, 1966, 1977, 1969, 1976, 1978, 1995, 1996; Zambian Cup 1965, 1966, 1974, 1977, 1984, 1991, 1994, 1995. Notable player: Kalusha **Bwalya**.

Muharraq *club* Bahrain national league club. *Keynotes* Muharraq's 24 domestic league titles is an Asian club record. **Asian Cup-winners Cup** runners-up 1990 (0–1 agg., v **Piroozi** of Iran); **Arab Club Champions Cup** runners-up 1994 (v **Esperance Tunis** of Tunisia); Bahrain League champions 1957, 1958, 1960, 1961, 1962, 1963, 1964, 1965, 1966, 1967, 1970, 1971, 1973, 1974, 1976, 1980, 1983, 1984, 1986, 1988, 1991, 1992, 1995, 1999.

Müller, Gerd *player* Striker. West **Germany** international (62 caps, 68 goals, 1966-74). Born 3 November 1945, in Nördlingen. *Clubs* TSV Nördlingen, **Bayern Munich** *Keynotes* Nicknamed "der Bomber", Müller is the all-time top scorer for Germany; 21 goals clear of his nearest rival, Rudi Völler. Only four players in the world have scored more international goals, and very few have matched his goal-scoring ratio of 1.1 goals per match. He made his international debut on 12 December 1966, a 1–2 defeat by **France** (in Paris, European Championship qualifier). Müller scored the 43rd-minute winning goal in the 1974 **World Cup** final (2–1, v **Netherlands**, in Munich). In England, however, he is most remembered for the extra-time goal that knocked **England** out of the 1970 World Cup finals (3–2, in León, Mexico) – a volley past England's goalkeeper Peter Bonetti. The match was seen as revenge for West Germany's 1966 World Cup final defeat by England. Müller was top scorer in the 1970 tournament with 10 goals, including two in extra time against **Italy** in the semi-final (a match which West Germany eventually lost 3-4). Müller scored 14 goals in two World Cup finals tournaments – the competition record. He also scored two to help West Germany to the **European Championship** in 1972 (3–0, v **Soviet Union**, in Brussels). Müller moved to Bayern Munich from his local club TSV Nördlingen in 1964. He scored 365 goals in the German **Bundesliga**. At 21 years of age, Müller was top scorer in the 1967 **European Cup-winners Cup**, with nine goals for Bayern Munich. He was top scorer again in the 1974 **European Cup** (nine goals – including two goals in the final; a 4–0 defeat of **Atlético Madrid**); and again in 1975 (six goals, including Bayern Munich's second in the 2–0 defeat of **Leeds United**). He completed a hat-trick of European Cup-winner's medals when helping Bayern to the trophy in 1976, with a 1–0 win over **Saint-Etienne**. *Honours* World Cup (West Germany, 1974); World Cup Golden Boot 1970; European Championship (West Germany, 1972); European Cup (Bayern Munich, 1974, 1975, 1976); European Cup-winners Cup (Bayern Munich 1967); German Bundesliga championship (Bayern Munich 1969, 1972, 1973, 1974); *France Football* **European Footballer of the Year** 1970, runner-up 1972; **European Golden Boot** 1970 (38 league goals for Bayern Munich), 1972 (40 league goals for Bayern Munich).

Mullery, Alan *player-manager* Midfield. **England** international (35 caps). Born 23 November 1941. Career ca. 1957-76. *Clubs* (player) **Fulham** (twice), **Tottenham Hotspur**, (manager) **Brighton & Hove Albion** (twice), **Charlton Athletic**, **Crystal Palace**, **Queens Park Rangers**, **Barnet** (director of football). *Keynotes* Joined Fulham in 1957, turning professional in December 1958 and moving to Tottenham Hotspur for £72,500 in March 1964. He captained the club to its 1972 **UEFA Cup** triumph against **Wolverhampton Wanderers** (3–2 agg.). Mullery has the unenviable distinction of being the first England player to be dismissed when he was sent off against **former-Yugoslavia** in the semi-final of the 1968 **European Championship** (5 June). Voted **Footballer of the Year** in 1975 and awarded the MBE in 1976. In Mullery's first spell as manager of Brighton, he guided the club to two successive promotions and a place in Division One in 1981-82. Became a television pundit for

BSkyB. Included in the **Football League Centenary 100 players**. *Honours* **FA Cup** (Tottenham Hotspur 1967); **League Cup** (Tottenham Hotspur 1971); UEFA Cup (Tottenham Hotspur 1972).

Mundialito *competition* literally, the little World Cup. Informal name for the former non-FIFA international women's tournament organised by the Italy-based **Federation of Independent European Female Football**. Two editions were played, in Italy in 1970, and in Mexico in 1971, with **Denmark**, **women** winning both competitions.

Munich air crash *disaster* air disaster on 6 February 1958, in which 23 people were killed, including eight **Manchester United** players, along with club officials and journalists. Manchester United was travelling back from its **European Cup** quarter-final away leg against **Red Star Belgrade**. The plane, an Elizabethan airliner, had stopped off at Munich to refuel. It already had made two attempts to take off in snowy conditions; the plane eventually crashed into the airport's perimeter fencing. The dead players were: Roger Byrne, Geoff Bent, Eddie Colman, Mark Jones, David Pegg, Tommy Taylor, Liam "Billy" Whelan and Duncan **Edwards** (who died two weeks later in hospital). Walter Crickmer (club secretary), Bert Whalley (coach), Tom Curry (trainer) and journalist and former England goalkeeper Frank **Swift** were also killed. Johnny Berry and Jackie Blanchflower survived but never played again, while Bobby **Charlton**, Dennis Viollet, Billy Foulkes and Harry Gregg recovered in time for the 1958 **FA Cup** final (which United lost 0–2, v **Bolton Wanderers**). The United manager Matt **Busby** also survived. A stadium clock at **Old Trafford** honours those who died. A tribute match to mark the 40th anniversary of the disaster was staged at Old Trafford on 18 August 1998. Among those playing was Eric **Cantona**, who played for the Cantona All-Stars in the first half and for Manchester United in the second. United won 8–4. See also **Busby Babes**.

Municipal (Club Deportivo Municipal) *club* Guatemala national league club based in Guatemala City, founded 1936. Ground: Estadio Mateo Flores, capacity: 50,000. Strip: red shirts, blue shorts. **CONCA-CAF Champions Cup** 1974 (4–2 agg., v **Transvaal** of Surinam; **Torneo Grandes de Centroamerica** – finalist 1998 (v **Saprissa** of Costa Rica), semi-final 1997); Guatemala national champions 1943, 1947, 1951, 1955, 1964, 1966, 1970, 1973, 1976, 1992; Guatemala Cup 1995, 1996.

Municipal (Stade) *ground* French football ground situated in Toulouse, Midi-Pyrénées; home of Toulouse Football Club. Ground capacity: 37,532 all seated. *History* Opened in 1949. Refurbished for the 1998 **World Cup** at a cost of £17 million. During the tournament, Stade Municipal staged one match from each of groups B (**Austria** v **Cameroon**), C (**Denmark** v **South Africa**), D (**Nigeria** v **Paraguay**), G (**England** v **Romania**) and H (**Argentina** v **Japan**); and a second round game (**Netherlands** v **Yugoslavia**) – total attendance 217,900; average attendance 36,316.

Mura Murska Sobota *club* Slovenian national league club based in Murska Sobota, founded 1946. Ground: Fazanerija, capacity: 5,000. Strip: black shirts with white sleeves, black shorts. Pre-independence Slovenian league champions 1970; Slovenian league runners-up 1994; Slovenian Cup 1995.

muscle injury *medical* an injury to a **muscle**, caused either directly by a blow or cut, or through overuse or overstretching. See **contusion**, **haematoma**, **rupture**, **strain**, **tear**.

muscle *medical* a collection of muscle fibres that, by its contraction, causes movement.

music *misc.* home teams generally run on to the field of play accompanied by a "favourite" piece of music selected to rouse the home supporters. **Sunderland** players, for example, enter to the sound of Prokofiev's "Dance of the Knights" from Romeo and Juliet.

MUTV *n.* subscription television channel dedicated to **Manchester United** which first broadcast on 10 September 1998 and cost between £8 to £10 million to establish. The station broadcasts six hours a day, seven days a week, from a studio inside **Old Trafford**. It is the world's first daily football club channel.

Mwanza Pamba SC (also called Pamba SC) *club* Tanzanian national league club based in Mwanza. Ground: Kirumba, capacity: 11,000. Strip: red shirts, white shorts. The club holds the record for the biggest victory in the **African Cup-winners Cup** (12–1, v Anse Boileau of **Seychelles**, 1990, preliminary round: Pamba won 17–1 on aggregate). Tanzania and Zanzibar Union League champions 1990; Tanzanian Cup 1992.

Myanmar *country AFC* republic in southeast Asia on Bay of Bengal, bordered by **India**, **China**, **Laos** and **Thailand**. Independence from Britain in 1948, former name Burma; renamed Myanmar in 1989. Area: 678,000 sq km (261,720 sq miles). Population: 42,330,000. Language: Burmese. Capital: Yangon (formerly known as Rangoon). *Dossier* Myanmar Football Confederation (Yangon) formed in 1947, affiliated to **FIFA** in 1957 and **Asian Football Confederation** (AFC) in 1958, president: Colonel Thoung Htike; general secretary: Naw Tawng. Season played from May to February. National stadium: Aung Sang Memorial Stadium, Yangon, capacity: 45,000. National strip: red shirts, white shorts and red socks. *International tournament record* **Olympic Games** – qualified for finals tournament 1972 (third in its first-round group of four nations); **Women's World Cup** – never entered; **World Cup** – never entered; **Asean Tiger Cup** – played in first tournament in 1996 (third in its five-nation group); **Asian Cup of Nations** – runners-up 1968 (qualified for the five-nation finals tournament after winning a group tournament played in Myanmar, then won two and drew one of its four final-tournament games in Tehran, losing 1–3 to the hosts and tournament-winners **Iran**);· **Asian Games** – entered first tournament in 1951, winners/gold medal 1966 (1–0 v Iran, in Bangkok, Thailand), joint-winners/shared gold 1970 (0–0 v **South Korea**, in Bangkok), third place 1958 (5–4, v **Indonesia**, in

Manila, the Philippines, third/fourth play-off), second round group stage 1974, also qualified for finals tournament 1951, 1958, 1978, 1982, 1994; **Asian Women's Championship** – never entered; **Asian Youth Championship** (under-19) – winners 1961 (shared with Indonesia), 1963 (shared with South Korea), 1964, 1966 (both shared with **Israel**), 1968, 1969 (shared with **Thailand**), 1970**South East Asian Games** – winners 1965 (shared with Thailand), 1967, 1969, 1971, 1973; **Under-17 World Championship** – never qualified; **World Youth Cup** (under-20) – never qualified. *Record against British and Irish national teams* none played. *Record in international club tournaments* **Asian Champion Teams Cup** – **Finance and Revenue** (quarter-final 1998). Other leading club: Mandalay (league champions 1998).

N

Nacional (Club Nacional de Fútbol) *club* Uruguayan Primera League club based in Montevideo, founded 1899 (after merger of Montevideo FC and Defensa). Ground: technically, Nacional's stadium is Parque Central, capacity: 15,000, however, the club plays all its home games at Estadio Centenario (the national stadium), capacity: 75,000. Strip: white shirts, blue shorts. *Keynotes* By 1998, Nacional had won 37 domestic league titles; only **Rangers** (47), **Peñarol** (45) and **Linfield** (42) had won more domestic championships. **World Club Cup** 1971 (3–2 agg., v **Panathinaikos** – Panathinaikos was **European Cup** runners-up, **Ajax** withdrew from the World Club Cup), 1980 (1–0 v **Nottingham Forest**, in Tokyo, Japan), 1988 (2–2, 7–6 pens., v **PSV Eindhoven**, in Tokyo); **Copa Inter America** winners 1972 (3–2 ag., v **Cruz Azul** of Mexico), 1989 (5–1 agg., v Club Deportivo **Olimpia** of Honduras), runners-up 1981 (4–4 agg., 1–2 playoff v **UNAM** of Mexico – playoff in Los Angeles, USA); **Copa Libertadores** winners 1971 (0–1, 1–0, 2–0 playoff, v **Estudiantes**), 1980 (0–0, 1–0, v **Internacional Porto Allegre** of Brazil), 1988 (3–1 agg., v **Newell's Old Boys** of Argentina), runners-up 1964 (0–0, 0–1, v **Independiente** of Argentina), 1967 (0–0, 0–0, 1–2 playoff, v **Racing Club** of Argentina), 1969 (0–1, 0–2, v Estudiantes); **Supercopa** runners-up 1990 (3–6 agg., v **Olimpia** of Paraguay); **Recopa** winners 1988 (1–0 v **Racing Club** of Argentina); Uruguayan amateur league (played from 1900-31) champions 1902, 1903, 1912, 1915, 1916, 1917, 1919, 1920, 1922, 1923, 1924; **Copa Uruguaya** (Uruguay's professional league, started in 1932) champions 1933, 1934, 1939, 1940, 1941, 1942, 1943, 1946, 1947, 1950, 1952, 1955, 1956, 1957, 1963, 1966, 1969, 1970, 1971, 1972, 1977, 1980, 1983, 1992, 1998; **Pre-Libertadores Liguilla** winners 1982, 1990, 1992, 1993, 1996.

Nacional (Club Nacional) *club* Paraguay national league club based in the capital Asuncion, founded in 1904 by students at the National College of Asuncion. Ground: Estadio Arsenio Erico, capacity: 10,000. Strip: white shirts with blue and red trim, blue shorts. Paraguay League champions 1909, 1911, 1924, 1926, 1942, 1946.

Nacional (Estadio) *ground* Chilean national stadium situated in Santiago; home of **Chile** national side and **Universidad de Chile**. Ground capacity: 80,000. *History* Infamous as the stadium in which thousands of political prisoners were held, many of whom were never seen again, during the military coup which overthrew Salvador Allende's democratically-elected government in September 1973; an incident portrayed in the 1982 Constantin Costa-Gavras film *Missing*. These events provoked controversy during the 1974 **World Cup** qualifyng campaign. Chile and the **Soviet Union** had to meet in a playoff to secure a place in the finals. The Soviet Union refused to play the return leg at the Nacional and the Chileans countered by rejecting pleas to switch the tie elsewhere. As a result, the match was held without the the Soviet Union, and after Chile scored direct from the kick-off the tie was awarded to the South Americans. The stadium opened before **World War II**, staging the 1941 (17th edition) and 1945 (19th edition) **Copa America** tournaments, both of which were unofficial or "extraordinarios" series. Nacional was the venue for the 1962 World Cup final (**Brazil** v **Czechoslovakia**). During the tournament, it also staged all of the group 2 fixtures (Chile v **Switzerland**, **Italy** v West **Germany**, Chile v Italy, West Germany v Switzerland, West Germany v Chile, Italy v Switzerland), a quarter-final tie (**former-Yugoslavia** v West Germany), a semi-final (Brazil v Chile) and the 3rd place playoff (Chile v Yugoslavia) – total attendance 663,771; average attendance 66,377. The stadium also hosted the 1955 (24th edition) and 1991 (36th edition) Copa America tournaments, including the final round matches in 1991. Nacional was also a venue during the 1975 (31st edition) and 1979 (32nd edition) series, staging the second leg of the 1979 final (Chile v **Paraguay**, 55,000). Chilean club side Club Social y Deportivo **Colo Colo** played the home leg of the **Copa Libertadores** at Nacional in 1973 (v **Independiente**, 77,000) and 1991 (v **Olimpia**, 64,000). The stadium also staged the Copa Libertadores final playoffs in 1965 (**Peñarol** v Independiente), 1966 (Peñarol v **River Plate**), 1967 (**Racing Club** v Nacional Montevideo), 1974 (Independiente v **São Paulo**), 1976 (River Plate v Cruzeiro).

Nadi al Difftayn *club* former name of Jordan club **Wihdat FC**.

Nagoya Grampus Eight *club* Japanese **J-League** club based in Nagoya, formerly Toyota FC (until 1991).

Ground: Nagoya Mizuho Athletics Stadium, capacity: 27,000. Strip: red shirts and red shorts. **Asian Cup-winners Cup** runners-up 1997 (1–3, v **Al Hilal** of Saudi Arabia, in Riyadh, Saudi Arabia); J-league runners-up 1996. Nagoya was Gary **Lineker**'s last professional club.

Nakata, Hidetoshi *player* Midfield. **Japan** international (22 caps). Born 1977. *Clubs* **Bellmare Hiratsuka**, Perugia (Italy). *Keynotes* Nakata played in the 1998 **World Cup** finals. His move to the Italian club Perugia before the 1998-99 season helped secure a multi-million pound contract for the club to have its games broadcast in Japan for several years, as well as thousands of replica shirt sales in Japan. *Honours* Asian Football Confederation **Asian Footballer of the Year** 1998.

Nakivubo Villa (Villa SC) *club* Ugandan national league club based in the capital Kampala. Ground: Nakivubo (national stadium until 1997) capacity: 25,000. Strip: red shirts, blue shorts. **African Cup of Champion Clubs** runners-up 1991 (2-6 agg., v **Club Africain** of Tunisia); **African Cup-winners Cup** quarter-final 1984; **CAF Cup** runners-up 1992 (0-3 agg., v **Shooting Stars** of Nigeria); **East and Central African Club Championship** winners 1987, 1990, runners-up 1999; Ugandan league champions 1982, 1984, 1987, 1990, 1992, 1994, 1998; Ugandan Cup 1983, 1986, 1988, 1989, 1998.

Namibia *country CAF* republic in southwest Africa on the Atlantic Ocean and bordered by **Angola**, **Botswana**, **South Africa** and **Zambia**. One of the driest countries in the world, with the Kalahari desert in the northeast and the Namib desert on the Atlantic coast. Annexed by Germany in 1884 as German Southwest Africa, administered by South Africa (by League of Nations Mandate) as British South Africa from 1920 to 1946. Name changed to South West Africa. South Africa continued to exert rule over the country – including the imposition of apartheid – in contravention of a United Nations decision in 1966 that the mandate be terminated, and an International Court of Justice ruling in 1971 that South Africa give up the territory. The name Namibia was recognised by the United Nations in 1968. Area: 825,419 sq km (318,614 sq miles). Population: 1,510,000 (1992 est.). Languages: tribal languages, Afrikaans, German and English. Capital: Windhoek. *Dossier* Namibia Football Association (Windhoek) formed in 1989, affiliated to **FIFA** in 1992 and **Confédération Africaine de Football** (CAF) in 1990, member of the **Confederation of Southern African Football Associations** (COSAFA), president: Immanuel Namaseb; general secretary: Barry Rukoro. Season played from February to November. National stadium: Independence Katutura, Windhoek, capacity: 40,000. National strip: blue, red, green, yellow and white shirts, blue, red, green, yellow and white shorts and blue, red, green, yellow and white socks. Nicknames of national team: the Desert Rats and the Brave Warriors. First international game: May 1989, v

Angola (0–1, Windhoek, friendly). Biggest victory: 6–0 v Botswana (25 August 1996, Windhoek, **African Cup of Nations** qualifier). Biggest defeat: 1–7, v **Egypt** (8 November 1996, away, World Cup qualifier). *International tournament record* **Olympic Games** – first entered 1996, never qualified for finals tournament; **Women's World Cup** – first entered 1999; **World Cup** – first entered 1994, reached second round of qualifying tournament in 1998 (finished last in its group of four nations); African Cup of Nations – first entered 1996, never qualified for finals tournament; **COSAFA Championship** – runners-up 1997 (final round league of five nations); COSAFA Youth Tournament (under 20) – semi-final 1994; **Under-17 World Championship** – never qualified; **World Youth Cup** (under-20) – never qualified. *Record against British and Irish national teams* none played. *History* National league first played 1985; first won by Benfica (of Tsumeb). *League system* Sixteen clubs play in the national league. There are four regional leagues: the Namibia Soccer Confederation League; the Central Nambia FA League; the Northern Namibia FA League; and the Amateur Soccer Association League. *Record in international club tournaments* no major success. Leading clubs: **Black Africans Nashua**, **Blue Waters**, **MP Tigers**, **Orlando Pirates**, **Liverpool**, **Chief Santos**. Namibia has many clubs named after popular international teams: eg Arsenal and Leeds United (from Windhoek), Benfica, Monaco and Rangers (from Tsumeb), Chelsea (from Grootfontein), and Manchester United; as well as the dramatically named Touch and Go (based in Otavi), Try Again (from Keetmanshoop), Hot Flames and Young Ones (from Windhoek) and Bingo (from Rundu).

Napier City Rovers *club* New Zealand national league club based in Napier. New Zealand National League champions 1989, 1992, 1993, 1998; (New Zealand) Chatham Cup 1985, 1993.

Napoli (SSC) *club* Italian league. *Dossier* Ground: **San Paolo** (Stadio), Naples, Campania, capacity: 80,000 all seated. Strip: light blue shirts with single white and black stripe, white shorts, light blue socks. Nickname: Bluerchiati (Blue and hoops). Record win: 8–1 v Pro Pratia (**Serie A** 1955-56). Record defeat: 1–11 v Alessandria (**Campionato Nazionale**). *History* Formed in 1926 from the merger of Poths' Naples FC (formed by sailor William Poths at the turn of the century) and Internazionale. The merged club was called Internapoli; only later did it become Napoli. The club's official name is Società Sportiva Calcio Napoli. The club won its first major trophy, the Italian Cup (**Coppa Italia**), in 1962 (2–1 v SPAL Ferrara). Diego **Maradona**'s arrival in 1984 transformed Napoli. The club won the League and Cup **double** in 1986-87, the **UEFA Cup** in 1989 (5–4 agg. v **Stuttgart VfB**) and a second league title in 1989-90. Since Maradona left in 1991, the club has failed to win any silverware, although it did reach the Italian Cup final in 1997 (1–3 agg. v Vicenza). *Honours* Italian League 1986-87, 1989-90; Italian Cup 1962 (2–1 v SPAL Ferrara), 1976 (4–0 v

Verona), 1987 (4–0 agg. v Atalanta); **UEFA Cup** 1989 (5–4 agg. v Stuttgart VFB); **Anglo-Italian Cup** 1975 (4–1 v **Southampton**).

narrowing the angle *tactics* reducing the target the attacker has to aim at by quickly closing him/her down. Goalkeepers narrow-the-angle in a one-on-one situation by coming off the goal line quickly and creating as large an obstacle as possible.

NASL Soccer Bowl *competition* see **North American Soccer League**.

National Asset Register *n.* UK record of publicly-owned assests published on 24 November 1997. **Ipswich Town**'s **Portman Road** ground's car park is owned by the Inland Revenue.

National Association Football League *competition* former United States football league – though restricted to eastern US – founded 1906, folded 1921, when replaced by the **American Soccer League**. First won by West Hudson (1906), which won the championship another five times. Bethlehem Steel was the last winner, in 1921.

National Bucharest *club* Romanian national league club based in Bucharest, founded 1934 (as Lafayette, later known as Grafica, Spartac and Progresul in 1954; current name adopted 1989). Ground: Stadionul Cotroceni, capacity: 16,000 (a brand new **all-seater stadium**). Strip: white shirts, blue shorts. *History* During the communist years, it was the official club of the Romanian union of hairdressers. The club's original stadium, Stadionul Republica, was demolished in the mid 1980s to make way for a huge palace and urban development by order of Nicolae Ceausescu, Romania's former communist dictator. **UEFA Cup** second round 1997; Romanian league runners-up 1997; Romanian Cup 1960, runners-up 1997.

National Federation of Football Supporters Clubs (NatFed) *confederation* umbrella body of supporters' clubs. Formed in 1927 under the motto "To help not hinder" it sought to promote close relations between clubs and supporters' clubs. In 1953, the NatFed claimed to have 500,000 members and, in 1956, it was instrumental in persuading the then government to relax gaming laws to enable supporters to raise financial assistance. By 1988, its membership was at an all-time low following the creation in 1985 of the **Football Supporters Association**.

National Football Intelligence Unit *misc.* autonomous police department established in Britain to combat organised football **hooliganism**.

National Football Museum *n.* museum housing football memorabilia, including archive films, photographs and publications, which is located at **Preston North End**'s **Deepdale** ground.

National Printing Agency *club* Somalia national league club based in the capital Mogadishu. **African Cup of Champion Clubs** second round 1984; Somalia league champions 1983.

National Professional Football League *competition* former South African professional league founded in 1959, exclusively for all-white football clubs (during South Africa's strict apartheid years of racial segregation). Changed name to the National Football League and, in 1978, merged with the non-white **National Professional Soccer League (sense 1)**.

National Professional Soccer League *competition* **1**. former name for South Africa's National Soccer League (NSL) which, until 1977, was contested by non-white clubs. Founded in 1971. It merged with the all-white **National Football League** in 1978 and became the NSL in 1985. **2**. former independent professional football league of the United States of America, founded 1967. Merged the following year with the **United Soccer Association** to form the **North American Soccer League**. Only winners: Oakland Clippers (1967).

National Soccer League *competition* see **National Professional Soccer League (sense 1).**

National Vocational Qualifications *misc.* see **coaching qualification** and **National Youth Training Scheme** (Scotland).

National Youth Training Scheme (Scotland) *misc.* vocational training programme launched by the **Scottish Football Association** in 1997. Trainees ("skillseekers") train for Scottish Vocational Qualifications (SVQ) in "Sport, recreation and allied occupations: coaching, teaching and instruction – context of association football". In the first year of the scheme, all the trainees were young players registered with professional senior league clubs. The coaching qualifications are at SVQ levels II and III. About 80 hours' tuition is needed to attain the level-two qualification. See also **coaching qualification**.

national identity-card scheme *n.* government proposed legislation requiring all football supporters to carry/show identity cards as a condition of stadium admission. The proposal was dropped in 1990 following a campaign led by the **Football Supporters Association**, opposition from clubs, the football authorities and the police, and strong criticism by the **Taylor Report**. *History* The 1987-92 Thatcher/Major government proposed the introduction of a computerised national identity scheme as a key part of the **Football Spectators Act**. The government's move was in response to growing crowd disturbances, such as the **Heysel Stadium tragedy** and rioting by **Millwall** supporters at **Luton Town**'s **Kenilworth Road** ground in March 1985 (**FA Cup**, sixth round). Luton's home-fans-only membership scheme introduced in the wake of the Millwall match and as an alternative to the **Football Association**'s order to install **perimeter fencing** in front of the Family Stand at Kenilworth Road had a strong influence on government thinking (Luton chairman David Evans was at the time a Conservative MP). The **Football League**'s proposal that all League clubs introduce partial membership schemes had been supported in Lord Justice **Popplewell**'s final report on the **Bradford City fire**, but was not widely supported (one club refused to comply in any way). The then government responded by seeking to establish a national identity-card scheme supported by law. However, the Taylor Report concluded that a computerised national identity-card scheme would present considerable safety dangers by increasing congestion outside grounds and would be very difficult to enforce. As a result, the government shelved its proposals. **Torquay United** introduced an identity-card scheme for home supporters following crowd trouble in November 1986 when **Wolverhampton Wanderers'** fans rampaged through the town centre. **Colchester United** also banned away supporters from its **Layer Road** ground.

Nationwide Football Conference *competition* see Football Conference.

Nationwide Football League *competition* see Football League.

Nauru *country no international affiliation* island republic in the southwest Pacific in Polynesia, 2,100 km northeast of **Australia**. Independence in 1968 from its previous joint-administrators Australia, **New Zealand** and Britain. Area: 21,2 sq km (8 sq miles). Population: 8,100 (1983 census). Language: Nauruan and English. Capital: Yaren. *Dossier* Football association affiliated neither to **FIFA** nor to the **Oceania Football Confederation**.

Navbakhor Namangan *club* Uzbekistan league club based in Namangan, founded 1978 (as Tekstilschik, later Automobilist – current name adopted 1988). Ground: Navbakhor Stadium, capacity: 40,000. **Asian Cup of Champion Teams** quarter-final 1998; Uzbekistan league champions 1996, third 1993, 1994, 1995; Uzbekistan Cup 1992, 1995, 1998, runners-up 1993.

Ndaye, Pierre Mulumba *player* **Congo Democratic Republic** (Zaire) international. *Clubs* AS Bantou, Renaissance, Union Tskisto, **Vita Club Kinshasa**. *Keynotes* Top scorer **African Cup of Nations** 1974 (nine goals) and scored all four of Zaire's goals in the final against Zambia (2–2, 2–0 replay, in Cairo, Egypt). *Honours* African Cup of Nations (Zaire, 1974); **African Cup of Champion Clubs** (Vita Club Kinshasa, 1973); Zaire league championship (Vita Club Kinshasa, 1970, 1971, 1972, 1973, 1975).

near post *n.* the **goal post** that is nearest to the ball as it is played from the wing (for example at a **corner kick**). A defender might, for example, be "defending the near post". *adj.* **near-post** (eg near-post header, near-post corner). Compare **far post**.

Necaxa (full name: Club Impulsora del Deportivo Necaxa) *club* Mexican national league club, based in Mexico City, founded 1923. *Keynotes* The club was founded as a merger of two older clubs (Luz y Fuerza and El Tranvias). Its name was changed to Atlético Espanol in 1971 – when it was bought by businessmen from the the Spanish community in Mexico City – reverting to Necaxa in 1982, after being taken over by a television company. Ground: Estadio Azteca, capacity: 110,000. Strip: red and white striped shirts and white shorts. **CONCACAF Champion Clubs Cup** 1975 (as

Atlético Espanol) (5-1 agg., v **Transvaal** of Surinam), runners-up 1996 (final league of four in Guatemala); **CONCACAF Cup-winners Cup** 1994 (3-0, v **Aurora** of Guatemala, in Miami, USA), finalist 1998 (v **Olimpia** of Honduras); Mexican League Champions 1933, 1935, 1937, 1938, 1995, 1996, 1998 (apertura); Mexican Cup (Copa Mexico and its predecessor the Copa Eliminatoria) 1925, 1926, 1933, 1960, 1966, 1995.

Neeskens, Johan *player* Midfield. **Netherlands** international (49 caps, 17 goals, 1970-81). Born 15 September 1951. *Clubs* Harlem, **Ajax**, **Barcelona**, New York Cosmos. *Keynotes* Neeskens was, essentially, a midfield player but also played in defence (for example, the 1971 **European Cup** final) and occasionally as striker. He made his international debut on 11 November 1970 (0–1, v **East Germany**, in Dresden, **European Championship** qualifier). He was the joint second-highest scorer in the 1974 **World Cup** finals, with five goals, including a penalty in the second minute against West Germany in the final (1–2, in Munich) – the first penalty in a World Cup final. He was one of the outstanding players of the 1974 tournament, alongside Johan **Cruyff**. His performance in the final was slightly marred, however, by some crude tackling on West Germany's Hoeness, and a subsequent caution. He played in three successive European Cup final winning teams (1971, 2–0, v **Panathinaikos**; 1972, 2–0, v **Internazionale**; 1973, 1–0, v **Juventus**). Joined Barcelona in 1974 and went on to win the **European Cup-winners Cup** in 1979 (4–3, v Fortuna Dusseldorf). *Honours* World Cup runner-up (Netherlands, 1974, 1978); European Cup (Ajax, 1971, 1972, 1973); European Cup-winners Cup (Barcelona, 1979); Dutch league championship (Ajax, 1970, 1972, 1973); Dutch Cup (1970, 1971, 1972); Spanish Cup (Barcelona 1978).

Neftchi Baku *club* Azerbaijan national league and former-Soviet Union league club, based in the capital Baku, founded 1937 (as Neftjanik, until 1968). Ground: National Tofik Bakhramov (the national stadium) capacity: 37,000. Strip: white shirts, maroon shorts. Third in former Soviet Union League Championship 1966, Azerbaijan League Champions 1992, runners-up 1997 (even though Neftchi finished top of the league in 1997, the Azerbaijan football association awarded the championship to rivals **Karabakh Agdam**, based on junior league results as well as the national league; a decision not accepted by **the Union of European Football Associations** which awarded the **European Cup** place to Neftchi Baku); Azerbaijan Cup 1996.

Neftchi Fergana *club* Uzbekistan league club based in Fergana, founded 1960 (as Spartak). Ground: Spartak, capacity: 15,000. **Asian Champion Teams Cup** semi-final 1994; Uzbekistan league champions 1992 (shared with **Pachtakor Tashkent**), 1993, 1994, 1995, 1997, runners-up 1996; Uzbekistan Cup 1994, 1996.

negative *adj.* of a style of play that tends to stifle the opposition team's attempts to score, rather than creating any chances for one's own team.

negligence *legal* term that refers to a lack of proper care and attention. Several football-related incidents have led court proceedings and findings of guilt on the grounds of negligence. *Keynotes* After part of a stand collapsed at **Blackburn Rovers' Ewood Park** ground in 1896, injuring five people, a court judgement was made in favour of the spectators on the grounds of negligent construction for which the club committee members were made personally liable (one spectator won £25 compensation). Factual evidence uncovered by the **Popplewell Committee of Inquiry** into the 1985 **Bradford City fire** led to court action (*Fletcher and Britton v Bradford City AFC* and others). These proceedings found in favour of the fire's victims due to negligence on the part of the club and the local Fire Authority. Also in 1985, a player injured by foul play sued for wrongful assault and negligence (*Condon v Basi*, 1985). The case was proved and the decision upheld by the Court of Appeal on the grounds that the duty owed by one competitor to play according to the rules was breached on this occasion by violent foul play. In October 1998, **Bradford City** striker Gordon Watson sued **Huddersfield Town** and its defender Kevin Gray on the grounds of negligence following a tackle by Gray which resulted in a double fracture of his opponent's leg during a First Division encounter on 1 February 1997. Watson was supported by his club, which brought similar action for recklessness against both Gray and Huddersfield. Watson was kept out of the game for 18 months following the incident, having joined the club for a then record fee of £575,000 from **Southampton** only a few weeks earlier. Watson's complaint was upheld although the action brought by his club was dismissed. The 27-year-old Watson's victory meant he became the first player in English league football to win damages (£909,143) as a result of the actions of a fellow professional.

Nehoda, Zdenek *player* Striker. **Czechoslovakia** international (90 caps, 31 goals, 1971-87). Born 9 May 1952. *Clubs* **Dukla Prague**, Amaliendorf, SV Darmstadt, **Standard Club Liege**, FC Grenoble Dauphiné. *Keynotes* Nehoda was the most capped player in the former Czechoslovakia's history and its second highest goalscorer; he scored in extra time for his country in the 1976 **European Championship** semi-final against **Netherlands** (3–1), and in the **penalty shoot-out** in the final against West **Germany** (2–2, 5–3 pens.). He also played for the Czechoslovakian side that finished third in the 1980 tournament. *Honours* European Championship (Czechoslovakia, 1976); Czechoslovakian league championship (Dukla Prague, 1977, 1979, 1982).

Nejedly, Oldrich *player* Striker. **Czechoslovakia** international (44 caps, 28 goals, 1931-38). Born 13 December 1909. *Club* **Sparta Prague**. *Keynotes* Nejedly was third-highest goalscorer in the former-Czechoslovakia's history. He was the top scorer in the 1934 **World Cup** finals in Italy (five goals), and scored twice at the 1938 finals. *Honours* World Cup runner-up

(Czechoslovakia, 1934); World Cup **Golden Boot** 1934; **Mitropa Cup** (Sparta Prague, 1935); Czechoslovakia league championship (Sparta Prague, 1932, 1936, 1938).

Nelson *club* former-English league. *Dossier* Ground: Seedhill Ground, Lancashire. Record attendance: 14,979 v **Bradford City** (27 April 1929, Division Three (North)). Best average attendance: 8,795 (1923-24). *Keynotes* Founder members of Division Three (North) in 1921-22, winning the title the following season. Nelson holds the **Football League** record of consecutive away defeats, losing 24 away matches until the club failed **re-election** in 1930-31 and was replaced by **Chester**. *League record* Division Two 1923-24; Division Three (North) 1921-22 to 1922-23, 1924-25 to 1930-31.

Neman Grodno *club* Belarus national league club, founded 1964. Ground: Neman, capacity: 14,000. Belarus Cup 1993.

Nepal *country* AFC kingdom in the Himalayan Mountains, sandwiched between **India** and **China**. Mountainous in the north (including Mount Everest at 8,872 m, 29,108 feet, on the border with China), with Ganges plain in the south. Independence from Britain in 1923. Area: 141,415 sq km (54,585 sq miles). Population: 19,280,000 (1993 est.). Languages: Nepali, Maithir, Bhojpuri and various dialects. Capital: Kathmandu. *Dossier* All-Nepal Football Association (Kathmandu) formed in 1951, affiliated to **FIFA** in 1970 and **Asian Football Confederation** (AFC) in 1971, president: Ganesh Thapa; general secretary: Lok Bahadur Shahi. National stadium: Dasarath Rangashala, Kathmandu, capacity: 35,000. National strip: red shirts, red shorts and red socks. *International tournament record* **Olympic Games** – never qualified for finals tournament; **Women's World Cup** – never entered; **World Cup** – first entered 1986, last in qualifying group first round in 1986, 1990 and 1998, did not enter in 1994; **Asian Cup of Nations** – first entered 1984, last in qualifying group first round in both 1984 and 1988, did not enter in 1992, failed to qualify for finals tournament again in 1996; **Asian Games** – first entered 1954, never past first round; **Asian Women's Football Championship** – first entered 1986; **South Asian Gold Cup** – semifinal 1995 (1–2, v **Sri Lanka**, in Sri Lanka), semifinal/fourth 1999 (0-2 v Maldives, in India) hosts 1997; South Asian Confederation Games – winners twice, runners-up once; **Under-17 World Championship** – never qualified; **World Youth Cup** (under-20) – never qualified. *Record against British and Irish national team* none played. *History* A Kathmandu regional football association was founded in 1951 and, in 1973, the All-Nepal Football Association (ANFA) took overall control of the country's 20 regional associations. A semi-professional domestic league, the ANFA League, began in 1996. Disaster struck at the Dasarath Rangashala, Kathmandu, in March 1988: more than 100 people died and 300 were injured in a stadium disaster. The spectators were crushed as the crowd rushed towards the locked stadium exits to take cover from a hailstorm. Nepal suffered its biggest World Cup defeat in 1990, a 0–9 defeat by **South Korea** (15 May 1990, in Seoul, World Cup qualifier). *League system* The ANFA League has a complex structure. Each of the 20 regional associations holds its own competition in the first part of the season; the winners from each region (including the top four clubs from the Kathmandu league), plus the Army and Police select teams, play in four groups. The top two clubs in each of the four groups go into an eight-club knockout tournament: the winning club is declared national champions and qualifies for the **Asian Cup-winners Cup**. The first championship, in 1997, was won by the Tribhuwan Army Club, followed by Mahendra Police in 1998. The qualifying berth for the **Asian Champion Teams Cup** goes to the winners of the 12-club Kathmandu league. *Record in international club tournaments* Asian Champion Teams Cup – Kathmandu SC, Mahendra Police, New Road Team (NRT Club), Ranipokhari and Manang Marsyangdi have all played but failed to progress beyond first round or first-round group stage; Asian Cup-winners Cup – Tribhuwan Army Club played in the 1997 tournament but was defeated in the first round.

net *n.* the wide mesh fitted to the back of the **crossbar** and **goalposts**, and secured to the pitch, essentially to capture the ball when a **goal** (sense **2.**) is scored – helping to establish that the ball did, in fact, cross the line between the goalposts and under the crossbar. The term net is often used to describe the entire **goal** (sense **1.**) The **Laws of the game** do not, themselves, make nets compulsory. An obligation to supply nets may, however, be stipulated by the **competition rules** of a particular league or tournament. *Keynotes* Developed and patented by Liverpool-based City engineer J A Brodie in 1890 and were described as "a huge pocket into which the ball goes when a goal is scored". Goal nets made one of their first appearances in January 1891 at the Town Ground (home at the time of **Nottingham Forest**) for a representative match between teams from the North and the South of England. The **FA Cup** final that year between **Blackburn Rovers** and **Notts County** at the Kennington Oval was the first to use goal nets, although the **Football Association** did not officially sanction their use until February 1892. **Raith Rovers**' 1894-95 **Scottish FA Cup** victory over Fifth King's Rifle Volunteers (6–3, first round) was replayed by order of the Scottish FA after Raith, the home club, provided no goal nets – it lost the second encounter (3–4). The design of goal nets has changed over the years. In the 1960s and 1970s, it was common for goal nets to be supported by angled metal **stanchions**. Stanchions would either be full-length, from the crossbar to the ground, or a 45-degree corner stanchion attached to cross bar and post; nets would be pegged around the bottom. On occasions, however, stanchions have been problematic. **Chelsea**'s Alan Hudson was attributed with scoring a goal in a **Division One** match against **Ipswich Town** on 26 September 1970, although the ball actually hit the outside   of

the metal stanchion and bounced back into play. The referee, Roy Capey, awarded a "goal" rather than a goal-kick to Ipswich in the belief that the ball had struck the stanchion inside of the goal. Although the BBC's **Match of the Day** television cameras clearly showed that it was not a goal, a Football League statement said: "It would be impossible to order a replay, as Ipswich are suggesting, because the Laws of the Game state categorically that the referee's decision on all matters is final" (see **phantom goals**, **rematch**). It is now more common for nets to be suspended by taut (or elasticated) ropes attached to two or three independent posts with pegs around the bottom. At **Real Madrid**'s **Bernabéu Stadium** the goal nets and posts are supported by the perimeter fencing. Before the club's **Champions League** semi-final first leg match with **Borussia Dortmund** the fencing at the south end gave way under the weight of supporters climbing on it, forcing the goal to collapse and delaying the kick-off by 75 minutes – a freestanding goal from Real's training ground was eventually erected to allow the match to start (1 April 1998). **The Union of European Football Associations** subsequently instructed Real to play its next two home European ties at least 190 miles away from Bernabéu Stadium and fined the club £512,000 as punishment for the incident. Although most goal nets are white, some clubs have introduced coloured nets that reflect their team colours. For example, the goal nets at **Norwich City**'s **Carrow Road**'s goal nets are yellow and green, while **Celtic Park**'s are green and white.

net gate receipts *n. pl.* see **gate receipts.**

Netherlands (also called Holland) *country* UEFA kingdom in west Europe on the North Sea, and bordered by **Belgium** and **Germany**. Around two-fifths of the land is reclaimed from the sea. Occupied by Germany in **World War II**. Founder member of the European Union. Area: 41,160 sq km (15,890 sq miles). Population: 15,420,000 (1995 census). Language: Dutch. Capital: Amsterdam (Government based in The Hague). *Dossier* Football association (Koninklijke Nederlandsche Voetbalbond, Zeist), formed in 1889, affiliated to **FIFA** in 1904 (founder member) and founder member of the **Union of European Football Associations** (UEFA) in 1954, president: Dr M Sprengers; general secretary: Harry Been. Season played from August to May. National stadium: Olympisch Stadion, Amsterdam, capacity: 59,000. National strip: orange shirts, white shorts and orange socks. Website: *http://www.soccer.boa.nl/natelf.html* (national team site). National team nickname: de Oranje. First international game: 30 April 1905 v Belgium (4–1, Antwerp, Belgium, friendly). Biggest victories: 9–0 v **Finland** (4 July 1912, in Stockholm, Sweden, **Olympic Games** third/fourth playoff; Vos scored five of the goals); and 9–0 v **Norway** (1 November 1972, Rotterdam, **World Cup** qualifier). Biggest defeat: 2–12 v **England** (21 December 1907, Darlington, England, friendly). Most capped players: Ruud **Krol** (83 appearances, 1969–83), Ronald Koeman (77 appearances,

1983-1995), Aaron Winter (77 appearances, 1987-), Frank Rijkaard (73 appearances, 1981–94), Hans van Breukelen (72 appearances, 1980–92), Jan Wouters (70 appearances, 1982-1994), Dennis **Bergkamp** (668appearances, 1990-), Ruud **Gullit** (66 appearances, 1981–1994). Leading goalscorers: Dennis Bergkamp (36 goals, 1990-), Faas Wilkes (35 goals, 1946–61), Johan **Cruyff** (33, 1966–77), Abe Lenstra (33 goals, 1940–59), Bep Bakhuys (28 goals, 1928–37), Kick Smit (26 goals, 1934–46), Marco **van Basten** (24 goals, 1983–92). Other notable international players: Frank and Ronald **de Boer**, Johan **Neeskens**, Robby Rensenbrink, Johnny Rep. *International tournament record* Olympic Games – third/bronze medal, 1908 (2–0, v **Sweden**, in London, third/fourth play-off; lost 0–4 v eventual winners England in semi-final), third/bronze medal 1912 (9–0, v Finland, in Stockholm, third/fourth play-off; lost 1–4 v **Denmark** in semi-final), third/bronze medal 1920 (1–3 v **Spain**, in Antwerp, second/third play-off; lost 0–3 v eventual winners Belgium in semi-final), fourth 1924 (1–1, 1-3 replay, v Sweden, in Paris, third/fourth play-off; lost 1–2 v eventual winners **Uruguay** in semi-final); World Cup – runners-up 1974 (1–2 v West **Germany**, in Munich, Germany) and 1978 (1–3, v **Argentina**, in Buenos Aires, Argentina), semi-final/fourth 1998 (1–2, v **Croatia**, in Paris, third/fourth playoff), quarter-final 1994, also qualified for finals tournament 1934, 1938, 1990; **European Championship** – winners 1988 (2–0 v **Soviet Union**, in Munich, Germany), third place 1976 (3–2 v **Yugoslavia**, in Zagreb, third/fourth play-off), semi-final 1992, quarter-final 1996, also qualified for finals tournament 1980, co-hosts 2000 (with Belgium); **Under-17 World Championship** – never qualified; **World Youth Cup** (under-20) – quarter-final 1983, also qualified 1995; **Women's World Cup/ European Championship for Women** – see **Netherlands, women**. *World Cup performance* (finals and qualifiers to end of 1998 tournament) played 108, won 58, drawn 27, lost 22, scored 225 goals, conceded 97 goals; win rate: 54%; goals scored per game: 2.08. *Record against British and Irish national teams* v England, played 13, won three, drawn five, lost five; v **Northern Ireland**, played five, won two, drawn two, lost one; v **Scotland**, played 13, won five, drawn three, lost five; v **Wales**, played five, won five, drawn none, lost none; v **Republic of Ireland**, played 15, won nine, drawn one, lost five. *History* The country is registered as the Netherlands with FIFA, though is often known as Holland. Football was introduced in the 1860s, supposedly by English textile workers. Haarlemse FC of Amsterdam was Holland's first club, founded in 1879. One of the oldest existing clubs, **Sparta Rotterdam**, was founded in 1888. Netherlands has the second-oldest football association in continental Europe, founded in 1889 (the same year as Denmark). Its league and cup competitions date from 1898 and 1899, respectively, although the current national league, the Eredivisie, started in 1956-57.

Professional football was officially introduced in 1956. Dutch clubs have been in 15 major European club competition finals (**European Cup, Cup-winners Cup** and **UEFA/Fairs Cup**), winning 10 (they lag behind England, **Italy**, Spain and Germany in European competition success). Amsterdam club **Ajax** were **World Club Cup** winners in 1972 and European Cup winners three years running – 1971, 1972, 1973 – and again in 1995. Leading Dutch internationals Johan Cruyff, Gerry Muhren and Johan Neeskens played in all three of the 1970s European Cup winning sides. Ajax, coached by Rinus **Michels**, pioneered the **total football** playing system during this era: Michels also coached the national side that reached the World Cup final in 1974, applying the same principles to the Dutch squad. Ajax is one of only four clubs to have won all three major European titles (along with **Juventus, Bayern Munich** and **Barcelona**). Ajax's club rivals **Feyenoord** were European champions in 1970 – the first Dutch club to win the trophy – with **PSV Eindhoven** winners in 1988. Despite Dutch football's reputation of being dominated by the "big three" clubs (Ajax, Feyenoord and PSV), the Dutch league is the holder of the world-record sequence of 11 seasons when the title was won by 11 different clubs: 1943 **ADO Den Haag**; 1944 De Volewijckers; 1945 not held; 1946 Haarlem; 1947 Ajax; 1948 BVV Hertogenbosch (now FC Den Bosch); 1949 SVV Schiedam; 1950 Limburg Brunssue; 1951 PSV Eindhoven; 1952 **Willem II Tilburg**; 1953 RCH Haarlem; 1954 Eindhoven. This beat the previous best sequence of nine different champions in nine seasons (1919 to 1927). Nevertheless, the big three clubs have dominated the professional Eredivisie (premier league): since 1960, the league championship has been won by a club outside these three on only two occasions: 1964 (DWS Amsterdam) and 1981 (**AZ 67 Alkmaar**). Club football has been hampered by a continual emigration of Dutch players, particularly to the Spanish, Italian and English leagues. This is partly blamed on the lack of club competition in Netherlands and the financial disincentives – by way of high taxation – for players to stay at Dutch clubs. Compulsory club **membership schemes** were introduced in 1996-97 in an effort to combat **hooliganism**: spectators must hold a club membership card in order to see premier league matches. **All-seater stadiums** became compulsory at premier league grounds for the start of the 1998-99 season. Netherlands played its first international game: in 1905 (above) and its first competition match in 1908: it was given a bye straight into the semi-final of the Olympic Games (0–4, v England, at White City, London, 22 October 1908). Netherlands was bronze medalist in three consecutive Olympic Games football tournaments, 1908, 1912 and 1920. Holland's only major international title was the 1988 European Championship: a 2–0 victory against the Soviet Union. The 1988 winning team included the famous and immensely gifted trio of Marco van Basten, Ruud Gullit and Frank Rijkaard, with Gullit and van Basten scoring the goals. The trio played their club football in Italy for **Milan**. Netherlands has twice been the losing finalist in the World Cup, losing on each occasion to the home nation: in 1974 against West Germany – with another famous trio, Cruyff, Neeskens and Johnny Rep – and in 1978 against Argentina. At the 1998 World Cup finals in France, Netherlands lost on penalties in the semi-final against **Brazil** (1–1, 2–4 pens., in Marseille). Netherlands also lost on penalties in the semi-final of the 1992 European Championship semi-final 1992 (2–2, 4–5 pens., v eventual winners Denmark, in Gothenburg), and again in the quarter-final in 1996 (0–0, 4–5 pens., v **France**, in England). Netherlands co-hosts the 2000 European Championship finals with Belgium. *World Cup final teams and scorers* 1974 (runners-up): Jongbloed (goalkeeper), Suurbier, Rijsbergen (De Jong), Haan, Krol, Jansen, Neeskens (1), Van Hanegem, Rep, Cruyff, Rensenbrink (R Van de Kerkhof); 1978 (runners-up): Jongbloed (goalkeeper), Krol, Poortvliet, Brandts, Jansen (Suurbier), W Van de Kerkhof, Neeskens, Haan, Rep (Nanninga (1)), Rensenbrink, R Van de Kerkhof. *European Championship winning team and scorers* 1988: Van Breukelen (goalkeeper), Van Aerle, Rijkaard, R Koeman, Van Tiggelen, Vanenburg, Wouters, Muhren, E Koeman, Gullit (1), Van Basten (1). *League system* Eighteen clubs play in the national premier league, the Eredivisie. Three points are awarded for a victory, with one for a draw: final positions for clubs level on points are determined by **goal difference**. The bottom club is automatically relegated to the first division, the Eerste Divisie, with the first-division champions automatically promoted. The remaining two promotion/relegation places are decided by a playoff system (the Nacompetitie), played in June. There are two playoff groups of four clubs, played as mini-leagues, the clubs playing each other at home and away. The two group winners qualify for the next season's premier league. While the competition itself is straightforward, the composition of the groups is complex, with six clubs coming from the first division and two from the premier league. The first-division season is divided into quarters: the clubs heading the table at the end of the first, second and third periods qualify for the playoffs, along with the runners-up and third-placed clubs at the end of the season. However, if any of these "period champions" also feature in the top three positions at the end of the season (as is usually the case), the remaining places are taken by the fourth, fifth, and if necessary, sixth and seventh-placed clubs. The six first division clubs are joined in the playoffs by the 16th- and 17th-placed teams in the premier league; one in each group. There are 18 clubs in the first division, from which there is no relegation. The Dutch Cup involves premier league, first division and amateur league clubs, with the final played in May. An amateur league championship is decided by an end-of-season playoff between the Sunday league and Saturday league champions. *Record in international club tournaments* World Club Cup – Ajax (winners 1972, 1995), Feyenoord (winners 1970); European Cup – Ajax (winners 1971, 1972, 1973 and 1995, runners-up 1969, 1996, semi-final 1980, 1997), Feyenoord (winners 1970, semi-final 1963), PSV Eindhoven (winners 1988, semi-final 1976, champions league 1993); UEFA Cup/Fairs Cup – Ajax (winners 1992), Feyenoord (winners 1974) and PSV Eindhoven (winners 1978), AZ 67 Alkmaar (runners-up 1981) and **FC Twente Enschede** (runners-up 1975, semi-final 1973); **European Cup-winners Cup** – Ajax (winners 1987, runners-up 1988), Feyenoord (semi-final, 1981, 1992), PSV Eindhoven (semi-final, 1975) and FC Twente Enschede (semi-final 1978); **European Supercup** – Ajax (winners 1972, 1973, 1996). Other leading clubs: Sparta Rotterdam, ADO Den Haag, Willem II Tilburg, **Go Ahead Eagles**, **Roda JC Kerkrade**, **FC Groningen**, **FC Utrecht**.

Netherlands Antilles   *country* CONCACAF self-governing part of the Netherlands Realm (full-internal autonomy, though remains an overseas region of the **Netherlands**). Comprises two groups of islands in the Caribbean – Curacao and Bonaire, lying off the coast of **Venezuela**, and St Eustatius, Saba and part of St Maarten in the Leeward Islands. Area: 993 sq km (383 sq miles). Population: 191,000. Languages: Dutch, Papiamento (a creole version of Spanish) and English. Capital: Willemstad (Curacao). *Dossier* Football association (Nederlands Antiliaanse Voetbal Unie, Curacao) formed in 1921, affiliated to **FIFA** in 1932 and founder member of **Confederación Norte-Centroamericana y del Caribe de Fútbol** (CONCACAF) in 1961, president: Andres Constansia; general secretary: Stanley Coffy. Season played from August to February. National stadium: Korsou, Willemstad, capacity: 12,000. National strip: white shirts with red and blue stripes, white shorts and red, white and blue hooped socks. Best victory: 2–1 v **Mexico** (April 1963, San Salvador, El Salvador, **CONCACAF Championship** first round group) *International tournament record* **World Cup** – reached second round of the qualifying tournament in 1962, 1974 and 1990; **Caribbean Nations Cup** – third in its first-round group 1998; **CCCF Championship** – runners-up 1960 (a final league of five nations, held in Havana, Cuba, with the Netherlands Antilles finishing level on points with winners Costa Rica, the tournament decided on goal difference); **Central American and Caribbean Games** – winners 1950 and 1962; CONCACAF Championship – third place 1963 (held in San Salvador, El Salvador, the final round was decided on a league of four nations), third place 1969 (in San Jose, Costa Rica, final league of six nations); fifth 1965 (in Guatemala City, Guatemala); **Gold Cup** – never qualified; **Under-17 World Championship** – never qualified; **World Youth Cup** (under-20) – never qualified. *Record against British and Irish national teams* none played. *Record in international club tournaments* **CONCACAF Champions Cup** – **Jong Colombia** (runners-up 1967, 1979); **CONCACAF Cup-winners Cup** – Jong Colombia (semi-final/fourth 1995). Other leading clubs: Sport Unie Brion Trappers (Curacao), Sithoc (Curacao) and Juventus.

Netherlands, women *country/women* women's football in the Netherlands is administered by the national football association, the Koninklijke Nederlandsche Voetbalbond (KNVB), Zeist. *History* Women's football was first played in Netherlands in the 19th century. Its development, however, was suppressed by the national association. In 1896, for example, **Sparta Rotterdam**'s attempt to organise a women's fixture against an **England XI** was scuppered by the KNVB. Like the German and English associations, the KNVB imposed a ban, in 1955, on women's fixtures being staged at grounds affiliated to the national association. In the same year, however, a national women's association, the Dutch Ladies Soccer Association, was established, along with a national league of 14 clubs. Women's football came under the auspices of the KNVB in 1971, following a recommendation by the **Union of European Football Associations** in November 1971 (see **women's football**). By 1996, there were around 1,000 women's teams. *Dossier* First international match: September 1956, v West **Germany**, 1–2, in Essen. First official international match: November 1973, v England (0–1, in Reading). *International tournament record* **Women's World Cup** – entered first tournament in 1991, never qualified for finals tournament; **European Championship for Women**, entered first tournament in 1982-84, quarter final 1989, 1991 and 1993. Leading club: SV Saestum.

netto *informal* take-home pay (after tax and deductions).

network *misc.* Italian term for the merger of a football club with a large corporation, such as the 1986 purchase of **AC Milan** by Silvio Berlusconi's Fininvest corporation.

Neuchâtel Xamax FC *club* Swiss national league club based in Neuchâtel, founded 1970 (after merger of FC Neuchâtel with Cantonal Neuchâtel). Ground: Maladiere, capacity: 20,000. Strip: red and black striped shirts, black shorts. Swiss league champions 1916 (as Cantonal, note: three regional leagues operated until 1933, with the national championship decided by an inter-league playoff), 1987, 1988; Swiss Cup runners-up 1950 (as Cantonal), 1974, 1985, 1990.

neutral assistant referee *rules* assistant **referee** appointed from the international list of assistant referees to officiate at **international "A" matches**. He or she must be from a neutral country.

neutral venue *regulations* a ground that is not the home stadium of either of the teams involved in a fixture. *Keynotes* Neutral venues are commonly stipulated under **competition rules** for cup finals and **playoffs** and, occasionally, by order of a governing body as a disciplinary sanction against a particular club (eg as a punishment for crowd trouble). Neutral venues may also be used simply because there is no other practical choice: **Albania**, for example, was forced to play its "home matches" for the 1998 **World Cup** qualifying tournament in **Spain** because of the civil war in its own country. *Regulations* **Football League** clubs decide which

team will wear its **home strip** for a match at a neutral venue by mutual agreement or by **tossing a coin** (Football League regulation 35). Where two **Scottish Football League** clubs are engaged in a match at neutral venue both clubs must change their strips if their colours are similar (Scottish Football League rule 66). Clubs which host matches played under the auspices of the Scottish Football League are entitled to 15% of the **gate receipts** if its ground is used as a neutral venue (Scottish Football League rule 42).

New Brighton *club* former-English league. *Dossier* Ground: Sandheys Park and Tower Athletic Ground, New Brighton, Merseyside. Record attendance: 14,291 v **Tranmere Rovers** (Tower Athletic Ground, 21 September 1946, Division Three (North)). Best average attendance: 6,861 (1948-49). *Keynotes* Joined the **Football League** with the expansion of the Northern and Southern sections in 1923-24. The club finished third in Division Three (North) in 1924-25 – its highest League position. New Brighton failed re-election in 1950-51, finishing bottom and being the worst-supported League club. It was replaced by **Workington**. *League record* Division Three (North) 1923-24 to 1950-51.

New Brighton Tower *club* former English league. *Dossier* Ground: Tower Atletic Grounds, New Brighton, Merseyside. Record attendance: 10,000. Best average attendance: 3,575 (1898-99). *Keynotes* Elected to the **Football League** in 1898-99. The club played three seasons in Division Two, finishing fourth in 1900-01 – its highest League position. Tower folded after resigning its League status at the end of the 1900-01 season. *League record* Division Two 1898-99 to 1900-01.

New Caledonia *country associate member of OFC* Group of islands in the south Pacific between **Australia** and **Fiji**. A French Overseas Territory. Area: 19,105 sq km (7,375 sq miles). Population: 164,173. Language: French. Capital: Nouméa. *Dossier* Football association is not affiliated to **FIFA**, and is only an associate member of the **Oceania Football Confederation** (OFC). Hosted the second **Oceania Cup** in 1980. Biggest victory: 8–0 v **Papua New Guinea** (February 1980, Noumea, Oceania Cup group stage). Biggest defeat: 0–8 v Australia (February 1980, Noumea, Oceania Cup group stage). Notable international player: Christian Karembeu – a World Cup winner with **France** in 1998 – is from New Caledonia. He was **Oceania Footballer of the Year** in 1995. *International tournament record* **World Cup** – never entered; Oceania Cup – entered first tournament in 1973, third 1973 (2–1 v New Hebrides (now **Vanuatu**) in New Zealand, third/fourth play-off), 1980 (as hosts, 2–1, v Fiji, in Noumea, third/fourth play-off); **Olympic Games** – never entered; **Women's World Cup** – never entered. *Record against British and Irish national teams* none played. **League system** Ten clubs compete in each of three regional leagues. The national championship is decided by a playoff competition.

New Den *ground* English football ground situated in south London; home of **Millwall**. *Dossier* Ground capacity: 20,146 all seated. Pitch dimensions: 100m x 68m. Record attendance: 20,093 v **Arsenal** (10 January 1994, **FA Cup**, third round). *History* The New Den was opened by former Labour Party leader John Smith on 4 August 1993 (v **Sporting Lisbon**, friendly) and the ground is named after the club's previous home the **Den**. Situated on the site of former playing fields called Senegal Fields and close to London Bridge station, the New Den is only 400 metres from its predecessor. Built at a cost of £15.5 million on land freely given by Lewisham Council, which had been trying to relocate the club since 1988, the ground contains a council-run sports centre consisting of a **créche**, five-a-side pitches and a bar. Millwall received £3.75 million towards the costs of construction from the **Football Trust** – at the time the largest grant to one club. The stadium is the first in the UK to outsource its facilities management to a third party. On 2 December 1998, Millwall was found guilty by the **Football Association** of failing to control its fans and warned about its future conduct, following a series of **pitch invasions** at the New Den during the Second Division match against **Manchester City** on 29 September that year.

New England Revolution *club* United States football club and founder member of **Major League Soccer**, based in Boston, Massachusetts. Member of the league's **Eastern Conference**. Founded: 1996. Ground: Foxboro Stadium (Foxboro), capacity: 60,310. Notable player: Alexi Lalas.

New Radiant *club* Maldives national league club. **Asian Champion Teams Cup** quarter-final 1997; **Asian Cup-winners Cup** quarter-final 1996; Maldives league champions 1995, 1997; Maldives Cup 1994, 1996, 1997, 1998.

New Zealand *country OFC* Commonwealth nation in the south Pacific, south-east of **Australia**. Comprises North and South Islands and several smaller islands. Became a dominion in 1907, though the British monarch is still head of state. The South Island is mainly mountainous. Area: 265,150 sq km (102,350 sq miles). Population: 3,660,000 (1996 census). Languages: English and Maori. Capital: Wellington. *Dossier* Football association (Soccer New Zealand, Auckland) formed in 1891 affiliated to **FIFA** in 1948 and **Oceania Football Confederation** (OFC) in 1966, president: Jock Irvine; general secretary: F John Morton. Season played from October to May. National stadium: Mount Smart, Auckland, capacity: 45,000. National strip: white shirts with black trim, white shorts and white socks. Nickname: The All Whites. Biggest victory: 13–0 v **Fiji** (16 August 1981, Auckland, **World Cup** qualifier – the second highest margin of victory in a World Cup match; the record is held by **Iran**). Notable international players: Wynton Rufer (member of **Werder Bremen**'s German league championship-winning team in 1993), Sumner and Wooddin (the two scorers of New Zealand's only goals in a World Cup finals tournament – in the 2–5 defeat by **Scotland**, 15 June 1982, in Malaga, Spain). *International tournament record* **Olympic**

Games – never qualified for finals tournament; World Cup – first entered 1970, qualified from Asia-Oceania groups for finals tournament in 1982 (finished last in its first-round group of four, with no points, behind **Brazil**, **Soviet Union** and Scotland); **Oceania Cup** 1973 (2–1, v **Tahiti** (French Polynesia), in New Zealand), 1998 (1–0, v Australia, in Australia); **Under-17 World Championship** – qualified for finals tournament 1997; **World Youth Cup** (under-20) – never qualified; **Women's World Cup/Asian Women's Championship/Oceania Women's Tournament** – see **New Zealand, women**. *World Cup performance* (finals and qualifiers to end of 1998 tournament) played 54, won 23, drawn 12, lost 19, scored 119 goals, conceded 70 goals; win rate 43%; goals scored per game 2.20. *Record against British and Irish national teams* v **England**, played two, lost two; v Scotland, played one, lost one. *History* Football was introduced by the British in the 19th century, with the original football association formed in 1891. The first national competition, the Brown Shield, was a challenge competition for the various provincial football associations; first won by Wellington in 1892 (9–2, v Canterbury). The competition has continued in various forms, and is now played whenever there is a challenger to the holders. A second competition for provincial associations was started in 1926, with a trophy presented by the English **Football Association** – the Football Association Trophy. A national league was inaugurated in 1970 (local leagues existed before then), with the winners receiving the original Football Association Trophy (replaced in 1984 by a sponsor's trophy). The premier national cup competition, the Chatham Cup, has been competed for since 1923, when a trophy was donated by the British ship HMS Chatham. It was modelled on the English **FA Cup** and was first won by Seacliff (of Dunedin, 4–0, v YMCA of Wellington). New Zealand hosted the first Oceania Cup in 1973 (17–24 February 1973). Aside from winning the 1973 and 1998 Oceania Cup, New Zealand's best international achievement was in qualifying for the World Cup finals in 1982, in Spain: although it lost all three games, conceded 12 goals and scored only two. It has scored an average 2.20 goals per game in all its World Cup matches – and is third in the all-time **World Cup goal-scoring averages**, behind Germany and Brazil. *League system* Three points awarded for a win with one for a draw. Twelve clubs compete in the North Island Soccer League; the bottom club is automatically relegated, the 11th-placed club enters a playoff with the top two regional league clubs. There is a separate South Island Soccer League with eight clubs in the top flight. Championship playoffs introduced in 1993. Leading clubs: **Christchurch United**, **Mount Wellington**, **Napier City Rovers**, **North Shore United**, **Waitakere City**.

New Zealand, women *country/women* women's football in New Zealand is governed by the Women's Soccer Association of New Zealand, Christchurch, affiliated to the national football association, Soccer New

Zealand. Association football is one of the most popular women's team games in the country, with more than 8,500 senior and youth players. Women's football is well organised at national and junior level, with schoolgirl, under-17, under-20 and senior national teams. *History* In 1980, New Zealand joined **Australia**, **Fiji** and **Papua New Guinea** in founding the Oceania Women's Football Association. The national team won the first **Asian Women's Championship** in 1975 (the only time it has entered), and qualified for the first **Women's World Cup** in China in 1971. *League system* Women's football is organised by regional leagues, though there is a national knockout competition. *International tournament record* Women's World Cup – entered first tournament in 1991, qualified for finals tournament 1991 (last in its group of four with no points from its three games), runners-up in the Oceania qualifying group 1995 (behind Australia) and again in 1999 qualifying tournament; Oceania Women's Tournament (World Cup qualifier) – runners-up 1998 (1–3, v Australia); Asian Women's Championship – winners of the first tournament in 1975 (3–1, v **Thailand**, in Hong Kong); New Zealand has not entered since.

Newcastle United *club* English league. *Dossier* Ground: **St James' Park**, Newcastle-upon-Tyne. Strip: black and white striped shirts, black shorts, black socks. Website: *http://www.newcastle-utd.co.uk* Nickname: Magpies. Ground capacity: 36,843 all seated. Record attendance: 68,386 v **Chelsea** (3 September 1930, Division One). Best average attendance: 56,283 (1947-48). Biggest win: 13–0 v **Newport County** (5 October 1946, Division Two). Biggest defeat: 0–9 v **Bolton Wanderers** (15 April 1895, Division Two). *History* The club was founded in 1881 in the Byker district of Newcastle and initially called Stanley before adopting the name Newcastle East End. Originally, East End played its matches at Heaton, but in May 1892 local rivals Newcastle West End folded and the club took over the lease of St James' Park. East End played its first game at the ground on 3 September 1892 (v **Celtic**, friendly), and, in February 1893, the club changed its name to Newcastle United. The club joined the **Football League** that year and was promoted to Division One five years later. In 1904-05, United won its first League Championship, and over the following five seasons, the club either finished first or fourth in Division One. In addition, between 1905 and 1911, the club reached five **FA Cup** finals (1905, 0–2 v **Aston Villa**; 1906, 0–1 v **Everton**; 1908, 1–3 v **Wolverhampton Wanderers**; 1910, 2–0 replay v **Barnsley**; 1911, 0–1 replay v **Bradford City**), winning the trophy only once. The Newcastle side of the period included James "Gentleman Jim" Howie, **centre-forward** Bill "Cockles" Appleyard and **Ireland** international Bill McCracken, who, along with other quick full-backs of the time, was instrumental in provoking a change to the **offside** law in 1925. A further FA Cup triumph in 1924 was followed by a second League title in 1926-27 – with a team captained by Scottish international striker Hughie

Gallacher, who set a club record of 36 goals during the season. In 1933-34 United was relegated, and missed the drop to Division Three (North) in 1937-38 only on **goal average**, either side of **World War II**. The club returned to the top flight in 1948-49 and, in the early 1950s, it won the FA Cup three times (1951, 1952, 1955), thanks in part to a director-manager, Stan Seymour, and with a side that included striker Jackie **Milburn** and wing-half, and future manager Joe Harvey. Newcastle's consecutive FA Cup wins meant that it became the first club in the 20th century to retain the trophy – **Blackburn Rovers** (1890, 1891, and again in 1884, 1885, 1886) and **Wanderers** (1872, 1873, and again in 1876, 1877, 1878) had achieved the same feat earlier, while **Tottenham Hotspur** twice did the same (1960, 1961 and 1981, 1982). Harvey's return to the club as manager in 1962 was followed by promotion back to the top flight as Division Two Champions in 1964-65. Four years later, with a team captained by Bobby Moncur and including the strike partnership of Wyn Davies and Bryan "Pop" Robson, United won the **UEFA** (Fairs) **Cup**. Despite a **Wembley** appearance in the 1974 FA Cup final (0–3 v **Liverpool**) and victory in the **Anglo-Italian Cup** in 1973 (also the **Texaco Cup** in 1974 and 1975), and a succession of managers, including Osvaldo **Ardiles**, Jack Charlton, Kenny **Dalglish**, Kevin **Keegan**, Gordon Lee and Jim Smith, Newcastle's next 30 years were devoid of major honours. Relegation in 1977-78 was followed by promotion to the top flight in 1984-85 and a further period in Division Two (from 1992-93 Division One) that also included only narrowly missing relegation to what would have been Division Three in 1991-92 for the first time in the club's history. The next season, with Keegan as manager, the club took the Division One title, winning the first 11 matches of the season – a club record. The club's financial difficulties, which resulted from the £5.5 million cost of the replacement for the ground's west stand, led to a four-year power-struggle for United, with Sir John Hall, a local property developer, and his Magpie Group finally wresting control of the club in 1992 from the then chairman, Gordon McKeag. On the club's return to the top flight, United finished third in its first season, and second behind **Manchester United** in 1995-96 and 1996-97. United paid a UK record **transfer fee** of £15 million to bring Alan **Shearer** to St James' Park in July 1996. Keegan sensationally resigned as manager on 8 January 1997, to be replaced, just as he had been as a player at Liverpool nearly 20 years previously, by Kenny Dalglish, who was replaced two games into the 1998-99 season by ex-Chelsea boss Rud **Gullit**. The club reached the FA Cup final in 1998 (0–2 v Arsenal) and again in 1999 (0–2 v Manchester United). In April 1997, Newcastle became a plc and floated on the stock market (flotation price = 135p). Hall's grand plan for the club, although he resigned as club chairman in 1997, is to create a **sporting club** similar to that which exists at **Barcelona**. Hall resigned as chairman in 1997. In March 1998, following press reports of disparaging comments about the club's supporters, Tyneside womenfolk and Alan Shearer, among others, allegedly made by the new chairman Freddie Shepherd and vice-chairman Douglas Hall, the pair resigned as directors of both the club and **Newcastle United plc**, but were reinstated in July 1998. In December 1998, NTL, a Hampshire-based telecommunications business, took a 6% stake in the club and agreed an option to buy a fur-ther 51% share at a later date. NTL abandoned its takeover plans in April 1999 following a Competition Commission ruling to reject BSkyB's proposed pur-chase of Manchester United. *League record* **Premier League** 1993-94–; Division One 1898-99 to 1933-34, 1948-49 to 1960-61, 1965-66 to 1977-78, 1984-85 to 1988-89; First Division 1992-93; Division Two 1893-94 to 1897-98, 1934-35 to 1947-48, 1961-62 to 1964-65, 1978-79 to 1983-84, 1989-90 to 1991-92. *Honours* League 1904-05, 1906-07,1908-09, 1926-27; First Division 1992-93; Division Two 1964-65; FA Cup 1910 (2–0 replay v Barnsley), 1924 (2–0 v Aston Villa – *Team* Bradley, Hampson, Hudspeth, Mooney, Spencer, Gibson, Low, Cowan, Harris (1), McDonald, Seymour (1)), 1932 (2–1 v Arsenal – *Team* McInroy, Nelson, Fairhurst, McKenzie, Davidson, Weaver, Boyd, Richardson, Allen (2), McMenemy, Lang), 1951 (2–0 v **Blackpool** – *Team* Fairbrother (goalkeeper), Cowell, Corbett, Harvey, Brennan, Crowe, Walker, Taylor, Milburn (2), G Robledo, Mitchell), 1952 (1–0 v Arsenal – *Team* Simpson (goalkeeper), Cowell, McMichael, Harvey, Brennan. E Robledo, Walker, Foulkes, Milburn, G Robledo (1), Mitchell), 1955 (3–1 v **Manchester City** – *Team* Simpson, Cowell, Batty, Scoular, Stokoe, Casey, White, Milburn (1), Keeble, Hannah (1), Mitchell (1)); **FA Charity Shield** 1909 (2–0 v **Northampton Town**); **Sheriff of London's Charity Shield** 1907 (5–2 v **Corinthians**); Texaco Cup 1974 (2–1 v **Burnley**), 1975 (3–1 agg. v Southampton); UEFA (Fairs) Cup 1969 (6–2 agg. v **Újpesti Dózsa** – *Team* first leg (home) McFaul, Craig, Clark, Gibb, Burton, Moncur (2), Scott (1), Robson, Davies, Arentoft, Sinclair (Foggon); second leg (away) McFaul, Craig, Clark, Gibb, Burton, Moncur (1), Scott, (Foggon (1)), Arentoft (1), Robson, Davies, Sinclair); Anglo-Italian Cup 1973 (2–1 v **Fiorentina**). *Records* Alf **McMichael** is Newcastle's most-capped player (40 for **Northern Ireland**); Jim Lawrence holds the record for club appearances (432, 1904-22); Jackie Milburn is Newcastle's record league goalscorer (177, 1946-57).

Newcastle United plc *n.* publicly-quoted business which owns **Newcastle United**. The club became a fully listed company on the London Stock Exchange in April 1997 (flotation price = 135p) in September 1995. Newcastle had a market capitalisation – the market value of the company's issued share capital (eg the quoted price of its shares multiplied by the number of shares outstanding) – of £193.4 million on flotation.

Newell's Old Boys (Club Atlético) *club* Argentinean national league club, based in Rosario, founded in 1903 by pupils of the Anglo-Argentine Commercial School.

Ground: Parque Independienca, capacity: 31,000. Strip: red and black halved shirts, black shorts. **Copa Libertadores** runners-up 1988 (1–3 agg., v **Nacional** of Uruguay), 1992 (1–1 agg., 2–3 pens., v **São Paulo**); Argentinean league champions 1974, 1988, 1992. Notable players: Diego **Maradona**, Gabriel **Batistuta**, Amerigo Gallego.

Newport County *club* former-English league. *Dossier* Ground: Somerton Park, Gwent. Record atten-dance: 24,268 v **Cardiff City** (16 October 1937, Division Three (South)). Best average attendance: 12,505 (1946-47). *Keynotes* Formed in 1912 by employees of the Lysaght iron foundry. The club was a founder member of Division Three in 1920-21. Newport played only one season, 1946-47, outside of the bottom two divisions – having won the Division Three (South) Championship on the eve of **World War II** – in its 60-year **Football League** tenure. The club lost its League status for one season in 1931-32 and was relegated to the **Football Conference** in 1987-88 and replaced by **Lincoln City**. Newport's solitary **Welsh Cup** victory in 1980 (5–1 agg. v **Shrewsbury Town**) provided the club with entry into the following season's **European Cup-winners Cup** competition in which it reached the quarter-final (2–3 agg. v **Carl Zeiss Jena**). The club was reformed in 1989 as Newport AFC. *League record* Division Three 1920-21, 1958-59 to 1961-62, 1980-81 to 1987-88; Division Three (South) 1921-22 to 1930-31 (suspended for one season), 1932-33 to 1938-39, 1946-47 to 1957-58; Division Four 1962-63 to 1979-80. *Honours* Division Three (South) 1938-39; Welsh Cup (5–1 agg. v Shrewsbury Town).

Newry Town FC *club* Northern Ireland national league club based in Newry, founded 1923 Ground: the Showgrounds, capacity: 5,000. Strip: blue and white striped shirts, white shorts. Northern Ireland league third place 1928.

Newton Cup *competition* former annual and later occasional fixture between **Uruguay** and **Argentina**, first played 1906, named after an Englishman, Richard Newton. Uruguay won the trophy seven times (1913, 1915, 1917, 1919, 1920, 1924, 1929); Argentina won it 15 times (1906, 1907, 1908, 1911, 1916, 1918, 1924, 1927, 1928, 1937, 1942, 1945, 1968, 1971, 1975; the fixture was drawn on six drawn occasions. See also **Lipton Cup**.

Newtown *club* Welsh league. Ground: Latham Park, Powys. Strip: red shirts, white shorts. Nickname: The Robins. Ground capacity: 5,000. *Keynotes* Formed in 1875. Qualified for the **UEFA Cup** in 1996-97, losing in the first preliminary round (1–7, **Skonta Riga**, agg.) *Honours* **Welsh Cup** 1879 (1–0 v **Wrexham**), 1895 (3–2 v Wrexham).

Nicaragua *country CONCACAF* republic in Central America, on the Caribbean Sea and Pacific Ocean, lying to the south of **Honduras** and to the north of **Costa Rica**. Largest of the Central American republics. Tropical climate. Area: 148,000 sq km (57,130 sq miles). Population: 4,400,000 (1994 est.). Languages: Spanish,

Indian and English. Capital: Managua. Civil war and revolution affected the country throughout the 20th century. *Dossier* Football association (Federación Nicaragüense de Fútbol, Managua) formed in 1931, affiliated to **FIFA** in 1950 and **Confederación Norte-Centroamericana y del Caribe de Fútbol** (CONCACAF) in 1968, president: Julio Rocha Lopez; general secretary: Rolando Lopez Sanders. Season played from September to June. National stadium: Estadio Nacional, Managua, capacity: 30,000. National strip: blue and white striped shirts, blue shorts and blue and white striped socks. *International tournament record* **Women's World Cup** – never entered; **World Cup** – entered for the first time in 1994 and again in 1998, but failed to get past first round of qualifying tournaments; **CCCF Championship** – finished bottom of five nations in 1941 (no points), of four in 1943 (no points), of six in 1946 (two points) and of four in first round group in 1961 (no points); **CONCACAF Championship** – finished bottom of five nations in its first round group in 1963 (no points), of six in 1967 (one point); **Gold Cup** – never qualified; **Under-17 World Championship** – never qualified; **World Youth Cup** (under-20) – never qualified. *Record against British and Irish national teams* none played. *League system* Ten clubs compete in the first division, playing each other three times in the first phase of the season. The national championship (the Campeonato Nacional) is decided by an end-of-season knockout tournament for the top clubs, with a final at the end of May. The bottom four clubs enter a relegation playoff. *Record in international club tournaments* **Diriangen FC** has represented Nicaragua in the **CONCACAF Champions Cup** more than any other club. Other leading clubs: **America FC**, **Juventus FC**, Masachapa, Real Esteli, Walter Ferreti.

Nice *club* see **Olympique Gymnaste Club de Nice**.

Nicholson, Bill *player-manager* Defender/midfield. **England** international (1 cap). Born 26 January 1919. Career ca. 1936-55. *Clubs* (player) **Tottenham Hotspur**. *Honours* League Championship (Tottenham Hotpsur 1950-51); Division Two (Tottenham Hotpsur 1949-50). *Clubs* (manager) Tottenham Hotspur (1958-74). *Honours* League Championship (Tottenham Hotpsur 1960-61); **FA Cup** (1961, 1962, 1967); **League Cup** (1971, 1973); **European Cup-winners Cup** (1963); **UEFA Cup** (1972). *Keynotes* A one-club player and manager with Tottenham Hotspur in a career which spanned more than 40 years. He joined Spurs as an amateur in March 1936, turning professional in August 1938. During **World War II**, Nicholson guested for several clubs, including **Sunderland** and **Newcastle United**. As a player, Nicholson won successive titles, Division Two in 1949-50 and the **Football League** Championship the following season. Nicholson retired in 1955, joining the Spurs coaching staff and, in October 1958, he was appointed manager. Prior to taking up the manager's reins at **White Hart Lane**, Nicholson was part of the England coaching team at the 1958 **World Cup** finals. In his first League match

as manager, Nicholson saw his side beat **Everton** 10-4, in the highest-scoring Division One match this century. Nicholson created one of the finest sides in English football, leading Tottenham to the first League and FA Cup **double** of the 20th century in 1960-61. In his 16-year managerial career, Nicholson won eight major trophies with the club. He left Spurs in August 1974, becoming football consultant at **West Ham United** before returning to White Hart Lane in July 1976 in an administrative capacity.

nickname *n.* informal and unofficial name given to a player or team, either out of affection or in derision. *Keynotes* Brazilian players are the most famous recipients of nicknames, many playing under their pet names. These include former **World Footballer of the Year Zico** (real name Artur Antunes Coimbra), **Bebeto** (real name José Roberto Gama de Oliveira) and, most famously, **Pelé** (real name Edson Arantes do Nascimento). Pelé attributes the name to a childhood taunt from another schoolboy, but does not know what it meant! Ghanaian international Abedi **Pelé** (real name Abedi Ayew), was nicknamed after the star Brazilian. Nicknames are often given by fans to key players in recognition of a spurious trait, such as Psycho (Stuart Pearce), Chopper (Ron Harris) and Razor (Neil Ruddock). Others are given by the press in recognition of an outstanding player or team: Ferenc **Puskás** – the "Galloping Major" – was one of the **Magnificent Magyars**, the notable Hungarian national team of the 1950s; Austrian international Ernst **Ocwirk** was nicknamed "Clockwork Ocwirk" after his display against England in 1951. The post-war Swedish forward trio of Gunnar **Gren**, Gunnar **Nordhal** and Nils **Liedholm** came to be known as the **Gre-no-li** by appreciative **AC Milan** supporters. Club nicknames often have their origins in a local industry or landmark: Toffees – Everton, after the Ancient Everton Toffee House, said to have been opposite the ground; Cobblers – Northampton, because of the local shoe and boot industry; and Hatters – Luton, because of the millinery industry. **Reading**'s **Elm Park** was originally owned by biscuit manufacturer, Huntley and Palmer, and until the company departed from the town in 1974 the club's nickname was the "Biscuitmen". Some are more obscure **Peterborough United**'s nickname, the Posh, is derived from the club's formation. In 1921, the manager of Fletton United is reported to have said that he wanted "Posh players for a Posh new team" and the moniker stuck when Peterborough & Fletton United was established in 1923. For a time **Burnley** was known as the "Royalites" after Prince Albert saw the club's local derby with **Bolton Wanderers** at **Turf Moor** in October 1886 – which is believed to be the first occasion that a member of the British royal family attended a football match. In 1884, Bolton Wanderers sported a strip consisting of white shirts with red spots and the nickname "The Spots" remained for many years. **Darlington**'s Quaker nickname is derived from John Beaumont Pease, a Quaker and slavery abolitionist, who was the original owner of the club's **Feethams**

Ground. **Chelsea** changed its nickname from the Pensioners – after the local nursing home for retired military veterans – to the unimaginative Blues in an attempt to modernise its image. Some of the most evocative nicknames are those of the various African national teams: Desert Warriors (**Algeria**); Black Panthers (**Angola**); Zebras (**Botswana**); Indomitable Lions (**Cameroon**); Red Devils (**Congo**); Leopards (**Congo Democratic Republic**); Pharoes (**Egypt**); Scorpions (**Gambia**); Black Stars (**Ghana**); Elephants (**Ivory Coast**); Crocodiles (**Lesotho**); Lone Star (**Liberia**); Eagles (**Mali**); Atlas Lions (**Morocco**); Mambas (**Mozambique**); Desert Rats (**Namibia**); Super Eagles (**Nigeria**); Lions (**Senegal**); Bafana Bafana (**South Africa**); Cranes (**Uganda**); Mighty Zambia (**Zambia**); and Warriors (**Zimbabwe**). **Jamaica**'s nickname, Reggae Boyz, is said to have been coined in 1995 by a journalist when the team travelled to Africa to play Zambia in a friendly.

Nielsen, Poul *player* Striker. **Denmark** international (38 caps, 52 goals, 1910-25). Born 25 December 1891. *Club* KB. *Keynotes* Nicknamed Tist, Poul Nielsen is Denmark's all-time top scorer, with 52 goals in only 38 matches (1.37 goals per match). He made his international debut as an 18-year-old on 5 May 1910 against **England** amateurs (2–1, in Copenhagen, friendly). *Honours* **Olympic Games** silver medal (Denmark, 1912).

Nielsen, Sophus *player* Striker. **Denmark** international *Keynotes* Scored a world international record 10 goals in one match (17–1, Denmark v France, 22 October 1908, White City, London, **Olympic Games** semi-final). *Honours* Olympic Games silver medal (Denmark, 1908).

Niger *country CAF* republic in west Africa, bordered by **Benin**, **Burkina Faso**, **Chad**, **Libya**, **Mali** and **Nigeria**. Landlocked country with much of the land within the Sahara Desert. Independence from **France** in 1960. Drought has caused major hardship to the population, which relies heavily on agriculture. Area: 1,186,410 sq km (457,955 sq miles). Population: 9,460,000 (1996 est.). Languages: French, Hausa, Djerma and other native languages. Capital: Niamey. *Dossier* Football association (Fédération Nigerienne de Football, Niamey) formed in 1967, affiliated to **FIFA** and **Confédération Africaine de Football** (CAF) in 1967, member of the **West African Football Union**, president: Amadou Hima Souley; general secretary: Inoussa Soungaize. Season played from October to July. National stadium: Stade 29 Juillet, Niamey, capacity: 30,000. National strip: orange shirts, white shorts and green socks. First international game: 1967, v Burkina Faso (2–3, Niamey, friendly). Biggest victory: 7–1 v **Mauritania** (14 October 1990, Niamey, **African Cup of Nations** qualifier). Biggest defeat: 1–9 v **Ghana** (21 September 1969, Niamey, African Cup of Nations qualifier). *International tournament record* **Olympic Games** – first entered 1968, never qualified for finals tournament; **Women's World Cup** – never entered. *Record*

against British and Irish national teams none played; **World Cup** – first entered 1978, reached third round of qualifying tournament in 1982 (lost 1–4 agg., v eventual qualifiers **Algeria**); African Cup of Nations – first entered 1970, reached second round of qualifying tournament in 1970 after a walkover against Nigeria, never qualified for finals tournament; **CSSA Zone 3 Championship** – third 1986 (in Ghana). *History* National league started in 1966, first won by **Secteur 6**. *Record in international club tournaments* **African Cup of Champion Clubs** – Olympique Niamey (second round 1978); **African Cup-winners Cup** – Olympic Niamey (second round 1991); **CAF Cup** – Zumunta Athletic Club (quarter final 1993); **West African Football Union General Eyadema Cup** – ASFAN (runners-up 1996), JS Ténéré (runners-up 1998). Other leading clubs: **Sahel FC**, **Liberté**.

Nigeria *country CAF* federal republic in west Africa on the Gulf of Guinea, and bordered by **Benin**, **Cameroon**, **Chad** and **Niger**. The most populous country in Africa. Tropical rainforest in the south, highlands in the east and semi-desert in the north. Oil exports contribute heavily to its wealth. Independence from Britain in 1960, became a republic in 1963. Consists of 30 states. Area: 923,850 sq km (356,605 sq miles). Population: 97,220,000 (1995 est.). Languages: English, Hausa, Yoruba, Ibo and other regional languages. Capital: Abuja (a new town created in the 1970s, that replaced the former capital Lagos in 1992 – Lagos remains the chief port and largest city). *Dossier* Nigeria Football Association (Lagos) formed in 1945, affiliated to **FIFA** and the **Confédération Africaine de Football** (CAF) in 1958, member of the **West African Football Union**, president: Colonel Abdulmumini Aminu; general secretary: Sani Ahmed Toro. Season played from February to November. National stadium: Surulere, Lagos, capacity: 80,000. National strip: green shirts, white shorts and green socks. Website: *http://home5.swipnet.se/~w-58456/* (unofficial). Nickname of national team: Super Eagles. First international game: 1950, v **Ghana** (0–1, Accra, friendly). Biggest victories: 7–1 v **Burkina Faso** (27 July 1991, Lagos, qualifier) and 6–0 v **Ethiopia** (24 July 1993, Lagos, African Cup of Nations qualifier). Biggest defeat: 0–7 v Ghana (0–1, Accra, friendly). Highest crowd: 80,000 v **Algeria** (22 March 1980, Surulere Stadium, Lagos, African Cup of Nations final, see below). Most capped players: Peter Rufai (70 appearances, ca. 1985-; also Nigeria's most-capped goalkeeper). Leading goalscorer: Rashidi **Yekini** (41 goals in 67 appearances, ca. 1981-). Other notable international players: Daniel Amokachi, Emmanuel **Amunike**, Celestine **Babayaro**, Finidi George, Nwankwo **Kanu**, Victor **Ikpeba Nosa**. *International tournament record* **Olympic Games** – winners (gold medal) 1996 (3–2, v **Argentina**, final Atlanta, USA); **Women's World Cup** – entered first tournament in 1991, qualified for final tournament in 1991, 1995 (finished last in first-round groups in both years) and 1999;

World Cup – finals tournament second round 1994 (won its first-round group of four nations), second round 1998 (won its first-round group ahead of **Paraguay**, **Spain** and **Bulgaria**), reached the final round of the African qualifying tournament in 1970, 1978 and again in 1982; African Cup of Nations – winners 1980 (3–0, v **Algeria**, in Lagos), winners 1994 (2–1, v **Zambia**, in Tunis, Tunisia), runners-up 1984 (1–3, v **Cameroon**, in Abidjan, the Ivory Coast), runners-up 1988 (0–1, v Cameroon, in Casablanca, Morocco), runners-up 1990 (0–1, v host nation Algeria, in Algiers), third 1974 (four-nation final round group, Addis Ababa, Ethiopia), third 1978 (awarded third place after third/fourth play-off match against **Tunisia** was abandoned after 30 minutes; 1–2, v **Uganda** in Kumasi, Ghana, semi-final), third 1992 (2–1, v Cameroon, in Dakar, Senegal, third/fourth play-off) joint-hosts 2000; **Afro-Asian Cup of Nations** – winners 1995 (5–2, agg., v **Uzbekistan**); **African Games** – winners 1973 (v Ghana, in Nigeria), runners-up 1978 (v Algeria, in Algeria); **African under-17 championship** – runners-up 1995; **African Women's Tournament** – winners 1998 (2–0, v Ghana, in Lagos); **African Youth Cup/Junior African Nations Cup** (under 20) – winners 1983, 1985, 1987, 1989; **Confederations Cup** (Intercontinental Championship) – fourth place 1995 (1–1, 4–5 pens., v **Mexico**, in Riyadh, Saudi Arabia, third/fourth play-off); **Under-17 World Championship** – winners 1985 (2–0, v West **Germany**, in Beijing, China), winners 1993 (2–1, v Ghana, in Tokyo, Japan), runners-up 1987 (1–1, 1–3 pens., v **Soviet Union**, in Toronto, Canada); **World Youth Cup** (under-20) – runners-up 1989 (0–2, v **Portugal**, in Riyadh, Saudi Arabia), third place 1985, hosts and quarter-final 1999; **All-Africa Games** – hosts 2003. *World Cup performance* (finals and qualifiers to end of 1998 tournament) played 64, won 31, drawn 16, lost 17, scored 106 goals, conceded 70 goals; win rate: 48%; goals scored per game: 1.65. *Record against British and Irish national teams* v **England** – lost one (16 November 1994, 0–1, **Wembley**, friendly). *History* Nigeria is one of the most successful footballing nations in Africa. It has twice qualified for the World Cup finals tournament, and reached the second round in 1994 and 1998. In 1994, it lost 1–2 to an extra-time penalty against **Italy** in the second round in Boston, USA: Italy had equalised in the 89th minute through Roberto **Baggio**, after Amunike had scored in the 26th minute of normal time. In 1998, it again went out in the second round (1–4 v **Denmark**). Nigeria went close to qualifying in three previous tournaments. In 1970 it reached the final, fourth-round, stage of the African qualifying tournament, finishing as runners-up in a three-nation final group, with only one nation qualifying. It also reached the fourth-round final stage in 1978, this time finishing third of three nations, again with just one to qualify. In 1982, Africa was granted two qualifying berths. Nigeria, however, lost to Algeria (1–4 agg.) in the fourth round, final qualifying stage. It has won the

African Cup of Nations twice: as hosts in 1980, 3–0 against Algeria (Segun Odegbami scored twice, Muda Lawal scored the third); and 1994, 2–1 against Zambia, (Emmanuel Amunike scored both goals in the final in Tunis). It has been runners-up on three occasions. Nigeria's two greatest senior victories were, arguably: the 3–0 victory over Bulgaria (the eventual World Cup semi-finalists) in the 1994 World Cup first round (21 June 1994, Dallas, USA); and the 3–2 victory over **Spain** in the 1998 World Cup finals (13 June 1998, in Nantes, France, first round; Adepoju, Lawal and Oliseh scoring for Nigeria). The World Cup campaign was marred, however, by the deaths of five spectators at the home qualifying tie against **Guinea** on 6 April 1997. The deaths occurred as the 40,000 spectators tried to leave Surulere stadium at the end of the game; several of the gates remained closed and the five fans were crushed to death. Nigerian president Sani Abacha, who seized power in a coup on 17 October 1993, instructed the national side to withdraw from the 1996 African Cup of Nations finals tournament in **South Africa**, preventing the team from defending its title. Abacha was reacting to criticism levelled at the country by South African president Nelson **Mandela**, over human rights issues (including Nigeria's execution of the writer Ken Saro-Wiwa and eight other Ogoni activists). Nigeria's withdrawal from the tournament was subsequently punished by CAF, which imposed a two-year ban. In 1996, Nigeria became the first African nation to win the Olympic Games gold medal, beating Argentina 3–2 in the final at Sanford Stadium in Athens, Georgia, USA, in front of 86,117 spectators. Celestine Babayaro, Daniel Amokachi and Amunike scored for Nigeria. Nigeria had already beaten Brazil 4–3 in the semi-final, with Kanu (2), Ikpeba and Brazil's Roberto Carlos (own goal) scoring for Nigeria. Nigeria became the first African nation to win a FIFA world tournament when it won the Under-17 World Championship in 1985 (2–0, v West Germany). The final in Beijing was watched by 80,000 spectators. It won the tournament again in 1993 (2–1, v Ghana). Nigeria is the most successful nation in African women's football. It hosted the World Youth Cup in April 1999 and reached the quarter-final. It qualified for the first Women's World Cup finals in 1991, winning the final of the African qualifying competition (6–0 agg., v Cameroon), but finished bottom of its four-nation first-round group in the finals tournament. It qualified again in 1995, winning the African qualifying competition final (11–2 agg., v South Africa), but again finished bottom of its four-nation first-round group in the finals tournament (including a 0–8 defeat by **Norway**, the eventual winners of the tournament). Nigeria was awarded a bye to the second stage of the 1999 African qualifying tournament because of its success in the 1991 and 1995 tournaments. At club level, the Nigerian FA Challenge Cup was introduced in 1945, with a league founded in 1972. Professional football was officially introduced in 1989, with a professional "Super League" started in 1992. No Nigerian club has won the **African Cup of Champion**

Clubs, though three have reached the final (see below). Three Nigerian clubs have won the **African Cup-winners Cup**, **IICC Shooting Stars**, **Enugu Rangers** and **BCC Lions**. *League system* Eighteen clubs play in the Super League. Three points are awarded for a victory, with one for a draw: final positions for clubs level on points are determined by **goal difference**. *Record in international club tournaments* African Cup of Champion Clubs – Enugu Rangers International (runners-up 1975, semi-final 1976, 1978, 1982), **Iwuanyanwu Nationale** (runners-up 1988, semi-final 1990), IICC Shooting Stars (runners-up 1996), **Bendel Insurance** (semi-final 1980), **Stationery Stores** (semi-final 1993), Eagle Cement (of Port Harcourt, quarter-final "champions-league" stage 1998); African Cup-winners Cup – IICC Shooting Stars (winners 1976), Enugu Rangers (winners 1977), BCC Lions (winners 1990, runners-up 1991), Stationery Stores (runners-up 1981), **Leventis United** (runners-up 1985), Ranchers Bees DIC (runners-up 1988), Bendel United (runners-up 1989), **Julius Berger** (runners-up 1995), El Kanemi Warriors (semi-final 1993), Bendel Insurance (semi-final 19879), Abiola Babes Mashood (semi-final 1987), Katsina (quarter-final 1996); **CAF Cup** – IICC Shooting Stars (winners 1992), Bendel Insurance (winners 1994), Jasper United (semi-final 1997); **West African Football Union General Eyadema Cup** – New Nigeria Bank (winners 1983, 1984, runners-up 1985, 1988), Bendel Insurance (winners 1993, 1994, 1995), IICC Shooting Stars (winners 1999). Other leading club: Udoji United FC (of Awka, league champions 1996).

Ninety Two Club *n.* association of supporters who have visited every every **Premier League** and **Football League** ground. Founded in 1978; the name is derived from the fact that since 1950-51, when the regional bottom two divisions were expanded to 24 clubs each, there have been 92 clubs in the Football League and Premier League.

Ninian Park *ground* Welsh football ground (English league) situated in Cardiff, South Glamorgan; home of **Cardiff City**. *Dossier* Ground capacity: 14,660. Pitch dimensions: 104m x 71m. Record ground attendance: 61,566 **Wales** v **England**, 14 October 1961. Record club attendance: 57,893 v **Arsenal** (22 April 1953, Division One). Best average attendance: 37,933 (1952-53). *History* Cardiff played its first match at Ninian Park on 1 September 1910 (v **Aston Villa**, friendly). Cardiff was granted a seven-year lease on the site by the local council on condition that the club provided guarantees for the £90-a-year rent. Lord Ninian Crichton Stuart, who later became an MP, acted as a guarantor and the ground, which was provisionally called Sloper Park and was built on the site of a rubbish tip, was named in his honour – making it one of only four current **Football League** grounds to be named after an individual (the others being **Dean Court**, Madejski Stadium and **Adams Park**). On 18 January 1937, Ninian Park's main stand

was destroyed by fire after thieves bungled a robbery attempt. Ninian Park staged its first Wales international fixture on 6 March 1911 (v **Scotland**) and up to May 1976, when a pitch invasion (v **former-Yugoslavia**, **European Championship** qualifier, 22 May) led to **UEFA** banning its use for international matches for two years, it had staged 67 Wales games. Thereafter, Ninian Park was no longer the principal Welsh venue, staging only 15 further internationals between 1978 and 1989, when **FIFA** stipulated that **World Cup** matches should be played at all-seater stadiums, forcing the **Football Association of Wales** to play major games at Cardiff Arms Park (home of Welsh rugby). Between 1976 and 1997, Ninian Park's capacity was cut from 46,000 to fewer than 15,000. The first floodlit match at Ninian Park took place on 5 October 1960 (v **Grasshopper-Club Zürich**, friendly).

Nissa Ashkhabad *club* Turkmenistan national league club. Ground: Nissa Stadium. **Asian Champion Teams Cup** third round 1997; Turkmenistan league champions 1996 (in fact, the 1996 season was never completed, but Nissa was allowed to compete in the Asian Champion Teams' Cup in 1997), runners-up 1994, 1995; Turkmenistan Cup 1998, runners-up 1996.

Nithsdale Wanderers *club* former-Scottish league. *Dossier* Ground: Crawick Holm, Sanquar, Dumfries and Galloway. *Keynotes* Played two seasons in **Scottish Football League** Division Two. *League record* Division Two 1925-26 to 1926-27.

Niue *country associate member of OFC* island and self-governing overseas territory of **New Zealand**. Situated in the south Pacific between **Tonga** and the **Cook Islands**. Full internal self-government since 1974. Area: 259 sq km (100 sq miles). Population: 2,250. Capital Alofi. *Dossier* Football association is not affiliated to **FIFA**, but is an associate member of the **Oceania Football Confederation** (OFC).

NK Hajduk Split *club* see **Hajduk Split**.

N'Kkono, Thomas *player* Goalkeeper. **Cameroon** international. *France Football* **African Footballer of the Year** 1979, 1982. Clubs **Canon Yaoundé**, **Espanyol**. *Keynotes* Played in the 1988 **UEFA Cup** final for Espanyol against Bayer Leverkusen (3–3 agg., 2–3 pens.). *Honours* **African Cup of Nations** runner-up (Cameroon, 1986); **African Cup of Champion Clubs** (Canon Yaoundé, 1978, 1980); African Cup-winners Cup (Canon Yaoundé, 1979); Cameroon league championship (Canon Yaoundé, 1979, 1980).

NK Osijek *club* Croatia national league and former-Yugoslavia league club based in Osijek, founded 1947. Ground: Gradski, capacity: 30,000. Strip: white shirts, white shorts.

NK Rijeka *club* Croatia national league and former-Yugoslavia league club based in Rijeka, founded 1946. Ground: Kantrida, capacity: 21,000. Strip: white shirts, white shorts. Former-Yugoslavia Cup 1978, 1979.

Nkana FC (also known as Nkana Red Devils) *club* Zambian national league club based in Kitwe, founded as Rokana Mine, changed name to Rokana United and later Nkana Red Devils, adopted current name 1993. Ground: Scriveners, capacity: 12,000. Strip: red shirts, white shorts. **African Cup of Champion Clubs** runners-up 1990 (1–1 agg., 3–5 pens., v **JS Kabylie** of Algeria), **African Cup-winners Cup** quarter-final 1998; Zambian league champions 1982, 1983, 1985, 1986, 1988, 1989, 1990, 1992, 1993; Zambian Cup 1975 (as Rokana United).

no home victories during a season *record* no English **Football League** or **Premier League** club has gone through an entire season without winning at least one home game. **Crystal Palace** had played 15 **Premier League** fixtures at **Selhurst Park** during the 1997-98 season before winning one, finally breaking its duck against **Derby County** on 18 April 1998 (3–1). The club recorded a second home victory (1–0 v **Sheffield Wednesday**) on the final day of the season.

no opposition *misc.* matches in which only one team turns up. *Keynotes* In 1973 the **Soviet Union** refused to play the second leg of a **World Cup** qualifying match against **Chile** at the **Nacional** Stadium in Santiago, because it had housed several thousand political prisoners during a military coup. Chile countered by rejecting pleas to switch the tie elsewhere. As a result, the match was held without the Soviet Union team, and after Chile scored direct from the kick-off the tie was awarded to the South Americans, who thus qualified for the 1974 tournament. **Scotland**'s 1998 World Cup qualifying match in **Estonia** involved only the Scots after the Estonians refused to turn up following **FIFA**'s decision to bring forward the kick-off time because the Tallinn stadium's **floodlights** were of a poor standard. The match subsequently was replayed at a neutral venue.

No-Names *club* former-English club. *Keynotes* Founded in Kilburn, North London, by former pupils of Harrow School ca. 1859.

no-score-draw *n.* in **pools** betting, a match finishing 0–0.

non-contract player *regulations* senior player who has neither a **full** nor **monthly contract** with a club that holds his **registration**. The player's registration will expire at the end of the season (FA Premier League rule K.20, Football League regulation 51.2). **Football League** clubs may be entitled to receive a **transfer fee** or **compensation fee** for a non-contract player if, firstly the player is under 24 years old and, secondly, if it has made the player a written offer of a contract within the season (ie while the player is still registered at the club) (Football League rule 51.4). The registration of a non-contract player in the **Premier League** is not transferable (so no compensation fee is payable) (FA Premier League rule K.8). Compare **contract player**, **out-of-contract player**

non-league *adj.* organised football competition outside of the major professional leagues and cups.

non-UK players *n. pl.* see **foreign players.**

Nordahl, Gunnar *player* Striker. **Sweden** international (33 caps, 43 goals, ca. 1942-48). Born 19 October 1921, died 1995. Career ca. 1940-57. *Clubs* Degerfors IF, **IFK Norrköping, AC Milan, Roma**. *Keynotes* One of the **Gre-no-li** trio. Nordahl is Sweden's second-highest all-time international goalscorer – in spite of an international career shortened by Sweden's ban on professionals from its national squad until the late 1950s. Top scorer in the 1948 Olympic Games football finals tournament (seven goals). After winning the Olympic Games gold medal with Sweden in 1948, Nordahl never played for his country again. He had scored an average of 1.3 goals per game for his country. His strike record for his clubs was equally impressive: Nordahl scored 93 goals in 92 games for IFK Norköpping, helping his club win four successive championships. He joined Milan in 1949 and later played for Roma. He scored 225 goals in 257 **Serie A** matches and was league top scorer five times. Nordahl's four brothers also played senior league football in Sweden. *Honours* **Olympic Games** gold medal (Sweden, 1948); Swedish league championship (IFK Norköpping 1945, 1946, 1947, 1948); Italian Serie A championship (AC Milan, 1951, 1955).

Norma Tallinn *club* former Estonian national league club based in the capital Tallinn, founded 1959, dissolved 1997 (though largely absorbed by **Lantana Tallinn**).The club had, traditionally, been associated with ethnic Russian supporters. Estonian regional league champions 1964, 1967, 1970, 1979, 1989; Estonian league champions 1992, 1993; Estonian Cup 1962, 1965, 1971, 1973, 1974, 1989, 1994.

normal playing time *rules* the **duration of play** of a match, including any time added by the referee for any playing time lost owing to the assessment of **injuries** to players and their transport from the field of play, **time wasting, substitutions** and other causes. Unless otherwise agreed – and within the rules of a particular competition – there are two equal periods of 45 minutes (Law VII). Normal playing time does not include **extra time**, nor does it include any additional time allowed in either period of play in order that a **penalty kick** be taken after the expiration of the normal period of play.

Norris, Sir Henry *official* former chairman of **Fulham** and, later, **Arsenal**. Member of Parliament. Norris engineered Arsenal's move to **Highbury** Stadium and is believed to have heavily influenced the other club chairmen in Arsenal's successful, and highly controversial, election to the first division in 1919 (see Arsenal for details). Banned from football in 1927 for alleged financial irregularities.

North American Championship *competition* former international football competition contested by members of the **North American Football Confederation** (**Cuba, Mexico** and the **United States of America**). Played twice in 1947 (Havana, Cuba) and 1949 (Mexico City, Mexico); the latter doubled as a **World Cup** qualifying group, with two of the three nations qualifying for the 1950 World Cup finals in Brazil. Mexico won both competitions, winning all its matches. Cuba was second in 1947, with USA runners-up in 1949. A North American Championship was reconvened with a tournament in March 1991, involving **Canada**, Mexico and USA. Mexico won the tournament on goal difference from USA.

North American Football Confederation *confederation* former football confederation comprising **Cuba**, **Mexico** and the **United States of America**, founded 1939. A **North American Championship** was held twice (1947 and 1949). Cuba and Mexico were founder members, in 1961, of the **Confederación Norte-Centroamericana y del Caribe de Fútbol** (CONCACAF), the current regional federation.

North American Soccer League (NASL) *competition* former professional football league of the United States of America, founded in 1968 by a merger of the **United Soccer Association** and the **National Professional Soccer League**. The league was under the auspices of the **United States Soccer Confederation**. The NASL sold club **franchises** across the United States and Canada. With the exception of 1969, the league was decided by a final playoff: the NASL Soccer Bowl. Six points were awarded for a win, four for a **shoot-out win**, plus a bonus point scored for every goal (maximum three bonus points). First winners: Atlanta Chiefs. Other winners: Kansas City Spurs (1969), Rochester Lancers (1970), Dallas Tornado (1971), **New York Cosmos** (1972, 1977, 1978, 1980, 1982), Philadelphia Atoms 1973, Los Angeles Aztecs (1974), Tampa Bay Rowdies (1975), Toronto Metros (1976), Vancouver Whitecaps (1979), Chicago Sting (1981, 1984 – the last winners), Tulsa Roughnecks (1983). Disbanded 1984. Notable former players: **Pelé**, Franz **Beckenbauer**, Rodney Marsh, Teofilo **Cubillas**.

North Korea (Democratic People's Republic of Korea) *country AFC* republic in east Asia, occupying the north part of the Korean peninsula, on the Sea of Japan and the Yellow Sea. Bordered by **China** and **South Korea**. Formed after second world war with the occupation of the region by **Soviet Union** troops. Invaded South Korea in 1950 in an attempt at reunifying Korea. The three-year Korean War that followed in 1950–53 ended in stalemate. Area: 122,310 sq km (47,210 sq miles). Population: 23,260,000 (1995 est.). Language: Korean. Capital: P'yongyang. *Dossier* Football Association of the Democratic People's Republic of Korea (P'yongyang) formed in 1945 affiliated to **FIFA** in 1958 and **Asian Football Confederation** (AFC) in 1974, president: Choe Ryong Hae; general secretary: Li Chang Son. Season played from March to November, National stadium: Moranbong, P'yongyang, capacity: 90,000. National strip: white shirts, white shorts and white socks. Best victory: 1–0, v **Italy** (19 July 1966, **Ayresome Park**, Middlesbrough, **World Cup** first round). Notable international players: **Pak Doo Ik**, **Seung-zin**. *International tournament record Olympic Games* – qualified for finals tournament 1976; **Women's World Cup** – qualified for finals tournament in 1999; World Cup – first entered 1966 (quarter-final), has not qualified for finals tournament since then;

Asian Cup of Nations – first entered 1972, semi-final/fourth 1980 (0–3, v **Iran**, in Kuwait, third/fourth playoff), also qualified for finals tournament 1992; **Asian Games** – first entered 1974, joint-winners/shared gold medal 1978 (0–0, v **South Korea**, in Bangkok, Thailand), runners-up/silver medal 1990 (0–0, 1–4 pens., v **Iran**, in Beijing, China), semi-final/fourth 1974 (1–2, v **Malaysia**, in Tehran, Iran), semi-final 1982, second round 1998; Asian Games (women) – runners-up 1998 (0–1, v China, in Thailand); **Asian Youth Championship** (under-19) – joint-winners 1976 (shared with Iran); **Asian Women's Championship** – first entered 1989, runners-up 1993 (0–3, v **China**, in Malaysia), 1997 (0–3, v China, in China), semi-final/fourth 1991; **Dynasty Cup** – entered first tournament in 1990, third 1990, 1992; **Under-17 World Championship** – never qualified; **World Youth Cup** (under-20) – never qualified. *Record against British and Irish national teams* none played. *History* As well as success in the 1978 Asian Games, when North Korea shared the gold medal in the football competition, its greatest tournament was the 1966 World Cup. Star player Pak Doo Ik scored a memorable goal in the 42nd minute against Italy in the first round group stage, a result which knocked Italy out of the tournament. A late equaliser by Seung-zin against **Chile** (1–1) helped North Korea to qualify for the quarter-final. North Korea went out of the tournament 3–5 against **Portugal** (23 July, quarter-final at Goodison Park, Liverpool), although it had been leading 3–0 after only 22 minutes. *Record in international club tournaments* **Asian Champion Teams Cup** – **April 25th** (semi-final/third 1990, also reached finals tournament in 1988), **P'yongyang** (qualified for finals tournament 1991). Other leading club: Chadongcha FC.

North Shore United *club* New Zealand national league club, based in Auckland. New Zealand National League champions 1977, 1994; (New Zealand) Chatham Cup 1952, 1960, 1963, 1967, 1979, 1986.

North v South *misc.* representative match between two sides, one drawn from the North of England and the other from southern-based clubs. *Keynotes* In December 1870, the **Football Association** organised one of the first **representative** matches, North of England v South of England, designed to promote the Association and its rules outside its power base in Southern England. The match was played at the Oval, the South winning 1-0.

North Yemen *former country* see **Yemen** (sense 2).

Northampton Town *club* English league. *Dossier* Ground: **Sixfields Stadium**, Northampton. Strip: claret shirts with white trim, white shorts and claret socks. Nickname: the Cobblers. Ground capacity: 7,653. Record attendance (at Sixfields): 7,461 v **Barnet** (15 October 1994, Third Division). Record attendance at former **County Ground**; 24,523 v **Fulham** (23 April 1966, Division One). Best average attendance: 18,633 (County Ground, 1965-66). Biggest win: 10–0 v **Walsall** (5 November 1927, Division Three (South)), v

Sutton Town (7 December 1907, **FA Cup**, preliminary round). Biggest defeat: 0–11 v **Southampton** (28 December 1901, **Southern League**). *History* Formed in 1897 at Northamptonshire County Cricket Ground by local teachers. In 1909, Northampton turned professional and joined the Southern League, which, under the managership of Herbert **Chapman**, the club won in 1909. It was as Southern League Champions that Northampton contested the 1909 **Charity Shield** (0–2 v **Newcastle United**). The club was a **founder member** of **Football League** Division Three in 1920-21. Aside from two FA Cup fifth round appearances, in 1934 (0–4 v **Preston North End**) and 1950 (2–4 v **Derby County**), Northampton achieved little of merit until the club won promotion to Division Three in 1960-61. Over the next nine seasons, Northampton experienced a meteoric rise to Division One (1965-66) before dropping again in a similarly dramatic fashion, so that by 1969-70 the club was back playing in Division Four, even applying for re-election in 1971-72. In 1970, the club again reached the fifth round of the FA Cup (2–8 v **Manchester United**), having reached the quarter-final stage of the **League Cup** in both 1965 (0–1 v **Plymouth Argyle**) and 1967 (1–3 v **West Bromwich Albion**). Northampton survived relegation from the Football League in 1993-94 only because **Football Conference** Champions Kidderminster's ground failed to meet Football League standards. In 1996-97, Northampton made its first **Wembley** appearance, winning the Third Division end-of-season **playoff** (1–0 v **Swansea City**). In a return Wembley visit the following season, the club narrowly missed further playoff success and promotion to the First Division by losing to **Grimsby Town** (0–1). In March 1992, Northampton, over £1 million in debt, was placed in the hands of an administrator – Barry Ward, who subsequently became club chairman. By 1993, the club was saved and, with the support of the local council, pursued plans to relocate to a new **all-seater stadium**. Although the club's final match at the County Ground was supposed to take place on 30 April 1994, the new Sixfields Stadium not ready in time, so the old ground staged a further five home matches, the last occurring on 11 October (v **Mansfield Town**). Sixfields Stadium hosted its first game on 15 October 1994 (v Barnet, Third Division). *League record* Division One 1965-66; Division Two 1963-64 to 1964-65, 1966-67; Second Division 1997-98–; Division Three 1920-21, 1961-62 to 1962-63, 1967-68 to 1968-69, 1976-77, 1987-88 to 1989-90; Third Division 1992-93 to 1996-97, 1999-00; Division Three (South) 1921-22 to 1957-58; Division Four 1958-59 to 1960-61, 1969-70 to 1975-76, 1977-78 to 1986-87, 1990-91 to 1991-92. *Honours* Division Three 1962-63; Division Four 1986-87; Southern League 1909. *Records* E Lloyd Davies is Northampton's most capped player (12 (16) for **Wales**); Tommy Fowler holds the record for club League appearances (521, 1946-61); Jack English is Northampton's record League goalscorer (135, 1947-60).

Northern *club* former-Scottish league. *Dossier* Ground: Hyde Park, Glasgow, Strathclyde. *Keynotes* Played only one season in **Scottish Football League** Division Two, achieving only nine points from 18 fixtures. *League record* Division Two 1893-94.

Northern Ireland *country UEFA* constituent region of the United Kingdom, in the north-east of Ireland, comprising the six counties of Antrim, Armagh, Down, Fermanagh, Derry/Londonderry and Tyrone. The region was created in 1921 on the establishment of the Irish Free State (see **Ireland, Republic of, Ireland**), in an attempt by the British Government to mollify the large Protestant and Loyalist population, and its leaders, in the Northeast while agreeing to an independent Ireland in the south. The division has created political, community and religious tension ever since, as well as terrorist action from both Republican and Loyalist groups. British troops were introduced in the late 1960s. There have been various attempts to deliver a peaceful solution, including the 1998 Good Friday Agreement drawn up between the British and Irish governments and political parties in Northern Ireland. Area: 14,150 sq km (5,640 sq miles). Population: 1,570,000 (1991 census). Languages: English. Capital: Belfast. *Dossier* **Irish Football Association** (Belfast) formed in 1880, affiliated to **FIFA** 1911, permanent member of the **International FA Board**, and founder member of the **Union of European Football Associations** (UEFA) in 1954, president: Jim Boyce; general secretary: David Bowen. Season played from August to May. National stadium: Windsor Park, Belfast, capacity: 28,000. National strip: green shirts, white shorts, green socks. First international game: 20 October 1923 v **England** (2–1, Belfast, **Home International Championship**). First international game v **Scotland** 1 March 1924 (0–2, Glasgow, Home International Championship); v **Wales** 15 March 1924 (0–1, Belfast, Home International Championship); v Republic of Ireland 20 September 1978 (0–0, Dublin, **European Championship** qualifier). First international game against non-UK opposition: 12 May 1951 v **France** (2–2, Belfast, friendly). Biggest victory: 7–0 v Wales (1 February 1930, Belfast, Home International Championship). Biggest defeats: 0–7 v England (16 November 1938, Manchester, Home International Championship), 2–9 v England (16 November 1949, Manchester, Home International Championship and **World Cup** qualifier). Most capped players: Pat **Jennings** (119 appearances, 1964-86), Mal Donaghy (91 appearances, 1980-95), Sammy McIlroy (88 appearances, 1972-87), Jimmy Nichol (73 appearances, 1976-86), David McCreery (67 appearances, 1976-90), Nigel Worthington (66 appearances, 1984-97), Martin O'Neill (64 appearances, 1972-85), Gerry Armstrong (63 appearances, 1977-86). Leading goalscorers: Colin Clarke (13 goals in 38 appearances, 1986-93), Gerry Armstrong (12 goals in 63 appearances), Joe Bambrick (12 goals, in 11 appearances, 1929-38), Billy Gillespie (12 goals in 25 appearances, 1913-31; eight for all-

Ireland), Jimmy Quinn (12 goals in 46 appearances, 1984-96), Billy **Bingham** (10 goals in 56 appearances, 1951-64). Other notable international player: Danny **Blanchflower** (56 appearances, two goals, 1954-58), George **Best** (37 appearances 1964-78, 9 goals), Derek Dougan (43 appearances, 1959-73), Peter **Doherty** (16 caps). National team coaches/managers: Billy Bingham (1967-71 and 1980-93), Terry Neill (1971-1975), Dave Clements (1975-76, as player-manager), Danny Blanchflower (1976-79), Bryan Hamilton (1994-97), Lawrie McMenemy 1998- (the first non-Irish manager of the national side). *International tournament record* **Olympic Games** – never entered; **Women's World Cup** – see **Northern Ireland, women**; World Cup – first entered 1950, quarter-final 1958, second round 1982, also qualified for finals tournament 1986; European Championship – first entered 1964 (second round – no qualifying tournament), thereafter never qualified for finals tournament; **European Championship for Women** – see Northern Ireland, women; Home International Championship (British Championship) winners 1980, 1984 (the last championship), shared 1956, 1958, 1959, 1964; **Under-17 World Championship** – never qualified; **World Youth Cup** (under-20) – never qualified. *World Cup performance* (finals and qualifiers to end of 1998 tournament) played 97, won 31, drawn 25, lost 41, scored 102 goals, conceded 121 goals; win rate 32%; goals scored per game 1.05. *Record against British and Republic of Ireland national teams* v England, played 58 won three, drawn 12, lost 43; v Republic of Ireland, played eight, won one, drawn four, lost three; v Scotland played 56, won 14, drawn 12, lost 30; v Wales, played 53, won 14, drawn 14, lost 25. *History* The Irish League is the third oldest league competition in the world, founded in 1890; teams competed from the whole of Ireland until 1921. The **Irish FA Cup** started 1881, and was first won by Moyola Park (1–0, v Cliftonville); again this was the all-Ireland cup until 1921. The first known club was the now-defunct Ulster FC, founded in Belfast in 1878 (the club already existed as a rugby club). Of the major clubs still in existence, the oldest is **Cliftonville** FC, from Newtownabbey, founded in 1879; followed by **Distillery** FC in 1880, **Glentoran** in 1882, and **Linfield FC** in 1886. Domestic football in Northern Ireland has been largely dominated by two clubs: Linfield FC (42 Irish League championships and 35 Irish FA Cups by 1998) and Glentoran (19 Irish League championships and 17 Irish FA Cups by 1998). By 1999, only two clubs in the world had won more domestic league championships than Linfield: **Rangers** (47) and **Peñarol** (45). Linfield holds the world record for the most domestic cup triumphs (35 by 1998, four more than **Al Ahly** of Egypt and five more than **Celtic**). Club football has been affected by the political situation in Northern Ireland. Most notably, **Derry City**, from Derry/Londonderry – a predominantly Catholic club – withdrew from the Northern Ireland league in 1972 and plays in the Republic of Ireland. Two rival Belfast clubs,

Cliftonville, with a traditionally Catholic following, and Linfield, with a large Protestant fan base, were forced by the police to play their derby matches at a neutral venue, Windsor Park, from 1970 to 1998. In November 1998, police allowed the league fixture to be played at Cliftonville's ground Solitude, with a restricted crowd of 1,500. The best performances of Northern Irish clubs in European club competitions are Linfield's quarter-final appearance in the **European Cup** in 1967 (2–3 agg., v **CSKA Sofia**), and Glentoran's quarter-final of the **European Cup-winners Cup** in 1974 (0–7 agg., v **Borussia Mönchengladbach**). Although Ireland played its first match in 1882 (above), it was not until 12 May 1951 that Northern Ireland played a match against a nation from outside the United Kingdom (2–2, v France, in Belfast, friendly), and another 18 months before it played a fixture outside the British Isles (1–3, v France, in Paris, friendly, 11 November 1952). Northern Ireland qualified for the 1958 World Cup finals in Sweden. It reached the quarter final – after winning a first-round group playoff against **Czechoslovakia** (2–1, in Malmö) – losing 0–4 against France in Norrköping. Peter McParland scored five of his country's six goals in the tournament. The team also included Danny Blanchflower, Derek Dougan and Billy Bingham. Bingham later became the country's longest-serving manager. The 1958 World Cup was the only occasion in which all four home nations reached the finals: Northern Ireland joined Wales in the last eight, while Scotland and England were eliminated in the first round. Bingham lead Northern Ireland to two World Cup finals tournaments, 1982 and 1986. At the 1982 finals in Spain, Northern Ireland topped its first-round group to qualify for the second round; its three first-round matches included a victory over the host country (1–0, in Valencia, Gerry Armstrong scoring the goal). The tournament was also notable for the debut of Norman Whiteside; at 17 years and 42 days he was the youngest player ever to appear in the World Cup finals (v **former-Yugoslavia**, 17 June 1982, in Zaragoza, first round). Northern Ireland has never qualified for the European Championship finals tournament (it reached the second round in 1964, but there were no qualifiers). It missed out on the 1996 tournament playoffs on goal difference to the Republic of Ireland. Arguably Northern Ireland's best player of all time, George Best, was never able to play for Northern Ireland in the finals of a major championship. *League system* The Irish Premier division has 10 clubs (increased from eight for the 1997-98 season), playing each other four times each season. The bottom club is automatically relegated. Three points are awarded for a victory, with one for a draw: final positions for clubs level on points are determined by **goal difference**. There are eight clubs in the First Division. *Record in international club tournaments* **European Cup** – **Linfield** (quarter-final 1967); European Cup-winners Cup – Glentoran (quarter-final 1974); **UEFA Cup** – **Coleraine** (second round 1970, 1971), **Portadown** (second round 1975).

Northern Ireland, women *country/women* women's football in Northern Ireland is administered by the Irish Football Association, Belfast. *History* The former Northern Ireland Women's Football Association was founded in November 1976, with a three-division league formed in may 1977. The Northern Ireland national women's team took part in its first international match in 1977, against the Republic of Ireland (see **Ireland, Republic of, women**). *League system* The national league has three divisions: Premier, First and Second Divisions. There are 23 clubs in the national structure. *Dossier* First international match: 1977, 1–4, v Republic of Ireland. *International tournament record* **Women's World Cup** – never qualified (did not enter 1999); **European Championship for Women** – entered first tournament 1984, never beyond first-round group stage.

Northern Mariana Islands *country associate member of OFC* self-governing commonwealth of the **United States of America** in the west Pacific. A chain of volcanic and coral islands forming part of the Mariana Islands (the other part being **Guam**). Area: 471 sq km (182 sq miles). Population: 45,200. Languages: Chamorro, English. Capital: Saipan. *Dossier* Football association is not affiliated to **FIFA**, but is an associate member of the **Oceania Football Confederation** (OFC).

Northwich Victoria *club* former-English league. *Dossier* Ground: Drill Field, Northwich, Cheshire. Record attendance: 4,000. Best average attendance: 2,500 (1892-93). *Keynotes* Founded in 1874 and **founder members** of **Football League** Division Two in 1892-93. The club's Drill Field ground, its home since 1875, is believed to be the **oldest ground** in continuous use by one club in the world. The club was forced to move its home **FA Cup** fourth round tie against **Oldham Athletic** in 1976-77 to **Manchester City**'s **Maine Road** after more tickets were sold than the Drill Field ground could accommodate. Victoria resigned its League status in 1893-94. It plays in the **Football Conference**. *League record* Division Two 1892-93 to 1893-94.

Norway *country UEFA* kingdom of northwest Europe in Scandinavia, bordered by **Sweden**, **Finland** and the Russian Confederation. Mountainous country running from 58 to 72 degrees north (into the Arctic Circle), characterised by fjords, fertile valleys, glaciers and vast forests. Independence from Sweden in 1905, occupied by German forces in **World War II**. Area: 323,895 sq km (125,025 sq miles). Population: 4,400,000 (1996 est.). Languages: Norwegian, Saami (Lappish), Finnish. Capital: Oslo. *Dossier* Football association (Norges Fotballforbund, Oslo) formed in 1902, affiliated to **FIFA** in 1908 and founder member of **Union of European Football Associations** (UEFA) in 1954, president: Per Ravn Omdal; general secretary: Trygve Bornø. Season played from mid-April to mid-October. National stadium: Ullevål Stadion, Oslo, capacity: 26,000. National strip: red shirts, white shorts and blue socks. First international game: 12 July 1908, v Sweden (3–11, Gothenburg, Sweden, friendly). Biggest victory: 11–0 v **United States of America** (6 August 1948, Oslo, friendly). Biggest defeat: 0–12 v **Denmark** (7 October 1917, Copenhagen, Denmark, friendly). Most capped players: Thorbjørn Svenssen (104 appearances, 1947–62), Erik Thorstvedt (92 appearances, 1982-96), Svein Grondalen (77 appearances, 1973–84), Kjetil Rekdal (76 appearances, 1987-). Leading goalscorers: Jørgen Juve (33 goals, 1928–37), Einar Gundersen (26 goals, 1917–28). Other notable international players: Jan Åge Fjørtoft (20 international goals, 1986-97), Tore Andre Flo, Ole Gunnar Solskjaer. Website: *http://www.unik.no/~larsa/football/html* (unofficial). *International tournament record* **Olympic Games** – third/bronze medal 1936 (3–2, v **Poland**, Berlin, third/fourth playoff); **World Cup** – first entered 1938, second round 1998, also qualified for finals tournament 1938, 1994; **European Championship** – first round 1960 and 1964, has since failed to qualify for the finals tournament; **Scandinavian Championship** – winners 1932; **Women's World Cup/European Championship for Women/** Olympic Games (women)/**Algarve Cup** – see **Norway, women**. *World Cup performance* (finals and qualifiers to end of 1998 tournament) played 84, won 30, drawn 18, lost 36, scored 117 goals, conceded 127 goals; win rate: 36%; goals scored per game: 1.51. *Record against British and Irish national teams* v **England**, played 10, won two, drawn three, lost five; v **Northern Ireland**, played four, won three, drawn none, lost one; v **Scotland**, played 12, won one, drawn four, lost seven; v **Wales**, played six, won three, drawn two, lost one; v **Republic of Ireland**, played 15, won two, drawn seven, lost six. *History* The first clubs were founded at the end of the 19th century, with **Kongsvinger IL** (founded 1892), **Odd SK Skien** (1894), **SOFK Lyn Oslo** (1896) and **Viking FK Stavanger** (1899) among the first. The Norwegian Cup has been played since 1902 (first won by Grane Nordstrand) and the league since 1937-8 (first won by **Fredrikstad FK**). The national championship was decided by end-of-season playoffs until 1961, after which the champions were the club which topped the table at the end of the season. Domestic football remains largely part-time, a factor which has contributed to the continuous exodus of leading players to foreign clubs, such as Rune Bratseth, a member of **Werder Bremen**'s victorious 1992 **European Cup-winners Cup** side, and Henning Berg, Jan Age Fjortoft, Tore Andre Flo, Frode Grodas, Egil Ostenstad, Ole Gunnar Solskjaer and Eric Thorstvedt, who all play, or have played, in England. Seventeen of Norway's 22-man squad for the 1998 World Cup finals played for foreign clubs, including 11 in England. Despite this, Norwegian clubs have performed well in recent European club competitions: **SK Brann** reached the quarter-final of the European Cup-winners Cup in 1997 while, in the same year, **Rosenborg BK** reached the quarter-finals of the **European Cup**/Champions League, qualifying from the league stage (with three wins from its six matches, including a 2–1 victory away to **AC Milan)**, before losing to **Juventus** in the quarter-final. Aside from the Olympic Games bronze medal in 1936, Norway's best achievement at international level was in qualifying for the second round of the World Cup in 1998, under coach Egil Olsen. It had already won its European qualifying group, winning six of its eight matches, with no defeats, scoring 21 goals with only two conceded. In the finals tournament in France, it finished runners-up in its first-round group of four nations, including a 2–1 victory over eventual runners-up **Brazil**. It was defeated 0–1 by **Italy** in the second round. The victory over Brazil was the second over the country in just over a year (Norway beat Brazil 4–2 in a friendly in Oslo, 30 May 1997). Norway's only appearances in the European Championship finals were in 1960 and 1964. From 1968 to 1988 Norway finished last in each of its qualifying groups. The Norwegian women's team is one of the most successful in the world: it won the second women's World Cup in 1995, finished runners-up in the inaugural event in 1991 – in front of 65,000 spectators in Guangzhou, China – and was third in the first Olympic Games tournament in Atlanta, USA (a feat which matched that of the men's Olympic squad of 1936). It won the European Championship for Women in 1993 (see Norway, women). *League system* There are 14 clubs in the national first division, the Tippeliga. Three points are awarded for a victory, with one for a draw: final positions for clubs level on points are determined by **goal difference** and, if necessary, by **goals scored**. The bottom three clubs are automatically relegated to the second division. The second division is divided into two sections of 12 clubs: the champions of both sections are automatically promoted; the third promotion place is decided by a two-leg playoff between the two section runners-up. The Norwegian Cup final is played at the end of October. *Record in international club tournaments* **European Cup/Champions League** – Rosenborg BK (quarter-final 1997, champions league 1998, second round 1987), Fredrikstad FK (second round 1961), Lyn Oslo (second round 1965), Valerengens (second round 1967), **Lillestrøm SK** (second round 1979); European Cup-winners Cup – SOFK Lyn Oslo (quarter-final 1969), SK Brann (quarter-final 1997); **UEFA Cup** – Valerengens (second round 1966), FK Skied Oslo (second round 1970), Rosenborg (second round 1972), Viking FK Stavanger (second round 1973, 1983), Start Kristiansand (second round 1978), Kongsvinger IL (second round 1994). Other leading clubs: **Tromsø IL**, Odd Sk Skien.

Norway, women *country/women* women's football in Norway is controlled by the national association, the Norges Fotballforbund, in Oslo. *History* Women's football has been administered by the national football association since 1975. In 1988, Norway won the first **FIFA** women's tournament in Guangzhou, China. Norway hosted the 1987 **European Championship for Women** in 1987, and won the competition in 1993. It competed in the first **Women's World Cup** in 1991, losing in the final against United States of America, women, and won the tournament in 1995. Norway was bronze medalist at the first **Olympic Games** women's football tournament in 1996, in Atlanta, USA. One in three Norwegians is thought to have watched the 1995 Women's World Cup final on television, while nearly half the population watched television coverage of the 1996 Olympic Games semi-final against hosts **United States of America** (Norway lost 1–2, the match settled by a **golden goal)**. Regional leagues began in 1979, with the first national league championship played in 1987, with 10 teams competing. By 1995, there were an estimated 64,000 players and 1,830 clubs registered with the national association. Norway's most capped player, Heidi **Store**, had, by June 1997, played a world-record 148 times for the national side. *Dossier* First official international match: 1978, v **Sweden**. Most capped player: Heidi Store (148 appearances). *League system* Ten clubs compete in the National League. Below the National League are six regional First Divisions. *International tournament record* Olympic Games (women) – semi-final/bronze medal 1996 (2–0, v **Brazil** third/fourth playoff, in Atlanta, USA); Women's World Cup – winners 1995 (2–0, v **Germany**, Stockholm, Sweden), runners-up 1991 (1–2, v United States of America, Guangzhou, China); European Championship for Women – winners 1993 (1–0 v **Italy**, Cesena, Italy), runners-up 1989 (1–4 v West Germany, Osnabruck, Germany), runners-up 1989 (1–3 v West Germany, Aalborg, Denmark), semi-final 1987 (as hosts), semi-final 1995; FIFA women's tournament – winners 1988 (v Sweden, in Guangzhou, China); **Algarve Cup** – winners 1998 (4–1, v **Denmark)**.

Norwich City *club* English league. *Dossier* Ground: **Carrow Road**, Norwich, Norfolk. Strip: yellow shirts with green trim, green shorts with yellow trim, yellow socks with green trim. Nickname: Canaries. Ground capacity: 21,994 all seated. Record attendance: 43,984 v **Leicester City** (30 March 1963, **FA Cup**, sixth round). Best average attendance: 28,420 (1972-73). Biggest win: 10–2 v **Coventry City** (15 March 1930, Division Three (South)), 8–0 v **Sutton United** (28 January 1989, FA Cup, fourth round). Biggest defeat: 2–10 v **Swindon Town** (5 September 1908, **Southern League)**. *History* Founded in 1902 largely at the instigation of two local school teachers who called a meeting at the Criterion Cafe. Norwich turned professional and joined the Southern League in 1905 after the **Football Association** barred the club from competing in the 1904 **FA Amateur** Cup because it already believed the club to be professional. Between 1908 and 1935, Norwich played at a venue called the Nest (where, in 1909, **Reading** refused to play a cup-tie because the pitch was too short and which, in 1935, was declared unfit for large crowds by the Football Association) before settling at Carrow Road. As a founder member of Division Three in 1920-21, the club had to wait more than a decade before gaining promotion to Division Two, winning the Division Three (South) Championship in 1933-34. In the first two seasons after **World War II**, Norwich finished joint-bottom on points of Division Three (South), eventually gaining promotion to Division Two in 1959-60, after a series of near-misses in 1950-51, 1951-52 and 1952-53. Norwich has a history of FA Cup **giant-killing**: 1909 (3-2 v **Liverpool**, second round); 1911 (3-1 v **Sunderland**, first round), 1915 (3-2 v **Tottenham Hotspur**, second round), 1935 (2-1 replay v **Leeds United**, fourth round), 1951 (3-1 v Liverpool, third round), 1954 (2-1 v **Arsenal**, fourth round). Norwich's most famous FA Cup giantkilling run occurred in 1958-59. The club, then of Division Three, and under the managership of Archie Macaulay and with a team that included the striking partnership of Terry Bly and Terry Allcock, reached the FA Cup semi-finals (0-1 replay v **Luton Town**) defeating **Manchester United** (3-0, third round) and Tottenham Hotspur (1-0 replay, fifth round) on the way. In 1962, the club won its first major trophy, the **League Cup** (4-0 agg. v **Rochdale**). Ron Saunders was appointed manager in 1969 and, in 1971-72, the club finally secured a place in the top flight by winning the Division Two Championship. A year later, Norwich reached its first **Wembley** final, losing to Tottenham Hotspur (0-1) in the League Cup. The club reached the semi-final of the League Cup the following season (1-2 agg. v **Wolverhampton Wanderers**) and the final, again, in 1974-75 (0-1 v **Aston Villa**). Relegation in 1973-74 was followed by an immediate return to the top flight the next season – a feat that was repeated in 1980-81 and 1981-82. In 1985, the club reached its fourth League Cup final, lifting the trophy for a second time (1-0 v **Sunderland**). Norwich was also relegated, making it the only club to win the League Cup and lose its Division One status in the same season. In 1989 and 1992, the club reached the FA Cup semi-final stage, losing on both occasions (0-1 v **Everton**; 0-1 v Sunderland). Norwich finished third in the first season of the **Premier League** – the club's highest-ever League position, thus qualifying for European competition (**UEFA Cup**) for the first time. Celebrity cook Delia Smith is a director of the club. *League record* Premier League 1992-93 to 1994-95; Division One 1972-73 to 1973-74, 1975-76 to 1980-81, 1982-83 to 1984-85, 1986-87 to 1991-92; First Division 1993-94 to 1995-96–; Division Two 1934-35 to 1938-39, 1960-61 to 1971-72, 1974-75,1981-82, 1985-86; Division Three 1920-21, 1958-59 to 1959-60; Division Three (South) 1921-22 to 1933-34, 1946-47 to 1957-58. *Honours* Division Two 1971-72, 1985-86; Division Three (South) 1933-34; League Cup 1962 (4-0 agg. v Rochdale), 1985 (1-0 v Sunderland). *Records* Mark Bowen is Norwich's most capped player (35 (41) for **Wales**); Ron Ashman holds the record for club appearances (592 (1947-64); Johnny Gavin is Norwich's record league goalscorer (122, 1945-54, 1955-58).

not interfering with play *rules* see **interfering with play**.

Nottingham Forest *club* English league. *Dossier* Ground: **City Ground**, Nottingham. Strip: Red shirts with white trim, white shorts, red and white socks. Nickname: Reds. Ground capacity: 30,602 all seated. Record attendance: 49,946 v **Manchester United** (28 October 1967, Division One). Best average attendance: 32,715 (1967-68). Biggest win: 14-0 v **Clapton** (17 January 1891, **FA Cup**, first round). Biggest defeat: 1-9 v **Blackburn Rovers** (10 April 1937, Division Two). *History* Founded in 1865 by some shinty (a form of hockey) players, the club is the second oldest **Football League** or **Premier League** club (after neighbours **Notts County**). Forest is one of only two clubs to be named after the ground at which it was formed, in this case the Forest Recreation Ground (the other club is **Crystal Palace (2.)**). The club was also the last in the Football League to be run by an elected committee, not becoming a limited company run by a board of directors until 1982. The club turned professional in 1889 and played at several venues after leaving the Forest Recreation Ground, including, in 1880, Trent Bridge Cricket Ground, before settling at what later became known as the City Ground in 1898. Although the club was not a founder member of the League, joining the newly created two-tier structure as members of Division One in 1892-93, it was at the forefront of several important developments in the game. **Shinguards**, for example, were invented and patented in 1874 by Nottingham Forest and **England** centre-forward Sam Weller Widdowson. In 1878, a **referee** used a **whistle** during a match for the first time in a game between Forest and Sheffield Norfolk, while in January 1891 the **crossbar** and **goal nets** (see **net**) made their first full appearance at the club's Town Ground for a **representative match** between teams from the North and the South (goal net experiments had earlier taken place in Liverpool). Forest's application to join the Football League was supported by neighbours Notts County on the condition that they were allowed first choice of home fixtures against five selected clubs. Six years after joining the Football League, Forest won the FA Cup (3-1 v **Derby County**), having reached the semi-final stage on four previous occasions as a non-league (**Football Alliance**) club – 1879 (1-2 v **Old Etonians**), 1880 (0-1 v Oxford University), 1885 (0-3 replay v **Queen's Park**) and 1892 (2-6 second replay v **West Bromwich Albion**). Forest was relegated in 1905-06, but immediately returned to the top-flight as Division Two Champions the following season before slipping down again in 1910-11. In the 1930s, Forest only narrowly avoided relegation on **goal average** to Division Three (South) in two consecutive seasons (1937-38, 1938-39), before finally dropping out of Division Two in 1948-49. The club won the Division Three (South) Championship in 1950-51. Six years later it gained promotion to Division One and, in 1959, Forest won its second FA Cup (2-1 v **Luton Town**). In 1966-67, under the managership of Johnny Carey and with a side captained by Bobby McKinlay, who played a club record 614 games between 1951 and 1970, Forest finished League runners-up as well as being FA Cup semi-finalists (1–2 v **Tottenham Hotspur**). The appointment of Brian **Clough** as manager (a position he held for 18 years) in 1975 was the beginning of Forest's most successful period. Over part of 1977 and 1978 Forest was unbeaten for a League record 42 games and won the Championship, the club's only League title, and the **League Cup** (1–0 replay v **Liverpool**) in the same season. In the following season, Forest won the **European Cup** (1–0 v **Malmö FF**) – having beaten holders **Liverpool** (2–0 agg.) in the first round – the League Cup again (3–2 v **Southampton**), making it the first to retain the trophy, and finished second in the League. In 1979-80, Forest played in three Cup finals, winning the European Cup (1–0 v **Hamburg (SV)**) and the **European Super Cup** (2–1 agg. v **Barcelona**), and losing in the League Cup final (0–1 v **Wolverhampton Wanderers**). The club lost the European Super Cup encounter with **Valencia** on away goals in 1980-81 (2–2 agg.), and in 1983-84 was defeated in a **UEFA Cup** semi-final (2–3 agg. v **RSC Anderlecht**). Thirteen years later, allegations that the match referee had accepted bribes from Anderlecht officials surfaced and led to the Belgian club being banned from European competition for one year – this verdict was later overturned by the **Court of Arbitration for Sport** (CAS). Clough's Forest enjoyed further success in the League Cup, winning the trophy in consecutive seasons in 1989 (3–1 v Luton Town) and 1990 (1–0 v **Oldham Athletic**). The following season, Forest reached the FA Cup final (1–2 a.e.t. v Tottenham Hotspur) and, in 1992, another League Cup final (0–1 v Manchester United). Clough's reign as Forest manager ended with the club's relegation to the First Division in 1992-93. Forest immediatley won promotion, but after finishing third in its first season in the Premier League and despite reaching the semi-final stage of the UEFA Cup (2–7 agg. v **Bayern Munich**) the following year, the club was relegated again in 1996-97. Under the managership of Dave Bassett, Forest returned to the top flight in 1997-98, winning the First Division title. Bassett was dismissed early in 1999 and the club was relegated at the end of the season. The club was floated on the **Alternative Investment Market** in October 1997 (flotation price = 70p), which is a precursor to full floatation on the stock market. *League record* Premier League 1992-93, 1994-95 to 1996-97, 1998-99–; Division One 1892-93 to 1905-06, 1907-08 to 1910-11, 1922-23 to 1924-25, 1957-58 to 1971-72, 1977-78 to 1991-92; First Division 1993-94, 1997-98, 1999-00; Division Two 1906-07, 1911-12 to 1921-22, 1925-26 to 1948-49, 1951-52 to 1956-57, 1972-73 to 1976-77; Division Three (South) 1949-50 to 1950-51. *Honours* League 1977-78; First Division 1997-98; Division Two 1906-07, 1921-22; Dvision Three (South) 1950-51; FA Cup

1898 (3–1 v Derby County), 1959 (2–1 v Luton Town – *Team* Thomson, Whare, McDonald, Whitefoot, McKinlay, Burkitt, Dwight (1), Quigley, Wilson (1), Gray, Imlach); League Cup 1978 (1–0 replay v Liverpool), 1979 (3–2 v Southampton), 1989 (3–1 v Luton Town), 1990 (1–0 v Oldham Athletic). **FA Charity Shield** 1978 (5–0 v **Ipswich Town**); **Simod Cup** 1989 (4–3 v Everton); **Zenith Data Systems Cup** 1992 (3–2 v Southampton); **Anglo-Scottish Cup** 1977 (5–1 agg. v **Orient**); European Cup 1979 (1–0 v Malmö FF – *Team* **Shilton**, Anderson, Lloyd, Burns, Clark, Francis (1), McGovern, Bowyer, Robertson, Woodcock, Birtles), 1980 (1–0 v Hamburg (SV) – *Team* Shilton, Anderson, Gray (Gunn), Lloyd, Burns, O'Neill, McGovern, Bowyer, Mills (O'Hare), Robertson (1), Birtles); European Super Cup 1980 (2–1 agg. v Barcelona). *Records* Stuart **Pearce** is Forest's most capped player (76 for **England**); Bob McKinlay holds the record for club appearances (614, 1951-70); Grenville Morris is Forest's overall record goalscorer (199, 1898-1913).

Nottingham Forest plc *n.* publicly-quoted business which owns **Nottingham Forest**. The club became a listed company on the **Alternative Investment Market** in October 1997 (flotation price = 70p). Forest had a market capitalisation – the market value of the company's issued share capital (eg the quoted price of its shares multiplied by the number of shares outstanding) – of £31.8 million when it joined the AIM.

Notts County *club* English league. *Dossier* Ground: **Meadow Lane** (County Ground), Nottingham. Strip: black and white striped shirts, white shorts, black socks. Nickname: Magpies. Ground capacity: 20,300. Record attendance: 47,310 v **York City** (12 March 1955, **FA Cup**, sixth round). Best average attendance: 35,176 (1949-50). Record win: 15–0 v **Rotherham Town** (24 October 1885, FA Cup, first round, at Trent Bridge). Biggest defeat: 1–9 v **Blackburn Rovers** (16 November 1889, Division One), v **Aston Villa** (29 September 1888, Division One), v **Portsmouth** (9 April 1927, Division Two). *History* Founded in 1862 (formally constituted in December 1864 when the club began playing fixtures against other clubs rather than simply playing internal matches), the club is the oldest in the **Football League** or **Premier League**. Several of County's early venues were cricket grounds, including Trent Bridge and Beeston Cricket Ground, which it shared with the cricketers (although cricket generally took priority), as well as sharing **Nottingham Forest**'s facilities. The club finally moved to a ground of its own in 1910, when it became tenants at the council-owned Meadow Lane. County reached consecutive FA Cup semi-finals in 1883 (1–2 v **Old Etonians**) and 1884 (0–1 v Blackburn Rovers) In 1885, the club turned professional, becoming a founder member of the Football League in 1888-89. County was a FA Cup finalist in 1891 (1–3 v Blackburn Rovers) and won the competition three years later (4–1 v **Bolton Wanderers**), thus becoming the first club from outside the top flight to win the trophy. (Overall seven Division Two clubs have won the FA Cup: Notts County (1894), **Wolverhampton Wanderers** (1908), **Barnsley** (1912), **West Bromwich Albion** (1931), **Sunderland** (1973), **Southampton** (1976), **West Ham United** (1980).) County was relegated from Division One in 1892-93 via the end-of-season **test matches**, which, between 1892-93 and 1897-98, were used to determine promotion and relegation. The club won the Division Two Championship in 1896-97, 1913-14 and 1922-23. County finished third in Division One in 1890-91 and 1900-01 – the club's highest League position. It reached the FA Cup semi-final in 1921. (1–3 v **Huddersfield Town**). By 1930-31, the club was playing in Division Three (South), albeit for one season, regaining its higher grade status by winning the title. Relegation from Division Two in 1957-58 was immediately followed by further demotion to Division Four for the first time in the club's history. The club endured a further seven-season spell in the bottom division between 1964-65 and 1970-71, returning to Division Three as champions at the beginning of a period which, in 1983-84, culminated in a return to the top flight for the first time in 50 seasons. County was an end-of-season Division Three **playoff** semi-finalist in 1987-88 and, in 1989-90, the club won the playoff final (2–0 v **Tranmere Rovers**) – the club's first **Wembley** appearance. The following season the club was again victorious in the playoffs (3–1 v **Brighton & Hove Albion**). It made a third Wembley appearance in five years when it won the re-established **Anglo-Italian Cup** at the stadium in 1995 (2–1 v Ascoli). Relegation from Division One in 1991-92 was rapidly followed by further demotions, so that by 1997-98 the club was playing in the bottom division. During the 1997-98 season, County achieved a number of milestones. It became the first club to play 4,000 league matches (on 10 January 1998, v **Rochdale**). County's victory over **Mansfield Town** (2–0) on 31 January 1998 was the club's 10th in succession and its sixth consecutive away win, a record for the club going back 102 years. The home win over **Leyton Orient** on 28 March 1998 (1–0) ensured promotion to Division Two, and made the club only the second since **World War II** to win a division Championship as early as March (the other being **Middlesbrough** in 1973-74). County was a **League Cup** quarter-finalist in 1964 (0–1 v **Manchester City**), 1973 (1–3 v **Chelsea**) and 1976 (0–1 v **Newcastle United**). **Juventus**' strip is modelled on Notts County's colours. *League record* Division One (including Football League) 1888-89 to 1892-93, 1897-98 to 1912-13, 1914-15 to 1919-20, 1923-24 to 1925-26, 1981-82 to 1983-84, 1991-92; First Division 1992-93 to 1994-95; Division Two 1893-94 to 1896-97, 1913-14, 1920-21 to 1922-23, 1926-27 to 1929-30, 1931-32 to 1934-35, 1950-51 to 1957-58, 1973-74 to 1980-81, 1984-85, 1990-91; Second Division 1995-96 to 1996-97, 1998-99–; Division Three 1958-59, 1960-61 to 1963-64, 1971-72 to 1972-73, 1985-86 to 1989-

90; Third Division 1997-98; Division Three (South) 1930-31, 1935-36 to 1949-50; Division Four 1959-60, 1964-65 to 1970-71. *Honours* Division Two 1896-97, 1913-14, 1922-23; Division Three (South) 1930-31, 1949-50; Third Division 1997-98; Division Four 1970-71. FA Cup 1894 (4–1 v Bolton Wanderers); Anglo-Italian Cup 1995 (2–1 v Ascoli). *Records* Kevin Wilson is County's most capped player (15 (42) for **Northern Ireland**); Albert Iremonger holds the record for club League appearances (564, 1904-26); Les Bradd is County's record League goalscorer (124, 1967-78).

Nou Camp   *ground*   Spanish football ground situated in Barcelona, Catalonia; home of **Barcelona**. Ground capacity: 115,000. *History* Opened on 24 September 1957 (v Warsaw Select XI) and built at a cost 66 million pesetas. The new ground (camp nou in Catalan) initially had a 90,000 capacity, which was increased to 120,000 for the 1982 **World Cup**. Adjoining facilities include a mini stadium, the 16,500 capacity Mini-Estad, which was opened in 1982 and is the home of Barça's reserve **team**. The Nou Camp was redeveloped for both the 1982 World Cup and again for the 1992 **Olympic Games**. The conversion of terracing to seated accommodation has reduced the capacity slightly to around 118,000. During the 1982 World Cup, the stadium staged five matches: the opening game (**Belgium** v **Argentina**, group 3); all three second round group A fixtures (**Poland** v Belgium, **Soviet Union** v Belgium, Poland v Soviet Union); and a semi-final (**Italy** v Poland) – total attendance 250,000; average attendance 50,000. It also hosted the opening ceremony. The stadium was the venue of the 1992 Olympic Games final (**Spain** v Poland, 95,000), the 1989 **European Cup** final (**AC Milan** v **Steaua Bucharest**, 97,000) and the 1982 **European Cup-winners Cup** final (Barcelona v **Standard Club Liège**, 100,000). It was also the setting for the 1999 European Cup final (Manchester United v Bayern Munich, 90,000).

NSAID   *medical*   abbreviation for non-steroidal anti-inflammatory drug. A form of painkiller that works by suppressing the inflammatory response. Available over the counter at chemists. Ibuprofen is a typical example.

number of victories   *n. pl.*   method of determining the league position if two or more clubs are level on **points**. In the national league of **Belgium**, for example, this takes precedence over **goal difference**. See also **goal average**, **goals scored**.

number two   *n.*   another word for **assistant manager/coach**.

Nuremberg   (Nürnberg) (1. FC)   *club*   German league. *Dossier* Ground: Frankenstadion, Nuremberg, Bavaria. Strip: red and white striped shirts, black shorts, red and white socks. Ground capacity: 49,000. *History* Formed in 1900. In the inter-war period, Nuremberg, simply referred to as Der Club, was Germany's dominant club, winning six German Championships between 1920 and 1936. It also won the first German Cup (**DFB Dokal**) final in 1935 and, in 1948, the inaugural West German championship. Nuremberg's last major success of the 20th century was in 1967-68 when the club won its only **Bundesliga** title. It has since reached the German Cup final on only one occasion (1982, 2–4 v **Bayern Munich**). Nuremberg's best performance in European club competition occurred in 1963, when it was a **European Cup-winners Cup** semi-finalist (2–3 agg. **Atlético Madrid**). The club returned to the Bundesliga in 1998-99 after several years in the lower divisions, including a spell in Regionalliga Süd (one of the four regional third divisions). *Honours* German League 1920 (2–0 v SPVgg Fürth), 1921 (5–0 v Vorwärts Berlin), 1924 (3–0 v **Hamburg** (SV)), 1925 (1–0 v FSV Frankfurt), 1927 (2–0 v Hertha BSC Berlin), 1936 (2–1 v Fortuna Düsseldorf); West German League 1948 (2–1 v **Kaiserslautern** (1.FC)), 1961 (3–0 v **Borussia Dortmund**); Bundesliga 1967-68; German Cup 1935 (2–0 v **Schalke 04** FC), 1939 (2–0 v SV Waldhof Mannheim); West German Cup 1962 (2–1 v Fortuna Düsseldorf).

nursery club   *n.*   a club which acts as a junior partner in a first-refusal arrangement with a second - usually senior, or richer - club. The senior partner usually has first refusal on signing any young players; while others may be given match experience at the nursery club. The nursery club invariably benefits from financial or coaching assistance or investment from the senior club. *Keynotes* In November 1998, **Manchester United** and **Royal Antwerp** of Belgium reached a nursery – club agreement in which United invested in the Belgian club. **Arsenal** has a similar agreement with the French club

Saint Etienne. West Ham United established deals with the Perth club (Australia) Kingsway Olympics (subsequently called Sydney Hammers) and Sydney-based Blacktown City, which involved the establishment of two centres of excellence. The agreement allows West Ham to bring the best players to London subject to work-permit rules. One novel approach, adopted by German club Bonner, was to sign 15 members of the Cuban national squad. The so-called co-operation agreement, signed by Bonner and the Cuban football federation in December 1998, enables the Cubans to gain from German coaching and Bonner to field any of the players. **Roma (AS)** bought French club **Olympique Gymnaste Club de Nice** for around £2 million in 1998, enabling the Italian club's young players to gain experience in first-team football. In January 1999, **Ajax** became the first club to franchise its name by taking a 51% share in the South African club Ajax Cape Town, which had been formed from a merger between Seven Stars and **Cape Town Spurs**. The Dutch club invested £1.2 million in its South African counterpart, with the aim of nurturing young talented African players. *regulations* **Football League** clubs are prohibited from establishing nursery-club arrangements with other clubs (either as junior or senior partners). (Football League regulation 86). *vb.* to execute a nutmeg.

nutmeg   *n.*   ball played between an opponent's legs. Sometimes shortened to "nuts" or "megs" depending on individual preference.

O

O'Higgins (Club de Deportes) *club* Chilean national league club based in Rancagua, founded 1955. Ground: Estadio El Teniente, capacity: 25,000. Strip: sky blue shirts, white shorts. Chilean Cup (**Copa Chile**) runners-up 1983, 1994.

Oakwell *ground* English football ground situated in Barnsley, south Yorkshire; home of **Barnsley**. *Dossier* Ground capacity: 18,806 all seated. Pitch dimensions: 100.5m x 68.5m. Record attendance: 40,255 v **Stoke City** (15 February 1936, **FA Cup**, fifth round). Best average attendance: 21,262 (1947-48). *History* The ground derives its name from the oak trees that previously grew on the site. Oakwell was bought by the club for £1,376 in 1911. Barnsley played its first game at Oakwell on 8 September 1888 (v Fitzwilliam, friendly) on the same day that the **Football League** began. By the 1986-87 season, Oakwell had the lowest seating capacity of any ground in the top two divisions: in February 1993 it had 2,164 seats; in August 1995, it could seat 19,073. Oakwell staged its first floodlit match in February 1962 (v **Bolton Wanderers**, friendly). The ground was the venue for a **Football League** v League of Ireland **inter-League match** on 10 September 1969.

OB Odense (Odense Boldklub) *club* Danish national league club based in Odense, founded 1887. Ground: Odense Stadion, capacity: 16,000. Strip: blue and white striped shirts, blue shorts. Danish league champions 1977, 1982, 1989; Danish Cup 1983, 1991, 1993.

Obilic Belgrade *club* Yugoslavian and **former-Yugoslavia** national league club based in the capital Belgrade, founded 1924. Ground: Obilic, capacity: 3,000. Yugoslavian league champions 1998 (a year after promotion from the second division); Yugoslavian Cup runners-up 1998.

obstruction *rules* one of the offences listed as a **foul** under the **Laws of the game** (Law XII). A foul is committed if a player's progress is unfairly impeded. An example is where a player kicks the ball past an opposition player but is prevented from following the ball because the opposition player stands in the way while making no effort to play or chase after the ball. The referee should halt play (unless an **advantage** can be played) and award an **indirect free kick** from the spot where the offence took place (unless it took place within the **defending team**'s **goal area** – in which case it is

taken either from anywhere within that area if the offence is committed by an **attacking player** or, if the offence is committed by a **defending playe**r, from the **goal area line** at the point nearest to where the foul was committed). *vb.* **obstruct** to commit such an offence.

Obuassi Goldfields *club* Ghanaian professional league club based in Obuassi. Ground: Len Clay, capacity: 9,000. Strip: orange shirts, black shorts. **African Cup of Champion Clubs** – runners-up 1997 (1–1 agg., 4–5 pens., v **RAJA CA Casablanca**, of Morocco), quarter-final 1995; Ghanaian League champions 1994, 1995, 1996; Ghanaian Cup 1993.

Oceania Cup *competition* biennial tournament for member countries of the **Oceania Football Confederation** (OFC). *History* The huge geographical area covered by Oceania slowed the development of continent-wide tournaments and by the 1990s, only two editions had been played (1973 and 1980). It was rekindled in 1996 and scheduled as a biennial tournament, doubling up as the Oceania **World Cup** qualifying competition in alternate editions. The winners also qualify for the **Confederations Cup**. The tournament has two qualifying groups: Melanesian (**Fiji, New Caledonia, Papua New Guinea, Solomon Islands, Vanuatu**); and Polynesia (**American Samoa, Cook Islands, Tahiti/French Polynesia, Tonga, Western Samoa**). Two from each group qualify for the final stages, to be joined by **New Zealand** and **Australia**; divided into two round-robin groups of three. The tournament culminates with knockout semi-finals, third/fourth place playoff and final. *Winners, results (and venues)* 1973 New Zealand, 2–0, v Tahiti (in New Zealand); 1980 Australia, 4–2, v Tahiti/French Polynesia (in New Caledonia); 1996 Australia, 11–0 agg., v Tahiti/French Polynesia (World Cup qualifier, over two legs); 1998 New Zealand, 1–0, v Australia (in Australia). *Record win:* 16–0, Australia v Cook Islands (28 September 1998, in Australia, final tournament).

Oceania Football Confederation (OFC) *confederation* international football association for Oceania, based in Auckland, **New Zealand**, founded 1966. President: Charles Dempsey (New Zealand). General secretary: Josephine King (New Zealand). The OFC does not have an automatic berth at the 2002 **World Cup**

finals; the winner of the Oceania qualifying tournament must take part in a **playoff** against the fifth-placed nation in the **Confederación Sudamericana de Fútbol** (CONMEBOL) qualifying tournament. For the 1998 World Cup finals, the winner of the OFC tournament, **Australia**, was forced to playoff against the fourth-placed nation in the **Asian Football Confederation** qualifying tournament, **Iran** – which won over two legs. The OFC was allocated one automatic place at the 1999 **Women's World Cup** finals. *History* Only two **Oceania Cup** tournaments (1973 and 1980) were played before 1996, when it was rekindled as the **Oceania World Cup** qualifying competition. It is now scheduled as a biennial tournament. The OFC has had its own World Cup qualifying group since 1986, although it has never been given an automatic qualifying place: OFC qualifying tournament winners have, on each occasion, been required to playoff against a nation from another qualifying tournament. In 1986, for example, Australia lost to **Scotland** (runners-up in one of the UEFA qualifying groups); in 1990 temporary OFC members **Israel** (playing in the OFC group to avoid conflict with Arab nations in its region) lostto **Colombia** (winners of one of the CONMEBOL groups); in 1994 Australia first played off against CONCACAF runners-up **Canada**, and then against **Argentina** (runners-up in one of the CONMEBOL groups); in 1998 Australia lost a playoff against Iran (fourth place in the AFC tournament). Prior to 1986, countries from the region played in Asia/Oceania combined qualifying tournaments. The OFC has had an automatic berth in the Women's World Cup since the first tournament in 1991. *Full member countries* Australia, **Cook Islands**, Fiji, New Zealand, **Papua New Guinea**, **Solomon Islands**, **Tahiti/French Polynesia**, **Tonga**, **Vanuatu**, **Western Samoa**. *Provisional members* **American Samoa**, **New Caledonia**. *Associate members* **Niue Island**, **Northern Marianas**. *Competitions* The OFC runs the Oceania Cup and the Oceania qualifying tournaments for the **World Cup**, Women's World Cup and youth tournaments. There are no continent-wide club tournaments.

Oceania Footballer of the Year *award* annual award made by a panel of football writers to the player from a member country of the **Oceania Football Confederation**. *Winners and nationality* 1988 Frank Farina (**Australia**); 1989 Wynton Rufer (**New Zealand**); 1990 Wynton Rufer; 1991 Robert Slater (Australia); 1992 Wynton Rufer; 1993 Robert Slater; 1994 Aurelio Vidmar (Australia); 1995 Christian Karembeu (born in **New Caledonia**, plays for **France**); 1996 Paul Okon (Australia); 1997 Mark Bosnich (Australia); 1998 Christian Karembeu.

Oceania Women's Tournament *competition* international nations tournament for women, under the auspices of the **Oceania Football Confederation** (OFC), first played 1998; serves as a qualifier for the **Women's World Cup** (winners qualify). *Winner and result* 1998 **Australia**, 3–1, v **New Zealand**.

Ochilview Park *ground* Scottish football ground situated in Stenhousemuir, Lothian region; home of **Stenhousemuir**. Ground capacity: 3,520. Pitch dimensions: 103m x 68m. Record attendance: 12,500 v **East Fife** (11 March 1950, **Scottish FA Cup**, fourth round). *Keynotes* Stenhousemuir first played at Ochilview Park in 1890 and it remains one of the least developed of all **Scottish League** grounds. Ochilview Park has the distinction of being the setting for the first modern floodlit match in Scotland. This took place on 7 November 1951 (v **Hibernian**, friendly).

Ocwirk, Ernst *player-manager* Midfield. **Austria** international (62 caps, 1945-62). Born 7 March 1926, died 1980. *Clubs* Floridsdorfer, FK **Austria Vienna** (twice), **Sampdoria**. *Honours* **World Cup** third place (Austria, 1954); Austrian league championship (Austria Vienna, 1949, 1950, 1953; as manager of Austria Vienna, 1969, 1970). *Keynotes* Captain of the Austrian national team. In 1954 World Cup, he scored the final goal in the 3–1 defeat of **Uruguay** to take the third place in the tournament. He was nicknamed "Clockwork Ocwirk" by the English press and spectators after the 2–2 draw between **England** and Austria at **Wembley** on 28 November 1951 (friendly): Ocwirk was at the centre of Austria's precision play, exemplified by his accurate long pass that to set up Melchior for the first goal of the game. Ocwirk moved to Sampdoria in 1956 and was voted seventh in the first *France Football* **European Footballer of the Year** award in his first season in Italy. Returned to Austria Vienna in 1961. Later became coach of Austria Vienna, wining two league titles, and Sampdoria.

Odd Sk Skien (Sportsklubb) *club* Norwegian league club based in Skien, founded in 1894 (Norway's second-oldest football club). Ground: Falkum. Strip: white shirts, black shorts. Norwegian league runners-up 1951, 1957; Norwegian Cup 1903, 1904, 1905, 1906, 1913, 1915, 1919, 1922, 1924, 1926, 1931.

odds *n. pl.* the ratio offered by a bookmaker for a wager on the outcome of a particular event, such as the exact score in a match, the winners of a tournament, or the first player to score in a game. Odds of 6:1 (expressed as: six to one *against*), for example, mean that a successful £10 stake will win £60 (plus the return of the stake, and minus any betting tax). Odds of 10:11 (expressed as: eleven to 10 *on*) mean that a £10 stake will win only £9.09 (plus the return of the stake and minus any tax). When the bet is "evens" (1:1), a £10 bet will win £10 (plus the return of the stake and minus any tax). Also known as **price**.

OFC *abbrev.* **Oceania Football Confederation**

off-the-ball *n.* match incident that occurs away from the ball.

offensive or abusive language *rules* one of the listed infringements of the **Laws of the game** punishable by the offending player being **sent off** (Law XII). The offence is committed irrespective of whether the language is directed at another player (of either team), match official or other person. The **International FA**

Board specifically includes racist remarks under this offence.

Office of Fair Trading *misc.* British regulatory body to ensure competitive business practice. The OFT has occasionally ruled on UK football matters. In November 1978, the OFT ruled against ITV's bid to show match highlights on a Saturday evening after the commercial television channels had agreed a three-year deal with the **Football League.** The OFT claimed the deal, which would have ended **Match of the Day**, was a breach of the laws relating to restrictive practices. It has also investigated the television agreement between the **Premier League** clubs and BSkyB to determine whether the clubs had acted as a cartel and should alternatively sell the rights to matches individually. In November 1998, the OFT recommended that BSkyB's proposed takeover of **Manchester United** be referred to the Monopolies and Mergers Commission (now Competition Commission).

official *n.* **1.** a person designated with the responsibility of, or assisting with, enforcing the **Laws of the game**. The officials are the **referee**, two **assistant referees** and, for some matches, the **fourth official**. **2.** a senior representative of a football club, federation or governing body.

offside *rules* a potentially-illegal playing position taken up by a player relative to the ball, the field of play and the opposition players, as stipulated by the **Laws of the game** (Law XI). It is not an offence per se to be in an offside position. A player is in an offside position if, at the moment the ball touches, or is played by one of his/her team mates, all the following conditions are satisfied: (a) he/she is in the opposition's **half** of the field; (b) he or she is closer to the opponent's **goal line** than the ball; and (c) there are fewer than two **defending players** closer than him/her to the goal line (the goalkeeper is also counted as a defending player). The player can be penalised only if, as well as being in an offside position, the **referee** considers that he/she is **interfering with play** or an opponent, or can gain an advantage by being in that position. A player is not offside if he/she receives the ball directly from a **goal-kick**, a **corner-kick**, or a **throw-in**. Nor is a player offside if he or she is level with the second-last or last two opponents. The rule only applies to a player at the moment the ball is played by a team mate – once the ball has been played, the player does not become offside by, for example, running forward, even if there are subsequently fewer than two opposition players between the player and the goal line. The referee may penalise a player for being in an offside position – assuming the above criteria are satisfied – by stopping play and awarding an **indirect free-kick** to the opposition, taken from the position that the infringement occurred. The referee may choose not to halt play if an **advantage** can be played by the opposition team. It is one of the duties of the **assistant referees** to indicate to the referee when a player may be penalised for being in an offside position, by raising the **assistant ref-**

eree's flag. *History* The first offside rule, played at the English Public schools in the mid 19th century, meant that no attacking player could be in front of the ball when the ball was played (**rugby football** has retained this principle). This meant that players tended to dribble the ball forward rather than pass it. In 1867, the **Football Association** modified the rule so that a player would only be offside if, when the ball was played, he was both in front of the ball and one of the last three defending players – as played at that time by Charterhouse and Westminster schools (the so-called three-man offside rule). This favoured much greater positional and passing-based tactics. The offside rule was changed in 1925 by the **International FA Board** when the key number of defending players closer to the goal line than the attacking player was reduced from three to two (a central principle of the modern offside rule), and one which led to the development of contemporary **formations**. The rule was amended in 1990 so that an attacking player level with the key defending player was not deemed offside (previously, a player could be offside simply by being level with the second-last defending player). *adj.* usage: offside position; offside player. *adv.* usage: straying offside; caught offside See: **interfering with play**, **offside trap**, **onside**.

offside trap *tactics* strategy implemented by a defending team to increase the likelihood of the attacking players being caught **offside**. The trap is implemented by maintaining a straight line of defenders, parallel with the **goal line**, that quickly moves forward in unison before the ball is played by an attacking player; as the line moves forward, any attacking player in front of the line will be offside as soon as the ball is played. If the forward player is deemed to be interfering with play, the referee will give an **indirect free kick** to the defenders. The line may be held anywhere up to the **half-way line**, thus keeping the opposition players in their own half. *Keynotes* The strategy has created a counter-offensive strategy where forwards attempt to beat the offside trap by timing their forward run so that they are level with the line of defending players as the ball is played; the defenders are thus caught out of position and the attacker has a clear run towards goal.

OFK Beograd (Omladinski Futbal Klub Beograd) *club* Yugoslavian and **former-Yugoslavia** national league club based in the capital Belgrade, Serbia, founded 1911 (as BSK Beograd); the oldest top-flight club in Yugoslavia. Ground: Omladinski, capacity: 25,000. Strip: white shirts, white shorts. **European Cup-winners Cup** semi-final 1963; **UEFA Cup** quarter-final 1973; **Mitropa Cup** semi-final 1939 (as BSK Beograd); former Yugoslavia league champions (as BSK) 1931, 1933, 1935, 1936, 1939; former Yugoslavia Cup (as BSK) 1953, 1955, (as OSK) 1962, 1966. Notable former player: Slobodan Santrac (Yugoslavia's national team coach for the World Cup in 1998).

OGC Nice *club* France. See **Olympique Gymnaste Club de Nice**.

Ögryte Idrottssälskap (Ögryte IS Gothenburg) *club* Swedish national league club based in Gothenburg, founded 1887, the oldest remaining club in Sweden. Ground: Gamla Ullevi Stadium, capacity: 18,000. Strip: red shirts, red shorts. Swedish league champions 1896, 1897, 1898, 1899, 1902, 1904, 1905, 1906, 1907, 1909, 1913, 1926, 1928, 1985.

Okwahu United *club* Ghanaian professional league club based in Nkawkaw. Ground: Nkawkaw Sports, capacity: 15,000. Strip: red shirts, yellow shorts. Ghanaian Cup 1986. Notable former player: Anthony **Yeboah**.

Old Etonians *club* amateur football club founded in 1865, comprising former pupils of Eton College. *Keynotes* Old Etonians were twice winners of the **FA Cup** (1879, 1–0 v Clapham Rovers, and 1882, 1–0 v **Blackburn Rovers**). The club was also four-times runner-up, losing in the finals of 1875, 1876, 1881 and 1883. Old Etonians played in the first FA Cup Final to go to **extra time** (13 March 1875, v **Royal Engineers**). The match finished 1–1. Three days later, Old Etonians became the first team to lose an FA Cup final **replay** (0–2). It was the last all-**amateur** team to win the FA Cup. Lord Alfred **Kinnaird**, the club founder and one of its FA Cup winners, later became president of the **Football Association**. Old Etonians now play in the Arthurian League.

Old Show Ground *ground* former-English football ground situated in Scunthorpe, Humberside; former home of **Scunthorpe United**. *Dossier* Capacity (1998): 10,000. Record attendance: 23,935 v **Portsmouth** (30 January 1954, **FA Cup**, fourth round). *Keynotes* Brumby Hall, one of the clubs which would merge in 1899 to form Scunthorpe United, first played at the Old Show Ground in 1895 and it was United's home until 1988, when Scunthorpe moved to a new stadium, **Glanford Park**. The Old Show Ground is famous for having the first **cantilever stand** in the UK, which was opened 23 August 1958 with seats for 2,200 people. The first floodlit match at the Old Show Ground took place on 3 October 1957 (v **Rochdale**, Division Three (North)). It staged its final match on 18 May 1988 (v **Torquay United**, Division Four **playoff** semi-final).

Old Trafford *ground* English football ground situated in Manchester; home of **Manchester United**. *Dossier* Ground capacity: 56,387 all seated. Pitch dimensions: 106m x 69m. Record attendance: 76,962 **Wolverhampton Wanderers** v **Grimsby Town** (**FA Cup** semi-final, 25 March 1939). Club record attendance: 70,504 v **Aston Villa** (27 December 1920, **Division One**). Best average attendance: 57,552 (1967-68). *History* Manchester United benefactor and local brewer John Davies purchased the Old Trafford site after the club had won its first **Football League** title in 1908. The ground, built at a cost £60,000, was designed by Archibald **Leitch** and had a potential capacity of 80,000. Manchester United played its first match at Old Trafford on 19 February 1910 (v **Liverpool**, Division One). Old Trafford is one of only two English club grounds that has staged two League matches featuring different clubs on the same day (the other is **Hartlepool United**'s **Victoria Park** in August 1986): in May 1921 the ground was the venue for United v **Derby County** and later that day, the Division Two encounter between **Stockport County** and **Leicester City** (Stockport's **Edgeley Road** ground had been closed due to **crowd trouble**). Old Trafford's location, close to the Manchester Ship canal and Trafford Park docks, was classed as an industrial zone, which allowed the club, unlike many others, to develop the ground largely unhindered by the proximity of housing, and the planning controls that accompany residential areas. Despite massage rooms, a gymnasium and tip-up seats, Old Trafford failed to keep up with ground developments elsewhere. In the 1930s, the club almost followed its predecessor, Newton Heath, into bankruptcy, and this was followed by near relegation to the then Division Three (North). As a result, gates declined and Old Trafford had little development. United was forced to use **Manchester City**'s **Maine Road** ground between 1941 and 1949 because Old Trafford, due to its proximity to the docks, had suffered extensive bomb damage during **World War II**. After the war, the War Damage Commission awarded the club more than £22,000 to help rebuild the stands and United returned to Old Trafford in August 1949. However, the club was forced to play its midweek European fixtures at Maine Road in 1956 owing to the lack of floodlighting at Old Trafford; a problem that was eventually solved in March 1957, although two sections of roofing had to be demolished to prevent shadows. Ground development in the 1960s included the construction of private boxes (see **executive boxes**) – the first at a European football ground. During the 1967-68 season, Old Trafford attracted the highest average gate (57,759) ever recorded by an English league club. In 1973, the ground became fully covered, and two years later, in order to build on the success of the private facilities constructed nine years earlier, United erected an executive suite at the back of the main stand. As part of Old Trafford's transformation to an all-seater stadium following the recommendations of the **Taylor Report**, the Stretford End, the oldest undeveloped part of the ground, was demolished in May 1992 – its final match being Norman Whiteside's **testimonial** on 3 May. The first phase of the 10,000-plus all-seater Stretford End development was opened in September 1992 – with fans offered free plastic rain capes because there was no roof – and completed in the summer of 1993. The last terracing, at the Scoreboard End, was replaced in 1994. In 1995, United began the construction of new 25,500 seat three-tier north stand that was completed in May 1996, bringing Old Trafford's capacity up to 55,300 – the biggest club ground in England. The temporary floodlights used during the construction of the new north stand subsequently were used by **Chelsea** while **Stamford Bridge**'s new west stand was being built. Old Trafford's north stand houses a musuem and tour centre, including an interactive multi-media facility. In September 1998, United announced further redevelopment of Old Trafford with plans to expand its capacity to 67,500. Old Trafford has staged one FA Cup final (1915 Chelsea v **Sheffield United**), two final replays (1911 **Bradford City** v **Newcastle United**, 1970 Chelsea v **Leeds United**) and two **League Cup** final replays (1977 Aston Villa v **Everton**, 1978 **Nottingham Forest** v Liverpool). The ground also regularly hosts FA Cup semi-finals. In 1966, Old Trafford was used as a **World Cup** venue. The ground staged group 3 matches (**Portugal** v **Hungary**; Portugal v **Bulgaria**; Hungary v Bulgaria) – total attendance 79,453; average attendance 26,484. Old Trafford was also a **European Championship** venue in 1996, staging: group C matches (**Czech Republic** v **Germany**; Germany v **Russia**; **Italy** v Germany); a quarter final (Germany v Portugal); and a semi-final (Czech Republic v **France**). In addition, Old Trafford has staged two **England** internationals (v **Scotland**, 17 April 1926, v **South Africa**, 24 May 1997) and numerous Rugby League internationals and Cup finals, including the inaugural Super League Gand final (24 October 1998). The first floodlit match at Old Trafford occurred on 25 March 1957 (v **Bolton Wanderers**, Division One). In memory of the lives lost in the **Munich air disaster**, a commemorative clock stands outside Old Trafford.

oldest goalkeeper *record* **1. World Cup** finals tournament: Pat **Jennings** was the oldest goalkeeper at a World Cup finals match; he was 41 years old when playing for **Northern Ireland** against **Brazil** on his birthday in 1986 (0–3, 12 June, in Guadalajara, Mexico). Dino **Zoff**, at 40 years old, was the oldest keeper in a World Cup final when playing for **Italy** against West **Germany** in 1982 (3–1, 11 July, in Madrid, Spain). **2. Football League**: Neil McBain, at 51 years 120 days, for **New Brighton** (v **Hartlepool United**, 15 March 1947, Division Three North); Peter **Shilton** was the oldest first-choice (ie not an emergency stand-in) goalkeeper at 47 years 126 days, for **Leyton Orient** (1996–97, Third Division).

oldest ground *record* **Chesterfield** is thought to have played its earliest matches at the **Recreation Ground**, some time between 1866 and 1870, which would make it the **Football League**'s oldest venue. **Northwich Victoria** of the **Football Conference** claims to occupy the world's oldest football ground (Drill Field) in continuous use by one club, while Hallam claims the world's oldest ground (Sandgate), first used for football in 1860.

oldest player *record* **1. World**: **Uruguay** striker Hector **Scarone**, (career ca. 1917-53) retired from senior football aged 55 years. **2. World Cup finals**: Roger **Milla** of **Cameroon** played in the World Cup finals in 1994, and at the age of 42 years and 39 days he scored in his country's final group match (1–6, v **Russia**, 28 June 1994, in Detroit, USA, first round: coincidentally, the match in which Oleg **Salenko** scored a World Cup

finals record five goals in one game). **3. Football League**: Neil McBain, at 51 years 120 days, for **New Brighton** (v **Hartlepool United**, 15 March 1947, Division Three North). McBain was also the oldest goalkeeper, though he was only an emergency replacement (he was actually the New Brighton manager). **3.** Football League Division One: Stanley **Matthews**, at 50 years five days, was the oldest English top-flight player when he played his last league match for **Stoke City** (v **Fulham**, 3–1, 6 February 1965. **4.** FA **Premier League**: John Burridge, 43 years 147 days, for **Manchester City** (v **Newcastle United**, 29 April 1995). Burridge was also the oldest Premier League goalkeeper, and kept a clean sheet (he went on as half-time substitute and the game finished 0–0). **5. Football Association Women's Premier League**: Sue Buckett, of Southampton Saints, retired from league football in 1994 at the age of 51.

Oldham Athletic *club* English league. *Dossier* Ground: **Boundary Park**, Oldham, Greater Manchester. Strip: blue and red striped shirts, blue shorts with red trim, blue socks with red trim. Nickname: the Latics. Ground capacity: 13,559 all seated. Record attendance: 47,671 v **Sheffield Wednesday** (25 January 1930, **FA Cup**, fourth round). Best average attendance: 18,075 (1920-21). Biggest win: 11–0 v **Southport** (26 December 1962, Division Four). Biggest defeat: 4–13 v **Tranmere Rovers** (26 December 1935, Division Three (North)). *History* Founded in 1897 as Pine Villa, a pub team, the club took over the ground (Athletic Ground) in 1899 vacated by the town's first professional club, Oldham County, turned professional and adopted the name Oldham Athletic to reflect its new home. At the turn of the century, Oldham spent several seasons away from the Athletic Ground (later Boundary Park), at nearby Hudson Fold, before returning permanently in 1906. The club was elected to Division Two in 1907-08, finishing third in that season, and, in 1909-10, won promotion to Division One on **goal average**. The years immediately proceeding **World War I** were amongst Oldham's most successful periods, with the club an FA Cup semi-finalist in 1913 (0–1 v **Aston Villa**) and Division One runners-up in 1914-15 – the club's highest-ever position. Oldham lost its top-flight status in 1922-23, dropping to Division Three (North) in 1935-36. The club won the Division Three (North) title in 1952-53, but managed only one season in Division Two. Promotion from Division Four in 1970-71 (a year in which the club won the **Ford Sporting League**) was quickly followed in 1973-74 by the Division Three Championship. Under the managership of ex-**Everton** striker and former **England** international Joe Royle (1982-94), Oldham narrowly missed promotion to the Division One in 1986-87, losing at the semi-final stage of the end-of-season **playoffs**, before the club secured a return to the top flight in 1990-91 for the first time in 68 years by winning the Division Two title. In the same season, Oldham made its first **Wembley** appearance, reaching the **League Cup** final (0–1 v **Nottingham**

Forest), having defeated **Arsenal** (3–1, fourth round), **Southampton** (2–0 replay, fifth round) and **West Ham United** (6–3 agg. semi-final) on the way. The club was also an FA Cup semi-finalist (1–2 replay v **Manchester United**), having earlier disposed of both **Everton** (2–1 replay, fifth round) and Aston Villa (3–0, sixth round). Oldham made a further FA Cup semi-final appearance in 1994 (1–4 replay v Manchester United), but was relegated from the **Premier League** in the same season. Further demotion followed in 1996-97. Between 1986 and 1991, Oldham's Boundary Park ground had an **artificial pitch**. *League record* Premier League 1992-93 to 1993-94; Division One 1910-11 to 1922-23; First Division 1991-92, 1994-94 to 1996-97; Division Two 1907-08 to 1909-10, 1923-24 to 1934-35, 1953-54, 1974-75 to 1990-91; Second Division 1997-98–; Division Three 1963-64 to 1968-69, 1971-72 to 1973-74; Division Three (North) 1935-36 to 1952-53, 1954-55 to 1957-58; Divsion Four 1958-59 to 1962-63, 1969-70 to 1970-71. *Honours* Division Two 1990-91; Division Three 1973-74; Division Three (North) 1952-53. *Records* Gunnar Halle is Oldham's most capped player (61 for **Norway**); Ian Wood holds the record for club League appearances (525, 1966-80); Roger Palmer is Oldham's record League goalscorer (141, 1988-94).

Olimpia (Club Deportivo) *club* Honduras national league club based in the capital Tegucigalpa, formed 1927 (the club's basketball section was founded in 1912). Ground: Estadio Nacional "Tiburcio Carias Andino", capacity: 35,000. Strip: white shirts, white shorts. **CONCACAF Champions Cup** 1972 (2–0 agg., v **Robin Hood** of Surinam) and 1988 (4–0 agg., v **Defence Force** of Trinidad and Tobago), runners-up 1985 (1–2 agg., v Defence Force); **CONCACAF Cup-winners Cup** finalist 1998 (v **Necaxa** of Mexico); **Torneo Grandes de Centroamerica** semi-final 1998; Honduras League champions 1966, 1967, 1969, 1971, 1977, 1982, 1984, 1986, 1987, 1989, 1993, 1996, 1997; Honduras Cup 1995; **Campeonisimo** 1982, 1984, 1993.

Olimpia (Club Olimpia) *club* Paraguay national league club based in the capital Asuncion, founded in 1902 by William Paats, a Dutch physical education instructor in Asuncion, and his pupils. Ground: Estadio Manuel Ferreira, capacity: 40,000. Strip: white shirts with a black hoop, white shorts. *Keynotes* Olimpia qualified for the first **Copa Libertadores** in 1960. It was the first club from outside of **Brazil**, **Argentina** or **Uruguay** to win the Copa Libertadores (1979), and the first to have won the South American club "double", winning the Copa Libertadores and **Supercopa** in the same season (1990). There is a traditional rivalry with Club **Guarani**, dating back to 1903 (the game between the two is known as the "Viejo clasico", or Old Classic). It holds the national league record of six consecutive championships (1978 to 1983). By 1999, it had won 36 league championships; only five clubs in the world had won more domestic titles. *Honours* Copa Libertadores winners 1979 (2–0, 0–0, v **Boca Juniors**), 1990 (3–1

agg., v **Barcelona Sporting Club** of Peru), runners-up 1960 (the first Copa Libertadores, 0–1, 1–1, v **Peñarol**), 1989 (2–2 agg., 4–5 pens., v **Atlético Nacional Medellin** of Colombia), 1991 (0–3 agg., v **Colo Colo** of Chile); Supercopa winners 1990 (6–3 agg., v **Nacional Montevideo** of Uruguay); **Copa CONMEBOL** runners-up 1992; **Copa Mercosur** semi-final 1998; **Recopa** – Olimpia (winners 1990 – by default having won the Copa Libertadores and the Supercopa in the same season); **Copa Inter-America** winners 1979-80 (8–3 agg., v **Deportivo FAS** of El Salvador); **World Club Cup** 1979-80 (3–1 agg., v **Malmö FF** of Sweden); Paraguay League champions 1912, 1914, 1916, 1925, 1927, 1928, 1929, 1931, 1936, 1937, 1938, 1947, 1948, 1956, 1957, 1958, 1959, 1960, 1962, 1965, 1968, 1971, 1975, 1978, 1979, 1980, 1981, 1982, 1983, 1985, 1988, 1989, 1993, 1995, 1997, 1998.

Olimpico (Estadio Hernándo Siles) *ground* Bolivian national stadium situated in La Paz; home of **Bolivia** national side and clubs **Bolivar** Independiente Unificada, Club Deportivo Municipal, Club Chaco Petrolero. Ground capacity: 55,000 (29,000 seated). *History* At 3,800 metres (12,400 feet) above sea level, Estadio Hernando Siles is the highest national stadium in the world. The stadium partially staged the 1963 (29th edition) **Copa America**, which Bolivia won for the first and only occasion.

Olimpico (Stadio) *ground* Italian football ground situated in Rome, Lazio; home of **Lazio** and **Roma (AS)**. Ground capacity: 82,000 all seated. **Italy**'s national stadium and every third Italian international is played there. *History* Originally named Stadio dei Cipressi (Stadium of the Cypress trees) and built adjacent to the Foro Mussolini sports complex which the Fascist Italian dictator had constructed in the 1930s, but his planned 100,000 capacity stadium was never built. The Stadio Olimpico opened in 1953 (Italy v **Hungary**) and was the venue for athletics during the 1960 **Olympic Games**. The stadium was redeveloped and its capacity increased to 80,000 for the 1990 **World Cup** finals. Stadio Olimpico staged the 1990 World Cup final (West **Germany** v **Argentina**); the opening fixture (Italy v **Austria**) and two other group A matches (Italy v USA, Italy v **Czechoslovakia**); one second round game (Italy v **Uruguay**); and a quarter-final (Italy v **Republic of Ireland**) – total attendance 439,238; average attendance 73,063. It was also the venue for the 1960 Olympic Games final (**former-Yugoslavia** v **Denmark**, 40,000) and the 1968 **European Championship** final (Italy v former-Yugoslavia, 85,000 (+ replay, 85,000). The stadium has hosted three **European Cup** finals (1977 **Liverpool** v **Borussia Mönchengladbach**, 57,000; 1984 Liverpool v Roma (AS), 69,693; 1996 **Juventus** v **Ajax**, 67,000).

Olimpija Ljubljana *club* *Slovenia* Slovenian national league club based in the capital Ljubljana, founded 1911. Ground: Bezigrad, capacity: 18,000. Strip: green shirts, green shorts. **European Cup-**

winners Cup second round 1997; former-Yugoslavia Cup runners-up 1970 (it was the only Slovenian club to have any notable success in the former-Yugoslavian league); pre-independence Slovenian league champions 1947, 1952, 1962, 1987; Slovenian league champions 1992, 1993, 1994, 1995; pre-independence Slovenian Cup 1953, 1954, 1955, 1956, 1958, 1962, 1963, 1969, 1970, 1971, 1972, 1976, 1977, 1981, 1988; Slovenian Cup 1993, 1996.

Olimpik Tiranè *club* Albanian national league club, based in Tirana, founded 1950, formerly known as Klubi Sportiv Dinamo Tiranè. Ground: Selman Stèrmasi, capacity: 12,500. Strip: blue shirts, blue shorts. Albanian league champions 1950, 1951, 1952, 1953, 1955, 1956, 1960, 1967, 1973, 1975, 1976, 1977, 1980, 1986, 1990; Albanian Cup 1950, 1951, 1952, 1953, 1954, 1960, 1971, 1974, 1978, 1982, 1989, 1990.

Olympiakos *club* Greek national league club based in Athens, founded 1925. Ground: Yorgos Karaiskakis; capacity: 34,000. Strip: red and white striped shirts, white shorts. *Keynotes* Olympiakos won six consecutive league titles (1954 to 1959), a national record. The 1991 Karaiskakis stadium hosted the 1971 **European Cup-winners Cup** final and replay (**Chelsea** v **Real Madrid**, 3–2, agg.). Twenty-one spectators were crushed to death there on 8 February 1981 as the 40,000 crowd left the ground after a game between Olympiakos and AEK Athens; Olympiakos had won 6–0. **European Cup-winners Cup** quarter-final 1993; Greek league champions 1931, 1933, 1934, 1936, 1937, 1938, 1947, 1948, 1951, 1954, 1955, 1956, 1957, 1958, 1959, 1966, 1967, 1973, 1974, 1975, 1980, 1981, 1982, 1983, 1987, 1997, 1998, 1999; Greek Cup 1947, 1951, 1952, 1953, 1954, 1957, 1958, 1959, 1960, 1961, 1963, 1965, 1968, 1971, 1973, 1975, 1981, 1990, 1992, 1999.

Olympiastadion *ground* 1. German football ground situated in Munich, Bavaria; home of **Bayern Munich** and **Munich 1860**. Ground capacity: 64,000 all seated. *History* Built for the 1972 **Olympic Games** at a cost of Dm137 million. The stadium has an unusual-shaped glass roof which covers only two-thirds of its stands. Bayern Munich and Munich 1860 are both trying to find an alternative to the municipally-owned ground, the former planning to build a 100,000 capacity stadium at a cost of £175 million. Olympiastadion was the venue for the 1974 **World Cup** final (West **Germany** v **Netherlands**). During the tournament it also staged three group 4 matches (**Italy** v **Haiti**, **Poland** v Haiti, **Argentina** v Haiti) and the 3rd-place **playoff** (Poland v **Brazil**) – total attendance 252,433; average attendance 50,486. The stadium hosted the 1988 **European Championship** final (Netherlands v **Soviet Union**, 72,000) and the 1972 Olympic Games final (Poland v **Hungary**, 50,000). Olympiastadion has staged three **European Cup** finals (1979 **Nottingham Forest** v **Malmö FF**, 57,500; 1993 **Olympique de Marseille** v **AC Milan**, 64,400; 1997 **Borussia Dortmund** v

Juventus, 59,000). **2.** German football ground situated in Berlin; home of Hertha Berlin. Ground capacity: 76,000. *History* Built for Hitler for the 1936 Olympic Games. The ground was redeveloped in the 1960s and refurbished for the 1974 World Cup. Since German reunification, the stadium has staged the German Cup final (**DfB Pokal**). It occasionally hosts Germany's international matches. During the 1974 World Cup, Olympiastadion staged three group A fixtures (West Germany v Chile, **Chile** v **East Germany**, **Australia** v Chile) – total attendance 126,268; average attendance 42,089. The ground was the venue of the 1936 Olympic Games football final (Italy v **Austria**).

Olympic Games *competition* international sports tournament held every four years. The football tournament comes under the auspices of **FIFA** and, since 1992, has been open to players under 23 years of age (although a maximum number of over-age players can be included). Qualification for the finals tournament is via confederation qualification tournaments. The **European Under-21 Championship** serves as **UEFA**'s **Olympic Games** qualifier. The host nation qualifies automatically for the men's competition. The finals competition comprises first-round group games (four countries per group), followed by a straight knockout tournament. The top seven nations in the 1999 **Women's World Cup** qualify with the hosts (Australia) for the 2000 Olympic Games Women's football tournament in Sydney. Medals are awarded in both the men's and women's event: winners – gold; runners-up – silver; third place – bronze. *History* The modern Olympic Games are a revival of the ancient Greek Panhellenic Festival, held every fourth year in honour of Zeus, at ancient Olympia, from 786 BC to AD 394. The tournament lasted five days and included sports, festivities and sacrifices. Only men were allowed to compete. The modern Games were the brainchild of Baron Pierre de Coubertin and first played in 1896 in Athens. They are held every fourth year and include track and field athletics as well as a vast range of sports from equestrianism to synchronised swimming, gymnastics and shooting. Separate Winter Olympic Games have been held since 1924. Football was played at the first games, with teams known to have come from **Denmark**, Izmir (in West Turkey) and Athens. There is no complete record of the results. In the second Games in Paris, in 1900, only three teams took part, Club Francais (of Paris), Belgium Student XI and Upton Park FC (representing Great Britain). Upton Park beat Club Francais 4–0 in the "final". Football was also played at the 1904 Games in St Louis, USA, again with only three teams taking part: Galt FC of Ontario, Canada (the winners), St Rose Kickers and Christian Brothers College, both of St Louis. The first official football tournament was played at the fourth Games in London in 1908. Five countries took part: **England** (amateurs), **Sweden**, Denmark, **Netherlands**, **France** A, France B. England took the gold medal (2–0, v Denmark, at White City), with Frederick Chapman and Vivian **Woodward** scoring the goals, in front of 8,000 spectators. England was again victorious at the second official tournament in Sweden in 1912, when the tournament had grown to 11 nations. **Egypt** was the first African country to enter the football tournament, competing in the seventh Games in Antwerp, Belgium, in 1920. In 1924, **Uruguay** became the first South American nation to compete at the Olympics, at the Games in Paris, France. Uruguay won the tournament comfortably: opening with a 7–0 victory over **former-Yugoslavia**, followed by a 3–0 defeat of **United States of America**, a 5–1 win against France in the quarter-final, a 2–1 defeat of the Netherlands in the semi-final and a 3–0 victory over **Switzerland** in the final – 20 goals in five games, with only two conceded. Uruguay took the gold medal again in 1928, with South American neighbours **Argentina** taking silver medal, after a replay at the Olympic Stadium in Amsterdam, Netherlands. Until 1984, the Olympic Games football tournament was officially restricted to amateur participants: although the definition was, frequently, interpreted liberally. **Great Britain** and Denmark withdrew from the 1924 tournament, and did not enter in 1928, in protest at the International Olympic Committee's and FIFA's decision to allow players to be paid compensation in lieu of lost wages from their normal jobs. The nature of the Olympic Games changed dramatically with the international growth of professional football after **World War II**, with many leading nations no longer able to send their normal squads. Eastern European communist countries, however, continued to send their first-choice teams football in these countries was organised by the state, rather than along commercial lines, allowing their associations to argue that the players were not, actually, professional. Although Sweden won the first post-World War II Games in 1948 (against former-Yugoslavia in London), the next eight gold medalists were all from communist countries: **Hungary**; the **Soviet Union**; former-Yugoslavia; Hungary; Hungary; **Poland**; **East Germany**; and **Czechoslovakia**. From 1952 to 1980, only Denmark (silver medal 1960) broke the communist domination of the finals. Former-Yugoslavia appeared in four successive finals (1948 to 1960). FIFA, which presided over the football tournament qualification criteria (rather than the International Olympic Committee), changed its rules in 1984, allowing the selection of any player who had not taken part in a **World Cup** tournament match; a move which undermined the credibility of the competition. The 1984 gold medal went to France. The rules were changed, yet again, for the 1992 Games in Barcelona, Spain: selection was open to any player under 23 years of age. Regional qualifying tournaments were introduced in 1956. **Ghana** was the first African nation to win a medal at the Games (bronze medal, 1992) and, in 1996, **Nigeria** was the first African nation to take a gold medal. Although England took part in the 1908, 1912 and 1920 Games, the British and Northern Irish home nations do not now compete in the football tournament.

Great Britain (amateur sides) competed in the 1936, 1948, 1952, 1956 and 1960 finals tournaments. Great Britain is not affiliated to FIFA, so is no longer eligible to compete, and the United Kingdom constituent countries are not eligible to enter the Olympic Games in their own right. The International Olympic Committee agreed, at a meeting in 1993, to admit women's football as a full Olympic Sport at the 1996 Olympic Games in Atlanta, USA. The following nations competed in the first women's football tournament: Brazil, **China**, Denmark, **Japan**, Germany, **Norway**, Sweden and USA won the gold medal (2–1, v China); the bronze medal went to Norway (2–0, v Brazil). The 1996 final at the Sanford Stadium, Athens, Georgia, USA, was watched by 76,489 spectators. *Winners (men) (result, silver medal team, host city; bronze medal team):* 1908 England (2–0, v Denmark, in London, UK; bronze medal – Netherlands); 1912 England (4–2, v Denmark, in Stockholm, Sweden; bronze medal – Netherlands); 1920 **Belgium** (2–0, Czechoslovakia, in Antwerp, Belgium; bronze medal – Netherlands); 1924 Uruguay (3–0, v Switzerland, in Paris, France; bronze medal – Sweden); 1928 Uruguay (1–1, 2–1 replay, v Argentina, in Amsterdam, Netherlands; bronze medal – **Italy**); 1936 Italy (2–1, v **Austria**, in Berlin, Germany; bronze medal – Norway); 1948 Sweden (3–1, v **Yugoslavia**, in London, UK; bronze medal – Denmark); 1952 Hungary (2–0, v former-Yugoslavia, in Helsinki, Finland; bronze medal – Sweden); 1956 Soviet Union (1–0, v former-Yugoslavia, in Melbourne, Australia; bronze medal – **Bulgaria**); 1960 former-Yugoslavia (3–1, v Denmark, in Rome, Italy; bronze medal – Netherlands); 1964 Hungary (2–1, v Czechoslovakia, in Tokyo, Japan; bronze medal – East Germany); 1968 Hungary (4–1, v Bulgaria, in Mexico City, Mexico; bronze medal – Japan); 1972 Poland (2–1, v Hungary, in Munich, Germany; bronze medal – East Germany); 1976 East Germany (3–1, v Poland, in Montreal, Canada; bronze medal – Soviet Union); 1980 Czechoslovakia (1–0, v East Germany, in Moscow, Russia/former-Soviet Union; bronze medal – Soviet Union); 1984 France (2–0, v **Brazil**, in Los Angeles, USA; bronze medal – former-Yugoslavia); 1988 Soviet Union (2–1, v Brazil, in Seoul, South Korea; bronze medal – West **Germany**); 1992 **Spain** (3–2, v Poland, in Barcelona, Spain; bronze medal – Ghana); 1996 Nigeria (3–2, v Argentina, in Atlanta, United States of America; bronze medal – Brazil); 2000 (tournament in Sydney, Australia). *Winners (women) (result, silver medal team, host city; bronze medal team):* United States of America (2–1, v China, Athens, Georgia, USA; bronze medal – Norway).

Olympic Games football tournament: finals *competition* **stadiums** (and attendances where known) **1.** *men:* 1908 White City, London (8,000); 1912 Stockholm Stadion, Stockholm, Sweden (5,000); 1920 Olympisch, Antwerp, Belgium (35,000); 1924 Colombes, Paris, France (41,000); 1928 De Kuip, Rotterdam, Netherlands (18,000); 1936

Olympiastadion (2.), Berlin, Germany (90,000); 1948 **Wembley** Stadium, London (60,000); 1952 Olympiastadion, Helsinki, Finland (60,000); 1956 Melbourne Cricket Ground, Melbourne, Australia (120,000); 1960 Flamino, Rome, Italy (40,000); 1964 National Stadium, Tokyo, Japan (80,000); 1968 Azteca Stadium, Mexico City, Mexico; 1972 **Olympiastadion (1.)**, Munich, Germany (50,000); 1976 Olympic Stadium, Montreal, Canada (71,000); 1980 Centralny Lenina, Moscow, Soviet Union (70,000); 1984 **Rose Bowl**, Pasadena, USA (101,000); 1988 Olympic Stadium, Seoul, South Korea (73,000); 1992 **Nou Camp**, Barcelona, Spain (95,000); 1996 Sanford Stadium, Athens, Georgia, USA (86,117). **2.** women: 1996, Sanford Stadium, Athens, Georgia, USA (76,481).

Olympic Games, top scorer in finals tournament *record* Ferenc Bene scored 12 goals for **Hungary** in the 1964 finals in Japan; Bene scored one of Hungary's goals in the final against **Czechoslovakia** (2–1, National Stadium, Tokyo).

Olympique Casablanca *club* former Moroccan national league club, originally based in Casablanca. Club went bankrupt in 1995. **Arab Cup-winners Cup** 1991, 1993 and 1994; Moroccan League champions 1994; Moroccan Cup 1992.

Olympique Club Beja *club* Tunisian national league club based in Beja. Ground: Boujemaa Kemiti, capacity: 10,000. Strip: red shirts, black shorts. **African Cup-winners Cup** quarter-final 1994; Tunisian Cup 1993.

Olympique de Marseille *club* French national league club based in Marseille, formed 1899. France's most successful and best-supported club. Ground: Stade **Vélodrome** (founded as a cycle track), capacity: 60,000. Strip: white shirts, white shorts. *Keynotes* Marseille is the only French club to have lifted the **European Cup** (1993) but was stripped of the 1993-94 French league championship and the European title after players from French club Valenciennes admitted taking bribes before the two clubs' crucial end-of-season match: Marseille was subsequently relegated, expelled from the European Cup and **European Super Cup**, and banned from buying new players. The Marseille general manager, Jean-Pierre Bernes, was banned for life by the French football association. The scandal, and former president **Bernard Tapie**'s imprisonment for corruption, led to the club's near bankruptcy in 1995. The club's finances recovered and Marseilles returned to the top-flight in 1996 and reached the **UEFA Cup** final in 1999. European Cup 1993 (1–0, v **Milan**, in Munich, Germany), runners-up 1991 (0–0, 3–5 pens., v **Red Star Belgrade**, in Bari, Italy), semi-final 1990; UEFA Cup runners-up 1999 (0-3 v **Parma**, in Moscow); French league champions 1937, 1948, 1971, 1972, 1989, 1990, 1991, 1992; French Cup winners 1924, 1926, 1927, 1935, 1938, 1943, 1969, 1972, 1976, 1989. Notable former players: Alen Boksic, Eric **Cantona**, Tony Cascarino, Marcel **Desailly**, Jean-Pierre **Papin**, Chris Waddle.

Olympique Gymnaste Club de Nice *club* French national league club based in Nice, formed 1904. Ground: Ray, capacity: 18,500. Strip: blue and red striped shirts, black shorts. *Keynotes* OGC Nice was bought by Italian club **Roma (AS)** in 1998 in a **nursery-club** deal. French league champions 1951, 1952, 1956, 1959; French Cup 1952, 1954, 1997. Notable former player Just **Fontaine**.

Olympique Lyonnais *club* French national leauge club based in Lyon, formed 1950. Ground: Gerland, capacity: 43,000. Strip: white shirts, white shorts. French Cup 1964, 1967, 1973.

Olympique Niamey *club* Niger national league club, based in the capital Niamey. Ground: Seni Kountche, capacity: 7,000. **African Cup of Champion Clubs** second round 1978 (opposition given a walkover); **African Cup-winners Cup** second round 1991; Niger League champions 1974, 1976, 1977, 1978, 1989 and 1990; Niger Cup 1989 and 1991.

Omagh Town FC *club* Northern Ireland national league club based in Omagh, County Tyrone, founded 1964. Ground: St Julians Road, capacity: 8, 000. Strip: white shirts, black shorts.

Oman *country AFC* sultanate on the Arabian Peninsula, on the Arabian Sea. Bordered by **Saudi Arabia**, the **United Arab Emirates** and **Yemen**. Independence from Britain in 1951. Area: 271,950 sq km (104,970 sq miles). Population: 2,140,000 (1995 est.). Languages: Arabic, English and Urdu. Capital: Muscat. *Dossier* Oman Football Association (Muscat) formed in 1978, affiliated to **FIFA** in 1980 and **Asian Football Confederation** (AFC) in 1979, president: Sheik Saif b/Hashil Al Maskery; general secretary: Abdullah b/Mohammed BA Mukhalif. Season played from October to May. National stadium: El Shorta, Muscat, capacity: 45,000. National strip: red shirts with white sleeves, red and white shorts, red and white socks. Notable international players: Mohamed Amor al Kathiri (1996 **Under-17 World Championship** player of the tournament). *International tournament record* **Olympic Games** – never qualified for finals tournament; **Women's World Cup** – never entered; **World Cup** – first entered 1990 when last of four nations in its qualifying group, third of four nations in 1994, second of four nations in 1998; **Arabian Gulf Cup** – never won, hosts 1996; **Asian Championship** – first entered 1984 when finished third of five nations in qualifying tournament, has never qualified for finals tournament; **Asian Games** – second round 1998, first round 1986, 1994; **Asian Under-16 Championship** – winners 1996 (1–0, v **Thailand**, in Chiang Mai, Thailand); **Asian Women's Championship** – never entered; Under-17 World Championship – semi-final/fourth 1995 (0–2, v **Argentina**, in Guayaquil, Ecuador, third/fourth play-off), quarter-final 1997; **World Youth Cup** (under-20) – never qualified. *Record against British and Irish national teams* none played. *League system* Ten clubs compete in the Oman First Division, with 14 in the

Second Division. The bottom two clubs from the First Division are automatically relegated. *Record in international club tournaments* **Asian Champion Teams Cup** – **Omani Club** (runners-up 1993), **Al Fanja** (semi-final 1989); **Asian Cup-winners Cup** Al Fanja (quarter-final 1992), **Al Nasr** (quarter-final 1997). Other leading clubs: Dhofar (of Salala, league champions 1995, 1999), Sur (of Sur, league champions 1996).

Omani Club *club* Omani national league club, based in Muscat. **Asian Champion Teams Cup** runners-up 1993 (1–2 v **Thai Farmers Bank** of Thailand, Bangkok, Thailand); Oman league champions 1997.

Omonia Nicosia *club* Cyprus national league club based in the capital Nicosia, founded 1948. Ground: Makarion, capacity: 20,000. Strip: white shirts, white shorts. *Keynotes* Omonia's six consecutive league titles (1974 to 1979) is a national league record. **European Cup** second round 1973, 1980, 1986, 1988; **UEFA Cup** second round 1991; Cyprus league champions 1961, 1966, 1972, 1974, 1975, 1976, 1977, 1978, 1979, 1981, 1982, 1983, 1984, 1985, 1987, 1989, 1993; Cyprus Cup 1965, 1972, 1974, 1980, 1981, 1982, 1983, 1988, 1991, 1994.

OMTV *television* subscription television channel dedicated to **Olympique de Marseille**, which began broadcasting in January 1999.

on loan *misc.* see **temporary transfer**.

on-ball *adj.* player(s), attackers and defenders, with, or challenging for, the ball. Can also include those players in close proximity to the ball.

one hundred Premier League goals *record* Alan **Shearer** was the first player to score 100 **Premier League** goals, scoring 122 goals in 138 League games for **Blackburn Rovers** between 1992 and 1996.

one thousand first-class games *record* Pat **Jennings** was the first UK player to make 1,000 first-class appearances: he played his first match for **Watford** in May 1963 and his 1,000th for **Arsenal** in February 1983. He finally played in 1,097 matches and his full record is: 757 League games; 119 full internationals (**Northern Ireland**); 84 **FA Cup** ties; 72 **League Cup** fixtures; 55 European club games; two **Charity Shield**s; two representative internationals; one international under-23; two **Texaco Cup** games; two **Anglo-Italian** matches; one Super Cup game. **Pelé** played 1,365 matches in a career that lasted from 1956 to 1977, including 1,114 matches for **Santos** and 92 appearances for Brazil (1957-71).

one thousand Football League games *record* Peter **Shilton** became the first player to make 1,000 League appearances when he played for **Leyton Orient** against **Brighton & Hove Albion** at Brisbane Road on 22 December 1996. Shilton's playing record is: **Leicester City** 286 matches; **Stoke City** 110; **Nottingham Forest** 202; **Southampton** 188; **Derby County** 175; **Plymouth Argyle** 34; **Bolton Wanderers** one; and Leyton Orient six.

one-cup wonder *informal* team that has won a domestic cup only once. The 20 clubs to have done this in the **FA Cup** (up to and including 1999) are: **Barnsley**, Blackburn Olympic, **Blackpool**, **Bradford City**, **Burnley**, **Cardiff City**, **Charlton Athletic**, Clapham Rovers, **Coventry City**, **Derby County**, **Huddersfield Town**, **Ipswich Town**, **Leeds United**, **Notts County**, Old Carthusians, Oxford University, **Portsmouth**, **Royal Engineers**, **Southampton** and **Wimbledon**. By 1999, eight clubs had won the **Scottish FA Cup** only once: **Airdrieonians**, **Dumbarton**, **Dundee**, **Dundee United**, **East Fife**, **Greenock Morton**, **Partick Thistle** and **St Bernards**.

one-touch *adj.* passing movement or style of play in which the ball is played immediately to a team-mate. Usage: one-touch football.

one-two *n.* passing movement where a player in possession of the ball passes to a colleague, runs forward and immediately receives the ball back, usually to circumvent an opponent. Also called **wall pass**.

Oneida Football Club *club* former United States football club, based in Boston, founded 1862. The first football club in the United States, and thought to be the first outside England.

onion bag *n. informal* the **net**

onside *rules* not **offside**. adj. usage: onside player. adv. usage: played onside.

Operation Gandalf *misc.* code name of the £2 billion project to establish a breakaway European **Super League** initially consisting of as many as 80 clubs in a two-stage competition – a 32-club league and a knock-out cup for up to 50 other sides. Later, these plans were revised to include more clubs. In August 1998, **Ajax**, **Arsenal** and **Manchester United** all admitted participating in talks to form the league, which would operate outside the **Union of European Football Associations**' jurisdiction. Both **FIFA** and UEFA had threatened to impose sanctions on any clubs joining a breakaway, but the European governing body later agreed to review plans for a European Super League.

Operation own goal *misc.* undercover police operation in 1986 which led to the imprisonment of five members of the Chelsea Head-hunters, a gang of football **hooligans**. The five were jailed for a total of 38 years at the Inner London Crown Court on 11 May 1987. The operation was carried out by six police officers infiltrating the gang.

opioid *medical* class of strong **analgesic** drugs, that include morphine and codeine (the main active constituents of opium), dihydrocodeine, heroin, methadone, pethidine and dextromoramide. Opioids mimic naturally occurring analgesics (endorphins and encephalins) and produce euphoria. Opioids are controlled drugs and are sometimes used illegally by sports players either to decrease pain after an injury or for their euphoric effects. Opioids can mask ongoing injuries and thus, in the long term, can lead to permanent damage. They can also be used to increase a player's pain threshold. All opioids are banned substances in sport.

Opta Index *n.* assessment system that rates a player's performance by awarding points for successful crosses, passes, tackles, shots on target etc.

Organizacion del Futbol del Interior *confederation* association of the Interior league system in **Uruguay**. Involves teams outside Montevideo and its surrounding area.

Organizacion Deportiva Centroamericano y del Caribe *confederation* see **Congreso Deportivo Centroamericano.**

Oriente Petrolero *club* Bolivian national league club based in Santa Cruz de la Sierra, founded 1955. Ground: Estadio Ramon "Tahuichi" Aguilera Costas, capacity: 40,000. Strip: green shirts, green shorts. Bolivian national league champions 1971, 1979, 1990.

Orlando Pirates *club* Namibian national league club, based in Walvis Bay. Ground: Khomasdal. Namibian League Champions 1990; Namibian Cup Winners 1986.

Orlando Pirates *club* South African **National Soccer League** club based in Soweto, founded 1937 (formerly Orlando Boys Club). Ground: Orlando Stadium, Soweto. Strip: white shirts, black shorts. **African Cup of Champion Clubs** winners 1995 (3–2 agg., v **ASEC Mimosas Abidjan** of Ivory Coast), quarter-final 1996, quarter-final "champions-league" stage 1997; **African Super Cup** 1996 (v **J S Kabylie** of Algeria); South Africa National Soccer League champions 1971, 1973, 1975, 1994; South African Cup ("Super Bowl") winners 1980, 1988, 1996; South African **Top Eight Cup** 1972, 1973, 1978, 1983, 1993, 1996.

Orsi, Raimundo *player* Striker. **Argentina** (1924-28) and **Italy** international (1929-34, 35 caps, 13 goals). Born 2 December 1901, died 1986. *Clubs* **Independiente, Juventus**. *Keynotes* Orsi was born in Argentina, though both his parents were Italian immigrants; Orsi joined Juventus in 1929, the year he played his first game for his parents' native country. He scored the 81st-minute equaliser for Italy in the 1934 World Cup final against **Czechoslovakia**; Italy went on to win in extra time (2–1, in Rome). It was his last international goal. *Honours* **Olympic Games** silver medal (Argentina, 1928); **World Cup** (Italy, 1934); Italian **Serie A** championship (Juventus, 1931, 1932, 1933, 1934, 1935).

Ortega, Alvaro *referee* former Colombian referee, shot dead by a Colombian drugs gang after a league game, apparently connected to a betting scandal.

Oryx Douala *club* Cameroon national league club based in Douala. Ground: Akwa, capacity: 12,000. **African Cup of Champion Clubs** winners 1964 (the first year the tournament was held: 2–1 v **Stade Malien** of Mali, in Accra); Cameroon league champions 1961, 1963, 1964, 1965, 1967; Cameroon Cup 1956, 1963, 1968, 1970.

OS Belenenses (Clube de Futebol OS Belenenses) *club* Portuguese national league club based in Lisbon, founded in 1919. Ground: Estádio do Restelo, capacity:

42,000. Strip: blue shirts, white shorts. Portuguease League champions 1946; Portuguese Cup 1927, 1929, 1933, 1942, 1960, 1989.

OS Operacios *club* Sao Tomé and Principe national league club based in Principe. Ground: Porto Real, capacity: 3,500. Sao Tomé and Principe league champions 1990; Sao Tomé and Principe Cup 1992.

osteoarthritis *medical* erosion of **cartilage** causing permanent degenerative changes in a **joint**. The cartilage becomes soft and frayed, while the bone becomes more dense and smooth, with bony outgrowths. The joint becomes painful and loses function. Osteoarthritis is more common on weight bearing joints, for example in the hip and knee.

osteochondritis *medical* inflammation of the **bone** and **cartilage**. Osteochondritis dessecans describes the separation of joint cartilage and its underlying bone, particularly of the knee.

out of play *rules* of the match ball which is no longer **in play** because it has completely crossed a **goal-line** or **touchline** (ie, it is no longer within the **field of play**) (Law IX). The ball is out of play only if the whole of it has crossed the line. The rule applies equally to a ball on the ground or in the air. The ball is also out of play when play has been stopped by the referee.

out-of-contract player *regulations* player whose **full contract** or **monthly contract** has expired. An out-of-contract player is free to seek a transfer to another club (FA Premier League rule L.10, Football League regulation 59.1, Scottish Football League rule 60), and a **compensation fee** will only be payable if, firstly, the player is under 24 years of age and, secondly, the player's original club has made an offer of a contract which is at least as good as the terms of the original contract. Compare **non-contract player**; see also **free transfer (2).**

outfield player *n.* any of the **players** taking part in a game of football, excluding the **goalkeeper.**

outside left *n.* another word for **left winger**.

outside right *n.* another word for **right winger**.

outswinger *n.* cross or corner that, because of the spin imparted on it, swings away from the goal. A right-footed player crossing the ball from the right side of the pitch with the inside of the foot will tend to make the ball swing outwards. Compare **inswinger**, see **swerve**.

over the moon *informal* of a player delighted by his/her performance or that of the team, or for winning an important game.

overhead kick *n.* a shot or clearance (for example) executed by a player kicking the ball over his/her head to send it in the opposite direction to which he/she is facing.

over the top *informal* term used used to describe a **tackle** in which a player goes over the ball, catching the opponent's legs. Usage: "he went over the top".

overlapping play *tactics* aspect of the game which involves a player, such as a wing-back, making a run, which is further forward of the **on-ball** player, to receive a pass.

overload *tactics* a term to describe a situation in which the numbers of defenders is greater than numbers of attackers, or vice versa.

overuse injury *medical* injury or degenerative change arising out of overuse. The point at which **muscles**, **tendons** and other soft tissues become overused varies according the extent of fitness and training of a particular individual.

Owairan, Saeed Al- *player* **Saudi Arabia** international (55 caps). Born 1968. *Club* **Al Hilal**. *Keynotes* 1994 **Asian Footballer of the Year**.

Owen, Michael *player* Striker. England international (13 caps, 4 goals). Born 14 December 1979. *Clubs* **Liverpool**. *Keynotes* Michael Owen is the youngest player to score for **England** in a full international. The Liverpool striker entered the record books with his goal against **Morocco** (20 May 1998) in the friendly pre-1998 **World Cup** tournament, the **King Hassan II Cup**, held in Casablanca. He scored a memorable goal for England in the 1998 World Cup finals against **Argentina** (2–2, 3–4 pens., in France, second round). Owen scored a record 12 goals in seven England schoolboy internationals in season 1994-95. *Honours World Soccer* **World Footballer of the Year** runner-up 1998, BBC sports personality of the year 1998.

own goal *n.* goal attributed to a defending player if he or she was the last to contact the ball before it crossed the goal line. In practice, own goals are attributed only if a genuine error has been made and not, for example, if a player merely makes contact with a shot en route to the goal.

own goal, fastest *record* **1. Football League** six seconds, Pat Kruse of **Torquay United** (v **Cambridge United**, 3 January 1977, Division Four; a header into his own net) **2. Premier League/First Division** 16 seconds, Steve Bould of **Arsenal**, v **Sheffield Wednesday**, in Sheffield, 17 February 1990).

own half *n.* see **half** (sense 2).

Oxford United *club* English league. *Dossier* Ground: **Manor Ground**, Oxford. Strip: gold shirts with blue sleeves, blue shorts, gold socks with blue trim. Nickname: the U's. Ground capacity: 9,572. Record attendance: 22,750 v **Preston North End** (29 February 1964, **FA Cup**, sixth round). Best average attendance: 11,637 (1968-69). Biggest win: 7–0 v **Barrow** (19 December 1964, Division Four). Biggest defeat: 0–7 v **Sunderland** (19 September 1998, First Division). *History* Founded by a doctor and a vicar in 1893 as Headington FC, the club has no connection with the Oxford United that played in the Oxfordshire Thursday League around the time of **World War I**. Headington added United to its name in 1894 and the club did not become Oxford United until 1960. Headington played at a number of venues, including several years at a ground (originally known as Mattock's Field and Sandy Lane) that would eventually become the Manor Ground, where the club finally settled in 1925. In 1949, the club turned professional and joined the **Southern League**. The club won the Southern League Championship as Headington United in 1952-53, and was runners-up the following year. As Oxford United, the club won two consecutive Southern League titles in 1960-61 and 1961-62, before being elected to the **Football League** in 1962-63. Ron Atkinson was a member of Oxford's double Southern League title-winning side, eventually making more than 600 appearances for the club. Oxford became the first Division Four club to reach the FA Cup quarter-finals in 1964 (only **Bradford City**, **Cambridge United** and **Colchester United** have matched this feat), defeating top-flight **Blackburn Rovers** (3–1) in the previous round. In 1964-65, Oxford won promotion from Division Four, winning the Division Three Championship three years later. The club was relegated in 1975-76 only to return to Division Two as champions in 1983-84, before securing promotion to the top flight, again as champions and under the managership of Jim Smith, the following season. In 1982, publishing magnate Robert Maxwell rescued the club from a perilous financial position, but almost immediately alienated the club's supporters (and those of nearby **Reading**) by proposing a merger between Oxford and Reading under the name of Thames Valley Royals. Oxford's three-season spell in Division One coincided with the club's only major honour, the **League Cup** in 1986 (3–0 v **Queens Park Rangers**). Relegation to Division Two in 1987-88 was followed by further demotion in 1993-94. The club won promotion to the First Division in 1995-96, but in 1997-98 further financial problems forced Oxford (£8 million in debt) to put a number of players up for sale and suspend work on the construction of a new stadium (at Minchery Farm). It was relegated the following season. *League record* Division One 1985-86 to 1987-88; First Division 1992-93 to 1993-94, 1996-97–; Divsion Two 1968-69 to 1975-76, 1984-85, 1988-89 to 1991-92; Second Division 1994-95 to 1995-96,1999-00; Divsion Three 1965-66 to 1967-68, 1976-77 to 1983-84; Divsion Four 1962-63 to 1964-65. *Honours* Division Two 1984-85; Division Three 1967-68, 1983-84; Southern League 1952-53 (as Headington United), 1960-61, 1961-62; League Cup 1986 (3–0 v Queens Park Rangers). *Records* Jim Magilton is Oxford's most capped player (18 (36) for **Northern Ireland**); John Shuker holds the record for club League appearances (478, 1962-77); Graham Atkinson is Oxford's overall record goalscorer (77, 1962-73).

P

P'yongyang *club* North Korea national league club. Qualified for the **Asian Champion Teams Cup** finals tournament in Doha Qatar, 1991 (lost in group stage).

Pachtakor Tashkent *club* Uzbekistan and former Soviet Union league club based in the capital Tashkent, founded 1956. Ground: Pachtakor (the national stadium), capacity: 54,000. Asian Cup-winners Cup quarter-final 1999; Soviet Union Cup runners-up 1968 (0–1 v **Torpedo Moscow**); Uzbekistan league champions 1992 (shared with **Neftchi Fergana**), 1998, runners-up 1993; Uzbekistan Cup 1993, 1997, runners-up 1996.

Paine, Terry *player* Winger. **England** international (19 caps). Born 23 March 1939. Career ca. 1956-77. *Clubs* **Southampton, Hereford United** (player/coach). *Honours* Division Three (Southampton 1959-60; Hereford United 1975-76). *Keynotes* Joined Southampton as an amateur in 1956, turning professional in February 1957. Paine played 824 **Football League** matches in total: 713 for Southampton – a club record – and 111 for Hereford. He scored 168 goals in his League career. Awarded the MBE in 1977. Included in the **Football League Centenary 100 players**.

pairing *n.* another club (usually a neighbour) that a league club nominates before a season's **fixture list** is drawn up, so as to avoid both clubs playing on the same day risking a loss of revenue, traffic congestion and conflict between rival fans, as well as at the insistence of local police. Pairings can be nominated from the same and/or different divisions.

Paisley, Bob *player-manager* born 21 January 1919; died 14 February 1996. *Clubs* **Liverpool**. *Keynotes* Succeeded Bill **Shankly** as Liverpool manager in 1974 after joining the **Anfield** coaching staff in 1954 when he retired as a player, and having won a League title with the club in 1946-47. As a player, Paisley also won an FA Amateur Cup winner's medal with Bishop Auckland in 1939 (v Willington). Paisley is the most successful club manager in the history of English football, winning 20 trophies, including six League Championships and three **European Cups**, between 1974 and 1983. Paisley won the **Manager of the Year** award on a record six occasions. He retired in 1983, later becoming special adviser to new manager Kenny **Dalglish** and eventually joining the Anfield board. *Honours* (manager) League Champions (Liverpool 1975-76, 1976-77,

1978-79, 1979-80, 1981-82, 1982-83); **League Cup** (Liverpool 1981, 1982, 1983); European Cup (Liverpool 1977, 1978, 1981); **UEFA Cup** (Liverpool 1973); **European Super Cup** (Liverpool 1977).

Pak Doo Ik *player* **North Korea** international player. *Keynotes* Scored North Korea's 42nd minute goal against **Italy** in the 1966 **World Cup** finals tournament (1–0, 19 July 1966, **Ayresome Park**, Middlesbrough, first round), probably Italy's most embarrassing defeat in its history.

Pakistan Army *club* Pakistan national league club, based in Karachi. Pakistan national champions 1994, 1996.

Pakistan *country AFC* republic in south Asia on the Arabian Sea, bordered by **Afghanistan, China, India** and **Iran**. More than half the population is occupied in agriculture. Climate varies from the dry Thar Desert in the east to the temperate mountains in the north and west with rainfall up to 900 mm. Independence from Britain in 1947. The republic was formerly known as West Pakistan, one of two constituent parts of the former-republic of Pakistan; East Pakistan (about 1,600 km away) became an independent republic as **Bangladesh** in 1971. Fast rising population (about 3% increase per year). Area: 803,940 sq km (310,320 sq miles). Population: 130,200,000 (1995 est.). Languages: Urdu, English, Punjabi, Sindhi, Pushtu, Baluchi. Capital: Islamabad. *Dossier* Pakistan Football Association (Lahore) formed in 1948, affiliated to **FIFA** in 1948 and **Asian Football Confederation** (AFC) in 1960, president: Mian Muhammad Azhar; general secretary: Ghulan Abbas Baloch. Season played from March to October. National stadium: Karachi Stadium, capacity: 86,000. National strip: green shirts, white shorts, green socks. *International tournament record* **Women's World Cup** – never entered; **World Cup** – first entered 1990, last in its first-round qualifying group 1990, 1994 and 1998 (has lost all 12 of its qualifying games in the three tournaments, scoring six goals and conceding 70); **Asian Cup of Nations** – first entered 1960, never qualified for finals tournament; **Asian Games** – first entered 1954, never beyond first round; **Asian Women's Championship** – never entered; **South Asian Gold Cup** – semi-final/third 1995 (1–0, v **Sri Lanka**, in Nepal), hosted first tournament in 1993;

Under-17 World Championship – never qualified; **World Youth Cup** (under-20) – never qualified. *Record against British and Irish national teams* none played. *History* Football association formed in 1948, with a national championship commencing the same year; first won by Karachi Red. *League system* The national championship involves the top clubs from the many regional leagues: 24 clubs are divided into eight regional mini-leagues of only three clubs. The eight mini-league winners qualified for a straight knockout competition. *Record in international club tournaments* **Asian Champion Teams Cup** – **WAPDA** – reached final tournament 1992. Other leading clubs: **Pakistan International Airlines**, Allied Bank Limited (national champions 1997, President's Cup 1997, 1998), Defence Lahore (national champions 1993), Punjab Red (national champions 1989, 1990).

Pakistan International Airlines *club* Pakistan national league club, based in Karachi. Pakistan national champions 1971, 1972, 1974, 1976, 1978, 1981, 1998.

Palestine 1. *country AFC* partially autonomous regions of **Israel**, established by agreement between Israel and the Palestine Liberation Organisation in 1993. Population: about 750,000 Palestinians live in the autonomous regions and in other parts of Israel. Capital: Jericho. *Dossier* Palestine Football Association (Jericho) provisionally affiliated to **FIFA** in 1995, fully affiliated 1998, affiliated to **Asian Football Confederation** 1998, president: Ahmed Afifi, general secretary Khalil Hamed. (Israel is affiliated to the **Union of European Football Associations**.) *International tournament record* **Asian Cup of Nations** – first entered 2000. *Record against British and Irish national teams* none played. *League system* There are two leagues in Palestine: in the West Bank and in Gaza. The West Bank has 18 clubs in its first division, while 14 play in the Gaza first division. Each has two lower divisions. The ethnic-Palestinian team **Wihdat FC** plays in the National League of Jordan. 1998 champions Khadamat Rajah became the first Palestinian side to qualify for the **Asian Champion Teams Cup** (1998 edition). *Record in international club tournaments* first entered 1998, Khadamat qualified for the Asian Champion Teams Cup (first round). **2.** pre-1948. Former British-administered mandated territory (under the trusteeship of the League of nations) in the Middle East between Jordan and the Mediterranean. The region was divided in 1948 when the nation of Israel was created. *History* Former Palestine Football Association formed in 1928. Played in the second and third **World Cup** qualifying tournaments. In the 1934 tournament it lost 2–11 to **Egypt** over two legs. In the 1938 Palestine lost 1–4 to **Greece** over two legs. The 1933 team was made up entirely of Jewish players.

Palestino *club* see **Club Palestino**.

Palmeiras (Sociedade Esportiva Palmeiras) *club* Brazilian national league and **São Paulo** state league club based in São Paulo, founded 1914 (as Palestra

Italia, until 1942). Ground: Palestra Italia "Parque Antarctica", capacity: 32,000. Strip: green and white striped shirts, white shorts. **Copa Libertadores** runners-up 1961 (0–1, 1–1, v **Peñarol**), 1968, (1–2, 3–1, 0–2 playoff in Montevideo, v **Estudiantes**); **Campeonato Brasileiro** champions 1972, 1973, 1993, 1994; São Paulo Tournament winners 1951, 1965; Roberto Gomez Pedrosa Tournament winners 1967, 1969; **Copa do Brasil** winners 1960, 1967, 1998; state league champions 21 times (to 1998).

Palmerston Park *ground* Scottish football ground situated in Dumfries and Galloway; home of **Queen of the South**. *Dossier* Ground capacity: 8,352. Pitch dimensions: 102m x 67m. Record attendance: 24,500 v **Heart of Midlothian** (23 February 1952, **Scottish FA Cup**, third round). *Keynotes* Queen of the South has played at Palmerston Park ever since the club was formed in 1919. The ground is actually closer to Carlisle and the English border than it is to any other **Scottish Football League** ground. Palmerston Park has the distinction of being the first Scottish League ground to install **floodlights** on pylons. The first floodlit match took place in October 1958 (v **Preston North End**, friendly).

Pamir Dushanbe *club* Tajikistan national league, and former-Soviet Union first division club based in the capital Dushanbe, founded 1947. Ground: Central Stadium (the national stadium), capacity: 22,000. Strip: blue shirts, blue shorts. Tajikistan league champions 1992, 1995; Tajikistan Cup 1992.

Pan African Sports Club *club* Tanzanian national league club based in Dar es Salaam, formed 1975 (as Zamalik). Ground: National Stadium, Dar es Salaam, capacity: 25,000. Strip: blue shirts, gold shorts. Tanzanian Mainland League champions 1982; Tanzania and Zanzibar Union League champions 1982, 1988.

Pan-American Championship *competition* former and short-lived international tournament contested by nations of South, Central and North America, organised by the former **Conferación Panamericana de Football**. It was held only three times: 1952 (winners **Brazil**, held in Santiago, Chile), 1956 (winners Brazil, held in Mexico City, Mexico), 1960 (winners **Argentina**, held in San Jose, Costa Rica). The seven countries that took part were Argentina (not 1952), Brazil, **Chile** (not 1960), **Costa Rica** (not 1952), **Mexico, Panama** (only 1952), **Peru** (not 1960) and **Uruguay** (only 1952).

Pan-American Games *competition* multi-sport games open to all nations of North, South and Central America, held every four years. Includes an amateur football tournament. Twelve nations compete in three first-round groups of four; the best-placed nations qualify for the knockout quarter-finals. *Winners* **Argentina** (1937, 1951, 1955, 1959, 1971, 1995), **Brazil** (1963, 1975 (shared) 1979, 1987), **Mexico** (1967, 1975 (shared), **Uruguay** (1983), **United States of America** (1991), 1999 tournament in Winnipeg, Canada.

Anfield remembers those who died at the **Hillsborough disaster**.

Bologna v Juventus, 19 April 1997.

Swerve: Roberto Carlos (Brazil) beats the French wall, Tournoi, 3 June 1997.

Treble champions: three-quarters of a million people turn out to salute the Manchester United team that won the European Cup, FA Cup and Premier League Championship in May 1999.

Rene **Higuita** (Colombia) demonstrates the **scorpion kick** against England in 1995.

Geoff Hurst scores the opening goal in England's 1966 World Cup triumph.

Diego Maradona scores the "greatest goal ever" and his second for Argentina against England in the 1986 World Cup.

African heroes: Tournament top scorer Hossam Hassan and goalkeeper El Sayed Nader celebrate Egypt's triumph in the 1998 **African Cup of Nations**.

Party time: a 0–0 draw against Mexico is enough to take Jamaica's "Reggae Boyz" to the 1998 World Cup finals and a national holiday is declared in celebration.

New kid off the blocks: Michael **Owen** scores one of the best goals of the 1998 World Cup finals – but, once again, England are out at the hands of Argentina.

US and Iran players pose for the cameras at the 1998 World Cup.

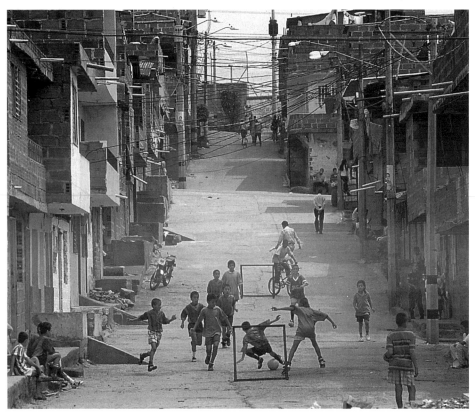

Street football: Barrio El Jardin, Colombia, 1998.

Panama *country CONCACAF* republic in Central America situated on the narrowest part of the isthmus between the Caribbean Sea and the Pacific Ocean, bordered by **Colombia** and **Costa Rica**. Area: 78,515 sq km (30,305 sq miles). Tropical climate. Population: 2,330,000 (1990 census). Independence from **Spain** in 1821 (in union with Colombia until 1903). Full control of the US-built Panama Canal, which cuts through the Central American isthmus, was passed from USA to Panama in 1990. Languages: Spanish and English. Capital: Panama City. *Dossier* Football association (Federación Panamena de Fútbol, Panama City, formed in 1937, affiliated to **FIFA** in 1938 and founder member of **Confederación Norte-Centroamericana y del Caribe de Fútbol** (CONCACAF) in 1961, president: Rogelio Paredes; general secretary: Arturo Durati. Season played from August to February. National stadium: Estadio Revolución, Panama City, capacity: 22,000. National strip: red shirts, blue shorts, white socks. *International tournament record* **Olympic Games** – reached qualifying tournament second round in 1992 (though it was given a walkover in the first round); **Women's World Cup** – had not entered before 1999; **World Cup** – first entered 1994 (eliminated in first round), second qualifying round 1998; **CCCF Championship** – winners 1951; **Gold Cup** – qualified for finals tournament 1993 (last in its group of four, Dallas, USA); **Under-17 World Championship** – never qualified; **World Youth Cup** (under-20) – never qualified. *Record against British and Irish national teams* none played. *League system* Twelve clubs compete in Panama's ANAPROF league first division. The league is played in two stages, with the champions of the first (league) stage qualifying for the **CONCACAF Champions Cup**. Three points are awarded for a victory, with one for a draw: final positions for clubs level on points are determined by **goal difference** and, if necessary, by **goals scored** and **number of victories**. The bottom club is automatically relegated. *Record in international club tournaments* no major success. Leading clubs: Arabe Unido (of Colón, league champions 1999), **Tauro FC**, **FC Euro Kickers**, Deportivo Pan de Azucar, **CD Plaza Amador**, **Panama Viejo FC**.

Panama Viejo FC *club* Panama national league club based in Panama City. Ground: Estadio Revolución (the national stadium), capacity: 22,000. Strip: yellow and green shirts, green shorts.

Panathinaikos *club* Greek national league club based in Athens, founded 1908. Ground: OAKA Spiros Louis (Olympic Stadium), capacity: 76,000 – the club moved from its old stadium, Apostolos Nikolaidis. Strip: green shirts, green shorts. **European Cup** runners-up 1971 0–2, v **Ajax**, at **Wembley**, London), semi-final 1985; Greek league champions 1930, 1949, 1953, 1960, 1961, 1962, 1964, 1965, 1969, 1970, 1972, 1977, 1984, 1986, 1990, 1991, 1995, 1996; Greek Cup 1940, 1948, 1955, 1967, 1969, 1977, 1982, 1984, 1986, 1988, 1989, 1991, 1993, 1994, 1995.

Pancev, Darko *player* Striker. **Macedonia** and **former-Yugoslavia** international (15 goals for former-Yugoslavia, ca. 1989-). *Club* **Red Star Belgrade**. *Keynotes* Pancev scored the crucial last penalty in Red Star Belgrade's **penalty shoot-out** victory over **Olympique de Marseille** (0–0, 5–3 pens.) in 1991. He was third in the *World Soccer* **World Footballer of the Year** award for 1991. He scored two hat-tricks in **European Championship** qualifiers for former-Yugoslavia. *Honours* **European Cup** (Red Star Belgrade, 1991); former-Yugoslavia league championship (Red Star Belgrade, 1990, 1991, 1992); *France Football* **European Footballer of the Year** runner-up 1991; **European Golden Boot** 1991 (34 league goals for Red Star Belgrade).

Pantheres Noires *club* Rwandan national league club based in the capital Kigali. Ground: Militaire Camp, capacity: 5,000. Rwandan League champions 1984, 1985, 1986, 1987; Rwandan Cup 1983.

PAOK Salonica *club* Greek national league club based in Thesalonika (Salonika), founded 1926. Ground: Toumbas, capacity: 41,000. Strip: black and white striped shirts, white shorts. **European Cup-winners Cup** quarter-final 1974; Greek league champions 1976, 1985; Greek Cup 1972, 1974.

Papin, Jean-Pierre *player* Striker. **France** international (54 caps, 30 goals, 1986-95). Born 5 November 1963. *Clubs* Valenciennes, **Club Brugge**, **Olympique de Marseille**, **AC Milan**, **Bayern Munich**. *Keynotes* Papin is the second-highest goalscorer for France and was French league top scorer in four consecutive seasons (1989, 1990, 1991, 1992). He made his international debut on 26 February 1986 (0–0, v **Northern Ireland**, friendly, in Paris). He was transferred from Marseille to Milan in 1992. Papin played in two **European Cup** finals: 1991 for Marseille (0–0, 3–5 pens., v **Red Star Belgrade**); 1993 for AC Milan against his former club Marseille (0–1). He scored twice for France in the 1992 **European Championship**. *Honours* French league championship (Olympique de Marseille, 1989, 1990, 1991, 1992); *World Soccer* **World Footballer of the Year** 1991; FIFA **World Footballer of the Year** runner-up 1991, *France Football* **European Footballer of the Year** 1991.

Papua New Guinea *country OFC* Commonwealth nation in the southwest Pacific, comprising the eastern half of New Guinea (the western part being part of **Indonesia**) and its neighbouring islands, including New Britain and the Admiralty Islands. Independence from **Australia** in 1975. Area: 462,840 sq km (178,655 sq miles). Population: 3,850,000 (1992 est.). Languages: English, Pidgin English and more than 700 native languages. Capital: Port Moresby. *Dossier* Papua New Guinea Football (Soccer) Association (Goroka) formed in 1962, affiliated to **FIFA** and **Oceania Football Confederation** in 1963, president: Peter Mommers, general secretary: Edirs Kumbruwah. Season played from February to November. National stadium: Sir Hubert Murray Stadium, Port Moresby, capacity:

20,000. National strip: red shirts, black shorts, red socks. Biggest defeat: 2–11 v Australia (February 1980, in New Caledonia, **Oceania Cup**). *International tournament record* **Olympic Games** – qualifying tournament first round 1992 (fourth of four nations); **Women's World Cup** – entered first tournament in 1991, finished third of three in its qualifying group (losing all four of its games, scoring none and conceding 47 goals, including a 0–16 home defeat by **New Zealand, women**), also took part in 1995 (again finishing bottom of its three-nation qualifying group; losing all its four matches, this time conceding 19 goals, with none scored); **World Cup** – first entered 1998 (won its first round group ahead of **Vanuatu** and the **Solomon Islands**, finished third of three in the second round group, behind **New Zealand** and **Fiji**); Oceania Cup – first entered 1980 (third of four nations in its group); **Oceania Women's Tournament** (Women's World Cup qualifier) – entered first tournament in 1998 (did not qualify for 1999 World Cup finals); **Under-17 World Championship** – never qualified; **World Youth Cup** (under-20) – never qualified. *Record against British and Irish national teams* none played.

Para *state* one of the 27 state leagues in **Brazil**, founded 1913. Leading clubs: Clube de Remo (Belem), Paysandu Sport Clube (Belem).

Paraguay *country CONMEBOL* landlocked republic in South America, bordered by **Bolivia**, **Brazil** and **Argentina**. Independence from **Spain** in 1811. Hot summers and mild winters. Area: 406,750 sq km (157,055 sq miles). Population: 4,900,000 (1995 est.). Languages: Guarani and Spanish. Capital: Asunción. *Dossier* Football association (Liga Paraguaya de Fútbol, Asunción) formed in 1906, affiliated to FIFA and **Confederación Sudamericana de Fútbol** (CONMEBOL) in 1921, president: Oscar Harrison; general secretary: Candio Arturo Filártiga. Current home of the CONMEBOL; the Paraguayan Dr Nicolás Leóz has been the CONMEBOL president since 1986. Season played from March to November. National stadium: Estadio de los Defensores del Chaco, Asunción, capacity: 60,000. National strip: red and white striped shirts, blue shorts, blue socks. First international game: 11 May 1919 v Argentina (1–5, Asunción, friendly). Biggest victory: 7–0 v Bolivia (30 April 1949, Rio de Janeiro, Brazil). Biggest defeat: 0–8 v Argentina (20 October 1926, Santiago, Chile, **Copa America**). Most capped players: Roberto Fernandez (78 appearances), Juan Torales (77 appearances). Leading goalscorers: Saturnini Arrúa (13 goals, ca. 1969-74), Julio César **Romero** (12 goals, 1979-86). Other notable international players: Raul Vicente **Amarilla**, José Luis **Chilavert**. *International tournament record* **Olympic Games** – quarter-final 1992; **Women's World Cup** – first entered 1999; **World Cup** – entered first tournament in 1930, finals tournament second round 1986 (0–3 v **England**, Mexico City, Mexico), 1998 (0–1, v **France**, in Lens, France), also played in finals tournament first round 1930 (no qualification tournament, second in

first-round group of three nations), 1950 (third in three-nation first-round group), 1958 (third in four-nation first-round group); **Atlantic Cup** – participated 1960 (fourth of four nations), 1976 (third of four nations); Copa America – winners 1953 (league of seven nations, Lima, Peru), 1979 (3–1 agg., v Chile – two-leg final and a third playoff match in Buenos Aires), runners-up 1922, 1929, 1947, 1949, quarter-final 1997, hosts 1999; **South American Youth Cup** (under-20) – winners 1971; **Under-17 World Championship** – never qualified; **World Youth Cup** (under-20) – qualified for the first tournament in 1977, quarter-final 1979, also qualified 1977, 1999. *World Cup performance* (finals and qualifiers to end of 1998 tournament) played 81, won 33, drawn 20, lost 28, scored 108 goals, conceded 98 goals; win rate: 41%; goals scored per game: 1.33. *Record against British and Irish national teams* v England, played one, lost one; v **Scotland**, played one, won one. *History* Football is said to have been introduced to the country in 1900, by William Paats, a Dutch physical education instructor in Asuncion. The oldest current club, Club **Olimpia**, was founded in 1902, apparently by Paats and his pupils. The first football association, the Liga Paraguaya de Fútbol, was established in 1906 by five clubs, General Diaz, Club **Guarani**, Club **Libertad**, Club **Nacional** and Club Olimpia. The league was founded in 1906 (first won by Club Guarani). Professional football was introduced in 1935. The country's most successful club, Olimpia, had, by 1997 won the domestic championship 36 times. It has won the **Copa Libertadores** twice, and been runners-up three times. In 1979-80, it won the **World Club Cup**, beating **Malmö FF** (3–1 agg.). Paraguay played its first international in 1919, and took part in the Copa America in 1921 (it won the tournament in 1953 and 1979). It has qualified for the World Cup finals on five occasions. Paraguay's 0–1 defeat by France in the 1998 World Cup finals (28 June 1998, in Lens, second round) meant it became the first country to lose by a **golden goal** in a World Cup finals match; the goal was scored in the 24th minute of sudden-death extra time. *League system* Thirteen clubs play in the national premier division, the Division de Honor. The season is divided into an **apertura** and a **clausura**, but each of these is divided into two stages. The first stage of both competitions is played on a straight league basis, with each club playing each other once. There are no drawn games: if scores are level at the end of normal time, the result is decided by a **penalty shoot-out**. However, a **shoot-out-win** is worth two points (with one for the loser), compared with three points for an outright win. The apertura and clausura tournaments both culminate with a playoff competition involving the top eight clubs: comprising two mini-leagues of four clubs, followed by knock-out semi-finals and a final. To complicate things still further, the eight clubs qualifying for the second stage mini-leagues carry over **bonus points** from the first stage: 3.0 bonus points for the club finishing first in the league, 2.5 for the second, 2.0 for the third, and so on. The winners and runners-up in each of the mini-leagues go through to the knockout stage. The overall national champions are decided by a two-leg final play-off between the apertura and clausura champions. The two clubs with the fewest total points from the first stages of the apertura and clausura leagues are auto-matically relegated. A regional second division, the Primera de Ascenso, comprises 10 clubs from the cap-ital Asuncion. It is also divided into apertura and clausura tournaments and culminates in a four-club final mini-league to decide one promotion place. An additional, national tournament, the "Division Intermedia", is played between the 10 clubs from the Primera de Ascenso and six clubs from Paraguay's provincial leagues. The 16 clubs are divided into two sections, the top four in each qualify for a knockout tournament: the winner is promoted to the first division. The points system for the Division Intermedia and the Primera de Ascenso is more conventional, with three points awarded for a win and one for a drawn game (there are no shoot-out wins). *Record in international club tournaments* Copa Libertadores – Club Olimpia (winners 1979, 1990, runners-up 1960, 1989, 1991), **Cerro Porteño** (semi-final 1993, 1998, quarter-final 1992); **Supercopa** – Club Olimpia (winners 1990); **Copa CONMEBOL** – Club Olimpia (runners-up 1992), Atlético Colegiales (semi-final 1995); **Copa Mercosur** – Club Olimpia (semi-final 1998); **Recopa** – Club Olimpia (winners 1990 – by default having won the Copa Libertadores and the Supercopa); **Copa Inter-America** – Club Olimpia (winners 1979-80), **World Club Cup** – Club Olimpia (winners 1979-80); Leading clubs: Club Guarani, Club Libertad, Club **Nacional**.

Paraiba *state* one of the 27 state leagues in **Brazil**, founded 1917. Leading clubs: Botafogo FC (of Joao Pessoa – not to be confused with **Botofogo** of Rio de Janeiro), Treze FC (Campina Grande), Campinense Clube (Campina Grande).

Parana *state* one of the 27 state leagues in **Brazil**, founded 1915. Leading club sides: Coritiba FC (Curitiba), Clube Atlético Paranaense (Curitiba), Paraná Clube (Curitiba).

Parc des Princes *ground* French sports stadium situated in Paris; home of **Paris Saint-Germain**. Ground capacity: 49,300 all seated. *History* The stadium was opened in July 1897 and was completely rebuilt in both 1932 and 1972. The 1970s version included, for the first time in a European stadium, integral **flood-lights** and **closed-circuit television**. The stadium underwent a £5.4 million refurbishment for the 1998 **World Cup**. Parc des Princes was the original home of **Racing Club de Paris**. During the 1998 World Cup, Parc des Princes staged one game from each of groups D (**Nigeria** v **Bulgaria**), E (**Belgium** v **South Korea**), F (**Germany** v **United States**) and H (**Argentina** v **Jamaica**); a second round match (**Brazil** v **Chile**); and the third place playoff (**Croatia** v

Netherlands) – total attendance 281,175; average attendance 47,362. Parc des Princes was also used during the 1938 World Cup (**Switzerland** v Germany (plus replay), round 1; **Hungary** v **Sweden**, semi-final) – total attendance 67,332; average attendance 22,444. The stadium was also the setting for the 1984 **European Championship** final (**France** v **Spain**). It has staged three **European Cup** finals (1956 **Real Madrid** v **Stade de Reims**, 38,000; 1975 **Bayern Munich** v **Leeds United**, 50,000; 1981 **Liverpool** v Real Madrid, 48,360); two **European Cup-winners Cup** finals (1978 **RSC Anderlecht** v FK Austria, 48,679; 1994 Real Zaragoza v **Arsenal**, 42,424); and the first one-leg **UEFA Cup** final (1998 **Internazionale** v **Lazio**, 45,000). The ground has reg-ularly staged international football matches as well as Rugby Union and Rugby League fixtures.

Parc Lescure *ground* French football ground situ-ated in Bordeaux, Aquitaine; home of Football Club des Girondins de Bordeaux (see **Bordeaux**). Ground capacity: 36,500 all seated. *History* Opened on 12 June 1938 as a venue for the **World Cup** (see below). Refurbished for the 1998 World Cup at a cost of more than £6 million. During the tournament, Parc Lescure staged one match from each of groups A (**Norway** v **Scotland**), B (**Chile** v **Italy**), C (**Saudia Arabia** v **South Africa**), E (**Belgium** v **Mexico**), and H (**Argentina** v **Croatia**); and a second-round game (Croatia v **Romania**) – total attendance 200,986; aver-age attendance 33,497. The ground is a listed building and was first used during the 1938 World Cup (**Brazil** v **Czechoslovakia** (plus replay), quarter final; Brazil v **Sweden**, third place playoff) – total attendance 52,662; average attendance 17,554.

Paris Saint-Germain *club* French national league club based in Paris, formed 1970 (as Paris FC). Ground: **Parc des Princes**, capacity: 49,000 all seated. Strip: blue shirts with red stripe, blue shorts. **European Cup-winners Cup** 1996 (1–0, v **Rapid Vienna**, in Brussels), runners-up 1997 (0–1, v **Barcelona**, in Rotterdam); French league champions 1986, 1994; French Cup 1982, 1983, 1993, 1998.

Parma (AC) *club* Italian league. *Dossier* Ground: Stadio Ennio Tardini, Emila-Romagna. Strip: white shirts, white shorts, white socks. Ground capacity: 27,500. Record win: 6–0 v Pro Sesto (**Serie C**, 1950-51). Record defeat: 1–7 v Padova, **Serie B** 1931-32; v Palermo (Serie B 1958-59). *History* Formed in 1913, ini-tially as Verdi FC in honour of the Italian composer, Guiseppe Verdi. The club is officially called Parma Associazione Calcio, a name it adopted in the early-1930s. Parma had not won a major trophy until it lifted the Italian Cup (**Coppa Italia**) in 1992 (2–1 agg. v **Juventus**) and did not achieve top-flight status until promotion to **Serie A** under Nevio Scala in 1989-90. Over the next three years, and in addition to its 1992 Italian Cup success, Parma won the **European Cup-winners Cup** (1993, 3–1 v **Royal Antwerp FC**), the **European Super Cup** (1994 2–1 v **AC Milan**, agg.)

and the **UEFA Cup** (1995 2–1 v Juventus, agg). The club also reached the European Cup-winners Cup final in 1994 (0–1 v **Arsenal**) and, in 1996-97, Parma finished second behind Juventus in Serie A. It won the UEFA Cup again in 1999 (3–0 v **Olympique de Marseille**, in Moscow) and, in the same season, won the Coppa Italia - the first club to achieve this in the same season. Parma is renowned for ending AC Milan's 58-game unbeaten run in Serie A on 21 March 1993. Industrial conglomerate Parmalat owns a substantial stake in the club. *Honours* Italian Cup 1992 (2–1 v Juventus, agg.); 1999 (3-3 agg., away goals, v Fiorentina); European Cup-winners Cup 1993 (3–1 v Royal Antwerp); UEFA Cup 1995 (2–1 v Juventus, agg.); 3–3 agg., away goals, v **Fiorentina** 1999 (3-0 v Olympique de Marseille, in Moscow); European Super Cup 1994 (2–1 v Milan, agg).

parry *vb.* to execute a **save** by deflecting a shot or header away from the goal with the hands without actually stopping or catching the ball.

part-time contract *regulations* professional **contract** of a player who is paid for working less than a full working week. Most professional players in the major English **non-league** and many in the lower divisions of the **Scottish Football League** are on part-time contracts. In the Scottish Football League, a part-time contract can be for any period over 28 days, provided that it ends on 15 May in the last year of service (Scottish Football League rule 54).

part-timer *n.* player who plays professional football but is not employed on a full-time basis. The player holds a **part-time contract**. *pl.* **part-timers** A team of part-time players. *Keynotes* Dutch international Johan de Kock was a part-time player with Roda JC while playing for his country in the 1996 **European Championship** finals. He also worked as a civil engineer.

Partick Thistle *club* Scottish league. *Dossier* Ground: **Firhill Park**, Glasgow, Strathclyde. Strip: red and yellow hooped shirts with black trim, black shorts with yellow side panels, red and yellow hooped socks. Nickname: Jags. Ground capacity: 20,876. Record attendance: 49,838 v **Rangers** (18 February 1922, Division One). Biggest win: 16–0 v Royal Albert (17 January 1931, **Scottish FA Cup**, first round). Biggest defeat: 0–10 v **Queen's Park** (3 December 1881, Scottish FA Cup). *History* Founded in 1876, the club adopted the name Partick Thistle to distinguish itself from local rivals Partick FC. It was a founder member of the **Scottish Football League** Division Two in 1893-94, finishing fifth in that inaugural season. Partick won the Division Two title in 1896-97 and again in 1899-00. Until the club lost its Premier Division status in 1981-82 it had been outside the top flight for only eight seasons in its league history. Since 1981-82, Partick has spent more time in the First Division than it has in the Premier. Partick has finished third in the top flight, the club's highest position, on three occasions (1947-48, 1953-54, 1962-63). The club won the Scottish FA Cup in 1921 (1–0 v Rangers) and, in 1930, it again reached the final (1–2 replay v Rangers). Partick was a **Scottish League Cup** finalist

on three occasions in the 1950s: 1953-54 (2–3 v **East Fife**), 1956-57 (0–3 v **Celtic**) and 1958-59 (1–5 v **Heart of Midlothian**). The club caused a major upset in 1971-72 by heavily defeating Celtic (4–1) in the League Cup final with all four of the club's goals coming in a 30-minute spell. Partick was relegated in 1995-96 after finishing second bottom of the Premier Division and losing the end-of-season playoff (2–3 agg. v **Dundee United**) and, in 1997-98, the club was demoted to the Second Division for the first time in the club's history. *League record* Premier Division 1976-77 to 1981-82, 1992-93 to 1995-96; Division One (A Division) 1897-98 to 1898-99, 1900-01, 1902-03 to 1914-15, 1921-22 to 1969-70, 1971-72 to 1974-75; First Division 1975-76, 1982-83 to 1991-92, 1996-97; Division Two 1893-94 to 1896-97, 1899-00, 1901-02, 1970-71; Second Division 1997-98–. *Honours* First Division 1975-76; Division Two 1896-97, 1899-00, 1970-71; Scottish FA Cup 1921 (1–0 v Rangers); Scottish League Cup 1971-72 (4–1 v Celtic). *Records* Alan Rough is Partick's most capped player (51 (53) for **Scotland**); he also holds the record for club appearances (410, 1969-82).

Partizan Belgrade (Serbo-Croatian name: FK Partizan Beograd) *club* Yugoslavian and **former-Yugoslavia** national league club based in the capital Belgrade, Serbia, founded 1945. Ground: JNA (literally, the former-Yugoslavian National Army), capacity: 50,000. Strip: black and white striped shirts, white shorts. *History* Partizan was formed as the army club and was the second most successful club in the former-Yugoslavia (behind **Red Star Belgrade**), winning 11 league championships and five Yugoslavian Cups. It became independent of the army in 1963. It reached the quarter-final of the very first **European Cup** in 1955-56 (losing 3–4 agg., to eventual winners **Real Madrid**). In autumn 1998, Partizan set a Yugoslavian league record of 12 consecutive league wins. **European Cup** runners-up 1966 (1–2, v **Glasgow Rangers**, Heysel Stadium, Brussels, Belgium), quarter-final 1956, 1964; **European Cup-winners Cup** quarter-final 1990; former-Yugoslavia league champions 1947, 1949, 1961, 1962, 1963, 1965, 1976, 1978, 1983, 1986, 1987; former-Yugoslavian league champions 1993, 1994, 1996, 1997; former-Yugoslavia Cup 1947, 1952, 1954, 1957, 1989; former-Yugoslavian Cup 1992, 1994, 1998. Notable former players: Predrag **Mijatovic**, Savo Milosevic, Darko **Pancev**.

Partizani Tiranè (Klub Sportiv) *club* Albanian national league club, based in Tirana, founded 1946. Ground: Selman Stèrmasi, capacity: 12,500. Strip: red shirts, red shorts. **European Cup-winners Cup** second round 1971; Albanian league champions 1947, 1948, 1949, 1954, 1957, 1958, 1959, 1961, 1963, 1964, 1971, 1979, 1981, 1987, 1993; Albanian Cup 1948 (the first winners), 1949, 1957, 1958, 1961, 1964, 1966, 1968, 1970, 1973, 1980, 1991, 1993, 1997.

passing game *tactics* playing style characterised by retaining possession of the ball until a goal-scoring opportunity arises.

Pas Club *club* Iranian league club based in Tehran. **Asian Champion Teams Cup** 1992 (1–0, v **Al Shabab** of Saudi Arabia, in Bahrain); Iranian League champions 1967, 1968, 1976, 1977, 1991, 1992.

pass to the goalkeeper *rules* a goalkeeper is guilty of a **foul** under the **Laws of the game** if he or she makes hand contact with the ball from a deliberate pass (Law XII) – it is often referred informally as the "back-pass rule", even though the ball is not necessarily passed backwards. The punishment for such an offence is for the opposing team to be awarded an **indirect free kick** from the spot where the offence took place (unless within the **goal area**, in which case it must be taken from the goal area line, parallel to the **goal line** at the point nearest to where the foul was committed). Note: an offence is not committed if the goalkeeper handles the ball which merely deflects off a defending player of his/her own team. Neither is it an offence if a player uses his head, chest or knee to pass the ball back to the goalkeeper. A player is not, however, allowed to deliberately circumvent the rule by, for example, flicking the ball onto the head or knee in order that the goalkeeper can handle it – this would be ruled as illegal handling by the goalkeeper; the outfield player can be **cautioned** for **unsporting behaviour** and an **indirect free kick** should be awarded. A goalkeeper is also prohibited from handling a ball directly from a **throw-in** taken by a team-mate. *Keynotes* The rule was introduced in 1992.

pass *vb.* to strike the ball into the path of a team-mate. *n.* the execution of this.

Passarella, Daniel *player* Defender. **Argentina** international (69 caps, 22 goals for Argentina). Born 25 May 1953. *Clubs* Sarmiento, **River Plate**, **Fiorentina**, **Internazionale**. *Keynotes* Captained Argentina to the 1978 **World Cup**. Later coached River Plate and the Argentinean national team. Played for River Plate in the 1976 **Copa Libertadores** (1–4, 2–1, 2–3 playoff, v **Cruzeiro**). *Honours* World Cup (Argentina 1978); Argentinean league championship (River Plate, 1975, 1977, 1979, 1980).

pasuckquakkohowog *n.* rudimentary game of football said to have been played by native American Indians first observed, according to folklore, by the Pilgrim Fathers in 1620 in Massachusetts. It is literally translated as "they gather to play football". The matches were played by as many as 1,000 participants, on beaches, with the goals up to one or two kilometres apart.

patella *medical* disc-like **bone** found in front of the knee joint between the **femur** and the **tibia**, otherwise known as the knee bone.

Pattern for Football *n.* draft blueprint for English league football prepared by the **Football League management committee** in 1961. The first draft was drawn up in 1959 by Alan **Hardaker** and Joe **Richards** (a package which included the adopted proposal for a **League Cup**). It included plans for an increase in the overall size of the league, five divisions of 20 clubs each, including two regional fourth divisions, and automatic relegation of any club seeking re-election two

years in succession. Largely rejected by the Football League **full members** in 1963.

pay-per-view *television* televised football matches for which viewers will pay to access. *Keynotes* On 22 May 1998, **Premier League** chairmen voted unanimously against BSkyB's proposal to begin two to four trial pay-per-view Premier League matches each weekend during the 1998-99 season, although it is expected that pay-per-view will form an integral part of digital television in the UK. In the **United States of America**, BSkyB's sister company Fox Sports began showing live **English Premier League** matches on a pay-per-view basis in August 1998. In December 1998, the **Football League** announced the first experimental pay-per-view match in England: **Oxford United** v **Sunderland** (27 February 1999, First Division). In **Italy**, **AC Milan**, **Internazionale**, **Juventus** and **Napoli** signed a £134 million deal with the French television broadcaster Telepu to televise matches on a pay-per-view basis from the 1999-00 season. This agreement provoked furore among other **Serie A** clubs. Dutch television station Channel 7 attempted to introduce pay-per-view for **Netherlands**' Premier League (Eredivisie) matches in 1996. The scheme, in association with the Koninklijke Nederlandse Voetbalbond (KNVB, the Dutch FA) collapsed after a successful legal challenge by leading clubs Ajax and Feyenoord, claiming that the KNVB had no right to sell coverage of their home games. Around 295,000 paying viewers, generating £2.5 million, watched **Barcelona** v **Real Madrid** in February 1999. In Germany, Premiere, a subscription channel, shows live **Bundesliga** football. The first pay-per-view sporting event to be screened in the UK was the Frank Bruno/Mike Tyson heavyweight boxing world title fight in 1996, which was televised by BSkyB.

payments to relegated clubs *regulations* UK. After **relegation** from a league, a club may still be entitled to receive a share of any revenue due to league clubs. A club relegated from the **Premier League** is entitled to receive payments for two seasons after its relegation (FA Premier League rules section C). This amounts to half of a Premier League club's basic (non-merit related) share of the **television money** and half of a club's share of **sponsorship money**. A club that **retires** from the **Football League** (ie one that is relegated to the **Football Conference**) may receive 50% of the basic Third Division share of the league's **pool account**, as compensation for losing its league membership (Football League Article 65): in 1998-99 this was set as £210,000. The promoted club, however, may have its basic award reduced by 50% for its first season; its merit-related award, under the "ladder principle", is not affected (see pool account).

Paz, Ruben *player* Striker. **Uruguay** international. *Clubs* **Peñarol**, **Racing Club**. *Keynotes* Uruguayan league top scorer 1981 (17 goals, with Peñarol). Paz helped Argentinean club Racing Club to the South American Supercopa in 1988 (3–2 agg., v **Cruzeiro**), and was a beaten finalist in 1992 (1–4 agg., v Cruzeiro).

Honours **Copa America** runner-up (Uruguay, 1989); **Supercopa** (Racing Club, 1988); *El Mundo* South American Footballer of the Year 1988.

pelada *n.* informal game of football played by Brazilian workers in their breaks.

Pelé *player* Real name: Edson Arantes do Nascimento. Striker. **Brazil** international (92 caps, 77 goals, 1957-71). Born 23 October 1940, in Tres Coracoes, Brazil. Career ca. 1956-77. *Clubs* Bauru (youth team), **Santos FC**, New York Cosmos. *Keynotes* Pelé was the most outstanding player of his generation and one of the most talented and respected players in football history. Only Ferenc Puskás has scored more international goals than Pelé. He is one of only three players to have scored in two **World Cup** finals (1958, 1970), along with **Vava** and Paul **Breitner**, and could score fine individual goals from solo runs, swerving shots, free-kicks and powerful headers. Pelé was coached by his father, a former player, and joined local club Bauru. He was transferred to Santos in 1956 and made his senior league debut as a 15-year-old. Pelé scored on his international debut aged 16 years, 257 days, on 7 July 1957 (1–2, v **Argentina**, in Rio de Janeiro). He rose to international fame at the 1958 World Cup final in Sweden, scoring a memorable individual goal in a brace for Brazil in its 5–2 victory over **Sweden** at the **Råsunda Stadion**, Stockholm. He was equal-second highest scorer in the tournament, with six goals, including a **hat-trick** in only 23 minutes against **France** in the semi-final (5–2). Injury meant that Pelé played only two matches in the 1962 finals; though Brazil went on to retain the World Cup. Brazil had a disappointing tournament in 1966 but returned to take the trophy in 1970 – with Pelé the player of the tournament and scorer of the opening goal in the 4–1 defeat of **Italy** in the final. He scored Brazil's 100th World Cup goal during the 1970 finals. Pelé was top scorer at the **Copa America** in 1959, with eight goals, including one in the crucial and final match against Argentina; a 1–1 draw was not, however, sufficient to take the trophy to Brazil (an honour Pelé never achieved). He spent most of his club playing career at the comparatively modest club Santos, but inspired his club to win the World Club Cup twice – scoring seven goals in the two editions – and **Copa Libertadores** in successive years (the first Brazilian club to win the trophy), as well as domestic honours. He was the first player to score a hat-trick in the **World Club Cup** (5–2,v Benfica, in Lisbon, 11 October 1962; he also scored two in the 3–2 first leg victory at **Maracaná**). Pelé scored 1,090 goals for Santos in 1,114 matches. He retired briefly in 1974, but joined New York Cosmos in the **North American Soccer League** in 1975. He played his last competitive match on 1 October 1977, an exhibition match at Giants Stadium, New Jersey, three weeks short of his 37th birthday. He played the first half for New York Cosmos (scoring from a free-kick), and the second half for his old club Santos. The match was watched by 77,000 spectators. By the time of his retirement, Pelé was credited with 1,282 goals in 1,365 matches for his two senior clubs and the national team; though many were scored in friendlies. Pelé scored the 1,000th goal of his career with a penalty for Santos against **Vasco da Gama** on 20 November 1969, at Maracaná (2–1), and lists this as one of his two favourite goals: the other was against **Wales** in the 1958 World Cup (1–0, in Nya Ullevi stadium, Gothenburg, quarter-final, 19 June 1958). He said that the moniker, "Pelé", "doesn't mean anything" and attributes it to a childhood nickname given to him by a "boy in the street". The nickname was taken up by other schoolchildren to tease him; despite his protestations that he wanted to be called by his real name, Edson. Pelé became Brazil's Sports Minister in 1994. He was awarded an honorary **knighthood** by the United Kingdom on 3 December 1997. *Honours* World Cup (Brazil, 1958, 1970); Copa America runner-up (Brazil, 1959); Copa Libertadores (Santos, 1962, 1963); World Club Cup (Santos, 1962, 1963); São Paulo Tournament (the inter-state championship and forerunner of the Brazilian national championship) (Santos, 1959, 1963, 1964); Roberto Gomez Pedrosa Tournament (another interstate Brazilian championship) (Santos, 1968); São Paulo state championship (Santos, 1958, 1960, 1961, 1962, 1964, 1965, 1967, 1968, 1969, 1973); North American Soccer League championship (New York Cosmos, 1977).

Pelé, Abedi (full name: Abedi "Pelé" Ayew) *player*. **Ghana** international. Born 5 January 1962. *Clubs* Real Tamale United (Ghana, twice), Sad Club (Qatar), Dragons Oueme (Benin), Niort (France), Mulhouse (France), **Olympique de Marseille** (twice), OSC Lille, **Olympique Lyonnais**, **Torino**, Munich 1860, **Al-Ain**. *Keynotes* Pelé played for Marseille in the 1993 European Cup final (1–0, v **AC Milan**), and was on the losing side in the 1991 final (0–0, 3–5 pens., v **Red Star Belgrade**). *Honours* **African Cup of Nations** (Ghana, 1982); **Olympic Games** bronze medal (Ghana, 1992); **European Cup** (Olympique de Marseille, 1993, Marseille later stripped of title); French championship 1989, 1991, 1992, 1993; Marseille later stripped of the 1993 title); **Confédération Africaine de Football** (CAF) **African Footballer of the Year** 1992, *Afrique Football* African Footballer of the Year 1991, 1992, *France Football* African Footballer of the Year 1991, 1992, 1993.

Pelister Bitola *club* Macedonian national league club, based in Bitola, formed in 1945. Ground: Gradski, capacity: 15,000. Strip: green and white striped shirts, green shorts. Macedonian Cup runners-up 1993 and 1994.

Pelita Jaya *club* Indonesian national league club. **Asian Champion Teams Cup** semi-final 1989 and 1990; Indonesian national champions 1989, 1990, 1994.

pen. *abbrev.* abbreviation for **penalty-kick**. The abbreviation is often used after a scorer's name in lists of results given in newspapers to indicate that his or her goal was from penalty-kick. *pl.* **pens**. penalties: used in a record of a match to indicate that the result was settled by a **penalty shoot-out**. In the following example from the 1998 **World Cup** finals – **Argentina** v **England**, 2–2, 4–3 pens. – Argentina beat England 4–3 in the shoot-out (the match had finished 2–2 after extra time).

penalty arc   *rules*   arc of a circle of radius 9.15 metres (10 yards) drawn outside the **penalty area** centring on the **penalty spot** (Law I). The penalty arc, which must be no more than 12 cm (5 inches) wide, marks out the minimum distance any player, excluding the penalty taker and goalkeeper, must be from the penalty spot when a penalty kick is taken (Law XIV). Also called the **"D"**.

penalty area   *rules*   area in front of each **goal** of the **field of play** delineated by **lines**. Two lines of 16.5 metres (18 yards) length run at right angles to the **goal line**, 16.5 metres (18 yards) from each **goal post**. They are joined by a line running parallel to the goal line (Law I). **Fouls** and deliberate **handballs** committed within the penalty area by the defending side result in a **penalty kick**. The penalty area, together with the penalty arc, also marks out the minimum distance any player, excluding the penalty taker and goalkeeper, must be from the **penalty spot** when a penalty kick is taken (Law XIV). Free-kicks to the **defending team** awarded within the penalty area must be kicked beyond the penalty area before another player can make contact with the ball (Law XIII). The ball is **in play** from a goal-kick only when it has travelled beyond the penalty area (Law XVI). *Keynotes* The current dimensions of the penalty area were laid down in 1902.

penalty area line   *rules*   any of the lines marking out the penalty area (Law 1).

penalty kick   *rules*   method of restarting a game after it has been stopped for a **foul** or **handball** committed by a **defending player** inside his or her own **penalty area** as specified under the **Laws of the game** (Law XIV). A penalty kick is taken from the **penalty spot** and, until the kick is taken, all other players (from both sides) except the defending goalkeeper must be on the **field of play** but outside the penalty area, behind and at least 9.15 metres (10 yards) from the penalty mark (the 9.15 metre mark is delineated by a circular line - the **penalty arc** or "D". The player taking the penalty kick must play the ball forward and is not allowed to touch it a second time until it has made contact with another player of either side. The ball is **in play** as soon as it moves forward after being kicked. If the ball rebounds from the cross bar or post the penalty taker may not strike it again until it has been touched by another player. The kicker may, however, strike the ball if it has rebounded off, or has been punched out by, the goalkeeper. The defending goalkeeper must face the kicker and remain on the goal line until the ball is kicked. A goal can be scored directly from a penalty kick without a second player coming into contact with it (compare **indirect free kick**). Time will always be allowed by the referee for a penalty kick to be taken even if normal playing time, including any **added time**, or **extra time** has elapsed; however, when a

match or half is extended purely to allow a kick to be taken, play will stop as soon as the kick has successfully entered the goal or has been saved by the goalkeeper – this rule also applies during a **penalty shoot-out**. If the goalkeeper moves off his line or a defending player encroaches into the penalty area or penalty arc then the kick must be retaken, unless a goal has been scored, in which case the goal will stand. If an **attacking player** (other than the penalty taker) enters the penalty area or penalty arc before the kick is taken, then the penalty must be retaken if the ball has gone into the goal; if the penalty is saved or is missed, then it will not be retaken; if the ball rebounds off the goalposts or crossbar and touches the attacking player, the referee will stop play and award an indirect free kick to the defending team. The kick will always be retaken if offences are committed simultaneously by players from both teams (for example, if the goalkeeper moves off the goal line *and* an attacking player enters the penalty area or penalty arc), irrespective of whether the penalty is scored or missed. If the penalty kick taker commits an offence – such as striking the ball twice without another player touching it – then the referee should award an indirect free-kick to the defending side. If the ball is stopped on its way to the goal by an outside agent, then it must be retaken; if it stopped by an outside agent after rebounding off the **post**, **crossbar** or goalkeeper, then the referee will stop play and restart it with a **drop ball**. *Keynotes* Penalty kicks were introduced in 1891 after it was realised that a free-kick gave insufficient advantage to a team denied an almost-certain goal by a foul – particularly a hand-ball – close to the goal line. They were proposed by William McCrum of the **Irish Football Association** and adopted by the **International FA Board** at its meeting on 2 June 1891. The first penalty was awarded at **Airdrieonians**' former Broomfield Park ground on 6 March 1891 (**Scottish Football League**), three days after the ruling was agreed. However, it was awarded by mistake because the rule did not become law until the following season. The first "legal" penalty to be successfully converted was by **Renton**'s Alex McCall against **Leith Athletic** on 22 August 1891 (Scottish Football League). **Wolverhampton Wanderers**' John Heath was the first player to convert one in a **Football League** game (14 September 1891, v **Accrington**). **Aston Villa**'s Charlie Wallace was the first player to miss a penalty in an **FA Cup** final when he shot wide (v **Sunderland** at Crystal Palace, 1913, 1–0); it was only the second penalty in a final in the competition's history. John **Aldridge** was the first player to miss a penalty in an FA Cup final at **Wembley** Stadium (**Liverpool** v **Wimbledon**, 1988, 0–1); Aldridge had scored 11 penalties earlier in the season. Dave Beasant, the Wimbledon goalkeeper, is the first player to have saved a penalty at a Wembley FA Cup final. Francis Lee holds the British record for the most penalty goals in a league season: 13 (for **Manchester City**, Division One, 1971-72). Mexican international Manuel Rocquetas Rosas scored the first penalty in the **World Cup** (19 July 1930, **Mexico** v **Argentina**, 3–6, at **Centenario**, Montevideo, first round). In the same match, Argentina's Fernando Paternoster became the first player to miss a World Cup penalty.

penalty mark   *rules*   formal name for **penalty spot**.

penalty point   *n.*   mark against a player's name for being **sent off** or **cautioned**. Penalty points were the basis of a now-defunct disciplinary system adopted by the **Football Association** in 1972 and abolished at the end of the 1996-97 season. The points system was originally introduced in England following an agreement by the FA and **Football League**. Initially, the points system was graded according to the offence: a maximum four penalty points could be meted out for persistent dissent, fouling from behind or deliberate tripping. Players would receive an automatic suspension after accumulating 21, 33 or 45 penalty points in a season. Players reaching 21 points in a season received an automatic two-match suspension (replacing the former system where suspensions were for a number of weeks rather than matches). The penalty was reduced to a one-match ban in 1973. A three-match ban was introduced for any player sent off (later reduced to two). Automatic suspension prevented "tactical appeals" that were used by clubs to delay a suspension of a player until after a key match. Penalty points were replaced by **automatic suspensions**.

penalty saves   *record*   the **Football League** record for the longest sequence of penalty saves is held by Roy Brown; he saved six consecutive penalties for **Notts County** in 1972-73. Only two goalkeepers, Dave Beasant (1988, **Wimbledon**) and Mark Crossley (1991, **Nottingham Forest**) have saved penalties in an **FA Cup** final at **Wembley** Stadium. Coincidentally both played for Nottingham Forest during the 1998-99 season.

penalty shoot-out   *rules*   method of deciding the outcome of a drawn match (ie when the scores are level) in a **knockout competition**. The method requires each team to take a set number of (usually five) **penalty kick**s after the completion of **normal playing time**, and any **extra time** added according to the particular rules of the competition. The rules governing penalty shoot-outs were drawn up by the **International FA Board** in 1970 following a proposal by **FIFA** to replace the system of **drawing lots** as a method of deciding the outcome of drawn matches. They are, therefore, in addition to, rather than part of the **Laws of the game**. Penalty shoot-outs are, technically, not part of the match – players, for example, are not credited with the goals scored in this way and the match is still recorded as a draw for the purposes of records and rankings. Penalty kicks taken in a shoot-out are governed by the same rules as those taken in normal playing time, except that the penalty kick ends as soon as the ball has either entered the goal, been saved by the goalkeeper, or been missed. The penalty kicker must not contact the ball twice and, once the ball is struck, no other player other

than the defending goalkeeper is allowed to make contact with it. All the kicks are taken from the same **penalty spot**; as chosen by the referee. The first penalty kick is taken by the team whose captain wins the toss (see **tossing a coin**). Initially, both teams are scheduled to take five kicks each; the referee records the names of each player who has taken one. Kicks are taken alternatively, with no player taking more than one. The winning team is the one that scores the most goals. If it becomes mathematically impossible for one team to score as many as the other within the initial five penalties, then the shoot-out is terminated. If the scores are level after five kicks, then the result is decided by **sudden death**, requiring one team to score and the other team to fail. A player can take a second penalty only if all his team-mates, including the goalkeeper, have taken one. Only players on the **field of play** at the end of the match (after normal time, or extra time if played) can take penalties. Players who have temporarily left the field (ie for treatment to an injury, but have not been formally substituted) are entitled to take penalties. An exception to this rule applies to a goalkeeper who, if injured during the shoot out, may be substituted if his or her team has not used up all its allotted **substitutes**. If all the substitutes have been used, then an injured goalkeeper can be replaced by one of the outfield players. If a team has fewer than 11 players on the field of play and the scores are level after all its players have taken a penalty, then a player can take a second kick. This creates a potential advantage for a team that, for example, had a player sent off; this team being entitled to nominate its first-choice penalty taker while the opposition is down to its last choice. During the shoot-out, all outfield players, except for the kicker, must remain in the centre circle. The goalkeeper not facing the penalty must wait outside the penalty area, on the field of play on the goal line where it meets the penalty area. Managers and coaches are not allowed on the field of play during the shoot-out.

Keynotes **The Union of European Football Associations** introduced the penalty shootout to decide tied European competition matches in 1970. Previously, drawn **European Cup**, **European Cup-winners Cup** and **UEFA** (Fairs) **Cup** games had been decided by **tossing a coin**. The first player to score in a penalty shoot-out in a British football match was **George Best** for **Manchester United** against **Hull City** at **Boothferry Park** on 5 August 1970, in a **Watney Cup** semi-final. United's **Denis Law** was the first player to miss a shoot-out penalty, in the same match. Law's penalty was saved by Hull goalkeeper Ian McKechnie. McKechnie took Hull's fifth penalty and failed to score, thus becoming the first goalkeeper to save, take and miss a penalty in a shoot-out! United won 4–3 in the shoot-out. Penalty shoot-outs were introduced for **FA Cup** ties in the 1991-92 season; shoot-outs take place if the score is level at the end of **extra-time** in the first **replay**. **Scunthorpe United** was the first club to be knocked out of the FA Cup following a penalty shootout. The club's 3–3 draw with **Rotherham**

United at **Millmoor** on 26 November 1991 ended with the home side winning 7–6 on penalties after Scunthorpe's Ian Helliwell missed from the spot. The first penalty shootout to decide a FA Cup semi-final occurred in 1992, when **Liverpool** defeated **Portsmouth** 3–1 on penalties in a replay at **Villa Park**.The first club to win promotion by a penalty shoot-out was **Torquay United** (5–4 pens., v **Blackpool**, **Wembley Stadium**, Division Four playoff final, 1991). Penalty shoot-outs were introduced for the **Scottish FA Cup** final in 1989-90 (with no replays); **Aberdeen** Beat **Celtic** 9–8 in the first final shoot-out after a 0–0 draw (1990). Penalties were first used in the **Scottish League Cup** final in 1988; **Rangers** beat Aberdeen 5–3 after a 3–3 draw. The highest scoring shoot-out on record for a senior match was in a league playoff between **Argentinos Juniors** and **Racing Club** on 20 November 1988; Argentinos won 20–19 (the match had finished 2–2). The longest penalty shootout in English football occurred in the 1997-98 FA Cup 1st qualifying round match between Littlehampton and Marlow. The replay finished 2–2, but Marlow won 11–10 on penalties. This equalled the score of the previous record penalty shoot-out, **Aldershot** v **Fulham**, **Freight Rover Trophy** (1987). However, all of the previous 21 penalty kicks had gone in before Littlehampton's goalkeeper, Mark Howells, shot wide, whereas seven other spot kicks were missed during the Aldershot v Fulham shoot-out. The highest penalty shootout score in international football is 11–10 (**North Korea** v **Hong Kong**, **Asian Cup of Nations** qualifier, 1975). The 1992 **African Cup of Nations** was won 11–10 on penalties by **Ivory Coast** after drawing 0–0 with **Ghana** in the final (in Dakar, Senegal). The first penalty shootout in the **World Cup** finals occurred in **Spain** on 8 July 1982 when West **Germany** defeated **France** on penalties 4–3 in the semi-finals following a 3–3 draw in normal time. **Valencia** won the first penalty shootout to decide a major European club competition final, defeating **Arsenal** 5–4 after a goalless draw in the 1980 European Cup-winners Cup final. One of the first players to be **sent off** during a penalty shoot-out was Dean Gibb, playing for non-league club Bedlington Terriers in an FA Cup second qualifying-round replay against Bamber Bridge. Gibb scored his penalty in the shoot-out and promptly made an abusive gesture at the Bamber Bridge supporters; he was booked and sent off for his second caution.

penalty spot *rules* point from which **penalty kick**s are taken, located within each **penalty area** of the **field of play** and indicated by a suitable mark. The penalty spot is 11 metres (12 yards) out from the mid point of each goal line (Law I) It marks the position from which a penalty kick is taken. Also called **penalty mark.**

Peñarol (Club Atlético Peñarol) *club* Uruguayan Primera League club based in Montevideo. Ground: technically, Peñarol's stadium is Estadio Las Acacias, capacity: 10,000. However, the club plays all its home games at Estadio **Centenario** (the national stadium), capacity: 75,000. Strip: black and yellow striped shirts, black shorts. *History* Peñarol was founded by English rail workers in 1891 as the Central Uruguay Railway Cricket Club, adopting the current name from 1914. By 1998, it had won 45 domestic league titles, just three behind the world record held by **Rangers** of Scotland. Peñarol qualified for the first **Copa Libertadores** in 1960 and holds the record for the biggest victory in the competition (11–2, v Valencia of Venezuela, 1970, first-round group). *Honours* **World Club Cup** 1961 (0–1, 5–0, 2–1 playoff, v **Benfica**), 1966 (2–0, 2–0, v **Real Madrid**), 1982 (2–0 v **Aston Villa**, Tokyo, Japan), runners-up 1960 (the first tournament), 1987; Copa Libertadores winners 1960 (the first tournament; 1–0, 1–1, v **Olimpia** of Paraguay), 1961 (1–0, 1–1, v **Palmeiras** of Brazil), 1966 (2–0, 2–3, 4–2 playoff, v **River Plate** of Argentina – playoff in Santiago, Chile), 1982 (0–0, 1–0, v **Cobreloa** of Chile), 1987 (0–2, 2–1, 1–0 playoff, v **America Cali** of Colombia – playoff in Santiago, Chile), runners-up 1962 (1–2, 3–2, 0–3 playoff v **Santos** of Brazil), 1965 (0–1, 3–1, 1–4 v **Independiente** of Argentina), 1970 (0–1, 0–0, v **Estudiantes LP** of Argentina), 1983 (2–3 agg., v **Grêmio** of Brazil); **CONMEBOL Cup** runners-up 1993 (3–3 agg., 1–3 pens. v **Botafogo** of Brazil), 1994 (4–6 agg., v **São Paulo FC** of Brazil); Uruguayan amateur league (played from 1900-31) champions 1900, 1901, 1905, 1907, 1911, 1918, 1921, 1924, 1926, 1928, 1929; **Copa Uruguaya** (Uruguay's professional league, started in 1932) champions 1932, 1935, 1936, 1937, 1938, 1944, 1945, 1949, 1951, 1953, 1954, 1958, 1959, 1960, 1961, 1962, 1964, 1965, 1967, 1968, 1973, 1974, 1975, 1978, 1979, 1981, 1982, 1985, 1986, 1993, 1994, 1995, 1996, 1997; **Pre-Libertadores Liguilla** winners 1974, 1975, 1977, 1978, 1980, 1984, 1985, 1986, 1988, 1994, 1997.

pennant *n.* small tapering flag, usually triangular, in club/country colours and with club/country badge. Catains generally exchange pennants before international fixtures.

perimeter fencing *n.* security fencing separating the field of play from the spectators, and designed to combat **pitch invasions**. Overly-secure "prison-type" perimeter fencing was, however, implicated in the deaths of spectators at the **Hillsborough disaster** (see **Taylor Report**). *Keynotes* In 1895, and following a number of violent incidents, clubs were encouraged to put railings, rather than ropes, around the pitch. Although clubs were not obliged to install railings, the move was designed to prevent spectators entering the field of play. **Everton** first erected wire fencing behind both goals at **Goodison Park** in November 1963, but these had disappeared by the time the ground was used as a venue for the 1966 **World Cup**. **Chelsea** was the first club in the UK to erect perimeter fencing around the whole ground. The club erected 2.5-metre (eight-foot) wire barricades with a barbed-wire top (later removed) behind each goal (Shed End and North stand) in October

1972 following three pitch invasions by fans at Chelsea's opening game of the 1972-73 season, against **Leeds United**. The first match in which part of the **Stamford Bridge** crowd was behind the fencing took place on 14 October (v **West Bromwich Albion**, **Division One**). The club later added fencing on both sides of the ground. Increasing crowd disorder at football matches in the 1970s and 1980s resulted in many clubs following Chelsea's example. Following rioting by **Millwall** supporters at **Luton Town**'s **Kenilworth Road** ground in March 1985 (**FA Cup**, sixth round), the **Football Association** ordered the club to install perimeter fencing – instead, Luton became one of the first **Football League** clubs to introduce a **membership scheme**. Chelsea, dogged by continuing crowd problems, went a stage further in 1985 and installed an **electric fence**. The club was prevented from turning on the power by the local council. Until the barbed-wire-topped perimeter fencing at the visiting supporters' end of **Cambridge United**'s **Abbey Stadium** ground was removed in 1992, it was commonly known as the Concentration Camp End. **Swansea City**'s **Vetch Field** is one of only two grounds in the Football League to retain some perimeter fencing – the other being **Cardiff City**'s **Ninian Park**. Both Saint-Etienne and RC Lens were unwilling to remove perimeter fencing from their grounds despite a **FIFA** instruction that all World Cup 1998 venues should be fence-free.

Pernambuco *state* one of the 27 state leagues in **Brazil**, founded 1915. Leading clubs: Sport Club do Recife (Recife), Santa Cruz FC (Recife), Clube Nautico Capibaribe (Recife).

Persepolis *club* former name, until 1979, of Iranian club **Piroozi**.

Peru *country CONMEBOL* republic in South America on the Pacific Ocean, bordered by **Bolivia**, **Brazil**, **Chile**, **Colombia** and **Ecuador**. Physically, Peru varies from the dry but fertile coastal plain (the most populated area) to the Andes mountains and the Amazon lowlands. Independence from **Spain** in 1824. Area: 1,285,215 sq km (496,095 sq miles). Population: 23,850,000 (1995 est.). Languages: Spanish, Quechua, Aymara. Capital: Lima. *Dossier* Football association (Federación Peruana de Fútbol, Lima) founded in 1922, affiliated to **FIFA** in 1944 and **Confederación Sudamericana de Fútbol** (CONMEBOL) in 1926, president: Dr Nicolás Delfino Puccinelli; general secretary: Dr Javier Quintana Arraiza. Season played from February to December. National stadium: Estadio Nacional, Lima, capacity: 45,000. National strip: white shirts with red stripe, white shorts, white socks. First international game: 1 November 1927 (0–4, v **Uruguay**, Lima, **Copa America**, Peru as hosts). Biggest victory: 9–0 v Ecuador (11 August 1938, Bogota, Bolivar Games). Biggest defeat: 1–7 v Brazil (24 April 1949, Rio de Janeiro, Copa America); 0–6 v **Argentina** (21 June 1978, Argentina, World Cup finals tournament). Most capped players: Hector Chumpitaz (106 appearances, 1965-81), Rubén Diaz (89 appear-

ances, 1972-85), José Valasquez (82 appearances, 1972-85). Leading goalscorers: Teófilo **Cubillas** (26 goals in 81 games, 1968-82), Teodoro Fernandez (24 goals in 31 appearances, 1935-47), Hugo Sotil (18 goals in 63 games, 1970-79). *International tournament record* **Women's World Cup** – first entered 1999, never qualified for finals tournament; **World Cup** – finals tournament quarter-final 1970, finals tournament second round group stage 1978, also qualified for finals tournament 1982; Copa America – winners 1939 (first in league of five nations, hosts), 1975 (1–0 v Colombia, in Caracas, Venezuela, replay after two-leg final had not produced a winner), semi-final/fourth 1997 (0–1, v **Mexico**, in Oruro, Bolivia, third/fourth playoff); **South American Women's Championship** – third 1998 (3–3, 5–4 pens, v Peru, in Mar del Plata, Argentina, third/fourth playoff). *World Cup performance* (finals and qualifiers to end of 1998 tournament) played 72, won 23, drawn 19, lost 30, scored 92 goals, conceded 103 goals; win rate 32%; goals scored per game 1.28. *Record against British and Irish national teams* v **England**, played two, won one, lost one; v **Scotland**, played three, won one, drawn one, lost one. *History* Football was introduced by the British in the late 19th century, with the earliest teams growing out of tennis and cricket clubs: Lima still has a Club Lawn Tennis, playing in the national football league. The Liga Nacional de Futbol was founded in 1926, though until 1966 it was restricted to clubs in and around the capital, Lima. Provincial leagues operated from the 1920s. Professional football was officially introduced in 1931. The league system became truly national in 1972 when the Peru championship was decided by a tournament for the Lima clubs and the various provincial champions. A conventional national league of 14 clubs was formed in 1966, reduced to 12 clubs in 1997. The national team played its first game at the 1927 South American Championship, and has won the tournament twice. The 1970 World Cup squad was, perhaps, the finest in the country's history. It reached the quarter-final, losing 2–4 in a memorable game against Brazil, with Cubillas scoring one of the goals of the tournament. The 1970 squad also featured Hector Chumpitaz and Hugo Sotil. In 1964, more than 300 spectators were killed and 500 injured during a riot at the end of Peru's home match against Argentina: one of the world's worst stadium disasters (see **Lima disaster**). *League system* There are 12 clubs in the Peruvian national league, played in two parts, **apertura** and **clausura**. In each part, clubs play each other only once. Three points are awarded for a victory, with one for a draw: final positions for clubs level on points are determined by **goal difference**. The championship is decided by a playoff between the apertura and clausura champions (unless one club has won both competitions, thus becoming outright champions). The six clubs with the highest total points (excluding the champions) enter an end-of-season playoff league, with the winners gaining Peru's second **Copa Libertadores** berth. The two clubs with the fewest accumulated points in the apertura and clausura stages are automatically relegated. The champions of the second division (for clubs in the Lima metropolitan area only) are automatically promoted. The second promotion place is granted to the winners of the Copa Peru, a mini-league tournament for provincial league champions. *Record in international club tournaments* Copa Libertadores – **Universitario** (runners-up 1972, semi-final 1967, 1971, 1975), Defensor Lima (semi-final 1974), **Sporting Cristal** (runners-up 1997, quarter-final 1995), **Alianza** (semi-final 1976, 1978); **Copa CONMEBOL** – Universitario (semi-final 1997). Other leading clubs:**Deportivo Municipal**, **Sport Boys**.

Peterborough United *club* English league. *Dossier* Ground: **London Road**, Peterborough, Cambridgeshire. Strip: blue shirts, white shorts and white socks. Nickname: Posh. Ground capacity: 15,314. Record attendance: 30,096 v **Swansea** Town (20 February 1965, **FA Cup**, fifth round). Best average attendance: 14,203 (1960-61). Biggest win: 9–1 v **Barnet,** away (5 September 1998, Third Division). Biggest defeat: 1–8 v **Northampton Town** (18 December 1946, FA Cup, second round second replay). *History* Founded in 1934 from the remnants of Peterborough & Fletton United, which had been formed in 1923 at the London Road ground (a venue used previously by several clubs). The club joined the Midland League in 1935 and, before winning election to Football League Division Four in place of **Gateshead** in 1960-61, it had won the Midland League title on five occasions between 1956 and 1960. Peterborough, the last Midland League club to enter the Football League, won the Division Four Championship in its first League season, winning 28 fixtures and scoring a record 134 goals – 52 of which were scored by Terry Bly. In 1964-65, Peterborough was a FA Cup quarter finalist (1–5 v **Chelsea**), recording a famous victory over **Arsenal** (2–1, fourth round) in the process. The following season, the club reached the last four of the **League Cup** (3–6 agg. v **West Bromwich Albion**). The club enjoyed further League Cup success in 1991-92, reaching the last eight (0–1 replay v **Middlesbrough**) with victories over **Wimbledon** (4–2 agg., second round), **Newcastle United** (1–0, third round) and **Liverpool** (1–0, fourth round). Peterborough was docked 19 points and relegated in 1967-68 on the orders of the **Football Association** for allegedly offering illegal bonus payments to players. The club won the Division Four Championship in 1973-74 and missed further elevation in 1977-78 on **goal average**, only to be relegated the following season. Peterborough won promotion to the newly established First Division in 1991-92 via the end-of-season **playoffs** (2–1 v **Stockport County**), finishing 10th in 1992-93 – the club's highest League position. Relegation in 1993-94 was rapidly followed by further demotion, so that by 1997-98 the club was back playing in the bottom division. In January 1997, pizza franchise millionaire Peter Boizot bought 97% of the club's shares for more than £1 million,

effectively halving the club's debts. Ex-**Barnet**, **Birmingham City** and **Southend United** manager Barry Fry had taken a substantial financial interest in the club when he became Peterborough manager in May 1996. *League record* First Division 1992-93 to 1993-94; Second Division Two 1994-95 to 1996-97; Division Three 1961-62 to 1967-68 (demoted for financial irregularities), 1974-75 to 1978-79, 1991-92; Third Division 1997-98 to present; Division Four 1960-61, 1968-69 to 1973-74, 1979-80 to 1990-91. *Honours* Division Four 1960-61, 1973-74; Southern League 1924. *Records* Tony Millington is Peterborough's most capped player (8 (21) for **Wales**); Tommy Robson holds the record for most club League appearances (482, 1968-81); Jim Hall is Peterborough's record League goalscorer (122, 1967-75).

Peters, Martin *player* Midfield. **England** international (67 caps, 20 goals). Born 8 November 1943. Career ca. 1959-81. *Clubs* **West Ham United**, **Tottenham Hotspur**, **Norwich City**, **Sheffield United** (Player-manager). *Keynotes* Joined West Ham United as an apprentice in 1959, turning professional in November 1960. Peters made 302 **Football League** appearances for West Ham, scoring on 81 occasions. He was the UK's first £200,000 player when he moved across London to Tottenham Hotspur in March 1970, with Jimmy **Greaves** moving in the opposite direction. Peters played 189 League matches for Spurs before moving to Norwich City in March 1975 for £50,000. He went on to make 207 League appearances for Norwich, then became Sheffield United player-manager in July 1980. Peters was a member of the West Ham trio – with Geoff **Hurst** and Bobby **Moore** – in England's 1966 World Cup winning side, scoring the second of his country's four goals. Alf Ramsey once described Peters as being "10 years ahead of his time". Awarded the MBE in 1978. Appointed to the Spurs board in September 1998. Included in the **Football League Centenary 100 players**. *Honours* League Cup (Tottenham Hotspur 1971, 1973); **European Cup-winners Cup** (West Ham United 1965); **UEFA Cup** (Tottenham Hotspur 1972); **World Cup** (England 1966).

Petro Atlético *club* Angolan national league club, based in the capital Luanda, founded 1980. Ground: Coqueiros, capacity: 30,000. Strip: yellow shirts, blue shorts. *Keynotes* Petro holds the national league record of five consecutive league titles (1986 to 1990). **African Cup of Champion Clubs** quarter-final 1996; **CAF Cup** runners-up 1997 (1–2 agg, v **Espérance** of Tunisia); Angolan league champions 1982, 1984, 1986, 1987, 1988, 1989, 1990, 1992, 1994, 1995, 1997; Angolan Cup 1987.

PFA *abbrev.* Professional Footballer Association.

PFA Footballer of the Year *award* see **Footballer of the Year** (sense **2**.).

PG Notwane *club* Botswana national league club based in the capital Gaborone. Ground: National Stadium, capacity: 20,000. Strip: yellow shirts, blue shorts. Botswana league champions 1978, 1996; Botswana Cup 1995, 1997.

phantom goal *misc.* "goal" given that was never scored. **Chelsea**'s Alan Hudson was attributed with scoring a "goal" in a **Division One** match against **Ipswich Town** on 26 September 1970, although the ball hit the metal stanchion outside the net and bounced back into play. The referee, Roy Capey, awarded a "goal" rather than a goal-kick to Ipswich in the belief that the ball had struck the stanchion inside the goal. Although BBC television cameras clearly showed that it was not a goal, a Football League statement said: "It would be impossible to order a replay, as Ipswich are suggesting, because the Laws of the Game state categorically that the referee's decision on all matters is final."

Philippines *country AFC* republic comprising more than 7,000 islands on an archipelago between the Pacific Ocean and the South China Sea. The largest islands are Luzon and Mindanao. The capital Manila is on Luzon. Independence from the **United States of America** in 1946. Area: 300,000 sq km (115,800 sq miles). Population: 69,800,000 (1996 est.). Languages: Filipino, English, Spanish, Cebuano. Capital: Manila. *Dossier* Philippine Football Confederation (Manilla) formed in 1907 (as the Philippines Amateur Athletic Confederation), affiliated to **FIFA** in 1928 and founder member of the **Asian Football Confederation** (AFC) in 1954, president: René Adad; general secretary: Christopher Monfort. Season played from July to April. National stadium: Jose Rizal Memorial Stadium, Manila, capacity: 30,000. National strip: blue and red shirts, blue shorts, white socks. First international game: February 1913, v **China** (2–1, in Manila, **Far Eastern Games**). *International tournament record* **Olympic Games** – never qualified for finals tournament, in the 1992 qualifying tournament the Philippines lost all eight of its qualifying matches, conceding 51 goals and scoring only one; **Women's World Cup** – first entered 1999, failed to qualify for finals tournament; **World Cup** – first entered 1998 (last in its first-round qualifying group of four nations, losing all three group matches); **Asean Tiger Cup** – entered first tournament in 1996, lost all four of its group games, conceding 16 goals with none scored; **Asian Cup of Nations** – entered first tournament in 1956, finished last in each of its qualifying tournament groups in 1956, 1968, 1980, 1984 and 1996 (did not enter in 1976, 1988, 1992); **Asian Games** – first entered 1954, quarter-final 1958; **Asian Women's Championship** – first entered 1977; Far Eastern Games – winners 1913 (see result above); **Under-17 World Championship** – never qualified; **World Youth Cup** (under-20) – never qualified. *Record against British and Irish national teams* none played. *History* Football was introduced by the Spanish in the late 19th century. Although the Philippines has had little success in international football, the game has a long history in the country. The original Philippines football association was founded in 1907. The Philippines can claim to be the first Asian country to

play in and win an international fixture in Asia: it won the first Far Eastern Games tournament in 1914, a single fixture against China (see above). A semi-professional league began in 1994. *League system* Eight clubs qualify from the regional leagues and are divided into two mini-leagues of four clubs. The top two in each group enter knockout semi-finals and final. *Record in international club tournaments* no tournament success. Leading clubs: Philippines Air Force, Pa Team.

Philips Stadion *ground* Dutch football ground situated in Eindhoven; home of **PSV** (Philips Sport Vereinegeng) **Eindhoven**. Ground capacity: 30,000. *Keynotes* Eindhoven is home to the Dutch electrical conglomerate Philips, which owns and finances PSV, and hence gives its name to the club's stadium. Until the redevelopment of the **Feyenoord** Stadion and the building of the **Amsterdam ArenA**, the Philips Stadion was the best stadium in **Netherlands**. The ground received an investment of around £20 million to update facilities before the 2000 **European Championship**. The stadium includes a toys megastore and extensive corporate facilities as well as central heating in the stands.

photographer *misc.* photographers have taken photographs at football matches since the 19th century and football is now the most photographed sport in the world. According to the **International FA Board**, photographers must not use flash guns or their own artificial light sources.

photographers' line *rules* line marked behind the **goal line** at a football ground where photographers are allowed to perch. A decision by the **International FA Board** states that the line should be at an angle to the goal line, running from a point at least 6 metres behind the goal posts to a point at least 2 metres from the **corner flag**, running no closer than 3.5 metres from the point where the **goal area** line meets the goal line. Photographers must not pass over these lines.

physio *abbrev.* an abbreviated term for **physiotherapy** or **physiotherapist**.

physiotherapist *medical* a trained and qualified practitioner in **physiotherapy**. *Regulations* **Premier League** and **Football League** clubs are required to ensure that they have a qualified physiotherapist in attendance at each game (both clubs must provide one), to attend to injured players and match officials (FA Premier League rule H.6.2, Football League regulation 32.1).

physiotherapy *medical* a form of therapy that uses physical and exercise-based measures in building up muscles, correcting deformity and restoring function after disease or injury.

Piauí *state* one of the 27 state leagues in **Brazil**, founded 1918. Leading club sides: Esporte Clube Flamengo (of Teresina – not to be confused with **Flamengo** of Rio de Janeiro), River Atletico Clube (Teresina).

pilimatun *n.* early and rudimentary form of football played by native South American Indians in **Chile**.

Piñar del Rio *club* Cuba national league club based in Piñar del Rio. Strip: green shirts, black shorts. **CONCACAF Champions Cup** runners-up 1989 (2–4 agg., v **UNAM** of Mexico), 1990 (2–8 agg., v **América** of Mexico).

Pinto, Joao *player* **Portugal** international (70 caps, one goal, 1983-96). Born 1961. *Club* **Porto**. *Keynotes* Portugal's most-capped player. As well as his European Cup success with Porto in 1987 (2–1, v **Bayern Munich**), Pinto was on the losing side in the **European Cup-winners Cup** final in 1984 (1–2, v **Juventus**). *Honours* **European Cup** (Porto, 1987); European Super Cup (Porto, 1987); Portuguese league championship (Porto, 1984, 1988, 1991, 1994).

Piola, Silvio *player* Striker. **Italy** international (34 caps, 30 goals, 1935-1952). Born 29 September 1913, died 1996. Career ca. 1929-56. *Clubs* Pro Vercelli, **Lazio**, **Torino**, **Juventus**, Novara. *Keynotes* Piola is Italy's third-highest international goalscorer and scored twice in the 1938 **World Cup** final (4–2, v Hungary, in Paris). He was the third-highest scorer in the 1938 tournament with four goals (his other two goals came in the 3–1 quarter-final victory over the hosts **France**). He scored on his international debut on 24 March 1935 (2–0, v **Austria**, in Vienna, **Dr Gerö Cup**). Piola scored 356 senior goals, including 290 in Italy's **Serie A**, a league record. Gained some notoriety in Britain after deliberately handling the ball into the net in a friendly game against **England** (13 May 1939, 2–2, in Milan); the goal was allowed to stand. Moved from Pro Vercelli to Lazio in 1934 and subsequently to Torino in 1942 and later Juventus. Part of the three-man Italian national team coaching committee in 1953-54. *Honours* World Cup (Italy, 1938).

Piroozi *club* Iranian league club based in the capital Tehran, originally known as Shahin FC (until 1968), then as Persepolis; changed to current name in 1979 after the Islamic revolution. **Asian Champion Teams Cup** semi-final/third 1997 (4–1, v **Al Zawra** of Iraq, in Malaysia), semi-final/fourth place 1998 (1–4, v **Al-Hilal** of Saudi Arabia, in Hong Kong, third/fourth play-off); **Asian Cup-winners Cup** 1990 (1–0 agg., v **Al Muharraq** of Bahrain), runners-up 1992 (1–2 agg., v Nissan (now **Yokohama Marinos**) of Japan); Iranian League champions (as Shahin FC) 1960, (as Persepolis) 1973, 1975, 1977, (as Piroozi) 1988, 1995, 1996, 1997, 1998.

pitch *rules* another name for **field of play**.

pitch dimensions *n.* see **field of play**.

pitch inspection *n.* examination of the state of the **field of play** made by the referee. At all matches the referee decides if the pitch is playable. *Regulations* for **Premier League** matches, the referee must carry out a pitch inspection at every league match; if it is unfit for play the referee can instruct that the match be postponed, or the kick-off delayed (FA Premier League rule G.10). The referee's post-match report to the Premier League must include information on the condition of the pitch (FA Premier League rule G.11).

pitch invasion *misc.* a form of illegal mass demonstration by spectators at a football match, by large numbers running onto the pitch in protest, celebration or, in extreme cases, in an attempt to have the match abandoned. Football authorities, however, have the discretionary power to let a scoreline stand in the event that a match is abandoned. In Britain, invading the pitch is a criminal offence, even in celebration after a club's victory. *Keynotes* On 20 April 1901, **Newcastle United**'s home Division One fixture against local rivals **Sunderland** at **St James' Park** was abandoned after fans invaded the pitch and, amid fighting, broke the goalposts. The match was replayed on 24 April and Sunderland won 2–0. This is the first recorded case of a **Football League** match being abandoned due to crowd trouble. Also at St James' Park, Newcastle United's 1974 **FA Cup** quarter-final tie against **Nottingham Forest** was held up for 20 minutes after the crowd invaded the pitch. Before the interruption, Forest led 3–1 but after the restart Newcastle came back to win 4–3. The **Football Association** ordered the game to be replayed at a **neutral ground** and the clubs twice met at **Goodison Park** before Newcastle secured a 1–0 victory. The first pitch invasion at a **World Cup** match occurred in the first tournament in 1930. Argentinean fans ran on to the pitch to celebrate what they thought was a victory in their country's opening game, against **France**, when the referee blew the final whistle six minutes early. The French players argued with the referee, who then consulted the linesmen; the match eventually restarted, but the score remained 1–0 to the Argentineans (15 July 1930, at Central Park, Montevideo). On 27 April 1974, a pitch invasion at **Old Trafford** in a vital First Division relegation match for **Manchester United** against **Manchester City** led to the match being abandoned. The invasion, only five minutes away from full-time, was sparked by a goal for Manchester City by former United player Denis **Law**, which effectively meant that United would be relegated. Rioting on and off the pitch at a match in Lima, **Peru**, on 25 May 1964 led to more than 300 deaths and 500 injuries (see **Lima disaster**). The riot was triggered by the referee disallowing a goal for Peru in its match against **Argentina** at Estadio Nacional. A pitch invasion by home fans at **Gabon**'s **World Cup** qualifier against **Morocco** in April 1997 (in Libreville) lead to the match being abandoned after 55 minutes. Morocco was leading 4–0: the score was allowed to stand.

Pittodrie Stadium *ground* Scottish football ground situated in Aberdeen, in the Grampian region; home of **Aberdeen**. *Dossier* Ground capacity: 21,634 all seated. Pitch dimensions: 105m x 66m. Record attendance: 45,061 v **Heart of Midlothian** (13 March 1954, **Scottish FA Cup**, fourth round). (1948-49). *History* Aberdeen, a forerunner of the present club, first played at Pittodrie Park – it became Pittodrie Stadium in the 1960s – on 2 September 1899 (v **Dumbarton**). The present club played its first match, a North-East League fixture, at the ground on 15 August 1903 (v **Stenhousemuir**). There is some confusion over the origins of the Pittodrie name: one view is that the land was owned by Knight Erskine of Pittodrie village, while another holds that Pittodrie is derived from a Scottish/Gaelic word meaning "place of manure". Aberdeen bought the ground's freehold for £5,668 in 1905. Pittodrie became the UK's first **all-seater stadium** in 1978 when the final terracing, the South Side, was replaced with seating, creating a 24,000 capacity. In the mid-1980s, Pittodrie became the first Scottish ground to install executive boxes. The first floodlit match at Pittodrie took place on 21 October 1954 (v **Luton Town**, friendly). Pittodrie staged its first full **Scotland** international on 3 February 1900 (v **Wales**).

place-kick *rules* another name for **kick-off**.

Plainmoor *ground* English football ground situated in Torquay, Devon; home of **Torquay United**. *Dossier* Ground capacity: 6,003. Pitch dimensions: 102m x 68m. Record attendance: 21,908 v **Huddersfield Town** (29 January 1955, **FA Cup**, fourth round). Best average attendance: 9,096 (1967-68). *History* Torquay Town, as United was then known, first played at Plainmoor in 1910 after the club was formed from a merger between Torquay and Ellacombe. Babbacombe FC also used Plainmoor, and, in 1921, it merged with Town to form Torquay United. Torquay first used **floodlights** on 22 November 1954 (v **Birmingham City**), but the lights were fitted to poles and were deemed not of a sufficient standard for competitive games and were replaced in December 1960. A few days after the **Bradford fire**, Plainmoor's main stand was partially damaged by fire and demolished. Following crowd trouble in November 1986 when **Wolverhampton Wanderers** fans rampaged through the town, the club introduced an identity card scheme for home supporters, effectively banning away fans in a similar fashion to that at **Luton Town** and **Colchester United**. In 1992, the club agreed a new 90-year lease on the council-owned ground. Also in 1992, Plainmoor became the first **Football League** ground to stage a match with no uniformed police on duty, relying on stewards to police the crowd and saving the club a considerable sum in policing costs.

Plánicka, Frantisek *player* Goalkeeper. **Czechoslovakia** international (73 caps, 1926-38). Born 2 June 1904, died 1996. *Clubs* Slovan Prague, Bubenec, **Slavia Prague**. *Keynotes* When Czechoslovakia drew with **Brazil** in the quarter-final of the 1938 **World Cup**, Plánicka played the second half with a broken arm (1–1, in Bordeaux, France); he missed the replay, which Czechoslovakia lost 1–2. *Honours* World Cup runner-up (Czechoslovakia 1934; captain of the 1934 and 1938 Czechoslovakian World Cup sides); Czechoslovakia league championship (Slavia Prague) 1925, 1929, 1930, 1931, 1933, 1934, 1935, 1937; **Mitropa Cup** 1938 (Slavia Prague).

plantar ligament *medical* one of the **ligaments** on the underside of the foot.

Platini, Michel *player-manager* Striker. **France** international (72 caps, 41 goals, 1976-87). Born 21 June 1955. Career ca. 1972-87. Clubs AS Nancy-Lorraine, **Saint Étienne**, **Juventus**. *Keynotes* Platini scored on his international debut (27 March 1976, 2–2, v **Czechoslovakia**, in Paris, friendly) and is **France**'s all-time top goalscorer. He scored the opening goal in France's 2–0 victory over **Spain** in the 1984 **European Championship** final (27 June 1984, Paris) – a free-kick that Spain's goalkeeper Arconada failed to hold. He was the 1984 tournament's top scorer – in front of the home fans – with nine goals, including two hat-tricks in the first round (against **Belgium** in the 5–0 victory; and **former-Yugoslavia**, with France winning 3–2), and scored in all five of France's games. Platini holds the all-time record for the most goals in a European Championship finals. Platini scored once in the 1978 **World Cup** finals tournament, and twice in the 1982 finals tournament, including an equaliser against West **Germany** in the memorable semi-final at **Nou Camp**, Barcelona (3–3 after extra time, 4–5 pens.). His two goals at the 1986 tournament were similarly crucial: the opening goal in France's 2–0 victory over **Italy** in the second round; and the equaliser against **Brazil** in the quarter final – a match that France won on penalties (1–1, 4–3 pens.). Platini was French national team coach 1988-92 and director of the 1998 World Cup finals in France. At club level, Platini left France for Italy in 1982, with a transfer from Saint Etienne to Juventus, and played in the 1983 European Cup in Athens (0–1, v **Hamburg (SV)**). A year later, Platini helped Juventus to win the European Cup-winners Cup (2–1, v **Porto**, in Basle). He was top scorer in the 1985 European Cup, with seven goals, and scored the only goal – a penalty – in the ill-fated final against **Liverpool** (the **Heysel Stadium disaster**). Platini scored in Juventus' World Club Cup triumph in 1985 (2–2, 4–2 pens., v **Argentinos Juniors**). *Honours* World Cup third place (France, 1986), World Cup fourth place (France, 1982); European Championship (France, 1984); *World Soccer* **World Footballer of the Year** 1984, 1985, runner-up 1983; *France Football* **European Footballer of the Year** 1983, 1984, 1985; *World Soccer* World Coach of the Year 1991; **European Cup** (Juventus, 1985); **European Cup-winners Cup** 1984; **World Club Cup** (Juventus, 1985); Italian **Serie A** championship (Juventus, 1984, 1986).

play it simple *tactics* instruction by a manager or coach to avoid over-elaboration in passing and movement.

play to the whistle *tactics* instruction by a manager or coach to continue play until the referee indicates a halt in the match, regardless of a player's opinion of alleged infringements.

player *rules* individual member of a football team who takes an active part in a match. Except where special rules apply (eg **five-a-side**, **futsal**), a match consists of two teams of no more than 11 players each, including a **goalkeeper** (Law III). Any of the **outfield players** can change places with the goalkeeper provided that the referee is notified and the change occurs during a stoppage in play (Law III). Except where special rules apply, there must be at least seven players in both teams for a match to start; the **International FA Board** recommends that a match should not continue if there are fewer than seven players in either team (although the decision on whether or not domestic matches with fewer than seven players on either team should be abandoned is left to the national football associations). It is the responsibility of each team to field 11 players and a match will go ahead even if there is an imbalance in the number of players in the two teams. See **substitute**.

player's name *regulations* player's name may, according to **competition rules**, appear at the back of a player's shirt above the **shirt number**. **Premier League** clubs must display players' names (FA Premier League rule F.7). **Football League** clubs may display the names of players on their shirts, but it is not obligatory (Football League regulation 35.9). It is not obligatory for clubs in the **Scottish Football League** to display players' names on shirts.

player-manager *n.* club **manager** (coach) who is also registered as a **player**. *Keynotes* Arguably the most successful player-manager of all time is the former **Liverpool** manager Kenny **Dalglish**. As player manager, Dalglish achieved the **Football League** championship and **FA Cup double** with Liverpool in 1986, the League championship in 1988 and 1990, and the FA Cup in 1989 and won three manager-of-the-year awards while still registered as a player.

Players' Cash Benefit Scheme *n.* non-contributory cash benefit scheme set up in April 1980 which provides a lump sum payment to members of the **Professional Footballers Association** (PFA) on retirement at age 35/40, or earlier if forced to retire through injury. The PFA, the **Football League** and the **Premier League** are joint trustees of the scheme which is funded by a 5% levy on players' **transfer fees**. Payments are tax-free and based on a players' years of service and earnings in the Premier League/Football League. A death benefit is also payable worth up to four times a players' earnings up to a maximum of £800,000.

Players' Union *n.* former name (until 1958) of the **Professional Footballers Association**.

players' equipment *rules* compulsory equipment which must be worn by a **player**, consisting of a **shirt**, **shorts**, **socks**, **shin guards** and **football boots** (Law IV). Players are prohibited from wearing anything which poses a hazard to another player, including any kind of jewellery. A player can be ordered to leave the **field of play** if he or she is not wearing appropriate equipment, or if it is not fitted properly. He or she can only return to the field of play during a stoppage and after gaining permission from the referee who must be satisfied that the equipment is satisfactory. Goalkeepers must wear shirts that distinguish them from the other players and officials. Also called **kit**.

players, most used in a season *record* **Birmingham City** holds the **Football League** record

of using the most players in its first team in a single season (46 players, 1995-96).

playing distance *rules* the ball is within playing distance if a player can make contact with the ball from his or her current position. The relevance of this is that a player will be guilty of **obstruction** if he or she prevents an opposition player from making progress when not within playing distance of the ball.

playmaker *n.* player with a reputation for creating goalscoring opportunites.

playoff *n.* method of deciding winners, final rankings, qualifiers, **promotion** and **relegation**. **1.** Playoffs are used in the **Football League** to decide the third of the three promotion places in each division, or from the first division to the **Premier League**. The third-, fourth-, fifth- and sixth-ranked clubs at the end of the season take part in a playoff knock-out competition: third v sixth and fourth v fifth over two legs (home and away), with the two winners playing a final match at a **neutral venue** (eg **Wembley** Stadium) (Football League regulation 11.1). Playoffs can also be used in the Football League to separate final league rankings (in all divisions) for clubs that are level on **points**, **goals scored** and **goals conceded**; such games would be played at a neutral venue (Football League regulation 10.1); even if clubs are not involved in promotion or relegation, their league position is important in determining their merit-related share of the **pool account**. **2.** If, at the end of the season, clubs in the Premier League are level on points, **goal difference** and goals scored, and their league positions would have a bearing on deciding the championship, relegation or on qualification for a European competition, the final positions are decided by a playoff at a neutral venue (FA Premier League rule B.31). **3.** Playoffs for promotion from the **Scottish Football League** First Division to the former-Premier Division were abolished at the end of the 1997-98 season; one club only is now promoted automatically to the **Scottish Premier League**. **4.** Playoffs also may be used from time to time to separate qualifiers in the **World Cup** and **European Championship**. In the 1996 European Championships, for example, 15 qualifiers were required from eight groups (to join hosts England). A playoff at a neutral venue decided the final qualifying place: a match between the two nations with the worst records of the eight runners-up in each group (**Netherlands** v **Republic of Ireland**, 0–2, **Anfield**, 1996). **5. Playoffs** The final stages of the United States of America soccer league season (see **Major League Soccer**). *Keynotes* A playoff competition was first used to decide promotion and relegation between the first and second divisions of the Football league in the 1892-93 season (see **test match**). Playoffs were re-introduced by the Football League in 1986-87. The playoff finals were originally played over two legs, a single-match final at a neutral venue (Wembley Stadium) was introduced for the playoffs in the 1989-90 season. The playoffs also were contested by the club finishing one place above the relegation places alongside the three clubs immediately below the automatic promotion places. The system was changed in 1988-89, such that the playoffs involved only promotion contenders. The very last berth at the 1998 World Cup finals was decided by a playoff between the winners of the **Oceania Football Confederation** qualifying tournament and the fourth-placed nation in the **Asian Football Confederation** qualifying tournament: **Iran** qualified at the expense of **Australia** (3–3 agg., away goals, November 1997). *vb.* to take part in a playoff match.

Plough Lane *ground* English football ground that was situated in south-west London; former home of **Wimbledon**. *Dossier* Capacity (1991): 13,500. Record attendance: 18,080 (v HMS Victory, **FA Amateur Cup**, 2 March 1935). Best average attendance: 7,995 (1987-88). *Keynotes* Wimbledon played its first match at Plough Lane on 9 September 1912, and its final game, in front of 10,002 spectators, on 4 May 1991 (v **Crystal Palace**). The first floodlit match at Plough Lane took place on 3 October 1960 (v **Arsenal**, London Charity Cup).

ployvalent *misc.* French term for a player who can perform a number of roles.

Plymouth Argyle *club* English league. *Dossier* Ground: **Home Park**, Plymouth, Devon. Strip: green and black striped shirts, black shorts and black socks. Nickname: the Pilgrims. Ground capacity: 19,630. Record attendance: 43,596 v **Aston Villa** (10 October 1936, Division Two). Best average attendance: 23,375 (1946-47). Biggest win: 8–1 v **Millwall** (16 January 1932, Division Two). Biggest defeat: 0–9 v **Stoke City** (17 December 1960, Division Two). *History* Founded in 1886 as the football section of Argyle Athletic Club. The name Argyle comes from the popularity of the then monarch, Queen Victoria, and her love for Scotland. Argyle settled at Home Park in 1901, and following the success of a number of exhibition football matches, including one between The Wednesday (later **Sheffield Wednesday**) and **Notts County** on 24 April 1903, the club decided to concentrate on football. Argyle joined the Southern League in 1903, winning the title in 1913, and was a founder member of Division Three in 1920-21. In nine remarkable Division Three (South) seasons between 1921-22 and 1929-30, Argyle finished run-ners-up on six consecutive occasions (twice missing promotion by one point (1924-25, 1925-26) and once on **goal average** (1921-22)); third (1927-28); fourth (1928-29); and champions (1929-30, losing only four matches). Until relegation to the bottom division in 1994-95, Argyle alternated between divisions Two and Three, finishing fourth in Division Two in both 1931-32 and 1952-53 – the club's highest-ever **Football League** position. The club was a **League Cup** semi-finalist in 1965 (2–4 agg. v **Leicester City**) and again in 1974 (1–3 agg. v **Manchester City**). Argyle's most celebrated moment came in 1984 when the club reached the FA Cup semi-finals (0–1 v **Watford**) while in the Third Division. In 1994, Argyle, under the player-man-agership of former **England** goalkeeper Peter **Shilton**,

was a Second Division end-of-season **playoff** semi-finalist and two years later the club made its first **Wembley** appearance, winning the Third Division playoff final (1–0 v **Darlington**). By 1998-99, the club was back playing in the bottom division. *League record* Division Two 1930-31 to 1949-50, 1952-53 to 1955-56, 1959-60 to 1967-68, 1975-76 to 1976-77, 1986-87 to 1991-92; Second Division 1994-95, 1996-97 to 1997-98; Division Three 1920-21, 1958-59, 1968-69 to 1974-75, 1977-78 to 1985-86; Third Division 1995-96, 1998-99–; Division Three (South) 1921-22 to 1929-30, 1950-51 to 1951-52, 1956-57 to 1957-58. *Honours* Division Three 1958-59; Division Three (South) 1929-30, 1951-52; Southern League 1913. *Records* Moses Russell is Argyle's most capped player (20 (23) for **Wales**); Kevin Hodges holds the record for club League appearances (530, 1978-92); Sammy Black is Argyle's record League goalscorer (180, 1924-38).

Pohang Steelers *club* South Korean Pro-Football League club, based in P'ohang, formerly known as POSCO Dolphins, POSCO Atoms. **Asian Champion Teams Cup** 1996-97 (2–1 v **Ilhwa Chunma** of South Korea, in Malaysia), 1997-98 (0–0, 6–5 pens., v **Dalian FC** of China, in Hong Kong); **Asian Super Cup** 1998 (1-1, agg., away goals, v **Al Nasr** of Saudi Arabia); South Korean Pro-Football League champions 1986, 1988, 1992; Korean FA Cup 1996; Adidas Korea Cup 1993.

point – mark awarded to a club that either wins or draws a fixture in a league-based competition. The number of points awarded to the winning side depends on the **competition rules** of a particular league; commonly, one point is awarded to each side in a drawn match, with either two or three points awarded to a winning team (and none to the loser). In league-based competitions, the final positions are decided on the bases of points won throughout the tournament; if clubs are level on points, they may be separated by, for example, **goal dif-ference**, **goals scored**, **goal average**, **goals con-ceded**, **number of victories** and/or **playoffs**. Three points are awarded for a win in the **Premier League**, **Football League**, **Scottish Football League** and **Football Conference**. Three-points-for-a-win was introduced for the qualifying tournament and group stages of the 1998 **World Cup** and for the 1996 **European Championship**; just two points had been awarded in previous competitions. In the United States **Major League Soccer**, three points are awarded for a win, with one for a **shoot-out win** (there are no drawn games). The now-defunct **North American Soccer League** awarded six points for a win, four for a shoot-out win and a bonus point for every goal scored (up to a maximum of three). *History* The points system for the English Football League was drawn up partway through the first season of 1988-89. A meeting on 21 November 1888 decided that a win would be worth two points, with one for a draw. This was formalised at the first sub-com-mittee of the League on 11 January 1889. The allocation of points was revised at a meeting of the League in

February 1981. Since the beginning of the 1981-82 season three points have been awarded for a win; a draw remains as one point. The new system would have changed the outcome of only one English League Championship: in 1974-75, third-place **Ipswich Town** would have won the first division in place of **Derby County** had it been awarded three points for each win. The new system was designed "to encourage more attacking football". However, the average goals per game in the English Football League after the rule change was about 2.6–2.7 goals per game, compared with 2.5 before the change – only a minor improvement.

points deduction *n.* the removal of **points** as a punishment for infringing regulations. *Keynotes* In 1889, **Notts County** was fined £25 for fielding an ineligible player, the Cambridge University and England striker Tinsley Lindley, after successfully appealing against a one-point penalty. **Middlesbrough**'s relegation plight in 1996-97 was exacerbated when the **Football Association** docked the club three points for failing to fulfil a **Premier League** fixture against **Blackburn Rovers** at **Ewood Park**. **Peterborough United** received one of the harshest penalties for making **illegal payments** to players when, in 1967-68, it was fined 19 points, which effectively condemned the club to Division Four football the following season. Following three pitch invasions at the **Goldstone Ground** during the match against **Lincoln City** (10 October 1996), and further crowd trouble during a game against **Fulham** (26 October), the FA enforced the three-point deduction against **Brighton & Hove Albion**. In 1997-98, **Leyton Orient** had three points deducted for fielding suspended players.

points in a season, fewest *record* **1. Football League**: eight points from 34 games, 11.8%, **Doncaster Rovers** (1904-05, Division Two). **2. Premier League**: 27 points, 25%, **Ipswich Town** (1994-95); **3. Scottish Football League**: three points from 18 games, 8.3%, **Abercorn** (1896-97 – the club had won the Scottish Division Two title the previous season – but scored only 21 goals and conceded 88 in the top flight). The 20th century record is six points from 30 games, 10%, **Stirling Albion** (1954-55, Division One).

points in a season, most *record* the number of points awarded for a victory in English football changed from two to three in 1981. For comparison, the English league records are shown as the number of points originally awarded, the percentage of the total points available, and the equivalent number of points under the modern system. **1. Football League**: 74 points from 46 games, 80.4%, **Lincoln City** (1975-76, Division Four; equivalent to 106 points in modern points system). **Sunderland** won the 1998-99 First Division championship with 105 points in 46 games (76.1% - a record under the modern points system). **2.** Division One: 68 points from 42 games, 80.9%, **Liverpool** (1978-79, Division One; equivalent to 98 points). **3.** FA **Premier League**: 92 points from 42 games, 73%,

Manchester United (1993-94; three points for a win). **4. Scottish Football League** Division One. There have been a number of changes in the size of the Scottish Football League, making comparisons difficult. The following are calculated as a percentage of the total points available (in all record cases there were two points for a win and one for a draw): 36 points in 18 games, 100%, **Rangers** (1898-99); 63 in 34 games, 92.6%, **Celtic** (1967-68); 33 points 18 games, 91.7%, Celtic (1897-98); 76 points in 42 games, 90.5%, Rangers (1920-21). **5.** Scottish Football League Division Two: 67 points in 36 games, 93.1%, **Morton** (now **Greenock Morton**, 1963-64).

points, minus *record* **Port Glasgow Athletic**, formerly a **Scottish League** club, had seven points deducted for fielding an ineligible player in 1893-94. This meant that at one stage during the season the club registered minus one point.

Pokou, Laurent *player* Striker. **Ivory Coast** international. *Clubs* **Africa Sports**, **ASEC Abidjan**. *Keynotes* Pokou was top scorer in two consecutive **African Cup of Nations** finals tournaments, with six goals in 1968 and eight in 1970; he is the tournament's all-time top scorer. *Honours France Football* **African Footballer of the Year** runner-up 1970.

Poland *country* UEFA republic in East Europe, on the Baltic Sea, bordered by **Belarus**, the **Czech Republic**, **Germany**, **Lithuania**, **Slovakia** and **Ukraine**. Independent republic in 1918, occupied by Germany during **World War II**, with new boundaries drawn up in 1945. Communist republic from 1947-1989. Democracy returned in 1989; Poland was one of the first of the former Eastern Bloc countries to break from communism. Area: 312,685 sq km (120,695 sq miles). Population: 38,610,000 (1996 census). Languages Polish and minority German. Capital: Warsaw. *Dossier* Football association (Fédération Polonaise de Football, Warsaw), formed in 1919 affiliated to **FIFA** in 1923 and founder member of **Union of European Football Associations** (UEFA) in 1954, president: Dr Marian Dziurowicz; general secretary: Michael Listkiewicz. Season played from August to June with **winter break** from December to February. National stadium: Stadion Slaski, Chorzów, Katowice, capacity: 35,000. National strip: white shirts, red shorts, white and red socks. First international game: 18 December 1921 v **Hungary** (0–1, Budapest, friendly). Biggest victory: 9–0 v **Norway** (4 September 1963, Szczecin, friendly). Biggest defeat: 0–8 v **Denmark** (26 June 1948, Copenhagen, friendly). *Most capped players* Grzegorz **Lato** (95 appearances, 1971–80), Wladyslaw Zmuda (92 appearances, in the 1980s), Antoni Szymanowski (87 appearances), Kazimierz **Deyna** (83 appearances, ca. 1969–78), Zbigniew **Boniek** (80 appearances, ca. 1977–85), Wlodzimierz **Lubanski** (63 appearances, 1963–80). Leading goalscorers: Wlodzimierz Lubanski (44 goals, ca. 1963–80), Grzegorz Lato (42 goals, 1971–80), Kazimierz Deyna (33 goals, ca. 1969–78), Ernest Pol (39 goals, 1956-65). *International tournament record*

Olympic Games – winners/gold medal 1972 (2–1 v Hungary, Munich, Germany), runners-up/silver medal 1976 (1–3 v **East Germany**, Montreal, Canada), runners-up/silver medal 1992 (2–3 v **Spain**, Barcelona, Spain), fourth 1936; **Women's World Cup** – first entered 1991, has never qualified for finals tournament; **World Cup** – first entered 1934, third place 1974 (1–0 v **Brazil**, third/fourth playoff, Munich), 1982 (3–2 v **France**, third/fourth playoff, Alicante, Spain), also qualified for finals tournament 1938, 1978, 1986; **European Championship** – lost in first round in 1960 and 1964 (no qualifying tournaments), failed to qualify for finals tournaments 1968 to 1996; **European Championship for Women** – first entered 1991, has never qualified for finals tournament. *World Cup performance* (finals and qualifiers to end of 1998 tournament) played 91, won 45, drawn 16, lost 30, scored 154, conceded 110 goals; win rate 49%; goals scored per game 1.69; **European Under-16 Championship** winners 1993; **European Youth Championship** (under-18) runner-up 1981; **Under-17 World Championship** – fourth 1993; **World Youth Cup** (under-20) – third 1983, fourth 1979. *Record against British and Irish national teams* v **England**, played 14, won one, drawn five, lost eight; v **Northern Ireland**, played eight, won three, drawn five, lost one; v **Scotland**, played six, won three, drawn two, lost one; v **Wales**, played three, won one, drawn one, lost one; v **Republic of Ireland**, played 21, won 10, drawn six, lost five. *History* The Polish football association was founded just a year after the country was re-established as an independent state after **World War I**. The first clubs, however, were formed much earlier, with **Cracovia** and **Wisla Kraków** both founded in 1906, and **LKS Lódź** founded in 1908 (all three are still in existence). Two clubs have dominated domestic football: **Widzew Lódź**, founded in 1910, and **Legia Warsaw**, founded in 1916. Both have reached the semi-final of the **European Cup**. The national side played its first game in 1921, against Hungary, and its first competition match in 1924, at the **Olympic Games** in Paris, again versus Hungary (0–5). Its most successful period was the 1970s and early 1980s: when it won the Olympic Games gold medal (1972) and silver medal (1976) and twice finished third in the World Cup (1974 and 1982). Poland won the Olympic games silver medal again in 1992. Poland is often seen as England's **"bogey team"**, having shared the same European Championship and World Cup qualifying groups on numerous occasions since the 1974 World Cup: (European Championship: 1992, 2000; World Cup: 1974, 1990, 1994, 1998). Poland's record against England, however, is poor, winning only once in 13 games. Nevertheless, many England supporters remember the 1974 World Cup qualifying campaign when Poland qualified at England's expense, after a 2-0 win in the home leg (6 June 1973, in Chorzow) and a 1-1 draw at **Wembley** Stadium (17 October 1973). Lubanski and Banas scored in Chorzow, Domarski at Wembley. The Wembley game, however, is most noted for an outstanding performance by Poland's goalkeeper

Jan **Tomaszewski**. Poland's national stadium at Chorzow was closed by UEFA in 1993 following serious crowd trouble. Crowd violence and vandalism reached a peak in October 1996 with rioting by fans of Widzew Lódź and Legia Warsaw: a situation which led to the closure of both clubs' stadiums for the rest of the 1996-97 season. **Górnik Zabrze** runners-up in the 1970 **European Cup-winners Cup**, beaten 1–2 by **Manchester City**. Poland won the first **European Championships for Players with Learning Disabilities** (4–2, v **Belgium**, in Leicester, England, 1996), and the first **World Football Championships for Players with learning Disabilities** (4–0, v Brazil, in Leicester, 1998). *League system* Poland has two professional divisions. Eighteen clubs compete in the national first division, the bottom four are automatically relegated. Three points are awarded for a victory, with one for a draw: final positions for clubs level on points are determined by the respective results of the matches between those clubs. The second division is divided into two regional groups of 18 clubs (east and west). The winners and runners-up are automatically promoted, while the bottom four in each group are relegated. The domestic cup final is played at the end of June. *Record in international club tournaments* European Cup – Legia Warsaw (semi-final 1970, quarter-final 1971), Widzew Lódź (semi-final 1983, reached the Champions League in 1997), Górnik Zabrze (quarter final 1968), **Ruch Chorzów** (quarter final 1975), Wisla Kraków (quarter-final 1979); European Cup-winners Cup – Górnik Zabrze (runners-up 1970, quarter-final 1971), **Slask Wroclaw** (quarter-final 1977), Legia Warsaw (quarter-final 1982); **UEFA Cup** – Ruch Chorzów (quarter final 1974), **Stal Mielec** (quarter-final 1976), Legia Warsaw (third-round 1969, second round 1997, including two preliminary round victories). Other leading clubs: Cracovia, **Lech Poznan**, LKS Lodz, Amica Wronki (of Wronki, Polish Cup 1998).

Police Club *club* Iraqi league club, also known as Al Schurta. **Asian Champion Teams' Cup** runners-up 1971 (as Al Schurta, walkover, v **Maccabi Tel Aviv** – the Iraqi club refused to play in the final); **Asian Cup-winners Cup** quarter-final 1998; Iraq League champions 1980, 1998.

Police Club *club* Mauritius national league club, based in Port Louis. Ground: Sir Anerood Jugnauth, capacity: 18,000. Mauritius League champions 1971, 1972, 1981 and 1982; Mauritius Cup 1962, 1963, 1965 and 1984, runners-up 1967, 1969, 1977, 1980 and 1982.

Police FC *club* Trinidad and Tobago league club based in St James (Trinidad). Strip: shirts, shorts. **CONCACAF Champions Cup** runners-up 1991 (2–4 agg., v **Puebla** of Mexico).

police *misc.* football clubs are required to organise security at all senior fixtures and must cooperate with local police. Around 75 to 250 police officers are required at most **Premier League** matches. Police presence has reduced with the increase in private security services and club stewarding. In 1992, **Torquay United**'s **Plainmoor** became the first **Football League** ground to stage a match with no uniformed police on duty, relying on stewards to police the crowd and saving the club a considerable sum in policing costs.

political football   *n.*   a problem that is exploited by politicians as an issue for debate rather than resolution. Public transport, the health service and "green politics" are typical political footballs of the late 20th century.

politics, football and   *misc.*   political events that have affected football. *Keynotes* In December 1935, the Trades Union Congress (TUC) attempted to prevent **England** playing **Germany** at **White Hart Lane** (4 December) because of the nature of the Hitler Government and the ground's proximity to a large Jewish community. The TUC's protest was ignored and the then Home Secretary (Sir John Simon) announced that: "Wednesday's match has no political significance whatsoever... It is a game of football, which nobody need attend unless he wishes, and I hope that all who take an interest in it from any side will do their utmost to discourage the idea that a sporting fixture in this country has any political implications." **Northern Ireland** was forced during the 1970s to play several international matches at English club grounds because of increasing political problems in Ireland – it used **Boothferry Park**, **Craven Cottage**, **Goodison Park**, **Highfield Road** and **Hillsborough**, and switched its home matches against **Scotland** to **Hampden Park** during this period. Northern Ireland called off its planned friendly match against Malta, scheduled for 19 August 1998, following the bombing of Omagh town centre the previous weekend. The **Soviet Union** refused to play the second leg of its 1974 **World Cup** qualifying play-off against **Chile** in Santiago's Estadio **Nacional** because it was used to house political dissidents during the September 1973 military coup. Chile was awarded a place in the finals after the Soviet Union failed to turn up. Human rights pressure group Amnesty International attempted to get **FIFA** to cancel the 1978 World Cup because of abuses perpetrated by Argentina's military rulers, to no avail. War in the Balkans led to **former-Yugoslavia**'s expulsion from the 1992 **European Championship** in **Sweden**. **Denmark** was drafted in to replace former-Yugoslavia and went on to win the tournament. In 1990, ethnic tension in the region resulted in clashes between players/officials and the police, and crowd trouble at the Yugoslav Cup tie between the Croatian, Dinamo Zagreb (now **Croatia Zagreb**), and the Serbian, **Red Star Belgrade**. Continuing problems in the region forced the cancellation of England's friendly against former-Yugoslavia at Wembley on 18 November 1998. In addition, the **Republic of Ireland**'s European Championship 2000 qualifying fixture in Belgrade, scheduled for 10 October 1998, was postponed for one month due to the escalating political situation in the region and the possibility of Nato air strikes on military installations in Belgrade.

Similarly, Albania's Euro 2000 qualifier against Greece, also due to be played on 10 October, was postponed because of the political unrest in the region. **South Africa** was barred from virtually all international sport during apartheid. It entered the World Cup for the first time in 1994.

Polivalente   *misc.*   Spanish term for a player who can perform a number of roles.

Polster Toni   *player*   Striker. **Austria** international (94 caps, 44 goals, 1982–). Born 10 March 1964. *Clubs* **Austria Vienna**, **Sevilla**, Logroñes, Vallecano and **Cologne** (1.FC). *Keynotes* Austria's all-time record goalscorer and most capped player.

polypeptide hormones   *medical*   a class of drugs with similar effects to **anabolic steroids**; misused by athletes and players to stimulate the body's own natural steroids, thus promoting muscle growth and repair of damaged tissues. They are banned in football and most other sports.

Pontiac Silverdrome   *stadium*   US sports ground situated near Detroit, Michigan. Ground capacity: 72,700 all seated. *History* Permanently roofed stadium opened in 1978. Staged an indoor international on 19 June 1993 between **England** and **Germany** (US Cup). During the 1994 **World Cup**, the stadium staged two group A matches (**Switzerland** v **USA**, Switzerland v **Romania**) and two group B fixtures (**Sweden** v **Russia**, **Brazil** v Sweden) – total attendance 283,598; average 70,899.

pool account   *n.*   fund held by the **Football League**, into which all the league's income is paid; this includes revenue from television and sponsorship, a levy on member clubs' **gate receipts**, and money from the **Football Association**'s **FA Cup** gate-compensation fund (see **gate-compensation money**). Clubs are required to pay 3% of their net gate receipts into the pool account (Football League Article 57.3). The pool account is used to pay for Football League business, as well as prize money and gate-compensation money. The rest of the pool account money is shared out to the Football League's member clubs; partly as a fixed amount, and in part related to each club's performance. Each club thus receives a "basic award" (in 1998-99, First Division clubs received £620,000 each for the season, Second Division clubs £300,000 and Third Division clubs £210,000). Any remaining money is paid out to the clubs, with three-quarters going to First Division clubs, 18% to Second Division clubs, and 7% to clubs in the Third Division. This additional money is paid on merit, according to where the club finishes in its division – the "ladder principle": if there are 24 clubs in the division, the bottom club receives one share, whereas the top club receives 24 shares. The Football League may also deduct a 10% **Ground improvement levy** from the merit-related award; however, the levy is not applied to clubs that have already met the requirements of the **Taylor Report** (Football League Article 63.2). See also **payments to relegated clubs**.

Pools War *misc.* name given to the dispute between the English **Football League** and the **pools** companies in 1936. The dispute arose over the publication of **fixture lists** by the Football League, which were used by the pools companies to print their postal betting coupons. Key members of the Football League management committee – notably Will **Cuff**, John **McKenna** and Charles **Sutcliffe** – were at that time morally opposed to football as a vehicle for gambling and had refused to accept any money from the Pools Promoters Association (PPA) in lieu of its copyright to the fixtures list. The Football League went further and attempted to block the operation of the pools companies by scrapping the fixtures list for 29 February and 7 March 1936, releasing the new fixtures only at the last possible moment. Clubs with a long distance to travel were informed of the location of their away fixture on the Thursday evening before the game the following Saturday. Other fixtures were announced on the Friday evening. The **Scottish Football League** decided against a similar action. The pools companies responded by extending the deadline for the receipt of coupons, helped by the leaking of the fixtures to the newspapers (the League had, in fact, merely substituted one weekend's fixtures for those of another; once a few fixtures were known, the rest were deduced). The exercise proved highly disruptive to the clubs themselves and to spectators – with reports of serious adverse effects on attendances and travelling supporters. The dispute ended on 9 March, when the Football League agreed to restore the fixtures list. By 1936, the pools revenue was already approaching £30 million per year. The League continued to oppose pools betting and refused further offers of payments from the PPA. In 1959 the High Court ruled that copyright of its fixtures did indeed belong to the Football League. The ruling led to a 10-year agreement between the PPA and the Football League: pools operators would pay 0.5% of the total stake money to the Football League and the Scottish League (in 1959-60, this was about £275,000). Agreements also were reached with pools operators in other countries which also used the Football League fixtures list.

pools *n. pl.* organised system of betting on the results of football matches. Participants bet by postal coupon (or via a collection point/agent) on the results of many rather than individual matches, usually by predicting which matches will finish in a **score-draw**. The total prize money, or pool, is distributed to all those with a winning entry; the size of the payout, or dividend, depending on the number of winners and the amount of money in the pool. *Keynotes* The football pools were launched in 1923, by Littlewoods, initially in Manchester. By the 1950s the industry employed around 100,000 people, mostly as part-time collectors. The first £100,000 prize was won in 1950; the first £200,000 in 1957; the first £300,000 in 1959; the first £500,000 in 1972; and the first £1 million in 1987. The biggest pools payout was £2,924,622, on 19 November

1994, by Littlewoods Pools to a syndicate from Manchester. In Scotland, **Dundee United** began its own pools competition in 1956 which financed ground improvements at **Tannadice**. See **Pools War**.

pools panel *n.* body which forecasts the results of postponed matches for **pools** purposes. The surrogate scores replace the missing results on the pools coupons (and serve no other purpose). It meets at a hotel in Manchester throughout the league season. The pools panel first sat during the 1962-63 winter (when the season was extended by several weeks). During this period, only three out of 32 **FA Cup** ties were played on 5 January 1963 and the following week only eight **Football League** fixtures were played. As a result, the pools companies were forced to declare three successive coupons void. On 23 January the pools panel was used for the first time to forecast the results of postponed matches. Notable former players: Ted **Drake**, Tom **Finney**, Tommy **Lawton** and George Young, and ex-referee Arthur Ellis forecast seven draws, eight away victories and 23 home wins, with results broadcast on television.

pools, forerunners of *misc.* football-related competitions with prize money. Several newspapers/magazines ran football competitions before the **pools** began in 1923. In 1910, *The Racing and Football Outlook* offered readers a prize for correctly predicting six away wins. *The Umpire* offered a first prize of £300 for correctly forecasting the results of six matches.

Popplewell Committee of Inquiry into Crowd Safety and Control at Sports Grounds *misc.* government appointed inquiry set up to examine the **Bradford fire**. The commission's remit was later extended to include the **Heysel Stadium disaster**. The inquiry, chair by Mr Justice Popplewell, examined evidence from over 200 oral and written sources. Popplewell produced an interim (Cmnd 9585) and a final report (Cmnd 9710) which led to three new laws: Sporting Events Act 1986; Public Order Act 1986; and Fire Safety and Safety of Places of Sport Act 1987. In addition, Popplewell recommended a revised Green Guide (first published in 1973) which contained safety recommendations for grounds but had no force in law. This suggestion was followed with the publication of a revised Guide to Safety at Sports Grounds. Popplewell's final report also stressed the need for one authority to have responsibility for the structural safety of stadiums. Factual evidence uncovered by the inquiry led to court proceedings (*Fletcher and Britton v Bradford City AFC and others*) which found in favour of the fire's victims due to **negligence** on the part of the club and the local Fire Authority.

Poppy Appeal *misc.* annual campaign organised by the British Legion in remembrance of lives lost in the two World Wars. Over the weekend of 23–26 October 1998, all 46 **Premier League** and **Football League** matches played a recorded message by BBC sports presenter Des **Lynam** and held a minute's silence to help launch the 1998 Poppy Appeal.

Port Glasgow Athletic *club* former-Scottish league. *Dossier* Ground: Clune Park, Port Glasgow, Strathclyde. *Keynotes* Joined the **Scottish League** in 1893-94 in place of **Renton**. In that first season, the club was deducted seven points for fielding an **ineligible player** which at one point during the campaign meant the club was minus one point – the only occasion this has occurred in the UK. The club won the Division Two Championship in 1901-02, securing a place in the top flight via the **test matches** (6–0 v **Kilmarnock**). Athletic's highest League position was ninth, which the club achieved in 1903-04. The club was a **Scottish FA Cup** semi-finalist in both 1899 (2–4 v **Celtic**) and 1906 (0–2 v **Heart of Midlothian**). *League record* Division One 1902-03 to 1909-10; Division Two 1893-94 to 1901-02. *Honours* Division Two 1901-02.

Port Saigon *club* Vietnamese national league club based in Ho Chi Minh City (Saigon). Vietnam league champions 1994, 1997.

Port Vale *club* English league. *Dossier* Ground: **Vale Park**, Burslem, Stoke-on-Trent, Staffordshire. Strip: white shirts with black trim, black shorts, white socks with black trim. Nickname: Valiants. Ground capacity: 22,356. Record attendance: 50,000 v **Aston Villa** (20 February 1960, **FA Cup**, fifth round). Best average attendance: 20,869 (1954-55). Biggest win: 9–1 v **Chesterfield** (24 September 1932, Division Two). Biggest defeat: 0–10 v **Sheffield United** (10 December 1892, Division Two), v **Notts County** (26 February 1895, Division Two). *History* Founded in 1876 as Port Vale, a title that derives from the names of several landmarks in the Longport district of Stoke-on-Trent. After moving to a venue next to Burslem Station in 1884 the club adopted the prefix Burslem and turned professional. It was as Burslem Port Vale tha, in 1885, the club became the first to adopt limited company status. Vale joined the newly-expanded **Football League** in 1892, dropped out in 1896 and rejoined in 1898 before going bust in 1907 and resigning from the League. The club was reformed by local businessmen in 1913, switching to the Old Recreation Ground and dropping Burslem from its name. The Football League expelled **Leeds City** on 4 October 1919 for failing to cooperate with the football authorities who had accused the club of making **illegal payments** to players during **World War I**: its place in Division Two was taken by Vale. Continuing financial problems led to Vale's directors pursuing a merger with neighbours **Stoke City** (which itself went bankrupt in 1908) in 1926, but protest by supporters scuppered this plan. Following relegation to Division Three (North) in 1928-29, the club returned as champions the next season avoided relegation but was on **goal average** in 1931-32 but was relegated in 1935-36. At the start of the 1950-51 season, with the club in Division Three (South), Vale moved to a new ground, Vale Park, which it had planned to turn into a 70,000 capacity "Wembley of North" – a plan that never materialised. In 1953-54, Vale, then of Division Three (North), reached the **FA**

Cup semi-finals (1–2 v **West Bromwich Albion**), defeating Cup-holders **Blackpool** (2–0) in the fifth round. In the same season, the club won the Division Three (North) title by a margin of 11 points. After relegation to Division Four in 1958-59, the club spent the next 31 seasons alternating between bottom two divisions. Port Vale was found guilty by the Football League of paying unregistered players in 1967-68, as well as making a number of other illegal payments. The clubs was fined £2,000 by the **Football Association** and expelled by the Football League. However, the latter punishment was deferred until the end of the season; the club was able, therefore, to apply for **re-election** (and was successful). In 1988-89, Vale won promotion to Division Two via the end-of-season **playoffs** (2–1 agg. v **Bristol Rovers**). The club failed to reach the First Division through the same route in 1992-93 after reaching the playoff finals (0–3 v **West Bromwich Albion**). The following season, Vale returned to **Wembley** and won the **Autoglass Trophy** (2–1 v **Stockport County**). In 1996 it was an **Anglo-Italian Cup** finalist (2–5 v **Genoa**). *League record* First Division 1994-95–; Division Two 1892-93 to 1895-96 (failed re-election as Burslem Port Vale), 1898-99 to 1906-07 (resigned as Burslem Port Vale), 1919-20 (4 October 1919 – took over the fixtures of Leeds City) to 1928-29, 1930-31 to 1935-36, 1954-55 to 1956-57; Second Division 1989-90 to 1993-94; Division Three 1959-60 to 1964-65, 1970-71 to 1977-78, 1983-84, 1986-87 to 1988-89; Divsion Three (North) 1929-30, 1936-37 to 1937-38, 1952-53 to 1953-54; Divsion Three (South) 1938-39 to 1951-52, 1957-58; Division Four 1958-59, 1965-66 to 1969-70, 1978-79 to 1982-83, 1984-85 to 1985-86. *Honours* Division Three (North) 1929-30, 1953-54; Division Four 1958-59; Autoglass Trophy 1993 (2–1 v Stockport County). *Records* Sammy Morgan is Vale's most capped player (7 (18) for **Northern Ireland**); Roy Sproson holds the record for club appearances (761, 1950-72); Wilf Kirkham is Vale's record League goalscorer (154, 1923-29, 1931-33).

Portadown FC *club* Northern Ireland national league club based in Portadown, County Armagh, founded 1924. Ground: Shamrock Park, capacity: 15,000. Strip: red shirts, red shorts. *Keynotes* Portadown has a largely Protestant following and, in 1998, was barred, by the police, from playing its home matches against traditionally Catholic club **Cliftonville** at Shamrock Park, for security reasons. It won the 1999 **Irish FA Cup** after its opponent, Cliftonville was disqualified for fielding a **cup-tied** player in the semi-final. **UEFA Cup** second round 1975; Northern Ireland league champions 1990, 1991, 1996; **Irish FA Cup** (Northern Ireland) winners 1991, 1999 (walkover). Notable former players: Wilbur Cush (26 caps for Northern Ireland, 1951-62).

Porthmadog *club* Welsh league. Ground: **Y Traeth**, Gwynedd. Strip: red and black stripes on shirts, black shorts. Nickname: Port. Ground capacity: 4,000. Formed in 1884. *Keynotes* David Taylor, with 43 league goals for Porthmadog in 1993-94, was the unofficial **European Golden Boot** winner.

porteur d'eau *misc.* French term for midfield player who is constantly closing down opponents and breaking up attacks. See also **midfield dynamo.**

Portman Road *ground* English football ground situated in Ipswich, Suffolk; home of **Ipswich Town**. *Dossier* Ground capacity: 22,600 all seated. Pitch dimensions: 102m x 75m. Record attendance: 38,010 v **Leeds United** (8 March 1975, **FA Cup**, sixth round). Best average attendance: 26,672 (1976-77). *History* In September 1888, Ipswich Association Football Club merged with a local rugby club, Ipswich Football Club, to form Ipswich Town. The new club moved to the Corporation-owned Portman Road ground. Until 1907, the club played on what is now the training pitch. The first football match on today's pitch took place on 9 January 1907 (Suffolk County v Cambridge County). The ground was used by the army during **World War I** and whippet racing took place in 1922. In 1968, the club renewed Portman Road's lease with the council for further 99 years and, in 1970, inner-ground advertising was allowed for the first time. Between 1968 and 1984, three of Portman Road's four sides were redeveloped and, during summer 1992 it became the first **Premier League** ground to be all seated. The first floodlit match took place on 16 February 1960 (v **Arsenal**, friendly).The ground staged an England Under-21 intrnational in 1971. According to the National Asset Register, which was published on 24 November 1997, Portman Road's car park is owned by the Inland Revenue.

Porto (Futebol Clube do Porto) *club* Portuguese national league club based in Oporto (Portuguese name: Porto), founded in 1906. Ground: Estádio das Antas, capacity: 76,000. Strip: blue and white striped shirts, blue shorts. **European Cup** 1987 (2–1 v **Bayern Munich**, Vienna, Austria), quarter final 1997, Champions League 1998; **European Cup-winners Cup** runners-up 1984 (1–2, v **Juventus**, Basle, Switzerland); **World Club Cup** winners 1987 (2–1, v **Peñarol**, Tokyo); **European Supercup** – winners 1987-88 (2–0 agg. v **Ajax**); Portuguese League champions 1935, 1939, 1940, 1956, 1959, 1978, 1979, 1985, 1986, 1988, 1990, 1992, 1993, 1995, 1997, 1998, 1999; Portuguese Cup 1922, 1925, 1932, 1937, 1956, 1958, 1968, 1977, 1984, 1988, 1991, 1994, 1998.

Portsmouth Centenary tournament *competition* four-team pre-season tournament staged at **Portsmouth**'s **Fratton Park** ground in August 1998 to celebrate the club's 100th anniversary. Aside from Portsmouth, the tournament also involved **Genoa**, Sochaux and **Wimbledon**. Sochaux won the final (2–1 v Genoa).

Portsmouth *club* English league. *Dossier* Ground: **Fratton Park**, Portsmouth, Hampshire. Strip: blue shirts with white trim, white shorts, blue sock with white trim. Nickname: Pompey. Ground capacity: 19,179.

Record attendance: 51,385 v **Derby County** (26 February 1949, **FA Cup**, sixth round). Best average attendance: 37,082 (1948-49). Biggest win: 9–1 v **Notts County** (9 April 1927, Division Two). Biggest defeat: 0–10 v **Leicester City** (20 October 1928, Division One). *History* Founded 1898 by several local businessmen after the city's leading club, Royal Artillery, had been suspended by the **Football Association** for breaching amateur regulations. The businessmen, including Alderman J E Pink, established a limited company and, for £4,950, bought some land near Fratton railway station. Professional players were signed and the club joined the **Southern League**. In 1902, Portsmouth won the Southern League Championship and, after winning a second title in 1920, it was elected to the newly-formed **Football League** Division Three (South) in 1921-22. The club won the Division Three (South) Championship in 1923-24, finishing fourth in Division Two the following season. Promotion to the top flight was achieved in 1926-27. Portsmouth reached its first FA Cup final in 1929 (0–2 v **Bolton Wanderers**) and a second final in 1934 (1–2 v **Manchester City**). Either side of **World War II**, and under the managership of first Jack Tinn and later Bob Jackson, Portsmouth enjoyed its most successful period. The club won its first major trophy, the FA Cup, in 1939 (4–1 v **Wolverhampton Wanderers**) followed by consecutive League Championships in 1948-49 and 1949-50 It finished joint second on points in 1954-55 but, after narrowly missing relegation on **goal average** in 1957-58, the club was relegated the following season before slipping to Division Three in 1960-61. A quick return to Division Two as champions the next year was the beginning of a 13-year period of mid-table inconsistency that led to relegation in 1975-76 and, two years later, demotion to Division Four for the first time. Portsmouth staged the first **floodlit** Football League match on 22 February 1956 (v **Newcastle United**, Division One), although the **kick off** was delayed for 10 minutes after the lights failed. In 1982-83, Portsmouth returned to Division Two as Champions and ,in 1986-87, under the managership of Alan **Ball**, the club returned to the top flight, albeit for only one season. Portsmouth was a FA Cup semi-finalist in 1992, losing on penalities to **Liverpool** after a scoreless replay. The following year, Portsmouth narrowly missed promotion to the **Premier League**, reaching the end-of-season **playoffs**. In 1988, ex-**Queens Park Rangers**' chairman John Gregory bought the club for £2 million but, after failing to agree planning permission for a new ground he put the club up for sale in January 1995, only to take it off the market a year later after no suitable buyer had come forward. A consortium backed by American millionaire and US sports stadiums developer Vince Wolanin offered to buy the club in 1997 (the group submitted a further offer in March 1998), but this was rejected by the board. At the same time, Terry **Venables** – who had bought a 51% stake in Portsmouth for £1 in 1996, becoming the club's chairman as a result – received a reported £250,000 payment in Janaury 1998, with control of the club returning to the Gregory family. Alan Ball was reappointed manager in January 1998. The club was forced to borrow £150,000 from the **Professional Footballers Association** in November 1998, to pay its wage bill. The club was bought for a reported £4.5 million by a US based millionaire in May 1999. *League record* Division One 1927-28 to 1958-59, 1987-88; First Division 1992-93–; Division Two 1924-25 to 1926-27, 1959-60 to 1960-61, 1962-63 to 1975-76, 1983-84 to 1986-87, 1988-89 to 1991-92; Division Three 1920-21, 1961-62, 1976-77 to 1977-78,1980-81 to 1982-83; Division Three (South) 1921-22 to 1923-24; Division Four 1978-79 to 1979-80. *Honours* League 1948-49, 1949-50; Division Three 1961-62, 1982-83; Division Three (South) 1923-24; Southern League 1902, 1920; FA Cup 1939 (4–1 v Wolverhampton Wanderers – *Team* Walker, Morgan, Rochford, Guthrie, Rowe, Wharton, Worrall, McAlinden, Anderson (1), Barlow (1), Parker (2)). *Records* Jimmy **Dickinson** is Portsmouth's most capped player (48 for **England**); he also holds the record for club appearances (764, 1946-65); Peter Harris is Portsmouth's record League goalscorer (194, 1946-60).

Portugal *country UEFA* republic in south-west Europe bordered by the Atlantic Ocean and **Spain**. Includes the **Azores** and **Madeira**. Ruled by a military dictatorship from 1928 to 1968. Joined European Union in 1986. Former colonies chiefly in Africa as well as **Brazil**. Area: 91,360 sq km (35,370 sq miles). Population: 9,900,000 (1994 est.). Languages: Portuguese (the language also is spoken in **Angola**, Brazil and **Mozambique**). Capital: Lisbon (Portuguese name: Lisboa) *Dossier* Football association (Federaçã Portuguesa de Futebol, Lisbon), formed in 1914, affiliated to **FIFA** in 1923 and founder member of the **Union of European Football Associations** (UEFA) in 1954, president: Dr Gilberto Parca Madail; general secretary: António Eduardo Sequeira. Season played from August to June. National stadium: Estádio Nacional, capacity: 60,000. National strip: red shirts, green shorts, red socks. First international game: 18 December 1921 v Spain (1–3, Madrid, friendly). Biggest victory: 8–0 v **Liechtenstein** (18 December 1994, Lisbon, European Championship qualifier). Biggest defeat: 0–10 v **England** (25 May 1947, Lisbon, friendly). Most capped players: Joao **Pinto** (70 appearances, from 1983-96, one goal), Tamanini Nené (66 appearances, 1971-84), **Eusébio** Ferreira (64 appearances, 1961-73), Humberto Coelho (64 appearances, 1968-83). Leading goalscorers: Eusébio Ferreira (41 goals, 1961-73), Tamanini Nené (22 goals, 1971-84), Fernando Peyroteo (15 goals, 1938-49), Rui Jordao (15 goals, 1972-89). Other notable international players: Mario Esteves **Coluna**, Paolo **Futre**. *International tournament record* Olympic Games – first entered 1928, semifinal/fourth 1996 (0–5, v Brazil, in Athens, Georgia, USA, third/fourth playoff), quarter-final 1928; **Women's World Cup** – first entered 1995, never

qualified for finals tournament; **World Cup** – first entered 1934, third place 1966 (2–1 v **Soviet Union**, **Wembley** Stadium, London, third/fourth playoff), also qualified for finals tournament in 1986; European Championship – entered first tournament in 1960, semi-final 1984 (2–3 v **France**, Marseille, France), quarter final 1960 and 1996; **European Championship for Women** – first entered 1995, never beyond first-round group stage; **Algarve Cup** – permanent hosts; **European under-21 championship** runners-up 1994; **European under-16 Championship** – winners 1989 and 1995, runners-up 1988; **European Youth Championship** (under-18) – winners 1994, runners-up 1988, 1990, 1992, 1994; **Under-17 World Championship** – third place 1989 (3–0 v **Bahrain**, Scotland); **World Youth Cup** (under-20) – winners 1989 (2-0 v **Nigeria**, Riyadh, Saudi Arabia), winners 1991 (0–0, 4–2 pens. v Brazil, Lisbon – a match watched by 120,000 spectators at the Estádioda Luz), third place 1995 (3–2 v Spain, Doha, Qatar), quarter final 1979, also qualified 1999. *World Cup performance* (finals and qualifiers to end of 1998 tournament): played 92, won 42, drawn 20, lost 30, scored 138 goals, conceded 119 goals; win rate 46%; goals scored per game 1.5. *Record against British and Irish national teams* v England, played 17 times, won two, drawn six, lost nine; v **Northern Ireland**, played 10, won three, drawn five, lost two; v **Scotland**, played 13, won six, drawn three, lost four; v **Wales**, played two, won one, drawn none, lost one; v **Republic of Ireland**, played nine, won six, drawn none, lost three. *History* Football was introduced at the end of the 19th century, with four of the country's five most successful clubs formed in the 1900s: **Boavista FC** (1903), **Benfica** (1904), **Sporting Clube de Portugal** (1906), **Porto** (1906). **OS Belenenses** was formed in 1919. The Portuguese Cup has been played since 1922, first won by Porto. The national league was founded in 1934-35, with Porto, again, winning the first title. The "Big three" clubs, Porto, Benfica and Sporting, have dominated domestic football. They have won 62 league championships between them; OS Belenenses is the only club outside the three to have won the title, and that in only one year (1946). Benfica has been in seven **European Cup** finals, winning in 1961 and 1962. The most famous Portuguese player of all time, Eusébio – Mozambiquan by birth – appeared in Benfica's first five European Cup finals, scoring twice in the 5–2 defeat of **Real Madrid** in 1962, and was tournament top scorer in 1966 (eight goals) and 1968 (six goals). FC **Porto** was European Cup and **World Club Cup** champions in 1987. The national side played its first game in 1921, with its first competition match in 1928 (4–2, v **Chile**, in Amsterdam, Olympic Games first round). Portugal's World Cup history is highlighted by its third place in 1966. It has, however, qualified for the finals tournament only twice in 15 attempts since 1934. *League system* Eighteen clubs compete in the national first division, the I Divisao. Clubs play each other at home and away

(34 games in total). Three points are awarded for a victory, with one for a draw: final positions for clubs level on points are determined by **goal difference** and, if necessary, by **goals scored** and **number of victories**. The bottom three clubs are automatically relegated to the 18-club second division, the II Divisao de Honra. Below this, the II Divisao B is divided into three regional leagues, also of 18 clubs each: each regional champion is promoted, replacing the bottom three clubs from the II Divisao. A third tier, the III Divisao, is divided into six regional leagues. *Record in international club tournaments* European Cup – Benfica (winners 1961, 1962, runners-up 1963, 1965, 1968, 1988, 1990), Porto (winners 1987, Champions League and quarter-final 1997); **European Cup-winners Cup** – Sporting Clube de Portugal (winners 1964, semi-final 1974), Porto (runners-up 1984), Benfica (quarter-final 1997); **UEFA Cup** – Benfica (runners-up 1983), Sporting Clube de Portugal (semi-final 1991), **Vitória SC Setúbal** (quarter-final 1973), Boavista FC (third round 1997); World Club Cup – Porto (winners 1987); **European Supercup** – Porto (winners 1987-88). Other leading club: OS Belenenses.

Portuguesa (Associaçao Portuguesa de Deportes) *club* Brazilian national league and **São Paulo** state league club based in São Paulo, founded 1920. Ground: Oswaldo Teixeira Duarte "Caninde", capacity 25,000. Strip: green and red hooped shirts, white shorts. **Copa Libertadores** second-round group stage 1977; São Paulo Tournament winners 1952, 1955; state league champions three times (to 1998).

Portuguesa FC *club* Venezuelan national league club based in Acarigua, founded 1926, reformed 1996. Ground: Estadio General José Antonio Páez, capacity 20,000. Strip: red and black striped shirts, white shorts. **Copa Libertadores** semi-final 1977; Venezuelan league champions (**Torneo Clausura**) 1973, 1975, 1976, 1977, 1978; **Copa Venezuela** winners 1973, 1976, 1977.

POSCO Atoms *club* Former name of **Pohang Steelers**.

possession *n.* **1.** of a team, the act of keeping control of the ball through passing between team-mates. *Usage* "Liverpool was able to protect its 1–0 lead by keeping possession for the final five minutes of play." **2.** the proportion of playing time that one team is in control of the ball. **3.** *rules* taking control of the ball by a goalkeeper, by deliberately touching it with his or her hands or arms. Possession by a goalkeeper is important in respect of Law XII of the **Laws of the game**, which states that a **foul** is committed if the goalkeeper takes more than four **steps** after taking control of the ball without releasing it back into play, or if he/she handles the ball again after releasing it from his/her possession before another player has contacted the ball.

possession space *tactics* any area of the pitch outside of the **scoring space** (the **penalty box** and the area immediately outside and directly in front of the goal).

post *rules* another word for **goal post**.

Postel 2000 *club* Chad national league club based in the capital N'Djamena. Ground: Concorde (the national stadium), capacity 25,000. **African Cup of Champion Clubs** first round 1996 (after qualifying round); Chad league champions 1993, 1995; Chad Cup 1991.

postpone *vb.* to cancel a match and rearrange it for another date. *Regulations* **Premier League** matches can be postponed only if the match clashes with a fixture in another competition involving one or both teams (such as an **FA Cup** tie), or by instruction of the **referee**, the police or the league board (FA Premier League rule E.11). Premier League and **Football League** home clubs whose league matches are postponed because of a clash with the away club's **League Cup** or **FA Cup** tie are able to claim **gate compensation money** for lost revenue (FA Premier League rules section C, Football League Article 68.2). In the Football League, compensation is paid only to clubs when their match is postponed from a Saturday and rearranged for a day other than a Saturday (Football League Article 68.2).

Power Dynamos *club* Zambian national league club based in Kitwe, founded 1977. Ground: Garden Park, capacity 15,000. Strip: red shirts, yellow shorts. **African Cup-winners Cup** 1991 (5–4 agg., v **BCC Lions** of Nigeria), runners-up 1982 (0–4 agg., v **Al Mokaouloum** of Egypt); Zambian league champions 1984, 1991, 1994, 1997; Zambian Cup 1980, 1981, 1985, 1988, 1990, 1993, 1997.

power surge *misc.* significant increase in domestic electricity consumption at half-time and full-time. *Keynotes* In the UK, the electricity generating companies recorded a 1,100 mega watt rise in demand at full-time, in addition to a 1,000 mega watt increase at half-time, during **England**'s 1998 **World Cup** group G encounter with **Tunisia** (15 June, Stade Velodrome).

Praia Cruz (Sporting Club Praia Cruz) *club* Sao Tomé and Principe national league club based in Sao Tomé. Ground: Municipale, capacity 2,500. Sao Tomé and Principe league champions 1982, 1985, 1992; Sao Tomé and Principe Cup 1982.

pre-contract agreement *n.* a deal struck between a player and a club which is not his or her current employer. The fallout from the **Bosman ruling** allows players to negotiate a pre-contract agreement with another club six months before his or her existing deal finishes. *Keynote* Brian **Laudrup** signed a pre-contract agreement orior to his short-lived transfer to **Chelsea** while still a **Rangers** player.

Pre-Libertadores Liguilla *competition* semi-knockout and league-based tournament of **Uruguay** to see which two clubs qualify for the **Copa Libertadores**, first competed 1974. The competition involves the two top league clubs (ie the winners of the **apertura** and **clausura**), which automatically qualify for the "league", and six teams that qualify from a two-round (plus losers' playoff) knockout tournament (the

"Torneo Nacional") – involving the next seven teams from the **Primera A** division, and nine teams from the Interior league (see **Organizacion del Futbol del Interior**). The final eight teams are divided into two groups of four; the top two from each qualifying for knockout semi-finals and final. The top club automatically qualifies for the Copa Libertadores, while a second place is given to the winners of a playoff between the second-placed Liguilla club and the winners of the Uruguayan league championship (the **Copa Uruguaya**). All the matches are played at the national stadium, Estadio **Centenario**. The tournament is also used to determine Uruguay's two qualification berths for the **Copa CONMEBOL**. Previous winners: **Danubio** (1983); **Defensor-Sporting Club** (1976, 1979, 1981, 1989, 1991); **Nacional** (1982, 1990, 1992, 1993, 1996); **Peñarol** (1974, 1975, 1977, 1978, 1980, 1984, 1985, 1986, 1988, 1994, 1997); **Montevideo Wanderers** (1987); Bella Vista (1998).

pre-season *n.* period immediately preceding the start of a new season. *adj.* usage: pre-season friendly.

pre-season tournament *n.* a series of competitive fixtures that are held prior to the start of a new season and generally are used to help players' achieve match fitness. In contrast to **close-season tournaments**, which are usually contested by national sides, pre-season tournaments tend to be club affairs. See **Birra Moretti tournament**, **Carlsberg tournament**, **Makita Cup**, **Memorial Cecchi Gori tournament**, **Umbro Trophy**, **Watney Cup**.

preliminary round *n.* initial round of a knockout competition to determine the qualifying clubs for the competition proper: preliminary rounds may be essential to reduce the number of clubs to, for example, 128, 64, 32 or 16, such that they can be reduced by a series of eliminations to produce a final round of two clubs; or to select clubs qualifying for the group stages of an international tournament.

Premier League *competition* top flight in English league football; a single division of 20 clubs, formed in 1992 from the old **Football League** First Division. The Football Association Premier League Limited is a registered, limited company and has 100 shares, valued at £1 each. Each member club is issued with one share. Its registered office is in West London. Member clubs can send two delegates to the Premier League annual general meeting, only one of whom can vote. *League system* Three points are awarded for a victory and one for a drawn match. If teams have identical points, the final league positions are decided on **goal difference** (FA Premier League rule B.22). If clubs are level on points and goal difference then positions are decided on **goals scored** (FA Premier League rule B.23). If clubs are still level, and are involved in relegation, the championship or on qualification for a European competition, the clubs will **playoff** at a **neutral venue** (FA Premier League rule B.31). At the end of the season, the bottom three clubs in the league are relegated to the Football League Division One, replaced by the top two clubs in that

division plus the winner of the playoff between the third-, fourth-, fifth- and sixth-placed clubs. *History* The Premier League originally contained 22 clubs, all of which would have been entitled to play in the former First Division of the Football League at the beginning of the first Premier League season of 1992-93. The League was reduced to 20 clubs at the end of 1994-95, by relegating the bottom four clubs of the new league and promoting only two from the Football League. *Premier League champions* 1993 **Manchester United**; 1994 Manchester United; 1995 **Blackburn Rovers**; 1996 Manchester United; 1997 Manchester United; 1998 **Arsenal**.

Premier League (US) *n.* United States amateur football league – the "fourth division" in US football. Introduced in 1995, first winners: San Francisco United All Blacks. Part of the **United Systems of Independent Soccer Leagues**.

Premier League Board *n.* board of directors of the Football Association Premier League Limited (see **Premier League**).

Premier League Championship Trophy *n.* trophy awarded to the winner of the FA **Premier League**. *Regulations* The trophy is held by the champions until the following season's competition is completed, but returned at least three weeks before the end of the season (FA Premier League rule B26).

Premiership *competition* another name for the **Premier League**.

Prenton Park *ground* English football ground situated in Birkenhead, Merseyside; home of **Tranmere Rovers**. *Dossier* Ground capacity: 16,789 all seated. Pitch dimensions 100.5m x 64m. Record attendance: 24,424 v **Stoke City** (5 February 1972, **FA Cup**, fourth round). Best average attendance: 11,815 (1958-59). *History* Rovers played at several venues, including Steele's Field and Borough Road (later also called Prenton Park), before settling at its present home in 1912. The club played its first match at the ground on 9 March 1912 (v Lancaster, Lancashire Combination League). Until 1920, Rovers shared Prenton Park with an amateur club, Northern Nomads. The ground's car park was used to send up smoke screens to confuse German pilots bombing the nearby docks during **World War II**. Tranmere was refused permission to lay an **artificial pitch** in 1985 after failing to win the approval of the other **Football League** clubs. Following Peter Johnson's takeover of the club in 1987, Prenton Park underwent a complete refurbishment, including the installation in 1988 of an electronic scoreboard, which was bought from **Everton.** In 1994, Rovers embarked on the construction of three new stands built over a nine-month period, ensuring the ground met the **all-seater stadiums deadline**. Prenton Park's first floodlit match took place on 29 September 1958 (v **Rochdale**, Division Three). The ground staged the home leg of Republic of Ireland club **Shelbourne**'s 1998-99 **UEFA Cup** first round qualifying tie against **Rangers** on 22 July 1998. The tie was switched from Shelbourne's Tolka Park ground after requests from the Irish police and the **Football Association of Ireland** because of the potential for crowd trouble following heigthened sectarian tension in Northern Ireland at the time.

press box *misc.* enclosure or special area for journalists/reporters. *Keynotes* **Celtic Park** had the first press box at a UK football ground when the club opened one in 1894.

pressing game *tactics* style of play which involves a team defending by moving forward and attacking the opposition by putting **on-ball** opponents under immediate pressure. Teams often counteract opponents which play a **passing game** by adopting pressing tactics, limiting the opposition's time on the ball and forcing them into making errors.

Preston North End *club* English league. Ground: **Deepdale**, Preston, Lancashire. *Dossier* Strip: white and navy blue shirts, navy blue shorts and navy blue socks. Nickname: the Lilywhites or North End. Ground capacity: 21,412. Record attendance: 42,684 v **Arsenal** (23 April 1938, Division One). Best average attendance: 33,226 (1948-49). Biggest win: 26–0 v **Hyde** (15 October 1887, **FA Cup**, first round). Biggest defeat: 0–7 v **Blackpool** (1 May 1948, Division One). *History* North End cricket club was founded in 1863, and, in 1879, it began playing football, which became the main focus of attention from 1881. The cricket club adopted the name Preston North End in 1875 when it moved to Deepdale. The club reached the FA Cup final in 1888 (1–2 v **West Bromwich Albion**), having been a semi-finalist the previous year (1–3 v West Bromwich Albion). Preston was a founder member of the **Football League**, and the club's Jack Gordon is credited with scoring the first League goal, on 8 September 1888. Preston was the first **League Champions** in 1888-89, winning the title without losing a match and conceding only 15 goals. The club also lifted the **FA Cup** in 1889 (3–0 v **Wolverhampton Wanderers**), without conceding a goal, making Preston the first club to win the **double**. Preston retained the title the following season and was runners-up in 1890-91, 1891-92 and 1892-93. During this period, Preston, nicknamed the "Invicibles" and under the managership of William **Sudell**, was at the forefront of football's move towards professionalism, bringing in players on wages from Scotland. Preston was relegated in 1900-01, having narrowly avoided the drop in the previous two seasons, but returned as Division Two Champions in 1903-04. Thereafter, until relegation to Division Three in 1969-70, the club switched on 10 occasions between the top two divisions. Preston played in the last pre-**Wembley** FA Cup final, held at **Stamford Bridge**, in 1922 (0–1 v **Huddersfield Town**) and featured in two consecutive FA Cup finals in the late 1930s; losing in 1937 (1–3 v **Sunderland**) and winning the trophy a year later (1–0 a.e.t. v Huddersfield Town) in Wembley's first **extra-time** final: future Liverpool manager Bill **Shankly** played in both North End teams. During the 1950s, Preston almost recaptured its early football dominance,

finishing Division One runners-up in both 1952-53 (losing the title only on **goal average**) and 1957-58, and, in 1954, reaching a sixth FA Cup final (2–3 v West Bromwich Albion). Preston's side of the 1950s included Tom **Finney**, who made 433 League appearances between 1946 and 1960, scoring 187 goals, and Tommy **Docherty**. Preston, then a Division Two side, made its seventh FA Cup final appearance in 1964 (2–3 v **West Ham United**). Although Preston won promotion as Champions, after only one season in Division Three (1970-71) – the club, under the managership of ex-**Manchester United** and former **England** international Bobby **Charlton**, was again demoted in 1973-74, a season in which it was docked one point for fielding an **ineligible player**. A brief three-season spell in Division Two between 1978-79 and 1980-81 was followed by relegation to Division Four for the first time in 1984-85, with the club finishing 91st in the League the following year. The club reached the semi-finals of the Division Three **playoffs** in 1988-89. In 1993-94 and 1994-95, Preston narrowly missed promotion, losing on the first occasion in the final of the Third Division playoffs (2–4 v **Wycombe Wanderers**), and at the semi-final stage the following season. The club won the Third Division Championship in 1995-96. The club was floated on the **Alternative Investment Market** in October 1995 (flotation price = 400p), which is a precursor to full floatation on the stock market. *League record* Division One (including Football League) 1888-89 to 1900-01, 1904-05 to 1911-12, 1913-14, 1919-20 to 1924-25, 1934-35 to 1948-49, 1951-52 to 1960-61; Division Two 1901-02 to 1903-04, 1912-13, 1914-15, 1925-26 to 1933-34, 1949-50 to 1950-51, 1960-61 to 1969-70, 1971-72 to 1973-74, 1978-79 to 1980-81; Second Division 1992-93, 1996-97–; Division Three 1970-71, 1974-75 to 1977-78, 1981-82 to 1984-85, 1987-88 to 1991-92; Third Division 1993-94 to 1995-96; Division Four 1985-86 to 1986-87. *Honours* League 1888-89, 1889-90; Division Two 1903-04, 1912-13, 1950-51; Division Three 1970-71; Third Division 1995-96; FA Cup 1889 (3–0 v Wolverhampton Wanderers), 1938 (1–0 a.e.t. v Huddersfield Town – *Team* Holdcroft, Gallimore, A Beattie, Shankly, Smith, Batey, Watmough, Mutch (1, pen.), Maxwell, R Beattie, H O'Donnell). *Records* Tom Finney is Preston's most capped player (76 for England); Alan Kelly holds the record for club League appearances (447, 1961-75); Finney is also Preston's record League goalscorer (187, 1946-60).

Preston North End plc *n.* publicly-quoted business which owns **Preston North End**. The club became a listed company on the **Alternative Investment Market** in October 1995 (flotation price = 400p). Preston had a market capitalisation – the market value of the company's issued share capital (ie the quoted price of its shares multiplied by the number of shares outstanding) – of £8.2 million when it joined the AIM.

Prevoyance Yaoundé *club* Cameroon national league club based in the capital Yaoundé. Ground: Ahmadou Ahidjo (national stadium), capacity: 60,000.

Strip: black shirts, yellow shorts. Cameroon league runners-up 1995, 1996; Cameroon Cup 1990.

Pride Park *ground* English football ground situated in Derbyshire; home of **Derby County**. *Dossier* Ground capacity: 33,000 all seated. Pitch dimensions: 105m x 68.5m. Record attendance: 32,913 v **Liverpool** (13 March 1999, **Premier League**). *History* The ground is situated in a development zone, that also includes retail and office facilities, one mile from Derby's previous home, the **Baseball Ground**. The opening match at Pride Park took place on 4 August 1997 (v **Sampdoria**, friendly). **Floodlights** failed at the first league fixture (v **Wimbledon**, 13 August 1997, Premier League) and the game was abandoned after 56 minutes. Derby remained unbeaten at Pride Park until 7 February 1998, when it lost 0–1 to **Aston Villa** in a Premier League fixture.

Priestfield Stadium *ground* English football ground situated in Gillingham, Kent; home of **Gillingham**. *Dossier* Ground capacity: 10,600. Pitch dimensions: 104m x 69m. Record attendance: 23,002 v **Queens Park Rangers** (10 January 1948, **FA Cup**, third round). Best average attendance: 12,576 (1951-52). *History* New Brompton FC (later Gillingham) bought a piece of land near Gillingham Road, which eventually became Priestfield Stadium, at the club's foundation in 1893. Originally entitled the New Brompton Athletic Ground, the club adopted the Priestfield Stadium name in 1947. A wooden stand constructed at the ground by local shipyard workers in 1899 continued to be used until it was outlawed in the aftermath of the 1985 **Bradford fire** – having been the oldest stand in senior UK football. Priestfield was one of the last **Football League** grounds to install **floodlights**, staging its first floodlit fixture on 25 September 1963 (v **Bury**, **League Cup**). **Brighton & Hove Albion** moved to Priestfield on a temporary **groundshare** basis at the start of 1997-98, playing its first match at the stadium on 16 August 1997 (v **Macclesfield Town**, Third Division).

Primeiro de Agosto *club* Angolan national league club, based in the capital Luanda. Ground: Citadela (the national stadium), capacity: 60,000. Strip: red shirts, black shorts. **African Cup of Champion Clubs** quarter-final "champions-league" stage 1997; **African Cup-winners Cup** runners-up 1998 (2–4 agg., v **Espérance Tunis** of Tunisia); Angolan league champions 1979, 1980, 1981, 1991, 1993, 1996, 1998; Angolan Cup 1984, 1990, 1991, 1992, 1998.

Primeiro de Maio *club* Angolan national league club, based in Benguela, founded 1914. Ground: Sao Felipe. Strip: red shirts, white shorts. **CAF Cup** runners-up 1994 (1–3 agg., v **Bendel Insurance** of Nigeria); Angolan league champions 1983, 1985; Angolan Cup, 1982, 1983.

Primera A *competition* top-flight league in **Uruguay**, involves clubs mainly from the Montevideo area.

Primera Liga *competition* the top-flight national professional league of Spain, founded in 1929. By 1998,

the title had been won by only eight clubs: **Real Madrid** (27 championships), **Barcelona** (15), **Atlético Madrid** (nine), **Athletic Bilbao** (eight), **Valencia** (four), **Real Sociedad** (two), **Sevilla** (one) and **Real Betis** (one). *League system* The league comprises 20 clubs (reduced from 22 clubs at the end of the 1996-97 season). Three points are awarded for a victory, with one for a draw: final positions for clubs level on points are determined by the relative performance of the respective clubs in matches against each other. The bottom two clubs are automatically relegated, replaced by the champions and runners-up in the 22-club second division (Segunda Division A). A third promotion/relegation place is decided by playoffs between the third- and fourth-bottom clubs in the Primera Liga and the third- and fourth-placed sides in the second division.

Prince Louis *club* Burundi national league club based in the capital Bujumbura. Stadium: Prince Louis Rwigasore (national stadium), capacity: 20,000. Burundi league champions 1980, 1981; Burundi Cup 1992.

Princetown Rules *misc.* former set of football laws drawn up in the **United States of America** in 1873 by Princetown, Columbia, Rutgers and Yale Universities. Based on the English **Football Association** Laws of 1863.

private medical insurance *regulations* financial provision for medical expenses and healthcare for sick or injured players. **Premier League** and **Football League** clubs are required to provide **private medical insurance** for **contract players** and **trainees** under an agreement with the **Professional Footballers' Association** (FA Premier League rule H.11, Football League regulation 50.1).

Pro League (US) *competition* United States professional football league – the "third division" in US' football. Introduced in 1995, first winners: Long Island Rough Riders. Part of the **United Systems of Independent Soccer Leagues**.

processional entry *regulations* formal marching of teams and officials on to the pitch before the start of play. The referee and assistant referees must lead the teams on to the pitch five minutes before the kick off of a **Premier League** or **Football League** match (FA Premier League rule G.10.12, Football League regulation 30.10).

Professional Football Negotiating and Consultative Committee *n.* organisation comprising representatives of the **Professional Footballers' Association**, the **Football Association**, the FA **Premier League** and the **Football League**. Its principal function is to deal with any issues concerning players' terms and conditions (such as pay, pensions, holiday entitlement and insurance). The Premier League and Football League are prohibited from making any changes to their regulations which might impact on players' terms and conditions, unless they have been fully discussed and agreed by the Committee.

Professional Footballers Association (PFA) *n.* football players' trade union founded in Manchester in

1907. The PFA has approximately 3,500 members made up of **Premier League** and **Football League** professionals, youth trainees and a smaller percentage of semi-professional players with **non-league** clubs. The main duties of the PFA are to protect and promote the interests of its members in negotiations with the governing football authorities – the **Football Association**, the Premier League and the Football League – with a view to the abolition of all restrictions which adversely affect the legal, social and financial position of all players. The PFA provides free legal advice and assistance where necessary in any action connected with the professional engagement of players and may represent a member at an **appeal** or **disciplinary hearing** conducted by the football authorities. The PFA has a place on the **Football League Appeals Committee** which may deal with claims for contractual monies, discipline and transfers. The PFA also assists players seeking new contracts and gives advice to those in the process of negotiating new contracts. Other PFA services provided to members include: the **Benevolent Fund**, **accident insurance**, the **Footballers Further Education & Vocational Training Society Ltd**, the **Players' Cash Benefit Scheme** and the PFA/Football League Players Retirement Income Scheme. The PFA has its own legal advisers and operates its own financial management and pensions company, PFA Investments. Under the PFA's structure, every football club appoints a delegate who is responsible for the collection of members' subscriptions and bringing to the notice of members information circulated from the PFA's headquarters based in Bishopsgate, Manchester. The PFA also holds area meetings throughout the country on matters of importance to its members. Responsibility for the overall management of the PFA lies with a management committee of eight members elected by delegates at the PFA's annual general meeting held in November or December. The Management Committee then selects a chairman from among themselves. Barry Horne was appointed PFA chairman in 1997. Earlier chairmen include Pat Nevin (1993-97), Brian Marwood (1990-1993), Garth Crooks (1988-1990), Steve Coppell (1982-1984) and Alan Gowling (1980-1982). Gordon Taylor has been the full-time Chief Executive/Treasurer of the Association since November 1981, and Brendan Batson is the Deputy Chief Executive. *History* The PFA was formed on 2 December 1907 at the Imperial Hotel, Manchester and its first meeting was chaired by Billy **Meredith**, a famous player of the era with both **Manchester City** and **Manchester United**, and **Wales**. The PFA has played an important role in protecting and promoting the interests of players, and particular periods of its history have signalled an advance in the conditions of its members. In 1961, the PFA, under the leadership of its then chairman Jimmy **Hill**, led a successful campaign, backed by the threat of a nationwide strike, to abolish the **maximum wage** for players. Following the 1963 High Court judgement in the case of *George Eastham v*

Newcastle United and the football authorities in 1963, which ruled that the **retain and transfer system** for professional footballers was unlawful, the PFA established a new procedure in negotiations with the **Football League** which allowed a player to join another club at the end of his contract. Substantial financial benefits for players were also established. Clubs could negotiate longer deals and players had greater control over the terms. In 1978, a player's right to move at the end of his contract was fully recognised and a more efficient procedure established (see **freedom of contract**). The Football League **Appeals Committee** with an independent chairman was set up to consider any dispute arising from the question of a **compensation** (transfer) **fee**. The PFA is represented on this committee. In 1981, the present standard **contract** was agreed. In 1992, the **Professional Football Negotiating and Consultative Committee** was set up with representatives of the PFA, the Football League and Premier League under an independent chairman Sir John Wood C.B.E. The functions of the committee are to discuss all matters affecting professional association football and to consider questions concerning player's remuneration and other terms and conditions of employment. No major changes in the regulations of the Leagues affecting a players' terms and conditions may be made without PFA agreement.

Professional Leagues Committee   *n.*   body representing the leading European Leagues, including the **Premier League**, which was established on 6 July 1998 under the chairmanship of Antonio Mattarese. The body's original remit was to lobby **the Union of European Football Associations** to drastically change the format of the three main European club competitions – **Champions League**, **European Cup-winners Cup** and **UEFA Cup**. UEFA subsequently expanded both the European Cup and UEFA Cup, and abolished the European Cup-winners Cup for the 1999-00 season.

professional foul   *n.*   deliberate **foul** committed in order to prevent a goal-scoring opportunity. The punishment for such an offence is for the offender to be **sent off** for **serious foul play**. *Keynotes* In May 1982, a **Football League** committee chaired by Sir Matt **Busby** recommended that the Laws of the game be amended to facilitate the dismissal off of a player who commits such an offence and that a **penalty kick** be awarded if the professional foul took place outside the penalty area and had prevented a near-certain goal. Bobby **Charlton** and Jimmy **Hill** were among the committee members. The proposals were accepted by the Football League clubs but, crucially, the notion of a penalty for a professional foul committed outside the penalty area was rejected by **FIFA**.

professional   *n.*   person who plays football for money. Professional players were officially allowed in English football in 1885, and in Scotland in 1893. *Regulations* In **Scottish Football League** rules, the term "professional player" is largely equivalent to that of "**contract player**" as used in the regulations of the English **Premier League** and **Football League**; ie a professional footballer who has a **full contract** or **monthly contract** with a club that holds his **registration**. The names of all professional players must be included in the **club list of players** submitted to the league at the end of each season (Scottish Football League rule 50(a)). Compare **amateur player**, **delayed transfer player**.

professional referee *n.* a referee paid a regular salary to officiate at matches. Compare **match fee**.

programme *n.* see **match programme**.

promotion *n.* Qualification for a higher division in a **league**, usually by winning the division, finishing as runner-up or winning a **playoff** competition. *Keynotes* Promotion and **relegation** between the two English **Football League** divisions was introduced in the 1898-89 season. The system in which the top two teams of the second division would automatically replace the bottom two of the first division was introduced by the English Football League in 1898-99, replacing the previous system of **test matches**. **Glossop North End** and **Manchester City** were the first two clubs to win promotion in this way, at the expense of **Bolton Wanderers** and **Sheffield Wednesday**. However, under the old test-match rules, **Darwen** and **Sheffield United** were the first to be promoted to the first division in the 1892-93 season, with **Accrington** and **Notts County** relegated. Promotion and relegation were introduced in Scotland in the 1921-22 season. Promotion is not mandatory in the **Scottish Football League**: "in the event of either or both clubs in the [Third/Second] Division refusing to go into the [Second/First] Division. . . then either or both of the two lowest clubs in the [Second/First] Division shall remain in that Division. No club shall be allowed to accept payment in respect of foregoing the right of promotion" (Scottish Football League rule 32). See **playoff.**

Prosinecki, Robert *player* Striker. **Croatia** and **former-Yugoslavian** international (34 caps, eight goals for Croatia; four goals for former-Yugoslavia, ca. 1989-). Born 12 January 1969. *Clubs* **Red Star Belgrade, Real Madrid, Barcelona, Sevilla**. *Honours* **European Cup** (Red Star Belgrade, 1991); *World Soccer* **World Footballer of the Year** runner-up 1991.

prostitute *misc.* commercial sex worker. Mexican prostitutes in Guadalajara wore Brazilian-style yellow shirts to attract business after **Brazil**'s 1–0 victory against **Spain** in the first round of the 1986 **World Cup** in Guadalajara, Mexico.

Protasov, Oleg *player* Striker. **Soviet Union** international (68 caps, 29 goals, 1984-92). *Clubs* **Dnepr Dnepropetrovsk, Dinamo Kiev** and **Olimpiakos**. *Keynotes* Protasov is the second-highest all-time Soviet goalscorer (10 goals behind Oleg **Blokhin**). *Honours* **European Championship** (Soviet Union, runner-up 1988).

protective gear *n.* equipment to protect specific parts of the body from injury or further damage. Aside from **shinguards**, jockstraps, gum shields and other common protective gear, several players have worn protective equipment during matches to prevent further injury. *Keynotes* **England** captain Bryan **Robson** famously wore a harness to protect a dislocated shoulder against **Morocco** during the 1986 **World Cup**. However, Robson fell in the Moroccan penalty box, was led from the pitch with the arm in a sling, and played no further part in the competition. **Tottenham Hotspur**'s Gary Mabbutt wore a protective face mask for several matches after he suffered a fractured eye socket and a broken cheek bone in a clash with **Wimbledon**'s John Fashanu in November 1993. Paul **Gascoigne** also sported a mask to protect a cheek bone, while playing for **Lazio**. **Juventus** striker Filippo Inzaghi wore a protective mouth guard during matches in April-May 1998 after damaging his teeth. Italian defender Fabio Cannavaro wore a protective strap across his face during his country's 1998 World Cup quarter-final match with **France** at **Stade de France** on 3 July. Dutchman René van de Kerkhof's protective plaster casting covering a wrist injury provoked controversy before the start of the 1978 World Cup final between **Netherlands** and **Argentina** at the **Monumental** in Buenos Aires on 25 June. Although van de Kerkhof had worn the cast in the preceding five matches, the Argentinian players complained that it presented a potential danger. The referee, Sergio Gonella, ordered it to be covered.

Provident Fund *n.* former players' retirement fund set up by the English **Football League** in 1949. The fund was based on a levy of gate receipts and, later, from broadcasting rights. Players received a lump sum on their 35th birthday proportional to their earnings, and equivalent to about one year's final salary.

PSM Ujung *club* Indonesian national league club. **Asian Cup-winners Cup quarter-final** 1998; Indonesian national league runners-up 1996.

PSV Eindhoven (Philips Sport Vereniging) *club* Dutch national league club, based in Eindhoven, and founded in 1913 by the Philips electric company. Ground: Philips Stadion, capacity: 30,000 all seated. Strip: red and thin white striped shirts and black shorts. **European Cup** 1988 (0–0, 6–5 pens, v **Benfica**, in Stuttgart), semi-final 1976, quarter-final 1993; **UEFA Cup** 1978 (3–0 agg., v **SC Bastia**); **European Cup-winners Cup** semi-final 1975; Dutch league champions 1929, 1935, 1951, 1963, 1975, 1976, 1978, 1986, 1987, 1988, 1989, 1991, 1992, 1997; Dutch Cup 1950, 1974, 1976, 1988, 1989, 1990, 1996. Notable former players: Ruud **Gullit**, Rene and Willy van de Kerkhof, Ronald Koeman, **Romario, Ronaldo** (bought for £6 million in 1994).

post-traumatic stress disorder *medical* an abnormal psychological reaction to a traumatic event such as the **Hillsborough disaster**, **Heysel Stadium disaster** or **Bradford fire**. Sufferers experience extreme psychological discomfort, such as anxiety or panic when reminded of the event. In serious cases sufferers are plagued with uncontrollable memories, thoughts and feelings on a regular basis, and can feel as if they are going through the trauma again.

public-address system *n.* apparatus for amplifying speech for transmission around a stadium. The system is used to convey information such as the names and numbers of the players, safety information and other public notices. A public address system is a mandatory requirement in most league **ground criteria**, and to satisfy local authority safety inspectors. It should be capable of conveying clear information to all spectator areas. *Keynotes* It is not uncommon for the public address system to announce the news that the partner of a spectator has gone into labour at a local hospital, giving rise to traditional cheers from both sets of supporters. One such announcement, however, was – unbeknown to the crowd – deliberately staged as part of the shooting of a film called *Life is a Roller Coaster*, set in the North-east of England. The announcement, at **St James' Park**, home of **Newcastle United**, was for a fictitious father-to-be played by actor Jonathon Spence, whose "wife" was in Newcastle's Royal Victoria Infirmary (Newcastle United v **Southampton**, 12 September 1998).

Puc, Antonin *player* Striker. **Czechoslovakia** international (34 goals, 59 caps, 1926–1938). *Club* **Slavia Prague**. *Keynotes* Puc is the highest goalscorer in the former-Czechoslovakia's history. He scored Czechoslovakia's goal in its 1–2 defeat by **Italy** in the 1934 World Cup final. *Honours* **World Cup** runner-up (Czechoslovakia, 1934).

Puebla (full name: Club de Fútbol Puebla de la Franja) *club* Mexican national league club, based in Puebla and founded in 1943. Ground: Estadio Cuahtemoc, capacity: 45,000. Strip: white shirts with blue sash and white shorts. **CONCACAF Champions Cup** 1991 (4–2 agg., v **Police FC** of Trinidad and Tobago); Mexican league champions 1983 and 1990; Mexican Cup (Copa Mexico) 1945, 1953, 1988 and 1990.

Puerto Rico *country CONCACAF* Commonwealth, the easternmost island of the Greater Antilles, situated between the **Dominican Republic** and the **US Virgin Islands**. Former Spanish colony, self-governing commonwealth within the **United States of America** since 1952. Languages: Spanish, English (official). Area: 8,960 sq km (3,460 sq miles). Population: 3,580,000. Capital: San Juan. *Dossier* Football association (Federacción Puertorriqueña de Fútbol, Hato Rey) formed in 1940, affiliated to **FIFA** in 1960 and **Confederación Norte-Centroamericana y del Caribe de Fútbol** (CONCACAF) in 1960, president: Dr Luis Russi Dilan; general secretary: Juan Manuel Villa Niella. Season played from June to March. National stadium: Sixto Escobar, San Juan, capacity: 12,000. National strip: blue shirts, blue and white shorts, blue and white socks. *International tournament record* **Women's World Cup** – first entered 1999, never qualified for finals tournament; **World Cup** – first entered 1974, never beyond first qualifying round; **Caribbean Nations Cup** – played in 1993 finals tournament, finishing third of four nations in its group;

CONCACAF Women's Championship – first entered 1998 (last in its first-round group of four nations, conceding 38 goals, with none scored, including a 1–21 defeat by **Canada**)**Gold Cup** – never qualified. *Record against British and Irish national teams* none played. Leading clubs: Guayama Cruz Azul. Nacional (of Carolina, league champions 1999).

pulled muscle *medical* a non-technical term for a **sprain** or **strain** injury to a **muscle**.

Pusan Daewoo Royals *club* South Korean Pro-Football League club based in Pusan, formerly Daewoo Royals (until 1996). **Asian Champion Teams Cup** 1985-86 (3–1, v **Al Ahly** of Saudi Arabia, in Jiddah, Saudi Arabia); **Asian Cup-winners Cup** quarter-final 1990; South Korean Pro-Football League champions 1984, 1987, 1991, 1997; Adidas Korea Cup 1997; Pro-Specs Cup 1997; Philip Morris Korea Cup 1998.

push and run *tactics* style of play which involves players passing the ball quickly and making runs to receive a return pass. Such a move tends to wrong-foot the opposition and makes it difficult for defenders to cover their **on-ball** team-mates. The **Tottenham Hotspur** side which won successive Second and First Division titles 1949-51, under manager Arthur Rowe, operated the push and run tactic.

push *rules* one of the offences listed as a **foul** under the **Laws of the game** (Law XII). The offence is committed if a player pushes an opponent in a reckless or careless manner, or, in the opinion of the referee, with excessive force. The punishment for deliberately pushing an opponent is for the opposing team to be awarded a **direct free kick**, taken from the point where the foul was committed (unless within the opponents' **goal area**, in which case it is taken from anywhere within that area). If the foul is committed in the offending side's penalty area, then the opponents are awarded a **penalty kick**. If a player pushes the referee, he or she will be **sent off** and is likely to receive further sanction (eg an additional suspension on top of the automatic one- or two-match ban for being sent off) by the relevant governing body.

Puskás, Ferenc *player* Striker. **Hungary** and **Spain** international (84 caps, 83 goals, 1945-56; four caps for Spain, no goals, 1961-62). Born 2 April 1927, in Kispest, Budapest. Career ca. 1943-66. *Clubs* Kispest AC/Honvéd SE (now **Kispest-Honvéd FC**), **Real Madrid**. *Keynotes* One of the **Magnificent Magyars**, Puskás is the world's all-time top international goalscorer. At 18 years of age, he scored on his international debut (20 August 1945, 5–2, v **Austria**, in Budapest, friendly). He was affectionately known as the "Galloping Major". Puskás is one of only three players to have scored in both a **World Cup** final (1954, 2–3, v West **Germany**) and **Olympic Games** final (1952, 2–0, v **Yugoslavia**). Only Zoltan **Czibor** (in the same years) and Pedro **Cea** have equalled this feat. Puskás had missed most of the 1954 World Cup finals tournament, having been injured in the first game, an 8–3 thrashing against a deliberately weak West German team (the West Germans made a tactical decision to avoid playing **Brazil** in the quarter-final; a task left for Hungary). Puskas returned and managed to limp his way through the final, this time against against a full-strength West German team, and put the Hungarians ahead after six minutes. Hungary slipped 2–3 behind in the 83rd minute and Puskás was denied a late equaliser by an **offside** decision. Puskás left Hungary after the **Soviet Union** quashed a nationalist uprising in 1956 and ended his Hungarian international career at the age of only 29: Puskás later played for Spain at the 1962 World Cup finals in Chile. He played four times for Spain, but failed to score. Puskás had scored four hat-tricks among his 83 goals for Hungary. He joined his local club Kispest AC in 1943 – following his father's playing career at the same club – as an inside-left. Puskás moved to Real Madrid in 1958 and helped the club win the 1959 European Cup (though he did not play in the final because of injury). Puskás won a **European Cup** winner's medal in 1960 and scored four goals – one more than his team-mate Alfredo **Di Stefano** – in the 7–1 triumph over **Eintracht Frankfurt** at **Hampden Park**, Glasgow. Puskás was tournament top scorer with 12 goals and the first player to score a hat-trick in a European Cup final (15 minutes earlier than Di Stefano!). He scored another hat-trick in the 1962 final, this time on the losing side (3–5, v **Benfica**, in Amsterdam), but was, once again, tournament top scorer; jointly with Real Madrid team-mates Di Stefano and Tejada, with seven goals each. He was in the losing team again in 1964, in Real Madrid's 1–3 defeat by **Internazionale**, but was joint top scorer for the tournament with seven goals. Puskás later managed **Panathinaikos**, taking the club to the European Cup final in 1971 (0–2, v **Ajax**) – its only European final. He became caretaker coach of the Hungarian national team in 1993. *Honours* Olympic Games gold medal (Hungary, 1952 – Puskás was captain); World Cup runner-up (Hungary, 1954); **Dr Gerö Cup** (Hungary, 1953); European Cup (Real Madrid, 1960); Hungarian league championship (Honvéd SE, 1950, 1950, 1952, 1954, 1955); Spanish league championship (Real Madrid 1961, 1962, 1963, 1964, 1965). *France*

Football **European Footballer of the Year** runner-up 1960.

pyramid structure *n.* relationship between various leagues that are linked by **promotion** and **relegation**; the top of the pyramid is the national premier or first division, beneath which are a number of other national and regional leagues and **feeder leagues**. The structure is pyramid-shaped because of the increasing number of leagues at the equivalent level at regional and local level. **1. England**: the relationship between the various amateur, semi-professional and professional leagues affiliated (directly, or indirectly via **county football associations**) to the **Football Association**. There are about 100 leagues in the English league pyramid and most of these are regionally based. There are three national leagues: the **Football Conference**; the **Football League** (with its three divisions); and, ultimately, the FA **Premier League** (the top of the pyramid). Beneath the Football Conference are three regional leagues: Isthmian League, Northern Premier League and **Southern League**; the Premier Division champions of each are promoted to the Conference. There are three further divisions in the Isthmian League. Beneath the Northern Premier League is a first division, itself fed by four regional divisions. Beneath the Southern League Premier Division are two regional divisions (southern and midland), each fed by a number of regional leagues. Each of the regional leagues is fed by further county and district leagues. Theoretically, it is possible for any club – given sufficient time – to progress through the entire pyramid from the lowest amateur level up to the Premier League, provided that its stadium meets the **ground criteria** of the league into which it is promoted. **2. Scotland**: there is no continuous pyramid in Scottish league football, and no automatic promotion to and relegation from the **Scottish Football League** (the Scottish Football League does, however, feed directly into the **Scottish Premier League**). **3.** Overseas: other countries, such as **Italy** (see **Serie A**) and **Russia** also have vast pyramid structures.

Pyunik Yerevan *club* Armenian national league club, based in the capital Yerevan. Armenian league champions 1996, 1997; Armenian Cup 1996.

Q

Qatar *country AFC* state in the Middle East, in the Gulf of Arabia, on the Qatar Peninsula. Bordered by **Saudi Arabia** and the **United Arab Emirates**. Ruling monarchy (the Sheikh). Area: 11,435 sq km (4,415 sq miles). Population: 539,000 (1994 census: about three-quarters of the resident population are foreign nationals). Languages: Arabic, English. Capital: Doha (Ad Dawhah). *Dossier* Qatar Football Association (Doha) formed in 1960, affiliated to **FIFA** in 1970, and **Asian Football Confederation** (AFC) in 1972, president: Sheikh Saud Bin Khaled Al-Thani; general secretary: Hamad Hajes Alkaabi. Season played from October to May. National stadium: Khalifa International Stadium, Doha, capacity: 50,000. National strip: white shirts, white shorts, white socks. *International tournament record* **Olympic Games** – quarter final 1992 (0–2 v **Poland**, Barcelona, Spain – Qatar qualified for the finals having won an Asia first round qualifying group of five nations, and a second round group of six), also qualified for finals tournament 1984; **Women's World Cup** – never entered; **World Cup** – first entered 1978, never qualified for finals tournament but reached the qualifying tournament second-round groups in 1990, 1998 (in 1998, Qatar won all three of its first round group matches, scoring 14 goals with none conceded, finished fourth of five nations in the second stage, only two points behind **Iran**, which qualified for the finals tournament); **Arab Cup of Nations** – runners-up 1998 (1–3, v Saudi Arabia, in Doha, Qatar); **Arabian Gulf Cup** – winners 1992, runners-up 1996, hosts 1992; **Asian Cup of Nations**– first entered 1976, qualified for finals tournament in 1980, 1984, 1988, 1992, but failed to get beyond first round; **Asian Games** – first entered 1978, quarter-final 1998; **Asian Under-16 Championship** – winners 1990 (v United Arab Emirates, in UAE), runners-up 1984, 1986, 1992, 1994, 1998, hosts 1984, 1986, 1994; **Asian Women's Championship** – never entered; **Under-17 World Championship** – fourth place 1991 (1–1, 1–4 pens., v **Argentina**, third/fourth playoff, also lost semi-final on penalties, 0–0, 2–4 pens., v tournament winners **Ghana**); **World Youth Cup** (under-20) – runners-up 1981 (0–4 v West **Germany**, Sydney, Australia; Qatar beat **England** 2–1 in the semi-final), hosts 1995. *World Cup performance* (finals and qualifiers to end of 1998 tournament) played 42, won 20, drawn 8, lost 14, scored 69 goals, conceded 41 goals; win rate 48%; goals scored per game 1.64. *Record against British and Irish national teams* none played (at senior level). *History* National league and cup competition (the Emir's Cup) began in 1973. **Al Saad** won the **Asian Champion Teams Cup** in 1988. Qatar has around 2,000 registered players. The national side has had considerable success at junior level, including fourth place in the 1991 Under-17 World Championship and victory in the Asian Under-16 Championship in 1990 (see above). Qatar hosted the 10th World Youth Cup (under-20) in 1995. *League system* Nine clubs compete in the national First Division. Three points are awarded for a win, with one for a draw. *Record in international club tournaments* Asian Champion Teams Cup – Al Saad (winners 1988), **Al Arabi** (runners-up 1994), **Al Rayyan** (semi-final 1991, quarter-final 1997); **Asian Cup-winners Cup** – Al Arabi (semi-final 1993), **Al Ittihad** (quarter-final 1998); **Arab Cup-winners Cup** – Al Saad (runners-up 1992). Other leading club: **Al Ahly**. Al Wakra (league champions 1999).

QPR *club abbrev.* for **Queens Park Rangers**.

quadruple hat trick *record* twelve goals by one player in a single match. This feat has been achieved by only one player at senior level in Scottish or English league football. John Petrie scored a British record 13 goals for **Arbroath** (v Bon Accord, **Scottish FA Cup** first round, 12 September 1985).

qualified medical practitioner *n.* see **doctor.**

qualifying tournament *n.* discrete tournament, the winners (finalists or set number of best-placed teams) of which qualify for the main competition.

Quang Nam Danang *club* Vietnamese national league club based in Da Nang. **Asian Cup-winners Cup** semi-final 1992 (reached the semi-final after two walkovers, lost to eventual winners Nissan – now **Yokohama Marinos** – of Japan, 1–4 agg.); Vietnam league champions 1992, 1993.

Queen of the South *club* Scottish league. *Dossier* Ground: **Palmerston Park**, Dumfries, Dumfries and Galloway. Strip: blue shirts with white trim, blue shorts, blue socks with white trim. Nickname: Doonhamers. Ground capacity: 8,352. Record attendance: 24,500 v **Heart of Midlothian** (23 February 1952, **Scottish FA**

Cup, third round). Biggest win: 11–1 v **Stranraer** (16 January 1932, Scottish FA Cup, first round). Biggest defeat: 2–10 v **Dundee** (1 December 1962, Division One). *History* Founded in 1919, Queen of the South joined the **Scottish Football League** in 1925-26, winning promotion to Division One in 1932-33. The club's name is derived from the title given to the town of Dumfries, close to the English border, where the club is located. The following season, Queen of the South finished fourth, which is the club's highest League position. The club's best period came shortly after **World War II**. It won the Division Two Championship and was a **Scottish League Cup** finalist (1–3 v **Hibernian**) in 1950-51, having reached the semi-final of the Scottish FA Cup the previous season (0–3 replay v **Rangers**). The club also appeared in the last four of the Scottish League Cup in 1960-61. Queen of the South reached its first final in 1997-98, when it played in the last **Scottish League Challenge Cup** final (0–1 v **Falkirk**). *League record* Division One (A Division) 1933-34 to 1949-50, 1951-52 1958-59, 1962-63 to 1963-64; First Division 1975-76 to 1978-79, 1981-82, 1986-87 to 1988-89; Division Two (B Division) 1925-26 to 1932-33, 1950-51, 1959-60 to 1961-62, 1964-65 to 1974-75; Second Division 1979-80 to 1980-81, 1982-83 to 1985-86, 1989-90**QPR** club abbrev. for Queens Park Rangers. *Honours* Division Two 1950-51. *Records* Billy Houliston is Queen of the South's most capped player (3 for **Scotland**); Allan Ball holds the record for club League appearances (731, 1963-82); Jim Patterson is Queen of the South's record League goalscorer (250, 1949-63).

Queen's Park *club* Scottish league. *Dossier* Ground: **Hampden Park**, Glasgow, Strathclyde. Strip: white and black hooped shirts, white shorts with black stripe, black socks with white hoops. Nickname: Spiders. Ground capacity: 52,000. Record club attendance: 95,772 v **Rangers** (18 January 1930, **Scottish FA Cup**). Biggest win: 16–0 v St Peters (29 August 1885, Scottish FA Cup, 1st rd). Biggest defeat: 0–9 v **Motherwell** (26 April 1926, Division One). *History* Founded in July 1867, Queen's Park is Scotland's oldest football club and it was the dominant force in the early years of Scottish football, pioneering the **passing game**. Queen's Park won the Scottish FA Cup on 10 occasions in the competition's first 20 years – 1874 (2–0 v Clydesdale), 1875 (3–0 v **Renton**), 1876 (2–0 v 3rd Lanark Rifle Volunteers), 1880 (3–0 v Thornliebank), 1881 (3–1 replay v **Dumbarton**), 1882 (4–1 v Dumbarton), 1884 (walkover), 1886 (3–1 v Renton), 1890 (2–1 replay v **Vale of Leven**), 1893 (2–1 replay v **Celtic**). It was also a finalist on two other occasions: 1892 (1–5 replay v Celtic) and 1900 (3–4 v Celtic). Uniquely, Queen's Park also appeared in two English **FA Cup** finals: 1884 (1–2 v **Blackburn Rovers**) and 1885 (0–2 v Blackburn Rovers). The club has the distinction of being the only senior club in the UK to retain its amateur status. Aside from one season spent in Division Two (1922-23), the club, which joined the **Scottish Football League** only

in 1900-01, managed to maintain its place in the top flight until after **World War II**. Since relegation to the B Division in 1947-48, Queen's Park has spent only two seasons in the top flight and, with the reorganisation in 1994-95, the club joined the new Third Division. *League record* Division One (A Division) 1900-01 to 1914-15, 1921-22, 1923-24 to 1947-48, 1956-57 to 1957-58; First Division 1981-82 to 1982-83; Scottish League 1915-16 to 1920-21; Division Two (B Division) 1922-23, 1948-49 to 1955-56, 1958-59 to 1974-75; Second Division 1975-76 to 1980-81, 1983-84 to 1993-94; Third Division 1994-95 to present. *Honours* Division Two 1922-23, 1955-56; Second Division 1980-81; Scottish FA Cup 1874 (2–0 v Clydesdale), 1875 (3–0 v Renton), 1876 (2–0 v 3rd Lanark Rifle Volunteers), 1880 (3–0 v Thornliebank), 1881 (3–1 replay v Dumbarton), 1882 (4–1 v Dumbarton), 1884 (walkover v Vale of Leven), 1886 (3–1 v Renton), 1890 (2–1 replay v Vale of Leven), 1893 (2–1 replay v Celtic). *Records* Walter Arnott is Queen's Park's most capped player (14 for **Scotland**); J B McAlpine holds the record for club League appearances (473); he is also the club's record League goalscorer (163).

Queens Park Rangers *club* English league. Ground: **Loftus Road**, west London. *Dossier* Strip: blue and white hooped shirts, white shorts, white socks. Nickname: Rangers or R's. Ground capacity: 19,148 all seated. Record attendance: 35,353 v **Leeds United** (27 April 1974, Division One). Best average attendance: 23,850 (1975-76). Biggest win: 8–1 v **Bristol Rovers** (27 November 1937, **FA Cup**, first round); v **Crewe Alexandra** (3 October 1983, **League Cup**, 1st rd). Biggest defeat: 1–8 v **Mansfield Town** (15 March 1965, Division Three), v **Manchester United** (19 March 1969, Division One). *History* Founded in 1886 from the merger of St Jude's and Christchurch Rangers, and attaching the name Queens Park, which was the west London district in which most of the players lived, to Rangers. The club turned professional in 1898 and joined the **Southern League**, winning the title in 1908 and 1912. It was as Southern League Champions that QPR contested the first **Charity Shield** match in 1908 (0–4 replay v Manchester United). QPR also appeared in the 1912 Charity Shield (1–2 v **Blackburn Rovers**). Before settling at Loftus Road (which had previously been the home of amateur club Shepherd's Bush FC) in 1917, the club had played at 11 other venues – QPR's total of 12 grounds is greater than that of any other **Football League** or **Premier League** club. QPR joined the newly created Division Three in 1920-21 and finished third. The club won promotion to Division Two as Division Three (South) Champions just after **World War II** (1947-48). QPR, under the managership of Alex Stock and with a side that included striker Rodney Marsh, achieved a unique double in 1966-67, winning both the Division Three Championship and the League Cup (3–2 v **West Bromwich Albion**) – the first Division Three side to win the trophy. The following season, the club won a place in the top flight for the first time, albeit for only one season. Dave Sexton's appointment as manager in 1974, after Gordon Jago had led the club back to the top division, was followed, in 1975-76, by QPR's highest-ever final League position (runners-up) and, for the first time, European competition qualification. The club reached the quarter-final of the **UEFA Cup** in 1976-77, going out on away goals (3–3 agg. v **AEK Athens**). Relegation in 1979-80 was followed, in 1982, by Rangers' one and only **FA Cup** final appearance (0–1 replay v **Tottenham Hotspur**). In 1981, QPR became first club to install an **artificial pitch** (the pitch was returned to grass in 1987). In 1986, the club reached its second League Cup final (0–3 v **Oxford United**). In 1991-92, QPR won promotion to the newly-established **Premier League** under the managership of former-captain Gerry **Francis**, but lost its place in the top flight again in 1995-96. QPR almost merged with west London neighbours **Fulham** (both clubs were owned by Marler Estates (see also **Stamford Bridge**) in 1987 but the Football League refused to sanction the move. QPR's holding company, Loftus Road, which also owns Rugby Union club Wasps, floated on the **Alternative Investment Market**, which is a precursor to full floatation on the stock market, in October 1996 (flotation price = 72p). *League record* Premier League 1992-93 to 1995-96; Division One 1968-69, 1973-74 to 1978-79, 1983-84 to 1991-92; First Division 1996-97–; Division Two 1948-49 to 1951-52, 1967-68, 1969-70 to 1972-73, 1979-80 to 1982-83; Division Three 1920-21, 1958-59 to 1966-67; Division Three (South) 1921-22 to 1947-48, 1952-53 to 1957-58. *Honours* Division Two 1982-83; Division Three 1966-67; Division Three (South) 1947-48; Southern League 1908, 1912; League Cup 1967 (3–2 v West Bromwich Albion). *Records* Alan McDonald is QPR's most capped player (52 for **Northern Ireland**); Tony Ingham holds the record for club appearances (519, 1950-63); George Goddard is QPR's record League goalscorer (172, 1926-34).

Quilmes Athletic Club *club* Argentinean national league club, based in Quilmes, Buenos Aires, founded 27 November 1887. Ground: Estadio Centenario Jose L Meiszner, capacity: 20,000. Strip: white shirts, blue shorts. *Keynotes* Quilmes is one of the two oldest Argentinean clubs still in existence, formed just a few months after **Gimnasia y Esgrima La Plata**. Argentinean league champions 1912 (two leagues operated prior to 1927), 1978. Notable player: Ubaldo Fillol.

R

Racecourse Ground *ground* Welsh football ground (English league) situated in Wrexham, Clwyd; home of **Wrexham**. *Dossier* Ground capacity: 9,200. Pitch dimensions: 101m x 65m. Record attendance: 34,445 v **Manchester United** (26 January 1957, **FA Cup**, 4th rd). Best average attendance: 11,651 (1977-78). *History* The Racecourse Ground derives its name from the horse racing which was first staged there in 1807. It also staged cricket which continued after horse racing was banned for a time in 1858; the final horse races took place in August 1912. The first football match to be staged at the Racecourse Ground was a practice game on 5 October 1872, several weeks after Wrexham had been founded. The cricket pitch on which Wrexham played staged **Wales'** first home international fixture, on 5 March 1877 (v **Scotland**). Wrexham has twice played elsewhere: when the ground was waterlogged; and between 1880-83 at Rhosddu Recreation Ground after the cricket club increased the club's rent. Wrexham was banned from the FA Cup in February 1884 following crowd trouble at the Racecourse Ground. Much of the ground's development over the years has been funded by the **supporters' club**, including the erection of floodlights in 1959 and later, a £4,000 structure at the Town End, called the Pigeon Loft, bought from the local Majestic Cinema. The Racecourse Ground was extensively redeveloped between 1972 and 1980, including the construction of the Yale Stand, which housed the new changing rooms. At the time of the stand's opening, in 1972, the ground had three sets of changing rooms. Capacity was at one stage based on the number of toilets, rather than on the number of turnstiles, seats and safety exits, as is commonly the case. Over the years, the Racecourse Ground has staged numerous Wales international games and **Welsh Cup** finals. On 30 August 1997, Racecourse Ground staged its first Rugby Union international, when Wales met Romania in a friendly. The first floodlit match at the Racecourse took place on 30 September 1959 (v **Swindon**, Division Three).

Racing Bafoussam *club* Cameroon national league club based in Bafoussam. Ground: Omnisports, capacity: 35,000. Strip: red shirts, white shorts. **African Cup-winners Cup** quarter-final 1990. Cameroon league champions 1989, 1992, 1993, 1995; Cameroon Cup 1996.

Racing Club *club* Argentinean national league club, based in Avellaneda, Buenos Aires, founded 1903. Ground: Estadio Presidente Peron, capacity: 56,000. Strip: sky blue and white striped shirts, black shorts. *Keynotes* The club was formed by French immigrants and won the league championship nine times between 1913 and 1925. Its seven consecutive domestic league titles (1913 to 1919) is an Argentinean record, a **CONMEBOL** club record and a joint South American record (with **Robin Hood** of **Surinam**; Surinam is not in CONMEBOL). It also holds the South American club record of 39 league games without defeat (1965 to 1966). In 1999, a bill before the Argentine Congress declared racing part of the country's national heritage, saving the club from bankruptcy. Racing club has won both the **Copa Libertadores** and the **World Club Cup**, and won the first **Supercopa** in 1988. World Club Cup 1967 (0–1, 2–1, 1–0 replay in Montevideo, v **Celtic**); Copa Libertadores winners 1967 (0–0, 0–0, 2–1 playoff, v **Nacional** of Uruguay), semi-final 1968, 1997; Supercopa winners 1988 (3–2 agg., v **Cruzeiro**), runners-up 1992 (1–4 agg., v Cruzeiro); **Copa Mercosur** quarter-final 1998; Argentinean League champions 1913, 1914, 1915, 1916, 1917, 1918, 1919, 1921, 1925 (two leagues operated prior to 1927), 1949, 1950, 1951, 1958, 1961, 1966.

Racing Club *club* Haitian national league club based in the capital Porte-au-Prince, founded 1923. Strip: yellow shirts, blue shorts. **CONCACAF Champions Cup** 1963 (v **Guadalajara** of Mexico, walkover in the final).

Racing Club de Paris *club* French league club based in Paris, formed 1932. Ground: **Stade Colombe**, capacity: 30,000. Strip: sky blue and white hooped shirts, white shorts. Racing's Stade Colombe hosted the 1938 **World Cup** final. The club was dissolved in 1966 and reformed in 1982 (as Matra Racing). Became Racing 92 in 1991. French league champions 1936; French Cup 1936, 1939, 1940, 1945, 1949.

racism *n.* prejudice against or antagonism towards players/officials/supporters of other races. *Rules* Racist remarks are considered as offensive or abusive language; a player guilty of this will be sent off (Law XII). On 30 March 1998, the **Football Taskforce** published a report which found that while racism in the professional game had diminished it was still widespread at an amateur level. The report recommended an end to the anomaly in existing legislation which allows the police to act against racist chanting by more than one but does not specifically make racist abuse by an individual illegal – the government agreed that the law would be amended at the earliest opportunity. The **Football (Offences) Act** 1991 made racist chanting a criminal offence. The Act stipulates that it is illegal to engage in racist chanting (eg, phrase sung in unison by more than one individual) two hours prior to a match and one hour afterwards. However, some supporters persist in racially abusing players from an ethnic minority and the law has been difficult to enforce. *Keynotes* In February 1998, **Leeds United** apologised to **Leicester City** for the racist chanting of some of its supporters at a **Filbert Street** encounter between the two clubs (7 February 1998, **Premier League**). **Cardiff City** fans were also accused of racist chanting during the club's fourth round **FA Cup** replay against **Reading** at **Elm Park** (3 February 1998). The **Union of European Football Associations** fined the **Football Association** £27,000 in October 1998 for racist chanting by a section of **England** fans at the **European Championship** 2000 qualifying match in Stockholm against **Sweden** on 5 September. During the 1997-98 season, 31 people were arrested for racist or indecent chanting. Some players and managers have made or have been accused of making racist comments to black and other players from ethnic backgrounds. Although the Football Association has investigated some of these allegations, it generally takes no action unless the victim of the abuse officially reports it or the incident is included in a referee's official match report. In November 1997, **Chester City** manager Kevin Ratcliffe was found guilty of racial discrimination by an **employment tribunal**. The **tribunal** ruled that Ratcliffe had verbally abused a former Chester apprentice, James Hussaney. In the US, **New England Revolution** player Edward Gorter was fined a Major League Soccer League record £13,000 and suspended for two matches in October 1998 after racially insulting team-mate David Nakhid.

Radio 5 Live   *radio*   BBC 24-hour sports and news channel. Radio 5 broadcasts live football commentary and in May 1998 agreed a two-year extension (until summer 2001) to its contract to broadcast **Premier League** fixtures.

radio   *misc.*   radio commentary of matches dates from 1927 and was introduced for **Football League** matches during World War II (when regional competitions operated). **Blackpool**'s game against **Manchester United** on 14 October 1939 was broadcast to front-line troops in France.

Radnicki Beograd (Rad Beograd)   *club*   Yugoslavian and **former-Yugoslavia** national league club based in the capital Belgrade, Serbia, founded 1920 by the communists. Ground: Stadion Radnicki, capacity: 4,000. Strip: red and white shirts, blue shorts. Former-Yugoslavia league third place 1956, 1958; former-Yugoslavian Cup runners-up 1957.

Radnicki Nis (FK Radnicki Nis)   *club*   Yugoslavian and **former-Yugoslavia** national league club based in Nis, founded 1923. Ground: Cair, capacity: 20,000. Strip: blue shirts with white sleeves, blue shorts. **UEFA Cup** semi-final 1982; has never won a major Yugoslavian or former-Yugoslavian competition, third in the former-Yugoslavia league 1980, 1981.

Rail Club Nationaux Kadiogo (RCK)   *club*   Faso Burkina Faso national league club based in Ouagadougou. Stadium: Municipale, capacity: 4,000. Strip: red shirts, white shorts. **African Cup-winners Cup** semi-final 1978, 1980; Burkina Faso Cup 1975, 1976, 1977, 1978, 1979, 1980, 1994.

Raith Rovers   *club*   Scottish league. *Dossier* Ground: **Stark's Park**, Kirkcaldy, Fife. Strip: navy blue shirts with white shoulder stripe and white trim, white shorts with navy blue and red trim, navy socks with red and white trim. Nickname: Rovers. Ground capacity: 10,721 all seated. Record attendance: 31,306 v **Heart of Midlothian** (7 February 1953, **Scottish FA Cup**, 2nd rd). Biggest win: 10–1 v Coldstream (13 February 1954, Scottish FA Cup, 2nd rd). Biggest defeat: 2–11 v **Morton** (18 March 1936, Division Two). *History* Founded in 1883, the club's name is derived from the local laird of Raith. The club joined the **Scottish League** in 1902-03 – the first Fife club to do so – and won election to Division One as Champions in 1909-10. Raith has spent much of its League career alternating between the two divisions. In 1921-22, the club recorded it highest League position, finishing third in Division One. Raith was a Scottish FA Cup finalist in 1913 (0–2 v **Falkirk**) and in 1948-49, the club reached the Scottish League Cup final (0–2 v **Rangers**). In 1994-95, the club won the Scottish League Cup (2–2, 6–5 pens v **Celtic**) and promotion, as First Division Champions, to the Premier Division for the first time since the League was restructured in 1975-76. Raith's League Cup triumph ensured the club qualified for European competition (**UEFA Cup**) for the first time the following season. The club was forced to switch its tie against **Bayern Munich** to **Hibernian**'s **Easter Road** due to its own ground's limited capacity. Rovers has the distinction of holding the UK club record for the most League goals scored in one season; 142 in 1937-38. *League record* Premier Division 1993-94, 1995-96 to 1996-97; Division One (A Division) 1910-11 to 1914-15, 1921-22 to 1925-26, 1927-28 to 1928-29, 1938-39, 1949-50 to 1962-63, 1967-68 to 1969-70; First Division 1976-77, 1978-79 to 1983-84, 1987-88 to 1992-93, 1994-95, 1997-98–; Scottish League 1915-16 to 1920-21; Division Two (B Division) 1902-03 to 1909-10, 1926-27, 1929-30 to 1937-38, 1946-47 to 1948-49, 1963-64 to 1966-67, 1970-71 to 1974-75; Second Division 1975-76, 1984-85 to 1986-87. *Honours* First Division 1992-93, 1994-95; Division Two 1907-08, 1909-10 (shared with Leith); Scottish League Cup 1994-95 (2–2, 6–5 pens v Celtic). *Records* David Morris is Raith's most capped player (6 for **Scotland**); Willie McNaught holds the record for club League appearances (430); Gordon Dalziel is Raith's record League goalscorer (154, 1987-94).

RAJA CA Casablanca (RAJA Club Athletism) *club* Moroccan national league club, based in Casablanca. Ground: Derejega, capacity: 15,000. Strip: green shirts and white shorts. **African Cup of Champion Clubs** – winners 1989 (Mouloudia d'Oran on penalties after drawing 1–1 in two-leg final), 1997 (1–1 agg., 5–4 pens., v **Obuassi Goldfields**, of Ghana), quarter-final "champions-league" stage 1998; **Afro-Asian Club Cup** 1998-99; **Arab Club Champions Cup** runners-up 1996); Moroccan League champions 1988 and 1996, 1997, 1998; Moroccan Cup 1968, 1974, 1977, 1982 and 1988 and 1996.

Ramsey Alf *player-manager* Right-back. **England** international (32 caps). Born 21 January 1920; died 28 April 1999. Career ca. 1943–55. *Clubs* (player) **Portsmouth**, **Southampton**, **Tottenham Hotspur**. *Honours* League Championship (Tottenham Hotspur 1950-51); Division Two (Tottenham Hotspur 1949-50). *Clubs* (manager) **Ipswich Town**. Also England manager (stats: played 113, won 69, drawn 27, lost 17, goals for 224, goals against 99). *Honours* League Championship (Ipswich Town 1961-62); Division Two (Ipswich Town 1960-61); Division Three (South) (Ipswich Town 1956-57); **World Cup** (England 1966). *Keynotes* Retired from playing in August 1955 and immmediately joined Ipswich Town, just relegated to Division Three (South), as manager. He led the Suffolk club to the Division Two title and League Championship in consecutive seasons between 1960 and 1962. Coincidentally, Ramsey had earlier achieved the same feat as a player with Tottenham Hotspur. He is one of only nine men to have won the Championship as player and manager. Ramsey was appointed England manager in April 1963, leading the country to its only World Cup success three years later with a side nicknamed the "Wingless Wonders" after the manager had discarded traditional wingers in favour of a 4–4–2 **formation**. Ramsey was dismissed as England manager in May 1974 following England's failure to secure a place at that year's World Cup finals. In the mid-1970s, Ramsey sat on the board of **Birmingham City**.

Randers Freja *club* Danish league club based in Randers, founded 1898. Ground: Randers Stadion, capacity: 20,000. Strip: blue and white striped shirts, blue shorts. **European Cup-winners Cup** quarter-final 1969; Danish Cup 1967, 1968, 1973.

Rangers (Hong Kong) *club* Hong Kong league club. Hong Kong League champions 1971; Hong Kong Cup 1995.

Rangers *club* Scottish league. *Dossier* Ground: **Ibrox Stadium**, Glasgow, Strathclyde. Strip: blue shirts with white trim, white shorts with blue and red trim, black socks with red tops. Nickname: Gers. Ground capacity: 50,500 all seated. Record attendance: 118,567 v **Celtic** (2 January 1939, Division One). Biggest win: 14–2 v Blairgowrie (20 January 1934, **Scottish FA Cup**, 1st rd). Biggest defeat: 2–10 v **Airdrieonians** (1886).

History Founded in the Gareloch area west of Glasgow in 1872, Rangers soon became the city's most popular club and a bastion of Scottish Protestantism in contrast to the Catholic origins of its arch-rivals **Celtic**. The club played in its first Scottish FA Cup final in 1877 (2–3 second replay v **Vale of Leven**) and in a second final two years later (1–1 v Vale of Leven) when the trophy was awarded to the opposition because Rangers refused to play a replay. Rangers was a founder member of the Scottish League, sharing the inaugural Championship in 1890-91 with **Dumbarton** after both clubs finished with 29 points. It was not until 1898-99 that the club won its first outright title, a year in which the club won all 18 League fixtures – a record. Since then the club has won the Championship a record number of times, the 1996-97 success being the club's 47th title triumph and the last of a nine-in-a-row sequence which equalled Celtic's record established between 1965-66 and 1973-74. It won the title again in 1998-99. To the end of 1998-99, Rangers had won the Scottish FA Cup 28 times and been runners-up on a further 17 occasions. Altogether the club has won the **Scottish League** and Cup **double** 14 times (1928-29, 1929-30, 1933-34, 1934-35, 1948-49, 1949-50, 1952-53, 1962-63, 1963-64, 1975-76, 1977-78, 1991-92, 1992-93, 1995-96). In addition, Rangers has won the Scottish League Cup a record 21 times. Altogether the club has won the domestic **treble** – Scottish League Championship, Scottish FA Cup and Scottish League Cup – on six occasions (1948-49, 1963-64, 1975-76, 1977-78, 1992-93, 1998-99). In 1959-60, Rangers was a **European Cup** semi-finalist (4–12 agg. v **Eintracht Frankfurt**) and the following season, the club reached the first final of the **European Cup-winners Cup** (1–4 agg. v **Fiorentina**). Rangers was a European Cup-winners Cup finalist again in 1966-67 (0–1 v **Bayern Munich**) and the club finally won the trophy in 1971-72 (3–2 v **Dinamo Moscow**). It was a **UEFA** (Fairs) **Cup** semi-finalist in 1968-69 (2–0 agg. **Newcastle United**) and, in 1973, it contested the **European Super Cup** (3–6 agg. v **Ajax**). Rangers reached the semi-final stage (four groups of four clubs) of the restructured European Cup in 1992-93. The club's most successful period came between 1920-21 and 1953-54, when, under the managership of Will Struth, Rangers won 18 League titles, 10 Scottish FA Cups and 2 Scottish League Cups. The record during the Graeme **Souness**/Walter Smith era, between 1986-87 and 1997-98, is almost as impressive, with the club winning 10 League Championships, including nine consecutive titles, three Scottish FA Cups and seven Scottish League Cup trophies. Much of Rangers' current success has been achieved due to the finance made available, first by David Holmes and later by steel magnate David Murray, to buy players and extensively redevelop Ibrox Stadium. The ground has twice been the scene of large-scale fatalities among spectators: on 5 April 1902 (**Scotland** v **England**), 26 people died and 500 were injured when a wooden terrace collapsed; and on 2 January 1971 (Rangers v Celtic) 66 people were killed and 145 injured on a stairway (see **disaster**). The club, together with **Aberdeen** and Celtic, has never played outside the top division. Rangers and Celtic's nine-year run in the league is one short of the world record 10-year run held by **Berlin FC and Dynamo Tbilisi**. Rangers has won more championships (48 by 1999) than any other club in the world – three more than **Peñarol** of **Uruguay**. *League record* Premier League 1998-99 to present; Premier Division 1975-76 to 1997-98; Division One (A Division) 1893-94 to 1914-15, 1921-22 to 1974-75; Scottish League 1890-91 to 1892-93, 1915-16 to 1920-21. *Honours* Premier League 1998-99; Premier Division 1975-76, 1977-78, 1986-87, 1988-89, 1989-90, 1990-91, 1991-92, 1992-93, 1993-94, 1994-95, 1995-96, 1996-97, 1998-9; Division One (A Division) 1899-00, 1900-01, 1901-02, 1910-11, 1911-12, 1912-13, 1922-23, 1923-24, 1924-25, 1926-27, 1927-28, 1928-29, 1929-30, 1930-31, 1932-33, 1933-34, 1934-35, 1936-37, 1938-39, 1946-47, 1948-49, 1949-50, 1952-53, 1955-56, 1956-57, 1958-59, 1960-61, 1962-63, 1963-64, 1974-75; Scottish League 1917-18, 1919-20, 1920-21; Scottish FA Cup 1894 (3–1 v Celtic), 1897 (5–1 v Dumbarton), 1898 (2–0 v **Kilmarnock**), 1903 (2–0 second replay v **Heart of Midlothian**), 1928 4–0 v Celtic), 1930 (2–1 v replay v **Partick Thistle**), 1932 (3–0 replay v Kilmarnock), 1934 (5–0 v **St Mirren**), 1935 (2–1 v **Hamilton Academicals**), 1936 (1–0 v **Third Lanark**), 1948 (1–0 replay v (**Greenock**) **Morton**), 1949 (4–1 v **Clyde**), 1950 (3–0 v **East Fife**), 1953 (1–0 replay v Aberdeen), 1960 (2–0 v Kilmarnock), 1962 (2–0 v St Mirren), 1963 (3–0 replay v Celtic), 1964 (3–1 v **Dundee**), 1966 (1–0 replay v Celtic), 1973 (3–2 v Celtic), 1976 (3–1 v Heart of Midlothian), 1978 (2–1 v Aberdeen), 1979 (3–2 second replay v **Hibernian**), 1981 (4–1 replay v **Dundee United**), 1992 (2–1 v Airdrieonians), 1993 (2–1 v Aberdeen), 1996 (5–1 v Heart of Midlothian); 1999 (1-0 v Celtic); Scottish League Cup 1946-47 (4–0 v Aberdeen), 1948-49 (2–0 v **Raith Rovers**), 1960-61 (2–0 v Kilmarnock), 1961-62 (3–1 v Heart of Midlothian), 1963-64 (5–0 v Morton), 1964-65 (2–1 v Celtic), 1970-71 (1–0 v Celtic), 1975-76 (1–0 v Celtic), 1977-78 (2–1 v Celtic), 1978-79 (2–1 v Aberdeen), 1981-82 (2–1 v Dundee United), 1983-84 (3–2 a.e.t. v Celtic), 1984-85, (1–0 v Dundee United); 1986-87 (2–1 v Celtic), 1987-88 (3–3, 5–3 pens v Aberdeen), 1988-89 (3–2 v Aberdeen), 1990-91 (2–1 v Celtic), 1992-93 (2–1 v Aberdeen), 1993-94 (2–1 v Hibernian), 1996-97 (4–3 v Heart of Midlothian), 1998-99 (2–1 v St Johnstone); European Cup-winners Cup 1971-72 (3–2 v Dinamo Moscow – *Team* McCloy (goal-keeper), Jardine, Johnstone, Smith, Mathieson, Greig, Conn, MacDonald, McLean, Stein (1), Johnston (2).). *Records* Ally **McCoist** is Rangers most capped player (59 for Scotland); John Greig holds the record for club League appearances (496, 1962-78); McCoist is also the club's record League goalscorer (250, 1985-98).

Rapid Bucharest *club* Romanian national league club based in the capital Bucharest, founded in 1923. Ground: Stadionul Giulesti, capacity: 18,000. Strip: white and maroon shirts, white shorts. *Keynotes* Rapid's Romanian Cup triumph in 1940, against Venus Bucharest, was acheived after a world-record three replays (2–2, 4–4, 2–2, 2–1). **European Cup-winners Cup** quarter-final 1973; Romanian League champions 1967; Romanian Cup 1935, 1937, 1938, 1939, 1940, 1941, 1942, 1972, 1975, 1998.

Rapid Vienna (SK Rapid Wien) *club* Austrian national league club, based in Vienna, founded 1898. Ground: Gerhard **Hanappi** Stadion, capacity: 19,600. Strip: green and white striped shirts, white shorts. **European Cup** semi-finalists 1961; **European Cup-winners Cup** runners-up 1985; winners **Mitropa Cup** 1930 and 1950, runners-up 1927 and 1928; Austrian League Champions 1912 (the first league champions), 1913, 1916, 1917, 1919, 1920, 1921, 1923, 1929, 1930, 1935, 1938, 1940, 1941, 1946, 1948, 1951, 1952, 1954, 1956, 1957, 1960, 1964, 1967, 1968, 1982, 1983, 1987, 1988, 1996; Austrian Cup 1919, 1920, 1927, 1946, 1961, 1968, 1969, 1972, 1976, 1983, 1984, 1985, 1987, 1995; German League Champions 1941, German Cup 1938.

Råsunda Stadion *ground* Swedish football ground situated in Stockholm; Swedish national stadium and home of **AIK Stockholm** (Allmänna Idrottsklubben – General Sports Club). Ground capacity: 36,000 all seated. *History* Built before World War I, although the site was first used for football at the turn of the century. It is situated in the Stockholm suburb of Solna. Råsunda was redeveloped before World War II and upgraded for the 1992 **European Championship**. The stadium staged eight fixtures during the 1958 **World Cup**: **Sweden** v **Mexico**, Mexico v **Wales**, Sweden v **Hungary**, Sweden v Wales, group 3; Wales v Hungary, group 3 **playoff**; Sweden v **Soviet Union**, quarter-final; **Brazil** v **France**, semi-final; Brazil v Sweden, final – total attendance 223,954; average attendance 27,994. Råsunda hosted the 1992 European Championship final (**Denmark** v **Germany**, 37,000) and the 1998 **European Cup-winners Cup** final (**Chelsea** v **Stuttgart (VfB)**, 30,216).

Ravelli, Thomas *player* Goalkeeper. **Sweden** international (143 caps, 1981-). Born 13 August 1959 in Sweden, of Austrian parents. *Clubs* Östers IF, **IFK Göteborg**, **Tampa Bay Mutiny**. *Keynotes* The most-capped player in the world, Ravelli made his international debut on 15 February 1981 (1–2, v **Finland**). He played for Sweden in the semi-finals of both the 1992 **European Championship** and 1994 **World Cup**. In 143 internationals, Ravelli conceded 143 goals. He was a semi-professional for most of his career, accepting his first full-time professional contract at the age of 38 when he moved to Tampa Bay Mutiny in the United States **Major League Soccer**. His twin brother Andreas played in midfield, also at international level. *Honours* World Cup third place (Sweden, 1994); Swedish league championship (Östers IF, 1980, 1981, IFK Göteborg, 1990, 1991, 1993, 1994, 1995, 1996).

Razak, Karim Abdul *player* Striker. **Ghana** international. *Club* **Asante Kotoko**. *Honours* **African Cup of Nations** (Ghana, 1978); *France Football* **African Footballer of the Year** 1978.

RC Lens *club* French league club based in Lens, formed 1906. Ground: **Felix-Bollaert**, capacity: 41,649 (a 1998 **World Cup** finals venue, and the first stadium to host a **golden goal** in a World Cup match: 1–0, **France** v **Paraguay**, 28 June 1998). Strip: yellow shirts, red shorts. French league champions 1998; French Cup runners-up 1998.

read *vb.* to judge the pace of the ball or, more generally, to be aware of the position of team-mates and opposition.

re-election *n.* former system of re-instatement or relegation from the English **Football League**. Introduced in the first league season 1888-89, when the bottom four clubs were formally required to retire and reapply for membership. All League clubs would vote either on their reinstatement, or replacement by a new club. In the first season, **Stoke City**, **Burnley**, **Derby County** and **Notts County** were re-elected. Between 1892-93 and 1897-98, movement between the two divisions was determined by a series of test matches. This was replaced by **promotion** and **relegation**. The re-election system was modified in 1976, when it was decided that from 1977 the Southern and Northern Leagues would agree on a list of clubs to be proposed for election; the Football League Management Committee would vet the list and choose two to challenge the four clubs due for re-election. The result would prevent the dilution of the vote among the non-league applicants. **Wimbledon** was the immediate beneficiary, replacing **Workington** for the 1977-78 season. Wimbledon had won three **Southern League** championships in succession. The following season **Southport** was replaced by **Wigan Athletic**; but no new clubs were elected over the next eight years, until the system was revised again in 1986-87 and automatic promotion and relegation was introduced between Division Four (Third Division) and the **Football Conference**, provided that the promoted club could meet the Football League's **ground criteria**. **Scarborough** was the first club to be directly promoted from the Conference, at the expense of **Lincoln City**.

reacher area/space *tactics* notional area of the pitch – 32m, spanning approximately from the **goal line** out from the defending team's (the "final third"). The term originated with Charles Reep of the Football Association, who examined the source of goals. His research found that most goals are scored from in-play and restart situations within the reacher area. Reep suggested that to win a 42-game league, a team should attempt to secure at least 140 (54%) of the 260 average reachers (when the ball enters the reacher area) achieved during a match. This theory is based on the notion that, on average, 6.5 reachers produce one shot and nine shots produce one goal.

Reading *club* English league. *Dossier* Ground: **Madejski Stadium**, Reading, Berkshire. Strip: blue and white hooped shirts, white shorts, white socks. Nickname: Royals. Ground capacity: 25,000. Record attendance: 33,042 v **Brentford** (**Elm Park**, 19 February 1927, **FA Cup**, 5th rd). Best average attendance: 15,973 (Elm Park, 1950-51). Biggest win: 10–2 v **Crystal Palace** (4 September 1946, Division Three (South)). Biggest defeat: 0–18 v **Preston North End** (1893-84, FA Cup, 1st rd). *History* Reading was founded in 1871, making it the oldest **Football League** club south of Nottingham. The club amalgamated with Reading Hornets in 1877 and, in 1889, Earley FC, before settling at **Elm Park** in 1894. The ground was adjacent to biscuit manufacturer Huntley and Palmer's sports ground, and until the company departed from the town in 1974 the club's nickname was the "Biscuitmen". Reading was a founder member of the Southern League in 1894 and, in 1920-21, it joined the newly-established Division Three. The club won the Division Three (South) title in 1925-26. The following season, the club was an **FA Cup** semi-finalist (0–3 v **Cardiff City**) and, in 1938, Reading lifted the **Division Three (South) Cup** (6–1 v **Bristol City**). Until Reading's promotion to the First Division in 1994-95, the club had spent all but seven of its 66-season League history in the bottom two divisions. In the club's centenary year, 1970-71, it was relegated to Division Four for the first time. Reading won the **Simod Cup** in 1988 (4–1 v **Luton Town**). The club narrowly missed promotion to the Premier League in 1994-95, losing in the final of the end-of-season **play-offs** (3–4 v **Bolton Wanderers**). Reading reached the quarter-final stage of the **League Cup** in 1996 (1–2 v **Leeds United**). The previous year, the club had announced plans to relocate to a new £37 million stadium alongside the M4 at Smallmead. In 1983, the club almost ceased to exist after **Oxford United** chairman Robert Maxwell announced a merger between the clubs, with the new one to be called Thames Valley Royals. A boardroom coup at Reading eventually scuppered this plan and multi-millionaire auto magazine publisher John Madejski bought the club in September 1990. Reading moved to its new 25,000-capacity purpose-built ground, Madejski Stadium, in August 1998. *League record* First Division 1994-95 to 1997-98; Division Two 1926-27 to 1930-31, 1986-87 to 1987-88; Second Division 1992-93 to 1993-94, 1998-99–; Division Three 1920-21, 1958-59 to 1970-71,1976-77, 1979-80 to 1982-83,1984-85 to 1985-86, 1988-89 to 1991-92; Division Three (South) 1921-22 to 1925-26, 1931-32 to 1957-58; Division Four 1971-72 to 1975-76, 1977-78 to 1978-79, 1983-84. *Honours* Division Two 1993-94; Division Three 1985-86; Division Three (South) 1925-26; Division Four 1979-80; Simod Cup 1988 (4–1 v Luton Town); Division Three (South) Cup 1938 (6–1 v Bristol City). *Records* Jimmy Quinn is Reading's most capped player (17 (46) for **Northern Ireland**); Martin Hicks holds the record for club appearances (500, 1978-91); Ronnie Blackman is Reading's record League goalscorer (158, 1947-54).

Real Bamako (full name AS Real de Bamako) *club* Mali national league club, based in the capital Bamako. Ground: Mamadou Konate, capacity: 10,000. Strip: black shirts and white shorts **African Cup of Champion Clubs** runner up 1966 (4–5 agg., v **Stade Abidjan** of Ivory Coast); Mali League champions 1964, 1969, 1980, 1981, 1983, 1986, 1991; Mali Cup 1962, 1964, 1966, 1967, 1968, 1969, 1980, 1989, 1991.

Real Betis Balompié *club* Spanish league. *Dossier* Ground: Benito Vilamarín (Estadio), Sevilla Andalucía. Strip: green and white striped shirts, white shorts, green socks with white trim. Nickname: Verdiblancos. Ground capacity: 47,500. *History* Formed in 1907 by a break-away group of **Sevilla** members. The club merged with Sevilla Balompié in 1914, receiving royal patronage and adopting the name Real Betis **Balompié**. Although Betis won its only Spanish League (**Primera Liga**) title in 1934-35 and its one domestic Cup (**Copa del Ray**) in 1977, the club has upstaged its local rivals, Sevilla, since returning to the Primera Liga in 1994-95. The club reached the Copa del Ray final in 1997 (2–3 v **Barcelona**) and the last eight of the **European Cup-winners Cup** in 1998 (2–5 agg. v **Chelsea**). Brazilian international **Denilson** de Oliveira joined the club from **São Paulo** after the 1998 **World Cup** in a then world record deal worth £21.5 million. *Honours* Spanish League 1934-35; Spanish Cup 1977 (2–2, 11–9 pens. v **Athletic Bilbao**).

Real España *club* Honduras national league club based in San Pedro Sula, formed 1925. Ground: Estadio Francisco Morazan, capacity: 20,000. Strip: yellow and black striped shirts, black shorts. **Torneo Grandes de Centroamerica** semi-final 1998; Honduras league champions 1974, 1975, 1976, 1980, 1988, 1990, 1994; Honduras Cup 1992; **Campeonisimo** 1994.

Real Madrid (CF) *club* Spanish league. *Dossier* Ground: **Bernabéu** (Estadio Santiágo), Madrid, Castille. Strip: white shirts with purple trim, white shorts with purple trim, white socks with purple trim. Nickname: Meringues. Ground capacity: 106,000. *History* Formed in 1902 as Madrid FC by students. The official name of the club is Real Madrid Club de Fútbol. The club was granted its royal (**Real**) blessing by King Alfredo XIII in 1920 and turned professional in 1929 when the national Spanish league began. Don Santiágo Bernabéu, who took over as club president in 1943 (until his death in 1978), masterminded Real's rise after the Spanish Civil war that culminated in European dominance in the late 1950s, winning five **European Cup**s between 1956 and 1960 (see below). Real added a sixth European Cup in 1966 and was a finalist in 1981 (0–1 v **Liverpool**). Real secured its seventh European Cup in 1998, although Jupp Heynckes, who had led the club to victory, was sacked only eight days later. The club reached the **European Cup-winners Cup** final in 1971 (1–2 a.e.t. replay v **Chelsea**) and won consecutive **UEFA Cup**s in 1985 and 1986. Madrid was Spanish dictator Franco's favourite team. At its 1998 annual general meeting, the club announced that it was

£81 million in debt. Famous foreign players who have worn the white of Real include: Roberto Carlos, Lawrie Cunningham, **Didi**, Pedrag **Mijatovic**, Ferenc **Puskás**, Héctor Rial, José Santamaria, Hugo **Sánchez**, Bernd Schuster, Clarence Seedorf, and Alfredo di **Stéfano**. *Honours* Spanish League 1929-30, 1930-31, 1931-32, 1932-33, 1953-54, 1954-55, 1956-57, 1957-58, 1960-61, 1961-62, 1962-63, 1963-64, 1964-65, 1966-67, 1967-68, 1968-69, 1971-72, 1974-75, 1975-76, 1977-78, 1978-79, 1979-80, 1985-86, 1986-87, 1987-88, 1988-89, 1989-90, 1994-95, 1996-97; Spanish Cup 1905 (1–0 v **Athletic Bilbao**), 1906 (4–1 v Athletic Bilbao), 1907 (1–0 v Vizcaya Bilbao), 1908 2–1 v Vigo Sporting), 1917 (2–1 replay v Arenas Guecho Bilbao), 1934 (2–1 v **Valencia**), 1936 (2–1 v **Barcelona**), 1946 (3–1 v Valencia), 1947 (2–0 v **Espanyol**), 1962 (2–1 v **Sevilla**), 1970 (3–1 v Valencia), 1974 (4–0 v Barcelona), 1975 (0–0, 4–3 pens v **Atlético Madrid**), 1980 (6–1 v Castilla), 1982 (2–1 v Sporting Gijón), 1989 (1–0 v Real Valladolid), 1993 (2–0 v **Real Zaragoza**); European Cup (Champions League) 1956 (4–3 v **Stade de Reims**), 1957 (2–0 v **Fiorentina**), 1958 (3–2 a.e.t. v **AC Milan**), 1959 (2–0 v Stade de Reims), 1960 (7–3 v **Eintracht Frankfurt**), 1966 (2–1 v **Partizan Belgrade**), 1998 (1–0 v **Juventus**); UEFA Cup 1985 (3–1 agg. **Videoton FC Fehérrarh**), 1986 (5–3 agg. v **Cologne**); **World Club Cup** 1960 (5–1 agg. v Club Atletico **Peñarol**), 1998-99 (2–1 v **Vasco da Gama**).

Real *n.* royal seal of approval (Spanish).

Real Olympique Banjul *club* Gambian national league club based in the capital Banjul. Ground: Box Bar (the national stadium), capacity: 10,000. Strip: green shirts, black shorts. **African Cup of Champion Clubs** second round 1979, 1995; Gambian League champions 1975, 1978, 1983, 1994, 1997, 1998; Gambian Cup 1997.

Real Olympique Castel *club* republic Central African Republic national league club based in the capital Bangui. Ground: Municipale, capacity: 15,000. Strip: green shirts, black shorts. **African Cup of Champion Clubs** second round 1974; Central African Republic league champions 1971, 1973, 1975, 1979, 1982; Central African Republic Cup 1989.

Real Republicans *club* Sierra Leone national league club based in the capital Freetown. Ground: Brookfields, capacity: 36,000. Strip: white shirts, black shorts. Sierra Leone league champions 1981, 1983, 1984; Sierra Leone Cup 1986.

Real Santa Cruz *club* Bolivian national league club based in Santa Cruz de la Sierra, founded 1962. Ground: Estadio Ramon "Tahuichi" Aguilera Costas, capacity: 40,000. Strip: white shirts, white shorts.

Real Sociedad (DF) *club* Spanish league. *Dossier* Ground: Anotea (Estadio), San Sebastián, Basque Provinces. Strip: blue and white striped shirts, white shorts, white socks. Ground capacity: 29,350. *History* Formed in 1909 as part of a cycling club known as Ciclista de San Sebastián. The club's official name is

Real Sociedad de Fútbol. As Ciclista de San Sebastián, it won the Spanish Cup (**Copa del Ray**) in 1909, reaching the final as Real Sociedad on a further three occasions – 1913 (1–2 replay v **Barcelona**), 1928 (1–3 replay v Barcelona) and 1951 (0–3 v Barcelona) – before finally winning the trophy again in 1987. The following season, the club reached another final (0–1 v Barcelona). Sociedad won consecutive Spanish League (**Primera Liga**) titles in 1980-81 and 1981-82, and, in 1983, it reached the semi-final stage of the **European Cup** (2–3 agg. v **Hamburg (SV)**). *Honours* Spanish League 1980-81, 1981-82; Spanish Cup 1909 (3–1 v Vigo Sporting), 1987 (2–2, 4–3 pens. v **Atlético Madrid**).

Real Zaragoza *club* Spanish league. *Dossier* Ground: La Romareda, Zaragoza, Aragón. Strip: white shirts with blue trim, blue shorts, white socks with blue tops. Ground capacity: 34,741. *History* A Zaragoza football club was established in 1903, but folded after three years. In 1921, Zaragoza DC was formed and following a merger in 1925 adopted the name Zaragoza CD, becoming Real Zaragoza CD (Club Deportivo) in 1952 when the club was granted royal patronage. Zaragoza reached the **UEFA** (Fairs) **Cup** final in both 1964 and 1966, winning on the first occasion in a one-off match against fellow Spanish club **Valencia** and losing two years later, also against domestic opposition, **Barcelona** (3–4 agg.). Before Zaragoza's 1995 **European Cup-winners Cup** victory, the club had twice reached the semi-final stage of the competition: 1965 (2–3 agg. v **West Ham United**); 1987 (2–6 agg. v **Ajax**). The club finished second in the Spanish League (**Primera Liga**) in 1974-75 – its highest position. *Honours* Spanish Cup 1964 (2–1 v **Atlético Madrid**), 1966 (2–0 v **Athletic Bilbao**), 1986 (1–0 v Barcelona), 1994 (0–0, 5–4 pens. v Celta Vigo); European Cup-winners Cup 1995 (2–1 v Arsenal); UEFA (Fairs) Cup 1964 (2–1 v Valencia).

rearranged fixture *n.* football match played on a different date to that originally scheduled. Can arise because of a clash of fixtures between two competitions (such as a league match and cup tie) or a postponement due to bad weather or illness to a team, or at the request of the police because of fears of **hooliganism** or crowd trouble or because neighbouring teams are scheduled in cup competitions to play at home on the same day. Matches may also be rearranged by permission of the governing body because of severe **fixture congestion** or for premium live television coverage. **Notts County** were the first club to rearrange a **Football League** match. On 17 November 1888 Notts County played its **FA Cup** third qualifying round v Derby Midland, rescheduling its league game against **Derby County**.

Recopa *competition* annual international club tournament for member countries of the **Confederación Sudamericana de Fútbol** (CONMEBOL, the South American confederation), first played 1988. The tournament originally consisted of a playoff between the winners of the **Copa Libertadores** and the **Supercopa**.

History Although the tournament was once played over two legs, it is now staged as a single fixture in Japan. The tournament was won in 1990 by **Olimpia**, without it playing the match: the club had won the Copa Libertadores and Supercopa in the same season, a rare "double". **São Paulo** repeated the double in 1993; the Recopa, however, was competed that year between São Paulo and the winners of the **Copa CONMEBOL**, **Botafogo**. *Winners, results and runners-up:* 1988 **Nacional** (Uruguay), 1–0 agg., v **Racing Club**; 1989 **Boca Juniors** 1–0, v Atletico Nacional Medellin (at the Orange Bowl, Miami, USA); 1990 Olimpia (no contest, see above); 1991 **Colo Colo**, 0–0, 5–4 pens., v **Cruzeiro** (in Kobe, Japan); 1992 São Paulo, 0–0 agg., 4–2 pens., v Cruzeiro; 1993 São Paulo, 3–1, v Botafogo (in Kobe, Japan); 1994 **Independiente** 1–0, v **Velez Sarsfield** (National Stadium, Tokyo); 1995 **Grêmio**, 4–1, v Independiente (in Kobe); 1996 Velez Sarsfield, 1–1, 4–2 pens., v River Plate (National Stadium, Tokyo); 1997 not played.

record attendance *record* see **attendance, highest.**

Recreation Ground *ground* English football ground situated in Chesterfield, Derbyshire; home of **Chesterfield**. *Dossier* Ground capacity: 8,880. Pitch dimensions: 103m x 65m. Record attendance: 30,968 v **Newcastle United** (7 April 1939, Division Two). Best average attendance: 15,372 (1947-48). *History* Chesterfield is thought to have played its earliest matches at the Recreation Ground, which would make it the **Football League**'s oldest venue, although the club played at a ground in Spital for several seasons in the 1880s before returning to its present home around 1887. The Recreation Ground was the last Football League venue to install floodlights, finally staging its first floodlit match on 18 October 1967 (**Sheffield Wednesday**, friendly) after two previous attempts ended in failure.

Recreation Park *ground* Scottish football ground situated in Alloa, Central region; home of **Alloa Athletic**. *Dossier* Ground capacity: 4,111. Pitch dimensions: 100.5m x 68.5m. Record attendance: 15,467 v **Celtic** (February 1955, **Scottish FA Cup**). *Keynotes* Alloa first played at Recreation Park in 1895. Floodlights were first erected at the ground in 1979, making the club the second last in Scotland to install lights. **Rangers** has played its reserve matches at the ground.

Red Boys Differdange *club* Luxembourg national league club based in Differdange, formed in 1907. Ground: Thillenberg, capacity: 6,500. Strip: red shirts and red shorts. Luxembourg League Champions 1923, 1926, 1931, 1932, 1933, 1979; Luxembourg Cup 1925, 1926, 1927, 1929, 1930, 1931, 1934, 1936, 1952, 1953, 1958, 1972, 1979, 1982, 1985.

Red Star 93 *club* French league club based in Paris, formed by Jules **Rimet** in 1897. Ground: Saint-Ouen, capacity: 12,000. Strip: white shirts, white shorts. The origin of the club's English name is unknown. French Cup, 1921, 1922, 1923, 1928, 1942.

Red Star Belgrade (Serbo-Croatian: FK Crvena Zvezda Beograd) *club* Yugoslavian and **former-Yugoslavia** national league club based in the capital Belgrade, Serbia, founded 1945. Ground: **Crvena Zvezda stadium**, capacity: 97,000. Strip: red and white striped shirts, red shorts. *History* Founded by the communists, originally as the club of the University of Belgrade. Its ground, the national stadium, was built on the original site of pre-**World War II** club Jugoslavija. Red Star reached the semi-final of its first European Cup campaign in 1957. A year later, Red Star went out of the competition in the ill-fated quarter-final tie against **Manchester United** (4-5 agg.), the afternoon before the **Munich air crash**: eight Manchester players were killed on their journey home from the second leg in Belgrade. In 1991, the club became the first and only former-Yugoslavian club to win the **European Cup**. It added the **World Club Cup** in December 1991. Red Star played its only **European Super Cup** match in November 1991, against Manchester United. Only one leg was played (at **Old Trafford**): Red Star lost 0–1. Red Star reached the quarter-final group stage of the 1992 European Cup, finishing as runner-up in its group. All Yugoslavian clubs were banned from European competitions (because of the Civil War) until the 1995-96 season. World Club Cup 1991 (3–0, v **Colo Colo**, of Chile, in Tokyo); European Cup 1991 (0–0, 5–3 pens., v **Olympique de Marseille**, in Bari, Italy), semi-final 1957, 1962, 1971, quarter-final 1958, 1974, 1981, 1982, 1987, quarter-final group 1992 (second in its group of four); **European Cup-winners Cup** semi-final 1975, quarter-final 1972, 1986; **UEFA Cup/Fairs Cup** runners-up 1979 (1–2 agg., v **Borussia Mönchengladbach**), quarter-final 1963; European Super Cup runners-up 1991 (0–1 v Manchester United, Mitropa Cup 1968; Former-Yugoslavia League champions 1951, 1953, 1956, 1957, 1959, 1960, 1964, 1968, 1969, 1970, 1973, 1977, 1980, 1981, 1984, 1988, 1990, 1991, 1992; Yugoslavian league champions 1995; former-Yugoslavia Cup 1948, 1949, 1950, 1958, 1959, 1964, 1968, 1970, 1971, 1982, 1985, 1990; Yugoslavian Cup 1993, 1995, 1996, 1997.

red card *rules* red-coloured card used by a referee to signal to a player that he or she is being **sent off** for an offence under the **Laws of the game** (Law XII). *Keynotes* Red cards were introduced to English football on 2 October 1976. The first red card in the English **Football League** was meted out to David **Wagstaffe** of **Blackburn Rovers** (v **Leyton Orient**, 2 October 1976). George **Best** received a red card on the same day – for foul and abusive language – while playing for **Fulham** in its league game at **Southampton**. The system was stopped by the **Football Association** in January 1981, and reinstated in 1987. The first player to receive a red card in a **World Cup** finals tournament match was Carlos Caszely of **Chile**, in the 1974 World Cup (Chile v West **Germany**, 0–1, **Olimpiastadion**, Berlin, 14 June 1974). Compare **yellow card**.

Reebok Stadium *ground* English football ground situated in Bolton, Greater Manchester; home of **Bolton Wanderers**. *Dossier* Ground capacity: 25,000 all seated. Pitch dimensions: 104m x 68m. Record attendance: 25,000 (sell-out on several occasions during 1997-98 season; first, v **Manchester United**, 20 September 1997, **Premier League**). *History* Built at a cost of £35 million and situated five miles from Bolton's previous ground, **Burnden Park**. The Reebok Stadium staged its first League game on 2 September 1997 (v **Everton**, Premier League) and attracted a crowd of 23,131. Bolton has retained the old centre-spot from **Burnden Park**.

referee *rules* the person appointed to officiate and adjudicate over a game of football. The referee's authority is granted by the **Laws of the game** and these begin when he or she enters the **field of play**. The referee is the final arbiter on the enforcement of the laws during play and when play has been suspended. The referee controls the match with the assistance of the **assistant referees** and, in certain matches with the **fourth official**. His or her decision on issues affecting the outcome of the game is final. Only disciplinary matters can be appealed against (appeals are dealt with by the relevant governing body). The referee's duties are to: decide that a game can be played (taking into account the state of the pitch, the weather and any instruction from the police regarding safety or public order); allow the full or agreed time (see **duration of play**), adding all time lost for the assessment of **injuries**, the removal of injured players, substitutions, and **wasted time**; suspend or **abandon** the match where necessary because of outside interference (this, for example, might be on the advice of the police for safety or public order reasons, or because of very poor weather); stop play to allow a seriously injured player to be removed from the field of play (life-threatening injuries, such as choking, would, in practice, be treated on the field); ensure that players with bleeding wounds leave the field of play for treatment (a new rule introduced for the 1997-98 season following increasing concerns about the risk of transmitting blood-borne diseases); where necessary **caution** a player (which includes showing the player a **yellow card**) for **dangerous play**, **dissent**, persistent infringement of the Laws, delaying the restart of play, failing to retreat at least 9.15 m (10 yards) from a free-kick or corner kick, **unsporting behaviour**, or for entering, re-entering or leaving the field of play without the referee's permission; **send off** a player (after showing the player a **red card**) if the player is guilty of **serious foul play**, **violent conduct**, **spitting** at an opponent, official or any other person, or using **offensive** or **abusive language**, or who commits a cautionable offence after already having been cautioned; check that the ball fulfils the required technical standards; ensure that the players' equipment meets the requirements of the Laws of the game; maintain a record of the game (including the score, and the name of the scorers and players cautioned); submit the names of any cautioned or sent-off player to the competent authority; stop play for infringements of the laws, but refrain from so doing if this would give an advantage to the abused team (see **advantage**); restrict people other than the players and assistant referees from entering the field of play without his or her permission and signal; signal the restart of play after **stoppages**; and discipline team officials for misconduct (and this can include expelling them from the **technical area**) (Law V). The referee is responsible for interpreting the rules and it is the referee's opinion which decides, for example, if an injury requires immediate treatment or that an incident of misconduct warrants a caution. The referee is, however, obliged to take the advice of the assistant referees over incidents which the referee did not see – a decision may only be overturned on the advice of the assistant if play has not already recommenced. The referee is also required to report any misconduct on behalf of spectators (en masse), officials, players, substitutes and others, during, after or before the match, to the relevant authority. The referee must wear a shirt or jersey distinctive in colour from the playing teams. It is the duty of the referee to allow play to flow and not to interfere to the extent that insignificant and non-deliberate infringements are penalised. According to the **International FA Board**, a referee or assistant referee is not liable for any injury to players, officials or spectators or any loss or damage to property, or financial loss, in connection with any decision carried out under the Laws. See **international referee,** assistant referee, fourth official. – *vb.* to adjudicate over a game. *Keynotes* Match officials were introduced at the inception of the **FA Cup** in 1872. Before then, disputes over the rules were generally settled by the club captains. FA Cup matches were adjudicated by two "umpires", with a referee – who was not on the field of play – appointed to rule on any points where the umpires disagreed. The role of umpires was written into the Laws of the game in 1874, and referees in 1880. The decision that referees and (at the time, umpires) should be neutral was taken at a **Football League** sub-committee meeting on 11 January 1889. Umpires previously had been members of the competing clubs. The retirement age for referees in the Football League and FA Premier League is 48 years.

referee's notebook *n.* pocket book kept by the referee to record the score in a game of football, as well as the names of players who have received a **caution** or who have been **sent off**.

referee, woman *official* a female **referee**. Although the playing of football is strictly divided into the men's and women's game, women are neither barred from qualifying as **Football Association** referees and **referee's assistants**, nor from officiating at men's matches. *History* Pat Dunn was the first woman to qualify with the Football Association as a referee and, by 1974, there were 29 women referees. Women referees were initially restricted to officiating at women's matches. Elizabeth **Forsdick** was the first referee's assistant (then known as "linesman") at a men's **FA Cup**

match (October 1981). Kim George was the first woman to referee an **FA Cup** match (February 1989, preliminary round). Wendy **Toms** was the first woman to referee a senior men's league match (Woking v Telford, 31 August 1996, **Football Conference**). Linda Bailey (referee), Karen Ford and Anne Smart (referee's assistants) were the first women to take all three officials' positions at a senior FA-affiliated men's game (26 October 1996, Broomfield United v Kent University, Kent County League). Three women officiated at a full-international match in 1985 (**Sweden** v **Norway**), the first international match to be refereed by a woman. Claudia **Vasconcelos** was the first woman to officiate at a **FIFA** tournament (the 1991 **Women's World Cup** finals in China). Ingrid Jonsson refereed the second **Women's World Cup** final in 1995 (**Norway** v **Germany**, at **Råsunda Stadion**, Stockholm). By 1996, 40 women referees were listed on the FIFA register of international referees; 45 women were listed as referee's assistants. The decision by FIFA, in 1996, to rename "linesmen" as referee's assistants partly reflects a desire to remove gender-stereotyping from the role of match officials. In 1998, the US **Major League Soccer** appointed Nancy Lay and Sandra Hunt as its first two women referees. Carolina Domenech became the first woman to referee a first-class match in **Spain**, when she took charge of the Third Division match between Sabadell and Ontinyent. See also **Sex Discrimination Act**.

referees' officer *official* appointment by the **Premier League** to help improve relations between referees, managers and players. The first appointee to the post was Philip Don, a former referee, who took up office before the 1998-99 season.

register *regulations* to document a player's **registration** with a football club according to the particular rules of a league governing body.

registration *regulations* documents submitted to, and held by, the relevant league certifying a player's eligibility to play for his or her club. A player is only allowed to be registered with one club at any one time. The registration document must be signed by the player, witnessed by another person, signed by a club official, and submitted to a league governing body, such as the **Premier League**, **Football League**, **Scottish Premier League** or **Scottish Football League**, for its approval. Registration documents must be received – as originals or by fax – and approved by midday on the last working day prior to a player's first match for a club (FA Premier League rule K.15, Football League regulation 37.2). In the Scottish Football League, the documents must be received before the player can play for his club; they can be faxed, but the original registration documents and the contracts of service must be received within 14 days (Scottish Football League rules 44 and 45). A club continues to hold the registration of a **contract player** (or **professional player** in Scotland), even after the player's contract has expired, until the player signs for a new club or until the registration is formally cancelled (eg owing to permanent disability or mutual consent) provided that the player's name is included in the **club list of players** submitted for registration each year. If a player is registered as a **non-contract** player with a club, the registration will automatically expire at the end of the season. The player is then entitled to sign for a new club (though the original club may offer to re-register the player) (FA Premier League rule K.20, Football League regulation 51). If clubs cease to be members of their league for a reason other than relegation (for example, through insolvency), their players' registrations will automatically be transferred to the league; any subsequent **transfer fees** or **compensation fees** will go to the league, which may, at its discretion, pay an amount to any club owed money for previous transfers by the defunct club and the club itself (FA Premier League rules K.29 and 30, Football League regulation 58.1). In the Scottish Football League, **trialists** are allowed to play up to three games for a club without being registered (Scottish Football League rule 49). There are a number of different types of registration, the definitions vary according to the rules of the respective league. In the Premier League, for example, there are five basic kinds of registration: **full contract, monthly-contract, non-contract, temporary** (loan) and **student**. As well as contract, monthly-contract, non-contract and on-loan players, the Football League requires registration of **trainees**, those on **scholarship agreements** and, until they are phased out, **associated schoolboys**. Youth players at Football League clubs will also need to be registered with a **Football Academy** or **Centre of Excellence**. The Scottish Football League lists **professional players** (with various types of contract), **delayed-transfer players**, **apprentices**, **trainees**, **associated schoolboys** and **amateur players**. *vb.* **register**.

Reipas Lahti *club* Finnish league club based in Lahti, founded 1891 (Finland's oldest major club). Ground: Keskusurheilukenttä (shared with **Kuusysi Lahti**), capacity: 15,000. Strip: orange and black striped shirts, black shorts. *Keynotes* With **Cardiff City**, it holds the record of having qualified for the **European Cup-winners Cup** in five successive seasons, 1973-74 to 1977-78, though only once progressed to the second round (1974-75). Finnish League champions 1963, 1967, 1970; Finnish Cup 1972, 1973, 1974, 1975, 1976, 1978.

release *regulations* to cancel a player's **registration**. See **free transfer** (sense 3).

relegation *competition rules* demotion from a higher to a lower division in a league. Relegation may be automatic if a club finishes in the bottom one, two or three places (for example) or if it loses a relegation **playoff** competition. *Keynotes* The system in which the top two teams of the second division would automatically replace the bottom two of the first division was introduced by the English **Football League** in 1898-99, replacing the previous system of **test matches**. **Bolton Wanderers** and **Sheffield Wednesday** were the first clubs to be relegated in this way, and were replaced by **Glossop North End** and **Manchester City** from the second division. However, under the old test-match rules, **Accrington** and **Notts County** were the first to be relegated from the first division in the 1892-93 season, with **Darwen** and **Sheffield United** promoted. Relegation was introduced in **Scotland** in the 1921-22 season. Although relegation in most countries is decided over a single season, either by automatic relegation on league position (usually the bottom one, two or three clubs), or through relegation playoffs, in some North and South American countries it is decided by performance over two or more seasons. In **Uruguay**, for example, the two clubs with the lowest total points accumulated over the past three seasons are relegated. In **Mexico**, the relegated clubs are those with the worst performance over two seasons.

rematch *n.* match played again following an incident which contravenes the written or unwritten laws of the game, and making the result questionable. *Keynotes* In February 1999, the **Football Association**, backed belatedly by **FIFA**, ordered a rematch of **Arsenal**'s **FA Cup** fifth round tie with **Sheffield United**. Arsenal had "won" the game at **Highbury**, but the winning goal was scored in controversial fashion. Arsenal offered to replay the match because Marc Overmars' goal was scored following a throw-in after United goalkeeper Alan Kelly had deliberately kicked the ball into touch to allow an injured team-mate medical treatment. Usually, under the unwritten rules of sportsmanship, the ball is returned to the other side in such a situation. In the rematch, Arsenal again won 2-1 (23 February 1999). The result of the first match remains on record. **UEFA** ruled that **Spartak Moscow**'s home 1997-98 **UEFA Cup** match against **Sion** of Switzerland be played again after it was found that the **goalposts** for the original encounter (1 October 1997, Lokomotiv Stadium, Moscow) were 2 cm taller than permitted. In the German **Bundesliga**, a match between 1860 Munich and Karlsruhe (5 August 1997, 2-2), was initially ordered to be replayed after a television recording indicated that Karlsruhe's 87th-minute equaliser had been scored after the referee had stopped play for a foul. FIFA was called in to examine the decision and ruled that the match could not be replayed.

Renaissance *club* Chad national league club based in the capital N'Djamena. Ground: Concorde (the national stadium), capacity: 25,000. **African Cup-winners Cup** first round 1997 (after preliminary round); Chad League champions 1989; Chad Cup 1990, 1996.

Reno FC *club* Jamaica league club based in Savannah del Mar. Strip: blue shirts, white shorts. Jamaica league champions 1990, 1991.

Renton *club* former-Scottish league. *Dossier* Ground: Tontine Park, Renton, Strathclyde. *Keynotes* Joined the expanded **Scottish League** in its second season, 1891-92, having been a very successful club in the **Scottish FA Cup** in the first few years of the competition. The club had initially been a founder member of the Scottish League in 1890-91, but was expelled for playing against Edinburgh Saints, a team almost entirely made up of players from **St Bernards**, which had been suspended for being professional. Renton was a Scottish FA Cup semi-finalist (1874, 0–2 v **Queen's Park**) and then a finalist (1875, 0–3 Queen's Park) in the competition's first two years. Following a further semi-final appearance in 1878 (0–1 replay v **Third Lanark** Rifle Volunteers), the club reached the final three times in four years, winning the trophy twice: 1885 (3–1 replay v **Vale of Leven**); 1886 (1–3 v Queen's Park); 1888 (6–1 v **Cambuslang**). Renton played **West Bromwich Albion** in 1888 in an unofficial "Championship of the World" between the winners of their countries respective cups (4–1). In 1895, the club reached the final of the Scottish FA Cup again (1–2 v St Bernards). Renton resigned from the Scottish League after four months of the 1897-98 season. *League record* Divison One 1893-94; Scottish League 1891-92 to 1892-93; Division Two 1894-95 to 1897-98. *Honours* Scottish FA Cup 1885 (3–1 replay v Vale of Leven), 1888 (6–1 v Cambuslang).

replay 1. *competition rules* **rematch** between two sides where a previous game failed to result in a winning score. Whether or not a rematch is required depends on the rules of a particular competition. Games may also be decided by **extra time**, **golden goal**, **away goals** or **penalty kicks**. **2.** *rules* rematch between two teams where a previous game had been abandoned by the **referee** because of poor weather or for public order or safety reasons. Such a match must be replayed in full (and starting with the score at 0-0), unless the competition rules state that a result should stand at the point a match is stopped. **3.** *rules* see **action replay**. *Keynotes* The first **FA Cup** final to go to a replay was the 1875 match between **Royal Engineers** and **Old Etonians**. Royal Engineers won the replay 2–0, following a 1–1 draw. From 1999, the **Football Association** scrapped final replays, preferring the match to be settled by a **penalty shoot-out**, though replays continued for other ties. Semi-final replays were scrapped from the 1999-00 season; the last FA Cup semi-final replay was between **Arsenal** and **Manchester United** (1–2 a.e.t., at **Villa Park**, 14 April 1999). Overall, 14 FA Cup finals have gone to a replay, including 1910-11-12 and 1981-82-83. In Scotland, the 1876 **Scottish FA Cup** between **Queen's Park** and **Third Lanark** Rifle Volunteers was the first to go to a replay. Queen's Park emerged victorious, winning the replay 2–0, following a 1–1 draw in the first encounter.

replica kit *misc.* shirts, shorts and socks which can be bought by supporters and other consumers. Replica kits, especially shirts, are now commonly sported by fans, providing clubs/national federations with additional finance. *Keynotes* Perugia's purchase of **Japan** 1998 **World Cup** star Hidetoshi Nakata for £2million was a sound investment given that around 500,000 replica shirts bearing his name are likely to be sold in Japan.

report on referees *regulations* report made by the clubs involved in a fixture on the conduct and efficiency of the referee and assistant referees. **Premier League**, **Football League** and **Scottish Football League** clubs must submit a report on the officials at every match, and send this to the league within six days (England) – or three days (Scotland) – of the match (FA Premier League rule G.13.1, Football League regulation 33.1, Scottish Football League rule 67).

representative match *n.* match played by teams selected from players of a particular affiliation, such as the **Football League** or **Scottish League** (see **Inter-League match**), rather than their nationality. Compare **international match**.

Republic of Ireland *country* see **Ireland, Republic of.**

Requins de L'Atlantique *club* Benin national league club based in Cotonou. Ground: Quartier Akpakpa, capacity: 10,000. Strip: red shirts, white shorts. **West African Club Cup** semi-final 1983; Benin League champions 1985, 1987, 1990; Benin Cup 1978, 1981, 1983, 1989.

reserve match *n.* match played between two **reserve** teams. *Keynotes* The Old firm **derby** between **Celtic** and **Rangers** scheduled for Monday 1 September 1997 was preceded by a reserve game on Saturday 30 August at **Ibrox Park**, watched by 33,800 fans.

reserve *n.* player who is not picked for the **first team** but is part of the **squad**.

reserve team *n.* team comprising **reserve** players. Reserve teams generally play in lower leagues or special reserve leagues. British football clubs are barred from entering a second or reserve team in their national football leagues. Some countries allow reserve teams to play in the national league, but bar them from promotion to the top flight. In **Spain**, for example, **Atlético Madrid**'s reserve team, the B side, currently play in the Segunda División A, the tier below the Primera Liga. Reserve sides in Spain cannot be promoted.

restart of play *rules* resumption of play in a game of football after the **half-time interval**, after a **goal** has been scored or after any other stoppage by the **referee**. Play is restarted after the half-time interval with a **kick-off** taken by the team that won the toss (see **tossing a coin**) (Law VIII). The game is similarly restarted with a kick-off after a goal is scored, with the team that conceded the goal taking the kick (Law VIII). Where play is halted for an infringement of the Laws of the game, play will be restarted, as appropriate, by a **free kick** or **penalty kick**. Where the ball has gone out of the **field of play**, the game is restarted, where appropriate, by a **throw-in**, **goal kick** or **corner kick**. If a game is restarted for any other reason, for example a temporary suspension of play, and the ball had not already gone over the touch or goal lines, then play may be restarted by a **drop-ball** (Law VIII).

restraint of trade (also freedom of contract) *legal* action which interferes with free market conditions (eg, where supply and demand are allowed to operate without regulation). In football, both the football authorities and the clubs have attempted to retain a players' services and, as a result, limit their earnings even after their contract had expired (see **retain-and-transfer system**). The first challenge to the employment restrictions placed on footballers was mounted in 1913 when **Aston Villa**'s Lawrence Kingaby sought to have his contractual status established after Villa prevented his free movement by placing a transfer fee on him. However, instead of challenging the restraint of trade this imposed on Kingaby (already established in law for other trades), the player claimed damages for 1. loss of employment; and 2. maliciously charging an excessive transfer fee. The judge ruled that there was no case to answer and that the transfer fee was permissible under the terms of Kingaby's contract (*Kingaby v Aston Villa*, 1913). The first challenge in the UK to the restraint of trade inherent in the retain and transfer system was mounted in 1955 by the **Professional Footballers Association** (PFA) in Aldershot Football Club v Ralph Banks. **Aldershot** player Banks sought a transfer and the club imposed a transfer fee, wanting to recoup the £500 it had paid **Bolton Wanderers** for his services. Although his 12-month contract had terminated, FA rules stated that Aldershot retained his registration. In addition, the club also claimed possession of Banks' accommodation, a house which the club owned. The court upheld the club's position and granted it a possession order for the house. Banks was later given a **free transfer**. In 1962, George **Eastham** (Eastham v Newcastle United, Football Association and Football League) successfully challenged the FA's ruling that a club retained a player's services after his employment contract had expired. In 1972, former **Manchester United** player John Cooke had his proposed transfer from **Sligo Rovers** to **Wigan Athletic** (then non-League) blocked by **FIFA** on the same grounds that had been declared a restraint of trade in the Eastham case. The Football Association upheld FIFA's decision, refusing to register the transfer. The FA was successfully sued (Cooke v Football Association, 1972). Belgian Jean-Marc **Bosman** successfully argued that the rules on transfers of players and the limits on the number of **European Union** (EU) nationals allowed to play in club matches were contrary to the **Treaty of Rome** – the founding articles of the European Community. The European Communities Court of Justice ruled in Bosman's favour on 15 December 1995 (Case C-415/93 Bosman). It concluded that **UEFA** rules governing the number of non-domestic EU nationals eligible to play during a club match were contrary to the freedom of movement of workers within the Union as contained in article 85 of the Treaty of Rome. The Court also found that free circulation of players was constrained by the UEFA system of transfers, which prevents a player employed by a club in one member state moving to a new club in a another member state unless a transfer fee is paid for his or her services.

result   *n.*   the final **score** and outcome of any **penalty shoot-out** (if required) of a football match. *Regulations* **Football League** clubs must send the result to the Football League Executive within six days of a league match; the notification must also include the names of the players competing and a report on the performance of the referee (Football League regulation 33.1). Both clubs must send these details. For **Premier League** matches, both clubs' secretaries are required to send the result on a standard form (printed in the **league handbook**), which also requires the names of all the players and nominated substitutes, and the details of any substitutions; the report must be sent within six days (FA Premier League rule E.34). **Scottish Football League** clubs must send the result, attendance and report on the referee's and assistant referees' performance within three days of the game (Scottish Football League rule 67). The reports must be on official league forms.

retain-and-transfer system   *misc.*   former players' contract system that prevented the movement of players from one club to another unless agreed by the club that held the player's **registration** documents; with a fee payable to that club. *History* The system was introduced in England in 1889 when the original **Football League** rules were drawn up. Players whose contracts had expired would not be paid until a new deal had been negotiated – clear pressure on the player to re-sign. Players' contracts were also limited to one year. The system remained in place despite a legal challenge in 1910 brought by the Players Union in support of Lawrence Kingaby (see **restraint of trade**). Efforts to change the transfer rules by the **Professional Footballers Association** (PFA), under the chairmanship of Jimmy **Hill**, led to a threat of industrial action in 1961 (along with disagreement over the **maximum wage**). As a result, the Football League agreed to amend the retain-and-transfer system as follows: players could not be transferred during their contract period without their consent; they would be given advanced notice of a new contract and time to negotiate new terms; if agreement was not reached they would continue to be paid, albeit on the minimum wage after the first month, and on their old terms – on a month-by-month contract – after the second month; and players could ask the Football League Management Committee to adjudicate if they had not re-signed or had not been transferred by 31 August. Although this was an improvement, it still did not allow players to move freely at the end of their contracts. In 1960, another player's dispute gave rise to a further legal challenge of the system the case of George Eastham. He had been denied a transfer on three occasions by his club **Newcastle United** and kept under the retain-and-transfer rule. Although he was eventually allowed to sign for **Arsenal**, Eastham was persuaded by the PFA to take legal action against the **Football Association**, Football League and Newcastle United. The case was heard in the High Court in June 1963. The High Court judge Mr Justice Wilberforce ruled that the retain-and-transfer system was indeed an unlawful restraint of trade. (The judgement also allowed clubs to negotiate longer contracts with players, hitherto limited to just two years.) In 1964, and in consultation with the PFA, the Football League Management Committee drew up new transfer regulations. Under the new rules, players were given greater control over their contracts by being granted the right to take their case to an independent tribunal if the Football League Management Committee was unable to settle a dispute between club and player. Players were allowed union representation at these tribunals from the PFA. Players were also entitled to a percentage of any transfer fee (unless they had requested the transfer). The transfer system was overhauled again in 1978 when the Football League and Professional Footballers Association agreed a new **freedom-of-contract** system (itself modified in 1995 by the **Bosman ruling**).

retire *regulations* to relinquish membership of the **Football League** or **Scottish Football League**. A club that is relegated from the Football League (to the **Football Conference**) is required to resign its membership of the league (Football League regulation 13.1). The club may, however, receive financial compensation for losing its league membership (see **payments to relegated clubs**). There is no automatic relegation from the Scottish Football League; a club that wishes to resign from the league must give two full seasons' notice, except with prior approval at a league general meeting (Scottish Football League rule 21). The membership of a club that is promoted to the **Scottish Premier League** is automatically terminated (Scottish Football League rule 21). **Wigan Borough** was the first club to retire from the Football League during a season, after only 12 games of the 1931-32 campaign; the club was insolvent with £20,000 debts. Its results were declared null and void.

Réunion *country associate member of CAF* island and French overseas region in the Indian Ocean, 650 km (400 miles) east of **Madagascar** and 180 km (110 miles) south-west of **Mauritius**. Became a French colony in 1642. Area: 2,510 sq km (969 sq miles). Population: 624,000. Languages: French. Capital: Saint-Denis. *Dossier* Football association (Fédération Sportive Réunionaise, Saint Denis) formed in 1925 and affiliated to the French Football Federation. It is not affiliated to FIFA but became an associate member of the **Confédération Africaine de Football** (CAF) in 1992, president: Yves Etheve; general secretary: Ismael Locate. Season played from March to November. National stadium: Stade de l'Est, Saint Denis, capacity: 10,000. National strip: white shirts, red shorts, green socks. First international game: 1947 v Mauritius (1–2, neutral venue, **Indian Ocean Games**). Biggest victory: 9–0 v the **Maldives** (twice: 26 August 1979, Saint Denis; and 30 August 1985, neutral venue, Indian Ocean Games). Biggest defeat: 2–15 v Mauritius (1950, neutral venue, Indian Ocean Games). *International tournament record* World Cup – never entered; African Cup of

Nations – never entered; **Olympic Games** – never entered; Indian Ocean Games – winners 1979, 1998 (3–3, 7–6 pens., in Saint-Denis) runners-up 1954, 1957, 1963, 1985, 1993. *Record against British and Irish national teams* none played. *History* National league championship started in 1950; first won by SS Patriote (of Saint-Denis). There are two domestic cup competitions: the Coupe de la Réunion (first won by Bourbon in 1957), and the Coupe de France. *Record in international club tournaments* **African Cup of Champion Clubs** – Saint-Pierroise (second round 1995); **African Cup-winners Cup** – USS Tamponnaise (quarter-final 1994), **Saint-Louisienne** (semi-final 1997); **CAF Cup** – Saint-Denis (semi-final 1994), USS Tamponnaise (quarter-final 1996).

Revie, Don *player-manager* Inside-forward. **England** international (6 caps). Born 10 July 1927; died 26 May 1989. Career ca 1944–63. *Clubs* (player) **Leicester City**, **Hull City**, **Manchester City**, **Sunderland**, **Leeds United**. *Honours* FA Cup (Manchester City 1956). *Clubs* (manager) Leeds United. Also **England** (*record* played 30, won 15, drawn 8, lost 7, goals for 52, goals against 16) and coach of the **United Arab Emirates**. *Honours* League Championship (Leeds United 1968-69, 1973-74); Division Two (Leeds United 1963-64); **FA Cup** (Leeds United 1972); **League Cup** (Leeds United 1968); **UEFA** (Fairs) **Cup** (Leeds United 1968, 1971). *Keynotes* As a player Revie was inspired by the Hungarian demolition of England at **Wembley** in 1953. He developed the so-called Revie plan in which he would play the same deep-lying centre-forward role performed so successfully by Nandor Hidegkuti for **Hungary**. In 1955, Revie was voted **Footballer of the Year** by the football writers and, in 1956, he won an FA Cup winner's medal (v **Birmingham City**). Revie became player-manager at Leeds in March 1961, having joined the club as a player from Sunderland in November 1958. Although Leeds only just escaped relegation from Division Two in Revie's first full season in charge, he transformed them into one of Europe's strongest clubs, securing the club's first League title in 1968-69 and another in 1973-74, its only FA Cup victory (1972 v **Arsenal**), the League Cup in 1968 (also v Arsenal), and twice leading it to European success (UEFA (Fairs) Cup 1968 v **Ferencváros**, 1971 v **Juventus**). Revie was appointed England manager in April 1974 but failed to secure the country a place in the 1978 **World Cup** finals. The **Football Association** banned Revie from the game for ten years after he controversially quit as England manager in July 1977. The courts later ruled that the FA had acted contrary to natural justice and overturned the ban (Revie v Football Association, 1979). Revie was awarded a CBE in 1970.

Review Body for Scottish Football *n.* committee headed by **Scottish Football Association** secretary Ernie Walker that was set up in 1995 to look at the structure and future of Scottish football. The committee recommended the creation of a **Premier League**, which began in 1998-99.

Rhayader Town *club* Welsh league. Ground: The Weirglodd, Rhayader, Powys. Strip: red and white shirts, red shorts. Nickname: Thin Red Line. Ground capacity: 1,500. Formed in 1879.

Rheinstadion *ground* German sports stadium situated in Düsseldorf, Nordheim-Westfalen; home of Fortuna Düsseldorf. Ground capacity: 55,850. *History* Opened in 1926 and completely redeveloped for the 1974 **World Cup**. During the tournament, the Rheinstadion staged two group 3 fixtures (**Bulgaria** v **Sweden**, Sweden v **Uruguay**) and three second round group B matches (**West Germany** v **Yugoslavia**, West Germany v Sweden, Sweden v Yugoslavia) – total attendance 222,446; average attendance 44,489. The stadium was a venue for the 1988 **European Championship** and it staged the 1981 **European Cup-winners Cup** final (**Dynamo Tbilisi** v **Carl Zeiss Jena**, 9,000).

Rhyl *club* Welsh league. Ground: Belle Vue, Rhyl, Flintshire. Strip: white shirts, white shorts. Nickname: Lilywhites. Ground capacity: 4,000. Formed in 1883. *Honours* Welsh League 1925-26 (Northern Division); **Welsh Cup** 1952 (4–3 v Merthyr Tydfil), 1953 (2–1 v **Chester**).

RICE *medical* abbreviation for rest, ice, compression and elevation: the easiest way to remember how to treat **soft tissue injuries**. Any injured part of the body must not be put under further strain and must be rested. Ice packs in the form of crushed ice cubes wrapped in a wet towel, packs of frozen peas, and commercial preparations will help to stop further swelling by dissipating heat from the site of the injury. Ice should not be applied directly to the skin. Compression in the form of a bandage or elasticated bandage will work against any swelling and stop it from progressing further. Elevation of the injury, such as resting a foot above the level of the pelvis, will allow for the slow backtrack of fluid that will tend to accumulate at an injury site.

Richards, Viv (Isaac Vivian Alexander) *player* **Antigua and Barbuda** international. Born 1952. *Keynotes* Although Richards played football for his country, he is celebrated as one of the most successful cricketers of all time, captaining the West Indies from 1986 and scoring a record 1,710 runs in test cricket in a single season.

Richards, Sir Joe *official* former president of the **Football League** (1957-66) and the first to be knighted (1966). Former member of the **Football League management committee** (1948-66). Steered the formation of the Fourth Division (launched 1958). Co-author, with Alan **Hardaker**, of the **Pattern for Football**. Former chairman of **Barnsley**.

right back *n.* **defender** who plays on the right side of a **formation**.

right half *n.* **midfielder** who plays on the right side of a **formation**.

right wing *n.* the right side of a **formation**.

right winger *n.* **attacker** who plays on the right side of a **formation**.

Rimet, Jules *n.* the third president of **FIFA** (1921-54) who, in 1928, with fellow Frenchman Henri Delaunay (then general secretary of the Fédération Française de Football), proposed the organisation of the FIFA **World Cup**. Made honorary president of FIFA in 1954.

Rinder, Fred *official* former chairman of **Aston Villa** (1894-1925), member of the **Football League management committee** from 1917, vice-president 1930, and life member 1938. Credited with transforming Aston Villa to a significant business, including the move to **Villa Park** and the development of the ground (including the £90,000 Trinity Road stand).

Rio Branco Cup *competition* former annual and later occasional fixture between **Uruguay** and **Brazil**, first played 1931. It was last contested in 1967. Uruguay won the trophy three times (1940, 1946, 1948); Brazil won it four times (1931, 1932, 1947, 1958); with one tied tournament (1967).

Rio de Janeiro *state* one of the 27 state leagues in **Brazil**, founded 1905 (the third-oldest league in Brazil). Leading clubs: **Botafogo**, **Flamengo**, **Fluminense**, **Vasco da Gama**.

Rio Grande do Norte *state* one of the 27 state leagues in **Brazil**, founded 1920. Leading clubs: ABC Futebol Clube (Natal), America Futebol Clube (Natal).

Rio Grande do Sul *state* one of the 27 state leagues in **Brazil**, founded 1919. Leading clubs: **Grêmio** (Porto Alegre), **Internacional** (Porto Alegre).

Riodairibord Wanderers *club* Zimbabwe national league club based in Kadoma, founded by a merger of two former clubs, Rio Tinto and Dairibord. Ground: Kadoma, capacity: 12,000. Strip: yellow shirts, white shorts. **East and Central African Club Championship** runners-up 1982 (then known as Rio Tinto, 0–1, v **AFC Leopards** of Kenya, in Kenya); Zimbabwe Cup runners-up 1982.

rituals *misc.* regular set routine performed by an individual, several players or the entire team. *Keynotes* Prior to every match **France** played during the 1998 **World Cup**, defender Laurent Blanc would kiss the shaven head of goalkeeper Fabien Barthez. Frank Leboeuf, who replaced Blanc in the final against **Brazil**, maintained the good luck kiss ritual. Before every match, Paul Ince puts his shirt on as he leaves the tunnel. Leboeuf's team-mate Emmanuel Petit takes some grass from the pitch and allows the wind to blow it from his hand in memory of his brother Olivier, who died while playing football.

Riva, Luigi (Gigi) *player* Striker. **Italy** international (42 caps, 35 goals, 1965-74). Born 7 November 1944. *Clubs* Legnano, Cagliari. *Keynotes* Riva joined Cagliari in 1963. He made his international debut on 27 June 1965 (1–2, v **Hungary**, in Budapest, friendly), and scored his first international goal on 1 November 1965 – one of a hat-trick in the 5–0 defeat of Cyprus (in Cosenza, **European Championship** qualifier). Riva scored one of the extra-time goals that helped Italy defeat **West Germany** in the 1970 **World Cup** semi-final (4–3, at Azteca Stadium, Mexico City). Despite missing the first match of the 1968 European Championship final, Riva played in the replay and scored the opening goal in Italy's 2–0 defeat of **Yugoslavia** (at Olympic Stadium, Rome). He suffered two broken legs in his playing career, but still managed to become Italy's all-time top scorer. He was **Serie A** top scorer in three seasons, including 21 goals from only 28 games in 1969-70, the only occasion that Cagliari has won the Italian championship. *Honours* World Cup runner-up (Italy, 1970); European Championship 1968; Serie A championship (Cagliari, 1970); *France Football* European Footballer of the Year runner-up 1969.

Rivelino Roberto   *player* Winger. **Brazil** international (94 caps, 1965-78, 26 goals). Born 1 January 1946. *Clubs* **Corinthians**, **Fluminense** *Keynotes* Rivelino played in the 1970 and 1974 **World Cup** finals tournaments and was renowned for a fierce left-foot shot and for his skill at free kicks. He once scored a goal from the half-way line for Corinthians in a league game against Rio Preto; the opposition goalkeeper was making his routine start-of-the-game prayers when Rivelino took his long-distance shot just after the kick-off. *Honours* World Cup (Brazil, 1970); **South American Footballer of the Year** (*El Mundo*), runner-up 1977.

River Plate 1. (Club Atlético) *club* Argentinean national league club, based in Buenos Aires, founded 1901. Ground: Estadio Antonio Vespucio Liberti "Monumental" de Nunez, capacity: 78,500. Strip: white shirts with a red sash, black shorts. *History* River Plate was founded in 1905 as a merger of two clubs, Santa Rosa and Rosales. The club was dominant in the 1940s and 1950s, winning the championship nine times in the two decades. It has won the **Copa Libertadores** on two occasions, adding the **Supercopa** in 1997. Seventy-four spectators died at its stadium in June 1968, during a match against **Boca Juniors**; Boca fans caused panic among the home fans as they threw burning paper into the crowd beneath them. **World Club Cup** 1986 (1–0, v **Steaua Bucharest**); Copa Libertadores winners 1986 (2–1, 1–0, v **America de Cali**), 1996 (2–1 agg., v América de Cali), runners-up 1966 (0–2, 3–2, 2–4 playoff, v **Peñarol**), 1976 (1–4, 2–1, 2–3 playoff, v **Cruzeiro**), semi-final 1970, 1990, 1995, 1998; Supercopa winners 1997 (2–1 agg., v **São Paulo**), runners-up 1991 (2–3 agg., v Cruzeiro), semi-final 1988; **Copa Mercosur** quarter-final 1998; Argentinean League champions 1920 (two leagues operated prior to 1927), 1932, 1936, 1937, 1941, 1942, 1945, 1947, 1952, 1953, 1955, 1956, 1957, 1975, 1977, 1979, 1980, 1986, 1990, 1992, 1994 (**apertura**), 1995 (apertura), 1997, (apertura), 1997 (**clausura**); Argentinean National Championship (a pre-national-league tournament operating from 1967 to 1985) winners 1975, 1979, 1981. Notable players: Gabriel **Batistuta**, Alfredo **Di Stefano**, Mario **Kempes**, Bernabe **Ferreyra**, Ubaldo Fillol, José Manuel **Moreno**, Daniel **Passarella**, Oscar **Ruggeri**. **2.** (Club Atlético River Plate) *club* Uruguayan Primera League club based in Montevideo, founded 1932.

Ground: Parque Federico Saroldi, capacity: 11,000. Strip: red and white striped shirts, white shorts. **Copa Uruguaya** (Uruguay's professional league) runners-up 1992. **3.** *club* former Uruguayan league club, based in Montevideo, founded 1902, disbanded 1920. Uruguayan amateur league (played from 1900-31) champions 1908, 1910, 1913, 1914.

Rivera, Gianni   *player* Inside-forward. **Italy** international (60 caps, 14 goals). Born 18 August 1943. *Clubs* Alessandria, **AC Milan**. *Keynotes* Rivera was bought by AC Milan in 1959 for £65,000 (at the age of 16), although his transfer was deliberately delayed until 1960, when he was considered ready for the move. He went on as a substitute to replace Boninsegna in the 1970 **World Cup** final, when Italy lost 1–4 against **Brazil** (Azteca, Mexico City). Became president of AC Milan. *Honours* World Cup runner-up (Italy, 1970); *France Football* **European Footballer of the Year** 1969, runner-up 1963; **World Club Cup** (AC Milan, 1969); **European Cup** (AC Milan, 1963, 1969); **European Cup-winners Cup** (AC Milan, 1968, 1973); Italian **Serie A** championship (AC Milan, 1962, 1968).

Riverside (Cellnet) **Stadium** *ground* English football ground situated in Middlesbrough; home of **Middlesbrough**. *Dossier* Ground capacity: 35,000 all seated. Pitch dimensions: 105m x 68m. Record attendance: 34,687 v **Tottenham Hotspur** (20 February 1999, **Premier League**). *History* Middlesbrough played its first match at the Riverside Stadium on 26 August 1995 (v **Chelsea**, Premier League). Developed jointly by the Teesside Development Corporation (TDC), the biggest quango of its kind, Middlesbrough Borough Council and the football club at an initial cost of around £18 million (£12 million for the stadium plus £6 million on the infrastructure). The ground is built on the site of a former oil storage facility. The TDC paid for much of the surrounding infrastructure and the club was responsible for the actual stadium. The **Football Trust** contributed £3 million of the stadium costs and a 10-year sponsorship deal with mobile phone company Cellnet yielded a further £4 million – hence the ground's official title: Cellnet Riverside Stadium. British Steel, a major local employer, withdrew its £10,000 sponsorship in 1995 after it was disclosed that much of the stadium was being built with German-made steel. The club banned smoking at the Riverside in 1998-99. In December 1998, Boro anounced plans to increase the capacity to 42,000.

Robin Hood *club* Surinam national league club based in the capital Paramaribo, founded 1945. Strip: green shirts, red shorts. *Keynotes* Robin Hood jointly holds the South American club record of seven consecutive league titles (1983 to 1989) – equal with **Racing Club** of Argentina. This is also a joint CONCACAF club record, matched by Club Deportivo Hercules of El Salvador. Its 23 league titles is a CONCACAF club record. **CONCACAF Champions Cup** runners-up 1972, 1976, 1977, 1982, 1983; Surinam League champions 1953, 1954, 1955, 1956, 1959, 1961, 1964, 1971, 1975, 1976, 1979, 1980, 1981, 1983, 1984, 1985, 1986, 1987, 1988, 1989, 1992, 1993, 1994.

Robo-Cup *misc.* competition organised to coincide with the 1998 **World Cup** finals, to find the most efficient football-playing robot. Teams from **England** and **Denmark** were required to create a computer programme for a small robot on wheels. The programmes had to be "self-thinking" and were required to manoeuvre a tennis ball past the other robot and into the opposition goal. The final, at the Science Museum in London, was won by Static, a programme designed by a team from Aarhus University in Denmark, which beat Robonaldo, from Westfield College, London, 1–0 (12 July 1998).

Robson, Bobby *player-manager* Right-half/Inside-forward. **England** international (20 caps). Born 18 February 1933. Career ca. 1950–68. *Clubs* (player) **Fulham** (twice), **West Bromwich Albion**, Vancouver Royals. *Clubs* (manager) Vancouver Royals, Fulham, **Ipswich Town**, **PSV Eindhoven** (twice), **Sporting Lisbon**, **Porto (FC)**, **Barcelona**. Also England manager (*record* P95, W47, D30, L18, F154, A60). *Honours* **FA Cup** (Ipswich Town 1978); **UEFA Cup** (Ipswich Town 1981); Dutch League (PSV Eindhoven 1990-91, 1991-92); Portuguese League (Porto (FC) 1994-95, 1995-96); Portugese Cup (Porto (FC) 1994); Spanish Cup (Barcelona 1997); **European Cup-winners Cup** (Barcelona 1997). *Keynotes* Robson finished his playing career in Canada with Vancouver Royals. He had a brief spell as player-coach of the Royals before becoming Fulham manager in January 1968. He was appointed Ipswich Town manager in January 1969. Robson, who had scored twice on his England debut (4–0 v **France**, 27 November 1957), became manager of the national side in July 1982. During Robson's eight years as England boss he endured an uneasy relationship with the press. The country's failure to qualify for the 1984 **European Championship** and England's poor showing at the 1988 tournament were low points. Yet he led England to the quarter-final stage of the 1986 **World Cup** (2–1 v **Argentina**) and, at the 1990 tournament, to the semi-finals (1–1, 3–4 pens. v West **Germany**). He resigned as England manager after the 1990 World Cup and subsequently has been a highly successful manager on the continent.

Robson, Bryan *player-manager* Midfield. **England** international (90 caps, 26 goals). Born 11 January 1957. Career ca. 1971–96. *Clubs* (player) **West Bromwich Albion, Manchester United**. *Honours* League Championship (Manchester United 1992-93); **FA Cup** (Manchester United 1983, 1985, 1990); **League Cup** (Manchester United 1992); **European Cup-winners Cup** (Manchester United 1991). *Clubs* (manager) **Middlesbrough**. First Division (Middlesbrough 1994-95). *Keynotes* Known as "Captain Marvel" due to his courageous displays, Robson joined West Bromwich Albion in 1972, having had trials with **Burnley, Coventry City** and **Newcastle United**. He turned professional in August 1974. Transferred to Manchester United for a record £1.5 million in October 1981, scoring 74 goals in 345 **Football League** appearances for the club. Robson suffered a series of injuries as a player, including a broken leg three times and a repeatedly dislocated shoulder (during the 1986 **World Cup** finals as well as on several other occasions). He scored England's quickest World Cup goal, after only 27 seconds against **France** on 16 June 1982. As Middlesbrough manager, Robson took the club to the Premier League in his first season and, in 1996-97, Boro reached two **Wembley** finals: FA Cup (0–2 v **Chelsea**); League Cup (0–1 replay v **Leicester City**). The following season, the club was again a League Cup finalist (0–2 a.e.t. v Chelsea). Included in the **Football League Centenary 100 players**.

Rochdale *club* English league. *Dossier* Ground: **Spotland**, Rochdale, Greater Manchester. Strip: white shirts with blue trim, blue shorts and white socks. Nickname: Dale. Ground capacity: 9,195. Record attendance: 24,231 v **Notts County** (10 December 1949, **FA Cup**, 2nd rd). Best average attendance: 8,616 (1948-49). Biggest win: 8–1 v **Chesterfield** (18 December 1926, Division Three (North)). Biggest defeat: 0–8 v **Wrexham** (28 December 1929, Division Three (North)), v **Leyton Orient** (20 October 1987, Division Four), 1–9 v **Tranmere Rovers** (25 December 1931, Division Three (North)). *History* Founded in 1907 as Rochdale AFC largely at the behest of Harvey Rigg, the former secretary of a rugby club. He needed a team to help pay the rent at a ground called St Clements (later known as Spotland) following the demise of two earlier football clubs, another Rochdale AFC and Rochdale Town, which had both used the venue. The club was a founder member of Division Three (North) in 1921-22, but has spent only six seasons (1958-59, 1969-70 to 1973-74) of its 72-season League career outside the bottom division. Rochdale finished ninth in Division Three in 1969-70, which is the club's highest League position. Rochdale's most celebrated achievement came in the second **League Cup** competition, when the club, under the managership of Tony Collins, reached the final (0–4 agg. v **Norwich City**) – a feat no other bottom-division club has repeated. In 1990, the club reached the fifth round of the FA Cup (0–1 v **Crystal Palace**). *League record* Division Three 1958-59, 1969-70 to 1973-74; Third Division 1992-93–; Division Three (North) 1921-22 to 1957-58; Division Four 1959-60 to 1968-69, 1974-75 to 1991-92. *Records* Graham Smith holds the record for club League appearances (317, 1966-74); Reg Jenkins is Rochdale's record League goalscorer (119, 1964-73).

Roda JC Kerkrade *club* Netherlands national league club, based in Heerlen, and founded in 1914 (merged with Rapid Heerlem in 1962). Ground: Gemeentelijk Sportpark Kaalheide, capacity: 25,000. Strip: yellow shirts and black shorts. **European Cup-winners Cup** quarter-final 1998; Dutch Cup 1997.

Rodriguez, Rodolfo *player* Goalkeeper. **Uruguay** international (78 caps, 1976-86). *Honours* **Copa**

America (Uruguay, 1983). *Keynotes* Uruguay's most-capped player.

Roi Baudouin (Stade du) (formerly Heysel) *ground* Belgian football ground situated in Brussels; **Belgium** national stadium. Ground capacity: 50,000 all seated. *History* Heysel Stadium opened in 1930 as part of the Parc des Expositions, marking the country's 100th anniversary. Following the **Heysel Stadium disaster**, when 39 people, mainly Italians, were trampled or crushed to death before the 1985 **European Cup** final between **Liverpool** and **Juventus** on 29 May, the ground has been almost entirely rebuilt and renamed Stade du Roi Baudouin (King Baudouin Stadium). The partially-completed stadium, with a 40,000 capacity, was opened in 1996 (Belgium v **Germany**) and the reconstruction was completed in 1998. It staged the opening match of the 2000 **European Championship**, which is jointly hosted by Belgium and **Netherlands**. Heysel has staged more European finals (five **European Cups**, including one replay, and three **European Cup-winners Cups**) than any other ground: European Cup (1958 **Real Madrid** v **AC Milan**, 67,000; 1966 Real Madrid v **Partizan Belgrade**, 55,000; 1974 **Bayern Munich** v **Atlético Madrid**, 65,000 (+ replay, 65,000); 1985 Juventus v Liverpool, 58,000); European Cup-winners Cup (1964 **Sporting Lisbon** v **MTK Hungaria FC** (as MTK Budapest), 9,000; 1976 **RSC Anderlecht** v **West Ham United**, 58,000; 1980 **Valencia** v **Arsenal**, 40,000). Under its new name, the stadium has hosted a European Cup-winners Cup final (1996 **Paris St-Germain** v **Rapid Vienna**, 37,500).

Roker Park *ground* English football ground that was situated in Sunderland, Tyne & Wear; former home of **Sunderland**. *Dossier* Capacity (1997): 22,657. Pitch dimensions 103m x 68m. Record attendance: 75,118 v **Derby County** (6 March 1933, FA Cup, 6th rd replay). Best average attendance: 47,785 (1949-50). *History* Sunderland played its first match at Roker Park on 10 September 1898 (v **Liverpool**, Division One). The club initially rented some farmland, but in 1908 bought the freehold for £10,000. Roker Park suffered bomb damage in March 1943 in an incident that also resulted in the death of a policeman. In December 1952, Roker Park became only the second Division One ground to install **floodlights** (v **Dundee**, 11 December, friendly). The recommendations of the **Taylor Report** and its requirement for all-seater stadiums led Sunderland, in conjunction with the local council, to study alternative sites for a new stadium. Initially a 300-acre site adjacent to the Nissan car plant was favoured as the best possible site. The Japanese car manufacturer objected to Sunderland's plans to build a huge leisure complex, including a 40,000-capacity stadium, on the site, but in May 1994 an alternative 23-acre site, the former Wearmouth colliery, became available (see Stadium of Light). Sunderland played its final League match at Roker Park on 3 May 1997 (v **Everton**, Premier League, 22,052). In 1966, Roker Park was used as a **World Cup**

venue. The ground staged group 4 fixtures (**Chile** v **Italy**; Italy v **Soviet Union**; Chile v Soviet Union) and a quarter-final tie (Soviet Union v **Hungary**) – total attendance 93,122; average attendance 23,280. Roker Park has hosted three England international matches (v Ireland, 18 February 1899, v Ireland, 23 October 1920; v **Wales**, 15 November 1950). Roker Park also was the venue of a **Football League** v Irish League match on 12 October 1907 and a Football League v Scottish League encounter on 18 March 1964. The 1955 **FA Cup** semi-final replay (**Newcastle United** v **York City**) and two **FA Amateur Cup** finals (1926 Northern Nomads v Stockton, 1939 Bishop Auckland v Willington) were held at Roker Park. The site is now a housing estate.

Rollin, Jack *misc.* editor of **Rothmans Football Yearbook**, which was published for the 29th time in 1998. Now succeeded by his daughter Glenda.

Roma (AS) *club* Italian league. *Dossier* Ground: **Olimpico** (Stadio), Rome, Lazio. Strip: burgundy shirts with yellow trim, burgundy shorts with yellow trim, burgundy socks. Nickname: I Lupi (the Wolves). Ground capacity: 82,922 all seated. Record win: 9–0 v Cremonese (**Serie A** 1929-30). Record defeat: 1–7 v Torino (Serie A). *History* Formed in 1927 following the merger of the Alba, Fortitudo, Roman and Pro Roma clubs. The full name of the club is Associazione Sportiva Roma, hence the title AS Roma. Before moving to Stadio Olimpico via Stadio del Partito Nazionale Fascista (PNF), Roma played at Campo Testaccio. The club won its first League Championship in 1941-42 and a second in 1982-83. The latter triumph followed two consecutive Italian Cup victories in 1980 (0–0, 3–2 pens. v **Torino**) and 1981 (2–2, 5–3 pens. v Torino). Roma reached the 1984 **European Cup** final (1–1, 2–4 pens. v **Liverpool**) and, in 1991, the **UEFA Cup** final (1–2 agg. v **Internazionale**). The club's only European success was achieved in 1961, when it won the **UEFA** (Fairs) **Cup** (4–2 agg. v **Birmingham City**). *Honours* Italian League 1941-42, 1982-83; Italian Cup 1964 (1–0 agg. v Torino), 1969 (league basis), 1980 (0–0, 3–2 pens. v Torino), 1981 (2–2, 5–3 pens. v Torino), 1984 (2–1 agg. v Hella Verona), 1986 (3–2 agg. v **Sampdoria**), 1991 (4–2 agg. v Sampdoria). UEFA (Fairs) Cup 1961 (4–2 agg. v Birmingham City); **Anglo-Italian Cup** 1972 (3–1 v **Blackpool**).

Romania *country UEFA* country in south-east Europe on the Black Sea, next to **Bulgaria**, **Hungary**, **Moldova**, **Ukraine** and **former-Yugoslavia**. Became a communist state after **World War II**. Communist dictator Nicolae Ceausescu overthrown and executed in 1989. Non-communist administration followed. Area: 237,500 sq km (91,699 sq miles). Population: 22,730,000 (1994 census). Languages: Romanian, with minority German and Hungarian. Capital: Bucharest. *Dossier* Football association (Fédération Roumaine de Football, Bucharest) formed in 1909, affiliated to **FIFA** in 1930 and founder member of the **Union of European Football Associations** (UEFA) in 1954, president: Mircea Sandu; general secretary: Adalbert Kassai. Season played from August to June with a **winter break** in January and February. National stadium: Stadionul National (formerly Stadionul 23 August), Bucharest, capacity: 70,000. National strip: yellow shirts, yellow shorts, yellow socks. First international game: 8 June 1922 v **Yugoslavia** (2–1, Belgrade, friendly). Biggest victory: 9–0 v **Finland** (14 October 1973, Bucharest, **World Cup** qualifier). Biggest defeat: 0–9 v **Hungary** (6 June 1948, Budapest, Balkan and Central European Championship). Record attendance: 100,000 v **Czechoslovakia** (0–2, 22 May 1960, Stadionul 23 August, Bucharest, **European Championship** quarter-final first leg). Most capped players: Georghe **Hagi** (115 appearances, 1983-), Ladislau Bölöni (104, 1975-88), Michael Klein (90, 1981-91). Leading goalscorers: Georghe Hagi (33 goals, 1983-), Iuliu Bodola (30, 1931-39), Anghel Iordanescu (26, 1971-81), Ladislau Bölöni (25, 1975-88). Other notable international players: Ilie Dumitrescu, Dan Petrescu, Marius Lacatus, Viorel **Moldovan**, Florin Raducioiu. *International tournament record* **Olympic Games** – first entered 1924, quarter-final 1964; **Women's World Cup** – first entered 1995, never qualified for finals tournament; World Cup – entered first tournament in 1930, quarter-final 1994, second round 1990, 1998, also qualified for finals tournament 1930 (no qualifying tournament), 1934, 1938 (walkover in qualifying tournament) and 1970; **Balkan Cup** 1931, 1933, 1936, 1980; **European Championship** – entered first tournament in 1960, quarter-final 1960, 1972, also qualified for finals tournament in 1984 and 1996; **European Under-18 Junior Championship** winners 1962; **European Championship for Women** – first entered 1993, never progressed beyond first-round group stage; **World Youth Cup** (under-20) – third 1981 (1–0 v **England**, in Sydney, Australia, third/fourth playoff). *World Cup performance* (finals and qualifiers to end of 1998 tournament) played 95, won 50, drawn 20, lost 25, scored 177 goals, conceded 102 goals. win rate: 53%; goals scored per game: 1.86. *Record against British and Irish national teams* v **England**, played 10, won two, drawn six, lost two; v **Northern Ireland**, played three, won none, drawn none, lost three; v **Scotland**, played five, won one, drawn two, lost two; v **Wales**, played five, won three, drawn one, lost one; v **Republic of Ireland**, played four, won two, drawn one, lost one. *History* Football was introduced at the end of the 19th century. Romania's football association was founded in 1908, the second in Eastern Europe (after Czechoslovakia), at the instigation of the then Prince Carol (heir to the former monarchy). The national championship was started in 1910, with the Romanian Cup first played in 1934. The championship was settled by a final playoff until 1934, when a straight league system was introduced. The 1940 Cup final, won by **Rapid Bucharest** against Venus Bucharest, went to a world record three replays (2–2, 4–4, 2–2, 2–1). **Steaua Bucharest** and **Dinamo Bucharest** have dominated club football: since 1951 the championship has been won only 13 times by a club outside the "big two"; and since 1980 only **Universitatea Craiova** has managed to break the domination (winning in 1980, 1981 and 1991). Steaua holds the European record of 104 consecutive league games without defeat (1986 to 1989), four short of the world record held by **ASEC Mimosas Abidjan** of **Ivory Coast**). In 1986, Steaua became the only Eastern European club to win the **European Cup** (0-0, 2-0 pens v **Barcelona**); it reached the final again in 1989 (0–4, v **AC Milan**). Romania played its first international in 1922, and its first international competition match in 1924 (0-6, v **Netherlands**, in Paris, Olympic Games first round). Along with **Belgium**, **France** and **Yugoslavia**, it was one of only four European countries to enter the first World Cup, in **Uruguay** in 1930. Its appearance was partly because the former Prince Carol, who had become **King Carol II**, intervened to ensure that the players were not only paid but had their regular jobs preserved for their return after a three-month absence. Romania, like several other countries, initially had declined the invitation to participate. It won its opening game (3–1, v **Peru**), but was eliminated after a 0–4 defeat by the host and eventual champions Uruguay, in front of 80,000 spectators at **Centenario Estadio**, Montevideo. Although Romania has entered all but two World Cup competitions (not in 1950 and 1962), and has entered all the European Championships, it has never progressed beyond the quarter-final in a major senior international tournament. Viorel Moldovan has the unusual honour of having scored the 2,000th goal in the 1998 World Cup tournament – the first competition to have broken the 2,000 barrier in qualifiers and finals– (2–1, v England, 22 June, in Toulouse, France). Michael **Owen**'s goal for England in the same match was the 100th goal conceded by Romania in all World Cup matches (qualifiers and finals). *League system* Eighteen clubs play in the first division (the Divizia Nationala). Three points are awarded for a victory, with one for a draw: final positions for clubs level on points are determined by **goal difference**. The bottom three clubs are relegated to the second division. Divizia A is divided into two regional leagues of 18 clubs: both champions are promoted, along with the winner of a playoff between the two regional-league runners-up. The third tier (Divizia B), comprises four regional leagues. *Record in international club tournaments* European Cup – Steaua Bucharest (winners 1986, runners-up 1989 semi-final 1988, qualified for **Champions League** 1997), Dinamo Bucharest (semi-final 1984); **European Cup-winners Cup** – Dinamo Bucharest (semi-final 1990, quarter-final 1989) Rapid Bucharest (quarter-final 1973), Steaua Bucharest (quarter-final 1993); **UEFA Cup** – Universitatea Craiova (semi-final 1983), Victoria Bucharest (quarter-final 1989; club now defunct), **National Bucharest** second round 1997; **European Super Cup** – Steaua Bucharest (winners 1986). Other notable club: **UTA Arad**.

Romario (full name: Romario da Souza Faria) *player* Striker. **Brazil** international (62 caps, 44 goals, 1987-98). Born 29 January 1966. *Clubs* Olario, **Vasco da Gama**, **PSV Eindhoven**, **Barcelona**, **Flamengo** (twice), **Valencia**. *Keynotes* Although the 1994 **World Cup** final against **Italy** finished goalless, Romario scored a penalty for Brazil in the shoot-out after Marcio Santos had missed; Brazil went on to win 3–2 on penalties. Romario scored Brazil's opening goal in the 3–2 defeat of **Netherlands** in the quarter-final, and the only goal – an 81st-minute header – in the 1–0 defeat of **Sweden** in the semi-final; he was Brazil's top scorer in the tournament with five goals. Romario scored Brazil's goal in the 1988 **Olympic Games** football final (1–2, v **Soviet Union**); he was top scorer in the tournament with seven goals. Romario joined PSV Eindhoven from **Vasco da Gama** in 1989, scoring 98 league goals in his five seasons in Netherlands. He was transferred to **Barcelona** for £3 million in 1993 and played in the 1994 **European Cup** final (0–4, v AC Milan). *Honours* World Cup (Brazil, 1994); Olympic Games silver medal (Brazil, 1988); Rio de Janeiro state championship 1987, 1988; Dutch League championship 1991, 1992; Spanish League championship (Barcelona, 1994); **FIFA World Footballer of the Year** 1994.

Romero, Julio César *player* Striker. **Paraguay** international. Clubs Sportivo Luqueno, **New York Cosmos**, **Fluminense**. *Honours El Mundo* South American Footballer of the Year 1985. *Keynotes* Paraguay's all-time second-highest goalscorer.

Ronaldo (full name: Ronaldo Luiz Nazario da Lima) *player* Striker. **Brazil** international (44 caps, 29 goals). Born 1976, in Rio de Janeiro. *Clubs* São Cristovão, **Cruzeiro**, **PSV Eindhoven**, **Barcelona**, **Internazionale**. *Keynotes* Ronaldo was transferred from Cruzeiro to PSV in 1994, and from PSV to Barcelona for £12.5 million in July 1996. He became the world's most expensive player in June 1997 with a £18 million transfer to Internazionale. By the end of the 1997-98 season, when he was still only 21, Ronaldo had scored 228 goals in 263 league matches in Brazil, **Netherlands**, **Spain** and **Italy**. Although Ronaldo helped Brazil reach the final of the 1998 **World Cup**, the strain of virtually three years playing, training and promotional work – apparently without a break – left Ronaldo obviously fatigued by the end of the tournament. He did not take part in training for the final, was reported to have been in hospital on the day, and was rumoured to have suffered a fit; his absence from the squad was shrouded in mystery. Brazil coach Mario **Zagallo** was heavily criticised for playing a clearly unfit Ronaldo in the final. Despite his lacklustre performance on the last day, however, Ronaldo was chosen for **FIFA**'s 22-man all-star squad of the 1998 World Cup tournament. He is the first player to win FIFA's **World Footballer of the Year** award in successive seasons. *Honours* World Cup runner-up (Brazil, 1998); **Olympic Games** bronze medal (Brazil, 1996); **Copa America** (Brazil, 1997); **Copa del Ray** (Barcelona, 1996);

European Cup-winners Cup Barcelona, 1997); **UEFA Cup** (Internazionale, 1998); FIFA World Footballer of the Year 1996, 1997; *World Soccer* Footballer of the Year 1996, 1997, third 1998;*France Football* European Footballer of the Year 1997, 1998; **European Golden Boot** 1997 (34 goals for Barcelona; the Golden Boot was awarded under a new league-rating system introduced by the organisers, weighted in favour of Europe's top-ranked leagues).

Rondonia *state* one of the 27 state leagues in **Brazil**, founded 1945. Leading clubs: Sociedade Esportiva Ariquemes (Ariquemes), Ferroviario AC, Flamengo (of Porto Velho – not to be confused with **Flamengo** of Rio de Janeiro).

Roots Hall *ground* English football ground situated in Southend, Essex; home of **Southend United**. *Dossier* Ground capacity: 12,306. Pitch dimensions: 100.5m x 68m. Record attendance: 31,090 v **Liverpool** (10 January 1979, **FA Cup**, third round). Best average attendance: 12,089 (1949-50). *History* Southend first played at Roots Hall between 1906 and 1916 before moving there for a second time in 1955. At the time of the first match the pitch was 33 metres higher than the current one. Roots Hall was turned into allotments during **World War I** and in the inter-war period sand was excavated from the site. The club established a trust fund in 1950 to raise the £11,258 required to buy the site from the local council. Southend returned to Roots Hall on 20 August 1955 (v **Norwich City**, Division Three (South)). In 1984-85, Roots Hall staged the Rugby League fixtures of the Kent-based Invicta club. Plans to sell the ground for redevelopment as a retail superstore and move the club to a new stadium were rejected in 1989. The first floodlit match at Roots Hall took place on 31 August 1959 (v **Charlton Athletic** Reserves, **Football Combination**).

RoPS Rovaniemi (Rovaniemen Palloseura) *club* Finnish national league club based in Rovaniemi, founded 1950. Ground: Keskuskenttä, capacity: 4,000. Strip: blue shirts, white shorts. **European Cup-winners Cup** quarter-final 1988; Finnish Cup 1986.

Roraima *state* one of the 27 state leagues in **Brazil**, founded 1995. Leading clubs: Atletico Roraima Clube (Boa Vista), Bare.

Rosario Central (Club Atlético) *club* Argentinean national league club, based in Rosario, founded in 1889 by British employees of Central Argentine Railway. It is Argentina's third oldest surviving club. Ground: Estadio Gigante de Arroyito "Cordiviola", capacity: 50,000. Strip: blue and yellow striped shirts, blue shorts. **Copa CONMEBOL** winners 1995 (4–4 agg., 4–3 pens., v **Atlético Mineiro**), runners-up 1998 (0–1 agg., v **Santos**), semi-final 1996; Argentinean League champions 1987; Argentinean National Championship (a pre-national-league tournament operating from 1967 to 1985) winners 1971, 1973, 1980. Notable former player: Mario **Kempes**.

Rose Bowl *ground* US sports ground situated in Pasadena, California; home of UCLA and soccer club

Los Angeles Galaxy. Ground capacity: 100,092 all seated. *History* Principally a venue for American college football and the largest sports stadium in Southern California. The Rose Bowl was first used for football (**soccer**) during the 1984 Los Angeles **Olympic Games**, staging the football final (**France v Brazil**, 101,799) and the bronze medal playoff. The stadium staged a double-header of two football matches on 16 June 1996 when a crowd of 92,216 watched the friendly international between **USA v Mexico** followed by the **Major League Soccer** encounter between **Los Angeles Galaxy** v **Tampa Bay Mutiny**. In addition to the 1994 **World Cup** final (Brazil v **Italy,** 75,000), the stadium was the venue for seven other fixtures during the tournament: **Romania** v **Colombia**, **USA** v Colombia, Romania v USA, group A; **Cameroon** v **Sweden**, group B; Romania v **Argentina**, second round; Brazil v **Bulgaria**, semi-final; Sweden v Bulgaria, 3rd place playoff – total attendance 715,835; average attendance 89,479.

Rosenborg BK Trondheim (Ball Klub) *club* Norwegian national league club based in Trondheim, founded in 1917. Ground: Lerkendal, capacity: 28,000. Strip: white shirts, black shorts. *Keynotes* Rosenborg BK holds the Norwegian record of seven consecutive league titles (1992 to 1998). **European Cup/Champions League** quarter-final 1997 (qualified from the Champions League, winning three of its six matches, including a 2-1 victory away to **AC Milan**, before losing 1-3 agg. against **Juventus** in the quarter-final), qualified for champions league 1998, second round 1987; **UEFA Cup** second round 1972; Norwegian League champions 1967, 1969, 1971, 1985, 1988, 1990, 1992, 1993, 1994, 1995, 1996, 1997, 1998; Norwegian Cup 1960, 1964, 1971, 1988, 1990, 1992, 1995.

Ross County *club* Scottish league. *Dossier* Ground: **Victoria Park**, Dingwall, Highlands. Strip: navy blue shirts with white pinstripes, white shorts with navy blue trim, red socks with navy blue hoops. Ground capacity: 5,400. Record attendance: 8,000 v **Rangers** (28 February 1966, **Scottish FA Cup**). Biggest win: 11–0 v St Cuthbert Wanderers (December 1993, Scottish FA Cup). Biggest defeat: 1–10 v Inverness Thistle (Highland League). *History* Founded in 1929, the club played in the Highland League until 1994-95 when it joined the Third Division along with **Inverness Caledonian Thistle** following the expansion of the **Scottish League** from 38 to 40 clubs. On three occasions since the Third Division was established, Ross has narrowly missed promotion, finishing third in 1994-95, 1996-97 and 1997-98. In 1998-99 County finally won promotion, taking the Third Division title. Ross has the distinction of the being the most northerly senior club in the UK. *League record* Second Division 1999-00; Third Division 1994-95 to 1998-99. *Records* William Herd holds the record for club League appearances (124, 1995-98); Derek Adams is the record League goalscorer (38, 1996-98).

Rossi, Paolo *player* Striker. **Italy** international (48 caps, 20 goals, 1977-86). Born 23 September 1956. *Career* ca. 1980–89. *Clubs* Prato, **Juventus** (twice – returned after his spell at Perugia), Como, Vicenza, Perugia, **AC Milan**. *Keynotes* Rossi made his international debut on 21 December 1977 (1–0, v **Belgium**, in Liege, friendly). In 1979, Perugia paid a then world-record £3.5 million for Rossi's transfer from Vicenza. The following year, however, he was suspended for three years (later reduced to two) for alleged **match fixing**. The ban was rescinded in time for Rossi to play in the 1982 **World Cup** finals; he scored the opening goal in Italy's 3–1 defeat of **West Germany** (**Bernabeu**, Madrid) and was tournament top scorer with six goals. Rossi played in the 1985 **European Cup** final, the match of the **Heysel Stadium disaster**. He retired from playing in 1986. *Honours* World Cup (Italy, 1982); World Cup **Golden Boot** 1982; *World Soccer* **World Footballer of the Year** 1982; *France Football* European Footballer of the Year 1982; European Cup (Juventus, 1985); **European Cup-winners Cup** (Juventus, 1984); Italian Serie A championship (Juventus, 1982, 1984).

Rotherham United *club* English league. *Dossier* Ground: **Millmoor Ground**, Rotherham, south Yorkshire. Strip: red shirts with white sleeves with red trim, white shorts with red trim, and red socks with white trim. Nickname: Merry Millers. Ground capacity: 11,514. Record attendance: 25,170 v **Sheffield United** (13 December 1952, Division Two). Best average attendance: 18,770 (1951-52). Biggest win: 8–0 v **Oldham Athletic** (26 May 1947, Division Three (North)). Biggest defeat: 1–11 v **Bradford City** (25 August 1928, Division Three (North)). *History* Founded in 1925 from a merger between Rotherham County (formed as Thornhill in 1882) and Rotherham Town (formed in 1905, although an older but unrelated Rotherham Town was founded around 1882 and spent three seasons in Division Two between 1893 and 1896). In 1925-26, the new club took County's place in the League (Division Three (North)), which it had joined in 1919-20, and continued to play at Millmoor. In 1951-52, Rotherham won the Division Three (North) Championship and in 1954-55, the club only narrowly missed promotion to the top flight on goal average, finishing on the same number of points as both **Birmingham City** and **Luton Town**, and despite winning more games and scoring more goals than either of its rivals – this is Rotherham's highest League position. Rotherham has spent much of the period since relegation from Division Two in 1967-68 alternating between the bottom two divisions. The club enjoyed a two-season return to Division Two, following promotion as Division Three Champions in 1980-81. In 1987-88, the club lost its Division Three status in the end-of-season **playoffs**, but made an immediate return, winning the Division Four Championship in 1988-89. The club reached the fifth round of the **FA Cup** in 1952-53 (1–3 v **Aston Villa**) and 1968 (0–2 replay v **Leicester City**). Rotherham was a **League Cup**

finalist in the inaugural competition in 1960-61 (2–3 agg. a.e.t. v Aston Villa). In 1996, Rotherham made a first and successful **Wembley** appearance, winning the **Auto Windscreens Shield** (2–1 v **Shrewsbury Town**). *League record* Division Two 1951-52 to 1967-68, 1981-82 to 1982-83; Second Division 1992-93 to 1996-97; Division Three 1968-69 to 1972-73, 1975-76 to 1980-81, 1983-84 to 1987-88, 1989-90 to 1990-91; Third Division 1997-98–; Division Three (North) 1925-26 to 1950-51; Division Four 1973-74 to 1974-75, 1988-89, 1991-92. *Honours* Division Three 1980-81; Division Three (North) 1950-51; Division Four 1988-89; Auto Windscreens Shield 1996 (2–1 v Shrewsbury Town). *Records* Shaun Goater is Rotherham's most capped player (18 for **Bermuda**); Danny Williams holds the record for club League appearances (459, 1946-62); Gladstone Guest is Rotherham's record League goalscorer (130, 1946-56).

Rothmans Football Yearbook *publication* football yearbook first published in 1970. The book contains information on all the Premier/Football League clubs and those in the Scottish Premier/Football Leagues; it also records all league and cup results from the previous season; and provides coverage of European club and international competitions.

Rotor Volgograd *club* Russian national league and former Soviet Union league club based in Volgograd, founded in 1929 (formerly known as Traktor Stalingrad, Torpedo Stalingrad, Stal Stalingrad, Stal Volgograd, and Barrikady Volgograd, adopting current name in 1975). Ground: Central Stadium, capacity: 30,000. Strip: blue shirts, blue shorts. **Far East Club Championship** winners 1998 (3–2, v **Dalian Wanda** of China); Russian League runners-up 1993; Russian Cup runners-up 1995; no Soviet Union League or Cup honours.

rouge *n.* former rule adopted in some early football codes (eg at Eton College and **Sheffield rules**), where a point was scored if the ball crossed the goal line between either of two outer posts each side of the "inner" goal. Compare **Australian rules**.

Rous, Stanley *n.* sixth president of **FIFA** (1961-74). Nationality: English. Made honorary president of FIFA in 1974.

route one football *tactics* style of football characterised by direct long and high passes up the field of play, usually with the intention of exploiting the heading skills of tall attackers. It contrasts a more patient style of play with short passes and slow build-up.

Rowley, Arthur *player* Striker. Career ca. 1946–65. *Clubs* **West Bromwich Albion**, **Fulham**, **Leicester City**, **Shrewsbury Town**. *Keynotes* Retired in February 1965, while player-manager of Shrewsbury Town, having scored a record 434 **Football League** goals in his career. Overall, Rowley made 619 League appearances between 1946 and 1965, scoring four goals for WBA, 27 for Fulham, 251 for Leicester City and 152 for Shrewsbury. During the 1956-57 season, Rowley scored 44 Division Two goals for Leicester, which remains a club record, as does his overall goal tally for

Shrewsbury. He became Shrewsbury player-manager in 1958 and following his retirement from playing in 1965 he was manager for a further three years. His brother Jack, who made six appearances for **England** and who later coached **Ajax**, score twice for **Manchester United** in the **FA Cup** final. Included in the **Football League Centenary 100 players**.

Royal Antwerp FC *club* Belgium national league club based in Antwerp, founded 1880; Belgium's oldest club. Ground: Bosuil Stadium, capacity: 20,000. Strip: red shirts, red shorts. **European Cup-winners Cup** runners-up 1993 (1–3 v **Parma**, **Wembley Stadium**); Belgium league champions 1929, 1931, 1944, 1957; Belgium Cup 1955, 1992. *Keynotes* In November 1998, Royal Antwerp signed a **nursery club**-type deal with **Manchester United**.

Royal Engineers *club* former English club. *Keynotes* Army side credited with introducing **formations** into football tactics. Prior to the mid-1870s, most clubs relied on only rudimentary playing positions, with an emphasis on individual dribbling skills. Royal Engineers played in a 1-2-4-3 formation, comprising a three-quarter back (in front of the goalkeeper), two half backs, four wingers and three centres. The club adopted a strategy of short passes. Its effectiveness was demonstrated over four seasons: from 1871 to 1875, the club lost only three games in 86 played (with 74 wins and nine draws), conceding 21 goals and scoring 244. Royal Engineers appeared in four of the first seven **FA Cup** finals, winning the trophy in 1875 (2–0 v **Old Etonians**, replay).

Royal Lesotho Defence Force (RLDF) *club* Lesotho national League team, based in the capital Maseru. Ground: National, capacity: 20,000. Strip: green shirts, and yellow shorts. Lesotho League champions 1983, 1984, 1987, 1990, 1994, 1997, 1998; Lesotho Cup 1985, 1986, 1988, 1990.

royal box *n.* stadium enclosure or designated seating area reserved for visiting members of the royal family. The **FA Cup** trophy and medals are presented from the royal box at **Wembley** Stadium.

royalty, and football. *misc.* **Burnley's Turf Moor** ground is believed to have been the venue for the first football match attended by a member of the British royal family. Prince Albert saw the local derby between Burnley and **Bolton Wanderers** at the ground in October 1886, having earlier opened a nearby hospital. George V was the first reigning monarch to attend an **FA Cup** final, when, in 1914, he watched Burnley defeat **Liverpool** (1–0) in the last final to be staged at **Crystal Palace**. At the turn of the century (January 1901) football matches were cancelled during the mourning period for Queen Victoria. In 1935, two representative matches were staged to celebrate the Jubilee of King George V (Football League XI v **West Bromwich Albion**, 8 May 1935, at the **Hawthorns** and Football League v Wales & Ireland, 11 May 1935, at **Goodison Park**). Both matches were also used to experiment with the use of **two referees**. King George VI visited Norwich City's

Carrow Road ground on 29 October 1938 during a match with **Millwall** – this is the first occasion a reigning monarch watched a Division Two game. The royal family is generally represented at major football matches at Wembley. Queen Elizabeth II, the current monarch, presented the **Jules Rimet** trophy to **England** captain **Bobby Moore** in 1966 and the Henri Delaunay Cup to **Germany** skipper Jürgen **Klinsmann**, following his nation's success at the 1996 **European Championship**. Up to 1998, the Queen has also been present at 10 FA Cup finals. **King Carol II**, former king of Romania (born 1893, died 1953), was noted for his positive intervention with the Romanian squad for the first **World Cup** in 1930. Romania had initially declined the invitation to travel to Uruguay because its players were unable to take the necessary three months off work; King Carol II ruled that each player should have his job retained, on full pay, until they returned. He was deposed by the Romanian Iron Guard in 1940, and fled to South America.

RSC Anderlecht (Royal Sporting Club) *club* Belgium national league club based in Brussels, founded 1908. Ground: Stade Constant Vanden Stock, capacity: 28,000. Strip: white shirts, white shorts. *History* Anderlecht is by far the most successful club in Belgium football, having won the Belgium league 24 times by 1998, and the cup eight times. Its five consecutive league titles (1964 to 1968) is a national record. It has won three European club competitions (see below) and is the only Belgium club to win a major European trophy. It has appeared in European club competitions every season since 1964-65; an achievement bettered only by **Barcelona** and **Benfica**. It entered the first **European Cup** in 1955, losing 4–10 (agg.) to Vörös Lobogó in the first round. Its worst defeat, perhaps, was the 0–10 humiliation by **Manchester United** in the 1956 European Cup first round (at **Maine Road**, Manchester United did not then have lights at Old Trafford), losing the tie 0–12 overall. It reached the final of the **UEFA/Fairs Cup** in 1970, the first of its four European finals, narrowly losing to **Arsenal** over two legs. In 1997, the club was found guilty of bribing the referee in the 1984 3–2 defeat of **Nottingham Forest** in the UEFA Cup semi-final. Anderlecht was banned for 12 months from European competitions, but this was overturned in May 1998 by the **Court of Arbitration in Sport**, ruling that the UEFA executive committee was not empowered to impose such a ban. *Honours* **European Cup-winners Cup** 1976 (4–2 v **West Ham United**, Heysel Stadium, Brussels), 1978 (4–0 v **FK Austria Vienna**, Paris), runners-up 1977 (0–2, v **Hamburger SV**, Amsterdam), 1990 (0–2, v **Sampdoria**, Gothenburg); UEFA Cup/Fairs Cup 1983 (2–1 agg., v Benfica), runners-up 1970 (3–4 agg., v Arsenal), 1984 (2–2 agg., 3–4 pens., v **Tottenham Hotspur**); **European Super Cup** 1976 (5–3 agg., v **Bayern Munich**), 1978 (4–3 agg., v **Liverpool**); Belgium League winners 1947, 1949, 1950, 1951, 1954, 1955, 1956, 1959, 1962, 1964, 1965, 1966, 1967, 1968, 1972, 1974, 1981, 1985, 1986, 1987, 1991, 1993, 1994, 1995; Belgium Cup 1965, 1972, 1973, 1975, 1976, 1988, 1989, 1994.

Ruch Chorzów *club* Polish national league side based in Chorzów, Katowice, founded in 1920 (known as Unia Chorzów from 1950-55). Ground: Ruch, capacity: 40,000. Strip: blue shirts, blue shorts. **European Cup** quarter-final 1975; **UEFA Cup** quarter final 1974; Polish League champions 1933, 1934, 1935, 1936, 1938, 1952, 1953, 1960, 1968, 1974, 1975, 1979, 1989 (1952 and 1953 as Unia Chorzów); Polish Cup 1951 (as Unia), 1974, 1996.

rugby football *n.* type of football played with an oval ball where handling is allowed by all the players. The ball can be kicked or handled, but players cannot use their hands to propel the ball forward. Players are ruled offside if they are in front of the ball when it is kicked forward by a team-mate. The principal objective is to carry or kick the ball towards the opposition goal, and for an attacking player to touch the ball down in the area behind the try-line, thus scoring a try. Points are also scored by kicking the ball between two posts and over a crossbar; either from a set kick following a try (a conversion) or from a penalty kick. Players can also score a drop-goal by kicking the ball over the crossbar during open play. Players running with the ball can be tackled by an opposition player by grasping and holding, but not tripping. There are two rugby codes: rugby union (played with 15 players on each team), and rugby league (with 13 players). Both codes allow professionalism. *History* Rugby football shares common origins with **association football** and, in the mid-19th century, the English public schools were playing several variations on a common theme. The rugby code originates from a game played at Rugby School – the first formal rules were drawn up by the school in 1846. The principal difference from other early football codes was that in rugby, if the ball was caught cleanly, the player had the option of running with the ball. Attempts were made to draw up a unified football code but exponents were largely divided into those that supported the handling codes, and those that favoured a game centred on kicking. An irreparable schism occurred at a **Football Association** meeting on 1 December 1863, only five weeks after the formation of the FA. Founder members Blackheath FC resigned from the FA, unable to accept that handling and running with the ball would be prohibited from the FA's new rules, and opted to continue independently of the FA. Many clubs throughout Britain continued to operate under Rugby rules and, in 1870 Scottish rugby clubs issued a challenge to any English club to take on a Scottish representative team. The challenge was rejected by the FA, but accepted by Blackheath FC, which organised a committee to select the English side. Both Blackheath and Richmond wrote to *The Times* on Christmas Eve 1870, proposing that a common set of rules should be drawn up and, on 26 January 1871, 21 clubs, including Blackheath, Richmond and Harlequins, founded the Rugby Football

Union (RFU). The first **England** v **Scotland** game was played on 27 March 1871, in Edinburgh (the match won by Scotland). Three months later, on 24 June, a set of 59 rules was adopted by the RFU.

Rugby Park *ground* Scottish football ground situated in Kilmarnock, Strathclyde; home of **Kilmarnock**. *Dossier* Ground capacity: 18,128. Pitch dimensions: 104m x 66m. Record attendance: 35,995 v **Rangers** (10 March 1962, **Scottish FA Cup**). *Keynotes* Kilmarnock first played at Rugby Park on 26 August 1899 (v **Celtic**). The ground was used by the army during World War II for coal and oil storage. In the 1990s, Kilmarnock pursued plans to relocate to a new purpose-built 20,000 capacity stadium, but when these failed the club decided to completely redevelop Rugby Park. Between 1994 and 1995, Rugby Park was transformed into a 18,000 capacity all-seater stadium. The first floodlit match at Rugby Park took place in October 1953 (v **Manchester United**, friendly). Rugby Park has staged two full **Scotland** international fixtures: v **Wales**, 24 March 1894; v Wales, 5 March 1910.

Rummenigge, Karl-Heinz *player* Striker. West **Germany** international (95 caps, 45 goals, 1976–86). Born 25 September 1955. *Clubs* Lippstadt, **Bayern Munich**, **Internazionale**, **Servette FC Geneve**. *Keynotes* Rummenigge was the second-highest goalscorer in the 1982 **World Cup** finals, with five goals. In the match of the tournament, the semi-final against France, a partially fit Rummenigge, brought on as a substitute, scored the first of West Germany's goals in extra time that helped his team claw back to 3–3 after the French had taken a 3–1 lead: West Germany went on to win 5–4 in a **penalty shoot-out**. Rummenigge was in the losing side in two successive World Cup finals; having lost the 1982 final 1–3 against **Italy**, West Germany lost 2–3 against **Argentina**. Rummenigge scored for Germany but his team was already two goals behind. He also scored three goals in the 1978 finals in Argentina, including two in the first-round match against **Mexico** (6–0). Rummenigge was in the triumphant, and impressive, West German team that won the 1980 **European Championship**, and scored his country's opening goal in the finals in Italy (1–0, v **Czechoslovakia**). West Germany beat **Belgium** 2–1 in the final in Rome. Rummenigge has a winner's (1976) and runner's up (1982) medal in the European Cup. *Honours* World Cup runner-up (West Germany 1982, 1990); European Championship (West Germany, 1980); **World Club Cup** (Bayern Munich, 1976); **European Cup** (Bayern Munich, 1976); German **Bundesliga** championship (Bayern Munich, 1980, 1981). *France Football* **European Footballer of the Year** 1980, 1981, runner-up 1979; *World Soccer* **World Footballer of the Year** runner-up 1982.

run the line *vb.* to undertake the job of the **assistant referee** or, more usually, **club linesman**.

runner-up *n.* team that finishes second in a league or cup competition. *Keynotes* (Up to and including 1997-98) **Everton** has been runner-up seven times in the **FA**

Cup, while **Leicester City**, with four appearances in the final, has never won the tournament. **Manchester United** hold the record for most runner-up positions in the English top-flight (12), followed by **Liverpool** and **Aston Villa** (10 each). Nine clubs have been runners-up once but have never won the championship: **Blackpool**, **Bristol City**, **Cardiff City**, **Charlton Athletic**, Leicester City, **Oldham Athletic**, **Queens Park Rangers**, **Southampton** and **Watford**. **Rangers** has been a **Scottish FA Cup** runner-up on 18 occasions, while **Celtic** has been a runner-up 17 times. **Hamilton Academicals** has been runners-up twice, but has never won the trophy. Both Celtic and Rangers had been runners-up in the Scottish Premier/First/ Division One on 24 occasions. **Airdrieonians** was runner-up in four consecutive seasons in the Scottish Division One from 1922-23 to 1925-26, but has never won the title.

running off the ball *tactics* player moving into space to receive a pass or as a decoy to entice an opponent out of position.

rupture *medical* **1.** complete tearing of a **ligament** through injury. Such injuries may require surgery. Some are immobilised with a dressing and left to heal of their own accord. **2.** severe injury to a muscle when all of the muscle fibres are torn. Surgery may be required.

rush goalie *informal* in unofficial (kickabout) matches **1.** where the nearest or covering player automatically assumes the goalkeeper role. **2.** where the goalkeeper of a team, especially one with fewer players, is allowed to play outside of his/her penalty area. Compare **stick goalie**.

Rush Ian *player* Striker. **Wales** international (73 caps, 28 goals). Born 20 October 1961. Career ca. 1978-. *Clubs* (player) **Chester**, **Liverpool** (twice), **Juventus**, **Leeds United**, **Newcastle United**, **Wrexham**. *Honours* League Championship (Liverpool 1981-82, 1982-83, 1983-84, 1985-86, 1989-90); **FA Cup** (Liverpool 1986, 1989, 1992); **League Cup** (Liverpool 1981, 1982, 1983, 1984, 1995); **European Cup** (Liverpool 1984). *Keynotes* Joined Liverpool from Chester for £300,000 in 1980 and in two spells with the club scored 233 goals in 469 **Football League** appearances. In 1987, Rush was transferred to Juventus for £3.2 million, but he scored only 7 goals in 29 **Serie A** starts and returned to Merseyside after only one season with the Italian club. Rush holds the post-war record for most FA Cup goals, scoring 42 (39 for Liverpool and three for Chester), including a record five in finals - two in 1986 (3–1 v **Everton**) and 1989 (3–2 v Everton) and one in 1992 (2–0 v **Sunderland**). With Geoff **Hurst**, Rush shares the record as the highest scorer in the League Cup with 49 goals. Rush is Wales's record goalscorer with 28 goals in 73 international games. He won his first cap, against **Scotland,** on 21 May 1980. Voted **PFA Young Footballer of the Year** in 1983 and, in 1984, both **Footballer of the Year** and **PFA Footballer of the Year**. Included in the **Football League Centenary 100 players**.

Russia (Russian Federation) *country UEFA* vast federation of eastern Europe and northern Asia; by area, the largest country in the world. It stretches from the Arctic Ocean to China. Neighbouring countries: **Azerbaijan**, **Belarus**, **China**, **Estonia**, **Finland**, **Georgia**, **Kazakhstan**, **Latvia**, **Lithuania**, **Mongolia** and **Norway**. Dramatic climatic and geographical variation. An empire prior to 1917 when revolution led to the removal of Russia's ruling monarchy (then Tsar Nicholas II). A communist state was established after the Bolsheviks came to power in October 1917. Russia became the centre of the Union of Soviet Socialist Republics (see **Soviet Union**). The Soviet Union broke up ca. 1989-1991, with the establishment of the Russian Federation in 1991. Area: 17,078,005 sq km (6,592,110 sq miles). Population: 147,500,000 (1996 est.). Languages: Russian. Capital: Moscow. *Dossier* Football Union of Russia (Moscow) formed in 1912 affiliated to FIFA in 1912 and founder member (as the Soviet Union) of the **Union of European Football Associations** (UEFA) in 1954, president: Dr Vlacheslav Koloskov; general secretary: Vladimir Radionov. Season played from the beginning of March to the beginning of November. National stadium: Luzhniki, Moscow, capacity: 96,000. Strip: white shirts, blue shorts, red socks. First international game: 30 June 1912 v Finland (1–2, Stockholm, Olympic Games). Biggest victory: 7–0 v **San Marino** (7 June 1995, Serravalle, San Marino, **European Championship** qualifier) (note: the Soviet Union beat Finland 10–0 in 1957). Biggest defeat: 0–16 v **Germany** (1 July 1912, Stockholm, **Olympic Games** consolation tournament) Most capped players: Victor Onopko (58 appearances, 1992-), Valeri Karpin (37 appearances, 1992-97), Yuri Nikiforov (39 appearances, 1992-). Leading goalscorers: Igor Kolyvanov (12 goals, 1993-), Dimitri Radchenko (nine goals, 1992-97), Igor Simutenkov (nine goals, 1994-). Other notable international players: Andrei Kanchelskis, Lev Yashin, Oleg **Salenko**. *International tournament record* Olympic Games – entered as pre-Soviet Russia in 1912, lost in first round; **Women's World Cup** – first entered 1995, qualified for finals tournament 1999; **World Cup** – first entered as an independent state in the 1998 tournament, finished second in qualifying group of five, losing playoff with **Italy**; European Championship – first entered as an independent state in 1996, qualified for finals tournament 1996, last in four-nation first-round group stage; **European Championship for Women** – first entered 1995, quarter-final 1995; **Under-17 World Championship** – never qualified; **World Youth Cup** (under-20) – quarter-final 1995. *World Cup performance* (finals and qualifiers to end of 1998 tournament – includes all results for the former Soviet Union and Commonwealth of Independent States) played 104, won 61, drawn 20, lost 23, scored 205, conceded 83 goals; win rate 59%; goals scored per game 1.97. *Record against British and Irish national teams* v **England**, none played; v **Northern Ireland**, none played; v **Scotland**, played

two, drawn two; v **Wales**, none played; v **Republic of Ireland**, played two, won one, drawn one, lost one. *History* Football is said to have been introduced in 1887, by two English cotton mill owners, Clement and Harry Charnock, whose Morozov mill club at Orekhovo Zuyevo, to the east of Moscow, played in the same team colours (blue and white) as **Blackburn Rovers**. Regional leagues formed in St Petersburg and Moscow around the turn of the century. A Russian football association, the All-Russian Football Union, was established in 1912. Pre-Soviet Russia played eight games from 1912 to 1917, including two in the Olympic Games of 1912. Russia's existing league clubs all date, officially at least, from the Soviet era, with the most successful, **Spartak Moscow**, **Dinamo Moscow**, **CSKA Moscow** and **Torpedo Moscow**, all founded between 1922 and 1924. Soviet clubs were largely organised alongside major employers or trade unions: CSKA, for example, was originally an army club; Dinamo was linked to the electrical workers' union (though the club was formed from the original Morozov mill club), while Torpedo was the car workers' club. **Lokomotiv Moscow** (founded in 1923) was the railway workers' club, and played in special tournaments for railway clubs across the European communist countries. Lokomotiv won the first Soviet Cup in 1936 (2-0 v **Dinamo Tbilisi** of Georgia). Only Spartak was considered independent, though technically linked to a food producers' co-operative. The big four Moscow clubs, Spartak, Dinamo, CSKA and Torpedo, flourished in the Soviet Union football league and Cup competitions, winning 33 Soviet league titles and 27 Soviet Cups between them: Dinamo won the first championship in 1936. The most successful Soviet club, however, was **Dinamo Kiev**, from the **Ukraine**. No Russian club has ever won a major European club title. CSKA Moscow holds the honour of being the last Soviet League champions (1991), with Spartak the last Cup (1992). Russian clubs had only modest success in European club competitions during the Soviet era, particularly when compared with Dinamo Kiev's two **European Cup-winners Cup** triumphs. However, Spartak Moscow reached the semi-final of the European Cup in 1991 and qualified for the **Champions League** in 1995. Dinamo Moscow reached the final of the European Cup-winners Cup in 1972. The post-Soviet Russian league championship was started in 1992, first won by Spartak Moscow (also winners in 1993, 1994 and 1996). The first winner of the new Russian Cup was Torpedo Moscow, in 1993. A new Russian Football Federation was established in 1992, after the creation of the Russian Federation in 1991, with Russia's first post-Soviet match played on 17 August 1992 v **Mexico** (2–0, in Moscow, friendly). Although the former Soviet countries (minus the Baltic states) played in the European Championship finals in Sweden collectively as the **Commonwealth of Independent States**, the 1994 World Cup qualifying group place, that had originally been earmarked for the Soviet Union, was controversially awarded to Russia, to the chagrin of the Ukraine. Russia qualified in its own right for the 1996 European Championships – an impressive qualifying campaign of eight wins and two draws, with 34 goals scored and only five conceded – but registered just one point from its three first-round group games at the finals in England. It failed to qualify for the 1998 World Cup finals, beaten in a qualifying playoff by Italy (1–2, agg.). A number of key Soviet internationals played for Russia after the break-up of the union, despite being born in the Ukraine. These include Andrei Kanchelskis, and Viktor Onopko, Russia's most capped player. Russia and Ukraine played each other for the first time on 5 September 1998: Onopko scored one of the goals for Russia (2–3, in Kiev, European Championship qualifier). *League system* Eighteen clubs play in the Russian premier division (the Vischaya): the bottom three are automatically relegated to the first division. Three points are awarded for a victory, with one for a draw: final positions for clubs level on points are determined by the number of matches won (rather than **goal difference**) and, if necessary, by the results of matches between the relevant clubs. However, if two or more clubs are level on points at the top of the league, the title is settled by a championship playoff. There are 22 clubs in the first division, the bottom five relegated to the three regional second divisions (western, eastern and central zones of 16 to 22 clubs). A fourth-tier third division is comprised of six regional leagues, each with 13 to 20 clubs. The amateur fourth division comprises at least 10 zones, from Siberia to Moscow, with a national amateur championship at the end of the season. The domestic Cup final is played in June, with preliminary qualifying matches starting in the May of the previous season (in order to cope with the vast number of eligible clubs). *Record in international club tournaments* **European Cup/Champions League** – Spartak Moscow (semi-final 1991, quarter-final group stage 1994, qualified for Champions League 1995), CSKA Moscow (quarter-final group stage 1993); European Cup-winners Cup – Dinamo Moscow (runners-up 1972, semi-final 1985), Spartak Moscow (semi-final 1993), Lokomotiv Moscow (semi-final 1998); **UEFA Cup** – Spartak Moscow (semi-final 1998, quarter-final 1984), Torpedo Moscow

(quarter-final 1991). Other leading clubs: **Alania Vladikavkaz**, **Rotor Volgograd**. See **Soviet Union**.

Rwanda *country CAF* republic in central Africa, bordered by **Burundi**, **Tanzania**, **Uganda** and **Zaire**. Tropical climate, subsistence agriculture. Part of the Belgium territory of Ruanda-Urindi from 1916. Independence from Belgium in 1962. Civil war from 1990, between ethnic Tutsis and Hutus. Languages: French, Bantu and tribal languages. Area: 26,330 sq km (10,165 sq miles). Population: 7,460,000 (1993 est.). Capital: Kigali. *Dossier* Football association (Fédération Rwandaise de Football Amateur, Kigali) formed in 1972, affiliated to **FIFA** in 1976 and **Confédération Africaine de Football** (CAF) in 1976, president: Lt Col César Kayizari; general secretary: Jean Bosco Gasherebuka. Season played from August to March. National stadium: Stade Amahoro, Kigali, capacity: 35,000. National strip: red, green and yellow shirts, green shorts, red socks. First international game: 29 June 1976 v Burundi (2–6, neutral venue, Central African Games). Biggest defeat: 1–6 v **Congo Democratic Republic** (Zaire) (July 1976, neutral venue, friendly). *International tournament record* **Olympic Games** – first entered 1988, never qualified for finals tournament; **World Cup** – first entered 1998 (lost in first qualifying round to eventual qualifiers **Tunisia**, 1–5 agg.); **African Cup of Nations** – first entered 1982, never past first round stage of qualifying tournament; **East and Central African Championship** – never reached final, hosts 1998. *History* Rwandan league championship played from 1981, Cup from 1980. *Record against British and Irish national teams* never played. *Record in international club tournaments* **African Cup-winners Cup** – **Etincelles** (second round 1989); **East and Central African Club Championship** Rayon Sports (third place, 1999). Other leading clubs: FC APR (Kigali, League champions 1995, 1996), **Kiyovou Sports**, **Pantheres Noires**, Mukungwa Ruhengeri (of Ruhengeri, league champions 1988, 1989), Mukura Valley Sports (of Butare, Rwandan Cup 1980, 1986, 1992), Rayon Sports (of Butare, League champions 1981, 1997).

S

Safety of Sports Ground Act 1975 *legal* legislation requiring (the then) **Division One** and **Division Two** football grounds (plus **Wembley** and Murrayfield in Edinburgh) to meet specified safety standards. The Act was the result of an inquiry (Lord Wheatley, Cmnd 4952, 1972) into the 1971 **Ibrox Park disaster** in which 66 people died (see **Wheatley Report**). It introduced a system of certification of sports grounds, with the local authority listing the improvements that must be made to a stadium in order to be granted a crowd capacity and safety certificate.All stadiums accommodating more than 10,000 spectators are required to hold a current safety certificate covering, for example, entrances and exits and means of escape in the event of fire. Clubs failing to meet the standards of the legislation could have their ground capacities reduced or their licences to hold matches withdrawn. The Act required many clubs to make major and expensive improvements. Financial assistance came from the newly founded **Football Grounds Improvement Trust**. The Act was criticised for ignoring the stadiums in the lower divisions. It followed the 1973 **Green Guide** which contained safety recommendations for grounds but had no force in law and was likened to a Highway Code for crowd safety. Other football-related safety legislation includes the Fire Safety and Safety of Places of Sport Act 1987 (see **Bradford fire**), **Football Spectators** Act 1989, and the Football (Offences) Act 1991.

safety certificate *n.* written approval that a club's ground has passed standards for crowd safety and crowd control. Safety certificates are issued by local authorities.

SAFF Cup *competition* see **South Asian Football Confederation Cup.**

sag-back defence *tactics* the tactic of defending the **scoring space**.

sagging *tactics* aspect of play which involves a defender covering a team-mate who is marking/engaging an **onball** attacker by moving towards the ball/goal and giving greater depth to the defence. See also **covering**.

Saharan Arab Democratic Republic *n. country* see **Western Sahara.**

Sahel FC *club* Niger national league club, based in the capital Niamey. Ground: Stade 29 Juillet, Niamey, capacity: 30,000 (Niger's national stadium). Strip: green shirts and yellow shorts. Niger League champions 1987, 1991, 1992, 1994 and 1996; Niger Cup 1974, 1985, 1986, 1987, 1992, 1993 and 1996.

St Andrews *ground* English football ground situated in Birmingham, west Midlands; home of **Birmingham City**. *Dossier* Ground capacity: 27,500 all seated. Pitch dimensions: 105m x 68.5m. Record attendance: 66,844 v Everton (11 February 1939, **FA Cup**, fifth round). Best average attendance: 38,453 (1948-49). *History* Birmingham City, then plain Birmingham, played its first match at St Andrews on 26 December 1906 (v **Middlesbrough**, Division One). The club, founded as Small Heath Alliance in 1875, had previously played its matches at Muntz Road. Initially, Birmingham signed a 21-year lease for St Andrews and it took the club 10 months to prepare the ground for football, including the construction of an estimated 48,000-capacity end terrace at Tilton Road, known as the **Kop**. When Birmingham moved to St Andrews in 1906, it displaced a gypsy camp and legend has it that the gypsies placed a curse on the ground which several managers have since attempted to exorcise. St Andrews was the only **Football League** ground during World War II to be shut because of air-raids and, although the ban was lifted in March 1940, the ground was hit by 20 bombs. In January 1942, the main stand burned down and the club was forced to play at Leamington and at **Villa Park**. A fan was killed when a wall collasped following rioting involving City and **Leeds United** supporters on 11 May 1985 – the same day as the **Bradford City fire**. Further crowd trouble occurred during the club's Division Three encounter with **Stoke City** in February 1992. David Sullivan's purchase of the club in March 1993 was followed in April 1994 by the first major construction work at St Andrews for almost 30 years, involving the demolition of the Tilton Road end. Floodlights were erected in 1956, with the first floodlit match on 31 October (v **Borussia Dortmund**, friendly). St Andrews staged one of two Football League v **Scottish League** World War I "Victory" matches on 22 February 1919 (the other match took place at **Ibrox Stadium** on 5 April 1919). The ground has been the venue for several FA Cup semi-finals.

St Bernards *club* former Scottish league. *Dossier* Ground: Royal Gynasium Ground/Powderhall Stadium.

Keynotes Founder member of the new two-tier **Scottish League** in 1893-94, finishing third in Division One – the club's highest League position. The club had been suspended for professionalism when the Scottish League was formed in 1890-91. Following relegation to Division Two in 1900-01, the club was twice denied a return to the top flight despite winning the Championship (1900-01, 1906-07) because automatic promotion/relegation was not introduced in Scotland until 1921-22. St Bernards won the **Scottish FA Cup** in 1895 (2–1 v **Renton**) and reached the semi-final stage on three other occasions: 1893 (0–5 v **Celtic**), 1896 (0–1 v **Heart of Midlothian**), 1938 (1–2 second replay v **East Fife**). St Bernards never returned to League football after World War II. *League record* Division One 1893-94 to 1899-00; Division Two 1900-01 to 1938-39. *Honours* Division Two 1900-01, 1906-07; Scottish FA Cup 1895 (2–1 v Renton).

St Catherine's Roma Wolves *club* **Canadian Professional Soccer League (Ontario Division)** club based in St Catherine's, Ontario. Ground: Roma Club. Strip: red shirts, black shorts. Canadian National Soccer League champions 1995; Canadian Professional Soccer League (Ontario Division) champions 1997, 1998.

St Francis *club* republic of Ireland national league club. Strip: shirts, shorts. Republic of Ireland **FAI Cup** runners-up 1990.

St Gallen FC (Fussball-Club) *club* Swiss national league club based in Sion, founded 1879. It is the oldest club in Switzerland and one of the oldest in the world outside the United Kingdom. Ground: Espenmoos, capacity: 14,000. Strip: green shirts, green shorts. Swiss national champions 1904; Swiss Cup 1969, runners-up 1945, 1977.

St Georges *club* Ethiopian national league club based in Addis Ababa, founded 1936. Ground: Saba, capacity: 20,000. Strip: yellow shirts, red shorts. **African Cup of Champion Clubs** semi-final 1967; Ethiopian League champions 1950, 1966, 1967, 1968, 1971, 1975, 1987, 1991, 1992, 1994, 1995, 1996; Ethiopian Cup 1972, 1974, 1977.

St Helena *country no international affiliation* island and United Kingdom dependent territory, in the South Atlantic, about 1,200 km west of Africa. Area: 122 sq km (47 sq miles). Population: 5,600. Capital: Jamestown. Dependent territories: Ascension Islands and Tristan da Cunha. *Dossier* Football association, neither affiliated to **FIFA** nor to **Confédération Africaine de Football** (CAF).

St Jakob Stadion *ground* Swiss sports ground situated in Basle; home of FC Basel. Ground capacity: 42,000. *History* During the 1954 **World Cup**, St Jakob staged six matches: **Hungary** v **West Germany**, group 2; **Uruguay** v **Scotland**, group 3; **Belgium** v **England**, group 4; **Switzerland** v **Italy**, group 4 playoff; Uruguay v England, quarter-final; West Germany v **Austria**, semi-final – total attendance 226,000; average attendance 53,006. The stadium has

been the venue for four **European Cup-winners Cup** finals (1969 **Slovan Bratislava** v **Barcelona**, 40,000; 1975 **Dinamo Kiev** v **Ferencváros**, 13,000; 1979 Barcelona v Fortuna Düsseldorf, 58,000; 1984 **Juventus** v **Porto**, 60,000).

St James Gate *club* republic of Ireland national league club based in Dublin, founded 1913. Ground: Iveagh Grounds. Strip: black and white hooped shirts, white shorts. Republic of Ireland League champions 1922 (the first championship), 1940; Republic of Ireland **FAI Cup** 1922 (the first FAI Cup), 1938, runners-up 1934, 1937. Notable former player: J O'Reilly (20 caps for the Republic of Ireland, formerly with **Aberdeen**).

St James Park *ground* English football ground situated in Exeter, Devon; home of **Exeter City**. *Dossier* Ground capacity: 10,570. Pitch dimensions: 104m x 67m. Record attendance: 20,984 v **Sunderland** (4 March 1931, **FA Cup**, sixth round replay). Best average attendance: 10,339 (1952-53). *History* Exeter United, which merged with St Sidwell's Old Boys to form Exeter City in 1904, first played at St James Park – then St James' Field – on 20 October 1894 (v Tavistock). The ground had previously been used for rugby but, at just over 91 metres, it did not meet the **Football Association**'s minimum pitch length, leading to several clubs, including **Burnley**, **Reading** and **Nelson**, refusing to play FA Cup ties at the ground in 1910. With the help of the local MP, Henry Duke, the club was able to acquire some more land, enabling St James Park to be extended. The first match on the new pitch occurred on 14 October 1911 (v **West Ham United**). The club bought the 3.5 acre site for £5,000 in 1921 and, 75 years later, in May 1996, financial needs meant that the ground's freehold was sold to property developers Beazer Homes – sponsors at one time of the **Southern League** – for £600,000. The first floodlit match at St James Park took place on 9 March 1953 (v **Plymouth Argyle**).

St James' Park *ground* English football ground situated in Newcastle, Tyne & Wear; home of **Newcastle United**. *Dossier* Ground capacity: 36,843 all seated. Pitch dimensions: 105m x 68m. Record attendance: 68,386 v **Chelsea** (3 September 1930, Division One). Best average attendance: 56,283 (1947-48). *History* Built on the fringes of Town Moor, an expanse of land to which the Freemen of the City had been granted grazing rights in perpetuity since 1357. As a result, St James' Park's freehold is jointly owned by the City Council and the Freemen of the City, which over the years has, together with the inner-city location, made it difficult to develop and expand the ground. The name is derived from the nearby St James' Terrace. Newcastle Rangers first began using the site for football in 1880 and six years later, another local team, Newcastle West End, took over the lease. When West End folded in May 1892, its local rivals Newcastle East End moved in and played its first game at the ground on 3 September 1892 (v **Celtic**, friendly). In February 1893, East End changed its name to Newcastle United. Almost immediately, the club was confronted by the restrictions placed on the ground's development by the freeholders when it was forced to demolish a stand it had erected. After leasing a further four acres of land in 1899, the club was able to double the ground's capacity to 30,000 and reduce the pronounced slope of the pitch. Success on the pitch – the club won its first League Championship and appeared in its first **FA Cup** final in 1905 – enabled United to develop St James' Park at a cost of £12,000. This development involved the construction of a west stand that included a players' swimming pool, but faced considerable objections from local residents. Indeed, a proposal to cover the east terracing in 1930 was rejected by the council because of objections from residents of the adjacent Leazes Terrace – something that continued after World War II. In 1947-48, United's average gate was 56,299 (a League record until bettered by **Manchester United** in 1968-69), despite being in Division Two. St James' Park was initially selected as a venue for the 1996 **World Cup** on condition that the ground be given more seating. However, the failure of the club and the council to agree the building plans meant that the **Football Association** switched the North East's World Cup slot to **Middlesbrough**'s **Aryesome Park**. The continual feud between United and the City Council over the development of St James' Park led, in 1966, to the club investigating plans to move to nearby Gosforth, while the council made a proposal to turn the ground into a 63,000 capacity, multi-purpose stadium – neither plan was pursued. Three years later, Minister of Sport Denis Howell was asked to mediate between the two parties, whose relationship had deteriorated to the point where the club dropped the council's coat of arms from the players' shirts. In 1971, the club signed a 99-year lease for the ground and, at last, there was approval to build a new east stand as part of a plan to transform St James' Park into a 47,000 plus stadium with seated and terrace accommodation on all four sides. Relegation in 1977-78 put these plans on hold, and ten years later the council ordered the closure of the 80-year old west stand, which, in the aftermath of the **Bradford City fire**, was deemed a fire hazard. The financial difficulties that resulted from the £5.5 million cost of the replacement stand led to a four-year power-struggle for the club that eventually ended when Sir John Hall and his Magpie Group took control in 1992. Since then St James' Park has been transformed into a 36,843 all-seater stadium at a cost of £23.5 million. The constraints of the ground's inner-city location led the club to investigate the possibility of moving to a new venue across the River Tyne at Gateshead, but it eventually decided to increase St James' capacity to 51,000. The club deems it necessary to expand St James' Park because for League matches every seat at the ground, other than the 1,800 allocated to away supporters, belongs to a **season-ticket** holder; a further 12,000 people are on waiting list. St James' Park was used as a **European Championship** venue in 1996, hosting group B matches (**France** v **Romania**; **Bulgaria** v

Romania; Bulgaria v France). The ground has also staged four **England** internationals (v **Wales**, 18 March 1901, v **Scotland**, 6 April 1907, v Wales, 15 November 1933, v **Norway**, 9 November 1938) and two wartime internationals (v Scotland, 2 December 1939, v Scotland, 8 February 1941). The first floodlit match at St James' Park occurred on 25 February 1953 (v **Celtic**, friendly). The first floodlit FA Cup tie between two football League clubs took place at the ground on 28 November 1955 (**Carlisle United** v **Darlington**, 1st round replay).

St Johnstone *club* Scottish league. *Dossier* Ground: **McDiarmid Park**, Perth, Tayside. Strip: blue and white striped shirts, blue shorts with white pinstripes, blue socks with white hoops. Nickname: Saints. Ground capacity: 10,673 all seated. Record attendance: 10,504 v **Rangers** (20 October 1990, Premier Division). Biggest win: 9–0 v **Albion Rovers** (9 March 1946, **Scottish League Cup**). Biggest defeat: 1–10 v **Third Lanark** (24 January 1903, **Scottish FA Cup**). *History* Founded in 1884 by members of St Johnstone cricket club. From 1885 the club played at the Recreation Ground before opening Muirton Park on 25 December 1924 (v **Queen's Park**). The club moved to the new 10,600 capacity McDiarmid Park in August 1989. St Johnstone joined the **Scottish Football League** in 1912-13, winning promotion to the top flight as Division Two Champions in 1923-24. Third place in Division One, achieved in 1970-71, is the club's highest League position. The club has been a Scottish FA Cup semi-finalist on four occasions: 1934, 1968, 1989 and 1991. The Saints reached the Scottish League Cup final in 1969 (0–1 v **Celtic**), and, in 1971-72, it competed in Europe for the first, reaching the third round of the **UEFA Cup** (2–5 agg. v **Zeljeznicar Sarajevo**). The club was a **Scottish League Challenge Cup** finalist in 1996-97 (0–1 v **Stranraer**) and, in 1998-99, it again reached the final of the League Cup (1–2 v Rangers). *League record* Premier League 1998-99–; Premier Division 1975-76, 1983-84, 1990-91 to 1993-94, 1997-98; Division One 1924-25, 1929-30, 1932-33 to 1938-39, 1960-61 to 1961-62, 1963-64 to 1974-75; First Division 1976-77 to 1982-83, 1984-85, 1988-89 to 1989-90, 1994-95 to 1996-97; Division Two (B Division) 1912-13 to 1923-24, 1930-31 to 1931-32, 1946-47 to 1959-60, 1962-63; Second Division 1985-86 to 1987-88. *Honours* First Division 1982-83, 1989-90, 1996-97; Division Two 1923-24, 1959-60, 1962-63. *Records* George O'Boyle is St Johnstone's most capped player (10 for **Northern Ireland**); Drew Rutherford holds the record for club League appearances (298); John Brogan is St Johnstone's record League goalscorer (140, 1977-83).

St Joseph Warriors *club* Liberian national league club, based in the capital Monrovia. Strip: blue shirts and white shorts. **West African Cup** semi final 1984; Liberian National League champions 1976, 1978 and 1979.

St Kitts-Nevis (full title: St Christopher-Nevis) *country* CONCACAF island and Commonwealth state in the leeward Islands of the West Indies. Comprises two islands, St Christopher and Nevis. Area: 262 sq km (101 sq miles). Population: 43,350 (1995 est.). Languages: English. Capital: Basseterre, on St Christopher Island. *Dossier* St Kitts-Nevis Amateur Football Association (Basseterre) formed in 1932, affiliated to **FIFA** in 1992 and **Confederación Norte-Centroamericana y del Caribe de Fútbol** (CONCACAF) in 1992, president: Peter Jenkins; general secretary: Ian Liburd. National stadium: Warner Park, capacity: 8,000. National strip: green and yellow shirts, red shorts, yellow socks. *International tournament record* **World Cup** – first entered 1998, qualifying tournament first-round group stage; **Caribbean Nations Cup** – runners-up 1997 (0–4, v **Trinidad and Tobago**, in St Kitts), semi-final/fourth 1993 (2–3, v Trinidad and Tobago, in Jamaica, third/fourth playoff); **Gold Cup** – never qualified (lost in 1997 final-qualifying playoff against Cuba). *Record against British and Irish national teams* none played. Leading club: Suzuki Newtown United.

St Louis *club* Seychelles national league club based in the capital Victoria. *Keynotes* St Louis is the most successful side in the country: its eight league titles in eight years (1985 to 1992) is just one behind the African club record held by **Hafia FC** of **Guinea**. Seychelles League champions 1979, 1980, 1981, 1983, 1985, 1986, 1987, 1988, 1989, 1990, 1991, 1992, Seychelles Cup 1988, 1996.

St Lucia *country CONCACAF* Commonwealth country in the Windward Islands of the West Indies. Full independence from Britain 1979. Area: 617 sq km (238 sq miles). Population: 140,900 (1995 est.). Languages: English and French patois. Capital: Castries. *Dossier* St Lucia Football Association (Castries) formed in 1979, affiliated to **FIFA** and **Confederación Norte-Centroamericana y del Caribe de Fútbol** (CONCACAF) in 1988, president: Mark Louis; general secretary: Lyndon Cooper. National stadium: Mindo Philip Park, Castries, capacity: 5,000. National strip: blue and white shirts, black shorts, blue socks. Biggest victory: 9–0 v **Aruba** (1991, St Lucia, **Olympic Games** Central and North America regional qualifying tournament, preliminary round). *International tournament record* Olympic Games – never qualified for finals tournament; **World Cup** – first entered 1998, qualifying tournament first-round group stage; **Caribbean Nations Cup** – third place 1991 (4–1 v **Guyana**, in Jamaica, third/fourth playoff); **Gold Cup** – never qualified for finals tournament. *Record against British and Irish national teams* none played. Leading club: Mabauya Valley (league champions 1999).

St Mirren *club* Scottish league. *Dossier* Ground: **St Mirren Park**, Paisley, Strathclyde. Strip: black and white striped shirts, white shorts, white socks. Nickname: Buddies. Ground capacity: 15,410. Record attendance: 47,438 v **Celtic** (20 August 1949, **Scottish League Cup**). Biggest win: 15–0 v Glasgow University (30 January 1960, **Scottish FA Cup**, first round). Biggest defeat: 0–9 v **Rangers** (4 December 1897,

Division One). *History* Founded in 1877 by some Paisley cricketers and rugby players. The club's name is derived from the patron saint of Paisley. St Mirren was a founder member of the **Scottish Football League** in 1890-91, finishing third in 1892-93, a position equalled in 1979-80 and the club's highest League placing. Before being relegated from Division One in 1970-71, the club had spent only two seasons (1935-36, 1967-68) outside the top flight. St Mirren reached its first major final in 1908 when it contested the Scottish FA Cup at **Hampden Park** (1–5 v Celtic). The club won the trophy in 1926 (2–0 v Celtic), 1959 (3–1 v **Aberdeen**), 1987 (1–0 a.e.t. v **Dundee United**) and, aside from 1908, was a runner-up in 1934 (0–5 v Rangers) and 1962 (0–2 v Rangers). St Mirren was a Scottish League Cup finalist in 1955-56 (1–2 v Aberdeen). In 1980, St Mirren became the first (and only) Scottish winners of the **Anglo-Scottish Cup** (5–1 agg. v **Bristol City**). The club was a **Scottish League Challenge Cup** finalist in 1993-94 (0–3 **Falkirk**). The club has competed in European competition on four occasions (**UEFA Cup** 1908-81, 1983-84 and 1985-86; **European Cup-winners Cup** 1987-88), although it has never progressed further than the second round. *League record* Premier Division 1977-78 to 1991-92; Division One (A Division) 1893-94 to 1914-15, 1921-22 to 1934-35, 1936-37 to 1966-67, 1968-69 to 1970-71; First Division 1975-76 to 1976-77, 1992-93–; Scottish League 1890-91 to 1892-93, 1915-16 to 1920-21; Division Two 1935-36, 1967-68, 1971-72 to 1974-75. *Honours* First Division 1976-77; Division Two 1967-68; Scottish FA Cup 1926 (2–0 v Celtic), 1959 (3–1 v Aberdeen), 1987 (1–0 a.e.t. v Dundee United); Anglo-Scottish Cup 1980 (5–1 agg. v Bristol City). *Records* Godmundor Torfason is St Mirren's most capped player (29 for **Iceland**); Tony Fitzpatrick holds the record for club League appearances (351, 1973-88); David McCrae is St Mirren's record League goalscorer (221).

St Mirren Park *ground* Scottish football ground situated in Paisley, Strathclyde region; home of **St Mirren.** *Dossier* Ground capacity: 15,410. Pitch dimensions: 102m x 67m. Record attendance: 47,438 v **Celtic** (20 August 1949, **Scottish League Cup**). *Keynotes* St Mirren first played at St Mirren Park, originally called Love Street, in 1894. The club returned in 1905 and bought the freehold for £3,900. Greyhound racing and speedway have both been tried at St Mirren Park but without much success, although a greyhound named St Mirren won on the first occasion the dogs were staged. The first floodlit match at St Mirren Park took place on 13 February 1959 (v **Peebles**, Scottish FA Cup).

St Patrick's Athletic *club* Republic of Ireland national league club based in Dublin, founded 1929. Ground: Harold's Cross, capacity: 10,000. Strip: red shirts, white shorts. Republic of Ireland league champions 1952, 1955, 1956, 1990, 1996, 1998, 1999; Republic of Ireland **FAI Cup** 1959, 1961, runners-up 1954, 1967, 1974, 1980.

St Vincent and the Grenadines *country* CONCACAF islands and islets in the Lesser Antilles in the West Indies. A Commonwealth state. Area: 389 sq km (159 sq miles). Population: 109,000 (1994 est.). Language: English. Capital: Kingstown. *Dossier* St Vincent and the Grenadines Football Confederation (Kingstown) formed in 1979 affiliated to **FIFA** and **Confederación Norte-Centroamericana y del Caribe de Fútbol** (CONCACAF) in 1988, president: Louis Daisley; general secretary: Earl Bennett. National strip: green shirts with yellow border, blue shorts, yellow socks. Biggest defeat: 3–11, v **Honduras** (1997, away, **World Cup** qualifier). *International tournament record* **Women's World Cup** – had not entered before 1999; World Cup – qualifying tournament second round 1994 qualifying tournament second round group 1998; **Caribbean Nations Cup** – runners-up 1995 (0–5 v **Trinidad and Tobago**, in the Cayman Islands); **Gold Cup** – qualified 1996; **Under-17 World Championship** – never qualified; **World Youth Cup** (under-20) – never qualified. *Record against British and Irish national teams* none played. *Record in international club tournaments* **Caribbean Club Championship** – Chelsea FC (of Lowmans, quarter-final 1998; also, St Vincent League champions 1998). Other leading club: Stubborn Youth SC.

Saint Etienne (Association Sportive) *club* French national league club based in Saint Étienne, formed 1920. Ground: **Geoffroy-Guichard**, capacity: 35,924. Strip: green shirts, white shorts. **European Cup** runners-up 1976 (0–1, v **Bayern Munich**, **Hampden Park**, Glasgow); French League champions 1957, 1964, 1967, 1968, 1969, 1970, 1974, 1975, 1976, 1981; French Cup 1962, 1968, 1970, 1974, 1975, 1977. Notable former player: Michel **Platini**.

Saint-Denis (Club Sportif de Saint-Denis) *club* Réunion national league club based in the capital Saint-Denis, founded in 1969. Ground: Stade de l'Est (national stadium), capacity: 10,000. Strip: yellow shirts, green shorts. **CAF Cup** – semi-final 1994 (2–4 agg. v **Bendel Insurance** of Nigeria, the eventual winners); Réunion League champions 1980, 1984, 1987, 1995, 1996; Coupe de la Réunion winners 1974, 1975, 1977, 1978, 1979, 1985, 1986, 1988.

Saint-Louisienne (Societe Sportive Saint-Louisienne) *club* Réunion national league club based in Saint-Louis, founded in 1936. Ground: Theophile Hoareau, capacity: 2,500. Strip: green shirts, white shorts. Its eight consecutive league titles (1963 to 1970) is just one short of the African club record held by **Hafia FC** of **Guinea**. **African Cup-winners Cup** semi-final 1997; Réunion League champions 1958, 1963, 1964, 1965, 1966, 1967, 1968, 1969, 1970, 1982, 1988, 1997, 1998; Coupe de la Réunion winners 1964, 1968, 1969, 1970, 1981, 1987, 1995.

Saint-Pierroise (Jeuness Sportive Saint-Pierroise) *club* Réunion national league club based in Saint-Pierre, founded in 1950. Ground: Cayenne, capacity: 5,000. Strip: white shirts, black shorts. *Keynotes* The club has won the Réunion league championship more than any other, and is the only one to have won the domestic "triple" (league championship, Coupe de France and Coupe de la Réunion), in 1971 and 1989. **African Cup of Champion Clubs** – second round 1995; Réunion League champions 1956, 1957, 1959, 1960, 1961, 1971, 1972, 1973, 1975, 1976, 1978, 1989, 1990, 1993, 1994; Coupe de la Réunion winners 1959, 1962, 1971, 1980, 1984, 1989, 1992, 1994.

Salas, (José) Marcelo *player* Striker. **Chile** international (44 caps, 31 goals, 1994-). Born 24 December 1974. *Clubs* (include) **River Plate**, **Lazio**. *Keynotes* Salas scored both goals in River Plate's second-leg victory over **São Paulo** in the 1997 Supercopa final (2–0 agg.). He was sold by River Plate to Italian club Lazio in February 1998 for £12 million. He is Chile's all-time top international goalscorer. *Honours El Pais* **South American Footballer of the Year** 1997; **Supercopa** (River Plate, 1997); Argentinean league championship (River Plate, 1997 **apertura** and **clausura**).

Salenko, Oleg *player* **Russia** international. *Keynotes* Salenko was joint top scorer in the 1994 World Cup finals with six goals (the same as Hristo **Stoichkov**) He holds the record for the most goals (five) scored in a single World Cup finals match (6–1 v **Cameroon**, 28 June 1994, first-round group stage, in Detroit, USA). Salenko was one of several **Ukraine** nationals who elected to play for Russia when it was awarded the former **Soviet Union**'s place in the 1994 World Cup qualifiers. He subsequently remained with the Russian team. *Honours* World Cup **Golden Boot** 1994.

Salgaocar *club* Indian club based in Goa. Ground: Nehru Stadium, capacity: 25,000. Indian National League champions 1999; Confederation Cup 1988, 1989, 1998; Indian Super Cup 1998.

Sammer, Matthias *player* Defender. **East Germany** (23 caps, six goals, 1988-90) and **Germany** international (51 caps, eight goals, 1990-). Born 5 September 1967. *Clubs* **Dynamo Dresden**, **Stuttgart (VfB)**, **Internazionale**, **Borussia Dortmund**. *Keynotes* Sammer and Andreas Thom were the first former East Germans to play for the unified Germany in 1990 and, in 1996, he became the first player from East Germany to be voted European Footballer of the Year. Both Sammer and Thom played in the 1992 **European Championship** final (0–2, v **Denmark**, in Gothenburg). Sammer played in the 1996 final when Germany beat the **Czech Republic** 2–0, at **Wembley** Stadium. Sammer, an attacking sweeper, was transferred to Internazionale at the start of the 1992-93 season, but returned to Germany, with Borussia Dortmund, after only 11 appearances for Inter. He captained Borussia Dortmund to the 1997 European Cup victory over **Juventus** (3–1, in Munich). A knee injury kept him out of the 1998 **World Cup** finals. Sammer scored both East Germany's goals in the last match ever played by the former country (2–0 **Belgium**, friendly, Brussels). *Honours* **European Cup** (Borussia Dortmund, 1997); (East German League championship (Dynamo Dresden, 1989, 1990); German **Bundesliga** championship (VfB Stuttgart, 1992, Borussia Dortmund, 1995, 1996); *France Football* European Footballer of the Year 1996.

Samoa *country OFC* see **Western Somoa.**

Sampdoria *club* Italian league. *Dossier* Ground: **Luigi Ferraris**, Genoa, Liguira. Strip: blue shirts with black, red and white hoops, white shorts, blue and white hooped socks. Website: *http://www.sampdoria.it/* Nickname: Bluerchiati (Blue and hoops). Ground capacity: 42,000 all seated. Record win: 7–0 v Pro Patria (**Serie A** 1955-56). Record defeat: 1–7 v **Internazionale** (Serie A 1955-56); v Udinese (Serie A 1960-61). *History* Formed in 1946 from the merger of Andrea Doria and Sampierdarenese. The club's full name is Sampdoria Unione Calcio. Andrea Doria and Sampierdarenese had merged in 1927 to form Dominante (later called Liguria after the region in which Genoa is situated) but had separated immediately after **World War II**. Sampdoria's strip is a mixture of Andrea Doria's red and black colours and Sampierdarenese's blue and white colours. The club won its first major trophy, the Italian Cup (**Coppa Italia**), in 1985 (3–1 agg. v **AC Milan**) with a team including Trevor **Francis**, Roberto Mancini, Graeme **Souness**, Pietro Vierchowod and Gianluca **Vialli**. Sampdoria reached the **European Cup-winners Cup** final in both 1989 and 1990, losing on the first occasion (0–2 v **Barcelona**) and lifting the trophy the following year with two extra time goals from Vialli (2–0 a.e.t. v **RSC Anderlecht**). The next season, Sampdoria won its first Italian League title and, in 1992, it reached the **European Cup** final (0–1 a.e.t. v Barcelona). In December 1998, former **England** international David Platt was appointed manager, although his assistant Giorgio Veneri was temporarily in charge of first-team affairs until Platt received his coaching licence. Platt's reign lasted for only a few games. *Honours* Italian League 1990-91; Italian Cup 1985 (3–1 agg. v AC Milan), 1988 (3–2 agg. v **Torino**), 1989 (4–1 agg. v **Napoli**), 1994 (6–1 agg. v Ancona); European Cup-winners Cup 1990 (2–0 v RSC Anderlecht).

Samsung *club* see **Suwon Samsung Bluewings**.

sandwich *vb.* illegal challenge executed by two players simultaneously charging into an opponent.

San Jose Clash *club* United States football club and founder member of **Major League Soccer**, based in San Jose, California. Member of the league's **Western Conference**. Founded: 1996. Ground: Spartan Stadium, capacity: 30,010.

San José *club* Bolivian national league club based in Oruro, founded 1949. Ground: Estadio "Monumental" Jesus Bermudez, capacity: 40,000. Strip: white shirts with a sky blue V, sky blue shorts. Bolivian national league champions 1995.

San Lorenzo de Almagro (Club Atlético) *club* Argentinean national league club, based in Almagro, Buenos Aires, founded 1908. The club is named after one its founders, Lorenzo Massa, a local priest. Ground: Estadio. Pedro Bidegain "El Gasometro", capacity:

39,000. Strip: red and blue striped shirts, white shorts. San Lorenzo qualified for the first **Copa Libertadores** in 1960. Copa Libertadores semi-final 1960, 1988; **Copa CONMEBOL** semi-final 1993; **Copa Mercosur** semi-final 1998; Argentinean League champions 1923, 1924 (two leagues operated prior to 1927), 1927, 1933, 1946, 1959, 1968, 1972, 1995 (**clausura**); Argentinean National Championship (a pre-national-league tournament operating from 1967 to 1985) winners 1972, 1974. Notable player: Oscar **Ruggeri**.

San Mamés *ground* Spanish football ground situated in Bilbao, Basque region; home of **Athletic Bilbao**. Ground capacity: 46,223. *History* Built in 1913 and immediately referred to as La Catedral (The Cathedral). In keeping with the club's English origins, the ground was laid with English turf. It staged Spain's first full home international in 1921 (v **Belgium**, 9 October, 2-0, friendly). The stadium was substantially redeveloped in the 1950s and was refurbished for the 1982 **World Cup**. San Mamés became a all-seater stadium in 1997. During the 1982 World Cup, San Mamés staged three group 4 matches (**England** v **France**, England v **Czechoslovakia**, England v **Kuwait**) – total attendance 119,354; average attendance 39,784.

San Marino *country UEFA* indepenent republic and enclave within northern **Italy**, south of Rimini. Independent since 1862. Area: 61 sq km (24 sq miles). Population: 24,000 (1993 census). Languages: Italian. Capital: San Marino. *Dossier* Football association (Federazione Sammarinese Giuoco Calcio, San Marino) formed in 1931 affiliated to **FIFA** and **Union of European Football Associations** (UEFA) in 1988, president: Giorgio Crescentini; general secretary: Luciano Casadei. League season played from the end of September to May with a **winter break** in January: the Cup final is played in July. National stadium: Olimpico, Serravalle, capacity: 7,000. National strip: light blue shirts, light blue shorts, light blue socks. First international game: 14 November 1990 v **Switzerland** (0–4, in San Marino, **European Championship** qualifier). Biggest victory: none to date. Biggest defeat: 0–10 v **Norway** (9 September 1992, Oslo, **World Cup** qualifier). Most capped players: William Guerra (34 appearances, 1990-97). Other notable international players: Massimo Bonini (former **Juventus** midfelder, appointed San Marino national coach in 1996), Davide **Gualtier**, Waldes Pasolini (scorer of San Marino's first ever international goal: v **Romania**, 27 March 1991, in Serraville, European Championship). *International tournament record* **Olympic Games** – first entered 1992 (last in its qualifying group), never qualified for finals tournament; **Women's World Cup** – never entered; World Cup – first entered 1994, last in its qualifying group 1994 and 1998 (in 1998, played eight, lost eight, conceded 42 goals, scored none); European Championship – first entered 1992, last in its qualifying group 1992 and 1996 (in 1996, it played 10, lost 10, scored two, conceded 36). *World Cup performance* (finals and qualifiers to end of 1998 tournament) played

20, won 2, drawn 1, lost 17, scored 12 goals, conceded 77 goals; win rate 10%; goals scored per game 0.60. *Record against British and Irish national teams* v England, played two, lost two; v **Northern Ireland**, none played; v **Scotland**, played four, lost four; v **Wales**, played two, lost two; v **Republic of Ireland**, none played. *History* San Marino has had a football association since 1931, though it did not join UEFA and FIFA until 1988. San Marino played in the 1992 European Championships and earned its first point in an international tournament on 10 March 1993 (0–0, v **Turkey**, in Serravalle, World Cup qualifier). San Marino holds the record for the fastest goal ever scored in a World Cup match and the fastest goal against England – Davide Gualtieri scored after nine seconds (1–7 v **England**, 17 November 1993, Bologna – technically a home match for San Marino – World Cup qualifier). The away fixture in the same competition (17 February, 0–6, v England, **Wembley** Stadium, World Cup qualifier) was also notable because England goalkeeper Chris Woods did not make a single save and touched the ball only six times. San Marino's national league was restructured in 1996-97. *League system* The national first division has 16 clubs divided into two groups of eight. Each club plays every other club in its group at home and away. Each club also plays one match against each team in the other group (22 games in total). Three points are awarded for a victory, with one for a draw: final positions for clubs level on points are determined by **goal difference**. At the end of the initial series, the top three clubs in each group qualify for an end-of-season playoff tournament, comprising a series of eliminators, a knockout semi-final and final. These matches can all go to **extra time** or **penalties** if scores are level at the end of normal time. *Record in international club tournaments* never entered. Leading clubs: **Domagnano**, **Faetano**, **Folgore**, **La Fiorita**, **Libertas**, **Tre Fiori**.

San Paolo (Stadio) *ground* Italian football ground situated in Naples, Campania; home of **Napoli** and regular Italian international venue. Ground capacity: 72,000 all seated. *History* Built in 1959 in an area to the west of the city known as Campi Flegrei. Named after St Paul, the stadium set a then Italian record for **season ticket** sales (70,000) in the mid-1980s with the arrival of Diego **Maradona**. San Paolo has been closed by the authorities more times because of crowd problems than any other Italian club stadium. The ground was extensively redeveloped in the 1980s and underwent more refurbishment for the 1990 **World Cup**. During the tournament, San Paolo staged two group B matches (**Argentina** v **Soviet Union**, Argentina v **Romania**), a second-round fixture (**Cameroon** v **Colombia**), a quarter-final tie (**England** v Cameroon) and a semi-final (Argentina v **Italy**) – total attendance 273,701; average attendance 54,740.

San Siro (Stadio Giuseppe Meazza) *ground* Italian football ground situated in Milan, Lombardy; home of **AC Milan** and **Internazionale**. Ground capacity: 85,500 all seated. *History* First opened in September

1926 as the 35,000 capacity home of AC Milan (v Internazionale). The stadium was originally called Calcistico San Siro after the west Milanese suburb in which it is situated. Bought by the local council before World War II, the stadium was refurbished after hostilities ceased and Inter left its own stadium, Arena, to share the revamped 82,000 capacity ground in 1955. San Siro was renamed Stadio Giuseppe **Meazza** in 1979 in honour of the Italian international striker who played in the country's 1934 and 1938 **World Cup** triumphs and for both Milan clubs. The stadium was redeveloped for the 1990 World Cup at a cost of £50 million. This included the construction of a third tier and a plexiglass roof. As San Siro, the stadium staged three matches during the 1934 World Cup (**Switzerland** v **Netherlands**, round 1; **Germany** v **Sweden**, quarterfinal; **Italy** v **Austria**, semi-final) – total attendance 96,000; average attendance 32,000. During the 1990 World Cup, Stadio Giuseppe Meazza was the venue for three group D fixtures (**West Germany** v **Yugoslavia**, West Germany v **United Arab Emirates**, **Colombia** v West Germany), one second-round match (West Germany v Netherlands) and a quarter-final (West Germany v Czechoslovakia) – total attendance 366,348; average attendance 73,269. It has also hosted two **European Cup** finals (1965 Internazionale v **Benfica**, 80,000; 1970 **Feyenoord** v **Celtic**, 50,000).

Sanchez, Hugo   *player*   Striker. **Mexico** international (57 caps, 26 goals, 1977-1998). Born 11 June 1958. *Clubs* **UNAM**, **Real Madrid**, **América**, Rayo Vallecano (Spain). *Keynotes* Mexican league top scorer 1979 (26 goals) and top scorer in the Spanish Primera division five seasons in succession. Voted eighth in the 1987 *World Soccer* **World Footballer of the Year** award; the first Mexican to appear in the annual top 10. Captained Mexico's 1986 **World Cup** team. Sanchez scored Real Madrid's first goal in the 1986 UEFA Cup final (6–3 agg., v **Cologne** (1.FC)). *Honours* **CONCACAF Champions Cup** (UNAM, 1980, 1982); **UEFA Cup** (Real Madrid, 1986); Mexican League championship (UNAM, 1977, 1981); Spanish League championship (Real Madrid, 1986, 1987, 1988, 1989, 1990); **European Golden Boot** 1990 (38 league goals for Real Madrid; award shared with Hristo **Stoichkov**).

Sanfrecce Hiroshima FC   *club*   Japanese **J-League** club based in Hiroshima, formerly Toyo Kogyo (1938–81) and Mazda FC (1981–92). Ground: Hiroshima Big Arch, capacity: 50,000. Strip: purple shirts and white shorts. **Asian Champion Teams Cup** semi final/third 1968 (as Toyo Kogyo – 2–0, v Mysore State of India); Japanese national league champions 1965, 1966, 1967, 1968, 1970; Emperor's Cup 1966, 1968, 1970.

Santa Catarina   *state*   one of the 27 state leagues in **Brazil**, founded 1924. Leading clubs: Avai FC (Avai), Figueirense FC (Florianopolis), Joinville Esporte Clube (Joinville), Criciuma Esporte Clube (Criciuma).

Santiago Wanderers   *club*   Chilean national league club based in Valparaiso, founded 1892. Ground:

Estadio Playa Ancha, capacity: 18,500. Strip: green shirts, green shorts. Chilean League champions 1958, 1968; Chilean Cup (**Copa Chile**) winners 1959, 1961.

Santos *club* Jamaica league club based in the capital Kingston. Strip: green and yellow striped shirts, white shorts. Jamaica league champions 1974, 1975, 1976, 1977, 1980.

Santos Djalma *player* Defender. **Brazil** international (100 caps, three goals, 1952-68). *Born* 27 February 1929. Clubs **Portuguesa**, **Palmeiras**, Clube Atlético Paranaense. *Honours* **World Cup** (Brazil, 1958, 1962); **Copa America** runner-up (Brazil, 1953, 1957, 1959). *Keynotes.* Santos is Brazil's all-time most-capped player and appeared in four World Cup finals tournaments (1954, 1958, 1962 and 1966), gaining two winner's medals. He scored the first of only three international goals in the 1954 World Cup quarter-final (2–4, v **Hungary**, in Berne). He gained a **Copa Libertadores** runner-up medal with Palmeiras in 1961 (1–2 agg., v **Peñarol**).

Santos FC Futebol Clube *club* Brazilian national league and **São Paulo** state league club based in Santos, founded 1912. Ground: Urbano Caldeira "Vila Belmiro", capacity: 25,000. Strip: white shirts (or black and white stripes), white shorts. **Copa Libertadores** winners 1962 (2–1, 2–3, 3–0 playoff in Buenos Aires, v **Peñarol**), 1963 (3–2, 2–1, v **Boca Juniors**), semi-final 1964, 1965; **Supercopa** semi-final 1996; **World Club Cup** 1962 (3–2, 5–2, v **Benfica**), 1963 (2–4, 4–2, 1–0 playoff in **Maracana** Stadium, Rio de Janeiro, v **AC Milan**: 351,000 watched the three-match final, including 150,000 for the second leg at Maracana); **Campeonato Brasileiro** runners-up 1983; São Paulo Tournament winners 1959, 1963, 1964; Roberto Gomez Pedrosa Tournament winners 1968; **Copa do Brasil** winners 1961, 1962, 1963, 1964, 1965 (a tournament record of five consecutive trophies); state league champions 15 times (to 1998). Notable former player: **Pelé**.

Santos, Nilton *player* Defender. **Brazil** international (83 caps, 1949-63). Born 16 May 1927. Career ca. 1948-63. *Clubs* **Flecheiras**, **Botafogo**. *Keynotes* Santos was a forerunner of the modern **wing-back**. Sent off for fighting with **Hungary**'s captain Jozsef **Boszik**, in the notorious **Battle of Berne** at the 1954 **World Cup** finals. He scored in Brazil's 3-0 over **Austria** in the 1958 World Cup (first round, in Uddevalla, **Sweden**), on the way to his country's triumph in the final. *Honours* World Cup (Brazil, 1958, 1962); **Copa America** (Brazil 1949); São Paulo Tournament (the inter-state championship and forerunner of the Brazilian national championship) (Botafogo, 1962); Rio state championship 1948, 1957, 1961, 1962.

São Paulo *state* one of the 27 state leagues in **Brazil**, founded 1901 (the oldest league in Brazil). Leading clubs: **Palmeiras** (formerly Palestra Italia),**Santos**, Sao Paulo FC, **Corinthians**, **Portuguesa**.

Sao Tomé and Príncipe *country CAF* island republic very close to the equator in the Gulf of Guinea,

200 km (125 miles) off the coast of **Gabon**, West Africa. Comprises the islands of Príncipe and Sao Tomé, and several small islands. Independence from Portugal in 1975. Area: 964 sq km (372 sq miles). Population: 131,000 (1995 est.). Capital: Sao Tomé. Languages: Fang (Bantu) and Portuguese (the official language). *Dossier* Football association (Federação Santomense de Futebol, (Sao Tomé) formed in 1975, affiliated to **FIFA** and **Confédération Africaine de Football** (CAF) in 1986 president: Manuel Dende; general secretary: Ricardino Barros. Season played from April to March. National stadium: Estadio 12 de Julho, Sao Tomé, capacity: 5,000. National strip: green and yellow shirts, green and yellow shirts shorts, green and yellow shirts socks. First international game: 29 June 1976 v **Chad** (0–5, neutral venue, Central African Games). Biggest defeat: 0–11 v **Congo** (7 July 1976, neutral venue, Central African Games). *International tournament record* **Olympic Games** – never entered; **World Cup** – never entered; **African Nations Cup** – never entered. *Record against British and Irish national teams* none played. *History* National league championship began in 1977; first won by **Vitória Riboque**. *Record in international club tournaments* none. Leading clubs Vitoria Riboque, **Desportivo Guadeloupe**, **OS Operacios**, **Praia Cruz**.

São Paulo FC *club* Brazilian national league and **São Paulo** state league club based in São Paulo, founded 1930. Ground: Cicero Pompeu de Toledo, capacity: 88,000. Strip: white shirts with one red and one white hoop, white shorts. **Copa Libertadores** winners 1992 (1–1 agg., 3–2 pens., v **Newell's Old Boys**), 1993 (5–3 agg., v **Universidad Catolica** of Chile), runners-up 1974 (2–1, 0–2, 1–0 playoff in Santiago, Chile, v **Independiente**), 1994 (1–1 agg., 3–5 pens., v **Velez Sarsfield**); **Copa CONMEBOL** winners 1994 (6–4 agg., v **Peñarol**); **Supacopa** winners 1993 (4–4 agg., 5–3 pens., v **Flamengo**), semi-final 1994; **World Club Cup** 1992 (2–1 v **Barcelona**, Tokyo), 1993 (3–2, v **AC Milan**, Tokyo); **Recopa** winners 1992 (0–0 agg., 4–2 pens., v **Cruzeiro**), 1993 (3–1, v **Botafogo**, in Kobe, Japan); **Master de la Copa CONMEBOL** winners 1996 São Paulo(3–0, v **Atlético Mineiro**); **Campeonato Brasileiro** champions 1977, 1986, 1991; state league champions 19 times (to 1998). Notable former players: Cafú, Careca, **Denilson**, Junior, Juninho, Mirandinha, Rai.

Saprissa *club* see **Deportivo Saprissa**.

Sárosi, György *player* Striker/midfield. **Hungary** international (75 caps, 42 goals, 1931-40). Born 12 September 1912, in Budapest, died 1993. *Clubs* **Ferencváros**. *Keynotes* Sárosi was an all-round sportsman, excelling in swimming, tennis and fencing as well as football. He scored 349 goals for his club, in only 383 games. He scored a 65th-minute opportunist goal for Hungary in the 1938 **World Cup** final against Italy to bring the score to 2-3; but it was not enough to stop **Italy** from retaining the championship (2-4, in Paris). He scored four goals in the tournament, making him joint-third top scorer in the 1938 World Cup finals. He is fifth in Hungary's all-time list of goalscorers. Sárosi later moved to Italy where he coached Padova, Lucchese, Bari, Juventus, **Genoa**, **Roma**, Bologna and Brescia, and Lugano in Switzerland. *Honours* World Cup runner-up (Hungary, 1938, as captain); Hungarian championship (Ferencváros, 1932, 1934, 1938, 1940, 1941); **Mitropa Cup** (Ferencváros, 1937); **Serie A** championship as manager (**Juventus**, 1952).

Sarrià Estadia *ground* former Spanish football ground situated in **Barcelona**; former-home of **Espanyol** (RCD). Capacity (1997): 41,000. Espanyol sold the ground due to financial difficulties and moved to the Estadia Olimpic (Montjuic) at the start of the 1997-98 **Primera Liga** campaign. The ground, which opened in 1923, was demolished on 20 September 1997. Sarrià hosted one of the most memorable **World Cup** matches when **Italy** defeated **Brazil** 3–2 in the second round (group C) of the 1982 finals. During the tournament, Sarrià also staged two other group C second round matches (Italy v **Argentina**, Brazil v Argentina) – total attendance 127,000; average attendance 42,333. The stadium also hosted the 1964 **UEFA** (Fairs) **Cup** final (**Real Zaragoza** v **Valencia**, 50,000), which was played as a one-off match.

satellite centre of excellence/football academy *regulations* **UK**. A **centre of excellence** or **football academy** run by a **football club** that is not based at its main facility. Each club is allowed one main centre or academy and one satellite facility. Satellite facilities are open only to players in the under-nine to under-16 age groups.

Saudi Arabia *country AFC* kingdom on the Arabian Peninsula, bordered by **Iraq**, **Jordan**, **Kuwait**, **Oman**, **Qatar**, **United Arab Emirates** and **Yemen**. Area: 2,400,900 sq km (926,745 sq miles). Population: 16,900,000 (1992 est.). The majority of the land area is desert. It has a quarter of the world's known oil reserves. Language: Arabic. Capital: Riyadh (Ar Riyad). *Dossier* Saudi Arabian Football Confederation (Riyadh) formed in 1959 affiliated to **FIFA** in 1959 and **Asian Football Confederation** (AFC) in 1972, president: Bin Abdulaziz Faisal Bin Fahad; general secretary: Bin Daham Abd Rahman Abd. Season played from November to May. National stadium: King Fahd Stadium, Riyadh, capacity: 70,000. National strip: white shirts, green shorts, white socks. Best victory: 1–0, v **Belgium** (29 June 1994, in Washington, USA, **World Cup** first round). *International tournament record* **Olympic Games** – qualified for finals tournament 1984, 1996; **Women's World Cup** – never entered; World Cup – first entered 1978, second round of finals tournament 1994, also qualified for finals tournament 1998; **Afro-Asian Nations Cup** – runners-up 1985 (the first tournament, 3–5 agg., v **Cameroon**); **Arab Cup of Nations** – winners 1998 (3–1, v Qatar, in Doha, Qatar), runners-up 1992 (2–3, v Egypt, in Syria); **Arabian Gulf Cup** – winners 1994; **Asian Cup of Nations** – winners 1984 (2–0 v **China**, Singapore),

1988 (0–0, 4–3 pens., v **South Korea**, Doha, Qatar), 1996 (0–0, 4–2 pens., v United Arab Emirates, in the UAE), runners-up 1992 (0–1 v **Japan**, Hiroshima, Japan); **Asian Games** – runners-up 1986 (0–2 v South Korea, Seoul), semi-final 1982, quarter-final 1990, 1994, hosts 1992, 1995, 1998; **Asian Under-16 Championship** winners 1984, 1988; **Asian Women's Championship** – never entered; **Asian Youth Cup** (under-19) winners 1986, 1992; **Confederations Cup** – runners-up 1992 (1–3 v **Argentina**, Riyadh); **Under-17 World Championship** – winners 1989 (2–2, 5–4 pens., v **Scotland**, **Hampden Park**, Glasgow); **World Youth Cup** (under-20) – qualified 1985, 1987, 1989, 1993, 1999. *World Cup performance* (finals and qualifiers to end of 1998 tournament) played 57, won 26, drawn 14, lost 17, scored 84 goals, conceded 60 goals; win rate: 46%; goals scored per game: 1.47. *Record against British and Irish national teams* v **England**, played two, drawn two; v **Scotland**, played one, drawn one; v **Wales**, played one, drawn one. Most capped players: Majed **Abdullah** (142 appearances, 1978-95: the World's second-most capped player); Mohammed Al-Deyea (100 appearances). Leading goalscorers: Youssef Al-Thyniyan (45 goals, from 88 appearances). Other notable international players: Saeed al-**Owairan**, Sami al-Jaber (scored the goal in Saudi's 1–0 defeat of Qatar, which clinched qualification for the 1998 World Cup finals; had achieved 88 caps and 23 goals by the age of 25). *History* National cup competition started in 1958, league championship began in 1975 (first won by **Al Nasr**). Saudi Arabian clubs have won the **Asian Champion Teams' Cup**, the **Asian Cup-winners Cup**, the **Asian Super Cup**, the **Arab Club Champions Cup** and the **Arab Cup-winners Cup**. Leading club **Al Hilal** has one all three Asian club cups and the Arab Club Champions Cup. Saudi Arabia is the most successful nation in the Asian Cup of Nations, with three championships and one runners-up; a record marginally better than that of **Iran** (which has also won the championship three times, but has played in only three finals). It has never won the Asian Games (runner-up 1986), but has qualified twice for both the World Cup finals and for the Olympic Games football tournament finals. At youth level, Saudi Arabia is one of only six nations to have won the Under-17 World Championship, and is, thus, the only Asian nation to have won a FIFA world tournament (men). Its 1989 victory was against the host nation Scotland, at Hampden Park, and was settled on penalties after a 2–2 draw (Al-Reshoudie and Al-Terair scored for Saudi Arabia). Saudi Arabia hosted and sponsored the Confederations Cup between 1992 and 1997. *League system* Twelve clubs compete in the national first division. The top four enter a knockout championship play off. The bottom club is relegated, while the 10th and 11th placed clubs enter a relegation playoff. *Record in international club tournaments* Asian Champion Teams' Cup – Al Hilal (winners 1991, runners-up 1986, 1987, semi-final/third 1998), **Al Ahly** (runners-up 1985), **Al Shabab** (runners-up 1992), **Al Ittifaq** (winners 1999, semi-final 1988), Al Nasr (runners-up 1996, quarter-final 1997); **Asian Cup-winners Cup** – **Al Qadisiyah** (winners 1993), Al Hilal (winners 1996, semi-final 1990), Al Nasr (winners 1998, runners-up 1991), **Al Ittihad** (winners 1999 semi-final 1992, 1994), Al Riyadh (semi-final 1996); **Asian Super Cup** – Al Hilal (winners 1997); **Arab Club Champions Cup** – Al Ittifaq (winners 1984), Al Shabab (winners 1993, runners-up 1998), Al Hilal (winners 1995, runners-up 1992); **Arab Cup-winners Cup** – Al Qadsia (runners-up 1993), Al Shabab (runners-up 1994, 1997); **Arab Super Cup** – Al Shabab (winners 1995).

save *vb.* (by a **goalkeeper**) to prevent the ball from entering the goal; a goalkeeper may use any part of his/her body provided that the ball is not handled outside the penalty area or that a foul is not committed. *n.* the execution of this.

Savicevic, Dejan *player* Midfield. **former-Yugoslavia** and **Yugoslavia** international. Born 15 September 1966 (51 caps, 19 goals, 1986-). *Clubs* **Red Star Belgrade, AC Milan.** *Keynotes* Savicevic was the last player to score for former Yugoslavia (13 November 1991, 2–0, v **Austria**, in Vienna, **European Championship** qualifier). Transferred to AC Milan from Red Star Belgrade in 1992 for £4 million. Scored with a volley from the edge of the penalty area for Milan in the 1994 **European Cup** final (4–0, v **Barcelona**); his second European Cup medal. *Honours* European Cup (Red Star Belgrade, 1991, AC Milan 1994); Yugoslavian League championship (Red Star Belgrade, 1988, 1990, 1991, 1992); Italian **Serie A** championship (AC Milan, 1993, 1994, 1996); *France Football* **European Footballer of the Year** runner-up 1991.

SC Bastia (Sporting Club Bastia) *club* French national league club based in Bastia, formed 1962. Ground: Amand-Cesari-Furiani, capacity: 10,000. Strip: blue and white striped shirts, white shorts. **UEFA Cup** runners-up 1978 (0–3 agg., v **PSV Eindhoven**); French Cup 1981.

SCAF Tocages (Stade Central Africaine) *club* Central African Republic national league club based in the capital Bangui. Ground: Centrafricaine, capacity: 2,000. Strip: green shirts, red shorts. **African Cup of Champion Clubs** second round 1985; Central African Republic league champions 1977, 1985, 1989; Central African Republic Cup 1984.

Scandinavian Championship *competition* former international nations tournament, played over four years, contested by the Scandinavian countries. The tournament was staged from 1924 to 1971. Each country played the other three countries once a year and the tournament consisted of each nation playing each other twice at home and twice away. **Denmark** (winners 1928), **Finland** (winners 1963), **Norway** (winners 1932); and **Sweden** (winners 1936, 1947, 1951, 1955, 1959, 1967, 1971).

Scarborough *club* English league. *Dossier* Ground: **McCain Stadium**, Scarborough, north Yorkshire. Strip: red shirts with thin white stripes, white shorts with red trim, and red socks. Nickname: Boro. Ground capacity: 6,899. Record League attendance: 7,314 v **Wolverhampton Wanderers** (15 August 1987, Division Three). Best average attendance: 2,962 (1988-89). Biggest win: 6–0 v **Rhyl** Athletic (29 November 1930, **FA Cup**, first round). Biggest defeat: 1–7 v **Wigan Athletic** (11 March 1997, Third Division). *History* Founded in 1879 as Scarborough Cricketers FC and becoming plain Scarborough in 1887. The club played at several venues, including the Recreation Ground, before settling in 1898 at the Athletic Ground (or Seamer Road), which in 1988 became McCain Stadium after the club sold the name rights to a frozen food company. Scarborough won the **FA Challenge Trophy** three times in five seasons in 1973 (2–1 v Wigan Athletic), 1976 (3–2 a.e.t. v Stafford Rangers) and 1977 (2–1 v Dagenham). In 1986-87, Scarborough became the first non-League club to gain automatic entry to the Football League when, as **Football Conference** Champions, it replaced **Lincoln City** in Division Four. Scarborough was a Division Four end-of-season **playoff** semi-finalist in 1988-89 and in 1992-93, the club reached the last 16 of the **League Cup** (0–1 v **Arsenal**), having enjoyed a memorable two-legged victory over **Coventry City** (3–2 agg.) in the second round. A further famous League Cup giantkilling act occurred in 1989-90, when Scarborough defeated **Chelsea** over two legs (3–2 agg., second round). The club's 5th place in Division Four in 1988-89 is its highest League position. Scarborough lost its Football League status in dramatic fashion on the last day of the 1998-99 season. Scarborough needed to equal or better the result of relegation rivals **Carlisle United**. It secured a 1-1 draw at home to **Peterborough United**, but Carlisle scored a winning goal in the fifth minute of injury time in its game against **Plymouth Argyle** (2-1). The Yorkshire club was relegated to the Football Conference. *League record* Third Division 1992-93 to present; Division Four 1987-88 to 1991-92. *Honours* Football Conference 1986-87. FA Challenge Trophy 1973 (2–1 v Wigan Athletic), 1976 (3–2 a.e.t. v Stafford Rangers), 1977 (2–1 v Dagenham). *Records* Ian Ironside holds the record for club League appearances (183, 1988-91, 1992, 1994-97); Darren Foreman is Scarborough's record League goalscorer (35, 1991-95).

scarf *misc.* long, narrow piece of fabric usually worn around the neck by supporters as a visible illustration of support for their team. *Keynotes* Football scarves are traditionally made of wool and reflect team colours. In the 1970s, printed silk scarves were popular, while the recent return to woollen scarves has been accompanied by a greater diversity of design. Although scarves are generally worn around the neck, they are also tied around the wrist or waist or attached to belts and left to dangle. Scarves are sometimes twirled around the head or held aloft. Such actions provide an exciting and colourful spectacle when a large group of supporters engage in the same demonstration. Fans in **Liverpool**'s **Kop**, for example, are renowned for holding scarves aloft during the rendition of the football anthem, *You'll never walk alone*.

Scarone, Hector *player* Striker. **Uruguay** international (29 goals, 1917-30). Born 21 June 1898. *Clubs* Sportsman (Uruguay), **Nacional** (twice), **Barcelona**, **Internazionale**, Palermo. *Keynotes* Uruguay's record goalscorer and joint top scorer in the 1926 and 1927 **Copa America** tournaments (six and three goals, respectively). He retired aged 55 years. *Honours* **World Cup** (Uruguay, 1930 – the first tournament); **Olympic Games** gold medal (Uruguay, 1924, 1928); Copa America (Uruguay, 1917, 1920, 1923, 1924, 1926; runner-up 1919, 1927).

Schalke (04) *club* German league. *Dossier* Ground: Parkstadion, Essen. Strip: blue shirts with thin white stripes down one side, white shorts, blue socks. Ground capacity: 70,600. *History* Formed in 1904 and officially called FC Schalke 04 Gelsenkirchen after the town close to Dortmund. Schalke's best period occurred before and during **World War II**, when it won six German Championships, including consecutive titles in both 1934-35 and 1939-40, and one domestic cup. Aside from winning six titles between 1933 and 1942, the club also appeared in three further national **playoff** finals: 1933 (0–3 v Fortuna Düsseldorf), 1938 (3–4 replay v Hannover 96), 1941 (3–4 v **Rapid Vienna**). It was also a German Cup finalist on four occasions: 1935 (0–2 v **Nuremberg** (1.FC)), 1936 (1–2 v VfB Leipzeig), 1941 (1–2 v Dresdner SC) and 1942 (1–2 v Dresdner SC). On the domestic front, Schalke has won only one West German title and one West German Cup since the war. In 1997, Schalke, in its first European club competition for 19 years, lifted the **UEFA Cup**, defeating **Internazionale** on penalties. Schalke was the club supported by the U-boat crew in the highly acclaimed television series, Das Boot. *Honours* German League 1934 (2–1 v Nuremberg (1.FC)), 1935 (6–4 v **Stuttgart** (VfB)), 1937 (2–0 v Nuremberg (1.FC)), 1939 (9–0 v Admira Vienna), 1940 (1–0 v Dresdner SC), 1942 (2–0 v First Vienna FC); West German League 1958 (3–0 v **Hamburg SV**); German Cup 1937 (2–1 v Fortuna Düsseldorf); West German Cup 1971-72 (5–0 v **Kaiserslautern** (1.FC)); UEFA Cup 1997 (1–1, 4–1 pens. v Internazionale).

Schiaffino, Juan *player* Striker. **Uruguay** international (12 goals, 1945-54; and four caps for **Italy** ca. 1954-55). Born 28 July 1925, in Montevideo. Career ca. 1944-1960. *Clubs* **Peñarol, AC Milan, Roma**. *Keynotes* Uruguayan league joint top scorer 1945 (20 goals, for Peñarol). Schiaffino scored the 66th-minute equaliser in Uruguay's crucial final-round 2–1 victory over **Brazil** in the 1950 **World Cup** finals. He was the second highest scorer in the 1950 tournament, with five goals, four of them in the 8–0 victory over **Bolivia** in the first round. After the World Cup finals in 1954, where he helped Uruguay to fourth place, Schiaffino was

transferred to Milan for a then world record fee of £72,000. He scored the opening goal for Milan in the 1958 **European Cup** against **Real Madrid** in Brussels; his club eventually losing 2–3, after extra-time. Later became manager of Peñarol and, in 1975, coach of the Uruguayan national team. *Honours* World Cup (Uruguay, 1950; fourth place 1954); Uruguayan League championship (Peñarol, 1944, 1945, 1949, 1951, 1953, 1954); Italian **Serie A** championship (AC Milan, 1955, 1957).

Schmeichel, Peter *player* Goalkeeper. **Denmark** international (110 caps). Born 18 November 1963. Career ca. 1983-. *Clubs* Hvidovre, **Brøndby**, **Manchester United**. *Keynotes* Transferred to Manchester United for £550,000 from Brøndby in August 1991. Schmeichel famously scored for United during a 1995-96 **UEFA Cup** tie against **Rotor Volgograd**. He also "scored" against **Wimbledon** in a 1997 **FA Cup** fourth round replay, but this was ruled out for offside. In October 1998, Schmeichel left United at the end of the 1998-99 season. Included in the **Football League Centenary 100 players**. *Honours* Danish League (Brøndby 1985, 1987, 1988, 1990, 1991), Danish Cup (Brøndby 1989), **Premier League** (Manchester United 1992-93, 1993-94, 1995-96, 1996-97, 1998-99), FA Cup (Manchester United 1994, 1996, 1999), **European Cup** (Manchester United 1999) **European Super Cup** (Manchester United 1991), **European Championship** (Denmark 1992).

scholarship agreement *regulations* agreement between a club and a **student** player of 14 years of age (or who will be 14 in the calendar year) and under 18 years, under which the player will undergo an approved programme of education designed by the club and suitable to the player's needs (FA Premier League rules M.48-51, Football League youth development rule 11). A scholarship agreement constitutes one category of **registration**. The agreements are drawn up by the FA and must be signed by both the player and the club. See also **trainee** (sense **1**).

Schön, Helmut *player-manager* Striker. **Germany** international (16 caps, 17 goals). Born 15 September 1915; died 23 February 1996. *Clubs/country* (manager) West Germany. *Honours* **World Cup** (West Germany 1974); **European Championship** (West Germany 1972). *Keynotes* Schön played for Dresden in the inter-war period. He became national coach of the short-lived independent state of Saarland after **World War II**, before becoming assistant to the West German coach Sepp Herberger in 1955. Schön took full control of the national side in 1963. He led West Germany to four World Cup finals and his record reads: runners-up (1966, 2–4 a.e.t. v **England**); third (1970, v 1–0 v **Uruguay**); winners (1974, 2–1 v **Netherlands**); second/semi-final stage (1978, third place). Schön's West Germany also won the 1972 European Championships (3–0 v **USSR**) and was a finalist in 1976 (2–2, 4–5 pens. v **Czechoslovakia**). Under Schön's managership, West Germany recorded 87 victories in 139 matches. He gave international debuts to two future national managers, Franz **Beckenbauer** and Bertie Vogts.

schwalbe *n.* *German* informal name for a dive (sense **2.**) (German: literally the name of a swallow).

scissors kick *n.* kick executed by jumping into the air raising one leg and then striking the ball with the second leg, in a scissors motion.

score 1. *vb. rules* to gain a point or **goal** in a game of football. A goal is scored when the whole of the ball has crossed the **goal line**, under the **crossbar** and between the **goalposts** assuming no other infringements had taken place prior to this (Law X). The team scoring the most goals in a game wins the match. If no goals are scored or each side scores the same number of goals then the game is a **draw** (sense **1**). **2.** *n. rules* the current or final goal tally in a match.

score, highest by one team (British clubs) *record* (home teams listed first; the English league records are for all divisions before and after the league's restructuring in 1992). **1.** UK domestic competition: 36–0, **Arbroath** v Bon Accord (12 September 1885, **Scottish FA Cup** first round; record in 20th century; 20–0, **Stirling Albion** v Selkirk (8 December 1984, Scottish FA Cup first round). **2.** FA **Premier League**: 9–0, **Manchester United** v **Ipswich Town** (4 March 1995); United also holds the record for the highest Premiership score away from home: 1–8, v **Nottingham Forest** (6 February 1999). **3. Football League** Division One: 12–2, **Aston Villa** v **Accrington** (12 March 1892); 12–0, **West Bromwich Albion** v **Darwen** (4 April 1892); **Nottingham Forest** v **Leicester Fosse** (21 April 1909). **4.** First Division: 7–0, **Bolton Wanderers** v **Swindon Town** (8 March 1997); 0–7, **Stoke City** v **Birmingham City** (10 January 1998). **5.** Division Two: 13–0, **Newcastle United** v **Newport County** (5 October 1946). **6.** Second Division: 1–8, **Hartlepool United** v **Plymouth Argyle** (7 May 1994); **7.** Division Three: 10–0, **Gillingham** v **Chesterfield** (5 September 1987). **8.** Third Division (South): 12–0, **Luton Town** v **Bristol Rovers** (13 April 1936); a match in which Luton's emergency centre-forward Joe **Payne** set an Football League scoring record by netting 10 goals. **9.** Third Division (North) 13–0, **Stockport County** v **Halifax Town** (6 January 1934); 13–4, **Tranmere Rovers** v **Oldham Athletic** (26 December 1935). **10.** Third Division: 1–9, **Barnet** v **Peterborough United** (5 September 1998). **11.** Division Four: 11–0, Oldham Athletic v **Southport** (26 December 1962). **12. FA Cup**: 26–0, Preston North End v Hyde (15 October 1887, first round). **13. League Cup**: 10–0 **West Ham United** v **Bury** (25 October 1983, second round); 10–0, **Liverpool** v **Fulham** (23 September 1986, second round). **14. Scottish Football League** (all divisions): 15–1, **Airdrieonians** v Dundee Wanderers (1 December 1894, Division Two). **15. Scottish Premier Division/League**: 8–0, **Aberdeen** v **Motherwell** (26 March 1979); 1–8, **Kilmarnock** v **Rangers** (6 September 1980); 8–3, **Celtic** v **Hamilton Academicals** (3 January 1987); 0–8, Hamilton Academicals v Celtic (5 November 1988). **16.** Scottish Football League Division One: 11–0, Celtic v **Dundee** (26 October 1895); 1–11 Airdrieonians v **Hibernian** (24 October 1959). **17. Scottish FA Cup**: see above (**1**). **17. FA Women's Challenge Cup** 40–0, Norwich v Milton Keynes (1983).

score, highest by one team (international club competitions) *record* (home teams listed first). **1. European Cup**: 12–2, **Feyenoord** v **KR Reykjavik** (1969-70, first round); **2. European Cup-winners Cup**: 16–1, **Sporting Clube de Portugal** v **Apoel Nicosia** (1963-64, second round); **3. UEFA Cup**: 14–0, **Ajax** v **Red Boys** of Luxembourg (1984-85, first round); **4. Copa Libertadores**: 11–2, **Peñarol** v Valencia of Venezuela (1970, first–round group); **5. African Cup-winners Cup**: 12–1, **Mwanza Pamba SC** of Tanzania v Anse Boileau of Seychelles (1990, preliminary round); **6. African Cup of Champion Clubs**: 9–0, **Kabwe Warriors** of Zambia v Majanta Meseru of Lesotho (1972, first round).

score, highest by one team (internationals) *record* (home teams listed first). **1. World Cup** (all): 0–17, **Maldives** v **Iran** (2 June 1997, in Damascus, Syria, first round qualifier). **2.** UK international: 0–13, **Ireland** v **England** (18 February 1882, friendly, Belfast). **3.** World Cup finals: 10–1, **Hungary** v **El Salvador** (15 June 1982, in Elche, Spain, first round group – Hungary still failed to qualify for the second round!); **4. Oceania Cup**: 16–0, **Australia** v **Cook Islands** (28 September 1998, final tournament).

score, most goals in one match *record* **1. Football League**: 17 (13–4, **Tranmere Rovers** v **Oldham Athletic**, 26 December 1935, Third Division (North)). **2.** English top flight (Football League Division One, Premier Division or **Premier League**): 14 (12–2, **Aston Villa** v **Accrington**, 12 March 1892, Division One); (10–4, **Tottenham Hotspur** v **Everton**, 11 October 1958). **3. FA Cup**: 26 (26–0, **Preston North End** v Hyde, 15 October 1887, first round). **4. Scottish Football League**: 16 (15–1, **Airdrieonians** v Dundee Wanderers, 1 December 1894, Division Two). **5.** Scottish top flight (Scottish League Division One or Premier League): 12 (1–11, Airdrieonians v **Hibernian**, 24 October 1959, Division One). **6. Scottish FA Cup** 36 (36–0, **Arbroath** v Bon Accord, 12 September 1885, first round).

score-draw *n.* in **pools** betting, a drawn match where the sides score at least one goal each.

score-sheet *n.* document of the score and scorers in a football match. **get on the score-sheet** *informal* to score.

scorers, most in one game *record* see **goals, most scorers in one match**.

scoring space *n.* area of the pitch in which the majority of goals are scored. George Wilkinson referred to a square section of the pitch – the penalty box and the area immediately outside and directly in front of the goal – as the "critical scoring space". See also **reacher area/space**.

scorpion kick *n.* theatrical kick pioneered by the **Colombia** goalkeeper Rene **Higuita**. Higuita has been known to wait for a high ball struck goal-bound into his own goal area then, diving forward, he kicks the ball firmly with his heels giving him a scorpion shape; he pulled off the stunt at **Wembley** Stadium in Colombia's 0–0 draw with **England** (autumn 1995, friendly).

Scotland *country UEFA* constituent country of the United Kingdom, consisting of the central Lowlands – which include the main population centres of Glasgow and Edinburgh – the Highlands in the north, the Southern Uplands, and about 800 islands, including Orkneys, Shetlands and the Western Isles. Scotland was an independent country until 1603. Area: 78,750 sq km (30,400 sq miles). Population: 5,000,000 (1991 census). Languages: English, Gaelic. Capital: Edinburgh. *Dossier* The **Scottish Football Association** (Glasgow) formed in 1873, affiliated to **FIFA** in 1910 (until 1920, rejoined 1924 until 1928, rejoined 1946), permanent member of the **International FA Board**, and founder member of the **Union of European Football Associations** (UEFA) in 1954, president: John McGinn; general secretary: awaiting appointment. Season played from August to May. National stadium: **Hampden Park**, Glasgow, capacity: 52,000. National strip: dark blue shirts, white shorts, red socks with dark blue tops. First international game: 30 November 1872, v **England** (0–0, Glasgow, friendly); an unofficial game was played on 5 March 1870 (1–1 v England, London). First game v **Wales**, 25 March 1876 (4–0, Glasgow, friendly); v **Ireland**, 26 January 1884 (5–0, Belfast, **Home International Championship**); v **Northern Ireland**, 1 March 1924 (2–0, Glasgow, Home International Championship); v **Republic of Ireland**, 3 May 1961 (4–1, Glasgow, **World Cup** qualifier). First international game outside the British Isles: 28 May 1929 v **Norway** (7–3, Oslo, friendly). Biggest victory: 11–0 v Ireland (23 February 1901, Glasgow, Home International Championship). Biggest defeats: 0–7 v **Uruguay** (19 June 1954, Basle, World Cup first round); 3–9 v England (15 April 1961, **Wembley** Stadium, Home International Championship). Record attendance: 149,547 (17 April 1937, 3–1, v England, Hampden Park, Home International Championship). Lowest home attendance: 7,843 (6 May 1969, 1–1, v Northern Ireland, Home International Championship). National coaches/managers: Andy Beattie 1954-58; Sir Matt **Busby** 1958; Dawson Walker 1958; Andy Beattie 1959-60; Ian McColl 1960-65; Jock **Stein** 1965; John Prentice 1966; Malcolm MacDonald 1966-67; Bobby Brown 1967-71; Tommy **Docherty** 1971-72; Willie Ormond 1973-77; Ally MacLeod 1977-78; Jock Stein 1978-85; Alex **Ferguson** (**caretaker manager**) 1985-86; Andy Roxburgh 1986-93; Craig Brown 1993-. Most capped players: Kenny **Dalglish** (102 appearances, 1971-86), Jim Leighton (90 appearances, 1983-98), Alex McLeish (77 appearances, 1980-93), Paul McStay (76 appearances, 1984-97), Willie Miller (65 appearances, 1975-90), Danny McGrain (62 appear-

ances, 1973-82). Leading goalscorers: Denis **Law** (30 goals in 55 appearances, 1959-74), Kenny Dalglish (30 goals in 102 appearances), Hughie **Gallacher** (23 goals in 20 appearances, 1924-35), Lawrie Reilly (22 goals in 38 appearances, 1949-57), Ally **McCoist** (19 goals in 59 appearances, 1986-). Other notable international players: Billy **Bremner**, Charlie **Cooke**, Alan **Hansen**, Billy **Liddell**, Dave **Mackay**, Frank **McLintock**, Graeme **Souness**, Alex **Young**. Website: *http://www.scottishfa.co.uk* (official site). *International tournament record* **Olympic Games** – never entered; **Women's World Cup** – see **Scotland, women**; World Cup – first entered 1950 (qualified for finals tournament, but withdrew before the main tournament), qualified for finals tournament (first round) 1954, 1958, 1974, 1978, 1982, 1986, 1990, 1998; **European Championship** – first entered 1968, qualified for finals tournament (first round) 1992, 1996; **European Championship for Women** – see **Scotland, women**; **European Junior Championship**/**European Youth Championship** (under-18) – winners 1982; Home International Championship (British Championship) winners 40 times, and winners of the first championship in 1884; **Under-17 World Championship** – runners-up and hosts 1989 (2–2, 4–4 pens., v **Saudi Arabia**, Hampden Park); **World Youth Cup** (under-20) – quarter-final 1983, 1987. *World Cup performance* Finals and qualifiers to end of 1998 tournament: played 102, won 48, drawn 22, lost 32, scored 165 goals, conceded 129 goals; win rate: 47%; goals scored per game: 1.61. Performance in qualifiers: played 79, won 44, drawn 15, lost 20, scored 140 goals, conceded 88 goals; win rate: 56%; goals scored per game: 1.77. Performance in finals tournaments played 23, won four, drawn seven, lost 12, scored 25 goals, conceded 41 goals; win rate: 17%; goals scored per game: 1.08. *Record against other British and Irish national teams* v England played 108, won 40, lost 44, drawn 24; v all-Ireland played 36, won 31, lost one, drawn four; v Northern Ireland played 56, won 30, lost 14, drawn 12; v Republic of Ireland played six, won two, lost two, drawn two; v Wales played 101, won 60, lost 18, drawn 23. *History* Scotland's first club, **Queen's Park**, was founded in Glasgow in 1867, though its first tournament game was against English opposition. It competed in the first (English) **FA Cup** in 1872; reaching the semi-finals without playing a match. Although Queen's Park drew 0–0 against the first FA Cup winners, the **Wanderers**, at the semi-final in London, it could not afford to stay on for a replay so had to withdraw from the competition. Scotland has the second oldest Cup and league competitions in the World. The **Scottish FA Cup** started in 1874, and was first won by Queen's Park (2–0, v Clydesdale). Queen's Park won 10 of the first 20 Scottish FA Cup finals, and was beaten in only one final (1–5, v **Celtic** in 1892). It played its last Scottish FA Cup final in 1900 (3–4, v Celtic). Queen's Park's record of 10 Scottish Cup triumphs has kept the club at fifth place in the all-time Scottish club rankings. It continues to play in the Scottish Football League and has remained a strictly-amateur side since its foundation. The Scottish League and Cup have been dominated by Celtic and **Rangers**, the Glasgow "Old Firm". Rangers has won the Scottish League championship a world-record 48 times (one shared), with 27 Scottish FA Cups and 21 Scottish League Cups. Celtic is ranked second in the all-time list, with 36 League titles, 30 Scottish FA Cups and 10 League Cups. Both clubs share the record for most successive titles, with nine each: Celtic 1966-74; Rangers 1989-97. After the "big two", come **Aberdeen** (four league titles, seven Scottish FA Cups, six Scottish League Cups), **Heart of Midlothian** (four league titles, six Scottish FA Cups, four Scottish League Cups), Queen's Park (10 Scottish FA Cups), and **Hibernian** (four league titles, two Scottish FA Cups, two Scottish League Cups). The Scottish Football League began in 1890-91, the first title shared between **Dumbarton** and Rangers with 29 points each, ahead of Celtic on 21 points. It was expanded to two divisions in 1893-94, at the same time as professional football was legalised. Between 1946-47 and 1955-56, Division One was called the 'A' Division and Division Two the 'B' Division. The Scottish Football League was reorganised before the start of the 1975-76 season. The two divisions were replaced by a Premier Division of 10 clubs, and a First and Second Division of 14 clubs each. The reorganisation created a smaller top flight, enabling the bigger clubs to play each other four times in a season. The League was reorganised again before the 1994-95 season, maintaining the Premier Division, but creating three lower divisions. Two clubs joined Division Three from the Highland League, **Ross County** and **Inverness Caledonian Thistle** (a controversial merger of Inverness Thistle and Inverness Caledonian; the move was not welcomed by all the supporters of the two former rivals). The Premier Division clubs resigned from the Scottish Football League at the end of the 1997-98 season to form the **Scottish Premier League**; a move which gave greater financial autonomy to the top-flight, particularly benefiting from television revenue. The lower divisions were largely unaffected (save for a loss of trickle-down revenue from the top flight). Promotion/relegation between the Scottish Premier League and Scottish Football League First Division was retained, though the number of promotion/relegation places was reduced to one; previously, there existed the possibility of the second-placed club gaining promotion if it could beat the second-bottom club in the Premier Division in an end-of-season play-off. It has been proposed that the Scottish Premier League be expanded to 12 clubs from 2000-01, with a possible second promotion/relegation place and the reintroduction of playoffs. The **Scottish League Cup** was first played in 1947 (Rangers v Aberdeen, 4–0). The Edinburgh club Hibernian was the joint-first British club to enter a European club competition, reaching the semi-final of the first **European Cup** in 1955-56: it lost 0–3 agg., v **Stade de Reims** (English club

Birmingham City, and a **London Select XI** had entered the Inter-City Fairs Cup, now the **UEFA Cup**, in the same year). It is worth noting that, while representing Scotland in the competition, Hibernian had finished only fifth in the 1954-55 Scottish championship. Celtic was the first British team to win the European Cup, with a 2–1 victory over **Internazionale**, at the **Estádio Nacional**, Lisbon, Portugal, in 1967; Gemmell and Chalmers scored for Celtic. Two Scottish clubs have won the **European Cup-winners Cup**: Rangers in 1972, and Aberdeen in 1983, the latter under the managership of Alex Ferguson. Scotland took part in the first official international match in the World, a game against England on 30 November 1872 (St Andrew's Day). The match took place at the West of Scotland Cricket Club, Partick, and was organised by Queen's Park. A crowd of 4,000 spectators watched a goalless draw. The gate receipts came to £103. A nominally-Scottish side had played an unofficial game against England in London on 5 March 1870 (1–1); the match featured players based in London, some with only tenuous claims to a Scottish birthright. The popularity of the once-annual fixture against England was demonstrated at Hampden Park on 17 April 1937; the match attracted the highest official attendance for any in the British Isles: 149,547. It was the first **all-ticket** match in Scotland, and raised £24,000 in gate receipts. By 1998, Scotland had played in the World Cup finals on eight occasions, two behind England. Scotland had qualified for the finals tournament nine times, having withdrawn before the finals in 1950, compared with eight by England (England progressed to the finals automatically in 1966 and 1970). It has, however, never progressed beyond the first round in the finals. Scotland's game against **Brazil** in the 1998 World Cup finals in **France** (1–2, 10 June 1998, in St-Denis, France) was not only the opening game of the tournament, but also Scotland's 100th world Cup match (qualifiers and finals). Scotland qualified for the European Championship finals tournaments in 1992 and 1996 but has never progressed beyond the first-round group stages. Scotland holds the European nation's record of 13 consecutive victories (7 April 1897 to 21 March 1885). Hughie Gallacher jointly holds the record for the most goals in a game for Scotland; he scored five in his country's 7–3 victory over Ireland on 23 February 1929. The record had been set up in the previous century by Charlie Heggie, who scored five in Scotland's 7–2 defeat of Ireland on 20 March 1886. Arguably Scotland's greatest player, Kenny Dalglish, played a record 102 times for his country in an international career that lasted exactly 15 years and two days (10 November 1971 to 12 November 1986). Dalglish is also the joint top scorer for Scotland, with 30 goals; a record he shares with another Scottish hero, Denis Law. Scotland hosted and was runners-up in the 1989 Under-17 World Championship. Scottish football has had two notable black points, both involving serious loss of life, and both occurring at Rangers' **Ibrox Stadium**. The first incident, in April 1902, occurred when a new stand collapsed six minutes into an international match between Scotland and England: 26 people died and more than 500 were injured. The second disaster occurred on 2 January 1971, close to the end of a game between Rangers and Celtic: 66 died and around 145 were injured as crush barriers collapsed under the weight of a crowd of spectators trying to return to the terraces after Rangers scored a late equaliser. This second **Ibrox Park Disaster** led to a public inquiry and publication of the **Wheatley Report** into stadium safety. Scottish football has not been immune from football **hooliganism**: the worst case resulted in 60 arrests at Ibrox Stadium following disorder at a league game early in the 1975-76 season. *League system* There are 10 clubs in the Scottish Premier League (with a proposed expansion to 12 clubs from 2000-01), and in each of the Scottish Football League Divisions One, Two and Three. The 10 clubs play each other four times in a season (twice at home and twice away). Three points are awarded for a victory, with one for a draw: final positions for clubs level on points are determined by **goal difference**; if clubs are level on points and goal difference, their respective positions are decided by **goals scored**. If the clubs are still level, and are involved in promotion, relegation, the championship, or qualification for a European tournament, their final positions are determined by a **playoff**. One club is promoted from the First Division to the Premier League (the number of promoted clubs may be affected by the proposed expansion of the Premier League in 2000-01); there are two promotion/relegation places between the First and Second, and Second and Third Divisions; promotion/relegation is decided on final league positions, there is no playoff system. There is no relegation from the Third Division. Beneath the Scottish Football League are three amateur and semi-professional regional leagues: the **Highland League**, **South of Scotland League** and **East of Scotland League** (their member clubs also compete in the **Scottish Qualifying Cup**). Separate amateur/semi-professional leagues are run by the **Scottish Junior Football Association** which, despite its name, is for adult clubs playing outside the five leagues named above. *Record in international club tournaments* European Cup – Celtic (winners 1967, runners-up 1970, semi-final 1974), Hibernian (semi-final 1956), Rangers (semi-final 1960, second in its quarter final group 1993), **Dundee United** (semi-final 1984); European Cup-winners Cup – Rangers (winners 1972, runners-up 1961, 1967), Aberdeen (winners 1983, semi-final 1984), Celtic (semi-final 1964, 1966), **Dunfermline Athletic** (semi-final 1969); UEFA Cup/Fairs Cup – Dundee United (runners-up 1987), Hibernian (semi-final 1961), **Kilmarnock** (semi-final 1967), **Dundee** (semi-final 1968), Rangers (semi-final 1969); **European Supercup** – Aberdeen (winners 1983).

Scotland, women *country/women* women's football in Scotland is administered by the Scottish Women's Football Association (SWFA), in Glasgow,

founded on 17 September 1972, affiliated to the **Scottish Football Association** (SFA) in July 1999. *History* The first Scottish women's league was formed in 1968, in Glasgow. Scotland's first competitive campaign, the 1984 **European Championship for Women** qualifying tournament, included two defeats by **England** (0–4 at **Dumbarton**, and 0–2 at **Elland Road**, Leeds). Leading club Stewarton Thistle played in the first English Women's FA Cup final (now the **FA Women's Challenge Cup**) in 1971, losing 1–4 against Southampton (at Crystal Palace National Sports Centre in London). The SWFA was the last women's association in Europe to affiliate to its national association. *Dossier* First official international match: November 1972, v England, 2–3, in Greenock. Biggest victory: 7–1, v **Faeroe Islands**, (1995, European Championship for Women qualifier). *League system* There are 31 clubs in the SWFA league, a 10-club Premier Division, and two regional divisions, North East (11 clubs), West (10 clubs). In 1997-98, the 10 Premier Division clubs were: Aberdeen LFC, Ayr United LFC, Clyde LFC, Cove Rangers LFC, Cumbernauld AFC, Dundee United LFC, Guilianos LFC, Maryhill Eagles LFC, Stirling Albion LFC, Stewarton Thistle LFC. *International tournament record* **Women's World Cup** – never qualified for finals tournament; European Championship for Women – entered first tournament in 1984, never qualified for finals tournament.

Scott, Elisha *player* Goalkeeper. **Northern Ireland** international (31 caps). Career ca. 1911-22. *Clubs* Belfast Celtic, **Liverpool**. *Keynotes* Played 429 games for Liverpool during a 22-year career which began in 1911-12. During his championship-winning seasons, Scott conceded only 66 goals in 81 games. Included in the **Football League Centenary 100 players**. *Honours* League Championship (Liverpool 1921-22, 1922-23).

Scottish Emergency Cup *competition* a Scottish cup competition played in 1940, at the beginning of **World War II**. *Winners* **Rangers**.

Scottish FA Cup *competition* annual Scottish knockout competition which began in 1873-74. *History* The idea for the competition came from **Queen's Park** players as they travelled back from competing in the first **FA Cup** competition. A meeting was held in Glasgow on 13 March 1873, attended by eight clubs and the inaugural competition attracted 16 entrants, including Alexandria Athletic, Blythwood, Clydesdale, **Dumbarton**, Eastern, Queen's Park, **Renton, Third Lanark** Rifle Volunteers. **Rangers** was ineligible for the first competition because its entry form arrived too late. In the early years, several finals were less than straightforward. Queen's Park won the first three Scottish FA Cup finals and the club was awarded the trophy in 1884 because **Vale of Leven**, which had asked for the game to be postponed, failed to appear for the final. In 1879, Rangers refused to participate in the replay of the final because a "goal" had been disallowed in the first match. The cup was awarded to Vale of Leven. The 1880 final between Queen's Park and Dumbarton was replayed after the latter's complaint about supporters on the pitch was upheld. Third Lanark's victory over Celtic in the 1889 final was put on hold because the result of first match was declared void owing to a snowstorm during the game. The 1892 final between **Celtic** and Queen's park was replayed following crowd trouble. *Records* (Up to and including 1998) Celtic has won the Scottish FA Cup a record 30 times, with the club's first victory recorded in 1892. The club also holds the record for final appearances, 41. **East Fife** is the only non-top-flight club to have won the trophy, achieving its success in 1938 when in Division Two. The first final to go to a replay was the 1876 encounter between Queen's Park and Third Lanark Rifle Volunteers. Renton's 6–1 victory over **Cambuslang** in 1888 and Celtic's triumph over **Hibernian** by the same score in 1972 is the biggest winning margin in a Cup final. In 1990, Aberdeen won the first Scottish FA Cup final to be decided by a **penalty shootout** (0–0, 9–8 pens. v Celtic). The 1937 final at **Hampden Park** between Celtic and **Aberdeen** attracted a record UK attendance for a club match, with 146,433 spectators. *Final results* 1874, Queen's Park 2–0 Clydesdale; 1875, Queen's Park 3–0 Renton; 1876, Queen's Park 2–0 replay Third Lanark Rifles Volunteer; 1877, Vale of Leven 3–2 Rangers (second replay); 1878, Vale of Leven 1–0 Third Lanark Rifles Volunteer; 1879, Vale of Leven 1–1 Rangers (walkover in replay); 1880, Queen's Park 3–0 Thornlibank; 1881, Queen's Park 3–1 Dumbarton; 1882, Queen's Park 4–1 Dumbarton (replay); 1883, Dumbarton 2–1 Vale of Leven (replay); 1884, Queen's Park v Vale of Leven (walkover); 1885, Renton 3–1 Vale of Leven (replay); 1886, Queen's Park 3–1 Renton; 1887, Hibernian 2–1 Dumbarton; 1888, Renton 6–1 Cambuslang; 1889, Third Lanark 2–1 Celtic ; 1890, Queen's Park 2–1 Vale of Leven (replay); 1891, Hearts 1–0 Dumbarton; 1892, Celtic 5–1 Queen's Park; 1893, Queen's Park 2-1 Celtic; 1894, Rangers 3–1 Celtic; 1895, St Bernard's 2–1 Renton; 1896, Hearts 3–1 Hibernian; 1897, Rangers 5–1 Dumbarton; 1898, Rangers 2–0 Kilmarnock; 1899, Celtic 2–0 Rangers; 1900, Celtic 4–3 Queen's Park; 1901, Hearts 4–3 Celtic; 1902, Hibernian 1–0 Celtic; 1903, Rangers 2–0 Hearts (second replay); 1904, Celtic 3–2 Rangers; 1905, Third Lanark 3–1 Rangers (replay); 1906, Hearts 1–0 Third Lanark; 1907, Celtic 3–0 Hearts; 1908, Celtic 5–1 St Mirren; 1909, Celtic v Rangers (cup withheld after crowd rioting); 1910, Dundee 2–1 Clyde (second replay); 1911, Celtic 2–0 Hamilton Academical (replay); 1912, Celtic 2–0 Clyde; 1913, Falkirk 2–0 Raith Rovers; 1914, Celtic 4–1 Hibernian (replay); 1920, Kilmarnock 3-2 Albion Rovers; 1921, Partick Thistle 1–0 Rangers; 1922, Morton 1-0 Rangers; 1923, Celtic 1–0 Hibernian; 1924, Airdrieonians 2–0 Hibernian; 1925, Celtic 2–1 Dundee; 1926, St Mirren 2–0 Celtic; 1927, Celtic 3-1 East Fife; 1928, Rangers 4–0 Celtic; 1929, Kilmarnock 2–0 Rangers; 1930, Rangers 2–1 Partick Thistle (replay); 1931, Celtic 4–2 Motherwell (replay); 1932, Rangers 3–0 Kilmarnock (replay); 1933, Celtic 1–0 Motherwell;

1934, Rangers 5–0 St Mirren; 1935, Rangers 2–1 Hamilton Academical; 1936, Rangers 1–0 Third Lanark; 1937, Celtic 2-1 Aberdeen; 1938, East Fife 4–2 Kilmarnock (replay); 1939, Clyde 4–0 Motherwell; 1947, Aberdeen 2-1 Hibernian; 1948, Rangers 1–0 Morton (replay); 1949, Rangers 4–1 Clyde; 1950, Rangers 3–0 East Fife; 1951, Celtic 1–0 Motherwell; 1952, Motherwell 4–0 Dundee; 1953, Rangers 1–0 Aberdeen (replay); 1954, Celtic 2–1 Aberdeen; 1955, Clyde 1–0 Celtic (replay); 1956, Hearts 3–1 Celtic; 1957, Falkirk 2-1 Kilmarnock (replay); 1958, Clyde 1–0 Hibernian; 1959, St Mirren 3-1 Aberdeen; 1960, Rangers 2–0 Kilmarnock; 1961, Dunfermline Athletic 2–0 Celtic (replay); 1962, Rangers 2–0 St Mirren; 1963, Rangers 3–0 Celtic (replay); 1964, Rangers 3–1 Dundee; 1965, Celtic 3–2 Dunfermline Athletic; 1966, Rangers 1–0 Celtic (replay); 1967, Celtic 2–0 Aberdeen; 1968, Dunfermline Athletic 3–1 Hearts; 1969, Celtic 4–0 Rangers; 1970, Aberdeen 3–1 Celtic; 1971, Celtic 2–1 Rangers (replay); 1972, Celtic 6–1 Hibernian; 1973, Rangers 3–2 Celtic; 1974, Celtic 3–0 Dundee United; 1975, Celtic 3–1 Airdrieonians; 1976, Rangers 3–1 Hearts; 1977, Celtic 1-0 Rangers; 1978, Rangers 2-1 Aberdeen; 1979, Rangers 3–2 Hibernian (second replay); 1980, Celtic 1–0 Rangers; 1981, Rangers 4–1 Dundee United (replay); 1982, Aberdeen 4–1 Rangers; 1983, Aberdeen 1–0 Rangers; 1984, Aberdeen 2–1 Celtic; 1985, Celtic 2-1 Dundee United; 1986, Aberdeen 3–0 Hearts; 1987, St Mirren 1–0 Dundee United; 1988, Celtic 2–1 Dundee United; 1989, Celtic 1–0 Rangers; 1990, Aberdeen v Celtic (9–8 pens.); 1991, Motherwell 4–3 Dundee United; 1992, Rangers 2-1 Airdrieonians ; 1993, Rangers 2–1 Aberdeen; 1994, Dundee United 1–0 Rangers; 1995, Celtic 1–0 Airdrieonians; 1996, Rangers 5–1 Hearts; 1997, Kilmarnock 1–0 Falkirk; 1998, Hearts 2-1 Rangers.

Scottish FA Cup winner's medals *record* Charles Campbell played on the winning side in eight Scottish FA Cup finals (1874, 1875, 1876, 1880, 1881, 1882, 1884, 1886, all for **Queens Park**). Bob McPhail made nine Scottish FA Cup final appearances 1924-36, winning one with Airdrie and winning six, drawing one and losing one with Rangers.

Scottish Football Association *confederation* the national football confederation of Scotland, headquarters in Park Gardens, Glasgow. Formed in 1873, it is the world's second oldest football confederation. It is a permanent member of the **International FA Board**, and founder member of the **Union of European Football Associations** (UEFA) in 1954. President: John McGinn. General secretary: awaiting appointment. There are 75 member clubs and three associate member clubs as well as several affiliated associations. Governing bodies currently affiliated to the Scottish FA include: the **Scottish Football League**, the **Scottish Premier League**, the **Highland League**, the **East of Scotland League**, the **South of Scotland League**, the **Scottish Junior FA**, the Scottish Amateur FA (founded 1909), the **Scottish Youth Football**

Association, the Scottish Welfare Football Association (founded 1918), the **Scottish Women's Football Association** the **Scottish Schools Football Association** and the various regional football associations. *History* Founded in March 1873 – at the same time as a Scottish (Rugby) Football Union was formed. Affiliated to **FIFA** in 1910, resigned in 1920 along with the other home nations (England, Wales, Ireland), with Britain refusing to associate with its former enemies from **World War I**. It rejoined FIFA in 1924, but resigned again in 1928, also with the other home nations, in a dispute over the definition of "amateur" in the **Olympic Games** football tournament. It rejoined FIFA in 1946.

Scottish Football League Appeals Committee *regulations (Scotland)* tribunal in Scotland, set up to adjudicate in disputes between a club and a player on matters not explicitly covered by league regulations (Scottish Football League rule 65). Players may request personal hearings and can be represented by the Scottish Professional Footballers Association. The committee does not rule on disputes arising over **compensation fees**; these are adjudicated by the Scottish Football League **Compensation Tribunal**.

Scottish Football League *competition* the second tier of Scottish domestic league football, existing directly below the **Scottish Premier League**. There are three divisions of mostly professional and semi-professional clubs. Its headquarters are in Glasgow. President: J Oliver. General secretary: Peter Donald. The Scottish Football League also controls and runs the **Scottish Football League Cup**. *History* The Scottish Football League began in 1890-91, and is the second oldest national league in the World (created two years after the English **Football League**). The first title was shared between **Dumbarton** and **Rangers**. The league was expanded in 1893-94 to two divisions. Division One continued through **World War I**, while Division Two was suspended from 1916-17 through to 1920-21. Both divisions were suspended during **World War II**, and were replaced by regional competitions: the Scottish North-East and Scottish Southern leagues ran from 1941 to 1945. The Scottish Football League was reorganised before the start of the 1975-76 season. The two divisions were replaced by a Premier Division of 10 clubs, and First and Second Divisions of 14 clubs each. The top-flight clubs then played each other four times in a season, instead of twice. The League was reorganised again before the 1994-95 season, maintaining the Premier Division, but creating three lower divisions of 10 clubs. Two clubs joined the new Division Three from the Highland League, **Ross County** and **Inverness Caledonian Thistle**, thus making a total of 40 clubs in the four divisions. The Premier Division clubs resigned from the Scottish Football League at the end of the 1997-98 season to form the Scottish Premier League. Promotion/relegation between the Scottish Premier League and Scottish Football League First Division was retained; however, the number of promotion/relegation places was reduced to one (the playoff

between the First Division runners-up and second-bottom Premier Division clubs was abolished). By the reorganisation at the end of the 1997-98 season, only 11 clubs had ever won the Scottish championship: Rangers (47 championships, including one shared), **Celtic** (36), **Aberdeen** (four), **Heart of Midlothian** (four), **Hibernian** (four), Dumbarton (two, including one shared), **Dundee** (one), **Dundee United** (one), **Kilmarnock** (one), **Motherwell** (one) and **Third Lanark** (one). Rangers and Celtic hold the record for most successive titles, with nine each: Celtic 1966-74; Rangers 1989-97 (one behind the world record held by **Dynamo Berlin**). By 1998, Rangers had won more championships (47) than any other club in the world – two more than **Peñarol** of Uruguay. *League system* There are 10 clubs in each of the First, Second and Third Divisions. The 10 clubs in each division play each other four times in a season: twice at home and twice away (Scottish Football League rule 27). Three points are awarded for a victory, with one for a draw: final positions for clubs level on points are determined by **goal difference**; if clubs are level on points and goal difference, their respective positions are decided by **goals scored** (Scottish Football League rule 30). If the clubs are still level, and are involved in promotion, relegation, or the divisional championships, their final positions are determined by a **playoff** (Scottish Football League rule 30). Divisional championship trophies are awarded for each of the three divisions. Championship trophies are held until the end of the following season, but must be given back to the Scottish Football League by 1 May in the following season (Scottish Football League rule 34). Sixteen gold medals and a commemorative flag are given to each of the divisional champions. *Promotion/relegation* The champion club in Division One is promoted to the Scottish Premier League, provided that it meets the membership criteria (eg stadium standards) of the top-flight league (Scottish Football League rule 31; Scottish Premier League rule A2.3). The top two clubs in the Second Division are automatically promoted to the First Division, at the expense of the bottom two clubs from the First; provided that the promoted clubs' grounds meet the standards required of the First Division (Scottish Football League rule 31). Similarly, the top two clubs in the Third Division replace the bottom two in the Second Division, subject again to the promoted clubs fulfilling minimum ground standards. Membership criteria include that the promoted club's stadium meets specified accommodation and safety standards. Under the rules of the Scottish Football League, promotion is not mandatory: "in the event of either or both clubs in the [Third/Second] Division refusing to go into the [Second/First] Division... then either or both of the two lowest clubs in the [Second/First] Division shall remain in that Division. No club shall be allowed to accept payment in respect of foregoing the right of promotion" (Scottish Football League rule 32). There is no relegation from the Third Division. Beneath the Scottish Football League (though there is no direct promotion/relegation) are the regional **Highland League**, **South of Scotland League** and **East of Scotland League**.

Scottish Football League Trading Account *n.* fund held by the **Scottish Football League**, into which all the league's income is paid. At the end of each financial year, any surplus in the account is shared out to the Scottish Football League's member clubs: 75% shared equally between all 30 member clubs and 25% related to each club's end-of-season league position (the "ladder principle"). With 10 clubs in each division, the bottom club receives one share of the division's merit allocation, whereas the top club receives 10 shares (Scottish Football League rule 35).

Scottish Junior Cup *competition* annual Scottish knockout tournament for member clubs of the **Scottish Junior Football Association**.

Scottish Junior Football Association *confederation* governing body for **junior football clubs** in Scotland, based in Glasgow, founded 1886. President: J Grant. General secretary: T Johnston. Member clubs are those playing outside the Scottish senior league system (ie, clubs not competing in either the **Scottish Premier League**, **Scottish Football League**, **Highland League**, **East of Scotland League** or **South of Scotland League**); they are not youth clubs. The Scottish Junior FA is not responsible for youth football. Its aim is "to foster and develop the game of association football among all junior football clubs in Scotland." The Scottish Junior FA is affiliated to the **Scottish Football Association** and runs an annual Scottish Junior Cup for all member clubs. Scottish junior clubs must be independent of senior clubs and their players may be registered as professionals or amateurs. Clubs whose players are transferred to senior clubs may be entitled to a **transfer fee** or **compensation fee** (see also **delayed transfer player**). Scottish junior clubs cannot enter the **Scottish FA Cup**.

Scottish Juvenile Football Association *confederation* see **Scottish Youth Football Association**.

Scottish League Challenge Cup (formerly B&Q Cup until 1995) *competition* knockout Scottish Cup competition open to lower tier Scottish League clubs which began in 1991, as the B&Q Centenary Cup, and ended in 1998. The final was played in the first half of the season and drawn games were settled by a **penalty shootout**. *Final results* 1991, **Dundee** 3–2 **Ayr United** (at **Fir Park**); 1992, **Hamilton Academicals** 1–0 Ayr United (at Fir Park); 1993, Hamilton Academicals 3–2 Morton (at **St Mirren Park**); 1994, Falkirk 3–0 St Mirren (at Fir Park); 1995, **Airdrieonians** 3–2 Dundee (at **McDiarmid Park**); 1996, **Stenhousemuir** 0–0 Dundee United (5–4 pens., at McDiarmid Park); 1997, Stranraer 1–0 St Johnstone (at **Broadwood Stadium**); 1998, Falkirk 1–0 Queen of the South (Fir Park).

Scottish League Cup *competition* annual Scottish knockout competition which began in 1946-47 and involves Scottish League clubs. *History* The competi-

tion extended the popular World War II Scottish Southern League Cup tournament which started in 1940-41 – one novelty of this competition was that **Rangers** won the 1943 trophy on corners following a 1–1 draw with **Falkirk**. Originally the League Cup was played on a group-based system in which the winners went into the knock-out quarter-final stage. Between 1977-78 and 1979-80, a knockout format was introduced for all rounds. The 1983-84 season brought the introduction at the quarter-final stage of four groups of four teams, with the winners going on to the semi-finals. The competition is now a straight knockout event, with the two top-tier clubs entering at the second-round stage. The Scottish League Cup differs from its English equivalent in that since 1949-50 (with the exception of 1977-78, 1978-79 and 1983-84) it is completed in the first half of season, with the final generally played in October each year. *Records* (Up to and including 1999) Rangers has won the trophy a record 21 times, the first being in 1946-47. **Celtic**'s 7–1 victory over Rangers in 1957-58 is the record winning margin in the final. The first final to go to a **penalty shoot-out** was the 1987-88 match between Rangers and **Aberdeen**. Ally **McCoist** holds the record for League Cup medals, having been on the winning side on nine occasions – all with Rangers. *Final results* 1946, Aberdeen 3–2 Rangers; 1947, Rangers 4–0 Aberdeen; 1948, **East Fife** 4–1 Falkirk (replay); 1949, Rangers 2–0 **Raith Rovers**; 1950, East Fife 3–0 **Dunfermline Athletic**; 1951, **Motherwell** 3–0 Hibernian; 1952, **Dundee** 3–2 **Rangers**; 1953, Dundee 2–0 **Kilmarnock**; 1954, East Fife 3–2 **Partick Thistle**; 1955, **Hearts** 4–2 **Motherwell**; 1956, Aberdeen 2–1 **St Mirren**; 1957, Celtic 3–0 Partick Thistle (replay); 1958, Celtic 7–1 Rangers; 1959, Hearts 5–1 Partick Thistle; 1960, Hearts 2–1 **Third Lanark**; 1961, Rangers 2–0 Kilmarnock; 1962, Rangers 3–1 Hearts (replay); 1963, Hearts 1–0 Kilmarnock; 1964, Rangers 5–0 **Morton**; 1965, Rangers 2–1 Celtic; 1966, Celtic 2–1 Rangers; 1967, Celtic 1–0 Rangers; 1968, Celtic 5–3 Dundee; 1969, Celtic 6–2 Hibernian; 1970, Celtic 1–0 **St Johnstone**; 1971, Rangers 1–0 Celtic; 1972, Partick Thistle 4–1 Celtic; 1973, Hibernian 2-1 Celtic; 1974, Dundee 1–0 Celtic; 1975, Celtic 6–3 Hibernian; 1976, Rangers 1–0 Celtic; 1977, Aberdeen 2–1 Celtic; 1978, Rangers 2–1 Celtic; 1979, Rangers 2–1 Aberdeen; 1960, **Dundee United** 3–0 Aberdeen (replay); 1981, Dundee United 3–0 Dundee; 1982, Rangers 2–1 Dundee United; 1983, Celtic 2–1 Rangers; 1984, Rangers 3–2 Celtic; 1985, Rangers 1–0 Dundee United; 1986, Aberdeen 3–0 Hibernian; 1987, Rangers 2–1 Celtic; 1988, Rangers 3–3 Aberdeen (5–3 pens.); 1989, Rangers 3–2 Aberdeen; 1990, Aberdeen 2–1 Rangers; 1991, Rangers 2–1 Celtic; 1992, Hibernian 2–0 Dunfermline Athletic; 1993, Rangers 2–1 Aberdeen; 1994, Rangers 2–1 Hibernian; 1995, Raith Rovers 2–2 Celtic (6–5 pens.); 1996, Aberdeen 2–0 Dundee; 1997, Rangers 4–3 Hearts; 1998, Celtic 3–0 Dundee United; 1999, Rangers 2–1 St Johnstone.

Scottish manager of the year *award* annual accolade to the most outstanding manager in Scottish league football. *Winners* 1987, Jim McLean (**Dundee United**); 1988, Billy McNeill (**Celtic**); 1989, Graeme Souness (**Rangers**); 1990, Andy Roxburgh (**Scotland**); 1991, Alex Totten (**St Johnstone**); 1992, Walter Smith (Rangers); 1993, Walter Smith (Rangers); 1994, Walter Smith (Rangers); 1995, Jimmy Nicholl (**Raith Rovers**); 1996, Walter Smith (Rangers); 1997, Walter Smith (Rangers); 1998, Wim Jansen (Celtic).

Scottish Premier League *competition* the top flight of Scottish league football. Its headquarters are in Glasgow. Chief executive: R Mitchell. *History* The Scottish Premier League was founded before the start of the 1998-99 season, with the 10 clubs from the former Scottish Premier Division joining on resigning from the **Scottish Football League**. The 10 clubs that competed in the first season of the new league were: **Aberdeen, Celtic, Dundee, Dundee United, Dunfermline Athletic, Heart of Midlothian, Kilmarnock, Motherwell, Rangers** and **St Johnstone**. The move gave the top flight greater financial autonomy, while still retaining promotion and relegation from and to the Scottish Football League First Division. The Scottish Premier League is a limited company. *League system* Ten clubs play each other four times in a season (twice at home and twice away). Three points are awarded for a victory, with one for a draw: final positions for clubs level on points are determined by **goal difference**; if clubs are level on points and goal difference, their respective positions are decided by **goals scored**. If the clubs are still level, and are involved in relegation, the championship, or qualification for a European tournament, their final positions are determined by a playoff. There is just one promotion/relegation place: the bottom club in the Premier League is automatically relegated to the Scottish Football League First Division; the champion club of the First Division is promoted, provided that it meets the membership criteria of the top-flight league (Scottish Premier League rule A2.3, Scottish Football League rule 31).

Scottish Qualifying Cup *competition* annual Scottish knockout tournament for Scottish **senior football clubs** outside of the **Scottish Football League** and **Scottish Premier League**. There are two regional tournaments: north – with all member clubs of the **Highland League**; and south – contested by member clubs of the **East of Scotland League** and the **South of Scotland League**. The two finals take place at neutral grounds at the beginning of November. The semi-finalists from both sections qualify for the **Scottish FA Cup**.

Scottish Schools Football Association *confederation* the national governing body for schools football in **Scotland**, founded 1903, affiliated to the **Scottish Football Association**.

Scottish Summer Cup *competition* Scottish regional cup competition played during **World War II**. *Winners* 1941 **Hibernian**; 1942 **Rangers**; 1943 **St Mirren**; 1944 **Motherwell**; 1945 **Partick Thistle**.

Scottish Victory Cup *competition* Scottish cup competition played in 1945-46, immediately after World War II, and before the full resumption of the **Scottish FA Cup**. *Winners* **Rangers**.

Scottish Vocational Qualification *misc.* see **National Youth Training Scheme (Scotland)**.

Scottish Youth Football Association *confederation* national governing body for youth football in Scotland, formed in 1999 by the amalgamation of the Association of Scottish Youth Football Clubs (founded 1927), the Scottish Juvenile Football Association (founded 1899) and the youth division of the Scottish Amateur Football Association. The amalgamation was in keeping with recommendations of the Scottish Football Independent Review Commission. There are more than 50,000 registered players at this level. Schools' football is run by the Scottish Schools' Football Association and its regional associations. Compare **Scottish Junior Football Association**.

scout *n.* an official of a club whose duties are to search for new footballing talent, at other clubs, particularly lower-division, non-league and junior teams. The scout will make recommendations to a club as to whether a player is worth signing, either as a contract player or as a junior. Large clubs usually have a network of scouts working around the country, and, may have scouts visiting or working in other countries. *vb.* to perform the role of a scout.

Screen Sport Super Cup *competition* former mini-league competition, sponsored by the European satellite television sports channel Screen Sport, involving the six **Football League** clubs that would have qualified for European competition had **the Union of European Football Associations** not banned English clubs as a result of the **Heysel Stadium disaster**. The competition lasted for only one season (1985-86), although the two-legged final was held over to the following season. The six clubs were **Everton (European Cup), Manchester United (European Cup-winners Cup), Liverpool, Norwich City, Southampton and Tottenham (UEFA Cup)**. *Final result* Liverpool 7–2 Everton (agg.).

screening the ball *tactics* placing the body between an opponent and the ball.

screw-in studs *n. pl* type of **studs** that are attached to the main part of a **football boot** by a threaded screw. They are made of metal or plastic. Screw-in studs were legalised by the **International FA Board** in 1951, replacing traditional leather studs fixed to the boots by nails. Compare **moulded studs**.

scrimmage *tactics* 1. rush by several players to force the ball into the goal. This was a popular way of scoring in football's early years. 2. the term is also used in **American Football** to describe the time that the ball is in play before it is declared as dead.

Scudetto *n.* Italian 1. green, red and white shield worn on the shirts of Italy's national champions for the whole of the following season. A club that wins the Scudetto 10 times is granted the right to wear a gold star above its club badge: an honour granted to the big-three clubs, **Juventus**, **AC Milan** and **Internazionale**. Juventus now has the right to wear two stars following a championship title. **2.** informal name for the Liga Calcio **Serie A** championship and the earlier **Campionato Nazionale**. By 1998, the Scudetto had been won by: Juventus (25 times); AC Milan (15); **Internazionale** (13); **Genoa 1893** (9); **Torino** (8); **Bologna** (7) and Pro Vercelli (7); no other club has won more than two Scudettos.

Scunthorpe United *club* English league. *Dossier* Ground: **Glanford Park**, Scunthorpe, Humberside. Strip: white shirts with claret and sky blue trim, sky blue shorts with claret and white trim, and sky blue socks with claret and white trim. Nickname: Iron. Ground capacity: 9,183. Record attendance: 8,775 v **Rotherham United** (1 May 1989, Division Four). Best average attendance: 12,377 (**Old Show Ground**, 1958-59). Biggest win: 9–0 v Boston United (21 November 1953, **FA Cup**, first round). Biggest defeat: 0–8 v **Carlisle United** (25 December 1952, Division Three (North)). *History* Founded in 1899 from a merger of local clubs including Brumby Hall (formed around 1895). United in turn amalgamated with Lindsey United in 1910 to form Scunthorpe & Lindsey United – reverting to Scunthorpe United in 1956. Brumby Hall first played at the Old Show Ground in 1895 and it was United's home until 1988, when Scunthorpe became the first League club to open a new stadium, Glanford Park, since **Southend United** did so in 1955. The club joined the expanded Division Three (North) in 1950-51, having previously won the Midland Counties League on two occasions (1927 and 1939). Scunthorpe won the Division Three (North) Championship in 1957-58 and enjoyed a six-season period in Division Two during which the club finished fourth in 1961-62 – its highest League position. Following relegation in 1963-64, the club has mainly been in Division Four (Third Division) with only occasional forays into the higher grade. During the 1973-74 season the club's home match against **Exeter City** was never played because the visitors failed to arrive (2 April 1974): Scunthorpe was awarded two points as a result. The club reached the fifth round of the FA Cup in 1958 (0–1 v **Liverpool**) and 1970 (1–3 v **Swindon Town**). Scunthorpe was a Division Four end-of-season playoff semi-finalist in 1987-88, 1988-89 and 1990-91, and in 1991-92, the club was a losing finalist (1–1, 3–4 pens. v **Blackpool**). In 1998-99, Scunthorpe successfully achieved promotion, winning the Third Division playoff (1-0 v Leyton Orient). *League record* Division Two 1958-59 to 1963-64; Division Three 1964-65 to 1967-68, 1972-73, 1983-84; Second Division 1999-00 –; Third Division 1992-93 to 1998-99; Division Three (North) 1950-51 to 1957-58; Division Four 1968-69 to 1971-72, 1973-74 to 1982-83, 1984-85 to 1991-92. *Honours* Division Three (North) 1957-58. *Records* Jack Brownsword holds the record for club League appearances (595, 1950-65); Steve Cammack is Scunthorpe's record League goalscorer (110, 1979-81, 1981-86).

Sealand Road *ground* football ground situated in Chester, Cheshire; former home of **Chester City**. *Dossier* Capacity (1990): 8,747. Pitch dimensions: 104m x 69m. Record attendance: 20,500 v **Chelsea** (16 January 1952, **FA Cup**, third round replay). *Keynotes* Chester played its first match at Sealand Road on 15 December 1906 (v Bangor) and it was the club's home until 1990, with the final game there taking place on 28 April 1990 (v **Rotherham United**, Division Three). The first floodlit match at Sealand Road took place on 12 October 1960 (v **Leyton Orient**, **League Cup**).

season *n.* period of the year in which the main club league and cup competitions are played. The league season starts on the date of the first league match, and closes on a day stipulated by the relevant football authority (the **Premier League**, **Football League**, or **Scottish Football League**, for example). Compare **close season**.

season ticket *n.* admission ticket that entitles the holder to attend all of a club's League and some cup matches each season. Season tickets are usually sold for a particular seat number in the stadium. Season ticket holders are often entitled to additional benefits, such as priority in the purchase of cup tickets. *Keynotes* Every seat at **Newcastle United**'s **St James' Park** ground (other than the 1,800 seats for visiting fans) belongs to a season-ticket holder; a further 12,000 people are on the waiting list to buy. **Napoli**'s **San Paulo** stadium set a then Italian record for **season ticket** sales (70,000) in the mid-1980s with the arrival of Diego **Maradona**. **Juventus** sold a record 40,338 season tickets for the 1997-98 season. In July 1998, **Internazionale** reported that two months before the start of the season the club had sold a record 50,000 season tickets. **Ajax**'s **Amsterdam ArenA** has 46,000 season ticket holders, among its 51,700 capacity.

seat lettering *n.* words, badges and logos picked out in different coloured seats at football grounds. *Keynotes* The Executive Stand at **Nottingham Forest**'s **City Ground**, which was opened in August 1980, has the name "FOREST" picked out in white seats against a backdrop of red. This is thought to be the first occasion that seat lettering was used. Since then the use of seat lettering has become commonplace.

Seba United *club* Jamaica league club based in Montego Bay. Strip: red and green striped shirts, green shorts. Jamaica League champions 1987, 1997; Jamaica Cup 1992 and 1995.

Second Class League *competition* original name of the English **Football League** Division Two.

second cautionable offence *rules* infringement of the **Laws of the game** committed after a player has already received a **caution** for a previous offence in the same match. A player committing such a second offence will be **sent off**. A player should also be sent off for committing a second offence before the referee has recorded the initial caution.

second half *n.* see **half** (sense 1).

second strip *n.* another name for **away strip**. *Keynotes* **Manchester United** changed from its all grey strip, which manager Alex **Ferguson** claimed made his players indistinguishable from the crowd, at half-time during a **Premier League** match against **Southampton** at the **Dell**. **Chelsea** was forced to wear **Coventry City**'s second strip (red and black checks), with the badge and sponsors name blacked out, after the club arrived at **Highfield Road** to find that its blue strip clashed with Coventry's first strip, forcing the match to be delayed by 15 minutes (9 April 1997). Referee Steve Dunn asked **Sheffield United**'s players to replace their black socks during half-time in the club's 1997 sixth-round **FA Cup** tie against Coventry City because he also was wearing black socks. A set of white socks were brought under police escort from Coventry's training ground. Referee David Elleray was forced to change his top during the Premier League clash between **Aston Villa** and **Wimbledon** at **Villa Park** on 12 September 1998 because of a clash, while **Norwich City** players changed their kit at half-time in a First Division encounter with **Barnsley** at the **Oakwell Ground** due to a clash with the match official's colours (8 September 1998). **FIFA** instructed the 32 nations competing in the 1998 **World Cup** to wear strips which would be distinguishable on black and white television sets, because viewers in many countries had no access to colour sets. **Sunderland**'s supporters were allowed to choose the club's 1998-99 second strip. Fans had the option of four designs and over 11,000 of them stated their preference via a specially constructed polling booth at the club's **Stadium of Light**.

Secteur 6 *club* Niger national league club, based in the capital Niamey. Ground: Musulman, capacity: 1,500. *Keynotes* Secteur 6 holds the national league record of five consecutive titles (1966 to 1970). Niger League champions 1966, 1967, 1968, 1969 and 1970.

seeding *misc.* arrangements to ensure big clubs/countries are not drawn to meet each other in the early or qualifying stages of tournaments/competitions. *Keynotes* The League Champions of the strongest **UEFA** countries, for example, are seeded for the **Champions League** stage of the **European Cup**. A similar system operates in the **UEFA Cup**. In 1998-99, a seeding system, consisting of four groups containing the 16 strongest clubs, was established for the second round of the UEFA Cup, ensuring that the big clubs were kept apart.

Seeldrayers, Rodolphe *n.* fourth president of **FIFA** (1954-55). Nationality: Belgian.

Seeler, Uwe *player* Striker. **West Germany** international (72 caps, 43 goals, 1954–70). Born 5 November 1936, in Hamburg. Career ca. 1952-71. *Club* **Hamburg SV**. *Keynotes* Seeler made his debut for West Germany at only 17 years 345 days (v **France**, in Hanover, 16 October 1954, 1–3; as a substitute) and played in four **World Cup** finals tournaments (21 matches in total, 1958–70) – scoring in all four (a feat he shares with **Pelé**). His late back-headed equaliser for

West Germany against **England** in the 1970 World Cup quarter-final is, perhaps, the goal most remembered by England supporters; West Germany went on to win the match in extra time, putting the holders out of the competition (3–2, in León, Mexico). Seeler played in the 1968 **European Cup-winners Cup** final against **AC Milan** (0–2, at Feyenoord, Rotterdam); he was the tournament's top scorer with six goals. He later became president of Hamburg SV. *Honours* World Cup runner-up (West Germany, 1966; captain).

SEIB Diourbel (Société Electique et Industrial de Baol) *club* Senegal national league club, based in Diourbel. Ground: Ely Manal Fall, capacity: 3,000. Strip: red shirts, white shorts. West African Cup semi-final 1986; Senegal League champions 1980, 1983, 1987.

Seiko *club* Hong Kong league club. *Keynotes* Seiko holds the national league record of seven consecutive titles (1979 to 1985). Hong Kong League champions 1973, 1975, 1979, 1980, 1981, 1982, 1983, 1984, 1985; Hong Kong Cup 1975, 1976, 1978, 1980, 1981, 1986.

Sekondi Hasaacas *club* Ghanaian League club based in Sekondi, formed 1929. Ground: Gyandu Park, capacity: 15,000. Strip: green shirts, white shorts. **African Cup-winners Cup** semi-final 1981, **West African Football Union General Eyadema Cup** 1982; Ghanaian Cup 1980, 1985.

Selangor FA *club* Malaysian national league football team, based in Petaling Jaya, in the state of Selangor. Ground: Shah Alam Stadium, capacity: 80,000. Strip: red and yellow shirts, red and yellow shorts. *Keynotes* Selangor's 29 outright domestic cups (plus two shared) is an Asian club record;only three clubs in the world have won more domestic cups (**Linfield**, **Al Ahly**, **Celtic**). **Asian Champion Teams Cup** – played in the first tournament in 1967, runners up 1967 (1–2 v **Hapoel Tel-Aviv** in final in Bangkok, Thailand); Malaysia Cup: 1922, 1927, 1928 (joint), 1929 (joint), 1935, 1936, 1938, 1949, 1956, 1959, 1961, 1962, 1963, 1966, 1968, 1969, 1971, 1972, 1973, 1975, 1976, 1978, 1979, 1981, 1982, 1984, 1986, 1995, 1996, 1997, 1998.

Select League (US) *competition* former United States professional football league – the former top division of the **United Systems of Independent Soccer Leagues** (USISL). Merged in 1997 with the A-League, to form a new A-League, but under the administration of the USISL. Only winners: California Jaguars (1996).

Selhurst Park *ground* English football ground situated in south London; home of both **Crystal Palace** and **Wimbledon**. *Dossier* Ground capacity: 26,400 all seated. Pitch dimensions: 100.5m x 68m. Record attendance: 51,482 Palace v **Burnley** (11 May 1979, Division Two). Best average attendance: 30,167 (Palace, 1972-73). *History* Following the Admiralty's takeover of the Crystal Palace ground in 1915, the football club played at several venues before settling at Selhurst Park in 1924. Selhurst Park is situated on a former brickfield that belonged to the London Brighton and South Coast

Railway Company. The club bought the site for £2,750 in 1922 and played its first match at the ground on 30 August 1924 (v **Sheffield Wednesday**, Division Two). Archibald **Leitch** was responsible for the ground's development, including designing its main stand. Although the club's owners had grand plans for Selhurst Park in the early 1950s, the ground was virtually the same from 1924 until 1969. Then, to coincide with Palace's first season in the top flight, a new stand, named after chairman Arthur Wait, was built. In September 1985, **Charlton Athletic** moved to Selhurst Park in the first long-term **groundshare** between two English league clubs. When Charlton returned to The **Valley** in 1991, **Wimbledon** took its place at Selhurst Park, agreeing a seven-year groundshare with Palace. Wimbledon's match against Sheffield Wednesday on 2 October 1991 attracted a crowd of only 3,121 – the lowest-ever post-World War II Division One attendance. Selhurst Park became an all-seater stadium in August 1995, when the Holmesdale End, which seats over 8,000 spectators, was opened. The first floodlit match to be played at Selhurst Park took place on 28 September 1953 (Palace v **Chelsea**, friendly). **Millwall** has played several "home" matches at the ground due to the temporary closure of the **Den** following **crowd trouble**. Selhurst Park also staged an **England** international on 1 March 1926 (v **Wales**) and an **Olympic football** match (**South Korea** v **Sweden**) during the 1948 London Olympics.

Semaine Anglaise *misc.* French term for a midweek football match – a rare feature of French football.

Semassi Sokode AC (Athletic Club) *club* Togo national league club based in Sokode-Tchaoudjo, founded 1978. Ground: Sokode, capacity: 15,000. Strip: red shirts, white shorts. **African Cup of Champion Clubs** semi-final 1984; Togo league champions 1978, 1979, 1981, 1982, 1983, 1993, 1994, 1995; Togo Cup 1980, 1982, 1983, 1990, 1991.

send off *rules* to punish an individual player by sending him or her off the field of play for one of a number of offences listed in the **Laws of the game** (Law XII). A referee is the only official allowed to send off a player and, in doing so, shows the offending player a **red card** and records the player's name. A player may be sent off in addition to his or her team being punished by way of a **free kick** or **penalty kick**. A player may be sent off for **violent conduct**; **serious foul play**; using **offensive** or **abusive language**; or for a **second cautionable offence**. A player will be sent off for **serious foul play** if, in the opinion of the referee, he or she commits a **foul** or **handball** that prevents an opposition player from taking a clear opportunity to score a goal (a "**professional foul**"; see also **last man**). If a player is sent off before play starts, then he or she may be replaced by one of the **substitutes**. After play has started, a player who has been sent off cannot be replaced. The implications of being sent off vary according to the rules of a particular competition; however, players sent off will receive an **automatic suspension**, the length of which

is defined by the **competition rules**. *Keynotes* **Umpires** were first given powers to send off players in 1873. The record for the highest number of sendings off in a single match in English league football was set by **Chesterfield** and **Plymouth Argyle** on 22 February 1997, when five players were dismissed. Chesterfield, the home side, had two players dismissed, and Plymouth three; two from each side were sent off in a fight in the last minute of play. The record was equalled on 3 December 1997 (**Wigan Athletic** v **Bristol Rovers**), when Bristol Rovers had four players sent off and Wigan one (the home side eventually won 3–0). Other British clubs to have four players dismissed in a single match are **Hereford United** (away v **Northampton Town**, 6 September 1992, Third Division), **Stranraer** (away v **Airdreonians**, 3 December 1994 Scottish First Division) and **Hearts of Midlothian** (away v **Rangers**, 14 September 1996, Scottish Premier Division). The fastest sending off in world football was that of **Bologna** player Giuseppe Lorenzo, dismissed after 10 seconds against **Parma** (9 December 1990, Italian league). The fastest sending off in British football was Mark Smith of **Crewe Alexandra** after 19 seconds (v **Darlington**, at Darlington, 12 March 1994, Third Division); **Blackburn Rovers**' goalkeeper Tim Flowers was sent off after 72 seconds, a record for the FA **Premier League** (v **Leeds United**, 1 February 1995). Kevin Moran of **Manchester United** is the only player to be sent off in an **FA Cup** final (v **Everton**, May 1985, at **Wembley** Stadium, 1–0). Jock Buchanan of Rangers was the first player to be sent off in a **Scottish** FA Cup final (v **Kilmarnock**, May 1929, 0–2). In 1994-95, 376 players were sent off in English league and cup football; this compares with 183 in the 1984-85 season. There have been three occasions when 13 players were sent off in **Football League** matches on one day (14 December 1985, 19 August 1995 and 9 September 1995). Fifteen players were sent off in English league and cup football on 20 November 1982 (12 in the FA Cup and three in the Football League). There have never been more than four players sent off on any one day in Scottish league or cup football. Eight players were sent off in four separate incidents during a Brazilian **Supercopa** quarter-final between **Grêmio** (four) and **Peñarol** (four) in October 1993. Gremio won 2-0. Brazilian club America Futebol Clube (of Três Rios) had five players dismissed in a Brazilian domestic cup match against Itaperuna Esporte Clube (23 November 1991; the match was abandoned – because there were fewer than seven players on the America FC team – and the tie awarded to Itaperuna). Scottish international winger Willie Johnston was sent off 21 times in his first-class career (once with **Scotland**, seven times with Rangers, six times with **West Bromwich Albion**, four times with the **Vancouver Whitecaps** and three times with Hearts of Midlothian) – a record for a British-born player. **Colchester United** was the first Football League club to have its goalkeeper (John Keeley) and substitute goalkeeper (Nathan Munson) sent off in same match – both for professional fouls (16 October 1993, 0–5, v **Hereford United**, Third Division). **Italy**'s substitute Giuseppe Bergomi was sent off despite going on in the 89th minute of his country's **European Championship** qualifier against **Norway** in 1991.

sending off *rules* the act of being **sent off**, also called dismissal.

Senegal *country CAF* republic in West Africa on the Atlantic Ocean. A flat dry country, bordered by **Gambia**, **Guinea**, **Guinea-Bissau**, **Mali** and **Mauritania**. Area: 196,720 sq km (75,935 sq miles). Population: 7,970,000 (1993 est.). Languages: French, native languages and dialects. Capital: Dakar. *Dossier* Football association (Fédération Sénégalaise de Football, Dakar) formed in 1960, affiliated to **FIFA** in 1962 and **Confédération Africaine de Football** (CAF) in 1963, president: Alioune Gueye; general secretary: Doudou Sene. Season played from October to July. National stadium: Stade de l'Amite, Dakar, capacity: 60,000. National strip: green shirts, yellow shorts, red socks. Nickname of national team: the Lions. First international game: 1962 v **Ivory Coast** (1–1, Dakar, friendly). Biggest victory: 6–0 v **Mauritania** (13 February 1984, neutral venue, **Amilcar Cabral Cup**). Biggest defeat: 0–4 v Mali (1965, Mali, African Games qualifier), 0–4 v **Congo Democratic Republic** (Zaire) (30 January 1969, Zaire, friendly), 0–4 v **Tunisia** (15 July 1995, in Tunisia, **African Nations Cup** qualifier). Notable international players: Sagna, Cheikh Seck, Francois Bocande, Roger Mendy. *International tournament record* **Olympic Games** – first entered 1972, never qualified for finals tournament; **Women's World Cup** – never qualified for finals tournament; **World Cup** – first entered 1970, qualifying tournament second round group stage 1994; **African Cup of Nations** – first entered 1965, fourth place 1990 (0–1 v **Zambia**, Algiers, Algeria third/fourth playoff), quarter-finals 1992, 1994, also qualified for finals tournament 1968, 1986, hosts 1992; **African Youth Cup** (under-20) – qualified for finals tournament 1995; **Amilcar Cabral Cup** – winners 1979, 1980, 1983, 1984, 1985, 1986, 1991 (1–0, v Cape Verde), runners-up 1982, 1993, 1997; **CEDEAO Cup** – winners 1985, runners-up 1991. *Record against British and Irish national teams* none played. *History* National league commenced in 1960, first won by ASC Jeanne d'Arc. *Record in international club tournaments* **African Cup of Champion Clubs** – ASC Jeanne d'Arc (semi-final1974), **US Goreé** (semi-final 1979, 1985), **ASC Diaraf** (semi-final 1983, quarter-final 1996); **African Cup-winners Cup** – ASC Jeanne d'Arc (semi-final 1975); **CAF Cup** – ASC Jeanne d'Arc (runners-up 1998); West African Football Union General Eyadema Cup – **SEIB Diourbel** (semi-final 1986), AS Police (winners 1979, 1980). Other leading clubs: **ASC Ndiambour**, ASC Yeggo (of Dakar, Senegal Cup 1998), AS Douanes (of Dakar, League champions 1993, 1997, Senegal Cup 1986, 1997), Sonacos (of Diourbel, League champions 1996).

senior football club *misc.* **1. Scotland.** Scottish club that plays in one of the major leagues affiliated to the **Scottish Football Association**: **Scottish Premier League**, **Scottish Football League**, **Highland League**, **East of Scotland League** and **South of Scotland League**. Senior clubs are eligible to enter the Scottish FA Cup (the Highland League, East of Scotland League and South of Scotland League clubs doing so via the **Scottish Qualifying Cup**). **2. England**. Technically, the term senior football club also applies to adult football clubs at the higher levels of English football, though the expression is rarely used except in football administration. Compare **junior football club**.

Sergipe *state* one of the 27 state leagues in **Brazil**, founded 1918. Leading clubs: CS Sergipe (Aracaju), Associacao Desportiva Confianca (Aracaju), Associacao Olimpica Itabaiana (Aracaju).

Serie A *competition* the Italian national league premier division. *History* Although an Italian national championship, the **Campionato Nazionale**, was introduced in 1898, a true national league, the Liga Calcio, did not begin until 1929-30. The Milan club **Internazionale** won the first championship in 1929-30 (then playing as Ambrosiana-Inter). The Championship was not played from 1944 to 1945, but resumed immediately after World War II in 1946. The national champions wear a championship shield, the **Scudetto**, on their shirts for the following season (the championship is informally called the Scudetto). A club that wins the championship 10 times is granted the right to wear a gold star above its club badge: an honour granted to the big-three clubs, **Juventus**, **AC Milan** and Internazionale. Juventus now has the right to wear two stars, having won the championship 25 times to 1998. By 1998, the Liga Calcio championship (Campionato Nazionale and Serie A) had been won by: Juventus (25 times); AC Milan (15); Internazionale (13); **Genoa 1893** (9); **Torino** (8); **Bologna** (7) and Pro Vercelli (7); no other club had won more than two titles. Gabriel **Batistuta** scored in each of Fiorentina's first 11 matches in Serie A in the 1994-95 season – a Serie A record. *League system* Serie A, has 18 clubs, playing each other twice (home and away) in a season. Three points are awarded for a victory, with one for a draw: final positions for clubs level on points are determined by **goal difference**. The bottom three clubs are automatically relegated, while the fourth relegation place is determined by a **playoff** (spareggio) between the 14th and 15th placed club at a neutral venue. Twenty clubs compete in **Serie B**, with the top four clubs automatically promoted to Serie A, and the bottom four automatically relegated to Serie C1 (there is no playoff). Serie C1 is divided into two regional divisions of 18 clubs (Girone A and B). The four clubs promoted to Serie B are decided as follows: the two divisional champions are promoted automatically, with one further place in each division decided by a playoff series between the second-, third-, fourth- and fifth-placed clubs. Below Serie C1 is the Serie C2, comprising three regional divisions. There is a national women's Serie A of 16 clubs. There are also three regional Serie B divisions.

Serie B *competition* Italian national football league second division. See **Serie A**.

Serie C1 *competition* Italian national football league third divisions; comprised of two regional divisions. See **Serie A**.

serious foul play *rules* one of the offences listed in the **Laws of the game**, punishable by the offending player being **sent off** (Law XII). Serious foul play includes a dangerous and illegal **tackle from behind**; any other reckless and dangerous foul tackle, and where, in the opinion of the referee, a player commits a **foul** or **handball** that prevents an opposition player from taking a clear opportunity to score a goal (a "**professional foul**"). If a player attempts to prevent a goal by illegally handling the ball, but the ball still goes in the net, then a goal is awarded and the player is guilty of the lesser offence of **unsporting behaviour** and should receive a **caution**. See **last man**, **moving away from goal**.

Servette FC Geneve (Football Club) *club* Swiss national league club based in Geneva, founded 1890. Ground: Charmilles, capacity: 30,000. Strip: orange shirts, orange shorts. **European Cup-winners Cup** quarter-final 1967, 1979; Swiss national champions 1907, 1918, 1922, 1925, 1926, 1930, 1933 (three regional leagues operated until 1933, with the national championship decided by an inter-league playoff), 1934, 1940, 1946, 1950, 1961, 1962, 1979, 1985, 1994; Swiss Cup 1928, 1949, 1971, 1978, 1979, 1984.

set out their stall *informal* to make clear a team's strategy for a match – for example to play defensively for a draw or to seek an **away goal** – usually evident in the early minutes of the game, or even through the team selection.

set piece *n.* term referring to a **corner** or **free kick**. Compare **open play**.

set play *n.* rehearsed strategy executed at a **corner** or **free kick**.

Seung-zin *player* Striker. **North Korea** international. *Keynotes* Seung-zin scored the late equaliser in Korea's 1–1 draw against **Chile** which helped the country to qualify for the **World Cup** quarter-finals of 1966 (15 July 1966, **Ayresome Park**, Middlesbrough). Seung-zin also opened the scoring after one minute in the 3–5 defeat by **Portugal** in the quarter-final at **Goodison Park** (23 July 1966), a match in which Korea had been leading 3–0 after 22 minutes.

Sever's disease *medical* an **overuse injury** affecting the heel bone and **Achilles' tendon**

Sevilla (FC) *club* Spanish league. *Dossier* Ground: Sánchez Pizjuán (Estadio), Sevilla, Andalucía. Strip: white shirts with red trim, white shorts with red trim, white socks. Ground capacity: 70,000. *History* Formed by employees, some English, of Rio Tinto mines in 1905. The club's official name is Sevilla Fútbol Club. Sevilla's ground, which is situated in the Nervión district, was renamed after a former president. The club's only honours, one domestic title (**Primera Liga**) and

three Spanish Cup (**Copa del Rey**) victories, were all won within a 13-year period between 1935 and 1949. Diego **Maradona** had a 26-match career with Sevilla in 1992-93, while the 1998 World Cup **golden boot** winner Davor **Suker** also played for the Andalucían club before departing to **Real Madrid** in 1996. Sevilla was almost automatically relegated in 1994-95 for financial irregularities, but the club retained its Primera Liga status, after being reinstated by the Spanish football authorities – which turned the Spanish top flight into a 22-club league. *Honours* Spanish League 1945-46; Spanish Cup 1935 (3–0 v Sabadell), 1939 (6–2 v Racing Ferrol), 1948 (4–1 v Celta Vigo).

Sex Discrimination Act *legal* UK statute laid before Parliament in 1975, for the purposes of preventing unfair discrimination by virtue of sex, particularly with regard to employment, education or housing. Section 44 of the Act specifically exempts competitive sports from its general principles where physical strength, stamina or physique is an issue: put simply, it is perfectly lawful for a football team to restrict its membership to one sex. The majority of sports are played on this basis. Section 44 states: "Nothing in parts II to IV [the general duties of the Act] shall, in relation to any sport, game or other activity of a competitive nature where the physical strength, stamina or physique of the average woman puts her at a disadvantage to the average man, render unlawful any act related to the participation of a person as a competitor in events involving that activity which are confined to competitors of one sex." The main point to note is that the act refers to the "average woman", discrimination is, therefore, justified irrespective of the strengths of any individual competitor. Football clearly falls under this definition. There are some sports, however, where women are not at an obvious physical disadvantage; darts and snooker, for example. Preventing a woman from gaining a professional licence in such sports would probably fall foul of the law, if the discrimination was because of the applicant's sex rather than any justifiable qualification criteria. It would also be unlawful for the Football Association to prohibit a women from officiating, as a **referee** or **referee's assistant**, at a men's match if, again, the discrimination was by virtue of her sex (see **referee, woman**). In football, any argument for discrimination based on physical strength falls down at early junior level where girls and boys under 11 years of age are of similar average strength and physique; a principle clearly taken on board by the English Schools Football Association which, in 1990, ruled that mixed competitive matches could be played in schools, by children up to the age of 11 years. Education legislation in the **United States of America** requires that colleges provide equal funding to men and women, including sports budgets. Funding for men's sports continues to outweigh women's funding by three to one, although women's collegiate football has benefited with an increase in the number of women's teams during the 1990s. See also **Bennett v Football Association Ltd and Nottinghamshire FA**.

sexy football *informal* term describing exciting and penetrative football. It was first coined to describe the preferred style of play adopted by Ruud **Gullit** on becoming **Chelsea** manager in 1996.

Seychelles *country CAF* republic and archipelago in the Indian Ocean, off east Africa, comprising 37 granite and 49 coral islands and many islets: the world's largest tropical lagoon. Independence from Britain in 1976. Area: 404 sq km (156 sq miles). Population: 73,850 (1994 est.). Languages: Creole, English and French. Capital: Victoria (on the largest island, Mahé). *Dossier* Seychelles Football Confederation (Victoria) formed in 1979 affiliated to **FIFA** and **Confédération Africaine de Football** (CAF) in 1986, president: Suketu Patel; general secretary: Wilhem Boniface. National stadium: People's Stadium, Victoria, capacity: 7,000. National strip: red shirts, blue shorts, white socks. First international game: 13 March 1974 v **Reunion** (0–2, Reunion, friendly). Biggest victory: has not won by more than a single goal. Biggest defeat: 0–6 v **Madagascar** (27 August 1990, neutral venue, **Indian Ocean Games**). *International tournament record* **Olympic Games** – never entered; **Women's World Cup** – never entered **World Cup** – never entered; **African Cup of Nations** – first entered 1990 (lost in preliminary round of qualifying tournament), never qualified for finals tournament; **Indian Ocean Games** – runners-up 1979, third place 1990; **Under-17 World Championship** – never entered; **World Youth Cup** (under-20) – never entered. *Record against British and Irish national teams* none played. *History* National league championship commenced in 1979. Seychelles club Anse Boileau has the unenviable distinction of losing an African Cup-winners Cup match by the biggest margin (1-12 v Mwanza Pamba SC of Tanzania, 1990, preliminary round; it lost 1-17 on aggregate). *Record in international club tournaments* **African Cup of Champion Clubs** – no teams past first round; **African Cup-winners Cup** – no teams past first round. Leading clubs: **St Louis**, St Michel United (league champions 1996, 1997, Seychelles Cup 1997), Red Star (of Anse aux Pins, league champions 1998, Seychelles Cup 1995).

SFA *abbrev.* **Scottish Football Association**

Shakhter Donetsk *club* Ukraine national league and former-Soviet Union league club based in Donetsk (formerly Stalino – the town was originally named Yuzovka, literally "Hughesovka", after John Hughes, the Welshman who founded an ironworks there in 1872). The club was founded in 1936 (as Stachanovec Stalino, changed name in 1946 to Shakhter Donetsk). Ground: Shakhter, capacity: 41,000. Strip: orange and black striped shirts, black shorts. **European Cup-winners-Cup** quarter-final 1983; **UEFA Cup** third round 1977; Ukraine league runners-up 1994, 1997, 1998; Ukraine Cup 1995, 1997, runners-up 1996; former-Soviet Union league runners-up 1975, 1979; former Soviet Union Cup 1961, 1962, 1980, 1983.

Shackleton, Len *player* Inside-forward. **England** international (5 caps). Born 3 May 1922. Career ca. 1938-57. *Clubs* **Bradford Park Avenue**, **Newcastle**

United, Sunderland. *Keynotes* Member of **Arsenal's** ground staff before turning professional with Bradford Park Avenue in December 1940. Moved to Newcastle United for £13,000 in October 1946 and, in February 1948, to Sunderland for £20,050. He made 384 **Football League** appearances, scoring 126 goals. On his debut for Newcastle he scored six goals in a Division Two encounter with **Newport County** (13-0, 5 October 1946). Shackleton retired through injury in September 1957, after publishing an autobiography entitled "Clown Prince of Soccer" (a tag that had followed him throughout his career). This provoked controversy, especially the chapter devoted to "the average club director's knowledge of football" – which consisted of a blank page. Included in the **Football League Centenary 100 players**.

Shahin FC *club* former name, until 1968, of **Piroozi**.

Shamrock Rovers *club* Republic of Ireland national league club based in the capital Dublin, on the east coast, founded 1899. Ground: Royal Dublin Society Showgrounds, capacity: 22,000. Strip: green and white hooped shirts, green shorts. **European Cup-winners Cup** second round 1963, 1967, 1979; **UEFA Cup/Fairs Cup** second round 1966, 1983; Republic of Ireland League champions 1923, 1925, 1927, 1932, 1938, 1939, 1954, 1957, 1959, 1964, 1984, 1985, 1986, 1987 1994; Republic of Ireland **FAI Cup** 1925, 1929, 1930, 1931, 1932, 1933, 1936, 1940, 1944, 1945, 1948, 1955, 1956, 1962, 1964, 1965, 1966, 1967, 1968, 1969, 1978, 1985, 1986, 1987, runners up 1922 (the first FAI Cup), 1926, 1946, 1957, 1958, 1984, 1991. Notable former players: Tommy Eglington (24 caps for the Republic of Ireland, later with **Everton**), Peter Farrell (28 caps for the Republic of Ireland, later with Everton), Johnny **Giles** (59 appearances for the Republic of Ireland), Paddy Mulligan (50 caps for the Republic of Ireland, later with **Chelsea**, **Crystal Palace**, and **West Bromwich Albion**), Frank O'Neill (20 caps for the Republic of Ireland), Ray **Treacy** (42 caps for the Republic of Ireland, formerly with **West Bromwich Albion**, **Charlton Athletic**, **Swindon Town** and **Preston North End**).

Shanghai Shenua Chinese national league club based in Shanghai. Ground: Shanghai Stadium, capacity: 80,000. Chinese league champions 1961, 1962, 1983, 1995, runners-up 1996; Chinese Cup 1998.

Shankly, Bill *manager* born 2 September 1913; died 29 September 1981. *Clubs* **Carlisle United**, **Grimsby Town, Workington, Huddersfield Town, Liverpool**. *Honours* League (Liverpool 1963-64, 1965-66, 1972-73); Division Two Champions (Liverpool 1961-62); **FA Cup** (Liverpool 1965, 1974); **UEFA Cup** (Liverpool 1973). *Keynotes* Shankly retired from playing in March 1949, having won five caps for Scotland as a right-half during a career with Carlisle United and **Preston North End**. He won an FA Cup winner's medal with Preston in 1938 (v Huddersfield Town). He joined Liverpool as manager in December

1959, retiring in July 1974. Shankly led Liverpool to its first FA Cup victory (1965, v **Leeds United**) and, in 1973, to its first success in European competition (UEFA Cup, v **Borussia Mönchengladbach**). In 1974, he was awarded an OBE. Shankly is credited with uttering the immortal witticism: "Some people say football is a matter or life and death. They're wrong. It's much more important than that."

shape   *n.*   the notional quality of retaining a **formation** during a game of football. A team that retains its shape, for example, is one that keeps its players in their allotted position, holds its defensive line and maintains control in the midfield.

Shareholders United Against Murdoch (SUAM) *misc.* group of **Manchester United** shareholders campaigning against the proposed takeover of the club by BSkyB. The bid was rejected by the Competition Commission in April 1999.

Shay   *ground*   English football ground situated in Halifax, west Yorkshire; home of **Halifax Town**. *Dossier* Ground capacity: 7,449. Pitch dimensions 100.5m x 64m. Record attendance: 36,885 v **Tottenham Hotspur** (14 February 1953, **FA Cup**, fifth round). Best average attendance: 10,525 (1922-23). *Keynotes* Halifax first played at the Shay in 1921-22 and the name is derived from the Shay Syke district in which it is situated. The ground hosted baseball and speedway for a period after World War II. The Shay was the setting on 16 November 1985 for the lowest-ever attendance at an FA Cup tie between two **Football League** clubs, when only 1,501 turned up to watch Halifax play **Scunthorpe United** (first round). The first floodlit match at the Shay took place on 14 February 1953 (v **Red Star Belgrade**, friendly).

Shearer, Alan   *player*   Striker. **England** international (49 caps, 22 goals). Born 13 August 1970. Career ca. 1987-. *Clubs* **Southampton**, **Blackburn Rovers**, **Newcastle United**. *Keynotes* Joined Southampton as ann apprentice in April 1988, going on to score 23 goals in 118 **Football League** appearances for the club. He became the youngest player to score a Division One hattrick when he scored three for Southampton against **Arsenal** on 9 April 1988 at the age of 17 years and 140 days. Shearer moved to Blackburn Rovers for a record £3.6 million in July 1992 and achieved a phenomenal scoring rate, netting 122 goals in 138 League games. Thus, Shearer was the first player to score 100 **Premier League** goals. He became the world's most expensive player when he transferred to Newcastle United for £15 million in July 1996. Shearer topped the Premier League goalscoring charts for three consecutive seasons between 1995-96 and 1997-98. Shearer made his England debut against **France** on 19 February 1992. He won the **Golden Boot** award for five goals at the 1996 **European Championship**, having gone 13 internationals without scoring prior to the tournament. Voted **Footballer of the Year** in 1994 and **PFA Footballer of the Year** in both 1995 and 1997. Included in the **Football League Centenary 100 players**. *Honours*

League Championship (Blackburn Rovers 1994-95).

Sheffield FC   *club*   former English club. *Keynotes* Established in 1857 by members of Sheffield Cricket Club, it was one of the earliest football clubs outside London. The club adopted its own set of rules (**Sheffield rules**) before coming into line with those of the **Football Association**. Joined the FA shortly after is formation in 1863. Sheffield took part in the first recorded **charity match** (1862).

Sheffield Football Association   *confederation*   early regional football association founded in Sheffield in 1868, with local clubs including The Wednesday (later **Sheffield Wednesday**) but not Sheffield FC, which had joined the **Football Association**. Adopted and modified the **Sheffield rules**.

Sheffield rules   *n. pl.*   early set of rules dating from 1857, established by **Sheffield FC**. The 11 rules outlawed running with the ball while handling it, and did not, in the original code, include an **offside** rule (most codes at that time prohibited players from being in front of the ball when it was passed). The rules were modified to include scoring points for outer goals or **rouges** (abolished in 1868). The Sheffield rules were adopted by the **Sheffield Football Association** formed in 1868, which introduced a standard width goal of eight yards (7.3 metres), though opting for a crossbar height of nine feet (2.74 metres) – the Football Association had chosen eight feet (2.44 metres). The Sheffield FA also introduced an offside rule: ruling that an attacking player was offside if, when the ball was played, he was both in front of the ball and the last defender (at that time the **Football Association** ruled that a player would be offside only if he was both in front of the ball and one or both of the last two defenders). In 1870, the Sheffield FA introduced **free-kicks** for handling and offsides, as well as **corner kicks** (adopted by the Football Association in 1872). The Sheffield FA amended its rules on 26 February 1877, bringing them into line with those of the Football Association; adopting **throw-in**s, free-kicks for fouls, the FA's version of the offside rule, and 11-a-side matches. These amendments effectively unified Association Football rules across the country.

Sheffield United   *club*   English league. *Dossier* Ground: **Bramall Lane**, Sheffield, south Yorkshire. Strip: red and white striped shirts, black shorts, red socks with white trim. Nickname: Blades. Ground capacity: 30,370 all seated. Record attendance: 68,287 v **Leeds United** (15 February 1936, **FA Cup**, fifth round). Best average attendance: 35,094 (1947-48). Biggest win: 10–0 v Burslem **Port Vale** (10 December 1892, Division Two). Biggest defeat: 0–13 v **Bolton Wanderers** (1 February 1890, FA Cup, second round). *History* Founded in September 1889 by the ground committee to make better use of Bramall Lane's facilities – the ground had first been used for football in December 1862 and had been regularly used by The Wednesday (later **Sheffield Wednesday**) until 1887 – and generate additional income. United was elected to the newly-established Division Two in 1892, becoming a limited company (also involving a cricket club) in 1899. In United's first League season, it did not win away until 10 December 1892. Then it won 10–0 at Burslem Port Vale (still United's biggest victory and the only double-figure away win in **Football League** history). At the end of the season, United won promotion to the top flight by winning in the **test matches** (1–0 **Accrington**), that between 1892-93 and 1897-98 were used to determine promotion and relegation. Five years later, United won its only League Championship, having been runners-up the previous season. The following year, despite taking four matches to defeat **Liverpool** in the semi-finals, the club lifted the FA Cup (4–1 v **Derby County**). At the turn of the century, the club was again runners-up in the League, and reached consecutive FA Cup finals over the next two seasons, losing in 1901 (1–3 replay v **Tottenham Hotspur**) and winning a year later (2–1 replay v **Southampton**). The 1902 FA Cup-winning team contained 22-stone goalkeeper, Willie "Fatty" **Foulke**, and the first player to be transferred for £1,000, Alf **Common**. An FA Cup semi-final defeat in 1914 (0–1 replay v **Burnley**) was followed by a further success in the competition in the so-called **Khaki Cup final** of 1915 (3–0 v **Chelsea**). United recorded its fourth FA Cup final victory in 1925 (1–0 v **Cardiff City**), having lost at the semi-final stage the previous year (0–1 v **Bolton Wanderers**). The club appeared in a further FA Cup semi-final in 1928 (0–1 second replay v **Huddersfield Town**) and, in 1936, as a Second Division club reached another final (0–1 v **Arsenal**) as a Second Division club. United had maintained top-flight status until 1933-34, and for the next 45 years, until it was relegated to Division Three in 1979-80, the club alternated between the top two divisions, never finishing higher than fifth (1961-62) in Division One. In 1960-61, United again reached the FA Cup semi-final stage (0–2 second replay v **Leicester City**). In the summer of 1973, Yorkshire County Cricket Club played its final match at Bramall Lane enabling the ground to be fully enclosed for the first time in 118 years. Within a decade of playing in Division Four (1981-82), United, under the managership of Dave **Bassett**, won promotion back to the top flight – ironically local rivals Sheffield Wednesday went in the opposite direction. In 1993, United lost to Wednesday in an FA Cup semi-final (1–2), which following supporters' protests had been played at **Wembley**. The following season United lost its place in the Premier League, after defeat on the final day of the season (2–3 v Chelsea). United narrowly missed promotion back to the Premier League via the end-of-season playoffs in 1996-97, when the club lost in the final (0–1 v **Crystal Palace**). During an extraordinary few days in March 1998, United's manager, Nigel Spackman, resigned in protest at having to sell players. This precipitated the departure of the club chairman, Mike McDonald, and its chief executive. Ex-United player Steve Thompson was appointed temporary manager and within two weeks he had led the club to an FA Cup semi-final (0–1 v **Newcastle United**). He was replaced by ex-**Manchester United** captain Steve Bruce in summer 1998. In January 1997, Sheffield United floated on the London Stock Exchange (flotation price = 60p). *League record* Premier League 1992-93 to 1993-94; Division One 1893-94 to 1933-34, 1946-47 to 1948-49, 1953-54 to 1955-56, 1961-62 to 1967-68, 1971-72 to 1975-76; First Division 1990-91 to 1991-92, 1994-95–; Division Two 1892-93 to 1893-94, 1934-35 to 1938-39, 1949-50 to 1952-53, 1956-57 to 1960-61, 1968-69 to 1970-71, 1976-77 to 1978-79, 1984-85 to 1987-88, 1989-90; Division Three 1979-80 to 1980-81, 1982-83 to 1983-84, 1988-89; Division Four 1981-82. *Honours* League 1897-88; Division Two 1952-53; Division Four 1981-82; FA Cup 1899 (4–1 v Derby County), 1902 (2–1 replay v Southampton), 1915 (3–0 v Chelsea), 1925 (1–0 v Cardiff City). *Records* Billy Gillespie is United's most capped player (25 for **Northern Ireland**); Joe Shaw holds the record for club appearances (629, 1948-66); Harry Johnson is United's record League goalscorer (205, 1919-30).

Sheffield United plc *n.* publicly-quoted business which owns **Sheffield United**. The club became a fully listed company on the London Stock Exchange in January 1997 (flotation price = 60p). Sheffield United had a market capitalisation – the market value of the company's issued share capital (eg, the quoted price of its shares multiplied by the number of shares outstanding) – of £29.8 million on floatation.

Sheffield Wednesday *club* English league. *Dossier* Ground: **Hillsborough**, Sheffield, south Yorkshire. Strip: blue and white striped shirts with white and yellow trim, blue shorts, blue socks with white and yellow trim. Website: *http://www.swfc.co.uk* Nickname: Wednesday or Owls. Ground capacity: 39,859 all seater. Record attendance: 72,841 v **Manchester City** (17 February 1934, **FA Cup**, fifth round). Best average attendance: 42,634 (1952-53). Biggest win: 12–0 v Halliwell (17 January 1891, FA Cup, first round). Biggest defeat: 0–10 v **Aston Villa** (5 October 1912, Division One). *History* Founded in 1867 as the football arm of the Wednesday Cricket Club, the club was called The Wednesday until 1929, although it severed its links with the cricketers in 1883. The name Wednesday derives from the fact that weekly half-day closing in Sheffield traditionally occurred on that day; thus providing people with the opportunity to pursue sporting activities. The Wednesday's early venues included **Bramall Lane** – before neighbours **Sheffield United** was formed and moved into the ground – and Olive Grove, prior to the club finding a permanent home at Hillsborough in 1899. To help raise the £5,000 purchase price of the site the club became a **limited company**. Hillsborough is situated in the Owlerton district of Sheffield; hence the club's nickname. The Wednesday reached the quarter-final stage of the FA Cup on nine consecutive occasions between 1887-88 and 1895-96, making it to the final in 1890 (1–6 v **Blackburn Rovers**) and winning the trophy in 1896. Despite its early formation, Wednesday did not join the League until

1892-93, when Division One was expanded from 14 to 16 clubs. Wednesday was relegated at the end of the 1898-99 season, but bounced back to Division One at the first attempt before going on to win its first League Championship in 1902-03, which the club successfully defended the following season. During Wednesday's relegation season the club was involved in the shortest League match, after the football authorities ordered the final 11 minutes of a game that had been abandoned due to bad light to be played (v Aston Villa, 13 March 1899, Division One): during the replayed time Wednesday scored a further goal to win 4–1; the two sides then played a benefit match. During the 1899-00 season, the club conceded the lowest number of goals (22) in Division Two for a 34-game season – a record the club holds with Woolwich **Arsenal** (1903-04) – as well as winning all its home matches. Wednesday's team of the late-1920s and early-1930s, when the club again won two consecutive League titles, included **full-back** Ernie Blenkinsop and **inside-forward** Jimmy Seed. After winning the title in 1928-29 the club replaced the "The" with Sheffield and following the second Championship triumph the next season, Wednesday finished third in Division One in four out of seven seasons before being relegated in 1936-37. Wednesday also won the FA Cup for a third time in 1935, but this was the club's last major honour until it won the **League Cup** in 1991. The club did not regain its place in the top flight until 1950 and on one occasion (1946–47) only narrowly avoided relegation to the then Division Three (North). Ironically, Wednesday won promotion on **goal average**, beating arch-rivals Sheffield United into third place. Throughout the 1950s, Wednesday regularly alternated between the top two divisions, with relegation generally followed by immediate promotion – this occurred in 1950-51 and 1951-52, 1954-55 and 1955-56, 1957-58 and 1958-59. In 1966, Wednesday reached the FA Cup final (2–3 v **Everton**). The appointment of former Wednesday player Derek Dooley as manager in 1971 failed to bring success to the club and he was sacked two years later after Wednesday, once again, only narrowly avoided relegation to Division Three. Dooley had played for Wednesday in the early 1950s, scoring 46 goals in 30 Division Two games during the 1951-52 season, but a broken leg, which was amputated, ended his career in 1953. Dooley's successor, Steve Burtenshaw, failed to stop the club's decline and Wednesday was relegated to Division Three for the first time in its history in 1974-75, the club finishing 11 points behind its nearest rivals. The following season the club finished one place above the relegation zone, and spent a further four seasons in Division Two before being promoted. Over the past 20 years, a succession of managers – Len Ashurst, Jackie Charlton, Howard Wilkinson, Peter Eustace, Ron Atkinson, Trevor **Francis**, David Pleat – have attempted to turn Wednesday into the powerful footballing force it was in the late 1920s, without much success. Atkinson led the club to its first trophy in 56 years, the League Cup in 1991, and in 1993 Francis's team reached the

final of both the FA Cup (1–2 a.e.t/replay v **Arsenal**) and League Cup (also 1–2 v Arsenal). Thus, Wednesday is one of only two clubs (the other is **Middlesbrough**, 1997) that have lost both the FA Cup final and the League Cup final in the same season. *League record* Premier League 1992-93–; Division One 1892-93 to 1898-99,1900-01 to 1919-20, 1926-27 to 1936-37, 1950-51, 1952-53 to 1954-55, 1956-57 to 1957-58, 1959-60 to 1969-70, 1984-85 to 1989-90, 1991-92; Division Two 1899-00, 1920-21 to 1925-26, 1937-38 to 1949-50, 1951-52, 1955-56, 1958-59, 1970-71 to 1974-75, 1980-81 to 1983-84, 1990-91; Division Three 1975-76 to 1979-80. *Honours* League 1902-03, 1903-04, 1928-29, 1929-30; Division Two 1899-00, 1925-26, 1951-52, 1955-56, 1958-59; FA Cup 1896 (2–1 v **Wolverhampton Wanderers**), 1907 (2–1 v **Everton**), 1935 (4–2 v **West Bromwich Albion** – *Team* Brown, Nibloe, Catlin, Sharp, Millership, Burrows, Hooper (1), Surtees, Palethorpe (1), Starling, Rimmer (2)); **League Cup** 1991 (1–0 v **Manchester United**); **FA Charity Shield** 1935 (1–0 v **Arsenal**); **Sheriff of London's Charity Shield** 1905 (2–1 v Corinthians). *Records* Nigel Worthington is Wednesday's most capped player (50 (66) for **Northern Ireland**); Andy Wilson holds the record for club appearances (502, 1900-20); he is Wednesday's record league goalscorer (199, 1900-20).

Shelbourne FC *club* Republic of Ireland national league club based in the capital Dublin, on the east coast, founded 1895. Ground: Tolka Park (shared with **Home Farm FC**), capacity: 9,000. Strip: red shirts, white shorts. Known as Reds United from 1934 to 1936. **UEFA Cup/Fairs Cup** second round 1965; all-Ireland League runners-up 1907; **Irish FA Cup** (all-Ireland) winners 1906, 1911, 1920, runners-up 1905, 1907, 1908; Republic of Ireland League champions 1926, 1929, 1931, 1944, 1947, 1953, 1962, 1992; Republic of Ireland **FAI Cup** 1939, 1960, 1963, 1993, 1996, 1997, runners-up 1923, 1925, 1944, 1949, 1951, 1962, 1973, 1975, 1995, 1998; FAI League Cup runners-up 1998. Notable former players: Val Harris (20 caps for Northern Ireland, later with **Everton**), Joe **Haverty** (32 caps for the Republic of Ireland, formerly with **Arsenal**, **Blackburn Rovers**, **Millwall**, **Celtic** and **Bristol Rovers**).

Shell Caribbean Cup *competition* former name, until 1999, of the **Caribbean Nations Cup** (Copa Caribe).

Sheriff of London's Charity Shield *competition* annual match between the best professional team and the best amateur club (usually **Corinthians**), which was a precursor for the current **FA Charity Shield** game. Ten Sheriff of London's Charity Shield matches were played between 1898 and 1907. The match has been revived on three occasions, between 1931 and 1934 (although the 1932 match was not played), in 1965 and 1966, and again in 1983 (to celebrate Corinthians centenary). The trophy was sold an auction for £40,000 in 1998, making it one of the most expensive football items ever to be sold in this way. *Results* 1898,Corinthians 2–2 Sheffield United (shared trophy); 1899, **Aston Villa** 1–1 **Queen's Park** (shared trophy); 1900, Corinthians 2–1 Aston Villa; 1901, Aston Villa 1–0 Corinthians; 1902, **Tottenham Hotspur** 5–2 Corinthians; 1903, **Sunderland** 3–0 Corinthians; 1904, Corinthians 10–3 **Bury**; 1905, The (**Sheffield**) **Wednesday** 2–1 Corinthians; 1906, **Liverpool** 5–1 Corinthians; 1907, **Newcastle United** 5–2 Corinthians; 1931, **Arsenal** 5–3 Corinthians; 1933, Arsenal 9–2 Corinthians; 1934, Tottenham Hotspur 7–4 Corinthians; 1965, Arsenal 7–0 Corinthian Casuals; 1966, Arsenal 5–2 Corinthian Casuals.

Sherpa Van Trophy *competition* the former **Associate Members Cup** between 1987-88 and 1988-89, and a competition open only to clubs from Divisions Three and Four. *Final results* 1987-88, **Wolverhampton Wanderers** 2–0 **Burnley**; 1988-89, Bolton Wanderers 4–1 **Torquay United**.

shield *vb.* to use one's body to keep another player from touching the ball while retaining **control**.

Shielfield Park *ground* Scottish football ground situated in Berwick-upon-Tweed, Northumberland (England); home of **Berwick Rangers**. *Dossier* Ground capacity: 4,131. Pitch dimensions: 102m x 69m. Record attendance: 13,365 v **Rangers** (28 January 1967, **Scottish FA Cup**, first round). *Keynotes* Berwick Rangers first played on the current pitch at Shielfield Park in 1954 (v **Aston Villa**, friendly). The club had previously played on a pitch directly behind the ground's main stand. Berwick sold the ground to the local council in 1985 and, since 1995, Shielfield has been leased by the **supporters' club**. The first floodlit match at the ground took place in 1972 (v **St Mirren**).

Shilton, Peter *player* Goalkeeper. **England** international (125 caps). Born 18 October 1949. Career ca. 1965-97. *Clubs* **Leicester City**, **Stoke City**, **Nottingham Forest**, **Southampton**, **Derby County**, **Plymouth Argyle** (player-manager), **Bolton Wanderers**, **Leyton Orient**. *Keynotes* England's most capped player, made his international debut against **East Germany** on 25 November 1970 and his final appearance against **Italy** on 7 July 1990. This would have been more but under Ron Greenwood's managership Shilton alternated with Ray **Clemence**. Joined Leicester City in 1965, turning professional in September 1966 and making 286 **Football League** appearances for the club. Shilton was understudy in the Leicester goal to Gordon **Banks** and, in November 1974, he followed his predecessor by joining Stoke City in a £325,000 deal. Shilton was transferred to Nottingham Forest for £270,000 in September 1977. He played in 202 League games for Forest; 188 for Southampton, which he joined for £300,000 in August 1982; and 175 for Derby County following a £90,000 move in June 1987. Shilton became the first player to make 1,000 League appearances when he played for Leyton Orient against **Brighton & Hove Albion** at **Brisbane Road** on 22 December 1996. Voted **PFA**

Footballer of the Year in 1978 and awarded the MBE in 1986. Included in the **Football League Centenary 100 players**. *Honours* League Championship (Nottingham Forest 1977-78); Division Two (Leicester City 1970-71); **League Cup** (Nottingham Forest 1979); **European Cup** (Nottingham Forest 1979, 1980).

Shimizu S-Pulse *club* Japanese **J-League** club based in Shimizu, Shizuoka, formed 1991. Ground: Nihondaira, capacity: 20,300. Strip: orange shirts and orange shorts. Japanese League Cup 1996.

shin *vb. informal* to make an illegal tackle designed to hurt or injure the opponent.

shinguard (shinpad) *n.* protective pad worn over the shin, inside the sock. *Rules* shinguards are a compulsory part of the **players equipment**. *Keynotes* Invented and patented in 1874 by **Nottingham Forest** and **England** centre-forward Sam Weller Widdowson. Shinguards were first mentioned in the rules of the game in 1880. Widdowson twice served on the **FA Committee**, 1888 to 1892 and 1893 to 1894, and he appeared three times for Nottinghamshire County Cricket Club. He died on 9 May 1927.

shinpad *n.* another name for **shinguard**.

shin-splints *medical* sharp pain, swelling and tenderness at the front of the **tibia** (shin bone), caused by overexertion.

Shirak Gyumri *club* Armenian national league club, based in Gyumri. Armenian League champions 1994; Armenian Cup runners-up 1993, 1994.

shirt numbers *rules/regulations* unique numbers displayed on **shirts** and allocated to individual players to differentiate them from their team-mates. Shirt numbering may be on a match-by-match basis or by way of fixed **squad numbers**; in either case, no two team-mates may display the same shirt number. Shirt numbers are given in the **match programme**. **Premier League**, **Football League** and **Scottish Football League** rules require that the shirt numbers are included in the **teamsheet** given to the referee before a match (FA Premier League rule E.18, Football League regulation 30.7, Scottish Football League rule 29). Players cannot change their shirt number during a match, unless an outfield player takes over as the goalkeeper (Football League regulation 30.7, Scottish Football League rule 29). Premier League clubs allocate **squad numbers** to their players (FA Premier League rule F.4); shirt numbers may also appear on the front *left* leg of the players' shorts (rule F.8). In the Football League and Scottish Football League, shirts must be numbered 1-14; Football League and Scottish Football League clubs do not adopt squad numbers. Premier League clubs must display the name of the player above the shirt number (FA Premier League rule F.7). Football League clubs must display the player's number, but the addition of his name is optional (Football League regulation 35.9); since the start of the 1999-00 season, Football League clubs have been required to display players' numbers on the front *right* leg of their shorts (Football League regulation 30.8). Players' names are not obligatory on the shirts of players in the Scottish Football League. *History* Shirt numbering was first suggested in 1907 but was rejected by the Football Association. Shirt numbers were first used in a **Football League** match on 25 August 1928: by **Arsenal** (v **Sheffield Wednesday**, at **Hillsborough**) and by **Chelsea** (v **Swansea**, at **Stamford Bridge**). They were first used in an **FA Cup** final in 1933; with **Everton** players numbered 1–11, and **Manchester City** 12–22; Everton's goalkeeper, Sagar, was numbered 1, with Manchester City's keeper, Langford, numbered 22. Everton won the match 3–0. Shirt numbers were made obligatory for Football League matches in 1939, when the system required that numerals would be at least eight inches in height, of a colour that contrasted the shirt, and would be stitched to the back of the shirt. The rule required that the right back would wear number 2; left back 3; right half-back 4; centre half-back 5; left half-back 6; outside right 7; inside right 8; centre forward 9; inside left 10 and outside left 11. The goalkeeper did not wear a shirt number. **Scotland** and **England** first played in numbered shirts on 17 April 1937 (3–1, at Hampden Park, Glasgow, **Home International Championship**). They were introduced for **World Cup** matches at the 1938 tournament in France. 529. *Keynotes* One unusual shirt number is sported by Internazionale's Chilean striker Ivan Zamorano, whose shirt has the number 18, but with a + sign between the two figures (ie 1 + 8) to create the traditional "number nine" of the centre-forward.

shirt *rules/regulations* part of a **player's equipment**, compulsory under the **Laws of the game** (Law IV). The goalkeeper must wear a shirt which distinguishes him or her from the other players and the referee. Also called jersey. *Keynotes* Goalkeepers were first required to wear shirts of a different colour to their teammates in 1909 (though the idea had first been proposed in 1898). They were given a choice from scarlet, blue or white, with green added to the list in 1912. In 1939, the **Football League** made it obligatory for shirts to display the individual **number** of each player.

shirt sponsorship *n.* company name or logo on club shirt. *Regulations* the design of the sponsor's logo must have the approval of the relevant league board or governing body (eg. FA Premier League rule 22, Scottish Football League rule 87). For televised games, they must also comply with rules laid down by the **Union of European Football Associations** (UEFA). The FA **Premier League** prohibits advertisements in any way connected to the tobacco industry (FA Premier League rule F.22). *Keynotes* Most clubs/national sides have major business sponsorship deals which include emblazoning the company name on the club strip. Non-League Kettering Town first appeared in a kit with a sponsor's (Kettering Tyres) name on it in 1976. However, the early days of club sponsorship were controversial. Until 1983, television companies refused to broadcast games in which the teams wore shirts bearing sponsors' names. On 22 October 1980, the showing of television highlights

of **Aston Villa**'s match with **Brighton & Hove Albion** was scrapped after Albion refused to wear shirts that did not bear its sponsor's name. In November 1980, UEFA fined **Nottingham Forest** £7,000 for having a sponsor's name on the club's shirts, while the **Football Association** refused to sanction **Coventry City**'s proposed change of name to Coventry Talbot following a £250,000 sponsorship deal with the car company. Nowadays it is unusual for club shirts not to have a sponsor's name. Arsenal's 18-year deal with the Japanese electrical business JVC, the longest in English football, finished at the end of the 1998-99 season. **Barcelona** refuse to have a sponsor's name on the club's blue and red striped shirts, although the **Barcelona Foundation** receives financial backing from Coca-Cola, Agfa and Black & Decker among others.

shoot-out *n.* chiefly US system for deciding drawn association football games in the **United States of America**. Contrasting the **penalty shoot-out** employed in most Football Association, **FIFA** and **UEFA** tournaments, the shoot-out consists of one-against-one play, with an attacking player starting with the ball 32 metres (35 yards) from the goal, with only the goalkeeper to beat. The attacking player has five seconds from the referee's whistle to dribble the ball and score. Once the goalkeeper has made contact with the ball, the attacking player must not strike the ball again.

shoot-out win *n.* victory in United States league football after a **shoot-out**. Only one point is awarded for such a victory, instead of three for a win in normal playing time (there being no draws in US league football). The system is in operation in the US **Major League Soccer**, **A-League/Select League**, **Pro-League** and **Premier Leagues**. **Paraguay** operates a similar system for its top-flight Division de Honor: a shoot-out-win is awarded two points, with one for the loser; three points are awarded for an outright win. In contrast to the US system, the shoot-out is by conventional penalty kicks.

shooting boots *informal* reference to a player in goalscoring form, "he has his shooting boots on".

short-lived transfers *misc.* transferred players whose career with their new club lasted for a very short period. *Keynotes* David Unsworth lasted only six days at **Villa Park** following his £3 million move from **West Ham United** in July 1998. Unsworth then rejoined his former club, **Everton**. Asa Hartford's time at **Nottingham Forest** following his £400,000 transfer from **Manchester City** in June 1979 lasted only two months before he joined Everton for £100,000. Clive Allen moved to **Crystal Palace** in summer 1980 as part of a deal which took Kenny Sansom to **Arsenal** and only two months after he had joined the **Highbury** club for £1.2 million from **Queens Park Rangers**. Having moved to **Upton Park** from **Oxford United** for £1 million in June 1994, Joey Beauchamp's West Ham United career endured only the close season before he was off to **Swindon Town**. In August 1998, **Coventry City** made a £750,000 profit on the sale of Croatian international

Robert Jarni to **Real Madrid**, having signed him only a few days earlier from **Real Betis** Balompié. In 1933 Jim McCambridge signed for three clubs in three countries in three weeks. He left **Cardiff City** to become player-manager of **Ballymena United**, but changed his mind and signed for **Bristol Rovers**.

shorts *rules/regulations* short trousers, finishing at or above the knee, forming part of a **player's equipment**, compulsory under the **Laws of the game** (Law IV). If **thermal shorts** are worn under the shorts, these must be of the same colour as the shorts. **Premier League** clubs may include the players' **squad numbers** on the front *left* leg of the shorts (FA Premier League rule F.8). Since the start of the 1999-00 season, **Football League** clubs have been required to display players' **shirt numbers** on the front *right* leg of their shorts (Football League regulation 30.8). See also **knickerbockers**.

shot *vb.* to strike the ball firmly with either foot towards the opposition goal in an attempt to score. *n.* the execution of this.

Shrewsbury Town *club* English league. *Dossier* Ground: **Gay Meadow**, Shrewsbury, Shropshire. Strip: blue shirts with white trim, blue shorts, and blue socks with white trim. Nickname: Town or Shrews. Ground capacity: 8,000. Record attendance: 18,917 v **Walsall** (26 April 1961, Division Three). Best average attendance: 9,799 (1951-52). Biggest win: 7–0 v **Swindon Town** (6 May 1955, Division Three (South)). Biggest defeat: 1–8 v **Norwich City** (13 September 1952, Division Three (South), v **Coventry City** (22 October 1963, Division Three). *History* Founded in 1886. Shrewsbury played at several grounds, including at Monkmoor Racecourse and at Barracks Ground, before settling at Gay Meadow in 1910. As early as 1891, Shrewsbury won the **Welsh Cup** (5–2 v **Wrexham**), but the club had to wait 64 years before joining the **Football League** when it joined the expanded Division Three (North) in 1950-51. The following season the club competed in Division Three (South). Aside from 1891, the club made three further appearances in the Welsh Cup final as a non-league side: lifting the trophy in 1938 (2–1 replay v **Swansea** Town); and losing in both 1931 (0–7 v Wrexham) and 1948 (0–3 v Lovells Athletic). In 1959-60 and again in 1967-68, the club narrowly missed promotion to Division Two, finishing third on both occasions. In the inaugural **League Cup** competition in 1960-61, Shrewsbury reached the semi-final stage (3–4 agg. v **Rotherham United**). Shrewsbury's best period occurred between 1977 and 1985, during which the club reached five Welsh Cup finals – lifting the trophy in 1977 (4–2 agg. v **Cardiff City**), 1979 (2–1 agg. v Wrexham), 1984 (2–1 agg. v Wrexham), 1985 (5–1 agg. v **Bangor City**); and losing in 1980 (1–5 agg. v **Newport County**) – and the FA Cup quarter-finals in both 1979 (1–3 replay v **Wolverhampton Wanderers**) and 1982 (2–5 v **Leicester City**). Also, the club twice finished eighth in Division Two (1983-84, 1984-85) – the club's highest-ever League position. In 1995-96, Shrewsbury made its first **Wembley** appearance, reaching the final of the **Auto Windscreens Shield** (1–2 v Rotherham United). *League record* Division Two 1979-80 to 1988-89; Second Division 1994-95 to 1996-97; Division Three 1959-60 to 1973-74, 1975-76 to 1978-79, 1989-90 to 1991-92; Third Division 1993-94, 1997-98–; Division Three (North) 1950-51; Division Three (South) 1951-52 to 1957-58; Division Four 1958-59; 1974-75. *Honours* Division Three 1978-79. Third Division 1993-94; Welsh Cup 1891, 1938 (2–1 replay v Swansea Town), 1977 (4–2 agg. v Cardiff City), 1979 (2–1 agg. v Wrexham), 1984 (2–1 agg. v Wrexham), 1985 (5–1 agg. v Bangor City). *Records* Jimmy McLaughlin (5 (12) for **Northern Ireland**) and Bernard McNally (5 for Northern Ireland) are Shrewsbury's most capped players; Colin Griffith holds the record for club League appearances (406, 1975-89); Arthur **Rowley** is Shrewsbury's record League goalscorer (152, 1958-65 – Rowley holds the League record for the highest individual number of goals (434)).

shutout *n.* US and Canada. Another word for **clean sheet**.

sick as a parrot *informal* of a player disappointed by his/her performance or that of the team, or for losing an important game.

side *n.* **1.** either of two imaginary divisions of the field of play looking from one goal line towards the other, divided on the left and right sides of an imaginary line drawn from one penalty spot to the other. Usage: football commentators often describe an incident on the "far side" or "near side" of play, respective of where they are situated. **2.** another term for **team.**

side volley *vb.* to kick a moving ball before it hits the ground and before it travels across the body. *n.* the execution of this.

side-stepping *n.* ploy to draw the defender out of position in a one-on-one situation by **feinting** to go either side of the player. The next step depends on the defender's reaction: if the player moves in the direction of the feint, the attacker takes the opposite pathway; if the defender maintains his position, the attacker can take the ball in the direction of the feint. Stanley **Matthews** was a great exponent of the classic side-step. See also **dribble**.

sidefoot *vb.* to execute a measured pass or shot with the inside of the foot; the effect is usually one of accuracy without particular power.

Sierra Leone *country CAF* republic in West Africa on the Atlantic Ocean, bordered by **Guinea** and **Liberia**. Independence from Britain in 1961. Area: 73,325 sq km (27,920 sq miles). Population: 4,460,000 (1993 est.). Languages: English, Krio Temne, Mende. Capital: Freetown. *Dossier* Sierra Leone Football Association (Freetown) formed in 1923, affiliated to **FIFA** and **Confédération Africaine de Football** (CAF) in 1967, president: Justice M E Tolla Thompson; general secretary: Alimu Bah. Season played from February to December. National stadium: Siaka Stevens,

Freetown, capacity: 30,000. National strip: green white and blue shirts, white shorts, blue socks. Nickname of national team: Leone Stars. First international game: 1954 v **Ghana** (0–2, Ghana, friendly). Biggest victory: 5–1 v **Niger** (7 March 1976, Freetown, **World Cup** qualifier), 5–1 v Niger (4 June 1995, Freetown, **African Nations Cup** qualifier). Biggest defeat: 0–5 v **Malawi** (6 July 1978, Malawi, friendly). *International tournament record* **Olympic Games** – first entered 1980, never qualified for finals tournament; **World Cup** – first entered 1974, reached second round of CAF qualifying tournament 1998 (second in its group of four nations, behind **Morocco** and ahead of Ghana and **Gabon**); **African Cup of Nations** – qualified for finals tournament first round group stage 1994, 1996; **Amilcar Cabral Cup** – winners 1993 (2–0, v **Senegal**), 1995 (0–0, 4–2 pens., v **Mauritania**), runners-up 1984, 1986. *Record against British and Irish national teams* none played. *History* There is a long history of football in Sierra Leone, the game probably introduced by the British during the colonial years. Its football association was founded in 1923, 38 years before independence from Britain. International matches date back to 1954, though its first documented international competition match was in 1972 (1–1, v Ghana, African Games qualifier). Although Sierra Leone took part in the second-round group stage of the 1998 World Cup qualifying competition, it actually lost its first round (0–2 agg., v **Burundi**). Burundi, however, withdrew from the tournament, its second-round place given to Sierra Leone. Sierra Leone international Mohammed Kallon held the distinction of being the youngest player ever to appear in the African Cup of Nations finals tournament: he was 16 years three months at the start of the 1996 tournament. *Record in international club tournaments* **African Cup of Champion Clubs** – **Mighty Blackpool** (quarter-final 1989); **CAF Cup** – **Diamond Stars** (quarter-final 1994), Ports Authority (quarter-final 1996); **West African Football Union General Eyadema Cup** – **East End Lions** (winners 1996). Other leading club: **Real Republicans**.

signing-on fee   *n.*   fee paid to a player as a bonus for agreeing a contract with a new club. *Regulations* only **contract players** (on contracts lasting at least three months) may receive such a fee and they must be paid in annual instalments over the period of the contract (FA Premier League rules J.15 and 16, **Football League** regulation 55.13). *Keynotes* The English Football League ruled in 1891 that signing-on fees should be limited to a maximum of £10, a move designed to stop clubs poaching players from each other and from clubs in the former **Alliance League**. In 1910, the Football league ruled that players could be paid a percentage of the transfer fee (the amount depending on years of service - from 10% after one year, to 50% after five years) to compensate for loss of accrued benefits (such as a right to service-linked pay and long-service awards). Perhaps the most unusual signing-on fee was that of Valentin Bargan, a goalkeeper who, in September 1998, signed for Stemnic Buda in the

Romanian fourth division for a truck-load of firewood and about £6.50. See **transfer fee**.

Sileks Kratovo   *club*   Macedonian national league club, based in Kratovo. Macedonian League champions 1996, 1997, 1998, runners-up 1993, 1994 and 1995; Macedonian Cup 1994, 1997, runners-up 1995.

Silures   *club*   former Burkina Faso national league club based in Ouagadougou, disbanded 1982. *Keynotes* Silures' eight domestic league titles in eight years is only one behind the African club record held by **Hafia FC** of **Guinea**). **African Champion Clubs Cup** quarter-final 1978; Burkina Faso league champions 1974, 1975, 1976, 1977, 1978, 1979, 1980, 1981.

silverware   *n. informal*   another term for trophies.

Simba FC   *club*   Ugandan national league club based in the capital Kampala (associated with the Ugandan Army). Ground: Lugogo, capacity: 5,000. Strip: yellow shirts, green shorts. **African Cup of Champion Clubs** runners-up 1972 (4-7 agg., v **Hafia Conakry** of Guinea); Ugandan league champions 1971, 1972, 1973; Ugandan Cup 1977.

Simba SC   (Sports Club)   *club*   Tanzanian national league club based in Dar es Salaam, founded 1930 (as Qora School and formerly known as Dar Sunderland). Ground: National Stadium, Dar es Salaam, capacity: 25,000. Strip: red shirts, white shorts. *Keynotes* Simba SC holds the national league record of five consecutive titles (1976 to 1980). **African Cup of Champion Clubs** semi-final 1974; **CAF Cup** runners-up 1993 (0–2 agg., v **Stella Club Abidjan** of Ivory Coast); **East and Central African Club Championship** winners, 1974, 1991, 1992, 1995, 1996; Tanzanian Mainland League champions 1965, 1966 (both as Dar Sunderland), 1972, 1973, 1976, 1977, 1978, 1979, 1980, 1984, 1990, 1994, 1995; Tanzania and Zanzibar Union League champions 1993, 1994, 1995.

Simod Cup   *competition*   renamed **Full Members Cup** from 1988, and a competition open only to clubs from Divisions One and Two. *Final results* 1987-88 **Reading** 4–1 **Luton Town**, 1988-89 **Nottingham Forest** 4–3 **Everton**.

Simonsen, Allan   *player*   Striker. **Denmark** international player (21 goals, ca. 1972-83). *Clubs* **Vejle BK**, **Borussia Mönchengladbach**, **Barcelona**, **Charlton Athletic**. *Keynotes* Simonsen was a prolific goalscorer and has the rare distinction of scoring in the finals of all three major European club tournaments. He scored twice for Borussia Mönchengladbach in the 1975 **UEFA Cup** final (5–1 agg., v FC Twente Enschede), and once in the 1979 final (2–1 agg., v **Red Star Belgrade**) when he finished as tournament top scorer with nine goals. He also scored in the 1977 European Cup final (1–3, v **Liverpool**), and after his transfer to Barcelona he scored in the 1982 European Cup-winners Cup final (2–1 v **Standard Club Liege**). Simonsen also had gone on as a substitute in the 1973 UEFA Cup final defeat by Liverpool (2–3 agg.) but did not score. He later became coach of the **Faeroe Islands**. *Honours France* UEFA Cup (Borussia Mönchengladbach, 1975,

1979); ; **European Cup-winners Cup** (Barcelona, 1982); German **Bundesliga** championship (Borussia Mönchengladbach, 1975, 1976, 1977). *Football* **European Footballer of the Year** 1977.

simple fracture *medical* another word for **closed fracture**.

Sincil Bank *ground* English football ground situated in Lincoln, Lincolnshire; home of **Lincoln City**. *Dossier* Ground capacity: 10,918. Pitch dimensions: 100.5m x 68.5m. Record attendance: 23,196 v **Derby County** (15 September 1967, **League Cup**, fourth round). Best average attendance: 16,775 (1952-53). *History* Lincoln City played its first match at Sincil Bank on 2 September 1895 (v **Gainsborough Trinity**, friendly), sub-letting the ground from Stamp End Cricket Club. The club took over the lease the following season, buying the freehold for £4,875 in 1929. In February 1908, during a match against **Leeds City**, the ground's main stand was toppled by a freak storm but the game was delayed by only 37 minutes, while a fire destroyed the South Park Stand in September 1929. Despite using the ground for an assortment of activities to raise money, including greyhound racing, boxing matches and concerts, the club was forced to sell Sincil Bank to the local council for £225,000 in 1982. Since 1985, the ground has undergone extensive redevelopment, including the construction of the £1 million 6,000 capacity Linpave Stand, which opened in March 1995. The first floodlit match at Sincil Bank took place on 31 January 1962 (v **Barnsley**, Division Three).

Sindelar, Matthias *player* Striker. **Austria** international (43 caps, 27 goals, 1926-37). Born 18 February 1903, in Kozlau, Czechoslovakia, died 1939. Career ca. 1920-38. *Clubs* Hertha (Vienna, the club was dissolved inn 1940), FK **Austria Vienna**. *Keynotes* A slightly built centre-forward, Sindelar was known for his close control and shooting ability. He was a star member of the Austria Vienna club team and the so-called national **Wunderteam**. Sindelar scored both goals in the crucial 2–1 victory over **Italy** in Vienna in the 1931-32 Dr Gerö Cup; a match that sealed the championship. He was also in the side that finished runner-up to Italy in the 1933-35 edition of the tournament. Sindelar scored the opening goal in Austria's 3–2 extra-time victory over **France** in the 1934 World Cup first round; Austria eventually losing to the host nation Italy in the semi-final (0–1, in Milan). Sindelar did not play in the **Olympic Games** final in 1936 (when Austria lost 1–2 against Italy). Austria withdrew from the 1938 World Cup (the nation having been absorbed into Germany's Third Reich) and the situation disturbed him so much that he committed suicide in January 1939, with his girl-friend: 20,000 people were reported to have turned out for the funeral of the man affectionately known as Der Papieriener (Man of Paper) because of his slim build. In 1998 a public poll voted Sindelar the Austrian Player of the Century – almost 60 years after he had last kicked a ball. *Honours* **World Cup** fourth place 1934; **Dr Gerö Cup** (Austria, 1932); Austrian Cup (FK Austria Vienna,

1933, 1935, 1936); **Mitropa Cup** (FK Austria Vienna, 1933, 1936).

Singapore Armed Forces *club* Singapore S-League club, based in Singapore. **Asian Cup-winners Cup** second round 1997; Singapore League champions 1978, 1981, 1986, 1997, 1998.

Singapore *country AFC* republic in South -East Asia, an island connected to the Malay Peninsula by a man-made causeway. Tropical climate. Major financial services and electronics industries. Independence from Britain in 1959, initially joined the Malaysian confederation, but became an independent republic in 1965. Area: 616 sq km (238 sq miles). Population: 2,990,000 (1995 est.). Languages: Malay, Mandarin, Tamil, English. Capital: Singapore. *Dossier* Football Association of Singapore (Singapore) formed in 1892, affiliated to **FIFA** in 1952 and founder member of the **Asian Football Confederation** (AFC) in 1954, president: Ibrahim Othman; general secretaries: John Koh and Eng Yoon Tan. Season played from April to August. National stadium: National Stadium, Singapore, capacity: 65,000. National strip: red shirts, red shorts, red socks. *International tournament record* **Olympic Games** – never qualified for finals tournament; **Women's World Cup** – entered first tournament in 1991, but has never reached finals tournament (in 1991 it lost all four games, conceding 21 goals, with none scored); **World Cup** – first entered 1978, never progressed beyond first-round group stage of qualifying tournament (last in its 1998 qualifying group); **Asean Tiger Cup** – hosted first tournament in 1996 (third in its five-nation first round group); **Asian Cup of Nations** – first entered 1960, qualified as hosts in 1984 but failed to progress beyond first-round group stage; **Asian Games** – fourth place 1966 (0–2, v Japan, Bangkok, third/fourth playoff); **Asian Women's Championship** – played in the first championship in 1975 and most championships since then, but with little success; **Under-17 World Championship** – never qualified; **World Youth Cup** (under-20) – never qualified. *Record against British and Irish national teams* none played. *History* The Football Association of Singapore was founded in 1892. The Singapore national side played in the Malaysian league and cup competitions from 1921 until 1994 (winning both in 1994). A professional S-League began in April 1996 (costing £5 million to set up), replacing the national amateur club league. *League system* Eleven professional clubs play in the Singapore S-League. Three points are awarded for a win, with one for a draw. Each club is required to have three to five foreign players. *Record in international club tournaments* **Asian Champion Teams Cup** – **Geylang United** and Tiong Bahru have played in the qualifying or first-round group stages but neither has qualified for the knock-out stages; **Asian Cup-winners Cup** – Singapore Armed Forces (second round 1997).

single-entity ownership *n.* see **franchise**.

Sion (Football-Club Sion) *club* Swiss national league club based in Sion, founded 1909. Ground: Tourbillon, capacity: 19,000. Strip: white shirts, white shorts. **European Cup-winners Cup** quarter-final 1987; Swiss League champions 1992, 1997; Swiss Cup 1965, 1974, 1980, 1982, 1986, 1991, 1995, 1997.

Sir Norman Chester Centre for Football Research *misc.* football research centre based in the Sociology Department of **Leicester University**, Leicester, founded 1987. It is funded by the **Football Trust**. Its research has ranged from the analysis of racism in football to hooliganism and ground safety.

Sitora Dushanbe *club* Tajikistan national league club based in the capital Dushanbe. Ground: Frunze, capacity: 20,000. Tajikistan League champions 1993, 1994, runners-up 1996; Tajikistan Cup 1993.

sitter *n.* easy opportunity to score a goal. The term is more often used with a missed opportunity to score, as in "he missed a sitter".

Sivori, Omar Enrique *player* Striker. **Argentina** international (18 caps, nine goals, 1955-57); also played for **Italy** (nine caps, eight goals, 1959-1961). Born 2 October 1935 in Buenos Aires. *Clubs* **River Plate**, **Juventus**, **Napoli**. *Keynotes* Played in a renowned Argentina forward line at the 1957 Copa America alongside Corbatta, Maschio, Angelillo and Cruz; the five playing a major role in the crucial game against runners-up **Brazil** in the penultimate match of the tournament (3–0, at Estadio Nacional, Lima, Peru). Immediately after the tournament, Maschio went to **Bologna**, Angelillo to **Internazionale** and Sivori to Juventus, with none of the three ever playing again for Argentina. Sivori's transfer from River Plate in 1957 was for a world record £91,000. He scored 144 goals in eight seasons at Juventus before moving to Napoli in 1965. Sivori scored eight goals in only nine matches for his adopted Italy, including four in one match, with his former Argentine partner Angelillo also on the score sheet (6–0, v **Israel**, 4 November 1961, in Turin, **World Cup** qualifier). He became national coach of Argentina in 1973. *Honours* **Copa America** (Argentina, 1957); *France Football* **European Footballer of the Year** 1961; Argentina league championship (River Plate, 1955, 1956, 1957); Italian **Serie A** championship (Juventus, 1958, 1960, 1961).

Six-O-Six *radio* **Radio 5 Live** football phone-in programme, transmitted each Saturday evening during the season and hosted by David **Mellor**.

six-pointer *n. informal* league match whose significance to both teams is worth more than the three points awarded for victory. This is because both clubs are either challenging for the title or a European position, or are engaged in a relegation/promotion battle.

six-yard area *n.* another word for **goal area**. Also called six-yard box.

six-yard line *n.* another name for **goal area line**.

Sixfields Stadium *ground* English football ground situated in Northampton, Northamptonshire; home of **Northampton Town**. *Dossier* Ground capacity: 7,653

all seated. Pitch dimensions: 106m x 66m. Record attendance: 7,461 v **Barnet** (15 October 1994, Third Division). *History* Opened several months behind schedule on 15 October 1994 (v Barnet, Third Division). Sixfields Stadium cost £5.25 million (plus around £6 million in infrastructure costs). Named after the area in which the ground is situated and endorsed through a competition run by the local newspaper, *The Chronicle and Echo*, the ground is owned by the local council. The management of the stadium complex, which is also used by other local sports clubs, including the Phoenix Athletics Club, is outsourced to a private company. Northampton Town pays a percentage of gate receipts to the council and contributes to the costs of policing the stadium on match days. Several weeks after the stadium opened the **kick-off** of Northampton's match with **Fulham** was delayed when the visiting goalkeeper sank into the goalmouth, after heavy rain had dislodged the top soil where a rugby post was usually positioned.

SK Brann (Sportsklubben) *club* Norwegian national league club based in Minde, Bergen, founded in 1908. Ground: Brann, capacity: 24,000. Strip: red shirts with white sleeves, white shorts. **European Cup-winners Cup** quarter-final 1997 (SK beat **PSV Eindhoven** 4-3 agg., in the second round, before losing 1-4 agg. against **Liverpool** in the quarter-final); Norwegian League champions 1962, 1963; Norwegian Cup 1923, 1925, 1976, 1982.

SK Sturm Graz *club* Austrian national league club based in Graz, founded 1909. Ground: Arnold Schwarzenegger Stadion, capacity: 15,500. Strip: white shorts, black shorts. **European Cup** champions-league stage 1998-99; Austrian league champions 1998; Austrian Cup 1996, 1997, 1999.

SK Tiranè (Klubi Sportiv SK Tiranè) *club* Albanian national league club, based in Tirana, founded 1920 (as Agmi, various names since, including 17 Nèntori, Puna Tiranè). Ground: Selman Stèrmasi, capacity: 12,500. Strip: blue and white striped shirts, white shorts. **European Cup** (as 17 Nèntori) second round 1983, 1989, 1990; **European Cup-winners Cup** (as 17 Nèntori) second round 1987; Albanian League champions 1930 (the first champions),1931, 1932, 1934, 1936, 1937, 1965, 1966, 1968, 1970, 1982, 1985, 1988, 1989, 1995, 1996, 1997; Albanian Cup 1963, 1976, 1977, 1983, 1984, 1986, 1994, 1996.

SKA-PVO Bishkek (formerly Alga-PVO Bishkek, Alga Frunze and Alga Bishkek) *club* Kyrgyzstan national league club based in the capital Bishkek, founded 1960. Ground: Spartak, capacity: 25,000 (the national stadium). Kyrghizian League champions 1992 and 1993, Kyrghizian Cup 1992 and 1993, 1997, 1998.

skin *vb. informal* **1.** to make a deliberately dangerous tackle. **2.** to easily pass an opponent or ride a challenge.

Skonto Riga *club* Latvian national league club based in the capital Riga, founded 1991. Ground: Daugava, capacity: 15,000. *Keynotes* Skonto Riga's eight consecutive league titles (1991 to 1998), is a

Latvian record and only two behind the world record for consecutive titles in succesive years held by **FC Berlin** and **Dynamo Tbilisi**. **European Cup** first round 1993, 1994 (both after wining preliminary round); **UEFA Cup** first round 1995 (after beating **Aberdeen** 1–0 agg., in preliminary round); Latvian League champions 1991, 1992, 1993, 1994, 1995, 1996, 1997, 1998; Latvian Cup 1992, 1995, 1997, 1998, runners-up 1991, 1996.

Slask Wroclaw *club* Polish national league side based in Wroclaw, founded in 1947. Ground Slask, capacity: 15,000. Strip: green shirts, white shorts. **European Cup-winners Cup** (quarter-final 1977); Polish League champions 1977; Polish Cup 1987.

Slavia Prague *club* Czech Republic and former Czechoslovakia league club based in Prague, founded 1893. The joint oldest club in the Czech Republic with **Sparta Prague**. Ground: Dr Vacka, capacity: 16,300 (5,000 seated). Strip: red and white halved shirts, white shorts. **European Cup-winners Cup** quarter-final 1998; **Mitropa Cup** 1938, runners-up 1929; pre-1925 Czech League champions 1897, 1898, 1899, 1913, 1918, 1924; Pohár Dobrocinnosti (Czech cup competition from 1906–1916) winners 1908, 1910, 1911, 1912; World War II Czech regional league champions 1940, 1941, 1942, 1943; former Czechoslovakia League champions 1925, 1929, 1930, 1931, 1933, 1934, 1935, 1937, 1940, 1941, 1942, 1943, 1947; former Czechoslovakia Cup runners-up 1974 (Slavia never won the competition); Czech Republic League champions 1996; Czech Republic Cup 1997. Notable former players: Antonín **Puc**, John Madden (former **Celtic** and Scottish international player – one of the stars of Slavia's six-times championship winning team of the 1930s).

Slavia Sofia *club* Bulgarian national league club based in the capital Sofia, formed 1913. Ground: Slavia Stadium, capacity: 32,000. Strip: white shirts, white shorts. **European Cup-winners Cup** semi-final 1967; Bulgarian League champions 1928, 1930, 1936, 1939, 1941, 1943, 1996; Bulgarian Cup/Soviet Army Cup 1963, 1964, 1966, 1975, 1980; Republic Cup 1996.

slice *vb.* to miskick the ball in such a way that it spins away in an unintended direction. *n.* the execution of such a kick. *adj.* **sliced**.

sliding tackle *n.* tackle made by sliding along the ground towards the opponent.

Sliema Wanderers *club* Maltese national league club, based in Sliema and formed in 1909. Ground: Ta'Qali Stadium, Valletta, capacity: 18,000 (all Maltese premier league games are played here). Strip: blue shirts and black shorts. **European Cup** – second round 1971/72, lost 1–7 to **Celtic** over two legs); **European Cup-winners Cup** – second round 1969; Maltese League champions 1920, 1923, 1924, 1926, 1930, 1933, 1934, 1936, 1938, 1939, 1940, 1949, 1954, 1956, 1957, 1964, 1965, 1966, 1971, 1972, 1976, 1989, 1996; Maltese FA Trophy winners 1935, 1936, 1937, 1940, 1946, 1948, 1951, 1952, 1956, 1959, 1963, 1965, 1968, 1969, 1974, 1979, 1990.

Sligo Rovers *club* Republic of Ireland national league club based in Sligo, County Sligo on the north-west coast, founded 1908. Ground: The Showgrounds, capacity: 10,000. Strip: red and white striped shirts, white shorts. Republic of Ireland League champions 1937, 1977; Republic of Ireland **FAI Cup** 1983, 1994, runners-up 1939, 1940, 1970 (one of only two FAI Cup finals to require two replays, Sligo losing 0–0, 0–0, 1–2 to **Bohemians**), 1978, 1981; FAI League Cup 1998.

slipped disc *medical* displacement of the intervertebral discs (the discs are interposed between each vertebrae in the spinal column).

Sloga Jugomagnat Skopje *club* Macedonian national league club, based in the capital Skopje. Macedonian League runners-up 1998; Macedonian Cup runners-up 1997.

slope *n.* the gradient of a pitch. **Ground criteria** of the **Football League** require that the slope, in any direction, of a league ground must not exceed 1:41 (1.4 degrees).

Slovakia (Slovak Republic) *country UEFA* republic in East Central Europe, neighbouring **Austria**, **Czech Republic**, **Hungary**, **Poland** and **Ukraine**. Independence from the Hapsburg empire of Austro-Hungary in 1918 as part of Czechoslovakia. Briefly existed as an independent state, though close ally of Nazi Germany, from 1939-45. Communist country from 1948, with Slovak Socialist Republic established in 1968 (remaining part of Czechoslovakia). Independence from Czechoslovakia in 1993. Area: 49,035 sq km (18,932 sq miles). Population: 5,370,000 (1995 est.). Languages: Slovak and Hungarian. Capital: Bratislava. *Dossier* Slovak Football Association (Bratislava) formed in 1993, affiliated to **FIFA** in 1994 and **Union of European Football Associations** (UEFA) in 1993, president: Milan Sluzanic; general secretary: Peter Zidovsky. Season played from August to June with a winter break. National stadium: Tehelné Pole, Bratislava, capacity: 33,000. National strip: blue shirts, blue shorts, blue socks. First international game: 27 August 1939 v **Germany** (2–0, Bratislava, friendly). First post-independence game: 16 November 1993 v **Slovenia** (2–0, Prievidza, Slovenia, friendly). Biggest victory: 6–0 v **Malta** (22 September 1996, Bratislava, **World Cup** qualifier). Biggest defeat: 0–6 v **Argentina** (22 June 1995, Mendoza, Argentina, friendly). Most capped players: Dusan Tittel (41 appearances, 1994-). Leading goalscorers: Peter Dubovsky (10 goals, 1994-). *International tournament record* **Women's World Cup** – first entered 1995, never qualified for finals tournament; World Cup – first entered as an independent nation 1998 (fourth in six-nation qualifying group, played 10, won five, drew one, lost four); **European Championship** – first entered 1996 (third in six-nation qualifying group, played 10, won four, drew two, lost four); **European Championship for Women** – first entered 1995 tournament (second of three nations in first-round group); **Under-17 World Championship** – never qualified; **World Youth Cup** (under-20) – never qualified. *World Cup performance* (finals and qualifiers to end of 1998 tournament) played 10, won 5, drawn 1, lost 4, scored 18 goals, conceded 14 goals; win rate 50%; goals scored per game 1.80. *Record against British and Irish national teams* v **Northern Ireland**, played one, lost one. *History* Football has been played in the region since the latter part of the 19th century, with some of the earliest clubs still in existence: **Artmedia Petrzalka**, founded as Pozsonyi Torna Egyesulet - an ethnic Hungarian club - in 1892; Tatran Presov, founded in 1898; Chemlon Humenne, founded 1903; DAC Dunajska Streda, founded 1904; MSK Zilina, founded in 1908; and FC Nitra, founded in 1909. The country's most successful club, **Slovan Bratislava**, which won the Czechoslovakian league eight times and cup five times, was founded in 1919. A Slovakian national league operated during the country's brief period as an independent state during World War II: Slovan won four of the six championships. Slovan is the only Slovakian club to have won a European club championship: in 1969 it won the **European Cup-winners Cup**, beating **Barcelona** 3–2 in Basle. Slovan has continued as one of the major clubs in the Slovak championship, along with (**1.**) **FC Inter Bratislava Kosice**, and the second-most successful Slovak club in the former Czechoslovakian league, **Spartak Trnava**. Slovakia's league championship restarted in 1993, originally with a championship playoff mini league at the end of the season. It was restructured in 1996-97. The Slovak Cup has been played since 1970. Slovakia played 16 international matches between 1939 and 1943, against Germany, **Bulgaria**, **Croatia** and **Romania**. The national side re-emerged in 1993, with a friendly against Slovenia, and played its first international competition match after independence on 7 September 1994, v **France** (0-0, in Bratislava, European Championship qualifier). *League system* Sixteen clubs play in the national first division. Three points are awarded for a victory, with one for a draw: final positions for clubs level on points are determined by **goal difference**. The bottom two clubs are automatically relegated to the 18-club second division. The bottom four clubs are relegated from the second division, replaced by the champions of the four regional third divisions. The domestic Cup final is played as a single match in June. *Record in international club tournaments* **European Cup** – Spartak Trnava (semi-final 1969, quarter-final 1973, 1974), **Kosice** (1.FC) (qualified for Champions League 1997, 1998, lost all six matches in both years); European Cup-winners Cup – Slovan Bratislava (winners 1969, quarter-final 1963). **UEFA Cup** – **Inter Bratislava** (third round 1976). Mitropa Cup – Spartak Trnava (winners 1967), Inter Bratislava (winners 1969), Tatran Presor (winners 1981). Other leading club: **FK Lokomotiva Kosice**.

Slovan Bratislava (SK Slovan Bratislava) *club* Slovakian national league club, based in the capital Bratislava, founded 1919 as 1. CSK Bratislavia (First Czechoslovak Sports Club), changed name to SK Bratislava in 1939, NV in 1949, TJ Slovan CHZJD in 1952, and reverted to SK Slovan Bratislava in 1990. Ground: Tehelné Pole (national stadium), capacity: 32,000. Strip: blue and white shirts, white shorts. *History* Slovan was the only former-Czechoslovakian club to win a European club competition, doing so in 1968-1969, the year of the **Eastern-Bloc boycott**. **European Cup-winners Cup** – winners 1969 (3-2, v **Barcelona**, in Basle, Switzerland), quarter-final 1963; Former Czechoslovakian League winners 1949, 1950, 1951 (as NV Bratislava), 1955, 1970, 1974, 1975, 1992; Czechoslovakian Cup 1962, 1963, 1968, 1974, 1982; Slovakian League winners 1940, 1941, 1942, 1944 (as SK Bratislava), 1994, 1995; 1996, Slovakian Cup 1970, 1972, 1974, 1976, 1982, 1983, 1989, 1994, 1997.

Slovenia *country UEFA* republic in Southeast Europe, on the Adriatic Sea, east of **Italy** and south of **Austria**, also bordered by **Croatia** and **Hungary**. Became part of a united kingdom with Croatia and Serbia in 1918, (renamed Yugoslavia in 1929) and a Yugoslav Socialist federal republic after World War II. Declared independent from **former-Yugoslavia** in 1991. Area: 20,250 sq km (7,815 sq miles). Population: 1,980,000 (1995 est.). Languages: Slovene. Capital: Ljubljana. *Dossier* Football Association of Slovenia (Ljubljana) formed in 1920, affiliated to **FIFA** in 1992 and **Union of European Football Associations** (UEFA) in 1993, president: Rudi Zavrl; general secretary: Dane Jost. Season played from August to June with a **winter break**. National stadium: Bezigrad, Ljubljana, capacity: 22,000. National strip: green shirts, white shorts, white socks. First international game: 19 June 1991 v Croatia (0–1, Murska Sobota, Slovenia, friendly). Biggest victory: 3–0 v **Cyprus** (27 April 1994, Maribor, Slovenia, friendly) and 3–0 v **Estonia** (29 March 1995, Maribor, **European Championship** qualifier). Biggest defeat: 0–4 v Denmark (30 April 1997, in Copenhagen, **World Cup** qualifier). Most capped players: **1.** *former-Yugoslavia:* Branko Oblak (46 appearances for former-Yugoslavia, 1970-77); **2.** *Slovenia:* Robert Englaro (33 appearances, 1993-), Ales Ceh (33 appearances, 1993-), Marinko Galic (33 appearances, 1993-). Leading goalscorers: Primoz Gliha (10 goals, 1994-), Zlatko Zahovic (nine goals, 1994-). Other notable players: Srecko Katanec (31 appearances for former-Yugoslavia, 1983-90, Italian league championship winner's medal with **Sampdoria**). *International tournament record* **Women's World Cup** – first entered 1995, never qualified for finals tournament; World Cup – first entered 1998 (fifth of five nations in qualifying group – played eight, won none, drew one, lost seven); European Championship – first entered 1996 (fifth of six nations in qualifying group – played 10, won three, drew two, lost five); **European**

Championship for Women – first entered 1995 (last in first round group of three nations, losing all six matches, conceding 60 goals with none scored, including a 0–17 defeat by Spain); **Under-17 World Championship** – never qualified; **World Youth Cup** (under-20) – never qualified. *World Cup performance* (finals and qualifiers to end of 1998 tournament) played 8, won 0, drawn 1, lost 7, scored 5 goals, conceded 20 goals; win rate 0%; goals scored per game 0.62. *Record against British and Irish national teams* none played. *History* Slovenia's two oldest existing clubs, **Olimpija Ljubljana** and SET Vevce (of Ljubljana) were both founded in 1911. Only Olimpija played in the former-Yugoslavia first division (its best achievement was as former-Yugoslavia Cup runners-up in 1970). A Slovenian league has been played since World War II, with a Cup played since the 1950s: Olimpija and Maribor Branik (now **Maribor Teatanik**) were the two most successful clubs in the pre-independence era and have continued their success in the national league and cup. The national side played its first game in 1991, and its first competition match on 7 September 1994, v **Italy** (1-1, in Maribor, European Championship qualifier). *League system* Ten clubs compete in the national first division, playing each other three times (33 games). Three points are awarded for a victory, with one for a draw: final positions for clubs level on points are determined by **goal difference**. The bottom club is automatically relegated to the 16-club second division. The champions of the second division are promoted, while a second promotion/relegation place is decided by a two-leg **playoff** between the runners up in the second division and the second-bottom club from the first. The Slovenian Cup final is played over two legs in May and June. *Record in international club tournaments* **UEFA Cup** – Maribor Teatanik (second round 1994), **European Cup-winners Cup** – Olimpija Ljubljana (second round 1997), Primorje Ajdovscina (second round 1998). Other leading club: **Mura Murska Sobota**.

slutspil *n.* Danish. Second of the two phases in the Danish football league season, from March to June, after the winter break. See: **grundspil**.

Small Simba *club* Zanzibar league club (club of the Zanzibar army). Ground: Amaan, capacity: 10,000. Strip: red shirts, white shorts. Zanzibar Island League champions 1983, 1986, 1988, 1991, 1995.

Smith, Tommy *player* Defender/Midfield. **England** international (1 cap). Born 5 April 1945. Career ca. 1960-79. *Clubs* **Liverpool**, **Swansea City** (player/coach). *Keynotes* Joined Liverpool in 1960, turning professional in April 1962. Scored a memorable header for Liverpool in the club's 1977 European Cup final triumph (3–1 v **Borussia Mönchengladbach**, Rome). Smith was Liverpool captain for several years. In August 1978, he left **Anfield** to join his former team-mate John Toshack at Swansea City but was forced to retire from the game through injury a year later. Included in the **Football League Centenary 100 players**.

Smith, Arthur *misc.* British playwright and author of the stageplay **An evening with Gary Lineker**, and the television comedy play *My summer with Des*, about a man's relationship with a fantasy woman played out under the backdrop of the 1996 **European Championship**; Des being the BBC television presenter Desmond **Lynam**. *Honours* League Championship (Liverpool 1965-66, 1972-73, 1975-76, 1976-77); **FA Cup** (Liverpool 1965, 1974); **European Cup** (Liverpool 1977); **UEFA Cup** (Liverpool 1973, 1976).

Snatch of the day *misc.* attempt in 1978 by London Weekend Television to buy exclusive rights to televise English **Football League** matches, which effectively would have ended the BBC's **Match of the Day** highlights on Saturday evenings. The BBC sued the Football League for breach of contract (a clause in its original contract stated that the League must discuss any new deals with the BBC once its existing contract had expired) and was supported by the **Office of Fair Trading**. A four-year deal was thrashed out between the League, BBC and ITV in which both networks would show highlights, with league clubs benefiting from greater television revenue.

Soccer Bowl *competition* see **North American Soccer League**.

Soccer – the Fight for Survival *misc.* report on the future of football in England, produced by the Secretaries, Managers and Coaches Associations in 1980. Compiled by Alan Dicks, Harry Haslam, Bill Nicholson, Ron Saunders, Graham **Taylor** and Terry **Venables** and the then **Arsenal** secretary Ken Friar. The report was discussed by club chairmen at a seminar in Solihull. The seminar led to a number of proposals later accepted by the **Football League** at an extraordinary general meeting in February 1981, most notably the awarding of three points for a win – the first change to the points system since the league was founded in 1888 (the change introduced from 1981-82) – and that clubs could not buy players if they had payments outstanding on previous purchases. It also proposed that clubs could appoint a paid director, previously barred by **Football Association** rules. This was eventually passed by the FA in 1982, widening the scope of people who could afford to be involved in football business; a job previously confined largely to wealthy volunteers. Malcolm Macdonald of **Fulham** and Terry Venables of **Queens Park Rangers** became the first club managers to be appointed directors. Terry Cooper was the first player to be appointed to an English Football League club's board of directors (as player-manager of **Bristol City**).

soccer *n.* another word for **Association football** (derived from three letters in asSOCiation). Soccer is the preferred term in the **United States of America** and **Canada** – to avoid confusion with **American Football** – and in **Australia**, to distinguish it from **rugby football** and **Australian rules**.

Soccer's hard men *misc.* video released in autumn 1992 featuring television footage of apparently deliberate foul play. The video also featured comments by then

Wimbledon player Vinnie Jones, who was fined a record £20,000 and given a six-month suspended sentence by a **Football Association** disciplinary committee for bringing the game into disrepute.

socks *rules* a textile covering for the foot, worn under the football **boots** and over the **shinpads**. They are part of a **players' equipment**, compulsory under the **Laws of the game** (Law IV). *Keynotes* **Football League** clubs were required to register the colour of their socks in 1937.

SOFK Lyn Oslo (Ski og Fotball Klubb) *club* Norwegian national league club based in Oslo, founded in 1896. Ground: Ullevål, capacity: 23,000 (the national stadium). Strip: red and white striped shirts, blue shorts. **European Cup** second round 1965; **European Cup-winners Cup** quarter-final 1969; Norwegian league champions 1964, 1968; Norwegian Cup 1908, 1909, 1910, 1911, 1945, 1946, 1967, 1968.

soft-tissue injury *medical* injury to a **tendon**, **ligament** or **muscle**.

Solomon Islands *country OFC* Commonwealth country in the West Pacific to the east of New Guinea. It comprises hundreds of islands and islets, the largest of which is Guadalcanal. Other main islands are Choiseul, Malaita, New Georgia, San Cristobal and Santa Isabel. Independence from Britain in 1978. Area: 29,790 sq km (11,500 sq miles). Population: 349,500 (1993 est.). Languages: English, Pidgin English and at least 120 Melanesian languages and dialects. Capital: Honiara. *Dossier* Solomon Islands Football Confederation (Honiara, on Guadalcanal) formed in 1978 affiliated to **FIFA** and **Oceania Football Confederation** (OFC) in 1988, president: Allan Boso; general secretary: Patrick Turanga. Season played from May to December. National stadium: Lawson Tawa, Honaria, capacity: 12,000. National strip: green, yellow and blue shirts, green, yellow and blue shorts, white socks. Biggest victory: 9–0 v **Tonga** (1997, Honaria, **World Cup** qualifier). Biggest defeat: 0–13, v **Australia** (1997, in Australia, World Cup qualifier). *International tournament record* World Cup – first entered 1994 (third of three nations in first-round qualifying group), never qualified for finals tournament (in 1998 it was second in its first-round group of three); **Oceania Cup** – first entered 1980 (last in first-round group of four nations). *Record against British and Irish national teams* none played.

Somalia *country CAF* republic in North-East Africa, on the Indian Ocean, east of **Ethiopia**. Independence from Britain and Italy in 1960. Civil war and severe famine in the 1990s. Area: 6,300,000 sq km (243,180 sq miles). Population: 9,200,000 (1992 est.). Languages: Somali, Arabic, English, Italian. Capital: Mogadishu. *Dossier* Somali Football Confederation (Mogadishu) formed in 1951, affiliated to **FIFA** in 1960 and **Confédération Africaine de Football** (CAF) in 1968, member of the **Confederation of East and Central African Football Associations** (COCEFA), president: Weheliye Addo; general secretary: Dr Yasin Abukar Arif. Season played from November to July.

National stadium: Cons, Mogadishu, capacity: 40,000. National strip: sky blue and white shirts, white and sky blue shorts, white and sky blue socks. First international game: 1960 v **Cameroon** (2–9, neutral venue, friendly). Biggest victory: 5–2 v **Mauritania** (7 August 1985, neutral venue, Pan Arab Games). Biggest defeat: 2–9 v Cameroon (above). *International tournament record* **Olympic Games** – first entered 1992 (qualifying tournament); **Women's World Cup** – never entered **World Cup** – first entered 1982, never progressed beyond qualifying tournament; **African Cup of Nations** – first entered 1974, never beyond qualifying tournament preliminary round; **Under-17 World Championship** – never qualified; **World Youth Cup** (under-20) – never qualified. *Record against British and Irish national teams* none played. *Record in international club tournaments* **African Cup of Champion Clubs** – **Horsed** (second round 1981), **National Printing Agency** (second round 1984); **Lavori Publici** (second round 1981), Horsed (second round 1988); **East and Central African Club Championship** – Horsed (runners-up 1977, lost to Luo Union of Kenya). Other leading club: **Mogadishu Municipality**.

Somerset Park *ground* Scottish football ground situated in Ayr, Strathclyde region; home of **Ayr United**. *Dossier* Ground capacity: 12,128. Pitch dimensions: 100.5m x 66m. Record attendance: 25,225 v **Rangers** (13 September 1969, Division One). *Keynotes* Ayr FC first played at Somerset Park in 1888 and United continued to play there when the club merged with Ayr Parkhouse in 1910. United bought the site for £2,500 in 1920. Floodlights were not installed until 1970 because the ground lay under the flight path of nearby Prestwick Airport.

songs *n. pl.* **1.** records made by players, clubs or musicians that are usually, although not exclusively, linked to a specific match or tournament. There is a long tradition of **FA Cup** finalists recording a club song prior to the match. The 1972 **Chelsea** squad's *Blue is the Colour* (recorded prior to the 1972 League Cup final) was one of the more successful of the genre, reaching number five and staying 12 weeks in the British singles charts. Other examples are *Good Old Arsenal*, which reached number 16 during a seven-week stint in the charts in 1971, **Manchester United**'s *Glory Glory Man United* (no. 13, five weeks in chart) and **West Ham United**'s *I'm Forever Blowing Bubbles* (no. 31, two weeks in chart). **Liverpool** have had five chart singles, with the *Anfield Rap (Red Machine In Full Effect)* reaching number three in the charts in 1988. The **England** and **Scotland** teams have also been associated with songs before major international tournaments. The 1970 England **World Cup** squad's *Back Home* reached number one and was in the charts for a total of 17 weeks. In 1990 the England squad teamed up with the successful pop group New Order to record *World in Motion*, which included a rap by John **Barnes**. It reached number one in Britain (12 weeks in chart) and, ironically, achieved major success in Europe, reaching number one in the German singles chart. The England Squad also released *This Time (We'll Get It Right)/England We'll Fly The Flag* in 1982 (no.2, 13 weeks in chart). The 1986 record *We've Got The Whole World At Our Feet/When We Are Far From Home* failed to make the top-50 UK singles, as did the 1988 release *All The Way*. Scotland's *We Have A Dream* (recorded with musician B A Robertson) reached number five in 1982 (nine weeks in chart), but the 1974 *Easy Easy* (no.20, four weeks) and *Say It With Pride* released in 1990 (no.45, three weeks in chart) were less successful. In 1978, Rod Stewart's *Ole Ola (Muhler Brasileira)*, recorded for Scotland's World Cup campaign, reached number four (six weeks in chart). England's 1996 **European Championship** campaign was accompanied by an album, *The Beautiful Game*, that included the number-one single *Three Lions*, (recorded with Baddiel, Skinner and the Lightning Seeds). Scotland had two rival songs for Euro 96: *Purple Heather* by Rod Stewart and Primal Scream's *The Big Man And The Scream Team Meet The Barmy Army*. An instrumental version of the latter was included on *The Beautiful Game* – the FA considered that its lyrical content was too offensive for inclusion in the official Euro '96 album. Individual players have also made records. These include Glenn (**Hoddle**) and Chris (Waddle) with *Diamond Lights*, which reached no.12 in the charts in 1987 (eight weeks in chart), Kevin **Keegan**'s *Head Over Heel' In Love* (no.31, six weeks in chart) and Paul **Gascoigne**'s version of *Fog On The Tyne* (recorded with Lindisfarne) which reached number two (eight weeks in chart). Gascoigne (recording as Gazza) also released Geordie Boys (Gazza Rap) which reached no.34 in the charts in 1990. Football songs have not been restricted to players and teams. In 1989, the Barmy Army (an Adrian Sherwood/On U Sound project) released an album of songs about, and dedicated to, football: *The English Disease*. The most famous track, *Sharp As A Needle* – a tribute to Kenny **Dalglish** – achieved cult status. The album also featured crowd recordings from West Ham United, **Liverpool**, **Manchester City**, **Blackburn Rovers**, **Stockport County**, **Crewe Alexandra**, **Leyton Orient**, **Wimbledon** and **Nottingham Forest**. The Wedding Present released its popular album *George Best*, with **Best** appearing on the album cover. Perhaps the most successful international "football song" was the adopted anthem *Nessun Dorma* (from the opera Turandot), sung by Luciano Pavarotti as the official song of the 1990 World Cup in Italy. *Nessun Dorma* reached number two in the UK charts but was also a major hit worldwide. **2.** anthems sung by football spectators, either in praise of their own team, as antagonism for their opponents or opposing spectators, or simply as part of football folklore. Popular anthems include Liverpool fans' rendition of *You'll Never Walk Alone* (previously recorded by Gerry and the Pacemakers), *When The Saints Go Marching In*, sung at Southampton (and adapted by many other teams' fans),

Chelsea fans' *One Man Went To Mow*, and Arsenal spectators' *One-Nil To The Arsenal*. A number of songs are traditional to all clubs' fans, such as the creations *Wem-b-le-y*, *There's Only One [player's name]*, and *We're On the March With [manager's name] Army*. Top players such as George Best, Charlie George and Eric **Cantona** have been the butt of many short-lived crowd songs.

soule, la *n*. French. Early and rudimentary form of football played in Brittany, northwest France.

Souness, Graeme *player-manager* Midfield. **Scotland** international (54 caps, 3 goals). Born 6 May 1953. Career ca. 1969-91. *Clubs* (player) Tottenham Hotspur, **Middlesbrough**, **Liverpool**, **Sampdoria**. *Honours* League Championship (Liverpool 1978-79, 1979-80, 1981-82, 1982-83, 1983-84); Division Two (Middlesbrough 1973-74); **League Cup** (Liverpool 1981 (first game only), 1982, 1983, 1984); Italian Cup (Sampdoria 1985). *Clubs* (manager) **Rangers** (player-manager), Liverpool, **Galatasaray**, **Southampton**, **Torino**, **Benfica**. *Honours* Scottish League (Rangers 1986-87, 1988-89, 1989-90, 1990-91); **FA Cup** (Liverpool 1992); Scottish League Cup (Rangers 1986-87, 1987-88, 1988-89, 1990-91); Turkish Cup (Galatasaray 1996). *Keynotes* Joined Tottenham Hotspur as an apprentice in 1969, turning professional in May 1970. Souness never made a League start for Spurs and was transferred to Middlesbrough for £30,000 in January 1973. He moved to Liverpool for a **Football League** record of £352,000 in January 1978, going on to make 247 League appearances for the club, many as captain. In June 1984, Souness joined Sampdoria for £650,000 and, in 1985, was a member of the side which won the club's first silverware, La **Coppa Italia** (3–1 agg. v **AC Milan**). He became Rangers' first player-manager in 1986, winning four League Championships with the club and laying the foundations for its record-equalling nine consecutive League title victories. Known as a "hard" player, Souness was found guilty of **violent play** on his debut, the opening match of the 1986-87 season, against **Hibernian**. He was suspended for three matches, while Rangers and Hibernian were fined £5,000 and £1,000 respectively. Souness replaced Kenny **Dalglish** as Liverpool manager in 1991, but his sole FA Cup final victory (v **Sunderland**) in 1992 – the year in which he suffered a serious heart attack – was not enough to meet either the expectations of the **Anfield** board or those of the club's fans, and he was dismissed in 1994. Included in the **Football League Centenary 100 players**.

South Africa *country CAF* republic in the deep south of Africa and member of the Commonwealth, bordered by **Namibia**, **Botswana** and **Zimbabwe** to the north and by **Swaziland** and **Mozambique** to the northeast. The country of **Lesotho** is an enclave within South Africa. Formed as a Union in 1910 from two Boer states, Transvaal and Orange Free State, and two former British colonies, Natal and Cape Province. Racial segregation (apartheid) introduced by an all-white Government in 1948. There followed 43 years of legislatively enforced segregation and political disempowerment of black people. South Africa was banned from international sport for a significant part of the apartheid years. Apartheid laws repealed in 1991. Free elections in April 1994, with Nelson **Mandela**, leader of the African National Congress inaugurated as the country's first black president in May 1994. Area: 1,220,845 sq km (471,369 sq miles). Population: 41,540,000 (1995 est.). Languages: English, Bantu, various other African languages, Afrikaans. Capital: Pretoria. *Dossier* South African Football Association (Johannesburg) formed in 1892 (as the Football Association of South Africa) and again in 1991, affiliated to **FIFA** in 1910, 1926 and 1952 (suspended 1964, expelled 1976), rejoined in 1992, founder members of **Confédération Africaine de Football** (CAF) in 1957 (suspended 1964), re-affiliated 1992, member of the **Confederation of Southern African Football Associations** (COSAFA), president: Molefi Oliphant; general secretary: Danny Jordaan. National stadium: Soccer City, Johannesburg, capacity: 80,000. National strip: gold and black shirts, green shorts, white socks. Nickname of national team: Bafana Bafana (The Boys). First international game: 9 July 1906 v **Argentina** (1–0, in Buenos Aires, Argentina, friendly) and, post-apartheid: 7 July 1992 v **Cameroon** (1–0, home, friendly). Biggest victory: 8–0 v **Australia** (17 September 1955, in Australia, friendly). Biggest defeat (post-apartheid): 0–4 v **Nigeria** (10 October 1992, in Nigeria, **World Cup** qualifier) and 0–4 v **Mexico** (6 October 1993, in Los Angeles, USA, friendly). Record attendance: 80,000 (31 January 1996 v **Ghana**, 3–0, Soccer City, Johannesburg, **African Cup of Nations** semi-final; and 3 February 1996, v **Tunisia**, 2–0, Soccer City, Johannesburg, African Cup of Nations final). Most capped player: Sizwe Motuang (50 appearances to 1998). Leading goalscorer: Phil Masinga (14 goals, to 1998). Website: *http://www.bafanaclub.com/* (unofficial site). *International tournament record* **Olympic Games** – first entered 1996 (failed to qualify for finals tournament); **Women's World Cup** – first entered 1995, reached final of Africa qualifying group (2–11 agg., v Nigeria; thus failing to qualify for finals tournament); **World Cup** – first entered 1994, qualified for finals tournament 1998; African Cup of Nations – South Africa withdrew from the first tournament in 1957, it first competed in 1994 (third of four-nation qualifying group, with one win and two draws), winners 1996 (above), runners-up 1998 (0–2, v Egypt, in Burkina Faso); **African Youth Cup** – runners-up 1997 (0–1, v **Morocco**, in Morocco); **All-Africa Games** – hosts 1999; **Under-17 World Championship** – never qualified; **World Youth Cup** (under-20) – never qualified. *World Cup performance* (finals and qualifiers to end of 1998 tournament) played 15, won 8, drawn 4, lost 3, scored 16 goals, conceded 13 goals; win rate: 53%; goals scored per game: 1.07. *Record against British and Irish national teams* v **England**, played one, lost one. *History* A football asso-

ciation was founded by the British in 1882 in the then-British colony of Natal – the joint-earliest association outside the UK (along with an association of New South Wales, Australia, founded in the same year). The original Football Association of South Africa was founded in 1892 and, in the same year, a tournament (the Currie Cup) was organised for representative sides of the four South African Provinces. The first club, Pietermaritzburg County, was founded in 1879. The first professional whites-only league, the National Professional Football league, started in 1959 (later known as the National Football League). A non-white National Professional Soccer League was formed in 1971: the two merged in 1978 to form the National Soccer League. Other leagues in operation at various times included the South African Soccer League (ca. 1965), the Federated Professional League (ca.1969-90), and the whites-only Datsun League (ca. 1977). A National Football League Cup was started in 1959, the Federated Professional League Cup from 1969, the National Professional Soccer League Cup from 1971. South African domestic football suffered one of its worst days on 13 January 1991, when 40 spectators were crushed to death as part of the 20,000 crowd at a friendly match between **Kaizer Chiefs** and **Orlando Pirates** (in Orkney, near Johannesburg) tried desperately to escape fighting that had broken out when the referee awarded a goal to the Chiefs. More than 50 fans were injured. After reaffiliating with FIFA in 1992, South Africa played three friendly matches against Cameroon (1–0, 1–2, and 2–2, 7, 9 and 11 July 1992, all in South Africa). Its first post-apartheid international competition match took place on 16 August 1992, v Zimbabwe (1-4, in Zimbabwe, African Cup of Nations, qualifier). It won the African Cup of Nations in 1996 (as hosts) and was runners-up in 1998. South Africa qualified for the World Cup finals tournament, at only the second attempt, in 1998. *League system* There are 18 clubs in the National Soccer League, playing each other at home and away. Three points are awarded for a victory, with one for a draw; final positions for clubs level on points are determined by **goal difference**. The bottom two clubs are automatically relegated to the second division. *Record in international club tournaments* **African Cup of Champion Clubs** – Orlando Pirates (winners 1995, quarter-final 1996, quarter-final "champions-league" stage 1997), **Manning Rangers** (quarter-final "champions-league" stage 1998); **African Cup-winners Cup** – **Jomo Cosmos** (semi-final 1993, quarter-final 1997) Pretoria City (quarter-final 1996; withdrew); **African Super Cup** – Orlando Pirates (winners 1996). Other leading clubs: Kaizer Chiefs, **Mamelodi Sundowns, Wits University**.

South American Championship *competition* see **Copa America.**

South American Club Championship *competition* former South American champion clubs tournament, played just once, in 1947. The following clubs took part in a league format, representing seven nations: **Colo**

Colo, **Emelec**, Litoral (of Bolivia), **Municipal**, **Nacional**, **River Plate**, **Vasco da Gama**. Vasco da Gama won the tournament, with four wins and two draws, followed by River Plate. Ecuador club Emelec finished last, with one draw in its six games. See also **Copa Libertadores**.

South American Footballer of the Year *award* annual award to the South American national voted best Footballer of the Year. Since 1986, the official **CON-MEBOL** award has been organised by the Uruguayan magazine *El Pais*, which bars players from non-South American clubs. Pre-1986 winners are from the Venezuelan journal *El Mundo*. *Winners, nationalities and clubs* 1971 Tostao (**Brazil**, **Cruzeiro**); 1972 Teófilo **Cubillas** (**Peru**, **Alianza**); 1973 **Pelé** (Brazil, **Santos**); 1974 Elías **Figueroa** (**Chile**, **Internacional**); 1975 Elías Figueroa (Internacional); 1976 Elías Figueroa (Internacional); 1977 **Zico** (Brazil, **Flamengo**); 1978 Mario **Kempes** (**Argentina**, **Valencia**); 1979 Diego **Maradona** (Argentina, **Argentinos Juniors**); 1980 Diego Maradona (**Boca Juniors**); 1981 Zico (Flamengo); 1982 Zico (Flamengo); 1983 Socrates (Brazil, **Corinthians**); 1984 Enzo **Francescoli** (**Uruguay**, **River Plate**); 1985 Julio César **Romero** (**Paraguay**, **Fluminense**); 1986 Antonio Alzamendi (Uruguay, River Plate); 1987 Carlos **Valderrama** (**Colombia**, **Deportivo Cali**); 1988 Rubén **Paz** (Uruguay, **Racing Club**); 1989 Bebeto (Brazil, **Vasco da Gama**); 1990 Raúl **Amarilla** (Paraguay, Olimpia, Paraguay); 1991 Oscar Ruggeri (Argentina, **Velez Sarsfield**); 1992 Rai (Brazil, **São Paulo**); 1993 Carlos Valderrama (**Atlético Junior**); 1994 Cafu (Brazil, São Paulo); 1995 Enzo Francescoli (River Plate); 1996 José Luis **Chilavert** (Paraguay, Vélez Sarsfield); 1997 Marcelo **Salas** (Chile, River Plate); 1998 Martin Palermo (Argentina, Boca Juniors).

South American Under-17 Championship *competition* international nations' youth tournament, for players under 17 years old, first played 1985. It features the member countries of the **Confederación Sudamericana de Fútbol** (CONMEBOL, the South American confederation), and is played approximately every two years. It serves as the qualifying tournament for the **Under-17 World Championship**. *Winners:* 1985 **Argentina**; 1986 **Bolivia**; 1988 **Brazil**; 1991 Brazil; 1993 **Colombia**.

South American Women's Championship *competition* women's international nations tournament for member countries of the **Confederación Sudamericana de Fútbol** (CONMEBOL); serves as a qualifier for the **Women's World Cup** (one automatic berth; runners-up playoff with third-place nation in the CONCACAF qualifying group). *Winners (and venues)* 1991 **Brazil** (league of three, in Maringa, Brazil); 1995 Brazil (league of five, in Uberlândia, Brazil)); 1998 Brazil, 7–1, v **Argentina** (in Mar del Plata, Argentina).

South American Youth Cup (under-20) *competition* international nations' tournament, for players under 20, first played 1954. It features the member countries of the

Confederación Sudamericana de Fútbol (CON-MEBOL, the South American confederation), and is now played approximately every two years. Since 1977, it has served as the qualifying tournament for the **World Youth Cup** (under-20). *Winners* 1954 **Uruguay**; 1958 Uruguay; 1964 Uruguay; 1967 **Argentina**; 1971 **Paraguay**; 1974 **Brazil**; 1975 Uruguay; 1977 Uruguay; 1979 Uruguay; 1981 Uruguay; 1983 Brazil; 1985 Brazil; 1987 **Colombia**; 1988 Brazil; 1991 Brazil; 1992 Brazil; 1995 Brazil; 1997 Argentina.

South Asian Football Confederation Cup *competition* see **South Asian Gold Cup**.

South Asian Football Confederation *confederation* regional football association, affiliated to the **Asian Football Confederation** (AFC). *Member countries* **Bangladesh**, **India**, the **Maldives**, **Nepal**, **Pakistan**, **Sri Lanka**. Organises the **South Asian Gold Cup**.

South Asian Gold Cup *competition* regional nations tournament for member countries of the **South Asian Football Confederation**, first played 1993. Formerly known as the South Asian Association of Regional Co-operation Tournament and the South Asian Football Confederation Cup. The tournament is played as two mini-leagues of three countries: the winners qualify for the final, with the runners-up playing off for third place. Winners (result and host city): 1993 **India** (v **Sri Lanka**, in Lahore, Pakistan); 1995 Sri Lanka (1–0, v India, in Colombo, Sri Lanka); 1997 India (5–1, v the **Maldives**, in Kathmandu, Nepal); India (2–0, v Bangladesh, in Margoa, India).

South China *club* Hong Kong League club. **Asian Cup-winners Cup** runners-up 1993 (2–6 agg., v **Al-Qadisiyah** of Saudi Arabia), quarter-final 1997; Hong Kong League champions 1949, 1951, 1952, 1953, 195, 1957, 1958, 1959, 1960, 1961, 1962, 1966, 1968, 1969, 1972, 1974, 1976, 1977, 1978, 1986, 1987, 1988, 1990, 1991, 1992, 1997; Hong Kong Cup 1985, 1987, 1988, 1990, 1991, 1997.

South East Asian Games *competition* regional sports competition. The football tournament is played in two round-robin groups of five nations: the group winners qualify for the final; the runners-up play off for third place. *Winners* 1959 South **Vietnam**; 1961 **Malaysia**; 1965 **Myanmar** and **Thailand** (shared); 1967, 1969, 1971, 1973 Myanmar; 1975 Thailand; 1977, 1999 Malaysia; 1981, 1983, 1985 Thailand; 1987 Indonesia; 1989 Malaysia; 1991 **Indonesia**; 1193-95 result unknown; 1997 Indoinesia.

South Korea *country AFC* republic in east Asia, occupying the south part of the Korean peninsula, on the East China Sea, the Sea of Japan and the Yellow Sea. Bordered by **North Korea**. Established as a republic in 1948. Area: 98,445 sq km (38,000 sq miles). Population: 44,610,000 (1995 census). Language: Korean. Capital: Seoul. *Dossier* Korea Football Association (Seoul) formed in 1928 affiliated to **FIFA** in 1948 and founder member of **Asian Football Confederation** (AFC) in 1954, president Dr

Mung Joon Chung, general secretary Jung Nam Kim. Season played from March to November. National stadium: Olympic Stadium, Seoul, capacity: 100,000. National strip: red shirts, black shorts and red socks. Most capped players: Soon-Ho Choi (113 appearances, 1980-91), Park Kyung Hoon (108 appearances), Hong Myung-bo (97, to 1998). Leading goalscorers: Sun-Hong Hwang (45 goals, in 78 appearances, to 1998). Other notable players: **Cha Bum Kun**. Website: http://*www.kfa.or.kr* *International tournament record* **Olympic Games** – first entered 1948, qualified for finals tournament 1948, 1964, 1988 (as hosts), 1992, 1996; **Women's World Cup** – entered first tournament in 1991, never qualified for finals tournament; **World Cup** – first entered 1954, qualified for finals tournament 1954, 1986, 1990, 1994, 1998 (never progressed beyond first round, and never won a game in the finals tournament), co-hosts (with Japan) 2002; **Afro-Asian Nations Cup** – winners 1991 (2–2, 4–3 pens., v **Egypt**); **Asian Cup of Nations** – first entered 1956, winners 1956 (four-nation league tournament in Hong Kong), 1960 (four-nation final league tournament in Seoul), runners-up 1972 (1–2, v **Iran**, in Bangkok, Thailand), 1980 (0–3, v Kuwait, in Kuwait), 1988 (0–0, 3–4 pens., v **Saudi Arabia**, in Doha, Qatar), third 1964 (four-nation league), also qualified for finals tournament 1984; **Asian Games** – first entered 1954, winners/gold medal 1970 (joint-winners, 0–0, v **Burma**, in Bangkok), 1978 (joint-winners, 0–0, v North Korea, in Bangkok), 1986 (2–0, v **Saudi Arabia**, in Seoul), runners-up 1954 (2–5, v **Taiwan**, in Manila), 1958 (2–3, v Taiwan, in Tokyo), 1962 (1–2, v **India**, in Djakarta, Indonesia), semi-final/third 1990 (1–0, v **Thailand**, in Beijing, China), fourth 1994 (1–2, v **Kuwait**, in Hiroshima, Japan), quarter-final 1998, second stage 1974, also qualified for finals tournament 1966, 1982; **Asian Under-16 Championship** – winners 1986; **Asian Women's Championship** – first entered 1991, no major success; **Asian Youth Championship** (under-19) – winners 1978 (joint-winners with Iraq), 1980, 1982, 1990, 1996 1998; **Dynasty Cup** – entered first tournament in 1990, winners 1990 (1–1, 5–4, pens., v **China**, in Beijing), runners-up 1992 (2–2, 5–6 pens., v Japan, in China), 1995 (2–2 agg., 3–5 pens., v Japan, in Hong Kong); **Under-17 World Championship** – never qualified; **World Youth Cup** (under-20) – semi-final/fourth 1983, quarter-final 1991, also qualified 1979, 1981, 1993, 1999. *World Cup performance* (finals and qualifiers to end of 1998 tournament) played 90, won 48, drawn 23, lost 19, scored 169 goals, conceded 93 goals; win rate: 53%; goals scored per game: 1.88. *Record against British and Irish national teams* none played. *History* The Korean Football Association was formed in 1928 (at that time representing the whole of Korea). The South Korean Pro-Football League was established in 1983, as a fully-professional national competition. The Korean FA Cup was first played in 1996, when it was won by **Pohang Steelers** (0–0,

7–6 pens. v **Suwon Samsung Bluewings**). The Korean FA Cup was predated by the Adidas Korea Cup, first won, in 1992, by **Chunan Ilhwa Chunma** (the competition is played in mini-leagues, followed by a knockout stage). Other domestic cups have included the Pro-Specs Cup (1997, won by **Pusan Daewoo Royals**) and Philip Morris Korea Cup (1998, also won by Pusan Daewoo Royals). South Korean clubs have performed well in Asian club tournaments, winning the **Asian Champion Teams Cup** four times and the **Asian Super Cup** twice (by 1998). The 1996-97 Asian Champion Teams Cup final was between two South Korean clubs: Pohang Steelers beating reigning champions Chunan Ilhwa Chunma. South Korea is the most successful Asian nation in World Cup history, having qualified for the finals tournament five times, the first time in 1956. In 1994, although South Korea failed to win any of its three games, it earned a credible draw with **Spain** (2–2, first round group, in Dallas). Jung-won scored a 90th-minute equaliser, after Myong-Bo had pulled a goal back in the 84th minute. South Korea drew against **Bolivia** (0-0) and was narrowly defeated, 2–3, by **Germany** in the same group stage. South Korea managed a 1-1 draw with **Belgium** in the 1998 finals, but was well beaten (0-5) by **Netherlands**. In 1988, the spectators at the Olympic Games football tournament in Seoul were awarded the FIFA **Fair Play award** for sportsmanship. *League system* Ten clubs compete in the Pro-football League. Three points are awarded for a win, with one for a draw. After each club has played each other at home and away, the top four enter a knockout playoff tournament to decide the championship. *Record in international club tournaments* Asian Champion Teams Cup – Pusan Daewoo **Royals** (winners 1985-86), Chunan Ilhwa Chunma (winners 1995-96, runners-up 1996-97, semi-final/fourth 1994), Pohang Steelers (winners 1996-97, 1997-98); **Asian Cup-winners Cup** – Daewoo Royals (quarter finals 1990); **Samsung** (runners-up 1998), Chunnam Dragons (runners-up 1999), Pohang Steelers (winners 1998); **Ulsan Hyundai Horang-i** (semi-final/third 1997); Asian Super Cup – Ilhwa Chunma (winners 1996); **Afro-Asian Club Championship** – Ilhwa Chunma (winners 1996). Other leading clubs: Anyang LG Cheetahs (formerly Lucky Goldstar, league champions 1985, 1990), Chunnam Dragons (Korean FA Cup 1997), Halleluyah Eagles (league champions 1983; no longer in professional league), Puchon SK (formerly Yukong Elephants, league champions 1989, Adidas Korea Cup 1994, 1996).

South Melbourne *club* Australian national league club, based in Melbourne (formerly South Melbourne Hellas). Ground: Middle Park. Strip: blue shirts, blue shorts. Australian League champions 1984, 1991, 1998; **Australian Cup** 1990, 1996.

South of Scotland League *competition* Scottish amateur and semi-professional league for **senior football clubs** in the South of Scotland. The league is directly affiliated to the **Scottish Football Association**. Although the league is, technically, at a level directly below the **Scottish Football League** there is no direct promotion. Member clubs compete in the **Scottish Qualifying Cup** (southern section); the semi-finalists qualifying for the **Scottish FA Cup**.

South Vietnam *former country* see **Vietnam**.

South Yemen *former country* see **Yemen** (sense 3).

Southall, Neville *player* Goalkeeper. **Wales** international (92 caps). Born 16 September 1958. Career ca. 1980-. *Clubs* **Bury**, **Everton**, **Port Vale**, **Stoke City**, **Doncaster Rovers**, **Torquay United**. *Keynotes* Transferred to Everton from Bury for £150,000 in 1981. Played a record 750 matches for Everton, including a record 578 **Football League** appearances. Joined Stoke City on a free transfer in 1998 before joining Doncaster Rovers in August 1998. Later appeared for Torquay United. Southall is Wales' most capped international, with 92 appearances. He made his Wales debut against **Northern Ireland** on 27 May 1982. Voted **Footballer of the Year** in 1985. Included in the **Football League Centenary 100 players**. *Honours* League Championship (Everton 1984-85, 1986-87); **FA Cup** (Everton 1984, 1985, 1995); **European Cup-winners Cup** (1985).

Southampton *club* English league. *Dossier* Ground: The **Dell**, Hampshire. Strip: red and white striped shirts, black shorts, red and white striped socks. Website: *http://www.soton.ac.uk/-saints/* Nickname: Saints. Ground capacity: 15,300 all seated. Record attendance: 31,044 v **Manchester United** (8 October 1969, Division One). Best average attendance: 25,527 (1966-67). Biggest win: 9–3 v **Wolverhampton Wanderers** (18 September 1965, Division Two), 7–1 v **Ipswich Town** (7 January 1961, **FA Cup**, 3rd). Biggest defeat: 0–8 v **Tottenham Hotspur** (28 March 1936, Division Two), 0–8 v **Everton** (20 November 1971, Division One). *History* Founded in 1885 by members of Deanery FC and St Mary's YMCA, and initially named Southampton St Mary's; hence the nickname, Saints. In 1894, Southampton turned professional and entered the **Southern League**. A year later, the club became a **limited company** and dropped the St Mary's from its name. The club won the Southern League Championship on five occasions between 1897 and 1904. During this period Southampton also reached two FA Cup finals (1900, 0–4 v **Bury**; 1902, 1–2 replay v **Sheffield United**) and an FA Cup semi-final (1898, 0–2 v **Nottingham Forest**). Also, it was the first professional football club to go on on an overseas tour, when it visited **Hungary** in 1901 (beating sides from Budapest 8–0 and 13–0). The club was a founder member of Division Three in 1920-21, finishing second in its first season and winning promotion to Division Two the following year from Division Three (South) – Division Three had been regionally split that season. Between 1947-48 and 1949-50, the club narrowly missed gaining a place in Division One on three consecutive occasions: in 1947-48, the club finished

third behind **Birmingham City** and **Newcastle United**; in April 1949, Southampton was eight points clear, but finally finished third behind **Fulham** and **West Bromwich Albion**; and the next season the club finished fourth despite accumulating the same number of points as **Sheffield Wednesday** and Sheffield United, who finished second and third respectively, but missing promotion on **goal average**. Southampton finally won promotion in 1965-66 under the managership of former player Ted Bates, who managed the club for 18 years (1955-73). Bates's era as Southampton manager ended in 1973, when he was replaced by Lawrie McMenemy, and despite being relegated to Division Two at the end of the season, the club won the FA Cup two years later – its only major honour as a League club. Southampton's victory in the 1976 FA Cup final was the sixth by a team from Division Two (overall seven Division Two clubs have won the FA Cup: also **Notts County** (1894), Wolverhampton Wanderers (1908), **Barnsley** (1912), West Bromwich Albion (1931), **Sunderland** (1973), **West Ham United** (1980)). The following season the club reached the quarter finals of the **European Cup-winners Cup** (2–3 agg. v **RSC Anderlecht**). In 1977-78, the club returned to the top flight, finishing second behind **Liverpool** in 1983-84, the club's highest ever League position. In 1979, Southampton reached the **League Cup** final (2–3 v Nottingham Forest). McMenemy departed in 1985 (he later returned to a position on the board) and a succession of managers – Chris Nicholl, Ian Branfoot, Alan **Ball**, Dave Merrington, Graeme **Souness**, David Jones – have followed in quick succession. A number of notable players, including Alan Ball, Kevin **Keegan**, Jim McCalliog, Peter Osgood and Peter **Shilton**, have joined Southampton in the twilight of their careers. The club has also discovered some outstanding players, namely Alan **Shearer**, sold to **Blackburn Rovers** for £3.6 million in July 1992, a then record. Southampton, under the name Southampton Leisure, floated on the stock market in January 1997 (flotation price = 150p). *League record* Premier League 1992-93–; Division One 1966-67 to 1973-74, 1978-79 to 1991-92; Division Two 1922-23 to 1952-53, 1960-61 to 1965-66, 1974-75 to 1977-78; Division Three 1920-21, 1958-59 to 1959-60; Division Three (South) 1921-22, 1953-54 to 1957-58. *Honours* Division Three 1959-60; Division Three (South) 1921-22; Southern League 1897, 1898, 1899, 1903, 1904; FA Cup 1976 (1–0 v Manchester United – *Team* Turner, Rodrigues, Peach, Holmes, Blyth, Steele, Gilchrist, Channon, Osgood, McCalliog, Stokes (1)). *Records* Peter Shilton is Southampton's most capped player (49 (125) for **England**); Terry **Paine** holds the record for club appearances (713, 1956-74; Mick Channon is Southampton's record league goalscorer (185, 1966-77, 1979-82).

Southampton Leisure Holdings plc *n.* publicly-quoted business which owns **Southampton**. Southampton Leisure, which also has interests in property development and in providing care facilities, became a fully listed company on the London Stock Exchange in January 1997 (floatation price = 150p). Southampton Leisure had a market capitalisation – the market value of the company's issued share capital (eg, the quoted price of its shares multiplied by the number of shares outstanding) – of £7.9 million on floatation.

Southampton WFC *club* former women's football club, based in Southampton, founded 1966, folded 1986. Southampton was the most successful English women's club in the 1970s, appearing in a record nine consecutive Women's FA Cup finals (now **FA Women's Challenge Cup**) 1971-1978, winning the first three editions of the tournament (1971-73). Southampton won the trophy eight times, and was beaten finalist twice.

Southend United *club* English league. *Dossier* Ground: **Roots Hall**, Essex. Strip: blue shirts, blue shorts, blue socks. Nickname: Shrimpers. Ground capacity: 12,306. Record attendance: 31,090 v **Liverpool** (10 January 1979, **FA Cup**, third round). Best average attendance: 12,089 (1949-50). Biggest win: 10–1 v Golders Green (24 November 1934, FA Cup, first round), v **Brentford** (7 December 1968, FA Cup, second round), v **Aldershot** (6 November 1990, **Leyland Daf Cup**, preliminary round). Biggest defeat: 1–9 v **Brighton & Hove Albion** (27 November 1965, Division Three). *History* Founded in 1906 as a professional outfit to rival the longer-established amateur club Southend Athletic. Southend has played at various venues, including a pitch at Roots Hall between 1906 and 1916 which was 33 metres higher than the current one, at The Kursaal and at the Southend Stadium, before moving to Roots Hall for a second time in 1955. The club joined the Second Division of the **Southern League** in 1906, finishing runners-up twice, and reformed as a limited company in 1919, becoming founder members of Division Three in 1920-21. In the club's first League season it reached the third round of the FA Cup – equivalent to today's fifth round – (1–4 v **Tottenham Hotspur**). Until Southend won promotion to Division Two in 1990-91, the club had spent the preceding 64 seasons in one or other of the bottom two divisions, winning the Division Four Championship in 1980-81 – the club's only major honour. Southend has reached the FA Cup fifth round on four occasions: 1926 (0–1 v **Nottingham Forest**), 1952 (1–2 v **Sheffield United**), 1976 (0–1 v **Derby County**) and 1993 (0–2 v **Sheffield Wednesday**). During Southend's five-season tenure of the First Division, it finished 13th in 1994-95 – the club's highest-ever League position. Relegation from the First Division in 1996-97 was followed by further demotion in 1997-98. *League record* Division One 1992-93 to 1996-97; Division Two 1991-92; Second Division 1997-98; Division Three 1920-21, 1958-59 to 1965-66, 1972-73 to 1975-76, 1978-79 to 1979-80, 1981-82 to 1983-84, 1987-88 to 1988-89, 1990-91; Division Three (South) 1921-22 to 1957-58; Third Division 1998-99–. Division Four 1966-67 to

1971-72, 1976-77 to 1977-78, 1980-81, 1984-85 to 1986-87, 1989-90. *Honours* Division Four 1980-81. *Records* George MacKenzie is Southend's most capped player (9 for **Republic of Ireland**); Sandy Anderson holds the record for club League appearances (451, 1950-63); Roy Hollis is Southend's record League goalscorer (122, 1953-60).

Southern League *competition* one of the three English leagues directly below the **Football Conference** (see **pyramid system**). *History* The Southern League was formed in 1894, originally as a rival league to the then largely midlands-and-north-based **Football League**. It started with two divisions of nine and seven clubs. At the time of its formation, only one club from the south, Woolwich **Arsenal**, was playing in the Football League.

Southport *club* former English league. *Dossier* Ground: Haig Avenue, Merseyside. Record League attendance: 14,766 v **Rochdale** (27 December 1949, Division Three (North)). Best average attendance: 8,034 (1947-48). *Keynotes* Founded as Southport Vulcan, a name adopted in honour of its sponsors (a local factory) during the regional competitions of World War I. This is the only case of a club under the jurisdiction of the English **Football League** using a sponsor's name in its title. Founder members of Division Three (North) in 1921-22, spending only four seasons outside the bottom flight in a 50-season League career. Southport lost its League status in 1977-78 and was replaced by **Wigan Athletic**, having previously applied for re-election five times. The club was on the receiving end of one of the League's biggest defeats, losing 11–0 against **Oldham Athletic** on 26 December 1962 (Division Four). It finished eighth in Division Three in 1968-69, the club's highest League position. Southport currently plays in Football Conference League. *League record* Division Three 1967-68 to 1969-70, 1973-74; Division Three (North) 1921-22 to 1957-58; Division Four 1958-59 to 1966-67, 1970-71 to 1972-73, 1975-76 to 1977-78. *Honours* Division Four 1972-73.

Soviet Union (Union of Soviet Socialist Republics) *former country former UEFA* former communist country of Eastern Europe comprising **Armenia**, **Azerbaijan**, **Belarus**, **Estonia**, **Georgia**, **Kazakhstan**, **Kyrgyzstan**, **Latvia**, **Lithuania**, **Moldova**, **Russia**, **Tajikistan**, **Turkmenistan**, **Ukraine** and **Uzbekistan**. Founded after the overthrowing of the Tsarist monarchy and Bolshevik revolution in 1917. Became a communist dictatorship under Josef Stalin (general secretary from 1922 until his death in 1953). Soviet citizens suffered extensive hardships during World War II under German occupation and abuse of human rights during the Stalin era. Invaded **Czechoslovakia** in 1968 and **Afghanistan** in 1979. Tense political conflict with the United States of America after World War II – the so-called Cold War – characterised by the proliferation of nuclear arms and the space race. All sports were organised and controlled by the Committee of Physical Culture and Sport.

Participation in sport was originally perceived for the supposed individual and societal benefits – team building, health, strength and morale, for example – but became one of the tools by which the Soviet Union attempted to express the success of the communist system, as much to its own citizens as to the West. Liberalisation under President Mikhail Gorbachev from 1985, economic crisis and the rise of nationalism in the constituent republics led to the break-up of the Union from 1989 to 1991. Former area: 22,402,202 sq km (8,649,489 sq miles). Former population: 284,500,000 (1988 est., at that time the third largest in the World). Languages: Russian (official) and the various languages of the constituent republics. Former capital: Moscow. *Dossier* A Russian Football Association was formed in 1912, with the Soviet Union Confederation (Moscow) affiliated to **FIFA** in 1946 and a founder member of the **Union of European Football Associations** (UEFA) in 1954. National strip: red, red, red socks. First international game: as the Soviet Union: 15 July 1952 v **Bulgaria** (2–1, Kotka, Finland, **Olympic Games**). Biggest victory: 11–1 v **India** (16 September 1955, Moscow, friendly) and 10–0 v **Finland** (15 August 1957, Helsinki, **World Cup** qualifier). Biggest defeat: 0–5 v **England** (22 October 1958, London, friendly). Most capped players: Oleg **Blokhin** (110 appearances, 1972–1988), Rinat Dasayev (97 appearances, 1979–90), Albert Shesternev (91 appearances, 1961-71), Vladimir Bessonov (85 appearances, 1977–90), Anatoly Demyanenko (80 appearances, 1981-90), Lev **Yashin** (79 appearances, 1954-67), Sergei Aleinkov (77 appearances, 1984-92). Leading goalscorers: Oleg Blokhin (35 goals, 1972–1988), Oleg Protasov (29 goals, 1984-92), Valentin Ivanov (26 goals, 1955-65), Eduard Streltsov (25 goals, 1955-67), Viktor Kolotov (22 goals, 1970-78). Other notable international player: Anatoly **Byshovets**. *International tournament record* Olympic Games – winners/gold medal) 1956 (1–0 v Yugoslavia, Melbourne, Australia) and 1988 (2–1 v **Brazil**, Seoul, South Korea), equal-third/shared bronze medal 1972 (2–2, v **East Germany**, in Munich, third/fourth playoff), third/bronze medal 1976 (2–0, v Brazil, in Montreal, Canada, third/fourth playoff), 1980 (2–0, v Yugoslavia, in Moscow, third/fourth playoff), hosts 1980; World Cup – fourth 1966 (1–2 v **Portugal**, **Wembley** Stadium, London, third/fourth playoff; 1–2 v West **Germany**, **Goodison Park**, semi-final), quarter final 1958, 1962, 1970, second round 1982, 1986, also qualified for finals tournament in 1990, (withdrew from the tournament in 1974 for refusing to play a qualifying playoff match with **Chile** following a right-wing military coup in that country – Chile actually kicked off the "match" in its national stadium in Santiago with no opposition); **European Championship** – winners 1960 (2–1 v **Yugoslavia**, Paris – the first tournament), runners-up 1964 (1–2 v **Spain**, Madrid), 1972 (0–3 v West Germany, Brussels), 1988 (0–2 v **Netherlands**, Munich), semi-final (fourth, 0–2 v England third/fourth playoff, Rome; the Soviet Union lost to **Italy** in the

semi-final on the **toss of a coin** after a 0–0 draw) 1968, quarter final 1976, also qualified 1992; **European Junior Championship** (under-18) – winners 1966 (joint-winners with Italy), 1967, 1976, 1978; **European Under-23 Championship** – winners 1976, runners up 1972; **European Under-21 Championship** – winners 1980, 1990; **European Under-16 Championship** winners 1985, runners-up 1984, 1987; **European Youth Championship** (under-18) – winners 1988, 1990, runners-up 1984; **Under-17 World Championship** – winners 1987 (1–1, 4–2 pens., v Nigeria, Toronto, Canada); **World Youth Cup** (under-20) – winners 1977 (2–2, 9–8 pens., v **Mexico**, Tunis, Tunisia), 1994 (4–0, v **Japan**, Lagos, Nigeria), runners-up 1979 (1–3 v **Argentina**, Tokyo, Japan). *Record against British and Irish national teams* v England, played 11, won three, drawn three, lost five; v **Northern Ireland**, played four, won two, drawn two, lost none; v **Scotland**, played four, won three, drawn one, lost none; v **Wales**, played five, won two, drawn two, lost one; v **Republic of Ireland**, played eight, won four, drawn one, lost three. *History* Officially-organised clubs date from the 1920s and, although some had roots in older sports clubs, they were largely linked to trade unions and major employers (see **Russia** for details). The most successful clubs in Soviet league and cup competitions were **Dinamo Kiev**, **Schakhter Donetsk** and **Dnepr Dnepropetrovsk** (all Ukraine), **Spartak Moscow**, **Dinamo Moscow**, **CSKA Moscow**, **Torpedo Moscow** and Zenit Leningrad (now **Zenit St Petersburg**) (all Russia), **Dinamo Tbilisi** (Georgia), and **Ararat Yerevan** (Armenia). Soviet clubs won only three major European club trophies, with none won by any of the Russian clubs. Dinamo Kiev won the **European Cup-winners Cup** in 1975 and 1986. Dinamo Tbilisi won the same competition in 1981. The Soviet Union withdrew its clubs from the 1968-69 **European Cup** and European Cup-winners Cup in protest at UEFA's decision to divide the tournaments' qualifying rounds into Communist and non-Communist countries (see **Eastern-Bloc boycott**). The Soviet Union played no international matches until the 1952 Olympic Games in Helsinki. **Sweden** was the first western country to visit the Soviet Union (8 September 1954, 7–0, in Moscow, friendly). It won the first European Championship of 1960, a 2-1 victory over Yugoslavia, and was runner-up at the second championship in 1964. The Soviet goalkeeper in both finals, Lev Yashin, is considered to have been one of the most talented of all time. The Soviet Union played its final international match on 13 November 1991 (3–0, v **Cyprus**, in Larnaca, European Championship qualifier); its last goal was scored by former **Rangers** striker Mikhailichenko. Having qualified for the European Championship finals, its place in the tournament in Sweden was taken by the ephemeral **Commonwealth of Independent States** (CIS), a body formed on 21 December 1991, comprising 11 of the final 12 Soviet Republics (Georgia did not join, the three Baltic States,

Estonia, Latvia and Lithuania, had already left the union). The CIS played 12 games, including the three first-round group games in the European Championship. Controversially, the Soviet Union's allocated place in the 1994 World Cup qualifying tournament was given to Russia, leaving the remaining 11 republics out of the World Cup until the 1998 tournament. The initials on the Soviet Union's famous red shirts, CCCP, were commonly misinterpreted as roman letters; they were, in fact, Cyrillic script (the phonetic alphabet of Russian, Bulgarian and Serbo-Croat), translated as SSSR. *European Championship winning team and scorers:* 1960 Yashin (goalkeeper), Tchekeli, Maslenkin, Kroutikov, Voinov, Netto, Metreveli (1), Ivanov, Ponedelnik (1), Bubukin, Meshki. *Record in international club tournaments* European Cup – Dinamo Kiev (semi-final 1977, 1987), Spartak Moscow (semi-final 1991); European Cup-winners Cup – Dinamo Kiev (winners 1975, 1986), Dinamo Tbilisi (winners 1981), Dinamo Moscow (runners-up 1972); **UEFA Cup** – Spartak Moscow (quarter-final 1984), **Dinamo Minsk** (quarter-final 1985), **Torpedo Moscow** (quarter-final 1991). See **Commonwealth of Independent States**, **Russia.**

space *n.* during play, an area of the pitch unoccupied by players. **run into space** *vb.* to run into an unmarked position on the field of play. **create space** *vb.* tactical use of passing and players running off the ball to create goalscoring opportunities.

Spagnolo, Victor *misc.* supporter of Italian club **Genoa (1893)** who was stabbed to death by **AC Milan** fans on 5 February 1995. A plaque outside **Luigi Ferraris** stadium in Genoa acts as a reminder of his death.

Spain *country UEFA* kingdom in Southwest Europe, on the Iberian Peninsula. On the Atlantic Ocean and Mediterranean Sea, bordered by **Portugal**, **France** and **Andorra**. A civil war from 1936-39 led to the defeat of the former Republican government by the right-wing Nationalist military forces of General Francisco Franco. He declared himself head of state for life in 1947. His death in 1975 led to the liberalisation of Spain and a return to democratic elections. Franco attempted to suppress the culture and language of Catalonia (northeast Spain, eg **Barcelona**, Gerona, Tarragona), the Basque Country (central-north Spain, eg Bilbao, San Sebastian) and Galicia (northwest Spain, eg La Coruna). Joined European Community in 1986. Colonial history includes former territories in Africa and South America. Population: 40,460,000 (1995 est.). Area: 504,880 sq km (194,885 sq miles). Capital: Madrid. Languages: Spanish (Castilian), Catalan, Basque, Galician. *Dossier* Football association (Real Federación Espanyola de Fútbol, Madrid) formed in 1913 (after Spain joined **FIFA**; regional associations operated before the national organisation), affiliated to FIFA in 1904 and founder member of the **Union of European Football Associations** (UEFA) in 1954, president: Angel Maria Villar Llona; general secretary: Gerardo González Otero.

Season played from September to June. National stadium: there is no single national football stadium; international matches are played at several major club grounds; the 1964 **European Championship** final and the 1982 **World Cup** final were, however, played at **Bernabéu** Stadium, Madrid (capacity: 106,000). National strip: red shirts, blue shorts, blue socks with red, blue and yellow border. First international game: 28 August 1920 v **Denmark** (0–1, Brussels, **Olympic Games** first round). Biggest victory: 13–0 v **Bulgaria** (21 May 1933, Madrid, friendly). Biggest defeat: 1–7 v **England** (9 December 1931, **Highbury**, London, friendly). Most capped players: Andoni **Zubizaretta** (126 appearances, to 1998), Jose Antonio **Camacho** (81 appearances, 1975-88), Rafael Gordillo (75 appearances, 1978-88), Emilio **Butragueño** (69 appearances, 1984-92). Leading goalscorers: Emilio Butragueño (26 goals, 1984-92), Alfredo **Di Stéfano** (23 goals, 1957-61; Di Stéfano was a naturalised Spaniard – he also played eight times for his native **Argentina**), Miguel Gonzalez (21 goals, 1985-93), Julio Salinas (22 goals, 1986-96). Other notable international players: Luis **Enrique,** Francisco **Gento**. Website: *http://www.sportec.com/www/rfef/main.htm* (official site). *International tournament record* Olympic Games – winners/gold medal 1992 (3–2, v **Poland**, Barcelona), runners-up/silver medal 1920 (1–3, v **Netherlands**, in Antwerp, second/third play-off), quarter-final 1928, 1968, 1996, hosts 1992; **Women's World Cup** – entered first tournament in 1991, never qualified for finals tournament; World Cup – first entered 1934, fourth place 1950 (fourth in final round group of four nations in **Brazil** – including a 1–6 defeat by the hosts in front of 152,000 spectators at the **Maracana** Stadium, Rio de Janeiro, the second-highest attendance for a World Cup match), quarter-final 1934, 1986, 1994, also qualified for finals tournament 1950, 1962, 1966, 1978, 1982 (automatic), 1990, 1998, hosts 1982; European Championship – winners 1964 (2–1, v **Soviet Union**, Madrid), runners-up 1984 (0–2, v **France**, Paris), quarter-final 1960, 1968, 1976, 1996, also qualified for finals tournament 1980, 1988, hosts 1964; **European Championship for Women** – first entered 1987, never past first-round group stages; **European Under-21 Championship** – winners 1986 (3–3 agg., 3–0 pens., v **Italy**), runners-up 1984 (0–3 agg., v England); **European Under-16 Championship** – winners 1986, 1988, 1991, runners-up 1995; **European Junior/Youth** (under-18) Championship winners 1952, 1954, 1995; **Under-17 World Championship** – runners-up 1991 (0–1 v **Ghana**, Florence, Italy), semi-final/fourth 1997 (1–2, v Germany, in Egypt, third/fourth playoff) 1999; **World Youth Cup** (under-20) – runners-up 1985 (0–1, v Brazil, Moscow), fourth 1995 (2–3, v Portugal, Qatar, third/fourth play-off), quarter-final 1979, also qualified 1999. *World Cup performance* (finals and qualifiers to end of 1998 tournament) played 109, won 60, drawn 24, lost 25, scored 213 goals, conceded 104 goals; win rate:

55%; goals scored per game: 1.95. *Record against British and Irish national teams* v England, played 18, won five, drawn three, lost 10; v **Northern Ireland**, played 13, won eight, drawn four, lost one; v **Scotland**, played 10, won four, drawn three, lost three; v **Wales**, played five, won two, drawn two, lost one; v **Republic of Ireland**, played 23, won 13, drawn six, lost four. *History* Modern football is said to have been introduced in the area around Bilbao by British mine workers and sailors towards the end of the 19th century. The first club, **Athletic Club Bilbao**, was founded in 1898. **Barcelona** (1899), **Espanyol** (1900). **Real Madrid** (1902), **Atletico de Madrid** (1903), Deportivo La Coruna (1904), Sporting Gijon (1905), **Sevilla** (1905) and **Real Betis** (1907) were formed over the next decade. Two clubs, Real Club Recreativo de Huelva and Gimnasia de Tarragona, were founded as sports clubs in 1880 and 1886, respectively, with football sections formed later. The earliest league championship was played in the Catalonia region from 1901 and first won by Hispania FC (see **Catalonia Championship**). Regional leagues operated in other parts of Spain and continued after the national professional league was formed in 1929. Regional championships were abolished by the post-Civil War military government in 1940. Regional champions and (sometimes) runners-up competed for the Spanish Cup, the **Copa del Rey**, founded in 1902 by King Alfonso XIII. A **Mediterranean League** (Liga Mediterrania) involving clubs from Catalonia and Valencia was played for one season, 1936-37, during the Civil War. Real Madrid (27 national championships to 1998), Barcelona (15), Atlético Madrid (nine) and Atlético Bilbao (eight) have dominated the league. Valencia (four), **Real Sociedad** (two), Sevilla (one) and Real Betis (one) are the only other clubs to have claimed the title. Real Madrid holds the national league record of five consecutive titles (1961 to 1965 and 1986 to 1990). The fervent rivalry between Spain's biggest clubs, Barcelona (in Catalonia) and Real Madrid (from the capital), has its roots in the Spanish Civil War and the subsequent suppression of Catalonian cultural identity during the Franco years. Real Madrid won the European Cup a tournament-record five times in succession (1956-60) and again in 1966 and 1998. It is the most successful club in the competition's history. Barcelona has won the competition just once (1992), but scores a victory over its rivals by being one of only four clubs (with **Juventus**, **Bayern Munich** and **Ajax**) to have won all three major European club competitions (see below). Real Madrid has won nine premier European club competitions, excluding the **European Super Cup** this is more than any other European club; Barcelona is second with eight, ahead of **AC Milan**, with seven. Atlético Madrid (European Cup-winners Cup), **Real Zaragoza** (**UEFA Cup** and European Cup-winners Cup), **Valencia** (UEFA Cup and Cup-winners Cup) have also triumphed in Europe. By 1998 Spanish clubs had, collectively, appeared in 42 European Cup, UEFA Cup/Fairs Cup and European Cup-winners Cup finals, lagging behind Italian clubs (50), and marginally ahead of English clubs (39). English clubs, however, had won 26 cups, Italian clubs 26, and Spanish clubs 23. Barcelona has played in European club competitions in every season since the first Fairs (now UEFA) Cup started in 1955; no other European club has matched this achievement. Ever since the presence of Argentinian Alfredo Di Stefano and Hungarian Ferenc **Puskas** in Real Madrid's team of the 1950s, Spain has attracted some of the top overseas players (curiously, both Di Stefano and Puskas were later able to play for the Spanish national team). Puskas's Hungarian national team-mates Zoltan **Czibor** and Sandor **Kocsis**, both played for Barcelona in the 1950s and early 1960s. Johann **Cruyff**, Mario **Kempes**, Diego **Maradona**, Gary **Lineker**, Hristo **Stoichkov**, Roberto Carlos and **Ronaldo** have all played in the Spanish league. Like Italy, Spain's concern over the impact of the foreign-players influx on opportunities for Spanish-born players, and the national team, led to a lengthy ban – from 1963 to 1973 – on the signing of new players from overseas. Spain played its first international in 1920 at the Olympic Games in Belgium, and won the silver medal. Nine years later, it became the first country from continental Europe to beat **England** in a fully-recognised international match outside the Olympic Games (15 May 1929, 4–3, in Madrid, friendly). England avenged the defeat with a 7–1 victory over Spain two years later in London. Spain finished fourth in the 1950 World Cup. Spain's triumph at the 1964 European Nations Cup (now known as the European Championship) is its only major tournament success, though it was runners-up in the European Championship of 1984. The 1964 final at **Bernabéu**, Madrid was watched by 105,000 spectators. Having won its qualifying group with eight wins and two draws, Spain's exit at the first-round stage in the 1998 World Cup finals in France was particularly disappointing: the squad was considered one of Spain's finest and was thought to be a contender for the title. A 6–1 victory in the final group game over **Bulgaria** (24 June 1998, in Lens) was small consolation. In the same match, Andoni Zubizarreta's 126th and last appearance for Spain made him the second most-capped goalkeeper of all time, one more than the 125 appearances of England's Peter **Shilton**, but still 17 behind the record held by Thomas **Ravelli** of **Sweden**. Not long before the 1998 tournament, Spain had played 31 consecutive matches without defeat (7 September 1994 to 28 January 1998), an all-time record for a European nation, and only five behind the world record set by Brazil. In 1991, the Spanish Football Association was awarded FIFA's **Fair Play Award** for sportsmanship. *European Championship winning team and scorers:* 1964 Iribar (goalkeeper), Rivilla, Olivella, Calleja, Zoco, Fusté, Amancio, Pereda (1), Marcelino (1), Suárez, Lapetra. *League system* Twenty clubs play in the national premier division, the **Primera Liga** (reduced from 22 clubs at the end of the 1996-97 season). Three points are awarded for a victory, with one for a draw: final positions for clubs level on points are determined by the relative performance of the respective clubs in matches against each other. The bottom two clubs are automatically relegated, replaced by the champions and runners-up in the 22-club second division (Segunda Division A). A third promotion/relegation place is decided by playoffs between the third- and fourth-bottom clubs in the Primera Liga and the third- and fourth-placed sides in the Segunda Division A. The bottom four clubs in the Segunda Division A are relegated automatically. There are four regional divisions of 20 clubs in the Segunda Division B, and 17 regional Tercera Division leagues. Unlike the situation in England and Scotland, Spanish league clubs are permitted to have reserve sides in the lower leagues. Reserve sides cannot, however, be promoted to the Primera Liga. Record in international club tournaments (winners and runners-up only): **World Club Cup** – Real Madrid (winners 1960, 1998), Atlético Madrid (winners 1974); European Cup/Champions League – Real Madrid (winners 1956, 1957, 1958, 1959, 1960, 1966, 1998, runners-up 1962, 1964, 1981), Atlético Madrid (runners-up 1974), Barcelona (winners 1992, runners-up 1961, 1986, 1994); European Cup-winners Cup – Atlético Madrid (winners 1962, runners-up 1963, 1986), Barcelona (winners 1979, 1982, 1989, 1997, runners-up 1969, 1991), **Real Zaragoza** (winners 1995), **Valencia** (winners 1980), Real Madrid (runners-up 1971, 1983), RCD Mallorca (finallists 1999); **UEFA Cup/Fairs Cup** – Barcelona (winners 1958, 1960, 1966, runners-up 1962), Real Madrid (winners 1985, 1986), Real Zaragoza (winners 1964, runners-up 1966), Valencia (winners 1962, 1963, runners-up 1964), Athletic Bilbao (runners-up 1977), Espanyol (runners-up 1988). Other leading clubs: Sevilla, Real Sociedad, Real Betis Balompié, Deportivo la Coruña, UD Las Palmas, CD Tenerife.

spareggio *misc.* Italian. **Playoff** to determine which of the 14th and 15th clubs in Italy's **Serie A** league is relegated to the **Serie B** (four clubs are relegated in total). A single match played at a neutral venue.

Sparta Prague *club* Czech Republic and former-Czechoslovakia league club based in Prague, founded 1893. The joint-oldest club in the Czech Republic with **Slavia Prague**. Ground: Stadión Letná, capacity: 22,000 all seated. Strip: claret shirts, white shorts. *Keynotes* Sparta holds the former-Czechoslovakia League record of five consecutive championships (1919 to 1923, and 1987 to 1991). **European Cup** champions-league stage 1998; **European Cup-winners Cup** semi-final 1973; **Mitropa Cup** 1927, 1935, runners-up 1930, 1936; pre-1925 Czech League champions 1912, 1917, 1919, 1920, 1921, 1922, 1923; Pohár Dobrocinnosti (Czech cup competition from 1906–1916) winners 1909, 1915; World War II Czech regional League champions 1939, 1944; former Czechoslovakia League champions 1926, 1927, 1932, 1936, 1938, 1946, 1948, 1952, 1954, 1965, 1967, 1984, 1985, 1987, 1988, 1989, 1990, 1991, 1993 (the

last ever Czechoslovakia championship); former Czechoslovakia Cup 1964, 1972, 1976, 1980, 1984, 1988, 1989, 1992; Czech Republic League champions 1994, 1995, 1997, 1998; Czech Republic Cup 1996. Notable former player: Oldrich **Nejedly**.

Sparta Rotterdam *club* Dutch national league club, based in Rotterdam, and founded in 1888. Ground: Het Kasteel, capacity: 13,000. Strip: red and white striped shirts and black shorts. Dutch League champions 1909, 1911, 1912, 1913, 1915, 1959; Dutch Cup 1958, 1962, 1966.

Spartak Moscow *club* Russian national league and former Soviet Union league club, founded in 1922 (known as Moskovski Klub Sporta until 1935). Ground: Lokomotiv (ground shared with **Lokomotiv Moscow**), capacity: 24,000: Spartak's original hone, the recently-reconstructed **Luzhniki Stadium**, capacity: 96,000, is now home to Torpedo Moscow and the national side. Strip: red shirts with horizontal white stripe, white shorts. *History* During the Soviet era, Spartak was one of the few independent clubs, though technically it was affiliated to a food producers' cooperative (compare **CSKA Moscow**, the army club, and **Lokomotiv Moscow**, the railway workers' club). Its early success – and relative political independence – was built up by Nikolai Starostin who was sent to a Soviet labour camp for 10 years for alleged anti-Soviet crimes. Three hundred and forty spectators were crushed to death at the Luzhniki Stadium during a **UEFA Cup** second match against Dutch club Haarlem in 1982: the worst stadium disaster in Europe. The club's championship victory in 1998 was marred by a riot of 1,500 celebrating fans in one of Moscow's shopping districts. Spartak is the favourite club of Russia's first democratically-elected president, Boris Yeltsin. **European Cup** semi-final 1991, quarter-final group stage 1994 (third in its league of four), qualified for Champions League 1995 (third in its group of four); **European Cup-winners Cup** semi-final 1993; UEFA Cup semi-final 1998, quarter-final 1984; Russian League champions 1992, 1993, 1994, 1996, 1997, 1998; Russian Cup 1994, 1998; Soviet Union League champions 1936, 1938, 1939, 1952, 1953, 1956, 1958, 1962, 1969, 1979, 1987, 1989; Soviet Union Cup 1938, 1939, 1946, 1947, 1950, 1958, 1963, 1965, 1971, 1992 (the last Soviet Cup final).

Spartak Subotica *club* Yugoslavian and **former-Yugoslavia** national league club based in Subotica, Serbia, founded 1945. Ground: Gradski, capacity: 28,000. Strip: blue shirts, blue shorts. Former-Yugoslavia Cup runners-up 1962; Yugoslavian Cup runners-up 1994.

Spartak Trnava *club* Slovakian national league club, based in Trnava, founded 1925 (as Rapid Trnava). Ground: Spartak, capacity: 24,000. Strip: red and black striped shirts, black shorts. **European Cup** – semi-final 1969, quarter-final 1973, 1974; **Mitropa Cup** 1967; former Czechoslovakian League winners 1968, 1969, 1971, 1972, 1973; Czechoslovakian Cup 1951 (as Kovosmalt Trnava – unofficial tournament) 1967, 1971, 1975, 1986; Slovakian League runners-up 1997, 1998; Slovakian Cup 1971, 1975, 1986, 1991, 1998.

spectator   *n.*   person who attends a match; not necessarily with any allegiance to a particular club. *rules* If a spectator enters the field of play and makes contact with the ball or interferes with the play (in the opinion of the referee), then the match must be stopped and restarted with a **drop ball**. Compare **supporter**.

spectators, women   *n. pl.*   women who attend football matches. *History* Despite claims that more women now attend football matches in Great Britain than, say, in the 1970s, it is hard to find concrete data to support a longer-term trend. Although much of the historical evidence on women spectators is anecdotal, it is clear that women have always made up a substantial minority of football spectators. The fact that fewer women than men attended the first **Football League** matches has been attributed more to women's historical lack of opportunities than to any more subtle differences in men's and women's preferences for entertainment. While the emancipation of the working classes in the late 19th century – through better working conditions and, in particular, shorter **working hours** – led to the dramatic rise in popularity of football among men (who now had Saturday afternoons off, with money to spend) it had less of an impact on women who still bore the majority of childcare responsibilities. Put simply, men were able to go to the match, while women stayed at home with the children. Women, however, began to make up a greater share of football crowds after **World War I**, partly because of a change in women's perception of their role in society, partly owing to the increased popularity of **women's football**, and partly because the sport itself was considered more respectable and, therefore, no longer "unsuitable for ladies". **Brentford FC** was one of the first clubs to actively encourage women spectators, with special transport laid on for women by the City Corporation. The wider appeal of football in the 1960s, enhanced by the 1966 **World Cup**, also contributed to the encouragement of more women spectators. The so-called "English disease" of football **hooliganism** in the 1970s, however, discouraged many people, and perhaps disproportionately women, from attending matches. The dramatic improvement in ground conditions, coupled with renewed respectability of football in the 1990s is said to have contributed to more women attending matches regularly, rather than occasionally. British football clubs and the **Football Association** actively tried to increase the number of women attending matches in the 1990s. The FA's **Blueprint for the Future of Football**, for example, states: "In consultation with supporter groups, to improve spectator facilities and conditions inside stadiums in ways which do least to alienate 'traditional fans', but will also prove more attractive to under-represented groups (particularly black spectators, women, children, older spectators etc) stadiums which will prove to be hooligan hostile but safe and supporter friendly." In 1995-96, only 13% of Premier

League crowds were women (**fan survey** by the **Sir Norman Chester Centre for Football Research**).

Spencer Alberto Pedro   *player*   Striker. **Ecuador** and **Uruguay** international. Born 1937. *Clubs* **Barcelona** Sporting Club (of Guayaquil), **Peñarol**. *Keynotes* Spencer scored more goals than any other player in the history of the Copa Libertadores (54 goals). He won three Copa Libertadores winner's medals with Peñarol (1960, 1961 and 1966), scoring in all three winning finals. Spencer played international football for his birthright country Ecuador, and for Uruguay. His only goal for Uruguay was against **England** in 1964 (6 May, 1–2, **Wembley** Stadium). Spencer was Uruguay league top scorer in 1961 (18 goals), 1962 (16 goals) and 1967 (11 goals) – all with Peñarol – and scored all the goals in Peñarol's defeat of **Real Madrid** (2-0, 2-0) in the 1966 World Club Cup. *Honours* **World Club Cup** (Peñarol, 1961, 1966); **Copa Libertadores** (Peñarol, 1960, 1961 and 1966); Copa Uruguaya (Peñarol, 1959, 1960, 1961, 1962, 1964, 1965, 1967, 1968).

spinal injury   *medical*   injury to the spinal cord or vertebrae. Injuries include fractured vertebrae and **slipped disc**. A player sustaining a spinal injury will need to be stretchered off and taken immediately to hospital. Spinal injuries in football are rare. *Keynotes* One notorious example was that of the former **Manchester City** goalkeeper Bert **Trautmann** who fractured cervical vertebrae (the neck vertebrae) in the 1956 **FA Cup** final (v **Birmingham City**, 3–1). Trautmann continued to play the remaining 15 minutes of the game after receiving the injury.

Spion Kop   *n.*   (Afrikaans: "look-out") site of Boer War battle, January 1890. A failed attempt by soldiers from the 2nd Royal Lancaster Regiment and the 2nd Royal Lancashire Fusiliers to capture the Spion Kop hill resulted in 322 British fatalities. Spectators' mounds at football grounds became known as Kops in memory of the event. The Kop at **Anfield** dates from 1906.

spitting 1.   *rules*   one of the listed infringements of the **Laws of the game** punishable by the offending player being **sent off** (Law XII). The offence is committed by a player who projects saliva deliberately at another player (of either team), match official or other person. **2.** habit adopted by many players, presumably to clear their mouths of saliva built up during exertion. Although unsightly, it is not an infringement of the Laws of the game unless a player spits at another person, as above. *Keynotes* **Iraq** international defender Barmeer Shaker was suspended from international matches for one year after spitting at the **referee** during his country's 1–2 defeat by **Belgium** in the 1986 **World Cup** (1–2, 8 June 1986, in Toluca, **Mexico**, first round).

sponsored tournaments   *misc.*   competitions financially supported by business. *Keynotes* The **Football League** first received overtures from businesses wishing to sponsor matches and competitions in 1892 (a firm called Hudson & Co. offered to donate a cup worth £500 to the winners of a competition contested solely by Football League clubs), it was a further 78 years before the first sponsored tournaments began with the **Ford Sporting League**, **Texaco Cup** and **Watney Cup**. At around the same time the **Dryborough Cup** began in Scotland, while the **Blaxnit Cup** brought together leading clubs from **Northern Ireland** and the **Republic of Ireland**. The Football League first considered sponsorship for its main league and **League Cup** competitions in 1980. A year later, it appointed a marketing firm, CSS Promotions, to investigate the commercial potential of sponsorship. In 1982, the Football League signed a £2 million four-year deal with the National Dairy Council to sponsor the League Cup, when the competition became the Milk Cup. Since then, the League Cup has had several further sponsors: Littlewoods Challenge Cup (1986-87 to 1989-90); Rumbelows Cup (1990-91 to 1991-92); Coca-Cola Cup (1992-93 to 1998); Worthington Cup (1998-). In 1983, the Football League agreed a deal with electronics firm Canon for sponsorship of the League itself. It was worth £3.3 million over three seasons, Mitre Sports signed a match-ball deal worth £500,000 in 1984. By 1987 every league club had singed sponsorship deals. Problems with shirt sponsorship arose in 1981 because television companies refused to broadcast games with clubs wearing shirts displaying sponsors' names – a situation overturned when new television contracts were negotiated in 1983 (see television). In September 1994, the **Football Association** announced that **pools** company Littlewoods would have its name attached to the **FA Cup** as part of a £14 million four-year sponsorship deal. Since 1998-99, financial services company AXA has had its name attached to both the FA Cup and the **FA Charity Shield**. CSI, the sports marketing company, sponsors the **FA Women's Cup**. The Coca-Cola Company first began sponsoring football in 1975, when the soft drinks company officially sponsored the FIFA **World Youth Championship**. FIFA's international **ranking** system is sponsored by Coca-Cola and are officially entitled the FIFA/Coca-Cola **World Rankings**. FIFA received £20 million from each of the 12 principal corporate sponsors of the 1998 **World Cup**. A further 33 companies paid a total of £100 million to use the World Cup in their own advertising. Sainsbury's was the official **England** supermarket for the 1998 World Cup, while Nestle's *Cheerios* was the tournaments's official breakfast cereal. Air France, the French national air-carrier, painted action footballers on 16 aircraft as part of the company's support for the 1998 tournament.

sponsorship money *regulations* monies paid out to clubs as a share of the overall sum negotiated between the football authority and any sponsoring company. **Premier League** clubs receive an equal share of the pot for any commercial contracts negotiated by the Premier League, after any agreed deductions (FA Premier League rules section C). See also **payments to relegated clubs.**

Spora Luxembourg *club* Luxembourg national league club, based in Luxembourg City, founded 1933 (after merger of Racing Club and Sporting Club,

founded in 1907 and 1908, respectively). Racing Club were the first Luxembourg League champions in 1910. Ground: Municipal, capacity: 9,200. Strip: yellow shirts, yellow shorts. Luxembourg League champions 1925, 1928, 1929, 1934, 1935, 1936, 1938, 1949, 1956, 1961, 1989 (Racing Club, 1910; Sporting Club, 1911, 1919); Luxembourg Cup 1928, 1932, 1940, 1950, 1957, 1965, 1966, 1980 (Racing Club 1922).

Sport Boys *club* Peruvian national League club based in Callao, Lima, founded in 1927. Ground: Estadio Miguel Grau, capacity: 18,000. Strip: pink shirts, black shorts. Peru League champions 1935, 1937, 1942, 1951, 1958, 1984, 1998.

Sporting Clube Bissau *club* Guinea-Bissau national league club based in the capital Bissau. Strip: green shirts, white shorts. Ground: Lino Correia, capacity: 8,000. **African Cup of Champion Clubs** second round 1984; **African Cup-winners Cup** second round 1977; Guinea-Bissau League champions 1983, 1984, 1986, 1987, 1990, 1991, 1992; Guinea-Bissau Cup 1976, 1987, 1991.

Sporting Clube de Portugal *club* Portuguese national league club based in Lisbon, founded in 1906, also known as Sporting Lisbon. Ground: José Alvalade, capacity: 52,500. Strip: green and white hooped shirts, black shorts. Sporting Club holds the record for the biggest victory in a **European Cup-winners Cup** match (16–1, v **Apoel Nicosia**, 1963-64, second round): it went on to win the trophy. European Cup-winners Cup – winners 1964 (1–0 v **MTK Budapest**, Antwerp, Belgium), semi-final 1974; **European Cup** – qualifed for **Champions League** 1998; **UEFA Cup** semi-final 1991; Portuguese League champions 1941, 1944, 1947, 1948, 1949, 1951, 1952, 1953, 1954, 1958, 1962, 1966, 1970, 1974, 1980, 1982; Portuguese Cup 1923, 1934, 1936, 1938, 1941, 1945, 1946, 1948, 1954, 1963, 1971, 1973, 1974, 1978, 1982, 1995.

Sporting Clube de Praia *club* Cape Verde Islands national league club based in the capital Praia. Ground: Varzea (the national stadium), capacity: 15,000. Strip: green shirts, white shorts. **African Cup of Champions Clubs** first round 1992 (after preliminary round); Cape Verde League champions 1960, 1968, 1985, 1991, 1997.

Sporting Cristal *club* Peruvian national league club based in the capital Lima, founded in 1922 (as Sporting Tabaco until 1955). Ground: Estadio San Martin de Porras, capacity: 15,000. Strip: sky blue shirts, white shorts. **Copa Libertadores** runners-up 1997 (0-1 agg., v **Cruzeiro** of Brazil), quarter-final 1995; Peru League champions 1956, 1961, 1968, 1970, 1972, 1979, 1980, 1983, 1988, 1991, 1994, 1995, 1996.

Sports Report 1. *television* former BBC television show, which included up to 30 minutes of recorded Football League football highlights on Saturday night. Superseded by **Match of the Day**. **2.** *radio* BBC radio sports programme that is on the air at 5 pm every Saturday and includes a full check on the day's football, racing and other sporting results. On 3 January 1998, the programme celebrated its fiftieth anniversary.

spot kick *rules* another name for **penalty kick**.

spot-the-ball *n.* weekly competitions run by some newspapers and by **pools** companies where, for a small entrance fee, competitors place a cross on a photograph of a football game from which the ball has been erased. The winner is the entrant who has placed the cross closest to the centre of the ball. In 1975, a levy was placed on spot-the-ball competitions operated by pools companies to finance the **Football Grounds Improvement Trust** and later the **Football Trust**.

Spotland *ground* English football ground situated in Greater Manchester; home of **Rochdale**. *Dossier* Ground capacity: 9,195. Pitch dimensions: 104m x 69m. Record attendance: 24,231 v **Notts County** (10 December 1949, **FA Cup**, second round). Best average attendance: 8,616 (1948-49). *History* Rochdale first played at Spotland, then known as St Clements, on 3 September 1907 (v **Oldham Athletic**, friendly). Spotland, a name derived from the area in which the ground is situated, had been used since 1878 for rugby and a football club called Rochdale AFC was invited to use the ground to help pay the rent after St Clements Rugby Club folded. Rochdale AFC and another football club, Rochdale Town, which also used the ground, both disbanded, leaving the way free for the formation of the current Rochdale to fill the void. Rochdale bought Spotland's freehold for £1,700 in 1914, selling the ground to a private company for £175,000 in 1980 and repurchasing it three years later after the new owners went bankrupt. **Coventry City** refused to play an FA Cup tie under Spotland's "outdated" **floodlights** in 1970, forcing the game to be played on a Monday afternoon. The floodlights, which were erected in 1954, were inaugurated on 2 February (v **St Mirren**, friendly) and replaced in August 1971. In 1988, Rochdale Hornets Rugby League Club agreed a **groundshare** of Spotland. Since the March 1990 the ground has been jointly owned by Rochdale, Rochdale Hornets and the local council – the first **Football League** ground to be owned in such a way. This move led to a change of name for the ground, but Denehurst Park Stadium has failed to catch on.

sprain *medical* a mild or moderate injury to a **muscle**, **ligament**, **tendon** or **joint capsule** due to sudden traction. Damage is restricted, at most, to some torn fibres rather than a complete rupture. Very mild sprains may be treated with ice or pain relieving sprays such that players can continue to play. Moderate injuries will require **RICE**. and possible physiotherapy. *vb.* **sprain**, **sprained**.

spread betting *n.* form of gambling where the punter attempts to predict whether the size of the outcome of an event will be higher or lower than the "spread" offered by the betting company. The fundamental difference between this and conventional gambling is that the potential gains or losses are not fixed in advance. Football spreads are one of the most common offered by the companies, and are not restricted just to the result of a match. Spreads can be offered on, for example, the number of bookings meted out in a championship, the number of corners in a match, or the time (in seconds) of the first throw in. A spread consists of a narrow range of possible outcomes predicted by the betting company. The company may, for example, have offered 160-165 goals as its prediction for the total number of goals scored in the 1998 **World Cup** finals. A punter might think that this was an overestimate and "sell" at 160 goals. Alternatively, if the punter felt it would be a high-scoring tournament, he or she might "buy" at 165 goals. There were, in fact, 171 goals scored overall, so the buyers would have won, and the sellers would have lost. Because there were six more goals than the top end of the spread, a buyer would have won six times his or her stake – £60 for a £10 stake. Sellers, however, would have lost 11 times their stake (the bottom end of the spread was 11 goals fewer than the total scored). Had there been 150 goals, sellers would have won 10 times their stake, and buyers would have lost 15 times their stake (a loss of £150 for a £10 stake). A further possibility is for the punter to close the bet even before the event has finished, or even taken place, because the "market" has moved. For example, after the first week of the World Cup a spread company might have felt that it had underestimated the total goals and increased its spread to 170-175 goals. A punter who had bought at 165 could have cashed in at that point and sold at 170: an instant gain of five times the stake, regardless of the total goals tally. In Britain, all spread betting companies are licensed by the Security and Futures Authority and the bets are legally binding (conventional gambling debts cannot be enforced by UK law). Spread betting is by account only; accounts are offered only to people with a good credit rating. *History* Spread betting originated in the futures financial market (futures are commodities bought at an agreed price regardless of their actual value at a set delivery date: the trader's skill is in buying at a relatively low price predicting that the world market for the commodity will push the price up by the time the product - coffee, cereals, or metals, for example - is produced and delivered). In Britain, a company called IG Index was set up in 1975 to offer City traders the chance to bet on the overall future movement of the Financial Times Share Index. Sports' spreads were only a small part of the business. In 1992, Sporting Index was launched solely to offer sports spreads, again mainly to City traders. It is reported to have taken £2 million in the 1994 World Cup, and around £10 million in 1998. By 1998 there were five licensed spread betting companies in the UK: City Index, IG Index, Ladbrokes Sporting Spreads, Sporting Index and William Hill Index.

spring ligament *medical* a **ligament** in the ankle that supports the **talus**.

Springfield Park *ground* English football ground situated in Greater Manchester; former home of **Wigan**

Athletic (until end 1998-99). Dossier Ground capacity: 7,290. Pitch dimensions: 104m x 66m. Record attendance: 30,611 Wigan Borough v **Sheffield Wednesday** (12 January 1929, **FA Cup**, third round). Best average attendance: 6,701 (1978-79). *Keynotes* Athletic bought Springfield Park for £2,850 in May 1932. Springfield Park was first used for football on 1 September 1897 (Wigan County v **Burton Swifts**) and it was **Wigan Borough**'s home between November 1920 and October 1931, when the club folded. It was while Borough was tenants at Springfield that the ground's record attendance was achieved (see above). The biggest crowd recorded by Wigan Athletic was 27,526 on 12 December 1953 (**Hereford United**, FA Cup, second round). In 1902, Wigan Rugby League Club also played at Springfield Park. The first floodlit match there took place on 24 October 1966 (v **Manchester City**, friendly).

Spurs *club* nickname of Tottenham Hotspur.

squad *n.* **1.** all the registered players at a football club eligible to play for the first team. **2.** the players selected for a national team, from which the final 11 players and named substitutes can be chosen. International **competition rules** generally restrict the number of players in each national squad for the finals tournament: 22 players, for example, were eligible to play for each country in the 1998 **World Cup** finals; their names were submitted before the tournament started.

squad number *regulations* individual **shirt number** that, if required by **competition rules**, is allocated to every member of a club's first team squad at the beginning of the season (or upon transfer to the club). Each player has a different number which is retained throughout the season unless that player ceases playing for the club. Squad numbers are obligatory in the **Premier League** (FA Premier League rule F.1), must be displayed at the back of a player's shirt (rule F.7), may be displayed on the front left hand side of a player's shorts (rule F.8), and must be included in the **teamsheet** given to the referee before the start of a match (rule E.18). Premier League clubs must allocate squad numbers sequentially; a new player signed midway through a season may thus end up with the highest shirt number in the team. If players leave, however, their squad numbers can be reallocated (FA Premier League rule F.5). Squad numbers may also be allocated for international fixtures. They remain fixed for the duration of the **World Cup** and **European Championship** finals tournaments. Squad numbers are not used in the **Football League** and **Scottish Football League** (shirts are simply numbered from one to 14 for the 11 players and three substitutes).

squad rotation *n.* the practice of regularly changing a team's lineup to combat or exploit the strengths and weaknesses of the opposition or to rest players for more important fixtures. *Keynotes* **Chelsea**'s Gianluca **Vialli** was criticised for his use of the squad rotation system at **Stamford Bridge** in 1998-99, although there was little evidence that he changed his side more frequently than other major clubs.

square ball *n.* a pass played sideways, parallel with the goal lines.

Sri Lanka *country AFC* republic and large island in the Indian Ocean, Southeast of **India**. Independence from Britain in 1948. Name changed from Ceylon in 1972. Ongoing political differences between the government and Tamil separatists in north Sri Lanka has led to periodic terrorist activity by the Tamil Tigers and other Tamil groups. Area: 65,610 sq km (25,325 sq miles). Population: 17,900,000 (1994 census). Languages: Sinhala, Tamil, English. Capital: Colombo. *Dossier* Football Confederation of Sri Lanka (Colombo) formed in 1939, affiliated to **FIFA** in 1950 and **Asian Football Confederation** (AFC) in 1958, president: Manilal Fernando; general secretary: G A K Abeysekera. Season played from September to March. National stadium: Sugathadasa, Colombo, capacity: 25,000. National strip: maroon and gold shirts, white shorts, white socks. Biggest defeat: 1–12 v **East Germany** (12 January 1964, Colombo, friendly). *International tournament record* **Olympic Games** – last of four nations in 1992 qualifying tournament first round group stage; **Women's World Cup** – never entered; **World Cup** – first entered 1994, never progressed beyond qualifying tournament first-round group stage (second of four nations in 1998); **Asian Cup of Nations** – first entered 1980, never beyond qualifying tournament first round group stage; **Asian Games** – never entered; **Asian Women's Championship** – never entered; **South Asian Football Confederation Cup** – winners 1995 (1–0, v India, in Colombo), runners-up 1993 (v India, in Lahore, Pakistan), semi-final 1997, hosts 1995; **Under-17 World Championship** – never qualified; **World Youth Cup** (under-20) – never qualified. *Record against British and Irish national teams* none played. *League system* There are two top-flight groups of nine clubs; three points are awarded for a win, with one for a draw. The top two clubs in each group enter a knockout semi-final and final to decide the championship. *Record in international club tournaments* **Asian Champions Teams Cup** – no Sri Lankan club has progressed beyond qualifying group stage; **Asian Cup-winners Cup** – no Sri Lankan club has progressed beyond first round or qualifying group stage. Leading clubs: Saunders SC (of Colombo, national champions 1997, 1998, Sri Lanka Cup 1987, 1992, 1997), Old Benedictines (of Colombo, Sri Lanka Cup 1996), Pettah United (national champions 1996), Renown SC (of Colombo, Sri Lanka Cup 1989, 1990, 1993, 1994), York SC (of Kandy, Sri Lanka Cup 1991), Ratnarns (of Colombo, league champions 1998).

Stábile, Guillermo *player* Striker, **Argentina** (31 caps). Born 17 January 1906. *Clubs* **Huracan**, **Genoa**, **Napoli**, Red Star Paris. Stábile scored the first hat-trick in the **World Cup** (19 July 1930, Argentina v **Mexico**, 6–3, at **Centenario**, Montevideo, first round), and was top scorer in that year's finals with eight goals.

Stade Abidjan *club* Ivory Coast national league club based in the capital Abidjan, founded 1936. Ground: Robert Champroux, capacity: 10,000. Strip: blue shirts, white shorts. **African Cup of Champion Clubs** winners 1966 (5–4 agg., v **AS Real Bamako**); **West African Football Union General Eyadema Cup** 1977; Ivory Coast League champions 1962, 1963, 1965, 1966, 1969; Ivory Coast Cup 1971, 1976, 1984, 1993, 1994; Ivory Coast Super Cup (Coupe Houphouët-Boigny) winners 1985.

Stade de France *ground* French sports stadium situated at Saint-Denis, Paris. Ground capacity: 80,000 all seated. *History* Built for the 1998 **World Cup** on the site of a former gasworks and at a cost of more than £270 million. Stade de France has a roof of filtered glass, eight levels and four tiers. The lower tier is fitted on air cushions and is retractable, providing a reduced capacity of 25,000. It has 148 private boxes, three panoramic restaurants, 43 cafes and snack bars, two 120sq cm screens, 454 floodlights, 670 toilets, 17 shops and 36 lifts. The stadium was officially opened on 28 January 1998 with a friendly match between the home nation and **Spain**. Le Grand Stade, as it is popularly known, was the venue of the 1998 World Cup final (**Brazil** v **France**) and the competition's **opening ceremony**. It also staged one match from each of groups A (Brazil v **Scotland**), B (**Austria** v **Italy**), C (France v **Saudia Arabia**), E (**Belgium** v **Netherlands**) and G (**Romania** v **Tunisia**); one second-round match (**Nigeria** v **Denmark**); a quarter-final (Italy v France); and a semi-final (France v **Croatia**) – total attendance 692,500; average attendance 76,944.

Stade de Reims *club* French league club based in Reims, formed 1931. Ground: Auguste Delaune, capacity: 18,000. Strip: red shirts with white sleeves, white shorts. **European Cup** runners-up 1956 (3–4, v **Real Madrid**, **Parc des Princes**, Paris), 1959 (0–2, v Real Madrid, Stuttgart); French League champions 1949, 1953, 1955, 1958, 1960, 1962; French Cup 1958. Notable former players: Raymond **Kopa**, Just **Fontaine**.

Stade Malien *club* Mali national league club, based in the capital Bamako. Ground: Mamadou Konate, capacity: 10,000. Strip: blue shirts and white shorts. *Keynotes* Stade Malien has won the Mali Cup 14 times, a national record shared with **Djoliba Athletic Club**; only bettered in Africa by **Al Ahly** of Egypt. **African Cup of Champion Clubs** runner-up in the first tournament of 1964 (1–2, v **Oryx Douala** of Cameroon, in Accra); **West African Club Champions Cup** runner-up 1984; Mali League champions 1970, 1972, 1984, 1987, 1989, 1993, 1995; Mali Cup 1961, 1963, 1970, 1972, 1982, 1984, 1985, 1986, 1988, 1990, 1992, 1994, 1995, 1997.

Stade Tunisien Le Bardo *club* Tunisian national league club based in the capital Tunis, formerly known as US Tunisienne. Ground: Stade Olympique El Menzah (the national stadium), capacity: 50,000. Strip: red shirts, green shorts. **African Cup-winners Cup** quarter-final 1993; **Arab Cup-winners Cup** 1989; Tunisian League champions 1929, 1930, 1932, (all as US Tunisienne), 1957, 1961, 1962, 1965; Tunisian Cup 1929, 1930, 1932, 1933, 1934 (all as US Tunisienne), 1957, 1958, 1960, 1962, 1966.

Stadium of Light *ground* English football ground situated in Sunderland, Tyne & Wear; home of **Sunderland**. *Dossier* Ground capacity: 41,590 all seated. Pitch dimensions 105m x 68m. Record attendance: 41,505 v **Bolton Wanderers** (20 March 1999, First Division). *History* Sunderland moved to Stadium of Light at the start of the 1997-98 season, having just been relegated from the Premier League and having played at **Roker Park** since 1898. The name of Sunderland's new ground remained a secret until it was unveiled by the club's directors at a midnight news conference on 29 July 1997. The following evening the stadium was officially opened with a friendly match between Sunderland and **Ajax**. Crowd capacity was limited to 41,000 due to unfinished building works. Sunderland's first league fixture at the ground took place on 15 August 1997 (v **Manchester City**, First Division). The stadium is built on the site of the former Wearmouth colliery, which closed in 1993, as part of a huge shakeout of the mining industry following the 1984-85 miner's strike. The Stadium of Light holds the record for the biggest First Division **attendance** (see above) since the formation of the **Premier League** in 1992. Pre-match entertainment at the Stadium of Light before the home side's Division One match against **Portsmouth** on 21 March 1998 included the Young Northern Symphonia orchestra playing Prokofiev's Romeo and Juliet, and a troupe of ballet dancers. The entertainment coincided with the launch by the club of a compact disc featuring music for players to run out to before a game. By 1999, the stadium was served by a new Metro system. The club plans to increase the ground's capacity to around 64,000. See also **Estadio da Luz**.

stadium tour *n.* organised visit to a football stadium. According to the English Tourist Board (ETB) tours of football stadiums are one of the fastest growing areas of tourism with over 500,000 people visiting a soccer ground in 1997. ETB figures show that **Wembley** and **Old Trafford** are the most popular attractions. Stadium visits typically include a tour of the dressing rooms, trophy room and bootroom.

Stair Stadium *ground* Scottish football ground situated in Stranraer, Dumfries and Galloway; home of **Stranraer**. Ground capacity: 6,100. Pitch dimensions: 100.5m x 64m. Record attendance: 6,500 v **Rangers** (24 January 1948, **Scottish FA Cup**, first round). *Keynotes* Stranraer first played at Stair Park in 1905. Originally it was part of a public park which was bequeathed to Wigtown District Council by the Ear of Stair (hence the name). Stranraer enclosed the pitch and, in 1909, built a pavilion. In August 1981, Stair Park became the last senior football ground in the UK to install floodlights.

Stal Mielec *club* Polish national league side based in Mielec, founded in 1939. Ground: Stal, capacity: 30,000. Strip: blue shirts, blue shorts. **UEFA Cup** – quarter-final 1976; Polish League champions 1973, 1976. Notable former player: Grzegorz **Lato**.

Stalybridge Celtic *club* former English league. *Dossier* Ground: Bower Fold, Greater Manchester. Record attendance: 9,753 v **West Bromwich Albion** (17 January 1923, **FA Cup** first round replay). Best average attendance: 5,250 (1921-22). *Keynotes* Founder members of Division Three (North) in 1921-22. The club won its first League fixture 6–0 (v **Chesterfield**) and finished seventh that season – its highest League position. Stalybridge resigned its League status after only two seasons. The club currently plays in the Nortern League. *League record* Division Three (North) 1921-22 to 1922-23.

Stamford Bridge *ground* English football ground situated in west London; home of **Chelsea**. *Dossier* Ground capacity: 35,000 all seated (42,000 eventually). Pitch dimensions: 103m x 68m. Record attendance: 82,905 v **Arsenal** (12 October 1935, **Division One**). Best average attendance: 48,260 (1954-55). *History* Stamford Bridge derives its name from the bridge that spans the railway line alongside the ground. From 1876 until 1904, when Gus and Joe Mears bought it, Stamford Bridge was the headquarters of the London Athletic Club. The Mears brothers, with Fred Parker, were intent on establishing a sports stadium that would include not only athletics but cycling, and provide a home for **Fulham**. Archibald **Leitch** was hired to redevelop Stamford Bridge after Gus Mears and Parker had visited grounds that he had been responsible for designing, including **Hampden Park**, **Ibrox** and **Celtic Park** in Glasgow. Fulham turned down the offer to rent the ground so Mears and Parker decided to form their own football club. In May 1905, the Chelsea Football and Athletic Company was established and the club rented the ground from Mears for an annual fee of £2,000. At the time, Stamford Bridge, with a capacity of between 60,000 and 70,000, was England's second largest venue after **Crystal Palace**. The Leitch-designed east stand was demolished in 1972 as Chelsea, under the chairmanship of Brian Mears (the son of Gus Mears' nephew, Joe junior), embarked upon a £5.5 million redevelopment of Stamford Bridge following the club's success in the **FA Cup** (1970) and the **European Cup-winners Cup** (1971). The redevelopment, which began in June 1972, but resulted only in the construction of the 11,500 seat East stand (the largest single stand that had been built in England at the time), caused the club severe financial problems. In 1979, the club's debts and Stamford Bridge were transfered to SB Property (SBP) in which the Mears family held a majority share. In April 1982, the former **Oldham Athletic** chairman Ken Bates bought the club for a nominal amount. Several months later, he signed a seven-year lease with SBP allowing Chelsea to remain at Stamford Bridge, and providing the club with the option of buying the ground by August 1988. The Mears' stake in SBP was sold to property company **Marler Estates**, which would eventually also own **Craven Cottage** and **Loftus Road**. Marler's initial redevelopment plans for Stamford Bridge included a stadium as its centrepiece, but later the company sought planning permission for a scheme that precluded any sports ground. These plans were passed by the then Tory-controlled Hammersmith and Fulham council in March 1986, but two months later control of the council changed to Labour and the new administration adopted a policy to preserve football at all three of the borough's grounds. Chelsea exercised its option to buy Stamford Bridge in August 1988, but there was no agreement as to its valuation between the club and Marler Estates, which was subsequently bought by another property company, Cabra Estates. Although Chelsea's lease expired in August 1989, ongoing court proceedings meant that the club remained at the ground until in 1991 when the High Court ruled that Stamford Bridge's valuation would be based on its 1988 value and which an independent valuer set at £22.85 million. The Royal Bank of Scotland (RBS), as Cabra's main creditor, became Chelsea's new landlord in December 1992 following the decline in the property market. The bank granted Chelsea a 20-year lease with the option of buying the ground for £16.5 million by the year 2012. Matthew Harding, a lifelong Chelsea supporter and newly appointed club director who died in 1997, bought the ground's freehold from RBS in April 1995. Chelsea began the redevelopment of Stamford Bridge in December 1993. In December 1997, **Chelsea Village** agreed a £75 million loan (bond) with SBC Warburg Dillon Read enabling the club to clear its debts and buy Stamford Bridge from the late Matthew Harding's estate. Under the title Chelsea Village (also the name of the holding company that owns the club), the redeveloped ground consists of a 42,000 stadium, a 160-bedroom hotel, underground car park and the largest club **super-store** in the country. The temporary floodlights used during the construction of the new west stand at Stamford Bridge were first used by **Manchester United** while **Old Trafford**'s enlarged north stand was being built. Stamford Bridge has been the venue for several sports, including American football, athletics (the AAA Championship were held at the ground throughout the 1920s), baseball, greyhound racing and speedway, and the ground has hosted some major football matches. Immediately prior to the FA Cup final moving permanently to **Wembley** in 1923, Stamford Bridge staged three finals (1920 **Aston Villa** v **Huddersfield Town**, 1921 **Tottenham Hotspur** v **Wolverhampton Wanderers**, 1922 Huddersfield Town v **Preston North End**). It has also staged four **FA Amateur Cup** finals (1907, 1935 replay, 1946, 1948), 10 **FA Cup** semi-finals and eight **FA Charity Shield** matches (including the first one in 1908, Manchester United v **Queens Park Rangers**). **England** have played three international matches at Stamford Bridge (v **Scotland**,

5 April 1913, v **Wales**, 20 November 1929, v **Austria**, 7 December 1932), as well as a victory international after **World War II** (v **Switzerland**, 11 May 1946). Stamford Bridge was the venue for the first leg of the 1958 **UEFA** (Fairs) **Cup** final between a composite **London XI** and one from **Barcelona** (5 March 1958). Although the official record attendance for a football match at Stamford Bridge is 82,905 (v Arsenal, Division One, 12 October 1935, the second-highest club attendance in England), Chelsea played **Dinamo Moscow** on 13 November 1945 in the first of a series of post-war goodwill friendlies between UK clubs (Dinamo also played Arsenal, **Cardiff City** and **Rangers**) the Russian champions attracted a crowd officially totalling 74,496 but unofficially estimated to be in the region of 100,000. This match also resulted in a court case after overflowing supporters trespassed in neighbouring gardens and led to the Metropolitan Police having to pay compensation (Munday v Metropolitan Police Receiver, 1949). The first floodlit match took place on 19 March 1957 (v **Sparta Prague**, friendly). Stamford Bridge was the first football stadium in England to erect perimeter fencing around the whole of the ground.

stamps *misc.* postage stamps to commemorate football players and occasions. *Keynotes* The Royal Mail issued special commemorative stamps for both the 1966 **World Cup** and the 1996 **European Championship**. The former consisted of three stamps, 4d, 6d and 1s 3d (pre-decimal coinage), each depicting a piece of football action. A special version of the 4d stamp, which was the main postage value of the period, was issued after **England**'s victory with the words "England winners" added. The Euro' 96 collection featured five footballers from the English game – Dixie **Dean** 19p, Bobby **Moore** 25p, Duncan **Edwards** 35p, Billy **Wright** 41p, Danny **Blanchflower** 60p – and the series was entitled "Football Legends". It was at the 1966 British National Stamp Exhibition that the Jules Rimet trophy was stolen (see **World Cup trophies**). The **USA** commemorated its hosting of the 1994 World Cup with a set of three stamps – 29c, 40c and 50c. **Hungary**'s 6–3 victory over England at **Wembley** on 25 November 1953 was commemorated by Magyar Posta, the Hungarian postal service, with a special stamp.

stanchion *n.* physical support that keeps the **net** taught behind the goal posts.

stand *n.* permanent or temporary structure built to accommodate spectators at a sports ground. See **terrace**.

Standard Club Liege *club* Belgium national league club based in Liege, founded 1898. Ground: Sclessin, capacity: 25,000. Strip: red shirts, white shorts. **European Cup-winners Cup** runners-up 1982 (1–2, v **Barcelona**, **Nou Camp**, Barcelona); Belgium league champions 1958, 1961, 1963, 1969, 1970, 1971, 1982, 1983; Belgium Cup 1954, 1966, 1967, 1981, 1993.

standard situation *misc.* German term for **set piece**.

standby official *rules* see **reserve official**.

Stanley Matthews football boots *trademark* a range of **football boots** manufactured in the 1950s by the Co-operative Wholesale Society (CWS). The prototype was developed by J Grainge of the CWS factory in Heckmondwike, West Yorkshire, at the request of England player Stanley **Matthews**, who wanted the CWS to create a lightweight football shoe similar to those worn by the **Brazil** national team at the 1950 **World Cup** finals. The boot was characterised by being made of soft, lightweight leather, without the hard toe caps and ankle supports present on traditional British designs. The prototype weighed around 700 grams – light by the standards of the day – which was reduced to 280 grams in later models. It was probably the first British boot that, as the manufacturers claimed, you could "bend it double". The boot was a major commercial success, with more than 500,000 sold in the 1950s.

stanozolol *medical* a type of **anabolic steroid**.

Stark's Park *ground* Scottish football ground situated in Kirkcaldy, Fife region; home of **Raith Rovers**. *Dossier* Ground capacity: 10,721 all seated. Pitch dimensions: 103m x 64m. Record attendance: 31,306 v **Heart of Midlothian** (7 February 1953, **Scottish FA Cup**, second round). *Keynotes* Raith Rovers has played at Stark's Park since 1891, playing its first match there in August. The ground had previously been used by several other Kirkcaldy clubs, including Rangers and Union. Although Raith contemplated relocating to a purpose-built out-of-town stadium, the club decided in 1995 to redevelop Stark's Park. Raith's League Cup triumph in 1994-95 ensured the club qualified for European competition (**UEFA Cup**) for the first time the following season. However, the club was forced to switch its tie against **Bayern Munich** to **Hibernian**'s **Easter Road** ground due to Stark's Park's limited capacity. The first floodlit match at Stark's Park took place in August 1960 (v Petach Tikva (Israel), friendly).

start of play *rules* rcommencement of play in a game of football. It must be signalled by the **referee**, upon which a player takes a **kick-off** (or place-kick) from the **centre spot**, moving the ball into the opposing team's half of the **field of play** (Law VIII). Every player must be in his or her own half of the field and all opposition players must be at least 10 yards (9.15 metres) from the ball until it is kicked off. The game starts as soon as the ball has moved. It must then be kicked by a different player (ie the player taking the kick-off cannot touch the ball twice – if a player breaks this rule an **indirect free kick** will be awarded to the other team). The start of play is preceded by **tossing a coin** to determine the **choice of ends** – the team winning the toss chooses ends, the team losing the toss takes the kick-off (Law VIII). After the **half-time interval**, the game is restarted with the teams changing ends, and the kick-off is taken by the team that did not take the kick-off at the start of play (ie the team that won the toss) (Law VIII) .

starting line-up *n.* the 11 players that start a football match (not including any named **substitutes**).

Station Park *ground* Scottish football ground situated in Forfar, Tayside region; home of **Forfar Athletic**. *Dossier* Ground capacity: 8,732. Pitch dimensions: 105m x 63m. Record attendance: 10,780 v **Rangers** (2 February 1970, **Scottish FA Cup**, second round). *Keynotes* Forfar first played at Station Park in 1888, but did not purchase the ground until 1956. Despite the name, the ground is, courtesy of railways rationalisation in the 1960s, further from a station than any other in the UK. The first floodlit match at Station Park took place on 11 October 1971 (v **Aberdeen**).

Stationery Stores *club* Nigerian national league club based in Lagos, founded 1958. Ground: Surulere, capacity: 80,000 (the national stadium). Strip: yellow shirts, maroon shorts. **African Cup of Champion Clubs** semi-final 1993; **African Cup-winners Cup** runners-up 1981 (1–2 agg., v **Union Douala** of Cameroon); Nigerian league champions 1977, 1992; Nigerian FA Challenge Cup 1967, 1968, 1982, 1990.

Steaua Bucharest *club* Romanian national league club based in the capital Bucharest, founded in 1947. Formerly known as Armata, CSCA and CCA – reflecting its connection with the army – adopting current name in 1962. Ground: Stadionul Ghencea, capacity: 30,000. Strip: red shirts, blue shorts. *Keynotes* Steaua is the only club from a former communist country to have won the **European Cup**, and is noted for its youth development programme. Steaua holds the European record of 104 consecutive league games without defeat (1986 to 1989), four short of the world record held by **ASEC Mimosas Abidjan** of **Ivory Coast**). Its six consecutive titles (1993 to 1998) is a Romanian league record. European Cup 1986 (0–0, 2–0 pens., v **Barcelona**, Seville, Spain), runners-up 1989 (0–4, v **AC Milan**, at **Nou Camp**, Barcelona) semi-final 1988, qualified for Champions league 1997; **European Cup-winners Cup** quarter-final 1993; **European Super Cup** 1986 (1–0 v **Dinamo Kiev**, Monte Carlo, Monaco); Romanian League champions 1951, 1952, 1953, 1956, 1960, 1961, 1968, 1976, 1978, 1985, 1986, 1987, 1988, 1989, 1993, 1994, 1995; 1996, 1997, 1998; Romanian Cup 1949, 1950, 1951, 1952, 1955, 1962, 1966, 1967, 1969, 1970, 1971, 1976, 1979, 1985, 1987, 1988, 1989, 1992, 1996, 1997. Notable players: Marius **Lacatus**, Gheorghe **Hagi**, Anghel **Iordanescu**.

Stein, Jock *manager* born 5 October 1923;. died 10 November 1985. *Clubs* **Dunfermline Athletic**, **Hibernian**, **Celtic**, **Leeds United**. Also **Scotland** manager. *Honours* Scottish League (Celtic 1965-66, 1966-67, 1967-68, 1968-69, 1969-70, 1970-71, 1971-72, 1972-73, 1973-74, 1976-77); **Scottish FA Cup** (Dunfermline Athletic 1961, Celtic 1965, 1967, 1969, 1971, 1972, 1974, 1975, 1977); **Scottish League Cup** (Celtic 1965-66, 1966-67, 1967-68, 1968-69, 1969-70, 1974-75); **European Cup** (Celtic 1967). *Keynotes* Stein was appointed Celtic manager in 1965 after successfully leading Dunfermline Athletic to the Scottish FA Cup in 1961 and a brief spell in charge at Hibernian. Stein had played for Celtic in the early-1950s, winning a Scottish League and Cup **double** with the club in 1953-54 before becoming an assistant coach when injury forced his retirement from the game in 1955. Stein was the first manager to lead a British club to success in the European Cup (1967, 2–1 v **Internazionale**). He also led Celtic to a record nine consecutive Scottish League titles between 1965-66 and 1974-75, and a second European Cup final appearance (1970, v **Feyenoord**). Stein spent a few months as manager of Leeds United before becoming Scotland coach in 1978, and was awarded a CBE in 1979. He died of a heart attack at **Cardiff City**'s **Ninian Park** ground moments after Scotland had secured a place in the 1986 **World Cup** finals by drawing with **Wales**.

Stella Abidjan *club* Ivory Coast national league club based in the capital Abidjan, founded 1936. Ground: Parc des Sports, capacity: 10,000. Strip: green shirts, white shorts. **African Cup-winners Cup** runners-up 1975 (1–5 agg., v **Tonnerre Yaoundé** of Cameroon); African **CAF Cup** 1993 (2–0 agg., v **SC Simba** of Tanzania); **West African Football Union General Eyadema Cup** 1981, runners-up 1987; Ivory Coast League champions 1979, 1981, 1984; Ivory Coast Cup 1974, 1975; Ivory Coast Super Cup (Coupe Houphouët-Boigny) winners 1974, 1984.

Stenhousemuir *club* Scottish league. *Dossier* Ground: **Ochilview Park**, Falkirk, Lothian. Strip: maroon shirts with sky blue pattern, white shorts with maroon trim, maroon socks with white and sky blue trim. Nickname: Warriors. Ground capacity: 3,520. Record attendance: 12,500 v **East Fife** (11 March 1950, **Scottish FA Cup**, fourth round). Biggest win: 9–2 v **Dundee United** (19 April 1937, Division Two). Biggest defeat: 2–11 v **Dunfermline Athletic** (27 September 1930, Division Two). *History* Founded in 1884 as a local village team. The club joined the **Scottish Football League** with the reformation of Division Two in 1920-21. Until the restructuring of the Scottish League in 1994-95 created a Third Division, Stenhousemuir had always played in the bottom division. However, its third-place Second Division finish in 1993-94 meant the club was no longer in the lowest tier. Stenhousemuir's victory in the 1995-96 **Scottish League Challenge Cup** (0–0, 5–4 pens v **Dundee United**) was the club's first major honour in its 114 year history. The club was relegated to the Third Division in 1997-98. Its promotion the following season was a milestone; it was the first promotion for Stenhousemuir since joining the league in 1921-22. *League record* Division Two (B Division) 1921-22 to 1993-94; Second Division 1994-95 to 1997-98, 1999-00–; Third Division 1998-99. *Honours* Scottish League Challenge Cup 1995-96 (0–0, 5–4 pens v Dundee United). *Records* Archie Ross holds the record for club League appearances (360).

Stephenson, Clement *player* Inside-forward. **England** international (1 cap). Born 36 February 1890. Career ca. 1910-1929. *Clubs* Blyth Spartans, **Aston**

Villa, Huddersfield Town. *Keynotes* Bought by Huddersfield for £3,000 from Aston Villa in March 1921, he captained the side to three consecutive League titles between 1924 and 1926. He was Huddersfield manager between 1929 and 1942. Included in the **Football League Centenary 100 players**. *Honours* League Championship (Huddersfield Town 1923-24, 1924-25, 1925-26); **FA Cup** (Aston Villa 1913, 1920; Huddersfield Town 1922).

steps *rules* one of the offences listed as a **foul** under the **Laws of the game** (Law XII) A goalkeeper commits such an offence if he or she: takes more than four steps in any direction while controlling the ball with his or her hands, before releasing it back into play (Law XII). The punishment for such an offence is for the opposing team to be awarded an **indirect free kick** from the spot where the offence took place (unless within the **goal area**, in which case it must be taken from the **goal line** at the point nearest to where the foul was committed).

steward *misc.* non-police official appointed to keep crowd order and supervise seating. *Keynotes* In 1992, **Torquay United**'s **Plainmoor** ground became the first in the **Football League** to stage a match with no uniformed police on duty, relying on stewards to police the crowd and saving the club a considerable sum in policing costs.

stick goalie *informal* in unofficial (kickabout) matches where the goalkeeper of a team, especially one that has more players than the opposition, must remain in his/her penalty area. Compare **rush goalie**.

Stiles, Nobby (Norbert) *player* Defender/Midfield. **England** international (28 caps, 1 goal). Born 18 May 1942. Career ca. 1957-75. *Clubs* **Manchester United**, **Middlesbrough**, **Preston North End** (player-manager). Also, **Vancouver Whitecaps** and **West Bromwich Albion** manager. *Keynotes* Joined Manchester United in 1957, turning professional in June 1958. He played an influential part in England's 1966 World Cup success, especially in the semi-final against **Portugal** when he effectively nullified the threat posed by **Eusebio**. During the tournament, Stiles, whose participation was controversial, provoked further anger following an horrendous sliding tackle on Simon of **France** which he later admitted was: "A bad, bad tackle. I got stick and deserved to get stick." The **Football Association**'s **international committee** demanded that he be dropped from England's team but Alf **Ramsey** retained his services. Included in the **Football League Centenary 100 players**. *Honours* League Championship (Manchester United 1964-65, 1966-67); **European Cup** (Manchester United 1968); **World Cup** (England 1966). He received an **FA Cup** winner's medal although he did not play in United's 1963 triumph.

stimulant *medical* a class of drug that increases physiological function, such as heart rate. They give the feeling of increased energy and arousal. They include legal chemicals, for example caffeine in coffee and some soft drinks, to prescribed or illegal drugs, such as **amphetamines, ephedrine** and **cocaine**. Most stimulants are banned in most sports, although caffeine is allowed up to a certain level. They can have dangerous side-effects when misused, including psychological dependence, insomnia, digestive disorders, respiratory problems and depression.

Stirling Albion *club* Scottish league. *Dossier* Ground: **Forthbank Stadium**, Stirling, Central. Strip: red and white halved shirts, red and white halved shorts, red socks with white top. Nickname: Binos. Ground capacity: 3,808. Record attendance: 3,808 v **Aberdeen** (15 February 1996, **Scottish FA Cup**, fourth round). Biggest win: 20–0 v Selkirk (8 December 1984, Scottish FA Cup, first round). Biggest defeat: 0–9 v **Dundee United** (30 December 1967, Division One). *History* Founded in 1945 by the former chairman of **King's Park** and a group of local businessmen. The club was established at a ground near Annfield House, taking the name Annfield Park. Initially the only spectators' and officials' seats were in the back of "Albion" lorries, which is where the club derives its name. Stirling joined the **Scottish Football League** in 1947-48, winning promotion from Division Two as runners-up in 1948-49 and 1950-51. Between 1952-53 and 1964-65, the club won the Division Two Championship on four occasions, but its tenure of the top flight never lasted for more than three seasons on each occasion. The club was a Scottish FA Cup quarter-finalist in 1949-50 (1–5 v **Partick Thistle**), 1958-59 (1–3 v **Celtic**), 1961-62 (0–6 v **Motherwell**). Annfield Road is the only Scottish football ground to have installed an **artificial pitch**. The plastic pitch experiment took place between 1987 and 1990. Stirling moved to the new purpose-built Forthbank Stadium in April 1993, having been forced to share **Stenhousemuir**'s **Ochilview Park** for most of the 1992-93 season. *League record* Division One (A Division) 1949-50, 1951-52, 1953-54 to 1955-56, 1958-59 to 1959-60, 1961-62, 1965-66 to 1967-68; First Division 1977-78 to 1980-81, 1991-92 to 1993-94, 1996-97 to 1997-98; Division Two (B Division) 1947-48 to 1948-49, 1950-51, 1952-53, 1956-57 to 1957-58, 1960-61, 1962-63 to 1964-65, 1968-69 to 1974-75; Second Division 1975-76 to 1976-77, 1981-82 to 1990-91, 1994-95 to 1995-96, 1998-99–. *Honours* Division Two 1952-53, 1957-58, 1960-61, 1964-65; Second Division 1976-77, 1990-91, 1995-96. *Records* Matt McPhee holds the record for club League appearances (504, 1967-81); Billy Steele is Stirling's record League goalscorer (129, 1971-83).

stock market *misc.* market in which shares are bought and sold. *Keynotes* Since **Tottenham Hotspur** became the first UK club to float on the stock market in October 1983, several other UK clubs have followed. In October 1989, **Millwall** became a plc named **Millwall Holdings** which was floated on the stock market with a £5 million share issue. Aside from Tottenham Hotspur and Millwall, at the start of the 1998-99 season 10 other UK clubs were quoted on the London Stock Exchange:

Aston Villa, Bolton Wanderers (Burnden Leisure), Leeds United (Leeds Sporting), Heart of Midlothian, Leicester City, Manchester United, Newcastle United, Sheffield United, Southampton (Southampton Leisure) and Sunderland. A number of other clubs, including some foreign, also announced their intention to become public limited companies. In March 1998, Lazio became the first Serie A club to begin the process of transferring to a plc when the club formally applied for a stock market floatation. The club finally made its Milan bourse debut on 6 May 1998. On 1 June 1998, both FC Porto and Sporting Clube de Portugal were launched on the Lisbon bourse. Several UK clubs are listed on the Alternative Investment Market, which is a precursor to a full stock market listing. As of the start of the 1998-99 season, these clubs were: Birmingham City, Celtic, Charlton Athletic, Chelsea (Chelsea Village), Queens Park Rangers (Loftus Road), Nottingham Forest, Preston North End, West Bromwich Albion. Football share prices tend to move in line with the club's performance on the pitch. For example, following Tottenham Hotspur's elimination from the 1997-98 FA Cup competition (1–3 v Barnsley, replay, 4 February 1998), £2 million was wiped off the club's stock market value, with shares falling to 63p – a two-year low. Manchester United's share price fell by £26 million on the day after the club was eliminated from the Champions League on away goals (1–1 agg. v Monaco, 19 March 1998) at the quarter-final stage, while Aston Villa's share price declined after the club was knocked out of the UEFA Cup, also on away goals (2–2 agg. v Atlético Madrid, 17 March 1998). Sunderland's shares fell by more than 20% on the day after the club had failed to secure Premiership football, losing the final of the 1997-98 end-of-season First Division playoff (4–4, 6–7 pens. v Charlton Athletic, 25 May 1998). Other significant events may also adversely affect the share price of a club. Ruud Gullit's surprise dismissal as Chelsea's player-manager in February 1998 precipitated an estimated 7% fall in the value of Chelsea Village, the club's holding company. Also, following press reports of alleged comments made by Newcastle United's chairman Freddie Shepherd and vice-chairman Douglas Hall, the club's share price fell by around £9 million on the morning of 16 March 1998. Manchester United's share price jumped by more than 30% on 7 September 1998 following the announcement that BSkyB had made a bid for the club. On the same day, the share price of other quoted clubs also rose: Aston Villa (up 55p), Chelsea Village (up 7p), Leicester City (up 4p) and Newcastle United (up 5p). See also English National Investment Company.

stockings *rules* another name for socks.

Stockport County *club* English league. *Dossier* Ground: Edgeley Park, Greater Manchester. Strip: white shirts with two blue stripes, white shorts with two blue stripes, and white socks. Nickname: County or Hatters. Ground capacity: 11,540. Record attendance: 27,833 v Liverpool (11 February 1950, FA Cup, fifth round). Best average attendance: 14,399 (1937-38). Biggest win: 13–0 v Halifax Town (6 January 1934, Division Three (North)). Biggest defeat: 1–8 v Chesterfield (19 April 1902, Division Two). *History* Founded as Heaton Norris Rovers (the club played its first matches on Heaton Norris Recreation Ground) in 1883 by members of Wycliffe Congregational Church. The club amalgamated with rivals Heaton Norris in 1885 and, in 1890, adopted the name Stockport County – the town had became a county borough the previous year. County joined Division Two in 1900-01, failed re-election in 1903-04 (although the club finished five points clear of bottom-placed Leicester Fosse), and returned to the League in 1905-06 after winning the Lancashire Combination League. Relegation in 1920-21 was followed by an immediate return to Division Two as Division Three (North) Champions. At the end of the 1920-21 season, County was forced to play home matches at Old Trafford after Edgeley Park had been closed following crowd trouble. In 1926-27, Stockport had two points deducted for fielding an ineligble player, Joe Smith (v Stoke City, Division Three (North)), 19 March 1927). Between 1926-27 and 1991-92, County spent all but one season (1937-38) in the bottom two divisions. During that time, the club won the Division Four Championship (1966-67). County reached the end-of-season playoffs on four occasions between 1989-90 and 1993-94. In 1989-90, County lost at the semi-final stage of the Division Four playoffs and, in 1991-92, the club was defeated in the Division Three playoff final (1–2 v Peterborough United). The following season, County was a Second Division playoff semi-final loser and, in 1993-94, the club reached the playoff final (1–2 v Burnley). The club reached consecutive Autoglass Trophy finals in 1992 (0–1 Stoke City) and 1993 (1–2 v Port Vale). County won promotion to the First Division in 1996-97 and, in the same season, the club was a League Cup semi-finalists (1–2 agg. v Middlesbrough). *League record* First Division 1997-98–; Division Two 1900-01 to 1903-04 (failed re-election), 1905-06 to 1920-21, 1922-23 to 1925-26, 1937-38, 1958-59; Second Division 1992-93 to 1996-97; Division Three 1958-59, 1967-68 to 1969-70,1991-92; Division Three (North) 1921-22, 1926-27 to 1936-37, 1938-39 to 1957-58; Division Four 1959-60 to 1966-67, 1970-71 to 1990-91. *Honours* Division Three (North) 1921-22, 1936-37; Division Four 1966-67; Division Three (North) Cup 1935 (2–0 v Walsall). *Records* Martin Nash is County's most capped player (8 for Canada); Andy Thorpe holds the record for club appearances (489, 1978-86, 1988-92); Jack Connor is County's record League goalscorer (132, 1951-56).

Stoichkov, Hristo *player* Striker/midfield. Bulgaria international (76 caps, 37 goals, 1987–98). Born 8 February 1966. *Clubs* CSKA Sofia, Barcelona (twice), Parma. *Keynotes* Stoichkov is Bulgaria's second highest all-time goalscorer. He was joint top scorer (with Oleg **Salenko**) at the 1994 World Cup finals (six goals) and scored in every round as Bulgaria reached the semi-final. Stoichkov was one of several players suspended by the Bulgarian authorities after fighting broke out at the 1985 Bulgarian Cup final between CSKA and **Levski Sofia** – in front of the Communist Party leadership. Stoichkov was sold by CSKA Sofia to Barcelona in 1990 for a then Bulgarian record fee of £2 million. He played for Barcelona in two European Cup finals: 1992 (1–0, v **Sampdoria**) and 1994 (0–4, v **AC Milan**). Stoichkov also scored in Barcelona's 3–1 aggregate win over **Werder Bremen** in the 1992 European Super Cup, and in the 1992 **World Club Cup** (1–2, v **São Paulo**). After a comparatively unsuccessful spell in Italy with Parma, he returned to Barcelona and was as an 84th-minute substitute in the 1997 UEFA Cup final (1–0, v **Paris St Germain**). *Honours* **World Cup** fourth place (Bulgaria, 1994); World Cup **Golden Boot** 1994; **European Cup** (Barcelona, 1992); **European Super Cup** (Barcelona, 1992); **UEFA Cup** (Barcelona, 1997); Bulgarian League championship (CSKA Sofia, 1987, 1989, 1990); European **Golden Boot** winner 1990 (38 goals for CSKA Sofia, shared with Hugo **Sanchez**); **FIFA World Footballer of the Year** runner-up 1992, 1994; *France Football* **European Footballer of the Year** 1994.

Stoke City *club* English league. *Dossier* Ground: **Britannia Stadium**, Stoke-on-Trent, Staffordshire. Strip: red and white striped shirts, white shorts, red socks. Nickname: the Potters. Ground capacity: 24,054. Record attendance: 26,664 v **Manchester City** (3 May 1998, First Division). Best average attendance: 31,590 (**Victoria Ground**, 1947-48). Biggest win: 10–3 v **West Bromwich Albion** (4 February 1937, Division One). Biggest defeat: 0–10 v **Preston North End** (14 September 1889, Division One). *History* Founded as Stoke Ramblers in 1868 by employees of the North Staffordshire Railway Company. Ramblers was dropped from the club's name in 1875 and, in 1878, it merged with Stoke Victoria Athletic Club. Stoke played at several grounds, including the County Cricket Ground, Sweeting's Field and Athletic Ground, before settling at the Victoria Ground in 1883, when the club adopted its red and white striped shirts – it had previously sported red and blue stripes. Stoke was a founder member of the Football League in 1888, finishing bottom in the first two seasons and dropping out in 1889-90 before rejoining when the League expanded from 12 to 14 clubs in 1891-92. The club retained its Division One status in 1897-98 via the **test matches**, that from 1892-93 had been used to determine promotion and relegation. The club was an **FA Cup** semi-finalists in 1899 (1–3 v **Derby County**). Following one season in Division Two in 1906-07, the club, £1,100 in debt, went into liquidation and resigned from the League. A new **limited company** football club was founded but it had to wait until 1919-20 to gain League status. The club spent one season back in the top flight in 1922-23 and, in 1925, added the City prefix to its name. After relega-

tion from Division Two in 1925-26, the club bounced back immediately, winning the Division Three (North) Championship. With a young Stanley **Matthews** in the side, Stoke won promotion to Division One as Champions in 1932-33. Either side of World War II, Stoke twice achieved its highest-ever League position, finishing fourth in both 1935-36 and 1946-47. Matthews returned to Stoke from **Blackpool** in October 1961, aged 46, and the club, under the managership of Tony Waddington, won promotion to Division One in 1963-64. The promotion-winning side had the highest average age of any team in the League at the time. Stoke's victory in the 1972 League Cup final (2–1 v **Chelsea**) was the club's first major trophy success in its then 109-year history. Stoke required 11 matches, involving 18 hours of football, to get to the final. The club appeared in two consecutive FA Cup semi-finals in 1971 (0–2 replay v **Arsenal**) and 1972 (1–2 replay v Arsenal). Prior to the start of 1973-74 season, Stoke won the **Watney Cup** (2–0 v **Hull City**). A further spell in Division Two from the mid-1980s was followed by a period in Division Three. The club recorded a second **Wembley** Cup triumph in 1992 by winning the **Autoglass Trophy** (1–0 v **Stockport County**). Stoke reached the Division Three end-of-season playoffs in 1991-92 and, in 1996, having returned to the First Division as Champions in 1992-93, failed to gain promotion to the Premier League following defeat at the semi-final playoff stage. At the start of the 1997-98 season, Stoke moved to the new Britannia Stadium, but was relegated to the Second Division at the end of the campaign. *League record* Division One (including Football League) 1888-89 to 1889-90 (not re-elected), 1891-92 to 1906-07, 1922-23, 1933-34 to 1952-53, 1963-64 to 1976-77, 1979-80 to 1984-85; First Division 1993-94 to 1997-98; Division Two 1907-08 (resigned for financial reasons), 1919-20 to 1921-22, 1923-24 to 1925-26, 1927-28 to 1932-33, 1953-54 to 1962-63, 1977-78 to 1978-79, 1985-86 to 1989-90; Second Division 1992-93, 1998-99–; Division Three 1990-91 to 1991-92; Division Three (North) 1926-27. *Honours* Division Two 1932-33, 1962-63, 1992-93; Division Three (North) 1926-27; League Cup 1972 (2–1 v Chelsea); Watney Cup 1973 (2–0 v Hull City); Autoglass Trophy 1992 (1–0 v Stockport County). *Records* Gordon Banks is Stoke's most-capped player (36 (73) for **England**); Eric Skeels holds the record for club appearances (506, 1958-76); Freddie Steele is Stoke's record League goalscorer (142, 1934-49).

Stonewall FC *club* leading English gay men's football club. Four-times winners of the **Gay Games** football tournament. Also Gay European champions.

stoppages *n. pl.* any of the delays recorded by a **referee** that contribute to **added time**, such as for **injuries**, **time-wasting**, **substitutions** or time taken to **caution** or **send off** a player.

stopper *n.* one of a centre-back pairing who is strong in the air and a good tackler. See **covering centre-back**.

Store, Heidi   *player*   Norwegian women's international striker; by June 1997, she had made a world record 148 appearances for **Norway**.

strain   *medical*   minor injury to a **muscle** when some of the muscle fibres are overstretched. Mild strains are treated by **RICE**.

stranieri   *n.*   Italian for overseas player.

Stranraer   *club*   Scottish league. *Dossier* Ground: **Stair Park**, Stranraer, Dumfries and Galloway. Strip: blue shirts with white trim, white shorts, blue socks with red top. Nickname: Blues. Ground capacity: 6,100. Record attendance: 6,500 v **Rangers** (24 January 1948, **Scottish FA Cup**, first round). Biggest win: 7–0 v **Brechin City** (6 February 1965, Division Two). Biggest defeat: 1–11 v **Queen of the South** (16 January 1932, Scottish FA Cup, first round). *History* Stranraer is the third oldest club in the **Scottish Football League**, having been founded in 1870. Stranraer joined the League in 1955-56 and the club remained in the bottom division until 1993-94, when it won the Second Division Championship. The previous season, Stranraer had missed promotion on **goal difference**. Although the club was relegated from the First Division after only one season, it regained a place in the higher level by winning the Second Division title in 1997-98. It was relegated again the following year. Stranraer's **Scottish League Challenge Cup** final victory in 1996–97 was the club's first cup trophy in 126 years (1–0 v **St Johnstone**). *League record* First Division 1994-95, 1998-99–; Division Two (B Division) 1955-56 to 1974-75; Second Division 1975-76 to 1993-94, 1995-96 to 1997-98, 1999-00–. *Honours* Second Division C1993-94; Scottish League Challenge Cup 1996-97 (1–0 v St Johnstone). *Records* Danny McDonald holds the record for club League appearances (256).

streaker   *misc.*   individual who runs naked on to a football pitch. *Keynote* The first female streaker at a major football match was Variana Scotney, who ran on to the pitch at **Highbury** during an **Arsenal-Tottenham Hotspur derby** in 1981-82.

Streich, Joachim   *player*   Striker. **East Germany** international (98 caps, 55 goals, 1969–1984; excludes **Olympic Games**). Born 13 April 1951. *Clubs* **Hansa Rostock**, **Magdeburg** (1.FC). *Keynotes* Streich made his international debut in a friendly against **Iraq** on 8 December 1969 (1-1, in Baghdad). He holds the record for the most appearances and most goals for the former East Germany and is the world's seventh-highest international goalscorer.

stress fracture   *medical*   a fine, hairline crack appearing in a bone without injury. This can occur through over-exercising, such as extended training runs. It commonly occurs in athletes and football players in the **tibia**, **fibula** and second **metatarsal**. Treatment is by **RICE**, the emphasis being on rest. Treatment is often augmented with painkillers, and may be followed up with **physiotherapy**.

stretcher   *n.*   apparatus for transferring an injured person in order that he/she can receive medical attention at an appropriate location. In its simplest form, a stretcher comprises a canvas stretched between two poles. Stretchers are used in football to transfer an injured played from the **field of play**. *Regulations* **Premier League** home clubs must provide at least two stretchers and trained stretcher bearers (FA Premier League rule H.6.4).

striker   *n.*   player who operates as an attacker and whose role is primarily to score goals and **assist** scoring opportunities. Also called **attacker**.

striking an opponent   *rules*   one of the offences listed as a **foul** under the **Laws of the game** (Law XII). The offence is also committed if an attempt is made to strike the opponent. The punishment for deliberately striking or attempting to strike an opponent is for the opposing team to be awarded a **direct free kick**, taken from the point where the foul was committed (unless within the opponents' **goal area**, in which case it is taken from anywhere within that area). If the foul is committed in the offending side's penalty area, then the opponents are awarded a **penalty kick**. A player guilty of striking an opponent will be **sent off** for **violent conduct** (Law XII).

strip   *rules*   the jersey or **shirts**, **shorts** and **socks** worn by members of a team; the team's uniform. Each member of the team (except the **goalkeeper**) must wear the same strip and it must be distinguishable from the opposing team and match officials. The goalkeeper must wear a shirt which distinguishes him or her from the rest of the players and officials. *regulations* **1. Premier League** clubs are required to register their **home strip** and **away strip** (including those of the goalkeeper) during the **close season** (FA Premier League rule F.15): they are then printed in the **league handbook**. Changes are permitted only with the consent of the **Premier League Board** (FA Premier League rule F.18). Premier League clubs are entitled to register a **third strip**, but it may be worn at league matches only with the consent of the Premier League Board (FA Premier League rules F.19-21). Clubs are, where possible, required to use their first-choice, home strip both at home and away. Second choice colours should be used, however, by the **away club** if they clash with those of the **home club**. **2. Football League** clubs are required to register their **home strip** with the Football League during the **close season**. They must play all their home games in this strip (Football League regulation 35). When playing away, they must simply ensure that their strip does not clash with that of their opponents. **3. Scottish Football League** clubs must register and submit for approval with the league their first-, second- and, where applicable, third-choice strip (Scottish Football League rule 66). Scottish Football League clubs are required to play in their first-choice strip wherever possible; the home club wears its first-choice kit in the event that both clubs in a fixture have similar playing colours. A club is, however, allowed to play up to four of its home league matches in a second- or third-choice strip provided that the league and match officials are notified at least two days in advance of the game. Where two clubs are engaged in a match at **neutral venue** both clubs must change their strips if their colours are similar. It is prohibited to change the registered strips during a season, without the written permission of the Scottish Football League Management Committee. *Keynotes* The word *strip* does not originate from stripping (eg removing one's clothes), but from *stripe*, thought to have been coined in the fifteenth century. The first team required to change its shirts owing to a clash of strips was **Sunderland** in 1890, at a game against **Wolverhampton Wanderers**: the home team was asked to make the change. By 1891, Football League clubs were required to register their strip with the league and to have a set of white shirts in case of a clash. The rule was changed in 1921 such that the away team would be required to change its strip in the event of a clash.

strongest side *regulations* see **full-strength team.**

student *regulations* a player under 21 years of age who is in full-time education and whose **registration** is held by a league club with a licensed **Football Academy** or **Centre of Excellence** (FA Premier League rule K.4, Football League regulation 53 and special Football League youth development rule 8). There are 13 student age-groups, starting with under-nine, and ending with under-21. The youngest players can be registered after the third Saturday in the April immediately preceding the child's ninth birthday, or at any time in the year in which the child will reach the age of nine (FA Premier League rule M.38, Football League youth development rule 8). Premier League players under 17 years of age can only be registered as students (FA Premier League rule K.4). Premier League clubs must include the names of students in their **club list of players** to retain their registration. Premier League and Football League clubs can hold the registration of 40 students in each age group under-9 to under-12; 30 in each of the under-13 and under-14 age groups; 20 in each age group under-15 and under-16; and 15 in each age group under-17 to under-21 (FA Premier League rule M.37). Restrictions are placed on the number of games played by students in a season (FA Premier League rules 67 and 70, Football League youth development rule 19). Registration as a student terminates when the student completes full-time education. Clubs may offer players of 14 years of age (or who will be 14 in the calendar year) a **Scholarship Agreement**. Football League clubs (but not Premier League clubs) can offer players a trainee agreement (see **trainee**, sense **1).** once they have reached the legal school-leaving age (Football League youth development rule 12). A club is barred from making an approach or **inducement** to a student registered with another club (FA Premier League rules 52-55, Football League youth development rule 14). If a student player is registered as a student with a new club (ie different to the one where he had originally been

registered), the new club must pay **compensation** to the original club for the player's training and development, provided that the former club either held the player's registration, intended to retain the registration or intended to offer the player a scholarship agreement (FA Premier League rule 57, Football League youth development rule 15.1). If a student player is registered as a **contract player** with a new club, the new club must also pay compensation to the original club for the player's training and development, provided that the player had either been offered or had entered into a scholarship agreement or had been offered, but declined, a contract (FA Premier League rule 58, Football League youth development rule 15.2). Student registrations replaced the former "**associated schoolboy**" registrations in England at the end of July 1998.

studs *n. pl.* rounded short protrusions on the soles of **football boots** to give extra grip. There are two main types: **screw-in studs**, made of plastic or metal, and **moulded studs**, made of plastic. *History* Studs were originally made from laminated leather, cut from thick hide using a cork borer and nailed in place. Leather studs or bars were officially sanctioned in 1891, until that time, players had been using all sorts of accessories – some dangerous – to give themselves added grip. Screw-in studs were pioneered in the late 1940s, and sanctioned by the **International FA Board** in 1951. Studs of different materials – eg aluminium, plastic and rubber – to suit different playing conditions were developed in the 1950s and made legal in 1955. Referees and assistants in England were first required to inspect players' studs in 1970. The Football League even issued official stud gauges to each official.

Stuttgart (VfB) *club* German league. *Dossier* Ground: **Gottlieb-Daimler stadion**, Stuttgart Baden-Württemberg. Strip: white shirts with red band, white shorts, red socks. Ground capacity: 70,000. *History* Originally formed in 1893, merging with FV 93 and KC Cannstadt in 1912. The club is officially called Verein für Ballspiel Stuttgart. Stuttgart reached its first German League national **playoff** in 1935 (4–6 v **Schalke 04**) and, in the post-war period, the club won a West German title in both 1950 and 1952. Stuttgart won further titles in 1983-84 and 1991-92. The club was ordered by **UEFA** to replay its 1992-93 **European Cup** (Champions League) first-round fixture with **Leeds United** for fielding an **ineligible player** in the away leg, losing the **playoff** in **Barcelona** (1–2). During the 1950s, Stuttgart also won two West German Cups. The club next won the cup in 1997, having reached the final for a third time in 1986 (2–5 v **Bayern Munich**). Stuttgart was a **UEFA Cup** finalist in 1989 (4–5 agg. v **Napoli**) and it reached the **European Cup-winners Cup** final in 1998 (0–1 v **Chelsea**). *Honours* West German League 1950 (2–1 v Kickers Offenbach), 1952 (3–2 v Saarbrücken (1.FC)); **Bundesliga** 1983-84, 1991-92; West German Cup 1954 (1–0 v **Cologne** (1.FC)), 1958 (4–3 v Fortuna Düsseldorf); German Cup 1997 (2–0 v Energie Cottbus).

stylish *adj.* of a style of play characterised by exemplary **control** and creative footwork.

Suárez, Luisito *player* Striker. **Spain** international (32 caps, 14 goals, 1957-72). Born 2 May 1935 in La Coruña. *Clubs* Deportivo de La Coruña, **Barcelona**, **Internazionale**, **Sampdoria**. *Keynotes* Suárez played for his local club Deportivo de La Coruña, but was signed by Barcelona in 1953; he was subsequently transferred from Barcelona to Internazionale for £210,000. As well as his two European Cup winner's medals with Inter, Suárez played for runners-up Barcelona in the 1962 final against **Benfica** (2–3, **Wankdorf Stadion**, Berne). He played in the second leg of the first Fairs Cup final in 1958, and scored in the 8–2 aggregate defeat of the London Select XI. Suárez became the Spanish national team coach in 1989 – which included the 1990 **World Cup** finals tournament – and had two spells as coach at Internazionale. *Honours* **European Championship** 1964; **European Cup** (Inter, 1964, 1965); Spanish league championship (Barcelona, 1959, 1960); **UEFA/Fairs Cup** (Barcelona, 1958; Italian **Serie A** championship (Inter, 1963, 1965, 1966); *France Football* **European Footballer of the Year** 1960 (while at Barcelona), runner-up 1961 and 1964 (while at Inter).

sub *abbrev.* **substitute**.

Subbuteo *trademark* toy football game. Small plastic model players with rounded bases are used to "kick" a plastic ball on a felt pitch. Each model player is operated by flicking its base with the forefinger or middle finger to strike the ball. Possession is retained until the operator is unable to reach the ball with one of his or her players or until the ball strikes an opposition player or goes out of play according to conventional association rules. The goalkeeper is mounted on a stalk operated from behind the goal. Teams are available in club and national team colours. Black players were introduced to UK editions in the 1990s, thus reflecting efforts to reduce **racism** in football. The game is played worldwide, with local, national and international tournaments.

substitute board *n.* display board held up by a **fourth official** to indicate that a **substitution** is to be made. Modern substitute boards have a digital display to show the number of the player to be withdrawn and of the player coming on (see **indicator board**). Display boards are also used to indicate the amount of **added time** (though they do not override the decision of the referee, the ultimate arbiter of total playing time). *Keynotes* Substitute boards were introduced in the **Football League** in 1975.

substitute *rules* a designated member of a team who may replace any of the **players** during the course of a game for tactical reasons or because a player is injured (Law III). The number of substitutes allowed in a match is governed by the particular rules of the competition but, in any match played under **FIFA**, the international federations (**UEFA, CAF, CONMEBOL, CONCACAF, AFC** or **OFC**) or a national association the number must not exceed three players chosen from no more than seven nominated individuals (in most competitions, their names are given to the referee before the match). For other matches, such as friendly matches, up to five substitutions may be made if the two teams agree in advance and the referee is informed. The referee must be informed of a substitution before it is made and the substitute can enter the **field of play** only during a **stoppage**, from the halfway line, after the substituted player has left and after the referee has signalled his or her permission. An individual who has been substituted cannot take any further part in the game. *Regulations* Five substitutes may be named in **Premier League** matches, whose names and shirt numbers must be included in the **teamsheet** (FA Premier League rule E.18.1) and on the form submitted to the League as notification of the match **result** (rule E.34); only three substitutes can be used in a match (rule E.22). In **Football League** and **Scottish Football League** matches, clubs can name and play three substitutes (Football League regulation 30.4, Scottish Football League rule 29). *History* Substitutes were introduced into the English **Football League** in 1965-66, but only for genuine injuries, and only one substitution per club could be made in a game. The first player to be brought on as a substitute in a league match was Keith Peacock, for **Charlton Athletic** against **Bolton Wanderers** (21 August 1965, at Bolton). From 1986, clubs were allowed to use two substitutes for **FA Cup** and **League Cup** games; the rule extended to Football League games in 1987-88. The Premier League allowed two substitutions from three named substitutes (two outfield plus one goalkeeper) in 1992-93; this was introduced by the Football League the following season. Both the Football League and Premier League allowed three substitutions from three named substitutes of any position in 1995-96. *vb.* to make a substitution.

substitute, fastest goal *record* **1. Football League** three seconds after going on to the field, Phil Starbuck, for **Huddersfield Town** (v **Wigan Athletic**, 12 April 1993, Second Division) **2. Premier League** 13 seconds after going on to the field, Jamie Cureton for **Norwich City** (v **Chelsea**, 10 December 1994).

Suchitepequez (Club Deportivo) *club* Guatemala national league club based in Mazatenango. Ground: Estadio Carlos Salazar. Strip: blue and white diagonal halved shirts, blue shorts. Guatemala national champions 1983, 1989; Guatemala Cup 1993, 1994, 1998.

Sudan *country CAF* republic in Northeast Africa, south of **Egypt** and on the Red Sea. Large areas of desert. Independence from Britain and Egypt in 1956. Civil war between the Islamic government and the Sudan People's Liberation Army, led to widespread famine in the south in the late 1990s. Up to 1.2 million people were thought to be starving in the 1998 famine. Area: 2,505,815 sq km (967,245 sq miles) – the largest country in Africa. Population: 28,900,000 (1996 est.). Languages: Arabic and tribal languages. Capital:

Khartoum. *Dossier* Sudan Football Association (Khartoum) formed in 1936, affiliated to **FIFA** in 1948 and founder member of **Confédération Africaine de Football** (CAF) in 1957, president Omer Albakri Abuhuraz; general secretary: Majdi Shams Eldein. Member of both the **Arab Football Union** and the **Confederation of East and Central African Football Associations**. Season played from July to June. National stadium: Municipal, Khartoum, capacity: 60,000. National strip: green shirts, white shorts, green socks. First international game: 1956 v **Ethiopia** (1–2, in Ethiopia, friendly). Biggest victory: 4–0, v **Nigeria** (28 November 1963, Khumasi, Ghana, **African Cup of Nations** finals tournament, first round group), and 4–0, v **Uganda** (4 June 1971, Khartoum, **Olympic Games** qualifier). Biggest defeat: 0–5, v **Cameroon** (14 August 1983, in Cameroon, African Cup of Nations qualifier). *International tournament record* **World Cup** – first entered 1958, qualifying tournament third round 1958, 1970; African Cup of Nations – winners 1970 (1–0, v **Ghana**, Khartoum), runners-up 1959 (just three nations in tournament, in Cairo, Egypt), 1963 (0–3 v Ghana, Accra, Ghana), third place 1957 (only three nations in competition, in Khartoum), has not qualified for finals tournament since 1976; hosts of first tournament in 1957 and again in 1970 (finals in Khartoum); Olympic Games – first round group stage 1972 (last in four-nation group); **East and Central African Championship** – winners 1980 (1–0 v **Tanzania**, Khartoum), runners-up 1990 (0–2 v **Uganda**, Zanzibar); **World Youth Cup** (under-20) – never qualified; **Under-17 World Championship** – never qualified; **Women's World Cup** – never entered. *Record against British and Irish national teams* none played. *History* Football was introduced by the British during the colonial years. The country's two oldest clubs, **El Hilal** and **El Mourada**, were founded in 1930, with **El Merreikh Sports Club** founded a year later. The Sudan Football Association was established in 1936. The Khartoum-Omdurman Premier League dates from 1951. The capital Khartoum and Omdurman (or Umm Durman) are the country's two largest cities; the league, however, also involves clubs from Wad Madani, El Obied and Port Sudan. A domestic cup has been played since 1970. Sudanese clubs have entered African club competitions since their inception, with Al Hilal reaching the semi-final of the **African Cup of Champion Clubs** in 1966, the second year of the competition; the club were twice runners-up, in 1987 and 1992. El Merreikh's triumph in the 1989 **African Cup-winners Cup** is the only African club title won by a Sudanese club. It has entered the World Cup since the 1958 tournament, the second African country to enter (after Egypt in 1934). Its first entry in 1958 started with a two-leg victory over Syria (2–1 agg.) and was followed by a walkover in the second round. It withdrew from the final qualifying round, refusing to play **Israel** (just as Egypt had done in the second round). It has never qualified for the World Cup finals, though

reached the third and final round in 1970 (finishing third in the final group of three behind Nigeria and qualifiers **Morocco**). *Record in international club tournaments* African Cup of Champion Clubs – El Hilal (runners-up 1987, 1992); African Cup-winners Cup – El Merreikh (winners 1989, semi-final 1990); **CAF Cup** – El Mourada (semi-final 1994), El Hilal (quarter-final 1998); East and Central African Club Championship – El Merreikh (winners 1986, 1994, runners-up 1987, 1993), El Mourada (third place 1995), El Hilal (semi-final 1988).

sudden death *n.* of a **penalty shoot-out** where the next team to miss a penalty will lose the match, provided that the other team scores. **2.** another term for **golden goal**.

sudden-death overtime *n.* chiefly US. Another term for **golden goal**.

Sudell, Major William *official* first treasurer of the **Football League** and credited with creating its name. Born 1849, died 1911. Sudell was honorary treasurer of the league until 1992. Former manager and chairman of Preston Nelson (later **Preston North End**). Left Preston North End in 1893. Imprisoned in 1895 for embezzlement of money from the Peel Hall cotton mill - allegedly to finance the football club.

suicide *medical* the act of intentionally killing oneself, often as a result of depression. Honduran fan Domingo Padilla fatally shot himself after his country's first-round elimination from the 1982 **World Cup** finals in **Spain**. Former **Norwich City** and **Nottingham Forest** striker Justin Fashanu committed suicide in 1998; a warrant for his arrest had been issued in the United States of America for alleged sex offences.

Suker, Davor *player* Striker. **Croatia** international (50 caps, 41 goals, 1992-). Born 1 January 1968. *Clubs* (include) **Sevilla**, **Real Madrid**. *Keynotes* Croatia's top scorer. Suker scored one of the goals of the tournament at the 1996 **European Championship** finals in England: a chip with the outside of his left foot over the fast-retreating Danish goalkeeper Peter **Schmeichel** and into the net (3–0, v **Denmark**, first round). Suker was top scorer at the 1998 World Cup finals with six goals and was chosen for **FIFA**'s 22-man 1998 World Cup all-star squad. He scored in Croatia's 2–1 victory over **Netherlands** in the third/fourth playoff, to help his country to its greatest footballing achievement. He was an 89th-minute substitute in the 1998 European Cup final (1–0, v **Juventus**). Suker is the all-time record goalscorer in the **European Championship**. *Honours* World Cup, third place (Croatia, 1998); **European Cup** (Real Madrid, 1998); Spanish league championship (Real Madrid, 1997); **European Footballer of the Year** runner-up 1998.

summer break *n.* mid-season break in **Sweden**'s national league. The league runs from April to October, with a break in July to coincide with the main holiday period. It contrasts many northern European countries which have a **winter break** to avoid the worst winter weather.

summer wages *n. pl.* historically, these were wages paid to a player in the **close season**. Before the players' **maximum wage** was abolished, it was common for players to be paid a lower wage when no competitive games were played.

sunburn *medical* erythema (redness of the skin) owing to dilation of the capillaries at the surface of the skin, sometimes with blistering, caused by excessive exposure to ultraviolet light - particularly UVB (260 nm-320 nm wavelength). Sunburn can be a problem for players and spectators alike. *Keynotes* Researchers at St Luke's hospital in Bradford found the 1998 **England** World Cup strip to be too thin: it gave protection against ultraviolet irradiation equivalent to a suncream factor of only 5-10. Skin specialist Dr Andrew Wright claimed that this may be too low to give adequate protection for fair-skinned players as well as fans wearing replica kit, particularly in the summer sun. The wearing of an additional layer of clothing underneath was advised.

Sunday fixture *n.* a match played on a Sunday. *Keynotes* **Football League** clubs were prohibited from playing on Sundays for many years. Sunday fixtures were first allowed in England on 6 January 1974 – an FA dispensation granted owing to a national fuel crisis (caused by the miners' strike in the winter of 1973-74; clubs were not allowed to use electricity for floodlighting all at the same time). The first match was **Cambridge United** v **Oldham Athletic** (2–2, FA Cup third round), an 11 am kick-off. **Millwall** v **Fulham** (20 January 1974) was the first Football League fixture to be played on a Sunday. In 1983, a two-year contract between the English Football League and the television companies allowed five Sunday fixtures a season to be screened live on the ITV television network (these were complemented by five live matches on Friday evenings on BBC).

Sunday, Ibrahim *player* Midfield. **Ghana** international. *Clubs* Accra Standfast (Ghana), Kofiridua Corner Stars (Ghana), **Asante Kotoko**. *Honours* **African Cup of Nations** runner-up (Ghana, 1968, 1970); **African Cup of Champion Clubs** (Asante Kotoko, 1970); *France Football* **African Footballer of the Year** 1971.

Sunderland *club* English league. *Dossier* Ground: **Stadium of Light**, Sunderland, Tyne & Wear. Strip: red and white striped shirts, black shorts, red and white socks. Nickname: Rokermen. Ground capacity: 41,590. Record attendance: 41,505 v **Bolton Wanderers** (20 March 1999, First Division). Best average attendance: 47,785 (**Roker Park**, 1949-50). Biggest win: 11–1 v **Fairfield** (2 February 1895, **FA Cup**, first round). Biggest defeat: 0–8 v **West Ham United** (19 October 1968, Division One), v **Watford** (25 September 1982, Division One). *History* Founded as Sunderland and District Teachers Association FC in 1879 largely at the instigation of Jimmy Allan, a teacher at Hendon School. Lack of finance forced the club to accept non-teacher members and, in 1890, the club adopted the title Sunderland AFC. The club played its first matches at Blue House Field which was near to

Allan's school, not moving to Roker Park until 1898. Sunderland was expelled from the FA Cup competition in 1888 after it fielded three ineligible Scottish players. At that time, Allan and others formed a new club, Sunderland Albion (folded in 1892), but Sunderland, backed by shipyard owner Richard Thompson, assembled the so-called "Team of All Talents" and achieved **Football League** status. Sunderland's election (it replaced **Stoke**) to the League was achieved only after the club agreed to pay a proportion of the visitors' travelling expenses, due to the long distances that opponents would have to travel to play in the North-East. Between 1891-92 and 1894-95, the club won three League Championships in four seasons (finishing second in the other). In 1890–91, Sunderland was deducted two points for fielding an ineligible player, Ned Doig (v **West Bromwich Albion**, Football League, 20 September 1890). The club was the first to score 100 Football League goals in a season (1892-93). Another League Championship was won in 1901-02. Sunderland's success inspired **Athletic Bilbao** to adopt the same strip when the Basque club was formed in 1902. Sunderland continued to enjoy League success, winning further titles in 1912-13 and 1935-36. The club narrowly missed winning the double in 1913, losing in the FA Cup final (0–1 v **Aston Villa**). In 1937, Sunderland won the FA Cup for the first time (3–1 v **Preston North End**), having lost at the semifinal stage in 1931 (0–2 v **Birmingham**). The club reached the FA Cup semi-finals again the following season (1–3 v **Huddersfield Town**) and, in the mid-1950s, two consecutive semi-finals (1955 0–1 v **Manchester City**, 1956 0–3 v **Birmingham City**). Having spent a record 68 years in the top flight, Sunderland was relegated in 1957-58. The club returned to Division One in 1963-64, having missed promotion on **goal average** the previous season. Under the managership of Bob Stokoe, who was appointed in November 1972 when the club was third bottom of Division Two, and with a side that included Jim Montgomery, Ian **Porterfield** and Dennis Tueart, Sunderland became in 1973 the first Division Two team for 42 years to win the FA Cup (the only other Division Two clubs to win the FA Cup are: **Notts County** (1894), **Wolverhampton Wanderers** (1908), **Barnsley** (1912), West Bromwich Albion (1931), **Southampton** (1976), **West Ham United** (1980). Sunderland's victory over Leeds, the overwhelming favourites, in 1973 was the club's first major trophy since its 1937 FA Cup triumph. A five-season spell back in the top flight between 1980-81 and 1984-85 was followed in 1987-88 by relegation to Division Three, via the end-of-season **playoffs**, for the first time in the club's history. Sunderland joined the elite again in 1990, albeit for only one season, despite losing in the Division Two end-of-season playoff final against **Swindon Town** (0–1), because the Wiltshire side was denied promotion due to financial irregularities. Sunderland won the First Division Championship in 1995-96 but, again, the club's stay in the topflight lasted for only one season. Sunderland's one season in the **Premier League** in 1996-97 coincided with its move from Roker Park, the club's home for 99 years, to the new Stadium of Light. The season, and particularly manager Peter Reid's performance, was also recorded for the BBC television documentary, *Premier Passions*, which was shown in 1998. Sunderland failed to immediately regain a position in the topflight, losing in the 1997-98 First Division playoff final (4–4, 6–7 pens. v **Charlton Athletic**). The club was promoted as champions the following season, with 105 points from 46 games; a Football League record under the modern three-points-for-a-win system. Sunderland's record is marginally inferior to Lincoln City's Football League record of 74 points from 46 games in 1975-76 (Division Four) – under the modern system Lincoln would have won 106 points from its 46 games (see points in a season, most). Sunderland floated on the London Stock Exchange in December 1996 (flotation price = 585p). *League record* Premier League 1996-97, 1999-00; Division One (including Football League) 1890-91 to 1957-58, 1964-65 to 1969-70, 1976-77, 1980-81 to 1984-85, 1990-91; First Division 1992-93 to 1995-96, 1997-98 to 1998-99; Division Two 1958-59 to 1963-64, 1970-71 to 1975-76, 1977-78 to 1979-80, 1985-86 to 1986-87, 1988-89 to 1989-90, 1991-92; Division Three 1987-88. *Honours* League 1891-92, 1892-93, 1894-95, 1901-02, 1912-13, 1935-36; First Division 1995-96, 1998-99; Division Two 1975-76; Division Three 1987-88; FA Cup 1937 (3–1 v Preston North End – *Team* Mapson, Gorman, Hall, Thomson, Johnston, McNab, Duns, Carter (1), Gurney (1), Gallacher, Burbanks (1)), 1973 (1–0 v Leeds United – *Team* Montgomery, Malone, Guthrie, Horswill, Watson, Pitt, Kerr, Hughes, Halom, Porterfield (1), Tueart); **FA Charity Shield** 1936 (2–1 v **Arsenal**); **Sheriff of London's Charity Shield** 1903 (3–0 v Corinthians). *Records* Charlie Hurley is Sunderland's most capped player (38 (40) for **Republic of Ireland**); Jim Montgomery holds the record for club appearances (537, 1962-77); Charles **Buchan** is Sunderland's record League goalscorer (209, 1911-25).

Sunderland plc *n.* publicly-quoted business which owns **Sunderland**. The club became a fully listed company on the London Stock Exchange in December 1996 (flotation price = 585p). Sunderland had a market capitalisation – the market value of the company's issued share capital (eg, the quoted price of its shares multiplied by the number of shares outstanding) – of £47.7 million when it floated.

Sunrise Flacq United SC (Sports Club) *club* Mauritius national league club, based in Flacq and founded in 1948. Ground: St Francois Xavier, capacity: 5,000. Strip: yellow shirts and red shorts. **African Cup of Champion Clubs** second round 1988, 1990, 1991 and 1993; Mauritius League champions 1987, 1989, 1990, 1991, 1992 and 1995, 1996, 1997; Mauritius Cup 1985, 1987, 1992, 1993, 1996.

Super League *misc.* **1.** continental-based club league (See **Copa Mercosur**, **Copa Merconorte**) **2.** proposal in the 1980s for a breakaway league involving the leading clubs in the English **Football League**, fuelled by a desire to receive a larger share of television and sponsorship money. It was formally proposed on 30 September 1985 by the so-called **Big Five** clubs (**Arsenal, Everton, Liverpool, Manchester United** and **Tottenham Hotspur**). They proposed a new league of 18-20 invited clubs, existing outside the Football League. The proposal was opposed by the **Professional Footballers Association** and clubs from the lower divisions. A compromise package of proposals ("the **Heathrow Agreement**") was negotiated between the clubs preventing the breakaway league, but giving a greater share of the revenue to the First Division clubs. It also involved a smaller First Division (20 clubs), promotion and relegation **playoffs**, automatic promotion and relegation from the **Football Conference** (at that time known as the Gola League) to and from the Fourth Division, and greater representation of First Division clubs on the **Football League Management Committee**. The Football League finally accepted the compromise at its Extraordinary General Meeting of 28 April 1986. See **Premier League**.

Supercopa (Trofeo João Havelange) *competition* former annual South American club tournament for all former winners of the **Copa Libertadores** and the former **South American Champions Cup**, first played 1988. By 1997 there had been 17 former winners; a preliminary round was used to eliminate one of these, leaving 16 clubs in the tournament proper. The first round was divided into four mini-leagues of four clubs, each club playing each other at home and away (six games in all); three points are awarded for a win, and one for a draw. The winners of each group qualified for the knockout semi-finals. The semi-finals and final were played over two legs, the winners decided on the **aggregate score**, with **penalties**, if necessary. The tournament was replaced in 1998 by the revamped **Supercopa Masters** – a slimmer tournament for previous winners of the Supercopa. *Winners, scores and runners-up:* 1988 **Racing Club**, 3–2 agg., v **Cruzeiro**; 1989 **Boca Juniors**, 0–0 agg., 5–3 pens., v **Independiente**; 1990 **Olimpia** 6–3 agg., v **Nacional** (Uruguay); 1991 Cruzeiro, 3–2 agg., v **River Plate**; 1992 Cruzeiro, 4–1 agg., v Racing Club; 1993 **São Paulo**, 4–4 agg., 5–3 pens., v **Flamengo**; 1994 Independiente, 2–1 agg., v Boca Juniors; 1995 Independiente, 2–1 agg., v Flamengo; 1996 **Velez Sarsfield** 3–0 agg., v Cruzeiro; 1997 River Plate, 2–1 agg., v São Paulo.

Supercopa Masters *competition* annual South American club knockout tournament for all former winners of the **Supercopa**, first played 1992. The eight eligible clubs are: **Cruzeiro, São Paulo, Boca Juniors, River Plate, Velez Sarsfield, Rácing Club, Independiente,** and **Olimpia**. The tournament had a slow start; by 1997, only two finals had been played.

It was revamped in 1998, however, in order to replace the Supercopa. *Winners* 1992 Boca Juniors; 1993 not played; 1994 Cruzeiro; 1995-97 not played.

Superga aircrash *disaster* plane crash on 4 May 1949 on the Superga Hill outside Turin. The plane was returning from Lisbon transporting the **Torino** team – the best in Italy at the time, including 10 members of the national side. All the crew and passengers were killed, including Italy's captain, Valentino **Mazzola**,and the club's English manager, Leslie Lievesley. In all, there were 31 fatalities. Torino had been playing a friendly in Lisbon. The dead football heroes were given a state funeral. After the tragedy, the remaining four matches were was played – and won – by Torino's youth team and, out of respect, their opponents also put out youth teams; Torino won the 1948-49 championship, making it five in a row; the last time the trophy went to the club for 27 years.

superhooligan gangs *misc.* groups of supporters with a reputation for violence towards fans from other clubs. Superhooligan gangs differ from other trouble-makers and ordinary fans because they typically wear no club colours, they travel to matches by regular transport, rather than by **football specials**, to hinder detection by the police and opposing fans, and they leave "calling cards" with their victims. Several super-hooligan gangs emerged in the early 1980s, including the Baby Squad (**Leicester City**), Bushwhackers (**Millwall**), Gooners (**Arsenal**), Headhunters (**Chelsea**), Inter City Firm (**West Ham United**) and Service Crew (**Leeds United**). In **Italy**, supporters known as **Ultras** – groups of organised supporters – that follow all the major **Serie A** clubs also have a violent reputation. Although most ultra gangs are associated with right-wing politics, such as **Lazio**'s Irriducibili and **Roma**'s Boys Roma, both **AC Milan**'s Fossa del Leoin and Brigate Rossonere and **Fiorentina**'s Collettivo Autonomo Viola have left-wing leanings. The death of **Genoa** supporter Victor **Spagnulo** following a clash between home supporters and AC Milan fans, including members of a Milan grouping called Barbour, prior to a **Serie A** match between the clubs on 5 February 1995 led the suspension of sports events the following weekend. The **Ajax** F-side, named after an area of the club's former ground, De Mere, where they would congregate, regularly clash with their bitter rivals from **Feyenoord**. The two groups fought a pre-arranged battle in March 1997 and F-side member Carl Procaine later died from head injuries sustained in the melee. Football gangs in **Argentina** are known as *barras bravas* and, between 1990 and early-1998, 37 people died as a result of football-related violence in the country. In May 1998, an Argentine judge ordered the country's Division One programme to be halted for two weeks in an attempt to stop the escalating violence at matches. The same judge also suspended all Division Two matches in November 1998 in a further effort to combat crowd trouble. See also **hooliganism, football.**

super-sub *n.* substitute who regularly comes off the bench to score or make a positive contribution to the match. *Keynotes* **Liverpool**'s David Fairclough earned the nickname super-sub in the late-1970s. On one occasion, Fairclough scored a wonderful individual goal to take Liverpool to the 1977 European Cup semi-final (3–2 agg. v **Saint Etienne**).

support *n.* to follow the fortunes of a particular club, taking pleasure from its successes, and disappointment at its failures.

supporter *n.* person who **supports** a club. Also called fan. Supporters often demonstrate their allegiance to their club, by wearing club colours, joining supporters clubs or membership schemes and adding vocal encouragement or disdain at the good or bad performance of its players. Compare **spectator**.

supporters' club *n.* association of supporters following one club which can be officially recognised or which can be an independent organisation. **Barcelona** has more than 100,000 members of its official supporters' club. There are branches in Central, North and South America and more than 1,000 in Spain, including almost 400 in Catalonia, the region in which Barcelona is located. A Supporters' Club Congress is held every year at which the Barça president is required to attend and answer questions. In the UK, many clubs have refused to acknowledge supporters' club despite the finance they have often generated, especially helping to fund ground developments and rescuing bankrupt clubs. *Keynotes* Much of the work to enclose **Shrewsbury Town**'s **Gay Meadow** during the 1930s was funded by the **supporters' club**. **Lincoln City's** supporters' club has contributed around £1.6 million to club funds between 1945 and 1996. **Portsmouth**'s supporters' club provided the finances in 1962 to enable the club to erect **floodlights** on corner pylons. **Swindon** fans provided the £4,300 required to roof the Town End at the club's **County Ground** in 1932. **Queens Park Rangers'** supporters' club raised the finance to roof the **Loftus Road** End of the club's ground in 1938. **Tranmere Rovers'** supporters' club gave £15,000 towards the cost of installing floodlights at **Prenton Park** in 1958. **Ipswich Town**'s supporters club gave the club £42,000 over a 12-month period in 1965, yet the club later removed recognition and created its own supporters' association.

supporters' panel *n.* body of supporters established at each **Premier League** club to aid communication and discover what the fans' concerns are.

Surinam *country CONCACAF* republic on the north coast of South America, between **Guyana** and **French Guiana**. Independence from the **Netherlands** in 1975. Area: 163,820 sq km (63,235 sq miles). Population: 4,070,000 (1995 est.). Languages: Dutch, English, Spanish. Capital: Paramaribo. *Dossier* Football association (Surinaamse Voetbal Bond, Paramaribo) formed in 1920, affiliated to **FIFA** in 1929 and founder member of **Confederación Norte-Centroamericana y del**

Caribe de Fútbol (CONCACAF) in 1961, president: Erik Tjon Kie Sim; general secretary: Roel Goede. Surinam is affiliated to the North and Central American and Caribbean confederation, and enters the Caribbean nations and club tournaments, in spite of its location in South America. Season played from autumn to spring. National stadium: Surinam Stadion, Paramaribo, capacity: 21,000. National strip: red, green and white shirts, white or green shorts, white or green socks. *International tournament record* **World Cup** – first entered 1962, reached final round of the qualifying tournament in 1978 (last of six-nation league tournament held in Mexico), qualifying tournament second-round group stage 1986; **Gold Cup** – never qualified; **Caribbean Nations Cup** – fourth place 1994 (0–2, v **Guadeloupe**, Trinidad, third/fourth playoff, in Trinidad), 1996 (1–1, 2–3 pens., v **Martinique**, in Trinidad, third/fourth playoff); **Olympic Games** – qualifying tournament second round 1992; **World Youth Cup** (under-20) – never qualified; **Under-17 World Championship** – never qualified; **Women's World Cup** – had not entered before 1999. *Record against British and Irish national teams* none played. *History* League championship first played 1950. By 1997, only four clubs had won the league title: **Robin Hood** (23 championships), **SV Transvaal** (16), **Leo Victor** (three), Voorwaarts (three). Robin Hood jointly holds the South American club record of seven consecutive league tiles (1983 to 1989); equal with **Racing Club** of Argentina. Its 23 league titles is a CONCACAF club record. *League system* Ten clubs play in Surinam's national first division, playing each other three times in a season (27 games in total). Three points are awarded for a victory, with one for a draw. The bottom club is automatically relegated to the second division; the second- and third-bottom clubs enter a relegation playoff to decide the second relegation place. The champions of the second division and the winner of the second division playoffs are promoted. *Record in international club tournaments* **CONCACAF Champions Cup** – SV Transvaal (winners 1973, 1981, runners-up 1974, 1975, 1986), Robin Hood (runners-up 1972, 1976, 1977, 1982, 1983). Other leading clubs: Leo Victor SV, Voorwaarts (of Paramaribo, league champions 1952, 1957, 1977), SNL (of Paramaribo, league champions 1999).

suspension *n.* punishment meted out in the form of a short-term ban to a player for misconduct, such as for being **sent off** or for collecting a certain number of **cautions**. The length of the suspension – which can be anything from a single match to five or more games – depends on the **competition rules** of a tournament and may vary according to the severity of the incident; it may also be at the discretion of the relevant governing body (eg, **Football Association** or **Scottish Football Association**). *Regulations* Clubs also may impose suspensions or fines on players, though the details must be forwarded in writing to their league and football association (FA Premier League rule J.20, Football League regulation 55.7, Scottish Football

League rule 55). Aside from suspensions imposed for failing a **drug** test, several players have received lengthy bans after being found guilty of misconduct charges or for bringing the game into disrepute. *Keynotes* **Oldham Athletic's** left-back Billy Cook was suspended for 12 months following his refusal to leave the pitch after being dismissed against **Middlesbrough** on Easter Monday 1915. The referee gave Cook one minute to leave the field and after he refused the match was abandoned. The 4–1 result in Middlesbrough's favour was allowed to stand and Oldham was fined £350. More recently, Eric **Cantona** received an eight-month suspension following his altercation with **Crystal Palace** supporter Matthew Simmons on 25 January 1995. Willie Johnston, the Scotland and **West Bromwich Albion** player, was banned for five games after he attempted to kick the referee following his dismissal, the tenth of his career, during a match with **Brighton & Hove Albion** on 22 September 1976. **Chelsea** striker Peter Osgood was banned for eight matches after receiving a second trio of bookings in a 12-month period in 1971. **Real Madrid's** Juanito was suspended for two years after he butted referee Adolf Prokop during the club's 1979 **European Cup** tie with **Grasshopper Zurich**. **Queens Park Rangers** defender Mark Dennis was banned for 53 days (later amended to an eight-match ban) after he was sent off for the 11th time in his career against **Tottenham Hotspur** in November 1987. **Torquay United's** Dave Caldwell received the same punishment following his fifth dismissal during the 1987-88 season. Kevin **Keegan** and Billy **Bremner**, the first domestic players sent off in a match at **Wembley** (1974 FA **Charity Shield**), were each suspended for ten matches. **Arsenal's** Paul Davis received a nine-match ban and a record £3,000 fine after televsion footage captured him punching **Southampton's** Glenn Cockerill in an off-the-ball incident during a match at **Highbury** in October 1988. Cockerill's jaw was broken. Frank Sinclair, on loan at West Bromwich Albion from Chelsea, also received a nine-match suspension after a clash of heads with referee Paul Alcock in January 1992. The same referee figured in an incident that led to one of the longest bans being imposed on a player in England. **Sheffield Wednesday's** Paolo Di Canio pushed Alcock to the ground after the referee had dismissed him during a **Premier League** match against Arsenal on 26 September 1998. Di Canio was suspended for 11 matches – three for the dismissal and an additional eight games for his actions – and fined £10,000. **Lazio** defender Jose Antonio Chamot was suspended for one match by the Italian football authorities in April 1998 after giving referee Pierluigi Collina "an overly firm handshake" following a **Serie A** encounter with **Juventus**. Club officials also can be suspended from football. In 1997-98, the Spanish football confederation suspended **Atlético Madrid's** president, Jesus Gil, for the duration of the season following his criticism of the authorities.

Sutcliffe 1. Charles Edward *official/referee.* former director of **Burnley FC** and **Football League** referee. *Born* 1864, in Burnley, England, died 1939. Member of the **Football League management committee** 1898-1939, president of the Football League 1936-39. Compiled the Football League **fixture list** from 1919-39. Credited with the foundation of the **Football Mutual Insurance Confederation** and with maintaining the integrity of the Football League during **World War I**, after the national league programme was suspended. In 1915, he devised a new system for drawing up the Football League fixture list; it remained in place until 1967. Co-author (with J A Brierley and Fred **Howarth**) of *The story of the Football League* (1938). **2**. His son Harold (1903-67), compiled the Football League fixture list from 1939 until 1967.

Suwon Samsung Bluewings *club* South Korean Pro-Football League club, based in Suwon, near Seoul, joined South Korean Pro-Football League in 1996. **Asian Cup-winners Cup** runners-up 1998 (0-1, v **Al-Nasr** of **Saudi Arabia**, in Riyadh, Saudi Arabia); South Korean Pro-Football League champions 1998, runners-up 1996 (its first season in the league).

SV Austria Salzburg *club* Austrian national league club, based in Salzburg, founded 1933 from merger of Rapid Salzburg and Hertha (founded 1904). Ground: Lehen, capacity: 14,500. Strip: white shirts, white shorts. **UEFA Cup** runners-up 1994; Austrian League Champions 1994, 1995, 1997; Austrian Cup runners-up 1974, 1980, 1981.

SV Transvaal *club* Surinam national league club based in the capital Paramaribo, founded 1921. Strip: green and white striped shirts, green shorts. **CONCACAF Champions Cup** 1973, 1981, runners-up 1974, 1975, 1986; Surinam league champions 1950, 1951, 1962, 1965, 1966, 1967, 1968, 1969, 1970, 1973, 1974, 1990, 1991, 1995, 1996, 1997.

Swansea City *club* English league. *Dossier* Ground: **Vetch Field**, Swansea, west Glamorgan. Strip: white shirts with black shoulders and stripes on sleeves, white shorts with black trim, and white socks with black trim. Nickname: Swans. Ground capacity: 11,477. Record attendance: 32,796 v **Arsenal** (17 February 1968, **FA Cup**, fourth round). Best average attendance: 22,535 (1948-49). Biggest win: 12–0 v Sliema W (Malta) (15 September 1982, **European Cup-winners Cup**, first round first leg). Biggest defeat: 0–8 v **Liverpool** (9 January 1990, FA Cup, third round). *History* Founded in June 1912 as Swansea Town (a name the club retained until February 1970 when it became Swansea City) to be the town's entrant to the expanding **Southern League**. Vetch Field has been the club's home since its formation. Swansea's first **Welsh Cup** victory occurred in 1913 (1–0 replay v Pontypridd) and the club has won the trophy on a further eight occasions (see below). Swansea is one of six Welsh clubs playing in the English **pyramid** (**Cardiff City** and **Wrexham**, and non-league Colwyn Bay, Merthyr Tydfil and Newport AFC). The club was a

founder member of Division Three in 1920-21, and in 1924-25 it won the Division Three (South) Championship. A further Division Three (South) title was won in 1948-49, but apart from that and the previous season, the club spent 31 seasons between 1925-26 and 1964-65, when it was relegated, in Division Two. Swansea was a FA Cup semi-finalist in 1926 (0–3 v **Bolton Wanderers**) and 1964 (1–2 v **Preston North End**), and reached the last 16 of the **League Cup** in 1964-65 (2–3 v **Chelsea**) and 1976-77 (1–5 replay v Bolton Wanderers). Swansea's 1964 FA Cup campaign included victories over **Sheffield United** (4–0 replay, fourth round), **Stoke City** (2–0 replay, fifth round) and Liverpool (2–1, sixth round). Under the managership of former Liverpool and **Wales** international striker John Toshack (1978-1984), Swansea went from Division Four to Division One in four seasons between 1977-78 and 1980-81, finishing sixth in its first season (1981-82) in the top flight – the club's highest League position. The following season Swansea was relegated and the club's demise thereafter was just as rapid as its previous rise, so that by 1986-87 it was back playing in Division Four. Swansea won promotion to Division Three via the end-of-season **playoffs** (5–4 agg. v **Torquay United**) in 1987-88 and in 1992-93, the club was a Second Division playoff semi-finalist. The club won the **Autoglass Trophy** in 1994 (1–1, 3–1 pens. v **Huddersfield Town**) and, following relegation to the bottom division in 1995-96, it returned to **Wembley** in the 1996-97 Third Division playoff final (0–1 v **Northampton Town**). The club has qualified for the **European Cup-winners Cup** on seven occasions (1961-62, 1966-67, 1981-82, 1982-83, 1983-84, 1989-90, 1991-92), but only in 1982-83 did it progress to the second round (0–3 agg. v **Paris St Germain**). Swansea's 1961-62 European Cup-winners Cup qualification meant the club became the first Welsh side to play in a European club competition (3–7 agg., v Motor Jena, preliminary round). *League record* Division One 1981-82 to 1982-83; Division Two 1925-26 to 1946-47, 1949-50 to 1964-65, 1979-80 to 1980-81, 1983-84; Second Division 1992-93 to 1995-96; Division Three 1920-21, 1965-66 to 1966-67, 1970-71 to 1972-73, 1978-79, 1984-85 to 1985-86, 1988-89 to 1991-92; Third Division 1996-97–; Division Three (South) 1921-22 to 1924-25, 1947-48 to 1948-49; Division Four 1967-68 to 1969-70, 1973-74 to 1977-78, 1986-87 to 1987-88. *Honours* Division Three (South) 1924-25, 1948-49; Welsh Cup 1913 (1–0 replay v Pontypridd), 1932 (2–0 replay v Wrexham), 1950 (4–1 v Wrexham), 1961 (3–1 v **Bangor City**), 1966 (5–2 agg. v **Chester**), 1981 (2–1 agg. v Hereford United), 1982 (2–1 agg. v Cardiff City), 1983 (4–1 agg. v Wrexham), 1989 (5–0 v Kidderminster Harriers); Autoglass Trophy winners 1994 (1–1, 3–1 pens. v Huddersfield Town). *Records* Ivor **Allchurch** is Swansea's most capped player (42 (68) for Wales, and his brother Len won 11 caps); Wilfred Milne holds the record for club League appearances (585, 1919-37); Ivor Allchurch is also

Swansea's record League goalscorer (166, 1949-58, 1965-68).

swapping shirts *misc.* tradition at major football fixtures, such as cup finals and internationals, for players to swap shirts with members of the opposition team. The practice is thought to have become popular at the 1954 **World Cup** finals in Switzerland.

Swaziland *country CAF* kingdom in Southeast Africa, next to **Mozambique** and **South Africa**. Independence from Britain in 1968. Consists of mountains in the west and a plateau to the east. Area: 17,365 sq km (6,705 sq miles). Population: 850,600 (1993 est.). Languages: English, Siswati. Capital: Mbabane. *Dossier* National Football Association of Swaziland (Mbabane) formed in 1968, affiliated to **FIFA** and **Confédération Africaine de Football** (CAF) in 1976, member of the **Confederation of Southern African Football Associations** (COSAFA), president: A B Mthethwa; general secretary: M M Vilakazi. Season played from March to October. National stadium: Somholo, Mbabane, capacity: 15,000. National strip: blue shirts, gold shorts, white socks. Nickname of national team: Sihlangu (the shield). First international game: 1 May 1968 v **Malawi** (2–0, Mbabane, friendly). Biggest victory: has never won by more than two goals. Biggest defeat: 1–9 v **Zambia** (1978, in Zambia, friendly). Notable international players: Denis Matse, Robson Diakubi, Bongi Diamini, Bright Zondo (all former Swaziland players of the year). *International tournament record* **World Cup** – first entered 1994, never past first round of qualifying tournament; **African Cup of Nations** – first entered 1986, never past first-round group stage of qualifying tournament; **Olympic Games** – lost in preliminary round of qualifying tournament 1992; **World Youth Cup** (under-20) – never qualified; **Under-17 World Championship** – never entered; COSAFA Under-20 Championship – third place 1995 (1–3 v **Lesotho**, in Lesotho, third/fourth playoff), semi-final 1986, hosts 1993; **Women's World Cup** – never entered. *Record against British and Irish national teams* none played. *League system* Sixteen clubs compete in the national first division, playing each other at home and away. Three points are awarded for a victory, with one for a draw. *Record in international club tournaments* **African Cup of Champion Clubs** – never past first round; **African Cup-winners Cup** – **Mbabane Highlanders** (second round 1986), **Eleven Men In Flight** (second round 1994); **CAF Cup** – **Manzini Wanderers** (second round 1993), **Moneni Pirates** (second round 1994); COSAFA Club Championship – Mbabane Highlanders (winners 1992). Other leading clubs: **Denver Sundowns**, Mbabane Swallows.

Sweden *country UEFA* kingdom in Scandinavia, in North Europe, bordered by **Norway** and **Finland**. Member of the European Union. Neutral in World Wars I and II. Area: 449,790 sq km (173,620 sq miles). Population: 8,840,000 (1996 est.). Languages: Swedish, Finnish, Lapish. Capital: Stockholm. *Dossier* Football association (Svenska Fotbollförbundet, Solna)

formed in 1904, founder member of **FIFA** in 1904 and founder member of the **Union of European Football Associations** (UEFA) in 1954, president: Lars-Åke Lagrell; general secretary: Lars-Christer Olsson. Season played from April to October, with a **summer break** in July. National stadium: **Råsunda Stadion**, Solna, Stockholm, capacity: 36,000 all seated. National strip: yellow shirts, blue shorts, yellow socks. First international game: 12 July 1908 v **Norway** (11–3, Gothenburg, friendly). Biggest victory: 12–0 v **Latvia** (29 May 1927, Stockholm, friendly). Biggest defeats: 1–12 v England Amateurs (20 October 1908, London, Olympic Games first round), and 0–10 v **Denmark** (5 October 1913, Stockholm, friendly). Most capped players: Thomas **Ravelli** (143 appearances, 1981-1998; the most capped player in the world), Bjorn Nordqvist (115 appearances, 1963-78), Orvar Bergmark (94 appearances, 1951-1966), Ronnie Hellström (77 appearances, 1966-80), Roland Nilsson (96 appearances, 1986-). Leading goalscorers: Sven Rydell (49 goals, 1923-32; in only 43 games), Gunnar **Nordahl** (43 goals, ca. 1942-58), Gunnar **Gren** (32 goals, ca. 1940-58), Kennet Andersson (30 goals, 1990-), Martin Dahlin (29 goals, 1991-), Agne Simonsson (27 goals, ca. 1957-66), Tomas Brolin (25 goals, ca. 1990-97). Other notable international players: Nils **Liedholm**. Website: *http://*www.svenskfotboll.se (official site). *International tournament record* **Olympic Games** – winners/gold medal, 1948 (3–1, v **Yugoslavia**, London), third place/bronze medal, 1924 (3–1 v **Netherlands**, Paris, third/fourth playoff), 1952 (2–0 v **West German**y, Helsinki, Finland, third/fourth playoff), quarter-final 1988, 1992; **World Cup** – first entered 1934, runners-up 1958 (2–5 v **Brazil**, Stockholm), third place 1950 (third in the four-nation final group, Brazil), 1994 (4–0, v **Bulgaria**, Los Angeles, USA, third/fourth playoff), fourth place 1938 (2–4 v Brazil, Bordeaux, **France**, third/fourth playoff), quarter-final 1934, also qualified for finals tournament 1970, 1974 (second round), 1978, 1990, hosts 1958; **European Championship** – first entered 1968, semi-final 1992 (2–3 v **Germany**, Stockholm, semi-final), quarter-final 1964, hosts 1992; **European Under-21 Championship** – runners-up 1992 (1–2 agg., v **Italy**); **Scandinavian Championship** – winners 1936, 1947, 1951, 1955, 1959, 1967, 1971; **Under-17 World Championship** – never qualified; **World Youth Cup** (under-20) – qualified for finals tournament 1991 (third in its first-round group of four); **Women's World Cup/European Championship for Women/Olympic Games** (women) – see **Sweden, women**. *World Cup performance* (finals and qualifiers to end of 1998 tournament) played 115, won 60, drawn 21, lost 34, scored 222 goals, conceded 142 goals; win rate 52%; goals scored per game 1.93. *Record against British and Irish national teams* v **England**, played, 16 won five, drawn five, lost six; v **Northern Ireland**, played five, won three, drawn none, lost two; v **Scotland**, played 10, won four, drawn one, lost five; v

Wales, played five, won four, drawn one, lost none; v **Republic of Ireland**, played seven, won four, drawn one, lost two. *History* Football was introduced by British workers in the 1870s. First clubs formed in the late 19th century: **Ögryte Idrottssälskap**, of Gothenburg, founded in 1887, is the oldest still in existence. Other current clubs founded before the turn of the century include **AIK Stockholm**, **Djurgårdens IF Stockholm** (both founded in 1891), GAIS **Göteborg** (1894), Lulea FF/IFK (1895), Hammarby IF, **IFK Norrköping**, IFK Eskilstuna (all 1897), and IFK Malmö (1899). The Swedish football association was formed in 1904, and is a founder member of FIFA. It was, however, preceded by the Swedish Sports and Athletic Association, formed in 1885, as Swedish football's first governing body. A knockout championship was founded in 1895, but was initially based in and around Gothenburg: clubs from Stockholm were admitted in 1900. The Swedish national league started in 1925, first won by GAIS Göteborg. From 1982 to 1990, inclusively, the championship was decided by a two-leg playoff between the top two clubs: IFK Göteborg appeared in six of the nine playoffs, winning five of them. The championship reverted to a conventional "European" style in 1991. The Swedish Cup, the Svenska Kupa, was first played in 1941 (Helsingborg IF beat IK Sleipner 3–1 in the first final). IFK Göteborg has twice won the **UEFA Cup**, 4-0 on aggregate in 1982 against **Hamburg (SV)**, and 2-1 in 1987 against **Dundee United**. **Malmö FF** reached the final of the European Cup in 1979 (beaten 0–1 by **Nottingham Forest** in Munich). With a population of only 8.8 million, and its clubs still largely part-time, Sweden's record in international tournaments is impressive. Sweden hosted the 1958 World Cup and was beaten in the final by Brazil. It was third in 1950 and 1994 (Sweden was also the top scorer at the tournament with 15 goals), and was fourth in 1938. At the 1950 finals in Brazil, Sweden's final-round group match against Brazil, which it lost 1–7, attracted 138,000 spectators to **Maracana Stadium**, Rio de Janeiro. Professional players were banned from the 1950 and 1954 World Cup squads. Sweden failed to qualify for the 1998 finals, finishing third in its qualifying group, behind **Austria** and **Scotland**. Sweden was Olympic Gold medal winners in 1948 - with its **"Gre-no-li"** forward trio of Gunnar Gren, Nils Liedholm, Gunnar Nordhal - and bronze medalists in 1924 and 1952. Sweden hosted the 1992 European Championships when it reached the semi-final, its best in the competition. The Swedish women's team has won the European Championship for Women (1984) and finished third in the first Women's World Cup in 1991. *World Cup final team and scorers* 1958 (runners-up) Svensson (goalkeeper), Bergmark, Axbom, Börjesson, Gustavsson, Parling, Hamrin, Gren, Simonsson (1), Liedholm (1), Skoglund. *League system* Fourteen clubs compete in the national premier league, the Allsvenskan. Three points are awarded for a victory, with one for a draw: final positions for clubs level on points are determined by **goal difference**. The bottom two clubs are automatically relegated, replaced by the champions of the two regional first divisions. Two additional promotion/relegation places are decided by two-leg playoffs between the two first-division runners-up and the third- and fourth-bottom clubs in the premier league. There are 14 clubs in each of the first divisions (north and south). European Cup and UEFA Cup places are decided from the previous year's league positions (because Sweden's league season overlaps with the start of both tournaments). One UEFA berth was, however, awarded to the current-year cup winners: the Swedish Cup final is played over two legs at the end of May, with the tournament starting in March of the previous year. *Record in international club tournaments* European Cup – Malmö FF (runners-up 1979), **IFK Göteborg** (quarter-final 1995, also qualified for **Champions League** 1996, 1997, 1998); **European Cup-winners Cup** – **Åtvidabergs FF** (quarter-final 1972), IFK Göteborg (IFK Gothenburg) (quarter-final 1980), Malmö FF (quarter-final 1975, 1987), AIK Stockholm (quarter-final 1997); UEFA Cup – IFK Göteborg (winners 1982, 1987). Other leading clubs: IFK Norrköping, Ögryte Idrottssälskap (Ögryte IS Gothenburg), Djurgårdens IF Stockholm, **Halmstads BK**, **Helsingborgs IF**.

Sweden, women *country/women* women's football in Sweden is administered by the national football association, the Svenska Fotbollförbundet, in Solna. Football is the most popular participative sport for women in the country, with more than 160,000 players at senior and youth level. *History* Women's football came under the auspices of the national football association in 1978. Sweden won the first **European Championship for Women** in 1984, a two-leg victory over **England**, and was runners-up to Norway in the first **FIFA** women's tournament in Guangzhou, China, in 1988. It hosted the 1995 **Women's World Cup**. Regional women's club competitions started in 1970, with a national championship first played in 1972 (won by Oxabacks IF). The national cup competition, the Folksam Cup, started in 1981, first won by Jitex. By 1996, there were 3,242 registered clubs. *Dossier* First international match: 1973, v **Finland** (0–0). Most capped player: Pia Sundhage (146 appearances, retired 1996). *League system* There are 12 clubs in the national Premier Division and three regional First Divisions of 10 clubs. *International tournament record* **Olympic Games** (women) – played in the first tournament in 1996 (first round, Atlanta, USA); FIFA women's tournament – runners-up 1988 (v Norway, in Guangzhou, China); Women's World Cup – entered first tournament in 1991, third place 1991 (4–0 v **Germany**, in China, third/fourth playoff), quarter-final 1995, hosts 1995; **Algarve Cup** – has entered since the first tournament in 1989; European Championship for Women – entered first championship in 1984, winners 1984 (1–1 agg., 4–3 pens., v England), runners-up 1987 (1–2, v **Norway**, Oslo), runners-up 1995 (2–3, v Germany, Kaiserslautern), third place 1989

(2–1, v **Italy**, in West Germany, third/fourth playoff), quarter-final 1991, 1993. Leading clubs: Alvsjo Alk, Oxaback IF, Tyreso FF.

sweeper   *n.*   player who operates either behind or in front of the defence (depending on the opposition), covering for **on-ball** team-mates and intercepting the opposition's through passes or loose balls, for example. There are three types of sweeper: one, the sweeper plays behind the back-line, providing cover for the defenders; two, the sweeper plays behind the back-line, and as well as providing cover, brings the ball out of defence and initiates **counter-attacks**; three, the sweeper plays in front of the back-four, preventing through balls being played and engaging **on-ball** forwards and attacking midfield opponents (see **ball-winner**). Sweepers (rear or front) are generally astute readers of the game with great tactical awareness. The former **AC Milan** and **Italy** captain Franco **Baresi** is considered to be one of the modern game's finest exponents of the sweeper's art. See also **libero**.

sweetener   *n. informal*   another word for **signing-on fee**.

swerve   *n.*   the deviation of a ball in flight from a straight-line course, generally caused by side spin on the ball and by wind. The tremendous force and spin with which Roberto Carlos struck his famous "double-swerve" free kick for **Brazil** against **France** in the four-nation **Tornoi** in France in 1997 allowed the shot to benefit from two aerodynamic phenomena. Firstly, side spin imparts an increase in the speed of the air flow on one side of the ball, causing a relative decrease in air pressure from one side of the ball to the other; the ball thus swerves towards the side of lowest pressure (a principle that also explains the lift on an aeroplane wing). Secondly, above a certain critical velocity, the resistance to the movement of a sphere through air – or "drag" – is suddenly reduced as the aerodynamic characteristics are enhanced. In the case of Carlos's kick, the ball swerved as a result of its side spin and, as the ball slowed through the critical velocity, the drag suddenly increased causing a further change in the flight of the ball. Judging a ball that changes course mid-flight is problematic for goalkeepers.

swerving pass   *n.*   pass which curls/bends in order to reach its target.

Swift, Frank   *player*   Goalkeeper. **England** international (19 caps). Born 24 December 1913. Career ca. 1931-50. *Clubs* **Manchester City**. *Keynotes* The first goalkeeper to captain England this century, after making 14 wartime appearances for his country. He fainted at the end of Manchester City's 1934 FA Cup final victory over **Portsmouth** (2–1), when he was only 20, later admitting that his failure to wear gloves had resulted in Pompey's goal. He retired from playing in 1949, becoming a football journalist. Swift died in the **Munich air disaster** after he had travelled with the **Manchester United** side to Belgrade to report on the match for the *News of the World*. Included in the **Football League Centenary 100 players**. *Honours* League Championship (Manchester City 1936-37); Division

Two (Manchester City 1946-47); **FA Cup** (Manchester City 1934).

Swindon Town   *club*   English league. *Dossier* Ground: **County Ground**, Swindon, Wiltshire. Strip: red shirts with white trim, red shorts, red socks. Nickname: Robins. Ground capacity: 15,728. Record attendance: 32,000 v **Arsenal** (15 January 1972, **FA Cup**, third round). Best average attendance: 20,075 (1969-70). Biggest win: 10–1 v **Farnham United** (28 November 1925, FA Cup, first round replay). Biggest defeat: 1–10 v **Manchester City** (25 January 1930, FA Cup, fourth round replay). *History* Founded by Reverend William Pitt in 1881 as the football section of Spartans Cricket Club and adopting the name Swindon Town some time before 1893 when the club merged with St Mark's Young Men's Friendly Society. The club turned professional and became a founder member of the **Southern League** in 1894, and settling at the County Ground a year later. Between 1909-10 and 1913-14, Swindon won two Southern League titles (1910-11 and 1913-14), appeared in two FA Cup semi-finals in 1910 (0–2 **Newcastle United**) and 1912 (0–1 replay v **Barnsley**), and, in the intervening year, reached a quarter-final (1–3 v **Chelsea**). It was as Southern League Champions that Swindon contested the 1911 **FA Charity Shield** (4–8 v **Manchester United**). Swindon was a founder member of Division Three in 1920-21, finishing fourth in the inaugural season. In 1963-63, after 42 years as a Division Three club, Swindon won promotion to Division Two, dropping again two season's later. The club achieved a notable **double** in 1968-69, winning promotion from Division Three and lifting the **League Cup** (3–1 a.e.t. v **Arsenal**). At the start of the 1969-70 season, the club added the **Anglo-Italian League Cup-winners Cup** (5–2 agg. v **Roma (AS)**). The following year, Swindon won the **Anglo-Italian Cup** (3–0 v **Napoli**, match abandoned after 76 minutes) and reached the FA Cup quarter-finals (0–2 v **Leeds United**). By 1982-83, the club was in Division Four, rising again in 1985-86 and winning the divisional title with a then divisional record 102 points. Under the managership of Osvaldo **Ardiles**, Swindon won promotion to the top flight via the Division Two end-of-season **playoffs** in 1989-90 (1–0 v **Sunderland**), but the club's elevation was denied by the **Football League** after an investigation uncovered financial irregularities committed during the mid-1980s (Sunderland was promoted instead). Initially Swindon's punishment included demotion to Division Three but its Division Two status was restored on appeal. Player-manager Glenn **Hoddle** led Swindon to the Premier League in 1992-93 via the First Division playoffs (4–3 v **Leicester City**). The club was relegated from the Premier League to the Second Division in consecutive seasons in 1993-94 and 1994-95, before immediately returning as champions to the First Division. *League record* Premier League 1993-94; First Division 1992-93, 1994-95, 1996-97–; Division Two 1963-64 to 1964-65, 1969-70 to 1973-74, 1987-88 to 1991-92;

Second Division 1995-96; Division Three 1920-21, 1958-59 to 1962-63, 1965-66 to 1968-69, 1974-75 to 1981-82, 1986-87; Division Three (South) 1921-22 to 1957-58; Division Four 1982-83 to 1985-86. *Honours* Second Division 1995-96; Division Four 1985-86; Southern League 1910-11, 1913-14; League Cup 1969 (3–1 a.e.t. v Arsenal); Anglo-Italian Cup 1970 (3–0 v Napoli, match abandoned after 76 minutes); Anglo-Italian League Cup-winners Cup 1969 (5–2 agg. v Roma, AS). *Records* Rod Thomas is Swindon's most capped player (30 (50) for **Wales**); John Trollope holds the record for club appearances (770, 1960-80); Harry Morris is Swindon's record League goalscorer (216, 1926-33).

Switzerland *country UEFA* landlocked republic in West Europe, situated between **Austria**, **France**, **Germany** and **Italy**. Includes parts of the Alps and Jura Mountains. Area: 41,285 sq km (15,935 sq miles). Population: 7,020,000 (1995 est.). Languages: German, French, Italian, Romansch. Capital: Berne. *Dossier* Football association (Schweizerischer Fussball-Verband, Berne) formed in 1895, founder member of **FIFA** in 1904 and founder member of the **Union of European Football Associations** (UEFA) in 1954, president: Marcel Mathier; general secretary: Peter Gillieron. Season played from July to June, with a **winter break** from the beginning of December to the end of February. National stadium: **Wankdorf**, Berne, capacity: 37,551. National strip: red shirts, white shorts, red socks. First international game: 12 February 1902 v France (0–1, Paris, friendly). Biggest victory: 9–0 v **Lithuania** (25 May 1924, Paris, Olympic Games preliminary round). Biggest defeats: 0–9 v England Amateurs (20 May 1909, Basle, friendly) and 0–8 v **Hungary** (25 October 1959, Budapest, Hungary, Dr Gerö Cup). Most capped players: Heinz Hermann (117 appearances, 1978–91), Alain Geiger (112 appearances, 1980-96). Leading goalscorers: Max Abegglen (32 goals, 1922-37), his younger brother André Abegglen (30 goals, 1927-43), Jacques Fatton (29 goals, 1946-55). Other notable international players: Kubilay Türkyilmaz, Christophe Bonvin. Website: *http://www.fussballverband.ch* (official site). *International tournament record* Olympic Games – runners-up/silver medal 1924 (0–3 v **Uruguay**, Paris); **Women's World Cup** – entered first tournament in 1991, never qualified for finals tournament; **World Cup** – first entered 1934, quarter-final 1934, 1938, 1954, second round 1994, also qualified 1950, 1962, 1966, hosts 1954; **European Championship** – first entered 1964 (lost in first round – no qualifying tournament), qualified for finals tournament 1996 (last of four nations in first-round group stage, losing two and drawing one of its three matches); **European Championship for Women** – first competed 1984, never past the first-round group stage (in the 1989 tournament, Switzerland lost 0–10 at home to West Germany, having drawn 0–0 away); **Dr Gerö Cup** – Switzerland finished bottom of the five- or six-nation league in each of the six

tournaments staged, winning only five games and drawing eight of the 50 games it played; **Under-17 World Championship** – never qualified; **World Youth Cup** (under-20) – never qualified. *World Cup performance* (finals and qualifiers to end of 1998 tournament) played 100, won 38, drawn 21, lost 41, scored 139 goals, conceded 153 goals; win rate 38%; goals scored per game 1.39. *Record against British and Irish national teams* v **England**, played 18, won three, drawn four, lost 11; v **Northern Ireland**, played three, won one, drawn one, lost two; v **Scotland**, played 14, won four, drawn three, lost seven; v **Wales**, played four, won three, drawn none, lost one; v **Republic of Ireland**, played 11, won three, drawn one, lost seven. *History* Football is thought to have been introduced in the late 1850s by English students in Geneva. The oldest surviving clubs are **St Gallen FC** (1879), **Grasshopper-Club Zurich** (1886), **Servette FC Geneve** (1890), FC Basel (1893), Basel Sportclub Old Boys (1894) and FC La Chaux-de-Fonds (1894). Switzerland is a founder member of FIFA. Its football association was founded in 1895, one of the earliest outside the United Kingdom. The national championship dates back to 1898: until 1933 it was decided by a playoff between the winners of the various regional leagues. A true national league started in 1934 and has been played continuously ever since. The Swiss Cup has been played since 1926. Both **BSC Young Boys** and **FC Zurich** have reached the semi-final of the **European Cup**. The Swiss national team played its first game in 1905 (above) and its first international tournament match in 1924 (25 May, 9-0, v Lithuania, in Paris, Olympic Games preliminary round). Its only notable success was the Olympic Games silver medal at the same tournament. It hosted the 1954 World Cup finals. Roy Hodgson coached the national side from 1991, and took Switzerland to the 1994 World Cup finals, the first time it had qualified since 1966. He also coached Switzerland through the 1996 European Championship qualifying tournament – the first time Switzerland had qualified – though his appointment as manager of **Blackburn Rovers** meant that he did not coach the side at the finals tournament. The headquarters of FIFA (Zurich) and UEFA (Berne) are both located in Switzerland. *League system* There are 12 clubs in the national first division (the National League A), playing each other twice in the first phase of the season from mid-July to the beginning of December. Three points are awarded for a victory, with one for a draw: final positions for clubs level on points are determined by **goal difference**. After the winter break, the top eight clubs from the first phase in the season qualify for a championship league, again playing each other at home and away. Once again, three points are awarded for a victory, and one for a draw. However, the final points total is determined by a sum and the total from the second phase to half the club's total from the first phase: final positions for clubs level on points are determined by their respective positions at the end of the first phase. The bottom four clubs enter a similar second-phase league, along with the top four clubs from the first phase of the second division. The top four in the promotion/relegation league qualify for the first division the following season. The promotion/relegation league is determined by points scored in the second phase only: final positions for clubs level on points are determined by **goal difference**. There are 12 clubs in the second division (the National League B). The Swiss Cup final is played at the beginning of June. *Record in international club tournaments* European Cup/Champions League – BSC Young Boys Bern (semi final 1959), FC Zurich (semi-final 1964, 1977); **European Cup-winners Cup** – BSC Young Boys Bern (quarter-final 1988), FC Zurich (quarter-final 1974), Grasshopper-Club Zurich (quarter-final 1990), Lausanne-Sports (quarter-final 1965), Servette FC Geneve (quarter-final 1967, 1979), **Sion** (quarter-final 1987); **UEFA/Fairs Cup** – Grasshopper-Club Zurich (semi-final 1978), Lausanne-Sports (semi-final 1958); **Mitropa Cup** – Grasshopper-Club Zurich (quarter-final 1937). Other leading clubs: **Neuchatel Xamax FC, FC Lugano, FC Luzern.**

switch play *tactic* constantly moving the ball from one side of the pitch to the other in order to create a scoring opportunity.

Sydney City Hakoah *club* former Australian national league club, based in Sydney, dissolved 1987. Australian League champions 1977, 1980, 1981, 1982; **Australian Cup** 1986.

Sydney United *club* Australian national league club, based in Sydney (formerly Sydney Croatia). Ground: Croatian Sports Centre. Strip: red shirts, white shorts. **Australian Cup** 1987.

synovial fluid *medical* fluid found inside flexible **joints**.

synovitis *medical* inflammation of the synovial membrane of a **joint**. Can be caused by direct injury or by infection. Often associated with an effusion within the synovial cavity.

synthetic pitch *n.* another word for **artificial pitch**.

Syria *country AFC* Arab republic in West Asia, next to **Israel**, **Iraq**, **Jordan**, the **Lebanon** and **Turkey**, on the Mediterranean Sea. Independence from France 1946. Brief merger with Egypt to form the United Arab Republic (1958-61). Six-Day War with Israel in 1967. Area: 185,680 sq km (71,675 sq miles). Population: 14,620,000 (1996 est.). Languages: Arabic. Capital: Damascus. *Dossier* Syrian Football Confederation (Damascus) formed in 1936, affiliated to **FIFA** in 1937

and **Asian Football Confederation** (AFC) in 1970, member of the **Arab Football Union**, president: Al-Ameer Al-Fattah; general secretary: Toufik Sarhan. Season played from September to May. National stadium: Al Abassiyne, Damascus, capacity: 45,000. National strip: white shirts, white shorts, white socks. Biggest victory: 12–0 v **Maldives** (4 June 1997, in Damascus, **World Cup** qualifier), and 12–0 v Maldives (9 June 1997, in Tehran, World Cup qualifier). *International tournament record* **Olympic Games** – never qualified for finals tournament; **Women's World Cup** – never entered; World Cup – first entered 1950, reached qualifying tournament third (final) round 1986 (1–3 agg., v **Iraq**); **Arab Cup of Nations** – runners-up 1966 (1–2, v Iraq, in Iraq), 1988 (1–1, 3–4 pens., v Iraq, in Jordan), hosts 1992; Arab Games – silver medal/runners-up 1997 (0–1, v **Jordan**); **Asian Cup of Nations** – first entered 1980, qualified for finals tournament 1980, 1984, 1988, 1996, never past first round; **Asian Games** – first entered 1982, qualified for finals tournament 1982 (third of five nations in first round group); **Asian Women's Championship** – never entered; **Asian Youth Cup** (under-20) – winners 1994 (2–1, v **Japan**, in Djakarta, Indonesia); Mediterranean Games – winners/gold medal 1987; **Under-17 World Championship** – never qualified; **World Youth Cup** (under-20) – quarter-final 1991, also qualified for finals tournament 1995 (third of four nations in first-round group). *Record against British and Irish national teams* none. *History* Football was introduced by the French in the 1920s. The football association was founded in 1936. Syria's cup competition started in 1966, with a national league following a year later. Syria was one of the earliest countries in Asia to enter the World Cup; its first qualifying campaign was for the 1950 tournament. In the 1998 World Cup qualifying tournament Syria finished third of its four-nation group, with just seven points from its five games (its opening match against Kyrgyzstan was abandoned). However, it scored 27 goals, with 24 of these coming in the space of five days: Syria scored a unique 12–0 double victory against Maldives (4 June 1997, in Damascus and 9 June 1997, in Tehran). *League system* Fourteen clubs compete in the national first division. *Record in international club tournaments* **Asian Champion Teams Cup** – Al Ittihad (semi-final, fourth, 1985); **Arab Cup-winners Cup** – Al Jaish (runners-up 1998). Other leading clubs: **Al Foutoua, Jablah**, Teshrin (of Latakia, League champions 1982, 1997).

T

Táchira (Unión Atlético Táchira) *club* Venezuelan national league club based in San Cristóbal, founded 1975 (as Deportivo Táchira). Ground: Estadio Peublo Nuevo, capacity: 30,000. Strip: yellow and black striped shirts, black shorts. Venezuelan League champions (**Torneo Clausura**) 1979, 1981, 1984, 1986; **Copa Venezuela** winners 1986, 1999.

tackle from behind *rules* challenge for the ball made by one player from behind an opponent in possession of the ball. It is important that the player makes contact with the ball before any contact is made with the opponent. Failure to do this should result in a **direct free kick** being awarded to the opposition team (Law XII). Any tackle from behind that endangers the safety of an opponent is ruled as serious foul play; a player guilty of this offence will be sent off. *Keynotes* The International FA Board introduced the ruling that a player should be sent off for any dangerous tackle from behind prior to the 1998 **World Cup** finals. Its directive applied to all football matches. A year after its directive was issued, the Board noted that referees were not implementing it uniformly. At its 1999 meeting, the Board decided that referees would be monitored and sanctioned if they failed to punish players for these infringements.

tackle *vb.* to take possession of the ball away from an opposing player who has control of it. Legal tackles require that the player makes contact with the ball before, or without making contact with the opposition player, and must not be in a fashion that would endanger the safety of the opposition player (see **foul** for details). *n.* the execution of this.

Tackle, Darren *player* fictitious journeyman footballer and *Guardian* columnist *Keynotes*. Tackle plays for the fictional club the Greens which plays at the Daihatsu Studium. Tackle is "author" of a weekly column 'The Diary of Darren Tackle', which chronicles the life of a professional Premier League player, including his alleged habits of drug taking, gambling and spurned attempts at womanising.

tactics *n. pl.* the playing strategy of a team.

Tahiti/French Polynesia (formerly French Oceania) *country OFC* registered with **FIFA** as Tahiti. Overseas territory of **France** in the South Pacific. French Polynesia consists of five archipelagos, including the Society Islands, the largest of which is Tahiti, the Tuamotu group, the Gambier group, the Tubuai Islands and the Marquesas Islands. Self-governing since 1977. Area: 3,940 sq km (1,520 sq miles). Population: 199,031. Languages: Tahitian and French. Capital: Papeete (on Tahiti). *Dossier* Football association (Fédération Tahitienne de Football, Papeete) formed in 1989, affiliated to FIFA in 1990 and **Oceania Football Confederation** (OFC) in 1990, president: Reynald Temarii; general secretary: Luc Dimitri Pitoeff. Season played from February to October. National stadium: Stade Olympique, Papeete, capacity: 15,000. National strip: white shirts, red shorts, white socks. Biggest victory: 12–0, v **American Samoa** (7 September 1998, **Oceania Cup** Polynesian qualifying group). *International tournament record* **Women's World Cup** – first entered 1999, did not qualify for World Cup finals tournament; **World Cup** – first entered 1994, participated in first-round group stage of Oceania qualifying tournament 1994, 1998, never qualified for next stage; Oceania Cup – runners-up 1973 (0–2 v **New Zealand**, in New Zealand), 1980 (2–4 v **Australia**, in Noumea, New Caledonia), 1996 (0–11 agg., v Australia, doubling as World Cup qualifier), fourth 1998 (2–4, v Fiji, in Australia, third/fourth playoff); **Oceania Women's Tournament** (World Cup qualifier) – first entered 1998; **Under-17 World Championship** – never entered; **World Youth Cup** (under-20) – never entered. *Record against British and Irish national teams* none played. *History* French Polynesia finished as runners-up in the first three Oceania Cup tournaments, finished fourth in 1998, and has consistently been the strongest of the Polynesian/Melanesian countries. The Tahiti Cup was first played in 1938; first won by Marine. A national league started in 1948; first won by Fei Pi. The Supercup (Coupe des Champions) has been played since 1995. Leading club **Central Sport** holds the Oceania club record of eight consecutive national league titles (1972 to 1979). Its 19 league titles is also an Oceania club record. *League system* Twelve clubs. Other leading clubs: AS Pirae (of Pirae, 1989, 1991, 1993, 1995, 1998 Tahiti Cup winners four times to 1998, Supercup 1996), AS Venus (of Mahina, League champions 1953, 1990, 1992, 1997, Tahiti Cup winners five times to 1998, Supercup 1995), Excelsior (of Papeete, League champions 1952, 1956, 1957, 1959, 1960, 1986, 1988, Tahiti Cup winners four times to 1998), Fei Pi (of Papeete, League champions

1948, 1949, 1950, 1951, 1968, 1970, 1971, Tahiti Cup winners five times to 1998), Jeunes Tahitiens (of Papeete, league champions 1954, 1961, 1987, Tahiti Cup winners five times to 1998).

Taiwan (Chinese Taipei, Republic of China) *country AFC* island republic in Southeast Asia, between the East China and South China Seas. Became part of **China** in 1683 and ceded to **Japan** in 1895; returned to China in 1945. When, under Mao Zedong, mainland China became a communist People's Republic in 1949, The former nationalist government of China fled to Taiwan island. The nationalists, under Chiang Kei-Shek, claimed sovereignty over mainland China up until the 1970s. Free elections introduced in 1991. Improved relations with China since state of "civil war" with the mainland officially ended in 1991. Former name: Formosa. The country is registered with **FIFA** as Chinese Taipei. Area: 35,990 sq km (13,890 sq miles). Population: 21,500,000 (1996 est.). Languages: Mandarin, Taiwanese. Capital: Taipei. *Dossier* Chinese Taipei Football Association (Taipei) formed in 1936, affiliated to FIFA in 1954 and founder member of the **Asian Football Confederation** (AFC) in 1954, president: Chang Chia-Hsiang; general secretary: Yeh Ming-Shan. Season played from August to March. National stadium: Chung-Shan, Taipai, capacity: 30,000. National strip: blue shirts, white shorts, red socks. *International tournament record* **Olympic Games** – played in the 1960 finals tournament (last in first-round group of four nations, behind **Italy**, **Brazil** and **Great Britain**); **Women's World Cup** – quarter-final 1991 (finals tournament was played in the People's Republic of China); **World Cup** – first entered 1958, never progressed beyond first qualifying round, has played in both the Asian and Oceania qualifying groups (the latter in 1978, 1986 and 1990); **Asian Cup of Nations** – first entered 1956, third 1960 (third in four-nation final tournament, in South Korea), fourth 1968 (fourth in five-nation final tournament, in Iran); **Asian Games** – first entered 1954, winners 1954 (5–2 v **South Korea**, Manila, Philippines), 1958 (3–2 v South Korea, Tokyo, Japan); **Asian Games** (women) – fourth 1998 (1–2, v Japan, in Thailand, third/fourth playoff), **Asian Women's Championship** – winners 1977 (3-0, v Thailand, in Taiwan), 1979 (v **India**, in India), 1981 (5-0, v Thailand, in Hong Kong), runners-up 1989 (0-1, v People's Republic of China, in Hong Kong), third 1991 (0-0, 5-4 pens., v **North Korea**, in Japan, third/fourth playoff), third 1995 (3-0 v North Korea, in Sabah, Malaysia, third/fourth playoff), fourth 1997 (0–2 v Japan, in Guangdong, China, third/fourth playoff); **Under-17 World Championship** – never qualified; **World Youth Cup** (under-20) – never qualified. *Record against British and Irish national teams* none played. *History* Although football is long-established in Taiwan, with its football association founded in 1936, the sport lags behind baseball and basketball in popularity. In the 1954 and 1958 Asian Games, the tournament-winning Taiwanese side played as the "Republic of China" with a team picked from players playing in **Hong Kong**. The nation was banned by the Indonesian Government from taking part in the 1962

games held in Indonesia. It was expelled from the AFC in 1975 (after the People's Republic of China had joined the AFC in 1974) and rejoined in 1990. It was unable to compete in either the Asian Cup of Nations or the football tournament of the Asian Games during that period. Taiwan has a strong record in international women's tournaments and qualified for the first Women's World Cup in 1991. It just missed qualifying for 1995 – finishing third in the 1994 Asian Games women's tournament (two qualified for World Cup finals) – and just failed to qualify for the 1999 finals after losing the AFC qualifying group third/fourth playoff against Japan at the tournament in China (three Asian nations qualified). *League system* Eight clubs compete in the national first division. Three points are awarded for a win, with one for a draw. *Record in international club tournaments* No major success. Leading clubs: 1994 Ta Tung (of Taipei, League champions 1994), Taipower (of Taipei, League champions 1995, 1996, 1997, 1998).

Taj Club *club* former nameof Iranian club, until 1979, of **Esteghlal Sports Club**.

Tajikistan *country AFC* republic in North Asia, has borders with **Afghanistan**, **China**, **Kyrgyzstan** and **Uzbekistan**. The country is mountainous, with more than half the land above 3,000 metres (10,000 feet). In 1921, became part of the Turkestan Soviet Socialist Autonomous Republic, and fully integrated with the **Soviet Union** in 1929. Independence from Soviet Union in 1991; former member of the ephemeral **Commonwealth of Independent States**. Area: 143,100 sq km (55,235 sq miles). Population: 5,700,000 (1994 est.). Languages: Tajik, Russian, Uzbek. Capital: Dushanbe. *Dossier* Tajikistan Football Confederation (Dushanbe) formed in 1991, affiliated to **FIFA** and **Asian Football Confederation** (AFC) in 1994, president: Khodja Karimov; general secretary: Abdukarim Shehov. Season played from April to November. National stadium: Central Stadium, Dushambe, capacity: 22,000. National strip: green shirts, white shorts, green socks. *International tournament record* **Olympic Games** – never qualified for finals tournament; **Women's World Cup** – never entered; **World Cup** – first entered 1998 (second in its first-round qualifying group of four nations); **Asian Cup of Nations** – first entered 1996 (lost 4-5 agg., v Uzbekistan in the qualifying tournament, losing to a **golden goal** in extra time of the second leg in Tashkent); **Asian Games** – never entered; **Asian Women's Championship** – never entered; **Under-17 World Championship** – never qualified; **World Youth Cup** (under-20) – never qualified. *Record against British and Irish national teams* none played. *League system* There are 16 clubs in the national Premier Division, playing each other twice in a season. Three points are awarded for a win, with one for a draw; clubs level on points are separated on **goal difference**. Ten clubs compete in the First Division. Because the season overlaps with the Asian club tournaments, champions and cup winners from the previous year qualify for the **Asian Cup of Champion Teams** and

Asian Cup-winners Cup. *Record in international club tournaments* **Asian Champion Teams Cup** – **Dinamo Dushanbe** (second round 1997). Other leading clubs: **Pamir Dushanbe**, **Sitora Dushanbe**, **Vakhsh Kurgan-Tyube**, Varzob Dushanbe (League champions 1998), FK Khujand (Tajikistan Cup 1998).

take his legs *informal* instruction sometimes voiced by fans for one of their team's players to trip an opponent who is running into a goalscoring position.

Tallinna Sadam *club* Estonian national league club based in the capital Tallinn, founded 1992. In 1998, the club merged with Levadia Maardu. Ground: Kadriorg, capacity: 6,000. Strip: blue shirts, blue shorts. Estonian League champions; Estonian Cup 1996, 1997.

talofibular ligaments *medical* two of the ligaments attached to the **fibula** and ankle. The most important in terms of footballers' injuries is the **anterior talofibular ligament**.

talus *medical* the ankle bone. Joined to the **fibula** by the **talofibular ligament**. Can be injured by forced inversion of the foot.

Tampa Bay Mutiny *club* United States football club and founder member of **Major League Soccer**, based in Tampa, Florida. Member of the league's **Eastern Conference**. Founded: 1996. Ground: Houlihan's Stadium, capacity: 74,300. Finished first in the 1996 Eastern Conference table, but lost to **DC United** in Eastern Conference final. Notable players: Carlos **Valderrama**, Thomas **Ravelli**.

Tannadice Park *ground* Scottish football ground situated in Dundee, Tayside region; home of **Dundee United**. Ground capacity: 12,616 all seated. Pitch dimensions: 100.5m x 68m. Record attendance: 28,000 v **Barcelona** (16 November 1966, **UEFA** (Fairs) **Cup**). *History* Tannadice Park, originally called Clepington Park, was home to Dundee Wanderers, when the then Dundee Hibernian reached an agreement with its owners and moved there in 1909. Wanderers removed most of the ground's fixtures and fittings before decamping elsewhere, leaving Dundee Hibernian with little more than an empty shell. The club renamed the ground Tannadice Park after spending around £3,000 on preparing it for football. Dundee Hibernian played its first match at the newly-christened Tannadice on 18 August 1909 (v **Hibernian**, friendly). When the club was refounded as Dundee United in 1924, the new board bought the ground for £2,500. United's own pools competition, which began in 1956, financed many ground developments. In 1990, the local authority proposed that United and **Dundee** should share a council-developed new stadium at Caird Park. Both clubs declined the offer and United began a major redevelopment to turn Tannadice into a 14,000 plus all-seater stadium. The first floodlit match at Tannadice took place on 10 November 1962 (v **Rangers**).

Tanzania (United Republic of) *country CAF* republic in East Africa on the Indian Ocean, includes the island of **Zanzibar**. Its neighbours are **Burundi**, **Kenya**, **Malawi**, **Mozambique**, **Rwanda**, **Uganda**

and **Zaire**. The mainland region of Tanganyika gained independence from Britain in 1961 (it had been a German colony until World War I). Tanganyika joined with the former island republic of Zanzibar in 1964 to form the United Republic of Tanzania. Area: 939,760 sq km (362,750 sq miles). Population: 29,700,000 (1994 est.). Languages: Swahili, English. Capital: Dodoma. *Dossier* Football Association of Tanzania (Dar es Salaam) formed in 1930, affiliated to **FIFA** in 1964 and **Confédération Africaine de Football** (CAF) in 1960, member of the **Confederation of East and Central African Football Associations** (CECAFA), president: Ahamad Muhidin Ndolanga; general secretary: Ismail Aden Rage. Zanzibar is an independent member of CECAFA, but not of FIFA and CAF. Season played from September to August. National stadium: National Stadium, Dar es Salaam, capacity: 25,000. National strip: yellow shirts with black stripes, yellow shorts, yellow socks. First international game: 1963, v **Ethiopia** (0–4, Addis Ababa, friendly). Biggest victory: 7–0 v **Somalia** (1 December 1995, in Uganda). **East and Central African Championship**). Biggest defeat: 0–7 v Ethiopia (1969, in Ethiopia, African Cup of Nations). *International tournament record* **Olympic Games** – first entered 1968, never qualified for finals tournament; **Women's World Cup** – never entered; **World Cup** – first entered 1974, qualifying tournament second round 1982; **African Cup of Nations** – first entered 1968, qualified for finals tournament 1980 (first round); East African Challenge Cup – winners 1965, 1966; **East and Central African Championship** – winners 1974, 1994 (2–2, 4–3 pens., v Uganda, in Kenya), runners-up 1973, 1980, 1981, 1992; **Gossage Cup** – won four times by Tanganyika and once by Zanzibar; **Under-17 World Championship** – never qualified; **World Youth Cup** (under-20) – never qualified. *Record against British and Irish national teams* none played. *League system* Clubs from the mainland play in the Tanzanian Mainland League and compete in a combined Tanzania and Zanzibar Union League. *Record in international club tournaments* **African Cup of Champion Clubs** – **Simba SC** (semi-final 1974), **Young Africans SC** (quarter-final "champions-league" stage 1998); **African Cup-winners Cup** – Rangers International (quarter-final 1977); **CAF Cup** – Simba SC (runners-up 1993); **East and Central African Club Championship** – Simba SC (winners, 1974, 1991, 1992, 1995, 1996), Young Africans SC (winners, 1975, 1993, 1999); East African Super Cup – Malindi (runners-up 1994), Young Africans (runners-up 1996). Other leading clubs: **Mwanza Pamba SC**, **Pan African Sports Club**. See also **Zanzibar**.

Tapie, Bernard *official* former politician and former president (1985-93) of **Olympique de Marseille**. Tapie was jailed on corruption charges, including the bribery of opposition players in the 1993-93 French league championship.

tap-in *n.* goal that is scored from close range with considerable ease.

Taraz Dzhambul *club* Kazakhstan national league club based in Zhambyl, founded 1961 (as Metallist, various names since then). Ground: Khimik, capacity: 23,000. **Asian Champion Teams' Cup** second round 1998; Kazakhstan League champions 1996, runners-up 1995; Kazakhstan Cup runners-up 1993.

target player *n.* attacking player who provides an outlet for passes played out of defence and who holds the ball up by screening it from the opposition in order for team-mates to join the attack. **Wales** international Mark **Hughes** is considered to be one of the best exponents of target play in the modern game. Also called **target man**.

tarsal bone *medical* any of the seven bones of the ankle, including the larger **talus** (ankle bone).

tarsus *medical* the seven bones of the ankle.

Tauro FC *club* Panama national league club based in Panama City. Ground: Estadio Pedregal. Strip: black and white striped shirts, black shorts. Panama League champions 1996, 1997.

Tavria Simferopol *club* Ukraine national league and former Soviet Union league club based in Simferopol, founded 1958 (as Avangard) Ground: Lokomotiv, capacity: 24,000. Strip: red shirts, red shorts. Ukraine League champions 1992; Ukraine cup runners-up 1994; never won former-Soviet Union league or Cup.

Taylor, Graham *manager* born 15 September 1944. *Clubs* **Lincoln City**, **Watford** (twice), **Aston Villa**, **Wolverhampton Wanderers**. Also **England** manager (*record* played 38, won 18, drawn 13, lost 7, goals for 62, goals against32). *Honours* Division Four (Lincoln City 1975-76; Watford 1977-78); Second Division (Watford 1997-98). *Keynotes* Appeared for **Grimsby Town** and Lincoln City as a player, becoming the Red Imps' manager at the age of 28 in 1972 when a hip injury forced his retirement. Taylor was appointed Watford manager in 1977 and over the following decade he led the club to Division One, finishing runners-up in 1982-83, and to the 1984 **FA Cup** final (0–2 v **Everton**). He moved to Aston Villa in 1987, taking the club back to the top flight in his first season in charge. Taylor became England's seventh manager in 1990. Under Taylor's managership, England qualified for the 1992 **European Championship** finals, but finished bottom of its group. The tournament culminated in a 2–1 defeat by hosts **Sweden**, a match in which Gary **Lineker** was controversially substituted. The press coverage following the game was vitriolic; *The Sun* leading with the headline "Swedes 2 Turnips 1". Taylor's relationship with the media never recovered: he resigned in 1993, following England's failure to reach the 1994 **World Cup**, and returned to club management. Having returned to Watford in May 1997 following a spell as manager of Wolverhampton Wanderers, Taylor led the club to the **Premier League** in 1999.

Taylor Report *legal* official inquiry and report into the **Hillsborough disaster** of 1989, led by Lord Justice Peter **Taylor**. Taylor highlighted antiquated grounds, poor facilities, **hooliganism**, excessive alcohol drinking and poor leadership as factors having a negative effect on football in Britain at that time. Taylor described some of the conditions at grounds as "squalid" and was highly critical of the "caging" of fans behind security fences. The 104-page report, published on 29 January 1990, gave a plan for radical modernisation of grounds and accommodation which signalled the end of standing terraces and the arrival, in Britain, of **all seated** stadiums. Its 76 recommendations included that First Division (now **Premier League**) and Second Division (now Division One) grounds should be all seated by August 1994; with all other **Football League** grounds brought to this standard by 1999. It also recommended the removal of "prison-type" perimeter fencing, and that there should be more pitchside gates that are clearly marked and never locked. It suggested an overhaul of police operations at football grounds and an improvement of communications between the police and the emergency services. It recommended new criminal offences for certain football-related behaviour, including unauthorised **pitch invasions**, racial abuse and **ticket touting**. In the Budget of March 1990, the Treasury's share of the tax on pools betting was cut by 2.5%, with the £100 million raised made available to the **Football Trust** to allocate to clubs for ground improvements. The Taylor Report rejected the Thatcher Government's proposed **national membership scheme** for football supporters on the grounds of poor effectiveness and safety.

Taylor, Tommy *player* Striker. **England** international (19 caps, 16 goals). Born 29 January 1932. Career ca. 1949-58. *Clubs* **Barnsley**, **Manchester United**. *Keynotes* Joined Manchester United from Barnsley for £29,999 in March 1953. Taylor scored 112 goals in 163 **Football League** appearances for United. He also scored the club's only goal in the 1957 **FA Cup** final (1–2 v **Aston Villa**). Taylor scored twice for England against **Brazil** on 9 May 1956. Overall Taylor made 212 **Football League** appearances and scored 138 goals in a career ended in 1958 when he died in the **Munich air crash**. Included in the **Football League Centenary 100 players**. *Honours* League Championship (Manchester United 1955-56, 1956-57).

Taylor, Peter *official* (1931-97). British judge and Lord Chief Justice 1992-96. Author of the **Taylor Report**, the public inquiry into the 1989 **Hillsborough disaster**. Taylor said at the time of his report: "The years of patching up grounds, of having periodic disasters and narrowly avoiding many others by muddling through on a wing and a prayer must be over." Taylor was a lifelong supporter of **Newcastle United**.

TB Tvoroyri (Tvoroyrar Boltfelag) *club* Faeroe Islands national league club based in Tvoroyri, founded 1892; the nation's oldest major club. Ground: Sevmyra, capacity: 4,000. Strip: black and white striped shirts, black shorts. Faeroe Islands League champions 1943, 1949, 1951, 1976, 1977, 1980, 1987; Cup 1977, 1978, 1979, 1980.

tchoekah *n.* early and rudimentary form of football played by native South American Indians in Patagonia (the southernmost parts of **Argentina** and **Chile**).

team *n.* the 11 players and named substitutes chosen to take part in a game of football.

team-sheet *regulations* record given to the referee in advance of a fixture listing the names of the players and **substitutes**. **Competition rules** may make this obligatory. The **Premier League**, for example, requires that the list be given at least one hour prior to the **kick off time**, and that it should also include the players' **shirt numbers** and the colour of the **strip** and goalkeeper's strip (FA Premier League rule E.18). **Football League** and **Scottish Football League** clubs are required to hand the team-sheet to the referee at least 45 minutes before kick-off, also including the names and numbers of players, substitutes and the colour of the goalkeeper's shirt: the list must also be given to a representative of the opposition (Football League regulation 30.5, Scottish Football League rule 29). Any player or substitute injured or incapacitated before the kick-off may be replaced, but the referee must be notified of the change. Clubs may be fined for breaching these rules. Premier League **referees** are required to send the team sheets, along with their match reports, to the league as soon as is practicable after a game (FA Premier League rule G.11).

tear *medical* injury to a **muscle** when many of the muscle fibres are broken. Essentially the same as a **sprain**. Partial tears can normally be treated by the application of **ice** as a first-aid measure, followed by rest, **elevation** and, in some cases, **physiotherapy**.

technical area *rules* area surrounding the **designated seating facility** (or "dugout") to accommodate club personnel and substitutes (Law V). This area extends to one metre either side of the designated seating facility, extending forward to a distance up to one metre away from the touchline. Markings are not always required, though the area may be delineated by solid or broken white lines. The significance of the technical area varies between competitions. For example, the number of people who are allowed to occupy the technical area may be limited, and teams may be required to name these occupants before the start of the match. The club **coach** and officials must remain within the technical area, except in special circumstances, such as the **club doctor** treating a player when given permission to do so by the referee. The coach is allowed to convey tactical information to the players provided that he or she remains within the technical area. Anyone misbehaving in the technical area may be reported to the referee by the **fourth** official.

Tele Sporting Club *club* Eritrea national league club, based in the capital Asmara, formerly in the Ethiopian national league. Ground: Ras Asula (the national stadium, and shared with **Eritrea Shoe Factory**), capacity: 25,000. **African Cup of Champion Clubs** second round 1970, 1974; Ethiopian League champions 1969, 1970, 1972, 1973; Ethiopian Cup winners.

telegram claims *n. pl* former system for registering a claim for prize money in **pools** betting. When the **dividend forecast** was high, pools companies would ask those who thought they had a winning coupon to contact them by telegram to claim a share of the **dividend**. The system is no longer used and, in reality, was merely used to speed the claims process; it was never compulsory.

television, football and *n.* live transmission or recorded highlights of football matches. *Keynotes* Film of the Division One clash between **Arsenal** and **Everton** on 29 August 1936 was the first match on television. The first live match to be televised was an experimental broadcast by the BBC of the Arsenal v Arsenal Reserves match at **Highbury** on 16 September 1937. The first **FA Cup** final to be televised was the 1937 match between **Sunderland** and **Preston North End** on 30 April, which the BBC showed in parts. The following year, the final was televised live in its entirety. Between 1938 and 1997 (when its contract ended, and with the exception of the 1952 match), the BBC has shown the FA Cup final live every year. Other than the final, the first live transmission of a game took place on 8 February 1947, when the BBC televised the FA Cup fifth-round encounter between **Charlton Athletic** and **Blackburn Rovers**. The first **Football League** match to be televised live was the Division One match between **Bolton Wanderers** and **Blackpool** (9 September 1960), although plans to regularly transmit Friday night fixtures were dropped. In **Scotland**, the first **Scottish FA Cup** final to be shown live was the 1955 match between **Clyde** and **Celtic** on 23 April, and the first live Scottish League match was the game between Clyde and **Aberdeen** on 3 September 1955. BBC television's **Match of the Day** programme made its debut on 22 August 1964, showing highlights of the **Liverpool** v Arsenal game from **Anfield** on BBC2. Anfield was also the venue for the first colour transmission of a football match, the Liverpool v **West Ham United** fixture of 15 November 1969. The first FA Cup final on colour television was the 1968 final. The 1954 **World Cup** in Switzerland was the first finals tournament to be televised. Televised football has often been criticised for reducing attendance at matches. For example, aggregate attendance at Football League matches fell by 2 million over the 1951-52 season and the decline was blamed on increasing television coverage. Concern that live broadcasts were adversely affecting Football League gate receipts led to an agreement with the **Football Association** that, from the 1954-55 season, the Cup final would be played on the Saturday after the completion of the league programme. *Regulations* Clubs are not allowed to televise, record or transmit league games without the written consent of the league (FA Premier League rules section C, Football League regulation 66.1, Scottish Football League rule 71). Premier League clubs, however, are permitted to relay **closed-circuit television** pictures within the ground where the match is being played. Premier League clubs are required to provide the referee and the League with a VHS video recording of each league match (FA Premier League rule G.14).

television audience *n.* number of people/households watching a match. *Keynotes* The first big television audience for a televised match was in 1948, when the BBC claimed that more than 1 million people had tuned in to watch that year's **FA Cup** final. Largest television audience for a domestic match: FA Cup final 1970 (**Chelsea** v **Leeds United**) – combined ITV/BBC audience of 26 million. Biggest worldwide television audience: 2.7 billion, 1990 **World Cup** final 1990 (**Germany** v **Argentina**). The British Independent Television (ITV) network audience for the 1998 World Cup finals second round game **England** v **Argentina** on 30 June 1998 (2–2, 3–4 pens., in St Etienne, France) was estimated at 26,000,000 the biggest ever for an ITV programme. More than 20,000 Glastonbury music festival revellers are estimated to have watched England's 1998 World Cup group G match with **Colombia** (26 June) on a big screen in the so-called "Field of Vision" – possibly the biggest gathering to watch an England international match outside the game's venue.

television blackout *n.* period from August to December 1985 when no televised **Football League** matches – highlights or live coverage – were broadcast owing to a breakdown in contract negotiations between the Football League and the television networks. The blackout was blamed for a 10% fall in attendance on the first day of the season. A £1.3 million contract was finally reached between the two sides in December 1985, and a similar deal was struck with the **Football Association** soon after, allowing League games and **FA Cup** matches to be televised again.

television gantry *n.* permanent or temporary overhead platforms used to televise football matches.

television income *regulations* monies paid out to clubs as a share of the overall sum negotiated between the football authority and the broadcasting company. The **Premier League**'s domestic television earnings are largely shared out by the clubs, though an amount is also given to the **Professional Footballers Association** for benevolence, educational and insurance purposes. The remaining pot is shared as follows (FA Premier League rule D8.1): 50% divided equally to all Premier League clubs; 25% divided to all clubs but weighted according to their respective league position (ie the top clubs receive more); and 25% divided equally between the home and away clubs whose matches are broadcast. In the 1997-98 season, for example, the payouts ranged from £4,263,289 for the bottom club, **Barnsley**, to £9,714,004 for the league champions **Arsenal**. See also **relegated club**. *Keynotes* A two-year deal, worth about £5.4 million, thrashed out by the English **Football League** in 1983 allowed 10 matches to be screened live; five each for the BBC (on Friday evening) and ITV network (on Sunday afternoon). In February 1985, a four-year deal worth £19 million (with huge projected additional earnings on sponsorship and pitchside advertising) was rejected by the Football

League's club chairmen, despite approval by the **Football League Management Committee** and its Television Negotiating Committee. Football was not shown on television from August to December 1985. Broadcasting was restored for 1986 in a short-term deal to last until the end of the season. A two-year deal worth £6.2 million was agreed in 1986. Television companies were allowed to broadcast 14 league games – plus two League Cup semi-final legs and the final – in both the 1986-87 and 1987-88 seasons. In 1996, British Sky Broadcasting (BSkyB) reached a four-year deal with the Premier League governing body worth £670 million, plus an additional £73 million from the BBC to show recorded highlights. The Sky deal guarantees every Premier League club at least three live screenings during a season. Over the 1996-97 season, Premiership football received £93 million from television, equivalent to 20% of total income. By comparison, **Serie A** clubs received £122 million (32% of total income) from television and D1 (France) sides £63 million (30% of total income). Top English clubs have seen a substantial increase in the money derived from television since the Premier League was established in 1992-93. Payouts to the three Premiership clubs each season earning the most television money since the League's creation are as follows: 1992-93, **Manchester United** (£2,413,660), **Aston Villa** (£2,268,495), **Blackburn Rovers** (£2,036,098); 1993-94, Manchester United (£2,611,115), Blackburn Rovers (£2,460,125), **Leeds United** (£2,100,215); 1994-95 Manchester United (£2,938,460), Blackburn Rovers (£2,716,475), **Liverpool** (£2,261,790); 1995-96, **Newcastle United** (£3,103,520), Manchester United (£2,990,420), Liverpool (£2,482,550); 1996-97, Manchester United (£6,291,045), Liverpool (£5,774,430), Arsenal (£5,668,430); 1997-98, Arsenal (£9,714,004), Manchester United (£9,523,451), Liverpool (£8,771,628).

Tempete *club* Haitian national league club based in St Marc, founded 1970. Strip: blue shirts, white shorts.

temporary registration *regulations* to **register** a player with a new club on a temporary basis; also called loan. Such transfers can be made only with the permission of the league or leagues concerned and, in the **Premier League**, are limited to two per club at any one time and five in a season (FA Premier League rule L.7). In the Premier League and **Football League**, temporary transfers must normally be for a minimum of four weeks and are limited to a maximum of three months (FA Premier League rule F.6, Football League rule 48.2). Loan periods may only be extended at the discretion of the league. The temporary transfer of a goalkeeper may be for a period less than four weeks but, again, only at the discretion of the league. The Football League can sanction longer-term loan periods for players under-23 years of age, lasting up to the end of the season (Football League regulation 49.1). Football League clubs may sign up to eight players on a temporary basis in a season, with no more than two at a time, and only two from any one club (Football League regulation 48.1). Players cannot be recalled during the loan period, unless – and only in the case of goalkeepers – there is a recall clause in the loan contract. Temporary transfers must be made by the **transfer deadline**: the Football League makes an exception to this rule for the temporary transfer of a goalkeeper, but only if an independent medical practitioner certifies that all the club's professional goalkeepers are medically unfit to play (Football League regulation 37.5). Clubs in the **Scottish Football League** are restricted to five temporary transfers per season and four at any one time (Scottish Football League rule 47(d)); at any one time, clubs are permitted only one on-loan player over 21 (rule 47(d)); temporary transfers are not permitted between clubs in the same division (rule 47(b)); with the exception of the goalkeeper, loans cannot be for periods of less than 28 days (rule 47(e)); loan periods are restricted to a maximum of three months, with the exception of players under 21 who may be loaned for a whole season (rule 47(f)); and, with the exception of the **Scottish Football League Cup** or **Scottish FA Cup**, clubs are not allowed to attach riders to a temporary transfer that stipulates which clubs the player is or is not allowed to play against (rules 47(g) and (h)). **FIFA** regulations stipulate that any temporary transfer of a player to a club in a different country must be for a minimum of three months. The above rules may be relaxed in extenuating circumstances at the discretion of the relevant league governing body.

temporary seating   *n.*   short-term spectator seating accommodation used while permanent facilities are being erected, or installed for individual matches. *Keynotes* A notable example of temporary seating was in place at **Northampton Town**'s **County Ground** for its 1970 fifth round **FA Cup** tie with **Manchester United** – the only occasion in the club's 97-year tenancy of the ground when it was fully enclosed. **Borussia Dortmund** has retained an area of terracing, known as the Südtribune, at its ground, the **Westfalenstadion**, installing removable seats to comply with **UEFA** regulations for European competition matches.

tendon   *medical*   a discrete band of tough connective tissue by which a **muscle** is attached to a **bone**. They are surrounded by a tendon sheath.

tenosynovitis   *medical*   inflammation of a **tendon** sheath. The tendons of the foot are particularly susceptible to this form of **overuse injury**.

ten-yard mile   *misc.*   moving a free kick ten yards (9.15m) forward for a secondary offence, such as continuing dissent, failure to retreat the original ten yards or delaying the kick. **FIFA** agreed a trial of the ten-yard rule in **Jersey** in 1998, and this was extended to the 1999-00 **Auto Windscreens Shield** competition.

terrace   *n.*   tiered area around all or part of a football pitch for spectators to stand. Made obsolete at many UK grounds by the implemetation of the **Taylor Report**.

test match   *n.*   formerly, one of a series of end-of-season playoff matches that decided which teams would

be promoted or relegated between the two divisions of the English **Football League**. Test matches were replaced by automatic **promotion** and **relegation** in 1898-99. *Keynotes* The format of test matches initially consisted of the bottom three teams in Division One playing the top three sides in Division Two, with the winners either retaining their place in the top flight or gaining promotion. All the matches were played at **neutral venue**. The system was revised at the end of the 1895-96 season so that the bottom two sides in Division One and the top two clubs in Division Two played each other twice on a home-and-away basis in a mini-league format: where a Division Two team finished higher than a Division One club, it would replace the lowest top-flight finisher. Test matches were largely abandoned because the results of some matches were considered suspicious. For example, in 1897-98 incumbent Division One club **Stoke** met Division Two champions **Burnley** with both clubs needing only a draw to ensure a place in the top flight the following season. The match ended 0–0. Test matches also produced some "unfair" outcomes. In 1892-93, **Sheffield United** and **Darwen**, second and third in Division Two, won promotion, while Small Heath (later **Birmingham**), which had finished top and six points clear of Darwen, failed to secure a place in Division One. Also, **Notts County** was relegated from Division One, along with **Accrington** (which, as a result, went out of business), despite finishing six points clear of bottom-placed Newton Heath (later **Manchester United**), which retained top-flight status. Stoke and Burnley finished top of the last test match series, but the Football League decided to increase the number of clubs in Division One from 16 to 18, so both clubs were joined by fellow participants, **Blackburn Rovers** and **Newcastle United**, in the top flight the following season. *Test match results* 1892-93, Sheffield United 1–0 Accrington; Darwen 3–0 Notts County; Newton Heath 5–2 Small Heath (replay) – Darwen and Sheffield United replaced Accrington and Notts County in Division One; 1893-94, Small Heath 3–1 Darwen; **Liverpool** 2–0 Newton Heath; **Preston North End** 4–0 Notts County – Liverpool and Small Heath replaced Darwen and Newton Heath in Division One; 1894-95, Bury 1–0 Liverpool; Stoke 3–0 Newton Heath; **Derby County** 2–1 Notts County – Bury replaced Liverpool in Division One; 1895-96, **Manchester City** 1–1 **West Bromwich Albion**; West Bromwich Albion 6–1 Manchester City; Liverpool 4–0 Small Heath; Small Heath 0–0 Liverpool; Liverpool 2–0 West Bromwich Albion; West Bromwich Albion 2–0 Liverpool; Manchester City 3–0 Small Heath; Small Heath 8–0 Manchester City – Liverpool replaced Small Heath in Division One; 1896-97, Notts County 1–0 **Sunderland**; Sunderland 0–0 Notts County; Newton Heath 2–0 Burnley; Burnley 2–0 Newton Heath; Burnley 0–1 Notts County; Notts County 1–1 Burnley; Sunderland 2–0 Newton Heath; Newton Heath 1–1 Sunderland – Notts County replaced Burnley in Division One; 1897-98, Newcastle United 2–1 Stoke; Stoke 1–0

Newcastle United; Burnley 2–0 Blackburn Rovers, Blackburn Rovers; 1–0 Burnley; Newcastle United 4–0 Blackburn Rovers; Blackburn Rovers 4–3 Newcastle United; Burnley 0–2 Stoke; Stoke City 0–0 Burnley. In Scotland, test matches were used intermittently to decide which team would seek **re-election** before automatic promotion and relegation was established in 1921-22. Test matches were usually one-off games, but at the end of the 1914-15 season **Cowdenbeath**, **Leith Athletic** and **St Bernards** were involved in a series of matches to decide the top three places in the Scottish Division Two after all three clubs had finished with 37 points. Cowdenbeath eventually took the Scottish Division Two Championship.

testimonial *n.* match arranged for the financial benefit of a long-serving player; profits on gate receipts are given to the player. *Regulations* **Premier League** and **Football League** rules limit testimonials to players that have completed at least 10 years' service (FA Premier League rule J.30, Football League regulation 26). *Keynotes* Both Mark **Hughes** (of **Manchester United**, v **Celtic**, May 1994, 42,079 spectators) and Ally **McCoist** (of **Rangers**, v **Newcastle United**, 3 August 1993) received around £500,000 in testimonial proceeds. A crowd of 25,000 attended Pat **Jennings'** testimonial at **Highbury** on 8 May 1985 between **Arsenal** (for which Jennings played 237 league games) and **Tottenham Hotspur** (472 league games); he received about £100,000. Bobby **Charlton'**s testimonial match, a game between Manchester United and Celtic, which took place at **Old Trafford** on 18 September 1972, attracted a crowd of 60,538 – the biggest attendance for a friendly match in England aside from the traditional season **curtain-raiser**, the **Charity Shield**.

Texaco Cup *competition* early 1970s knockout competition originally named the International League Board Competition, but following sponsorship by the US oil company, renamed the Texaco Cup. In 1970-71, the competition involved 16 invited clubs, six each from the English and Scottish Leagues, and two each from **Northern Ireland** and the **Republic of Ireland**. Political problems in Northern Ireland prevented the Irish clubs participating in following seasons, so the competition involved nine English and seven Scottish participants. All matches, except for the 1973-74 final, were played over two legs. Each club received £1,000, 1st round winners a further £1,500, 2nd round winners £2,000, runners-up £2,500 and the competition's winners £3,500. *Final results* 1970-71, **Wolverhampton Wanderers** 4–1 **Heart of Midlothian** (agg.); 1971-72, **Derby County** 2–1 **Airdrieonians** (agg.); 1972-73, **Ipswich Town** 4–2 **Norwich City** (agg.); 1973-74, **Newcastle United** 2–1 **Burnley** (agg.); 1974-75, **Newcastle United** 3–1 **Southampton** (agg.). In 1976, the Texaco Cup became the **Anglo-Scottish Cup**, and in 1981, after Scottish sides withdrew, the competition ceased.

Thai Farmers Bank *club* Thailand national league club, based in Bangkok. **Asian Champion Teams Cup** 1994 (2–1 v **Omani Club** of Oman, Bangkok), 1995 (1–0 v Al Arabi of Qatar, Bangkok), semi-final/third 1996, played in the first tournament in 1967 (second round); **Afro-Asian Club Cup** 1994 (v **SC Zamalek** of Egypt), runners-up 1995 (v **Espérance** of Tunisia); Thailand professional league champions 1993, 1995.

Thailand *country AFC* kingdom in South East Asia, next to **Cambodia**, **Laos**, **Malaysia** and **Myanmar**. Independence as Siam in 1896 by agreement between English and French governments, occupied by Japanese during **World War II**. Adopted the name of Thailand in 1939. Area: 514,000 sq km (198,405 sq miles). Population: 58,340,000 (1993 census). Languages: Thai. Capital: Bangkok. *Dossier* Football Association of Thailand (Bangkok) formed in 1916, affiliated to **FIFA** in 1925 and **Asian Football Confederation** (AFC) in 1957, president: Vijit Getkaew; general secretary: Worawi Makudi. Season played from November to April. National stadium: Suphachalasai, Bangkok, capacity: 45,000. National strip: red shirts, red shorts, red socks. *International tournament record* **Olympic Games** – qualified for finals tournament 1956 (0–9, v **Great Britain**, preliminary round, in Melbourne), 1968 (lost all three of its first-round group matches); **Women's World Cup** – entered first tournament in 1991, never qualified for finals tournament; **World Cup** – first entered 1974, never past first qualifying round; **Asean Tiger Cup** – winners 1996 (1–0, v **Malaysia**, in Singapore); **Asian Cup of Nations** – third place 1972 (2–2, 5–3 pens., v Cambodia, Bangkok, third/fourth playoff), also qualified for finals tournament 1992, 1996, hosts 1972; **Asian Games** – fourth 1990 (0–1 v **South Korea**, Beijing, China, third/fourth playoff), 1998 (0–3, v **China**, in Bangkok, third/fourth playoff), second-round group stage 1966, 1970, 1978, hosts 1978; **Asian Under-16 Championship** – runners-up 1996 (0–1, v **Oman**, in Chiang Mai, Thailand); **Asian Women's Championship** – entered first tournament in 1975, winners 1983 (3–0, v **India**, in Bangkok), runners-up 1975 (1–3, v **New Zealand**, in Hong Kong), 1977 (0–3, v **Taiwan**, in Taiwan), 1981 (0–5, v Taiwan, in Hong Kong); **Asian Youth Championship** (under 19) – winners 1962, 1969 (joint champions with Myanmar); **South East Asia Games** – winners/gold medal 1965 (joint-champions with Burma), 1975, 1981, 1983, 1985, 1995, runners-up 1997; **Under-17 World Championship** – qualified for finals tournament 1997; **World Youth Cup** (under-20) – never qualified. *Record against British and Irish national teams* v **Northern Ireland**, played one, drew one. *History* The Football Association of Thailand was founded in 1916. The football league became professional in 1995. Thailand hosted the first ever Asian **Champion Teams Cup** in 1967 (in Bangkok): the country's leading club, **Thai Farmers Bank**, has won the tournament twice. Thailand finished third in the 1972 Asean Cup of Nations and won the inaugural Asean Tiger Cup in 1996. In 1998, Thailand was fined £25,000 and banned from all international football by the AFC following an Asean Tiger Cup group match against Indonesia: both sides had attempted to lose the match to avoid playing hosts **Vietnam** in Hanoi in the semi-final (both had already qualified). Thailand somehow managed to win the match 3–2, after Indonesia scored a deliberate own-goal in injury time (31 August 1998). Indonesia was also fined and suspended. Thailand's national women's team won the Asian Women's Championship in 1983. League system Twelve clubs compete in the national first division; three points are awarded for a win, with one for a draw. The bottom club is automatically relegated, while the 11th-placed club enters a relegation/promotion playoff. *Record in international club tournaments* **Asian Champion Teams Cup** – Thai Farmers Bank (winners 1994, 1995, semi-final/third 1996), **Bangkok Bank** (qualified for finals tournament 1967, 1968, 1971, 1985, 1987, 1991); Air Force (qualified for finals tournament 1988, but withdrew), **Port Authority** (qualified for finals tournament 1991); **Afro-Asian Club Cup** – Thai Farmers Bank (winners 1994, runners-up 1995); **Asian Cup-winners Cup** – **TOT Thailand** (fourth 1995), Royal Thai Air Force (second round 1997). Other leading clubs: Sinthana (Bec T-S, of Bangkok, national champions 1998).

Thames *club* former English league. *Dossier* Ground: West Ham Stadium, London. Record League attendance: 8,275 v **Exeter City** (29 August 1931, Division Three (South)). Best average attendance: 2,623 (1931-32). *Keynotes* Founded in 1928 to play at the 50,000 capacity West Ham Stadium on Prince Regent Lane which also staged greyhound and speedway racing. Thames' home match with **Luton Town** on 6 December 1930 attracted only 469 spectators, thought to be the lowest attendance at a **Football League** match played on a Saturday afternoon. The club folded in 1932 and was replaced by **Newport County**. *League record* Division Three (South) 1930-31 to 1931-32.

The Strongest *club* Bolivian national league club based in La Paz, founded 1908. Ground: Estadio Achumani "Rafael Mendoza Castellon", capacity: 40,000. Strip: yellow and black striped shirts, black shorts. Bolivian national League champions 1964, 1974, 1977, 1986, 1989, 1993; 12-times winners of the former La Paz regional league;

theatre/visual arts, football and *misc.* football as a subject of stageplays or television drama. One of the most successful football-related stageplays was Arthur **Smith**'s *An evening with Gary Lineker*, successful in provincial and West End theatre. Smith also wrote the 1998 BBC television comedy play *My summer with Des*, about a man's relationship with a fantasy woman played out under the backdrop of the 1996 **European Championship**; Des being the BBC television presenter Desmond **Lynam**. It starred Neil Morrissey and Rachel Wise, with appearances from England goalkeepers David Seaman and Peter **Shilton**.

thermal shorts *n.* close-fitting underwear warn underneath a player's **shorts** to provide extra warmth, particularly to protect strained muscles. *Rules* Because thermal shorts are, more often, visible (by extending further than the players' shorts), the **Laws of the game** state that they must be of the same colour as the team shorts (Law IV).

Third Division (North) v Division Three (South) *competition* series of six matches in the 1950s between representative teams from Division Three (North) and Division Three (South). *Final results* 1955 South 2–0 North; 1955, North 3–3 South; 1956, South 2–1 North; 1957, North 2–1 South; 1957, North 2–2 South; 1958, South 1–0 North. The competition ceased with the establishment of Divisions Three and Four in 1958-59.

Third Division Cup *competition* former regional cup competition between clubs in the newly-created Division Three (North) and Division Three (South). It was first mooted in 1932 and began a year later, although there was little interest in the competition. A proposed relaunch in 1939-40, that would involve only those clubs finishing second and third in the Southern and Northern sections of Division Three, was interrupted by World War II, and the competition survived only one season after hostilities were over. *Final results* (Northern Section) 1933-34, **Darlington** 4–3 **Stockport County**; 1934-35, Stockport County 2–0 **Walsall**; 1935-36, **Chester City** 2–1 Darlington; 1936-37, Chester City 3–1 **Southport**; 1937-38, Southport 4–1 **Bradford City**; 1938-39, Bradford City 3–0 **Accrington**; 1945-46, **Rotherham** 5–4 (agg.) Chester City; (Southern Section) 1933-34, **Exeter City** 1–0 **Torquay United**, 1934-35, **Bristol Rovers** 3–2 **Watford**, 1935-36, **Coventry City** 5–2 **Swindon Town** (agg.); 1936-37, **Millwall** 3–3 Watford (each club shared the trophy for six months); 1937-38, **Reading** 6–2 **Bristol City**, 1938-39, Torquay United v **Queens Park Rangers** or **Port Vale** (matches not played due to the war); 1945-46, **Bournemouth** 1–0 Walsall.

Third Lanark *club* former Scottish league. *Dossier* Ground: Cathkin Park, Glasgow, Strathclyde. Nickname: Hi-Hi's. Record attendance: 45,455 v **Rangers** (27 February 1954, **Scottish FA Cup**, third round). Biggest win: 10–0 v **Clackmannan** (21 January 1928, Scottish FA Cup, first round). Biggest defeat: 0–8 v **Hibernian** (1947-48, Division One), v **Motherwell** (1924-25, Division One), v **St Mirren** (1960-61, Scottish FA Cup, third round). *Keynotes* Founded in 1872 by members of the Third Lanark Rifle Volunteers, a name the club discarded and replaced with Third Lanark in 1878. As Third Lanark Rifles, the club reached two Scottish FA Cup finals: 1876 (0–2 v **Queen's Park**), 1878 (0–1 v **Vale of Leven**). Third Lanark won the trophy twice, 1889 (3–1 replay v **Celtic**) and 1905 (3–1 v Rangers), and reached the final on a further two occasions, in 1906 (0–1 v **Heart of Midlothian**) and 1936 (0-1 v Rangers). The club won the League Championship in 1903-04 and the Division Two title twice (1930-31, 1934-35). Third Lanark reached the **Scottish League Cup** final in 1960 (1–2 v Heart of Midlothian). Just six years before the club was dissolved in the courts, it finished third in Division One (1960-61). *League record* Division One (A Division) 1893-94 to 1914-15, 1921-22 to 1924-25, 1928-29, 1931-32 to 1933-34, 1935-36 to 1952-53, 1957-58 to 1964-65; Scottish League 1890-91 to 1892-93, 1915-16 to 1920-21; Division Two (B Division) 1925-26 to 1927-28, 1929-30 to 1930-31, 1934-35, 1953-54 to 1956-57, 1965-66 to 1966-67. *Honours* League Champions 1903-04; Division Two 1930-31, 1934-35; Scottish FA Cup 1889 (3–1 replay v Celtic), 1905 (3–1 v Rangers).

third strip *regulations* an additional **strip** registered by clubs in addition to their **home** and **away strips**. The third strip may only be worn at **Premier League** matches with the consent of the Premier League Board (FA Premier League rules F.19-21). **Scottish Football League** clubs may, at their discretion, register a third-choice strip that is distinctive in colour and design from their home and away strips. A club is permitted to play up to four home league fixtures in any season with a strip other than its home colours, provided that it gives two days' notice to the league, officials and opponents (Scottish Football League rule 66).

Thistle *club* former Scottish league. *Dossier* Ground: Beechwood Park/Braewood Park, Glasgow, Strathclyde. *Keynotes* Played only one season in Scottish Division Two, finishing bottom with only seven points. *League record* Division Two 1893-94.

Three Tenors *misc.* Jose Carreras, Placido Domingo and Luciano Pavarotti. As well as being, perhaps, the three leading operatic tenors of the late 20th century, the three are noted for their interest in football and staging a special concert prior to the 1990, 1994 and 1998 **World Cup** finals, including a concert in front of the Eiffel Tower with the Orchestre de Paris, conducted by James Levine, for the 1998 finals in Paris (10 July 1998). They released a single for the 1998 tournament, a version of the Gerry and the Pacemakers 1963 hit, "You'll never walk alone". Pavarotti's version of Nessun Dorma was the official music of the 1990 World Cup.

three-five-two *tactics* system of play/formation. A system consisting of three defenders, five midfielders and two attackers. The defensive line is made up of two central defenders and a free player – known as a **sweeper** – who plays behind the other two, covering any open space, forward runs by opponents and through passes. The five midfield players will typically include two **wing-backs**, who push forward down the flanks when the team is attacking, but who also provide defensive cover.

three-man plays *tactics* aspect of play in which three players form a triangle within a specific playing area. This provides the **on-ball** player with two passing alternatives, two decoy team-mates and two players to make runs and create space. The players can also interchange. The triangle can have a defensive or an attacking emphasis depending on the position of the players (eg two forward and one back, or vice versa). Triangulation can occur in any part of the pitch and

among any three players so long as they have developed a basic understanding of the tactic and its application.

through ball *n.* pass played between defenders into space for an attacker who has made a forward run.

throw-in *rules* method of restarting a game after the ball has crossed either of the two **touchlines** (Law XV). The rule applies even if the ball curves out of play and back in without touching the ground – it does not, therefore, have to bounce outside the **field of play**. The game is restarted by a player throwing the ball into play from the point where it crossed the touchline and is awarded against the team that touched the ball last before it left the field of play. The player must have both feet on the ground, either on the touchline or outside it, must use both hands, and must be facing the field of play. The ball must be thrown from behind and over the thrower's head. Failure to observe these rules results in the throw in being awarded to the opposite side (the infringement is known as a **foul throw**). The thrower must not touch the ball again until it has contacted another player (of either side) – an **indirect free kick** will be awarded if the thrower touches the ball twice (though, if the player handles the ball, a direct free kick will be awarded). A goal cannot be scored from a throw-in unless the ball is first touched by a second player, from either side, before going into the goal. A goal kick is awarded if a player throws the ball directly into the opponent's goal; a corner kick is given if the ball goes into his or her own team's goal. A goalkeeper is not allowed to handle a ball received directly from a throw-in – an infringement of this rule will result in an indirect free kick awarded to the opposition. See also **kick in**, **long throw**.

Tianjin Football Club *club* Chinese national league club based in Tianjin (Tientsin), 112 km southeast of Beijing. Chinese League champions 1957, 1960, 1980.

tibia *medical* the larger of the two long **bones** in the leg below the knee.

tibiofibular ligament *medical* either of the anterior or posterior **ligaments** binding the **tibia** and **fibula** at the ankle.

ticket allocation *n.* the proportion of match tickets made available to supporters, clubs, officials, sponsors etc for away fixtures, finals, semi-finals, tournaments. *UK regulations* Unless otherwise agreed by the **Premier League Board**, or by the two clubs, the home club at a **Premier League** match must make available 3,000 tickets or the equivalent of 10% of the ground capacity (whichever is the smallest) to the away club. Home clubs in the **Football League** must make at least 2,000 places available for visiting fans, or the equivalent of 10% of the ground capacity (whichever is the smallest): this figure may only be reduced by written agreement of the Football League Executive (Football League regulation 31.2). Premier League, Football League and **Scottish Football League** clubs are not allowed to charge away supporters more than home fans for seats of comparable quality (FA Premier League rule I.20, Football League regulation 31.2, Scottish Football League rule 80). *Keynotes* The

Football Association has been regularly criticised for its allocation of **FA Cup** final tickets. Clubs reaching the final often have trouble satisfying demand for tickets from their own supporters. In 1950, Liverpool had to resort to a ballot to distribute its 8,000 ticket allocation after receiving more than 100,000 applications. In 1996, the FA shared 51,000 tickets between the participating clubs (**Manchester United** and **Liverpool**). The **League Cup** final, by contrast, has come to be known as the people's final because of the higher proportion of tickets made available to fans of the competing clubs. The 1998 **European Cup** (Champions League) finalists **Juventus** and **Real Madrid** each received just over 28% (14,500) of available tickets for the match held at **Amsterdam ArenA** (capacity: 51,500) on 20 May. **Chelsea** and **Stuttgart (VfB)** each received almost 30% (11,000) of the 37,000 tickets for the 1998 **European Cup-winners Cup** final held at **Råsunda Stadion** in Stockholm on 13 May. The 1998 **World Cup** organising committee (CFO) attracted widespread criticism for its ticket allocation policy for the finals, with the European Commission threatening legal action in March 1998. Ticket allocation for major competitions varies. The ticket allocation for competing nations in the 1996 **European Championship**, with the exception of **England**, the host nation, for the last 16 (second round) matches in stadiums with a 40,000 or more capacity amounted to 7,000, or at least 17.5% of the available number of tickets. At the same stage of the 1998 World Cup, the ticket allocation for competing nations was considerably less. For example, for the **Argentina** v England match at the 36,000 capacity Stade **Geoffroy-Guichard** in St Etienne on 30 June the official ticket allocation to each country was 2,079, or less than 6% of the total number of tickets available. Nations qualifying for the 2000 European Championship, to be jointly held in **Belgium** and **Netherlands**, will get at least 16% of all match tickets. Supporters are guaranteed 74% of tickets for the tournament; 14% will go to the organisers, administrations and sponsors, FIFA, UEFA and the host cities will receive 4%; and the media will get an 8% allocation.

ticket tout   *n.*   person who illegally sells match tickets, usually in the vicinity of grounds. *vb.* **tout**.

tifosi   *n.*   groups of club-sponsored travelling supporters that follow Italian clubs. The concept was first developed by **Internazionale** manager Helenio **Herrera** in the early 1960s. Herrera missed the atmosphere of the **Nou Camp** when he moved from **Barcelona** to **San Siro** in 1960 and he convinced Internazionale president Angelo Morrati to encourage supporters' clubs. Internazionale's first **European Cup** victory in 1964 was achieved at Prater Stadio (now **Ernst Happel Stadio**) in Vienna and is thought to be the first occasion when there was a mass movement of supporters to a major European club match.

Tiga Berlian   *club*   Indonesian national league club. **Asian Champion Teams Cup** semi-final 1985; Indonesian national champions 1985 and 1986; Indonesian Cup 1987, 1988,1989.

tight   *tactics*   of a team adopting close **man-to-man** marking in defence giving little oportunity for the opposition to create goalscoring chances.

Tiligul Tiraspol   *club*   Moldovan national league side based in Tiraspol. Ground: Municipal, capacity: 12,000. Strip: red shirts and red shorts. Moldovan League runners-up 1992, 1993, 1994 1995, 1996; Moldovan Cup 1993, 1994, 1995, runners-up 1992, 1996.

time-wasting 1.   *rules*   deliberate act by a player to hold up the play – such as, taking an excessive amount of time to take a goal kick or throw in, or feigning injury – particularly towards the end of a game. The referee should account for this in the **added time** at the end of the **duration of play** (Law VII) and may also **caution** such an offender for **delaying the restart of play** (Law XII). If a goalkeeper uses tactics which, in the referee's opinion, are designed to waste time, the referee may award an **indirect free kick** to the opposing team from the spot where the offence took place (unless within the **goal area**, in which case it must be taken from the **goal area line** at the point nearest to where the foul was committed) (Law X11). A goalkeeper is considered to be time-wasting if he/she holds the ball in his/her hands for more than 5-6 seconds. **2.**   *tactics*   conduct within the rules of the game to use up playing time in a manner that prevents the opposition from having a scoring opportunity. This might include, for example, guarding the ball close to the corner flag in the opposition's half of the field of play, kicking the ball high into the crowd for a throw-in, or continually playing the ball back to the goalkeeper. Team coaches will often attempt to waste time near to the end of play by making a substitution in the hope that the referee will not adequately compensate for this in added time.

timing of goals   *misc.*   official method of timing goals. In 1997, **FIFA** introduced a standardised system for timing goals and this is applicable at all official matches. FIFA produced the following examples to explain the system: A **goal** scored after 32 minutes and 15 seconds is recorded as 33 – because it was scored in the 33rd minute. Goals scored during time added on for stoppages are recorded as follows: a goal scored after 46 minutes and 30 seconds of the **first half** is recorded as 47+. The + sign indicates that the goal was scored before **half-time**, rather than two minutes into the **second half**. The timing of a goal scored after 90 minutes follows the same system. For example, a goal scored after 92 minutes and 45 seconds would be recorded as 93+.

Timoumi, Mohamed   *player*   former **Morocco** international. *Club* **FAR Rabat**. *Honours* **African Cup of Champion Clubs** (FAR Rabat, 1985); *France Football* **African Footballer of the Year** 1985.

TIPS   *n.*   appraisal system used by Amsterdam club **Ajax**. Players are assessed according to the following criteria: T for technique; I for intelligence; P for personality; and S for speed.

title *n.* another word for **league championship**.

title race *n.* the closing stages of the **league championship**, as the leading clubs compete for the top position.

Tocantins *state* one of the 27 state leagues in **Brazil**, founded 1993. Leading clubs: Tocantinopolos Esporte Clube (Tocantinopolos), Intercap Esporte Clube (Paraiso), Uniao (Araguaina), Gurupi Esporte Clube (Gurupi).

Today League *competition* title of the English **Football League** in the 1986-87 season, under the sponsorship of the now-defunct *Today* daily newspaper. The deal was originally scheduled to last two years at £2 million a season.

Togo *country CAF* republic in West Africa, next to **Benin**, **Burkina Faso** and **Ghana**. In 1922, the former German colony of Togoland was divided into French Togoland and British Togoland. The latter merged with Ghana in 1956; French Togoland became independent Republic of Togo in 1990. Area: 56,800 sq km (21,930 sq miles). Population: 3,500,000 (1991 est.). Languages: French, Kabre, Ewe. Capital: Lomé. *Dossier* Football association (Fédération Togolaise de Football, Lomé) formed in 1960, affiliated to **FIFA** in 1962 and **Confédération Africaine de Football** (CAF) in 1963, member of the **West African Football Union**, president: Séyl Memene; general secretary: Duevi Anani Tsibiaku. Season played from October to July. National stadium: Stade Général Etienne Eyadema, Lomé, capacity: 20,000. National strip: white shirts, green shorts, red socks with yellow and green stripes. Nickname of national team: Les Aiglons (the Eaglets). First international game: 1956 v Ghana (1–1, Lomé, friendly). Biggest victory: 4–0 v Benin (1972), v **Cameroon** (1975), v **Mali** (1980), v **Mauritania** (1983), v **Liberia** (1983). Biggest defeat: 0–7 v **Morocco** (1979, in Morocco, African Nations Cup qualifier). *International tournament record* **Olympic Games** – first entered 1972, never qualified for finals tournament; **Women's World Cup** – never qualified; **World Cup** – first entered 1974, second qualifying round 1978, 1982; **African Cup of Nations** – first entered 1968, qualified for finals tournament 1972 (first round), 1984 (first round); **African under-20 Youth Championship** – runners up 1987 (v **Nigeria**); **CEDEAO Tournament** – runners-up 1983 (0–1, v **Ivory Coast**, in Ivory Coast); **Under-17 World Championship** – never qualified; **West African Championship** – runners-up 1982, 1983, 1984, 1986 (each time against Ghana); **World Youth Cup** (under-20) – qualified 1987 (last in first-round group of four nations). *Record against British and Irish national teams* none played. *History* League championship dates from 1964-65. *League system* Ten clubs compete in the national first division, playing each other at home and away (18 games in total). Three points are awarded for a victory, with one for a draw: final positions for clubs level on points are determined by **goal difference**. *Record in international club tournaments* **African Cup**

of Champion Clubs – **Etoile Filante** (runners-up 1968) **Semassi Sokode AC** (semi-final 1984); African Cup-winners Cup – **Agaza Lomé** (runners-up 1983, semi-final 1994); **CAF Cup** – Omnisports Agaza Lomé (quarter-final 1995). Other leading clubs: **ASKO Kara**, Dynamic (of Lomé, League champions 1970, 1971, 1997).

Toluca (full name: Club Deportivo Toluca) *club* Mexican national league club, based in Toluca and founded in 1917. Ground: Estadio Mexico '70 "La Bombonera", capacity: 31,000. Strip: red shirts, white shorts. Nickname: the Red Devils. **CONCACAF Champion Cup** 1968 (walkover in final), runners-up 1998 (0–1, v **DC United**, in Washington DC); Mexican league champions 1967, 1968, 1975, 1998 (clausura); Mexican Cup (Copa Mexico) winners 1956, 1989.

Tomaszewski, Jan *player* Goalkeeper. **Poland** international (65 caps). *Clubs* **Legia Warsaw**, **LKS Lodz**, Beerschot (Belgium), Hercules. *Honours* **World Cup** third place (Poland, 1974); **Olympic Games** silver medal (Poland, 1976). *Keynotes* Tomaszewski is especially noted for an outstanding performance in the 1974 World Cup qualifying game against **England**: the away game at **Wembley** Stadium (17 October 1973) finished 1-1 and ended England's chances of going to the finals, allowing Poland not only to qualify, but to go on to the semi-finals and finish in third place.

Toms, Wendy *official* first woman to referee a professional national-league match in England (Woking v Telford United, **Football Conference**, 30 August 1996). Andy Ellis of Woking was the first of four players to be booked in the match, which ended 0–0.

Tonga *country OFC* island kingdom in the Southwest Pacific Ocean, comprising three groups of coral and volcanic islands. British protectorate from 1900, independence from Britain in 1970. Formerly known as the Friendly Islands. Area: 699 sq km (270 sq miles). Population: 130,000 (1991 est.). Languages: Tongan, English. Capital: Nuku'Alofa. *Dossier* Tonga Football Association (Nuku'Alofa) formed in 1965, affiliated to **FIFA** in 1994 and **Oceania Football Confederation** (OFC), president: Honorable Ve'Ehala; general secretary: 'Ahongalu Fusimalohi. National strip: red shirts, white shorts, red and white socks. Biggest victory 2–0. Biggest defeat: 0–9, v **Solomon Islands** (1 March 1997, in the Solomon Islands, World Cup first-round playoff). *International tournament record* **World Cup** – first entered 1998, qualifying round first-round playoff; **Oceania Cup** – first entered 1996 (never qualified for finals tournament); **Olympic Games** – never entered; **Women's World Cup** – never entered. *Record against British and Irish national teams* none played. *History* Football Association formed in 1965, while still a British protectorate. Tonga entered the 1998 World Cup and hosted the three-nation Polynesian qualifying group of the OFC. It won both its matches, against the Cook Islands and Western Samoa, but lost the two-leg playoff against the Melanesian group winners the Solomon Islands (0–13 agg.). Leading clubs: Kolofo'ou, Lotoha'apoai (League champions 1998).

Tonnerre Yaoundé (Tonnerre Kalara Yaoundé) *club* Cameroon national league club based in Yaoundé, founded 1938. Ground: Ahmadou Ahidjo (national stadium), capacity: 60,000. Strip: white shirts, black shirts. **African Cup-winners Cup** 1975 (5–1 agg., v **Stella Abidjan** of Ivory Coast), runners-up 1976 (2–4 agg., v **Shooting Stars** of Nigeria); Cameroon League champions 1981, 1983, 1984, 1987, 1988; Cameroon Cup 1958, 1974, 1987, 1989, 1991. Notable former player: Roger **Milla**.

Top-Eight Cup *competition* annual tournament for South African National Soccer League clubs; contested by the top-eight clubs from the previous league season. First played 1972, won by **Orlando Pirates**.

top flight *n.* the highest division in a league; used chiefly to distinguish the premier division from the first division in leagues where both styles exist – including the English and Scottish Football Leagues. *adj.* **top-flight** *usage* top-flight team.

top scorer *n.* player who scores the most goals in a season or competition, or who has scored most goals in the history of a club or country. *Keynotes* In the 1979-80 season, Colin Garwood finished as top scorer for two clubs. He scored 17 goals for Portsmouth (24 matches, Division Four) and 10 for Aldershot (16 games, Division Four). See **golden boot**, **goals** (various entries).

Torino *club* Italian league. *Dossier* Ground: **Delle Alpi** (Stadio), Turin, Piemonte. Strip: claret shirts, white shorts, claret socks. Nickname: La Granata (Clarets). Ground capacity: 71,000 all seated. *History* Formed in 1906 from the merger of FC Torinese (which had merged with Internazionale Torino in 1900) and a breakaway group of **Juventus** members. The club is officially known as Torino Calcio. In 1949, disaster struck Torino when a plane transporting the team – the best in Italy at the time, winning five League titles between 1943 and 1949, and which included 10 members of the national side – from Lisbon crashed into the Superga hill outside Turin. Since that disaster, Torino has won only one Italian League title, in 1975-7, winning all its home games in the process. In 1992, Torino appeared in its only European final, the **UEFA Cup**, in which the club lost on the **away goals** rule (2–2 agg. v **Ajax**). Before moving to Stadio delle Alpi in 1990, Torino shared Stadio Comunale in Turin with Juventus, having previously played at Campo Filadelfia. Internationals, Denis **Law** (Scotland) and Joe Baker (England) both played for Torino in the early 1960s. In 1997, Graeme **Souness** took over as manager of the club for a short spell. Torino was relegated to Serie B in 1995-96, and the club only narrowly missed a return to the top flight in 1997-98, losing a penalty shootout in the playoffs. *Honours* Italian League 1927 (league playoff), 1928 (league playoff), 1942-43, 1945-46, 1946-47, 1947-48, 1948-49, 1975-76. Italian Cup 1936 (5–1 v Alessandria), 1943 (4–0 v Venezia), 1968 (league basis), 1971 (0–0, 5–3 pens. v **AC Milan**), 1993 (5–5 v **Roma (AS)** won on away goals).

torn cartilage *medical* injury to the **cartilage**. In footballers, the knee cartilage is susceptible to a weight-bearing rotational force, resulting in the displacement of the central part of the cartilage. The injury is characterised by an inability to straighten the knee joint, reduced flexion and extension and a feeling of instability in the knee. The knee should be immobilised and the injured player stretchered off the field of play and taken to hospital.

Torneo   Apertura *competition* see   **Copa Venezuela**.

Torneo Clausura *competition* national club tournament of Venezuela, played in the second half of the season (the **clausura**). The two-stage league involves the top six teams from each group in the **Copa Venezuela** (played over the first half of the season, the **apertura**). The first stage of the Torneo clausura is played in two groups, made up of the first-, fourth- and sixth-placed teams in one apertura group, with the second-, third- and fifth-placed teams in the other group. Each group of six teams plays each other twice, with the top three in each group qualifying for the final league. These final six teams play each other twice, the winners declared champions, with the first and second teams both qualifying for the **Copa Libertadores**. The next two playoff for a place in the **Copa CONMEBOL**.

Torneo Grandes de Centroamerica (UNCAF Club Cup) *competition* annual international club tournament for champion and runners-up clubs of the Central American nations, **Costa Rica**, **El Salvador**, **Guatemala**, **Honduras**, under the auspices of the regional confederation UNCAF. It is played in two mini-leagues of four clubs, playing each other home and away. The top two in each group qualify for knockout semi-finals and a final. *Winners* 1996 **Alajuelense** (of Costa Rica) (played in a league format as three clubs withdrew); 1997 **Alianza** (of El Salvador), 1–0, v **Deportivo Saprissa** (of Costa Rica); 1998 final between **Municipal** (of Guatemala) and Saprissa.

Torneo Nacional *competition* Uruguay's knock-out competition to decide which six teams from its **Primera A** and Interior leagues join the league winners in the country's **Pre-Libertadores Liguilla**.

Toronto Croatia *club* **Canadian Professional Soccer League (Ontario Division)** club based in Toronto, Ontario. Ground: Centennial Stadium. Strip: red shirts, white shorts. Canadian National Soccer League champions 1970, 1971, 1972, 1973, 1992.

Toronto Italia *club* former club of the now-defunct **Canadian National Soccer League** and former **Eastern Canada Professional Soccer League**, based in Woodbridge, Ontario. Ground: Rainbow Creek Stadium. Disbanded 1997. Canadian National Soccer League champions 1957, 1960, 1975, 1976, 1984, 1988, 1989, 1994, 1996; Eastern Canada Professional Soccer League champions 1962, 1963, 1965. Notable player: Lalo Maradona (striker), brother of Diego **Maradona**.

Toronto Lynx *club* Canadian club playing in the **American A-League**. Based in Toronto, Ontario, founded 1997. Ground: Varsity Stadium, capacity: 21,700. Strip: purple and white shirts, white shorts.

Torpedo Moscow (full name: Torpedo-Luzhniki Moscow) *club* Russian national league and former Soviet Union league club, founded in 1924 as Proletarskkaja Kuznica. Became AMO in 1931, changed name to ZIS in 1932, and Torpedo in 1936. In 1996, it adopted the name Torpedo-Luzhniki. Ground: Luzhniki stadium, capacity: 96,000 (it moved from its Torpedo Stadium, capacity: 16,500, in 1997). Strip: white shirts, black shorts. **UEFA Cup** – quarter-final 1991; Russian Cup 1993; Soviet Union League champions 1960, 1965, 1976; Soviet Union Cup 1949, 1952, 1960, 1968, 1972, 1986.

Torquay United *club* English league. *Dossier* Ground: **Plainmoor**, Torquay, Devon. Strip: yellow and navy blue striped shirts, navy blue shorts, and yellow socks. Nickname: the Gulls. Ground capacity: 6,003. Record attendance: 21,908 v **Huddersfield Town** (29 January 1955, **FA Cup**, fourth round). Best average attendance: 9,096 (1967-68). Biggest win: 9–0 v **Swindon Town** (8 March 1952, Division Three (South)). Biggest defeat: 2–10 v **Fulham** (7 September 1931, Division Three (South)), v **Luton Town** (2 September 1933, Division Three (South)). *History* Founded in 1898 as Torquay by old boys of two local colleges. The club became Torquay Town in 1910, when it moved to Plainmoor and merged with Ellacombe FC, and in 1921, after amalgamating with Babbacombe FC, Torquay United. Torquay was elected to Division Three (South) in 1927-28, replacing **Aberdare Athletic**, but the club finished bottom of the division and was forced to apply for re-election. The club's entire 64-season League career (up to and including season 1998-99) has been spent in one or other of the bottom two divisions. Torquay missed promotion to Division Two on **goal average** in 1956-57 and in 1967-68, the club finished fourth in Division Three – its highest League position. In 1987-88, Torquay was a Division Four end-of-season **playoff** finalist (4–5 agg. v **Swansea City**). Its first **Wembley** appearance took place in 1989 when the club reached the final of the **Sherpa Van Trophy** (1–4 v **Bolton Wanderers**). Two years later, the club made a victorious return trip to the stadium, winning the 1990-91 Division Four playoff final (2–2, 5–4 pens. v **Blackpool**). The club was a Third Division playoff semi-finalist in 1993-94 and finalist in 1997-98 (0–1 v **Colchester United**). During the 1997-98 season, Torquay set a club record of eight consecutive victories. *League record* Division Three 1960-61 to 1961-62, 1966-67 to 1971-72, 1991-92; Third Division 1992-93–; Division Three (South) 1927-28 to 1957-58; Division Four 1958-59 to 1959-60, 1962-63 to 1965-66, 1972-73 to 1990-91. *Records* Dennis Lewis holds the record for club League appearances (443, 1947-59); Sammy Collins is Torquay's record League goalscorer (204, 1948-58).

tossing a coin *rules* **1.** method of determining which team in a match will be given the **choice of ends** before the **start of play** – the team winning the toss chooses ends, the team losing the toss takes the **kick-off** (Law VIII). The coin is spun by the referee, and one of the team captains chooses which side of the coin will land uppermost. After the **half-time interval**, the game is restarted with the teams changing ends, and the kick-off is taken by the team that won the toss. **2.** method of determining which team will take the first kick in a **penalty shoot-out**. **3.** *Regulations* a toss of a coin may be used to decide which club will wear its **home strip** when a **Football League** match is played at a neutral venue (Football League regulation 35.3). **4.** a very rare method of determining the outcome of a drawn game which, in certain tournaments, should normally be settled by a penalty shoot-out; the result of the match may technically be decided by the toss of a coin or by **drawing lots** if the light fails before the penalty shoot-out has been completed. *History* Tossing a coin to decide which team kicks off was included in the very first set of **Laws of the game** adopted by the **Football Association** in 1863. One of the first recorded incidents of a match result being decided by tossing a coin was the FA Cup first round fixture between **Sheffield FC** and Shropshire Wanderers in October 1873. The first match, and the replay in November, were drawn; Sheffield FC was awarded the match on the toss of a coin. One important game which was decided on the toss of a coin occurred in 1968: **Italy** qualified for the final of the 1968 **European Championship** after winning its semi-final on the toss of a coin (0–0 v **Soviet Union**, Naples, Italy). It went on to win the tournament, after a replay against **Yugoslavia**. It is traditional in British league football for the referee to give the coin used in the toss to one of the **ballboys/ballgirls**.

TOT Thailand *club* Thailand national league club. **Asian Cup-winners Cup** fourth 1995 (1–1, 0–3 pens., v Al Ittihad of Saudi Arabia, third/fourth playoff, Sharjah, United Arab Emirates).

Total Network Solutions *club* Welsh league. Ground: **Saints**, Treflan, Llansantffraid, Powys. Strip: green shirts, black shorts. Nickname: Saints. Ground capacity: 1,500. *Keynotes* Formed in 1959 and previously known as Llansantffraid. Qualified for the **European Cup-winners Cup** in 1996-97 (1–6 v **Ruch Chorzow**, agg. preliminary round). *Honours* **Welsh Cup** 1996 (3–3, 3–2 pens. v **Barry Town**).

total football *tactics* style of play adopted by **Netherlands** during the 1974 **World Cup** finals that was earlier honed by Dutch coach Rinus **Michels** during his spell at **Ajax**. The approach is based on a 4–3–3 system but with players constantly interchanging so that all outfield players can take part in an attack, with their regular position covered by a team-mate. The concept of total football requires highly flexible players who are able to adapt to different roles. Total football enables a team to alter its **formation** several times during a match.

Tottenham Hotspur *club* English league. *Dossier* Ground: **White Hart Lane**, north London. Strip: white shirts with navy blue trim, navy blue shorts, white socks. Website: *http://www.spurs.co.uk* Nickname: Spurs or Lillywhites. Ground capacity: 36,200 all seated. Record attendance: 75,038 v **Sunderland** (5 March 1938, **FA Cup**, sixth round). Best average attendance: 55,509 (1967-68). Biggest win: 13–2 v **Crewe Alexandra** (3 February 1960, FA Cup, fourth round replay). Biggest defeat: 0–7 v **Liverpool** (2 September 1978, Division One). *History* The club was founded in 1882 as Hotspur FC by a group of local cricketers, and in 1885 the name was prefixed with Tottenham. The name Hotspur originates from Shakespeare's Harry Hotspur, a character who was based on a member of the Northumberland family which owned large parts of land in the Tottenham area of London. Tottenham's first enclosed ground was at Northumberland Park, which was located behind the Northumberland Arms public house, and was only a short distance from the club's present home, White Hart Lane, which it moved to in 1899. Tottenham was a Southern League club when it won its first FA Cup in 1901 (3–1 replay v **Sheffield United**) – this is the only occasion since the formation of the **Football League** that a non-league club has won the cup. Tottenham was elected to Division Two in 1908-09, winning promotion to the top flight in the club's first season. Relegation followed in 1914-15 and although the League expanded after **World War I**, Tottenham failed to secure a place in Division One (see **Arsenal**). The club returned to the top flight as Division Two Champions in 1920-21 and the following season Tottenham won its second FA Cup trophy (1–0 v **Wolverhampton Wanderers**). Under the managership of former player Arthur Rowe, whose **push-and-run** style (short passing and quick movement) teams included England internationals Eddie Baily, Ted Ditchburn, Alf **Ramsey** and future manager Bill **Nicholson**, Tottenham won the Division Two title and the League Championship in successive seasons in 1949-50 and 1950-51 – a feat matched only by **Everton** (1930-31, 1931-32), **Ipswich Town** (1960-61, 1961-62), Liverpool (1904-05, 1905-06). Nicholson became manager in October 1958 and in his first match in charge Tottenham recorded its then biggest win (10–4 v Everton, 11 October 1958). In 1960-61, the club became the first this century to win the League Championship and FA Cup **double** (2–0 v **Leicester City**), with a side that included Scottish internationals Bill Brown, Dave **Mackay** and John White, **Northern Ireland** captain Danny **Blanchflower,** England internationals Maurice Norman and Bobby Smith, and **Wales** winger Cliff **Jones**. The following season the club retained the FA Cup (3–1 v **Burnley**) – only the second team this century to achieve this feat (**Newcastle United** was the first in 1951 and 1952, while **Blackburn Rovers** and Wanderers, each on two occasions, had achieved the same feat in the 1800s; Tottenham did the same again in 1980 and 1981) – and reached the semi-finals of the **European Cup** (3–4 agg. v **Benfica**). In 1963, Tottenham became the first

English club to win a major European competition when it lifted the **European Cup-winners Cup** (5–1 v **Atlético Madrid**). In 1967, Tottenham won the first all-London FA Cup final (2–1 v **Chelsea**) and the club's **UEFA Cup** victory in 1972 was achieved by contesting the first all-English final in a European competition (3–2 agg. v Wolverhampton Wanderers). Tottenham's victory in the 1973 **League Cup** final (1–0 v **Norwich City**) meant that Nicholson had led the club to seven finals in four competitions (FA Cup three times, League Cup twice and European Cup-winners Cup and UEFA Cup once) and won every one. Indeed, until losing to **Coventry City** (2–3 a.e.t.) in 1987, Tottenham had won every FA Cup final the club had contested. Tottenham's record of eight FA Cup triumphs is bettered only by **Manchester United** with nine. Following the club's back-to-back FA Cup victories in 1981 and 1982, it reached the League Cup final (1–3 a.e.t. Liverpool, making it the first to reach three consecutive **Wembley** Cup finals), the semi-final of the European Cup-winners Cup (1–2 agg. v **Barcelona**) in 1982 and, in 1984, it won the UEFA Cup for a second time (2–2, 4–2 pens. v **Anderlecht**). Tottenham's 1991 FA Cup victory (2–1 v **Nottingham Forest**) was followed in 1999 by a League Cup triumph (1–0, vLeicester City). Despite teams that over the years have included Osvaldo **Ardiles**, Martin Chivers, Paul **Gascoigne**, Jimmy **Greaves**, Glenn **Hoddle**, Jürgen **Klinsmann**, Gary **Lineker**, Martin **Peters**, Terry **Venables**, Ricardo Villa and Chris Waddle, Tottenham has failed to mount a serious Championship challenge since it won the double. The club has also experienced serious off-the-field problems. By the end of 1982, when businessman and Tottenham supporter Irving Scholar took control of the club, it was more than £5.5 million in debt (then the highest in English football). The following year, Tottenham became the first English club to float on the Stock Exchange (October 1983, floatation price = 100p), but by 1991 the club had accumulated debts amounting to £18 million despite the sale of Waddle to **Olympique de Marseille** for £4.25 million in July 1989 and the sale of its training ground for housing development. In June 1991, a partnership involving, as chairman, electronics millionaire Alan Sugar and former Tottenham player Terry **Venables**, who at the time was the manager but, as a result, became chief executive, bought the club. Venables was sacked amid acrimonious circumstances in June 1993. In 1994, Tottenham was fined £600,000, banned from the 1994-95 FA Cup competition and deducted 12 points from the forthcoming League campaign, for financial irregularities committed during the 1980s. The points reduction was initially reduced to six on condition that the club pay an additional £900,000 fine and, in December 1994, an FA arbitration tribunal lifted the points deduction entirely and rescinded the ban on FA Cup participation, although the club still had to pay a £1.5 million fine for financial misdemeanours. Tottenham also had lost two points for failing to play the opening fixture of the 1988-89 season against Coventry City because redevelopment of White Hart Lane's East Stand was unfinished. The punishment was later commuted to a £15,000 fine. Amid controversy, George **Graham** was appointed manager in October 1998, replacing Swiss national Christian Gross, who, had succeeded former-England captain Gerry Francis in November 1997. *League record* Premier League 1992-93–; Division One 1909-10 to 1914-15, 1920-21 to 1927-28, 1933-34 to 1934-35, 1950-51 to 1976-77, 1978-79 to 1991-92; Division Two 1908-09, 1919-20, 1928-29 to 1932-33, 1935-36 to 1949-50, 1977-78. *Honours* League 1950-51, 1960-61; Division Two Champions 1919-20, 1949-50; Southern League 1900; FA Cup 1901 (3–1 replay v Sheffield United), 1921 (1–0 v Wolverhampton Wanderers), 1961 (2–0 v Leicester City – *Team* Brown, Baker, Henry, Blanchflower, Norman, Mackay, Jones, White, Smith (1), Allen, Dyson (1)), 1962 (3–1 v Burnley – *Team* Brown, Baker, Henry, Blanchflower (1, pen.), Norman, Mackay, Medwin, White, Smith (1), Greaves (1), Jones), 1967 (2–1 v Chelsea – *Team* Jennings, Kinnear, Knowles, Mullery, England, Mackay, Robertson (1), Greaves, Gilzean, Venables, Saul (1)), 1981 (3–2 replay v **Manchester City** – *Team* Aleksic, Hughton, Miller, Roberts, Perryman, Villa (Brooke), Ardiles, Archibald, Galvin, Hoddle (1), Crooks; replay Aleksic, Hughton, Miller, Roberts, Perryman, Villa (2), Ardiles, Archibald, Galvin, Hoddle, Crooks (1)), 1982 (1–0 replay v **Queens Park Rangers** – *Team* Clemence, Hughton, Miller, Price, Hazard, (Brooke), Perryman, Roberts, Archibald, Galvin, Hoddle (1), Crooks; replay Clemence, Hughton, Miller, Price, Hazard (Brooke), Perryman, Roberts, Archibald, Galvin, Hoddle (1, pen), Crooks), 1991 (2–1 v **Nottingham Forest** – *Team* Thorstvedt, Edinburgh, Van den Hauwe, Sedgley, Howells, Mabbutt, Stewart (1), Gascoigne (Nayim), Samways (Walsh), Lineker, Allen, plus 1 o.g.); League Cup 1971 (2–0 v **Aston Villa**), 1973 (1–0 v **Norwich City**); **FA Charity Shield** 1921 (2–0 v Burnley), 1951 (2–1 v Newcastle United), 1961 (3–2 v FA XI), 1962 (5–1 v **Ipswich Town**), 1967 (3–3 v Manchester United (each club held the trophy for six months)), 1981 (2–2 v Aston Villa (each club held the trophy for six months)), 1991 (0–0 Arsenal (each club held the trophy for six months)); **Sheriff of London's Charity Shield** 1902 (5–2 v **Corinthians**), 1934 (7–4 v Corinthians); European Cup-winners Cup 1963 (5–1 v **Atlético Madrid** – *Team* Brown, Baker, Henry, Blanchflower, Norman, Marchi, Jones, White (1), Smith, Greaves (2), Dyson (2)); UEFA Cup 1972 (3–2 agg. v Wolverhampton Wanderers – *Team* first leg (away) Jennings, Kinnear, Knowles, Mullery, England, Beal, Gilzean, Perryman, Chivers (2), Peters, Coates; second leg (home) Jennings, Kinnear, Knowles, Mullery (1), England, Beal, Gilzean, Perryman, Chivers, Peters, Coates), 1984 (2–2 agg. 4–2 pens. v Anderlecht – *Team* Parks, Thomas, Roberts, Hughton, Perryman, Miller (1), Stevens (Mabbutt), Hazard, Galvin, Archibald, Falco; second leg (home) Parks, Thomas, Hughton, Roberts (1), Miller

(Ardiles), Mabbutt (Dick), Hazard, Stevens, Galvin, Archibald, Falco); **Anglo-Italian League Cup-winners Cup** 1971 (3–0 agg. v **Torino**). *Records* Pat **Jennings** is Tottenham's most capped player (74 (119) for **Northern Ireland**); Steve Perryman holds the record for club appearances (655, 1969-88); Jimmy Greaves is Tottenham's record league goalscorer (220, 1961-70).

Tottenham Hotspur plc *n.* publicly-quoted business which owns **Tottenham Hotspur**. The club became a fully listed company on the London Stock Exchange in October 1983 (floatation price = 100p). Tottenham had a market capitalisation – the market value of the company's issued share capital (eg, the quoted price of its shares multiplied by the number of shares outstanding) – of £9.2 million on floatation. It was the first football club to seek a stock market listing and, in 1991, Alan Sugar took a majority shareholding in the club (40.5%) for around £8 million.

touchdown *misc.* early football codes did not include **goal-kicks** or **corner-kicks**. Instead, if the ball went out of play behind the goal line, players from either team could attempt to touch the ball down thus winning a free kick: if the attacking team won the touchdown it could take a free kick at goal. The principle was dropped from **association football** by the **Football Association** in 1872, but retained in **rugby football**. In **American Football**, a touchdown is scored by an attacking player being in possession of the ball in the opposition's end zone.

touchline ban *n.* punishment meted out by a football governing body to a coach or manager prohibiting that person from coaching from the **technical area** for a set period. Essentially, it means that the coach or manager has to watch matches from the stands. *Keynotes* In May 1990, then-**Rangers** manager Graeme **Souness** was banned for two seasons by the **Scottish Football Association** for various offences, including a breach of a previous touchline ban.

touchline *rules* either of the two longer boundary **lines** of the **field of play** (Law I). They run at right angles to the **goal lines**.

Tourbillon *club* Chad national league club based in the capital N'Djamena. Ground: Concorde (the national stadium), capacity: 25,000. **African Cup of Champion Clubs** first round 1992 (victory in preliminary round); **CAF Cup** first round 1993 (victory in preliminary round); Chad League champions 1991, 1997; Chad Cup 1989.

Tournoi de France *competition* one-off end-of-season four-nation tournament held in **France** in June 1997. The four countries participating were **Brazil**, **England**, France and **Italy**. *Results* France 1–1 Brazil; England 2–0 Italy; France 0–1 England; Italy 3–3 Brazil; Brazil 1–0 England; France 1–1 Italy. England winners.

Toute Puissant Mazembe *club* Congo Democratic Republic (formerly Zaire) national league club based in Lubumbashi, founded 1933 (formerly known as Toute Puissant Englebert). Ground: Mobutu, capacity: 40,000.

Strip: black shirts, white shorts. **African Cup of Champion Clubs** winners 1967 (3–3 agg., v **Asante Kotoko** of Ghana; awarded trophy because Asante refused to participate in a playoff), 1968 (6–4 agg., v **Etoile Filante** of Togo), runners-up 1969 (3–5 agg., v Al Ismaili of Egypt), 1970 (2–3 agg., v Asante Kotoko); **African Cup-winners Cup** 1980 (4–1 agg., v **Africa Sports** of Ivory Coast); Congo DR league champions 1966, 1967, 1969, 1976, 1987; Congo DR Cup 1966, 1967, 1976, 1979. Notable former players: Raymonde Tschimenu **Bwanga**, Mwamba **Kazadi**.

Township Rollers *club* Botswana national league club based in the capital Gaborone. Ground: the National Stadium, capacity: 20,000. Strip: royal blue shirts, gold shorts. Botswana League champions 1979, 1980, 1982, 1983, 1984, 1985, 1987, 1995; Botswana Cup 1993, 1994, 1996.

Toyota Cup Competition *n.* sponsor's name for the **World Club Cup**.

TPS Turku (Turun Palloseura) *club* Finnish national league club based in Turku, founded 1922. Ground: Kupittaa, capacity: 10,000. Strip: black and white striped shirts, white shorts. **UEFA Cup** third rouund 1989; Finnish League champions 1928, 1939, 1941, 1949, 1968, 1971, 1972, 1975; Finnish Cup 1991, 1994.

Trabzonspor Kolübü PK *club* Turkish national league club based in Trabzon, founded 1967. Ground: Avni Aker, capacity: 27,000. Strip: light blue shirts, light blue shorts. *Keynotes* Trabzonspor won the 1980 League championship with only 25 goals from 30 games – a world record for a national championship-winning side of 0.833 goals per game. Turkish League champions 1976, 1977, 1979, 1980, 1981, 1984; Turkish Cup 1977, 1978, 1984, 1992, 1995.

tracksuit trousers *n. pl.* leggings or sports trousers. *Regulations* These may be worn by goalkeepers (Football League regulation 35.5 stipulates that they may be worn only in adverse weather conditions and must be "acceptable to the referee").

trainee *regulations* **1. England** player aged 16-18 years old who is registered, and has signed a "trainee agreement" with a **Football League** club. As part of their tuition, trainees are required to take lessons and an exam in the **Laws of the game**. Trainees are only entitled to receive a stipulated training rate of payment, plus board and lodgings. The names of all registered trainees must be included in the **club list of players** (Football League regulation 60) – see also **student player**. FA **Premier League** rules were amended prior to the 1998-99 season abolishing trainee contracts; Premier League players under 17 years of age can now be registered only as student players (FA Premier League rule K.4). **2. Scotland** A player who, when aged under 21, signs a full professional registration form and contract of service with a **Scottish Football League** club while undertaking a formal course of training provided jointly by the **Scottish Football Association**, the Scottish Football League and the Scottish Professional Footballers Association; the training is obligatory

unless a dispensation is granted (Scottish Football League rule 63). Since August 1997, trainees have been able to take part in the **National Youth Training Scheme (Scotland)** and obtain a Scottish Vocational Qualification. See also **apprentice**.

train *vb.* to coach, or be coached, in footballing skills, tactics and fitness. **training** *n.* the execution of this.

trainer *n.* **1.** a practitioner in fitness training. **2.** informal name for **physiotherapist**.

training ground *n.* facility used by clubs for coaching and training. Training grounds generally are situated away from club stadiums.

Tranmere Rovers *club* English league. *Dossier* Ground: **Prenton Park**, Birkenhead, Merseyside. Strip: white shirts with blue and green trim, white shorts, white socks with blue and green trim. Nickname: Rovers. Ground capacity: 16,789 all seated. Record attendance: 24,424 v **Stoke City** (5 February 1972, **FA Cup**, fourth round). Best average attendance: 11,815 (1958-59). Biggest win: 13–0 v Oswestry United (10 October 1914, FA Cup, second preliminary round). Biggest defeat: 1–9 v **Tottenham Hotspur** (14 January 1953, FA Cup, third round replay). *History* Founded as Belmont FC in 1884 by members of two cricket clubs, adopting the name Tranmere Rovers the following year. The club played at several venues, including Steele's Field and Borough Road (later also called Prenton Park), before settling at its present home in 1912. Tranmere joined the newly-established Division Three (North) in 1921-22. It won the **Welsh Cup** in 1935 (1–0 v **Chester**), having reached the final of the competition the previous season (0–3 replay v **Bristol City**). The club's 13–4 (including nine goals by "Bunny" Bell) victory over **Oldham Athletic** on 26 December 1935 is the only time that 17 goals have been scored in a **Football League** match. In the late 1930s the club was experiencing financial problems which led to an offer of assistance from nearby Lever Brothers on condition the club move to the company's sports ground, the Oval, and change its name to Port Sunlight after the area in which the company is located; Rovers refused. The club almost ceased to exist in 1982, requiring a £200,000 loan from Wirral Borough Council to continue. Peter Johnson, who in June 1994 took over at **Everton**, became Rovers' chairman in 1987 and proceeded to turn the club round. Until Tranmere won promotion to Division Two via the end-of-season **playoffs** in 1990-91 (1–0 v **Bolton Wanderers**), the club had spent only one (1938-39) of its previous 63-season League history outside the bottom two divisions. The club had failed at the same stage the previous season (0–2 v **Notts County**). Tranmere reached two consecutive **Leyland Daf Trophy** finals, winning in 1991 (2–1 v **Bristol Rovers**) and losing the following year (2–3 v **Birmingham City**). Tranmere failed to win promotion to the Premier League through the playoffs by losing at the semi-final stage in three consecutive seasons,1992-93, 1993-94 and 1994-95. In 1994 the club also reached the semi-final stage of the League Cup, losing on penalties (4–4 agg. v **Aston Villa**). *League record* First Division 1992-93–; Division Two 1938-39, 1991-92; Second Division 1992-93; Division Three 1958-59 to 1960-61, 1967-68 to 1974-75, 1976-77 to 1978-79, 1989-90 to 1990-91; Division Three (North) 1921-22 to 1937-38, 1946-47 to 1957-58; Division Four 1961-62 to 1966-67, 1975-76, 1979-80 to 1988-89. *Honours* Division Three (North) 1937-38; Welsh Cup 1935 (1–0 v Chester); Leyland Daf Cup 1990 (2–1 v Bristol Rovers). *Records* John Aldridge is Tranmere's most capped player (30 (69) for **Republic of Ireland**); Harold Bell holds the record for club appearances (595, 1946-64, including a League record 401 consecutive appearances); Ian Muir is Tranmere's record League goalscorer (142, 1985-95).

transfer *regulations* to **register** a player with a new club. Transfers must be in writing, on official forms obtained from the relevant league governing body, and with the governing body's approval. A transferred player cannot be re-registered with the original club within 12 months without the permission of the league governing body (FA Premier League rule K.16, Football League regulation 41.5) – **temporary transfers** are not subject to this restriction. Transfers must be made before the **transfer deadline** except at the discretion of the league. **1. Contract player** (or **professional player** in Scotland): if a player is transferred while still under contract, the clubs must agree a **compensation fee** (Premier League) or **transfer fee** (**Football League/Scottish Football League**), or **free transfer** (sense **1.**) and the player must agree a contract of service with the new club. Without these agreements the transfer cannot go ahead. **2. Out-of-contract player**: if the player's contract has already expired, then he is free to join any other club; his former club may still be able to seek a compensation fee, either agreed by the clubs or settled by the **Football League Appeals Committee** or Scottish Football League **Compensation Tribunal**, but only if it has made the player a written offer of a new contract – which is at least as good as the previous contract – and the player is under 24 years of age (FA Premier League rule L.12, Football League regulation 59.3, Scottish Football League rule 60). **3. Non-contract player**: a non-contract player is free to move to another club; if a non-contract player is transferred from a Football League club, the club may be entitled to receive a compensation fee if it has made the player a written offer of a contract within the current season (ie while the player is still registered at the club) and the player is under 24 years of age (Football League regulation 51.4). Premier League clubs are not entitled to receive compensation fees for non-contract players (FA Premier League rule K.8). See also **freedom of contract**, **temporary transfer**.

transfer agreement *regulations* the written agreement drawn up between two clubs for the transfer of a player's registration. The transfer agreement will, for example, include the details of any **compensation fee** (**Premier League**) or **transfer fee** (**Football League**). The Premier League has a standard transfer agreement form, published in its **league handbook**.

transfer deadline *regulations* fixed time and date after which transfers will not be permitted, except at the discretion of the league governing body. In England, the deadline is 5 pm on the fourth Thursday in March (FA Premier League rule L.1, Football League regulation 37.4). In Scotland, the deadline is 31 March (Scottish Football League rule 47).

transfer fee *regulations* **1. Premier League** another term for **compensation fee** (sense **1**). **2. Football League** fee agreed between two clubs for the **transfer** of a **contract player** who is currently registered with the selling club (Football League regulations 41.2 and 42.1). The transfer fee is paid by the buying club directly to the league for immediate forwarding to the player's original club – ie the league acts as the intermediary (Football League regulation 44.1). The club paying the transfer fee must pay a deposit to the league when the relevant transfer document are submitted. The full payment must be made within a timescale agreed by the clubs, and certainly within the period of a player's contract (Football League regulation 44.2). If a player is transferred before the balance is paid, then any subsequent transfer fee must be used immediately to settle the outstanding balance. Clubs are allowed to agree conditional payments, such as if a player makes a certain number of first-team or international appearances (Football League regulation 45.1). **3. Scottish Football League** fee agreed between two clubs for the transfer of a professional player who is currently registered with, and is under contract to the selling club (Scottish Football League rule 47). Unless otherwise agreed, the buying club must pay at least 50% of the fee when the transfer agreement is signed, with the balance paid within 12 months (Scottish Football League rule 47.ii). If a player is transferred before the balance is paid, then any subsequent transfer fee must be used immediately to settle the outstanding balance. Scottish Football League clubs are also allowed to agree conditional payments, as above (Scottish Football League rule 47.i). Compare compensation fee (senses **2.** and **3.**), **free transfer** *History* A Football League rule introduced in 1899 abolished a previous system whereby transfer lists were published; the details of any transfer (including the fees exchanged) was deemed to be confidential. An impasse existed between the **Football Association** (FA) – which, in 1899, imposed a maximum transfer fee of £10, to cover expenses – and the Football League, which had not ruled for a restriction. The FA considered that transferring players for profit was "unsportsmanlike". In February 1905, **Middlesbrough** paid **Sunderland** a record £1,000 for Alf **Common** (Middlesbrough had, for financial comparison, paid £10,000 for a new stadium, **Ayresome Park**, only six years before). In March the same year, the FA attempted to control transfer-fee inflation by imposing a limit of £350, to come into effect in

1908. The rule was abandoned as unworkable shortly after coming into force. In 1910, the Football league ruled that players could be paid a percentage of the transfer fee (the amount depending on years of service) to compensate for loss of accrued benefits (such as a right to service-linked pay and long-service awards). See **retain-and transfer system**.

transfer fee, highest *record* **1.** World: Brazilian **Denilson** became the world's most expensive player following his £21.5 million move from **São Paulo** to **Real Betis** after the 1998 **World Cup**. **2.** United Kingdom: Alan **Shearer** is the UK's most expensive player. The **England** captain was transferred from **Blackburn Rovers** to **Newcastle United** for a record £15 million in July 1996 – a then world record. **3.** UK goalkeeper: Steve Simonsen became the most expensive UK goalkeeper in September 1998 when he moved from **Tranmere Rovers** to **Everton** for £3.3 million. **4.** Italy: Christian Vieri's £19 million move to **Lazio** from **Atlético Madrid** in summer 1998 is an Italian record.

transfer levy *n.* fixed percentage of a **compensation fee** or **transfer fee** paid by the buying club to the relevant league and used for league purposes. The **Premier League** and **Football League** charge the buying club a 5% levy to fund benefit plans for players (FA Premier League rules L.32 and 33, Football League regulations 44.2.8-10). The Football League may also deduct an additional 5% **Ground improvement levy** from the transfer fee, but only if the club selling the player does not meet the requirements of the **Taylor report** (Football League regulation 44.2.11).

transfer list *regulations* a list containing the names and details of players whose **registrations** a **Scottish Football League** club is prepared to transfer (Scottish Football League rule 50(c)). The list must be submitted to the Scottish Football League no later than 15 May in any season, and must include the transfer fee being asked (if there is one) and any relevant information justifying the fee. Clubs may approach and sign any player whose name appears on a transfer list, without seeking the consent of the club, provided that the new club pays the **transfer fee** stipulated by the player's original club (Scottish Football League rule 52). See **transfer request**.

transfer market *n.* informal name for the collective buying and selling of players.

transfer request *n.* formal request by a player that he/she be made available for transfer. A player transferred after making a written request will not normally be entitled to any remaining instalments of a **signing-on fee** (FA Premier League rule J.17.2, Football League regulation 55.14).

transfer window *n.* official time period in which players can be transferred. In **Spain**, for example, the transfer window each season lasts from mid-December to mid-January. See also **transfer deadline**.

Traoré, Abdoulaye *player* **Ivory Coast** international. Born 4 March 1963. *Clubs* **ASEC Abidjan**, Al Khalij

(Saudi Arabia). *Keynotes* Joint record holder for appearing in six consecutive **African Cup of Nations** finals tournaments: 1986, 1988, 1990, 1992, 1994, 1996. *Honours* African Cup of Nations (Ivory Coast, 1992).

trap *vb.* to control the ball with the feet, bringing it to an immediate standstill.

Trapattoni, Giovanni *player-manager* Midfield. Born 17 March 1939. *Clubs* (manager) **AC Milan**, **Juventus**, **Internazionale**, **Bayern Munich**, Cagliari, **Fiorentina**. *Keynotes* As a player Trapattoni was a wing-half with AC Milan, where he made 274 appearances and won two European Cup winner's medals (1963, 2–1 v **Benfica**; 1969, 4–1 v **Ajax**) and a European Cup-winner's Cup medal (1968, 2–0 v **Hamburg (SV)**). He was youth coach at the **San Siro** before becoming Juventus manager in 1976. Trapattoni fashioned a highly successful Juventus team which was sound in defence and occasionally devastating on the **counter attack**. During Trapattoni's decade as Juve manager, the club won six **Serie A** titles, two Italian Cups, each of the three major European club competitions, a **European Super Cup** and a **World Club Cup**, making him the most successful manager in the history of the club and the pre-eminent Italian coach of his generation. He brought Liam **Brady**, Michel **Platini** and Zbigniew **Boniek** to Juventus. Trapattoni was considered too defence-minded to be considered as national coach, although Juventus players, including Dion **Zoff**, Claudio Gentile, Gaetano Scirea, Antonio Cabrini, Marco Tardelli and Paolo **Rossi**, provided the core of Italy's 1982 **World Cup** winning side. After a spell back at the San Siro as coach of Internazionale, where he won a further Serie A title, Trapattoni replaced Franz **Beckenbauer** (who became club president) as Bayern Munich manager. He took the club to the semifinal stage of the **European Cup** in 1995 (0–5 agg. v **Ajax**), but a disappointing sixth place in the **Bundesliga**. Trapattoni departed, only to return in the summer of 1996 and, using the same defensive tactics he had employed at Juventus, Bayern won the 1996-97 Bundesliga title. Thus Trapattoni has the distinction of being the first foreign manager to win the German championship. He became Fiorentina manager in 1998 and the club's victory over Udinese on 4 October was Trapattoni's 327th in Serie A – a record.

Trautmann Bert *player* Goalkeeper. Career ca 1949–64. *Club* **Manchester City**. *Honours* **FA Cup** (Manchester City 1956). *Keynotes* Ex-German prisoner of war, who was captured in 1945. Rather than be repatriated after hostilities ended he joined non-League St Helens Town. Was an **FA Cup** finalist in consecutive years with Manchester City, receiving a loser's medal in 1955 (1–3 v **Newcastle United**) and a winner's medal the following season (3–1 v **Birmingham City**). X-rays taken three days after the 1956 final revealed that Trautmann had played the last 15 minutes with a broken neck. He was voted **Footballer of the Year** in 1956. He later managed **Stockport County** (1965-66). Included in the **Football League Centenary 100**

players. *Honours* Italian League (Juventus 1976-77, 1977-78, 1980-81, 1981-82, 1983-84, 1985-86; Internazionale 1988-89); German League (Bayern Munich 1996-97); Italian Cup (Juventus 1979, 1983); **European Cup** (Juventus 1985); **European Cup-winners Cup** (Juventus 1984); **UEFA Cup** (Juventus 1977); **European Super Cup** (Juventus 1984); **World Club Cup** (Juventus 1985).

Travadores de Praia *club* Cape Verde Islands national league club based in the capital Praia. Ground: Varzea (the national stadium), capacity: 15,000. **African Cup of Champions Clubs** first round 1995; Cape Verde League champions 1994, 1996.

Tre Fiori *club* San Marino league club based in Fiorentino, founded 1949. Ground: Fiorentino, capacity: 2,000. San Marino League champions 1988, 1993, 1994, 1995; San Marino Cup 1966, 1971, 1974, 1975, 1985, runners-up 1986, 1992.

treatment *medical* medical attention given to a player on or off the field of play.

treatment table *medical* **physiotherapist**'s workbench.

Treaty of Rome *legal* treaty signed on 25 March 1957 that laid down the principles for the European Economic Community (now the European Union, EU). Various articles of the Treaty have implications for the business of football and for players' **freedom of contract** (see **Bosman ruling**). Article 52 of the Treaty says that any business in the EU should be free to locate itself in any member state – a principle that has been used to argue that a football club should be able to relocate to another EU member state while still retaining membership of its original domestic league. Conversely, it is suggested that any such relocation could be in breach of Article 86 of the Treaty, which forbids a business from exploiting a dominant position in the market. *Keynotes* One club considering the application of the Treaty principles was English league club **Wimbledon**, which in the late 1990s considered a relocation to a purpose-built stadium in Dublin in the **Republic of Ireland**, while still playing in the FA **Premier League**. The **Football Association of Ireland** and the **Union of European Football Associations** (UEFA) were said to be opposed to the plans.

treble *n.* winning three honours in one season. *Keynotes* No English League division team has ever achieved a treble of domestic honours. **Liverpool**, however, won the League Championship, the **League Cup** and the **European Cup** in 1984. Manchester United won the League, **FA Cup** and European Cup in 1998-99.The domestic treble is less elusive in **Scotland**. **Rangers** have won the Scottish domestic treble (League/Premier Championship; **Scottish FA Cup** and **Scottish League Cup**) on five occasions, while **Celtic** have won the treble twice, including the 1966-67 season, when they also became the first British club to win the European Cup. **Barry Town** completed a Welsh domestic treble by winning the League of Wales, the **Welsh FA Cup**, and the League of Wales

Cup in 1996-97. See also **double**, **double-double**, **grand slam**.

trialist *regulations* a player who is not formally registered with a club but is allowed to play in a **Scottish Football League** match up to and including 31 March in any season for the purposes of testing the player's suitability for the club prior to him being offered a formal contract or, at least, being registered with that club (Scottish Football League rule 49). Trialists are allowed a maximum of three matches for any one club in any season. No more than two trialists can play for one club in any match. Clubs must attach of the words "not registered" to the names of any trialists in the teamsheet included with the report of the match **result** (as submitted to the league); they must also include details of the player's previous club, place and date of birth, and address.

Tricolore *n.* ball developed by sports manufacturers Adidas for the 1998 **World Cup**. The ball differs from previous designs in that it is slightly smaller (68.5–69.5cm circumference compared to 71cm), lighter (420–445g compared to 450g), absorbs less water (up to 45g compared with up to 200g) and is made of polyurethane rather than leather. It is claimed that the ball travels faster and is more accurate than past footballs. Its pace is generated by a lining consisting of millions of gas-filled bubbles which absorb less energy than normal balls.

tridente *tactics* Italian term for a three-pronged attack. First used to describe the attacking trio Alessandro del Piero, Fabrizio Ravanelli and Gianluca Vialli at **Juventus** in the mid-1990s.

Trinidad and Tobago *country CONCACAF* independent republic in the West Indies. It comprises the two southernmost islands of the Lesser Antilles. The islands lie only 11 km and 30 km (7 and 19 miles) respectively from the coast of **Venezuela**. The climate is humid and tropical. It gained independence from Britain in 1962. Area: 5,130 sq km (1,980 sq miles). Population: 1,270,000 (1996 est.). Languages: English, Hindi, French, Spanish. Capital: Port of Spain. *Dossier* Trinidad and Tobago Football Association (Port of Spain) formed in 1908, affiliated to **FIFA** in 1963 and **Confederación Norte-Centroamericana y del Caribe de Fútbol** (CONCACAF) in 1964, president: Oliver Camps; general secretary: Richard Groden. Season played from January to December. National stadium: Queen's Park Oval, Port of Spain, capacity: 25,000. National strip: red shirts, black shorts, white socks. Biggest victory: 8–0 v **Dominican Republic** (23 June 1996, Port of Spain, World Cup qualifier). Best victory: 2–1, v **Republic of Ireland** (30 May 1982, in Port of Spain, friendly). Notable international player: Dwight Yorke (of **Aston Villa** and **Manchester United**). *International tournament record* Olympic Games – never qualified for finals tournament; **Women's World Cup** – first entered 1991, never qualified for finals tournament; **World Cup** – first entered 1964, runner-up in second and final qualifying round 1974 (only one nation to qualify), reached third round of CONCACAF qualifying tournament in 1990 (third in final-round group of five nations, with two to qualify), qualified from the three-round Caribbean zone tournament 1998 (finished last in its four-nation CONCACAF semi-final round); **Caribbean Nations Cup** – winners 1989 (2–1 v **Grenada**, in Bridgetown, Barbados), 1992 (3–1 v **Jamaica**, in Jamaica), 1994 (7–2 v **Martinique**, in Trinidad), 1995 (5–0 v **St Vincent**, in Cayman Islands), 1996 (2–0, v Cuba, in Trinidad), 1997 (4–0, v **St Kitts and Nevis**, in Antigua and St Kitts), runners-up 1991 (0–2 v Jamaica, in Jamaica), 1998 (1–2, v Jamaica, in Trinidad), third place 1993 (3–2 v St Kitts and Nevis, in Jamaica, third/fourth playoff); **CONCACAF Championship** – entered 1967, 1969, 1971, hosts 1971; **CONCACAF Women's Championship** – entered first tournament in 1991, third 1991 (4–2, v **Haiti**), fourth 1994 (league of five), third in its first-round group of four 1998; **Gold Cup** – qualified 1991, 1996, 1998; **Under-17 World Championship** – never qualified for finals tournament; **World Youth Cup** (under-20) – qualified for finals tournament 1991 (last of four-nation first-round group). *Record against British and Irish national teams* v Republic of Ireland, played one, won one. *History* Trinidad and Tobago was the second country in the Caribbean to establish a football association, founded in 1908 (four years after Haiti). It narrowly missed qualifying for the 1974 World Cup finals in Germany. Having won its three-nation first-round group, it qualified for a final six-nation qualifying group in Haiti and was runner-up ahead of Mexico, but two points behind Haiti, the only nation to qualify. It also went close to qualifying for 1990 World Cup finals tournament in Italy. Having reached the third and final round of the CONCACAF qualifying tournament in 1990, with victories over **Guyana** (5–0 agg.) and **Honduras** (1–1 agg., **away goals**), it needed a victory in its final match against the **United States of America**, but lost 0–1 in Port of Spain. Trinidad and Tobago won the Caribbean Nations Cup in 1989, 1992, 1994 and 1995; it was runners-up in 1998. At club level, **Defence Force**, from Chaguanas, won the CONCACAF Champions Cup in 1985 (joint winners 1978). **Police Club**, from St James, was runners-up in 1987. The majority of the national league clubs are from Trinidad. In 1989, Trinidad and Tobago spectators were awarded the FIFA **Fair Play award** for sportsmanship. *League system* Twelve clubs compete in the national first division, playing each other at home and away. Three points are awarded for a win in normal time. Two points are awarded for a victory in sudden-death overtime or penalties; there are no draws. Final positions for clubs level on points are determined by **goal difference**. *Record in international club tournaments* **CONCACAF Champions Cup** – **Defence Force** (winners 1985, joint-winners 1978, runners-up 1987, 1988), **Police FC** (runners-up 1991), United

Petrotin (quarter-final 1997); **Joe Public** (quarter-final 1998); **Caribbean Club Championship** – Joe Public (winners 1998), Courts Caledonia AIA (runners-up 1998). Other leading club: Trinity Falcons.

triple hat-trick   *record*   nine goals by one player in a single match. *Keynotes* Bunny Bell was the first to achieve a triple hat-trick in the English or Scottish football leagues (nine goals for **Tranmere Rovers** v **Oldham Athletic**, Division Three (North), 26 December 1935); Joe Payne scored 10 goals for **Luton Town** against **Bristol Rovers** (Division Three (South), 13 April 1936); Ted MacDougall scored nine for **Bournemouth** in an **FA Cup** tie against Margate (20 November 1971). See also **hat-trick**, **double hat-trick**, **quadruple hat-trick**.

tripping an opponent   *rules*   one of the offences listed as a **foul** under the **Laws of the game** (Law XII). A player commits the offence by causing the opposing player to stumble or fall entangling the feet or legs. The player is not guilty if he or she plays the ball first and only trips the opponent during the same movement. It is also an offence to attempt to trip an opponent. The punishment for a trip is for the opposing team to be awarded a **direct free kick**, taken from the point where the foul was committed (unless within the opponents' **goal area**, in which case it is taken from anywhere within that area). However, if the foul is committed in the offending side's **penalty area**, then the opponents are awarded a **penalty kick**. *Keynotes* Tripping was defined by the **Football Association** in the rules of the game adopted at its foundation in 1863 as "throwing an adversary by use of the legs" and rule 14 stated that "neither tripping nor **hacking** shall allowed and no player shall use his hands to hold an adversary". See **tackle from behind**. The **Laws** do not distinguish between trips commited with or without intent; they are all ruled as fouls – though, in practice, referees may show some leniency for minor events.

Tromsø IL (Idrettslag)   *club*   Norwegian national league club based in Tromsø, a small island in the Arctic Ocean off the northwest coast of mainland Norway, 70 degrees north, inside the Arctic Circle. Founded in 1920; the most northerly league football club in the world, about 350 miles from the North Pole. Ground: Alfheim, capacity: 11,000. Strip: red and white striped shirts, white shorts. Norwegian League runners-up 1990; Norwegian Cup 1986, 1996.

T-shirt message   *n.*   slogan written on a t-shirt worn under a player's shirt. *Keynotes* **Liverpool** striker Robbie Fowler wore one in support of striking Liverpool dock workers during a **European Cup-winners Cup** match against Brann Bergen at **Anfield**. Fowler was fined £900 by UEFA because his t-shirt message was deemed to be "politically motivated". **Chelsea** captain Dennis Wise exposed a t-shirt after scoring against **Derby County** on 18 January 1997 with the message "Cheer-up Luca, we love you. XX", a reference to teammate Gianluca **Vialli**'s continued place on the bench. Ian Wright, then of **Arsenal** unveiled the message "Just done it" (a play on Nike's "Just do it" slogan) after he scored his 179th goal for the club, against **Bolton Wanderers** on 13 September 1997, thereby breaking Cliff **Bastin**'s 58-year-old club record (178). Wright also wore a t-shirt under his **West Ham United** shirt with a slogan in support of striking Essex firefighters on 9 September 1998 (v **Wimbledon**, Premier League)

tsu chu *n.* ancient Chinese ball game dating from around 2500 BC, to 220 AD, an early form of football. A stuffed animal-skin ball is thought to have been kicked between two bamboo posts up to 10 metres high. Some accounts suggest that the ball had to be struck through a gap in a net stretched between the posts. The games could form part of festivities. Other accounts indicate that tsu chu was used as part of soldiers' training around 250-200 BC. Frescoes from AD 25-220 indicate that women also took part in the game.

Tully, Walter *player* Inside-forward/wing-half. Career ca. 1908-14. *Clubs* Clapton, **Tottenham Hotspur**, **Northampton Town**. *Keynotes* First outfield black player in the English game. Joined Spurs in 1908, later moving to Northampton. His transfer to Northampton followed a particularly nasty incident in 1909 in which Tully was racially abused during a game at **Bristol City**. Tully played 110 matches for Northampton before World War I curtailed his career. He enlisted with the 17th (1st Football) Battalion of the Middlesex Regiment. Tully, who became the British Army's first black officer, was killed in action on 25 March 1918. A garden dedicated to him, the Walter Tully Memorial Garden, stands next to Northampton's **Sixfields Stadium**.

Tunisia *country CAF* republic in north Africa on the Mediterranean Sea, next to **Algeria** and **Libya**. Desert in the south of the country. Independence from **France** in 1956. Area: 164,150 sq km (63,360 sq miles). Population: 8,800,000 (1994 est.). Languages: Arabic, French. Capital: Tunis. *Dossier* Football association (Fédération Tunisienne de Football, Tunis), formed in 1956, affiliated to **FIFA** and **Confédération Africaine de Football** (CAF) in 1960, member of the **Arab Football Union**, president: Dr Tarek Ben M'Barek; general secretary: Amor Darragi. Season played from August to May. National stadium: Stade Olympique el Menzah, Tunis, capacity: 50,000. National strip: red shirts, white shorts, red socks. First documented international game: 1938 v France B (2–3, Tunis); post-independence: 1 June 1957 (1–2 v Algeria, neutral venue, friendly). Biggest victories: 5–0, v **Rwanda** (1983), **Nigeria** (1984), **Guinea** (1988), **Angola** (1988) and **Benin** (1993). Biggest defeat: 1–10 v **Hungary** (24 July 1960, in Hungary, friendly – unconfirmed result) and 0–8 v Algeria (8 April 1958, v Algeria, in Algeria, friendly). Notable international players: Tarak **Dhiab**, Faouzi Rouissi, Adel Sellimi. *International tournament record* **Olympic Games** – first entered 1960, qualified for finals tournament 1960 (first round), 1988 (first round), 1996 (first round); **Women's World Cup** – never entered; **World Cup** – first entered 1962, qualified for finals tournament 1978 (first round), 1998 (first

round); **African Cup of Nations** – first entered 1962, runners-up 1965 (2–3, v **Ghana**, Tunis, Tunisia), third 1962 (3–0, v **Uganda**, Addis Ababa, Ethiopia, third/fourth playoff), fourth 1978 (match abandoned v Nigeria, Accra, Ghana, third/fourth playoff – game awarded to Nigeria), quarter-final 1998, also qualified for finals tournament 1963, 1982, 1994 (as hosts 2000); **African Youth Cup** (under-20) runners-up 1985 (2–3 agg., v Nigeria); **All-African Games** (under-23 years) – runners-up 1991 (v **Cameroon**, in Egypt); **All-Arab Games** – runners-up 1957; **Arab Nations Cup** – winners 1962 (tournament in the Lebanon); **Under-17 World Championship** – qualified for finals tournament 1993; **World Youth Cup** (under-20) – qualified for finals tournament 1985, hosts of the first tournament in 1977. *World Cup performance* (finals and qualifiers to end of 1998 tournament) played 62, won 27, drawn 17, lost 18, scored 84 goals, conceded 53 goals win rate: 44%; goals scored per game: 1.35. *Record against British and Irish national teams* v **England**, played two, won none, drawn one, lost one; v **Wales**, played one, won one. *History* Football in Tunisia dates back to the country's French colonial past. An independent football association was formed in 1956, immediately after the country achieved independence. The Tunisian league championship (founded as the Ligue Tunisie) and Tunisian Cup started around 1921. One of the earliest clubs, Racing Club Tunis, won the **North African Club Championship** in 1919, the first year it was played. Two Tunisian clubs have won the **African Cup of Champion Clubs**: **Club Africain** (1991) and **Espérance** (1994). Tunisia has qualified for two World Cup finals tournaments and two Olympic Games football final tournaments. In 1978, it became the first African nation to win a match at a World Cup finals tournament (3–1, v **Mexico**, in Rosario, Argentina). It drew 0–0 with **West Germany** and lost 0–1 to **Poland** in its other first-round games. In 1998 it earned only one point from its three first-round group games at the finals in France (1–1, v Romania, at **Stade de France**). *League system* The national first division has 16 clubs, divided into two groups of eight. The top four in each group at the end of the first phase enter a championship group; the bottom four enter a relegation group. The group winners and runners-up take two and one bonus points, respectively, to the final group. Bonus points are also awarded to the fifth and sixth placed clubs entering the relegation group. Three points are awarded for a victory, with one for a draw: final positions for clubs level on points are determined by **goal difference**. Two clubs are relegated to the second division. *Record in international club tournaments* African Cup of Champion Clubs – Club Africain (winners 1991, quarter-final champions-league stage 1997), Espérance (winners 1994), **CS Sfaxien** (semi-final 1996), **ES Sahel** (quarter-final champions-league stage 1998); **African Cup-winners Cup** – **CA Bizerte** (winners 1988), Espérance (finalists 1998, runners-up 1987), Club Africain (runners-up 1990), ES Sahel (winners

1997), **Stade Tunisien Le Bardo** (quarter-final 1993), **Olympique Club Beja** (quarter-final 1994); **CAF Cup** – ES Sahel (winners 1995), CA Bizerte (semi-final 1992), Espérance (winners 1997), CS Sfaxien (winners 1998), Jeunesse Sportive Kairouaniase (quarter-final 1994); **African Super Cup** – Espérance (winners 1994), ES Sahel (winners 1997); **Afro-Asian Club Cup** – Club Africain (winners 1992), Espérance (winners 1995); **North African Club Championship** – Racing Club Tunis (winners 1919 – the first tournament); **Arab Club Champions Cup** – Espérance (winners 1994, runners-up 1987, 1995), CS Sfaxien (runners-up 1986), CA Bizerte (semi-final 1994); Club Africain (winners 1997); **Arab Cup-winners Cup** – Stade Tunisien Le Bardo (winners 1989), Club Africain (winners 1995), ES Sahel (runners-up 1995), Avenir Sportif La Marsa (semi-final 1995); **Arab Super Cup** – Espérance (winners 1996).

Turan Tauz *club* Azerbaijan national league club, based in Tauz, founded 1992. Ground: Shekhar, capacity: 10,000. Azerbaijan League champions 1994.

Turf Moor *ground* English football ground situated in Burnley, Lancashire; home of **Burnley**. *Dossier* Ground capacity: 22,546. Pitch dimensions 104m x 66m. Record attendance: 54,775 v **Huddersfield Town** (23 February 1924, **FA Cup**, third round). Best average attendance: 33,621 (1947-48). *History* Burnley played its first match at Turf Moor on 17 February 1883 (v Rawtenstall, friendly), and only two other **Football League** clubs (**Preston North End** and **Stoke City**) have played continuously at their present grounds for longer. Turf Moor was the venue for the first visit of a member of the royal family to a football match when Prince Albert watched Burnley play **Bolton Wanderers** in October 1886. One spectator was killed at Turf Moor in 1924 when the ground recorded its largest attendance. A further death occurred in February 1992 when Burnley apprentice Ben Lee was killed after the roof of the Long Side stand gave way as he was trying to retrieve a football. The Long Side, the last remaining large terracing at a Football League ground, was demolished in 1995. The £180,000 Cricket Field Stand, which opened in 1969, included the country's first oil-fired heating for spectators, but the cost of running the system was so high it was abandoned after only two seasons. Turf Moor has staged one full **England** international (v **Wales**, 28 November 1927) and it was the venue of a **Inter-League** fixture held to experiment with the change in the **offside law** in 1925 (Football League v **Scottish League**, 27 April 1925). Turf Moor hosted an earlier Football League v Scottish League encounter on 21 March 1914, and has been used for some FA Cup semi-finals. The first floodlit match at Turf Moor took place on 16 December 1957 (v **Blackburn Rovers**, friendly).

Turkey *country UEFA* republic in South East Europe and the most westerly part of Asia. It lies between the Black Sea and the Mediterranean Sea, and is bordered by **Armenia**, **Bulgaria**, **Georgia**, **Greece**, **Iran**, **Iraq** and **Syria**. The two halves of the country are separated by the Bosphorus, a strait linking the Black Sea with the Sea of Marmara, which is spanned by two bridges. Its largest city, Istanbul (population 6.6 million), is in Europe (although its metropolitan area straddles the Bosphorus), whereas the capital Ankara (2.6 million) is in Anatolia (or Asia Minor), the Asian part of the country. Ankara replaced Istanbul as capital in 1923, when Turkey became a republic (Istanbul was, at that time, in allied occupied territory). Area: 779,450 sq km (300,870 sq miles). Population: 62,530,000 (1995 est.). Languages: Turkish, Kurdish. Capital: Ankara. *Dossier* Football association (Türkiye Futbol Federasyonu, Istanbul), formed in 1923, affiliated to **FIFA** in 1923 and **Union of European Football Associations** (UEFA) in 1962, president: Abdullah Kigili; general secretary: Aydin Torunoglu. Season played from August to the end of May, with a three-week break from the end of December. National stadium: Inönü Stadi, Istanbul, capacity: 45,000. National strip: white shirts, white shorts, red and white socks. First international game: 26 October 1923. Biggest victory: 7–0 v **Syria** (20 November 1949, Ankara, **World Cup** qualifier), 7– 0 v **South Korea** (20 June 1954, Geneva, Switzerland, World Cup first round). Biggest defeat: 0–8 v **Poland** (23 April 1968, friendly, Chorzów, Poland), 0–8 v **England** (14 November 1984, Istanbul, World Cup qualifier), 0–8 v England (14 October 1987, **Wembley** Stadium, European Championship qualifier). Most capped players: Oguz Cetin (69 appearances, to 1997), Recep Cetin (56 appearances, to 1997), Bülent Korkmaz (55 appearances, to 1998). Leading goalscorers: **Hakan** Sükür (22 goals in 41 games, 1992-), **Lefter** Kücükandonyadis (21 goals, 1948-62), Cemil Turan (19 goals, 1971-78), Metin Oktay (19 goals, 1955-65). Other notable players: Tanju Colak, Ridvan Dilman. *International tournament record* Olympic Games – first entered 1924, quarter-final 1948; **Women's World Cup** – never entered; World Cup – first entered 1950, but withdrew after qualifying for finals tournament, also qualified for finals tournament 1954 (first round); **European Championship** – entered first tournament in 1960 (first round – no qualifying tournament), qualified for finals tournament 1996 (fourth of three nations in first round group, losing all three games; **European Championship for Women** – never entered; **European Under-16 Championship** – winners 1994 (1–0 v **Denmark**); **European Youth Championship** (under 18) – winners 1992 (2–1 v Poland), runners-up 1993 (0–1 v England); **Under-17 World Championship** – never qualified; **World Youth Cup** (under-20) – qualified for finals tournament 1993 (last in four-nation first-round group). *World Cup performance* (finals and qualifiers to end of 1998 tournament) played 75, won 20, drawn 9, lost 46, scored 92 goals, conceded 145 goals; win rate 27%; goals scored per game 1.23. *Record against British and Irish national teams* v England, played eight, won none, drawn one, lost seven; v **Northern Ireland**, played nine, won two, drawn two, lost five; v **Scotland**, played one, won one; v **Wales**, played six, won one, drawn one, lost four; v **Republic of Ireland**, played nine, won one, drawn three, lost five. *History* Modern football has been played in Turkey since the end of the 19th century, said to have been played by the British and Greek communities. The first official clubs were founded at the beginning of the 20th century: **Besiktas** (1903), **Galatasaray** (1905) and **Fenerbahçe** (1907). The first league was started in Istanbul in 1905. The Turkish Football Confederation was founded in 1923 and official regional leagues were started in 1924. The leading regional competition, the Istanbul league, in operation from 1924 to 1958, was dominated by the "big three" of Galatasaray, Fenerbahçe and Besiktas. From 1937 to 1950, a national championship, of sorts, was decided by a playoff competition between the main Istanbul clubs and the top regional sides. Professional football was introduced in 1951, and a national professional league replaced the regional competitions in 1959. The national championship also has been dominated by Galatasaray, Fenerbahçe and Besiktas. Trabzonspor is the only club to have taken the national championship away from Istanbul's big three, winning in 1976, 1977, 1979, 1980, 1981 and 1984. Crowd violence at a match between Kayserispor Kulübü and Siwas in September 1971 led to the partial collapse of a stand at Kayseri stadium, resulting in 44 fatalities. Turkey qualified for the 1954 World Cup finals – the only occasion it played in the finals tournament – after winning the home leg (1–0) and losing the away leg (1–4) of its qualifying tie with **Spain**; a playoff in Rome finished 2–2, and Turkey went through to the finals in Switzerland after a blind Italian boy drew lots from a hat. *League system* Eighteen clubs compete in the national first division, playing each other at home and away. Three points are awarded for a victory, with one for a draw: final positions for clubs level on points are determined by **goal difference**. The bottom three clubs are automatically relegated. There is no national second division. There are, however, five regional leagues, with the season played in two phases. The champions and runners-up in the first phase of each league (running from August to December) qualify for a promotion league of 10 clubs. These 10 play each other at home and away (18 games in all, from January to May), with the champions and runners-up promoted to the first division. The third-, fourth- and fifth-placed clubs qualify for a playoff tournament. The five regional leagues continue through the second phase of the season (minus the top two clubs from the first phase) and the second-phase champions of each league join the end of season playoff. The playoff tournament thus has eight clubs: it is a straight knockout, with a single-match final (settled on penalties, if necessary); the winner is promoted. The Turkish Cup final is played in mid-April. *Record in international club tournaments* **European Cup** – Galatasaray (semi-final 1989, quarter-final 1994, qualified for Champions League 1995, 1998), Besiktas (qualified for Champions League 1998); **European**

Cup-winners Cup – Fenerbahçe (quarter-final 1964), **Göztepe Izmir** (quarter-final 1969), **Bursaspor** (quarter-final 1975), Galatasaray (quarter-final 1992); **UEFA Cup** – Göztepe Izmir (semi-final 1969), Besiktas (third round 1997). Other leading clubs: **Trabzonspor**, **Altay** Spor Kolübü, **MKE Ankaragücü** Kolübü, **Gençlerbirligi** Spor Kolübü.

Turkish Republic of Northern Cyprus   *country no international affiliation*   see **Cyprus (2).**

Turkmenistan   *country AFC*   republic of North Asia, on the CaspianSea, bordered by **Afghanistan**, **Iran**, **Kazakhstan** and **Uzbekistan**. In 1925, became part of the Turkestan Soviet Socialist Autonomous Republic, with Tajikistan and Uzbekistan, and fully integrated with the **Soviet Union** in 1925. Independence from Soviet Union in 1991; former member of the ephemeral **Commonwealth of Independent States**. Area: 488,100 sq km (188,405 sq miles). Population: 4,500,000 (1995 est.). Languages: Turkmen, Russian, Uzbek. Capital: Ashkhabad. *Dossier* Turkmenistan Football Confederation (Ashkhabad) formed in 1992 affiliated to **FIFA** and **Asian Football Confederation** (AFC) in 1994, president: Boris Shikmuradov; general secretary: Kakjan Ataev. Season played from August to May. National stadium: Central Stadium, Ashkhabad, capacity: 12,000. National strip: green shirts, white shorts, green socks. *International tournament record* **Olympic Games** – never qualified for finals tournament; **Women's World Cup** – never entered; **World Cup** – first entered 1998 (third in its qualifying group of four nations); **Asian Cup of Nations** – first entered 1996 (last in its group of four nations); **Asian Games** – first entered 1994, quarter-final 1994, 1998; **Asian Women's Championship** – never entered. *Record against British and Irish national teams* none played. *History* A league and cup competition has been played since 1992 (after full independence). The 1996 season was not completed owing to clashes with the national side's fixture list (the leaders at the nominal finish to the season, **Nissa Ashkhabad**, were awarded the 1997 place in the **Asian Champion Teams Cup**). Until 1997 football had been played from April to November. Then a new league was launched, with a championship starting in the autumn and finishing in the spring. In 1998, the football association organised the **Turkmenistan President's Cup**. *League system* Twelve clubs compete in the national Premier Division. Three points are awarded for a win, with one for a draw. *Record in international club tournaments* **Kopetdag Ashkhabad** (quarter-final 1999); **Asian Champion Teams Cup** – Nissa Ashkhabad (third round 1997); **Asian Cup-winners Cup** – Kopetdag Ashkhabad (semi-final/fourth 1998).

Turkmenistan President's Cup   *competition*   international invitation club tournament played in Ashkhabad, **Turkmenistan**, first played 1998. The first edition featured eight leading clubs, one each from **Armenia**, **China**, **Iran**, **Russia**, South **Korea** and **Ukraine**, and two from the host nation. The tournament involved two mini-leagues of four clubs, culminating in semi-finals and final.*Winner and score* **Esteghlal** (Iran) 0–0, 7–6 pens., v **Zenit St Petersburg** (Russia).

Turks and Caicos *country CONCACAF* British Crown Colony in the West Indies. An archipelago of around 30 islands (six inhabited) in the Southeast Bahamas. Jamaican dependency from 1873 to 1962, self-government from 1976. Area: 430 sq km (166 sq miles). Population: 15,000. Languages: English. Capital: Cockburn Town, on Grand Turk Island. *Dossier* Football Association of Turks and Caicos (Cockburn Town), affiliated to **FIFA** in 1998, associate member of **Confederación Norte-Centroamericana y del Caribe de Fútbol** (CONCACAF) in 1997, full member 1998. *International tournament record* **World Cup** – never entered; **CONCACAF Championship** – never entered; **Gold Cup** – never entered; **Caribbean Nations Cup** – never entered. *Keynotes* In 1998 Turks and Caicos became the 200th member of FIFA.

turnstile *n.* mechanical gate used at football grounds to admit one spectator at a time. The operation of the turnstile is generally controlled by the club's ticket staff. Match **attendance** is recorded by counting devices attached to the turnstile mechanism.

turnover *vb.* to continually change a team's line-up to accommodate all squad members. Common in a club with a large squad of big-name players. The term was first applied to the **AC Milan** squad of the early 1990s, which included Zvonimir Boban, Ruud **Gullit,** Jean-Pierre **Papin,** Marco **Van Basten** and Dejan Savicevic. See **squad rotation.**

Tuvalu *country no international affiliation* island and Commonwealth country in the Southwest Pacific Ocean, in Polynesia, formerly known as the Ellice Islands. Independence from Britain 1978. Area: 25 sq km (10 sq miles). Population: 10,000 (1991 census). Languages: Tuvaluan, English. Capital: Funafuti. *Dossier* Football association neither affiliated to **FIFA** nor to the **Oceania Football Confederation.** *International tournament record* none.

Twerton Park *ground* English football ground situated in Bath, Avon; home of non-league Bath City and former home of **Bristol Rovers.** *Dossier* Ground capacity: 8,900. Record attendance: 9,464 v **Liverpool** (8 February 1992, **FA Cup,** fourth round). *Keynotes* Bristol Rovers played its first match at Twerton Park on 27 August 1986 (v **Reading, League Cup**), exactly 54 years after Bath made its first appearance at the ground, ironically against Bristol Rovers Reserves (27 August 1932). Rovers' match attendances were 23% down on the final **Eastville** average in the club's first season at Twerton Park. The first floodlit match at Twerton Park took place on 16 December 1964 (v **Arsenal**, friendly).

twin towers *n.* two 38.5-metre (126-feet) high domed structures which form part of the entrance to **Wembley** Stadium. The towers have listed building status. **Darlington**'s **Feethams** ground also has twin towers at its entrance.

two referees *misc.* the use of two match referees to officiate at a game. *Keynotes* **West Bromwich Albion**'s **Hawthorns Ground** was the setting for an experiment with two referees. The idea had first been proposed by **Everton** chairman Will **Cuff** at the 1935 annual meeting of the **Football League**. Two matches were held at the Hawthorns using the dual control plan (**England** v The Rest, 27 March 1935 and Football League XI v West Bromwich Albion, 8 May 1935). Everton's **Goodison Park** staged a further trial using two referees (Football League v Wales & Ireland, 11 May 1935). Both the Football League XI v The Rest match at the Hawthorns and the Football League v Wales & Ireland encounter at Goodison Park were staged to celebrate the Jubilee of King George V. A proposal to try the two referees system in selected matches during the 1937-38 season was defeated at the **Football Association**'s annual general meeting in 1937. The idea was resurrected in March 1999, when FIFA's technical committee decided to experiment with two referees at designated leagues during the 1999-00 season.

two-a-side football *n.* see **jorky-ball.**

two-leg *adj.* match played over two games, at the home grounds of both competing clubs. See **aggregate, away goals**.

Tynecastle Park *ground* Scottish football ground situated in Edinburgh, Lothian region; home of **Heart of Midlothian**. *Dossier* Ground capacity: 18,300. Pitch dimensions: 99m x 67m. Record attendance: 53,396 v **Rangers** (13 February, 1932 **Scottish FA Cup**, third round). *History* Hearts played its first match at Tynecastle in April 1881, moving across the road to the present ground in March 1886 (v **Bolton Wanderers**, friendly). The club bought the ground in 1926. In the early 1990s, Hearts considered a number of sites for a possible new ground, but plans for £25 million stadium at Millerhill were rejected and a proposal for a shared 27,000 capacity facility with **Hibernian** at Hermiston was also shelved. As a result, Tynecastle has been significantly redeveloped. The first floodlit match at Tynecastle took place in October 1957 (v **Newcastle United**, friendly). The ground has staged eight full **Scotland** internationals: v **Wales**, 26 March 1892; v Wales, 3 March 1906; v Wales, 2 March 1912; v Wales, 14 February 1925; v Wales, 26 October 1932; v **Northern Ireland**, 13 November 1935; v Wales, 9 November 1938; v **Estonia**, 10 October 1998.

U

UCD *club* see **University College Dublin FC**.

UDEAC Tournament (Tournament of the Union Douaniere et Economique des États de l'Afrique Centrale) *competition* international tournament for member countries of the **Union of Football Associations of Central Africa**. *Winners* **Cameroon** (1984, 1986, 1987, 1989), **Gabon** (1985, 1988, **Congo** (1990).

UEFA 2000 taskforce *n.* body established by UEFA in 1998 to examine the future of the game in Europe. The taskforce recommended the formation of a 32-club **European Cup** (Champions League) competition and the merging of the **European Cup-winners Cup** and the **UEFA Cup** competitions to form a 96-club knockout competition.

UEFA *abbrev.* **Union of European Football Associations**.

UEFA Cup *competition* European-wide club knock-out competition which began as the International Inter-Cities Fairs Cup in 1955 and was commonly known as the Fairs Cup until 1971-72, when it became the UEFA Cup. Both the 1964 (**Real Zaragoza** v **Valencia**) and 1965 (**Ferencváros** v **Juventus**) finals were one-off matches, otherwise all finals up to 1998 (**Internazionale** v **Lazio**), when UEFA adopted a one-match format, have been played over two legs. The 1998 final was also the first to attract sponsorship similar to that given to the **European Cup**. Three clubs per country were able to enter the 1961-62 competition. The number of entrants from a particular country is now based on the past performance of its clubs in European competition. An additional place is available to the country which tops the UEFA Fair Play League. In 1995-96, UEFA revamped its long- running summer competition the **Intertoto Cup** to provide another route into the UEFA Cup for three clubs each season. Although some clubs and countries were disparaging of the Intertoto, **Bordeaux**, having qualified via this method of entry, reached the 1996 UEFA Cup final (v **Bayern Munich**). Also, clubs which enter the qualifying rounds of the European Cup, and which fail to progress beyond these qualifying stages, automatically go into the UEFA Cup. A seeding system, consisting of four groups containing the 16 strongest clubs, was established for the second round of the 1998-99 competition, ensuring that the big clubs were kept apart. In 1967, the **Football League** established an automatic UEFA Cup place for the **League Cup** winners (although this applied only to Division One clubs). This was withdrawn by UEFA before the start of the 1997-98 competition, only to be reinstated following protestations by the League, including the threat of court proceedings. From 1999-00, the UEFA Cup merged with the **European Cup-winners Cup** as part of a revamp of European club competitions. English participants are the fourth-placed **Premier League** club and both the **FA Cup** and League Cup winners. In addition, the third-placed Premiership club, should it fail to progress beyond the European Cup qualifying stage, will join the UEFA Cup. *History* Initially a tournament for European cities staging industrial trade fairs and based on an idea put forward by FIFA vice-president Ernst Thommen. The **Union of European Football Associations** (UEFA), founded in 1954, agreed plans for the inaugural competition with the 12 European cities holding trade fairs in April 1955 and the first ties were held the following month with both representative teams and club sides. For example, Birmingham was represented by **Birmingham City**, while London entered a "**London Select XI**". The 12 entrants were organised into four groups of three with each side playing the others home and away, with the group winners going into the semi-finals. The first tournament lasted almost three years (1955-58) and was disrupted by the withdrawals of the Vienna and Cologne sides before **Barcelona** met London Select XI in the two-legged final in March 1958, with the first match staged at **Stamford Bridge**. The second tournament, which lasted for two seasons (1958-60), was played on a two-legged knockout basis between 16 teams, most of which were club sides. The 1960-61 final (**Roma** (AS) v Birmingham City) was held over to the following season after the Roma (AS) v **Hibernian** semi-final went to a third match. *Records* (Up to and including 1998) **Leeds United** was the first club to lift the trophy without actually winning the tie, when in 1971 it beat Juventus - which won eight and drew four of its 12 games - on the **away goals** rule after the aggregate scores finished 3–3. Since then, Juventus in 1977 (v **Athletic Bilbao**) and **Eintracht Frankfurt** in 1980 (v **Borussia Mönchengladbach**) have won the UEFA

Cup in the same manner. In 1984, **Tottenham Hotspur**, having become the first club to win the renamed UEFA Cup in 1972, was the first to win the trophy in a **penalty-shootout**, beating **RSC Anderlecht** 4–3 on spot kicks. Both Bayer Leverkusen in 1988 (3–2 pens v Espanyol) and **Schalke (04)** in 1997 (4–1 pens v Internazionale) have since done the same. In 1971, Barcelona became the permanent holders of the Fairs Cup trophy after the club, as the competition's first winner, defeated the holders, Leeds United, in a specially-arranged **playoff** match (2–1, 22 September). Three clubs, all Spanish, have won the trophy in consecutive competitions – Barcelona 1958 and 1960; Valencia 1962 and 1963; **Real Madrid** 1985 and 1986. Internazionale's appearance in the 1998 final was the club's fourth during the 1990s. Italian clubs have won the UEFA Cup on nine occasions, recording seven victories between 1989 and 1998. Between 1968 and 1973, English clubs (**Arsenal**, Leeds United (twice), **Liverpool**, **Newcastle United** and Tottenham Hotspur) won the trophy for six consecutive seasons. The competition has produced nine finals between clubs from the same country (1962, 1964, 1966, 1972, 1980, 1990, 1991, 1995, 1998). The largest aggregate attendance at a UEFA Cup final occurred in 1989 when 150,000 watched **Napoli** and **Stuttgart VfB** at **San Paolo** stadium (83,000) and **Gottlieb-Daimler Stadion** (67,000). The lowest aggregate of 42,000 was recorded in 1978 when **Bastia** and **PSV Eindhoven** met. *Final results* 1958, Barcelona 8–2 agg. London Select XI; 1960, Barcelona 4–1 Birmingham City (agg.); 1961, Roma (AS) 4–2 Birmingham City (agg.); 1962, Valencia 7–3 Barcelona (agg.); 1963, Valencia 4–1 **Croatia Zagreb** (as **Dynamo Zagreb**) (agg.); 1964, Real Zaragoza 2–1 Valencia (**Nou Camp**) (agg.); 1965, Ferencváros 1–0 Juventus (Comunale Stadio, Turin); 1966, Barcelona 4–3 Real Zaragoza (agg.); 1967, Dynamo Zagreb 2–0 Leeds United (agg.); 1968, Leeds United 1–0 Ferencváros (agg.); 1969, Newcastle United 6–2 **Ujpesti Torna Egylet** (as **Ujpest Dozsa)** (agg.); 1970, Arsenal 4–3 Anderlecht (agg.); 1971, Leeds United 3–3 Juventus (agg. Leeds won on away goals); 1972, Tottenham Hotspur 3–2 **Wolverhampton Wanderers** (agg.); 1973, Liverpool 3-2 Borussia Mönchengladbach (agg.); 1974, Feyenoord 4–2 Tottenham Hotspur (agg.); 1975, Borussia Mönchengladbach 5–1 **FC Twente Enschede** (agg.); 1976, Liverpool 4–3 Brugge (agg.); 1977, Juventus 2–2 Athletic Bilbao (agg. Juventus won on away goals); 1978, PSV Eindhoven 3–0 Bastia (agg.); 1979, Borussia Monchengladbach 2–1 **Red Star Belgrade** (agg.); 1980, Eintracht Frankfurt 3–3 Borussia Monchengladbach (agg. Eintracht won on away goals); 1981, **Ipswich Town** 5–4 **AZ 67 Alkmaar** (agg.); 1982, **IFK Gotënburg** 4–0 **Hamburg** (SV) (agg.); 1983, RSC Anderlecht 2–1 **Benfica** (agg.); 1984, Tottenham Hotspur 2–2 Anderlecht (agg. 4–3 pens.); 1985 Real Madrid 3–1 **FC Feherrar** (as **Videoton)** (agg.); 1986, Real Madrid 5–3 **Cologne** (agg.); 1987,

IFK Gotënburg 2–1 **Dundee United** (agg.); 1988, Bayer Leverkusen 3–3 **Espanyol** (agg. 3–2 pens.); 1989, Napoli 5–4 Stuttgart VfB (agg.); 1990, Juventus 3–1 **Fiorentina** (agg.); 1991, Internazionale 2-1 Roma (AS) (agg.); 1992, **Ajax** 2–2 **Torino** (agg. Ajax win on away goals); 1993, Juventus 6–1 **Borussia Dortmund** (agg.); 1994, Internazionale 2–0 **Salzburg** (agg.); 1995, **Parma** 2-1 Juventus (agg.); 1996, Bayern Munich 5–1 Bordeaux (agg.); 1997, Schalke (04) 1–1 Internazionale (agg. 4–1 pens.); 1998 Internazionale 3–0, v **Lazio** (**Parc des Prince**s); 1999 Parmar 3–1 Olympique de Marseille (**Luzhniki Stadium**).

UEFA Pro Licence *misc.* see **coaching qualification**.

UEFA Under-18 European Championship of Women's Football *competition* international women's youth tournament, first played 1997 in Spain. *Winners* 1997 **Netherlands**.

Uganda *country CAF* republic in east Africa, next to **Kenya**, **Rwanda**, **Sudan**, **Tanzania** and **Congo Democratic Republic** (Zaire). Independence from Britain in 1962. Civil war followed by military dictatorship under General Idi Amin, 1971-78. Area: 236,580 sq km (91,320 sq miles). Population: 16,670,000 (1991 census). Languages: English and tribal languages. Capital: Kampala. *Dossier* Confederation of Uganda Football Associations (FUFA, Kampala) formed in 1924, affiliated to **FIFA** and to **Confédération Africaine de Football** (CAF) in 1959, member of the Confederation of East and Central African Football Associations (CECAFA), president: Twaha Kakaire; general secretary: Christopher Rwanika. Season played from January to November. National stadium: Nakivubo, Kampala, capacity: 25,000 (Mandela Stadium, Kampala, capacity: 50,000 planned). National strip: yellow shirts with black stripes, black shorts with yellow stripes, yellow and red socks. Nickname of national team: the Cranes. First international game: 1930, v **Kenya** (0–0, friendly – earlier games may have been played in the **Gossage Cup**, which dates from 1927). Biggest victory: 7–0, v **Zanzibar** (30 September 1969, Kampala, **East and Central African Championship**) Biggest defeat: 0–6, v Egypt (30 July 1995, Cairo, **African Cup of Nations** qualifier). *International tournament record* **Olympic Games** – first entered 1964, never qualified for finals tournament; **Women's World Cup** – never entered; **World Cup** – first entered 1978 (qualifying tournament second round); African Cup of Nations – first entered 1962, runners-up 1978 (0–2, v **Ghana**, Accra, Ghana, fourth 1962 (0–3, v **Tunisia**, Addis Ababa, Ethiopia, third/fourth playoff), also qualified for finals tournament 1974, 1976; East and Central African Championship – winners 1973, 1976, 1977, 1989, 1990, 1992 (1–0, v Tanzania, in Tanzania), 1996 (1–0, v Sudan B, in Sudan), runners-up 1974, 1982, 1994; Gossage Cup – winners 26 times (from 1927 to 1972); **Under-17 World Championship** – never qualified; **World Youth Cup** (under-20) – never qualified. *Record against British and Irish national teams* none played. *History* Football introduced by the British, with the first football association founded in 1924, the fifth oldest association in Africa. International matches date back to the 1920s, when representative sides from Uganda took part in the annual Gossage Cup, with Kenya and Tanganyika (now **Tanzania**). Uganda's best international achievement was as runners-up in the 1978 African Cup of Nations (above). A national league dates from 1966, first won by Express FC (now **Express Red Eagles**). Two club sides, **Simba FC** (1972), **Nakivubo Villa** (1991), have reached the final of the **African Cup of Champion Clubs**, both beaten over two legs. In the 1996 season, Ugandan club Bushenyi finished bottom of the National First Division with only two points from 30 games (two draws, 28 defeats); it conceded 113 goals and scored only nine. Bushenyi had been promoted the previous season. *League system* Twenty-two clubs compete in the FUFA National League First Division. Three points are awarded for a victory, with one for a draw; final positions for clubs level on points are determined by **goal difference**. The bottom three clubs are relegated to the Second Division. *Record in international club tournaments* African Cup of Champion Clubs – Simba FC (runners-up 1972), Nakivubo Villa (runners-up 1991), Express Red Eagles (semi-final 1995); **African Cup-winners Cup** – Nakivubo Villa (quarter-final 1984), **Kampala City Council SC** (quarter-final 1985); **CAF Cup** – Nakivubo Villa (runners-up 1992), Kampala City Council SC (semi-final 1997); East and Central African Club Championship – Kampala City Council (winners 1978), Nakivubo Villa (winners 1987, 1990, runners-up 1999), Express Red Eagles (runners-up 1994, 1995); East African Super Cup – **Uganda Electricity Board** (winners 1996), Express Red Eagles (winners 1997).

Uganda Electricity Board *club* Ugandan national league club based in Jinja. Ground: Jinja, capacity: 8,000. East African Super Cup 1996; Ugandan league runners-up 1995; Ugandan Cup 1996; Ugandan Supercup (Cup winners v league champions) 1996.

Újpesti Dózsa *club* former name (1957-90) of Hungarian club **Újpesti Torna Egylet**.

Újpesti Torna Egylet (Újpesti TE) *club* Hungarian national league club based in Budapest founded 1885, formerly known as Budapest Dósza (1949-57) and **Újpesti Dózsa** (1957-90). Ground: Megyeri Úti, capacity: 32,000. Strip: white shirts, white shorts. **European Cup** – semi-final (as Újpesti Dózsa) 1974; **UEFA Cup** – runners-up (as Újpesti Dózsa) 1969 (2–6 agg., v **Newcastle United**); **Mitropa Cup** – winners (as Újpesti Dózsa) 1929, 1939; Hungarian league champions 1930, 1931, 1933, 1935, 1939, 1945, 1946, 1947, 1960, 1969, 1970, 1971, 1972, 1973, 1974, 1975, 1978, 1979, 1990, 1998; Hungarian Cup 1969, 1970, 1975, 1982, 1983, 1987, 1992. Notable former players: László **Fazekas**, András Torocsik.

Ukraine *country UEFA* republic in East Europe, on the Black Sea, bordered by **Belarus**, **Hungary**, **Moldova**, **Poland**, **Romania**, **Russia** and **Slovakia**.

Ukraine was the second largest republic by area in the former Soviet Union. Became an independent People's Republic in 1918, overtaken by Soviet Union in 1920. Occupied by **Germany** during **World War II**. Independence from Soviet Union in 1991, former member of the ephemeral **Commonwealth of Independent States**. Area: 603,700 sq km 233,030 sq miles). Population: 52,120,000 (1994 est.). Languages: Ukrainian, Russian. Capital: Kiev. *Dossier* Football Confederation of Ukraine (Kiev) formed in 1991, affiliated to **FIFA** in 1992 and **Union of European Football Associations** (UEFA) in 1993, president: Valery Pustovoitenko; general secretary: Anatoly Popov. Season played from the end of July until the middle of June with a **winter break** from mid-November to mid-March. National stadium: Central Republican Stadium (Dinamo Kiev's stadium), capacity: 100,000. National strip: yellow or blue shirts, blue shorts, yellow socks. First international game: 29 April 1992, v Hungary (1–3, in Uzhgorod, friendly). Biggest victory: 3–0 v **Estonia** (13 November 1994, in Kiev, European Championship qualifier). Biggest defeat: 0–4 v **Croatia** (25 March 1995, in Zagreb, Croatia, **European Championship** qualifier). Record attendance: 82,000, v Russia (5 September 1998, 3–2, in Kiev, European Championship qualifier). Notable international players: Igor **Belanov** (former-Soviet Union international), Andriy Shevchenko. *International tournament record* **Women's World Cup** – first entered 1995, never qualified for finals tournament; **World Cup** – first entered 1998 (second in six-nation qualifying group – won six, drawn two, lost two; lost to Croatia 1–3 agg., in playoff); European Championship – first entered 1996 (fourth in six-nation qualifying group); **European Championship for Women** – first entered 1995 (first round); **Under-17 World Championship** – never qualified; **World Youth Cup** (under-20) – never qualified. *World Cup performance* (finals and qualifiers to end of 1998 tournament) played 12, won 6, drawn 3, lost 3, scored 11 goals, conceded 9 goals; win rate 50%; goals scored per game 0.92. *Record against British and Irish national teams* v **Northern Ireland**, played two, won two. *History* Ukraine's oldest existing clubs, Torpedo Zaporozhye and SK Nikolayev (originally known as Metallist), were both founded in 1920. **Dinamo Kiev**, was founded in 1927 and was the most successful club in the former Soviet Union, with 13 Soviet league championships and nine Soviet Cups. It was twice winners of the **European Cup-winners Cup** (1975 and 1986) and once the **European Super Cup** (1975). With **Dinamo Tbilisi**, it was one of only two Soviet clubs to win a European trophy. Since independence, Dinamo has dominated the domestic league, winning six successive titles, including the first Ukrainian championship in 1993. Ukraine played its first international match in 1992 (above) but missed the 1994 World Cup: the former Soviet Union's qualification berth was given, controversially, to Russia. Several notable Ukrainian-born players, including Victor

Onopko, Andrei Kanchelskis and Oleg **Salenko**, elected to play for Russia in the 1994 World Cup qualifiers, and subsequently remained with the Russian team. However, Ukraine's star player Yuri Kalitvintsev was born in Russia. Ukraine's first international competition match was on 7 September 1994, v **Lithuania** (0–2, in Kiev, European Championship qualifier). It reached the qualifying playoff matches for the 1998 World Cup, losing 1–3 over two legs to Croatia. Ukraine and Russia played each other for the first time on 5 September 1998 (3–2, in Kiev,. European Championship qualifier). *League system* Sixteen clubs play in the national premier division (reduced from 18 before the 1996-97 season). Three points are awarded for a victory, with one for a draw: final positions for clubs level on points are determined by **goal difference** and, if necessary, by **goals scored**. The bottom two clubs are automatically relegated to the first division. There are 24 clubs in the first division, the top two are automatically promoted. The second division is divided into two regional divisions of 20 or 21 clubs. Some of the major clubs, such as Dinamo Kiev, **Shachter Donetsk** and CSKA Kiev, have reserve sides in the lower league. These are ineligible for promotion to the premier division. The winter break, lasting from mid-November to mid-March, is the longest in Europe. The Ukrainian Cup final is played at the end of May. *Record in international club tournaments* European Cup – Dinamo Kiev (semi-final 1977, 1987, 1999; Champions League and quarter-final 1998; European Cup-winners Cup – Dinamo Kiev (winners 1975, 1986); **Shachter Donetsk** (quarter-final 1983); **UEFA Cup** – Shachter Donetsk (third round 1977); European Super Cup – Dinamo Kiev (winners 1975). Other leading clubs: **Dnepr Dnepropetrovsk, Chernomorets Odessa, Tavria Simferopol, Metalist Kharkov**.

Ullevi (Gamla and Nya) *grounds* Swedish football/sports grounds situated in Gothenberg; home of **IFK Götenberg,** Örgryte IS and GAIS. Ground capacities: 18,000 (Gamla), 30,000 all seated (Nya). *History* Two stadiums bear the Norse god of sport's name, Ullevi, the Gamla (old) and Nya (new). All of Gothenberg's three main clubs play at Gamla Ullevi, while Neya Ullevi, which is adjacent and was built for the 1958 **World Cup**, hosts international fixtures, the occasional European final and IFK's big European matches. It also hosts other sporting events, notably athletics meetings. **UEFA** instructed IFK to play its 1996 **Champions League** qualifier against **Ferencváros** at Idrottsparken in Norrköping following several incidents of crowd trouble at Nya Ullevi. The ground was refurbished for the 1992 **European Championship**. During the 1958 World Cup tournament, Nya Ullevi staged seven fixtures: **England** v **Soviet Union**, **Brazil** v England, Brazil v Soviet Union, group 4; Soviet Union v England, group 4 **playoff**; Brazil v **Wales**, quarter-final; **Sweden** v **West Germany**, semi-final; **France** v West Germany, 3rd place playoff – total attendance 272,230; average attendance 32,490. The ground

has also hosted two **European Cup-winners Cup** finals (1983 **Aberdeen** v **Real Madrid**, 17,804; 1990 **Sampdoria** v **Anderlecht**, 20,103).

Ulsan Hyundai Horang-i (formerly Hyundai Tigers) *club* South Korean Pro-Football League club, based in Ulsan. **Asian Cup-winners Cup** semi-final/third 1997 (1–0, v **Esteghlal Sports Club**, third/fourth playoff, in Riyadh, Saudi Arabia); South Korean Pro-Football League champions 1986, 1996, runners-up 1988; Adidas Korea Cup 1995, 1998.

Ultras *misc.* groups of organised and extremely loyal supporters that follow all the major clubs in **Italy**. These groups include: Forever Ultras Inter (**Internazionale**); Fossa del Leoni (**AC Milan**); Colletivo Autonomo Viola (**Fiorentina**); Lo Juventus Club (**Juventus**); and Fossi dei Grifone (**Genoa**).

Umbro Cup *competition* pre-season knockout tournament sponsored by the sportswear company and involving four invited club sides. In 1996, the tournament was played at **Nottingham Forest**'s **City Ground** and involved, in addition to Forest, **Ajax, Chelsea** and **Manchester United**; Chelsea winners. **Goodison Park** was the venue for the 1997 tournament, which involved Ajax, Chelsea, **Everton** and **Newcastle United**; Chelsea winners. Renamed the Gelderland Tournament in 1998 and staged in Arnhem, Netherlands. The tournament involved **Atlético Madrid**, Chelsea, Club de Regatas **Flamengo**, Vitesse Arnhem; Atlético winners.

Umbro International Tournament *competition* international tournament between four invited national teams – **Brazil, England** (the hosts), **Japan** and **Sweden** – that took place at the end of the 1994-95 season: England 2–1 Japan (3 June, **Wembley**), Brazil 1–0 Sweden (4 June, **Villa Park**), Brazil 3–0 Japan (6 June, **Goodison Park**), England 3–3 Sweden (8 June, **Elland Road**), Brazil 3–1 England (final, 11 June, **Wembley**).

umpire *n.* formerly, one of two officials who adjudicated on the rules of the game in 19th century football matches. See **referee**; *history*.

UNAM (full name: Club Universidad Nacional Autónoma de Mexico) *club* Mexican national league club, based in Mexico City and founded in 1954. Known as "Los Pumas". Ground: Estadio Ciudad Universitaria, capacity: 72,000. Strip: dark blue shirts, with a gold puma face on the chest, and dark blue shorts; or white shirts, with a black puma's face on the chest, and white shorts. **CONCACAF Champion Clubs Cup** 1980 (2–0, v Universidad de Honduras, of Honduras, in Tegucigalpa, Honduras), 1982 (2–1 agg., v **Robin Hood** of Surinam) and 1989 (4–2 agg., v **Pinar del Rio** of Cuba); **Copa Inter Americana** winners 1980; Mexican League Champions 1977, 1981 and 1991; Mexican Cup (Copa Mexico) winners 1975. Notable former players: Jorge **Campos**, Hugo **Sanchez**.

unbeaten at home (club) *record* **1.** World – domestic league: **Real Madrid** played 122 league games at home without defeat (17 February 1957 to 7

March 1965). **2. Football League** club: 85 matches in various competitions, **Liverpool** (January 1978 to January 1981). **3.** European club competitions: **Manchester United** played 56 matches in all European competitions at its **Old Trafford** ground without defeat (1957 to 1996).

unbeaten in international matches *record* The five longest runs of international matches without defeat are: **Brazil**, 37 matches (16 December 1993 to 18 January 1996; 30 victories); **Hungary**, 31 matches (4 June 1950 to 30 June 1954; 27 victories – includes five **Olympic Games** matches); **Argentina**, 31 matches (19 February 1991 to 15 August 1993); **Spain**, 31 matches (7 September 1994 to 28 January 1998); **France**, 30 matches (16 February 1994 to 9 November 1996). *Keynotes* **England** achieved 20 games undefeated (15 March 1890 to 4 April 1896; though the record would extend to 36 matches if amateur internationals were included). **Scotland**'s best run is 22 games without defeat (7 April 1879 to 17 March 1888).

unbeaten in league matches *record* the following statistics are for national leagues only. **1.** World/Africa: **ASEC Mimosas Abidjan** was unbeaten for 108 Ivory Coast league matches (1988 to 19 June 1994). **2.** Europe: **Steaua Bucharest**, 104 games without defeat in the Romanian league (17 August 1986 to 10 September 1989). **3.** Asia: **Dalian Wanda** of China, 55 matches (1996 to 21 December 1997). **4.** South America: **Racing Club** of Argentina, 39 matches (1965 to 1966). **5. Football League**: 42 matches, **Nottingham Forest** (November 1977 to 9 December 1978; Forest's sequence consisted of the final 26 matches of the 1977-78 season and the first 16 of 1978-79, and comprised 21 victories and 21 draws. It came to an end, 0-2, at **Anfield** against **Liverpool**. **6.** FA **Premier League**: 25 matches, Nottingham Forest (1994-95/1995-96). **7. Scottish Football League**: 62 matches, Celtic (13 November 1915- to 21 April 1917, wartime league). **8. Serie A** (Italian league): 58 matches, **AC Milan** (ended by **Parma** on 21 March 1993). **9. France**: 32 matches, **Nantes** (ended by a 0–2 defeat by Strasbourg in 1995). *Keynotes* The British all-league record is 153 games unbeaten, held by Penlake Junior FC (including 152 victories, Warrington Hilden Friendly League, 1981-86).

UNCAF Club Cup *competition* see **Torneo Grandes de Centroamerica**.

UNCAF Cup *competition* international nations competition of Central America, contested by **Costa Rica**, **El Salvador**, **Guatemala**, **Honduras**, **Nicaragua** and **Panama**, first played 1991. *Winners* Costa Rica (1991, final tournaments in San José, Costa Rica, 1997, 1999, finals tournament in San José), Honduras (1992, final tournament Tegucigalpa, Honduras). The top three nations qualify for **CONCACAF Gold Cup** in alternate years.

unconscious *medical* not conscious, lacking normal sensory awareness. Unconsciousness can be caused, for example, by oxygen starvation, certain drugs or a severe blow to the head. *Keynotes* **Uruguay** international Juan Hohberg was knocked unconscious after scoring an 87th-minute equaliser in his country's **World Cup** semi-final against **Hungary** in 1954; the injury occurred as his players jumped on him in celebration. Hohberg recovered but Uruguay lost in extra-time (2–4, in Lausanne, Switzerland). **Yugoslavia**'s Rajko Mitic knocked himself out before the start of his country's World Cup game against **Brazil** at the **Maracana Stadium**, Rio de Janeiro. Mitic walked into an iron girder as he left the dressing room; Yugoslavia started with 10 players and was 0–1 behind by the time Mitic went on. Yugoslavia lost the match 0–2 (1 July 1950, first round).

Under-17 World Championship *competition* biennial international nations tournament for players under-17 years of age. The finals take place at a host country, with qualification decided by regional competitions run by the various confederations. The first finals took place in **China**, in 1985. Winners (result, runners-up, venue): 1985 **Nigeria** (2–0, v West **Germany**, at Workers Stadium, Beijing, China); 1987 **Soviet Union** (1–1, 3–1 pens., v Nigeria, at Varsity Stadium, Toronto, Canada); 1989 **Saudi Arabia** (2–2, 5–4 pens., v **Scotland**, at **Hampden Park**, Glasgow); 1991 **Ghana** (1–0, v **Spain**, at Comunale, Florence, Italy); 1993 Nigeria (2–1, v Ghana, at National Stadium, Tokyo, Japan); 1995 Ghana (3–2 v **Brazil**, Estadio Modelo, Guayaquil Ecuador); 1997 Brazil (2–1, v Ghana, Nasser International Stadium, Cairo, Egypt).

Underhill Stadium *ground* English football ground situated in Hertfordshire; home of **Barnet**. *Dossier* Ground capacity: 4,057. Pitch dimensions: 102m x 66m. Record League attendance: 5,090 v **Crewe Alexandra** (17 August 1991, Division Four); This was the club's first game in the Football League – a 4-7 defeat. Best average attendance: 3,643 (1991-92). *Keynotes* Barnet played its first match at Underhill Stadium as Barnet Alston on 14 September 1907 (v **Crystal Palace**, London League). It remained largely undeveloped until the 1960s when **floodlights** were installed and two terraces were built. The biggest attendance at Underhill was recorded on 23 February 1952, when 11,026 watched Barnet play **Wycombe Wanderers** in the fourth round of the **FA Amateur Cup**. At the time of Barnet's elevation to the **Football League** Underhill had a capacity of 9,766, but by December 1993 that was down to 3,219 – the lowest in the League. The first floodlit match at Underhill took place on 2 October 1962 (v **Arsenal**, friendly).

undersoil heating *misc.* heating system under the turf which helps to prevent a frozen pitch. *Keynotes* In 1958, **Everton** became the first **Football League club** to install undersoil heating. The **Goodison Park** system, which cost around £16,000, involved 20 miles of electrical wiring under the pitch. **Arsenal** followed Everton's example in 1964 and installed an undersoil heating system at **Highbury**. Undersoil heating was installed at **Oldham Athletic**'s **Boundary Park**

ground in 1980. The ground, over 465 metres above sea level (the third highest in the Football League), was prone to freezing. The heating enabled Oldham to switch its 1981 Boxing Day fixture against **Blackburn Rovers**, which had been scheduled for **Ewood Park**, to Boundary Park – this was the first occasion that the Football League allowed such a change.

ungentlemanly conduct *rules* obsolete name for **unsporting behaviour**.

unintentional *adj.* *rules* of a **handball** which, in the opinion of the referee, was committed without intent (Law XII of the **Laws of the game**). *Keynotes* If a ball is struck so hard that a player is unable to get his or her hand or arm out of the way, then the referee will rule that the handball was unintentional and a **foul** will not have been committed. Mistimed tackles, however, are always ruled as fouls if a player fails to make contact with ball before tripping an opponent, even if they are committed without obvious intent. The Laws governing **tripping an opponent** (Law XII) do not distinguish between unintentional and intentional.

Union Douala (Union Sportif Douala) *club* Cameroon national league club based in Douala. Ground: Reunification, capacity: 50,000. Strip: green shirts, white shorts. **African Cup of Champion Clubs** winners 1979 (1–1 agg., 5–3 pens v **Hearts of Oak** of Ghana); **African Cup-winners Cup** 1981 (2–0 agg., v **Stationery Stores** of Nigeria); Cameroon league champions 1969, 1976, 1978, 1990; Cameroon Cup 1961, 1969, 1980, 1985, 1997.

Union Espanola *club* Chilean national league club based in Santiago, founded 1935. Ground: Estadio Santa Laura, capacity: 28,500. Strip: red shirts, blue shorts. **Copa Libertadores** runners-up 1975 (1–0, 1–3, 0–2 playoff, v **Independiente**); Chilean league champions 1943, 1951, 1973, 1975, 1977; Chilean Cup (**Copa Chile**) winners 1992, 1993.

Union of European Football Associations (UEFA) *confederation* international football association for Europe (though it also includes **Israel** – for political expediency – and **Russia** and **Turkey**, two other countries straddling Europe and Asia). *Dossier* UEFA's headquarters are based in Nyon (a small town between Lausanne and Geneva), **Switzerland**. It was founded in 1954 and affiliated to **FIFA** 1954. President: Lennart Johansson (Sweden). General secretary: Gerhard Aigner (Germany). *Keynotes* UEFA has 51 member countries, including one provisional member. UEFA is allocated 15 automatic berths at the 2002 **World Cup** finals (including **France** as reigning champions). UEFA was allocated 15 of the 32 places at the 1998 World Cup finals (this included the host nation, France). It was allocated six places for the 1999 **Women's World Cup** finals. *Full member countries* **Albania, Andorra, Armenia, Austria, Azerbaijan, Belarus, Belgium, Bulgaria, Croatia, Cyprus, Czech Republic, Denmark, England, Estonia, Faroe Islands, Finland**, France, **Georgia, Germany, Greece, Hungary, Iceland**, Israel, **Italy, Latvia, Liechtenstein, Lithuania, Luxembourg, Macedonia, Malta, Moldova, Netherlands, Northern Ireland, Norway, Poland, Portugal, Republic of Ireland, Romania**, Russia, **San Marino, Scotland, Slovakia, Slovenia, Spain, Sweden**, Switzerland, Turkey, **Ukraine, Wales, Yugoslavia**. *Provisional member* **Bosnia-Herzegovina**. *Competitions (selection)* **European Championship, European Championship for Women, European Under-21 Championship; European Youth Championship** (under-18); **European Cup/Champions League; European Cup-winners Cup; UEFA Cup; European Under-21 Championship; European Youth Championship** (under-18). Website: *http://www.uefa.com* (official site). *History* Considering that football was well established throughout Europe by the end of the 19th century, it is perhaps surprising that a European confederation was founded only in 1954; 38 years after the establishment of the South American confederation, the **Confederación Sudamericana de Fútbol** (CONMEBOL). The absence of a European football confederation delayed the development of continent-wide club and nations tournaments, although regional competitions such as the **Mitropa Cup** for clubs, and the various regional nations tournaments, notably the **Dr Gerö Cup**, the British **Home International Championships**, the **Scandinavian Championship**, the **Balkan Cup** and the **Baltic Championship**, were established many years before. The formation of the confederation quickly led to a number of new European tournaments, including the European Cup (first played 1955-56), the UEFA Cup (first played as the International Inter-Cities Fairs Cup 1955-58), the European Cup-winners Cup (first played 1960-61), and the European Championship (first played as the European Nations Cup 1959-60). There were 34 original members of UEFA; the break-up of the Soviet Union around 1989-91 led to the admission of a number of new independent nations. By 1998 there were 51 member countries. In November 1971, UEFA recommended that all football played in each member country should come under the auspices of a single national association: the recommendation has been adopted by virtually all UEFA members. UEFA instigated a Committee for Women's Football at its Congress in 1972. UEFA now organises a number of international women's tournaments, at senior and youth level (see above).

Union of Football Associations of Central Africa (UFACA) *confederation* international football association of central Africa, based in Yaoundé, founded 1979. *Member countries* **Cameroon, Central African Republic, Chad, Congo, Equatorial Guinea, Gabon**. *Nations tournaments* **UDEAC Tournament** (Tournament of the Union Douaniere et Economique des États de l'Afrique Centrale).

Union of Soviet Socialist Republics (USSR) see **Soviet Union**.

Union Sportive Luxembourg *club* Luxembourg national league club, based in Luxembourg City (the capital city), formed in 1908 (formerly US Hollerich, until 1920). Ground: Achille Hammerel, capacity: 6,000. Strip: white shirts, blue shorts. Luxembourg league champions 1912, 1914, 1915, 1916, 1917, 1927, 1962, 1971, 1990, 1991, 1992, runners-up 10 times (to 1998); Luxembourg Cup 1947, 1959, 1963, 1964, 1969, 1970, 1986, 1989, 1991, 1996, runners-up 11 times (to 1997).

United Arab Emirates *country AFC* confederation of the seven emirates of Abu Dhabi, Ajman, Dubai, Fujairah, Ras al Khaimah, Sharjah and Umm al Qaiwain. Situated on the Arabia Gulf, in Southwest Asia, next to **Oman** and **Saudi Arabia**. Area: 75,150 sq km (29,010 sq miles). Population: 2,400,000 (1996 est.). Languages: Arabic, English. Capital: Abu Dhabi. *Dossier* United Arab Emirates Football Association (Abu Dhabi) formed in 1971, affiliated to **FIFA** in 1972 and **Asian Football Confederation** (AFC) in 1974, member of the **Arab Football Union**, president: Sheikh Bin Zayed Abdulla; general secretary: Ahmed Nasser Al Fardan. Season played from October to May. National stadium: Zayed Sports City, Abu Dhabi, capacity: 60,000. National strip: white shirts, white shorts, white socks. Notable international players: Khalid Mubarak – the first Emirates player to score in a **World Cup** finals match (1–5 v West **Germany**, 15 June 1994, in Milan, Italy, first-round group match) – and Jumaa, the only other Emirates player to have scored in a World Cup finals (1–4 v **Yugoslavia**, 19 June, 1994, in Bologna, Italy, first-round group match). *International tournament record* **Olympic Games** – never qualified for finals tournament; **Women's World Cup** – never entered; **World Cup** – first entered 1986, qualified for finals tournament 1990 (finished last in its four-nation first-round group, losing each of its three matches, scoring two goals and conceding 11); **Arabian Gulf Cup** – never won, hosts 1994; **Asian Cup of Nations** – first entered 1980, runners-up 1996 (0–0, 2–4 pens., v Saudi Arabia, in Abu Dhabi); fourth place 1992 (1–1, 3–4 pens., v **China**, in Hiroshima, Japan), also qualified for finals tournament 1980, 1984, 1988, hosts 1996; **Asian Games** – first entered 1986, quarter-final 1994, second round 1998; **Asian Under-16 Championship** – runners-up 1990 (0–2, v **Qatar**, in United Arab Emirates); **Asian Women's Championship** – never entered; **Under-17 World Championship** – qualified for the 1991 tournament (first-round group stage); **World Youth Cup** (under-20) – never qualified. *World Cup performance* (finals and qualifiers to end of 1998 tournament) played 36, won 17, drawn 10, lost 9, scored 58 goals, conceded 39 goals; win rate 47%; goals scored per game 1.61. *Record against British and Irish national teams* none played. *History* A national league and Cup were founded in 1974. The UAE has around 5,000 registered players. The UAE qualified for the 1990 World Cup finals tournament in **Italy** and was runner-up in the 1996 Asian Cup of Nations. There are two league trophies: the UAE Super League is played at the end of the regular league season and features the top six sides in the First Division.

League system There are 12 clubs in the national league first division. They play each other three times in a season (33 games). Three points are awarded for a win, with one for a draw. The bottom two clubs are relegated automatically. *Record in international club tournaments* **Asian Champion Teams Cup** – Al-Anin (third place 1999), **Al Shabab** (semi-final 1991), **Al Wasl** (semi-final 1992); **Asian Cup-winners Cup** – Al Shaab (runners-up 1995, semi-final 1990); **Arab Club Champions Cup** – **Al Arabi** (runners-up 1993), hosts 1988. Other leading club: **Al Sharjah**, Al Wahda (league champions 1999).

United colours of Football *publication* fanzine produced by the **Football Supporters Association** and supported by the Campaign for Racial Equality (CRE) and **Professional Footballers Association** (PFA) that was given away free to supporters in the first few weeks of the 1994-95 season as part of the continuing campaign – **Let's kick racism out of football** – to eradicate racism from the game. Around 110,000 copies of the fanzine were distributed.

United Kingdom (UK)   see **Great Britain, England, Northern Ireland, Scotland, Wales**

United Soccer Association *competition* **1.** former professional football league of the **United States of America**, founded 1967. Merged the following year with the **National Professional Soccer League** to form the **North American Soccer League**. Each of its 12 teams was a representative side from an overseas club playing for a US city. The only winner was **Los Angeles Wolves** (1967). **2.** former professional football league of the United States of America, founded 1984. Existed for only two seasons; won by Fort Lauderdale Sun (1984 and 1985 – the latter as South Florida Sun).

United States Football Association *confederation* former name of the **United States Soccer Confederation**.

United States of America (USA) *country CONCACAF* country in North America, between **Mexico** and **Canada**, and including Alaska and the Pacific island of Hawaii. It is the most powerful economic and military country in the world, and the fourth biggest by area (after **Russia, Canada** and **China**). Military and nuclear-weapons stand-off (the Cold War) with the former-Soviet Union from 1945-90. Area: 9,363,130 sq km (3,614,170 sq miles). Population: 265,620,000 (1996 est.). Languages: English, Spanish. Capital: Washington, DC. *Dossier* **American Football Association**, founded in 1884, replaced in 1913 by the **United States Soccer Confederation** (Chicago; originally known as the United States Football Association), affiliated to **FIFA** in 1913 and founder member of **Confederación Norte-Centroamericana y del Caribe de Fútbol** (CONCACAF) in 1961, president: Alan Rothenberg; general secretary: Hank Steinbrecher. The United States was an original member of the ephemeral **North American Football Confederation**. Season played from 1

April to September, with the **playoffs** in October. National stadium: **Rose Bowl**, Los Angeles, capacity: 100,092. National strip: white shirts, white shorts, white socks. First international game: 28 November 1885 v Canada (0–1, Newark, US, friendly). Biggest victory: 8–1 v **Cayman Islands** (14 November 1993, Mission Viejo, California, friendly), 7–0 v **El Salvador** (5 December 1993, Los Angeles, friendly). Biggest defeat: 0–10 v **England** (27 May 1964, New York, friendly), 0–10 v **Italy** (4 April 1975, Rome, friendly). Record attendance: 93,000 v **Colombia** (22 June 1994, Pasadena Rose Bowl, Los Angeles, World Cup first-round group match), 93,000 v **Romania** (26 June 1994, Pasadena Rose Bowl, **World Cup** first-round group match). Most capped players: Marcelo **Balboa** (125 appearances, 1988-), Cobi **Jones** (114, 1992-), Paul Caligiuri (110, 1984-98). Leading goalscorers: Eric **Wynalda** (32 goals in 102 appearances, 1990-), Bruce Murray (21 in 93 appearances, 1985-93). Other notable international players: Joe Gaetjens (scored the goal for the USA that beat England, 1–0, in the 1950 World Cup finals in Belo Horizonte, Brazil), Mia **Hamm** (the United States' most-capped woman player). Website: *http://www.us-soccer.com/* (official site). *International tournament record* **Olympic Games** – hosted the third Olympic Games in 1904, with football as a demonstration sport at the games (US representative sides were second and third in the three-team competition), also played at the finals tournament of 1924, 1928, 1936, 1948, 1952, 1956, 1972, 1984 (hosts), 1988, 1992 and 1996 (hosts); World Cup – entered first tournament in 1930, semi-final 1930 (1–6, v **Argentina**, at Centenario Stadium, Montevideo, Uruguay), second round 1994, also qualified for finals tournament 1934, 1950, 1990, 1998, hosts 1994; **CONCACAF** under-17 championship – winners 1983, 1992; CONCACAF youth championship (under-20) – winners 1982; **Gold Cup** – winners 1991 (0–0, 4–3 pens., v **Honduras**, in Los Angeles, USA), runners-up 1993 (0–4 v Mexico, at Azteca Stadium, Mexico City – 120,000 spectators), 1998 (0–1, v Mexico, in Los Angeles), semi-final/third 1996 (3–0, v **Guatemala**, in California); **North American Championship** – runners-up 1949, 1991; **Pan American Games** (under-23) – winners 1991; **South American Championship** – first invited 1993, fourth place 1995 (0–1, v Colombia, in Moldonado, Uruguay, third/fourth playoff); **Under-17 World Championship** – quarter-final 1991, 1993, also qualified for finals tournament 1985, 1987, 1989, 1997; **US Cup** (invitation) – winners 1992, 1995, runners-up 1999; **World Youth Cup** (under-20) – semi-final 1989, quarter-final 1993 (fourth place, 0–2 v **Brazil**, Riyadh, Saudi Arabia), also qualified for finals tournament 1981, 1983, 1987, 1999; **Women's World Cup/Women's Olympic Games/CONCACAF Women's Championship** – see **United States of America, women**. *World Cup performance* (finals and qualifiers to end of 1998 tournament)

played 84, won 30, drawn 19, lost 35, scored 118 goals, conceded 146 goals; win rate: 36%; goals scored per game: 1.40. *Record against British and Irish national teams* v England played seven, won two, lost five; v **Scotland** played four, won one, drawn one, lost two; v **Northern Ireland** none played; v **Wales** none played; v **Republic of Ireland** played five, won two, drawn one, lost two. *History* American Indians are said to have played a rudimentary game of football known as Pasuckquakkohowog – first observed, according to folklore, by the Pilgrim Fathers in 1620 in Massachusetts. European settlers are believed to have played a form of football in Virginia from 1609. US colleges played European football from around 1820, with an annual game started at Harvard College in 1827. Princeton College played its own version of football, "ballown", with Yale College playing a game called "rough-house" football. The first US club, Oneidas, was founded in Boston in 1862. It was the first club in the world outside England. Oneidas had 17 founder members, all born in England or of English parents, and played its games on Boston Common. Just as in England, interest polarised into clubs wishing to play either the dribbling or the handling codes of football; **American Football** (the US handling code) was established in US colleges around 1876. Princetown and Rutgers Universities played the first intercollegiate match on 6 November 1876 in New Brunswick (Rutgers won 6–4). Interest in association football grew in the late 1870s as many British immigrants arrived to work in US industries. The American Football Association (AFA) was formed in 1884. The first national domestic cup, the **American Cup**, was played in 1884 under the auspices of the AFA; first won by Kearny O N T (1–0, v New York). It was gradually overshadowed by the **US Open Challenge Cup** – first played in 1914 – organised by the new national confederation, the United States Football Association. The **US Amateur Cup** started in 1924. The first US league, the **American League of Professional Football**, was founded 1894 but folded after one season. A new national league, the **National Association Football League**, was founded in 1906 and lasted until 1922. It was replaced by the **American Soccer League (1.)** – 1921-33; followed by the **American Soccer League (2.)** – 1933–83. The **United Soccer Association** and the **National Professional Soccer League** were independently founded 1967, and merged in 1968 to form the **North American Soccer League** – folded 1984. The **United Soccer League** lasted from 1984 to 1985, followed by the **Western Soccer League** (WSL) from 1985 to 1989; and the American Soccer League (ASL) **(3.)** 1988-89. A new professional **A-League** was founded in 1990 after the merger of ASL and WSL. The **United Systems of Independent Soccer Leagues** (USISL) was founded in 1986, with the USISL **Pro League** and **Premier League** started in 1995. The USISL **Select League** started in 1996. In

1996, the **Major League Soccer** was founded (the official first division of US soccer). In 1997, the Select League and old A-League merged to form a new A-League, becoming the official US "second division": the Pro and Premier Leagues becoming the third and fourth divisions, respectively. The United States' first international game was against Canada in 1885 (above), with the fixture repeated annually. The United States has entered every World Cup since the first in 1930, and has played in six finals tournaments (it has qualified four times: there was no qualifying tournament in 1930, and it qualified automatically as hosts in 1994). Its best performance was in reaching the semifinal in 1930: its defeat by Argentina at Centenario Stadium in Montevideo was watched by 80,000 spectators. The US hosted the 1994 tournament – a huge operation that even included the growing of natural turf in vast glasshouses for temporary laying in some of the stadiums which, normally, have synthetic surfaces for American football matches. The US qualified from the first-round group stage, despite finishing only in third place in its four-nation group, and was beaten by Brazil in the second round (0–1, Stanford Stadium, San Francisco). In preparation for the 1994 World Cup, a specially groomed US national team played 52 international games between 30 January 1993 and 4 June 1994 (an average of one game every 9.5 days), and 44 of these were friendlies. The US national team – without its European-based players – trained together at its base in **Mission Viejo**, near Los Angeles. The preparation was somewhat disrupted, however, when the overseas-based players rejoined the squad just prior to the World Cup, seven or eight immediately gaining first-choice status. Although USA qualified for the 1998 World Cup finals tournament in France, it finished bottom of its group of four nations with no points. The final group match was against **Iran** (1–2, 21 June 1998, in Lyon), a match preceded by magnanimous diplomacy both on and off the pitch. Before the game US president Bill Clinton announced on television: "The World Cup is beloved across our planet because it offers a chance for people to be judged not by where they grew up, the colour of their skin, or the way they choose to worship, but by their spirit, skill and strength. May today's game between American and Iranian athletes be another step toward ending the estrangement between our nations." USA has an excellent record in the CONCACAF Gold Cup, winning the first competition in 1991, with the final staged at Los Angeles Coliseum. It has been runners-up twice: its defeat by Mexico in 1993, at Azteca Stadium, Mexico City, was watched by 120,000 spectators. USA has been invited by the **Confederación Sudamericana de Fútbol** to take part in the South American Championship (the **Copa America**) since 1993, and was fourth in 1995. The United States competed in football tournaments of the Olympic Games even before football was an official Olympic event. When USA hosted the third Olympic Games in 1904, football

was included as a demonstration sport. There were only three teams in the football competition, two representing the United States. Christian Brothers and St Rose, both of St Louis, finished second and third, respectively, behind Galt FC of Canada. The US Olympic team has, however, been noted as much by the margin of its defeats as by any success at the Games: in 1928 it lost 2–11 to Argentina in the first round; in 1948 it lost 0–9 to Italy in the first round; in 1952 it was beaten 0–8 by Italy in the preliminary round; in 1956 it lost 1–9 to **Yugoslavia** in the first round; and in 1972 it was beaten 0–7 by West **Germany** in one of its first-round group matches. By contrast, the American women's team has consistently been among the top three or four nations in the world, with an impressive goals tally and defensive record. The United States won the gold medal at the first Women's Olympic Games football tournament in 1996; its final victory over China, in Athens, Georgia, USA, was watched by 76,481 spectators. USA also won the first Women's World Cup, held in China in 1991. In the CONCACAF women's qualifying tournament, the US team had won two of its first-round matches 12–0 (v Mexico and v **Martinique**), drew the third 0-0 with **Trinidad and Tobago**, won its second-round match 10–0 against **Haiti**, and beat Canada 5–0 in the final match: a qualifying-tournament total of 49 goals for, none against. At the finals tournament in China, the 2–1 victory over Norway in the final was watched by 65,000 spectators at Tianhe Stadium, Guangzhou. In total, the team scored 64 goals and conceded five, in its five qualifying and six finals-tournament games. The US was third in 1995 and is hosts for the 1999 finals. US Soccer claimed that the 1999 Women's World Cup would be "biggest and most successful women's sporting event ever". The United States hosts two annual international invitation tournaments: the **US Cup** (men), first played 1992, and the **US Women's Cup**, first played 1994. *League system* see: **Major League Soccer**, **United Systems of Independent Soccer Leagues**, **Pro League**, **Premier League** and **Select League**. *Record in international club tournaments* **CONCACAF Champions Cup** – **DC United** (winners 1998, semifinal 1997), (runners-up 1997), Rochester Lancers (fourth 1971), Seattle Sounders (fourth 1996); **Copa Inter Americana** – DC United (winners 1998). Other leading clubs: **Chicago Fire**, **Colorado Rapids**, **Dallas Burn**, **Kansas City Wiz**, **Los Angeles Galaxy**, **San Jose Clash**, **Columbus Crew**, **DC United**, **Metrostars**, **Miami Fusion**, **New England Revolution**, **Tampa Bay Mutiny**.

United States of America, women   *country/women* women's football in the USA comes under the auspices of the national association, US Soccer, based in Chicago. Association football is one of the most popular participative sports for women in the country, with an estimated 9,000,000 players at senior and youth level. *History* Intercollegiate matches date back to the 1950s, with women's football particularly strong in the northern states. The first United States national women's championship took place in 1980. By 1991, it was estimated that 39% of all football players in the United States were women. The American women's team has been consistently among the top three or four nations in the world, with an impressive goal tally and defensive record. The United States won the gold medal at the first Women's **Olympic Games** football tournament in 1996; the final victory over **China**, in Athens, Georgia, USA, was watched by 76,481 spectators, the world record crowd for a women's sporting event. USA also won the first **Women's World Cup**, held in China in 1991. In the CONCACAF women's qualifying tournament (the **CONCACAF Women's Championship**), the US team had won two of its first-round matches 12–0 (v **Mexico** and v **Martinique**), drew the third 0–0 with **Trinidad and Tobago**, won its second-round match 10–0 against **Haiti**, and beat **Canada** 5–0 in the final match: a qualifying-tournament total of 49 goals, for, and none against. At the finals tournament in China, the United States' 2–1 victory over **Norway** in the final was watched by 65,000 spectators at Tianhe Stadium, Guangzhou. In total, the team scored 64 goals, and conceded only five, in its five qualifying- and six finals-tournament games. The US was third in the 1995 World Cup – this time scoring 36 goals, with one conceded in its four qualifying games – and hosts the 1999 finals. US Soccer claimed that the 1999 Women's World Cup would be the "biggest and most successful women's sporting event ever". The United States is undefeated in the four-nation **US Women's Cup**, the annual international invitation tournament first played in 1994. It won all its 12 matches in the four editions from 1994 to 1997. The most celebrated US international, Mia **Hamm** had played 145 times for the national side by 1998 and is the country's record goalscorer scoring her 100th international goal in September 1998 (4–1, v Russia). She is one of seven US players to have more than 100 caps for the national side. *Dossier* First international match: 1985, v Italy (0–1, in **Italy**). Most capped player: Mia Hamm (145 appearances). *League system* There are many youth and college leagues run by several different governing bodies. The top level of women's association football in the USA is the collegiate leagues, also run by two independent associations: the National Collegiate Athletic Association (NCAA) and the National Association of Intercollegiate Athletics. The NCAA runs three division; scholarships can be offered by colleges in the top two divisions. The 1998 US women's squad was entirely composed of college players. *International tournament record* Women's World Cup – winners of first tournament in 1991 (2–1 v **Norway**, at Tianhe Stadium, Guangzhou, China), third place 1995 (2–0 v China, in Sweden, third/fourth play-off; 0–1, v Norway, semi-final), hosts 1999; **Algarve Cup** – runners-up 1999, semi-final/third 1998; CONCACAF Women's Championship – winners 1991 (5–0, v Canada); 1994 (league of five nations); 1998 did not enter (because it qualified automatically for the 1999 Women's World Cup as the host nation); Goodwill Games women's football tournament – winners 1998, (2–0, v China, in New York, USA); US Women's Cup (international invitation tournament) – winners 1994, 1995, 1996, 1997, 1998; Women's Olympic Games football tournament – winners/gold medal of first tournament in 1996 (2–1, v China, in Athens, Georgia state, USA).

United States Soccer Confederation *confederation* football confederation of the **United States of America**, based in Chicago. Formed in 1913 (as United States Football Association) from the American Amateur Football Association. Affiliated to **FIFA** in 1913, founded the **US Open Challenge Cup**, first played 1914.

United Systems of Independent Soccer Leagues *competition* multi-divisional league system developed in the United States to provide a nationwide football structure, founded 1986 as the Southwest Indoor Soccer League (became the Southwest Independent Soccer League in 1990, the Sunbelt Independent Soccer League in 1992, the United States Interregional Soccer League in 1992, with the current name adopted in 1994). An outdoor league started in 1989 (first winners – Colorado Comets). A **Pro League** and **Premier League** were introduced in 1995, with the top **Select League** added in 1996. The component leagues exist beneath the **Major League Soccer** (officially, the United States "first division"). The top division in the USISL's structure is the **A-League** (formed in 1997 from the USISL's former Select League and the formerly independent A-League). The A-League – now officially the US's second division – has 26 teams. Beneath the A-League are the Pro-League (officially the United States' third division) and Premier League (an amateur league – the "fourth division"). (Ironically, the term "Premier League" is used to describe the fourth division in American soccer – contrasting the use of the term to describe the top division in English and Scottish football.) Each of the USISL's leagues is divided into regional "conferences" each with its own regional divisions. There is a system of qualified promotions, whereby a club that wins its league can be promoted to the higher league if it meets certain standards, such as stadium quality. However, the ceiling to this is the A-League; there are no promotions to Major League Soccer.

Universidad Autonoma de Guadalajara "Los Tecos" *club* Mexican national league club, based in Guadalajara and founded in 1971. Ground: Estadio Trez de Marzo, capacity: 30,000. Strip: white shirts with an owl motif on the chest, white shorts. **CONCACAF Cup-winners Cup** 1995 (2–1, v **Luis Angel Firpo**, of El Salvador); Mexican League champions 1994.

Universidad Autonoma de Nuevo León (Club Deportivo) *club* Mexican national league club, based in Monterrey and founded in 1967. Known as "Los Tigres". Ground: Estadio Universitaria, capacity: 43,000.

Strip: gold shirts with a blue hoop and gold shorts. Mexican League Champions 1978 and 1982; Mexican Cup (Copa Mexico) winners 1976 and 1992.

Universidad Catolica *club* Chilean national league club based in the capital Santiago, founded 1935. Ground: Estadio San Carlos de Apoquindo, capacity: 20,000. Strip: white shirts with single blue hoop, blue shorts. **Copa Libertadores** runners-up 1993 (3–5 agg., v **São Paulo**), semi-final 1962, 1969; **Copa Inter Americana** winners 1994; Chilean League champions 1949, 1954, 1961, 1966, 1997 (apertura tournament); Chilean Cup (**Copa Chile**) winners 1983, 1991.

Universidad de Chile *club* Chilean national league club based in the capital Santiago, founded 1928. Ground: Estadio Nacional, capacity: 80,000. Strip: blue shirts with a red "U" over the heart, blue shorts. Universidad de Chile qualified for the first **Copa Libertadores** in 1960. Copa Libertadores semi-final 1970, 1996; **Copa CONMEBOL** semi-final 1994; Chilean League champions 1940, 1959, 1962, 1964, 1965, 1967, 1969, 1994, 1995; Chilean Cup (**Copa Chile**) winners 1979, 1998.

Universidad de los Andes (ULA Mérida) *club* former name, until 1996, of Venezuelan club **Atlético Zulia**.

Universidad Nacional Autonoma de Honduras (UNAH) *club* Honduran national league club based in the capital Tegucigalpa. **CONCACAF Champions Cup** runners-up 1980 (three-club final tournament in Tegucigalpa, behind **UNAM** of **Mexico**).

Universitario (Club Universitario de Deportes) *club* Peruvian national League club based in the capital Lima, founded in 1924. Ground: Estadio Teodoro "Lolo" Fernandez, capacity: 12,000. Strip: cream shirts, cream shorts. **Copa Libertadores** runners-up 1972 (0–0, 1–2, v **Independiente** of **Argentina**), semi-final 1967, 1971, 1975; **Copa CONMEBOL** semi-final 1997; Peru League champions 1929, 1934, 1939, 1941, 1945, 1946, 1949, 1959, 1960, 1964, 1966, 1967, 1969, 1971, 1974, 1982, 1987, 1990, 1992, 1993, 1998.

Universitatea Craiova *club* Romanian national league club based in Craiova, founded in 1948. Known as Stiinta Craiova from 1950 to 1966. Ground: Stadionul Central, capacity: 35,000. Strip: blue and white striped shirts, white shorts. The only club, in the 1980s and 1990s, to have broken the league championship domination by the Romanian "big two", **Steaua Bucharest** and **Dinamo Bucharest**. **UEFA Cup** – semi-final 1983; Romanian League champions 1974, 1980, 1981, 1991; Romanian Cup 1977, 1978, 1981, 1983, 1991, 1993, 1994.

Universitate Riga *club* Latvian national league club based in the capital Riga (formerly RAF Jelgava), founded 1988. Ground: LU, capacity: 6,000. Latvian regional league champions 1988, 1989 (as RAF Jelgava); Latvian regional cup winners 1988; Latvian Cup 1993, 1996.

University College Dublin FC (UCD) *club* Republic of Ireland national league club based in the capital Dublin, founded 1895. Ground: Belfield, capacity: 10,000. Strip: sky blue shirts, white shorts. Republic of Ireland **FAI Cup** 1984.

unsporting behaviour *rules* one of the listed infringements of the **Laws of the game**, punishable by a **caution** and, if the game is stopped specifically for that offence, by an **indirect free kick** (Law XII). Unsporting behaviour includes obstructing an opponent without bodily contact (ie by a tactic designed to delay an opposing player or make him or her change course - for example, by stepping from side to side or moving the arms up and down to prevent the opponent from going forward); deliberately distracting an opponent at, or impeding a player from taking, a **free-kick** or **throw-in**; and trying to trick the referee over the rule governing a **pass to the goalkeeper**. It is also unsporting behaviour to pretend to be fouled (see **dive**, sense **2.**) or to undertake "any simulating behaviour intended to deceive the referee". A goalkeeper can be guilty of unsporting behaviour for lying on the ball longer than necessary in order to waste time. A player may be guilty of unsporting behaviour on or off the field of play, irrespective of whether the conduct is aimed at an opposing player, a team-mate, a match official or any other person. A player who illegally handles the ball in an attempt to stop a goal is guilty of unsporting behaviour if the ball still goes in the net and a goal is scored. This is a lesser offence than **serious foul play** where an obvious opportunity to score a goal is prevented by a player handling the ball illegally.

Upton Park *ground* English football ground situated in east London; home of **West Ham United**. *Dossier* Ground capacity: 26,012 all seated. Pitch dimensions: 102m x 66m. Record attendance: 42,322 v **Tottenham Hotspur** (17 October 1970, Divsion One). Best average attendance: 31,125 (1968-69). *History* West Ham moved to Upton Park in 1904 after playing at grounds in Canning Town and East Ham, and at the Memorial Recreation Ground in Plaistow. The ground is officially called Boleyn Ground, derived from a house known as Boleyn Castle (named after Henry VIII's second wife, Anne Boleyn) which until the 1950s was situated next to the ground – West Ham had also merged with Boleyn Castle FC in 1904. West Ham played its first match at Upton Park on 2 September 1904 (v **Millwall**, Southern League). West Ham's success in 1923 (promotion to Division One and an **FA Cup** final appearance) enabled the club to construct a double-decker stand which opened in 1925. On 18 April 1936, a crowd of 43,528 watched West Ham play London rivals **Charlton Athletic** (Division Two). Had the figure been verified before the club's offices were destroyed by bombing during **World War II** it would have been the ground's record attendance. The ground's proximity to the Royal Victoria and the Royal Albert docks at Silvertown and the industrial areas of Stratford meant that the ground suffered regular bomb damage during the war, including being hit by a V1 flying bomb in 1944. As in the 1920s, West Ham's success on the pitch in the 1960s ushered in a period of redevelopment at Upton Park, which included the construction of a new east stand. In order to raise the estimated £13 million necessary to fulfil the **Taylor Report**'s recommendations, the club launched a bond scheme (see **debentures**) which would give those purchasing one the right to buy a **season ticket**. Although a survey of supporters indicated that 70% were interested in a bond, fewer than 5% of fans actually bought one. The scheme was met with match boycotts and pitch protests, and average gates in 1992-93 were 25% down on the previous season, despite the club winning promotion back to the **Premier League** at the first attempt. West Ham increased its borrowings and reduced season ticket prices to ameliorate the fans' protests. In February 1994, the new north stand, or **Bobby Moore** stand as it was named, opened at a cost of £5.5 million, while at the opposite end of the ground the Centenary Stand was completed exactly one year later. Upton Park staged its first floodlit match on 16 April 1953 (v Tottenham Hotspur, friendly). The ground was the venue for five **FA Amateur Cup** Finals (1930, 1932, 1934, 1936 replay, 1937).

Upton Park Cup *competition* annual match between the champion clubs of **Jersey** and **Guernsey** to decide the champions of the **Channel Islands**. The venue alternates between the two islands. First played 1907, in Guernsey, and won by Northerners AC St Sampsons (of Guernsey).

Urawa Red Diamonds *club* Japanese **J-League** club based in Urawa, formerly Mitsubishi Motors FC (1951-1992). Ground: Urawa Komaba Stadium, capacity: 21,500. Strip: red shirts and white shorts. Japanese National League champions 1969, 1973, 1978, 1982; Emperor's Cup 1972, 1974, 1979, 1981; Japanese League Cup 1978.

Uruguay *country* CONMEBOL republic in South America, on the Atlantic Coast, south of **Brazil**, and to the east of **Argentina**. Independence from Brazil 1930. Military government from 1976 to 1984, democratic elections 1986. Area: 186,925 sq km (72,155 sq miles). Population: 3,200,000 (1996 est.). Languages: Spanish. Capital: Montevideo. *Dossier* Football association (Asociación Uruguaya de Fútbol, Montevideo) formed in 1900 affiliated to **FIFA** in 1923 and **Confederación Sudamericana de Fútbol** (CONMEBOL) in 1916, president: Eugenio Figueredo Aguerre; general secretary: Dr Victor Della Valle. Season played from February to December. National stadium: Estadio **Centenario**, Montevideo, capacity: 80,000. National strip: sky blue shirts with white collars and cuffs, black shorts, black socks with sky blue borders. First international game: 16 May 1901 v Argentina (2–3, Montevideo, friendly). Biggest victory: 9–0 v **Bolivia** (6 November 1927, Lima, South American Championship). Biggest defeat: 0–6 v Argentina (20 July 1902, Montevideo, friendly). Record attendance: 93,000 v **Yugoslavia** (27 July 1930, 6–1, Estadio Centenario, Montevideo, **World Cup** semi-final); 93,000 v Argentina (30 July 1930, 4–2, Centenario Stadium, Montevideo, World Cup final). Most capped

players: Rodolfo **Rodriguez** (78 appearances, 1976-86), Angel **Romano** (69 appearances, 1911-27), Enzo **Francescoli** (65 appearances, 1983-). Leading goalscorers: Hector **Scarone** (29 goals, 1917-30), Angel Romano (28 goals, 1911-27.) Other notable international players: Hugo de León, Daniel Fonseca, Atilio **Garcia**, Ladislao **Mazurkiewicz**, Ruben **Paz**, Juan **Schiaffino**, Ruben Sosa. *International tournament record* **Olympic Games** – first entered 1924, winners/gold medal 1924 (3–0 v **Switzerland**, in Paris, **France**), 1928 (1–1, 2–1 replay, v Argentina, in Amsterdam, **Netherlands** – the only time in Olympic history that the final has been decided by a replay); **Women's World Cup** – first entered 1999; World Cup – hosted and won first tournament,1930 (4–2, v Argentina, at Centenario Stadium, Montevideo), 1950 (first of four-nation final group tournament in Brazil: 2–2 v **Spain**, 3–2 v **Sweden**, 2–1 v Brazil), fourth 1954 (1–3 v **Austria**, in Zurich, Switzerland, third/fourth playoff), 1970 (0–1 v West **Germany**, at Azteca Stadium, Mexico City, Mexico, third/fourth playoff), quarter-final 1966, second round 1986, 1990, also qualified for finals tournament 1962, 1974; **Atlantic Cup** – third 1956, 1960, fourth 1976; **Confederations Cup** (Intercontinental Championship) – fourth 1998 (0–1, v **Czech Republic**, in Riyadh, Saudi Arabia, third/fourth playoff); **Copa America** – entered first tournament in 1910, winners 14 times; 1916 (first in four-nation group, Buenos Aires, Argentina), 1917 (first in four-nation group, Montevideo), 1920 (first in four-nation group, Viña del Mar, **Chile**), 1923 (first in four-nation group, Montevideo), 1924 (first in four-nation group, Montevideo), 1926 (first in five-nation group, Santiago, Chile), 1935 (first in four-nation group, Lima, **Peru**), 1942 (first in seven-nation group, Montevideo), 1956 (first in six-nation group, Montevideo), 1959 (first in five-nation group, Guayaquil, **Ecuador**), 1967 (first in six-nation group, Montevideo), 1983 (3–1 agg., v Brazil), 1987 (1–0 v Chile, Buenos Aires, Argentina), 1995 (1–1, 5–3 pens., v Brazil, in Montevideo), runners-up 1910 (only three nations in tournament), 1919, 1927, 1939, 1941, 1989; **Lipton Cup** (v Argentina) – winners 1910, 1911, 1912, 1919, 1922, 1927, 1968 (Argentina won the cup nine times, with the fixture drawn on 11 occasions); **Newton Cup** (also v Argentina) – winners 1913, 1915, 1917, 1919, 1920, 1924, 1929 (the cup was won 15 times by Argentina, with six drawn matches); **Pan-American Championships** – entered only once, in 1952 (third of six nations); **Pan American Games** – winners 1983; **Rio Branco Cup** (v Brazil) – winners 1940, 1946, 1948 (Brazil won the cup four times, with one tied game); **South American Youth Cup** (under-20) – winners 1954, 1958, 1964, 1975, 1977, 1979, 1981; **Under-17 World Championship** – never qualified; **World Youth Cup** (under-20) – qualified for first finals tournament 1977, runners-up 1997 (1–2, v Argentina, in Kuala Lumpur, Malaysia), third 1979 (1–1, 5–3 pens., v **Poland**, in Japan, third/fourth playoff), fourth 1977 (0–4 v Brazil, in Tunisia, third/fourth playoff), 1999 (0–1 v **Mali**, third/fourth playoff), in Nigeria, quarter-final 1981,

1983, 1993, also qualified 1999. *World Cup performance* (finals and qualifiers to end of 1998 tournament) played 95, won 45, drawn 21, lost 29, scored 141 goals, conceded 106 goals; win rate 47%; goals scored per game 1.48. *Record against British and Irish national teams* v **England**, played nine, won four, drawn three, lost two; v **Northern Ireland**, played two, won none, drawn none, lost two; v **Scotland**, played four, won two, drawn one, lost one; v **Wales**, played one, won none, drawn one, lost one; v **Republic of Ireland**, played two, won one, drawn one, lost two. *History* Football was introduced to Uruguay in the 19th century, with matches between resident Britons and British sailors in Montevideo recorded in 1878. The first club, Albion Football Club, was founded in Montevideo in 1886, by an Englishman, William Poole, a professor at the city's university. The country's most successful club, **Peñarol**, was founded in 1891 as the Central Uruguyan Railway Cricket Club. The other half of Uruguay's "big two", **Nacional**, was founded in 1899 and was the first club organised by native Uruguayans. An amateur league was started in 1900, with just four clubs in the inaugural championship: Albion FC, Central Uruguyan Railway Cricket Club (Peñarol), Uruguay Athletic Club and Deutscher Fussaball Klub. The title was won by the Central Uruguyan Railway Cricket Club. A professional league started in 1932 (again, first won by Peñarol). By 1997, Peñarol and Nacional had won the championship 80 times between them. Only **Wanderers** (four titles), the former River Plate club (not the modern club of the same name), **Defensor** (three), and five other one-time winners have taken the title away from the big two. Most of Uruguay's leading clubs are in Montevideo. Peñarol won the first two **Copa Libertadores**, in 1960 and 1961, and won the title again in 1966 and 1982. Nacional won the trophy in 1971 and 1980. Peñarol played in the first **World Club Cup** in 1960 but, having drawn the home leg 0–0, the club lost the away leg against **Real Madrid**, 1–5. Peñarol won the tournament three times, in 1961, 1966 and 1982; the latter against **Aston Villa** (2–0, in Tokyo). Nacional has also won the World Club Cup three times, in 1971, 1980 – 1–0, v **Nottingham Forest** (in Tokyo, Japan) – and 1988. Uruguay played its first international match in 1901 and played in the first South American Championship in 1910. In 1930 it hosted the first World Cup. Uruguay, in its national centenary year, won the first title, adding to its Olympic Gold medals of 1924 and 1928. Thirteen countries competed in the event, staged at three grounds in Montevideo: Pocitos, Central Park and Centenario. The first game, on 13 July, was played at Pocitos: 1,000 people watched **France** beat Mexico (4–1). Uruguay did not enter the World Cup in 1934 or 1938, but won the tournament in its second participation in 1950. The final match at **Maracana**, Rio de Janeiro, was played in front of the highest-ever crowd for a football match; the attendance recorded at 199,000 (although there has been some debate about the actual tally). Uruguay beat Brazil 2-1. It was, in fact, the last game in the final league of four nations (the only World Cup tournament where a true final

was not played). *World Cup final teams and scorers* 1930 (winners) Ballesteros (goalkeeper), Nasazzi, Mascheroni, JL Andrade, Fernandez, Gestido, Dorado (1), Scarone, Castro (1), Cea (1), Iriarte (1); 1950 (winners) Máspoli (goalkeeper), Gonzáles, Tejera, Gambetta, Varela, VR Andrade, Ghiggia (1), Peréz, Miguez, Schiaffino (1), Morán. *League system* The Uruguay league has three top divisions: Primera A (with 12 clubs), B and C, played in two halves of 11 games each: the **apertura** and **clausura**. Three points are awarded for a victory, with one for a draw: If necessary, the championship – "Copa Uruguaya" – is decided by a **playoff** of the top teams from the apertura and clausura league tables (there may be no need, if one team wins both league halves). There is a regional "Interior" league system run by the **Organizacion del Futbol del Interior**. There is no "cup" competition but, since 1974, eight clubs have competed in the **Pre-Libertadores Liguilla** – a complicated tournament that decides which two teams qualify for the Copa Libertadores, giving a chance of qualification to clubs from both the Primera and Interior leagues. *Record in international club tournaments* World Club Cup – Peñarol (winners 1961, 1966, 1982, runners-up 1960, 1987); **Nacional** (winners 1971, 1981, 1988); **Copa Inter America** – Nacional (winners 1972, 1989, runners-up 1981; Copa Libertadores – Peñarol (winners 1960, 1961, 1966, 1982, 1987, runners-up 1962, 1965, 1970, 1983), Nacional (winners 1971, 1980, 1988, runners-up 1964, 1967, 1969); **Supercopa** – Nacional (runners-up 1990); **Copa CONMEBOL** – Peñarol (runners-up 1993, 1994). Other leading clubs: **Danubio**, **Defensor-Sporting Club**, **Liverpool FC**, **Wanderers**, **River Plate**, **Bella Vista**.

US Amateur Cup *competition* United States club knockout competition, inaugurated 1924, open to amateur clubs. First won, in 1924, by Fleisher Yarn of Pennsylvania (3–0 v Swedish American of Michigan).

US Cup *competition* annual international invitation tournament organised by US Soccer, the national association of the **United States of America** (USA), first played 1992. The tournament involves four nations, including perennial hosts USA. It is played on a league basis, at various venues, over a week or two weeks in June. The first tournament was won by USA, ahead of **Italy**, **Ireland** and **Portugal**. Other nations which have competed are: **Bolivia**, **Brazil**, **Colombia**, **Denmark**, **England**, **Germany**, **Guatemala**, **Mexico**, **Nigeria** and **Peru**. *Winners:* 1992 USA; 1993 Germany; 1995 USA; 1996 Mexico; 1997 Mexico; 1998 not played; 1999 Mexico.

US Goreé (Union Sportive) *club* Senegalese national league club, based in Dakar. Ground: Demba Diop, capacity: 30,000. Strip: white shirts, blue shorts. **African Cup of Champion Clubs** semi-final 1979, 1985; Senegal League champions 1978, 1981, 1984; Senegal Cup 1965, 1972, 1992.

US Mbila Nzambi *club* Gabon national league club based in Libreville. Ground: Parc des Princes, capacity: 35,000. Strip: red shirts, white shorts. **African Cup of**

Champion Clubs quarter-final 1981; Gabon League champions 1980, 1981; Gabon Cup 1987, 1991.

US Open Challenge Cup *competition* United States club knockout competition, inaugurated 1914. First won by Brooklyn Field Club of New York (2–1 v Brooklyn Celtic, also of New York). The tournament overshadowed the former **American Cup** (first played in 1885). *Winners (since 1980)* 1980 New York Pancyprian Freedoms; 1981 Los Angeles Maccabee; 1982 New York Pancyprian Freedoms; 1983 New York Pancyprian Freedoms; 1984 New York A O Krete; 1985 San Francisco Greek-American; 1986 St Louis Kutis; 1987 Washington Club Espana; 1988 St Louis Busch Seniors; 1989 St Petersburg Kickers; 1990 Chicago Eagles; 1991 Brooklyn Italians; 1992 San Jose Oaks; 1993 CD Mexico; 1994 Greek-Americans; 1995 Richmond Kickers; 1996 **DC United**; 1997 **Dallas Burn**; 1998 **Chicago Fire**.

US Robert *club* Martinique national league club. **CONCACAF Champions Cup** semi-final/fourth 1994 (0–0, 2–4 pens., v **Alianza** of **Mexico**, third/fourth playoff).

US Virgin Islands *country associate member of CONCACAF* part of the Virgin Islands, a group of around 100 small islands, in the Leeward Islands of the West Indies. The US Virgin islands are an unincorporated territory of the **United States of America** and comprise St Croix, St John, St Thomas and a further 50 or so islets. Area: 345 sq km (133 sq miles). Population: 102,000. Languages: English. Capital: Charlotte Amalie (on St Thomas). *Dossier* Football association, not affiliated to **FIFA**, but is an associate member of the **Confederación Norte-Centroamericana y del Caribe de Fútbol** (CONCACAF). *International tournament record* Olympic Games – never entered; **Women's World Cup** – never entered; World Cup – never entered; **Caribbean Nations Cup** – never entered; **Gold Cup** – never entered. *Record against British and Irish national teams* none played. *League system* Two separate leagues operate in St Croix and in St Thomas/St John. Leading clubs: St John United/of Cruz Bay) and Hell-o-Nights (of Groveplace).

US Women's Cup *competition* annual international women's invitation tournament, formerly known as the Chiquita Cup, first played 1994. The four-nation tournament is run by US Soccer, the United States' national football association, and is played in various stadiums in Eastern USA on a league basis, over seven to nine days in May, June, July or August. The first edition featured **USA**, **Germany**, **China** and **Norway**; in 1995 USA, Norway, **Australia** and **Taiwan** (Chinese Taipei); in 1996 USA, **Canada**, China and **Japan**; 1997 USA, Australia, Canada, **Italy**. Winners 1994 USA; 1995 USA; 1996 USA; 1997 USA.

USA *country* see **United States of America**.

USM Algiers (Union Sportive de la Medina d'Algiers) *club* Algerian national League club, based in the capital El Djezaïr (Algiers), formerly known as USK Algiers. Ground: Bologhine, capacity: 30,000. Strip: red shirts,

black shorts. *Keynotes* USM lost a world-record five consecutive domestic cup finals (1969 to 1973). **African Cup of Champion Clubs** quarter-final "champions league" stage 1997; **African Cup-winners Cup** quarter-final 1998; Algerian League champions 1963, 1996 (having been promoted the previous season); Algerian Cup 1996, 1997.

USS Tamponnaise (Union Sportive Stade) *club* Réunion national league club based in Le Tampon, founded in 1982. Ground: Roland Garros, capacity: 1,500. Strip: blue shirts, blue shorts. **African Cup-winners Cup** quarter-final 1994; **CAF Cup** quarter-final 1996; Réunion League champions 1991, 1992; Coupe de la Réunion winners 1991, 1993.

UTA Arad *club* Romanian national league club based in Arad, founded in 1943 (formerly known as IT Arad and Flamura Rosie). Ground: UTA, capacity: 15,000. Strip: red shirts, red shorts. Romanian League champions 1947, 1948, 1950, 1954, 1969, 1970; Romanian Cup 1948, 1953.

utility player *n.* player who can operate in a number of positions.

Uzbekistan *country AFC* republic in North Asia, next to **Afghanistan**, **Kazakhstan**, **Kyrgyzstan**, **Tajikistan** and **Turkmenistan**. In 1921, became part of the Turkestan Soviet Socialist Autonomous Republic, with Tajikistan and Turkmenistan, and fully integrated with the **Soviet Union** in 1925. Independence from Soviet Union in 1991; former member of the ephemeral **Commonwealth of Independent States**. Area: 447,400 sq km (172,695 sq miles). Population: 22,200,000 (1994 census). Languages: Uzbek, Russian, Turkish. Capital: Tashkent. *Dossier* Uzbekistan Football Confederation (Tashkent) formed in 1946 affiliated to **FIFA** and **Asian Football Confederation** (AFC) in 1994, president: Zakirjon Almatov; general secretary: Zakirdjon Kurbanov. Season played from March to November. National stadium: Pachtakor, Tashkent, capacity: 54,000. National strip: blue shirts, white shorts, green socks. Most capped players: Andrey Fedorov (30 appearances to 1999), Sergey Lebedev (29 appearances to 1999), Igor Shkvyrin (28 appearances to 1999). Leading goalscorer: Igor Shkvyrin (20 goals). *International tournament record* Olympic Games – never qualified for finals tournament; **Women's World Cup** – first entered 1999 (third in its qualifying group of four nations); **World Cup** – first entered 1998 (second round of qualifying tournament; first in its four-nation first-round group, with five wins and one draw); **Afro-Asian Nations Cup** – runners-up 1995 (3–5 agg., v **Nigeria**; **Asian Cup of Nations** – first entered 1996, finals tournament first round; **Asian Games** – first entered 1994, winners/gold medal 1994 (4–2 v **China**, in Hiroshima, Japan), quarter-final 1998; **Asian Women's Championship** – first entered 1995; **Under-17 World Championship** – never qualified; **World Youth Cup** (under-20) – never qualified. *Record against British and Irish national teams* none played. *History* The Uzbekistan Football Association was established in 1946. During the Soviet years, clubs played in Uzbekistan and Soviet Union tournaments: **Pachtakor Tashkent** was Soviet Union Cup runners-up in 1968. Uzbekistan national league and cup competitions began in 1992. *League system* Sixteen clubs play in the national Premier Division, playing each other twice per season. Three points are awarded for a win, with one for a draw. The Cup of Uzbekistan is also part played in a league format. In 1996, for example, 42 clubs were divided into eight mini-leagues; the top two clubs in each progressed to a second stage of four mini-leagues of four clubs each. The top two clubs of each mini-league quali-fied for a straight knockout tournament involving eight clubs. The final was played at the end of the season in November. Because the season overlaps with the Asian club tournaments, champions from the previous year qualify for the **Asian Cup of Champion Teams** and **Asian Cup-winners Cup**. *Record in international club tournaments* **Asian Champion Teams Cup – Neftchi Fergana** (semi-final 1994), **Navbakhor Namangan** (quarter-final 1998); Asian cup-winners Cup – Pachtakor Tashkent (quarter-final 1999). Other leading club: **MHSK Tashkent**.

V

Vakhsh Kurgan-Tyube *club* Tajikistan national league club based in Qurghonteppa, formed 1960. Ground: Pakhtakor, capacity: 8,000. Tajikistan League champions 1997; Tajikistan Cup 1997.

Valderrama, Carlos *player* Midfield. **Colombia** international (111 caps, 10 goals, 1985-98). Born 2 September 1961. *Clubs* **Millonarios**, **Deportivo Cali**, **Atlético Nacional Medellin**, Montpellier HSC (France), Real Valladolid Deportivo (Spain), **Atlético Junior**, **Miami Fusion**. *Honours El Mundo* **South American Footballer of the Year** 1987; *El Pais* **South American Footballer of the Year** 1987, 1993. *Keynotes* Valderrama made his debut for Colombia on 27 October 1985, at 24 years of age (0–3, v **Paraguay**). Aside from being Colombia's most capped player, he is also noted for his long curly blonde hairstyle.

Vale of Leven *club* former Scottish league. *Dossier* Ground: Millburn Park, Alexandria, Strathclyde. *Keynotes* Founder members of the **Scottish League** in 1890-91, having been a successful **Scottish FA Cup** side in the years preceding the formation of the League. In the late-1870s, Vale won the Cup in three consecutive years: 1877 (3–2 second replay v **Rangers**), 1878 (1–0 v **Third Lanark** Volunteers), 1879 (1–1 v Rangers – awarded the trophy because Rangers refused to play a replay). Vale appeared in three more finals during the following decade: 1883 (1–2 second replay v **Dumbarton**), 1885 (1–3 v **Renton**), 1890 (1–2 second replay v **Queen's Park**). The club dropped into the regional Leagues for several seasons after finishing bottom of the Scottish League with only five points in 1891-92. Vale's ninth position in the Scottish League in the inaugural season was the club's highest finish. The club failed to gain re-election in 1923-24. *League record* Scottish League 1890-91 to 1891-92; Division Two 1905-06 to 1914-15, 1921-22 to 1923-24. *Honours* Scottish FA Cup 1877 (3–2 second replay v Rangers), 1878 (1–0 v Third Lanark Volunteers), 1879 (1–1 v Rangers – awarded the trophy because Rangers refused to play a replay).

Vale Park *ground* English football ground situated in Burslem, Stoke-on-Trent, Staffordshire; home of **Port Vale**. *Dossier* Ground capacity: 22,356. Pitch dimensions 104m x 70m. Record attendance: 50,000 v **Aston Villa** (20 February 1960, **FA Cup**, fifth round). Best average attendance: 20,869 (1954-55). *History* Vale moved to Vale Park, which the club planned to turn into a 70,000 capacity "Wembley of North", in 1950. Lack of finance prevented the realisation of this aim and one stand still has not been properly developed. The club played its first match at Vale Park on 24 August 1950 (v **Newport County**, Division Three (South)) before, a then club record attendance, 30,042. Vale Park staged its first floodlit match on 24 September 1958 (v **West Bromwich Albion**, friendly).

Valencia (CF) *club* Spanish league. *Dossier* Ground: Luis Casanova (Estadio – also known as La Mestalla), Valencia. Strip: white shirts, black shorts, black socks. Website: *http://www.valenciacf.es/* Nickname: Los Ches. Ground capacity:: 49,291. *History* Valencia was refounded in 1919, having been formed originally in 1902 by foreign residents of the city. The club's official name is Valencia Club de Fútbol. Valencia enjoyed a golden period during the 1940s, winning the Spanish League (**Primera Liga**) on three occasions and the Spanish Cup (**Copa del Ray**) twice during the decade. It reached three consecutive **UEFA** (Fairs) **Cup** finals between 1962 and 1964, winning the trophy on the first two occasions and losing the 1964 one-off final against fellow Spanish side **Real Zaragoza** (1–2). Under Alfredo di **Stéfano**'s managership, the club won a further League Championship in 1970-71, beating **Barcelona** on **goal difference**. Valencia also reached three successive domestic cup finals in 1970 (1–3 v **Real Madrid**), 1971 (3–4 v **Barcelona**) and 1972 (1–2 v **Atlético Madrid**). Since winning the Copa del Ray in 1979 and the **European Cup-winners Cup** – defeating **Arsenal** on penalties – and the **European Super Cup** the following year, Valencia's only achievement of note was to reach the domestic cup final in 1995 (1–2 v Deportivo La Coruña). *Honours* Spanish League 1941-42, 1943-44, 1946-47, 1970-71; Spanish Cup 1941 (3–1 v RCD **Espanyol**), 1949 (1–0 v **Athletic Bilbao**), 1954 (3–0 v Barcelona), 1967 (2–1 v Athletic Bilbao), 1979 (2–0 v Real Madrid); European Cup-winners Cup 1980 (0–0, 5–4 pens. v Arsenal); UEFA (Fairs) Cup 1962 (7–3 agg. v Barcelona), 1963 (4–1 v Dynamo Zagreb); European Super Cup 1980 (2–2 away goals v **Nottingham Forest**).

valgus *medical* position in which the knee is bent inwards. Excessive force in this position can cause injury to the **medial collateral ligament**.

Valletta FC *club* Maltese national league club, based in the capital Valletta and formed in 1904. Ground: Ta'Qali Stadium, Valletta, capacity: 18,000 (all Maltese premier league games are played here). Strip: white shirts and white shorts. Maltese League champions 1915, 1932, 1945, 1946, 1948, 1959, 1960, 1963, 1974, 1978, 1980, 1984, 1990, 1992, 1998, 1999; Maltese FA Trophy 1960, 1964, 1975, 1977, 1978, 1991, 1995, 1996.

Valley *ground* English football ground situated in south London; home of **Charlton Athletic**. *Dossier* Ground capacity: 20,000 all seated. Pitch dimensions: 101m x 67m. Record attendance: 75,031 v **Aston Villa** (12 February 1938, **FA Cup**, fifth round). Best average attendance: 40,216 (1948-49). *History* After playing at numerous grounds, including Siemens Meadow, Woolwich Common, Pound Park and Horn Lane, Charlton finally settled at The Valley in 1919 – supporters helped to raise the finance to buy the site and to prepare it for football (the area had been left without a football club following Woolwich **Arsenal**'s move to north London before **World War I**). Charlton played its first match at the Valley on 13 September 1919 (v Summerstown), and it was the ground's potential that helped win the club election to the **Football League** in 1921-22. Several fans were hurt when barriers collapsed during an FA Cup fourth round-tie with **Bolton Wanderers** in March 1923. Charlton departed the Valley in 1923, but because of the poor facilities at its new ground, known as the Mount, it still played several matches at the ground and returned there the following season. **Millwall** used the Valley for a season during **World War II** after its own ground, the **Den**, was bombed. The Glikstein family, which first had become involved with Charlton by investing £100,000 in 1931, sold the club to Mark Hulyer for the nominal sum of £1,000 in 1981, starting a series of events which ultimately led to the club's departure to share **Crystal Palace**'s **Selhurst Park** ground, and an emotional return. Property development company Sunley bought the club in 1984, agreeing a £2 million investment only a few minutes before a Football League deadline elapsed (see Charlton Athletic). In September 1985, the new owners announced the groundshare with Palace, with the "final" game taking place on 21 September (v **Stoke City**, Division Two). The move provoked much anger among Charlton supporters, some of whom campaigned to return the club to the Valley – which eventually occurred in December 1992 (see **Valley Party**). After much financial wrangling – including, in April 1992, the creation of the Charlton Investment Plan, which offered a 10-year saving on tickets in return for investments of between £33 and £10,000 – and failed planning proposals, and one season (1991-92) sharing **West Ham United**'s **Upton Park**, Charlton returned to a three-sided Valley on 5 December 1992 (v **Portsmouth**,

Division Two). A new East Stand was opened on 2 April 1994 and the temporary west stand seating (subsequently re-erected at **Chelsea**'s **Stamford Bridge** when the Shed was demolished) was replaced with permanent facilties that summer, completing a fully-enclosed all-seater stadium with a 15,222 capacity. The club's promotion to the Premier League in 1998-99 led to further development, increasing capacity to 20,000. The first floodlit match at the Valley took place on 20 September 1961 (v **Rotherham United**, Division Two). The Valley staged an under-21 **Inter-League** match between representative teams from the Football League and Italy's **Serie B** (10 March 1998). The ground hosted two sellout rock concerts by The Who in 1974 and 1976.

Valley Parade *ground* English football ground situated in Bradford, west Yorkshire; home of **Bradford City**. *Dossier* Ground capacity: 18,018. Pitch dimensions: 100.5m x 67m. Record attendance: 39,146 v **Burnley** (11 March 1911, **FA Cup**, fourth round). Best average attendance: 22,585 (1920-21). *History* Valley Parade orginally staged rugby fixtures, and it was during a rugby match between Manningham and Heckmondwicke on Christmas Day in 1888 that one of the first recorded deaths of a supporter at an English sports ground occurred. When Rugby League club Manningham swapped codes and became a football club in 1903, the newly-named Bradford City continued to play at Valley Parade. City's first match took place on 5 September 1903 (v Gainsborough, Division Two). Archibald **Leitch** engineered a complete redevelopment of the ground from 1908, including the construction of the Main Stand. On 11 May 1985, during the club's final match of the season (v **Lincoln City**, 11 May 1985), with 11,000 supporters celebrating the team's Division Three Championship success, this stand burned down, killing 56 people and injuring more than 200 others (see **Bradford fire**). The first floodlit match at Valley Parade, under lights financed from supporters' donations, took place on 20 December 1954 (v **Hull City**, friendly). Valley Parade staged an **Inter-League** match between the **Football League** and the Irish League on 10 October 1903, and in 1904 the ground was the venue for the **FA Amateur Cup** final (Sheffield v Ealing). In 1991, Valley Parade hosted the **World Student Games** football final and the 3rd-place **playoff**. City's biggest crowd at Valley Parade (39,146 v Burnley (11 March 1911, FA Cup, fourth round)) is the longest surviving record attendance of any club in the Football League. **Bradford Park Avenue** shared Valley Parade during the 1973-74 season before the club folded.

Valley Party *n.* one-issue political party established in 1990 by disgruntled **Charlton Athletic** supporters to contest the May 1990 local elections in the London Borough of Greenwich as part of a campaign to return the club to its former home, the **Valley**. *History* In September 1985, Charlton's owners announced that the club would be leaving the Valley to share **Crystal Palace**'s **Selhurst Park** ground, with the "final" game taking place on 21 September (v **Stoke City**, Division Two). The move provoked anger among Charlton supporters, some of whom campaigned to return the club to the Valley. Greenwich council's planning committee rejected the club's proposal for a 25,000 all-seater Valley Stadium in January 1990. Local elections took place the following May and supporters campaigning for Charlton's return to the Valley established their own party to contest 60 of the borough's 62 seats – the two not contested were held by pro-Valley councillors. The Valley Party polled 14,838 votes (10.9% of the total) and, although the party won no seats, it did succeed in helping to unseat the former chairman of the planning committee. Several months later, the council and the club reached a compromise plan for the Valley which was passed at a meeting on 2 April 1991. Charlton returned to a three-sided Valley on 5 Decmber 1992 (v **Portsmouth**, Division Two).

Valur (Knattspyrnufélagid Valur) *club* Icelandic national league club based in Reykjavik, founded 1911. Ground: Hlídarendi, capacity: 2,000. Strip: red shirts, white shorts. **European Cup** second round 1968; Icelandic League winners 1930, 1933, 1935, 1936, 1937, 1938, 1940, 1942, 1943, 1944, 1945, 1956, 1966, 1967, 1976, 1978, 1980, 1985, 1987; Icelandic Cup 1965, 1974, 1976, 1977, 1988, 1990, 1991, 1992.

van Basten, Marco *player* Striker. **Netherlands** international (58 caps, 24 goals, 1983-92). Born 31 October 1964. Career ca. 1981-1994. *Clubs* **Ajax**, **AC Milan**. *Keynotes* Van Basten made his international debut on 7 September 1983 (3–0, v **Iceland** in Groningen, **European Championship** qualifier). He scored the second goal in Netherlands' 2–0 victory over the **Soviet Union** in the 1988 European Championship final in Munich; he had scored a hat-trick in the 3–1 first-round victory over **England** (in Dusseldorf), and the 88th-minute winner in the semi-final against hosts **Germany** (2–1, in Hamburg). Van Basten scored 128 goals in 133 games in five years at Ajax, including a goal on his debut in 1981-82, as a 17-year-old. He also scored the only goal in Ajax's **European Cup-winners Cup** triumph in 1987 (1–0, v **Lokomotiv Leipzig**). Van Basten continued to win trophies and score goals after his move to Milan in 1987; he was top scorer in the 1989 **European Cup** with 10 goals, including two in the final against **Steaua Bucharest** (his Dutch strike partner Ruud **Gullit** also scored two in the 4–0 victory). Van Basten was in the Milan side that retained the trophy the following year, but was on the losing side in the 1993 final against **Olympique de Marseille** (0–1); a match in which he was substituted by Eranio. Van Basten also scored in the 1989 European Supercup (2–1, v **Barcelona**). His career was ended prematurely through persistent ankle injuries. *Honours* European Championship (Netherlands 1988); **World Club Cup** (AC Milan 1989, 1990); European Cup (Milan, 1989, 1990); European Cup-winners Cup (Ajax, 1987); **European Super Cup** (Milan, 1989, 1990); European **Golden Boot** 1986 (37 goals); Dutch League (Ajax,

1982, 1983, 1985); Italian League (AC Milan 1988, 1992, 1993); *World Soccer* **World Footballer of the Year** 1988, 1992, runner-up 1989; **FIFA World Footballer of the Year** 1992; *France Football* **European Footballer of the Year** 1988, 1989, 1992.

Vancouver 86ers *club* Canadian club playing in the **American A-League** and formerly in the now-defunct **Canadian Soccer League**. Based in Vancouver, British Columbia, founded 1987. Ground: Swangard Stadium, capacity: 6,900. Strip: black shirts, white shorts. Canadian Soccer League champions 1988, 1989, 1990, 1991; A-League runners-up 1997.

Vanuatu *country OFC* island republic in the South Pacific, in Melanesia. Independence from France and Britain in 1980. Area: 14,765 sq km (5,700 sq miles). Population: 160,000 (1996 est.). Languages: Bislama, English, French and Melanesian. Capital: Port Villa. *Dossier* Vanuatu Football Confederation (Port Villa) formed in 1934, affiliated to **FIFA** and to **Oceania Football Confederation** (OFC) in 1988, president: Tinsley Lulu; general secretary: Jacques Tronquet. Season played from March to September. National strip: gold or black shirts, black shorts, gold or black socks. *International tournament record* **Olympic Games** – never entered; **Women's World Cup** – never entered; **World Cup** – first entered 1994, never progressed beyond first qualifying round; **Oceania Cup** – first entered 1996, never qualified for final stages. *Record against British and Irish national teams* none played. *Record in international club tournaments* none.

Varela, Obdulio *player* Midfield. **Uruguay** international. Born 20 September 1917, died 1995. Career ca. 1937-1955. *Clubs* **Montevideo Wanderers**, **Peñarol**. *Keynotes* Varela captained Uruguay to victory in the 1950 **World Cup** finals, scoring a crucial 73rd-minute equaliser against **Spain** in the final round of matches (2–2, in Sao Paulo); had Uruguay lost that match, it would have lost the World Cup to **Brazil** by virtue of an inferior **goal difference**. Varela also played in the 1954 World Cup finals when Uruguay finished fourth: he scored in the 4–2 quarter-final defeat of **England**. Varela joined Peñarol from Montevideo Wanderers in 1942, later becoming coach. *Honours* World Cup (Uruguay, 1950); **Copa America** (Uruguay, 1944); Uruguayan league championship (Peñarol, 1944, 1945, 1949, 1951, 1953, 1954).

Varsity match *competition* annual fixture between Cambridge and Oxford Universities, first played 1874. Now played at Fulham's **Craven Cottage** stadium, on the day of the annual university boat race. *Winners* (Up to and including 1999) Cambridge 45; Oxford 44. Draws: 26.

varus *medical* position in which the knee is bent outwards. Excessive force in this position can cause injury to the **lateral collateral ligament**.

Vasas DH (Danubius Hotels) *club* Hungarian national league club based in Budapest, founded 1911 as Vasas, later known as Kinizsi Vasas (1943-45) and Vasas SC (1946-95). Ground: Fáy Útcai, capacity:

18,000. Strip: red and white chequered shirts, blue shorts. **European Cup** semi-final 1958; **Mitropa Cup** 1956, 1957, 1960, 1962, 1965, 1970, 1983; Hungarian League champions 1957, 1961, 1962, 1965, 1966, 1977; Hungarian Cup 1955, 1973, 1981, 1986.

Vasco da Gama (Clube de Regatas Vasco da Gama) *club* Brazilian national league and **Rio de Janeiro** state league club based in Rio de Janeiro, founded 1898. The club has a strong following among Rio's Portuguese community. Ground: San Januario, capacity: 40,000. Strip: white shirts with a black sash, white shorts. **Campeonato Sudamericano de Campeones** winners 1948 (the only year the tournament was played); **Copa Libertadores** winners 1998 (4–1 agg., v **Barcelona Sporting Club**); **Copa CONMEBOL** semi-final 1996; **Campeonato Brasileiro** champions 1974, 1989, 1997; São Paulo Tournament winners 1958; **Copa do Brasil** runners-up 1965; state league champions 20 times (to 1998). Notable former players: Bebeto, Mazinho, Geovani Silva, Tostão.

Vasco Volcanoes (formerly Vasco da Gama) *club* Bermuda national league champions 1996, 1999, runners-up 1997.

Vasconcelos, Claudia *referee* Brazilian referee, the first woman to officiate at a **FIFA** tournament (the 1991 **Women's World Cup** finals in **China**).

Vatican City *country no international affiliation* papal state in the centre of Rome, **Italy**; the smallest country in the world. Seat of the head of the Roman Catholic Church. Area: 0.44 sq km (0.17 sq miles). Population: 1,000. Languages: Italian, Latin. Capital: Vatican City. *Dossier* No affiliated football association. The country's head of State, Pope John Paul II, is a lifelong supporter of **Cracovia** and a former goalkeeper.

Vaughton *misc.* Birmingham-based firm that has supplied medals and trophies to the **Football League** almost continuously since 1891.

Vauxhall Conference *competition* see **Football Conference**.

Vava *player* Real name: Edevaldo Izito Neto. Striker. **Brazil** international. *Keynotes* One of only three players to have scored in two **World Cup** finals (1958, 1962), along with **Pelé** and Paul **Breitner**. *Honours* World Cup (Brazil, 1958, 1962).

Vejle BK (Boldklub) *club* Danish national league club based in Vejle, founded 1891. Ground: Vejle Stadion, capacity: 18,500. Strip: red shirts, white shorts. **European Cup-winners Cup** quarter-final 1978; Danish League champions 1958, 1971, 1972, 1978, 1984; Danish Cup 1958, 1959, 1972, 1975, 1977, 1981.

Velez Mostar *club* Bosnia-Herzegovina and **Yugoslavia** national league club based in Mostar, founded 1922. Ground: Gradski, capacity: 21,000 (pre-civil war). Strip: red shirts, red shorts. **European Cup-winners Cup** second round 1982, 1987; **UEFA Cup** quarter-final 1975; former Yugoslavia League runners-up 1973, 1974, 1987; former Yugoslavia Cup 1981, 1986. Notable former player: Dusan Bajevic (scored 29

goals, former-Yugoslavia striker,1970-77, and fifth in the former country's all-time goal-scoring list).

Velez Sarsfield *club* Argentinean national league club, based in Buenos Aires, founded 1910. Ground: Estadio José Amalfitani, capacity: 50,000. Strip: white shirts with a blue "V", blue shorts. **World Club Cup** 1994 (2–0, v **Milan**); **Copa Libertadores** winners 1994 (1–1 agg., 5–3 pens., v **São Paulo**); **Supercopa** winners 1996 (3–0 agg., v **Cruzeiro**); **Recopa** winners 1997 (1–1, 4–2 pens., v **River Plate**); **Copa Mercosur** quarter-final 1998; **Copa Inter America** 1996 (2–0 agg., v Cartagines of Costa Rica); Argentinean league champions 1993 (**clausura**), 1996 (A= **apertura**) 1996 (clausura); Argentinean National Championship (a pre-national-league tournament operating from 1967 to 1985) winners 1968. Notable player: José Luis **Chilavert**.

Vélodrome (Stade) *ground* French football ground situated in Marseille, Provence Alpes-Côte d'Azur; home of **Olympique de Marseille**. Ground capacity: 60,000 all seated. *History* Opened on 13 June 1937 (Olympique de Marseille v **Torino**). Refurbished for the 1998 **World Cup** at a cost of £39 million. During the tournament, Stade Vélodrome staged one match from each of groups A (**Brazil** v **Norway**), C (**France** v **South Africa**), E (**Netherlands** v **South Korea**) and G (**England** v **Tunisia**); a second round game (**Italy** v Norway); a quarter-final (**Argentina** v Netherlands); and a semi-final (Brazil v Netherlands) – total attendance 394,164; average attendance 56,309. In December 1997, the ground was the venue of the draw for the final stages of the competition, which was preceded by an exhibition match between a Europe XI and a Rest of the World XI. Stade Vélodrome was used during the 1938 World Cup (Italy v Norway, round 1; Italy v Brazil, semi-final) – total attendance 51,826; average attendance 25,913.

Venables, Terry *player-manager* Midfield. **England** international (2 caps). Born 6 January 1943. Career ca. 1960-75. *Clubs* (player) **Chelsea**, **Tottenham Hotspur**, **Queens Park Rangers**, **Crystal Palace**. *Honours* **FA Cup** (Tottenham Hotspur 1967); **League Cup** (Chelsea 1965). *Clubs/country* (manager) Crystal Palace (twice), Queens Park Rangers, **Barcelona**, Tottenham Hotspur, England (record: played 38, won 18, drawn 13, lost 7, goals for 62, goals against 32), **Australia**. *Honours* Division Two (Crystal Palace 1978-79; Queens Park Rangers 1982-83); FA Cup (Tottenham Hotspur 1991); Spanish League (Barcelona 1984-85). *Keynotes* As a player, Venables holds the distinction of being the first to be capped at five levels – schoolboy, youth, amateur, Under-23 and full international. Venables scored from the penalty spot for Chelsea during the first leg of the 1965 League Cup final at **Leicester City**. He became Palace manager in June 1976, following a spell as coach alongside Malcolm Allison. In three seasons, Venables took Palace to the top flight, winning promotion from Division Three in 1976-77 and the Division Two Championship in 1978-79. Succeeded Tommy **Docherty** as Queens Park

Rangers' manager in October 1980 and took a major shareholding in the club. Under Venables, QPR reached its first FA Cup final in 1982, ironically against his former club as a player and future employer Tottenham Hotspur (0–1 replay). He became Barcelona's manager in May 1984, leading the club to its first Spanish League title in 11 years in 1984-85. The following season, Venables took the club to the **European Cup** final (0–0, 0–2 pens. v **Steau Bucharest**). He released a pop record featuring him singing a Catalan version of "My Way". Appointed Tottenham Hotspur's manager in September 1987, and, in June 1991 he joined with electronics millionaire Alan Sugar to buy the club. As a result, Venables became chief executive, but was sacked amid acrimonious circumstances in June 1993. The legal ramifications of his departure from Tottenham forced him to resign as England coach, having been appointed as successor to Graham **Taylor** and having helped the team to the semi-final stage of the 1996 **European Championship** (1–1, 5–6 pens. v **Germany**). After taking charge of the Austrialia national side, Venables went within a whisker of leading the country to the 1998 **World Cup**, losing the playoff against **Iran** on away goals. Venables bought a 51% stake in **Portsmouth** for £1 in 1996, becoming the club's chairman as a result, and receiving a reported £250,000 payment in January 1998, when he left the club. He became Palace manager for a second time in summer 1998, but left early the following year. Venables became the first Briton to win the **World Manager of the Year** in 1985. Co-author of a novel, "They used to play on grass", and co-creator of the *Hazel* television series.

Venezuela *country CONMEBOL* republic in South America, next to the Caribbean Sea, **Brazil**, **Colombia** and **Guyana**. Independence from **Spain** in 1830. Area: 912,045 sq km (352,050 sq miles). Population: 20,410,000 (1993 est.). Languages: Spanish. Capital: Caracas. *Dossier* Football association (Federación Venezolana de Fútbol, Candelaria, Caracas) formed in 1926, affiliated to **FIFA** and **Confederación Sudamericana de Fútbol** (CONMEBOL) in 1952, president: Rafael Esquivel Melo; general secretary: Serafin Boutureira. Season played from September to June. National stadium: Estadio Olimpico, Caracas, capacity: 30,000. National strip: dark red shirts, white shorts, white socks with black border. First international game: 10 February 1938 v **Panama** (1–2, Panama City, **Central American and Caribbean Games**). Biggest victory: 6–0 v **Puerto Rico** (26 December 1946, Barranquilla, Colombia, Central American and Caribbean Games) Biggest defeat: 0–11 v **Argentina** (10 August 1975, Rosario, Argentina, Copa America first round). *International tournament record* **Olympic Games** – never qualified for finals tournament; **Women's World Cup** – first entered 1991 (third of three nations in South American qualifying group), did not enter 1995; **World Cup** – first entered 1966, finished last in each of its CONMEBOL qualifier groups 1966-1998 (in 1998, it drew three games and lost 13 of its 16 qualifiers); Central American and Caribbean

Games winners 1982; **South American Championship** – first entered 1967, has never progressed to second stage of tournament; **Under-17 World Championship** – never qualified for finals tournament; **World Youth Cup** (under-20) – never qualified. *Record against British and Irish national teams* none played. *History* Football association founded in 1926. Founder member of the former **Confederacion Centroamericano y del Caribe de Fútbol** (CCCF) in 1938, but never played in the **CCCF Championship**. Caracas regional league started 1921, later became Venezuelan amateur league. Professional league began 1956. Three clubs have reached the semi-final of the **Copa Lbertadores**: **Portuguesa FC**, Atlético San Cristabal (as Deportivo San Cristobal) and **Universidad de los Andes**. Venezuela's record in the **Copa America** is poor. Its worst year was 1975, when it lost 0-4 and 1-5, against Brazil, and 1-5 and 0-11 against Argentina. In the final placings (based on the comparative results of all the nations in each tournament), it was placed fifth of six nations in 1967 and ninth of 12 in 1993; it has finished last of 10 or 12 nations in all other years to 1997. Venezuelan striker Dolgetta was the top scorer at the 1993 tournament in **Ecuador**, with four goals. Venezuela's only international tournament success was the 1982 triumph in the Central American and Caribbean Games. *League system* League played in two stages: the **Torneo Apertura** or "**Copa Venezuela**" and **Torneo Clausura**. The Copa Venezuela is played by geographical region: the Grupo Centro Oriental and the Grupo Centro Occidental. Each has nine teams, playing each other twice. The Copa is decided by a two-leg playoff between the winners of each group. The top six teams in each group qualify for the Torneo Clausura. The first stage of the Torneo Clausura is also played in two groups, made up of the first, fourth and sixth placed teams in one Apertura group, with the second, third and fifth teams in the other group. Each group of six teams plays each other twice, with the top three in each group qualifying for the final league. These final six teams play each other twice, with the winners declared champions and the first and second both qualifying for the Copa Libertadores. The next two playoff for a place in the **Copa CON-MEBOL**. *Record in international club tournaments* Copa Libertadores – Portuguesa FC (of Acariga) (semi-final 1977), Atlético San Cristabal (then known as Deportivo San Cristobal) (semi-final 1983), **Atlético Zulia** (then known as Universidad de los Andes, semi-final 1984); Copa CONMEBOL – **Caracas FC** (quarter-final 1993), **Minerven FC** (quarter-final 1994), Mineros Guayana (quarter-final 1995). Other leading clubs: **Táchira**, **Deportivo Italia**.

venues, switching *misc.* moving a match to the opponents or another ground. *Keynotes* In the early years, clubs would sell their right to stage a match after being drawn at home in the **FA Cup**. **Notts County** and **Nottingham Forest** were both drawn at home in the first round of the 1910 FA Cup competition. County, which had drawn **Bradford City**, agreed to switch its match to **Valley Parade** for £1,000. City won the game (4–2) but failed to recover the payment from match receipts. In 1911, non-League **Northampton Town** sold its right to stage a second round FA Cup replay against **Newcastle United** for £900 following a 1–1 draw at **St James' Park**. Newcastle won the second match 1–0. More recently several European fixtures have been switched to prevent **crowd trouble**. For example, the first leg of **Chelsea**'s second-round **European Cup-winners Cup** match with FC Copenhagen, originally scheduled to be played in Denmark on 2 October 1998, was switched to **Stamford Bridge** because **Brøndy** and **Manchester United** were involved in a **European Cup** encounter at the same stadium the previous night. Greek champions **Panathinaikos** was forced to switch its Champions League game with **Dinamo Kiev** to **AEK**'s ground (Nikos Goumas stadium) in September 1998 because the Rolling Stones rock group was playing a concert at its own Olimpiakos stadium on the same night.

Verdy Kawasaki *club* Japanese **J-League** club based in Inagi, formerly Yomiuri Nippon (1969-92). Ground: Todoroki Stadium, capacity: 25,000. Strip: green shirts, white shorts. **Asian Champion Teams Cup** 1987 (as Yomiuri Nippon – walkover in final after **Al Hilal** of Saudi Arabia withdrew), semi-final/third 1993, semi-final/fourth 1992, quarter-final 1998; **Asian Cup-winners Cup** quarter-final 1998, J League winners 1993 and 1994; Japanese League Cup 1979, 1985, 1991, 1992, 1993, 1994; Japanese National League champions 1983, 1984, 1987, 1991, 1992; Emperor's Cup 1985, 1987, 1988.

verrou *tactics* forerunner of the **catenaccio** system.

Vetch Field *ground* Welsh football ground (English league) situated in Swansea, west Glamorgan; home of **Swansea City**. *Dossier* Ground capacity: 11,477. Pitch dimensions: 102m x 68m. Record attendance: 32,796 v **Arsenal** (17 February 1968, **FA Cup**, fourth round). Best average attendance: 22,535 (1948-49). *History* Vetch Field was used by Swansea Villa during the 1880s and became a sports ground in 1891. Only when the ground's owners, the Gas Light Company, had its plans to build a gas works on the site rejected was a football club formed, in June 1912, to play at Vetch Field. Swansea Town, as City was known until 1970, first played at Vetch Field on 7 September 1912 (v **Cardiff City**, Southern League). The ground was not quite ready for Swansea's Southern League debut so its first match was played at a local recreation ground. In its first season, Vetch Field had no turf and players were forced to wear knee pads to protect them from the clinker surface. The name Vetch Field is derived from its former use as a field to grow cattle fodder known as vetch. Swansea sold the ground to the local council for £50,000 in 1974, agreeing only a five-year lease and with the proviso that should the club lose its **Football League** status it would also lose the ground. Vetch Field is one of only two grounds in the Football League to retain some

perimeter fencing – the other being Cardiff City. The local council ruled Vetch Field as unsafe in 1997, forcing Swansea to postpone its home Third Division fixture with **Chester City** (22 November). The first floodlit match at Vetch Field took place on 10 October 1960 (v **Heart of Midlothian**).

VfB Leipzig *club* German and former East German national league club based in Leipzig. Founded 1896 (known as **Lokomotive Leipzig** from 1966-91). Winners of the first German league championship in 1903. Ground: Zentralstadion, capacity: 39,000. Strip: blue shirts, white shorts. **European Cup-winners Cup** runners-up 1987 (as Lokomotive, 0–1, v **Ajax**, in Athens); **UEFA Cup** semi-final 1974; former-East German League runners-up 1967, 1986, 1988; German League champions 1903, 1906, 1913; German Cup 1936; former-East German Cup 1957, 1976, 1986, 1987.

Vialli, Gianluca *player-manager* Striker. **Italy** international (59 caps, 16 goals). Born 9 July 1964. Career 1981-. *Clubs* Cremonese, **Sampdoria**, **Juventus**, **Chelsea** (player-manager). *Keynotes* Vialli began his career with Cremonese before moving to Sampdoria in 1984, where he struck up a good partnership with Roberto Mancini, helping to win the Genoa club's first silverware, the Italian Cup, in 1985, and, in 1990-91, its first Italian Championship. He played 333 League games for Sampdoria and scored 140 goals. Following Sampdoria's 1992 **European Cup** final defeat (0–1 a.e.t. v **Barcelona**), Vialli moved to Juventus for a then world record £12 million. At Juventus, Vialli joined the small group of players who have won all three major European club competitions, captaining the club to its 1996 European Cup triumph (1–1, 4–2 pens. v **Ajax**). During his four-year spell at Stadio **Delle Alpi**, Vialli scored 25 goals in 137 appearances. He signed for Chelsea on a free transfer two months after Juventus' European Cup victory and earned an **FA Cup** winner's medal after going on for two minutes in the 1997 final against **Middlesbrough**. Vialli succeeded Ruud **Gullit** as Chelsea player-manager in February 1998, leading to club to two Cup triumphs – **League Cup** (2–0 a.e.t. v Middlesbrough) and European Cup-winners Cup (1–0 v **Stuttgart (VfB)** – in his first few months in charge. *Honours* Italian League (Sampdoria 1990-91, Juventus 1994-95); Italian Cup (Sampdoria 1985, 1988, 1989; Juventus 1995); FA Cup (Chelsea 1997); European Cup (Juventus 1996); **European Cup-winners Cup** (Sampdoria 1990); **UEFA Cup** (Juventus 1993).

Vicarage Road *ground* English football ground situated in Hertfordshire; home of **Watford**. *Dossier* Ground capacity: 22,000. Pitch dimensions: 105m x 68.5m. Record attendance: 34,099 v **Manchester United** (3 February 1969, **FA Cup**, fourth round replay). Best average attendance: 18,246 (1984-85). *History* Watford played its first match at Vicarage Road on 30 August 1922 (v **Millwall**, Division Three). The ground was built on the site of a former gravel pit and bought for £2,750 by Benskins Brewery for Watford's use in 1921. The owners initially leased the ground to the club for £150 per season, with the club signing a 150-year extension in 1968. To help pay creditors, Watford staged greyhound racing at Vicarage Road from October 1928, leading to a reprimand from the **Football League** in December 1930 for switching on the track-side lighting used to illuminate the dogs during an after-noon football match. The stadium was one of the few Football League grounds not to erect **perimeter fenc-ing**. On 18 October 1986, a new stand, officially named after the club president and former **FIFA** secretary Stanley **Rous**, was opened, and its construction meant that the pitch was moved and relaid. In April 1991, non-League Wealdstone agreed a £2.5 million one-off pay-ment to share Vicarage Road on a 127-year lease after selling its own Lower Mead ground. Wealdstone's tenure lasted only two seasons before the club moved on. Watford now share Vicarage Road with Rugby Union club Saracens. The ground staged its first Rugby Union match on 13 August 1997, when Saracens played a European Conference match against a French club, Castres. The highest Vicarage Road attendance at a rugby match was recorded on 19 April 1998 when 20,000 spectators watched Saracens play Newcastle in the Allied Dunbar Premiership. Vicarage Road staged its first floodlit match on 13 October 1953 (v **Luton Town**, friendly).

Vicente Calderón (Estadio) *ground* Spanish foot-ball ground situated in Madrid, Castille; home of **Atlético Madrid**. Ground capacity: 62,000. *History* Opened in 1966 thanks largely to the financial support of the club's president, Vincente Calderón. After vacating its previous ground, Metropolitano, Atlético had been forced to share **Real Madrid**'s Estadio Santiágo **Bernabéu** for one season because of the financial problems encountered building the new ground. Estadio Vincente Calderón is situated next to the Manzanares river, in the south-east of the city, and is built over a highway. Originally called Estadio Manzanares, it was renamed after Calderón in 1971. The ground was refur-bished for the 1982 **World Cup**. During the tourna-ment, the stadium staged all three second-round group D matches (**France** v **Austria**, Austria v **Northern Ireland**, France v Northern Ireland) – total attendance 84,000; average attendance 28,000.

Victoria (Club Deportivo) *club* Honduras national league club based in La Ceiba, formed 1935. Ground: Estadio Municipal Ceibeno. Strip: blue shirts, white shorts. Honduras League champions 1995.

Victoria Ground *ground* English football ground situated in Stoke, Staffordshire; former home of **Stoke City**. *Dossier* Capacity (1997): 24,071. Pitch dimen-sions 106m x 69m. Record attendance: 51,380 v **Arsenal** (29 March 1937, Division One).Best average attendance: 31,590 (Victoria Ground 1947-48). *History* Stoke played at several grounds, including the County Cricket Ground, Sweeting's Field and Athletic Ground, before settling at Victoria Ground in 1883. The club played its first match there on 24 September 1883 and

appeared in red and white striped shirts for the first time. The ground initially included an athletics track, which remained until 1930. The ground hosted a floodlit match between City and **Crewe Alexandra**, using Wells (oil-fired) lights in February 1890. Stoke was forced to play one match at **Port Vale**'s **Vale Park** in 1976 after the roof of the Butler Street stand was damaged by high winds. In March 1996, the club decided, with the sup-port of the local council, to relocate to a new community sports stadium entitled **Britannia Stadium** after the club's sponsors, Britannia Building Society. That year the Victoria Ground had the largest (9,700 capacity) sur-viving terrace in the UK. Stoke's final League match at Victoria Ground took place on 4 May 1997 (v **West Bromwich Albion**, 22,500). The Victoria Ground staged the first **Football League** v **Irish League** match to take place in England, on 9 November 1895. It was also the venue of a Football League v Southern League encounter on 9 October 1911, and for three **England** matches (v **Wales**, 23 February 1889 and 13 March 1893; v **Northern Ireland**, 18 November 1936) and a **World War I** "Victory" international (v Wales, 18 October 1919). Aside from the 1890 experiment, Victoria Ground's first floodlit match took place on 10 October 1956 (v Port Vale, Division Two).

Victoria Park 1. *ground* English football ground situated in Cleveland; home of **Hartlepool United**. *Dossier* Ground capacity: 7,229. Pitch dimensions: 101m x 68.5m. Record attendance: 17.426 v **Manchester United** (5 January 1957, **FA Cup**, third round). Best average attendance: 9,265 (1951-52). *History* The then Hartlepools United took over the Victoria Ground (as it was known until the 1990s) which had been the home of West Hartlepool rugby club since 1886, in 1908, playing its first match there on 2 September (v **Newcastle United** Reserves). For a time, United shared the ground with West Hartlepool FC, an amateur club which folded in 1910. Although the ground was unscathed during **World War II**, its wooden stand had been destroyed by a bomb dropped from a German Zeppelin on 27 November 1916, forcing the club to play three matches elsewhere. United sold the ground to the local council for £10,000 in 1971. The Victoria Ground is one of only two English club grounds that has staged two League matches featuring different clubs on the same day (the other is **Old Trafford** in May 1921): on 23 August 1983, Hartlepool played **Cardiff City** in Division Four and later that day, the ground was used for the Division Three match between **Middlesbrough** and **Port Vale** (Boro's **Ayresome Park** ground had been shut on 1 August after the club went into liquidation). The first floodlit match at Victoria Ground took place on 6 January 1967 (v **Southend United**, Division Four). **2.** *ground* Scottish foot-ball ground situated originally in Highland region; home of **Ross County**. *Dossier* Ground capacity: 5,400. Pitch dimensions: 100.5m x 68.5m. Record attendance: 8,000 v **Rangers** (28 February 1966, **Scottish FA Cup**). *Keynotes* Ross County has played at Victoria Park since the club was formed in 1929. Victoria Park is the most northerly senior football ground in the UK.

victories, consecutive (club) *record* **1. Football League**: 14 consecutive victories, **Manchester United** (1904-05, Division Two); 14, **Bristol City** (1905-06, Division Two); 14 **Preston North End** (1950-51, Division Two); **Bradford Park Avenue** holds the league record of 25 successive home victories in the Football League (1926-27 (18) and 1927-28 (7), Division Three North). **2.** Division One: 13 matches, **Tottenham Hotspur** (1959-60/1960-61; the run consisted of the final two matches of 1959-60, followed by a record 11-match winning sequence at the beginning of 1960-61; Spurs went on to win the championship). **Premier League**: 10 matches, **Arsenal** (1997-98; Arsenal won the championship).

victories, consecutive (countries) *record* the world record for consecutive victories by an international team is 14 games, held jointly by **Australia** (27 October 1996 to 22 November 1997) and **Brazil** (10 June to 14 December 1997). *Keynotes* Australia's winning sequence came to an end in the first of a two-leg playoff against **Iran** to determine the final place at the 1998 **World Cup** finals (1–1, in Tehran; Australia drew the second leg 2–2 and was eliminated from the tournament on **away goals**).

victories, most in a season (club) *record* **1. Football League** 33 victories from 42 matches, **Doncaster Rovers** (Third Division North, 1946-47) **2.** English top flight (FA **Premier League**/former First Division) 31 victories from 42 matches, **Tottenham Hotspur** (1960-61).

Victory Soccer Club *club* Maldives national league club. **Asian Champion Teams Cup** second round 1998; Maldives league champions 1986, 1987, 1988, 1993.

video evidence *misc.* video footage used in disciplinary hearings, either to support the imposition of sanctions against players who have committed serious – usually violent – infringements of the rules, or for players appealing against such sanctions. Televised football recordings have been allowed in disciplinary hearings by the English FA since December 1990. They were first allowed for domestic matches in Scotland in the 1996-97 season. *Keynotes* **Coventry City** player Dion **Dublin** lost his appeal to the Football Association against a sending-off (v **Blackburn Rovers**, 28 September 1997) despite presenting video evidence of the offence. Referee Rob Styles subsequently withdrew one caution he had imposed on **Birmingham City** striker Peter Ndlovu for "diving" in the First Division match between City and **Huddersfield Town** (31 October 1998) after studying a video of the incident. **Arsenal**'s Paul Davis received a nine-match ban and a record £3,000 fine after televsion footage captured him punching **Southampton**'s Glenn Cockerill in an off-the-ball incident during a match at **Highbury** in October 1988. At the 1994 **World Cup**, **Italy** defender Mauro Tassotti was given an eight-match suspension

after **FIFA** studied video evidence of an **off-the-ball** incident in which he elbowed **Spain**'s Luis Enrique.

video recording *regulations* a television recording of a football match. **Premier League** clubs are required to provide the referee and the League with a VHS video recording of each league match (FA Premier League rule G.14).

Videoton FC Fehérvar *club* Hungarian national league club based in Székesfehérvar, founded 1941 as Vadásztöltténgyár (1941-48), previously known as Videoton (1968-93), Dolgozók (1949-50), Vasas (1950-68), Parmalat FC (1994–96). Ground: Sóstói, capacity: 18,000. Strip: blue and red striped shirts, blue shorts. **UEFA Cup** – runners-up (as Videoton) 1985 (1–3 agg., v **Real Madrid**).

Vietnam *country AFC* republic in Southeast Asia, next to the South China Sea. It is bordered by **Cambodia**, **China** and **Laos**. Formerly part of the French colonies of Indo China. War of independence 1946; the country was divided in 1954 into North and South Vietnam. There followed the Vietnam War between the communist North and the United States-aided South. The war resulted in the deaths of 500,000 civilians, 1,000,000 North Vietnamense soldiers, 200,000 South Vietnamese soldiers and nearly 57,000 United States soldiers. A fifth of the country's agricultural land and half of the forests were destroyed. Area: 329,566 sq km (127,246 sq miles). Population: 74,000,000 (1995 est.). Languages: Vietnamese, French, Chinese. Capital: Hanoi. *Dossier* Vietnam Football Confederation (Hanoi) formed in 1962, affiliated to **FIFA** in 1964 and **Asian Football Confederation** (AFC) in 1954 (initially as the former South Vietnam), president: Mai Van Muon; general secretary: Professor PhamNgoc Vien. Season played from November to May. National stadium: Stade Hang Day, Hamoi, capacity: 40,000. National strip: red shirts, red shorts, red socks. First international game: South Vietnam played in the second football tournament of the **Asian Games** in 1954. *International tournament record* **Olympic Games** – never entered; **Women's World Cup** – never entered; **World Cup** – South Vietnam first entered 1974, united Vietnam first entered in 1994, never beyond qualifying tournament first round group stage (last in its group in 1994 and 1998); **Asean Tiger Cup** – played in the first tournament in 1996, semi-final/third (3–2, v **Indonesia**, in Singapore, third/fourth playoff), final 1998 (0–1, v Singapore, in Vietnam); **Asian Champions Cup** – South Vietnam first entered 1956, united Vietnam first entered in 1996, fourth 1956 (final tournament in Hong Kong), 1960 (final tournament in South Korea); Asian Games – South Vietnam first entered 1958, fourth 1962 (1–4 v **Malaysia**, in Jakarta, Indonesia), quarter-final 1958, also entered 1998 (last in its first-round group of three nations); **Asian Women's Championship** – never entered; **South East Asian Games** – South Vietnam won first tournament in 1959, third place 1997; **Under-17 World Championship** – never qualified; **World Youth Cup (under-20)** – never qualified. *Record against British and Irish national teams* none played. *History* Football introduced by French traders, now played by an estimated 300,000. Former South Vietnam club Vietnam Customs SC played in the first **Asian Champion Teams Cup** in 1967, in Bangkok. Vietnamese national championship has been played regularly since 1981. A new league structure was introduced in 1996. *League system* Twelve clubs play in the national First Division; the top four sides play off in an end-of-season knockout. *Record in international club tournaments* Asian Champion Teams Cup – Vietnam Customs SC (first round 1967; the first ever tournament), Vietnam Police (first round group 1968); **Asian Cup-winners Cup** – **Quang Nam Danang** (semi-final 1992). Other leading clubs: Cau Lac Bo Quan Doi (Vietnam League champions 1982, 1983, 1987), Cong An Hanoi (League champions 1984, 1988), Dong Thap (League champions), Hai Quan (Vietnam Cup 1997), **Ho Chi Minh City Police**, Port Saigon.

Viking FK Stavanger (FotballKlubb) *club* Norwegian national League club based in Stavanger, founded in 1899. Ground: Stavanager, capacity: 18,000. Strip: blue shirts, white shorts. **UEFA Cup** second round 1973, 1983; Norwegian League champions 1958, 1972, 1973, 1974, 1975, 1979, 1982, 1991; Norwegian Cup 1953, 1959, 1979, 1989.

Vikingur (Knattspyrnufélagid Vikingur) *club* Icelandic national league club based in Reykjavik, founded 1908. Ground: Vikingsvöllur, capacity: 2,000. Strip: red and black striped shirts, black shorts. Icelandic League winners 1920, 1924, 1981, 1982, 1991; Icelandic Cup 1971.

Viktoria Zizkov *club* Czech Republic and former Czechoslovakia league club based in Prague, founded 1903. Ground: FK Viktoria, capacity: 8,000. Strip: red and white striped shirts, red shorts. Pohár Dobrocinnosti (Czech Cup competition from 1906–1916) winners 1913, 1914, 1916; former Czechoslovakia League champions 1928; Czech Republic Cup 1994.

Villa Park *ground* English football ground situated in Birmingham, west Midlands; home of **Aston Villa**. *Dossier* Ground capacity: 40,310 all seated. Pitch dimensions: 105m x 66m. Record attendance: 76,588 v **Derby County** (2 March 1946, **FA Cup**, sixth round). Best average attendance: 47,320 (1948-49). *History* Villa Park was built on the site of the mid-Victorian Aston Lower Grounds amusement park. Aston Villa played its first match at Villa Park on 17 April 1897 (v **Blackburn**, friendly), one week after the club became only the second to achieve the **double**. The land was owned by the Midlands brewing company, Flowers, and was rented to Villa for £250. The club also had the option to buy the land within 21 years at the price of 5 shillings a square yard and, in 1911, Villa paid almost £12,000 to buy the land and other facilities. The club turned the previous structures, including an aquarium and a skating rink, into offices, a gymnasium, a practice pitch and car park. Until 1914, Villa Park also had a cycle track around the pitch that was often used on

match days to accommodate extra spectators. The redevelopment of Villa Park's Witton End (now the North Stand) in the 1970s caused the club substantial financial difficulties, and a police inquiry and a report found that normal building procedures had not been followed. The roof extension to the Holte End, which was completed in August 1990, was demolished in 1994 after it was discovered that converting the stand to an **all seated** facility would be impossible with the roof in place. Before demolition in 1994, the Holte End was the largest end terrace in the country, while the new all-seater stand, with its 13,462 seats, is the biggest end stand. Villa Park hosted its first floodlit match in November 1958 (v **Heart of Midlothian**, friendly). Until Villa Park's floodlights were incorporated into its stands they were arranged to spell out the club's initials, "AV". The ground staged its first **England** international on 8 April 1899 (v **Scotland**). In addition to staging five other England internationals between 1902 and 1958, two wartime internationals (v **Wales**, 25 October 1941, v Scotland, 3 February 1945) were held at Villa Park during World War II. In 1966, Villa Park was selected as a **World Cup** venue and staged three group 2 matches (**Argentina** v **Spain**; Argentina v **West Germany**; West Germany v Spain) – total attendance 134,512; average attendance 44,837. During the 1996 **European Championship**, Villa Park was the venue for three group A matches (**Netherlands** v Scotland; **Switzerland** v Netherlands; Scotland v Switzerland), as well as one quarter-final (**Czech Republic** v **Croatia**). It also staged the **Brazil** v **Sweden** fixture in the 1995 **Umbro International Tournament** (4 June 1995). In 1999, Villa Park staged its first European club final, the last in the **European Cup-winners Cup** (**Lazio**, 2–1, v Real Mallorca).. Villa Park is regularly used (more than any other league ground) as a **neutral venue** to stage FA Cup semi-finals.

Villa SC *club* see **Nakivubo Villa**.

violent conduct *rules* one of the listed infringements of the **Laws of the game**, punishable by the offending player being **sent off** (Law XII). Violent conduct includes deliberately striking, butting or kicking another player (opponent or team-mate), match official or other person.

Violet Kickers *club* Jamaica league club based in St James County. Strip: blue shirts, blue shorts. Jamaica League champions 1994, 1996.

Violette AC *club* Haitian national league club based in the capital Porte-au-Prince, founded 1918. Strip: green shirts, white shorts. **CONCACAF Champions Cup** 1984 (declared champions by default after, having won the Caribbean stage, the Central and Northern group tournament was incomplete).

Virgin Islands *country* see **British Virgin Islands**, **US Virgin Islands**.

virtual reality replay *television* technology developed by BSkyB to recreate match incidents in pseudo-three-dimensional computer images.

visiting club *regulations* the **away club**

visiting supporters *n. pl.* supporters of the **away club**. *Regulations* **Premier League**, **Football League** and **Scottish Football League** clubs must make provision for a reasonable number of visiting fans and are not allowed to charge them more than home fans for seats of comparable quality (FA Premier League rule I.20, Football League regulation 31.2, Scottish Football League rule 80). Unless otherwise agreed by the **Premier League Board**, or by the two clubs, the home club at a Premier League match must make available 3,000 tickets or the equivalent of 10% of the ground capacity (whichever is the smallest) to the away club. Home clubs in the Football League must make at least 2,000 places available for visiting fans, or the equivalent of 10% of the ground capacity (whichever is the smallest): this figure may only be reduced by written agreement of the Football League Executive (Football League regulation 31.2).

visually impaired football *n.* association football adapted to meet the needs of visually-impaired people. Tournaments are **five-a-side**, in a closed court (ie the ball can rebound off the walls) with players wearing protective headbands and using a ball which is fitted with ball bearings so it can be heard by the players. The goalkeeper is usually fully-sighted. Games involving totally blind players require silence when the ball is in play. Tournaments may be categorised according to the degree of visual impairment: B1, for players whose sight is absent or limited to the perception of light and dark; B2 for players with a visual acuity of no more than 2/60 and a field of vision less than 5 degrees (players in this category are able to read the biggest letter in an optician's chart at no more than 2 metres, and have a very narrow field of vision); and B3, for players with a visual acuity of no more than 6/60, and a field of vision less than 20 degrees (players can read the top letter of the chart at six metres, and have a slightly wider field of vision). *History* Football for blind and visually-impaired people is known to have been played in schools from the 1930s, with various regional and international competitions dating from the 1960s. The first European Championships, organised by the International Blind Sports Confederation (IBSF), were held in Santa Coloma de Gramanet, Barcelona, **Spain**, in September 1997. IBSF organised a simultaneous South American Championship in Asuncion, **Paraguay**. Outside South America and Europe, the sport has also become popular in **Australia**, **Egypt**, the **Ivory Coast**, **South Africa**, **Malaysia**, and the **United States of America**. The first World Championships took place in São Paulo, **Brazil**, in September 1998. Six countries took part: **Argentina**, Brazil, **Great Britain**, **Greece**, Spain, **Colombia**. It was played according to **Futsal** rules. Brazil beat Argentina in the final (the Great Britain team finished fifth). Football in the B1 category is set for inclusion at the Paralympic Games. IBSF website: *http://www.ibsa.es*

Vita Club Kinshasa (Association Sportive Vita Club) *club* Congo Democratic Republic (formerly Zaire) national league club based in the capital Kinshasa, founded 1935. Ground: 24 Septembre, capacity: 25,000. Strip: yellow shirts, black shorts. **African Cup of Champion Clubs** winners 1973 (5–4 agg., v **Asante Kotoko** of Ghana), runners-up 1981 (0–5 agg., v **JE Tizi-Ouzou** of Algeria); **CAF Cup** semi-final 1996; Congo DR League champions 1970, 1971, 1972, 1973, 1975, 1977, 1980, 1988, 1993, 1997; Congo DR Cup 1971, 1972, 1973, 1975, 1977, 1981, 1982, 1983. Notable former player: **Pierre Mulumba Ndaye**.

Vital'O Sports Club *club* Burundi national league club based in the capital Bujumbura, founded 1966. Stadium: Prince Louis Rwigasore (national stadium), capacity: 20,000. Strip: purple shirts, white shorts. **African Cup of Champion Clubs** quarter-final 1985; **East and Central African Club Championship** fourth 1999; Burundi League champions 1979, 1983, 1984, 1990, 1992, 1993, 1998; Burundi Cup 1991, 1993, 1995, 1997.

Vitoria Riboque *club* Sao Tomé and Principe national league club based in Sao Tomé. Ground: Estadio 12 de Julho, Sao Tomé, capacity: 5,000. Strip: yellow shirts, green shorts. Sao Tomé and Principe league champions 1977, 1978, 1979, 1986, 1989; Sao Tomé and Principe Cup 1984, 1985, 1986, 1988, 1990.

Vitória SC Setúbal *club* Portuguese national league club based in **Setúbal**, founded in 1910. Ground: Estádio do Bonfim, capacity: 30,700. Strip: green and white striped shirts, white shorts. **UEFA Cup** quarter-final 1973; Portuguese League runners-up 1972; Portuguese Cup 1965, 1967.

Vllaznia Shkodër (Klubi Sportiv) *club* Albanian national League club, based in Shkoder, founded 1919 (as Bashkimi). Ground: Loro Boriçi, capacity: 15,000. Strip: blue and red striped shirts, blue shorts. **European Cup-winners Cup** second round 1988; Albanian League champions 1945, 1946, 1972, 1974, 1978, 1983, 1992, 1998; Albanian Cup 1965, 1972, 1979, 1981, 1987.

Vojvodina Novi Sad *club* Yugoslavian and **former-Yugoslavia** national league club based in Novi Sad, Serbia, founded 1914. Ground: Gradski, capacity: 22,000. Strip: red and white (in halves) shirts, white shorts. **European Cup** quarter-final 1967 (lost to eventual winners **Celtic**, 1–3 agg.); **UEFA Cup** quarter-final 1968; **Mitropa Cup** 1997; former Yugoslavia League champions 1966, 1989, runners-up 1957, 1962, 1975; Yugoslavian League third place 1992, 1993, 1994, 1995; former-Yugoslavia Cup runners-up 1951.

volley *vb.* to kick a moving ball before it hits the ground. *n.* the execution of this.

Vorwärts Berlin *club* see **FC Victoria 9**.

W

WAC Casablanca (Wydad Athletic Casablanca) *club* Moroccan national league club based in Casablanca. Ground: Derejega, capacity: 15,000. Strip: red shirts and white shorts. **African Cup of Champion Clubs** – winners 1992 (2–0 agg., v **El Hilal** of Sudan), **African Cup-winners Cup** semi-final 1998; **Afro-Asian Club Cup** – winners 1992 (2–0 agg., v **Pass Club** of **Iran**); **Arab Club Champions Cup** 1992 (v **Al Hilal** of **Saudi Arabia**); **Arab Cup-winners Cup** 1991, 1992, 1993; North African Championship winners 1948, 1951; North African Cup 1949; Moroccan League champions 1948, 1949, 1950, 1951, 1957, 1966, 1969, 1976, 1977, 1978, 1986, 1990, 1991, 1993; Moroccan Cup 1970, 1978, 1979, 1981, 1989, 1991 and 1994, 1998.

Waitakere City *club* New Zealand national league club based in Waitakere. New Zealand National League champions 1990, 1992, 1995, 1996, 1997; (New Zealand) Chatham Cup 1994, 1995, 1996.

Wales *country UEFA* Welsh name: Cymru. Principality and constituent country of the United Kingdom, bordered by **England** to its east, and the Irish Sea to the west. Area: 20,760 sq km (8,015 sq miles). Population: 2,800,000 (1991 census). Languages: English, Welsh (about one-fifth of the population speak Welsh). Capital: Cardiff. An elected Welsh Assembly was introduced in 1999, with limited administrative and tax-raising powers. *Dossier* The **Football Association of Wales** (Cardiff) formed in 1876, affiliated to **FIFA** in 1910, permanent member of the **International FA Board**, and founder member of the **Union of European Football Associations** (UEFA) in 1954, president: John Hughes; general secretary: David Collins. Season played from August to May. National stadium: Cardiff Arms Park (the official home ground of the Welsh Rugby Football Union). National strip: red shirts, red shorts, red socks. First international game: 25 March 1876 v **Scotland** (0–4, Glasgow, friendly). First game v England 18 January 1879 (1–2, London, friendly); v **Ireland** 25 February 1882 (7–1, Wrexham, friendly); v **Northern Ireland** 15 March 1924 (1–0, Belfast, **Home International Championship**); v **Republic of Ireland** 28 September 1960 (3–2, Dublin, friendly). First international outside home countries: 25 May 1933 v **France** (1–1, Paris, friendly). Biggest victory: 11–0 v Ireland (3 March 1888, Wrexham, Home International Championship). Biggest defeat: 0–9 v Scotland (23 March 1878, Glasgow, friendly). National team coaches/managers: Mike Smith (1974-79), Mike England (1980-88), David Williams (**caretaker manager** 1988), Terry Yorath (1988-93), John Toshack (1994), Mike Smith (1994-95), Bobby Gould (1995-). Most capped players: Neville **Southall** (92 , 1982-97), Peter Nicholas (73, 1979-92), Ian **Rush** (73, 1980-97), Joey Jones (72, 1976-86), Ivor **Allchurch** (68 apearances, 1951-66), Brian Flynn (66, 1975-84), Mark **Hughes** (66, 1984-), Dean Saunders (64, 1986-), David Phillips (62, 1984-). Leading goalscorers: Ian Rush (28 goals in 73), Ivor Allchurch (23 goals in 68), Trevor Ford (23 goals in 38, 1947-57), Dean Saunders (21 goals in 64), L Mark Hughes (16 goals in 66), John **Charles** (15 goals in 38, 1950-65), Cliff **Jones** (15 goals in 59, 1954-69), John Toshack (13 goals in 40 appearances, 1969-80). Other notable international players: Ryan **Giggs** (22 appearances, five goals, 1991-), A J (Jack) Kelsey, Billy **Meredith**. Website: *http://www.faw.co.uk* (official site). *International tournament record* **Olympic Games** – never entered; **Women's World Cup** – see **Wales, women**; **World Cup** – first entered 1950, quarter-final 1958; **European Championship** – first entered 1964 (first round: no qualifying tournament), quarter-final 1976; **European Championship for Women** – see **Wales, women**; **Home International Championship** (British Championship) winners 12 times, the first in 1907; **Under-17 World Championship** – never qualified; **World Youth Cup** (under-20) – never qualified. *World Cup performance* (finals and qualifiers to end of 1998 tournament) played 75, won 24, drawn 15, lost 36, scored 104 goals, conceded 109 goals; win rate 32%; goals scored per game 1.39. *Record against other British and Irish national teams* v England played 97, won 14, lost 62, drawn 21; v all-Ireland played 37, won 17, lost 13, drawn seven; v Northern Ireland played 53, won 25, lost 14, drawn 14; v Republic of Ireland played nine, won five, lost three, drawn one; v Scotland played 101, won 18, lost 60, drawn 23. *History* The first football club in Wales was the now-defunct **Druids**, founded circa 1870. **Wrexham** was formed in 1875. The **Welsh FA Cup** was first played in 1878 and is the

World's third-oldest Cup competition. The first final was between Wrexham and Druids (1–0). By the time of its last final appearance in 1904, Druids had won the Welsh Cup eight times and had been in 13 finals. Wrexham heads the all-time ranking in the Welsh Cup, with 23 final victories by 1998, followed by **Cardiff City** (22) and **Swansea City** (10). The Welsh Cup was suspended during **World War I** and **World War II**. At the beginning of the 1920s, Welsh clubs joined the English **Football League**: Cardiff City (1920-21), **Newport County** (1920-21), Swansea City (1920-21) and Wrexham (1921-22). Aberdare (1926-27), Cardiff City, Merthyr Town (1920-21), Swansea City and Wrexham remain in the English league; Aberdare (1926-27) and Merthyr (1929-30) lasted only a few seasons, while Newport County **retired** from the league in 1988. Cardiff City were the Football League runners-up in the 1923-24 season, losing to **Huddersfield Town** on **goal average**. Ironically, had the league been played under modern rules – with clubs level on points separated by **goal difference** and **goals scored** – then Cardiff City would have taken the championship out of England. Both Cardiff City and Huddersfield Town finished the season on 57 points. Cardiff had an inferior goal average (1.794 v 1.818) identical goal difference (+27), but superior goals scored (61 v 60). Cardiff City missed a penalty on the last day of the season which, had it been scored, would have increased its goal average to 1.824, marginally above that of Huddersfield. In 1927, Cardiff City became the only Welsh club to lift the English **FA Cup**, beating **Arsenal** 1–0 at **Wembley** Stadium; Hughie Ferguson scored the goal in the 75th minute. It was beaten finalist in the 1925 FA Cup (0–1 v **Sheffield United**). A Welsh national league – the **League of Wales** – started in 1992-93, and was first won by **Cwmbran Town**. Full professional club **Barry Town** is the most successful Welsh League club, having won the title in 1996, 1997, 1998. It won the domestic "treble" (league, Welsh League Cup, Welsh FA Cup) in 1997, and holds a league record of 38 games without defeat (including 33 victories, 1997-98). A number of Welsh clubs have performed well in European club competitions: the best achievement by Cardiff City, which reached the semi-final of the **European Cup-winners Cup** in 1968 (it lost 3–4 agg., v **Hamburg SV**). Wrexham reached the quarter-final of the same competition in 1976, with Newport County reaching the quarter-final in 1981. **Bangor City** was unlucky to lose to the Italian club **Napoli** in the 1962-63 European Cup-winners Cup preliminary round: Bangor had drawn with the Italian side over two legs (2–0, 1–3), but went out of the tournament 1–2 in the replay. The Welsh club would have won had the modern **away-goals** rule been applicable at the time. Bangor had another glamourous tie in 1985: having reached the second round, the club lost against **Atletico Madrid** (0–3 agg.). Wales played its first international game in 1876, against Scotland. However, it took five years to notch its first victory (1–0, v England, 26 February 1881, in Blackburn, friendly).

William Henry Davies was the first Welshman to score for his country, in the 1–2 defeat by England on 18 January 1879. Wales did not play a match outside the British Isles until 1933, when it travelled to Paris for a friendly against France (1–1, 25 May); it was also Wales' first opposition from outside the home nations. Wales first entered the World Cup in 1950, and has qualified only once for the finals tournament., reaching the quarter-final in 1958, and being eliminated 0–1 by the eventual World champions **Brazil** (19 June 1958, in Gothenburg, Sweden); **Pelé** scored Brazil's goal. Although the 1958 World Cup was, perhaps, the country's best international achievement, it had qualified for the finals somewhat fortuitously. Wales had finished runners-up in its qualifying group to **Czechoslovakia** and should not have progressed to the finals; it qualified after a **playoff** against **Israel** (4–0 agg.). Israel had not played a single match in its Asia/Africa qualifying group because all its opponents had withdrawn in political protest; FIFA ruled that it could not progress to the finals without playing a qualifying tournament match and ordered a playoff against a European group runner-up. The 1958 Welsh squad included Ivor Allchurch, John Charles and Jack Kelsey. Wales reached the quarter-final of the European Championship in 1976 having won its four-nation qualifying group. Wales narrowly missed out in the 1994 World Cup finals. It needed to beat Romania in the final qualifying game at home in Cardiff, but lost 1–2 and missed a late penalty. On 16 October 1991, Ryan Giggs became Wales' youngest capped player at 17 years 321 days (1–4, v **Germany**, in Nuremburg, European Championship qualifier); his record was beaten on 3 June 1998 by Ryan Green, at 17 years 218 days old (v **Malta**, in Valetta, friendly). *League system* seventeen clubs compete in the League of Wales national Premier Division, with three points awarded for a draw and one for a win; clubs level on points are separated on goal difference. The bottom two clubs are relegated. The First Division is divided into two regional leagues, north and south. Each has 20 clubs, with the champions in each promoted to the Premier Division, subject to meeting league ground and financial criteria. *Record in international club tournaments* European Cup-winners Cup – Cardiff City (semi-final 1968, quarter-final 1965, 1971, second round 1989), Wrexham (quarter-final 1976, second round 1973, 1985, 1987, 1991), Newport County (quarter-final 1981), Swansea City (second round 1983), Bangor City (second round 1986); **UEFA Cup** – Barry Town (first round 1997; after winning first and second preliminary rounds). No Welsh club has progressed beyond the preliminary rounds of the **European Cup**. Other leading clubs: **Ebbw Vale**, **Connah's Quay**, **Inter CableTel**, **Newtown**.

Wales, women *country/women* women's football in Wales is administered by the **Football Association of Wales**, in Cardiff. *History* Wales' first international game was against the **Republic of Ireland** in 1973. The national women's team took part in its first international women's tournaments in 1976. Welsh women's football was taken under the aegis of the national association in 1993, with its subsequent entry into the European Championship for Women (1993-95 edition). *International tournament record* **Women's World Cup** – never qualified for finals tournament; **European Championship for Women** – first entered 1995 (last in its group of four nations).

walkover *n.* situation where a club wins a round of a knockout tournament because the opposition fails to turn up for the match, or withdraws. Compare **bye**.

wall pass *n.* another term for **one-two**.

wall *tactics* another word for **defensive wall**.

Wallidan Leader *club* Gambian national league club based in the capital Banjul. Ground: Box Bar (the national stadium), capacity: 10,000. Strip: blue shirts, white shorts. *Keynotes* Its national club record of eight consecutive league titles (1985 to 1992) is only one behind the African club record held by **Hafia FC** of **Guinea**. **African Cup-winners Cup** second round 1995; Gambian league champions 1974, 1977, 1979, 1985, 1986, 1987, 1988, 1989, 1990, 1991, 1992, 1995; Gambian Cup 1976, 1978, 1981, 1984, 1986, 1987, 1991, 1993, 1994, 1998.

Walsall *club* English league. *Dossier* Ground: **Bescot Stadium**, Walsall, West Midlands, capacity: 9,000. Strip: red shirts, black shorts and red socks. Nickname: the Saddlers. Record attendance: 10,628 **England** v **Switzerland** (20 May 1991, **'B' International**). Best average attendance: 12,089 (Fellows Park, 1949-50). Biggest win: 10–0 v **Darwen** (4 March 1899, Division Two). Biggest defeat: 0–12 v **Small Heath** (17 December 1892, Division Two), v Darwen (26 December 1896, Division Two). *History* Formed in 1888 as Walsall Town Swifts from an amalgamation of Walsall Swifts (founded in 1877) and Walsall Town (1879). The club moved to its Hillary Street ground (later named **Fellows Park**) in 1896 after playing at a ground on West Bromwich Road for several seasons. As early as 1889, Walsall reached the second round of the **FA Cup** – equivalent to today's fifth round – (1–6 v **Wolverhampton Wanderers**). Walsall was a **founder member** of Division Two in 1892-93, failed re-election in 1894-95, but returned in 1896-97. The club again failed re-election in 1900-01, remaining outside the League until the formation of Division Three (North) in 1921-22. In 1933, Walsall produced one of the biggest-ever FA Cup shocks, knocking out the imminent League Champions and, at the time, considered the best team in England, **Arsenal** (2–0, third round), and, in 1939, Walsall reached the FA Cup fifth round (0–3 v **Huddersfield Town**). Between 1951-52 and 1954-55, Walsall made four consecutive applications to retain its League status, finishing bottom of Division Three (South) on three occasions and second from bottom once. Walsall reached the FA Cup fifth round in 1975 (1–2 v **Birmingham City**), 1978 (1–4 v Arsenal) and again in 1987 (0–1 second replay v **Watford**). Aside from the club's 1933 victory over

Arsenal, Walsall's most significant Cup success came in 1984 when the club was a **League Cup** semi-finalist (2–4 agg. v **Liverpool**). Walsall won promotion to Division Two in 1987-88 via the end-of-season **play-offs** (4–0 replay v **Bristol City**). In 1990, Walsall moved to a new ground, Bescot Stadium, with the final League match played at Fellows Park on 11 May (v **Rotherham United**, Division Three). Unfortunately for the club the move to the new ground coincided with relegation to Division Four. Walsall was a Third Division end-of-season playoff semi-finalist in 1992-93. By 1995-96, the club was back playing in the Second Division. It won automatic promotion to the First Division in 1998-99 as Second Division runners up. *League record* Division One 1999-00; Division Two 1892-93 to 1894-95 (failed re-election), 1896-97 to 1900-01 (failed re-election), 1961-62 to 1962-63, 1988-89; Second Division 1995-96 to present; Division Three 1960-61, 1963-64 to 1978-79, 1980-81 to 1987-88, 1989-90; Third Division 1992-93 to 1994-95; Division Three (North) 1921-22 to 1926-27, 1931-32 to 1935-36; Division Three (South) 1927-28 to 1930-31, 1936-37 to 1957-58; Division Four 1958-59 to 1959-60, 1979-80, 1990-91 to 1991-92. *Honours* Division Four 1959-60. *Records* Mick Kearns is Walsall's most capped player (15 (18) for **Republic of Ireland**); Colin Harrison holds the record for club League appearances (467, 1964-82); Tony Richards (184, 1954-63) and Colin Taylor (184, 1958-63) are Walsall's record league goalscorers.

Walter, 1. Fritz *player* Striker. **Germany**/West Germany international (61 caps, 33 goals, 1940-58). Born 31 October 1921. *Clubs* **Kaiserslautern**. *Keynotes* Captain of West Germany's 1954 **World Cup** winning team; his half-cleared cross set up the chance for Helmut Rahn to score the 83rd-minute winner at **Wankdorf Stadion** (3-2, v **Hungary**, Berne, **Switzerland**). Fifth in West Germany's all-time list of goalscorers. *Honours* World Cup (West Germany 1954); West German Championship (Kaiserslautern, 1951, 1953). **2.** His brother, Otmar *player* Striker. West Germany international. *Keynotes* Played alongside his brother Fritz Walter in the 1954 World Cup final. Both brothers scored two goals each in the semi-final; a 6-1 defeat of **Austria**. See also **brothers**. *Honours* World Cup (West Germany 1954).

Wanderers *club* former English club. *Keynotes* Founded as **Forest** in 1859, the club took the Wanderers title in 1864, having moved from East London to Batterseas Park. As Wanderers, the club appeared in five of the first seven **FA Cup** finals, winning the inaugural competition in 1872 (1–0 v **Royal Engineers**) and the trophy on a further four occasions (1873, 2–0 v Oxford University; 1876, 3–0 v **Old Etonians**, replay; 1877, 2–1 v Oxford University; 1878, 3–1 v Royal Engineers). Charles Wollaston played in all five of the Wanderers' FA Cup triumphs, while a future president of **Football Association**, Lord Kinnaird, played in three of them, two as goalkeeper. The club disbanded in 1881.

Wankdorf Stadion *ground* Swiss sports ground situated in Berne, capacity: 37,551; Swiss national stadium and home of **BSC Young Boys**. *History* Opened in 1925 and completely redeveloped for the 1954 **World Cup**. The stadium stages the Swiss Cup final. During the 1954 World Cup, Wankdorf staged five matches, including the final: **West Germany** v **Turkey**, group 2; **Uruguay** v **Czechoslovakia**, group 3; **England** v **Switzerland**, group 4; **Hungary** v **Brazil**, quarter-final; West Germany v Hungary, final – total attendance 193,972; average attendance 62,477. Wankdorf also has hosted a **European Cup** final (1961 **Benfica** v **Barcelona**, 28,000) and a **European Cup-winners Cup** final (1989 Barcelona v **Sampdoria**, 45,000).

Wankie *club* Zimbabwe national league club based in Wankie (home of the world's largest coal mine). Ground: Wankie, capacity: 10,000. Strip: red shirts, red shorts. Zimbabwe Cup 1970, 1973, 1991.

WAPDA *club* Pakistan national league club, based in Lahore. **Asian Champion Teams Cup** finals tournament 1992; Pakistan national champions 1983, 1991, 1992.

war *n.* see **World War I**, **World War II**, **Fútbol war**.

warm-up *n.* gentle exercise before the start of a game or before a substitute enters the **field of play**. It is important to gently stretch and warm the muscles before undertaking vigorous exercise in order to reduce the risk of muscle **strain**. *vb.* **warm up** to carry out this exercise.

Wartime football *misc.* football during the two World Wars. *Keynotes* During **World War I** the **Football League** was abandoned after the 1914-15 season (restarting in 1919-20), but in the north of the country and the Midlands the Football League established regional tournaments – **Midland Regional Tournament** and the **Lancashire Regional Tournament**. The competitions were divided into a Principal Tournament and an additional Subsidiary Tournament which took place towards the end of the season after the main competition had been completed. *Principal tournament winners* Lancashire Region 1915-16, **Manchester City**; 1916-17, **Liverpool**; 1917-18, **Stoke City**; 1918-19, **Everton**; Midlands Region 1915-16, **Nottingham Forest**; 1916-17, **Leeds City**; 1917-18, Leeds City; 1918-19, Nottingham Forest. In seasons 1917-18 and 1918-19, the two winners of the regional tournaments played each other in a final over two-legs, with the winners declared **League Champions**. *Final results* 1917-18, Leeds City 2–1 Stoke City (agg.); 1918-19, Nottingham Forest 1–0 Everton. In addition, five clubs from the south joined with **Southern League** teams in a **London Combination** league. As with the Football League's regional competition, the London Combination was divided into a Principal Tournament and an additional Supplementary Tournament. The London Combination was continued as the **Football Combination** after the war as a league competition for the reserve sides of Southern-based clubs. *Principal tournament winners* 1915-16, **Chelsea**; 1916-17, **West Ham United**; 1917-18, Chelsea; 1918-19, **Brentford**. The **FA Cup** was abandoned during World War I, with the last final before the temporary cessation being **Sheffield United**'s 3–0 triumph over Chelsea at **Old Trafford** in 1915 in what is known as the **Khaki final** due to the large number of soldiers present. The final was the last big match in England for four years. In **Scotland**, the **Scottish League** continued uninterrupted throughout World War I, although the **Scottish FA Cup** was abandoned for the duration of hostilities. During **World War II** a more elaborate (but less consistent in England) system of regional competitions was developed in both England and Scotland. *Regional League results* 1939-40, South A – **Arsenal**; South B – **Queens Park Rangers**; South C – **Tottenham Hotspur**; South D – **Crystal Palace**; Western – Stoke City; South-western – **Plymouth Argyle**; Midland – **Wolverhampton Wanderers**; East Midland – **Chesterfield**; North-west – **Bury**; North-east **Huddersfield Town**; Scottish West and South – **Rangers**; Scottish East and North – **Falkirk**. See World War I and World War II.

waste time *rules* see **time-wasting**.

Waterford United *club* Republic of Ireland national league club based in Waterford, in Waterford County on the South coast. Founded in 1921 as Waterford FC. Ground: Kilcohan Park, capacity: 12,000. Strip: blue shirts, blue shorts. **European Cup** second round 1971; **European Cup-winners Cup** second round 1981; Republic of Ireland League champions; 1966, 1968, 1969, 1970, 1972, 1973; Republic of Ireland **FAI Cup** 1937, 1980, runners-up 1941, 1959, 1968, 1972, 1979, 1986. Notable former players: Shay Brennan (19 caps for the Republic of Ireland, formerly with **Manchester United**).

Waterhouse *club* Jamaica league club based in the capital Kingston. **Caribbean Club Championship** semi-final 1998; Jamaica League champions 1998; Jamaica Federation Cup 1998.

Watford *club* English league. *Dossier* Ground: **Vicarage Road**, Watford, Hertfordshire. Strip: yellow shirts with black and red trim, black shorts, and black socks with yellow trim. Nickname: the Hornets. Ground capacity: 22,000. Record attendance: 34,099 v **Manchester United** (3 February 1969, **FA Cup**, fourth round replay). Best average attendance: 18,246 (1984-85). Biggest win: 10–1 v **Lowestoft Town** (27 November 1926, FA Cup, first round). Biggest defeat: 0–10 v **Wolverhampton Wanderers** (13 January 1912, FA Cup, first round replay). *History* Founded in 1881 as Watford Rovers, becoming West Herts in 1890. In 1898, the club absorbed another local team, Watford St Mary's, and became Watford. Watford played at several venues, including at Cassiobury Park and at Cassio Road (West Herts Sports Ground), before settling at Vicarage Road in 1922. The club won the Southern League Championship in 1915 and, in 1920-21, it was a founder member of Division Three. The club was an FA Cup quarter-finalist in 1932 (0–5 v **Newcastle United**). In 1959-60, Watford won promotion to Division Three and narrowly missed further elevation in 1963-64 and again in 1966-67, finishing third on both occasions, before lifting the Division Three Championship on **goal average** in 1968-69. Watford reached the FA Cup semi-finals in 1970 (1–5 v **Chelsea**), having disposed of **Stoke City** (1–0, fourth round) and **Liverpool** (1–0, sixth round) . After dropping to Division Four in 1975-76 the club embarked on its most successful period. Singer-songwriter and erstwhile supporter Elton John became chairman in 1976 and, in 1977, future **England** manager Graham **Taylor** was appointed manager. Taylor adopted a very successful **long ball** game based on two strong central attackers, Luther Blissett and Ross Jenkins, supported by two quick wingers, John **Barnes** and Nigel Callaghan. Under Taylor, who was assisted by ex-**Arsenal** manager Bertie Mee, Watford progressed from Division Four to Division One runners-up in six seasons between 1977-78 and 1982-83, as well as being a **League Cup** semi-finalist in 1979 (1–3 agg. v **Nottingham Forest**). The League Cup success featured a victory over Manchester United at **Old Trafford** (2–1, third round). In 1983-84, the club reached the FA Cup final (0–2 v **Everton**) and competed in European competition for the first time, reaching the last 16 of the **UEFA Cup** (2–7 agg. v **Sparta Prague**). Taylor left in 1987 and Watford was relegated in 1987-88, although the club almost made an immediate return, reaching the semi-final stage of the end-of-season Division Two **playoffs**. Elton John sold the club to former **West Ham United** director Jack Petchey in 1990. Both Taylor and John returned to the club in 1997 after it had been relegated to the Second Division and, in 1997-98, Watford won promotion as Champions. The club won a second successive promotion, securing a place in the **Premier League** for the first time, by winning the 1998-99 First Division playoffs (2-0 v Bolton Wanderers). *League record* Premier League 1999-00 –; Division One 1982-83 to 1987-88; First Division1992-93 to 1995-96, 1998-99–; Division Two 1969-70 to 1971-72, 1979-80 to 1981-82, 1988-89 to 1991-92; Second Division 1996-97 to 1997-98; Division Three 1920-21, 1960-61 to 1968-69, 1972-73 to 1974-75, 1978-79; Division Three (South) 1921-22 to 1957-58; Division Four 1958-59 to 1959-60, 1975-76 to 1977-78. *Honours* Second Division 1997-98, Division Three 1968-69, Division Four 1977-78, Southern League 1915, **Division Three (South) Cup** 1937 (1–1 v **Millwall** (shared trophy)). *Records* John Barnes (31 (79) for England) and Kenny Jackett (31 for **Wales**) are Watford's most capped players; Luther Blissett holds the record for club League appearances (415, 1976-83, 1984-88, 1991-92); he is also Watford's record League goalscorer (158, 1976-83, 1984-88, 1991-92).

Watney Cup *competition* early 1970s pre-season English knockout tournament sponsored by brewing company Watney Mann. The tournament involved the two clubs from each of the four divisions that had scored the most goals in the previous season, barring promoted clubs and those that had qualified for European competition. It was the first sponsored competition for **Football League** clubs. The tournament also introduced the **penalty shootout**, which had been pioneered in the **North American Soccer League**, to decide drawn matches. From 1971, the competition also experimented with the **offside** laws, with attacking players offside only in the **penalty area**. Each club received £4,000 for participating, with a further £500 payments awarded for qualifying from the 1st round and for reaching the semi-finals. Winning teams picked up an additional £1,000, while all participants received a share of television money. *Final results* 1970, **Derby County** 4–1 **Manchester United**; 1971, **Colchester United** 4–4 **West Bromwich Albion** (4–3 pens); 1972, **Bristol Rovers** 0–0 **Sheffield United** (7–6 pens); 1973, **Stoke City** 2–0 **Hull City**.

Watson Hutton, Alexander *official* founder of the Argentine Football Association League in 1893, and the so-called "father of Argentine football". Hutton was born in Edinburgh, Scotland, and became director of the English High School in Buenos Aires. A fledgling Argentine Association Football League had existed in 1891, but Watson Hutton's is the true forerunner of the modern league in **Argentina**. English High School, later became Alumni (an old boys' club), won 10 championships between 1900 and 1911.

WBA *club* abbreviation for **West Bromwich Albion**.

Weah, George Opong *player* Striker. **Liberia** international. Born 1 October 1966. *Clubs* Young Survivors, Bongrange Bonguine, **Mighty Barolle** and **Invincible Eleven** (all of Liberia), **Tonnerre Yaoundé** (of Cameroon), **AS Monaco**, **Paris Saint-Germain** and **Milan**. *Keynotes* Weah was the first African to receive the **FIFA World Footballer of the Year** award. Joined AS Monaco in 1988, and Paris St Germain in 1992. Top scorer in the 1995 **European Cup** tournament, with seven goals (for Paris St Germain). Transferred to AC Milan in 1995. In 1996, Weah was awarded FIFA's **Fairplay Award** for sportsmanship. *Honours* Cameroon League championship (Tonnerre Yaoundé, 1987, 1988); French league championship (Paris St Germain, 1994); Italian **Serie A** championship (Milan, 1996); FIFA World Footballer of the Year 1995; **Confédération Africaine de Football** (CAF) Footballer of the Year 1995; *France Football* **African Footballer of the Year** 1994.

wedging *tactics* two defenders acting in unison to limit the **goalscoring**, dribbling and passing opportunities available to twin attackers through a combination of **marking** and **sagging** tactics.

Welsh Cup *competition* annual Welsh-knockout competition founded in 1877. Since the **League of Wales** was established by the **Football Association of Wales** in 1992, the Welsh Cup has been exclusively open to Welsh clubs, having previously allowed bordering English clubs to enter. Welsh winners of the competition have since 1961 qualified for **European Cup-winners Cup**. From 1996-97, only those clubs playing in the League of Wales could win a place in Europe the following season by lifting the Welsh Cup. The three Welsh Football League clubs, **Cardiff City**, **Swansea City** and **Wrexham**, and their non-League colleagues that play in the English pyramid system – Colwyn Bay, Merthyr Tydfil and Newport AFC – no longer compete in the competition. The Football Association of Wales runs an additional invitation competition - the FAW invitation Cup - which includes the English league clubs from Wales. Between 1962 and 1985, the final was played on a home and away basis (although several finals required a third match to settle the tie, but not on an aggregate basis), otherwise it has been a one-off match. *Keynotes* Wrexham, the first winners of the competition in 1878, was forced to wait almost a year before receiving the trophy and medals because the Welsh Football Association was so short of money. The 1934 final between **Bristol City** and **Tranmere Rovers** was the first all-English contest, and a Welsh club did not regain the trophy until **Lovells Athletic**'s victory in 1948. *Records* (Up to and including 1998) Wrexham has won the competition a record 23 times and it has also been a finalist on a further 22 occasions – also a record. The first final to go to a replay was the 1898 match between Druids and Wrexham. *Final results* 1878, Wrexham 1–0 Druids; 1879, **Newtown** 2–1 Wrexham; 1880, Druids 2–1 Ruthin; 1881, Druids 2–0 Newtown White; 1882, Druids 2–1 Northwich Victoria; 1883 Wrexham 1–0 Druids; 1884, Oswestry 3–2 Druids; 1885, Druids 2–0 Oswestry; 1886, Druids 5–2 Newtown; 1887, Chirk 4–2 Davenham; 1888, Chirk 5–0 Newtown; 1889, **Bangor City** 2–1 Northwich Victoria; 1890, Chirk 1–0 Wrexham; 1891, **Shrewsbury Town** 5–2 Wrexham; 1892, Chirk 2–1 Westminster Rovers; 1893, Wrexham 2–1 Chirk; 1894, Chirk 2–0 Westminster Rovers; 1895, Newtown 3–2 Wrexham; 1896, Bangor City 3–1 Wrexham; 1897, Wrexham 2–0 Newtown; 1898, Druids 2–1 Wrexham; 1899, Druids 1–0 Wrexham; 1900, AberwystwythTown 3–0 Druids; 1901, Oswestry 1–0 Druids ; 1902, Wellington 1–0 Wrexham; 1903, Wrexharn 8–0 Aberaman; 1904, Druids 3–2 Aberdare; 1905, Wrexham 3–0 Aberdare; 1906, Wellington 3–2 Whitchurch; 1907, Oswestry 2–0 Whitchurch; 1908, Chester 3–1 Connah's Quay; 1909, Wrexham 1–0 **Chester**; 1910, Wrexham 2–0 Chester; 1911, Wrexham 6–1 Connah's Quay; 1912 **Cardiff City** 3–0 Pontypridd; 1913, **Swansea** Town 1–0 Pontypridd; 1914, Wrexham 3–0 Llanelli; 1915, Wrexham 1–0 Swansea; 1920, Cardiff City 2–1 Wrexham; 1921, Wrexham 3–1 Pontypridd; 1922, Cardiff City 2–0 Ton Pentre; 1923, Cardiff City 3–2 Aberdare; 1924, Wrexham 1–0 Merthyr; 1925 Wrexham 3–1 Flint; 1926, Ebbw Vale 3–2 Swansea; 1927, Cardiff City 2–0 Rhyl; 1928, Cardiff City 2–0 Bangor City; 1929, Connah's Quay 3–0 Cardiff City; 1930, Cardiff City 4–2 Rhyl; 1931, Wrexham 7–0 Shrewsbury Town; 1932, Swansea 2–0 Wrexham; 1933, Chester 2–0 Wrexham; 1934, Bristol City 3–0 Tranmere Rovers; 1935, Tranmere Rovers 1–0 Chester; 1936, **Crewe Alexandra** 2–0 Chester; 1937, Crewe Alexandra 3–1 Rhyl; 1938, Shrewsbury Town 2–1 Swansea; 1939, South Liverpool 2-1 Cardiff City; 1940, Wellington 4–0 Swansea; 1947, Chester 5–1 Merthyr; 1948, Lovells 3–0 Shrewsbury Town; 1949, Merthyr 2–0 Swansea; 1950, Swansea 4–1 Wrexham; 1951, Merthyr 3–2 Cardiff City; 1952, Rhyl 4–3 Merthyr; 1953, Rhyl 2–1 Chester; 1954, Flint 2–1 Chester; 1955, Barry 4–3 Chester; 1956, Cardiff City 3–2 Swansea; 1957, Wrexham 2–1 Swansea; 1958, Wrexham 2–0 Chester; 1959, Cardiff City 2–0 Lovells Athletic; 1960, Wrexham 1–0 Cardiff City; 1961, Swansea 3–1 Bangor City; 1962, Bangor City 3–1 Wrexham; 1963, Borough United 2–1 Newport (agg.); 1964, Cardiff City 2–0 Bangor City; 1965, Cardiff Clty 3–0 Wrexham; 1966, Swansea 2–1 Chester; 1967, Cardiff City 4–3 Wrexham (agg.); 1968, Cardiff City 6–1 Hereford (agg.); 1969, Cardiff City 5–1 Swansea (agg.); 1970, Cardiff City 5–0 Chester (agg.); 1971, Cardiff City 4–1 Wrexham (agg.); 1972, Wrexham 3–2 Cardiff City (agg.); 1973, Cardiff City 5–1 Bangor City (agg.); 1974, Cardiff City 2–0 Stourbridge (agg.); 1975, Wrexham 5–2 Cardiff City (agg.); 1976, Cardiff City 6–5 Hereford (agg.); 1977, Shrewsbury Town 4–2 Cardiff City (agg.); 1978, Wrexham 3–1 Bangor City (agg.); 1979, Shrewsbury Town 2–1 Wrexham (agg.); 1980, Newport County 5–1 Shrewsbury Town (agg.); 1981, Swansea City 2–1 Hereford United (agg.); 1982, Swansea City 2–1 Cardiff (agg.); 1983, Swansea City 4–1 Wrexham (agg.); 1984, Shrewsbury Town 2–0 Wrexham (agg.); 1985, Shrewsbury Town 5–1 Bangor City (agg.); 1986, Wrexham 2–1 Kidderminster Harriers; 1987, Merthyr 1–0 Newport County; 1988, Cardiff City 2–0 Wrexham; 1989, Swansea City 5–0 Kidderminster Harriers; 1990, Hereford United 2–1 Wrexham; 1991, Swansea City 2–0 Wrexham; 1992, Cardiff City 1–0 Hednesford; 1993, Cardiff City 5–0 Rhyl; 1994, **Barry Town** 2-1 Cardiff City; 1995, Wrexham 2–1 Cardiff City; 1996, **Llansantffraid** 3–3 Barry Town (3–2 pens.); 1997, Barry Town 2–1 **Cwmbran**; 1998, Bangor City 1–1 Connah's Quay (5–3 pens.); 1999, **Inter CableTel** (Cardiff) 1–1 Carmarthen (4–2 pens.).

Welshpool Town *club* Welsh league. Ground: **Maesydre**, Welshpool, Powys. Strip: white shirts, black shorts. Nickname: Maes-y-Dre. Ground capacity: 1,500. Formed in 1878.

Wembley *ground* English sports stadium situated in London; regular home of **England** national side and venue for both the **FA Cup** final (since 1923) and the **League Cup** final (since 1967). Current capacity: 79,045 all seated (for FA Cup finals). *History* Built as the centre-piece of the British Empire Exhibition at a cost of £750,000, Wembley was constructed on the site of "Watkin's Folly" – a tower built by Sir Edward Watkin and intended to rise to a height of 1,150 feet but which reached only 200 feet before being abandoned.

Designed by architects John Simpson and Maxwell Ayrton, the stadium features two distinctive 126-feet white towers – the renowned **twin towers**, which are listed buildings. The stadium forms part of a 73-acre complex that also includes Wembley Arena (opened in 1934) and a conference centre (opened in 1977). Cup winners and losers both climb Wembley's famed 39 steps to receive their medals. *History* Wembley took only 300 working days to complete (January 1922 to April 1923) and was finished just four days before the stadium staged its first event, the 1923 FA Cup final **Bolton Wanderers** v **West Ham United**). The match, which became known as the **White horse final**, attracted an estimated crowd of around 200,000, although the official attendance was put at a record 126, 047. The **Football Association** was forced to reimburse some ticket holders who could not gain admission and the chaotic events led to the establishment of a government-appointed body, Departmental Committee on Crowds. Thereafter the final was made an **all-ticket** affair. England played its first international at the stadium on 12 April 1924 before 37,250 spectators (v **Scotland**) and 11 days later the Empire Exhibition, which attracted around 30 million visitors, was opened. When the Exhibition closed in October 1925, the stadium's owners put the site up for sale at £350,000. Jimmy White, a speculator, bought it for £300,000 and nine months later Arthur Elvin, who had sold some of Exhibition's attractions, offered White £122,500 for the stadium. White committed suicide to avoid his creditors before the deal was agreed, enabling Elvin to purchase the site from the official receiver for the bid price and sell it on to a syndicate at a healthy £27,500 profit. Elvin became managing director of Wembley Stadium and Greyhound Racecourse Company Limited. Wembley underwent a facelift for the 1948 Olympic Games, including the construction of Olympic Way connecting the stadium with Wembley Park Station. The 100,000 capacity (44,000 seated; night matches 92,000) stadium was originally uncovered at both ends, and it was not until 1963 that roofs were erected to protect all spectators. At the same time, Wembley erected a suspended **press box** and a **television gantry**. Since the stadium became all-seater in 1990, its capacity is between 79,045 (for FA Cup finals) and 82,600 (rock concerts). The last 100,000 attendance was the 1985 FA Cup final (**Manchester United** v **Everton**). After the 1999 FA Cup final, Wembley was demolished and redeveloped as the UK's Millennium Stadium with the completion date the 2002 FA Cup final. Funding for the £320 million project, which will create a 88,000 capacity stadium and stage athletics and rugby as well as football, comes from the FA and the English Sports Council. Aside from the FA Cup and League Cup finals and England fixtures, Wembley has hosted a number of other football matches. Wembley was the setting for nine matches during the 1966 **World Cup**: England v **Uruguay**, **France** v **Mexico**, England v Mexico, Mexico v Uruguay, England v France (group 1); England v **Argentina**

(quarter-final); England v **Portugal** (semi-final); Portugal v **USSR** (3rd place playoff); England v West **Germany** (final) – total attendance = 748,800; average attendance = 83,200. During the tournament, a group 1 fixture (Uruguay v France, 45, 662) was played at White City stadium in west London because Wembley was hosting a pre-arranged greyhound meeting on the same evening. The stadium staged six matches during the 1996 **European Championship**: three group A fixtures (England v **Switzerland**, England v Scotland, England v **Netherlands**); a quarter-final (England v **Spain**); a semi-final (England v Germany); and the final (Germany v **Czech Republic**). Wembley was also the setting for the 1948 **Olympic Games** final (**Sweden** v **Yugoslavia**, 60,000). The stadium has hosted five **European Cup** finals (1963, **AC Milan** v Benfica, 45,000; 1968, Manchester United v Benfica, 100,000; 1970, **Feyenoord** v **Panathinaikos**, 90,000; 1978, **Liverpool** v **Brugge (FC)**, 92,000; 1992, **Barcelona** v **Sampdoria**, 70,827) and two **European Cup-winners Cup** finals (1965, West Ham United v **Munich 1860**, 100,000; 1993, **Parma** v **Antwerp**, 37,393). Both **UEFA** and the Football Association granted **Arsenal** permission to hold its 1998-99 **Champions League** matches at Wembley, with the first game taking place on 30 September 1998 and attracting a crowd of 73,455 (v Panathinaikos). In 1949, Wembley staged its first **FA Amateur Cup** final (Bromley v Romford), an event it continued to host until the competition's demise in 1974. Clapton **Orient** played two Division Three (South) fixtures at Wembley in 1930-31 (v **Brentford**, v **Southend United**) after the club's Lea Bridge ground was banned for not meeting the required standards. Argonauts, an amateur club which first applied to join the **Football League** in 1928, provisionally booked Wembley Stadium as its home ground in 1930, hoping to gain admission to Division Three (South). On 13 October 1928, Wembley hosted the Southern League match between the Ealing Association and **Ipswich Town** because the nearby Corfton Road ground was unfit. Greyhound racing was first staged in December 1927 and, in 1929, the stadium also became the regular venue (with the exception of 1932) of the Rugby League Cup final. Between 1931 and 1956, speedway was added to the sporting activities at Wembley (it continued to host the World Championships until 1981). A one-off American Football exhibition match was staged at the stadium in 1986 (Dallas Cowboys v Chicago Bears). On 7 March 1998, Wembley staged its first Five Nations Rugby international when **Wales**, which had switched to the stadium while Cardiff Arms Park was being redeveloped, played Scotland. Wembley regularly hosts non-sporting events, such as the 1985 Live Aid concert. Wembley installed floodlights in 1955 and the first match under lights took place that year (London v Frankfurt, **UEFA** (Fairs) **Cup**). On 30 November 1955, England made its first partially floodlit appearance at the stadium (v Spain), when the lights were turned on in the second half. The first all-floodlit international fixture occurred on 20 November 1963 (v **Northern Ireland**). In addition to FA Cup finals, Wembley hosted its first final replay in 1981 (**Tottenham Hotspur** v **Manchester City**). England played its 100th international at Wembley on 12 March 1975 (v West Germany).

Werder Bremen (SV) *club* German league. *Dossier* Ground: Weserstadion, Bremen. Strip: green and white striped shirts, green shorts, green socks. Ground capacity: 38,659. *History* Formed in 1899 and officially called Sport-Verein Werder Bremen. Between 1991 and 1994, the club won one **Bundesliga** title, two domestic Cups and the **European Cup-winners Cup** in successive seasons. Werder won its first Bundesliga Championship in 1964-65, having previously won only one trophy, the West German Cup in 1961. Werder's 1991 Cup victory followed two successive appearances in the final: 1989 (1–4 v **Borussia Dortmund**) and 1990 (2–3 v **Kaiserslautern** (1.FC)). *Honours* Bundesliga 1964-65, 1987-88, 1992-93; West German Cup 1961 (0–2 v Kaiserslautern (1.FC)), 1991 (1–1, 4–3 pens. v **Cologne** (1.FC)), 1994 (3–1 v Rot-Weiss Essen); European Cup-winners Cup 1992 (2–0 v **Monaco**).

West African Championship *competition* see **CSSA Zone 3 Tournament**.

West African Football Union (WAFU) *confederation* international football association of West Africa, based in Abidjan, Ivory Coast, founded 1975. Member countries: **Benin**, **Burkina Faso**, **Cape Verde**, **Gambia**, **Ghana**, **Guinea**, **Guinea Bissau**, **Côte d'Ivoire**, **Liberia**, **Mali**, **Mauritania**, **Niger**, **Nigeria**, **Senegal**, **Sierra Leone**, **Togo**. *Nations tournaments* **CEDEAO Tournament**. *International club tournaments* **West African Football Union General Eyadema Cup** .

West African Football Union General Eyadema Cup *competition* international club tournament for the league runners-up clubs of member nations of the **West African Football Union**. *Winners:* 1977 **Stade Abidjan** (Côte d'Ivoire); 1978 **ASFA Dakar** (Senegal); 1979 **AS Police** (Senegal); 1980 AS Police; 1981 **Stella Abidjan** (Côte d'Ivoire); 1982 **Sekondi Hasaacas** (Ghana); 1983 New Nigeria Bank (Nigeria); 1984 New Nigeria Bank; 1985 **Africa Sports Nationale** (Côte d'Ivoire); 1986 Africa Sports; 1987 Cornerstones Kumasi; 1988 ASFAG Conkary (Guinea); 1989 Ranchers Bees (Nigeria); 1990 **ASEC Mimosas Abidjan** (Ivory Coast); 1991 Africa Sports; 1992 **Stade Malien** (Mali); 1993 **Bendel Insurance** (Nigeria); 1994 Bendel Insurance; 1995 Bendel Insurance; 1996 **East End Lions** (of Sierra Leone); 1997 Ghapoa (Ghana); 1998 IICC **Shooting Stars** (Nigeria).

West Bromwich Albion *club* English league. *Dossier* Ground: The **Hawthorns**, West Bromwich, west Midlands. Strip: blue and white striped shirts, white shorts, white socks with blue trim. Nickname: Throstles or Baggies. Ground capacity: 25,396. Record attendance: 64,815 v **Arsenal** (6 March 1937, **FA Cup**, sixth round). Best average attendance: 38,910 (1949-50). Biggest win: 12–0 v **Darwen** (4 April 1892,

Division One). Biggest defeat: 3–10 v **Stoke City** (4 February 1937, Division One). *History* Founded as West Bromwich Strollers by employees at Salter's Spring Works in 1879. Strollers was replaced with Albion in 1881 and the club turned professional four years later. In 1886, Albion reached the first of three consecutive FA Cup finals (0–2 replay v **Blackburn Rovers**). The following season Albion lost again in the final (0–2 **Aston Villa**), before the club finally lifted the trophy in 1888 (2–1 v **Preston North End**). The club was a founder member of the **Football League** in 1888 and, in 1892, it won a second FA Cup (3–0 v Aston Villa). In 1895, Albion reached its fifth FA Cup final in 10 seasons (0–1 Aston Villa). The next year, the club avoided relegation despite finishing bottom of Division One by winning in the **test matches** that between 1892-93 and 1897-98 were used to determine promotion and relegation. Albion finally settled at The Hawthorns in 1900. After spending all but two seasons in Division Two between 1901-02 and 1910-11, the club reached a sixth FA Cup final in 1912 (0–1 replay v **Barnsley**) and, in 1919-20, Albion won its one and only League Championship. The team included seven internationals, among them **England** left-back Jesse Pennington. West Brom's victory in the 1931 FA Cup final (2–1 v **Birmingham**, with an all-English side) was only the fourth by a team from Division Two (overall seven Division Two clubs have won the FA Cup: **Notts County** (1894), **Wolverhampton Wanderers** (1908), **Barnsley** (1912), **Sunderland** (1973), **Southampton** (1976), **West Ham United** (1980)). The Cup triumph also coincided with the club's return to the top flight following a four-season spell in Division Two – thus becoming the first club to win promotion and the FA Cup in the same season. In 1935, the club again reached the FA Cup final (2–4 v **Sheffield Wednesday**). Albion narrowly missed winning the double in 1953-54, finishing runners-up in the League and achieving a fourth FA Cup success (3–2 v Preston North End). Between 1965-66 and 1960-70, the club was a **League Cup** finalist in three out of five seasons, winning in 1966 (5–3 agg. v West Ham United), and losing in 1967 (2–3 v **Queens Park Rangers**) and 1970 (1–2 a.e.t. v **Manchester City**). Following a further FA Cup triumph in 1968 (1–0 a.e.t. v **Everton**), Albion reached the quarter-finals of the **European Cup-winners Cup** (0–1 agg. v **Dunfermline Athletic**). In 1978-79, under the managership of Ron Atkinson and with a side that included future England captain Bryan **Robson**, Laurie Cunningham and Cyrille Regis, Albion finished third in Division One and reached the **UEFA Cup** quarter-finals (1–2 agg. v **Red Star Belgrade**). Relegation in 1986-87 was followed by demotion to Division Three for the first time in the club's history in 1991-92. Albion won promotion to the First Division via the end-of-season **playoffs** in 1992-93 (3–0 v **Port Vale**). West Brom floated on the **Alternative Investment Market** in January 1997 (floatation price = 280p), which is a precursor to full floatation on the stock market. Overall the club has appeared in 10 FA Cup finals and 17 semi-finals. *League record* Division One (including Football League) 1888-89 to 1900-01, 1902-03 to 1903-04, 1911-12 to 1926-27, 1931-32 to 1937-38, 1949-50 to 1972-73, 1976-77 to 1985-86; First Division 1993-94 to present; Division Two 1901-02, 1904-05 to 1910-11, 1927-28 to 1930-31, 1938-39 to 1948-49, 1973-74 to 1975-76, 1986-87 to 1990-91; Second Division 1992-93; Division Three 1991-92. *Honours* League 1919-20; Division Two 1901-02, 1910-11; FA Cup 1888: (2–1 v Preston North End), 1892 (3–0 v Aston Villa), 1931 (2–1 v Birmingham – *Team* Pearson, Shaw, Trentham, Magee, W Richardson, Edwards, Glidden, Carter, WG Richardson (2), Sandford, Wood), 1954 (3–2 v Preston North End – *Team* Sanders, Kennedy, Millard, Dudley, Dugdale, Barlow, Griffin (1), Ryan, Allen (2, 1 pen.), Nicholls, Lee), 1968 (1–0 a.e.t. v Everton – *Team* Osborne, Fraser, Williams, Brown, Talbut, Kaye (Clarke), Lovett, Collard, Astle (1), Hope, Clark); League Cup 1966 (5–3 agg. v West Ham United); **FA Charity Shield** 1920 (2–0 v **Tottenham Hotspur**), 1954 (4–4 v Wolverhampton Wanderers (each club held the trophy for six months)). *Records* Stuart Williams is West Brom's most capped player (33 (43) for **Wales**); Tony Brown holds the record for club appearances (574, 1963-80); he is also Albion's record League goalscorer (218, 1963-79).

West Bromwich Albion plc *n.* publicly-quoted business which owns **West Bromwich Albion**. The club became a listed company on the **Alternative Investment Market** in January 1997 (floatation price = 280p). West Bromwich had a market capitalisation – the market value of the company's issued share capital (eg, the quoted price of its shares multiplied by the number of shares outstanding) – of £20.5 million when it joined the AIM.

Westfalenstadion *ground* German football ground situated in Dortmund; home of **Borussia Dortmund**. Ground capacity: 69,000. *History* Built for the 1974 **World Cup** and part of sports complex situated in Westfalenpark. The ground was recently redeveloped, increasing the capacity to 69,000. Borussia has retained an area of terracing known as the Südtribune, installing removable seats to comply with **UEFA** regulations for European competition matches. Around 10,000 Dortmund fans watched on a giant screen at Westfalen the club's 1997 **World Club Cup** match against **Cruzeiro** Esporte Clube of **Brazil** in Tokyo. During the 1974 World Cup, Westfalen staged one group 2 fixture (**Scotland** v **Zaire**), two group 3 matches (**Netherlands** v **Sweden**, Netherlands v **Bulgaria**) and a second round group A game (Netherlands v Brazil) – total attendance 182,900; average attendance 45,725.

West Germany *former country* see **Germany**.

West Ham United *club* English league. *Dossier* Ground: **Upton Park**, east London. Strip: claret and light blue halved shirts, white shorts, light blue socks with claret trim. Website: *http://www.westhamunited.*

co.uk Nickname: Hammers. Ground capacity: 26,012 all seated. Record attendance: 42,322 v **Tottenham Hotspur** (17 October 1970, Divsion One). Best average attendance: 31,125 (1968-69). Biggest win: 10–0 v **Bury** (25 October 1983, **League Cup**, second round 2nd leg). Biggest defeat: 2–8 v **Blackburn Rovers** (26 December 1963, Division One). *History* Founded in 1895 as Thames Ironworks by shipyard workers employed by the company of the same name. The club joined the **Southern League** in 1898, but its decision to begin using professional players led Thames Ironworks' owner and club benefactor Arnold Hills to disown it. As a result, in 1900 Thames Ironworks was disbanded and re-formed as West Ham United. West Ham played its matches at the Hills-owned Memorial Recreation Ground and when the club's lease expired in 1904 it was forced to move, eventually settling at Boleyn Ground (more commonly known as Upton Park) and merging with Boleyn Castle FC. The club was elected to Division Two in 1919-20 following the expansion of the **Football League** after **World War I**. In 1923, the club won promotion to Division One and reached the **FA Cup** final (0–2 **Bolton Wanderers**) – the first **Wembley** final (see **White horse final**). Relegation followed in 1931-32 and for the next 26 years the club remained in Division Two, only narrowly avoiding the drop to Division Three (South) in 1932-33 and, in contrast, missing promotion on **goal average** in 1933-34. Under Ted Fenton's managership, and with a side that included future high-profile coaches such as Malcolm Allison, Jimmy Bloomfield, John Bond, Noel Cantwell, Frank O'Farrell and Dave Sexton, West Ham returned to the top flight in 1958. West Ham won the FA Cup, its first major trophy, in 1964 (3–2 v **Preston North End**) with a side managed by Ron **Greenwood** (who later became general manager), and which contained Geoff **Hurst** and Bobby **Moore**. In 1965, West Ham triumphed in the **European Cup-winners Cup** (2–0 v Munich 1860), and the following season the club reached the semi-final stage of the same competition (2–5 agg. v **Borussia Dortmund**) and the League Cup final (3–5 agg. v **West Bromwich Albion**). The club won two further FA Cup finals in 1975 (2–0 v **Fulham**) and 1980 (1–0 v **Arsenal**), both against London opposition, and, on the first occasion, against a Fulham side that contained West Ham's former-captain Moore. West Ham's victory in the 1980 FA Cup final was the seventh by a team from Division Two (the others are: **Notts County** (1894), **Wolverhampton Wanderers** (1908), **Barnsley** (1912), West Bromwich Albion (1931), **Sunderland** (1973), **Southampton** (1976)). In 1981, the club won the Division Two Championship for the second time and reached the League Cup final (1–2 replay v **Liverpool**). West Ham's highest-ever League position was achieved in 1985-86 when the club finished third in Division One. *League record* Premier League 1993–94–; Division One 1923-24 to 1931-32, 1958-59 to 1977-78, 1981-82 to 1988-89, 1991-92; First Division 1992-93; Division Two 1919-20 to

1922-23, 1932-33 to 1957-58, 1978-79 to 1980-81, 1989-90 to 1990-91. *Honours* Division Two 1957-58, 1980-81; FA Cup 1964 (3–2 v Preston North End – *Team* Standen, Bond, Burkett, Bovington, Brown, Moore, Brabrook, Boyce (1), Byrne, Hurst (1), Sissons (1)), 1975 (2–0 v Fulham – *Team* Day, McDowell, Lampard, Bonds, T Taylor, Lock, Jennings, Paddon, A Taylor (2), Brooking, Holland), 1980 (1–0 v Arsenal – *Team* Parkes, Stewart, Lampard, Bonds, Martin, Devonshire, Allen, Pearson, Cross, Brooking (1), Pike); European Cup-winners Cup 1965 (2–0 v Munich 1860 – *Team* Standen, Kirkup, Burkett, Peters, Brown, Moore, Sealey (2), Boyce, Hurst, Dear, Sissons). *Records* Bobby Moore is West Ham's most capped player (108 for **England**); Billy Bonds holds the record for club appearances (663, 1967-88); Vic Watson is West Ham's record league goalscorer (298, 1920-35).

West Refa'a *club* Bahrain national league club. Bahrain League champions 1982, 1987, 1990, 1993, 1997, 1998.

Western Conference *n.* one of the two regional divisions of the United States **Major League Soccer**. The clubs are: **Chicago Fire** (Chicago, Illinois), **Colorado Rapids** (Denver, Colorado), **Dallas Burn** (Dallas, Texas), **Kansas City Wiz** (Kansas City, Missouri), **Los Angeles Galaxy** (Los Angeles, California), **San Jose Clash** (San Jose, California). The first-, second-, third- and fourth-placed clubs in the conference contest a playoff competition. The winners of this play a championship final with the winners of the **Eastern Conference**. Conferences and conference playoffs are also in operation in the other US football leagues, eg the **A-League/Select League**, **Pro-League** and **Premier Leagues**.

Western Sahara *country no international affiliation* country/disputed territory in North Africa, formerly know as Spanish Sahara. Ceded by **Spain** to **Morocco** and **Mauritania** in 1975 (the territory was divided, the southern part going to Mauritania). The independence movement of Western Sahara (the Polisario) declared independence as the Saharan Arab Democratic Republic. Mauritania withdrew in 1979 and Morocco claimed the entire region. Internal war throughout 1980s. The independence of the state is recognised by some, but not all countries. Area: 266,000 sq km (102,675 sq miles). Population: 250,000. Capital: La'Youn (or Laayoune). *Dossier* Football association (Haut Council du Sport Sahraoui) founded in 1979. National stadium: El Aauin, capacity: 5,000. National strip: white shirts, black shorts. Season played from September to June. *International tournament record* has played only friendly matches. *League system* Fourteen clubs participate in a national league: some clubs, including Jeunesse Club Sportif El Aauin, compete in the Moroccan league.

Western Samoa *country OFC* country in the Southwest Pacific Ocean, comprising the islands of Savai'i, Upolu and a number of smaller islands and islets. Independence from Britain in 1962. Area: 2,840 sq km (1,095 sq miles). Population: 163,000 (1994 est.). Languages: English, Samoan. Capital: Apia. *Dossier* Samoa Football (Soccer) Association (Apia) formed in 1968, affiliated to **FIFA** and the **Oceania Football Confederation** (OFC) in 1986, president: Tautulu Roebuck; general secretary: Luapule Ropati Enosa. Season played from June to September. National stadium: Apia Park, Apia, capacity: 12,000. National strip: royal blue shirts, white shorts, royal blue and white socks. *International tournament record* **Olympic Games** – never entered; **Oceania Women's Tournament/Women's World Cup** – first entered 1998 (did not qualify for 1999 World Cup finals); **World Cup** – first entered 1998 (second in its first-round qualifying group of three); **Oceania Championship** – never entered. *Record against British and Irish national teams* none played. *History* Western Samoa first entered the World Cup at the 1998 tournament. At the Polynesian qualifying tournament in **Tonga**, in November 1996, Western Samoa defeated the Cook Islands (2–1), but lost 0–1 to Tonga, which qualified for the next stage. Association football lags behind rugby in popularity. *Record in international club tournaments* never entered.

Western Soccer League *n.* former United States professional football league, founded 1985 (as Western Soccer Alliance). Merged with **American Soccer League** (sense **3.**) to form the **A-League**. Won by San Jose Earthquakes (1985), Hollywood Kickers (1986), San Diego Nomads (1987, 1989), Seattle Storm (1988).

Whadadah *club* Jamaica league club based in Montego Bay. Strip: green shirts, yellow shorts. Jamaica League champions 1988, 1992.

Wharton, Arthur *player* Goalkeeper. Career ca. 1889-. *Clubs* **Preston North End**. *Keynotes* First black professional footballer in the English game. Joined Preston in 1886, turning professional in 1889. Principally a goalkeeper, Wharton, an accomplished athlete, could also play effectively on the wing. In the 1886 AAA amateur athletics championships, Wharton became the first UK athlete to run the 100 yards in under 10 seconds.

Wheatley Report *legal* UK Government report carried out under the chair of Lord Wheatley in the wake of the **Ibrox Park disaster** of 1971. The report made recommendations for the safety at sports grounds, including a requirement that grounds with a capacity of 10,000 or more should be licensed by the local authority. Initially, the findings were implemented as a voluntary "Green Guide", and later brought in formally in the **Safety of Sports Ground Act 1975**.

When Saturday Comes *publication* national **fanzine**-cum-football magazine that first appeared in March 1986 as an off-shoot of another fanzine, Snipe.

whistle *n.* portable instrument used by the referee to signify the start and restart or halting of play. It is used to start the match, during normal play to help implement the rules of the game, and at the end of the game – the **final whistle**. The traditional referee's whistle is of the "pea" type; a short shrill whistle with a small ball in its barrel to create a warbling effect. *vb.* to indicate a halt or start of play. *Keynotes* The referee's whistle was introduced in 1878. Referees in local games often take a spare whistle with a different tone, in case their first choice is too similar to one used for a match on a neighbouring pitch.

White Hart Lane *ground* English football ground situated in north London; home of **Tottenham Hotspur**. *Dossier* Ground capacity: 36,200 all seated. Pitch dimensions: 100.5m x 67m. Record attendance: 75,038 v **Sunderland** (5 March 1938, **FA Cup**, sixth round). Best average attendance: 55,509 (1967-68). *History* Tottenham Hotspur moved to White Hart Lane in 1899 after previously playing at Tottenham marshes and Northumberland Park. The ground was situated on a disused nursery owned by a brewery company that lay behind the White Hart Inn and which was close to White Hart Lane station. Tottenham initially named the ground the High Road Ground, eventually switching to the present title after **World War I**. The club played its first match at White Hart Lane on 4 September 1899 (v **Notts County**, friendly) and it bought the freehold to the site for £8,900 in 1905. Redevelopment followed and the ground opened a new stand, designed by Archibald **Leitch,** for the visit of **Manchester United** on 11 September 1909, Tottenham first match in Division One. The stand had a spurred cockerel perched on a ball on its roof – chosen to reflect the fact that fighting cocks wore spurs, as did Shakespeare's Harry Hotspur character from which the club draws its name (see Tottenham Hotspur). By 1923, more than 30,000 fans in the 50,000-capacity ground were under covered accommodation, and in 1934 Barclays Bank financed the building of a new Leitch-designed East Stand. Local rivals **Arsenal** played some matches at White Hart Lane during **World War II** after **Highbury** was damaged by bombs. Redevelopment of the ground, which began in 1980 with the construction of a new west stand, was the start of a period of upheaval at the club that led to two changes of ownership and resulted in severe financial difficulties. The cost of the stand escalated, especially after the club decided to almost double, to 72, the number of **executive boxes** built. Irving Scholar, a property developer and long-time Tottenham supporter, who had been brought in with Paul Bobroff by the then club chairman, Sidney Wale, to manage the development, took control of the club in November 1982, with debts running at more than £5.5 million. The escalating cost of necessary safety improvements in the wake of the **Bradford City fire**, coupled with declining gates and an £8 million-plus refurbishment of the east stand, including the construction of a new roof, resulted in mounting debt. And although Tottenham became the first English club in 1983 to float on the Stock Exchange, by 1991 the club had accumulated debts amounting to £18 million. The east stand's refit involved erecting seats and executive boxes on the middle tier, which was known as The Shelf. The club's plans greatly angered those Tottenham supporters who regularly stood on the

terrace and they campaigned to preserve the area (see **Left On The Shelf**). In June 1991, a partnership involving, as chairman, electronics millionaire Alan Sugar and former Tottenham player Terry Venables, who at the time was the manager but, as a result, became chief executive, bought the club. Thereafter a considerable sum of money has been spent on redeveloping the ground to meet the requirements of the **Taylor Report**, so that by August 1994 White Hart Lane had been converted into an all seated stadium. During the 1997-98 season redevelopment of the North Stand was completed bringing the ground's capacity up to more than 36,000. White Hart Lane staged its first floodlit match on 29 September 1953 (v **Racing Club de Paris**, friendly). The ground has been the venue for four **England** internationals (v **France**, 6 December 1933, v **Germany**, 4 December 1935, v **Czechoslovakia**, 1 December 1937, v **Italy**, 30 November 1949). White Hart Lane was used for the 1948 **Olympic Games** and it has also staged a number of FA Cup semi-final ties. In September 1991, White Hart Lane staged a boxing contest between Chris Eubank and Michael Watson.

White horse final *misc.* 1923 **FA Cup** final between **Bolton Wanderers** and **West Ham United** and the first to be held at **Wembley**. The official record attendance for the match was put at 126,047, but the actual number of fans was around 200,000. The sheer size of the crowd led to thousands of fans encroaching on to the pitch and it required mounted police, in particular constable George Scorey on his 13-year-old white horse, Billy, to clear it before the match could take place. Thereafter, although Scorey was only one of a team of mounted policemen on duty that day, it has always been referred to as the "White horse final".

Widzew Lódź *club* Polish national league side based in Lódź, founded in 1910. Ground: Widzew, capacity: 20,000. Strip: white shirts, white shorts. **European Cup** semi-final 1983, qualified for **Champions League** 1997; Polish League champions 1981, 1982, 1996, 1997; Polish Cup 1985. Zbigniew **Boniek**.

Wigan Athletic *club* English league. *Dossier* Ground: (until 1998-99) **Springfield Park**, Wigan, Greater Manchester. Strip: blue and black striped shirts, black shorts, and black socks with blue trim. Nickname: Latics. Ground capacity: 7,290. Record attendance: 27,526 v Hereford United (12 December 1953, **FA Cup**, second round). Best average attendance: 6,701 (1978-79). Biggest win: 7–1 v **Scarborough** (11 March 1997, Division Three). Biggest defeat: 1–6 v **Bristol Rovers** (3 March 1990, Division Three). *History* Founded in May 1932 following the demise of **Wigan Borough** the previous year. Athletic bought Springfield Park, which had been Borough's home, but the club was unable to take its predecessor's place in the **Football League**, eventually joining the Northern Premier League. Athletic enjoyed some success in the FA Cup as a non-League club. In 1934-35, Wigan set a record for the biggest winning margin by a non-League club over League opponents, defeating **Carlisle United** 6–1 (first round) at the Cumbrian side's **Brunton Park** ground (since equalled by several other non-League clubs – see **giantkilling**). In 1978-79, the club was elected to Division Four in the place of **Southport** and it won promotion to a higher grade in 1981-82. Wigan recorded a famous **League Cup** victory over **Chelsea** (4–2, third round) in 1981-82, before losing in a replay to **Aston Villa** (1–2 replay, fourth round). The club was a Division Three end-of-season **playoff** semi-finalist in 1986-87 and, in the same season, it reached the quarter-final stage of the FA Cup (0–2 v **Leeds United**). Two years earlier, the club had appeared at **Wembley** for the first time, winning the **Freight Rover Trophy** (3–1 v **Brentford**). Wigan won the Third Division Championship in 1996-97. Wigan returned to Wembly in 1999, winning the **Auto Windscreens Shield** (1–0, v **Millwall**). Since 1990, Wigan has pursued relocation plans and the possibility of developing a stadium to share with either Wigan Rugby League Club or Orrell Rugby Union club. In 1995, former Blackburn player Dave Whelan, owner of the JJB Sports retail chain, bought the club. *League record* Second Division 1992-93, 1997-98–; Division Three 1982-83 to 1991-92; Third Division 1993-94 to 1996-97; Division Four 1978-79 to 1981-82. *Honours* Division Three 1996-97; Freight Rover Trophy 1985 (3–1 v Brentford); Auto Windscreens Shield 1999 (1–0, v Millwall). *Records* Roy Carroll and Pat McGibbon are Wigan's most capped players (both 1 for **Northern Ireland**); Kevin Langley holds the record for club League appearances (317, 1981-86, 1990-94); David Lowe is Wigan's record League goalscorer (65, 1982-87, 1995-98).

Wigan Borough *club* former English league. *Dossier* Ground: **Springfield Park**, Wigan, Greater Manchester. Record attendance: 30,611 v **Sheffield Wednesday** (12 January 1929, **FA Cup**, third round). Best average attendance: 10,155 (1922-23). *Keynotes* Became Wigan's fourth attempt at establishing a viable football club in the town when the club was formed in November 1920. Borough joined the **Football League** in 1921-22 with the formation of Division Three (North). It was while Borough was in existence that Springfield Park recorded its highest attendance (see above). Financial problems forced Borough to resign from the League on 26 October 1931 after completing 12 fixtures and the results were declared void. The club finished fourth in Division Three (North) in 1928-29, its highest League position. Borough is not connected to present day **Wigan Athletic**. *League record* Division Three (North) 1921-22 to 1931-32.

Wihdat FC (Al Wahadat, Al Wehdat) *club* Jordan national league club based in Wihdat, in Amman. Ground: Amman Stadium, capacity: 30,000. Strip: green, red, black, white (the colours of the Palestinian national flag). *History* The club was founded at the Palestinian refugee camp of Wihdat, in Amman (around 38,000 people live in shelters set up by the United Nations Relief and Works Agency for Palestinian

Refugees). The club is seen as a symbol of Palestinian nationalism – with many supporters" songs dating to the civil war in Jordan (1970-71) between ethnic Jordanians and Palestinians – and hence attracts fervent support. Following fighting between its supporters and those of the Jordanian club **Al Ramthla** in 1986 the club was forced to change its name from Wihdat FC to Nadi al Difftayn ("the club of Two Banks"). Furthermore, it was initially relegated to the third division with four players banned for allegedly inciting trouble among supporters – sanctions later withdrawn after an appeal. The club reverted to its original name in 1990. Intense rivalry exists between Wihdat and the other largely ethnic Jordanian **Al Faisali**. Qualified for National League of Jordan in 1975. **Asian Champion Teams Cup** finals tournament 1989 (withdrew after winning first-round group of five clubs); Jordanian league champions 1980, 1987, 1988, 1991, 1994, 1995, 1996, 1997; Jordanian Cup 1983, 1986, 1989, 1996, 1997.

Wilberforce (Mr Justice Wilberforce) *misc.* High Court judge in the *George Eastham case*, ruling, in 1963, that the **retain and transfer** system was an unlawful restraint of trade.

Willem II Tilburg *club* Dutch national league club, based in Tilburg, and founded in 1896 (as Tilburgia, until 1908). Ground: Willem II, capacity: 15,000. Strip: red, white and blue shirts and white shorts. Dutch league champions 1916, 1952, 1955; Dutch Cup 1944, 1963.

Wimbledon *club* English league. Ground: **Selhurst Park**, south London. *Dossier* Strip: navy blue shirts with white and yellow trim, navy blue shorts, navy blue socks. Website: *http://www.wimbledon-fc.co.uk* Nickname: Dons. Ground capacity: 26,400 all seated. Record attendance: 30,115 v **Manchester United** (9 May 1993, Premier League). Best average attendance: 16,675 (1997-98). Biggest win: 6–0 v **Newport County** (3 September 1983, Division Three). Biggest defeat: 0–8 v **Everton** (29 August 1978, **League Cup**, second round). *History* Founded in 1889 as Wimbledon Old Centrals by former Central School students. Initially played in the local south London leagues before joining the Southern Surburban League in 1902. The club ceased to exist for a short time in 1910 before re-emerging in 1912 after combining with Wimbledon Borough. Until the club was elected to the **Football League** in place of **Workington** in 1977, Wimbledon had played mainly in the Isthmian League and the **Southern League**. It was as an Isthmian League side that the club won the **FA Amateur Cup** in 1963, with striker Eddie Reynolds scoring all four of Wimbledon's goals with his head in the final (4–2 v Sutton United). In 1964, the club turned professional and subsequently joined the Southern League. In the club's first six seasons in the Football League (1977-78 to 1983-84) it failed on only one occasion, the first year, to be either promoted or relegated. By 1986-87, Wimbledon had reached the top flight, winning the **FA Cup** two years later (1–0 v **Liverpool**) with Dave Beasant becoming the first goalkeeper to save a penalty in a **Wembley** final. The Cup final team became known as the "Crazy Gang", and, besides Beasant, included Alan Cork, Vinnie Jones, Lawrie Sanchez (the goalscorer) and Dennis Wise. In 1991, Wimbledon was forced to leave Plough Lane, the club's home since 1912, because there was no prospect of the ground being redeveloped to meet the requirements of the **Taylor Report** and because the club had failed to find a suitable site for a new stadium. The club agreed a seven-year **groundshare** of **Selhurst Park** with **Crystal Palace**, a club owned at the time by former Wimbledon chairman Ron Noades. Wimbledon chairman Sam Hamman has attempted to find a suitable site for a ground in the club's home borough of Merton, but in 1997 he outlined plans to relocate to Dublin, although the **Football Association**, **UEFA** and the **Football Association of Ireland** have all dismissed the idea. The club achieved its highest-ever League position in 1990-91, when it finished seventh. Wimbledon is the only club to have won both the FA Cup and the FA Amateur Cup. *League record* Premier League 1992-93–; Division One 1986-87 to 1991-92; Division Two 1984-85 to 1985-86; Division Three 1979-80, 1981-82, 1983-84; Division Four 1977-78 to 1978-79, 1980-81, 1982-83. *Honours* Division Four 1982-83; Southern League 1975, 1976, 1977; FA Cup 1988 (1–0 v Liverpool – *Team* Beasant, Goodyear, Phelan, Jones, Young, Thorn, Gibson (Scales), Cork (Cunningham), Fashanu, Sanchez (1), Wise); FA Amateur Cup 1963 (4–2 v Sutton United). *Records* Kenny Cunningham is Wimbledon's most capped player (16 for **Republic of Ireland**); Alan Cork holds the record for club appearances (430, 1977-92); he is also the club's record league goalscorer (145, 1977-92).

win bonus *n.* additional payment awarded to members of a winning team. Made legal by the **Football League** in 1920 (players could be paid £2 for a win and £1 for a draw on top of their salaries).

winding-up order *n.* court order preventing a club from trading normally and which is typically awarded after a club fails to pay its creditors. *Keynotes* In July 1983, **Leeds United** sued **Charlton Athletic** for non payment of £30,000 in transfer fees. As a consequence, Charlton faced a winding-up order in the High Court. **Middlesbrough** almost went out of business in the summer of 1986 after the Inland Revenue was granted a winding-up order for non-payment of tax arrears. An official receiver also was appointed, who sacked manager Bruce Rioch and the entire non-playing staff. A new board of directors, including millionaire Steve Gibson (who took control of the club in March 1994), saved the club from bankruptcy by re-forming it and paying off its debts. Boro was forced to play the first "home" game of the 1986-87 season at **Hartlepool United**'s **Victoria Ground**. A winding up order against **Wolverhampton Wanderers** was set aside in the Appeal Court in August 1986 after the club, £1.8 million in debt, was saved from bankruptcy by the joint efforts of the local council, Wolverhampton

Metropolitan Borough Council, and Gallaghers, a development company. While the council bought Molineux, the club's training ground and its social club for £1.1 million, Gallaghers paid off the club's debt in return for developing a retail store on an unused part of the site. **Aldershot** had a winding-up order for debts of £1.2 million frozen for 12 hours on 20 March 1992 so the club could fulfil a Division Four fixture against **Cardiff City**. The club subsequently was re-formed as Aldershot Town. In March 1998, **Chester City**'s existence came under threat when the Inland Revenue served a second winding-up order in the High Court for failing to settle a tax demand (the previous bill for unpaid taxes had been paid in January 1998).

wing back *n.* defender on the left/right side of the **formation** who, when given the opportunity, runs or takes the ball forward into an attacking position.

wing *n.* the side of a **formation**.

winger *n.* **striker** who plays on the side of the **formation**.

winter break *n.* period in the season in many northern European football leagues where no matches are scheduled owing to seasonal poor weather. After many years of discussion, the Scottish Premier League introduced a three-week break in January for its inaugural season in 1998-99. Scottish football has been plagued by postponed matches during the winter months. **Ukraine** and **Georgia** have the longest winter breaks: from mid-November to mid-March. Other leagues in which a winter break is taken include: **Austria**, **Denmark**, **Germany**, **Poland**, **Romania** and **Switzerland**.

Winter Championship *misc.* Spanish name given to the first half (19 matches) of the League programme in **Spain**'s **Primera Liga** each season.

Wisla Kraków *club* Polish national league side based in Krakow, founded in 1906. Ground: Wisla, capacity: 15,000. Strip: red shirts with blue sash, white shorts. *History* Poland's second-oldest club (founded in the same year as **Cracovia**). Accused of match fixing and had two points deducted in 1993 (see **Legia Warszaw**). **European Cup** quarter-final 1979; Polish League champions 1927, 1928, 1949, 1950, 1951, 1978 (1949–51 as Gwardia Kraków, 1999); Polish Cup 1926, 1954 (latter as Gwardia).

Withdean Stadium *ground* sports ground situated in Brighton, East Sussex; temporary home of **Brighton & Hove Albion**. *Dossier* Present capacity: 6,000. *Keynotes* Opened as an international tennis venue by the Lawn Tennis Association (LTA) in 1936, hosting the England v New Zealand Davis Cup tennis match in 1939. The complex also included a zoo and, during World War II, it was used as a mortuary. In 1955, the stadium became an athletics venue. Withdean was designated a centre of excellence by the LTA in 1993. Brighton moved to Withdean on a temporary three-year basis in 1999, having played its 1997-98 and 1998-99 home matches at **Gillingham**'s **Priestfield Stadium** – a 150-mile round trip for Brighton supporters. Average attendance at League matches plummeted from the 5,877 recorded at Goldstone during 1996-97 to 2,327 at Priestfield in 1997-98. The club overcame considerable opposition from local residents to its use of Withdean Stadium, promising, among other things, to limit the number of cars entering the area and to clear litter.

Wits University *club* South African **National Soccer League** club based in Johannesburg, founded 1902. Ground: Milpark Asics. Strip: gold shirts with blue sleeves, blue shorts. South African Cup ("Super Bowl") winners 1978 (the first tournament); South African **Top Eight Cup** 1984, 1995.

W–M formation *tactics* system of play/formation. A system consisting of a defensive formation arranged in a shape resembling a W – right back and left back, with a centre-half playing slightly ahead of them, and supported by a right-half and a left-half further forward; and an attacking formation arranged in a shape resembling an M – a centre-forward, right-winger and left-winger in a forward line supported by an inside-right and an inside-left playing behind them. The W–M formation was the first, and the most popular, of the modern systems of play and was established after the **offside** rule was changed in 1925-26. It is a rigid system (defenders defended, attackers attacked) with very little interplay or changing or roles.

Wolverhampton Wanderers *club* English league. *Dossier* Ground: **Molineux**, Wolverhampton, West Midlands. Strip: gold shirts with black trim, black shorts with gold trim, gold socks with black trim. Nickname: Wolves. Ground capacity: 28,525. Record attendance: 61,315 v **Liverpool** (11 February 1939, **FA Cup**, fifth round). Best average attendance: 45,466 (1949-50). Biggest win: 14–0 v Cresswell's Brewery (13 November 1886, FA Cup, second round). Biggest defeat: 1–10 v **Newton Heath** (15 October 1892, Division One). *History* St Luke's School in the Blakenhall district of Wolverhampton founded a football club in 1877 and some time within the following two years members of Blakenhall Wanderers Cricket Club joined them to form Wolverhampton Wanderers. The club was a founder member of the **Football League** in 1888, finishing third in the League's first season. The following season Wolves reached the FA Cup final (0–3 **Preston North End**) and the club moved to its present home, Molineux Grounds (the club had first played there in 1886 in a Walsall Cup semi-final). In six out of the next seven seasons, Wolves reached at least the last eight of the FA Cup, winning the trophy for the first time in 1893 (1–0 v **Everton**) and reaching a further final in 1896 (1–2 v The **Wednesday**). The club enjoyed another FA Cup success in 1908 (3–1 v **Newcastle United**), but it had been relegated in 1905-06 and did not regain a place in Division One until 1932-33, having spent one season in Division Three (North) in 1923-24, thus becoming the first founder members to drop to the bottom division. Wolves' victory in the 1908 FA Cup final was only the second for a team from Division Two (overall seven Division Two clubs have won the FA Cup: **Notts**

County (1894), **Barnsley** (1912), **West Bromwich Albion** (1931), **Sunderland** (1973), **Southampton** (1976), **West Ham United** (1980). Between 1917 and 1944 the club was managed by Major Frank Buckley. He led Wolves to the FA Cup final in 1939 (1–4 v **Portsmouth**) and second place in Division One in consecutive seasons in 1937-38 and 1938-39. Buckley provoked controversy before World War II when he claimed that the club's players, who were at the time renowned for being quick, had been receiving monkey gland treatment to give them more stamina (they had in fact been given injections against colds). Stan **Cullis**'s appointment as manager in 1948 was followed by a period of unprecedented success for the club. Cullis, a former Wolves captain, assembled a team that included England internationals Peter Broadbent, Ron **Flowers**, Jimmy Mullen, Bert **Williams** and Billy **Wright**, and adopted a highly-effective **long-ball game** that depended on pace and stamina. In 1949, Wolves secured its third FA Cup victory (3–1 v **Leicester City**) and in 1953-54 the club won its first League Championship. Wolves won two further titles in consecutive seasons in 1957-58 and 1958-59, and missed a third successive triumph by one point the following season. Had the club won the title in 1959-60 Wolves would have become the first club this century to win the **double**; it also lifted the FA Cup that season (3–0 v **Blackburn Rovers**). During the 1950s, the club also twice finished runners-up in Division One (1954-55, 1959-60) and became the only top-flight club to score 100 Football League goals in three succesive seasons (1957-58, 1958-59, 1959-60). At this time, Wolves also staged a number of floodlit friendlies against foreign opposition, including, in December 1954, Hungarian champions-elect Honvéd, whose side contained eight players from the Hungarian national team that had become the first to defeat **England** on home ground in November 1953 (Wolves won the match 3–2). In 1959-60, the club reached the **European Cup** quarter-finals (2–9 agg. v **Barcelona**) and, in 1960-61, the semi-final stage of the **European Cup-winners Cup** (1–3 v **Rangers**). Under the managership of Bill McGarry and with a side including Derek **Dougan**, Mike Bailey, Kenny Hibbitt, Jim McCalliog and Dave Wagstaffe, Wolves reached the final of the **UEFA Cup** in 1972, the first European final between two English clubs, but lost to **Tottenham Hotspur** (2–3 agg.). In 1974, the club won the **League Cup** (2–1 v **Manchester City**) and, in 1980, it lifted the trophy for a second time (1–0 v **Nottingham Forest**). The club went from Division One to Division Four in consecutive seasons between 1983-84 and 1986-87, before returning to Division Two in 1989-90. Wolves became the first and only club to win all four divisional championships when taking the Division Three and Division Four titles in consecutive seasons in 1987-88 and 1988-89 (the club also won the Division Three (North) title in 1923-24). The club almost went out of business in 1982, but a financial package put together by former striker Dougan and local businessmen, the Bhatti brothers, temporarily saved the club. In July 1986, Wolves, £1.8 million in debt, went into receivership, but the club was again saved, this time by the joint efforts of the local council, Wolverhampton Metropolitan Borough Council, and Gallaghers, a development company. While the council bought Molineux, the club's training ground and its social club for £1.1 million, Gallaghers paid off the club's debt in return for developing a retail store on an unused part of the site. As a result, a **winding-up order** was set aside in the Appeal Court. In May 1990, long-term Wolves fan and millionaire Jack Hayward bought the club for £2.1 million. Despite a succession of managers, including ex-England boss Graham **Taylor**, and some high-profile signings the club has been unable to regain top-flight status. In 1998, the club reached the FA Cup semi-final stage (0–1 v **Arsenal**). *League record* Division One (including Football League) 1888-89 to 1905-06, 1932-33 to 1964-65, 1967-68 to 1975-76, 1977-78 to 1981-82, 1983-84, 1991-92; First Division 1992-93 to present; Division Two 1906-07 to 1922-23, 1924-25 to 1931-32, 1965-66 to 1966-67, 1976-77, 1982-83, 1984-85, 1989-90 to 1991-92; Division Three 1985-86, 1988-89; Division Three (North) 1923-24; Division Four 1986-87 to 1987-88. *Honours* League 1953-54, 1957-58, 1958-59; Division Two 1931-32, 1976-77; Division Three 1988-89; Division Three (North) 1923-24; Division Four 1987-88; FA Cup 1893 (1–0 v Everton), 1908 (3–1 v Newcastle United), 1949 (3–1 v Leicester City – *Team* Williams, Pritchard, Springthorpe, Crook, Shorthouse, Wright, Hancocks, Smyth (1), Pye (2), Dunn, Mullen), 1960 (3–0 v Blackburn Rovers – *Team* Finlayson, Showell, Harris, Clamp, Slater, Flowers, Deeley (2), Stobart, Murray, Broadbent, Horne, plus 1o.g.); League Cup 1974 (2–1 v Manchester City), 1980 (1–0 v Nottingham Forest); **FA Charity Shield** 1959 (3–1 v Nottingham Forest); **Texaco Cup** 1971 (4–1 agg. v **Heart of Midlothian**); **Sherpa Van Trophy** 1988 (2–0 v **Burnley**). *Records* Billy Wright is Wolves' most capped player (105 for England); Derek Parkin holds the record for club appearances (501, 1967-82); Steve Bull is its record League goalscorer (247, 1986–98).

Wolves *club* nickname of **Wolverhampton Wanderers**.

Wome, Pierre Nlend *player* Midfielder. **Cameroon** international. Born 26 March 1979. *Clubs* **Canon Youndé**, **Vicenza**, Lucchese. *Keynotes* At 16 years old, Wome became the youngest player ever to play in the **African Cup of Nations** tournament (1996).

women spectators *misc.* See **spectators, women**.

Women's FA National Cup *competition* former name, until 1992-93, of the **FA Women's Challenge Cup**

women's football *n.* football played by all-women teams. Although casual matches sometimes involve mixed male and female teams, organised football at senior level, and all youth levels over 11 years of age, is divided by sex. Sex discrimination legislation in the United Kingdom does not extend to the participation of people in competitive sports (see **Sex Discrimination Act**). Women's football, for many years held back by outdated attitudes – including by some national associations – has experienced a phenomenal rise in popularity since the 1980s. There are more than 30,000,000 registered female players world-wide, with more than half of the world's national football associations organising women's tournaments. In Britain, there are more than 30,000 registered female players (youth and senior levels), and in excess of 50,000 women playing the game at some level. *History* The first recorded women's representative match in England under Association rules was played on 23 March 1895 at Crouch End, London (South of England v North of England, 1–7). Early opposition to women's football was voiced by the **Football Association** which, in 1902, instructed its members not to arrange fixtures with women's teams: it was considered offensive, inappropriate and medically dangerous. With many factories forced to take on female employees during **World War I**, women's football blossomed. Notable early clubs include **Dick, Kerr's Ladies**, a factory-based team from Preston which attracted crowds of tens of thousands, raising money for war victims and their families. There were an estimated 150 women's clubs in England by 1920. Despite its popularity – or perhaps because of it – on 5 December 1921, the FA requested that its member clubs refuse the use of their grounds for women's fixtures. The FA said at the time, "the Council feel impelled to express their strong opinion that the game of football is quite unsuitable for females and ought not to be encouraged." It also laid allegations of misappropriation of receipts to "other than charitable objects." The FA also barred FA referees and linesmen from officiating at women's matches. Only five days after the ban was announced, representatives from 25 women's clubs met in Blackburn to form the **English Ladies Football Association** (ELFA). Women's football remained popular in the north of England and in the Midlands, with some clubs also emerging around London, the south and southwest. However, ELFA's administrative resources were limited and it became increasingly difficult to find grounds that were not affiliated to the FA. The English FA was not the only national association to frown upon the women's game. In 1955, **Germany**'s football association, the Deutscher Fussball-Bund, banned women's clubs from playing on grounds belonging to clubs affiliated to its leagues. In the same year, the **Netherlands** football association, the Koninklijke Nederlandsche Voetbalbond (KNVB), introduced a ban on women's fixtures at affiliated stadiums – the intervention of the KNVB dates back to 1896 when it prevented a women's match between **Sparta Rotterdam** and an England XI. Women's football in England enjoyed a mini-boom after World War II, with **Manchester Corinthians**, formed in 1949, challenging the eminence of Dick, Kerr's Ladies as the top women's side. The FA's ban continued to disrupt the development of women's football and the Corinthians and its contemporary clubs were forced to play matches on rugby and cricket grounds, and other recreation pitches. An **International Ladies Football Association** was founded in 1957 and organised a European women's championship in 1957, with representative sides from **Austria**, England, Germany, **Luxembourg** and the Netherlands. Manchester Corinthians, representing England, won the final 4–1, at Poststadium, Berlin, in front of 37,000 spectators. The ban on women's clubs playing on German affiliated grounds was lifted in 1970, under pressure from the growing popularity of women's football in the country – there were more than 1,000 German women's clubs by 1971. In England, the FA's ban was lifted in January 1970, after the formation of a new **Women's Football Association** in November 1969. In 1969, the **Italy**-based **Confederation of Independent European Female Football** (FIEFF) organised a four-nation European tournament in Italy, followed by a world tournament (the "**Mundialito**") in 1970, in Italy, and in 1971, in Mexico. The **Union of European Football Associations** (UEFA) soon sought to control the women's game and, in November 1971, recommended that all football played in each member country should come under the auspices of a single national association. In response, the WFA and FA agreed, in February 1972, that: "All clubs be affiliated to a Women's Football Association, which shall be supervised and controlled within the National Association." In spite of this dictate, it was not until July 1993 that the Football Association established a Women's Football Committee and a Women's Football Co-ordinator. English women's club football in the 1970s was dominated by **Southampton WFC**, which played in nine consecutive Women's FA Cup finals from 1971 to 1979, winning seven. **Doncaster Belles** appeared in 11 finals from 1982 to 1994, winning six. A national league in England, the WFA National League, began in 1991, initially with eight clubs in each of three divisions (Premier, Northern and Southern). The league came under the auspices of the FA in 1994, and was renamed the **Football Association Women's Premier League** (FAWPL). The **FA Women's Challenge Cup** – open to all women's clubs in England – was first played in 1971 (originally known as the Women's FA National Cup). The **FA Women's Premier League Cup** (for FAWPL member clubs) started in 1992-93. The FA took control of the Women's national squad in 1993. The growth in women's football in England is indicated by the rapid rise in the number of women players and in the number of registered clubs. In 1989 there were just 263 clubs registered with the FA in England, with around 7,000 registered players. By 1996-97 there were 600 clubs with 14,000 registered players; by 1998, the number of registered women's teams had risen to 700. Girls' football also has dramatically increased in popularity, but not without controversy. In 1978, 12-year-old Theresa Bennett failed to prove, in court, that she should be allowed to play for a boys' club in a local junior league (see **Bennett v Football Association Ltd and Nottinghamshire FA**). In 1991, the Football Association repealed its rule that banned mixed football in schools for under-11s (rule 21(a)(111) of the Football Association rules allows mixed games in the youngest age group). The number of girls teams increased from 80 in 1989 to more than 1,000 by 1998, accompanied by a 15-fold increase in the number of girls playing, to more than 15,000. In 1998 there were 60 female youth leagues. In the under-12 age-group, 685 schools entered the 1997-98 **ESFA Five-a-side Competition** girls' tournament. Britain's first coaching facility for women, the **Women's Football Academy of the North**, was opened in 1998. Women's football is one of the most popular participative sports in many countries, notably **Brazil**, **China**, **Denmark**, **Germany**, **Japan**, the Netherlands, **New Zealand**, **Norway**, **Sweden** and the **United States of America**. Japan launched the world's first women's professional league in 1992. In Norway, there are an estimated 64,000 female players and 1,830 clubs (1995 figures). In the United States, around 39% of all association football players are women (1991 estimate). In Germany, by 1995 there were 490,000 registered women playing football, and 120,000 junior (under-16) players. The **European Championship for Women** began in 1982, with the first **Women's World Cup** finals played in 1991. The Women's World Cup was preceded, in 1988, by a trial, invitation-only tournament run by **FIFA** in Guangzhou, China. Other international tournaments include the **International Women's Football Tournament**, for invited nations, held in China since 1983. The United States has been proactive in developing the women's game and holds its own international invitation tournament, the **US Women's Cup**. The Scandinavian countries, in association with **Portugal**'s football association, the Federação Portuguesa de Futebol, have organised the **Algarve Cup** since 1989. The **Asian Women's Football Championship** has been played since 1975. Women's football became an Olympic sport at the 1996 **Olympic Games** in Atlanta, USA. *Dossier* Record attendance (England): 53,000, **Goodison Park**, 26 December 1920, Dick, Kerr's Ladies v St Helen's Ladies, 4–0, friendly; World : 76,481, Sanford Stadium, Athens, Georgia, USA, 1 August 1996, United States of America v China, 2–1, Olympic Games women's final. First official international match in the UK: November 1972, Scotland v England, 2–3, in Greenock, friendly. *Keynotes* Despite the growing popularity of women's football, psychologists maintain that many men still attempt to preserve the "masculine identity" of the game by using "denigrating and disempowering behaviour to distance women from the real, male form of the game". A study carried out in 1998 by the Centre for Communication Studies at Manchester Metropolitan University found that some referees even resort to patronising language to preserve the game's masculinity. The Centre followed the behaviour of referees at 28 five-aside league matches involving men's and women's teams and found that they did not view fouls by women as deliberate, merely that they were "a bit clumsy"; women were further patronised by male referees, being told that "it's a contact sport" when appealing for fouls. See also: **England, women**; **France, women**; **Northern Ireland, women**; **Republic of Ireland, women**; **Scotland, women**; **Wales, women**; **ESFA Girls' Under-16 Trophy** and **spectators, women**.

Women's Football Academy of the North *misc.* Britain's first football coaching facility for women, based in Peterlee, County Durham, opened September 1998.

Women's Football Association (WFA) *confederation* former association for women's football in England, founded November 1969, with 44 member clubs. It was affiliated to the **Football Association** in 1983. The WFA was dissolved in 1993, and women's football in England came fully under the auspices of the Football Association. Women's football in England is now administrated by the women's section of the Football Association, based in Potters Bar, Hertfordshire. The WFA founded the Women's Football Association National Cup (now known as the **FA Women's Challenge Cup**) in 1971, and the Women's Football Association National League in 1991 (now the **Football Association Women's Premier League**).

Women's World Cup *competition* international tournament for national women's teams, run by **FIFA**, first played 1991. *Qualification system* Qualification for the finals tournaments is through regional competitions run by the various international confederations. Sixteen nations compete in the 1999 finals tournament; qualification took place over two years in the six confederation qualification tournaments, involving around 70 nations. **UEFA**, the largest group, has six places, **AFC** has two, **CAF** two, **CONCACAF** two, **CONMEBOL** one, and **OFC** one; an additional place was decided by a playoff between the CONMEBOL runners-up and the CONCACAF third-placed nation (**Mexico** qualifed, 6–3 agg., v **Argentina**). The hosts, but not the reigning champions also qualify. Europe is the only region with qualifying tournaments played on a home-and-away basis. The other confederations have qualifying championships played at a single host nation. The **European Championship for Women** served as the European qualifying tournament for the first two Women's World Cup (1991, 1995); a separate European qualifying tournament was staged for the 1999 finals, with 34 European nations taking part. The European qualifying tournament is seeded, with the top 16 nations placed in four first-stream groups of four. Only nations in the top stream can qualify for the finals. The remaining 18 nations are grouped into four second-stream groups. The winners of the first-stream groups qualify automatically for the finals tournament. The remaining two places in the finals tournaments are determined by a series of playoffs between the first-stream group runners-up. Nations in the four second-stream groups cannot qualify for the

World Cup finals. The winners of each of these groups, however, playoff against the four fourth-placed nations in the first-stream groups; the playoff winners are promoted to/relegated from the first-stream group for the next international tournament (the 1998 playoff winners qualified for the top stream for the 1999-2001 European Championship for Women). The **CONCACAF Women's Championship** serves as the North and Central America/Caribbean qualifying tournament. The top seven finishers in the 1999 World Cup qualify with the hosts (**Australia**) for the 2000 Olympic Games Women's football tournament in Sydney. *Winners* (result, runners-up, venue, attendance; third place) 1991 **United States of America** (2–1, v **Norway**, Tianhe Stadium, Guangzhou, China, 65,000; third place **Sweden**); 1995 Norway (2–0, v **Germany**, Råsunda Stadium, Stockholm, 17,000; third place United States); 1999, finals in the United States. *History* Forty-six nations competed in the qualifying rounds for the 12-nation finals in **China**, 16-30 November 1991. The first finals were watched by 512,000 spectators. Fifty-six nations took part in the second qualifying tournament in 1995, with a predicted 74 participants in 1999. The **mission statement** of the 1999 Women's World Cup promised: "To stage a breakthrough for women's sport and inspire the next generation of female athletes."

Woodward, Vivian *player* Striker. **England** international (23 caps, 29 goals). Born 3 June 1879. Career ca. 1901-1914. *Clubs* **Tottenham Hotspur**, **Chelsea**. *Keynotes* Woodward made 67 appearances for England: 23 full caps and 44 amateur caps. He scored the second goal in England's 1908 **Olympic Games** victory (2–0 v **Denmark**) and he captained the side to a further gold medal four years' later (4–2 v Denmark). Woodward scored six goals for England in a amateur international against **Netherlands** (11 December 1909). Included in the **Football League Centenary 100 players**. *Honours* Olympic Games (England 1908, 1912).

woodwork 1. *n.* **goal posts** and **crossbar**. **2.** hit the **woodwork**, to **shoot** or **head** against a goal post or crossbar.

Woolfall, D B *official* second president of **FIFA** (1906-18) and the first Englishman to take this position.

workmanlike *adj.* of a team or player that achieves results through hard work and good organisation rather than creative play.

work permit *n.* legal document issued by the Department for Education and Employment (DfEE) to allow a player from outside the **European Union** (EU) or **European Economic Area** (EEA) to be registered and play for a club in the United Kingdom. Work permits are only issued to non-EU/EEA citizens if they have an "acceptable international reputation", usually meaning that they should have played in about 75% of their country's recent competitive matches. The DfEE also requires evidence that clubs have sought to find suitable players from within the EU, before looking for players from other overseas countries. Overseas players should also be paid at the top-end of the club's wage spectrum (so as to stop clubs from importing "cheap labour" rather than paying regular wages to EU citizens). Permits are issued to last until the end of the following June and extensions are considered at the end of each season: players should have established themselves as regular first-team players, playing in around 75% of club games. However, if players have not reached this requirement, but have a current work permit, they may be transferred once, and would be expected to play around 75% of the games for their new club's first team. *Keynotes* Brad **Friedel**, US international goalkeeper, was finally given clearance in December 1997 to play for **Liverpool** following an appeal after he was initially refused a work permit. Friedel failed to meet the DfEE's criteria for granting a work permit because he had not played in at least 75% of the USA's most recent international matches. In December 1997, **Tottenham Hotspur** also had a work permit refused for Swiss national Fritz Schmid, a fitness expert. The newly-appointed Spurs manager and fellow Swiss, Christian Gross, had wanted to bring him to **White Hart Lane**. The DfEE refused Tottenham's request on two grounds: that Schmid could not bring skills not already available in the UK; and that he has not established international reputation in his field.

working hours *misc.* The sociological impact of shortening working hours in British industry during the 19th century – enshrined for example in the Ten Hour Day Act 1847– was that working men had more free time. Many working class men now had time to devote to leisure activities: giving rise to increased popularity of sport, notably cricket and football. By the mid 19th century, Saturdays were gradually becoming half-days in British industry, giving rise to the traditional Saturday afternoon football fixture (Sundays were reserved as church days). See also **spectators**, **women**.

Workington *club* former English league. *Dossier* Ground: Borough Park, Workington, Cumbria. Record League attendance: 18,633 v **Carlisle United** (26 December 1963, Division Four). Best average attendance: 8,372 (1953-54). *Keynotes* Formed in 1884 and re-founded in 1921. Workington replaced **New Brighton** in Division Three (North) in 1951-52. Following promotion to Division Three in 1964-65, the club finished fifth in the next season – its highest League position. Having applied for re-election on four previous occasions, Workington lost its League status in 1976-77 – having finished in the bottom two of Division Four in four consecutive seasons – and was replaced by **Wimbledon**. Prior to joining the League, the club had reached the fourth round of the **FA Cup** in 1934 (1–2 v **Preston North End**). Workington was a **League Cup** quarter-finalist twice: 1963-64 (0–6 v **West Ham United**) and 1964-65 (0–2 replay v **Chelsea**). *League record* Division Three 1964-65 to 1966-67; Division Three (North) 1951-52 to 1957-58; Division Four 1958-59 to 1963-64, 1967-68 to 1976-77.

World Army Cup *competition* biennial tournament between national army teams, first played 1946 (won by **England**). **Italy** has won the trophy eight times,

followed by **Greece** (six), **France** (five), **Belgium** (four), **Iraq** and **Turkey** (three each). World Club Championship competition proposed international club tournament under the auspices of **FIFA**. The tournament is designed to be competed on a mini-league basis by eight clubs comprising: the champion club from each of the six continental confederations (CAF, AFC, OFC, UEFA, CONCACAF, CONMEBOL), the winners of the **World Club Cup** and the champion club of the host nation. The first edition was planned for January 2000.

World Club Cup (Copa Intercontinental) *competition* annual match between the winners of the **European Cup** and the **Copa Libertadores**. Champion clubs from Asia, north and central America, Africa and Oceania are not involved. The winners receive two trophies: the Toyota Cup (given by the sponsors) and the Intercontinental Cup (the original trophy). *History* The idea for the competition was first mooted in 1958, by the then **Union of European Football Associations** general secretary Henri Delaunay. It started in 1960, originally over two legs. From 1960-68, if both sides had won a match then a replay would be played, regardless of the **aggregate score**: replays were required in 1961, 1963, 1964 and 1967. The result was decided on aggregate scores from 1969-79. During the late 1960s and 1970s the fixture developed a reputation for on-field violent conduct – most notoriously by **Argentina**'s **Estudiantes La Plata** – and several European champions refused to take part; their places were taken by the European Cup runners-up (see results below). Since 1980, the fixture has been played as a single match, at the National Stadium in Tokyo, Japan, with the match decided on **penalties** in the event of a draw. Of the 37 fixtures up to and including 1998, South American clubs had won 20, European clubs 17. Argentinean and Italian clubs had won the trophy seven times each, followed by clubs from **Brazil** and **Uruguay** (six each), **Netherlands** and **Spain** (three each), **Germany** (two), and **Paraguay**, **Portugal** and **Yugoslavia** (one each). English clubs have been in five editions, but have lost on each occasion. One Scottish club, **Celtic**, has appeared in one edition. *Winners and results* 1960 **Real Madrid**, 0–0, 5–1, v **Peñarol**; 1961 Peñarol, 0–1, 5–0, 2–1 replay (in Montevideo), v **Benfica**; 1962 **Santos**, 3–2, 5–2, v Benfica; 1963, Santos, 2–4, 4–2, 1–0 replay (in Rio de Janeiro), v **AC Milan**; 1964 **Internazionale**, 0–1, 2–0, 1–0 replay (in Milan), v **Independiente**; 1965 Internazionale, 3–0, 0–0, v Independiente; 1966, Peñarol, 2–0, 2–0, v Real Madrid; 1967 **Racing Club**, 0–1, 2–1, 1–0 replay (in Montevideo), v Celtic; 1968 **Estudiantes**, 1–0, 1–1, v **Manchester United**; 1969 Milan, 4–2 agg., v Estudiantes; 1970 **Feyenoord**, 3–2 agg., v Estudiantes; 1971 **Nacional** (Montevideo), 3–2 agg., v **Panathinaikos** (European Cup runners-up – the European champions, Ajax, refused to play); 1972 **Ajax**, 4–1 agg., v Independiente; 1973 Independiente, 1–0 (single match in Rome) v **Juventus** (European Cup runners-up – Ajax refused to play); 1974 **Atletico**

Madrid (European Cup runners-up – Bayern Muncih refused to play), 2–1 agg., v Independiente; 1975 no tournament; 1976 Bayern Munich, 2–0 agg., v **Cruzeiro**; 1977 **Boca Juniors**, 5–2 agg., v **Borussia Mönchengladbach** (European Cup runners-up – Liverpool refused to play); 1978 no tournament; 1979 **Olimpia** (Asuncion), 3–1, v **Malmö** (European Cup runners-up – Nottingham Forest refused to play); 1980 Nacional, 1–0, v **Nottingham Forest**; 1981 **Flamengo**, 3–0, v **Liverpool**; 1982 Peñarol, 2–0, v **Aston Villa**; 1983 **Gremio**, 2–1, v **Hamburg (SV)**; 1984 Independiente, 1–0, v Liverpool; 1985 Juventus, 2–2, 4–2 pens., v **Argentinos Juniors**; 1986 **River Plate**, 1–0, v **Steaua Bucharest**; 1987 **Porto**, 2–1, v Peñarol; 1988 Nacional 2–2, 7–6 pens., v **PSV Eindhoven**; 1989 Milan, 1–0, v **Atlético Nacional Medellin**; 1990 Milan, 3–0, v Olimpia; 1991 **Red Star Belgrade**, 3–0, v **Colo Colo**; 1992 **São Paulo**, 2–1, v **Barcelona**; São Paulo, 3–2, v AC Milan; 1994 **Velez Sarsfield**, 2–0, v AC Milan; 1995 Ajax, 0–0, 4–3 pens., v Gremio; 1996 Juventus, 1–0, v River Plate; 1997 **Borussia Dortmund**, 2–0, v Cruzeiro; 1998 Real Madrid, 2–1, v Vasco da Gama. See also **Afro-Asian Club Cup**, **Copa Inter America**.

World Cup (Coupe de Monde) *competition* four-yearly international tournament, which was first played in 1930. The 1998 tournament, in France, was contested by 32 countries and the largest ever World Cup. In addition to **Brazil** and **France**, both of which qualified automatically as holders and host nation respectively, the other 30 finalists qualified via group matches played in each of the six **FIFA** confederations. A record total of 643 qualifying matches was played in the 1998 tournament and the qualifying and finals involved a record 172 nations. The format for the 1998 finals consisted of eight groups of four, with the top two countries in each section going forward to the second-round knockout stage. The 2002 event, to be jointly staged by **Japan** and **South Korea**, will also involve 32 nations. Aside from the two hosts and France, the holders, 14 participants will come from UEFA; five from AFC; three from CONCACAF; two from ASF; and four from CONMEBOL. In addition, a further place is available to either a nation from OCEANIA or CONMEBOL, which will be decided by a playoff. *History* Since its formation in 1904, FIFA has had the right to stage a world contest, but football's governing body did not endorse such a competition until 1929. At the FIFA Congress that year, the secretary of the French confederation, Henri Delaunay proposed that a world championship, or "International Championship" as it was then described, be established and 25 members voted to hold the competition within the following 12 months. The decision was taken in part because the growing professionalism of football (both **Czechoslovakia** and **Hungary**, for example, had established professional leagues in the mid-1920s) was no longer compatable with the amateur ethos of the Olympics. Jules **Rimet**, FIFA president between 1920 and 1954, was instrumental in establishing the tournament and the first trophy was later renamed in his honour (see **World Cup trophies**). The first tournament in **Uruguay** attracted only 13 entrants, with only four European countries (**Belgium**, France, **Romania** and **Yugoslavia**) taking part despite a promise from the host nation to fund the expenses of all those participating. France played **Mexico** in the opening World Cup fixture on 13 July 1930 and, after 19 minutes, French player Lucien **Laurent** scored the first World Cup goal. Uruguay won the inaugural tournament. Amid controversy, FIFA allowed fascist **Italy** to stage the second tournament in 1934 and again the host nation was victorious. Qualifying matches were introduced for the 1934 tournament, as was the third-place playoff. France staged the 1938 competition, with Italy again emerging as victors. FIFA changed the tournament's format for the 1950 finals, which were held in Brazil. There was no final as such but four leagues of four countries, with the winners of each section going into a further group stage. The victorious team, Uruguay, finished top of the final pool table, its last match with Brazil effectively proving to be a final despite the league system. Leagues were partially retained for the 1954 tournament in **Switzerland**. Two teams in each group of four were seeded and they played only the non-seeded countries, with the top two sides in each group going on to contest the quarter-finals and knockout stage. West **Germany** won the trophy, defeating Hungary 3–2 in the final – after being 0–2 down. **Sweden** hosted the 1958 tournament in which Brazil became the first nation to win the World Cup on another continent. The South Americans retained the trophy at the following tournament in **Chile**. **Goal average** was first used to separate teams level on points for the first time at the 1962 competition. In 1966, **England** became the third host nation to win the World Cup. FIFA allocated only one place to all the nations from Africa, Asia and Oceania, which led to all African nations and all Asian countries, apart from Korea, withdrawing from the tournament. FIFA again attracted controversy for its choice of venue for the 1970 tournament, following the shooting of peaceful demonstrators in Mexico City prior to the 1968 **Olympic Games**. European nations were also concerned about altitude problems, with Mexico City being more than 7,000 feet above sea level. Brazil emerged victorious and retained the Jules Rimet trophy outright, having won three times. At the 1974 tournament, held in West Germany and which the host nation won, FIFA introduced a second-phase league system and a new trophy (see World Cup trophies). More controversy surrounded FIFA's decision to stage the 1978 tournament in **Argentina**, which at the time was ruled by a military dictatorship. Again the host nation won the trophy. The number of nations competing in the finals was raised from 16 to 24, allowing greater representation from Africa, Asia and Central America, for the 1982 tournament in **Spain**. Italy, having made a slow start to the tournament, beat West Germany in the final. Mexico again hosted the 1986 finals after both Colombia, FIFA's preferred choice, and Brazil pulled out. Again West Germany was beaten finalists, with Argentina taking the trophy for a second time. A repeat of the 1986 final between Argentina and West Germany occurred in Italia'90, but with the Germans winning on this occasion. A penalty six minutes from the end decided the match, after Argentina had had two men sent off. In order to help establish football in the United States, FIFA granted the 1994 tournament to the USA, and Brazil won the competition for a record fourth time in the first final to be decided by a **penalty shootout**. The expanded 1998 tournament contained the first final between the host nation and the holders, with France prevailing over Brazil. The **golden goal** extra-time system was adopted for the 1998 competition. *Records* Brazil has won the World Cup a record four times, and together with West Germany (three victories) has appeared in a record six finals. Italy also has recorded three World Cup triumphs, and Argentina and Uruguay have both won twice. Czechoslovakia, **Netherlands** and Hungary have all twice been losing finalists. Only Brazil has appeared in all 16 World Cup finals. France's Just **Fontaine** is the record goalscorer in one tournament with 13 goals in 1958. *Final results* 1930, Uruguay 4–2 Argentina (Uruguay); 1934, Italy 2–1 Czechoslovakia; 1938, Italy 4–2 Hungary (France); 1950, Uruguay 2–1 Brazil (deciding match, Brazil); 1954, West Germany 3–2 Hungary (Switzerland); 1958, Brazil 5–2 Sweden (Sweden); 1962, Brazil 3–1 Czechoslovakia (Chile); 1966, England 4–2 West Germany (England); 1970, Brazil 4–1 Italy (Mexico); 1974, West Germany 2–1 Netherlands (West Germany); 1978, Argentina 3–1 Netherlands (Argentina); 1982, Italy 3–1 West Germany (Spain); 1986, Argentina 3–2 West Germany (Mexico); 1990, West Germany 1–0 Argentina (Italy); 1994, Brazil 0–0 Italy (3–2 pens; USA); 1998, France 3–0 Brazil (France).

World Cup rally *misc.* road rally from London to Mexico City held to coincide with the 1970 **World Cup**.

World Cup trophies *misc.* trophy awarded to the winning nation. There have been two **World Cup** trophies since the tournament was established in 1930. The first trophy, the Coupe de Monde de Football Assocation (renamed after World War II in honour **FIFA** president Jules **Rimet**), was won outright by **Brazil** following its third tournament victory in 1970. The Coupe Jules Rimet, as it was officially named, was 35 cm high and weighed around 3.8 kg. It was made of silver and was gold plated with a base of lapis lazuli. The trophy, by French sculptor Abel Lafleur, depicted a goddess of Victory holding up a eight-sided chalice. It was stolen on two occasions. In 1966, the trophy disappeared from a philatelic exhibition prior to the **England** tournament and was later found by a dog named "Pickles". In 1983, the trophy was stolen in Rio de Janeiro and is thought to have been melted down. The second World Cup trophy, made by the Italian sculptor Silvio Gazzaniga, was first presented in 1974. It stands 36 cm high, weighs 4,970 grammes and is made of solid gold. Its base is produced from malachite. No country can win the second trophy outright, although victors each receive a gold-plated copy.

World Football Championships for Players with Learning Disabilities *competition* international nation's tournament for people with learning disabilities, first played July-August 1998, in Leicester. The tournament comprised fifteen nations (from five continents) divided into four first-round groups. The competing countries were **Brazil**, **Burkina** Faso, **England**, **Germany**, **India**, **Mali**, **Mexico**, **Netherlands**, **Poland**, **Portugal**, **Russia**, **Scotland**, **South Africa**, **Spain** and **Sweden**. The group winners and runners-up qualified for the knockout stages. The championships, played over 18 days, were organised by the **Association of Football Players with Learning Disabilities** and cost more than £1.2 million to stage. They were sanctioned by the **Football Association** and **FIFA**. The tournament's patron was Gary **Lineker**. *Winners:* Poland, 4–0, v Brazil (third place: Germany, 5–3, v Portugal).

World Footballer of the Year (World Soccer) *award* annual accolade awarded by *World Soccer* to the best player as voted for by the magazine's readers. *Results* 1982, Paolo **Rossi** (**Juventus** and **Italy**); 1983 **Zico**, (Udinese and **Brazil**); 1984, Michel **Platini** (Juventus and **France**); 1985, Michel Platini (Juventus and France); 1986 Diego **Maradona**, (**Napoli** and **Argentina**); 1987, Ruud **Gullit** (**AC Milan** and **Netherlands**); 1988, Marco **Van Basten** (AC Milan and Netherlands); 1989, Ruud Gullit (AC Milan and Netherlands); 1990, Lothar **Matthäus** (**Internazionale** and **West Germany**); 1991, Jean-Pierre **Papin** (**Olympique de Marseille** and France); 1992, Marco Van Basten (AC Milan and Netherlands); 1993, Roberto **Baggio** (Juventus and Italy); 1994, Paolo **Maldini** (AC Milan and Italy); 1995, Gianluca **Vialli** (Juventus and Italy); 1996, **Ronaldo** (**Barcelona** and Brazil); 1997 Ronaldo (Barcelona, Internazionale and Brazil); 1998, Zinedine **Zidane** (Juventus and France). See also **FIFA World Footballer of the Year**.

World Soccer *publication* monthly magazine covering football around the globe, first published in 1960. It is the oldest continually published football magazine in the UK and 40% of its readership is based overseas.

World Team of the Year *award* annual award made by **FIFA** to the national team that heads the annual **FIFA world rankings**. *Winners* 1993 **Germany**; 1994 **Brazil**; 1995 Brazil; 1996 Brazil; 1997 Brazil; 1998 Brazil.

World Under-17 Championship *competition* see **Under-17 World Championship**.

World War I *n.* war between the Allied Forces of, among others, Britain and its Empire, France, Italy, Russia and the United States of America; and the Central European Powers of, among others, Austria-Hungary, Germany and Turkey, lasting from 1914 until 1918. An estimated 10 million people died, and around 20 million were injured. *Football* The English **Football League** and **Scottish Football League** programmes continued after the outbreak of war in August 1914: both governing bodies believed that the country needed a distraction from the war and that, in any case, the conflict was not expected to last beyond the end of the year. There were many who opposed the staging of football matches during the war, including the Dean of Lincoln who complained at the time of people "still gazing at football" while "their fellow-men are giving themselves in their country's peril". The league and clubs were also hit financially: gate receipts were well down on the pre-war period and players were forced to take a wage cut in order to finance a Football League relief fund to help support clubs in difficulty. A percentage of gate receipts was also levied for the relief fund. While the football programme continued, the **Football Association** agreed that matches were not to be played close to munitions factories during working hours; this followed a Parliamentary debate into an alleged high number of defective shells being produced in the factories. As a consequence, an **FA Cup** second-round replay between **Bradford City** and **Norwich** was played **behind closed doors** at Lincoln. **Everton** finished as Division One champions, with **Celtic** winning the Scottish championship. The season ended with the so-called **Khaki Cup final**, won by **Sheffield United** (the **Scottish FA Cup** had been suspended). By 1915, with many players already on active service or working in armament factories, combined with the logistical and financial difficulties of staging the matches, a decision was taken to suspend or curtail all major league competitions throughout the country. The full Football League, Southern League, Scottish Football League and Irish League programmes were officially suspended before the 1915-16 season; the formal announcement was made at a joint conference on 3 July 1915. The FA Cup also came to a stop. The Scottish Division One did, in fact, continue – albeit with its players restricted to a £2-per-week salary, and required to work for the war effort if they were not in active service. The Scottish Division Two and the Scottish FA Cup were suspended for the duration of the war. English regional competitions, organised under the jurisdiction of the Football League, operated during the war years with players receiving no more than their expenses. These included the Lancashire Regional Tournament, Midland Regional Tournament and the London Combination League. Matches could be played only on Saturdays – so as not to interfere with war work – and no trophies or medals were given to the competition winners. The national league programmes restarted in 1919. Forty-four Football League professionals are listed as having died on active service. See Donald **Bell**, **Footballers Battalion, Wartime football.**

World War II *n.* a war between the Allied Forces of, amongst others, Britain and its empire and Commonwealth, China, France, Russia and the United States of America, and the Axis Powers of, chiefly, Germany, Italy and Japan. It was precipitated by the German invasion of Poland in 1939. It ended with the unconditional surrender of Germany in May 1945 and the capitulation of Japan after the Americans had dropped nuclear bombs on Hiroshima and Nagasaki in August the same year. Fifty-five million people died; more than a third were Russians. At least six million Jews were exterminated in the Holocaust. *Football* Although the 1939-40 English **Football League** season began, it was suspended the day after Britain's formal declaration of war against Germany on 3 September; only three rounds of matches had been played (**Blackpool** were top of Division One). Regional leagues and a Football League (War) Cup Competition were organised, starting in October 1939 and lasting throughout the war years. The fixtures were allowed to go ahead only with the permission of the War Office, and no teams were allowed to travel more than 50 miles. Gates for these regional matches were restricted to 8,000 spectators, and all matches were **all-ticket**. Players were limited to a maximum match fee of 30 shillings (£1.50). **Aston Villa**, **Exeter City**, **Derby County**, **Ipswich Town**, **Gateshead** and **Sunderland** stopped playing altogether during World War II, while **Notts County** fielded 132 players in a single season, such was the state of flux with players often unavailable or stationed in the area for only short periods. Albert Stubbins of Newcastle was the war-time leading goalscorer with 226 goals from 1939 to 1946. Scottish football was also regionalised, with Scottish North-East and Scottish Southern leagues in operation from 1941 to 1945. A number of war-time internationals were played between the home nations. These included a 1-1 draw between **England** and **Scotland** at **Hampden Park**, in May 1940, which attracted a crowd of 75,000. England's 8–0 victory over Scotland on 16 October 1943 was watched by 60,000 at **Maine Road**; Stanley **Matthews**, Denis **Compton** and Tommy **Lawton** were among the England team. England had already scored eight goals against **Wales** the previous month; Stan **Mortensen** was England's reserve - there were no official substitutes then - but went on as a replacement for an injured Welsh player (25 September 1943, 8–3, at **Wembley** Stadium). Football was also played in Germany's prisoner-of-war camps, with playing equipment supplied by the International Red Cross. One of the larger camps, Stalag Luft I, had 60 teams at its peak, playing in five leagues. In **Germany**, the regular football programme continued through to 1944. The league and cup were expanded to include the whole of Hitler's Third-Reich Germany, with three Austrian clubs, **Rapid Vienna**, Admira Wien (now **Admira-Wacker**), and **First Vienna** successful in both competitions. The expansion of Germany led to Austria's withdrawal from the 1938 **World Cup**; the nation having been absorbed into Germany. The World Cup did not resume until 1950 (**Argentina**, **Brazil** and Germany had all bid to stage the World Cup in 1942). The full English and Scottish league programmes restarted in 1946-47.

World Youth Cup (under-20) *competition* biennial international nations tournament for players under 20 years of age. The finals take place at a host country, with qualification decided by regional competitions run by the various confederations. *History* The first finals took place in Tunisia, in 1977. The highest crowd was 110,000 for the 1983 final at Azteca Stadium, Mexico City, Mexico. *Winners* (result, runners-up, venue) 1977 **Soviet Union** (2–2, 9–8 pens., v **Mexico**, in Tunis, Tunisia); 1979 **Argentina** (3–1, v Soviet Union, at the National Stadium, Tokyo, Japan); 1981 West **Germany** (4–0, v **Qatar**, at Sydney Cricket Ground, Sydney, Australia); 1983 **Brazil** (1–0, v Argentina, at the Azteca Stadium, Mexico City, Mexico); 1985 Brazil (1–0, v **Spain**, at the Centralny Lenina, Moscow, Russia/former-Soviet Union); 1987 **Yugoslavia** (1–1, 5–4 pens., v West Germany, at the Estadio **Nacional**, Santiago, Chile); 1989 **Portugal** (2–0, v **Nigeria**, at the King Fahd Stadium, Riyadh, Saudi Arabia); 1991 Portugal (0–0, 4–2 pens., v Brazil, at the **Estádio da Lu**z, Lisbon, Portugal); 1993 Brazil (2–1, v **Ghana**, in Sydney, Australia); 1995 Argentina (2–0, v Brazil, at the Khalifa International Stadium, Doha, Qatar); 1997 Argentina (2–1, v **Uruguay**, at the Shah Alam Stadium, Kuala Lumpur, Malaysia); 1992, Spain (4–0, v **Japan**, at the Surulere Stadium, Lagos, Nigeria)..

world ranking *n.* international ordering of national sides by classification first published by **FIFA** in August 1993 and updated on a monthly basis. FIFA's system, officially entitled the FIFA/Coca-Cola World Rankings, is based on an evaluation of all **World Cup** finals, World Cup qualifiers, continental championship finals (eg, **European Championships**), continental championship qualifiers and friendly matches played by senior national sides. Placings are not solely determined by results, but are based on five criteria: 1. result; 2. number of goals; 3. venue (home or away); 4. importance of the match; 5. strength of opposition. Points 4 and 5 are measured using a multiplication factor and certain considerations are taken into account when assessing a teams' performance. Rankings are determined as follows: *Results* Two points are awarded for each match and these are divided between the teams in accordance with their predetermined strengths. For example, where a strong nation plays a much weaker one, the points will be divided equally between the two if the former wins (eg, one apiece); if the latter wins, it will receive three points and the stronger nation will have one point deducted. The points awarded for matches between countries with only a small difference in terms of strength are as follows: if the slightly stronger nation wins it will receive 1.9 and the losers 0.10; if the slightly weaker nation triumphs it receives 2.1 and the losers will be deducted 0.10; a drawn match is split 0.9 to the stronger country and 1.1 to the weaker one. In matches between sides of equal strength, the winners will receive two points and the losers will have two points deducted; a drawn match will result in both countries receiving one point apiece. *Number of goals* The points awarded for the number of goals scored are also determined by the relative strengths and weakness of the two countries: weaker sides receive greater reward for scoring against a stronger nation than where the stronger country scores against the weaker one. *Venue* Nations winning away from home receive a bonus of 0.3 points (there are no bonus points for matches played at a neutral venue). *Importance of match* A multiplying factor awards bonus points to winners depending on the nature of fixture. The multiplying factor is as follows: friendlies x 1.0; continental championship qualifiers x 1.1; continental championship finals and World Cup qualifiers x 1.25; World Cup finals x 1.5. *Regional strength* A multiplying factor awards bonus points to winners of matches between nations from the same confederation and is based on an annually determined assessment of each of the six FIFA confederations, which is a measure of the past performance of national sides in intercontinental matches. The multiplying factor for 1997 was as follows: **Confédération Africaine de Football** (CAF) x 0.95; **Asian Football Confederation** (AFC) x 0.90 **Union of European Football Associations** (UEFA) is x 1.0; **Confederación Norte-Centroamericana y del Caribe de Fútbol** (CONCACAF) x 0.90; **Confederación Sudamericana de Fútbol** (CONMEBOL) x 1.0; **Oceania Football Confederation** (OFC) x 0.85. Matches between countries from different confederations have a regional strength factor of one. The FIFA system also takes into account the number of games played during the evaluation period and a country's previous results to determine a team's overall position, as well as a formulation that is based on a combination of the best eight results achieved in a ranking period and the overall total of all results played during that time. A country's score for a 12-month period is added to its existing score from each of the previous five years, which are devalued each year and are eventually eliminated from the equation (eg, the previous year's value is higher than that of five years ago). Countries that top the FIFA/Coca-Cola World Rankings each year receive the **Top team of the year** award. A **Best mover of the year** award goes to the country making the best progress in terms of the net number of points gained over the year.

Wrexham *club* English league. *Dossier* Ground: **Racecourse Ground**, Wrexham, Clwyd. Strip: red shirts, white shorts and red socks. Nickname: Robins. Ground capacity: 9,200. Record attendance: 34,445 v **Manchester United** (26 January 1957, **FA Cup**, fourth round). Best average attendance: 11,651 (1977-78). Biggest win: 10–1 v **Hartlepools United** (3 March 1962, Division Four). Biggest defeat: 0–9 v **Brentford** (15 October 1963, Division Three). *History* Founded in September 1872 by a group of cricketers who played at the Racecourse Ground. In 1878, the club was the first winners of the **Welsh Cup** (1–0 v Druids). Wrexham was disbanded in March 1884 after being expelled from the English **Football Association** following crowd trouble at an FA Cup tie with Oswestry (3–4, second round). A month later a new club was formed called Wrexham Olympic, which reverted to plain Wrexham in 1887. Aside from the Racecourse

Ground, the club played at two other venues (Salisbury Park Road and Rhosddu Recreation ground) in the early years before making the ground its permanent home in 1883. Wrexham is one of six Welsh clubs playing in the English **pyramid system** (**Cardiff City** and **Swansea City**, and non-league Colwyn Bay, Merthyr Tydfil and Newport AFC). Prior to the club becoming an original member of Division Three (North) in 1921-22, it won the Welsh Cup on 12 occasions (see below). Wrexham joined Division Three in 1958-59 when the bottom 12 clubs in northern and southern sections formed Division Four. Wrexham reached the quarter-final stage of the inaugural **League Cup** competition in 1960-61 (0–3 v **Aston Villa**). The club was relegated in 1963-64, returning to Division Three as runners-up in 1969-70. In 1974, Wrexham was an FA Cup quarter-finalist (0–1 v **Burnley**), having disposed of **Middlesbrough** (1–0, fourth round) and **Southampton** (1–0, fifth round). Wrexham reached the quarter-finals of the **European Cup-winners Cup** in 1975-76 (1–2 agg. v **Anderlecht**) and, in 1976-77, the club lifted its first and only Football League trophy, winning the Division Three Championship. The next season, Wrexham was both an FA Cup (2–3 v **Arsenal**) and a League Cup (1–3 v **Liverpool**) quarter-finalist, but by 1983-84 the club was back playing in Division Four following two consecutive demotions. Wrexham narrowly missed promotion to Division Three via the end-of-season **playoffs** in 1988-89, losing in the final (1–2 agg. v **Leyton Orient**). In 1990-91, Wrexham finished bottom of the League and was forced to apply for re-election. One of the club's most famous FA Cup victories occurred in 1992, when it defeated the reigning League Champions Arsenal (2–1, third round). Wrexham won promotion to the Second Division in 1992-93 and in 1997, the club was again an FA Cup quarter-finalist (0–1 v **Chesterfield**), having recorded victories over **West Ham United** (0–1 replay, third round) and **Birmingham City** (3–1, fifth round) on the way. In 1997-98, Wrexham missed entering the Second Division playoffs on goals scored. Wrexham's 23 Welsh Cup victories is more than any other club and it has also been a finalist on a further 22 occasions – also a record. *League record* Division Two 1978-79 to 1981-82; First Division 1993-94 to present; Division Three 1958-59 to 1959-60, 1962-63 to 1963-64, 1970-71 to 1977-78, 1982-83; Third Division 1992-93; Division Three (North) 1921-22 to 1957-58; Division Four 1960-61 to 1961-62, 1964-65 to 1969-70, 1983-84 to 1991-92. *Honours* Division Three 1977-78; Welsh Cup 1878 (1–0 v Druids), 1883 (1–0 v Druids), 1893 (2–1 v Chirk), 1897 (2–0 v **Newtown**), 1903 (8–0 v Aberaman), 1905 (3–0 v Aberdare Athletic), 1909 (1–0 v **Chester**), 1910 (2–1 v Chester), 1911 (6–1 v **Connah's Quay**), 1914 (1–0 replay v LLlanelli), 1915 (1–0 replay v **Swansea Town**), 1921 (3–1 replay v Pontypridd), 1924 (1–0 replay v Merthyr Town), 1925 (3–1 v Flint), 1931 (7–0 v **Shrewsbury Town**), 1957 (2–1 v Swansea Town), 1958 (2–0 replay v Chester),

1960 (1–0 v Cardiff City), 1972 (3–2 agg. v Cardiff City), 1975 (5–2 agg. v Cardiff City), 1978 (3–1 agg. v **Bangor City**), 1986 (3–2 agg. v Kidderminster Harriers), 1995 (2–1 v Cardiff City). *Records* Dai Davies is Wrexham's most capped player (28 (51) for **Wales**); Arfon Griffiths holds the record for club League appearances (592, 1959-61, 1962-79); Tom Bamford is Wrexham's record League goalscorer (175, 1928-34).

Wright, Billy *player-manager* Defender. **England** international (105 caps, 3 goals). Born 6 February 1924. Career ca. 1938-59. *Clubs* (player) **Wolverhampton Wanderers**. *Honours* League Championship (Wolverhampton Wanderers 1953-54, 1957-58, 1958-59); **FA Cup** (Wolverhampton Wanderers 1949). *Clubs* (manager) **Arsenal**. Also, England Youth team manager. *Keynotes* Joined Wolverhampton Wanderers in 1938, turning professional in 1941. Wright made 491 **Football League** appearances for Wolves, scoring 13 goals. First player in the World to win 100 caps for his country (for which he was made a **Football Association** life member). He appeared in all but three of England's first 108 postwar matches, and was captain on 90 occasions. Wright was never booked throughout his club and international career. He was voted **Footballer of the Year** in 1952 and was awarded the CBE in 1959. Moved to television after being sacked as Arsenal manager in June 1966. Included in the **Football League Centenary 100 players**.

wrist injury *medical* damage to the wrist caused, for example by the hand being forced backwards due to a fall or, infrequently, by a goalkeeper attempting to stop a ball struck with great force. Wrist injuries include both **fractures** and **ligament** damage (**sprains**, **tears** and **rupture**).

Wunderteam *misc.* nickname of the highly successful Austrian national team of the 1930s, under the management of Hugo Meisl and Scottish trainer Jimmy Hogan. One hundred and one goals were scored in 30 games from 1931-34. Star players included Johann Horvath, Anton Schall, Matthias **Sindelar** and Karl Zischek.

Wycombe Wanderers *club* English league. *Dossier* Ground: **Adams Park**, Wycombe, Buckinghamshire. Strip: light blue and navy blue quartered shirts, navy blue shorts, navy blue socks. Nickname: the Saddlers. Ground capacity: 10,000. Record attendance: 9,002 v **West Ham United** (7 January 1995, **FA Cup**, third round). Biggest win: 5–0 v **Hitchin Town** (3 December 1994, FA Cup second round). Biggest defeat: 0–5 v **Walsall** (7 November 1995, **Auto Windscreens Shield**, first round). *History* Founded in 1884 as North Town Wanderers by workers employed in the furniture industry. The club adopted the name Wycombe Wanderers in 1887. It played at several venues, including at The Rye and at Spring Meadow, before settling at Loakes Park where the club remained, except for one season (1899), until moving to a purpose-built stadium, Adams Park in 1990. Wycombe entered the Isthmian League in 1921 and won the **FA Amateur Cup** in 1931 (1–0 v Hayes). In 1975, the club reached the third round of the FA Cup (0–1 replay v **Middlesbrough**). Wycombe won the **FA Challenge Trophy** in 1991 (2–1 v Kidderminster Harriers) and 1993 (4–1 v Runcorn). Wycombe narrowly missed promotion to the League on **goal difference** in 1991-92. The club was promoted to the Third Division in 1992-93 (displacing **Halifax Town**) as Football Conference Champions, immediately winning promotion to the Second Division via the end-of-season **play-offs** (4–2 v **Preston North End**). *League record* Second Division 1994-95 to present; Third Division 1993-94. *Honours* Football Conference 1992-93; FA Amateur Cup 1931 (1–0 v Hayes); FA Trophy 1991 (2–1 v Kidderminster Harriers), 1993 (4–1 v Runcorn). *Records* Dave Carroll holds the record for club League appearances (210, 1993-98); he is also Wycombe's record League goalscorer (31, 1995-98).

Wynalda, Eric *player* Striker. **United States of America** international (98 caps, 31 goals, 1990-). Born 9 June 1969. *Clubs* San Diego State University, San Francisco Bay Blackhawks, FC Saarbruecken (Germany), Bochum (Germany), **San José Clash**. *Keynotes* Wynalda is the USA's top goalscorer. Played in the 1990, 1994 and 1998 **World Cup** finals teams.

Xelaju MC (Mario Camposeco) *club* Guatemala national league club based in Quezaltenango. Ground: Estadio Mario Camposeco. Strip: red and blue broad striped shirts, blue shorts. Guatemala national champions 1962, 1996.

X-ray *medical* image produced by exposing a photographic film to X-rays. Useful in injury diagnosis because bones are relatively opaque to X-rays (compared to soft tissues); **fractures** and **hairline fractures** can be diagnosed without surgery. More complex techniques – such as contrast X-rays and computerised tomography – have been developed for organ and tissue imaging.

Y

yard short of pace *informal* clichéd phrase used to describe a player who lacks the necessary speed to keep up with the game.

Yashin, Lev *player* Goalkeeper. **Soviet Union** international (75 caps 1954-67). Born 22 October 1929, died 1990. Career ca. 1949-70 *Clubs* **Dinamo Moscow** *Keynotes* Considered one of the greatest goalkeepers of all time. Yashin, once a goalminder for Dinamo's ice hockey team, made his debut as a footballer for Dinamo in 1951 and went on to play 326 matches in the Soviet league. Awarded the Order of Lenin in 1968. Retired from playing in 1970. Later became coach of Dinamo. In 1998, Yashin was named in a poll of 130 European football writers as the goalkeeper for the all-time "Europe XI". *Honours* **Olympic Games** gold medal (Soviet Union, 1956); **European Championship** (Soviet Union, 1960 - the first championship); Soviet Union league championship (Dinamo Moscow, 1954, 1955, 1957, 1959, 1963); *France Football* **European Footballer of the Year** 1963.

Yekini, Rashidi *player* Striker. **Nigeria** international (67 caps, 41 goals). Born 12 August 1962. *Clubs* **IICC Shooting Stars**, Abiola Babies (Nigeria), **Africa Sports** (Ivory Coast), **Vitória SC Setúbal**, **Olympiakos**, Sporting Gijon (Spain), FC Zurich (Switzerland). *Keynotes* Yekini was top scorer at the **African Cup of Nations** final tournament in 1992 and 1994, with four and five goals, respectively. *Honours* African Cup of Nations (Nigeria, 1994, runner-up 1988, 1990, third place 1992); **African Footballer of the Year** 1993.

yellow card *rules* yellow-coloured card used by a referee to signal to a player that he or she is to receive a **caution** for an offence under the **Laws of the game** (Law XII). *Keynotes* Yellow cards were introduced to the **Football League** on 2 October 1976. The system was stopped by the **Football Association** in January 1981, and reinstated in 1987. See: **red card**.

Yemen 1. Republic of Yemen *country AFC* republic in South West Asia, on the Arabian and Red Seas, next to **Oman** and **Saudi Arabia**. Independence in 1918. Country divided in 1962 into South Yemen (Democratic republic of Yemen) and North Yemen (Yemen Arab Republic). War between the two in 1971-72 and again in 1979. Reunited as Republic of Yemen in 1990. Area: 527,970 sq km (328,065 sq miles). Population: 15,800,000 (1995 est.). Languages: Arabic. Capital: Sana'a. *Dossier* Yemen Football Association (Sana'a) formed in 1962, affiliated to **FIFA** and **Asian Football Confederation** (AFC) in 1980 (see **3.** South Yemen, below), president: Ali Ahmed Al-Ashwal; general secretary: Mujahed Ali Al-Saraha. Season played from October to April. National stadium: Sana'a Stadium, capacity: 50,000. National strip: green shirts, green shorts, green socks. *International tournament record* **Olympic Games** – Republic of Yemen first entered 1992, never passed first qualifying round; **Women's World Cup** – never entered; **World Cup** – Republic of Yemen first entered 1994, never progressed beyond first qualifying round (second in its group of four nations in 1998); **Asian Cup of Nations** – Republic of Yemen first entered 1994, never progressed beyond first qualifying round; **Asian Games** – Republic of Yemen first entered 1990, never past first round; **Asian Women's Championship** – never entered; **Under-17 World Championship** – never qualified; **World Youth Cup (under-20)** – never qualified. *Record against British and Irish national teams* none played. *History* Following reunification, the Yemen national league began in 1990 (first won by Al Tilal). *League system* Fourteen clubs compete in the national First Division (increased from 12 in 1998-99. The bottom two clubs are relegated automatically. Three points are awarded for a win, with one for a draw). *Record in international club tournaments*: no major success in international tournaments. Leading clubs: Al Wehda (Yemen league champions 1997, 1998, "Unity Cup" winners 1998), Ahli (Yemen Cup 1997), Al Tilal (Yemen league champions 1990). **2. North Yemen** *former country* former country in southwest Arabia on the Red Sea, declared a republic in 1962 as the Yemen Arab Republic. Formally united with South Yemen in May 1990. *Dossier* Football association formed 1962, affiliated to **FIFA** (the 150th member of FIFA) and AFC in 1980. *International tournament record* **World Cup** – North Yemen entered 1986 and 1990, never progressed beyond first qualifying round; **Asian Cup of Nations** – entered in 1984 and 1988, never past first qualifying round; **Asian Games** – never entered. **3. South Yemen** *former country* former country on the south coast of the Arabian Peninsular, declared independence from British protection in 1967 as the People's Democratic Republic of Yemen. Consisted of the former British territory of Aden and surrounding desert areas. Unified with North Yemen in 1990. *Dossier* Football association formed 1940, affiliated to **FIFA** and AFC in 1967. *International tournament record* **World Cup** – South Yemen entered once in 1986 (4–7 agg., v **Bahrain**, first-round qualifier); **Asian Cup of Nations** – reached final tournament in 1976 after walkover in qualifying tournament, finished last in its three-nation first round group (with two defeats, including 0–8 v **Iran**), also entered 1988 (last in its qualifying group); **Asian Games** – entered 1982 (first round).

Yemen Arabic Republic *former country* see **Yemen** (sense 2).

Yokohama Flugels *club* former Japanese **J-League** club based in Yokohama, formerly All Nippon Airways (1984-1992). Ground: Mitsuzawa Stadium, capacity: 15,050. *Keynotes* At the end of the 1997-98 season, the Flugels, a founder member of the J League, ceased to function as a separate club, merging with neighbours **Yokohama Marinos** after incurring debts of around £5 million. Flugels final competitive match was the 1998 Emporer's Cup final, which the club won (2–1 v **Shimizu S-Pulse**). **Asian Cup-winners Cup** 1995 (2–1, v **Al Shaab** of the United Arab Emirates, in Sharjah, United Arab Emirates), semi-final 1996; **Asian Super Cup** 1995 (4–3 agg., v **Thai Farmers Bank** of Thailand); Emperor's Cup 1994, 1999.

Yokohama Marinos *club* Japanese **J-League** club based in Yokohama, formerly Nissan Football Club (1972-92) Ground: Mitsuzawa Stadium, capacity: 15,050. Strip: blue shirts and white shorts. *Keynotes* At the end of the 1997-98 season, the club absorbed its neighbours **Yokohama Flugels**, a founder member of the J League, and winners of both the **Asian Cup-winners Cup** and **Asian Super Cup** in 1995, which had accrued debts of around £5 million. **Asian Champion Teams Cup** runners-up 1989 (2–3 agg., v **Liaoning** of China), quarter-final 1997; **Asian Cup-winners Cup** 1992 (6–1 agg., v **Al Nasr** of Saudi Arabia), 1993 (2–1, v **Piroozi** of Iran), semi-final 1994; J-League champions 1995; Japanese National League champions 1989, 1990; Emperor's Cup 1984, 1986, 1989, 1990, 1992, 1993; Japanese League Cup 1988, 1989, 1990.

York City *club* English league. *Dossier* Ground: **Bootham Crescent**, York, Yorkshire. Strip: red shirts, blue shorts and red socks. Nickname: Minstermen. Ground capacity: 9,534. Record attendance: 28,123 v **Huddersfield Town** (5 March 1938, **FA Cup**, sixth round). Best average attendance: 10,412 (1948-49). Biggest win: 9–1 v **Southport** (2 February 1957, Division Three (North)). Biggest defeat: 0–12 v **Chester** (1 February 1936, Division Three (North)). *History* Founded in 1922 after the original York City, formed in 1908, ceased to exist in 1917. The club played at Fulfordgate before taking over Yorkshire County Cricket Club's Bootham Crescent ground in 1932. York was

elected to Division Three (North) in 1929-30, replacing **Ashington**. The club enjoyed the first of many cup **giantkilling** performances in 1938, reaching the FA Cup quarter-finals (1–2 replay v Huddersfield Town), following victories over Division One opponents **Middlesbrough** (1–0, fifth round) and **West Bromwich Albion** (3–2, fourth round). In 1955, York went a stage further, becoming only the third Division Three side to reach the FA Cup semi-finals (0–2 replay v **Newcastle United**). In earlier rounds, the club defeated **Blackpool** (2–0, third round) and **Tottenham Hotspur** (3–1, fifth round). York won promotion to Division Three in 1958-59, the first season of newly established Division Four, but survived only one term. In 1961-62, the club was a **League Cup** quarter-finalist (1–2 v **Rochdale**). Promotion to Division Three in 1970-71 was followed in 1973-74 by elevation to Division Two, albeit for only two seasons, for the first time in the club's history. By 1977-78 the club was back playing in Division Four. In 1983-84, York secured its first domestic trophy, winning the Division Four Championship – 16 points clear of its nearest rivals. The club won promotion to the Second Division in 1992-93 via the end-of-season **playoffs** (1–1, 5–3 pens. v **Crewe Alexandra**) and the following season it almost repeated the feat, reaching the semi-final stage of the playoffs. Other notable giantkilling feats by York include victories over **Arsenal** (1–0, FA Cup, third round 1985) and **Manchester United** (3–0, League Cup, third round 1st leg, 1995-96) *League record* Division Two 1974-75 to 1975-76; Second Division 1993-94, 1998-99; Division Three 1959-60, 1965-66, 1971-72 to 1973-74, 1976-77, 1984-85 to 1987-88; Third Division 1992-93, 1999-00; Division Three (North) 1929-30 to 1957-58; Division Four 1958-59, 1960-61 to 1964-65, 1966-67 to 1970-71, 1977-78 to 1983-84, 1988-89 to 1991-92. *Honours* Division Four 1983-84. *Records* Peter Scott is York's most capped player (7 (10) for **Northern Ireland**); Barry Jackson holds the record for club League appearances (481, 1958-70); Norman Wilkinson is York's record League goalscorer (125, 1954-66).

Young Africans SC *club* Tanzanian national league club based in Dar es Salaam. Ground: National Stadium, Dar es Salaam, capacity: 25,000. Strip: yellow shirts, green shorts. **African Cup of Champion Clubs** quarter-final "champions-league" stage 1998; **East and Central African Club Championship** winners, 1975, 1993, 1999; Tanzanian Mainland League champions 1968, 1969, 1970, 1971, 1974, 1981, 1983, 1985, 1987, 1989, 1991, 1992, 1993, 1996, 1997,1998; East African Super Cup runners-up 1996; Tanzania and Zanzibar Union League champions 1981, 1983, 1987, 1991, 1996.

Young, Alex *player* Striker. **Scotland** international (8 caps). Born 3 February 1937. Career ca. 1955-69. *Clubs* **Heart of Midlothian**, **Everton**, **Glentoran** (player-manager), **Stockport County**. *Keynotes* Joined Everton from Heart of Midlothian for £42,000 in

November 1960. While at Goodison Park, Young was the inspiration for a television play, *The Golden Vision*. Retired through injury in 1969. Included in the **Football League Centenary 100 players**. *Honours* League Championship (Everton 1962-63); **FA Cup** (Everton 1966); Scottish League (Heart of Midlothian 1957-58, 1959-60); Scottish FA Cup (Heart of Midlothian 1956); Scottish League Cup (Heart of Midlothian 1960).

Young Boys Berne *club* see **BSC Young Boys**.

Young Footballer of the Year (England) *award* **Professional Footballers Association** accolade for the best young player in English league football each season. *Winners* 1974, Kevin Beattie (**Ipswich Town**); 1975, Mervyn Day (**West Ham United**); 1976, Peter Barnes (**Manchester City**); 1977, Andy **Gray (Aston Villa)**; 1978, Tony Woodcock (**Nottingham Forest**); 1979, Cyrille Regis (**West Bromwich Albion**); 1980, Glenn **Hoddle (Tottenham Hotspur)**; 1981, Gary Shaw (Aston Villa); 1982, Steve Moran (**Southampton**); 1983, Ian **Rush (Liverpool)**; 1984, Paul Walsh (**Luton Town**); 1985, Mark **Hughes (Manchester United)**; 1986, Tony Cottee (West Ham United); 1987, Tony **Adams (Arsenal)**; 1988, Paul **Gascoigne (Newcastle United)**; 1989, Paul Merson (Arsenal); 1990, Matthew Le Tissier (Southampton); 1991, Lee Sharpe (Manchester United); 1992, Ryan **Giggs** (Manchester United); 1993, Ryan Giggs (Manchester United); 1994, Andy Cole (Newcastle United); 1995, Robbie Fowler (Liverpool); 1996, Robbie Fowler (Liverpool); 1997, David Beckham (Manchester United); 1998, Michael Owen (Liverpool).

Young player of the year (Scotland) *award* **Scottish Professional Footballers Association** accolade for the best young player in Scottish league football. *Winners* 1978, Graeme Payne (**Dundee United**); 1979, Ray Stewart (Dundee United); 1980, John McDonald (**Rangers**); 1981, Charlie Nicholas (**Celtic**); 1982, Frank McAvennie (**St Mirren**); 1983, Paul McStay (Celtic); 1984, John Robertson (**Heart of Midlothian**); 1985, Craig Levein (Heart of Midlothian); 1986, Craig Levein (Heart of Midlothian); 1987, Robert Fleck (Rangers); 1988, John Collins (**Hibernian**); 1989, Billy McKinlay (Dundee United); 1990, Scott Crabbe (Heart of Midlothian); 1991, Eoin Jess (**Aberdeen**); 1992, Philip O'Donnell (**Motherwell**); 1993, Eoin Jess (Aberdeen); 1994, Philip O'Donnell (Motherwell); 1995, Charlie Miller (Rangers); 1996, Jackie McNamara (Celtic); 1997, Robbie Winters (Dundee United); 1998, Gary Naysmith (Heart of Midlothian).

youngest player *record* **1. World Cup finals** 17 years 41 days, Norman Whiteside for **Northern Ireland** (v **Yugoslavia**, 17 June 1982, 0–0, in Spain, World Cup first round). **Pelé** was the youngest to play in a World Cup final, at 17 years, 237 days (29 June 1958, **Brazil** v **Sweden**, 5–2, Råsunda Stadium, Stockholm); Pelé scored twice, giving him a total of six goals for the tournament. **2. FA Cup** (any match), 15

years 88 days, Andrew Awford, for Worcester City (10 October 1987, FA Cup qualifier). **3. FA Cup final** 17 years 245 days, James Prinsep for **Clapham Rovers** (v **Old Etonians**, 29 March 1879, at Kennington Oval); Paul Allen of **West Ham United** was the youngest FA Cup final player in the 20th century, at 17 years 265 days (v **Arsenal**, May 1980, at **Wembley** Stadium) – Allen was notoriously fouled by Arsenal's Willie Young when in an almost certain goal-scoring position; the youngest FA Cup final goalscorer was Norman Whiteside, at 18 years, 19 days, for **Manchester United** (v **Brighton and Hove Albion**, 26 May 1983, 4–0, replay at Wembley Stadium); David Nish was the youngest FA Cup final captain, at 21 years, seven months, for **Leicester City** (v **Manchester City**, 26 April 1969, at Wembley Stadium). **4. Football League**: 15 years 158 days, Albert Geldard of **Bradford Park Avenue** (v **Millwall**, 16 September 1929, Division Two); and 15 years 158 days, Ken Roberts of **Wrexham** (v Bradford Park Avenue, 1 September 1951, Division Three North); Ronnie Dix was the youngest Football League goalscorer at 15 years 180 days, for **Bristol Rovers** (v **Norwich City**, 3 March 1928, Division Three South). **5.** Division One: 15 years 185 days, Derek Forster of **Sunderland** (v Leicester City, 22 August 1964), Forster was also the youngest goalkeeper; Jason Dozzell was the youngest Division One scorer at 16 years 57 days, for **Ipswich Town** (v **Coventry City**, 4 February 1984). **6.** FA **Premier League**: 17 years three days, Neil Finn, for West Ham United (v Manchester City, 1 January 1996), Finn was also the youngest goalkeeper; Andy Turner was the youngest Premier League scorer at 17 years 166 days, for **Tottenham Hotspur** (v Everton, 5 September 1992). **7. Scottish Football League**: 15 years, Ronnie Simpson for **Queens Park** (1946-47), Simpson was also the youngest goalkeeper. **8. FA Women's Challenge Cup final** 13 years, Sharon Roberts for **Southampton WFC**, 1978 Cup final. *Keynotes* Michael **Owen** is the youngest player to score for **England** in a full international. The **Liverpool** striker entered the record books with his goal against **Morocco** (20 May 1998) in the friendly pre-1998 World Cup tournament, the **King Hassan II Cup**, held in Casablanca. At 16 years of age, Ryan Stepp became the youngest player to score in the **Asian Cup of Nations**, when he scored for **Guam** against **Taiwan** in the 1996 qualifying tournament. Ryan Green of **Wolverhampton Wanderers** became the youngest player to appear for **Wales** in a full international on 3 June 1998 (v Malta, friendly). Green was 17 years and 218 days old, whereas Ryan **Giggs** (Manchester United) was 17 years and 321 days old when he made his international debut (v West Germany, 16 October 1991).

youngest referee for an FA Cup final *record* Kevin Howley refereed the 1960 FA Cup final at **Wembley** aged 35 (**Wolverhampton Wanderers** v **Blackburn Rovers**, 3–0); the match, however, was remembered for the poor behaviour of the Blackburn fans, some of whom threw objects at Mr Howley.

Yugoslavia, Federal Republic of *country UEFA* federal republic of Southeast Europe, on the Adriatic Sea, consisting of the republics of Montenegro and Serbia, and the autonomous regions of Kosovo and Vojvodina. Federal Republic of Yugoslavia declared in 1992, from the remaining republics of the former Socialist Federal Republic of Yugoslavia (see **former-Yugoslavia**). Area: 102,170 sq km (39,435 sq miles). Population: 10,540,000 (1995 est.). Languages: Serbo-Croat, Macedonian, Albanian, Hungarian. Capital: Belgrade (Beograd). *Dossier* Yugoslav Football Association (Belgrade) formed in 1919, affiliated to **FIFA** in 1919 and founder member of the **Union of European Football Associations** (UEFA) in 1954, president: Miljan Miljanic; general secretary: Branko Bulatovic. Season played from August to May. National stadium: **Crvena Zvezda** Stadion, Belgrade, capacity: 97,000. National strip: blue shirts, white shorts, red socks. First international game: (former-Yugoslavia): 28 August 1920 v **Czechoslovakia** (0–7, Antwerp in Belgium, **Olympic Games** first round); (Federal Republic of Yugoslavia): 23 December 1994 v **Brazil** (0–2, in Porto Allegre, Brazil, friendly). Biggest victory (former-Yugoslavia): 10–0 v **Venezuela** (14 June 1972, Curitiba in Brazil, Brazilian tournament to celebrate 150th anniversary of its independence); (Federal Republic of Yugoslavia): 8–1, v **Faroe Islands** (6 October 1996, in Toftir, Faroe Islands, **World Cup** qualifier). Biggest defeats (former-Yugoslavia): 0–7 v Czechoslovakia (as above), 0–7 v **Uruguay** (26 May 1924, in Paris, Olympic Games first round), 0–7 v Czechoslovakia (28 October 1925, Prague, friendly). Most capped players (former-Yugoslavia): Dragan **Dzajic** (85 appearances, 1964-79), Zlatko Vujovic (70 appearances, 1979-90); Federal Republic of Yugoslavia: Dragan Stojkovic (71 appearances 1984-; includes appearances for former Yugoslavia; Dejan **Savicevic** (51 appearances, 1986-; includes appearances for former Yugoslavia). Leading goalscorers (former-Yugoslavia): Stjepan **Bobek** (38 goals, 1946-56), Milan Galic (37 goals, 1959-65); Federal Republic of Yugoslavia: Dejan Savicevic (20 goals, 1986-), Predrag **Mijatovic** (16 goals, 1994-); Savo Milosevic (17 goals, 1994-). *International tournament record* (former Yugoslavia to 1992, Federal Republic of Yugoslavia from 1994) Olympic Games – first entered 1920, winners/gold medal 1960 (3–1, v Denmark, in Rome, Italy), runners-up/silver medal 1948 (1–3, v **Sweden**, at **Wembley** Stadium, London), 1952 (0–2, v **Hungary**, in Helsinki, Finland), 1956 (0–1 v **Soviet Union**, at Melbourne Cricket Ground, Melbourne, Australia), semi-final 1980 (fourth, 0–2 v Soviet Union, in Moscow, third/fourth playoff), sixth 1964; **Women's World Cup** – never qualified; World Cup – first entered 1930, semi-final 1930 (1–6, v eventual winners **Uruguay**, Montevideo), 1962 (fourth, 0–1, v **Chile**, in Santiago, third/fourth playoff), quarter-final 1954, 1958,

1990, second round 1974, 1998, also qualified for finals tournament 1950, 1986, did not enter 1994; **Balkan Cup** – winners 1934; **Dr Gerö Cup/International Cup** – fourth 1955-60; **European Championship** – first entered 1960, runners-up 1960 (1–2, v Soviet Union, in Paris, France), 1968 (0–2, v **Italy**, in Rome), semi-final 1976 (fourth, 2–3, v Netherlands, in Belgrade), quarter-final 1972, second round 1964, also qualified for finals tournament 1984, 1992 (though did not compete in finals tournament due to civil war – place taken by eventual winners **Denmark**), did not enter 1996; **European Junior Championship/European Youth Championship** (under-18) – winners 1951, runners-up 1979; **European Under-21 Championship** – winners 1978, runners-up 1990; **European Under-16 Championship** – runners-up 1990; **Under-17 World Championship** – never qualified; **World Youth Cup** (under-20) – qualified for finals tournament 1979 (first round group stage). *World Cup performance* (finals and qualifiers to end of 1998 tournament includes matches played by former Yugoslavia and Federal Republic of Yugoslavia) played 116, won 63, drawn 26, lost 27, scored 232 goals, conceded 123 goals. win rate: 54%; goals scored per game: 2.00. *Record against British and Irish national teams* 1. Former Yugoslavia: v **England**, played 14, won four, drawn five, lost five; v **Northern Ireland**, played seven, won five, drawn one, lost one; v **Scotland**, played eight, won one, drawn five, lost two; v **Wales**, played seven, won four, drawn three, lost none; v **Republic of Ireland**, played two, won one, drawn none, lost one; 2. none played by the Federal Republic of Yugoslavia. *History* The first clubs in the modern Yugoslavia were founded before World War I. **OFK Beograd** was founded as BSK Beograd in 1911 (just after Croatian club **Hajduk Split**, also in 1911), with FK **Vojvodina Novi Sad** founded in 1914. Yugoslavia's most famous club, Red Star Belgrade (FK **Crvena Zvezda Beograd**), was founded by the Communists in 1945 at Belgrade University, taking the ground of pre-World War II club Jugoslavija. The national league was founded in 1923, and has been played without a break since the end of World War II, continuing through the civil war and surviving the transition to the new Federal Republic league in 1992. The Yugoslavian Cup was first played in 1957. Yugoslavia's two leading clubs, Red Star Belgrade and former army club **Partizan Belgrade**, were also the most successful in the former Yugoslavia. By the final season of former Yugoslavia, Red Star had won the league 18 times and Cup 12 times; Partizan was league champions 11 times, and Cup winners five times. The two have continued to dominate the domestic competitions since the new Federal Republic was formed, though the balance has shifted slightly in favour of Partizan. One or other won the league championship and Cup every year from 1992 to 1997, but newly promoted FK **Obilic**, also from Belgrade, broke the sequence by winning the 1998 league title. The major clubs are nearly all from Serbia (half of the 1997-98 Division A clubs came from Belgrade), though FK **Buducnost Podgorica** (formerly known as FK Buducnost Titograd) is from the Montenegron capital, Podgorica. Red Star Belgrade won the **European Cup**, the continent's premier club competition, in 1991, with a 5–3 penalty victory over **Olympique de Marseille** in Bari, Italy, after a 0–0 draw. It added the **World Club Championship** in the same year, with a 3-0 victory over South American champions **Colo Colo**, from Chile, at the Japanese National Stadium in Tokyo. Partizan Belgrade reached the quarter-final of the first European Cup in 1955-56, losing 3-4 (agg.) to the eventual winners, **Real Madrid**. Red Star reached the quarter-final league stage of the European Cup in 1992, but no Yugoslavian club could enter European competitions again until 1995-96, when a ban on the national side and clubs was lifted. National team matches date back to the 1920 Olympic Games, a competition in which the country contested a record four finals in succession. Former Yugoslavia won the Gold medal at the 1960 Olympic Games, and was silver medalists in 1948, 1952 and 1956. Its best achievement in the European Championship was as runners-up in the first championship, 1960. It reached the semi-final of the 1976 tournament. Former Yugoslavia qualified for the 1992 European Championship but was barred from the finals tournament owing to the civil war in the region. The temporary international ban also prevented it from competing in the 1996 tournament. Former Yugoslavia finished fourth in the 1962 World Cup in Chile, and was semi-finalists in the first World Cup in 1930. The first senior tournament competed in by the new Federal Republic of Yugoslavia was the 1998 World Cup. It finished second in its qualifying tournament group, behind **Spain** and ahead of the **Czech Republic**, with seven wins and one defeat (scoring 29 goals, conceding seven, in its 10 games). Yugoslavia qualified for the finals tournament with a 12–1 aggregate victory over **Hungary** in the playoffs, winning the first leg 7–1 in Budapest. Real Madrid striker Predrag Mijatovic scored seven of the goals, giving him a tally of 14 for the qualifiers (the top scorer in the UEFA qualifying groups: he added another goal in the finals tournament). Yugoslavia qualified for the second round of the finals tournament in France (second in its first-round group), but lost to Netherlands (1–2, in Toulouse) with Edgar Davids scoring the 90th-minute winner. *League system* Yugoslavia's league system was restructured prior to the 1998-99 season – on the recommendation of UEFA. The Yugoslavian top flight, A Division, has 18 clubs (increased from 10 in 1996-97, and 12 in 1997-98). Clubs play each other twice in a season. Three points are awarded for a victory, with one for a draw: final positions for clubs level on points are determined by **goal difference**. The domestic Cup final is played over two legs in May. More than 2,000 clubs, the majority of which are amateur or semi-professional, enter the tournament. *Record in international club tournaments* World Club Championship – **Red Star Belgrade** (FK Crvena Zvezda Beograd) (winners 1991); European Cup – Red Star Belgrade (winners 1991, semi-final 1957, 1962, 1971, quarter-final 1958, 1974, 1981, 1982, 1987, quarter-final group 1992), Partizan Belgrade (FK Partizan Beograd) (runners-up 1966, quarter-final 1956, 1964), Vojvodina Novi Sad (quarter-final 1967); **European Cup-winners Cup** – OFK Beograd (semi-final 1963), Red Star Belgrade (semi-final 1975, quarter-final 1972, 1986), Partizan Belgrade (quarter-final 1990); **UEFA Cup/Fairs Cup** – Red Star Belgrade (runners-up 1979, quarter-final 1963), **Radnicki Nis** (semi-final 1982); Vojvodina Novi Sad (quarter-final 1968), , OFK Beograd (quarter-final 1973); UEFA Cup/Fairs Cup – Belgrade Select XI (a Belgrade representative side – semi-final 1960, quarter-final 1961). Other leading clubs: **Spartak Subotica**, **Budocnost Podgorica,** FK **Obilic Beograd**.

Z

Zabaleta, Aitor *n.* **Real Sociedad** supporter who died from knife wounds following a clash with **Atlético Madrid** fans before the 1998-99 **UEFA Cup** tie at the **Vicente Calderon** Stadio. The following week, Sociedad's players all wore Zabaleta's name on their shirts for the Primera Liga match with **Real Madrid**.

Zagallo, Mario Lobo *player-manager* Striker. **Brazil** international. Born 1931. *Clubs* (as player) América FC (Brazil), **Flamengo**, **Botafogo**; (as manager) Botafogo, **Fluminense**, Flamengo, Brazil (three times), **Kuwait**, **Saudi Arabia**, **United Arab Emirates**. *Keynotes* Zagallo, a left winger, scored in Brazil's 5-2 defeat of **Sweden** in the 1958 **World Cup** final (at **Råsunda Stadium**, Stockholm). He ignored the advice of doctors who had diagnosed a spinal-cord injury and went on to win a second World Cup winner's medal in 1962. He was appointed Botafogo manager in 1967, following two seasons as youth team coach. Zagallo was drafted in to manage the Brazil national side only three months before the 1970 World Cup, which the country won in some style (4–1 v **Italy**). Zagallo became a club coach, first at Fluminense and later across Rio de Janerio at Flamengo, before returning to manage the national side prior to the 1974 World Cup. Following a seven-year spell in the Middle East managing a string of national sides, Zagallo became assistant to Carlos Alberto Parreira with the national side. The partnership brought Brazil its first World Cup victory since 1970 in USA 1994. Zagallo was in sole charge for the 1998 World Cup, when the holders reached the final (0–3 v **France**). *Honours* (as player) World Cup (Brazil, 1958, 1962); (as manager) World Cup (Brazil 1970, 1994).

Zagreb (NK Zagreb) *club* Croatia national league and former Yugoslavia league club based in the capital Zagreb, founded 1945. Ground: Stadion NK Zagreb, capacity 18,000 (10,000 seats). Strip: white shirts, white shorts.

Zaire *country CAF* see **Congo Democratic Republic.**

Zaki, Badou *player* **Morocco** international. *Clubs* AS Salé (Morocco), **Real Mallorca**. *Keynotes* Became coach of his former club AS Salé. *Honours France Football* **African Footballer of the Year** 1986.

Zalgiris Vilnius *club* Lithuanian national league, and former Soviet Union league club, founded in 1947 and based in the Lithuanian capital Vilnius. Known as Spartak Vilnius until 1962. Ground: Vingis, capacity 13,000. Strip: green shirts and white shorts. **UEFA Cup** second round 1990; former-Soviet Union league third place 1987; **Baltic League** winners 1990; Lithuanian League Champions 1991, 1992, runners-up 1993, 1994, 1995, 1997, 1998; Lithuanian Cup 1991, 1993, 1994, 1997, runners-up 1992, 1995. Sister club: Zalgiris-Volmeta Vilnius.

Zamalek Sporting Club *club* Egyptian national league club based in the capital Cairo, founded 1925. Ground: Hassan Helmi, capacity: 40,000. Strip: white shirts with two red hoops, red shorts. *Keynotes* Zamalek played in the regional Cairo league before joining the inaugural national league in 1948. It is the most successful club in the **African Cup of Champion Clubs**, with four titles to 1997. It has won a record eight African club competitions (including **African Super Cup** and **Afro-Asian Club Cup**; compare record held by **Al Ahly**). Egypt's worst stadium disaster was at Zanalek's ground: 49 spectators died from crushing at a match against **Dukla Prague** in February 1974. The club finished league runners-up in 1999, having been deducted nine points for failing to play one of its matches. African Cup of Champion Clubs winners 1984 (2–0 agg., v **IICC Shooting Stars** of Nigeria), 1986 (2–2 agg., 4–2 pens., v **Africa Sports** of the Ivory Coast), 1993 (0–0 agg., 7–6 pens., v **Asante Kotoko** of Ghana), 1996, (3–3 agg., 5–4 pens., v IICC Shooting Stars), runners-up 1994 (1–3 agg., v **Esperance** of Tunisia), quarter-final "champions-league" stage 1997; African Super Cup 1993 (1–0, v Al Ahly of Egypt), 1996 (0–0, 4–2 pens., v **Al Mokaouloum** of Egypt); Afro-Asian Club Cup – winners 1987, 1997); Cairo league champions 1940, 1941, 1944, 1945, 1946, 1947, 1949, 1951, 1952, 1953; Egyptian league champions 1960, 1964, 1965, 1978, 1984, 1988, 1992, 1993; Egyptian Cup 1932, 1935, 1938, 1941, 1943 (shared), 1944, 1952, 1955, 1957, 1958 (shared), 1959, 1960, 1962, 1975, 1977, 1979, 1987, 1988, 1989.

Zambia *country CAF* republic in central Africa, south of **Congo Democratic Republic** (Zaire) and **Tanzania**. Independence from Britain in 1964. Formerly known as Northern Rhodesia. Area: 752,615 sq km (290, 510 sq miles). Population: 8,940,000 (1993 est.). Languages: English and African languages. Capital: Lusaka. *Dossier* Football Association of Zambia (Lusaka) formed in 1929, affiliated to **FIFA** and the **Confédération Africaine de Football** (CAF) in 1964, member of the **Confederation of Southern African Football Associations** (COSAFA), president: T D Mulonga; general secretary: J Mazumba. Season played from March to November. National stadium: Independence Stadium, Lusaka, capacity: 30,000. National strip: copper and black shirts, green shorts, red socks. Nickname of national team: the Mighty Zambia. First international game: 4 July 1964 v **Tanzania** (1–0, neutral venue, friendly). Biggest victory: 9–0 v **Kenya** (13 November 1978, in Malawi, East and Central African Championship). Biggest defeat: 1–10 v **Congo Democratic Republic** (Zaire) (22 November 1969, Kinshasa, Congo DR, friendly) and 0–9 v **Belgium** (4 June 1994, in Brussels, friendly). Notable international players: Kalusha **Bwalya**, Peter Kaumba. *International tournament record* **Olympic Games** – quarter final 1988 (won its first-round group of four nations, including a 4–0 victory against **Italy**, September 1988, Soeul, South Korea), also qualified for finals tournament 1980; **Women's World Cup** – entered the first tournament in 1991 (though Zambia did not play a game), first qualifying round 1995; **World Cup** – first entered 1969, reached fourth and final qualifying round 1974 (second in three-nation playoff group, with only one nation, Congo DR, qualifying for finals); **African Cup of Nations** – first entered 1970, runners-up 1974 (2–2, 0–2 replay, v Congo DR, in Cairo, Egypt), 1994 (1-2, v **Nigeria**, in Tunis, Tunisia), semi-final/third 1982 (2-0, v **Algeria**, in Tripoli, Libya, third/fourth playoff), 1990 (1-0, v **Senegal**, in Algiers, Algeria, third/fourth playoff), quarter-final 1992, also qualified for finals tournament 1978, 1986; **COSAFA Championship** – winners 1997 (final round league of five nations), 1998 (final round league); **COSAFA Youth Tournament** (under-20) – winners 1986, 1993, 1995. **East and Central African Championship** – winners 1984 (0–0, 3–0 pens., v **Malawi**, in Uganda), 1991 (2–0,v Kenya, in Uganda), runners-up 1976 (0–2, v **Uganda**, in Zanzibar), 1977 (0–0, 3–5 pens., v Uganda, in Somalia), 1978 (2–3, v Malawi, in Malawi), 1988 (1–3, v Malawi in Malawi); **Under-17 World Championship** – never qualified; **World Youth Cup** (under-20) – qualified 1999. *Record against British and Irish national teams* none played. *History* Football was introduced to Zambia by the British during the colonial era. Zambia's football association was founded in 1929, as the Northern Rhodesian Football Association. The current Zambian national league and Cup date from 1962. **Power Dynamos** was the first Zambian club to win an African club tournament, the **African Cup-winners Cup** in 1991. Another Zambian club, **Kabwe Warriors**, holds the record for the biggest victory in the **African Cup of Champion Clubs** (9–0, v Majanta Meseru of Lesotho, 1972, first round). Zambia has been runners-up twice in the African Cup of Nations (1974 and 1994). The 1970

final went to a replay, with Zambia eventually losing 0-2 to Zaire (now Congo Democratic Republic). It has reached the semi-finals on two other occasions. Zambia's best international achievement was in reaching the Olympic Games quarter-final in Seoul, in 1988. It topped its four-nation first round group, having beaten both Italy and **Guatemala** 4-0, with a 2-2 draw against **Iraq**, but lost 0-4 in the semi-final against West **Germany**. It has twice won the East and Central African Championship. Eighteen national squad players were killed in an air crash off the coast of Gabon in April 1993. The squad was on its way to Senegal for a World Cup qualifier. The Zambian government agreed to compensate the families of the dead players in 1998, after a long legal battle. In 1993, the Football Association of Zambia was awarded FIFA's **Fairplay Award** for sportsmanship. *League system* Sixteen teams play each other at home and away. Three points are awarded for a victory, with one for a draw: final positions for clubs level on points are determined by **goal difference**. *Record in international club tournaments* African Cup of Champion Clubs – **Nkana FC** (runners-up 1990), **Mufulira Wanderers** (semi-final 1977); African Cup-winners Cup – Power Dynamos (winners 1991, runners-up 1982), Nkana FC (quarter-final 1998); **East and Central African Cup – Green Buffaloes** (semi-final 1980), Kabwe Warriors (semi-final 1981) **CAF Cup** – Nchanga Rangers (of Chingola, semi-final 1998). Other leading club: Konkola Blades (of Chililabombwe, Zambian Cup 1998).

Zanzibar *country no separate affiliation* island and constituent part of the republic of **Tanzania**. Area: 1,658 sq km (640 sq miles). Population: 571,000. British protectorate from 1890 to 1963, when gained independence. Joined with Tanganyika to form the republic of Tanzania in 1964. Languages: Kiswahili and English. Chief town: Zanzibar. *Dossier* Football association formed in 1964, neither independently affiliated to **FIFA** nor to the **Confédération Africaine de Football** (CAF) (see Tanzania), but is an independent member of the **Confederation of East and Central African Football Associations** (CECAFA). Season played from September to August. National stadium: Amaan, capacity: 10,000. National strip: red shirts, white shorts, socks. First international game: 4 October 1967 v **Kenya** (0–6, in Kenya, **Gossage Cup**). Biggest victory: 3–0 v **Tanzania** (3 October 1969, in Uganda, Gossage Cup). Biggest defeat: 0–8 v **Zambia** (21 November 1992, in Uganda, **East and Central African Championship**). *International tournament record* **Olympic Games** – not eligible (see Tanzania); **Women's World Cup** – never eligible; **World Cup** – not eligible (see Tanzania); **African Cup of Nations** – not eligible (see Tanzania); **East and Central African Championship** – winners 1995 (1–0 v Uganda "B", in Uganda: note, Uganda, as hosts, entered two teams; Uganda "A" was beaten by Zanzibar at the group stage), hosts 1976, 1990; Gossage Cup – winners once (date unknown). *Record against British and Irish national* *teams* none played. *League system* Clubs play in the Zanzibar Island League and compete in a combined Tanzania and Zanzibar Union League. *Record in international club tournaments* **African Cup-winners Cup** – **KMKM Zanzibar** (quarter-final 1977); **Malindi Sports Club** (quarter-final 1994); **CAF Cup** – Malindi Sports Club (semi-final 1995; **East and Central African Club Championship** – KMKM Zanzibar (semi-final 1983). Other leading clubs: **Small Simba**, Mhlandege (Zanzibar league champions 1996, 1998). See also **Tanzania**

Zeljeznicar Sarajevo *club* **Bosnia-Herzegovina** and **former Yugoslavia** national league club based in Sarajevo, founded 1921. Ground: Grbavica, capacity: 26,000 (pre-civil war). Strip: sky blue shirts, sky blue shorts. **UEFA Cup** semi-final 1985, quarter-final 1972; former Yugoslavia league champions 1972, runners-up 1971; former Yugoslavia Cup runners-up 1981; Bosnia League champions 1998; Bosnian Cup runners-up 1997. Notable former player: Bahtic (joint-top scorer in the 1984-85 UEFA Cup with seven goals).

Zenit St Petersburg *club* Russian national league and former **Soviet Union** league club based in St Petersburg, founded in 1931 as Stalinets Leningrad (became Zenit Leningrad in 1940, adopted current name in 1991). Ground: Petrovski, capacity: 25,000. Strip: white shirts, white shorts. Soviet Union League champions 1984; Soviet Cup 1944.

Zenith Data Systems Cup *competition* the former **Full Members' Cup** (**Simod Cup**), from 1990, and a competition open only to clubs from Divisions One and Two. The competition ceased in 1992. *Final results* 1989-90 **Chelsea** 1–0 **Middlesbrough**, 1990-91 **Crystal Palace** 4–1 **Everton**, 1991-92 **Nottingham Forest** 3–2 **Southampton**.

Zico *player* Real name: Artur Antunes Coimbra. Striker. **Brazil** international (71 caps, 48 goals, 1971-86). Born 3 March 1953. Career ca. 1970-1993. *Clubs* **Flamengo** (twice), **Udinese**, **Kashima Antlers**. *Keynotes* Zico is Brazil's second highest goalscorer (after **Pelé**), making his debut on 25 February 1976 (2–1, v **Uruguay**, in Montevideo), and scoring his first international goal two days later (2–1, v **Argentina**, in Buenos Aires). He was top scorer in the 1981 **Copa Libertadores**, with 11 goals, including all four of Flamengo's in the final against Cobreloa (2–1, 0–1, 2–0 playoff). He finished his international career at the 1986 **World Cup** finals but later played club football in the Japanese **J-League**. Assistant coach of 1998 Brazilian World Cup squad. *Honours* **World Club Championship** (Flamengo, 1981); Copa Libertadores (Flamengo, 1981); *World Soccer* **World Footballer of the Year** 1983; *El Mundo* South American Footballer of the Year 1977, 1981, 1982, runner-up 1976, 1980.

Zidane, Zinedine *player* Midfielder. **France** international (45 caps, 11 goals). Born 23 June 1972. Career ca. 1989-. *Clubs* Cannes, **Bordeaux**, **Juventus**. *Keynotes* Zidane made his French League debut for Cannes in 1989, moving to Bordeaux three seasons later. Zidane inspired Bordeaux to the **UEFA Cup** final in 1996 (1–5 v **Bayern Munich** (agg.)), scoring a spectacular goal from 35 yards in the third round against **Real Betis**. He joined Juventus before the 1996 **European Championship**. Zidane appeared in the 1997 and 1998 **European Cup** (Champions League) finals with Juventus, but was a loser on both occasions. He made his international debut for France in August 1994, scoring twice in a 2–2 draw with the **Czech Republic**. Zidane headed two more goals for France in the 1998 World Cup victory over **Brazil**. *Honours* Italian League (Juventus 1996-97, 1997-98); **World Cup** (France 1998); *World Soccer* **World Footballer of the Year** 1998; **FIFA World Footballer of the Year** 1998; **European Footballer of the Year** 1998.

Zimbabwe *country AFC* republic in southern central Africa, north of **South Africa**, and bordering **Botswana**, **Mozambique** and **Zambia**. Became the self-Governing British colony of Southern Rhodesia in 1923. Unilateral declaration of independence under white government (led by Ian Smith) 1965, full independence 1980, under new prime minister, and former independence fighter, Robert Mugabe. Area: 390,310 sq km (150,660 sq miles). Population: 11,500,000 (1995 est.). Languages: English, Shona, Sindebele and other native languages. Capital: Harare. *Dossier* Zimbabwe Football Association founded in 1965, affiliated to **FIFA** in 1965 and **Confédération Africaine de Football** (CAF) in 1980, member of the **Confederation of Southern African Football Associations** (COSAFA), president: L Mugabe; general secretary: P Hwata. Season played from January to November. National stadium: Rufaro Stadium, capacity: 60,000. National strip: green shirts, gold shorts, green and gold socks. Nickname of national team: the Warriors. First international game: (as Rhodesia) 15 July 1950 v **Australia** (0–5, home, friendly), first as Zimbabwe: May 1979 v **Mozambique** (6–0, in Harare, friendly). Biggest victory: 6–0 v Mozambique (as above). Biggest defeat: 0–7 v **South Africa** (1977, in South Africa). Other notable international players: Peter Ndlovu, Bruce **Grobbelaar**. *International tournament record* **Olympic Games** – third and final qualifying round 1992; **Women's World Cup** – entered in 1991, but withdrew without playing a match; **World Cup** – first entered 1970 (as Rhodesia), never past second qualifying round; **African Cup of Nations** – first entered 1982, never qualified for finals tournament; **COSAFA Championship** – runners-up 1998 (final round league of five nations); **COSAFA Youth Tournament** (under-20) – winners 1991, runners-up 1986, 1993; **East and Central African Championship** – winners 1985 (2–0 v **Kenya**, in Zimbabwe), runners-up 1983 (0–1 v Kenya, in Kenya), 1987 (1–1, 4–5 pens.), v **Ethiopia**, in Ethiopia); **Under-17 World Championship** – never qualified; **World Youth Cup** (under-20) – never qualified. *Record against British and Irish national teams* none played. *History* Football was introduced in the late

19th century, allegedly by British railway workers. National league and Cup competitions date from 1962, with the National Professional Soccer League founded in 1992. No Zimbabwean club has won a major African or regional club tournament. Zimbabwe (as Southern Rhodesia) was part of a Football Association of Southern Africa (which included Lesotho, Malawi, South Africa and Zambia) from 1957 to 1964. The national football association was formed in 1965, as the Rhodesian Football Association, and was affiliated to FIFA in the same year. CAF, however, refused admission until the country had established a new majority-rule constitution after the elections in March 1980. Zimababwe, as Rhodesia, was also suspended by FIFA in the 1970s. The first recorded international match was against Australia in 1950 (above), though representative sides played teams from South Africa from 1908. Its first competition match was in the 1970 World Cup qualifiers (23 November 1969, 1–1, v Australia): a series of three games was played over one week, all in Lourenco Marques, Mozambique; Zimbabwe lost the third match (1–3), after a goalless draw in the second. Zimbabwe had been barred from playing in the Africa qualifying group and was playing in an Asia-Oceania qualifying competition. Zimbabwe has never qualified for the World Cup or African Cup of Nations finals tournaments and its best achievement was in winning the East and Central African Championship in 1985 (Zimbabwe is no longer eligible to play in this tournament as it is now a member of the southern African confederation, COSAFA). *League system* Sixteen clubs compete in the National Professional Soccer League, each playing each other twice. Three points are awarded for a victory, with one for a draw; final positions for clubs level on points are determined by **goal difference**. *Record in international club tournaments* **African Cup of Champion Clubs** – **Dynamos Harare** (runners-up 1998, quarter-final 1981, 1984, 1987, 1995), **Black Rhinos** (quarter-final 1985), **Zimbabwe Saints** (quarter-final 1989); **African Cup-winners Cup** – **Blackpool** (semi-final 1995), **CAPS United** (quarter-final 1982, 1983), Dynamos Harare (quarter-final 1991); East and Central African Club Championship – **Riodairibord Wanderers** (then known as Rio Tinto, runners-up 1982, 0–1, v **AFC Leopards** of Kenya, in Kenya). Other leading clubs: **Black Aces, Bulawayo Highlanders, Wankie**.

Zimbabwe Saints *club* Zimbabwe national league club based in Bulawayo. Ground: Barbour Fields (shared with **Bulawayo Highlanders**), capacity: 10,000. Strip: blue shirts, red shorts. **African Cup of Champion Clubs** quarter-final 1989; Zimbabwe league champions 1977, 1988; Zimbabwe Cup 1977, 1979, 1987.

Zimbru Chisinau *club* Moldovan national league side based in the capital Chisinau (Kishnev) and formed in 1947. Various previous names (Dinamo, Burevestnik, Moldova, Avintul and Nistrul) until current one adopted in 1991. Ground: Republican (the national stadium),

capacity: 22,000, or Zimbur Stadium, or Speia municipal stadium. Strip: yellow shirts and yellow shorts. *Keynotes* Zimbru holds the national league record of five consecutive league titles (1992 to 1996). Moldovan League champions 1992, 1993, 1994, 1995, 1996, 1998, runners-up 1997; Moldovan Cup 1997, 1998, runners-up 1995. Notable player: Iurie Miterev – Moldova's top international goalscorer; he also scored nine goals in one league match in Zimbru's league-record 15–1 victory against Ciuhur Ocnita (19 June 1997, in Chisinau).

Zoff, Dino *player* Goalkeeper. **Italy** international (112 caps, no goals, 1968-83). Born 1942. *Clubs* Udinese, Mantova Nuova AC, **Napoli, Juventus**. *Keynotes* Zoff was 26 years old when he made his international debut (10 April 1968, 2-0, v **Bulgaria**). He played 112 times for his country – in an international career that spanned 15 years – and conceded only 91 goals (0.81 per match). Zoff was manager of Juventus – where he won the **UEFA Cup** and Italian Cup in 1990 – and later **Lazio** (at which he was also president). He became Italy's national team coach in 1998. Zoff holds a world record for the longest **clean sheet** in senior-level international football: in 1973-74, he played 1,143 minutes for Italy without conceding a goal. *Honours* World Cup (Italy, 1982; as captain); **European Championship** (Italy, 1968); UEFA Cup (Juventus, 1977); Italian League (Juventus, 1972, 1973, 1975, 1977, 1978, 1981, 1982); *France Football* **European Footballer of the Year** runner-up 1973.

Zola, Gianfranco *player* Striker. **Italy** international (35 caps, 9 goals). Born 5 July 1966. *Clubs* Nuorese, Torres, **Napoli, Parma, Chelsea**. *Keynotes* Zola was transferred to Chelsea from Parma for £4.5 million in November 1996; he won the Carling Premiership Player of the Month for December 1996, seven weeks after joining the club. *Honours* **La Coppa Italia** (Napoli 1992), **European Cup-winners Cup** (Parma 1993, Chelsea 1998), **UEFA Cup** (Parma 1995), **European Super Cup** (Chelsea 1998), **FA Cup** (Chelsea 1997), **League Cup** (Chelsea 1998); **Football Writers' Footballer of the Year** 1997.

zone 14 *tactics* area in front of the penalty arc identified by football analysts as critical for creating goalscoring opportunities. The area was identified by scientists at the Research Institute for Sport and Exercise Sciences at Liverpool John Moores University, who divided each half of the pitch into 18 zones. By analysing matches at the 1998 **World Cup** finals, they found that winning teams made significantly more successful passes from zone 14 than losing teams and, in particular, that the passes were more often played forward, from the zone into the penalty area. The area is roughly equivalent to the **hole**, as described by football tacticians.

zone defence *tactics* a defensive system which involves each defender covering a designated, and overlapping, area/sector. Typically each member of a zone defence will move as a unit to the edge of their designated sectors and towards the ball to repel an attack. The role of a member of a zone defence is to engage an **onball** attacker in their sector or to cover opponents and their onball teammates.

Zongo, Mamadou *player* Striker. **Burkina Faso** international (1996-). Born 8 October 1980. Career ca. 1995-. *Clubs* RC Bobo Dioulasso, **ASEC Abidjan**. *Keynotes* At just 16 years of age, Zongo became Burkina footballer of the year and league top scorer before moving to Ivory Coast club ASEC Abidjan; played in 1998 **African Nations Cup** finals tournament aged 17 years.

Zubizaretta, Andoni *player* Goalkeeper. **Spain** international (126 caps, 1983-1998). Born 23 October 1961. *Clubs* **Athletic Bilbao**, **Barcelona**, **Valencia**. *Keynotes* Zubizaretta made his international debut on 23 January 1985 (3–1, v **Finland**) and went on to become Spain's most capped player. His 126th and last appearance at the 1998 **World Cup** finals made him the second most-capped goalkeeper of all time, one more than Peter **Shilton**, but still 13 behind the record held by Thomas **Ravelli** of **Sweden**. Zubizaretta conceded 107 international goals (0.85 goals per game). He was transferred in 1985 from Bilbao to Barcelona for £1.2 million, at the time a world record **transfer fee** for a goalkeeper. Zubizaretta won two European club medals with Barcelona, but let in four goals in the 1994 **European Cup** final (0–4, v **Milan**). *Honours* **European Cup-winners Cup** (Barcelona, 1989), European Cup (Barcelona, 1992); Spanish League championship (Athletic League Bilbao, 1983, 1984, Barcelona, 1991, 1992, 1993, 1994).

Zumunta Athletic Club *club* Niger national league club, based in the capital Niamey. Ground: Seni Kountche, capacity: 7,000. Strip: yellow shirts and black shorts. **CAF Cup** quarter-final 1993 (lost 1–2 to Insurance FC of Ethiopia in two-leg quarter-final); Niger League champions 1985, 1986, 1988 and 1993; Niger Cup 1977 and 1994.

zwiskampf *misc.* German term used to describe a challenge for the ball.

Bibliography

Anon, *90 minutes: Newsletter of the United States National Soccer Hall of Fame*, vol. 7 (National Soccer Hall of Fame, Oneonta, NY, 1995)

Gary Armstrong and Richard Giulianotti, *Entering the Field: New Perspectives on World Football* (Berg, Oxford International Publishers Ltd, 1997)

Barry Baker, *The African Football Guide 1996–97* (Heart Books, Rijmenam, 1996)

David J. Ball, 'Assessing the risks', Sports Exercise and Injury, pp3–9, vol. 4 (1), (Churchill Livingstone, Edinburgh, 1998)

Gavin Barber, 'Fan power and democracy', Factsheet 7 (Sir Norman Chester Centre for Football Research, Leicester, 1995)

Norman Barrett, *The Daily Telegraph Football Chronicle*, 3rd edn (Ebury Press, London, 1996)

Stephen Bradbury, 'Racism and Football', Factsheet 6 (Sir Norman Chester Centre for Football Research, Leicester, 1995)

British Psychological Society, 'Sexism and Women's Football', Media Release, 10 September 1998 (British Psychological Society, Leicester, 1998)

Eric Brown, (ed.) *News of the World Football Annual 1998–99* (Invincible Press, London, 1998)

Bryon Butler, *Football League 1888–1988: the Official Illustrated History* (Queen Anne Press, London, 1987)

Bryon Butler, *Official Illustrated History of the FA Cup* (Headline Books, London, 1996)

Christopher Cook, (ed.) *Pears Cyclopaedia 1990–91*, 99th edn (Pelham Books Ltd, London, 1990)

Peterjon Cresswell and Simon Evans, *European Football: A Fans' Handbook* (Rough Guides, London, 1997)

Mark Curren and Laurence Redmond, 'Why Support Football', Factsheet 3 (Sir Norman Chester Centre for Football Research, Leicester, 1991)

Gerry Boon (ed.), *Deloitte & Touche Annual Review of Football Finance* (Deloitte & Touche, Manchester 1997, 1998)

John H Dirckx, (ed.) *Steadman's Concise Medical and Allied Health Dictionary* 3rd edn (Williams and Wilkins, Baltimore, 1997)

Jim Drewett and Alex Leith, *Virgin Book of Football Records* (Virgin Publishing Ltd, London, 1997)

English Schools Football Association, *English Schools Football Association Handbook 1998–99* (English Schools Football Association, Stafford, 1998)

FA Premier League, *FA Premier League Handbook 1997–98* (FA Premier League Ltd, London, 1997)

FA Premier League, *FA Premier League Handbook 1998–99* (FA Premier League Ltd, London, 1998)

FA Premier League, 'FA Premier League Fan Survey' (Sir Norman Chester Centre for Football Research, Leicester, 1996)

FA Premier League, 'Football After Taylor', Factsheet 2, (Sir Norman Chester Centre for Football Research, Leicester, 1993)

FIFA, 'Amendments to the Laws of the game', FIFA Circular no. 585 (FIFA, Zurich, 1996)

FIFA, 'Amendments to the Laws of the game', FIFA Circular no. 644 (FIFA, Zurich, 1998)

FIFA, 'The Laws of the Game' (FIFA, Zurich, 1998)

FIFA, *FIFA Directory 1998* (FIFA, Zurich, 1998)

Football Association, Annual Report & Accounts (Football Association, London, 1995, 1996, 1997)

Football Association, 'Information on the amendments to the laws of the game and instructions of the International FA Board 1996/97' (Football Association, London, 1996)

Football Association, 'Information on the amendments to the laws of the game and instructions of the International FA Board 1998/99' (Football Association, London, 1998)

Football Association, 'Woman's football competitions', Girls' and women's football Factsheet 2 (Football Association, London, 1996)

Football Association, 'Woman's football history', Girls' and women's football Factsheet 1 (Football Association, London, 1996)

Football League, *Football League Handbook* (The Football League Limited, Lytham St Annes, 1998)

Cris Freddi, *Complete Book of the World Cup* (Willow, London, 1998)

Brian Glanville, '100 Greatest Footballers of All Time', (*The Sunday Times Magazine* 9 (nos. 5–8), 1997)

Maurice Golesworthy, *Encyclopaedia of Association Football* (Robert Hale, London, 1963)

Edward Grayson, *Sport and the Law* (Butterworths, London, 1988)

Liz Green, 'Women and Football', Factsheet 5 (Sir Norman Chester Centre for Football Research, Leicester, 1993)

Mike Hammond, (ed.) *The European Football Handbook* (Sports Projects, Smethwick, annual editions: 1990–98)

Graham Hart, *Guinness Football Encyclopaedia* (Guinness Publishing, London, 1995)

Tessa Hayward, 'A History of Female Football Fans', Factsheet 9 (Sir Norman Chester Centre for Football Research, Leicester, 1995)

Barry J Hugman, (ed.) *Official PFA Footballers Factfile* (Queen Anne Press, London, 1996, 1997, 1998)

Brian Hunter, (ed.) *Statesman's Yearbook 1997/98*, 134th edn (Macmillan, London, 1997)

John S Hunter, 'Phenomenon of Football' (Letter to *The Times*, 13 June 1997)

Simon Inglis, *Football Grounds of Great Britain* (Willow, London, 1987)

Simon Inglis, *League Football and the Men Who Made It: Official Centenary History of the Football League 1888–1988* (Willow, London, 1988)

Simon Inglis, *Football Grounds of Britain* (Willow, London, 1996)

Douglas Lamming, *Scottish Football Internationalists' Who's Who 1872–1986* (Hutton Press, East Yorkshire, 1987)

Douglas Lamming, *English Football Internationalists' Who's Who* (Hutton Press, East Yorkshire, 1990)

Michael Lewis, *World Cup Soccer* (Moyer Bell, London, 1994)

Sue Lopez, *Women on the Ball* (Scarlet Press, London, 1997)

Margus Luik and Eduard Nisenboim, *Football in Former Soviet Union Republics* (VH Sportmedia AG, Tallinn, 1997)

Ian McArthur and David Kemp, *Elegance Borne of Brutality: An Eclectic History of the Football Boot* (Two Heads Publishing, London, 1995)

Stephen McGarrigle, *The Complete Who's Who of Irish International Football* (Mainstream, Edinburgh, 1996)

Chris Nawrat and Steve Hutchings, *The Sunday Times Illustrated History of Football* (Hamlyn, London, 1996)

Guy Oliver, *The Guinness Book of World Soccer*, 2nd edn (Guinness Publishing, Enfield, 1995)

Steve Pearce, *The Shoot Ultimate Stats and Facts Guide to English Cup Football* (Boxtree, London, 1997)

Steve Pearce, *The Shoot Ultimate Stats and Facts Guide to English League Football* (Boxtree, London, 1997)

Steve Pearce and Tim Barnett, *The Shoot Ultimate Stats and Facts Guide to International Football* (Boxtree, London, 1997)

Mark Perryman, *'Football United: New Labour, the task force, and the future of the game'* (Fabian Society, London, 1997)

Premier League, Annual Report & Accounts (FA Premier League, London, 1994, 1995, 1996, 1997)

Andy Pringle and Neil Fissler, *Where Are They Now* (Two Heads Publishing, London, 1996)

Keir Radnedge, *Ultimate Encyclopaedia of Soccer* (Carlton Books, London, 1996)

Filippo M Ricci, *The Phillys African Football Yearbook 1998* (self-published, Rome, 1998)

Jonathan Rice, *Curiosities of Football* (Pavilion Books, London, 1996)

Jack Rollin, *Guinness Football Factbook* (Guinness Publishing, London, 1993)

Jack Rollin, (ed.) *The Rothmans Football Yearbook* (Headline Books, London, annual editions: 1970–1998)

Albert Sarpong, 'Black Footballers in Britain', Factsheet 4 (Sir Norman Chester Centre for Football Research, Leicester, 1995)

Scottish Football League, *Scottish Football League Handbook 1998–99* (The Scottish Football League, Glasgow, 1998)

Albert Sewell, (ed.) *News of the World Football Annual 1997–98* (Invincible Press, London, 1997)

Dennis Signy, *A Pictorial History of Soccer* (Hamlyn, London, 1969)

Alan G Smith, *Soccer Injuries – Prevention and First Aid* (Crowood Press, Marlborough, 1989)

Bruce Smith, *World Cup Pocket Annual 1998* (Virgin Publishing Ltd, London, 1998)

Phil Soar, *Hamlyn A–Z of Football Records* (Hamlyn, London, 1984)

David Stockley, *Drug Warning* (Optima Books, London, 1992)

Brian Tabner, *Through the Turnstiles* (Yore Publications, Middlesex, 1992)

The Times *Atlas of the World*, 3rd edn, (Times Books, London, 1995)

Dag Tuastad, 'The Political Role of Football for Palestinians in Jordan', in Gary Armstrong and Richard Giulianotti (eds.) Entering the Field: New Perspectives on World Football (Berg, Oxford International Publishers Ltd, 1997)

US Soccer, *1998 Media Guide* (US Soccer Communications Department, Chicago, 1998)

Serge Van Hoof, Michael Parr and Carlos Yametti, *The North and Latin American Football Guide 96/97* (Heart Books, Rijmenam, 1997)

Serge Van Hoof, Michael Parr and Carlos Yametti, *The North and Latin American Football Guide 97/98* (Heart Books, Rijmenam, 1998)

W H G Wilkinson, *Soccer Tactics: Top Team Strategies Explained* (Crowood Press, Marlborough, 1996)

Graham Williams, *The Code War* (Yore Publications, Harefield, 1994).

John Williams, 'Football and Football Hooliganism', Factsheet 1 (Sir Norman Chester Centre for Football Research, Leicester, 1993)

Russ Williams, *Football Babylon* (Virgin Publishing, London, 1996)

Rob Woolard, *A–Z of Asian Football 97–98* (EFP International (HK) Ltd, Hong Kong, 1997)

Elizabeth Wyse, (ed.) *Guinness Book of Records* (Guinness Publishing Ltd, Enfield, 1998)

Websites

Asian Football Confederation: http://www.asian-football.com

Association of Football Statisticians: http://innotts.co.uk/~soccerstats/

Confederacion Sudamericana de Fútbol: http://www.conmebol.com

Confèdèration Africaine de Football: http://www.cafonline.com

FIFA: http://www.fifa.com

J-League: http://www.j-league.or.jp

Korea Football Association: http://www. kfa.or.kr

Rec.Sport.Soccer Statistics Foundation: www.risc.uni-linz.ac.at/non-official/rsssf

Union of European Football Associations: www.uefa.com

US Soccer: http://www.us-soccer.com

Acknowledgments

We should like to thank the following individuals and organisations for their help in producing this book: the Association of Football Players with Learning Difficulties; the Bangladesh Football Federation; the BBC Press Office; Malcolm Berry, chief executive of the English Schools Football Association; Dean Braithwaite; Terry Brisco; Cliff Butler at Manchester United; Mike Darling; Anne-Marie Dargan; J D Dent, secretary of the Football League; Doncaster Belles; East Fife; Carol Dunne at the Ladies Football Association of Ireland; the Fèdèration Malienne de Foot-Ball; the FIFA Media Advisory; the Football Association; the Football Association of Malaysia; John Foster at the National Union of Journalists; Mike Foster, Secretary of the FA Premier League; Carlos Giron at CONCACAF; Mark Gleeson; Gavin Griffiths (football for blind and visually impaired players); Dr Richard Hawkins at the Football Association Medical Education Centre; the International Blind Sports Federation; Lindsay Jackson at the FA Women's section; J A Kirkpatrick, deputy secretary of the Scottish Football League; Lloyd Lewis; Pille Liimal; Maureen McGonicle at the Scottish Women's Football Association; Helen Miller at Sunderland AFC; Jim Moorhouse at US Soccer; Fiona Neathey; Indrek Petersoo; Ants Pïldoja; Dave Prole; the Rec.Sport.Soccer Statistics Foundation; The Royal Geographical Society, London; Lynda Ryan; Patrick Ryan; the Scottish Football League; the Scottish Junior Football Association; Simon Shaw; Colin Sherwood; Madeline Weston; Clare Wheatley at Arsenal Ladies and the many football clubs that helped with our research. Thanks are also due to the football coverage of: BBC Radio 5 Live, BBC Sport, Carlton Sport, *Daily Telegraph*, *Evening Standard*, *Financial Times*, Football Mundial, *FourFourTwo*, The *Guardian*, *Independent*, *Independent on Sunday*, ITN, *Mirror*, *Observer*, Sky Sports, *Sunday Telegraph*, *Sunday Times*, *The Times*, When Saturday Comes and *World Soccer*.

We should especially like to thank Verity Willcocks and Charlie Carman at Boxtree, Ruth Gladwin for her help and support at the outset of the project, Gavin Hamilton at *World Soccer*.

Special recognition is reserved for the following people who provided advice, support, encouragement, inspiration and love, and without whom this book would not have been possible:
Charlie, Ezra, Hannah, Rachel, Dave, Liz, Jeanne and Bill.